Collins

Collins
Dictionary
English-Portuguese
Português-Inglês

HarperCollins Publishers
Westerhill Road
Bishopbriggs
Glasgow
G64 2QT
Great Britain

Third Edition 2006

Reprint 10 9 8 7 6 5 4 3

© HarperCollins Publishers 1991, 2001, 2006

ISBN 978-0-00-722426-5

Collins® and Bank of English®
are registered trademarks of
HarperCollins Publishers Limited

www.collinslanguage.com

A catalogue record for this book is
available from the British Library

HarperCollins Publishers,
10 East 53rd Street,
New York, NY 10022

COLLINS PORTUGUESE CONCISE DICTIONARY
Second US Edition 2001

ISBN 978-0-06-093694-5

www.harpercollins.com

HarperCollins books may be purchased for
educational, business, or sales promotional
use. For information, please write to:
Special Markets Department,
HarperCollins Publishers,
10 East 53rd Street,
New York, NY 10022

Typeset by Thomas Callan

Printed in Italy by LEGO Spa, Lavis (Trento),
ITALY

Acknowledgements
We would like to thank those authors and
publishers who kindly gave permission for
copyright material to be used in the Collins
Word Web. We would also like to thank
Times Newspapers Ltd for providing
valuable data.

EDITORS
John Whitlam
Vitoria Davies
Mike Harland

When you buy a Collins dictionary or
thesaurus and register on
www.collinslanguage.com for the free
online and digital services, you will not be
charged by HarperCollins for access to
Collins free Online Dictionary content or
Collins free Online Thesaurus content on
that website. However, your operator's
charges for using the internet on your
computer will apply. Costs vary from
operator to operator. HarperCollins is not
responsible for any charges levied by online
service providers for accessing Collins free
Online Dictionary or Collins free Online
Thesaurus on www.collinslanguage.com
using these services.

HarperCollins does not warrant
that the functions contained in
www.collinslanguage.com content will be
uninterrupted or error free, that defects will be
corrected, or that www.collinslanguage.com
or the server that makes it available are free
of viruses or bugs. HarperCollins is not
responsible for any access difficulties that
may be experienced due to problems with
network, web, online or mobile phone
connections.

ÍNDICE		CONTENTS	
Introdução	v	Introduction	v
Abreviaturas usadas neste dicionário	vi	Abbreviations used in this dictionary	vi
Pronúncia	viii	Pronunciation guide	viii
Ortografia do português	xiii	Portuguese spelling	xiii
Verbos portugueses	xiv	Portuguese verb forms	xiv
Verbos ingleses	xvii	English verb forms	xvii
Números	xx	Numbers	xx
INGLÊS–PORTUGUÊS	1	ENGLISH–PORTUGUESE	1
PORTUGUÊS–INGLÊS	405	PORTUGUESE–ENGLISH	405

contributors/colaboradores
Carlos Ramires,
Nelly Wanderley Fernandes Porto,
Ana Maria de Mello e Souza,
Adriana Ceschin Rieche, Lígia Xavier,
Amos Maidantchik, Helio Leoncio Martins,
Jane Horwood

consultant/assessor
Dr Euzi Rodrigues Moraes

editorial staff/redação
Gerry Breslin, Joyce Littlejohn

William Collins' dream of knowledge
for all began with the publication of
his first book in 1819. A self-educated
mill worker, he not only enriched
millions of lives, but also founded a
flourishing publishing house. Today,
staying true to this spirit, Collins books
are packed with inspiration, innovation,
and practical expertise.
They place you at the centre of a world
of possibility and give you exactly what
you need to explore it.

Language is the key to this exploration,
and at the heart of Collins Dictionaries
is language as it is really used. New
words, phrases, and meanings spring
up every day, and all of them are
captured and analysed by the Collins
Word Web. Constantly updated, and
with over 2.5 billion entries, this living
language resource is unique to our
dictionaries.

Words are tools for life. And a Collins
Dictionary makes them work for you.

Collins. Do more.

INTRODUÇÃO

PARA COMPREENDER O INGLÊS

Este novo dicionário, completamente atualizado, fornece ao leitor uma cobertura ampla e prática dos usos lingüísticos mais comuns, incluindo a terminologia relativa à área empresarial e à microinformática, além de uma seleção abrangente de abreviaturas, siglas e topônimos encontrados freqüentemente na imprensa. Para facilitar as consultas do leitor, as formas irregulares de verbos e substantivos ingleses foram incluídas, com indicações que fazem referência à forma básica, onde uma tradução é dada.

PARA EXPRESSAR-SE EM INGLÊS

A fim de ajudar o leitor a expressar-se correta e idiomaticamente em inglês, foram incluídas várias indicações para orientá-lo quanto à tradução mais apropriada em um determinado contexto. Todas as palavras de uso mais comum receberam um tratamento detalhado, com muitos exemplos de utilização típica.

UM COMPANHEIRO DE TRABALHO

Todo o cuidado foi tomado para fazer deste novo dicionário da editora Collins uma obra totalmente confiável, fácil de ser usada e útil para o trabalho e estudos do leitor. Esperamos que ele seja um companheiro de longos anos no atendimento das necessidades de expressão numa língua estrangeira.

INTRODUCTION

UNDERSTANDING PORTUGUESE

This new and thoroughly up-to-date dictionary provides the user with wide-ranging, practical coverage of current usage, including terminology relevant to business and office automation, and a comprehensive selection of abbreviations, acronyms and geographical names commonly found in the press. You will also find, for ease of consultation, irregular forms of Portuguese verbs and nouns with a cross-reference to the basic form where a translation is given.

SELF-EXPRESSION IN PORTUGUESE

To help you express yourself correctly and idiomatically in Portuguese, numerous indications – think of them as signposts – guide you to the most appropriate translation for your context. All the most commonly used words are given detailed treatment, with many examples of typical usage.

A WORKING COMPANION

Much care has been taken to make this new Collins dictionary thoroughly reliable, easy to use and relevant to your work and study. We hope it will become a long-serving companion for all your foreign language needs.

ABREVIATURAS — ABBREVIATIONS

abreviatura	ab(b)r	abbreviation
adjetivo	adj	adjective
administração	Admin	administration
advérbio, locução adverbial	adv	adverb, adverbial phrase
aeronáutica	Aer	flying, air travel
agricultura	Agr	agriculture
anatomia	Anat	anatomy
arquitetura	Arq, Arch	architecture
artigo definido	art def	definite article
artigo indefinido	art indef	indefinite article
uso atributivo do substantivo	atr	compound element
automobilismo	Aut(o)	the motor car and motoring
auxiliar	aux	auxiliary
aeronáutica	Aviat	flying, air travel
biologia	Bio	biology
botânica, flores	Bot	botany
português do Brasil	BR	Brazilian Portuguese
inglês britânico	Brit	British English
química	Chem	chemistry
linguagem coloquial (!chulo)	col(!)	colloquial (offensive!)
comércio, finanças, bancos	Com(m)	commerce, finance, banking
comparativo	compar	comparative
computação	Comput	computing
conjunção	conj	conjunction
construção	Constr	building
uso atributivo do substantivo	cpd	compound element
cozinha	Culin	cookery
artigo definido	def art	definite article
economia	Econ	economics
educação, escola e universidade	Educ	schooling, schools and universities
eletricidade, eletrônica	Elet, Elec	electricity, electronics
especialmente	esp	especially
exclamação	excl	exclamation
feminino	f	feminine
ferrovia	Ferro	railways
uso figurado	fig	figurative use
física	Fís	physics
fisiologia	Fisiol	physiology
fotografia	Foto	photography
(verbo inglês) do qual a partícula é inseparável	fus	(phrasal verb) where the particle is inseparable
geralmente	gen	generally
geometria	Geom	geometry
geografia, geologia	Geo	geography, geology
geralmente	ger	generally
impessoal	impess, impers	impersonal
artigo indefinido	indef art	indefinite article
linguagem coloquial (!chulo)	inf(!)	colloquial (offensive!)

infinitivo	*infin*	infinitive
invariável	*inv*	invariable
irregular	*irreg*	irregular
jurídico	*Jur*	law
gramática, lingüística	*Ling*	grammar, linguistics
masculino	*m*	masculine
matemática	*Mat(h)*	mathematics
medicina	*Med*	medicine
ou masculino ou feminino, dependendo do sexo da pessoa	*m/f*	masculine/feminine
militar, exército	*Mil*	military matters
música	*Mús, Mus*	music
substantivo	*n*	noun
navegação, náutica	*Náut, Naut*	sailing, navigation
adjetivo ou substantivo numérico	*num*	numeral adjective or noun
	o.s.	oneself
pejorativo	*pej*	pejorative
fotografia	*Phot*	photography
física	*Phys*	physics
fisiologia	*Physiol*	physiology
plural	*pl*	plural
política	*Pol*	politics
particípio passado	*pp*	past participle
preposição	*prep*	preposition
pronome	*pron*	pronoun
psicologia, psiquiatria	*Psico, Psych*	psychology, psychiatry
português de Portugal	*PT*	European Portuguese
pretérito	*pt*	past tense
química	*Quím*	chemistry
religião e cultos	*Rel*	religion, church services
	sb	somebody
educação, escola e universidade	*Sch*	schooling, schools and universities
singular	*sg*	singular
	sth	something
sujeito (gramatical)	*su(b)j*	(grammatical) subject
subjuntivo, conjuntivo	*sub(jun)*	subjunctive
superlativo	*superl*	superlative
também	*tb*	also
técnica, tecnologia	*Tec(h)*	technical term, technology
telecomunicações	*Tel*	telecommunications
tipografia, imprensa	*Tip*	typography, printing
televisão	*TV*	television
tipografia, imprensa	*Typ*	typography, printing
inglês americano	*US*	American English
ver	*V*	see
verbo	*vb*	verb
verbo intransitivo	*vi*	intransitive verb
verbo reflexivo	*vr*	reflexive verb
verbo transitivo	*vt*	transitive verb
zoologia	*Zool*	zoology
marca registrada	®	registered trademark
equivalente cultural	≈	cultural equivalent

PORTUGUESE PRONUNCIATION

The rules given below refer to Portuguese as spoken in the city and surrounding region of Rio de Janeiro, Brazil.

CONSONANTS

c	[k]	café	*c* before *a, o, u* is pronounced as in *c*at
ce, ci	[s]	cego	*c* before *e* or *i*, as in re*c*eive
ç	[s]	raça	*ç* is pronounced as in re*c*eive
ch	[ʃ]	chave	*ch* is pronounced as in *sh*ock
d	[d]	data	as in English EXCEPT *d* before an *i* sound or final
de, di	[dʒ]	difícil, cidade	unstressed *e* is pronounced as in ju*dge*
g	[g]	gado	*g* before *a, o, u* as in *g*ap
ge, gi	[ʒ]	gíria	*g* before *e* or *i*, as *s* in lei*s*ure
h		humano	*h* is always silent in Portuguese
j	[ʒ]	jogo	*j* is pronounced as *s* in lei*s*ure
l	[l]	limpo, janela	as in English EXCEPT *l* after a vowel tends to
	[w]	falta, total	become *w*
lh	[ʎ]	trabalho	*lh* is pronounced like the *lli* in mi*lli*on
m	[m]	animal, massa	as in English EXCEPT *m* at the end of a syllable,
	[ãw]	cantam	preceded by a vowel nasalizes the preceding vowel
	[ĩ]	sim	
n	[n]	nadar, penal	as in English EXCEPT *n* at the end of a syllable,
	[ã]	cansar	preceded by a vowel and followed by a consonant,
	[ẽ]	alento	nasalizes the preceding vowel
nh	[ɲ]	tamanho	*nh* is pronounced like the *ni* in o*ni*on
q	[k]	queijo	*qu* before *i* or *e* is pronounced as in *k*ick
q	[kw]	quanto	*qu* before *a* or *o*, or *qü* before *e* or *i*, is pronounced as
		cinqüenta	in *qu*een
-r-	[r]	compra	*r* preceded by a consonant (except *n*) and followed
			by a vowel is pronounced with a single trill
r-, -r-	[x]	rato, arpão	inital *r, r* followed by a consonant and *rr* pronounced
rr	[x]	borracha	similar to the Scottish *ch* in lo*ch*
-r	[*]	pintar, dizer	word-final *r* before a word beginning with a
			consonant or at the end of a sentence is
			pronounced [x]; before a word beginning with a
			vowel it ispronounced [r]. In colloquial speech
			this variable sound is often not pronounced at all
s-	[s]	sol	as in English EXCEPT intervocalic *s* is pronounced
-s-	[z]	mesa	as in ro*s*e
-s-	[ʒ]	rasgar, desmaio	*s* before *b, d, g, l, m, n, r,* and *v*, as in lei*s*ure
-s-, -s	[ʃ]	escada, livros	*s* before *c, f, p, qu, t* and finally, as in *s*ugar
-ss-	[s]	nosso	double *s* is always pronounced as in bo*ss*
t	[t]	todo	as in English EXCEPT *t* followed by an *i* sound or
te, ti	[tʃ]	amante, tipo	final unstressed *e* is pronounced as *ch* in *ch*eer
x-	[ʃ]	xarope	initial *x* or *x* before a consonant (except *c*) is
		explorar	pronounced as in *s*ugar
-xce-,	[s]	exceto	*x* before *ce* or *ci* is unpronounced
-xci-		excitar	

ex-	[z]	exame	x in the prefix ex before a vowel is pronounced as z in squeeze
-x-	[ʃ]	relaxar	x in any other position may be pronounced
	[ks]	fixo	as in sugar, axe or sail
	[s]	auxiliar	
z-, -z-	[z]	zangar	as in English EXCEPT final z is pronounced as
-z	[ʒ]	cartaz	in leisure

b, f, k, p, v, w are pronounced as in English.

VOWELS

a, á, à, â	[a]	mata	a is normally pronounced as in father
ã	[ã]	irmã	ã is pronounced approximately as in sung
e	[e]	vejo	unstressed (except final) e is pronounced like e in they, stressed e is pronounced either as in they or as in bet
-e	[i]	fome	final e is pronounced as in money
é	[ɛ]	miséria	é is pronounced as in bet
ê	[e]	pêlo	ê is pronounced as in they
i	[i]	vida	i is pronounced as in mean
o	[o]	locomotiva	unstressed (except final) o is pronounced as in local;
	[ɔ]	loja	stressed o is pronounced either as in local or as
	[o]	globo	in rock
-o	[u]	livro	final o is pronounced as in foot
ó	[ɔ]	óleo	ó is pronounced as in rock
ô	[o]	colônia	ô is pronounced as in local
u	[u]	luva	u is pronounced as in rule; it is silent in gue, gui, que and qui

DIPHTHONGS

ãe	[ãj]	mãe	nasalized, approximately as in flying
ai	[aj]	vai	as in ride
ao, au	[aw]	aos, auxílio	as in shout
ão	[ãw]	vão	nasalized, approximately as in round
ei	[ej]	feira	as in they
eu	[ew]	deusa	both elements pronounced
oi	[oj]	boi	as in toy
ou	[o]	cenoura	as in local
õe	[õj]	aviões	nasalized, approximately as in 'boing!'

STRESS

The rules of stress in Portuguese are as follows:

(a) when a word ends in a, e, o, m (except im, um and their plural forms) or s, the second last syllable is stressed: camarada, camaradas, parte, partem
(b) when a word ends in i, u, im (and plural), um (and plural), n or a consonant other than m or s, the stress falls on the last syllable: vendi, algum, alguns, falar
(c) when the rules set out in (a) and (b) are not applicable, an acute or circumflex accent appears over the stressed vowel: ótica, ânimo, inglês

In the phonetic transcription, the symbol ['] precedes the syllable on which the stress falls.

EUROPEAN PRONUNCIATION

The pronunciation of Brazilian Portuguese differs quite markedly from the Portuguese spoken in Portugal itself and in the African and island states. The more phonetic nature of Brazilian means that words nearly always retain their set pronunciation; in European Portuguese, on the other hand, vowels can often be unpronounced or weakened and consonants can change their sound, all depending on their position within a word or whether they are being elided with a following word. The major differences in pronunciation of European Portuguese are as follows:-

CONSONANTS: as in Brazilian, except:

-b-	[β]	cuba	*b* between vowels is a softer sound, closer to have
d	[d]	dança, difícil	as in English EXCEPT *d* between vowels is softer,
-d-	[ð]	fado, cidade	approximately as in the
-g-	[ɣ]	saga	*g* between vowels is a softer sound, approximately as in lager
gu	[ɣw]	aguentar	in certain words *gu* is pronounced as in Gwent
qu	[kw]	tranquilo	in certain words *qu* is pronounced as in quoits
r-, rr	[ʀ]		initial *r* and double *r* are pronounced either like the
	[rr]		French *r* or strongly trilled as in Scottish Rory; pronunciation varies according to region
-r-, -r	[r]	rato, arma	*r* in any other position is slightly trilled
t	[t]	todo, amante	*t* is pronounced as in English
z	[ʒ]	zangar	as in English EXCEPT final *z* is pronounced as *sh* in flash
	[ʃ]	cartaz	

VOWELS: as in Brazilian, except:

a	[a]	falar	stressed *a* is pronounced either as in father or as
	[ɐ]	cama	*u* in further
-a-, -a	[ə]	falar, fala	unstressed or final *a* is pronounced as *e* in further
e	[ə]	medir	unstressed *e* is a very short *i* sound as in rabbit
-e	[ə]	arte, regime	final *e* is barely pronounced; these would sound like English *art* and *regime*
o	[u]	poço, poder	unstressed or final *o* is pronounced as in foot

PRONÚNCIA INGLESA

Em geral, damos a pronúncia de cada verbete em colchetes logo após a palavra em questão. Todavia, quando a verbete for composto de duas ou mais palavras, e cada uma delas aparecer em outro lugar no dicionário, o leitor encontrará a pronúncia de cada palavra na sua posição alfabética.

VOGAIS

	Exemplo Inglês	Explicação
[aː]	father	Entre o *a* de p*a*dre e o *o* de n*ó*; como em f*a*da
[ʌ]	but, come	Aproximadamente como o primeiro *a* de c*a*ma
[æ]	man, cat	Som entre o *a* de l*á* e o *e* de p*é*
[ə]	father, ago	Som parecido com o *e* final pronuncia do em Portugal
[əː]	bird, heard	Entre o *e* aberto e o *o* fechado
[ɛ]	get, bed	Como em p*é*
[ɪ]	it, big	Mais breve do que em s*i*
[iː]	tea, see	Como em f*i*no
[ɔ]	hot, wash	Como em p*ó*
[ɔː]	saw, all	Como o *o* de p*o*rte
[u]	put, book	Som breve e mais fechado do que em b*u*rro
[uː]	too, you	Som aberto como em j*u*ro

DITONGOS

	Exemplo Inglês	Explicação
[aɪ]	fly, high	Como em b*ai*le
[au]	how, house	Como em c*au*sa
[ɛə]	there, bear	Como o *e* de a*e*roporto
[eɪ]	day, obey	Como o *ei* de l*ei*
[ɪə]	here, hear	Como *ia* de companh*ia*
[əu]	go, note	[ə] seguido de um *u* breve
[ɔɪ]	boy, oil	Como em b*ói*a
[uə]	poor, sure	Como *ua* em s*ua*

CONSOANTES

	Exemplo Inglês	Explicação
[d]	mended	Como em *d*a*d*o, an*d*ar
[g]	get, big	Como em *g*rande
[dʒ]	gin, judge	Como em ida*d*e
[ŋ]	sing	Como em ci*n*co
[h]	house, he	*h* aspirado
[j]	young, yes	Como em *i*ogurte
[k]	come, mock	Como em *c*ama
[r]	red, tread	*r* como em pa*r*a, mas pronunciado no céu da boca
[s]	sand, yes	Como em *s*ala
[z]	rose, zebra	Como em *z*ebra
[ʃ]	she, machine	Como em *ch*apéu
[tʃ]	chin, rich	Como *t* em *t*imbre
[w]	water, which	Como o *u* em ág*u*a

[ʒ]	vision	Como em já
[θ]	think, myth	Sem equivalente, aproximadamente como um s
		pronunciado entre os dentes
[ð]	this, the	Sem equivalente, aproximadamente como um z
		pronunciado entre os dentes

b, f, l, m, n, p, t, v pronunciam-se como em português.

O signo [*] indica que o r final escrito pronuncia-se apenas em inglês britânico, exceto quando a palavra seguinte começa por uma vogal. O signo ['] indica a sílaba acentuada.

PORTUGUESE SPELLING

The spelling of Portuguese as it is used in Europe differs significantly from that of Brazilian Portuguese. The differences, which affect consonant groups and accents, follow general patterns but do not on the whole conform to fixed rules. Limited space makes it impossible to cover all European forms in the dictionary text, but major differences in spelling and vocabulary have been included. In addition, the following guide is intended as a broad outline of these differences.

The following changes in spelling are consistent:

- Brazilian *gü* and *qü* become European *gu* and *qu*, e.g. agüentar (BR), aguentar (PT); cinqüenta (BR), cinquenta (PT).
- Brazilian -*éia* becomes European -*eia*, e.g. idéia (BR), ideia (PT).
- European spelling links forms of the verb *haver de* with a hyphen, e.g. *hei de* (BR), *hei-de* (PT).
- The numbers dezesseis (BR), dezessete(BR), dezenove (BR) become dezasseis (PT), dezassete (PT), dezanove (PT).
- Adverbial forms of adjectives ending in *m* take double *m* in European spelling, single *m* in Brazilian, e.g. comumente (BR), comummente (PT).
- European spelling adds an acute accent to the final *a* in first person plural preterite forms of irregular -*ar* verbs to distinguish them from the present tense, e.g. amamos (BR), amámos (PT).
- Brazilian conosco becomes European connosco.

The following changes may take place, but are not consistent:

CONSONANT CHANGES
- Brazilian *c* and *ç* double to *cc* and *cç*, acionista (BR), accionista (PT), seção (BR), secção (PT).
- Brazilian *t* becomes *ct*, e.g. elétrico (BR), eléctrico (PT).
- European spelling adds *b* to certain words, e.g. súdito (BR), súbdito (PT), sutilizar (BR), subtilizar (PT).
- European spelling changes *ç*, *t* to *pç*, *pt* , e.g. exceção (BR), excepção (PT), ótimo (BR), óptimo (PT).
- Brazilian -*n*- becomes -*mn*-, e.g. anistia (BR), amnistia (PT).
- Brazilian *tr* becomes *t*, e.g. registro (BR), registo (PT).

ACCENTUATION CHANGES
- Brazilian *ôo* loses circumflex accent, e.g. vôo (BR), voo (PT).
- European spelling changes circumflex accent on *e* and *o* to acute, e.g. tênis (BR), ténis (PT), abdômen (BR), abdómen (PT).

PORTUGUESE VERB FORMS

1 Gerund. 2 Imperative. 3 Present. 4 Imperfect. 5 Preterite. 6 Future.
7 Present subjunctive. 8 Imperfect subjunctive. 9 Future subjunctive.
10 Past participle. 11 Pluperfect. 12 Personal infinitive.

etc indicates that the irregular root is used for all persons of the tense, e.g. **ouvir 7**
ouça ouça, ouças, ouça, ouçamos, ouçais, ouçam.

abrir 10 aberto
acudir 2 acode 3 acudo, acodes, acode,
   acodem
aderir 3 adiro 7 adira
advertir 3 advirto 7 advirta *etc*
agir 3 ajo 7 aja *etc*
agradecer 3 agradeço 7 agradeça *etc*
agredir 2 agride 3 agrido, agrides, agride,
   agridem 7 agrida *etc*
AMAR 1 amando 2 ama, amai 3 amo,
   amas, ama, amamos, amais, amam
   4 amava, amavas, amava, amávamos,
   amavéis, amavam 5 amei, amaste,
   amou, amamos (*PT*: amámos),
   amastes, amaram 6 amarei, amarás,
   amará, amaremos, amareis, amarão
   7 ame, ames, ame, amemos, ameis,
   amem
   8 amasse, amasses, amasse,
   amássemos, amásseis, amassem
   9 amar, amares, amar, ámarmos,
   amardes, amarem 10 amado 11 amara,
   amaras, amara, amáramos, amáreis,
   amaram 12 amar, amares, amar,
   amarmos, amardes, amarem
ansiar 2 anseia 3 anseio, anseias, anseia,
   anseiam 7 anseie *etc*
apreçar 7 aprece *etc*
arrancar 7 arranque *etc*
arruinar 2 arruína 3 arruíno, arruínas,
   arruína, arruínam 7 arruíne, arruínes,
   arruíne, arruínem
aspergir 3 aspirjo 7 aspirja *etc*
atribuir 3 atribuo, atribuis, atribui,
   atribuímos, atribuís, atribuem
averiguar 7 averigúe, averigúes,
   averigúe, averigúem
boiar 2 bóia, bóias, bóia, bóiam 7 bóie,
   bóies, bóie, bóiem

bulir 2 bole 3 bulo, boles, bole, bolem
caber 3 caibo 5 coube *etc* 7 caiba *etc*
   8 coubesse *etc* 9 couber *etc*
cair 2 cai 3 caio, cais, cai, caímos, caís,
   caem 4 caía *etc* 5 caí, caíste 7 caia *etc*
   8 caisse *etc*
cobrir 3 cubro 7 cubra *etc* 10 coberto
colorir 3 coluro 7 colura *etc*
compelir 3 compilo 7 compila *etc*
crer 2 crê 3 creio, crês, crê, cremos,
   credes, crêem 5 cri, creste, creu,
   cremos, crestes, creram 7 creia *etc*
cuspir 2 cospe 3 cuspo, cospes, cospe,
   cospem
dar 2 dá 3 dou, dás, dá, damos, dais, dão
   5 dei, deste, deu, demos, destes, deram
   7 dê, dês, dê, demos, deis, dêem 8 desse
   etc 9 der *etc* 11 dera *etc*
deduzir 2 deduz 3 deduzo, deduzes, deduz
denegrir 2 denigre 3 denigro, denigres,
   denigre, denigrem 7 denigre *etc*
despir 3 dispo 7 dispa *etc*
dizer 2 diz (dize) 3 digo, dizes, diz, dizemos,
   dizeis, dizem 5 disse *etc* 6 direi *etc* 7 diga
   etc 8 dissesse *etc* 9 disser *etc* 10 dito
doer 2 dói 3 dôo (*BR*), doo (*PT*), dóis, dói
dormir 3 durmo 7 durma *etc*
escrever 10 escrito
ESTAR 2 está 3 estou, estás, está,
   estamos, estais, estão 4 estava *etc*
   5 estive, estiveste, esteve, estivemos,
   estivestes, estiveram 7 esteja *etc*
   8 estivesse *etc* 9 estiver *etc* 11 estivera *etc*
extorquir 3 exturco 7 exturca *etc*
FAZER 2 faço 3 faz, fizeste, fez, fizemos,
   fizestes, fizeram 6 farei *etc* 7 faça *etc*
   8 fizesse *etc* 9 fizer *etc* 10 feito 11 fizera *etc*
ferir 3 firo 7 fira *etc*
fluir 3 fluo, fluis, flui, fluímos, fluís, fluem

fugir 2 foge 3 fujo, foges, foge, fogem
  7 fuja *etc*
ganhar 10 ganho
gastar 10 gasto
gerir 3 giro 7 gira *etc*
haver 2 há 3 hei, hás, há, havemos, haveis,
  hão 4 havia *etc* 5 houve, houveste,
  houve, houvemos, houvestes,
  houveram 7 haja *etc* 8 houvesse *etc*
  9 houver *etc* 11 houvera *etc*
ir 1 indo 2 vai 3 vou, vais, vai, vamos,
  ides, vão 4 ia *etc* 5 fui, foste, foi, fomos,
  fostes, foram 7 vá, vás, vá, vamos,
  vades, vão 8 fosse, fosses, fosse,
  fôssemos, fôsseis, fossem 9 for *etc*
  10 ido 11 fora *etc*
ler 2 lê 3 leio, lês, lê, lemos, ledes, lêem
  5 li, leste, leu, lemos, lestes, leram
  7 leia *etc*
medir 3 meço, 7 meça *etc*
mentir 3 minto 7 minta *etc*
ouvir 3 ouço 7 ouça *etc*
pagar 10 pago
parar 2 pára 3 paro, paras, pára
parir 3 pairo 7 paira *etc*
pecar 7 peque *etc*
pedir 3 peço 7 peça *etc*
perder 3 perco 7 perca *etc*
poder 3 posso 5 pude, pudeste, pôde,
  pudemos, pudestes, puderam 7 possa
  etc 8 pudesse *etc* 9 puder *etc* 11 pudera *etc*
polir 2 pule 3 pulo, pules, pule, pulem
  7 pula *etc*
pôr 1 pondo 2 põe 3 ponho, pões, põe,
  pomos, pondes, põem 4 punha *etc*
  5 pus, puseste, pôs, pusemos, pusestes,
  puseram 6 porei *etc* 7 ponha *etc*
  8 pusesse *etc* 9 puser *etc* 10 posto
  11 pusera *etc*
preferir 3 prefiro 7 prefire *etc*
pervenir 2 previne 3 previno, prevines,
  previne, previnem 7 previna *etc*
prover 2 provê 3 provejo, provês, provê,
  provemos, provedes, provêem 5 provi,
  proveste, proveu, provemos, provestes,
  proveram 7 proveja *etc* 8 provesse *etc*
  9 prover *etc*
querer 3 quero, queres, quer 5 quis,
  quiseste, quis, quisemos, quisestes,

quiseram 7 queira *etc* 8 quisesse *etc*
  9 quiser *etc* 11 quisera *etc*
refletir 3 reflito 7 reflita *etc*
repetir 3 repito 7 repita *etc*
requerer 3 requeiro, requeres, requer 7
  requeira *etc*
reunir 2 reúne 3 reúno, reúnes, reúne,
  reúnem 7 reúna *etc*
rir 2 ri 3 rio, ris, ri, rimos, rides, ridem
  5 ri, riste, riu, rimos, ristes, riram
  7 ria *etc*
saber 3 sei, sabes, sabe, sabemos,
  sabeis, sabem 5 soube, soubeste, soube,
  soubemos, soubestes, souberam 7 saiba
  etc 8 soubesse *etc* 9 souber *etc* 11 soubera
  etc
seguir 3 sigo 7 siga *etc*
sentir 3 sinto 7 sinta *etc*
ser 2 sê 3 sou, és, é, somos, sois, são 4 era
  etc 5 fui, foste, foi, fomos, fostes, foram
  7 seja *etc* 8 fosse *etc* 9 for *etc* 11 fora *etc*
servir 3 sirvo 7 sirva *etc*
subir 2 sobe 3 subo, sobes, sobe, sobem
suster 2 sustém 3 sustenho, sustens,
  sustém, sustendes, sustêm 5 sustive,
  sustiveste, susteve, sustivemos,
  sustivestes, sustiveram 7 sustenha *etc*
ter 2 tem 3 tenho, tens, tem, temos,
  tendes, têm 4 tinha *etc* 5 tive, tiveste,
  teve, tivemos, tivestes, tiveram 6 terei
  etc 7 tenha *etc* 8 tivesse *etc* 9 tiver *etc*
  11 tivera *etc*
torcer 3 torço 7 torça *etc*
tossir 3 tusso 7 tussa *etc*
trair 2 trai 3 traio, trais, trai, traímos,
  traís, traem 7 traia *etc*
trazer 2 (traze) traz 3 trago, trazes, traz,
  5 trouxe, trouxeste, trouxe, trouxemos,
  trouxestes, trouxeram 6 trarei *etc*
  7 traga *etc* 8 trouxesse *etc* 9 trouxer *etc*
  11 trouxera *etc*
UNIR 1 unindo 2 une, uni 3 uno, unes,
  une, unimos, unis, unem 4 unia,
  unias, uníamos, uníeis, uniam 5 uni,
  uniste, uniu, unimos, unistes, uniram
  6 unirei, unirás, unirá, uniremos,
  unireis, unirão 7 una, unas, una,
  unamos, unais, unam 8 unisse,
  unisses, unisse, uníssemos, unísseis,

unissem 9 unir, unires, unir, unirmos, unirdes, unirem 10 unido 11 unira, uniras, unira, uníramos, uníreis, uniram 12 unir, unires, unir, unirmos, unirdes, unirem

valer 3 valho 7 valha *etc*

ver 2 vê 3 vejo, vês, vê, vemos, vedes, vêem 4 via *etc* 5 vi, viste, viu, vimos, vistes, viram 7 veja *etc* 8 visse *etc* 9 vir *etc* 10 visto 11 vira

vir 1 vindo, 2 vem 3 venho, vens, vem, vimos, vindes, vêm 4 vinha *etc* 5 vim, vieste, veio, viemos, viestes, vieram 7 venha *etc* 8 viesse *etc* 9 vier *etc* 10 vindo 11 viera *etc*

VIVER 1 vivendo 2 vive, vivei 3 vivo, vives, vive, vivemos, viveis, vivem 4 vivia, vivias, vivia, vivíamos, vivíeis, viviam 5 vivi, viveste, viveu, vivemos, vivestes, viveram 6 viverei, viverás, viverá, viveremos, vivereis, viverão 7 viva, vivas, viva, vivamos, vivais, vivam 8 vivesse, vivesses, vivesse, vivêssemos, vivêsseis, vivessem 9 viver, viveres, viver, vivermos, viverdes, viverem 10 vivido 11 vivera, viveras, vivera, vivêramos, vivêreis, viveram 12 viver, viveres, viver, vivermos, viverdes, viverem

VERBOS IRREGULARES EM INGLÊS

PRESENT	PT	PP	PRESENT	PT	PP
arise	arose	arisen	find	found	found
awake	awoke	awoken	fling	flung	flung
be (am, is, are; being)	was, were	been	fly	flew	flown
			forbid	forbad(e)	forbidden
bear	bore	born(e)	forecast	forecast	forecast
beat	beat	beaten	forget	forgot	forgotten
begin	began	begun	forgive	forgave	forgiven
bend	bent	bent	freeze	froze	frozen
bet	bet, betted	bet, betted	get	got	got, (US) goten
bid (at auction)	bid	bid	give	gave	given
bind	bound	bound	go (goes)	went	gone
bite	bit	bitten	grind	ground	ground
bleed	bled	bled	grow	grew	grown
blow	blew	blown	hang	hung	hung
break	broke	broken	hang (execute)	hanged	hanged
breed	bred	bred	have	had	had
bring	brought	brought	hear	heard	heard
build	built	built	hide	hid	hidden
burn	burnt, burned	burnt, burned	hit	hit	hit
			hold	held	held
burst	burst	burst	hurt	hurt	hurt
buy	bought	bought	keep	kept	kept
can	could	(been able)	kneel	knelt, kneeled	knelt, kneeled
cast	cast	cast			
catch	caught	caught	know	knew	known
choose	chose	chosen	lay	laid	laid
cling	clung	clung	lead	led	led
come	came	come	lean	leant, leaned	leant, leaned
cost	cost	cost			
creep	crept	crept	leap	leapt, leaped	leapt, leaped
cut	cut	cut			
deal	dealt	dealt	learn	learnt, learned	learnt, learned
dig	dug	dug			
do (does)	did	done	leave	left	left
draw	drew	drawn	lend	lent	lent
dream	dreamed, dreamt	dreamed, dreamt	let	let	let
			lie (lying)	lay	lain
drink	drank	drunk	light	lit, lighted	lit, lighted
drive	drove	driven			
eat	ate	eaten	lose	lost	lost
fall	fell	fallen	make	made	made
feed	fed	fed	may	might	–
feel	felt	felt	mean	meant	meant
fight	fought	fought	meet	met	met

xvii

PRESENT	PT	PP	PRESENT	PT	PP
mistake	mistook	mistaken	speed	sped,	sped,
mow	mowed	mown,		speeded	speeded
		mowed	spell	spelt,	spelt,
must	(had to)	(had to)		spelled	spelled
pay	paid	paid	spend	spent	spent
put	put	put	spill	spilt,	spilt,
quit	quit,	quit,		spilled	spilled
	quitted	quitted	spin	spun	spun
read	read	read	spit	spat	spat
rid	rid	rid	spoil	spoiled,	spoiled,
ride	rode	ridden		spoilt	spoilt
ring	rang	rung	spread	spread	spread
rise	rose	risen	spring	sprang	sprung
run	ran	run	stand	stood	stood
saw	sawed	sawed,	steal	stole	stolen
		sawn	stick	stuck	stuck
say	said	said	sting	stung	stung
see	saw	seen	stink	stank	stunk
sell	sold	sold	stride	strode	stridden
send	sent	sent	strike	struck	struck
set	set	set	swear	swore	sworn
sew	sewed	sewn	sweep	swept	swept
shake	shook	shaken	swell	swelled	swollen,
shear	sheared	shorn,			swelled
		sheared	swim	swam	swum
shed	shed	shed	swing	swung	swung
shine	shone	shone	take	took	taken
shoot	shot	shot	teach	taught	taught
show	showed	shown	tear	tore	torn
shrink	shrank	shrunk	tell	told	told
shut	shut	shut	think	thought	thought
sing	sang	sung	throw	threw	thrown
sink	sank	sunk	thrust	thrust	thrust
sit	sat	sat	tread	trod	trodden
sleep	slept	slept	wake	woke,	woken,
slide	slid	slid		waked	waked
sling	slung	slung	wear	wore	worn
slit	slit	slit	weave	wove	woven
smell	smelt,	smelt,	weep	wept	wept
	smelled	smelled	win	won	won
sow	sowed	sown,	wind	wound	wound
		sowed	wring	wrung	wrung
speak	spoke	spoken	write	wrote	written

NÚMEROS

NUMBERS

NÚMEROS CARDINAIS

CARDINAL NUMBERS

um (uma)	1	one
dois (duas)	2	two
três	3	three
quatro	4	four
cinco	5	five
seis	6	six
sete	7	seven
oito	8	eight
nove	9	nine
dez	10	ten
onze	11	eleven
doze	12	twelve
treze	13	thirteen
catorze	14	fourteen
quinze	15	fifteen
dezesseis (BR), dezasseis (PT)	16	sixteen
dezessete (BR), dezassete (PT)	17	seventeen
dezoito	18	eighteen
dezenove (BR), dezanove (PT)	19	nineteen
vinte	20	twenty
vinte e um (uma)	21	twenty-one
trinta	30	thirty
quarenta	40	forty
cinqüenta (BR), cinquenta (PT)	50	fifty
sessenta	60	sixty
setenta	70	seventy
oitenta	80	eighty
noventa	90	ninety
cem	100	a hundred
cento e um (uma)	101	a hundred and one
duzentos(-as)	200	two hundred
trezentos(-as)	300	three hundred
quinhentos(-as)	500	five hundred
mil	1.000/1,000	a thousand
um milhão	1.000.000/1,000,000	a million

NÚMEROS

NUMBERS

NUMBERS

FRAÇÕES ETC		FRACTIONS ETC
zero vírgula cinco	0,5/0.5	zero point five
três vírgula quatro	3,4/3.4	three point four
dez por cento	10%	ten per cent
cem por cento	100%	a hundred per cent

NÚMEROS ORDINAIS		ORDINAL NUMBERS
primeiro	1°/1st	first
segundo	2°/2nd	second
terceiro	3°/3rd	third
quarto	4°/4th	fourth
quinto	5°/5th	fifth
sexto	6°/6th	sixth
sétimo	7°/7th	seventh
oitavo	8°/8th	eighth
nono	9°/9th	ninth
décimo	10°/10th	tenth
décimo primeiro	11°/11th	eleventh
vigésimo	20°/20th	twentieth
trigésimo	30°/30th	thirtieth
quadragésimo	40°/40th	fortieth
qüinquagésimo(BR), quinquagésimo(PT)	50°/50th	fiftieth
centésimo	100°/100th	hundredth
centésimo primeiro	101°/101st	hundred-and-first
milésimo	1000°/1000th	thousandth

Aa

A, a [eɪ] N (letter) A, a m; (Mus): **A** lá m; **A for Andrew** (Brit) or **Able** (US) A de Antônio; **A road** (Brit: Aut) via expressa; **A shares** (Brit: Stock Exchange) ações fpl preferenciais a

O KEYWORD

a [eɪ, ə] INDEF ART (before vowel or silent h: an)
1 um(a); **a book/girl/mirror** um livro/uma menina/um espelho; **an apple** uma maçã; **she's a doctor** ela é médica
2 (instead of the number "one") um(a); **a year ago** há um ano, um ano atrás; **a hundred/thousand** etc **pounds** cem/mil etc libras
3 (in expressing ratios, prices etc): **3 a day/week** 3 por dia/semana; **10 km an hour** 10 km por hora; **30p a kilo** 30p o quilo

a. ABBR = **acre**
AA N ABBR (= Alcoholics Anonymous) AA m; (Brit: = Automobile Association) ≈ TCB m (BR), ≈ ACP m (PT); (US: = Associate in/of Arts) título universitário; (: = anti-aircraft) AA
AAA N ABBR (= American Automobile Association) ≈ TCB m (BR), ≈ ACP m (PT); (Brit) = **Amateur Athletics Association**
AAUP N ABBR (= American Association of University Professors) sindicato universitário
AB ABBR (Brit) = **able-bodied seaman**; (Canadian) = **Alberta**
abaci ['æbəsaɪ] NPL of **abacus**
aback [ə'bæk] ADV: **to be taken ~** ficar surpreendido, sobressaltar-se
abacus ['æbəkəs] (pl **abaci**) N ábaco
abandon [ə'bændən] VT abandonar ■ N (wild behaviour): **with ~** com desenfreio; **to ~ ship** abandonar o navio
abandoned [ə'bændənd] ADJ (child, house) abandonado; (unrestrained) desenfreado
abase [ə'beɪs] VT: **to ~ o.s. (so far as to do)** rebaixar-se (até o ponto de fazer)
abashed [ə'bæʃt] ADJ envergonhado
abate [ə'beɪt] VI (lessen) diminuir; (calm down) acalmar-se
abatement [ə'beɪtmənt] N see **noise**
abattoir ['æbətwɑːʳ] (Brit) N matadouro
abbey ['æbɪ] N abadia, mosteiro

abbot ['æbət] N abade m
abbreviate [ə'briːvɪeɪt] VT (essay) resumir; (word) abreviar
abbreviation [əbriːvɪ'eɪʃən] N (short form) abreviatura; (act) abreviação f
ABC N ABBR (= American Broadcasting Company) rede de televisão
abdicate ['æbdɪkeɪt] VT abdicar, renunciar a ■ VI abdicar, renunciar ao trono
abdication [æbdɪ'keɪʃən] N abdicação f
abdomen ['æbdəmən] N abdômen m
abdominal [æb'dɔmɪnl] ADJ abdominal
abduct [æb'dʌkt] VT seqüestrar
abduction [æb'dʌkʃən] N seqüestro
Aberdonian [æbə'dəunɪən] ADJ de Aberdeen ■ N natural m/f de Aberdeen
aberration [æbə'reɪʃən] N aberração f; **in a moment of mental ~** num momento de desatino
abet [ə'bɛt] VT see **aid**
abeyance [ə'beɪəns] N: **in ~** (law) em desuso; (matter) suspenso
abhor [əb'hɔːʳ] VT detestar, odiar
abhorrent [əb'hɔrənt] ADJ detestável, repugnante
abide [ə'baɪd] VT agüentar, suportar; **I can't ~ him** eu não o soporto
▶ **abide by** VT FUS (promise, word) cumprir; (law, rules) ater-se a
ability [ə'bɪlɪtɪ] N habilidade f, capacidade f; (talent) talento; (skill) perícia; **to the best of my ~** o melhor que eu puder or pudesse
abject ['æbdʒɛkt] ADJ (poverty) miserável; (coward) desprezível, vil; **an ~ apology** um pedido de desculpa humilde
ablaze [ə'bleɪz] ADJ em chamas; **~ with light** resplandecente
able ['eɪbl] ADJ capaz; (skilled) hábil, competente; **to be ~ to do sth** poder fazer algo
able-bodied [-'bɔdɪd] ADJ são(-sã); **~ seaman** (Brit) marinheiro experimentado
ably ['eɪblɪ] ADV habilmente
ABM N ABBR = **anti-ballistic missile**
abnormal [æb'nɔːməl] ADJ anormal
abnormality [æbnɔː'mælɪtɪ] N anormalidade f
aboard [ə'bɔːd] ADV a bordo ■ PREP a bordo de; (train) dentro de

abode [ə'bəud] N (old) residência, domicílio; (Law): **of no fixed ~** sem domicílio fixo

abolish [ə'bɔlɪʃ] VT abolir

abolition [æbə'lɪʃən] N abolição f

abominable [ə'bɔmɪnəbl] ADJ abominável, detestável

aborigine [æbə'rɪdʒɪnɪ] N aborígene m/f

abort [ə'bɔ:t] VT (Med) abortar; (plan) fracassar

abortion [ə'bɔ:ʃən] N aborto; **to have an ~** fazer um aborto

abortive [ə'bɔ:tɪv] ADJ (failed) fracassado; (fruitless) inútil

abound [ə'baund] VI: **to ~ (in** or **with)** abundar (em)

◯ KEYWORD

about [ə'baut] ADV 1 (approximately) aproximadamente; **it takes about 10 hours** leva mais ou menos 10 horas; **at about 2 o'clock** aproximadamente às duas horas; **it's just about finished** está quase terminado

2 (referring to place) por toda parte, por todo lado; **to run/walk** etc **about** correr/andar etc por todos os lados

3: **to be about to do sth** estar a ponto de fazer algo

■ PREP 1 (relating to) acerca de, sobre; **a book about London** um livro sobre Londres; **what is it about?** do que se trata?, é sobre o quê?; **we talked about it** nós falamos sobre isso; **what** or **how about doing this?** que tal se fizermos isso?

2 (place) em redor de, por; **to walk about the town** andar pela cidade

about face N (Mil) meia-volta; (fig) reviravolta

about turn N = **about face**

above [ə'bʌv] ADV em or por cima, acima ■ PREP acima de, por cima de; **mentioned ~** acima mencionado; **costing ~ £10** que custa mais de £10; **~ all** sobretudo

aboveboard [ə'bʌv'bɔ:d] ADJ legítimo, limpo

abrasion [ə'breɪʒən] N (on skin) esfoladura

abrasive [ə'breɪzɪv] ADJ abrasivo; (fig: person) cáustico; (: manner) mordaz

abreast [ə'brɛst] ADV lado a lado; **to keep ~ of** (fig) estar a par de

abridge [ə'brɪdʒ] VT resumir, abreviar

abroad [ə'brɔ:d] ADV (be abroad) no estrangeiro; (go abroad) ao estrangeiro; **there is a rumour ~ that ...** (fig) corre o boato de que ...

abrupt [ə'brʌpt] ADJ (sudden) brusco; (curt) ríspido

abruptly [ə'brʌptlɪ] ADV bruscamente

abscess ['æbsɪs] N abscesso (BR), abcesso (PT)

abscond [əb'skɔnd] VI: **to ~ with** sumir com; **to ~ from** fugir de

absence ['æbsəns] N ausência; **in the ~ of** (person) na ausência de; (thing) na falta de

absent ['æbsənt] ADJ ausente; **~ without leave** ausente sem permissão oficial; **to be ~** faltar

absentee [æbsən'ti:] N ausente m/f

absenteeism [æbsən'ti:ɪzəm] N absenteísmo

absent-minded ADJ distraído

absent-mindedness [-'maɪndɪdnɪs] N distração f

absolute ['æbsəlu:t] ADJ absoluto

absolutely [æbsə'lu:tlɪ] ADV absolutamente; **oh, yes, ~!** claro que sim!

absolve [əb'zɔlv] VT: **to ~ sb (from)** (sin etc) absolver alguém (de); (blame) isentar alguém (de); **to ~ sb from** (oath) desobrigar alguém de

absorb [əb'zɔ:b] VT absorver; (group, business) incorporar; (changes) assimilar; (information) digerir; **to be ~ed in a book** estar absorvido num livro

absorbent [əb'zɔ:bənt] ADJ absorvente; **absorbent cotton** [əb'zɔ:bənt-] (US) N algodão m hidrófilo

absorbing [əb'zɔ:bɪŋ] ADJ (book, film etc) absorvente, cativante

absorption [əb'zɔ:pʃən] N absorção f; (interest) fascinação f

abstain [əb'steɪn] VI: **to ~ (from)** abster-se (de)

abstemious [əb'sti:mɪəs] ADJ abstinente

abstention [əb'stɛnʃən] N abstenção f

abstinence ['æbstɪnəns] N abstinência, sobriedade f

abstract [adj, n 'æbstrækt, vt æb'strækt] ADJ abstrato ■ N resumo ■ VT (remove) abstrair; (summarize) resumir; (steal) surripiar

absurd [əb'sə:d] ADJ absurdo

absurdity [əb'sə:dɪtɪ] N absurdo

ABTA ['æbtə] N ABBR = **Association of British Travel Agents.**

Abu Dhabi ['æbu:'dɑ:bɪ] N Abu Dabi (no article)

abundance [ə'bʌndəns] N abundância

abundant [ə'bʌndənt] ADJ abundante

abuse [n ə'bju:s, vt ə'bju:z] N (insults) insultos mpl; (misuse: ill-treatment) maus-tratos mpl, abuso ■ VT insultar; maltratar; abusar; **open to ~** aberto ao abuso

abusive [ə'bju:sɪv] ADJ ofensivo

abysmal [ə'bɪzməl] ADJ (ignorance) profundo, total; (very bad) péssimo

abyss [ə'bɪs] N abismo

AC N ABBR (US) = **athletic club** ■ ABBR (= alternating current) CA

a/c ABBR (Banking etc: = account) c/

academic [ækə'dɛmɪk] ADJ acadêmico; (pej: issue) teórico ■ N universitário(-a); **academic year** N ano letivo; **academic freedom** N liberdade de cátedra

academy [ə'kædəmɪ] N (learned body) academia; (school) instituto, academia, colégio; **military/ naval ~** academia militar/escola naval; **academy of music** N conservatório

ACAS ['eɪkæs] (Brit) N ABBR (= Advisory, Conciliation and Arbitration Service) ≈ Justiça do Trabalho

accede [æk'si:d] VI: **to ~ to** (request) consentir em, aceder a; (throne) subir a

accelerate [æk'sɛləreɪt] VT, VI acelerar

acceleration [æksɛlə'reɪʃən] N aceleração f

accelerator [æk'sɛləreɪtəʳ] N acelerador m
accent ['æksɛnt] N (written) acento;
(pronunciation) sotaque m; (fig: emphasis) ênfase f
accentuate [æk'sɛntjueɪt] VT (syllable) acentuar;
(need, difference etc) ressaltar, salientar
accept [ək'sɛpt] VT aceitar; (responsibility)
assumir
acceptable [ək'sɛptəbl] ADJ (offer) bem-vindo;
(risk) assumir, aceitável
acceptance [ək'sɛptəns] N aceitação f; to meet
with general ~ ter aprovação geral
access ['æksɛs] N acesso ◼ VT (Comput) acessar;
to have ~ to ter acesso a; the burglars gained
~ through a window os ladrões conseguiram
entrar por uma janela
accessible [æk'sɛsəbl] ADJ acessível; (available)
disponível
accession [æk'sɛʃən] N acessão f; (of king)
elevação f ao trono; (to library) aquisição f
accessory [æk'sɛsərɪ] N acessório; (Law): ~ to
cúmplice m/f de; toilet accessories (Brit)
artigos de toalete
access road N via de acesso
access time N (Comput) tempo de acesso
accident ['æksɪdənt] N acidente m; (chance)
casualidade f; to meet with or have an ~ sofrer
or ter um acidente; ~s at work acidentes de
trabalho; by ~ (unintentionally) sem querer; (by
coincidence) por acaso
accidental [æksɪ'dɛntl] ADJ acidental
accidentally [æksɪ'dɛntəlɪ] ADV (by accident) sem
querer; (by chance) casualmente
accident insurance N seguro contra acidentes
accident-prone ADJ com tendência para sofrer
or causar acidente, desastrado
acclaim [ə'kleɪm] VT aclamar; to be ~ed for
one's achievements ser aclamado por seus
fatas ◼ N aclamação f
acclamation [æklə'meɪʃən] N (approval)
aclamação f; (applause) aplausos mpl
acclimate [ə'klaɪmət] (US) VT = acclimatize
acclimatize [ə'klaɪmətaɪz] (Brit) VT: to become
~d (to) aclimatar-se (a)
accolade ['ækəleɪd] N louvor m, honra
accommodate [ə'kɔmədeɪt] VT alojar; (reconcile:
subj: car, hotel, etc) acomodar, conciliar; (oblige,
help) comprazer a; (adapt): to ~ one's plans to
acomodar seus projetos a; this car ~s 4 people
este carro tem lugar para 4 pessoas
accommodating [ə'kɔmədeɪtɪŋ] ADJ
complacente, serviçal
accommodation [əkɔmə'deɪʃən] (Brit) N
alojamento; (space) lugar m (BR), sítio (PT); he's
found ~ ele já encontrou um lugar para morar;
"~ to let" "aluga se (apartamento etc)"; they
have ~ for 500 têm lugar para 500 pessoas;
seating ~ lugares mpl sentados
accommodations [əkɔmə'deɪʃənz] (US) NPL
= accommodation
accompaniment [ə'kʌmpənɪmənt] N
acompanhamento
accompanist [ə'kʌmpənɪst] N

acompanhador(a) m/f, acompanhante m/f
accompany [ə'kʌmpənɪ] VT acompanhar
accomplice [ə'kʌmplɪs] N cúmplice m/f
accomplish [ə'kʌmplɪʃ] VT (task) concluir; (goal)
alcançar
accomplished [ə'kʌmplɪʃt] ADJ (person)
talentoso; (performance) brilhante
accomplishment [ə'kʌmplɪʃmənt] N (bringing
about) realização f; (achievement) proeza;
accomplishments NPL (skills) talentos mpl
accord [ə'kɔːd] N tratado ◼ VT conceder; of his
own ~ por sua iniciativa; with one ~ de comum
acordo
accordance [ə'kɔːdəns] N: in ~ with de acordo
com, conforme
according [ə'kɔːdɪŋ] PREP: ~ to segundo; (in
accordance with) conforme; ~ to plan como
previsto
accordingly [ə'kɔːdɪŋlɪ] ADV (thus) por
conseguinte; (appropriately) do modo devido
accordion [ə'kɔːdɪən] N acordeão m
accost [ə'kɔst] VT abordar
account [ə'kaunt] N conta; (report) relato;
accounts NPL (books, department) contabilidade
f; "~ payee only" (Brit) "cheque não endossável"
(a ser creditado na conta do favorecido); to keep an ~
of anotar, registrar; to bring sb to ~ for sth/
for having done sth chamar alguém a contas
por algo/por ter feito algo; by all ~s segundo
dizem todos; of little ~ sem importância; on
his own ~ por sua conta; to pay £5 on ~ pagar
£5 por conta; to buy sth on ~ comprar algo
a crédito; of no ~ sem importância; on ~ por
conta; on no ~ de modo nenhum; on ~ of por
causa de; to take into ~, take ~ of levar em
conta
▶ **account for** VT FUS (explain) explicar VT
(represent) representar; all the children were
~ed for nenhuma das crianças faltava; 4
people are still not ~ed for 4 pessoas ainda
não foram encontradas
accountability [əkauntə'bɪlɪtɪ] N
responsabilidade f
accountable [ə'kauntəbl] ADJ: ~ (to)
responsável (por)
accountancy [ə'kauntənsɪ] N contabilidade f
accountant [ə'kauntənt] N contador(a) m/f (BR),
contabilista m/f (PT)
accounting [ə'kauntɪŋ] N contabilidade f;
accounting period N exercício
account number N número de conta
account payable N conta a pagar
account receivable N conta a receber
accredited [ə'krɛdɪtɪd] ADJ (agent) autorizado
accretion [ə'kriːʃən] N acresção f
accrue [ə'kruː] VI aumentar; (mount up)
acumular-se; to ~ to advir a
accrued interest [ə'kruːd-] N juros mpl
acumulados
accumulate [ə'kjuːmjuleɪt] VT acumular ◼ VI
acumular-se
accumulation [əkjuːmju'leɪʃən] N

acumulação f
accuracy ['ækjʊrəsɪ] N exatidão f, precisão f
accurate ['ækjʊrɪt] ADJ (number) exato;
(description) correto; (person, device) preciso; (shot)
certeiro
accurately ['ækjʊrətlɪ] ADV com precisão
accusation [ækju'zeɪʃən] N acusação f; (instance)
incriminação f
accusative [ə'kjuːzətɪv] N (Ling) acusativo
accuse [ə'kjuːz] VT: to ~ sb (of sth) acusar
alguém (de algo)
accused [ə'kjuːzd] N: the ~ acusado(-a)
accustom [ə'kʌstəm] VT acostumar; to ~ o.s. to
sth acostumar-se a algo
accustomed [ə'kʌstəmd] ADJ (usual) habitual; ~
to acostumado a
AC/DC ABBR (= alternating current/direct current)
CA/CC
ACE [eɪs] N ABBR = American Council on
Education
ace [eɪs] N ás m; to be or come within an ~ of
doing (Brit) não fazer por um triz
acerbic [ə'səːbɪk] ADJ (also fig) acerbo
acetate ['æsɪteɪt] N acetato
ache [eɪk] N dor f ■ VI doer; (yearn): to ~ to do
sth ansiar por fazer algo; I've got (a) stomach
~ eu estou com dor de barriga; my head ~s dói-
me a cabeça; I'm aching all over estou todo
dolorido
achieve [ə'tʃiːv] VT (reach) alcançar; (realize)
realizar; (victory, success) obter
achievement [ə'tʃiːvmənt] N (of aims) realização
f; (success) proeza
acid ['æsɪd] ADJ ácido, azedo ■ N ácido
acidity [ə'sɪdɪtɪ] N acidez f
acid rain N chuva ácida
acknowledge [ək'nɔlɪdʒ] VT (fact) reconhecer;
(person) cumprimentar; (also: acknowledge
receipt of) acusar o recebimento de (BR) or a
recepção de (PT)
acknowledgement [ək'nɔlɪdʒmənt] N
(of letter) notificação f de recebimento;
acknowledgements NPL (in book)
agradecimentos mpl
ACLU N ABBR (= American Civil Liberties Union)
associação que defende os direitos humanos
acme ['ækmɪ] N acme m
acne ['æknɪ] N acne f
acorn ['eɪkɔːn] N bolota
acoustic [ə'kuːstɪk] ADJ acústico; acoustic
coupler N (Comput) acoplador m acústico
acoustics [ə'kuːstɪks] N, NPL acústica
acquaint [ə'kweɪnt] VT: to ~ sb with sth (inform)
pôr alguém ao corrente de alguma coisa; to be
~ed with (person) conhecer; (fact) saber
acquaintance [ə'kweɪntəns] N conhecimento;
(person) conhecido(-a); to make sb's ~ conhecer
alguém
acquiesce [ækwɪ'ɛs] VI: to ~ (to) condescender
(a); (request) ceder(a)
acquire [ə'kwaɪər] VT adquirir; (interest, skill)
desenvolver

acquired [ə'kwaɪəd] ADJ adquirido; an ~ taste
um gosto cultivado
acquisition [ækwɪ'zɪʃən] N aquisição f
acquisitive [ə'kwɪzɪtɪv] ADJ cobiçoso
acquit [ə'kwɪt] VT absolver; to ~ o.s. well
desempenhar-se bem
acquittal [ə'kwɪtəl] N absolvição f
acre ['eɪkər] N acre m (= 4047m²)
acreage ['eɪkərɪdʒ] N extensão f (em acres)
acrid ['ækrɪd] ADJ (smell) acre; (fig) mordaz
acrimonious [ækrɪ'məʊnɪəs] ADJ (remark)
mordaz; (argument) acrimonioso
acrobat ['ækrəbæt] N acrobata m/f
acrobatic [ækrə'bætɪk] ADJ acrobático
acrobatics [ækrə'bætɪks] NPL acrobacia
Acropolis [ə'krɔpəlɪs] N: the ~ a Acrópole
across [ə'krɔs] PREP (from one side to the other of)
de um lado para outro de; (on the other side of) no
outro lado de; (crosswise) através de ■ ADV de um
lado ao outro; to walk ~ (the road) atravessar
(a rua); to run/swim ~ atravessar correndo/a
nado; the lake is 12 km ~ o lago tem 12 km de
largura; ~ from em frente de; to get sth ~ (to
sb) conseguir comunicar algo (a alguém)
acrylic [ə'krɪlɪk] ADJ acrílico ■ N acrílico
ACT N ABBR (= American College Test) ≈ vestibular m
act [ækt] N ação f; (Theatre) ato; (in show) número;
(Law) lei f ■ VI tomar ação; (behave, have effect)
agir; (Theatre) representar; (pretend) fingir ■ VT
(part) representar; in the ~ of no ato de; ~ of
God (Law) força maior; to catch sb in the ~
apanhar alguém em flagrante, flagrar alguém;
it's only an ~ é só encenação; to ~ Hamlet (Brit)
representar Hamlet; to ~ the fool (Brit) fazer-se
de bobo; to ~ as servir de; it ~s as a deterrent
serve para dissuadir; ~ing in my capacity as
chairman, I ... na qualidade de presidente,
eu ...
▶ **act on** VT FUS: to ~ on sth agir de acordo com
algo
▶ **act out** VT (event) representar; (fantasy)
realizar
acting ['æktɪŋ] ADJ interino ■ N (performance)
representação f, atuação f; (activity): to do some
~ fazer teatro
action ['ækʃən] N ação f; (Mil) batalha, combate
m; (Law) ação judicial; to bring an ~ against
sb (Law) intentar ação judicial contra alguém;
killed in ~ (Mil) morto em combate; out of ~
(person) fora de combate; (thing) com defeito; to
take ~ tomar atitude; to put a plan into ~ pôr
um plano em ação; action replay (Brit) N (TV)
replay m
activate ['æktɪveɪt] VT (mechanism) acionar;
(Chem, Phys) ativar
active ['æktɪv] ADJ ativo; (volcano) em atividade;
active duty (US) N (Mil) ativa
actively ['æktɪvlɪ] ADV ativamente
active partner N (Comm) comanditado(-a)
active service N (Mil) ativa
activist ['æktɪvɪst] N ativista m/f, militante m/f
activity [æk'tɪvɪtɪ] N atividade f

actor ['æktə^r] N ator m
actress ['æktrɪs] N atriz f
actual ['æktjuəl] ADJ real
actually ['æktjuəlɪ] ADV realmente; (in fact) na verdade; (even) mesmo
actuary ['æktjuərɪ] N atuário(-a)
actuate ['æktjueɪt] VT atuar, acionar
acuity [ə'kju:ɪtɪ] N acuidade f
acumen ['ækjumən] N perspicácia; **business ~** tino para os negócios
acupuncture ['ækjupʌŋktʃə^r] N acupuntura
acute [ə'kju:t] ADJ agudo; (person) perspicaz
ad [æd] N ABBR = **advertisement**
A.D. ADV ABBR (= Anno Domini) d.C. ■ N ABBR (US: Mil) = **active duty**
adamant ['ædəmənt] ADJ inflexível
Adam's apple ['ædəmz-] N pomo-de-Adão m (BR), maçã-de-Adão f (PT)
adapt [ə'dæpt] VT adaptar ■ VI: **to ~ (to)** adaptar-se (a)
adaptability [ədæptə'bɪlɪtɪ] N adaptabilidade f
adaptable [ə'dæptəbl] ADJ (device) ajustável; (person) adaptável
adaptation [ædæp'teɪʃən] N adaptação f
adapter [ə'dæptə^r] N (Elec) adaptador m; = **adapter**
ADC N ABBR (Mil) = **aide-de-camp**; (US: = Aid to Dependent Children) auxílio a crianças dependentes
add [æd] VT acrescentar; (figures: also: **add up**) somar ■ VI: **to ~ to** (increase) aumentar
▶ **add on** VT acrescentar, adicionar
▶ **add up** VT (figures) somar ■ VI (fig): **it doesn't ~ up** não faz sentido; **it doesn't ~ up to much** é pouca coisa
adder ['ædə^r] N víbora
addict ['ædɪkt] N viciado(-a); **heroin ~** viciado(-a) em heroína; **drug ~** toxicômano(-a)
addicted [ə'dɪktɪd] ADJ: **to be/become ~ to** ser/ficar viciado em
addiction [ə'dɪkʃən] N (Med) dependência
adding machine ['ædɪŋ-] N máquina de somar
Addis Ababa ['ædɪs'æbəbə] N Adis-Abeba
addition [ə'dɪʃən] N (adding up) adição f; (thing added) acréscimo; **in ~** além disso; **in ~ to** além de
additional [ə'dɪʃənl] ADJ adicional
additive ['ædɪtɪv] N aditivo
address [ə'drɛs] N endereço; (speech) discurso ■ VT (letter) endereçar; (speak to) dirigir-se a, dirigir a palavra a; **form of ~** tratamento; **to ~ (o.s. to)** (problem, issue) enfocar; **absolute/relative ~** (Comput) endereço absoluto/relativo
addressee [ædrɛ'si:] N destinatário(-a)
Aden ['eɪdən] N Áden (no article); **Gulf of ~** golfo de Áden
adenoids ['ædɪnɔɪdz] NPL adenóides fpl
adept ['ædɛpt] ADJ: **~ at** hábil or competente em
adequate ['ædɪkwɪt] ADJ (enough) suficiente; (suitable) adequado; (satisfactory) satisfatório; **to feel ~ to the task** sentir-se à altura da tarefa
adequately ['ædɪkwɪtlɪ] ADV adequadamente
adhere [əd'hɪə^r] VI: **to ~ to** aderir a; (abide by)

ater-se a
adhesion [əd'hi:ʒən] N adesão f
adhesive [əd'hi:zɪv] ADJ, N adesivo; **adhesive tape** M (Brit) durex® m, fita adesiva; (US) esparadrapo
ad hoc [-hɔk] ADJ (decision) para o caso; (committee) ad hoc
ad infinitum [-ɪnfɪ'naɪtəm] ADV ad infinitum
adjacent [ə'dʒeɪsənt] ADJ: **~ (to)** adjacente (a)
adjective ['ædʒɛktɪv] N adjetivo
adjoin [ə'dʒɔɪn] VT ser contíguo a
adjoining [ə'dʒɔɪnɪŋ] ADJ adjacente
adjourn [ə'dʒə:n] VT (postpone) adiar; (session) suspender ■ VI encerrar a sessão; (go) deslocar-se; **they ~ed to the pub** (Brit: inf) deslocaram-se para o bar
adjournment [ə'dʒə:nmənt] N (period) recesso
Adjt ABBR (Mil: = adjutant) Ajte
adjudicate [ə'dʒu:dɪkeɪt] VT, VI julgar
adjudication [ədʒu:dɪ'keɪʃən] N julgamento
adjust [ə'dʒʌst] VT (change) ajustar; (clothes) arrumar; (machine) regular ■ VI: **to ~ (to)** adaptar-se (a)
adjustable [ə'dʒʌstəbl] ADJ ajustável
adjuster [ə'dʒʌstə^r] N see **loss**
adjustment [ə'dʒʌstmənt] N ajuste m; (of engine) regulagem f; (of prices, wages) reajuste m; (of person) adaptação f
adjutant ['ædʒətənt] N ajudante m
ad-lib [-lɪb] VT, VI improvisar ■ N improviso; (Theatre) caco ■ ADV: **ad lib** à vontade
adman ['ædmæn] (inf: irreg) N publicitário
admin ['ædmɪn] (inf) N ABBR = **administration**
administer [əd'mɪnɪstə^r] VT administrar; (justice) aplicar; (drug) ministrar
administration [ədmɪnɪs'treɪʃən] N administração f; (US: government) governo
administrative [əd'mɪnɪstrətɪv] ADJ administrativo
administrator [əd'mɪnɪstreɪtə^r] N administrador(a) m/f
admirable ['ædmərəbl] ADJ admirável
admiral ['ædmərəl] N almirante m
Admiralty ['ædmərəltɪ] (Brit) N (also: **Admiralty Board**) Ministério da Marinha, Almirantado
admiration [ædmə'reɪʃən] N admiração f
admire [əd'maɪə^r] VT (respect) respeitar; (appreciate) admirar
admirer [əd'maɪrə^r] N (suitor) pretendente m/f; (fan) admirador(a) m/f
admission [əd'mɪʃən] N (admittance) entrada; (fee) ingresso; (enrolment) admissão f; (confession) confissão f; **"~ free", "free ~"** "entrada gratuita", "ingresso gratuito"; **by his own ~ he drinks too much** ele mesmo reconhece que bebe demais
admit [əd'mɪt] VT admitir; (acknowledge) reconhecer; (accept) aceitar; (confess) confessar; **"children not ~ted"** "entrada proibida a menores de idade"; **this ticket ~s two** este ingresso é válido para duas pessoas; **I must ~ that ...** devo admitir or reconhecer que ...

▶ **admit of** VT FUS admitir
▶ **admit to** VT FUS confessar
admittance [əd'mɪtəns] N entrada; **"no ~"** "entrada proibida"
admittedly [əd'mɪtədlɪ] ADV evidentemente
admonish [əd'mɔnɪʃ] VT admoestar
ad nauseam [æd'nɔːsɪæm] ADV sem parar
ado [ə'duː] N: **without further** or **(any) more ~** sem mais cerimônias
adolescence [ædəu'lɛsns] N adolescência
adolescent [ædəu'lɛsnt] ADJ, N adolescente m/f
adopt [ə'dɔpt] VT adotar
adopted [ə'dɔptɪd] ADJ adotivo
adoption [ə'dɔpʃən] N adoção f
adoptive [ə'dɔptɪv] ADJ adotivo
adorable [ə'dɔːrəbl] ADJ encantador(a)
adoration [ædə'reɪʃən] N adoração f
adore [ə'dɔːˈ] VT adorar
adoring [ə'dɔːrɪŋ] ADJ devotado
adoringly [ə'dɔːrɪŋlɪ] ADV com adoração
adorn [ə'dɔːn] VT adornar, enfeitar
adornment [ə'dɔːnmənt] N enfeite m, adorno
ADP N ABBR = **automatic data processing**
adrenalin [ə'drɛnəlɪn] N adrenalina
Adriatic (Sea) [eɪdrɪ'ætɪk-] N (mar m) Adriático
adrift [ə'drɪft] ADV à deriva; **to come ~** desprender-se
adroit [ə'drɔɪt] ADJ hábil
ADT (US) ABBR (= Atlantic Daylight Time) hora de verão de Nova Iorque.
adult ['ædʌlt] N adulto(-a) ■ ADJ adulto; (literature, education) para adultos; **adult education** N educação f para adultos
adulterate [ə'dʌltəreɪt] VT adulterar
adulterer [ə'dʌltərəˈ] N adúltero
adulteress [ə'dʌltərɪs] N adúltera
adultery [ə'dʌltərɪ] N adultério
adulthood ['ædʌlthud] N idade f adulta
advance [əd'vɑːns] N avanço; (money: payment in advance) adiantamento; (: loan) empréstimo; (Mil) avançada ■ ADJ antecipado ■ VT (develop) desenvolver, promover; (money) adiantar ■ VI (move forward) avançar; (progress) progredir; **in ~** com antecedência; **to make ~s to sb** (gen) fazer propostas a alguém; (amorously) fazer propostas amorosas a alguém
advanced [əd'vɑːnst] ADJ avançado; (studies, country) adiantado; **~ in years** de idade avançada
advancement [əd'vɑːnsmənt] N (improvement) progresso; (in rank) promoção f
advance notice N aviso prévio
advantage [əd'vɑːntɪdʒ] N vantagem f; (supremacy) supremacia; (advantage) benefício; (Tennis) o primeiro ponto marcado depois do empate de 40 iguais; **to take ~ of** (use) aproveitar, aproveitar-se de; (gain by) tirar proveito de; **it's to our ~ (to do)** é vantajoso para nós (fazer)
advantageous [ædvən'teɪdʒəs] ADJ: **~ (to)** vantajoso (para)
advent ['ædvənt] N advento, chegada; **A~** (Rel) Advento

Advent calendar N calendário do Advento
adventure [əd'vɛntʃəˈ] N aventura
adventurous [əd'vɛntʃərəs] ADJ aventureiro
adverb ['ædvəːb] N advérbio
adversary ['ædvəsərɪ] N adversário(-a)
adverse ['ædvəːs] ADJ (effect) contrário; (weather, publicity) desfavorável; **~ to** contrário a
adversity [əd'vəːsɪtɪ] N adversidade f
advert ['ædvəːt] (Brit) N ABBR = **advertisement**
advertise ['ædvətaɪz] VI anunciar, fazer propaganda; (in newspaper etc) anunciar ■ VT (event, job) anunciar; (product) fazer a propaganda de; **to ~ for** (staff) procurar
advertisement [əd'vəːtɪsmənt] N (classified) anúncio; (display, TV) propaganda, anúncio
advertiser ['ædvətaɪzəˈ] N anunciante m/f
advertising ['ædvətaɪzɪŋ] N publicidade f; **advertising agency** N agência de publicidade; **advertising campaign** N campanha publicitária
advice [əd'vaɪs] N conselhos mpl; (notification) aviso; **piece of ~** conselho; **to ask (sb) for ~** pedir conselho (a alguém); **to take legal ~** consultar um advogado; **advice note** (Brit) N aviso
advisable [əd'vaɪzəbl] ADJ aconselhável
advise [əd'vaɪz] VT aconselhar; (inform): **to ~ sb of sth** avisar alguém de algo; **to ~ sb against sth** desaconselhar algo a alguém; **to ~ sb against doing sth** aconselhar alguém a não fazer algo; **you would be well/ill ~d to go** seria melhor você ir/você não ir
advisedly [əd'vaɪzɪdlɪ] ADV de propósito
adviser [əd'vaɪzəˈ] N conselheiro(-a); (consultant) consultor(a) m/f; (political) assessor(a) m/f
advisor [əa'vaɪzəˈ] N = **adviser**
advisory [əd'vaɪzərɪ] ADJ consultivo; **in an ~ capacity** na qualidade de assessor(a) or consultor(a)
advocate [vt 'ædvəkeɪt, n 'ædvəkɪt] VT defender; (recommend) advogar ■ N advogado(-a); (supporter) defensor(a) m/f
advt. ABBR = **advertisement**
AEA (Brit) N ABBR (= Atomic Energy Authority) ≈ CNEN f
AEC (US) N ABBR (= Atomic Energy Commission) ≈ CNEN f
Aegean [iː'dʒiːən] N: **the ~ (Sea)** Egeu (o mar)
aegis ['iːdʒɪs] N: **under the ~ of** sob a égide de
aeon ['iːən] N eternidade f
aerial ['ɛərɪəl] N antena ■ ADJ aéreo
aerobatics [ɛərəu'bætɪks] NPL acrobacias fpl aéreas
aerobics [ɛə'rəubɪks] N ginástica
aerodrome ['ɛərədrəum] (Brit) N aeródromo
aerodynamic [ɛərəudaɪ'næmɪk] ADJ aerodinâmico
aerodynamics [ɛərəudaɪ'næmɪks] N, NPL aerodinâmica
aeronautics [ɛərə'nɔːtɪks] N aeronáutica
aeroplane ['ɛərəpleɪn] (Brit) N avião m
aerosol ['ɛərəsɔl] N aerossol m

aerospace industry ['ɛərəuspeɪs-] N indústria aeroespacial

aesthetic [iːs'θɛtɪk] ADJ estético

aesthetics [iːs'θɛtɪks] N, NPL estética

afar [ə'fɑːʳ] ADV: **from ~** de longe

AFB (US) N ABBR = **Air Force Base**

AFDC (US) N ABBR (= *Aid to Families with Dependent Children*) auxílio-família m

affable ['æfəbl] ADJ afável; (*behaviour*) simpático

affair [ə'fɛəʳ] N (*matter*) assunte; (*business*) negócio; (*question*) questão f; (*also*: **love affair**) caso; **~s** (*matters*) assuntos mpl; (*personal concerns*) vida; **that is my ~** isso é comigo; **the Watergate ~** o caso Watergate

affect [ə'fɛkt] VT afetar; (*move*) comover

affectation [æfɛk'teɪʃən] N afetação f

affected [ə'fɛktɪd] ADJ afetado

affection [ə'fɛkʃən] N afeto, afeição f

affectionate [ə'fɛkʃənət] ADJ afetuoso, carinhoso

affectionately [ə'fɛkʃənətlɪ] ADV carinhosamente

affidavit [æfɪ'deɪvɪt] N (*Law*) declaração f escrita e juramentada

affiliated [ə'fɪlɪeɪtɪd] ADJ: **~ (to)** afiliado (a); **~ company** filial f

affinity [ə'fɪnɪtɪ] N afinidade f; **to have an ~ with** (*rapport*) ter afinidade com; (*resemblance*) ter semelhanca com

affirm [ə'fəːm] VT afirmar

affirmation [æfə'meɪʃən] N afirmação f

affirmative [ə'fəːmətɪv] ADJ afirmativo ■ N: **in the ~** afirmativamente

affix [ə'fɪks] VT (*signature*) apor; (*stamp*) colar

afflict [ə'flɪkt] VT afligir; **to be ~ed with** sofrer de

affliction [ə'flɪkʃən] N aflição f; (*illness*) doença

affluence ['æfluəns] N riqueza

affluent ['æfluənt] ADJ rico; **the ~ society** a sociedade de abundância

afford [ə'fɔːd] VT (*provide*) fornecer; (*goods etc*) ter dinheiro suficiente para; (*permit o.s.*): **I can't ~ the time** não tenho tempo; **can we ~ a car?** temos dinheiro para comprar um carro?; **we can ~ to wait** podemos permitir-nos esperar

affray [ə'freɪ] (*Brit*) N (*Law*) desordem f, tumulto

affront [ə'frʌnt] N ofensa

affronted [ə'frʌntɪd] ADJ afrontado, ofendido

Afghan ['æfgæn] ADJ, N afegão(-gã) m/f

Afghanistan [æf'gænɪstæn] N Afeganistão m

afield [ə'fiːld] ADV: **far ~** muito longe

AFL-CIO N ABBR (= *American Federation of Labor and Congress of Industrial Organizations*) *confederação sindical*

afloat [ə'fləut] ADV (*floating*) flutuando; (*at sea*) no mar; **to stay ~** continuar flutuando; **to keep/get ~** (*business*) manter financeiramente equilibrado/estabelecer

afoot [ə'fut] ADV: **there is something ~** está acontecendo algo

aforementioned [ə'fɔːmɛnʃənd] ADJ acima mencionado

aforesaid [ə'fɔːsɛd] ADJ supracitado, referido

afraid [ə'freɪd] ADJ (*frightened*) assustado; (*fearful*) receoso; **to be ~ of/to** ter medo de; **I am ~ that** lamento que; **I'm ~ so/not** receio que sim/não

afresh [ə'frɛʃ] ADV de novo

Africa ['æfrɪkə] N África

African ['æfrɪkən] ADJ, N africano(-a)

Afrikaans [æfrɪ'kɑːns] N (*Ling*) afrikaan m

Afrikaner [æfrɪ'kɑːnəʳ] N africânder m/f

Afro-American ['æfrəu-] ADJ afro-americano

AFT N ABBR (= *American Federation of Teachers*) *sindicato dos professores*

aft [ɑːft] ADV a ré

after ['ɑːftəʳ] PREP (*time*) depois de ■ ADV depois ■ CONJ depois que; **~ dinner** depois do jantar; **the day ~ tomorrow** depois de amanhã; **day ~ day** dia após dia; **time ~ time** repetidas vezes; **a quarter ~ two** (*US*) duas e quinze; **what are you ~?** o que você quer?; **who are you ~?** quem procura?; **~ he left done** depois que ele se foi; **~ having done** tendo feito; **the police are ~ him** a polícia está atrás dele; **to ask ~ sb** perguntar por alguém; **~ all** afinal (de contas); **~ you!** passe primeiro!

afterbirth ['ɑːftəbəːθ] N placenta

aftercare ['ɑːftəkɛəʳ] (*Brit*) N (*Med*) assistência pós-operatória

after-effects NPL (*of illness etc*) efeitos mpl secundários

afterlife ['ɑːftəlaɪf] N vida após a morte

aftermath ['ɑːftəmæθ] N conseqüências fpl; **in the ~ of** no período depois de

afternoon [ɑːftə'nuːn] N tarde f; **good ~!** boa tarde!

afters ['ɑːftəz] (*Brit*: *inf*) N (*dessert*) sobremesa

after-sales service (*Brit*) N serviço pós-vendas; (*of computers etc*) assistência técnica

after-shave (lotion) N loção f após-barba

aftershock ['ɑːftəʃɔk] N abalo secundário

afterthought ['ɑːftəθɔːt] N reflexão f posterior or tardia

afterwards ['ɑːftəwədz] ADV depois; **immediately ~** logo depois

again [ə'gɛn] ADV (*once more*) outra vez; (*repeatedly*) de novo; **to do sth ~** voltar a fazer algo; **~ and ~** repetidas vezes; **now and ~** de vez em quando

against [ə'gɛnst] PREP contra; (*compared to*) em contraste com; **~ a blue background** sobre um fundo azul; (**as**) ~ (*Brit*) em contraste com

age [eɪdʒ] N idade f; (*old age*) velhice f; (*period*) época ■ VT, VI envelhecer; **he's 20 years of ~** ele tem 20 anos de idade; **at the ~ of 20** aos 20 anos de idade; **under ~** menor de idade; **to come of ~** atingir a maioridade; **it's been ~s since I saw him** faz muito tempo que eu não o vejo

aged[1] [eɪdʒd] ADJ: **~ 10** de 10 anos de idade

aged[2] ['eɪdʒɪd] ADJ idoso ■ NPL: **the ~** os idosos

age group N faixa etária; **the 40 to 50 ~** a faixa etária dos 40 aos 50 anos

ageless ['eɪdʒlɪs] ADJ (*eternal*) eterno; (*ever young*)

sempre jovem
age limit N idade f mínima/máxima
agency ['eɪdʒənsɪ] N agência; (government body) órgão m; **through** or **by the ~ of** por meio de
agenda [ə'dʒɛndə] N ordem f do dia
agent ['eɪdʒənt] N agente m/f; (spy) agente m/f secreto(-a)
aggravate ['ægrəveɪt] VT agravar; (annoy) irritar
aggravation [ægrɪ'veɪʃən] N irritação f
aggregate ['ægrɪgət] N (whole) conjunto; **on ~** (Sport) no total dos pontos
aggression [ə'grɛʃən] N agressão f
aggressive [ə'grɛsɪv] ADJ agressivo
aggressiveness [ə'grɛsɪvnɪs] N agressividade f
aggrieved [ə'gri:vd] ADJ aflito
aghast [ə'gɑ:st] ADJ horrorizado
agile ['ædʒaɪl] ADJ ágil
agitate ['ædʒɪteɪt] VT agitar; (trouble) perturbar
■ VI: **to ~ for/against** fazer agitação a favor de/contra de
how long ~?
agitation [ædʒɪ'teɪʃən] N agitação f
agitator ['ædʒɪteɪtə'] N agitador(a) m/f
AGM N ABBR (= annual general meeting) AGO f
agnostic [æg'nɔstɪk] N agnóstico
ago [ə'gəu] ADV: **2 days ~** há 2 dias (atrás); **not long ~** há pouco tempo; **as long ~ as 1960** já em 1960; **how long ~?** há quanto tempo?
agog [ə'gɔg] ADJ (eager) ávido; (impatient): **~ to** ansioso para; (excited): **(all) ~** entusiasmado
agonize ['ægənaɪz] VI: **to ~ over sth** agoniar-se or angustiar-se com algo
agonizing ['ægənaɪzɪŋ] ADJ (pain) agudo; (wait) angustiante
agony ['ægənɪ] N (pain) dor f; (distress) angústia; **to be in ~** sofrer dores terríveis; **agony column** N correspondência sentimental
agree [ə'gri:] VT (price, date) combinar ■ VI concordar; (correspond) corresponder; (statements etc) combinar; **to ~ (with)** (person, Ling) concordar (com); **to ~ to do** aceitar fazer; **to ~ to do** aceitar fazer; **to ~ to sth** consentir algo; **to ~ that** (admit) concordar or admitir que; **it was ~d that ...** foi combinado que ...; **they ~ on this** concordam or estão de acordo nisso; **garlic doesn't ~ with me** não me dou bem com o alho
agreeable [ə'gri:əbl] ADJ agradável; (willing) disposto; **are you ~ to this?** você concorda or está de acordo com isso?
agreed [ə'gri:d] ADJ (time, place) combinado; **to be ~** concordar, estar de acordo
agreement [ə'gri:mənt] N acordo; (Comm) contrato; **in ~** de acordo; **by mutual ~** de comum acordo
agricultural [ægrɪ'kʌltʃərəl] ADJ (of crops) agrícola; (of crops and cattle) agropecuário
agriculture ['ægrɪkʌltʃə'] N (of crops) agricultura; (of crops and cattle) agropecuária
aground [ə'graund] ADV: **to run ~** encalhar
ahead [ə'hɛd] ADV adiante; **go right** or **straight ~** siga em frente; **go ~!** (fig) vá em frente!; (: speak) pode falar!; **~ of** na frente de; (fig: schedule etc) antes de; **~ of time** antes do tempo; **to go ~**

(with) prosseguir (com); **to be ~ of sb** (fig) ter vantagem sobre alguém
AI N ABBR = **Amnesty International**; (Comput) = **artificial intelligence**
AIB (Brit) N ABBR (= Accident Investigation Bureau) comissão de inquérito sobre acidentes.
AID N ABBR = **artificial insemination by donor**; (US) = **Agency for International Development**
aid [eɪd] N ajuda ■ VT ajudar; **with the ~ of** com a ajuda de; **in ~ of** em benefício de; **to ~ and abet** (Law) ser cúmplice de; see also **hearing**
aide [eɪd] N (person) assessor(a) m/f
AIDS [eɪdz] N ABBR (= acquired immune deficiency syndrome) AIDS f (BR), SIDA f (PT)
AIH N ABBR = **artificial insemination by husband**
ailing ['eɪlɪŋ] ADJ enfermo
ailment ['eɪlmənt] N achaque m
aim [eɪm] VT: **to ~ sth (at)** (gun, camera, blow) apontar algo (para); (missile, remark) dirigir algo (a) ■ VI (also: **take aim**) apontar ■ N (skill) pontaria; (objective) objetivo, meta; **to ~ at** (with weapon) mirar; **to ~ to do** pretender fazer
aimless ['eɪmlɪs] ADJ sem objetivo
aimlessly ['eɪmlɪslɪ] ADV à toa
ain't [eɪnt] (inf) = **am not; aren't; isn't**
air [ɛə'] N ar m; (appearance) aparência, aspeto ■ VT arejar; (grievances, ideas) discutir ■ CPD (currents, attack etc) aéreo; **to throw sth into the ~** jogar algo para cima; **by ~** (travel) de avião; (send) por via aérea; **to be on the ~** (Radio, TV: programme, station) estar no ar; **air base** N base f aérea; **air bed** ['ɛəbɛd] (Brit) N colchão m de ar
airborne ['ɛəbɔ:n] ADJ (in the air) no ar; (plane) em vôo; (troops) aerotransportado
air cargo N frete m aéreo
air-conditioned [-kən'dɪʃənd] ADJ com ar condicionado
air conditioning [-kən'dɪʃənɪŋ] N ar condicionado
air-cooled [-ku:ld] ADJ refrigerado a ar
aircraft ['ɛəkrɑ:ft] N INV aeronave f; **aircraft carrier** N porta-aviões m inv
air cushion N almofada de ar
airfield ['ɛəfi:ld] N campo de aviação
Air Force N Força Aérea, Aeronáutica
air freight N frete m aéreo
air freshener [-'frɛʃnə'] N perfumador m de ar
air gun ['ɛəgʌn] N espingarda de ar comprimido
air hostess (Brit) N aeromoça (BR), hospedeira (PT)
airily ['ɛərɪlɪ] ADV levianamente
airing ['ɛərɪŋ] N: **to give an ~ to** arejar; (fig: ideas, views) discutir
air letter (Brit) N aerograma m
airlift ['ɛəlɪft] N ponte aérea
airline ['ɛəlaɪn] N linha aérea
airliner ['ɛəlaɪnə'] N avião m de passageiros
airlock ['ɛəlɔk] N (blockage) entupimento de ar
airmail ['ɛəmeɪl] N: **by ~** por via aérea
air mattress N colchão m de ar
airplane ['ɛəpleɪn] (US) N avião m

air pocket N bolsa de ar
airport ['ɛəpɔːt] N aeroporto
air raid N ataque m aéreo
airsick ['ɛəsɪk] ADJ: **to be ~** enjoar-se (no avião)
airspace ['ɛəspeɪs] N espaço aéreo
airstrip ['ɛəstrɪp] N pista (de aterrissar)
air terminal N terminal m aéreo
airtight ['ɛətaɪt] ADJ hermético
air traffic control N controle m de tráfego aéreo
air traffic controller N controlador(a) m/f de tráfego aéreo
airy ['ɛərɪ] ADJ (room) arejado; (manner) leviano
aisle [aɪl] N (of church) nave f; (of theatre etc) corredor m, coxia
ajar [ə'dʒɑː'] ADJ entreaberto
AK (US) ABBR (Post) = **Alaska**
aka ABBR (= also known as) vulgo
akin [ə'kɪn] ADJ: **~ to** parecido com
AL (US) ABBR (Post) = **Alabama**
ALA N ABBR = **American Library Association**
à la carte [æla:'kɑːt] ADJ, ADV à la carte
alacrity [ə'lækrɪtɪ] N alacridade f; **with ~** prontamente
alarm [ə'lɑːm] N alarme m; (anxiety) inquietação f ■ VT alarmar, inquietar; **alarm call** N (in hotel etc) sinal m de alarme; **alarm clock** N despertador m
alarming [ə'lɑːmɪŋ] ADJ alarmante
alarmist [ə'lɑːmɪst] ADJ, N alarmista m/f
alas [ə'læs] EXCL ai, ai de mim
Alaska [ə'læskə] N Alasca m
Albania [æl'beɪnɪə] N Albânia
Albanian [æl'beɪnɪən] ADJ albanês(-esa) ■ N albanês(-esa) m/f; (Ling) albanês m
albeit [ɔːl'biːɪt] CONJ embora
album ['ælbəm] N (for stamps etc) álbum m; (record) elepê m
albumen ['ælbjumɪn] N albumina; (of egg) albume m
alchemy ['ælkɪmɪ] N alquimia
alcohol ['ælkəhɔl] N álcool m
alcoholic [ælkə'hɔlɪk] ADJ alcoólico ■ N alcoólatra m/f
alcoholism ['ælkəhɔlɪzəm] N alcoolismo
alcove ['ælkəuv] N alcova
Ald. ABBR = **alderman**
alderman ['ɔːldəmən] (irreg) N vereador m
ale [eɪl] N cerveja
alert [ə'ləːt] ADJ atento; (to danger, opportunity) alerta; (sharp) esperto; (watchful) vigilante ■ N alerta ■ VT: **to ~ sb (to sth)** alertar alguém (de or sobre algo); **to be on the ~** estar alerta; (Mil) ficar de prontidão
Aleutian Islands [ə'luːʃən-] NPL ilhas fpl Aleútas
Alexandria [ælɪg'zɑːndrɪə] N Alexandria
alfresco [æl'freskəu] ADJ, ADV ao ar livre
Algarve [æl'gɑːv] M: **the ~** o Algarve
algebra ['ældʒɪbrə] N álgebra
Algeria [æl'dʒɪərɪə] N Argélia
Algerian [æl'dʒɪərɪən] ADJ, N argelino(-a)
Algiers [æl'dʒɪəz] N Argel
algorithm ['ælgərɪðəm] N algoritmo

alias ['eɪlɪəs] ADV também chamado ■ N (of criminal) alcunha; (of writer) pseudônimo
alibi ['ælɪbaɪ] N álibi m
alien ['eɪlɪən] N estrangeiro(-a); (from space) alienígena m/f ■ ADJ: **~ to** alheio a
alienate ['eɪlɪəneɪt] VT alienar
alienation [eɪlɪə'neɪʃən] N alienação f
alight [ə'laɪt] ADJ em chamas; (eyes) aceso; (expression) intento ■ VI (passenger) descer (de um veículo); (bird) pousar
align [ə'laɪn] VT alinhar
alignment [ə'laɪnmənt] N alinhamento
alike [ə'laɪk] ADJ semelhante; (identical) igual ■ ADV similarmente; igualmente; **to look ~** parecer-se
alimony ['ælɪmənɪ] N (payment) pensão f alimentícia
alive [ə'laɪv] ADJ vivo; (lively) alegre; **to be ~ with** fervilhar de; **~ to** sensível a
alkali ['ælkəlaɪ] N álcali m

◯ **KEYWORD**

all [ɔːl] ADJ (singular) todo(ɐ); (plural) todoɐ(aɐ); **all day/night** o dia inteiro/a noite inteira; **all men** todos os homens; **all five came** todos os cinco vieram; **all the books/food** todos os livros/toda a comida; **all the time/his life** o tempo todo/toda a sua vida
■ PRON **1** tudo; **I ate it all, I ate all of it** comi tudo; **all of us/the boys went** todos nós fomos/ todos os meninos foram; **we all sat down** nós todos sentamos; **is that all?** é só isso?; (in shop) mais alguma coisa?
2 (in phrases): **above all** sobretudo; **after all** afinal (de contas); **not at all** (in answer to question) em absoluto, absolutamente não; **I'm not at all tired** não estou nada cansado; **anything at all will do** qualquer coisa serve; **all in all** ao todo
■ ADV todo, completamente; **all alone** completamente só; **it's not as hard as all that** não é tão difícil assim; **all the more** ainda mais; **all the better** tanto melhor, melhor ainda; **all but** quase; **the score is 2 all** o escore é 2 a 2

allay [ə'leɪ] VT (fears) acalmar; (pain) aliviar
all clear N sinal m de tudo limpo; (after air raid) sinal de fim de alerta aérea
allegation [ælɪ'geɪʃən] N alegação f
allege [ə'lɛdʒ] VT alegar; **he is ~d to have said** afirma-se que ele disse
alleged [ə'lɛdʒd] ADJ pretenso
allegedly [ə'lɛdʒɪdlɪ] ADV segundo dizem
allegiance [ə'liːdʒəns] N lealdade f
allegory ['ælɪgərɪ] N alegoria
all-embracing [-ɪm'breɪsɪŋ] ADJ universal
allergic [ə'ləːdʒɪk] ADJ: **~ (to)** alérgico (a)
allergy ['ælədʒɪ] N alergia
alleviate [ə'liːvɪeɪt] VT (pain) aliviar; (difficulty) minorar

alley ['ælɪ] N (*street*) viela; (*in garden*) passeio

alliance [əˈlaɪəns] N aliança

allied ['ælaɪd] ADJ aliado; (*related*) afim, aparentado

alligator ['ælɪɡeɪtəʳ] N aligátor *m*; (*in Brazil*) jacaré *m*

all-important ADJ importantíssimo

all-in (*Brit*) ADJ, ADV (*charge*) tudo incluído; **all-in wrestling** (*Brit*) N luta livre

alliteration [əlɪtəˈreɪʃən] N aliteração *f*

all-night ADJ (*café*) aberto toda a noite; (*party*) que dura toda a noite

allocate ['æləkeɪt] VT (*earmark*) destinar; (*share out*) distribuir

allocation [æləˈkeɪʃən] N (*of money*) repartição *f*; (*distribution*) distribuição *f*; (*money*) verbas *fpl*

allot [əˈlɔt] VT distribuir, repartir; **to ~ to** designar para; **in the ~ted time** no tempo designado

allotment [əˈlɔtmənt] N (*share*) partilha; (*garden*) lote *m*

all-out ADJ (*effort etc*) máximo; (*attack etc*) irrestrito ■ ADV: **all out** com toda a força

allow [əˈlau] VT (*practice, behaviour*) permitir; (*sum to spend etc*) dar, conceder; (*claim, goal*) admitir; (*sum, time estimated*) calcular; (*concede*): **to ~ that** reconhecer que; **to ~ sb to do** permitir a alguém fazer; **he is ~ed to do** é permitido que ele faça, ele pode fazer; **smoking is not ~ed** é proibido fumar; **we must ~ 3 days for the journey** temos que calcular três dias para a viagem

▸ **allow for** VT FUS levar em conta

allowance [əˈlauəns] N ajuda de custo; (*welfare, payment*) pensão *f*, auxílio; (*Tax*) abatimento; **to make ~s for** levar em consideração

alloy ['ælɔɪ] N liga

all right ADV (*well*) bem; (*correctly*) corretamente; (*as answer*) está bem!

all-round ADJ (*view*) geral, amplo; (*person*) consumado

all-rounder (*Brit*) N: **to be a good ~** ser homem/mulher para tudo

allspice ['ɔːlspaɪs] N pimenta da Jamaica

all-time ADJ (*record*) de todos os tempos

allude [əˈluːd] VI: **to ~ to** aludir a

alluring [əˈljuərɪŋ] ADJ tentador(a)

allusion [əˈluːʒən] N alusão *f*

alluvium [əˈluːvɪəm] N aluvião *m*

ally [n 'ælaɪ, vt əˈlaɪ] N aliado ■ VT: **to ~ o.s. with** aliar-se com

almighty [ɔːlˈmaɪtɪ] ADJ onipotente; (*row etc*) a maior

almond ['ɑːmənd] N (*fruit*) amêndoa; (*tree*) amendoeira

almost ['ɔːlməust] ADV quase

alms [ɑːmz] NPL esmolas *fpl*, esmola

aloft [əˈlɔft] ADV em cima

alone [əˈləun] ADJ só, sozinho ■ ADV só, somente; **to leave sb ~** deixar alguém em paz; **to leave sth ~** não tocar em algo; **let ~ ...** sem falar em ...

along [əˈlɔŋ] PREP por, ao longo de ■ ADV: **is he coming ~?** ele vem conosco?; **he was hopping/limping ~** ele/ia pulando/coxeando; **~ with** junto com; **all ~** (*all the time*) o tempo tudo

alongside [əlɔŋˈsaɪd] PREP ao lado de ■ ADV (*Naut*) encostado

aloof [əˈluːf] ADJ afastado, altivo ■ ADV: **to stand ~** afastar-se

aloofness [əˈluːfnɪs] N afastamento, altivez *f*

aloud [əˈlaud] ADV em voz alta

alphabet ['ælfəbet] N alfabeto

alphabetical [ælfəˈbetɪkəl] ADJ alfabético; **in ~ order** em ordem alfabética

alphanumeric ['ælfənjuːˈmerɪk] ADJ alfanumérico

alpine ['ælpaɪn] ADJ alpino

Alps [ælps] NPL: **the ~** os Alpes

already [ɔːlˈredɪ] ADV já

alright ['ɔːlraɪt] (*Brit*) ADV = **all right**

Alsatian [ælˈseɪʃən] (*Brit*) N (*dog*) pastor *m* alemão

also ['ɔːlsəu] ADV também; (*moreover*) além disso

altar ['ɔltəʳ] N altar *m*

alter ['ɔltəʳ] VT alterar ■ VI modificar-se

alteration [ɔltəˈreɪʃən] N (*to plan*) mudança; (*to clothe*) conserto; (*to build*) reforma; **timetable subject to ~** horário sujeito a mudanças

alternate [*adj* ɔlˈtəːnɪt, *vi* ˈɔltəːneɪt] ADJ alternado; (*US: alternative*) alternativo ■ VI: **to ~ with** alternar-se (com); **on ~ days** em dias alternados

alternately [ɔlˈtəːnɪtlɪ] ADV alternadamente

alternating ['ɔltəːneɪtɪŋ] ADJ: **~ current** corrente *f* alternada

alternative [ɔlˈtəːnətɪv] ADJ alternativo ■ N alternativa

alternatively [ɔlˈtəːnətɪvlɪ] ADV: **~ one could ...** por outro lado se podia ...

alternator ['ɔltəːneɪtəʳ] N (*Aut*) alternador *m*

although [ɔːlˈðəu] CONJ embora; (*given that*) se bem que

altitude ['æltɪtjuːd] N altitude *f*

alto ['æltəu] N (*female*) contralto *f*; (*male*) alto

altogether [ɔːltəˈɡeðəʳ] ADV (*completely*) totalmente; (*on the whole*) no total; **how much is that ~?** qual é a soma total?

altruistic [æltruˈɪstɪk] ADJ (*person*) altruísta; (*behaviour*) altruístico

aluminium [æljuˈmɪnɪəm] (*Brit*) N alumínio

aluminum [əˈluːmɪnəm] (*US*) N = **aluminium**

always ['ɔːlweɪz] ADV sempre

AM ABBR = **amplitude modulation**

am [æm] VB *see* **be**

a.m. ADV ABBR (= *ante meridiem*) da manhã

AMA N ABBR = **American Medical Association**

amalgam [əˈmælɡəm] N amálgama *m*

amalgamate [əˈmælɡəmeɪt] VI amalgamar-se ■ VT amalgamar, unir

amalgamation [əmælɡəˈmeɪʃən] N (*Comm*) amalgamação *f*, união *f*

amass [əˈmæs] VT acumular

amateur ['æmətəʳ] ADJ, N amador(a) *m/f*;

amateur dramatics N teatro amador

amateurish ['æmətərɪʃ] (pej) ADJ amador(a)

amaze [ə'meɪz] VT pasmar; **to be ~d (at)** espantar-se (de or com)

amazement [ə'meɪzmənt] N pasmo, espanto; **to my ~** para o meu espanto

amazing [ə'meɪzɪŋ] ADJ (surprising) surpreendente; (fantastic) fantástico; (incredible) incrível

amazingly [ə'meɪzɪŋlɪ] ADV (surprisingly) surpreendentemente; (incredibly) incrivelmente

Amazon ['æməzən] N (Geo) Amazonas m; (Mythology) amazona f ■ CPD amazônico, do Amazonas; **the ~ basin** a bacia amazônica; **the ~ jungle** a selva amazônica

Amazonian [æmə'zeunɪən] ADJ (of river, region) amazônico; (of state) amazonense ■ N amazonense m/f

ambassador [æm'bæsədə^r] N embaixador/ embaixatriz m/f

amber ['æmbə^r] N âmbar m; **at ~** (Brit: Aut) em amarelo

ambidextrous [æmbɪ'dɛkstrəs] ADJ ambidestro

ambience ['æmbɪəns] N ambiente m

ambiguity [æmbɪ'gjuɪtɪ] N ambigüidade f

ambiguous [æm'bɪgjuəs] ADJ ambíguo

ambition [æm'bɪʃən] N ambição f

ambitious [æm'bɪʃəs] ADJ ambicioso; (plan) grandioso

ambivalent [æm'bɪvələnt] ADJ ambivalente; (pej) equívoco

amble ['æmbl] VI (also: **amble along**) andar a furta-passo

ambulance ['æmbjuləns] N ambulância

ambush ['æmbuʃ] N emboscada ■ VT emboscar

ameba [ə'mi:bə] (US) N = **amoeba**

ameliorate [ə'mi:lɪəreɪt] VT melhorar

amen ['ɑ:'mɛn] EXCL amém

amenable [ə'mi:nəbl] ADJ: **~ to** (advice etc) receptivo a

amend [ə'mɛnd] VT (law, text) emendar; (habits) corrigir

amendment [ə'mɛndmənt] N (to law etc) emenda; (text) correção f

amends [ə'mɛndz] N: **to make ~** compensar; **to make ~ to sb for sth** compensar alguém por algo

amenity [ə'mi:nɪtɪ] N amenidade f; **amenities** NPL (features, facilities) atrações fpl, comodidades fpl

America [ə'mɛrɪkə] N (continent) América; (USA) Estados Unidos mpl

American [ə'mɛrɪkən] ADJ americano; (from USA) norte-americano, estadunidense ■ N americano(-a); (from USA) norte-americano(-a)

americanize [ə'mɛrɪkənaɪz] VT americanizar

amethyst ['æmɪθɪst] N ametista

Amex ['æmɛks] N ABBR = **American Stock Exchange**

amiable ['eɪmɪəbl] ADJ amável

amicable ['æmɪkəbl] ADJ amigável; (person) amigo

amid(st) [ə'mɪd(st)] PREP em meio a

amiss [ə'mɪs] ADV: **to take sth ~** levar algo a mal; **there's something ~** aí tem coisa

ammo ['æməu] (inf) N ABBR = **ammunition**

ammonia [ə'məunɪə] N (gas) amoníaco; (liquid) amônia

ammunition [æmju'nɪʃən] N munição f; (fig) argumentos mpl; **ammunition dump** N depósito de munições

amnesia [æm'ni:zɪə] N amnésia

amnesty ['æmnɪstɪ] N anistia; **to grant an ~ to** anistiar

amoeba [ə'mi:bə] (US ameba) N ameba

amok [ə'mɔk] ADV: **to run ~** enlouquecer

among(st) [ə'mʌŋ(st)] PREP entre, no meio de

amoral [æ'mɔrəl] ADJ amoral

amorous ['æmərəs] ADJ amoroso; (in love) apaixonado, enamorado

amorphous [ə'mɔ:fəs] ADJ amorfo

amortization [əmɔ:taɪ'zeɪʃən] N amortização f

amount [ə'maunt] N quantidade f; (of money etc) quantia, importância, montante m ■ VI: **to ~ to** (reach) chegar a; (total) montar a; (be same as) equivaler a, significar; **this ~s to a refusal** isto equivale a uma recusa; **the total ~** (of money) o total

amp(ère) ['æmp(ɛə^r)] N ampère m; **a 13 amp plug** um pino de tomada de 13 ampères

ampersand ['æmpəsænd] N "e" m comercial

amphibian [æm'fɪbɪən] N anfíbio

amphibious [æm'fɪbɪəs] ADJ anfíbio

amphitheatre ['æmfɪθɪətə^r] (US **amphitheater**) N anfiteatro

ample ['æmpl] ADJ amplo; (abundant) abundante; (enough) suficiente; **this is ~** isso é mais do que suficiente; **to have ~ time/room** ter tempo/lugar de sobra

amplifier ['æmplɪfaɪə^r] N amplificador m

amplify ['æmplɪfaɪ] VT amplificar

amply ['æmplɪ] ADV amplamente

ampoule ['æmpu:l] (US **ampule**) N (Med) ampola

amputate ['æmpjuteɪt] VT amputar

Amsterdam ['æmstədæm] N Amsterdã (BR), Amsterdão (PT)

amt ABBR = **amount**

amuck [ə'mʌk] ADV = **amok**

amuse [ə'mju:z] VT divertir; (distract) distrair; **to ~ o.s. with sth/by doing sth** divertir-se com algo/em fazer algo; **to be ~d at** achar graça em; **he was not ~d** ele ficou sem graça

amusement [ə'mju:zmənt] N diversão f, diversão f; (pleasure) divertimento; (pastime) passatempo; (laughter) riso; **much to my ~** para grande diversão minha; **amusement arcade** N fliperama m

amusing [ə'mju:zɪŋ] ADJ divertido

an [æn, ən, n] INDEF ART see **a**

ANA N ABBR = **American Newspaper Association; American Nurses Association**

anachronism [ə'nækrənɪzəm] N anacronismo

anaemia [ə'ni:mɪə] (US **anemia**) N anemia

anaemic [ə'ni:mɪk] (US **anemic**) ADJ anêmico

anaesthetic [ænɪs'θetɪk] (US **anesthetic**) ADJ, N anestésico; **under** ~ sob anestesia; **local/general** ~ anestesia local/geral

anaesthetist [æ'ni:sθɪtɪst] (US **anesthetist**) N anestesista m/f

anagram ['ænəgræm] N anagrama m

analgesic [ænæl'dʒi:sɪk] ADJ anaalgésica ■ N analgésico

analog(ue) ['ænəlɔg] ADJ (watch, computer) analógico

analogy [ə'nælədʒɪ] N analogia; **to draw** or **make an** ~ **between** fazer uma analogia entre

analyse ['ænəlaɪz] (US **analyze**) VT analizar

analyses [ə'næləsi:z] NPL of **analysis**

analysis [ə'næləsɪs] (pl **analyses**) N análise f; **in the last** or **final** ~ em última análise

analyst ['ænəlɪst] N analista m/f; (psychoanalyst) psicanalista m/f

analytic(al) [ænə'lɪtɪk(əl)] ADJ analítico

analyze ['ænəlaɪz] (US) VT = **analyse**

anarchic [ə'nɑ:kɪk] ADJ anárquico

anarchist ['ænəkɪst] ADJ, N anarquista m/f

anarchy ['ænəkɪ] N anarquia

anathema [ə'næθɪmə] N: **it is ~ to him** ele tem horror disso

anatomical [ænə'tɔmɪkəl] ADJ anatômico

anatomy [ə'nætəmɪ] N anatomia

ANC N ABBR (= African National Congress) CNA m

ancestor ['ænsɪstər] N antepassado

ancestral [æn'sestrəl] ADJ ancestral

ancestry ['ænsɪstrɪ] N ascendência, ancestrais mpl

anchor ['æŋkər] N âncora ■ VI (also: **to drop anchor**) ancorar, fundear ■ VT (boat) ancorar; (fig): **to** ~ **sth to** firmar algo em; **to weigh** ~ levantar âncoras; **to drop** ~ fundear

anchorage ['æŋkərɪdʒ] N ancoradouro

anchovy ['æntʃəvɪ] N enchova

ancient ['eɪnʃənt] ADJ antigo; (person, car) velho; ~ **monument** monumento antigo

ancillary [æn'sɪlərɪ] ADJ auxiliar

and [ænd] CONJ e; ~ **so on** e assim por diante; **try** ~ **come** tente vir; **he talked** ~ **talked** ele falou sem parar; **better** ~ **better** cada vez melhor

Andes ['ændi:z] NPL: **the** ~ os Andes

anecdote ['ænɪkdəut] N anedota

anemia etc [ə'ni:mɪə] (US) N = **anaemia** etc

anemic [ə'ni:mɪk] (US) ADJ = **anaemic**

anemone [ə'nemənɪ] N (Bot) anêmona

anesthetic etc [ænɪs'θetɪk] (US) ADJ, N = **anaesthetic** etc

anesthetist [æ'ni:sθɪtɪst] (US) N = **anaesthetist**

anew [ə'nju:] ADV de novo

angel ['eɪndʒəl] N anjo

anger ['æŋgər] N raiva ■ VT zangar

angina [æn'dʒaɪnə] N angina (de peito)

angle ['æŋgl] N ângulo; **from their** ~ do ponto de vista deles; (viewpoint) ■ VI: **to** ~ **for** (fish, compliments) pescar

angler ['æŋglər] N pescador(a) m/f de vara (BR) or à linha (PT)

Anglican ['æŋglɪkən] ADJ, N anglicano(-a)

anglicize ['æŋglɪsaɪz] VT anglicizar

angling ['æŋglɪŋ] N pesca à vara (BR) or à linha (PT)

Anglo- ['æŋgləu] PREFIX anglo-

Anglo-Brazilian ADJ anglo-brasileiro

Anglo-Portuguese ADJ anglo-português(-esa)

Anglo-Saxon [-'sæksən] ADJ anglo-saxão(-xôni(c)a) ■ N anglo-saxão(-xôni(c)a) m/f; (Ling) anglo-saxão m

Angola [æŋ'gəulə] N Angola (no article)

Angolan [æŋ'gəulən] ADJ, N angolano(-a)

angrily ['æŋgrɪlɪ] ADV com raiva

angry ['æŋgrɪ] ADJ zangado; **to be** ~ **with sb/at sth** estar zangado com alguém/algo; **to get** ~ zangar-se; **to make sb** ~ zangar alguém

anguish ['æŋgwɪʃ] N (physical) dor f, sofrimento; (mental) angústia

angular ['æŋgjulər] ADJ (shape) angular; (features) anguloso

animal ['ænɪməl] N animal m, bicho ■ ADJ animal

animate [vt 'ænɪmeɪt, adj 'ænɪmɪt] ADJ animado ■ VT animar

animated ['ænɪmeɪtɪd] ADJ animado

animation [ænɪ'meɪʃən] N animação f

animosity [ænɪ'mɔsɪtɪ] N animosidade f

aniseed ['ænɪsi:d] N erva-doce f, anis f

Ankara ['æŋkərə] N Ancara

ankle ['æŋkl] N tornozelo; **ankle sock** N soquete f

annex [n 'æneks, vt æ'neks] N (also: Brit: annexe: building) anexo ■ VT anexar

annexation [æneks'eɪʃən] N anexação f

annexe ['æneks] (Brit) N = **annex**

annihilate [ə'naɪəleɪt] VT aniquilar

anniversary [ænɪ'və:sərɪ] N aniversário

annotate ['ænəuteɪt] VT anotar

announce [ə'nauns] VT anunciar; **he ~d that he wasn't going** ele declarou que não iria

announcement [ə'naunsmənt] N anúncio; (official) comunicação f; (in letter etc) aviso; **to make an** ~ anunciar alguma coisa

announcer [ə'naunsər] N (Radio, TV) locutor(a) m/f

annoy [ə'nɔɪ] VT aborrecer; **to be ~ed (at sth/with sb)** aborrecer-se (com algo/alguém); **don't get ~ed!** não se aborreça!

annoyance [ə'nɔɪəns] N aborrecimento; (thing) moléstia

annoying [ə'nɔɪɪŋ] ADJ irritante; (person) importuno

annual ['ænjuəl] ADJ anual ■ N (Bot) anual f; (book) anuário; **annual general meeting** (Brit) N assembléia geral ordinária

annually ['ænjuəlɪ] ADV anualmente

annual report N relatório anual

annuity [ə'nju:ɪtɪ] N anuidade f or renda anual; **life** ~ renda vitalícia

annul [ə'nʌl] VT anular; (law) revogar

annulment [ə'nʌlmənt] N anulação f; (of law) revogação f

annum ['ænəm] N *see* **per**

Annunciation [ənʌnsɪ'eɪʃən] N Anunciação *f*

anode ['ænəʊd] N anodo

anoint [ə'nɔɪnt] VT ungir

anomalous [ə'nɔmələs] ADJ anômalo

anomaly [ə'nɔməlɪ] N anomalia

anon [ə'nɔn] ADV daqui a pouco

anon. [ə'nɔn] ABBR = **anonymous**

anonymity [ænə'nɪmɪtɪ] N anonimato

anonymous [ə'nɔnɪməs] ADJ anônimo; **to remain ~** ficar no anonimato

anorak ['ænəræk] N anoraque *m* (BR), anorak *m* (PT)

anorexia [ænə'rɛksɪə] N (*Med: also:* **anorexia nervosa**) anorexia

another [ə'nʌðə^r] ADJ: **~ book** (*one more*) outro livro, mais um livro; (*a different one*) um outro livro, um livro diferente ■ PRON outro; **~ drink?** outra bebida?, mais uma bebida?; **in ~ 5 years** daqui a 5 anos; *see also* **one**

ANSI N ABBR (= *American National Standards Institute*) instituto de padrões

answer ['ɑ:nsə^r] N resposta; (*to problem*) solução *f* ■ VI responder ■ VT (*reply to*) responder a; (*problem*) resolver; **in ~ to your letter** em resposta *or* respondendo à sua carta; **to ~ the phone** atender o telefone; **to ~ the bell** *or* **the door** atender à porta

► **answer back** VI replicar, retrucar

► **answer for** VT FUS responder por, responsabilizar-se por

► **answer to** VT FUS (*description*) corresponder a; (*needs*) satisfazer

answerable ['ɑ:nsərəbl] ADJ: **~ (to sb/for sth)** responsável (perante alguém/por algo); **I am ~ to no-one** não tenho que dar satisfações a ninguém

answering machine ['ɑ:nsərɪŋ-] N secretária eletrônica

ant [ænt] N formiga

ANTA N ABBR = **American National Theater and Academy**

antacid [ænt'æsɪd] ADJ antiácido

antagonism [æn'tægənɪzəm] N antagonismo

antagonist [æn'tægənɪst] N antagonista *m/f*, adversário(-a)

antagonistic [æntægə'nɪstɪk] ADJ antagônico, hostil; (*opposed*) oposto, contrário

antagonize [æn'tægənaɪz] VT contrariar, hostilizar

Antarctic [ænt'ɑ:ktɪk] ADJ antártico ■ N: **the ~** o Antártico

Antarctica [æn'tɑ:ktɪkə] N Antártica

Antarctic Circle N Círculo Polar Antártico

Antarctic Ocean N oceano Antártico

ante ['æntɪ] N: **to up the ~** apostar mais alto

ante... ['æntɪ] PREFIX ante..., pré...

anteater ['ænti:tə^r] N tamanduá *m*

antecedent [æntɪ'si:dənt] N antecedente *m*

antechamber ['æntɪtʃeɪmbə^r] N antecâmara

antelope ['æntɪləʊp] N antílope *m*

antenatal ['æntɪ'neɪtl] ADJ pré-natal;

antenatal clinic N clínica pré-natal

antenna [æn'tɛnə] (*pl* **antennae**) N antena

antennae [æn'tɛni:] NPL *of* **antenna**

anthem ['ænθəm] N motete *m*; **national ~** hino nacional

ant hill N formigueiro

anthology [æn'θɔlədʒɪ] N antologia

anthropologist [ænθrə'pɔlədʒɪst] N antropologista *m/f*, antropólogo(-a)

anthropology [ænθrə'pɔlədʒɪ] N antropologia

anti... [æntɪ] PREFIX anti...

anti-aircraft ADJ antiaéreo; **anti-aircraft defence** N defesa antiaérea

anti-ballistic missile ['æntɪbə'lɪstɪk-] N míssil *m* antimíssil

antibiotic [æntɪbaɪ'ɔtɪk] ADJ, N antibiótico

antibody ['æntɪbɔdɪ] N anticorpo

anticipate [æn'tɪsɪpeɪt] VT (*foresee*) prever; (*expect*) esperar; (*forestall*) antecipar; (*look forward to*) aguardar, esperar; **this is worse than I ~d** isso é pior do que eu esperava; **as ~d** como previsto

anticipation [æntɪsɪ'peɪʃən] N (*expectation*) expectativa; (*eagerness*) entusiasmo; **thanking you in ~** antecipadamente grato(s), agradeço (*or* agradecemos) antecipadamente a atenção de V.S^a

anticlimax [æntɪ'klaɪmæks] N desapontamento

anticlockwise [æntɪ'klɔkwaɪz] (*Brit*) ADV em sentido anti-horário

antics ['æntɪks] NPL bobices *fpl*; (*of child*) travessuras *fpl*

anticyclone [æntɪ'saɪkləʊn] N anticiclone *m*

antidote ['æntɪdəʊt] N antídoto

antifreeze ['æntɪfri:z] N anticongelante *m*

antiglobalization N, MOD antiglobalização *m*; **~ protesters** manifestantes antiglobalização

antihistamine [æntɪ'hɪstəmi:n] N anti-histamínico

Antilles [æn'tɪli:z] NPL: **the ~** as Antilhas

antipathy [æn'tɪpəθɪ] N antipatia

Antipodean [æntɪpə'di:ən] ADJ australiano e neozelandês

Antipodes [æn'tɪpədi:z] NPL: **the ~** a Austrália e a Nova Zelândia

antiquarian [æntɪ'kwɛərɪən] ADJ: **~ bookshop** livraria de livros usados, sebo (BR) ■ N antiquário(-a)

antiquated ['æntɪkweɪtɪd] ADJ antiquado

antique [æn'ti:k] N antiguidade *f* ■ ADJ antigo; **antique dealer** N antiquário(-a); **antique shop** N loja de antiguidades

antiquity [æn'tɪkwɪtɪ] N antiguidade *f*

anti-Semitic [-sɪ'mɪtɪk] ADJ (*person*) anti-semita; (*views, publications etc*) anti-semítico

anti-Semitism [-'sɛmɪtɪzəm] N anti-semitismo

antiseptic [æntɪ'sɛptɪk] ADJ, N anti-séptico

antisocial [æntɪ'səʊʃəl] ADJ insociável; (*against society*) anti-social

antitank ['æntɪ'tæŋk] ADJ antitanque *inv*

antitheses [æn'tɪθɪsi:z] NPL *of* **antithesis**

antithesis [æn'tɪθɪsɪs] (*pl* antitheses) N antítese *f*

antitrust legislation ['æntɪ'trʌst-] N legislação *f* antitruste

antlers ['æntləz] NPL esgalhos *mpl*, chifres *mpl*

antivirus ['æntɪvaɪərəs] ADJ antivirus *inv*; ~ software programa (de) antivírus

Antwerp ['æntwə:p] N Antuérpia

anus ['eɪnəs] N ânus *m*

anvil ['ænvɪl] N bigorna

anxiety [æŋ'zaɪətɪ] N (*worry*) inquietude *f*; (*eagerness*) ânsia; (*Med*) ansiedade *f*; ~ to do ânsia de fazer

anxious ['æŋkʃəs] ADJ (*worried*) preocupado, apreensivo; (*worrying*) angustiante; (*keen*) ansioso; ~ to do/for sth ansioso para fazer/por algo; to be ~ that desejar que; I'm very ~ about you estou muito preocupado com você

anxiously ['æŋkʃəslɪ] ADV ansiosamente

O KEYWORD

any ['enɪ] ADJ 1 (*in questions etc*) algum(a); have you any butter/children? você tem manteiga/filhos?; if there are any tickets left se houver alguns bilhetes sobrando

2 (*with negative*) nenhum(a); I haven't any money/books não tenho dinheiro/livros

3 (*no matter which*) qualquer; choose any book you like escolha qualquer livro que quiser

4 (*in phrases*): in any case em todo o caso; any day now qualquer dia desses; at any moment a qualquer momento; at any rate de qualquer modo; any time a qualquer momento; (*whenever*) quando quer que seja

■ PRON 1 (*in questions etc*) algum(a); have you got any? tem algum?; can any of you sing? algum de vocês sabe cantar?

2 (*with negative*) nenhum(a); I haven't any (of them) não tenho nenhum (deles)

3 (*no matter which one(s)*): take any of those books (you like) leve qualquer um desses livros (que você quiser)

■ ADV 1 (*in questions etc*) algo; do you want any more soup/sandwiches? quer mais sopa/sanduíches?; are you feeling any better? você está se sentindo melhor?

2 (*with negative*) nada; I can't hear him any more não consigo mais ouvi-lo

anybody ['enɪbɔdɪ] PRON qualquer um, qualquer pessoa; (*in interrogative sentences*) alguém; (*in negative sentences*): I don't see ~ não vejo ninguém

anyhow ['enɪhau] ADV 1 (*at any rate*) de qualquer modo, de qualquer maneira; I shall go ~ eu irei de qualquer jeito 2 (*haphazard*) de qualquer jeito; do it ~ you like de qualquer jeito; do it ~ you like faça do jeito que você quiser; she leaves things just ~ ela deixa as coisas de qualquer maneira

anyone ['enɪwʌn] PRON 1 (*in questions etc*)

alguém; can you see ~? você pode ver alguém?; if ~ should phone ... se alguém telefonar 2 (*with negative*) ninguém; I can't see ~ não vejo ninguém 3 (*no matter who*) quem quer que seja; ~ could do it qualquer um(a) podeira fazer isso; I could teach ~ to do it eu podeira ensimar qualquer um(a) a fazer isso

anyplace ['enɪpleɪs] (*US*) ADV em qualquer parte; (*negative sense*) em parte nenhuma; (*everywhere*) em *or* por toda a parte

anything ['enɪθɪŋ] PRON 1 (*in questions etc*) alguma coisa; can you see ~? você pode ver alguma coisa?; if ~ happens to me ... se alguma coisa me acontecer ... 2 (*with negative*) nada; I can't see ~ naõ posso ver nada 3 (*no matter what*) qualquer coisa; you can say ~ you like você pode dizer o que quiser; ~ will do qualquer coisa serve

anytime ['enɪtaɪm] ADV (*at any moment*) a qualquer momento; (*whenever*) não importa quando

anyway ['enɪweɪ] ADV 1 (*at any rate*) de qualquer modo; I shall go ~ eu irei de qualquer jeito 2 (*besides*) além disso; ~, I couldn't come even if I wanted to além disso, mesmo se eu quisesse, não poderia vir

anywhere ['enɪwɛəʳ] ADV (*in questions etc*) em algum lugar; can you see him ~? vocî pode vê-lo em algum lugar? 2 (*with negative*) em parte nenhuma; I can't see him ~ não o vejo em parte nenhuma 3 (*no matter where*) não importa onde/onde quer que seja; ~ in the world em qualquer lugar do mundo; put the books down ~ colegue os livros em qualquer lugar

Anzac ['ænzæk] N ABBR (= *Australia-New Zealand Army Corps*) soldado da tropa ANZAC

apart [ə'pɑ:t] ADV à parte, à distância; (*separately*) separado; 10 miles ~ separados por 10 milhas; to take ~ desmembrar; they are living ~ estão separados; ~ from além de, à parte de

apartheid [ə'pɑ:teɪt] N apartheid *m*

apartment [ə'pɑ:tmənt] (*US*) N apartamento; apartment building (*US*) N prédio *or* edifício (de apartamentos)

apathetic [æpə'θetɪk] ADJ apático

apathy ['æpəθɪ] N apatia, indiferença

APB (*US*) N ABBR (= *all points bulletin*) expressão usada pela polícia significando "descubram e prendam o suspeito"

ape [eɪp] N macaco ■ VT macaquear, imitar

Apennines ['æpənaɪnz] NPL: the ~ os Apeninos

aperitif [ə'perɪtɪv] N aperitivo

aperture ['æpətʃuəʳ] N orifício; (*Phot*) abertura

APEX ['eɪpeks] N (*Brit*: = *Association of Professional, Executive, Clerical and Computer Staff*) sindicato de funcionários comerciais; (*Aviat*: = *advance passenger excursion*) APEX *f*

apex ['eɪpeks] N ápice *m*

aphid ['eɪfɪd] N pulgão *m*

aphrodisiac [æfrəu'dɪzɪæk] ADJ afrodisíaco ■ N afrodisíaco

API N ABBR = **American Press Institute**

apiece [ə'piːs] ADV (for each person) cada um, por cabeça; (for each item) cada

aplomb [ə'plɔm] N desenvoltura

APO (US) N ABBR (= Army Post Office) serviço postal do exército

apocalypse [ə'pɔkəlɪps] N apocalipse m

apolitical [eɪpə'lɪtɪkl] ADJ apolítico

apologetic [əpɔlə'dʒetɪk] ADJ cheio de desculpas

apologetically [əpɔlə'dʒetɪklɪ] ADV (say) desculpando-se; (smile) como quem pede desculpas

apologize [ə'pɔlədʒaɪz] VI: **to ~ (for sth to sb)** desculpar-se or pedir desculpas (por or de algo a alguém)

apology [ə'pɔlədʒɪ] N desculpas fpl; **please accept my apologies for ...** peço desculpas por ...; **to send one's apologies** apresentar desculpas

apoplectic [æpə'plɛktɪk] ADJ (Med) apopléctico; (inf): **~ with rage** enraivecido

apoplexy ['æpəplɛksɪ] N (Med) apoplexia

apostle [ə'pɔsl] N apóstolo

apostrophe [ə'pɔstrəfɪ] N apóstrofo

appal [ə'pɔːl] VT horrorizar

Appalachian Mountains [æpə'leɪʃən-] NPL: **the ~** os montes Apalaches

appalling [ə'pɔːlɪŋ] ADJ (shocking) chocante; (awful) terrível; **she's an ~ cook** ela é uma péssima cozinheira

apparatus [æpə'reɪtəs] N aparelho; (in gym) aparelhos mpl; (organization) aparato

apparel [ə'pærl] (US) N vestuário, roupa

apparent [ə'pærənt] ADJ aparente; (obvious) claro, patente; **it is ~ that ...** é claro or evidente que ...

apparently [ə'pærəntlɪ] ADV aparentemente, pelo(s) visto(s)

apparition [æpə'rɪʃən] N aparição f; (ghost) fantasma m

appeal [ə'piːl] VI (Law) apelar, recorrer ■ N (Law) recurso, apelação f; (request) pedido; (plea) súplica; (charm) atração f; **to ~ (to sb) for** suplicar (a alguém); **to ~ to** (subj: person) suplicar a; (be attractive to) atrair; **to ~ to sb for mercy** pedir misericórdia a alguém; **it doesn't ~ to me** não me atrai; **right of ~** direito a recorrer or apelar

appealing [ə'piːlɪŋ] ADJ (attractive) atraente; (touching) comovedor(a), comovente

appear [ə'pɪəʳ] VI (come into view) aparecer; (be present) comparecer; (Law) apresentar-se, comparecer; (publication) ser publicado; (seem) parecer; **it would ~ that ...** pareceria que ...; **to ~ in "Hamlet"** trabalhar em "Hamlet"; **to ~ on TV** (person, news item) sair na televisão; (programme) passar na televisão

appearance [ə'pɪərəns] N (coming into view) aparecimento; (presence) comparecimento; (look, aspect) aparência; **to put in** or **make an ~** comparecer; **in order of ~** (Theatre) por ordem de entrar em cena; **to keep up ~s** manter as aparências; **to all ~s** ao que tudo indica

appease [ə'piːz] VT (pacify) apaziguar; (satisfy) satisfazer

appeasement [ə'piːzmənt] N apaziguamento

append [ə'pɛnd] VT anexar

appendage [ə'pɛndɪdʒ] N apêndice m

appendices [ə'pɛndɪsiːz] NPL of **appendix**

appendicitis [əpɛndɪ'saɪtɪs] N apendicite f

appendix [ə'pɛndɪks] (pl **appendices**) N apêndice m; **to have one's ~ out** tirar o apêndice

appetite ['æpɪtaɪt] N apetite m; (fig) desejo; **that walk has given me an ~** essa caminhada me abriu o apetite

appetizer ['æpɪtaɪzəʳ] N (food) tira-gosto; (drink) aperitivo

appetizing ['æpɪtaɪzɪŋ] ADJ apetitoso

applaud [ə'plɔːd] VI aplaudir ■ VT aplaudir; (praise) admirar

applause [ə'plɔːz] N aplausos mpl

apple ['æpl] N maçã f; (also: **apple tree**) macieira; **she's the ~ of his eye** ela é a menina dos olhos dele; **apple tree** N macieira; **apple turnover** N pastel m de maçã

appliance [ə'plaɪəns] N (Tech) aparelho; **electrical** or **domestic ~s** eletrodomésticos mpl

applicable [ə'plɪkəbl] ADJ aplicável; (relevant) apropriado; **the law is ~ from January** a lei entrará em vigor a partir de janeiro; **to be ~ to** valer para

applicant ['æplɪkənt] N: **~ (for)** (for post) candidato(-a) (a); (Admin: for benefit etc) requerente m/f (de)

application [æplɪ'keɪʃən] N aplicação f; (for a job, a grant etc) candidatura, requerimento; **on ~** a pedido; **application form** N (formulário de) requerimento; (hard work) esforço; **application program** N (Comput) aplicativo

applications package N (Comput) pacote m de aplicações

applied [ə'plaɪd] ADJ aplicado

apply [ə'plaɪ] VT (paint etc) usar; (law etc) pôr em prática ■ VI: **to ~ to** apresentar-se a; (be suitable for) ser aplicável a; (be relevant to) dizer respeito a; (ask) pedir; **to ~ for** (permit, grant, job) solicitar, pedir; **to ~ the brakes** frear (BR), travar (PT); **to ~ o.s. to** aplicar-se a, dedicar-se a

appoint [ə'pɔɪnt] VT (to post) nomear; (date, place) marcar

appointed [ə'pɔɪntɪd] ADJ: **at the ~ time** à hora marcada

appointee [əpɔɪn'tiː] N nomeado(-a)

appointment [ə'pɔɪntmənt] N (engagement) encontro, marcado, compromisso; (at doctors etc) hora marcada; (act) nomeação f; (post) cargo; **to make an ~ (with) sb** marcar um encontro (com) alguém; (with doctor, hairdresser etc) marcar hora (com); **"~s (vacant)"** (Press) "ofertas de emprego"; **by ~** com hora marcada

apportion [ə'pɔːʃən] VT repartir, distribuir; (blame) pôr; **to ~ sth to sb** atribuir algo a alguém

appraisal [ə'preɪzl] N avaliação f

appraise [ə'preɪz] VT avaliar

appreciable [ə'priːʃəbl] ADJ apreciável, notável

appreciate [ə'priːʃieɪt] VT (like) apreciar, estimar; (be grateful for) agradecer; (understand) compreender ■ VI (Comm) valorizar-se; **I ~ your help** agradeço-lhe a or pela sua ajuda

appreciation [əpriːʃi'eɪʃən] N apreciação f, estima; (understanding) compreensão f; (gratitude) agradecimento; (Comm) valorização f

appreciative [ə'priːʃiətɪv] ADJ (person) agradecido; (comment) elogioso

apprehend [æpri'hɛnd] VT (understand) perceber, compreender; (arrest) prender

apprehension [æpri'hɛnʃən] N apreensão f

apprehensive [æpri'hɛnsɪv] ADJ apreensivo, receoso

apprentice [ə'prɛntɪs] N aprendiz m/f ■ VT: **to be ~d** ser aprendiz de

apprenticeship [ə'prɛntɪsʃɪp] N aprendizado, aprendizagem f; **to serve one's ~** fazer seu aprendizado

appro. ['æprəu] (Brit: inf) ABBR (Comm) = **approval**

approach [ə'prəutʃ] VI aproximar-se ■ VT aproximar-se de; (be approximate) aproximar-se a; (ask, apply to) dirigir-se a; (subject, passer-by) abordar ■ N aproximação f; (access) acesso; (proposal) proposição f; (to problem, situation) enfoque m; **to ~ sb about sth** falar com alguém sobre algo

approachable [ə'prəutʃəbl] ADJ (person) tratável; (place) acessível

approach road N via de acesso

approbation [æprə'beɪʃən] N aprovação f

appropriate [vt ə'prəuprieɪt, adj ə'prəupriit] ADJ (apt) apropriado; (relevant) adequado ■ VT (take) apropriar-se de; (allot): **to ~ sth for** destinar algo a; **it would not be ~ for me to comment** não seria conveniente eu comentar

appropriately [ə'prəupriitli] ADV adequadamente

appropriation [əprəupri'eɪʃən] N (confiscation) apropriação f; (of funds for sth) dotação f

approval [ə'pruːvəl] N aprovação f; (permission) consentimento; **on ~** (Comm) a contento; **to meet with sb's ~** (proposal etc) ser aprovado por alguém, obter a aprovação de alguém

approve [ə'pruːv] VT (publication, product) autorizar; (motion, decision) aprovar
  ▸ **approve of** VT FUS aprovar

approved school [ə'pruːvd-] (Brit) N reformatório

approvingly [ə'pruːvɪŋli] ADV com aprovação

approx. ABBR = **approximately**

approximate [adj ə'prɔksɪmɪt, vt ə'prɔksɪmeɪt] ADJ aproximado ■ VT aproximar

approximately [ə'prɔksɪmɪtli] ADV aproximadamente

approximation [əprɔksɪ'meɪʃən] N aproximação f

apr N ABBR (= annual percentage rate) taxa de juros anual

Apr. ABBR = **April**

apricot ['eɪprɪkɔt] N damasco

April ['eɪprəl] N abril m; see also **July**; **April Fool's Day** N Primeiro-de-abril m

apron ['eɪprən] N avental m; (Aviat) pátio de estacionamento

apse [æps] N (Archit) abside f

APT (Brit) N ABBR = **advanced passenger train**

apt [æpt] ADJ (suitable) adequado; (appropriate) a propósito, apropriado; (likely): **~ to do** sujeito a fazer

Apt. ABBR (= apartment) ap., apto

aptitude ['æptɪtjuːd] N aptidão f, talento; **aptitude test** N teste m de aptidão

aptly ['æptli] ADV (express) acertadamente; **~ named** apropriadamente chamado

aqualung ['ækwəlʌŋ] N aparelho respiratório autônomo

aquarium [ə'kwɛəriəm] N aquário

Aquarius [ə'kwɛəriəs] N Aquário

aquatic [ə'kwætɪk] ADJ aquático

aqueduct ['ækwɪdʌkt] N aqueduto

AR (US) ABBR (Post) = **Arkansas**

ARA (Brit) N ABBR = **Associate of the Royal Academy**

Arab ['ærəb] ADJ, N árabe m/f

Arabia [ə'reɪbɪə] N Arábia

Arabian [ə'reɪbɪən] ADJ árabe; **Arabian Desert** N deserto da Arábia; **Arabian Sea** N mar m Arábico

Arabic ['ærəbɪk] ADJ árabe ■ N (Ling) árabe m; (numerals) arábico; **Arabic numerals** NPL algarismos mpl arábicos

arable ['ærəbl] ADJ cultivável

ARAM (Brit) N ABBR = **Associate of the Royal Academy of Music**

arbiter ['ɑːbɪtə'] N árbitro

arbitrary ['ɑːbɪtrəri] ADJ arbitrário

arbitrate ['ɑːbɪtreɪt] VI arbitrar

arbitration [ɑːbɪ'treɪʃən] N arbitragem f; **the dispute went to ~** o litígio foi submetido a arbitragem

arbitrator ['ɑːbɪtreɪtə'] N árbitro

ARC N ABBR = **American Red Cross**

arc [ɑːk] N arco

arcade [ɑː'keɪd] N arcada; (round a square) arcos mpl; (passage with shops) galeria

arch [ɑːtʃ] N arco; (of foot) curvatura ■ VT arquear, curvar ■ ADJ malicioso ■ PREFIX: ~(-) arce..., arqui...; **pointed ~** ogiva

archaeological [ɑːkiə'lɔdʒɪkl] (US **archeological**) ADJ arqueológico

archaeologist [ɑːkɪ'ɔlədʒɪst] (US **archeologist**) N arqueólogo(-a)

archaeology [ɑːkɪ'ɔlədʒɪ] (US **archeology**) N arqueologia

archaic [ɑː'keɪɪk] ADJ arcaico

archangel ['ɑːkeɪndʒəl] N arcanjo

archbishop [ɑːtʃ'bɪʃəp] N arcebispo

arch-enemy N arquiinimigo(-a)

archeology *etc* [ɑːkɪ'ɔlədʒɪ] (*US*) = **archaeology** *etc*

archer ['ɑːtʃəʳ] N arqueiro(-a)

archery ['ɑːtʃərɪ] N tiro de arco

archetypal ['ɑːkɪtaɪpəl] ADJ arquetípico

archetype ['ɑːkɪtaɪp] N arquétipo

archipelago [ɑːkɪ'pɛlɪgəu] N arquipélago

architect ['ɑːkɪtɛkt] N arquiteto(-a)

architectural [ɑːkɪ'tɛktʃərəl] ADJ arquitetônico

architecture ['ɑːkɪtɛktʃəʳ] N arquitetura

archives ['ɑːkaɪvz] NPL arquivo

archivist ['ɑːkɪvɪst] N arquivista *m/f*

archway ['ɑːtʃweɪ] N arco

ARCM (*Brit*) N ABBR = **Associate of the Royal College of Music**

Arctic ['ɑːktɪk] ADJ ártico ■ N: **the ~** o Ártico; **Arctic Circle** N Círculo Polar Ártico; **Arctic Ocean** N oceano Ártico

ARD (*US*) N ABBR (*Med*) = **acute respiratory disease**

ardent ['ɑːdənt] ADJ (*admirer*) ardente; (*discussion*) acalorado; (*fervent*) fervoroso

ardour ['ɑːdəʳ] (*US* **ardor**) N (*passion*) ardor *m*; (*fervour*) fervor *m*

arduous ['ɑːdjuəs] ADJ árduo

are [ɑːʳ] VB *see* **be**

area ['ɛərɪə] N (*zone*) zona, região *f*; (*part of place*) região; (*in room, of knowledge, experience*) área; (*Mat*) superfície *f*, extensão *f*; **dining ~** área de jantar; **the London ~** a região de Londres; **area code** (*US*) N (*Tel*) código DDD or de área

arena [ə'riːnə] N arena; (*of circus*) picadeiro (BR), pista (PT); (*for bullfight*) arena (BR), praça (PT)

aren't [ɑːnt] = **are not**

Argentina [ɑːdʒən'tiːnə] N Argentina

Argentinian [ɑːdʒən'tɪnɪən] ADJ, N argentino(-a)

arguable ['ɑːgjuəbl] ADJ discutível

arguably ['ɑːgjuəblɪ] ADV possivelmente

argue ['ɑːgjuː] VI (*quarrel*) discutir; (*reason*) argumentar; **to ~ about sth (with sb)** discutir sobre algo (com alguém); **to ~ that** sustentar que

argument ['ɑːgjumənt] N (*reasons*) argumento; (*quarrel*) briga, discussão *f*; (*debate*) debate *m*; **~ for/against** argumento a favor de/contra

argumentative [ɑːgju'mɛntətɪv] ADJ (*person*) que gosta de discutir

aria ['ɑːrɪə] N (*Mus*) ária

ARIBA (*Brit*) N ABBR = **Associate of the Royal Institute of British Architects**

arid ['ærɪd] ADJ árido

aridity [ə'rɪdɪtɪ] N aridez *f*

Aries ['ɛərɪz] N Áries *m*

arise [ə'raɪz] (*pt* **arose**, *pp* **arisen**) VI (*rise up*) levantar-se, erguer-se; (*emerge*) surgir; **to ~ from** resultar de; **should the need ~** se for necessário

arisen [ə'rɪzn] *of* **arise**

aristocracy [ærɪs'tɔkrəsɪ] N aristocracia

aristocrat ['ærɪstəkræt] N aristocrata *m/f*

aristocratic [ærɪstə'krætɪk] ADJ aristocrático

arithmetic [ə'rɪθmətɪk] N aritmética

arithmetical [ærɪθ'mɛtɪkl] ADJ aritmético

ark [ɑːk] N: **Noah's A~** arca de Noé

arm [ɑːm] N (*of organization etc*) braço, divisão *f* ■ VT armar; **arms** NPL (*weapons*) armas *fpl*; (*Heraldry*) brasão *m*; **~ in ~** de braços dados

armaments ['ɑːməmənts] NPL (*weapons*) armamento

armband ['ɑːmbænd] N faixa de braço, braçadeira; (*for swimming*) bóia de braço

armchair ['ɑːmtʃɛəʳ] N poltrona

armed [ɑːmd] ADJ armado; **the ~ forces** as forças armadas; **armed robbery** N assalto à mão armada

Armenia [ɑː'miːnɪə] N Armênia

Armenian [ɑː'miːnɪən] ADJ armênio ■ N armênio(-a); (*Ling*) armênio

armful ['ɑːmful] N braçada

armistice ['ɑːmɪstɪs] N armistício

armour ['ɑːməʳ] (*US* **armor**) N armadura; (*also*: **armour plating**) blindagem *f*

armo(u)red car ['ɑːməd-] N carro blindado

armo(u)ry ['ɑːmərɪ] N arsenal *m*

armpit ['ɑːmpɪt] N sovaco

armrest ['ɑːmrɛst] N braço (de poltrona)

arms control N controle *m* de armas

arms race N corrida armamentista

army ['ɑːmɪ] N exército

aroma [ə'rəumə] N aroma

aromatic [ærə'mætɪk] ADJ aromático

arose [ə'rəuz] PT *of* **arise**

around [ə'raund] ADV em volta; (*in the area*) perto ■ PREP em volta de; (*near*) perto de; (*fig: about*) cerca de; **is he ~?** ele está por aí?

arouse [ə'rauz] VT despertar; (*anger*) provocar

arrange [ə'reɪndʒ] VT arranjar; (*organize*) organizar; (*put in order*) arrumar ■ VI: **we have ~d for a car to pick you up** providenciamos um carro para buscá-lo; **it was ~d that ...** foi combinado que ...; **to ~ to do sth** combinar em or ficar de fazer algo

arrangement [ə'reɪndʒmənt] N (*agreement*) acordo; (*order, lay out*) dispocição *f*; **arrangements** NPL (*plans*) planos *mpl*; (*preparations*) preparativos *mpl*; **to come to an ~ (with sb)** chegar a um acordo (com alguém); **home deliveries by ~** entregas a domicílio por convênio; **I'll make all the necessary ~s** eu vou tomar todas as providências necessárias

array [ə'reɪ] N: **~ of** (*of things, people*) variedade *f* de; (*Math, Comput*) tabela

arrears [ə'rɪəz] NPL atrasos *mpl*; **to be in ~ with one's rent** atrasar o aluguel

arrest [ə'rɛst] VT prender, deter; (*sb's attention*) chamar, prender ■ N detenção *f*, prisão *f*; **under ~** preso

arresting [ə'rɛstɪŋ] ADJ (*fig: beauty*) cativante; (: *painting, novel*) impressionante

arrival [ə'raɪvəl] N chegada; **new ~** recém-chegado; (*baby*) recém-nascido

arrive [ə'raɪv] VI chegar

▸ **arrive at** VT FUS (*fig*) chegar a

arrogance ['ærəgəns] N arrogância
arrogant ['ærəgənt] ADJ arrogante
arrow ['ærəu] N flecha; (sign) seta
arse [ɑ:s] (Brit: inf!) N cu m (!)
arsenal ['ɑ:sɪnl] N arsenal m
arsenic ['ɑ:snɪk] N arsênico
arson ['ɑ:sn] N incêndio premeditado
art [ɑ:t] N arte f; (craft) ofício; (skill) habilidade
f, jeito; **Arts** NPL (Sch) letras fpl; **work of** ~ obra
de arte
artefact ['ɑ:tɪfækt] N artefato
arterial [ɑ:'tɪərɪəl] ADJ (Anat) arterial; ~ **road**
estrada mestra
artery ['ɑ:tərɪ] N (Med) artéria; (fig) estrada
principal
artful ['ɑ:tful] ADJ ardiloso, esperto
art gallery N museu m de belas artes; (small,
private) galeria de arte
arthritis [ɑ:'θraɪtɪs] N artrite f
artichoke ['ɑ:tɪtʃəuk] N (globe artichoke)
alcachofra; (also: **Jerusalem artichoke**)
topinambo
article ['ɑ:tɪkl] N artigo; **articles** NPL (Brit:
Law: training) contrato de aprendizagem; **~s of**
clothing peças fpl de vestuário
articles of association NPL (Comm) estatutos
mpl sociais
articulate [adj ɑ:'tɪkjulɪt, vt ɑ:'tɪkjuleɪt] ADJ
(speech) bem articulado; (writing) bem escrito;
(person) eloqüente ▪ VT expressar
articulated lorry [ɑ:'tɪkjuleɪtɪd-] (Brit) N
caminhão m ou camião m (PT) articulado,
jamanta
artifice ['ɑ:tɪfɪs] N ardil m, artifício
artificial [ɑ:tɪ'fɪʃəl] ADJ artificial; (limb) postiço;
(person, manner) afetado; **artificial insemination**
[-ɪnsɛmɪ'neɪʃən] N inseminação f artificial;
artificial intelligence N inteligência artificial;
artificial respiration N respiração f artificial
artillery [ɑ:'tɪlərɪ] N artilharia
artisan ['ɑ:tɪzæn] N artesão(-sã) m/f
artist ['ɑ:tɪst] N artista m/f; (Mus) intérprete m/f
artistic [ɑ:'tɪstɪk] ADJ artístico
artistry ['ɑ:tɪstrɪ] N arte f, mestria
artless ['ɑ:tlɪs] ADJ (innocent) natural, simples;
(clumsy) desajeitado
art school N ≈ escola de artes
ARV N ABBR (= American Revised Version) tradução
norte-americana da Bíblia
AS (US) N ABBR (Sch: = Associate in/of Science) título
universitário ▪ ABBR (Post) = **American Samoa**

○ KEYWORD

as [æz, əz] CONJ **1** (referring to time) quando; **as**
the years went by no decorrer dos anos; **he**
came in as I was leaving ele chegou quando
eu estava saindo; **as from tomorrow** a partir
de amanhã
2 (in comparisons) tão como, tanto(s) como; **as big**
as tão grande como; **twice as big as** duas vezes
maior que; **as much/many as** tanto/tantos

como; **as much money/many books as** tanto
dinheiro quanto/tantos livros quanto; **as soon**
as logo que, assim que
3 (since, because) como; **as you can't come, I'll**
go without you como você não pode vir, eu vou
sem você
4 (referring to manner, way) como; **do as you wish**
faça como quiser; **as she said** como ela disse
5 (concerning): **as for** or **to that** quanto a isso
6: **as if** or **though** como se; **he looked as if he**
was ill ele parecia doente
▪ PREP (in the capacity of): **he works as a driver**
ele trabalha como motorista; **he gave it to me**
as a present ele me deu isso de presente; see
also **long; such; well**

ASA N ABBR (= American Standards Association)
associação de padronização
a.s.a.p. ABBR = **as soon as possible**
asbestos [æz'bɛstəs] N asbesto, amianto
ascend [ə'sɛnd] VT subir; (throne) ascender
ascendancy [ə'sɛndənsɪ] N predomínio,
ascendência
ascendant [ə'sɛndənt] N: **to be in the** ~ estar
em alta
Ascension [ə'sɛnʃən] N (Rel): **the** ~ a Ascensão;
Ascension Island N ilha da Ascensão
ascent [ə'sɛnt] N subida; (slope) rampa;
(promotion) ascensão f
ascertain [æsə'teɪn] VT averiguar, verificar
ascetic [ə'sɛtɪk] ADJ ascético
asceticism [ə'sɛtɪsɪzəm] N ascetismo
ASCII ['æski:] N ABBR (= American Standard Code for
Information Interchange) ASCII m
ascribe [ə'skraɪb] VT: **to** ~ **sth to** atribuir algo a
ASCU (US) N ABBR = **Association of State**
Colleges and Universities
ASE N ABBR = **American Stock Exchange**
ASH [æʃ] (Brit) N ABBR (= Action on Smoking and
Health) liga antitabagista
ash [æʃ] N cinza; (tree, wood) freixo
ashamed [ə'ʃeɪmd] ADJ envergonhado; **to be** ~
of ter vergonha de; **to be** ~ (**of o.s.**) **for having**
done ter vergonha de ter feito
ashen ['æʃn] ADJ cinzento
ashore [ə'ʃɔ:ʳ] ADV em terra; **to go** ~ descer à
terra, desembarcar
ashtray ['æʃtreɪ] N cinzeiro
Ash Wednesday N quarta-feira de cinzas
Asia ['eɪʃə] N Ásia; **Asia Minor** N Ásia Menor
Asian ['eɪʃən] ADJ, N asiático(-a)
Asiatic [eɪsɪ'ætɪk] ADJ asiático(-a)
aside [ə'saɪd] ADV à parte, de lado ▪ N aparte m;
~ **from** além de
ask [ɑ:sk] VT perguntar; (invite) convidar; **to** ~
sb sth perguntar algo a alguém; **to** ~ **sb for**
sth pedir algo a alguém; **to** ~ **sb to do sth**
pedir para alguém fazer algo; **to** ~ **sb the time**
perguntar as horas a alguém; **to** ~ **sb about**
sth perguntar a alguém sobre algo; **to** ~ **about**
the price perguntar pelo preço; **to** ~ (**sb**) **a**
question fazer uma pergunta (a alguém); **to** ~

sb out to dinner convidar alguém para jantar
▶ **ask after** VT FUS perguntar por
▶ **ask for** VT FUS pedir; **it's just ~ing for it** or **trouble** é procurar encrenca
askance [ə'skɑːns] ADV: **to look ~ at sb, sth** olhar alguém/algo de soslaio
askew [ə'skjuː] ADV torto
asking price ['ɑːskɪŋ-] N preço pedido
asleep [ə'sliːp] ADJ dormindo; **to fall ~** dormir, adormecer
ASLEF ['æzlɛf] (Brit) N ABBR (= Associated Society of Locomotive Engineers and Firemen) sindicato dos ferroviários
asp [æsp] N áspide m or f
asparagus [əs'pærəgəs] N aspargo (BR), espargo (PT); **asparagus tips** NPL aspargos mpl
ASPCA N ABBR = American Society for the Prevention of Cruelty to Animals
aspect ['æspɛkt] N aspecto; (direction in which a building etc faces) direção f
aspersions [əs'pəːʃənz] NPL: **to cast ~ on** difamar, caluniar
asphalt ['æsfælt] N asfalto
asphyxiate [æs'fɪksɪeɪt] VT asfixiar ▪ VI asfixiar-se
asphyxiation [æsfɪksɪ'eɪʃən] N astixia
aspirations [æspə'reɪʃəns] N (hopes) esperança; (ambitions) aspirações fpl
aspire [əs'paɪəʳ] VI: **to ~ to** aspirar a
aspirin ['æsprɪn] N aspirina
ass [æs] N jumento, burro; (inf) imbecil m/f; (US: inf!) cu m (!)
assail [ə'seɪl] VT assaltar, atacar
assailant [ə'seɪlənt] N (attacker) assaltante m/f, atacante m/f; (aggressor) agressor(a) m/f
assassin [ə'sæsɪn] N assassino(-a)
assassinate [ə'sæsɪneɪt] VT assassinar
assassination [əsæsɪ'neɪʃən] N assassinato, assassínio
assault [ə'sɔːlt] N assalto; (Law): **~ (and battery)** vias fpl de fato ▪ VT assaltar, atacar; (sexually) agredir, violar
assemble [ə'sɛmbl] VT (people) reunir; (objects) juntar; (Tech) montar ▪ VI reunir-se
assembly [ə'sɛmblɪ] N (meeting) reunião f; (institution) assembléia; (people) congregação f; (construction) montagem f; **assembly language** N (Comput) linguagem f de montagem; **assembly line** N linha de montagem
assent [ə'sɛnt] N aprovação f ▪ VI: **to ~ (to sth)** consentir or assentir (em algo)
assert [ə'səːt] VT afirmar; (claim etc) fazer valer; **to ~ o.s.** impor-se
assertion [ə'səːʃən] N afirmação f
assertive [ə'səːtɪv] ADJ (vigorous) enérgico; (forceful) agressivo; (dogmatic) peremptório
assess [ə'sɛs] VT avaliar; (tax, damages) fixar; (property etc: for tax) taxar
assessment [ə'sɛsmənt] N avaliação f
assessor [ə'sɛsəʳ] N avaliador(a) m/f; (of tax) avaliador(a) do fisco
asset ['æsɛt] N (property) bem m; (quality)

vantagem f, trunfo; **assets** NPL (property, funds) bens mpl; (Comm) ativo
asset-stripping [-'strɪpɪŋ] N (Comm) venda em parcelas do patrimônio social
assiduous [ə'sɪdjuəs] ADJ assíduo
assign [ə'saɪn] VT (date) fixar; **to ~ (to)** (task) designar (a); (resources) destinar (a); (cause, meaning) atribuir (a)
assignment [ə'saɪnmənt] N tarefa
assimilate [ə'sɪmɪleɪt] VT assimilar; (absorb: immigrants) integrar
assimilation [əsɪmɪ'leɪʃən] N assimilação f
assist [ə'sɪst] VT ajudar; (progress etc) auxiliar; (injured person etc) socorrer
assistance [ə'sɪstəns] N ajuda, auxílio; (welfare) subsídio; (to injured person) socorro
assistant [ə'sɪstənt] N assistente m/f, auxiliar m/f; (Brit: also: shop assistant) vendedor(a) m/f; **assistant manager** N subgerente m/f
assizes [ə'saɪzɪz] NPL sessão f de tribunal superior
associate [adj ə'səuʃɪɪt, vt, vi ə'səuʃɪeɪt] ADJ associado; (professor, director etc) adjunto ▪ N (colleague) colega m/f; (at work, member) sócio(-a); (in crime) cúmplice m/f ▪ VI: **to ~ with sb** associar-se com alguém ▪ VT associar; **~ company** companhia ligada; **~ director** diretor(a) m/f associado(-a)
associated company [ə'səuʃɪeɪtɪd-] N companhia ligada
association [əsəusɪ'eɪʃən] N associação f; (link) ligação f; (Comm) sociedade f; **in ~ with** em parceria com
association football (Brit) N futebol m
assorted [ə'sɔːtɪd] ADJ sortido; **in ~ sizes** em vários tamanhos
assortment [ə'sɔːtmənt] N (of shapes, colours) sortimento; (of books, people) variedade f
Asst. ABBR = **assistant**
assuage [ə'sweɪdʒ] VT (grief, pain) aliviar, abrandar; (thirst) matar
assume [ə'sjuːm] VT (suppose) supor, presumir; (responsibilities etc) assumir; (attitude, name) adotar, tomar
assumed name [ə'sjuːmd-] N nome m falso
assumption [ə'sʌmpʃən] N (supposition) suposição f, presunção f; **on the ~ that** na suposição or hipótese que; (on condition that) com a condição de que
assurance [ə'ʃuərəns] N garantia; (confidence) confiança; (insurance) seguro
assure [ə'ʃuəʳ] VT assegurar; (guarantee) garantir; **to ~ sb that** garantir or assegurar a alguém que
AST (US) ABBR (= Atlantic Standard Time) hora de inverno de Nova Iorque
asterisk ['æstərɪsk] N asterisco
astern [ə'stəːn] ADV à popa; (direction) à ré
asteroid ['æstərɔɪd] N asteróide m
asthma ['æsmə] N asma
asthmatic [æs'mætɪk] ADJ, N asmático(-a)
astigmatism [ə'stɪgmətɪzəm] N astigmatismo
astir [ə'stəːʳ] ADV em agitação

astonish [ə'stɒnɪʃ] VT assombrar, espantar
astonishing [ə'stɒnɪʃɪŋ] ADJ espantoso, surpreendente
astonishingly [ə'stɒnɪʃɪŋlɪ] ADV surpreendentemente
astonishment [ə'stɒnɪʃmənt] N assombro, espanto; **to my** ~ para minha grande surpresa
astound [ə'staund] VT pasmar, estarrecer
astray [ə'streɪ] ADV: **to go** ~ (*person*) perder-se; (*letter etc*) extraviar-se; **to go** ~ **in one's calculations** cometer um erro em seus cálculos; **to lead** ~ (*morally*) desencaminhar
astride [ə'straɪd] PREP montado *or* a cavalo sobre
astringent [ə'strɪndʒənt] ADJ adstringente ■ N adstringente *m*
astrologer [əs'trɒlədʒəʳ] N astrólogo(-a)
astrology [əs'trɒlədʒɪ] N astrologia
astronaut ['æstrənɔːt] N astronauta *m/f*
astronomer [əs'trɒnəməʳ] N astrônomo(-a)
astronomical [æstrə'nɒmɪkəl] ADJ astronômico
astronomy [əs'trɒnəmɪ] N astronomia
astrophysics ['æstrəu'fɪzɪks] N astrofísica
astute [əs'tjuːt] ADJ astuto
asunder [ə'sʌndəʳ] ADV: **to put** ~ separar; **to tear** ~ rasgar
ASV N ABBR (= *American Standard Version*) tradução da Bíblia
asylum [ə'saɪləm] N (*refuge*) asilo; (*hospital*) manicômio; *see also* **political asylum**
asymmetric(al) [eɪsɪ'mɛtrɪk(l)] ADJ assimétrico

O **KEYWORD**

at [æt] PREP **1** (*referring to position*) em; (*referring to direction*) a; **at the top** em cima; **at home/ school** em casa/ na escola; **at the baker's** na padaria; **to look at sth** olhar para algo
2 (*referring to time*): **at 4 o'clock** às quatro horas; **at night** à noite; **at Christmas** no Natal; **at times** às vezes
3 (*referring to rates, speed etc*): **at £1 a kilo** a uma libra o quilo; **two at a time** de dois em dois
4 (*referring to manner*): **at a stroke** de um golpe; **at peace** em paz
5 (*referring to activity*): **to be at work** estar no trabalho; **to play at cowboys** brincar de mocinho; **to be good at sth** ser bom em algo
6 (*referring to cause*): **to be shocked/surprised/ annoyed at sth** ficar chocado/surpreso/ chateado com algo; **I went at his suggestion** eu fui por causa da sugestão dele
7 (= *symbol*) arroba

ate [eɪt] PT *of* **eat**
atheism ['eɪθɪɪzəm] N ateísmo
atheist ['eɪθɪɪst] N ateu(-atéia) *m/f*
Athenian [ə'θiːnɪən] ADJ, N ateniense *m/f*
Athens ['æθɪnz] N Atenas
athlete ['æθliːt] N atleta *m/f*
athletic [æθ'lɛtɪk] ADJ atlético
athletics [æθ'lɛtɪks] N atletismo

Atlantic [ət'læntɪk] ADJ atlântico ■ N: **the** ~ **(Ocean)** o (oceano) Atlântico
atlas ['ætləs] N atlas *m inv*
Atlas Mountains NPL: **the** ~ os montes Atlas
A.T.M. ABBR (= *Automatic Telling Machine*) caixa automática *or* eletrônica
atmosphere ['ætməsfɪəʳ] N atmosfera; (*fig*) ambiente *m*
atmospheric [ætməs'fɛrɪk] ADJ atmosférico
atmospherics [ætməs'fɛrɪks] NPL (*Radio*) estática
atoll ['ætɒl] N atol *m*
atom ['ætəm] N átomo
atomic [ə'tɒmɪk] ADJ atômico
atom(ic) bomb N bomba atômica
atomizer ['ætəmaɪzəʳ] N atomizador *m*, pulverizador *m*
atone [ə'təun] VI: **to** ~ **for** (*sin*) expiar; (*mistake*) reparar
atonement [ə'təunmənt] N expiação *f*
ATP N ABBR (= *Association of Tennis Professionals*) Associação *f* de Tenistas Profissionais
atrocious [ə'trəuʃəs] ADJ atroz; (*very bad*) péssimo
atrocity [ə'trɒsɪtɪ] N atrocidade *f*
atrophy ['ætrəfɪ] N atrofia ■ VT atrofiar ■ VI atrofiar-se
attach [ə'tætʃ] VT (*fasten*) prender; (*document, letter*) juntar, anexar; (*importance etc*) dar; (*employee, troops*) adir; **to be** ~**ed to sb/sth** (*to like*) ter afeição por alguém/algo; **the** ~**ed letter** a carta junta *or* anexa
attaché [ə'tæʃeɪ] N adido(-a); **attaché case** N pasta
attachment [ə'tætʃmənt] N (*tool*) acessório; (*love*): ~ **(to)** afeição *f* (por); (*to e-mail*) anexo
attack [ə'tæk] VT atacar; (*subj: criminal*) assaltar; (*task etc*) empreender ■ N ataque *m*; (*mugging etc*) assalto; (*on sb's life*) atentado; **heart** ~ ataque cardíaco *or* de coração
attacker [ə'tækəʳ] N agressor(a) *m/f*; (*criminal*) assaltante *m/f*
attain [ə'teɪn] VT (*also*: **attain to**: *happiness, results*) alcançar, atingir; (: *knowledge*) obter
attainments [ə'teɪnmənts] NPL feito
attempt [ə'tɛmpt] N tentativa ■ VT tentar; **to make an** ~ **on sb's life** atentar contra a vida de alguém; **he made no** ~ **to help** ele não fez nada para ajudar
attempted [ə'tɛmptɪd] ADJ: ~ **theft** *etc* (*Law*) tentativa de roubo *etc*
attend [ə'tɛnd] VT (*lectures*) assistir a; (*party*) presenciar; (*school*) cursar; (*church*) ir a; (*course*) fazer; (*patient*) tratar; **to** ~ **(up)on** acompanhar, servir
▶ **attend to** VT FUS (*matter*) encarregar-se de; (*speech etc*) prestar atenção a; (*needs, customer*) atender a; (*patient*) tratar de
attendance [ə'tɛndəns] N (*being present*) comparecimento; (*people present*) assistência
attendant [ə'tɛndənt] N servidor(a) *m/f*; (*Theatre*) arrumador(a) *m/f* ■ ADJ concomitante

attention [ə'tɛnʃən] N atenção f; (care) cuidados mpl ■ EXCL (Mil) sentido!; **at ~** (Mil) em posição de sentido; **for the ~ of ...** (Admin) atenção ...; **it has come to my ~ that ...** constatei que ...

attentive [ə'tɛntɪv] ADJ atento; (polite) cortês

attentively [ə'tɛntɪvlɪ] ADV atentamente

attenuate [ə'tɛnjueɪt] VT atenuar ■ VI atenuar-se

attest [ə'tɛst] VI: **to ~ to** atestar

attic ['ætɪk] N sótão m

attire [ə'taɪə^r] N traje m, roupa

attitude ['ætɪtjuːd] N atitude f; (view): **~ (to)** atitude (para com)

attorney [ə'təːnɪ] N (US: lawyer) advogado(-a); (having proxy) procurador(a) m/f

Attorney General N (Brit) procurador(a) m/f geral da Justiça; (US) Secretário de Justiça

attract [ə'trækt] VT atrair, chamar

attraction [ə'trækʃən] N atração f; (good point) atrativo; **~ towards sth** atração por algo

attractive [ə'træktɪv] ADJ atraente; (idea, offer) interessante

attribute [n 'ætrɪbjuːt, vt ə'trɪbjuːt] N atributo ■ VT: **to ~ sth to** atribuir algo a

attrition [ə'trɪʃən] N: **war of ~** guerra de atrição

Atty. Gen. ABBR = **Attorney General**

ATV N ABBR (= all terrain vehicle) veículo todo-terreno

aubergine ['əubəʒiːn] N berinjela

auburn ['ɔːbən] ADJ castanho-avermelhado

auction ['ɔːkʃən] N (also: **sale by auction**) leilão m ■ VT leiloar; **to sell by ~** vender em leilão; **to put up for ~** pôr em leilão

auctioneer [ɔːkʃə'nɪə^r] N leiloeiro(-a)

auction room N local m de leilão

audacious [ɔː'deɪʃəs] ADJ audaz, atrevido; (pej) descarado

audacity [ɔː'dæsɪtɪ] N audácia, atrevimento; (pej) descaramento

audible ['ɔːdɪbl] ADJ audível

audience ['ɔːdɪəns] N (in theatre, concert etc) platéia; (of TV, radio programme) audiência; (of speech etc) auditório; (of writer, magazine) público; (interview) audiência

audio-typist ['ɔːdɪəu-] N datilógrafo(-a) (de textos ditados em fita)

audio-visual [ɔːdɪəu'-] ADJ audiovisual; **audio-visual aid** ['ɔːdɪəu-] N recursos mpl audiovisuais

audit ['ɔːdɪt] VT fazer a auditoria de ■ N auditoria

audition [ɔː'dɪʃən] N audição f

auditor ['ɔːdɪtə^r] N auditor(a) m/f

auditorium [ɔːdɪ'tɔːrɪəm] (pl **auditoria**) N auditório

Aug. ABBR = **August**

augment [ɔːg'mɛnt] VT, VI aumentar

augur ['ɔːgə^r] VI: **it ~s well** é de bom augúrio ■ VT (be a sign of) augurar, pressagiar

August ['ɔːgəst] N agosto; see also **July**

august [ɔː'gʌst] ADJ augusto, imponente

aunt [ɑːnt] N tia

auntie ['ɑːntɪ] N titia

aunty ['ɑːntɪ] N titia

au pair ['əu'pɛə^r] N (also: **au pair girl**) au pair f

aura ['ɔːrə] N (of person) ar m, aspecto; (of place) ambiente m

auspices ['ɔːspɪsɪz] NPL: **under the ~ of** sob os auspícios de

auspicious [ɔːs'pɪʃəs] ADJ favorável; (occasion) propício

austere [ɔs'tɪə^r] ADJ austero; (manner) severo

austerity [ɔ'stɛrətɪ] N simplicidade f; (Econ) privação f

Australasia [ɔːstrə'leɪzɪə] N Australásia

Australia [ɔs'treɪlɪə] N Austrália

Australian [ɔs'treɪlɪən] ADJ, N australiano(-a)

Austria ['ɔstrɪə] N Áustria

Austrian ['ɔstrɪən] ADJ, N austríaco(-a)

AUT (Brit) N ABBR (= Association of University Teachers) sindicato universitário

authentic [ɔː'θɛntɪk] ADJ autêntico

authenticate [ɔː'θɛntɪkeɪt] VT autenticar

authenticity [ɔːθɛn'tɪsɪtɪ] N autenticidade f

author ['ɔːθə] N autor(a) m/f

authoritarian [ɔːθɔrɪ'tɛərɪən] ADJ autoritário

authoritative [ɔː'θɔrɪtətɪv] ADJ (account) autorizado; (manner) autoritário

authority [ɔː'θɔrɪtɪ] N autoridade f; (government body) jurisdição f; (permission) autorização f; **the authorities** NPL (ruling body) as autoridades; **to have ~ to do sth** ter autorização para fazer algo

authorization [ɔːθəraɪ'zeɪʃən] N autorização f

authorize ['ɔːθəraɪz] VT autorizar

authorized capital ['ɔːθəraɪzd-] N (Comm) capital m autorizado

authorship ['ɔːθəʃɪp] N autoria

autistic [ɔː'tɪstɪk] ADJ autista

auto ['ɔːtəu] (US) N carro, automóvel m ■ CPD (industry) automobilístico

autobiographical [ɔːtəbaɪə'græfɪkl] ADJ autobiográfico

autobiography [ɔːtəbaɪ'ɔgrəfɪ] N autobiografia

autocratic [ɔːtə'krætɪk] ADJ autocrático

autograph ['ɔːtəgrɑːf] N autógrafo ■ VT (photo etc) autografar

automat ['ɔːtəmæt] N (vending machine) autômato; (US: restaurant) restaurante m automático

automata [ɔː'tɔmətə] NPL of **automaton**

automated ['ɔːtəmeɪtɪd] ADJ automatizado

automatic [ɔːtə'mætɪk] ADJ automático ■ N (gun) pistola automática; (washing machine) máquina de lavar roupa automática; (Brit: car) carro automático

automatically [ɔːtə'mætɪklɪ] ADV automaticamente

automatic data processing N processamento automático de dados

automation [ɔːtə'meɪʃən] N automação f

automaton [ɔː'tɔmətən] (pl **automata**) N autômato

automobile ['ɔːtəməbiːl] (US) N carro, automóvel m ■ CPD (industry, accident)

automobilístico
autonomous [ɔ:'tɔnəməs] ADJ autônomo
autonomy [ɔ:'tɔnəmɪ] N autonomia
autopsy ['ɔ:tɔpsɪ] N autópsia
autumn ['ɔ:təm] N outono
auxiliary [ɔ:g'zɪlɪərɪ] ADJ, N auxiliar m/f
AV ABBR = **audiovisual**
Av. ABBR (= avenue) Av., Avda
avail [ə'veɪl] VT: **to ~ o.s. of** aproveitar, valer-se
de ▪ N: **to no ~** em vão, inutilmente
availability [əveɪlə'bɪlɪtɪ] N disponibilidade f
available [ə'veɪləbl] ADJ disponível; (time) livre;
every ~ **means** todos os recursos à sua (or nossa
etc) disposição; **is the manager ~?** o gerente
pode me atender?; (on phone) queria falar com
o gerente; **to make sth ~ to sb** pôr algo à
disposição de alguém
avalanche ['ævəlɑ:nʃ] N avalanche f
avant-garde ['ævãŋ'gɑ:d] ADJ de vanguarda
avarice ['ævərɪs] N avareza
avaricious [ævə'rɪʃəs] ADJ avarento, avaro
avdp. ABBR = **avoirdupoids**
Ave. ABBR (= avenue) Av., Avda
avenge [ə'vendʒ] VT vingar
avenue ['ævənju:] N avenida; (drive) caminho;
(means) solução f
average ['ævərɪdʒ] N média ▪ ADJ (mean)
médio; (ordinary) regular ▪ VT alcançar uma
média de; (calculate) calcular a média de; **on ~**
em média; **above/below (the) ~** acima/abaixo
da média
▸ **average out** VT calcular a média de ▪ VI: **to ~
out at** dar uma média de
averse [ə'və:s] ADJ: **to be ~ to sth/doing sth**
ser avesso or pouco disposto a algo/a fazer algo;
I wouldn't be ~ to a drink eu aceitaria uma
bebida; **aversion** [ə'və:ʃən] N aversão f
avert [ə'və:t] VT prevenir; (blow, one's eyes) desviar
aviary ['eɪvɪərɪ] N aviário, viveiro de aves
aviation [eɪvɪ'eɪʃən] N aviação f
avid ['ævɪd] ADJ ávido
avidly ['ævɪdlɪ] ADV avidamente
avocado [ævə'kɑ:dəu] N (also: Brit: avocado pear)
abacate m
avoid [ə'vɔɪd] VT evitar
avoidable [ə'vɔɪdəbl] ADJ evitável
avoidance [ə'vɔɪdəns] N evitação f
avowed [ə'vaud] ADJ confesso, declarado
AVP (US) N ABBR = **assistant vice-president**
AWACS ['eɪwæks] N ABBR (= airborne warning and
control system) AWACS m (sistema aerotransportado
de alerta e de controle)
await [ə'weɪt] VT esperar, aguardar; **~ing
attention/delivery** (Comm) a ser(em)
atendido(s)/entregue(s); **long ~ed** longamente
esperado
awake [ə'weɪk] (pt awoke, pp awaked) ADJ
acordado ▪ VT, VI despertar, acordar; **~ to**
atento a; **to be ~** estar acordado; **he was still ~**
ele ainda estava acordado
awakening [ə'weɪkənɪŋ] N despertar m
award [ə'wɔ:d] N (prize) prêmio, condecoração f;

(Law: damages) sentença; (act) concessão f ▪ VT
outorgar, conceder; adjudicar
aware [ə'weəʳ] ADJ: ~ **of** (conscious) consciente
de; (informed) informado de or sobre; **to become
~ of** reparar em, saber de; **politically/socially
~** conscientizado politicamente/socialmente;
I am fully ~ that ... eu compreendo
perfeitamente que ...
awareness [ə'weənɪs] N consciência; (knowledge)
conhecimento; **to develop people's ~ (of)**
conscientizar o público (de)
awash [ə'wɔʃ] ADJ: ~ **with** (also fig) inundado de
away [ə'weɪ] ADV fora; (faraway) muito longe;
two kilometres ~ a dois quilômetros de
distância; **two hours ~ by car** a duas horas de
carro; **the holiday was two weeks ~** faltavam
duas semanas para as férias; ~ **from** longe de;
he's ~ for a week está ausente uma semana;
he's ~ in Miami ele foi para Miami; **to take
~** levar; **to work/pedal** etc ~ trabalhar/pedalar
etc sem parar; **to fade ~** (colour) desvanecer-se;
(enthusiasm, sound) diminuir; **away game** N
(Sport) jogo de fora; **away match** N (Sport) jogo
de fora
awe [ɔ:] N temor m respeitoso
awe-inspiring ADJ imponente
awesome ['ɔ:səm] ADJ ≈ awe-inspiring
awestruck ['ɔ:strʌk] ADJ pasmado
awful ['ɔ:fəl] ADJ terrível, horrível; (quantity): **an ~
lot of** um monte de
awfully ['ɔ:fəlɪ] ADV (very) muito
awhile [ə'waɪl] ADV por algum tempo, um pouco
awkward ['ɔ:kwəd] ADJ (person, movement)
desajeitado; (shape) incômodo; (problem) difícil;
(situation) embaraçoso, delicado
awkwardness ['ɔ:kwədnəs] N (embarrassment)
embaraço
awl [ɔ:l] N sovela
awning ['ɔ:nɪŋ] N toldo
awoke [ə'wəuk] PT of **awake**
awoken [ə'wəukən] PP of **awake**
AWOL ['eɪwɔl] ABBR (Mil) = **absent without
leave**
awry [ə'raɪ] ADV: **to be ~** estar de viés or de
esguelha; **to go ~** sair mal
axe [æks] (US ax) N machado ▪ VT (employee)
despedir; (project etc) abandonar; (jobs) reduzir;
to have an ~ to grind (fig) ter interesse pessoal,
puxar a brasa para a sua sardinha (inf)
axes¹ ['æksɪz] NPL of **ax(e)**
axes² ['æksi:z] NPL of **axis**
axiom ['æksɪəm] N axioma m
axiomatic [æksɪəu'mætɪk] ADJ axiomático
axis ['æksɪs] (pl axes) N eixo
axle ['æksl] N (also: axle tree: Aut) eixo
ay(e) [aɪ] EXCL (yes) sim ▪ N: **the ~s** os votos a
favor
AYH N ABBR = **American Youth Hostels**
AZ (US) ABBR (Post) = **Arizona**
azalea [ə'zeɪlɪə] N azaléia
Azores [ə'zɔ:z] NPL: **the ~** os Açores
Aztec ['æztɛk] ADJ, N asteca m/f

Bb

B, b [biː] N (*letter*) B, b m; (*Mus*): **B** si m; **B for Benjamin** (*Brit*) *or* **Baker** (*US*) B de Beatriz; **B road** (*Brit: Aut*) via secundária

b. ABBR = **born**

BA N ABBR = **British Academy**; (*Sch*) = **Bachelor of Arts**

babble ['bæbl] VI balbuciar; (*brook*) murmurinhar ■ N balbucio

baboon [bə'buːn] N babuíno

baby ['beɪbɪ] N neném m/f, nenê m/f, bebê m/f; (*US: Inf*) querido(-a); **baby carriage** (*US*) N carrinho de bebê; **baby grand** N (*also:* **baby grand piano**) piano de ¼ de cauda

babyhood ['beɪbɪhud] N primeira infância

babyish ['beɪbɪʃ] ADJ infantil

baby-minder (*Brit*) N ≈ babá f

baby-sit (*irreg*) VI tomar conta da(s) criança(s)

baby-sitter N baby-sitter m/f

bachelor ['bætʃələʳ] N solteiro; (*Sch*): **B~ of Arts/Science** ≈ bacharel m em Letras/Ciências; **B~ of Arts/Science degree** ≈ bacharelado em Letras/Ciências

bachelorhood ['bætʃələhud] N celibato

bachelor party (*US*) N despedida de solteiro

back [bæk] N (*of person*) costas fpl; (*of animal*) lombo; (*of hand*) dorso; (*of car, train*) parte f traseira; (*of house*) fundos mpl; (*of chair*) encosto; (*of page*) verso; (*of book*) lombada; (*of crowd*) fundo; (*of coin*) reverso; (*Football*) zagueiro (BR), defesa m (PT) ■ VT (*financially*) patrocinar; (*candidate: also:* **back up**) apoiar; (*horse: at races*) apostar em; (*car*) recuar ■ VI (*car etc: also:* **back up**) dar marcha-ré (BR), fazer marcha atrás (PT) ■ CPD (*payment*) atrasado; (*Aut: seats, wheels*) de trás ■ ADV (*not forward*) para trás; (*returned*) de volta; **he's ~** ele voltou; (*restitution*): **throw the ball ~** devolva a bola; (*again*): **he called ~** chamou de novo; **to have one's ~ to the wall** (*fig*) estar acuado; **to break the ~ of a job** (*Brit*) fazer o mais difícil de um trabalho; **at the ~ of my mind was the thought that ...** no meu íntimo havia a idéia que ...; **- to front** pelo avesso, às avessas; **~ garden/room** jardim m /quarto dos fundos; **to take a ~ seat** (*fig*) colocar-se em segundo plano; **when will you be ~?** quando você estará de volta?; **he ran ~** recuou correndo; **can I have it ~?** pode devolvê-lo?

▶ **back down** VI desistir

▶ **back on to** VT FUS: **the house ~s on to the golf course** a casa dá fundas para o campo de golfe

▶ **back out** VI (*of promise*) voltar atrás, recuar

▶ **back up** VT (*support*) apoiar; (*Comput*) tirar um backup de

backache ['bækeɪk] N dor f nas costas

backbencher [bæk'bentʃəʳ] (*Brit*) N membro do parlamento sem pasta

backbiting ['bækbaɪtɪŋ] N maledicência

backbone ['bækbəun] N coluna vertebral; (*fig*) esteio; **he's the ~ of the organization** ele é o pilar *or* esteio da organização

backchat ['bæktʃæt] (*Brit: inf*) N insolências fpl

backcloth ['bækklɔθ] (*Brit*) N pano de fundo

backcomb ['bækkəum] (*Brit*) VT encrespar

backdate [bæk'deɪt] VT (*letter*) antedatar; **~d pay rise** aumento de vencimento com efeito retroativo

backdrop ['bækdrɔp] N = **backcloth**

backer ['bækəʳ] N (*supporter*) partidário(-a); (*Comm: in partnership*) comanditário(-a); (: *financier*) financiador(a) m/f

backfire [bæk'faɪəʳ] VI (*Aut*) engasgar; (*plan*) sair pela culatra

backgammon [bæk'gæmən] N gamão m

background ['bækgraund] N fundo; (*of events*) antecedentes mpl; (*basic knowledge*) bases fpl; (*experience*) conhecimentos mpl, experiência ■ CPD (*noise, music*) de fundo; **~ reading** leitura de fundo; **family ~** antecedentes mpl familiares

backhand ['bækhænd] N (*Tennis: also:* **backhand stroke**) revés m

backhanded ['bækhændɪd] ADJ (*fig*) ambíguo

backhander ['bækhændəʳ] (*Brit*) N (*bribe*) propina, peita (PT)

backing ['bækɪŋ] N (*fig*) apoio; (*Comm*) patrocínio; (*Mus*) fundo (musical)

backlash ['bæklæʃ] N reação f

backlog ['bæklɔg] N: **~ of work** atrasos mpl

back number N (*of magazine etc*) número atrasado

backpack ['bækpæk] N mochila

backpacker ['bækpækəʳ] N excursionista m/f com mochila

back pay N salário atrasado

backpedal ['bækpɛdl] vi (fig) recuar, voltar atrás
backside [bæk'saɪd] (inf) n traseiro
backslash ['bækslæʃ] n contrabarra
backslide ['bækslaɪd] (irreg) vi ter uma recaída
backspace ['bækspeɪs] vi (Typing) retroceder
backstage [bæk'steɪdʒ] ADV nos bastidores
back-street ADJ (abortion) clandestino; ~ **abortionist** aborteiro(-a)
backstroke ['bækstrəuk] n nado de costas
backtrack ['bæktræk] vi (fig) = **backpedal**
backup ['bækʌp] ADJ (train, plane) reserva inv; (Comput) de backup ▪ n (support) apoio; (Comput: also: **backup file**) backup m; (US: congestion) congestionamento
backward ['bækwəd] ADJ (movement) para trás; (person, country) atrasado; (shy) tímido; ~ **and forward movement** movimento de vaivém
backwards ['bækwədz] ADV (move, go) para trás; (read a list) às avessas; (fall) de costas; **to know sth** ~ (Brit) or ~ **and forwards** (US) (inf) saber algo de cor e salteado
backwater ['bækwɔ:tər] n (fig: backward place) lugar m atrasado; (: remote place) fim-do-mundo m
backyard [bæk'jɑ:d] n quintal m
bacon ['beɪkən] n toucinho, bacon m
bacteria [bæk'tɪərɪə] NPL bactérias fpl
bacteriology [bæktɪərɪ'ɔlədʒɪ] n bacteriologia
bad [bæd] ADJ mau(-má), ruim; (child) levado; (mistake, injury) grave; (meat, food) estragado; **his** ~ **leg** sua perna machucada; **to go** ~ estragar-se; **to have a** ~ **time of it** passar um mau pedaço; **I feel** ~ **about it** (guilty) eu me sinto culpado (por isso); **in** ~ **faith** de má fé
bade [bæd] PT of **bid**
badge [bædʒ] n (of school etc) emblema m; (policeman's) crachá m
badger ['bædʒər] n texugo ▪ vt acossar
badly ['bædlɪ] ADV mal; ~ **wounded** gravemente ferido; **he needs it** ~ faz-lhe grande falta; **things are going** ~ as coisas vão mal; **to be** ~ **off (for money)** estar com pouco dinheiro
bad-mannered [-'mænəd] ADJ mal-educado, sem modas
badminton ['bædmɪntən] n badminton m
bad-tempered ADJ mal humorado; (temporary) de mau humor
baffle ['bæfl] vt (puzzle) deixar perplexo, desconcertar
baffled ['bæfld] ADJ perplexo
baffling ['bæflɪŋ] ADJ desconcertante
bag [bæg] n saco, bolsa; (handbag) bolsa; (satchel, shopping bag) sacola; (case) mala; (of hunter) caça ▪ vt (inf: take) pegar; (game) matar; (Tech) ensacar; ~**s of** ... (inf: lots of) ... de sobra; **to pack one's** ~**s** fazer as malas; ~**s under the eyes** olheiras fpl
bagful ['bægful] n saco cheio
baggage ['bægɪdʒ] n bagagem f; **baggage checkroom** [-'tʃɛkru:m] (US) n depósito de bagagem; **baggage claim** n (at airport) recebimento de bagagem

baggy ['bægɪ] ADJ folgado, largo
Baghdad [bæg'dæd] n Bagdá f
bagpipes ['bægpaɪps] NPL gaita de foles
bag-snatcher [-'snætʃər] (Brit) n trombadinha m
bag-snatching [-'snætʃɪŋ] (Brit) n roubo de bolsa
Bahamas [bə'hɑ:məz] NPL: **the** ~ as Bahamas
Bahrain [bɑ:'reɪn] n Barein m
bail [beɪl] n (payment) fiança; (release) liberdade f sob fiança ▪ vt (prisoner: gen: grant bail to) libertar sob fiança; (boat: also: **bail out**) baldear a água de; **on** ~ sob fiança; **to be released on** ~ ser posto em liberdade mediante fiança; see also **bale**
  ▸ **bail out** vt (prisoner) afiançar; (fig: help out) socorrer
bailiff ['beɪlɪf] n (Law: Brit) oficial m/f de justiça (BR) or de diligências (PT); (: US) funcionário encarregado de acompanhar presos no tribunal
bait [beɪt] n isca, engodo; (for criminal etc) atrativo, chamariz m ▪ vt iscar, cevar; (person) apoquentar
bake [beɪk] vt cozinhar ao forno; (Tech: clay etc) cozer ▪ vi assar; (be hot) fazer um calor terrível
baked beans [beɪkt-] NPL feijão m cozido com molho de tomate
baker ['beɪkər] n padeiro(-a)
bakery ['beɪkərɪ] n (for bread) padaria; (for cakes) confeitaria
baking ['beɪkɪŋ] n (act) cozimento; (batch) fornada; **baking powder** n fermento em pó; **baking tin** n (for cake) fôrma; (for meat) assadeira; **baking tray** n tabuleiro
balaclava [bælə'klɑ:və] n (also: **balaclava helmet**) capuz f
balance ['bæləns] n equilíbrio; (scales) balança; (Comm) balanço; (remainder) resto, saldo ▪ vt equilibrar; (budget) nivelar; (account) fazer o balanço de; (compensate) contrabalançar; (pros and cons) pesar; ~ **of trade/payments** comercial/balanço de pagamentos; ~ **carried forward** transporte; ~ **brought forward** transporte; **to** ~ **the books** fazer o balanço dos livros
balanced ['bælənst] ADJ (report) objetivo; (personality, diet) equilibrado
balance sheet n balanço geral
balcony ['bælkənɪ] n (open) varanda; (closed) galeria; (in theatre) balcão m
bald [bɔ:ld] ADJ calvo, careca; (tyre) careca
baldness ['bɔ:ldnɪs] n calvície f
bale [beɪl] n (Agr) fardo
  ▸ **bale out** vi (of a plane) atirar-se de pára-quedas ▪ vt (Naut: water) baldear; (: boat) baldear a água de
Balearic Islands [bælɪ'ærɪk-] NPL: **the** ~ as ilhas Baleares
baleful ['beɪlful] ADJ (look) triste; (sinister) funesto, sinistro
balk [bɔ:k] vi: **to** ~ **(at)** (subj: person) relutar (contra); (: horse) refugar, empacar (diante de);

to ~ at doing relutar em fazer
Balkan ['bɔːlkən] ADJ balcânico ■ N: **the ~s** os
　Balcãs
ball [bɔːl] N bola; (of wool, string) novelo; (dance)
　baile m; **to play ~ with sb** jogar bola com
　alguém; (fig) fazer o jogo de alguém; **to be on**
　the ~ (fig: competent) ser competente or batuta
　(inf); (: alert) estar alerta; **to start the ~ rolling**
　(fig) dar começo, dar o pontapé inicial; **the ~ is**
　in their court (fig) é a vez deles de agir
ballad ['bæləd] N balada
ballast ['bæləst] N lastro
ball bearings NPL rolimã m
ball cock N torneira com bóia
ballerina [bælə'riːnə] N bailarina
ballet ['bæleɪ] N balé m; **ballet dancer** N
　bailarino(-a)
ballistic [bə'lɪstɪk] ADJ balístico
ballistics [bə'lɪstɪks] N balística
balloon [bə'luːn] N balão m; (hot air balloon) balão
　de ar quente ■ VI (sails etc) inflar(-se); (prices)
　disparar
balloonist [bə'luːnɪst] N aeróstata m/f
ballot ['bælət] N votação f; **ballot box** N urna;
　ballot paper N cédula eleitoral
ballpark ['bɔːlpaːk] (US) N estádio de beisebol;
　ballpark figure (inf) N número aproximado
ballpoint (pen) ['bɔːlpɔɪnt-] N (caneta)
　esferográfica
balls [bɔːlz] (inf!) NPL colhões mpl (!), ovos mpl (!)
balm [baːm] N bálsamo
balmy ['baːmɪ] ADJ (breeze, air) suave, fragrante;
　(Brit: inf) = **barmy**
BALPA ['bælpə] N ABBR (= British Airline Pilots'
　Association) sindicato dos aeronautas
balsam ['bɔːlsəm] N bálsamo
balsa (wood) ['bɔːlsə-] N pau-de-balsa m
Baltic ['bɔːltɪk] N: **the ~ (Sea)** o (mar) Báltico
balustrade ['bæləstreɪd] N balaustrada
bamboo [bæm'buː] N bambu m
bamboozle [bæm'buːzl] (inf) VT embromar,
　trapacear
ban [bæn] N proibição f, interdição f; (suspension,
　exclusion) exclusão f ■ VT proibir, interditar;
　(exclude) excluir; **he was ~ned from driving**
　(Brit) cassaram-lhe a carteira de motorista
banal [bə'naːl] ADJ banal
banana [bə'naːnə] N banana
band [bænd] N (group) bando, banda; (gang)
　quadrilha; (at a dance) orquestra; (Mil) banda;
　(strip) faixa, cinta
　▸ **band together** VI juntar-se, associar-se
bandage ['bændɪdʒ] N atadura (BR), ligadura
　(PT) ■ VT enfaixar
Band-Aid® ['bændeɪd] (US) N esparadrapo
bandit ['bændɪt] N bandido
bandstand ['bændstænd] N coreto
bandwagon ['bændwægən] N: **to jump on the ~**
　(fig) entrar na roda, ir na onda
bandy ['bændɪ] VT (jokes, insults) trocar
　▸ **bandy about** VT usar a torto e a direito
bandy-legged ADJ cambaio, de pernas tortas

bane [beɪn] N: **it** (or **he** etc) **is the ~ of my life** é a
　maldição da minha vida
bang [bæŋ] N estalo; (of door) estrondo; (of gun,
　exhaust) explosão f; (blow) pancada ■ EXCL bum!,
　bumba! ■ VT bater com força; (door) fechar com
　violência ■ VI produzir estrondo; (door) bater;
　(fireworks) soltar ■ ADV (Brit: inf): **to be ~ on**
　time chegar na hora exata; **to ~ at the door**
　bater à porta com violência; **to ~ into sth** bater
　em algo
banger ['bæŋəʳ] N (Brit: car: also: **old banger**)
　calhambeque m, lata-velha; (: inf: sausage)
　salsicha; (firework) bomba (de São João)
Bangkok [bæŋ'kɔk] N Bangcoc
Bangladesh [bæŋglə'dɛʃ] N Bangladesh m (no
　article)
bangle ['bæŋgl] N bracelete m
bangs [bæŋz] (US) NPL (fringe) franja
banish ['bænɪʃ] VT banir
banister(s) ['bænɪstə(z)] N(PL) corrimão m
banjo ['bændʒəu] (pl banjoes or banjos) N banjo
bank [bæŋk] N banco; (of river, lake) margem f;
　(of earth) rampa, ladeira ■ VI (Aviat) ladear-se;
　(Comm): **they ~ with Pitt's** eles têm conta no
　banco Pitt's
　▸ **bank on** VT FUS contar com, apostar em
bank: bank account N conta bancária; **bank**
　card N cartão m de garantia de cheques; **bank**
　charges (Brit) NPL encargos mpl bancários;
　bank draft N saque m bancário
banker ['bæŋkəʳ] N banqueiro(-a); **~'s card** (Brit)
　cartão m de garantia de cheques; **~'s order** (Brit)
　ordem f bancária
banker's card (Brit) N = **bank card**
bank giro N transferência bancária
Bank holiday (Brit) N feriado nacional
banking ['bæŋkɪŋ] N transações fpl bancárias;
　(job) profissão f de banqueiro; **banking hours**
　NPL horário de banco
bank loan N empréstimo bancário
bank manager N gerente m/f de banco
banknote ['bæŋknəut] N nota (bancária)
bank rate N taxa bancária
bankrupt ['bæŋkrʌpt] N falido(-a), quebrado(-a)
　■ ADJ falido, quebrado; **to go ~** falir; **to be ~**
　estar falido/quebrado
bankruptcy ['bæŋkrʌptsɪ] N falência;
　(fraudulent) bancarrota
bank statement N extrato bancário
banner ['bænəʳ] N faixa
bannister(s) ['bænɪstə(z)] N(PL) = **banister(s)**
banns [bænz] NPL proclamas fpl
banquet ['bæŋkwɪt] N banquete m
bantamweight ['bæntəmweɪt] N peso-galo
banter ['bæntəʳ] N caçoada
baptism ['bæptɪzəm] N batismo
Baptist ['bæptɪst] N batista m/f
baptize [bæp'taɪz] VT batizar
bar [baːʳ] N (gen, of chocolate) barra; (rod) vara;
　(of window etc) grade f; (fig: hindrance) obstáculo;
　(prohibition) impedimento; (pub) bar m; (counter:
　in pub) balcão m ■ VT (road) obstruir; (window)

trancar; (*person*) excluir; (*activity*) proibir ■ PREP:
~ **none** sem exceção; ~ **of soap** sabonete *m*;
behind ~s (*prisoner*) atrás das grades; **the B~**
(*Law: profession*) a advocacia; (*people*) o corpo de
advogados

Barbados [baː'beɪdɔs] N Barbados *m* (*no article*)

barbaric [baː'bærɪk] ADJ bárbaro

barbarous ['baːbərəs] ADJ bárbaro

barbecue ['baːbɪkjuː] N churrasco

barbed wire ['baːbd-] N arame *m* farpado

barber ['baːbər] N barbeiro, cabeleireiro

barbiturate [baː'bɪtjurɪt] N barbitúrico

Barcelona [baːsə'ləunə] N Barcelona

bar chart N gráfico de barras

bar code N código de barras

bare [bɛər] ADJ despido; (*head*) descoberto; (*trees,
vegetation*) sem vegetação; (*minimum*) básico
■ VT (*body, teeth*) mostrar; **the ~ essentials** o
imprescindível

bareback ['bɛəbæk] ADV em pêlo, sem arreios

barefaced ['bɛəfeɪst] ADJ descarado

barefoot ['bɛəfut] ADJ, ADV descalço

bareheaded [bɛə'hɛdɪd] ADJ, ADV de cabeça
descoberta

barely ['bɛəlɪ] ADV apenas, mal

Barents Sea ['bærənts-] N: **the ~** o mar de
Barents

bargain ['baːgɪn] N (*deal*) negócio; (*agreement*)
acordo; (*good buy*) pechincha ■ VI (*trade*)
negociar; (*haggle*) regatear; (*negotiate*): **to ~ (with
sb**) pechinchar (com alguém); **into the ~** ainda
por cima
  ▶ **bargain for** (*inf*) VT FUS: **he got more than
  he ~ed for** ele conseguiu mais do que pediu

bargaining ['baːgənɪŋ] N (*haggling*) regateio;
(*talks*) negociações *fpl*

barge [baːdʒ] N barcaça
  ▶ **barge in** VI irromper
  ▶ **barge into** VT FUS (*collide with*) atropelar;
  (*interrupt*) intrometer-se em

baritone ['bærɪtəun] N barítono

barium meal ['bɛərɪəm-] N contraste *m* de bário

bark [baːk] N (*of tree*) casca; (*of dog*) latido ■ VI
latir

barley ['baːlɪ] N cevada; **barley sugar** N
maltose *f*

barmaid ['baːmeɪd] N garçonete *f* (BR),
empregada (de bar) (PT)

barman ['baːmən] (*irreg*) N garçom *m* (BR),
empregado (de bar) (PT)

barmy ['baːmɪ] (*Brit: inf*) ADJ maluco

barn [baːn] N celeiro

barnacle ['baːnəkl] N craca

barometer [bə'rɒmɪtər] N barômetro

baron ['bærən] N barão *m*; (*of press, industry*)
magnata *m*

baroness ['bærənɪs] N baronesa

barracks ['bærəks] NPL quartel *m*, caserna

barrage ['bæraːʒ] N (*Mil*) fogo de barragem;
(*dam*) barragem *f*; (*fig*): **a ~ of questions** uma
saraivada de perguntas

barrel ['bærəl] N barril *m*; (*of gun*) cano; **barrel**

organ N realejo

barren ['bærən] ADJ (*sterile*) estéril; (*land*) árido

barricade [bærɪ'keɪd] N barricada ■ VT
barricar; **to ~ o.s. (in)** basrricar-se (em)

barrier ['bærɪər] N barreira; (*fig: to progress etc*)
obstáculo; (*Brit: also*: **crash barrier**) cerca entre
as pistas; **barrier cream** (*Brit*) N creme *m*
protetor

barring ['baːrɪŋ] PREP exceto, salvo

barrister ['bærɪstər] (*Brit*) N advogado(-a),
causídico(-a)

barrow ['bærəu] N (*wheelbarrow*) carrinho (de
mão)

bar stool N tamborete *m* de bar

Bart. (*Brit*) ABBR = **baronet**

bartender ['baːtɛndər] (*US*) N garçom *m* (BR),
empregado (de bar) (PT)

barter ['baːtər] N permuta, troca ■ VT: **to ~ sth
for sth** trocar algo por algo

base [beɪs] N base *f* ■ VT (*troops*): **to be ~d at**
estar estacionado em; (*opinion, belief*): **to ~ sth
on** basear *or* fundamentar algo em ■ ADJ
(*thoughts*) sujo, baixo, vil; **coffee-~d** à base de
café; **a Rio-~d firm** uma empresa sediada
no Rio; **I'm ~d in London** estou sediado em
Londres

baseball ['beɪsbɔːl] N beisebol *m*

baseboard ['beɪsbɔːd] (*US*) N rodapé *m*

base camp N base *f* de operações

Basel ['baːzl] N = **Basle**

basement ['beɪsmənt] N (*in house*) porão *m*; (*in
shop etc*) subsolo

base rate N taxa de base

bases[1] ['beɪsɪz] NPL *of* **base**

bases[2] ['beɪsiːz] NPL *of* **basis**

bash [bæʃ] (*inf*) VT (*with fist*) dar soco *or* murro
em; (*with object*) bater em ■ N (*Brit*): **I'll have a ~
(at it)** vou tentar (fazê-lo); **~ed in** amassado
  ▶ **bash up** (*inf*) VT (*car*) arrebentar; (*Brit: person*)
  dar uma surra em, espancar

bashful ['bæʃful] ADJ tímido, envergonhado

bashing ['bæʃɪŋ] (*inf*) N surra; **Paki-~**
espancamento de asiáticos por motivos racistas; **queer-**
~ *espancamento de homossexuais*

BASIC ['beɪsɪk] N (*Comput*) BASIC *m*

basic ['beɪsɪk] ADJ básico; (*facilities*) mínimo;
(*vocabulary, rate*) de base

basically ['beɪsɪkəlɪ] ADV basicamente; (*really*)
no fundo

basic rate N (*of tax*) alíquota de base

basics ['beɪsɪks] NPL: **the ~** o essencial

basil ['bæzl] N manjericão *m*

basin ['beɪsn] N (*vessel*) bacia; (*dock, Geo*) bacia;
(*also*: **washbasin**) pia

basis ['beɪsɪs] (*pl* **bases**) N base *f*; **on a part-time
~** num esquema de meio-expediente; **on a trial
~** em experiência; **on the ~ of what you've said**
com base no que você disse

bask [baːsk] VI: **to ~ in the sun** tomar sol

basket ['baːskɪt] N cesto; (*with handle*) cesta

basketball ['baːskɪtbɔːl] N basquete(bol) *m*;
basketball player N jogador(a) *m/f* de basquete

basketwork ['bɑ:skɪtwə:k] N obra de verga, trabalho de vime

Basle [bɑ:l] N Basiléia

Basque [bæsk] ADJ, N basco(-a)

bass [beɪs] N (Mus) baixo; **bass clef** N clave f de fá

bassoon [bə'su:n] N fagote m

bastard ['bɑ:stəd] N bastardo(-a); (inf!) filho-da-puta m (!)

baste [beɪst] VT (Culin) untar; (Sewing) alinhavar

bastion ['bæstɪən] N baluarte m

bat [bæt] N (Zool) morcego; (for ball games) bastão m; (Brit: for table tennis) raquete f ■ VT: **he didn't ~ an eyelid** ele nem pestanejou; **off one's own ~** por iniciativa própria

batch [bætʃ] N (of bread) fornada; (of papers) monte m; (lot) remessa, lote m; **batch processing** N (Comput) processamento batch or em lote

bated ['beɪtɪd] ADJ: **with ~ breath** contendo a respiração

bath [bɑ:θ, pl bɑ:ðz] N banho; (bathtub) banheira ■ VT banhar; **to have a ~** tomar banho (de banheira); see also **baths**; **bath chair** N cadeira de rodas

bathe [beɪð] VI banhar-se; (US: have a bath) tomar um banho ■ VT banhar; (wound) lavar

bather ['beɪðəʳ] N banhista m/f

bathing ['beɪðɪŋ] N banho; **bathing cap** N touca de banho; **bathing costume** (US **bathing suit**) N (woman's) maiô m (BR), fato de banho (PT)

bath mat N tapete m de banheiro

bathrobe ['bɑ:θrəub] N roupão m de banho

bathroom ['bɑ:θrum] N banheiro (BR), casa de banho (PT)

baths [bɑ:θs] NPL (also: **swimming baths**) banhos mpl públicos

bath towel N toalha de banho

bathtub ['bɑ:θtʌb] N banheira

batman ['bætmən] N (Brit: irreg) N ordenança m

baton ['bætən] N (Mus) batuta; (Athletics) bastão m; (truncheon) cassetete m

battalion [bə'tælɪən] N batalhão m

batten ['bætn] N (Carpentry) ripa
▶ **batten down** VT (Naut): **to ~ down the hatches** correr as escotilhas

batter ['bætəʳ] VT espancar; (subj: wind, rain) castigar ■ N massa (mole)

battered ['bætəd] ADJ (hat, pan) amassado, surrado; **~ wife/child** mulher/criança seviciada

battering ram ['bætərɪŋ] N aríete m

battery ['bætərɪ] N bateria; (of torch) pilha; **battery charger** N carregador m de bateria; **battery farming** N criação f intensiva

battle ['bætl] N batalha; (fig) luta ■ VI lutar; **that's half the ~** (fig) é meio caminho andado; **it's a** or **we're fighting a losing ~** estamos lutando em vão; **battle dress** N uniforme m de combate

battlefield ['bætlfi:ld] N campo de batalha

battlements ['bætlmənts] NPL ameias fpl

battleship ['bætlʃɪp] N couraçado

bauble ['bɔ:bl] N bugiganga

baud [bɔ:d] N (Comput) baud m; **baud rate** N (Comput) índice m de baud, taxa de transmissão

baulk [bɔ:lk] VI = **balk**

bauxite ['bɔ:ksaɪt] N bauxita

bawdy ['bɔ:dɪ] ADJ indecente; (joke) imoral

bawl [bɔ:l] VI gritar; (child) berrar

bay [beɪ] N (Geo) baía; (Bot) louro; (Brit: for parking) área de estacionamento; (: for loading) vão m de carregamento ■ VI ladrar; **to hold sb at ~** manter alguém a distância; **the B~ of Biscay** o golfo de Biscaia; **bay leaf** (irreg) N louro

bayonet ['beɪənɪt] N baioneta

bay tree N loureiro

bay window N janela saliente

bazaar [bə'zɑ:ʳ] N bazar m

bazooka [bə'zu:kə] N bazuca

BB (Brit) N ABBR (= Boys' Brigade) movimento de meninos

B & B N ABBR = **bed and breakfast**

BBB (US) N ABBR (= Better Business Bureau) organização de defesa ao consumidor

BBC N ABBR (= British Broadcasting Corporation) companhia britânica de rádio e televisão

BBE (US) N ABBR (= Benevolent and Protective Order of Elks) associação beneficente

B.C. ADV ABBR (= before Christ) a.C ■ ABBR (Canadian) = **British Columbia**

BCG N ABBR (= Bacillus Calmette-Guérin) BCG m

BD N ABBR (= Bachelor of Divinity) título universitário

B/D ABBR = **bank draft**

BDS N ABBR (= Bachelor of Dental Surgery) título universitário

○ **KEYWORD**

be [bi:] (pt **were**, pp **been**) AUX VB **1** (with present participle: forming continuous tense) estar; **what are you doing?** o que você está fazendo (BR) or a fazer (PT)?; **it is raining** está chovendo (BR) or a chover (PT); **I've been waiting for you for hours** há horas que eu espero por você

2 (with pp: forming passives): **to be killed** ser morto; **the box had been opened** a caixa tinha sido aberta; **the thief was nowhere to be seen** ninguém viu o ladrão

3 (in tag questions): **it was fun, wasn't it?** foi divertido, não foi?; **she's back again, is she?** ela voltou novamente, é?

4 (+ to + infin): **the house is to be sold** a casa está à venda; **you're to be congratulated for all your work** você devia ser cumprimentado pelo seu trabalho; **he's not to open it** ele não pode abrir isso

■ VB + COMPLEMENT **1** (gen): **I'm English** sou inglês; **I'm tired** estou cansado; **I'm hot/cold** estou com calor/frio; **he's a doctor** ele é médico; **2 and 2 are 4** dois e dois são quatro; **she's tall/pretty** ela é alta/bonita; **be careful!** tome cuidado!; **be quiet!** fique quieto!, fique calado!; **be good!** seja bonzinho!

2 (of health) estar; **how are you?** como está?;

he's very ill ele está muito doente

3 *(of age)*: how old are you? quantos anos você tem?; I'm twenty (years old) tenho vinte anos

4 *(cost)* ser; how much was the meal? quanto foi a refeição?; that'll be £5.75, please são £5.75, por favor

■ vi 1 *(exist, occur etc)* exister, haver; the best singer that ever was o maior cantor de todos os tempos; is there a God? Deus existe?; be that as it may ... de qualquer forma ...; so be it que seja assim

2 *(referring to place)* estar; I won't be here tomorrow eu não estarei aqui amanhã; Edinburgh is in Scotland Edinburgo é or fica na Escócia; it's on the table está na mesa

3 *(referring to movement)* ir; where have you been? onde você foi?; I've been to the post office/to China fui ao correio/à China; I've been in the garden estava no quintal

■ IMPERS VB 1 *(referring to time)* ser; it's 8 o'clock são 8 horas; it's the 28th of April é 28 de abril

2 *(referring to distance)* ficar; it's 10 km to the village fica a 10 km do lugarejo

3 *(referring to the weather)* estar; it's too hot/cold está quente/frio demais

4 *(emphatic)*: it's only me sou eu!; it's only the postman é apenas o carteiro; it was Maria who paid the bill foi Maria quem pagou a conta

B/E ABBR = bill of exchange

beach [biːtʃ] N praia ■ VT puxar para a terra *or* praia, encalhar

beachcomber ['biːtʃkəumər] N vagabundo(-a) de praia

beachwear ['biːtʃwɛər] N roupa de praia

beacon ['biːkən] N *(lighthouse)* farol *m*; *(marker)* baliza; *(also:* radio beacon*)* radiofarol *m*

bead [biːd] N *(of necklace)* conta; *(of sweat)* gota; **beads** NPL *(necklace)* colar *m*

beady ['biːdɪ] ADJ: ~ eyes olhinhos vivos

beagle ['biːgl] N bigle *m*

beak [biːk] N bico

beaker ['biːkər] N copo com bico

beam [biːm] N *(Arch)* viga; *(of light)* raio; *(Naut)* através *m*; *(Radio)* feixe *m* direcional ■ VI brilhar; *(smile)* sorrir; to drive on full *or* main ~ *(Brit)*, to drive on high ~ *(US)* transitar com os faróis altos

beaming ['biːmɪŋ] ADJ *(sun, smile)* radiante

bean [biːn] N feijão *m*; *(of coffee)* grão *m*; runner/broad ~ vagem *f*/fava; bean shoots NPL brotos *mpl* de feijão; bean sprouts NPL brotos *mpl* de feijão

bear [bɛər] *(pt* bore, *pp* borne*)* N urso; *(Stock Exchange)* baixista *m/f* ■ VT *(carry, support)* arcar com; *(tolerate)* suportar; *(fruit)* dar; *(name, title)* trazer; *(traces, signs)* apresentar, trazer; *(children)* ter, dar à luz; *(Comm: interest)* render ■ VI: to ~ right/left virar à direita/à esquerda; to ~ the responsibility of assumir a responsabilidade de; to ~ comparison with comparar-se a;

I can't ~ him eu não o agüento; to bring pressure to ~ on sb exercer pressão sobre alguém

▶ **bear out** VT *(theory, suspicion)* confirmar, corroborar

▶ **bear up** VI agüentar, resistir

▶ **bear with** VT FUS *(sb's moods, temper)* ter paciência com; ~ with me a minute só um momentinho, por favor

bearable ['bɛərəbl] ADJ suportável, tolerável

beard [bɪəd] N barba

bearded ['bɪədɪd] ADJ barbado, barbudo

bearer ['bɛərər] N portador(a) *m/f*; *(of title)* detentor(a) *m/f*

bearing ['bɛərɪŋ] N porte *m*, comportamento; *(connection)* relação *f*; **bearings** NPL *(also:* ball bearings*)* rolimã *m*; to take a ~ fazer marcação; to find one's ~s orientar-se

beast [biːst] N bicho; *(inf)* fera

beastly ['biːstlɪ] ADJ horrível

beat [biːt] N *(of heart)* batida; *(Mus)* ritmo, compasso; *(of policeman)* ronda ■ VT *(hit)* bater em; *(eggs)* bater; *(defeat)* vencer, derrotar; *(better)* superar, ultrapassar; *(drum)* tocar; *(rhythm)* marcar ■ VI *(heart)* bater; to ~ about the bush falar com rodeios (BR), fazer rodeios (PT); to ~ it *(inf)* cair fora; off the ~en track fora de mão; to ~ time marcar o compasso; that ~s everything! isso é o cúmulo!

▶ **beat down** VT *(door)* arrombar; *(price)* conseguir que seja abatido; *(seller)* conseguir que abata o preço ■ VI *(rain)* cair a cântaros; *(sun)* bater de chapa

▶ **beat off** VT repelir

▶ **beat up** VT *(inf: person)* espancar; *(eggs)* bater

beaten ['biːtn] PP *of* beat

beater ['biːtər] N *(for eggs, cream)* batedeira

beating ['biːtɪŋ] N batida; *(thrashing)* surra; to take a ~ levar uma surra

beat-up [-ʌp] ADJ *(car)* caindo aos pedaços; *(suitcase etc)* surrado

beautician [bjuːˈtɪʃən] N esteticista *m/f*

beautiful ['bjuːtɪful] ADJ belo, lindo, formoso

beautify ['bjuːtɪfaɪ] VT embelezar

beauty ['bjuːtɪ] N beleza; *(person)* beldade *f*, beleza; the ~ of it is that ... o atrativo disso é que ...; beauty contest N concurso de beleza; beauty queen N miss *f*, rainha de beleza; beauty salon [-sælɔn] N salão *m* de beleza; beauty spot N sinal *m* *(de beleza na pele)*; *(Brit: Tourism)* lugar *m* de beleza excepcional

beaver ['biːvər] N castor *m*

becalmed [bɪˈkɑːmd] ADJ parado devido a calmaria

became [bɪˈkeɪm] PT *of* become

because [bɪˈkɔz] CONJ porque; ~ of por causa de

beck [bɛk] N: to be at sb's ~ and call estar às ordens de alguém

beckon ['bɛkən] VT *(also:* beckon to*)* chamar com sinais, acenar para

become [bɪˈkʌm] *(irreg: like* come*)* VT *(suit)* favorecer a ■ VI *(+n)* virar, fazer-se, tornar-se;

(+ *adj*) tornar-se, ficar; **to ~ fat/thin** ficar gordo/ magro; **to ~ angry** zangar-se, ficar com raiva; **it became known that** soube-se que; **what has ~ of him?** o que é feito dele?, o que aconteceu a ele?

becoming [bɪˈkʌmɪŋ] ADJ (*behaviour*) decoroso; (*clothes*) favorecedor(a), elegante

BEd N ABBR (= *Bachelor of Education*) habilitação ao magistério

bed [bɛd] N cama; (*of flowers*) canteiro; (*of coal, clay*) camada, base *f*; (*of sea, lake*) fundo; (*of river*) leito; **to go to ~** ir dormir, deitar(-se)
  ▶ **bed down** VI dormir

bed and breakfast N (*place*) pensão *f*; (*terms*) cama e café da manhã (BR) *or* pequeno almoço (PT)

bedbug [ˈbɛdbʌg] N percevejo

bedclothes [ˈbɛdkləʊðz] NPL roupa de cama

bed cover N colcha

bedding [ˈbɛdɪŋ] N roupa de cama

bedevil [bɪˈdɛvl] VT (*harass*) acossar; **to be ~led by** ser vítima de

bedfellow [ˈbɛdfɛləʊ] N: **they are strange ~s** (*fig*) eles formam uma dupla estranha

bedlam [ˈbɛdləm] N confusão *f*

bedpan [ˈbɛdpæn] N comadre *f*

bedpost [ˈbɛdpəʊst] N pé *m* de cama

bedraggled [bɪˈdrægld] ADJ molhado, ensopado; (*dirty*) enlameado

bedridden [ˈbɛdrɪdn] ADJ acamado

bedrock [ˈbɛdrɔk] N (*fig*) fundamento, alicerce *m*; (*Geo*) leito de rocha firme

bedroom [ˈbɛdrum] N quarto, dormitório

Beds (*Brit*) ABBR = **Bedfordshire**

bedside [ˈbɛdsaɪd] N: **at sb's ~** a cabeceira de alguém ■ CPD (*book, lamp*) de cabeceira

bedsit(ter) [ˈbɛdsɪt(əʳ)] (*Brit*) N conjugado

● **BEDSIT**
●
●
● Um *bedsit* é um quarto mobiliado cujo
● aluguel inclui uso de cozinha e banheiro
● comuns. Esse sistema de alojamento é
● muito comum na Grã-Bretanha entre
● estudantes, jovens profissionais liberais etc.

bedspread [ˈbɛdsprɛd] N colcha

bedtime [ˈbɛdtaɪm] N na hora de ir para cama

bee [biː] N abelha; **to have a ~ in one's bonnet (about sth)** estar obcecado (por algo)

beech [biːtʃ] N faia

beef [biːf] N carne *f* de vaca; **roast ~** rosbife *m*
  ▶ **beef up** (*inf*) VT (*support*) reforçar; (*essay*) desenvolver mais

beefburger [ˈbiːfbəːgəʳ] N hambúrguer *m*

beefeater [ˈbiːfiːtəʳ] N alabardeiro (*da guarda da Torre de Londres*)

beehive [ˈbiːhaɪv] N colméia

beeline [ˈbiːlaɪn] N: **to make a ~ for** ir direto a

been [biːn] PP *of* **be**

beer [bɪəʳ] N cerveja; **beer can** N lata de cerveja

beet [biːt] (US) N beterraba

beetle [ˈbiːtl] N besouro

beetroot [ˈbiːtruːt] (*Brit*) N beterraba

befall [bɪˈfɔːl] (*irreg: like* **fall**) VT acontecer a

befit [bɪˈfɪt] VT convir a

before [bɪˈfɔːʳ] PREP (*of time*) antes de; (*of space*) diante de ■ CONJ antes que ■ ADV antes, anteriormente; à frente, na dianteira; **~ going** antes de sair; **~ she goes** antes dela sair; **the week ~** a semana anterior; **I've seen it ~** eu já vi isso (antes); **I've never seen it ~** nunca vi isso antes

beforehand [bɪˈfɔːhænd] ADV antes

befriend [bɪˈfrɛnd] VT fazer amizade com

befuddled [bɪˈfʌdld] ADJ atordoado, aturdido

beg [bɛg] VI mendigar, pedir esmola ■ VT (*also*: **beg for**) mendigar; (*favour*) pedir; (*entreat*) suplicar; **to ~ sb to do sth** implorar a alguém para fazer algo; **that ~s the question of ...** isso dá por resolvida a questão de ...; *see also* **pardon**

began [bɪˈgæn] PT *of* **begin**

beggar [ˈbɛgəʳ] N (*also*: **beggarman**; **beggarwoman**) mendigo(-a)

begin [bɪˈgɪn] (*pt* **began**, *pp* **begun**) VT, VI começar, iniciar; **to ~ doing** *or* **to do sth** começar a fazer algo; **~ning (from) Monday** a partir de segunda-feira; **I can't ~ to thank you** não sei como agradecer-lhe; **to ~ with** em primeiro lugar

beginner [bɪˈgɪnəʳ] N principiante *m/f*

beginning [bɪˈgɪnɪŋ] N início, começo; **right from the ~** desde o início

begrudge [bɪˈgrʌdʒ] VT: **to ~ sb sth** (*envy*) invejar algo de alguém; (*give grudgingly*) dar algo a alguém de má vontade

beguile [bɪˈgaɪl] VT (*enchant*) encantar

beguiling [bɪˈgaɪlɪŋ] ADJ (*charming*) sedutor(a), encantador(a)

begun [bɪˈgʌn] PP *of* **begin**

behalf [bɪˈhɑːf] N: **on** *or* **in** (US) **~ of** (*as representative of*) em nome de; (*for benefit of*) no interesse de; (*in aid of*) em favor de; **on my/his ~** em meu nome/no nome dele

behave [bɪˈheɪv] VI comportar-se; (*well: also*: **behave o.s.**) comportar-se (bem)

behaviour [bɪˈheɪvjəʳ] (US **behavior**) N comportamento

behead [bɪˈhɛd] VT decapitar, degolar

beheld [bɪˈhɛld] PT, PP *of* **behold**

behind [bɪˈhaɪnd] PREP atrás de ■ ADV atrás; (*move*) para trás ■ N traseiro; (*time*) atrasado; **to be ~ (schedule) with sth** estar atrasado *or* com atraso em algo; **~ the scenes** nos bastidores; **to leave sth ~** (*forget*) esquecer algo; (*run ahead of*) deixar algo para trás

behold [bɪˈhəʊld] (*irreg: like* **hold**) VT contemplar

beige [beɪʒ] ADJ bege

Beijing [beɪˈʒɪŋ] M Pequim

being [ˈbiːɪŋ] N (*state*) existência; (*entity*) ser *m*; **to come into ~** nascer, aparecer

Beirut [beɪˈruːt] N Beirute

belated [bɪˈleɪtɪd] ADJ atrasado

belch [bɛltʃ] VI arrotar ■ VT (*also*: **belch out**:

smoke etc) vomitar

beleaguered [bɪ'liːgəd] ADJ *(city, fig)* assediado; *(army)* cercado

Belfast ['bɛlfɑːst] N Belfast

belfry ['bɛlfrɪ] N campanário

Belgian ['bɛldʒən] ADJ, N belga *m/f*

Belgium ['bɛldʒəm] N Bélgica

Belgrade [bɛl'greɪd] N Belgrado

belie [bɪ'laɪ] VT *(contradict)* contradizer; *(disprove)* desmentir; *(obscure)* ocultar

belief [bɪ'liːf] N *(opinion)* opinião *f*; *(trust, faith)* fé *f*; *(acceptance as true)* crença, convicção *f*; **it's beyond ~** é inacreditável; **in the ~ that** na convicção de que

believe [bɪ'liːv] VT: **to ~ sth/sb** acreditar algo/em alguém ■ VI: **to ~ in** *(God, ghosts)* crer em; *(method, person)* acreditar em; **I ~ (that) ...** *(think)* eu acho que ...; **I don't ~ in corporal punishment** não sou partidário de castigos corporais; **he is ~d to be abroad** acredita-se que ele esteja no exterior

believer [bɪ'liːvə'] N *(Rel)* crente *m/f*, fiel *m/f*; *(in idea, activity)*: **~ in** partidário(-a) de

belittle [bɪ'lɪtl] VT diminuir, depreciar

Belize [bɛ'liːz] N Belize *m (no article)*

bell [bɛl] N sino; *(small, doorbell)* campainha; *(animal's, on toy)* guizo, sininho; **that rings a ~** *(fig)* tenho uma vaga lembrança disso; **the name rings a ~** o nome não me é estranho

bell-bottoms NPL calça boca-de-sino

bellboy ['bɛlbɔɪ] *(Brit)* N boy *m* (de hotel) (BR), groom *m* (PT)

bellhop ['bɛlhɔp] *(US)* N = **bellboy**

belligerent [bɪ'lɪdʒərənt] ADJ *(at war)* beligerante; *(fig)* agressivo

bellow ['bɛləu] VI mugir; *(person)* bramar ■ VT *(orders)* gritar, berrar

bellows ['bɛləuz] NPL fole *m*

bell push *(Brit)* N botão *m* de campainha

belly ['bɛlɪ] N barriga, ventre *m*

bellyache ['bɛlɪeɪk] *(inf)* N dor *f* de barriga ■ VI bufar

belly button ['bɛlɪbʌtn] N umbigo

belong [bɪ'lɔŋ] VI: **to ~ to** pertencer a; *(club etc)* ser sócio de; **the book ~s here** o livro fica guardado aqui

belongings [bɪ'lɔŋɪŋz] NPL pertences *mpl*

beloved [bɪ'lʌvɪd] ADJ querido, amado ■ N bem-amado(-a)

below [bɪ'ləu] PREP *(beneath)* embaixo de; *(lower than, less than)* abaixo de; *(covered by)* debaixo de ■ ADV em baixo; **see ~** ver abaixo; **temperatures ~ normal** temperaturas abaixo da normal

belt [bɛlt] N cinto; *(of land)* faixa; *(Tech)* correia ■ VT *(thrash)* surrar ■ VI *(Brit: inf)*: **to ~ along** ir a toda, correr; **industrial ~** zona industrial
  ‣ **belt out** VT *(song)* cantar a plenos pulmões
  ‣ **belt up** *(Brit: inf)* VI calar a boca

beltway ['bɛltweɪ] *(US)* N via circular

bemoan [bɪ'məun] VT lamentar

bemused [bɪ'mjuːzd] ADJ bestificado,

estupidificado

bench [bɛntʃ] N banco; *(work bench)* bancada (de carpinteiro); *(Brit: Pol)* assento num Parlamento; **the B~** *(Law)* o tribunal; *(people)* os magistrados, o corpo de magistrados; **bench mark** N referência

bend [bɛnd] *(pt, pp)* VT *(leg, arm)* dobrar; *(pipe)* curvar ■ VI dobrar-se, inclinar-se ■ N curva; *(in pipe)* curvatura; **bends** NPL mal-dos-mergulhadores *m*
  ‣ **bend down** VI abaixar-se; *(squat)* agachar-se
  ‣ **bend over** VI debruçar-se

beneath [bɪ'niːθ] PREP *(position)* abaixo de; *(covered by)* debaixo de; *(unworthy of)* indigno de ■ ADV em baixo

benefactor ['bɛnɪfæktə'] N benfeitor(a) *m/f*

benefactress ['bɛnɪfæktrɪs] N benfeitora

beneficial [bɛnɪ'fɪʃəl] ADJ: **~ (to)** benéfico (a)

beneficiary [bɛnɪ'fɪʃərɪ] N *(Law)* beneficiário(-a)

benefit ['bɛnɪfɪt] N benefício, vantagem *f*; *(as part of salary etc)* benefício; *(money)* subsídio, auxílio ■ VT beneficiar ■ VI: **to ~ from sth** beneficiar-se de algo; **benefit (performance)** N apresentação *f* beneficente

Benelux ['bɛnɪlʌks] N Benelux *m*

benevolent [bɪ'nɛvələnt] ADJ benévolo

BEng N ABBR (= *Bachelor of Engineering*) título *universitário*

benign [bɪ'naɪn] ADJ *(person, smile)* afável, bondoso; *(Med)* benigno

bent [bɛnt] PT, PP *of* **bend** ■ N inclinação *f* ■ ADJ *(wire, pipe)* torto; *(inf: dishonest)* corrupto; **to be ~ on** estar empenhado em; **to have a ~ for** ter queda para

bequeath [bɪ'kwiːð] VT legar

bequest [bɪ'kwɛst] N legado

bereaved [bɪ'riːvd] NPL: **the ~** os enlutados ■ ADJ enlutado

bereavement [bɪ'riːvmənt] N luto

beret ['bɛreɪ] N boina

Bering Sea ['beɪrɪŋ-] N: **the ~** o mar de Bering

Berks *(Brit)* ABBR = **Berkshire**

Berlin [bəː'lɪn] N Berlim; **East/West ~** Berlim Oriental/Ocidental

berm [bəːm] *(US)* N acostamento (BR), berma (PT)

Bermuda [bəː'mjuːdə] N Bermudas *fpl*; **Bermuda shorts** NPL bermuda

Bern [bəːn] N Berna

berry ['bɛrɪ] N baga

berserk [bə'səːk] ADJ: **to go ~** perder as estribeiras

berth [bəːθ] N *(bed)* beliche *m*; *(cabin)* cabine *f*; *(on train)* leito; *(for ship)* ancoradouro ■ VI *(in harbour)* atracar, encostar-se; *(at anchor)* ancorar; **to give sb a wide ~** *(fig)* evitar alguém

beseech [bɪ'siːtʃ] *(pt, pp* **besought**) VT suplicar, implorar

beset [bɪ'sɛt] *(pt, pp* **beset**) VT *(subj: problems, difficulties)* acossar ■ ADJ: **a policy ~ with dangers** uma política cercada de perigos

besetting [bɪ'sɛtɪŋ] ADJ: **his ~ sin** seu grande

vício

beside [bɪ'saɪd] PREP *(next to)* junto de, ao lado de, ao pé de; *(compared with)* em comparação com; **to be ~ o.s. (with anger)** estar fora de si; **that's ~ the point** isso não tem nada a ver

besides [bɪ'saɪdz] ADV além disso ■ PREP *(as well as)* além de; *(except)* salvo, exceto

besiege [bɪ'si:dʒ] VT *(town)* sitiar, pôr cerco a; *(fig)* assediar

besotted [bɪ'sɔtɪd] *(Brit)* ADJ: **~ with** gamado em, louco por

besought [bɪ'sɔ:t] PT, PP *of* **beseech**

bespectacled [bɪ'spɛktɪkld] ADJ de óculos

bespoke [bɪ'spəuk] *(Brit)* ADJ *(garment)* feito sob medida; **~ software** software *m* sob medida; **~ tailor** alfaiate *m* que confecciona roupa sob medida

best [bɛst] ADJ melhor ■ ADV (o) melhor; **the ~ part of** *(quantity)* a maior parte de; **at ~** na melhor das hipóteses; **to make the ~ of sth** tirar o maior partido possível de algo; **to do one's ~** fazer o possível; **to the ~ of my knowledge** que eu saiba; **to the ~ of my ability** o melhor que eu puder; **he's not exactly patient at the ~ of times** mesmo nos seus melhores momentos ele não é muito paciente; **the ~ thing to do is ...** o melhor é ...; **best man** N padrinho de casamento

bestow [bɪ'stəu] VT *(affection)* dar, oferecer; *(honour, title)*: **to ~ sth on sb** outorgar algo a alguém

bestseller ['bɛst'sɛləʳ] N *(book)* best-seller *m*

bet [bɛt] *(pt, pp* **betted)** N aposta ■ VT: **to ~ sb sth** apostar algo con alguém ■ VI: **to ~ (on)** apostar (em); **to ~ money on sth** apostar dinheiro em algo; **it's a safe ~** *(fig)* é coisa segura, é dinheiro ganho

Bethlehem ['bɛθlɪhɛm] N Belém

betray [bɪ'treɪ] VT trair; *(denounce)* delatar

betrayal [bɪ'treɪəl] N traição *f*

better ['bɛtəʳ] ADJ, ADV melhor ■ VT melhorar; *(go above)* superar ■ N: **to get the ~ of sb** vencer alguém; **you had ~ do it** é melhor você fazer isso; **he thought ~ of it** pensou melhor, mudou de opinião; **to get ~** melhorar; **that's ~!** isso!

betting ['bɛtɪŋ] N jogo; **betting shop** *(Brit)* N agência de apostas

between [bɪ'twi:n] PREP no meio de, entre ■ ADV no meio; **the road ~ here and London** a estrada daqui a Londres; **we only had 5 ~ us** juntos só tínhamos 5; **~ you and me** cá entre nós

bevel ['bɛvəl] N *(also:* **bevel edge)** bisel *m*

beverage ['bɛvərɪdʒ] N bebida

bevy ['bɛvɪ] N: **a ~ of** um grupo *or* bando de

bewail [bɪ'weɪl] VT lamentar

beware [bɪ'wɛəʳ] VT, VI: **to ~ (of)** precaver-se (de), ter cuidado (com); **"~ of the dog"** "cuidado com o cachorro" ■ EXCL cuidado!

bewildered [bɪ'wɪldəd] ADJ atordeado; *(confused)* confuso

bewildering [bɪ'wɪldərɪŋ] ADJ atordoador(a),

desnorteante

bewitching [bɪ'wɪtʃɪŋ] ADJ encantador(a), sedutor(a)

beyond [bɪ'jɔnd] PREP *(in space, exceeding)* além de; *(exceeding)* acima de, fora de; *(date)* mais tarde que; *(above)* acima ■ ADV além; *(in time)* mais longe, mais adiante; **~ doubt** fora de qualquer dúvida; **to be ~ repair** no ter conserto

b/f ABBR = **brought forward**

BFPO N ABBR (= *British Forces Post Office)* serviço postal do exército

bhp N ABBR *(Aut:* = *brake horsepower)* potência efetiva ao freio

bi... [baɪ] PREFIX bi...

biannual [baɪ'ænjuəl] ADJ semestral

bias ['baɪəs] N *(prejudice)* preconceito; *(preference)* prevenção *f*

bias(s)ed ['baɪəst] ADJ parcial; **to be bias(s)ed against** ter preconceito contra

bib [bɪb] N babadouro, babador *m*

Bible ['baɪbl] N Bíblia

bibliography [bɪblɪ'ɔɡrəfɪ] N bibliografia

bicarbonate of soda [baɪ'kɑ:bənɪt-] N bicarbonato de sódio

bicentenary [baɪsɛn'ti:nərɪ] N bicentenário

bicentennial [baɪsɛn'tɛnɪəl] N bicentenário

biceps ['baɪsɛps] N bíceps *m inv*

bicker ['bɪkəʳ] VI brigar

bicycle ['baɪsɪkl] N bicicleta; **bicycle path** N ciclovia; **bicycle pump** N bomba de bicicleta; **bicycle track** N ciclovia

bid [bɪd] *(pt* **bid,** *pp* **bid)** N oferta; *(at auction)* lance *m*; *(attempt)* tentativa ■ VI fazer uma oferta; fazer lance; *(Comm)* licitar, fazer uma licitação ■ VT *(price)* oferecer; *(order)* mandar, ordenar; **to ~ sb good day** dar bom dia a alguém

bidder ['bɪdəʳ] N *(Comm)* licitante *m*; **the highest ~** quem oferece mais

bidding ['bɪdɪŋ] N *(at auction)* lances *mpl*; *(Comm)* licitação *f*; *(order)* ordem *f*

bide [baɪd] VT: **to ~ one's time** esperar o momento adequado

bidet ['bi:deɪ] N bidê *m*

bidirectional ['baɪdɪ'rɛkʃənl] ADJ bidirecional

biennial [baɪ'ɛnɪəl] ADJ bienal ■ N *(plant)* planta bienal

bier [bɪəʳ] N féretro

bifocals [baɪ'fəuklz] NPL óculos *mpl* bifocais

big [bɪɡ] ADJ grande; *(bulky)* volumoso; **~ brother/sister** irmão(-irmã mais velho/a); **to do things in a ~ way** fazer as coisas em grande escala

bigamy ['bɪɡəmɪ] N bigamia

big dipper [-'dɪpəʳ] N montanha-russa

big end N *(Aut)* cabeça de biela

bigheaded ['bɪɡ'hɛdɪd] ADJ convencido

big-hearted ['bɪɡ'hɑːtɪd] ADJ magnânimo

bigot ['bɪɡət] N fanático, intolerante *m/f*

bigoted ['bɪɡətɪd] ADJ fanático, intolerante

bigotry ['bɪɡətrɪ] N fanatismo, intolerância

big toe N dedão *m* do pé

big top N tenda de circo

big wheel N (at fair) roda gigante

bigwig ['bɪgwɪg] (inf) N mandachuva m

bike [baɪk] N bicicleta

bikini [bɪ'ki:nɪ] N biquíni m

bilateral [baɪ'lætrəl] ADJ bilateral

bile [baɪl] N bílis f

bilingual [baɪ'lɪŋgwəl] ADJ bilíngüe

bilious ['bɪlɪəs] ADJ bilioso

bill [bɪl] N conta; (invoice) fatura; (Pol) projeto de lei; (US: banknote) bilhete m, nota; (in restaurant) conta, notinha; (notice) cartaz m; (of bird) bico ■ VT (item) faturar; (customer) enviar fatura a; **may I have the ~ please?** a conta or a notinha, por favor?; **"stick** or **post no ~s"** é proibido afixar cartazes"; **to fit** or **fill the ~** (fig) servir; **~ of exchange** letra de câmbio; **~ of lading** conhecimento de carga; **~ of sale** nota de venda; (formal) escritura de venda

billboard ['bɪlbɔ:d] N quadro para cartazes

billet ['bɪlɪt] N alojamento ■ VT alojar, quartelar

billfold ['bɪlfəuld] (US) N carteira (para notas)

billiards ['bɪlɪədz] N bilhar m

billion ['bɪlɪən] N (Brit: = 1,000,000,000,000) trilhão m; (US: = 1,000,000,000) bilhão m

billow ['bɪləu] N (of smoke) bulcão m ■ VI (smoke) redemoinhar; (sail) enfunar-se

billy goat ['bɪlɪ-] N bode m

bin [bɪn] N caixa; (Brit: also: **dustbin; litter bin**) lata de lixo; see also **breadbin**

binary ['baɪnərɪ] ADJ binário

bind [baɪnd] (pt, pp) VT atar, amarrar; (wound) enfaixar; (oblige) obrigar; (book) encadernar ■ N (inf) saco

▶ **bind over** VT (Law) pôr em liberdade condicional

▶ **bind up** VT (wound) enfaixar; **to be bound up with** estar vinculado a

binder ['baɪndəʳ] N (file) fichário

binding ['baɪndɪŋ] ADJ (contract) sujeitante ■ N (of book) encadernação f

binge [bɪndʒ] (inf) N: **to go on a ~** tomar uma bebedeira

bingo ['bɪŋgəu] N bingo

binoculars [bɪ'nɔkjuləz] NPL binóculo

bio ... [baɪəu] PREFIX bio ...

biochemistry [baɪə'kemɪstrɪ] N bioquímica

biodegradable ['baɪəudɪ'greɪdəbl] ADJ biodegradável

biographer [baɪ'ɔgrəfəʳ] N biógrafo(-a)

biographic(al) [baɪə'græfɪk(l)] ADJ biográfico

biography [baɪ'ɔgrəfɪ] N biografia

biological [baɪə'lɔdʒɪkəl] ADJ biológico

biologist [baɪ'ɔlədʒɪst] N biólogo(-a)

biology [baɪ'ɔlədʒɪ] N biologia

biometric ['baɪəu'metrɪk] ADJ biométrico(-a)

biophysics ['baɪəu'fɪzɪks] N biofísica

biopsy ['baɪɔpsɪ] N biopsia

biotechnology ['baɪəutek'nɔlədʒɪ] N biotecnia

birch [bə:tʃ] N bétula; (cane) vara de vidoeiro

bird [bə:d] N ave f, pássaro; (Brit: inf: girl) gatinha

birdcage ['bə:dkeɪdʒ] N gaiola

bird's-eye view N vista aérea; (overview) vista geral

bird flu N gripe f do frango

bird watcher [-'wɔtʃəʳ] N ornitófilo(-a)

Biro® ['baɪərəu] N caneta esferográfica

birth [bə:θ] N nascimento; (Med) parto; **to give ~ to** dar à luz, parir; **birth certificate** N certidão f de nascimento; **birth control** N controle m de natalidade; (methods) métodos mpl anticoncepcionais

birthday ['bə:θdeɪ] N aniversário (BR), dia m de anos (PT) ■ CPD de aniversário; see also **happy**

birthmark ['bə:θmɑ:k] N nevo

birthplace ['bə:θpleɪs] N lugar m de nascimento

birth rate N índice m de natalidade f

Biscay ['bɪskeɪ] N: **the Bay of ~** o golfo de Biscaia

biscuit ['bɪskɪt] N (Brit) bolacha, biscoito; (US) pão m doce

bisect [baɪ'sekt] VT dividir ao meio

bishop ['bɪʃəp] N bispo; (Xadrez) peça de jogo de xadrez

bit [bɪt] PT of **bite** ■ N pedaço, bocado; (of tool) broca; (of horse) freio; (Comput) bit m; **a ~ of** (a little) um pouco de; **a ~ mad/dangerous** um pouco doido/perigoso; **~ by ~** pouco a pouco; **to come to ~s** (break) cair aos pedaços; **bring all your ~s and pieces** traz todos os teus troços; **to do one's ~** fazer sua parte

bitch [bɪtʃ] N (dog) cadela, cachorra; (inf!: woman) cadela (!), vagabunda (!)

bite [baɪt] (pt bit, pp bitten) VT, VI morder; (insect etc) picar ■ N mordida; (insect bite) picada; (mouthful) bocado; **to ~ one's nails** roer as unhas; **let's have a ~ (to eat)** (inf) vamos fazer uma boquinha

biting ['baɪtɪŋ] ADJ (wind) penetrante; (wit) mordaz

bit part N (Theatre) ponta

bitten ['bɪtn] PP of **bite**

bitter ['bɪtəʳ] ADJ amargo; (wind, criticism) cortante, penetrante; (battle) encarniçado ■ N (Brit: beer) cerveja amarga; **to the ~ end** até o fim

bitterly ['bɪtəlɪ] ADV (complain, weep) amargamente; (criticize) asperamente; (oppose) implacavelmente; (jealous, disappointed) extremamente; **it's ~ cold** faz um frio glacial

bitterness ['bɪtənɪs] N amargor m; (anger) rancor m

bittersweet ['bɪtəswi:t] ADJ agridoce

bitty ['bɪtɪ] (Brit: inf) ADJ sem nexo

bitumen ['bɪtjumɪn] N betume m

bivouac ['bɪvuæk] N bivaque m

bizarre [bɪ'zɑːʳ] ADJ esquisito

bk ABBR = **bank; book**

BL N ABBR = **Bachelor of Laws**; (= Bachelor of Letters) título universitário; (US: = Bachelor of Literature) título universitário

bl ABBR = **bill of lading**

blab [blæb] VI dar or bater com a língua nos dentes ■ VT (also: **blab out**) revelar, badalar

black [blæk] ADJ preto; (humour) negro ■ N

(*colour*) cor *f* preta; (*person*): **B~** negro(-a), preto(-a) ■ VT (*shoes*) lustrar (BR), engraxar (PT); (*Brit: Industry*) boicotar; **to give sb a ~ eye** esmurrar alguém e deixá-lo de olho roxo; **~ and blue** contuso, contundido; **there it is in ~ and white** (*fig*) aí está preto no branco; **to be in the ~** (*in credit*) estar com saldo credor

▶ **black out** VI (*faint*) desmaiar

black belt (US) N zona de negros

blackberry ['blækbərı] N amora preta (BR), amora silvestre (PT)

blackbird ['blækbɔːd] N melro

blackboard ['blækbɔːd] N quadro(-negro)

black box N (*Aviat*) caixa preta

black coffee N café *m* preto

Black Country (*Brit*) N: **the ~** *zona industrial na região central da Inglaterra*

blackcurrant [blæk'kʌrənt] N groselha negra

black economy (*Brit*) N economia invisível

blacken ['blækən] VT enegrecer; (*fig*) denegrir

Black Forest N: **the ~** a Floresta Negra

blackhead ['blækhɛd] N cravo

black ice N gelo negro

blackjack ['blækdʒæk] N (*Cards*) vinte-e-um *m*; (*US: truncheon*) cassetete *m*

blackleg ['blæklɛg] (*Brit*) N fura-greve *m/f*

blacklist ['blæklɪst] N lista negra ■ VT colocar na lista negra

blackmail ['blækmeɪl] N chantagem *f* ■ VT fazer chantagem a

blackmailer ['blækmeɪləʳ] N chantagista *m/f*

black market N mercado *ou* câmbio negro

blackout ['blækaut] N blecaute *m*; (*fainting*) desmaio; (*of radio signal*) desvanecimento

Black Sea N: **the ~** o mar Negro

black sheep N (*fig*) ovelha negra

blacksmith ['blæksmɪθ] N ferreiro

black spot N (*Aut*) lugar *m* perigoso; (*for unemployment etc*) área crítica

bladder ['blædəʳ] N bexiga

blade [bleɪd] N folha; (*of knife, sword*) lâmina; (*of oar, rotor*) pá *f*; **a ~ of grass** uma folha de relva

blame [bleɪm] N culpa ■ VT: **to ~ sb for sth** culpar alguém por algo; **to be to ~** ter a culpa

blameless ['bleɪmlɪs] ADJ (*person*) inocente

blanch [blɑːntʃ] VI (*person, face*) empalidecer ■ VT (*Culin*) escaldar

bland [blænd] ADJ suave; (*taste*) brando

blank [blæŋk] ADJ em branco; (*shot*) sem bala; (*look*) sem expressão ■ N (*of memory*): **to go ~** dar um branco, on form, espaço em branco; (*cartridge*) bala de festim; **we drew a ~** (*fig*) chegamos a lugar nenhum; **blank cheque** (US **blank check**) N cheque *m* em branco; **to give sb a blank cheque to do ...** dar carta branca a alguém para fazer ...

blanket ['blæŋkɪt] N (*for bed*) cobertor *m*; (*for travelling etc*) manta; (*of snow, fog*) camada ■ ADJ (*statement, agreement*) global, geral; **to give ~ cover** (*subj: insurance policy*) dar cobertura geral

blare [blɛəʳ] VI (*horn, radio*) clangorar

blasé ['blɑːzeɪ] ADJ indiferente

blasphemous ['blæsfɪməs] ADJ blasfemo

blasphemy ['blæsfɪmɪ] N blasfêmia

blast [blɑːst] N (*of wind*) rajada; (*of whistle*) toque *m*; (*of explosive*) explosão *f*; (*shock wave*) sopro; (*of air, steam*) jato ■ VT (*blow up*) fazer voar; (*blow open*) abrir com uma carga explosiva ■ EXCL (*Brit: inf*) droga!; (**at**) **full ~** (*play music etc*) no volume máximo; (*fig*) a todo vapor

▶ **blast off** N (*Space*) decolar

blast-off N (*Space*) lançamento

blatant ['bleɪtənt] ADJ descarado

blatantly ['bleɪtəntlɪ] ADV (*lie*) descaradamente; **it's ~ obvious** é de toda a evidência, está na cara

blaze [bleɪz] N (*fire*) fogo; (*in building etc*) incêndio; (*flames*) chamas *fpl*; (*fig: of colour*) esplendor *m*; (: *of glory, publicity*) explosão *f* ■ VI (*fire*) arder; (*guns*) descarregar; (*eyes*) brilhar ■ VT: **to ~ a trail** (*fig*) abrir (um) caminho; **in a ~ of publicity** numa explosão de publicidade

blazer ['bleɪzəʳ] N casaco esportivo, blazer *m*

bleach [bliːtʃ] N (*also*: **household bleach**) água sanitária ■ VT (*linen*) branquear

bleached [bliːtʃt] ADJ (*hair*) oxigenado; (*linen*) branqueado, alvejado

bleachers ['bliːtʃəz] (US) NPL (*Sport*) arquibancada descoberta

bleak [bliːk] ADJ (*countryside*) desolado; (*prospect*) desanimador(a), sombrio; (*weather*) ruim; (*smile*) sem graça, amarelo

bleary-eyed ['blɪərɪ'aɪd] ADJ de olhos injetados

bleat [bliːt] VI balir ■ N balido

bled [blɛd] PT, PP of **bleed**

bleed [bliːd] (*pt, pp* **bled**) VT, VI sangrar; **my nose is ~ing** eu estou sangrando do nariz

bleeper ['bliːpəʳ] N (*of doctor etc*) bip *m*

blemish ['blɛmɪʃ] N mancha; (*on reputation*) mácula

blend [blɛnd] N mistura ■ VT misturar ■ VI (*colours etc: also*: **blend in**) combinar-se, misturar-se

blender ['blɛndəʳ] N (*Culin*) liqüidificador *m*

bless [blɛs] (*pt, pp* **blest**) VT abençoar; **~ you!** (*after sneeze*) saúde!

blessed[1] [blɛst] PT, PP of **bless**; **to be ~ with** estar dotado de

blessed[2] ['blɛsɪd] ADJ (*Rel: holy*) bendito, bento; (*happy*) afortunado; **it rains every ~ day** chove cada santo dia

blessing ['blɛsɪŋ] N bênção *f*; (*godsend*) graça, dádiva; (*approval*) aprovação *f*; **to count one's ~s** dar graças a Deus; **it was a ~ in disguise** Deus escreve certo por linhas tortas

blest [blɛst] PT, PP of **bless**

blew [bluː] PT of **blow**

blight [blaɪt] VT (*hopes etc*) frustrar, gorar ■ N (*of plants*) ferrugem *f*

blimey ['blaɪmɪ] (*Brit: inf*) EXCL nossa!

blind [blaɪnd] ADJ cego ■ N (*for window*) persiana; (: *also*: **Venetian blind**) veneziana ■ VT cegar; (*dazzle*) deslumbrar; **the blind** NPL (*blind people*) os cegos; **to turn a ~ eye (on**

or **to)** fazer vista grossa (a); **blind alley** N becosem-saída *m*; **blind corner** (*Brit*) N curva sem visibilidade
blindfold ['blaɪndfəuld] N venda ▪ ADJ, ADV com os olhos vendados, às cegas ▪ VT vendar os olhos a
blindly ['blaɪndlɪ] ADV às cegas; (*without thinking*) cegamente
blindness ['blaɪndnɪs] N cegueira
blind spot N (*Aut*) local *m* pouco visível; (*fig*) ponto fraco
blink [blɪŋk] VI piscar ▪ N (*inf*): **the TV's on the** ~ a TV está com defeito
blinkers ['blɪŋkəz] NPL antolhos *mpl*
blinking ['blɪŋkɪŋ] (*Brit: inf*) ADJ: **this** ~ ... este danado ...
bliss [blɪs] N felicidade *f*
blissful ['blɪsful] ADJ (*event, day*) maravilhoso; (*sigh, smile*) contente; **in** ~ **ignorance** numa bendita ignorância
blissfully ['blɪsfulɪ] ADJ (*smile*) ditosamente; (*happy*) maravilhosamente
blister ['blɪstə'] N (*on skin*) bolha; (*in paint, rubber*) empola ▪ VI (*paint*) empolar-se
blithe [blaɪð] ADJ alegre
blithely ['blaɪðlɪ] ADV (*unconcernedly*) tranqüilamente; (*joyfully*) alegremente
blithering ['blɪðərɪŋ] (*inf*) ADJ: **this** ~ **idiot** esta besta quadrada
BLit(t) N ABBR (= *Bachelor of Literature*) título universitário
blitz [blɪts] N bombardeio aéreo; (*fig*): **to have a** ~ **on sth** dar um jeito em algo
blizzard ['blɪzəd] N nevasca
BLM (*US*) N ABBR = **Bureau of Land Management**
bloated ['bləutɪd] ADJ (*swollen*) inchado; (*full*) empanturrado
blob [blɔb] N (*drop*) gota; (*stain, spot*) mancha; (*indistinct shape*) ponto
bloc [blɔk] N (*Pol*) bloco
block [blɔk] N (*of wood*) bloco; (*of stone*) laje *f*; (*in pipes*) entupimento; (*toy*) cubo; (*of buildings*) quarteirão *m* ▪ VT obstruir, bloquear; (*pipe*) entupir; (*progress*) impedir; (*Comput*) blocar; ~ **of flats** (*Brit*) prédio (de apartamentos); **3** ~**s from here** a três quarteirões daqui; **mental** ~ bloqueio; ~ **and tackle** (*Tech*) talha
  ▶ **block up** VT (*hole*) tampar; (*pipe*) entupir; (*road*) bloquear
blockade [blɔ'keɪd] N bloqueio ▪ VT bloquear
blockage ['blɔkɪdʒ] N obstrução *f*
block booking N reserva em bloco
blockbuster ['blɔkbʌstə'] N grande sucesso
block capitals NPL letras *fpl* de forma
blockhead ['blɔkhɛd] N imbecil *m/f*
block letters NPL letras *fpl* maiúsculas
block release (*Brit*) N licença para fins de aperfeiçoamento profissional
block vote (*Brit*) N voto em bloco
blog ['blɔg] N (*inf: Internet journal*) blog *m*, blogue *f*
blogger ['blɔgər] N (*inf: person*) blogueiro(a)

bloke [bləuk] (*Brit: inf*) N cara *m* (*BR*), gajo (*PT*)
blond(e) [blɔnd] ADJ, N louro(-a)
blood [blʌd] N sangue *m*
bloodcurdling ['blʌdkə:dlɪŋ] ADJ horripilante, de fazer gelar o sangue nas veias
blood donor N doador(a) *m/f* de sangue
blood group N grupo sangüíneo
bloodhound ['blʌdhaund] N sabujo
bloodless ['blʌdlɪs] ADJ (*victory*) incruento; (*pale*) pálido
bloodletting ['blʌdlɛtɪŋ] N (*Med*) sangria; (*fig*) derramamento de sangue
blood poisoning N toxemia
blood pressure N pressão *f* arterial *or* sangüínea
bloodshed ['blʌdʃɛd] N matança, carnificina
bloodshot ['blʌdʃɔt] ADJ (*eyes*) injetado
bloodstained ['blʌdsteɪnd] ADJ manchado de sangue
bloodstream ['blʌdstri:m] N corrente *f* sangüínea
blood test N exame *m* de sangue
bloodthirsty ['blʌdθə:stɪ] ADJ sangüinário
blood transfusion N transfusão *f* de sangue
blood vessel N vaso sangüíneo
bloody ['blʌdɪ] ADJ sangrento; (*nose*) ensangüentado; (*Brit: inf!*): **this** ~ ... essa droga de ..., esse maldito ...; ~ **strong/good** forte/bom pra burro (*inf*)
bloody-minded ['blʌdɪ'maɪndɪd] (*Brit: inf*) ADJ espírito de porco *inv*
bloom [blu:m] N flor *f*; (*fig*) florescimento, viço ▪ VI florescer
blooming ['blu:mɪŋ] (*inf*) ADJ: **this** ~ ... esse maldito ..., esse miserável ...
blossom ['blɔsəm] N flor *f* ▪ VI florescer; (*fig*) desabrochar-se; **to** ~ **into** (*fig*) tornar-se
blot [blɔt] N borrão *m*; (*fig*) mancha ▪ VT borrar; (*ink*) secar; **a** ~ **on the landscape** um aleijão na paisagem; **to** ~ **one's copy book** (*fig*) manchar sua reputação
  ▶ **blot out** VT (*view*) tapar; (*memory*) apagar
blotchy ['blɔtʃɪ] ADJ (*complexion*) cheio de manchas
blotter ['blɔtə'] N mata-borrão *m*
blotting paper ['blɔtɪŋ-] N mata-borrão *m*
blouse [blauz] N blusa
blow [bləu] (*pt* **blew**, *pp* **blown**) N golpe *m*; (*punch*) soco ▪ VI soprar ▪ VT (*subj: wind*) soprar; (*instrument*) tocar; (*fuse*) queimar; (*glass*) soprar; **to** ~ **one's nose** assoar o nariz; **to come to** ~**s** chegar às vias de fato
  ▶ **blow away** VT levar, arrancar ▪ VI ser levado pelo vento
  ▶ **blow down** VT derrubar
  ▶ **blow off** VT levar ▪ VI ser levado
  ▶ **blow out** VI (*candle*) apagar; (*tyre*) estourar ▪ VT (*candle*) apagar
  ▶ **blow over** VI passar
  ▶ **blow up** VI explodir; (*fig*) perder a paciência ▪ VT explodir; (*tyre*) encher; (*Phot*) ampliar
blow-dry N escova ▪ VT fazer escova em

blowlamp ['bləulæmp] (*Brit*) N maçarico

blown [bləun] PP *of* **blow**

blow-out N (*of tyre*) furo; (*inf: big meal*) regabofe *m*

blowtorch ['bləutɔːtʃ] N = **blowlamp**

blowzy ['blauzɪ] (*Brit*) ADJ balofa

BLS (*US*) N ABBR = **Bureau of Labor Statistics**

blubber ['blʌbəʳ] N óleo de baleia ▪ VI (*pej*) choramingar

blue [bluː] ADJ azul; (*depressed*) deprimido; **blues** N (*Mus*): **the ~s** o blues; **to have the ~s** (*inf: feeling*) estar na fossa, estar de baixo astral; (**only**) **once in a ~ moon** uma vez na vida e outra na morte; **out of the ~** (*fig*) de estalo, inesperadamente; **blue baby** N criança azul; **blue film** N filme picante

bluebell ['bluːbɛl] N campainha

bluebottle ['bluːbɔtl] N varejeira azul

blue cheese N queijo tipo roquefort

blue-chip ADJ: **~ investment** investimento de primeira ordem

blue-collar worker N operário(-a)

blue jeans NPL jeans *m* (BR), jeans *mpl* (PT)

blueprint ['bluːprɪnt] N anteprojeto; (*fig*): **~ (for)** esquema *m* (de)

bluff [blʌf] VI blefar ▪ N blefe *m*; (*crag*) penhasco ▪ ADJ (*person*) brusco; **to call sb's ~** pagar para ver alguém

blunder ['blʌndəʳ] N gafe *f* ▪ VI cometer *or* fazer uma gafe; **to ~ into sb/sth** esbarrar com alguém/algo

blunt [blʌnt] ADJ (*knife*) cego; (*pencil*) rombudo; (*person*) franco, direto ▪ VT embotar; **~ instrument** (*Law*) arma imprópria

bluntly ['blʌntlɪ] ADV sem rodeios

bluntness ['blʌntnɪs] N (*of person*) franqueza, rudeza

blur [bləːʳ] N borrão *m* ▪ VT borrar, nublar; (*vision*) embaçar

blurb [bləːb] N (*for book*) dizeres *mpl* de propaganda

blurred [bləːd] ADJ indistinto, borrado

blurt out [bləːt-] VT (*reveal*) deixar escapar; (*say*) balbuciar

blush [blʌʃ] VI corar, ruborizar-se ▪ N rubor *m*, vermelhidão *f*

blusher ['blʌʃəʳ] N blusher *m*

bluster ['blʌstəʳ] N fanfarronada, bazófia ▪ VI fanfarronar

blustering ['blʌstərɪŋ] ADJ (*person*) fanfarrão(-rona)

blustery ['blʌstərɪ] ADJ (*weather*) borrascoso, tormentoso

Blvd ABBR = **boulevard**

BM N ABBR = **British Museum**; (*Sch*: = *Bachelor of Medicine*) *título universitário*

BMA N ABBR = **British Medical Association**

BMJ N ABBR = **British Medical Journal**

BMus N ABBR (= *Bachelor of Music*) *título universitário*

BO N ABBR (*inf*: = *body odour*) fartum *m*, c.c. *m*; (*US*) = **box office**

boar [bɔːʳ] N javali *m*

board [bɔːd] N (*wooden*) tábua; (*cardboard*) quadro; (*notice board*) quadro de avisos; (*for chess etc*) tabuleiro; (*committee*) junta, conselho; (*in firm*) diretoria, conselho administrativo; (*Naut, Aviat*): **on ~** a bordo ▪ VT embarcar em; **full ~** (*Brit*) pensão *f* completa; **half ~** (*Brit*) meiapensão *f*; **~ and lodging** casa e comida; **above ~** (*fig*) limpo; **across the ~** ADJ geral ▪ ADV de uma maneira geral; **to go by the ~** ficar abandonado, dançar (*inf*)
▶ **board up** VT (*door*) entabuar

boarder ['bɔːdəʳ] N hóspede *m/f*; (*Sch*) interno(-a)

board game N jogo de tabuleiro

boarding card ['bɔːdɪŋ-] N = **boarding pass**

boarding house ['bɔːdɪŋ-] N pensão *m*

boarding pass ['bɔːdɪŋ-] (*Brit*) N (*Aviat, Naut*) cartão *m* de embarque

boarding school ['bɔːdɪŋ-] N internato

board meeting N reunião *f* da diretoria

board room N sala da diretoria

boardwalk ['bɔːdwɔːk] (*US*) N passeio de tábuas

boast [bəust] VI contar vantagem; **to ~ (about** *or* **of)** gabar-se (de), jactar-se (de) ▪ VT ostentar ▪ N jactância, bazófia

boastful ['bəustful] ADJ vaidoso, jactancioso

boastfulness ['bəustfulnɪs] N bazófia, jactância

boat [bəut] N barco; (*small*) bote *m*; (*big*) navio; **to go by ~** ir de barco; **to be in the same ~** (*fig*) estar no mesmo barco

boater ['bəutəʳ] N (*hat*) chapéu *m* de palha

boating ['bəutɪŋ] N passeio de barco

boatman ['bəutmən] (*irreg*) N barqueiro

boatswain ['bəusn] N contramestre *m*

bob [bɔb] VI (*boat, cork on water: also:* **bob up and down**) balouçar-se ▪ N (*Brit: inf*) = **shilling**
▶ **bob up** VI aparecer, surgir

bobbin ['bɔbɪn] N bobina, carretel *m*

bobby ['bɔbɪ] (*Brit: inf*) N policial *m/f* (BR), polícia *m* (PT)

bobsleigh ['bɔbsleɪ] N bob *m*, trenó *m* duplo

bode [bəud] VI: **to ~ well/ill (for)** ser de bom/mau agouro (para)

bodice ['bɔdɪs] N corpete *m*

bodily ['bɔdɪlɪ] ADJ corporal; (*pain*) físico; (*needs*) material ▪ ADV (*lift*) em peso

body ['bɔdɪ] N corpo; (*corpse*) cadáver *m*; (*of car*) carroceria; (*of plane*) fuselagem *f*; (*fig: group*) grupo; (: *organization*) organização *f*; (*quantity*) conjunto; (*of wine*) corpo; **in a ~** todos juntos

body-building N musculação *f*

bodyguard ['bɔdɪɡɑːd] N guarda-costas *m inv*

body repairs NPL lanternagem *f*

bodywork ['bɔdɪwəːk] N lataria

boffin ['bɔfɪn] (*Brit*) N cientista *m/f*

bog [bɔɡ] N pântano, atoleiro ▪ VT: **to get ~ged down (in)** (*fig*) atolar-se (em)

bogey ['bəuɡɪ] N (*worry*) espectro; (*Brit: inf: dried mucus*) meleca

boggle ['bɔɡl] VI: **the mind ~s** (*wonder*) não dá para imaginar; (*innuendo*) nem quero pensar

bogie ['bəuɡɪ] N (*Rail*) truque *m*

Bogotá [bɔgə'tɑː] N Bogotá
bogus ['bəugəs] ADJ falso; (*workman etc*) farsante
Bohemia [bəu'hiːmɪə] N Boêmia
Bohemian [bəu'hiːmɪən] ADJ, N boêmio(-a)
boil [bɔɪl] VT ferver; (*eggs*) cozinhar ▪ VI ferver
 ▪ N (*Med*) furúnculo; **to bring to the** (*Brit*) *or* **a** (*US*) ~ deixar ferver; **to come to the** (*Brit*) *or* **a** (*US*) ~ começar a ferver
 ▶ **boil down to** VT FUS (*fig*) reduzir-se a
 ▶ **boil over** VI transbordar
boiled egg [bɔɪld-] N ovo cozido
boiled potatoes [bɔɪld-] NPL batatas *fpl* cozidas
boiler ['bɔɪləʳ] N caldeira; (*for central heating*) boiler *m*; **boiler suit** (*Brit*) N macacão *m* (BR), fato macaco (PT)
boiling ['bɔɪlɪŋ] ADJ: **it's** ~ (*weather*) está um calor horrível; **I'm** ~ (**hot**) (*inf*) estou morrendo de calor; **boiling point** N ponto de ebulição
boisterous ['bɔɪstərəs] ADJ (*noisy*) barulhento; (*excitable*) agitado; (*crowd*) turbulento
bold [bəuld] ADJ corajoso; (*pej*) atrevido, insolente; (*outline, colour*) forte
boldness ['bəuldnɪs] N arrojo, coragem *f*; (*cheek*) audácia, descaramento
bold type N (*Typ*) negrito
Bolivia [bə'lɪvɪə] N Bolívia
Bolivian [bə'lɪvɪən] ADJ, N boliviano(-a)
bollard ['bɔləd] N (*Brit: Aut*) poste *m* de sinalização; (*Naut*) poste de amarração
bolster ['bəulstəʳ] N travesseiro
 ▶ **bolster up** VT sustentar
bolt [bəult] N (*lock*) trinco, ferrolho; (*with nut*) parafuso, cavilha ▪ ADV: ~ **upright** direito como um fuso ▪ VT (*door*) fechar a ferrolho, trancar; (*food*) engolir às pressas ▪ VI fugir; (*horse*) disparar; **to be a** ~ **from the blue** (*fig*) cair como uma bomba, ser uma bomba
bomb [bɔm] N bomba ▪ VT bombardear
bombard [bɔm'bɑːd] VT bombardear
bombardment [bɔm'bɑːdmənt] N bombardeio
bombastic [bɔm'bæstɪk] ADJ bombástico
bomb disposal N: ~ **expert** perito(-a) em desmontagem de explosivos; ~ **unit** unidade *f* de desmontagem de explosivos
bomber ['bɔməʳ] N (*Aviat*) bombardeiro; (*terrorist*) terrorista *m/f*
bombing ['bɔmɪŋ] N bombardeio; (*by terrorists*) atentado a bomba
bombshell ['bɔmʃel] N granada de artilharia; (*fig*) bomba
bomb site N zona bombardeada
bona fide ['bəunə'faɪdɪ] ADJ genuíno, autêntico
bonanza [bə'nænzə] N boom *m*
bond [bɔnd] N (*binding promise*) compromisso; (*link*) vínculo, laço; (*Finance*) obrigação *f*; (*Comm*): **in** ~ (*goods*) retido sob caução na alfândega
bondage ['bɔndɪdʒ] N escravidão *f*
bonded warehouse ['bɔndɪd-] N depósito da alfândega, entreposto aduaneiro
bone [bəun] N osso; (*of fish*) espinha ▪ VT desossar; tirar as espinhas de; **bone china** N porcelana com mistura de cinza de ossos

bone-dry ADJ completamente seco
bone idle ADJ preguiçoso
boner ['bəunəʳ] (*US*) N gafe *f*
bonfire ['bɔnfaɪəʳ] N fogueira
Bonn [bɔn] N Bonn
bonnet ['bɔnɪt] N toucado; (*Brit: of car*) capô *m*
bonny ['bɔnɪ] (*Scottish*) ADJ bonitinho
bonus ['bəunəs] N (*payment*) bônus *m*; (*fig*) gratificação *f*; (*on salary*) prêmio, gratificação *f*
bony ['bəunɪ] ADJ (*arm, face, Med: tissue*) ossudo; (*meat*) cheio de ossos; (*fish*) cheio de espinhas
boo [buː] VT vaiar ▪ N vaia ▪ EXCL ruuh!, bu!
boob [buːb] (*inf*) N (*breast*) seio; (*Brit: mistake*) besteira, gafe *f*
booby prize ['buːbɪ-] N prêmio de consolação
booby trap ['buːbɪ-] N armadilha explosiva
booby-trapped ['buːbɪtræpt] ADJ que tem armadilha explosiva
book [buk] N livro; (*of stamps, tickets*) talão *m*; (*notebook*) caderno ▪ VT reservar; (*driver*) autuar; (*football player*) mostrar o cartão amarelo a; **books** NPL (*Comm*) contas *fpl*, contabilidade *f*; **to keep the** ~**s** fazer a escrituração *or* contabilidade; **by the** ~ de acordo com o regulamento, corretamente; **to throw the** ~ **at sb** condenar alguém à pena máxima
 ▶ **book in** (*Brit*) VI (*at hotel*) registrar (BR), registar (PT)
 ▶ **book up** VT reservar; **all seats are** ~**ed up** todos os lugares estão tomados; **the hotel is** ~**ed up** o hotel está lotado
bookable ['bukəbl] ADJ: **seats are** ~ lugares podem ser reservados
bookcase ['bukkeɪs] N estante *f* (para livros)
book ends NPL suportes *mpl* de livros
booking ['bukɪŋ] (*Brit*) N reserva; **booking office** (*Brit*) N (*Rail, Theatre*) bilheteria (BR), bilheteira (PT)
book-keeping N escrituração *f*, contabilidade *f*
booklet ['buklɪt] N livrinho, brochura
bookmaker ['bukmeɪkəʳ] N book(maker) *m* (BR), agenciador *m* de apostas (PT)
bookseller ['buksɛləʳ] N livreiro(-a)
bookshop ['bukʃɔp] N livraria
bookstall ['bukstɔːl] N banca de livros
bookstore ['bukstɔːʳ] N = **bookshop**
book token N vale *m* para livro
book value N valor *m* contábil
boom [buːm] N (*noise*) barulho, estrondo; (*in sales etc*) aumento rápido; (*Econ*) boom *m*, fase *f* or aumento de prosperidade ▪ VI (*sound*) retumbar; (*business*) tomar surto
boomerang ['buːməræŋ] N bumerangue *m*
boom town N cidade *f* de rápido crescimento econômico
boon [buːn] N dádiva, benefício
boorish ['buərɪʃ] ADJ rude
boost [buːst] N estímulo ▪ VT estimular; **to give a** ~ **to sb's spirits** *or* **to sb** dar uma força a alguém
booster ['buːstəʳ] N (*Med*) revacinação *f*; (*TV*) amplificador *m* (de sinal); (*Elec*) sobrevoltador

m; (*also*: **booster rocket**) foguete *m* auxiliar; **booster seat** N (*Aut: for children*) assento de carro para crianças maiores

boot [buːt] N bota; (*for football*) chuteira; (*for walking*) bota (para caminhar); (*ankle boot*) botina; (*Brit: of car*) porta-malas *m* (BR), mala (BR) (*inf*), porta-bagagem *m* (PT) ▪ VT (*kick*) dar pontapé em; (*Comput*) dar carga em; **to ~ ...** (*in addition*) ainda por cima ...; **to give sb the ~** (*inf*) botar alguém na rua

booth [buːð] N (*at fair*) barraca; (*telephone booth, voting booth*) cabine *f*

bootleg [ˈbuːtlɛg] ADJ de contrabando; **~ recording** gravação *f* pirata

booty [ˈbuːtɪ] N despojos *mpl*, pilhagem *f*

booze [buːz] (*inf*) N bebida alcoólica ▪ VI embebedar-se

boozer [ˈbuːzər] (*inf*) N (*person*) beberrão(-beberrona) *m/f*; (*Brit: pub*) pub *m*

border [ˈbɔːdər] N margem *f*; (*for flowers*) borda; (*of a country*) fronteira; (*on cloth etc*) debrum *m*, remate *m* ▪ VT (*also*: **border on**) limitar-se com ▪ CPD (*town, region*) fronteiriço; **the B~s** a região fronteiriça entre a Escócia e a Inglaterra
▸ **border on** VT FUS (*fig*) chegar às raias de

borderline [ˈbɔːdəlaɪn] N (*fig*) fronteira; **borderline case** N caso-limite *m*

bore [bɔːr] PT *of* **bear** ▪ VT (*hole*) abrir; (*well*) cavar; (*person*) aborrecer ▪ N (*person*) chato(-a), maçante *m/f*; (*of gun*) calibre *m*; **what a ~!** que chato! (BR), que maçada! (PT); **to be ~d to tears** *or* **~d to death** *or* **~d stiff** estar muito entediado

bored [bɔːd] ADJ entediado

boredom [ˈbɔːdəm] N tédio, aborrecimento

boring [ˈbɔːrɪŋ] ADJ chato, maçante

born [bɔːn] ADJ: **to be ~** nascer; **I was ~ in 1960** nasci em 1960; **~ blind** cego de nascença; **a ~ leader** um líder nato

borne [bɔːn] PP *of* **bear**

Borneo [ˈbɔːnɪəu] N Bornéu

borough [ˈbʌrə] N município

borrow [ˈbɒrəu] VT: **to ~ sth (from sb)** pedir algo emprestado a alguém; **may I ~ your car?** você pode me emprestar o seu carro?

borrower [ˈbɒrəuər] N tomador(a) *m/f* de empréstimo

borrowing [ˈbɒrəuɪŋ] N empréstimo(s) *m(pl)*

borstal [ˈbɔːstl] (*Brit*) N reformatório (de menores)

bosom [ˈbuzəm] N peito; **bosom friend** N amigo(-a) íntimo(-a) *or* do peito

boss [bɒs] N chefe *m/f*; (*employer*) patrão(-troa) *m/f*; (*in agriculture, industry etc*) capataz *m* ▪ VT (*also*: **boss about; boss around**) mandar em

bossy [ˈbɒsɪ] ADJ mandão(-dona)

bosun [ˈbəusn] N contramestre *m*

botanical [bəˈtænɪkl] ADJ botânico

botanist [ˈbɒtənɪst] N botânico(-a)

botany [ˈbɒtənɪ] N botânica

botch [bɒtʃ] VT (*also*: **botch up**) estropiar, atamancar

both [bəuθ] ADJ, PRON ambos(-as), os dois/as duas ▪ ADV: **~ A and B** tanto A como B; **~ of us went, we ~ went** nós dois fomos, ambos fomos

bother [ˈbɒðər] VT (*worry*) preocupar; (*irritate*) incomodar, molestar; (*disturb*) atrapalhar ▪ VI (*also*: **bother o.s.**) preocupar-se ▪ N (*trouble*) preocupação *f*; (*nuisance*) amolação *f*, inconveniente *m* ▪ EXCL bolas!; **to ~ about** preocupar-se com; **I'm sorry to ~ you** lamento incomodá-lo; **please don't ~** por favor, não se preocupe, não se dê ao trabalho; **don't ~** não vale a pena; **to ~ doing** dar-se ao trabalho de fazer; **it's no ~** não tem problema

Botswana [bɒtˈswɑːnə] N Botsuana

bottle [ˈbɒtl] N garrafa; (*of perfume, medicine*) frasco; (*baby's*) mamadeira (BR), biberão *m* (PT) ▪ VT engarrafar
▸ **bottle up** VT conter, refrear

bottleneck [ˈbɒtlnɛk] N (*traffic*) engarrafamento; (*fig*) obstáculo, problema *m*

bottle-opener N abridor *m* (de garrafas) (BR), abre-garrafas *m inv* (PT)

bottom [ˈbɒtəm] N (*of container, sea*) fundo; (*buttocks*) traseiro, bunda (*inf*); (*of page, list*) pé *m*; (*of class*) nível *m* mais baixo; (*of mountain, hill*) sopé *m* ▪ ADJ (*low*) inferior, mais baixo; (*last*) último; **to get to the ~ of sth** (*fig*) tirar algo a limpo

bottomless [ˈbɒtəmlɪs] ADJ sem fundo; (*fig*) insondável; (*funds*) ilimitado

bough [bau] N ramo

bought [bɔːt] PT, PP *of* **buy**

boulder [ˈbəuldər] N pedregulho, matacão *m*

bounce [bauns] VI (*ball*) saltar, quicar; (*cheque*) ser devolvido (*por insuficiência de fundos*) ▪ VT fazer saltar ▪ N (*rebound*) salto; **he's got plenty of ~** (*fig*) ele tem pique

bouncer [ˈbaunsər] (*inf*) N leão-de-chácara *m*

bound [baund] PT, PP *of* **bind** ▪ N (*leap*) pulo, salto; (*gen pl: limit*) limite *m* ▪ VI (*leap*) pular, saltar ▪ VT (*border*) demarcar; (*limit*) limitar ▪ ADJ: **~ by** (*law, regulation*) limitado por; **to be ~ to do sth** (*obliged*) ter a obrigação de fazer algo; (*likely*) na certa ir fazer algo; **~ for** com destino a; **out of ~s** fora dos limites

boundary [ˈbaundrɪ] N limite *m*, fronteira

boundless [ˈbaundlɪs] ADJ ilimitado

bountiful [ˈbauntɪful] ADJ (*person*) generoso; (*supply*) farto

bounty [ˈbauntɪ] N (*generosity*) generosidade *f*; (*wealth*) fartura

bouquet [ˈbukeɪ] N (*of flowers*) buquê *m*, ramalhete *m*; (*of wine*) buquê *m*, aroma *m*

bourbon [ˈbuəbən] (US) N (*also*: **bourbon whiskey**) uísque *m* (BR) *or* whisky *m* (PT) (norte-americano)

bourgeois [ˈbuəʒwɑː] ADJ burguês(-guesa)

bout [baut] N período; (*of malaria etc*) ataque *m*; (*of activity*) explosão *f*; (*Boxing etc*) combate *m*

boutique [buːˈtiːk] N butique *f*

bow¹ [bəu] N (*knot*) laço; (*weapon, Mus*) arco

bow² [bau] N (*of the body*) reverência; (*of the

head) inclinação *f*; (*Naut: also*: **bows**) proa ■ VI curvar-se, fazer uma reverência; (*yield*): **to ~ to** *or* **before** ceder ante, submeter-se a; **to ~ to the inevitable** curvar-se ao inevitável

bowels ['bauəlz] NPL intestinos *mpl*, tripas *fpl*; (*fig*) entranhas *fpl*

bowl [bəul] N tigela; (*for washing*) bacia; (*ball*) bola; (*of pipe*) fornilho; (*US: stadium*) estádio ■ VI (*Cricket*) arremessar a bola

▶ **bowl over** VT (*fig*) impressionar, comover

bow-legged ADJ cambaio, de pernas tortas

bowler ['bəuləʳ] N jogador(a) *m/f* de bolas; (*Cricket*) lançador *m* (da bola); (*Brit: also*: **bowler hat**) chapéu-coco *m*

bowling ['bəuliŋ] N (*game*) boliche *m*; **bowling alley** N boliche *m*; **bowling green** N gramado (BR) *or* relvado (PT) para jogo de bolas

bowls [bəulz] N jogo de bolas

bow tie ['bəu-] N gravata-borboleta

box [bɒks] N caixa; (*crate*) caixote *m*; (*for jewels*) estojo; (*for money*) cofre *m*; (*Theatre*) camarote *m* ■ VT encaixotar; (*Sport*) boxear contra ■ VI (*Sport*) boxear

boxer ['bɒksəʳ] N (*person*) boxeador *m*, pugilista *m*; (*dog*) boxer *m*; **boxer shorts** NPL cueca samba-canção

boxing ['bɒksiŋ] N (*Sport*) boxe *m*, pugilismo

Boxing Day (*Brit*) N *Dia de Santo Estêvão* (*26 de dezembro*)

boxing gloves NPL luvas *fpl* de boxe

boxing ring N ringue *m* de boxe

box number N (*for advertisements*) caixa postal

box office N bilheteria (BR), bilheteira (PT)

boxroom ['bɒksrum] N quarto pequeno

boy [bɔi] N (*young*) menino, garoto; (*older*) moço, rapaz *m*; (*son*) filho; (*servant*) criado

boycott ['bɔikɒt] N boicote *m*, boicotagem *f* ■ VT boicotar

boyfriend ['bɔifrɛnd] N namorado

boyish ['bɔiiʃ] ADJ (*man*) jovial; (*looks*) pueril; (*woman*) como ares de menino

Bp ABBR = **bishop**

BR ABBR = **British Rail**

bra [brɑː] N sutiã *m* (BR), soutien *m* (PT)

brace [breis] N reforço, braçadeira; (*on teeth*) aparelho; (*tool*) arco de pua; (*Typ: also*: **brace bracket**) chave *f* ■ VT firmar, reforçar; (*knees, shoulders*) retesar; **braces** NPL (*Brit*) suspensórios *mpl*; **to ~ o.s.** (*for weight, fig*) preparar-se

bracelet ['breislit] N pulseira

bracing ['breisiŋ] ADJ tonificante

bracken ['brækən] N samambaia (BR), feto (PT)

bracket ['brækit] N (*Tech*) suporte *m*; (*group*) classe *f*, categoria; (*range*) faixa; (*also*: **brace bracket**) chave *f*; (*also*: **round bracket**) parêntese *m*; (*also*: **square bracket**) colchete *m* ■ VT pôr entre parênteses; (*fig: also*: **bracket together**) agrupar; **in ~s** entre parênteses (*or* colchetes)

brackish ['brækiʃ] ADJ (*water*) salobro

brag [bræg] VI gabar-se, contar vantagem

braid [breid] N (*trimming*) galão *m*; (*of hair*) trança

Braille [breil] N braile *m*

brain [brein] N cérebro; **brains** NPL (*Culin*) miolos *mpl*; (*intelligence*) inteligência, miolos; **he's got ~s** ele é inteligente

brainchild ['breintʃaild] N idéia original

brainless ['breinlis] ADJ estúpido, desmiolado

brainstorm ['breinstɔːm] N (*fig*) momento de distração; (*US: brainwave*) idéia luminosa

brainwash ['breinwɔʃ] VT fazer uma lavagem cerebral em

brainwave ['breinweiv] N inspiração *f*, idéia luminosa *or* brilhante

brainy ['breini] ADJ inteligente

braise [breiz] VT assar na panela

brake [breik] N freio (BR), travão *m* (PT) ■ VT, VI frear (BR), travar (PT); **brake fluid** N óleo de freio (BR) *or* dos travões (PT); **brake light** N farol *m* do freio (BR), farolim *m* de travagem (PT); **brake pedal** N pedal *m* do freio (BR), travão *m* de pé (PT)

bramble ['bræmbl] N amora-preta

bran [bræn] N farelo

branch [brɑːntʃ] N ramo, galho; (*road*) ramal *m*; (*Comm*) sucursal *f*, filial *f*; (: *bank*) agência ■ VI bifurcar-se

▶ **branch out** VI (*fig*) diversificar suas atividades; **to ~ out into** estender suas atividades a

branch line N (*Rail*) ramal *m*

branch manager N gerente *m/f* de sucursal *or* filial

brand [brænd] N marca; (*fig: type*) tipo ■ VT (*cattle*) marcar com ferro quente; (*fig: pej*): **to ~ sb a communist** *etc* estigmatizar alguém de comunista *etc*

brandish ['brændiʃ] VT brandir

brand name N marca de fábrica, griffe *f*

brand-new ADJ novo em folha, novinho

brandy ['brændi] N conhaque *m*

brash [bræʃ] ADJ (*rough*) grosseiro; (*forward*) descarado

Brasilia [brə'ziliə] N Brasília

brass [brɑːs] N latão *m*; **the ~** (*Mus*) os metais; **the top ~** as altas patentes; **brass band** N banda de música

brassiere ['bræsiəʳ] N sutiã *m* (BR), soutien *m* (PT)

brass tacks NPL: **to get down to ~** passar ao que interessa, entrar no assunto principal

brat [bræt] (*pej*) N pirralho, fedelho, malcriado

bravado [brə'vɑːdəu] N bravata

brave [breiv] ADJ valente, corajoso ■ N guerreiro pele-vermelha ■ VT (*face up to*) desafiar; (*resist*) encarar

bravery ['breivəri] N coragem *f*, bravura

bravo [brɑː'vəu] EXCL bravo!

brawl [brɔːl] N briga, pancadaria ■ VI brigar

brawn [brɔːn] N força; (*meat*) patê *m* de carne

brawny ['brɔːni] ADJ musculoso, carnudo

bray [brei] N zurro, ornejo ■ VI zurrar, ornejar

brazen ['breizn] ADJ descarado ■ VT: **to ~ it out** defender-se descaradamente

brazier ['breɪzɪə^r] N braseiro
Brazil [brə'zɪl] N Brasil m
Brazilian [brə'zɪljən] ADJ, N brasileiro(-a)
Brazil nut N castanha-do-pará f
bread [brɛd] N pão m; (inf: money) grana; **to earn one's daily ~** ganhar o pão or a vida; **to know which side one's ~ is buttered (on)** saber o que lhe convém; **bread and butter** N pão m com manteiga; (fig) ganha-pão m
breadbin ['brɛdbɪn] (Brit) N caixa de pão
breadboard ['brɛdbɔːd] N tábua de pão; (Comput) breadboard m
breadbox ['brɛdbɒks] (US) N caixa de pão
breadcrumbs ['brɛdkrʌmz] NPL migalhas fpl; (Culin) farinha de rosca
breadline ['brɛdlaɪn] N: **to be on the ~** viver na miséria
breadth [brɛtθ] N largura; (fig) amplitude f
breadwinner ['brɛdwɪnə^r] N arrimo de família
break [breɪk] (pt **broke**, pp **broken**) VT quebrar (BR), partir (PT); (split) partir; (promise) quebrar; (word) faltar a; (fall) amortecer; (journey) interromper; (law) violar, transgredir; (record) bater; (news) revelar ■ VI quebrar-se, partir-se; (storm) começar subitamente; (weather) mudar; (dawn) amanhecer; (story, news) revelar ■ N (gap) abertura; (crack) fenda; (fracture) fratura; (breakdown) ruptura, rompimento; (rest) descanso; (interval) intervalo; (at school) recreio; (chance) oportunidade f; **to ~ one's leg** etc quebrar a perna etc; **to ~ with sb** romper com alguém; **to ~ the news to sb** dar a notícia a alguém; **to ~ even** sair sem ganhar nem perder; **to ~ free** or **loose** soltar-se; **to ~ open** (door etc) arrombar; **to take a ~** (few minutes) descansar um pouco, fazer uma pausa; (holiday) tirar férias para descansar; **without a ~** sem parar
▶ **break down** VT (door etc) arrombar; (figures, data) analisar; (resistance) acabar com ■ VI (go awry) desarranjar-se; (machine, Aut) enguiçar, pifar (inf); (Med) sofrer uma crise nervosa; (person: cry) desatar a chorar; (talks) fracassar
▶ **break in** VT (horse etc) domar; (US: car) fazer a rodagem de ■ VI (burglar) forçar uma entrada; (interrupt) interromper
▶ **break into** VT FUS (house) arrombar
▶ **break off** VI (speaker) parar-se, deter-se; (branch) partir ■ VT (talks) suspender; (relations) cortar; (engagement) terminar, acabar com
▶ **break out** VI (war) estourar; (prisoner) libertar-se; **to ~ out in spots/a rash** aparecer coberto de manchas/brotvejas
▶ **break through** VI: **the sun broke through** o sol apareceu, o tempo abriu ■ VT FUS (defences, barrier) transpor; (crowd) abrir passagem por
▶ **break up** VI despedaçar-se; (ship) partir-se; (partnership) acabar; (marriage) desmanchar-se; (friends) separar-se, brigar, falhar; **you're ~ing up** sua voz está falhando ■ VT (rocks) partir; (biscuit etc) quebrar; (journey) romper; (fight) intervir em; (marriage) desmanchar
breakable ['breɪkəbl] ADJ quebradiço, frágil

■ N: **~s** artigos mpl frágeis
breakage ['breɪkɪdʒ] N quebradura; (Comm) quebra; **to pay for ~s** pagar indenização por quebras
breakaway ['breɪkəweɪ] ADJ (group etc) dissidente
breakdown ['breɪkdaun] N (Aut) enguiço, avaria; (in communications) interrupção f; (of marriage) fracasso, término; (machine) enguiço; (Med: also: **nervous breakdown**) esgotamento nervoso; (of figures) discriminação f, desdobramento; **breakdown service** (Brit) N auto-socorro (BR), pronto socorro (PT); **breakdown van** (Brit) N reboque m (BR), pronto socorro (PT)
breaker ['breɪkə^r] N onda grande
breakeven ['breɪk'iːvn] CPD: **~ chart** gráfico do ponto de equilíbrio; **~ point** ponto de equilíbrio
breakfast ['brɛkfəst] N café m da manhã (BR), pequeno almoço (PT); **breakfast cereal** N cereais mpl
break-in N roubo com arrombamento
breaking point ['breɪkɪŋ-] N limite m
breakthrough ['breɪkθruː] N ruptura; (fig) avanço, novo progresso
break-up N (of partnership, marriage) dissolução f; **break-up value** N (Comm) valor m de liquidação
breakwater ['breɪkwɔːtə^r] N quebra-mar m
breast [brɛst] N (of woman) peito, seio; (chest, meat) peito
breast-feed (irreg: like **feed**) VT, VI amamentar
breast pocket N bolso sobre o peito
breast-stroke ['brɛststrəuk] N nado de peito
breath [brɛθ] N fôlego, respiração f; **to go out for a ~ of air** sair para tomar fôlego; **out of ~** ofegante, sem fôlego
Breathalyser® ['brɛθəlaɪzə^r] N bafômetro
breathe [briːð] VT, VI respirar; **I won't ~ a word about it** não vou abrir a boca, eu sou um túmulo
▶ **breathe in** VT, VI inspirar
▶ **breathe out** VT, VI expirar
breather ['briːðə^r] N pausa
breathing ['briːðɪŋ] N respiração f; **breathing space** N (fig) descanso, repouso
breathless ['brɛθlɪs] ADJ sem fôlego; (Med) ofegante
breathtaking ['brɛθteɪkɪŋ] ADJ comovedor(a), emocionante
bred [brɛd] PT, PP of **breed**
-bred [brɛd] SUFFIX: **well/ill-** bem-/mal-educado
breed [briːd] (pt, pp **bred**) VT (animals) criar; (plants) miltiplicar; (hate, suspicion) gerar ■ VI criar, reproduzir ■ N raça
breeder ['briːdə^r] N (person) criador(a) m/f; (Phys: also: **breeder reactor**) reator m regenerador
breeding ['briːdɪŋ] N reprodução f; (raising) criação f; (upbringing) educação f
breeze [briːz] N brisa, aragem f
breezy ['briːzɪ] ADJ (person) despreocupado, animado; (weather) ventoso
Breton ['brɛtən] ADJ bretão(-tã) ■ N bretão(-tã);

(*Ling*) bretão m

brevity ['brevɪtɪ] N brevidade f

brew [bru:] VT (*tea*) fazer; (*beer*) fermentar; (*plot*) armar, tramar ∎ VI (*tea*) fazer-se, preparar-se; (*beer*) fermentar; (*storm, fig*) armar-se

brewer ['bru:əʳ] N cervejeiro(-a)

brewery ['bruərɪ] N cervejaria

briar ['braɪəʳ] N (*thorny bush*) urze-branca f; (*wild rose*) roseira-brava

bribe [braɪb] N suborno ∎ VT subornar; **to ~ sb to do sth** subornar alguém para fazer algo

bribery ['braɪbərɪ] N suborno

bric-a-brac ['brɪkəbræk] N bricabraque m

brick [brɪk] N tijolo

bricklayer ['brɪkleɪəʳ] N pedreiro

brickwork ['brɪkwə:k] N alvenaria

brickworks ['brɪkwə:kz] N fábrica de tijolos

bridal ['braɪdl] ADJ nupcial

bride [braɪd] N noiva

bridegroom ['braɪdgrum] N noivo

bridesmaid ['braɪdzmeɪd] N dama de honra

bridge [brɪdʒ] N (*Archit, Dentistry*) ponte f; (*Naut*) ponte de comando; (*Cards*) bridge m; (*of nose*) cavalete m ∎ VT (*river*) lançar uma ponte sobre; (*gap*) transpor

bridging loan ['brɪdʒɪŋ-] (*Brit*) N empréstimo a curto prazo

bridle ['braɪdl] N cabeçada, freio ∎ VT enfrear; (*fig*) refrear, conter; **bridle path** N senda

brief [bri:f] ADJ breve ∎ N (*Law*) causa; (*task*) tarefa ∎ VT (*inform*) informar; (*instruct*) instruir; **briefs** NPL (*for men*) cueca (BR), cuecas fpl (PT); (*for women*) calcinha (BR), cuecas fpl (PT); **in ~** ... em resumo ...; **to ~ sb about sth** informar alguém sobre algo

briefcase ['bri:fkeɪs] N pasta

briefing ['bri:fɪŋ] N instruções fpl; (*Press*) informações fpl

briefly ['bri:flɪ] ADV (*glance*) rapidamente; (*say*) em poucas palavras; **to glimpse ~** vislumbrar

briefness ['bri:fnɪs] N brevidade f

Brig. ABBR (= *brigadier*) brig

brigade [brɪ'geɪd] N (*Mil*) brigada

brigadier [brɪgə'dɪəʳ] N general m de brigada, brigadeiro

bright [braɪt] ADJ claro, brilhante; (*weather*) resplandecente; (*person: clever*) inteligente; (: *lively*) alegre, animado; (*colour*) vivo; (*future*) promissor(a), favorável; **to look on the ~ side** considerar o lado positivo

brighten ['braɪtn] (*also: brighten up*) VT (*room*) tornar mais alegre; (*event*) animar, alegrar ∎ VI (*weather*) clarear; (*person*) animar-se, alegrar-se; (*face*) iluminar-se; (*prospects*) tornar-se animado *or* favorável

brightly ['braɪtlɪ] ADV brilhantemente

brightness ['braɪtnɪs] N claridade f

brilliance ['brɪljəns] N brilho, claridade f

brilliant ['brɪljənt] ADJ brilhante; (*clever*) inteligente; (*inf: great*) sensacional

brim [brɪm] N borda; (*of hat*) aba

brimful ['brɪmful] ADJ cheio até as bordas; (*fig*) repleto

brine [braɪn] N (*Culin*) salmoura

bring [brɪŋ] (*pt, pp* **brought**) VT trazer; **to ~ sth to an end** acabar com algo; **I can't ~ myself to fire him** não posso me resolver a despedi-lo
- ▶ **bring about** VT ocasionar, produzir
- ▶ **bring back** VT (*restore*) restabelecer; (*return*) devolver
- ▶ **bring down** VT (*price*) abaixar; (*Mil: plane*) abater, derrubar; (*government, plane*) derrubar
- ▶ **bring forward** VT adiantar; (*Bookkeeping*) transportar
- ▶ **bring in** VT (*person*) fazer entrar; (*object*) trazer; (*Pol: legislation*) introduzir; (: *bill*) apresentar; (*Law: verdict*) pronunciar; (*produce: income*) render; (*harvest*) recolher
- ▶ **bring off** VT (*task, plan*) levar a cabo; (*deal*) fechar
- ▶ **bring out** VT (*object*) tirar; (*meaning*) salientar; (*new product, book*) lançar
- ▶ **bring round** VT (*unconscious person*) fazer voltar a si; (*convince*) convencer
- ▶ **bring to** VT (*unconscious person*) fazer voltar a si
- ▶ **bring up** VT (*person*) educar, criar; (*carry up*) subir; (*question*) introduzir; (*food*) vomitar

brink [brɪŋk] N beira; **on the ~ of doing** a ponto de fazer, à beira de fazer; **she was on the ~ of tears** ela estava à beira de desatar em prantos

brisk [brɪsk] ADJ vigoroso; (*tone, person*) enérgico; (*speedy*) rápido; (*trade, business*) ativo

bristle ['brɪsl] N (*of animal*) pêlo rijo; (*of beard*) pêlo de barba curta; (*of brush*) cerda ∎ VI (*in anger*) encolerizar-se; **to ~ with** estar cheio de

bristly ['brɪslɪ] ADJ (*beard, hair*) eriçado

Brit [brɪt] (*inf*) N ABBR (= *British person*) britânico(-a)

Britain ['brɪtən] N (*also: Great Britain*) Grã-Bretanha; **in ~** na Grã-Bretanha

British ['brɪtɪʃ] ADJ britânico ∎ NPL: **the ~** os britânicos; **British Isles** NPL: **the British Isles** as ilhas Britânicas; **British Rail** N companhia ferroviária britânica

Briton ['brɪtən] N britânico(-a)

Brittany ['brɪtənɪ] N Bretanha

brittle ['brɪtl] ADJ quebradiço, frágil

Br(o). ABBR (*Rel*: = *brother*) Fr

broach [brəutʃ] VT (*subject*) abordar, tocar em

broad [brɔ:d] ADJ (*street, range*) amplo; (*shoulders, smile*) largo; (*distinction, outline*) geral; (*accent*) carregado ∎ N (US: *inf*) sujeita; **~ hint** indireta transparente; **in ~ daylight** em pleno luz do dia

broadband ['brɔ:dbænd] N banda larga

broad bean N fava

broadcast ['brɔ:dkɑ:st] (*pt, pp* **broadcast**) N transmissão f ∎ VT (*Radio, TV*) transmitir ∎ VI transmitir

broadcasting ['brɔ:dkɑ:stɪŋ] N radiodifusão f, transmissão f; **broadcasting station** N emissora

broaden ['brɔ:dən] VT alargar ∎ VI alargar-se; **to ~ one's mind** abrir os horizontes

broadly ['brɔ:dlɪ] ADV em geral

broad-minded ADJ tolerante, liberal

broccoli ['brɔkəlɪ] N brócolis mpl (BR), brócolos mpl (PT)

brochure ['brəʊʃjuəʳ] N folheto, brochura

brogue [brəug] N (accent) sotaque m regional; (shoe) chanca

broil [brɔɪl] (US) VT grelhar

broke [brəuk] PT of break ■ ADJ (inf) sem um vintém, duro; (: company): **to go ~** quebrar

broken ['brəukən] PP of break ■ ADJ quebrado; (marriage) desfeito; **~ leg** perna quebrada; **a ~ home** um lar desfeito; **children from ~ homes** filhos de pais separados; **in ~ English** num inglês mascavado

broken-down ADJ (car) enguiçado; (machine) com defeito; (house) desmoronado, caindo aos pedaços

broken-hearted ADJ com o coração partido

broker ['brəukəʳ] N corretor(a) m/f

brokerage ['brəukrɪdʒ] N corretagem f

brolly ['brɔlɪ] (Brit: inf) N guarda-chuva m

bronchitis [brɔŋ'kaɪtɪs] N bronquite f

bronze [brɔnz] N bronze m; (sculpture) estátua feita de bronze

bronzed ['brɔnzd] ADJ bronzeado

brooch [brəutʃ] N broche m

brood [bru:d] N ninhada; (children) filhos mpl; (pej) prole f ■ VI (hen) chocar; (person) cismar, remoer

broody ['bru:dɪ] ADJ (fig) taciturno, melancólico

brook [bruk] N arroio, ribeiro

broom [brum] N vassoura; (Bot) giesta-das-vassouras

broomstick ['brumstɪk] N cabo de vassoura

Bros. ABBR (Comm: = brothers) Irmãos

broth [brɔθ] N caldo

brothel ['brɔθəl] N bordel m

brother ['brʌðəʳ] N irmão m

brotherhood ['brʌðəhud] N (association, Rel) confraria

brother-in-law (pl brothers-in-law) N cunhado

brotherly ['brʌðəlɪ] ADJ fraternal, fraterno

brought [brɔ:t] PT, PP of bring

brow [brau] N (forehead) fronte f, testa; (rare: gen: eyebrow) sobrancelha; (of hill) cimo, cume m

browbeat ['braubi:t] (irreg: like beat) VT intimidar, amedrontar

brown [braun] ADJ marrom (BR), castanho (PT); (hair) castanho; (tanned) bronzeado, moreno; (rice, bread, flour) integral ■ N (colour) cor f marrom (BR) or castanho (PT) ■ VT tostar; (tan) bronzear; (Culin) dourar; **to go ~** (person) bronzear-se, ficar moreno; (leaves) secar; **brown bread** N pão m integral

Brownie ['braunɪ] N (also: Brownie Guide) fadinha de bandeirante

brownie ['braunɪ] (US) N (cake) docinho de chocolate com amêndoas

brown paper N papel m pardo

brown sugar N açúcar m mascavo

browse [brauz] VI (in shop) dar uma olhada; (among books) folhear livros; (animal) pastar; **to ~ through a book** folhear um livro

bruise [bru:z] N hematoma m, contusão f ■ VT machucar; (fig) magoar ■ VI (fruit) amassar

Brum [brʌm] (inf) N ABBR = **Birmingham**

Brummagem ['brʌmədʒəm] (inf) N = **Birmingham**

Brummie ['brʌmɪ] (inf) N natural m/f de Birmingham

brunch [brʌntʃ] N brunch m

brunette [bru:'nɛt] N morena

brunt [brʌnt] N: **the ~ of** (greater part) a maior parte de

brush [brʌʃ] N escova; (for painting, shaving etc) pincel m; (Bot) mato rasteiro; (quarrel) bate-boca m ■ VT (sweep) varrer; (groom) escovar; (also: **brush past**; **brush against**) tocar ao passar, roçar; **to have a ~ with sb** bater boca com alguém; **to have a ~ with the police** ser indiciado pela polícia
▶ **brush aside** VT afastar, não fazer caso de
▶ **brush up** VT (knowledge) retocar, revisar

brushed [brʌʃt] ADJ (Tech: steel, chrome etc) escovado; (nylon, denim etc) felpudo

brush-off (inf) N: **to give sb the ~** dar o fora em alguém

brushwood ['brʌʃwud] N (bushes) mato; (sticks) lenha, gravetos mpl

brusque [bru:sk] ADJ ríspido; (apology) abrupto

Brussels ['brʌslz] N Bruxelas; **Brussels sprout** N couve-de-bruxelas f

brutal ['bru:tl] ADJ brutal

brutality [bru:'tælɪtɪ] N brutalidade f

brute [bru:t] N bruto; (person) animal m ■ ADJ: **by ~ force** por força bruta

brutish ['bru:tɪʃ] ADJ grosseiro, bruto

BS (US) N ABBR = **Bachelor of Science**

bs ABBR = **bill of sale**

BSA N ABBR = **Boy Scouts of America**

BSc N ABBR = **Bachelor of Science**

BSI N ABBR (= British Standards Institution) instituto britânico de padrões

BST ABBR (= British Summer Time) hora de verão

Bt. (Brit) ABBR = **baronet**

btu N ABBR (= British thermal unit) BTU f (1054.2 joules)

bubble ['bʌbl] N bolha (BR), borbulha (PT) ■ VI borbulhar; **bubble bath** N banho de espuma; **bubble gum** N chiclete m (de bola) (BR), pastilha elástica (PT)

Bucharest [bu:kə'rɛst] N Bucareste

buck [bʌk] N (rabbit) macho; (deer) cervo; (US: inf) dólar m ■ VI corcovear; **to pass the ~** fazer o jogo de empurra
▶ **buck up** VI (cheer up) animar-se, cobrar ânimo ■ VT: **to ~ one's ideas up** tomar jeito

bucket ['bʌkɪt] N balde m ■ VI (Brit: inf): **the rain is ~ing down** está chovendo a cântaros

buckle ['bʌkl] N fivela ■ VT afivelar ■ VI torcer-se, cambar-se
▶ **buckle down** VI empenhar-se

Bucks [bʌks] (Brit) ABBR = **Buckinghamshire**

bud [bʌd] N broto; (of flower) botão m ■ VI brotar,

desabrochar; (fig) florescer

Budapest [bjuːdəˈpɛst] N Budapeste

Buddha [ˈbudə] N Buda m

Buddhism [ˈbudɪzəm] N budismo

Buddhist [ˈbudɪst] ADJ (person) budista; (scripture, thought etc) budístico ■ N budista m/f

budding [ˈbʌdɪŋ] ADJ (flower) em botão; (passion etc) nascente; (poet etc) em ascensão

buddy [ˈbʌdɪ] (US) N camarada m, companheiro

budge [bʌdʒ] VT mover ■ VI mexer-se

budgerigar [ˈbʌdʒərɪgɑːʳ] N periquito

budget [ˈbʌdʒɪt] N orçamento ■ VI: **to ~ for sth** incluir algo no orçamento; **she works out her ~ every month** ela calcula seu orçamento todos es meses; **I'm on a tight ~** estou com o orçamento apertado

budgie [ˈbʌdʒɪ] N = **budgerigar**

Buenos Aires [ˈbwɛnəˈsaɪrɪz] N Buenos Aires

buff [bʌf] ADJ (colour) cor de camurça ■ N (inf: enthusiast) aficionado(-a)

buffalo [ˈbafələu] (pl **buffalo** or **buffaloes**) N (Brit) búfalo; (US: bison) bisão m

buffer [ˈbʌfəʳ] N pára-choque m; (Comput) buffer m, memória intermediária

buffering [ˈbʌfərɪŋ] N (Comput) buffering m, armazenamento intermediário

buffer state N estado-tampão m

buffet¹ [ˈbufeɪ] (Brit) N (in station) bar m; (food) bufê m

buffet² [ˈbafɪt] VT (subj: wind etc) fustigar; **buffet car** (Brit) N vagão-restaurante m; **buffet lunch** N almoço americano

buffoon [bəˈfuːn] N bufão m

bug [bʌg] N (esp US: insect) bicho; (fig: germ) micróbio; (spy device) microfone m oculto; (tap) escuta clandestina; (Comput: of program) erro; (: of equipment) defeito ■ VT (inf: annoy) apoquentar, incomodar; (room) colocar microfones em; (phone) grampear; **I've got the travel ~** peguei a mania de viajar

bugbear [ˈbʌgbɛəʳ] N pesadelo, fantasma m

bugger [ˈbʌgəʳ] (inf!) N filho-da-puta m (!) ■ VT: **~ (it)!** merda! (!); **~ all** (nothing) chongas (!)
  ▶ **bugger off** (inf!) VI: **~ off!** vai a merda! (!)

buggy [ˈbʌgɪ] N (for baby) carrinho (desdobrável) de bebê

bugle [ˈbjuːgl] N trompa, corneta

build [bɪld] (pt, pp **built**) N (of person) talhe m, estatura ■ VT construir, edificar
  ▶ **build on** VT FUS (fig) explorar, aproveitar
  ▶ **build up** VT (Med) fortalecer; (stocks) acumular; (business) desenvolver; (reputation) estabelecer

builder [ˈbɪldəʳ] N (contractor) construtor(a) m/f, empreiteiro(-a); (worker) pedreiro

building [ˈbɪldɪŋ] N (act, industry) construção f; (residential, offices) edifício, prédio; **building contractor** N empreiteiro(-a) de obras; (company) construtora; **building industry** N construção f; **building site** N terreno de construção; **building society** (Brit) N sociedade f de crédito imobiliário, financiadora; **building**

trade N construção f

build-up N (of gas etc) acumulação f; (publicity): **to give sb/sth a good ~** fazer muita propaganda de alguém/algo

built [bɪlt] PT, PP of **build** ■ ADJ: **~-in** (cupboard) embutido; (device) incorporado, embutido

built-up area N zona urbanizada

bulb [bʌlb] N (Bot) bulbo; (Elec) lâmpada

bulbous [ˈbʌlbəs] ADJ bojudo

Bulgaria [bʌlˈgɛərɪə] N Bulgária

Bulgarian [bʌlˈgɛərɪən] ADJ búlgaro ■ N búlgaro(-a); (Ling) búlgaro

bulge [bʌldʒ] N bojo, saliência; (in birth rate, sales) disparo ■ VI inchar-se; (pocket etc) fazer bojo; **to be bulging with** estar abarrotado de

bulk [bʌlk] N (mass) massa, volume m; **in ~** (Comm) a granel; **the ~ of** a maior parte de; **bulk buying** [-ˈbaɪɪŋ] N compra a granel

bulkhead [ˈbʌlkhɛd] N anteparo

bulky [ˈbʌlkɪ] ADJ volumoso; (person) corpulento

bull [bul] N touro; (Stock Exchange) altista m/f; (Rel) bula

bulldog [ˈbuldɔg] N buldogue m

bulldoze [ˈbuldəuz] VT arrasar (com buldôzer); **I was ~d into doing it** (fig: inf) fui forçado or obrigado a fazê-lo

bulldozer [ˈbuldəuzəʳ] N buldôzer m, escavadora

bullet [ˈbulɪt] N bala

bulletin [ˈbulɪtɪn] N noticiário; (journal) boletim m; **bulletin board** N (US) quadro de anúncios; (Comput) informativo

bulletproof [ˈbulɪtpruːf] ADJ à prova de balas; **~-vest** colete m à prova de balas

bullet wound N ferida de bala

bullfight [ˈbulfaɪt] N tourada

bullfighter [ˈbulfaɪtəʳ] N toureiro

bullfighting [ˈbulfaɪtɪŋ] N (art) tauromaquia

bullion [ˈbuljən] N ouro (or prata) em barras

bullock [ˈbuləк] N boi m, novilho

bullring [ˈbulrɪŋ] N praça de touros

bull's-eye N centro do alvo, mosca (do alvo) (BR)

bully [ˈbulɪ] N fanfarrão m, valentão m ■ VT intimidar, tiranizar

bullying [ˈbulɪɪŋ] N provocação f, implicância

bum [bʌm] N (inf: backside) bum-bum m; (esp US: tramp) vagabundo(-a), vadio(-a)
  ▶ **bum around** (inf) VI vadiar

bumblebee [ˈbʌmblbiː] N mamangaba

bumf [bʌmf] (inf) N (forms etc) papelada

bump [bʌmp] N (blow) choque m, embate m, baque m; (in car: minor accident) batida; (jolt) sacudida; (on head) galo; (on road) elevação f; (sound) baque ■ VT (strike) bater contra, dar encontrão em ■ VI dar sacudidas
  ▶ **bump along** VI mover-se aos solavancos
  ▶ **bump into** VT FUS chocar-se com or contra, colidir com; (inf: person) dar com, topar com

bumper [ˈbʌmpəʳ] N (Brit) pára-choque m ■ ADJ: **~ crop/harvest** supersafra; **bumper cars** NPL carros mpl de trombada

bumph [bʌmf] N = **bumf**

bumptious [ˈbʌmpʃəs] ADJ presunçoso

bumpy ['bʌmpɪ] ADJ (road) acidentado, cheio de altos e baixos; (journey) cheio de solavancos; (flight) turbulento

bun [bʌn] N pão m doce (BR), pãozinho (PT); (in hair) coque m

bunch [bʌntʃ] N (of flowers) ramo; (of keys) molho; (of bananas, grapes) cacho; (of people) grupo; **bunches** NPL (in hair) cachos mpl

bundle ['bʌndl] N trouxa, embrulho; (of sticks) feixe m; (of papers) maço ▪ VT (also: **bundle up**) embrulhar, atar; (put): **to ~ sth/sb into** meter or enfiar algo/alguém correndo em
▸ **bundle off** VT (person) despachar sem cerimônia
▸ **bundle out** VT expulsar sem cerimônia

bung [bʌŋ] N tampão m, batoque m ▪ VT (also: **bung up**: pipe, hole) tapar; (Brit: inf: throw) jogar; **my nose is ~ed up** estou com o nariz entupido

bungalow ['bʌŋgələu] N bangalô m, chalé m

bungle ['bʌŋgl] VT estropear, estragar

bunion ['bʌnjən] N joanete m

bunk [bʌŋk] N beliche m; **bunk beds** NPL beliche m, cama-beliche f

bunker ['bʌŋkəʳ] N (coal store) carvoeira; (Mil) abrigo, casamata; (Golf) bunker m

bunny ['bʌnɪ] N (also: **bunny rabbit**) coelhinho; **bunny girl** (Brit) N coelhinha; **bunny hill** (US) N (Ski) pista para principiantes

bunting ['bʌntɪŋ] N bandeiras fpl

buoy [bɔɪ] N bóia
▸ **buoy up** VT fazer boiar; (fig) animar

buoyancy ['bɔɪənsɪ] N flutuabilidade f

buoyant ['bɔɪənt] ADJ flutuante; (person) alegre; (Comm: market) animado; (: currency, prices) firme

burden ['bə:dn] N (responsibility) responsabilidade f, fardo; (load) carga ▪ VT carregar; (oppress) sobrecarregar; (trouble): **to be a ~ to sb** ser um estorvo para alguém; **to be a ~ to sb** ser um fardo para alguém

bureau [bjuə'rəu] (pl **bureaux**) N (Brit: desk) secretária, escrivaninha; (US: chest of drawers) cômoda; (office) escritório, agência

bureaucracy [bjuə'rɔkrəsɪ] N burocracia

bureaucrat ['bjuərəkræt] N burocrata m/f

bureaucratic [bjuərə'krætɪk] ADJ burocrático

bureaux [bjuə'rəuz] NPL of **bureau**

burgeon ['bə:dʒən] VI florescer

burglar ['bə:gləʳ] N ladrão/ladrona m/f; **burglar alarm** N alarma de roubo

burglarize ['bə:gləraɪz] (US) VT assaltar, arrombar

burglary ['bə:glərɪ] N roubo

burgle ['bə:gl] VT assaltar, arrombar

Burgundy ['bə:gəndɪ] N (wine) borgonha m

burial ['berɪəl] N enterro; **burial ground** N cemitério

burly ['bə:lɪ] ADJ robusto, forte

Burma ['bə:mə] N Birmânia

Burmese [bə:'mi:z] ADJ birmanês(-esa) ▪ N INV birmanês(-esa) m/f; (Ling) birmanês m

burn [bə:n] (pt, pp **burnt**) VT queimar; (house) incendiar ▪ VI queimar-se, arder; (sting) arder,

picar ▪ N queimadura; **the cigarette ~t a hole in her dress** o cigarro fez um buraco no vestido dela; **I've ~t myself!** eu me queimei!
▸ **burn down** VT incendiar
▸ **burn out** VT (subj: writer etc): **to ~ o.s. out** desgastar-se

burner ['bə:nəʳ] N (on cooker, heater) bico de gás, fogo

burning ['bə:nɪŋ] ADJ ardente; (hot: sand etc) abrasador(a); (ambition) grande

burnish ['bə:nɪʃ] VT polir, lustrar

burnt [bə:nt] PT, PP of **burn; burnt sugar** (Brit) N caramelo

burp [bə:p] (inf) N arroto ▪ VI arrotar

burrow ['bʌrəu] N toca, lura ▪ VI fazer uma toca, cavar; (rummage) esquadrinhar

bursar ['bə:səʳ] N tesoureiro(-a); (Brit: student) bolsista m/f (BR), bolseiro(-a) (PT)

bursary ['bə:sərɪ] (Brit) N (Sch) bolsa

burst [bə:st] (pt, pp **burst**) VT (balloon, pipe) arrebentar; (banks etc) romper ▪ VI estourar; (tyre) furar; (bomb) estourar, explodir ▪ N estouro; (of shots) rajada; **to ~ into flames** incendiar-se de repente; **to ~ into tears** desatar a chorar; **to ~ out laughing** cair na gargalhada; **to be ~ing with** (subj: room, container) estar abarrotado de; (: emotion) estar tomado de; **to be ~ing with health/energy** estar esbanjando saúde/energia; **the door ~ open** a porta abriu-se de repente; **a ~ of applause** una salva de palmas; **a ~ of energy/speed/enthusiasm** uma explosão de energia/velocidade/ entusiasmo
▸ **burst into** VT FUS (room etc) irromper em
▸ **burst out of** VT FUS sair precipitadamente de

bury ['berɪ] VT enterrar; (at funeral) sepultar; **to ~ one's head in one's hands** cobrir o rosto com as mãos; **to ~ one's head in the sand** (fig) bancar avestruz; **to ~ the hatchet** (fig) fazer as pazes

bus [bʌs] N ônibus m inv (BR), autocarro (PT)

bush [buʃ] N arbusto, mata; (scrubland) sertão m; **to beat about the ~** ser evasivo

bushel ['buʃl] N alqueire m

bushy ['buʃɪ] ADJ (thick) espesso

busily ['bɪzɪlɪ] ADV atarefadamente

business ['bɪznɪs] N (matter) negócio; (trading) comércio, negócios mpl; (firm) empresa; (occupation) profissão f; (affair) assunto; **to be away on ~** estar fora a negócios; **he's in the insurance ~** ele trabalha com seguros; **to do ~ with sb** fazer negócios com alguém; **it's my ~ to ...** encarrego-me de ...; **it's none of my ~** eu não tenho nada com isto; **that's my ~** isso é cá comigo; **he means ~** fala a sério; **business address** N endereço profissional; **business card** N cartão m de visita

businesslike ['bɪznɪslaɪk] ADJ eficiente, metódico, sério

businessman ['bɪznɪsmən] (irreg) N homem m de negócios

business trip N viagem f de negócios
businesswoman ['bɪznɪswumən] (*irreg*) N mulher f de negócios
busker [bʌskər] (*Brit*) N artista m/f de rua
bus lane N pista reservada aos ônibus (BR) *or* autocarros (PT)
bus shelter N abrigo
bus station N rodoviária
bus-stop N ponto de ônibus (BR), paragem f de autocarro (PT)
bust [bʌst] N (*Anat*) busto ■ ADJ (*inf: broken*) quebrado ■ VT (*inf: Police: arrest*) prender, grampear; **to go ~** falir
bustle ['bʌsl] N animação f, movimento ■ VI apressar-se, andar azafamado
bustling ['bʌslɪŋ] ADJ (*town*) animado, movimentado
bust-up (*Brit: inf*) N bate-boca m
busy ['bɪzɪ] ADJ (*person*) ocupado, atarefado; (*shop, street*) animado, movimentado; (*US: Tel*) ocupado (BR), impedido (PT) ■ VT: **to ~ o.s. with** ocupar-se em *or* de
busybody ['bɪzɪbɔdɪ] N intrometido(-a)
busy signal (*US*) N sinal m de ocupado (BR) *or* impedido (PT)

 KEYWORD

but [bʌt] CONJ **1** (*yet*) mas, porém; **he's not very bright, but he's hard-working** ele não é muito inteligente mas é trabalhador; **he's tired but Paul isn't** ele está cansado mas Paul não; **the trip was enjoyable but tiring** a viagem foi agradável porém cansativa
2 (*however*) mas; **I'd love to come, but I'm busy** eu adoraria vir, mas estou ocupado
3 (*showing disagreement, surprise etc*) mas; **but that's far too expensive!** mas isso é caro demais!
■ PREP (*apart from, except*) exceto, menos; **he was/we've had nothing but trouble** ele só deu problema/nós só tivemos problema; **no-one but him** só ele, ninguém a não ser ele; **who but a lunatic would do such a thing?** quem, exceto um louco, faria tal coisa?; **but for** sem, se não fosse; **but for you** se não fosse você; **(I'll do) anything but that** (eu faria) qualquer coisa menos isso
■ ADV (*just, only*) apenas; **she's but a child** ela é apenas uma criança; **had I but known** se eu soubesse; **I can but try** a única coisa que eu posso fazer é tentar; **all but finished** quase acabado

butane ['bju:teɪn] N butano
butcher ['butʃər] N açougueiro (BR), homem m do talho (PT) ■ VT (*prisoners etc*) chacinar, massacrar; (*cattle etc for meat*) abater e carnear
butcher's (shop) N açougue m (BR), talho (PT)
butler ['bʌtlər] N mordomo
butt [bʌt] N (*cask*) tonel m; (*for rain*) barril m; (*thick end*) cabo, extremidade f; (*of gun*) coronha; (*of

**cigarette*) toco (BR), ponta (PT); (*Brit: fig: target*) alvo ■ VT (*subj: goat*) marrar; (: *person*) dar uma cabeçada em
▶ **butt in** VI (*interrupt*) interromper
butter ['bʌtər] N manteiga ■ VT untar com manteiga; **butter bean** N fava
buttercup ['bʌtəkʌp] N botão-de-ouro m, ranúnculo
butter dish N manteigueira
butterfingers ['bʌtəfɪŋgəz] (*inf*) N mão-furada m/f
butterfly ['bʌtəflaɪ] N borboleta; (*Swimming: also:* **butterfly stroke**) nado borboleta
buttocks ['bʌtəks] NPL nádegas fpl
button ['bʌtn] N botão m; (*US: badge*) emblema m ■ VT (*also:* **button up**) abotoar ■ VI ter botões
buttonhole ['bʌtnhəul] N casa de botão, botoeira; (*flower*) flor f na lapela ■ VT obrigar a ouvir
buttress ['bʌtrɪs] N contraforte m
buxom ['bʌksəm] ADJ (*baby*) saudável; (*woman*) rechonchudo
buy [baɪ] (*pt, pp* **bought**) VT comprar ■ N compra; **to ~ sb sth/sth from sb** comprar algo para alguém/algo a alguém; **to ~ sb a drink** pagar um drinque para alguém
▶ **buy back** VT comprar de volta; (*Comm*) recomprar
▶ **buy in** (*Brit*) VT (*goods*) comprar, abastecer-se com
▶ **buy into** (*Brit*) VT FUS (*Comm*) comprar ações de
▶ **buy off** VT (*partner*) comprar a parte de; (*business*) comprar o fundo de comércio de
▶ **buy up** VT comprar em grande quantidade
buyer ['baɪər] N comprador(a) m/f; **~'s market** mercado de comprador
buzz [bʌz] N zumbido; (*inf: phone call*): **to give sb a ~** dar uma ligada para alguém ■ VI zumbir ■ VT (*call on intercom*) chamar no interfone; (*Aviat: plane, building*) voar baixo sobre
▶ **buzz off** (*inf*) VI cair fora
buzzard ['bʌzəd] N abutre m, urubu m
buzzer ['bʌzər] N cigarra, vibrador m; (*doorbell*) campainha
buzz word N modismo

 KEYWORD

by [baɪ] PREP **1** (*referring to cause, agent*) por, de; **killed by lightning** morto por um raio; **a painting by Picasso** um quadro de Picasso
2 (*referring to method, manner, means*) de, com; **by bus/car/train** de ônibus/carro/trem; **to pay by cheque** pagar com cheque; **by moonlight/candlelight** sob o luar/à luz de vela; **by saving hard, he ...** economizando muito, ele ...
3 (*via, through*) por, via; **we came by Dover** viemos por *ou* via Dover
4 (*close to*) perto de, ao pé de; **the house by**

the river a casa perto do rio; **a holiday by the sea** férias à beira-mar; **she sat by his bed** ela sentou-se ao lado de seu leito **5** (past) por; **she rushed by me** ela passou por mim correndo **6** (not later than): **by 4 o'clock** antes das quatro; **by this time tomorrow** esta mesma hora amanhã; **by the time I got here it was too late** quando eu cheguei aqui, já era tarde demais **7** (during): **by daylight** durante o dia **8** (amount) por; **by the kilometre** por quilômetro; **paid by the hour** pago por hora **9** (Math, measure) por; **to divide/multiply by 3** dividir/multiplicar por 3; **it's broader by a metre** tem um metro a mais de largura **10** (according to) segundo, de acordo com; **it's all right by me** por mim tudo bem **11**: **(all) by oneself** etc (completamente) só, sozinho; **he did it (all) by himself** ele fêz tudo sozinho **12**: **by the way** a propósito; **this wasn't my idea, by the way** a propósito, essa não era a minha idéia ■ ADV **1** see **go; pass** etc. **2**: **by and by** logo, mais tarde; **by and large**

(on the whole) em geral; **Britain has a poor image abroad, by and large** de uma maneira geral, a Grã-Bretanha tem uma imagem ruim no exterior

bye(-bye) ['baɪ('baɪ)] EXCL até logo (BR), tchau (BR), adeus (PT)

by(e)-law N lei f de município

by-election (Brit) N eleição f parlamentar complementar

bygone ['baɪgɔn] ADJ passado, antigo ■ N: **let ~s be ~s** o que passou passou

bypass ['baɪpɑːs] N via secundária, desvio; (Med) ponte f de safena ■ VT evitar

by-product N subproduto, produto derivado; (of situation) subproduto

byre ['baɪəʳ] (Brit) N estábulo (de vacas)

bystander ['baɪstændəʳ] N circunstante m/f; (observer) espectador(a) m/f; **a crowd of ~s** um grupo de curiosos

byte [baɪt] N (Comput) byte m

byway ['baɪweɪ] N caminho secundário

byword ['baɪwəːd] N: **to be a ~ for** ser sinônimo de

by-your-leave N: **without so much as a ~** sem mais aquela

Cc

C, c [si:] N (letter) C, c m; (Sch: mark) ≈ 5, 6; (Mus): **C** dó m; **C for Charlie** C de Carlos

C. ABBR = **Celsius**; (= centigrade) C

c ABBR (= century) séc.; (= circa) ca.; (US etc: = cent) cent

CA N ABBR = **Central America**; (Brit) = **chartered accountant** ■ ABBR (US: Post) = **California**

ca. ABBR (= circa) ca

c/a ABBR = **capital account; credit account**; (= current account) c/c

CAA N ABBR (Brit) = **Civil Aviation Authority**; (US: = Civil Aeronautics Authority) ≈ DAC m

CAB (Brit) N ABBR (= Citizens' Advice Bureau) serviço de informação do consumidor

cab [kæb] N táxi m; (of truck etc) boléia; (of train) cabina de maquinista; (horse-drawn) cabriolé m

cabaret ['kæbəreɪ] N cabaré m

cabbage ['kæbɪdʒ] N repolho (BR), couve f (PT)

cabin ['kæbɪn] N cabana; (on ship) camarote m; (on plane) cabina de passageiros; **cabin cruiser** N lancha a motor com cabine

cabinet ['kæbɪnɪt] N (Pol) gabinete m; (furniture) armário; (also: **display cabinet**) armário com vitrina; **~ reshuffle** reforma ministerial

cabinet-maker N marceneiro(-a)

cabinet minister N ministro(-a) (integrante do gabinete)

cable ['keɪbl] N cabo; (telegram) cabograma m ■ VT enviar cabograma para

cable-car N bonde m (BR), teleférico (PT)

cablegram ['keɪblgræm] N cabograma m

cable railway (Brit) N funicular m

cable television N televisão f a cabo

cache [kæʃ] N esconderijo; **a ~ of arms** etc um depósito secreto de armas etc

cackle ['kækl] VI gargalhar; (hen) cacarejar

cacti ['kæktaɪ] NPL of **cactus**

cactus ['kæktəs] (pl **cacti**) N cacto

CAD N ABBR (= computer-aided design) CAD m

caddie ['kædɪ] N corregador m de tracos

caddy ['kædɪ] N = **caddie**

cadet [kə'dɛt] N (Mil) cadete m

cadge [kædʒ] (inf) VT: **to ~ (from** or **off)** filar (de)

cadre ['kɑ:də'] N funcionários mpl qualificados

Caesarean [si:'zɛərɪən] (US **Cesarean**) ADJ, N: **~ (section)** cesariana

CAF (Brit) ABBR (= cost and freight) custo e frete

café ['kæfeɪ] N café m

cafeteria [kæfɪ'tɪərɪə] N lanchonete f

caffein(e) ['kæfi:n] N cafeína

cage [keɪdʒ] N (bird cage) gaiola; (for large animals) jaula; (of lift) cabina ■ VT engaiolar; enjaular

cagey ['keɪdʒɪ] (inf) ADJ cuidadoso, reservado, desconfiado

cagoule [kə'gu:l] N casaco de náilon

CAI N ABBR (= computer-aided instruction) CAI m

Cairo ['kaɪərəu] N o Cairo

cajole [kə'dʒəul] VT lisonjear

cake [keɪk] N (large) bolo; (small) doce m, bolinho; **it's a piece of ~** (inf) é moleza or sopa; **he wants to have his ~ and eat it (too)** (fig) ele quer chupar cana e assoviar ao mesmo tempo; **cake mix** N massa pronta de bolo; **cake of soap** N sabonete m

caked [keɪkt] ADJ: **~ with** encrostado de

cake shop N confeitaria

calamitous [kə'læmɪtəs] ADJ calamitoso

calamity [kə'læmɪtɪ] N calamidade f

calcium ['kælsɪəm] N cálcio

calculate ['kælkjuleɪt] VT calcular; (estimate: chances, effect) avaliar

▶ **calculate on** VT FUS: **to ~ on sth/on doing sth** contar com algo/em fazer algo

calculated ['kælkjuleɪtɪd] ADJ (insult, action) intencional; **a ~ risk** um risco calculado

calculating ['kælkjuleɪtɪŋ] ADJ (scheming) maquinador(a), calculista; (clever) matreiro

calculation [kælkju'leɪʃən] N cálculo

calculator ['kælkjuleɪtə'] N calculador m

calculus ['kælkjuləs] N cálculo; **integral/ differential ~** cálculo integral/diferencial

calendar ['kæləndə'] N calendário; **calendar month** N mês m civil; **calendar year** N ano civil

calf [kɑ:f] (pl **calves**) N (of cow) bezerro, vitela; (of other animals) cria; (also: **calfskin**) pele f or couro de bezerro; (Anat) barriga-da-perna

caliber ['kælɪbə'] (US) N = **calibre**

calibrate ['kælɪbreɪt] VT calibrar

calibre ['kælɪbə'] (US **caliber**) N (of person) capacidade f, compêtencia, calibre m

calico ['kælɪkəu] N (Brit) morim m; (US) chita

California [kælɪ'fɔ:nɪə] N Califórnia

calipers ['kælɪpəz] (US) NPL = **callipers**

call [kɔ:l] VT chamar; (*label*) qualificar, descrever; (*Tel*) telefonar a, ligar para; (*summon: witness*) citar; (*announce: flight*) anunciar; (*meeting, strike*) convocar ▪ VI chamar; (*shout*) gritar; (*Tel*) telefonar; (*visit: also:* **call in; call round**) dar um pulo ▪ N (*shout, announcement*) chamada; (*also:* **telephone call**) chamada, telefonema *m*; (*of bird*) canto; (*visit*) visita; (*fig: appeal*) chamamento, apelo; **to be ~ed** chamar-se; **she's ~ed Suzanna** ela se chama Suzanna; **to ~ (for)** passar (para buscar); **who is ~ing?** (*Tel*) quem fala?; **London ~ing** (*Radio*) aqui fala Londres; **on ~** (*nurse, doctor etc*) de plantão; **please give me a ~ at 7** acorde-me às 7.00 por favor; **to make a ~** telefonar; **to pay a ~ on sb** visitar alguém, dar um pulo na casa de alguém; **there's not much ~ for these items** não há muita procura para esses artigos
▸ **call at** VT FUS (*subj: ship*) fazer escala em; (*: train*) parar em
▸ **call back** VI (*return*) voltar, passar de novo; (*Tel*) ligar de volta ▪ VT (*Tel*) ligar de volta para
▸ **call for** VT FUS (*demand*) requerer, exigir; (*fetch*) ir buscar
▸ **call in** VT (*doctor, expert, police*) chamar
▸ **call off** VT (*cancel*) cancelar
▸ **call on** VT FUS (*visit*) visitar; (*appeal to*) pedir; (*turn to*) recorrer a; **to ~ on sb to do** pedir para alguém fazer
▸ **call out** VI gritar, bradar ▪ VT (*doctor, police, troops*) chamar
▸ **call up** VT (*Mil*) chamar às fileiras; (*Tel*) dar uma ligada
call box (*Brit*) N cabine *f* telefônica
caller ['kɔ:lə^r] N visita *m/f*; (*Tel*) chamador(a) *m/f*
call girl N call girl *f*, prostituta
call-in (*US*) N (*Radio*) programa com participação dos ouvintes; (*TV*) programa com participação dos espectadores
calling ['kɔ:lɪŋ] N vocação *f*; (*trade*) profissão *f*
calling card (*US*) N cartão *m* de visita
callipers ['kælɪpəz] (*US* **calipers**) NPL (*Math*) compasso de calibre; (*Med*) aparelho ortopédico
callous ['kæləs] ADJ cruel, insensível
callousness ['kæləsnɪs] N crueldade *f*, insensibilidade *f*
callow ['kæləu] ADJ inexperiente
calm [kɑ:m] ADJ calmo; (*peaceful*) tranqüilo; (*weather*) estável ▪ N calma ▪ VT acalmar; (*fears, grief*) abrandar
▸ **calm down** VT acalmar, tranqüilizar ▪ VI acalmar-se
calmly ['kɑ:mlɪ] ADV tranqüilamente, com calma
calmness ['kɑ:mnɪs] N tranqüilidade *f*
Calor gas ® ['kælə^r-] N butano
calorie ['kælərɪ] N caloria
calve [kɑ:v] VI parir
calves [kɑ:vz] NPL *of* **calf**
CAM N ABBR (= *computer-aided manufacture*) CAM *m*
camber ['kæmbə^r] N (*of road*) abaulamento

Cambodia [kæm'bəudjə] N Camboja
Cambodian [kæm'bəudiən] ADJ, N cambojano(-a)
Cambs (*Brit*) ABBR = **Cambridgeshire**
came [keɪm] PT *of* **come**
camel ['kæməl] N camelo
cameo ['kæmɪəu] N camafeu *m*
camera ['kæmərə] N máquina fotográfica; (*Cinema, TV*) câmera; **in ~** (*Law*) em câmara
cameraman ['kæmərəmən] (*irreg*) N cinegrafista *m*
camera phone N celular *m* com câmera
Cameroon [kæmə'ru:n] N Camarões *m*
Cameroun [kæmə'ru:n] N = **Cameroon**
camouflage ['kæməfla:ʒ] N camuflagem *f* ▪ VT camuflar
camp [kæmp] N campo, acampamento; (*Mil*) acampamento; (*for prisoners*) campo; (*faction*) facção *f* ▪ VI acampar ▪ ADJ afeminado; **to go ~ing** fazer camping (BR), fazer campismo (PT)
campaign [kæm'peɪn] N (*Mil, Pol etc*) campanha ▪ VI fazer campanha
campaigner [kæm'peɪnə^r] N: **~ for** partidário(-a) de; **~ against** oponente *m/f* de
camp-bed (*Brit*) N cama de campanha
camper ['kæmpə^r] N campista *m/f*; (*vehicle*) reboque *m*
camping ['kæmpɪŋ] N camping *m* (BR), campismo (PT); **to go ~** acampar; **camping site** N camping *m* (BR), parque *m* de campismo (PT)
campsite ['kæmpsaɪt] N camping *m* (BR), parque *m* de campismo (PT)
campus ['kæmpəs] N campus *m*, cidade *f* universitária
camshaft ['kæmʃɑ:ft] N eixo de ressaltos
can¹ [kæn] N (*of oil, food*) lata ▪ VT enlatar; (*preserve*) conservar em latas; **to carry the ~** (*Brit: inf*) assumir a responsabilidade

🔵 **KEYWORD**

can² [kæn] (*negative* **can't, cannot,** *conditional* **could**) AUX VB **1** (*be able to*) poder; **you can do it if you try** se você tentar, você consegue fazê-lo; **I'll help you all I can** ajudarei você em tudo que eu puder; **she couldn't sleep that night** ela não conseguiu dormir aquela noite; **I can't go on any longer** não posso continuar mais; **can you hear me?** você está me ouvindo?; **I can see you tomorrow, if you're free** posso vê-lo amanhã, se você estiver livre
2 (*know how to*) saber; **I can swim** sei nadar; **can you speak Portuguese?** você fala português?
3 (*may*): **can I use your phone?** posso usar o telefone?; **could I have a word with you?** será que eu podia falar com você?; **you can smoke if you like** você pode fumar se quiser; **can I help you with that?** posso ajudá-lo?
4 (*expressing disbelief, puzzlement*): **it CAN'T be true!** não pode ser verdade!; **what CAN he want?** o que é que ele quer?

5 (expressing possibility, suggestion etc): **he could be in the library** ele talvez esteja na biblioteca; **they could have forgotten** eles podiam ter esquecido

Canada ['kænədə] N Canadá m
Canadian [kə'neɪdɪən] ADJ, N canadense m/f
canal [kə'næl] N canal m
Canaries [kə'nɛərɪz] NPL = **Canary Islands**
canary [kə'nɛərɪ] N canário
Canary Islands NPL: **the ~** as (ilhas) Canárias
Canberra ['kænbərə] N Canberra
cancel ['kænsəl] VT cancelar; (contract) anular; (cross out) riscar, invalidar; (stamp) contra-selar
▸ **cancel out** VT anular; **they ~ each other out** eles se anulam
cancellation [kænsə'leɪʃən] N cancelamento; (of contract) anulação f
cancer ['kænsər] N câncer m (BR), cancro (PT); **C~** (Astrology) Câncer
cancerous ['kænsrəs] ADJ canceroso
cancer patient N canceroso(-a)
cancer research N pesquisa sobre o câncer (BR) or cancro (PT)
candid ['kændɪd] ADJ franco, sincero
candidacy ['kændɪdəsɪ] N candidatura
candidate ['kændɪdeɪt] N candidato(-a)
candidature ['kændɪdətʃər] (Brit) N = **candidacy**
candied ['kændɪd] ADJ cristalizado; **~ apple** (US) macã f do amor
candle ['kændl] N vela; (in church) círio; **candle holder** N (single) castiçal m; (bigger, more ornate) candelabro, lustre m
candlelight ['kændllaɪt] N: **by ~** à luz de vela; (dinner) à luz de velas
candlestick ['kændlstɪk] N (plain) castiçal m; (bigger, ornate) candelabro, lustre m
candour ['kændər] (US **candor**) N franqueza
candy ['kændɪ] N (also: **sugar candy**) açúcar m cristalizado; (US) bala (BR), rebuçado (PT)
candy-floss [-flɔs] (Brit) N algodão-doce m
candy store (US) N confeitaria
cane [keɪn] N (Bot) cana; (stick) bengala; (for chairs etc) palhinha ▪ VT (Brit: Sch) castigar (com bengala)
canine ['kænaɪn] ADJ canino
canister ['kænɪstər] N lata
cannabis ['kænəbɪs] N (also: **cannabis plant**) cânhamo; (drug) maconha
canned [kænd] ADJ (food) em lata, enlatado; (inf: music) gravado; (Brit: inf: drunk) bêbado; (US: inf: worker) despedido
cannibal ['kænɪbəl] N canibal m/f
cannibalism ['kænɪbəlɪzəm] N canibalismo
cannon ['kænən] (pl inv or **cannons**) N canhão m
cannonball ['kænənbɔːl] N bala (de canhão)
cannon fodder N bucha para canhão
cannot ['kænɔt] = **can not**
canny ['kænɪ] ADJ astuto
canoe [kə'nuː] N canoa
canoeing [kə'nuːɪŋ] N (Sport) canoagem f
canoeist [kə'nuːɪst] N canoísta m/f

canon ['kænən] N (clergyman) cônego; (standard) cânone m
canonize ['kænənaɪz] VT canonizar
can opener N abridor m de latas (BR), abre-latas m inv (PT)
canopy ['kænəpɪ] N dossel m; (Arch) baldaquino
cant [kænt] N jargão m
can't [kɑːnt] = **can not**
Cantab. (Brit) ABBR = **cantabrigiensis; of Cambridge**
cantankerous [kæn'tæŋkərəs] ADJ rabugento, irritável
canteen [kæn'tiːn] N cantina; (bottle) cantil m; (Brit: of cutlery) jogo (de talheres)
canter ['kæntər] N meio galope ▪ VI ir a meio galope
cantilever ['kæntɪliːvər] N cantiléver m
canvas ['kænvəs] N (material) lona; (for painting) tela; (Naut) velas fpl; **under ~** (camping) em barracas
canvass ['kænvəs] VI (Pol): **to ~ for** fazer campanha por ▪ VT (Pol: district) fazer campanha em; (: person) angariar; (investigate: opinions) sondar
canvasser ['kænvəsər] N cabo eleitoral
canvassing ['kænvəsɪŋ] N (Pol) angariação f de votos; (Comm) pesquisa de mercado
canyon ['kænjən] N canhão m, garganta, desfiladeiro
CAP N ABBR (= Common Agricultural Policy) PAC f
cap [kæp] N gorro; (peaked) boné m; (of pen, bottle) tampa; (contraceptive: also: **Dutch cap**) diafragma m; (for toy gun) cartucho; (Brit: Football): **he won his England ~** ele foi escalado para jogar na seleção inglesa ▪ VT (outdo) superar; **and to ~ it all, he ...** (Brit) e para completar or culminar, ele ...
capability [keɪpə'bɪlɪtɪ] N capacidade f
capable ['keɪpəbl] ADJ (of sth) capaz; (competent) competente, hábil; **~ of** (interpretation etc) susceptível de, passível de
capacious [kə'peɪʃəs] ADJ vasto
capacity [kə'pæsɪtɪ] N capacidade f; (of stadium etc) lotação f; (role) condição f, posição f; **filled to ~** lotado; **in his ~ as** em sua condição de; **this work is beyond my ~** este trabalho está além das minhas limitações; **in an advisory ~** na condição de consultor; **to work at full ~** trabalhar com máximo rendimento
cape [keɪp] N capa; (Geo) cabo
Cape of Good Hope N Cabo da Boa Esperança
caper ['keɪpər] N (Culin: gen: **capers**) alcaparra; (prank) travessura
Cape Town N Cidade f do Cabo
capita ['kæpɪtə] see **per capita**
capital ['kæpɪtl] N (also: **capital city**) capital f; (money) capital m; (also: **capital letter**) maiúscula; **capital account** N conta de capital; **capital allowance** N desconto para depreciação; **capital assets** NPL bens mpl imobilizados, ativo fixo; **capital expenditure** N despesas fpl or dispêndio de capital; **capital**

gains tax N imposto sobre ganhos de capital;
capital goods NPL bens *mpl* de capital
capital-intensive ADJ intensivo de capital
capitalism ['kæpɪtəlɪzəm] N capitalismo
capitalist ['kæpɪtəlɪst] ADJ, N capitalista *m/f*
capitalize ['kæpɪtəlaɪz] VT capitalizar ■ VI: **to ~
on** (*fig*) aproveitar, explorar
capital punishment N pena de morte
capital transfer tax (*Brit*) N imposto sobre
transferências de capital
Capitol ['kæpɪtl] N *ver abaixo*

● **CAPITOL**
●
● O Capitólio (*Capitol*) é a sede do Congresso
● dos Estados Unidos, localizado no monte
● Capitólio (*Capitol Hill*), em Washington.

capitulate [kə'pɪtjuleɪt] VI capitular
capitulation [kəpɪtju'leɪʃən] N capitulação *f*
capricious [kə'prɪʃəs] ADJ caprichoso
Capricorn ['kæprɪkɔːn] N Capricórnio
caps [kæps] ABBR = **capital letters**
capsize [kæp'saɪz] VT, VI emborcar, virar
capstan ['kæpstən] N cabrestante *m*
capsule ['kæpsjuːl] N cápsula
Capt. ABBR (= *captain*) Cap
captain ['kæptɪn] N capitão *m* ■ VT capitanear,
ser o capitão de
caption ['kæpʃən] N (*heading*) título; (*to picture*)
legenda
captivate ['kæptɪveɪt] VT cativar
captive ['kæptɪv] ADJ, N cativo(-a)
captivity [kæp'tɪvɪtɪ] N cativeiro
captor ['kæptər] N capturador(a) *m/f*
capture ['kæptʃər] VT prender, aprisionar;
(*person*) capturar; (*place*) tomar; (*attention*) atrair,
chamar ■ N captura; (*of place*) tomada; (*thing
taken*) presa
car [kɑːr] N carro, automóvel *m*; (*Rail*) vagão *m*;
by ~ de carro
Caracas [kə'rækəs] N Caracas
carafe [kə'ræf] N garrafa de mesa
caramel ['kærəməl] N (*sweet*) caramelo; (*burnt
sugar*) caramelado
carat ['kærət] N quilate *m*; **18 ~ gold** ouro de 18
quilates
caravan ['kærəvæn] N reboque *m* (BR), trailer *m*
(BR), rulote *f* (PT); (*in desert*) caravana; **caravan
site** (*Brit*) N parque *m* de campismo
caraway ['kærəweɪ] N: **~ seed** sementes *fpl* de
alcaravia
carbohydrate [kɑːbəu'haɪdreɪt] N hidrato de
carbono; (*food*) carboidrato
carbolic acid [kɑː'bɔlɪk-] N ácido carbólico,
fenol *m*
carbon ['kɑːbən] N carbono
carbonated ['kɑːbəneɪtɪd] ADJ (*drink*) gasoso
carbon copy N cópia de papel carbono
carbon dioxide N dióxido de carbono
carbon monoxide N monóxido de carbono
carbon paper N papel *m* carbono

carbon ribbon N fita carbono
carburettor [kɑːbju'rɛtər] (*US* **carburetor**) N
carburador *m*
carcass ['kɑːkəs] N carcaça
carcinogenic [kɑːsɪnə'dʒɛnɪk] ADJ
carcinogênico
card [kɑːd] N (*also:* **playing card**) carta; (*visiting
card, postcard etc*) cartão *m*; (*membership card etc*)
carteira; (*thin cardboard*) cartolina; **to play ~s**
jogar cartas
cardamom ['kɑːdəməm] N cardamomo
cardboard ['kɑːdbɔːd] N cartão *m*, papelão *m*;
cardboard box N caixa de papelão
card-carrying member [-'kærɪɪŋ-] N membro
ativo
card game N jogo de cartas
cardiac ['kɑːdɪæk] ADJ cardíaco
cardigan ['kɑːdɪgən] N casaco de lã, cardigã *m*
cardinal ['kɑːdɪnl] ADJ cardeal; (*Math*) cardinal
■ N (*Rel*) cardeal *m*; (*Math*) número cardinal
card index N index *m* fichário
Cards (*Brit*) ABBR = **Cardiganshire**
cardsharp ['kɑːdʃɑːp] N batoteiro(-a),
trapaceiro(-a)
card vote (*Brit*) N votação *f* de delegados
CARE [kɛər] N ABBR (= *Cooperative for American
Relief Everywhere*) associação beneficente
care [kɛər] N cuidado; (*worry*) preocupação *f*;
(*charge*) encargo, custódia ■ VI: **to ~ about**
(*person, animal*) preocupar-se com; (*thing, idea*)
ter interesse em; **would you ~ to/for ...?** você
quer ...?; **I wouldn't ~ to do it** eu não gostaria
de fazê-lo; **~ of** (*on letter*) aos cuidados de; **in
sb's ~** a cargo de alguém; **"with ~"** "frágil";
to take ~ (to do) cuidar-se *or* ter o cuidado (de
fazer); **to take ~ of** (*person*) cuidar de; (*situation*)
encarregar-se de; **the child has been taken
into ~** a criança foi entregue aos cuidados da
Assistência Social; **I don't ~** não me importa; **I
couldn't ~ less** não dou a mínima
▶ **care for** VT FUS cuidar de; (*like*) gostar de
careen [kə'riːn] VI (*ship*) dar de quilha, querenar
■ VT querenar
career [kə'rɪər] N carreira ■ VI (*also:* **career
along**) correr a toda velocidade; **career girl** N
moça disposta a fazer carreira; **careers officer**
N orientador(a) *m/f* vocacional; **career woman**
(*irreg*) N mulher *f* com profissão liberal
carefree ['kɛəfriː] ADJ despreocupado
careful ['kɛəful] ADJ (*thorough*) cuidadoso;
(*cautious*) cauteloso; (**be**) **~!** tenha cuidado!
carefully ['kɛəfulɪ] ADV cuidadosamente,
cautelosamente
careless ['kɛəlɪs] ADJ descuidado; (*heedless*)
desatento
carelessly ['kɛəlɪslɪ] ADV sem cuidado; (*without
worry*) sem preocupação
carelessness ['kɛəlɪsnɪs] N descuido, falta de
atenção
caress [kə'rɛs] N carícia ■ VT acariciar
caretaker ['kɛəteɪkər] N zelador(a) *m/f*;
caretaker government (*Brit*) N governo

interino

car-ferry N barca para carros (BR), barco de passagem (PT)

cargo ['kɑːɡəʊ] (pl **cargoes**) N carga; (freight) frete m; **cargo boat** N cargueiro; **cargo plane** N avião m de carga

car hire (Brit) N aluguel m (BR) or aluguer m (PT) de carros

Caribbean [kærɪ'biːən] ADJ caraíba; **the ~ (Sea)** o Caribe

caricature ['kærɪkətjʊər] N caricatura

caring ['kɛərɪŋ] ADJ (person) bondoso; (society) humanitário

carnage ['kɑːnɪdʒ] N carnificina, matança

carnal ['kɑːnl] ADJ carnal

carnation [kɑː'neɪʃən] N cravo

carnival ['kɑːnɪvəl] N carnaval m; (US: funfair) parque m de diversões

carnivorous [kɑː'nɪvərəs] ADJ carnívoro

carol ['kærəl] N: **(Christmas) ~** cântico de Natal

carouse [kə'raʊz] VI farrear

carousel [kærə'sɛl] (US) N carrossel m

carp [kɑːp] N INV (fish) carpa
  ▶ **carp at** VT FUS criticar

car park (Brit) N estacionamento

carpenter ['kɑːpɪntər] N carpinteiro

carpentry ['kɑːpɪntrɪ] N carpintaria

carpet ['kɑːpɪt] N tapete m ▪ VT atapetar; (with fitted carpet) acarpetar; **fitted ~** (Brit) carpete m; **carpet slippers** NPL chinelos mpl; **carpet sweeper** [-'swiːpər] N limpador m de tapetes

car rental (US) N aluguel m (BR) or aluguer m (PT) de carros

carriage ['kærɪdʒ] N carruagem f; (Brit: Rail) vagão m; (of goods) transporte m; (: cost) porte m; (of typewriter) carro; (bearing) porte m; **~ forward** frete a pagar; **~ free** franco de porte; **~ paid** frete or porte pago; **carriage return** N retorno do carro

carriageway ['kærɪdʒweɪ] (Brit) N (part of road) pista

carrier ['kærɪər] N transportador(a) m/f; (company) empresa de transportes, transportadora; (Med) portador(a) m/f; (Naut) porta-aviões m inv; **carrier bag** (Brit) N saco, sacola; **carrier pigeon** N pombo-correio

carrion ['kærɪən] N carniça

carrot ['kærət] N cenoura

carry ['kærɪ] VT carregar; (take) levar; (transport) transportar; (a motion, bill) aprovar; (involve: responsibilities etc) implicar; (Math: figure) levar; (Comm: interest) render ▪ VI (sound) projetar-se; **to get carried away** (fig) exagerar
  ▶ **carry forward** VT transportar
  ▶ **carry on** VI (continue) seguir, continuar; (inf: complain) queixar-se, criar caso ▪ VT prosseguir, continuar
  ▶ **carry out** VT (orders) cumprir; (investigation) levar a cabo, realizar; (idea, threat) executar

carrycot ['kærɪkɒt] (Brit) N moisés m inv

carry-on (inf) N alvoroço, rebuliço

cart [kɑːt] N carroça, carreta; (US: for luggage)

carrinho ▪ VT transportar (em carroça)

carte blanche ['kɑːt'blɒnʃ] N: **to give sb ~** dar carta branca a alguém

cartel [kɑː'tɛl] N (Comm) cartel m

cartilage ['kɑːtɪlɪdʒ] N cartilagem f

cartographer [kɑː'tɒɡrəfər] N cartógrafo(-a)

cartography [kɑː'tɒɡrəfɪ] N cartografia

carton ['kɑːtən] N (box) caixa (de papelão); (of yogurt) pote m; (of milk) caixa; (packet) pacote m

cartoon [kɑː'tuːn] N (drawing) desenho; (Press) charge f; (satirical) caricatura; (Brit: comic strip) história em quadrinhos (BR), banda desenhada (PT); (film) desenho animado

cartoonist [kɑː'tuːnɪst] N caricaturista m/f, cartunista m/f; (Press) chargista m/f

cartridge ['kɑːtrɪdʒ] N cartucho; (of record player) cápsula

cartwheel ['kɑːtwiːl] N pirueta, cabriola; **to turn a ~** fazer uma pirueta

carve [kɑːv] VT (meat) trinchar; (wood, stone) cinzelar, esculpir; (initials, design) gravar
  ▶ **carve up** dividir, repartir

carving ['kɑːvɪŋ] N (object) escultura; (design) talha, entalhe m

carving knife (irreg) N trinchante m, faca de trinchar

car wash N lavagem f de carros

cascade [kæs'keɪd] N cascata ▪ VI cascatear, cair em cascata

case [keɪs] N (instance, investigation, Med) caso; (for spectacles etc) estojo; (Law) causa; (Brit: also: **suitcase**) mala; (of wine etc) caixa; (Typ): **lower/upper ~** caixa baixa/alta; **to have a good ~** ter bons argumentos; **there's a strong ~ for ...** há bons argumentos para ...; **in ~ (of)** em caso (de); **in any ~** em todo o caso; **just in ~** CONJ se por acaso ▪ ADV por via das dúvidas

case history N (Med) anamnese f

case study N (Med) caso clínico; (Sociology) estudo sociológico

cash [kæʃ] N dinheiro (em espécie) ▪ VT descontar; **to pay (in) ~** pagar em dinheiro; **~ on delivery** pagamento contra entrega; **to be short of ~** estar sem dinheiro
  ▶ **cash in** VT (insurance policy etc) resgatar
  ▶ **cash in on** VT FUS lucrar com, explorar

cash account N conta de caixa

cash-book N livro-caixa m

cash box N cofre m

cash card (Brit) N cartão m de saque

cash desk (Brit) N caixa

cash discount N desconto para pagamento à vista

cash dispenser N caixa automática or eletrônica

cashew [kæ'ʃuː] N (also: **cashew nut**) castanha de caju

cash flow N fluxo de caixa

cashier [kæ'ʃɪər] N caixa m/f ▪ VT (Mil) exonerar

cashmere ['kæʃmɪər] N caxemira, cachemira

cash payment N (in money) pagamento em dinheiro; (in one go) pagamento à vista

cash price N preço à vista
cash register N caixa registradora
cash sale N venda à vista
casing ['keɪsɪŋ] N invólucro; (*of boiler etc*) revestimento
casino [kə'si:nəu] N casino
cask [kɑ:sk] N barril *m*
casket ['kɑ:skɪt] N cofre *m*, porta-jóias *m inv*; (*US: coffin*) caixão *m*
Caspian Sea ['kæspɪən-] N: **the ~** o mar Cáspio
casserole ['kæsərəul] N panela de ir ao forno; (*food*) ensopado (BR) no forno, guisado (PT) no forno
cassette [kæ'sɛt] N fita-cassete *f*; **cassette deck** N toca-fitas *m inv*; **cassette player** N toca-fitas *m inv*; **cassette recorder** N gravador *m*
cassock ['kæsək] N sotaina, batina
cast [kɑ:st] (*pt, pp* **cast**) VT (*throw*) lançar, atirar; (*skin*) mudar, perder; (*metal*) fundir; (*Theatre*): **to ~ sb as Hamlet** dar a alguém o papel de Hamlet ■ VI (*Fishing*) lançar ■ N (*Theatre*) elenco; (*mould*) forma, molde *m*; (*also*: **plaster cast**) gesso; **to ~ loose** soltar; **to ~ one's vote** votar
▸ **cast aside** VT rejeitar
▸ **cast away** VT desperdiçar
▸ **cast down** VT abater, desalentar
▸ **cast off** VI (*Naut*) soltar o cabo; (*Knitting*) rematar os pontos ■ VT (*Knitting*) rematar
▸ **cast on** VT (*Knitting*) montar ■ VI montar os pontos
castanets [kæstə'nɛts] NPL castanholas *fpl*
castaway ['kɑ:stəwəɪ] N náufrago(-a)
caste [kɑ:st] N casta
caster sugar ['kɑ:stəʳ-] (*Brit*) N açucar *m* branco refinado
casting vote ['kɑ:stɪŋ-] (*Brit*) N voto decisivo, voto de minerva
cast iron N ferro fundido ■ ADJ: **cast-iron** (*fig: will*) de ferro; (: *alibi*) forte
castle ['kɑ:sl] N castelo; (*Chess*) torre *f*
castor ['kɑ:stəʳ] N (*wheel*) rodízio; **castor oil** N óleo de rícino; **castor sugar** (*Brit*) N = **caster sugar**
castrate [kæs'treɪt] VT castrar
casual ['kæʒjul] ADJ (*by chance*) fortuito; (*irregular: work etc*) eventual; (*unconcerned*) despreocupado; (*informal: clothes etc*) descontraído, informal; **~ wear** roupas *fpl* esportivas; **casual labour** N mão-de-obra *f* ocasional
casually ['kæʒjulɪ] ADV (*in a relaxed way*) casualmente; (*dress*) informalmente
casualty ['kæʒjultɪ] N (*wounded*) ferido(-a); (*dead*) morto(-a); (*of situation: victim*) vítima; (*Med: department*) pronto-socorro; (*Mil*) baixa; **casualties** NPL perdas *fpl*; **casualty ward** (*Brit*) N setor *m* de emergência, pronto-socorro
cat [kæt] N gato
catacombs ['kætəku:mz] NPL catacumbas *fpl*
Catalan ['kætəlæn] ADJ catalão(-lã) ■ N catalão(-lã) *m/f*; (*Ling*) catalão *m*
catalogue ['kætələg] (*US* **catalog**) N catálogo ■ VT catalogar

Catalonia [kætə'ləunɪə] N Catalunha
catalyst ['kætəlɪst] N catalisador *m*
catapult ['kætəpʌlt] (*Brit*) N catapulta; (*sling*) atiradeira
cataract ['kætərækt] N (*also: Med*) catarata
catarrh [kə'tɑ:ʳ] N catarro
catastrophe [kə'tæstrəfɪ] N catástrofe *f*
catastrophic [kætə'strɔfɪk] ADJ catastrófico
catcall ['kætkɔ:l] N assobio
catch [kætʃ] (*pt, pp* **caught**) VT (*ball, train, illness*) pegar (BR), apanhar (PT); (*fish*) pescar; (*arrest*) prender, deter; (*person: by surprise*) flagrar, surpreender; (*attention*) atrair; (*hear*) ouvir; (*understand*) compreender; (*get entangled*) prender; (*also*: **catch up**) alcançar ■ VI (*fire*) pegar; (*in branches etc*) ficar preso, prender-se ■ N (*fish etc*) pesca; (*act of catching*) captura; (*game*) manha, armadilha; (*of lock*) trinco, lingüeta; **to ~ sb's attention** or **eye** chamar a atenção de alguém; **to ~ fire** pegar fogo; (*building*) incendiar-se; **to ~ sight of** avistar
▸ **catch on** VI (*understand*) entender (BR), perceber (PT); (*grow popular*) pegar
▸ **catch out** (*Brit*) VT (*with trick question*) apanhar em erro
▸ **catch up** VI equiparar-se; (*make up for lost time*) recuperar o tempo perdido ■ VT (*also*: **catch up with**) alcançar
catching ['kætʃɪŋ] ADJ (*Med*) contagioso
catchment area ['kætʃmənt-] N (*Brit*) área atendida por um hospital, uma escola etc
catch phrase N clichê *m*, slogan *m*
catch-22 [-twentɪ'tu:] N: **it's a ~ situation** é uma situação do tipo se correr, o bicho pega, se ficar, o bicho come
catchy ['kætʃɪ] ADJ (*tune*) que pega fácil, que gruda no ouvido
catechism ['kætɪkɪzəm] N (*Rel*) catecismo
categoric(al) [kætɪ'gɔrɪk(əl)] ADJ categórico, terminante
categorize ['kætɪgəraɪz] VT classificar
category ['kætɪgərɪ] N categoria
cater ['keɪtəʳ] VI preparar comida
▸ **cater for** VT FUS (*needs*) atender a; (*consumers*) satisfazer
caterer ['keɪtərəʳ] N (*service*) serviço de bufê
catering ['keɪtərɪŋ] N serviço de bufê; (*trade*) abastecimento
caterpillar ['kætəpɪləʳ] N lagarta ■ CPD (*vehicle*) de lagartas; **caterpillar track** N lagarta
cathedral [kə'θi:drəl] N catedral *f*
cathode ['kæθəud] N cátodo; **cathode ray tube** N tubo de raios catódicos
catholic ['kæθəlɪk] ADJ eclético
Catholic ['kæθəlɪk] ADJ, N (*Rel*) católico(-a)
cat's-eye (*Brit*) N (*Aut*) catadióptrico
catsup ['kætsəp] (*US*) N ketchup *m*
cattle ['kætl] NPL gado
catty ['kætɪ] ADJ malicioso
Caucasian [kɔ:'keɪʒn] ADJ, N caucasóide *m/f*
Caucasus ['kɔ:kəsəs] N Cáucaso
caucus ['kɔ:kəs] N (*Pol: group*) panelinha (de

políticos); (: US) comitê m eleitoral (para indicar candidatos)

caught [kɔ:t] PT, PP of **catch**

cauliflower ['kɔlıflauə'] N couve-flor f

cause [kɔ:z] N causa; (reason) motivo, razão f ▪ VT causar, provocar; **there is no ~ for concern** não há motivo de preocupação; **to ~ sth to be done** fazer com que algo seja feito; **to ~ sb to do sth** fazer com que alguém faça algo

causeway ['kɔ:zweı] N (road) calçada; (embankment) banqueta

caustic ['kɔ:stık] ADJ cáustico; (fig) mordaz

caution ['kɔ:ʃən] N cautela, prudência; (warning) aviso ▪ VT acautelar, avisar

cautious ['kɔ:ʃəs] ADJ cauteloso, prudente, precavido

cautiously ['kɔ:ʃəslı] ADV com cautela

cautiousness ['kɔ:ʃəsnıs] N cautela, prudência

cavalier [kævə'lıə'] ADJ arrogante ▪ N (knight) cavaleiro

cavalry ['kævəlrı] N cavalaria

cave [keıv] N caverna, gruta
▸ **cave in** VI dar de si; (roof etc) ceder

caveman ['keıvmæn] (irreg) N troglodita m, homem m das cavernas

cavern ['kævən] N caverna

caviar(e) ['kævıɑ:'] N caviar m

cavity ['kævıtı] N cavidade f; (in tooth) cárie f

cavort [kə'vɔ:t] VI cabriolar

cayenne [keı'ɛn] N (also: **cayenne pepper**) pimenta-de-caiena

CB N ABBR = **Citizens' Band (Radio)**; (Brit: = Companion of (the Order of the Bath)) título honorífico

CBC N ABBR = **Canadian Broadcasting Corporation**

CBE N ABBR (= Companion of (the Order of) the British Empire) título honorífico

CBI N ABBR (= Confederation of British Industry) federação de indústria

CBS (US) N ABBR (= Columbia Broadcasting System) emissora de televisão

CC (Brit) = **County Council**

cc ABBR (= cubic centimetre) cc; (on letter etc) = **carbon copy**

CCA (US) N ABBR (= Circuit Court of Appeals) tribunal de recursos itinerante

CCU (US) N ABBR (= coronary care unit) unidade de cardiologia

CD N ABBR (= compact disc) disco laser; (Mil: Brit) = **Civil Defence (Corps)**; (US) = **Civil Defense** ▪ ABBR (Brit: = Corps Diplomatique) CD

CD burner, CD writer N gravador m inv de CD

CDC (US) N ABBR = **center for disease control**

CD player N toca-discos m inv laser

Cdr. ABBR (= commander) Com

CDT (US) N ABBR (= Central Daylight Time) hora de verão do centro

cease [si:s] VT, VI cessar

ceasefire [si:s'faıə'] N cessar-fogo m

ceaseless ['si:slıs] ADJ contínuo, incessante

ceaselessly ['si:slıslı] ADV sem parar, sem cessar

CED (US) N ABBR = **Committee for Economic Development**

cedar ['si:də'] N cedro

cede [si:d] VT ceder

cedilla [sı'dılə] N cedilha

CEEB (US) N ABBR (= College Entry Examination Board) comissão de admissão ao ensino superior

ceiling ['si:lıŋ] N (also fig) teto

celebrate ['sɛlıbreıt] VT celebrar ▪ VI celebrar; (birthday, anniversary etc) festejar; (Rel: mass) rezar

celebrated ['sɛlıbreıtıd] ADJ célebre

celebration [sɛlı'breıʃən] N (act) celebração f; (party) festa

celebrity [sı'lɛbrıtı] N celebridade f

celeriac [sə'lɛrıæk] N aipo-rábano

celery ['sɛlərı] N aipo

celestial [sı'lɛstıəl] ADJ (of sky) celeste; (divine) celestial

celibacy ['sɛlıbəsı] N celibato

cell [sɛl] N cela; (Bio) célula; (Elec) pilha, elemento

cellar ['sɛlə'] N porão m; (for wine) adega

'cellist ['tʃɛlıst] N violoncelista m/f

'cello ['tʃɛləu] N violoncelo

cellophane® ['sɛləfeın] N celofane m

cellular ['sɛljulə'] ADJ celular

cellulose ['sɛljuləus] N celulose f

Celsius ['sɛlsıəs] ADJ Célsius inv

Celt [kɛlt] ADJ, N celta m/f

Celtic ['kɛltık] ADJ celta ▪ N (Ling) celta m

cement [sə'mɛnt] N cimento ▪ VT cimentar; (fig) cimentar, fortalecer; **cement mixer** N betoneira

cemetery ['sɛmıtrı] N cemitério

cenotaph ['sɛnətɑ:f] N cenotáfio

censor ['sɛnsə'] N (person) censor(a) m/f; (concept): **the ~** a censura ▪ VT censurar

censorship ['sɛnsəʃıp] N censura

censure ['sɛnʃə'] VT criticar

census ['sɛnsəs] N censo

cent [sɛnt] N (US etc: coin) cêntimo; see also **per**

centenary [sɛn'ti:nərı] N centenário

centennial [sɛn'tɛnıəl] N centenário

center etc ['sɛntə'] (US) = **centre etc**

centigrade ['sɛntıgreıd] ADJ centígrado

centilitre ['sɛntıli:tə'] (US **centiliter**) N centilitro

centimetre ['sɛntımi:tə'] (US **centimeter**) N centímetro

centipede ['sɛntıpi:d] N centopéia

central ['sɛntrəl] ADJ central

Central African Republic N República Centro-Africana

Central America N América Central

Central American ADJ centro-americano

central heating N aquecimento central

centralize ['sɛntrəlaız] VT centralizar

central processing unit N (Comput) unidade f central de processamento

central reservation (Brit) N (Aut) canteiro divisor

centre ['sɛntə'] (US **center**) N centro; (of room, circle etc) meio ▪ VT centrar ▪ VI (concentrate): **to**

~ **(on)** concentrar (em)
centrefold ['sɛntəfəʊld] (*US* **centerfold**) N
poster *m* central
centre-forward N (*Sport*) centro-avante *m*,
centro
centre-half N (*Sport*: *centro*) médio
centrepiece ['sɛntəpi:s] (*US* **centerpiece**) N
centro de mesa
centre spread (*Brit*) N páginas *fpl* centrais
centrifugal [sɛntrɪ'fju:gl] ADJ centrífugo
centrifuge ['sɛntrɪfju:3] N centrífuga
century ['sɛntjʊrɪ] N século; **20th** ~ século vinte
CEO (*US*) N ABBR = **chief executive officer**
ceramic [sɪ'ræmɪk] ADJ cerâmico
ceramics [sɪ'ræmɪks] N cerâmica
cereal ['si:rɪəl] N cereal *m*
cerebral ['sɛrɪbrəl] ADJ cerebral; (*intellectual*)
intelectual
ceremonial [sɛrɪ'məʊnɪəl] N cerimonial *m*;
(*rite*) rito
ceremony ['sɛrɪmənɪ] N cerimônia; (*ritual*) rito;
to stand on ~ fazer cerimônia
cert [sə:t] (*Brit*: *inf*) N: **it's a dead** ~ é barbada, é
coisa certa
certain ['sə:tən] ADJ (*sure*) seguro; (*person*): **a ~ Mr
Smith** un certo Sr. Smith; (*particular*): ~ **days/
places** certos dias/lugares; (*some*): **a ~ coldness/
pleasure** uma certa frieza/um certo prazer; **to
make ~ of** assegurar-se de; **for** ~ com certeza
certainly ['sə:tənlɪ] ADV certamente, com
certeza
certainty ['sə:təntɪ] N certeza
certificate [sə'tɪfɪkɪt] N certidão *f*, diploma *m*
certified mail ['sə:tɪfaɪd-] (*US*) N correio
registrado
certified public accountant ['sə:tɪfaɪd-] (*US*) N
perito-contador *m* /perita-contadora *f*
certify ['sə:tɪfaɪ] VT certificar ▪ VI: **to ~ to**
atestar
cervical ['sə:vɪkl] ADJ: ~ **cancer** câncer *m* (BR) *or*
cancro (PT) do colo do útero; ~ **smear** exame *m*
de lâmina, esfregaço
cervix ['sə:vɪks] N cerviz *f*
Cesarean [sɪ'zɛərɪən] (*US*) ADJ, N = **Caesarean**
cessation [sə'seɪʃən] N cessação *f*, suspensão *f*
cesspit ['sɛspɪt] N fossa séptica
CET ABBR (= *Central European Time*) *hora da Europa
Central*
Ceylon [sɪ'lɔn] N (*old*) Ceilão *m*
cf. ABBR (= *compare*) cf
c/f ABBR (*Comm*: = *carry forward*) a transportar
CG (*US*) N ABBR = **coastguard**
cg ABBR (= *centigram*) cg
CH (*Brit*) N ABBR (= *Companion of Honour*) *título
honorífico*
ch (*Brit*) ABBR = **central heating**
ch. ABBR (= *chapter*) cap
Chad [tʃæd] N Chad *m*
chafe [tʃeɪf] VT (*rub*) roçar; (*wear*) gastar; (*irritate*)
irritar ▪ VI (*fig*): **to ~ at sth** irritar-se com algo
chaffinch ['tʃæfɪntʃ] N tentilhão *m*
chagrin ['ʃægrɪn] N desgosto

chain [tʃeɪn] N corrente *f*; (*of islands*) grupo; (*of
mountains*) cordilheira; (*of shops*) cadeia; (*of events*)
série *f* ▪ VT (*also*: **chain up**) acorrentar; **chain
reaction** N reação *f* em cadeia
chain-smoke VI fumar um (cigarro) atrás do
outro
chain store N magazine *m* (BR), grande
armazem *f* (PT)
chair [tʃɛər] N cadeira; (*armchair*) poltrona; (*of
university*) cátedra; (*of meeting*) presidência, mesa
▪ VT (*meeting*) presidir; **the** ~ (*US*: *electric chair*) a
cadeira elétrica
chairlift ['tʃɛəlɪft] N teleférico
chairman ['tʃɛəmən] (*irreg*) N presidente *m*
chairperson ['tʃɛəpə:sn] N presidente *m/f*
chairwoman ['tʃɛəwʊmən] (*irreg*) N presidenta,
presidente *f*
chalet ['ʃæleɪ] N chalé *m*
chalice ['tʃælɪs] N cálice *m*
chalk [tʃɔ:k] N (*Geo*) greda; (*for writing*) giz *m*
▶ **chalk up** VT escrever a giz; (*fig*: *success*) obter
challenge ['tʃælɪndʒ] N desafio ▪ VT desafiar;
(*statement, right*) disputar, contestar; **to ~ sb
to sth/to do sth** desafiar alguém para algo/a
fazer algo
challenger ['tʃælɪndʒər] N (*Sport*) competidor(a)
m/f
challenging ['tʃælɪndʒɪŋ] ADJ desafiante; (*tone*)
de desafio; **chamber** ['tʃeɪmbər] N câmara; (*Brit:
Law*: *gen pl*) sala de audiências
chamber of commerce ▪ N câmara de
comércio
chambermaid ['tʃeɪmbəmeɪd] N arrumadeira
(BR), empregada (PT)
chamber music N música de câmara
chamberpot ['tʃeɪmbəpɔt] N urinol *m*
chameleon [kə'mi:lɪən] N camaleão *m*
chamois ['ʃæmwɑ:] N camurça; **chamois
leather** ['ʃæmɪ-] N camurça
champagne [ʃæm'peɪn] N champanhe *m or f*
champion ['tʃæmpɪən] N campeão(-peã) *m/f*; (*of
cause*) defensor(a) *m/f* ▪ VT defender, lutar por
championship ['tʃæmpɪənʃɪp] N campeonato
chance [tʃɑ:ns] N (*luck*) acaso, casualidade *f*;
(*opportunity*) oportunidade, ocasião *f*; (*likelihood*)
chance *f*; (*risk*) risco ▪ VT arriscar ▪ ADJ
fortuito, casual; **there is little ~ of his coming**
é pouco provável que ele venha; **to take a ~**
arriscar-se; **it's the ~ of a lifetime** é uma
chance que só se tem uma vez na vida; **by** ~ por
acaso; **to ~ it** arriscar-se; **to ~ to do** fazer por
acaso
▶ **chance (up)on** VT FUS dar com, encontrar
por acaso
chancel ['tʃɑ:nsəl] N coro, capela-mor *f*
chancellor ['tʃɑ:nsələr] N chanceler *m*; **C~ of
the Exchequer** (*Brit*) Ministro da Economia
(Fazenda e Planejamento)
chandelier [ʃændə'lɪər] N lustre *m*
change [tʃeɪndʒ] VT (*alter*) mudar; (*wheel, bulb,
money*) trocar; (*replace*) substituir; (*clothes,
house*) mudar de, trocar de; (*nappy*) mudar,

trocar; (*transform*): **to ~ sb into** transformar alguém em ■ VI mudar(-se); (*change clothes*) trocar-se; (*trains*) fazer baldeação (BR), mudar (PT); (*be transformed*): **to ~ into** transformar-se em ■ N mudança; (*exchange, money returned*) troca; (*difference*) diferença; (*of clothes*) muda; (*modification*) modificação f; (*transformation*) transformação f; (*coins: also:* **small change**) trocado; **to ~ gear** (*Aut*) trocar de marcha; **to ~ one's mind** mudar de idéia; **for a ~** para variar; **she ~d into an old skirt** ela (trocou de roupa e) vestiu uma saia velha; **a ~ of clothes** uma muda de roupa; **to give sb ~ for** *or* **of £10** trocar £10 para alguém

changeable ['tʃeɪndʒəbl] ADJ (*weather, mood*) instável; (*mood*) instável, inconstante

change machine N *máquina que fornece trocado*

changeover ['tʃeɪndʒəuvə'] N (*to new system*) mudança

changing ['tʃeɪndʒɪŋ] ADJ variável; **changing room** (*Brit*) N (*Sport*) vestiário; (*in shop*) cabine f de provas

channel ['tʃænl] N (*of river*) leito; (*of boats*) canal; (*of sea*) canal, estreito; (*groove*) ranhura; (*fig: medium*) meio, via ■ VT (*money, resources*): **to ~ (into)** canalizar (para); **to go through the usual ~s** seguir os trâmites normais; **green/red ~** (*Customs*) canal verde/vermelho; **the (English) C~** o Canal da Mancha

Channel Islands NPL: **the ~** as ilhas Anglo-Normandas

chant [tʃɑːnt] N (*of crowd*) canto; (*Rel*) cântico ■ VT cantar; (*word, slogan*) entoar

chaos ['keɪɔs] N caos m

chaotic [keɪ'ɔtɪk] ADJ caótico

chap [tʃæp] N (*Brit: inf: man*) sujeito (BR), tipo (PT); (*term of address*): **old ~** meu velho ■ VT (*skin*) rachar

chapel ['tʃæpəl] N capela

chaperon(e) ['ʃæpərəun] N mulher f acompanhante ■ VT acompanhar

chaplain ['tʃæplɪn] N capelão m

chapped [tʃæpt] ADJ ressecado

chapter ['tʃæptə'] N capítulo

char [tʃɑː'] VT (*burn*) tostar, queimar ■ VI (*Brit*) trabalhar como diarista ■ N (*Brit*) = **charlady**

character ['kærɪktə'] N caráter m; (*in novel, film*) personagem m/f; (*role*) papel m; (*eccentric*): **to be a (real) ~** ser um número; (*letter*) letra; **a person of good ~** uma pessoa de bom caráter; **character code** N (*Comput*) código de caráter

characteristic [kærɪktə'rɪstɪk] ADJ característico ■ N característica

characterize ['kærɪktəraɪz] VT caracterizar

charade [ʃə'rɑːd] N charada

charcoal ['tʃɑːkəul] N carvão m de lenha; (*Art*) carvão m

charge [tʃɑːdʒ] N (*of gun, electrical, Mil: attack*) carga; (*Law*) encargo, acusação f; (*fee*) preço, custo; (*responsibility*) encargo; (*task*) incumbência ■ VT (*battery*) carregar; (*Mil: enemy*) atacar; (*price*) cobrar; (*customer*) cobrar dinheiro de; (*sb*

with task) incumbir, encarregar; (*Law*): **to ~ sb (with)** acusar alguém (de) ■ VI precipitar-se; (*make pay*) cobrar; **charges** NPL: **bank/labour ~s** taxas *fpl* cobradas pelo banco/custos *mpl* de mão-de-obra; **free of ~** grátis; **is there a ~?** se tem que pagar?; **there's no ~** é de graça; **extra ~** sobretaxa; **to reverse the ~s** (*Brit: Tel*) ligar a cobrar; **how much do you ~?** quanto você cobra?; **to ~ an expense (up) to sb's account** pôr a despesa na conta de alguém; **to take ~ of** encarregar-se de, tomar conta de; **to be in ~ of** estar a cargo de *or* encarregado de; **they ~d us £10 for the dinner** eles nos cobraram £10 pelo jantar; **to ~ in/out** precipitar-se para dentro/fora; **charge account** N conta de crédito; **charge card** N cartão m de crédito (*emitido por uma loja*)

chargé d'affaires ['ʃɑː.ʒeɪdæ'fɛə'] N encarregado(-a) de negócios

chargehand ['tʃɑːdʒhænd] (*Brit*) N capataz m

charger ['tʃɑːdʒə'] N (*also:* **battery charger**) carregador m; (*old: warhorse*) cavalo de batalha

charisma [kə'rɪzmə] N carisma m

charitable ['tʃærɪtəbl] ADJ caritativo; (*organization*) beneficente

charity ['tʃærɪtɪ] N caridade f; (*organization*) obra de caridade; (*kindness*) compaixão f; (*money, gifts*) donativo

charlady ['tʃɑːleɪdɪ] (*Brit*) N diarista

charlatan ['tʃɑːlətən] N charlatão m

charm [tʃɑːm] N (*quality*) charme m; (*attraction*) encanto, atrativo; (*spell*) feitiço; (*talisman*) amuleto; (*on bracelet*) berloque m ■ VT encantar, deliciar; **charm bracelet** N pulseira de berloques

charming ['tʃɑːmɪŋ] ADJ encantador(a)

chart [tʃɑːt] N (*table*) quadro; (*graph*) gráfico; (*diagram*) diagrama m; (*map*) carta de navegação; (*weather chart*) carta meteorológica *or* de tempo ■ VT fazer um gráfico de; (*course, progress*) traçar; **charts** NPL (*hit parade*) paradas *fpl* (de sucesso); **to be in the ~s** (*record, pop group*) estar nas paradas (de sucesso)

charter ['tʃɑːtə'] VT fretar ■ N (*document*) carta, alvará m; **on ~** (*plane*) fretado

chartered accountant ['tʃɑːtəd-] (*Brit*) N perito-contador m /perita-contadora f

charter flight N vôo charter *or* fretado

charwoman ['tʃɑːwumən] (*irreg*) N = **charlady**

chase [tʃeɪs] VT (*pursue*) perseguir; (*hunt*) caçar, dar caça a; (*also:* **chase away**) enxotar ■ VI: **to ~ after** correr atrás de ■ N perseguição f, caça
  ▶ **chase down** (*US*) VT = **chase up**
  ▶ **chase up** (*Brit*) VT (*person*) ficar atrás de; (*information*) pesquisar

chasm ['kæzəm] N abismo

chassis ['ʃæsɪ] N chassi m

chaste [tʃeɪst] ADJ casto

chastened ['tʃeɪsnd] ADJ: **to be ~ by an experience** aprender uma lição com uma experiência

chastening ['tʃeɪsnɪŋ] ADJ: **it was a ~**

experience foi uma lição

chastise [tʃæs'taɪz] VT castigar

chastity ['tʃæstɪtɪ] N castidade f

chat [tʃæt] VI (also: **have a chat**) conversar, bater papo (BR), cavaquear (PT); (on the Internet) bater papo, conversar ▪ N conversa, bate-papo m (BR), cavaqueira (PT)
> **chat up** (Brit: inf) VT (girl) paquerar

chatroom N sala f de bate-papo

chat show (Brit) N programa m de entrevistas

chattel ['tʃætl] N see **goods**

chatter ['tʃætəʳ] VI (person) tagarelar; (animal) emitir sons; (teeth) tiritar ▪ N tagarelice f; emissão f de sons; (of birds) chilro; (of people) tagarelice f

chatterbox ['tʃætəbɔks] N tagarela m/f

chatty ['tʃætɪ] ADJ (style) informal; (person) conversador(a)

chauffeur ['ʃəufəʳ] N chofer m, motorista m/f

chauvinism ['ʃəuvɪnɪzəm] N (also: **male chauvinism**) machismo; (nationalism) chauvinismo

chauvinist ['ʃəuvɪnɪst] N (also: **male chauvinist**) machista m; (nationalist) chauvinista m/f

ChE ABBR = **chemical engineer**

cheap [tʃiːp] ADJ barato; (ticket etc) a preço reduzido; (poor quality) barato, de pouca qualidade; (behaviour) vulgar; (joke) de mau gosto ▪ ADV barato; **a ~ trick** uma sujeira, uma sacanagem

cheapen ['tʃiːpən] VT baixar o preço de, rebaixar; **to ~ o.s.** rebaixar-se

cheaply ['tʃiːplɪ] ADV barato, por baixo preço

cheat [tʃiːt] VI trapacear; (at cards) roubar (BR), fazer batota (PT); (in exam) colar (BR), cabular (PT) ▪ VT defraudar, enganar ▪ N fraude f; (person) trapaceiro(-a); **to ~ sb (out of sth)** passar o conto do vigário em alguém; **to ~ on sb** (inf: husband, wife etc) passar alguém para trás

cheating ['tʃiːtɪŋ] N trapaça

check [tʃɛk] VT (examine) controlar; (facts) verificar; (count) contar; (halt) conter, impedir; (restrain) parar, refrear ▪ VI verificar ▪ N (inspection) controle m, inspeção f; (curb) freio; (US: bill) conta; (Chess) xeque m; (token) ficha, talão m; (pattern: gen pl) xadrez m; (US) = **cheque** ▪ ADJ (also: **checked**: pattern, cloth) xadrez inv; **to ~ with sb** perguntar a alguém; **to keep a ~ on sb/sth** controlar alguém/algo
> **check in** VI (in hotel) registrar-se; (in airport) apresentar-se ▪ VT (luggage) entregar
> **check off** VT checar
> **check out** VI (of hotel) pagar a conta e sair ▪ VT (story) verificar; (person) investigar; **~ it out** (see for yourself) confira
> **check up** VI: **to ~ up on sth** verificar algo; **to ~ up on sb** investigar alguém

checkbook ['tʃɛkbuk] (US) N = **chequebook**

checkered ['tʃɛkəd] (US) ADJ = **chequered**

checkers ['tʃɛkəz] (US) N (jogo de) damas fpl

check guarantee card (US) N cartão m (de garantia) de cheques

check-in (desk) N (at airport) check-in m

checking account ['tʃɛkɪŋ-] (US) N conta corrente

checklist ['tʃɛklɪst] N lista de conferência

checkmate ['tʃɛkmeɪt] N xeque-mate m

checkout ['tʃɛkaut] N caixa

checkpoint ['tʃɛkpɔɪnt] N (ponto de) controle m

checkroom ['tʃɛkrum] (US) N depósito de bagagem

checkup ['tʃɛkʌp] N (Med) check-up m; (of machine) revisão f

cheek [tʃiːk] N bochecha; (impudence) folga, descaramento; **what a ~!** que folga!

cheekbone ['tʃiːkbəun] N maçã f do rosto

cheeky ['tʃiːkɪ] ADJ insolente, descarado

cheep [tʃiːp] N (of bird) pio ▪ VI piar

cheer [tʃɪəʳ] VT dar vivas a, aplaudir; (gladden) alegrar, animar ▪ VI gritar com entusiasmo ▪ N (gen pl) gritos mpl de entusiasmo; **cheers** NPL (of crowd) aplausos mpl; **~s!** saúde!
> **cheer on** VT torcer por
> **cheer up** VI animar-se, alegrar-se VT alegrar, animar

cheerful ['tʃɪəful] ADJ alegre

cheerfulness ['tʃɪəfulnɪs] N alegria

cheerio [tʃɪərɪ'əu] (Brit) EXCL tchau (BR), adeus (PT)

cheerless ['tʃɪəlɪs] ADJ triste, sombrio

cheese [tʃiːz] N queijo

cheeseboard ['tʃiːzbɔːd] N (in restaurant) sortimento de queijos

cheesecake ['tʃiːzkeɪk] N queijada, torta de queijo

cheetah ['tʃiːtə] N chitá m

chef [ʃɛf] N cozinheiro-chefe/cozinheira-chefe m/f

chemical ['kɛmɪkəl] ADJ químico ▪ N produto químico

chemist ['kɛmɪst] N (Brit: pharmacist) farmacêutico(-a); (scientist) químico(-a)

chemistry ['kɛmɪstrɪ] N química

chemist's shop (Brit) N farmácia

cheque [tʃɛk] (Brit) N cheque m; **to pay by ~** pagar com cheque

chequebook ['tʃɛkbuk] (Brit) N talão m (BR) or livro (PT) de cheques

cheque card (Brit) N cartão m (de garantia) de cheques

chequered ['tʃɛkəd] (US **checkered**) ADJ (fig) variado, acidentado

cherish ['tʃɛrɪʃ] VT (person) tratar com carinho; (memory) lembrar (com prazer); (love) apreciar; (protect) cuidar; (hope etc) acalentar

cheroot [ʃə'ruːt] N charuto

cherry ['tʃɛrɪ] N cereja; (also: **cherry tree**) cerejeira

Ches (Brit) ABBR = **Cheshire**

chess [tʃɛs] N xadrez m

chessboard ['tʃɛsbɔːd] N tabuleiro de xadrez

chessman ['tʃɛsmæn] (irreg) N peça, pedra (de xadrez)

chessplayer ['tʃɛspleɪəʳ] N xadrezista m/f

chest [tʃɛst] N (Anat) peito; (box) caixa, cofre m;

to get sth or it off one's ~ (inf) desabafar; **chest measurement** N medida de peito; **chest of drawers** N cômoda

chestnut ['tʃɛsnʌt] N castanha; (also: **chestnut tree**) castanheiro; (colour) castanho ■ ADJ castanho

chew [tʃuː] VT mastigar

chewing gum ['tʃuːɪŋ-] N chiclete m (BR), pastilha elástica (PT)

chic [ʃɪk] ADJ elegante, chique

chick [tʃɪk] N pinto; (inf: girl) broto

chicken ['tʃɪkɪn] N galinha; (food) galinha, frango; (inf: coward) covarde m/f, galinha
▶ **chicken out** (inf) VI agalinhar-se

chicken feed N (fig) dinheiro miúdo

chickenpox ['tʃɪkɪnpɔks] N catapora (BR), varicela (PT)

chickpea ['tʃɪkpiː] N grão-de-bico m

chicory ['tʃɪkərɪ] N chicória

chide [tʃaɪd] VT repreender, censurar

chief [tʃiːf] N (of tribe) cacique m, morubixaba m; (of organization) chefe m/f ■ ADJ principal; **C~ of Staff** (Mil) chefe m do Estado-Maior; **chief constable** (Brit) N chefe m/f de polícia; **chief executive** (US **chief executive officer**) N diretor(a) m/f geral

chiefly ['tʃiːflɪ] ADV principalmente

chiffon ['ʃɪfɔn] N gaze f

chilblain ['tʃɪlbleɪn] N frieira

child [tʃaɪld] (pl **children**) N criança; (offspring) filho(-a); **do you have any ~ren?** você tem filhos?

childbirth ['tʃaɪldbəːθ] N parto

childhood ['tʃaɪldhud] N infância

childish ['tʃaɪldɪʃ] ADJ infantil

childless ['tʃaɪldlɪs] ADJ sem filhos

childlike ['tʃaɪldlaɪk] ADJ infantil, ingênuo

child minder (Brit) N cuidadora de crianças

children ['tʃɪldrən] NPL of **child**

Chile ['tʃɪlɪ] N Chile m

Chilean ['tʃɪlɪən] ADJ, N chileno(-a)

chili ['tʃɪlɪ] (US) N = **chilli**

chill [tʃɪl] N frio, friagem f; (Med) resfriamento ■ VT (Culin) semi-congelar; (person) congelar ■ ADJ frio, glacial; **"serve ~ed"** "servir fresco"

chilli ['tʃɪlɪ] (US **chili**) N pimentão m picante

chilly ['tʃɪlɪ] ADJ frio; (person) friorento; **to feel ~** estar com frio

chime [tʃaɪm] N (of bell) repique m; (of clock) soar m ■ VI repicar; soar

chimney ['tʃɪmnɪ] N chaminé f; **chimney sweep** N limpador m de chaminés

chimpanzee [tʃɪmpæn'ziː] N chimpanzé m

chin [tʃɪn] N queixo

China ['tʃaɪnə] N China

china ['tʃaɪnə] N porcelana; (crockery) louça fina

Chinese [tʃaɪ'niːz] ADJ chinês(-esa) ■ N INV chinês(-esa) m/f; (Ling) chinês m

chink [tʃɪŋk] N (opening) fenda, fissura; (noise) tinir m

chip [tʃɪp] N (gen pl: Brit: Culin) batata frita; (: US: also: **potato chip**) batatinha frita; (of wood) lasca;

(of glass, stone) lasca, pedaço; (at poker) ficha; (Comput: also: **microchip**) chip m ■ VT (cup, plate) lascar; **when the ~s are down** (fig) na hora H
▶ **chip in** (inf) VI interromper; (contribute) compartilhar as despesas

chipboard ['tʃɪpbɔːd] N compensado

chipmunk ['tʃɪpmʌŋk] N tâmia m

chippings ['tʃɪpɪŋz] NPL: **"loose ~"** "projeção de cascalho"

chiropodist [kɪ'rɔpədɪst] (Brit) N pedicuro(-a)

chiropody [kɪ'rɔpədɪ] (Brit) N quiropodia

chirp [tʃəːp] VI chilrar, piar; (cricket) chilrear ■ N chilro

chirpy ['tʃəːpɪ] ADJ alegre, animado

chisel ['tʃɪzl] N (for wood) formão m; (for stone) cinzel m

chit [tʃɪt] N talão m

chitchat ['tʃɪttʃæt] N conversa fiada

chivalrous ['ʃɪvəlrəs] ADJ cavalheiresco

chivalry ['ʃɪvəlrɪ] N cavalheirismo

chives [tʃaɪvz] NPL cebolinha

chloride ['klɔːraɪd] N cloreto

chlorinate ['klɔrɪneɪt] VT clorar

chlorine ['klɔːriːn] N cloro

chock [tʃɔk] N cunha

chock-a-block ADJ abarrotado, apinhado

chock-full ADJ = **chock-a-block**

chocolate ['tʃɔklɪt] N chocolate m

choice [tʃɔɪs] N (selection) seleção f; (option) escolha; (preference) preferência ■ ADJ seleto, escolhido; **by** or **from ~** de preferência; **a wide ~** uma grande variedade

choir ['kwaɪər] N coro

choirboy ['kwaɪəbɔɪ] N menino de coro

choke [tʃəuk] VI sufocar-se; (on food) engasgar ■ VT estrangular; (block) obstruir ■ N (Aut) afogador m (BR), ar m (PT)

choker ['tʃəukər] N (necklace) colar m curto

cholera ['kɔlərə] N cólera m

cholesterol [kə'lestərɔl] N colesterol m

choose [tʃuːz] (pt **chose**, pp **chosen**) VT escolher ■ VI: **to ~ between** escolher entre; **to ~ to do** optar por fazer

choosy ['tʃuːzɪ] ADJ exigente

chop [tʃɔp] VT (wood) cortar, talhar; (Culin: also: **chop up**) cortar em pedaços; (meat) picar ■ N golpe m; (Culin) costeleta; **chops** NPL (inf: jaws) beiços mpl; **to get the ~** (Brit: inf: project) ser cancelado; (: person: be sacked) ser posto na rua
▶ **chop down** VT (tree) abater, derrubar

choppy ['tʃɔpɪ] ADJ (sea) agitado

chopsticks ['tʃɔpstɪks] NPL pauzinhos mpl, palitos mpl

choral ['kɔːrəl] ADJ coral

chord [kɔːd] N (Mus) acorde m

chore [tʃɔːr] N tarefa; (routine task) trabalho de rotina; **household ~s** afazeres mpl domésticos

choreographer [kɔrɪ'ɔɡrəfər] N coreógrafo(-a)

chorister ['kɔrɪstər] N corista m/f

chortle ['tʃɔːtl] VI rir, gargalhar

chorus ['kɔːrəs] N (group) coro; (song) coral m; (refrain) estribilho

chose [tʃəuz] PT of **choose**
chosen ['tʃəuzn] PP of **choose**
chowder ['tʃaudəʳ] N sopa (de peixe)
Christ [kraist] N Cristo
christen ['krɪsn] VT batizar; (nickname) apelidar
christening ['krɪsnɪŋ] N batismo
Christian ['krɪstɪən] ADJ, N cristão(-tã) m/f
Christianity [krɪstɪ'ænɪtɪ] N cristianismo
Christian name N prenome m, nome m de batismo
Christmas ['krɪsməs] N Natal m; **Happy** or **Merry ~!** Feliz Natal!; **Christmas card** N cartão m de Natal; **Christmas cracker** N ver abaixo; **Christmas Day** N dia m de Natal; **Christmas Eve** N véspera de Natal; **Christmas Island** N ilha de Christmas; **Christmas tree** N árvore f de Natal

CHRISTMAS CRACKER

Um cilindro de papelão que ao ser aberto faz estourar uma bombinha. Contém um presente surpresa e um chapéu de papel que cada convidado coloca na cabeça durante a ceia de Natal.

chrome [krəum] N = **chromium**
chromium ['krəumɪəm] N cromo
chromosome ['krəuməsəum] N cromossomo
chronic ['krɔnɪk] ADJ crônico; (fig: drunkenness) inveterado
chronicle ['krɔnɪkl] N crônica
chronological [krɔnə'lɔdʒɪkəl] ADJ cronológico
chrysanthemum [krɪ'sænθəməm] N crisântemo
chubby ['tʃʌbɪ] ADJ roliço, gorducho
chuck [tʃʌk] VT jogar (BR), deitar (PT); (Brit: also: chuck up; in: job) largar; (: person) acabar com
▶ **chuck out** VT (thing) jogar (BR) or deitar (PT) fora; (person) expulsar
chuckle ['tʃʌkl] VI rir
chug [tʃʌg] VI mover-se fazendo ruído de descarga; (car, boat: also: chug along) ir indo
chum [tʃʌm] N camarada m/f
chump [tʃʌmp] (inf) N imbecil m/f, boboca m/f
chunk [tʃʌŋk] N pedaço, naco
chunky ['tʃʌŋkɪ] ADJ (furniture) pesado; (person) atarracado; (knitwear) grosso
church [tʃəːtʃ] N igreja; **the C~ of England** a Igreja Anglicana
churchyard ['tʃəːtʃjɑːd] N adro, cemitério
churlish ['tʃəːlɪʃ] ADJ (silence) constrangedor(a); (behaviour) grosseiro, rude
churn [tʃəːn] N (for butter) batedeira; (also: milk churn) lata, vasilha ■ VT bater, agitar
▶ **churn out** VT produzir em série
chute [ʃuːt] N rampa; (also: rubbish chute) despejador m
chutney ['tʃʌtnɪ] N conserva picante
CIA (US) N ABBR (= Central Intelligence Agency) CIA f
CID (Brit) N ABBR = **Criminal Investigation Department**

cider ['saidəʳ] N sidra
CIF ABBR (= cost, insurance and freight) CIF
cigar [sɪ'gɑːʳ] N charuto
cigarette [sɪgə'rɛt] N cigarro; **cigarette case** N cigarreira; **cigarette end** N ponta de cigarro, guimba (BR); **cigarette holder** N piteira (BR), boquilha (PT)
C-in-C ABBR = **commander-in-chief**
cinch [sɪntʃ] (inf) N: **it's a ~** é sopa, é moleza
Cinderella [sɪndə'rɛlə] N Gata Borralheira
cinders ['sɪndəz] NPL cinzas fpl
cine-camera ['sɪnɪ-] (Brit) N câmera (cinematográfica)
cine-film ['sɪnɪ-] (Brit) N filme m cinematográfico
cinema ['sɪnəmə] N cinema m
cine-projector ['sɪnɪ-] (Brit) N projetor m cinematográfico
cinnamon ['sɪnəmən] N canela
cipher ['saifəʳ] N cifra; **in ~** cifrado
circa ['səːkə] PREP cerca de
circle ['səːkl] N círculo; (in cinema) balcão m ■ VI dar voltas ■ VT (surround) rodear, cercar; (move round) dar a volta de
circuit ['səːkɪt] N circuito; (tour, lap) volta; (track) pista; **circuit board** N placa
circuitous [səː'kjuɪtəs] ADJ tortuoso
circular ['səːkjuləʳ] ADJ circular ■ N (carta) circular f
circulate ['səːkjuleɪt] VT, VI circular
circulation [səːkju'leɪʃən] N circulação f; (of newspaper, book etc) tiragem f
circumcise ['səːkəmsaɪz] VT circuncidar
circumference [sə'kʌmfərəns] N circunferência
circumflex ['səːkəmflɛks] N (also: circumflex accent) (acento) circunflexo
circumscribe ['səːkəmskraɪb] VT circunscrever
circumspect ['səːkəmspɛkt] ADJ prudente, cauteloso
circumstances ['səːkəmstənsɪz] NPL circunstâncias fpl; (conditions) condições fpl; (financial condition) situação f econômica; **in the ~** em tais circunstâncias, assim sendo, neste caso; **under no ~** de modo algum, de jeito nenhum
circumstantial [səːkəm'stænʃl] ADJ (report) circunstanciado; **~ evidence** prova circunstancial
circumvent [səːkəm'vɛnt] VT (rule etc) driblar, burlar
circus ['səːkəs] N circo; (also: Circus: in place names) praça
cistern ['sɪstən] N tanque m; (in toilet) caixa d'água
citation [saɪ'teɪʃən] N (commendation) menção f; (US: Law) intimação f; (quotation) citação f
cite [saɪt] VT citar; (Law) intimar
citizen ['sɪtɪzn] N (of country) cidadão(-dã) m/f; (of town) habitante m/f
citizenship ['sɪtɪznʃɪp] N cidadania
citric acid ['sɪtrɪk-] N ácido cítrico

citrus fruit ['sɪtrəs-] N citrino
city ['sɪtɪ] N cidade f; **the C-** centro financeiro de Londres.; **city centre** N centro (da cidade)
civic ['sɪvɪk] ADJ cívico, municipal; **civic centre** (Brit) N sede f do município
civil ['sɪvɪl] ADJ civil; (polite) delicado, cortês; **civil disobedience** N resistência passiva; **civil engineer** N engenheiro(-a) civil; **civil engineering** N engenharia civil
civilian [sɪ'vɪlɪən] ADJ, N civil m/f
civilization [sɪvɪlaɪ'zeɪʃən] N civilização f
civilized ['sɪvɪlaɪzd] ADJ civilizado
civil law N direito civil
civil rights NPL direitos mpl civis
civil servant N funcionário(-a) público(-a)
Civil Service N administração f pública
civil war N guerra civil
cl ABBR (= centilitre) cl
clad [klæd] ADJ: ~ **(in)** vestido (de)
claim [kleɪm] VT exigir, reclamar; (rights etc) reivindicar; (assert): **to ~ that** afirmar que ■ VI (for insurance) reclamar ■ N reclamação f; (Law) direito; (pretension) pretensão f; (wage claim etc) reivindicação f; **(insurance)** ~ reclamação f; **to put in a ~ for** (pay rise etc) reivindicar
claimant ['kleɪmənt] N (Admin, Law) requerente m/f
claim form N formulário de requerimento; (Insurance) formulário para reclamações
clairvoyant [klɛə'vɔɪənt] N clarividente m/f
clam [klæm] N molusco
▶ **clam up** (inf) VI ficar calado
clamber ['klæmbər] VI subir; (up hill etc) escalar
clammy ['klæmɪ] ADJ (hands, face) úmido e pegajoso; (sticky) pegajoso
clamour ['klæmər] (US **clamor**) N clamor m ■ VI: **to ~ for** clamar
clamp [klæmp] N grampo ■ VT (two things together) grampear
▶ **clamp down on** VT FUS suprimir, proibir
clan [klæn] N clã m
clandestine [klæn'dɛstɪn] ADJ clandestino
clang [klæŋ] N retintim m, som metálico ■ VI retinir
clansman ['klænzmən] (irreg) N membro de um clã escocês
clap [klæp] VI bater palmas, aplaudir ■ VT (performer) aplaudir ■ N (of hands) palmas fpl; **to ~ one's hands** bater palmas; **a ~ of thunder** uma trovoada
clapping ['klæpɪŋ] N aplausos mpl, palmas fpl
claret ['klærət] N clarete m
clarification [klærɪfɪ'keɪʃən] N esclarecimento
clarify ['klærɪfaɪ] VT esclarecer
clarinet [klærɪ'nɛt] N clarinete m
clarity ['klærɪtɪ] N clareza
clash [klæʃ] N (of metal) estridor m; (with police, fig) choque m ■ VI (gangs, beliefs) chocar-se; (disagree) entrar em conflito, ter uma desavença; (colours) não combinar; (dates, events) coincidir; (weapons, cymbals etc) bater ruidosamente
clasp [klɑːsp] N fecho; (embrace) abraço ■ VT

(hold) prender; (hand) apertar; (embrace) abraçar
class [klɑːs] N classe f; (lesson) aula; (type) tipo ■ CPD de classe ■ VT classificar
class-conscious ADJ que tem consciência de classe
class consciousness N consciência de classe
classic ['klæsɪk] ADJ clássico ■ N (author, work, race etc) clássico; **classics** NPL (Sch) línguas fpl clássicas
classical ['klæsɪkl] ADJ clássico
classification [klæsɪfɪ'keɪʃən] N classificação f
classified ['klæsɪfaɪd] ADJ (information) secreto; **classified advertisement** N classificado
classify ['klæsɪfaɪ] VT classificar
classmate ['klɑːsmeɪt] N colega m/f de aula
classroom ['klɑːsrum] N sala de aula
classy ['klɑːsɪ] (inf) ADJ (person) classudo; (flat, clothes) chique, incrementado
clatter ['klætər] N ruído, barulho; (of hooves) tropel m ■ VI fazer barulho or ruído
clause [klɔːz] N cláusula; (Ling) oração f
claustrophobia [klɔːstrə'fəubɪə] N claustrofobia
claw [klɔː] N (of animal) pata; (of bird of prey) garra; (of lobster) pinça; (Tech) unha ■ VT arranhar
▶ **claw at** VT FUS arranhar; (tear) rasgar
clay [kleɪ] N argila
clean [kliːn] ADJ limpo; (clear) nítido, bem definido ■ VT limpar; (hands, face etc) lavar ■ ADV: **he ~ forgot** ele esqueceu completamente; **to come ~** (inf: own up) abrir o jogo; **to ~ one's teeth** (Brit) escovar os dentes; ~ **driving licence** (Brit), ~ **record** (US) carteira de motorista sem infrações
▶ **clean off** VT tirar
▶ **clean out** VT limpar
▶ **clean up** VT limpar, assear ■ VI (fig: make profit): **to ~ up on** faturar com, lucrar com
clean-cut ADJ (person) alinhado
cleaner ['kliːnər] N (person) faxineiro(-a); (product) limpador m
cleaner's ['kliːnəz] N (also: **dry cleaner's**) tinturaria
cleaning ['kliːnɪŋ] N limpeza; **cleaning lady** N faxineira
cleanliness ['klɛnlɪnɪs] N limpeza
cleanly ['kliːnlɪ] ADV perfeitamente; (without mess) limpamente
cleanse [klɛnz] VT limpar; (purify) purificar
cleanser ['klɛnzər] N limpador m; (for face) creme m de limpeza
clean-shaven [-'ʃeɪvn] ADJ sem barba, de cara raspada
cleansing department ['klɛnzɪŋ-] (Brit) N departamento de limpeza
clean-up N limpeza geral
clear [klɪər] ADJ claro; (footprint, photograph) nítido; (obvious) evidente; (glass, water) transparente; (road, way) limpo, livre; (conscience) tranqüilo; (skin) macio; (profit) líquido; (majority) absoluto ■ VT (space) abrir; (desk etc) limpar; (room) esvaziar; (Law: suspect) absolver; (fence,

wall) saltar, transpor; (*obstacle*) salvar, passar sobre; (*debt*) liquidar; (*woodland*) desmatar; (*cheque*) compensar; (*Comm: goods*) liquidar ■ VI (*weather*) abrir; (*sky*) clarear; (*fog etc*) dissipar-se ■ ADV: ~ **of** a salvo de ■ N: **to be in the ~** (*out of debt*) estar sem dívidas; (*out of suspicion*) estar livre de suspeita; (*out of danger*) estar fora de perigo; **to ~ the table** tirar a mesa; **to ~ one's throat** pigarrear; **to ~ a profit** fazer um lucro líquido; **let me make myself ~** deixe-me explicar melhor; **do I make myself ~?** entendeu?; **to make o.s. ~** fazer-se entender bem; **to make it ~ to sb that ...** deixar bem claro para alguém que; **I have a ~ day tomorrow** (*Brit*) não tenho compromisso amanhã; **to keep ~ of sb/sth** evitar alguém/ algo
  ▶ **clear off** (*inf*) VI (*leave*) cair fora
  ▶ **clear up** VT limpar; (*mystery*) resolver, esclarecer
clearance ['klıərəns] N (*of trees, slums*) remoção *f*; (*permission*) permissão *f*; **clearance sale** N (*Comm*) liquidação *f*
clear-cut ADJ bem definido, nítido
clearing ['klıərıŋ] N (*in wood*) clareira; (*Brit: Banking*) compensação *f*; **clearing bank** (*Brit*) N câmara de compensação
clearly ['klıəlı] ADV (*distinctly*) distintamente; (*obviously*) claramente; (*coherently*) coerentemente
clearway ['klıəweɪ] (*Brit*) N *estrada onde não se pode estacionar*
cleavage ['kli:vɪdʒ] N (*of dress*) decote *m*; (*of woman*) colo
cleaver ['kli:və] N cutelo (de açougueiro)
clef [klɛf] N (*Mus*) clave *f*
cleft [klɛft] N (*in rock*) fissura
clemency ['klɛmənsı] N clemência
clement ['klɛmənt] ADJ (*weather*) ameno
clench [klɛntʃ] VT apertar, cerrar; (*teeth*) trincar
clergy ['klɜːdʒı] N clero
clergyman ['klɜːdʒımən] (*irreg*) N clérigo, pastor *m*
clerical ['klɛrıkəl] ADJ de escritório; (*Rel*) clerical
clerk [klɑːk, (*US*) klɜːrk] N auxiliar *m/f* de escritório; (*US: sales person*) balconista *m/f*; **C~ of Court** (*Law*) escrivão(-vã) *m/f* (do tribunal)
clever ['klɛvəʳ] ADJ (*mentally*) inteligente; (*deft, crafty*) hábil; (*device, arrangement*) engenhoso
clew [klu:] (*US*) N = **clue**
cliché ['kli:ʃeɪ] N clichê *m*, frase *f* feita
click [klık] VT (*tongue*) estalar; (*heels*) bater; (*Comput*) clicar em ■ VI (*make sound*) estalar; (*Comput*) clicar
client ['klaɪənt] N cliente *m/f*
clientele [kli:ɑːn'tɛl] N clientela
cliff [klıf] N penhasco
cliffhanger ['klıfhæŋəʳ] N (*TV, fig*) história de suspense
climactic [klaɪ'mæktık] ADJ culminante
climate ['klaɪmıt] N clima *m*
climax ['klaɪmæks] N clímax *m*, ponto

culminante; (*sexual*) clímax
climb [klaɪm] VI subir; (*plant*) trepar; (*plane*) ganhar altitude; (*prices etc*) escalar; (*move with effort*): **to ~ over a wall/into a car** passar por cima de um mura/entrar num carro ■ VT (*stairs*) subir; (*tree*) trepar em; (*hill*) escalar ■ N subida; (*of prices etc*) escalada; **to ~ over a wall** passar por cima de um muro
  ▶ **climb down** VI descer; (*Brit: fig*) recuar, ceder
climb-down (*Brit*) N retração *f*
climber ['klaɪməʳ] N alpinista *m/f*; (*plant*) trepadeira
climbing ['klaɪmıŋ] N alpinismo
clinch [klıntʃ] VT (*deal*) fechar; (*argument*) decidir, resolver
cling [klıŋ] (*pt, pp* **clung**) VI: **to ~ to** pegar-se a, aderir a; (*hold on to: support, idea*) agarrar-se a; (*clothes*) ajustar-se a
clinic ['klınık] N clínica; (*consultation*) consulta
clinical ['klınıkl] ADJ clínico; (*fig*) frio, impessoal
clink [klıŋk] VI tinir
clip [klıp] N (*for hair*) grampo (*BR*), gancho (*PT*); (*also:* **paper clip**) mola, clipe *m*; (*TV, Cinema*) clipe; (*on necklace etc*) fecho; (*Aut: holding hose etc*) braçadeira ■ VT (*cut*) aparar; (*also:* **clip together**: *papers*) grampear
clippers ['klıpəz] NPL (*for gardening*) podadeira; (*for hair*) máquina; (*also:* **nail clippers**) alicate *m* de unhas
clipping ['klıpıŋ] N recorte *m*
clique [kli:k] N panelinha
cloak [kləuk] N capa, manto ■ VT (*fig*) encobrir
cloakroom ['kləukrum] N vestiário; (*Brit: WC*) sanitários *mpl* (*BR*), lavatórios *mpl* (*PT*)
clock [klɔk] N relógio; (*in taxi*) taxímetro; **round the ~** (*work etc*) dia e noite, ininterruptamente; **30,000 on the ~** (*Brit: Aut*) 30, 000 km rodados; **to work against the ~** trabalhar contra o tempo
  ▶ **clock in** (*Brit*) VI assinar o ponto na entrada
  ▶ **clock off** (*Brit*) VI assinar o ponto na saída
  ▶ **clock on** (*Brit*) VI = **clock in**
  ▶ **clock out** (*Brit*) VI = **clock off**
  ▶ **clock up** VT (*miles, hours etc*) fazer
clockwise ['klɔkwaɪz] ADV em sentido horário
clockwork ['klɔkwɜːk] N mecanismo de relógio ■ ADJ de corda
clog [klɔg] N tamanco ■ VT entupir ■ VI (*also:* **clog up**) entupir-se
cloister ['klɔɪstəʳ] N claustro
clone [kləun] N clone *m*
close [*adj, adv* kləus, *vb, n* kləuz] ADJ próximo; (*print, weave*) denso, compacto; (*friend*) íntimo; (*connection*) estreito; (*examination*) minucioso; (*weather*) abafado; (*atmosphere*) sufocante; (*room*) mal arejado ■ ADV perto ■ VT (*shut*) fechar; (*end*) acabar, concluir ■ VI (*shop, door etc*) fechar; (*end*) concluir-se, terminar-se ■ N (*end*) fim *m*, conclusão *f*, terminação *f*; **~ by, ~ at hand** perto, pertinho; **how ~ is Edinburgh to Glasgow?** qual é a distância entre Edimburgo e Glasgow?; **to have a ~ shave** (*fig*) livrar-se por um triz; **at ~**

quarters de perto; **to bring sth to a ~** dar fim a algo

▶ **close down** VT, VI fechar definitivamente

▶ **close in** VI (hunters) apertar o cerco; (night, fog) cair; **the days are closing in** os dias estão ficando mais curtos; **to ~ in on sb** aproximar-se de alguém, cercar alguém

▶ **close off** VT (area) isolar

closed [kləuzd] ADJ fechado

closed-circuit ADJ: **~ television** televisão f de circuito fechado

closed shop N estabelecimento industrial que só admite empregados sindicalizados

close-knit ADJ (family, community) muito unido

closely ['kləuslɪ] ADV (exactly) fielmente; (carefully) rigorosamente; (watch) de perto; **we are ~ related** somos parentes próximos; **a ~ guarded secret** um segredo bem guardado

closet ['klɔzɪt] N (cupboard) armário; (walk-in) closet m

close-up [kləus-] N close m, close-up m

closing ['kləuzɪŋ] ADJ (stages, remarks) final; **~ price** (Stock Exchange) cotação f de fechamento

closing-down sale (Brit) N liquidação f (por motivo de fechamento)

closure ['kləuʒər] N (of factory etc) fechamento

clot [klɔt] N (gen: blood clot) coágulo; (inf: idiot) imbecil m/f ■ VI (blood) coagular-se

cloth [klɔθ] N (material) tecido, fazenda; (rag) pano; (also: **tablecloth**) toalha

clothe [kləuð] VT vestir; (fig) revestir

clothes [kləuðz] NPL roupa; **to take one's ~ off** tirar a roupa; **clothes brush** N escova (para a roupa); **clothes line** N corda (para estender a roupa); **clothes peg** (US **clothes pin**) N pregador m

clothing ['kləuðɪŋ] N = **clothes**

clotted cream ['klɔtɪd-] (Brit) N creme m coalhado

cloud [klaud] N nuvem f ■ VT (liquid) turvar; **to ~ the issue** confundir or complicar as coisas; **every ~ has a silver lining** (proverb) Deus escreve certo por linhas tortas

▶ **cloud over** VI (also: fig) fechar

cloudburst ['klaudbə:st] N aguaceiro

cloud-cuckoo-land (Brit) N: **to live in ~** viver no mundo da lua

cloudy ['klaudɪ] ADJ nublado; (liquid) turvo

clout [klaut] VT dar uma bofetada em ■ N (blow) bofetada; (fig) influência

clove [kləuv] N cravo; **clove of garlic** N dente m de alho

clover ['kləuvər] N trevo

cloverleaf ['kləuvəli:f] (irreg) N (Aut) trevo rodoviário

clown [klaun] N palhaço ■ VI (also: **clown about; clown around**) fazer palhaçadas

cloying ['klɔɪɪŋ] ADJ (taste, smell) enjoativo, nauseabundo

club [klʌb] N (society) clube m; (weapon) cacete m; (also: **golf club**) taco ■ VT esbordoar ■ VI: **to ~ together** cotizar-se; **clubs** NPL (Cards) paus

mpl; **club car** (US) N (Rail) vagão-restaurante m

clubhouse ['klʌbhaus] N sede f do clube

cluck [klʌk] VI cacarejar

clue [klu:] N indício, pista; (in crossword) definição f; **I haven't a ~** não faço idéia

clued up [klu:d-] (US **clued in**) (inf) ADJ entendido

clueless ['klu:lɪs] (inf) ADJ burro

clump [klʌmp] N (of trees etc) grupo

clumsy ['klʌmzɪ] ADJ (person) desajeitado; (movement) deselegante, mal-feito; (attempt) inábel

clung [klʌŋ] PT, PP of **cling**

cluster ['klʌstər] N grupo; (of flowers) ramo ■ VI agrupar-se, apinhar-se

clutch [klʌtʃ] N (grip, grasp) garra; (Aut) embreagem f (BR), embraiagem f (PT); (pedal) pedal m de embreagem (BR) or embraiagem (PT) ■ VT empunhar, pegar em ■ VI: **to ~ at** agarrar-se a

clutter ['klʌtər] VT (also: **clutter up**) abarrotar, encher desordenadamente ■ N bagunça, desordem f

CM (US) ABBR (Post) = **North Mariana Islands**

cm ABBR (= centimetre) cm

CNAA (Brit) N ABBR (= Council for National Academic Awards) órgão não universitário que outorga diplomas

CND N ABBR = **Campaign for Nuclear Disarmament**

CO N ABBR (= commanding officer) Com.; (Brit) = **Commonwealth Office** ■ ABBR (US: Post) = **Colorado**

Co. ABBR = **county**; (: = company) Cia

c/o ABBR (= care of) a/c

coach [kəutʃ] N (bus) ônibus m (BR), autocarro (PT); (horse-drawn) carruagem f, coche m; (of train) vagão m; (Sport) treinador(a) m/f, instrutor(a) m/f; (tutor) professor(a) m/f particular ■ VT (Sport) treinar; (student) preparar, ensinar; **coach trip** N passeio de ônibus (BR) or autocarro (PT)

coagulate [kəu'ægjuleɪt] VI coagular-se ■ VT coagular

coal [kəul] N carvão m; **coal face** N frente f de carvão

coalfield ['kəulfi:ld] N região f carbonífera

coalition [kəuə'lɪʃən] N coalizão f, coligação f

coalman ['kəulmæn] (irreg) N carvoeiro

coal merchant N = **coalman**

coalmine ['kəulmaɪn] N mina de carvão

coal miner N mineiro de carvão

coal mining N mineração f de carvão

coarse [kɔ:s] ADJ grosso, áspero; (vulgar) grosseiro, ordinário

coast [kəust] N costa, litoral m ■ VI (Aut) ir em ponto morto

coastal ['kəustəl] ADJ costeiro

coaster ['kəustər] N embarcação f costeira, barco de cabotagem; (for glass) descanso

coastguard ['kəustgɑ:d] N (person) guarda encarregado de policiar a costa

coastline ['kəustlaɪn] N litoral m

coat [kəut] N (jacket) casaco; (overcoat) sobretudo;

(of animal) pelo; (of paint) demão f, camada ■ VT
cobrir, revestir; **coat hanger** N cabide m
coating ['kəutɪŋ] N camada
coat of arms N brasão m
co-author [kəu-] N co-autor(a) m/f
coax [kəuks] VT persuadir com meiguice
cob [kɔb] N see **corn**
cobbler ['kɔbləʳ] N sapateiro
cobbles ['kɔblz] NPL pedras fpl arredondadas
cobblestones ['kɔblstəunz] NPL = **cobbles**
COBOL ['kəubɔl] N COBOL m
cobra ['kəubrə] N naja
cobweb ['kɔbwɛb] N teia de aranha
cocaine [kɔ'keɪn] N cocaína
cock [kɔk] N (rooster) galo; (male bird) macho ■ VT
(gun) engatilhar; **to ~ one's ears** (fig) prestar
atenção
cock-a-hoop ADJ exultante, eufórico
cockerel ['kɔkərəl] N frango, galo pequeno
cock-eyed [-aɪd] ADJ (crooked) torto; (fig: idea)
absurdo
cockle ['kɔkl] N berbigao m
cockney ['kɔknɪ] N londrino(-a) (nativo dos bairros
populares do leste de Londres)
cockpit ['kɔkpɪt] N (in aircraft) cabina
cockroach ['kɔkrəutʃ] N barata
cocktail ['kɔkteɪl] N coquetel m (BR), cocktail m
(PT); **cocktail cabinet** N móvel-bar m; **cocktail
party** N coquetel (BR), cocktail (BR); **cocktail
shaker** [-ʃeɪkəʳ] N coqueteleira
cocoa ['kəukəu] N cacau m; (drink) chocolate m
coconut ['kəukənʌt] N coco
cocoon [kə'ku:n] N casulo
COD ABBR (Brit) = **cash on delivery**; (US)
= **collect on delivery**
cod [kɔd] N INV bacalhau m
code [kəud] N cifra; (dialling code, post code)
código; **code of practice** N deontologia
codeine ['kəudi:n] N codeína
codicil ['kɔdɪsɪl] N codicilo
codify ['kəudɪfaɪ] VT codificar
cod-liver oil N óleo de fígado de bacalhau
co-driver [kəu-] N (in race) co-piloto; (in lorry)
segundo motorista m
co-ed ['kəu'ɛd] ADJ ABBR = **coeducational** ■ N
(US: female student) aluna de escola mista; (Brit:
school) escola mista
coeducational ['kəuedju'keɪʃənl] ADJ misto
coerce [kəu'ə:s] VT coagir
coercion [kəu'ə:ʃən] N coerção f
coexistence ['kəuɪg'zɪstəns] N coexistência
C. of C. N ABBR = **chamber of commerce**
C of E ABBR = **Church of England**
coffee ['kɔfɪ] N café m; **white ~** (Brit) or **~ with
cream** (US) café com leite; **coffee bar** (Brit) N
café m, lanchonete f; **coffee bean** N grão m
de café; **coffee break** N hora do café; **coffee
cake** (US) N pão m doce com passas; **coffee cup**
N xícara (BR) or chávena (PT) de café; **coffee
grounds** NPL borras fpl de café; **coffee plant** N
pé m de café
coffeepot ['kɔfɪpɔt] N cafeteira

coffee table N mesinha de centro
coffin ['kɔfɪn] N caixão m
C of I ABBR = **Church of Ireland**
C of S ABBR = **Church of Scotland**
cog [kɔg] N (tooth) dente m; (wheel) roda dentada
cogent ['kəudʒənt] ADJ convincente
cognac ['kɔnjæk] N conhaque m
cogwheel ['kɔgwi:l] N roda dentada
cohabit [kəu'hæbɪt] VI (formal): **to ~ (with sb)**
coabitar (com alguém)
coherent [kəu'hɪərənt] ADJ coerente
cohesion [kəu'hi:ʒən] N coesão f
cohesive [kəu'hi:sɪv] ADJ coeso
COI (Brit) N ABBR (= Central Office of Information)
serviço de informação governamental
coil [kɔɪl] N rolo; (rope) corda enrolada; (of smoke)
espiral f; (Elec) bobina; (contraceptive) DIU m ■ VT
enrolar ■ VI enrolar-se, espiralar-se
coin [kɔɪn] N moeda ■ VT (word) cunhar, criar
coinage ['kɔɪnɪdʒ] N moeda, sistema m
monetário
coin box (Brit) N telefone m público
coincide [kəuɪn'saɪd] VI coincidir
coincidence [kəu'ɪnsɪdəns] N coincidência
coin-operated [-'ɔpəreɪtɪd] ADJ (machine,
laundry) automático, que funciona com moedas
Coke® [kəuk] N coca
coke [kəuk] N (coal) coque m
Col. ABBR (= colonel) Cel
COLA (US) N ABBR (= cost-of-living adjustment)
≈ URP f
colander ['kɔləndəʳ] N coador m, passador m
cold [kəuld] ADJ frio ■ N frio; (Med) resfriado
(BR), constipação f (PT); **it's ~** está frio; **to be
~** estar com frio; **to catch ~** resfriar-se (BR),
apanhar constipação (PT); **to catch a ~** apanhar
um resfriado; **in ~ blood** a sangue frio; **to have
~ feet** (fig) estar com medo; **to give sb the ~
shoulder** tratar alguém com frieza, dar uma
fria em alguém (inf)
cold-blooded [-'blʌdɪd] ADJ (Zool) de sangue
frio; (murder) a sangue frio
cold cream N creme m de limpeza
coldly ['kəuldlɪ] ADV friamente
cold-shoulder VT tratar com frieza
cold sore N herpes m labial
coleslaw ['kəulslɔ:] N salada de repolho cru
colic ['kɔlɪk] N cólica
collaborate [kə'læbəreɪt] VI colaborar
collaboration [kəlæbə'reɪʃən] N colaboração f
collaborator [kə'læbəreɪtəʳ] N colaborador(a)
m/f
collage [kɔ'lɑ:ʒ] N colagem f
collagen ['kɔlədʒən] N colágeno
collapse [kə'læps] VI cair, tombar; (roof) dar de si,
desabar; (building) desabar; (Med) desmaiar ■ N
desabamento, desmoronamento; (of government)
queda; (Med) colapso
collapsible [kə'læpsəbl] ADJ dobrável
collar ['kɔləʳ] N (of shirt) colarinho; (of coat etc)
gola; (for dog) coleira; (Tech) aro, colar m ■ VT (inf:
person) prender

collarbone ['kɔləbəun] N clavícula
collate [kɔ'leɪt] VT cotejar
collateral [kə'lætrəl] N garantia subsidiária or pignoratícia
collation [kə'leɪʃən] N colação f
colleague ['kɔli:g] N colega m/f
collect [kə'lɛkt] VT reunir; (as a hobby) colecionar; (gather) recolher; (wages, debts) cobrar; (donations, subscriptions) colher; (mail) coletar; (Brit: call for) (ir) buscar ■ VI (people) reunir-se; (dust, dirt) acumular-se ■ ADV: **to call ~** (US: Tel) ligar a cobrar; **to ~ one's thoughts** refletir; **~ on delivery** (US: Comm) pagamento na entrega
collected [kə'lɛktɪd] ADJ: **~ works** obra completa
collection [kə'lɛkʃən] N coleção f; (of people) grupo; (of donations) arrecadação f; (of post, for charity) coleta; (of writings) coletânea
collective [kə'lɛktɪv] ADJ coletivo; **collective bargaining** N negociação f coletiva
collector [kə'lɛktəʳ] N colecionador(a) m/f; (of taxes etc) cobrador(a) m/f; **~'s item** or **piece** peça de coleção
college ['kɔlɪdʒ] N colégio; (of university) faculdade f; (of technology, agriculture) instituto, escola; **to go to ~** fazer faculdade; **college of education** N faculdade f de educação

COLLEGE

Além de "universidade", college também se refere a um centro de educação superior para jovens que terminaram a educação obrigatória, secondary school. Alguns oferecem cursos de especialização em matérias técnicas, artísticas ou comerciais, outros oferecem disciplinas universitárias.

collide [kə'laɪd] VI: **to ~ (with)** colidir (com)
collie ['kɔlɪ] N collie m
colliery ['kɔlɪərɪ] (Brit) N mina de carvão
collision [kə'lɪʒən] N colisão m; **to be on a ~ course** estar em curso de colisão
colloquial [kə'ləukwɪəl] ADJ coloquial
collusion [kə'lu:ʒən] N colusão f, conluio; **in ~ with** em conluio com
cologne [kə'ləun] N (also: **eau-de-cologne**) (água de) colônia
Colombia [kə'lɔmbɪə] N Colômbia
Colombian [kə'lɔmbɪən] ADJ, N colombiano(-a)
colon ['kəulən] N (sign) dois pontos; (Med) cólon m
colonel ['kɔ:nl] N coronel m
colonial [kə'ləunɪəl] ADJ colonial
colonize ['kɔlənaɪz] VT colonizar
colony ['kɔlənɪ] N colônia
color etc ['kʌləʳ] (US) = **colour** etc
Colorado beetle [kɔlə'rɑ:dəu-] N besouro da batata, dorífora
colossal [kə'lɔsl] ADJ colossal
colour ['kʌləʳ] (US **color**) N cor f ■ VT colorir; (with crayons) colorir, pintar; (dye) tingir; (fig: account) falsear ■ VI (blush) corar; **colours** NPL

(of party, club) cores fpl; **in ~** (photograph etc) a cores
colo(u)r bar N discriminação f racial
colo(u)r-blind ['kʌləblaɪnd] ADJ daltônico
colo(u)red ['kʌləd] ADJ colorido; (person) de cor
colo(u)reds ['kʌlədz] NPL gente f de cor
colo(u)r film N filme m a cores
colo(u)rful ['kʌləful] ADJ colorido; (account) vivido; (personality) vivo, animado
colo(u)ring ['kʌlərɪŋ] N colorido; (complexion) tez f; (in food) colorante m
colo(u)rless ['kʌləlɪs] ADJ sem cor, pálido
colo(u)r scheme N distribuição f de cores
colour supplement (Brit) N (Press) revista, suplemento a cores
colo(u)r television N televisão f a cores
colt [kəult] N potro
column ['kɔləm] N coluna; (of smoke) faixa; (of people) fila; **the editorial** ~ o editorial
columnist ['kɔləmnɪst] N cronista m/f
coma ['kəumə] N coma m; **to be in a ~** estar em coma
comb [kəum] N pente m; (ornamental) crista; (of cock) crista ■ VT (hair) pentear; (area) vasculhar
combat ['kɔmbæt] N combate m ■ VT combater
combination [kɔmbɪ'neɪʃən] N combinação f; (of safe) segredo; **combination lock** N fechadura de combinação
combine [vt, vi kəm'baɪn, n 'kɔmbaɪn] VT combinar; (qualities) reunir ■ VI combinar-se ■ N (Econ) associação f; (pej) monopólio; **a ~d effort** um esforço conjunto
combine (harvester) N ceifeira debulhadora
combo ['kɔmbəu] N (Jazz etc) conjunto
combustible [kəm'bʌstɪbl] ADJ combustível
combustion [kəm'bʌstʃən] N combustão f

🔘 KEYWORD

come [kʌm] (pt **came**, pp **come**) VI **1** (movement towards) vir; **come here!** vem aqui!; **I've only come for an hour** eu só vim por uma hora; **come with me** vem comigo; **are you coming to my party?** você vem à minha festa?; **to come running** vir correndo
2 (arrive) chegar; **he's just come from Aberdeen** ele acabou de chegar de Aberdeen; **she's come here to work** ela veio aqui para trabalhar; **they came to a river** eles chegaram num rio; **to come home** chegar em casa
3 (reach): **to come to** chegar a; **the bill came to £40** a conta deu £40; **her hair came to her waist** o cabelo dela batia na cintura; **to come to power** chegar ao poder; **to come to a decision** chegar a uma decisão
4 (occur): **an idea came to me** uma idéia me ocorreu
5 (be, become) ficar; **to come loose/undone** soltar-se/desfazer-se; **I've come to like him** passei a gostar dele
▶ **come about** VI suceder, acontecer
▶ **come across** VT FUS (person) topar com; (thing) encontrar

▶ **come away** VI (*leave*) ir-se embora; (*become detached*) desprender-se, soltar-se

▶ **come back** VI (*return*) voltar

▶ **come by** VT FUS (*acquire*) conseguir

▶ **come down** VI (*price*) baixar; (*tree*) cair; (*building*) desmoronar-se

▶ **come forward** VI (*volunteer*) apresentar-se

▶ **come from** VT FUS (*place, source etc: subj: person*) ser de; (: *thing*) originar-se de

▶ **come in** VI (*visitor*) entrar; (*on deal etc*) participar; (*be involved*) estar envolvido

▶ **come in for** VT FUS (*criticism etc*) merecer

▶ **come into** VT FUS (*money*) herdar; (*fashion*) ser; (*be involved*) estar envolvido em

▶ **come off** VI (*button*) desprender-se, soltar-se; (*attempt*) dar certo

▶ **come on** VI (*pupil, work, project*) avançar; (*lights, electricity*) ser ligado; **come on!** vamos!, vai!

▶ **come out** VI (*fact*) vir à tona; (*book*) ser publicado; (*stain, sun*) sair

▶ **come round** VI (*after faint, operation*) voltar a si

▶ **come to** VI (*regain consciousness*) voltar a si

▶ **come up** VI (*sun*) nascer; (*problem, in conversation*) surgir; (*event*) acontecer

▶ **come up against** VT FUS (*resistance, difficulties*) enfrentar, esbarrar em

▶ **come up with** VT FUS (*idea*) propor, sugerir; (*money*) contribuir

▶ **come upon** VT FUS (*find*) encontrar, achar

comeback ['kʌmbæk] N (*of film star etc*) volta; (*reaction*) reação f; (*response*) resposta

comedian [kə'miːdɪən] N cômico, humorista m

comedienne [kəmiːdɪ'ɛn] N cômica, humorista

comedown ['kʌmdaun] (*inf*) N revés m, humilhação f

comedy ['kɔmɪdɪ] N comédia; (*humour*) humor m

comet ['kɔmɪt] N cometa m

comeuppance [kʌm'ʌpəns] N: **to get one's ~ (for sth)** pagar (por algo)

comfort ['kʌmfət] N comodidade f, conforto; (*well-being*) bem-estar m; (*solace*) consolo; (*relief*) alívio ■ VT consolar, confortar; **comforts** NPL (*of home etc*) conforto

comfortable ['kʌmfətəbl] ADJ confortável; (*financially*) tranqüilo; (*walk, climb etc*) fácil; **I don't feel very ~ about it** não estou completamente conformado com isso

comfortably ['kʌmfətəblɪ] ADV confortavelmente

comforter ['kʌmfətəʳ] (US) N edredom m (BR), edredão m (PT)

comfort station (US) N banheiro (BR), lavatórios mpl (PT)

comic ['kɔmɪk] ADJ (*also:* **comical**) cômico ■ N (*person*) humorista m/f; (*Brit: magazine*) revista em quadrinhos (BR), revista de banda desenhada (PT), gibi m (BR) (*inf*)

comical ['kɔmɪkl] ADJ engraçado, cômico

comic strip N história em quadrinhos (BR), banda desenhada (PT)

coming ['kʌmɪŋ] N vinda, chegada ■ ADJ que

vem, vindouro; **in the ~ weeks** nas próximas semanas

coming(s) and going(s) N(PL) vaivém m, azáfama

Comintern ['kɔmɪntəːn] N Comintern m

comma ['kɔmə] N vírgula

command [kə'mɑːnd] N ordem f, mandado; (*control*) controle m; (*Mil: authority*) comando; (*mastery*) domínio; (*Comput*) comando ■ VT (*troops*) mandar; (*give orders to*) mandar, ordenar; (*dispose of*) dispor de; (*deserve*) merecer; **to ~ sb to do** mandar alguém fazer; **to have/take ~ of** ter/assumir o controle de; **to have at one's ~** (*money, resources etc*) dispor de

commandeer [kɔmən'dɪəʳ] VT requisitar

commander [kə'mɑːndəʳ] N (*Mil*) comandante m/f

commander-in-chief N (*Mil*) comandante-em-chefe m/f, comandante-chefe m/f

commanding [kə'mɑːndɪŋ] ADJ (*appearance*) imponente; (*voice, tone*) autoritário, imperioso; (*lead, position*) dominante; **commanding officer** N comandante m/f

commandment [kə'mɑːndmənt] N (*Rel*) mandamento

command module N (*Space*) módulo de comando

commando [kə'mɑːndəu] N (*group*) comando; (*soldier*) soldado

commemorate [kə'mɛməreɪt] VT (*with monument*) comemorar; (*with celebration*) celebrar

commemoration [kəmɛmə'reɪʃən] N comemoração f

commemorative [kə'mɛmərətɪv] ADJ comemorativo

commence [kə'mɛns] VT, VI começar, iniciar

commend [kə'mɛnd] VT (*praise*) elogiar, louvar; (*entrust*) encomendar; (*recommend*): **to ~ sth to sb** recomendar algo a alguém

commendable [kə'mɛndəbl] ADJ louvável

commendation [kɔmɛn'deɪʃən] N elogio, louvor m

commensurate [kə'mɛnʃərɪt] ADJ: **~ with** compatível com

comment ['kɔmɛnt] N comentário ■ VI comentar; **to ~ on sth** comentar algo; **to ~ that** observar que; **"no ~"** "sem comentário"

commentary ['kɔməntərɪ] N comentário

commentator ['kɔmənteɪtəʳ] N comentarista m/f

commerce ['kɔməːs] N comércio

commercial [kə'məːʃəl] ADJ comercial ■ N anúncio, comercial m; **commercial bank** N banco comercial; **commercial break** N intervalo para os comerciais; **commercial college** N escola de comércio

commercialism [kə'məːʃəlɪzəm] N mercantilismo

commercialize [kə'məːʃəlaɪz] VT comercializar

commercial radio N rádio f comercial

commercial television N televisão f comercial

commercial traveller N caixeiro/a-viajante m/f
commercial vehicle N veículo utilitário
commiserate [kə'mɪzəreɪt] VI: **to ~ with**
comiserar-se de, condoer-se de
commission [kə'mɪʃən] N (body, fee) comissão
f; (act) incumbência; (order for work of art etc)
empreitada, encomenda ■ VT (Mil) dar patente
oficial a; (work of art) encomendar; (artist)
incumbir; **out of ~** (Naut) fora do serviço ativo;
(not working) com defeito; **to ~ sb to do sth**
mandar alguém fazer algo; **to ~ sth from sb**
encomendar algo a alguém; **~ of inquiry** (Brit)
comissão de inquérito
commissionaire [kəmɪʃə'nɛər] (Brit) N porteiro
commissioner [kə'mɪʃənər] N comissário(-a)
commit [kə'mɪt] VT (act) cometer; (money,
resources) alocar; (to sb's care) entregar; **to ~ o.s.**
(to do) comprometer-se (a fazer); **to ~ suicide**
suicidar-se; **to ~ to writing** pôr por escrito,
pôr no papel; **to ~ sb for trial** levar alguém a
julgamento
commitment [kə'mɪtmənt] N (obligation)
compromisso; (political etc) engajamento;
(undertaking) promessa
committed [kə'mɪtɪd] ADJ (writer, politician etc)
engajado
committee [kə'mɪtɪ] N comitê m; **to be on**
a ~ ser membro de um comitê; **committee**
meeting N reunião f de comitê
commodity [kə'mɔdɪtɪ] N mercadoria;
commodities NPL (Comm) commodities mpl;
commodity exchange N bolsa de mercadorias
common ['kɔmən] ADJ comum; (vulgar) vulgar
■ N terrenos baldios mpl; **Commons** NPL (Brit:
Pol): **the (House of) C~s** a Câmara dos Comuns;
to have sth in ~ (with sb) tel algo em comum
(con alguém); **in ~ use** de uso corrente; **it's**
~ knowledge that todos sabem que; **to the ~**
good para o bem comum
commoner ['kɔmənər] N plebeu(-béia) m/f
common ground N (fig) consenso
common law N lei f consuetudinária ■ ADJ:
common-law wife concubina
commonly ['kɔmənlɪ] ADV geralmente
Common Market N Mercado Comum
commonplace ['kɔmənpleɪs] ADJ vulgar, trivial
■ N lugar-comum m
common room N sala comum; (Sch) sala dos
professores (or estudantes)
common sense N bom senso
Commonwealth ['kɔmənwɛlθ] N: **the ~** a
Comunidade Britânica
commotion [kə'məuʃən] N tumulto, confusão f
communal ['kɔmju:nl] ADJ (life) comunal;
(shared) comun
commune [n 'kɔmju:n, vi kə'mju:n] N (group)
comuna ■ VI: **to ~ with** comunicar-se
communicate [kə'mju:nɪkeɪt] VT comunicar
■ VI: **to ~ (with)** comunicar-se (com)
communication [kəmju:nɪ'keɪʃən] N
comunicação f; (letter, call) mensagem f;
communication cord (Brit) N sinal m de

alarme; **communications network** N rede f de
comunicações; **communications satellite** N
satélite m de comunicações
communicative [kə'mju:nɪkətɪv] ADJ
comunicativo
communion [kə'mju:nɪən] N (also: **Holy**
Communion) comunhão f
communiqué [kə'mju:nɪkeɪ] N comunicado
communism ['kɔmjunɪzəm] N comunismo
communist ['kɔmjunɪst] ADJ, N comunista m/f
community [kə'mju:nɪtɪ] N comunidade f;
(within larger group) sociedade f; **community**
centre N centro social; **community**
chest (US) N fundo de assistência social;
community health centre N centro de saúde
comunitário; **community service** N serviços
mpl comunitários; **community spirit** N espírito
comunitário
commutation ticket [kɔmju'teɪʃən-] (US) N
passe m, bilhete m de assinatura
commute [kə'mju:t] VI viajar diariamente ■ VT
comutar
commuter [kə'mju:tər] N viajante m/f habitual
compact [adj kəm'pækt, n 'kɔmpækt] ADJ
compacto; (style) conciso ■ N (pact) pacto; (also:
powder compact) estojo; **compact disk** N disco
laser
companion [kəm'pænɪən] N companheiro(-a)
companionship [kəm'pænɪənʃɪp] N
companhia, companheirismo; (spirit)
camaradagem f
companionway [kəm'pænjənweɪ] N (Naut)
escada de tombadilho
company ['kʌmpənɪ] N companhia; (Comm)
sociedade f, companhia; **he's good ~** ele é
uma boa companhia; **we have ~** temos visita;
to keep sb ~ fazer companhia a alguém;
to part ~ with separar-se de; **Smith and**
C~ Smith e Companhia; **company car** N
carro da companhia; **company director** N
administrador(a) m/f de companhia; **company**
secretary (Brit) N (Comm) secretário(-a) geral
(de uma companhia)
comparable ['kɔmpərəbl] ADJ comparável
comparative [kəm'pærətɪv] ADJ comparativo;
(relative) relativo
comparatively [kəm'pærətɪvlɪ] ADJ (relatively)
relativamente
compare [kəm'pɛər] VT: **to ~ sb/sth with/to**
comparar alguém(-also com/a); (contrast): **to**
~ (to/with) comparar (a/com) ■ VI: **to ~ with**
comparar-se com; **how do the prices ~?** qual é
a diferença entre os preços?; **~d with** or **to** em
comparação com
comparison [kəm'pærɪsn] N comparação f;
in ~ (with) em comparação (com), comparado
(com)
compartment [kəm'pɑ:tmənt] N (Rail, of fridge)
compartimento; (of wallet) divisão f
compass ['kʌmpəs] N bússola; **within the ~ of**
no âmbito de
compasses ['kʌmpəsɪz] NPL compasso

compassion [kəm'pæʃən] N compaixão f
compassionate [kəm'pæʃənət] ADJ
compassivo; **on ~ grounds** por motivos
humanitários
compatibility [kɔmpætɪ'bɪlɪtɪ] N
compatibilidade f
compatible [kəm'pætɪbl] ADJ compatível
compel [kəm'pɛl] VT obrigar
compelling [kəm'pɛlɪŋ] ADJ (fig: argument)
convincente
compendium [kəm'pɛndɪəm] N compêndio
compensate ['kɔmpənseɪt] VT (employee, victim)
indenizar ■ VI: **to ~ for** compensar
compensation [kɔmpən'seɪʃən] N
compensação f; (damages) indenização f
compère ['kɔmpɛəʳ] N apresentador(a) m/f
compete [kəm'pi:t] VI (take part) competir; (vie):
to ~ (with) competir (com), fazer competição
(com)
competence ['kɔmpɪtəns] N competência,
capacidade f
competent ['kɔmpɪtənt] ADJ competente
competition [kɔmpɪ'tɪʃən] N (contest) concurso;
(Econ) concorrência; (rivalry) competição f; **in ~
with** em competição com
competitive [kəm'pɛtɪtɪv] ADJ competitivo;
(person) competidor(a); **competitive
examination** N concurso
competitor [kəm'pɛtɪtəʳ] N (rival) competidor(a)
m/f; (participant, Econ) concorrente m/f; **our ~s**
(Comm) a (nossa) concorrência
compile [kəm'paɪl] VT compilar, compor
complacency [kəm'pleɪsnsɪ] N satisfação f
consigo mesmo
complacent [kəm'pleɪsənt] ADJ relaxado,
acomodado
complain [kəm'pleɪn] VI queixar-se; (in shop etc)
reclamar; **to ~ of** (pain) queixar-se de
complaint [kəm'pleɪnt] N (objection) objeção f;
(criticism) queixa; (in shop etc) reclamação f; (Jur)
querela; (Med) achaque m, doença
complement ['kɔmplɪmənt] N complemento;
(esp ship's crew) tripulação f ■ VT complementar
complementary [kɔmplɪ'mɛntərɪ] ADJ
complementar
complete [kəm'pli:t] ADJ completo; (finished)
acabado ■ VT (finish: building, task) acabar;
(: set, group) completar; (a form) preencher; **a ~
disaster** um desastre total
completely [kəm'pli:tlɪ] ADV completamente
completion [kəm'pli:ʃən] N conclusão f,
término; (of contract etc) realização f; **to be
nearing ~** estar quase pronto; **on ~ of contract**
na assinatura do contrato; (for house) na
escritura
complex ['kɔmplɛks] ADJ complexo ■ N (Psych,
of ideas etc) complexo; (of buildings) conjunto
complexion [kəm'plɛkʃən] N (of face) cor f, tez f;
(fig) aspecto
complexity [kəm'plɛksɪtɪ] N complexidade f
compliance [kəm'plaɪəns] N (submission)
submissão f; (agreement) conformidade f; **in ~**

with de acordo com, conforme
compliant [kəm'plaɪənt] ADJ complacente,
submisso
complicate ['kɔmplɪkeɪt] VT complicar
complicated ['kɔmplɪkeɪtɪd] ADJ complicado
complication [kɔmplɪ'keɪʃən] N problema f;
(Med) complicação f
compliment [n 'kɔmplɪmənt, vt 'kɔmplɪmɛnt]
N (formal) cumprimento; (praise) elogio ■ VT
elogiar; **compliments** NPL cumprimentos mpl;
to pay sb a ~ elogiar alguém; **to ~ sb (on sth/
on doing sth)** cumprimentar or elogiar alguém
(por algo/por ter feito algo)
complimentary [kɔmplɪ'mɛntərɪ] ADJ
lisonjeiro; (free) gratuito; **complimentary
ticket** N entrada de favor or de cortesia
compliments slip N memorando
comply [kəm'plaɪ] VI: **to ~ with** cumprir com
component [kəm'pəunənt] ADJ componente
■ N (part) peça; (element) componente m
compose [kəm'pəuz] VT compor; **to be ~d of**
compor-se de; **to ~ o.s.** tranqüilizar-se
composed [kəm'pəuzd] ADJ calmo
composer [kəm'pəuzəʳ] N (Mus)
compositor(a) m/f
composite ['kɔmpəzɪt] ADJ composto
composition [kɔmpə'zɪʃən] N composição f
compost ['kɔmpɔst] N adubo
composure [kəm'pəuʒəʳ] N serenidade f, calma
compound [n, adj 'kɔmpaund, vt kəm'paund]
N (Chem, Ling) composto; (enclosure) recinto
■ ADJ composto; (fracture) complicado ■ VT (fig:
problem etc) agravar; **compound interest** N juro
composto
comprehend [kɔmprɪ'hɛnd] VT compreender
comprehension [kɔmprɪ'hɛnʃən] N
compreensão f
comprehensive [kɔmprɪ'hɛnsɪv] ADJ
abrangente; (Insurance) total; **comprehensive
insurance policy** N apólice f de seguro com
cobertura total; **comprehensive (school)** (Brit)
N escola secundária de amplo programa

⬤ **COMPREHENSIVE SCHOOL**
⬤
⬤ Criadas na década de 1960 pelo governo
⬤ trabalhista da época, as comprehensive
⬤ schools são estabelecimentos de ensino
⬤ secundário polivalentes concebidos para
⬤ acolher todos os alunos sem distinção e
⬤ lhes oferecer oportunidades iguais, em
⬤ oposição ao sistema seletivo das grammar
⬤ schools. A maioria dos estudantes britânicos
⬤ freqüenta atualmente uma comprehensive
⬤ school, mas as grammar schools não
⬤ desapareceram de todo.

compress [vt kəm'prɛs, n 'kɔmprɛs] VT
comprimir; (text, information etc) reduzir ■ N
(Med) compressa
compression [kəm'prɛʃən] N compressão f
comprise [kəm'praɪz] VT (also: **be comprised of**)

compreender, constar de; (constitute) constituir

compromise ['kɔmprəmaɪz] N meio-termo ■ VT comprometer ■ VI chegar a um meio-termo ■ CPD (decision, solution) de meio-termo

compulsion [kəm'pʌlʃən] N compulsão f; (force) coação f, força; **under ~** sob coação, à força

compulsive [kəm'pʌlsɪv] ADJ compulsório; **he's a ~ smoker** ele não pode deixar de fumar

compulsory [kəm'pʌlsərɪ] ADJ obrigatório; (retirement) compulsório; **compulsory purchase** N compra compulsória

compunction [kəm'pʌŋkʃən] N compunção; **to have no ~ about doing sth** não hesitar em fazer algo

computer [kəm'pju:tər] N computador m

computerize [kəm'pju:təraɪz] VT informatizar, computadorizar

computer language N linguagem f de máquina

computer peripheral N periférico

computer program N programa m de computador

computer progra(m)mer N programador(a) m/f

computer program(m)ing N programação f

computer science N informática, computação f

computer scientist N cientista m/f da computação

computing [kəm'pju:tɪŋ] N computação f; (science) informática

comrade ['kɔmrɪd] N camarada m/f

comradeship ['kɔmrɪdʃɪp] N camaradagem f

comsat ['kɔmsæt] N ABBR = **communications satellite**

con [kɔn] VT enganar; (cheat) trapacear ■ N vigarice f; **cons** NPL see **convenience**; **pro**; **to ~ sb into doing sth** convencer alguém a fazer algo (por artimanhas)

concave [kɔn'keɪv] ADJ côncavo

conceal [kən'si:l] VT ocultar; (information) omitir

concede [kən'si:d] VT (admit) reconhecer, admitir ■ VI ceder

conceit [kən'si:t] N presunção f

conceited [kən'si:tɪd] ADJ vaidoso

conceivable [kən'si:vəbl] ADJ concebível; **it is ~ that** é possível que

conceivably [kən'si:vəblɪ] ADV: **he may ~ be right** é possível que ele tenha razão

conceive [kən'si:v] VT conceber ■ VI conceber, engravidar; **to ~ of sth/of doing sth** conceber algo/fazer idéia de fazer algo

concentrate ['kɔnsəntreɪt] VI concentrar-se ■ VT concentrar

concentration [kɔnsən'treɪʃən] N concentração f; **concentration camp** N campo de concentração

concentric [kɔn'sɛntrɪk] ADJ concêntrico

concept ['kɔnsɛpt] N conceito

conception [kən'sɛpʃən] N (idea) conceito, idéia; (Bio) concepção f

concern [kən'sə:n] N (matter) assunto; (Comm)

empresa; (anxiety) preocupação f ■ VT (worry) preocupar; (involve) envolver; (relate to) dizer respeito a; **to be ~ed (about)** preocupar-se (com); **"to whom it may ~"** "a quem interessar possa"; **as far as I'm ~ed** no que me diz respeito, quanto a mim; **to be ~ed with** (person: involved with) ocupar-se de; (book: be about) tratar de; **the department ~ed** (under discussion) o departamento em questão; (relevant) o departamento competente

concerning [kən'sə:nɪŋ] PREP sobre, a respeito de, acerca de

concert ['kɔnsət] N concerto; **in ~** de comum acordo

concerted [kən'sə:tɪd] ADJ (joint) conjunto; (strong) sério

concert hall N sala de concertos

concertina [kɔnsə'ti:nə] N sanfona ■ VI engavetar-se

concert master (US) N primeiro violino de uma orquestra

concerto [kən'tʃə:təu] N concerto

concession [kən'sɛʃən] N concessão f; **tax ~** redução no imposto

concessionaire [kənseʃə'nɛər] N concessionário(-a)

concessionary [kən'sɛʃənrɪ] ADJ (ticket, fare) a preço reduzido

conciliation [kənsɪlɪ'eɪʃən] N conciliação f

conciliatory [kən'sɪlɪətrɪ] ADJ conciliador(a)

concise [kən'saɪs] ADJ conciso

conclave ['kɔnkleɪv] N conclave m

conclude [kən'klu:d] VT (finish) acabar, concluir; (treaty etc) firmar; (agreement) chegar a; (decide) decidir; **to ~ that** chegar à conclusão de que ■ VI terminar, acabar

conclusion [kən'klu:ʒən] N conclusão f; **to come to the ~ that** chegar à conclusão de que

conclusive [kən'klu:sɪv] ADJ conclusivo, decisivo

concoct [kən'kɔkt] VT (excuse) fabricar; (plot) tramar; (meal) preparar

concoction [kən'kɔkʃən] N (mixture) mistura

concord ['kɔŋkɔ:d] N (harmony) concórdia; (treaty) acordo

concourse ['kɔŋkɔ:s] N (hall) saguão m; (crowd) multidão f

concrete ['kɔŋkri:t] N concreto (BR), betão m (PT) ■ ADJ concreto; **concrete mixer** N betoneira

concur [kən'kə:r] VI estar de acordo, concordar

concurrently [kən'kʌrntlɪ] ADV ao mesmo tempo, simultaneamente

concussion [kən'kʌʃən] N (Med) concussão f cerebral

condemn [kən'dɛm] VT (denounce) denunciar; (prisoner, building) condenar

condemnation [kɔndɛm'neɪʃən] N condenação f; (blame) censura

condensation [kɔndɛn'seɪʃən] N condensação f

condense [kən'dɛns] VI condensar-se ■ VT condensar

condensed milk [kən'dɛnst-] N leite m condensado
condescend [kɔndɪ'sɛnd] VI condescender, dignar-se; **to ~ to do sth** condescender a fazer algo
condescending [kɔndɪ'sɛndɪŋ] ADJ condescendente
condition [kən'dɪʃən] N condição f; (health) estado de saúde; (Med: illness) doença ■ VT condicionar; **conditions** NPL (circumstances) circunstâncias fpl; **on ~ that** com a condição (de) que; **in good/poor ~** em bom/mau estado (de conservação); **a heart ~** um problema no coração; **weather ~s** condições fpl meteorológicas
conditional [kən'dɪʃənl] ADJ condicional; **to be ~ upon** depender de
conditioner [kən'dɪʃənəʳ] N (for hair) condicionador m; (for fabrics) amaciante m
condo ['kɔndəu] (US: inf) N ABBR = **condominium**
condolences [kən'dəulənsɪz] NPL pêsames mpl
condom ['kɔndɔm] N preservativo, camisa-de-Venus f
condominium [kɔndə'mɪnɪəm] (US) N (building) edifício; (rooms) apartamento
condone [kən'dəun] VT admitir, aceitar
conducive [kən'dju:sɪv] ADJ: **~ to** conducente para or a
conduct [n 'kɔndʌkt, vt, vi kən'dʌkt] N conduta, comportamento ■ VT conduzir; (manage) dirigir; (Mus) reger ■ VI (Mus) reger uma orquestra; **to ~ o.s.** comportar-se
conducted tour [kən'dʌktɪd-] N viagem f organizada; (of building etc) visita guiada
conductor [kən'dʌktəʳ] N (of orchestra) regente m/f; (on bus) cobrador(a) m/f; (US: Rail) revisor(a) m/f; (Elec) condutor m
conductress [kən'dʌktrɪs] N (on bus) cobradora
conduit ['kɔndɪt] N conduto
cone [kəun] N cone m; (Bot) pinha; (for ice-cream) casquinha; **pine ~** pinha
confectioner [kən'fɛkʃənəʳ] N confeiteiro(-a) (BR), pasteleiro(-a) (PT)
confectioner's (shop) N confeitaria (BR), pastelaria (PT); (sweet shop) confeitaria
confectionery [kən'fɛkʃnərɪ] N (cakes) bolos mpl; (sweets) doces mpl
confederate [kən'fɛdrɪt] ADJ confederado ■ N cúmplice m/f; (US: History) confederado(-a) (sulista)
confederation [kənfɛdə'reɪʃən] N confederação f
confer [kən'fəːʳ] VT: **to ~ on** outorgar a ■ VI conferenciar
conference ['kɔnfərns] N (meeting) congresso; **to be in ~** estar em conferência; **conference room** N sala de conferência
confess [kən'fɛs] VT confessar ■ VI (admit) admitir
confession [kən'fɛʃən] N admissão f; (Rel) confissão f
confessional [kən'fɛʃənl] N confessionário

confessor [kən'fɛsəʳ] N confessor m
confetti [kən'fɛtɪ] N confete m
confide [kən'faɪd] VI: **to ~ in** confiar em, fiar-se em
confidence ['kɔnfɪdns] N confiança; (faith) fé f; (secret) confidência; **to have (every) ~ that** ter certeza de que; **motion of no ~** moção de não confiança; **in ~** em confidência; **confidence trick** N conto do vigário
confident ['kɔnfɪdnt] ADJ confiante, convicto; (positive) seguro
confidential [kɔnfɪ'dɛnʃəl] ADJ confidencial; (secretary) de confiança
confidentiality ['kɔnfɪdɛnʃɪ'ælɪtɪ] N sigilo
configuration [kən'fɪgju'reɪʃən] N (also: Comput) configuração f
confine [kən'faɪn] VT (shut up) encarcerar; (limit): **to ~ (to)** confinar (a); **to ~ o.s. to (doing) sth** limitar-se a (fazer) algo
confined [kən'faɪnd] ADJ (space) reduzido
confinement [kən'faɪnmənt] N (imprisonment) prisão f; (enclosure) reclusão f; (Med) parto
confines ['kɔnfaɪnz] NPL confins mpl
confirm [kən'fəːm] VT confirmar
confirmation [kɔnfə'meɪʃən] N confirmação f; (Rel) crisma
confirmed [kən'fəːmd] ADJ inveterado
confiscate ['kɔnfɪskeɪt] VT confiscar
confiscation [kɔnfɪs'keɪʃən] N confiscação f
conflagration [kɔnflə'greɪʃən] N conflagração f
conflict [n 'kɔnflɪkt, vi kən'flɪkt] N (disagreement) divergência; (of interests, loyalties) conflito; (fighting) combate m ■ VI estar em conflito; (opinions) divergir
conflicting [kən'flɪktɪŋ] ADJ (reports) divergente; (interests) oposto; (account) discrepante
conform [kən'fɔːm] VI conformar-se; **to ~ to** ajustar-se a, acomodar-se a
conformist [kən'fɔːmɪst] N conformista m/f
confound [kən'faund] VT confundir; (amaze) desconcertar
confounded [kən'faundɪd] ADJ maldito
confront [kən'frʌnt] VT (problems) enfrentar; (enemy, danger) defrontar-se com
confrontation [kɔnfrən'teɪʃən] N confrontação f
confuse [kən'fju:z] VT (perplex) desconcertar; (mix up) confundir, misturar; (complicate) complicar
confused [kən'fju:zd] ADJ confuso; (person) perplexo, confuso
confusing [kən'fju:zɪŋ] ADJ confuso
confusion [kən'fju:ʒən] N (mix-up) mal-entendido; (perplexity) perplexidade f; (disorder) confusão f
congeal [kən'dʒi:l] VI (freeze) congelar-se; (coagulate) coagular-se
congenial [kən'dʒi:nɪəl] ADJ simpático, agradável
congenital [kən'dʒɛnɪtl] ADJ congênito
conger eel ['kɔŋgeʳ-] N congro
congested [kən'dʒɛstɪd] ADJ congestionado

congestion [kən'dʒɛstʃən] N (Med) congestão f;
(traffic) congestionamento

conglomerate [kən'glɔmərɪt] N (Comm)
conglomerado

conglomeration [kənglɔmə'reɪʃən] N
conglomeração f, aglomeração f

Congo ['kɔŋgəu] N (state) Congo

congratulate [kən'grætjuleɪt] VT parabenizar;
to ~ sb (on) felicitar or parabenizar alguém
(por)

congratulations [kəngrætju'leɪʃənz] NPL: **~
(on)** parabéns mpl (por) ■ EXCL parabéns!

congregate ['kɔŋgrɪgeɪt] VI reunir-se

congregation [kɔŋgrɪ'geɪʃən] N (in church) fiéis
mpl; (assembly) congregação f, reunião f

congress ['kɔŋgrɛs] N congresso; (US): **C~**
Congresso

● **CONGRESS**
●
● O Congresso é o Parlamento dos Estados
● Unidos. Consiste na House of Representatives
● e no Senado Senate. Os representantes e
● senadores são eleitos por sufrágio universal
● direto. O Congresso se reúne no Capitol, em
● Washington.

congressman ['kɔŋgrɛsmən] (US: irreg) N
deputado

congresswoman ['kɔŋgrɛswumən] (US: irreg) N
deputada

conical ['kɔnɪkl] ADJ cônico

conifer ['kɔnɪfəʳ] N conífera

coniferous [kə'nɪfərəs] ADJ (forest) conífero

conjecture [kən'dʒɛktʃəʳ] N conjetura ■ VT, VI
conjeturar

conjugal ['kɔndʒugl] ADJ conjugal

conjugate ['kɔndʒugeɪt] VT conjugar

conjugation [kɔndʒu'geɪʃən] N conjugação f

conjunction [kən'dʒʌŋkʃən] N conjunção f; **in ~
with** junto com

conjunctivitis [kəndʒʌŋktɪ'vaɪtɪs] N
conjuntivite f

conjure ['kʌndʒəʳ] VI fazer truques ■ VT fazer
aparecer

▶ **conjure up** VT (ghost, spirit) fazer aparecer,
invocar; (memories) evocar

conjurer ['kʌndʒərəʳ] N mágico(-a),
prestidigitador(a) m/f

conjuring trick ['kʌndʒərɪŋ-] N mágica

conker ['kɔŋkəʳ] (Brit) N castanha-da-índia

conk out [kɔŋk-] (inf) VI pifar

con man ['kɔn-] (irreg) N vigarista m

connect [kə'nɛkt] VT (Elec, Tel) ligar; (fig:
associate) associar; (join): **to ~ sth (to)** juntar
or unir algo (a) ■ VI: **to ~ with** (train) conectar
com; **to be ~ed with** estar relacionado com;
I'm trying to ~ you (Tel) estou tentando
completar a ligação

connection [kə'nɛkʃən] N ligação f; (Elec, Rail)
conexão f; (Tel) ligação f; (fig) relação f; **in ~
with** com relação a; **what is the ~ between**

them? qual é a relação entre eles?; **business ~s**
contatos de trabalho

connexion [kə'nɛkʃən] (Brit) N = **connection**

conning tower ['kɔnɪŋ-] N torre f de comando

connive [kə'naɪv] VI: **to ~ at** ser conivente em

connoisseur [kɔnɪ'sɜʳ] N conhecedor(a) m/f,
apreciador(a) m/f

connotation [kɔnə'teɪʃən] N conotação f

connubial [kə'nju:bɪəl] ADJ conjugal

conquer ['kɔŋkəʳ] VT conquistar; (enemy) vencer;
(feelings) superar

conqueror ['kɔŋkərəʳ] N conquistador(a) m/f

conquest ['kɔŋkwɛst] N conquista

cons [kɔnz] NPL see **convenience**

conscience ['kɔnʃəns] N consciência; **in all ~**
em sã consciência

conscientious [kɔnʃɪ'ɛnʃəs] ADJ consciencioso;
(objection) de consciência; **conscientious
objector** N aquele que faz uma objeção de consciência
à sua participação nas forças armadas

conscious ['kɔnʃəs] ADJ: **~ (of)** consciente (de);
(deliberate: insult, error) intencional; **to become
~ of** tornar-se consciente de, conscientizar-se de

consciousness ['kɔnʃəsnɪs] N consciência; **to
lose/regain ~** perder/recuperar os sentidos

conscript ['kɔnskrɪpt] N recruta m/f

conscription [kən'skrɪpʃən] N serviço militar
obrigatório

consecrate ['kɔnsɪkreɪt] VT consagrar

consecutive [kən'sɛkjutɪv] ADJ consecutivo

consensus [kən'sɛnsəs] N consenso; **the ~ (of
opinion)** o consenso (de opiniões)

consent [kən'sɛnt] N consentimento ■ VI:
to ~ to consentir em; **age of ~** maioridade; **by
common ~** de comum acordo

consequence ['kɔnsɪkwəns] N conseqüência;
(significance): **of ~** de importância; **in ~** por
conseqüência

consequently ['kɔnsɪkwəntlɪ] ADV por
conseguinte

conservation [kɔnsə'veɪʃən] N (Of the
environment) preservação f; (of energy, paintings
etc) conservação f; (also: **nature conservation**)
proteção f do meio ambiente; **energy ~**
conservação da energia

conservationist [kɔnsə'veɪʃənɪst] N
conservacionista m/f

conservative [kən'sə:vətɪv] ADJ conservador(a);
(cautious) moderado; (Brit: Pol): **C~** conservador(a)
■ N (Brit: Pol) conservador(a) m/f

conservatory [kən'sə:vətrɪ] N (Mus)
conservatório; (greenhouse) estufa

conserve [kən'sə:v] VT conservar; (preserve)
preservar; (supplies, energy) poupar ■ N conserva

consider [kən'sɪdəʳ] VT (believe) acreditar; (take
into account) levar em consideração; (study)
estudar, examinar; **to ~ doing sth** pensar em
fazer algo; **~ yourself lucky** dê-se por sortudo;
all things ~ed afinal de contas

considerable [kən'sɪdərəbl] ADJ considerável;
(sum) importante

considerably [kən'sɪdərəblɪ] ADV

considerávelmente
considerate [kənˈsɪdərɪt] ADJ atencioso
consideration [kənsɪdəˈreɪʃən] N consideração
f; *(deliberation)* deliberação f; *(factor)* fator
m; *(reward)* remuneração f; **out of ~ for** em
consideração a; **to be under ~** estar em
apreciação; **my first ~ is my family** minha
maior preocupação é a minha família
considering [kənˈsɪdərɪŋ] PREP em vista de
■ CONJ: **~ (that)** apesar de que, considerando
que
consign [kənˈsaɪn] VT consignar; **to ~ to** *(to
a place)* relegar para; *(to sb's care, to poverty)*
confiar a
consignee [kɔnsaɪˈniː] N consignatário(-a)
consignment [kənˈsaɪnmənt] N consignação f;
consignment note N *(Comm)* guia de remessa
consignor [kənˈsaɪnəʳ] N consignador(a) m/f
consist [kənˈsɪst] VI: **to ~ of** *(comprise)*
compreender
consistency [kənˈsɪstənsɪ] N *(of policies etc)*
coerência; *(thickness)* consistência
consistent [kənˈsɪstənt] ADJ *(person)* coerente,
estável; *(argument, idea)* sólido; *(even)* constante; **~
with** compatível com, de acordo com
consolation [kɔnsəˈleɪʃən] N conforto
console [vt kənˈsəul, n ˈkɔnsəul] VT confortar
■ N consolo
consolidate [kənˈsɔlɪdeɪt] VT consolidar
consols [ˈkɔnsɔlz] *(Brit)* NPL *(Stock Exchange)*
consolidados mpl
consommé [kənˈsɔmeɪ] N consomê m, caldo
consonant [ˈkɔnsənənt] N consoante f
consort [n ˈkɔnsɔːt, vi kənˈsɔːt] N consorte m/f
■ VI: **to ~ with** ter ligações com, conviver com;
prince ~ príncipe m consorte
consortia [kənˈsɔːtɪə] NPL of **consortium**
consortium [kənˈsɔːtɪəm] *(pl* **consortiums** *or*
consortia) N consórcio
conspicuous [kənˈspɪkjuəs] ADJ *(noticeable)*
conspícuo; *(visible)* visível; *(garish)* berrante;
(outstanding) notável; **to make o.s. ~** fazer-se
notar
conspiracy [kənˈspɪrəsɪ] N conspiração f, trama
conspiratorial [kənspɪrəˈtɔːrɪəl] ADJ
conspirador(a)
conspire [kənˈspaɪəʳ] VI conspirar
constable [ˈkʌnstəbl] *(Brit)* N policial m/f (BR),
polícia m/f (PT); **chief ~** chefe m/f de polícia
constabulary [kənˈstæbjulərɪ] N polícia
(distrital)
constant [ˈkɔnstənt] ADJ constante; *(loyal)* leal,
fiel
constantly [ˈkɔnstəntlɪ] ADV constantemente
constellation [kɔnstəˈleɪʃən] N constelação f
consternation [kɔnstəˈneɪʃən] N consternação f
constipated [ˈkɔnstɪpeɪtəd] ADJ com prisão de
ventre
constipation [kɔnstɪˈpeɪʃən] N prisão f de
ventre
constituency [kənˈstɪtjuənsɪ] N *(Pol)* distrito
eleitoral; *(people)* eleitorado; **constituency**

party N partido local
constituent [kənˈstɪtjuənt] N *(Pol)* eleitor(a)
m/f; *(component)* componente m
constitute [ˈkɔnstɪtjuːt] VT *(represent)*
representar; *(make up)* constituir
constitution [kɔnstɪˈtjuːʃən] N constituição f;
(health) compleição f
constitutional [kɔnstɪˈtjuːʃənl] ADJ
constitucional
constrain [kənˈstreɪn] VT obrigar
constrained [kənˈstreɪnd] ADJ: **to feel ~ to ...**
sentir-se compelido a ...
constraint [kənˈstreɪnt] N *(compulsion)* coação
f, pressão f; *(restriction)* limitação f; *(shyness)*
constrangimento
constrict [kənˈstrɪkt] VT apertar, constringir
construct [kənˈstrʌkt] VT construir
construction [kənˈstrʌkʃən] N construção
f; *(structure)* estrutura; *(fig: interpretation)*
interpretação f; **under ~** em construção;
construction industry N construção f
constructive [kənˈstrʌktɪv] ADJ construtivo
construe [kənˈstruː] VT interpretar
consul [ˈkɔnsl] N cônsul m/f
consulate [ˈkɔnsjulɪt] N consulado
consult [kənˈsʌlt] VT, VI consultar
consultancy [kənˈsʌltənsɪ] N consultoria;
consultancy fee N honorário de consultor
consultant [kənˈsʌltənt] N *(Med: médico/a)*
especialista m/f; *(other specialist)* assessor(a)
m/f, consultor(a) m/f ■ CPD: **~ engineer**
engenheiro-consultor/engenheira-consultora
m/f; **~ paediatrician** pediatra m/f; **legal/
management ~** assessor jurídico/consultor em
administração
consultation [kɔnsəlˈteɪʃən] N *(Med)* consulta;
(discussion) discussão f; **in ~ with** em consulta
com
consulting room [kənˈsʌltɪŋ-] *(Brit)* N
consultório
consume [kənˈsjuːm] VT *(eat)* comer; *(drink)*
beber; *(fire etc, Comm)* consumir
consumer [kənˈsjuːməʳ] N consumidor(a) m/f;
consumer credit N crédito ao consumidor;
consumer durables NPL bens mpl de consumo
duráveis; **consumer goods** NPL bens mpl de
consumo
consumerism [kənˈsjuːmərɪzəm] N *(Econ)*
consumismo; *(consumer protection)* proteção f ao
consumidor
consumer society N sociedade f de consumo
consummate [ˈkɔnsʌmeɪt] VT consumar
consumption [kənˈsʌmpʃən] N consumação f;
(buying) consumo; *(Med)* tuberculose f; **not fit
for human ~** impróprio para consumo
cont. ABBR = **continued**
contact [ˈkɔntækt] N contato ■ VT entrar *or*
pôr-se em contato com; **to be in ~ with sb** estar
em contato com alguém; **he has good ~s** tem
boas relações; **contact lenses** NPL lentes fpl de
contato
contagious [kənˈteɪdʒəs] ADJ contagioso; *(fig:*

laughter etc) contagiante
contain [kən'teɪn] VT conter; **to ~ o.s.** conter-se
container [kən'teɪnə^r] N recipiente *m*; (*for shipping etc*) container *m*, cofre *m* de carga
containerize [kən'teɪnəraɪz] VT containerizar
contaminate [kən'tæmɪneɪt] VT contaminar
contamination [kəntæmɪ'neɪʃən] N
contaminação *f*
cont'd ABBR = **continued**
contemplate ['kɔntəmpleɪt] VT (*idea*)
considerar; (*person, painting etc*) contemplar;
(*expect*) contar com; (*intend*) pretender, pensar
em
contemplation [kɔntəm'pleɪʃən] N
contemplação *f*
contemporary [kən'tɛmpərərɪ] ADJ
contemporâneo; (*design etc*) moderno ■ N
contemporâneo(-a)
contempt [kən'tɛmpt] N desprezo; **contempt
of court** (*Law*) N desacato à autoridade do
tribunal
contemptible [kən'tɛmptəbl] ADJ desprezível
contemptuous [kən'tɛmptjuəs] ADJ
desdenhoso
contend [kən'tɛnd] VT (*assert*): **to ~ that**
afirmar que ■ VI: **to ~ with** (*struggle*) lutar com;
(*difficulty*) enfrentar; (*compete*): **to ~ for** competir
por; **to have to ~ with** arcar com, lidar com;
he has a lot to ~ with ele tem muito o que
enfrentar
contender [kən'tɛndə^r] N contendor(a) *m/f*
content [*adj, vt* kən'tɛnt, *n* 'kɔntɛnt] ADJ (*happy*)
contente; (*satisfied*) satisfeito ■ VT contentar,
satisfazer ■ N conteúdo; (*fat content, moisture
content etc*) quantidade *f*; **contents** NPL (*of
packet, book*) conteúdo; (**table of**) **~s** índice *m*
das matérias; **to be ~ with** estar contente or
satisfeito com; **to ~ o.s. with sth/with doing
sth** contentar-se com algo/em fazer algo
contented [kən'tɛntɪd] ADJ contente, satisfeito
contentedly [kən'tɛntɪdlɪ] ADV contentemente
contention [kən'tɛnʃən] N (*assertion*) asserção
f; (*disagreement*) contenda; **bone of ~** pomo da
discórdia
contentious [kən'tɛnʃəs] ADJ controvertido
contentment [kən'tɛntmənt] N
contentamento
contest [*n* 'kɔntɛst, *vt* kən'tɛst] N contenda;
(*competition*) concurso ■ VT (*dispute*) disputar;
(*legal case*) defender; (*Pol*) ser candidato a;
(*competition*) disputar; (*statement, decision*)
contestar
contestant [kən'tɛstənt] N competidor(a) *m/f*;
(*in fight*) adversário(-a)
context ['kɔntɛkst] N contexto; **in/out of ~** em/
fora de contexto
continent ['kɔntɪnənt] N continente *m*; **the
C~** (*Brit*) o continente europeu; **on the C~** na
Europa (*continental*)
continental [kɔntɪ'nɛntl] ADJ continental ■ N
(*Brit*) europeu(-péia) *m/f*; **continental breakfast**
N café *m* da manhã (BR), pequeno almoço (PT)

(*de pão, geléia e café*); **continental quilt** (*Brit*) N
edredom *m* (BR), edredão *m* (PT)
contingency [kən'tɪndʒənsɪ] N contingência;
contingency plan N plano de contingência
contingent [kən'tɪndʒənt] N contingente *m*
■ ADJ contingente; **to be ~ upon** depender de
continual [kən'tɪnjuəl] ADJ contínuo
continually [kən'tɪnjuəlɪ] ADV constantemente
continuation [kəntɪnju'eɪʃən] N
prolongamento; (*after interruption*) continuação
f, retomada
continue [kən'tɪnju:] VI prosseguir, continuar
■ VT continuar; (*start again*) recomeçar,
retomar; **to be ~d** (*story*) segue; **~d on page 10**
continua na página 10
continuity [kɔntɪ'njuːɪtɪ] N (*also: Cinema, TV*)
continuidade *f*; **continuity girl** N (*Cinema*)
continuista
continuous [kən'tɪnjuəs] ADJ contínuo; **~
performance** (*Cinema*) sessão *f* contínua; **~
stationery** (*Comput*) formulários *mpl* contínuos
continuously [kən'tɪnjuəslɪ] ADV (*repeatedly*)
repetidamente; (*uninterruptedly*) continuamente
contort [kən'tɔːt] VT contorcer
contortion [kən'tɔːʃən] N contorção *f*
contortionist [kən'tɔːʃənɪst] N
contorcionista *m/f*
contour ['kɔntuə^r] N (*outline: gen pl*) contorno;
(*also:* **contour line**) curva de nível
contraband ['kɔntrəbænd] N contrabando
■ ADJ de contrabando, contrabandeado
contraception [kɔntrə'sɛpʃən] N
anticoncepção *f*
contraceptive [kɔntrə'sɛptɪv] ADJ
anticoncepcional ■ N anticoncepcional *f*
contract [*n, cpd* 'kɔntrækt, *vt, vi* kən'trækt] N
contrato ■ CPD (*price, date*) contratual; (*work*)
de empreitada ■ VI (*become smaller*) contrair-
se, encolher-se; (*Comm*): **to ~ to do sth**
comprometer-se por contrato a fazer algo ■ VT
contrair; **~ of employment** or **service** contrato
de trabalho, ≈ vínculo empregatício
▶ **contract in** VI comprometer-se por contrato
▶ **contract out** VI desobrigar-se por contrato;
(*from pension scheme*) optar por não participar
contraction [kən'trækʃən] N contração *f*
contractor [kən'træktə^r] N contratante *m/f*
contractual [kən'træktʃuəl] ADJ contratual
contradict [kɔntrə'dɪkt] VT contradizer,
desmentir
contradiction [kɔntrə'dɪkʃən] N contradição *f*;
to be in ~ with contradizer
contradictory [kɔntrə'dɪktərɪ] ADJ
contraditório
contralto [kən'træltəu] N contralto
contraption [kən'træpʃən] (*pej*) N engenhoca,
geringonça
contrary[1] ['kɔntrərɪ] ADJ contrário ■ N
contrário; **on the ~** muito pelo contrário;
unless you hear to the ~ salvo aviso contrário;
~ to what we thought ao contrário do que
pensamos

contrary² [kən'trɛərɪ] ADJ teimoso

contrast [n 'kɔntrɑːst, vt kən'trɑːst] N contraste m ▪ VT comparar; **in ~ to** or **with** em contraste com, ao contrário de

contrasting [kən'trɑːstɪŋ] ADJ contrastante

contravene [kɔntrə'viːn] VT infringir

contravention [kəntrə'vɛnʃən] N contravenção f, infração f

contribute [kən'trɪbjuːt] VT contribuir ▪ VI dar; **to ~ to** (charity) contribuir para; (newspaper) escrever para; (discussion) participar de

contribution [kɔntrɪ'bjuːʃən] N (donation) doação f; (Brit: for social security) contribuição f; (to debate) intervenção f; (to journal) colaboração f

contributor [kən'trɪbjuːtə'] N (to newspaper) colaborador(a) m/f

contributory [kən'trɪbjutərɪ] ADJ: **it was a ~ factor in ...** era um fator que contribuiu para ...; **contributory pension scheme** (Brit) N sistema m de pensão contributária

contrite ['kɔntraɪt] ADJ arrependido, contrito

contrivance [kən'traɪvəns] N (scheme) maquinação f; (device) aparelho, dispositivo

contrive [kən'traɪv] VT (invent) idealizar; (carry out) efetuar; (plot) tramar ▪ VI: **to ~ to do** chegar a fazer

control [kən'trəul] VT controlar; (traffic etc) dirigir; (machinery) regular; (temper) dominar ▪ N controle m; (of car) direção f (BR), condução f (PT); (check) freio, controle; **controls** NPL (of vehicle) mando; (on radio, television etc) controle; **to take ~ of** assumir o controle de; **to be in ~ of** ter o controle de; (in charge of) ser responsável por; **to ~ o.s.** controlar-se; **out of/under ~** fora de/ sob controle; **through circumstances beyond our ~** por motivos alheios à nossa vontade; **control key** N (Comput) tecla de controle

controller [kən'trəulə'] N controlador(a) m/f

controlling interest [kən'trəulɪŋ-] N (Comm) controle m acionário

control panel N painel m de instrumentos

control point N ponto de controle

control room N sala de comando; (Radio, TV) sala de controle

control tower N (Aviat) torre f de controle

control unit N (Comput) unidade f de controle

controversial [kɔntrə'vəːʃl] ADJ controvertido, polêmico

controversy ['kɔntrəvəːsɪ] N controvérsia, polêmica

conurbation [kɔnə'beɪʃən] N conurbação f

convalesce [kɔnvə'lɛs] VI convalescer

convalescence [kɔnvə'lɛsns] N convalescença

convalescent [kɔnvə'lɛsnt] ADJ, N convalescente m/f

convector [kən'vɛktə'] N (heater) aquecedor m de convecção

convene [kən'viːn] VT convocar ▪ VI convocar-se

convener [kən'viːnə'] N organizador(a) m/f

convenience [kən'viːnɪəns] N (easiness) facilidade f; (suitability) conveniência; (comfort) comodidade f; (advantage) vantagem f, conveniência; **at your ~** quando lhe convier; **at your earliest ~** (Comm) o mais cedo que lhe for possível; **all modern ~s** (also: Brit: all mod cons) com todos os confortos; **convenience foods** NPL alimentos mpl semiprontos

convenient [kən'viːnɪənt] ADJ conveniente; (useful) útil; (place) acessível; (time) oportuno, conveniente; **if it is ~ to you** se isso lhe convier, se isso não lhe for incômodo

conveniently [kən'viːnɪəntlɪ] ADV convenientemente

convent ['kɔnvənt] N convento

convention [kən'vɛnʃən] N (custom) costume m; (agreement) convenção f; (meeting) assembléia

conventional [kən'vɛnʃənl] ADJ convencional

convent school N colégio de freiras

converge [kən'vəːdʒ] VI convergir; (people): **to ~ on** convergir para

conversant [kən'vəːsnt] ADJ: **to be ~ with** estar familiarizado com

conversation [kɔnvə'seɪʃən] N conversação f, conversa

conversational [kɔnvə'seɪʃənl] ADJ de conversa; (familiar) familiar; (talkative) loquaz; (Comput) conversacional, interativo

conversationalist [kɔnvə'seɪʃnəlɪst] N conversador(a) m/f; **she's a good ~** ela tem muita conversa

converse [n 'kɔnvəːs, vi kən'vəːs] N inverso ▪ VI conversar

conversely [kɔn'vəːslɪ] ADV pelo contrário, inversamente

conversion [kən'vəːʃən] N conversão f; (Brit: of house) transformação f; **conversion table** N tabela de conversão

convert [vt kən'vəːt, n 'kɔnvəːt] VT converter ▪ N convertido(-a)

convertible [kən'vəːtəbl] ADJ convertível ▪ N conversível m

convex [kɔn'vɛks] ADJ convexo

convey [kən'veɪ] VT transportar, levar; (thanks) expressar; (information) deixar claro

conveyance [kən'veɪəns] N (of goods) transporte m; (vehicle) meio de transporte, veículo

conveyancing [kən'veɪənsɪŋ] N (Law) transferência de bens imóveis

conveyor belt [kənveɪə'-] N correia transportadora

convict [vt kən'vɪkt, n 'kɔnvɪkt] VT condenar; (sentence) declarar culpado ▪ N presidiário

conviction [kən'vɪkʃən] N condenação f; (belief) convicção f; (certainty) certeza

convince [kən'vɪns] VT (assure) assegurar; (persuade) convencer; **to ~ sb of sth/that** convencer alguém de algo/de que

convinced [kən'vɪnst] ADJ: **~ of/that** convencido de/de que

convincing [kən'vɪnsɪŋ] ADJ convincente

convincingly [kən'vɪnsɪŋlɪ] ADV convincentemente

convivial [kən'vɪvɪəl] ADJ jovial, alegre

convoluted ['kɔnvəluːtɪd] ADJ (*shape*) curvilíneo; (*argument*) complicado

convoy ['kɔnvɔɪ] N escolta

convulse [kən'vʌls] VT convulsionar; **to be ~d with laughter/pain** morrer de rir/dor

convulsion [kən'vʌlʃən] N convulsão f; (*laughter*) ataque m, acesso

coo [kuː] VI arrulhar; (*person*) falar suavemente

cook [kuk] VT cozinhar; (*meal*) preparar ■ VI cozinhar ■ N cozinheiro(-a)
▸ **cook up** (*inf*) VT (*excuse, story*) bolar

cookbook ['kukbuk] N livro de receitas

cooker ['kukəʳ] N fogão m

cookery ['kukərɪ] N (*dishes*) cozinha; (*art*) culinária; **cookery book** (*Brit*) N = **cookbook**

cookie ['kukɪ] (*US*) N bolacha, biscoito

cooking ['kukɪŋ] N cozinha ■ CPD (*apples, chocolate*) para cozinhar; (*utensils, salt*) de cozinha

cookout ['kukaut] (*US*) N churrasco

cool [kuːl] ADJ fresco; (*not hot*) tépido; (*calm*) calmo; (*unfriendly*) frio ■ VT resfriar ■ VI esfriar; **it's ~** (*weather*) está fresco
▸ **cool down** VI esfriar; (*fig: person, situation*) acalmar-se

cool box (*Brit*) N mala frigorífica

cooler ['kuːləʳ] (*US*) N mala frigorífica

cooling tower ['kuːlɪŋ-] N torre f de esfriamento

coolly ['kuːlɪ] ADV (*calmly*) calmamente; (*audaciously*) descaradamente; (*unenthusiastically*) friamente

coolness ['kuːlnɪs] N frescura; (*hostility*) frieza; (*indifference*) indiferença

coop [kuːp] N (*for poultry*) galinheiro; (*for rabbits*) capoeira
▸ **coop up** VT (*fig*) confinar

co-op ['kəuɔp] N ABBR = **cooperative (society)**

cooperate [kəu'ɔpəreit] VI colaborar; (*assist*) ajudar

cooperation [kəuɔpə'reɪʃən] N cooperação f, colaboração f

cooperative [kəu'ɔpərətɪv] ADJ cooperativo ■ N cooperativa

coopt [kəu'ɔpt] VT: **to ~ sb onto a committee** cooptar alguém para fazer parte de um comitê

coordinate [vt kəu'ɔːdɪneɪt, n kəu'ɔːdɪnət] VT coordenar ■ N (*Math*) coordenada; **coordinates** NPL (*clothes*) coordenados mpl

coordination [kəuɔːdɪ'neɪʃən] N coordenação f

coot [kuːt] N galeirão m

co-ownership [kəu-] N co-propriedade f, condomínio

cop [kɔp] (*inf*) N policial m/f (BR), polícia m/f (PT), tira m (*inf*)

cope [kəup] VI sair-se, dar-se; **to ~ with** poder com, arcar com; (*problem*) estar à altura de

Copenhagen ['kəupn'heɪgən] N Copenhague

copier ['kɔpɪəʳ] N (*also: photocopier*) copiador m

co-pilot [kəu-] N co-piloto(-a)

copious ['kəupɪəs] ADJ copioso, abundante

copper ['kɔpəʳ] N (*metal*) cobre m; (*inf: policeman/ woman*) polícia m/f; **coppers** NPL (*coins*) moedas fpl de pouco valor

coppice ['kɔpɪs] N bosquete m

copse [kɔps] N = **coppice**

copulate ['kɔpjuleɪt] VI copular

copulation [kɔpju'leɪʃən] N cópula

copy ['kɔpɪ] N cópia; (*duplicate*) duplicata; (*of book etc*) exemplar m; (*of writing*) originais mpl ■ VT copiar; (*imitate*) imitar; **to make good ~** (*Press*) fazer uma boa matéria
▸ **copy out** VT copiar

copycat ['kɔpɪkæt] (*inf*) N macaco

copyright ['kɔpɪraɪt] N direitos mpl de autor, direitos autorais, copirraite m; **~ reserved** todos os direitos reservados

copy typist N datilógrafo(-a)

copywriter ['kɔpɪraɪtəʳ] N redator(a) m/f de material publicitário

coral ['kɔrəl] N coral m; **coral reef** N recife m de coral

Coral Sea N: **the ~** o mar de Coral

cord [kɔːd] N corda; (*Elec*) fio, cabo; (*fabric*) veludo cotelê; **cords** NPL (*trousers*) calça (BR) *or* calças fpl (PT) de veludo cotelê

cordial ['kɔːdɪəl] ADJ cordial ■ N cordial m

cordless ['kɔːdlɪs] ADJ sem fio

cordon ['kɔːdn] N cordão m
▸ **cordon off** VT isolar

corduroy ['kɔːdərɔɪ] N veludo cotelê

CORE [kɔːʳ] (*US*) N ABBR = **Congress of Racial Equality**

core [kɔːʳ] N centro, núcleo; (*of fruit*) caroço; (*of problem*) âmago ■ VT descaroçar; **rotten to the ~** completamente podre

Corfu [kɔː'fuː] N Corfu f (*no article*)

coriander [kɔrɪ'ændəʳ] N coentro

cork [kɔːk] N rolha; (*tree*) cortiça

corkage ['kɔːkɪdʒ] N *taxa cobrada num restaurante pela abertura das garrafas levadas pelo cliente*

corked [kɔːkt] (*Brit*) ADJ que tem gosto de rolha

corkscrew ['kɔːkskruː] N saca-rolhas m inv

corky ['kɔːkɪ] (*US*) ADJ que tem gosto de rolha

cormorant ['kɔːmərnt] N cormorão m, corvo marinho

corn [kɔːn] N (*Brit: wheat*) trigo; (*US: maize*) milho; (*cereals*) grão m, cereal m; (*on foot*) calo; **~ on the cob** (*Culin*) espiga de milho

cornea ['kɔːnɪə] N córnea

corned beef ['kɔːnd-] N carne f de boi enlatada

corner ['kɔːnəʳ] N (*outside*) esquina; (*inside*) canto; (*in road*) curva; (*Football etc: also:* **corner kick**) córner m ■ VT (*trap*) encurralar; (*Comm*) açambarcar, monopolizar ■ VI (*in car*) fazer uma curva; **to cut ~s** (*fig*) matar o serviço; **corner flag** N (*Football*) bandeira de escanteio; **corner kick** N (*Football*) córner m

cornerstone ['kɔːnəstəun] N pedra angular; (*fig*) base f, fundamento

cornet ['kɔːnɪt] N (*Mus*) cornetim m; (*Brit: of ice-cream*) casquinha

cornflakes ['kɔːnfleɪks] NPL flocos mpl de milho

cornflour ['kɔːnflauəʳ] (*Brit*) N farinha de milho,

maisena®
cornice ['kɔːnɪs] N cornija
Cornish ['kɔːnɪʃ] ADJ de Cornualha ∎ N (Ling) córnico
corn oil N óleo de milho
cornstarch ['kɔːnstɑːtʃ] (US) N = cornflour
cornucopia [kɔːnjuˈkəupɪə] N cornucópia
Cornwall ['kɔːnwəl] N Cornualha
corny ['kɔːnɪ] (inf) ADJ velho, gasto
corollary [kəˈrɔlərɪ] N corolário
coronary ['kɔrənərɪ] N: ~ (thrombosis) trombose f (coronária)
coronation [kɔrəˈneɪʃən] N coroação f
coroner ['kɔrənəʳ] N magistrado que investiga mortes suspeitas
coronet ['kɔrənɪt] N coroa aberta, diadema m
Corp. ABBR = corporation
corporal ['kɔːpərl] N cabo ∎ ADJ corpóreo; ~ punishment castigo corporal
corporate ['kɔːpərɪt] ADJ corporativo; (action, ownership) coletivo; (Comm: of a company) da empresa; corporate identity N imagem f da empresa; corporate image N imagem f da empresa
corporation [kɔːpəˈreɪʃən] N (of town) município, junta; (Comm) sociedade f; corporation tax N imposto sobre a renda de sociedades
corps [kɔːʳ, pl kɔːz] (pl corps) N (Mil) unidade f; (diplomatic) corpo; the press ~ a imprensa
corpse [kɔːps] N cadáver m
corpuscle ['kɔːpʌsl] N corpúsculo
corral [kəˈrɑːl] N curral m
correct [kəˈrɛkt] ADJ exato; (proper) correto ∎ VT corrigir; you are ~ você tem razão
correction [kəˈrɛkʃən] N correção f; (erasure) emenda
correlate ['kɔrɪleɪt] VT correlacionar ∎ VI: to ~ with corresponder a
correlation [kɔrɪˈleɪʃən] N correlação f
correspond [kɔrɪsˈpɔnd] VI (write): to ~ (with) corresponder-se (com); (be equal to): to ~ to corresponder a; (be in accordance): to ~ (with) corresponder a
correspondence [kɔrɪsˈpɔndəns] N correspondência; (relationship) relação f; correspondence course N curso por correspondência
correspondent [kɔrɪsˈpɔndənt] N correspondente m/f
corresponding [kɔrɪsˈpɔndɪŋ] ADJ correspondente
corridor ['kɔrɪdɔːʳ] N corredor m
corroborate [kəˈrɔbəreɪt] VT corroborar
corrode [kəˈrəud] VT corroer ∎ VI corroer-se
corrosion [kəˈrəuʒən] N corrosão f
corrosive [kəˈrəuzɪv] ADJ corrosivo
corrugated ['kɔrəgeɪtɪd] ADJ corrugado; corrugated iron N chapa ondulada or corrugada
corrupt [kəˈrʌpt] ADJ corrupto ∎ VT corromper; (bribe) subornar; (data) corromper, destruir; ~ practices corrupção f

corruption [kəˈrʌpʃən] N corrupção f; (of data) destruição f
corset ['kɔːsɪt] N espartilho; (Med) colete m
Corsica ['kɔːsɪkə] N Córsega
Corsican ['kɔːsɪkən] ADJ, N córsico(-a)
cortège [kɔːˈtɛːʒ] N séquito, cortejo
cortisone ['kɔːtɪzəun] N cortisona
coruscating ['kɔrəskeɪtɪŋ] ADJ cintilante
c.o.s. ABBR (= cash on shipment) pagamento na expedição
cosh [kɔʃ] (Brit) N cassetete m
cosignatory ['kəuˈsɪgnətərɪ] N co-signatário(-a)
cosiness ['kəuzɪnɪs] (US coziness) N conforto; (atmosphere) aconchego, conforto
cos lettuce [kɔs-] N alface m (cos)
cosmetic [kɔzˈmɛtɪk] N cosmético ∎ ADJ (preparation) cosmético; (fig: measure, improvement) simbólico, superficial; ~ surgery cirurgia plástica embelezadora
cosmic ['kɔzmɪk] ADJ cósmico
cosmonaut ['kɔzmənɔːt] N cosmonauta m/f
cosmopolitan [kɔzməˈpɔlɪtn] ADJ cosmopolita
cosmos ['kɔzmɔs] N cosmo
cosset ['kɔsɪt] VT paparicar
cost [kɔst] (pt, pp cost) N (gen) custo; (price) preço ∎ VI custar ∎ VT custar; (determine cost of) determinar o custo de; costs NPL (Law, Comm) custas fpl; at the ~ of à custa de; how much does it ~? quanto custa?; it ~s £5/too much custa £5/é muito caro; to ~ sb time/effort custar tempo/esforço a alguém; it ~ him his life/job custou-lhe a vida/o emprego; the ~ of living o custo de vida; at all ~s custe o que custar; cost accountant N contador(a) m/f de custos
co-star [kəu-] N co-estrela m/f
Costa Rica [kɔstəˈriːkə] N Costa Rica
Costa Rican ['kɔstəˈriːkən] ADJ, N costarriquenho(-a)
cost centre N centro de custo
cost control N controle m dos custos
cost-effective ADJ rentável
cost-effectiveness N rentabilidade f
costly ['kɔstlɪ] ADJ (expensive) caro, custoso; (valuable) suntuoso
cost-of-living ADJ: ~ allowance ajuda de custo; ~ index índice m de preços ao consumidor
cost price (Brit) N preço de custo
costume ['kɔstjuːm] N traje m; (Brit: woman's: also: swimming costume) maiô m (BR), fato de banho (PT); (man's) calção m (de banho) (BR), calções mpl de banho (PT); costume jewellery N bijuteria
cosy ['kəuzi] (US cozy) ADJ cômodo; (atmosphere) aconchegante; (life) folgado, confortável
cot [kɔt] N (Brit: child's) cama (de criança), berço; (US: campbed) cama de lona
Cotswolds ['kɔtswəuldz] NPL: the ~ região de colinas em Gloucestershire
cottage ['kɔtɪdʒ] N casa de campo; (rustic) cabana; cottage cheese N ricota (BR), queijo creme (PT); cottage industry N indústria

artesanal; **cottage pie** N *prato de carne picada com batata*
cotton ['kɔtn] N algodão *m*; (*thread*) fio, linha
■ CPD de algodão
▶ **cotton on** (*inf*) VI: **to ~ on (to sth)** sacar (algo)
cotton candy (*US*) N algodão *m* doce
cotton wool (*Brit*) N algodão *m* (hidrófilo)
couch [kautʃ] N sofá *m*; (*doctor's*) cama; (*psychiatrist's*) divã *m* ■ VT formular
couchette [kuː'ʃɛt] N leito
cough [kɔf] VI tossir ■ N tosse *f*
▶ **cough up** VT expelir; (*inf: money*) desembolsar
cough drop N pastilha para a tosse
cough mixture N xarope *m* (para a tosse)
cough syrup N xarope *m* (para a tosse)
could [kud] PT *of* **can**
couldn't ['kudnt] = **could not**
council ['kaunsl] N conselho; **city** *or* **town ~** câmara municipal; **C~ of Europe** Conselho da Europa; **council estate** (*Brit*) N conjunto habitacional; **council house** (*Brit*) N casa popular
councillor ['kaunsələr] N vereador(a) *m/f*
counsel ['kaunsl] N (*advice*) conselho; (*lawyer*) advogado(-a) ■ VT: **to ~ sth/sb to do sth** aconselhar algo/alguém a fazer algo; ~ **for the defence/the prosecution** advogado(-a) *m/f* de defesa/promotor(a) *m/f* público(-a)
counsellor ['kaunsələr] (*US* **counselor**) N conselheiro(-a); (*US: Law*) advogado(-a)
count [kaunt] VT contar; (*include*) incluir ■ VI contar ■ N conta; (*of votes etc*) contagem *f*; (*of pollen, alcohol*) nível *m*; (*nobleman*) conde *m*; (*sum*) total *m*, soma; **not ~ing the children** sem contar as crianças; **10 ~ing him** 10 contando com ele; **it ~s for very little** conta muito pouco; ~ **yourself lucky** considere-se sortudo; **that doesn't ~!** isso não vale!
▶ **count on** VT FUS contar com; **to ~ on doing sth** contar em fazer algo
▶ **count up** VT contar
countdown ['kauntdaun] N contagem *f* regressiva
countenance ['kauntɪnəns] N expressão *f* ■ VT tolerar
counter ['kauntər] N (*in shop*) balcão *m*; (*in post office etc*) guichê *m*; (*in games*) ficha ■ VT contrariar; (*blow*) parar ■ ADV: ~ **to** ao contrário de; **to buy under the ~** (*fig*) comprar por baixo do pano or da mesa
counteract [kauntər'ækt] VT neutralizar
counterattack ['kauntərətæk] N contra-ataque *m* ■ VI contra-atacar
counterbalance [kauntə'bæləns] N contrapeso
counter-clockwise ADV ao contrário dos ponteiros do relógio
counter-espionage N contra-espionagem *f*
counterfeit ['kauntəfɪt] N falsificação *f* ■ VT falsificar ■ ADJ falso, falsificado
counterfoil ['kauntəfɔɪl] N canhoto (BR), talão *m* (PT)

counterintelligence ['kauntərɪn'tɛlɪdʒəns] N contra-informacão *f*
countermand ['kauntəmɑːnd] VT revogar
countermeasure ['kauntəmɛʒər] N contramedida
counteroffensive ['kauntərə'fɛnsɪv] N contraofensiva
counterpane ['kauntəpeɪn] N colcha
counterpart ['kauntəpɑːt] N contrapartida; (*of person*) sósia *m/f*; (: *opposite number*) homólogo(-a)
counterproductive ['kauntəprə'dʌktɪv] ADJ contraproducente
counterproposal ['kauntəprə'pəuzl] N contraproposta
countersign ['kauntəsaɪn] VT autenticar
countersink ['kauntəsɪŋk] (*irreg: like* **sink**) VT escarear
countess ['kauntɪs] N condessa
countless ['kauntlɪs] ADJ inumerável
countrified ['kʌntrɪfaɪd] ADJ bucólico, rústico
country ['kʌntrɪ] N país *m*; (*nation*) nação *f*; (*native land*) terra; (*as opposed to town*) campo; (*region*) região *f*, terra; **in the ~** no campo; (*esp in Brazil*) no interior; **mountainous ~** região montanhosa; **country and western (music)** N música country; **country dancing** (*Brit*) N dança regional; **country house** (*irreg*) N casa de campo
countryman ['kʌntrɪmən] N (*national*) compatriota *m*; (*rural*) camponês *m*
countryside ['kʌntrɪsaɪd] N campo
country-wide ADJ em todo o país; (*problem*) de escala nacional ■ ADV em todo o país
county ['kauntɪ] N condado; **county town** (Brit) N capital *f* do condado
coup [kuː] N golpe *m* de mestre; (*also*: **coup d'état**) golpe (de estado)
coupé ['kuːpeɪ] N (*Aut*) cupê *m*
couple ['kʌpl] N (*of things, people*) par *m*; (*married couple, courting couple*) casal *m* ■ VT (*ideas, names*) unir, juntar; (*machinery*) ligar, juntar; **a ~ of** um par de; (*a few*) alguns/algumas
couplet ['kʌplɪt] N dístico
coupling ['kʌplɪŋ] N (*Rail*) engate *m*
coupon ['kuːpɔn] N cupom *m* (BR), cupão *m* (PT); (*pools coupon*) talão *m*; (*voucher*) vale *m*
courage ['kʌrɪdʒ] N coragem *f*
courageous [kə'reɪdʒəs] ADJ corajoso
courgette [kuə'ʒɛt] (Brit) N abobrinha
courier ['kurɪər] N correio; (*diplomatic*) mala; (*for tourists*) guia *m/f*, agente *m/f* de turismo
course [kɔːs] N (*direction*) direção *f*; (*process*) desenvolvimento; (*of river, Sch*) curso; (*of ship*) rumo; (*of bullet*) trajetória; (*fig*) procedimento; (*Golf*) campo; (*part of meal*) prato; **of ~** naturalmente; (*certainly*) certamente; **of ~!** claro!, lógico!; **(no) of ~ not!** claro que não!; **in due ~** oportunamente, no devido tempo; **first ~** entrada; **in the ~ of the next few days** no decorrer dos próximos dias; **the best ~ would be to do ...** o melhor seria fazer ...; **we have no other ~ but to ...** não temos nenhuma outra

opção, senão ...; **course of action** N atitude f

court [kɔ:t] N (royal) corte f; (Law) tribunal m; (Tennis etc) quadra ■ VT (woman) cortejar, namorar; (danger etc) procurar; **out of ~** (Law: settle) extrajudicialmente; **to take to ~** demandar, levar a julgamento; **~ of appeal** tribunal de recursos

courteous ['kə:tɪəs] ADJ cortês(-esa)

courtesan [kɔ:tɪ'zæn] N cortesã f

courtesy ['kə:təsɪ] N cortesia; **(by) ~ of** com permissão de; **courtesy coach** N ônibus m (BR) or autocarro (PT) gratuito; **courtesy light** N (Aut) luz f interior

court-house (US) N palácio de justiça

courtier ['kɔ:tɪəʳ] N cortesão m

court martial (pl **courts martial**) N conselho de guerra ■ VT submeter a conselho de guerra

courtroom ['kɔ:trum] N sala de tribunal

court shoe N escarpim m

courtyard ['kɔ:tjɑ:d] N pátio

cousin ['kʌzn] N primo(-a) m/f; **first ~** primo(-mã) irmão(-a)

cove [kəuv] N angra, enseada

covenant ['kʌvənənt] N convênio ■ VT: **to ~ £2000 per year to a charity** comprometer-se a doar £2000 por ano para uma obra de caridade

Coventry ['kɔvəntrɪ] N: **to send sb to ~** (fig) relegar alguém ao ostracismo

cover ['kʌvəʳ] VT (gen, Press, costs) cobrir; (with lid) tapar; (chairs etc) revestir; (distance) percorrer; (include) abranger; (protect) abrigar; (issues) tratar ■ N (gen, Press, Comm) cobertura; (lid) tampa; (for chair etc) capa; (for bed) cobertor m; (envelope) envelope m; (of book, magazine) capa; (shelter) abrigo; (Insurance) cobertura; **to take ~** abrigar-se; **under ~** (indoors) abrigado; **under ~ of** sob o abrigo de; (fig) sob capa de; **under separate ~** (Comm) em separado; **£10 will ~ everything** £10 vão dar para tudo

▶ **cover up** VT (person, object): **to ~ up (with)** cobrir (com); (fig: truth, facts) abafar, encobrir ■ VI: **to ~ up for sb** (fig) cobrir alguém

coverage ['kʌvərɪdʒ] N (Press, Insurance) cobertura

cover charge N couvert m

covering ['kʌvərɪŋ] N cobertura; (of snow, dust etc) comada; **covering letter** (US **cover letter**) N carta de cobertura

cover note N (Insurance) nota de cobertura

cover price N preço de capa

covert ['kəuvə:t] ADJ (threat) velado; (action) oculto, secreto

cover-up N encobrimento (dos fatos)

covet ['kʌvɪt] VT cobiçar

cow [kau] N vaca ■ CPD fêmea ■ VT intimidar

coward ['kauəd] N covarde m/f

cowardice ['kauədɪs] N covardia

cowardly ['kauədlɪ] ADJ covarde

cowboy ['kaubɔɪ] N vaqueiro

cower ['kauəʳ] VI encolher-se (de medo)

cowshed ['kauʃɛd] N estábulo

cowslip ['kauslɪp] N (Bot) primavera

cox [kɔks] N ABBR = **coxswain**

coxswain ['kɔksn] N timoneiro(-a)

coy [kɔɪ] ADJ tímido

coyote [kɔɪ'əutɪ] N coiote m

coziness ['kəuzɪnɪs] (US) N = **cosiness**

cozy ['kəuzɪ] (US) ADJ = **cosy**

CP N ABBR (= Communist Party) PC m

cp. ABBR (= compare) cp

c/p (Brit) ABBR = **carriage paid**

CPA (US) N ABBR = **certified public accountant**

CPI N ABBR (= Consumer Price Index) IPC m

Cpl. ABBR = **Corporal**

CP/M N ABBR (= Central Program for Microprocessors) CP/M m

c.p.s. ABBR (= characters per second) c.p.s

CPSA (Brit) N ABBR (= Civil and Public Services Association) sindicato dos funcionários públicos

CPU N ABBR (= Central Processing Unit) CPU f

cr. ABBR = **credit; creditor**

crab [kræb] N caranguejo; **crab apple** N maçã ácida

crack [kræk] N rachadura; (gap) brecha; (noise) estalo; (joke) piada; (Drugs) crack m; (inf: attempt): **to have a ~ (at sth)** tentar (fazer algo) ■ VT quebrar; (nut) partir, descascar; (wall) rachar; (safe) arrombar; (whip etc) estalar; (knuckles) estalar, partir; (joke) soltar; (mystery) resolver; (code) decifrar ■ ADJ (expert) de primeira classe; **to get ~ing** (inf) pôr mãos à obra

▶ **crack down on** VT FUS (crime) ser linha dura com; (spending) cortar

▶ **crack up** VI (Psych) sofrer um colapso nervoso

crackdown ['krækdaun] N: **~ (on)** (on crime) endurecimento (em relação a); (on spending) arrocho (a)

cracked [krækt] (inf) ADJ doido

cracker ['krækəʳ] N (biscuit) biscoito; (Christmas cracker) busca-pé-surpresa m; (firework) busca-pé m; **a ~ of a ...** (Brit: inf) um(a) ... sensacional

crackers ['krækəz] (Brit: inf) ADJ: **he's ~** ele é maluco

crackle ['krækl] VI crepitar

crackling ['kræklɪŋ] N (of fire) crepitação f; (of leaves etc) estalidos mpl; (of pork) torresmo

cradle ['kreɪdl] N berço ■ VT (child) embalar; (object) segurar com cuidado

craft [krɑ:ft] N (skill) arte f; (trade) ofício; (cunning) astúcia; (boat) barco

craftsman ['krɑ:ftsmən] (irreg) N artífice m, artesão m

craftsmanship ['krɑ:ftsmənʃɪp] N (quality) qualidada f

craftsmen ['krɑ:ftsmɛn] NPL of **craftsman**

crafty ['krɑ:ftɪ] ADJ astuto, malandro, esperto

crag [kræg] N penhasco

cram [kræm] VT (fill): **to ~ sth with** encher or abarrotar algo de; (put): **to ~ sth into** enfiar algo em ■ VI (for exams) estudar na última hora

cramming ['kræmɪŋ] N (for exams) virada final

cramp [kræmp] N (Med) cãibra; (Tech) grampo ■ VT (limit) restringir; (annoy) estorvar

cramped [kræmpt] ADJ apertado, confinado

crampon ['kræmpən] N gato de ferro

cranberry ['krænbərɪ] N oxicoco

crane [kreɪn] N (*Tech*) guindaste *m*; (*bird*) grou *m* ■ VT, VI: **to ~ forward, to ~ one's neck** espichar-se, espichar o pescoço

crania ['kreɪnɪə] NPL *of* **cranium**

cranium ['kreɪnɪəm] (*pl* **crania**) N crânio

crank [kræŋk] N manivela; (*person*) excêntrico(-a)

crankshaft ['kræŋkʃɑːft] N virabrequim *m*

cranky ['kræŋkɪ] ADJ (*eccentric*) excêntrico; (*bad-tempered*) irritadiço

cranny ['krænɪ] N *see* **nook**

crap [kræp] (*inf!*) N papo furado; **to have a ~** cagar (*!*)

crash [kræʃ] N (*noise*) estrondo; (*of cars etc*) batida; (*of plane*) desastre *m* de avião; (*Comm*) falência, quebra; (*Stock Exchange*) craque *m* ■ VT (*car*) colidir; (*plane*) cair, espatifar ■ VI bater; cair, espatifar-se; (*two cars*) colidir, bater; (*Comm*) falir, quebrar; (*fall noisily*) cair (com estrondo); (*fig*) despencar; **to ~ into** bater em; **he ~ed into a wall** ele bateu com o carro num muro; **crash barrier** (*Brit*) N (*Aut*) cerca de proteção; **crash course** N curso intensivo; **crash helmet** N capacete *m*; **crash landing** N aterrissagem *f* forçada (BR), aterragem *f* forçosa (PT)

crass [kræs] ADJ grosseiro

crate [kreɪt] N caixote *m*; (*inf: old car*) lata-velha; (*for bottles*) engradado

crater ['kreɪtəʳ] N cratera

cravat(e) [krə'væt] N gravata

crave [kreɪv] VT, VI: **to ~ for** ansiar por

craving ['kreɪvɪŋ] N (*of pregnant woman*) desejo

crawl [krɔːl] VI arrastar-se; (*child*) engatinhar; (*vehicle*) arrastar-se a passo de tartaruga ■ N rastejo; (*Swimming*) crawl *m*; **to ~ to sb** (*inf*) puxar o saco de alguém

crayfish ['kreɪfɪʃ] N INV (*freshwater*) camarão *m* d'água doce; (*saltwater*) lagostim *m*

crayon ['kreɪən] N lápis *m* de cera, crayon *m*

craze [kreɪz] N mania; (*fashion*) moda

crazed [kreɪzd] ADJ (*look, person*) enlouquecido; (*pottery, glaze*) craquelê

crazy ['kreɪzɪ] ADJ (*person*) louco, maluco, doido; (*idea*) disparatado; **to go ~** enlouquecer; **to be ~ about sb/sth** (*inf*) ser louco por alguém/algo; **crazy paving** (*Brit*) N pavimento irregular

creak [kriːk] VI chiar, ranger; (*door etc*) ranger

cream [kriːm] N (*of milk*) nata; (*artificial, cosmetic*) creme *m*; (*élite*): **the ~ of** a fina flor de ■ ADJ (*colour*) creme *inv*

▶ **cream off** VT (*fig*) tirar

cream cake N bolo de creme

cream cheese N ricota (BR), queijo creme (PT)

creamery ['kriːmərɪ] N (*shop*) leiteria; (*factory*) fábrica de laticínios

creamy ['kriːmɪ] ADJ (*colour*) cor de creme; (*taste*) cremoso

crease [kriːs] N (*fold*) dobra, vinco; (*in trousers*) vinco; (*wrinkle*) ruga ■ VT (*fold*) dobrar, vincar; (*wrinkle*) amassar, amarrotar ■ VI (*wrinkle up*)

amassar-se, amarrotar-se

crease-resistant ADJ: **a ~ fabric** um tecido que não amarrota

create [kriː'eɪt] VT criar; (*produce*) produzir

creation [kriː'eɪʃən] N criação *f*

creative [kriː'eɪtɪv] ADJ criativo; (*inventive*) inventivo

creativity [kriːeɪ'tɪvɪtɪ] N criatividade *f*

creator [kriː'eɪtəʳ] N criador(a) *m/f*; (*inventor*) inventor(a) *m/f*

creature ['kriːtʃəʳ] N (*animal*) animal *m*, bicho; (*living thing*) criatura

crèche [krɛʃ] N creche *f*

credence ['kriːdns] N: **to lend** *or* **give ~ to** dar crédito a

credentials [krɪ'dɛnʃlz] NPL credenciais *fpl*

credibility [krɛdɪ'bɪlɪtɪ] N credibilidade *f*

credible ['krɛdɪbl] ADJ acreditável; (*trustworthy*) digno de crédito

credit ['krɛdɪt] N (*gen, Comm*) crédito; (*merit*) mérito ■ VT (*believe: also:* **give credit to**) acreditar; (*Comm*) creditar ■ CPD creditício; **credits** NPL (*Cinema, TV*) crédito; **to ~ sb with sth** (*fig*) atribuir algo a alguém; **to ~ £5 to sb** creditar £5 a alguém; **to be in ~** (*person, bank account*) ter fundos; on ~ a crédito; **to one's ~** honra lhe seja; **to take the ~ for sth** atribuir-se o mérito de; **it does him ~** é motivo de honra para ele; **he's a ~ to his family** ele é um orgulho para a família

creditable ['krɛdɪtəbl] ADJ louvável

credit account N conta de crédito

credit agency (*Brit*) N agência de crédito

credit balance N saldo credor

credit bureau (*US: irreg*) N = **credit agency**

credit card N cartão *m* de crédito

credit control N controle *m* de crédito

credit facilities NPL crediário

credit limit N limite *m* de crédito

credit note N nota de crédito

creditor ['krɛdɪtəʳ] N credor(a) *m/f*

credit transfer N transferência

creditworthy ['krɛdɪtwəːðɪ] ADJ merecedor(a) de crédito

credulity [krɪ'djuːlɪtɪ] N credulidade *f*

creed [kriːd] N credo

creek [kriːk] N enseada; (*US*) riacho

creel [kriːl] N cesto de pescador

creep [kriːp] (*pt, pp* **crept**) VI (*animal*) rastejar; (*person*) deslizar(-se); (*plant*) trepar ■ N (*inf*) puxa-saco *m*; **it gives me the ~s** me dá arrepios; **to ~ up on sb** pegar alguém de surpresa

creeper ['kriːpəʳ] N trepadeira; **creepers** NPL (*US: for baby*) macacão *m* (BR), fato macaco (PT)

creepy ['kriːpɪ] ADJ (*frightening*) horripilante

creepy-crawly [-'krɔːlɪ] (*inf*) N bichinho

cremate [krɪ'meɪt] VT cremar

cremation [krɔ'meɪʃən] N cremação *f*

crematoria [krɛmə'tɔːrɪə] NPL *of* **crematorium**

crematorium [krɛmə'tɔːrɪəm] (*pl* **crematoria**) N crematório

creosote ['krɪəsəut] N creosoto

crêpe [kreɪp] N (fabric) crepe m; (paper) papel crepom m; **crêpe bandage** (Brit) N atadura de crepe; **crêpe paper** N papel m crepom; **crêpe sole** N sola de crepe

crept [krɛpt] PT, PP of **creep**

crescendo [krɪˈʃɛndəu] N crescendo

crescent [ˈkrɛsnt] N meia-lua; (street) rua semicircular

cress [krɛs] N agrião m

crest [krɛst] N (of bird) crista; (of hill) cimo, topo; (of helmet) cimeira; (of coat of arms) timbre m

crestfallen [ˈkrɛstfɔːlən] ADJ abatido, cabisbaixo

Crete [kriːt] N Creta

crevasse [krɪˈvæs] N fenda

crevice [ˈkrɛvɪs] N (crack) fenda; (gap) greta

crew [kruː] N (of ship etc) tripulação f; (gang) bando, quadrilha; (Mil) guarnição f; (Cinema) equipe f

crew-cut N corte m à escovinha

crew-neck N gola arredondada

crib [krɪb] N manjedoira, presépio; (US: cot) berço ∎ VT (inf) colar

cribbage [ˈkrɪbɪdʒ] N jogo de cartas

crick [krɪk] N cãibra; ~ **in the neck** torcicolo

cricket [ˈkrɪkɪt] N (insect) grilo; (game) criquete m, cricket m

cricketer [ˈkrɪkɪtər] N jogador(a) m/f de criquete

crime [kraɪm] N (no pl: illegal activities) crime m; (offence) delito; (crime in general) criminalidade f; (fig) pecado, maldade f; **crime wave** N onda de criminalidade

criminal [ˈkrɪmɪnl] N criminoso ∎ ADJ criminal; (law) penal; (morally wrong) imoral; **the C~ Investigation Department** (Brit) a Brigada de Investigação Criminal

crimp [krɪmp] VT (hair) frisar

crimson [ˈkrɪmzn] ADJ carmesim inv

cringe [krɪndʒ] VI encolher-se

crinkle [ˈkrɪŋkl] VT amassar, enrugar

cripple [ˈkrɪpl] N coxo(-a), aleijado(-a) ∎ VT aleijar; (ship, plane) inutilizar; (industry, exports) paralisar

crippling [ˈkrɪplɪŋ] ADJ (disease) devastador(a); (taxation, debts) excessivo

crises [ˈkraɪsiːz] NPL of **crisis**

crisis [ˈkraɪsɪs] (pl **crises**) N crise f

crisp [krɪsp] ADJ (crunchy) crocante; (vegetables, fruit) fresco; (bacon etc) torrado; (manner) seco

crisps [krɪsps] (Brit) NPL batatinhas fpl fritas

criss-cross [krɪs-] ADJ (design) entrecruzado; (pattern) em xadrez ∎ VT entrecruzar; ~ **pattern** padrão m em xadrez m

criteria [kraɪˈtɪərɪə] NPL of **criterion**

criterion [kraɪˈtɪərɪən] (pl **criteria**) N critério

critic [ˈkrɪtɪk] N crítico(-a)

critical [ˈkrɪtɪkl] ADJ crítico; (illness) grave; **to be ~ of sth/sb** criticar algo/alguém

critically [ˈkrɪtɪkəlɪ] ADV (examine) criteriosamente; (speak) criticamente; (ill) gravemente

criticism [ˈkrɪtɪsɪzm] N crítica

criticize [ˈkrɪtɪsaɪz] VT criticar

critique [krɪˈtiːk] N crítica

croak [krəuk] VI (frog) coaxar; (bird) crocitar; (person) falar lugubremente ∎ N grasnido

crochet [ˈkrəuʃeɪ] N crochê m

crock [krɔk] N jarro; (inf: also: **old crock**: person) caco velho; (: car) calhambeque m

crockery [ˈkrɔkərɪ] N louça

crocodile [ˈkrɔkədaɪl] N crocodilo

crocus [ˈkrəukəs] N açafrão-da-primavera m

croft [krɔft] (Brit) N pequena chácara

crofter [ˈkrɔftər] (Brit) N arrendatário

croissant [ˈkrwasã] N croissant m

crone [krəun] N velha encarquilhada

crony [ˈkrəunɪ] (inf: pej) N camarada m/f, compadre m

crook [kruk] N (inf: criminal) vigarista m/f; (of shepherd) cajado; (of arm) curva

crooked [ˈkrukɪd] ADJ (bent) torto; (path) tortuoso; (dishonest) desonesto

crop [krɔp] N (produce) colheita; (amount produced) safra; (riding crop) chicotinho; (of bird) papo ∎ VT cortar

▶ **crop up** VI surgir

cropper [ˈkrɔpər] N: **to come a** ~ (inf) dar com os burros n'água, entrar pelo cano

crop spraying [-ˈspreɪɪŋ] N pulverização f das culturas

croquet [ˈkrəukeɪ] (Brit) N croquet m, croquê m

croquette [krəˈkɛt] N croquete m

cross [krɔs] N cruz f; (hybrid) cruzamento ∎ VT cruzar; (street etc) atravessar; (thwart: person, plan) contrariar ∎ VI atravessar ∎ ADJ zangado, mal-humorado; **to ~ o.s.** persignar-se; **they've got their lines ~ed** eles têm um mal-entendido

▶ **cross out** VT riscar

▶ **cross over** VI atravessar

crossbar [ˈkrɔsbaːr] N travessa; (Sport) barra transversal

crossbreed [ˈkrɔsbriːd] N raça cruzada

cross-Channel ferry N barca que faz a travessia do Canal da Mancha

cross-check N conferição f ∎ VT conferir

cross-country (race) N corrida pelo campo

cross-examination N interrogatório; (Law) repergunta

cross-examine VT interrogar; (Law) reperguntar

cross-eyed [-aɪd] ADJ vesgo

crossfire [ˈkrɔsfaɪər] N fogo cruzado

crossing [ˈkrɔsɪŋ] N (road) cruzamento; (rail) passagem f de nível; (sea passage) travessia; (also: **pedestrian crossing**) faixa (para pedestres) (BR), passadeira (PT); **crossing guard** (US) N guarda m/f para pedestres

cross-purposes NPL: **to be at** ~ **(with sb)** não entender-se (com alguém); **we're (talking) at** ~ não falamos da mesma coisa

cross-reference N referência remissiva

crossroads [ˈkrɔsrəudz] N cruzamento

cross section N (of object) corte m transversal; (of population) grupo representativo

crosswalk ['krɔswɔːk] (US) N faixa (para pedestres) (BR), passadeira (PT)
crosswind ['krɔswɪnd] N vento costal
crosswise ['krɔswaɪz] ADV transversalmente
crossword ['krɔswəːd] N palavras fpl cruzadas
crotch [krɔtʃ] N (of garment) fundilho
crotchet ['krɔtʃɪt] N (Mus) semínima
crotchety ['krɔtʃɪtɪ] ADJ (person) rabugento
crouch [krautʃ] VI agachar-se
croup [kruːp] N (Med) crupe m
croupier ['kruːpɪə] N crupiê m/f
crouton ['kruːtɔn] N crouton m
crow [krəu] N (bird) corvo; (of cock) canto, cocoricó m ■ VI (cock) cantar, cocoricar; (fig) contar vantagem
crowbar ['krəubɑːʳ] N pé-de-cabra m
crowd [kraud] N multidão f; (Sport) público, galera (inf); (unruly) tropel m; (common herd) turba, vulgo ■ VT (fill) apinhar ■ VI (gather) reunir-se; (cram): **to ~ in** encher de; **~s of people** um grande número de pessoas
crowded ['kraudɪd] ADJ (full) lotado; (well-attended) concorrido; (densely populated) densamente populado
crowd scene N (Cinema, Theatre) cena de multidão
crown [kraun] N coroa; (of head, hill) topo; (of hat) copa ■ VT coroar; (tooth) pôr uma coroa artificial em; (fig) rematar; **crown court** (Brit) N Tribunal m de Justiça
crowning ['kraunɪŋ] ADJ (achievement, glory) supremo
crown jewels NPL jóias fpl reais
crown prince N príncipe m herdeiro
crow's-feet NPL pés-de-galinha mpl
crow's-nest N (on ship) cesto de gávea
crucial ['kruːʃl] ADJ (decision) vital; (vote) decisivo; **~ to** vital para
crucifix ['kruːsɪfɪks] N crucifixo
crucifixion [kruːsɪ'fɪkʃən] N crucificação f
crucify ['kruːsɪfaɪ] VT crucificar
crude [kruːd] ADJ (materials) bruto; (fig: basic) tosco; (: vulgar) grosseiro; **crude (oil)** N petróleo em bruto
cruel ['kruəl] ADJ cruel
cruelty ['kruəltɪ] N crueldade f
cruet ['kruːɪt] N galheta
cruise [kruːz] N cruzeiro ■ VI (ship) fazer um cruzeiro; (aircraft) voar; (car): **to ~ at ... km/h** ira ... km por hora; **cruise missile** N míssil m Cruise
cruiser ['kruːzəʳ] N cruzador m
cruising speed ['kruːzɪŋ-] N velocidade f de cruzeiro
crumb [krʌm] N (of bread) migalha; (of cake) farelo
crumble ['krʌmbl] VT esfarelar ■ VI (building, fig) desmoronar-se; (plaster, earth) esfacelar-se; (fig) desintegrar-se
crumbly ['krʌmblɪ] ADJ farelento
crummy ['krʌmɪ] (inf) ADJ mixa; (unwell) podre
crumpet ['krʌmpɪt] N bolo leve
crumple ['krʌmpl] VT (paper) amassar; (material)

amarrotar
crunch [krʌntʃ] VT (food etc) mastigar; (underfoot) esmagar ■ N (fig): **the ~** a momento decisivo
crunchy ['krʌntʃɪ] ADJ crocante
crusade [kruː'seɪd] N cruzada; (campaign) campanha ■ VI (fig): **to ~ for/against** batalhar por/contra
crusader [kruː'seɪdəʳ] N cruzado; (fig): **~ (for)** batalhador(a) m/f (por)
crush [krʌʃ] N (people) esmagamento; (crowd) aglomeração f; (love): **to have a ~ on sb** ter um rabicho por alguém; (drink): **lemon ~** limonada ■ VT (press) esmagar; (squeeze) espremer; (paper) amassar; (cloth) enrugar; (army, opposition) aniquilar; (hopes) destruir; (person) arrasar
crushing ['krʌʃɪŋ] ADJ (burden) esmagador(a)
crust [krʌst] N côdea; (of bread, pastry) casca; (of snow, ice) crosta; (of earth) camada
crustacean [krʌs'teɪʃən] N crustáceo
crusty ['krʌstɪ] ADJ cascudo
crutch [krʌtʃ] N muleta; (of garment: also: crotch) fundilho
crux [krʌks] N ponto crucial
cry [kraɪ] VI chorar; (shout: also: cry out) gritar ■ N grito; **to ~ for help** gritar por socorro; **it's a far ~ from ...** (fig) é totalmente diferente de ...
  ▶ **cry off** VI desistir
crying ['kraɪɪŋ] ADJ (fig) flagrante
crypt [krɪpt] N cripta
cryptic ['krɪptɪk] ADJ enigmático
crystal ['krɪstl] N cristal m
crystal-clear ADJ cristalino, claro
crystallize ['krɪstəlaɪz] VT cristalizar ■ VI cristalizar-se
CSA N ABBR = **Confederate States of America**
CSC N ABBR (= Civil Service Commission) comissão de recrutamento de funcionários públicos
CSE (Brit) N ABBR = **Certificate of Secondary Education**
CS gas (Brit) N gás m CS
CST (US) N ABBR (= Central Standard Time) fuso horário
CT (US) ABBR (Post) = **Connecticut**
ct ABBR = **carat**
cu. ABBR = **cubic**
cub [kʌb] N filhote m; (also: cub scout) lobinho
Cuba ['kjuːbə] N Cuba
Cuban ['kjuːbən] ADJ, N cubano(-a)
cubbyhole ['kʌbɪhəul] N esconderijo
cube [kjuːb] N cubo ■ VT (Math) elevar ao cubo; **cube root** N raiz f cúbica
cubic ['kjuːbɪk] ADJ cúbico; **~ metre etc** metro cúbico etc
cubicle ['kjuːbɪkl] N cubículo; (shower cubicle) boxe m
cuckoo ['kuku:] N cuco; **cuckoo clock** N relógio de cuco
cucumber ['kjuːkʌmbəʳ] N pepino
cud [kʌd] N: **to chew the ~** ruminar
cuddle ['kʌdl] VT abraçar ■ VI abraçar-se
cuddly ['kʌdlɪ] ADJ fofo
cudgel ['kʌdʒəl] N cacete m ■ VT: **to ~ one's**

brains quebrar a cabeça

cue [kju:] N (*Snooker*) taco; (*Theatre etc*) deixa

cuff [kʌf] N (*of shirt, coat etc*) punho; (*US: on trousers*) bainha; (*blow*) bofetada ■ vT esbofetear; **off the ~** de improviso; **cuff links** NPL abotoaduras *fpl*

cu. in. ABBR = **cubic inches**

cuisine [kwɪ'zi:n] N cozinha

cul-de-sac ['kʌldəsæk] N beco sem saída

culinary ['kʌlɪnərɪ] ADJ culinário

cull [kʌl] vT (*flowers*) escolher; (*story, idea*) escolher, selecionar; (*kill*) matar seletivamente ■ N (*of animals*) matança seletiva

culminate ['kʌlmɪneɪt] vI: **to ~ in** terminar em; (*lead to*) resultar em

culmination [kʌlmɪ'neɪʃən] N (*of career*) auge *m*; (*of process*) conclusão *f*

culottes [kju:'lɔts] NPL saia-calça

culpable ['kʌlpəbl] ADJ culpável

culprit ['kʌlprɪt] N culpado(-a)

cult [kʌlt] N culto; **cult figure** N ídolo

cultivate ['kʌltɪveɪt] vT (*also fig*) cultivar

cultivation [kʌltɪ'veɪʃən] N cultivo; (*fig*) cultura

cultural ['kʌltʃərəl] ADJ cultural

culture ['kʌltʃəʳ] N (*also fig*) cultura

cultured ['kʌltʃəd] ADJ culto

cumbersome ['kʌmbəsəm] ADJ pesado, desajeitado; (*person*) lente, ineficiente

cumin ['kʌmɪn] N cominho

cumulative ['kju:mjulətɪv] ADJ cumulativo

cunning ['kʌnɪŋ] N astúcia ■ ADJ astuto, malandro; (*device, idea*) engenhoso

cup [kʌp] N xícara (BR), chávena (PT); (*prize, of bra*) taça

cupboard ['kʌbəd] N armário; (*for crockery*) guarda-louça

cup final (*Brit*) N final *f*

Cupid ['kju:pɪd] N Cupido

cupidity [kju:'pɪdɪtɪ] N cupidez *f*

cupola ['kju:pələ] N cúpula

cup tie (*Brit*) N jogo eliminatório

curable ['kjuərəbl] ADJ curável

curate ['kjuəːrɪt] N coadjutor *m*

curator [kjuə'reɪtəʳ] N diretor(a) *m/f*

curb [kə:b] vT refrear ■ N freio; (*US*) = **kerb**

curdle ['kə:dl] vI coalhar

curds [kə:dz] NPL coalho

cure [kjuəʳ] vT curar ■ N tratamento, cura; **to be ~d of sth** sarar(-se) de algo

cure-all N (*fig*) panacéia

curfew ['kə:fju:] N toque *m* de recolher

curio ['kjuərɪəu] N antiguidade *f*

curiosity [kjuərɪ'ɔsɪtɪ] N curiosidade *f*

curious ['kjuərɪəs] ADJ (*interested*) curioso; (*nosy*) abelhudo; (*unusual*) estranho

curiously ['kjuərɪəslɪ] ADV curiosamente; **~ enough, ...** por estranho que pareça, ...

curl [kə:l] N (*of hair*) cacho ■ vT (*hair: loosely*) frisar; (: *tightly*) encrespar; (*paper*) enrolar; (*lip*) torcer ■ vI (*hair*) encaracolar

▶ **curl up** vI frisar-se; (*person*) encaracolar-se

curler ['kə:ləʳ] N rolo, bobe *m*

curlew ['kə:lu:] N maçarico

curling ['kə:lɪŋ] N (*Sport*) curling *m*; **curling tongs** (*US* **curling irons**) NPL ferros *mpl* de frisar cabelo

curly ['kə:lɪ] ADJ cacheado, crespo

currant ['kʌrnt] N passa de corinto; (*blackcurrant, redcurrant*) groselha

currency ['kʌrnsɪ] N moeda; **foreign ~** câmbio, divisas; **to gain ~** (*fig*) consagrar-se

current ['kʌrnt] N corrente *f*; (*in river*) correnteza ■ ADJ corrente; (*present*) atual; (*accepted*) corrente; **in ~ usage** de uso corrente; **current account** (*Brit*) N conta corrente; **current affairs** NPL atualidades *fpl*; **current assets** NPL (*Comm*) ativo corrente; **current liabilities** NPL (*Comm*) passivo corrente

currently ['kʌrntlɪ] ADV atualmente

curricula [kə'rɪkjulə] NPL *of* **curriculum**

curriculum [kə'rɪkjuləm] (*pl* **curriculums** *or* **curricula**) N programa *m* de estudos; **curriculum vitae** [-'vi:taɪ] N curriculum vitae *m*, currículo

curry ['kʌrɪ] N caril *m* ■ vT: **to ~ favour with** captar simpatia de; **curry powder** N pós *mpl* de caril, curry *m*

curse [kə:s] vI xingar (BR), praguejar (PT) ■ vT (*swear at*) xingar (BR); (*bemoan*) amaldiçoar ■ N maldição *f*; (*swearword*) palavrão *m* (BR), baixo calão *m* (PT); (*problem*) castigo

cursor ['kə:səʳ] N (*Comput*) cursor *m*

cursory ['kə:sərɪ] ADJ rápido, superficial

curt [kə:t] ADJ seco, brusco

curtail [kə:'teɪl] vT (*freedom, rights*) restringir; (*visit etc*) abreviar, encurtar; (*expenses etc*) reduzir

curtain ['kə:tn] N cortina; (*Theatre*) pano; **curtain call** N (*Theatre*) chamada à ribalta; **curtain ring** N argola

curts(e)y ['kə:tsɪ] N mesura, reverência ■ vI fazer reverência

curvature ['kə:vətʃəʳ] N curvatura

curve [kə:v] N curva ■ vT encurvar, torcer ■ vI encurvar-se, torcer-se; (*road*) fazer (uma) curva

curved [kə:vd] ADJ curvado, curvo

cushion ['kuʃən] N almofada; (*Snooker*) tabela ■ vT (*seat*) escorar com almofada; (*shock, fall etc*) amortecer

cushy ['kuʃɪ] (*inf*) ADJ: **a ~ job** uma boca; **to have a ~ time** estar na moleza

custard ['kʌstəd] N (*for pouring*) nata, creme *m*; **custard powder** (*Brit*) N pó *m* para fazer creme

custodian [kʌs'təudɪən] N guarda *m/f*

custody ['kʌstədɪ] N custódia; (*for offenders*) prisão *f* preventiva; **to take into ~** deter

custom ['kʌstəm] N (*tradition*) tradição *f*; (*convention*) costume *m*; (*habit*) hábito; (*Comm*) clientela

customary ['kʌstəmərɪ] ADJ costumeiro; **it is ~ to do it** é costume fazê-lo

custom-built ADJ feito sob encomenda

customer ['kʌstəməʳ] N cliente *m/f*; **he's an awkward ~** (*inf*) ele é um cara difícil

customized ['kʌstəmaɪzd] ADJ (*car etc*) feito sob

encomenda
custom-made ADJ (car) feito sob encomenda;
(clothes) feito sob medida
customs ['kʌstəmz] NPL alfândega
Customs and Excise (Brit) N autoridades fpl
alfandegárias
customs duty N imposto alfandegário
customs officer N inspetor(a) m/f da alfândega,
aduaneiro(-a)
cut [kʌt] (pt, pp **cut**) VT cortar; (price) baixar;
(record) gravar; (reduce) reduzir; (inf: class) matar
■ VI cortar; (intersect) interceptar-se ■ N corte
m; (in spending) redução f; (of garment) tacho; **cold
cuts** NPL (US) frios mpl sortidos; **to ~ a tooth**
estar com um dente nascendo; **to ~ one's
finger** cortar o dedo; **to get one's hair ~** cortar
o cabelo; **to ~ sth short** abreviar algo; **to ~ sb
dead** fingir que não conhece alguém
▶ **cut back** VT (plants) podar; (production,
expenditure) cortar
▶ **cut down** VT (tree) derrubar; (reduce) reduzir;
to ~ sb down to size (fig) abaixar a crista de
alguém, colocar alguém no seu lugar
▶ **cut in** VI: **to ~ in (on)** interromper; (Aut)
cortar
▶ **cut off** VT (piece, Tel) cortar; (person, village)
isolar; (supply) suspender; (retreat) impedir;
(troops) cercar; **we've been ~ off** (Tel) fomos
cortados
▶ **cut out** VT (shape) recortar; (activity etc)
suprimir; (remove) remover
▶ **cut through** VI abrir caminho
▶ **cut up** VT cortar em pedaços
cut-and-dried ADJ (also: **cut-and-dry**) todo
resolvido
cutaway ['kʌtəweɪ] ADJ, N: **~ (drawing)** vista
diagramática
cutback ['kʌtbæk] N redução f, corte m
cute [kju:t] ADJ bonitinho, gracinha; (shrewd)
astuto
cut glass N cristal m lapidado; **cuticle** ['kju:tɪkl]
N cutícula
cuticle remover ■ N produto para tirar as
cutículas
cutlery ['kʌtlərɪ] N talheres mpl
cutlet ['kʌtlɪt] N costeleta
cutoff ['kʌtɔf] N (also: **cutoff point**) ponto de
corte; **cutoff switch** N interruptor m
cutout ['kʌtaut] N (shape) figura para recortar;
(switch) interruptor m
cut-price (US **cut-rate**) ADJ a preço reduzido

cut-throat N assassino(-a) ■ ADJ feroz
cutting ['kʌtɪŋ] ADJ cortante; (remark) mordaz
■ N (Brit: from newspaper) recorte m; (: Rail) corte
m; (Cinema) corte m; (from plant) muda
cuttlefish ['kʌtlfɪʃ] N sita
cut-up ADJ arrasado, aflito
CV N ABBR = **curriculum vitae**
C & W N ABBR = **country and western (music)**
cwo ABBR (Comm) = **cash with order**
cwt ABBR = **hundredweight**
cyanide ['saɪənaɪd] N cianeto
cybercafé ['saɪbəkæfeɪ] N cibercafé m
cybernetics [saɪbə'nɛtɪks] N cibernética
cyberspace ['saɪbəspeɪs] N ciberespaço
cyclamen ['sɪkləmən] N cíclame m
cycle ['saɪkl] N ciclo; (bicycle) bicicleta ■ VI
andar de bicicleta; **cycle lane, cycle path** N
ciclovia f; **cycle race** N corrida de bicicletas;
cycle rack N engradado para guardar
bicicletas
cycling ['saɪklɪŋ] N ciclismo
cyclist ['saɪklɪst] N ciclista m/f
cyclone ['saɪkləun] N ciclone m
cygnet ['sɪgnɪt] N cisne m novo
cylinder ['sɪlɪndəʳ] N cilindro; (of gas) bujão m;
cylinder capacity N capacidade f cilíndrica,
cilindrada; **cylinder head** N cilíndrico
cylinder-head gasket N culatra
cymbals ['sɪmblz] NPL pratos mpl
cynic ['sɪnɪk] N cínico(-a)
cynical ['sɪnɪkl] ADJ cínico, sarcástico
cynicism ['sɪnɪsɪzəm] N cinismo
CYO (US) N ABBR = **Catholic Youth Organization**
cypress ['saɪprɪs] N cipreste m
Cypriot ['sɪprɪət] ADJ, N cipriota m/f
Cyprus ['saɪprəs] N Chipre f
cyst [sɪst] N cisto
cystitis [sɪs'taɪtɪs] N cistite f
CZ (US) N ABBR (= Canal Zone) zona do canal do
Panamá
czar [zɑ:ʳ] N czar m
Czech [tʃɛk] ADJ tcheco ■ N tcheco(-a); (Ling)
tcheco
Czechoslovak [tʃɛkə'sləuvæk] ADJ, N
= **Czechoslovakian**
Czechoslovakia [tʃɛkəslə'vækɪə] N
Tchecoslováquia
Czechoslovakian [tʃɛkəslə'vækɪən] ADJ, N
tchecoslovaco(-a); **Czech Republic** N: **the
Czech Republic** a República Tcheca

Dd

D, d [di:] N (*letter*) D, d *m*; (*Mus*): **D** ré *m*; **D for David** (*Brit*) *or* **Dog** (*US*) D de dado

D (*US*) ABBR (*Pol*) = **democrat(ic)**

d (*Brit*) ABBR (*old*) = **penny**

d. ABBR = **died**

DA (*US*) N ABBR = **district attorney**

dab [dæb] VT (*eyes, wound*) tocar (de leve); (*paint, cream*) aplicar de leve ■ N (*of paint*) pincelada; (*of liquid*) gota; (*amount*) pequena quantidade *f*

dabble ['dæbl] VI: **to ~ in** interessar-se por

dachshund ['dækshund] N bassê *m*

dad [dæd] (*inf*) N papai *m*

daddy ['dædɪ] N = **dad**

daddy-long-legs N INV pernilongo

daffodil ['dæfədɪl] N narciso-dos-prados *m*

daft [dɑ:ft] ADJ bobo, besta; **to be ~ about** ser louco por

dagger ['dægə'] N punhal *m*, adaga; **to look ~s at sb** olhar feio para alguém; **to be at ~s drawn with sb** andar às turras com alguém

dahlia ['deɪljə] N dália

daily ['deɪlɪ] ADJ diário ■ N (*paper*) jornal *m*, diário; (*Brit: domestic help*) diarista (BR), mulher *f* a dias (PT) ■ ADV diariamente; **twice ~** duas vezes por dia

dainty ['deɪntɪ] ADJ delicado; (*tasteful*) elegante, gracioso

dairy ['dɛərɪ] N leiteria ■ ADJ (*industry*) de laticínios; (*cattle*) leiteiro; **dairy cow** N vaca leiteira; **dairy farm** N fazenda de gado leiteiro; **dairy products** NPL laticínios *mpl*; **dairy store** (*US*) N leiteria

dais ['deɪɪs] N estrado

daisy ['deɪzɪ] N margarida; **daisy wheel** N (*on printer*) margarida

daisy-wheel printer N impressora margarida

Dakar ['dækə'] N Dacar

dale [deɪl] (*Brit*) N vale *m*

dally ['dælɪ] VI vadiar

dalmatian [dæl'meɪʃən] N (*dog*) dálmata *m*

dam [dæm] N represa, barragem *f* ■ VT represar

damage ['dæmɪdʒ] N (*physical*) danos *mpl*; (*harm*) prejuízo; (*dents etc*) avaria ■ VT (*spoil, break*) danificar; (*harm*) prejudicar; **damages** NPL (*Law*) indenização *f* por perdas e danos; **to pay £5,000 in ~s** pagar £5,000 de indenização; **~ to property** danos materiais

damaging ['dæmɪdʒɪŋ] ADJ: **~ (to)** prejudicial (a)

Damascus [də'mɑːskəs] N Damasco

dame [deɪm] N (*title*) título honorífico dado a uma membra da Ordem do Império Britânico; título honorífico dado à esposa de um cavalheiro ou baronete; (*US: inf*) dona; (*Theatre*) dama

damn [dæm] VT condenar; (*curse*) maldizer ■ N (*inf*): **I don't give a ~** não dou a mínima, estou me lixando ■ ADJ (*inf: also: **damned***) donado, maldito; **~ (it)!** (*que*) droga!

damnable ['dæmnəbl] (*inf*) ADJ (*behaviour*) condenável; (*weather*) horrível

damnation [dæm'neɪʃən] N (*Rel*) danação *f* ■ EXCL (*inf*) droga!

damning ['dæmɪŋ] ADJ (*evidence*) prejudicial; (*criticism*) condenador(a)

damp [dæmp] ADJ úmido ■ N umidade *f* ■ VT (*also: **dampen**: cloth, rag*) umedecer; (: *enthusiasm etc*) jogar água fria em

dampcourse ['dæmpkɔːs] N impermeabilização *f*

damper ['dæmpə'] N (*Mus*) abafador *m*; (*of fire*) registro; **to put a ~ on** (*fig: atmosphere*) criar um mal-estar em; (: *party*) acabar com a animação de; (: *enthusiasm*) cortar

dampness ['dæmpnɪs] N umidade *f*

damson ['dæmzən] N ameixa pequena

dance [dɑːns] N dança; (*party etc*) baile *m* ■ VI dançar; **to ~ about** saltitar; **dance hall** N salão *m* de baile

dancer ['dɑːnsə'] N dançarino(-a); (*professional*) bailarino(-a)

dancing ['dɑːnsɪŋ] N dança

D and C N ABBR (*Med*: = *dilation and curettage*) dilatação *f* e curetagem *f*

dandelion ['dændɪlaɪən] N dente-de-leão *m*

dandruff ['dændrəf] N caspa

dandy ['dændɪ] N dândi *m* ■ ADJ (*US: inf*) bacana

Dane [deɪn] N dinamarquês(-esa) *m/f*

danger ['deɪndʒə'] N perigo; (*risk*) risco; (*possibility*): **there is a ~ of ...** há o risco de ...; **"~!"** (*on sign*) "perigo!"; **to be in ~ of** correr o risco de; **in ~** em perigo; **out of ~** fora de perigo; **danger list** N (*Med*): **on the danger list** na lista dos pacientes graves

dangerous ['deɪndʒərəs] ADJ perigoso

dangerously ['deɪndʒərəslɪ] ADV

perigosamente; ~ **ill** gravemente doente
danger zone N zona de perigo
dangle ['dæŋgl] VT balançar ■ VI pender
balançando
Danish ['deɪnɪʃ] ADJ dinamarquês(-esa) ■ N
(Ling) dinamarquês m; **Danish pastry** N doce m
(de massa com frutas)
dank [dæŋk] ADJ frio e úmido
Danube ['dænjuːb] N: **the** ~ o Danúbio
dapper ['dæpəʳ] ADJ garboso; (appearance)
esmerado
dare [dɛəʳ] VT: **to** ~ **sb to do sth** desafiar alguém
a fazer algo ■ VI: **to** ~ **(to) do sth** atrever-se a
fazer algo, ousar fazer algo; **I** ~ **say** (I suppose)
acho provável que; **I** ~**n't tell him** (Brit) eu não
ouso dizê-lo a ele; **I** ~ **say he'll turn up** acho
provável que ele venha
daredevil ['dɛədɛvl] N intrépido, atrevido
Dar-es-Salaam ['dɑːrɛssə'lɑːm] N Dar-es-
Salaam
daring ['dɛərɪŋ] ADJ (audacious) audacioso; (bold)
ousado ■ N atrevimento, audácia, ousadia;
(courage) coragem f, destemor m
dark [dɑːk] ADJ (gen, hair) escuro; (complexion)
moreno; (cheerless) triste, sombrio; (fig) sombrio
■ N escuro; **in the** ~ no escuro; **in the** ~
about (fig) no escuro sobre; **after** ~ depois de
escurecer; **it is/is getting** ~ está escuro/está
escurecendo; **dark chocolate** N chocolate m
amargo
darken ['dɑːkən] VT escurecer; (colour) fazer
mais escuro ■ VI escurecer(-se)
dark glasses NPL óculos mpl escuros
darkly ['dɑːklɪ] ADV (gloomily) sombriamente; (in
a sinister way) sinistramente
darkness ['dɑːknɪs] N escuridão f
dark room N câmara escura
darling ['dɑːlɪŋ] ADJ querido ■ N querido(-a);
(favourite): **to be the** ~ **of** ser o queridinho de
darn [dɑːn] VT cerzir
dart [dɑːt] N dardo; (in sewing) alinhavo ■ VI
precipitar-se; **to** ~ **away/along** ir-se/seguir
precipitadamente
dartboard ['dɑːtbɔːd] N alvo (para jogo de
dardos)
darts N (game) jogo de dardos
dash [dæʃ] N (sign) hífen m; (: long) travessão
m; (rush) correria; (small quantity) pontinha
■ VT (throw) arremessar; (hopes) frustrar ■ VI
precipitar-se, ir depressa
▶ **dash away** VI sair apressado
▶ **dash off** VT (letter, essay) escrever a toda ■ VI
= **dash away**
dashboard ['dæʃbɔːd] N painel m de
instrumentos
dashing ['dæʃɪŋ] ADJ arrojado
dastardly ['dæstədlɪ] ADJ vil
data ['deɪtə] NPL dados mpl
database ['deɪtəbeɪs] N banco de dados
data capture N entrada de dados
data processing N processamento de dados
data transmission N transmissão f de dados

date [deɪt] N (day) data; (with friend) encontro;
(fruit) tâmara; (tree) tamareira ■ VT datar;
(person) namorar; **what's the** ~ **today?** que dia
é hoje?; ~ **of birth** data de nascimento; **closing**
~ data de encerramento; **to** ~ até agora; **out**
of ~ desatualizado; **up to** ~ (correspondence etc)
em dia; (dictionary, phone book etc) atualizado;
(method, technology) moderno; **to bring up to**
~ (correspondence, person) pôr em dia; (method)
modernizar; **letter** ~**d 5th July** (Brit) or **July 5th**
(US) carta datada de 5 de julho
dated ['deɪtɪd] ADJ antiquado
dateline ['deɪtlaɪn] N meridiano or linha de data
date rape N estupro cometido pelo
acompanhante da vítima, geralmente após
encontro romântico
date stamp N carimbo datador
daub [dɔːb] VT borrar
daughter ['dɔːtəʳ] N filha
daughter-in-law (pl **daughters-in-law**) N nora
daunt [dɔːnt] VT desalentar, desencorajar
daunting ['dɔːntɪŋ] ADJ desanimador(a)
dauntless ['dɔːntlɪs] ADJ intrépido, destemido
dawdle ['dɔːdl] VI (waste time) fazer cera; (go slow)
vadiar
dawn [dɔːn] N alvorada, amanhecer m; (of
period, situation) início ■ VI (day)
amanhecer; (fig): **it** ~**ed on him that** ...
começou a perceber que ...; **at** ~ ao amanhecer;
from ~ **to dusk** de manhã à noite; **dawn**
chorus (Brit) N canto dos pássaros na alvorada
day [deɪ] N dia m; (working day) jornada, dia útil;
the ~ **before/after** a véspera/o dia seguinte;
the ~ **before yesterday** anteontem; **the** ~ **after**
tomorrow depois de amanhã; **the following**
~ o dia seguinte; **(on) the** ~ **that** ... o dia em
que ...; ~ **by** ~ dia a dia; **by** ~ de dia; **paid by the**
~ pago por dia; **these** ~**s, in the present** ~ hoje
em dia
daybook ['deɪbuk] (Brit) N diário
day boy N (Sch) externo
daybreak ['deɪbreɪk] N amanhecer m
daydream ['deɪdriːm] N devaneio ■ VI
devanear
day girl N (Sch) externa
daylight ['deɪlaɪt] N luz f (do dia)
Daylight Saving Time (US) N hora de verão
day release N: **to be on** ~ ter licença de um
dia por semana para fins de aperfeiçoamento
profissional
day return (Brit) N (ticket) bilhete m de ida e
volta no mesmo dia
day shift N turno diurno
daytime ['deɪtaɪm] N dia m ■ ADJ de dia, diurno
day-to-day ADJ (life, expenses) cotidiano; **the**
~ **routine** o dia-a-dia; **on a** ~ **basis** dia a dia,
diariamente
day trip N excursão f (de um dia)
day tripper N excursionista m/f
daze [deɪz] VT (stun) aturdir ■ N: **in a** ~ aturdido
dazzle ['dæzl] VT (bewitch) deslumbrar; (blind)
ofuscar

dazzling ['dæzlɪŋ] ADJ deslumbrante, ofuscante

DC ABBR (Elec) = **direct current**; (US: Post) = **District of Columbia**

DD N ABBR (= Doctor of Divinity) título universitário

dd. ABBR (Comm: = delivered) entregue

D/D ABBR = **direct debit**

D-day ['di:deɪ] N o dia D

DDS (US) N ABBR (= Doctor of Dental Science; = Doctor of Dental Surgery) títulos universitários

DDT N ABBR (= dichlorodiphenyltrichloroethane) DDT m

DE (US) ABBR (Post) = **Delaware**

DEA (US) N ABBR (= Drug Enforcement Administration) = Conselho Nacional de Entorpecentes

deacon ['di:kən] N diácono

dead [dɛd] ADJ morto; (deceased) falecido; (numb) dormente; (telephone) cortado; (Elec) sem corrente ■ ADV (very) totalmente; (completely) completamente; (exactly) absolutamente ■ NPL: **the ~** os mortos; **to shoot sb ~** matar alguém a tiro; **the line has gone ~** (Tel) caiu a ligação; **~ tired** morto de cansado; **to stop ~** estacar; **~ on time** na hora em ponto

deaden ['dɛdn] VT (blow, sound) amortecer; (pain) anestesiar

dead end N beco sem saída ■ ADJ: **a dead-end job** um emprego sem perspectivas

dead heat N (Sport) empate m; **to finish in a ~** (race) ser empatado

dead-letter office N seção f de cartas não reclamadas

deadline ['dɛdlaɪn] N prazo final; **to work to a ~** trabalhar com prazo estabelecido

deadlock ['dɛdlɔk] N impasse m

dead loss (inf) N: **to be a ~** não ser de nada

deadly ['dɛdlɪ] ADJ mortal, fatal; (weapon) mortífero ■ ADV: **~ dull** tediosíssimo, chatíssimo

deadpan [dɛd'pæn] ADJ sem expressão

Dead Sea N: **the ~** o mar Morto

deaf [dɛf] ADJ surdo

deaf-aid (Brit) N aparelho para a surdez

deaf-and-dumb ADJ surdo-mudo; **~ alphabet** alfabeto de surdos-mudos

deafen ['dɛfn] VT ensurdecer

deafening ['dɛfnɪŋ] ADJ ensurdecedor(a)

deaf-mute N surdo-mudo/surda-muda

deafness ['dɛfnɪs] N surdez f

deal [di:l] (pt, pp **dealt**) N (agreement) acordo; (business) negócio ■ VT (cards, blows) dar; **to strike a ~ with sb** fechar um negócio com alguém; **it's a ~!** (inf) negócio fechado; **he got a fair/bad ~ from them** ele foi/não foi bem tratado por eles; **a good ~** bastante; **a good** or **great ~ (of)** bastante, muito
  ▸ **deal in** VT FUS (Comm) negociar em or com
  ▸ **deal with** VT FUS (people) tratar com; (problem) ocupar-se de; (subject) tratar de; (Comm) negociar; (punish) castigar

dealer ['di:lə'] N negociante m/f; (for cars) concessionário(-a); (for products) revendedor(a)

m/f; (Cards) carteador(a) m/f, banqueiro(-a)

dealership ['di:ləʃɪp] N concessionária

dealings ['di:lɪŋz] NPL transações fpl

dealt [dɛlt] PT, PP of **deal**

dean [di:n] N (Rel) decano; (Sch: Brit) reitor(a) m/f; (: US) orientador(a) m/f de estudos

dear [dɪə'] ADJ querido, caro; (expensive) caro ■ N: **my ~** meu querido/minha querida ■ EXCL: **~ me!** ai, meu Deus!; **D~ Sir/Madam** (in letter) Ilmo. Senhor/Exma. Senhora (BR), Exmo. Senhor/Exma. Senhora (PT); **D~ Mr/Mrs X** Caro Sr./Cara Sra.

dearly ['dɪəlɪ] ADV (love) ternamente; (pay) caro

dearth [də:θ] N escassez f

death [dɛθ] N morte f; (Admin) óbito

deathbed ['dɛθbɛd] N leito de morte

death certificate N certidão f de óbito

death duties NPL (Brit) impostos mpl sobre inventário

deathly ['dɛθlɪ] ADJ (colour) pálido; (silence) profundo ■ ADV (quiet) completamente

death penalty N pena de morte

death rate N (índice m de) mortalidade f

death sentence N sentença de morte

death toll N número de mortos (en acidentes)

deathtrap ['dɛθtræp] N perigo

deb [dɛb] (inf) N ABBR = **debutante**

debacle [deɪ'ba:kl] N fracasso

debar [dɪ'ba:'] VT (exclude) excluir; **to ~ sb from doing sth** proibir a alguém fazer algo or que faça algo

debase [dɪ'beɪs] VT degradar; (value) desvalorizar; (quality) piorar

debatable [dɪ'beɪtəbl] ADJ discutível

debate [dɪ'beɪt] N debate m ■ VT debater ■ VI (consider): **to ~ whether** perguntar-se se

debauchery [dɪ'bɔ:tʃərɪ] N decadência

debenture [dɪ'bɛntʃə'] N (Comm) debênture f

debilitate [dɪ'bɪlɪteɪt] VT debilitar

debit ['dɛbɪt] N débito ■ VT: **to ~ a sum to sb** or **to sb's account** lançar uma quantia ao débito de alguém or à conta de alguém; see also **direct debit**; **debit balance** N saldo devedor; **debit note** N nota de débito

debrief [di:'bri:f] VT interrogar

debriefing [di:'bri:fɪŋ] N interrogatório

debris ['dɛbri:] N escombros mpl

debt [dɛt] N (sum) dívida; (state) endividamento; **to be in ~** ter dívidas, estar endividado; **bad ~** dívida incobrável; **debt collector** N cobrador(a) m/f de dívidas

debtor ['dɛtə'] N devedor(a) m/f

debug ['di:'bʌg] VT (Comput) depurar

debunk [di:'bʌŋk] VT (myths, ideas) desmascarar

début ['deɪbju:] N estréia

debutante ['dɛbjutænt] N debutante f

Dec. ABBR (= December) dez

decade ['dɛkeɪd] N década

decadence ['dɛkədəns] N decadência

decadent ['dɛkədənt] ADJ decadente

decaf ['di:kæf] (inf) N descafeinado m

decaffeinated [dɪ'kæfɪneɪtɪd] ADJ descafeinado

decamp [dɪ'kæmp] (*inf*) VI safar-se

decant [dɪ'kænt] VT (*wine*) decantar

decanter [dɪ'kæntə'] N garrafa ornamental

decarbonize [di:'ka:bənaɪz] VT (*Aut*) descarbonizar

decay [dɪ'keɪ] N decadência; (*of building*) ruína; (*fig*) deterioração f; (*rotting*) podridão f; (*also:* **tooth decay**) cárie f ▪ VI (*rot*) apodrecer-se; (*fig*) decair

decease [dɪ'si:s] N falecimento, óbito

deceased [dɪ'si:st] N: **the ~** o falecido (a falecida)

deceit [dɪ'si:t] N engano; (*duplicity*) fraude f

deceitful [dɪ'si:tful] ADJ enganador(a)

deceive [dɪ'si:v] VT enganar

decelerate [di:'sɛləreɪt] VT moderar a marcha de, desacelerar ▪ VI diminuir a velocidade

December [dɪ'sɛmbə'] N dezembro; *see also* **July**

decency ['di:sənsɪ] N decência; (*kindness*) bondade f

decent ['di:sənt] ADJ (*proper*) decente; (*kind, honest*) honesto, amável

decently ['di:səntlɪ] ADV (*respectably*) decentemente; (*kindly*) gentilmente

decentralization ['di:sɛntrəlaɪ'zeɪʃən] N descentralização f

decentralize [di:'sɛntrəlaɪz] VT descentralizar

deception [dɪ'sɛpʃən] N engano; (*deceitful act*) fraude f

deceptive [dɪ'sɛptɪv] ADJ enganador(a)

decibel ['dɛsɪbɛl] N decibel m

decide [dɪ'saɪd] VT (*person*) convencer; (*question, argument*) resolver ▪ VI decidir; **to ~ to do/that** decidir fazer/que; **to ~ on sth** decidir-se por algo; **to ~ on doing** decidir fazer; **to ~ against doing** decidir não fazer

decided [dɪ'saɪdɪd] ADJ (*resolute*) decidido; (*clear, definite*) claro, definido

decidedly [dɪ'saɪdɪdlɪ] ADV (*distinctly*) claramente; (*emphatically*) decididamente

deciding [dɪ'saɪdɪŋ] ADJ decisivo

deciduous [dɪ'sɪdjuəs] ADJ decíduo

decimal ['dɛsɪməl] ADJ decimal ▪ N decimal m; **to 3 ~ places** com 3 casas decimais

decimalize ['dɛsɪməlaɪz] (*Brit*) VT decimalizar

decimal point N vírgula de decimais

decimate ['dɛsɪmeɪt] VT dizimar

decipher [dɪ'saɪfə'] VT decifrar

decision [dɪ'sɪʒən] N (*choice*) escolha; (*act of choosing*) decisão f; (*decisiveness*) resolução f; **to make a ~** tomar uma decisão

decisive [dɪ'saɪsɪv] ADJ (*action*) decisivo; (*person*) decidido; (*manner, reply*) categórico

deck [dɛk] N (*Naut*) convés m; (*of bus*): **top ~** andar m de cima; (*of cards*) baralho; **to go up on ~** subir ao convés; **below ~** abaixo do convés principal; **record/cassette ~** toca-discos m inv/ toca-fitas m inv; **deck chair** N cadeira de lona, espreguiçadeira; **deck hand** N taifeiro(-a)

declaration [dɛklə'reɪʃən] N declaração f; (*public announcement*) pronunciamento

declare [dɪ'klɛə'] VT (*intention*) revelar; (*result*) divulgar; (*income, at customs*) declarar

declassify [di:'klæsɪfaɪ] VT tornar público

decline [dɪ'klaɪn] N declínio; (*lessening*) diminuição f, baixa ▪ VT recusar ▪ VI diminuir; (*fall*) baixar; **~ in living standards** queda dos padrões de vida; **to ~ to do sth** recusar-se a fazer algo

declutch ['di:'klʌtʃ] (*Brit*) VI debrear

decode [di:'kəud] VT decifrar; (*TV signal etc*) decodificar

decoder [di:'kəudə'] N decodificador m

decompose [di:kəm'pəuz] VI decompor-se

decomposition [di:kɔmpə'zɪʃən] N decomposição f

decompression [di:kəm'prɛʃən] N descompressão f; **decompression chamber** N câmara de descompressão

decongestant [di:kən'dʒɛstənt] N descongestionante m

decontaminate [di:kən'tæmɪneɪt] VT descontaminar

decontrol [di:kən'trəul] VT (*prices etc*) liberar

décor ['deɪkɔ:'] N decoração f; (*Theatre*) cenário

decorate ['dɛkəreɪt] VT (*adorn*): **to ~ (with)** adornar (com); (*give medal to*) condecorar; (*paint*) pintar; (*paper*) decorar com papel

decoration [dɛkə'reɪʃən] N decoração f, adorno; (*on tree, dress etc*) enfeite m; (*act*) decoração; (*medal*) condecoração f

decorative ['dɛkərətɪv] ADJ decorativo

decorator ['dɛkəreɪtə'] N (*painter*) pintor(a) m/f

decorum [dɪ'kɔ:rəm] N decoro

decoy ['di:kɔɪ] N engodo, chamariz m

decrease [n 'di:kri:s, vt, vi di:'kri:s] N: **~ (in)** diminuição f (de) ▪ VT reduzir ▪ VI diminuir; **to be on the ~** estar diminuindo

decreasing [di:'kri:sɪŋ] ADJ decrescente

decree [dɪ'kri:] N decreto ▪ VT: **to ~ (that)** decretar (que); **~ absolute** sentença final de divórcio; **decree nisi** N ordem f provisória de divórcio

decrepit [dɪ'krɛpɪt] ADJ decrépito; (*building*) (que está) caindo aos pedaços

decry [dɪ'kraɪ] VT execrar; (*disparage*) denegrir

dedicate ['dɛdɪkeɪt] VT dedicar

dedicated ['dɛdɪkeɪtɪd] ADJ (*person, Comput*) dedicado; **~ word processor** processador m de texto dedicado

dedication [dɛdɪ'keɪʃən] N (*devotion*) dedicação f; (*in book*) dedicatória; (*on radio*) mensagem f

deduce [dɪ'dju:s] VT deduzir

deduct [dɪ'dʌkt] VT deduzir; (*from wage etc*) descontar

deduction [dɪ'dʌkʃən] N (*deducting*) redução f; (*amount*) subtração f; (*deducing*) dedução f; (*from wage etc*) desconto; (*conclusion*) conclusão f, dedução f; **deed** [di:d] N feito; (*Law*) escritura, título

deed of covenant ▪ N escritura de transferência

deem [di:m] VT julgar, estimar; **to ~ it wise to do** julgar prudente fazer

deep [di:p] ADJ profundo; (*in measurements*)

de profundidade; (*voice*) baixo, grave; (*person*) fechado; (*breath*) fundo; (*colour*) forte, carregado ■ ADV: **the spectators stood 20 ~** os espectadores formaram-se em 20 fileiras; **knee-~ in water** com água até os joelhos; **to be 4 metres ~** ter 4 metros de profundidade; **he took a ~ breath** ele respirou fundo

deepen ['di:pən] VT aprofundar ■ VI (*mystery*) aumentar

deep-freeze N congelador *m*, freezer *m* (BR)

deep-fry VT fritar em recipiente fundo

deeply ['di:plɪ] ADV (*breathe*) fundo; (*interested, moved*) profundamente

deep-rooted [-'ru:tɪd] ADJ (*prejudice*) enraizado; (*affection*) profundo

deep-sea diver N escafandrista *m/f*

deep-sea diving N mergulho com escafandro

deep-sea fishing N pesca de alto-mar

deep-seated [-'si:tɪd] ADJ (*beliefs etc*) arraigado

deep-set ADJ (*eyes*) fundo

deer [dɪər] N INV veado, cervo

deerskin ['dɪəskɪn] N camurça, pele *f* de cervo

deerstalker ['dɪəstɔ:kər] N *tipo de chapéu como o de Sherlock Holmes*

deface [dɪ'feɪs] VT desfigurar

defamation [defə'meɪʃən] N difamação *f*

defamatory [dɪ'fæmətrɪ] ADJ difamatório

default [dɪ'fɔ:lt] VI (*Law*) inadimplir; (*Sport*) não comparecer ■ N (*Comput: also:* **default value**) valor *m* de default; **by ~** (*win*) por desistência; (*Law*) à revelia; (*Sport*) por ausência; **to ~ on a debt** deixar de pagar uma dívida

defaulter [dɪ'fɔ:ltər] N (*in debt*) devedor(a) *m/f* inadimplente

default option N (*Comput*) opção *f* de default

defeat [dɪ'fi:t] N derrota; (*failure*) malogro ■ VT derrotar, vencer; (*fig: efforts*) frustrar

defeatism [dɪ'fi:tɪzm] N derrotismo

defeatist [dɪ'fi:tɪst] ADJ, N derrotista *m/f*

defect [n 'di:fɛkt, vi dɪ'fɛkt] N defeito ■ VI: **to ~ to the enemy** desertar para se juntar ao inimigo; **physical/mental ~** defeito físico/ mental

defective [dɪ'fɛktɪv] ADJ defeituoso

defector [dɪ'fɛktər] N trânsfuga *m/f*

defence [dɪ'fɛns] (US **defense**) N defesa; **in ~ of** em defesa de; **witness for the ~** testemunha de defesa; **the Ministry of D~** (*Brit*), **the Department of Defense** (*US*) o Ministério da Defesa

defenceless [dɪ'fɛnslɪs] ADJ indefeso

defend [dɪ'fɛnd] VT defender; (*Law*) contestar

defendant [dɪ'fɛndənt] N acusado(-a); (*in civil case*) réu(-ré) *m/f*

defender [dɪ'fɛndər] N defensor(a) *m/f*

defending champion [dɪ'fɛndɪŋ-] N (*Sport*) atual campeâo(-peã) *m/f*

defending counsel [dɪ'fɛndɪŋ-] N (*Law*) advogado(-a) de defesa

defense [dɪ'fɛns] (US) N = **defence**

defensive [dɪ'fɛnsɪv] ADJ defensivo ■ N: **on the ~** na defensiva

defer [dɪ'fə:r] VT (*postpone*) adiar ■ VI (*submit*): **to ~ to** submeter-se a

deference ['dɛfərəns] N deferência; **out of** *or* **in ~ to** por *or* em deferência a

defiance [dɪ'faɪəns] N desafio; (*rebellion*) rebeldia; **in ~ of** sem respeito por; (*despite*) a despeito de

defiant [dɪ'faɪənt] ADJ (*insolent*) desafiante, insolente; (*challenging*) desafiador(a)

defiantly [dɪ'faɪəntlɪ] ADV desafiadoramente

deficiency [dɪ'fɪʃənsɪ] N (*lack*) deficiência, falta; (*defect*) defeito; (*Comm*) déficit *m*; **deficiency disease** N doença de carência

deficient [dɪ'fɪʃənt] ADJ (*inadequate*) deficiente; (*incomplete*) incompleto; (*defective*) imperfeito; (*defective*): **~ in** falto de, carente de

deficit ['dɛfɪsɪt] N déficit *m*

defile [vt, vi dɪ'faɪl, n 'di:faɪl] VT (*memory*) desonrar; (*statue etc*) profanar ■ VI desfilar ■ N desfile *m*

define [dɪ'faɪn] VT definir

definite ['dɛfɪnɪt] ADJ (*fixed*) definitivo; (*clear, obvious*) claro, categórico; (*certain*) certo; (*Ling*) definido; **he was ~ about it** ele foi categórico

definitely ['dɛfɪnɪtlɪ] ADV sem dúvida

definition [dɛfɪ'nɪʃən] N definição *f*

definitive [dɪ'fɪnɪtɪv] ADJ conclusivo

deflate [di:'fleɪt] VT esvaziar; (*person*) fazer perder o rebolado; (*Econ*) deflacionar

deflation [di:'fleɪʃən] N (*Econ*) deflação *f*

deflationary [di:'fleɪʃənrɪ] ADJ (*Econ*) deflacionário

deflect [dɪ'flɛkt] VT desviar

defog ['di:'fɔg] (US) VT desembaçar

defogger ['di:'fɔgər] (US) N (*Aut*) desembaçador *m*

deform [dɪ'fɔ:m] VT distorcer

deformed [dɪ'fɔ:md] ADJ deformado

deformity [dɪ'fɔ:mɪtɪ] N deformidade *f*

defraud [dɪ'frɔ:d] VT: **to ~ sb (of sth)** trapacear alguém (por causa de algo)

defray [dɪ'freɪ] VT (*costs, expenses*) correr com

defrost [di:'frɔst] VT descongelar

deft [dɛft] ADJ (*hands*) destro; (*movement*) hábil

defunct [dɪ'fʌŋkt] ADJ extinto

defuse [di:'fju:z] VT tirar o estopim *or* a espoleta de; (*situation*) neutralizar

defy [dɪ'faɪ] VT desafiar; (*resist*) opor-se a; (*order*) desobedecer

degenerate [vi dɪ'dʒɛnəreɪt, adj dɪ'dʒɛnərɪt] VI deteriorar ■ ADJ degenerado

degradation [degrə'deɪʃən] N degradação *f*

degrade [dɪ'greɪd] VT degradar

degrading [dɪ'greɪdɪŋ] ADJ degradante

degree [dɪ'gri:] N grau *m*; (*Sch*) diploma *m*, título; **~ in maths** formatura em matemática; **10 ~s below (zero)** 10 graus abaixo de zero; **a considerable ~ of risk** um grau considerável de risco; **by ~s** (*gradually*) pouco a pouco; **to some ~, to a certain ~** até certo ponto

dehydrated [di:haɪ'dreɪtɪd] ADJ desidratado; (*milk*) em pó

dehydration [di:haɪ'dreɪʃən] N desidratação f
de-ice VT (windscreen) descongelar
de-icer [-'aɪsəʳ] N descongelador m
deign [deɪn] VI: **to ~ to do** dignar-se a fazer
deity ['di:ɪtɪ] N divindade f, deidade f
dejected [dɪ'dʒɛktɪd] ADJ (depressed) deprimado; (face) triste
dejection [dɪ'dʒɛkʃən] N desânimo
del. ABBR = **delete**
delay [dɪ'leɪ] VT (decision etc) retardar, atrasar; (train, person) atrasar ▪ VI hesitar ▪ N demora; (postponement) adiamento; **to be ~ed** estar atrasado; **without ~** sem demora or atraso
delayed-action [dɪ'leɪd-] ADJ de retardo, de ação retardada
delectable [dɪ'lɛktəbl] ADJ (person) gostoso; (food) delicioso
delegate [n 'dɛlɪgɪt, vt 'dɛlɪgeɪt] N delegado(-a) ▪ VT (person) autorizar, task, delegar; **to ~ sth to sb/sb to do sth** delegar algo a alguém/alguém para fazer algo
delegation [dɛlɪ'geɪʃən] N (group) delegação f; (by leader) autorização f
delete [dɪ'li:t] VT eliminar, riscar; (Comput) deletar
Delhi ['dɛlɪ] N Délhi
deliberate [adj dɪ'lɪbərɪt, vi dɪ'lɪbəreɪt] ADJ (intentional) intencional; (slow) pausado, lento ▪ VI deliberar; (consider) considerar
deliberately [dɪ'lɪbərɪtlɪ] ADV (on purpose) de propósito; (slowly) lentamente
deliberation [dɪlɪbə'reɪʃən] N deliberação f
delicacy ['dɛlɪkəsɪ] N delicadeza; (of problem) dificuldade f; (choice food) iguaria
delicate ['dɛlɪkɪt] ADJ delicado; (health) frágil; (skilled) fino
delicately ['dɛlɪkɪtlɪ] ADV delicadamente
delicatessen [dɛlɪkə'tɛsn] N delicatessen m
delicious [dɪ'lɪʃəs] ADJ delicioso; (food) saboroso
delight [dɪ'laɪt] N (feeling) prazer m, deleite m; (person) encanto; (experience) delícia ▪ VT encantar, deleitar; **to take (a) ~ in** deleitar-se com
delighted [dɪ'laɪtɪd] ADJ: **~ (at or with sth)** encantado (com algo); **to be ~ to do sth/that** ter muito prazer em fazer algo/ficar muito contente que; **I'd be ~** eu adoraria
delightful [dɪ'laɪtful] ADJ encantador(a), delicioso
delimit [di:'lɪmɪt] VT delimitar
delineate [dɪ'lɪnɪeɪt] VT delinear; (fig: describe) descrever, definir
delinquency [dɪ'lɪŋkwənsɪ] N delinqüência
delinquent [dɪ'lɪŋkwənt] ADJ, N delinqüente m/f
delirious [dɪ'lɪrɪəs] ADJ delirante; **to be ~** delirar
delirium [dɪ'lɪrɪəm] N delírio
deliver [dɪ'lɪvəʳ] VT (distribute) distribuir; (hand over) entregar; (message) comunicar; (speech) proferir; (free) livrar; (Med) partejar; **to ~ the goods** (fig) dar conta do recado
deliverance [dɪ'lɪvrəns] N libertação f,

livramento
delivery [dɪ'lɪvərɪ] N entrega; (of mail) distribuição f; (of speaker) enunciação f; (Med) parto; **to take ~ of** receber; **delivery note** N guia or nota de entrega; **delivery van** (US **delivery truck**) N furgão m de entrega
delta ['dɛltə] N delta m
delude [dɪ'lu:d] VT iludir, enganar; **to ~ o.s.** iludir-se
deluge ['dɛlju:dʒ] N dilúvio; (fig) enxurrada ▪ VT (fig): **to ~ (with)** inundar (de)
delusion [dɪ'lu:ʒən] N ilusão f; **to have ~s of grandeur** ter mania de grandeza
de luxe [də'lʌks] ADJ de luxo
delve [dɛlv] VI: **to ~ into** (subject) investigar, pesquisar; (cupboard etc) vasculhar
Dem. (US) ABBR (Pol) = **democrat(ic)**
demagogue ['dɛməgɔg] N demagogo(-a)
demand [dɪ'mɑ:nd] VT exigir; (rights) reivindicar, reclamar ▪ N exigência; (claim) reivindicação f; (Econ) procura; **to ~ sth (from or of sb)** exigir algo (de alguém); **to be in ~** estar em demando; **on ~** à vista
demanding [dɪ'mɑ:ndɪŋ] ADJ (boss) exigente; (work) absorvente
demarcation [di:mɑ:'keɪʃən] N demarcação f; **demarcation dispute** N (Industry) dissídio coletivo
demean [dɪ'mi:n] VT: **to ~ o.s.** rebaixar-se
demeanour [dɪ'mi:nəʳ] (US **demeanor**) N conduta, comportamento
demented [dɪ'mɛntɪd] ADJ demente, doido
demilitarized zone [di:'mɪlɪtəraɪzd-] N zona desmilitarizada
demise [dɪ'maɪz] N falecimento
demist [di:'mɪst] (Brit) VT desembaçar
demister [di:'mɪstəʳ] (Brit) N (Aut) desembaçador m de pára-brisa
demo ['dɛməu] (inf) N ABBR (= demonstration) passeata
demobilize [di:'məubɪlaɪz] VT desmobilizar
democracy [dɪ'mɔkrəsɪ] N democracia
democrat ['dɛməkræt] N democrata m/f
democratic [dɛmə'krætɪk] ADJ democrático
demography [dɪ'mɔgraəfɪ] N demografia
demolish [dɪ'mɔlɪʃ] VT demolir, derrubar; (fig: argument) refutar, contestar
demolition [dɛmə'lɪʃən] N demolição f; (of argument) contestação f
demon ['di:mən] N demônio ▪ CPD: **a ~ squash player** um(a) craque em squash
demonstrate ['dɛmənstreɪt] VT demonstrar ▪ VI: **to ~ (for/against)** manifestar-se (a favor de/contra)
demonstration [dɛmən'streɪʃən] N (Pol) manifestação f; (: march) passeata; (proof) demonstração f; (exhibition) exibição f; **to hold a ~** realizar uma passeata
demonstrative [dɪ'mɔnstrətɪv] ADJ demonstrativo
demonstrator ['dɛmənstreɪtəʳ] N (Pol) manifestante m/f; (Comm: sales person)

demonstrador(a) *m/f*; (: *car, computer etc*) modelo de demonstração

demoralize [dɪ'mɔrəlaɪz] VT desmoralizar

demote [dɪ'məut] VT rebaixar de posto

demotion [dɪ'məuʃən] N rebaixamento

demur [dɪ'məːʳ] VI: **to ~ (at sth)** objetar (a algo), opor-se (a algo) ▪ N: **without ~** sem objeção

demure [dɪ'mjuəʳ] ADJ recatado

demurrage [dɪ'mʌrɪdʒ] N sobreestadia

den [dɛn] N (*of animal*) covil *m*; (*of thieves*) antro, esconderijo; (*room*) aposento privado, cantinho

denationalization ['diːnæʃnəlaɪ'zeɪʃən] N desnacionalização *f*, desestatização *f*

denationalize [diː'næʃnəlaɪz] NT desnacionalizar, desestatizar

denial [dɪ'naɪəl] N refutação *f*; (*refusal*) negativa; (*of report etc*) desmentido

denier ['dɛnɪəʳ] N denier *m*; **15 ~ stockings** meias de 15 denieres

denigrate ['dɛnɪgreɪt] VT denegrir

denim ['dɛnɪm] N brim *m*, zuarte *m*; **denims** NPL jeans *m* (BR), jeans *mpl* (PT); **denim jacket** N jaqueta de brim

denizen ['dɛnɪzn] N habitante *m/f*

Denmark ['dɛnmɑːk] N Dinamarca

denomination [dɪnɔmɪ'neɪʃən] N valor *m*, denominação *f*; (*Rel*) confissão *f*, seita

denominator [dɪ'nɔmɪneɪtəʳ] N denominador *m*

denote [dɪ'nəut] VT (*indicate*) denotar, indicar; (*represent*) representar; (*mean*) significar

denounce [dɪ'nauns] VT denunciar

dense [dɛns] ADJ (*crowd*) denso; (*smoke, foliage etc*) denso, espesso; (*inf: stupid*) estúpido, bronco

densely ['dɛnslɪ] ADV: **~ populated** com grande densidade de população; **~ wooded** coberto de florestas densas

density ['dɛnsɪtɪ] N densidade *f*; **single/double ~ disk** (*Comput*) disco de densidade simples/dupla

dent [dɛnt] N amolgadura, depressão *f* ▪ VT (*also*: **make a dent in**) amolgar, dentar; **to make a ~ in** (*fig*) reduzir

dental ['dɛntl] ADJ (*treatment*) dentário; (*hygiene*) dental; **dental surgeon** N cirurgião(-giã) *m/f* dentista

dentist ['dɛntɪst] N dentista *m/f*; **~'s surgery** (*Brit*) consultório dentário

dentistry ['dɛntɪstrɪ] N odontologia

dentures ['dɛntʃəz] NPL dentadura

denunciation [dɪnʌnsɪ'eɪʃən] N denúncia

deny [dɪ'naɪ] VT negar; (*report*) desmentir; (*refuse*) recusar; **he denies having said it** ele nega ter dito isso

deodorant [diː'əudərənt] N desodorante *m* (BR), desodorizante *m* (PT)

depart [dɪ'pɑːt] VI ir-se, partir; (*train etc*) sair; **to ~ from** (*fig: differ from*) afastar-se de

department [dɪ'pɑːtmənt] N departamento; (*Comm*) seção *f*; (*Pol*) repartição *f*; **that's not my ~** (*fig*) este não é o meu departamento; **D~ of State** (US) Departamento de Estado

departmental [diːpɑːt'mɛntl] ADJ departamental; **~ manager** chefe *m/f* de serviço

department store N magazine *m* (BR), grande armazém *m* (PT)

departure [dɪ'pɑːtʃəʳ] N partida, ida; (*of train etc*) saída; (*of employee*) saída; (*fig*): **~ from** afastamento de; **a new ~** uma nova orientação; **departure lounge** N sala de embarque

departures board (US **departure board**) N horário de saídas

depend [dɪ'pɛnd] VI: **to ~ (up)on** depender de; (*rely on*) contar com; **it ~s** depende; **~ing on the result ...** dependendo do resultado ...

dependable [dɪ'pɛndəbl] ADJ (*person*) de confiança, seguro; (*watch, car*) confiável

dependant [dɪ'pɛndənt] N dependente *m/f*

dependence [dɪ'pɛndəns] N dependência

dependent [dɪ'pɛndənt] ADJ: **to be ~ (on)** depender (de), ser dependente (de) ▪ N = **dependant**.

depict [dɪ'pɪkt] VT (*in picture*) retratar, representar; (*describe*) descrever

depilatory [dɪ'pɪlətrɪ] N (*also*: **depilatory cream**) depilatório

depleted [dɪ'pliːtɪd] ADJ esgotado

deplorable [dɪ'plɔːrəbl] ADJ (*disgraceful*) deplorável; (*regrettable*) lamentável

deplore [dɪ'plɔːʳ] VT (*condemn*) deplorar; (*regret*) lamentar

deploy [dɪ'plɔɪ] VT dispor; (*missiles*) instalar

depopulate [diː'pɔpjuleɪt] VT despovoar

depopulation ['diːpɔpju'leɪʃən] N despovoamento

deport [dɪ'pɔːt] VT deportar

deportation [dɪpɔː'teɪʃən] N deportação *f*; **deportation order** N ordem *f* de deportação

deportment [dɪ'pɔːtmənt] N comportamento; (*way of walking*) modo de andar

depose [dɪ'pəuz] VT depor

deposit [dɪ'pɔzɪt] N (*Comm, Geo*) depósito; (*Chem*) sedimento; (*of ore, oil*) jazida; (*down payment*) sinal *m*; (*for hired goods etc*) caução *f* ▪ VT depositar; (*luggage*) guardar; **to put down a ~ of £50** pagar um sinal de £50; **deposit account** N conta de depósito a prazo

depositor [dɪ'pɔzɪtəʳ] N depositante *m/f*

depository [dɪ'pɔzɪtərɪ] N (*person*) depositário(-a); (*place*) depósito

depot ['dɛpəu] N (*storehouse*) depósito, armazém *m*; (*for vehicles*) garagem *f*, parque *m*; (US) estação *f*

depraved [dɪ'preɪvd] ADJ depravado, viciado

depravity [dɪ'prævɪtɪ] N depravação *f*, vício

deprecate ['dɛprɪkeɪt] VT desaprovar

deprecating ['dɛprɪkeɪtɪŋ] ADJ desaprovador(a)

depreciate [dɪ'priːʃɪeɪt] VT depreciar ▪ VI depreciar-se, desvalorizar-se

depreciation [dɪpriːʃɪ'eɪʃən] N depreciação *f*

depress [dɪ'prɛs] VT deprimir; (*press down*) apertar

depressant [dɪ'prɛsnt] N (*Med*) depressor *m*

depressed [dɪ'prɛst] ADJ (person) deprimido; (area, market, trade) em depressão

depressing [dɪ'prɛsɪŋ] ADJ deprimente

depression [dɪ'prɛʃən] N (also: Econ) depressão f; (hollow) achatamento

deprivation [dɛprɪ'veɪʃən] N privação f; (loss) perda

deprive [dɪ'praɪv] VT: **to ~ sb of** privar alguém de

deprived [dɪ'prəɪvd] ADJ carente

dept. ABBR (= department) depto

depth [dɛpθ] N profundidade f; (of feeling) intensidade f; (of room etc) comprimento; **in the ~s of despair** no auge do deespero; **at a ~ of 3 metres** a uma profundidade de 3 metros; **to be out of one's ~** (Brit: swimmer) estar sem pé; (fig) estar voando; **to study sth in ~** estudar algo em profundidade; **depth charge** N carga de profundidade

deputation [dɛpju'teɪʃən] N delegação f

deputize ['dɛpjutaɪz] VI: **to ~ for sb** substituir alguém; **deputy** ['dɛpjutɪ] ADJ: **deputy chairman** vice-presidente(-a) m/f ▪ N (assistant) ajunto; (replacement) substituto(-a), suplente m/f; (Pol: MP) deputado(-a); (second in command) vice m/f

deputy head (Brit: Sch) ▪ N diretor adjunto/ diretora adjunta m/f

deputy leader (Brit: Pol) ▪ N vice-líder m/f

derail [dɪ'reɪl] VT descarrilhar; **to be ~ed** descarrilhar

derailment [dɪ'reɪlmənt] N descarrilhamento

deranged [dɪ'reɪndʒd] ADJ (person) louco, transtornado

derby ['də:bɪ] (US) N chapéu-coco

deregulate [dɪ'rɛgjuleɪt] VT liberar

deregulation [dɪ'rɛgju'leɪʃən] N liberação f

derelict ['dɛrɪlɪkt] ADJ abandonado

deride [dɪ'raɪd] VT ridicularizar, zombar de

derision [dɪ'rɪʒən] N irrisão f, escárnio

derisive [dɪ'raɪsɪv] ADJ zombeteiro

derisory [dɪ'raɪsərɪ] ADJ (sum) irrisório; (person, smile) zombeteiro

derivation [dɛrɪ'veɪʃən] N derivação f

derivative [dɪ'rɪvətɪv] N derivado ▪ ADJ derivado; (work) pouco original

derive [dɪ'raɪv] VT: **to ~ (from)** obter or tirar (de) ▪ VI: **to ~ from** derivar-se de

dermatitis [də:mə'taɪtɪs] N dermatite f

dermatology [də:mə'tolədʒɪ] N dermatologia

derogatory [dɪ'rɔgətərɪ] ADJ depreciativo

derrick ['dɛrɪk] N (crane) guindaste m; (oil derrick) torre f de perfurar

derv [də:v] (Brit) N gasóleo

DES (Brit) N ABBR (= Department of Education and Science) Ministério da Educação e das Ciências

desalination [di:sælɪ'neɪʃən] N dessalinização f

descend [dɪ'sɛnd] VT, VI descer; **to ~ from** descer de; (to descend to) descambar em; **in ~ing order** em ordem decrescente

▶ **descend on** VT FUS (subj: enemy, angry person) cair sobre; (: misfortune) abater-se sobre; (: gloom,

silence) invadir; **visitors ~ed (up)on us** visitas invadiram nossa casa

descendant [dɪ'sɛndənt] N descendente m/f

descent [dɪ'sɛnt] N descida; (slope) declive m, ladeira; (origin) descendência

describe [dɪs'kraɪb] VT descrever

description [dɪs'krɪpʃən] N descrição f; (sort) classe f, espécie f; **of every ~** de toda a sorte, de todo o tipo

descriptive [dɪs'krɪptɪv] ADJ descritivo

desecrate ['dɛsɪkreɪt] VT profanar

desert [n 'dɛzət, vt, vi dɪ'zə:t] N deserto ▪ VT (place) desertar; (partner, family) abandonar ▪ VI (Mil) desertar

deserter [dɪ'zə:tər] N desertor m

desertion [dɪ'zə:ʃən] N (Mil) deserção f; (Law) abandono do lar

desert island N ilha deserta

deserts [dɪ'zə:ts] NPL: **to get one's just ~** receber o que merece

deserve [dɪ'zə:v] VT merecer

deservedly [dɪ'zə:vɪdlɪ] ADJ merecidamente

deserving [dɪ'zə:vɪŋ] ADJ (person) merecedor(a), digno; (action, cause) meritório

desiccated ['dɛsɪkeɪtɪd] ADJ dessecado

design [dɪ'zaɪn] N (sketch) desenho, esboço; (layout, shape) plano, projeto; (pattern) desenho, padrão m; (of dress, car etc) modelo; (art) design m; (intention) propósito, intenção f ▪ VT desenhar; (plan) projetar; **to have ~s on** ter a mira em; **well-~ed** bem projetado; **to be ~ed for sb/sth** (intended) ser destinado a alguém/algo

designate [vt 'dɛzɪgneɪt, adj 'dɛzɪgnɪt] VT (point to) apontar; (appoint) nomear; (destine) designar ▪ ADJ designado

designation [dɛzɪg'neɪʃən] N (appointment) nomeação f; (name) designação f

designer [dɪ'zaɪnər] N (Art) artista m/f gráfico(-a); (Tech) desenhista m/f, projetista m/f; (fashion designer) estilista m/f

desirability [dɪzaɪrə'bɪlɪtɪ] N necessidade f

desirable [dɪ'zaɪərəbl] ADJ (proper) desejável; (attractive) atraente

desire [dɪ'zaɪər] N anseio; (sexual) desejo ▪ VT querer; (lust after) desejar, cobiçar; **to ~ to do sth/that** desejar fazer algo/que

desirous [dɪ'zaɪərəs] ADJ: **~ of** desejoso de

desk [dɛsk] N (in office) mesa, secretária; (for pupil) carteira f; (at airport) balcão m; (in hotel) recepção f; (Brit: in shop, restaurant) caixa

desk-top publishing N editoração f eletrônica, desktop publishing m

desolate ['dɛsəlɪt] ADJ (place) deserto; (person) desolado

desolation [dɛsə'leɪʃən] N (of place) desolação f; (of person) aflição f

despair [dɪs'pɛər] N desesperança ▪ VI: **to ~ of** desesperar-se de; **to be in ~** estar desesperado

despatch [dɪs'pætʃ] N, VT = **dispatch**

desperate ['dɛspərɪt] ADJ desesperado; (situation) desperador(a); **to be ~ for sth/to do** estar louco por algo/para fazer

desperately ['dɛspərɪtlɪ] ADV desesperadamente; (very: unhappy) terrívelmente; (: ill) gravemente

desperation [dɛspə'reɪʃən] N desespero, desesperança; **in (sheer) ~** desesperado

despicable [dɪs'pɪkəbl] ADJ desprezível

despise [dɪs'paɪz] VT desprezar

despite [dɪs'paɪt] PREP apesar de, a despeito de

despondent [dɪs'pɔndənt] ADJ abatido, desanimado

despot ['dɛspɔt] N déspota m/f

dessert [dɪ'zə:t] N sobremesa

dessertspoon [dɪ'zə:tspu:n] N colher f de sobremesa

destabilize [di:'steɪbɪlaɪz] VT desestabilizar

destination [dɛstɪ'neɪʃən] N destino

destine ['dɛstɪn] VT destinar

destined ['dɛstɪnd] ADJ: **to be ~ to do sth** estar destinado a fazer algo; **~ for** com destino a

destiny ['dɛstɪnɪ] N destino

destitute ['dɛstɪtju:t] ADJ indigente, necessitado; **~ of** desprovido de

destroy [dɪs'trɔɪ] VT destruir; (animal) matar

destroyer [dɪs'trɔɪər] N (Naut) contratorpedeiro

destruction [dɪs'trʌkʃən] N destruição f

destructive [dɪs'trʌktɪv] ADJ (capacity, criticism) destrutivo; (force, child) destruidor(a)

desultory ['dɛsəltərɪ] ADJ (reading, conversation) desconexo; (contact) irregular

detach [dɪ'tætʃ] VT separar; (unstick) desprender

detachable [dɪ'tætʃəbl] ADJ separável; (Tech) desmontável

detached [dɪ'tætʃt] ADJ (attitude) imparcial, objetivo; (house) independente, isolado

detachment [dɪ'tætʃmənt] N distanciamento; (Mil) destacamento; (fig) objetividade f, imparcialidade f

detail ['di:teɪl] N detalhe m; (trifle) bobagem f; (Mil) destacamento ■ VT detalhar; (Mil): **to ~ sb (for)** destacar alguém (para); **in ~** pormenorizado, em detalhe; **to go into ~(s)** entrar em detalhes

detailed ['di:teɪld] ADJ detalhado

detain [dɪ'teɪn] VT deter; (in captivity) prender; (in hospital) hospitalizar

detainee [di:teɪ'ni:] N detido(-a)

detect [dɪ'tɛkt] VT perceber; (Med, Police) identificar; (Mil, Radar, Tech) detectar

detection [dɪ'tɛkʃən] N descoberta; (Med, Police) identificação f; (Mil, Radar, Tech) detecção f; **to escape ~** evitar ser descoberto; **crime ~** investigação f de crimes

detective [dɪ'tɛktɪv] N detetive m/f; **private ~** detetive particular; **detective story** N romance m policial

detector [dɪ'tɛktər] N detetor m

detention [dɪ'tɛnʃən] N detenção f, prisão f; (Sch) castigo

deter [dɪ'tə:r] VT (discourage) desanimar; (dissuade) dissuadir; (prevent) impedir

detergent [dɪ'tə:dʒənt] N detergente m

deteriorate [dɪ'tɪərɪəreɪt] VI deteriorar-se

deterioration [dɪtɪərɪə'reɪʃən] N deterioração f

determination [dɪtə:mɪ'neɪʃən] N determinação f; (resolve) resolução f

determine [dɪ'tə:mɪn] VT determinar; (facts) descobrir; (limits etc) demarcar; **to ~ to do** resolver fazer, determinar-se de fazer

determined [dɪ'tə:mɪnd] ADJ (person) resoluto; (quantity) determinado; (effort) grande; **~ to do** decido a fazer

deterrence [dɪ'tɛrəns] N dissuasão f

deterrent [dɪ'tɛrənt] N dissuasivo

detest [dɪ'tɛst] VT detestar

detestable [dɪ'tɛstəbl] ADJ detestável

detonate ['dɛtəneɪt] VI explodir, estalar ■ VT detonar

detonator ['dɛtəneɪtər] N detonador m

detour ['di:tuər] N desvio

detract [dɪ'trækt] VI: **to ~ from** (merits, reputation) depreciar; (quality, pleasure) diminuir

detractor [dɪ'træktər] N detrator(a) m/f

detriment ['dɛtrɪmənt] N: **to the ~ of** em detrimento de; **without ~ to** sem detrimento de

detrimental [dɛtrɪ'mɛntl] ADJ: **~ (to)** prejudicial (a)

deuce [dju:s] N (Tennis) empate m, iguais

devaluation [dɪvælju'eɪʃən] N desvalorização f

devalue [dɪ'vælju:] VT desvalorizar

devastate ['dɛvəsteɪt] VT devastar; (fig): **to be ~d by** estar arrasado com; **he was ~d by the news** as notícias deixaram-no desolado

devastating ['dɛvəsteɪtɪŋ] ADJ devastador(a); (fig) assolador(a)

devastation [dɛvəs'teɪʃən] N devastação f

develop [dɪ'vɛləp] VT desenvolver; (Phot) revelar; (disease) contrair; (resources) explotar; (engine trouble) começar a ter ■ VI desenvolver-se; (advance) progredir; (evolve) evoluir; (appear) aparecer

developer [dɪ'vɛləpər] N (Phot) revelador m; (also: **property developer**) empresário(-a) de imóveis

developing country [dɪ'vɛləpɪŋ-] N país m em desenvolvimento

development [dɪ'vɛləpmənt] N desenvolvimento; (advance) progresso; (of land) urbanização f; **development area** N zona a ser urbanizada

deviate ['di:vɪeɪt] VI desviar-se

deviation [di:vɪ'eɪʃən] N desvio

device [dɪ'vaɪs] N (scheme) estratagema m, plano; (apparatus) aparelho, dispositivo; **explosive ~** dispositivo explosivo

devil ['dɛvl] N diabo

devilish ['dɛvlɪʃ] ADJ diabólico

devil-may-care ADJ despreocupado

devious ['di:vɪəs] ADJ (means) intricado, indireto; (person) malandro, esperto

devise [dɪ'vaɪz] VT (plan) criar; (machine) inventar

devoid [dɪ'vɔɪd] ADJ: **~ of** destituído de

devolution [di:və'lu:ʃən] N (Pol) descentralização f

devolve [dɪ'vɔlv] VI: **to ~ (up)on** passar a ser da

competência de

devote [dɪ'vəʊt] VT: **to ~ sth to** dedicar algo a

devoted [dɪ'vəʊtɪd] ADJ (loyal: friendship) leal; (: partner) fiel; **to be ~ to** (love) estar devotado a; **the book is ~ to politics** o livro trata de política

devotee [dɛvəʊ'tiː] N adepto(-a), entusiasta m/f; (Rel) devoto

devotion [dɪ'vəʊʃən] N devoção f; (to duty) dedicação f

devour [dɪ'vauəʳ] VT devorar

devout [dɪ'vaut] ADJ devoto

dew [djuː] N orvalho

dexterity [dɛks'tɛrɪtɪ] N destreza

dext(e)rous ['dɛkstrəs] ADJ destro

dg ABBR (= decigram) dg

diabetes [daɪə'biːtiːz] N diabete f

diabetic [da'ə'bɛtɪk] ADJ (person) diabético; (chocolate, jam) para diabéticos ■ N diabético(-a)

diabolical [daɪə'bɒlɪkl] ADJ diabólico; (inf: dreadful) horrível

diagnose [daɪəg'nəʊz] VT diagnosticar

diagnoses [daɪəg'nəsiːz] NPL of **diagnosis**

diagnosis [daɪəg'nəʊsɪs] (pl **diagnoses**) N diagnóstico

diagonal [daɪ'ægənl] ADJ diagonal ■ N diagonal f

diagram ['daɪəgræm] N diagrama m, esquema m

dial ['daɪəl] N disco ■ VT (number) discar (BR), marcar (PT); **to ~ a wrong number** discar (BR) or marcar (PT) um número errado; **can I ~ London direct?** é possível discar direto para Londres?

dial. ABBR = **dialect**

dial code (US) N = **dialling code**

dialect ['daɪəlɛkt] N dialeto

dialling code ['daɪəlɪŋ-] (Brit) N código de discagem

dialling tone ['daɪəlɪŋ-] (Brit) N sinal m de discagem (BR) or de marcar (PT)

dialogue ['daɪəlɒg] (US **dialog**) N diálogo; (conversation) conversa

dial tone (US) N = **dialling tone**

dialysis [daɪ'ælɪsɪs] N diálise f

diameter [daɪ'æmɪtəʳ] N diâmetro

diametrically [daɪə'mɛtrɪklɪ] ADV: **~ opposed (to)** diametralmente oposto (a)

diamond ['daɪəmənd] N diamante m; (shape) losango, rombo; **diamonds** NPL (Cards) ouros mpl; **diamond ring** N anel m de brilhante

diaper ['daɪəpəʳ] (US) N fralda

diaphragm ['daɪəfræm] N diafragma m

diarrhoea [daɪə'riːə] (US **diarrhea**) N diarréia

diary ['daɪərɪ] N (daily account) diário; (engagements book) agenda; **to keep a ~** ter um diário

diatribe ['daɪətraɪb] N diatribe f

dice [daɪs] NPL of **die** ■ N INV dado ■ VT (Culin) cortar em cubos

dicey ['daɪsɪ] (inf) ADJ: **it's a bit ~** é um pouco arriscado

dichotomy [daɪ'kɒtəmɪ] N dicotomia

Dictaphone® ['dɪktəfəʊn] N ditafone® m, máquina de ditar

dictate [dɪk'teɪt] VT ditar ■ VI: **to ~ to** (person) dar ordens a; **I won't be ~d to** não vou acatar ordens

dictates ['dɪkteɪts] NPL ditames mpl

dictation [dɪk'teɪʃən] N ditado; **at ~ speed** com a velocidade de ditado

dictator [dɪk'teɪtəʳ] N ditador(a) m/f

dictatorship [dɪk'teɪtəʃɪp] N ditadura

diction ['dɪkʃən] N dicção f

dictionary ['dɪkʃənrɪ] N dicionário

did [dɪd] PT of **do**

didactic [daɪ'dæktɪk] ADJ didático

didn't ['dɪdənt] = **did not**

die [daɪ] N (pl **dice**) dado; (pl **dies**) cunho, molde m ■ VI morrer; (fig: fade) murchar; **to ~ of** or **from** morrer de; **to be dying for sth/to do sth** estar louco por algo/para fazer algo

▶ **die away** VI (sound, light) extinguir-se lentamente

▶ **die down** VI (fire) apagar-se; (wind) abrandar; (excitement) diminuir

▶ **die out** VI desaparecer; (animal, bird) extinguir-se

diehard ['daɪhɑːd] N reacionário(-a), reaça m/f (inf)

diesel ['diːzl] N diesel m; (also: **diesel oil**) óleo diesel; **diesel engine** ['diːzəl-] N motor m diesel; **diesel (fuel)** N óleo diesel

diet ['daɪət] N dieta; (restricted food) regime m ■ VI (also: **be on a diet**) estar de dieta, fazer regime; **to live on a ~ of** alimentar-se de

dietician [daɪə'tɪʃən] N dietista m/f

differ ['dɪfəʳ] VI (be different): **to ~ from sth** ser diferente de algo, diferenciar-se de algo; (disagree): **to ~ (about)** discordar (sobre)

difference ['dɪfərəns] N diferença; (disagreement) divergência; (quarrel) desacordo; **it makes no ~ to me** não faz diferença para mim, para mim dá no mesmo; **to settle one's ~s** resolver as diferenças

different ['dɪfərənt] ADJ diferente

differential [dɪfə'rɛnʃəl] N (Aut) diferencial m; **wage/price ~s** diferenças de salário/preço

differentiate [dɪfə'rɛnʃɪeɪt] VT diferenciar, distinguir ■ VI: **to ~ (between)** distinguir (entre)

differently ['dɪfərəntlɪ] ADV de outro modo, de forma diferente

difficult ['dɪfɪkəlt] ADJ difícil; **~ to understand** difícil de (se) entender

difficulty ['dɪfɪkəltɪ] N dificuldade f; **to have difficulties with** ter problemas com; **to be in ~** estar em dificuldade

diffidence ['dɪfɪdəns] N timidez f

diffident ['dɪfɪdənt] ADJ tímido

diffuse [adj dɪ'fjuːs, vt dɪ'fjuːz] ADJ difuso ■ VT difundir

dig [dɪg] (pt, pp **dug**) VT (hole, garden) cavar; (coal) escavar; (nails etc) cravar ■ N (prod) pontada;

(archaeological) excavação f; (remark) alfinetada; **to ~ into one's pockets for sth** enfiar as mãos nos bolsos à procura de algo; **to ~ one's nails into** cravar as unhas em

▶ **dig in** vi (Mil) cavar trincheiras; (inf: eat) atacar ▪ vt (compost) misturar; (knife, claw) cravar; **to ~ in one's heels** (fig) bater o pé; **~ in!** vai lá!

▶ **dig into** vt fus (savings) gastar

▶ **dig out** vt escavar

▶ **dig up** vt (plant) arrancar; (information) trazer à tona

digest [vt daɪ'dʒɛst, n 'daɪdʒɛst] vt (food) digerir; (facts) assimilar ▪ n sumário

digestible [dɪ'dʒɛstəbl] adj digerível

digestion [dɪ'dʒɛstʃən] n digestão f

digestive [dɪ'dʒɛstɪv] adj digestivo

digit ['dɪdʒɪt] n (Math) dígito; (finger) dedo

digital ['dɪdʒɪtəl] adj digital; **digital camera** n câmara digital; **digital computer** n computador m digital; **digital TV** n televisão f digital

dignified ['dɪgnɪfaɪd] adj digno

dignitary ['dɪgnɪtərɪ] n dignitário(-a)

dignity ['dɪgnɪtɪ] n dignidade f

digress [daɪ'grɛs] vi: **to ~ from** afastar-se de

digression [daɪ'grɛʃən] n digressão f

digs [dɪgz] (Brit: inf) npl pensão f, alojamento

dike [daɪk] n = **dyke**

dilapidated [dɪ'læpɪdeɪtɪd] adj arruinado

dilate [daɪ'leɪt] vt dilatar ▪ vi dilatar-se

dilatory ['dɪlətərɪ] adj retardio

dilemma [daɪ'lɛmə] n dilema m; **to be in a ~** estar num dilema

diligent ['dɪlɪdʒənt] adj (worker) diligente; (research) cuidadoso

dill [dɪl] n endro, aneto

dilly-dally ['dɪlɪ'dælɪ] vi (loiter) vadiar; (hesitate) vacilar

dilute [daɪ'luːt] vt diluir ▪ adj diluído

dim [dɪm] adj (light, eyesight) fraco; (outline) indistinto; (memory) vago; (room) escuro; (inf: person) burro ▪ vt (light) diminuir; (US: Aut) baixar; **to take a ~ view of sth** desaprovar algo

dime [daɪm] (US) n moeda de dez centavos.

dimension [dɪ'mɛnʃən] n dimensão f; (measurement) medida; (also: dimensions: scale, size) famanho

-dimensional [dɪ'mɛnʃənl] suffix: **two~** bidimensional

diminish [dɪ'mɪnɪʃ] vt, vi diminuir

diminished [dɪ'mɪnɪʃt] adj: **~ responsibility** (Law) responsabilidade f reduzida

diminutive [dɪ'mɪnjutɪv] adj diminuto ▪ n (Ling) diminutivo

dimly ['dɪmlɪ] adv fracamente; (not clearly) indistintamente

dimmers ['dɪməz] (US) npl (Aut: headlights) faróis mpl baixos

dimple ['dɪmpl] n covinha

dim-witted [-'wɪtɪd] (inf) adj burro

din [dɪn] n zoeira ▪ vt: **to ~ sth into sb** (inf)

meter algo na cabeça de alguém, repisar algo a alguém

dine [daɪn] vi jantar

diner ['daɪnər] n (person) comensal m/f; (Rail) vagão-restaurante m; (US: eating place) lanchonete f

dinghy ['dɪŋgɪ] n dingue m, bote m; **rubber ~** bote de borracha; (also: sailing dinghy) barco a vela

dingy ['dɪndʒɪ] adj (room) sombrio, lúgubre; (clothes, curtains etc) sujo; (dull) descolorido

dining car ['daɪnɪŋ-] (Brit) n (Rail) vagão-restaurante m

dining room ['daɪnɪŋ-] n sala de jantar

dinner ['dɪnər] n (evening meal) jantar m; (lunch) almoço; (banquet) banquete m; **~'s ready!** está na mesa!; **dinner jacket** n smoking m; **dinner party** n jantar m; **dinner time** n (midday) hora de almoço; (evening) hora de jantar

dinosaur ['daɪnəsɔːr] n dinossauro

dint [dɪnt] n: **by ~ of** à força de

diocese ['daɪəsɪs] n diocese f

dioxide [daɪ'ɔksaɪd] n dióxido

Dip. (Brit) abbr = **diploma**

dip [dɪp] n (slope) inclinação f; (in sea) mergulho; (Culin) pasta para servir com salgadinhos ▪ vt (in water) mergulhar; (ladle etc) meter; (Brit: Aut: lights) baixar ▪ vi (ground, road) descer subitamente

diphtheria [dɪf'θɪərɪə] n difteria

diphthong ['dɪfθɔŋ] n ditongo

diploma [dɪ'pləumə] n diploma m

diplomacy [dɪ'pləuməsɪ] n diplomacia

diplomat ['dɪpləmæt] (Brit) n diplomata m/f

diplomatic [dɪplə'mætɪk] adj diplomático; **to break off ~ relations (with)** romper relações diplomáticas (com)

dipstick ['dɪpstɪk] n (Aut) vareta medidora

dipswitch ['dɪpswɪtʃ] (Brit) n (Aut) interruptor m de luz alta e baixa

dire [daɪər] adj terrível; (very bad) péssimo

direct [daɪ'rɛkt] adj direto; (route) reto; (manner) franco, sincero ▪ vt dirigir; (order): **to ~ sb to do sth** ordenar alguém para fazer algo ▪ adv direto; **can you ~ me to ...?** pode me indicar o caminho a ...?; **direct cost** n (Comm) custo direto; **direct current** n (Elec) corrente f contínua; **direct debit** (Brit) n (Banking) débito direto; **direct dialling** n (Tel) discagem f direta (BR), marcação f directa (PT); **direct hit** n (Mil) acerto direto

direction [dɪ'rɛkʃən] n (way) indicação f; (TV, Radio, Cinema) direção f; **directions** npl (to a place) indicação f; (instructions) instruções fpl; **~s for use** modo de usar; **to ask for ~s** pedir uma indicação, perguntar o caminho; **sense of ~** senso de direção; **in the ~ of** na direção de

directive [dɪ'rɛktɪv] n diretriz f

direct labour n mão-de-obra direta

directly [dɪ'rɛktlɪ] adv (in a straight line) diretamente; (at once) imediatamente

direct mail n mala direta

direct mailshot (Brit) N mailing m
directness [daɪ'rɛktnɪs] N (of person, speech) franqueza
director [dɪ'rɛktər] N diretor m; **D~ of Public Prosecutions** (Brit) = procurador(a) m/f de República
directory [dɪ'rɛktərɪ] N (Tel) lista (telefônica); (also: **street directory**) lista de endereços; (Comm) anuário comercial; (Comput) diretório; **directory enquiries** (US **directory assistance**) N (serviço de) informações fpl (BR), serviço informativo (PT)
dirt [dəːt] N sujeira (BR), sujidade (PT); **to treat sb like ~** espezinhar alguém
dirt-cheap ADJ baratíssimo
dirt road N estrada de terra
dirty ['dəːtɪ] ADJ sujo; (joke) indecente ■ VT sujar; **dirty trick** N golpe m baixo, sujeira
disability [dɪsə'bɪlɪtɪ] N incapacidade f; **disability allowance** N pensão f de invalidez
disable [dɪs'eɪbl] VT (subj: illness, accident) incapacitar; (tank, gun) inutilizar
disabled [dɪs'eɪbld] ADJ deficiente ■ NPL: **the ~** os deficientes
disadvantage [dɪsəd'vɑːntɪdʒ] N desvantagem f; (prejudice) inconveniente m
disadvantaged [dɪsəd'vɑːntɪdʒd] ADJ (person) menos favorecido
disadvantageous [dɪsædvɑːn'teɪdʒəs] ADJ desvantajoso
disaffected [dɪsə'fɛktɪd] ADJ: ~ **(to or towards)** descontente (de)
disaffection [dɪsə'fɛkʃən] N descontentamento
disagree [dɪsə'griː] VI (differ) diferir; (be against, think otherwise): **to ~ (with)** não concordar (com), discordar (de); **garlic ~s with me** o alho me faz mal, o alho não me convém
disagreeable [dɪsə'grɪəbl] ADJ desagradável
disagreement [dɪsə'griːmənt] N desacordo; (quarrel) desavença
disallow ['dɪsə'lau] VT não admitir; (Law) vetar, proibir; (Brit: goal) anular
disappear [dɪsə'pɪər] VI desaparecer, sumir; (custom etc) acabar
disappearance [dɪsə'pɪərəns] N desaparecimento, desaparição f
disappoint [dɪsə'pɔɪnt] VT (cause to regret) desapontar; (let down) decepcionar; (hopes) frustrar
disappointed [dɪsə'pɔɪntɪd] ADJ decepcionado; (with oneself) desapontado
disappointing [dɪsə'pɔɪntɪŋ] ADJ decepcionante
disappointment [dɪsə'pɔɪntmənt] N decepção f; (cause) desapontamento
disapproval [dɪsə'pruːvəl] N desaprovação f
disapprove [dɪsə'pruːv] VI: **to ~ of** desaprovar
disapproving [dɪsə'pruːvɪŋ] ADJ desaprovativo, de desaprovação
disarm [dɪs'ɑːm] VT desarmar
disarmament [dɪs'ɑːməmənt] N desarmamento

disarming [dɪs'ɑːmɪŋ] ADJ (smile) encantador(a)
disarray [dɪsə'reɪ] N desordem f; **in ~** (troops) desbaratado; (organization) desorganizado, caótico; (thoughts) confuso; (clothes) em desalinho; **to throw into ~** (troops) desbaratar; (government etc) deixar em polvorosa
disaster [dɪ'zɑːstər] N (accident) desastre m; (natural) catástrofe f
disastrous [dɪ'zɑːstrəs] ADJ desastroso
disband [dɪs'bænd] VT dispersar ■ VI dispersar-se, desfazer-se
disbelief [dɪsbə'liːf] N incredulidade f; **in ~** com incredulidade, incrédulo
disbelieve ['dɪsbə'liːv] VT não acreditar em
disc [dɪsk] N disco; (Comput) = **disk**
disc. ABBR (Comm) = **discount**
discard [dɪs'kɑːd] VT (old things) desfazer-se de; (fig) descartar
disc brake N freio de disco (BR), travão m de discos (PT)
discern [dɪ'səːn] VT perceber; (identify) identificar
discernible [dɪ'səːnəbl] ADJ perceptível; (object) visível
discerning [dɪ'səːnɪŋ] ADJ perspicaz
discharge [vt dɪs'tʃɑːdʒ, n 'dɪstʃɑːdʒ] VT (duties) cumprir, desempenhar; (settle: debt) saldar, quitar; (patient) dar alta a; (employee) despedir; (soldier) dar baixa em, dispensar; (defendant) pôr em liberdade; (waste etc) descarregar, despejar ■ N (Elec) descarga; (dismissal) despedida; (of duty) desempenho; (of debt) quitação f; (from hospital) alta; (from army) baixa; (Law) absolvição f; (Med) secreção f; (also: **vaginal discharge**) corrimento; **to ~ one's gun** descarregar a arma, disparar; **~d bankrupt** falido(-a) reabilitado(-a)
disciple [dɪ'saɪpl] N discípulo(-a)
disciplinary ['dɪsɪplɪnərɪ] ADJ disciplinar; **to take ~ action against sb** mover ação disciplinar contra alguém
discipline ['dɪsɪplɪn] N disciplina; (self-discipline) auto-disciplina ■ VT disciplinar; (punish) punir; **to ~ o.s. to do sth** disciplinar-se para fazer algo
disc jockey N (on radio) radialista m/f; (in discothèque) discotecário(-a)
disclaim [dɪs'kleɪm] VT negar
disclaimer [dɪs'kleɪmər] N desmentido; **to issue a ~** publicar um desmentido
disclose [dɪs'kləuz] VT revelar
disclosure [dɪs'kləuʒər] N revelação f
disco ['dɪskəu] N ABBR = **discothèque**
discolour [dɪs'kʌlər] (US **discolor**) VT descolorar; (fade: fabric) desbotar; (yellow: teeth) amarelar; (stain) manchar ■ VI (fabric) desbotar; (teeth etc) amarelar
discolo(u)ration [dɪskʌlə'reɪʃən] N (of fabric) desbotamento; (stain) mancha
discolo(u)red [dɪs'kʌləd] ADJ descolorado; (teeth etc) amarelado
discomfort [dɪs'kʌmfət] N (unease) inquietação f; (physical) desconforto

disconcert [dɪskən'sə:t] VT desconcertar
disconnect [dɪskə'nɛkt] VT desligar; (pipe, tap) desmembrar; (gas, water) cortar
disconnected [dɪskə'nɛktɪd] ADJ (speech, thoughts) desconexo, incoerente
disconsolate [dɪs'kɔnsəlɪt] ADJ desconsolado, inconsolável
discontent [dɪskən'tɛnt] N descontentamento
discontented ['dɪskən'tɛntɪd] ADJ descontente
discontinue [dɪskən'tɪnju:] VT interromper; (payments) suspender; **"~d"** (Comm) "fora de linha"
discord ['dɪskɔ:d] N discórdia; (Mus) dissonância
discordant [dɪs'kɔ:dənt] ADJ dissonante
discothèque ['dɪskəutɛk] N discoteca
discount [n 'dɪskaunt, vt dɪs'kaunt] N desconto ■ VT descontar; (idea) ignorar; **to give sb a ~ on sth** dar or conceder um desconto a alguém por algo; **~ for cash** desconto por pagamento à vista; **at a ~** com desconto; **discount house** N (Finance) agência corretora de descontos; (Comm: also: **discount store**) loja de descontos; **discount rate** N taxa de desconto
discourage [dɪs'kʌrɪdʒ] VT (dishearten) desanimar; (dissuade) dissuadir; (deter) desincentivar; (theft etc) desencorajar; (advise against): **to ~ sth/sb from doing** desaconselhar algo/alguém a fazer
discouragement [dɪs'kʌrɪdʒmənt] N (depression) desânimo, desalento; **to act as a ~ to sb** dissuadir alguém
discouraging [dɪs'kʌrɪdʒɪŋ] ADJ desanimador(a)
discourteous [dɪs'kə:tɪəs] ADJ descortês
discover [dɪs'kʌvər] VT descobrir; (missing person) encontrar; (mistake) achar
discovery [dɪs'kʌvərɪ] N (act) descobrimento, descoberta; (of object etc) achado; (thing found) descoberta
discredit [dɪs'krɛdɪt] VT desacreditar; (claim) desmerecer ■ N descrédito
discreet [dɪ'skri:t] ADJ discreto; (careful) cauteloso
discreetly [dɪ'skri:tlɪ] ADV discretamente
discrepancy [dɪ'skrɛpənsɪ] N (difference) diferença; (disagreement) discrepância
discretion [dɪ'skrɛʃən] N discrição f; **at the ~ of** ao arbítrio de; **use your ~** aja segundo o seu critério
discretionary [dɪ'skrɛʃənrɪ] ADJ (powers) discricionário
discriminate [dɪ'skrɪmɪneɪt] VI: **to ~ between** fazer distinção entre; **to ~ against** discriminar contra
discriminating [dɪ'skrɪmɪneɪtɪŋ] ADJ (public, audience) criterioso
discrimination [dɪskrɪmɪ'neɪʃən] N (discernment) discernimento; (bias) discriminação f; **racial/ sexual ~** discriminação racial/sexual
discus ['dɪskəs] N disco; (event) arremesso do disco
discuss [dɪ'skʌs] VT discutir; (analyse) analisar

discussion [dɪ'skʌʃən] N discussão f; (debate) debate m; **under ~** em discussão
disdain [dɪs'deɪn] N desdém m ■ VT desdenhar
disease [dɪ'zi:z] N doença
diseased [dɪ'zi:zd] ADJ doente
disembark [dɪsɪm'ba:k] VT, VI desembarcar
disembarkation [dɪsɛmba:'keɪʃən] N desembarque m
disembodied ['dɪsɪm'bɔdɪd] ADJ desencarnado
disembowel ['dɪsɪm'bauəl] VT estripar, eviscerar
disenchanted ['dɪsɪn'tʃɑ:ntɪd] ADJ: **~ (with)** desencantado (de)
disenfranchise ['dɪsɪn'fræntʃaɪz] VT privar do privilégio do voto; (Comm) retirar a concessão de
disengage [dɪsɪn'geɪdʒ] VT soltar; (Tech) desengrenar; (Aut): **to ~ the clutch** desembrear
disentangle [dɪsɪn'tæŋgl] VT (from wreckage) desvencilhar; (wool, wire) desembaraçar
disfavour [dɪs'feɪvər] (US **disfavor**) N desfavor m
disfigure [dɪs'fɪgər] VT (person) desfigurar; (object) estragar, enfear
disgorge [dɪs'gɔ:dʒ] VT descarregar, despejar
disgrace [dɪs'greɪs] N ignomínia; (downfall) queda; (shame) vergonha, desonra ■ VT (family) envergonhar; (name, country) desonrar
disgraceful [dɪs'greɪsful] ADJ vergonhoso; (behaviour) escandaloso
disgruntled [dɪs'grʌntld] ADJ descontente
disguise [dɪs'gaɪz] N disfarce m ■ VT disfarçar; **to ~ o.s. (as)** disfarçar-se (de); **in ~** disfarçado; **there's no disguising the fact that ...** não há como esconder o fato de que ...
disgust [dɪs'gʌst] N repugnância ■ VT repugnar a, dar nojo em
disgusting [dɪs'gʌstɪŋ] ADJ (revolting) repugnante; (unacceptable) inaceitável
dish [dɪʃ] N prato; (serving dish) travessa; **to do** or **wash the ~es** lavar os pratos or a louça
▶ **dish out** VT repartir
▶ **dish up** VT servir; (facts, statistics) apresentar
dishcloth ['dɪʃklɔθ] N pano de prato or de louça
dishearten [dɪs'hɑ:tn] VT desanimar
dishevelled [dɪ'ʃɛvəld] (US **disheveled**) ADJ (hair) despenteado; (clothes) desalinhado
dishonest [dɪs'ɔnɪst] ADJ (person) desonesto; (means) fraudulento
dishonesty [dɪs'ɔnɪstɪ] N desonestidade f
dishonour [dɪs'ɔnər] (US **dishonor**) N desonra
dishono(u)rable [dɪs'ɔnərəbl] ADJ (person) desonesto, vil; (behaviour) desonroso
dish soap (US) N detergente m
dishtowel [dɪʃ'tauəl] (US) N pano de prato
dishwasher ['dɪʃwɔʃər] N máquina de lavar louça or pratos
disillusion [dɪsɪ'lu:ʒən] VT desiludir ■ N desilusão f; **to become ~ed** ficar desiludido, desiludir-se
disillusionment [dɪsɪ'lu:ʒənmənt] N desilusão f
disincentive [dɪsɪn'sɛntɪv] N desincentivo; **to be a ~ to sb** desincentivar alguém
disinclined ['dɪsɪn'klaɪnd] ADJ: **to be ~ to do**

estar pouco disposto a fazer

disinfect [dɪsɪn'fɛkt] vt desinfetar

disinfectant [dɪsɪn'fɛktənt] n desinfetante m

disinflation [dɪsɪn'fleɪʃən] n desinflação f

disinherit [dɪsɪn'hɛrɪt] vt deserdar

disintegrate [dɪs'ɪntɪgreɪt] vi desintegrar-se

disinterested [dɪs'ɪntrəstɪd] ADJ imparcial

disjointed [dɪs'dʒɔɪntɪd] ADJ desconexo

disk [dɪsk] n (*Comput*) disco; **single-/double-sided** ~ disquete de face simples/dupla; **disk drive** n unidade f de disco

diskette [dɪs'kɛt] (*US*) n = **disk**

disk operating system n sistema m operacional residente em disco

dislike [dɪs'laɪk] n desagrado ■ vt antipatizar com, não gostar de; **to take a ~ to sb/sth** tomar antipatia por alguém/algo; **I ~ the idea** não gosto da idéia

dislocate ['dɪsləkeɪt] vt deslocar; **he has ~d his shoulder** ele deslocou o ombro

dislodge [dɪs'lɔdʒ] vt mover, deslocar; (*enemy*) desalojar

disloyal [dɪs'lɔɪəl] ADJ desleal

dismal ['dɪzml] ADJ (*dull*) sombrio, lúgubre; (*depressing*) deprimente; (*very bad*) horrível

dismantle [dɪs'mæntl] vt desmontar, desmantelar

dismay [dɪs'meɪ] n consternação f ■ vt consternar; **much to my** ~ para minha grande consternação

dismiss [dɪs'mɪs] vt (*worker*) despedir; (*pupils*) dispensar; (*soldiers*) dar baixa a; (*official*) demitir; (*Law, possibility*) rejeitar ■ vi (*Mil*) sair de forma

dismissal [dɪs'mɪsəl] n (*of worker*) despedida; (*of official*) demissão f

dismount [dɪs'maunt] vi (*from horse*) desmontar; (*from bicycle*) descer

disobedience [dɪsə'biːdɪəns] n desobediência

disobedient [dɪsə'biːdɪənt] ADJ desobediente

disobey [dɪsə'beɪ] vt desobedecer a; (*rules*) transgredir, desrespeitar

disorder [dɪs'ɔːdər] n desordem f; (*rioting*) distúrbios mpl, tumulto; (*Med*) distúrbio; **stomach** ~ problema estomacal

disorderly [dɪs'ɔːdəlɪ] ADJ (*untidy*) desarrumado; (*meeting*) tumultuado; (*behaviour*) escandaloso; **disorderly conduct** n (*Law*) perturbação f da ordem, ofensa à moral

disorganized [dɪs'ɔːgənaɪzd] ADJ desorganizado

disorientated [dɪs'ɔːrɪɛnteɪtəd] ADJ desorientado

disown [dɪs'əun] vt repudiar; (*child*) rejeitar

disparaging [dɪs'pærɪdʒɪŋ] ADJ depreciativo; **to be ~ about sb/sth** fazer pouco de alguém/algo, depreciar alguém/algo

disparate ['dɪspərɪt] ADJ (*groups*) diverso; (*levels*) desigual

disparity [dɪs'pærɪtɪ] n desigualdade f

dispassionate [dɪs'pæʃənət] ADJ (*calm*) calmo, controlado; (*impartial*) imparcial

dispatch [dɪs'pætʃ] vt (*person, business*) despachar; (*send: parcel etc*) expedir; (: *messenger*) enviar ■ n (*sending*) remessa; (*speed*) rapidez f, urgência; (*Press*) comunicado; (*Mil*) parte f; **dispatch department** n (serviço de) expedição f; **dispatch rider** n (*Mil*) estafeta m/f

dispel [dɪs'pɛl] vt dissipar

dispensary [dɪs'pɛnsərɪ] n dispensário, farmácia

dispense [dɪs'pɛns] vt (*give out*) dispensar; (*medicine*) preparar (e vender); **to ~ sb from** dispensar alguém de

▶ **dispense with** vt FUS prescindir de

dispenser [dɪs'pɛnsər] n (*device*) distribuidor m automático

dispensing chemist [dɪs'pɛnsɪŋ-] (*Brit*) n farmácia

dispersal [dɪs'pəːsl] n dispersão f

disperse [dɪs'pəːs] vt (*objects*) espalhar; (*crowd*) dispersar ■ vi dispersar-se

dispirited [dɪs'pɪrɪtɪd] ADJ desanimado

displace [dɪs'pleɪs] vt (*shift*) deslocar

displaced person [dɪs'pleɪst-] n (*Pol*) deslocado(-a) de guerra

displacement [dɪs'pleɪsmənt] n deslocamento

display [dɪs'pleɪ] n (*in shop*) mostra; (*exhibition*) exposição f; (*Comput: information*) apresentação f visual; (: *device*) display m; (*Mil*) parada; (*of feeling*) manifestação f; (*pej*) ostentação f; (*show, spectacle*) espetáculo ■ vt mostrar; (*goods*) expor; (*feelings, tastes*) manifestar; (*ostentatiously*) ostentar; (*results, departure times*) expor; **on** ~ (*visible*) à mostra; (*goods, paintings etc*) em exposição; **display advertising** n anúncios mpl

displease [dɪs'pliːz] vt desagradar, desgostar; (*Offend*) ofender; (*annoy*) aborrecer

displeased [dɪs'pliːz] ADJ: ~ **with** descontente com; (*disappointed*) aborrecido

displeasure [dɪs'plɛʒər] n desgosto

disposable [dɪs'pəuzəbl] ADJ descartável; (*income*) disponível; **disposable nappy** (*Brit*) n fralda descartável

disposal [dɪs'pəuzl] n (*availability, arrangement*) disposição f; (*of rubbish*) destruição f; (*of property etc: by selling*) venda, traspasse m; (: *by giving away*) cessão f; **at sb's** ~ à disposição de alguém; **to put sth at sb's** ~ pôr algo à disposição de alguém

dispose [dɪs'pəuz]: **to ~ of** vt FUS (*time, money*) dispor de; (*unwanted goods*) desfazer-se de; (*throw away*) jogar (BR) or tirar (PT) fora; (*Comm: stock*) vender; (*problem, task*) lidar; (*argument*) derrubar

disposed [dɪs'pəuzd] ADJ: ~ **to do** disposto a fazer; **to be well ~ towards sb** estar predisposto a favor de alguém

disposition [dɪspə'zɪʃən] n (*inclination*) disposição f; (*temperament*) índole f

dispossess ['dɪspəzɛs] vt: **to ~ sb (of)** despojar alguém (de)

disproportion [dɪsprə'pɔːʃən] n desproporção f

disproportionate [dɪsprə'pɔːʃənət] ADJ desproporcionado

disprove [dɪs'pruːv] vt refutar

dispute [dɪs'pjuːt] N disputa; (*verbal*) discussão f; (*domestic*) briga; (*also*: **industrial dispute**) conflito, disputa ▪ VT disputar; (*argue*) discutir; (*question*) questionar; **to be in** or **under ~** (*matter*) estar em discussão; (*territory*) estar em disputa, ser disputado

disqualification [dɪskwɔlɪfɪ'keɪʃən] N (*Law*) inabilitação f, incapacitação f; (*Sport*) desclassificação f; **~ (from driving)** (*Brit*) cassação f da carteira (de motorista)

disqualify [dɪs'kwɔlɪfaɪ] VT (*Sport*) desclassificar; **to ~ sb for sth/from doing sth** desqualificar alguém para algo/de fazer algo; **to ~ sb (from driving)** (*Brit*) cassar a carteira (de motorista) a alguém

disquiet [dɪs'kwaɪət] N inquietação f

disquieting [dɪs'kwaɪətɪŋ] ADJ inquietante, alarmante

disregard [dɪsrɪ'gɑːd] VT ignorar ▪ N (*indifference*): **~ (for)** (*feelings*) desconsideração f (por); (*danger*) indiferença (a); (*money*) menosprezo (por)

disrepair [dɪsrɪ'pɛəʳ] N: **to fall into ~** ficar dilapidado

disreputable [dɪs'rɛpjutəbl] ADJ (*person*) de má fama; (*behaviour*) vergonhoso

disrepute ['dɪsrɪ'pjuːt] N descrédito, desonra; **to bring into ~** desacreditar, desprestigiar

disrespect [dɪsrɪ'spɛkt] N: **~ (for)** desrespeito (por)

disrespectful [dɪsrɪ'spɛktful] ADJ desrespeitoso

disrupt [dɪs'rʌpt] VT (*plans*) desfazer; (*conversation, proceedings*) perturbar, interromper

disruption [dɪs'rʌpʃən] N (*interruption*) interrupção f; (*disturbance*) perturbação f

disruptive [dɪs'rʌptɪv] ADJ (*influence*) maléfico; (*strike*) perturbador(a)

dissatisfaction [dɪssætɪs'fækʃən] N descontentamento

dissatisfied [dɪs'sætɪsfaɪd] ADJ: **~ (with)** descontente (com)

dissect [dɪ'sɛkt] VT dissecar

disseminate [dɪ'sɛmɪneɪt] VT divulgar

dissent [dɪ'sɛnt] N dissensão f

dissenter [dɪ'sɛntəʳ] N (*Rel, Pol etc*) dissidente m/f

dissertation [dɪsə'teɪʃən] N (*also*: *Sch*) dissertação f, tese f

disservice [dɪs'səːvɪs] N: **to do sb a ~** prejudicar alguém

dissident ['dɪsɪdnt] ADJ, N dissidente m/f

dissimilar [dɪ'sɪmɪləʳ] ADJ: **~ (to)** dessemelhante (de), diferente (de)

dissipate ['dɪsɪpeɪt] VT dissipar; (*money, effort*) desperdiçar ▪ VI dissipar-se

dissipated ['dɪsɪpeɪtɪd] ADJ (*person*) dissoluto

dissociate [dɪ'səuʃɪeɪt] VT dissociar, separar; **to ~ o.s. from** desassociar-se de, distanciar-se de

dissolute ['dɪsəluːt] ADJ dissoluto

dissolution [dɪsə'luːʃən] N dissolução f

dissolve [dɪ'zɔlv] VT dissolver ▪ VI dissolver-se; (*fig: problem etc*) desaparecer; **to ~ in(to) tears** debulhar-se em lágrimas

dissuade [dɪ'sweɪd] VT: **to ~ sb (from)** dissuadir alguém (de)

distance ['dɪstns] N distância; **in the ~** ao longe; **what's the ~ to London?** qual é a distância daqui a Londres?; **it's within walking ~** pode-se ir a pé, dá para ir a pé (*inf*)

distant ['dɪstnt] ADJ distante; (*manner*) afastado, reservado

distaste [dɪs'teɪst] N repugnância

distasteful [dɪs'teɪstful] ADJ repugnante

Dist. Atty. (*US*) ABBR = **district attorney**

distemper [dɪs'tɛmpəʳ] N (*paint*) tinta plástica; (*of dogs*) cinomose f

distended [dɪs'tɛndɪd] ADJ inchado

distil [dɪs'tɪl] (*US* **distill**) VT destilar

distillery [dɪs'tɪlərɪ] N destilaria

distinct [dɪs'tɪŋkt] ADJ (*different*) distinto; (*clear*) claro; (*unmistakable*) nítido; **as ~ from** em oposição a

distinction [dɪs'tɪŋkʃən] N (*difference*) diferença; (*honour*) honra; (*in exam*) distinção f; **to draw a ~ between** fazer distinção entre; **a writer of ~** um escritor de destaque

distinctive [dɪs'tɪŋktɪv] ADJ distintivo

distinctly [dɪs'tɪŋktlɪ] ADV claramente, nitidamente

distinguish [dɪs'tɪŋgwɪʃ] VT distinguir; (*differentiate*) diferenciar; (*identify*) identificar ▪ VI: **to ~ between** (*concepts*) distinguir entre, fazer distinção entre; **to ~ o.s.** distinguir-se

distinguished [dɪs'tɪŋgwɪʃt] ADJ (*eminent*) eminente; (*in appearance*) distinto; (*career*) notável

distinguishing [dɪs'tɪŋgwɪʃɪŋ] ADJ (*feature*) distintivo

distort [dɪs'tɔːt] VT distorcer

distortion [dɪs'tɔːʃən] N detorção f; (*of sound*) deturpação f

distract [dɪs'trækt] VT distrair; (*attention*) desviar; (*bewilder*) aturdir

distracted [dɪs'træktɪd] ADJ distraído; (*anxious*) aturdido

distraction [dɪs'trækʃən] N distração f; (*confusion*) aturdimento, perplexidade f; (*amusement*) divertimento; **to drive sb to ~** deixar alguém louco

distraught [dɪs'trɔːt] ADJ desesperado

distress [dɪs'trɛs] N (*anguish*) angústia; (*misfortune*) desgraça; (*want*) miséria; (*pain*) dor f ▪ VT (*cause anguish*) afligir; **in ~** (*ship*) em perigo; **~ed area** (*Brit*) área de baixo nível socio-econômico

distressing [dɪs'trɛsɪŋ] ADJ angustiante

distress signal N sinal m de socorro

distribute [dɪs'trɪbjuːt] VT distribuir; (*share out*) repartir, dividir

distribution [dɪstrɪ'bjuːʃən] N distribuição f; (*of profits etc*) repartição f; **distribution cost** N custo de distribuição

distributor [dɪs'trɪbjutəʳ] N (*Aut*) distribuidor m; (*Comm*) distribuidor(a) m/f; (*: company*) distribuidora

district ['dɪstrɪkt] N (*of country*) região *f*; (*of town*) zona; (*Admin*) distrito; **district attorney** (*US*) N promotor(a) *m/f* público(-a); **district council** (*Brit*) N ≈ município (BR), câmara municipal (PT); **district nurse** (*Brit*) N enfermeiro/a do Serviço Nacional que visita os pacientes em casa

distrust [dɪs'trʌst] N desconfiança ■ VT desconfiar de

distrustful [dɪs'trʌstful] ADJ desconfiado

disturb [dɪs'tə:b] VT (*disorganize*) perturbar; (*upset*) incomodar; (*interrupt*) atrapalhar; **sorry to ~ you** desculpe incomodá-lo

disturbance [dɪs'tə:bəns] N perturbação *f*; (*upheaval*) convulsão *f*; (*political, violent*) distúrbio; (*of mind*) transtorno; **to cause a ~** perturbar a ordem

disturbed [dɪs'tə:bd] ADJ perturbado; (*child*) infeliz; **to be mentally/emotionally ~** ter problemas psicológicos/emocionais

disturbing [dɪs'tə:bɪŋ] ADJ perturbador(a)

disuse [dɪs'ju:s] N: **to fall into ~** cair em desuso

disused [dɪs'ju:zd] ADJ abandonado

ditch [dɪtʃ] N fosso; (*irrigation ditch*) rego ■ VT (*inf: partner*) abandonar; (: *car, plan etc*) desfazer-se de

dither ['dɪðəʳ] VI vacilar

ditto ['dɪtəu] ADV idem

divan [dɪ'væn] N (*also*: **divan bed**) divã ■

dive [daɪv] N (*from board*) salto; (*underwater, of submarine*) mergulho; (*Aviat*) picada; (*pej: café, bar etc*) espelunca ■ VI mergulhar; picar; **to ~ into** (*bag, drawer etc*) enfiar a mão; (*shop, car etc*) enfiar-se em

diver ['daɪvəʳ] N (*Sport*) saltador(a) *m/f*; (*underwater*) mergulhador(a) *m/f*

diverge [daɪ'və:dʒ] VI divergir

divergent [daɪ'və:dʒənt] ADJ divergente

diverse [daɪ'və:s] ADJ diverso; (*group*) heterogêneo

diversification [daɪvə:sɪfɪ'keɪʃən] N diversificação *f*

diversify [daɪ'və:sɪfaɪ] VT, VI diversificar

diversion [daɪ'və:ʃən] N (*Brit: Aut*) desvio; (*distraction, Mil*) diversão *f*; (*of funds*) desvio

diversity [daɪ'və:sɪtɪ] N diversidade *f*

divert [daɪ'və:t] VT desviar; (*amuse*) divertir

divest [daɪ'vɛst] VT: **to ~ sb of sth** privar alguém de algo

divide [dɪ'vaɪd] VT (*Math*) dividir; (*separate*) separar; (*share out*) repartir ■ VI dividir-se; (*road*) bifurcar-se; **to ~ (between** or **among)** dividir or repartir (entre); **40 ~d by 5** 40 dividido por 5 ▸ **divide out** VT: **to ~ out (between** or **among)** distribuir or repartir (entre)

divided [dɪ'vaɪdɪd] ADJ (*fig*) dividido; **divided highway** (*US*) N pista dupla; **divided skirt** N saia-calça

dividend ['dɪvɪdɛnd] N dividendo; (*fig*) lucro; **to pay ~s** valer a pena; **dividend cover** N cobertura para pagamento de dividendos

dividers [dɪ'vaɪdəz] NPL compasso de ponta seca; (*between pages*) divisórias *fpl*

divine [dɪ'vaɪn] ADJ (*also fig*) divino ■ VT (*future,*

truth) adivinhar; (*water, metal*) descobrir

diving ['daɪvɪŋ] N (*Sport*) salto; (*underwater*) mergulho; **diving board** N trampolim *m*; **diving suit** N escafandro

divinity [dɪ'vɪnɪtɪ] N divindade *f*; (*Sch*) teologia

division [dɪ'vɪʒən] N divisão *f*; (*sharing out*) repartição *f*; (*disagreement*) discórdia; (*Football*) grupo; (*Brit: Pol*) votação *f*; **~ of labour** divisão do trabalho

divisive [dɪ'vaɪsɪv] ADJ que causa divisão

divorce [dɪ'vɔ:s] N divórcio ■ VT divorciar-se de; (*dissociate*) desligar-se

divorced [dɪ'vɔ:st] ADJ divorciado

divorcee [dɪvɔ:'si:] N divorciado(-a)

divulge [daɪ'vʌldʒ] VT (*information*) divulgar; (*secret*) revelar

DIY (*Brit*) ADJ ABBR, N ABBR = **do-it-yourself**

dizziness ['dɪzɪnɪs] N vertigem *f*, tontura

dizzy ['dɪzɪ] ADJ (*person*) tonto; (*height*) vertiginoso; **to feel ~** sentir-se tonto, sentir-se atordoado; **to make sb ~** dar vertigem a alguém

DJ N ABBR = **disc jockey**

Djakarta [dʒə'kɑ:tə] N Jacarta

DJIA (*US*) N ABBR (*Stock Exchange*) = **Dow Jones Industrial Average**

dl ABBR (= *decilitre*) dl

DLit(t) N ABBR = **Doctor of Literature**; (= *Doctor of Letters*) títulos universitários

DLO N ABBR = **dead-letter office**

dm ABBR (= *decimetre*) dm

DMus N ABBR (= *Doctor of Music*) título universitário

DMZ N ABBR = **demilitarized zone**

DNA N ABBR (= *deoxyribonucleic acid*) ADN *m*

○ KEYWORD

do [du:] (*pt* **did**, *pp* **done**) VB AUX **1** (*in negative constructions*): **I don't understand** eu não compreendo

2 (*to form questions*): **didn't you know?** você não sabia?; **what do you think?** o que você acha?

3 (*for emphasis, in polite expressions*): **people do make mistakes sometimes** é impossível não cometer erros de vez em quando; **she does seem rather late** ela está muito atrasada; **do sit down/help yourself** sente-se/sirva-se; **do take care!** tome cuidado!; **oh do shut up!** cale a boca!

4 (*used to avoid repeating vb*): **she swims better than I do** ela nada melhor que eu; **do you agree?** — **yes, I do/no, I don't** você concorda? — sim, concordo/não, não concordo; **she lives in Glasgow** — **so do I** ela mora em Glasgow — eu também; **who broke it?** — **I did** quem quebrou isso? — (fui) eu

5 (*in question tags*): **you like him, don't you?** você gosta dele, não é?; **he laughed, didn't he?** ele riu, não foi?

■ VT **1** (*gen: carry out, perform etc*) fazer; **what are you doing tonight?** o que você vai fazer hoje à noite?; **to do the washing-up/cooking** lavar a louça/cozinhar; **to do one's teeth/**

nails escovar os dentes/fazer as unhas; **to do one's hair** (comb) pentear-se; (style) fazer um penteado; **we're doing Othello at school** (studying) nós estamos estudando Otelo na escola; (performing) nós vamos encenar Otelo na escola

2 (Aut etc): **the car was doing 100** o carro estava a 100 por hora; **we've done 200 km already** nós já fizemos 200 km; **he can do 100 in that car** ele consegue dar 100 nesse carro

■ VI **1** (act, behave) fazer; **do as I do** faça como eu faço

2 (get on, fare) ir; **how do you do?** como você está indo?

3 (suit) servir; **will it do?** serve?

4 (be sufficient) bastar; **will £10 do?** £10 dá?; **that'll do** é suficiente; **that'll do!** (in annoyance) basta!, chega!; **to make do (with)** contentar-se(com)

■ N (inf: party etc) festa; **we're having a little do on Saturday** nós vamos dar uma festinha no sábado; **it was rather a do** foi uma festança

▶ **do away with** VT FUS (kill) matar; (abolish: law etc) abolir; (withdraw) retirar

▶ **do up** VT (laces) atar; (zip) fechar; (dress, skirt) abotoar; (renovate: room, house) arrumar, renovar

▶ **do with** VT FUS (need): **I could do with a drink/some help** eu bem que gostaria de tomar alguma coisa/eu bem que precisaria de uma ajuda; (be connected) ter a ver com; **what has it got to do with you?** o que é que isso tem a ver com você?

▶ **do without** VI: **if you're late for tea then you'll do without** se você chegar atrasado ficará sem almoço

■ VT FUS passar sem; **I can do without a car** eu posso ficar sem um carro; **we'll have to do without a holiday this year** não poderemos ter férias esse ano

do. ABBR = ditto

DOA ABBR (= dead on arrival) ≈ já era cadáver

d.o.b. ABBR = date of birth

docile ['dəusaıl] ADJ dócil

dock [dɔk] N (Naut) doca; (wharf) cais m; (Law) banco (dos réus) ■ VI (arrive) chegar; (Law: enter dock) entrar no estaleiro; (Space) unir-se no espaço ■ VT (pay etc) deduzir; **docks** NPL docas fpl; **dock dues** NPL direitos mpl portuários

docker ['dɔkər] N portuário, estivador m

docket ['dɔkıt] N (of delivery etc) guia

dockyard ['dɔkjɑːd] N estaleiro

doctor ['dɔktər] N médico(-a); (PhD etc) doutor(a) m/f ■ VT (fig) tratar, falsificar; (drink etc) falsificar; (cat) castrar; **~'s office** (US) consultório

doctorate ['dɔktərıt] N doutorado

Doctor of Philosophy N (degree) doutorado; (person) doutor(a) m/f

doctrine ['dɔktrın] N doutrina

document [n 'dɔkjumənt, vt 'dɔkjumɛnt] N documento ■ VT documentar

documentary [dɔkju'mɛntərı] ADJ documental ■ N documentário

documentation [dɔkjumɛn'teıʃən] N documentação f

DOD (US) N ABBR = **Department of Defense**

doddering ['dɔdərıŋ] ADJ (senile) caquético, caduco

Dodecanese (Islands) [dəudıkə'niːz-] N(PL) (ilhas fpl do) Dodecaneso

dodge [dɔdʒ] N (of body) evasiva; (trick) trapaça ■ VT esquivar-se de, evitar; (tax) sonegar; (blow) furtar-se a ■ VI: **to ~ out of the way** esquivar-se; **to ~ the traffic** ziguezaguear por entre os carros

dodgems ['dɔdʒəmz] (Brit) NPL carros mpl de choque

dodgy ['dɔdʒı] ADJ arriscado

DOE N ABBR (Brit) = **Department of the Environment**; (US) = **Department of Energy**

doe [dəu] N (deer) corça; (rabbit) coelha

does [dʌz] VB see **do**

doesn't ['dʌznt] = **does not**

dog [dɔg] N cachorro, cão m ■ VT (subj: person) seguir; (: bad luck) perseguir; **to go to the ~s** (nation etc) degringolar; **dog biscuits** NPL biscoitos mpl para cachorro; **dog collar** N coleira de cachorro; (of priest) gola de padre

dog-eared [-ıəd] ADJ surrado

dog food N ração f para cachorro

dogged ['dɔgıd] ADJ tenaz, persistente

dogma ['dɔgmə] N dogma m

dogmatic [dɔg'mætık] ADJ dogmático

do-gooder [-'gudər] (pej) N bom(boa) samaritano(-a)

dogsbody ['dɔgzbɔdı] (Brit: inf) N faz-tudo m/f

doing ['duıŋ] N: **this is your ~** foi você que fez isso; **doings** NPL (events) acontecimentos mpl; (activities) atividades fpl

do-it-yourself N sistema m faça-você-mesmo ■ ADJ do tipo faça-você-mesmo

doldrums ['dɔldrəmz] NPL: **to be in the ~** (person) estar abatido; (business) estar parado or estagnado

dole [dəul] (Brit) N (payment) subsídio de desemprego; **on the ~** desempregado

▶ **dole out** VT distribuir

doleful ['dəulful] ADJ triste, lúgubre

doll [dɔl] N boneca; (US: inf: woman) mulher f juven e bonita

▶ **doll up** VT: **to ~ o.s. up** embonecar-se (BR), ataviar-se (PT)

dollar ['dɔlər] N dólar m; **dollar area** N zona do dólar

dolled up [dɔld-] (inf) ADJ embonecado

dolphin ['dɔlfın] N golfinho

domain [də'meın] N domínio; (fig) campo

dome [dəum] N (Arch) cúpula; (shape) abóbada

domestic [də'mɛstık] ADJ doméstico; (national) nacional; (home-loving) caseiro; (strife) interno

domesticated [də'mɛstıkeıtıd] ADJ domesticado; (home-loving) prendado; **he's very ~** ele é muito prendado (no lar)

domesticity [dɔmɛs'tɪsɪtɪ] N vida caseira
domestic servant N empregado(-a) doméstico(-a)
domicile ['dɔmɪsaɪl] N domicílio
dominant ['dɔmɪnənt] ADJ dominante
dominate ['dɔmɪneɪt] VT dominar
domination [dɔmɪ'neɪʃən] N dominação f
domineering [dɔmɪ'nɪərɪŋ] ADJ dominante, mandão(-dona)
Dominican Republic [də'mɪnɪkən-] N República Dominicana
dominion [də'mɪnɪən] N domínio; (territory) império
domino ['dɔmɪnəu] (pl dominoes) N peça de dominó; **dominoes** N (game) dominó m
don [dɔn] N (Brit) professor(a) m/f universitário(-a) ■ VT vestir
donate [də'neɪt] VT doar
donation [də'neɪʃən] N doação f; (contribution) contribuição f
done [dʌn] PP of **do**
donkey ['dɔŋkɪ] N burro
donkey-work (Brit: inf) N labuta
donor ['dəunər] N doador(a) m/f
don't [dəunt] = **do not**
doodle ['du:dl] N rabisco ■ VI rabiscar
doom [du:m] N (fate) destino; (ruin) ruína ■ VT: **to be ~ed to failure** estar destinado or fadado ao fracasso
doomsday ['du:mzdeɪ] N o Juízo Final
door [dɔ:r] N porta; (entry) entrada; **next ~** na casa ao lado; **to go from ~ to ~** ir de porta em porta
doorbell ['dɔ:bɛl] N campainha
door handle N maçaneta (BR), puxador m (PT); (of car) maçaneta
door knocker N aldrava
doorman ['dɔ:mæn] (irreg) N porteiro
doormat ['dɔ:mæt] N capacho
doormen ['dɔ:mɛn] NPL of **doorman**
doorpost ['dɔ:pəust] N batente m de porta
doorstep ['dɔ:stɛp] N degrau m da porta, soleira
door-to-door ADJ: **~ selling** venda de porta em porta
doorway ['dɔ:weɪ] N vão m da porta, entrada
dope [dəup] N (inf: person) imbecil m/f; (: drugs) malconha; (information) dica, macete m ■ VT (horse etc) dopar
dopey ['dəupɪ] (inf) ADJ (groggy) zonzo; (stupid) imbecil
dormant ['dɔ:mənt] ADJ inativo; (latent) latente
dormer ['dɔ:mər] N (also: **dormer window**) água-furtada, trapeira
dormice ['dɔ:maɪs] NPL of **dormouse**
dormitory ['dɔ:mɪtrɪ] N dormitório; (US) prédio numa universidade onde os estudantes moram
dormouse ['dɔ:maus] (pl dormice) N rato (de campo)
DOS [dɔs] N ABBR (= disk operating system) DOS m
dosage ['dəusɪdʒ] N dosagem, posologia; (on label) posologia
dose [dəus] N dose f; (Brit: bout) ataque m ■ VT:

to ~ o.s. medicar-se; **a ~ of flu** uma gripe
doss house ['dɔs-] (Brit) N pensão f barata or de malta (PT)
dossier ['dɔsɪeɪ] N dossiê
DOT (US) N ABBR = **Department of Transportation**
dot [dɔt] N ponto; (speck) marca sequeria ■ VT: **~ted with** salpicado de; **on the ~** em ponto; **dot command** N (Comput) comando precedido de um ponto
dote [dəut]: **to ~ on** VT FUS adorar, idolatrar
dot-matrix printer N impressora matricial
dotted line ['dɔtɪd-] N linha pontilhada; **to sign on the ~** (fig) firmar o compromisso
dotty ['dɔtɪ] (inf) ADJ lelé, doido
double ['dʌbl] ADJ duplo ■ ADV (twice): **to cost ~** (sth) custar o dobro (de algo) ■ N dobro; (person) duplo(-a); (Cinema) substituto(-a) ■ VT dobrar; (efforts) duplicar ■ VI dobrar; (have two uses): **to ~ as** servir também de; **~ five two six (5526)** (Brit: Tel) cinco cinco dois meia; **it's spelt with a ~ "1"** escreve-se com dois ls; **at the ~** (Brit), **on the ~** em passo acelerado
▶ **double back** VI (person) voltar atrás
▶ **double up** VI (bend over) dobrar-se; (share room) dividir o quarto
double bass N contrabaixo
double bed N cama de casal
double bend (Brit) N curva dupla, curva em "s"
double-breasted [-'brɛstɪd] ADJ trespassado
double-check VT, VI verificar de novo
double-click VI (Comput) dar um clique duplo
double-clutch (US) VI fazer embreagem dupla
double cream (Brit) N creme m de leite
double-cross [dʌbl'krɔs] VT (trick) enganar; (betray) atraiçoar
double-decker [dʌbl'dɛkər] N ônibus m (BR) or autocarro (PT) de dois andares
double declutch (Brit) VI fazer embreagem dupla
double exposure N (Phot) dupla exposição f
double glazing [-'gleɪzɪŋ] (Brit) N (janelas fpl de) vidro duplo
double room N quarto de casal
doubles N (Tennis) dupla
doubly ['dʌblɪ] ADV duplamente
doubt [daut] N dúvida ■ VT duvidar; (suspect) desconfiar de; **without (a) ~** sem dúvida; **beyond ~** ADV sem dúvida alguma ■ ADJ indubitável; **there is no ~ that** não há dúvida que; **to ~ that ...** duvidar que ...; **I ~ it very much** duvido muito
doubtful ['dautful] ADJ duvidoso; **to be ~ about sth** ter dúvidas or estar em dúvida sobre algo; **I'm a bit ~** duvido
doubtless ['dautlɪs] ADV sem dúvida
dough [dəu] N massa; (inf: money) grana
doughnut ['dəunʌt] (US donut) N sonho (BR), bola de Berlim (PT)
dour [duər] ADJ austero
douse [dauz] VT (with water) encharcar; (flames) apagar

dove [dʌv] N pomba

dovetail ['dʌvteɪl] VI (fig) encaixar-se ■ N: ~ **joint** sambladura em cauda de andorinha

dowager ['dauədʒəʳ] N mulher que herda o título do marido falecido

dowdy ['daudɪ] ADJ desalinhado; (inelegant) deselegante, pouco elegante

Dow-Jones average ['dau'dʒəunz-] (US) N índice m da bolsa de valores de Nova Iorque

down [daun] N (fluff) lanugem f; (feathers) penugem f; (hill) colina ■ ADV abaixo; (downwards) para baixo; (on the ground) por terra ■ PREP por, abaixo ■ VT (inf: drink) tomar de um gole só; (: food) devorar; **Downs** NPL (Brit): **the ~ chapada gredosa do sul da Inglaterra; ~ there** lá em baixo; **~ here** aqui em baixo; **the price of meat is ~** o preço da carne baixou; **I've got it ~ in my diary** já o anotei na minha agenda; **to pay £2 ~** pagar £2 de entrada; **England are two goals ~** a Inglaterra está perdendo por dois gols; **to ~ tools** (Brit) cruzar os braços; **~ with X!** abaixo X!

down-and-out N (tramp) vagabundo(-a)

down-at-heel ADJ descuidado, desmazelado; (appearance) deselegante

downbeat ['daunbiːt] N (Mus) tempo forte ■ ADJ sombrio, negativo

downcast ['daunkɑːst] ADJ abatido

downer ['daunəʳ] (inf) N (drug) calmante m; **to be on a ~** (depressed) estar na fossa, estar de baixo astral

downfall ['daunfɔːl] N queda, ruína

downgrade ['daungreɪd] VT (reduce) reduzir; (devalue) desvalorizar, depreciar

downhearted [daun'hɑːtɪd] ADJ desanimado

downhill ['daun'hɪl] ADV para baixo ■ N (Ski: also: **downhill race**) descida; **to go ~** descer, ir morro abaixo; (fig: business) degringolar

Downing Street ['daunɪŋ-] (Brit) N: **10 ~** residência do primeiro-ministro

● **DOWNING STREET**

● Downing Street é a rua de Westminster
● (Londres) onde estão localizadas as
● residências oficiais do Primeiro-ministro
● (número 10) e do Ministro da Fazenda
● (número 11). O termo Downing Street é
● freqüentemente utilizado para designar o
● governo britânico.

download ['daunləud] VT (Comput) baixar, fazer o download de

down-market ADJ destinado a consumidores de renda baixa

down payment N entrada, sinal m

downplay ['daunpleɪ] (US) VT minimizar

downpour ['daunpɔːʳ] N aguaceiro

downright ['daunraɪt] ADJ (lie) patente; (refusal) categórico ■ ADV francamente

downstairs ['daun'stɛəz] ADV (below) lá em baixo; (direction) para baixo; **to come or go ~** descer

downstream ['daun'striːm] ADV água or rio abaixo

downtime ['dauntaɪm] N (of machine, person) tempo ocioso

down-to-earth ADJ prático, realista

downtown ['daun'taun] ADV no centro da cidade ■ ADJ (US): **~ Chicago** o centro comercial de Chicago

downtrodden ['dauntrɔdn] ADJ oprimido

down under ADV na Austrália (or Nova Zelândia)

downward ['daunwəd] ADJ, ADV para baixo; **a ~ trend** uma tendência para a baixa

downwards ['daunwədz] ADV = **downward**

dowry ['daurɪ] N dote m

doz. ABBR (= dozen) dz

doze [dəuz] VI dormitar
▶ **doze off** VI cochilar

dozen ['dʌzn] N dúzia; **a ~ books** uma dúzia de livros; **80p a ~** 80p a dúzia; **~s of times** milhares de vezes

DPh N ABBR (= Doctor of Philosophy) título universitário

DPhil N ABBR = **DPh**

DPP (Brit) N ABBR = **Director of Public Prosecutions**

DPT N ABBR (Med: = diphtheria, pertussis, tetanus) espécie de vacina

Dr ABBR (= doctor) Dr(a)

Dr. ABBR (in street names) = **drive**; (= doctor) Dr(a)

dr ABBR (Comm) = **debtor**

drab [dræb] ADJ sombrio

draft [drɑːft] N (first copy) rascunho; (Pol: of bill) projeto de lei; (bank draft) saque m, letra; (US: call-up) recrutamento ■ VT (plan) esboçar; (speech, letter) rascunhar; see also **draught**

draftsman etc ['drɑːftsmən] (US) N = **draughtsman** etc

drag [dræg] VT arrastar; (river) dragar ■ VI arrastar-se ■ N (inf) chatice f (BR), maçada (PT); (of cigarette) tragada; (Aviat, Naut) resistência; (women's clothing): **in ~** em travesti
▶ **drag away** VT: **to ~ away (from)** desgrudar (de)
▶ **drag on** VI arrastar-se

dragnet ['drægnet] N rede f de arrasto; (by police) diligência policial

dragon ['drægən] N dragão m

dragonfly ['drægənflaɪ] N libélula

dragoon [drə'guːn] N (cavalryman) dragão m ■ VT: **to ~ sb into doing sth** (Brit) forçar alguém a fazer algo

drain [dreɪn] N (drain pipe) cano de esgoto; (underground) esgoto; (in street) bueiro; (source of loss) sorvedouro ■ VT (land, marshes, Med) drenar; (reservoir) esvaziar; (vegetables) coar; (fig) esgotar ■ VI (water) escorrer, escoar-se; **to feel ~ed** sentir-se esgotado or estafado

drainage ['dreɪnɪdʒ] N (act) drenagem f; (Med, Agr) dreno; (system) esgoto

drainboard ['dreɪnbɔːd] (US) N = **draining board**

draining board ['dreɪnɪŋ-] (Brit) N escorredor m

drainpipe ['dreɪnpaɪp] N cano de esgoto
drake [dreɪk] N pato (macho)
dram [dræm] N (drink) trago
drama ['drɑːmə] N (art) teatro; (play, event) drama m
dramatic [drə'mætɪk] ADJ dramático; (theatrical) teatral
dramatically [drə'mætɪklɪ] ADV dramaticamente
dramatist ['dræmətɪst] N dramaturgo(-a)
dramatize ['dræmətaɪz] VT dramatizar
drank [dræŋk] PT of drink
drape [dreɪp] VT ornar, cobrir ■ VI cair
draper ['dreɪpəʳ] (Brit) N fanqueiro(-a)
drapes [dreɪps] (US) NPL cortinas fpl
drastic ['dræstɪk] ADJ drástico
drastically ['dræstɪklɪ] ADV drasticamente
draught [drɑːft] (US draft) N (of air) corrente f; (drink) trago; (Naut) calado; (beer) chope m; on ~ (beer) de barril
draughtboard ['drɑːftbɔːd] (Brit) N tabuleiro de damas
draughts (Brit) N (jogo de) damas fpl
draughtsman ['drɑːftsmən] (US draftsman) (irreg) N desenhista m/f industrial
draughtsmanship ['drɑːftsmənʃɪp] (US draftsmanship) N (art) desenho industrial; (technique) habilidade f de desenhista
draughtsmen ['drɑːftsmɛn] (US draftsmen) NPL of draughtsman
draw [drɔː] (pt drew, pp drawn) VT (picture) desenhar; (cart) puxar; (curtain) fechar; (gun) sacar; (attract) atrair; (money) tirar; (: from bank) sacar; (wages) receber; (comparison, distinction) fazer ■ VI (Sport) empatar ■ N (Sport) empate m; (lottery) sorteio; (attraction) atração f; to ~ to a close tender para o fim; to ~ near aproximar-se
▶ **draw back** VI (move back): to ~ back (from) recuar (de)
▶ **draw in** VI (Brit: car) encostar; (: train) entrar na estação ■ VT (involve) envolver
▶ **draw on** VT FUS (resources) recorrer a, lançar mão de; (person, imagination) recorrer a
▶ **draw out** VI (car, train) sair ■ VT (lengthen) esticar, alargar; (money) sacar; (confession, truth) arrancar; (shy person) desacanhar, desinibir
▶ **draw up** VI (stop) parar(-se) ■ VT (chair etc) puxar; (document) redigir; (plans) esboçar
drawback ['drɔːbæk] N inconveniente m, desvantagem f
drawbridge ['drɔːbrɪdʒ] N ponte f levadiça
drawee [drɔː'iː] N sacado
drawer¹ ['drɔːʳ] N gaveta
drawer² ['drɔːəʳ] N (of cheque) sacador(a) m/f, emitente m/f
drawing ['drɔːɪŋ] N desenho; **drawing board** N prancheta; **drawing pin** (Brit) N tachinha (BR), pionés m (PT); **drawing room** N sala de visitas
drawl [drɔːl] N fala arrastada
drawn [drɔːn] PP of draw ■ ADJ (haggard) abatido
drawstring ['drɔːstrɪŋ] N cordão m

dread [drɛd] N medo, pavor m ■ VT temer, recear, ter medo de
dreadful ['drɛdful] ADJ terrível
dream [driːm] (pt, pp dreamt) N sonho ■ VT, VI sonhar; **to have a ~ about sb/sth, to ~ about sb/sth** sonhar com alguém/algo; **sweet ~s!** sonha com os anjos!
▶ **dream up** VT inventar, bolar (inf)
dreamer ['driːməʳ] N sonhador(a) m/f
dreamt [drɛmt] PT, PP of dream
dreamy ['driːmɪ] ADJ (expression, person) sonhador(a), distraído; (music) sentimental
dreary ['drɪərɪ] ADJ (talk, time) monótono; (weather) sombrio
dredge [drɛdʒ] VT dragar
▶ **dredge up** VT tirar do fundo; (fig: unpleasant facts) trazer à tona, descobrir
dredger ['drɛdʒəʳ] N (ship) draga; (Brit: also: **sugar dredger**) polvilhador m
dregs [drɛgz] NPL lia; (of humanity) escória, ralé f
drench [drɛntʃ] VT encharcar; **to get ~ed** encharcar-se
dress [drɛs] N vestido; (no pl: clothing) traje m ■ VT vestir; (wound) fazer curativo em; (Culin) preparar, temperar ■ VI vestir-se; **to ~ o.s., to get ~ed** vestir-se; **to ~ a shop window** adornar uma vitrina
▶ **dress up** VI vestir-se com elegância; (in fancy dress) fantasiar-se
dress circle (Brit) N balcão m nobre
dress designer N estilista m/f
dresser ['drɛsəʳ] N (Theatre) camareiro(-a); (also: **window dresser**) vitrinista m/f; (Brit: cupboard) aparador m; (US: chest of drawers) cômoda de espelho
dressing ['drɛsɪŋ] N (Med) curativo; (Culin) molho; **dressing gown** (Brit) N roupão m; (woman's) peignoir m; **dressing room** N (Theatre) camarim m; (Sport) vestiário; **dressing table** N penteadeira (BR), toucador m (PT)
dressmaker ['drɛsmeɪkəʳ] N costureiro(-a)
dressmaking ['drɛsmeɪkɪŋ] N (arte f da) costura
dress rehearsal N ensaio geral
dress shirt N camisa social
dressy ['drɛsɪ] (inf) ADJ (clothes) chique
drew [druː] PT of draw
dribble ['drɪbl] VI gotejar, pingar; (baby) babar ■ VT (ball) driblar
dried [draɪd] ADJ seco; (eggs, milk) em pó
drier ['draɪəʳ] N = dryer
drift [drɪft] N (of current etc) força; (of snow, sand etc) monte m; (distance off course) deriva; (meaning) sentido ■ VI (boat) derivar; (sand, snow) amontoar-se; **to let things ~** deixar o barco correr; **to ~ apart** (friends, lovers) afastar-se um do outro; **I get** or **catch your ~** eu entendo mais ou menos o que você está dizendo
drifter ['drɪftəʳ] N nômade m/f
driftwood ['drɪftwud] N madeira flutuante
drill [drɪl] N furadeira; (bit, of dentist) broca; (for mining etc) broca, furadeira; (Mil) exercícios mpl militares ■ VT furar, brocar; (Mil) exercitar

■ vɪ (for oil) perfurar

drilling ['drɪlɪŋ] N (for oil) perfuração f; **drilling rig** N torre f de perfurar

drily ['draɪlɪ] ADV = **dryly**

drink [drɪŋk] (pt **drank**, pp **drunk**) N bebida
■ vт, vɪ beber; **to have a ~** tomar uma bebida; **a ~ of water** um copo d'água; **would you like something to ~?** você quer beber or tomar alguma coisa?; **to ~ to sb/sth** brindar alguém/algo
▶ **drink in** vт embeber-se em

drinkable ['drɪŋkəbl] ADJ (not dangerous) potável; (palatable) bebível

drinker ['drɪŋkə^r] N bebedor(a) m/f

drinking ['drɪŋkɪŋ] N (drunkenness) alcoolismo; **drinking fountain** N bebedouro; **drinking water** N água potável

drip [drɪp] N gotejar m; (one drip) gota, pingo; (Med) gota a gota m; (inf: person) mané m, banana m ■ vɪ gotejar, pingar

drip-dry ADJ (shirt) de lavar e vestir

drip-feed (irreg) vт alimentar intravenosamente

dripping ['drɪpɪŋ] N gordura ■ ADJ: **~ wet** encharcado

drive [draɪv] (pt **drove**, pp **driven**) N passeio (de automóvel); (journey) trajeto, percurso; (also: **driveway**) entrada; (energy) energia, vigor m; (Psych) impulso; (Sport) drive m; (campaign) campanha; (Tech) propulsão f; (Comput: also: **disk drive**) unidade f de disco ■ vт conduzir; (car) dirigir (BR), guiar (PT); (urge) fazer trabalhar; (by power) impelir; (push) empurrar; (Tech: motor) acionar; (nail): **to ~ sth into** cravar algo em ■ vɪ (Aut: at controls) dirigir (BR), guiar (PT); (: travel) ir de carro; **to go for a ~** dar um passeio (de carro); **it's 3 hours' ~ from London** são 3 horas de carro de lá a Londres; **left-/right-hand ~** direção à esquerda/direita; **front-/rear-wheel ~** (Aut) tração dianteira/traseira; **to ~ sb to do sth** impelir alguém a fazer algo; **to ~ sb mad** deixar alguém louco
▶ **drive at** vт Fus (fig: intend, mean) querer dizer; **what are you driving at?** onde é que voce queria chegar?
▶ **drive on** vɪ seguir adiante ■ vт impelir

drive-in ADJ drive-in ■ N (cinema) drive-in m; **drive-in window** (US) N balcão m drive-in

drivel ['drɪvl] (inf) N bobagem f, besteira

driven ['drɪvn] PP of **drive**

driver ['draɪvə^r] N motorista m/f; (Rail) maquinista m

driver's license (US) N carteira de motorista (BR), carta de condução (PT)

driveway ['draɪvweɪ] N entrada

driving ['draɪvɪŋ] N direção f (BR), condução f (PT) ■ ADJ: **~ rain** chuva torrencial; **driving force** N (fig) mola; **driving instructor** N instrutor(a) m/f de auto-escola (BR) or de condução (PT); **driving lesson** N aula de direção (BR) or de condução (PT); **driving licence** (Brit) N carteira de motorista (BR),

carta de condução (PT); **driving mirror** (Brit) N retrovisor m; **driving school** N auto-escola f; **driving test** N exame m de motorista

drizzle ['drɪzl] N chuvisco ■ vɪ chuviscar

droll [drəul] ADJ engraçado

dromedary ['drɔmədərɪ] N dromedário

drone [drəun] N (sound) zumbido; (male bee) zangão m ■ vɪ (bee, engine) zumbir; (also: **drone on**) falar monotonamente

drool [druːl] vɪ babar(-se); **to ~ over sth** babar por algo

droop [druːp] vɪ pender

drop [drɔp] N (of water) gota; (lessening) diminuição f; (fall: distance) declive m; (: in prices) baixa, queda; (: in salary) redução f; (also: **parachute drop**) salto ■ vт (allow to fall) deixar cair; (voice, eyes, price) baixar; (set down from car) deixar (saltar/descer); (omit) omitir ■ vɪ cair; (price, temperature) baixar; (wind) parar; **drops** NPL (Med) gotas fpl; **cough ~s** pastilhas para tosse; **a ~ of 10%** uma queda de 10%; **to ~ sb a line** escrever (umas linhas) para alguém
▶ **drop in** (inf) vɪ (visit): **to ~ in (on)** dar um pulo (na casa de)
▶ **drop off** vɪ (sleep) cochilar vт (passenger) deixar (saltar)
▶ **drop out** vɪ (withdraw) retirar-se; (student etc) largar tudo

droplet ['drɔplɪt] N gotícula

drop-out N pessoa que abandona o trabalho, os estudos etc

dropper ['drɔpə^r] N conta-gotas m inv

droppings ['drɔpɪŋz] NPL fezes fpl (de animal)

dross [drɔs] N escória

drought [draut] N seca

drove [drəuv] PT of **drive** ■ N: **~s of people** uma quantidade de gente

drown [draun] vт afogar; (also: **drown out**: sound) encobrir ■ vɪ afogar-se

drowse [drauz] vɪ dormitar

drowsy ['drauzɪ] ADJ sonolento; **to be ~** estar com sono

drudge [drʌdʒ] N burro-de-carga m

drudgery ['drʌdʒərɪ] N trabalho enfadonho

drug [drʌg] N remédio, medicamento; (narcotic) droga; (: Med, Admin) entorpecente m ■ vт drogar; **to be on ~s** (an addict) estar viciado em drogas; (Med) estar sob medicação; **hard/soft ~s** drogas pesadas/leves; **drug addict** N toxicômano(-a)

druggist ['drʌgɪst] (US) N farmacêutico(-a)

drug peddler N traficante m/f de drogas

drugstore ['drʌgstɔː] (US) N drogaria

drum [drʌm] N tambor m; (large) bombo; (for oil, petrol) tambor, barril m ■ vɪ (with fingers) tamborilar ■ vт: **to ~ sth into sb** incutir algo em alguém; **drums** NPL (kit) bateria
▶ **drum up** vт (enthusiasm, support) angariar

drummer ['drʌmə^r] N baterista m/f

drum roll N rufo de tambor

drumstick ['drʌmstɪk] N (Mus) baqueta; (of chicken) perna

drunk [drʌŋk] PP *of* **drink** ■ ADJ bêbado ■ N
(*also*: **drunkard**) bêbado(-a); **to get ~** ficar
bêbado, encher a cara (*inf*)
drunkard ['drʌŋkəd] N beberrão(-beberrona) *m/f*
drunken ['drʌŋkən] ADJ (*laughter*) de bêbado;
(*party*) cheic de bêbado; (*person*) bêbado; **~
driving** embriaguez *f* no volante
drunkenness ['drʌŋkənnɪs] N embriaguez *f*
dry [draɪ] ADJ seco; (*day*) sem chuva;
(*uninteresting*) insípido; (*humour*) irônico ■ VT
secar, enxugar; (*tears*) limpar ■ VI secar; **on ~
land** em terra firme; **to ~ one's hands/hair/
eyes** enxugar as maõs o cabelo/as lágrimas
▶ **dry up** VI secar completamente; (*supply*)
esgotar-se; (*in speech*) calar-se; (*dishes*) enxugar
(a louça)
dry-clean VT lavar a seco
dry-cleaner N tintureiro(-a)
dry-cleaner's N tinturaria, lavanderia
dry-cleaning N lavagem *f* a seco
dry dock N (*Naut*) dique *m* seco
dryer ['draɪə'] N secador *m*; (*also*: **spin-dryer**)
secadora
dry goods NPL (*Comm*) fazendas *fpl* e artigos *mpl*
de armarinho
dry goods store (US) N armarinho
dry ice N gelo seco
dryness ['draɪnɪs] N secura
dry rot N putrefação *f* fungosa
dry run N (*fig*) ensaio, prova
dry ski slope N pista de esqui artificial
DSc N ABBR (= *Doctor of Science*) título universitário
DSS (Brit) N ABBR (= *Department of Social Security*)
≈ INAMPS *m*
DST (US) ABBR (= *Daylight Saving Time*) hora de verão
DT N ABBR (*Comput*) = **data transmission**
DTI (Brit) N = **Department of Trade and Industry**
DTP N ABBR (= *desktop publishing*) DTP *m*
DT's (*inf*) NPL ABBR (= *delirium tremens*) delirium
· tremens *m*
dual ['djuəl] ADJ dual, duplo; **dual carriageway**
(Brit) N pista dupla
dual-control ADJ de duplo comando
dual nationality N dupla nacionalidade *f*
dual-purpose ADJ de duplo uso
dubbed [dʌbd] ADJ (*Cinema*) dublado; (*nicknamed*)
apelidado
dubious ['dju:bɪəs] ADJ duvidoso; (*reputation,
company*) suspeitoso; **I'm very ~ about it** eu
tenho muitas dúvidas a respeito
Dublin ['dʌblɪn] N Dublin
Dubliner ['dʌblɪnə'] N natural *m/f* de Dublin
duchess ['dʌtʃɪs] N duquesa
duck [dʌk] N pato ■ VI (*also*: **duck down**)
abaixar-se repentinamente ■ VT mergulhar
duckling ['dʌklɪŋ] N patinho
duct [dʌkt] N conduto, canal *m*; (*Anat*) ducto
dud [dʌd] N (*shell*) bomba falhada; (*object, tool*):
it's a ~ não presta ■ ADJ (*Brit: coin, note*) falso; **~
cheque** cheque *m* sem fundos, cheque *m* voador
(*inf*)
due [dju:] ADJ (*proper*) devido; (*expected*) esperado;

(*fitting*) conveniente, oportuno ■ N: **to give
sb his** (*or* **her**) **~** ser justo com alguém ■ ADV:
~ north exatamente ao norte; **dues** NPL (*for
club, union*) quota; (*in harbour*) direitos *mpl*; **in ~
course** no devido tempo; (*eventually*) no final; **~
to** devido a; **the rent is ~ on the 30th** o aluguel
vence no dia 30; **the train is ~ at 8** o trem deve
chegar às 8; **I am ~ 6 days' leave** eu tenho
direito a 6 dias de folga; **due date** N (*data de*)
vencimento
duel ['djuəl] N duelo; (*fig*) batalha
duet [dju:'ɛt] N dueto
duff [dʌf] (*Brit: inf*) ADJ de nada
duffel bag ['dʌfl-] N mochila
duffel coat ['dʌfl-] N casaco de baeta
duffer ['dʌfə'] (*inf*) N zero (à esquerda)
duffle bag ['dʌfl-] N = **duffelbag**
duffle coat ['dʌfl-] N = **duffelcoat**
dug [dʌg] PT, PP *of* **dig**
duke [dju:k] N duque *m*
dull [dʌl] ADJ (*light*) sombrio; (*intelligence, wit*)
lento; (*boring*) enfadonho; (*sound, pain*) surdo;
(*weather, day*) nublado, carregado; (*blade*)
embotado, cego ■ VT (*pain, grief*) aliviar; (*mind,
senses*) entorpecer
duly ['dju:lɪ] ADV devidamente; (*on time*) no
devido tempo
dumb [dʌm] ADJ mudo; (*pej: stupid*) estúpido; **to
be struck ~** (*fig*) ficar pasmo
dumbbell ['dʌmbɛl] N (*Sport*) haltere *m*
dumbfounded [dʌm'faundɪd] ADJ pasmado
dummy ['dʌmɪ] N (*tailor's model*) manequim *m*;
(*mock-up*) modelo; (*Brit: for baby*) chupeta; (*Cards*)
morto ■ ADJ falso; **dummy run** N prova, ensaio
dump [dʌmp] N (*heap*) montão *m*; (*also*: **rubbish
dump**) depósito de lixo; (*inf: place*) chiqueiro;
(*Mil*) depósito; (*Comput*) dump *m*, descarga ■ VT
(*put down*) depositar, descarregar; (*get rid of*)
desfazer-se de; (*Comm: goods*) fazer dumping
de; (*Comput*) tirar um dump de; **to be (down) in
the ~s** (*inf*) estar na fossa
dumping ['dʌmpɪŋ] N (*Econ*) dumping *m*; (*of
rubbish*): **"no ~"** "proibido jogar lixo" (BR),
"proibido deitar lixo" (PT)
dumpling ['dʌmplɪŋ] N bolinho cozido
dumpy ['dʌmpɪ] ADJ gorducho
dunce [dʌns] N burro, ignorante *m/f*
dune [dju:n] N duna
dung [dʌŋ] N estrume *m*
dungarees [dʌŋgə'ri:z] NPL macacão *m* (BR),
fato macaco (PT)
dungeon ['dʌndʒən] N calabouço
dunk [dʌŋk] VT mergulhar
duo ['dju:əu] N (*gen*) dupla; (*Mus*) duo
duodenal [dju:ə'di:nl] ADJ duodenal
dupe [dju:p] N (*victim*) otário(-a), trouxa *m/f* ■ VT
enganar
duplex ['dju:plɛks] (US) N (*house*) casa geminada;
(*also*: **duplex apartment**) duplex *m*
duplicate [n 'dju:plɪkət, vt 'dju:plɪkeɪt] N (*of
document*) duplicata; (*of key*) cópia ■ VT duplicar;
(*photocopy*) multigrafar; (*repeat*) reproduzir; **in ~**

em duplicata; ~ **key** cópia de chave
duplicating machine ['dju:plɪkeɪtɪŋ-] N
duplicador m
duplicator ['dju:plɪkeɪtə^r] N duplicador m
duplicity [dju:'plɪsɪtɪ] N falsidade f
durability [djuərə'bɪlɪtɪ] N durabilidade f,
solidez f
durable ['djuərəbl] ADJ durável; (clothes, metal)
resistente
duration [djuə'reɪʃən] N duração f
duress [djuə'rɛs] N: **under** ~ sob coação
during ['djuərɪŋ] PREP durante
dusk [dʌsk] N crepúsculo, anoitecer m
dusky ['dʌskɪ] ADJ (sky, room) sombrio; (person,
complexion) moreno
dust [dʌst] N pó m, poeira ■ VT (furniture) tirar o
pó de; (cake etc): **to** ~ **with** polvilhar com
▶ **dust off** VT (dirt) tirar
dustbin ['dʌstbɪn] N (Brit) lata de lixo
duster ['dʌstə^r] N pano de pó
dust jacket N sobrecapa
dustman ['dʌstmən] (Brit: irreg) N lixeiro, gari
m (BR) (inf)
dustpan ['dʌstpæn] N pá f de lixo
dusty ['dʌstɪ] ADJ empoeirado
Dutch [dʌtʃ] ADJ holandês(-esa) ■ N (Ling)
holandês m ■ ADV: **let's go** ~ (inf) cada um paga
o seu, vamos rachar; **the Dutch** NPL (people) os
holandeses
Dutch auction N leilão m em que os ertantes
oferecem cada vez menos
Dutchman ['dʌtʃmən] (irreg) N holandês m
dutiable ['dju:tɪəbl] ADJ (taxable) tributável; (by
customs) sujeito a impostos alfandegários
dutiful ['dju:tɪful] ADJ (child) respeitoso; (husband,
wife) atencioso; (employee) zeloso, consciente
duty ['dju:tɪ] N dever m; (tax) taxa; (customs) taxa
alfandegária; **duties** NPL funções fpl; **to make
it one's** ~ **to do sth** dar-se a responsabilidade
de fazer algo; **to pay** ~ **on sth** pagar imposto
sobre algo; **on** ~ de serviço; (at night etc) de
plantão; **off** ~ de folga

duty-free ADJ livre de impostos; ~ **shop** duty-
free f
duty officer N (Mil etc) oficial m de serviço
duvet ['du:veɪ] (Brit) N edredom m (BR), edredão
m (PT)
DV ABBR (= Deo volente) se Deus quiser
DVD N ABBR (= digital versatile or video disc) DVD m;
DVD burner, DVD writer N gravador m de DVD
DVM (US) N ABBR (= Doctor of Veterinary Medicine)
título universitário
dwarf [dwɔ:f] (pl dwarves) N anão(-anã) m/f
■ VT ananicar
dwarves [dwɔ:vz] NPL of **dwarf**
dwell [dwɛl] (pt, pp dwelt) VI morar
▶ **dwell on** VT FUS estender-se sobre
dweller ['dwɛlə^r] N habitante m/f
dwelling ['dwɛlɪŋ] N residência
dwelt [dwɛlt] PT, PP of **dwell**
dwindle ['dwɪndl] VI diminuir
dwindling ['dwɪndlɪŋ] ADJ descrescente,
minguante
dye [daɪ] N tintura, tinta ■ VT tingir; **hair** ~
tintura para o cabelo
dyestuffs ['daɪstʌfs] NPL corantes mpl
dying ['daɪɪŋ] ADJ moribundo, agonizante;
(moments) final; (words) último
dyke [daɪk] (Brit) N (embankment) dique m,
represa
dynamic [daɪ'næmɪk] ADJ dinâmico
dynamics [daɪ'næmɪks] N, NPL dinâmica
dynamite ['daɪnəmaɪt] N dinamite f ■ VT
dinamitar
dynamo ['daɪnəməu] N dínamo
dynasty ['dɪnəstɪ] N dinastia
dysentery ['dɪsntrɪ] N disenteria
dyslexia [dɪs'lɛksɪə] N dislexia
dyslexic [dɪs'lɛksɪk] ADJ, N dislético(-a),
disléxico(-a)
dyspepsia [dɪs'pɛpsɪə] N dispepsia
dystrophy ['dɪstrəfɪ] N distrofia; see also
muscular dystrophy

Ee

E, e [iː] N (letter) E, e m; (Mus): **E** mi m; **E for Edward** (Brit) or **Easy** (US) E de Eliane

E ABBR (= east) E

E111 N ABBR (also: **form E111**) formulário E111

ea. ABBR = **each**

E.A. (US) N ABBR (= educational age) idade educacional

each [iːtʃ] ADJ cada inv ■ PRON cada um(a); **~ one** cada um; **~ other** um ao outro; **they hate ~ other** (eles) se odeiam; **you are jealous of ~ other** vocês têm ciume um do outro; **~ day** cada dia; **they have 2 books ~** eles têm 2 livros cada um; **they cost £5 ~** custam £5 cada; **~ of us** cada um de nós

eager [ˈiːgər] ADJ ávido; (hopeful) desejoso; (ambitious) ambicioso; (pupil) empolgado; **to be ~ to do sth** ansiar por fazer algo; **to be ~ for** ansiar por

eagle [ˈiːgl] N águia

E and OE ABBR (= errors and omissions excepted) SEO

ear [ɪər] N (external) orelha; (inner, fig) ouvido; (of corn) espiga; **to play by ~** tocar de ouvido; **up to one's ~s in debt** endividado até o pescoço

earache [ˈɪəreɪk] N dor f de ouvidos

eardrum [ˈɪədrʌm] N tímpano

earl [əːl] N conde m

earlier [ˈəːlɪər] ADJ (date etc) mais adiantado; (edition etc) anterior ■ ADV mais cedo

early [ˈəːlɪ] ADV cedo; (before time) com antecedência ■ ADJ (sooner than expected) prematuro; (reply) pronto; (Christians, settlers) primeiro; (man) primitivo; (life, work) juvenil; **have an ~ night/start** vá para cama cedo/saia de manhã cedo; **in the ~ or ~ in the spring/19th century** no princípio da primavera/do século dezenove; **as ~ as possible** o mais cedo possível; **you're ~!** você chegou cedo!; **~ in the morning** de manhã cedo; **she's in her ~ forties** ela tem pouco mais de 40 anos; **at your earliest convenience** (Comm) o mais cedo que lhe for possível; **early retirement** N aposentadoria antecipada; **early warning system** N sistema m de alerta antecipado

earmark [ˈɪəmɑːk] VT: **to ~ sth for** reservar or destinar algo para

earn [əːn] VT ganhar; (Comm: interest) render; (praise, reward) merecer; **to ~ one's living** ganhar a vida

earned income [əːnd-] N rendimento do trabalho individual

earnest [ˈəːnɪst] ADJ (wish) intenso; (manner) sério ■ N (also: **earnest money**) sinal m em dinheiro; **in ~** a sério

earnings [ˈəːnɪŋz] NPL (personal) vencimentos mpl, salário, ordenado; (of company) lucro

ear nose and throat specialist N otorrinolaringologista m/f, otorrino m/f

earphones [ˈɪəfəʊnz] NPL fones mpl de ouvido

earplugs [ˈɪəplʌgz] NPL borrachinhas fpl (de ouvido)

earring [ˈɪərɪŋ] N brinco

earshot [ˈɪəʃɔt] N: **out of/within ~** fora do/ao alcance do ouvido or da voz

earth [əːθ] N terra; (Brit: Elec) fio terra ■ VT (Brit: Elec) ligar à terra; **what on ~!** que diabo!

earthenware [ˈəːθənwɛər] N louça de barro ■ ADJ de barro

earthly [ˈəːθlɪ] ADJ terrestre; **~ paradise** paraíso terrestre; **there is no ~ reason to think ...** não há a mínima razão para se pensar que ...

earthquake [ˈəːθkweɪk] N terremoto (BR), terramoto (PT)

earth tremor N tremor m, abalo sísmico

earthworks [ˈəːθwəːks] NPL trabalhos mpl de terraplenagem

earthworm [ˈəːθwəːm] N minhoca

earthy [ˈəːθɪ] ADJ (fig: vulgar) grosseiro; (: natural) natural

earwax [ˈɪəwæks] N cerume m

earwig [ˈɪəwɪg] N lacrainha

ease [iːz] N facilidade f; (relaxed state) sossego ■ VT facilitar; (relieve: pressure) afrouxar; (pain, tension) aliviar; (help pass): **to ~ sth in/out** meter/tirar algo com cuidado ■ VI (situation) abrandar; **at ~!** (Mil) descansar!; **to be at ~** estar à vontade; **with ~** com facilidade

▶ **ease off** VI acalmar-se; (at work) deixar de trabalhar tanto; (wind) baixar; (rain) moderar-se

▶ **ease up** VI = **ease off**

easel [ˈiːzl] N cavalete m

easily [ˈiːzɪlɪ] ADV facilmente, fácil (inf)

easiness ['i:zɪnɪs] N facilidade f; (of manner) desenvoltura

east [i:st] N leste m ■ ADJ (region) leste; (wind) do leste ■ ADV para o leste; **the E~** o Oriente; (Pol) o leste

Easter ['i:stəʳ] N Páscoa ■ ADJ (holidays) da Páscoa; (traditions) pascal; **Easter egg** N ovo de Páscoa; **Easter Island** N ilha da Páscoa

easterly ['i:stəlɪ] ADJ (to the east) para o leste; (from the east) do Leste

Easter Monday N Segunda-Feira da Páscoa

eastern ['i:stən] ADJ do leste, oriental; **E~ Europe** a Europa Oriental; **the E~ bloc** (Pol) o Bloco Oriental

Easter Sunday N Domingo da Páscoa

East Germany N Alemanha Oriental

eastward(s) ['i:stwəd(z)] ADV ao leste

easy ['i:zɪ] ADJ fácil; (comfortable) folgado, cômodo; (relaxed) natural, complacente; (victim, prey) desprotegido ■ ADV: **to take it** or **things ~** (not worry) levar as coisas com calma; (go slowly) ir devagar; (rest) descansar; **payment on ~ terms** (Comm) pagamento facilitado; **that's easier said than done** é mais fácil falar do que fazer; **I'm ~** (inf) para mim, tanto faz; **easy chair** N poltrona

easy-going ADJ pacato, fácil

eat [i:t] (pt ate, pp eaten) VT, VI comer
▶ **eat away** VT corroer
▶ **eat away at** VT FUS corroer
▶ **eat into** VT FUS = **eat away at**
▶ **eat out** VI jantar fora
▶ **eat up** VT (food) acabar; **it ~s up electricity** consome eletricidade demais

eatable ['i:təbl] ADJ comestível

eau de Cologne [əudə-] N (água de) Colônia

eaves [i:vz] NPL beira, beiral m

eavesdrop ['i:vzdrɔp] VI: **to ~ (on)** escutar às escondidas

ebb [ɛb] N refluxo ■ VI baixar; (fig: also: ebb away) declinar; **the ~ and flow** o fluxo e refluxo; **to be at a low ~** (fig: person) estar de maré baixa; (: business, relations etc) ir mal; **ebb tide** N baixa-mar f, maré f vazante

ebony ['ɛbənɪ] N ébano

ebullient [ɪ'bʌlɪənt] ADJ vivo, enérgico

EC N ABBR (= European Community) CE f

ECB N ABBR (= European Central Bank) BCE m, Banco Central Europeu

eccentric [ɪk'sɛntrɪk] ADJ, N excêntrico(-a)

ecclesiastic(al) [ɪkliːzɪ'æstɪk(əl)] ADJ eclesiástico

ECG N ABBR (= electrocardiogram) eletro

ECGD N ABBR (= Export Credits Guarantee Department) serviço de garantia financeira para exportações

echo ['ɛkəu] (pl echoes) N eco ■ VT (sound) ecoar, repetir ■ VI ressoar, repetir

éclair [eɪ'klɛəʳ] N (Culin) bomba

eclipse [ɪ'klɪps] N eclipse m ■ VT eclipsar

ECM (US) N ABBR = **European Common Market**

ecologist [ɪ'kɔlədʒɪst] N ecologista m/f

ecology [ɪ'kɔlədʒɪ] N ecologia

economic [i:kə'nɔmɪk] ADJ econômico; (business etc) rentável

economical [i:kə'nɔmɪkəl] ADJ econômico; (proposition etc) rentável

economically [i:kə'nɔmɪklɪ] ADV economicamente

economics [i:kə'nɔmɪks] N economia ■ NPL aspectos mpl econômicos

economist [ɪ'kɔnəmɪst] N economista m/f

economize [ɪ'kɔnəmaɪz] VI economizar, fazer economias

economy [ɪ'kɔnəmɪ] N economia; **economies of scale** economias de escala; **economy class** N (Aviat) classe f econômica; **economy size** N tamanho econômico

ECSC N ABBR (= European Coal and Steel Community) CECA f

ecstasy ['ɛkstəsɪ] N êxtase m; **to go into ecstasies over** extasiar-se com

ecstatic [ɛks'tætɪk] ADJ extasiado

ECT N ABBR = **electroconvulsive therapy**

ECU N ABBR (= European Currency Unit) ECU f

Ecuador ['ɛkwədɔ:ʳ] N Equador m

Ecuadorian [ɛkwə'dɔ:rɪən] ADJ, N equatoriano(-a)

ecumenical [i:kju'mɛnɪkl] ADJ ecumênico

eczema ['ɛksɪmə] N eczema m

eddy ['ɛdɪ] N rodamoinho

edge [ɛdʒ] N (of knife etc) fio; (of table, chair etc) borda; (of lake etc) margem f ■ VT (trim) embainhar ■ VI: **to ~ forward** avançar pouco a pouco; **on ~** (fig) = **edgy**; **to have the ~ on** (fig) levar vantagem sobre; **to ~ away from** afastar-se pouco a pouco de

edgeways ['ɛdʒweɪz] ADV lateralmente; **he couldn't get a word in ~** não pôde entrar na conversa

edging ['ɛdʒɪŋ] N (Sewing) debrum m; (of path) borda

edgy ['ɛdʒɪ] ADJ nervoso, inquieto

edible ['ɛdɪbl] ADJ comestível

edict ['i:dɪkt] N édito

edifice ['ɛdɪfɪs] N edifício

edifying ['ɛdɪfaɪɪŋ] ADJ edificante

Edinburgh ['ɛdɪnbərə] N Edimburgo

edit ['ɛdɪt] VT (be editor of) dirigir; (cut) cortar, redigir; (Comput, TV) editar; (Cinema) montar

edition [ɪ'dɪʃən] N (gen) edição f; (number printed) tiragem f

editor ['ɛdɪtəʳ] N redator(a) m/f; (of newspaper) diretor(a) m/f; (of column): **foreign/political ~ editor(a)** m/f; (of book) organizador(a) m/f da edição; (also: **film editor**) montador(a) m/f

editorial [ɛdɪ'tɔ:rɪəl] ADJ editorial ■ N editorial m; **the ~ staff** a redação

EDP N ABBR = **electronic data processing**

EDT (US) ABBR (= Eastern Daylight Time) hora de verão de Nova Iorque

educate ['ɛdjukeɪt] VT educar; **~d at ... que cursou...**

education [ɛdju'keɪʃən] N educação f; (schooling)

ensino; (science) pedagogia; **primary** (Brit) or **elementary** (US) ~ ensino de 1° /2° grau
educational [ɛdju'keɪʃənl] ADJ (policy, experience) educacional; (teaching) docente; (toy etc) educativo; ~ **technology** tecnologia educacional
Edwardian [ɛd'wɔːdɪən] ADJ da época do rei Eduardo VII, dos anos 1900
EE ABBR = **electrical engineer**
EEC N ABBR (= European Economic Community) CEE f
EEG N ABBR (= electroencephalogram) eletro
eel [iːl] N enguia
EENT (US) N ABBR (Med) = **eye, ear, nose and throat**
EEOC (US) N ABBR = **Equal Employment Opportunity Commission**
eerie ['ɪərɪ] ADJ (strange) estranho; (mysterious) misterioso
EET N ABBR (= Eastern European Time) hora da Europa Oriental
effect [ɪ'fɛkt] N efeito ■ VT (repairs) fazer; (savings) efetuar; **effects** NPL (Theatre) efeitos mpl; (property) bens mpl móveis, pertences mpl; **to take** ~ (law) entrar em vigor; (drug) fazer efeito; **to put into** ~ (plan) pôr em ação or prática; **to have an** ~ **on sb/sth** produzir efeito em alguém/algo; **in** ~ em vigor; his letter is to the ~ that ... a carta dele informa que ...
effective [ɪ'fɛktɪv] ADJ (successful) eficaz; (striking) impressionante; (actual) efetivo; **to become** ~ (Law) entrar em vigor; ~ **date** data de entrada em vigor
effectively [ɪ'fɛktɪvlɪ] ADV (successfully) eficazmente; (in reality) efetivamente
effectiveness [ɪ'fɛktɪvnɪs] N eficácia
effeminate [ɪ'fɛmɪnɪt] ADJ efeminado
effervescent [ɛfə'vɛsnt] ADJ efervescente
efficacy ['ɛfɪkəsɪ] N eficácia
efficiency [ɪ'fɪʃənsɪ] N eficiência; (of machine) rendimento; **efficiency apartment** (US) N kitchenette f
efficient [ɪ'fɪʃənt] ADJ eficiente; (machine) rentável
efficiently [ɪ'fɪʃəntlɪ] ADV eficientemente
effigy ['ɛfɪdʒɪ] N efígie f
effluent ['ɛfluənt] N efluente m
effort ['ɛfət] N esforço; **to make an** ~ **to** esforçar-se para
effortless ['ɛfətlɪs] ADJ fácil
effrontery [ɪ'frʌntərɪ] N descaramento
effusive [ɪ'fjuːsɪv] ADJ efusivo; (welcome) caloroso
EFL N ABBR (Sch) = **English as a foreign language**
EFTA ['ɛftə] N ABBR (= European Free Trade Association) AELC f
e.g. ADV ABBR (= exempli gratia) p. ex.
egalitarian [ɪgælɪ'tɛərɪən] ADJ igualitário
egg [ɛg] N ovo; **hard-boiled/soft-boiled** ~ ovo duro/mole
▶ **egg on** VT incitar

eggcup ['ɛgkʌp] N oveiro
eggplant ['ɛgplɑːnt] (esp US) N beringela
eggshell ['ɛgʃɛl] N casca de ovo
egg white N clara (de ovo)
egg yolk N gema
ego ['iːgəu] N ego
egoism ['iːgəuɪzəm] N egoísmo
egoist ['iːgəuɪst] N egoísta m/f
egotism ['ɛgəutɪzəm] N egotismo m
egotist ['ɛgəutɪst] N egotista m/f
Egypt ['iːdʒɪpt] N Egito
Egyptian [ɪ'dʒɪpʃən] ADJ, N egípcio(-a)
eiderdown ['aɪdədaun] N edredom m (BR), edredão m (PT)
eight [eɪt] NUM oito; see also **five**
eighteen ['eɪ'tiːn] NUM dezoito; see also **five**
eighth [eɪtθ] NUM oitavo; see also **fifth**
eighty ['eɪtɪ] NUM oitenta; see also **fifty**
Eire ['ɛərə] N (República da) Irlanda
EIS N ABBR (= Educational Institute of Scotland) sindicato dos professores escoceses
either ['aɪðə'] ADJ (one or other) um ou outro; (each) cada; (any) qualquer; (both) ambos ■ PRON: ~ **(of them)** qualquer (dos dois) ■ ADV: **no, I don't** ~ eu também não ■ CONJ: ~ **yes or no** ou sim ou não; **on** ~ **side** de ambos os lados; **I don't like** ~ não gosto nem de um nem do outro; **I haven't seen** ~ **one or the other** eu não vi nem um nem o outro
ejaculation [ɪdʒækju'leɪʃən] N (Physiology) ejaculação f
eject [ɪ'dʒɛkt] VT expulsar ■ VI (pilot) ser ejetado
ejector seat [ɪ'dʒɛktəʳ-] N assento ejetor
eke [iːk] **to** ~ **out** VT (money) economizar; (food) economizar em; (add to) complementar
EKG (US) N ABBR (= electrocardiogram) eletro
el [ɛl] (US: inf) N ABBR = **elevated railroad**
elaborate [adj ɪ'læbərɪt, vt, vi ɪ'læbəreɪt] ADJ complicado; (decorated) rebuscado ■ VT elaborar; (expand) expandir; (refine) aperfeiçoar ■ VI: **to** ~ **on** acrescentar detalhes a
elapse [ɪ'læps] VI transcorrer
elastic [ɪ'læstɪk] ADJ elástico; (adaptable) flexível, adaptável ■ N elástico; **elastic band** (Brit) N elástico
elasticity [ɪlæs'tɪsɪtɪ] N elasticidade f
elated [ɪ'leɪtɪd] ADJ: **to be** ~ rejubilar-se
elation [ɪ'leɪʃən] N exaltação f
elbow ['ɛlbəu] N cotovelo ■ VT: **to** ~ **one's way through the crowd** abrir passagem pela multidão com os cotovelos; **elbow room** N (fig) liberdade f
elder ['ɛldəʳ] ADJ mais velho ■ N (tree) sabugueiro; (person) o(-a mais velho/a); (of tribe) ancião; (of church) presbítero
elderly ['ɛldəlɪ] ADJ idoso, de idade ■ NPL: **the** ~ as pessoas de idade, os idosos
eldest ['ɛldɪst] ADJ mais velho ■ N o(-a mais velho/a)
elect [ɪ'lɛkt] VT eleger ■ ADJ: **the president** ~ o presidente eleito; **to** ~ **to do** (choose) optar por

fazer

election [ɪ'lɛkʃən] N (*voting*) votação f; (*installation*) eleição f; **to hold an ~** realizar uma eleição; **election campaign** N campanha eleitoral

electioneering [ɪlɛkʃə'nɪərɪŋ] N campanha *or* propaganda eleitoral

elector [ɪ'lɛktəʳ] N eleitor(a) m/f

electoral [ɪ'lɛktərəl] ADJ eleitoral; **electoral college** N colégio eleitoral; **electoral roll** (*Brit*) N lista de eleitores

electorate [ɪ'lɛktərɪt] N eleitorado

electric [ɪ'lɛktrɪk] ADJ elétrico

electrical [ɪ'lɛktrɪkəl] ADJ elétrico; **electrical engineer** N engenheiro(-a) eletricista; **electrical failure** N pane f elétrica

electric blanket N cobertor m elétrico

electric chair (*US*) N cadeira elétrica

electric cooker N fogão m elétrico

electric current N corrente f elétrica

electric fire (*Brit*) N aquecimento elétrico

electrician [ɪlɛk'trɪʃən] N eletricista m/f

electricity [ɪlɛk'trɪsɪtɪ] N eletricidade f; **electricity board** (*Brit*) N empresa de energia elétrica

electric light N luz f elétrica

electric shock N choque m elétrico

electrify [ɪ'lɛktrɪfaɪ] VT (*fence, Rail*) eletrificar; (*audience*) eletrizar

electro... [ɪ'lɛktrəu] PREFIX eletro...

electrocardiogram [ɪ'lɛktrəu'kɑ:dɪəgræm] N eletrocardiograma m

electro-convulsive therapy N eletrochoques mpl

electrocute [ɪ'lɛktrəkju:t] VT eletrocutar

electrode [ɪ'lɛktrəud] N eletrodo (BR), eléctrodo (PT)

electroencephalogram [ɪ'lɛktrəuen'sɛfələgræm] N eletroencefalograma m

electrolysis [ɪlɛk'trɔlɪsɪs] N eletrólise f

electromagnetic [ɪlɛktrəumæg'nɛtɪk] ADJ eletromagnético

electron [ɪ'lɛktrɔn] N elétron m (BR), electrão m (PT)

electronic [ɪlɛk'trɔnɪk] ADJ eletrônico; **electronic data processing** N processamento de dados eletrônico; **electronic mail** N correio eletrônico

electronics [ɪlɛk'trɔnɪks] N eletrônica

electron microscope N microscópio eletrônico

electroplated [ɪ'lɛktrəu'pleɪtɪd] ADJ galvanizado

electrotherapy [ɪ'lɛktrəu'θɛrəpɪ] N eletroterapia

elegance ['ɛlɪgəns] N elegância

elegant ['ɛlɪgənt] ADJ (*person, building*) elegante; (*idea*) refinado

element ['ɛlɪmənt] N elemento; **to brave the ~s** enfrentar intempérie

elementary [ɛlɪ'mɛntərɪ] ADJ (*gen*) elementar; (*primitive*) rudimentar; (*school, education*)

primário; **elementary school** (*US*) N *ver* abaixo

● **ELEMENTARY SCHOOL**
●
● Nos Estados Unidos e no Canadá, uma
● *elementary school* (também chamada de *grade*
● *school* ou *grammar school* nos Estados Unidos)
● é uma escola pública onde os alunos passam
● de seis a oito dos primeiros anos escolares.

elephant ['ɛlɪfənt] N elefante m

elevate ['ɛlɪveɪt] VT elevar; (*in rank*) promover

elevated railroad (*US*) N ferrovia elevada

elevation [ɛlɪ'veɪʃən] N elevação f; (*land*) eminência; (*height*) altura

elevator ['ɛlɪveɪtəʳ] (*US*) N elevador m

eleven [ɪ'lɛvn] NUM onze; *see also* **five**

elevenses [ɪ'lɛvənzɪz] (*Brit*) NPL refeição leve da manhã

eleventh [ɪ'lɛvnθ] NUM décimo-primeiro; **at the ~ hour** (*fig*) no último momento, na hora H; *see also* **fifth**

elf [ɛlf] (*pl* **elves**) N elfo, duende m

elicit [ɪ'lɪsɪt] VT: **to ~ (from)** (*information*) extrair (de); (*response, reaction*) provocar (de)

eligible ['ɛlɪdʒəbl] ADJ elegível, apto; **to be ~ for sth** (*job etc*) ter qualificações para algo; (*pension etc*) ter direito a algo

eliminate [ɪ'lɪmɪneɪt] VT (*poverty, smoking*) erradicar; (*candidate, team*) eliminar; (*strike out*) suprimir; (*suspect*) eliminar, excluir

elimination [ɪlɪmɪ'neɪʃən] N eliminação f; **by a process of ~** por eliminação

élite [eɪ'li:t] N elite f

élitist [eɪ'li:tɪst] (*pej*) ADJ elitista

elixir [ɪ'lɪksəʳ] N elixir m

Elizabethan [ɪlɪzə'bi:θən] ADJ elisabetano

ellipse [ɪ'lɪps] N elipse f

elliptical [ɪ'lɪptɪkl] ADJ elíptico

elm [ɛlm] N olmo

elocution [ɛlə'kju:ʃən] N elocução f

elongated ['i:lɔŋgeɪtɪd] ADJ alongado

elope [ɪ'ləup] VI fugir

elopement [ɪ'ləupmənt] N fuga do lar paterno

eloquence ['ɛləkwəns] N eloqüência

eloquent ['ɛləkwənt] ADJ eloqüente

else [ɛls] ADV outro, mais; **something ~** outra coisa; **somewhere ~** em outro lugar (BR), noutro sítio (PT); **everywhere ~** por todo o lado (menos aqui); **everyone ~** todos os outros; **where ~?** onde mais?; **what ~ can we do?** que mais podemos fazer?; **or ~** senão; **there was little ~ to do** não havia outra coisa a fazer; **nobody ~ spoke** ninguém mais falou

elsewhere [ɛls'wɛəʳ] ADV (*be*) em outro lugar (BR), noutro sítio (PT); (*go*) para outro lugar (BR), a outro sítio (PT)

ELT N ABBR (*Sch*) = **English Language Teaching**

elucidate [ɪ'lu:sɪdeɪt] VT esclarecer, elucidar

elude [ɪ'lu:d] VT (*pursuer*) escapar de, esquivar-se de; (*subj: fact, idea*) evadir

elusive [ɪ'lu:sɪv] ADJ esquivo; (*quality*)

indefinével; (answer) evasivo
elves [ɛlvz] NPL of **elf**
emaciated [ɪ'meɪsɪeɪtɪd] ADJ emaciado, macilento
e-mail ['i:meɪl] N e-mail m, correio eletrônico ■ VT (person) enviar um e-mail a; **e-mail account** N conta de e-mail, conta de correio eletrônico; **e-mail address** N e-mail m, endereço eletrônico
emanate ['ɛmaneɪt] VI: to ~ from emanar de
emancipate [ɪ'mænsɪpeɪt] VT libertar; (women) emancipar
emancipated [ɪ'mænsɪpeɪtɪd] ADJ emancipado
emancipation [ɪmænsɪ'peɪʃən] N emancipação f
emasculate [ɪ'mæskjuleɪt] VT emascular
embalm [ɪm'bɑ:m] VT embalsamar
embankment [ɪm'bæŋkmənt] N aterro; (of river) dique m
embargo [ɪm'bɑ:gəu] (pl embargoes) N (Naut) embargo; (Comm) proibição f ■ VT boicotear; to put an ~ on sth proibir algo
embark [ɪm'bɑ:k] VI embarcar ■ VT embarcar; to ~ on (fig) empreender, começar
embarkation [ɛmbɑ:'keɪʃən] N (of people, goods) embarque m; **embarkation card** N cartão m de embarque
embarrass [ɪm'bærəs] VT (politician) embaraçar; (emotionally) constranger
embarrassed [ɪm'bærəst] ADJ (laugh, silence) descomfortável; to be financially ~ estar com dificuldades financeiras
embarrassing [ɪm'bærəsɪŋ] ADJ embaraçoso, constrangedor(a)
embarrassment [ɪm'bærəsmənt] N embaraço, constrangimento; (financial) dificuldades fpl
embassy ['ɛmbəsɪ] N embaixada
embed [ɪm'bɛd] VT embutir; (teeth etc) cravar
embedded [ɪm'bɛdɪd] ADJ encravado
embellish [ɪm'bɛlɪʃ] VT embelezar; (fig: story) florear
embers ['ɛmbəz] NPL brasa, borralho, cinzas fpl
embezzle [ɪm'bɛzl] VT desviar
embezzlement [ɪm'bɛzlmənt] N desvio (de fundos)
embezzler [ɪm'bɛzlə'] N malversador(a) m/f
embitter [ɪm'bɪtə'] VT (person) amargurar; (relations) azedar
embittered [ɪm'bɪtəd] ADJ amargurado
emblem ['ɛmbləm] N emblema m
embodiment [ɪm'bɔdɪmənt] N encarnação f
embody [ɪm'bɔdɪ] VT (features) incorporar; (ideas) expressar
embolden [ɪm'bəuldn] VT encorajar, animar
embolism ['ɛmbəlɪzəm] N embolia
embossed [ɪm'bɔst] ADJ realçado; ~ with ornado com relevos de
embrace [ɪm'breɪs] VT abraçar, dar um abraço em; (include) abarcar, abranger; (adopt: idea) adotar ■ VI abraçar-se ■ N abraço
embroider [ɪm'brɔɪdə'] VT bordar; (fig: story) florear

embroidery [ɪm'brɔɪdərɪ] N bordado
embroil [ɪm'brɔɪl] VT: to become ~ed (in sth) ficar envolvido (em algo)
embryo ['ɛmbrɪəu] N (fig) embrião m
emend [ɪ'mɛnd] VT emendar
emerald ['ɛmərəld] N esmeralda
emerge [ɪ'mə:dʒ] VI sair; (from sleep) acordar; (fact, idea) emergir; it ~s that ... (Brit) veio à tona que ...
emergence [ɪ'mə:dʒəns] N surgimento, aparecimento; (of a nation) nascimento
emergency [ɪ'mə:dʒənsɪ] N emergência; in an ~ em caso de urgência; state of ~ estado de emergência; **emergency cord** (US) N sinal m de alarme; **emergency exit** N saída de emergência; **emergency landing** N aterrissagem f forçada (BR), aterragem f forçosa (PT); **emergency lane** (US) N (Aut) acostamento (BR), berma (PT); **emergency meeting** N reunião f extraordinária; **emergency road service** (US) N auto-socorro (BR), pronto socorro (PT); **emergency services** NPL serviços mpl de emergência; **emergency stop** (Brit) N (Aut) parada de emergência
emergent [ɪ'mə:dʒənt] ADJ (nation) em desenvolvimento; (group) emergente
emery board ['ɛmərɪ-] N lixa de unhas
emery paper ['ɛmərɪ-] N lixa or papel m de esmeril
emetic [ɪ'mɛtɪk] N emético
emigrant ['ɛmɪgrənt] N emigrante m/f
emigrate ['ɛmɪgreɪt] VI emigrar
emigration [ɛmɪ'greɪʃən] N emigração f
émigré ['ɛmɪgreɪ] N emigrado(-a)
eminence ['ɛmɪnəns] N eminência
eminent ['ɛmɪnənt] ADJ eminente
eminently ['ɛmɪnəntlɪ] ADV eminentemente
emirate ['ɛmɪrɪt] N emirado
emission [ɪ'mɪʃən] N emissão f
emit [ɪ'mɪt] VT (gen) emitir; (smoke) soltar; (smell) exalar; (sound) produzir
emolument [ɪ'mɔljumənt] N (often pl: formal: fee) honorário; (salary) remuneração f
emotion [ɪ'məuʃən] N emoção f
emotional [ɪ'məuʃənəl] ADJ (needs, exhaustion) emocional; (person) sentimental, emotivo; (scene) comovente; (tone) emocionante
emotionally [ɪ'məuʃənəlɪ] ADV (disturbed, involved) emocionalmente; (behave) emotivamente; (speak) com emoção
emotive [ɪ'məutɪv] ADJ que sensibiliza; ~ power capacidade f de comover
empathy ['ɛmpəθɪ] N empatia; to feel ~ with sb ter afinidade com alguém
emperor ['ɛmpərə'] N imperador m
emphases ['ɛmfəsi:z] NPL of **emphasis**
emphasis ['ɛmfəsɪs] (pl emphases) N ênfase f; (stress) acentuação f; to lay or place ~ on sth dar ênfase a; the ~ is on reading a leitura ocupa um lugar de destaque
emphasize ['ɛmfəsaɪz] VT (word, point) enfatizar, acentuar; (feature) salientar

emphatic [ɛm'fætɪk] ADJ (*statement*) vigoroso, expressivo; (*person*) convincente; (*manner*) enfático

emphatically [ɛm'fætɪkəlɪ] ADV com ênfase; (*certainly*) certamente

empire ['ɛmpaɪə^r] N império

empirical [ɛm'pɪrɪkl] ADJ empírico

employ [ɪm'plɔɪ] VT empregar; (*tool*) utilizar; **he's ~ed in a bank** ele trabalha num banco

employee [ɪmplɔɪ'i:] N empregado(-a)

employer [ɪm'plɔɪə^r] N empregador(a) m/f, patrão(-troa) m/f

employment [ɪm'plɔɪmənt] N (*gen*) emprego; (*work*) trabalho; **to find ~** encontrar um emprego; **without ~** sem emprego, desempregado; **place of ~** local de trabalho; **employment agency** N agência de empregos; **employment exchange** (*Brit*) N bolsa de trabalho

empower [ɪm'pauə^r] VT: **to ~ sb to do sth** autorizar alguém para fazer algo

empress ['ɛmprɪs] N imperatriz f

emptiness ['ɛmptɪnɪs] N vazio, vácuo

empty ['ɛmptɪ] ADJ vazio; (*place*) deserto; (*house*) desocupado; (*threat*) vão(vã) ■ N (*bottle*) vazio ■ VT esvaziar; (*place*) evacuar ■ VI esvaziar-se; (*place*) ficar deserto; **on an ~ stomach** em jejum, com o estômago vazio; **to ~ into** (*river*) desaguar em

empty-handed [-'hændɪd] ADJ de mãos vazias

empty-headed [-'hɛdɪd] ADJ de cabeça oca

EMS N ABBR (= *European Monetary System*) SME m

EMT N ABBR = **emergency medical technician**

emulate ['ɛmjuleɪt] VT (*person*) emular com

emulsion [ɪ'mʌlʃən] N emulsão f; (*also*: **emulsion paint**) tinta plástica

enable [ɪ'neɪbl] VT: **to ~ sb to do sth** (*allow*) permitir que alguém faça algo; (*make possible*) tornar possível; (*prepare*) capacitar alguém para fazer algo

enact [ɪn'ækt] VT (*law*) pôr em vigor, promulgar; (*play*) representar; (*role*) fazer

enamel [ɪ'næməl] N esmalte m; **enamel paint** N esmalte m

enamoured [ɪ'næməd] ADJ: **to be ~ of** (*person*) estar apaixonado por; (*activity etc*) ser louco por; (*idea*) encantar-se com

encampment [ɪn'kæmpmənt] N acampamento

encased [ɪn'keɪst] ADJ: **~ in** (*enclosed*) encaixado em; (*covered*) revestido de

enchant [ɪn'tʃɑ:nt] VT encantar

enchanted [ɪn'tʃɑ:ntɪd] ADJ encantado

enchanting [ɪn'tʃɑ:ntɪŋ] ADJ encantador(a)

encircle [ɪn'sə:kl] VT cercar, circundar; (*waist*) rodear

enc(l). ABBR (*in letters etc*) = **enclosed**; **enclosure**

enclave ['ɛnkleɪv] N: **an ~ of** um encrave de

enclose [ɪn'kləuz] VT (*land*) cercar; (*with letter etc*) anexar (BR), enviar junto (PT); **please find ~d** segue junto

enclosure [ɪn'kləuʒə^r] N cercado; (*Comm*)

documento anexo

encoder [ɪn'kəudə^r] N (*Comput*) codificador m

encompass [ɪn'kʌmpəs] VT abranger, encerrar

encore [ɔŋ'kɔ:^r] EXCL bis!, outra! ■ N bis m

encounter [ɪn'kauntə^r] N encontro ■ VT encontrar, topar com; (*difficulty*) enfrentar

encourage [ɪn'kʌrɪdʒ] VT (*activity*) encorajar; (*growth*) estimular; (*person*): **to ~ sb to do sth** animar alguém a fazer algo

encouragement [ɪn'kʌrɪdʒmənt] N estímulo

encouraging [ɪn'kʌrɪdʒɪŋ] ADJ animador(a)

encroach [ɪn'krəutʃ] VI: **to ~ (up)on** invadir; (*time*) ocupar

encrusted [ɪn'krʌstəd] ADJ: **~ with** incrustado de

encumber [ɪn'kʌmbə^r] VT: **to be ~ed with** (*carry*) estar carregado de; (*debts*) estar sobrecarregado de

encyclop(a)edia [ɛnsaɪkləu'pi:dɪə] N enciclopédia

end [ɛnd] N (*gen, also aim*) fim m; (*of table, line, rope etc*) ponta; (*of street, town*) final m; (*Sport*) ponta ■ VT acabar, terminar; (*also*: **bring to an end**, **put an end to**) acabar com, pôr fim a ■ VI terminar, acabar; **from ~ to ~** de ponta a ponta; **to come to an ~** acabar; **to be at an ~** estar no fim, estar terminado; **in the ~** ao fim, por fim, finalmente; **on ~** (*object*) na ponta; **to stand on ~** (*hair*) arrepiar-se; **for hours on ~** por horas a fio; **at the ~ of the day** (*Brit: fig*) no final das contas; **to this ~**, **with this ~ in view** a este fim

▶ **end up** VI: **to ~ up in** terminar em; (*place*) ir parar em

endanger [ɪn'deɪndʒə^r] VT pôr em perigo; **an ~ed species** uma espécie ameaçada de extinção

endear [ɪn'dɪə^r] VT: **to ~ o.s. to sb** conquistar a afeição de alguém, cativar alguém

endearing [ɪn'dɪərɪŋ] ADJ simpático, atrativo

endearment [ɪn'dɪəmənt] N: **to whisper ~s** sussurrar palavras carinhosas; **term of ~** palavra carinhosa

endeavour [ɪn'dɛvə^r] N esforço; (*US* **endeavor**) (*attempt*) tentativa; (*striving*) empenho ■ VI: **to ~ to do** esforçar-se para fazer; (*try*) tentar fazer

endemic [ɛn'dɛmɪk] ADJ endêmico

ending ['ɛndɪŋ] N fim m, conclusão f; (*of book*) desenlace m; (*Ling*) terminação f

endive ['ɛndaɪv] N (*curly*) chicória; (*smooth, flat*) endívia

endless ['ɛndlɪs] ADJ interminável; (*possibilities*) infinito

endorse [ɪn'dɔ:s] VT (*cheque*) endossar; (*approve*) aprovar

endorsee [ɪndɔ:'si:] N endossado(-a), endossatário(-a)

endorsement [ɪn'dɔ:smənt] N (*Brit: on driving licence*) descrição f das multas; (*approval*) aval m; (*signature*) endosso

endorser [ɪn'dɔ:sə^r] N endossante m/f, endossado(a) m/f

endow [ɪn'dau] VT (*provide with money*) dotar; (: *institution*) fundar; **to be ~ed with** ser dotado de

endowment [ɪnˈdaumənt] N dotação f;
endowment assurance N seguro dotal
end product N (Industry) produto final; (fig)
resultado
end result N resultado final
endurable [ɪnˈdjuərəbl] ADJ suportável
endurance [ɪnˈdjuərəns] N resistência
endurance test N teste m de resistência
endure [ɪnˈdjuəʳ] VT (bear) agüentar, suportar
■ VI (last) durar; (resist) resistir
end user N (Comput) usuário(-a) (BR) or utente
m/f (PT)
enema [ˈɛnɪmə] N (Med) enema m, clister m
enemy [ˈɛnəmɪ] ADJ, N inimigo(-a); **to make an
~ of sb** fazer de alguém um inimigo
energetic [ɛnəˈdʒɛtɪk] ADJ energético
energy [ˈɛnədʒɪ] N energia; **Department of E~**
Ministério da Energia; **energy crisis** N crise f
de energia
energy-saving ADJ (policy) de economia de
energia; (device) que economiza energia
enervating [ˈɛnəveɪtɪŋ] ADJ enervante
enforce [ɪnˈfɔːs] VT (Law) fazer cumprir
enforced [ɪnˈfɔːst] ADJ forçoso
enfranchise [ɪnˈfræntʃaɪz] VT conferir o direito
de voto a; (set free) emancipar
engage [ɪnˈɡeɪdʒ] VT (attention) chamar; (interest)
atrair; (lawyer) contratar; (clutch) engrenar ■ VI
(Tech) engrenar; **to ~ in** dedicar-se a, ocupar-se
com; **to ~ sb in conversation** travar conversa
com alguém
engaged [ɪnˈɡeɪdʒd] ADJ (Brit: phone) ocupado
(BR), impedido (PT); (: toilet) ocupado; (betrothed)
noivo; **to get ~** ficar noivo; **he is ~ in research**
dedica-se à pesquisa; **engaged tone** (Brit) N
(Tel) sinal m de ocupado (BR) or de impedido (PT)
engagement [ɪnˈɡeɪdʒmənt] N (appointment)
encontro; (booking) contrato; (battle) combate m;
(to marry) noivado; **I have a previous ~** já tenho
compromisso; **engagement ring** N aliança de
noivado
engaging [ɪnˈɡeɪdʒɪŋ] ADJ atraente, simpático
engender [ɪnˈdʒɛndəʳ] VT engendrar, gerar
engine [ˈɛndʒɪn] N (Aut) motor m; (Rail)
locomotiva; **engine driver** (Brit) N maquinista
m/f
engineer [ɛndʒɪˈnɪəʳ] N engenheiro(-a); (US:
Rail) maquinista m/f; (Brit: for repairs) técnico(-a);
(: for domestic appliances) consertador(a) m/f (de
aparelhos domésticos)
engineering [ɛndʒɪˈnɪərɪŋ] N engenharia
■ CPD: **~ works** or **factory** fábrica de construção
de máquinas
engine failure N falha do motor
engine trouble N enguiço
England [ˈɪŋɡlənd] N Inglaterra
English [ˈɪŋɡlɪʃ] ADJ inglês(-esa) ■ N (Ling)
inglês m; **the English** NPL (people) os ingleses;
an ~ speaker uma pessoa de língua inglesa;
English Channel N: **the English Channel** o
Canal da Mancha

Englishman [ˈɪŋɡlɪʃmən] (irreg) N inglês m
English-speaking ADJ de língua inglesa
Englishwoman [ˈɪŋɡlɪʃwumən] (irreg) N inglesa
engrave [ɪnˈɡreɪv] VT gravar
engraving [ɪnˈɡreɪvɪŋ] N gravura
engrossed [ɪnˈɡrəust] ADJ: **~ in** absorto em
engulf [ɪnˈɡʌlf] VT (subj: fire, water) engolfar,
tragar; (: panic, fear) tomar conta de
enhance [ɪnˈhɑːns] VT (gen) ressaltar, salientar;
(beauty) realçar; (position) melhorar; (add to)
aumentar
enigma [ɪˈnɪɡmə] N enigma m
enigmatic [ɛnɪɡˈmætɪk] ADJ enigmático
enjoy [ɪnˈdʒɔɪ] VT (like) gostar de; (have: health,
privilege) desfrutar de; (food) comer com gosto; **to
~ o.s.** divertir-se
enjoyable [ɪnˈdʒɔɪəbl] ADJ (pleasant) agradável;
(amusing) divertido
enjoyment [ɪnˈdʒɔɪmənt] N (joy) prazer m; (use)
gozo
enlarge [ɪnˈlɑːdʒ] VT aumentar; (broaden)
estender, alargar; (Phot) ampliar ■ VI: **to ~ on**
(subject) desenvolver, estender-se sobre
enlarged [ɪnˈlɑːdʒd] ADJ (edition) ampliado; (Med:
organ, gland) dilatado, hipertrofiado
enlargement [ɪnˈlɑːdʒmənt] N (Phot)
ampliação f
enlighten [ɪnˈlaɪtn] VT (inform) informar,
instruir
enlightened [ɪnˈlaɪtnd] ADJ (cultured) culto;
(knowledgeable) bem informado; (tolerant)
compreensivo
enlightening [ɪnˈlaɪtnɪŋ] ADJ esclarecedor(a)
enlightenment [ɪnˈlaɪtənmənt] N
esclarecimento; (History): **the E~** o Século das
Luzes
enlist [ɪnˈlɪst] VT alistar; (support) conseguir,
aliciar ■ VI alistar-se; **~ed man** (US: Mil)
praça m
enliven [ɪnˈlaɪvn] VT animar, agitar
enmity [ˈɛnmɪtɪ] N inimizade f
ennoble [ɪˈnəubl] VT (with title) nobilitar
enormity [ɪˈnɔːmɪtɪ] N enormidade f
enormous [ɪˈnɔːməs] ADJ enorme
enormously [ɪˈnɔːməslɪ] ADV imensamente
enough [ɪˈnʌf] ADJ: **~ time/books** tempo
suficiente/livros suficientes ■ PRON: **have
you got ~?** você tem o suficiente? ■ ADV:
big ~ suficientemente grande; **will 5 be ~?** 5
chegam?; **~! basta!, chega!; that's ~, thanks**
chega, obrigado; **I've had ~!** não agüento mais!;
I've had ~ of him estou farto dele; **he has not
worked ~** não tem trabalhado o suficiente; **it's
hot ~ (as it is)!** já está tão quente!; **he was kind
~ to lend me the money** ele teve a gentileza de
me emprestar o dinheiro; **which, funnily** or
oddly ~ ... o que, por estranho que pareça ...
enquire [ɪnˈkwaɪəʳ] VT, VI = **inquire**
enrage [ɪnˈreɪdʒ] VT enfurecer, enraivecer
enrich [ɪnˈrɪtʃ] VT enriquecer
enrol [ɪnˈrəul] (US **enroll**) VT inscrever; (Sch)
matricular ■ VI inscrever-se; matricular-se

enrol(l)ment [ɪn'rəulmənt] N inscrição f; (Sch) matrícula

en route [ɔn-] ADV (on the way) no caminho; ~ **for** or **to** a caminho de

ensconced [ɪn'skɔnst] ADJ: ~ **in** acomodado em

enshrine [ɪn'ʃraɪn] VT (fig) conservar, resguardar

ensign ['ɛnsaɪn] N (flag) bandeira; (Mil) insígnia; (US: Naut) guarda-marinha m

enslave [ɪn'sleɪv] VT escravizar

ensue [ɪn'sju:] VI seguir-se; (result) resultar; (happen) acontecer

ensure [ɪn'ʃuəʳ] VT assegurar; **to ~ that** verificar-se que

ENT N ABBR (= Ear, Nose & Throat) otorrinolaringologia

entail [ɪn'teɪl] VT (involve) implicar; (result in) acarretar

entangle [ɪn'tæŋɡl] VT enredar, emaranhar; **to get ~d in sth** (fig) ficar enrolado em algo

enter ['ɛntəʳ] VT (room) entrar em; (club) ficar or fazer-se sócio de; (army) alistar-se em; (competition) inscrever-se em; (sb for a competition) inscrever; (write down) completar; (Comput) entrar com ■ VI entrar
  ▸ **enter for** VT FUS inscrever-se em
  ▸ **enter into** VT FUS (relations) estabelecer; (plans) fazer parte de; (debate, negotiations) entrar em; (agreement) chegar a, firmar
  ▸ **enter up** VT lançar
  ▸ **enter (up)on** VT FUS (career) entrar para

enteritis [ɛntə'raɪtɪs] N enterite f

enterprise ['ɛntəpraɪz] N empresa; (undertaking) empreendimento; (initiative) iniciativa; **free/private ~** livre-empresa/empresa privada

enterprising ['ɛntəpraɪzɪŋ] ADJ empreendedor(a)

entertain [ɛntə'teɪn] VT (amuse) divertir, entreter; (invite: guest) receber (em casa); (idea, plan) estudar

entertainer [ɛntə'teɪnəʳ] N artista m/f

entertaining [ɛntə'teɪnɪŋ] ADJ divertido ■ N: **to do a lot of ~** receber com freqüência

entertainment [ɛntə'teɪnmənt] N (amusement) entretenimento, diversão f; (show) espetáculo; **entertainment allowance** N verba de representação

enthralled [ɪn'θrɔ:ld] ADJ encantado, cativado

enthralling [ɪn'θrɔ:lɪŋ] ADJ cativante, encantador(a)

enthuse [ɪn'θu:z] VI: **to ~ about** or **over** entusiasmar-se com or por

enthusiasm [ɪn'θu:zɪæzəm] N entusiasmo

enthusiast [ɪn'θu:zɪæst] N entusiasta m/f; **a jazz** etc ~ um(-a) aficionado(a) de jazz etc

enthusiastic [ɪnθu:zɪ'æstɪk] ADJ entusiasmado; **to be ~ about** entusiasmar-se por

entice [ɪn'taɪs] VT atrair, tentar; (seduce) seduzir

enticing [ɪn'taɪsɪŋ] ADJ sedutor(a), tentador(a)

entire [ɪn'taɪəʳ] ADJ inteiro

entirely [ɪn'taɪəlɪ] ADV totalmente, completamente

entirety [ɪn'taɪərətɪ] N: **in its ~** na sua totalidade

entitle [ɪn'taɪtl] VT: **to ~ sb to sth** dar a alguém direito a algo; **to ~ sb to do** dar a alguém direito de fazer

entitled [ɪn'taɪtld] ADJ (book etc) intitulado; **to be ~ to sth/to do sth** ter direito a algo/de fazer algo

entity ['ɛntɪtɪ] N ente m

entourage [ɔntu'ra:ʒ] N séquito

entrails ['ɛntreɪlz] NPL entranhas fpl

entrance [n 'ɛntrəns, vt ɪn'tra:ns] N entrada; (arrival) chegada ■ VT encantar, fascinar; **to gain ~ to** (university etc) ser admitido em; **entrance examination** N exame m de admissão; **entrance fee** N jóia; (to museum etc) (preço da) entrada; **entrance ramp** (US) N (Aut) entrada (para a rodovia)

entrancing [ɪn'tra:nsɪŋ] ADJ encantador(a), fascinante

entrant ['ɛntrənt] N participante m/f; (Brit: in exam) candidato(-a)

entreat [ɛn'tri:t] VT: **to ~ sb to do** suplicar con alguém para fazer

entreaty [ɛn'tri:tɪ] N rogo, súplica

entrée ['ɔntreɪ] N (Culin) entrada

entrenched [ɛn'trɛntʃd] ADJ (position, power) fortalecido; (idea) arraigado

entrepreneur [ɔntrəprə'nə:] N empresário(-a)

entrepreneurial [ɔntrəprə'nə:rɪəl] ADJ empreendedor(a)

entrust [ɪn'trʌst] VT: **to ~ sth to sb** confiar algo a alguém

entry ['ɛntrɪ] N entrada; (permission to enter) acesso; (in register) registro, assentamento; (in account) lançamento; (in dictionary) verbete m; **"no ~"** "entrada proibida"; (Aut) "contramão" (BR), "entrada proibida" (PT); **single/double ~ book-keeping** escrituração por partidas simples/dobradas; **entry form** N formulário de inscrição; **entry phone** (Brit) N interfone m (em apartamento)

entwine [ɪn'twaɪn] VT entrelaçar

enumerate [ɪ'nju:məreɪt] VT enumerar

enunciate [ɪ'nʌnsɪeɪt] VT pronunciar; (principle etc) enunciar

envelop [ɪn'vɛləp] VT envolver

envelope ['ɛnvələup] N envelope m

enviable ['ɛnvɪəbl] ADJ invejável

envious ['ɛnvɪəs] ADJ invejoso; (look) de inveja

environment [ɪn'vaɪərnmənt] N meio ambiente m; **Department of the E~** (Brit) Ministério da Habitação, Urbanismo e Meio Ambiente

environmental [ɪnvaɪərn'mɛntl] ADJ ambiental; **~ studies** (Sch) ecologia

environmentalist [ɪnvaɪərn'mɛntəlɪst] N ecologista m/f

Environmental Protection Agency (US) N ≈ Secretaria Especial do Meio Ambiente

envisage [ɪn'vɪzɪdʒ] VT (foresee) prever; (imagine) conceber, imaginar

envision [ɪn'vɪʒən] (US) VT = **envisage**

envoy ['ɛnvɔɪ] N enviado(-a)
envy ['ɛnvɪ] N inveja ▪ VT ter inveja de; **to ~ sb
sth** invejar alguém por algo, cobiçar algo de
alguém
enzyme ['ɛnzaɪm] N enzima
EPA (US) N ABBR (= Environmental Protection Agency)
≈ SEMA
ephemeral [ɪ'fɛmərl] ADJ efêmero
epic ['ɛpɪk] N epopéia ▪ ADJ épico
epicentre ['ɛpɪsɛntər'] (US **epicenter**) N
epicentro
epidemic [ɛpɪ'dɛmɪk] N epidemia
epilepsy ['ɛpɪlɛpsɪ] N epilepsia
epileptic [ɛpɪ'lɛptɪk] ADJ, N epilético(-a)
epilogue ['ɛpɪlɔg] N epílogo
episcopal [ɪ'pɪskəpl] ADJ episcopal
episode ['ɛpɪsəud] N episódio; (instalment)
capítulo
epistle [ɪ'pɪsl] N epístola
epitaph ['ɛpɪtɑːf] N epitáfio
epithet ['ɛpɪθɛt] N epíteto
epitome [ɪ'pɪtəmɪ] N epítome m
epitomize [ɪ'pɪtəmaɪz] VT epitomar, resumir
epoch ['iːpɔk] N época
epoch-making ADJ que marca época, marcante
eponymous [ɪ'pɔnɪməs] ADJ epônimo
equable ['ɛkwəbl] ADJ (climate) uniforme; (temper,
reply) equânime; (character) tranqüilo, calmo
equal ['iːkwl] ADJ igual; (treatment) equitativo,
equivalente ▪ N igual m/f ▪ VT ser igual a; **to
be ~ to** (task) estar à altura de; **~ to doing** capaz
de fazer
equality [iː'kwɔlɪtɪ] N igualdade f
equalize ['iːkwəlaɪz] VT, VI igualar; (Sport)
empatar
equalizer ['iːkwəlaɪzər'] N gol m (BR) ou golo (PT)
de empate
equally ['iːkwəlɪ] ADV igualmente; (share etc)
por igual
Equal Opportunities Commission (US **Equal
Employment Opportunity Commission**)
N comissão para a não-discriminação no
trabalho
equal(s) sign N sinal m de igualdade
equanimity [ɛkwə'nɪmɪtɪ] N equanimidade f
equate [ɪ'kweɪt] VT: **to ~ sth with** equiparar
algo com; **to ~ sth to** igualar algo a
equation [ɪ'kweɪʒən] N (Math) equação f
equator [ɪ'kweɪtər'] N equador m
equatorial [ɛkwə'tɔːrɪəl] ADJ equatorial
Equatorial Guinea N Guiné f Equatorial
equestrian [ɪ'kwɛstrɪən] ADJ eqüestre; (sport)
hípico ▪ N (man) ginete m; (woman) amazona
equilibrium [iːkwɪ'lɪbrɪəm] N equilíbrio
equinox ['iːkwɪnɔks] N equinócio
equip [ɪ'kwɪp] VT equipar; (person) prover,
munir; **to ~ sb/sth with** equipar alguém/algo
com, munir alguém/algo de; **to be well ~ped**
estar bem preparado ou equipado
equipment [ɪ'kwɪpmənt] N equipamento;
(machines etc) equipamentos mpl, aparelhagem f
equitable ['ɛkwɪtəbl] ADJ equitativo

equities ['ɛkwɪtɪz] (Brit) NPL (Comm) ações fpl
ordinárias
equity capital N capital m próprio
equivalent [ɪ'kwɪvəlnt] ADJ equivalente ▪ N
equivalente m; **to be ~ to** ser equivalente a
equivocal [ɪ'kwɪvəkl] ADJ equívoco; (open to
suspicion) ambíguo
equivocate [ɪ'kwɪvəkeɪt] VI sofismar
equivocation [ɪkwɪvə'keɪʃən] N sofismas mpl
ER (Brit) ABBR (= Elizabeth Regina) a rainha Elisabete
ERA (US) N ABBR (Pol: = equal rights amendment)
emenda sobre a igualdade das mulheres
era ['ɪərə] N era, época
eradicate [ɪ'rædɪkeɪt] VT erradicar, eliminar
erase [ɪ'reɪz] VT apagar
eraser [ɪ'reɪzər'] N borracha (de apagar)
erect [ɪ'rɛkt] ADJ (posture) ereto; (tail, ears)
levantado ▪ VT erigir, levantar; (assemble)
montar; (tent) armar
erection [ɪ'rɛkʃən] N construção f; (assembly)
montagem f; (structure) edifício; (Physio) ereção f
ergonomics [əːgə'nɔmɪks] N ergonomia
ERISA (US) N ABBR (= Employee Retirement Income
Security Act) lei referente às aposentadorias
ermine ['əːmɪn] N arminho
ERNIE ['əːnɪ] (Brit) N ABBR (= Electronic Random
Number Indicator Equipment) computador que serve
para o sorteio dos "premium bonds"
erode [ɪ'rəud] VT (Geo) causar erosão em;
(confidence) minar; (salary) corroer
erosion [ɪ'rəuʒən] N erosão f; (fig) corrosão f
erotic [ɪ'rɔtɪk] ADJ erótico
eroticism [ɪ'rɔtɪsɪzm] N erotismo
err [əːr'] VI errar, enganar-se; (Rel) pecar
errand ['ɛrnd] N recado, mensagem f; **to run
~s** fazer incumbências; **~ of mercy** missão f de
caridade; **errand boy** N mensageiro
erratic [ɪ'rætɪk] ADJ imprevisível
erroneous [ɪ'rəunɪəs] ADJ errôneo
error ['ɛrər'] N erro; **typing/spelling ~** erro de
datilografia/ortografia; **in ~** por engano; **~s and
omissions excepted** salvo erro ou omissão;
error message N (Comput) mensagem f de erro
erstwhile ['əːstwaɪl] ADJ antigo
erudite ['ɛrjudaɪt] ADJ erudito
erupt [ɪ'rʌpt] VI entrar em erupção; (fig)
explodir, estourar
eruption [ɪ'rʌpʃən] N erupção f; (fig) explosão f
ESA N ABBR (= European Space Agency) AEE f
escalate ['ɛskəleɪt] VI intensificar-se; (costs,
prices) disparar
escalation [ɛskə'leɪʃən] N escalada,
intensificação f; **escalation clause** N cláusula
de reajustamento
escalator ['ɛskəleɪtər'] N escada rolante
escapade [ɛskə'peɪd] N peripécia
escape [ɪ'skeɪp] N fuga; (from duties) escapatória;
(from chase) fuga, evasão f; (of gas) escapatória
▪ VI escapar; (flee) fugir, evadir-se; (leak) vazar,
escapar ▪ VT evitar, fugir de; (consequences)
fugir de; (elude): **his name ~s me** o nome dele
me foge à memória; **to ~ from** (place) escapar

de; (*person*) escapulir de; (*clutches*) livrar-se de;
to ~ to fugir para; **to ~ to safety** salvar-se; **to
~ notice** passar despercebido; **escape artist** N
ilusionista *m/f*; **escape clause** N cláusula que
permite revogação do contrato; **escape key** N
(*Comput*) tecla de saída; **escape route** N (*from
fire*) saída de emergência; (*of prisoners*) roteiro
da fuga

escapism [ɪ'skeɪpɪzəm] N escapismo, fuga à
realidade

escapist [ɪ'skeɪpɪst] ADJ (*person*) que foge da
realidade; (*literature*) de evasão

escapologist [ɛskə'pɒlədʒɪst] (*Brit*) N
ilusionista *m/f*

escarpment [ɪs'kɑːpmənt] N escarpa

eschew [ɪs'tʃuː] VT evitar

escort [n 'ɛskɔːt, vt ɪ'skɔːt] N acompanhante *m/f*;
(*Mil, Naut*) escolta ■ VT acompanhar; (*Mil, Naut*)
escoltar; **escort agency** N agência de escorte

Eskimo ['ɛskɪməu] ADJ esquimó ■ N esquimó
m/f; (*Ling*) esquimó *m*

ESL N ABBR (*Sch*) = **English as a Second
Language**

esophagus [iː'sɒfəgəs] (*US*) N = **oesophagus**

esoteric [ɛsə'tɛrɪk] ADJ esotérico

ESP N ABBR = **extrasensory perception**

esp. ABBR = **especially**

especially [ɪ'spɛʃlɪ] ADV (*gen*) especialmente;
(*above all*) sobretudo; (*particularly*) em particular

espionage ['ɛspɪənɑːʒ] N espionagem *f*

esplanade [ɛsplə'neɪd] N (*by sea*) avenida beira-
mar, esplanada

espouse [ɪ'spauz] VT (*policy, idea*) adotar; (*cause*)
abraçar

Esq. (*Brit*) ABBR (= *Esquire*) Sr

Esquire [ɪ'skwaɪər] (*Brit*) N (*abbr Esq.*): **J. Brown, ~**
Sr. J. Brown

essay ['ɛseɪ] N (*Sch, Literature*) ensaio

essence ['ɛsns] N essência; **in ~** em sua
essência; **speed is of the ~** a rapidez é
fundamental

essential [ɪ'sɛnʃl] ADJ (*necessary*) indispensável;
(*basic*) essencial ■ N elemento essencial; **it is ~
that** é indispensável que (+*sub*)

essentially [ɪ'sɛnʃəlɪ] ADV essencialmente

EST (*US*) ABBR (= *Eastern Standard Time*) hora de
inverno de Nova Iorque

est ABBR = **established**; **estimate(d)**

establish [ɪ'stæblɪʃ] VT estabelecer; (*facts*)
verificar; (*proof*) demonstrar; (*reputation*) firmar

established [ɪ'stæblɪʃt] ADJ consagrado; (*staff*)
fixo

establishment [ɪ'stæblɪʃmənt] N
estabelecimento; **the E~** a classe dirigente

estate [ɪ'steɪt] N (*land*) fazenda (BR),
propriedade *f* (PT); (*property*) propriedade; (*Law*)
herança; (*Pol*) estado; (*Brit: also:* **housing estate**)
conjunto habitacional; **estate agency** (*Brit*) N
imobiliária, corretora de imóveis; **estate agent**
(*Brit*) N corretor(a) *m/f* de imóveis (BR), agente
m/f imobiliário(-a) (PT); **estate car** (*Brit*) N
perua (BR), canadiana (PT)

esteem [ɪ'stiːm] N estima ■ VT estimar; **to
hold sb in high ~** estimar muito alguém

esthetic [ɪs'θɛtɪk] (*US*) ADJ = **aesthetic**

estimate [n 'ɛstɪmət, vt, vi 'ɛstɪmeɪt] N
(*assessment*) avaliação *f*; (*calculation*) cálculo;
(*Comm*) orçamento ■ VT estimar, avaliar,
calcular ■ VI (*Brit: Comm*): **to ~ for a job** orçar
uma obra; **at a rough ~** numa estimativa
aproximada

estimation [ɛstɪ'meɪʃən] N opinião *f*;
(*calculation*) cálculo; (*esteem*) apreço; **in my ~** na
minha opinião

Estonia [ɛ'stəunɪə] N Estônia

estranged [ɪ'streɪndʒd] ADJ (*couple*) separado;
(*husband, wife*) de quem se separou

estrangement [ɪ'streɪndʒmənt] N separação *f*

estrogen ['iːstrəudʒɛn] (*US*) N = **oestrogen**

estuary ['ɛstjuərɪ] N estuário

ET (*US*) ABBR (= *Eastern Time*) hora de Nova Iorque

ETA N ABBR = **estimated time of arrival**

et al. ABBR (= *et alii*) e outras pessoas

etc. ABBR (= *et cetera*) etc

etch [ɛtʃ] VT gravar com água-forte

etching ['ɛtʃɪŋ] N água-forte *f*

ETD N ABBR = **estimated time of departure**

eternal [ɪ'təːnl] ADJ eterno; (*unchanging*)
absoluto

eternity [ɪ'təːnɪtɪ] N eternidade *f*

ether ['iːθər] N éter *m*

ethereal [ɪ'θɪərɪəl] ADJ etéreo

ethical ['ɛθɪkl] ADJ ético; (*honest*) honrado

ethics ['ɛθɪks] N ética ■ NPL moral *f*

Ethiopia [iːθɪ'əupɪə] N Etiópia

Ethiopian [iːθɪ'əupɪən] ADJ, N etíope *m/f*

ethnic ['ɛθnɪk] ADJ étnico; (*culture*) folclórico;
(*food*) exótico

ethnology [ɛθ'nɒlədʒɪ] N etnologia

ethos ['iːθɒs] N sistema *m* de valores

e-ticket ['iːtɪkɪt] N bilhete eletrônico

etiquette ['ɛtɪkɛt] N etiqueta

ETV (*US*) N ABBR (= *Educational Television*) TV *f*
educativa

etymology [ɛtɪ'mɒlədʒɪ] N etimologia

EU ABBR (= *European Union*) UE *f*

eucalyptus [juːkə'lɪptəs] N eucalipto

euphemism ['juːfəmɪzm] N eufemismo

euphemistic [juːfə'mɪstɪk] ADJ eufêmico

euphoria [juː'fɔːrɪə] N euforia

Eurasia [juə'reɪʃə] N Eurásia

Eurasian [juə'reɪʃən] ADJ (*person*) eurasiático;
(*continent*) eurásio ■ N eurasiático(-a)

Euratom [juə'rætəm] N ABBR (= *European Atomic
Energy Community*) EURATOM *f*

euro ['juərəu] N (*currency*) euro *m*

Eurocheque ['juərəutʃɛk] N eurocheque *m*

Eurocrat ['juərəukræt] N eurocrata *m/f*,
funcionário(-a) da CEE

Eurodollar ['juərəudɒlər] N eurodólar *m*

Europe ['juərəp] N Europa

European [juərə'piːən] ADJ, N europeu(-péia);
European Court of Justice N Tribunal *m*
Europeu de Justiça; **European Union** N: **the**

European Union a União Européia

euthanasia [juːθəˈneɪzɪə] N eutanásia

evacuate [ɪˈvækjʊeɪt] VT evacuar

evacuation [ɪvækjuˈeɪʃən] N evacuação f

evade [ɪˈveɪd] VT (person) evitar; (question, duties) esquivar-se de; (tax) sonegar

evaluate [ɪˈvæljʊeɪt] VT avaliar; (evidence) interpretar

evangelist [ɪˈvændʒəlɪst] N evangelista m/f; (preacher) evangelizador(a) m/f

evangelize [ɪˈvændʒəlaɪz] VT evangelizar

evaporate [ɪˈvæpəreɪt] VI evaporar-se ■ VT evaporar

evaporated milk [ɪˈvæpəreɪtɪd-] N leite m desidratado

evaporation [ɪvæpəˈreɪʃən] N evaporação f

evasion [ɪˈveɪʒən] N evasão f, fuga; (of tax) sonegação f; (fig) evasiva

evasive [ɪˈveɪsɪv] ADJ evasivo

eve [iːv] N: **on the ~ of** na véspera de

even [ˈiːvn] ADJ (level) plano; (smooth) liso; (speed, temperature) uniforme; (equal, Sport) igual; (number) par; (nature) equilibrado ■ ADV até, mesmo; **~ if** mesmo que; **~ though** mesmo que, embora; **~ more** ainda mais; **~ faster** ainda mais rápido, mais rápido ainda; **~ so** mesmo assim; **never ~** nem sequer; **not ~** nem; **~ he was there** até ele esteve ali; **~ on Sundays** até nos domingos; **to get ~ with sb** ficar quite com alguém; **to break ~** sair sem lucros nem prejuízos

▶ **even out** VI nivelar-se

evening [ˈiːvnɪŋ] N (early) tarde f; (late) noite f; (before six) tarde f; (event) noitada; **in the ~** à noite; **this ~** hoje à noite; **tomorrow/ yesterday ~** amanhã/ontem à noite; **evening class** N aula noturna; **evening dress** N (man's) traje m de rigor (BR) or de cerimónia (PT); (woman's) vestido de noite

evenly [ˈiːvnlɪ] ADV uniformemente; (space) regularmente; (divide) por igual

evensong [ˈiːvnsɔŋ] N oração f da tarde

event [ɪˈvent] N acontecimento; (Sport) prova; **in the course of ~s** no decorrer dos acontecimentos; **in the ~ of** no caso de; **in the ~** de fato, na realidade; **at all ~s** (Brit), **in any ~** em todo o caso

eventful [ɪˈventfʊl] ADJ cheio de acontecimentos; (game etc) cheio de emoção, agitado

eventing [ɪˈventɪŋ] N (Horseriding) concurso completo (hipismo)

eventual [ɪˈventʃʊəl] ADJ (outcome) final; (resulting) definitivo

eventuality [ɪventʃʊˈælɪtɪ] N eventualidade f

eventually [ɪˈventʃʊəlɪ] ADV (finally) finalmente; (in time) por fim

ever [ˈevəʳ] ADV já, alguma vez; (in negative) nunca, jamais; (always) sempre; (at any time) em qualquer moment; (in question): **why ~ not?** por que nem sempre?; **the best ~** o melhor que já se viu; **have you ~ seen it?** você alguma vez

já viu isto?; **better than ~** melhor que nunca; **for ~** para sempre; **hardly ~** quase nunca; **~ since** ADV desde então ■ CONJ depois que; **~ so pretty** tão bonitinho; **thank you ~ so much** muitíssimo obrigado, obrigadão (inf); **yours ~** (Brit) (in letters) sempre seu/sua

Everest [ˈevərɪst] N (also: **Mount Everest**) o monte Everest

evergreen [ˈevəgriːn] N sempre-verde f

everlasting [evəˈlɑːstɪŋ] ADJ eterno, perpétuo

○ **KEYWORD**

every [ˈevrɪ] ADJ 1 (each) cada; **every one of them** cada um deles; **every shop in the town was closed** todas as lojas da cidade estavam fechadas

2 (all possible) todo(-a); **I gave you every assistance** eu lhe dei toda assistência; **I have every confidence in her** tenho absoluta confiança nela; **we wish you every success** desejamo-lhe o maior sucesso; **he's every bit as clever as his brother** ele é tão inteligente quanto o irmão

3 (showing recurrence) todo(-a); **every day/week** todo dia/toda semana; **every other car had been broken into** cada dois carros foram arrombados; **she visits me every other/third day** ele me visita cada dois/três dias; **every now and then** de vez em quando

everybody [ˈevrɪbɔdɪ] PRON todos, todo mundo (BR), toda a gente (PT); **~ knows about it** todo o mundo já sabe; **~ else** todos os outros

everyday [ˈevrɪdeɪ] ADJ (daily) diário; (usual) corrente; (common) comum; (routine) rotineiro

everyone [ˈevrɪwʌn] PRON = **everybody**

everything [ˈevrɪθɪŋ] PRON tudo; **~ is ready** tudo está pronto; **he did ~ possible** ele fez todo o possível

everywhere [ˈevrɪweəʳ] ADV (be) em todo lugar (BR), em toda a parte (PT); (go) a todo lugar (BR), a toda a parte (PT); (wherever): **~ you go you meet ...** aonde quer que se, encontra-se ...

evict [ɪˈvɪkt] VT despejar

eviction [ɪˈvɪkʃən] N despejo; **eviction notice** N notificação f de despejo

evidence [ˈevɪdəns] N (proof) prova(s) f(pl); (of witness) testemunho, depoimento; (indication) sinal m; (facts) dados mpl, evidência; **to give ~** testemunhar, prestar depoimento; **in ~** (obvious) em evidência, evidente

evident [ˈevɪdənt] ADJ evidente

evidently [ˈevɪdəntlɪ] ADV evidentemente; (apparently) aparentemente

evil [ˈiːvl] ADJ mau(-má); (person) perverso; (system, influence) nocivo; (smell) horrível ■ N mal m, maldade f

evildoer [ˈiːvlduːəʳ] N malfeitor(a) m/f

evince [ɪˈvɪns] VT evidenciar

evocative [ɪˈvɔkətɪv] ADJ evocativo, sugestivo

evoke [ɪˈvəuk] VT evocar

evolution [iːvəˈluːʃən] N evolução f; (*development*) desenvolvimento

evolve [ɪˈvɔlv] VT desenvolver ■ VI desenvolver-se

ewe [juː] N ovelha

ex- [ɛks] PREFIX (*former*) ex-; (*out of*): **the price ~ works** o preço na porta da fábrica

exacerbate [ɛksˈæsəbeɪt] VT (*pain, illness*) exacerbar; (*fig*) agravar

exact [ɪɡˈzækt] ADJ exato; (*person*) meticuloso ■ VT: **to ~ sth (from)** exigir algo (de)

exacting [ɪɡˈzæktɪŋ] ADJ exigente; (*conditions*) difícil

exactitude [ɪɡˈzæktɪtjuːd] N exatidão f

exactly [ɪɡˈzæktlɪ] ADV exatamente; (*time*) em ponto; (*indicating agreement*) isso mesmo

exaggerate [ɪɡˈzædʒəreɪt] VT, VI exagerar

exaggeration [ɪɡzædʒəˈreɪʃən] N exagero

exalted [ɪɡˈzɔːltɪd] ADJ exaltado

exam [ɪɡˈzæm] N ABBR = **examination**

examination [ɪɡzæmɪˈneɪʃən] N (*Sch, Med*) exame m; (*Law*) inquirição f; (*inquiry*) investigação f; **to sit** (*Brit*) or **take an ~** submeter-se a um exame; **the matter is under ~** o assunto está sendo examinado

examine [ɪɡˈzæmɪn] VT examinar; (*inspect*) inspecionar; (*Law: person*) interrogar; (*at customs: luggage*) revistar; (*passport*) controlar

examiner [ɪɡˈzæmɪnəʳ] N examinador(a) m/f

example [ɪɡˈzɑːmpl] N exemplo; **for ~** por exemplo; **to set a good/bad ~** dar um bom/mau exemplo

exasperate [ɪɡˈzɑːspəreɪt] VT exasperar, irritar

exasperating [ɪɡˈzɑːspəreɪtɪŋ] ADJ irritante

exasperation [ɪɡzɑːspəˈreɪʃən] N exasperação f, irritação f

excavate [ˈɛkskəveɪt] VT escavar

excavation [ɛkskəˈveɪʃən] N escavação f

excavator [ˈɛkskəveɪtəʳ] N (*machine*) escavadeira

exceed [ɪkˈsiːd] VT exceder; (*number*) ser superior a; (*speed limit*) ultrapassar; (*limits*) ir além de; (*powers*) exceder-se em; (*hopes*) superar

exceedingly [ɪkˈsiːdɪŋlɪ] ADV extremamente

excel [ɪkˈsɛl] VI sobressair, distinguir-se ■ VT superar; **to ~ o.s.** (*Brit*) destacar-se

excellence [ˈɛksələns] N excelência

Excellency [ˈɛksələnsɪ] N: **His ~** Sua Excelência

excellent [ˈɛksələnt] ADJ excelente

except [ɪkˈsɛpt] PREP (*also*: **except for, excepting**) exceto, a não ser ■ VT: **to ~ sb from** excluir alguém de; **~ if/when** a menos que, a não ser que; **~ that** exceto que

exception [ɪkˈsɛpʃən] N exceção f; **to take ~ to** ressentir-se de; **with the ~ of** à exceção de; **to make an ~** fazer exceção

exceptional [ɪkˈsɛpʃənl] ADJ excepcional

excerpt [ˈɛksəːpt] N trecho

excess [ɪkˈsɛs] N excesso; (*Comm*) excedente m; **in ~ of** mais de; **excess baggage** N excesso de bagagem; **excess fare** (*Brit*) N sobretaxa de excesso

excessive [ɪkˈsɛsɪv] ADJ excessivo

excess supply N oferta excedente

exchange [ɪksˈtʃeɪndʒ] N troca; (*of teachers, students*) intercâmbio; (*also*: **telephone exchange**) estação f telefônica (BR), central f telefónica (PT) ■ VT: **to ~ (for)** trocar (por); **in ~ for** em troca de; **foreign ~** (*Comm*) divisas fpl, câmbio; **exchange control** N controle m de câmbio; **exchange market** N mercado cambial or de câmbio; **exchange rate** N (*taxa de*) câmbio

Exchequer [ɪksˈtʃɛkəʳ] (*Brit*) N: **the ~** ≈ o Tesouro Nacional

excisable [ɪkˈsaɪzəbl] ADJ tributável

excise [n ˈɛksaɪz, vt ɛkˈsaɪz] N imposto de consumo ■ VT cortar (fora); **excise duties** NPL impostos mpl indiretos

excitable [ɪkˈsaɪtəbl] ADJ excitável; (*edgy*) nervoso

excite [ɪkˈsaɪt] VT (*stimulate, arouse*) excitar; (*awaken*) despertar; (*move*) entusiasmar; **to get ~d** entusiasmar-se

excitement [ɪkˈsaɪtmənt] N emoções fpl; (*anticipation*) expectativa; (*agitation*) agitação f

exciting [ɪkˈsaɪtɪŋ] ADJ emocionante, empolgante

excl. ABBR = **excluding; exclusive (of)**

exclaim [ɪkˈskleɪm] VI exclamar

exclamation [ɛkskləˈmeɪʃən] N exclamação f; **exclamation mark** N ponto de exclamação

exclude [ɪkˈskluːd] VT excluir; (*except*) excetuar

excluding [ɪkˈskluːdɪŋ] PREP: **~ tax** imposto excluído

exclusion [ɪkˈskluːʒən] N exclusão f; **to the ~ of** a ponto de excluir; **exclusion clause** N cláusula de exclusão

exclusive [ɪkˈskluːsɪv] ADJ exclusivo; (*club, district*) privativo; (*item of news*) com exclusividade; **~ of tax** sem incluir os impostos; **~ of postage** tarifas postais excluídas; **from 1st to 15th March** ~ entre o dia 1° e 15 de março; **~ rights** (*Comm*) exclusividade f

exclusively [ɪkˈskluːsɪvlɪ] ADV unicamente

excommunicate [ɛkskəˈmjuːnɪkeɪt] VT excomungar

excrement [ˈɛkskrəmənt] N excremento

excrete [ɪkˈskriːt] VI excretar

excruciating [ɪkˈskruːʃɪeɪtɪŋ] ADJ (*pain*) doloroso, martirizante

excursion [ɪkˈskəːʃən] N excursão f; **excursion ticket** N passagem f de excursão

excusable [ɪkˈskjuːzəbl] ADJ perdoável, excusável

excuse [n ɪkˈskjuːs, vt ɪkˈskjuːz] N desculpa; (*evasion*) pretexto ■ VT desculpar, perdoar; **to ~ sb from doing sth** dispensar alguém de fazer algo; **~ me!** (*attracting attention, apology*) desculpe!; (*asking permission*) (com) licença; **if you will ~ me ...** com a sua licença ...; **to make ~s for sb** apresentar desculpas por alguém; **to ~ o.s. for sth/for doing sth** desculpar-se de algo/de fazer algo

ex-directory (*Brit*) ADJ: **~ (phone) number** número que não figura na lista telefônica

execute ['ɛksɪkjuːt] VT (plan) realizar; (order) cumprir; (person, movement) executar
execution [ɛksɪ'kjuːʃən] N realização f; (killing) execução f
executioner [ɛksɪ'kjuːʃənər] N verdugo, carrasco
executive [ɪg'zɛkjutɪv] N (Comm, Pol) executivo ▪ ADJ executivo; **executive director** N diretor(a) m/f executivo(-a)
executor [ɪg'zɛkjutər] N executor(a) m/f testamentário(-a), testamenteiro(-a)
exemplary [ɪg'zɛmplərɪ] ADJ exemplar
exemplify [ɪg'zɛmplɪfaɪ] VT exemplificar; (illustrate) ilustrar
exempt [ɪg'zɛmpt] ADJ: ~ **from** isento de ▪ VT: **to ~ sb from** dispensar or isentar alguém de
exemption [ɪg'zɛmpʃən] N (from taxes etc) isenção f; (from military service) dispensa; (immunity) imunidade f
exercise ['ɛksəsaɪz] N exercício ▪ VT exercer; (right) valer-se de; (dog) levar para passear ▪ VI (also: **to take exercise**) fazer exercício; **exercise book** N caderno
exert [ɪg'zəːt] VT exercer; **to ~ o.s.** esforçar-se, empenhar-se
exertion [ɪg'zəːʃən] N esforço
ex gratia [-'greɪʃə] ADJ: ~ **payment** gratificação f
exhale [ɛks'heɪl] VT, VI expirar
exhaust [ɪg'zɔːst] N (Auto: also: **exhaust pipe**) escape m, exaustor m; (fumes) escapamento (de gás) ▪ VT esgotar; **to ~ o.s.** esgotar-se; ~ **manifold** (Aut etc) cano de descarga
exhausted [ɪg'zɔːstɪd] ADJ esgotado
exhausting [ɪg'zɔːstɪŋ] ADJ exaustivo, estafante
exhaustion [ɪg'zɔːstʃən] N exaustão f
exhaustive [ɪg'zɔːstɪv] ADJ exaustivo
exhibit [ɪg'zɪbɪt] N (Art) obra exposta; (Law) objeto exposto ▪ VT (courage etc) manifestar, mostrar; (quality, emotion) demonstrar; (film) apresentar; (paintings) expor
exhibition [ɛksɪ'bɪʃən] N exposição f
exhibitionist [ɛksɪ'bɪʃənɪst] N exibicionista m/f; (of talent etc) mostra
exhibitor [ɪg'zɪbɪtər] N expositor(a) m/f
exhilarating [ɪg'zɪləreɪtɪŋ] ADJ estimulante, tônico
exhilaration [ɪgzɪlə'reɪʃən] N euforia
exhort [ɪg'zɔːt] VT exortar
exile ['ɛksaɪl] N exílio; (person) exilado(-a) ▪ VT desterrar, exilar; **in ~** em exílio, exilado
exist [ɪg'zɪst] VI existir; (live) viver
existence [ɪg'zɪstəns] N existência; (life) vida; **to be in ~** existir
existentialism [ɛgzɪs'tɛnʃlɪzəm] N existencialismo
existing [ɪg'zɪstɪŋ] ADJ (laws) existente; (system, regime) atual
exit ['ɛksɪt] N saída ▪ VI (Comput, Theatre) sair; **exit ramp** (US) (Aut) saída da rodovia; **exit visa** N visto de saída
exodus ['ɛksədəs] N êxodo
ex officio [-ə'fɪʃɪəu] ADJ, ADV ex-officio, por

dever do cargo
exonerate [ɪg'zɒnəreɪt] VT: **to ~ from** (responsibility) desobrigar; (guilt) isentar
exorbitant [ɪg'zɔːbɪtənt] ADJ exorbitante
exorcize ['ɛksɔːsaɪz] VT exorcizar
exotic [ɪg'zɒtɪk] ADJ exótico
expand [ɪk'spænd] VT (widen) ampliar; (number) aumentar; (influence etc) estender ▪ VI (population, business) aumentar; (trade, gas etc) expandir-se; (metal) dilatar-se; **to ~ on** (notes, story etc) estender-se sobre
expanse [ɪk'spæns] N extensão f
expansion [ɪk'spænʃən] N (of town) desenvolvimento; (of trade) expansão f; (of population) aumento; (of metal) dilatação f
expansionism [ɪk'spænʃənɪzəm] N expansionismo
expansionist [ɪk'spænʃənɪst] ADJ expansionista
expatriate [n ɛks'pætrɪət, vt ɛks'pætrɪeɪt] N expatriado(-a) ▪ VT expatriar
expect [ɪk'spɛkt] VT (gen) esperar; (count on) contar com; (suppose) supor; (require) exigir ▪ VI: **to be ~ing** estar grávida; **to ~ sb to do** (anticipate) esperar que alguém faça; (demand) esperar de alguém que faça; **to ~ to do sth** esperar fazer algo; **as ~ed** como previsto; **I ~ so** suponho que sim
expectancy [ɪks'pɛktənsɪ] N expectativa; **life ~** expectativa de vida
expectant [ɪk'spɛktənt] ADJ expectante; ~ **mother** gestante f
expectantly [ɪk'spɛktəntlɪ] ADV cheio de expectativa
expectation [ɛkspɛk'teɪʃən] N (hope) esperança; (belief) expectativa; **in ~ of** na expectativa de; **against** or **contrary to all ~(s)** contra todas as expectativas; **to come** or **live up to one's ~s** corresponder à expectativa de alguém
expedience [ɛk'spiːdɪəns] N = **expediency**
expediency [ɛk'spiːdɪənsɪ] N conveniência; **for the sake of ~** por ser mais conveniente
expedient [ɛk'spiːdɪənt] ADJ conveniente, oportuno ▪ N expediente m, recurso
expedite ['ɛkspədaɪt] VT acelerar
expedition [ɛkspə'dɪʃən] N expedição f
expeditionary force [ɛkspə'dɪʃənrɪ-] N força expedicionária
expeditious [ɛkspə'dɪʃəs] ADJ eficiente
expel [ɪk'spɛl] VT expelir; (from place, school) expulsar
expend [ɪk'spɛnd] VT gastar; (use up) consumir
expendable [ɪk'spɛndəbl] ADJ prescindível
expenditure [ɪk'spɛndɪtʃər] N gastos mpl; (of energy) consumo
expense [ɪk'spɛns] N gasto, despesa; (high cost) custo; (expenditure) despesas fpl; **expenses** NPL (Comm: costs) despesas fpl; (: paid to employee) ajuda de custo; **at the ~ of** à custa de; **to go to the ~ of** fazer a despesa de; **to meet the ~ of** arcar com a despesa de; **expense account** N relatório de despesas

expensive [ɪk'spɛnsɪv] ADJ caro
experience [ɪk'spɪərɪəns] N experiência ■ VT
(situation) enfrentar; (feeling) sentir; **to learn by ~**
aprender com a experiência
experienced [ɪk'spɪərɪənst] ADJ experiente
experiment [ɪk'spɛrɪmənt] N experimento,
experiência ■ VI: **to ~ (with/on)** fazer
experiências (com/em)
experimental [ɪksperɪ'mɛntl] ADJ
experimental
expert ['ɛkspəːt] ADJ hábil, perito ■ N
perito(-a); (specialist) especialista m/f; **~ in** or **at**
doing sth perito em fazer algo; **an ~ on sth**
um perito em algo; **expert witness** (Law) N
perito(-a)
expertise [ɛkspəː'tiːz] N perícia
expire [ɪk'spaɪər] VI (gen) expirar; (end) terminar;
(run out) vencer
expiry [ɪk'spaɪərɪ] N expiração f, vencimento
explain [ɪk'spleɪn] VT explicar; (clarify)
esclarecer; (demonstrate) expor
▸ **explain away** VT justificar
explanation [ɛksplə'neɪʃən] N explicação f; **to**
find an ~ for sth achar uma explicação para
algo
explanatory [ɪk'splænətrɪ] ADJ explicativo
explicit [ɪk'splɪsɪt] ADJ explícito
explode [ɪk'spləud] VI estourar, explodir; (fig)
explodir ■ VT detonar, fazer explodir; (fig:
theory) derrubar; (: myth) destruir
exploit [n 'ɛksplɔɪt, vt ɪk'splɔɪt] N façanha ■ VT
explorar
exploitation [ɛksplɔɪ'teɪʃən] N exploração f
exploration [ɛksplə'reɪʃən] N exploração f
exploratory [ɪk'splɔrətrɪ] ADJ (talks)
exploratório, de pesquisa; (Med: operation)
exploratório
explore [ɪk'splɔːr] VT explorar; (fig) examinar,
pesquisar
explorer [ɪk'splɔːrər] N explorador(a) m/f
explosion [ɪk'spləuʒən] N explosão f
explosive [ɪk'spləusɪv] ADJ explosivo ■ N
explosivo
exponent [ɪk'spəunənt] N (of theory etc)
representante m/f, defensor(a) m/f; (of skill)
expoente m/f; (Math) expoente m
export [vt ɛk'spɔːt, n, cpd 'ɛkspɔːt] VT exportar
■ N exportação f ■ CPD de exportação
exportation [ɛkspɔː'teɪʃən] N exportação f
exporter [ɛk'spɔːtər] N exportador(a) m/f
export licence N licença de exportação
expose [ɪk'spəuz] VT expor; (unmask)
desmascarar
exposed [ɪk'spəuzd] ADJ exposto; (house etc)
desabrigado; (wire) descascado; (pipes, beams)
aparente
exposition [ɛkspə'zɪʃən] N exposição f
exposure [ɪk'spəuʒər] N exposição f; (publicity)
publicidade f; (Phot) revelação f; (: shot)
fotografia; **to die from ~** (Med) morrer de frio;
exposure meter N fotômetro
expound [ɪk'spaund] VT expor, explicar

express [ɪk'sprɛs] ADJ (definite) expresso,
explícito; (Brit: letter etc) urgente ■ N (train)
rápido ■ ADV (send) por via expressa ■ VT
exprimir, expressar; (quantity) representar; **to ~**
o.s. expressar-se
expression [ɪk'sprɛʃən] N expressão f
expressionism [ɪk'sprɛʃənɪzəm] N
expressionismo
expressive [ɪk'sprɛsɪv] ADJ expressivo
expressly [ɪk'sprɛslɪ] ADV expressamente
expressway [ɪk'sprɛsweɪ] (US) N rodovia (BR),
auto-estrada (PT)
expropriate [ɛks'prəuprɪeɪt] VT expropriar
expulsion [ɪk'spʌlʃən] N expulsão f; (of gas, liquid)
emissão f
exquisite [ɛk'skwɪzɪt] ADJ requintado
ex-serviceman (irreg) N veterano (de guerra)
ext ABBR (Tel: extension) r. (BR), int. (PT)
extemporize [ɪk'stɛmpəraɪz] VI improvisar
extend [ɪk'stɛnd] VT (visit, street) prolongar;
(building) aumentar; (offer) fazer; (hand) estender;
(Comm: credit) conceder; (: period of loan) prorrogar
■ VI (land) estender-se
extension [ɪk'stɛnʃən] N (Elec) extensão f;
(building) acréscimo, expansão f; (of rights)
ampliação f; (Tel) ramal m (BR), extensão f
(PT); (of deadline, campaign) prolongamento,
prorrogação f; **extension cable** N cabo de
extensão
extensive [ɪk'stɛnsɪv] ADJ extenso; (damage)
considerável; (broad) vasto, amplo; (frequent)
geral, comum
extensively [ɪk'stɛnsɪvlɪ] ADV (altered, damaged
etc) amplamente; **he's travelled ~** ele já viajou
bastante
extent [ɪk'stɛnt] N (breadth) extensão f; (of
damage etc) dimensão f; (scope) alcance m; **to**
some or **to a certain ~** até certo ponto; **to the**
~ of ... a ponto de ...; **to a large ~** em grande
parte; **to what ~?** até que ponto?; **to such an**
~ that ... a tal ponto que ...; **debts to the ~ of**
£5,000 dívidas da ordem de £5,000
extenuating [ɪks'tɛnjueɪtɪŋ] ADJ: **~**
circumstances circunstâncias fpl atenuantes
exterior [ɛk'stɪərɪər] ADJ externo ■ N exterior
m; (appearance) aspecto
exterminate [ɪk'stəːmɪneɪt] VT exterminar
extermination [ɪkstəːmɪ'neɪʃən] N extermínio
external [ɛk'stəːnl] ADJ externo; (foreign)
exterior ■ N: **the ~s** as aparências; **for ~ use**
only (Med) exclusivamente para uso externo
externally [ɛk'stəːnəlɪ] ADV por fora
extinct [ɪk'stɪŋkt] ADJ extinto
extinction [ɪk'stɪŋkʃən] N extinção f
extinguish [ɪk'stɪŋgwɪʃ] VT extinguir
extinguisher [ɪk'stɪŋgwɪʃər] N (also: **fire**
extinguisher) extintor m
extol [ɪk'stəul] (US **extoll**) VT (merits) exaltar;
(person) elogiar
extort [ɪk'stɔːt] VT: **to ~ sth (from sb)** extorquir
algo (a or de alguém)
extortion [ɪk'stɔːʃən] N extorsão f

extortionate [ɪkˈstɔːʃnət] ADJ extorsivo, excessivo

extra [ˈɛkstrə] ADJ adicional; (excessive) de mais, extra; (bonus: payment) extraordinário ■ ADV (in addition) adicionalmente ■ N (surcharge) extra m, suplemento; (Cinema, Theatre) figurante m/f; (newspaper) edição f extra; **the wine will cost ~** o vinho não está incluído no preço; **~ large sizes** tamanhos extra grandes

extra... [ɛkstrə] PREFIX extra...

extract [vt ɪkˈstrækt, n ˈɛkstrækt] VT tirar, extrair; (tooth) arrancar; (mineral) extrair; (money) extorquir; (promise) conseguir, obter; (confession) arrancar, obter ■ N extrato

extraction [ɪkˈstrækʃən] N extração f; (of tooth) arrancamento; (descent) descendência

extracurricular [ˈɛkstrəkəˈrɪkjuləʳ] ADJ (Sch) extracurricular

extradite [ˈɛkstrədaɪt] VT (from country) extraditar; (to country) obter a extradição de

extradition [ɛkstrəˈdɪʃən] N extradição f

extramarital [ɛkstrəˈmærɪtl] ADJ extramatrimonial

extramural [ɛkstrəˈmjuərl] ADJ (course) de extensão universitária

extraneous [ɛkˈstreɪnɪəs] ADJ: **~ to** alheio a

extraordinary [ɪkˈstrɔːdnrɪ] ADJ extraordinário; (odd) estranho; **extraordinary general meeting** N assembléia geral extraordinária

extrapolation [ɛkstræpəˈleɪʃən] N extrapolação f

extrasensory perception [ˈɛkstrəˈsɛnsərɪ-] N percepção f extra-sensorial

extra time N (Football) prorrogação f

extravagance [ɪkˈstrævəgəns] N extravagância; (no pl: spending) esbanjamento

extravagant [ɪkˈstrævəgənt] ADJ (lavish) extravagante; (wasteful) gastador(a), esbanjador(a); (price) exorbitante; (praise) excessivo; (odd) excêntrico, estranho

extreme [ɪkˈstriːm] ADJ extremo; (case) excessivo ■ N extremo; **the ~ left/right** (Pol) a extrema esquerda/direita; **~s of temperature** temperaturas extremas

extremely [ɪkˈstriːmlɪ] ADV muito, extremamente

extremist [ɪkˈstriːmɪst] ADJ, N extremista m/f

extremity [ɪkˈstremətɪ] N extremidade f; (need) apuro, necessidade f

extricate [ˈɛkstrɪkeɪt] VT: **to ~ sb/sth (from)** (trap) libertar alguém/algo de; (situation) livrar alguém/algo de

extrovert [ˈɛkstrəvəːt] N extrovertido(-a)

exuberance [ɪgˈzjuːbərəns] N exuberância

exuberant [ɪgˈzjuːbərnt] ADJ (person) eufórico; (style) exuberante

exude [ɪgˈzjuːd] VT exsudar; (confidence) esbanjar; **the charm** etc **he ~s** o charme que emana dele etc

exult [ɪgˈzʌlt] VI: **to ~ (in)** regozijar-se (em)

exultant [ɪgˈzʌltənt] ADJ exultante, triunfante

exultation [ɛgzʌlˈteɪʃən] N exultação f, regozijo

eye [aɪ] N olho; (of needle) buraco ■ VT olhar, observar; **as far as the ~ can see** a perder de vista; **to keep an ~ on** vigiar, ficar de olho em; **to have an ~ for sth** ter faro para algo; **in the public ~** conhecido pelo público; **with an ~ to doing** (Brit) com vista a fazer; **there's more to this than meets the ~** a coisa é mais complicada do que parece

eyeball [ˈaɪbɔːl] N globo ocular

eyebath [ˈaɪbɑːθ] (Brit) N copinho (para lavar o olho)

eyebrow [ˈaɪbrau] N sobrancelha; **eyebrow pencil** N lápis m de sobrancelha

eye-catching ADJ chamativo, vistoso

eye cup (US) N copinho (para lavar o olho)

eye drops NPL gotas fpl para os olhos

eyeglass [ˈaɪglɑːs] N monóculo; **eyeglasses** NPL (US) óculos mpl

eyelash [ˈaɪlæʃ] N cílio

eyelet [ˈaɪlɪt] N ilhós m

eye-level ADJ à altura dos olhos

eyelid [ˈaɪlɪd] N pálpebra

eyeliner [ˈaɪlaɪnəʳ] N delineador m

eye-opener N revelação f, grande surpresa

eye shadow N sombra de olhos

eyesight [ˈaɪsaɪt] N vista, visão f

eyesore [ˈaɪsɔːʳ] N monstruosidade f

eyestrain [ˈaɪstreɪn] N cansaço ocular

eyetooth [ˈaɪtuːθ] (irreg) N dente m canino superior; **to give one's eyeteeth for sth/to do sth** (fig) dar tudo por algo/para fazer algo

eyewash [ˈaɪwɔʃ] N colírio; (fig) disparates mpl, maluquices fpl

eye witness N testemunha f ocular

eyrie [ˈɪərɪ] N ninho de ave de rapina

Ff

F ABBR = **Fahrenheit**

F, f [ɛf] N (letter) F, f m; (Mus): **F** fá m; **F for Frederick** (Brit) or **Fox** (US) F de Francisco

FA (Brit) N ABBR (= Football Association) confederação de futebol

FAA (US) N ABBR = **Federal Aviation Administration**

fable ['feɪbl] N fábula

fabric ['fæbrɪk] N tecido, pano; (of building) estrutura

fabricate ['fæbrɪkeɪt] VT inventar

fabrication [fæbrɪ'keɪʃən] N invencionice f

fabric conditioner N amaciante m de pano

fabulous ['fæbjuləs] ADJ fabuloso; (inf: super) sensacional

façade [fə'sɑːd] N fachada

face [feɪs] N (Anat) cara, rosto; (grimace) careta; (of clock) mostrador m; (side, surface) superfície f; (of building) frente f, fachada ■ VT (facts, problem) enfrentar; (particular direction: building) dar para; **~ down** (person) de bruços; (card) virado para baixo; **to lose ~** perder o prestígio; **to save ~** salvar as aparências; **to make** or **pull a ~** fazer careta; **in the ~ of** (difficulties etc) diante de, à vista de; **on the ~ of it** a julgar pelas aparências, à primeira vista; **~ to ~** face a face; **we are ~d with serious problems** estamos enfrentando sérios problemas, temos sérios problemas pela frente

▶ **face up to** VT FUS enfrentar

face:face cloth (Brit) N pano de rosto;**face cream** N creme m facial;**face lift** N (operação f) plástica; (of façade) remodelamento;**face powder** N pó m de arroz

face-saving ADJ para salvar as aparências

facet ['fæsɪt] N faceta

facetious [fə'siːʃəs] ADJ jocoso

face-to-face ADV face a face, cara a cara

face value N (of coin, stamp) valor m nominal; **to take sth at ~** (fig) tomar algo em sentido literal

facia ['feɪʃə] N = **fascia**

facial ['feɪʃəl] ADJ facial

facile ['fæsaɪl] ADJ superficial

facilitate [fə'sɪlɪteɪt] VT facilitar

facilities [fə'sɪlɪtɪz] NPL facilidades fpl, instalações fpl; **credit ~** crediário

facing ['feɪsɪŋ] PREP de frente para ■ N (of wall etc) revestimento; (Sewing) forro

facsimile [fæk'sɪmɪlɪ] N (copy, machine, document) fac-símile m

fact [fækt] N fato; **in ~** realmente, na verdade; **to know for a ~ that ...** saber com certeza que ...; **~s and figures** dados e números

fact-finding ADJ: **a ~ tour** or **mission** uma missão de pesquisa

faction ['fækʃən] N facção f

factor ['fæktər] N fator m; (Comm) comissário financiador, empresa que compra contas a receber; (: agent) corretor(a) m/f ■ VI comprar contas a receber; **safety ~** fator de segurança

factory ['fæktərɪ] N fábrica;**factory farming** (Brit) N criação f intensiva;**factory ship** N navio-fábrica m

factual ['fæktjuəl] ADJ real, factual

faculty ['fækəltɪ] N faculdade f; (US: teaching staff) corpo docente

fad [fæd] (inf) N mania, modismo

fade [feɪd] VI (colour, cloth) desbotar; (sound, hope) desvanecer-se; (light) apagar-se; (flower) murchar

▶ **fade in** VT (sound) subir; (picture) clarear

▶ **fade out** VT (sound) abaixar; (picture) escurecer

faeces ['fiːsiːz] (US feces) NPL fezes fpl

fag [fæg] (inf) N (cigarette) cigarro; (US: homosexual) bicha; (chore): **what a ~!** que saco!; **fag end** (Brit: inf) N ponta de cigarro, guimba

fagged out [fægd-] (Brit: inf) ADJ estafado

fail [feɪl] VT (candidate) reprovar; (exam) não passar em, ser reprovado em; (subj: leader) fracassar; (: courage) carecer; (: memory) falhar ■ VI (candidate, attempt) fracassar; (business) falir; (supply) acabar; (engine, brakes, voice) falhar; (patient) enfraquecer-se; **to ~ to do sth** (neglect) deixar de fazer algo; (be unable) não conseguir fazer algo; **without ~** sem falta

failing ['feɪlɪŋ] N defeito ■ PREP na or à falta de; **~ that** senão

failsafe ['feɪlseɪf] ADJ (device etc) de segurança contra falhas;**failure** ['feɪljər] N fracasso; (in exam) reprovação f; (of crop) perda; (mechanical etc) falha; **his failure to turn up** o fato dele não ter vindo; **heart failure** parada cardíaca

failure rate ■ N taxa de reprovados

faint [feɪnt] ADJ fraco; (recollection) vago; (mark)

indistinto; (*smell, trace*) leve; (*dizzy*) tonto
■ N desmaio ■ VI desmaiar; **to feel ~** sentir
tonteira

faint-hearted ADJ pusilânime

faintly ['feɪntlɪ] ADV indistintamente,
vagamente

faintness ['feɪntnɪs] N fraqueza

fair [fɛəʳ] ADJ justo; (*hair*) louro; (*complexion*)
branco; (*weather*) bom; (*good enough*) razoável;
(*sizeable*) considerável ■ ADV: **to play ~** fazer
jogo limpo ■ N (*also*: **trade fair**) feira; (*Brit*:
funfair) parque *m* de diversões; **a ~ amount of
time** bastante tempo; **it's not ~!** não é justo!;
fair copy N cópia a limpo

fair-haired ADJ (de cabelo) louro

fairly ['fɛəlɪ] ADV (*justly*) com justiça; (*share*)
igualmente; (*quite*) bastante; **I'm ~ sure** tenho
quase certeza

fairness ['fɛənɪs] N justiça; (*impartiality*)
imparcialidade *f*; **in all ~** com toda a justiça

fair play N jogo limpo

fairy ['fɛərɪ] N fada; **fairy godmother** N fada-
madrinha; **fairy lights** (*Brit*) NPL lâmpadas *fpl*
coloridas de enfeite; **fairy tale** N conto de fadas

faith [feɪθ] N fé *f*; (*trust*) confiança; (*denomination*)
seita; **to have ~ in sb/sth** ter fé *or* confiança em
alguém/algo

faithful ['feɪθful] ADJ fiel; (*account*) exato

faithfully ['feɪθfulɪ] ADV fielmente; **yours ~**
(*Brit*: *in letters*) atenciosamente

faith healer N curandeiro(-a)

fake [feɪk] N (*painting etc*) falsificação *f*; (*person*)
impostor(a) *m/f* ■ ADJ falso ■ VT fingir;
(*painting etc*) falsificar; **his illness is a ~** sua
doença é fingimento *or* um embuste

falcon ['fɔːlkən] N falcão *m*

Falkland Islands ['fɔːlklənd-] NPL: **the ~** as
(ilhas) Malvinas *or* Falkland

fall [fɔːl] (*pt* **fell**, *pp* **fallen**) N queda; (*US*: *autumn*)
outono ■ VI cair; (*price*) baixar; **falls** NPL
(*waterfall*) cascata, queda d'água; **to ~ flat** (*on
one's face*) cair de cara no chão; (*plan*) falhar;
(*joke*) não agradar; **to ~ short of** (*sb's expectations*)
não corresponder a, ficar abaixo de; **a ~ of snow**
(*Brit*) uma nevasca

▸ **fall apart** VI cair aos pedaços; (*inf*: *emotionally*)
descontrolar-se completamente

▸ **fall back** VI retroceder

▸ **fall back on** VT FUS (*remedy etc*) recorrer a

▸ **fall behind** VI ficar para trás

▸ **fall down** VI (*person*) cair; (*building*) desabar;
(*hopes*) cair por terra

▸ **fall for** VT FUS (*trick*) cair em; (*person*)
enamorar-se de

▸ **fall in** VI (*roof*) ruir; (*Mil*) alinhar-se

▸ **fall in with** VT FUS (*sb's plans etc*) conformar-
se com

▸ **fall off** VI cair; (*diminish*) declinar, diminuir

▸ **fall out** VI (*hair, teeth*) cair; (*friends etc*) brigar;
(*Mil*) sair da fila

▸ **fall over** VI cair por terra, tombar

▸ **fall through** VI (*plan, project*) furar

fallacy ['fæləsɪ] N (*error*) erro; (*lie*) mentira,
falácia

fallback ['fɔːlbæk] ADJ: **~ position** alternativa

fallen ['fɔːlən] PP *of* **fall**

fallible ['fæləbl] ADJ (*person*) falível; (*memory*)
falha

falling-off ['fɔːlɪŋ-] N declínio

fallopian tube [fə'ləupɪən-] N (*Anat*) trompa de
Falópio

fallout ['fɔːlaut] N chuva radioativa; **fallout
shelter** N refúgio contra chuva radioativa

fallow ['fæləu] ADJ alqueivado, de pousio

false [fɔːls] ADJ falso; (*impression*: *hair, teeth etc*)
postiço; (*disloyal*) desleal, traidor(a); **false alarm**
N alarme *m* falso; **false pretences** NPL: **under
false pretences** sob falsos pretextos

falsehood ['fɔːlshud] N (*lie*) mentira; (*falseness*)
falsidade *f*

falsely ['fɔːlslɪ] ADV falsamente

false teeth (*Brit*) NPL dentadura postiça

falsify ['fɔːlsɪfaɪ] VT falsificar

falter ['fɔːltəʳ] VI (*engine*) falhar; (*person*) vacilar

fame [feɪm] N fama

familiar [fə'mɪlɪəʳ] ADJ (*well-known*) conhecido;
(*tone*) familiar, íntimo; **to be ~ with** (*subject*)
estar familiarizado com; **to make o.s. ~ with
sth** familiarizar-se com algo; **to be on ~ terms
with sb** ter intimidade com alguém

familiarity [fəmɪlɪ'ærɪtɪ] N familiaridade *f*

familiarize [fə'mɪlɪəraɪz] VT: **to ~ o.s. with**
familiarizar-se com

family ['fæmɪlɪ] N família; **family allowance**
(*Brit*) N abono-família *m*; **family business** N
negócio de família; **family doctor** N médico(-a)
da família; **family life** N vida familiar; **family
planning** N planejamento familiar; **family
planning clinic** clínica de planejamento
familiar; **family tree** N árvore *f* genealógica

famine ['fæmɪn] N fome *f*

famished ['fæmɪʃt] ADJ faminto; **I'm ~!** (*inf*)
estou morrendo de fome

famous ['feɪməs] ADJ famoso, célebre

famously ['feɪməslɪ] ADV (*get on*)
maravilhosamente

fan [fæn] N (*hand-held*) leque *m*; (*Elec*) ventilador
m; (*person*) fã, fan (PT); (*Sport*) torcedor(a) *m/f* (BR),
adepto(a) (PT) ■ VT abanar; (*fire, quarrel*) atiçar

▸ **fan out** VI espalhar-se

fanatic [fə'nætɪk] N fanático(-a)

fanatical [fə'nætɪkəl] ADJ fanático

fan belt N correia do ventilador (BR) *or* da
ventoinha (PT)

fancied ['fænsɪd] ADJ imaginário

fanciful ['fænsɪful] ADJ (*notion*) irreal; (*design*)
extravagante

fancy ['fænsɪ] N (*whim*) capricho; (*taste*)
inclinação *f*, gosto; (*imagination*) imaginação *f*;
(*fantasy*) fantasia ■ ADJ (*decorative*) ornamental;
(*luxury*) luxuoso; (*as decoration*) como decoração
■ VT (*feel like, want*) desejar, querer; (*imagine*)
imaginar; (*think*) acreditar, achar; **to take a ~ to**
tomar gosto por; **it took *or* caught my ~** gostei

disso; **when the ~ takes him** quando lhe dá na veneta; **to ~ that ...** imaginar que ...; **he fancies her** (inf) ele está a fim dela; **fancy dress** N fantasia; **fancy-dress ball** N baile m à fantasia; **fancy goods** NPL artigos mpl de fantasia

fanfare ['fænfeəʳ] N fanfarra

fanfold paper ['fænfəuld-] N formulários mpl contínuos

fang [fæŋ] N presa

fan heater (Brit) N aquecedor m de ventoinha

fanlight ['fænlaɪt] N (window) basculante f

fantasize ['fæntəsaɪz] VI fantasiar

fantastic [fæn'tæstɪk] ADJ (enormous) enorme; (strange, wonderful) fantástico

fantasy ['fæntəsɪ] N (dream) sonho; (unreality) fantasia; (imagination) imaginação f

FAO N ABBR (= Food and Agriculture Organization) FAO f

FAQ ABBR (= free at quay) posto no cais

far [fɑːʳ] ADJ (distant) distante ■ ADV (also far away, far off) longe; **the ~ side/end** o lado de lá/a outra ponta; **the ~ left/right** (Pol) a extrema esquerda/direita; **is it ~ to London?** Londres é longe daqui?; **it's not ~ (from here)** não é longe (daqui); **~ better** muito melhor; **~ from** longe de; **by ~** de longe; **go as ~ as the farm** vá até a (BR) or à (PT) fazenda; **as ~ as I know** que eu saiba; **as ~ as possible** na medida do possível; **how ~?** até onde?; (fig) até que ponto?

faraway ['fɑːrəweɪ] ADJ remoto, distante

farce [fɑːs] N farsa

farcical ['fɑːsɪkəl] ADJ farsante

fare [fɛəʳ] N (on trains, buses) preço (da passagem); (in taxi: cost) tarifa; (: passenger) passageiro(-a); (food) comida ■ VI sair-se; **half/full ~** meia/inteira passagem

Far East N: **the ~** o Extremo Oriente

farewell [fɛə'wel] EXCL adeus ■ N despedida ■ CPD (party etc) de despedida

far-fetched [-fɛtʃt] ADJ inverossímil

farm [fɑːm] N fazenda (BR), quinta (PT) ■ VT cultivar
   ▶ **farm out** VT (work etc) dar de empreitada

farmer ['fɑːməʳ] N fazendeiro(-a), agricultor m

farmhand ['fɑːmhænd] N lavrador(a) m/f, trabalhador(a) m/f rural

farmhouse ['fɑːmhaus] (irreg) N casa da fazenda (BR) or da quinta (PT)

farming ['fɑːmɪŋ] N agricultura; (tilling) cultura; (of animals) criação f; **intensive ~** cultura intensiva; **sheep ~** criação de ovelhas, ovinocultura

farm labourer N lavrador(a) m/f, trabalhador(a) m/f rural

farmland ['fɑːmlænd] N terra de cultivo

farm produce N produtos mpl agrícolas

farm worker N = **farmhand**

farmyard ['fɑːmjɑːd] N curral m

Faroe Islands ['fɛərəu-] NPL: **the ~ as** (ilhas) Faroë

Faroes ['fɛərəuz] NPL = **Faroe Islands**

far-reaching [-'riːtʃɪŋ] ADJ de grande alcance, abrangente

far-sighted ADJ presbita; (fig) previdente

fart [fɑːt] (inf!) N peido (!) ■ VI soltar um peido (!), peidar (!)

farther ['fɑːðəʳ] ADV mais longe ■ ADJ mais distante, mais afastado

farthest ['fɑːðɪst] SUPERL of **far**

FAS (Brit) ABBR (= free alongside ship) FAS

fascia ['feɪʃə] N (Aut) painel m

fascinate ['fæsɪneɪt] VT fascinar

fascinating ['fæsɪneɪtɪŋ] ADJ fascinante

fascination [fæsɪ'neɪʃən] N fascinação f, fascínio

fascism ['fæʃɪzəm] N fascismo

fascist ['fæʃɪst] ADJ, N fascista m/f

fashion ['fæʃən] N moda; (fashion industry) indústria da moda; (manner) maneira ■ VT modelar, dar feitio a; **in ~** na moda; **out of ~** fora da moda; **in the Greek ~** à grega, à maneira dos gregos; **after a ~** (finish, manage etc) até certo ponto

fashionable ['fæʃənəbl] ADJ da moda, elegante; (writer, café) da moda

fashion designer N estilista m/f

fashion show N desfile m de modas

fast [fɑːst] ADJ rápido; (dye, colour) firme, permanente; (Phot: film) de alta sensibilidade; (clock): **to be ~** estar adiantado ■ ADV rápido, rapidamente, depressa; (stuck, held) firmemente ■ N jejum m ■ VI jejuar; **my watch is 5 minutes ~** meu relógio está 5 minutos adiantado; **~ asleep** dormindo profundamente; **as ~ as I can** o mais rápido possível; **to make a boat ~** (Brit) amarrar um barco

fasten ['fɑːsn] VT fixar, prender; (coat) fechar; (belt) apertar ■ VI prender-se, fixar-se
   ▶ **fasten (up)on** VT FUS (idea) agarrar-se a

fastener ['fɑːsnəʳ] N presilha, fecho; (of door etc) fechadura; **zip ~** (Brit) fecho ecler (BR) or éclair (PT)

fastening ['fɑːsnɪŋ] N = **fastener**

fast food N fast food f

fastidious [fæs'tɪdɪəs] ADJ (fussy) meticuloso; (demanding) exigente

fast lane N (Aut) pista de velocidade

fat [fæt] ADJ gordo; (meat) com muita gordura; (greasy) gorduroso; (book) grosso; (wallet) recheado; (profit) grande ■ N (on person, Chem) gordura; (lard) banha, gordura; **to live off the ~ of the land** viver na abundância

fatal ['feɪtl] ADJ fatal; (injury) mortal; (consequence) funesto

fatalism ['feɪtəlɪzəm] N fatalismo

fatality [fə'tælɪtɪ] N (road death etc) vítima m/f

fatally ['feɪtlɪ] ADV: **~ injured** mortalmente ferido

fate [feɪt] N destino; (of person) sorte f

fated ['feɪtɪd] ADJ (person) condenado; (project) fadado ao fracasso

fateful ['feɪtful] ADJ fatídico

father ['fɑːðəʳ] N pai m

Father Christmas N Papai m Noel

fatherhood ['fɑ:ðəhud] N paternidade f
father-in-law (pl **fathers-in-law**) N sogro
fatherland ['fɑ:ðəlænd] N pátria
fatherly ['fɑ:ðəlɪ] ADJ paternal
fathom ['fæðəm] N braça ■ VT (Naut) sondar;
  (unravel) penetrar, deslindar; (understand)
  compreender
fatigue [fə'ti:g] N fadiga, cansaço; (Mil) faxina;
  metal ~ fadiga do metal
fatness ['fætnɪs] N gordura
fatten ['fætn] VT, VI engordar; **chocolate is
  ~ing** o chocolate engorda
fatty ['fætɪ] ADJ (food) gorduroso ■ N (inf)
  gorducho(-a)
fatuous ['fætjuəs] ADJ fátuo
faucet ['fɔ:sɪt] (US) N torneira
fault [fɔ:lt] N (error) defeito, falta; (blame) culpa;
  (defect) defeito; (Geo) falha; (Tennis) falta, bola
  fora ■ VT criticar; **it's my ~** é minha culpa; **to
  find ~ with** criticar, queixar-se de; **at ~** culpado;
  to a ~ em demasia
faultless ['fɔ:ltlɪs] ADJ (action) impecável; (person)
  irrepreensível
faulty ['fɔ:ltɪ] ADJ defeituoso
fauna ['fɔ:nə] N fauna
faux pas ['fəu'pɑ:] N INV gafe f
favour ['feɪvə'] (US **favor**) N favor m ■ VT
  (proposition) favorecer, aprovar; (person etc)
  favorecer; (assist) auxiliar; **to ask a ~ of** pedir
  um favor a; **to do sb a ~** fazer favor a alguém;
  to be in ~ of sth/of doing sth estar a favor de
  algo/de fazer algo; **to find ~ with** cair nas boas
  graças de; **in ~ of** em favor de
favo(u)rable ['feɪuərəbl] ADJ favorável
favo(u)rably ['feɪvərəblɪ] ADV favoravelmente
favo(u)rite ['feɪvərɪt] ADJ predileto ■ N
  favorito(-a)
favo(u)ritism ['feɪvərɪtɪzəm] N favoritismo
fawn [fɔ:n] N cervo novo, cervato ■ ADJ (also:
  fawn-coloured) castanho-claro inv ■ VI: **to ~
  (up)on** bajular
fax [fæks] N (document, machine) fax m, fac-símile
  m ■ VT enviar por fax or fac-símile
FBI (US) N ABBR (= Federal Bureau of Investigation)
  FBI m
FCC (US) N ABBR = **Federal Communications
  Commission**
FCO (Brit) N ABBR (= Foreign and Commonwealth
  Office) ministério das Relações Exteriores
FD (US) N ABBR = **fire department**
FDA (US) N ABBR (= Food and Drug Administration)
  órgão controlador de medicamentos e gêneros
  alimentícios
fear [fɪə'] N medo; (misgiving) temor m ■ VT ter
  medo de, temer ■ VI: **to ~ for** recear or temer
  por; **to ~ that** temer que; **~ of heights** medo das
  alturas, vertigem f; **for ~ of** com medo de
fearful ['fɪəful] ADJ medonho, temível; (cowardly)
  medroso; (awful) terrível; **to be ~ of** temer, ter
  medo de
fearfully ['fɪəfəlɪ] ADV (timidly) timidamente;
  (inf: very) muito, terrivelmente

fearless ['fɪəlɪs] ADJ sem medo, intrépido; (bold)
  audaz
fearsome ['fɪəsəm] ADJ (opponent) medonho,
  temível; (sight) espantoso
feasibility [fi:zə'bɪlɪtɪ] N viabilidade f;
  feasibility study N estudo de viabilidade
feasible ['fi:zəbl] ADJ viável
feast [fi:st] N banquete m; (Rel: also: **feast day**)
  festa ■ VI banquetear-se
feat [fi:t] N façanha, feito
feather ['fɛðə'] N pena, pluma ■ VT: **to ~ one's
  nest** (fig) acumular riquezas ■ CPD (bed etc) de
  penas
feather-weight N (Boxing) peso-pena m
feature ['fi:tʃə'] N característica; (Anat) feição
  f, traço; (article) reportagem f ■ VT (subj: film)
  apresentar ■ VI figurar; **features** NPL (of face)
  feições fpl; **it ~d prominently in ...** ocupou um
  lugar de destaque em ...; **feature film** N longa-
  metragem m
featureless ['fi:tʃəlɪs] ADJ anônimo
Feb. ABBR (= February) fev.
February ['fɛbruərɪ] N fevereiro; see also **July**
feces ['fi:si:z] (US) NPL = **faeces**
feckless ['fɛklɪs] ADJ displicente
Fed (US) ABBR = **federal; federation**
fed [fɛd] PT, PP of **feed**
Fed. [fɛd] (US: inf) N ABBR = **Federal Reserve
  Board**
federal ['fɛdərəl] ADJ federal
Federal Reserve Board (US) N órgão controlador
  do banco central dos EUA
Federal Trade Commission (US) N órgão
  regulador de práticas comerciais
federation [fɛdə'reɪʃən] N federação f
fed up ADJ: **to be ~** estar (de saco) cheio (BR),
  estar farto (PT)
fee [fi:] N taxa (BR), propina (PT); (of school)
  matrícula; (of doctor, lawyer) honorários mpl;
  entrance ~ (to club) jóia; (to museum etc) entrada;
  membership ~ (to join) jóia; (annual etc) quota;
  for a small ~ em troca de uma pequena taxa
feeble ['fi:bl] ADJ fraco, débil; (attempt) ineficaz
feeble-minded ADJ imbecil
feed [fi:d] (pt, pp **fed**) N comida; (of baby)
  alimento infantil; (of animal) ração f; (on printer)
  mecanismo alimentador ■ VT (gen, machine)
  alimentar; (baby: breastfeed) amamentar; (animal)
  dar de comer a; (data, information): **to ~ into**
  introduzir em
  ▶ **feed on** VT FUS alimentar-se de
feedback ['fi:dbæk] M (Elec) feedback m; (from
  person) reação f
feeder ['fi:də'] N (bib) babador m
feeding bottle ['fi:dɪŋ-] (Brit) N mamadeira
feel [fi:l] (pt, pp **felt**) N (sensation) sensação f; (sense
  of touch) tato; (impression) impressão f ■ VT (touch)
  tocar, apalpar; (anger, pain etc) sentir; (think,
  believe) achar, acreditar; **to get the ~ of sth** (fig)
  acostumar-se a algo; **to ~ (that)** achar (que);
  I ~ that you ought to do it eu acho que você
  deveria fazê-lo; **to ~ hungry/cold** estar com

fome/frio (BR), ter fome/frio (PT); **to ~ lonely/ better** sentir-se só/melhor; **to ~ sorry for** ter pena de; **I don't ~ well** não estou me sentindo bem; **it ~s soft** é macio; **it ~s colder here** sente-se mais frio aqui; **it ~s like velvet** parece veludo; **to ~ like** (*want*) querer; **to ~ about** *or* **around** apalpar, tatear; **I'm still ~ing my way** (*fig*) ainda estou me ambientando

feeler ['fi:lə^r] N (*of insect*) antena; **to put out ~s** *or* **a ~** (*fig*) sondar opiniões, lançar um balão-de-ensaio

feeling ['fi:lɪŋ] N sensação *f*; (*foreboding*) pressentimento; (*opinion*) opinião *f*; (*emotion*) sentimento; (*impression*) impressão *f*; **to hurt sb's ~s** magoar alguém; **~s ran high about it** os sentimentos se esquentaram a respeito disso; **what are your ~s about the matter?** qual é a sua opinião sobre o assunto?; **my ~ is that ...** eu acho que ...; **I have a ~ that ...** tenho a impressão de que ...

feet [fi:t] NPL *of* **foot**

feign [feɪn] VT fingir

felicitous [fɪ'lɪsɪtəs] ADJ feliz

feline ['fi:laɪn] ADJ felino

fell [fɛl] PT *of* **fall** ■ VT (*tree*) lançar por terra, derrubar ■ N (*Brit: mountain*) montanha; (: *moorland*): **the ~s** a charneca ■ ADJ: **with one ~ blow** de um só golpe

fellow ['fɛləu] N (*gen*) camarada *m/f*; (*inf: man*) cara *m* (BR), tipo *m* (PT); (*of learned society*) membro; (*of university*) membro do conselho universitário ■ CPD: **~ students** colegas *m/fpl* de curso; **his ~ workers** seus colegas de trabalho; **fellow citizen** N concidadão(-dã) *m/f*; **fellow countryman** (*irreg*) N compatriota *m*; **fellow feeling** N simpatia; **fellow men** NPL semelhantes *mpl*

fellowship ['fɛləuʃɪp] N (*comradeship*) amizade *f*; (*grant*) bolsa de estudo; (*society*) associação *f*

fellow traveller (*US* **fellow traveler**) N companheiro(-a) de viagem; (*Pol*) simpatizante *m/f*

fell-walking (*Brit*) N caminhadas *fpl* nas montanhas

felon ['fɛlən] N (*Law*) criminoso(-a)

felony ['fɛlənɪ] N (*Law*) crime *m*

felt [fɛlt] PT, PP *of* **feel** ■ N feltro

felt-tip pen N caneta pilot® (BR) *or* de feltro (PT)

female ['fi:meɪl] N (*pej: woman*) mulher *f*; (*Zool*) fêmea ■ ADJ (*Bio, Elec*) fêmeo(-a); (*sex, character*) feminino; (*vote etc*) das mulheres; (*child etc*) do sexo feminino; **male and ~ teachers** professores e professoras; **female impersonator** N (*Theatre*) travesti *m*

feminine ['fɛmɪnɪn] ADJ feminino; (*womanly*) feminil ■ N feminino

femininity [fɛmɪ'nɪnɪtɪ] N feminilidade *f*

feminism ['fɛmɪnɪzəm] N feminismo

feminist ['fɛmɪnɪst] N feminista *m/f*

fen [fɛn] (*Brit*) N: **the F~s** os pântanos de Norfolk

fence [fɛns] N cerca; (*Sport*) obstáculo; (*inf: person*) receptor(a) *m/f* ■ VT (*also:* **fence in**) cercar ■ VI

esgrimir; **to sit on the ~** (*fig*) ficar no muro

fencing ['fɛnsɪŋ] N (*sport*) esgrima

fend [fɛnd] VI: **to ~ for o.s.** defender-se, virar-se
► **fend off** VT (*attack, attacker*) defender-se de

fender ['fɛndə^r] N (*of fireplace*) guarda-fogo *m*; (*on boat*) defesa de embarcação; (*US: Aut*) pára-lama *m*; (: *Rail*) limpa-trilhos *m inv*

fennel ['fɛnl] N erva-doce *f*, funcho

ferment [*vi* fə'mɛnt, *n* 'fə:mɛnt] VI fermentar ■ N (*fig*) agitação *f*

fermentation [fə:mən'teɪʃən] N fermentação *f*

fern [fə:n] N samambaia (BR), feto (PT)

ferocious [fə'rəuʃəs] ADJ feroz

ferocity [fə'rɔsɪtɪ] N ferocidade *f*

ferret ['fɛrɪt] N furão *m*
► **ferret about** (*Brit*) VI = **ferret around**
► **ferret around** VI: **to ~ around in sth** vasculhar algo
► **ferret out** VT (*information*) desenterrar, descobrir

ferry ['fɛrɪ] N (*small*) barco (de travessia); (*large: also:* **ferryboat**) balsa ■ VT transportar; **to ~ sth/sb across** *or* **over** transportar algo/alguém para o outro lado

ferryman ['fɛrɪmən] (*irreg*) N barqueiro, balseiro

fertile ['fə:taɪl] ADJ fértil; (*Bio*) fecundo

fertility [fə'tɪlɪtɪ] N fertilidade *f*; (*Bio*) fecundidade *f*; **fertility drug** N droga que propicia a fecundação

fertilize ['fə:tɪlaɪz] VT fertilizar; (*Bio*) fecundar

fertilizer ['fə:tɪlaɪzə^r] N adubo, fertilizante *m*

fervent ['fə:vənt] ADJ ardente, apaixonado

fervour ['fə:və^r] (*US* **fervor**) N fervor *m*

fester ['fɛstə^r] VI inflamar-se

festival ['fɛstɪvəl] N (*Rel*) festa; (*Art, Mus*) festival *m*

festive ['fɛstɪv] ADJ festivo; **the ~ season** (*Brit: Christmas*) a época do Natal

festivities [fɛs'tɪvɪtɪz] NPL festas *fpl*, festividades *fpl*

festoon [fɛs'tu:n] VT: **to ~ with** engrinaldar de *or* com

fetch [fɛtʃ] VT ir buscar, trazer; (*Brit: sell for*) alcançar; **how much did it ~?** quanto rendeu?, por quanto foi vendido?
► **fetch up** (*US*) VI ir parar

fetching ['fɛtʃɪŋ] ADJ atraente

fête [feɪt] N festa

fetid ['fɛtɪd] ADJ fétido

fetish ['fɛtɪʃ] N fetiche *m*

fetter ['fɛtə^r] VT restringir, refrear

fetters ['fɛtəz] NPL grilhões *mpl*

fettle ['fɛtl] (*Brit*) N: **in fine ~** (*car etc*) em bom estado; (*person*) em forma

fetus ['fi:təs] (*US*) N = **foetus**

feud [fju:d] N (*hostility*) inimizade *f*; (*quarrel*) disputa, rixa ■ VI brigar; **a family ~** uma briga de família

feudal ['fju:dl] ADJ feudal

feudalism ['fju:dəlɪzəm] N feudalismo

fever ['fi:və^r] N febre *f*; **he has a ~** ele está com febre

feverish ['fi:vərɪʃ] ADJ febril; (activity) febril
few [fju:] ADJ, PRON poucos(-as); **a ~ ...**
alguns(-algumas) ...; **I know a ~** conheço
alguns; **quite a ~ ...** vários(-as) ...; **in the next ~**
days nos próximos dias; **in the past ~ days** nos
últimos dias; **every ~ days/months** cada dois
ou três dias/meses; **a ~ more ...** mais alguns/
algumas ...
fewer ['fju:əʳ] ADJ, PRON menos
fewest ['fju:ɪst] ADJ o menor número de
FFA N ABBR = **Future Farmers of America**
FH (Brit) ABBR = **fire hydrant**
FHA (US) N ABBR (= Federal Housing Administration)
secretaria federal da habitação
fiancé [fɪ'ā:ŋseɪ] N noivo
fiancée [fɪ'ā:ŋseɪ] N noiva
fiasco [fɪ'æskəu] N fiasco
fib [fɪb] N lorota
fibre ['faɪbəʳ] (US fiber) N fibra
fibreboard ['faɪbəbɔ:d] (US fiberboard) N
madeira compensada, compensado
fibre-glass (US fiber-glass) N fibra de vidro
fibrositis [faɪbrə'saɪtɪs] N aponeurosite f
FICA (US) N ABBR = **Federal Insurance**
Contributions Act
fickle ['fɪkl] ADJ inconstante; (weather) instável
fiction ['fɪkʃən] N ficção f; (invention) invenção f
fictional ['fɪkʃənl] ADJ de ficção
fictionalize ['fɪkʃnəlaɪz] VT romancear
fictitious [fɪk'tɪʃəs] ADJ fictício
fiddle ['fɪdl] N (Mus) violino; (cheating) fraude f,
embuste m; (swindle) trapaça ▪ VT (Brit: accounts)
falsificar
▶ **fiddle with** VT FUS brincar com
fiddler ['fɪdləʳ] N violinista m/f
fiddly ['fɪdlɪ] ADJ (task) espinhoso
fidelity [fɪ'dɛlɪtɪ] N fidelidade f
fidget ['fɪdʒɪt] VI estar irrequieto, mexer-se
fidgety ['fɪdʒɪtɪ] ADJ inquieto, nervoso
fiduciary [fɪ'dju:ʃɪərɪ] N fiduciário(-a)
field [fi:ld] N campo; (fig) área, esfera,
especialidade f; **to lead the ~** (Sport) tomar a
dianteira; (Comm) liderar; **to have a ~ day** (fig)
fazer a festa; **field glasses** NPL binóculo; **field**
marshal N marechal-de-campo
fieldwork ['fi:ldwə:k] N trabalho de campo
fiend [fi:nd] N demônio
fiendish ['fi:ndɪʃ] ADJ diabólico
fierce [fɪəs] ADJ feroz; (wind, attack) violento;
(heat) intenso; (fighting, enemy) feroz, violento
fiery ['faɪərɪ] ADJ (burning) ardente; (temperament)
fogoso
FIFA ['fi:fə] N ABBR (= Fédération Internationale de
Football Association) FIFA
fifteen [fɪf'ti:n] NUM quinze; see also **five**
fifth [fɪfθ] NUM quinto; **I was (the) ~ to arrive**
eu fui o quinto a chegar; **he came ~ in the**
competition ele tirou o quinto lugar; (in race)
ele chegou em quinto lugar; **Henry the F~**
Henrique Quinto; **the ~ of July, July the F~** dia
cinco de julho; **I wrote to him on the ~** eu lhe
escrevi no dia cinco

fiftieth ['fɪftɪɪθ] NUM qüinquagésimo; see also
fifth
fifty ['fɪftɪ] NUM cinqüenta; **about ~ people**
umas cinqüenta pessoas; **he'll be ~ (years old)**
next birthday ele fará cinqüenta anos no seu
próximo aniversário; **he's about ~** ele tem uns
cinqüenta anos; **the fifties** os anos 50; **to be**
in one's fifties estar na casa dos cinqüenta
anos; **the temperature was in the fifties** a
temperatura estava na faixa dos cinqüenta
graus; **to do ~** (Aut) ir a 50 (quilômetros por
hora)
fifty-fifty ['fɪftɪ'fɪftɪ] ADV: **to share** or **go ~ with**
sb dividir meio a meio com alguém, rachar
com alguém ▪ ADJ: **to have a ~ chance** ter 50%
de chance
fig [fɪg] N figo
fight [faɪt] (pt, pp fought) N briga; (Mil) combate
m; (struggle: against illness etc) luta ▪ VT lutar
contra; (cancer, alcoholism) combater; (election)
competir; (Law: case) defender ▪ VI brigar,
bater-se; (fig): **to ~ (for/against)** lutar (por/
contra)
▶ **fight back** VI revidar; (Sport, from illness etc)
reagir ▪ VT (tears) tentar reter
▶ **fight off** VT (attack, attacker) repelir; (illness,
sleep, urge) lutar contra
▶ **fight out** VT: **to ~ it out** resolver a questão
pela briga
fighter ['faɪtəʳ] N combatente m/f; (fig)
lutador(a) m/f; (plane) caça m; **fighter pilot** N
piloto de caça
fighting ['faɪtɪŋ] N (battle) batalha; (brawl) briga
figment ['fɪgmənt] N: **a ~ of the imagination**
um produto da imaginação
figurative ['fɪgjurətɪv] ADJ (expression) figurado;
(style) figurativo
figure ['fɪgəʳ] N (Drawing, Math) figura, desenho;
(numeral) algarismo; (number, cipher) número,
cifra; (outline) forma; (of woman) corpo; (person)
personagem m ▪ VT (esp US) imaginar ▪ VI
(appear) figurar; (US: make sense) fazer sentido;
public ~ personalidade f
▶ **figure on** (US) VT FUS: **to ~ on doing** contar
em fazer
▶ **figure out** VT compreender
figurehead ['fɪgəhɛd] N (Naut) carranca de proa;
(pej: leader) chefe m nominal
figure of speech N figura de linguagem
figure skating N movimentos mpl de patinação
Fiji (Islands) ['fi:dʒi:-] N(PL) (ilhas fpl) Fiji (no
article)
filament ['fɪləmənt] N filamento
filch [fɪltʃ] (inf) VT surripiar, afanar
file [faɪl] N (tool) lixa; (dossier) dossiê m, pasta;
(folder) pasta; (: binder) fichário; (Comput) arquivo;
(row) fila, coluna ▪ VT (wood, nails) lixar; (papers)
arquivar; (Law: claim) apresentar, dar entrada
em; (store) arquivar ▪ VI: **to ~ in/out** entrar/sair
em fila; **to ~ past** desfilar em frente de; **to ~ a**
suit against sb (Law) abrir processo contra
alguém; **file name** N (Comput) nome m do

arquivo

filibuster ['fɪlɪbʌstəʳ] *(esp US)* N *(Pol)* obstrucionista *m/f* ■ VI obstruir

filing ['faɪlɪŋ] N arquivamento; **filings** NPL *(of iron etc)* limalha; **filing cabinet** N fichário, arquivo; **filing clerk** N arquivista *m/f*

Filipino [fɪlɪ'piːnəu] N *(person)* filipino(-a); *(Ling)* filipino

fill [fɪl] VT encher; *(vacancy)* preencher; *(order)* atender ■ N: **to eat one's ~** encher-se *or* fartar-se de comer; **~ed with admiration** cheio de admiração

▶ **fill in** VT *(form)* preencher; *(need)* satisfazer; *(hole)* tapar; *(time)* encher; *(details, report)* escrever ■ VI: **to ~ in for sb** substituir alguém; **to ~ sb in on sth** *(inf)* dar as dicas a alguém sobre algo

▶ **fill out** VT preencher

▶ **fill up** VT encher ■ VI *(Aut)* abastecer o carro; **~ it up, please** *(Aut)* pode encher (o tanque), por favor

fillet ['fɪlɪt] N filete *m*, filé *m* ■ VT preparar em filés; **fillet steak** N filé *m*

filling ['fɪlɪŋ] N *(Culin)* recheio; *(for tooth)* obturação *f* (BR), chumbo (PT); **filling station** N posto de gasolina

fillip ['fɪlɪp] N estímulo, incentivo

filly ['fɪlɪ] N potranca

film [fɪlm] N filme *m*; *(of liquid etc)* camada fina, véu *m* ■ VT *(scene)* rodar, filmar ■ VI filmar; **film star** N astro/estrela do cinema; **film strip** N diafilme *m*; **film studio** N estúdio (de cinema)

filter ['fɪltəʳ] N filtro ■ VT filtrar; **filter coffee** N café *m* filtro; **filter lane** *(Brit)* N *(Aut)* pista para se dobrar à esquerda *(or* à direita); **filter tip** N filtro

filter-tipped ADJ filtrado

filth [fɪlθ] N sujeira (BR), sujidade *f* (PT)

filthy ['fɪlθɪ] ADJ sujo; *(language)* indecente, obsceno

fin [fɪn] N barbatana

final ['faɪnl] ADJ final, último; *(definitive)* definitivo ■ N *(Sport)* final *f*; **finals** NPL *(Sch)* exames *mpl* finais; **final demand** N *(on invoice etc)* demanda final

finale [fɪ'nɑːlɪ] N final *m*

finalist ['faɪnəlɪst] N *(Sport)* finalista *m/f*

finalize ['faɪnəlaɪz] VT concluir, completar

finally ['faɪnəlɪ] ADV *(lastly)* finalmente, por fim; *(eventually)* por fim; *(irrevocably)* definitivamente

finance [faɪ'næns] N *(money)* fundos *mpl*; *(money management)* finanças *fpl* ■ VT financiar; **finances** NPL *(finance finances)* finanças

financial [faɪ'nænʃəl] ADJ financeiro; **~ statement** demonstração financeira

financially [faɪ'nænʃəlɪ] ADV financeiramente

financial year N ano fiscal, exercício

financier [fɪ'nænsɪəʳ] N financista *m/f*; *(backer)* financiador(a) *m/f*

find [faɪnd] *(pt, pp* **found**) VT encontrar, achar; *(discover)* descobrir ■ N achado, descoberta; **to ~ sb guilty** *(Law)* declarar alguém culpado

▶ **find out** VT descobrir; *(person)* desmascarar ■ VI: **to ~ out about** informar-se sobre; *(by chance)* saber de

findings ['faɪndɪŋz] NPL *(Law)* veredito, decisão *f*; *(of report)* constatações *fpl*

fine [faɪn] ADJ fino; *(excellent)* excelente; *(good)* bom/boa; *(beautiful)* bonito ■ ADV *(well)* muito bem ■ N *(Law)* multa ■ VT *(Law)* multar; **to be ~** *(person)* estar bem; *(weather)* estar bom; **you're doing ~** você se dá bem; **to cut it ~** deixar pouca margem; *(arrive just in time)* chegar em cima da hora; **fine arts** NPL belas artes *fpl*

finely ['faɪnlɪ] ADV *(tune)* finamente; **~ chopped** picado

finery ['faɪnərɪ] N enfeites *mpl*

finesse [fɪ'nɛs] N sutileza

fine-tooth comb N: **to go through sth with a ~** *(fig)* passar o pente fino em algo

finger ['fɪŋgəʳ] N dedo ■ VT *(touch)* manusear; *(Mus)* dedilhar; **little/index ~** dedo mínimo/indicador

fingermark ['fɪŋgəmɑːk] N dedada

fingernail ['fɪŋgəneɪl] N unha

fingerprint ['fɪŋgəprɪnt] N impressão *f* digital ■ VT *(person)* tirar as impressões digitais de

fingerstall ['fɪŋgəstɔːl] N dedeira

fingertip ['fɪŋgətɪp] N ponta do dedo; **to have sth at one's ~s** ter algo à sua disposição, dispor de algo; *(knowledge)* saber algo na ponta da língua

finicky ['fɪnɪkɪ] ADJ *(fussy)* fresco, cheio de coisas

finish ['fɪnɪʃ] N *(end)* fim *m*; *(Sport)* chegada; *(on wood etc)* acabamento ■ VT, VI terminar, acabar; **to ~ doing sth** terminar de fazer algo; **to ~ with sb** *(end relationship)* acabar com alguém; **to ~ third** chegar no terceiro lugar

▶ **finish off** VT terminar; *(kill)* liquidar

▶ **finish up** VT acabar ■ VI acabar; *(in place)* ir parar

finished product ['fɪnɪʃt-] N produto acabado

finishing line ['fɪnɪʃɪŋ-] N linha de chegada, meta

finishing school ['fɪnɪʃɪŋ-] N escola de aperfeiçoamento (para moças)

finishing touches ['fɪnɪʃɪŋ-] NPL últimos retoques *mpl*

finite ['faɪnaɪt] ADJ finito

Finland ['fɪnlənd] N Finlândia

Finn [fɪn] N finlandês(-esa) *m/f*

Finnish ['fɪnɪʃ] ADJ finlandês(-esa) ■ N *(Ling)* finlandês *m*

fiord [fjɔːd] N = **fjord**

fir [fəːʳ] N abeto

fire [faɪəʳ] N fogo; *(accidental)* incêndio; *(gas fire, electric fire)* aquecedor *m* ■ VT *(gun)* disparar; *(arrow)* atirar; *(interest)* estimular; *(dismiss)* despedir; *(excite)*: **to ~ sb with enthusiasm** encher alguém de entusiasmo ■ VI disparar ■ CPD: **~ hazard**, **~ risk** perigo *or* risco de incêndio; **on ~** em chamas; **to set ~ to sth, set sth on ~** incendiar algo; **insured against ~** segurado contra fogo; **to come under ~ (from)**

(fig) ser atacado (por); **fire alarm** N alarme *m* de incêndio
firearm ['faɪərɑːm] N arma de fogo
fire brigade N (corpo de) bombeiros *mpl*
fire chief (US) N = **fire master**
fire department (US) N = **fire brigade**
fire drill N treinamento de incêndio
fire engine N carro de bombeiro
fire escape N escada de incêndio
fire extinguisher N extintor *m* de incêndio
fireguard ['faɪəgɑːd] (*Brit*) N guarda-fogo *m*
fire insurance N seguro contra fogo
fireman ['faɪəmɛn] (*irreg*) N bombeiro
fire master (*Brit*) N capitão *m* dos bombeiros
firemen ['faɪəmɛn] NPL *of* **fireman**
fireplace ['faɪəpleɪs] N lareira
fireproof ['faɪəpruːf] ADJ à prova de fogo
fire regulations NPL normas *fpl* preventivas contra incêndio
fire screen N guarda-fogo *m*
fireside ['faɪəsaɪd] N lugar *m* junto à lareira
fire station N posto de bombeiros
firewood ['faɪəwud] N lenha
fireworks ['faɪəwəːks] NPL fogos *mpl* de artifício; (*display*) queima de fugos
firing ['faɪərɪŋ] N (*Mil*) tiros *mpl*, tiroteio; **firing line** N (*Mil*) linha de fogo; **to be in the firing line** (*fig*) estar na linha de frente; **firing squad** N pelotão *m* de fuzilamento
firm [fəːm] ADJ firme ■ N firma; **to be a ~ believer in sth** ser partidário perseverante de algo; **to stand ~** *or* **take a ~ stand on sth** (*fig*) manter-se firme em algo
firmly ['fəːmlɪ] ADV firmemente
firmness ['fəːmnɪs] N firmeza
first [fəːst] ADJ primeiro ■ ADV (*before others*) primeiro; (*when listing reasons etc*) em primeiro lugar ■ N (*person: in race*) primeiro(-a); (*Aut*) primeira; (*Brit: Sch*) menção *f* honrosa; **the ~ of January** primeiro de janeiro (BR), dia um de Janeiro (PT); **at ~** no início; **~ of all** antes de tudo, antes de mais nada; **in the ~ place** em primeiro lugar; **I'll do it ~ thing tomorrow** vou fazê-lo amanhã cedo; **head ~** com a cabeça para a frente; **for the ~ time** pela primeira vez; **from the (very) ~** desde o início; *see also* **fifth**; **first aid** N primeiros socorros *mpl*
first-aid kit N estojo de premeiros socorros
first-aid post N pronto-socorro
first-class ADJ de primeira classe; **first-class mail** N correspondência prioritária
first-hand ADJ de primeira mão
first lady (US) N primeira dama
firstly ['fəːstlɪ] ADV primeiramente, em primeiro lugar
first name N primeiro nome *m*
first night N (*Theatre*) estréia
first-rate ADJ de primeira categoria
fir tree N abeto
FIS (*Brit*) N ABBR (= *Family Income Supplement*) abono-família *m*
fiscal ['fɪskəl] ADJ fiscal; **~ year** ano-fiscal

fish [fɪʃ] N INV peixe *m* ■ VT, VI pescar; **to go ~ing** ir pescar
▸ **fish out** VT (*from water*) pescar; (*from box etc*) tirar
fish bone N espinha de peixe
fisherman ['fɪʃəmən] (*irreg*) N pescador *m*
fishery ['fɪʃərɪ] N pescaria
fish factory (*Brit*) N fábrica de processamento de pescados
fish farm N viveiro (de piscicultura)
fish fingers (*Brit*) NPL filezinhos *mpl* de peixe
fish hook N anzol *m*
fishing boat ['fɪʃɪŋ-] N barco de pesca
fishing industry ['fɪʃɪŋ-] N indústria da pesca
fishing line ['fɪʃɪŋ-] N linha de pesca
fishing net ['fɪʃɪŋ-] N rede *f* de pesca
fishing rod ['fɪʃɪŋ-] N vara (de pesca)
fishing tackle ['fɪʃɪŋ-] N apetrechos *mpl* (de pesca)
fish market N mercado de peixe
fishmonger ['fɪʃmʌŋgəʳ] N peixeiro(-a); **~'s (shop)** peixaria
fish sticks (US) NPL = **fish fingers**
fishy ['fɪʃɪ] (*inf*) ADJ (*tale*) suspeito
fission ['fɪʃən] N fissão *f*; **nuclear ~** fissão nuclear
fissure ['fɪʃəʳ] N fenda, fissura
fist [fɪst] N punho
fistfight ['fɪstfaɪt] N briga de socos
fit [fɪt] ADJ (*healthy*) em (boa) forma; (*suitable*) adequado, apropriado ■ VT (*subj: clothes*) caber em; (*try on: clothes*) experimentar, provar; (*facts*) enquadrar-se *or* condizer com; (*accommodate*) ajustar, adaptar; (*correspond exactly*) encaixar em; (*put in, attach*) colocar; (*equip*) equipar; (*suit*) assentar bem ■ VI (*clothes*) servir; (*parts*) ajustar; (*in space, gap*) caber; (*correspond*) encaixar-se ■ N (*Med*) ataque *m*; **~ to** bom para; **~ for** adequado para; **a ~ of anger/pride** um acesso de raiva/orgulho; **to have a ~** (*Med*) sofrer *or* ter um ataque; (*fig: inf*) fazer escândalo; **this dress is a good/tight ~** este vestido tem um bom corte/está um pouco justo; **do as you think** *or* **see ~** faça como você achar melhor; **by ~s and starts** espasmodicamente
▸ **fit in** VI encaixar-se; (*fig: person*) dar-se bem (com todos)
▸ **fit out** (*Brit*) VT (*also*: **fit up**) equipar
fitful ['fɪtful] ADJ espasmódico, intermitente
fitment ['fɪtmənt] N móvel *m*
fitness ['fɪtnɪs] N (*Med*) saúde *f*, boa forma; (*of remark*) conveniência
fitted ['fɪtɪd] ADJ (*cupboards*) embutido; (*Brit: kitchen*) com armários embutidos; **~ carpet** carpete *m*
fitter ['fɪtəʳ] N ajustador(a) *m/f*, montador(a) *m/f*; (*also*: **gas fitter**) gasista *m/f*
fitting ['fɪtɪŋ] ADJ apropriado ■ N (*of dress*) prova; **fittings** NPL (*in building*) instalações *fpl*, acessórios *mpl*; **fitting room** N (*in shop*) cabine *f* (para experimentar roupa)
five [faɪv] NUM cinco; **she is ~ (years old)** ela

tem cinco anos; **they live at number ~/at ~ Green Street** eles moram no número cinco/na Green Street número cinco; **there are ~ of us** somos cinco; **all ~ of them came** todos os cinco vieram; **it costs ~ pounds** custa cinco libras; **~ and a quarter/half** cinco e um quarto/e meio; **it's ~ (o'clock)** são cinco horas; **to divide sth into ~** dividir algo em cinco partes; **they are sold in ~s** eles são vendidos em pacotes de cinco

five-day week N semana de cinco dias

fiver ['faɪvə^r] (inf) N (Brit) nota de cinco libras; (US) nota de cinco dólares

fix [fɪks] VT (secure) fixar, colocar; (arrange) arranjar; (mend) consertar; (meal, drink) preparar; (inf: game etc) arranjar ■ N: **to be in a ~** estar em apuros; **the fight was a ~** a luta foi uma marmelada; **to ~ sth in one's mind** gravar algo
▶ **fix up** VT (meeting) marcar; **to ~ sb up with sth** arranjar algo para alguém

fixation [fɪk'seɪʃən] N fixação f

fixative ['fɪksətɪv] N fixador m

fixed [fɪkst] ADJ (prices, smile) fixo; **how are you ~ for money?** (inf) a quantas ainda você em matéria de dinheiro?; **fixed assets** NPL ativo fixo

fixture ['fɪkstʃə^r] N coisa fixa; (furniture) móvel m fixo; (Sport) desafio, encontro

fizz [fɪz] VI efervescer

fizzle ['fɪzl] VI chiar; **fizzle out** VI fracassar; (interest) diminuir

fizzy ['fɪzɪ] ADJ (drink) com gás, gasoso; (gen) efervescente

fjord [fjɔːd] N fiorde m

FL (US) ABBR (Post) = **Florida**

flabbergasted ['flæbəgɑːstɪd] ADJ pasmado

flabby ['flæbɪ] ADJ flácido

flag [flæg] N bandeira; (for signalling) bandeirola; (flagstone) laje f ■ VI acabar-se, descair; **~ of convenience** bandeira de conveniência
▶ **flag down** VT: **to ~ sb down** fazer sinais a alguém para que pare

flagon ['flægən] N garrafão m

flagpole ['flægpəul] N mastro de bandeira

flagrant ['fleɪgrənt] ADJ flagrante

flagship ['flægʃɪp] N nau f capitânia; (fig) carro-chefe m

flag stop (US) N (for bus) parada facultativa

flair [flɛə^r] N (talent) talento; (style) habilidade f

flak [flæk] N (Mil) fogo antiaéreo; (inf: criticism) críticas fpl

flake [fleɪk] N (of rust, paint) lasca; (of snow, soap powder) floco ■ VI (also: **flake off**) lascar, descamar-se

flaky ['fleɪkɪ] ADJ (paintwork) laminoso; (skin) escamoso; (pastry) folhado

flamboyant [flæm'bɔɪənt] ADJ (dress) espalhafatoso; (person) extravagante

flame [fleɪm] N chama; **to burst into ~s** irromper em chamas; **old ~** (inf) velha paixão f

flamingo [flə'mɪŋgəu] (pl **flamingoes**) N flamingo

flammable ['flæməbl] ADJ inflamável

flan [flæn] (Brit) N torta

flange [flændʒ] N flange m

flank [flæŋk] N flanco; (of person) lado ■ VT ladear

flannel ['flænl] N (Brit: also: **face flannel**) pano; (fabric) flanela; (Brit: inf) conversa fiada; **flannels** NPL calça (BR) or calças fpl (PT) de flanela

flannelette [flænə'lɛt] N baetilha

flap [flæp] N (of pocket, table) aba; (of envelope) dobra; (wing movement) bater m; (Aviat) flap m ■ VT (arms) oscilar; (wings) bater ■ VI (sail, flag) ondular; (inf: also: **be in a flap**) estar atarantado

flapjack ['flæpdʒæk] N (US: pancake) panqueca; (Brit: biscuit) biscoito de aveia

flare [flɛə^r] N fogacho, chama; (Mil) sinal m luminoso; (in skirt etc) folga
▶ **flare up** VI chamejar; (fig: person) encolerizar-se; (: violence) irromper

flared ['flɛəd] ADJ (trousers) com roda; (skirt) rodado

flash [flæʃ] N (of lightning) clarão m; (also: **news flash**) notícias fpl de última hora; (Phot) flash m; (of inspiration) lampejo ■ VT (light, headlights) piscar; (torch) acender; (news, message) transmitir; (look, smile) brilhar ■ VI brilhar; (light on ambulance, eyes etc) piscar; **in a ~** num instante; **to ~ by** or **past** passar como um raio; **to ~ sth about** (fig: inf) ostentar or exibir algo

flashback ['flæʃbæk] N flashback m

flashbulb ['flæʃbʌlb] N lâmpada de flash

flash card N (Sch) cartão m

flashcube ['flæʃkjuːb] N cubo de flash

flasher ['flæʃə^r] N (Aut) pisca-pisca m

flashlight ['flæʃlaɪt] N lanterna de bolso

flash point N ponto de centelha

flashy ['flæʃɪ] (pej) ADJ espalhafatoso

flask [flɑːsk] N frasco; (also: **vacuum flask**) garrafa térmica (BR), termo (PT)

flat [flæt] ADJ plano; (smooth) liso; (battery) descarregado; (tyre) vazio; (beer) choco; (denial) categórico; (Mus) abemolado; (: voice) desafinado; (rate) único; (fee) fixo ■ N (Brit: apartment) apartamento; (Mus) bemol m; (Aut) pneu m furado; **~ out** (work) a toque de caixa; (race) a toda; **~ rate of pay** (Comm) salário fixo

flat-footed [-'futɪd] ADJ de pés chatos

flatly ['flætlɪ] ADV terminantemente

flatmate ['flætmeɪt] (Brit) N companheiro(-a) de apartamento

flatness ['flætnɪs] N (of land) planura, lisura

flatten ['flætən] VT (also: **flatten out**) aplanar; (smooth out) alisar; (demolish) arrasar; (defeat) derrubar

flatter ['flætə^r] VT lisonjear; (show to advantage) favorecer

flatterer ['flætərə^r] N lisonjeador(a) m/f

flattering ['flætərɪŋ] ADJ lisonjeiro; (clothes etc) favorecedor(a)

flattery ['flætərɪ] N bajulação f

flatulence ['flætjuləns] N flatulência

flaunt [flɔːnt] VT ostentar, pavonear

flavour ['fleɪvə'] (US **flavor**) N sabor m ▪ VT condimentar, aromatizar; **strawberry-~ed** com sabor de morango

flavo(u)ring ['fleɪvərɪŋ] N condimento; (synthetic) aromatizante m

flaw [flɔː] N (in cloth, glass) defeito; (in character) falha; (in argument) erro

flawless ['flɔːlɪs] ADJ impecável

flax [flæks] N linho

flaxen ['flæksən] ADJ da cor de linho

flea [fliː] N pulga; **flea market** N feira de quinquilharias

fleck [flɛk] N (mark) mancha, sinal m; (of dust) partícula; (of mud) salpico; (of paint) pontinho ▪ VT salpicar; **brown ~ed with white** marrom salpicado de branco

fled [flɛd] PT, PP of **flee**

fledg(e)ling ['flɛdʒlɪŋ] N ave f recém-emplumada

flee [fliː] (pt, pp **fled**) VT fugir de ▪ VI fugir

fleece [fliːs] N velo; (wool) lã f ▪ VT (inf) espoliar

fleecy ['fliːsɪ] ADJ (blanket) felpudo; (cloud) fofo

fleet [fliːt] N (gen, of lorries etc) frota; (of ships) esquadra

fleeting ['fliːtɪŋ] ADJ fugaz

Flemish ['flɛmɪʃ] ADJ flamengo ▪ N (Ling) flamengo; **the Flemish** NPL os flamengos

flesh [flɛʃ] N carne f; (of fruit) polpa; **of ~ and blood** de carne e osso; **flesh wound** N ferimento de superfície

flew [fluː] PT of **fly**

flex [flɛks] N fio ▪ VT (muscles) flexionar

flexibility [flɛksɪ'bɪlɪtɪ] N flexibilidade f

flexible ['flɛksɪbl] ADJ flexível

flick [flɪk] N pancada leve; (with finger) peteleco, piparote m; (with whip) chicotada ▪ VT dar um peteleco; (switch) apertar; **flicks** NPL (Brit: inf) cinema m

▸ **flick through** VT FUS folhear

flicker ['flɪkə'] VI (light, flame) tremular; (eyelids) tremer ▪ N tremulação f; **a ~ of light** um fio de luz

flick knife (Brit: irreg) N canivete m de mola

flier ['flaɪə'] N aviador(a) m/f

flight [flaɪt] N vôo m; (escape) fuga; (of steps) lance m; **to take ~** fugir, pôr-se em fuga; **to put to ~** pôr em fuga; **flight attendant** (US) N comissário(-a) de bordo; **flight crew** N tripulação f; **flight deck** N (Aviat) cabine f do piloto; (Naut) pista de aterrissagem (BR) or aterragem (PT); **flight recorder** N gravador m de vôo

flimsy ['flɪmzɪ] ADJ (thin) delgado, franzino; (weak) débil; (excuse) fraco

flinch [flɪntʃ] VI encolher-se; **to ~ from sth/from doing sth** vacilar diante de algo/em fazer algo

fling [flɪŋ] (pt, pp **flung**) VT lançar ▪ N (love affair) caso

flint [flɪnt] N pederneira; (in lighter) pedra

flip [flɪp] VT (turn over) dar a volta em; (throw)

jogar; **to ~ a coin** tirar cara ou coroa

▸ **flip through** VT FUS folhear

flippant ['flɪpənt] ADJ petulante, irreverente

flipper ['flɪpə'] N (of animal) nadadeira; (for swimmer) pé-de-pato, nadadeira

flip side N (of record) outro lado

flirt [flɜːt] VI flertar ▪ N namorador(a) m/f, paquerador(a) m/f

flirtation [flɜː'teɪʃən] N flerte m, paquera

flit [flɪt] VI esvoaçar

float [fləʊt] N bóia; (in procession) carro alegórico; (sum of money) caixa ▪ VI flutuar; (swimmer) boiar ▪ VT fazer flutuar; (company) lançar (na Bolsa)

floating ['fləʊtɪŋ] ADJ flutuante; **~ vote** voto oscilante; **~ voter** indeciso(-a)

flock [flɒk] N (of sheep, Rel) rebanho; (of birds) bando; (of people) multidão f ▪ VI: **to ~ to** afluir

floe [fləʊ] N (also: **ice floe**) banquisa

flog [flɒg] VT açoitar; (inf) vender

flood [flʌd] N enchente f, inundação f; (of words, tears etc) torrente m ▪ VT inundar, alagar; (Aut: carburettor) afogar ▪ VI place, alagar; (people, goods): **to ~ into** inundar; **to ~ the market** (Comm) inundar o mercado; **in ~** transbordante

flooding ['flʌdɪŋ] N inundação f

floodlight ['flʌdlaɪt] (irreg: like **light**) N refletor m, holofote m ▪ VT iluminar com holofotes

floodlit ['flʌdlɪt] PT, PP of **floodlight** ▪ ADJ iluminado (por holofotes)

flood tide N maré f enchente

floor [flɔː'] N chão m; (in house) soalho; (storey) andar m; (of sea) fundo; (dance floor) pista de dança ▪ VT (fig: confuse) confundir, pasmar; **ground ~** (Brit) or **first ~** (US) andar térreo (BR), rés-do-chão (PT); **first ~** (Brit) or **second ~** (US) primeiro andar; **top ~** último andar; **to have the ~** (speaker) ter a palavra

floorboard ['flɔːbɔːd] N tábua de assoalho

flooring ['flɔːrɪŋ] N piso

floor lamp (US) N abajur m de pé

floor show N show m

floorwalker ['flɔːwɔːkə'] (esp US) N supervisor(a) m/f (numa loja de departamentos)

flop [flɒp] N fracasso ▪ VI (fail) fracassar; (into chair etc) cair pesadamente

floppy ['flɒpɪ] ADJ frouxo, mole; **floppy (disk)** N disquete m

flora ['flɔːrə] N flora

floral ['flɔːrl] ADJ floral

Florence ['flɒrəns] N Florença

florid ['flɒrɪd] ADJ (style) florido; (complexion) corado

florist ['flɒrɪst] N florista m/f

florist's (shop) N floricultura

flotation [fləʊ'teɪʃən] N (of shares) emissão f; (of company) lançamento (na Bolsa)

flounce [flaʊns] N babado, debrum m

▸ **flounce out** VI sair indignado

flounder ['flaʊndə'] (pl **flounder**) N (Zool) linguado ▪ VI (swimmer) debater-se; (fig) atrapalhar-se

flour ['flaʊə'] N farinha

flourish ['flʌrɪʃ] vɪ florescer ■ vᴛ brandir, menear ■ ɴ floreio; (bold gesture): **with a ~** con gestos floreados; (of trumpets) fanfarra

flourishing ['flʌrɪʃɪŋ] ᴀᴅᴊ próspero

flout [flaut] vᴛ (law) desrespeitar; (offer) desprezar

flow [fləu] ɴ (of tide, traffic) fluxo; (direction) curso; (of river, Elec) corrente f; (of blood) circulação f ■ vɪ correr; (traffic) fluir; (blood, Elec) circular; (clothes, hair) andular; **flow chart** ɴ fluxograma m; **flow diagram** ɴ fluxograma m

flower ['flauəʳ] ɴ flor f ■ vɪ florescer, florir; **in ~** em flor; **flower bed** ɴ canteiro

flowerpot ['flauəpɔt] ɴ vaso

flowery ['flauərɪ] ᴀᴅᴊ (perfume) a base de flor; (pattern) florido; (speech) floreado

flown [fləun] ᴘᴘ of **fly**

flu [flu:] ɴ gripe f

fluctuate ['flʌktjueɪt] vɪ flutuar; (temperature) variar

fluctuation [flʌktju'eɪʃən] ɴ flutuação f, oscilação f

flue [flu:] ɴ fumeiro

fluency ['flu:ənsɪ] ɴ fluência

fluent ['flu:ənt] ᴀᴅᴊ (speech) fluente; **he speaks ~ French, he's ~ in French** ele fala francês fluentemente

fluently ['flu:əntlɪ] ᴀᴅᴠ fluentemente

fluff [flʌf] ɴ felpa, penugem f

fluffy ['flʌfɪ] ᴀᴅᴊ macio, fofo; **~ toy** brinquedo de pelúcia

fluid ['flu:ɪd] ᴀᴅᴊ fluido ■ ɴ fluido; (in diet) líquido; **fluid ounce** (Brit) ɴ (= 0.028 l) 0.05 pints

fluke [flu:k] (inf) ɴ sorte f

flummox ['flʌməks] vᴛ desconcertar

flung [flʌŋ] ᴘᴛ, ᴘᴘ of **fling**

flunky ['flʌŋkɪ] ɴ lacaio

fluorescent [fluə'resnt] ᴀᴅᴊ fluorescente

fluoride ['fluəraɪd] ɴ fluoreto ■ ᴄᴘᴅ: **~ toothpaste** pasta de dentes com flúor

fluorine ['fluəri:n] ɴ flúor m

flurry ['flʌrɪ] ɴ (of snow) lufada; (haste) agitação f; **~ of activity/excitement** muita atividade/animação

flush [flʌʃ] ɴ (on face) rubor m; (plenty) abundância ■ vᴛ lavar com água ■ vɪ ruborizar-se ■ ᴀᴅᴊ: **~ with** rente com; **to ~ the toilet** dar descarga; **hot ~es** (Med) calores
▶ **flush out** vᴛ leventar

flushed [flʌʃt] ᴀᴅᴊ ruborizado, corado

fluster ['flʌstəʳ] ɴ agitação f ■ vᴛ atrapalhar, desconcertar

flustered ['flʌstəd] ᴀᴅᴊ atrapalhado

flute [flu:t] ɴ flauta

fluted ['flu:tɪd] ᴀᴅᴊ acanelado

flutter ['flʌtəʳ] ɴ agitação f; (of wings) bater m; (inf: bet) aposta ■ vɪ esvoaçar

flux [flʌks] ɴ fluxo; **in a state of ~** mudando continuamente

fly [flaɪ] (pt **flew**, pp **flown**) ɴ (insect) mosca; (on trousers: also: **flies**) braguilha ■ vᴛ (plane) pilotar; (passengers, cargo) transportar (de avião);

(flag) hastear; (distances) percorrer; (kite) soltar, empinar ■ vɪ voar; (passengers) ir de avião; (escape) fugir; (flag) hastear-se; **to ~ open** abrir-se bruscamente; **to ~ off the handle** perder as estribeiras
▶ **fly away** vɪ voar
▶ **fly in** vɪ chegar
▶ **fly off** vɪ = **fly away**
▶ **fly out** vɪ sair (de avião)

fly-fishing ɴ pesca com iscas artificiais

flying ['flaɪɪŋ] ɴ (activity) aviação f ■ ᴀᴅᴊ: **~ visit** visita de médico; **with ~ colours** brilhantemente; **he doesn't like ~** ele não gosta de andar de avião; **flying buttress** ɴ arcobotante m; **flying saucer** ɴ disco voador; **flying start** ɴ: **to get off to a flying start** (in race) disparar; (fig) começar muito bem

fly leaf ['flaɪli:f] (irreg) ɴ guarda (num livro)

flyover ['flaɪəuvəʳ] (Brit) ɴ (bridge) viaduto

flypast ['flaɪpɑ:st] ɴ desfile m aéreo

fly sheet ɴ (for tent) duplo teto

flywheel ['flaɪwi:l] ɴ volante m

FM ᴀʙʙʀ (Brit: Mil) = **field marshal**; (Radio: = frequency modulation) FM

FMB (US) ɴ ᴀʙʙʀ = **Federal Maritime Board**

FMCS (US) ɴ ᴀʙʙʀ (= Federal Mediation and Conciliation Service) ≈ Justiça do Trabalho

FO (Brit) ɴ ᴀʙʙʀ = **Foreign Office**

foal [fəul] ɴ potro

foam [fəum] ɴ espuma ■ vɪ espumar; **foam rubber** ɴ espuma de borracha

FOB ᴀʙʙʀ (= free on board) FOB

fob [fɔb] vᴛ: **to ~ sb off with sth** despachar alguém com algo; **to ~ sth off on sb** impingir algo a alguém

foc (Brit) ᴀʙʙʀ = **free of charge**

focal ['fəukəl] ᴀᴅᴊ focal; **focal point** ɴ foco

focus ['fəukəs] (pl **focuses**) ɴ foco ■ vᴛ (field glasses etc) enfocar ■ vɪ: **to ~ on** enfocar, focalizar; **in/out of ~** em foco/fora de foco

fodder ['fɔdəʳ] ɴ forragem f

FOE ɴ ᴀʙʙʀ (= Friends of the Earth) organizacão ecologista; (US: = Fraternal Order of Eagles) associação beneficente

foe [fəu] ɴ inimigo

foetus ['fi:təs] (US **fetus**) ɴ feto

fog [fɔg] ɴ nevoeiro

fogbound ['fɔgbaund] ᴀᴅᴊ imobilizado pelo nevoeiro

foggy ['fɔgɪ] ᴀᴅᴊ nevoento

fog lamp (US **fog light**) ɴ farol m de neblina

foible ['fɔɪbl] ɴ fraqueza, ponto fraco

foil [fɔɪl] vᴛ frustrar ■ ɴ folha metálica; (also: **kitchen foil**) folha or papel m de alumínio; (complement) contraste m, complemento; (Fencing) florete m; **to act as a ~ to** (fig) dar realce a

foist [fɔɪst] vᴛ: **to ~ sth on sb** impingir algo a alguém

fold [fəuld] ɴ (bend, crease) dobra, vinco, prega; (of skin) ruga; (Agr) redil m, curral m ■ vᴛ dobrar; **to ~ one's arms** cruzar os braços

▶ **fold up** vi (*map etc*) dobrar; (*business*) abrir falência ■ vt (*map etc*) dobrar

folder ['fəuldə'] N (*for papers*) pasta; (: *binder*) fichário; (*brochure*) folheto

folding ['fəuldɪŋ] ADJ (*chair, bed*) dobrável

foliage ['fəulɪɪdʒ] N folhagem f

folk [fəuk] NPL gente f ■ CPD popular, folclórico; **folks** NPL (*family*) família, parentes *mpl*; (*people*) gente f

folklore ['fəuklɔ:'] N folclore m

folk song N canção f popular *or* folclórica

follow ['fɔləu] vt seguir ■ vi seguir; (*result*) resultar; **to ~ sb's advice** seguir o conselho de alguém; **I don't quite ~ you** não consigo acompanhar o seu raciocínio; **to ~ in sb's footsteps** seguir os passos de alguém; **it doesn't ~ that ...** (isso) não quer dizer que ...; **to ~ suit** fazer o mesmo

▶ **follow out** vt (*idea, plan*) levar a cabo, executar

▶ **follow through** vt levar a cabo, executar

▶ **follow up** vt (*letter*) responder a; (*offer*) levar adiante; (*case*) acompanhar

follower ['fɔləuə'] N seguidor(a) m/f; (*Pol*) partidário(-a)

following ['fɔləuɪŋ] ADJ seguinte ■ N adeptos *mpl*

follow-up N continuação f ■ CPD: **~ letter** carta suplementar de reforço

folly ['fɔlɪ] N loucura

fond [fɔnd] ADJ (*memory, look*) carinhoso; (*hopes*) absurdo, descabido; **to be ~ of** gostar de

fondle ['fɔndl] vt acariciar

fondly ['fɔndlɪ] ADV (*lovingly*) afetuosamente; (*naïvely*): **he ~ believed that ...** ele acreditava piamente que ...

fondness ['fɔndnɪs] N (*for things*) gosto, afeição f; (*for people*) carinho

font [fɔnt] N (*Rel*) pia batismal; (*Typ*) fonte f, família

food [fu:d] N comida; **food mixer** N batedeira; **food poisoning** N intoxicação f alimentar; **food processor** N multiprocessador m de cozinha

foodstuffs ['fu:dstʌfs] NPL gêneros *mpl* alimentícios

fool [fu:l] N tolo(-a); (*History: of king*) bobo; (*Culin*) puré m de frutas com creme ■ vt enganar ■ vi (*gen: fool around*) brincar; (*waste time*) fazer bagunça; **to make a ~ of sb** (*ridicule*) ridicularizar alguém; (*trick*) fazer alguém de bobo; **to make a ~ of o.s.** fazer papel de bobo, fazer-se de bobo; **you can't ~ me** você não pode me fazer de bobo

▶ **fool about** (*pej*) vi (*waste time*) fazer bagunça; (*behave foolishly*) fazer-se de bobo

▶ **fool around** (*pej*) vi (*waste time*) fazer bagunça; (*behave foolishly*) fazer-se de bobo

foolhardy ['fu:lha:dɪ] ADJ temerário

foolish ['fu:lɪʃ] ADJ bobo; (*stupid*) burro; (*careless*) imprudente

foolishly ['fu:lɪʃlɪ] ADV imprudentemente

foolishness ['fu:lɪʃnɪs] N tolice f

foolproof ['fu:lpru:f] ADJ (*plan etc*) infalível

foolscap ['fu:lskæp] N papel m ofício

foot [fut] (*pl* **feet**) N pé m; (*of animal*) pata; (*measure*) pé (304 mm; 12 inches) ■ vi (*bill*) pagar; **on ~ a pé; to find one's feet** (*fig*) ambientar-se; **to put one's ~ down** (*Aut*) acelerar; (*say no*) bater o pé

footage ['futɪdʒ] N (*Cinema: length*) ≈ metragem f; (: *material*) seqüências *fpl*

foot and mouth (disease) N febre f aftosa

football ['futbɔ:l] N bola; (*game: Brit*) futebol m; (: *US*) futebol norte-americano

footballer ['futbɔ:lə'] N futebolista m, jogador m de futebol

football ground N campo de futebol

football match (*Brit*) N partida de futebol

football player N jogador m de futebol

foot brake N freio (BR) *or* travão m (PT) de pé

footbridge ['futbrɪdʒ] N passarela

foothills ['futhɪlz] NPL contraforte m

foothold ['futhəuld] N apoio para o pé

footing ['futɪŋ] N (*fig*) posição f; **to lose one's ~** escorregar; **on an equal ~** em pé de igualdade

footlights ['futlaɪts] NPL ribalta

footman ['futmən] (*irreg*) N lacaio

footnote ['futnəut] N nota ao pé da página, nota de rodapé

footpath ['futpɑ:θ] N caminho, atalho; (*pavement*) calçada

footprint ['futprɪnt] N pegada

footrest ['futrest] N suporte m para os pés

footsore ['futsɔ:'] ADJ com os pés doloridos

footstep ['futstep] N passo

footwear ['futwɛə'] N calçados *mpl*

FOR ABBR (= *free on rail*) franco sobre vagão

 KEYWORD

for [fɔ:'] PREP **1** (*indicating destination, direction*) para; **the train for London** o trem para Londres; **he went for the paper** foi pegar o jornal; **is this for me?** é para mim?; **it's time for lunch** é hora de almoçar

2 (*indicating purpose*) para; **what's it for?** para quê serve?; **to pray for peace** orar pela paz

3 (*on behalf of, representing*) por; **the MP for Hove** o MP por Hove; **he works for the government/ a local firm** ele trabalha para o governo/uma firma local; **I'll ask him for you** vou pedir a ele por você; **G for George** G de George

4 (*because of*) por; **for this reason** por esta razão; **for fear of being criticised** com medo de ser criticado

5 (*with regard to*) com relação a ed s; **it's cold for July** está frio para julho; **for everyone who voted yes, 50 voted no** para cada um que votou sim, cinqüenta votaram não

6 (*in exchange for*) por; **it was sold for £5** foi vendido por £5

7 (*in favour of*) a favor de; **are you for or against us?** você está a favor de ou contra nós?; **I'm all**

for it concordo plenamente, tem todo o meu apoio; **vote for X** vote em X

8 (*referring to distance*): **there are roadworks for 5 km** há obras na estrada por 5 quilômetros; **we walked for miles** andamos quilômetros

9 (*referring to time*): **he was away for 2 years** esteve fora 2 anos; **she will be away for a month** ela ficará fora um mês; **I have known her for years** eu a conheço há anos; **can you do it for tomorrow?** você pode fazer isso para amanhã?

10 (*with infinite clause*): **it is not for me to decide** não cabe a mim decidir; **it would be best for you to leave** seria melhor que você fosse embora; **there is still time for you to do it** ainda há tempo para você fazer isso; **for this to be possible ...** para que isso seja possível ...

11 (*in spite of*) apesar de; **for all his complaints ...** apesar de suas reclamações, ...

■ CONJ (*since, as: rather formal*) pois, porque; **she was very angry, for he was late again** ela estava muito zangada pois ele se atrasou novamente

forage ['fɒrɪdʒ] N forragem *f* ■ VI ir à procura de alimentos;**forage cap** N casquete *m*

foray ['fɒreɪ] N incursão *f*

forbad(e) [fə'bæd] PT *of* **forbid**

forbearing [fɔː'bɛərɪŋ] ADJ indulgente

forbid [fə'bɪd] (*pt* **forbad(e)**, *pp* **forbidden**) VT proibir; **to ~ sb to do sth** proibir alguém de fazer algo

forbidden [fə'bɪdn] PP *of* **forbid** ■ ADJ proibido

forbidding [fə'bɪdɪŋ] ADJ (*look, prospect*) sombrio; (*severe*) severo

force [fɔːs] N força ■ VT (*gen, smile*) forçar; (*confession*) arrancar à força; **the Forces** NPL (*Brit*) as Forças Armadas; **to ~ sb to do** forçar alguém a fazer; **in ~** em vigor; **to come into ~** entrar em vigor; **a ~ 5 wind** um vento força 5; **the sales ~** (*Comm*) a equipe de vendas; **to join ~s** unir forças; **by ~** à força

▶ **force back** VT (*crowd, enemy*) fazer recuar; (*tears*) reprimir

▶ **force down** VT (*food*) forçar-se a comer

forced [fɔːst] ADJ forçado

force-feed ['fɔːsfiːd] (*irreg*) VT alimentar à força

forceful ['fɔːsful] ADJ enérgico, vigoroso

forcemeat ['fɔːsmiːt] (*Brit*) N (*Culin*) recheio

forceps ['fɔːsɛps] NPL fórceps *m inv*

forcibly ['fɔːsəblɪ] ADV à força

ford [fɔːd] N vau *m* ■ VT vadear

fore [fɔː'] N: **to bring to the ~** pôr em evidência; **to come to the ~** (*person*) salientar-se

forearm ['fɔːrɑːm] N antebraço

forebear ['fɔːbɛə'] N antepassado

foreboding [fɔː'bəudɪŋ] N mau presságio

forecast ['fɔːkɑːst] (*irreg: like* **cast**) N prognóstico, previsão *f*; (*also:* **weather forecast**) previsão do tempo ■ VT prognosticar, prever

foreclose [fɔː'kləuz] VT (*Law: also:* **foreclose on**) executar

foreclosure [fɔː'kləuʒə'] N execução *f* de uma hipoteca

forecourt ['fɔːkɔːt] N (*of garage*) área de estacionamento

forefathers ['fɔːfɑːðəz] NPL antepassados *mpl*

forefinger ['fɔːfɪŋgə'] N (dedo) indicador *m*

forefront ['fɔːfrʌnt] N: **in the ~ of** em primeiro plano em

forego (*irreg: like* **go**) VT (*give up*) renunciar a; (*go without*) abster-se de

foregoing ['fɔːgəuɪŋ] ADJ acima mencionado ■ N: **the ~** o supracitado

foregone ['fɔːgɒn] PP *of* **forego** ■ ADJ: **it's a ~ conclusion** é uma conclusão inevitável

foreground ['fɔːgraund] N primeiro plano ■ CPD (*Comput*) de primeiro plano

forehand ['fɔːhænd] N (*Tennis*) golpe *m* de frente

forehead ['fɒrɪd] N testa

foreign ['fɒrɪn] ADJ estrangeiro; (*trade*) exterior; **foreign body** N corpo estranho;**foreign currency** N câmbio, divisas *fpl*

foreigner ['fɒrɪnə'] N estrangeiro(-a)

foreign exchange N (*system*) câmbio; (*money*) divisas *fpl*

foreign exchange market N mercado de câmbio

foreign exchange rate N taxa de câmbio

foreign investment N investimento estrangeiro

Foreign Office (*Brit*) N Ministério das Relações Exteriores

foreign secretary (*Brit*) N ministro das Relações Exteriores

foreleg ['fɔːlɛg] N perna dianteira

foreman ['fɔːmən] (*irreg*) N capataz *m*; (*in construction*) contramestre *m*; (*Law: of jury*) primeiro jurado

foremost ['fɔːməust] ADJ principal ■ ADV: **first and ~** antes de mais nada

forename ['fɔːneɪm] N prenome *m*

forensic [fə'rɛnsɪk] ADJ forense; **~ medicine** medicina legal; **~ expert** perito(-a) criminal

forerunner ['fɔːrʌnə'] N precursor(a) *m/f*

foresee [fɔː'siː] (*irreg: like* **see**) VT prever

foreseeable [fɔː'siːəbl] ADJ previsível

foreshadow [fɔː'fædəu] VT prefigurar

foreshorten [fɔː'fɔːtn] VT escorçar

foresight ['fɔːsaɪt] N previdência

foreskin ['fɔːskɪn] N (*Anat*) prepúcio

forest ['fɒrɪst] N floresta

forestall [fɔː'stɔːl] VT prevenir

forestry ['fɒrɪstrɪ] N silvicultura

foretaste ['fɔːteɪst] N antegosto, antegozo; (*sample*) amostra

foretell [fɔː'tɛl] (*irreg: like* **tell**) VT predizer, profetizar

forethought ['fɔːθɔːt] N previdência

foretold [fɔː'təuld] PT, PP *of* **foretell**

forever [fə'rɛvə'] ADV para sempre; (*a long time*) muito tempo, um tempão (*inf*); **he's ~ forgetting my name** ele vive esquecendo o meu nome

forewarn [fɔː'wɔːn] VT prevenir
forewent PT of **forego**
foreword ['fɔːwəːd] N prefácio
forfeit ['fɔːfɪt] N prenda, perda; (fine) multa ■ VT perder (direito a); (one's life, health) pagar com
forgave [fə'geɪv] PT of **forgive**
forge [fɔːdʒ] N forja; (smithy) ferraria ■ VT (signature, money) falsificar; (metal) forjar
▶ **forge ahead** VI avançar constantemente
forger ['fɔːdʒəʳ] N falsificador(a) m/f
forgery ['fɔːdʒərɪ] N falsificação f
forget [fə'gɛt] (pt **forgot**, pp **forgotten**) VT, VI esquecer
forgetful [fə'gɛtful] ADJ esquecido
forgetfulness [fə'gɛtfulnɪs] N esquecimento
forget-me-not N miosótis m
forgive [fə'gɪv] (pt **forgave**, pp **forgiven**) VT perdoar; **to ~ sb for sth** perdoar algo a alguém, perdoar alguém de algo
forgiveness [fə'gɪvnɪs] N perdão m
forgiving [fə'gɪvɪŋ] ADJ clemente
forgo [fɔː'gəu] (irreg: like **go**) VT = **forego**
forgot [fə'gɔt] PT of **forget**
forgotten [fə'gɔtn] PP of **forget**
fork [fɔːk] N (for eating) garfo; (for gardening) forquilha; (of roads etc) bifurcação f ■ VI (road) bifurcar-se
▶ **fork out** (inf) VT (pay) desembolsar, morrer em ■ VI (pay) descolar uma grana
forked [fɔːkt] ADJ (lightning) em ziguezague
fork-lift truck N empilhadeira
forlorn [fə'lɔːn] ADJ (person, place) desolado; (attempt) desesperado; (hope) último
form [fɔːm] N forma; (type) tipo; (Sch) série f; (questionnaire) formulário ■ VT formar; (organization) criar; **in the ~ of** na forma de; **to ~ part of sth** fazer parte de algo; **to ~ a queue** (Brit) fazer fila; **to be in good ~** (Sport, fig) estar em forma; **in top ~** em plena forma
formal ['fɔːməl] ADJ (offer, receipt) oficial; (person etc) cerimonioso; (occasion, education) formal; (dress) a rigor (BR), de cerimônia (PT); (garden) simétrico
formalities [fɔː'mælɪtɪz] NPL (procedures) formalidades fpl
formality [fɔː'mælɪtɪ] N (of person) formalismo; (formal requirement) formalidade f; (ceremony) cerimônia
formalize ['fɔːməlaɪz] VT formalizar
formally ['fɔːməlɪ] ADV oficialmente, formalmente; (in a formal way) formalmente
format ['fɔːmæt] N formato ■ VT (Comput) formatar
formation [fɔː'meɪʃən] N formação f
formative ['fɔːmətɪv] ADJ (years) formativo
former ['fɔːməʳ] ADJ anterior; (earlier) antigo; (ex) ex-; **the ~ ... the latter ...** aquele ... este ...; **the ~ president** o ex-presidente
formerly ['fɔːməlɪ] ADV anteriormente
form feed N (on printer) alimentar formulário
formidable ['fɔːmɪdəbl] ADJ terrível, temível
formula ['fɔːmjulə] (pl **formulas** or **formulae**) N

fórmula; **F~ One** (Aut) Fórmula Um
formulate ['fɔːmjuleɪt] VT formular
fornicate ['fɔːnɪkeɪt] VI fornicar
forsake [fə'seɪk] (pt **forsook**, pp **forsaken**) VT abandonar; (plan) renunciar a
forsaken [fə'seɪkən] PP of **forsake**
forsook [fə'suk] PT of **forsake**
fort [fɔːt] N forte m; **to hold the ~** (fig) agüentar a mão
forte ['fɔːtɪ] N forte m
forth [fɔːθ] ADV para adiante; **back and ~** de cá para lá; **and so ~** e assim por diante
forthcoming ['fɔːθ'kʌmɪŋ] ADJ próximo, que está para aparecer; (help) disponível; (person) comunicativo; (book) a ser publicado
forthright ['fɔːθraɪt] ADJ franco
forthwith ['fɔːθ'wɪθ] ADV em seguida
fortieth ['fɔːtɪɪθ] NUM quadragésimo; see also **fifth**
fortification [fɔːtɪfɪ'keɪʃən] N fortificação f
fortified wine ['fɔːtɪfaɪd-] N vinho generoso
fortify ['fɔːtɪfaɪ] VT (city) fortificar; (person) fortalecer
fortitude ['fɔːtɪtjuːd] N fortaleza
fortnight ['fɔːtnaɪt] (Brit) N quinzena, quinze dias mpl
fortnightly ['fɔːtnaɪtlɪ] ADJ quinzenal ■ ADV quinzenalmente
FORTRAN 'fɔːtræn] N FORTRAN m
fortress ['fɔːtrɪs] N fortaleza
fortuitous [fɔː'tjuːɪtəs] ADJ fortuito
fortunate ['fɔːtʃənɪt] ADJ (event) feliz; (person): **to be ~** ter sorte; **it is ~ that ...** é uma sorte que ...
fortunately ['fɔːtʃənɪtlɪ] ADV felizmente
fortune ['fɔːtʃən] N sorte f; (wealth) fortuna; **to make a ~** fazer fortuna
fortune-teller N adivinho(-a)
forty ['fɔːtɪ] NUM quarenta; see also **fifty**
forum ['fɔːrəm] N foro
forward ['fɔːwəd] ADJ (movement) para a frente; (position) avançado; (front) dianteiro; (not shy) imodesto, presunçoso; (Comm: delivery) futuro; (: sales, exchange) a termo ■ N (Sport) atacante m ■ ADV para a frente ■ VT (letter) remeter; (goods, parcel) expedir; (career) promover; (plans) ativar; **to move ~** avançar; **"please ~"** por favor remeta a novo endereço"; **~ planning** planejamento para o futuro
forward(s) ['fɔːwəd(z)] ADV para a frente
forwent [fɔː'wɛnt] PT of **forgo**; **fossil** ['fɔsl] N fóssil m
fossil fuel ■ N combustível m fóssil
foster ['fɔstəʳ] VT adoptar; (activity) promover; **foster brother** N irmão m de criação; **foster child** (irreg) N filho adotivo; **foster mother** N mãe f adotiva
fought [fɔːt] PT, PP of **fight**
foul [faul] ADJ sujo, porco; (food) podre; (weather) horrível; (language) obsceno; (deed) infame ■ N (Sport) falta ■ VT (dirty) sujar; (block) entupir; (football player) cometer uma falta contra; (entangle: anchor, propeller) enredar; **foul play** N

(Sport) jogada suja; (Law) crime m

found [faund] PT, PP of **find** ■ VT (establish) fundar

foundation [faun'deɪʃən] N (act) fundação f; (base) base f; (also: **foundation cream**) creme m base; **foundations** NPL (of building) alicerces mpl; **to lay the ~s** (fig) lançar os alicerces; **foundation stone** N pedra fundamental

founder ['faundə'] N fundador(a) m/f ■ VI naufragar

founding ['faundɪŋ] N fundação f ■ ADJ fundador(a)

foundry ['faundrɪ] N fundição f

fount [faunt] N fonte f

fountain ['fauntɪn] N chafariz m; **fountain pen** N caneta-tinteiro f

four [fɔː'] NUM quatro; **on all ~s** de quatro; see also **five**

four-poster N (also: **four-poster bed**) cama com colunas

foursome ['fɔːsəm] N grupo de quatro pessoas

fourteen ['fɔː'tiːn] NUM catorze; see also **five**

fourteenth ['fɔː'tiːnθ] NUM décimo-quarto; see also **fifth**

fourth [fɔːθ] NUM quarto ■ N (Aut: also: **fourth gear**) quarta; see also **fifth**

four-wheel drive N (Aut): **with ~** com tração nas quatro rodas

fowl [faul] N ave f (doméstica)

fox [fɔks] N raposa ■ VT deixar perplexo; **fox fur** N raposa

foxglove ['fɔksglʌv] N (Bot) dedaleira

fox-hunting N caça à raposa

foxtrot ['fɔkstrɔt] N foxtrote m

foyer ['fɔɪeɪ] N saguão m

FP N ABBR (Brit) = **former pupil**; (US) = **fireplug**

FPA (Brit) N ABBR = **Family Planning Association**

Fr. ABBR (Rel: = father) P.; (: = friar) Fr.

fr. ABBR (= franc) fr.

fracas ['fræka:] N desordem f, rixa

fraction ['frækʃən] N fração f

fractionally ['frækʃnəlɪ] ADV ligeiramente

fractious ['frækʃəs] ADJ irascível

fracture ['fræktʃə'] N fratura ■ VT fraturar

fragile ['frædʒaɪl] ADJ frágil

fragment ['frægmənt] N fragmento

fragmentary ['frægməntərɪ] ADJ fragmentário

fragrance ['freɪgrəns] N fragrância

fragrant ['freɪgrənt] ADJ fragrante, perfumado

frail [freɪl] ADJ (person) fraco; (structure) frágil; (weak) delicado

frame [freɪm] N (of building) estrutura; (body) corpo; (Tech) armação f; (of picture, door) moldura; (of spectacles: also: **frames**) armação f, aro ■ VT enquadrar, encaixilhar; (picture) emoldurar; (reply) formular; (inf) incriminar; **frame of mind** N estado de espírito

framework ['freɪmwə:k] N armação f; (fig) sistema m, quadro

France [fra:ns] N França

franchise ['fræntʃaɪz] N (Pol) direito de voto; (Comm) concessão f

franchisee [fræntʃaɪ'ziː] N concessionário(-a)

franchiser ['fræntʃaɪzə'] N concedente m/f

frank [fræŋk] ADJ franco ■ VT (letter) franquear

Frankfurt ['fræŋkfə:t] N Frankfurt (BR), Francoforte (PT)

frankfurter ['fræŋkfə:tə'] N salsicha de cachorro quente

franking machine ['fræŋkɪŋ-] N máquina de selagem

frankly ['fræŋklɪ] ADV francamente; (candidly) abertamente

frankness ['fræŋknɪs] N franqueza

frantic ['fræntɪk] ADJ frenético; (person) fora de si

frantically ['fræntɪklɪ] ADV freneticamente

fraternal [frə'tə:nl] ADJ fraterno

fraternity [frə'tə:nɪtɪ] N (club) fraternidade f; (US) clube m de estudantes; (guild) confraria

fraternize ['frætənaɪz] VI confraternizar

fraud [frɔːd] N fraude f; (person) impostor(a) m/f

fraudulent ['frɔːdjulənt] ADJ fraudulento

fraught [frɔːt] ADJ tenso; **~ with** repleto de

fray [freɪ] N combate m, luta ■ VT esfiapar ■ VI esfiapar-se; **tempers were ~ed** estavam com os nervos em frangalhos

FRB (US) N ABBR = **Federal Reserve Board**

FRCM (Brit) N ABBR = **Fellow of the Royal College of Music**

FRCO (Brit) N ABBR = **Fellow of the Royal College of Organists**

FRCP (Brit) N ABBR = **Fellow of the Royal College of Physicians**

FRCS (Brit) N ABBR = **Fellow of the Royal College of Surgeons**

freak [friːk] N (person) anormal m/f; (event) anomalia; (thing) aberração f; (inf: enthusiast): **health ~** maníaco(-a) com a saúde

▶ **freak out** (inf) VI (on drugs) baratinar-se; (get angry) ficar uma fera

freakish ['friːkɪʃ] ADJ anormal

freckle ['frekl] N sarda

free [friː] ADJ livre; (seat) desocupada; (not fixed) solto; (costing nothing) gratis, gratuito; (liberal) generoso ■ VT (prisoner etc) pôr em liberdade; (jammed object) soltar; **to give sb a ~ hand** dar carta branca a alguém; **~ and easy** informal; **admission ~** entrada livre; **~ (of charge)** (for free) grátis, de graça

freebie ['friːbɪ] (inf) N brinde m; (trip etc): **it's a ~** está tudo pago

freedom ['friːdəm] N liberdade f; **freedom fighter** N lutador(a) m/f pela liberdade

free enterprise N livre iniciativa

free-for-all N quebra-quebra m

free gift N brinde m

freehold ['friːhəuld] N propriedade f livre e alodial

free kick N (tiro) livre m

freelance ['friːlaːns] ADJ autônomo

freelancer ['friːlaːnsə'] N free-lance m/f

freeloader ['friːləudə'] (pej) N sanguessuga m

freely ['friːlɪ] ADV livremente

freemason ['fri:meɪsən] N maçom m
freemasonry ['fri:meɪsnrɪ] N maçonaria
Freepost® ['fri:pəust] N porte m pago
free-range N (egg) caseiro
free sample N amostra grátis
free speech N liberdade f de expressão
free trade N livre comércio
freeway ['fri:weɪ] (US) N auto-estrada
freewheel [fri:'wi:l] VI ir em ponto morto
freewheeling [fri:'wi:lɪŋ] ADJ independente,
livre
free will N livre arbítrio; **of one's own ~** por sua
própria vontade
freeze [fri:z] (pt froze, pp frozen) VI gelar(-
se), congelar-se ■ VT gelar; (prices, food,
salaries) congelar ■ N geada; (on arms, wages)
congelamento
▶ **freeze over** VI (lake, river) gelar; (windscreen)
cobrir-se de gelo
▶ **freeze up** VI gelar
freeze-dried ADJ liofilizado
freezer ['fri:zəʳ] N congelador m, freezer m (BR)
freezing ['fri:zɪŋ] ADJ: ~ **(cold)** (weather) glacial;
(water) gelado; **3 degrees below ~** 3 graus
abaixo de zero; **freezing point** N ponto de
congelamento
freight [freɪt] N (goods) carga; (money charged)
frete m; ~ **forward** frete pago na chegada; ~
inward frete incluído no preço; **freight car** (US)
N vagão m de carga
freighter ['freɪtəʳ] N cargueiro
freight forwarder [-'fɔ:wədəʳ] N despachante
m/f
freight train (US) N trem m de carga
French [frɛntʃ] ADJ francês(-esa) ■ N (Ling)
francês m; **the French** NPL os franceses;
French bean (Brit) N feijão m comum
French-Canadian ADJ franco-canadense
■ N canadense m/f francês(-esa) or da parte
francesa; (Ling) francês m do Canadá
French dressing N (Culin) molho francês (de
salada)
French fried potatoes NPL batatas fpl fritas
French fries (US) NPL = **French fried potatoes**
French Guiana [-gaɪ'ænə] N Guiana Francesa
Frenchman ['frɛntʃmən] (irreg) N francês m
French Riviera N: **the ~** a Costa Azul
French window N porta-janela, janela de
batente
Frenchwoman ['frɛntʃwumən] (irreg) N
francesa
frenetic [frə'nɛtɪk] ADJ frenético
frenzy ['frɛnzɪ] N frenesi m
frequency ['fri:kwənsɪ] N freqüência;
frequency modulation N freqüência
modulada
frequent [adj 'fri:kwənt, vt frɪ'kwɛnt] ADJ
freqüente ■ VT freqüentar
frequently ['fri:kwəntlɪ] ADV freqüentemente,
a miúdo
fresco ['frɛskəu] N fresco
fresh [frɛʃ] ADJ fresco; (new) novo; (cheeky)

atrevido; **to make a ~ start** começar de novo
freshen ['frɛʃən] VI (wind, air) tornar-se mais
forte
▶ **freshen up** VI (person) lavar-se, refrescar-se
freshener ['frɛʃnəʳ] N: **skin ~** refrescante m da
pele; **air ~** purificador m de ar
fresher ['frɛʃəʳ] (Brit: inf) N (Sch) calouro(-a)
freshly ['frɛʃlɪ] ADV (newly) novamente; (recently)
recentemente, há pouco
freshman ['frɛʃmən] (US: irreg) N = **fresher**
freshness ['frɛʃnɪs] N frescor m
freshwater ['frɛʃwɔ:təʳ] ADJ de água doce
fret [frɛt] VI afligir-se
fretful ['frɛtful] ADJ irritável
Freudian ['frɔɪdɪən] ADJ freudiano; ~ **slip** ato
falho
FRG N ABBR (= Federal Republic of Germany) RFA f
Fri. ABBR (= Friday) sex
friar ['fraɪəʳ] N frade m; (before name) frei m
friction ['frɪkʃən] N fricção f; (between people)
atrito; **friction feed** N (on printer) alimentação f
por fricção
Friday ['fraɪdɪ] N sexta-feira f; see also **Tuesday**
fridge [frɪdʒ] N geladeira (BR), frigorífico (PT)
fried [fraɪd] PT, PP of **fry** ■ ADJ frito; ~ **egg** ovo
estrelado or frito
friend [frɛnd] N amigo(-a); **to make ~s with sb**
fazer amizade com alguém
friendliness ['frɛndlɪnɪs] N simpatia
friendly ['frɛndlɪ] ADJ (kind) simpático; (relations,
behaviour) amigável ■ N (also: **friendly match**)
amistoso; **to be ~ with** ser amigo de; **to be
~ to** ser simpático com; **friendly society** N
sociedade f mutuante, mútua
friendship ['frɛndʃɪp] N amizade f
frieze [fri:z] N friso
frigate ['frɪgɪt] N fragata
fright [fraɪt] N (terror) terror m; (scare) pavor m; **to
take ~** assustar-se
frighten ['fraɪtən] VT assustar
▶ **frighten away** VT espantar
▶ **frighten off** VT espantar
frightened ['fraɪtnd] ADJ: **to be ~ of** ter medo de
frightening ['fraɪtnɪŋ] ADJ assustador(a)
frightful ['fraɪtful] ADJ terrível, horrível
frightfully ['fraɪtfulɪ] ADV terrivelmente
frigid ['frɪdʒɪd] ADJ (Med) frígido, frio
frigidity [frɪ'dʒɪdɪtɪ] N (Med) frigidez f
frill [frɪl] N babado; **without ~s** (fig: car) sem
nenhum luxo; (: dinner) simples; (: service) sem
mordomias; (: holiday) sem extras
fringe [frɪndʒ] N franja; (on shawl etc) beira, orla;
(edge: of forest etc) margem f; (fig): **on the ~ of** à
margem de; **fringe benefits** NPL benefícios
mpl adicionais; **fringe theatre** N teatro de
vanguarda
frisk [frɪsk] VT revistar
frisky ['frɪskɪ] ADJ alegre, animado
fritter ['frɪtəʳ] N bolinho frito
▶ **fritter away** VT desperdiçar
frivolity [frɪ'vɔlɪtɪ] N frivolidade f
frivolous ['frɪvələs] ADJ frívolo; (activity) fútil

frizzy ['frɪzɪ] ADJ frisado
fro [frəʊ] ADV *see* **to**
frock [frɔk] N vestido
frog [frɔg] N rã f; **to have a ~ in one's throat** ter pigarro
frogman ['frɔgmən] (*irreg*) N homem-rã m
frogmarch ['frɔgmɑːtʃ] (*Brit*) VT: **to ~ sb in/out** arrastar alguém para dentro/para fora
frolic ['frɔlɪk] VI brincar

KEYWORD

from [frɔm] PREP **1** (*indicating starting place*) de; **where do you come from?** de onde você é?; **we flew from London to Glasgow** fomos de avião de Londres para Glasgow; **to escape from sth/ sb** escapar de algo/alguém
2 (*indicating origin etc*) de; **a letter/telephone call from my sister** uma carta/um telefonema da minha irmã; **tell him from me that ...** diga a ele que da minha parte ...; **to drink from the bottle** beber na garrafa
3 (*indicating time*): **from one o'clock to** *or* **until** *or* **till two** da uma hora até às duas; **from January (on)** a partir de janeiro
4 (*indicating distance*) de; **we're still a long way from home** ainda estamos muito longe de casa
5 (*indicating price, number etc*) de; **prices range from £10 to £50** os preços vão de £10 a £50; **the interest rate was increased from 9% to 10%** a taxa de juros foi aumentada de 9% para 10%
6 (*indicating difference*) de; **he can't tell red from green** ele não pode diferenciar vermelho do verde; **to be different from sb/sth** ser diferente de alguém/algo
7 (*because of/on the basis of*): **from what he says** pelo que ele diz; **from what I understand** pelo que eu entendo; **to act from conviction** agir por convicção; **weak from hunger** fraco de fome

frond [frɔnd] N fronde f
front [frʌnt] N (*of dress*) frente f; (*of vehicle*) parte f dianteira; (*of house*) fachada; (*of book*) capa; (*promenade: also*: **sea front**) orla marítima; (*Mil, Pol, Meteorology, of dress*) frente f; (*fig: appearances*) fachada; ■ ADJ dianteiro, da frente ■ VI: **to ~ onto sth** dar para algo; **in ~ (of)** em frente (de)
frontage ['frʌntɪdʒ] N fachada
frontal ['frʌntəl] ADJ frontal
front bench (*Brit*) N (*Pol*) *os dirigentes do partido no poder ou da oposição*
front desk (*US*) N (*in hotel, at doctor's*) recepção f
front door N porta principal; (*of car*) porta dianteira
frontier ['frʌntɪəʳ] N fronteira
frontispiece ['frʌntɪspiːs] N frontispício
front page N primeira página
front room (*Brit*) N salão m, sala de estar
front runner N (*fig*) favorito(-a)
front-wheel drive N tração f dianteira

frost [frɔst] N geada; (*also*: **hoarfrost**) gelo
frostbite ['frɔstbaɪt] N ulceração f produzida pelo frio
frosted ['frɔstɪd] ADJ (*glass*) fosco; (*esp US: cake*) com cobertura
frosting ['frɔstɪŋ] (*esp US*) N (*on cake*) glacê f
frosty ['frɔstɪ] ADJ (*window*) coberto de geada; (*welcome*) glacial
froth [frɔθ] N espuma
frown [fraun] N olhar m carrancudo, cara amarrada ■ VI franzir as sobrancelhas, amarrar a cara
▶ **frown on** VT FUS (*fig*) desaprovar, não ver com bons olhos
froze [frəʊz] PT *of* **freeze**
frozen ['frəʊzn] PP *of* **freeze** ■ ADJ congelado; **~ foods** congelados mpl
FRS N ABBR (*Brit*: = *Fellow of the Royal Society*) membro de associação promovedora de pesquisa científica; (*US*: = *Federal Reserve System*) banco central dos EUA
frugal ['fruːgəl] ADJ frugal
fruit [fruːt] N INV fruta; (*fig: results*) fruto
fruiterer ['fruːtərəʳ] N fruteiro(-a); **~'s (shop)** fruterio (BR), frutaria (PT)
fruitful ['fruːtful] ADJ proveitoso
fruition [fruːˈɪʃən] N: **to come to ~** realizar-se
fruit juice N suco (BR) *or* sumo (PT) de frutas
fruitless ['fruːtlɪs] ADJ inútil, vão(-vã)
fruit machine (*Brit*) N caça-níqueis m inv (BR), máquina de jogo (PT)
fruit salad N salada de frutas
frump [frʌmp] N careta (*mulher antiquada*)
frustrate [frʌsˈtreɪt] VT frustrar
frustrated [frʌsˈtreɪtɪd] ADJ frustrado
frustrating [frʌsˈtreɪtɪŋ] ADJ frustrante
frustration [frʌsˈtreɪʃən] N frustração f; (*disappointment*) decepção f
fry [fraɪ] (*pt, pp* **fried**) VT fritar; *see also* **small**
frying pan ['fraɪɪŋ-] N frigideira
FT (*Brit*) N ABBR (= *Financial Times*) jornal financeiro; **the FT index** o índice da Bolsa de Valores de Londres
ft. ABBR = **foot; feet**
FTC (*US*) N ABBR = **Federal Trade Commission**
fuchsia ['fjuːʃə] N fúcsia
fuck [fʌk] (*inf!*) VI trepar (!) ■ VT trepar com (!); **~ off** ! vai tomar no cu! (!)
fuddled ['fʌdld] ADJ (*muddled*) confuso, enrolado
fuddy-duddy ['fʌdɪdʌdɪ] (*pej*) ADJ, N careta m/f
fudge [fʌdʒ] N (*Culin*) ≈ doce m de leite ■ VT (*issue, problem*) evadir
fuel [fjuəl] N (*gen, for heating*) combustível m; (*for propelling*) carburante m; **fuel oil** N óleo combustível; **fuel pump** N (*Aut*) bomba de gasolina; **fuel tank** N depósito de combustível
fug [fʌg] (*Brit*) N bafio
fugitive ['fjuːdʒɪtɪv] N fugitivo(-a)
fulfil [ful'fɪl] (*US* **fulfill**) VT (*function*) cumprir; (*condition*) satisfazer; (*wish, desire*) realizar
fulfilled [ful'fɪld] ADJ (*person*) realizado
fulfil(l)ment [ful'fɪlmənt] N satisfação f; (*of wish,*

desire) realização *f*
full [ful] ADJ cheio; (*fig*) pleno; (*use, volume*) máximo; (*complete*) completo; (*information*) detalhado; (*price*) integral; (*skirt*) folgado ■ ADV: ~ **well** perfeitamente; **I'm ~ (up)** estou satisfeito; ~ **(up)** (*hotel etc*) lotado; ~ **employment** pleno emprego; ~ **fare** passagem completa; **a ~ two hours** duas horas completas; **at ~ speed** a toda a velocidade; **in ~** (*reproduce, quote*) integralmente; (*name*) por completo; ~ **employment** pleno emprego
fullback ['fulbæk] N zagueiro (BR), defesa *m* (PT)
full-blooded [-'blʌdɪd] ADJ (*vigorous*) vigoroso
full-cream (*Brit*) ADJ: ~ **milk** leite *m* integral
full-grown ADJ crescido, adulto
full-length ADJ (*portrait*) de corpo inteiro; (*coat*) longo; ~ **(feature) film** longa-metragem *m*
full moon N lua cheia
full-scale ADJ (*model*) em tamanho natural; (*war*) em grande escala
full-sized [-saɪzd] ADJ (*portrait etc*) em tamanho natural
full stop N ponto (final)
full-time ADJ (*work*) de tempo completo *or* integral ■ N: **full time** (*Sport*) final *m*
fully ['fulɪ] ADV completamente; (*at least*): ~ **as big as** pelo menos tão grande como
fully-fledged [-flɛdʒd] ADJ (*teacher, barrister*) diplomado; (*citizen, member*) verdadeiro
fulsome ['fulsəm] (*pej*) ADJ extravagante
fumble ['fʌmbl] VI atrapalhar-se ■ VT (*ball*) atrapalhar-se com, apanhar de (*inf*)
▶ **fumble with** VT FUS atrapalhar-se com, apanhar de (*inf*)
fume [fju:m] VI fumegar; (*be angry*) estar com raiva; **fumes** NPL gases *mpl*
fumigate ['fju:mɪgeɪt] VT fumigar; (*against pests etc*) pulverizar
fun [fʌn] N (*amusement*) divertimento; (*joy*) alegria; **to have ~** divertir-se; **for ~** de brincadeira; **it's not much ~** não tem graça; **to make ~ of** fazer troça de, zombar de
function ['fʌŋkʃən] N função *f*; (*reception, dinner*) recepção *f* ■ VI funcionar; **to ~ as** funcionar como
functional ['fʌŋkʃənəl] ADJ funcional; (*practical*) prático
function key N (*Comput*) tecla de função
fund [fʌnd] N fundo; (*source, store*) fonte *f*; **funds** NPL (*money*) fundos *mpl*
fundamental [fʌndə'mɛntl] ADJ fundamental
fundamentalist [fʌndə'mɛntəlɪst] N fundamentalista *m/f*
fundamentally [fʌndə'mɛntəlɪ] ADV fundamentalmente
fundamentals [fʌndə'mɛntlz] NPL fundamentos *mpl*
fund-raising [-'reɪzɪŋ] N angariação *f* de fundos
funeral ['fju:nərəl] N (*burial*) enterro; (*ceremony*) exéquias *fpl*; **funeral director** N agente *m/f* funerário(-a); **funeral parlour** N casa funerária; **funeral service** N missa fúnebre

funereal [fju:'nɪərɪəl] ADJ fúnebre, funéreo
funfair ['fʌnfeəʳ] (*Brit*) N parque *m* de diversões
fungi ['fʌŋgaɪ] NPL *of* **fungus**
fungus ['fʌŋgəs] (*pl* **fungi**) N fungo; (*mould*) bolor *m*, mofo
funicular [fju:'nɪkjuləʳ] N (*also*: **funicular railway**) funicular *m*
funnel ['fʌnl] N funil *m*; (*of ship*) chaminé *m*
funnily ['fʌnɪlɪ] ADV: ~ **enough** por incrível que pareça
funny ['fʌnɪ] ADJ engraçado, divertido; (*strange*) esquisito, estranho; **funny bone** N *parte sensível do cotovelo*
fur [fəːʳ] N pele *f*; (*Brit: in kettle etc*) depósito, crosta; **fur coat** N casaco de peles
furious ['fjuərɪəs] ADJ furioso; (*effort*) incrível
furiously ['fjuərɪəslɪ] ADV com fúria; (*argue*) com violência
furl [fəːl] VT enrolar; (*Naut*) colher
furlong ['fəːlɒŋ] N = *201.17m*
furlough ['fəːləu] N licença
furnace ['fəːnɪs] N forno
furnish ['fəːnɪʃ] VT mobiliar (BR), mobilar (PT); (*supply*): **to ~ sb with sth** fornecer algo a alguém; ~**ed flat** (*Brit*) *or* **apartment** (*US*) apartamento mobiliado (BR) *or* mobilado (PT)
furnishings ['fəːnɪʃɪŋz] NPL mobília
furniture ['fəːnɪtʃəʳ] N mobília, móveis *mpl*; **piece of ~** móvel; **furniture polish** N cera de lustrar móveis
furore [fjuə'rɔːrɪ] N furor *m*
furrier ['fʌrɪəʳ] N peleiro(-a)
furrow ['fʌrəu] N (*in field*) rego; (*in skin*) sulco
furry ['fəːrɪ] ADJ peludo; (*toy*) de pelúcia
further ['fəːðəʳ] ADJ (*new*) novo, adicional ■ ADV mais longe; (*more*) mais; (*moreover*) além disso ■ VT promover; **how much ~ is it?** quanto mais tem que se ir?; **until ~ notice** até novo aviso; ~ **to your letter of ...** (*Comm*) em resposta à sua carta do ...; **further education** (*Brit*) N educação *f* superior
furthermore [fəːðə'mɔːʳ] ADV além disso
furthermost ['fəːðəməust] ADJ mais distante
furthest ['fəːðɪst] SUPERL *of* **far**
furtive ['fəːtɪv] ADJ furtivo
furtively ['fəːtɪvlɪ] ADV furtivamente
fury ['fjuərɪ] N fúria
fuse [fju:z] (*US* **fuze**) N fusível *m*; (*for bomb etc*) espoleta, mecha ■ VT fundir; (*fig*) unir ■ VI (*metal*) fundir-se; unir-se; ~ **the lights** (*Brit*) (*Elec*) queimar as luzes; **a ~ has blown** queimou um fusível; **fuse box** N caixa de fusíveis
fuselage ['fju:zəlɑːʒ] N fuselagem *f*
fuse wire N fio fusível
fusillade [fju:zɪ'leɪd] N fuzilada; (*fig*) saraivada
fusion ['fju:ʒən] N fusão *f*
fuss [fʌs] N (*uproar*) rebuliço; (*excitement*) estardalhaço; (*complaining*) escândalo ■ VI criar caso; **to make a ~** criar caso; **to make a ~ of sb** paparicar alguém
▶ **fuss over** VT FUS (*person*) paparicar
fussy ['fʌsɪ] ADJ (*person*) exigente, complicado,

cheio de coisas (*inf*); (*dress, style*) espalhafatoso;
I'm not ~ (*inf*) para mim, tanto faz
futile ['fjuːtaɪl] ADJ (*existence*) fútil; (*attempt*)
inútil, fútil
futility [fjuːˈtɪlɪtɪ] N inutilidade *f*
future ['fjuːtʃəʳ] ADJ futuro ■ N futuro;
(*prospects*) perspectiva; **futures** NPL (*Comm*)
operações *fpl* a termo; **in (the) ~** no futuro; **in
the near/immediate ~** em futuro próximo/
imediato

futuristic [fjuːtʃəˈrɪstɪk] ADJ futurístico
fuze [fjuːz] (US) N, VT, VI = **fuse**
fuzzy ['fʌzɪ] ADJ (*Phot*) indistinto; (*hair*) frisado,
encrespado
fwd. ABBR = **forward**
fwy (US) ABBR = **freeway**
FY ABBR = **fiscal year**
FYI ABBR (= *for your information*) para seu
conhecimento

Gg

G, g [dʒiː] N (*letter*) G, g m; (: *Mus*): **G** sol m; **G for George** G de Gomes

G N ABBR (*Brit: Sch*) = **good**; (*US: Cinema*: = *general (audience)*) livre

g ABBR (= *gram; gravity*) g

GA (*US*) ABBR (*Post*) = **Georgia**

gab [gæb] (*inf*) N: **to have the gift of the ~** ter lábia, ser bom de bico

gabble ['gæbl] VI tagarelar

gaberdine [gæbə'diːn] N gabardina, gabardine f

gable ['geɪbl] N cumeeira

Gabon [gə'bɔn] N Gabão m

gad about [gæd-] (*inf*) VI badalar

gadget ['gædʒɪt] N aparelho, engenhoca; (*in kitchen*) pequeno utensílio

Gaelic ['geɪlɪk] ADJ gaélico(-a) ■ N (*Ling*) gaélico

gaffe [gæf] N gafe f

gag [gæg] N (*on mouth*) mordaça; (*joke*) piada ■ VT amordaçar

gaga ['gɑːgɑː] ADJ: **to go ~** ficar gagá

gaiety ['geɪɪtɪ] N alegria

gaily ['geɪlɪ] ADV alegremente; (*coloured*) vivamente

gain [geɪn] N ganho; (*profit*) lucro ■ VT ganhar ■ VI (*watch*) adiantar-se; (*benefit*): **to ~ from sth** tirar proveito de algo; **to ~ on sb** aproximar-se de alguém; **to ~ 3lbs (in weight)** engordar 3 libras; **to ~ ground** ganhar terreno

gainful ['geɪnful] ADJ lucrativo, proveitoso

gainsay [geɪn'seɪ] (*irreg: like* **say**) VT (*contradict*) contradizer; (*deny*) negar

gait [geɪt] N modo de andar

gal. ABBR = **gallon**

gala ['gɑːlə] N festa, gala; **swimming ~** festival de natação

Galapagos (Islands) [gə'læpəgəs-] NPL: **the Galapagos (Islands)** as ilhas Galápagos

galaxy ['gæləksɪ] N galáxia

gale [geɪl] N (*wind*) ventania; **~ force 10** vento de força 10

gall [gɔːl] N (*Anat*) fel m, bílis f; (*fig*) descaramento ■ VT irritar

gall. ABBR = **gallon**

gallant ['gælənt] ADJ valente; (*polite*) galante

gallantry ['gæləntrɪ] N valentia; (*courtesy*) galanteria

gall bladder [gɔːl-] N vesícula biliar

galleon ['gælɪən] N galeão m

gallery ['gælərɪ] N (*in theatre etc*) galeria; (*also*: **art gallery**: *public*) museu m; (: *private*) galeria (de arte)

galley ['gælɪ] N (*ship's kitchen*) cozinha; (*ship*) galé f; (*also*: **galley proof**) paquê m

Gallic ['gælɪk] ADJ francês(-esa)

galling ['gɔːlɪŋ] ADJ irritante

gallon ['gæln] N galão m (= 8 *pints*; *Brit* = 4.5l; *US* = 3.8l)

gallop ['gæləp] N galope m ■ VI galopar; **~ing inflation** inflação galopante

gallows ['gæləuz] N forca

gallstone ['gɔːlstəun] N cálculo biliar

galore [gə'lɔːʳ] ADV à beça

galvanize ['gælvənaɪz] VT galvanizar; (*person, support*) arrebatar; **to ~ sb into action** galvanizar *or* eletrizar alguém

Gambia ['gæmbɪə] N Gâmbia (*no article*)

gambit ['gæmbɪt] N (*fig*): (**opening**) **~** início (de conversa)

gamble ['gæmbl] N (*risk*) risco; (*bet*) aposta ■ VT: **to ~ on** apostar em ■ VI jogar, arriscar; (*Comm*) especular

gambler ['gæmbləʳ] N jogador(a) m/f

gambling ['gæmblɪŋ] N jogo

gambol ['gæmbl] VI cabriolar

game [geɪm] N jogo; (*match*) partida; (*esp Tennis*) jogada; (*strategy*) plano, esquema m; (*Hunting*) caça ■ ADJ valente; (*willing*): **to be ~ for anything** topar qualquer parada; **games** NPL (*Sch*) esporte m (BR), desporto (PT); **I'm ~** eu topo; **big ~** caça grossa; **game bird** N ave f de caça

gamekeeper ['geɪmkiːpəʳ] N guarda-caça m

gamely ['geɪmlɪ] ADV valentemente

game reserve N reserva de caça

gamesmanship ['geɪmzmənʃɪp] N tática

gammon ['gæmən] N (*bacon*) toucinho (defumado); (*ham*) presunto

gamut ['gæmət] N gama

gang [gæŋ] N bando, grupo; (*of criminals*) gangue f; (*of workmen*) turma ■ VI: **to ~ up on sb** conspirar contra alguém

Ganges ['gændʒiːz] N: **the ~** o Ganges

gangling ['gæŋglɪŋ] ADJ desengonçado

gangplank ['gæŋplæŋk] N prancha (de desembarque)

gangrene ['gæŋgri:n] N gangrena
gangster ['gæŋstər] N gângster m, bandido
gangway ['gæŋweɪ] N (Brit: in cinema, bus) corredor m; (on ship) passadiço; (on dock) portaló m
gantry ['gæntrɪ] N pórtico; (for rocket) guindaste m
GAO (US) N ABBR (= General Accounting Office) = Tribunal m de Contas da União
gaol [dʒeɪl] (Brit) N, VT = jail
gap [gæp] N brecha, fenda; (in trees, traffic) abertura; (in time) intervalo; (fig) lacuna; (difference): ~ (between) diferença (entre)
gape [geɪp] VI (person) estar or ficar boquiaberto; (hole) abrir-se
gaping ['geɪpɪŋ] ADJ (hole) muito aberto
garage ['gærɑ:ʒ] N garagem f; (for car repairs) oficina (mecânica)
garb [gɑ:b] N traje m
garbage ['gɑ:bɪdʒ] N (US) lixo; (inf: nonsense) disparates mpl; **the book/film is** ~ o livro/filme é uma droga; **garbage can** (US) N lata de lixo; **garbage disposal (unit)** N triturador m de lixo
garbled ['gɑ:bld] ADJ (account) deturpado, destorcido
garden ['gɑ:dn] N jardim m ■ VI jardinar; **gardens** NPL (public park) jardim público, parque m; **garden centre** N loja de jardinagem
gardener ['gɑ:dnər] N jardineiro(-a)
gardening ['gɑ:dnɪŋ] N jardinagem f
gargle ['gɑ:gl] VI gargarejar ■ N gargarejo
gargoyle ['gɑ:gɔɪl] N gárgula
garish ['gɛərɪʃ] ADJ vistoso, chamativo; (colour) berrante; (light) brilhante
garland ['gɑ:lənd] N guirlanda
garlic ['gɑ:lɪk] N alho
garment ['gɑ:mənt] N peça de roupa
garner ['gɑ:nər] VT acumular, amontoar
garnish ['gɑ:nɪʃ] VT adornar; (food) enfeitar
garret ['gærət] N mansarda
garrison ['gærɪsn] N guarnição f ■ VT guarnecer
garrulous ['gærjuləs] ADJ tagarela
garter ['gɑ:tər] N liga; **garter belt** (US) N cinta-liga
gas [gæs] N gás m; (US: gasoline) gasolina ■ VT asfixiar com gás; (Mil) gasear; **gas cooker** (Brit) N fogão m a gás; **gas cylinder** N bujão m de gás
gaseous ['gæsɪəs] ADJ gasoso
gas fire (Brit) N aquecedor m a gás
gash [gæʃ] N talho; (tear) corte m ■ VT talhar; cortar
gasket ['gæskɪt] N (Aut) junta, gaxeta
gas mask N máscara antigás
gas meter N medidor m de gás
gasoline ['gæsəli:n] (US) N gasolina
gasp [gɑ:sp] N arfada ■ VI arfar
▶ **gasp out** VT (say) dizer com voz entrecortada
gas ring N boca de gás
gas station (US) N posto de gasolina
gas stove N (cooker) fogão m a gás; (heater) aquecedor m a gás

gassy ['gæsɪ] ADJ gasoso
gas tank (US) N (Aut) tanque m de gasolina
gas tap N torneira do gás
gastric ['gæstrɪk] ADJ gástrico; **gastric ulcer** N úlcera gástrica
gastroenteritis ['gæstrəuɛntə'raɪtɪs] N gastrenterite f
gastronomy [gæs'trɔnəmɪ] N gastronomia
gasworks ['gæswə:ks] N, NPL usina de gás, gasômetro
gate [geɪt] N portão m; (Rail) barreira; (of town, castle) porta; (at airport) portão m; (of lock) comporta
gateau ['gætəu] (pl -x) N bolo com creme e frutas
gateaux ['gætəuz] NPL of **gateau**
gate-crash ['geɪtkræʃ] (Brit) VT entrar de penetra em
gateway ['geɪtweɪ] N portão m, passagem f
gather ['gæðər] VT (flowers, fruit) colher; (assemble) reunir; (pick up) colher; (Sewing) franzir; (understand) compreender ■ VI (assemble) reunir-se; (dust, clouds) acumular-se; **to ~ (from/that)** concluir or depreender (de/que); **as far as I can** ~ ao que eu entendo; **to ~ speed** acelerar(-se)
gathering ['gæðərɪŋ] N reunião f, assembléia
GATT [gæt] N (= General Agreement on Tariffs and Trade) GATT m
gauche [gəuʃ] ADJ desajeitado
gaudy ['gɔ:dɪ] ADJ chamativo; (pej) cafona
gauge [geɪdʒ] N (instrument) medidor m; (measure, fig) medida; (Rail) bitola ■ VT medir; (fig: sb's capabilities, character) avaliar; **to ~ the right moment** calcular o momento azado; **petrol** (Brit) or **gas** (US) ~ medidor de gasolina
gaunt [gɔ:nt] ADJ descarnado; (bare, stark) desolado
gauntlet ['gɔ:ntlɪt] N luva; (fig): **to run the** ~ expôr-se (à crítica); **to throw down the** ~ lançar um desafio
gauze [gɔ:z] N gaze f
gave [geɪv] PT of **give**
gawky ['gɔ:kɪ] ADJ desengonçado
gawp [gɔ:p] VI: **to ~ at** olhar boquiaberto para
gay [geɪ] ADJ (homosexual) gay; (old-fashioned: cheerful) alegre; (colour) vistoso; (music) vivo
gaze [geɪz] N olhar m fixo ■ VI: **to ~ at sth** fitar algo
gazelle [gə'zɛl] N gazela
gazette [gə'zɛt] N (newspaper) jornal m; (official publication) boletim m oficial
gazetteer [gæzə'tɪər] N dicionário geográfico
GB ABBR = **Great Britain**
GBH (Brit: inf) N ABBR (Law) = **grievous bodily harm**
GC (Brit) N ABBR (= George Cross) distinção militar
GCE (Brit) N ABBR = **General Certificate of Education**
GCHQ (Brit) N ABBR (= Government Communications Headquarters) centro de intercepção de radiotransmissões estrangeiras
GCSE (Brit) N ABBR = **General Certificate of**

Secondary Education

GDP N ABBR = **gross domestic product**

GDR N ABBR (= *German Democratic Republic*) RDA f

gear [gɪəʳ] N equipamento; (*Tech*) engrenagem f; (*Aut*) velocidade f, marcha (BR), mudança (PT) ■ VT (*fig: adapt*): **to ~ sth to** preparar algo para; **our service is ~ed to meet the needs of the disabled** o nosso serviço está adequado às necessidades dos deficientes físicos; **top** (*Brit*) or **high** (*US*)/**low ~** quarta/primeira (marcha); **in ~** engrenado; **out of ~** desengrenado

▶ **gear up** VI: **to ~ up to do** preparar-se para fazer

gearbox ['gɪəbɔks] N caixa de mudança (BR) or velocidades (PT)

gear lever (*US* **gear shift**) N alavanca de mudança (BR) or mudanças (PT)

GED (*US*) N ABBR (*Sch*) = **general educational development**

geese [giːs] NPL of **goose**

Geiger counter ['gaɪgə-] N contador m Geiger

gel [dʒɛl] N gel m

gelatin(e) ['dʒɛlətiːn] N gelatina

gelignite ['dʒɛlɪgnaɪt] N gelignite f

gem [dʒɛm] N jóia, gema

Gemini ['dʒɛmɪnaɪ] N Gêminis m, Gêmeos mpl

gen [dʒɛn] (*Brit: inf*) N: **to give sb the ~ on sth** pôr alguém a par de algo

Gen. ABBR (*Mil*: = *general*) Gen.

gen. ABBR = **general**; (= *generally*) ger.

gender ['dʒɛndəʳ] N gênero

gene [dʒiːn] N (*Bio*) gene m

genealogy [dʒiːnɪˈælədʒɪ] N genealogia

general ['dʒɛnərl] N general m ■ ADJ geral; **in ~** em geral; **the ~ public** o grande público; **~ audit** (*Comm*) exame m geral de auditoria; **general anaesthetic** (*US* **general anesthetic**) N anestesia geral; **general delivery** (*US*) N posta-restante f; **general election** N eleições fpl gerais

generalization [dʒɛnrəlaɪˈzeɪʃən] N generalização f

generalize ['dʒɛnrəlaɪz] VI generalizar

generally ['dʒɛnrəlɪ] ADV geralmente

general manager N diretor(a) m/f geral

general practitioner N clínico(-a) geral

general strike N greve f geral

generate ['dʒɛnəreɪt] VT gerar; (*fig*) produzir

generation [dʒɛnəˈreɪʃən] N geração f

generator ['dʒɛnəreɪtəʳ] N gerador m

generic [dʒəˈnɛrɪk] ADJ genérico

generosity [dʒɛnəˈrɔsɪtɪ] N generosidade f

generous ['dʒɛnərəs] ADJ generoso; (*measure etc*) abundante

genesis ['dʒɛnəsɪs] N gênese f

genetic [dʒəˈnɛtɪk] ADJ genético; **~ engineering** engenharia genética

genetics [dʒɪˈnɛtɪks] N genética

Geneva [dʒɪˈniːvə] N Genebra

genial ['dʒiːnɪəl] ADJ cordial, simpático

genitals ['dʒɛnɪtlz] NPL órgãos mpl genitais

genitive ['dʒɛnətɪv] N genitivo

genius ['dʒiːnɪəs] N gênio

genocide ['dʒɛnəʊsaɪd] N genocídio

gent [dʒɛnt] N ABBR = **gentleman**

genteel [dʒɛnˈtiːl] ADJ fino

gentle ['dʒɛntl] ADJ (*sweet*) amável, doce; (*touch, breeze*) leve, suave; (*landscape*) suave; (*animal*) manso

gentleman ['dʒɛntlmən] (*irreg*) N senhor m; (*referring to social position*) fidalgo; (*well-bred man*) cavalheiro; **~'s agreement** acordo de cavalheiros

gentlemanly ['dʒɛntlmənlɪ] ADJ cavalheiresco

gentlemen ['dʒɛntlmen] NPL of **gentleman**

gentleness ['dʒɛntlnɪs] N doçura, meiguice f; (*of touch*) suavidade f; (*of animal*) mansidão f

gently ['dʒɛntlɪ] ADV suavemente

gentry ['dʒɛntrɪ] N pequena nobreza

gents [dʒɛnts] N banheiro de homens (BR), casa de banho dos homens (PT)

genuine ['dʒɛnjuɪn] ADJ autêntico; (*person*) sincero

genuinely ['dʒɛnjuɪnlɪ] ADJ sinceramente, realmente

geographer [dʒɪˈɔgrəfəʳ] N geógrafo(-a)

geographic(al) [dʒɪəˈgræfɪk(l)] ADJ geográfico

geography [dʒɪˈɔgrəfɪ] N geografia

geological [dʒɪəˈlɔdʒɪkl] ADJ geológico

geologist [dʒɪˈɔlədʒɪst] N geólogo(-a)

geology [dʒɪˈɔlədʒɪ] N geologia

geometric(al) [dʒɪəˈmɛtrɪk(l)] ADJ geométrico

geometry [dʒɪˈɔmətrɪ] N geometria

Geordie ['dʒɔːdɪ] (*Brit: inf*) N natural m/f da cidade de Newcastle-upon-Tyne

geranium [dʒɪˈreɪnjəm] N gerânio

geriatric [dʒɛrɪˈætrɪk] ADJ geriátrico

germ [dʒəːm] N micróbio, bacilo; (*Bio, fig*) germe m

German ['dʒəːmən] ADJ alemão(-mã) ■ N alemão(-mã) m/f; (*Ling*) alemão m; **German measles** N rubéola

Germany ['dʒəːmənɪ] N Alemanha

germination [dʒəːmɪˈneɪʃən] N germinação f

germ warfare N guerra bacteriológica

gerrymandering ['dʒɛrɪmændərɪŋ] N *reorganização dos distritos eleitorais para garantir a vitória do próprio partido*

gestation [dʒɛsˈteɪʃən] N gestação f

gesticulate [dʒɛsˈtɪkjuleɪt] VI gesticular

gesture ['dʒɛstjəʳ] N gesto; **as a ~ of friendship** em sinal de amizade

○ KEYWORD

get [gɛt] (*pt, pp* **got**, *pp* **gotten**) (*US*) VI **1** (*become, be*): **to get old/tired/cold** envelhecer/cansar-se/resfriar-se; **to get annoyed/bored** aborrecer-se/amuar-se; **to get drunk** embebedar-se; **to get dirty** sujar-se; **to get killed/married** ser morto/casar-se; **when do I get paid?** quando eu recebo?, quando eu vou ser pago?; **it's getting late** está ficando tarde

2 (*go*): **to get to/from** ir para/de; **to get home** chegar em casa
3 (*begin*) começar a; **to get to know sb** começar a conhecer alguém; **let's get going** or **started** vamos lá!
■ MODAL AUX VB: **you've got to do it** você tem que fazê-lo
■ VT **1**: **to get sth done** (*do*) fazer algo; (*have done*) mandar fazer algo; **to get the washing/dishes done** lavar roupa/a louça; **to get one's hair cut** cortar o cabelo; **to get the car going** or **to go** fazer o carro andar; **to get sb to do sth** convencer alguém a fazer algo; **to get sth/sb ready** preparar algo/arrumar alguém; **to get sb drunk/into trouble** embebedar alguém/meter alguém em confusão
2 (*obtain: money, permission, results*) ter; (*find: job, flat*) achar; (*fetch: person, doctor, object*) buscar; **to get sth for sb** arranjar algo para alguém; (*fetch*) ir buscar algo para alguém; **he got a job in London** ele arrumou um emprego em Londres; **get me Mr Harris, please** (*Tel*) pode chamar o Sr Harris, por favor; **can I get you a drink?** você está servido?
3 (*receive: present, letter*) receber; (*acquire: reputation, prize*) ganhar; **how much did you get for the painting?** quanto você recebeu pela pintura?
4 (*catch*) agarrar; (*hit: target etc*) pegar; **to get sb by the arm/throat** agarrar alguém pelo braço/pela garganta; **get him!** pega ele!; **the bullet got him in the leg** a bala pegou na perna dele
5 (*take, move*) levar; **to get sth to sb** levar algo para alguém; **I can't get it in/out/through** não consigo enfiá-lo/tirá-lo/passá-lo; **do you think we'll get it through the door?** você acha que conseguiremos passar isto na porta?; **we must get him to a hospital** temos que levá-lo para um hospital
6 (*plane, bus etc*) pegar, tomar; **where do I get the train to Birmingham?** onde eu pego o trem para Birmingham?
7 (*understand*) entender; (*hear*) ouvir; **I've got it** entendi; **I don't get your meaning** não entendo o que você quer dizer
8 (*have, possess*): **to have got** ter; **how many have you got?** quantos você tem?
▸ **get about** VI (*news*) espalhar-se
▸ **get along** VI (*agree*) entender-se; (*depart*) ir embora; (*manage*) = **get by**
▸ **get around** = **get round**
▸ **get at** VT FUS (*attack, criticize*) atacar; (*reach*) alcançar; **what are you getting at?** o que você está querendo dizer?
▸ **get away** VI (*leave*) partir; (*escape*) escapar
▸ **get away with** VT FUS conseguir fazer impunemente
▸ **get back** VI (*return*) regressar, voltar
■ VT receber de volta, recobrar
▸ **get by** VI (*pass*) passar; (*manage*) virar-se
▸ **get down** VI descer
■ VT (*object*) abaixar, descer; (*depress: person*)

deprimir
▸ **get down to** VT FUS (*work*) pôr-se a(fazer)
▸ **get in** VI entrar; (*train*) chegar; (*arrive home*) voltar para casa
▸ **get into** VT FUS entrar em; (*vehicle*) subir em; (*clothes*) pôr, vestir, enfiar; **to get into bed/a rage** meter-se na cama/ficar com raiva
▸ **get off** VI (*from train etc*) saltar (BR), descer (PT); (*depart: person, car*) sair; (*escape*) escapar
■ VT (*remove: clothes, stain*) tirar; (*send off*) mandar
■ VT FUS (*train, bus*) saltar de (BR), sair de (PT)
▸ **get on** VI (*at exam etc*): **how are you getting on?** como vai?; (*agree*): **to get on (with)** entender-se(com)
■ VT FUS (*train etc*) subir em (BR), subir para (PT); (*horse*) montar em
▸ **get out** VI (*of place, vehicle*) sair
■ VT (*take out*) tirar
▸ **get out of** VT FUS (*duty etc*) escapar de
▸ **get over** VT FUS (*illness*) restabelecer-se de
▸ **get round** VT FUS rodear; (*fig: person*) convencer
▸ **get through** VI (*Tel*) completar a ligação
▸ **get through to** VT FUS (*Tel*) comunicar se com
▸ **get together** VI (*people*) reunir-se
■ VT reunir
▸ **get up** VI levantar-se
■ VT FUS levantar
▸ **get up to** VT FUS (*reach*) chegar a; (*Brit: prank etc*) fazer

getaway ['gɛtəweɪ] N fuga, escape *m*; **getaway car** N carro de fuga
get-together N reunião *f*
get-up (*inf*) N (*outfit*) roupa
get-well card N cartão *m* com votos de melhoras
geyser ['giːzəʳ] N (*Geo*) gêiser *m*; (*Brit*) aquecedor *m* de água
Ghana ['gɑːnə] N Gana (*no article*)
Ghanaian [gɑːˈneɪən] ADJ, N ganense *m/f*
ghastly ['gɑːstlɪ] ADJ horrível; (*building*) medonho; (*appearance*) horripilante; (*pale*) pálido
gherkin ['gɜːkɪn] N pepino em vinagre
ghetto ['gɛtəu] N gueto
ghost [gəust] N fantasma *m* ■ VT (*sb else's book*) escrever
ghostly ['gəustlɪ] ADJ fantasmal
ghostwriter ['gəustraɪtəʳ] N escritor(a) *m/f* cujos trabalhos são assinados por outrem
ghoul [guːl] N assombração *f*
ghoulish ['guːlɪʃ] ADJ (*tastes etc*) macabro
GHQ N ABBR (*Mil*) = **general headquarters**
GI (*US: inf*) N ABBR (= *government issue*) soldado do exército americano
giant ['dʒaɪənt] N gigante *m* ■ ADJ gigantesco, gigante; ~ **(size) packet** pacote tamanho gigante
gibber ['dʒɪbəʳ] VI algraviar
gibberish ['dʒɪbərɪʃ] N algaravia

gibe [dʒaɪb] N deboche *m* ■ VI: **to ~ at** debochar de

giblets ['dʒɪblɪts] NPL miúdos *mpl*

Gibraltar [dʒɪ'brɔːltəʳ] N Gibraltar *m (no article)*

giddiness ['gɪdɪnɪs] N vertigem *f*

giddy ['gɪdɪ] ADJ *(dizzy)* tonto; *(speed)* vertiginoso; *(frivolous)* frívolo; **it makes me ~ me dá vertigem; to be** *or* **feel ~** estar com vertigem

gift [gɪft] N presente *m*, dádiva; *(offering)* oferta; *(ability)* dom *m*, talento; *(Comm: also:* **free gift)** brinde *m*; **to have a ~ for sth** ter o dom de algo, ter facilidade para algo

gifted ['gɪftɪd] ADJ bem-dotado

gift token N vale *m* para presente

gift voucher N = gift token

gig [gɪg] *(inf)* N *(of musician)* show *m*

gigantic [dʒaɪ'gæntɪk] ADJ gigantesco

giggle ['gɪgl] VI dar risadinha boba ■ N risadinha boba

GIGO ['gaɪgəʊ] *(inf)* ABBR *(Comput: = garbage in, garbage out)* qualidade de entrada, qualidade de saída

gild [gɪld] VT dourar

gill [dʒɪl] N *(measure)* = 0.25 pints *(BRIT* = 0.148l, *US* = 0.118l)*

gills [gɪlz] NPL *(of fish)* guelras *fpl*, brânquias *fpl*

gilt [gɪlt] ADJ dourado ■ N dourado

gilt-edged [-'ɛdʒd] ADJ *(stocks, securities)* do Estado, de toda confiança

gimlet ['gɪmlɪt] N verruma

gimmick ['gɪmɪk] N truque *m or* macete *m* (publicitário)

gin [dʒɪn] N gim *m*, genebra

ginger ['dʒɪndʒəʳ] N gengibre *m*
   ▶ **ginger up** VT animar

ginger ale N cerveja de gengibre

ginger beer N cerveja de gengibre

gingerbread ['dʒɪndʒəbrɛd] N *(cake)* pão *m* de gengibre; *(biscuit)* biscoito de gengibre

ginger-haired ADJ ruivo

gingerly ['dʒɪndʒəlɪ] ADV cuidadosamente

gingham ['gɪŋəm] N riscadinho

gipsy ['dʒɪpsɪ] N cigano ■ CPD *(caravan, camp)* de ciganos

giraffe [dʒɪ'rɑːf] N girafa

girder ['gəːdəʳ] N viga, trave *f*

girdle ['gəːdl] N *(corset)* cinta ■ VT cintar

girl [gəːl] N *(small)* menina (BR), rapariga (PT); *(young woman)* jovem *f*, moça; *(daughter)* filha; **an English ~** uma moça inglesa

girlfriend ['gəːlfrɛnd] N *(of girl)* amiga; *(of boy)* namorada

girlish ['gəːlɪʃ] ADJ ameninado, de menina

Girl Scout *(US)* N escoteira

Giro ['dʒaɪrəʊ] N: **the National ~** *(Brit)* serviço bancário do correio

giro ['dʒaɪrəʊ] N *(bank giro)* transferência bancária; *(post office giro)* transferência postal; *(Brit: welfare cheque)* cheque do governo destinado a desempregados

girth [gəːθ] N circunferência; *(stoutness)* gordura;

(of horse) cilha

gist [dʒɪst] N essencial *m*

 KEYWORD

give [gɪv] *(pt* **gave**, *pp* **given)** VT **1** *(hand over)* dar; **to give sb sth, give sth to sb** dar algo a alguém; **give it to him, give him it** dê isso a ele/dê-lhe isso; **I'll give you £5 for it** dou-lhe £5 por isso
  2 *(used with n to replace a vb)*: **to give a cry/sigh/ push** *etc* dar um grito/suspiro/empurrão *etc*; **to give a groan/shrug/shout** dar um gemido/de ombros/um grito; **to give a speech/a lecture** fazer um discurso/uma palestra; **to give three cheers** dar três vivas
  3 *(tell, deliver: news, advice, message etc)* dar; **did you give him the message/the news?** você deu a mensagem/notícia a ele?; **to give the right/wrong answer** dar a resposta certa/ errada
  4 *(supply, provide: opportunity, surprise, job etc)* dar; *(bestow: title, honour, right)* conceder; **the sun gives warmth and light** o sol fornece calor e luz; **that's given me an idea** isso me deu uma idéia
  5 *(dedicate: time, one's life/attention)* dedicar; **she gave it all her attention** ela dedicou toda sua atenção a isto
  6 *(organize)*: **to give a party/dinner** *etc* dar uma festa/jantar *etc*
  ■ VI **1** *(also:* **give way**: *break, collapse)* dar folga; **his legs gave beneath him** suas pernas bambearam; **the roof/floor gave as I stepped on it** o telhado/chão desabou quando eu pisei nele
  2 *(stretch: fabric)* dar de si
  ▶ **give away** VT *(money, opportunity)* dar; *(secret, information)* revelar
  ▶ **give back** VT devolver
  ▶ **give in** VI *(yield)* ceder
  ■ VT *(essay etc)* entregar
  ▶ **give off** VT *(heat, smoke)* soltar
  ▶ **give out** VT *(distribute)* distribuir; *(make known)* divulgar
  ▶ **give up** VI *(surrender)* desistir, dar-se por vencido
  ■ VT *(job, boyfriend, habit)* renunciar a; *(idea, hope)* abandonar; **to give up smoking** deixar de fumar; **to give o.s. up** entregar-se
  ▶ **give way** VI *(yield)* ceder; *(break, collapse: rope)* arrebentar; *(: ladder)* quebrar; *(Brit: Aut)* dar a preferência (BR), dar prioridade (PT)

give-and-take N toma-lá-dá-cá *m*

giveaway ['gɪvəweɪ] CPD: **~ prices** preços de liquidação ■ N *(inf)*: **her expression was a ~** a expressão dela a atraiçoava; **the exam was a ~!** o exame foi sopa!

given ['gɪvn] PP *of* **give** ■ ADJ *(fixed: time, amount)* dado, determinado ■ CONJ: **~ the circumstances** ... dadas as circunstâncias ...; **~**

that ... dado que ..., já que ...

glacial ['gleɪsɪəl] ADJ (Geo) glaciário; (wind, weather) glacial

glacier ['glæsɪər] N glaciar m, geleira

glad [glæd] ADJ contente; **to be ~ about sth/ that** estar contente com algo/contente que; **I was ~ of his help** eu lhe agradeci (por) sua ajuda

gladden ['glædən] VT alegrar

glade [gleɪd] N clareira

gladioli [glædɪ'əʊlaɪ] NPL gladíolos mpl

gladly ['glædlɪ] ADV com muito prazer

glamorous ['glæmərəs] ADJ encantador(a), glamoroso

glamour ['glæmər] N encanto, glamour m

glance [glɑːns] N relance m, vista de olhos ▪ VI: **to ~ at** olhar (de relance)
  ▶ **glance off** VT FUS (bullet) ricochetear de

glancing ['glɑːnsɪŋ] ADJ (blow) oblíquo

gland [glænd] N glândula

glandular fever ['glændjulər-] (Brit) ADJ mononucleose f infecciosa

glare [glɛər] N (of anger) olhar m furioso; (of light) luminosidade f; (of publicity) foco ▪ VI brilhar; **to ~ at** olhar furiosamente para

glaring ['glɛərɪŋ] ADJ (mistake) notório

glass [glɑːs] N vidro, cristal m; (for drinking) copo; (: with stem) cálice m; (also: **looking glass**) espelho; **glasses** NPL (spectacles) óculos mpl

glass-blowing [-bləʊɪŋ] N modelagem f de vidro a quente

glass fibre N fibra de vidro

glasshouse ['glɑːshaus] N estufa

glassware ['glɑːswɛər] N objetos mpl de cristal

glassy ['glɑːsɪ] ADJ (eyes) vidrado

Glaswegian [glæs'wiːdʒən] ADJ de Glasgow ▪ N natural m/f de Glasgow

glaze [gleɪz] VT (door) envidraçar; (pottery) vitrificar; (Culin) glaçar ▪ N verniz m; (Culin) glacê m

glazed [gleɪzd] ADJ (eye) vidrado; (pottery) vitrificado

glazier ['gleɪzɪər] N vidraceiro(-a)

gleam [gliːm] N brilho ▪ VI brilhar; **a ~ of hope** um fio de esperança

gleaming ['gliːmɪŋ] ADJ brilhante

glean [gliːn] VT (information) colher

glee [gliː] N alegria, regozijo

gleeful ['gliːful] ADJ alegre

glen [glɛn] N vale m

glib [glɪb] ADJ (answer) pronto; (person) labioso

glide [glaɪd] VI deslizar; (Aviat, birds) planar ▪ N deslizamento; (Aviat) vôo planado

glider ['glaɪdər] N (Aviat) planador m

gliding ['glaɪdɪŋ] N (Aviat) vôo sem motor

glimmer ['glɪmər] N luz f trêmula; (of interest, hope) lampejo ▪ VI tremeluzir

glimpse [glɪmps] N vista rápida, vislumbre m ▪ VT vislumbrar, ver de relance; **to catch a ~ of** vislumbrar

glint [glɪnt] N brilho; (in the eye) cintilação f ▪ VI cintilar

glisten ['glɪsn] VI brilhar

glitter ['glɪtər] VI reluzir, brilhar ▪ N brilho

glitz [glɪts] (inf) N cafonice f

gloat [gləut] VI: **to ~ (over)** exultar (com)

global ['gləubl] ADJ (worldwide) mundial; (overall) global

globalization ['gləubəlaɪzeɪʃən] N globalização f

global warming ADJ aquecimento global

globe [gləub] N globo, esfera

globetrotter ['gləubtrɔtər] N pessoa que corre mundo

globule ['glɔbjuːl] N glóbulo

gloom [gluːm] N escuridão f; (sadness) tristeza

gloomy ['gluːmɪ] ADJ (dark) escuro; (sad) triste; (pessimistic) pessimista; **to feel ~** estar abatido

glorification [glɔːrɪfɪ'keɪʃən] N glorificação f

glorify ['glɔːrɪfaɪ] VT glorificar; (praise) adorar

glorious ['glɔːrɪəs] ADJ (weather) magnífico; (future) glorioso; (splendid) excelente

glory ['glɔːrɪ] N glória ▪ VI: **to ~ in** gloriar-se de; **glory hole** (inf) N zona

Glos (Brit) ABBR = **Gloucestershire**

gloss [glɔs] N (shine) brilho; (also: **gloss paint**) pintura brilhante, esmalte m
  ▶ **gloss over** VT FUS encobrir

glossary ['glɔsərɪ] N glossário

glossy ['glɔsɪ] ADJ lustroso ▪ N (also: **glossy magazine**) revista de luxo

glove [glʌv] N luva; **glove compartment** N (Aut) porta-luvas m inv

glow [gləu] VI (shine) brilhar; (fire) arder ▪ N brilho

glower ['glauər] VI: **to ~ at (sb)** olhar (alguém) de modo ameaçador

glowing ['gləuɪŋ] ADJ (fire) ardente; (complexion) afogueado; (report, description etc) entusiástico

glow-worm N pirilampo, vaga-lume m

glucose ['gluːkəus] N glicose f

glue [gluː] N cola ▪ VT colar

glue-sniffing [-snɪfɪŋ] N cheira-cola m

glum [glʌm] ADJ (mood) abatido; (person, tone) triste

glut [glʌt] N abundância, fartura ▪ VT (market) saturar

glutinous ['gluːtɪnəs] ADJ glutinoso

glutton ['glʌtn] N glutão(-ona) m/f; **a ~ for work/punishment** um(a) trabalhador(a) incansável/um(a) masoquista

gluttonous ['glʌtənəs] ADJ glutão(-ona)

gluttony ['glʌtənɪ] N gula

glycerin(e) ['glɪsəriːn] N glicerina

GM ADJ ABBR (= genetically modified) geneticamente modificado

gm ABBR (= gram) g

GMAT (US) N ABBR (= Graduate Management Admissions Test) exame de admissão aos cursos de pós-graduação

GMB (Brit) N ABBR (= General Municipal Boilermakers and Allied Trade Union) sindicato dos empregados dos municípios

GMT ABBR (= Greenwich Mean Time) GMT m

gnarled [nɑ:ld] ADJ (*tree*) nodoso; (*tree*) retorcido

gnash [næʃ] VT: **to ~ one's teeth** ranger os dentes

gnat [næt] N mosquito

gnaw [nɔ:] VT roer

gnome [nəum] N gnomo

GNP N ABBR = **gross national product**

 KEYWORD

go [gəu] (*pt* **went**, *pp* **gone**, *pl* **goes**) VI **1** ir; (*travel, move*) viajar; **a car went by** um carro passou; **he has gone to Aberdeen** ele foi para Aberdeen

2 (*depart*) partir, ir-se; **"I must go,"** she said "preciso ir" ela disse; **our plane went at 6pm** nosso avião partiu às 6 da tarde; **they came at 8 and went at 9** eles chegaram às 8 e foram às 9

3 (*attend*) ir; **she went to university in Rio** ela fez universidade no Rio; **she goes to her dancing class on Tuesdays** ela vai a aula de dança às terças-feiras; **he goes to the local church** ele freqüenta a igreja local

4 (*take part in an activity*) ir; **to go for a walk** ir passear

5 (*work*) funcionar; **the clock stopped going** o relógio parou de funcionar; **the bell went just then** a campainha acabou de tocar

6 (*become*): **to go pale/mouldy** ficar pálido/mofado

7 (*be sold*): **to go for £10** ser vendido por £10

8 (*fit, suit*): **to go with** acompanhar, combinar com

9 (*be about to, intend to*): **he's going to do it** ele vai fazê-lo; **we're going to leave in an hour** vamos partir dentro de uma hora; **are you going to come?** você vem?

10 (*time*) passar

11 (*event, activity*) ser; **how did it go?** como foi?

12 (*be given*) ir (ser dado); **the job is to go to someone else** o emprego vai ser dado para outra pessoa

13 (*break*) romper-se; **the fuse went** o fusível queimou; **the leg of the chair went** a perna da cadeira quebrou

14 (*be placed*): **where does this cup go?** onde é que põe esta xícara?; **the milk goes in the fridge** pode guardar o leite na geladeira

■ N **1** (*try*): **to have a go (at)** tentar

2 (*turn*) vez *f*; **whose go is it?** de quem é a vez?

3 (*move*): **to be on the go** ter muito para fazer

▶ **go about** VI (*also:* **go around:** *rumour*) espalhar-se

■ VT FUS: **how do I go about this?** como é que eu faço isto?

▶ **go ahead** VI (*make progress*) progredir; (*get going*) ir em frente

▶ **go along** VI ir

■ VT FUS ladear; **to go along with** (*agree with:* *plan, idea, policy*) concordar com

▶ **go away** VI (*leave*) ir-se, ir embora

▶ **go back** VI (*return*) voltar; (*go again*) ir de novo

▶ **go back on** VT FUS (*promise*) faltar com

▶ **go by** VI (*years, time*) passar

■ VT FUS (*book, rule*) guiar-se por

▶ **go down** VI (*descend*) descer, baixar; (*ship*) afundar; (*sun*) pôr-se

■ VT FUS (*stairs, ladder*) descer

▶ **go for** VT FUS (*fetch*) ir buscar; (*like*) gostar de; (*attack*) atacar

▶ **go in** VI (*enter*) entrar

▶ **go in for** VT FUS (*competition*) inscrever-se em; (*like*) gostar de

▶ **go into** VT FUS (*enter*) entrar em; (*investigate*) investigar; (*embark on*) embarcar em

▶ **go off** VI (*leave*) ir-se; (*food*) estragar, apodrecer; (*bomb, gun*) explodir; (*event*) realizar-se

■ VT FUS (*person, place, food etc*) deixar de gostar de

▶ **go on** VI (*continue*) seguir, continuar; (*happen*) acontecer, ocorrer; **to go on doing sth** continuar fazendo or a fazer algo

▶ **go out** VI (*leave: room, building*) sair; (*for entertainment*): **are you going out tonight?** você vai sair hoje à noite?; (*couple*): **they went out for 3 years** eles namoraram 3 anos; (*fire, light*) apagar-se

▶ **go over** VI (*ship*) soçobrar

■ VT FUS (*check*) revisar

▶ **go round** VI (*news, rumour*) circular

▶ **go through** VT FUS (*town etc*) atravessar; (*search through: files, papers*) vasculhar; (*examine: list, book, story*) percorrer de cabo a rabo

▶ **go up** VI (*ascend*) subir; (*price, level*) aumentar

▶ **go without** VT FUS (*food, treats*) passar sem

goad [gəud] VT aguilhoar

go-ahead ADJ empreendedor(a) ■ N luz *f* verde

goal [gəul] N meta, alvo; (*Sport*) gol *m* (BR), golo (PT)

goalkeeper ['gəulki:pəʳ] N goleiro(-a) (BR), guarda-redes *m/f inv* (PT)

goalpost ['gəulpəust] N trave *f*

goat [gəut] N cabra; (*also:* **billy goat**) bode *m*

gobble ['gɔbl] VT (*also:* **gobble down, gobble up**) engolir rapidamente, devorar

go-between N intermediário(-a)

Gobi Desert ['gəubɪ-] N Deserto de Gobi

goblet ['gɔblɪt] N cálice *m*

goblin ['gɔblɪn] N duende *m*

go-cart N kart *m* ■ CPD: **~ racing** kartismo

god [gɔd] N deus *m*; **G~** Deus

godchild ['gɔdtʃaɪld] (*irreg*) N afilhado(-a)

goddaughter ['gɔdɔ:təʳ] N afilhada

goddess ['gɔdɪs] N deusa

godfather ['gɔdfɑ:ðəʳ] N padrinho

god-forsaken [-fə'seɪkən] ADJ miserável, abandonado

godmother ['gɔdmʌðəʳ] N madrinha

godparents ['gɔdpɛərənts] NPL padrinhos *mpl*

godsend ['gɔdsɛnd] N dádiva do céu

godson ['gɔdsʌn] N afilhado

goes [gəuz] VB see **go**

go-getter [-'gɛtər] N pessoa dinâmica, pessoa furona (inf)

goggle ['gɔgl] VI: **to ~ at** olhar de olhos esbugalhados

goggles ['gɔglz] NPL óculos mpl de proteção

going ['gəuɪŋ] N (conditions) estado do terreno
■ ADJ: **the ~ rate** tarifa corrente or em vigor;
~ concern empresa em funcionamento, empresa com fundo de comérico; **it was slow ~ ia devagar**

goings-on (inf) NPL maquinações fpl

go-kart [-kɑːt] N = **go-cart**

gold [gəuld] N ouro ■ ADJ de ouro

golden ['gəuldən] ADJ (made of gold) de ouro; (gold in colour) dourado; **golden age** N idade f de ouro; **golden handshake** (Brit) N bolada; **golden rule** N regra de ouro

goldfish ['gəuldfɪʃ] N INV peixe-dourado m

gold leaf N ouro em folha

gold medal N (Sport) medalha de ouro

gold mine N mina de ouro

gold-plated [-'plɛitɪd] ADJ plaquê inv

gold-rush N corrida do ouro

goldsmith ['gəuldsmɪθ] N ourives m/f inv

gold standard N padrão-ouro m

golf [gɔlf] N golfe m; **golf ball** N bola de golfe; (on typewriter) esfera; **golf club** N clube m de golfe; (stick) taco; **golf course** N campo de golfe

golfer ['gɔlfər] N jogador(a) m/f de golfe, golfista m/f

gondola ['gɔndələ] N gôndola

gondolier [gɔndə'lɪər] N gondoleiro

gone [gɔn] PP of **go**

gong [gɔŋ] N gongo

good [gud] ADJ bom/boa; (kind) bom, bondoso; (well-behaved) educado; (useful) útil ■ N bem m; **goods** NPL (possessions) bens mpl; (Comm) mercadorias fpl; **~s and chattels** bens móveis; **~! bom!**; **to be ~ at** ser bom em; **to be ~ for** servir para; **it's ~ for you** faz-lhe bem; **would you be ~ enough to ...?** podia fazer-me o favor de ...?, poderia me fazer a gentileza de ...?; **it's a ~ thing you were there** ainda bem que você estava lá; **she is ~ with children/her hands** ela tem habilidade com crianças/com as mãos; **to feel ~** sentir-se bem, estar bom; **it's ~ to see you** é bom ver você; (formal) prazer em vê-lo; **he's up to no ~** ele tem más intenções; **for the common ~** para o bem comum; **that's very ~ of you** é muita bondade sua; **is this any ~?** (will it do?) será que isso serve?; (what's it like?) será que vale a pena?; **a ~ deal (of)** muito; **a ~ many** muitos; **to make ~** reparar; **it's no ~ complaining** não adianta se queixar; **for ~** (forever) para sempre, definitivamente; (once and for all) de uma vez por todas; **~ morning/afternoon!** bom dia/boa tarde!; **~ evening!** boa noite!; **~ night!** boa noite!

goodbye [gud'baɪ] EXCL até logo (BR), adeus (PT); **to say ~** despedir-se

good faith N boa fé

good-for-nothing ADJ imprestável

Good Friday N Sexta-Feira Santa

good-humoured [-'hjuːməd] ADJ (person) alegre; (remark, joke) sem malícia

good-looking [-'lukɪŋ] ADJ bonito

good-natured ADJ (person) de bom gênio; (pet) de boa índole; (discussion) cordial

goodness ['gudnɪs] N (of person) bondade f; **for ~ sake!** pelo amor de Deus!; **~ gracious!** meu Deus do céu!, nossa (senhora)!

goods train (Brit) N trem m de carga

goodwill [gud'wɪl] N boa vontade f; (Comm) fundo de comércio, aviamento

goody-goody ['gudɪgudɪ] (pej) N puxa-saco m

goose [guːs] (pl **geese**) N ganso

gooseberry ['guzbərɪ] N groselha; **to play ~** (Brit) ficar de vela, segurar a vela

gooseflesh ['guːsflɛʃ] N = **goose pimples**

goose pimples NPL pele f arrepiada

goose step N (Mil) passo de ganso

GOP (US: inf) N ABBR (Pol: = Grand Old Party) partido republicano

gore [gɔːr] VT escornar ■ N sangue m

gorge [gɔːdʒ] N desfiladeiro ■ VT: **to ~ o.s. (on)** empanturrar-se (de)

gorgeous ['gɔːdʒəs] ADJ magnífico, maravilhoso; (person) lindo

gorilla [gə'rɪlə] N gorila m

gormless ['gɔːmlɪs] (Brit: inf) ADJ burro

gorse [gɔːs] N tojo

gory ['gɔːrɪ] ADJ sangrento

go-slow (Brit) N greve f de trabalho lento, operação f tartaruga

gospel ['gɔspl] N evangelho

gossamer ['gɔsəmər] N (cobweb) teia de aranha; (cloth) tecido diáfano, gaze f fina

gossip ['gɔsɪp] N (scandal) fofocas fpl (BR), mexericos mpl (PT); (chat) conversa; (scandalmonger) fofoqueiro(-a) (BR), mexeriqueiro(-a) (PT) ■ VI (spread scandal) fofocar (BR), mexericar (PT); (chat) bater (um) papo (BR), cavaquear (PT); **a piece of ~** uma fofoca (BR), um mexerico (PT); **gossip column** N (Press) coluna social

got [gɔt] PT, PP of **get**

Gothic ['gɔθɪk] ADJ gótico

gotten ['gɔtn] (US) PP of **get**

gouge [gaudʒ] VT (also: **gouge out**: hole etc) abrir; (: initials) talhar; **to ~ sb's eyes out** arrancar os olhos de alguém

gourd [guəd] N cabaça, cucúrbita

gourmet ['guəmeɪ] N gourmet m, gastrônomo(-a)

gout [gaut] N gota

govern ['gʌvən] VT governar; (event) controlar

governess ['gʌvənɪs] N governanta

governing ['gʌvənɪŋ] ADJ (Pol) no governo, ao poder; **~ body** conselho de administração

government ['gʌvnmənt] N governo ■ CPD

(of administration) governamental; (of state) do Estado; **local** ~ governo municipal

governmental [gʌvn'mɛntl] ADJ governamental

government housing (US) N casas fpl populares

government stock N títulos mpl do governo

governor ['gʌvənəʳ] N governador(a) m/f; (of school, hospital, jail) diretor(a) m/f

Govt ABBR = **government**

gown [gaun] N vestido; (of teacher, judge) toga

GP N ABBR (Med) = **general practitioner**

GPO N ABBR (Brit: old) = **General Post Office**; (US) = **Government Printing Office**

gr. ABBR (Comm) = **gross**

grab [græb] VT agarrar ▪ VI: **to** ~ **at** tentar agarrar

grace [greɪs] N (Rel) graça; (gracefulness) elegância, fineza ▪ VT (honour) honrar; (adorn) adornar; **5 days'** ~ um prazo de 5 dias; **to say** ~ dar graças (antes de comer); **with a good/bad** ~ de bom/mau grado; **his sense of humour is his saving** ~ seu único mérito é seu senso de humor

graceful ['greɪsful] ADJ elegante, gracioso

gracious ['greɪʃəs] ADJ gracioso, afável; (benevolent) bondoso, complacente; (formal: God) misericordioso ▪ EXCL: **(good)** ~! meu Deus do céu!, nossa (senhora)!

gradation [grə'deɪʃn] N gradação f

grade [greɪd] N (quality) classe f, qualidade f; (degree) grau m; (US: Sch) série f, classe; (: gradient) declive m ▪ VT classificar; **to make the** ~ (fig) ter sucesso; **grade crossing** (US) N passagem f de nível; **grade school** (US) N escola primária

gradient ['greɪdɪənt] N declive m; (Geom) gradiente m

gradual ['grædjuəl] ADJ gradual, gradativo

gradually ['grædjuəlɪ] ADV gradualmente, gradativamente, pouco a pouco

graduate [n 'grædjuɪt, vi 'grædjueɪt] N graduado, licenciado; (US) diplomado do colégio ▪ VI formar-se, licenciar-se

graduated pension ['grædjueɪtɪd-] N aposentadoria calculada em função dos últimos salários

graduation [grædju'eɪʃən] N formatura

graffiti [grə'fi:tɪ] N, NPL pichações fpl

graft [grɑ:ft] N (Agr, Med) enxerto; (Brit: inf) trabalho pesado; (bribery) suborno ▪ VT enxertar; **hard** ~ (inf) labuta

grain [greɪn] N grão m; (no pl: cereals) cereais mpl; (US: corn) trigo; (in wood) veio, fibra; **it goes against the** ~ é contra a sua (or minha etc) natureza

gram [græm] N grama m

grammar ['græməʳ] N gramática; **grammar school** N (Brit) = liceo

grammatical [grə'mætɪkl] ADJ gramatical

gramme [græm] N = **gram**

gramophone ['græməfəun] (Brit) N (old)

gramofone m

granary ['grænərɪ] N celeiro

grand [grænd] ADJ esplêndido; (inf: wonderful) ótemo, formidável ▪ N (inf: thousand) mil libras fpl (or dólares mpl)

grandchild ['græntʃaɪld] (irreg) N neto(-a)

granddad ['grændæd] N vovô m

granddaughter ['grændɔ:təʳ] N neta

grandeur ['grændjəʳ] N grandeza, magnificência; (of event) grandiosidade f; (of house, style) imponência

grandfather ['grænfɑ:ðəʳ] N avô m

grandiose ['grændɪəuz] ADJ grandioso; (pej) pomposo; (house, style) imponente

grand jury (US) N júri m de instrução

grandma ['grænmɑ:] N avó f, vovó f

grandmother ['grænmʌðəʳ] N avó f

grandpa ['grænpɑ:] N = **granddad**

grandparents ['grændpɛərənts] NPL avós mpl

grand piano N piano de cauda

Grand Prix ['grɑ̃:'pri:] N (Aut) Grande Prêmio

grandson ['grænsʌn] N neto

grandstand ['grænstænd] N (Sport) tribuna principal

grand total N total m geral or global

granite ['grænɪt] N granito

granny ['grænɪ] (inf) N avó f, vovó f

grant [grɑ:nt] VT (concede) conceder; (a request etc) anuir a; (admit) admitir ▪ N (Sch) bolsa; (Admin) subvenção f, subsídio; **to take sth for** ~**ed** dar algo por certo; **to** ~ **that** admitir que

granulated sugar ['grænjuleɪtɪd-] N açúcar m granulado

granule ['grænju:l] N grânulo

grape [greɪp] N uva; **sour** ~**s** (fig) inveja; **a bunch of** ~**s** um cacho de uvas

grapefruit ['greɪpfru:t] (pl inv or **grapefruits**) N toranja, grapefruit m (BR)

grapevine ['greɪpvaɪn] N parreira; **I heard it on** or **through the** ~ (fig) um passarinho me contou

graph [grɑ:f] N gráfico

graphic ['græ:fɪk] ADJ gráfico; **graphic designer** N desenhista m/f industrial

graphics ['græfɪks] N (art) artes fpl gráficas ▪ NPL (drawings) dessenhos mpl; (: Comput) gráficos mpl

graphite ['græfaɪt] N grafita

graph paper N papel m quadriculado

grapple ['græpl] VI: **to** ~ **with sth** estar às voltas com algo

grappling iron ['græplɪŋ-] N (Naut) arpéu m

grasp [grɑ:sp] VT agarrar, segurar; (understand) compreender, entender ▪ N (grip) agarramento; (reach) alcance m; (understanding) compreensão f; **to have sth within one's** ~ ter algo ao seu alcance; **to have a good** ~ **of sth** (fig) ter um bom domínio de algo, dominar algo

▸ **grasp at** VT FUS (rope etc) tentar agarrar; (opportunity) agarrar

grasping ['grɑ:spɪŋ] ADJ avaro

grass [grɑːs] N grama (BR), relva (PT); (*uncultivated*) cupim *m*; (*lawn*) gramado (BR), relvado (PT); (Brit: inf: *informer*) dedo-duro *m*

grasshopper ['grɑːʃɔpəʳ] N gafanhoto

grassland ['grɑːslænd] N pradaria

grass roots NPL (*fig*) raízes *fpl*, base *f* ▪ ADJ: **grass-roots** popular

grass snake N serpente *f*

grassy ['grɑːsɪ] ADJ coberto de grama (BR) *or* de relva (PT)

grate [greɪt] N (*fireplace*) lareira; (*of iron*) grelha ▪ VI ranger ▪ VT (*Culin*) ralar

grateful ['greɪtful] ADJ agradecido, grato

gratefully ['greɪtfəlɪ] ADV agradecidamente

grater ['greɪtəʳ] N ralador *m*

gratification [grætɪfɪ'keɪʃən] N satisfação *f*

gratify ['grætɪfaɪ] VT gratificar; (*whim*) satisfazer

gratifying ['grætɪfaɪɪŋ] ADJ gratificante

grating ['greɪtɪŋ] N (*iron bars*) grade *f* ▪ ADJ (*noise*) áspero

gratitude ['grætɪtjuːd] N agradecimento

gratuitous [grə'tjuːɪtəs] ADJ gratuito

gratuity [grə'tjuːɪtɪ] N gratificação *f*, gorjeta

grave [greɪv] N cova, sepultura ▪ ADJ sério; (*mistake*) grave; **grave digger** N coveiro

gravel ['grævl] N cascalho

gravely ['greɪvlɪ] ADV gravemente; ~ **ill** gravemente doente

gravestone ['greɪvstəun] N lápide *f*

graveyard ['greɪvjɑːd] N cemitério

gravitate ['grævɪteɪt] VI: **to ~ towards** ser atraído por

gravity ['grævɪtɪ] N (*Phys*) gravidade *f*; (*seriousness*) seriedade *f*, gravidade *f*

gravy ['greɪvɪ] N molho (de carne); **gravy boat** N molheira; **gravy train** (*inf*) N: **to be on** *or* **ride the gravy train** ter achado uma mina

gray [greɪ] (US) ADJ = **grey**

graze [greɪz] VI pastar ▪ VT (*touch lightly*) roçar; (*scrape*) raspar; (*Med*) esfolar ▪ N (*Med*) esfoladura, arranhadura

grazing ['greɪzɪŋ] N (*pasture*) pasto, pastagem *f*

grease [griːs] N (*fat*) gordura; (*lubricant*) graxa, lubrificante *m* ▪ VT (*Culin: dish*) untar; (*Tech: brakes etc*) lubrificar, engraxar; **grease gun** N bomba de graxa

greasepaint [griːspeɪnt] N maquilagem *f* (para o teatro)

greaseproof paper ['griːspruːf-] (*Brit*) N papel *m* de cera (vegetal)

greasy ['griːzɪ] ADJ gordurento, gorduroso; (*skin, hair*) oleoso; (*hands, clothes*) engordurado; (*Brit: road, surface*) escorregadio

great [greɪt] ADJ grande; (*inf*) genial; (*pain, heat*) forte; (*important*) importante; **they're ~ friends** eles são grandes amigos; **we had a ~ time** nos divertimos à beça; **it was ~!** foi ótimo, foi um barato (*inf*); **the ~ thing is that ...** o melhor é que ...

Great Barrier Reef N: **the ~** a Grande Barreira

Great Britain N Grã-Bretanha

▣ **GREAT BRITAIN**

▢ A Grã-Bretanha, *Great Britain* ou *Britain* em
▢ inglês, designa a maior das ilhas britânicas
▢ e, portanto, engloba a Escócia e o País de
▢ Gales. Junto com a Irlanda, a ilha de Man e
▢ as ilhas Anglo-normandas, a Grã-Bretanha
▢ forma as ilhas Britânicas, ou *British Isles*.
▢ Reino Unido, em inglês *United Kingdom* ou
▢ *UK*, é o nome oficial da entidade política que
▢ compreende a Grã-Bretanha e a Irlanda do
▢ Norte.

great-grandchild (*irreg*) N bisneto(-a)

great-grandfather N bisavô *m*

great-grandmother N bisavó *f*

Great Lakes NPL: **the ~** os Grandes Lagos

greatly ['greɪtlɪ] ADV imensamente, muito

greatness ['greɪtnɪs] N grandeza

Grecian ['griːʃən] ADJ grego

Greece [griːs] N Grécia

greed [griːd] N (*also*: **greediness**) avidez *f*, cobiça; (*for food*) gula

greedily ['griːdɪlɪ] ADV com avidez; (*eat*) gulosamente

greedy ['griːdɪ] ADJ avarento; (*for food*) guloso

Greek [griːk] ADJ grego ▪ N grego(-a); (*Ling*) grego; **ancient/modern ~** grego clássico/moderno

green [griːn] ADJ verde; (*inexperienced*) inexperiente, ingênuo ▪ N verde *m*; (*stretch of grass*) gramado (BR), relvado (PT); (*on golf course*) green *m*; (*also*: **village green**) ≈ praça; **greens** NPL (*vegetables*) verduras *fpl*; **to have ~ fingers** (*Brit*) or **a ~ thumb** (US) ter mão boa (para plantar); **green belt** N (*round town*) cinturão *m* verde; **green card** N (*Brit: Aut*) carta verde; (US) autorização *f* de residência

greenery ['griːnərɪ] N verdura

greenfly ['griːnflaɪ] (*Brit*) N pulgão *m*

greengage ['griːngeɪdʒ] N rainha-cláudia

greengrocer ['griːngrəusəʳ] (*Brit*) N verdureiro(-a)

greenhouse ['griːnhaus] N estufa

greenish ['griːnɪʃ] ADJ esverdeado

Greenland ['griːnlənd] N Groenlândia

Greenlander ['griːnləndəʳ] N groenlandês(-esa) *m/f*

green pepper N pimentão *m* verde

greet [griːt] VT saudar; (*welcome*) acolher; (*news*) receber

greeting ['griːtɪŋ] N cumprimento; (*welcome*) acolhimento; **Christmas/birthday ~s** votos de boas festas/feliz aniversário

greeting(s) card N cartão *m* comemorativo

gregarious [grə'gɛərɪəs] ADJ gregário

grenade [grə'neɪd] N (*also*: **hand grenade**) granada

grew [gruː] PT *of* **grow**

grey [greɪ] (US **gray**) ADJ cinzento; (*dismal*)

sombrio; **to go ~** (*hair, person*) ficar grisalho
grey-haired ADJ grisalho
greyhound ['greɪhaund] N galgo
grid [grɪd] N grade *f*; (*Elec*) rede *f*; (*US: Aut*) cruzamento
griddle [grɪdl] N (*on cooker*) chapa de assar
gridiron ['grɪdaɪən] N grelha; (*US: Football*) campo
grief [gri:f] N dor *f*, pesar *m*; **to come to ~** fracassar
grievance ['gri:vəns] N motivo de queixa, agravo
grieve [gri:v] VI sofrer ∎ VT dar pena a, afligir; **to ~ for** chorar por
grievous ['gri:vəs] ADJ penoso; **~ bodily harm** (*Law*) lesão *f* corporal (grave)
grill [grɪl] N (*on cooker*) grelha; (*also:* **mixed grill**) prato de grelhados ∎ VT (*Brit*) grelhar; (*question*) interrogar cerradamente
grille [grɪl] N grade *f*; (*Aut*) grelha
grill(room) ['grɪl(rum)] N grill-room *m*, ~ churrascaria
grim [grɪm] ADJ sinistro, lúgubre; (*unpleasant*) desagradável; (*unattractive*) feio; (*stern*) severo; (*inf: dreadful*) horrível
grimace [grɪ'meɪs] N careta ∎ VI fazer caretas
grime [graɪm] N sujeira (BR), sujidade *f* (PT)
grimy ['graɪmɪ] ADJ sujo, encardido
grin [grɪn] N sorriso largo ∎ VI sorrir abertamente; **to ~ (at)** dar um sorriso largo (para)
grind [graɪnd] (*pt, pp* **ground**) VT (*crush*) triturar; (*coffee, pepper etc*) moer; (*make sharp*) afiar; (*US: meat*) picar; (*polish: gem*) lapidar; (*: lens*) polir ∎ VI (*car gears*) ranger ∎ N (*work*) trabalho (repetitivo e maçante); **to ~ one's teeth** ranger os dentes; **to ~ to a halt** (*vehicle*) parar com um ranger de freios; (*fig: work, production*) paralisar-se; (*: talks, process*) empacar; **the daily ~** (*inf*) a labuta diária
grinder ['graɪndə'] N (*machine: for coffee*) moinho; (*: for waste disposal*) triturador *m*
grindstone ['graɪndstəun] N: **to keep one's nose to the ~** trabalhar sem descanso
grip [grɪp] N (*of hands*) aperto; (*handle*) punho; (*of racquet etc*) cabo; (*of tyre, shoe*) aderência; (*holdall*) valise *f* ∎ VT agarrar; (*attention*) prender; **to come** *or* **get to ~s with** arcar com; **to ~ the road** (*Aut*) aderir à estrada; **to lose one's ~** perder a pega; (*fig*) perder a eficiência
gripe [graɪp] N (*Med*) cólicas *fpl*; (*inf: complaint*) queixa ∎ VI (*inf*) bufar
gripping ['grɪpɪŋ] ADJ absorvente, emocionante
grisly ['grɪzlɪ] ADJ horrendo, medonho
grist [grɪst] N (*fig*): **it's (all) ~ to his mill** ele se vale de tudo
gristle ['grɪsl] N cartilagem *f*; (*on meat*) nervo
grit [grɪt] N areia, grão *m* de areia; (*courage*) coragem *f* ∎ VT (*road*) pôr areia em; **grits** NPL (*US*) canjica; **to ~ one's teeth** cerrar os dentes; **to have a piece of ~ in one's eye** ter uma pedrinha no olho
grizzle ['grɪzl] (*Brit*) VI choramingar

grizzly ['grɪzlɪ] N (*also:* **grizzly bear**) urso pardo
groan [grəun] N gemido ∎ VI gemer
grocer ['grəusə'] N dono(-a) de mercearia
grocer's (shop) N mercearia
grocery ['grəusərɪ] N mercearia; **groceries** NPL comestíveis *mpl*
grog [grɔg] N grogue *m*
groggy ['grɔgɪ] ADJ grogue
groin [grɔɪn] N virilha
groom [gru:m] N cavalariço; (*also:* **bridegroom**) noivo ∎ VT (*horse*) tratar; (*fig*): **to ~ sb for sth** preparar alguém para algo; **well-~ed** bem-posto
groove [gru:v] N ranhura, entalhe *m*
grope [grəup] VI tatear; **to ~ for** procurar às cegas
gross [grəus] ADJ grosso; (*flagrant*) grave; (*vulgar*) vulgar; (*: building*) de mau-gosto; (*Comm*) bruto ∎ N INV (*twelve dozen*) grosa ∎ VT (*Comm*): **to ~ £500,000** dar uma receita bruta de £500,000;
gross domestic product N produto interno bruto
grossly ['grəuslɪ] ADV (*greatly*) enormemente, gritantemente
gross national product N produto nacional bruto
grotesque [grə'tɛsk] ADJ grotesco
grotto ['grɔtəu] N gruta
grotty ['grɔtɪ] (*Brit: inf*) ADJ vagabundo; (*room etc*) mixa; **I'm feeling ~** estou me sentindo podre
grouch [grautʃ] (*inf*) VI ralhar ∎ N (*person*) pessoa geniosa, rabugento(-a)
ground [graund] PT, PP of **grind** ∎ N terra, chão *m*; (*Sport*) campo; (*land*) terreno; (*reason: gen pl*) motivo, razão *f*; (*US: also:* **ground wire**) (ligação *f* à) terra, fio-terra *m* ∎ VT (*plane*) manter em terra; (*US: Elec*) ligar à terra ∎ VI (*ship*) encalhar ∎ ADJ (*coffee etc*) moído; (*US: meat*) picado; **grounds** NPL (*of coffee etc*) borra; (*gardens etc*) jardins *mpl*, parque *m*; **on the ~** no chão; **to the ~** por terra; **below ~** embaixo da terra; **to gain/lose ~** ganhar/perder terreno; **common ~** consenso; **he covered a lot of ~ in his lecture** sua palestra cobriu uma área considerável; **ground cloth** (*US*) N = **groundsheet**; **ground control** N (*Aviat, Space*) controle *m* de solo *or* terra; **ground floor** N andar *m* térreo (BR), rés-do-chão *m* (PT)
grounding ['graundɪŋ] N (*Sch*) conhecimentos *mpl* básicos
groundless ['graundlɪs] ADJ infundado
groundnut ['graundnʌt] N amendoim *m*
ground rent (*Brit*) N foro
groundsheet ['graundʃi:t] (*Brit*) N capa impermeável
grounds keeper (*US*) N (*Sport*) zelador *m* de um campo esportivo
groundsman ['graundzmən] (*irreg*) N (*Sport*) zelador *m* de um campo esportivo
ground staff N pessoal *m* de terra
ground swell N (*of opinion*) onda
ground-to-ground missile N míssil *m* terra-

terra

groundwork ['graundwə:k] N base f, preparação f

group [gru:p] N grupo; (also: **pop group**) conjunto ▪ VT (also: **group together**) agrupar ▪ VI (also: **group together**) agrupar-se

grouse [graus] N INV (bird) tetraz m, galo-silvestre m ▪ VI (complain) queixar-se, resmungar

grove [grəuv] N arvoredo

grovel ['grɔvl] VI (fig) humilhar-se; **to ~ (before)** abaixar-se (diante de)

grow [grəu] (pt **grew**, pp **grown**) VI crescer; (increase) aumentar; (develop): **to ~ (out of/from)** originar-se; (become) tornar-se ▪ VT plantar, cultivar; (beard) deixar crescer; **to ~ rich/weak** enriquecer(-se)/enfraquecer-se

▸ **grow apart** VI (fig) afastar-se (um do outro)

▸ **grow away from** VT FUS (fig) afastar-se de

▸ **grow on** VT FUS: **that painting is ~ing on me** estou gostando cada vez mais daquele quadro

▸ **grow out of** VT FUS (clothes) ficar muito grande para; (habit) superar com or perder o tempo

▸ **grow up** VI crescer, fazer-se homem/mulher

grower ['grəuəʳ] N cultivador(a) m/f, produtor(a) m/f

growing ['grəuɪŋ] ADJ crescente; **~ pains** (Med) dores fpl do crescimento; (fig) dificuldades fpl iniciais

growl [graul] VI rosnar

grown [grəun] PP of **grow** ▪ ADJ crescido, adulto

grown-up N adulto(-a), pessoa mais velha

growth [grəuθ] N crescimento; (what has grown) crescimento; (increase) aumento; (Med) abcesso, tumor m; **growth rate** N taxa de crescimento

GRSM (Brit) N ABBR = **Graduate of the Royal Schools of Music**

grub [grʌb] N larva, lagarta; (inf: food) comida, rango (BR)

grubby ['grʌbɪ] ADJ encardido

grudge [grʌdʒ] N motivo de rancor ▪ VT: **to ~ sb sth** dar algo a alguém de má vontade, invejar algo a alguém; **to bear sb a ~ for sth** guardar rancor de alguém por algo; **he ~s (giving) the money** ele dá dinheiro de má vontade

grudgingly ['grʌdʒɪŋlɪ] ADV de má vontade

gruelling ['gruəlɪŋ] (US **grueling**) ADJ duro, árduo

gruesome ['gru:səm] ADJ horrível

gruff [grʌf] ADJ (voice) rouco; (manner) brusco

grumble ['grʌmbl] VI resmungar, bufar

grumpy ['grʌmpɪ] ADJ rabugento

grunt [grʌnt] VI grunhir ▪ N grunhido

G-string N (garment) tapa-sexo m

GSUSA N ABBR = **Girl Scouts of the United States of America**

GU (US) ABBR (Post) = **Guam**

guarantee [gærən'ti:] N garantia ▪ VT garantir

guarantor [gærən'tɔːʳ] N fiador(a) m/f

guard [ga:d] N guarda; (one person) guarda m; (Brit: Rail) guarda-freio; (on machine) dispositivo de segurança; (also: **fireguard**) guarda-fogo ▪ VT guardar; (protect): **to ~ (against)** proteger (contra); (prisoner) vigiar; **to be on one's ~** estar prevenido

▸ **guard against** VT FUS prevenir-se contra; **to ~ against doing sth** guardar-se de fazer algo

guard dog M cão m de guarda

guarded ['ga:dɪd] ADJ (statement) cauteloso

guardian ['ga:dɪən] N protetor(a) m/f; (of minor) tutor(a) m/f

guard's van (Brit) N (Rail) vagão m de freio

Guatemala [gwɔtə'ma:lə] N Guatemala

Guernsey ['gə:nzɪ] N Guernsey f (no article)

guerrilla [gə'rɪlə] N guerrilheiro(-a); **guerrilla warfare** N guerrilha

guess [gɛs] VT, VI (estimate) avaliar, conjeturar; (correct answer) adivinhar; (US: suppose) achar, supor ▪ N suposição f, conjetura; **to take** or **have a ~** adivinhar, chutar (inf); **to keep sb ~ing** não contar a alguém; **my ~ is that ...** meu palpite é que ...; **to ~ right/wrong** acertar/errar

guesstimate ['gɛstɪmɪt] (inf) N estimativa aproximada

guesswork ['gɛswə:k] N conjeturas fpl; **I got the answer by ~** obtive a resposta por adivinhação

guest [gɛst] N convidado(-a); (in hotel) hóspede m/f; **be my ~** fique à vontade

guest-house N pensão f

guest room N quarto de hóspedes

guffaw [gʌ'fɔː] N gargalhada ▪ VI dar gargalhadas

guidance ['gaɪdəns] N orientação f; (advice) conselhos mpl; **under the ~ of** sob a direção de, orientado por; **vocational** or **careers ~** orientação vocacional; **marriage ~** aconselhamento conjugal

guide [gaɪd] N (person) guia m/f; (book, fig) guia m; (Brit: also: **girl guide**) escoteira ▪ VT guiar; **to be ~d by sb/sth** orientar-se com alguém/por algo

guidebook ['gaɪdbuk] N guia m

guided missile ['gaɪdɪd-] N (internally controlled) míssil m guiado; (remote-controlled) míssil m teleguiado

guide dog N cão m de guia

guidelines ['gaɪdlaɪnz] NPL (advice) orientação f; (fig) princípios mpl gerais, diretrizes fpl

guild [gɪld] N grêmio

guildhall ['gɪldhɔ:l] (Brit) N sede f da prefeitura

guile [gaɪl] N astúcia

guileless ['gaɪllɪs] ADJ ingênuo, cândido

guillotine ['gɪləti:n] N guilhotina

guilt [gɪlt] N culpa

guilty ['gɪltɪ] ADJ culpado; **to plead ~/not ~** declarar-se culpado/inocente

Guinea ['gɪnɪ] N: **Republic of ~** (República da) Guiné f

guinea ['gɪnɪ] (Brit) N guinéu m (= 21 shillings: antiga unidade monetária equivalente a £1.05); **guinea pig** N porquinho-da-Índia m, cobaia; (fig) cobaia

guise [gaɪz] N: **in** or **under the ~ of** sob a aparência de, sob o pretexto de

guitar [gɪ'tɑː'] N violão m

guitarist [gɪ'tɑːrɪst] N violonista m/f

gulch [gʌltʃ] (US) N ravina

gulf [gʌlf] N golfo; (abyss: also fig) abismo; **the (Persian) G ~** o Golfo Pérsico

Gulf States NPL: **the ~** (in Middle East) os países do Golfo Pérsico

Gulf Stream N: **the ~** a corrente do Golfo

gull [gʌl] N gaivota

gullet ['gʌlɪt] N esôfago

gullibility [gʌlə'bɪlɪtɪ] N credulidade f

gullible ['gʌlɪbl] ADJ crédulo

gully ['gʌlɪ] N barranco

gulp [gʌlp] VI engolir em seco ■ VT (also: **gulp down**) engolir ■ N (of drink) gole m; **at one ~** de um gole só

gum [gʌm] N (Anat) gengiva; (glue) goma; (also: **gum drop**) bala de goma; (also: **chewing-gum**) chiclete m (BR), pastilha elástica (PT) ■ VT colar
▶ **gum up** VT: **to ~ up the works** (inf) estragar tudo

gumboil ['gʌmbɔɪl] N abscesso gengival, parúlide f

gumboots ['gʌmbuːts] (Brit) NPL botas fpl de borracha, galochas fpl

gumption ['gʌmpʃən] N juízo, bom senso

gun [gʌn] N (gen) arma (de fogo); (revolver) revólver m; (small) pistola; (rifle) espingarda; (cannon) canhão m ■ VT (also: **gun down**) balear; **to stick to one's ~s** (fig) não dar o braço a torcer, ser durão (inf)

gunboat ['gʌnbəut] N canhoneira

gun dog N cão m de caça

gunfire ['gʌnfaɪə'] N tiroteio

gunk [gʌŋk] (inf) N sujeira (BR), sujidade f (PT)

gunman ['gʌnmən] (irreg) N pistoleiro

gunner ['gʌnə'] N artilheiro

gunpoint ['gʌnpɔɪnt] N: **at ~** sob a ameaça de uma arma

gunpowder ['gʌnpaudə'] N pólvora

gunrunner ['gʌnrʌnə'] N contrabandista m/f de armas

gunrunning ['gʌnrʌnɪŋ] N contrabando de armas

gunshot ['gʌnʃɔt] N tiro (de arma de fogo); **within ~** ao alcance do tiro

gunsmith ['gʌnsmɪθ] N armeiro(-a)

gurgle ['gəːgl] VI (baby) balbuciar; (water) gorgolejar ■ N gorgolejo

guru ['guruː] N guru m

gush [gʌʃ] VI jorrar; (fig) alvoroçar-se ■ N jorro

gusset ['gʌsɪt] N nesga; (of tights, pants) entreperna

gust [gʌst] N (of wind) rajada

gusto ['gʌstəu] N: **with ~** com garra

gut [gʌt] N intestino, tripa; (Mus etc) corda de tripa ■ VT (poultry, fish) estripar; (building) destruir o interior de; **guts** NPL (Anat) entranhas fpl; (inf: courage) coragem f, raça (inf); **to hate sb's ~s** ter alguém atravessado na garganta, não poder ver alguém nem pintado; **gut reaction** N reação f instintiva

gutter ['gʌtə'] N (of roof) calha; (in street) sarjeta

guttural ['gʌtərl] ADJ gutural

guy [gaɪ] N (also: **guyrope**) corda; (inf: man) cara m (BR), tipo (PT)

Guyana [gaɪ'ænə] N Guiana

Guy Fawkes' Night N ver abaixo

● **GUY FAWKES' NIGHT**

A Guy Fawkes' Night, também chamada de bonfire night, é a ocasião em que se comemora o fracasso da conspiração (a Gunpowder Plot) contra James I e o Parlamento, em 5 de novembro de 1605. Um dos conspiradores, Guy Fawkes, foi surpreendido no porão do Parlamento quando estava prestes a atear fogo a explosivos. Todo ano, no dia 5 de novembro, as crianças preparam antecipadamente um boneco de Guy Fawkes e pedem às pessoas que passam na rua a penny for the Guy (uma moedinha para o Guy), com o qual compram fogos de artifício.

guzzle ['gʌzl] VI comer or beber com gula ■ VT engolir com gula

gym [dʒɪm] N (also: **gymnasium**) ginásio; (also: **gymnastics**) ginástica

gymkhana [dʒɪm'kɑːnə] N gincana

gymnasium [dʒɪm'neɪzɪəm] N ginásio

gymnast ['dʒɪmnæst] N ginasta m/f

gymnastics [dʒɪm'næstɪks] N ginástica

gym shoes NPL tênis mpl

gym slip (Brit) N uniforme m escolar

gynaecologist [gaɪnɪ'kɔlədʒɪst] (US **gynecologist**) N ginecologista m/f

gynaecology [gaɪnə'kɔlədʒɪ] (US **gynecology**) N ginecologia

gypsy ['dʒɪpsɪ] N, CPD = **gipsy**

gyrate [dʒaɪ'reɪt] VI girar

gyroscope ['dʒaɪərəskəup] N giroscópio

Hh

H, h [eɪtʃ] N (*letter*) H, h *m*; **H for Harry** (*Brit*), **H for How** (*US*) H de Henrique

habeas corpus ['heɪbɪəs'kɔːpəs] N (*Law*) habeas-corpus *m*

haberdashery ['hæbə'dæʃərɪ] (*Brit*) N armarinho

habit ['hæbɪt] N hábito, costume *m*; (*addiction*) vício; (*Rel*) hábito; **to get out of/into the ~ of doing sth** perder/criar o hábito de fazer algo

habitable ['hæbɪtəbl] ADJ habitável

habitat ['hæbɪtæt] N habitat *m*

habitation [hæbɪ'teɪʃən] N habitação *f*

habitual [hə'bɪtjuəl] ADJ habitual, costumeiro; (*drinker, liar*) inveterado

habitually [hə'bɪtjuəlɪ] ADV habitualmente

hack [hæk] VT (*cut*) cortar; (*chop*) talhar ■ N corte *m*; (*axe blow*) talho; (*pej: writer*) escrevinhador(a) *m/f*; (*old horse*) metungo

hacker ['hækə'] N (*Comput*) pirata (de dados de computador)

hackles ['hæklz] NPL: **to make sb's ~ rise** (*fig*) enfurecer alguém

hackney cab ['hæknɪ-] N fiacre *m*

hackneyed ['hæknɪd] ADJ corriqueiro, batido

had [hæd] PT, PP *of* have

haddock ['hædək] (*pl* haddocks *or* haddock) N hadoque *m* (BR), eglefim *m* (PT)

hadn't ['hædnt] = **had not**

haematology ['hiːmə'tɔlədʒɪ] (*US* hematology) N hematologia

haemoglobin ['hiːmə'gləubɪn] (*US* hemoglobin) N hemoglobina

haemophilia ['hiːmə'fɪlɪə] (*US* hemophilia) N hemofilia

haemorrhage ['hɛmərɪdʒ] (*US* hemorrhage) N hemorragia

haemorrhoids ['hɛmərɔɪdz] (*US* hemorrhoids) NPL hemorróidas *fpl*

hag [hæg] N (*ugly*) bruxa; (*nasty*) megera; (*witch*) bruxa

haggard ['hægəd] ADJ emaciado, macilento

haggis ['hægɪs] N *miúdos de carneiro com aveia, cozidos no estômago do animal*

haggle ['hægl] VI (*bargain*) pechinchar, regatear; **to ~ over** discutir sobre

haggling ['hæglɪŋ] N regateio

Hague [heɪg] N: **The ~** Haia

hail [heɪl] N (*weather*) granizo; (*of objects*) chuva; (*of criticism*) torrente *f* ■ VT (*greet*) cumprimentar, saudar; (*call*) chamar ■ VI chover granizo; (*originate*): **he ~s from Scotland** ele é originário da Escócia

hailstone ['heɪlstəun] N pedra de granizo

hailstorm ['heɪlstɔːm] N tempestade *f* de granizo

hair [hɛə'] N (*of human*) cabelo; (*of animal, on legs*) pêlo; (*one hair*) fio de cabelo, pêlo; (*head of hair*) cabeleira; **grey ~** cabelo grisalho; **to do one's ~** pentear-se

hairbrush ['hɛəbrʌʃ] N escova de cabelo

haircut ['hɛəkʌt] N corte *m* de cabelo

hairdo ['hɛəduː] N penteado

hairdresser ['hɛədrɛsə'] N cabeleireiro(-a)

hairdresser's N cabeleireiro

hair dryer N secador *m* de cabelo

-haired [hɛəd] SUFFIX: **fair/long~** de cabelo louro/comprido

hairgrip ['hɛəgrɪp] N grampo (BR), gancho (PT)

hairline ['hɛəlaɪn] N contorno do couro cabeludo; **hairline fracture** N fratura muito fina

hairnet ['hɛənɛt] N rede *f* de cabelo

hair oil N óleo para o cabelo

hairpiece ['hɛəpiːs] N aplique *m*

hairpin ['hɛəpɪn] N grampo (BR), gancho (PT), pinça; **hairpin bend** (*US* hairpin curve) N curva fechada

hair-raising [-'reɪzɪŋ] ADJ horripilante, de arrepiar os cabelos

hair remover N (creme *m*) depilatório

hair spray N laquê *m* (BR), laca (PT)

hairstyle ['hɛəstaɪl] N penteado

hairy ['hɛərɪ] ADJ cabeludo, peludo; (*inf: situation*) perigoso

Haiti ['heɪtɪ] N Haiti *m*

hake [heɪk] (*pl* hakes *or* hake) N abrótea

halcyon ['hælsɪən] ADJ tranqüilo

hale [heɪl] ADJ: **~ and hearty** robusto, em ótima forma

half [hɑːf] (*pl* halves) N metade *f*; (*Sport: of match*) tempo; (*of ground*) lado ■ ADJ meio ■ ADV meio, pela metade; **~-an-hour** meia hora; **~ a pound** meia libra; **two and a ~** dois e meio; **~ a dozen** meia-dúzia; **a week and a ~** uma semana e meia; ~ **(of it)** a metade; ~ **(of)** a metade de; ~ **the amount of** a metade de; **to cut sth in** ~ cortar algo ao meio; ~ **past three** três e meia; ~ **asleep/empty/closed** meio adormecido/ vazio/fechado; **to go halves (with sb)** rachar as despesas (com alguém)

half-back N (*Sport*) meio-de-campo

half-baked (*inf*) ADJ (*idea, scheme*) mal planejado

half-breed N mestiço(-a)

half-brother N meio-irmão m

half-caste N mestiço(-a)

half-hearted ADJ irresoluto, indiferente

half-hour N meia hora

half-mast; at ~ ADV (*flag*) a meio-pau

halfpenny ['heɪpnɪ] N meio pêni m

half-price ADJ pela metade do preço ■ ADV (*also*: **at half-price**) pela metade do preço

half term (*Brit*) N (*Sch*) dias de folga no meio do semestre

half-time N meio tempo

halfway [hɑːf'weɪ] ADV a meio caminho; (*in time*) no meio; **to meet sb** ~ (*fig*) chegar a um meio-termo com alguém

half-yearly ADV semestralmente ■ ADJ semestral

halibut ['hælɪbət] N INV hipoglosso

halitosis [hælɪ'təʊsɪs] N halitose f, mau hálito

hall [hɔːl] N (*for concerts*) sala; (*entrance way*) hall m, entrada; (*corridor*) corredor m; **town** ~ prefeitura (BR), câmara municipal (PT)

hallmark ['hɔːlmɑːk] N (*also fig*) marca

hallo [hə'ləʊ] EXCL = **hello**

hall of residence (*Brit*) (*pl* **halls of residence**) N residência universitária

Hallowe'en ['hæləʊ'iːn] N Dia m das Bruxas (31 de outubro)

● **HALLOWE'EN**

● Segundo a tradição, *Hallowe'en* é a noite dos
● fantasmas e dos bruxos. Na Escócia e nos
● Estados Unidos, sobretudo (bem menos
● na Inglaterra), as crianças, para festejar o
● *Hallowe'en*, se fantasiam e batem de porta em
● porta pedindo prendas (chocolates, maçãs
● etc).

hallucination [h
əluːsɪ'neɪʃən] N alucinação f

hallway ['hɔːlweɪ] N hall m, entrada; (*corridor*) corredor m

halo ['heɪləʊ] N (*of saint etc*) auréola; (*of sun*) halo m

halt [hɔːlt] N (*stop*) parada (BR), paragem f (PT); (*Rail*) pequena parada; (*Mil*) alto ■ VI parar; (*Mil*) fazer alto ■ VT deter; (*process*) interromper; **to call a** ~ **to sth** (*fig*) pôr um fim a algo

halter ['hɔːltəʳ] N (*for horse*) cabresto

halter-neck ['hɔːltənɛk] ADJ (*dress*) frente-única inv

halve [hɑːv] VT (*divide*) dividir ao meio; (*reduce by half*) reduzir à metade

halves [hɑːvz] NPL *of* **half**

ham [hæm] N presunto, fiambre m (PT); (*inf*:

actor, actress) canastrão(-trona) m/f; (: *also*: **radio ham**) rádio-amador(a) m/f

hamburger ['hæmbə:gəʳ] N hambúrguer m

ham-fisted [-'fɪstɪd] (*Brit*) ADJ desajeitado

ham-handed [-'hændɪd] (*US*) ADJ desajeitado

hamlet ['hæmlɪt] N aldeola, lugarejo

hammer ['hæməʳ] N martelo ■ VT martelar; (*fig*) dar uma surra em ■ VI (*on door*) bater insistentemente; **to** ~ **a point home to sb** fincar uma idéia na mente de alguém

▸ **hammer out** VT (*metal*) malhar; (*fig: solution*) elaborar

hammock ['hæmək] N rede f

hamper ['hæmpəʳ] VT dificultar, atrapalhar ■ N cesto

hamster ['hæmstəʳ] N hamster m

hamstring ['hæmstrɪŋ] N (*Anat*) tendão m do jarrete

hand [hænd] N mão f; (*of clock*) ponteiro; (*writing*) letra; (*applause*) aplauso; (*of cards*) cartas fpl; (*worker*) trabalhador m; (*measurement*) palmo ■ VT (*give*) dar, passar; (*deliver*) entregar; **to give** *or* **lend sb a** ~ dar uma mãozinha a alguém, dar uma ajuda a alguém; **at** ~ à mão, disponível; **in** ~ livre; (*situation*) sob controle; (*Comm*) em caixa, à disposição; **to be on** ~ (*person*) estar disponível; (*emergency services*) estar num estado de prontidão; **to** ~ (*information*) à mão; **to force sb's** ~ forçar alguém a agir; **to have a free** ~ ter carta branca; **to have sth in one's** ~ ter algo na mão; **on the one** ~ ..., **on the other** ~ ... por um lado ..., por outro (lado) ...

▸ **hand down** VT passar; (*tradition, heirloom*) transmitir; (*US: sentence, verdict*) proferir

▸ **hand in** VT entregar

▸ **hand out** VT distribuir

▸ **hand over** VT (*deliver*) entregar; (*surrender*) ceder; (*powers etc*) transmitir

▸ **hand round** (*Brit*) VT (*information*) fazer circular; (*chocolates*) oferecer

handbag ['hændbæg] N bolsa

handball ['hændbɔːl] N handebol m

hand basin ['hændbeɪsn] N pia (BR), lavatório (PT)

handbook ['hændbuk] N manual m

handbrake ['hændbreɪk] N freio (BR) *or* travão m (PT) de mão

hand cream N creme m para as mãos

handcuffs ['hændkʌfs] NPL algemas fpl

handful ['hændful] N punhado; (*of people*) grupo

handicap ['hændɪkæp] N (*Med*) incapacidade f; (*disadvantage*) desvantagem f; (*Sport*) handicap m ■ VT prejudicar; **mentally/physically ~ped** deficiente mental/físico

handicraft ['hændɪkrɑːft] N artesanato, trabalho manual

handiwork ['hændɪwəːk] N obra; **this looks like his** ~ (*pej*) isso parece coisa dele

handkerchief ['hæŋkətʃɪf] N lenço

handle ['hændl] N (*of door etc*) maçaneta; (*of*

bag etc) alça; *(of cup etc)* asa; *(of knife etc)* cabo; *(for winding)* manivela; *(inf: name)* título ∎ VT manusear; *(deal with)* tratar de; *(treat: people)* lidar com; **"~ with care"** "cuidado — frágil"; **to fly off the ~** perder as estribeiras
handlebar(s) ['hɑːndlbɑː(z)] N(PL) guidom m (BR), guidão m (PT)
handling charges ['hændlɪŋ-] NPL taxa de manuseio; *(Banking)* comissão f
hand-luggage N bagagem f de mão
handmade ['hændmeɪd] ADJ feito a mão
handout ['hændaut] N *(money, food)* doação f, esmola; *(leaflet)* folheto; *(at lecture)* apostila
hand-picked [-'pɪkt] ADJ *(fruit)* colhido à mão; *(staff)* escolhido a dedo
handrail ['hændreɪl] N *(on staircase)* corrimão m
handsfree kit ['hændzfriː-] N viva-voz m
handshake ['hændʃeɪk] N aperto de mão; *(Comput)* handshake m
handsome ['hænsəm] ADJ bonito; *(woman)* vistoso; *(gift)* generoso; *(building)* imponente, elegante; *(profit)* considerável
handstand ['hændstænd] N: **to do a ~** plantar bananeira
hand-to-mouth ADJ *(existence)* ao deus-dará
handwriting ['hændraɪtɪŋ] N letra, caligrafia
handwritten ['hændrɪtn] ADJ escrito à mão, manuscrito
handy ['hændɪ] ADJ *(close at hand)* à mão; *(useful)* útil; *(skilful)* habilidoso, hábil; **to come in ~** ser útil
handyman ['hændɪmæn] *(irreg)* N faz-tudo m; *(in hotel etc)* biscateiro
hang [hæŋ] *(pt, pp hung)* VT pendurar; *(on wall etc)* prender; *(head)* baixar; *(criminal)* *(pt, pp hanged)* enforcar ∎ VI estar pendurado; *(hair, drapery)* cair ∎ N *(inf)*: **to get the ~ of (doing) sth** pegar o jeito de (fazer) algo
▸ **hang about** VI vadiar, vagabundear; ~ **about!** *(inf)* 'pera aí!
▸ **hang around** VI = **hang about**
▸ **hang back** VI *(hesitate)*: **to ~ back from (doing) sth** vacilar em (fazer) algo
▸ **hang on** VI *(wait)* esperar ∎ VT FUS *(depend on)* depender de; **to ~ on to** *(keep hold of)* não soltar, segurar; *(keep)* ficar com
▸ **hang out** VT *(washing)* estender ∎ VI *(be visible)* aparecer; *(inf: spend time)* fazer ponto
▸ **hang together** VI *(argument etc)* ser coerente
▸ **hang up** VT *(coat)* pendurar ∎ VI *(Tel)* desligar; **to ~ up on sb** bater o telefone na cara de alguém
hangar ['hæŋəʳ] N hangar m
hangdog ['hæŋdɔg] ADJ *(look, expression)* envergonhado
hanger ['hæŋəʳ] N cabide m
hanger-on N parasita m/f, filão(-lona) m/f
hang-gliding N vôo livre
hanging ['hæŋɪŋ] N enforcamento
hangman ['hæŋmən] *(irreg)* N carrasco
hangover ['hæŋəuvəʳ] N *(after drinking)* ressaca; **to have a ~** estar de ressaca

hang-up N grilo
hank [hæŋk] N meada
hanker ['hæŋkəʳ] VI: **to ~ after** *(miss)* sentir saudade de; *(long for)* ansiar por
hankie ['hæŋkɪ] N ABBR = **handkerchief**
hanky ['hæŋkɪ] N ABBR = **handkerchief**
Hants *(Brit)* ABBR = **Hampshire**
haphazard [hæp'hæzəd] ADJ *(random)* fortuito; *(disorganized)* desorganizado
hapless ['hæplɪs] ADJ desafortunado
happen ['hæpən] VI acontecer; **what's ~ing?** o que é que está acontecendo?; **she ~ed to be in London** aconteceu que estava em Londres; **if anything ~ed to him** se lhe acontecesse alguma coisa; **as it ~s** ... acontece que ...
▸ **happen (up)on** VT FUS dar com
happening ['hæpənɪŋ] N acontecimento, ocorrência
happily ['hæpɪlɪ] ADV *(luckily)* felizmente; *(cheerfully)* alegremente
happiness ['hæpɪnɪs] N felicidade f; *(joy)* alegria
happy ['hæpɪ] ADJ fcliz; *(cheerful)* contente; **to be ~ (with)** estar contente (com), **to be ~** ser feliz; **to be ~ to do** *(willing)* estar disposto a fazer; **yes, I'd be ~ to** sim, com muito prazer; **~ birthday!** feliz aniversário; *(said to somebody)* parabéns!; **~ Christmas/New Year** feliz Natal/ Ano Novo
happy-go-lucky ADJ despreocupado
harangue [hə'ræŋ] VT arengar
harass ['hærəs] VT *(bother)* importunar; *(pursue)* acossar
harassed ['hærəst] ADJ chateado
harassment ['hærəsmənt] N perseguição f; *(worry)* preocupação f
harbour ['hɑːbəʳ] *(US harbor)* N porto ∎ VT *(hope etc)* abrigar; *(hide)* esconder; **to ~ a grudge against sb** guardar rancor a alguém
harbo(u)r dues NPL direitos mpl portuários
harbo(u)r master N capitão m do porto
hard [hɑːd] ADJ duro; *(difficult)* difícil; *(work)* árduo; *(person)* severo, cruel; *(facts)* verdadeiro ∎ ADV *(work)* muito, diligentemente; *(think, try)* seriamente; **to look ~ at** olhar firme or fixamente para; **~ luck!** azar!; **no ~ feelings!** sem ressentimentos!; **to be ~ of hearing** ser surdo; **to be ~ done by** ser tratado injustamente; **to be ~ on sb** ser rigoroso com alguém; **I find it ~ to believe that ...** acho difícil acreditar que ...
hard-and-fast ADJ rígido
hardback ['hɑːdbæk] N livro de capa dura
hardboard ['hɑːdbɔːd] N madeira compensada
hard-boiled egg [-'bɔɪld-] N ovo cozido
hard cash N dinheiro vivo or em espécie
hard copy N *(Comput)* cópia impressa
hard-core ADJ *(pornography)* pesado; *(supporters)* ferrenho
hard court N *(Tennis)* quadra de cimento
hard disk N *(Comput)* disco rígido
harden ['hɑːdən] VT endurecer; *(steel)* temperar;

(fig) tornar insensível ■ VI endurecer-se

hardened ['hɑːdnd] ADJ *(criminal, drinker)* inveterado; **to be ~ to sth** ser insensível a algo

hardening ['hɑːdnɪŋ] N endurecimento

hard-headed [-'hɛdɪd] ADJ prático

hard-hearted ADJ empedernido, insensível

hard labour N trabalhos *mpl* forçados

hardliner [hɑːd'laɪnər] N intransigente *m/f*

hardly ['hɑːdlɪ] ADV *(scarcely)* apenas; *(no sooner)* mal; **that can ~ be true** dificilmente pode ser verdade; **~ ever** quase nunca; **I can ~ believe it** mal posso acreditar nisso

hardness ['hɑːdnɪs] N dureza

hard sell N venda agressiva

hardship ['hɑːdʃɪp] N *(difficulty)* privação *f*

hard shoulder *(Brit)* N *(Aut)* acostamento (BR), berma (PT)

hard up *(inf)* ADJ duro (BR), liso (PT)

hardware ['hɑːdwɛər] N ferragens *fpl*; *(Comput)* hardware *m*; **hardware shop** N loja de ferragens

hard-wearing [-'wɛərɪŋ] ADJ resistente

hard-working ADJ trabalhador(a); *(student)* aplicado

hardy ['hɑːdɪ] ADJ forte; *(plant)* ■ resistente

hare [hɛər] N lebre *f*

hare-brained [-breɪnd] ADJ maluco, absurdo

harelip ['hɛəlɪp] N *(Med)* lábio leporino

harem [hɑː'riːm] N harém *m*

hark back [hɑːk-] VI: **to ~ back to** *(reminisce)* recordar; *(be reminiscent of)* lembrar

harm [hɑːm] N mal *m*; *(damage)* dano ■ VT *(person)* fazer mal a, prejudicar; *(thing)* danificar; **to mean no ~** ter boas intenções; **there's no ~ in trying** não faz mal tentar; **out of ~'s way** a salvo

harmful ['hɑːmful] ADJ prejudicial, nocivo; *(plant, weed)* daninho

harmless ['hɑːmlɪs] ADJ inofensivo; *(activity)* inofensivo

harmonic [hɑː'mɔnɪk] ADJ harmônico

harmonica [hɑː'mɔnɪkə] N gaita de boca, harmônica

harmonics [hɑː'mɔnɪks] NPL harmônicos *mpl*

harmonious [hɑː'məunɪəs] ADJ harmonioso

harmonium [hɑː'məunɪəm] N harmônio

harmonize ['hɑːmənaɪz] VT, VI harmonizar

harmony ['hɑːmənɪ] N harmonia

harness ['hɑːnɪs] N *(for horse)* arreios *mpl*; *(for child)* correia; *(safety harness)* correia de segurança ■ VT *(horse)* arrear, pôr arreios em; *(resources)* aproveitar

harp [hɑːp] N harpa ■ VI: **to ~ on about** bater sempre na mesma tecla sobre

harpist ['hɑːpɪst] N harpista *m/f*

harpoon [hɑː'puːn] N arpão *m* ■ VT arpoar

harpsichord ['hɑːpsɪkɔːd] N cravo, clavecino

harrow ['hærəu] N *(Agr)* grade *f*, rastelo

harrowing ['hærəuɪŋ] ADJ doloroso, pungente

harry ['hærɪ] VT *(Mil, fig)* assolar

harsh [hɑːʃ] ADJ *(life)* duro; *(judge, criticism)* severo; *(rough: surface, taste)* áspero; *(: sound)* desarmonioso

harshly ['hɑːʃlɪ] ADV severamente

harshness ['hɑːʃnɪs] N dureza, severidade *f*; *(roughness)* aspereza

harvest ['hɑːvɪst] N colheita; *(of grapes)* vindima ■ VT, VI colher

harvester ['hɑːvɪstər] N *(machine)* segadora; *(also:* **combine harvester)** ceifeira-debulhadora; *(person)* segador(a) *m/f*

has [hæz] VB *see* **have**

has-been *(inf)* N *(person)*: **he/she's a ~** ele/ela já era

hash [hæʃ] N *(Culin)* picadinho; *(fig: mess)* confusão *f* ■ N ABBR *(inf)* = **hashish**

hashish ['hæʃɪʃ] N haxixe *m*

hasn't ['hæznt] = **has not**

hassle ['hæsl] *(inf)* N *(fuss, problems)* complicação *f* ■ VT molestar, chatear

haste [heɪst] N pressa; **in ~** às pressas

hasten ['heɪsn] VT acelerar ■ VI: **to ~ to do sth** apressar-se em fazer algo

hastily ['heɪstɪlɪ] ADV depressa

hasty ['heɪstɪ] ADJ apressado; *(rash)* precipitado

hat [hæt] N chapéu *m*

hatbox ['hætbɔks] N chapeleira

hatch [hætʃ] N *(Naut: also:* **hatchway)** escotilha; *(also:* **service hatch)** comunicação *f* entre a cozinha e a sala de jantar ■ VI sair do ovo, chocar ■ VT chocar; *(plot)* tramar, arquitetar

hatchback ['hætʃbæk] N *(Aut)* camionete *f*, hatch *m*

hatchet ['hætʃɪt] N machadinha

hate [heɪt] VT odiar, detestar ■ N ódio; **to ~ to do** *or* **doing** odiar *or* detestar fazer; **I ~ to trouble you, but ...** desculpe incomodá-lo, mas ...

hateful ['heɪtful] ADJ odioso

hatred ['heɪtrɪd] N ódio

hat trick *(Brit)* N *(Sport, fig)* três vitórias *(or* gols *etc)* consecutivas

haughty ['hɔːtɪ] ADJ soberbo, arrogante

haul [hɔːl] VT puxar; *(by lorry)* carregar, fretar; *(Naut)* levar à orça ■ N *(of fish)* redada; *(of stolen goods etc)* pilhagem *f*, presa

haulage ['hɔːlɪdʒ] N transporte *m* (rodoviário); *(costs)* gasto com transporte; **haulage contractor** *(Brit)* N *(firm)* transportadora; *(person)* transportador(a) *m/f*

hauler ['hɔːlər] *(US)* N = **haulier**

haulier ['hɔːljər] *(Brit)* N *(firm)* transportadora; *(person)* transportador(a) *m/f*

haunch [hɔːntʃ] N anca, quadril *m*; *(of meat)* quarto traseiro

haunt [hɔːnt] VT *(subj: ghost)* assombrar; *(: problem, memory)* perseguir; *(frequent)* freqüentar; *(obsess)* obcecar ■ N lugar *m* freqüentado; *(haunted house)* casa mal-assombrada

haunted ['hɔːntɪd] ADJ *(castle etc)* mal-assombrado

haunting ['hɔːntɪŋ] ADJ *(sight, music)* obcecante

Havana [hə'vænə] N Havana

○ KEYWORD

have [hæv] (*pt, pp* had) AUX VB **1** (*gen*) ter; **to have arrived/gone/eaten/slept** ter chegado/ido/comido/dormido; **he has been kind/promoted** ele foi bondoso/promovido; **having finished** *or* **when he had finished, he left** quando ele terminou, foi embora

2 (*in tag questions*): **you've done it, haven't you?** você fez isto, não foi?; **he hasn't done it, has he?** ele não fez isto, fez?

3 (*in short questions and answers*): **you've made a mistake — no I haven't/so I have** você fez um erro — não, eu não fiz/sim, eu fiz; **I've been there before, have you?** eu já estive lá, e você?

■ MODAL AUX VB (*be obliged*): **to have (got) to do sth** ter que fazer algo; **I haven't got** *or* **I don't have to wear glasses** eu não preciso usar óculos; **this has to be a mistake** isto tem que ser um erro

■ VT **1** (*possess*) ter; **he has (got) blue eyes/dark hair** ele tem olhos azuis/cabelo escuro

2 (*referring to meals etc*): **to have breakfast** tomar café (BR), tomar o pequeno almoço (PT); **to have lunch/dinner** almoçar/jantar; **to have a drink/a cigarette** tomar um drinque/fumar um cigarro

3 (*receive, obtain etc*): **may I have your address?** pode me dar seu endereço?; **you can have it for 5 pounds** você pode levá-lo por 5 libras; **I must have it by tomorrow** preciso ter isto até amanhã; **to have a baby** dar à luz (BR), ter um nenê *or* bebê (PT)

4 (*maintain, allow*): **he will have it that he is right** ele vai insistir que ele está certo; **I won't have it/this nonsense!** não vou agüentar isso/este absurdo!; **we can't have that** não podemos permitir isto

5: **to have sth done** mandar fazer algo; **to have one's hair cut** ir cortar o cabelo; **to have sb do sth** mandar alguém fazer algo; **he soon had them all laughing/working** logo ele tinha feito com que todos rissem/trabalhassem

6 (*experience, suffer*): **to have a cold/flu** estar resfriado (BR) *or* constipado (PT)/com gripe; **she had her bag stolen/her arm broken** ela teve sua bolsa roubada/ela quebrou o braço; **to have an operation** fazer uma operação

7 (+ *n: take, hold etc*): **to have a swim/walk/bath/rest** ir nadar/passear/tomar um banho/descansar; **let's have a look** vamos dar uma olhada; **to have a party** fazer uma festa; **to have a meeting** ter um encontro; **let me have a try** deixe-me tentar

8 (*inf: dupe*): **he's been had** ele comprou gato por lebre

▶ **have out** VT: **to have it out with sb** (*settle a problem*) explicar-se com alguém

haven ['heɪvn] N porto; (*fig*) abrigo, refúgio

haven't ['hævnt] = **have not**

haversack ['hævəsæk] N mochila

havoc ['hævək] N destruição *f*; **to play ~ with** (*fig*) estragar

Hawaii [hə'waɪiː] N Havaí *m*

Hawaiian [ha'waɪjən] ADJ, N havaiano(-a)

hawk [hɔːk] N falcão *m* ■ VT (*goods for sale*) mascatear

hawker ['hɔːkə^r] N camelô *m*, mascate *m*

hawthorn ['hɔːθɔːn] N pilriteiro, estripeiro

hay [heɪ] N feno; **hay fever** N febre *f* do feno

haystack ['heɪstæk] N palheiro

haywire ['heɪwaɪə^r] (*inf*) ADJ: **to go ~** (*person*) ficar maluco; (*plan*) desorganizar-se, degringolar

hazard ['hæzəd] N (*danger*) perigo, risco; (*chance*) acaso ■ VT aventurar, arriscar; **to be a health/fire ~** ser um risco para a saúde/de incêndio; **to ~ a guess** arriscar um palpite

hazardous ['hæzədəs] ADJ (*dangerous*) perigoso; (*risky*) arriscado

hazard pay (US) N adicional *m* por insalubridade

hazard warning lights NPL (*Aut*) pisca-alerta *m*

haze [heɪz] N névoa

hazel [heɪzl] N (*tree*) aveleira ■ ADJ (*eyes*) castanho-claro *inv*

hazelnut ['heɪzlnʌt] N avelã *f*

hazy ['heɪzɪ] ADJ nublado; (*idea*) confuso

H-bomb N bomba de hidrogênio

h & c (*Brit*) ABBR = **hot and cold (water)**

HE ABBR = **high explosive**; (*Rel, Diplomacy*) = **His (or Her) Excellency**

he [hiː] PRON ele; **he who ...** quem ..., aquele que ...; **he-bear** *etc* N urso macho *etc*

head [hɛd] N cabeça; (*of table*) cabeceira; (*of queue*) frente *f*; (*of organization*) chefe *m/f*; (*of school*) diretor(a) *m/f* ■ VT (*list*) encabeçar; (*group*) liderar; **~s or tails** cara ou coroa; **~ first** de cabeça; **~ over heels** de pernas para o ar; **~ over heels in love** apaixonadíssimo; **to ~ the ball** cabecear a bola; **£10 a** *or* **per ~** £10 por pessoa *or* cabeça; **to sit at the ~ of the table** sentar-se à cabeceira da mesa; **to have a ~ for business** ter tino para negócios; **to have no ~ for heights** não suportar alturas; **to come to a ~** (*fig: situation etc*) chegar a um ponto crítico; **on your ~ be it** você que arque com as conseqüências

▶ **head for** VT FUS dirigir-se a; (*disaster*) estar procurando

▶ **head off** VT (*danger, threat*) desviar

headache ['hɛdeɪk] N dor *f* de cabeça; **to have a ~** estar com dor de cabeça

head cold N resfriado (BR), constipação *f* (PT)

headdress ['hɛddrɛs] N (*of Indian etc*) cocar *m*; (*of bride*) grinalda

header ['hɛdə^r] N (*Brit: inf: Football*) cabeçada; (*on page*) cabeçalho

headhunter ['hɛdhʌntə^r] N caçador *m* de cabeças

heading ['hɛdɪŋ] N título, cabeçalho; (*subject title*) rubrica

headlamp ['hɛdlæmp] (*Brit*) N = **headlight**

headland ['hɛdlənd] N promontório

headlight ['hɛdlaɪt] N farol m

headline ['hɛdlaɪn] N manchete f

headlong ['hɛdlɔŋ] ADV (fall) de cabeça; (rush) precipitadamente

headmaster [hɛd'mɑːstəʳ] N diretor m (de escola)

headmistress [hɛd'mɪstrɪs] N diretora f (de escola)

head office N matriz f

head-on ADJ (collision) de frente; (confrontation) direto

headphones ['hɛdfəunz] NPL fones mpl de ouvido

headquarters [hɛd'kwɔːtəz] NPL (of business etc) sede f; (Mil) quartel m general

headrest ['hɛdrɛst] N apoio para a cabeça

headroom ['hɛdrum] N (in car) espaço (para a cabeça); (under bridge) vão m livre

headscarf ['hɛdskɑːf] (irreg) N lenço de cabeça

headset ['hɛdsɛt] N fones mpl de ouvido

headstone ['hɛdstəun] N lápide f de ponta cabeça

headstrong ['hɛdstrɔŋ] ADJ voluntarioso, teimoso

head waiter N maitre m (BR), chefe m de mesa (PT)

headway ['hɛdweɪ] N progresso; **to make ~** avançar

headwind ['hɛdwɪnd] N vento contrário

heady ['hɛdɪ] ADJ (exciting) emocionante; (intoxicating) estonteante

heal [hiːl] VT curar ■ VI cicatrizar

health [hɛlθ] N saúde f; **good ~!** saúde!; **Department of H~** (US) ≈ Ministério da Saúde; **health centre** (Brit) N posto de saúde; **health food(s)** N(PL) alimentos mpl naturais; **health food shop** N loja de comida natural; **health hazard** N risco para a saúde

Health Service (Brit) N: **the ~** o Serviço Nacional da Saúde, ≈ a Previdência Social

healthy ['hɛlθɪ] ADJ (person) saudável; (air, walk) sadio; (economy) próspero, forte

heap [hiːp] N pilha, montão m ■ VT amontoar, empilhar; (plate) encher; **~s (of)** (inf: lots) um monte (de); **to ~ favours/praise/gifts etc on sb** cobrir or cumular alguém de favores/elogios/presentes etc

hear [hɪəʳ] (pt, pp **heard**) VT ouvir; (listen to) escutar; (news) saber; (lecture) assistir a ■ VI ouvir; **to ~ about** ouvir falar de; **when did you ~ about this?** quando você soube disso?; **to ~ from sb** ter notícias de alguém; **I've never ~d of the book** eu nunca ouvi falar no livro
  ▶ **hear out** VT ouvir sem interromper

heard [həːd] PT, PP of **hear**

hearing ['hɪərɪŋ] N (sense) audição f; (Law) audiência; **to give sb a ~** (Brit) ouvir alguém; **hearing aid** N aparelho para a surdez

hearsay ['hɪəseɪ] N boato, ouvir-dizer m; **by ~** por ouvir dizer

hearse [həːs] N carro fúnebre

heart [hɑːt] N coração m; (of problem, city) centro; **hearts** NPL (Cards) copas fpl; **to lose/take ~** perder o ânimo/criar coragem; **at ~** no fundo; **by ~** (learn, know) de cor; **to set one's ~ on sth/ on doing sth** decidir-se por algo/a fazer algo; **the ~ of the matter** a essência da questão; **heart attack** N ataque m de coração

heartbeat ['hɑːtbiːt] N batida do coração

heartbreak ['hɑːtbreɪk] N desgosto, dor f

heartbreaking ['hɑːtbreɪkɪŋ] ADJ desolador(a)

heartbroken ['hɑːtbrəukən] ADJ: **to be ~** estar inconsolável

heartburn ['hɑːtbəːn] N azia

-hearted ['hɑːtɪd] SUFFIX: **kind~** bondoso

heartening ['hɑːtnɪŋ] ADJ animador(a)

heart failure N parada cardíaca

heartfelt ['hɑːtfɛlt] ADJ (cordial) cordial; (deeply felt) sincero

hearth [hɑːθ] N lar m; (fireplace) lareira

heartily ['hɑːtɪlɪ] ADV sinceramente, cordialmente; (laugh) a gargalhadas, com vontade; (eat) apetitosamente; **I ~ agree** concordo completamente; **to be ~ sick of** (Brit) estar farto de

heartland ['hɑːtlænd] N coração m (do país)

heartless ['hɑːtlɪs] ADJ cruel, sem coração

heart-to-heart N (conversation) franco, sincero ■ N conversa franca

heart transplant N transplante m de coração

heartwarming ['hɑːtwɔːmɪŋ] ADJ emocionante

hearty ['hɑːtɪ] ADJ (person) energético; (laugh) animado; (appetite) bom/boa; (welcome) sincero; (dislike) absoluto

heat [hiːt] N calor m; (excitement) ardor m; (Sport: also: **qualifying heat**) (prova) eliminatória; (Zool): **in ~, on ~** (Brit) no cio ■ VT esquentar; (room, house) aquecer; (fig) acalorar
  ▶ **heat up** VI aquecer-se, esquentar ■ VT esquentar

heated ['hiːtɪd] ADJ aquecido; (fig) acalorado

heater ['hiːtəʳ] N aquecedor m

heath [hiːθ] (Brit) N charneca

heathen ['hiːðn] ADJ, N pagão/pagã m/f

heather ['hɛðəʳ] N urze f

heating ['hiːtɪŋ] N aquecimento, calefação f

heat-resistant ADJ resistente ao calor

heatstroke ['hiːtstrəuk] N insolação f

heat wave N onda de calor

heave [hiːv] VT (pull) puxar; (push) empurrar (com esforço); (lift) levantar (com esforço) ■ VI (water) agitar-se; (retch) ter ânsias de vômito ■ N puxão m; empurrão m; **to ~ a sigh** soltar um suspiro
  ▶ **heave to** VI (Naut) capear

heaven ['hɛvn] N céu m, paraíso; **~ forbid!** Deus me livre!; **thank ~!** graças a Deus!; **for ~'s sake!** pelo amor de Deus!

heavenly ['hɛvnlɪ] ADJ celestial; (Rel) divino

heavily ['hɛvɪlɪ] ADV pesadamente; (drink, smoke) excessivamente; (sleep, depend) profundamente

heavy ['hɛvɪ] ADJ pesado; (work) duro; (responsibility) grande; (sea) violento; (rain, meal) forte; (*drinker, smoker*) inveterado; (*weather*) carregado; **it's ~ going** é difícil; **heavy cream** (*US*) N creme *m* de leite

heavy-duty ADJ de serviço pesado

heavy goods vehicle (*Brit*) N caminhão *m* de carga pesada

heavy-handed [-'hændɪd] ADJ (*fig*) desajeitado, sem tato

heavyweight ['hɛvɪweɪt] N (*Sport*) peso-pesado

Hebrew ['hi:bru:] ADJ hebreu/hebréia; (*Ling*) hebraico ■ N (*Ling*) hebraico

Hebrides ['hɛbrɪdi:z] N: **the ~** as (ilhas) Hébridas

heckle ['hɛkl] VT apartear

heckler ['hɛklə^r] N pessoa que aparteia

hectare ['hɛktɛə^r] (*Brit*) N hectare *m*

hectic ['hɛktɪk] ADJ agitado

hector ['hɛktə^r] VT importunar, implicar com

he'd [hi:d] = **he would; he had**

hedge [hɛdʒ] N cerca viva, sebe *f* ■ VI dar evasivas ■ VT: **to ~ one's bets** (*fig*) resguardar-se; **as a ~ against inflation** para precaver-se da inflação

▶ **hedge in** VT cercar com uma sebe

hedgehog ['hɛdʒhɔg] N ouriço

hedgerow ['hɛdʒrəu] N cercas *fpl* vivas, sebes *fpl*

hedonism ['hi:dənɪzm] N hedonismo

heed [hi:d] VT (*also:* **take heed of:** *attend to*) prestar atenção a; (: *bear in mind*) levar em consideração

heedless ['hi:dlɪs] ADJ desatento, negligente

heel [hi:l] N (*of shoe*) salto; (*of foot*) calcanhar *m* ■ VT (*shoe*) pôr salto em; **to take to one's ~s** dar no pé *or* aos calcanhares

hefty ['hɛftɪ] ADJ (*person*) robusto; (*parcel*) pesado; (*piece*) grande; (*profit*) alto

heifer ['hɛfə^r] N novilha, bezerra

height [haɪt] N (*of person*) estatura; (*of building, tree*) altura; (*of plane*) altitude *f*; (*high ground*) monte *m*; (*altitude*) altitude *f*; (*fig: of power*) auge *m*; (: *of luxury*) máximo; (: *of stupidity*) cúmulo; **what ~ are you?** quanto você tem de altura?; **of average ~** de estatura mediana; **to be afraid of ~s** ter medo de alturas; **it's the ~ of fashion** é a última palavra *or* moda

heighten ['haɪtən] VT elevar; (*fig*) aumentar

heinous ['hi:nəs] ADJ hediondo, abominável

heir [ɛə^r] N herdeiro; **heir apparent** N herdeiro presuntivo

heiress ['ɛərɪs] N herdeira

heirloom ['ɛəlu:m] N relíquia de família

heist [haɪst] (*US: inf*) N (*hold-up*) assalto

held [hɛld] PT, PP *of* **hold**

helicopter ['hɛlɪkɔptə^r] N helicóptero

heliport ['hɛlɪpɔ:t] N (*Aviat*) heliporto

helium ['hi:lɪəm] N hélio

hell [hɛl] N inferno; **a ~ of a ...** (*inf*) um ... danado; **~!** (*inf*) droga!

he'll [hi:l] = **he will; he shall**

hellish ['hɛlɪʃ] ADJ infernal; (*inf*) terrível

hello [hə'ləu] EXCL oi! (BR), olá! (PT); (*on phone*) alô! (BR), está! (PT); (*surprise*) ora essa!

helm [hɛlm] N (*Naut*) timão *m*, leme *m*

helmet ['hɛlmɪt] N capacete *m*

helmsman ['hɛlmzmən] (*irreg*) N timoneiro

help [hɛlp] N ajuda; (*charwoman*) faxineira; (*assistant*) auxiliar *m/f* ■ VT ajudar; **~!** socorro!; **~ yourself** sirva-se; **can I ~ you?** (*in shop*) deseja alguma coisa?; **with the ~ of** com a ajuda de; **to be of ~ to sb** ajudar alguém, ser útil a alguém; **to ~ sb (to) do sth** ajudar alguém a fazer algo; **he can't ~ it** não tem culpa

helper ['hɛlpə^r] N ajudante *m/f*

helpful ['hɛlpful] ADJ (*person*) prestativo; (*advice*) útil

helping ['hɛlpɪŋ] N porção *f*

helpless ['hɛlplɪs] ADJ (*incapable*) incapaz; (*defenceless*) indefeso; (*baby*) desamparado

helplessly ['hɛlplɪslɪ] ADV (*watch*) sem poder fazer nada

Helsinki [hɛl'sɪŋkɪ] N Helsinque

helter-skelter ['hɛltə'skɛltə^r] (*Brit*) N (*at amusement park*) tobogã *m*

hem [hɛm] N bainha ■ VT embainhar

▶ **hem in** VT cercar, encurralar; **to feel ~med in** sentir-se acuado

he-man (*irreg*) N macho

hematology ['hi:mə'tɔlədʒɪ] (*US*) N = **haematology**

hemisphere ['hɛmɪsfɪə^r] N hemisfério

hemlock ['hɛmlɔk] N cicuta

hemoglobin ['hi:mə'gləubɪn] (*US*) N = **haemoglobin**

hemophilia ['hi:mə'fɪlɪə] (*US*) N = **haemophilia**

hemorrhage ['hɛmərɪdʒ] (*US*) N = **haemorrhage**

hemorrhoids ['hɛmərɔɪdʒ] (*US*) NPL = **haemorrhoids**

hemp [hɛmp] N cânhamo

hen [hɛn] N galinha; (*female bird*) fêmea

hence [hɛns] ADV (*therefore*) daí, portanto; **2 years ~** daqui a 2 anos

henceforth ['hɛns'fɔ:θ] ADV de agora em diante, doravante

henchman ['hɛntʃmən] (*pej: irreg*) N jagunço, capanga *m*

henna ['hɛnə] N hena

hen party (*inf*) N reunião *f* de mulheres

henpecked ['hɛnpɛkt] ADJ dominado pela esposa

hepatitis [hɛpə'taɪtɪs] N hepatite *f*

her [hə:^r] PRON (*direct*) a; (*indirect*) lhe; (*stressed, after prep*) ela ■ ADJ seu/sua, dela; **~ name** o nome dela; **I see ~** vejo-a, vejo ela (BR) (*inf*); **give ~ a book** dá-lhe um livro, dá um livro a ela; *see also* **me; my**

herald ['hɛrəld] N (*forerunner*) precursor(a) *m/f* ■ VT anunciar

heraldic [hɛ'rældɪk] ADJ heráldico

heraldry ['hɛrəldrɪ] N heráldica

herb [hə:b] N erva

herbaceous [hə:'beɪʃəs] ADJ herbáceo

herbal ['hə:bəl] ADJ herbáceo; **~ tea** tisana

herd [hə:d] N rebanho ■ VT (*drive: animals, people*) conduzir; (*gather*) arrebanhar

here [hɪəʳ] ADV aqui; (to this place) para cá; (at this point) nesse ponto ■ EXCL tomal; ~! (present) presente!; ~ is/are aqui está/estão; ~ he/she is! aqui está ele/ela!; ~ she comes lá vem ela; come ~! vem cá!; ~ and t~ aqui e ali

hereabouts ['hɪərə'bauts] ADV por aqui

hereafter [hɪər'ɑːftəʳ] ADV daqui por diante ■ N: the ~ a vida de além-túmulo

hereby [hɪə'baɪ] ADV (in letter) por este meio

hereditary [hɪ'rɛdɪtrɪ] ADJ hereditário

heredity [hɪ'rɛdɪtɪ] N hereditariedade f

heresy ['hɛrəsɪ] N heresia

heretic ['hɛrətɪk] N herege m/f

heretical [hɪ'rɛtɪkl] ADJ herético

herewith [hɪə'wɪð] ADV em anexo, junto

heritage ['hɛrɪtɪdʒ] N herança; (fig) patrimônio; **our national** ~ nosso patrimônio nacional

hermetically [həː'mɛtɪklɪ] ADV hermeticamente; ~ **sealed** hermeticamente fechado

hermit ['həːmɪt] N eremita m/f

hernia ['həːnɪə] N hérnia

hero ['hɪərəu] (pl heroes) N herói m; (of book, film) protagonista m

heroic [hɪ'rəuɪk] ADJ heróico

heroin ['hɛrəuɪn] N heroína; **heroin addict** N viciado(-a) em heroína

heroine ['hɛrəuɪn] N heroína; (of book, film) protagonista

heroism ['hɛrəuɪzm] N heroísmo

heron ['hɛrən] N garça

hero worship N culto de heróis

herring ['hɛrɪŋ] (pl herrings or herring) N arenque m

hers [həːz] PRON (o) seu/(a) sua, (o/a) dela; **a friend of** ~ uma amiga dela; **this is** ~ isto é dela; see also **mine**

herself [həː'sɛlf] PRON (reflexive) se; (emphatic) ela mesma; (after prep) si (mesma); see also **oneself**

Herts (Brit) ABBR = **Hertfordshire**

he's [hiːz] = **he is; he has**

hesitant ['hɛzɪtənt] ADJ hesitante, indeciso; **to be ~ about doing sth** hesitar em fazer algo

hesitate ['hɛzɪteɪt] VI hesitar; **to ~ to do** hesitar em fazer; **don't ~ to phone** não deixe de telefonar

hesitation [hɛzɪ'teɪʃən] N hesitação f, indecisão f; **I have no ~ in saying (that)** ... não hesito em dizer (que) ...

hessian ['hɛsɪən] N aniagem f

heterogeneous ['hɛtərə'dʒiːnɪəs] ADJ heterogêneo

heterosexual ['hɛtərəu'sɛksjuəl] ADJ, N heterossexual m/f

het up [hɛt-] (inf) ADJ excitado

HEW (US) N ABBR (= Department of Health, Education and Welfare) ministério da saúde, da educação e da previdência social

hew [hjuː] (pp hewed) VT cortar (com machado)

hex [hɛks] (US) N feitiço ■ VT enfeitiçar

hexagon ['hɛksəgən] N hexágono

hexagonal [hɛk'sægənl] ADJ hexagonal

hey [heɪ] EXCL eh! ei!

heyday ['heɪdeɪ] N: **the ~ of** o auge or apogeu de

HF N ABBR (= high frequency) HF f

HGV (Brit) N ABBR = **heavy goods vehicle**

HI (US) ABBR (Post) = **Hawaii**

hi [haɪ] EXCL oi!

hiatus [haɪ'eɪtəs] N hiato

hibernate ['haɪbəneɪt] VI hibernar

hibernation [haɪbə'neɪʃən] N hibernação f

hiccough ['hɪkʌp] VI soluçar ■ NPL soluço; **to have (the) ~s** estar com soluço

hiccup ['hɪkʌp] VI = **hiccough**

hiccups ['hɪkʌps] NPL = **hiccoughs**

hid [hɪd] PT of **hide**

hidden ['hɪdn] PP of hide ■ ADJ (costs) oculto

hide [haɪd] (pt hid, pp hidden) N (skin) pele f ■ VT esconder, ocultar; (view) obscurecer ■ VI: **to ~ (from sb)** esconder-se or ocultar-se (de alguém)

hide-and-seek N esconde-esconde m

hideaway ['haɪdəweɪ] N esconderijo

hideous ['hɪdɪəs] ADJ horrível

hide-out N esconderijo

hiding ['haɪdɪŋ] N (beating) surra; **to be in ~** (concealed) estar escondido; **hiding place** N esconderijo

hierarchy ['haɪərɑːkɪ] N hierarquia

hieroglyphic [haɪərə'glɪfɪk] ADJ hieroglífico

hieroglyphics [haɪərə'glɪfɪks] NPL hieroglifos mpl

hi-fi ['haɪfaɪ] ABBR = **high fidelity** ■ N altafidelidade f; (system) som m ■ ADJ de alta-fidelidade

higgledy-piggledy ['hɪgldɪ'pɪgldɪ] ADV desordenadamente

high [haɪ] ADJ alto; (number) grande; (price) alto, elevado; (wind) forte; (voice) agudo; (opinion) ótimo; (principles) nobre; (inf: person: on drugs) alto, baratinado; (Brit: Culin: meat, game) faisandé inv; (: spoilt) estragado ■ ADV alto, a grande altura ■ N: **exports have reached a new ~** as exportações atingiram um novo pico; **it is 20 m ~** tem 20 m de altura; ~ **in the air** nas alturas; **to pay a ~ price for sth** pagar caro por algo

highball ['haɪbɔːl] (US) N uísque com soda

highboy ['haɪbɔɪ] (US) N comoda alta

highbrow ['haɪbrau] ADJ intelectual, erudito

highchair ['haɪtʃɛəʳ] N cadeira alta (para criança)

high-class ADJ (neighbourhood) nobre; (hotel) de primeira categoria; (person) da classe alta; (performance etc) de alto nível

high court N (Law) tribunal m superior

higher ['haɪəʳ] ADJ (form of life, study etc) superior ■ ADV mais alto; **higher education** N ensino superior

high finance N altas finanças fpl

high-flier N estudante m/f (or empregado(-a)) talentoso(-a) e ambicioso(-a)

high-flying ADJ (fig) ambicioso, talentoso

high-handed ['hændɪd] ADJ despótico

high-heeled ['-hiːld] ADJ de salto alto

highjack ['haɪdʒæk] N, VT = **hijack**

high jump N (Sport) salto em altura
highlands ['haɪləndz] NPL serrania, serra; **the H~** (in Scotland) a Alta Escócia
high-level ADJ de alto nível; **~ language** (Comput) linguagem f de alto nível
highlight ['haɪlaɪt] N (fig: of event) ponto alto; (in hair) mecha ■ VT realçar, ressaltar; **the ~s of the match** os melhores lances do jogo
highlighter ['haɪlaɪtər] N (pen) caneta marca-texto
highly ['haɪlɪ] ADV altamente; (very) muito; **~ paid** muito bem pago; **to speak ~ of** falar elogiosamente de; **highly strung** ADJ tenso, irritadiço
High Mass N missa cantada
highness ['haɪnɪs] N altura; **Her** (or **His**) **H~** Sua Alteza
high-pitched ADJ agudo
high-powered ADJ (engine) muito potente, de alta potência; (fig: person) dinâmico; (: job, businessman) muito importante
high-pressure ADJ de alta pressão
high-rise ADJ alto
high-rise block N edifício alto, espigão m
high school N (Brit) escola secundária; (US) científico

● HIGH SCHOOL

● Uma high school é um estabelecimento de
● ensino secundário. Nos Estados Unidos,
● existem a Junior High School, que equivale
● aproximadamente aos dois últimos anos
● do primeiro grau, e a Senior High School, que
● corresponde ao segundo grau. Na Grã-
● Bretanha, esse termo às vezes é utilizado
● para as escolas secundárias.

high season (Brit) N alta estação f
high spirits NPL alegria; **to be in ~** estar alegre
high street (Brit) N rua principal
highway ['haɪweɪ] (US) N (between states, towns) estrada; (main road) rodovia
Highway Code (Brit) N Código Nacional de Trânsito
highwayman ['haɪweɪmən] (irreg) N salteador m de estrada
hijack ['haɪdʒæk] VT seqüestrar ■ N (also: hijacking) seqüestro (de avião)
hijacker ['haɪdʒækər] N seqüestrador(a) m/f (de avião)
hike [haɪk] VI (go walking) caminhar ■ N caminhada, excursão f a pé; (inf: in prices etc) aumento ■ VT (inf) aumentar
hiker ['haɪkər] N caminhante m/f, andarilho(-a)
hiking ['haɪkɪŋ] N excursões fpl a pé, caminhar m
hilarious [hɪ'lɛərɪəs] ADJ (behaviour, event) hilariante
hilarity [hɪ'lærɪtɪ] N hilaridade f
hill [hɪl] N colina; (high) montanha; (slope) ladeira, rampa

hillbilly ['hɪlbɪlɪ] (US) N montanhês(-esa) m/f; (pej) caipira m/f, jeca m/f
hillock ['hɪlək] N morro pequeno
hillside ['hɪlsaɪd] N vertente f
hill start N (Aut) partida em ladeira
hilly ['hɪlɪ] ADJ montanhoso; (uneven) acidentado
hilt [hɪlt] N (of sword) punho, guarda; **to the ~** (fig: support) plenamente
him [hɪm] PRON (direct) o; (indirect) lhe; (stressed, after prep) ele; **I see ~** vejo-o, vejo ele (BR) (inf); **give ~ a book** dá-lhe um livro, dá um livro a ele; see also **mine**
Himalayas [hɪmə'leɪəz] NPL: **the ~** o Himalaia
himself [hɪm'sɛlf] PRON (reflexive) se; (emphatic) ele mesmo; (after prep) si (mesmo); see also **oneself**
hind [haɪnd] ADJ traseiro ■ N corça
hinder ['hɪndər] VT atrapalhar; (delay) retardar
hindquarters ['haɪnd'kwɔːtəz] NPL (Zool) quartos mpl traseiros
hindrance ['hɪndrəns] N (nuisance) estorvo; (interruption) impedimento
hindsight ['haɪndsaɪt] N: **with (the benefit of) ~** em retrospecto
Hindu ['hɪnduː] ADJ, N hindu m/f
hinge [hɪndʒ] N dobradiça ■ VI (fig): **to ~ on** depender de
hint [hɪnt] N (suggestion) sugestão f; (advice) palpite m, dica; (sign) sinal m ■ VT: **to ~ that** insinuar que ■ VI dar indiretas; **to ~ at** fazer alusão a; (clue) dar uma indireta; **give me a ~** (clue) dá uma pista
hip [hɪp] N quadril m; **hip flask** N cantil m
hippie ['hɪpɪ] N hippie m/f
hip pocket N bolso traseiro
hippopotami [hɪpə'pɒtəmaɪ] NPL of hippopotamus
hippopotamus [hɪpə'pɒtəməs] (pl hippopotamuses or hippopotami) N hipopótamo
hippy ['hɪpɪ] N = **hippie**
hire ['haɪər] VT (Brit: car, equipment) alugar; (worker) contratar ■ N aluguel m; (of person) contratação f; **for ~** aluga-se; (taxi) livre; **on ~** alugado
  ▶ **hire out** VT alugar
hire(d) car ['haɪəd-] (Brit) N carro alugado
hire purchase (Brit) N compra a prazo; **to buy sth on ~** comprar algo a prazo or pelo crediário
his [hɪz] PRON (o) seu/(a) sua, (o/a) dele ■ ADJ seu/sua, dele; **~ name** o nome dele; **it's ~** é dele; see also **my; mine**
Hispanic [hɪs'pænɪk] ADJ hispânico
hiss [hɪs] VI (snake, fat) assoviar; (gas) silvar; (boo) vaiar ■ N silvo; vaia
histogram ['hɪstəgræm] N histograma m
historian [hɪ'stɔːrɪən] N historiador(a) m/f
historic(al) [hɪ'stɔrɪk(l)] ADJ histórico
history ['hɪstərɪ] N história; (of illness etc) histórico; **medical ~** (of patient) histórico médico
histrionics [hɪstrɪ'ɒnɪks] N teatro
hit [hɪt] (pt, pp hit) VT (strike: person, thing) bater

em; (*reach: target*) acertar, alcançar; (*collide with: car*) bater em, colidir com; (*fig: affect*) atingir
■ N (*blow*) golpe *m*; (*success*) sucesso, grande êxito; (*song*) sucesso; (*Internet visit*) visita; **to ~ it off with sb** dar-se bem com alguém; **to ~ the headlines** virar *or* fazer manchete; **to ~ the road** (*inf*) dar o fora, mandar-se
▶ **hit back** VI: **to ~ back at sb** revidar ao ataque (*or* à crítica *etc*) de alguém
▶ **hit out at** VT FUS tentar bater em; (*fig*) criticar veementemente
▶ **hit (up)on** VT FUS (*answer*) descobrir

hit-and-run driver N *motorista que atropela alguém e foge da cena do acidente*

hitch [hɪtʃ] VT (*fasten*) atar, amarrar; (*also*: **hitch up**) levantar ■ N (*difficulty*) dificuldade *f*; **to ~ a lift** pegar carona (BR), arranjar uma boleia (PT); **technical** ~ probleminha técnico
▶ **hitch up** VT (*horse, cart*) atrelar; *see also* **hitch**

hitch-hike VI pegar carona (BR), andar à boleia (PT)

hitch-hiker N pessoa que pega carona (BR) *or* anda à boleia (PT)

hi-tech ADJ tecnologicamente avançado ■ N alta tecnologia

hitherto [hɪðə'tu:] ADV até agora

hit-man ['hɪtmæn] (*irreg*) N sicário

hit-or-miss ADJ aleatório; **it's ~ whether ...** não é nada certo que ...

hit parade N parada de sucessos

hive [haɪv] N colméia; **the shop was a ~ of activity** (*fig*) a loja fervilhava de atividade
▶ **hive off** (*inf*) VT transferir

hl ABBR (= *hectolitre*) hl

HM ABBR (= *His* (*or* Her) Majesty) SM

HMG (Brit) ABBR = **His** (*or* **Her) Majesty's Government**

HMI (Brit) ABBR (Sch) = **His** (*or* **Her) Majesty's Inspector**

HMO (US) N ABBR (= *health maintenance organization*) *órgão que garante a manutenção de sáude*

HMS (Brit) ABBR = **His** (*or* **Her) Majesty's Ship**

HMSO (Brit) N ABBR (= *His* (*or* Her) Majesty's Stationery Office) *imprensa do governo*

HNC (Brit) N ABBR = **Higher National Certificate**

HND (Brit) N ABBR = **Higher National Diploma**

hoard [hɔ:d] N provisão *f*; (*of money*) tesouro ■ VT acumular

hoarding ['hɔ:dɪŋ] (Brit) N tapume *m*, outdoor *m*

hoarfrost ['hɔ:frɔst] N geada

hoarse [hɔ:s] ADJ rouco

hoax [həuks] N trote *m*

hob [hɔb] N *parte de cima do fogão*

hobble ['hɔbl] VI coxear

hobby ['hɔbɪ] N hobby *m*, passatempo predileto

hobby-horse N cavalinho-de-pau; (*fig*) tema *m* favorito

hobnob ['hɔbnɔb] VI: **to ~ with** ter intimidade com

hobo ['həubəu] (*pl* **hobos** *or* **hoboes**) (US) N vagabundo

hock [hɔk] N (Brit: *wine*) vinho branco do Reno;

(*of animal, Culin*) jarrete *m*; (*inf*): **to be in ~** (*person*) estar endividado; (*object*) estar no prego *or* empenhado

hockey ['hɔkɪ] N hóquei *m*

hocus-pocus ['həukəs'pəukəs] N (*trickery*) tapeação *f*; (*words*) embromação *f*

hodgepodge ['hɔdʒpɔdʒ] N = **hotchpotch**

hoe [həu] N enxada ■ VT trabalhar com enxada, capinar

hog [hɔg] N porco; (*person*) glutão(-ona) *m/f* ■ VT (*fig*) monopolizar; **to go the whole ~** ir até o fim

hoist [hɔɪst] N (*lift*) guincho; (*crane*) guindaste *m* ■ VT içar

hold [həuld] (*pt, pp* **held**) VT segurar; (*contain*) conter; (*keep back*) reter; (*believe*) sustentar; (*have*) ter; (*record etc*) deter; (*take weight*) agüentar; (*meeting*) realizar; (*detain*) deter; (*consider*): **to ~ sb responsible (for sth)** responsabilizar alguém (por algo) ■ VI (*withstand pressure*) resistir; (*be valid*) ser válido ■ N (*handle*) apoio (para a mão); (*fig: grasp*) influência, domínio; (*of ship*) porão *m*; (*of plane*) compartimento para cargo; **to ~ office** (Pol) exercer um cargo; **he ~s the view that ...** ele sustenta que ...; **~ the line!** (Tel) não desligue!; **to ~ one's own** (*fig*) virar-se, sair-se bem; **to ~ firm** *or* **fast** agüentar; **to catch** *or* **get (a) ~ of** agarrar, pegar; **to get ~ of** (*fig*) arranjar; **to get ~ of o.s.** controlar-se
▶ **hold back** VT reter; (*secret*) manter, guardar; **to ~ sb back from doing sth** impedir alguém de fazer algo
▶ **hold down** VT (*person*) segurar; (*job*) manter
▶ **hold forth** VI discursar, deitar falação
▶ **hold off** VT (*enemy*) afastar, repelir ■ VI (*rain*): **if the rain ~s off** se não chover
▶ **hold on** VI agarrar-se; (*wait*) esperar; **~ on!** espera aí!; (Tel) não desligue!
▶ **hold on to** VT FUS agarrar-se a; (*keep*) guardar, ficar com
▶ **hold out** VT estender ■ VI (*resist*) resistir; **to ~ out (against)** defender-se (contra)
▶ **hold over** VT (*meeting etc*) adiar
▶ **hold up** VT (*raise*) levantar; (*support*) apoiar; (*delay*) atrasar; (*traffic*) reter; (*rob*) assaltar

holdall ['həuldɔ:l] (Brit) N bolsa de viagem

holder ['həuldəʳ] N (*of ticket*) portador(a) *m/f*; (*of record*) detentor(a) *m/f*; (*of office, title etc*) titular *m/f*

holding ['həuldɪŋ] N (*share*) participação *f*; **holdings** NPL posses *fpl*; **holding company** N holding *f*

hold-up ['həuldʌp] N (*robbery*) assalto; (*delay*) demora; (Brit: *in traffic*) engarrafamento

hole [həul] N buraco; (*small: in sock etc*) furo ■ VT esburacar; **~ in the heart** (Med) defeito na membrana cardíaca; **to pick ~s (in)** (*fig*) botar defeito (em)
▶ **hole up** VI esconder-se

holiday ['hɔlədɪ] N (Brit: *vacation*) férias *fpl*; (*day off*) dia *m* de folga; (*public holiday*) feriado; **to be on ~** estar de férias; **tomorrow is a ~** amanhã é feriado; **holiday camp** (Brit) N colônia de férias

holiday-maker (Brit) N pessoa (que está) de férias

holiday pay N salário de férias

holiday resort N local m de férias

holiday season N temporada de férias

holiness ['həulɪnɪs] N santidade f

Holland ['hɔlənd] N Holanda

hollow ['hɔləu] ADJ oco, vazio; (cheeks) côncavo; (eyes) fundo; (sound) surdo; (laugh, claim) falso ■ N buraco; (in ground) cavidade f, depressão f ■ VT: **to ~ out** escavar

holly ['hɔlɪ] N azevinho

hollyhock ['hɔlɪhɔk] N malva-rosa

holocaust ['hɔləkɔːst] N holocausto

hologram ['hɔləgræm] N holograma m

holster ['həulstər] N coldre m

holy ['həulɪ] ADJ sagrado; (person) santo; (water) bento; **Holy Ghost** N Espírito Santo; **Holy Land** N: **the Holy Land** a Terra Santa; **holy orders** NPL ordens fpl sacras; **Holy Spirit** N = **Holy Ghost**

homage ['hɔmɪdʒ] N homenagem f; **to pay ~ to** prestar homenagem a, homenagear

home [həum] N casa, lar m; (country) pátria; (institution) asilo ■ CPD (domestic) caseiro, doméstico; (of family) familiar; (heating, computer etc) residencial; (Econ, Pol) nacional, interno; (Sport: team) de casa; (: game) no próprio campo ■ ADV (direction) para casa; (right in: nail etc) até o fundo; **to go/come ~** ir/vir para casa; **at ~** em casa; **make yourself at ~** fique à vontade; **near my ~** perto da minha casa
  ▸ **home in on** VT FUS (missiles) dirigir-se automaticamente para

home address N endereço residencial

home-brew N (wine) vinho feito em casa; (beer) cerveja feita em casa

homecoming ['həumkʌmɪŋ] N regresso ao lar

home computer N computador m residencial

Home Counties NPL os condados por volta de Londres

home economics N economia doméstica

home-grown ADJ (not foreign) nacional; (from garden) plantado em casa

homeland ['həumlænd] N terra (natal)

homeless ['həumlɪs] ADJ sem casa, desabrigado ■ NPL: **the ~** os desabrigados

home loan N crédito imobiliário, financiamento habitacional

homely ['həumlɪ] ADJ (domestic) caseiro; (simple) simples inv

home-made ADJ caseiro

Home Office (Brit) N Ministério do Interior

homeopathy etc [həumɪ'ɔpəθɪ] (US) = **homoeopathy etc**

home page N (Comput) home page f, página inicial

home rule N autonomia

Home Secretary (Brit) N Ministro do Interior

homesick ['həumsɪk] ADJ: **to be ~** estar com saudades (do lar)

homestead ['həumstɛd] N propriedade f; (farm) fazenda

home town N cidade f natal

homeward ['həumwəd] ADJ (journey) para casa, para a terra natal

homeward(s) ['həumwəd(z)] ADV para casa

homework ['həumwəːk] N dever m de casa

homicidal [hɔmɪ'saɪdl] ADJ homicida

homicide ['hɔmɪsaɪd] (US) N homicídio

homily ['hɔmɪlɪ] N homilia

homing ['həumɪŋ] ADJ (device, missile) de correção de rumo; **~ pigeon** pombo- correio

homoeopath ['həumɪəpæθ] (US homeopath) N homeopata m/f

homoeopathic [həumɪə'pæθɪk] (US homeopathic) ADJ homeopático

homoeopathy [həumɪ'ɔpəθɪ] (US homeopathy) N homeopatia

homogeneous [hɔməu'dʒiːnɪəs] ADJ homogêneo

homogenize [hə'mɔdʒənaɪz] VT homogeneizar

homosexual [hɔməu'sɛksjuəl] ADJ, N homossexual m/f

homosexuality [hɔməsɛksju'ælɪtɪ] N homossexualismo

Hon. ABBR = **honourable**; **honorary**

Honduras [hɔn'djuərəs] N Honduras (no article)

hone [həun] VT amolar, afiar

honest ['ɔnɪst] ADJ (truthful) franco; (trustworthy) honesto; (sincere) sincero, franco; **to be quite ~ with you ...** para falar a verdade ...

honestly ['ɔnɪstlɪ] ADV honestamente, francamente

honesty ['ɔnɪstɪ] N honestidade f, sinceridade f

honey ['hʌnɪ] N mel m; (US: inf: darling) querido(-a)

honeycomb ['hʌnɪkəum] N favo de mel; (pattern) em forma de favo ■ VT (fig): **to ~ with** crivar de

honeymoon ['hʌnɪmuːn] N lua-de-mel f; (trip) viagem f de lua-de-mel

honeysuckle ['hʌnɪsʌkl] N madressilva

Hong Kong ['hɔŋ'kɔŋ] N Hong Kong (no article)

honk [hɔŋk] N buzinada ■ VI (Aut) buzinar

Honolulu [hɔnə'luːluː] N Honolulu

honor ['ɔnər] (US) VT, N = **honour**

honorary ['ɔnərərɪ] ADJ (unpaid) não remunerado; (duty, title) honorário

honour ['ɔnər] (US honor) VT honrar ■ N honra; **in ~ of** em honra de

hono(u)rable ['ɔnərəbl] ADJ honrado

hono(u)r-bound ADJ: **to be hono(u)r-bound to do** estar moralmente obrigado a fazer

hono(u)rs degree N (Sch) diploma m com distinção

Hons. ABBR (Sch) = **hono(u)rs degree**

hood [hud] N capuz m; (of cooker) tampa; (Brit: Aut) capota; (US: Aut) capô m; (inf: hoodlum) pinta-brava m

hooded ['hudɪd] ADJ encapuzado, mascarado

hoodlum ['huːdləm] N pinta-brava m

hoodwink ['hudwɪŋk] VT tapear

hoof [huːf] (pl hooves) N casco, pata

hook [huk] N gancho; (on dress) colchete m;
(for fishing) anzol m ■ VT (fasten) prender com
gancho (or colchete); (fish) fisgar; ~ **and eye**
colchete m; **by ~ or by crook** custe o que custar;
to be ~ed (on) (inf) estar viciado (em); (person)
estar fissurado (em)
▶ **hook up** VT ligar
hooligan ['hu:lɪgən] N desordeiro(-a),
bagunceiro(-a)
hooliganism ['hu:lɪgənɪzm] N vandalismo
hoop [hu:p] N arco
hooray [hu:'reɪ] EXCL = **hurrah**
hoot [hu:t] VI (Aut) buzinar; (siren) tocar; (owl)
piar ■ VT (jeer at) vaiar ■ N buzinada; toque m
de sirena; **to ~ with laughter** morrer de rir
hooter ['hu:təʳ] N (Brit: Aut) buzina; (Naut,
factory) sirena
hoover® ['hu:vəʳ] (Brit) aspirador m (de pó) VT
passar o aspirador em
hooves [hu:vz] NPL of **hoof**
hop [hɔp] VI saltar, pular; (on one foot) pular num
pé só ■ N salto, pulo
hope [həup] VT: **to ~ that/to do** esperar que/
fazer ■ VI esperar ■ N esperança; **I ~ so/not**
espero que sim/não
hopeful ['həupful] ADJ (person) otimista,
esperançoso; (situation) promissor(a); **I'm ~
that she'll manage to come** acredito que ela
conseguirá vir
hopefully ['həupfulɪ] ADV (with hope)
esperançosamente; (one hopes): **~, they'll come
back** é de esperar or esperamos que voltem
hopeless ['həuplɪs] ADJ desesperado,
irremediável; (useless) inútil; (bad) péssimo
hopelessly ['həupləslɪ] ADV (confused, involved)
irremediavelmente
hopper ['hɔpəʳ] N tremonha
hops [hɔps] NPL (Bot) lúpulo
horde [hɔ:d] N multidão f
horizon [hə'raɪzn] N horizonte m
horizontal [hɔrɪ'zɔntl] ADJ horizontal
hormone ['hɔ:məun] N hormônio
horn [hɔ:n] N corno, chifre m; (material) chifre;
(Mus) trompa; (Aut) buzina
horned [hɔ:nd] ADJ (animal) com chifres,
chifrudo
hornet ['hɔ:nɪt] N vespão m
horny ['hɔ:nɪ] ADJ (material) córneo; (hands)
calejado; (inf: aroused) excitado (sexualmente),
com tesão (BR) (inf!)
horoscope ['hɔrəskəup] N horóscopo
horrendous [hə'rɛndɔs] ADJ horrendo
horrible ['hɔrɪbl] ADJ horrível; (terrifying) terrível
horrid ['hɔrɪd] ADJ horrível
horrific [hə'rɪfɪk] ADJ horroroso
horrify ['hɔrɪfaɪ] VT horrorizar
horrifying ['hɔrɪfaɪɪŋ] ADJ horripilante
horror ['hɔrəʳ] N horror m; **horror film** N
filme m de terror
horror-striken ADJ = **horror-struck**
horror-struck ADJ horrorizado
hors d'œuvre [ɔ:'də:vrə] N entrada

horse [hɔ:s] N cavalo
horseback ['hɔ:sbæk]: **on ~** ADJ, ADV a cavalo
horsebox ['hɔ:sbɔks] N reboque m (para
transportar cavalos)
horse chestnut N castanha-da-índia
horse-drawn ADJ puxado a cavalo
horsefly ['hɔ:sflaɪ] N mutuca
horseman ['hɔ:smən] (irreg) N cavaleiro; (skilled)
ginete m
horsemanship ['hɔ:smənʃɪp] N equitação f
horsemen ['hɔ:smən] NPL of **horseman**
horseplay ['hɔ:spleɪ] N zona, bagunça
(brincadeiras etc)
horsepower ['hɔ:spauəʳ] N cavalo-vapor m
horse-racing N corridas fpl de cavalo, turfe m
horseradish ['hɔ:srædɪʃ] N rábano-bastardo
horseshoe ['hɔ:sʃu:] N ferradura
horse show N concurso hípico
horse-trading N regateio
horse trials NPL = **horse show**
horsewhip ['hɔ:swɪp] VT chicotear
horsewoman ['hɔ:swumən] (irreg) N amazona
horsey ['hɔ:sɪ] ADJ aficionado por cavalos;
(appearance) com cara de cavalo
horticulture ['hɔ:tɪkʌltʃəʳ] N horticultura
hose [həuz] N (also: **hosepipe**) mangueira
▶ **hose down** VT lavar com mangueira
hosiery ['həuzɪərɪ] N meias fpl e roupa de baixo
hospice ['hɔspɪs] N asilo
hospitable ['hɔspɪtəbl] ADJ hospitaleiro
hospital ['hɔspɪtl] N hospital m
hospitality [hɔspɪ'tælɪtɪ] N hospitalidade f
hospitalize ['hɔspɪtəlaɪz] VT hospitalizar
host [həust] N anfitrião m; (in hotel etc)
hospedeiro; (TV, Radio) apresentador(a) m/f; (Rel)
hóstia; (large number): **a ~ of** uma multidão de
■ VT (TV programme) apresentar, animar
hostage ['hɔstɪdʒ] N refém m
host country N país m anfitrião
hostel ['hɔstl] N hospedaria; (for students)
residência; (for the homeless) albergue m, abrigo;
(also: **youth hostel**) albergue da juventude
hostelling ['hɔstlɪŋ] N: **to go (youth) ~** viajar de
férias pernoitando em albergues de juventude
hostess ['həustɪs] N anfitriã f; (Brit: air hostess)
aeromoça (BR), hospedeira de bordo (PT); (TV,
Radio) apresentadora; (in nightclub) taxi-girl f
hostile ['hɔstaɪl] ADJ hostil
hostility [hɔ'stɪlɪtɪ] N hostilidade f
hot [hɔt] ADJ quente; (as opposed to only warm)
muito quente; (spicy) picante; (fierce) ardente;
to be ~ (person) estar com calor; (thing, weather)
estar quente
▶ **hot up** (Brit: inf) VI (party, debate) esquentar
■ VT (~ pace) acelerar; (engine) envenenar
hot-air balloon N balão m de ar quente
hotbed ['hɔtbɛd] N (fig) foco, ninho
hotchpotch ['hɔtʃpɔtʃ] (Brit) N mixórdia, salada
hot dog N cachorro-quente m
hotel [həu'tɛl] N hotel m
hotelier [hɔ'tɛljeɪ] N hoteleiro(-a); (manager)
gerente m/f

hotel industry N indústria hoteleira
hotel room N quarto de hotel
hotfoot ['hɔtfut] ADV a mil, a toda
hot-headed [-'hedɪd] ADJ impetuoso
hothouse ['hɔthaus] N estufa
hot line N (Pol) telefone m vermelho, linha direta
hotly ['hɔtlɪ] ADV ardentemente, apaixonadamente
hotplate ['hɔtpleɪt] N (on cooker) chapa elétrica
hotpot ['hɔtpɔt] (Brit) N (Culin) ragu m
hot seat N (fig) posição f de responsabilidade
hot spot N área de tensão
hot spring N fonte f termal
hot-tempered ADJ esquentado, de pavio curto
hot-water bottle N bolsa de água quente
hound [haund] VT acossar, perseguir ■ N cão m de caça, sabujo
hour ['auəʳ] N hora; **at 30 miles an** ~ = a 50 km por hora; **lunch** ~ hora do almoço; **to pay sb by the** ~ pagar alguém por hora
hourly ['auəlɪ] ADV de hora em hora ■ ADJ de hora em hora; (rate) por hora
house [n haus, pl hauzɪz, vt hauz] N (gen, firm) casa; (Pol) câmara; (Theatre) assistência, lotação f ■ VT (person) alojar; (collection) abrigar; **to/at my** ~ para a/na minha casa; **the H** ~ **(of Commons)** (Brit) a Câmara dos Comuns; **the H** ~ **(of Representatives)** (US) a Câmara de Deputados; **on the** ~ (fig) por conta da casa; **house arrest** N prisão f domiciliar
houseboat ['hausbəut] N casa flutuante
housebound ['hausbaund] ADJ preso em casa
housebreaking ['hausbreɪkɪŋ] N arrombamento de domicílio
house-broken (US) ADJ = **house-trained**
housecoat ['hauskəut] N roupão m
household ['haushəuld] N família; (house) casa
householder ['haushəuldəʳ] N (owner) dono(-a) de casa; (head of family) chefe m/f de família
household name N nome m conhecido por todos
house-hunting ['haushʌntɪŋ] N: **to go** ~ procurar casa para morar
housekeeper ['hauski:pəʳ] N governanta
housekeeping ['hauski:pɪŋ] N (work) trabalhos mpl domésticos; (money) economia doméstica; (Comput) gestão f dos discos
houseman ['hausmən] (Brit: irreg) N (Med) interno
house-proud ADJ preocupado com a aparência da casa
house-to-house ADJ (enquiries) de porta em porta; (search) de casa em casa
house-trained (Brit) ADJ (animal) domesticado
house-warming (party) [-'wɔ:mɪŋ-] N festa de inauguração de uma casa
housewife ['hauswaɪf] (irreg) N dona de casa
housework ['hauswə:k] N trabalhos mpl domésticos
housing ['hauzɪŋ] N (provision) alojamento; (houses) residências fpl; (as issue) habitação f

■ CPD (problem, shortage) habitacional; **housing association** N organização beneficente que vende ou aluga casas; **housing conditions** NPL condições fpl de habitação; **housing development** N conjunto residencial; **housing estate** (Brit) N = **housing development**
hovel ['hɔvl] N casebre m
hover ['hɔvəʳ] VI pairar; (person) rondar
hovercraft ['hɔvəkrɑ:ft] N aerobarco
hoverport ['hɔvəpɔ:t] N porto para aerobarcos

 KEYWORD

how [hau] ADV **1** (in what way) como; **how was the film?** que tal o filme?; **how are you?** como vai?
2 (to what degree) quanto; **how much milk/many people?** quanto de leite/quantas pessoas?; **how long have you been here?** há quanto tempo você está aqui?; **how old are you?** quantos anos você tem?; **how tall is he?** qual é a altura dele?; **how lovely/awful!** que ótimo/terrível!

however [hau'ɛvəʳ] ADV de qualquer modo; (+ adj) por mais ... que; (in questions) como ■ CONJ no entanto, contudo, todavia
howitzer ['hauɪtsəʳ] N (Mil) morteiro, obus m
howl [haul] N uivo ■ VI uivar
howler ['hauləʳ] N besteira, erro
H.P. (Brit) N ABBR = **hire purchase**
h.p. ABBR (Aut: = horsepower) CV
HQ N ABBR (= headquarters) QG m
HR (US) N ABBR = **House of Representatives**
HRH ABBR (= His (or Her) Royal Highness) SAR
hr(s) ABBR (= hour(s)) h(s)
HS (US) ABBR = **high school**
HST (US) ABBR (= Hawaiian Standard Time) hora do Havaí
HTML N ABBR (= Hypertext Mark-up Language) HTML f
hub [hʌb] N (of wheel) cubo; (fig) centro
hubbub ['hʌbʌb] N algazarra, vozerio
hubcap ['hʌbkæp] N (Aut) calota
HUD (US) N ABBR (= Department of Housing and Urban Development) ministério do urbanismo e da habitação
huddle ['hʌdl] VI: **to** ~ **together** aconchegar-se
hue [hju:] N cor f, matiz m; **hue and cry** N clamor m público
huff [hʌf] N: **in a** ~ com raiva; **to take the** ~ ficar sem graça
hug [hʌg] VT abraçar; (thing) agarrar, prender ■ N abraço; **to give sb a** ~ dar um abraço em alguém, abraçar alguém
huge [hju:dʒ] ADJ enorme, imenso
hulk [hʌlk] N (wreck) navio velho; (hull) casco, carcaça; (person) brutamontes m inv; (building) trambolho
hulking ['hʌlkɪŋ] ADJ pesado, grandão(-ona)
hull [hʌl] N (of ship) casco
hullabaloo ['hʌləbə'lu:] (inf) N algazarra

hullo [hə'ləu] EXCL = **hello**
hum [hʌm] VT (*tune*) cantarolar ■ VI cantarolar; (*insect, machine etc*) zumbir ■ N zumbido
human ['hju:mən] ADJ humano ■ N (*also:* **human being**) ser *m* humano
humane [hju:'meɪn] ADJ humano
humanism ['hju:mənɪzm] N humanismo
humanitarian [hju:mænɪ'teərɪən] ADJ humanitário
humanity [hju:'mænɪtɪ] N humanidade *f*
humanly ['hju:mən'lɪ] ADV humanamente
humanoid ['hju:mənɔɪd] ADJ, N humanóide *m/f*
humble ['hʌmbl] ADJ humilde ■ VT humilhar
humbly ['hʌmblɪ] ADV humildemente
humbug ['hʌmbʌg] N fraude *f*, embuste *m*; (*Brit: sweet*) bala de hortelã
humdrum ['hʌmdrʌm] ADJ (*boring*) monótono, enfadonho; (*routine*) rotineiro
humid ['hju:mɪd] ADJ úmido
humidifier [hju:'mɪdɪfaɪər] N umidificador *m*
humidity [hju:'mɪdɪtɪ] N umidade *f*
humiliate [hju:'mɪlɪeɪt] VT humilhar
humiliation [hju:mɪlɪ'eɪʃən] N humilhação *f*
humility [hju:'mɪlɪtɪ] N humildade *f*
humor ['hju:mər] (US) N, VT = **humour**
humorist ['hju:mərɪst] N humorista *m/f*
humorous ['hju:mərəs] ADJ humorístico; (*person*) engraçado
humour ['hju:mə'] (US **humor**) N humorismo, senso de humor; (*mood*) humor *m* ■ VT (*person*) fazer a vontade de; **to be in a good/bad ~** senso de humor; **to be in a good/bad ~** estar de bom/mau humor
humo(u)rless ['hju:məlɛs] ADJ sem senso de humor
hump [hʌmp] N (*in ground*) elevação *f*; (*camel's*) corcova, giba; (*deformity*) corainda
humpback ['hʌmpbæk] N corcunda *m/f*
humpbacked ['hʌmpbækt] ADJ: **~ bridge** ponte pequena e muito arqueada
humus ['hju:məs] N húmus *m*, humo
hunch [hʌntʃ] N (*premonition*) pressentimento, palpite *m*
hunchback ['hʌntʃbæk] N corcunda *m/f*
hunched [hʌntʃt] ADJ corcunda
hundred ['hʌndrəd] NUM cem; (*before lower numbers*) cento; (*collective*) centena; **~s of people** centenas de pessoas; **I'm a ~ per cent sure** tenho certeza absoluta
hundredweight ['hʌndrədweɪt] N (*Brit*) 50.8 kg; 112 lb; (US) = 45.3 kg; 100 lb
hung [hʌŋ] PT, PP *of* **hang**
Hungarian [hʌŋ'gɛərɪən] ADJ húngaro ■ N húngaro(-a); (*Ling*) húngaro
Hungary ['hʌŋgərɪ] N Hungria
hunger ['hʌŋgər] N fome *f* ■ VI: **to ~ for** ter fome de; (*desire*) desejar ardentemente; **hunger strike** N greve *f* de fome
hungrily ['hʌŋgrəlɪ] ADV (*eat*) vorazmente; (*fig*) avidamente
hungry ['hʌŋgrɪ] ADJ faminto, esfomeado; (*keen*) **~ for** (*fig*) ávido de, ansioso por; **to be ~** estar com fome

hung up (*inf*) ADJ complexado, grilado
hunk [hʌŋk] N naco; (*inf: man*) gatão *m*
hunt [hʌnt] VT (*seek*) buscar, perseguir; (*Sport*) caçar ■ VI caçar ■ N caça, caçada
▶ **hunt down** VT acossar
hunter ['hʌntər] N caçador(a) *m/f*; (*Brit: horse*) cavalo de caça
hunting ['hʌntɪŋ] N caça
hurdle ['hə:dl] N (*Sport*) barreira; (*fig*) obstáculo
hurl [hə:l] VT arremessar, lançar; (*abuse*) gritar
hurrah [hu'rɑ:] EXCL oba!, viva!
hurray [hu'reɪ] EXCL = **hurrah**
hurricane ['hʌrɪkən] N furacão *m*
hurried ['hʌrɪd] ADJ (*fast*) apressado; (*rushed*) feito às pressas
hurriedly ['hʌrɪdlɪ] ADV depressa, apressadamente
hurry ['hʌrɪ] N pressa ■ VI (*also:* **hurry up**) apressar-se ■ VT (*also:* **hurry up:** *person*) apressar; (: *work*) acelerar; **to be in a ~** estar com pressa; **to do sth in a ~** fazer algo às pressas; **to ~ in/out** entrar/sair correndo; **to ~ home** correr para casa
▶ **hurry along** VI andar às pressas
▶ **hurry away** VI sair correndo
▶ **hurry off** VI sair correndo
▶ **hurry up** VI apressar-se
hurt [hə:t] (*pt, pp* **hurt**) VT machucar; (*injure*) ferir; (*damage: business etc*) prejudicar; (*fig*) magoar ■ VI doer ■ ADJ machucado, ferido; **I ~ my arm** machuquei o braço; **where does it ~?** onde é que dói?
hurtful ['hə:tful] ADJ (*remark*) que magoa, ofensivo
hurtle ['hə:tl] VI correr; **to ~ past** passar como um raio; **to ~ down** cair com violência
husband ['hʌzbənd] N marido, esposo
hush [hʌʃ] N silêncio, quietude *f* ■ VT silenciar, fazer calar; **~!** silêncio!, psiu!
▶ **hush up** VT (*fact*) abafar, encobrir
hushed [hʌʃt] ADJ (*tone*) baixo
hush-hush ADJ secreto
husk [hʌsk] N (*of wheat*) casca; (*of maize*) palha
husky ['hʌskɪ] ADJ rouco; (*burly*) robusto ■ N cão *m* esquimó
hustings ['hʌstɪŋz] (*Brit*) NPL (*Pol*) campanha (eleitoral)
hustle ['hʌsl] VT (*push*) empurrar; (*hurry*) apressar ■ N agitação *f*, atividade *f* febril; **~ and bustle** grande movimento
hut [hʌt] N cabana, choupana; (*shed*) alpendre *m*
hutch [hʌtʃ] N coelheira
hyacinth ['haɪəsɪnθ] N jacinto
hybrid ['haɪbrɪd] ADJ, N híbrido; (*mixture*) combinação *f*
hydrant ['haɪdrənt] N (*also:* **fire hydrant**) hidrante *m*
hydraulic [haɪ'drɔ:lɪk] ADJ hidráulico
hydraulics [haɪ'drɔ:lɪks] N hidráulica
hydrochloric acid ['haɪdrəu'klɔrɪk-] N ácido clorídrico

hydroelectric [haɪdrəʊɪ'lɛktrɪk] ADJ
  hidroelétrico
hydrofoil ['haɪdrəfɔɪl] N hidrofoil m, aliscafo
hydrogen ['haɪdrədʒən] N hidrogênio;
  hydrogen bomb N bomba de hidrogênio
hydrophobia ['haɪdrə'fəubɪə] N hidrofobia
hydroplane ['haɪdrəpleɪn] N lancha planadora
hyena [haɪ'i:nə] N hiena
hygiene ['haɪdʒi:n] N higiene f
hygienic [haɪ'dʒi:nɪk] ADJ higiênico
hymn [hɪm] N hino
hype [haɪp] (inf) N tititi m, falatório
hyperactive ['haɪpər'æktɪv] ADJ hiperativo
hypermarket ['haɪpəmɑ:kɪt] (Brit) N
  hipermercado
hypertension ['haɪpə'tɛnʃən] N (Med)
  hipertensão f
hyphen ['haɪfn] N hífen m
hypnosis [hɪp'nəusɪs] N hipnose f
hypnotic [hɪp'nɒtɪk] ADJ hipnótico
hypnotism ['hɪpnətɪzm] N hipnotismo
hypnotist ['hɪpnətɪst] N hipnotizador(a) m/f
hypnotize ['hɪpnətaɪz] VT hipnotizar

hypoallergenic ['haɪpəuæələ'dʒɛnɪk] ADJ
  hipoalergênico
hypochondriac [haɪpə'kɒndrɪæk] N
  hipocondríaco(-a)
hypocrisy [hɪ'pɒkrɪsɪ] N hipocrisia
hypocrite ['hɪpəkrɪt] N hipócrita m/f
hypocritical [hɪpə'krɪtɪkl] ADJ hipócrita
hypodermic [haɪpə'də:mɪk] ADJ hipodérmico
  ■ N seringa hipodérmica
hypothermia [haɪpə'θə:mɪə] N hipotermia
hypotheses [haɪ'pɒθɪsi:z] NPL of **hypothesis**
hypothesis [haɪ'pɒθɪsɪs] (pl **hypotheses**) N
  hipótese f
hypothetic(al) [haɪpəu'θɛtɪk(l)] ADJ hipotético
hysterectomy [hɪstə'rɛktəmɪ] N histerectomia
hysteria [hɪ'stɪərɪə] N histeria
hysterical [hɪ'stɛrɪkl] ADJ histérico; (funny)
  hilariante
hysterics [hɪ'stɛrɪks] NPL (nervous) crise f
  histérica; (laughter) ataque m de riso; **to be in** or
  have - ter uma crise histérica
Hz ABBR (= hertz) Hz

I i

I, i [aɪ] N (letter) I, i m; **I for Isaac** (Brit) or **Item** (US) I de Irene

I [aɪ] PRON eu ■ ABBR = **island**; (= isle) I

IA (US) ABBR (Post) = **Iowa**

IAEA N ABBR (= International Atomic Energy Agency) IAEA f

IBA (Brit) N (= Independent Broadcasting Authority) órgão que supervisiona as emissoras comerciais de TV

Iberian [aɪˈbɪərɪən] ADJ ibérico;**Iberian Peninsula** N: **the Iberian Peninsula** a península Ibérica

IBEW (US) N ABBR (= International Brotherhood of Electrical Workers) sindicato internacional dos eletricistas

i/c (Brit) ABBR = **in charge**

ICC N ABBR = **International Chamber of Commerce**; (US) = **Interstate Commerce Commission**

ice [aɪs] N gelo; (ice cream) sorvete m ■ VT (cake) cobrir com glacê; (drink) gelar ■ VI (also: **ice over**, **ice up**) gelar; **to put sth on** ~ (fig) engavetar algo;**ice age** N era glacial;**ice axe** N picareta para o gelo

iceberg [ˈaɪsbəːg] N iceberg m; **this is just the tip of the** ~ isso é só a ponta do iceberg

icebox [ˈaɪsbɔks] N (US) geladeira; (Brit: in fridge) congelador m; (insulated box) geladeira portátil

icebreaker [ˈaɪsbreɪkəʳ] N navio quebra-gelo m

ice bucket N balde m de gelo

ice-cold ADJ gelado

ice cream N sorvete m (BR), gelado (PT)

ice cube N pedra de gelo

iced [aɪst] ADJ (drink) gelado; (cake) glaçado

ice hockey N hóquei m sobre o gelo

Iceland [ˈaɪslənd] N Islândia

Icelander [ˈaɪsləndəʳ] N islandês(-esa) m/f

Icelandic [aɪsˈlændɪk] ADJ islandês(-esa) ■ N (Ling) islandês m

ice lolly (Brit) N picolé m

ice pick N furador m de gelo

ice rink N pista de gelo, rinque m

ice-skate N patim m (para o gelo) ■ VI patinar no gelo

ice-skating N patinação f no gelo

icicle [ˈaɪsɪkl] N pingente m de gelo

icing [ˈaɪsɪŋ] N (Culin) glacê m; (Aviat etc) formação f de gelo;**icing sugar** (Brit) N açúcar m

glacê

ICJ N ABBR = **International Court of Justice**

icon [ˈaɪkɔn] N (gen, Comput) ícone m

ICR (US) N ABBR = **Institute for Cancer Research**

ICU N ABBR (= intensive care unit) UTI f

icy [ˈaɪsɪ] ADJ gelado; (fig) glacial, indiferente

ID (US) ABBR (Post) = **Idaho**

I'd [aɪd] = **I would**; **I had**

ID card N = **identity card**

IDD (Brit) N ABBR (Tel: = international direct dialling) DDI f

idea [aɪˈdɪə] N idéia; **good** ~! boa idéia!; **to have an** ~ **that** ... ter a impressão de que ...; **I haven't the least** ~ não tenho a mínima idéia

ideal [aɪˈdɪəl] N ideal m ■ ADJ ideal

idealist [aɪˈdɪəlɪst] N idealista m/f

ideally [aɪˈdɪəlɪ] ADV de preferência; ~ **the book should have** ... seria ideal que o livro tivesse ...

identical [aɪˈdɛntɪkl] ADJ idêntico

identification [aɪdɛntɪfɪˈkeɪʃən] N identificação f; **means of** ~ documentos pessoais

identify [aɪˈdɛntɪfaɪ] VT identificar ■ VI: **to** ~ **with** identificar-se com

Identikit ® [aɪˈdɛntɪkɪt] N: **Identikit picture** retrato falado

identity [aɪˈdɛntɪtɪ] N identidade f;**identity card** N carteira de identidade;**identity parade** (Brit) N identificação f

ideological [aɪdɪəˈlɔdʒɪkəl] ADJ ideológico

ideology [aɪdɪˈɔlədʒɪ] N ideologia

idiocy [ˈɪdɪəsɪ] N idiotice f; (stupid act) estupidez f

idiom [ˈɪdɪəm] N expressão f idiomática; (style of speaking) idioma m, linguagem f

idiomatic [ɪdɪəˈmætɪk] ADJ idiomático

idiosyncrasy [ɪdɪəuˈsɪŋkrəsɪ] N idiossincrasia

idiot [ˈɪdɪət] N idiota m/f

idiotic [ɪdɪˈɔtɪk] ADJ idiota

idle [ˈaɪdl] ADJ ocioso; (lazy) preguiçoso; (unemployed) desempregado; (pointless) inútil, vão(-vã) ■ VI (machine) funcionar com a transmissão desligada
► **idle away** VT: **to** ~ **away the time** perder or desperdiçar tempo

idleness [ˈaɪdlnɪs] N ociosidade f; preguiça; (pointlessness) inutilidade f

idler [ˈaɪdləʳ] N preguiçoso(-a)

idle time N (*Comm*) tempo ocioso
idol ['aɪdl] N ídolo
idolize ['aɪdəlaɪz] VT idolatrar
idyllic [ɪ'dɪlɪk] ADJ idílico
i.e. ABBR (= *id est*) i.e., isto é

○ KEYWORD

if [ɪf] CONJ **1** (*conditional use*) se; **I'll go if you come with me** irei se você vier comigo; **if necessary** se necessário; **if I were you** se eu fôsse você
2 (*whenever*) quando
3 (*although*): (**even**) **if** mesmo que; **I like it,** (**even**) **if you don't** eu gosto disto, mesmo que você não goste
4 (*whether*) se
5: **if so/not** sendo assim/do contrário; **if only** se pelo menos; *see also* **as**

igloo ['ɪglu:] N iglu *m*
ignite [ɪg'naɪt] VT acender; (*set fire to*) incendiar ▪ VI acender
ignition [ɪg'nɪʃən] N (*Aut*) ignição *f*; **to switch on/off the ~** ligar/desligar o motor; **ignition key** N (*Aut*) chave *f* de ignição
ignoble [ɪg'nəubl] ADJ ignóbil
ignominious [ɪgnə'mɪnɪəs] ADJ vergonhoso, humilhante
ignoramus [ɪgnə'reɪməs] N ignorante *m/f*
ignorance ['ɪgnərəns] N ignorância; **to keep sb in ~ of sth** deixar alguém na ignorância de algo
ignorant ['ɪgnərənt] ADJ ignorante; **to be ~ of** ignorar
ignore [ɪg'nɔ:ʳ] VT (*person*) não fazer caso de; (*fact*) não levar em consideração, ignorar
ikon ['aɪkɒn] N = **icon**
IL (*US*) ABBR (*Post*) = **Illinois**
ILA (*US*) N ABBR (= *International Longshoremen's Association*) sindicato internacional dos portuários
I'll [aɪl] = **I will; I shall**
ill [ɪl] ADJ doente; (*slightly ill*) indisposto; (*bad*) mau(-má); (*harmful: effects*) nocivo ▪ N mal *m*; (*fig*) desgraça ▪ ADV: **to speak/think ~ of sb** falar/pensar mal de alguém; **to take** *or* **be taken ~** ficar doente
ill-advised [-əd'vaɪzd] ADJ pouco recomendado; (*misled*) mal aconselhado
ill-at-ease ADJ constrangido, pouco à vontade
ill-considered [-kən'sɪdəd] ADJ (*plan*) imponderado
ill-disposed ADJ: **to be ~ towards sb/sth** ser desfavorável a alguém/algo
illegal [ɪ'li:gl] ADJ ilegal
illegally [ɪ'li:gəlɪ] ADV ilegalmente
illegible [ɪ'ledʒɪbl] ADJ ilegível
illegitimate [ɪlɪ'dʒɪtɪmət] ADJ ilegítimo
ill-fated ADJ malfadado
ill-favoured [-'feɪvəd] (*US* **ill-favored**) ADJ desagradável
ill feeling N má vontade *f*, rancor *m*

ill-gotten ADJ (*gains etc*) mal adquirido
illicit [ɪ'lɪsɪt] ADJ ilícito
ill-informed ADJ mal informado
illiterate [ɪ'lɪtərət] ADJ analfabeto
ill-mannered [-'mænəd] ADJ mal-educado, grosseiro
illness ['ɪlnɪs] N doença
illogical [ɪ'lɒdʒɪkl] ADJ ilógico
ill-suited [-'su:tɪd] ADJ (*couple*) desajustado; **he is ~ to the job** ele é inadequado para o cargo
ill-timed [-taɪmd] ADJ inoportuno
ill-treat VT maltratar
ill-treatment N maus tratos *mpl*
illuminate [ɪ'lu:mɪneɪt] VT (*room, street*) iluminar, clarear; (*subject*) esclarecer; **~d sign** anúncio luminoso
illuminating [ɪ'lu:mɪneɪtɪŋ] ADJ esclarecedor
illumination [ɪlu:mɪ'neɪʃən] N iluminação *f*; **illuminations** NPL (*decorative lights*) luminárias *fpl*
illusion [ɪ'lu:ʒən] N ilusão *f*; **to be under the ~ that ...** estar com a ilusão de que ...
illusive [ɪ'lu:sɪv] ADJ ilusório
illusory [ɪ'lu:sərɪ] ADJ ilusório
illustrate ['ɪləstreɪt] VT ilustrar; (*subject*) esclarecer; (*point*) exemplificar
illustration [ɪlə'streɪʃən] N (*art*) ilustração *f*; (*example*) exemplo; (*explanation*) esclarecimento; (*in book*) gravura, ilustração
illustrator ['ɪləstreɪtəʳ] N ilustrador(a) *m/f*
illustrious [ɪ'lʌstrɪəs] ADJ ilustre
ill will N animosidade *f*
ILO N ABBR (= *International Labour Organization*) OIT *f*
ILWU (*US*) N ABBR (= *International Longshoremen's and Warehousemen's Union*) sindicato dos portuários
I'm [aɪm] = **I am**
image ['ɪmɪdʒ] N imagem *f*
imagery ['ɪmɪdʒərɪ] N imagens *fpl*
imaginable [ɪ'mædʒɪnəbl] ADJ imaginável, concebível
imaginary [ɪ'mædʒɪnərɪ] ADJ imaginário
imagination [ɪmædʒɪ'neɪʃən] N imaginação *f*; (*inventiveness*) inventividade *f*; (*illusion*) fantasia
imaginative [ɪ'mædʒɪnətɪv] ADJ imaginativo
imagine [ɪ'mædʒɪn] VT imaginar; (*delude o.s.*) fantasiar
imbalance [ɪm'bæləns] N desequilíbrio; (*inequality*) desigualdade *f*
imbecile ['ɪmbəsi:l] N imbecil *m/f*
imbue [ɪm'bju:] VT: **to ~ sth with** imbuir *or* impregnar algo de
IMF N ABBR (= *International Monetary Fund*) FMI *m*
imitate ['ɪmɪteɪt] VT imitar
imitation [ɪmɪ'teɪʃən] N imitação *f*; (*copy*) cópia; (*mimicry*) mímica
imitator ['ɪmɪteɪtəʳ] N imitador(a) *m/f*
immaculate [ɪ'mækjulət] ADJ impecável; (*Rel*) imaculado
immaterial [ɪmə'tɪərɪəl] ADJ irrelevante; **it is ~ whether ...** é indiferente se ...
immature [ɪmə'tjuəʳ] ADJ (*person, organism*)

imaturo; (*fruit*) verde; (*of one's youth*) juvenil

immaturity [ɪmə'tjuərɪtɪ] N imaturidade f

immeasurable [ɪ'mɛʒrəbl] ADJ incomensurável, imensurável

immediacy [ɪ'miːdɪəsɪ] N (*of events etc*) proximidade f; (*of needs*) urgência

immediate [ɪ'miːdɪət] ADJ imediato; (*pressing*) urgente, premente; (*neighbourhood, family*) próximo

immediately [ɪ'miːdɪətlɪ] ADV (*at once*) imediatamente; ~ **next to** bem junto a

immense [ɪ'mɛns] ADJ imenso; (*importance*) enorme

immensity [ɪ'mɛnsətɪ] N imensidade f

immerse [ɪ'məːs] VT (*submerge*) submergir; (*sink*) imergir, mergulhar; **to be ~d in** (*fig*) estar absorto em

immersion heater [ɪ'məːʃn-] (*Brit*) N aquecedor m de imersão

immigrant ['ɪmɪɡrənt] N imigrante m/f

immigrate ['ɪmɪɡreɪt] VI imigrar

immigration [ɪmɪ'ɡreɪʃən] N imigração f; **immigration authorities** NPL fiscais mpl de imigração, ≈ polícia federal; **immigration laws** NPL leis fpl imigratórias

imminent ['ɪmɪnənt] ADJ iminente

immobile [ɪ'məubaɪl] ADJ imóvel

immobilize [ɪ'məubɪlaɪz] VT imobilizar

immoderate [ɪ'mɔdərət] ADJ imoderado

immodest [ɪ'mɔdɪst] ADJ (*indecent*) indecente, impudico; (*person: boasting*) presumido, arrogante

immoral [ɪ'mɔrl] ADJ imoral

immorality [ɪmə'rælɪtɪ] N imoralidade f

immortal [ɪ'mɔːtl] ADJ imortal

immortalize [ɪ'mɔːtəlaɪz] VT imortalizar

immovable [ɪ'muːvəbl] ADJ (*object*) imóvel, fixo; (*person*) inflexível

immune [ɪ'mjuːn] ADJ: ~ **to** imune a, imunizado contra

immunity [ɪ'mjuːnɪtɪ] N (*Med*) imunidade f; (*Comm*) isenção f; **diplomatic** ~ imunidade diplomática

immunization [ɪmjunaɪ'zeɪʃən] N imunização f

immunize ['ɪmjunaɪz] VT imunizar

imp [ɪmp] N diabinho; criança levada

impact ['ɪmpækt] N impacto (BR), impacte m (BR)

impair [ɪm'pɛəʳ] VT prejudicar

impale [ɪm'peɪl] VT perfurar, empalar

impart [ɪm'pɑːt] VT (*make known*) comunicar; (*bestow*) dar

impartial [ɪm'pɑːʃl] ADJ imparcial

impartiality [ɪmpɑːʃɪ'ælɪtɪ] N imparcialidade f

impassable [ɪm'pɑːsəbl] ADJ (*barrier, river*) intransponível; (*road*) intransitável

impasse [æm'pɑːs] N (*fig*) impasse m

impassioned [ɪm'pæʃənd] ADJ ardente, veemente

impassive [ɪm'pæsɪv] ADJ impassível

impatience [ɪm'peɪʃəns] N impaciência

impatient [ɪm'peɪʃənt] ADJ impaciente; **to get**

or **grow** ~ impacientar-se

impeach [ɪm'piːtʃ] VT impugnar; (*public official*) levar a juízo

impeachment [ɪm'piːtʃmənt] N (*Law*) impeachment m

impeccable [ɪm'pɛkəbl] ADJ impecável

impecunious [ɪmpə'kjuːnɪəs] ADJ impecunioso, sem recursos

impede [ɪm'piːd] VT impedir, estorvar

impediment [ɪm'pɛdɪmənt] N obstáculo; (*also:* **speech impediment**) defeito (de fala)

impel [ɪm'pɛl] VT (*force*): **to ~ sb (to do sth)** impelir alguém (a fazer algo)

impending [ɪm'pɛndɪŋ] ADJ (*near*) iminente, próximo

impenetrable [ɪm'pɛnɪtrəbl] ADJ impenetrável; (*fig*) incompreensível

imperative [ɪm'pɛrətɪv] ADJ (*tone*) imperioso, obrigatório; (*necessary*) indispensável; (*pressing*) premente ■ N (*Ling*) imperativo

imperceptible [ɪmpə'sɛptɪbl] ADJ imperceptível

imperfect [ɪm'pəːfɪkt] ADJ imperfeito; (*goods etc*) defeituoso ■ N (*Ling: also:* **imperfect tense**) imperfeito

imperfection [ɪmpə'fɛkʃən] N (*blemish*) defeito; (*state*) imperfeição f

imperial [ɪm'pɪərɪəl] ADJ imperial

imperialism [ɪm'pɪərɪəlɪzəm] N imperialismo

imperil [ɪm'pɛrɪl] VT pôr em perigo, arriscar

imperious [ɪm'pɪərɪəs] ADJ imperioso

impersonal [ɪm'pəːsənl] ADJ impessoal

impersonate [ɪm'pəːsəneɪt] VT fazer-se passar por, personificar; (*Theatre*) imitar

impersonation [ɪmpəːsə'neɪʃən] N (*Law*) impostura; (*Theatre*) imitacão f

impersonator [ɪm'pəːsəneɪtəʳ] N impostor(a) m/f; (*Theatre*) imitador(a) m/f

impertinence [ɪm'pəːtɪnəns] N impertinência, insolência

impertinent [ɪm'pəːtɪnənt] ADJ impertinente, insolente

imperturbable [ɪmpə'təːbəbl] ADJ imperturbável, inabalável

impervious [ɪm'pəːvɪəs] ADJ impenetrável; (*fig*): ~ **to** insensível a

impetuous [ɪm'pɛtjuəs] ADJ impetuoso, precipitado

impetus ['ɪmpətəs] N ímpeto; (*fig*) impulso

impinge [ɪm'pɪndʒ]: **to ~ on** VT FUS impressionar, impingir em; (*affect*) afetar

impish ['ɪmpɪʃ] ADJ levado, travesso

implacable [ɪm'plækəbl] ADJ implacável, impiedoso

implant [*vt* ɪm'plɑːnt, *n* 'ɪmplɑːnt] VT (*Med*) implantar; (*fig*) inculcar ■ N implante m

implausible [ɪm'plɔːzɪbl] ADJ inverossímil (BR), inverosímil (PT)

implement [*n* 'ɪmplɪmənt, *vt* 'ɪmplɪmɛnt] N instrumento, ferramenta; (*for cooking*) utensílio ■ VT efetivar; (*carry out*) realizar, executar

implicate ['ɪmplɪkeɪt] VT (*compromise*) comprometer; (*involve*) implicar, envolver

implication [ɪmplɪˈkeɪʃən] N implicação f, conseqüência; (*involvement*) involvimento; **by ~** por conseqüência

implicit [ɪmˈplɪsɪt] ADJ implícito; (*complete*) absoluto

implicitly [ɪmˈplɪsɪtlɪ] ADV implicitamente; (*completely*) completamente

implore [ɪmˈplɔːʳ] VT (*person*) implorar, suplicar

imply [ɪmˈplaɪ] VT (*involve*) implicar; (*mean*) significar; (*hint*) dar a entender que; **it is implied** se subentende

impolite [ɪmpəˈlaɪt] ADJ indelicado, mal-educado

imponderable [ɪmˈpɒndərəbl] ADJ imponderável

import [vt ɪmˈpɔːt, n, cpd ˈɪmpɔːt] VT importar ▪ N (*Comm*) importação f; (: *article*) mercadoria importada; (*meaning*) significado, sentido ▪ CPD (*duty, licence etc*) de importação

importance [ɪmˈpɔːtəns] N importância; **to be of great/little ~** ser de grande/pouca importância

important [ɪmˈpɔːtənt] ADJ importante; **it is ~ that ...** é importante *or* importa que ...; **it's not ~** não tem importância, não importa

importantly [ɪmˈpɔːtəntlɪ] ADV: **but, more ~ ...** mas, o que é mais importante ...

importation [ɪmpɔːˈteɪʃən] N importação f

imported [ɪmˈpɔːtɪd] ADJ importado

importer [ɪmˈpɔːtəʳ] N importador(a) m/f

impose [ɪmˈpəʊz] VT impor ▪ VI: **to ~ on sb** abusar de alguém

imposing [ɪmˈpəʊzɪŋ] ADJ imponente

imposition [ɪmpəˈzɪʃən] N (*of tax etc*) imposição f; **to be an ~ on sb** (*person*) abusar de alguém

impossibility [ɪmpɒsɪˈbɪlɪtɪ] N impossibilidade f

impossible [ɪmˈpɒsɪbl] ADJ impossível; (*situation*) inviável; (*person*) insuportável; **it's ~ for me to leave** é-me impossível sair, não dá para eu sair (*inf*)

impostor [ɪmˈpɒstəʳ] N impostor(a) m/f

impotence [ˈɪmpətəns] N impotência

impotent [ˈɪmpətənt] ADJ impotente

impound [ɪmˈpaʊnd] VT confiscar

impoverished [ɪmˈpɒvərɪʃt] ADJ empobrecido; (*land*) esgotado

impracticable [ɪmˈpræktɪkəbl] ADJ impraticável, inexeqüível

impractical [ɪmˈpræktɪkl] ADJ pouco prático

imprecise [ɪmprɪˈsaɪs] ADJ impreciso, inexato

impregnable [ɪmˈpregnəbl] ADJ invulnerável; (*castle*) inexpugnável

impregnate [ˈɪmpregneɪt] VT (*gen*) impregnar; (*soak*) embeber; (*fertilize*) fecundar

impresario [ɪmprɪˈsɑːrɪəʊ] N empresário(-a)

impress [ɪmˈpres] VT impressionar; (*mark*) imprimir ▪ VI causar boa impressão; **to ~ sth on sb** inculcar algo em alguém; **it ~ed itself on me** fiquei com isso gravado (na memória)

impression [ɪmˈpreʃən] N impressão f; (*footprint etc*) marca; (*print run*) edição f; **to make a good/bad ~ on sb** causar boa/má impressão em

alguém; **to be under the ~ that** estar com a impressão de que

impressionable [ɪmˈpreʃənəbl] ADJ impressionável; (*sensitive*) sensível

impressionist [ɪmˈpreʃənɪst] N impressionista m/f

impressive [ɪmˈpresɪv] ADJ impressionante

imprint [ˈɪmprɪnt] N impressão f, marca; (*Publishing*) nome m (da coleção)

imprinted [ɪmˈprɪntɪd] ADJ: **~ on** imprimido em; (*fig*) gravado em

imprison [ɪmˈprɪzn] VT encarcerar

imprisonment [ɪmˈprɪzənmənt] N prisão f

improbable [ɪmˈprɒbəbl] ADJ improvável; (*story*) inverossímil (BR), inverosímil (PT)

impromptu [ɪmˈprɒmptjuː] ADJ improvisado ▪ ADV de improviso

improper [ɪmˈprɒpəʳ] ADJ (*unsuitable*) impróprio; (*dishonest*) desonesto; (*unseemly*) indecoroso; (*indecent*) indecente

impropriety [ɪmprəˈpraɪətɪ] N falta de decoro, inconveniência; (*indecency*) indecência; (*of language*) impropriedade f

improve [ɪmˈpruːv] VT melhorar ▪ VI melhorar; (*pupils*) progredir

▶ **improve (up)on** VT FUS melhorar

improvement [ɪmˈpruːvmənt] N melhora, melhoria; (*of pupils*) progresso; **to make ~s to** melhorar

improvisation [ɪmprəvaɪˈzeɪʃən] N improvisação f

improvise [ˈɪmprəvaɪz] VT, VI improvisar

imprudence [ɪmˈpruːdns] N imprudência

imprudent [ɪmˈpruːdnt] ADJ imprudente

impudent [ˈɪmpjudnt] ADJ insolente, impudente

impugn [ɪmˈpjuːn] VT impugnar, contestar

impulse [ˈɪmpʌls] N impulso, ímpeto; (*Elec*) impulso; **to act on ~** agir sem pensar *or* num impulso; **impulse buy** N compra por impulso

impulsive [ɪmˈpʌlsɪv] ADJ impulsivo

impunity [ɪmˈpjuːnɪtɪ] N: **with ~** impunemente

impure [ɪmˈpjʊəʳ] ADJ (*adulterated*) adulterado; (*not pure*) impuro

impurity [ɪmˈpjʊərɪtɪ] N impureza

IN (*US*) ABBR (*Post*) = **Indiana**

🔘 KEYWORD

in [ɪn] PREP 1 (*indicating place, position*) em; **in the house/garden** na casa/no jardim; **I have it in my hand** eu estou soft vousegurando isto; **in here/there** aqui dentro/lá dentro

2 (*with place names: of town, country, region*) em; **in London** em Londres; **in England/Japan/Canada/the United States** na Inglaterra/no Japão/no Canadá/nos Estados Unidos; **in Rio** no Rio

3 (*indicating time: during*) em; **in spring/autumn** na primavera/no outono; **in 1988** em 1988; **in May** em maio; **I'll see you in July** até julho; **in the morning** de manhã; **at 4 o'clock in the afternoon** às 4 da tarde

4 (*indicating time*: *in the space of*) em; **I did it in 3 hours/days** fiz isto em 3 horas/dias; **in 2 weeks** or **in 2 weeks' time** daqui a 2 semanas **5** (*indicating manner etc*): **in a loud/soft voice** em voz alta/numa voz suave; **written in pencil/ink** escrito a lápis/à caneta; **in English/ Portuguese** em inglês/português; **the boy in the blue shirt** o menino de camisa azul **6** (*indicating circumstances*): **in the sun** ao or sob o sol; **in the rain** na chuva; **a rise in prices** um aumento nos preços **7** (*indicating mood, state*): **in tears** aos prantos; **in anger/despair** com raiva/desesperado; **in good condition** em boas condições; **to live in luxury** viver no luxo **8** (*with ratios, numbers*): **1 in 10** 1 em 10, 1 em cada 10; **20 pence in the pound** vinte pênis numa libra; **they lined up in twos** eles se alinharam dois a dois **9** (*referring to people, works*) em; **in (the works of)** **Dickens** nas obras de Dickens **10** (*indicating profession etc*): **to be in teaching/ publishing** ser professor/trabalhar numa editora **11** (*after superl*): **the best pupil in the class** o melhor aluno da classe; **the biggest/smallest in Europe** o maior/menor na Europa **12** (*with present participle*): **in saying this** ao dizer isto

■ ADV: **to be in** (*person*: *at home*) estar em casa; (: *at work*) estar no trabalho; (*fashion*) estar na moda; (*ship, plane, train*): **it's in** chegou; **is he in?** ele está?; **to ask sb in** convidar alguém para entrar; **to run/limp** *etc* **in** entrar correndo/ mancando *etc*

■ N: **the ins and outs** (*of proposal, situation etc*) os cantos e recantos, os pormenores

in. ABBR = **inch(es)**
inability [ɪnəˈbɪlɪtɪ] N: ~ **(to do)** incapacidade f (de fazer); ~ **to pay** impossibilidade de pagar
inaccessible [ɪnækˈsɛsɪbl] ADJ inacessível
inaccuracy [ɪnˈækjurəsɪ] N inexatidão f, imprecisão f
inaccurate [ɪnˈækjurət] ADJ inexato, impreciso
inaction [ɪnˈækʃən] N inação f
inactivity [ɪnækˈtɪvɪtɪ] N inatividade f
inadequacy [ɪnˈædɪkwəsɪ] N (*insufficiency*) insuficiência
inadequate [ɪnˈædɪkwət] ADJ (*insufficient*) insuficiente; (*unsuitable*) inadequado; (*person*) impróprio
inadmissible [ɪnədˈmɪsəbl] ADJ inadmissível
inadvertent [ɪnədˈvəːtənt] ADJ (*mistake*) cometido sem querer
inadvertently [ɪnədˈvəːtntlɪ] ADV inadvertidamente, sem querer
inadvisable [ɪnədˈvaɪzəbl] ADJ desaconselhável, inoportuno
inane [ɪˈneɪn] ADJ tolo; (*fatuous*) vazio
inanimate [ɪnˈænɪmət] ADJ inanimado
inapplicable [ɪnˈæplɪkəbl] ADJ inaplicável

inappropriate [ɪnəˈprəuprɪət] ADJ inadequado; (*word, expression*) impróprio
inapt [ɪnˈæpt] ADJ inapto
inaptitude [ɪnˈæptɪtjuːd] N incapacidade f, inaptidão f
inarticulate [ɪnɑːˈtɪkjulət] ADJ (*person*) incapaz de expressar-se (bem); (*speech*) inarticulado
inasmuch as [ɪnəzˈmʌtʃ-] ADV, CONJ (*given that*) visto que; (*since*) desde que, já que
inattention [ɪnəˈtɛnʃən] N inatenção f
inattentive [ɪnəˈtɛntɪv] ADJ desatento
inaudible [ɪnˈɔːdɪbl] ADJ inaudível
inaugural [ɪˈnɔːgjurəl] ADJ (*speech*) inaugural; (: *of president*) de posse
inaugurate [ɪˈnɔːgjureɪt] VT inaugurar; (*president, official*) empossar
inauguration [ɪnɔːgjuˈreɪʃən] N inauguração f; (*of president, official*) posse f
inauspicious [ɪnɔːsˈpɪʃəs] ADJ infausto
in-between ADJ intermediário
inborn [ɪnˈbɔːn] ADJ (*feeling*) inato; (*defect*) congênito
inbred [ɪnˈbrɛd] ADJ inato; (*family*) de procriação consangüínea
inbreeding [ɪnˈbriːdɪŋ] N endogamia
Inc. ABBR = **incorporated**
Inca [ˈɪŋkə] ADJ (*also:* **Incan**) inca, incaico ■ N inca m/f
incalculable [ɪnˈkælkjuləbl] ADJ incalculável
incapability [ɪnkeɪpəˈbɪlɪtɪ] N incapacidade f
incapable [ɪnˈkeɪpəbl] ADJ: ~ **(of doing)** incapaz (de fazer)
incapacitate [ɪnkəˈpæsɪteɪt] VT incapacitar
incapacitated [ɪnkəˈpæsɪteɪtɪd] ADJ (*Law*) incapacitado
incapacity [ɪnkəˈpæsɪtɪ] N (*inability*) incapacidade f
incarcerate [ɪnˈkɑːsəreɪt] VT encarcerar
incarnate [*adj* ɪnˈkɑːnɪt, *vt* ˈɪnkɑːneɪt] ADJ encarnado, personificado ■ VT encarnar
incarnation [ɪnkɑːˈneɪʃən] N encarnação f
incendiary [ɪnˈsɛndɪərɪ] ADJ incendiário ■ N (*bomb*) bomba incendiária
incense [*n* ˈɪnsɛns, *vt* ɪnˈsɛns] N incenso ■ VT (*anger*) exasperar, enraivecer; **incense burner** N incensório
incentive [ɪnˈsɛntɪv] N incentivo, estímulo; **incentive scheme** N plano de incentivos
inception [ɪnˈsɛpʃən] N começo, início
incessant [ɪnˈsɛsnt] ADJ incessante, contínuo
incessantly [ɪnˈsɛsntlɪ] ADV constantemente
incest [ˈɪnsɛst] N incesto
inch [ɪntʃ] N polegada (= 25 mm; 12 in a foot); **to be within an ~ of** estar a um passo de; **he didn't give an ~** ele não cedeu nem um milímetro ► **inch forward** VI avançar palmo a palmo
inch tape (*Brit*) N fita métrica
incidence [ˈɪnsɪdns] N (*of crime, disease*) incidência
incident [ˈɪnsɪdnt] N incidente m, evento; (*in book*) episódio
incidental [ɪnsɪˈdɛntl] ADJ acessório, não

essencial; (*unplanned*) acidental, casual; ~
expenses despesas *fpl* adicionais

incidentally [ɪnsɪ'dɛntəlɪ] ADV (*by the way*) a
propósito

incidental music N música de cena *or* de fundo

incinerate [ɪn'sɪnəreɪt] VT incinerar

incinerator [ɪn'sɪnəreɪtəʳ] N incinerador *m*

incipient [ɪn'sɪpɪənt] ADJ incipiente

incision [ɪn'sɪʒən] N incisão *f*

incisive [ɪn'saɪsɪv] ADJ (*mind*) penetrante,
perspicaz; (*tone*) mordaz, sarcástico; (*remark etc*)
incisivo

incisor [ɪn'saɪzəʳ] N incisivo

incite [ɪn'saɪt] VT (*rioters*) incitar; (*violence*)
provocar

incl. ABBR = **including; inclusive (of)**

inclement [ɪn'klɛmənt] ADJ (*weather*)
inclemente

inclination [ɪnklɪ'neɪʃən] N (*tendency*) tendência;
(*disposition*) inclinação *f*

incline [n 'ɪnklaɪn, vt, vi ɪn'klaɪn] N inclinação
f, ladeira ■ VT (*slope*) inclinar; (*head*) curvar,
inclinar ■ VI inclinar-se; **to be ~d to** (*tend*)
tender a, ser propenso a; (*be willing*) estar
disposto a

include [ɪn'klu:d] VT incluir; **the service is/is
not ~d** o serviço está/não está incluído

including [ɪn'klu:dɪŋ] PREP inclusive; **~ tip**
gorjeta incluída

inclusion [ɪn'klu:ʒən] N inclusão *f*

inclusive [ɪn'klu:sɪv] ADJ incluído, incluso
■ ADV inclusive; **~ of** incluindo; **£50 ~ of all
surcharges** £50, incluídas todas as sobretaxas;
inclusive terms (*Brit*) NPL preço global

incognito [ɪnkɒg'ni:təu] ADV incógnito

incoherent [ɪnkəu'hɪərənt] ADJ incoerente

income ['ɪŋkʌm] N (*earnings*) renda,
rendimentos *mpl*; (*unearned*) renda; (*profit*)
lucro; **gross/net ~** renda bruta/líquida; **~ and
expenditure account** conta de receitas e
despesas; **income bracket** N faixa salarial;
income tax N imposto de renda (BR), imposto
complementar (PT); **income tax inspector** N
fiscal *m/f* do imposto de renda; **income tax
return** N declaração *f* do imposto de renda

incoming ['ɪnkʌmɪŋ] ADJ (*flight, passenger*) de
chegada; (*mail*) de entrada; (*government, tenant*)
novo; **~ tide** maré enchente

incommunicado [ɪnkəmjunɪ'ka:dəu] ADJ
incomunicável

incomparable [ɪn'kɒmpərəbl] ADJ
incomparável

incompatible [ɪnkəm'pætɪbl] ADJ incompatível

incompetence [ɪn'kɒmpɪtəns] N
incompetência

incompetent [ɪn'kɒmpɪtənt] ADJ incompetente

incomplete [ɪnkəm'pli:t] ADJ incompleto;
(*unfinished*) por terminar

incomprehensible [ɪnkɒmprɪ'hɛnsɪbl] ADJ
incompreensível

inconceivable [ɪnkən'si:vəbl] ADJ inconcebível

inconclusive [ɪnkən'klu:sɪv] ADJ inconclusivo;

(*argument*) pouco convincente

incongruous [ɪn'kɒŋgruəs] ADJ (*foolish*) ridículo,
absurdo; (*situation, figure*) incongruente; (*remark,
act*) impróprio

inconsequential [ɪnkɒnsɪ'kwɛnʃl] ADJ sem
importância

inconsiderable [ɪnkən'sɪdərəbl] ADJ: **not ~**
importante

inconsiderate [ɪnkən'sɪdərət] ADJ sem
consideração; **how ~ of him!** que falta de
consideração (de sua parte)!

inconsistency [ɪnkən'sɪstənsɪ] N
inconsistência

inconsistent [ɪnkən'sɪstnt] ADJ inconsistente; ~
with (*beliefs*) incompatível com

inconsolable [ɪnkən'səuləbl] ADJ inconsolável

inconspicuous [ɪnkən'spɪkjuəs] ADJ modesto,
discreto; (*more intensely: modest*) modesto; **to
make o.s. ~** não chamar a atenção

inconstant [ɪn'kɒnstnt] ADJ inconstante

incontinence [ɪn'kɒntɪnəns] N incontinência

incontinent [ɪn'kɒntɪnənt] ADJ incontinente

incontrovertible [ɪnkɒntrə'və:təbl] ADJ
incontestável

inconvenience [ɪnkən'vi:njəns] N (*quality*)
inconveniência; (*problem*) inconveniente *m* ■ VT
incomodar; **don't ~ yourself** não se incomode

inconvenient [ɪnkən'vi:njənt] ADJ
inconveniente, incômodo; (*time, place*)
inoportuno; **that time is very ~ for me** esse
horário me é muito inconveniente

incorporate [ɪn'kɔ:pəreɪt] VT incorporar;
(*contain*) compreender; (*add*) incluir

incorporated company [ɪn'kɔ:pəreɪtɪd-] (*US*) N
≈ sociedade *f* anônima

incorrect [ɪnkə'rɛkt] ADJ incorreto

incorrigible [ɪn'kɒrɪdʒɪbl] ADJ incorrigível

incorruptible [ɪnkə'rʌptɪbl] ADJ incorruptível;
(*not open to bribes*) insubornável

increase [n 'ɪnkri:s, vi, vt ɪn'kri:s] N aumento
■ VI, VT aumentar; **an ~ of 5%** um aumento de
5%; **to be on the ~** estar em crescimento *or* alta

increasing [ɪn'kri:sɪŋ] ADJ (*number*) crescente,
em aumento

increasingly [ɪn'kri:sɪŋlɪ] ADV (*more intensely*)
progressivamente; (*more often*) cada vez mais

incredible [ɪn'krɛdɪbl] ADJ inacreditável;
(*enormous*) incrível

incredulous [ɪn'krɛdjuləs] ADJ incrédulo

increment ['ɪnkrɪmənt] N aumento,
incremento

incriminate [ɪn'krɪmɪneɪt] VT incriminar

incriminating [ɪn'krɪmɪneɪtɪŋ] ADJ
incriminador(a)

incubate ['ɪnkjubeɪt] VT, VI incubar

incubation [ɪnkju'beɪʃən] N incubação *f*;
incubation period N período de incubação

incubator ['ɪnkjubeɪtəʳ] N incubadora; (*for eggs*)
chocadeira

inculcate ['ɪnkʌlkeɪt] VT: **to ~ sth in sb** inculcar
algo a alguém

incumbent [ɪn'kʌmbənt] N titular *m/f* ■ ADJ: **it**

is ~ on him to ... cabe a ele ...

incur [ɪn'kəːʳ] VT incorrer em; (*expenses*) contrair

incurable [ɪn'kjuərəbl] ADJ incurável; (*fig*) irremediável

incursion [ɪn'kəːʃən] N incursão *f*

indebted [ɪn'dɛtɪd] ADJ: **to be ~ to sb** estar em dívida com alguém, dever obrigação a alguém

indecency [ɪn'diːsnsɪ] N indecência

indecent [ɪn'diːsnt] ADJ indecente; **indecent assault** (*Brit*) N atentado contra o pudor; **indecent exposure** N exibição *f* obscena, exibicionismo

indecipherable [ɪndɪ'saɪfərəbl] ADJ indecifrável

indecision [ɪndɪ'sɪʒən] N indecisão *f*

indecisive [ɪndɪ'saɪsɪv] ADJ indeciso; (*discussion*) inconcludente, sem resultados

indeed [ɪn'diːd] ADV de fato; (*certainly*) certamente; (*furthermore*) aliás; **yes ~!** claro que sim!

indefatigable [ɪndɪ'fætɪɡəbl] ADJ incansável

indefensible [ɪndɪ'fɛnsɪbl] ADJ indefensível

indefinable [ɪndɪ'faɪnəbl] ADJ indefinível

indefinite [ɪn'dɛfɪnɪt] ADJ indefinido; (*uncertain*) impreciso; (*period, number*) indeterminado

indefinitely [ɪn'dɛfɪnɪtlɪ] ADV (*wait*) indefinidamente

indelible [ɪn'dɛlɪbl] ADJ indelével

indelicate [ɪn'dɛlɪkɪt] ADJ (*tactless*) inábil; (*not polite*) indelicado, rude

indemnify [ɪn'dɛmnɪfaɪ] VT indenizar, compensar

indemnity [ɪn'dɛmnɪtɪ] N (*insurance*) garantia, seguro; (*compensation*) indenização *f*

indent [ɪn'dɛnt] VT (*text*) recolher ■ VI: **to ~ for sth** (*Comm*) encomendar algo

indentation [ɪndɛn'teɪʃən] N entalhe *m*, recorte *m*; (*Typ*) parágrafo, recuo

indenture [ɪn'dɛntʃəʳ] N contrato de aprendizagem

independence [ɪndɪ'pɛndns] N independência; **Independence Day** N *ver abaixo*

● **INDEPENDENCE DAY**

● *Independence Day* é a festa nacional dos
● Estados Unidos. Todo dia 4 de julho os
● americanos comemoram a adoção, em 1776,
● da declaração de Independência escrita
● por Thomas Jefferson que proclamava a
● separação das 13 colônias americanas da
● Grã-Bretanha.

independent [ɪndɪ'pɛndnt] ADJ independente; (*business, school*) privado; (*inquiry*) imparcial; **to become ~** tornar-se independente

independently [ɪndɪ'pɛndntlɪ] ADV independentemente

indescribable [ɪndɪ'skraɪbəbl] ADJ indescritível

indestructible [ɪndɪ'strʌktəbl] ADJ indestrutível

indeterminate [ɪndɪ'təːmɪnɪt] ADJ indeterminado

index ['ɪndɛks] (*pl* **indexes**) N (*in book*) índice *m*; (*in library etc*) catálogo (*pl* **indices**) ['ɪndɪsiːz] (*ratio, sign*) índice *m*, expoente *m*; **index card** N ficha de arquivo

indexed ['ɪndɛkst] (*US*) ADJ = **index-linked**

index finger N dedo indicador

index-linked [-lɪŋkt] (*Brit*) ADJ vinculado ao índice (do custo de vida)

India ['ɪndɪə] N Índia

Indian ['ɪndɪən] ADJ, N (*from India*) indiano(-a); (*American, Brazilian*) índio(-a); **Red ~** índio(-a) pele vermelha; **Indian ink** N tinta nanquim; **Indian Ocean** N: **the Indian Ocean** o oceano Índico; **Indian summer** N (*fig*) veranico

India paper N papel *m* da China

India rubber N borracha

indicate ['ɪndɪkeɪt] VT (*show*) sugerir; (*point to*) indicar; (*mention*) mencionar ■ VI (*Brit: Aut*): **to ~ left/right** indicar para a esquerda/direita

indication [ɪndɪ'keɪʃən] N indício, sinal *m*

indicative [ɪn'dɪkətɪv] ADJ indicativo ■ N (*Ling*) indicativo; **to be ~ of sth** ser sintomático de algo

indicator ['ɪndɪkeɪtəʳ] N indicador *m*; (*Aut*) pisca-pisca *m*

indices ['ɪndɪsiːz] NPL *of* **index**

indict [ɪn'daɪt] VT acusar

indictable [ɪn'daɪtəbl] ADJ (*person*) culpado; **~ offence** crime sujeito às penas da lei

indictment [ɪn'daɪtmənt] N acusação *f*, denúncia

indifference [ɪn'dɪfrəns] N indiferença

indifferent [ɪn'dɪfrənt] ADJ indiferente; (*quality*) medíocre

indigenous [ɪn'dɪdʒɪnəs] ADJ indígena, nativo

indigestible [ɪndɪ'dʒɛstɪbl] ADJ indigesto

indigestion [ɪndɪ'dʒɛstʃən] N indigestão *f*

indignant [ɪn'dɪɡnənt] ADJ: **to be ~ about sth/with sb** estar indignado com algo/alguém, indignar-se de algo/alguém

indignation [ɪndɪɡ'neɪʃən] N indignação *f*

indignity [ɪn'dɪɡnɪtɪ] N indignidade *f*; (*insult*) ultraje *m*, afronta

indigo ['ɪndɪɡəu] ADJ cor de anil *inv* ■ N anil *m*

indirect [ɪndɪ'rɛkt] ADJ indireto

indirectly [ɪndɪ'rɛktlɪ] ADV indiretamente

indiscreet [ɪndɪ'skriːt] ADJ indiscreto; (*rash*) imprudente

indiscretion [ɪndɪ'skrɛʃən] N indiscrição *f*; imprudência

indiscriminate [ɪndɪ'skrɪmɪnət] ADJ indiscriminado

indispensable [ɪndɪ'spɛnsəbl] ADJ indispensável, imprescindível

indisposed [ɪndɪ'spəuzd] ADJ (*unwell*) indisposto

indisposition [ɪndɪspə'zɪʃən] N (*illness*) mal-estar *m*, indisposição *f*

indisputable [ɪndɪ'spjuːtəbl] ADJ incontestável

indistinct [ɪndɪ'stɪŋkt] ADJ indistinto; (*memory, noise*) confuso, vago

indistinguishable [ɪndɪ'stɪŋwɪʃəbl] ADJ indistinguível

individual [ɪndɪ'vɪdjuəl] N indivíduo ■ ADJ individual; (*personal*) pessoal; (*characteristic*) particular

individualist [ɪndɪ'vɪdjuəlɪst] N individualista *m/f*

individuality [ɪndɪvɪdju'ælɪtɪ] N individualidade *f*

individually [ɪndɪ'vɪdjuəlɪ] ADV individualmente, particularmente

indivisible [ɪndɪ'vɪzɪbl] ADJ indivisível

Indo-China ['ɪndəu-] N Indochina

indoctrinate [ɪn'dɔktrɪneɪt] VT doutrinar

indoctrination [ɪndɔktrɪ'neɪʃən] N doutrinação *f*

indolent ['ɪndələnt] ADJ indolente, preguiçoso

Indonesia [ɪndə'niːzɪə] N Indonésia

Indonesian [ɪndə'niːzɪən] ADJ indonésio ■ N indonésio(-a); (*Ling*) indonésio

indoor ['ɪndɔːʳ] ADJ (*inner*) interno, interior; (*inside*) dentro de casa; (*swimming pool*) coberto; (*games, sport*) de salão

indoors [ɪn'dɔːz] ADV em lugar fechado; (*at home*) em casa

indubitable [ɪn'djuːbɪtəbl] ADJ indubitável

induce [ɪn'djuːs] VT (*Med*) induzir; (*bring about*) causar, produzir; (*provoke*) provocar; **to ~ sb to do sth** induzir alguém a fazer algo

inducement [ɪn'djuːsmənt] N (*incentive*) incentivo

induct [ɪn'dʌkt] VT instalar

induction [ɪn'dʌkʃən] N (*Med: of birth*) indução *f*; **induction course** (*Brit*) N curso de indução

indulge [ɪn'dʌldʒ] VT (*desire*) satisfazer; (*whim*) condescender com; (*person*) comprazer; (*child*) fazer a vontade de ■ VI: **to ~ in** entregar-se a, satisfazer-se com

indulgence [ɪn'dʌldʒəns] N (*of desire*) satisfação *f*; (*leniency*) indulgência, tolerância

indulgent [ɪn'dʌldʒənt] ADJ indulgente

industrial [ɪn'dʌstrɪəl] ADJ industrial; (*injury*) de trabalho; (*dispute*) trabalhista; **industrial action** N greve *f*; **industrial design** N desenho industrial; **industrial estate** (*Brit*) N zona industrial

industrialist [ɪn'dʌstrɪəlɪst] N industrial *m/f*

industrialize [ɪn'dʌstrɪəlaɪz] VT industrializar

industrial park (*US*) N = **industrial estate**

industrial relations NPL relações *fpl* industriais

industrial tribunal (*Brit*) N = tribunal *m* do trabalho

industrial unrest (*Brit*) N agitação *f* operária

industrious [ɪn'dʌstrɪəs] ADJ trabalhador(a); (*student*) aplicado

industry ['ɪndəstrɪ] N indústria *f*; (*diligence*) aplicação *f*, diligência

inebriated [ɪ'niːbrɪeɪtɪd] ADJ embriagado, bêbado

inedible [ɪn'ɛdɪbl] ADJ não-comestível

ineffective [ɪnɪ'fɛktɪv] ADJ ineficaz

ineffectual [ɪnɪ'fɛktʃuəl] ADJ = **ineffective**

inefficiency [ɪnɪ'fɪʃənsɪ] N ineficiência

inefficient [ɪnɪ'fɪʃənt] ADJ ineficiente

inelegant [ɪn'ɛlɪgənt] ADJ deselegante

ineligible [ɪn'ɛlɪdʒɪbl] ADJ (*candidate*) inelegível; **to be ~ for sth** não estar qualificado para algo

inept [ɪ'nɛpt] ADJ inepto

ineptitude [ɪ'nɛptɪtjuːd] N inépcia, incompetência

inequality [ɪnɪ'kwɔlɪtɪ] N desigualdade *f*

inequitable [ɪn'ɛkwɪtəbl] ADJ injusto, iníquo

ineradicable [ɪnɪ'rædɪkəbl] ADJ inerradicável

inert [ɪ'nəːt] ADJ inerte; (*immobile*) imóvel

inertia [ɪ'nəːʃə] N inércia; (*laziness*) lerdeza

inertia-reel seat belt N cinto de segurança retrátil

inescapable [ɪnɪ'skeɪpəbl] ADJ inevitável

inessential [ɪnɪ'sɛnʃl] ADJ desnecessário

inestimable [ɪn'ɛstɪməbl] ADJ inestimável, incalculável

inevitable [ɪn'ɛvɪtəbl] ADJ inevitável; (*necessary*) forçoso, necessário

inevitably [ɪn'ɛvɪtəblɪ] ADV inevitavelmente

inexact [ɪnɪg'zækt] ADJ inexato

inexcusable [ɪnɪks'kjuːzəbl] ADJ imperdoável, indesculpável

inexhaustible [ɪnɪg'zɔːstɪbl] ADJ inesgotável, inexaurível

inexorable [ɪn'ɛksərəbl] ADJ inexorável

inexpensive [ɪnɪk'spɛnsɪv] ADJ barato, econômico

inexperience [ɪnɪk'spɪərɪəns] N inexperiência, falta de experiência

inexperienced [ɪnɪk'spɪərɪənst] ADJ inexperiente

inexplicable [ɪnɪk'splɪkəbl] ADJ inexplicável

inexpressible [ɪnɪk'sprɛsɪbl] ADJ inexprimível

inextricable [ɪnɪk'strɪkəbl] ADJ inextricável

infallibility [ɪnfælə'bɪlɪtɪ] N infalibilidade *f*

infallible [ɪn'fælɪbl] ADJ infalível

infamous ['ɪnfəməs] ADJ infame, abominável

infamy ['ɪnfəmɪ] N infâmia

infancy ['ɪnfənsɪ] N infância

infant ['ɪnfənt] N (*baby*) bebê *m*; (*young child*) criança

infantile ['ɪnfəntaɪl] ADJ infantil; (*pej*) acriançado

infant mortality N mortalidade *f* infantil

infantry ['ɪnfəntrɪ] N infantaria

infantryman ['ɪnfəntrɪmən] (*irreg*) N soldado de infantaria

infant school (*Brit*) N pré-escola

infatuated [ɪn'fætjueɪtɪd] ADJ: **~ with** apaixonado por

infatuation [ɪnfætju'eɪʃən] N gamação *f*, paixão *f* louca

infect [ɪn'fɛkt] VT (*wound*) infeccionar, infetar; (*person*) contagiar; (*food*) contaminar; (*fig: pej*) corromper, contaminar; **~ed with** (*illness*) contagiado por; **to become ~ed** (*wound*) infeccionar(-se), infetar(-se)

infection [ɪn'fɛkʃən] N infecção *f*; (*fig*) contágio

infectious [ɪn'fɛkʃəs] ADJ contagioso; (*fig*) infeccioso

infer [ɪn'fə:ʳ] VT deduzir, inferir

inference ['ɪnfərəns] N dedução f, inferência

inferior [ɪn'fɪərɪəʳ] ADJ inferior; (goods) de qualidade inferior ■ N inferior m/f; (in rank) subalterno(-a); **to feel ~** sentir-se inferior

inferiority [ɪnfɪərɪ'ɔrətɪ] N inferioridade f; **inferiority complex** N complexo de inferioridade

infernal [ɪn'fə:nl] ADJ infernal

infernally [ɪn'fə:nəlɪ] ADV (very) muito

inferno [ɪn'fə:nəu] N inferno; (fig) inferno de chamas

infertile [ɪn'fə:taɪl] ADJ infértil; (person, animal) estéril

infertility [ɪnfə'tɪlɪtɪ] N infertilidade f; (of person, animal) esterilidade f

infested [ɪn'fɛstɪd] ADJ: ~ **(with)** infestado (de), assolado (por)

infidelity [ɪnfɪ'dɛlɪtɪ] N infidelidade f

in-fighting N lutas fpl internas, conflitos mpl internos

infiltrate ['ɪnfɪltreɪt] VT (troops etc) infiltrar-se em ■ VI infiltrar-se

infinite ['ɪnfɪnɪt] ADJ infinito; (time, money) ilimitado

infinitely ['ɪnfɪnɪtlɪ] ADV infinitamente

infinitesimal [ɪnfɪnɪ'tɛsɪməl] ADJ infinitésimo

infinitive [ɪn'fɪnɪtɪv] N infinitivo

infinity [ɪn'fɪnɪtɪ] N (also: Math) infinito; (an infinity) infinidade f

infirm [ɪn'fə:m] ADJ enfermo, fraco

infirmary [ɪn'fə:mərɪ] N enfermaria, hospital m

infirmity [ɪn'fə:mɪtɪ] N fraqueza; (illness) enfermidade f, achaque m

inflame [ɪn'fleɪm] VT inflamar

inflamed [ɪn'fleɪmd] ADJ inflamado

inflammable [ɪn'flæməbl] (Brit) ADJ inflamável

inflammation [ɪnflə'meɪʃən] N inflamação f

inflammatory [ɪn'flæmətərɪ] ADJ (speech) incendiário

inflatable [ɪn'fleɪtəbl] ADJ inflável

inflate [ɪn'fleɪt] VT (tyre, balloon) inflar, encher; (price) inflar

inflated [ɪn'fleɪtɪd] ADJ (style) empolado, pomposo; (value) excessivo

inflation [ɪn'fleɪʃən] N (Econ) inflação f

inflationary [ɪn'fleɪʃənərɪ] ADJ inflacionário

inflexible [ɪn'flɛksɪbl] ADJ inflexível

inflict [ɪn'flɪkt] VT: **to ~ sth on sb** infligir algo em alguém; (tax etc) impor algo a alguém

infliction [ɪn'flɪkʃən] N imposição f, inflição f

in-flight ADJ (refuelling) em vôo; (movie) exibido durante o vôo; (service) de bordo

inflow ['ɪnfləu] N afluência

influence ['ɪnfluəns] N influência ■ VT influir em, influenciar; (persuade) persuadir; **under the ~ of alcohol** sob o efeito do álcool

influential [ɪnflu'ɛnʃl] ADJ influente

influenza [ɪnflu'ɛnzə] N gripe f

influx ['ɪnflʌks] N (of refugees) afluxo; (of funds) influxo

infomercial ['ɪnfəumə:ʃl] (US) N (for product)

infomercial m

inform [ɪn'fɔ:m] VT: **to ~ sb of sth** informar alguém de algo; (warn) avisar alguém de algo; (communicate) comunicar algo a alguém ■ VI: **~ on sb** delatar alguém; **to ~ sb about** informar alguém sobre

informal [ɪn'fɔ:ml] ADJ informal; (visit, discussion) extra-oficial; (intimate) familiar; **"dress ~"** "traje de passeio"

informality [ɪnfɔ:'mælɪtɪ] N falta de cerimônia; (intimacy) intimidade f; (familiarity) familiaridade f; (ease) informalidade f

informally [ɪn'fɔ:məlɪ] ADV sem formalidade; (unofficially) não oficialmente

informant [ɪn'fɔ:mənt] N informante m/f; (to police) delator(a) m/f

information [ɪnfə'meɪʃən] N informação f, informações fpl; (news) notícias fpl; (knowledge) conhecimento; **a piece of ~** uma informação; **for your ~** para a sua informação, para o seu governo; **information bureau** N balcão m de informações; **information office** N escritório de informações; **information processing** N processamento de informações; **information retrieval** N recuperação f de informações; **information technology** N informática

informative [ɪn'fɔ:mətɪv] ADJ informativo

informed [ɪn'fɔ:md] ADJ informado; **an ~ guess** um palpite baseado em conhecimento dos fatos

informer [ɪn'fɔ:məʳ] N delator(a) m/f

infra dig ['ɪnfrə-] (inf) ADJ ABBR (= infra dignitatem) abaixo da minha (or sua etc) dignidade

infra-red ['ɪnfrə-] ADJ infravermelho

infrastructure ['ɪnfrəstrʌktʃəʳ] N infraestrutura

infrequent [ɪn'fri:kwənt] ADJ infreqüente

infringe [ɪn'frɪndʒ] VT infringir, transgredir ■ VI: **to ~ on** violar

infringement [ɪn'frɪndʒmənt] N transgressão f; (of rights) violação f; (Sport) infração f

infuriate [ɪn'fjuərɪeɪt] VT enfurecer, enraivecer

infuriating [ɪn'fjuərɪeɪtɪŋ] ADJ de dar raiva, enfurecedor(a)

infuse [ɪn'fju:z] VT: **to ~ sb with sth** (fig) inspirar or infundir algo em alguém

infusion [ɪn'fju:ʒən] N (tea etc) infusão f

ingenious [ɪn'dʒi:njəs] ADJ engenhoso

ingenuity [ɪndʒɪ'nju:ɪtɪ] N engenho, habilidade f

ingenuous [ɪn'dʒɛnjuəs] ADJ ingênuo

ingot ['ɪŋgət] N lingote m

ingrained [ɪn'greɪnd] ADJ arraigado, enraizado

ingratiate [ɪn'greɪʃɪeɪt] VT: **to ~ o.s. with** cair nas (boas) graças de

ingratiating [ɪn'greɪʃɪeɪtɪŋ] ADJ insinuante

ingratitude [ɪn'grætɪtju:d] N ingratidão f

ingredient [ɪn'gri:dɪənt] N ingrediente m; (of situation) fator m

ingrowing toenail ['ɪngrəuɪŋ-] N unha encravada

ingrown toenail ['ɪngrəun-] N = **ingrowing**

toenail
inhabit [ɪn'hæbɪt] vt habitar; (occupy) ocupar
inhabitable [ɪn'hæbɪtəbl] ADJ habitável
inhabitant [ɪn'hæbɪtənt] N habitante m/f
inhale [ɪn'heɪl] vt inalar ▪ vi (in smoking) aspirar
inherent [ɪn'hɪərənt] ADJ: ~ **in** or **to** inerente a
inherently [ɪn'hɪərəntlɪ] ADV inerentemente, em si
inherit [ɪn'hɛrɪt] vt herdar
inheritance [ɪn'hɛrɪtəns] N herança; (fig) patrimônio
inhibit [ɪn'hɪbɪt] vt inibir; **to ~ sb from doing sth** impedir alguém de fazer algo
inhibited [ɪn'hɪbɪtɪd] ADJ inibido
inhibiting [ɪn'hɪbɪtɪŋ] ADJ constrangedor(a)
inhibition [ɪnhɪ'bɪʃən] N inibição f
inhospitable [ɪnhɔs'pɪtəbl] ADJ (person) inospitaleiro; (place) inóspito
inhuman [ɪn'hju:mən] ADJ inumano, desumano
inhumane [ɪnhju:'meɪn] ADJ desumano
inimitable [ɪ'nɪmɪtəbl] ADJ inimitável
iniquity [ɪ'nɪkwɪtɪ] N iniqüidade f; (injustice) injustiça
initial [ɪ'nɪʃl] ADJ inicial; (first) primeiro ▪ N inicial f ▪ vt marcar com iniciais; **initials** NPL (of name) iniciais fpl; (abbreviation) abreviatura, sigla
initialize [ɪ'nɪʃəlaɪz] vt (Comput) inicializar
initially [ɪ'nɪʃəlɪ] ADV inicialmente, no início; (first) primeiramente
initiate [ɪ'nɪʃɪeɪt] vt (start) iniciar, começar; (person) iniciar; **to ~ sb into a secret** revelar um segredo a alguém; **to ~ proceedings against sb** (Law) abrir um processo contra alguém
initiation [ɪnɪʃɪ'eɪʃən] N (into secret etc) iniciação f; (beginning) começo, início
initiative [ɪ'nɪʃətɪv] N iniciativa; **to take the ~** tomar a iniciativa
inject [ɪn'dʒɛkt] vt (liquid, fig: money) injetar; (person) dar uma injeção em; (fig: put in) introduzir
injection [ɪn'dʒɛkʃən] N injeção f; **to have an ~** tomar uma injeção
injudicious [ɪndʒu'dɪʃəs] ADJ imprudente
injunction [ɪn'dʒʌŋkʃən] N injunção f, ordem f
injure ['ɪndʒəʳ] vt ferir; (damage: reputation etc) prejudicar; (offend) ofender, magoar; **to ~ o.s.** ferir-se
injured ['ɪndʒəd] ADJ (person, leg) ferido; (feelings) ofendido, magoado; **~ party** (Law) parte f lesada
injurious [ɪn'dʒuərɪəs] ADJ: ~ (to) prejudicial (a)
injury ['ɪndʒərɪ] N ferida; (wrong) dano, prejuízo; **to escape without ~** escapar ileso; **injury time** N (Sport) desconto
injustice [ɪn'dʒʌstɪs] N injustiça; **to do sb an ~** fazer mau juízo de alguém
ink [ɪŋk] N tinta
ink-jet printer N impressora a tinta
inkling ['ɪŋklɪŋ] N suspeita; (idea): **to have an ~ of** ter uma vaga idéia de

ink pad N almofada de tinta
inky ['ɪŋkɪ] ADJ manchado de tinta
inlaid ['ɪnleɪd] ADJ (with gems) incrustado; (table etc) marchetado
inland [adj 'ɪnlənd, adv ɪn'lænd] ADJ interior, interno ▪ ADV para o interior; **~ waterways** hidrovias fpl
Inland Revenue (Brit) N ≈ fisco, ≈ receita federal (BR)
in-laws NPL sogros mpl
inlet ['ɪnlɛt] N (Geo) enseada, angra; (Tech) entrada; **inlet pipe** N tubo de admissão
inmate ['ɪnmeɪt] N (in prison) presidiário(-a); (in asylum) internado(-a)
inmost ['ɪnməust] ADJ mais íntimo
inn [ɪn] N hospedaria, taberna
innards ['ɪnədʒ] (inf) NPL entranhas fpl
innate [ɪ'neɪt] ADJ inato
inner ['ɪnəʳ] ADJ (place) interno; (feeling) interior; **inner city** N aglomeração f urbana, metrópole f
innermost ['ɪnəməust] ADJ mais íntimo
inner tube N (of tyre) câmara de ar
innings ['ɪnɪŋz] N (Sport) turno; (Brit: fig): **he's had a good ~** ele aproveitou bem a vida
innocence ['ɪnəsns] N inocência
innocent ['ɪnəsnt] ADJ inocente
innocuous [ɪ'nɔkjuəs] ADJ inócuo
innovation [ɪnəu'veɪʃən] N inovação f, novidade f
innuendo [ɪnju'ɛndəu] (pl innuendoes) N insinuação f, indireta
innumerable [ɪ'nju:mrəbl] ADJ incontável
inoculate [ɪ'nɔkjuleɪt] vt: **to ~ sb with sth** inocular algo em alguém; **to ~ sb against sth** vacinar alguém contra algo
inoculation [ɪnɔkju'leɪʃən] N inoculação f, vacinação f
inoffensive [ɪnə'fɛnsɪv] ADJ inofensivo
inopportune [ɪn'ɔpətju:n] ADJ inoportuno
inordinate [ɪn'ɔ:dɪnət] ADJ desmesurado, excessivo
inordinately [ɪn'ɔ:dɪnətlɪ] ADV desmedidamente, excessivamente
inorganic [ɪnɔ:'gænɪk] ADJ inorgânico
in-patient N paciente m/f interno(-a)
input ['ɪnput] N (information, Comput) entrada; (resources) investimento ▪ vt (Comput) entrar com
inquest ['ɪnkwɛst] N inquérito policial; (coroner's) inquérito judicial
inquire [ɪn'kwaɪəʳ] vi pedir informação ▪ vt (ask) perguntar; **to ~ about** pedir informações sobre; **to ~ when/where/whether** perguntar quando/onde/se
  ▸ **inquire after** vt fus (person) perguntar por
  ▸ **inquire into** vt fus investigar, indagar
inquiring [ɪn'kwaɪərɪŋ] ADJ (mind) inquiridor(a); (look) interrogativo
inquiry [ɪn'kwaɪərɪ] N pergunta; (Law) investigação f, inquérito; (commission) comissão f de inquérito; **to hold an ~ into sth** realizar uma investigação sobre algo; **inquiry desk** (Brit)

N balcão *m* de informações; **inquiry office** (*Brit*) N seção *f* de informações

inquisition [ɪnkwɪ'zɪʃən] N inquérito; (*Rel*): **the I~** a Inquisição

inquisitive [ɪn'kwɪzɪtɪv] ADJ (*curious*) curioso, perguntador(a); (*prying*) indiscreto, intrometido

inroads ['ɪnrəudz] NPL: **to make ~ into** (*savings, supplies*) consumir parte de

ins. ABBR = **inches**

insane [ɪn'seɪn] ADJ louco, doido; (*Med*) demente, insano

insanitary [ɪn'sænɪtərɪ] ADJ insalubre

insanity [ɪn'sænɪtɪ] N loucura; (*Med*) insanidade *f*, demência

insatiable [ɪn'seɪʃəbl] ADJ insaciável

inscribe [ɪn'skraɪb] VT inscrever; (*book etc*): **to ~ (to sb)** dedicar (a alguém)

inscription [ɪn'skrɪpʃən] N inscrição *f*; (*in book*) dedicatória

inscrutable [ɪn'skru:təbl] ADJ inescrutável, impenetrável

inseam measurement ['ɪnsi:m-] (*US*) N altura de entrepernas

insect ['ɪnsɛkt] N inseto; **insect bite** N picada de inseto

insecticide [ɪn'sɛktɪsaɪd] N inseticida *m*

insect repellent N repelente *m* contra insetos, insetífugo

insecure [ɪnsɪ'kjuə^r] ADJ inseguro

insecurity [ɪnsɪ'kjuərətɪ] N insegurança

insemination [ɪnsɛmɪ'neɪʃən] N: **artificial ~** inseminação *f* artificial

insensible [ɪn'sɛnsɪbl] ADJ impassível, insensível; (*unconscious*) inconsciente

insensitive [ɪn'sɛnsɪtɪv] ADJ insensível

insensitivity [ɪnsɛnsɪ'tɪvɪtɪ] N insensibilidade *f*

inseparable [ɪn'sɛprəbl] ADJ inseparável

insert [*vt* ɪn'sə:t, *n* 'ɪnsə:t] VT (*between things*) intercalar; (*into sth*) introduzir, inserir; (*in paper*) publicar; (: *advert*) pôr ▪ N folha solta

insertion [ɪn'sə:ʃən] N inserção *f*; (*publication*) publicação *f*; (*of pages*) matéria inserida

in-service ADJ (*training*) contínuo; (*course*) de aperfeiçoamento, de reciclagem

inshore [ɪn'ʃɔ:^r] ADJ perto da costa, costeiro ▪ ADV (*be*) perto da costa; (*move*) em direção à costa

inside ['ɪnsaɪd] N interior *m*; (*lining*) forro; (*of road: in Britain*) lado esquerdo (da estrada); (: *in US, Europe etc*) lado direito (da estrada) ▪ ADJ interior, interno; (*secret*) secreto ▪ ADV (*be*) dentro; (*go*) para dentro; (*inf: in prison*) na prisão ▪ PREP dentro de; (*of time*): **~ 10 minutes** em menos de 10 minutos; **insides** NPL (*inf*) entranhas *fpl*; **the ~ story** a verdade sobre os fatos; **inside forward** N (*Sport*) centro avante; **inside information** N informação *f* privilegiada; **inside lane** N (*Aut: in Britain*) pista da esquerda; (: *in US, Europe etc*) pista da direita; **inside leg measurement** (*Brit*) N altura de entrepernas; **inside out** ADV ás avezzas; (*know*) muito bem; **to turn sth inside out** virar

algo pelo avesso

insider [ɪn'saɪdə^r] N iniciado(-a); **insider dealing** N (*Stock Exchange*) uso de informações privilegiadas

insidious [ɪn'sɪdɪəs] ADJ insidioso; (*underground*) clandestino

insight ['ɪnsaɪt] N (*into situation*) insight *m*; (*quality*) discernimento; **an ~ into sth** uma idéia de algo

insignia [ɪn'sɪgnɪə] N INV insígnias *fpl*

insignificant [ɪnsɪg'nɪfɪknt] ADJ insignificante

insincere [ɪnsɪn'sɪə^r] ADJ insincero

insincerity [ɪnsɪn'sɛrɪtɪ] N insinceridade *f*

insinuate [ɪn'sɪnjueɪt] VT insinuar

insinuation [ɪnsɪnju'eɪʃən] N insinuação *f*; (*hint*) indireta

insipid [ɪn'sɪpɪd] ADJ insípido, insosso; (*person*) sem graça

insist [ɪn'sɪst] VI insistir; **to ~ on doing** insistir em fazer; (*stubbornly*) teimar em fazer; **to ~ that** insistir que; (*claim*) cismar que

insistence [ɪn'sɪstəns] N insistência; (*stubbornness*) teimosia

insistent [ɪn'sɪstənt] ADJ insistente, pertinaz; (*continual*) persistente

insole ['ɪnsəul] N palminha

insolence ['ɪnsələns] N insolência, atrevimento

insolent ['ɪnsələnt] ADJ insolente, atrevido

insoluble [ɪn'sɔljubl] ADJ insolúvel

insolvency [ɪn'sɔlvənsɪ] N insolvência

insolvent [ɪn'sɔlvənt] ADJ insolvente

insomnia [ɪn'sɔmnɪə] N insônia

insomniac [ɪn'sɔmnɪæk] N insone *m/f*

inspect [ɪn'spɛkt] VT inspecionar; (*building*) vistoriar; (*Brit: tickets*) fiscalizar; (*troops*) passar revista em

inspection [ɪn'spɛkʃən] N inspeção *f*; (*of building*) vistoria; (*Brit: of tickets*) fiscalização *f*

inspector [ɪn'spɛktə^r] N inspetor(a) *m/f*; (*Brit: on buses, trains*) fiscal *m*

inspiration [ɪnspə'reɪʃən] N inspiração *f*

inspire [ɪn'spaɪə^r] VT inspirar

inspired [ɪn'spaɪəd] ADJ (*writer, book etc*) inspirado; **in an ~ moment** num momento de inspiração

inspiring [ɪn'spaɪərɪŋ] ADJ inspirador(a)

inst. (*Brit*) ABBR (*Comm*) = **instant**

instability [ɪnstə'bɪlɪtɪ] N instabilidade *f*

install [ɪn'stɔ:l] VT instalar; (*official*) nomear

installation [ɪnstə'leɪʃən] N instalação *f*

installment [ɪn'stɔ:lmənt] (*US*) N = **instalment**; **installment plan** (*US*) N crediário

instalment [ɪn'stɔ:lmənt] (*Brit*) N (*of money*) prestação *f*; (*of story*) fascículo; (*of TV serial etc*) capítulo; **in ~s** (*pay*) a prestações; (*receive*) em várias vezes

instance ['ɪnstəns] N (*example*) exemplo; (*case*) caso; **for ~** por exemplo; **in many ~s** em muitos casos; **in that ~** naquele caso; **in the first ~** em primeiro lugar

instant ['ɪnstənt] N instante *m*, momento ▪ ADJ

imediato; (*coffee*) instantâneo; **of the 10th ~**
(*Brit: Comm*) de 10 do corrente
instantaneous [ɪnstən'teɪnɪəs] ADJ
instantâneo
instantly ['ɪnstəntlɪ] ADV imediatamente
instant messaging N sistema *m* de mensagens
instantâneas
instant replay (*US*) N (*TV*) replay *m*
instead [ɪn'stɛd] ADV em vez disso; **~ of** em vez
de, em lugar de
instep ['ɪnstɛp] N peito do pé; (*of shoe*) parte *f* de
dentro
instigate ['ɪnstɪgeɪt] VT (*rebellion, strike*)
fomentar; (*new ideas*) suscitar
instigation [ɪnstɪ'geɪʃən] N instigação *f*; **at sb's**
~ por incitação de alguém
instil [ɪn'stɪl] VT: **to ~ sth (into)** infundir or
incutir algo (em)
instinct ['ɪnstɪŋkt] N instinto
instinctive [ɪn'stɪŋktɪv] ADJ instintivo
instinctively [ɪn'stɪŋktɪvlɪ] ADV por instinto,
instintivamente
institute ['ɪnstɪtjuːt] N instituto; (*professional*
body) associação *f* ■ VT (*inquiry*) começar, iniciar;
(*proceedings*) instituir, estabelecer
institution [ɪnstɪ'tjuːʃən] N instituição *f*;
(*beginning*) início; (*organization*) instituto; (*Med:*
home) asilo; (*asylum*) manicômio; (*custom*)
costume *m*
institutional [ɪnstɪ'tjuːʃənəl] ADJ
institucional
instruct [ɪn'strʌkt] VT: **to ~ sb in sth** instruir
alguém em or sobre algo; **to ~ sb to do sth** dar
instruções a alguém para fazer algo
instruction [ɪn'strʌkʃən] N (*teaching*) instrução
f; **instructions** NPL ordens *fpl*; **~s (for use)**
modo de usar; **instruction book** N livro de
instruções
instructive [ɪn'strʌktɪv] ADJ instrutivo
instructor [ɪn'strʌktər] N instrutor(a) *m/f*
instrument ['ɪnstrumənt] N instrumento
instrumental [ɪnstru'mɛntl] ADJ (*Mus*)
instrumental; **to be ~ in** contribuir para
instrumentalist [ɪnstru'mɛntəlɪst] N
instrumentalista *m/f*
instrument panel N painel *m* de instrumentos
insubordinate [ɪnsə'bɔːdənɪt] ADJ
insubordinado
insubordination [ɪnsəbɔːdə'neɪʃən] N
insubordinação *f*
insufferable [ɪn'sʌfrəbl] ADJ insuportável
insufficient [ɪnsə'fɪʃənt] ADJ insuficiente
insufficiently [ɪnsə'fɪʃəntlɪ] ADV
insuficientemente
insular ['ɪnsjulər] ADJ insular; (*outlook*) estreito;
(*person*) de mente limitada
insulate ['ɪnsjuleɪt] VT isolar; (*protect: person,*
group) segregar
insulating tape ['ɪnsjuleɪtɪŋ-] N fita isolante
insulation [ɪnsju'leɪʃən] N isolamento
insulin ['ɪnsjulɪn] N insulina
insult [n 'ɪnsʌlt, vt ɪn'sʌlt] N insulto; (*offence*)

ofensa ■ VT insultar, ofender
insulting [ɪn'sʌltɪŋ] ADJ insultante, ofensivo
insuperable [ɪn'sjuːprəbl] ADJ insuperável
insurance [ɪn'ʃuərəns] N seguro; **fire/life ~**
seguro contra incêndio/de vida; **to take out ~**
(against) segurar-se or fazer seguro (contra);
insurance agent N agente *m/f* de seguros;
insurance broker N corretor(a) *m/f* de seguros;
insurance company N seguradora; **insurance**
policy N apólice *f* de seguro; **insurance**
premium N prêmio de seguro
insure [ɪn'ʃuər] VT segurar; **to ~ sb/sb's life**
segurar alguém/a vida de alguém; **to be ~d for**
£5000 estar segurado em £5000
insured [ɪn'ʃuəd] N: **the ~** o(-a segurado/a)
insurer [ɪn'ʃuərər] N (*person*) segurador(a) *m/f*;
(*company*) seguradora
insurgent [ɪn'sɜːdʒənt] ADJ, N insurgente *m/f*
insurmountable [ɪnsə'mauntəbl] ADJ
insuperável
insurrection [ɪnsə'rɛkʃən] N insurreição *f*
intact [ɪn'tækt] ADJ intacto, íntegro; (*unharmed*)
ileso, são e salvo
intake ['ɪnteɪk] N (*Tech*) entrada, tomada; (*: pipe*)
tubo de entrada; (*of food*) quantidade *f* ingerida;
(*Brit: Sch*): **an ~ of 200 a year** 200 matriculados
por ano
intangible [ɪn'tændʒɪbl] ADJ intangível
integral ['ɪntɪgrəl] ADJ (*whole*) integral, total;
(*part*) integrante, essencial
integrate ['ɪntɪgreɪt] VT integrar ■ VI integrar-
se
integrated circuit ['ɪntɪgreɪtɪd-] N (*Comput*)
circuito integrado
integration [ɪntɪ'greɪʃən] N integração *f*; **racial**
~ integração racial
integrity [ɪn'tɛgrɪtɪ] N integridade *f*,
honestidade *f*, retidão *f*
intellect ['ɪntəlɛkt] N intelecto; (*cleverness*)
inteligência
intellectual [ɪntə'lɛktjuəl] ADJ, N intelectual
m/f
intelligence [ɪn'tɛlɪdʒəns] N inteligência; (*Mil*
etc) informações *fpl*; **intelligence quotient**
N quociente *m* de inteligência; **intelligence**
service N serviço de informações; **intelligence**
test N teste *m* de inteligência
intelligent [ɪn'tɛlɪdʒənt] ADJ inteligente
intelligently [ɪn'tɛlɪdʒəntlɪ] ADV
inteligentemente
intelligentsia [ɪntɛlɪ'dʒəntsɪə] N: **the ~** a
intelligentsia
intelligible [ɪn'tɛlɪdʒɪbl] ADJ inteligível,
compreensível
intemperate [ɪn'tɛmpərət] ADJ imoderado;
(*with alcohol*) intemperado
intend [ɪn'tɛnd] VT (*gift etc*): **to ~ sth for** destinar
algo a; **to ~ to do sth** tencionar or pretender
fazer algo; (*plan*) planejar fazer algo
intended [ɪn'tɛndɪd] ADJ (*effect*) desejado; (*insult*)
intencional ■ N noivo(-a)
intense [ɪn'tɛns] ADJ intenso; (*person*) muito

emotivo

intensely [ɪn'tɛnslɪ] ADV intensamente; (very) extremamente

intensify [ɪn'tɛnsɪfaɪ] VT intensificar; (increase) aumentar

intensity [ɪn'tɛnsɪtɪ] N intensidade f; (of emotion) força, veemência

intensive [ɪn'tɛnsɪv] ADJ intensivo; **intensive care** N: **to be in intensive care** estar na UTI; **intensive care unit** N unidade f de tratamento intensivo

intent [ɪn'tɛnt] N intenção f ■ ADJ (absorbed) absorto; (attentive) atento; **to all ~s and purposes** para todos os efeitos; **to be ~ on doing sth** estar resolvido a fazer algo

intention [ɪn'tɛnʃən] N intenção f, propósito

intentional [ɪn'tɛnʃənl] ADJ intencional, propositado

intentionally [ɪn'tɛnʃənəlɪ] ADV de propósito

intently [ɪn'tɛntlɪ] ADV atentamente

inter [ɪn'təːʳ] VT enterrar

interact [ɪntər'ækt] VI interagir

interaction [ɪntər'ækʃən] N interação f, ação f recíproca

interactive [ɪntər'æktɪv] ADJ interativo

intercede [ɪntə'siːd] VI: **to ~ (with sb/on behalf of sb)** interceder (junto a alguém/em favor de alguém)

intercept [ɪntə'sɛpt] VT interceptar; (person) deter

interception [ɪntə'sɛpʃən] N interceptação f; (of person) detenção f

interchange [n 'ɪntətʃeɪndʒ, vt ɪntə'tʃeɪndʒ] N intercâmbio; (exchange) troca, permuta; (on motorway) trevo ■ VT intercambiar, trocar

interchangeable [ɪntə'tʃeɪndʒəbl] ADJ permutável

intercity (train) [ɪntə'sɪtɪ-] N expresso

intercom ['ɪntəkɔm] N interfone m

interconnect [ɪntəkə'nɛkt] VI interligar

intercontinental [ɪntəkɔntɪ'nɛntl] ADJ intercontinental

intercourse ['ɪntəkɔːs] N (social) relacionamento; **sexual ~** relações fpl sexuais

interdependent [ɪntədɪ'pɛndənt] ADJ interdependente

interest ['ɪntrɪst] N interesse m; (Comm: sum of money) juros mpl; (: in company) participação f ■ VT interessar; **to be ~ed in** interessar-se por, estar interessado em; **compound/simple ~** juros compostos/simples; **British ~s in the Middle East** os interesses britânicos no Oriente Médio

interested ['ɪntrɛstɪd] ADJ interessado; **to be ~ in** interessar-se por, estar interessado em

interest-free ADJ sem juros

interesting ['ɪntrɪstɪŋ] ADJ interessante

interest rate N taxa de juros

interface ['ɪntəfeɪs] N (Comput) interface f

interfere [ɪntə'fɪəʳ] VI: **to ~ in** (quarrel, other people's business) interferir or intrometer-se em; **to ~ with** (objects) mexer em; (hinder) impedir;

(plans) interferir; **don't ~** não se meta

interference [ɪntə'fɪərəns] N intromissão f; (Radio, TV) interferência

interfering [ɪntə'fɪərɪŋ] ADJ intrometido

interim ['ɪntərɪm] ADJ interino, provisório ■ N: **in the ~** neste ínterim, nesse meio tempo

interior [ɪn'tɪərɪəʳ] N interior m ■ ADJ interno; (ministry) do interior; **interior decorator** N decorador(a) m/f, arquiteto(-a) de interiores; **interior designer** N arquiteto(-a) de interiores

interject [ɪntə'dʒɛkt] VT inserir, interpor

interjection [ɪntə'dʒɛkʃən] N interrupção f; (Ling) interjeição f, exclamação f

interlock [ɪntə'lɔk] VI entrelaçar-se; (wheels etc) engatar-se, engrenar-se ■ VT engrenar

interloper ['ɪntələupəʳ] N intruso(-a)

interlude ['ɪntəluːd] N interlúdio; (rest) descanso; (Theatre) intervalo

intermarry [ɪntə'mærɪ] VI ligar-se por casamento

intermediary [ɪntə'miːdɪərɪ] N intermediário(-a)

intermediate [ɪntə'miːdɪət] ADJ intermediário

interminable [ɪn'təːmɪnəbl] ADJ interminável

intermission [ɪntə'mɪʃən] N intervalo

intermittent [ɪntə'mɪtnt] ADJ intermitente; (publication) periódico

intermittently [ɪntə'mɪtntlɪ] ADV intermitentemente, a intervalos

intern [vt ɪn'təːn, n 'ɪntəːn] VT internar; (enclose) encerrar ■ N (US) médico-interno/médica-interna

internal [ɪn'təːnl] ADJ interno; **~ injuries** ferimentos mpl internos

internally [ɪn'təːnəlɪ] ADV interiormente; **"not to be taken ~"** "uso externo"

Internal Revenue (Service) (US) N ≈ fisco, ≈ receita federal (BR)

international [ɪntə'næʃənl] ADJ internacional ■ N (Brit: Sport: game) jogo internacional; (: player) jogador(a) m/f internacional; **International Atomic Energy Agency** N Agência Internacional de Energia Atômica; **International Court of Justice** N Corte f Internacional de Justiça; **international date line** N linha internacional de mudança de data

internationally [ɪntə'næʃnəlɪ] ADV internacionalmente

International Monetary Fund N Fundo Monetário Internacional

internecine [ɪntə'niːsaɪn] ADJ mutuamente destrutivo

internee [ɪntəː'niː] N internado(-a)

Internet ['ɪntənet] N: **the ~** a Internet; **Internet café** N cibercafé m; **Internet Service Provider** N provedor de acesso à Internet

internment [ɪn'təːnmənt] N internamento

interplay ['ɪntəpleɪ] N interação f

Interpol ['ɪntəpɔl] N Interpol m

interpret [ɪn'təːprɪt] VT interpretar; (translate)

traduzir ▪ vi interpretar

interpretation [ɪntə:prɪ'teɪʃən] N interpretação f; (translation) tradução f

interpreter [ɪn'tə:prɪtə^r] N intérprete m/f

interpreting [ɪn'tə:prɪtɪŋ] N (profession) interpretação f

interrelated [ɪntərɪ'leɪtɪd] ADJ inter-relacionado

interrogate [ɪn'tɛrəʊgeɪt] VT interrogar

interrogation [ɪntɛrə'geɪʃən] N interrogatório

interrogative [ɪntə'rɔgətɪv] ADJ interrogativo ▪ N (Ling) interrogativo

interrogator [ɪn'tɛrəgeɪtə^r] N interrogador(a) m/f

interrupt [ɪntə'rʌpt] VT, VI interromper

interruption [ɪntə'rʌpʃən] N interrupção f

intersect [ɪntə'sɛkt] VT cruzar ▪ VI (roads) cruzar-se

intersection [ɪntə'sɛkʃən] N intersecção f; (of roads) cruzamento

intersperse [ɪntə'spə:s] VT entremear; **to ~ with** entremear com or de

intertwine [ɪntə'twaɪn] VT entrelaçar ▪ VI entrelaçar-se

interval ['ɪntəvl] N intervalo; (Brit: Sch) recreio; (: Theatre, Sport) intervalo; **sunny ~s** (in weather) períodos de melhoria; **at ~s** a intervalos

intervene [ɪntə'vi:n] VI intervir; (event) ocorrer; (time) decorrer

intervention [ɪntə'vɛnʃən] N intervenção f

interview ['ɪntəvju:] N entrevista ▪ VT entrevistar

interviewee [ɪntəvju:'i:] N entrevistado(-a)

interviewer ['ɪntəvju:ə^r] N entrevistador(a) m/f

intestate [ɪn'tɛsteɪt] ADJ intestado

intestinal [ɪn'tɛstɪnl] ADJ intestinal

intestine [ɪn'tɛstɪn] N intestino; **large/small ~** intestino grosso/delgado

intimacy ['ɪntɪməsɪ] N intimidade f

intimate [adj 'ɪntɪmət, vt 'ɪntɪmeɪt] ADJ íntimo; (knowledge) profundo ▪ VT insinuar, sugerir

intimately ['ɪntɪmətlɪ] ADV intimamente

intimation [ɪntɪ'meɪʃən] N insinuação f, sugestão f

intimidate [ɪn'tɪmɪdeɪt] VT amedrontar

intimidation [ɪntɪmɪ'deɪʃən] N intimidação f

🔘 **KEYWORD**

into ['ɪntu] PREP em **1** (indicating motion or direction) em; **come into the house/garden** venha para dentro/o jardim; **go into town** ir para a cidade; **he got into the car** ele entrou na carro; **throw it into the fire** jogue isto na fogueira; **research into cancer** pesquisa sobre o câncer; **he worked late into the night** ele trabalhou até altas horas; **the car bumped into the wall** o carro bateu no muro; **she poured tea into the cup** ela botou o chá na xícara

2 (indicating change of condition, result): **she burst into tears** ela desatou a chorar; **he**

was shocked into silence ele ficou mudo de choque; **into 3 pieces/French** em 3 pedaços/para o francês; **they got into trouble** eles se deram mal

intolerable [ɪn'tɔlərəbl] ADJ intolerável, insuportável

intolerance [ɪn'tɔlərəns] N intolerância

intolerant [ɪn'tɔlərənt] ADJ: **~ (of)** intolerante (com or para com)

intonation [ɪntəu'neɪʃən] N entonação f, inflexão f

intoxicate [ɪn'tɔksɪkeɪt] VT embriagar

intoxicated [ɪn'tɔksɪkeɪtɪd] ADJ embriagado

intoxication [ɪntɔksɪ'keɪʃən] N intoxicação f, embriaguez f

intractable [ɪn'træktəbl] ADJ (child, illness) intratável; (material) difícil de trabalhar; (problem) espinhoso

intranet ['ɪntrənet] N intranet f

intransigent [ɪn'trænsɪdʒənt] ADJ intransigente

intransitive [ɪn'trænsɪtɪv] ADJ intransitivo

intra-uterine device ['ɪntrə'ju:təraɪn-] N dispositivo intra-uterino

intravenous [ɪntrə'vi:nəs] ADJ intravenoso

in-tray N cesta para correspondência de entrada

intrepid [ɪn'trepɪd] ADJ intrépido

intricacy ['ɪntrɪkəsɪ] N complexidade f

intricate ['ɪntrɪkət] ADJ complexo, complicado

intrigue [ɪn'tri:g] N intriga ▪ VT intrigar ▪ VI fazer intriga

intriguing [ɪn'tri:gɪŋ] ADJ intrigante

intrinsic [ɪn'trɪnsɪk] ADJ intrínseco

introduce [ɪntrə'dju:s] VT introduzir; **to ~ sb (to sb)** apresentar alguém (a alguém); **to ~ sb to** (pastime, technique) iniciar alguém em; **may I ~ ...?** permita-me apresentar ...

introduction [ɪntrə'dʌkʃən] N introdução f; (of person) apresentação f; **a letter of ~** uma carta de recomendação

introductory [ɪntrə'dʌktərɪ] ADJ introdutório; **~ remarks** observações preliminares; **~ offer** oferta de lançamento

introspection [ɪntrəu'spɛkʃən] N introspecção f

introspective [ɪntrəu'spɛktɪv] ADJ introspectivo

introvert ['ɪntrəuvə:t] N introvertido(-a) ▪ ADJ (also: **introverted**) introvertido

intrude [ɪn'tru:d] VI: **to ~ (on or into)** intrometer-se (em)

intruder [ɪn'tru:də^r] N intruso(-a)

intrusion [ɪn'tru:ʒən] N intromissão f

intrusive [ɪn'tru:sɪv] ADJ intruso

intuition [ɪntju:'ɪʃən] N intuição f

intuitive [ɪn'tju:ɪtɪv] ADJ intuitivo

inundate ['ɪnʌndeɪt] VT: **to ~ with** inundar de

inure [ɪn'juə^r] VT: **to ~ (to)** habituar (a)

invade [ɪn'veɪd] VT invadir

invader [ɪn'veɪdə^r] N invasor(a) m/f

invalid [n 'ɪnvəlɪd, adj ɪn'vælɪd] N inválido(-a)

■ ADJ (not valid) inválido, nulo
invalidate [ɪn'vælɪdeɪt] VT invalidar, anular
invalid chair ['ɪnvəlɪd-] (Brit) N cadeira de rodas
invaluable [ɪn'væljuəbl] ADJ valioso, inestimável
invariable [ɪn'vɛərɪəbl] ADJ invariável
invariably [ɪn'vɛərɪəblɪ] ADV invariavelmente; **she is ~ late** ela sempre chega atrasada
invasion [ɪn'veɪʒən] N invasão f
invective [ɪn'vɛktɪv] N invectiva
inveigle [ɪn'viːgl] VT: **to ~ sb into (doing) sth** aliciar alguém para (fazer) algo
invent [ɪn'vɛnt] VT inventar
invention [ɪn'vɛnʃən] N invenção f; (inventiveness) engenho; (lie) ficção f, mentira
inventive [ɪn'vɛntɪv] ADJ engenhoso
inventiveness [ɪn'vɛntɪvnɪs] N engenhosidade f, inventiva
inventor [ɪn'vɛntəʳ] N inventor(a) m/f
inventory ['ɪnvəntrɪ] N inventário, relação f; **inventory control** N (Comm) controle m de estoques
inverse [ɪn'vəːs] ADJ, N inverso; **in ~ proportion to** em proporção inversa a
inversely [ɪn'vəːslɪ] ADV inversamente
invert [ɪn'vəːt] VT inverter
invertebrate [ɪn'vəːtɪbrət] N invertebrado
inverted commas [ɪn'vəːtɪd-] (Brit) NPL aspas fpl
invest [ɪn'vɛst] VT investir; (endow): **to ~ sb with sth** conferir algo a alguém, investir alguém de algo ■ VI investir; **to ~ in** investir em; (acquire) comprar
investigate [ɪn'vɛstɪgeɪt] VT investigar; (study) estudar, examinar
investigation [ɪnvɛstɪ'geɪʃən] N investigação f
investigative journalism [ɪn'vɛstɪgətɪv-] N jornalismo de investigação
investigator [ɪn'vɛstɪgeɪtəʳ] N investigador(a) m/f; **private ~** detetive particular
investiture [ɪn'vɛstɪtʃəʳ] N investidura
investment [ɪn'vɛstmənt] N investimento; **investment income** N rendimento de investimentos; **investment trust** N fundo mútuo
investor [ɪn'vɛstəʳ] N investidor(a) m/f
inveterate [ɪn'vɛtərət] ADJ inveterado
invidious [ɪn'vɪdɪəs] ADJ injusto; (task) desagradável
invigilate [ɪn'vɪdʒɪleɪt] (Brit) VT fiscalizar ■ VI fiscalizar o exame
invigilator [ɪn'vɪdʒɪleɪtəʳ] N fiscal m/f (de exame)
invigorating [ɪn'vɪgəreɪtɪŋ] ADJ revigorante
invincible [ɪn'vɪnsɪbl] ADJ invencível
inviolate [ɪn'vaɪələt] ADJ inviolado
invisible [ɪn'vɪzɪbl] ADJ invisível; **invisible assets** (Brit) NPL ativo intangível; **invisible ink** N tinta invisível; **invisible mending** N cerzidura
invitation [ɪnvɪ'teɪʃən] N convite m; **by ~ only** estritamente mediante convite; **at sb's ~** a convite de alguém

invite [ɪn'vaɪt] VT convidar; (opinions etc) solicitar, pedir; (trouble) pedir; **to ~ sb to do** convidar alguém para fazer; **to ~ sb to dinner** convidar alguém para jantar
▸ **invite out** VT convidar or chamar para sair
▸ **invite over** VT chamar
inviting [ɪn'vaɪtɪŋ] ADJ convidativo
invoice ['ɪnvɔɪs] N fatura ■ VT faturar; **to ~ sb for goods** faturar mercadorias em nome de alguém
invoke [ɪn'vəuk] VT invocar; (aid) implorar; (law) apelar para
involuntary [ɪn'vɔləntrɪ] ADJ involuntário
involve [ɪn'vɔlv] VT (entail) implicar; (require) exigir; **to ~ sb (in)** envolver alguém (em)
involved [ɪn'vɔlvd] ADJ envolvido; (emotionally) comprometido; (complex) complexo; **to be/get ~ in sth** estar/ficar envolvido em algo
involvement [ɪn'vɔlvmənt] N envolvimento; (obligation) compromisso
invulnerable [ɪn'vʌlnərəbl] ADJ invulnerável
inward ['ɪnwəd] ADJ (movement) interior, interno; (thought, feeling) íntimo
inwardly ['ɪnwədlɪ] ADV (feel, think etc) para si, para dentro
inward(s) ['ɪnwəd(z)] ADV para dentro
I/O ABBR (Comput: = input/output) E/S, I/O
IOC N ABBR (= International Olympic Committee) COI m
iodine ['aɪəudiːn] N iodo
ion ['aɪən] N íon m, ião m (PT)
Ionian Sea [aɪ'əunɪən-] N: **the ~** o mar Iônico
iota [aɪ'əutə] N (fig) pouquinho, tiquinho
IOU N ABBR (= I owe you) vale m
IOW (Brit) ABBR = Isle of Wight
IPA N ABBR (= International Phonetic Alphabet) AFI m
IQ N ABBR (= intelligence quotient) QI m
IRA N ABBR (= Irish Republican Army) IRA m; (US) = **individual retirement account**
Iran [ɪ'rɑːn] N Irã m (BR), Irão m (PT)
Iranian [ɪ'reɪnɪən] ADJ iraniano ■ N iraniano(-a); (Ling) iraniano
Iraq [ɪ'rɑːk] N Iraque m
Iraqi [ɪ'rɑːkɪ] ADJ, N iraquiano(-a)
irascible [ɪ'ræsɪbl] ADJ irascível
irate [aɪ'reɪt] ADJ irado, enfurecido
Ireland ['aɪələnd] N Irlanda; **Republic of ~** República da Irlanda
iris ['aɪrɪs] (pl **irises**) N íris f
Irish ['aɪrɪʃ] ADJ irlandês(-esa) ■ N (Ling) irlandês m; **the Irish** NPL os irlandeses
Irishman ['aɪrɪʃmən] (irreg) N irlandês m
Irish Sea N: **the ~** o mar da Irlanda
Irishwoman ['aɪrɪʃwumən] (irreg) N irlandesa
irk [əːk] VT aborrecer
irksome ['əːksəm] ADJ aborrecido
IRN (Brit) N ABBR (= Independent Radio News) agência de notícias radiofônicas
IRO (US) N ABBR = **International Refugee Organization**
iron ['aɪən] N ferro; (for clothes) ferro de passar

roupa ■ ADJ de ferro ■ VT (clothes) passar;
irons NPL (chains) grilhões mpl
▶ **iron out** VT (crease) tirar; (fig: problem) resolver
Iron Curtain N: **the ~** a cortina de ferro
iron foundry N fundição f
ironic(al) [aɪ'rɔnɪk(l)] ADJ irônico
ironically [aɪ'rɔnɪklɪ] ADV ironicamente
ironing ['aɪənɪŋ] N (activity) passar roupa;
(clothes) roupa passada; (to be ironed) roupa a
ser passada; **ironing board** N tábua de passar
roupa
ironmonger ['aɪənmʌŋgəʳ] (Brit) N ferreiro(-a)
ironmonger's (shop) (Brit) N loja de ferragens
iron ore N minério de ferro
ironworks ['aɪənwəːks] N siderúrgica
irony ['aɪrənɪ] N ironia; **the ~ of it is that ...** o
irônico é que ...
irrational [ɪ'ræʃənl] ADJ irracional
irreconcilable [ɪrɛkən'saɪləbl] ADJ (disagreement)
irreconciliável; (ideas) incompatível
irredeemable [ɪrɪ'diːməbl] ADJ (Comm)
irresgatável
irrefutable [ɪrɪ'fjuːtəbl] ADJ irrefutável
irregular [ɪ'rɛgjuləʳ] ADJ irregular; (surface)
desigual; (illegal) ilegal
irregularity [ɪrɛgju'lærɪtɪ] N irregularidade f;
(of surface) desigualdade f
irrelevance [ɪ'rɛləvəns] N irrelevância
irrelevant [ɪ'rɛləvənt] ADJ irrelevante
irreligious [ɪrɪ'lɪdʒəs] ADJ irreligioso
irreparable [ɪ'rɛprəbl] ADJ irreparável
irreplaceable [ɪrɪ'pleɪsəbl] ADJ insubstituível
irrepressible [ɪrɪ'prɛsəbl] ADJ irreprimível,
irrefreável
irreproachable [ɪrɪ'prəutʃəbl] ADJ
irrepreensível
irresistible [ɪrɪ'zɪstɪbl] ADJ irresistível
irresolute [ɪ'rɛzəluːt] ADJ irresoluto
irrespective [ɪrɪ'spɛktɪv]: **~ of** PREP
independente de, sem considerar
irresponsible [ɪrɪ'spɔnsɪbl] ADJ (act, person)
irresponsável
irretrievable [ɪrɪ'triːvəbl] ADJ (object)
irrecuperável; (loss, damage) irreparável
irreverent [ɪ'rɛvərnt] ADJ irreverente,
desrespeitoso
irrevocable [ɪ'rɛvəkəbl] ADJ irrevogável
irrigate ['ɪrɪgeɪt] VT irrigar
irrigation [ɪrɪ'geɪʃən] N irrigação f
irritable ['ɪrɪtəbl] ADJ irritável; (mood) de mal
humor, nervoso
irritate ['ɪrɪteɪt] VT irritar
irritating ['ɪrɪteɪtɪŋ] ADJ irritante
irritation [ɪrɪ'teɪʃən] N irritação f
IRS (US) N ABBR = **Internal Revenue Service**
is [ɪz] VB see **be**
ISBN N ABBR (= International Standard Book Number)
ISBN m
ISDN N ABBR (= Integrated Services Digital Network)
RDSI f, ISDN f
Islam ['ɪzlɑːm] N islamismo
Islamic [ɪz'læmɪk] ADJ islâmico(-a)

island ['aɪlənd] N ilha; (also: **traffic island**) abrigo
islander ['aɪləndəʳ] N ilhéu/ilhoa m/f
isle [aɪl] N ilhota, ilha
isn't ['ɪznt] = **is not**
isolate ['aɪsəleɪt] VT isolar
isolated ['aɪsəleɪtɪd] ADJ isolado
isolation [aɪsə'leɪʃən] N isolamento
isolationism [aɪsə'leɪʃənɪzm] N isolacionismo
isotope ['aɪsəutəup] N isótopo
ISP N ABBR (= Internet Service Provider) ISP m
Israel ['ɪzreɪl] N Israel
Israeli [ɪz'reɪlɪ] ADJ, N israelense m/f
issue ['ɪsjuː] N questão f, tema m; (outcome)
resultado; (of book) edição f; (of stamps) emissão
f; (of newspaper etc) número; (offspring) sucessão
f, descendência ■ VT (rations, equipment)
distribuir; (orders) dar; (certificate) emitir; (decree)
promulgar; (book) publicar; (cheques, banknotes,
stamps) emitir ■ VI: **to ~ from** (smell, liquid)
emanar de; **at ~** em debate; **to avoid the ~**
contornar o problema; **to take ~ with sb (over
sth)** discordar de alguém (sobre algo); **to make
an ~ of sth** criar caso com algo; **to confuse or
obscure the ~** complicar as coisas
Istanbul [ɪstæn'buːl] N Istambul
isthmus ['ɪsməs] N istmo
IT N ABBR = **information technology**

🔘 **KEYWORD**

it [ɪt] PRON **1** (specific: subject) ele/ela; (: direct object)
o(-a); (: indirect object) lhe; **it's on the table** está
em cima da mesa; **I can't find it** não consigo
achá-lo; **give it to me** dê-mo; **about/from it**
sobre/de isto; **did you go to it?** (party, concert etc)
você foi?
2 (impers) isto, isso; (after prep) ele, ela; **it's
raining** está chovendo (BR) or a chover (PT); **it's
cold today** está frio hoje; **it's Friday
tomorrow** amanhã é sexta-feira; **it's six
o'clock/the 10th of August** são seis horas/
hoje é (dia) 10 de agosto; **who is it? — it's me**
quem é? — sou eu

ITA (Brit) N ABBR (= initial teaching alphabet) alfabeto
modificado utilizado na alfabetização
Italian [ɪ'tæljən] ADJ italiano ■ N italiano(-a);
(Ling) italiano
italic [ɪ'tælɪk] ADJ itálico
italics [ɪ'tælɪks] NPL itálico
Italy ['ɪtəlɪ] N Itália
itch [ɪtʃ] N comichão f, coceira ■ VI (person) estar
com or sentir comichão or coceira; (part of body)
comichar, coçar; **I'm ~ing to do sth** estou louco
para fazer algo
itching ['ɪtʃɪŋ] N comichão f, coceira
itchy ['ɪtʃɪ] ADJ que coça; **to be ~** ; = **to itch**
it'd ['ɪtd] = **it would; it had**
item ['aɪtəm] N item m; (on agenda) assunto; (in
programme) número; (also: **news item**) notícia; **~s
of clothing** artigos de vestuário
itemize ['aɪtəmaɪz] VT detalhar, especificar

itinerant [ɪ'tɪnərənt] ADJ itinerante

itinerary [aɪ'tɪnərərɪ] N itinerário

it'll ['ɪtl] = **it will; it shall**

ITN (Brit) N ABBR (= Independent Television News) agência de notícias televisivas

its [ɪts] ADJ seu/sua, dele/dela ■ PRON o seu(-a) sua, o dele(-a) dela

it's [ɪts] = **it is; it has**

itself [ɪt'sɛlf] PRON (reflexive) si mesmo(-a); (emphatic) ele mesmo/ela mesma

ITV (Brit) N ABBR (= Independent Television) canal de televisão comercial

IUD N ABBR (= intra-uterine device) DIU m

I've [aɪv] = **I have**

ivory ['aɪvərɪ] N marfim m; (colour) cor f de marfim

Ivory Coast N Costa do Marfim

ivory tower N (fig) torre f de marfim

ivy ['aɪvɪ] N hera

Ivy League (US) N as grandes faculdades (Harvard, Yale, Princeton etc) do nordeste dos EUA

J j

J, j [dʒeɪ] N (*letter*) J, j *m*; **J for Jack** (*Brit*) or **Jig** (US) J de José

JA N ABBR = **judge advocate**

J/A ABBR = **joint account**

jab [dʒæb] VT (*elbow*) cutucar; (*punch*) esmurrar, socar ▪ N cotovelada, murro; (*Med: inf*) injeção *f*; **to ~ sth into sth** cravar algo em algo

jabber ['dʒæbə'] VT, VI tagarelar

jack [dʒæk] N (*Aut*) macaco; (*Bowls*) bola branca; (*Cards*) valete *m*
  ▸ **jack in** (*inf*) VT largar
  ▸ **jack up** VT (*Aut*) levantar com macaco; (*raise: prices*) aumentar

jackal ['dʒækl] N chacal *m*

jackass ['dʒækæs] N (*fig*) burro

jackdaw ['dʒækdɔ:] N gralha

jacket ['dʒækɪt] N jaqueta, casaco curto; (*of boiler etc*) capa, forro; (*of book*) sobrecapa; **potatoes in their ~s** (*Brit*) batatas com casca

jack-in-the-box N caixa de surpresas

jack-knife (*irreg: like* **knife**) N canivete *m* ▪ VI: **the lorry ~d** o reboque do caminhão deu uma guinada

jack-of-all-trades N pau *m* para toda obra, homem *m* dos sete instrumentos

jack plug N pino

jackpot ['dʒækpɔt] N bolada, sorte *f* grande

Jacuzzi® [dʒə'ku:zɪ] N jacuzzi® *m*, banheira de hidromassagem

jade [dʒeɪd] N (*stone*) jade *m*

jaded ['dʒeɪdɪd] ADJ (*tired*) cansado; (*fed-up*) aborrecido, amolado

jagged ['dʒægɪd] ADJ dentado, denteado

jaguar ['dʒægjuə'] N jaguar *m*

jail [dʒeɪl] N prisão *f*, cadeia ▪ VT encarcerar

jailbird ['dʒeɪlbə:d] N criminoso inveterado

jailbreak ['dʒeɪlbreɪk] N fuga da prisão

jailer ['dʒeɪlə'] N carcereiro

jalopy [dʒə'lɔpɪ] (*inf*) N calhambeque *m*

jam [dʒæm] N geléia; (*also:* **traffic jam**) engarrafamento; (*inf: difficulty*) apuro ▪ VT (*passage etc*) obstruir, atravancar; (*mechanism*) emperrar; (*Radio*) bloquear, interferir ▪ VI (*mechanism, drawer etc*) emperrar; **to get sb out of a ~** (*inf*) tirar alguém de uma enrascada; **to ~ sth into sth** forçar algo dentro de algo; **the telephone lines are ~med** as linhas telefônicas estão congestionadas

Jamaica [dʒə'meɪkə] N Jamaica

Jamaican [dʒə'meɪkən] ADJ, N jamaicano(-a) *m/f*

jamb ['dʒæm] N umbral *m*

jam-packed ADJ: **~ (with)** abarrotado (de)

jam session N jam session *m*

Jan. ABBR (= *January*) jan

jangle ['dʒæŋgl] VI soar estridentemente

janitor ['dʒænɪtə'] N (*caretaker*) zelador *m*; (*doorman*) porteiro

January ['dʒænjuərɪ] N janeiro; *see also* **July**

Japan [dʒə'pæn] N Japão *m*

Japanese [dʒæpə'ni:z] ADJ japonês(-esa) ▪ N INV japonês(-esa) *m/f*; (*Ling*) japonês *m*

jar [dʒɑ:'] N (*container, glass: large*) jarro; (*glass: small*) pote *m* ▪ VI (*sound*) ranger, chiar; (*colours*) destoar ▪ VT (*shake*) abalar

jargon ['dʒɑ:gən] N jargão *m*

jarring ['dʒɑ:rɪŋ] ADJ (*sound, colour*) destoante

Jas. ABBR = **James**

jasmin(e) ['dʒæzmɪn] N jasmim *m*

jaundice ['dʒɔ:ndɪs] N icterícia

jaundiced ['dʒɔ:ndɪst] ADJ (*fig: unenthusiastic*) desanimado; (*: embittered*) amargurado, despeitado; (*: disillusioned*) desiludido

jaunt [dʒɔ:nt] N excursão *f*

jaunty ['dʒɔ:ntɪ] ADJ alegre, jovial; (*step*) enérgico

Java ['dʒɑ:və] N Java (*no article*)

javelin ['dʒævlɪn] N dardo de arremesso

jaw [dʒɔ:] N mandíbula, maxilar *m*

jawbone ['dʒɔ:bəun] N osso maxilar, maxila

jay [dʒeɪ] N gaio

jaywalker ['dʒeɪwɔ:kə'] N pedestre *m/f* imprudente (BR), peão *m* imprudente (PT)

jazz [dʒæz] N jazz *m*
  ▸ **jazz up** VT (*liven up*) animar, avivar

jazz band N banda de jazz

jazzy ['dʒæzɪ] ADJ (*of Jazz*) jazzístico; (*bright*) de cor berrante

JCS (US) N ABBR = **Joint Chiefs of Staff**

JD (US) N ABBR (= *Doctor of Laws*) título universitário; (*: = Justice Department*) ministério da Justiça

jealous ['dʒɛləs] ADJ ciumento; (*envious*) invejoso; **to be ~** estar com ciúmes

jealously ['dʒɛləslɪ] ADV (*enviously*) invejosamente; (*guard*) zelosamente

jealousy ['dʒɛləsɪ] N ciúmes mpl; (envy) inveja
jeans [dʒiːnz] NPL jeans m (BR), jeans mpl (PT)
Jeep® [dʒiːp] N jipe® m
jeer [dʒɪər] VI: **to ~ (at)** (boo) vaiar; (mock) zombar (de)
jeering ['dʒɪərɪŋ] ADJ vaiador(a) ■ N vaias fpl
jeers ['dʒɪəz] NPL (boos) vaias fpl; (mocking) zombarias fpl
jelly ['dʒɛlɪ] N (jam) geléia
jellyfish ['dʒɛlɪfɪʃ] N INV água-viva
jeopardize ['dʒɛpədaɪz] VT arriscar, pôr em perigo
jeopardy ['dʒɛpədɪ] N: **to be in ~** estar em perigo, estar correndo risco
jerk [dʒəːk] N (jolt) solavanco, sacudida; (wrench) puxão m; (inf: idiot) babaca m ■ VT sacudir ■ VI (vehicle) dar um solavanco
jerkin ['dʒəːkɪn] N jaqueta
jerky ['dʒəːkɪ] ADJ espasmódico, aos arrancos
jerry-built ['dʒɛrɪ-] ADJ mal construído
jerry can ['dʒɛrɪ-] N lata
Jersey ['dʒəːzɪ] N Jersey (no article)
jersey ['dʒəːzɪ] N suéter m (BR), camisola (PT); (fabric) jérsei m, malha; **Jerusalem** [dʒə'ruːsələm] N Jerusalém
Jerusalem artichoke ■ N topinambo
jest [dʒɛst] N gracejo, brincadeira; **in ~** de brincadeira
jester ['dʒɛstər] N (History) bobo
Jesus (Christ) ['dʒiːzəskraɪst] N Jesus m (Cristo)
jet [dʒɛt] N (of gas, liquid) jato; (Aviat) (avião m a) jato; (stone) azeviche m
jet-black ADJ da cor do azeviche
jet engine N motor m a jato
jet lag N cansaço devido à diferença de fuso horário
jetsam ['dʒɛtsəm] N objetos mpl alijados ao mar
jettison ['dʒɛtɪsn] VT alijar
jetty ['dʒɛtɪ] N quebra-mar m, cais m
Jew [dʒuː] N judeu(-dia) m/f
jewel ['dʒuːəl] N jóia; (in watch) rubi m
jeweller ['dʒuːələr] (US **jeweler**) N joalheiro(-a)
jeweller's (shop) N joalheria
jewellery ['dʒuːəlrɪ] (US **jewelry**) N jóias fpl, pedrarias fpl
Jewess ['dʒuːɪs] N (offensive) judia
Jewish ['dʒuːɪʃ] ADJ judeu/judia
JFK (US) N ABBR = **John Fitzgerald Kennedy International Airport**
jib [dʒɪb] N (Naut) bujarrona; (of crane) lança ■ VI (horse) empacar; **to ~ at doing sth** relutar em fazer algo
jibe [dʒaɪb] N = **gibe**
jiffy ['dʒɪfɪ] (inf) N: **in a ~** num instante
jig [dʒɪg] N jiga
jigsaw ['dʒɪgsɔː] N (also: **jigsaw puzzle**) quebra-cabeça m; (tool) serra de vaivém
jilt [dʒɪlt] VT dar o fora em
jingle ['dʒɪŋgl] N (for advert) música de propaganda ■ VI tilintar, retinir
jingoism ['dʒɪŋgəuɪzm] N jingoísmo
jinx [dʒɪŋks] (inf) N caipora, pé m frio

jitters ['dʒɪtəz] (inf) NPL: **to get the ~** ficar muito nervoso
jittery ['dʒɪtərɪ] (inf) ADJ nervoso
jiu-jitsu [dʒuː'dʒɪtsuː] N jiu-jítsu m
job [dʒɔb] N trabalho; (task) tarefa; (duty) dever m; (post) emprego; (inf: difficulty): **you'll have a ~ to do that** não vai ser fácil você fazer isso; **it's not my ~** não faz parte das minhas funções; **a part-time/full-time ~** um trabalho de meio-expediente/de tempo integral; **it's a good ~ that ...** ainda bem que ...; **just the ~!** justo o que queria!
jobber ['dʒɔbər] (Brit) N (Stock Exchange) operador(a) m/f intermediário(-a)
jobbing ['dʒɔbɪŋ] (Brit) ADJ (workman) tarefeiro, pago por tarefa
job centre ['dʒɔbsɛntər] N agência de emprego
job creation scheme N plano para a criação de empregos
job description N descrição f do cargo
jobless ['dʒɔblɪs] ADJ desempregado
job lot N lote m (de mercadorias variadas)
job satisfaction N satisfação f profissional
job security N estabilidade f de emprego
job specification N especificação f do cargo
jockey ['dʒɔkɪ] N jóquei m ■ VI: **to ~ for position** manobrar para conseguir uma posição; **jockey box** (US) N (Aut) porta-luvas m inv
jocular ['dʒɔkjulər] ADJ (remark) jocoso, divertido; (person) alegre
jog [dʒɔg] VT empurrar, sacudir ■ VI (run) fazer jogging or cooper; **to ~ sb's memory** refrescar a memória de alguém
  ▸**jog along** VI ir levando
jogger ['dʒɔgər] N corredor(a) m/f, praticante m/f de jogging
jogging ['dʒɔgɪŋ] N jogging m
join [dʒɔɪn] VT (things) juntar, unir; (queue) entrar; (become member of) associar-se a; (meet) encontrar-se com; (accompany) juntar-se a ■ VI (roads, rivers) confluir ■ N junção f; **will you ~ us for dinner?** você janta conosco?; **I'll ~ you later** vou me encontrar com você mais tarde; **to ~ forces (with)** associar-se (com)
  ▸**join in** VI participar ■ VT FUS participar em
  ▸**join up** VI unir-se; (Mil) alistar-se
joiner ['dʒɔɪnər] (Brit) N marceneiro
joinery ['dʒɔɪnərɪ] N marcenaria
joint [dʒɔɪnt] N (Tech) junta, união f; (wood) encaixe m; (Anat) articulação f; (Brit: Culin) quarto; (inf: place) espelunca; (: marijuana cigarette) baseado ■ ADJ (common) comum; (combined) conjunto; (committee) misto; **by ~ agreement** por comum acordo; **~ responsibility** co-responsabilidade f; **joint account** N conta conjunta
jointly ['dʒɔɪntlɪ] ADV em comum; (collectively) coletivamente; (together) conjuntamente
joint ownership N co-propriedade f, condomínio
joint-stock company N sociedade f anônima

por ações
joint venture N joint venture *m*
joist [dʒɔɪst] N barrote *m*
joke [dʒəuk] N piada; (*also:* **practical joke**)
  brincadeira, peça ■ vɪ brincar; **to play a ~ on**
  pregar uma peça em
joker ['dʒəukər] N piadista *m/f*,
  brincalhão(-lhona) *m/f*; (*Cards*) curingão *m*
joking ['dʒəukɪŋ] N brincadeira
jollity ['dʒɔlɪtɪ] N alegria
jolly ['dʒɔlɪ] ADJ (*merry*) alegre; (*enjoyable*)
  divertido ■ ADV (*Brit: inf*) muito, extremamente
  ■ VT (*Brit*): **to ~ sb along** animar alguém; **~
  good!** (*Brit*) excelente!
jolt [dʒəult] N (*shake*) sacudida, solavanco; (*shock*)
  susto ■ VT sacudir; (*emotionally*) abalar
Jordan ['dʒɔːdən] N Jordânia; (*river*) Jordão *m*
Jordanian [dʒɔː'deɪnɪən] ADJ, N jordaniano(-a)
joss stick [dʒɔs-] N palito perfumado
jostle ['dʒɔsl] VT acotovelar, empurrar
jot [dʒɔt] N: **not one ~** nem um pouquinho
  ▸ **jot down** VT anotar
jotter ['dʒɔtər] (*Brit*) N bloco (de anotações)
journal [dʒəːnl] N (*paper*) jornal *m*; (*magazine*)
  revista; (*diary*) diário
journalese [dʒəː'nə'liːz] (*pej*) N linguagem *f*
  jornalística
journalism ['dʒəː'nəlɪzəm] N jornalismo
journalist ['dʒəː'nəlɪst] N jornalista *m/f*
journey ['dʒəːnɪ] N viagem *f*; (*distance covered*)
  trajeto ■ VI viajar; **return ~** volta; **a 5-hour ~** 5
  horas de viagem
jovial ['dʒəuvɪəl] ADJ jovial, alegre
jowl [dʒaul] N papada
joy [dʒɔɪ] N alegria
joyful ['dʒɔɪful] ADJ alegre
joyous ['dʒɔɪəs] ADJ alegre
joyride ['dʒɔɪraɪd] N passeio de carro; (*illegal*)
  passeio (*com veículo roubado*)
joystick ['dʒɔɪstɪk] N (*Aviat*) manche *m*, alavanca
  de controle; (*Comput*) joystick *m*
JP N ABBR = **Justice of the Peace**
Jr ABBR = **junior**
jubilant ['dʒuːbɪlnt] ADJ jubilante
jubilation [dʒuːbɪ'leɪʃən] N júbilo, regozijo
jubilee ['dʒuːbɪliː] N jubileu *m*; **silver ~** jubileu
  de prata
judge [dʒʌdʒ] N juiz/juíza *m/f*; (*in competition*)
  árbitro; (*fig: expert*) especialista *m/f*,
  conhecedor(a) *m/f* ■ VT julgar; (*competition*)
  arbitrar; (*estimate: weight, size etc*) avaliar;
  (*consider*) considerar ■ VI: **judging** *or* **to ~ by ...** a
  julgar por ...; **as far as I can ~** ao que me parece,
  no meu entender; **I ~d it necessary to inform
  him** julguei necessário informá-lo; **judge
  advocate** N (*Mil*) auditor *m* de guerra
Judge Advocate General N (*Mil*) procurador *m*
  geral da Justiça Militar
judg(e)ment ['dʒʌdʒmənt] N juízo;
  (*punishment*) decisão *f*, sentença; (*opinion*)
  opinião *f*; (*discernment*) discernimento; **in my
  judg(e)ment** na minha opinião; **to pass**

judg(e)ment on (*Law*) julgar, dar sentença
  sobre
judicial [dʒuː'dɪʃl] ADJ judicial; (*fair*) imparcial
judiciary [dʒuː'dɪʃɪərɪ] N poder *m* judiciário
judicious [dʒuː'dɪʃəs] ADJ judicioso
judo ['dʒuːdəu] N judô *m*
jug [dʒʌg] N jarro
jugged hare [dʒʌgd-] (*Brit*) N guisado de lebre
juggernaut ['dʒʌgənɔːt] (*Brit*) N (*huge truck*)
  jamanta
juggle ['dʒʌgl] VI fazer malabarismos
juggler ['dʒʌglər] N malabarista *m/f*
Jugoslav *etc* ['juːgəuslɑːv] = **Yugoslav** *etc*
jugular (vein) ['dʒʌgjulər-] N veia jugular
juice [dʒuːs] N suco (BR), sumo (PT); (*inf: petrol*):
  we've run out of ~ estamos sem gasolina
juicy ['dʒuːsɪ] ADJ suculento
jukebox ['dʒuːkbɔks] N juke-box *m*
Jul. ABBR (= *July*) jul
July [dʒuː'laɪ] N julho; **the first of ~** dia
  primeiro de julho; (**on**) **the eleventh of ~** (*no*)
  dia onze de julho; **in the month of ~** no mês de
  julho; **at the beginning/end of ~** no começo/
  fim de julho; **in the middle of ~** em meados
  de julho; **during ~** durante o mês de julho; **in ~
  of next year** em julho do ano que vem; **each** *or*
  every ~ todo ano em julho; **~ was wet this year**
  choveu muito em julho deste ano
jumble ['dʒʌmbl] N confusão *f*, mixórdia ■ VT
  (*also:* **jumble up**: *mix up*) misturar; (: *disarrange*)
  desorganizar; **jumble sale** (*Brit*) N venda de
  objetos usados, bazar *m*

● **JUMBLE SALE**
  As *jumble sales* têm lugar dentro de igrejas,
  salões de festa e escolas, onde são vendidos
  diversos tipos de mercadorias, em geral
  baratas e sobretudo de segunda mão, a
  fim de coletar dinheiro para uma obra de
  caridade, uma escola ou uma igreja.

jumbo (jet) ['dʒʌmbəu-] N avião *m* jumbo
jump [dʒʌmp] VI saltar, pular; (*start*)
  sobressaltar-se; (*increase*) disparar ■ VT pular,
  saltar ■ N pulo, salto; (*increase*) alta; (*fence*)
  obstáculo; **to ~ the queue** (*Brit*) furar a fila (BR),
  pôr-se à frente (PT); **to ~ for joy** pular de alegria
  ▸ **jump about** VI saltitar
  ▸ **jump at** VT FUS (*accept*) aceitar
  imediatamente; (*chance*) agarrar
  ▸ **jump down** VI pular para baixo
  ▸ **jump up** VI levantar-se num ímpeto
jumped-up [dʒʌmpt-] (*Brit: pej*) ADJ arrivista
jumper ['dʒʌmpər] N (*Brit: pullover*) suéter *m*
  (BR), camisola (PT); (*US: pinafore dress*) avental *m*;
  (*Sport*) saltador(a) *m/f*; **jumper cables** (US) NPL
  = **jump leads**
jump leads (US **jumper cables**) NPL cabos *mpl*
  para ligar a bateria
jumpy ['dʒʌmpɪ] ADJ nervoso
Jun. ABBR = **June**; **junior**

junction ['dʒʌŋkʃən] (Brit) N (of roads) cruzamento; (: on motorway) trevo; (Rail) entroncamento

juncture ['dʒʌŋktʃər] N: **at this ~** neste momento, nesta conjuntura

June [dʒuːn] N junho; see also **July**

jungle ['dʒʌŋgl] N selva, mato

junior ['dʒuːnɪər] ADJ (in age) mais novo or moço; (competition) juvenil; (position) subalterno ■ N jovem m/f; (Sport) júnior m; **he's ~ to me (by 2 years), he's (2 years) my ~** ele é (dois anos) mais novo do que eu; **he's ~ to me** (seniority) tenho mais antiguidade do que ele; **junior executive** N executivo(-a) júnior; **junior high school** (US) N ≈ colégio (2° e 3° ginasial); **junior minister** (Brit) N ministro(-a) subalterno(-a); **junior partner** N sócio(-a) minoritário(-a); **junior school** (Brit) N escola primária; **junior sizes** NPL tamanhos mpl para crianças

juniper ['dʒuːnɪpər] N junípero

junk [dʒʌŋk] N (cheap goods) tranqueira, velharias fpl; (lumber) trastes mpl; (rubbish) lixo; (ship) junco ■ VT (inf) jogar no lixo; **junk dealer** N belchior m

junket ['dʒʌŋkɪt] N (Culin) coalhada; (Brit: inf): **to go on a ~** viajar à custa do governo ■ VI (Brit: inf): **to go ~ing; = to go on a junket**

junk food N comida pronta de baixo valor nutritivo

junkie ['dʒʌŋkɪ] (inf) N drogado(-a)

junk room (US) N quarto de despejo

junk shop N loja de objetos usados

Junr ABBR = **junior**

junta ['dʒʌntə] N junta

Jupiter ['dʒuːpɪtər] N Júpiter m

jurisdiction [dʒuərɪs'dɪkʃən] N jurisdição f; **it falls** or **comes within/outside our ~** é/não é da nossa competência

jurisprudence [dʒuərɪs'pruːdəns] N jurisprudência

juror ['dʒuərər] N jurado(-a)

jury ['dʒuərɪ] N júri m; **jury box** N banca dos jurados

juryman ['dʒuərɪmən] (irreg) N = **juror**

just [dʒʌst] ADJ justo ■ ADV (exactly) justamente, exatamente; (only) apenas, somente; **he's ~ done it/left** ele acabou (BR) or acaba (PT) de fazê-lo/ir; **~ as I expected** exatamente como eu esperava; **~ right** perfeito; **~ two o'clock** duas (horas) em ponto; **she's ~ as clever as you** ela é tão inteligentecomo você; **it's ~ as good** é igualmente bom; **~ as well that ...** ainda bem que ...; **I was ~ about to phone** eu já ia telefonar; **we were ~ leaving** estávamos de saída; **~ as he was leaving** no momento em que ele saía; **~ before/enough** justo antes/o suficiente; **~ here** bem aqui; **it's ~ a mistake** não passa de um erro; **he ~ missed** falhou por pouco; **~ listen** escute aqui!; **~ ask someone the way** é só pedir uma indicação; **not ~ now** não neste momento; **~ a minute!, ~ one moment!** só um minuto!, espera aí!, peraí! (inf)

justice ['dʒʌstɪs] N justiça; (US: judge) juiz/ juíza m/f; **Lord Chief J~** (Brit) presidente do tribunal de recursos; **to do ~ to** (fig) apreciar devidamente; **this photo doesn't do you ~** esta foto não te faz justiça

Justice of the Peace N juiz/juíza m/f de paz

justifiable [dʒʌstɪ'faɪəbl] ADJ justificável

justifiably [dʒʌstɪ'faɪəblɪ] ADV justificadamente

justification [dʒʌstɪfɪ'keɪʃən] N (reason) justificativa; (action) justificação f

justify ['dʒʌstɪfaɪ] VT justificar; **to be justified in doing sth** ter razão de fazer algo

justly ['dʒʌstlɪ] ADV justamente; (with reason) com razão

justness ['dʒʌstnɪs] N justiça

jut [dʒʌt] VI (also: **jut out**) sobressair

jute [dʒuːt] N juta

juvenile ['dʒuːvənaɪl] ADJ juvenil; (court) de menores; (books) para adolescentes ■ N jovem m/f; (Law) menor m/f de idade; **juvenile delinquency** N delinqüência juvenil; **juvenile delinquent** N delinqüente m/f juvenil

juxtapose ['dʒʌkstəpəuz] VT justapor

juxtaposition [dʒʌkstəpə'zɪʃən] N justaposição f

Kk

K, k [keɪ] N (letter) K, k m; **K for King** K de Kátia
K ABBR (= kilobyte) K; (Brit: = Knight) título honorífico ■ N ABBR (= one thousand) mil
kaftan ['kæftæn] N cafetã m
Kalahari Desert [kælə'hɑːrɪ-] N deserto de Kalahari
kale [keɪl] N couve f
kaleidoscope [kə'laɪdəskəup] N calidoscópio, caleidoscópio
Kampala [kæm'pɑːlə] N Campala
Kampuchea [kæmpu'tʃɪə] N Kampuchea m, Camboja m
kangaroo [kæŋgə'ruː] N canguru m
kaput [kə'put] (inf) ADJ pifado
karate [kə'rɑːtɪ] N karatê m
Kashmir [kæʃ'mɪər] N Cachemira
KC (Brit) N ABBR (Law: = King's Counsel) título dado a certos advogados
kd ABBR (= knocked down) em pedaços
kebab [kə'bæb] N churrasquinho, espetinho
keel [kiːl] N quilha; **on an even ~** (fig) em equilíbrio
▶ **keel over** VI (Naut) emborcar; (person) desmaiar
keen [kiːn] ADJ (interest, desire) grande, vivo; (eye, intelligence) penetrante; (competition) acirrado, intenso; (edge) afiado; (eager) entusiasmado; **to be ~ to do** or **on doing sth** sentir muita vontade de fazer algo; **to be ~ on sth/sb** gostar de algo/alguém; **I'm not ~ on going** não estou a fim de ir
keenly ['kiːnlɪ] ADV (enthusiastically) com entusiasmo; (feel) profundamente, agudamente
keenness ['kiːnnɪs] N (eagerness) entusiasmo, interesse m; **~ to do** vontade de fazer
keep [kiːp] (pt, pp kept) VT (retain) ficar com; (maintain: house etc) cuidar; (detain) deter; (look after: shop etc) tomar conta de; (preserve) conservar; (hold back) reter; (accounts, diary) manter; (support: family etc) manter; (promise) cumprir; (chickens, bees etc) criar; (prevent): **to ~ sb from doing sth** impedir alguém de fazer algo ■ VI (food) conservar-se; (remain) ficar ■ N (of castle) torre f de menagem; (food etc): **to earn one's ~** ganhar a vida; (inf): **for ~s** para sempre; **to ~ doing sth** continuar fazendo algo; **to ~ sth**

from happening impedir que algo aconteça; **to ~ sb happy** manter alguém satisfeito; **to ~ a place tidy** manter um lugar limpo; **to ~ sb waiting** deixar alguém esperando; **to ~ an appointment** manter um compromisso; **to ~ a record of sth** anotar algo; **to ~ sth to o.s.** guardar algo para si mesmo; **to ~ sth (back) from sb** ocultar algo de alguém; **to ~ time** (clock) marcar a hora exata
▶ **keep away** VT: **to ~ sth/sb away from sb** manter algo/alguém afastado de alguém ■ VI: **to ~ away (from)** manter-se afastado (de)
▶ **keep back** VT (crowd, tears) conter; (money) reter ■ VI manter-se afastado
▶ **keep down** VT (control: prices, spending) limitar, controlar ■ VI não se levantar; **I can't ~ my food down** o que como não pára no estômago
▶ **keep in** VT (invalid, child) não deixar sair; (Sch) reter ■ VI: **to ~ in with sb** manter boas relações com alguém
▶ **keep off** VI não se aproximar ■ VT afastar; **"~ off the grass"** "não pise na grama"; **~ your hands off!** tira a mão!
▶ **keep on** VI: **to ~ on doing** continuar fazendo
▶ **keep out** VT impedir de entrar ■ VI (stay out) permanecer fora; **"~ out"** "entrada proibida"
▶ **keep up** VT manter ■ VI não atrasar-se, acompanhar; **to ~ up with** (pace) acompanhar; (level) manter-se ao nível de
keeper ['kiːpər] N guarda m, guardião(-diã) m/f
keep fit N ginástica
keeping ['kiːpɪŋ] N (care) cuidado; **in ~ with** de acordo com
keepsake ['kiːpseɪk] N lembrança
keg [kɛg] N barrilete m, barril m pequeno
kennel ['kɛnl] N casa de cachorro; **kennels** N (establishment) canil m
Kenya ['kɛnjə] N Quênia m
Kenyan ['kɛnjən] ADJ, N queniano(-a) m/f
kept [kɛpt] PT, PP of **keep**
kerb [kəːb] (Brit) N meio-fio (BR), borda do passeio (PT)
kernel ['kəːnl] N amêndoa; (fig) cerne m
kerosene ['kɛrəsiːn] N querosene m
ketchup ['kɛtʃəp] N molho de tomate, catsup m
kettle ['kɛtl] N chaleira; **kettle drums** NPL tímpanos mpl

key [ki:] N chave f; (Mus) clave f; (of piano, typewriter) tecla; (on map) legenda ■ CPD (issue etc) chave ■ VT (also: **key in**) digitar, teclar

keyboard ['ki:bɔ:d] N teclado ■ VT (text) teclar, digitar

keyed up [ki:d-] ADJ: **to be (all) ~** estar excitado or ligado (inf)

keyhole ['ki:həul] N buraco da fechadura

keynote ['ki:nəut] N (Mus) tônica; (fig) idéia fundamental ■ CPD: **~ speech** discurso programático

keypad ['ki:pæd] N teclado complementar

keyring ['ki:rɪŋ] N chaveiro

keystone ['ki:stəun] N pedra angular

keystroke ['ki:strəuk] N batida de tecla

kg ABBR (= kilogram) kg

~ KGB N ABBR KGB f

khaki ['kɑ:kɪ] ADJ cáqui

kibbutz [kɪ'buts] (pl **kibbutzim**) N kibutz m

kick [kɪk] VT (person) dar um pontapé em; (ball) chutar; (inf: habit) conseguir superar ■ VI (horse) dar coices ■ N (from person) pontapé m; (from animal) coice m, patada; (to ball) chute m; (of rifle) recuo; (inf: thrill): **he does it for ~s** faz isso para curtir
  ▶ **kick around** (inf) VI ficar por aí
  ▶ **kick off** VI (Sport) dar o pontapé inicial

kick-off N (Sport) chute m inicial

kick-start N (also: **kick-starter**) arranque m ■ VT dar partida em

kid [kɪd] N (inf: child) criança; (animal) cabrito; (leather) pelica ■ VI (inf) brincar

kidnap ['kɪdnæp] VT seqüestrar

kidnapper ['kɪdnæpəʳ] N seqüestrador(a) m/f

kidnapping ['kɪdnæpɪŋ] N seqüestro

kidney ['kɪdnɪ] N rim m; **kidney bean** N feijão m roxo; **kidney machine** N (Med) aparelho de hemodiálise

Kilimanjaro [kɪlɪmən'dʒɑːrəu] N: **Mount ~** Kilimanjaro

kill [kɪl] VT matar; (murder) assassinar; (destroy) destruir; (finish off) acabar com, aniquilar ■ N ato de matar; **to ~ time** matar o tempo
  ▶ **kill off** VT aniquilar; (fig) eliminar

killer ['kɪləʳ] N assassino(-a)

killing ['kɪlɪŋ] N (one) assassinato; (several) matança; (instance) morte f ■ ADJ (funny) divertido, engraçado; **to make a ~** (inf) faturar uma boa nota

killjoy ['kɪldʒɔɪ] N desmancha-prazeres m inv

kiln [kɪln] N forno

kilo ['ki:ləu] N quilo

kilobyte ['ki:ləubaɪt] N kilobyte m

kilogram(me) ['kɪləugræm] N quilograma m

kilometre ['kɪləmi:təʳ] (US **kilometer**) N quilômetro

kilowatt ['kɪləuwɔt] N quilowatt m

kilt [kɪlt] N saiote m escocês

kimono [kɪ'məunəu] N quimono

kin [kɪn] N parentela; see **kith, next**

kind [kaɪnd] ADJ (friendly) gentil; (generous) generoso; (good) bom/boa, bondoso, amável ■ N espécie f, classe f; (species) gênero; **in ~** (Comm) em espécie; **a ~ of** uma espécie de; **two of a ~** dois da mesma espécie; **would you be ~ enough to ...?, would you be so ~ as to ...?** pode me fazer a gentileza de ...?; **it's very ~ of you (to do)** é muito gentil da sua parte (fazer); **to repay sb in ~** (fig) pagar alguém na mesma moeda

kindergarten ['kɪndəgɑ:tn] N jardim m de infância

kind-hearted ADJ de bom coração, bondoso

kindle ['kɪndl] VT acender; (emotion) despertar

kindling ['kɪndlɪŋ] N gravetos mpl

kindly ['kaɪndlɪ] ADJ (good) bom/boa, bondoso; (gentle) gentil, carinhoso ■ ADV bondosamente, amavelmente; **will you ~ ...** você pode fazer o favor de ...; **he didn't take it ~** não gostou

kindness ['kaɪndnɪs] N bondade f, gentileza

kindred ['kɪndrɪd] ADJ aparentado; **~ spirit** pessoa com os mesmos gostos

kinetic [kɪ'nɛtɪk] ADJ cinético

king [kɪŋ] N rei m

kingdom ['kɪŋdəm] N reino

kingfisher ['kɪŋfɪʃəʳ] N martim-pescador m

kingpin ['kɪŋpɪn] N (Tech) pino mestre; (fig) mandachuva m

king-size(d) [-saɪz(d)] ADJ tamanho grande; (cigarettes) king-size

kink [kɪŋk] N (of rope) dobra, coca; (inf: fig) mania

kinky ['kɪŋkɪ] (pej) ADJ (odd) excêntrico, esquisito; (sexually) pervertido

kinship ['kɪnʃɪp] N parentesco

kinsman ['kɪnzmən] (irreg) N parente m

kinswoman ['kɪnzwumən] (irreg) N parenta

kiosk ['ki:ɔsk] N banca (BR), quiosque m (PT); (Brit: also: **telephone kiosk**) cabine f

kipper ['kɪpəʳ] N tipo de arenque defumado

kiss [kɪs] N beijo ■ VT beijar; **to ~ (each other)** beijar-se; **to ~ sb goodbye** despedir-se de alguém com beijos; **kiss of life** (Brit) N respiração f boca-a-boca

kit [kɪt] N apetrechos mpl; (clothes: for sport etc) kit m; (equipment) equipamento; (set of tools etc) caixa de ferramentas; (for assembly) kit m para montar
  ▶ **kit out** (Brit) VT equipar

kitbag ['kɪtbæg] N saco de viagem

kitchen ['kɪtʃɪn] N cozinha; **kitchen garden** N horta; **kitchen sink** N pia (de cozinha); **kitchen unit** (Brit) N módulo de cozinha

kitchenware ['kɪtʃɪnwɛəʳ] N bateria de cozinha

kite [kaɪt] N (toy) papagaio, pipa; (Zool) milhafre m

kith [kɪθ] N: **~ and kin** amigos e parentes mpl

kitten ['kɪtn] N gatinho

kitty ['kɪtɪ] N (pool of money) fundo comum, vaquinha; (Cards) bolo

KKK (US) N ABBR = **Ku Klux Klan**

Kleenex® ['kli:nɛks] N lenço de papel

kleptomaniac [klɛptəu'meɪnɪæk] N cleptomaníaco(-a)

km ABBR (= kilometre) km

km/h ABBR (= kilometres per hour) km/h

knack [næk] N: **to have the ~ of doing sth** ter um jeito or queda para fazer algo; **there's a ~ (to it)** tem um jeito

knapsack ['næpsæk] N mochila

knave [neɪv] N (Cards) valete m

knead [ni:d] VT amassar

knee [ni:] N joelho

kneecap ['ni:kæp] N rótula

knee-deep ADJ: **the water was ~** a água batia no joelho

kneel [ni:l] (pt, pp **knelt**) VI (also: **kneel down**) ajoelhar-se

kneepad ['ni:pæd] N joelheira

knell [nɛl] N dobre m de finados

knelt [nɛlt] PT, PP of **kneel**

knew [nju:] PT of **know**

knickers ['nɪkəz] (Brit) NPL calcinha (BR), cuecas fpl (PT)

knick-knack ['nɪk-] N bibelô m

knife [naɪf] (pl **knives**) N faca ■ VT esfaquear; **~, fork and spoon** talheɪ m

knight [naɪt] N cavaleiro; (Chess) cavalo

knighthood ['naɪthud] (Brit) N cavalaria; (title): **to get a ~** receber o título de Sir

knit [nɪt] VT tɪicotaɪ; (brows) fɪanzir ■ VI tricotar (BR), fazer malha (PT); (bones) consolidar-se; **to ~ together** (fig) unir, juntar

knitted ['nɪtɪd] ADJ de malha

knitting ['nɪtɪŋ] N ato de tricotar, trabalho de tricô (BR), malha (PT); **knitting machine** N máquina de tricotar; **knitting needle** N agulha de tricô (BR) or de malha (PT); **knitting pattern** N molde m para tricotar

knitwear ['nɪtwɛəʳ] N roupa de malha

knives [naɪvz] NPL of **knife**

knob [nɔb] N (of door) maçaneta; (of drawer) puxador m; (of stick) castão m; (on radio, TV etc) botão m; (lump) calombo; **a ~ of butter** (Brit) uma porção de manteiga

knobbly ['nɔblɪ] (Brit) ADJ (wood, surface) nodoso; (knees) ossudo

knobby ['nɔbɪ] (US) ADJ = **knobbly**

knock [nɔk] VT (strike) bater em; (bump into) colidir com; (inf: criticize) criticar, malhar ■ N pancada, golpe m; (on door) batida ■ VI: **to ~ at** or **on the door** bater à porta; **to ~ a hole into sth** abrir um buraco em algo; **to ~ a nail into** pregar um prego em
  ▶ **knock down** VT derrubar; (price) abater; (pedestrian) atropelar
  ▶ **knock off** VI (inf: finish) terminar ■ VT (inf: steal) abafar; (vase) derrubar; (from price): **to ~ off £10** fazer um desconto de £10
  ▶ **knock out** VT pôr nocaute, nocautear; (defeat) eliminar
  ▶ **knock over** VT (object) derrubar; (pedestrian) atropelar

knockdown ['nɔkdaun] ADJ (price) de liquidação, de queima (inf)

knocker ['nɔkəʳ] N (on door) aldrava

knocking ['nɔkɪŋ] N pancadas fpl

knock-kneed [-ni:d] ADJ cambaio

knockout ['nɔkaut] N (Boxing) nocaute m ■ CPD (competition) com eliminatórias

knock-up N (Tennis) bate-bola m

knot [nɔt] N nó m ■ VT dar nó em; **to tie a ~** dar or fazer um nó

knotty ['nɔtɪ] ADJ (fig) cabeludo, espinhoso

know [nəu] (pt **knew**, pp **known**) VT saber; (person, author, place) conhecer; (recognize) reconhecer ■ VI: **to ~ about** or **of sth** saber de algo; **to ~ that ...** saber que ...; **to ~ how to swim** saber nadar; **to get to ~ sth** (fact) saber, descobrir; (place) conhecer; **I don't ~ him** não o conheço; **to ~ right from wrong** saber distinguir o bem e o mal; **as far as I ~ ...** que eu saiba ...

know-all (Brit: pej) N sabichão(-chona) m/f

know-how N know-how m, experiência

knowing ['nəuɪŋ] ADJ (look: of complicity) de cumplicidade

knowingly ['nəuɪŋlɪ] ADV (purposely) de propósito; (spitefully) maliciosamente

know-it-all (US) N = **know-all**

knowledge ['nɔlɪdʒ] N conhecimento; (range of learning) saber m, conhecimentos mpl; **to have no ~ of** não ter conhecimento de; **not to my ~** que eu saiba, não; **without my ~** sem eu saber; **to have a working ~ of Portuguese** ter um conhecimento básico do português; **it's common ~ that ...** todos sabem que ...; **it has come to my ~ that ...** chegou ao meu conhecimento que ...

knowledgeable ['nɔlɪdʒəbl] ADJ entendido, versado

known [nəun] PP of **know** ■ ADJ (thief) famigerado; (fact) conhecido

knuckle ['nʌkl] N nó m
  ▶ **knuckle under** (inf) VI ceder

knuckleduster ['nʌkldʌstəʳ] N soco inglês

K.O. N ABBR = **knockout** ■ VT nocautear, pôr nocaute

koala [kəu'ɑ:lə] N (also: **koala bear**) coala m

kook [ku:k] (US: inf) N maluco(-a), biruta (inf)

Koran [kɔ'rɑ:n] N: **the ~** o Alcorão

Korea [kə'rɪə] N Coréia; **North/South ~** Coréia do Norte/Sul

Korean [kə'rɪən] ADJ coreano ■ N coreano(-a); (Ling) coreano

kosher ['kəuʃəʳ] ADJ kosher inv

kowtow ['kau'tau] VI: **to ~ to sb** bajular alguém

Kremlin ['krɛmlɪn] N: **the ~** o Kremlin

KS (US) ABBR (Post) = **Kansas**

Kt (Brit) ABBR (= Knight) título honorífico

Kuala Lumpur ['kwɑ:lə'lumpuəʳ] N Cuala Lumpur

kudos ['kju:dɔs] N glória, fama

Kuwait [ku'weɪt] N Kuweit m

Kuwaiti [ku'weɪtɪ] ADJ, N kuweitiano(-a)

kW ABBR (= kilowatt) kW

KY (US) ABBR (Post) = **Kentucky**

Ll

L, l [ɛl] N (letter) L, l m; **L for Lucy** (Brit) or **Love** (US) L de Lúcia

L ABBR (= lake) L; (: = large) G; (: = left) esq; (Brit: Aut: = learner) (condutor(a) m/f) aprendiz m/f

l ABBR (= litre) l

LA (US) N ABBR = **Los Angeles** ■ ABBR (Post) = **Louisiana**

lab [læb] N ABBR = **laboratory**

label ['leɪbl] N etiqueta, rótulo; (brand: of record) selo ■ VT etiquetar, rotular; **to ~ sb a ...** rotular alguém de ...

labor etc ['leɪbəʳ] (US) = **labour etc**

laboratory [lə'bɔrətərɪ] N laboratório

Labor Day (US) N Dia m do Trabalho

laborious [lə'bɔːrɪəs] ADJ laborioso

labor union (US) N sindicato

labour ['leɪbəʳ] (US **labor**) N (task) trabalho; (work force) mão-de-obra f; (workers) trabalhadores mpl; (Med): **to be in ~** estar em trabalho de parto ■ VI: **to ~ (at)** trabalhar (em) ■ VT insistir em; **L~, the L~ Party** (Brit) o Partido Trabalhista

labo(u)r camp N campo de trabalhos forçados

labo(u)r cost N custo de mão-de-obra

labo(u)red ['leɪbəd] ADJ (movement) forçado; (style) elaborado

labo(u)rer ['leɪbərəʳ] N operário; **farm labo(u)rer** trabalhador m rural, peão m; **day labo(u)rer** diarista m

labo(u)r force N mão-de-obra f

labo(u)r-intensive ADJ intensivo de mão-de-obra

labo(u)r market N mercado de trabalho

labo(u)r pains NPL dores fpl do parto

labo(u)r relations NPL relações fpl trabalhistas

labo(u)r-saving ADJ que poupa trabalho

labo(u)r unrest N agitação f operária

labyrinth ['læbɪrɪnθ] N labirinto

lace [leɪs] N renda; (of shoe etc) cadarço ■ VT (shoe) amarrar; (drink) misturar aguardente a

lace-making ['leɪsmeɪkɪŋ] N feitura de renda

laceration [læsə'reɪʃən] N laceração f

lace-up ADJ (shoes etc) de cordões

lack [læk] N falta ■ VT (money, confidence) faltar; (intelligence) carecer de; **through** or **for ~ of** por falta de; **to be ~ing** faltar; **to be ~ing in** carecer de

lackadaisical [lækə'deɪzɪkl] ADJ (careless)

descuidado; (indifferent) apático, indiferente

lackey ['lækɪ] N (fig) lacaio

lacklustre ['læklʌstəʳ] ADJ sem brilho, insosso

laconic [lə'kɔnɪk] ADJ lacônico

lacquer ['lækəʳ] N laca; (hair) fixador m

lacy ['leɪsɪ] ADJ rendado

lad [læd] N menino, rapaz m, moço; (Brit: in stable etc) empregado

ladder ['lædəʳ] N escada f de mão; (Brit: in tights) defeito (em forma de escada) ■ VT (Brit: tights) desfiar ■ VI (Brit: tights) desfiar

laden ['leɪdn] ADJ: **~ (with)** carregado (de); **fully ~** (truck, ship) completamente carregado, com a carga máxima

ladle ['leɪdl] N concha (de sopa)

lady ['leɪdɪ] N senhora; (distinguished, noble) dama; (in address): **ladies and gentlemen, ...** senhoras e senhores, ...; **young ~** senhorita; **L~ Smith** a lady Smith; **"ladies' (toilets)"** "senhoras"; **a ~ doctor** uma médica

ladybird ['leɪdɪbəːd] (Brit) N joaninha

ladybug ['leɪdɪbʌg] (US) N = **ladybird**

lady-in-waiting N dama de companhia

lady-killer ['leɪdɪkɪləʳ] N mulherengo

ladylike ['leɪdɪlaɪk] ADJ elegante, refinado

ladyship ['leɪdɪʃɪp] N: **your ~** Sua Senhoria

lag [læg] N (period of time) atraso, retardamento ■ VI (also: **lag behind**) ficar para trás ■ VT (pipes) revestir com isolante térmico

lager ['lɑːgəʳ] N cerveja leve e clara

lagging ['lægɪŋ] N revestimento

lagoon [lə'guːn] N lagoa

Lagos ['leɪgɔs] N Lagos

laid [leɪd] PT, PP of **lay**

laid-back (inf) ADJ descontraído

laid up ADJ: **to be ~ up with flu** ficar de cama com gripe

lain [leɪn] PP of **lie**

lair [lɛəʳ] N covil m, toca

laissez-faire [leseɪ'fɛəʳ] N laissez-faire m

laity ['leɪətɪ] N leigos mpl

lake [leɪk] N lago

Lake District (Brit) N: **the ~** a região dos Lagos

lamb [læm] N cordeiro; **lamb chop** N costeleta de cordeiro

lambskin ['læmskɪn] N pele f de cordeiro

lambswool ['læmzwul] N lã f de cordeiro

lame [leɪm] ADJ coxo, manco; (*excuse, argument*) pouco convincente, fraco; ~ **duck** (*fig*) pessoa incapaz

lamely ['leɪmlɪ] ADV (*fig*) sem convicção

lament [lə'ment] N lamento, queixa ▪ VT lamentar-se de

lamentable ['læməntəbl] ADJ lamentável

laminated ['læmɪneɪtɪd] ADJ laminado

lamp [læmp] N lâmpada

lamplight ['læmplaɪt] N: **by ~** à luz da lâmpada

lampoon [læm'puːn] VT satirizar

lamppost ['læmppəʊst] (*Brit*) N poste m

lampshade ['læmpʃeɪd] N abajur m, quebra-luz m

lance [lɑːns] N lança ▪ VT (*Med*) lancetar; **lance corporal** (*Brit*) N cabo

lancet ['lɑːnsɪt] N (*Med*) bisturi, lanceta

Lancs [læŋks] (*Brit*) ABBR = **Lancashire**

land [lænd] N terra; (*country*) país m; (*piece of land*) terreno; (*estate*) terras *fpl*, propriedades *fpl*; (*Agr*) solo ▪ VI (*from ship*) desembarcar; (*Aviat*) pousar, aterrissar (BR), aterrar (PT); (*fig: arrive unexpectedly*) cair, terminar ▪ VT (*obtain*) conseguir; (*passengers, goods*) desembarcar; **to go/travel by ~** ir/viajar por terra; **to own ~** ter propriedades; **to ~ on one's feet** (*fig*) dar-se bem, cair de pé; **to ~ sb with sth** (*inf*) sobrecarregar alguém com algo
  ▶ **land up** VI: **to ~ up in/at** ir parar em

landed gentry ['lændɪd-] N proprietários *mpl* de terras

landing ['lændɪŋ] N (*from ship*) desembarque m; (*Aviat*) pouso, aterrissagem *f* (BR), aterragem *f* (PT); (*of staircase*) patamar m; **landing card** N cartão m de desembarque; **landing craft** N navio para desembarque; **landing gear** N trem m de aterrissagem (BR) or de aterragem (PT); **landing stage** (*Brit*) N cais m de desembarque; **landing strip** N pista de aterrissagem (BR) or de aterragem (PT)

landlady ['lændleɪdɪ] N (*of rented property*) senhoria; (*of pub*) dona, proprietária

landlocked ['lændlɔkt] ADJ cercado de terra

landlord ['lændlɔːd] N senhorio, locador m; (*of pub etc*) dono, proprietário

landlubber ['lændlʌbər] N *pessoa desacostumada ao mar*

landmark ['lændmɑːk] N lugar m conhecido; (*fig*) marco

landowner ['lændəʊnər] N latifundiário(-a)

landscape ['lændskeɪp] N paisagem *f*; **landscape architect** N paisagista *m/f*

landscaped ['lændskeɪpt] ADJ projetado paisagisticamente

landscape gardener N paisagista *m/f*

landscape painting N (*Art: genre*) paisagismo; (*: picture*) paisagem *f*

landslide ['lændslaɪd] N (*Geo*) desmoronamento, desabamento; (*fig: Pol*) vitória esmagadora

lane [leɪn] N (*in country*) caminho, estrada estreita; (*in town*) ruela; (*Aut*) pista; (*in race*) raia; (*for air or sea traffic*) rota

language ['læŋgwɪdʒ] N língua; (*way one speaks, Comput, style*) linguagem *f*; **bad ~** palavrões *mpl*; **language laboratory** N laboratório de línguas; **language school** N escola de línguas

languid ['læŋgwɪd] ADJ lânguido

languish ['læŋgwɪʃ] VI elanguescer, debilitar-se

lank [læŋk] ADJ (*hair*) liso

lanky ['læŋkɪ] ADJ magricela

lanolin(e) ['lænəlɪn] N lanolina

lantern ['læntn] N lanterna

Laos [laus] N Laos m

lap [læp] N (*of track*) volta; (*of person*) colo ▪ VT (*also*: **lap up**) lamber ▪ VI (*waves*) marulhar
  ▶ **lap up** VT (*fig: food*) comer sofregamente; (*: compliments etc*) receber com sofreguidão

La Paz [læ'pæz] N La Paz

lapdog ['læpdɔg] N cãozinho de estimação

lapel [lə'pɛl] N lapela

Lapland ['læplænd] N Lapônia

Lapp [læp] ADJ, N lapão(-ona) *m/f*

lapse [læps] N lapso; (*bad behaviour*) deslize m ▪ VI (*expire*) caducar; (*law*) prescrever; (*morally*) decair; **to ~ into bad habits** adquirir maus hábitos; **~ of time** lapso, intervalo; **a ~ of memory** um lapso de memória

larceny ['lɑːsənɪ] N furto; **petty ~** delito leve

larch [lɑːtʃ] N lariço

lard [lɑːd] N banha de porco

larder ['lɑːdər] N despensa

large [lɑːdʒ] ADJ grande; (*fat*) gordo; **at ~** (*free*) em liberdade; (*generally*) em geral; **to make ~r** ampliar; **a ~ number of people** um grande número de pessoas; **by and ~** de modo geral; **on a ~ scale** em grande escala

largely ['lɑːdʒlɪ] ADV em grande parte; (*introducing reason*) principalmente

large-scale ADJ (*map*) em grande escala; (*fig*) importante, de grande alcance

largesse [lɑː'dʒɛs] N generosidade *f*

lark [lɑːk] N (*bird*) cotovia; (*joke*) brincadeira, peça
  ▶ **lark about** VI divertir-se, brincar

larva ['lɑːvə] (*pl* **larvae**) N larva

larvae ['lɑːviː] NPL *of* **larva**

laryngitis [lærɪn'dʒaɪtɪs] N laringite *f*

larynx ['lærɪŋks] N laringe *f*

lascivious [lə'sɪvɪəs] ADJ lascivo

laser ['leɪzər] N laser m; **laser beam** N raio laser; **laser printer** N impressora a laser

lash [læʃ] N chicote m, açoite m; (*blow*) chicotada; (*also*: **eyelash**) pestana, cílio ▪ VT chicotear, açoitar; (*subj*) rain, wind, castigar; (*tie*) atar
  ▶ **lash down** VT atar, amarrar ▪ VI (*rain*) cair em bátegas
  ▶ **lash out** VI: **to ~ out (at sb)** atacar (alguém) violentamente; **to ~ out at** or **against sb** (*criticize*) atacar alguém verbalmente; **to ~ out (on sth)** (*inf: spend*) esbanjar dinheiro (em algo)

lashings ['læʃɪŋz] (*Brit: inf*) NPL: **~ of** (*cream etc*) montes *mpl* de, um montão de

lass [læs] (*Brit*) N moça

lasso [læ'suː] N laço ▪ VT laçar

last [lɑ:st] ADJ último; (*final*) derradeiro ■ ADV em último lugar ■ VI (*endure*) durar; (*continue*) continuar; ~ **week** na semana passada; ~ **night** ontem à noite; **at** ~ finalmente; **at** ~! até que enfim!; ~ **but one** penúltimo; **the** ~ **time** a última vez; **it** ~**s (for) 2 hours** dura 2 horas
last-ditch ADJ desesperado, derradeiro
lasting ['lɑ:stɪŋ] ADJ duradouro
lastly ['lɑ:stlɪ] ADV (*last of all*) por fim, por último; (*finally*) finalmente
last-minute ADJ de última hora
latch [lætʃ] N trinco, fecho, tranca
▶ **latch on to** VT FUS (*cling to: person*) grudar em; (*: idea*) agarrar-se a
latchkey ['lætʃki:] N chave f de trinco
late [leɪt] ADJ (*not on time*) atrasado; (*far on in day etc*) tardio; (*hour*) avançado; (*recent*) recente; (*former*) antigo, ex-, anterior; (*dead*) falecido ■ ADV tarde; (*behind time, schedule*) atrasado; **to be** ~ estar atrasado, atrasar; **to be 10 minutes** ~ estar atrasado dez minutos; **to work** ~ trabalhar até tarde; ~ **in life** com idade avançada; **it was too** ~ já era tarde; **of** ~ recentemente; **in** ~ **May** no final de maio; **the** ~ **Mr X** o falecido Sr X
latecomer ['leɪtkʌmə^r] N retardatário(-a)
lately ['leɪtlɪ] ADV ultimamente
lateness ['leɪtnɪs] N (*of person*) atraso; (*of event*) hora avançada
latent ['leɪtnt] ADJ latente
later ['leɪtə^r] ADJ (*date etc*) posterior; (*version etc*) mais recente ■ ADV mais tarde, depois; ~ **on** mais tarde
lateral ['lætərl] ADJ lateral
latest ['leɪtɪst] ADJ último; **the** ~ **news** as últimas novidades; **at the** ~ no mais tardar
latex ['leɪtɛks] N látex m
lath [læθ, *pl* læðz] N ripa
lathe [leɪð] N torno
lather ['lɑ:ðə^r] N espuma (de sabão) ■ VT ensaboar ■ VI fazer espuma
Latin ['lætɪn] N (*Ling*) latim m ■ ADJ latino; **Latin America** N América Latina; **Latin American** ADJ, N latino-americano(-a)
latitude ['lætɪtju:d] N (*also fig*) latitude f
latrine [lə'tri:n] N latrina
latter ['lætə^r] ADJ último; (*of two*) segundo ■ N: **the** ~ o último, este
latterly ['lætəlɪ] ADV ultimamente
lattice ['lætɪs] N treliça; **lattice window** N janela com treliça de chumbo
Latvia ['lætvɪə] N Letônia
laudable ['lɔ:dəbl] ADJ louvável
laudatory ['lɔ:dətrɪ] ADJ laudatório, elogioso
laugh [lɑ:f] N riso, risada; (*loud*) gargalhada ■ VI rir, dar risada (*or* gargalhada); **(to do sth) for a** ~ (fazer algo) só de curtição
▶ **laugh at** VT FUS rir de
▶ **laugh off** VT disfarçar sorrindo
laughable ['lɑ:fəbl] ADJ ridículo, absurdo
laughing ['lɑ:fɪŋ] ADJ risonho; **this is no** ~ **matter** isto não é para rir; **laughing gas** N

laughing stock N alvo de riso
laughter ['lɑ:ftə^r] N riso, risada; (*people laughing*) risos mpl
launch [lɔ:ntʃ] N (*boat*) lancha; (*Comm, of rocket etc*) lançamento ■ VT (*ship, rocket, plan*) lançar
▶ **launch into** VT FUS lançar-se a
▶ **launch out** VI: **to** ~ **out (into)** lançar-se (a)
launching ['lɔ:ntʃɪŋ] N (*of rocket etc*) lançamento
launch(ing) pad N plataforma de lançamento
launder ['lɔ:ndə^r] VT lavar e passar; (*money*) lavar
launderette® [lɔ:n'drɛt] (*Brit*) N lavandaria automática
laundromat® ['lɔ:ndrəmæt] (*US*) N lavanderia automática
laundry ['lɔ:ndrɪ] N lavanderia; (*clothes*) roupa para lavar; **to do the** ~ lavar a roupa
laureate ['lɔ:rɪət] ADJ *see* **poet**
laurel ['lɔrl] N louro; (*Bot*) loureiro; **to rest on one's** ~**s** dormir sobre os louros
lava ['lɑ:və] N lava
lavatory ['lævətərɪ] N privada (BR), casa de banho (PT); **lavatories** NPL (*public*) sanitários mpl (BR), lavabos mpl (PT); **lavatory paper** (*Brit*) N papel m higiênico
lavender ['lævəndə^r] N lavanda
lavish ['lævɪʃ] ADJ (*amount*) generoso; (*person*): ~ **with** pródigo em, generoso com ■ VT: **to** ~ **sth on sb** encher or cobrir alguém de algo
lavishly ['lævɪʃlɪ] ADV (*give, spend*) prodigamente; (*furnished*) luxuosamente
law [lɔ:] N lei f; (*rule*) regra; (*Sch*) direito; **against the** ~ contra a lei; **to study** ~ estudar direito; **to go to** ~ (*Brit*) recorrer à justiça
law-abiding [-ə'baɪdɪŋ] ADJ obediente à lei
law and order N a ordem pública
lawbreaker ['lɔ:breɪkə^r] N infrator(a) m/f (da lei)
law court N tribunal m de justiça
lawful ['lɔ:ful] ADJ legal, lícito
lawfully ['lɔ:fulɪ] ADV legalmente
lawless ['lɔ:lɪs] ADJ (*act*) ilegal; (*person*) rebelde; (*country*) sem lei, desordenado
lawmaker ['lɔ:meɪkə^r] N legislador(a) m/f
lawn [lɔ:n] N gramado (BR), relvado (PT)
lawnmower ['lɔ:nməuə^r] N cortador m de grama (BR) or de relva (PT)
lawn tennis N tênis m de gramado (BR) or de relvado (PT)
law school (*US*) N faculdade f de direito
law student N estudante m/f de direito
lawsuit ['lɔ:su:t] N ação f judicial, processo; **to bring a** ~ **against** mover processo contra
lawyer ['lɔ:jə^r] N advogado(-a); (*for sales, wills etc*) notário(-a), tabelião(-liã) m/f
lax [læks] ADJ (*discipline*) relaxado; (*person*) negligente
laxative ['læksətɪv] N laxante m
laxity ['læksɪtɪ] N: **moral** ~ falta de escrúpulo or caráter
lay [leɪ] (*pt, pp* **laid**) PT *of* **lie** ■ ADJ leigo ■ VT (*place*) colocar; (*eggs, table*) pôr; (*trap*) armar; (*plan*) traçar; **to** ~ **the table** pôr a mesa; **to** ~ **the facts/one's proposals before sb** apresentar

os fatos/suas propostas a alguém; **to get laid**
(inf!) trepar (!)
▶ **lay aside** VT pôr de lado
▶ **lay by** VT = **lay aside**
▶ **lay down** VT (object) depositar; (flat) deitar;
(arms) depor; (rules etc) impor, estabelecer; **to
~ down the law** (pej) impor regras; **to ~ down
one's life** sacrificar voluntariamenta a vida
▶ **lay in** VT armazenar, abastecer-se de
▶ **lay into** (inf) VT FUS (attack) surrar, espancar;
(scold) dar uma bronca em
▶ **lay off** VT (workers) demitir
▶ **lay on** VT (water, gas) instalar; (meal,
entertainment) prover; (paint) aplicar
▶ **lay out** VT (spread out) dispor em ordem;
(design) planejar; (display) expor; (spend) esbanjar
▶ **lay up** VT (store) estocar; (ship) pôr fora de
serviço; (subj: illness) acometer
layabout ['leɪəbaut] (inf) N vadio(-a),
preguiçoso(-a)
lay-by (Brit) N acostamento
lay days NPL (Naut) dias mpl de estadia
layer ['leɪəʳ] N camada
layette [leɪ'ɛt] N enxoval m de bebê
layman ['leɪmən] (irreg) N leigo
lay-off N demissão f
layout ['leɪaut] N (of garden, building) desenho; (of
piece of writing) leiaute m; (disposition) disposição f;
(Press) composição f
laze [leɪz] VI descansar; (also: **laze about**) vadiar
laziness ['leɪzɪnɪs] N preguiça
lazy ['leɪzɪ] ADJ preguiçoso; (movement) lento
lb. ABBR (= pound (0.45 kg))
lbw ABBR (Cricket: = leg before wicket) falta em que o
batedor está com a perna em frente da meta
LC (US) N ABBR = **Library of Congress**
LCD N ABBR = **liquid crystal display**
Ld (Brit) ABBR (= lord) título honorífico
LDS N ABBR (= Licentiate in Dental Surgery) diploma
universitário; (: = Latter-day Saints) os Santos dos
Últimos Dias
LEA (Brit) N ABBR (= local education authority)
departamento de ensino do município
lead¹ [liːd] (pt, pp **led**) N (front position) dianteira;
(Sport) liderança; (fig) vantagem f; (clue) pista;
(Elec) fio; (for dog) correia; (in play, film) papel m
principal ■ VT conduzir; (guide) levar; (induce)
levar, induzir; (be leader of) chefiar; (start, guide:
activity) encabeçar; (Sport) liderar; (orchestra:
Brit) ser a primeira figura de; (: US) reger ■ VI
encabeçar; **to ~ sb astray** desencaminhar
alguém; **to be in the ~** (Sport: in race) estar na
frente; (: in match) estar ganhando; **to take
the ~** (Sport) disparar na frente; (fig) tomar a
dianteira; **to ~ the way** assumir a direção; **to ~
sb to believe that ...** levar alguém a acreditar
que ...; **to ~ sb to do sth** levar alguém a fazer
algo
▶ **lead away** VT levar
▶ **lead back** VI levar de volta
▶ **lead off** VI (in game etc) começar
▶ **lead on** VT (tease) provocar; **to ~ sb on to**

induzir alguém a
▶ **lead to** VT FUS levar a, conduzir a
▶ **lead up to** VT FUS conduzir a
lead² [lɛd] N chumbo; (in pencil) grafite f
leaded ['lɛdɪd] ADJ (petrol) com chumbo; **~
window** janela com pequenas lâminas de vidro presas
por tiras de chumbo
leaden ['lɛdən] ADJ (sky, sea) cor de chumbo,
cinzento
leader ['liːdəʳ] N líder m/f, chefe m/f; (of party,
union etc) líder m/f; (of gang) cabeça m/f; (of
newspaper) artigo de fundo; **they are ~s in their
field** são os líderes na área em que atuam; **the
L~ of the House** (Brit) o chefe dos ministros na
Câmara
leadership ['liːdəʃɪp] N liderança; (quality)
poder m de liderança; **under the ~ of ...** sob
a liderança de ...; (army) sob o comando de ...;
qualities of ~ qualidades de liderança
lead-free [lɛd-] ADJ sem chumbo
leading ['liːdɪŋ] ADJ (main) principal; (role) de
destaque; (first, front) primeiro, dianteiro; **a ~
question** uma pergunta capciosa; **~ role** papel
de destaque; **leading lady** N (Theatre) primeira
atriz f; **leading light** N (person) figura principal,
destaque m; **leading man** (irreg) N (Theatre)
ator m principal
lead pencil [lɛd-] N lápis f de grafite
lead poisoning [lɛd-] N saturnismo
lead singer N (in pop group) cantor(a) m/f
lead time [liːd-] N (Comm) prazo de entrega
lead weight [lɛd-] N peso de chumbo
leaf [liːf] (pl **leaves**) N folha; (of table) aba ■ VI: **to
~ through** (book) folhear; **to turn over a new ~**
mudar de vida, partir para outra (inf); **to take
a ~ out of sb's book** (fig) seguir o exemplo de
alguém
leaflet ['liːflɪt] N folheto
leafy ['liːfɪ] ADJ folhoso, folhudo
league [liːg] N liga; (Football: championship)
campeonato; (: table) classificação f; **to be in ~
with** estar de comum acordo com
leak [liːk] N (of liquid, gas) escape m, vazamento;
(hole) buraco, rombo; (in roof) goteira; (fig: of
information) vazamento ■ VI (ship) fazer água;
(shoe) deixar entrar água; (roof) gotejar; (pipe,
container, liquid) vazar; (gas) escapar; (fig: news)
vazar ■ VT (news) vazar; **the information
was ~ed to the enemy** as informações foram
passadas para o inimigo
▶ **leak out** VI vazar
leakage ['liːkɪdʒ] N (fig) vazamento
leaky ['liːkɪ] ADJ (pipe, shoe, boat) furado; (roof)
com goteira
lean [liːn] (pt, pp **leant**) ADJ magro ■ N (of meat)
carne f magra ■ VT: **to ~ sth on** encostar or
apoiar algo em ■ VI (slope) inclinar-se; **to ~
against** encostar-se or apoiar-se contra; **to ~ on**
encostar-se or apoiar-se em
▶ **lean back** VI (move body) inclinar-se para trás;
(against wall, in chair) recostar-se
▶ **lean forward** VI inclinar-se para frente

▶ **lean out** VI: **to ~ out (of)** inclinar-se para fora (de)

▶ **lean over** VI debruçar-se ■ VT FUS debruçar-se sobre

leaning ['li:nɪŋ] ADJ inclinado ■ N: **~ (towards)** inclinação f (para); **the L~ Tower of Pisa** a torre inclinada de Pisa

leant [lɛnt] PT, PP of **lean**

lean-to N alpendre m

leap [li:p] (pt, pp **leaped**) N salto, pulo ■ VI saltar

▶ **leap at** VT FUS: **to ~ at an offer** agarrar uma oferta

▶ **leap up** VI (person) levantar-se num ímpeto

leapfrog ['li:pfrɔg] N jogo de pular carniça

leapt [lɛpt] PT, PP of **leap**

leap year N ano bissexto

learn [lə:n] (pt, pp **learnt**) VT aprender; (by heart) decorar ■ VI aprender; **to ~ about sth** (Sch) instruir-se sobre algo; (hear, read) saber de algo; **we were sorry to ~ that ...** sentimos tomar conhecimento de que ...; **to ~ to do sth** aprender a fazer algo

learned ['lə:nɪd] ADJ erudito

learner ['lə:nə'] N principiante m/f; (Brit: also: **learner driver**) aprendiz m/f de motorista

learning ['lə:nɪŋ] N (process) aprendizagem f; (quality) erudição f; (knowledge) saber m

learnt [lə:nt] PT, PP of **learn**

lease [li:s] N arrendamento ■ VT arrendar; **on ~** em arrendamento

▶ **lease back** VT vender e alugar do comprador

leaseback ['li:sbæk] N venda de uma propriedade com a condição do comprador alugá-la ao vendedor

leasehold ['li:shəuld] N (contract) arrendamento ■ ADJ arrendado

leash [li:ʃ] N correia

least [li:st] ADJ: **the ~** + n o(-a) menor; (smallest amount of) a menor quantidade de ■ ADV: **the ~** + n o(-a) menos; **the ~ money** o menos dinheiro de todos; **the ~ expensive** o menos caro (a menos cara); **the ~ possible effort** o menor esforço possível; **at ~** pelo menos; **you could at ~ have written** você poderia pelo menos ter escrito; **not in the ~** de maneira nenhuma

leather ['lɛðə'] N couro ■ CPD de couro; **~ goods** artigos mpl de couro

leave [li:v] (pt, pp **left**) VT deixar; (go away from) abandonar ■ VI ir-se, sair; (train) sair ■ N (consent) permissão f, licença; (time off, Mil) licença; **to ~ sth to sb** (money etc) deixar algo para alguém; **to be left** sobrar; **there's some milk left over** sobrou um pouco de leite; **to ~ school** sair da escola; **~ it to me!** deixe comigo!; **on ~** de licença; **to take one's ~ of** despedir-se de

▶ **leave behind** VT (also fig) deixar para trás; (forget) esquecer

▶ **leave off** VT (lid, cover) não colocar; (heating) não ligar; (light) deixar apagado; (Brit: inf: stop): **to ~ off (doing sth)** parar (de fazer algo)

▶ **leave on** VT (coat etc) ficar com, não tirar; (lid) não tirar; (light, fire) deixar aceso; (radio) deixar ligado

▶ **leave out** VT omitir

leave of absence N licença excepcional

leaves [li:vz] NPL of **leaf**

Lebanese [lɛbə'ni:z] ADJ, N INV libanês(-esa) m/f

Lebanon ['lɛbənən] N Líbano

lecherous ['lɛtʃərəs] (pej) ADJ lascivo

lectern ['lɛktə:n] N atril m

lecture ['lɛktʃə'] N conferência, palestra; (Sch) aula ■ VI dar aulas, lecionar ■ VT (scold) passar um sermão em; **to give a ~ on** dar uma conferência sobre; **lecture hall** N salão m de conferências, anfiteatro

lecturer ['lɛktʃərə'] N conferencista m/f (BR), conferente m/f (PT); (Brit: at university) professor(a) m/f; **assistant ~** (Brit) assistente m/f; **senior ~** (Brit) lente m/f

lecture theatre N = **lecture hall**

LED N ABBR (= light-emitting diode) LED m

led [lɛd] PT, PP of **lead**

ledge [lɛdʒ] N (of window) peitoril m; (of mountain) saliência, proeminência

ledger ['lɛdʒə'] N livro-razão m, razão m

lee [li:] N sotavento; **in the ~ of** ao abrigo de

leech [li:tʃ] N sanguessuga

leek [li:k] N alho-poró m

leer [lɪə'] VI: **to ~ at sb** olhar maliciosamente para alguém

leeward ['li:wəd] ADJ de sotavento ■ ADV a sotavento ■ N sotavento; **to ~** para sotavento

leeway ['li:weɪ] N (fig): **to make up ~** reduzir o atraso; **to have some ~** ter certa liberdade de ação

left [lɛft] PT, PP of **leave** ■ ADJ esquerdo ■ N esquerda ■ ADV à esquerda; **on the ~** à esquerda; **to the ~** para a esquerda; **the L~** (Pol) a Esquerda

left-hand drive (Brit) N direção f do lado esquerdo

left-handed [-'hændɪd] ADJ canhoto; (scissors etc) para canhotos

left-hand side N lado esquerdo

leftist ['lɛftɪst] ADJ (Pol) esquerdista

left-luggage (office) (Brit) N depósito de bagagem

leftovers ['lɛftəuvəz] NPL sobras fpl

left wing N (Mil, Sport) ala esquerda; (Pol) esquerda ■ ADJ: **left-wing** (Pol) de esquerda, esquerdista

left-winger N (Pol) esquerdista m/f; (Sport) ponta-esquerda m/f

leg [lɛg] N perna; (of animal) pata; (of chair) pé m; (Culin: of meat) perna; (of journey) etapa; **1st/2nd ~** (Sport) primeiro/segundo turno; **to pull sb's ~** brincar or mexer com alguém; **to stretch one's ~s** esticar as pernas

legacy ['lɛgəsɪ] N legado; (fig) herança

legal ['li:gl] ADJ (lawful, of law) legal; (terminology, enquiry etc) jurídico; **to take ~ proceedings** or **action against sb** instaurar processo contra alguém; **legal adviser** N consultor(a) m/f jurídico(-a); **legal holiday** (US) N feriado

legality [lɪˈɡælɪtɪ] N legalidade f
legalize [ˈliːɡəlaɪz] VT legalizar
legally [ˈliːɡəlɪ] ADV legalmente; (*in terms of law*)
de acordo com a lei
legal tender N moeda corrente
legation [ləˈɡeɪʃən] N legação f
legend [ˈlɛdʒənd] N lenda; (*person*) mito
legendary [ˈlɛdʒəndərɪ] ADJ legendário
-legged [ˈlɛɡɪd] SUFFIX: **two~** de duas patas (*or
pernas*)
leggings [ˈlɛɡɪŋz] NPL (*over-trousers*) perneiras fpl;
(*women's*) legging f
legibility [lɛdʒɪˈbɪlɪtɪ] N legibilidade f
legible [ˈlɛdʒəbl] ADJ legível
legibly [ˈlɛdʒəblɪ] ADV legivelmente
legion [ˈliːdʒən] N legião f
legionnaire [liːdʒəˈnɛər] N legionário; **~'s
disease** doença rara parecida à pneumonia
legislate [ˈlɛdʒɪsleɪt] VI legislar
legislation [lɛdʒɪsˈleɪʃən] N legislação f; **a piece
of ~** uma lei
legislative [ˈlɛdʒɪslətɪv] ADJ legislativo
legislator [ˈlɛdʒɪsleɪtər] N legislador(a) m/f
legislature [ˈlɛdʒɪslətʃər] N legislatura
legitimacy [lɪˈdʒɪtɪməsɪ] N legitimidade f
legitimate [lɪˈdʒɪtɪmət] ADJ legítimo
legitimize [lɪˈdʒɪtɪmaɪz] VT legitimar
leg-room N espaço para as pernas
Leics (*Brit*) ABBR = **Leicestershire**
leisure [ˈlɛʒər] N lazer m; **at ~** desocupado, livre;
leisure centre N centro de lazer
leisurely [ˈlɛʒəlɪ] ADJ calmo, vagaroso
leisure suit (*Brit*) N jogging m
lemon [ˈlɛmən] N limão(-galego) m
lemonade [lɛməˈneɪd] N limonada
lemon cheese N coalho or pasta de limão
lemon curd N coalho or pasta de limão
lemon juice N suco (*BR*) or sumo (*PT*) de limão
lemon squeezer [-ˈskwiːzər] N espremedor m
de limão
lemon tea N chá m de limão
lend [lɛnd] (*pt, pp* **lent**) VT: **to ~ sth to sb**
emprestar algo a alguém; **to ~ a hand** dar uma
ajuda
lender [ˈlɛndər] N emprestador(a) m/f
lending library [ˈlɛndɪŋ] N biblioteca
circulante
length [lɛŋθ] N comprimento, extensão f; (*of
swimming pool*) extensão f; (*piece: of wood, string etc*)
comprimento; (*section: of road, pipe etc*) trecho;
(*amount of time*) duração f; **what ~ is it?** de que
comprimento é?; **it is 2 metres in ~** tem dois
metros de comprimento; **to fall full ~** cair
estirado; **at ~** (*at last*) finalmente, afinal;
(*lengthily*) por extenso; **to go to any ~(s) to do
sth** fazer qualquer coisa para fazer algo
lengthen [ˈlɛŋθən] VT encompridar, alongar
■ VI encompridar-se
lengthways [ˈlɛŋθweɪz] ADV
longitudinalmente, ao comprido
lengthy [ˈlɛŋθɪ] ADJ comprido, longo; (*meeting*)
prolongado

leniency [ˈliːnɪənsɪ] N indulgência
lenient [ˈliːnɪənt] ADJ indulgente
leniently [ˈliːnɪəntlɪ] ADV com indulgência
lens [lɛnz] N (*of spectacles*) lente f; (*of camera*)
objetiva
Lent [lɛnt] N Quaresma
lent [lɛnt] PT, PP *of* **lend**
lentil [ˈlɛntl] N lentilha
Leo [ˈliːəu] N Leão m
leopard [ˈlɛpəd] N leopardo
leotard [ˈliːətɑːd] N collant m
leper [ˈlɛpər] N leproso(-a); **leper colony** N
leprosário
leprosy [ˈlɛprəsɪ] N lepra
lesbian [ˈlɛzbɪən] ADJ lésbico ■ N lésbica
lesion [ˈliːʒən] N (*Med*) lesão f
Lesotho [lɪˈsuːtuː] N Lesoto
less [lɛs] ADJ, PRON, ADV menos ■ PREP: **~ 10%
discount** menos 10% de desconto; **~ than
that/you** menos que isso/você; **~ than half**
menos da metade; **~ than ever** menos do que
nunca; **~ than 1/a kilo/3 metres** menos de
um/um quilo/3 metros; **~ and ~** cada vez menos;
the ~ he works ... quanto menos trabalha ...;
income ~ expenses renda menos despesas
lessee [lɛˈsiː] N arrendatário(-a), locatário(-a)
lessen [ˈlɛsn] VI diminuir, minguar ■ VT
diminuir, reduzir
lesser [ˈlɛsər] ADJ menor; **to a ~ extent** or
degree nem tanto
lesson [ˈlɛsn] N aula; (*example, warning*) lição f; **a
maths ~** uma aula or uma lição de matemática;
to give ~s in dar aulas de; **to teach sb a ~** (*fig*)
dar uma lição em alguém
lessor [ˈlɛsər] N arrendador(a) m/f, locador(a) m/f
lest [lɛst] CONJ: **~ it happen** para que não
aconteça; **I was afraid ~ he forget** temi que ele
esquecesse
let [lɛt] (*pt, pp* **let**) VT (*allow*) deixar; (*Brit: lease*)
alugar; **to ~ sb do sth** deixar alguém fazer algo;
to ~ sb know sth avisar alguém de algo; **he ~
me go** ele me deixou ir; **~ the water boil and
... deixe ferver a água e ...; ~'s go!** vamos!; **~ him
come!** deixa ele vir!; **"to ~"** "aluga-se"
▶ **let down** VT (*lower*) abaixar; (*dress*)
encompridar; (*Brit: tyre*) esvaziar; (*hair*) soltar;
(*disappoint*) desapontar
▶ **let go** VT, VI soltar
▶ **let in** VT deixar entrar; (*visitor etc*) fazer
entrar; **what have you ~ yourself in for?** onde
você foi se meter?
▶ **let off** VT (*allow to leave*) deixar ir; (*culprit*)
perdoar; (*subj: bus driver*) deixar (saltar); (*firework
etc*) soltar; **to ~ off steam** (*fig*) desabafar
▶ **let on** VI revelar ■ VT (*inf*): **to ~ on that ...**
dizer por aí que ..., contar que ...
▶ **let out** VT deixar sair; (*dress*) alargar; (*scream*)
soltar; (*rent out*) alugar
▶ **let up** VI cessar, afrouxar
let-down N (*disappointment*) decepção f
lethal [ˈliːθl] ADJ letal; (*wound*) mortal
lethargic [lɛˈθɑːdʒɪk] ADJ letárgico

lethargy ['lɛθədʒɪ] N letargia
letter ['lɛtəʳ] N (of alphabet) letra; (correspondence) carta; **small/capital** ~ minúscula/maiúscula; **letter bomb** N carta-bomba
letterbox ['lɛtəbɔks] (Brit) N caixa do correio
letterhead ['lɛtəhɛd] N cabeçalho
lettering ['lɛtərɪŋ] N letras fpl
letter opener N corta-papel m
letterpress ['lɛtəprɛs] N (method) impressão f tipográfica
letter quality N qualidade f carta
letters patent N carta patente
lettuce ['lɛtɪs] N alface f
let-up N diminuição f, afrouxamento
leukaemia [lu:'ki:mɪə] (US **leukemia**) N leucemia
level ['lɛvl] ADJ (flat) plano; (flattened) nivelado; (uniform) uniforme ■ ADV no mesmo nível ■ N nível m; (height) altura; (flat place) plano; (also: **spirit level**) nível de bolha ■ VT aplanar; (gun) apontar; (accusation): **to ~ (against) sb** ser franco com alguém; **"A" ~s** NPL (Brit) = vestibular m; **"O" ~s** NPL (Brit) exames optativos feitos após o término do 10 Grau; **a ~ spoonful** (Culin) uma colherada rasa; **to be ~ with** estar no mesmo nível que; **to draw ~ with** (team) empatar com; (runner, car) alcançar; **on the ~** em nível; (fig: honest) sincero
▸ **level off** VI (prices etc) estabilizar-se ■ VT (ground) nivelar, aplanar
▸ **level out** VI, VT = **level off**
level crossing (Brit) N passagem f de nível
level-headed [-'hɛdɪd] ADJ sensato
levelling ['lɛvlɪŋ] (US **leveling**) ADJ (process) de nivelamento; (effect) nivelador(a)
lever ['li:vəʳ] N alavanca; (fig) estratagema m ■ VT: **to ~ up** levantar com alavanca
leverage ['li:vərɪdʒ] N força de uma alavanca; (fig: influence) influência
levity ['lɛvɪtɪ] N leviandade f, frivolidade f
levy ['lɛvɪ] N imposto, tributo ■ VT arrecadar, cobrar
lewd [lu:d] ADJ obsceno, lascivo
LI (US) ABBR = **Long Island**
liability [laɪə'bɪlətɪ] N responsabilidade f; (handicap) desvantagem f; **liabilities** NPL (Comm) exigibilidades fpl, obrigações fpl; (on balance sheet) passivo
liable ['laɪəbl] ADJ (subject): ~ **to** sujeito a; (responsible): ~ **for** responsável por; (likely): ~ **to do** capaz de fazer; **to be ~ to a fine** ser passível de or sujeito a uma multa
liaise [li:'eɪz] VI: **to ~ (with)** cooperar (com)
liaison [li:'eɪzɔn] N (coordination) ligação f; (affair) relação f amorosa
liar ['laɪəʳ] N mentiroso(-a)
libel ['laɪbl] N difamação f ■ VT caluniar, difamar
libellous ['laɪbləs] (US **libelous**) ADJ difamatório
liberal ['lɪbərl] ADJ liberal; (generous) generoso ■ N: **L~** (Pol) Liberal m/f

liberality [lɪbə'rælɪtɪ] N (generosity) generosidade f
liberalize ['lɪbərəlaɪz] VT liberalizar
liberal-minded ADJ liberal
liberate ['lɪbəreɪt] VT libertar
liberation [lɪbə'reɪʃən] N liberação f, libertação f
Liberia [laɪ'bɪərɪə] N Libéria
Liberian [laɪ'bɪərɪən] ADJ, N liberiano(-a)
liberty ['lɪbətɪ] N liberdade f; (criminal): **to be at ~** estar livre; **to be at ~ to do** ser livre de fazer; **to take the ~ of doing sth** tomar a liberdade de fazer algo
libido [lɪ'bi:dəu] N libido f
Libra ['li:brə] N Libra, Balança
librarian [laɪ'brɛərɪən] N bibliotecário(-a)
library ['laɪbrərɪ] N biblioteca; **library book** N livro de biblioteca
libretto [lɪ'brɛtəu] N libreto
Libya ['lɪbɪə] N Líbia
Libyan ['lɪbɪən] ADJ, N líbio(-a)
lice [laɪs] NPL of **louse**
licence ['laɪsns] (US **license**) N (gen, Comm) licença; (Aut) carta de motorista (BR), carta de condução (PT); (excessive freedom) libertinagem f; **produced under ~** fabricado sob licença; **licence number** (Brit) N (Aut) número da placa
license ['laɪsns] N (US) = **licence** ■ VT autorizar, dar licença a; (car) licenciar
licensed ['laɪsnst] ADJ (car) autorizado oficialmente; (for alcohol) autorizado para vender bebidas alcoólicas
licensee [laɪsən'si:] (Brit) N (in a pub) dono(-a)
license plate (US) N (Aut) placa (de identificação) (do carro)
licentious [laɪ'sɛnʃəs] ADJ licencioso
lichen ['laɪkən] N líquen m
lick [lɪk] VT lamber; (inf: defeat) arrasar, surrar ■ N lambida; **to ~ one's lips** (also fig) lamber os beiços; **a ~ of paint** uma mão de pintura
licorice ['lɪkərɪs] (US) N = **liquorice**
lid [lɪd] N (of box, case, pan) tampa; (eyelid) pálpebra; **to take the ~ off sth** (fig) desvendar algo
lido ['laɪdəu] N piscina pública ao ar livre
lie [laɪ] VI (pt lay, pp lain) (act) deitar-se; (state) estar deitado; (object: be situated) estar, encontrar-se; (fig: problem, cause) residir; (in race, league) ocupar (pt, pt **lied**) (tell lies) mentir ■ N mentira; **to ~ low** (fig) esconder-se; **to tell ~s** dizer mentiras, mentir
▸ **lie about** VI (things) estar espalhado; (people) vadiar
▸ **lie around** VI = **lie about**
▸ **lie back** VI recostar-se
▸ **lie down** VI deitar-se
Liechtenstein ['lɪktənstaɪn] N Liechtenstein m
lie detector N detector m de mentiras
lie-down (Brit) N: **to have a ~** descansar
lie-in (Brit) N: **to have a ~** dormir até tarde
lieu [lu:]: **in ~ of** PREP em vez de
Lieut. ABBR (= lieutenant) Ten
lieutenant [lɛf'tɛnənt, (US) lu:'tɛnənt] N (Mil)

tenente *m*

lieutenant-colonel N tenente-coronel *m*

life [laɪf] (*pl* **lives**) N vida ▪ CPD (*imprisonment*) perpétuo; (*style*) de vida; **true to ~** fiel à realidade; **to come to ~** (*fig*) animar-se; **to paint from ~** pintar copiando a natureza; **to be sent to prison for ~** ser condenado a prisão perpétua; **country/city ~** vida campestre/urbana; **life annuity** N renda vitalícia; **life assurance** (*Brit*) N = **life insurance**

lifebelt ['laɪfbɛlt] (*Brit*) N cinto salva-vidas

lifeblood ['laɪfblʌd] N (*fig*) força vital

lifeboat ['laɪfbəʊt] N barco salva-vidas

lifebuoy ['laɪfbɔɪ] N bóia salva-vidas

life expectancy N expectativa de vida

lifeguard ['laɪfgɑːd] N (guarda *m*) salva-vidas *m/f*

life imprisonment N prisão *f* perpétua

life insurance N seguro de vida

life jacket N colete *m* salva-vidas

lifeless ['laɪflɪs] ADJ sem vida; (*fig*) sem graça

lifelike ['laɪflaɪk] ADJ natural; (*realistic*) realista

lifeline ['laɪflaɪn] N corda salva-vidas

lifelong ['laɪflɒŋ] ADJ que dura todo a vida

life preserver [-prɪˈzəːvəʳ] (*US*) N = **lifebelt**; **life jacket**

life-raft N balsa salva-vidas

life-saver [-ˈseɪvəʳ] N (guarda *m*) salva-vidas *m/f*

life sentence N pena de prisão perpétua

life-size(d) [-saɪz(d)] ADJ de tamanho natural

life-span N vida, duração *f*

life style N estilo de vida

life support system N (*Med*) sistema *m* de respiração artificial

lifetime ['laɪftaɪm] N vida; **in his ~** durante a sua vida; **once in a ~** uma vez na vida; **the chance of a ~** uma oportunidade única

lift [lɪft] VT levantar; (*steal*) roubar ▪ VI (*fog*) dispersar-se, dissipar-se ▪ N (*Brit: elevator*) elevador *m*; **to give sb a ~** (*Brit*) dar uma carona para alguém (*BR*), dar uma boleia a alguém (*PT*)

▶ **lift off** VI (*rocket, helicopter*) decolar

▶ **lift out** VT tirar; (*troops etc*) evacuar de avião *or* helicóptero

▶ **lift up** VT levantar

lift-off ['lɪftɔf] N decolagem *f*

ligament ['lɪgəmənt] N ligamento

light [laɪt] (*pt, pp* **lit**) N luz *f*; (*lamp*) luz, lâmpada; (*daylight*) (luz do) dia *m*; (*Aut: headlight*) farol *m*; (: *rear light*) luz traseira; (*for cigarette etc*): **have you got a ~?** tem fogo? ▪ VT (*candle, cigarette, fire*) acender; (*room*) iluminar ▪ ADJ (*colour, room*) claro; (*not heavy, also fig*) leve; (*rain, traffic*) fraco; (*movement, action*) delicado ▪ ADV (*travel*) com pouca bagagem; **lights** NPL (*Aut*) sinal *m* de trânsito; **to turn the ~ on/off** acender/apagar a luz; **to cast** *or* **shed** *or* **throw ~ on** esclarecer; **to come to ~** vir à tona; **in the ~ of** à luz de; **to make ~ of sth** (*fig*) não levar algo a sério, fazer pouco caso de algo

▶ **light up** VI (*smoke*) acender um cigarro; (*face*) iluminar-se VT (*illuminate*) iluminar; (*cigarette etc*) acender

light bulb N lâmpada

lighten ['laɪtən] VI (*grow light*) clarear ▪ VT (*give light to*) iluminar; (*make lighter*) clarear; (*make less heavy*) tornar mais leve

lighter ['laɪtəʳ] N (*also: cigarette lighter*) isqueiro, acendedor *m*; (*boat*) chata

light-fingered [-ˈfɪŋgəd] ADJ gatuno; **to be ~** ter mão leve

light-headed [-ˈhɛdɪd] ADJ (*dizzy*) aturdido, tonto; (*excited*) exaltado; (*by nature*) estouvado

light-hearted ADJ alegre, despreocupado

lighthouse ['laɪthaʊs] N farol *m*

lighting ['laɪtɪŋ] N (*act, system*) iluminação *f*

lighting-up time (*Brit*) N hora oficial hora oficial do anoitecer

lightly ['laɪtlɪ] ADV (*touch*) ligeiramente; (*thoughtlessly*) despreocupadamente; (*slightly*) levemente; (*not seriously*) levianamente; **to get off ~** conseguir se safar, livrar a cara (*inf*)

light meter N (*Phot*) fotômetro

lightness ['laɪtnɪs] N claridade *f*; (*in weight*) leveza

lightning ['laɪtnɪŋ] N relâmpago, raio; **lightning conductor** N pára-raios *m inv*; **lightning rod** (*US*) N = **lightning conductor**; **lightning strike** (*Brit*) N greve *f* relâmpago

light pen N caneta leitora

lightship ['laɪtʃɪp] N navio-farol *m*

lightweight ['laɪtweɪt] ADJ (*suit*) leve; (*Boxing*) peso-leve

light year N ano-luz *m*

like [laɪk] VT gostar de ▪ PREP como; (*such as*) tal qual ▪ ADJ parecido, semelhante ▪ N: **the ~** coisas *fpl* parecidas; **his ~s and dis~s** seus gostos e aversões; **I would ~**, **I'd ~** (*eu*) (eu) gostaria de; **would you ~ a coffee?** você quer um café?; **to be** *or* **look ~ sb/sth** parecer-se com alguém/algo, parecer alguém/algo; **what does it look/taste/sound ~?** como é que é?/tem gosto de quê?/como é que soa?; **what's the weather ~?** como está o tempo?; **that's just ~ him** é típico dele; **something ~ that** uma coisa dessas; **do it ~ this** faça isso assim; **I feel ~ a drink** estou com vontade de tomar um drinque; **it is nothing ~ ...** não se parece nada com ...

likeable ['laɪkəbl] ADJ simpático, agradável

likelihood ['laɪklɪhud] N probabilidade *f*

likely ['laɪklɪ] ADJ provável; (*excuse*) plausível; **he's ~ to leave** é provável que ele se vá; **not ~!** (*inf*) nem morto!

like-minded ADJ da mesma opinião

liken ['laɪkən] VT: **to ~ sth to sth** comparar algo com algo

likeness ['laɪknɪs] N semelhança; **that's a good ~** tem uma grande semelhança

likewise ['laɪkwaɪz] ADV igualmente; **to do ~** fazer o mesmo

liking ['laɪkɪŋ] N afeição *f*, simpatia; **to take a ~ to sb** simpatizar com alguém; **to be to sb's ~** ser ao gosto de alguém

lilac ['laɪlək] N lilás m ∎ ADJ (colour) de cor lilás
lilt [lɪlt] N cadência
lilting ['lɪltɪŋ] N cadencioso; **lily** ['lɪlɪ] N lírio, açucena
lily of the valley ∎ N lírio-do-vale m
Lima ['li:mə] N Lima
limb [lɪm] N membro; **to be out on a ~** (fig) estar isolado
limber up ['lɪmbə^r-] VI (Sport) fazer aquecimento
limbo ['lɪmbəu] N: **to be in ~** (fig) viver na expectativa
lime [laɪm] N (tree) limeira; (fruit) limão m; (also: **lime juice**) suco (BR) or sumo (PT) de limão; (Geo) cal f
limelight ['laɪmlaɪt] N: **to be in the ~** (fig) ser o centro das atenções
limerick ['lɪmərɪk] N quintilha humorística
limestone ['laɪmstəun] N pedra calcária
limit ['lɪmɪt] N limite m ∎ VT limitar; **weight/speed ~** limite de peso/de velocidade
limitation [lɪmɪ'teɪʃən] N limitação f
limited ['lɪmɪtɪd] ADJ limitado; **to be ~ to** limitar-se a; **~ edition** edição f limitada; **limited (liability) company** (Brit) N = sociedade f anônima
limitless ['lɪmɪtlɪs] ADJ ilimitado
limousine ['lɪməzi:n] N limusine f
limp [lɪmp] N: **to have a ~** mancar, ser coxo ∎ VI mancar ∎ ADJ frouxo
limpet ['lɪmpɪt] N lapa
limpid ['lɪmpɪd] ADJ límpido, cristalino
linchpin ['lɪntʃpɪn] N cavilha; (fig) pivô m
Lincs [lɪŋks] (Brit) ABBR = **Lincolnshire**
line [laɪn] N linha; (straight line) reta; (rope) corda; (for fishing) linha; (US: queue) fila (BR), bicha (PT); (wire) fio; (row) fila, fileira; (of writing) linha; (on face) ruga; (speciality) ramo (de negócio); (Comm: type of goods) linha ∎ VT (road, room) encarreirar; (container, clothing): **to ~ sth (with)** forrar algo (de); **to ~ the streets** ladear as ruas; **in ~** em fila; **to cut in ~** (US) furar a fila (BR), pôr-se à frente (PT); **in his ~ of business** no ramo dele; **on the right ~s** no caminho certo; **a new ~ in cosmetics** uma nova linha de cosméticos; **hold the ~ please** (Brit: Tel) não desligue; **to be in ~ for sth** estar na bica para algo; **in ~ with** de acordo com; **to bring sth into ~ with sth** alinhar algo com algo; **to draw the ~ at doing sth** (fig) recusar-se a fazer algo; **to take the ~ that ...** ser de opinião que ...
▶ **line up** VI enfileirar-se ∎ VT enfileirar; (set up, have ready) preparar, arranjar; **to have sth/sb ~d up** ter algo programado/alguém em vista
linear ['lɪnɪə^r] ADJ linear
lined [laɪnd] ADJ (face) enrugado; (paper) pautado; (clothes) forrado
line feed N (Comput) entrelinha
linen ['lɪnɪn] N artigos de cama e mesa; (cloth) linho
line printer N impressora de linha
liner ['laɪnə^r] N navio de linha regular; (also: **bin liner**) saco para lata de lixo
linesman ['laɪnzmən] (irreg) N (Sport) juiz m de linha

line-up N formação f em linha, alinhamento; (Sport) escalação f
linger ['lɪŋgə^r] VI demorar-se, retardar-se; (smell, tradition) persistir
lingerie ['lænʒəri:] N lingerie f, roupa de baixo (de mulher)
lingering ['lɪŋgərɪŋ] ADJ persistente; (death) lento, vagaroso
lingo ['lɪŋgəu] (inf) (pl **lingoes**) N língua
linguist ['lɪŋgwɪst] N lingüista m/f
linguistic [lɪŋ'gwɪstɪk] ADJ lingüístico
linguistics [lɪŋ'gwɪstɪks] N lingüística
lining ['laɪnɪŋ] N forro; (Anat) parede f; (Tech) revestimento; (: of brakes) lona
link [lɪŋk] N (of a chain) elo; (connection) conexão f; (bond) vínculo, laço ∎ VT vincular, unir; (associate): **to ~ with** or **to** unir a; **links** NPL (Golf) campo de golfe; **rail ~** ligação ferroviária
▶ **link up** VT acoplar VI unir-se
link-up N ligação f; (in space) acoplamento; (of roads) junção f, confluência; (Radio, TV) transmissão f em rede
lino ['laɪnəu] N = **linoleum**
linoleum [lɪ'nəuliəm] N linóleo
linseed oil ['lɪnsi:d-] N óleo de linhaça
lint [lɪnt] N fibra de algodão; (thread) fio
lintel ['lɪntl] N verga
lion ['laɪən] N leão m; **lion cub** N filhote m de leão
lioness ['laɪənɪs] N leoa
lip [lɪp] N lábio; (of jug) bico; (of cup etc) borda; (insolence) insolência
lipread ['lɪpri:d] (irreg) VI ler os lábios
lip salve N pomada para os lábios
lip service N: **to pay ~ to sth** devotar-se a or elogiar algo falsamente
lipstick ['lɪpstɪk] N batom m
liquefy ['lɪkwɪfaɪ] VT liquefazer ∎ VI liquefazer-se
liqueur [lɪ'kjuə^r] N licor m
liquid ['lɪkwɪd] ADJ líquido ∎ N líquido; **liquid assets** NPL ativo disponível, disponibilidades fpl
liquidate ['lɪkwɪdeɪt] VT liquidar
liquidation [lɪkwɪ'deɪʃən] N: **to go into ~** entrar em liquidação
liquidator ['lɪkwɪdeɪtə^r] N liquidador(a) m/f
liquid crystal display N display m digital em cristal líquido
liquidity [lɪ'kwɪdətɪ] N (Comm) liquidez f
liquidize ['lɪkwɪdaɪz] (Brit) VT (Culin) liqüidificar, passar no liqüidificador
liquidizer ['lɪkwɪdaɪzə^r] (Brit) N (Culin) liqüidificador m
liquor ['lɪkə^r] N licor m, bebida alcoólica
liquorice ['lɪkərɪs] (Brit) N alcaçuz m
liquor store (US) N loja que vende bebidas alcoólicas
Lisbon ['lɪzbən] N Lisboa
lisp [lɪsp] N ceceio ∎ VI cecear, falar com a língua presa

lissom ['lɪsəm] ADJ gracioso, ágil

list [lɪst] N lista; (of ship) inclinação f ■ VT (write down) fazer uma lista or relação de; (enumerate) enumerar; (Comput) listar ■ VI (ship) inclinar-se, adernar; **shopping ~** lista de compras

listed building ['lɪstɪd-] (Brit) N prédio tombado

listed company ['lɪstɪd-] N = sociedade f de capital aberto, sociedade cotada na Bolsa

listen ['lɪsn] VI escutar, ouvir; (pay attention) prestar atenção; **to ~ to** escutar

listener ['lɪsnər] N ouvinte m/f

listing ['lɪstɪŋ] N (Comput) listagem f

listless ['lɪstlɪs] ADJ apático, indiferente

listlessly ['lɪstlɪslɪ] ADV apaticamente

list price N preço de tabela

lit [lɪt] PT, PP of **light**

litany ['lɪtənɪ] N ladainha, litania

liter ['liːtər] (US) N = **litre**

literacy ['lɪtərəsɪ] N capacidade f de ler e escrever, alfabetização f; **literacy campaign** N campanha de alfabetização

literal ['lɪtərl] ADJ literal

literally ['lɪtərəlɪ] ADV literalmente

literary ['lɪtərərɪ] ADJ literário

literate ['lɪtərət] ADJ alfabetizado, instruído; (educated) culto, letrado

literature ['lɪtərɪtʃər] N literatura; (brochures etc) folhetos mpl

lithe [laɪð] ADJ ágil

lithography [lɪ'θɒgrəfɪ] N litografia

Lithuania [lɪθju'eɪnɪə] N Lituânia

litigate ['lɪtɪgeɪt] VT, VI litigar

litigation [lɪtɪ'geɪʃən] N litígio

litmus paper ['lɪtməs-] N papel m de tornassol

litre ['liːtər] (US **liter**) N litro

litter ['lɪtər] N (rubbish) lixo; (paper) papéis mpl; (young animals) ninhada; (stretcher) maca, padiola ■ VT (subj: person) jogar lixo em; (: papers etc) estar espalhado por; **~ed with** (scattered) semeado de; (covered) coberto de; **litter bin** (Brit) N lata de lixo

litterbug ['lɪtəbʌg] N sujismundo

litter lout (Brit) N = **litterbug**

little ['lɪtl] ADJ (small) pequeno; (not much) pouco; **~ house** casinha ■ ADV pouco; **a ~** um pouco (de); **~ milk** pouco leite; **a ~ milk** um pouco de leite; **for a ~ while** por um instante; **with ~ difficulty** com pouca dificuldade; **as ~ as possible** o menos possível; **~ by ~** pouco a pouco; **to make ~ of** fazer pouco de; **little finger** N dedo mindinho

liturgy ['lɪtədʒɪ] N liturgia

live [vi, vt lɪv, adj laɪv] VI viver; (reside) morar ■ VT (a life) levar; (experience) viver ■ ADJ (animal) vivo; (wire) eletrizado; (broadcast) ao vivo; (shell) carregado; **to ~ in London** morar em Londres; **to ~ with sb** morar com alguém; **~ ammunition** munição de guerra

▶ **live down** VT redimir

▶ **live in** VI (maid) dormir no emprego; (student, nurse) ser interno(-a)

▶ **live off** VT FUS (land, fish etc) viver de; (pej: parents etc) viver às custas de

▶ **live on** VT FUS (food) viver de, alimentar-se de ■ VI continuar vivo; **to ~ on £50 a week** viver com £50 por semana

▶ **live out** VI (Brit: student) ser externo ■ VT: **to ~ out one's days** or **life** viver o resto de seus dias

▶ **live together** VI viver juntos

▶ **live up** (inf) VT: **to ~ it up** cair na farra

▶ **live up to** VT FUS (fulfil) cumprir; (justify) justificar

livelihood ['laɪvlɪhud] N meio de vida, subsistência

liveliness ['laɪvlɪnɪs] N vivacidade f

lively ['laɪvlɪ] ADJ vivo; (talk) animado; (pace) rápido; (party, tune) alegre

liven up ['laɪvn-] VT (room) dar nova vida a; (discussion, evening) animar ■ VI animar-se

liver ['lɪvər] N fígado

liverish ['lɪvərɪʃ] ADJ (fig) rabugento, mal-humorado

Liverpudlian [lɪvə'pʌdlɪən] ADJ de Liverpool ■ N natural m/f de Liverpool

livery ['lɪvərɪ] N libré f

lives [laɪvz] NPL of **life**

livestock ['laɪvstɔk] N gado

livid ['lɪvɪd] ADJ lívido; (inf: furious) furioso

living ['lɪvɪŋ] ADJ (alive) vivo ■ N: **to earn** or **make a ~** ganhar a vida; **cost of ~** custo de vida; **within ~ memory** na memória de pessoas ainda vivas; **living conditions** NPL condições fpl de vida; **living expenses** NPL despesas fpl para sobrevivência quotidiana; **living room** N sala de estar; **living standards** NPL padrão m or nível m de vida; **living wage** N salário de subsistência

lizard ['lɪzəd] N lagarto

llama ['lɑːmə] N lhama

LLB N ABBR (= Bachelor of Laws) título universitário

LLD N ABBR (= Doctor of Laws) título universitário

LMT (US) ABBR (= Local Mean Time) hora local

load [ləud] N carga; (weight) peso ■ VT (gen, Comput) carregar; (fig) cumular, encher; **a ~ of rubbish** um monte de besteira; **a ~ of, ~s of** (fig) um monte de, uma porção de

loaded ['ləudɪd] ADJ (vehicle): **to be ~ with** estar carregado de; (dice) viciado; (question, word) intencionado; (inf: rich) cheio da nota; (: drunk) de porre

loading bay ['ləudɪŋ-] N vão m de carregamento

loaf [ləuf] (pl **loaves**) N pão-de-forma m ■ VI (also: **loaf about**, **loaf around**) vadiar, vagabundar

loam [ləum] N marga

loan [ləun] N empréstimo ■ VT emprestar; **on ~** emprestado; **to raise a ~** levantar um empréstimo; **loan account** N conta de empréstimo; **loan capital** N capital-obrigações m

loath [ləuθ] ADJ: **to be ~ to do sth** estar pouco inclinado a fazer also, relutar em fazer algo

loathe [ləuð] VT detestar, odiar

loathing ['ləuðɪŋ] N ódio; **it fills me with ~** me dá (um) ódio

loathsome ['ləuðsəm] ADJ repugnante, asqueroso

loaves [ləuvz] NPL of **loaf**

lob [lɔb] N (Tennis) lobe m ■ VT: to ~ the ball dar um lobe

lobby ['lɔbɪ] N vestíbulo, saguão m; (Pol: pressure group) grupo de pressão, lobby m ■ VT pressionar

lobbyist ['lɔbɪɪst] N membro de um grupo de pressão

lobe [ləub] N lóbulo

lobster ['lɔbstə'] N lagostim m; (large) lagosta; **lobster pot** N armadilha para pegar lagosta

local ['ləukl] ADJ local ■ N (pub) bar m (local); **the locals** NPL (local inhabitants) os moradores locais; **local anaesthetic** (US **local anesthetic**) N anestesia local; **local authority** N município; **local call** N (Tel) ligação f local; **local government** N administração f municipal

locality [ləu'kælɪtɪ] N localidade f

localize ['ləukəlaɪz] VT localizar

locally ['ləukəlɪ] ADV nos arredores, na vizinhança

locate [ləu'keɪt] VT (find) localizar, situar; (situate): **to be ~d in** estar localizado em

location [ləu'keɪʃən] N local m, posição f; **on ~** (Cinema) em externas

loch [lɔx] N lago

lock [lɔk] N (of door, box) fechadura; (of canal) eclusa; (of hair) anel m, mecha ■ VT (with key) trancar; (immobilize) travar ■ VI (door etc) fechar-se à chave; (wheels) travar-se; ~ **stock and barrel** (fig) com tudo; **on full ~** (Brit: Aut) com o volante virado ao máximo
  ► **lock away** VT (valuables) guardar a sete chaves; (person) encarcerar
  ► **lock in** VT trancar dentro
  ► **lock out** VT trancar do lado de fora; (on purpose) deixar na rua; (: workers) recusar trabalho a
  ► **lock up** VT (criminal, mental patient) prender; (house) trancar ■ VI fechar tudo

locker ['lɔkə'] N compartimento com chave

locket ['lɔkɪt] N medalhão m

lockjaw ['lɔkdʒɔ:] N trismo

lockout ['lɔkaut] N greve f de patrões, lockout m

locksmith ['lɔksmɪθ] N serralheiro(-a)

lockup ['lɔkʌp] N (prison) prisão f; (cell) cela; (also: **lockup garage**) compartimento seguro

locomotive [ləukə'məutɪv] N locomotiva

locum ['ləukəm] N (Med) (médico(-a)) interino(-a)

locust ['ləukəst] N gafanhoto

lodge [lɔdʒ] N casa do guarda, guarita; (hunting lodge) pavilhão m de caça; (porter's) portaria; (Freemasonry) loja ■ VI (person): **to ~ (with)** alojar-se (na casa de) ■ VT (complaint) apresentar; **to ~ (itself) in/between** cravar-se em/entre

lodger ['lɔdʒə'] N inquilino(-a), hóspede m/f

lodging ['lɔdʒɪŋ] N alojamento; **lodgings** NPL quarto (mobiliado); see also **board**; **lodging house** (Brit) N casa de hóspedes

loft [lɔft] N sótão m

lofty ['lɔftɪ] ADJ alto, elevado; (haughty) altivo, arrogante; (sentiments, aims) nobre

log [lɔg] N (of wood) tora; (book) = **logbook** ■ N ABBR (= logarithm) log m ■ VT registrar
  ► **log in** VI (Comput) iniciar o uso, logar
  ► **log off** VI (Comput) encerrar o uso, dar logoff
  ► **log on** VI (Comput) iniciar o uso, logar
  ► **log out** VI (Comput) encerrar o uso, dar logoff

logarithm ['lɔgərɪðəm] N logaritmo

logbook ['lɔgbuk] N (Naut) diário de bordo; (Aviat) diário de vôo; (of car) documentação f (do carro)

log cabin N cabana de madeira

log fire N fogueira

loggerheads ['lɔgəhɛdz] NPL: **at ~ (with)** às turras (com)

logic ['lɔdʒɪk] N lógica

logical ['lɔdʒɪkl] ADJ lógico

logically ['lɔdʒɪkəlɪ] ADV logicamente

logistics [lɔ'dʒɪstɪks] N logística

logo ['ləugəu] N logotipo

loin [lɔɪn] N (Culin) (carne f de) lombo; **loins** NPL lombos mpl; **loin cloth** N tanga

loiter ['lɔɪtə'] VI perder tempo; (pej) vadiar, vagabundar

loll [lɔl] VI (also: **loll about**) refestelar-se, reclinar-se

lollipop ['lɔlɪpɔp] N pirulito (BR), chupa-chupa m (PT); (iced) picolé m; **lollipop lady** (Brit) N mulher que ajuda as crianças a atravessarem a rua; **lollipop man** (Brit: irreg) N homem que ajuda as crianças a atravessarem a rua

● **LOLLIPOP LADIES/MEN**
●
● Lollipop ladies/men são as pessoas que
● ajudam as crianças a atravessar a rua
● nas proximidades das escolas na hora
● da entrada e da saída. São facilmente
● localizados graças a suas longas capas
● brancas e à placa redonda com a qual pedem
● aos motoristas que parem. São chamados
● assim por causa da forma circular da placa,
● que lembra um pirulito (lollipop).

lollop ['lɔləp] (Brit) VI andar com pachorra

London ['lʌndən] N Londres

Londoner ['lʌndənə'] N londrino(-a)

lone [ləun] ADJ (person) solitário; (thing) único

loneliness ['ləunlɪnɪs] N solidão f, isolamento

lonely ['ləunlɪ] ADJ (person) só; (place, childhood) solitário, isolado; **to feel ~** sentir-se só

loner ['ləunə'] N solitário(-a)

lonesome ['ləunsəm] ADJ (person) só; (place, childhood) solitário

long [lɔŋ] ADJ longo; (road, hair, table) comprido ■ ADV muito tempo ■ N: **the ~ and the short of it is that ...** (fig) em poucas palavras ... ■ VI: **to ~ for sth** ansiar or suspirar por algo; **he had ~ understood that ...** fazia muito tempo que ele entendia ...; **how ~ is the street?** qual é a extensão da rua?; **how ~ is the lesson?** quanto dura a lição?; **6 metres ~ de** 6 metros de extensão, que mede 6 metros; **6 months ~ de** 6 meses de duração, que dura 6 meses; **all night ~ a** noite inteira; **he no ~er comes** ele não vem mais; **~ before/after** muito antes/depois; **before ~** (+*future*) dentro de pouco; (+*past*) pouco tempo depois; **~ ago** há muito tempo atrás; **don't be ~!** não demore!; **I shan't be ~** não vou demorar; **at ~ last** por fim, no final; **in the ~ run** no final de contas; **so** *or* **as ~ as** contanto que

long-distance ADJ (*travel*) de longa distância; (*call*) interurbano

longevity [lɔn'dʒɛvɪtɪ] N longevidade f

long-haired ADJ (*person*) cabeludo; (*animal*) peludo

longhand ['lɔŋhænd] N escrita usual

longing ['lɔŋɪŋ] N desejo, anseio; (*nostalgia*) saudade f ■ ADJ saudoso

longingly ['lɔŋɪŋlɪ] ADV ansiosamente; (*nostalgically*) saudosamente

longitude ['lɔŋgɪtjuːd] N longitude f

long johns [-dʒɔnz] NPL ceroulas fpl

long jump N salto em distância

long-life ADJ (*milk, batteries*) longa vida

long-lost ADJ perdido há muito (tempo)

long-playing record [-'pleɪɪŋ-] N elepê m (BR), LP m (PT)

long-range ADJ de longo alcance; (*forecast*) a longo prazo

longshoreman ['lɔŋʃɔːmən] (US: *irreg*) N estivador m, portuário

long-sighted ADJ presbita; (*fig*) previdente

long-standing ADJ de muito tempo

long-suffering ADJ paciente, resignado

long-term ADJ a longo prazo

long wave N (*Radio*) onda longa

long-winded [-'wɪndɪd] ADJ prolixo, cansativo

loo [luː] (*Brit: inf*) N banheiro (BR), casa de banho (PT)

loofah ['luːfə] N tipo de esponja

look [luk] VI olhar; (*seem*) parecer; (*building etc*): **to ~ south/(out) onto the sea** dar para o sul/o mar ■ N olhar m; (*glance*) olhada, vista de olhos; (*appearance*) aparência, aspecto; (*style*) visual m; **looks** NPL (*good looks*) físico, aparência; **~ (here)!** (*annoyance*) escuta aqui!; **~!** (*surprise*) olha!; **to ~ like sb** parecer-se com alguém; **it ~s like him** parece ele; **it ~s about 4 metres long** parece ter um 4 metros de comprimento; **it ~s all right to me** para mim está bem; **to have a ~ at sth** dar uma olhada em algo; **to have a ~ for sth** procurar algo; **to ~ ahead** olhar para a frente; (*fig*) pensar no futuro

▶ **look after** VT FUS cuidar de; (*deal with*) lidar com; (*luggage etc: watch over*) ficar de olho em

▶ **look around** VI olhar em torno; (*in shop*) dar uma olhada

▶ **look at** VT FUS olhar (para); (*read quickly*) ler rapidamente; (*consider*) considerar

▶ **look back** VI: **to ~ back at sth/sb** voltar-se

para ver algo/alguém; **to ~ back on** (*remember*) recordar, rever

▶ **look down on** VT FUS (*fig*) desdenhar, desprezar

▶ **look for** VT FUS procurar

▶ **look forward to** VT FUS aguardar com prazer, ansiar por; (*in letter*): **we ~ forward to hearing from you** no aguardo de suas notícias; **to ~ forward to doing sth** não ver a hora de fazer algo; **I'm not ~ing forward to it** não estou nada animado com isso

▶ **look in** VI: **to ~ in on sb** dar uma passada na casa de alguém

▶ **look into** VT FUS investigar

▶ **look on** VI assistir

▶ **look out** VI (*beware*): **to ~ out (for)** tomar cuidado (com)

▶ **look out for** VT FUS (*seek*) procurar; (*await*) esperar

▶ **look over** VT (*essay*) dar uma olhada em; (*town, building*) visitar; (*person*) olhar da cabeça aos pés

▶ **look round** VI virar a cabeça, voltar-se; **to ~ round for sth** procurar algo

▶ **look through** VT FUS (*papers, book*) examinar; (: *briefly*) folhear; (*telescope*) olhar através de

▶ **look to** VT FUS cuidar de; (*rely on*) contar com

▶ **look up** VI levantar os olhos; (*improve*) melhorar VT (*word*) procurar; (*friend*) visitar

▶ **look up to** VT FUS admirar, respeitar

lookout ['lukaut] N (*tower etc*) posto de observação, guarita; (*person*) vigia m; **to be on the ~ for** estar na expectativa de algo

look-up table N (*Comput*) tabela de pesquisa

loom [luːm] N tear m ■ VI (*also*: **loom up**) agigantar-se; (*event*) aproximar-se; (*threaten*) ameaçar

loony ['luːnɪ] (*inf*) ADJ meio doido ■ N debil m/f mental

loop [luːp] N laço; (*bend*) volta, curva; (*contraceptive*) DIU m ■ VT: **to ~ sth round sth** prender algo em torno de algo

loophole ['luːphəul] N escapatória

loose [luːs] ADJ (*not fixed*) solto; (*not tight*) frouxo; (*animal, hair*) solto; (*clothes*) folgado; (*morals, discipline*) relaxado; (*sense*) impreciso ■ N: **to be on the ~** estar solto ■ VT (*free*) soltar; (*slacken*) afrouxar; **~ connection** (*Elec*) conexão solta; **to tie up ~ ends (of sth)** (*fig*) amarrar (algo); **loose change** N trocado; **loose chippings** [-'tʃɪpɪŋz] NPL (*on road*) pedrinhas fpl soltas; **loose end** N: **to be at a loose end** (*Brit*) *or* **at loose ends** (*US*) (*fig*) não ter o que fazer

loose-fitting ADJ (*clothes*) folgado, largo

loose-leaf ADJ: **~ binder** *or* **folder** pasta de folhas soltas

loose-limbed [-'lɪmd] ADJ ágil

loosely ['luːslɪ] ADV frouxamente, folgadamente; (*not closely*) aproximativamente

loosen ['luːsən] VT (*free*) soltar; (*untie*) desatar; (*slacken*) afrouxar

▶ **loosen up** VI (*before game*) aquecer; (*inf: relax*)

descontrair-se

loot [luːt] N saque m, despojo ■ VT saquear, pilhar

looter ['luːtər] N saqueador(a) m/f

looting ['luːtɪŋ] N saque m, pilhagem f

lop off [lɔp-] VT cortar; (branches) podar

lop-sided [lɔp'saɪdɪd] ADJ torto

lord [lɔːd] N senhor m; **L~ Smith** Lord Smith; **the L~** (Rel) o Senhor; **good L~!** Deus meu!; **the (House of) L~s** (Brit) a Câmara dos Lordes

lordly ['lɔːdlɪ] ADJ senhorial; (arrogant) arrogante

lordship ['lɔːdʃɪp] (Brit) N: **Your L~** Vossa senhoria

lore [lɔːʳ] N sabedoria popular, tradições fpl

lorry ['lɔrɪ] (Brit) N caminhão m (BR), camião m (PT); **lorry driver** (Brit) N caminhoneiro (BR), camionista m/f (PT)

lose [luːz] (pt, pp lost) VT, VI perder; **to ~** (time) (clock) atrasar-se; **to ~ no time (in doing sth)** não demorar (a fazer algo); **to get lost** (person) perder-se; (thing) extraviar-se

loser ['luːzəʳ] N perdedor(a) m/f; (inf: failure) derrotado(-a), fracassado(-a); **to be a good/bad ~** ser bom/mau perdedor

loss [lɔs] N perda; (Comm): **to make a ~** sair com prejuízo; **to cut one's ~es** reduzir os prejuízos; **to sell sth at a ~** vender algo com prejuízo; **heavy ~es** (MIL) grandes perdas; **to be at a ~** estar perplexo; **to be at a ~ to do** ser incapaz de fazer; **to be a dead ~** ser totalmente inútil; **loss adjuster** N (Insurance) árbitro regulador de avarias; **loss leader** N (Comm) chamariz m

lost [lɔst] PT, PP of **lose** ■ ADJ perdido; **~ in thought** perdido em seus pensamentos; **~ and found property** (US) (objetos mpl) perdidos e achados mpl; **~ and found** (US) (seção f de) perdidos e achados mpl; **lost property** (Brit) N (objetos mpl) perdidos e achados mpl; **lost property office** or **department** (seção f de) perdidos e achados mpl

lot [lɔt] N (set of things) porção f; (at auctions) lote m; (destiny) destino, sorte f; **the ~** tudo, todos(-as); **a ~** muito, bastante; **a ~ of, ~s of** muito(s); **I read a ~** leio bastante; **to draw ~s** tirar à sorte; **parking ~** (US) estacionamento

lotion ['ləuʃən] N loção f

lottery ['lɔtərɪ] N loteria

loud [laud] ADJ (voice) alto; (shout) forte; (noise) barulhento; (support, condemnation) veemente; (gaudy) berrante ■ ADV alto; **out ~** em voz alta

loud-hailer [-'heɪləʳ] (Brit) N megafone m

loudly ['laudlɪ] ADV (noisily) ruidosamente; (aloud) em voz alta

loudspeaker [laud'spiːkəʳ] N alto-falante m

lounge [laundʒ] N sala de estar f; (of airport) salão m; (Brit: also: **lounge bar**) bar m social ■ VI recostar-se, espreguiçar-se

  ▸ **lounge about** VI ficar à-toa

  ▸ **lounge around** VI = **lounge about**

lounge suit (Brit) N terno (BR), fato (PT)

louse [laus] (pl lice) N piolho

  ▸ **louse up** (inf) VT estragar

lousy ['lauzɪ] (inf) ADJ ruim, péssimo; (ill): **to feel ~** sentir-se mal

lout [laut] N rústico, grosseiro

louvre ['luːvəʳ] (US **louver**) ADJ: **~ door** porta de veneziana; **~ window** veneziana

lovable ['lʌvəbl] ADJ adorável, simpático

love [lʌv] N amor m ■ VT amar; (care for) gostar; (activity): **to ~ to do** gostar (muito) de fazer; **~ (from) Anne** (on letter) um abraço or um beijo, Anne; **I ~ you** eu te amo; **I ~ coffee** adoro o café; **I'd ~ to come** gostaria muito de ir; **"15 ~"** (Tennis) "15 a zero"; **to be in ~ with** estar apaixonado por; **to fall in ~ with** apaixonar-se por; **to make ~** fazer amor; **~ at first sight** amor à primeira vista; **for the ~ of** pelo amor de; **to send one's ~ to sb** mandar um abraço para alguém; **love affair** N aventura (amorosa), caso (de amor); **love letter** N carta de amor; **love life** N vida sentimental

lovely ['lʌvlɪ] ADJ (delightful) encantador(a), delicioso; (beautiful) lindo, belo; (holiday, surprise) muito agradável, maravilhoso; **we had a ~ time** foi maravilhoso, nós nos divertimos muito

lover ['lʌvəʳ] N amante m/f; **a ~ of art/music** um(a) apreciador(a) de or um(a) amante de arte/música

lovesick ['lʌvsɪk] ADJ perdido de amor

love song N canção f de amor

loving ['lʌvɪŋ] ADJ carinhoso, afetuoso; (actions) dedicado

low [ləu] ADJ baixo; (depressed) deprimido; (ill) doente ■ ADV baixo ■ N (Meteorology) área de baixa pressão ■ VI (cow) mugir; **to turn (down) ~** baixar, diminuir; **to be ~ on** (supplies) ter pouco; **to reach a new** or **an all-time ~** cair para o seu nível mais baixo

low-alcohol ADJ de baixo teor alcoólico

lowbrow ['ləubrau] ADJ sem pretensões intelectuais

low-calorie ADJ baixo em calorias, de baixo teor calórico

low-cut ADJ (dress) decotado

low-down N (inf): **he gave me the ~ on it** me deu a dica sobre isso ■ ADJ (mean) vil, desprezível

lower¹ ['ləuəʳ] ADJ mais baixo; (less important) inferior ■ VT abaixar; (reduce) reduzir, diminuir; **to ~ o.s. to** (fig) rebaixar-se a

lower² ['lauəʳ] VI (sky, clouds) escurecer; (person): **to ~ at sb** olhar para alguém com raiva

low-fat ADJ magro

low-grade ADJ de baixa qualidade

low-key ADJ discreto

lowlands ['ləuləndz] NPL planície f

low-level ADJ de baixo nível, baixo; (flying) a baixa altura

lowly ['ləulɪ] ADJ humilde

low-lying ADJ de baixo nível

low-paid ADJ (person) de renda baixa; (work) mal pago

loyal ['lɔɪəl] ADJ leal

loyalist ['lɔɪəlɪst] N legalista m/f
loyalty ['lɔɪəltɪ] N lealdade f
lozenge ['lɔzɪndʒ] N (Med) pastilha; (Geom)
losango, rombo
LP N ABBR = **long-playing record**
L-plates ['ɛlpleɪts] (Brit) NPL placas fpl de
aprendiz de motorista

⊙ **L-PLATES**

⊙ As L-plates são placas quadradas com um
⊙ "L" vermelho que são colocadas na parte de
⊙ trás do carro para mostrar que a pessoa ao
⊙ volante ainda não tem carteira de motorista.
⊙ Até a obtenção da carteira, o motorista
⊙ aprendiz possui uma permissão provisória
⊙ e não tem direito de dirigir sem um
⊙ motorista qualificado ao lado. Os motoristas
⊙ aprendizes não podem dirigir em rodovias
⊙ mesmo que estejam acompanhados.

LPN (US) N ABBR (= Licensed Practical Nurse)
enfermeiro(-a) diplomado(-a)
LRAM (Brit) N ABBR = **Licentiate of the Royal
Academy of Music**
LSAT (US) N ABBR = **Law Schools Admissions
Test**
LSD N ABBR (= lysergic acid diethylamide) LSD m;
(Brit: = pounds, shillings and pence) sistema monetário
usado na Grã-Bretanha até 1971
LSE N ABBR = **London School of Economics**
LT ABBR (Elec: = low tension) BT
Lt. ABBR (= lieutenant) Ten
Ltd (Brit) ABBR (= limited (liability) company) SA
lubricant ['lu:brɪkənt] N lubrificante m
lubricate ['lu:brɪkeɪt] VT lubrificar
lucid ['lu:sɪd] ADJ lúcido
lucidity [lu:'sɪdɪtɪ] N lucidez f
luck [lʌk] N sorte f; **bad ~** azar m; **good ~!** boa
sorte!; **to be in ~** ter or dar sorte; **to be out of ~**
ter azar; **bar** or **hard** or **tough ~!** que azar!
luckily ['lʌkɪlɪ] ADV por sorte, felizmente
lucky ['lʌkɪ] ADJ (person) sortudo; (coincidence)
feliz; (situation) afortunado; (object) de sorte
lucrative ['lu:krətɪv] ADJ lucrativo
ludicrous ['lu:dɪkrəs] ADJ ridículo
ludo ['lu:dəu] N ludo
lug [lʌg] (inf) VT (drag) arrastar; (pull) puxar
luggage ['lʌgɪdʒ] N bagagem f; **luggage car** (US)
N (Rail) vagão m de bagagens; **luggage rack**
N (in train) rede f para bagagem; (on car) porta-
bagagem m, bagageiro; **luggage van** (Brit) N
(Rail) vagão m de bagagens
lugubrious [lu'gu:brɪəs] ADJ lúgubre
lukewarm ['lu:kwɔ:m] ADJ morno, tépido; (fig)
indiferente
lull [lʌl] N pausa, interrupção f ■ VT: **to ~ sb to
sleep** acalentar alguém; **to be ~ed into a false
sense of security** ser acalmado com uma falsa
sensação de segurança
lullaby ['lʌləbaɪ] N canção f de ninar
lumbago [lʌm'beɪgəu] N lumbago

lumber ['lʌmbəʳ] N (junk) trastes mpl velhos;
(wood) madeira serrada, tábua ■ VT: **to ~ sb
with sth/sb** empurrar algo/alguém para cima
de alguém ■ VI (also: **lumber about, lumber
along**) mover-se pesadamente
lumberjack ['lʌmbədʒæk] N madeireiro,
lenhador m
lumber room (Brit) N quarto de despejo
lumber yard N depósito de madeira
luminous ['lu:mɪnəs] ADJ luminoso
lump [lʌmp] N torrão m; (fragment) pedaço; (in
sauce) caroço; (in throat) nó m; (on body) galo,
caroço; (also: **sugar lump**) cubo de açúcar ■ VT:
to ~ together amontoar; **a ~ sum** uma quantia
global
lumpy ['lʌmpɪ] ADJ (sauce, bed) encaroçado
lunacy ['lu:nəsɪ] N loucura
lunar ['lu:nəʳ] ADJ lunar
lunatic ['lu:nətɪk] ADJ, N louco(-a); **lunatic
asylum** N manicômio, hospício
lunch [lʌntʃ] N almoço ■ VI almoçar; **to invite
sb for ~** convidar alguém para almoçar
luncheon ['lʌntʃən] N almoço formal; **luncheon
meat** N bolo de carne; **luncheon voucher** (Brit)
N vale m para refeição, ticket m restaurante
lunch hour N hora do almoço
lunch time N hora do almoço
lung [lʌŋ] N pulmão m; **lung cancer** N câncer m
(BR) or cancro (PT) de pulmão
lunge [lʌndʒ] VI (also: **lunge forward**) dar
estocada or bote; **to ~ at** arremeter-se contra
lupin ['lu:pɪn] N tremoço
lurch [lə:tʃ] VI balançar ■ N solavanco; **to leave
sb in the ~** deixar alguém em apuros, deixar
alguém na mão (inf)
lure [luəʳ] N (bait) isca; (decoy) chamariz m,
engodo ■ VT atrair, seduzir
lurid ['luərɪd] ADJ (account) sensacional; (detail)
horrível
lurk [lə:k] VI (hide) esconder-se; (wait) estar à
espreita
luscious ['lʌʃəs] ADJ (person, thing) atraente; (food)
delicioso
lush [lʌʃ] ADJ exuberante
lust [lʌst] N luxúria; (greed) cobiça
▶ **lust after** VT FUS cobiçar
▶ **lust for** VT FUS = **lust after**
luster ['lʌstəʳ] (US) N = **lustre**
lustful ['lʌstful] ADJ lascivo, sensual
lustre ['lʌstəʳ] (US luster) N lustre m, brilho
lusty ['lʌstɪ] ADJ robusto, forte
lute [lu:t] N alaúde m
Luxembourg ['lʌksəmbə:g] N Luxemburgo
luxuriant [lʌg'zjuərɪənt] ADJ luxuriante,
exuberante
luxurious [lʌg'zjuərɪəs] ADJ luxuoso
luxury ['lʌkʃərɪ] N luxo ■ CPD de luxo
LV (Brit) N ABBR = **luncheon voucher**
LW ABBR (Radio: = long wave) OL
lying ['laɪɪŋ] N mentira(s) f(pl) ■ ADJ mentiroso,
falso
lynch [lɪntʃ] VT linchar

lynching ['lɪntʃɪŋ] N linchamento
lynx [lɪŋks] N lince m
lyre ['laɪəʳ] N lira
lyric ['lɪrɪk] ADJ lírico

lyrical ['lɪrɪkəl] ADJ lírico
lyricism ['lɪrɪsɪzəm] N lirismo
lyrics ['lɪrɪks] NPL (of song) letra

Mm

M, m [ɛm] N (*letter*) M, m *m*; **M for Mary** (*Brit*) or
Mike (*US*) M de Maria
M N ABBR (*Brit*) = **motorway; the M8** ≈ BR 8 f;
(: = *medium*) M
m ABBR (= *metre*) m; (: = *mile*) mil.; = **million**
M.A. ABBR (*Sch*) = **Master of Arts**; (*US*) = **military
academy**; (: *Post*) = **Massachusetts**
mac [mæk] (*Brit*) N capa impermeável
macabre [mə'kɑ:brə] ADJ macabro
Macao [mə'kau] N Macau
macaroni [mækə'rəunɪ] N macarrão *m*
macaroon [mækə'ru:n] N biscoitinho de
amêndoas
mace [meɪs] N (*Bot*) macis *m*; (*sceptre*) bastão *m*
machinations [mækɪ'neɪʃənz] NPL
maquinações *fpl*, intrigas *fpl*
machine [mə'ʃi:n] N máquina ▪ VT (*dress etc*)
costurar à máquina; (*Tech*) usinar; **machine
code** N (*Comput*) código de máquina; **machine
gun** N metralhadora; **machine language** N
(*Comput*) linguagem *f* de máquina; **machine
readable** ADJ (*Comput*) legível por máquina
machinery [mə'ʃi:nərɪ] N maquinaria; (*fig*)
máquina
machine shop N oficina mecânica
machine tool N máquina-ferramenta *f*
machine washable ADJ (*garment*) lavável à
máquina
machinist [mə'ʃi:nɪst] N operário(-a) (de
máquina); (*Rail*) maquinista *m/f*
macho ['mætʃəu] ADJ machista
mackerel ['mækrl] N INV cavala
mackintosh ['mækɪntɔʃ] (*Brit*) N capa
impermeável
macro... ['mækrəu] PREFIX macro...
macro-economics N macroeconomia
mad [mæd] ADJ louco; (*foolish*) tolo; (*angry*)
furioso, brabo; (*keen*): **to be ~ about** ser louco
por; **to go ~** enlouquecer
madam ['mædəm] N senhora, madame *f*;
yes, ~ sim, senhora; **M~ Chairman** Senhora
Presidente; **can I help you, ~?** a senhora já foi
atendida?
madden ['mædn] VT exasperar
maddening ['mædnɪŋ] ADJ exasperante
made [meɪd] PT, PP *of* **make**
Madeira [mə'dɪərə] N (*Geo*) Madeira; (*wine*)

(*vinho*) Madeira *m*
Madeiran [mə'dɪərən] ADJ, N madeirense *m/f*
made-to-measure (*Brit*) ADJ feito sob medida
madly ['mædlɪ] ADV loucamente; **~ in love**
louco de amor
madman ['mædmən] (*irreg*) N louco
madness ['mædnɪs] N loucura; (*foolishness*)
tolice *f*
Madrid [mə'drɪd] N Madri (BR), Madrid (PT)
Mafia ['mæfɪə] N máfia
mag. [mæg] (*Brit: inf*) N ABBR = **magazine**
magazine [mægə'zi:n] N (*Press*) revista; (*Radio,
TV*) programa *m* de actualidades; (*Mil: store*)
depósito; (*of firearm*) câmara; **magazine rack** N
porta-revistas *m inv*
maggot ['mægət] N larva de inseto
magic ['mædʒɪk] N magia, mágica ▪ ADJ
mágico
magical ['mædʒɪkl] ADJ mágico
magician [mə'dʒɪʃən] N mago(-a); (*entertainer*)
mágico(-a)
magistrate ['mædʒɪstreɪt] N magistrado(-a),
juiz/juíza *m/f*
magnanimous [mæg'nænɪməs] ADJ
magnânimo
magnate ['mægneɪt] N magnata *m*
magnesium [mæg'ni:zɪəm] N magnésio
magnet ['mægnɪt] N ímã *m*, iman *m* (PT)
magnetic [mæg'nɛtɪk] ADJ magnético;
magnetic disk N (*Comput*) disco magnético;
magnetic tape N fita magnética
magnetism ['mægnɪtɪzəm] N magnetismo
magnification [mægnɪfɪ'keɪʃən] N aumento
magnificence [mæg'nɪfɪsns] N magnificência
magnificent [mæg'nɪfɪsnt] ADJ magnífico
magnify ['mægnɪfaɪ] VT aumentar
magnifying glass ['mægnɪfaɪɪŋ-] N lupa,
lente *f* de aumento
magnitude ['mægnɪtju:d] N magnitude *f*
magnolia [mæg'nəulɪə] N magnólia
magpie ['mægpaɪ] N pega
mahogany [mə'hɔgənɪ] N mogno, acaju *m*
▪ CPD de mogno *or* acaju
maid [meɪd] N empregada; (*old ~*) (*pej*) solteirona
maiden ['meɪdn] N moça, donzela ▪ ADJ (*aunt
etc*) solteirona; (*speech, voyage*) inaugural;
maiden name N nome *m* de solteira

mail [meɪl] N correio; (*letters*) cartas *fpl* ■ VT (*post*) pôr no correio; (*send*) mandar pelo correio; **by ~** pelo correio

mailbox ['meɪlbɔks] N (*US: for letters*) caixa do correio; (*Comput*) caixa de entrada

mailing list ['meɪlɪŋ-] N lista de clientes, mailing list *m*

mailman ['meɪlmæn] (*US: irreg*) N carteiro

mail order N pedido por reembolso postal; (*business*) venda por correspondência ■ CPD: **mail-order firm** or **house** firma de vendas por correspondência

mailshot ['meɪlʃɔt] (*Brit*) N mailing *m*

mail train N trem-correio, trem *m* postal

mail truck (*US*) N (*Aut*) = **mail van**

mail van (*Brit*) N (*Aut*) furgão *m* do correio; (*Rail*) vagão *m* postal

maim [meɪm] VT mutilar, aleijar

main [meɪn] ADJ principal ■ N (*pipe*) cano or esgoto principal; **the mains** NPL (*Elec, gas, water*) a rede; **in the ~** na maior parte; **main course** N (*Culin*) prato principal

mainframe ['meɪnfreɪm] N (*Comput*) mainframe *m*

mainland ['meɪnlənd] N: **the ~** o continente

mainline ['meɪnlaɪn] (*inf*) VT (*heroin*) picar-se com ■ VI picar-se, aplicar-se

main line N (*Rail*) linha-tronco *f* ■ ADJ: **main-line** de linha-tronco

mainly ['meɪnlɪ] ADV principalmente

main road N estrada principal

mainstay ['meɪnsteɪ] N (*fig*) esteio

mainstream ['meɪnstriːm] N corrente *f* principal

maintain [meɪn'teɪn] VT manter; (*keep up*) conservar (em bom estado); (*affirm*) sustentar, afirmar; **to ~ that ...** afirmar que ...

maintenance ['meɪntənəns] N manutenção *f*; (*Law: alimony*) alimentos *mpl*, pensão *f* alimentícia; **maintenance contract** N contrato de assistência técnica; **maintenance order** N (*Law*) ordem *f* de pensão

maisonette [meɪzə'nɛt] (*Brit*) N duplex *m*

maize [meɪz] N milho

Maj. ABBR (*Mil*) = **major**

majestic [mə'dʒɛstɪk] ADJ majestoso

majesty ['mædʒɪstɪ] N majestade *f*; (*title*): **Your M~** Sua Majestade

major ['meɪdʒər] N (*Mil*) major *m* ■ ADJ (*main*) principal; (*considerable*) importante; (*great*) grande; (*Mus*) maior ■ VI (*US: Sch*): **to ~ (in)** especializar-se (em); **a ~ operation** (*Med*) uma operação séria

Majorca [mə'jɔːkə] N Maiorca

major general N (*Mil*) general-de-divisão *m*

majority [mə'dʒɔrɪtɪ] N maioria ■ CPD (*verdict, holding*) majoritário

make [meɪk] (*pt, pp* **made**) VT fazer; (*manufacture*) fabricar, produzir; (*cause to be*): **to ~ sb sad** entristecer alguém, fazer alguém ficar triste; (*force*): **to ~ sb do sth** fazer com que alguém faça algo; (*equal*): **2 and 2 ~ 4** dois e dois são

quatro ■ N marca; **to ~ the bed** fazer a cama; **to ~ a fool of sb** fazer alguém de bobo; **to ~ a profit/loss** ter um lucro/uma perda; **to ~ it** (*arrive*) chegar; (*succeed*) ter sucesso; **what time do you ~ it?** que horas você tem?; **to ~ good** (*succeed*) dar-se bem; (*losses*) indenizar; **to ~ do with** contentar-se com

▸ **make for** VT FUS (*place*) dirigir-se a

▸ **make off** VI fugir

▸ **make out** VT (*decipher*) decifrar; (*understand*) compreender; (*see*) divisar, avistar; (*write out: prescription*) escrever; (: *form, cheque*) preencher; (*claim, imply*) afirmar; (*pretend*) fazer de conta; **to ~ out a case for sth** argumentar em favor de algo, defender algo

▸ **make over** VT (*assign*): **to ~ over (to)** transferir (para)

▸ **make up** VT (*constitute*) constituir; (*invent*) inventar; (*parcel*) embrulhar ■ VI reconciliar-se; (*with cosmetics*) maquilar-se (BR), maquilhar-se (PT); **to be made up of** compor-se de, ser composto de; **to ~ up one's mind** decidir-se

▸ **make up for** VT FUS compensar

make-believe ADJ fingido, simulado ■ N: **a world of ~** um mundo de faz-de-conta; **it's just ~** é pura ilusão

maker ['meɪkər] N (*of film, programme*) criador *m*; (*manufacturer*) fabricante *m/f*

makeshift ['meɪkʃɪft] ADJ provisório

make-up ['meɪkʌp] N maquilagem *f* (BR), maquilhagem *f* (PT); **make-up bag** N bolsa de maquilagem (BR), bolsa de maquilhagem (PT); **make-up remover** N removidor *m* de maquilagem

making ['meɪkɪŋ] N (*fig*): **in the ~** em vias de formação; **he has the ~s of an actor** ele tem tudo para ser ator

maladjusted [mælə'dʒʌstɪd] ADJ inadaptado, desajustado

malaise [mæ'leɪz] N mal-estar *m*, indisposição *f*

malaria [mə'lɛərɪə] N malária

Malawi [mə'lɑːwɪ] N Malavi *m*

Malay [mə'leɪ] ADJ malaio ■ N malaio(-a); (*Ling*) malaio

Malaya [mə'leɪə] N Malaia

Malayan [mə'leɪən] ADJ, N = **Malay**

Malaysia [mə'leɪzɪə] N Malaísia (BR), Malásia (PT)

Malaysian [mə'leɪzɪən] ADJ, N malásio(-a)

Maldives ['mɔːldaɪvz] NPL: **the ~** as ilhas Maldivas

male [meɪl] N (*Bio, Elec*) macho ■ ADJ (*sex, attitude*) masculino; (*animal*) macho; (*child etc*) do sexo masculino; **male chauvinist** N machista *m*; **male nurse** N enfermeiro

malevolence [mə'lɛvələns] N malevolência

malevolent [mə'lɛvələnt] ADJ malévolo

malfunction [mæl'fʌŋkʃən] N funcionamento defeituoso

malice ['mælɪs] N (*ill will*) malícia; (*rancour*) rancor *m*

malicious [mə'lɪʃəs] ADJ malevolente; (*Law*) com

intenção criminosa
malign [mə'laɪn] VT caluniar, difamar
malignant [mə'lɪgnənt] ADJ (Med) maligno
malingerer [mə'lɪŋgərəʳ] N doente m/f
fingido(-a)
mall [mɔːl] N (also: **shopping mall**) shopping m
malleable ['mælɪəbl] ADJ maleável
mallet ['mælɪt] N maço, marreta
malnutrition [mælnju:'trɪʃən] N desnutrição f
malpractice [mæl'præktɪs] N falta profissional
malt [mɔːlt] N malte m; (malt whisky) uísque m
de malte
Malta ['mɔːltə] N Malta
Maltese [mɔːl'tiːz] ADJ maltês(-esa) ■ N INV
maltês(-esa) m/f; (Ling) maltês m
maltreat [mæl'triːt] VT maltratar
mammal ['mæml] N mamífero
mammoth ['mæməθ] N mamute m ■ ADJ
gigantesco, imenso
man [mæn] (pl **men**) N homem m; (Chess) peça
■ VT (Naut) tripular; (Mil) guarnecer; (operate:
machine) operar; **an old** ~ um velho; **a young** ~
um jovem; ~ **and wife** marido e mulher
manacles ['mænəklz] NPL grilhões mpl
manage ['mænɪdʒ] VI arranjar-se, virar-se
■ VT (be in charge of) dirigir, administrar;
(business) gerenciar; (ship, person) controlar;
(device) manusear; (carry) carregar; **to** ~ **to do**
sth conseguir fazer algo; **to** ~ **without sb/sth**
passar sem alguém/algo; **can you** ~**?** você
consegue?
manageable ['mænɪdʒəbl] ADJ manejável; (task
etc) viável
management ['mænɪdʒmənt] N
administração f, direção f, gerência; **"under**
new ~**"** "sob nova direção"; **management**
accounting N contabilidade f administrativa
or gerencial; **management consultant** N
consultor(a) m/f em administração
manager ['mænɪdʒəʳ] N gerente m/f; (Sport)
técnico(-a); (of project) superintendente m/f; (of
department, unit) chefe m/f, diretor(a) m/f; (of
artist) empresário(-a); **sales** ~ gerente de vendas
manageress [mænɪdʒə'rɛs] N gerente f
managerial [mænə'dʒɪərɪəl] ADJ
administrativo, gerencial
managing director ['mænɪdʒɪŋ-] N diretor(a)
m/f geral, diretor-gerente/diretora-gerente m/f
Mancunian [mæŋ'kjuːnɪən] ADJ de Manchester
■ N natural m/f de Manchester
mandarin ['mændərɪn] N (also: **mandarin**
orange) tangerina; (person) mandarim m
mandate ['mændeɪt] N mandato
mandatory ['mændətərɪ] ADJ obrigatório;
(powers etc) mandatário
mandolin(e) ['mændəlɪn] N bandolim m
mane [meɪn] N (of horse) crina; (of lion) juba
maneuver etc [mə'nuːvəʳ] (US) = **manoeuvre** etc
manfully ['mænfəlɪ] ADV valentemente
manganese ['mæŋgəniːz] N manganês m
mangle ['mæŋgl] VT mutilar, estropiar ■ N
calandra

mango ['mæŋgəu] (pl **mangoes**) N manga
mangrove ['mæŋgrəuv] N mangue m
mangy ['meɪndʒɪ] ADJ sarnento, esfarrapado
manhandle ['mænhændl] VT (mistreat)
maltratar; (move by hand) manipular
manhole ['mænhəul] N poço de inspeção
manhood ['mænhud] N (age) idade f adulta;
(masculinity) virilidade f
man-hour N hora-homem f
manhunt ['mænhʌnt] N caça ao homem
mania ['meɪnɪə] N mania
maniac ['meɪnɪæk] N maníaco(-a); (fig) louco(-a)
manic ['mænɪk] ADJ maníaco
manic-depressive ADJ, N maníaco-
depressivo(-a)
manicure ['mænɪkjuəʳ] N manicure f (BR),
manicura (PT); **manicure set** N estojo de
manicure (BR) or manicura (PT)
manifest ['mænɪfest] VT manifestar, mostrar
■ ADJ manifesto, evidente ■ N (Aviat, Naut)
manifesto
manifestation [mænɪfɛs'teɪʃən] N
manifestação f
manifesto [mænɪ'fɛstəu] (pl **manifestos** or
manifestoes) N manifesto
manifold ['mænɪfəuld] ADJ múltiplo ■ N (Aut
etc) see **exhaust**
Manila [mə'nɪlə] N Manilha
manila [mə'nɪlə] ADJ: ~ **paper** papel-manilha m
manipulate [mə'nɪpjuleɪt] VT manipular
manipulation [mənɪpju'leɪʃən] N
manipulação f
mankind [mæn'kaɪnd] N humanidade f, raça
humana
manliness ['mænlɪnɪs] N virilidade f
manly ['mænlɪ] ADJ másculo, viril
man-made ADJ sintético, artificial
manna ['mænə] N maná m
mannequin ['mænɪkɪn] N manequim m
manner ['mænəʳ] N modo, maneira; (behaviour)
conduta, comportamento; (type): **all** ~ **of**
things todos os tipos de coisa; **manners** NPL
(conduct) boas maneiras fpl, educação f; **bad** ~**s**
falta de educação; **all** ~ **of** todo tipo de
mannerism ['mænərɪzəm] N maneirismo,
hábito
mannerly ['mænəlɪ] ADJ polido, educado
man(o)euvrable [mə'nuːvrəbl] (US
maneuverable) ADJ manobrável
manoeuvre [mə'nuːvəʳ] (US **maneuver**) VT
manobrar; (manipulate) manipular ■ VI
manobrar ■ N manobra; **to** ~ **sb into doing**
sth induzir alguém a fazer algo
manor ['mænəʳ] N (also: **manor house**) casa
senhorial, solar m
manpower ['mænpauəʳ] N potencial m
humano, mão-de-obra f
manservant ['mænsəvænt] (pl **menservants**)
N criado
mansion ['mænʃən] N mansão f, palacete m
manslaughter ['mænslɔːtəʳ] N homicídio
involuntário

mantelpiece ['mæntlpi:s] N consolo da lareira
mantle ['mæntl] N manto; (fig) camada
man-to-man ADJ, ADV de homem para homem
manual ['mænjuəl] ADJ manual ■ N manual m;
(Mus) teclado; **manual worker** N trabalhador(a)
m/f braçal
manufacture [mænju'fæktʃəʳ] VT manufaturar,
fabricar ■ N fabricação f
manufactured goods [mænju'fæktʃəd-] NPL
produtos mpl industrializados
manufacturer [mænju'fæktʃərəʳ] N fabricante
m/f
manufacturing industries [mænju'fæktʃərɪŋ]
NPL indústrias fpl de transformação
manure [mə'njuəʳ] N estrume m, adubo
manuscript ['mænjuskrɪpt] N manuscrito
many ['mɛnɪ] ADJ, PRON muitos(-as); **how ~?**
quantos(-as)?; **a great ~** muitíssimos; **twice as
~** ADJ duas vezes mais ■ PRON o dobro; **~ a time**
muitas vezes
map [mæp] N mapa m ■ VT fazer o mapa de
▶ **map out** VT traçar; (fig: career, holiday)
planejar
maple ['meɪpl] N bordo
mar [mɑːʳ] VT estragar
Mar. ABBR = **March**
marathon ['mærəθən] N maratona ■ ADJ: **a
~ session** uma sessão exaustiva; **marathon
runner** N corredor(a) m/f de maratona,
maratonista m/f
marauder [mə'rɔːdəʳ] N saqueador(a) m/f
marble ['mɑːbl] N mármore m; (toy) bola de
gude; **marbles** N (game) jogo de gude
March [mɑːtʃ] N março; see also **July**
march [mɑːtʃ] VI (Mil) marchar; (demonstrators)
desfilar ■ N marcha; (demonstration) passeata;
to ~ out of/into etc sair de/entrar em
marchando etc
marcher ['mɑːtʃəʳ] N (demonstrator)
manifestante m/f
marching ['mɑːtʃɪŋ] N: **to give sb his ~ orders**
(fig) dar um bilhete azul a alguém, mandar
passear alguém
march-past N desfile m
mare [mɛəʳ] N égua
marg. [mɑːdʒ] (inf) N ABBR = **margarine**
margarine [mɑːdʒə'riːn] N margarina
margin ['mɑːdʒɪn] N margem f
marginal ['mɑːdʒɪnl] ADJ marginal; **~ seat** (Pol)
cadeira ganha por pequena maioria
marginally ['mɑːdʒɪnəlɪ] ADV ligeiramente
marigold ['mærɪgəuld] N malmequer m
marijuana [mærɪ'wɑːnə] N maconha
marina [mə'riːnə] N marina
marinade [n mærɪ'neɪd, vt 'mærɪneɪd] N
escabeche m ■ VT = **marinate**
marinate ['mærɪneɪt] VT marinar, pôr em
escabeche
marine [mə'riːn] ADJ (in the sea) marinho;
(engineer) naval; (of seafaring) marítimo ■ N
fuzileiro naval; **marine insurance** N seguro
marítimo

marital ['mærɪtl] ADJ matrimonial, marital; **~
status** estado civil
maritime ['mærɪtaɪm] ADJ marítimo; **maritime
law** N direito marítimo
marjoram ['mɑːdʒərəm] N manjerona
mark [mɑːk] N marca, sinal m; (imprint)
impressão f; (stain) mancha; (Brit: Sch) nota;
(currency) marco; (Brit: Tech): **M~ 2 2° a** versão
■ VT (also: Sport: player) marcar; (stain) manchar;
(indicate) indicar; (commemorate) comemorar;
(Brit: Sch: grade) dar nota em; (: correct) corrigir; **to
~ time** marcar passo; **to be quick off the ~** (in
doing) (fig) não perder tempo (para fazer); **up
to the ~** (in efficiency) à altura das exigências
▶ **mark down** VT (prices, goods) rebaixar,
remarcar para baixo
▶ **mark off** VT (tick off) ticar
▶ **mark out** VT (trace) traçar; (designate) destinar
▶ **mark up** VT (price) aumentar, remarcar
marked [mɑːkt] ADJ acentuado
markedly ['mɑːkɪdlɪ] ADV marcadamente
marker ['mɑːkəʳ] N (sign) marcador m, marca;
(bookmark) marcador
market ['mɑːkɪt] N mercado ■ VT (Comm)
comercializar; **to be on the ~** estar à venda;
on the open ~ no mercado livre; **to play the ~**
especular na bolsa de valores
marketable ['mɑːkɪtəbl] ADJ comercializável
market analysis N análise f de mercado
market day N dia m de mercado
market demand N procura de mercado
market forces NPL forças fpl de mercado
market garden (Brit) N horta
marketing ['mɑːkɪtɪŋ] N marketing m
market leader N líder m do mercado
marketplace ['mɑːkɪtpleɪs] N mercado
market price N preço de mercado
market research N pesquisa de mercado
market value N valor m de mercado
marking ['mɑːkɪŋ] N (on animal) marcação f; (on
road) marca
marksman ['mɑːksmən] (irreg) N bom
atirador m
marksmanship ['mɑːksmənʃɪp] N boa pontaria
marksmen ['mɑːksmɛn] NPL of **marksman**
mark-up N (Comm: margin) margem f (de lucro),
markup m; (: increase) remarcação f, aumento
marmalade ['mɑːməleɪd] N geléia de laranja
maroon [mə'ruːn] VT: **to be ~ed** ficar
abandonado (numa ilha) ■ ADJ de cor
castanho-avermelhado, vinho inv
marquee [mɑː'kiː] N toldo, tenda
marquess ['mɑːkwɪs] N marquês m
marquis ['mɑːkwɪs] N = **marquess**
marriage ['mærɪdʒ] N casamento; **marriage
bureau** (irreg) N agência matrimonial;
marriage certificate N certidão f de
casamento; **marriage counselling** (US) N
= **marriage guidance; marriage guidance** (Brit)
N orientação f matrimonial
married ['mærɪd] ADJ casado; (life, love) conjugal;
to get ~ casar(-se)

marrow ['mærəu] N medula; (*vegetable*) abóbora

marry ['mærɪ] VT casar(-se) com; (*subj: father, priest etc*) casar, unir ■ VI (*also*) get married, casar(-se)

Mars [mɑːz] N (*planet*) Marte m

marsh [mɑːʃ] N pântano; (*salt marsh*) marisma

marshal ['mɑːʃl] N (*Mil: also:* **field marshal**) marechal m; (*at sports meeting etc*) oficial m ■ VT (*thoughts, support*) organizar; (*soldiers*) formar

marshalling yard ['mɑːʃlɪŋ-] N (*Rail*) local m de manobras

marshmallow [mɑːʃ'mæləu] N *espécie de doce de malvavisco*

marshy ['mɑːʃɪ] ADJ pantanoso

marsupial [mɑːˈsuːpɪəl] ADJ marsupial ■ N marsupial m

martial ['mɑːʃl] ADJ marcial; **martial arts** NPL artes *fpl* marciais; **martial law** N lei *f* marcial

Martian ['mɑːʃən] N marciano(-a)

martin ['mɑːtɪn] N (*also:* **house martin**) andorinha-de-casa

martyr ['mɑːtəʳ] N mártir m/f ■ VT martirizar

martyrdom ['mɑːtədəm] N martírio

marvel ['mɑːvl] N maravilha ■ VI: **to ~ (at)** maravilhar-se (de or com)

marvellous ['mɑːvələs] (US **marvelous**) ADJ maravilhoso

Marxism ['mɑːksɪzəm] N marxismo

Marxist ['mɑːksɪst] ADJ, N marxista m/f

marzipan ['mɑːzɪpæn] N maçapão m

mascara [mæsˈkɑːrə] N rímel m

mascot ['mæskət] N mascote f

masculine ['mæskjulɪn] ADJ, N masculino

masculinity [mæskjuˈlɪnɪtɪ] N masculinidade f

MASH [mæʃ] (US) N ABBR (*Mil*) = **mobile army surgical hospital**

mash [mæʃ] VT (*Culin*) fazer um purê de; (*crush*) amassar

mashed potatoes [mæʃt-] N purê m de batatas

mask [mɑːsk] N máscara ■ VT (*face*) encobrir; (*feelings*) esconder, ocultar

masochism ['mæsəkɪzəm] N masoquismo

masochist ['mæsəkɪst] N masoquista m/f

mason ['meɪsn] N (*also:* **stone mason**) pedreiro(-a); (*also:* **freemason**) maçom m

masonic [məˈsɔnɪk] ADJ maçônico

masonry ['meɪsənrɪ] N (*also:* **freemasonry**) maçonaria; (*building*) alvenaria

masquerade [mæskəˈreɪd] N baile m de máscaras; (*fig*) farsa, embuste m ■ VI: **to ~ as** disfarçar-se de, fazer-se passar por

mass [mæs] N (*of papers etc*) quantidade f; (*people*) multidão f; (*Phys*) massa; (*Rel*) missa; (*great quantity*) montão m ■ CPD de massa ■ VI reunir-se; (*Mil*) concentrar-se; **the masses** NPL (*ordinary people*) as massas; **~es of** (*inf*) montes de; **to go to ~** ir à missa

massacre ['mæsəkəʳ] N massacre m, carnificina ■ VT massacrar

massage ['mæsɑːʒ] N massagem f ■ VT fazer massagem em, massagear

masseur [mæˈsəːʳ] N massagista m

masseuse [mæˈsəːz] N massagista

massive ['mæsɪv] ADJ (*large*) enorme; (*support*) massivo

mass market N mercado de consumo em massa

mass media NPL meios *mpl* de comunicação de massa, mídia

mass meeting N concentração f de massa

mass-produce VT produzir em massa, fabricar em série

mass-production N produção f em massa, fabricação f em série

mast [mɑːst] N (*Naut*) mastro; (*Radio etc*) antena

master ['mɑːstəʳ] N mestre m; (*landowner*) senhor m, dono; (*fig: of situation*) dono; (*in secondary school*) professor m; (*title for boys*): **M~ X** o menino X ■ VT controlar; (*learn*) conhecer a fundo; **~ of ceremonies** mestre de cerimônias; **M~'s degree** mestrado; **master disk** N (*Comput*) disco mestre

masterful ['mɑːstəful] ADJ autoritário, imperioso

master key N chave f mestra

masterly ['mɑːstəlɪ] ADJ magistral

mastermind ['mɑːstəmaɪnd] N (*fig*) cabeça ■ VT dirigir, planejar

Master of Arts/Science N detentor(a) m/f de mestrado em letras/ciências; (*degree*) mestrado

masterpiece ['mɑːstəpiːs] N obra-prima

master plan N plano piloto

master stroke N golpe m de mestre

mastery ['mɑːstərɪ] N domínio

mastiff ['mæstɪf] N mastim m

masturbate ['mæstəbeɪt] VI masturbar-se

masturbation [mæstəˈbeɪʃən] N masturbação f

mat [mæt] N esteira; (*also:* **doormat**) capacho; (*also:* **table mat**) descanso ■ ADJ = **matt**

match [mætʃ] N fósforo; (*game*) jogo, partida; (*equal*) igual m/f ■ VT (*also:* **match up**) casar, emparelhar; (*go well with*) combinar com; (*equal*) igualar; (*correspond to*) corresponder a ■ VI combinar; (*couple*) formar um bom casal
▶ **match up** VT casar, emparelhar

matchbox ['mætʃbɔks] N caixa de fósforos

matching ['mætʃɪŋ] ADJ que combina (com)

matchless ['mætʃlɪs] ADJ sem igual, incomparável

mate [meɪt] N (*inf*) colega m/f; (*assistant*) ajudante m/f; (*Chess*) mate m; (*animal*) macho/ fêmea; (*in merchant navy*) imediato ■ VI acasalar-se ■ VT acasalar

material [məˈtɪərɪəl] N (*substance*) matéria; (*equipment*) material m; (*cloth*) pano, tecido; (*data*) dados *mpl* ■ ADJ material; (*important*) importante; **materials** NPL (*equipment*) material; **reading ~** (*material de*) leitura

materialistic [mətɪərɪəˈlɪstɪk] ADJ materialista

materialize [məˈtɪərɪəlaɪz] VI materializar-se, concretizar-se

materially [məˈtɪərɪəlɪ] ADV materialmente

maternal [məˈtəːnl] ADJ maternal

maternity [məˈtəːnɪtɪ] N maternidade f ■ CPD

de maternidade, de gravidez; **maternity
benefit** N auxílio-maternidade *m*; **maternity
dress** N vestido de gestante; **maternity
hospital** N maternidade *f*

matey ['meɪtɪ] (*Brit: inf*) ADJ chapinha

math [mæθ] (*US*) N = **maths**

mathematical [mæθə'mætɪkl] ADJ matemático

mathematician [mæθəmə'tɪʃən] N matemático(-a)

mathematics [mæθə'mætɪks] N matemática

maths [mæθs] (*US* **math**) N matemática

matinée ['mætɪneɪ] N matinê *f*

mating ['meɪtɪŋ] N acasalamento; **mating call**
N chamado do macho; **mating season** N época
de cio

matriarchal [meɪtrɪ'ɑːkl] ADJ matriarcal

matrices ['meɪtrɪsiːz] NPL *of* **matrix**

matriculation [mətrɪkju'leɪʃən] N matrícula

matrimonial [mætrɪ'məunɪəl] ADJ
matrimonial

matrimony ['mætrɪmənɪ] N matrimônio,
casamento

matrix ['meɪtrɪks] (*pl* **matrices**) N matriz *f*

matron ['meɪtrən] N (*in hospital*) enfermeira-
chefe *f*; (*in school*) inspetora

matronly ['meɪtrənlɪ] ADJ matronal; (*fig: figure*)
corpulento

matt [mæt] ADJ fosco, sem brilho

matted ['mætɪd] ADJ embaraçado

matter ['mætəʳ] N questão *f*, assunto; (*Phys*)
matéria; (*substance*) substância; (*content*)
conteúdo; (*reading matter etc*) material *m*; (*Med:
pus*) pus *m* ■ VI importar; **matters** NPL (*affairs*)
questões *fpl*; **it doesn't ~** não importa; (*I don't
mind*) tanto faz; **what's the ~?** o que (é que) há?,
qual é o problema?; **no ~ what** aconteça o que
acontecer; **as a ~ of course** o que é de se esperar;
(*routine*) por rotina; **as a ~ of fact** na realidade,
de fato; **it's a ~ of habit** é uma questão de
hábito; **printed ~** impressos; **reading ~** (*Brit*)
(*material de*) leitura

matter-of-fact [mætərə'fækt] ADJ prosaico,
prático

matting ['mætɪŋ] N esteira

mattress ['mætrɪs] N colchão *m*

mature [mə'tjuəʳ] ADJ maduro; (*cheese, wine*)
amadurecido ■ VI amadurecer

maturity [mə'tjuərɪtɪ] N maturidade *f*

maudlin ['mɔːdlɪn] ADJ (*film, book*) piegas *inv*;
(*person*) chorão(-rona)

maul [mɔːl] VT machucar, maltratar

Mauritania [mɔːrɪ'teɪnɪə] N Mauritânia

Mauritius [mə'rɪʃəs] N Maurício *f* (*no article*)

mausoleum [mɔːsə'lɪəm] N mausoléu *m*

mauve [məuv] ADJ cor de malva *inv*

maverick ['mævrɪk] N (*fig*) dissidente *m/f*

mawkish ['mɔːkɪʃ] ADJ piegas *inv*

max. ABBR = **maximum**

maxim ['mæksɪm] N máxima

maxima ['mæksɪmə] NPL *of* **maximum**

maximize ['mæksɪmaɪz] VT maximizar

maximum ['mæksɪməm] (*pl* **maxima** or

maximums) ADJ máximo ■ N máximo

May [meɪ] N maio; *see also* **July**

may [meɪ] (*conditional* **might**) AUX VB (*indicating
possibility*): **he ~ come** pode ser que ele venha, é
capaz de vir; (*be allowed to*): **~ I smoke?** posso
fumar?; (*wishes*): **~ God bless you!** que Deus
lhe abençoe; **he might be there** ele poderia
estar lá, ele é capaz de estar lá; **I might as well
go** mais vale que eu vá; **you might like to try**
talvez você queira tentar

maybe ['meɪbiː] ADV talvez; **~ he'll come** talvez
ele venha; **~ not** talvez não

May Day N dia *m* primeiro de maio

mayday ['meɪdeɪ] N S.O.S. *m* (*chamada de socorro
internacional*)

mayhem ['meɪhɛm] N caos *m*

mayonnaise [meɪə'neɪz] N maionese *f*

mayor [mɛəʳ] N prefeito (BR), presidente *m* do
município (PT)

mayoress ['mɛərɪs] N prefeita (BR), presidenta
do município (PT)

maypole ['meɪpəul] N *mastro erguido no dia primeiro
de maio*

maze [meɪz] N labirinto

MB ABBR (*Comput*) = **megabyte**; (*Canadian*)
= **Manitoba**

MBA N ABBR (= *Master of Business Administration*)
grau universitário

MBBS (*Brit*) N ABBR (= *Bachelor of Medicine and
Surgery*) *grau universitário*

MBChB (*Brit*) N ABBR (= *Bachelor of Medicine and
Surgery*) *grau universitário*

MBE (*Brit*) N ABBR (= *Member of the Order of the
British Empire*) *título honorífico*

MC N ABBR = **master of ceremonies**

MCAT (*US*) N ABBR = **Medical College
Admissions Test**

MCP (*Brit: inf*) N ABBR (= *male chauvinist pig*)
machista *m*

MD N ABBR = **Doctor of Medicine**; (*Comm*)
= **managing director** ■ ABBR (*US: Post*)
= **Maryland**

MDT (*US*) ABBR (= *Mountain Daylight Time*) *hora de
verão nas montanhas Rochosas*

ME (*US*) ABBR (*Post*) = **Maine** ■ N ABBR (*Med*)
= **medical examiner**

◯ KEYWORD

me [miː] PRON 1 (*direct*) me; **can you hear me?**
você pode me ouvir?; **he heard me** ele me
ouviu; **he heard ME!** (*not anyone else*) ele me
ouviu; **it's me** sou eu
2 (*indirect*) me; **he gave me the money, he gave
the money to me** ele deu o dinheiro para mim;
give them to me dê-me-os
3 (*stressed, after prep*) mim; **it's for me** é para
mim; **with me** comigo; **without me** sem mim

meadow ['mɛdəu] N prado, campina

meagre ['miːgəʳ] (*US* **meager**) ADJ escasso

meal [miːl] N refeição *f*; (*flour*) farinha; **to go**

out for a ~ jantar fora
mealtime ['mi:ltaɪm] N hora da refeição
mealy-mouthed ['mi:limauðd] ADJ insincero
mean [mi:n] (*pt, pp* **meant**) ADJ (*with money*) sovina, avarento, pão-duro *inv* (BR); (*unkind*) mesquinho; (*shabby*) malcuidado, dilapidado; (*of poor quality*) inferior; (*average*) médio ∎ VT (*signify*) significar, querer dizer; (*refer to*): **I thought you ~t her** eu pensei que você estivesse se referindo a ela; (*intend*): **to ~ to do sth** pretender *or* tencionar fazer algo ∎ N meio, meio termo; **means** NPL (*way, money*) meio; **by ~s of** por meio de, mediante; **by all ~s!** claro que sim!, pois não; **do you ~ it?** você está falando sério?; **what do you ~?** o que você quer dizer?; **to be ~t for** estar destinado a
meander [mɪ'ændə^r] VI (*river*) serpentear; (*person*) vadiar, perambular
meaning ['mi:nɪŋ] N sentido, significado
meaningful ['mi:nɪŋful] ADJ significativo; (*relationship*) sério
meaningless ['mi:nɪŋlɪs] ADJ sem sentido
meanness ['mi:nnɪs] N (*with money*) avareza, sovinice *f*; (*shabbiness*) pobreza, miséria; (*unkindness*) maldade *f*, mesquinharia
means test N (*Admin*) avaliação *f* de rendimento
meant [ment] PT, PP *of* **mean**
meantime ['mi:ntaɪm] ADV (*also*: **in the meantime**) entretanto, enquanto isso
meanwhile ['mi:nwaɪl] ADV = **meantime**
measles ['mi:zlz] N sarampo
measly ['mi:zlɪ] (*inf*) ADJ miserável
measure ['mɛʒə^r] VT medir; (*for clothes etc*) tirar as medidas de; (*consider*) avaliar, ponderar ∎ VI medir ∎ N medida; (*ruler: also*: **tape measure**) fita métrica; **a litre ~** um litro; **some ~ of success** certo grau de sucesso; **to take ~s to do sth** tomar medidas *or* providências para fazer algo
▶ **measure up** VI: **to ~ up (to)** corresponder (a)
measured ['mɛʒəd] ADJ medido, calculado; (*tone*) ponderado
measurement ['mɛʒəmənt] N (*act*) medição *f*; (*dimension*) medida; **measurements** NPL (*size*) medidas *fpl*; **to take sb's ~s** tirar as medidas de alguém; **chest/hip ~** medida de peito/quadris
meat [mi:t] N carne *f*; **cold ~s** (*Brit*) frios; **crab ~** caranguejo
meatball ['mi:tbɔ:l] N almôndega
meat pie N bolo de carne
meaty ['mi:tɪ] ADJ carnudo; (*fig*) substancial
Mecca ['mɛkə] N Meca; (*fig*): **a ~ (for)** a meca (de)
mechanic [mɪ'kænɪk] N mecânico
mechanical [mɪ'kænɪkl] ADJ mecânico;
  mechanical engineer N engenheiro(-a) mecânico(-a)
mechanics [mɪ'kænɪks] N mecânica ∎ NPL mecanismo
mechanical engineering N (*science*) mecânica; (*industry*) engenharia mecânica
mechanism ['mɛkənɪzəm] N mecanismo

mechanization [mɛkənaɪ'zeɪʃən] N mecanização *f*
MEd N ABBR (= *Master of Education*) grau universitário
medal ['mɛdl] N medalha
medalist ['mɛdəlɪst] (US) N = **medallist**
medallion [mɪ'dælɪən] N medalhão *m*
medallist ['mɛdəlɪst] (US **medalist**) N (*Sport*) ganhador(a) *m/f* de medalha
meddle ['mɛdl] VI: **to ~ in** meter-se em, intrometer-se em; **to ~ with sth** mexer em algo
meddlesome ['mɛdlsəm] ADJ intrometido
meddling ['mɛdlɪŋ] ADJ intrometido
media ['mi:dɪə] NPL meios *mpl* de comunicação, mídia
mediaeval [mɛdɪ'i:vl] ADJ = **medieval**
median ['mi:dɪən] (US) N (*also*: **median strip**) canteiro divisor
media research N pesquisa de audiência
mediate ['mi:dɪeɪt] VI mediar
mediation [mi:dɪ'eɪʃən] N mediação *f*
mediator ['mi:dɪeɪtə^r] N mediador(a) *m/f*
Medicaid ['mɛdɪkeɪd] (US) N programa de ajuda médica.
medical ['mɛdɪkl] ADJ médico ∎ N (*examination*) exame *m* médico; **medical certificate** N atestado médico; **medical student** N estudante *m/f* de medicina
Medicare ['mɛdɪkɛə^r] (US) N *sistema federal de seguro saúde*
medicated ['mɛdɪkeɪtɪd] ADJ medicinal, higienizado
medication [mɛdɪ'keɪʃən] N (*drugs etc*) medicação *f*
medicinal [mɛ'dɪsɪnl] ADJ medicinal
medicine ['mɛdsɪn] N medicina; (*drug*) remédio, medicamento; **medicine chest** N armário de remédios; **medicine man** (*irreg*) N curandeiro *m*, pajé *m*
medieval [mɛdɪ'i:vl] ADJ medieval
mediocre [mi:dɪ'əukə^r] ADJ medíocre
mediocrity [mi:dɪ'ɔkrɪtɪ] N mediocridade *f*
meditate ['mɛdɪteɪt] VI meditar
meditation [mɛdɪ'teɪʃən] N meditação *f*
Mediterranean [mɛdɪtə'reɪnɪən] ADJ mediterrâneo; **the ~ (Sea)** o (mar) Mediterrâneo
medium ['mi:dɪəm] (*pl* **mediums**) ADJ médio ∎ N (*means*) meio (*pl* **mediums**) (*person*) médium *m/f*; **the happy ~** o justo meio
medium-sized [-saɪzd] ADJ de tamanho médio
medium wave N (*Radio*) onda média
medley ['mɛdlɪ] N mistura; (*Mus*) pot-pourri *m*
meek [mi:k] ADJ manso, dócil
meet [mi:t] (*pt, pp* **met**) VT (*gen*) encontrar; (*accidentally*) topar com, dar de cara com; (*by arrangement*) encontrar-se com, ir ao encontro de; (*for the first time*) conhecer; (*go and fetch*) ir buscar; (*opponent, problem*) enfrentar; (*obligations*) cumprir; (*need*) satisfazer ∎ VI encontrar-se; (*for talks*) reunir-se; (*join: objects*)

unir-se; (get to know) conhecer-se ▪ N (Brit:
Hunting) reunião f de caçadores; (US: Sport)
promoção f, competição f; **pleased to ~ you!**
prazer em conhecê-lo/-la
▸ **meet up** vi: **to ~ up with sb** encontrar-se
com alguém
▸ **meet with** vt fus reunir-se com; (face:
difficulty) encontrar
meeting ['mi:tɪŋ] N encontro; (session: of
club, Comm) reunião f; (assembly: of people, Pol)
assembléia; (interview) entrevista; (Sport) corrida;
she's in or **at a ~** ela está em conferência; **to
call a ~** convocar uma reunião; **meeting place**
N ponto de encontro
megabyte ['mɛgəbait] N (Comput) megabyte m
megalomaniac [mɛgələu'meɪnɪæk] ADJ, N
megalomaníaco(-a)
megaphone ['mɛgəfəun] N megafone m
megapixel ['mɛgəpɪksl] N megapixel m
melancholy ['mɛlənkəlɪ] N melancolia ▪ ADJ
melancólico
melee ['mɛleɪ] N briga, refrega
mellow ['mɛləu] ADJ (sound) melodioso, suave;
(colour, wine) suave; (fruit) maduro ▪ vi (person)
amadurecer
melodious [mɪ'ləudɪəs] ADJ melodioso
melodrama ['mɛləudra:mə] ADJ melodrama m
melodramatic [mɛlədrə'mætɪk] ADJ
melodramático
melody ['mɛlədɪ] N melodia
melon ['mɛlən] N melão m
melt [mɛlt] vi (metal) fundir-se; (snow) derreter;
(fig) desvanecer-se ▪ vt derreter
▸ **melt away** vi desaparecer
▸ **melt down** vt fundir
meltdown ['mɛltdaun] N fusão f
melting point ['mɛltɪŋ-] N ponto de fusão
melting pot ['mɛltɪŋ-] N (fig) mistura
member ['mɛmbə^r] N membro(-a); (of club)
sócio(-a); (Anat) membro ▪ CPD: ~ **state**
estado membro; **M~ of Parliament**
(Brit) deputado(-a); **M~ of the European
Parliament** (Brit) Membro(-a) do
Parlamento Europeu; **M~ of the House of
Representatives** (US) membro(-a) da Câmara
dos representantes
membership ['mɛmbəʃɪp] N (state) adesão
f; (of club) associação f; (members) número de
sócios; **to seek ~ of** candidatar-se a sócio de;
membership card N carteira de sócio
membrane ['mɛmbreɪn] N membrana
memento [mə'mɛntəu] (pl **mementos** or
mementoes) N lembrança
memo ['mɛməu] N memorando, nota
memoirs ['mɛmwɑ:z] NPL memórias fpl
memo pad N bloco de memorando
memorable ['mɛmərəbl] ADJ memorável
memoranda [mɛmə'rændə] NPL of
memorandum
memorandum [mɛmə'rændəm] (pl
memoranda) N memorando
memorial [mɪ'mɔ:rɪəl] N monumento

comemorativo ▪ ADJ comemorativo; **Memorial
Day** (US) N ver abaixo

⬤ **MEMORIAL DAY**
⬤
⬤ Memorial Day é um feriado nos Estados
⬤ Unidos, a última segunda-feira de maio na
⬤ maior parte dos estados, em memória aos
⬤ soldados americanos mortos em combate.

memorize ['mɛmɛraiz] vt decorar, aprender
de cor
memory ['mɛmərɪ] N memória; (recollection)
lembrança; (of dead person): **in ~ of** em memória
de; **to have a good/bad ~** ter memória boa/
ruim; **loss of ~** perda de memória; **memory
card** N placa de memória
men [mɛn] NPL of **man**
menace ['mɛnəs] N ameaça; (nuisance) droga
▪ vt ameaçar
menacing ['mɛnəsɪŋ] ADJ ameaçador(a)
menagerie [mə'nædʒərɪ] N coleção f de animais
mend [mɛnd] vt consertar, reparar; (darn)
remendar ▪ N remendo; **to be on the ~** estar
melhorando
mending ['mɛndɪŋ] N conserto, reparo; (clothes)
roupas fpl por consertar
menial ['mi:nɪəl] ADJ (often pej) humilde,
subalterno
meningitis [mɛnɪn'dʒaitɪs] N meningite f
menopause ['mɛnəupɔ:z] N menopausa
menservants ['mɛnsə:vənts] NPL of
manservant
menstruate ['mɛnstrueɪt] vi menstruar
menstruation [mɛnstru'eɪʃən] N menstruação f
mental ['mɛntl] ADJ mental; **~ illness** doença
mental
mentality [mɛn'tælɪtɪ] N mentalidade f
mentally ['mɛntlɪ] ADV: **to be ~ handicapped**
ser deficiente mental
menthol ['mɛnθɔl] N mentol m
mention ['mɛnʃən] N menção f ▪ vt
mencionar; (speak of) falar de; **don't ~ it!** não
tem de quê!, de nada!; **I need hardly ~ that ...**
não preciso dizer que ...; **not to ~ ..., without
~ing ...** para não falar de ..., sem falar de ...
mentor ['mɛntɔ:^r] N mentor m
menu ['mɛnju:] N (set menu, Comput) menu m;
(printed) cardápio (BR), ementa (PT)
menu-driven ADJ (Comput) que se navega
através de menus
MEP N ABBR = **Member of the European
Parliament**
mercantile ['mə:kəntaɪl] ADJ mercantil; (law)
comercial
mercenary ['mə:sɪnərɪ] ADJ mercenário ▪ N
mercenário
merchandise ['mə:tʃəndaɪz] N mercadorias fpl
▪ vt comercializar
merchandiser ['mə:tʃəndaɪzə^r] N
comerciante m/f
merchant ['mə:tʃənt] N comerciante m/f;

timber/wine ~ negociante de madeira/vinhos; **merchant bank** (*Brit*) N banco mercantil

merchantman ['mə:tʃəntmən] (*irreg*) N navio mercante

merchant navy (*US* **merchant marine**) N marinha mercante

merciful ['mə:sɪful] ADJ (*person*) misericordioso, humano; (*release*) afortunado

mercifully ['mə:sɪflɪ] ADV misericordiosamente, generosamente; (*fortunately*) graças a Deus, felizmente

merciless ['mə:sɪlɪs] ADJ desumano, inclemente

mercurial [mə:'kjuərɪəl] ADJ volúvel; (*lively*) vivo

mercury ['mə:kjurɪ] N mercúrio

mercy ['mə:sɪ] N piedade *f*; (*Rel*) misericórdia; **to have ~ on sb** apiedar-se de alguém; **at the ~ of** à mercê de; **mercy killing** N eutanásia

mere [mɪə'] ADJ mero, simples *inv*

merely ['mɪəlɪ] ADV simplesmente, somente, apenas

merge [mə:dʒ] VT (*join*) unir; (*mix*) misturar; (*Comm*) fundir; (*Comput*) intercalar ■ VI unir-se; (*Comm*) fundir-se

merger ['mə:dʒə'] N (*Comm*) fusão *f*

meridian [mə'rɪdɪən] N meridiano

meringue [mə'ræŋ] N suspiro, merengue *m*

merit ['mɛrɪt] N mérito; (*advantage*) vantagem *f* ■ VT merecer

meritocracy [mɛrɪ'tɔkrəsɪ] N sistema *m* social baseado no mérito

mermaid ['mə:meɪd] N sereia

merrily ['mɛrɪlɪ] ADV alegremente, com alegria

merriment ['mɛrɪmənt] N alegria

merry ['mɛrɪ] ADJ alegre; **M~ Christmas!** Feliz Natal!

merry-go-round N carrossel *m*

mesh [mɛʃ] N malha; (*Tech*) engrenagem *f* ■ VI (*gears*) engrenar

mesmerize ['mɛzməraɪz] VT hipnotizar

mess [mɛs] N (*situation*) confusão *f*; (*of objects*) desordem *f*; (*in room*) bagunça; (*Mil*) rancho; **to be in a ~** (*untidy*) ser uma bagunça, estar numa bagunça; (*fig: marriage, life*) estar bagunçado; **to be/get o.s. in a ~** (*fig*) meter-se numa encrenca
▶ **mess about** (*inf*) VI perder tempo; (*pass the time*) vadiar
▶ **mess about with** (*inf*) VT FUS mexer com
▶ **mess around** (*inf*) VI = **mess about**
▶ **mess around with** (*inf*) VT FUS = **to mess about with**
▶ **mess up** VT (*disarrange*) desarrumar; (*spoil*) estragar; (*dirty*) sujar

message ['mɛsɪdʒ] N recado, mensagem *f*; **to get the ~** (*fig: inf*) sacar, pescar; **message switching** [-'swɪtʃɪŋ] N (*Comput*) troca de mensagens

messenger ['mɛsɪndʒə'] N mensageiro(-a)

Messiah [mɪ'saɪə] N Messias *m*

Messrs ['mɛsəz] ABBR (*on letters*: = *messieurs*) Srs

messy ['mɛsɪ] ADJ (*dirty*) sujo; (*untidy*) desarrumado; (*confused*) bagunçado

Met [mɛt] (*US*) N ABBR = **Metropolitan Opera**

met [mɛt] PT, PP *of* **meet** ■ ADJ ABBR = **meteorological**

metabolism [mɛ'tæbəlɪzəm] N metabolismo

metal ['mɛtl] N metal *m* ■ VT (*road*) empedrar

metallic [mɛ'tælɪk] ADJ metálico

metallurgy [mɛ'tælədʒɪ] N metalurgia

metalwork ['mɛtlwə:k] N (*craft*) trabalho em metal

metamorphosis [mɛtə'mɔ:fəsɪs] (*pl* **metamorphoses**) N metamorfose *f*

metaphor ['mɛtəfə'] N metáfora

metaphysics [mɛtə'fɪzɪks] N metafísica

meteor ['mi:tɪə'] N meteoro

meteoric [mi:tɪ'ɔrɪk] ADJ (*fig*) meteórico

meteorite ['mi:tɪəraɪt] N meteorito

meteorological [mi:tɪərə'lɔdʒɪkl] ADJ meteorológico

meteorology [mi:tɪə'rɔlədʒɪ] N meteorologia

meter ['mi:tə'] N (*instrument*) medidor *m*; (*also*: **parking meter**) parcômetro; (*US: unit*) = **metre**

methane ['mi:θeɪn] N metano

method ['mɛθəd] N método; **~ of payment** modalidade de pagamento

methodical [mɪ'θɔdɪkl] ADJ metódico

Methodist ['mɛθədɪst] ADJ, N metodista *m/f*

methodology [mɛθəd'ɔlədʒɪ] N metodologia

meths [mɛθs] (*Brit*) N = **methylated spirit**

methylated spirit ['mɛθɪleɪtɪd-] (*Brit*) N álcool *m* metílico or desnaturado

meticulous [mɛ'tɪkjuləs] ADJ meticuloso

metre ['mi:tə'] (*US* **meter**) N metro

metric ['mɛtrɪk] ADJ métrico; **to go ~** adotar o sistema métrico decimal

metrical ['mɛtrɪkl] ADJ métrico

metrication [mɛtrɪ'keɪʃən] N conversão *f* ao sistema métrico decimal

metric system N sistema *m* métrico decimal

metric ton N tonelada (métrica)

metronome ['mɛtrənəum] N metrônomo

metropolis [mɪ'trɔpəlɪs] N metrópole *f*

metropolitan [mɛtrə'pɔlɪtən] ADJ metropolitano

Metropolitan Police (*Brit*) N: **the ~** a polícia de Londres

mettle ['mɛtl] N (*spirit*) caráter *m*, têmpera; (*courage*) coragem *f*

mew [mju:] VI (*cat*) miar

mews [mju:z] (*Brit*) N: **~ cottage** pequena casa resultante de reforma de antigos estábulos

Mexican ['mɛksɪkən] ADJ, N mexicano(-a)

Mexico ['mɛksɪkəu] N México; **Mexico City** N Cidade *f* do México

mezzanine ['mɛtsəni:n] N sobreloja, mezanino

MFA (*US*) N ABBR (= *Master of Fine Arts*) grau universitário

mfr ABBR = **manufacture**; **manufacturer**

mg ABBR (= *milligram*) mg

Mgr ABBR = **Monseigneur**; **Monsignor**; (: ~ *manager*) dir

MHR (*US*) N ABBR = **Member of the House of**

Representatives Inglaterra

MHz ABBR (= megahertz) MHz

MI (US) ABBR (Post) = **Michigan**

MI5 (Brit) N ABBR (= Military Intelligence 5) ≈ SNI m

MI6 (Brit) N ABBR (= Military Intelligence 6) ≈ SNI m

MIA ABBR = **missing in action**

miaow [miːˈau] VI miar

mice [maɪs] NPL of **mouse**

micro... [ˈmaɪkrəu] PREFIX micro

microbe [ˈmaɪkrəub] N micróbio

microbiology [maɪkrəubaɪˈɔlədʒɪ] N microbiologia

microchip [ˈmaɪkrəutʃɪp] N microchip m

micro(computer) [ˈmaɪkrəu(kəmˈpjuːtər)] N micro(computador) m

microcosm [ˈmaɪkrəukɔzəm] N microcosmo

microeconomics [maɪkrəuiːkəˈnɔmɪks] N microeconomia

microfiche [ˈmaɪkrəufiːʃ] N microficha

microfilm [ˈmaɪkrəufɪlm] N microfilme m ▪ VT microfilmar

microlight [ˈmaɪkrəulaɪt] N ultraleve m

micrometer [maɪˈkrɔmɪtər] N micrômetro

microphone [ˈmaɪkrəfəun] N microfone m

microprocessor [maɪkrəuˈprəusesər] N microprocessador m

microscope [ˈmaɪkrəskəup] N microscópio; **under the ~** com microscópio

microscopic [maɪkrəˈskɔpɪk] ADJ microscópico

microwave [ˈmaɪkrəuweɪv] N (also: **microwave oven**) forno microondas

mid [mɪd] ADJ: **in ~ May** em meados de maio; **in ~ afternoon** no meio da tarde; **in ~ air** em pleno ar; **he's in his ~ thirties** ele tem por volta de trinta e cinco anos

midday [ˈmɪddeɪ] N meio-dia m

middle [ˈmɪdl] N meio; (waist) cintura ▪ ADJ meio; (quantity, size) médio, mediano; **in the ~ of the night** no meio da noite; **I'm in the ~ of reading it** estou no meio da leitura; **middle age** N meia-idade f ▪ CPD: **middle-age spread** barriga de meia-idade

middle-aged ADJ de meia-idade

Middle Ages NPL: **the ~** a Idade Média

middle class N: **the ~(es)** a classe média ▪ ADJ (also: **middle-class**) de classe média

Middle East N: **the ~** o Oriente Médio

middleman [ˈmɪdlmæn] (irreg) N intermediário; (Comm) atravessador m

middle management N escalão gerencial intermediário

middlemen [ˈmɪdlmɛn] NPL of **middleman**

middle name N segundo nome m

middle-of-the-road ADJ (policy) de meio-termo; (music) romântico

middleweight [ˈmɪdlweɪt] N (Boxing) peso médio

middling [ˈmɪdlɪŋ] ADJ mediano

midge [mɪdʒ] N mosquito

midget [ˈmɪdʒɪt] N anão(-anã) m/f ▪ ADJ minúsculo

Midlands [ˈmɪdləndz] NPL região central da

midnight [ˈmɪdnaɪt] N meia-noite f; **at ~** à meia-noite

midriff [ˈmɪdrɪf] N barriga

midst [mɪdst] N: **in the ~ of** no meio de, entre

midsummer [mɪdˈsʌmər] N: **a ~ day** um dia em pleno verão

midway [mɪdˈweɪ] ADJ, ADV: **~ (between)** no meio do caminho (entre)

midweek [mɪdˈwiːk] ADV no meio da semana

midwife [ˈmɪdwaɪf] (pl **midwives**) N parteira

midwifery [ˈmɪdwɪfərɪ] N trabalho de parteira, obstetrícia

midwinter [mɪdˈwɪntər] N: **in ~** em pleno inverno

midwives [ˈmɪdwaɪvz] NPL of **midwife**

might [maɪt] VB see **may** ▪ N poder m, força

mighty [ˈmaɪtɪ] ADJ poderoso, forte ▪ ADV (inf): **~ ... ...** pra burro

migraine [ˈmiːgreɪn] N enxaqueca

migrant [ˈmaɪgrənt] N (bird) ave f de arribação; (person) emigrante m/f; (fig) nômade m/f ▪ ADJ migratório; (worker) emigrante

migrate [maɪˈgreɪt] VI emigrar; (birds) arribar

migration [maɪˈgreɪʃən] N emigração f; (of birds) arribação f

mike [maɪk] N ABBR = **microphone**

mild [maɪld] ADJ (character) pacífico; (climate) temperado; (slight) ligeiro; (taste) suave; (illness) leve, benigno; (interest) pequeno ▪ N cerveja ligeira

mildew [ˈmɪldjuː] N mofo; (Bot) míldio

mildly [ˈmaɪldlɪ] ADV brandamente; (slightly) ligeiramente, um tanto; **to put it ~** (inf) para não dizer coisa pior

mildness [ˈmaɪldnɪs] N (softness) suavidade f; (gentleness) doçura; (quiet character) brandura

mile [maɪl] N milha (1609 m); **to do 30 ~s per gallon** ≈ fazer 10.64 quilômetros por litro

mileage [ˈmaɪlɪdʒ] N número de milhas; (Aut) ≈ quilometragem f; **mileage allowance** N ≈ ajuda de custo com base na quilometragem rodada

mileometer [maɪˈlɔmɪtər] (Brit) N ≈ conta-quilômetros m inv

milestone [ˈmaɪlstəun] N marco miliário; (event) marco

milieu [ˈmiːljəː] (pl **milieus** or **milieux**) N meio, meio social

milieux [ˈmiːljəːz] NPL of **milieu**

militant [ˈmɪlɪtnt] ADJ, N militante m/f

militarism [ˈmɪlɪtərɪzəm] N militarismo

militaristic [mɪlɪtəˈrɪstɪk] ADJ militarista

military [ˈmɪlɪtərɪ] ADJ militar ▪ N: **the ~** as forças armadas, os militares

militate [ˈmɪlɪteɪt] VI: **to ~ against** militar contra

militia [mɪˈlɪʃə] N milícia

milk [mɪlk] N leite m ▪ VT (cow) ordenhar; (fig) explorar, chupar; **milk chocolate** N chocolate m de leite; **milk float** (Brit) N furgão m de leiteiro

milking | **minimum**

milking ['mɪlkɪŋ] N ordenhação f, ordenha
milkman ['mɪlkman] (irreg) N leiteiro
milk shake N milk-shake m, leite m batido com sorvete
milk tooth (irreg) N dente m de leite
milk truck (US) N = **milk float**
milky ['mɪlkɪ] ADJ leitoso
Milky Way N Via Láctea
mill [mɪl] N (windmill etc) moinho; (coffee mill) moedor m de café; (factory) moinho, engenho; (spinning mill) fábrica de tecelagem, fiação f ▪ VT moer ▪ VI (also: **mill about**) aglomerar-se, remoinhar
millennia [mɪ'lɛnɪə] NPL of **millennium**
millennium [mɪ'lɛnɪəm] (pl **millenniums** or **millennia**) N milênio, milenário
miller ['mɪləʳ] N moleiro(-a)
millet ['mɪlɪt] N milhete m
milli... ['mɪlɪ] PREFIX mili...
milligram(me) ['mɪlɪɡræm] N miligrama m
millilitre ['mɪlɪliːtəʳ] (US **milliliter**) N mililitro
millimetre ['mɪlɪmiːtəʳ] (US **millimeter**) N milímetro
milliner ['mɪlɪnəʳ] N chapeleiro(-a) de senhoras
millinery ['mɪlɪnərɪ] N chapelaria de senhoras
million ['mɪljən] N milhão m; **a ~ times** um milhão de vezes
millionaire [mɪljə'nɛəʳ] N milionário(-a)
millipede ['mɪlɪpiːd] N embuá m
millstone ['mɪlstəun] N mó f, pedra (de moinho)
millwheel ['mɪlwiːl] N roda de azenha
milometer [maɪ'lɔmɪtəʳ] N = **mileometer**
mime [maɪm] N mimo; (actor) mímico(-a), comediante m/f ▪ VT imitar ▪ VI fazer mímica
mimic ['mɪmɪk] N mímico(-a), imitador(a) m/f ▪ VT imitar, parodiar
mimicry ['mɪmɪkrɪ] N imitação f; (Zool) mimetismo
Min. (Brit) ABBR (Pol) = **ministry**
min. ABBR = **minute**; (= minimum) min
minaret [mɪnə'rɛt] N minarete m
mince [mɪns] VT moer ▪ VI (in walking) andar com afetação ▪ N (Brit: Culin) carne f moída; **he does not ~ (his) words** ele não tem papas na língua
mincemeat ['mɪnsmiːt] N recheio de sebo e frutas picadas; (US: meat) carne f moída
mince pie N pastel com recheio de sebo e frutas picadas
mincer ['mɪnsəʳ] N moedor m de carne
mincing ['mɪnsɪŋ] ADJ afetado
mind [maɪnd] N mente f; (intellect) intelecto; (opinion): **to my ~** a meu ver; (sanity): **to be out of one's ~** estar fora de si ▪ VT (attend to, look after) tomar conta de, cuidar de; (be careful of) ter cuidado com; (object to): **I don't ~ the noise** o barulho não me incomoda; **do you ~ if ...?** você se incomoda se ...?; **it is on my ~** não me sai de cabeça; **to keep** or **bear sth in ~** levar algo em consideração, não esquecer-se de algo; **to make up one's ~** decidir-se; **I don't ~** (it doesn't worry me) eu nem ligo; (it's all the same to me) para

mim tanto faz; **~ you, ...** se bem que ...; **never ~!** não faz mal, não importa!; (don't worry) não se preocupe!; **to change one's ~** mudar de idéia; **to be in two ~s about sth** (Brit) estar dividido em relação a algo; **to have sb/sth in ~** ter alguém/algo em mente; **to have in ~ to do** pretender fazer; **it went right out of my ~** saiu-me totalmente da cabeça; **to bring** or **call sth to ~** lembrar algo; **"~ the step"** "cuidado com o degrau"
-minded ['maɪndɪd] SUFFIX: **fair~** imparcial, justo; **an industrially~ nation** uma nação de vocação industrial
minder ['maɪndəʳ] N (childminder) pessoa que toma conta de crianças; (bodyguard) guarda-costas m/f inv
mindful ['maɪndful] ADJ: **~ of** consciente de, atento a
mindless ['maɪndlɪs] ADJ estúpido; (violence, crime) insensato; (job) monótono

 KEYWORD

mine¹ [maɪn] PRON o meu (a minha); **that book is mine** esse livro é meu; **these cases are mine** estas caixas são minhas; **this is mine** este é meu; **yours is red, mine is green** o seu é vermelho, o meu é verde; **a friend of mine** um amigo meu

mine² N mina ▪ VT (coal) extrair, explorar; (ship, beach) minar; **mine detector** N detector m de minas
minefield ['maɪnfiːld] N campo minado; (fig) área delicada
miner ['maɪnəʳ] N mineiro
mineral ['mɪnərəl] ADJ mineral ▪ N mineral m; **minerals** NPL (Brit: soft drinks) refrigerantes mpl
mineralogy [mɪnə'rælədʒɪ] N mineralogia
mineral water N água mineral
minesweeper ['maɪnswiːpəʳ] N caça-minas m inv
mingle ['mɪŋɡl] VT misturar ▪ VI: **to ~ with** misturar-se com
mingy ['mɪndʒɪ] (inf) ADJ sovina, pão-duro inv (BR)
miniature ['mɪnətʃəʳ] ADJ em miniatura ▪ N miniatura
minibus ['mɪnɪbʌs] N microônibus m
minicab ['mɪnɪkæb] (Brit) N ≈ (táxi m) cooperativa
minicomputer ['mɪnɪkəm'pjuːtəʳ] N minicomputador m, míni m
MiniDisc® ['mɪnɪdɪsk] N MiniDisc® m
minim ['mɪnɪm] N (Mus) mínima
minima ['mɪnɪmə] NPL of **minimum**
minimal ['mɪnɪml] ADJ mínimo
minimize ['mɪnɪmaɪz] VT minimizar
minimum ['mɪnɪməm] (pl **minima**) ADJ mínimo ▪ N mínimo; **to reduce to a ~** reduzir ao minimo; **minimum lending rate** N (Econ) taxa mínima de empréstimos; **minimum wage** N

salário mínimo

mining ['maɪnɪŋ] N exploração f de minas ▪ ADJ mineiro

minion ['mɪnjən] (pej) N lacaio

miniskirt ['mɪnɪskə:t] N minissaia

minister ['mɪnɪstə^r] N (Brit: Pol) ministro(-a); (Rel) pastor m ▪ VI: **to ~ to sb** prestar assistência a alguém; **to ~ to sb's needs** atender às necessidades de alguém

ministerial [mɪnɪs'tɪərɪəl] (Brit) ADJ (Pol) ministerial

ministry ['mɪnɪstrɪ] N (Brit: Pol) ministério; (Rel): **to go into the ~** ingressar no sacerdócio

mink [mɪŋk] N marta; **mink coat** N casaco de marta

minnow ['mɪnəu] N peixinho (de água doce)

minor ['maɪnə^r] ADJ menor; (unimportant) de pouca importância; (inferior) inferior; (Mus) menor ▪ N (Law) menor m/f de idade

Minorca [mɪ'nɔ:kə] N Minorca

minority [maɪ'nɔrɪtɪ] N minoria; (age) menoridade f; **to be in a ~** estar em minoria

minster ['mɪnstə^r] N catedral f

minstrel ['mɪnstrəl] N menestrel m

mint [mɪnt] N (plant) hortelã f; (sweet) bala de hortelã ▪ VT (coins) cunhar; **the (Royal) M~** (Brit) or **the (US) M~** (US) ≈ a Casa da Moeda; **in ~ condition** em perfeito estado; **mint sauce** N molho de hortelã

minuet [mɪnju'ɛt] N minueto

miniscule ['mɪnəskju:l] ADJ minúsculo

minus ['maɪnəs] N (also: **minus sign**) sinal m de subtração ▪ PREP menos; (without) sem

minute[1] [maɪ'nju:t] ADJ miúdo, diminuto; (search) minucioso; **in ~ detail** por miúdo, em miúdos

minute[2] [n 'mɪnɪt] N minuto; (official record) ata; **minutes** NPL (of meeting) atas fpl; **it is 5 ~s past 3** são 3 e 5; **wait a ~!** (espere) minuto or minutinho!; **at the last ~** no último momento; **to leave sth till the last ~** deixar algo até em cima da hora; **up to the ~** (fashion) último; (news) de última hora; **up to the ~ technology** a última tecnologia; **minute book** N livro de atas; **minute hand** N ponteiro dos minutos

minutely [maɪ'nju:tlɪ] ADV (by a small amount) ligeiramente; (in detail) minuciosamente

miracle ['mɪrəkl] N milagre m

miraculous [mɪ'rækjuləs] ADJ milagroso

mirage ['mɪrɑ:ʒ] N miragem f

mire ['maɪə^r] N lamaçal m

mirror ['mɪrə^r] N espelho; (in car) retrovisor m ▪ VT refletir; **mirror image** N imagem f de espelho

mirth [mə:θ] N alegria; (laughter) risada

misadventure [mɪsəd'vɛntʃə^r] N desgraça, infortúnio; **death by ~** (Brit) morte acidental

misanthropist [mɪ'zænθrəpɪst] N misantropo(-a)

misapply [mɪsə'plaɪ] VT empregar mal

misapprehension [mɪsæprɪ'hɛnʃən] N mal-entendido, equívoco

misappropriate [mɪsə'prəuprɪeɪt] VT desviar

misappropriation [mɪsəprəuprɪ'eɪʃən] N desvio

misbehave [mɪsbɪ'heɪv] VI comportar-se mal

misbehaviour [mɪsbɪ'heɪvjə^r] (US **misbehavior**) N mau comportamento

misc. ABBR = **miscellaneous**

miscalculate [mɪs'kælkjuleɪt] VT calcular mal

miscalculation [mɪskælkju'leɪʃən] N erro de cálculo

miscarriage ['mɪskærɪdʒ] N (Med) aborto (espontâneo); (failure): **~ of justice** erro judicial

miscarry [mɪs'kærɪ] VI (Med) abortar espontaneamente; (fail: plans) fracassar

miscellaneous [mɪsɪ'leɪnɪəs] ADJ (items, expenses) diverso; (selection) variado

miscellany [mɪ'sɛlənɪ] N coletânea

mischance [mɪs'tʃɑ:ns] N infelicidade f, azar m

mischief ['mɪstʃɪf] N (naughtiness) travessura; (fun) diabrura; (harm) dano, prejuízo; (maliciousness) malícia

mischievous ['mɪstʃɪvəs] ADJ malicioso; (naughty) travesso; (playful) traquino

misconception [mɪskən'sɛpʃən] N concepção f errada, conceito errado

misconduct [mɪs'kɔndʌkt] N comportamento impróprio; **professional ~** má conduta profissional

misconstrue [mɪskən'stru:] VT interpretar mal

miscount [mɪs'kaunt] VT, VI contar mal

misdeed [mɪs'di:d] N delito, ofensa

misdemeanour [mɪsdɪ'mi:nə^r] (US **misdemeanor**) N má ação, contravenção f

misdirect [mɪsdɪ'rɛkt] VT (person) orientar or informar mal; (letter) endereçar mal

miser ['maɪzə^r] N avaro(-a), sovina m/f

miserable ['mɪzərəbl] ADJ (unhappy) triste; (wretched) miserável; (unpleasant: weather, person) deprimente; (contemptible: offer) desprezível; (: failure) humilhante; **to feel ~** estar na fossa, estar de baixo astral

miserably ['mɪzərəblɪ] ADV (smile, answer) tristemente; (fail, live, pay) miseravelmente

miserly ['maɪzəlɪ] ADJ avarento, mesquinho

misery ['mɪzərɪ] N (unhappiness) tristeza; (wretchedness) miséria

misfire [mɪs'faɪə^r] VI falhar

misfit ['mɪsfɪt] N (person) inadaptado(-a), deslocado(-a)

misfortune [mɪs'fɔ:tʃən] N desgraça, infortúnio

misgiving(s) [mɪs'gɪvɪŋ(z)] N(PL) (mistrust) desconfiança, receio; (apprehension) mau pressentimento; **to have misgiving(s)s about sth** ter desconfianças em relação a algo

misguided [mɪs'gaɪdɪd] ADJ enganado

mishandle [mɪs'hændl] VT (treat roughly) maltratar; (mismanage) manejar mal

mishap ['mɪshæp] N desgraça, contratempo

mishear [mɪs'hɪə^r] (irreg) VT ouvir mal

mishmash ['mɪʃmæʃ] (inf) N mixórdia, salada

misinform [mɪsɪn'fɔ:m] VT informar mal

misinterpret [mɪsɪn'tə:prɪt] VT interpretar mal

misinterpretation [mɪsɪntə:prɪ'teɪʃən] N

interpretação f errônea

misjudge [mɪs'dʒʌdʒ] VT fazer um juízo errado de, julgar mal

mislay [mɪs'leɪ] (irreg) VT extraviar, perder

mislead [mɪs'li:d] (irreg: like **lead**) VT induzir em erro, enganar

misleading [mɪs'li:dɪŋ] ADJ enganoso, errôneo

misled [mɪs'lɛd] PT, PP of **mislead**

mismanage [mɪs'mænɪdʒ] VT administrar mal; (situation) tratar de modo ineficiente

mismanagement [mɪs'mænɪdʒmənt] N má administração f

misnomer [mɪs'nəumə^r] N termo impróprio or errado

misogynist [mɪ'sɔdʒɪnɪst] N misógino

misplace [mɪs'pleɪs] VT (lose) extraviar, perder; (wrongly) colocar em lugar errado; **to be ~d** (trust etc) ser imerecido

misprint ['mɪsprɪnt] N erro tipográfico

mispronounce [mɪsprə'nauns] VT pronunciar mal

misquote [mɪs'kwəut] VT citar incorretamente

misread [mɪs'ri:d] (irreg) VT interpretar or ler mal

misrepresent [mɪsrɛprɪ'zɛnt] VT desvirtuar, deturpar

Miss [mɪs] N Senhorita (BR), a menina (PT); **Dear ~ Smith** Ilma. Srta. Smith (BR), Exma. Sra. Smith (PT)

miss [mɪs] VT (train, class, opportunity) perder; (fail to hit) errar, não acertar em; (fail to see): **you can't ~ it** e impossível não ver; (notice loss of: money etc) dar por falta de; (regret the absence of): **I ~ him** sinto a falta dele ■ VI falhar ■ N (shot) tiro perdido or errado; (fig): **that was a near ~** (near accident) essa foi por pouco; **the bus just ~ed the wall** o ônibus por pouco não bateu no muro; **you're ~ing the point** você não está entendendo

▶ **miss out** (Brit) VT omitir

▶ **miss out on** VT FUS perder, ficar por fora de

missal ['mɪsl] N missal m

misshapen [mɪs'ʃeɪpən] ADJ disforme

missile ['mɪsaɪl] N (weapon: Mil) míssil m; (: object thrown) projétil m; **missile base** N base f de mísseis; **missile launcher** [-'lɔ:ntʃə^r] N plataforma para lançamento de mísseis

missing ['mɪsɪŋ] ADJ (pupil) ausente; (thing) perdido; (removed) que está faltando; (Mil) desaparecido; **to be ~** estar desaparecido; **to go ~** desaparecer; **~ person** pessoa desaparecida

mission ['mɪʃən] N missão f; (official representatives) delegação f; **on a ~ to sb** em missão a alguém

missionary ['mɪʃənərɪ] N missionário(-a)

missive ['mɪsɪv] N missiva

misspell [mɪs'spɛl] VT (irreg: like **spell**) escrever errado, errar na ortografia de

misspent [mɪs'spɛnt] ADJ: **his ~ youth** sua juventude desperdiçada

mist [mɪst] N (light) neblina; (heavy) névoa; (at sea) bruma ■ VI (eyes: also: **mist over**) enevoar-se; (Brit: also: **mist over, mist up**: windows) embaçar

mistake [mɪs'teɪk] (irreg: like **take**) N erro, engano ■ VT entender or interpretar mal; **by ~** por engano; **to make a ~** fazer um erro; **to make a ~ about sb/sth** enganar-se a respeito de alguém/algo; **to ~ A for B** confundir A com B

mistaken [mɪs'teɪkən] PP of **mistake** ■ ADJ (idea etc) errado; (person) enganado; **to be ~** enganar-se, equivocar-se; **mistaken identity** N identidade f errada

mistakenly [mɪs'teɪkənlɪ] ADV por engano

mister ['mɪstə^r] (inf) N senhor m; see **Mr**

mistletoe ['mɪsltəu] N visco

mistook [mɪs'tuk] PT of **mistake**

mistranslation [mɪstræns'leɪʃən] N erro de tradução, tradução f incorreta

mistreat [mɪs'tri:t] VT maltratar

mistreatment [mɪs'tri:tmənt] N maus tratos mpl

mistress ['mɪstrɪs] N (lover) amante f; (of house) dona (da casa); (Brit: in school) professora, mestra; (of situation) dona; see **Mrs**

mistrust [mɪs'trʌst] VT desconfiar de ■ N: ~ **(of)** desconfiança (em relação a)

mistrustful [mɪs'trʌstful] ADJ: ~ **(of)** desconfiado (em relação a)

misty ['mɪstɪ] ADJ enevoado, nebuloso; (day) nublado; (glasses etc) embaçado

misty-eyed [-aɪd] ADJ (fig) sentimental

misunderstand [mɪsʌndə'stænd] (irreg) VT, VI entender or interpretar mal

misunderstanding [mɪsʌndə'stændɪŋ] N mal-entendido; (disagreement) desentendimento

misunderstood [mɪsʌndə'stud] PT, PP of **misunderstand**

misuse [n mɪs'ju:s, vt mɪs'ju:z] N uso impróprio; (of power) abuso; (of funds) desviar ■ VT (use wrongly) empregar mal; abusar de; desviar

MIT (US) N ABBR = **Massachusetts Institute of Technology**

mite [maɪt] N (small quantity) pingo; (Brit: small child) criancinha

miter ['maɪtə^r] (US) N = **mitre**

mitigate ['mɪtɪgeɪt] VT mitigar, atenuar; **mitigating circumstances** circunstâncias fpl atenuantes

mitigation [mɪtɪ'geɪʃən] N abrandamento, mitigação f

mitre ['maɪtə^r] (US **miter**) N mitra; (Carpentry) meia-esquadria

mitt(en) ['mɪt(n)] N mitene f

mix [mɪks] VT (gen) misturar; (combine) combinar ■ VI misturar-se; (people) entrosar-se ■ N mistura; (combination) combinação f; **to ~ sth with sth** misturar algo com algo; **to ~ business with pleasure** misturar trabalho com divertimento

▶ **mix in** VT misturar

▶ **mix up** VT (confuse: things) misturar; (: people) confundir; **to be ~ed up in sth** estar envolvido or metido em algo

mixed [mɪkst] ADJ misto; (*assorted*) sortido, variado; **mixed doubles** NPL (*Sport*) duplas *fpl* mistas; **mixed economy** N economia mista; **mixed grill** (*Brit*) N carnes *fpl* grelhadas

mixed-up ADJ (*confused*) confuso

mixer ['mɪksə'] N (*for food*) batedeira; (*person*) pessoa sociável

mixture ['mɪkstʃə'] N mistura; (*Med*) preparado

mix-up N trapalhada, confusão *f*

Mk (*Brit*) ABBR (*Tech*) = **mark**

mk ABBR = **mark** (*currency*)

mkt ABBR = **market**

MLitt N ABBR = **Master of Literature**; (= *Master of Letters*) grau universitário

MLR (*Brit*) N ABBR = **minimum lending rate**

mm ABBR (= *millimetre*) mm

MN ABBR (*Brit*) = **merchant navy**; (*US: Post*) = **Minnesota**

MO N ABBR (*Med*) = **medical officer**; (*US: inf*: = *modus operandi*) método ■ ABBR (*US: Post*) = **Missouri**

M.O. ABBR = **money order**

moan [məun] N gemido ■ VI gemer; (*inf*: *complain*): **to ~ (about)** queixar-se (de), bufar (sobre) (*inf*)

moaning ['məunɪŋ] N gemidos *mpl*; (*inf*: *complaining*) queixas *fpl*

moat [məut] N fosso

mob [mɔb] N multidão *f*; (*pej*): **the ~** (*masses*) o povinho; (*mafia*) a máfia ■ VT cercar

mob. ABBR (= *mobile phone*) cel.

mobile ['məubaɪl] ADJ móvel ■ N móvel *m*; **applicants must be ~** (*Brit*) os candidatos devem estar dispostos a aceitar qualquer deslocamento; **mobile home** N trailer *m*, casa móvel; **mobile shop** (*Brit*) N loja circulante

mobility [məu'bɪlɪtɪ] N mobilidade *f*

mobilize ['məubɪlaɪz] VT mobilizar ■ VI mobilizar-se; (*Mil*) ser mobilizado

moccasin ['mɔkəsɪn] N mocassim *m*

mock [mɔk] VT (*make ridiculous*) ridicularizar; (*laugh at*) zombar de, gozar de ■ ADJ falso, fingido; (*exam, battle*) simulado

mockery ['mɔkərɪ] N zombaria; **to make a ~ of sth** ridicularizar algo

mocking ['mɔkɪŋ] ADJ zombeteiro

mockingbird ['mɔkɪŋbəːd] N tordo-dos-remédios *m*

mock-up N maqueta, modelo

MOD (*Brit*) N ABBR = **Ministry of Defence**

mod cons [mɔd-] (*Brit*) NPL ABBR = **modern conveniences**; *see* **convenience**

mode [məud] N modo; (*of transport*) meio

model ['mɔdl] N modelo; (*Arch*) maqueta; (*person: for fashion, Art*) modelo *m/f* ■ ADJ (*car, toy*) de brinquedo; (*child, factory etc*) modelar ■ VT modelar; (*copy*): **to ~ o.s. on** mirar-se em ■ VI servir de modelo; (*in fashion*) trabalhar como modelo; **to ~ clothes** desfilar apresentando modelos; **to ~ sb/sth on** modelar alguém/algo a *or* por

modeller ['mɔdlə'] (*US* **modeler**) N modelador(a)

m/f; (*model maker*) maquetista *m/f*

model railway N trenzinho de brinquedo

modem ['məudɛm] N modem *m*

moderate [*adj, n* 'mɔdərət, *vi, vt* 'mɔdəreɪt] ADJ, N moderado(-a) ■ VI moderar-se, acalmar-se ■ VT moderar

moderately ['mɔdərətlɪ] ADV (*act*) com moderação, moderadamente; (*pleased, happy*) razoavelmente; **~ priced** de preço médio *or* razoável

moderation [mɔdə'reɪʃən] N moderação *f*; **in ~** com moderação

modern ['mɔdən] ADJ moderno; **~ languages** línguas *fpl* vivas

modernization [mɔdənaɪ'zeɪʃən] N modernização *f*

modernize ['mɔdənaɪz] VT modernizar, atualizar

modest ['mɔdɪst] ADJ modesto

modesty ['mɔdɪstɪ] N modéstia

modicum ['mɔdɪkəm] N: **a ~ of** um mínimo de

modification [mɔdɪfɪ'keɪʃən] N modificação *f*

modify ['mɔdɪfaɪ] VT modificar

Mods [mɔdz] (*Brit*) N ABBR (= (*Honour*) *Moderations*) *primeiro exame universitário (em Oxford)*

modular ['mɔdjulə'] ADJ (*filing, unit*) modular

modulate ['mɔdjuleɪt] VT modular

modulation [mɔdju'leɪʃən] N modulação *f*

module ['mɔdjuːl] N módulo

mogul ['məugl] N (*fig*) magnata *m*

MOH (*Brit*) N ABBR = **Medical Officer of Health**

mohair ['məuhɛə'] N mohair *m*, angorá *m*

Mohammed [mə'hæmɪd] N Maomé *m*

moist [mɔɪst] ADJ úmido (BR), húmido (PT), molhado

moisten ['mɔɪsn] VT umedecer (BR), humedecer (PT)

moisture ['mɔɪstʃə'] N umidade *f* (BR), humidade *f* (PT)

moisturize ['mɔɪstʃəraɪz] VT (*skin*) hidratar

moisturizer ['mɔɪstʃəraɪzə'] N creme *m* hidratante

molar ['məulə'] N molar *m*

molasses [məu'læsɪz] N melaço, melado

mold [məuld] (*US*) N, VT = **mould**

mole [məul] N (*animal*) toupeira; (*spot*) sinal *m*, lunar *m*; (*fig*) espião(-piã) *m/f*

molecule ['mɔlɪkjuːl] N molécula

molehill ['məulhɪl] N montículo (feito por uma toupeira)

molest [məu'lɛst] VT molestar; (*attack sexually*) atacar sexualmente

mollusc ['mɔləsk] N molusco

mollycoddle ['mɔlɪkɔdl] VT mimar

molt [məult] (*US*) VI = **moult**

molten ['məultən] ADJ fundido; (*lava*) liquefeito

mom [mɔm] (*US*) N = **mum**

moment ['məumənt] N momento; (*importance*) importância; **at the ~** neste momento; **for the ~** por enquanto; **in a ~** num instante; **"one ~ please"** (*Tel*) "não desligue"

momentarily ['məuməntrɪlɪ] ADV

momentaneamente; (US: soon) daqui a pouco

momentary ['məuməntəri] ADJ momentâneo

momentous [məu'mɛntəs] ADJ importantíssimo

momentum [məu'mɛntəm] N momento; (fig) ímpeto; **to gather** ~ ganhar ímpeto

mommy ['mɔmɪ] (US) N = **mummy**

Mon. ABBR (= Monday) seg., 2ª a

Monaco ['mɔnəkəu] N Mônaco (no article)

monarch ['mɔnək] N monarca m/f

monarchist ['mɔnəkɪst] N monarquista m/f

monarchy ['mɔnəkɪ] N monarquia

monastery ['mɔnəstərɪ] N mosteiro, convento

monastic [mə'næstɪk] ADJ monástico

Monday ['mʌndɪ] N segunda-feira; see also **Tuesday**

monetarist ['mʌnɪtərɪst] N monetarista m/f

monetary ['mʌnɪtərɪ] ADJ monetário

money ['mʌnɪ] N dinheiro; (currency) moeda; **to make** ~ ganhar dinheiro; **I've got no** ~ **left** não tenho mais dinheiro

moneyed ['mʌnɪd] ADJ rico, endinheirado

moneylender ['mʌnɪlɛndəʳ] N agiota m/f

moneymaking ['mʌnɪmeɪkɪŋ] ADJ lucrativo, rendoso

money market N mercado financeiro

money order N vale m (postal)

money-spinner (inf) N mina

money supply N meios mpl de pagamento, suprimento monetário

Mongol ['mɔŋgəl] N mongol m/f; (Ling) mongol m

mongol ['mɔŋgəl] ADJ, N (offensive) mongolóide m/f

Mongolia [mɔŋ'gəulɪə] N Mongólia

Mongolian [mɔŋ'gəulɪən] ADJ mongol ■ N mongol m/f; (Ling) mongol m

mongoose ['mɔŋguːs] N mangusto

mongrel ['mʌŋgrəl] N (dog) vira-lata m

monitor ['mɔnɪtəʳ] N (Sch) monitor(a) m/f; (TV, Comput) terminal m de vídeo ■ VT (heartbeat, pulse) controlar; (broadcasts, progress) monitorar

monk [mʌŋk] N monge m

monkey ['mʌŋkɪ] N macaco; **monkey business** N trapaça, travessura; **monkey nut** (Brit) N amendoim m; **monkey wrench** N chave f inglesa

mono ['mɔnəu] ADJ mono inv

mono... ['mɔnəu] PREFIX mono...

monochrome ['mɔnəkrəum] ADJ monocromático

monocle ['mɔnəkl] N monóculo

monogram ['mɔnəgræm] N monograma m

monolith ['mɔnəlɪθ] N monólito

monologue ['mɔnəlɔg] N monólogo

monoplane ['mɔnəpleɪn] N monoplano

monopolize [mə'nɔpəlaɪz] VT monopolizar

monopoly [mə'nɔpəlɪ] N monopólio; **Monopolies and Mergers Commission** (Brit) comissão de inquérito sobre os monopólios

monorail ['mɔnəureɪl] N monotrilho

monosodium glutamate [mɔnə'səudɪəm

'gluːtəmeɪt] N glutamato de monossódio

monosyllabic [mɔnəusɪ'læbɪk] ADJ monossilábico; (person) lacônico

monosyllable ['mɔnəsɪləbl] N monossílabo

monotone ['mɔnətəun] N monotonia; **to speak in a** ~ falar num tom monótono

monotonous [mə'nɔtənəs] ADJ monótono

monotony [mə'nɔtənɪ] N monotonia

monoxide [mɔ'nɔksaɪd] N see **carbon monoxide**

monsoon [mɔn'suːn] N monção f

monster ['mɔnstəʳ] N monstro

monstrosity [mɔns'trɔsɪtɪ] N monstruosidade f

monstrous ['mɔnstrəs] ADJ (huge) descomunal; (atrocious) monstruoso

montage [mɔn'tɑːʒ] N montagem f

Mont Blanc [mɔ̃blɑ̃] N Monte m Branco

Montevideo ['mɔntevi'deɪəu] N Montevidéu

month [mʌnθ] N mês m; **every** ~ todo mês; **300 dollars a** ~ 300 dólares mensais or por mês

monthly ['mʌnθlɪ] ADJ mensal ■ ADV mensalmente ■ N (magazine) revista mensal; **twice** ~ duas vezes por mês

monument ['mɔnjumənt] N monumento

monumental [mɔnju'mɛntl] ADJ monumental; (terrific) terrível; **monumental mason** N marmorista m/f

moo [muː] VI mugir

mood [muːd] N humor m; (of crowd) atmosfera; **to be in a good/bad** ~ estar de bom/mau humor; **to be in the** ~ **for** estar a fim or com vontade de

moody ['muːdɪ] ADJ (variable) caprichoso, de veneta; (sullen) rabugento

moon [muːn] N lua

moonbeam ['muːnbiːm] N raio de lua

moon landing N alunissagem f

moonlight ['muːnlaɪt] N luar m ■ VI ter dois empregos, ter um bico

moonlighting ['muːnlaɪtɪŋ] N trabalho adicional, bico

moonlit ['muːnlɪt] ADJ enluarado; **a** ~ **night** uma noite de lua

moonshot ['muːnʃɔt] N (Space) lançamento de nave para a lua

moonstruck ['muːnstrʌk] ADJ lunático, aluado

Moor [muəʳ] N mouro(-a)

moor [muəʳ] N charneca ■ VT (ship) amarrar ■ VI fundear, atracar

mooring ['muərɪŋ] N (place) ancoradouro; **moorings** NPL (chains) amarras fpl

Moorish ['muərɪʃ] ADJ mouro; (architecture) mourisco

moorland ['muələnd] N charneca

moose [muːs] N INV alce m

moot [muːt] VT levantar ■ ADJ: ~ **point** ponto discutível

mop [mɔp] N esfregão m; (for dishes) esponja com cabeça; (of hair) grenha ■ VT esfregar

▶ **mop up** VT limpar

mope [məup] VI estar or andar deprimido or desanimado

▶ **mope about** VI andar por aí desanimado

▶ **mope around** vi = **mope about**
moped ['məʊpɛd] N moto f pequena (BR), motorizada (PT)
moral ['mɔrl] ADJ moral ■ N moral f; **morals** NPL (principles) moralidade f, costumes mpl
morale [mɔ'rɑːl] N moral f, estado de espírito
morality [mə'rælıtı] N moralidade f; (correctness) retidão f, probidade f
moralize ['mɔrəlaız] vi: **to ~ (about)** dar lições de moral (sobre)
morally ['mɔrəlı] ADV moralmente
morass [mə'ræs] N pântano, brejo
moratorium [mɔrə'tɔːrıəm] (pl **moratoriums** or **moratoria**) N moratória
morbid ['mɔːbıd] ADJ mórbido

◯ **KEYWORD**

more [mɔːr] ADJ **1** (greater in number etc) mais; **more people/work/letters than we expected** mais pessoas/trabalho/cartas do que esperávamos; **I have more wine/money than you** tenho mais vinho/dinheiro do que você **2** (additional) mais; **do you want (some) more tea?** você quer mais chá?; **I have no** or **I don't have any more money** não tenho mais dinheiro; **it'll take a few more weeks** levará mais algumas semanas
■ PRON **1** (greater amount) mais; **more than 10** mais de 10; **it cost more than we expected** custou mais do que esperávamos **2** (further or additional amount) mais; **is there any more?** tem ainda mais?; **there's no more** não tem mais; **many/much more** muitos/muito mais
■ ADV mais; **more dangerous/difficult** etc **than** mais perigoso/difícil etc do que; **more easily/economically/quickly (than)** mais fácil/econômico/rápido(do que); **more and more** cada vez mais; **more or less** mais ou menos; **more than ever** mais do que nunca; **more beautiful than ever** mais bonito do que nunca

moreover [mɔː'rəʊvər] ADV além do mais, além disso
morgue [mɔːg] N necrotério
MORI ['mɔrı] (Brit) N ABBR (= Market and Opinion Research Institute) ≈ IBOPE m
moribund ['mɔrıbʌnd] ADJ agonizante
Mormon ['mɔːmən] N mórmon m/f
morning ['mɔːnıŋ] N manhã f; (early morning) madrugada ■ CPD da manhã; **good ~** bom dia; **in the ~** de manhã; **7 o'clock in the ~** (as) 7 da manhã; **3 o'clock in the ~** (as) 3 da madrugada; **tomorrow ~** amanhã de manhã; **this ~** hoje de manhã; **morning sickness** N náusea matinal
Moroccan [mə'rɔkən] ADJ, N marroquino(-a)
Morocco [mə'rɔkəʊ] N Marrocos m
moron ['mɔːrɔn] (inf) N débil mental m/f, idiota m/f
moronic [mə'rɔnık] ADJ imbecil, idiota

morose [mə'rəʊs] ADJ taciturno, rabugento
morphine ['mɔːfiːn] N morfina
Morse [mɔːs] N (also: **Morse code**) código Morse
morsel ['mɔːsl] N (of food) bocado
mortal ['mɔːtl] ADJ, N mortal m/f
mortality [mɔː'tælıtı] N mortalidade f; **mortality rate** N (taxa de) mortalidade f
mortar ['mɔːtər] N (cannon) morteiro; (Constr) argamassa; (dish) pilão m, almofariz m
mortgage ['mɔːgıdʒ] N hipoteca; (for house) financiamento ■ vt hipotecar; **to take out a ~** fazer um crédito imobiliário; **mortgage company** (US) N sociedade f de crédito imobiliário
mortgagee [mɔːgə'dʒiː] N credor(a) m/f hipotecário(-a)
mortgagor ['mɔːgədʒər] N devedor(a) m/f hipotecário(-a)
mortician [mɔː'tıʃən] (US) N agente m/f funerário(-a)
mortified ['mɔːtıfaıd] ADJ morto de vergonha
mortify ['mɔːtıfaı] vt motrificar
mortise lock ['mɔːtıs-] N fechadura embutida
mortuary ['mɔːtjuərı] N necrotério
mosaic [məʊ'zeıık] N mosaico
Moscow ['mɔskəʊ] N Moscou (BR), Moscovo (PT)
Moslem ['mɔzləm] ADJ, N = **Muslim**
mosque [mɔsk] N mesquita
mosquito [mɔs'kiːtəʊ] (pl **mosquitoes**) N mosquito; **mosquito net** N mosquiteiro
moss [mɔs] N musgo
mossy ['mɔsı] ADJ musgoso, musguento

◯ **KEYWORD**

most [məʊst] ADJ **1** (almost all: people, things etc) a maior parte de, a maioria de; **most people** a maioria das pessoas **2** (largest, greatest: interest) máximo; (money): **who has (the) most money?** quem é que tem mais dinheiro?; **he derived the most pleasure from her visit** ele teve o maior prazer em recebê-la
■ PRON (greatest quantity, number) a maior parte, a maioria; **most of it/them** a maioria dele/deles; **most of the money** a maior parte do dinheiro; **most of her friends** a maioria dos seus amigos; **do the most you can** faça o máximo que você puder; **I saw the most** vi mais; **to make the most of sth** aproveitar algo ao máximo; **at the (very) most** quando muito, no máximo
■ ADV (+vb) o mais; (+adj): **the most intelligent/expensive** etc o mais inteligente/ caro etc; (+adv: carefully, easily etc) o mais; (very: polite, interesting etc) muito; **a most interesting book** um livro interessantíssimo

mostly ['məʊstlı] ADV principalmente, na maior parte
MOT (Brit) N ABBR = **Ministry of Transport; the ~ (test)** vistoria anual dos veículos automotores

motel [məu'tɛl] N motel *m*

moth [mɔθ] N mariposa; (*clothes moth*) traça

mothball ['mɔθbɔ:l] N bola de naftalina

moth-eaten ADJ roído pelas traças

mother ['mʌðər] N mãe *f* ■ ADJ materno ■ VT (*care for*) cuidar de (como uma mãe); **mother board** N (*Comput*) placa-base *f*

motherhood ['mʌðəhud] N maternidade *f*

mother-in-law (*pl* mothers-in-law) N sogra

motherly ['mʌðəlɪ] ADJ maternal

mother-of-pearl N madrepérola

mother-to-be (*pl* mothers-to-be) N futura mamãe *f*

mother tongue N língua materna

mothproof ['mɔθpruːf] ADJ à prova de traças

motif [məu'tiːf] N motivo

motion ['məuʃən] N movimento; (*gesture*) gesto, sinal *m*; (*at meeting*) moção *f*; (*Brit: of bowels*) fezes *fpl* ■ VT, VI: **to ~ (to) sb to do sth** fazer sinal a alguém para que faça algo; **to be in ~** (*vehicle*) estar em movimento; **to set in ~** pôr em movimento; **to go through the ~s of doing sth** (*fig*) fazer algo automaticamente *or* sem convicção

motionless ['məuʃənlɪs] ADJ imóvel

motion picture N filme *m* (cinematográfico)

motivate ['məutɪveɪt] VT motivar

motivated ['məutɪveɪtɪd] ADJ: **~ (by)** motivado (por)

motivation [məutɪ'veɪʃən] N motivação *f*

motive ['məutɪv] N motivo ■ ADJ motor/motriz; **from the best (of) ~s** com as melhores intenções

motley ['mɔtlɪ] ADJ variado, heterogêneo

motor ['məutər] N motor *m*; (*Brit: inf: vehicle*) carro, automóvel *m* ■ CPD (*industry*) de automóvel ■ ADJ motor/motriz

motorbike ['məutəbaɪk] N moto(cicleta) *f*, motoca (*inf*)

motorboat ['məutəbəut] N barco a motor

motorcar ['məutəkaː] (*Brit*) N carro, automóvel *m*

motorcoach ['məutəkəutʃ] N ônibus *m* turístico

motorcycle ['məutəsaɪkl] N motocicleta; **motorcycle racing** N corrida de motocicleta

motorcyclist ['məutəsaɪklɪst] N motociclista *m/f*

motoring ['məutərɪŋ] (*Brit*) N automobilismo ■ ADJ (*accident, offence*) de trânsito; **~ holiday** passeio de carro

motorist ['məutərɪst] N motorista *m/f*

motorize ['məutəraɪz] VT motorizar

motor oil N óleo de motor

motor racing (*Brit*) N corrida de carros, automobilismo

motor scooter N lambreta (BR), motoreta (PT)

motor vehicle N automóvel *m*, veículo automotor

motorway ['məutəweɪ] (*Brit*) N rodovia (BR), autoestrada (PT)

mottled ['mɔtld] ADJ mosqueado, em furta cores

motto ['mɔtəu] (*pl* mottoes) N lema *m*

mould [məuld] (*US* mold) N molde *m*; (*mildew*) mofo, bolor *m* ■ VT moldar; (*fig*) moldar

mo(u)lder ['məuldər] VI (*decay*) desfazer-se

mo(u)lding ['məuldɪŋ] N moldura

mo(u)ldy ['məuldɪ] ADJ mofado

moult [məult] (*US* molt) VI mudar (de penas *etc*)

mound [maund] N (*of earth*) monte *m*; (*of blankets, leaves etc*) pilha, montanha

mount [maunt] N monte *m*; (*horse*) montaria; (*for jewel etc*) engaste *m*; (*for picture*) moldura ■ VT (*horse etc*) montar em, subir a; (*stairs*) subir; (*exhibition*) montar; (*attack*) montar, desfechar; (*picture*) emoldurar ■ VI (*increase*) aumentar
▶ **mount up** VI aumentar

mountain ['mauntɪn] N montanha ■ CPD de montanha; **to make a ~ out of a molehill** (*fig*) fazer um bicho de sete cabeças *or* um cavalo de batalha (de algo)

mountaineer [mauntɪ'nɪər] N alpinista *m/f*, montanhista *m/f*

mountaineering [mauntɪ'nɪərɪŋ] N alpinismo; **to go ~** praticar o alpinismo

mountainous ['mauntɪnəs] ADJ montanhoso

mountain rescue team N equipe *m* de socorro para alpinistas

mountainside ['mauntɪnsaɪd] N lado da montanha

mounted ['mauntɪd] ADJ montado

Mount Everest N monte *m* Everest

mourn [mɔːn] VT chorar, lamentar ■ VI: **to ~ for** chorar *or* lamentar a morte de

mourner ['mɔːnər] N parente(-a) *m/f or* amigo(-a) do defunto

mournful ['mɔːnful] ADJ desolado, triste

mourning ['mɔːnɪŋ] N luto ■ CPD (*dress*) de luto; **(to be) in ~** (estar) de luto

mouse [maus] (*pl* mice) N camundongo (BR), rato (PT); (*Comput*) mouse *m*; **mouse mat, mouse pad** N (*Comput*) mouse pad *m*

mousetrap ['maustræp] N ratoeira

mousse [muːs] N musse *f*

moustache [məs'taːʃ] (*US* mustache) N bigode *m*

mousy ['mausɪ] ADJ (*person*) tímido; (*hair*) pardacento

mouth [mauθ, *pl* mauðz] N boca; (*of cave, hole*) entrada; (*of river*) desembocadura

mouthful ['mauθful] N bocado

mouth organ N gaita

mouthpiece ['mauθpiːs] N (*of musical instrument*) bocal *m*; (*representative*) porta-voz *m/f*

mouth-to-mouth ADJ: **~ resuscitation** respiração *f* boca a boca

mouthwash ['mauθwɔʃ] N colutório

mouth-watering ADJ de dar água na boca

movable ['muːvəbl] ADJ móvel

move [muːv] N (*movement*) movimento; (*in game*) lance *m*, jogada; (*: turn to play*) turno, vez *f*; (*change: of house, job*) mudança ■ VT (*change position of*) mudar; (*: in game*) jogar; (*hand etc*) mexer, mover; (*from one place to another*) deslocar;

(*emotionally*) comover; (*Pol: resolution etc*) propor
■ vɪ mexer-se, mover-se; (*traffic*) circular;
(*also:* **move house**) mudar-se; (*develop: situation*)
desenvolver; **to ~ sb to do sth** convencer
alguém a fazer algo; **to get a ~ on** apressar-se;
to be ~d (*emotionally*) ficar comovido
▶ **move about** vɪ (*fidget*) mexer-se; (*travel*)
deslocar-se
▶ **move along** vɪ avançar
▶ **move around** vɪ = **move about**
▶ **move away** vɪ afastar-se
▶ **move back** vɪ (*step back*) recuar; (*return*) voltar
▶ **move down** vɪ abaixar; (*demote*) rebaixar
▶ **move forward** vɪ avançar ■ vɪ adiantar
▶ **move in** vɪ (*to a house*) instalar-se (numa
casa)
▶ **move off** vɪ partir
▶ **move on** vɪ ir andando ■ vɪ (*onlookers*)
afastar
▶ **move out** vɪ (*of house*) sair (de uma casa)
▶ **move over** vɪ afastar-se; **~ over!** (*towards
speaker*) chega mais para cá!; (*away from speaker*)
chega mais para lá!
▶ **move up** vɪ subir; (*employee*) ser promovido;
(*move aside*) chegar mais para lá *or* cá
moveable ['muːvəbl] ADJ = **movable**
movement ['muːvmənt] N movimento; (*gesture*)
gesto; (*of goods*) transporte *m*; (*in attitude, policy*)
mudança; (*Tech*) mecanismo; (*Med: also:* **bowel
movement**) defecação *f*
mover ['muːvə'] N autor(a) *m/f* de proposta
movie ['muːvɪ] N filme *m*; **to go to the ~s**
ir ao cinema; **movie camera** N câmara
cinematográfica
moviegoer ['muːvɪɡəʊə'] (*US*) N
freqüentador(a) *m/f* de cinema
moving ['muːvɪŋ] ADJ (*emotional*) comovente;
(*that moves*) móvel; (*in motion*) em movimento
■ N (*US*) mudança
mow [məʊ] (*pt* mowed, *pp* mown) vɪ (*grass*)
cortar; (*corn*) ceifar
▶ **mow down** vɪ ceifar; (*massacre*) chacinar
mower ['məʊə'] N ceifeira; (*also:* **lawnmower**)
cortador *m* de grama (BR) *or* de relva (PT)
mown [məʊn] PP *of* **mow**
Mozambique [məʊzəm'biːk] N Moçambique
m (*no article*)
MP N ABBR (= *Military Police*) PM *f*; (*Brit*) = **Member
of Parliament**; (*Canadian*) = **Mounted Police**
MP3 player N tocador *m* MP3
mpg N ABBR = **miles per gallon** (*30 mpg = 10.64
km/l*)
mph ABBR = **miles per hour** (*60 mph = 96 km/h*)
MPhil N ABBR (= *Master of Philosophy*) grau
universitário
MPS (*Brit*) N ABBR = **Member of the
Pharmaceutical Society**
Mr ['mɪstə'] (*US* Mr.) N: **Mr Smith** (o) Sr. Smith
MRC (*Brit*) N ABBR = **Medical Research Council**
MRCP (*Brit*) N ABBR = **Member of the Royal
College of Physicians**
MRCS (*Brit*) N ABBR = **Member of the Royal**

College of Surgeons
MRCVS (*Brit*) N ABBR = **Member of the Royal
College of Veterinary Surgeons**
Mrs ['mɪsɪz] (*US* Mrs.) N: **~ Smith** (a) Sra. Smith
MS N ABBR (= *manuscript*) ms; = **multiple
sclerosis**; (*US:* = *Master of Science*) grau universitário
■ ABBR (*US: Post*) = **Mississippi**
Ms [mɪz] (*US* Ms.) N (= *Miss or Mrs*): **Ms X** (a) Sa X

> **M s**
>
> *Ms* é um título utilizado em lugar de *Mrs*
> (senhora) ou de *Miss* (senhorita) para evitar
> a distinção tradicional entre mulheres
> casadas e solteiras. É aceito, portanto,
> como o equivalente de *Mr* (senhor) para
> os homens. Muitas vezes reprovado por
> ter surgido como manifestação de um
> feminismo exacerbado, é uma forma de
> tratamento muito comum hoje em dia.

MSA (*US*) N ABBR (= *Master of Science in Agriculture*)
grau universitário
MSc N ABBR = **Master of Science**
MSG N ABBR = **monosodium glutamate**
MST (*US*) ABBR (= *Mountain Standard Time*) hora de
inverno das montanhas Rochosas
MSW (*US*) N ABBR (= *Master of Social Work*) grau
universitário
MT N ABBR = **machine translation** ■ ABBR (*US:
Post*) = **Montana**
Mt ABBR (*Geo:* = *mount*) Mt

🄞 KEYWORD

much [mʌtʃ] ADJ (*time, money, effort*) muito; **how
much money/time do you need?** quanto
dinheiro/tempo você precisa?; **he's done so
much work for the charity** ele trabalhou
muito para a obra de caridade; **as much as**
tanto como
■ PRON muito; **there isn't much to do** não
há muito o que fazer; **much has been gained
from our discussions** nossas discussões
foram muito proveitosas; **how much does it
cost?** — **too much** quanto custa isso? — caro
demais; **how much is it?** quanto é?, quanto
custa?
■ ADV **1** (*greatly, a great deal*) muito; **thank you
very much** muito obrigado(-a); **we are very
much looking forward to your visit** estamos
aguardando a sua visita com muito ansiedade;
he is very much the gentleman/politician
ele é muito cavalheiro/político; **as much as**
tanto como; **I read as much as possible/as
I can/as ever** leio o máximo possível/que
eu posso/como nunca; **he is as much part
of the community as you** ele faz parte da
comunidade tanto quanto você
2 (*by far*) de longe; **I'm much better now** estou
bem melhor agora
3 (*almost*) quase; **the view is much as it was 10**

years ago a vista é quase a mesma que há dez anos; **how are you feeling?** — **much the same** como você está (se sentindo)? — do mesmo jeito

muck [mʌk] N (*dirt*) sujeira (BR), sujidade f (PT); (*manure*) estrume m; (*fig*) porcaria
▸ **muck about** (*inf*) VI (*fool about*) fazer besteiras; (*waste time*) fazer cera; (*tinker*) mexer
▸ **muck around** VI = **muck about**
▸ **muck in** (Brit: *inf*) VI dar uma ajuda
▸ **muck out** VT (*stable*) limpar
▸ **muck up** (*inf*) VT (*ruin*) estragar; (*dirty*) sujar
muckraking ['mʌkreɪkɪŋ] (*inf*) N (*Press*) sensacionalismo
mucky ['mʌkɪ] ADJ (*dirty*) sujo
mucus ['mjuːkəs] N muco
mud [mʌd] N lama
muddle ['mʌdl] N confusão f, bagunça; (*mix-up*) trapalhada ▪ VT (*also:* **muddle up:** *person, story*) confundir; (: *things*) misturar; **to be in a ~** (*person*) estar confuso; **to get in a ~** (*while explaining etc*) enrolar-se
▸ **muddle along** VI viver sem rumo
▸ **muddle through** VI virar-se
muddle-headed [-'hɛdɪd] ADJ (*person*) confuso
muddy ['mʌdɪ] ADJ (*road*) lamacento; (*person, clothes*) enlameado
mud flats NPL extensão f de terra lamacenta
mudguard ['mʌdɡɑːd] N pára-lama m
mudpack ['mʌdpæk] N máscara (de beleza)
mud-slinging [-slɪŋɪŋ] N difamação f, injúria
muesli ['mjuːzlɪ] N muesli m
muff [mʌf] N regalo ▪ VT (*chance*) desperdiçar, perder; (*lines*) estropiar
muffin ['mʌfɪn] N *bolinho redondo e chato*
muffle ['mʌfl] VT (*sound*) abafar; (*against cold*) agasalhar
muffled ['mʌfld] ADJ abafado, surdo
muffler ['mʌflər] N (*scarf*) cachecol m; (*US: Aut*) silencioso (BR), panela de escape (PT)
mufti ['mʌftɪ] N: **in ~** vestido à paisana
mug [mʌɡ] N (*cup*) caneca; (: *for beer*) caneco, canecão; (*inf: face*) careta; (: *fool*) bobo(-a) ▪ VT (*assault*) assaltar
▸ **mug up** (Brit: *inf*) VT (*also:* **mug up on**) decorar
mugger ['mʌɡər] N assaltante m/f
mugging ['mʌɡɪŋ] N assalto
muggy ['mʌɡɪ] ADJ abafado
mulatto [mjuː'lætəu] (*pl* **mulattoes**) N mulato(-a)
mulberry ['mʌlbrɪ] N (*fruit*) amora; (*tree*) amoreira
mule [mjuːl] N mula
mulled [mʌld] ADJ: **~ wine** quentão m
mull over [mʌl-] VT meditar sobre
multi... [mʌltɪ] PREFIX multi...
multi-access ADJ (*Comput*) de múltiplo acesso
multicoloured ['mʌltɪkʌləd] (US **multicolored**) ADI multicolor
multifarious [mʌltɪ'fɛərɪəs] ADJ diverso, variado

multilateral [mʌltɪ'lætrəl] ADJ (*Pol*) multilateral
multi-level (US) ADJ = **multistorey**
multimedia [mʌltɪ'miːdɪə] ADJ multimídia
multimillionaire [mʌltɪmɪljə'nɛər] N multimilionário(-a)
multinational [mʌltɪ'næʃənl] N multinacional f ▪ ADJ multinacional
multiple ['mʌltɪpl] ADJ múltiplo ▪ N múltiplo; **multiple choice** N múltipla escolha; **multiple crash** N engavetamento; **multiple sclerosis** N esclerose f múltipla
multiplication [mʌltɪplɪ'keɪʃən] N multiplicação f; **multiplication table** N tabela de multiplicação
multiplicity [mʌltɪ'plɪsɪtɪ] N multiplicidade f
multiply ['mʌltɪplaɪ] VT multiplicar ▪ VI multiplicar-se
multiracial [mʌltɪ'reɪʃl] ADJ multirracial
multistorey ['mʌltɪ'stɔːrɪ] (Brit) ADJ de vários andares
multitude ['mʌltɪtjuːd] N multidão f; (*large number*): **a ~ of** um grande número de
mum [mʌm] N (Brit: *inf*) mamãe f ▪ ADJ: **to keep ~** ficar calado; **~'s the word!** bico calado!
mumble ['mʌmbl] VT, VI resmungar, murmurar
mummify ['mʌmɪfaɪ] VT mumificar
mummy ['mʌmɪ] N (Brit: *mother*) mamãe f; (*embalmed*) múmia
mumps [mʌmps] N caxumba
munch [mʌntʃ] VT, VI mascar
mundane [mʌn'deɪn] ADJ banal, mundano
municipal [mjuː'nɪsɪpl] ADJ municipal
municipality [mjuːnɪsɪ'pælɪtɪ] N municipalidade f; (*area*) município
munitions [mjuː'nɪʃənz] NPL munições fpl
mural ['mjuərl] N mural m
murder ['məːdər] N assassinato; (*Law*) homicídio ▪ VT assassinar; (*spoil*) estragar; **to commit ~** cometer um assassinato
murderer ['məːdərər] N assassino
murderess ['məːdərɪs] N assassina
murderous ['məːdərəs] ADJ homicida
murk [məːk] N escuridão f
murky ['məːkɪ] ADJ escuro; (*water*) turvo; (*fig*) sombrio
murmur ['məːmər] N murmúrio ▪ VT, VI murmurar; **heart ~** (*Med*) sopro cardíaco *or* no coração
MusB(ac) N ABBR (= *Bachelor of Music*) grau universitário
muscle ['mʌsl] N músculo; (*fig: strength*) força (muscular)
▸ **muscle in** VI imiscuir-se, impor-se
muscular ['mʌskjulər] ADJ muscular; (*person*) musculoso; **muscular dystrophy** N distrofia muscular
MusD(oc) N ABBR (= *Doctor of Music*) grau universitário
muse [mjuːz] VI meditar ▪ N musa
museum [mjuː'zɪəm] N museu m

mush [mʌʃ] N pasta, papa; (fig) pieguice f
mushroom ['mʌʃrum] N cogumelo ▪ vi (fig)
crescer da noite para o dia, pipocar
mushy ['mʌʃi] ADJ mole; (pej) piegas inv
music ['mju:zik] N música; **music box** N
caixinha de música
musical ['mju:zikl] ADJ (of music, person) musical;
(harmonious) melodioso ▪ N (show) musical m;
musical instrument N instrumento musical
music hall N teatro de variedades
musician [mju:'zɪʃən] N músico(-a)
music stand N atril m, estante f de música
musk [mʌsk] N almíscar m
musket ['mʌskɪt] N mosquete m
muskrat ['mʌskræt] N rato almiscarado
musk rose N (Bot) rosa-moscada
Muslim ['mʌzlɪm] ADJ, N muçulmano(-a)
muslin ['mʌzlɪn] N musselina
musquash ['mʌskwɔʃ] N rato almiscarado; (fur)
pele f de rato almiscarado
mussel ['mʌsl] N mexilhão m
must [mʌst] AUX VB (obligation): **I ~ do it**
tenho que or devo fazer isso; (probability):
he ~ be there by now ele já deve estar lá;
(suggestion, invitation): **you ~ come and see
me soon** você tem que vir me ver em breve;
(indicating sth unwelcome): **why ~ he behave so
badly?** por que ele tem que se comportar tão
mal? ▪ N (necessity) necessidade f; **it's a ~ é**
imprescindível; **I ~ have made a mistake** eu
devo ter feito um erro
mustache ['mʌstæʃ] (US) N = **moustache**
mustard ['mʌstəd] N mostarda; **mustard gas** N
gás m de mostarda
muster ['mʌstəʳ] VT (support) reunir; (energy)
juntar; (Mil) formar; (also: **muster up**: strength,
courage) criar, juntar
mustiness ['mʌstɪnɪs] N mofo
mustn't ['mʌsnt] = **must not**
musty ['mʌsti] ADJ mofado, com cheiro de
bolor
mutant ['mju:tənt] ADJ, N mutante m/f
mutate [mju:'teɪt] VI sofrer mutação genética
mutation [mju:'teɪʃən] N mutação f
mute [mju:t] ADJ, N mudo(-a)
muted ['mju:tɪd] ADJ (colour) suave; (reaction)

moderado; (noise, Mus) abafado; (criticism) velado
mutilate ['mju:tɪleɪt] VT mutilar
mutilation [mju:tɪ'leɪʃən] N mutilação f
mutinous ['mju:tɪnəs] ADJ (troops) amotinado;
(attitude) rebelde
mutiny ['mju:tɪnɪ] N motim m, rebelião f ▪ vi
amotinar-se
mutter ['mʌtəʳ] VT, VI resmungar, murmurar
mutton ['mʌtn] N carne f de carneiro
mutual ['mju:tʃuəl] ADJ mútuo; (shared)
comum
mutually ['mju:tʃuəlɪ] ADV mutuamente,
reciprocamente
muzzle ['mʌzl] N (of animal) focinho; (guard: for
dog) focinheira; (of gun) boca ▪ VT (press etc)
amordaçar; (dog) pôr focinheira em
MVP (US) N ABBR (Sport) = **most valuable player**
MW ABBR (= medium wave) OM

○ **KEYWORD**

my [maɪ] ADJ meu/minha; **this is my house/
car/brother** esta é a minha casa/meu carro/
meu irmão; **I've washed my hair/cut my
finger** lavei meu cabelo/cortei meu dedo; **is
this my pen or yours?** esta caneta é minha
ou sua?

myopic [maɪ'ɔpɪk] ADJ míope
myriad ['mɪrɪəd] N miríade f
myself [maɪ'sɛlf] PRON (reflexive) me; (emphatic)
eu mesmo; (after prep) mim mesmo; see also
oneself
mysterious [mɪs'tɪərɪəs] ADJ misterioso
mystery ['mɪstərɪ] N mistério; **mystery story** N
romance m policial
mystic ['mɪstɪk] ADJ, N místico(-a)
mystical ['mɪstɪkl] ADJ místico
mystify ['mɪstɪfaɪ] VT (perplex) mistificar,
confundir; (disconcert) desconcertar
mystique [mɪs'ti:k] N mística
myth [mɪθ] N mito
mythical ['mɪθɪkəl] ADJ mítico
mythological [mɪθə'lɔdʒɪkl] ADJ mitológico
mythology [mɪ'θɔlədʒɪ] N mitologia

Nn

N, n [ɛn] N (*letter*) N, n *m*; **N for Nellie** (*Brit*) or **Nan** (*US*) N de Nair

N ABBR (= *north*) N

NA (*US*) N ABBR (= *Narcotics Anonymous*) associação de assistência aos toxicômanos; = **National Academy**

n/a ABBR = **not applicable**; (*Comm etc*) = **no account**

NAACP (*US*) N ABBR = **National Association for the Advancement of Colored People**

NAAFI ['næfɪ] (*Brit*) N ABBR (= *Navy, Army & Air Force Institute*) órgão responsável pelas lojas e cantinas do exército

nab [næb] (*inf*) VT pegar, prender

NACU (*US*) N ABBR = **National Association of Colleges and Universities**

nadir ['neɪdɪər] N (*Astronomy, fig*) nadir *m*

nag [næg] N (*pej: horse*) rocim *m* ■ VT ralhar, apoquentar

nagging ['nægɪŋ] ADJ (*doubt*) persistente; (*pain*) contínuo ■ N queixas *fpl*, censuras *fpl*, apoquentação *f*

nail [neɪl] N (*human*) unha; (*metal*) prego ■ VT pregar; **to ~ sb down to a date/price** conseguir que alguém se defina sobre a data/o preço; **to pay cash on the ~** (*Brit*) pagar na bucha*

nailbrush ['neɪlbrʌʃ] N escova de unhas

nailfile ['neɪlfaɪl] N lixa de unhas

nail polish N esmalte *m* (BR) or verniz *m* (PT) de unhas

nail polish remover N removedor *m* de esmalte (BR) or verniz (PT)

nail scissors NPL tesourinha de unhas

nail varnish (*Brit*) N = **nail polish**

Nairobi [naɪˈrəʊbɪ] N Nairóbi

naïve [naɪˈiːv] ADJ ingênuo

naïveté [naɪˈiːvteɪ] N = **naivety**

naïvety [naɪˈiːvətɪ] N ingenuidade *f*

naked ['neɪkɪd] ADJ nu(a); **with the ~ eye** a olho nu

nakedness ['neɪkɪdnɪs] N nudez *f*

NAM (*US*) N ABBR = **National Association of Manufacturers**

name [neɪm] N nome *m*; (*surname*) sobrenome *m*; (*reputation*) reputação *f*, fama ■ VT (*child*) pôr nome em; (*criminal*) apontar; (*appoint*) nomear; (*price*) fixar; (*date*) marcar; **what's your ~?** qual

é o seu nome?, como (você) se chama?; **my ~ is Peter** eu me chamo Peter; **by ~** de nome; **in the ~ of** em nome de; **to give one's ~ and address** (*to police etc*) dar o seu nome e endereço; **to make a ~ for o.s.** fazer nome; **to get (o.s.) a bad ~** fazer má reputação; **to call sb ~s** xingar alguém

name-dropping [-ˈdrɔpɪŋ] N: **she loves ~** ela adora esnobar conhecimento de gente importante

nameless ['neɪmlɪs] ADJ (*unknown*) sem nome; (*anonymous*) anônimo

namely ['neɪmlɪ] ADV a saber, isto é

nameplate ['neɪmpleɪt] N (*on door etc*) placa

namesake ['neɪmseɪk] N xará *m/f* (BR), homónimo(-a) (PT)

nanny ['nænɪ] N babá *f*; **nanny goat** N cabra

nap [næp] N (*sleep*) soneca; (*of cloth*) felpa ■ VI: **to be caught ~ping** ser pego de surpresa

NAPA (*US*) N ABBR (= *National Association of Performing Artists*) sindicato dos artistas de teatro e de cinema

napalm ['neɪpɑːm] N napalm *m*

nape [neɪp] N: **~ of the neck** nuca

napkin ['næpkɪn] N (*also: table napkin*) guardanapo

nappy ['næpɪ] (*Brit*) N fralda; **nappy liner** (*Brit*) N gaze *f*; **nappy rash** (*Brit*) N assadura

narcissi [nɑːˈsɪsaɪ] NPL of **narcissus**

narcissistic [nɑːsɪˈsɪstɪk] ADJ narcisista

narcissus [nɑːˈsɪsəs] (*pl* **narcissi**) N narciso

narcotic [nɑːˈkɔtɪk] ADJ narcótico ■ N narcótico; **narcotics** NPL (*drugs*) entorpecentes *mpl*

nark [nɑːk] (*Brit: inf*) VT encher o saco de

narrate [nəˈreɪt] VT narrar, contar

narration [nəˈreɪʃən] N narração *f*

narrative ['nærətɪv] N narrativa ■ ADJ narrativo

narrator [nəˈreɪtər] N narrador(a) *m/f*

narrow ['nærəʊ] ADJ estreito; (*shoe*) apertado; (*fig: majority*) pequeno; (*: ideas*) tacanho ■ VI (*road*) estreitar-se; (*difference*) diminuir; **to have a ~ escape** escapar por um triz; **to ~ sth down to** restringir or reduzir algo a; **narrow gauge** ADJ (*Rail*) de bitola estreita

narrowly ['nærəʊlɪ] ADV (*miss*) por pouco; **he**

~ missed injury/the tree por pouco não se machucou/não bateu na árvore

narrow-minded [-'maɪndɪd] ADJ de visão limitada, bitolado

NAS (US) N ABBR = **National Academy of Sciences**

NASA ['næsə] (US) N ABBR (= *National Aeronautics and Space Administration*) NASA f

nasal ['neɪzl] ADJ nasal

Nassau ['næsɔː] N (*in Bahamas*) Nassau'

nastily ['nɑːstɪlɪ] ADV (*say, act*) maldosamente

nastiness ['nɑːstɪnɪs] N (*malice*) maldade f; (*rudeness*) grosseria

nasturtium [nəs'təːʃəm] N chagas *fpl*, capuchinha

nasty ['nɑːstɪ] ADJ (*unpleasant: remark*) desagradável; (: *person*) mau, ruim; (*malicious*) maldoso; (*rude*) grosseiro, obsceno; (*revolting: taste, smell*) repugnante, asqueroso; (*wound, disease etc*) grave, sério; **to turn ~** (*situation, weather*) ficar feio; (*person*) engrossar

NAS/UWT (Brit) N ABBR (= *National Association of Schoolmasters/Union of Women Teachers*) sindicato dos professores

nation ['neɪʃən] N nação f

national ['næʃənl] ADJ, N nacional *m/f*; **national anthem** N hino nacional; **national debt** N dívida pública; **national dress** N traje *m* nacional

National Guard (US) N guarda nacional

National Health Service (Brit) N *serviço nacional de saúde*

National Insurance (Brit) N previdência social

nationalism ['næʃənəlɪzəm] N nacionalismo

nationalist ['næʃənəlɪst] ADJ, N nacionalista *m/f*

nationality [næʃə'nælɪtɪ] N nacionalidade f

nationalization [næʃənəlaɪ'zeɪʃən] N nacionalização f

nationalize ['næʃənəlaɪz] VT nacionalizar

nationally ['næʃənəlɪ] ADV (*nationwide*) de âmbito nacional; (*as a nation*) nacionalmente, como nação

national park N parque *m* nacional

national press N imprensa nacional

National Security Council (US) N conselho nacional de segurança

national service N (*Mil*) serviço militar

National Trust (Brit) N *ver abaixo*

● **NATIONAL TRUST**
●
● O *National Trust* é uma instituição
● independente, sem fins lucrativos,
● cuja missão é proteger e valorizar os
● monumentos e a paisagem da Grã-Bretanha
● devido a seu interesse histórico ou beleza
● natural.

nationwide ['neɪʃənwaɪd] ADJ de âmbito *or* a nível nacional ■ ADV em todo o país

native ['neɪtɪv] N (*local inhabitant*) natural *m/f*, nativo(-a); (*in colonies*) indígena *m/f*, nativo(-a)

■ ADJ (*indigenous*) indígena; (*of one's birth*) natal; (*language*) materno; (*innate*) inato, natural; **a ~ of Russia** um natural da Rússia; **a ~ speaker of Portuguese** uma pessoa de língua (materna) portuguesa

Nativity [nə'tɪvɪtɪ] N (*Rel*): **the ~** a Natividade

NATO ['neɪtəu] N ABBR (= *North Atlantic Treaty Organization*) OTAN f

natter ['nætər] (Brit) VI conversar fiado

natural ['nætʃrəl] ADJ natural; **death from ~ causes** morte f natural; **natural childbirth** N parto natural; **natural gas** N gás *m* natural

naturalist ['nætʃrəlɪst] N naturalista *m/f*

naturalization [nætʃrəlaɪ'zeɪʃən] N naturalização f

naturalize ['nætʃrəlaɪz] VT: **to become ~d** (*person*) naturalizar-se

naturally ['nætʃrəlɪ] ADV naturalmente; (*of course*) claro, evidentemente; (*instinctively*) por instinto, espontaneamente

naturalness ['nætʃrəlnɪs] N naturalidade f

natural resources NPL recursos *mpl* naturais

natural wastage N (*Industry*) afastamentos *mpl* naturais e voluntários

nature ['neɪtʃər] N natureza; (*character*) caráter *m*, índole f; **by ~** por natureza; **documents of a confidential ~** documentos de caráter confidencial

-natured ['neɪtʃəd] SUFFIX: **ill-** de mau caráter

nature reserve (Brit) N reserva natural

nature trail N *trilha de descoberta da natureza*

naturist ['neɪtʃərɪst] N naturista *m/f*

naught [nɔːt] N = **nought**

naughtiness ['nɔːtɪnɪs] N (*of child*) travessura, mau comportamento; (*of story etc*) picante *m*

naughty ['nɔːtɪ] ADJ (*child*) travesso, levado; (*story, film*) picante

nausea ['nɔːsɪə] N náusea

nauseate ['nɔːsɪeɪt] VT dar náuseas a; (*fig*) repugnar

nauseating ['nɔːsɪeɪtɪŋ] ADJ nauseabundo, enjoativo; (*fig*) nojento, repugnante

nauseous ['nɔːsɪəs] ADJ (*nauseating*) nauseabundo, enjoativo; (*feeling sick*): **to be ~** estar enjoado

nautical ['nɔːtɪkl] ADJ náutico; **nautical mile** N milha marítima (1853 m)

naval ['neɪvl] ADJ naval; **naval officer** N oficial *m* de marinha

nave [neɪv] N nave f

navel ['neɪvl] N umbigo

navigable ['nævɪgəbl] ADJ navegável

navigate ['nævɪgeɪt] VT (*ship*) pilotar; (*sea*) navegar ■ VI navegar; (*Aut*) ler o mapa

navigation [nævɪ'geɪʃən] N (*action*) navegação f; (*science*) náutica

navigator ['nævɪgeɪtər] N navegador(a) *m/f*

navvy ['nævɪ] (Brit) N trabalhador *m* braçal, cavouqueiro

navy ['neɪvɪ] N marinha (de guerra); (*ships*) armada, frota; **Department of the N~** (US) ministério da Marinha

navy(-blue) ADJ azul-marinho *inv*

Nazareth ['næzərəθ] N Nazaré

Nazi ['nɑːtsɪ] ADJ, N nazista *m/f*

Nazism ['nɑːtsɪzəm] N nazismo

NB ABBR (= *nota bene*) NB; (*Canada*) = **New Brunswick**

NBA (*US*) N ABBR = **National Basketball Association; National Boxing Association**

NBC (*US*) N ABBR (= *National Broadcasting Company*) *rede de televisão*

NBS (*US*) N ABBR (= *National Bureau of Standards*) *órgão de padronização*

NC ABBR (*Comm etc*) = **no charge**; (*US: Post*) = **North Carolina**

NCC N ABBR (*Brit*: = *Nature Conservancy Council*) *órgão de proteção à natureza*; (*US*) = **National Council of Churches**

NCCL (*Brit*) N ABBR (= *National Council for Civil Liberties*) *associação de defesa das liberdades civis*

NCO N ABBR = **non-commissioned officer**

ND (*US*) ABBR (*Post*) = **North Dakota**

NE (*US*) ABBR (*Post*) = **Nebraska; New England**

NEA (*US*) N ABBR = **National Education Association**

neap tide [niːp-] N maré *f* morta

near [nɪəʳ] ADJ (*place*) vizinho; (*time*) próximo; (*relation*) íntimo ■ ADV perto ■ PREP (*also*: **near to**: *space*) perto de; (: *time*) perto de, quase ■ VT aproximar-se de; **~ here/there** aqui/ali perto; **£25,000 or ~est offer** (*Brit*) £25,000 ou melhor oferta; **in the ~ future** no próximo futuro; **the building is ~ing completion** o edifício está quase pronto; **to come ~** aproximar-se

nearby [nɪə'baɪ] ADJ próximo, vizinho ■ ADV à mão, perto

Near East N: **the ~** o Oriente Próximo

nearer ['nɪərəʳ] ADJ que fica mais perto ■ ADV mais perto

nearly ['nɪəlɪ] ADV quase; **I ~ fell** quase que caí; **it's not ~ big enough** é pequeno demais

near miss N (*of planes*) quase-colisão *f*; (*shot*) tiro que passou de raspão

nearness ['nɪənɪs] N proximidade *f*; (*relationship*) intimidade *f*

nearside ['nɪəsaɪd] N (*Aut: right-hand drive*) lado esquerdo; (: *left-hand drive*) lado direito ■ ADJ esquerdo; direito

near-sighted [-'saɪtɪd] ADJ míope

neat [niːt] ADJ (*place*) arrumado, em ordem; (*person*) asseado, arrumado; (*work*) hábil; (*plan*) engenhoso, bem bolado; (*spirits*) puro

neatly ['niːtlɪ] ADV caprichosamente, com capricho; (*skilfully*) habilmente

neatness ['niːtnɪs] N (*tidiness*) asseio; (*skilfulness*) habilidade *f*

nebulous ['nɛbjuləs] ADJ nebuloso; (*fig*) vago, confuso

necessarily ['nɛsɪsrɪlɪ] ADV necessariamente; **not ~** não necessariamente

necessary ['nɛsɪsrɪ] ADJ necessário; **he did all that was ~** fez tudo o que foi necessário; **if ~** se necessário for

necessitate [nɪ'sɛsɪteɪt] VT exigir, tornar necessário

necessity [nɪ'sɛsɪtɪ] N (*thing needed*) necessidade *f*, requisito; (*compelling circumstances*) necessidade; **necessities** NPL (*essentials*) artigos *mpl* de primeira necessidade; **in case of ~** em caso de necessidade

neck [nɛk] N (*Anat*) pescoço; (*of garment*) gola; (*of bottle*) gargalo ■ VI (*inf*) ficar de agarramento; **~ and ~** emparelhados; **to stick one's ~ out** (*inf*) arriscar-se

necklace ['nɛklɪs] N colar *m*

neckline ['nɛklaɪn] N decote *m*

necktie ['nɛktaɪ] N (*esp US*) N gravata

nectar ['nɛktəʳ] N néctar *m*

nectarine ['nɛktərɪn] N nectarina

NEDC (*Brit*) N ABBR = **National Economic Development Council**

née [neɪ] ADJ: **~ Scott** em solteira Scott

need [niːd] N (*lack*) falta, carência; (*necessity*) necessidade *f*; (*thing needed*) requisito, necessidade ■ VT (*require*) precisar de; **I ~ to do it** preciso fazê-lo; **you don't ~ to go** você não precisa ir; **a signature is ~ed** é necessária uma assinatura; **to be in ~ of** *or* **have ~ of** estar precisando de; **£10 will meet my immediate ~s** £10 atenderão minhas necessidades mais prementes; **in case of ~** em caso de necessidade; **there's no ~ to do ...** não é preciso fazer ...; **there's no ~ for that** isso não é necessário

needle ['niːdl] N agulha ■ VT (*inf*) provocar, alfinetar

needlecord ['niːdlkɔːd] (*Brit*) N veludo cotelê

needless ['niːdlɪs] ADJ inútil, desnecessário; **~ to say ...** desnecessário dizer que ...

needlessly ['niːdlɪslɪ] ADV desnecessariamente, à toa

needlework ['niːdlwəːk] N trabalho de agulha, costura

needn't ['niːdnt] = **need not**

needy ['niːdɪ] ADJ necessitado, carente

negation [nɪ'geɪʃən] N negação *f*

negative ['nɛgətɪv] ADJ negativo ■ N (*Phot*) negativo; (*Ling*) negativa; **to answer in the ~** responder negativamente

neglect [nɪ'glɛkt] VT (*one's duty*) negligenciar, não cumprir com; (*child*) descuidar, esquecer-se de ■ N (*of child*) descuido, desatenção *f*; (*personal*) desleixo; (*of house etc*) abandono; (*of duty*) negligência; **to ~ to do sth** omitir de fazer algo

neglected [nɪ'glɛktɪd] ADJ abandonado

neglectful [nɪ'glɛktful] ADJ negligente; **to be ~ of sb/sth** descuidar de alguém/algo

negligee ['nɛglɪʒeɪ] N négligé *m*

negligence ['nɛglɪdʒəns] N negligência, descuido

negligent ['nɛglɪdʒənt] ADJ negligente

negligently ['nɛglɪdʒəntlɪ] ADV por negligência; (*offhandedly*) negligentemente

negligible ['nɛglɪdʒɪbl] ADJ insignificante, desprezível, ínfimo

negotiable [nɪ'gəuʃɪəbl] ADJ (cheque) negociável; (road) transitável

negotiate [nɪ'gəuʃɪeɪt] VI negociar ■ VT (treaty, transaction) negociar; (obstacle) contornar; (bend in road) fazer; **to ~ with sb for sth** negociar com alguém para obter algo

negotiation [nɪgəuʃɪ'eɪʃən] N negociação f; **to enter into ~s with sb** entrar em negociações com alguém

negotiator [nɪ'gəuʃɪeɪtəʳ] N negociador(a) m/f

Negress ['niːgrɪs] N negra

Negro ['niːgrəu] (pl **Negroes**) ADJ, N negro(-a)

neigh [neɪ] N relincho ■ VI relinchar

neighbour ['neɪbəʳ] (US **neighbor**) N vizinho(-a)

neighbo(u)rhood ['neɪbəhud] N (place) vizinhança, bairro; (people) vizinhos mpl

neighbo(u)ring ['neɪbərɪŋ] ADJ vizinho

neighbo(u)rly ['neɪbəlɪ] ADJ amistoso, prestativo

neither ['naɪðəʳ] CONJ: **I didn't move and ~ did he** não me movi nem ele ■ ADJ, PRON nenhum (dos dois), nem um nem outro ■ ADV: **~ good nor bad** nem bom nem mau; **~ story is true** nenhuma das estórias é verdade

neo... [niːəu] PREFIX neo-

neolithic [niːəu'lɪθɪk] ADJ neolítico

neologism [nɪ'ɔlədʒɪzəm] N neologismo

neon ['niːɔn] N neônio, néon m; **neon light** N luz f de neônio; **neon sign** N anúncio luminoso a neônio

Nepal [nɪ'pɔːl] N Nepal m

nephew ['nɛvjuː] N sobrinho

nepotism ['nɛpətɪzm] N nepotismo

nerve [nəːv] N (Anat) nervo; (courage) coragem f; (impudence) descaramento, atrevimento; **he gets on my ~s** ele me irrita, ele me dá nos nervos; **to have a fit of ~s** ter uma crise nervosa; **to lose one's ~** (self-confidence) perder o sangue frio; **nerve centre** (US **nerve center**) N (Anat) centro nervoso; (fig) centro de operações; **nerve gas** N gás m tóxico

nerve-racking [-'rækɪŋ] ADJ angustiante

nervous ['nəːvəs] ADJ (Anat) nervoso; (anxious) apreensivo; (timid) tímido, acanhado; **~ exhaustion** esgotamento nervoso; **nervous breakdown** N esgotamento nervoso

nervously ['nəːvəslɪ] ADV nervosamente; (timidly) timidamente

nervousness ['nəːvəsnɪs] N nervosismo; (timidity) timidez f

nest [nɛst] VI aninhar-se ■ N (of bird) ninho; (of wasp) vespeiro; **nest egg** N (fig) pé-de-meia m

nestle ['nɛsl] VI: **to ~ up to sb** aconchegar-se a alguém

nestling ['nɛstlɪŋ] N filhote m (de passarinho)

net [nɛt] N rede f; (fabric) filó m ■ ADJ (Comm) líquido ■ VT pegar na rede; (money: subj: person) faturar; (: deal, sale) render; **~ of tax** isento de impostos; **he earns £10,000 ~ per year** ele ganha £10,000 líquidas por ano; **the N~** (Internet) a Rede

netball ['nɛtbɔːl] N espécie de basquetebol

net curtains NPL cortinas fpl de voile

Netherlands ['nɛðələndz] NPL: **the ~** os Países Baixos

net profit N lucro líquido

nett [nɛt] ADJ = **net**

netting ['nɛtɪŋ] N rede f, redes fpl; (fabric) voile m

nettle ['nɛtl] N urtiga

network ['nɛtwəːk] N rede f; **there's no ~ coverage here** (Tel) aqui não tem cobertura ■ VT (Radio, TV) transmitir em rede; (computers) interligar

neuralgia [njuə'rældʒə] N neuralgia

neuroses [njuə'rəusiːz] NPL of **neurosis**

neurosis [njuə'rəusɪs] (pl **neuroses**) N neurose f

neurotic [njuə'rɔtɪk] ADJ, N neurótico(-a)

neuter ['njuːtəʳ] ADJ neutro ■ N neutro ■ VT (cat etc) castrar, capar

neutral ['njuːtrəl] ADJ neutro ■ N (Aut) ponto morto

neutrality [njuː'trælɪtɪ] N neutralidade f

neutralize ['njuːtrəlaɪz] VT neutralizar; **neutron bomb** N bomba de nêutrons (BR) ou neutrões (PT)

never ['nɛvəʳ] ADV nunca; **I ~ went** nunca fui; **~ again** nunca mais; **~ in my life** nunca na minha vida; see also **mind**

never-ending [-'ɛndɪŋ] ADJ sem fim, interminável

nevertheless [nɛvəðə'lɛs] ADV todavia, contudo

new [njuː] ADJ novo; **as good as ~** tal como novo

newborn ['njuːbɔːn] ADJ recém-nascido

newcomer ['njuːkʌməʳ] N recém-chegado(-a), novato(-a)

new-fangled [-'fæŋgld] (pej) ADJ ultramoderno

new-found ADJ (friend) novo; (enthusiasm) recente

Newfoundland ['njuːfənlənd] N Terra Nova

New Guinea N Nova Guiné f

newly ['njuːlɪ] ADV recém, novamente

newly-weds NPL recém-casados mpl

new moon N lua nova

newness ['njuːnɪs] N novidade f

news [njuːz] N notícias fpl; (Radio, TV) noticiário; **a piece of ~** uma notícia; **good/bad ~** boa/má notícia; **financial ~** noticiário financeiro; **news agency** N agência de notícias

newsagent ['njuːzeɪdʒənt] (Brit) N jornaleiro(-a)

news bulletin N (Radio, TV) noticiário

newscaster ['njuːzkɑːstəʳ] N locutor(a) m/f

newsdealer ['njuːzdiːləʳ] (US) N = **newsagent**

news flash N notícia de última hora

newsletter ['njuːzlɛtəʳ] N boletim m informativo

newspaper ['njuːzpeɪpəʳ] N jornal m; (material) papel m de jornal; **daily ~** diário; **weekly ~** semanário

newsprint ['njuːzprɪnt] N papel m de jornal

newsreader ['njuːzriːdəʳ] N = **newscaster**

newsreel ['njuːzriːl] N jornal m cinematográfico, atualidades fpl

newsroom ['nju:zru:m] N (Press) sala da redação; (TV) estúdio
news stand N banca de jornais
newt [nju:t] N tritão m
New Year N ano novo; **Happy ~!** Feliz Ano Novo!; **to wish sb a happy ~** desejar feliz ano novo a alguém
New Year's Day N dia m de ano novo
New Year's Eve N véspera de ano novo
New York [-jɔ:k] N Nova Iorque
New Zealand [-'zi:lənd] N Nova Zelândia ■ CPD neozelandês(-esa)
New Zealander [-'zi:ləndə'] N neozelandês(-esa) m/f
next [nɛkst] ADJ (in space) próximo, vizinho; (in time) seguinte, próximo ■ ADV depois; depois, logo; **the ~ day** o dia seguinte; **~ time** na próxima vez; **~ year** o ano que vem; **"turn to the ~ page"** "vire para a página seguinte"; **the week after ~** sem ser a semana que vem, a outra; **~ to** ao lado de; **~ to nothing** quase nada; **who's ~?** quem é o próximo?; **~ please!** próximo, por favor!; **when do we meet ~?** quando é que nós nos reencontramos?; **next door** ADV na casa do lado ■ ADJ vizinho
next-of-kin N parentes mpl mais próximos
NF N ABBR (Brit: Pol: = National Front) partido político da extrema direita ■ ABBR (Canada) = **Newfoundland**
NFL (US) N ABBR = **National Football League**
NG (US) ABBR = **National Guard**
NGO (US) N ABBR = **non-governmental organization**
NH (US) ABBR (Post) = **New Hampshire**
NHL (US) N ABBR = **National Hockey League**
NHS (Brit) N ABBR = **National Health Service**
NI ABBR = **Northern Ireland**; (Brit) = **National Insurance**
Niagara Falls [naɪ'ægrə-] NPL: **the ~** as cataratas do Niagara
nib [nɪb] N ponta or bico da pena
nibble ['nɪbl] VT mordiscar, beliscar; (Zool) roer
Nicaragua [nɪkə'rægjuə] N Nicarágua
Nicaraguan [nɪkə'rægjuən] ADJ, N nicaragüense m/f
nice [naɪs] ADJ (likeable) simpático; (kind) amável, atencioso; (pleasant) agradável; (attractive) bonito; (subtle) sutil, fino
nice-looking [-'lukɪŋ] ADJ bonito
nicely ['naɪslɪ] ADV agradavelmente, bem; **that will do ~** isso será perfeito
niceties ['naɪsɪtɪz] NPL sutilezas fpl
niche [ni:ʃ] N nicho
nick [nɪk] N (wound) corte m; (cut, indentation) entalhe m, incisão f; (Brit: inf): **in good ~** em bom estado ■ VT (cut) entalhar; (inf: steal) furtar; (: Brit: arrest) prender, arrochar; **in the ~ of time** na hora H, no momento exato; **to ~ o.s.** cortar-se
nickel ['nɪkl] N níquel m; (US) moeda de 5 centavos
nickname ['nɪkneɪm] N apelido (BR), alcunha

(PT) ■ VT apelidar de (BR), alcunhar de (PT)
Nicosia [nɪkə'si:ə] N Nicósia
nicotine ['nɪkəti:n] N nicotina
niece [ni:s] N sobrinha
nifty ['nɪftɪ] (inf) ADJ (car, jacket) chique; (gadget, tool) jeitoso
Niger ['naɪdʒə'] N (country, river) Níger m
Nigeria [naɪ'dʒɪərɪə] N Nigéria
Nigerian [naɪ'dʒɪərɪən] ADJ, N nigeriano(-a)
niggardly ['nɪgədlɪ] ADJ (person) avarento, sovina; (amount) miserável
nigger ['nɪgə'] (inf!) N (highly offensive) crioulo(-a), baiano(-a)
niggle ['nɪgl] VI (find fault) botar defeito; (fuss) fazer histórias ■ VT irritar
niggling ['nɪglɪŋ] ADJ (trifling) insignificante, mesquinho; (annoying) irritante; (pain, doubt) persistente
night [naɪt] N noite f; **at** or **by ~** à or de noite; **in** or **during the ~** durante a noite; **last ~** ontem à noite; **the ~ before last** anteontem à noite; **good ~!** boa noite!
night-bird N (Zool) ave f noturna; (fig) noctívago(-a)
nightcap ['naɪtkæp] N bebida tomada antes de dormir
nightclub ['naɪtklʌb] N boate f
nightdress ['naɪtdrɛs] N camisola (BR), camisa de noite (PT)
nightfall ['naɪtfɔ:l] N anoitecer m
nightgown ['naɪtgaun] N = **nightdress**
nightie ['naɪtɪ] N = **nightdress**
nightingale ['naɪtɪŋgeɪl] N rouxinol m
nightlife ['naɪtlaɪf] N vida noturna
nightly ['naɪtlɪ] ADJ noturno, de noite ■ ADV todas as noites, cada noite
nightmare ['naɪtmɛə'] N pesadelo
night porter N porteiro da noite
night safe N cofre m noturno
night school N escola noturna
nightshade ['naɪtʃeɪd] N: **deadly ~** (Bot) beladona
night shift N turno da noite
night-time N noite f
night watchman (irreg) N vigia m, guarda-noturno m
nihilism ['naɪɪlɪzm] N niilismo
nil [nɪl] N nada; (Brit: Sport) zero
Nile [naɪl] N: **the ~** o Nilo
nimble ['nɪmbl] ADJ (agile) ágil, ligeiro; (skilful) hábil, esperto
nine [naɪn] NUM nove; see also **five**
nineteen [naɪn'ti:n] NUM dezenove (BR), dezanove (PT); see also **five**
ninety ['naɪntɪ] NUM noventa; see also **fifty**
ninth [naɪnθ] NUM nono; see also **fifth**
nip [nɪp] VT (pinch) beliscar; (bite) morder ■ VI (Brit: inf): **to ~ out/down/up** dar uma saidinha/descida/subida ■ N (drink) gole m, trago; **to ~ into a shop** dar um pulo numa loja
nipple ['nɪpl] N (Anat) bico do seio, mamilo; (of bottle) bocal m, bico; (Tech) bocal (roscado)

nippy ['nɪpɪ] (*Brit*) ADJ (*person*) rápido, ágil; (*cold*) friozinho

nit [nɪt] N (*in hair*) lêndea, ovo de piolho; (*inf: idiot*) imbecil *m/f*, idiota *m/f*

nit-pick (*inf*) VI ser implicante

nitrate ['naɪtreɪt] N nitrato

nitrogen ['naɪtrədʒən] N nitrogênio

nitroglycerin(e) [naɪtrəu'glɪsəri:n] N nitroglicerina

nitty-gritty ['nɪtɪ'grɪtɪ] (*inf*) N: **to get down to the ~** chegar ao âmago

nitwit ['nɪtwɪt] (*inf*) N pateta *m/f*, bobalhão(-ona) *m/f*

NJ (*US*) ABBR (*Post*) = **New Jersey**

NLF N ABBR = **National Liberation Front**

NLQ ABBR (= *near letter quality*) qualidade *f* carta

NLRB (*US*) N ABBR (= *National Labor Relations Board*) *órgão de proteção aos trabalhadores*

NM (*US*) ABBR (*Post*) = **New Mexico**

 KEYWORD

no [nəu] (*pl* **noes**) ADV (*opposite of "yes"*) não; **are you coming? — no (I'm not)** você vem? — não(eu não); **no thank you** não obrigado
■ ADJ (*not any*) nenhum(a), não ... algum(a); **I have no more money/time/books** não tenho mais dinheiro/tempo/livros; **no other man would have done it** nenhum outro homem teria feito isto; **"no entry"** "entrada proibida"; **"no smoking"** "é proibido fumar"
■ N não *m*, negativa; **there were 20 noes and one "don't know"** houve 20 nãos e um "não sei"

no. ABBR (= *number*) n°

nobble ['nɔbl] (*Brit: inf*) VT (*bribe*) subornar; (*person: speak to*) agarrar; (*Racing: horse*) incapacitar (*com drogas*)

Nobel prize [nəu'bɛl-] N prêmio Nobel

nobility [nəu'bɪlɪtɪ] N nobreza

noble ['nəubl] ADJ (*person*) nobre; (*title*) de nobreza

nobleman ['nəublmən] (*irreg*) N nobre *m*, fidalgo

nobly ['nəublɪ] ADV nobremente

nobody ['nəubədɪ] PRON ninguém

no-claims bonus N bonificação *f* (*por não ter reclamado indenização*)

nocturnal [nɔk'tə:nəl] ADJ noturno

nod [nɔd] VI (*greeting*) cumprimentar com a cabeça; (*in agreement*) acenar (que sim) com a cabeça; (*doze*) cochilar, dormitar ■ VT: **to ~ one's head** inclinar a cabeça ■ N inclinação *f* da cabeça; **they ~ded their agreement** inclinaram a cabeça afirmando seu acordo
▶ **nod off** VI cochilar; **noise** [nɔɪz] N barulho

noise abatement ■ N luta contra a poluição sonora

noiseless ['nɔɪzlɪs] ADJ silencioso

noisily ['nɔɪzɪlɪ] ADV ruidosamente, com muito barulho

noisy ['nɔɪzɪ] ADJ barulhento

nomad ['nəumæd] N nômade *m/f*

nomadic [nəu'mædɪk] ADJ nômade

no man's land N terra de ninguém

nominal ['nɔmɪnl] ADJ nominal

nominate ['nɔmɪneɪt] VT (*propose*) propor; (*appoint*) nomear

nomination [nɔmɪ'neɪʃən] N (*proposal*) proposta; (*appointment*) nomeação *f*

nominee [nɔmɪ'ni:] N pessoa nomeada, candidato(-a)

non... [nɔn] PREFIX não-, des..., in..., anti-...

non-alcoholic ADJ não-alcoólico

non-breakable ADJ inquebrável

nonce word ['nɔns-] N palavra criada para a ocasião

nonchalant ['nɔnʃələnt] ADJ despreocupado

non-commissioned [-kə'mɪʃənd] ADJ: **~ officer** oficial *m* subalterno

non-committal [-kə'mɪtl] ADJ evasivo

nonconformist [nɔnkən'fɔ:mɪst] ADJ não-conformista, dissidente ■ N não-conformista *m/f*

non-contributory ADJ: **~ pension scheme** (*Brit*) *or* **plan** (*US*) caixa de aposentadoria não-contributária

non-cooperation N não-cooperação *f*

nondescript ['nɔndɪskrɪpt] ADJ qualquer; (*pej*) medíocre

none [nʌn] PRON (*person*) ninguém; (*thing*) nenhum(a), nada; **~ of you** nenhum de vocês; **I have ~** não tenho; **I've ~ left** não tenho mais; **~ at all** (*not one*) nem um só; **how much milk? — ~ at all** quanto leite? — nada; **he's ~ the worse for it** isso não o afetou

nonentity [nɔ'nɛntɪtɪ] N nulidade *f*, zero à esquerda *m*

non-essential ADJ não essencial, dispensável ■ NPL: **~s** desnecessários *mpl*

nonetheless [nʌnðə'lɛs] ADV no entanto, apesar disso, contudo

non-executive ADJ: **~ director** administrador(a) *m/f*, conselheiro(-a)

non-existent [-ɪg'zɪstənt] ADJ inexistente

non-fiction N literatura de não-ficção

non-flammable ADJ não inflamável

non-intervention N não-intervenção *f*

non obst. ABBR = **non obstante**; (= *notwithstanding*) não obstante

non-payment N falta de pagamento

nonplussed [nɔn'plʌst] ADJ perplexo, pasmado

non-profit-making ADJ sem fins lucrativos

nonsense ['nɔnsəns] N disparate *m*, besteira, absurdo; **~! bobagem!, que nada!; it's ~ to say ...** é um absurdo dizer que ...

non-shrink (*Brit*) ADJ que não encolhe

non-skid ADJ antiderrapante

non-smoker N não-fumante *m/f*

non-stick ADJ tefal®, não-aderente

non-stop ADJ ininterrupto; (*Rail*) direto; (*Aviat*) sem escala ■ ADV sem parar

non-taxable income N renda não-tributável

non-U (Brit: inf) ADJ ABBR (= non-upper class) que não se diz (or se faz)

non-volatile memory N (Comput) memória não volátil

non-voting shares NPL ações fpl sem direito de voto

non-white ADJ, N não-branco(-a)

noodles ['nuːdlz] NPL talharim m

nook [nuk] N canto, recanto; **~s and crannies** esconderijos mpl

noon [nuːn] N meio-dia m

no-one PRON = **nobody**

noose [nuːs] N laço corrediço; (hangman's) corda da forca

nor [nɔːʳ] CONJ = **neither** ■ ADV see **neither**

norm [nɔːm] N (convention) norma; (requirement) regra

normal ['nɔːml] ADJ normal ■ N: **to return to ~** normalizar-se

normality [nɔːˈmælɪtɪ] N normalidade f

normally ['nɔːməlɪ] ADV normalmente

Normandy ['nɔːməndɪ] N Normandia

north [nɔːθ] N norte m ■ ADJ do norte, setentrional ■ ADV ao or para o norte

North Africa N África do Norte

North African ADJ, N norte-africano(-a)

North America N América do Norte

North American ADJ, N norte-americano(-a)

Northants [nɔːˈθænts] (Brit) ABBR = **Northamptonshire**

northbound ['nɔːθbaund] ADJ em direção norte

north-east N nordeste m

northerly ['nɔːðəlɪ] ADJ (wind, course) norte

northern ['nɔːðən] ADJ do norte, setentrional

Northern Ireland N Irlanda do Norte

North Pole N: **the ~** o Pólo Norte

North Sea N: **the ~** o Mar do Norte

North Sea oil N petróleo do Mar do Norte

northward(s) ['nɔːθwəd(z)] ADV em direção norte

north-west N noroeste m

Norway ['nɔːweɪ] N Noruega

Norwegian [nɔːˈwiːdʒən] ADJ norueguês(-esa) ■ N norueguês(-esa) m/f; (Ling) norueguês m

nos. ABBR (= numbers) nº

nose [nəuz] N (Anat) nariz m; (Zool) focinho; (sense of smell: of person) olfato; (: of animal) faro ■ VI (also: **nose one's way**) avançar cautelosamente; **to turn up one's ~ at** desdenhar; **to pay through the ~ (for sth)** (inf) pagar os olhos da cara por algo
▸ **nose about** VI bisbilhotar
▸ **nose around** VI = **nose about**

nosebleed ['nəuzbliːd] N hemorragia nasal

nose-dive N (deliberate) vôo picado; (involuntary) parafuso

nose drops NPL gotas fpl para o nariz

nosey ['nəuzɪ] (inf) ADJ = **nosy**

nostalgia [nɒsˈtældʒɪə] N nostalgia

nostalgic [nɒsˈtældʒɪk] ADJ nostálgico

nostril ['nɒstrɪl] N narina

nosy ['nəuzɪ] (inf) ADJ intrometido, abelhudo

 KEYWORD

not [nɒt] ADV não; **he is not** or **isn't here** ele não está aqui; **you must not** or **mustn't do that** você não deve fazer isso; **it's too late, isn't it?** é muito tarde, não?; **he asked me not to do it** ele me pediu para não fazer isto; **not that (I don't like him/he isn't interesting)** não é que(eu não goste dele/ele não seja interessante); **not yet/now** ainda/agora não; see also **all; only**

notable ['nəutəbl] ADJ notável

notably ['nəutəblɪ] ADV (particularly) particularmente; (markedly) notavelmente

notary ['nəutərɪ] N (also: **notary public**) tabelião/tabelioa m/f, notário(-a)

notation [nəuˈteɪʃən] N notação f

notch [nɒtʃ] N (in wood) entalhe m; (in blade) corte m
▸ **notch up** VT (score) marcar; (victory) registrar

note [nəut] N (Mus, banknote) nota; (letter) nota, bilhete m; (record) nota, anotação f; (tone) tom m ■ VT (observe) observar, reparar em; (also: **note down**) anotar, tomar nota de; **just a quick ~ to let you know ...** apenas um bilhete rápido para avisá-lo ...; **to take ~s** tomar notas; **to compare ~s** (fig) trocar impressões; **to take ~ of** fazer caso de; **a person of ~** uma pessoa eminente

notebook ['nəutbuk] N caderno

note-case (Brit) N carteira

noted ['nəutɪd] ADJ célebre, conhecido

notepad ['nəutpæd] N bloco de anotações

notepaper ['nəutpeɪpəʳ] N papel m de carta

noteworthy ['nəutwəːθɪ] ADJ notável

nothing ['nʌθɪŋ] N nada; (zero) zero; **he does ~** ele não faz nada; **~ new/much** nada de novo; **for ~** (free) de graça, grátis; (in vain) em vão, por nada; **~ at all** absolutamente nada, coisa nenhuma

notice ['nəutɪs] N (sign) aviso, anúncio; (warning) aviso; (of leaving) aviso prévio; (Brit: review: of play etc) resenha ■ VT (observe) reparar em, notar; **without ~** sem aviso prévio; **advance ~** aviso prévio, preaviso; **to give sb ~ of sth** dar aviso a alguém de algo; **at short ~** de repente, em cima da hora; **until further ~** até nova ordem; **to hand in** or **give one's ~** (subj: employee) demitir, pedir a demissão; **to take ~ of** prestar atenção a, fazer caso de; **to bring sth to sb's ~** levar algo ao conhecimento de alguém; **it has come to my ~ that ...** tornei-me ciente que ...; **to escape** or **avoid ~** passar despercebido

noticeable ['nəutɪsəbl] ADJ evidente, visível

notice board (Brit) N quadro de avisos

notification [nəutɪfɪˈkeɪʃən] N aviso, notificação f

notify ['nəutɪfaɪ] VT avisar, notificar; **to ~ sth to sb** notificar algo a alguém; **to ~ sb of sth** avisar alguém de algo

notion ['nəuʃən] N noção f, idéia; **notions** NPL
(US) miudezas fpl

notoriety [nəutə'raɪətɪ] N notoriedade f, má
fama

notorious [nəu'tɔːrɪəs] ADJ notório

notoriously [nəu'tɔːrɪəslɪ] ADV notoriamente

Notts [nɔts] (Brit) ABBR = **Nottinghamshire**

notwithstanding [nɔtwɪθ'stændɪŋ] ADV no
entanto, não obstante ■ PREP: ~ **this** apesar
disto

nougat ['nuːgɑː] N torrone m, nugá m

nought [nɔːt] N zero

noun [naun] N substantivo

nourish ['nʌrɪʃ] VT nutrir, alimentar; (fig)
fomentar, alentar

nourishing ['nʌrɪʃɪŋ] ADJ nutritivo, alimentício

nourishment ['nʌrɪʃmənt] N alimento,
nutrimento

Nov. ABBR (= November) nov

Nova Scotia ['nəuvə'skəuʃə] N Nova Escócia

novel ['nɔvl] N romance m; (short) novela ■ ADJ
(new) novo, recente; (unexpected) insólito

novelist ['nɔvəlɪst] N romancista m/f

novelty ['nɔvəltɪ] N novidade f

November [nəu'vɛmbər] N novembro; see also
July

novice ['nɔvɪs] N principiante m/f, novato(-a);
(Rel) noviço(-a)

NOW [nau] (US) N ABBR = **National
Organization for Women**

now [nau] ADV (at the present time) agora; (these
days) atualmente, hoje em dia ■ CONJ: ~ **(that)**
agora que; **right** ~ agora mesmo; **by** ~ já;
just ~, **that's the fashion just** ~ é a moda
atualmente; **I saw her just** ~ eu a vi agora,
acabei de vê-la; ~ **and then**, ~ **and again** de vez
em quando; **from** ~ **on** de agora em diante; **in
3 days from** ~ daqui a 3 dias; **between** ~ **and
Monday** até segunda-feira; **that's all for** ~ por
agora é tudo

nowadays ['nauədeɪz] ADV hoje em dia

nowhere ['nəuwɛər] ADV (go) a lugar nenhum;
(be) em nenhum lugar; ~ **else** em nenhum
outro lugar

noxious ['nɔkʃəs] ADJ nocivo

nozzle ['nɔzl] N bico, bocal m; (Tech) tubeira;
(: hose) agulheta

NP N ABBR = **notary public**

NS (Canada) ABBR = **Nova Scotia**

NSC (US) N ABBR = **National Security Council**

NSF (US) N ABBR = **National Science Foundation**

NSPCC (Brit) N ABBR = **National Society for the
Prevention of Cruelty to Children**

NSW (Australia) ABBR = **New South Wales**

NT N ABBR (= New Testament) NT

nth [ɛnθ] ADJ: **for the** ~ **time** pela enésima vez

NUAAW (Brit) N ABBR (= National Union
of Agricultural and Allied Workers) sindicato da
agropecuária

nuance ['njuːɑːns] N nuança, matiz m

NUBE (Brit) N ABBR (= National Union of Bank
Employees) sindicato dos bancários

nubile ['njuːbaɪl] ADJ (woman) jovem e bela

nuclear ['njuːklɪər] ADJ nuclear; **nuclear
disarmament** N desarmamento nuclear

nuclei ['njuːklɪaɪ] NPL of **nucleus**

nucleus ['njuːklɪəs] (pl **nuclei**) N núcleo

nude [njuːd] ADJ nu(a) ■ N (Art) nu m; **in the** ~
nu, pelado

nudge [nʌdʒ] VT acotovelar, cutucar (BR)

nudist ['njuːdɪst] N nudista m/f; **nudist colony**
N colonia nudista

nudity ['njuːdɪtɪ] N nudez f

nugget ['nʌgɪt] N pepita

nuisance ['njuːsns] N amolação f,
aborrecimento; (person) chato; **what a ~!** que
saco! (BR), que chatice! (PT)

NUJ (Brit) N ABBR (= National Union of Journalists)
sindicato dos jornalistas

nuke [njuːk] (inf) N usina nuclear

null [nʌl] ADJ: ~ **and void** írrito e nulo

nullify ['nʌlɪfaɪ] VT anular, invalidar

NUM (Brit) N ABBR (= National Union of Mineworkers)
sindicato dos mineiros

numb [nʌm] ADJ dormente, entorpecido; (fig)
estupefato ■ VT adormecer, entorpecer; ~ **with
cold** tolhido de frio; ~ **with fear** paralisado de
medo

number ['nʌmbər] N número; (numeral)
algarismo ■ VT (pages etc) numerar; (amount
to) montar a; **a ~ of** vários, muitos; **to be ~ed
among** figurar entre; **they were ten in** ~ eram
em número de dez; **wrong ~** (Tel) engano

numbered account ['nʌmbəd-] N (in bank)
conta numerada

number plate (Brit) N placa (do carro)

Number Ten (Brit) N (= 10 Downing Street) residência
do primeiro-ministro

numbness ['nʌmnɪs] N torpor m, dormência;
(fig) insensibilidade f

numeral ['njuːmərəl] N algarismo

numerate ['njuːmərɪt] (Brit) ADJ: **to be ~** ter uma
noção básica da aritmética

numerical [njuː'mɛrɪkl] ADJ numérico

numerous ['njuːmərəs] ADJ numeroso

nun [nʌn] N freira

nuptial ['nʌpʃəl] ADJ nupcial

nurse [nəːs] N enfermeiro(-a); (also: **nursemaid**)
ama-seca, babá f ■ VT (patient) cuidar de, tratar
de; (baby: feed) criar, amamentar; (: Brit: rock)
embalar; (fig) alimentar; **wet ~** ama de leite

nursery ['nəːsərɪ] N (institution) creche f; (room)
quarto das crianças; (for plants) viveiro; **nursery
rhyme** N poesia infantil; **nursery school** N
escola maternal; **nursery slope** (Brit) N (Ski)
rampa para principiantes

nursing ['nəːsɪŋ] N (profession) enfermagem f;
(care) cuidado, assistência; **nursing home** N
sanatório, clínica de repouso; **nursing mother**
N lactante f

nurture ['nəːtʃər] VT alimentar

NUS (Brit) N ABBR (= National Union of Seamen)
sindicato dos marinheiros; (: = National Union of
Students) sindicato dos estudantes

NUT (Brit) N ABBR (= National Union of Teachers) sindicato dos professores

nut [nʌt] N (Tech) porca; (Bot) noz f ■ CPD (chocolate etc) de nozes

nutcase ['nʌtkeɪs] (inf) N doido(-a), biruta m/f

nutcrackers ['nʌtkrækəz] NPL quebra-nozes m inv

nutmeg ['nʌtmɛg] N noz-moscada

nutrient ['nju:trɪənt] N nutrimento ■ ADJ nutritivo

nutrition [nju:'trɪʃən] N (diet) alimentação f; (nourishment) nutrição f

nutritionist [nju:'trɪʃənɪst] N nutricionista m/f

nutritious [nju:'trɪʃəs] ADJ nutritivo

nuts [nʌts] (inf) ADJ: **he's ~** ele é doido

nutshell ['nʌtʃɛl] N casca de noz; **in a ~** (fig) em poucas palavras

nuzzle ['nʌzl] VI: **to ~ up to** aconchegar-se com

NV (US) ABBR (Post) = **Nevada**

NWT (Canada) ABBR = **Northwest Territories**

NY (US) ABBR (Post) = **New York**

NYC (US) ABBR (Post) = **New York City**

nylon ['naɪlɔn] N náilon m (BR), nylon m (PT) ■ ADJ de náilon; **nylons** NPL (stockings) meias fpl (de náilon)

nymph [nɪmf] N ninfa

nymphomaniac [nɪmfəu'meɪnɪæk] N ninfômana

NYSE (US) N ABBR = **New York Stock Exchange**

NZ ABBR = **New Zealand**

Oo

O, o [əu] N (*letter*) O, o *m*; (*US: Sch*)
= **outstanding; O for Olive** (*Brit*) *or* **oboe** (*US*)
O de Osvaldo
oaf [əuf] N imbecil *m/f*
oak [əuk] N carvalho ■ ADJ de carvalho
OAP (*Brit*) N *abbr* = **old-age pensioner**
oar [ɔːʳ] N remo; **to put** *or* **shove one's ~ in** (*fig*:
inf) meter o bedelho *or* a colher
oarsman ['ɔːzmən] (*irreg*) N remador *m*
oarswoman ['ɔːzwumən] (*irreg*) N remadora
OAS N ABBR (= *Organization of American States*)
OEA *f*
oases [əu'eɪsiːz] NPL *of* **oasis**
oasis [əu'eɪsɪs] (*pl* **oases**) N oásis *m inv*
oath [əuθ] N juramento; (*swear word*) palavrão *m*;
(*curse*) praga; **on** (*Brit*) *or* **under ~** sob juramento;
to take an ~ prestar juramento
oatmeal ['əutmiːl] N farinha *or* mingau *m* de
aveia
oats [əuts] N aveia
OAU N ABBR (= *Organization of African Unity*)
OUA *f*
obdurate ['ɔbdjurɪt] ADJ (*obstinate*) teimoso;
(*sinner*) empedernido; (*unyielding*) inflexível
obedience [ə'biːdɪəns] N obediência; **in ~ to** em
conformidade com
obedient [ə'biːdɪənt] ADJ obediente; **to be ~ to
sb/sth** obedecer a alguém/algo
obelisk ['ɔbɪlɪsk] N obelisco
obese [əu'biːs] ADJ obeso
obesity [əu'biːsɪtɪ] N obesidade *f*
obey [ə'beɪ] VT obedecer a; (*instructions,
regulations*) cumprir ■ VI obedecer
obituary [ə'bɪtjuərɪ] N necrológio
object [*n* 'ɔbdʒɪkt, *vi* əb'dʒɛkt] N (*gen, Ling*)
objeto; (*purpose*) objetivo ■ VI: **to ~ to** (*attitude*)
desaprovar, objetar a; (*proposal*) opor-se a; **I ~!**
protesto!; **he ~ed that ...** ele objetou que ...; **do
you ~ to my smoking?** você se incomoda que
eu fume?; **what's the ~ of doing that?** qual o
objetivo de fazer isso?; **expense is no ~** o preço
não é problema
objection [əb'dʒɛkʃən] N objeção *f*; (*drawback*)
inconveniente *m*; **I have no ~ to ...** não tenho
nada contra ...; **to make** *or* **raise an ~** fazer *or*
levantar uma objeção
objectionable [əb'dʒɛkʃənəbl] ADJ

desagradável; (*conduct*) censurável
objective [əb'dʒɛktɪv] ADJ objetivo ■ N
objetivo
objectivity [ɔbdʒɪk'tɪvɪtɪ] N objetividade *f*
object lesson N (*fig*): **~ (in)** demonstração *f* (de)
objector [əb'dʒɛktəʳ] N opositor(a) *m/f*
obligation [ɔblɪ'geɪʃən] N obrigação *f*;
(*debt*) dívida (de gratidão); **without ~** sem
compromisso; **to be under an ~ to do sth** ser
obrigado a fazer algo
obligatory [ə'blɪgətərɪ] ADJ obrigatório
oblige [ə'blaɪdʒ] VT (*do a favour for*) obsequiar,
fazer um favor a; (*force*): **to ~ sb to do sth**
obrigar *or* forçar alguém a fazer algo; **to be
~d to sb for doing sth** ficar agradecido por
alguém fazer algo; **anything to ~!** (*inf*) estou à
sua disposição!
obliging [ə'blaɪdʒɪŋ] ADJ prestativo
oblique [ə'bliːk] ADJ oblíquo; (*allusion*)
indireto
obliterate [ə'blɪtəreɪt] VT (*erase*) apagar; (*destroy*)
destruir
oblivion [ə'blɪvɪən] N esquecimento
oblivious [ə'blɪvɪəs] ADJ: **~ of** inconsciente de,
esquecido de
oblong ['ɔblɔŋ] ADJ oblongo, retangular ■ N
retângulo
obnoxious [əb'nɔkʃəs] ADJ odioso, detestável;
(*smell*) enjoativo
o.b.o (*US*) ABBR (= *or best offer*) ou melhor
oferta
oboe ['əubəu] N oboé *m*
obscene [əb'siːn] ADJ obsceno
obscenity [əb'sɛnɪtɪ] N obscenidade *f*
obscure [əb'skjuəʳ] ADJ obscuro, desconhecido;
(*difficult to understand*) pouco claro ■ VT ocultar,
escurecer; (*hide: sun etc*) esconder
obscurity [əb'skjuərɪtɪ] N obscuridade *f*;
(*darkness*) escuridão *f*
obsequious [əb'siːkwɪəs] ADJ obsequioso,
servil
observable [əb'zɜːvəbl] ADJ observável;
(*appreciable*) perceptível
observance [əb'zɜːvns] N observância,
cumprimento; (*ritual*) prática, hábito; **religious
~s** observância religiosa
observant [əb'zɜːvnt] ADJ observador(a)

observation [ɔbzə'veɪʃən] N observação
f; (by police etc) vigilância; (Med) exame m;
observation post N (Mil) posto de observação

observatory [əb'zə:vətrɪ] N observatório

observe [əb'zə:v] VT observar; (rule) cumprir

observer [əb'zə:vəʳ] N observador(a) m/f

obsess [əb'sɛs] VT obsedar, obcecar; **to be ~ed by** or **with sb/sth** estar obcecado por or com alguém/algo

obsession [əb'sɛʃən] N obsessão f, idéia fixa

obsessive [əb'sɛsɪv] ADJ obsessivo

obsolescence [ɔbsə'lɛsns] N obsolescência; **built-in** or **planned ~** (Comm) obsolescência pré-incorporada

obsolescent [ɔbsə'lɛsnt] ADJ obsolescente, antiquado

obsolete ['ɔbsəli:t] ADJ obsoleto; **to become ~** cair em desuso

obstacle ['ɔbstəkl] N obstáculo; (hindrance) estorvo, impedimento; **obstacle race** N corrida de obstáculos

obstetrician [ɔbstə'trɪʃən] N obstetra m/f

obstetrics [ɔb'stɛtrɪks] N obstetrícia

obstinacy ['ɔbstɪnəsɪ] N teimosia, obstinação f

obstinate ['ɔbstɪnɪt] ADJ obstinado

obstreperous [əb'strɛpərəs] ADJ turbulento

obstruct [əb'strʌkt] VT obstruir; (block: pipe) entupir; (hinder) estorvar

obstruction [əb'strʌkʃən] N obstrução f; (object) obstáculo

obstructive [əb'strʌktɪv] ADJ obstrutor(a)

obtain [əb'teɪn] VT (get) obter; (achieve) conseguir ■ VI prevalecer

obtainable [əb'teɪnəbl] ADJ disponível

obtrusive [əb'tru:sɪv] ADJ (person) intrometido, intruso; (building etc) que dá muito na vista

obtuse [əb'tju:s] ADJ obtuso

obverse ['ɔbvə:s] N (of medal, coin) obverso; (fig) contrapartida

obviate ['ɔbvɪeɪt] VT obviar a, prevenir

obvious ['ɔbvɪəs] ADJ (clear) óbvio, evidente; (unsubtle) nada sutil

obviously ['ɔbvɪəslɪ] ADV evidentemente; **~, he was not drunk** or **he was ~ not drunk** certamente ele não estava bêbado; **he was not ~ drunk** ele não aparentava estar bêbado; **~!** claro!, lógico!; **~ not!** (é) claro que não!

OCAS N ABBR (= Organization of Central American States) ODECA f

occasion [ə'keɪʒən] N ocasião f; (event) acontecimento ■ VT ocasionar, causar; **on that ~** naquela ocasião; **to rise to the ~** mostrar-se à altura da situação

occasional [ə'keɪʒənl] ADJ de vez em quando

occasionally [ə'keɪʒənəlɪ] ADV de vez em quando; **very ~** raramente

occasional table N mesinha

occult [ɔ'kʌlt] ADJ oculto ■ N: **the ~** as ciências ocultas

occupancy ['ɔkjupənsɪ] N ocupação f, posse f

occupant ['ɔkjupənt] N (of house) inquilino(-a); (of car) ocupante m/f

occupation [ɔkju'peɪʃən] N ocupação f; (job) profissão f; **unfit for ~** (house) inabitável

occupational [ɔkju'peɪʃənl] ADJ (accident) de trabalho; (disease) profissional; **occupational guidance** (Brit) N orientação f vocacional; **occupational hazard** N risco profissional; **occupational pension** N pensão f profissional; **occupational therapy** N terapia ocupacional

occupier ['ɔkjupaɪəʳ] N inquilino(-a)

occupy ['ɔkjupaɪ] VT ocupar; (house) morar em; **to ~ o.s. in doing** (as job) dedicar-se a fazer; (be busy with) ocupar-se de fazer; **to be occupied with sth** ocupar-se de algo

occur [ə'kə:ʳ] VI (event) ocorrer; (phenomenon) acontecer; (difficulty, opportunity) surgir; **to ~ to sb** ocorrer a alguém; **it ~s to me that ...** ocorre-me que ...

occurrence [ə'kʌrəns] N (event) ocorrência, acontecimento; (existence) existência

ocean ['əuʃən] N oceano; **~s of** (inf) um monte de; **ocean bed** N fundo do oceano

ocean-going [-'gəuɪŋ] ADJ de longo curso

Oceania [əuʃɪ'eɪnɪə] N Oceania

ocean liner N transatlântico

ochre ['əukəʳ] (US **ocher**) ADJ cor de ocre inv

o'clock [ə'klɔk] ADV: **it is 5 o'clock** são cinco horas

OCR N ABBR = **optical character reader**; **optical character recognition**

Oct. ABBR (= October) out

octagonal [ɔk'tægənl] ADJ octogonal

octane ['ɔkteɪn] N octano; **high-~ petrol** (Brit) or **gas** (US) gasolina de alto índice de octana

octave ['ɔktɪv] N oitava

October [ɔk'təubəʳ] N outubro; see also **July**

octogenarian [ɔktəudʒɪ'nɛərɪən] N octogenário(-a)

octopus ['ɔktəpəs] N polvo

odd [ɔd] ADJ (strange) estranho, esquisito; (number) ímpar; (sock etc) desemparelhado; (left over) avulso, de sobra; **60~** 60 e tantos; **at ~ times** às vezes, de vez em quando; **to be the ~ one out** ficar sobrando, ser a exceção

oddball ['ɔdbɔ:l] (inf) N excêntrico(-a), esquisito(-ona) m/f

oddity ['ɔdɪtɪ] N coisa estranha, esquisitice f; (person) excêntrico(-a)

odd-job man (irreg) N faz-tudo m

odd jobs NPL biscates mpl, bicos mpl

oddly ['ɔdlɪ] ADV curiosamente; see also **enough**

oddments ['ɔdmənts] (Brit) NPL (Comm) retalhos mpl

odds [ɔdz] NPL (in betting) pontos mpl de vantagem; **the ~ are against his coming** é pouco provável que ele venha; **it makes no ~** dá no mesmo; **to succeed against all the ~** conseguir contra todas as expectativas; **at ~** brigados(-as), de mal; **odds and ends** NPL miudezas fpl

ode [əud] N ode f

odious ['əudɪəs] ADJ odioso

odometer [əu'dɔmɪtəʳ] N conta-quilômetros m inv

odour ['əudəʳ] (US **odor**) N odor m, cheiro; (unpleasant) fedor m

odo(u)rless ['əudəlɪs] ADJ inodoro

OECD N ABBR (= Organization for Economic Cooperation and Development) OCDE f

oesophagus [iːˈsɔfəgəs] (US **esophagus**) N esôfago

oestrogen ['iːstrəudʒən] (US **estrogen**) N estrogênio

○ KEYWORD

of [ɔv, əv] PREP 1 (gen) de; **the history of France** a história da França; **a friend of ours** um amigo nosso; **a boy of 10** um menino de 10 anos; **that was very kind of you** foi muito gentil da sua parte; **the city of New York** a cidade de Nova Iorque

2 (expressing quantity, amount, dates etc) de; **a kilo of flour** um quilo de farinha; **how much of this do you need?** de quanto você precisa?; **3 of them** 3 deles; **3 of us went** 3 de nós foram; **a cup of tea/vase of flowers** uma xícara de chá/um vaso de flores; **the 5th of July** dia 5 de julho

3 (from, out of) de; **a statue of marble** uma estátua de mármore; **made of wood** feito de madeira

○ KEYWORD

off [ɔf] ADV 1 (referring to distance, time): **it's a long way off** fica bem longe; **the game is 3 days off** o jogo é daqui a 3 dias

2 (departure): **I'm off** estou de partida; **to go off to Paris/Italy** ir para Paris/a Itália; **I must be off** devo ir-me

3 (removal): **to take off one's hat/coat/clothes** tirar o chapéu/o casaco/a roupa; **the button came off** o botão caiu; **10% off** (Comm) 10% de abatimento or desconto

4 (not at work: on holiday): **to have a day off** tirar um dia de folga; (: sick): **to be off sick** estar ausente por motivo de saúde; **I'm off on Fridays** estou de folga às sextas-feiras

■ ADJ 1 (not turned on: machine, water, gas) desligado; (: light) apagado; (: tap) fechado

2 (cancelled: meeting, match, agreement) cancelado

3 (Brit: not fresh: food) passado; (: milk) talhado, anulado

4: **on the off chance** (just in case) ao acaso; **today I had an off day** (not as good as usual) hoje não foi o meu dia

■ PREP 1 (indicating motion, removal, etc) de; **the button came off my coat** o botão do meu casaco caiu

2 (distant from) de; **5 km off (the road)** a 5 km(da estrada); **off the coast** em frente à costa

3: **to be off meat** (no longer eat it) não comer mais carne; (no longer like it) enjoar de carne

offal ['ɔfl] N (Culin) sobras fpl, restos mpl

offbeat ['ɔfbiːt] ADJ excêntrico

off-centre (US **off-center**) ADJ descentrado, excêntrico

off-colour (Brit) ADJ (ill) indisposto

offence [ə'fɛns] (US **offense**) N (crime) delito; (insult) insulto, ofensa; **to give ~ to** ofender; **to take ~ at** ofender-se com, melindrar-se com; **to commit an ~** cometer uma infração

offend [ə'fɛnd] VT (person) ofender ■ VI: **to ~ against** (law, rule) pecar contra, transgredir

offender [ə'fɛndəʳ] N delinqüente m/f; (against regulations) infrator(a) m/f

offense [ə'fɛns] (US) N = **offence**

offensive [ə'fɛnsɪv] ADJ (weapon, remark) ofensivo; (smell etc) repugnante ■ N (Mil) ofensiva

offer ['ɔfəʳ] N oferta; (proposal) proposta ■ VT oferecer; (opportunity) proporcionar; **to make an ~ for sth** fazer uma oferta por algo; **to ~ sth to sb, ~ sb sth** oferecer algo a alguém; **to ~ to do sth** oferecer-se para fazer algo; **"on ~"** (Comm) "em oferta"

offering ['ɔfərɪŋ] N oferenda

offertory ['ɔfətərɪ] N (Rel) ofertório

off-hand [ɔfˈhænd] ADJ informal ■ ADV de improviso; **I can't tell you ~** não posso te dizer assim de improviso

office ['ɔfɪs] N (place) escritório; (room) gabinete m; (position) cargo, função f; **to take ~** tomar posse; **doctor's ~** (US) consultório; **through his good ~s** (fig) graças aos grandes préstimos dele; **O~ of Fair Trading** (Brit) órgão de proteção ao consumidor; **office automation** N automação f de escritórios; **office bearer** N (of club etc) detentor(a) m/f de um cargo; **office block** (US **office building**) N conjunto de escritórios; **office boy** N contínuo, bói m; **office building** (US) N conjunto de escritórios; **office hours** NPL (horas fpl de) expediente m; (US: Med) horas fpl de consulta; **office manager** N gerente m/f de escritório

officer ['ɔfɪsəʳ] N (Mil etc) oficial m/f; (of organization) diretor(a) m/f; (also: **police officer**) agente m/f policial or de polícia

office work N trabalho de escritório

office worker N empregado(-a) or funcionário(-a) de escritório

official [ə'fɪʃl] ADJ oficial ■ N oficial m/f; (civil servant) funcionário(-a) (público(-a))

officialdom [ə'fɪʃldəm] (pej) N burocracia

officially [ə'fɪʃəlɪ] ADV oficialmente

official receiver N síndico(-a) de massa falida

officiate [ə'fɪʃɪeɪt] VI (Rel) oficiar; **to ~ as Mayor** exercer as funções de prefeito; **to ~ at a marriage** celebrar um casamento

officious [ə'fɪʃəs] ADJ intrometido

offing ['ɔfɪŋ] N: **in the ~** (fig) em perspectiva

off-key ADJ, ADV desafinado

off-licence (Brit) N (shop) loja de bebidas alcoólicas

● OFF-LICENCE
●
● Uma loja off-licence vende bebidas alcóolicas
● (para viagem) nos horários em que os pubs
● estão fechados. Nesses estabelecimentos
● também se pode comprar bebidas não-
● alcoólicas, cigarros, batatas fritas, balas,
● chocolates etc.

off-limits (esp US) ADJ proibido

off line ADJ (Comput) fora de linha; (: switched off) desligado

off-load VT: **to ~ sth (onto)** (goods) descarregar algo (sobre); (job) descarregar algo (em)

off-peak ADJ (heating etc) de período de pouco consumo; (ticket, train) de período de pouco movimento

off-putting [-'putɪŋ] (Brit) ADJ desconcertante

off-season ADJ, ADV fora de estação or temporada

offset ['ɔfsɛt] (irreg: like set) VT (counteract) compensar, contrabalançar ■ N (also: **offset printing**) ofsete m

offshoot ['ɔfʃuːt] (fig) N desdobramento

offshore [ɔf'ʃɔːʳ] ADV a pouca distância da costa, ao largo ■ ADJ (breeze) de terra; (island) perto do litoral; (fishing) costeiro; **~ oilfield** campo petrolífero ao largo

offside ['ɔf'saɪd] N (Aut) lado do motorista ■ ADJ (Sport) impedido; (Aut) do lado do motorista

offspring ['ɔfsprɪŋ] N descendência, prole f

offstage ['ɔf'steɪdʒ] ADV nos bastidores

off-the-cuff ADJ improvisado ■ ADV de improviso

off-the-job training N treinamento fora do local de trabalho

off-the-peg (US **off-the-rack**) ADJ pronto

off-white ADJ quase branco

often ['ɔfn] ADV muitas vezes, freqüentemente; **how ~ do you go?** quantas vezes or com que freqüência você vai?; **as ~ as not** quase sempre; **very ~** com muita freqüência

ogle ['əugl] VT comer com os olhos

ogre ['əugəʳ] N ogre m

OH (US) ABBR (Post) = **Ohio**

oh [əu] EXCL oh!, ô!, ah!

OHMS (Brit) ABBR = **On His (or Her) Majesty's Service**

oil [ɔɪl] N (Culin) azeite m; (petroleum) petróleo; (for heating) óleo ■ VT (machine) lubrificar

oilcan ['ɔɪlkæn] N almotolia; (for storing) lata

oil change N mudança de óleo

oilfield ['ɔɪlfiːld] N campo petrolífero

oil filter N (Aut) filtro de óleo

oil-fired [-'faɪəd] ADJ que usa óleo combustível

oil gauge N indicador m do nível de óleo

oil industry N indústria petroleira

oil level N nível m de óleo

oil painting N pintura a óleo

oil refinery N refinaria de petróleo

oil rig N torre f de perfuração

oilskins ['ɔɪlskɪnz] NPL capa de oleado

oil slick N mancha de óleo

oil tanker N (ship) petroleiro; (truck) carro-tanque m de petróleo

oil well N poço petrolífero

oily ['ɔɪlɪ] ADJ oleoso; (food) gorduroso

ointment ['ɔɪntmənt] N pomada

OK (US) ABBR (Post) = **Oklahoma**

O.K. ['əu'keɪ] EXCL está bem, está bom, tá (bem or bom) (inf) ■ ADJ bom; (correct) certo ■ VT aprovar ■ N: **to give sth the O.K.** dar luz verde a algo; **is it O.K.?** tá bom?; **are you O.K.?** você está bem?; **are you O.K. for money?** você está bem de dinheiro?; **it's O.K. with** or **by me** para mim tudo bem

okay ['əu'keɪ] = **O.K.**

old [əuld] ADJ velho; (former) antigo, anterior; **how ~ are you?** quantos anos você tem?; **he's 10 years ~** ele tem 10 anos; **~er brother** irmão mais velho; **any ~ thing will do** qualquer coisa serve; **old age** N velhice f

old-age pensioner (Brit) N aposentado(-a) (BR), reformado(-a) (PT)

old-fashioned [-'fæʃnd] ADJ fora de moda; (person) antiquado; (values) absoleto, retrógrado

old maid N solteirona

old people's home N asilo de velhos

old-time ADJ antigo, do tempo antigo

old-timer N veterano

old wives' tale N conto da carochinha

olive ['ɔlɪv] N (fruit) azeitona; (tree) oliveira ■ ADJ (also: **olive-green**) verde-oliva inv; **olive oil** N azeite m de oliva

Olympic [əu'lɪmpɪk] ADJ olímpico; **the ~ Games**, **the ~s** os Jogos Olímpicos, as Olimpíadas

OM (Brit) N ABBR (= Order of Merit) título honorífico

Oman [əu'mɑːn] N Omã m (BR), Oman m (PT)

OMB (US) N ABBR (= Office of Management and Budget) serviço que assessora o presidente em assuntos orçamentários

omelet(te) ['ɔmlɪt] N omelete f (BR), omeleta (PT)

omen ['əumən] N presságio, agouro

ominous ['ɔmɪnəs] ADJ (menacing) preocupante; (event) de mau agouro

omission [əu'mɪʃən] N omissão f; (error) descuido, negligência

omit [əu'mɪt] VT omitir; (by mistake) esquecer; **to ~ to do sth** deixar de fazer algo

omnivorous [ɔm'nɪvərəs] ADJ onívoro

ON (Canada) ABBR = **Ontario**

◯ KEYWORD

on [ɔn] PREP **1** (indicating position) sobre, em(cima de); **on the wall** na parede; **on the left** à esquerda; **the house is on the main road** a casa fica na rua principal

2 (indicating means, method, condition etc): **on foot** a pé; **on the train/plane** no trem/no avião;

on the telephone/radio no telefone/rádio; **on television** na televisão; **to be on drugs** (addicted) ser viciado em drogas; (Med) estar sob medicação; **to be on holiday/business** estar de férias/a negócio
3 (referring to time): **on Friday** na sexta-feira; **a week on Friday** sem ser esta sexta-feira, a outra; **on arrival** ao chegar; **on seeing this** ao ver isto
4 (about, concerning) sobre
■ ADV **1** (referring to dress): **to have one's coat on** estar de casaco; **what's she got on?** o que ela está usando?; **she put her boots on** ela calçou as botas; **he put his gloves/hat on** ele colocou as luvas/o chapéu
2 (referring to covering): **screw the lid on tightly** atarraxar bem a tampa
3 (further, continuously): **to walk/drive on** continuar andando/dirigindo; **to go on** continuar(em frente); **to read on** continuar a ler
■ ADJ **1** (functioning, in operation: machine) em funcionamento; (light) aceso; (radio) ligado; (tap) aberto; (brakes: of car etc): **to be on** estar freado; (meeting): **is the meeting still on?** (in progress) a reunião ainda está sendo realizada?; (not cancelled) ainda vai haver reunião?; **there's a good film on at the cinema** tem um bom filme passando no cinema
2: **that's not on!** (inf: of behaviour) isso não se faz!

ONC (Brit) N ABBR = **Ordinary National Certificate**
once [wʌns] ADV uma vez; (formerly) outrora
■ CONJ depois que; **~ he had left/it was done** depois que ele saiu/foi feito; **at ~** imediatamente; (simultaneously) de uma vez, ao mesmo tempo; **all at ~** de repente; **~ a week** uma vez por semana; **~ more** mais uma vez; **I knew him ~** eu o conheci antigamente; **~ and for all** uma vez por todas, definitivamente; **~ upon a time** era uma vez
oncoming [ˈɔnkʌmɪŋ] ADJ (traffic) que vem de frente
OND (Brit) N ABBR = **Ordinary National Diploma**

 KEYWORD

one [wʌn] NUM um(a); **one hundred and fifty** cento e cinqüenta; **one by one** um por um
■ ADJ **1** (sole) único; **the one book which ...** o único livro que ...
2 (same) mesmo; **they came in the one car** eles vieram no mesmo carro
■ PRON **1** um(a); **this one** este/esta; **that one** esse/essa, aquele/aquela; **I've already got one/a red one** eu já tenho um/um vermelho
2: **one another** um ao outro; **do you two ever see one another?** vocês dois se vêem de vez em quando?; **the boys didn't dare look at one another** os meninos não ousaram olhar um para o outro

3 (impers): **one never knows** nunca se sabe; **to cut one's finger** cortar o dedo; **one needs to eat** é preciso comer

one-armed bandit N caça-níqueis m inv
one-day excursion (US) N bilhete m de ida e volta
one-man ADJ (business) individual; **one-man band** N homem-orquestra m
one-off (Brit: inf) N exemplar m único ■ ADJ único
one-piece ADJ: **~ bathing suit** maiô inteiro
onerous [ˈəʊnərəs] ADJ (task, duty) incômodo; (responsibility) pesado

○ **KEYWORD**

oneself [wʌnˈsɛlf] PRON (reflexive) se; (after prep, emphatic) si(mesmo/a); **by oneself** sozinho(-a); **to hurt oneself** ferir-se; **to keep sth for oneself** guardar algo para si mesmo; **to talk to oneself** falar consigo mesmo

one-sided [-ˈsaɪdɪd] ADJ (decision) unilateral; (judgement, account) parcial; (contest) desigual
one-time ADJ antigo
one-to-one ADJ (relationship) individual
one-upmanship [-ˈʌpmənʃɪp] N: **the art of ~** a arte de aparentar ser melhor do que os outros
one-way ADJ (street, traffic) de mão única (BR), de sentido único (PT)
ongoing [ˈɔngəʊɪŋ] ADJ (project) em andamento; (situation) existente
onion [ˈʌnjən] N cebola
on line ADJ (Comput) on-line, em linha; (: switched on) ligado
onlooker [ˈɔnlʊkəʳ] N espectador(a) m/f
only [ˈəʊnlɪ] ADV somente, apenas ■ ADJ único, só ■ CONJ só que, porém; **an ~ child** um filho único; **not ~ ... but also ...** não só ... mas também ...; **I ~ ate one** eu comi só um; **I saw her ~ yesterday** apenas ontem eu a vi; **I'd be ~ too pleased to help** eu teria muitíssimo prazer em ajudar; **I would come, ~ I'm very busy** eu iria, porém estou muito ocupado
ono ABBR (= or nearest offer) ou melhor oferta
onset [ˈɔnsɛt] N (beginning) começo; (attack) ataque m
onshore [ˈɔnʃɔːʳ] ADJ (wind) do mar
onslaught [ˈɔnslɔːt] N investida, arremetida
on-the-job training N treinamento no serviço
onto [ˈɔntu] PREP = **on to**
onus [ˈəʊnəs] N responsabilidade f; **the ~ is upon him to prove it** cabe a ele comprová-lo
onward(s) [ˈɔnwəd(z)] ADV (move) para diante, para a frente; **from this time onward(s)** de (ag)ora em diante
onyx [ˈɔnɪks] N ônix m
ooze [uːz] VI ressumar, filtrar-se; **to ~ a feeling** mostrar um sentimento exagerado
opacity [əʊˈpæsɪtɪ] N opacidade f
opal [ˈəʊpl] N opala

opaque [əu'peɪk] ADJ opaco, fosco

OPEC ['əupɛk] N ABBR (= Organization of Petroleum-Exporting Countries) OPEP f

open ['əupn] ADJ aberto; (car) descoberto; (road) livre; (fig: frank) aberto; (meeting) aberto, sem restrições; (admiration) declarado; (question) discutível; (enemy) assumido ■ VT abrir ■ VI (gen) abrir(-se); (shop) abrir; (book etc: commence) começar; **in the ~ (air)** ao ar livre; **the ~ sea** o largo; **~ ground** (among trees) clareira, abertura; (waste ground) terreno baldio; **to have an ~ mind (on sth)** ter uma cabeça aberta (a respeito de algo)
▸ **open on to** VT FUS (subj: room, door) dar para
▸ **open out** VT abrir ■ VI abrir-se
▸ **open up** VT abrir; (blocked road) desobstruir ■ VI (Comm) abrir

open-air ADJ a céu aberto

open-and-shut ADJ: **~ case** caso evidente

open day (Brit) N dia m de visita

open-ended [-'ɛndɪd] ADJ (fig) não limitado

opener ['əupnər] N (also: **can opener, tin opener**) abridor m de latas (BR), abre-latas m inv (PT)

open-heart surgery N cirurgia de coração aberto

opening ['əupnɪŋ] ADJ de abertura ■ N abertura; (start) início; (opportunity) oportunidade f; (job) vaga; **opening night** N (Theatre) estréia

openly ['əupənlɪ] ADV abertamente

open-minded [-'maɪndɪd] ADJ aberto, imparcial

open-necked [-nɛkt] ADJ aberto no colo

openness ['əupnnɪs] N abertura, sinceridade f

open-plan ADJ sem paredes divisórias

open sandwich N canapé m

open shop N empresa que admite trabalhadores não sindicalizados

Open University (Brit) N universidade que oferece curso universitário por correspondência

◉ **OPEN UNIVERSITY**
◉
◉ Fundada em 1969, a Open University oferece
◉ um tipo de ensino que compreende cursos
◉ (alguns blocos da programação da TV e do
◉ rádio são reservados para esse fim), deveres
◉ que são enviados pelo aluno ao diretor ou
◉ diretora de estudos e uma estada obrigatória
◉ em uma universidade de verão. É preciso
◉ cumprir um certo número de unidades ao
◉ longo de um período determinado e obter
◉ a média em um certo número delas para
◉ receber o diploma almejado.

opera ['ɔpərə] N ópera; **opera glasses** NPL binóculo de teatro; **opera house** N teatro lírico or de ópera; **opera singer** N cantor(a) m/f de ópera

operate ['ɔpəreɪt] VT (machine) fazer funcionar, pôr em funcionamento; (company) dirigir ■ VI funcionar; (drug) fazer efeito; (Med): **to ~ on sb** operar alguém

operatic [ɔpə'rætɪk] ADJ lírico, operístico

operating ['ɔpəreɪtɪŋ] ADJ (Comm: costs, profit) operacional; **operating system** N (Comput) sistema m operacional; **operating table** N mesa de operações; **operating theatre** N sala de operações

operation [ɔpə'reɪʃən] N operação f; (of machine) funcionamento; **to have an ~** fazer uma operação; **to be in ~** (system) estar em vigor; (machine) estar funcionando

operational [ɔpə'reɪʃənl] ADJ operacional; **when the service is fully ~** quando o serviço estiver com toda a sua eficácia

operative ['ɔpərətɪv] ADJ (measure) em vigor ■ N (in factory) operário(-a); **the ~ word** a palavra mais importante or atuante

operator ['ɔpəreɪtər] N (of machine) operador(a) m/f, manipulador(a) m/f; (Tel) telefonista m/f

operetta [ɔpə'rɛtə] N opereta

ophthalmic [ɔf'θælmɪk] ADJ oftálmico

ophthalmologist [ɔfθæl'mɔlədʒɪst] N oftalmologista m/f, oftalmólogo(-a)

opinion [ə'pɪnɪən] N opinião f; **in my ~** na minha opinião, a meu ver; **to seek a second ~** procurar uma segunda opinião

opinionated [ə'pɪnɪəneɪtɪd] ADJ opinioso

opinion poll N pesquisa, levantamento

opium ['əupɪəm] N ópio

opponent [ə'pəunənt] N oponente m/f; (Mil, Sport) adversário(-a)

opportune ['ɔpətjuːn] ADJ oportuno

opportunism [ɔpə'tjuːnɪzəm] N oportunismo

opportunist [ɔpə'tjuːnɪst] N (pej) oportunista m/f

opportunity [ɔpə'tjuːnɪtɪ] N oportunidade f; **to take the ~ of doing** aproveitar a oportunidade para fazer

oppose [ə'pəuz] VT opor-se a; **to be ~d to sth** opor-se a algo, estar contra algo; **as ~d to** em oposição a

opposing [ə'pəuzɪŋ] ADJ (side) oposto, contrário

opposite ['ɔpəzɪt] ADJ oposto; (house etc) em frente ■ ADV (lá) em frente ■ PREP em frente de, defronte de ■ N oposto, contrário; **the ~ sex** o sexo oposto; **opposite number** (Brit) N homólogo(-a)

opposition [ɔpə'zɪʃən] N oposição f

oppress [ə'prɛs] VT oprimir

oppression [ə'prɛʃən] N opressão f

oppressive [ə'prɛsɪv] ADJ opressivo

opprobrium [ə'prəubrɪəm] N (formal) opróbrio

opt [ɔpt] VI: **to ~ for** optar por; **to ~ to do** optar por fazer
▸ **opt out**; **to ~ out of doing sth** optar por não fazer algo

optical ['ɔptɪkl] ADJ ótico; **optical character reader** N leitora de caracteres óticos; **optical character recognition** N reconhecimento de caracteres óticos; **optical fibre** N fibra ótica; **optical illusion** N ilusão f ótica

optician [ɔp'tɪʃən] N oculista m/f

optics ['ɔptɪks] N ótica

optimism ['ɒptɪmɪzəm] N otimismo
optimist ['ɒptɪmɪst] N otimista m/f
optimistic [ɒptɪ'mɪstɪk] ADJ otimista
optimum ['ɒptɪməm] ADJ ótimo
option ['ɒpʃən] N opção f; **to keep one's ~s open** (fig) manter as opções em aberto; **I have no ~** não tenho opção or escolha
optional ['ɒpʃənəl] ADJ opcional, facultativo; **~ extras** acessórios mpl opcionais
opulence ['ɒpjuləns] N opulência
opulent ['ɒpjulənt] ADJ opulento
OR (US) ABBR (Post) = **Oregon**
or [ɔːʳ] CONJ ou; (with negative): **he hasn't seen or heard anything** ele não viu nem ouviu nada; **or else** senão; **either ..., or else** ou ..., ou (então)
oracle ['ɒrəkl] N oráculo
oral ['ɔːrəl] ADJ oral ▪ N exame m oral
orange ['ɒrɪndʒ] N (fruit) laranja ▪ ADJ cor de laranja inv, alaranjado
orangeade [ɒrɪndʒ'eɪd] N laranjada
oration [ɔː'reɪʃən] N oração f
orator ['ɒrətəʳ] N orador(a) m/f
oratorio [ɒrə'tɔːrɪəu] N oratório
orb [ɔːb] N orbe m
orbit ['ɔːbɪt] N órbita ▪ VT, VI orbitar; **to be/go into ~ (around)** estar/entrar em órbita (em torno de)
orchard ['ɔːtʃəd] N pomar m; **apple ~** pomar de macieiras
orchestra ['ɔːkɪstrə] N orquestra; (US: seating) platéia
orchestral [ɔː'kɛstrəl] ADJ orquestral; (concert) sinfônico
orchestrate ['ɔːkɪstreɪt] VT (Mus, fig) orquestrar
orchid ['ɔːkɪd] N orquídea
ordain [ɔː'deɪn] VT ordenar, decretar; (decide) decidir, mandar
ordeal [ɔː'diːl] N experiência penosa, provação f
order ['ɔːdəʳ] N (gen) ordem f; (Comm) encomenda; **good ~** bom estado ▪ VT (also: **put in order**) pôr em ordem, arrumar; (in restaurant) pedir; (Comm) encomendar; (command) mandar, ordenar; **in ~** em ordem; **in (working) ~** em bom estado; **in ~ of preference** por ordem de preferência; **in ~ to do/that** para fazer/que (+ sub); **on ~** (Comm) encomendado; **out of ~** com defeito, enguiçado; **to ~ sb to do sth** mandar alguém fazer algo; **to place an ~ for sth with sb** fazer uma encomenda a alguém para algo, encomendar algo a alguém; **made to ~** feito sob encomenda; **to be under ~s to do sth** ter ordens para fazer algo; **a point of ~** uma questão de ordem; **to the ~ of** (Banking) à ordem de; **order book** N livro de encomendas; **order form** N impresso para encomendas
orderly ['ɔːdəlɪ] N (Mil) ordenança m; (Med) servente m/f ▪ ADJ (room) arrumado, ordenado; (person) metódico
order number N número de encomenda
ordinal ['ɔːdɪnl] ADJ (number) ordinal
ordinary ['ɔːdnrɪ] ADJ comum, usual; (pej) ordinário, medíocre; **out of the ~** fora do comum, extraordinário; **ordinary seaman** (Brit: irreg) N marinheiro de segunda classe; **ordinary shares** NPL ações fpl ordinárias
ordination [ɔːdɪ'neɪʃən] N ordenação f
ordnance ['ɔːdnəns] N (Mil: unit) artilharia
Ordnance Survey (Brit) N serviço oficial de topografia e cartografia
ore [ɔːʳ] N minério
organ ['ɔːgən] N (gen) órgão m
organic [ɔː'gænɪk] ADJ orgânico
organism ['ɔːgənɪzəm] N organismo
organist ['ɔːgənɪst] N organista m/f
organization [ɔːgənaɪ'zeɪʃən] N organização f; **organization chart** N organograma m
organize ['ɔːgənaɪz] VT organizar; **to get ~d** organizar-se
organized labour ['ɔːgənaɪzd-] N mão-de-obra f sindicalizada
organizer ['ɔːgənaɪzəʳ] N organizador(a) m/f
orgasm ['ɔːgæzəm] N orgasmo
orgy ['ɔːdʒɪ] N orgia
Orient ['ɔːrɪənt] N: **the ~** o Oriente
oriental [ɔːrɪ'ɛntl] ADJ, N oriental m/f
orientate ['ɔːrɪənteɪt] VT: **to ~ o.s.** orientar-se
orifice ['ɒrɪfɪs] N orifício
origin ['ɒrɪdʒɪn] N origem f; (point of departure) procedência; **country of ~** país de origem
original [ə'rɪdʒɪnl] ADJ original ▪ N original m
originality [ərɪdʒɪ'nælɪtɪ] N originalidade f
originally [ə'rɪdʒɪnəlɪ] ADV (at first) originalmente; (with originality) com originalidade
originate [ə'rɪdʒɪneɪt] VI: **to ~ from** originar-se de, surgir de; **to ~ in** ter origem em
originator [ə'rɪdʒɪneɪtəʳ] N iniciador(a) m/f
Orkneys ['ɔːknɪz] NPL: **the ~** (also: **the Orkney Islands**) as ilhas Órcadas
ornament ['ɔːnəmənt] N ornamento; (trinket) quinquilharia; (on dress) enfeite m
ornamental [ɔːnə'mɛntl] ADJ decorativo, ornamental
ornamentation [ɔːnəmɛn'teɪʃən] N ornamentação f
ornate [ɔː'neɪt] ADJ enfeitado, requintado
ornithologist [ɔːnɪ'θɒlədʒɪst] N ornitólogo(-a)
ornithology [ɔːnɪ'θɒlədʒɪ] N ornitologia
orphan ['ɔːfn] N órfão/órfã m/f ▪ VT: **to be ~ed** ficar orfão
orphanage ['ɔːfənɪdʒ] N orfanato
orthodox ['ɔːθədɒks] ADJ ortodoxo
orthopaedic [ɔːθə'piːdɪk] (US **orthopedic**) ADJ ortopédico
OS (Brit) ABBR = **Ordnance Survey**; (Naut) = **ordinary seaman**; (Dress) = **outsize**
O/S ABBR = **out of stock**
oscillate ['ɒsɪleɪt] VI oscilar; (person) vacilar, hesitar
OSHA (US) N ABBR (= Occupational Safety and Health Administration) órgão que supervisiona a higiene e a segurança do trabalho
Oslo ['ɒzləu] N Oslo

ostensible [ɔs'tɛnsɪbl] ADJ aparente

ostensibly [ɔs'tɛnsɪblɪ] ADV aparentemente

ostentation [ɔstɛn'teɪʃən] N ostentação f

ostentatious [ɔstɛn'teɪʃəs] ADJ pomposo, espalhafatoso; (person) ostentoso

osteopath ['ɔstɪəpæθ] N osteopata m/f

ostracize ['ɔstrəsaɪz] VT condenar ao ostracismo

ostrich ['ɔstrɪtʃ] N avestruz m/f

OT N ABBR (= Old Testament) AT m

OTB (US) N ABBR (= off-track betting) apostas tomadas fora da pista de corridas

other ['ʌðəʳ] ADJ outro ■ PRON: **the ~ (one)** o outro(-a) outra ■ ADV (usually in negatives): **~ than** (apart from) além de; (anything but) exceto; **~s** (other people) outros; **some ~ people have still to arrive** outras pessoas ainda não chegaram; **the ~ day** outro dia; **some actor or ~** um certo ator; **somebody or ~** não sei quem, alguém; **the car was none ~ than John's** o carro não era nenhum outro senão o de João

otherwise ['ʌðəwaɪz] ADV de outra maneira ■ CONJ (if not) senão; **an ~ good piece of work** sob outros aspectos, um trabalho bem feito

OTT (inf) ABBR = **over the top;** see **top**

otter ['ɔtəʳ] N lontra

OU (Brit) N ABBR = **Open University**

ouch [autʃ] EXCL ai!

ought [ɔːt] (pt ought) AUX VB: **I ~ to do it** eu deveria fazê-lo; **this ~ to have been corrected** isto deveria ter sido corrigido; **he ~ to win** (probability) ele deve ganhar; **you ~ to go and see it** você deveria ir vê-lo

ounce [auns] N onça (= 28.35g)

our ['auəʳ] ADJ nosso; see also **my**

ours ['auəz] PRON (o) nosso/(a) nossa etc; see also **mine**

ourselves [auə'sɛlvz] PRON PL (reflexive, after prep) nós; (emphatic) nós mesmos(-as); **we did it (all) by ~** nós fizemos isso sozinhos; see also **oneself**

oust [aust] VT expulsar

🔵 **KEYWORD**

out [aut] ADV **1** (not in) fora; **(to stand) out in the rain/snow** (estar em pé) na chuva/neve; **it's cold out here/out in the desert** está frio aqui fora/faz frio lá no deserto; **out here/there** aqui/lá fora; **to go/come** etc **out** sair/vir etc para fora; **out loud** em voz alta

2 (not at home, absent) fora(de casa); **Mr Green is out at the moment** Sr. Green não está no momento; **to have a day/night out** passar o dia fora/sair à noite

3 (indicating distance): **the boat was 10 km out** o barco estava a 10 km da costa; **3 days out from Plymouth** 3 dias fora de Plymouth

4 (Sport): **the ball is/has gone out** a bola caiu fora; **out!** (Tennis etc) fora!

■ ADJ **1: to be out** (unconscious) estar inconsciente; (out of game) estar fora; (out of fashion) estar fora de moda

2 (have appeared: news, secret) do conhecimento público; (: flowers): **the flowers are out** as flores desabrocharam

3 (extinguished: light, fire) apagado; **before the week was out** (finished) antes da semana acabar

4: to be out to do sth (intend) pretender fazer algo; **to be out in one's calculations** (wrong) enganar-se nos cálculos

■ PREP: **out of 1** (outside, beyond): **out of** fora de; **to go out of the house** sair da casa; **to look out of the window** olhar pela janela

2 (cause, motive) por; **out of curiosity/fear/greed** por curiosidade/medo/ganância

3 (origin): **to drink sth out of a cup** beber algo na xícara; **to copy sth out of a book** copiar algo de um livro

4 (from among): **1 out of every 3 smokers** 1 entre 3 fumantes; **out of 100 cars sold, only one had any faults** dos 100 carros vendidos, só um tinha defeito

5 (without) sem; **to be out of milk/sugar/petrol** etc não ter leite/açúcar/gasolina etc

outage ['autɪdʒ] (esp US) N (power failure) blecaute m

out-and-out ADJ (liar etc) completo, rematado

outback ['autbæk] N (in Australia): **the ~** o interior

outbid [aut'bɪd] (pt, pp **outbidded**) VT sobrepujar

outboard ['autbɔːd] N (also: **outboard motor**) motor m de popa

outbreak ['autbreɪk] N (of war) deflagração f; (of disease) surto; (of violence etc) explosão f

outbuilding ['autbɪldɪŋ] N dependência

outburst ['autbəːst] N explosão f

outcast ['autkɑːst] N pária m/f

outclass [aut'klɑːs] VT ultrapassar, superar

outcome ['autkʌm] N resultado

outcrop ['autkrɔp] N afloramento

outcry ['autkraɪ] N clamor m (de protesto)

outdated [aut'deɪtɪd] ADJ antiquado, fora de moda

outdistance [aut'dɪstəns] VT deixar para trás

outdo [aut'duː] (irreg) VT ultrapassar, exceder

outdoor [aut'dɔːʳ] ADJ ao ar livre; (clothes) de sair

outdoors [aut'dɔːz] ADV ao ar livre

outer ['autəʳ] ADJ exterior, externo; **outer space** N espaço (exterior)

outfit ['autfɪt] N equipamento; (clothes) roupa, traje m; (inf: Comm) firma

outfitter's ['autfɪtəz] (Brit) N fornecedor m de roupas

outgoing ['autgəuɪŋ] ADJ (president, tenant) de saída; (character) extrovertido, sociável

outgoings ['autgəuɪŋz] (Brit) NPL despesas fpl

outgrow [aut'grəu] (irreg) VT: **he has ~n his clothes** a roupa ficou pequena para ele

outhouse ['authaus] N anexo

outing ['autɪŋ] N (going out) saída; (excursion) excursão f

outlandish [aut'lændɪʃ] ADJ estranho, bizarro

outlast [aut'lɑːst] VT sobreviver a

outlaw ['autlɔː] N fora-da-lei m/f; vt; (*person*) declarar fora da lei; (*practice*) declarar ilegal

outlay ['autleɪ] N despesas *fpl*

outlet ['autlɛt] N saída, escape *m*; (*of pipe*) desagüe *m*, escoadouro; (*US: Elec*) tomada; (*also:* **retail outlet**) posto de venda

outline ['autlaɪn] N (*shape*) contorno, perfil *m*; (*of plan*) traçado; (*sketch*) esboço, linhas *fpl* gerais ▪ vt (*theory, plan*) traçar, delinear

outlive [aut'lɪv] vt sobreviver a

outlook ['autluk] N (*attitude*) ponto de vista; (*fig: prospects*) perspectiva; (*: for weather*) previsão *f*

outlying ['autlaɪɪŋ] ADJ afastado, remoto

outmanoeuvre [autmə'nuːvəʳ] (*US* **outmaneuver**) vt (*rival etc*) passar a perna em

outmoded [aut'məudɪd] ADJ antiquado, fora de moda, obsoleto

outnumber [aut'nʌmbəʳ] vt exceder em número

out-of-date ADJ (*passport, ticket*) sem validade; (*theory, idea*) antiquado, superado; (*custom*) antiquado; (*clothes*) fora de moda

out-of-the-way ADJ remoto, afastado; (*fig*) insólito

outpatient ['autpeɪʃənt] N paciente *m/f* externo(-a) *or* de ambulatório

outpost ['autpəust] N posto avançado

output ['autput] N (*volume m* de) produção *f*; (*Tech*) rendimento; (*Comput*) saída ▪ vt (*Comput*) liberar

outrage ['autreɪdʒ] N (*scandal*) escândalo; (*atrocity*) atrocidade *f* ▪ vt ultrajar

outrageous [aut'reɪdʒəs] ADJ ultrajante, escandaloso

outrider ['autraɪdəʳ] N (*on motorcycle*) batedor(a) *m/f*

outright [*adv* aut'raɪt, *adj* 'autraɪt] ADV (*kill, win*) completamente; (*ask, refuse*) abertamente ▪ ADJ completo; franco

outrun [aut'rʌn] (*irreg*) vt ultrapassar

outset ['autsɛt] N início, princípio

outshine [aut'ʃaɪn] (*irreg*) vt (*fig*) eclipsar

outside [aut'saɪd] N exterior *m* ▪ ADJ exterior, externo; (*contractor etc*) de fora ▪ ADV (lá) fora ▪ PREP fora de; (*beyond*) além (dos limites) de; **at the ~** (*fig*) no máximo; **an ~ chance** uma possibilidade remota; **outside broadcast** N (*Radio, TV*) transmissão *f* de exteriores; **outside lane** N (*Aut: in Britain*) pista da direita; (*: in US, Europe*) pista da esquerda; **outside left** N (*Football*) extremo-esquerdo; **outside line** N (*Tel*) linha de saída

outsider [aut'saɪdəʳ] N (*stranger*) estranho(-a), forasteiro(-a); (*in race etc*) outsider *m*

outsize ['autsaɪz] ADJ enorme; (*clothes*) de tamanho extra-grande *or* especial

outskirts ['autskəːts] NPL arredores *mpl*, subúrbios *mpl*

outsmart [aut'smɑːt] vt passar a perna em

outspoken [aut'spəukən] ADJ franco, sem rodeios

outspread [aut'sprɛd] ADJ estendido

outstanding [aut'stændɪŋ] ADJ excepcional; (*work, debt*) pendente; **your account is still ~ a** sua conta ainda não está liquidada

outstay [aut'steɪ] vt: **to ~ one's welcome** abusar da hospitalidade (demorando mais tempo)

outstretched [aut'strɛtʃt] ADJ (*hand*) estendido; (*body*) esticado

outstrip [aut'strɪp] vt (*competitors, demand*) ultrapassar

out tray N cesta de saída

outvote [aut'vəut] vt: **to ~ sb (by ...)** vencer alguém (por ... votos); **to ~ sth (by ...)** rejeitar algo (por ... votos)

outward ['autwəd] ADJ (*sign, appearances*) externo; (*journey*) de ida

outwardly ['autwədlɪ] ADV para fora

outweigh [aut'weɪ] vt ter mais valor do que

outwit [aut'wɪt] vt passar a perna em

oval ['əuvl] ADJ ovalado ▪ N oval *m*; **Oval Office** N *ver abaixo*

 OVAL OFFICE

O Salão Oval (*Oval Office*) é o escritório particular do presidente dos Estados Unidos na Casa Branca, assim chamado devido a sua forma oval. Por extensão, o termo se refere à presidência em si.

ovary ['əuvərɪ] N ovário

ovation [əu'veɪʃən] N ovação *f*

oven ['ʌvn] N forno

ovenproof ['ʌvnpruːf] ADJ refratário

oven-ready ADJ pronto para o forno

ovenware ['ʌvnwɛəʳ] N louça refratária

○ **KEYWORD**

over ['əuvəʳ] ADV 1 (*across: walk, jump, fly etc*) por cima; **to cross over to the other side of the road** atravessar para o outro lado da rua; **over here** por aqui, cá; **over there** por ali, lá; **to ask sb over** (*to one's home*) convidar alguém

2: **to fall over** cair; **to knock over** derrubar; **to turn over** virar; **to bend over** curvar-se, debruçar-se

3 (*finished*): **to be over** estar acabado

4 (*excessively: clever, rich, fat etc*) muito, demais; **she's not over intelligent** ela não é superdotada

5 (*remaining: money, food etc*): **there are 3 over** tem 3 sobrando/sobraram 3; **is there any cake left over?** sobrou algum bolo?

6: **all over** (*everywhere*) por todos os lados; **over and over (again)** repetidamente

▪ PREP **1** (*on top of*) sobre; (*above*) acima de

2 (*on the other side of*) no outro lado de; **he jumped over the wall** ele pulou o muro

3 (*more than*) mais de; **over and above** além de; **this order is over and above what we have already ordered** esta encomenda está acima

do que já havíamos pedido
4 (*during*) durante; **let's discuss it over dinner**
vamos discutir isto durante o jantar

over... [əuvəʳ] PREFIX sobre..., super...
overabundant [əuvərə'bʌndənt] ADJ
superabundante
overact [əuvər'ækt] VI (*Theatre*) exagerar
overall N, ADJ [*n* 'əuvərɔːl, *adv* əuvər'ɔːl]
■ ADJ (*length*) total; (*study*) global ■ ADV (*view*)
globalmente; (*measure, paint*) totalmente;
overalls NPL macacão *m* (BR), (fato) macaco
(PT)
overanxious [əuvər'æŋkʃəs] ADJ muito ansioso
overawe [əuvər'ɔː] VT intimidar
overbalance [əuvə'bæləns] VI perder o
equilíbrio, desequilibrar-se
overbearing [əuvə'bɛəriŋ] ADJ autoritário,
dominador(a); (*arrogant*) arrogante
overboard ['əuvəbɔːd] ADV (*Naut*) ao mar;
man ~! homem ao mar!; **to go ~ for sth** (*fig*)
empolgar-se com algo
overbook [əuvə'buk] VI reservar em excesso
overcapitalize [əuvə'kæpitəlaiz] VT
sobrecapitalizar
overcast ['əuvəkɑːst] ADJ nublado, fechado
overcharge [əuvə'tʃɑːdʒ] VT: **to ~ sb** cobrar em
excesso a alguém
overcoat ['əuvəkəut] N sobretudo
overcome [əuvə'kʌm] (*irreg*) VT vencer,
dominar; (*difficulty*) superar ■ ADJ (*emotionally*)
assolado; **~ with grief** tomado pelador
overconfident [əuvə'kɔnfidənt] ADJ confiante
em excesso
overcrowded [əuvə'kraudid] ADJ superlotado;
(*country*) superpovoado
overcrowding [əuvə'kraudiŋ] N superlotação *f*;
(*in country*) superpovoamento
overdo [əuvə'duː] (*irreg*) VT exagerar; (*overcook*)
cozinhar demais; **to ~ it, to ~ things** (*work too
hard*) exceder-se; (*go too far*) exagerar
overdose ['əuvədəus] N overdose *f*, dose *f*
excessiva
overdraft ['əuvədrɑːft] N saldo negativo
overdrawn [əuvə'drɔːn] ADJ (*account*) sem
fundos, a descoberto
overdue [əuvə'djuː] ADJ atrasado; (*Comm*)
vencido; (*change*) tardio; **that change was long
~** essa mudança foi muito protelada
overestimate [əuvər'ɛstimeit] VT sobrestimar
overexcited [əuvərik'saitid] ADJ superexcitado
over-exertion [əuvəriɡ'zəːʃən] N estafa
overexpose [əuvərik'spəuz] VT (*Phot*) expor
demais (à luz)
overflow [*vi* əuvə'fləu, *n* 'əuvəfləu] VI
transbordar ■ N (*excess*) excesso; (*also*: **overflow
pipe**) tubo de descarga, ladrão *m*
overfly [əuvə'flai] (*irreg*) VT sobrevoar
overgenerous [əuvə'dʒɛnərəs] ADJ pródigo;
(*offer*) excessivo
overgrown [əuvə'ɡrəun] ADJ (*garden*) coberto de
vegetação; **he's just an ~ schoolboy** (*fig*) ele é

apenas um garotão de escola
overhang [*vt, vi* əuvə'hæŋ, *n* 'əuvəhæŋ] (*irreg*)
VT sobrepairar ■ VI sobressair ■ N saliência,
ressalto
overhaul [*vt* əuvə'hɔːl, *n* 'əuvəhɔːl] VT revisar
■ N revisão *f*
overhead [*adv* əuvə'hɛd, *adj, n* 'əuvəhɛd] ADV
por cima, em cima; (*in the sky*) no céu ■ ADJ
aéreo, elevado; (*railway*) suspenso ■ N (*US*)
= **overheads**; **overheads** NPL (*expenses*)
despesas *fpl* gerais
overhear [əuvə'hiəʳ] (*irreg*) VT ouvir por acaso
overheat [əuvə'hiːt] VI ficar superaquecido;
(*engine*) aquecer demais
overjoyed [əuvə'dʒɔid] ADJ: **to be ~ (a)** estar
muito alegre (com)
overkill ['əuvəkil] N (*fig*): **it would be ~** seria
exagero, seria matar mosquito com tiro de
canhão
overland ['əuvəlænd] ADJ, ADV por terra
overlap [*vi* əuvə'læp, *n* 'əuvəlæp] VI (*edges*)
sobrepor-se em parte; (*fig*) coincidir ■ N
sobreposição *f*
overleaf [əuvə'liːf] ADV no verso
overload [əuvə'ləud] VT sobrecarregar
overlook [əuvə'luk] VT (*have view on*) dar para;
(*miss*) omitir; (*forgive*) fazer vista grossa a
overlord ['əuvəlɔːd] N suserano
overmanning [əuvə'mæniŋ] N excesso de
pessoal
overnight [*adv* əuvə'nait, *adj* 'əuvənait] ADV
durante a noite; (*fig: suddenly*) da noite para o
dia ■ ADJ de uma (*or* de) noite; (*decision*) tomada
da noite para o dia; **to stay ~** passar a noite,
pernoitar; **if you travel ~ ...** se você viajar de
noite ...; **he'll be away ~** ele não voltará hoje
overpaid [əuvə'peid] PT, PP *of* **overpay**
overpass ['əuvəpɑːs] N (*road*) viaduto; (*esp US*)
passagem *f* superior
overpay [əuvə'pei] (*irreg*) VT: **to ~ sb by £50**
pagar £50 em excesso a alguém
overpower [əuvə'pauəʳ] VT dominar, subjugar;
(*fig*) assolar
overpowering [əuvə'pauəriŋ] ADJ (*heat, stench*)
sufocante
overproduction [əuvəprə'dʌkʃən] N superprodução *f*
overrate [əuvə'reit] VT sobrestimar,
supervalorizar
overreach [əuvə'riːtʃ] VT: **to ~ o.s.** exceder-se
overreact [əuvəri'ækt] VI reagir com exagero
override [əuvə'raid] (*irreg*) VT (*order, objection*) não
fazer caso de, ignorar; (*decision*) anular
overriding [əuvə'raidiŋ] ADJ primordial
overrule [əuvə'ruːl] VT (*decision*) anular; (*claim*)
indeferir
overrun [əuvə'rʌn] (*irreg*) VT (*country etc*) invadir;
(*time limit*) ultrapassar, exceder ■ VI ultrapassar
o devido tempo; **the town is ~ with tourists** a
cidade está infestada de turistas
overseas [əuvə'siːz] ADV ultra-mar; (*abroad*) no
estrangeiro, no exterior ■ ADJ (*trade*) exterior;

(*visitor*) estrangeiro
overseer ['əuvəsɪəʳ] N (*in factory*)
superintendente *m/f*; (*foreman*) capataz *m*
overshadow [əuvə'ʃædəu] VT ofuscar
overshoot [əuvə'ʃuːt] (*irreg*) VT passar
oversight ['əuvəsaɪt] N descuido; **due to an ~**
devido a um descuido *or* uma inadvertência
oversimplify [əuvə'sɪmplɪfaɪ] VT simplificar
demais
oversleep [əuvə'sliːp] (*irreg*) VI dormir além da
hora
overspend [əuvə'spɛnd] (*irreg*) VI gastar demais;
we have overspent by \$5000 gastamos \$5000
além dos nossos recursos
overspill ['əuvəspɪl] N excesso (de população)
overstaffed [əuvə'stɑːft] ADJ: **to be ~ ter um**
excesso de pessoal
overstate [əuvə'steɪt] VT exagerar
overstatement [əuvə'steɪtmənt] N exagero
overstep [əuvə'stɛp] VT: **to ~ the mark**
ultrapassar o limite
overstock [əuvə'stɔk] VT estocar em excesso
overstrike [*n* 'əuvəstraɪk, *vt* əuvə'straɪk] (*irreg*:
like **strike**) N (*on printer*) batida múltipla ■ VT
sobreimprimir
overt [əu'vəːt] ADJ aberto, indissimulado
overtake [əuvə'teɪk] (*irreg*) VT ultrapassar
overtaking [əuvə'teɪkɪŋ] N (*Aut*)
ultrapassagem *f*
overtax [əuvə'tæks] VT (*Econ*) sobrecarregar
de impostos; (*fig*: *strength, patience*) abusar de;
(: *person*) exigir demais de; **to ~ o.s.** exceder-se
overthrow [əuvə'θrəu] (*irreg*) VT (*government*)
derrubar
overtime ['əuvətaɪm] N horas *fpl* extras; **to do**
or **work ~** fazer horas extras; **overtime ban** N
recusa de fazer horas extras
overtone ['əuvətəun] N (*fig*: *also*: **overtones**)
implicação *f*, tom *m*
overture ['əuvətʃuəʳ] N (*Mus*) abertura; (*fig*)
proposta, oferta
overturn [əuvə'təːn] VT virar; (*system*) derrubar;
(*decision*) anular ■ VI virar; (*car*) capotar
overweight [əuvə'weɪt] ADJ gordo demais, com
excesso de peso; (*luggage*) com excesso de peso
overwhelm [əuvə'wɛlm] VT (*defeat*) esmagar,
assolar; (*affect deeply*) esmagar, sufocar
overwhelming [əuvə'wɛlmɪŋ] ADJ (*victory,*
defeat) esmagador(a); (*heat*) sufocante; (*desire*)

irresistível; **one's ~ impression is of heat** a
impressão mais forte é de calor
overwhelmingly [əuvə'wɛlmɪŋlɪ] ADV (*vote*) em
massa; (*win*) esmagadoramente
overwork [əuvə'wəːk] N excesso de trabalho
■ VT sobrecarregar de trabalho ■ VI trabalhar
demais
overwrite [əuvə'raɪt] (*irreg*) VT (*Comput*) gravar
em cima de
overwrought [əuvə'rɔːt] ADJ extenuado,
superexcitado
ovulation [ɔvju'leɪʃən] N ovulação *f*
owe [əu] VT dever; **to ~ sb sth, to ~ sth to sb**
dever algo a alguém
owing to ['əuɪŋ-] PREP devido a, por causa de
owl [aul] N coruja
own [əun] ADJ próprio ■ VI (*Brit*): **to ~ to**
(having done) sth confessar (ter feito) algo
■ VT possuir, ter; **a room of my ~** meu próprio
quarto; **can I have it for my (very) ~?** posso
ficar com isso para mim?; **to get one's ~ back** ir
à forra; **on one's ~** sozinho; **to come into one's**
~ revelar-se
▶ **own up** VI: **to ~ up to sth** confessar algo; **to ~**
up to having done sth confessar ter feito algo
own brand N (*Comm*) marca de distribuidora
owner ['əunəʳ] N dono(-a), proprietário(-a)
owner-occupier N proprietário(-a) com posse
e uso
ownership ['əunəʃɪp] N posse *f*; **it's under new**
~ (*shop etc*) está sob novo proprietário
ox [ɔks] (*pl* **oxen**) N boi *m*
oxen ['ɔksn] NPL *of* **ox**
Oxfam ['ɔksfæm] (*Brit*) N ABBR (= *Oxford*
Committee for Famine Relief) associação de assistência
oxide ['ɔksaɪd] N óxido
Oxon. ['ɔksn] (*Brit*) ABBR = **Oxoniensis; of**
Oxford
oxtail ['ɔksteɪl] N: **~ soup** sopa de rabada
oxyacetylene [ɔksɪə'sɛtɪliːn] N oxiacetileno
■ CPD: **~ burner, ~ torch** maçarico
oxiacetilênico
oxygen ['ɔksɪdʒən] N oxigênio; **oxygen mask**
N máscara de oxigênio; **oxygen tent** N tenda
de oxigênio
oyster ['ɔɪstəʳ] N ostra
oz. ABBR = **ounce(s)**
ozone ['əuzəun] N ozônio; **ozone layer** N
camada de ozônio

Pp

P, p [pi:] N (*letter*) P, p *m*; **P for Peter** P de Pedro
P ABBR = **president; prince**
p [pi:] ABBR (= *page*) p; (*Brit*) = **penny; pence**
PA N ABBR = **personal assistant; public address
system** ■ ABBR (*US: Post*) = **Pennsylvania**
pa [pɑ:] (*inf*) N papai *m*
p.a. ABBR = **per annum**
PAC (*US*) N ABBR = **political action committee**
pace [peɪs] N (*step*) passo; (*speed*) velocidade *f*;
(*rhythm*) ritmo ■ VI: **to ~ up and down** andar
de um lado para o outro; **to keep ~ with**
acompanhar o passo de; (*events*) manter-se
inteirado de *or* atualizado com; **to set the ~**
(*running*) regular a marcha; (*fig*) dar o tom; **to
put sb through his ~s** (*fig*) pôr alguém à prova
pacemaker ['peɪsmeɪkəʳ] N (*Med*) marcapasso *m*
pacific [pə'sɪfɪk] ADJ pacífico ■ N: **the P~
(Ocean)** o (Oceano) Pacífico
pacification [pæsɪfɪ'keɪʃən] N pacificação *f*
pacifier ['pæsɪfaɪəʳ] (*US*) N chupeta
pacifist ['pæsɪfɪst] N pacifista *m/f*
pacify ['pæsɪfaɪ] VT (*soothe*) acalmar, serenar;
(*country*) pacificar
pack [pæk] N pacote *m*, embrulho; (*US: packet*)
pacote *m*; (*: of cigarettes*) maço; (*of hounds*)
matilha; (*of thieves etc*) bando, quadrilha;
(*of cards*) baralho; (*bundle*) trouxa; (*backpack*)
mochila ■ VT (*wrap*) empacotar, embrulhar;
(*fill*) encher; (*in suitcase etc*) arrumar (na mala);
(*cram*): **to ~ into** entupir de, entulhar com; (*fig:
room etc*) lotar; (*Comput*) compactar ■ VI: **to ~
(one's bags)** fazer as malas; **to ~ into** (*room,
stadium*) apinhar-se em; **to send sb ~ing** (*inf*) dar
o fora em alguém
▶ **pack in** (*Brit: inf*) VI (*machine*) pifar ■ VT
(*boyfriend*) dar o fora em; **~ it in!** pára com isso!
▶ **pack off** VT (*person*) despedir
▶ **pack up** VI (*Brit: inf: machine*) pifar; (*: person*)
desistir, parar ■ VT (*belongings*) arrumar; (*goods,
presents*) empacotar, embrulhar
package ['pækɪdʒ] N pacote *m*; (*bulky*)
embrulho, fardo; (*also*: **package deal**) acordo
global, pacote; (*Comput*) pacote ■ VT (*goods*)
empacotar, acondicionar; **package holiday**
(*Brit*) N pacote *m* (de férias); **package tour** (*Brit*)
N excursão *f* organizada
packaging ['pækɪdʒɪŋ] N embalagem *f*

packed [pækt] ADJ (*crowded*) lotado, apinhado;
packed lunch (*Brit*) N merenda
packer ['pækəʳ] N (*person*) empacotador(a) *m/f*
packet ['pækɪt] N pacote *m*; (*of cigarettes*) maço;
(*of washing powder etc*) caixa; (*Naut*) paquete *m*;
packet switching [-'swɪtʃɪŋ] N (*Comput*)
chaveamento de pacote
pack ice N gelo flutuante
packing ['pækɪŋ] N embalagem *f*; (*internal*)
enchimento; (*act*) empacotamento; **packing
case** N caixa de embalagem
pact [pækt] N pacto; (*Comm*) convênio
pad [pæd] N (*of paper*) bloco; (*for inking*) almofada;
(*launch pad*) plataforma (de lançamento); (*to
prevent friction*) acolchoado; (*inf: home*) casa ■ VT
acolchoar, enchumaçar ■ VI: **to ~ in/about** *etc*
entrar/andar *etc* sem ruído
padding ['pædɪŋ] N enchimento; (*fig*)
palavreado inútil
paddle ['pædl] N (*oar*) remo curto; (*US: for table
tennis*) raquete *f* ■ VT remar ■ VI (*with feet*)
patinhar; **paddle steamer** N vapor *m* movido
a rodas
paddling pool ['pædlɪŋ-] (*Brit*) N lago de
recreação
paddock ['pædək] N cercado; (*at race course*)
paddock *m*
paddy field ['pædɪ-] N arrozal *m*
padlock ['pædlɔk] N cadeado ■ VT fechar com
cadeado
padre ['pɑ:drɪ] N capelão *m*, padre *m*
paediatrics [pi:dɪ'ætrɪks] (*US* **pediatrics**) N
pediatria
pagan ['peɪgən] ADJ, N pagão/pagã *m/f*
page [peɪdʒ] N página; (*also*: **page boy**)
mensageiro; (*at wedding*) pajem *m* ■ VT (*in hotel
etc*) mandar chamar
pageant ['pædʒənt] N (*procession*) cortejo
suntuoso; (*show*) desfile *m* alegórico
pageantry ['pædʒəntrɪ] N pompa, fausto
page break N quebra de página
pager ['peɪdʒəʳ] N bip *m*
paginate ['pædʒɪneɪt] VT paginar
pagination [pædʒɪ'neɪʃən] N paginação *f*
pagoda [pə'gəudə] N pagode *m*
paid [peɪd] PT, PP *of* **pay** ■ ADJ (*work*)
remunerado; (*holiday*) pago; (*official*) assalariado;

to put ~ to (*Brit*) acabar com
paid-up (*US* **paid-in**) ADJ (*member*) efetivo; (*shares*) integralizado; ~ **capital** capital *m* realizado
pail [peɪl] N balde *m*
pain [peɪn] N dor *f*; **to be in** ~ sofrer *or* sentir dor; **to have a ~ in** estar com uma dor em; **on ~ of death** sob pena de morte; **to take ~s to do sth** dar-se ao trabalho de fazer algo
pained [peɪnd] ADJ (*expression*) magoado, aflito
painful ['peɪnful] ADJ doloroso; (*laborious*) penoso; (*unpleasant*) desagradável
painfully ['peɪnfulɪ] ADV (*fig: very*) terrivelmente
painkiller ['peɪnkɪlə'] N analgésico
painless ['peɪnlɪs] ADJ sem dor, indolor
painstaking ['peɪnzteɪkɪŋ] ADJ (*work*) esmerado; (*person*) meticuloso
paint [peɪnt] N pintura ■ VT pintar; **to ~ the door blue** pintar a porta de azul; **to ~ the town red** (*fig*) cair na farra
paintbox ['peɪntbɔks] N estojo de tintas
paintbrush ['peɪntbrʌʃ] N (*artist's*) pincel *m*; (*decorator's*) broxa
painter ['peɪntə'] N pintor(a) *m/f*; (*decorator*) pintor(a) de paredes
painting ['peɪntɪŋ] N pintura; (*picture*) tela, quadro
paint-stripper N removedor *m* de tinta
paintwork ['peɪntwə:k] N pintura
pair [pɛə'] N (*of shoes, gloves etc*) par *m*; (*of people*) casal *m*; (*twosome*) dupla; **a ~ of scissors** uma tesoura; **a ~ of trousers** uma calça (BR), umas calças (PT)
▶ **pair off** VI formar pares
pajamas [pɪ'dʒɑ:məz] (*US*) NPL pijama *m*
Pakistan [pɑ:kɪ'stɑ:n] N Paquistão *m*
Pakistani [pɑ:kɪ'stɑ:nɪ] ADJ, N paquistanês(-esa) *m/f*
PAL [pæl] N ABBR (*TV: phase alternation line*) PAL *m*
pal [pæl] (*inf*) N camarada *m/f*, colega *m/f*
palace ['pæləs] N palácio
palatable ['pælɪtəbl] ADJ saboroso, apetitoso; (*acceptable*) aceitável
palate ['pælɪt] N paladar *m*
palatial [pə'leɪʃəl] ADJ suntuoso, magnífico
palaver [pə'lɑ:və'] (*inf*) N (*fuss*) confusão *f*; (*hindrances*) complicação *f*
pale [peɪl] ADJ (*face*) pálido; (*colour*) claro; (*light*) fraco ■ VI empalidecer ■ N: **to be beyond the ~** passar dos limites; **to grow** *or* **turn ~** empalidecer; ~ **blue** azul claro *inv*; **to ~ into insignificance (beside)** perder a importância (diante de)
paleness ['peɪlnɪs] N palidez *f*
Palestine ['pælɪstaɪn] N Palestina
Palestinian [pælɪs'tɪnɪən] ADJ, N palestino(-a)
palette ['pælɪt] N palheta
paling ['peɪlɪŋ] N (*stake*) estaca; **palings** NPL (*fence*) cerca
palisade [pælɪ'seɪd] N paliçada
pall [pɔ:l] N (*of smoke*) manto ■ VI perder a graça

pallet ['pælɪt] N (*for goods*) paleta
pallid ['pælɪd] ADJ pálido, descorado
pallor ['pælə'] N palidez *f*
pally ['pælɪ] (*inf*) ADJ chapinha
palm [pɑ:m] N (*hand, leaf*) palma; (*also*: **palm tree**) palmeira ■ VT: **to ~ sth off on sb** (*inf*) impingir algo a alguém
palmist ['pɑ:mɪst] N quiromante *m/f*
Palm Sunday N Domingo de Ramos
palpable ['pælpəbl] ADJ palpável
palpitations [pælpɪ'teɪʃənz] NPL palpitações *fpl*; **to have ~** sentir palpitações
paltry ['pɔ:ltrɪ] ADJ irrisório
pamper ['pæmpə'] VT paparicar, mimar
pamphlet ['pæmflət] N panfleto
pan [pæn] N (*also*: **saucepan**) panela (BR), caçarola (PT); (*also*: **frying pan**) frigideira; (*of lavatory*) vaso ■ VI (*Cinema*) tomar uma panorâmica ■ VT (*inf: book, film*) arrasar com; **to ~ for gold** batear à procura de ouro
panacea [pænə'sɪə] N panacéia
panache [pə'næʃ] N desenvoltura
Panama ['pænəmɑ:] N Panamá *m*; **Panama Canal** N canal *m* do Panamá
pancake ['pænkeɪk] N panqueca
Pancake Day (*Brit*) N terça-feira de Carnaval
pancreas ['pæŋkrɪəs] N pâncreas *m inv*
panda ['pændə] N panda *m/f*; **panda car** (*Brit*) N patrulhinha, carro policial
pandemonium [pændɪ'məunɪəm] N (*noise*) pandemônio; (*mess*) caos *m*
pander ['pændə'] VI: **to ~ to** favorecer
pane [peɪn] N vidraça, vidro
panel ['pænl] N (*of wood, Radio, TV*) painel *m*; (*of cloth*) pano; **panel game** (*Brit*) N jogo em painel
panelling ['pænlɪŋ] (*US* **paneling**) N painéis *mpl*
panellist ['pænəlɪst] (*US* **panelist**) N convidado(-a), integrante *m/f* do painel
pang [pæŋ] N: **a ~ of regret** uma sensação de pesar; **~s of hunger** fome aguda
panic ['pænɪk] N pânico ■ VI entrar em pânico
panicky ['pænɪkɪ] ADJ (*person*) assustadiço, apavorado
panic-stricken [-'strɪkən] ADJ tomado de pânico
pannier ['pænɪə'] N (*on bicycle*) cesta; (*on mule etc*) cesto, alcofa
panorama [pænə'rɑ:mə] N panorama *m*
panoramic [pænə'ræmɪk] ADJ panorâmico
pansy ['pænzɪ] N (*Bot*) amor-perfeito; (*inf: pej*) bicha (BR), maricas *m* (PT)
pant [pænt] VI arquejar, ofegar
pantechnicon [pæn'teknɪkən] (*Brit*) N caminhão *m* de mudanças
panther ['pænθə'] N pantera
panties ['pæntɪz] NPL calcinha (BR), cuecas *fpl* (PT)
pantihose ['pæntɪhəuz] (*US*) N meia-calça (BR), collants *mpl* (PT)
pantomime ['pæntəmaɪm] (*Brit*) N pantomima, *revista musical montada na época de*

Natal, baseada em contos de fada

● **PANTOMIME**
●
● Uma *pantomime*, também chamada
● simplesmente de *panto*, é um gênero de
● comédia em que o personagem principal em
● geral é um rapaz e na qual há sempre uma
● *dame*, isto é, uma mulher idosa representada
● por um homem, e um vilão. Na maior parte
● das vezes, a história é baseada em um conto
● de fadas, como "A gata borralheira" ou "O
● gato de botas", e a platéia é encorajada a
● participar prevenindo os heróis dos perigos
● que estão por vir. Esse tipo de espetáculo,
● voltado sobretudo para as crianças, visa
● também ao público adulto por meio de
● diversas brincadeiras que fazem alusão aos
● fatos atuais.

pantry ['pæntrɪ] N despensa
pants [pænts] NPL (*Brit: underwear: woman's*)
calcinha (BR), cuecas *fpl* (PT); (: *man's*) cueca
(BR), cuecas (PT); (*US: trousers*) calça (BR), calças
fpl (PT)
pantsuit ['pæntsuːt] (*US*) N terninho (de
mulher)
papacy ['peɪpəsɪ] N papado
papal ['peɪpəl] ADJ papal
paper ['peɪpəʳ] N papel *m*; (*also*: **newspaper**)
jornal *m*; (*also*: **wallpaper**) papel de parede;
(*study, article*) artigo, dissertação *f*; (*exam*) exame
m, prova ■ ADJ de papel ■ VT (*room*) revestir
(com papel de parede); **papers** NPL (*also*:
identity papers) documentos *mpl*; **a piece of ~**
um papel; **to put sth down on ~** pôr algo por
escrito; **paper advance** N (*on printer*) avançar
formulário
paperback ['peɪpəbæk] N livro de capa mole
■ ADJ: ~ **edition** edição *f* brochada
paper bag N saco de papel
paperboy ['peɪpəbɔɪ] N jornaleiro
paper clip N clipe *m*
paper hankie N lenço de papel
paper mill N fábrica de papel
paper money N papel-moeda *m*
paper profit N lucro fictício
paperweight ['peɪpəweɪt] N pesa-papéis *m inv*
paperwork ['peɪpəwəːk] N trabalho
burocrático; (*pej*) papelada
papier-mâché ['pæpɪeɪ'mæʃeɪ] N papel *m*
machê
paprika ['pæprɪkə] N páprica, pimentão-doce *m*
Pap smear [pæp-] N (*Med*) esfregaço
Pap test [pæp-] N (*Med*) esfregaço
par [pɑːʳ] N par *m*; (*equality of value*) paridade *f*,
igualdade *f*; (*Golf*) média *f*; **to be on a ~ with**
estar em pé de igualdade com; **at ~** ao par;
above/below ~ acima/abaixo do par; **to feel
below** *or* **under** *or* **not up to ~** estar aquém das
suas possibilidades
parable ['pærəbl] N parábola

parabola [pə'ræbələ] N parábola
parachute ['pærəʃuːt] N pára-quedas *m inv* ■ VI
saltar de pára-quedas; **parachute jump** N salto
de pára-quedas
parachutist ['pærəʃuːtɪst] N pára-quedista *m/f*
parade [pə'reɪd] N desfile *m* ■ VT desfilar; (*show
off*) exibir ■ VI desfilar; (*Mil*) passar revista;
parade ground N praça de armas
paradise ['pærədaɪs] N paraíso
paradox ['pærədɔks] N paradoxo
paradoxical [pærə'dɔksɪkl] ADJ paradoxal
paradoxically [pærə'dɔksɪklɪ] ADV
paradoxalmente
paraffin ['pærəfɪn] (*Brit*) N: ~ (**oil**) querosene *m*;
liquid ~ óleo de parafina; **paraffin heater** (*Brit*)
N aquecedor *m* a parafina; **paraffin lamp** (*Brit*)
N lâmpada de parafina
paragon ['pærəgən] N modelo
paragraph ['pærəgrɑːf] N parágrafo
Paraguay ['pærəgwaɪ] N Paraguai *m*
Paraguayan [pærə'gwaɪən] ADJ, N
paraguaio(-a)
parallel ['pærəlɛl] ADJ: ~ (**with** *or* **to**) (*lines
etc*) paralelo (a); (*fig*) correspondente (a) ■ N
paralela; correspondência
paralyse ['pærəlaɪz] (*Brit*) VT paralisar
paralyses [pə'rælɪsiːz] NPL *of* **paralysis**
paralysis [pə'rælɪsɪs] (*pl* **paralyses**) N paralisia
paralytic [pærə'lɪtɪk] ADJ paralítico; (*Brit: inf:
drunk*) de cara cheia
paralyze ['pærəlaɪz] (*US*) VT = **paralyse**
parameter [pə'ræmɪtəʳ] N parâmetro
paramilitary [pærə'mɪlɪtərɪ] ADJ paramilitar
paramount ['pærəmaunt] ADJ primordial; **of ~
importance** de suma importância
paranoia [pærə'nɔɪə] N paranóia
paranoid ['pærənɔɪd] ADJ paranóico
paranormal [pærə'nɔːməl] ADJ paranormal
parapet ['pærəpɪt] N parapeito, balaustrada
paraphernalia [pærəfə'neɪlɪə] N (*gear*)
acessórios *mpl*, parafernália, equipamento
paraphrase ['pærəfreɪz] VT parafrasear
paraplegic [pærə'pliːdʒɪk] N paraplégico(-a)
parapsychology [pærəsaɪ'kɔlədʒɪ] N
parapsicologia
parasite ['pærəsaɪt] N parasito(-a)
parasol ['pærəsɔl] N guarda-sol *m*, sombrinha
paratrooper ['pærətruːpəʳ] N pára-quedista *m/f*
parcel ['pɑːsl] N pacote *m* ■ VT (*also*: **parcel up**)
embrulhar, empacotar
▶ **parcel out** VT repartir, distribuir
parcel bomb (*Brit*) N pacote-bomba *m*
parcel post N serviço de encomenda postal
parch [pɑːtʃ] VT secar, ressecar
parched [pɑːtʃt] ADJ (*person*) morto de sede
parchment ['pɑːtʃmənt] N pergaminho
pardon ['pɑːdn] N perdão *m*; (*Law*) indulto ■ VT
perdoar; (*Law*) indultar; **~!** desculpe!; **~ me!, I
beg your ~** (*apologizing*) desculpe(-me); (**I beg
your**) **~?** (*Brit*), **~ me?** (*US*) (*not hearing*) como?,
como disse?
pare [pɛəʳ] VT (*Brit: nails*) aparar; (*fruit etc*)

descascar; (*fig: costs etc*) reduzir, cortar
parent ['pɛərənt] N (*father*) pai *m*; (*mother*) mãe *f*;
parents NPL (*mother and father*) pais *mpl*
parentage ['pɛərəntɪdʒ] N ascendência; **of unknown ~** de pais desconhecidos
parental [pə'rɛntl] ADJ paternal (*or* maternal), dos pais
parent company N (empresa) matriz *f*
parentheses [pə'rɛnθisiːz] NPL *of* **parenthesis**
parenthesis [pə'rɛnθisis] (*pl* **parentheses**) N parêntese *m*; **in parentheses** entre parênteses
parenthood ['pɛərənthud] N paternidade *f* (*or* maternidade *f*)
parenting ['pɛərəntɪŋ] N trabalho de ser pai (*or* mãe)
Paris ['pærɪs] N Paris
parish ['pærɪʃ] N paróquia, freguesia ■ ADJ paroquial; **parish council** (*Brit*) N ≈ junta da freguesia
parishioner [pə'rɪʃənər] N paroquiano(-a)
Parisian [pə'rɪzɪən] ADJ, N parisiense *m/f*
parity ['pærɪtɪ] N paridade *f*, igualdade *f*
park [paːk] N parque *m* ■ VT, VI estacionar
parka ['paːkə] N parka *m*
parking ['paːkɪŋ] N estacionamento; **"no ~"** "estacionamento proibido"; **parking lights** NPL luzes *fpl* de estacionamento; **parking lot** (*US*) N (parque *m* de) estacionamento; **parking meter** N parquímetro; **parking offence** (*Brit*) N = **parking offence**; **parking place** N vaga; **parking ticket** N multa por estacionamento proibido; **parking violation** (*US*) N infração *f* por estacionamento não permitido
parkway ['paːkweɪ] (*US*) N rodovia arborizada
parlance ['paːləns] N: **in common/modern ~** na linguagem cotidiana *or* corrente/moderna
parliament ['paːləmənt] (*Brit*) N parlamento
parliamentary [paːlə'mɛntərɪ] ADJ parlamentar
parlour ['paːlər] (*US* **parlor**) N sala de visitas, salão *m*, saleta
parlous ['paːləs] ADJ (*formal*) precário
Parmesan [paːmɪ'zæn] N (*also*: **Parmesan cheese**) parmesão *m*
parochial [pə'rəukɪəl] ADJ paroquial; (*pej*) provinciano
parody ['pærədɪ] N paródia ■ VT parodiar
parole [pə'rəul] N: **on ~** em liberdade condicional, sob promessa
paroxysm ['pærəksɪzəm] N paroxismo; (*of anger, coughing*) acesso
parquet ['paːkeɪ] N: **~ floor(ing)** parquete *m*, assoalho de tacos
parrot ['pærət] N papagaio; **parrot fashion** ADV mecanicamente, feito papagaio
parry ['pærɪ] VT aparar, desviar
parsimonious [paːsɪ'məunɪəs] ADJ sovina, parsimonioso
parsley ['paːslɪ] N salsa
parsnip ['paːsnɪp] N cherivia, pastinaga
parson ['paːsn] N padre *m*, clérigo; (*in Church of England*) pastor *m*

parsonage ['paːsnɪdʒ] N presbitério
part [paːt] N (*gen, Mus*) parte *f*; (*of machine*) peça; (*Theatre etc*) papel *m*; (*of serial*) capítulo; (*US: in hair*) risca, repartido ■ ADJ parcial ■ ADV = **partly** ■ VT dividir; (*break*) partir; (*hair*) repartir ■ VI (*people*) separar-se; (*roads*) bifurcar-se; (*crowd*) dispersar-se; (*break*) partir-se; **to take ~ in** participar de, tomar parte em; **to take sb's ~** defender alguém; **on his ~** da sua parte; **for my ~** pela minha parte; **for the most ~** na maior parte; **for the better ~ of the day** durante a maior parte do dia; **to be ~ and parcel of** fazer parte de; **to take sth in good ~** não se ofender com algo; **~ of speech** (*Ling*) categoria gramatical
▸ **part with** VT FUS ceder, entregar; (*money*) pagar
partake [paː'teɪk] (*irreg*) VI (*formal*): **to ~ of sth** participar de algo
part exchange (*Brit*) N: **in ~** como parte do pagamento
partial ['paːʃl] ADJ parcial; **to be ~ to** gostar de, ser apreciador(a) de
partially ['paːʃəlɪ] ADV parcialmente
participant [paː'tɪsɪpənt] N participante *m/f*
participate [paː'tɪsɪpeɪt] VI: **to ~ in** participar de
participation [paːtɪsɪ'peɪʃən] N participação *f*
participle ['paːtɪsɪpl] N particípio
particle ['paːtɪkl] N partícula; (*of dust*) grão *m*
particular [pə'tɪkjulər] ADJ (*special*) especial; (*specific*) específico; (*given*) determinado; (*fussy*) exigente, minucioso; **in ~** em particular; **I'm not ~** para mim tanto faz
particularly [pə'tɪkjulərlɪ] ADV em particular, especialmente
particulars [pə'tɪkjuləz] NPL detalhes *mpl*; (*personal details*) dados *mpl* pessoais
parting ['paːtɪŋ] N (*act*) separação *f*; (*farewell*) despedida; (*Brit: in hair*) risca, repartido ■ ADJ de despedida; **~ shot** (*fig*) flecha de parto
partisan [paːtɪ'zæn] ADJ partidário ■ N partidário(-a); (*in war*) guerrilheiro(-a)
partition [paː'tɪʃən] N (*Pol*) divisão *f*; (*wall*) tabique *m*, divisória ■ VT separar com tabique; (*fig*) dividir
partly ['paːtlɪ] ADV em parte
partner ['paːtnər] N (*Comm*) sócio(-a); (*Sport*) parceiro(-a); (*at dance*) par *m*; (*spouse*) cônjuge *m/f*; (*friend etc*) companheiro(-a) ■ VT acompanhar
partnership ['paːtnəʃɪp] N associação *f*, parceria; (*Comm*) sociedade *f*; **to go into** *or* **form a ~ (with)** associar-se (com), formar sociedade (com)
part payment N parcela, prestação *f*
partridge ['paːtrɪdʒ] N perdiz *f*
part-time ADJ, ADV de meio expediente
part-timer N (*also*: **part-time worker**) trabalhador(a) *m/f* de meio expediente
party ['paːtɪ] N (*Pol*) partido; (*celebration*) festa; (*group*) grupo; (*Law*) parte *f* interessada, litigante *m/f* ■ CPD (*Pol*) do partido, partidário; **dinner ~** jantar *m*; **to give** *or* **have** *or* **throw**

a ~ dar uma festa; **to be a ~ to a crime** ser cúmplice num crime; **party dress** N vestido de gala; **party line** N (Pol) linha partidária; (Tel) linha compartilhada

par value N (of share, bond) valor m nominal

pass [pɑːs] VT (time, object) passar; (exam) passar em; (place) passar por; (overtake, surpass) ultrapassar; (approve) aprovar; (candidate) aprovar ■ VI passar; (Sch) ser aprovado, passar ■ N (permit) passe m; (membership card) carteira; (in mountains) desfiladeiro; (Sport) passe m; (Sch: also: **pass mark**): **to get a ~ in** ser aprovado em; **to ~ sth through sth** passar algo por algo; **things have come to a pretty ~** (Brit) as coisas ficaram pretas; **to make a ~ at sb** tomar liberdade com alguém

▸ **pass away** VI falecer

▸ **pass by** VI passar ■ VT (ignore) passar por cima de

▸ **pass down** VT (customs, inheritance) passar

▸ **pass for** VT FUS passar por

▸ **pass on** VI (die) falecer ■ VT (hand on: news, illness) transmitir; (object) passar para; (price rises) repassar

▸ **pass out** VI desmaiar; (Brit: Mil) sair (de uma escola militar)

▸ **pass over** VT (ignore) passar por cima de

▸ **pass up** VT deixar passar

passable ['pɑːsəbl] ADJ (road) transitável; (work) aceitável

passage ['pæsɪdʒ] N (also: **passageway**: indoors) corredor m; (: outdoors) passagem f; (Anat) via; (act of passing) trânsito; (in book) passagem f, trecho; (fare) passagem (BR), bilhete m (PT); (by boat) travessia; (Mechanics, Med) conduto

passbook ['pɑːsbuk] N caderneta

passenger ['pæsɪndʒər] N passageiro(-a)

passer-by ['pɑːsə'-] (pl **passers-by**) N transeunte m/f

passing ['pɑːsɪŋ] ADJ (fleeting) passageiro, fugaz; **in ~** de passagem; **passing place** N trecho de ultrapassagem

passion ['pæʃən] N paixão f; **to have a ~ for sth** ser aficionado(-a) de algo

passionate ['pæʃənɪt] ADJ apaixonado

passive ['pæsɪv] ADJ (also: Ling) passivo

passkey ['pɑːskiː] N chave f mestra

Passover ['pɑːsəuvər] N Páscoa (dos judeus)

passport ['pɑːspɔːt] N passaporte m; **passport control** N controle m dos passaportes

password ['pɑːswəːd] N senha, contra-senha

past [pɑːst] PREP (drive, walk etc: in front of) por; (: beyond: further than) mais além de; (later than) depois de ■ ADJ passado; (president etc) ex-, anterior ■ N passado; **he's ~ forty** ele tem mais de quarenta anos; **ten/quarter ~ four** quatro e dez/quinze; **for the ~ few/3 days** nos últimos/3 dias; **to run ~** passar correndo (por); **it's ~ midnight** é mais de meia-noite; **in the ~** no passado; **I'm ~ caring** já não ligo mais; **he's ~ it** (Brit: inf: person) ele já passou da idade

pasta ['pæstə] N massa

paste [peɪst] N pasta; (glue) grude m, cola; (jewellery) vidro ■ VT (stick) grudar; (glue) colar; **tomato ~** massa de tomate

pastel ['pæstl] ADJ pastel; (painting) a pastel

pasteurized ['pæstəraɪzd] ADJ pasteurizado

pastille ['pæstl] N pastilha

pastime ['pɑːstaɪm] N passatempo

past master (Brit) N: **to be a ~ at** ser perito em

pastor ['pɑːstər] N pastor(a) m/f

pastoral ['pɑːstərl] ADJ pastoral

pastry ['peɪstrɪ] N massa; (cake) bolo

pasture ['pɑːstʃər] N (grass) pasto; (land) pastagem f, pasto

pasty [n 'pæstɪ, adj 'peɪstɪ] N empadão m de carne ■ ADJ pastoso; (complexion) pálido

pat [pæt] VT dar palmadinhas em; (dog etc) fazer festa em ■ N (of butter) porção f ■ ADV: **he knows it off ~** (Brit), **he has it down ~** (US) ele sabe isso de cor; **to give sb a ~ on the back** (fig) animar alguém

patch [pætʃ] N (of material) retalho; (eye patch) tapa-olho m; (area) área pequena; (spot) mancha; (mend) remendo; (of land) lote m, terreno ■ VT (clothes) remendar; **(to go through) a bad ~** (passar por) um mau pedaço

▸ **patch up** VT (mend temporarily) consertar provisoriamente; (quarrel) resolver

patchwork ['pætʃwəːk] N colcha de retalhos ■ ADJ (feito) de retalhos

patchy ['pætʃɪ] ADJ (colour) desigual; (information) incompleto

pate [peɪt] N: **a bald ~** uma calva, uma careca

pâté ['pæteɪ] N patê m

patent ['peɪtnt] N patente f ■ VT patentear ■ ADJ patente, evidente; **patent leather** N verniz m

patently ['peɪtntlɪ] ADV claramente

patent medicine N medicamento registrado

patent office N escritório de registro de patentes

paternal [pə'təːnl] ADJ paternal; (relation) paterno

paternity [pə'təːnɪtɪ] N paternidade f; **paternity suit** N (Law) processo de paternidade

path [pɑːθ] N caminho; (trail, track) trilha, senda; (trajectory) trajetória; (of planet) órbita

pathetic [pə'θetɪk] ADJ (pitiful) patético, digno de pena; (very bad) péssimo; (moving) comovente

pathological [pæθə'lɔdʒɪkl] ADJ patológico

pathologist [pə'θɔlədʒɪst] N patologista m/f

pathology [pə'θɔlədʒɪ] N patologia

pathos ['peɪθɔs] N patos m, patético

pathway ['pɑːθweɪ] N caminho, trilha

patience ['peɪʃns] N paciência; **to lose one's ~** perder a paciência

patient ['peɪʃnt] ADJ, N paciente m/f

patiently ['peɪʃntlɪ] ADV pacientemente

patio ['pætɪəu] N pátio

patriot ['peɪtrɪət] N patriota m/f

patriotic [pætrɪ'ɔtɪk] ADJ patriótico

patriotism ['pætrɪətɪzəm] N patriotismo

patrol [pə'trəul] N patrulha ■ VT patrulhar;

to be on ~ fazer ronda, patrulhar; **patrol boat** N barco de patrulha; **patrol car** N carro de patrulha

patrolman [pə'trəulmən] (US) N (irreg) guarda m, policial m (BR), polícia m (PT)

patron ['peɪtrən] N (customer) cliente m/f, freguês(-esa) m/f; (of charity) benfeitor(a) m/f; ~ **of the arts** mecenas m

patronage ['pætrənɪdʒ] N patrocínio m

patronize ['pætrənaɪz] VT (pej: look down on) tratar com ar de superioridade; (shop) ser cliente de; (business, artist) patrocinar

patronizing ['pætrənaɪzɪŋ] ADJ condescendente

patron saint N (santo(-a)) padroeiro(-a)

patter ['pætəʳ] N (of rain) tamborilada; (of feet) passos miúdos mpl; (sales talk) jargão m profissional ■ VI correr dando passinhos; (rain) tamborilar

pattern ['pætən] N modelo, padrão m; (Sewing) molde m; (design) desenho; (sample) amostra; **behaviour** ~ modo de comportamento

patterned ['pætənd] ADJ padronizado

paucity ['pɔːsɪtɪ] N penúria, escassez f

paunch [pɔːntʃ] N pança, barriga

pauper ['pɔːpəʳ] N pobre m/f; ~**'s grave** vala comum

pause [pɔːz] N pausa; (interval) intervalo ■ VI fazer uma pausa; **to** ~ **for breath** tomar fôlego; (fig) fazer uma pausa

pave [peɪv] VT pavimentar; **to** ~ **the way for** preparar o terreno para

pavement ['peɪvmənt] N (Brit) calçada (BR), passeio (PT); (US) pavimento

pavilion [pə'vɪlɪən] N pavilhão m; (for band etc) coreto; (Sport) barraca

paving ['peɪvɪŋ] N pavimento, calçamento; **paving stone** N laje f, paralelepípedo

paw [pɔː] N pata; (of cat) garra ■ VT passar a pata em; (touch) manusear; (amorously) apalpar

pawn [pɔːn] N (Chess) peão m; (fig) títere m ■ VT empenhar

pawnbroker ['pɔːnbrəukəʳ] N agiota m/f

pawnshop ['pɔːnʃɔp] N loja de penhores

pay [peɪ] (pt, pp **paid**) N salário; (of manual worker) paga ■ VT pagar; (debt) liquidar, saldar; (visit) fazer ■ VI pagar; (be profitable) valer a pena, render; **how much did you** ~ **for it?** quanto você pagou por isso?; **I paid £5 for that record** paguei or dei £5 por esse disco; **to** ~ **one's way** pagar sua parte; (company) render; **to** ~ **dividends** (fig) trazer vantagens or benefícios; **it won't** ~ **you to do that** não vale a pena você fazer isso; **to** ~ **attention (to)** prestar atenção (a); **to** ~ **one's respects to sb** fazer uma visita de cortesia a alguém

▶ **pay back** VT (money) devolver; (person) pagar; (debt) saldar

▶ **pay for** VT FUS pagar a; (fig) recompensar

▶ **pay in** VT depositar

▶ **pay off** VT (debts) saldar, liquidar; (mortgage) resgatar; (creditor) pagar, reembolsar; (worker) despedir ■ VI (plan, patience) valer a pena; **to** ~

sth off in instalments pagar algo a prazo

▶ **pay out** VT (money) pagar, desembolsar; (rope) dar

▶ **pay up** VT (debts) pagar, liquidar; (amount) pagar

payable ['peɪəbl] ADJ pagável; (cheque): ~ **to** em favor de, nominal

pay day N dia m do pagamento

PAYE (Brit) N ABBR (= pay as you earn) tributação na fonte

payee [peɪ'iː] N beneficiário(-a)

pay envelope (US) N = **pay packet**

paying ['peɪɪŋ] ADJ pagador(a); (business) rendoso; ~ **guest** pensionista m/f

payload ['peɪləud] N carga paga

payment ['peɪmənt] N pagamento; **advance** ~ (part sum) entrada; (total sum) pagamento adiantado; **deferred** ~, ~ **by instalments** pagamento a prazo; **monthly** ~ pagamento mensual; **in** ~ **for** or **of** em pagamento por; **on** ~ **of £5** contra pagamento de £5

pay packet (Brit) N envelope m de pagamento

pay phone ['peɪfəun] N telefone m público

payroll ['peɪrəul] N folha de pagamento; **to be on a firm's** ~ fazer parte do quadro de pessoal assalariado de uma firma

pay slip (Brit) N contracheque m

pay station (US) N cabine f telefônica, orelhão m (BR)

pay television N televisão f por assinatura

PBS (US) N ABBR = **Public Broadcasting Service**

PC N ABBR (= personal computer) PC m; (Brit) = **police constable** ■ ABBR (Brit) = **Privy Councillor**

pc ABBR = **per cent; postcard**

p/c ABBR = **petty cash**

PCB N ABBR = **printed circuit board**

PD (US) N ABBR = **police department**

pd ABBR = **paid**

PDA N ABBR (= personal digital assistant) PDA m (= assistente digital pessoal)

PDSA (Brit) N ABBR = **People's Dispensary for Sick Animals**

PDT (US) ABBR (= Pacific Daylight Time) hora de verão do Pacífico

PE N ABBR = **physical education** ■ ABBR (Canada) = **Prince Edward Island**

pea [piː] N ervilha

peace [piːs] N paz f; (calm) tranqüilidade f, quietude f; **to be at** ~ **with sb/sth** estar em paz com alguém/algo; **to keep the** ~ (subj: policeman) manter a ordem; (: citizen) não perturbar a ordem pública

peaceable ['piːsəbl] ADJ pacato

peaceful ['piːsful] ADJ (person) tranqüilo, pacífico; (place, time) tranqüilo, sossegado

peace-keeping [-'kiːpɪŋ] N pacificação f

peace offering N proposta de paz

peach [piːtʃ] N pêssego

peacock ['piːkɔk] N pavão m

peak [piːk] N (of mountain: top) cume m; (: point) pico; (of cap) pala, viseira; (fig: of career, fame) apogeu m; (: highest level) máximo

peak-hour ADJ (*traffic etc*) no horário de maior movimento, na hora de pique

peak hours NPL horário de maior movimento

peak period N período de pique

peaky ['pi:kɪ] (*Brit: inf*) ADJ adoentado

peal [pi:l] N (*of bells*) repique *m*, toque *m*; ~ **of laughter** gargalhada

peanut ['pi:nʌt] N amendoim *m*; **peanut butter** N manteiga de amendoim

pear [pɛəʳ] N pêra

pearl [pə:l] N pérola

pear tree N pereira

peasant ['pɛznt] N camponês(-esa) *m/f*

peat [pi:t] N turfa

pebble ['pɛbl] N seixo, calhau *m*

peck [pɛk] VT (*also*: **peck at**) bicar, dar bicadas em; (*food*) beliscar ▪ N bicada; (*kiss*) beijoca

pecking order ['pɛkɪŋ-] N ordem *f* de hierarquia

peckish ['pɛkɪʃ] (*Brit: inf*) ADJ: **I feel ~** estou a fim de comer alguma coisa

peculiar [pɪ'kju:lɪəʳ] ADJ (*odd*) estranho, esquisito; (*marked*) especial; (*belonging to*): ~ **to** próprio de

peculiarity [pɪkju:lɪ'ærɪtɪ] N (*distinctive feature*) peculiaridade *f*; (*oddity*) excentricidade *f*

pecuniary [pɪ'kju:nɪərɪ] ADJ pecuniário

pedal ['pɛdl] N pedal *m* ▪ VI pedalar; **pedal bin** (*Brit*) N lata de lixo com pedal

pedantic [pɪ'dæntɪk] ADJ pedante

peddle ['pɛdl] VT vender nas ruas, mascatear; (*drugs*) traficar, fazer tráfico de

peddler ['pɛdləʳ] N (*also*: **drugs peddler**) mascate *m/f*, camelô *m*

pedestal ['pɛdəstl] N pedestal *m*

pedestrian [pɪ'dɛstrɪən] N pedestre *m/f* (BR), peão *m* (PT) ▪ ADJ pedestre (BR), para peões (PT); (*fig*) prosaico; **pedestrian crossing** (*Brit*) N passagem *f* para pedestres (BR), passadeira (PT)

pediatrics [pi:dɪ'ætrɪks] (*US*) N = **paediatrics**

pedigree ['pɛdɪgri:] N (*of animal*) raça; (*fig*) genealogia ▪ CPD (*animal*) de raça

pedlar ['pɛdləʳ] N = **peddler**

pee [pi:] (*inf*) VI fazer xixi, mijar

peek [pi:k] VI: **to ~ at** espiar, espreitar; **to ~ over/into** espiar por cima de/dentro, espreitar por cima de/dentro

peel [pi:l] N casca ▪ VT descascar ▪ VI (*paint, skin*) descascar; (*wallpaper*) desprender-se
▶ **peel back** VT descascar

peeler ['pi:ləʳ] N (*potato etc peeler*) descascador *m*

peelings ['pi:lɪŋz] NPL cascas *fpl*

peep [pi:p] N (*Brit: look*) espiadela; (*sound*) pio ▪ VI (*Brit: look*) espreitar; (*sound*) piar
▶ **peep out** (*Brit*) VI mostrar-se, surgir

peephole ['pi:phəul] N vigia, olho mágico

peer [pɪəʳ] VI: **to ~ at** perscrutar, fitar ▪ N (*noble*) par *m/f*; (*equal*) igual *m/f*; (*contemporary*) contemporâneo(-a)

peerage ['pɪərɪdʒ] N pariato

peerless ['pɪəlɪs] ADJ sem igual

peeved [pi:vd] ADJ irritado

peevish ['pi:vɪʃ] ADJ rabugento

peg [pɛg] N cavilha; (*for coat etc*) cabide *m*; (*Brit: also*: **clothes peg**) pregador *m*; (*tent peg*) estaca ▪ VT (*clothes*) prender; (*Brit: groundsheet*) segurar com estacas; (*fig: prices, wages*) fixar, tabelar

pejorative [pɪ'dʒɔrətɪv] ADJ pejorativo

Pekin [pi:'kɪn] N Pequim

Peking [pi:'kɪŋ] N = **Pekin**

Pekin(g)ese [pi:kɪ'ni:z] N pequinês *m*

pelican ['pɛlɪkən] N pelicano; **pelican crossing** (*Brit*) N (*Aut*) passagem *f* sinalizada para pedestres (BR), passadeira para peões (PT)

pellet ['pɛlɪt] N bolinha; (*for shotgun*) pelota de chumbo

pell-mell ['pɛl'mɛl] ADV a esmo

pelmet ['pɛlmɪt] N sanefa

pelt [pɛlt] VT: **to ~ sb with sth** atirar algo em alguém ▪ VI (*rain: also*: **pelt down**) chover a cântaros; (*inf: run*) correr ▪ N pele *f* (não curtida)

pelvis ['pɛlvɪs] N pelvis *f*, bacia

pen [pɛn] N caneta; (*for sheep etc*) redil *m*, cercado; (*US: inf: prison*) cadeia; **to put ~ to paper** escrever ▶ **pen in** VT encurralar

penal ['pi:nl] ADJ penal

penalize ['pi:nəlaɪz] VT impor penalidade a; (*Sport*) penalizar; (*fig*) prejudicar

penal servitude [-'sə:vɪtju:d] N pena de trabalhos forçados

penalty ['pɛnltɪ] N pena, penalidade *f*; (*fine*) multa; (*Sport*) punição *f*; (*Football*) pênalti *m*; **to take a ~** cobrar um pênalti; **penalty area** (*Brit*) N área de pênalti; **penalty clause** N cláusula penal; **penalty kick** N (*Rugby*) chute *m* de pênalti; (*Football*) cobrança de pênalti

penance ['pɛnəns] N penitência

pence [pɛns] (*Brit*) NPL *of* **penny**

penchant ['pã:ʃã:ŋ] N pendor *m*, queda

pencil ['pɛnsl] N lápis *m* ▪ VT: **to ~ sth in** anotar algo a lápis; **pencil case** N lapiseira, porta-lápis *m inv*; **pencil sharpener** N apontador *m* (de lápis) (BR), apara-lápis *m inv* (PT)

pendant ['pɛndnt] N pingente *m*

pending ['pɛndɪŋ] PREP (*during*) durante; (*until*) até ▪ ADJ pendente

pendulum ['pɛndjuləm] N pêndulo

penetrate ['pɛnɪtreɪt] VT penetrar

penetrating ['pɛnɪtreɪtɪŋ] ADJ penetrante

penetration [pɛnɪ'treɪʃən] N penetração *f*

penfriend ['pɛnfrɛnd] (*Brit*) N amigo(-a) por correspondência, correspondente *m/f*

penguin ['pɛŋgwɪn] N pingüim *m*

penicillin [pɛnɪ'sɪlɪn] N penicilina

peninsula [pə'nɪnsjulə] N península

penis ['pi:nɪs] N pênis *m*

penitence ['pɛnɪtns] N penitência

penitent ['pɛnɪtnt] ADJ arrependido; (*Rel*) penitente

penitentiary [pɛnɪ'tɛnʃərɪ] (*US*) N penitenciária, presídio

penknife ['pɛnnaɪf] (*irreg*) N canivete *m*

pen name N pseudônimo

pennant ['pɛnənt] N flâmula

penniless ['pεnılıs] ADJ sem dinheiro, sem um tostão

Pennines ['pεnaınz] NPL: **the ~ as** Pennines

penny ['pεnı] (*pl* (*Brit*) **pence**) N pêni *m*; (*US*) cêntimo

penpal ['pεnpæl] N amigo(-a) por correspondência, correspondente *m/f*

pension ['pεnʃən] N pensão *f*; (*old-age pension*) aposentadoria, pensão de governo; (*Mil*) reserva
▶ **pension off** VT aposentar

pensionable ['pεnʃnəbl] ADJ (*person*) com direito a uma pensão; (*age*) de aposentadoria

pensioner ['pεnʃənər] (*Brit*) N aposentado(-a) (BR), reformado(-a) (PT)

pension fund N fundo da aposentadoria

pensive ['pεnsıv] ADJ pensativo; (*withdrawn*) absorto

pentagon ['pεntəgən] N: **the P~** (*US*) o Pentágono

● **PENTAGON**
●
●
● O Pentágono *Pentagon* é o nome dado
● aos escritórios do Ministério da Defesa
● americano, localizados em Arlington, no
● estado da Virgínia, por causa da forma
● pentagonal do edifício onde se encontram.
● Por extensão, o termo é utilizado também
● para se referir ao ministério.

Pentecost ['pεntıkɔst] N Pentecostes *m*

penthouse ['pεnthaus] (*irreg*) N cobertura

pent-up [pεnt-] ADJ (*feelings*) reprimido

penultimate [pe'nʌltımət] ADJ penúltimo

penury ['pεnjurı] N pobreza, miséria

people ['piːpl] NPL gente *f*, pessoas *fpl*; (*inhabitants*) habitantes *m/fpl*; (*citizens*) povo; (*Pol*): **the ~** o povo ■ N (*nation, race*) povo ■ VT povoar; **several ~ came** vieram várias pessoas; **I know ~ who ...** conheço gente que ...; **~ say that ...** dizem que ...; **old ~** os idosos; **young ~** os jovens; **a man of the ~** um homem do povo

pep [pεp] (*inf*) N pique *m*, energia, dinamismo
▶ **pep up** VT animar

pepper ['pεpər] N pimenta; (*vegetable*) pimentão *m* ■ VT apimentar; (*fig*): **to ~ with** salpicar de

peppermint ['pεpəmınt] N hortelã-pimenta; (*sweet*) bala de hortelã

pepper pot N pimenteiro

pep talk ['pεptɔːk] (*inf*) N conversa para levantar o espírito

per [pəːr] PREP por; **~ day/~son** por dia/pessoa; **~ annum** por ano; **as ~ your instructions** conforme suas instruções; **per capita** ADJ, ADV per capita, por pessoa

perceive [pə'siːv] VT perceber; (*notice*) notar; (*realize*) compreender

per cent N, ADV por cento; **a 20 ~ discount** um desconto de 20 por cento

percentage [pə'sεntıdʒ] N porcentagem *f*, percentagem *f*; **on a ~ basis** na base de percentagem

perceptible [pə'sεptıbl] ADJ perceptível, sensível

perception [pə'sεpʃən] N percepção *f*; (*insight*) perspicácia

perceptive [pə'sεptıv] ADJ perceptivo

perch [pəːtʃ] (*pl* **perches**) N (*for bird*) poleiro; (*fish*) perca ■ VI: **to ~ (on)** (*bird*) empoleirar-se (em); (*person*) encarapitar-se (em)

percolate ['pəːkəleıt] VT, VI passar

percolator ['pəːkəleıtər] N (*also*: **coffee percolator**) cafeteira de filtro

percussion [pə'kʌʃən] N percussão *f*

peremptory [pə'rεmptərı] ADJ peremptório; (*person: imperious*) autoritário

perennial [pə'rεnıəl] ADJ perene; (*fig*) constante ■ N planta perene

perfect [*adj, n* 'pəːfıkt, *vt* pə'fεkt] ADJ perfeito; (*utter*) completo ■ N (*also*: **perfect tense**) perfeito ■ VT aperfeiçoar; **a ~ stranger** uma pessoa completamente desconhecida

perfection [pə'fεkʃən] N perfeição *f*

perfectionist [pə'fεkʃənıst] N perfeccionista *m/f*

perfectly ['pəːfıktlı] ADV perfeitamente; **I'm ~ happy with the situation** estou completamente satisfeito com a situação; **you know ~ well** você sabe muito bem

perforate ['pəːfəreıt] VT perfurar

perforated ['pəːfəreıtıd] ADJ (*stamp*) picotado; **perforated ulcer** N (*Med*) úlcera perfurada

perforation [pəːfə'reıʃən] N perfuração *f*; (*line of holes*) picote *m*

perform [pə'fɔːm] VT (*carry out*) realizar, fazer; (*concert etc*) executar; (*piece of music*) interpretar ■ VI (*well, badly*) interpretar; (*animal*) fazer truques de amestramento; (*Theatre*) representar; (*Tech*) funcionar

performance [pə'fɔːməns] N (*of task*) cumprimento, realização *f*; (*of play, by artist*) atuação *f*; (*of engine, athlete, economy*) desempenho; (*of car*) performance *f*

performer [pə'fɔːmər] N (*actor*) artista *m/f*, ator/atriz *m/f*; (*Mus*) intérprete *m/f*

performing [pə'fɔːmıŋ] ADJ (*animal*) amestrado, adestrado

perfume ['pəːfjuːm] N perfume *m* ■ VT perfumar

perfunctory [pə'fʌŋktərı] ADJ superficial, negligente

perhaps [pə'hæps] ADV talvez; **~ he'll come** talvez ele venha; **~ so/not** talvez seja assim/talvez não

peril ['pεrıl] N perigo, risco

perilous ['pεrıləs] ADJ perigoso

perilously ['pεrıləslı] ADV: **they came ~ close to being caught** não foram presos por um triz

perimeter [pə'rımıtər] N perímetro; **perimeter wall** N muro periférico

period ['pıərıəd] N período; (*History*) época; (*time limit*) prazo; (*Sch*) aula; (*full stop*) ponto final; (*Med*) menstruação *f*, regra ■ ADJ (*costume, furniture*) da época; **for a ~ of three weeks** por um período de três semanas; **the holiday ~**

(Brit) o período de férias
periodic(al) [pɪərɪ'ɔdɪk(l)] ADJ periódico
periodical [pɪərɪ'ɔdɪkl] N periódico
periodically [pɪərɪ'ɔdɪklɪ] ADV periodicamente,
de vez em quando
period pains (Brit) NPL cólicas fpl menstruais
peripatetic [perɪpə'tetɪk] ADJ (salesman)
viajante; (teacher) que trabalha em vários
lugares
peripheral [pə'rɪfərəl] ADJ periférico ■ N
(Comput) periférico
periphery [pə'rɪfərɪ] N periferia
periscope ['perɪskəup] N periscópio
perish ['perɪʃ] VI perecer; (decay) deteriorar-se
perishable ['perɪʃəbl] ADJ perecível, deteriorável
perishables ['perɪʃəblz] NPL perecíveis mpl
perishing ['perɪʃɪŋ] (Brit: inf) ADJ (cold) gelado,
glacial
peritonitis [perɪtə'naɪtɪs] N peritonite f
perjure ['pə:dʒəʳ] VT: **to ~ o.s.** prestar falso
testemunho
perjury ['pə:dʒərɪ] N (Law) perjúrio, falso
testemunho
perk [pə:k] (inf) N mordomia, regalia
▶ **perk up** VI (cheer up) animar-se; (in health)
recuperar-se
perky ['pə:kɪ] ADJ (cheerful) animado, alegre
perm [pə:m] N permanente f ■ VT: **to have
one's hair ~ed** fazer permanente (no cabelo)
permanence ['pə:mənəns] N permanência,
continuidade f
permanent ['pə:mənənt] ADJ permanente;
I'm not ~ here não estou aqui em caráter
permanente
permanently ['pə:mənəntlɪ] ADV
permanentemente
permeable ['pə:mɪəbl] ADJ permeável
permeate ['pə:mɪeɪt] VI difundir-se ■ VT
penetrar; (subj: idea) difundir
permissible [pə'mɪsɪbl] ADJ permissível, lícito
permission [pə'mɪʃən] N permissão f;
(authorization) autorização f; **to give sb ~ to do
sth** dar permissão a alguém para fazer algo
permissive [pə'mɪsɪv] ADJ permissivo
permit [n 'pə:mɪt, vt pə'mɪt] N permissão f; (for
fishing, export etc) licença; (to enter) passe m ■ VT
permitir; (authorize) autorizar; **to ~ sb to do
sth** permitir a alguém fazer or que faça algo;
weather ~ting se o tempo permitir
permutation [pə:mju'teɪʃən] N permutação f
pernicious [pə:'nɪʃəs] ADJ nocivo; (Med)
pernicioso, maligno
pernickety [pə'nɪkɪtɪ] (inf) ADJ cheio de nove-
horas or luxo; (task) minucioso
perpendicular [pə:pən'dɪkjuləʳ] ADJ
perpendicular ■ N perpendicular f
perpetrate ['pə:pɪtreɪt] VT cometer
perpetual [pə'petjuəl] ADJ perpétuo
perpetuate [pə'petjueɪt] VT perpetuar
perpetuity [pə:pɪ'tju:ɪtɪ] N: **in ~** para sempre
perplex [pə'pleks] VT deixar perplexo
perplexing [pə:'pleksɪŋ] ADJ desconcertante

perquisites ['pə:kwɪzɪts] NPL (also: **perks**)
mordomias fpl, regalias fpl
persecute ['pə:sɪkju:t] VT importunar; (pursue)
perseguir
persecution [pə:sɪ'kju:ʃən] N perseguição f
perseverance [pə:sɪ'vɪərəns] N perseverança
persevere [pə:sɪ'vɪəʳ] VI perseverar
Persia ['pə:ʃə] N Pérsia
Persian ['pə:ʃən] ADJ persa ■ N (Ling) persa m;
the (~) Gulf o golfo Pérsico
persist [pə'sɪst] VI: **to ~ (in doing sth)** persistir
(em fazer algo)
persistence [pə'sɪstəns] N persistência; (of
disease) insistência; (obstinacy) teimosia
persistent [pə'sɪstənt] ADJ persistente;
(determined) teimoso; (disease) insistente,
persistente; **~ offender** (Law) infrator(a) m/f
contumaz
persnickety [pə'snɪkɪtɪ] (US: inf) ADJ
= **pernickety**
person ['pə:sn] N pessoa; **in ~** em pessoa; **on** or
about one's ~ consigo; **~ to ~ call** (Tel) chamada
pessoal
personable ['pə:sənəbl] ADJ atraente, bem
apessoado
personal ['pə:sənəl] ADJ pessoal; (private)
particular; (visit) em pessoa, pessoal; **~
belongings** or **effects** pertences mpl
particulares; **~ hygiene** higiene f íntima;
a ~ interview uma entrevista particular;
personal allowance N (Tax) abatimento da
renda de pessoa física; **personal assistant**
N secretário(-a) particular; **personal call** N
(Tel) chamada pessoal; **personal column** N
anúncios mpl pessoais; **personal computer**
N computador m pessoal; **personal details**
NPL (on form etc) dados mpl pessoais; **personal
identification number** N (Comput, Banking)
senha, número de identificação individual
personality [pə:sə'nælɪtɪ] N personalidade f
personally ['pə:sənəlɪ] ADV pessoalmente; **to
take sth ~** ofender-se
personal organizer N agenda
personal property N bens mpl móveis
personal stereo N Walkman® m
personify [pə:'sɔnɪfaɪ] VT personificar
personnel [pə:sə'nel] N pessoal m; **personnel
department** N departamento de pessoal;
personnel manager N gerente m/f de pessoal
perspective [pə'spektɪv] N perspectiva; **to get
sth into ~** colocar algo em perspectiva
Perspex® ['pə:speks] (Brit) N Blindex® m
perspicacity [pə:spɪ'kæsɪtɪ] N perspicácia
perspiration [pə:spɪ'reɪʃən] N transpiração f
perspire [pə'spaɪəʳ] VI transpirar
persuade [pə'sweɪd] VT persuadir; **to ~ sb to do
sth** persuadir alguém a fazer algo; **to ~ sb that/
of sth** persuadir alguém que/de algo
persuasion [pə'sweɪʒən] N persuasão f;
(persuasiveness) poder m de persuasão; (creed)
convicção f, crença
persuasive [pə'sweɪsɪv] ADJ persuasivo

pert [pə:t] ADJ atrevido, descarado
pertaining [pə:'teɪnɪŋ] PREP: ~ **to** relativo a
pertinent ['pə:tɪnənt] ADJ pertinente, a propósito
perturb [pə'tə:b] VT inquietar
perturbing [pə'tə:bɪŋ] ADJ inquietante
Peru [pə'ru:] N Peru m
perusal [pə'ru:zl] N leitura
peruse [pə'ru:z] VT ler com atenção, examinar
Peruvian [pə'ru:vjən] ADJ, N peruano(-a)
pervade [pə'veɪd] VT impregnar, penetrar em
pervasive [pə'veɪsɪv] ADJ (smell) penetrante; (influence, ideas, gloom) difundido
perverse [pə'və:s] ADJ perverso; (stubborn) teimoso; (wayward) caprichoso
perversion [pə'və:ʃən] N perversão f; (of truth) currupção f
perversity [pə'və:sɪtɪ] N perversidade f
pervert [n 'pə:və:t, vt pə'və:t] N pervertido(-a)
■ VT perverter, corromper; (truth) distorcer
pessary ['pɛsərɪ] N pessário
pessimism ['pɛsɪmɪzəm] N pessimismo
pessimist ['pɛsɪmɪst] N pessimista m/f
pessimistic [pɛsɪ'mɪstɪk] ADJ pessimista
pest [pɛst] N peste f, praga; (insect) inseto nocivo; (fig) peste f; **pest control** N dedetização f; (for mice) desratização f
pester ['pɛstə'] VT incomodar
pesticide ['pɛstɪsaɪd] N pesticida m
pestilent ['pɛstɪlənt] (inf) ADJ (exasperating) chato
pestle ['pɛsl] N mão f (de almofariz)
pet [pɛt] N animal m de estimação ■ CPD predileto ■ VT acariciar ■ VI (inf) acariciar-se; **teacher's** ~ (favourite) preferido(-a) do professor; ~ **lion** etc leão etc de estimação; **my** ~ **hate** a coisa que eu mais odeio
petal ['pɛtl] N pétala
peter out ['pi:tə'-] VI (conversation) esgotar-se; (road etc) acabar-se
petite [pə'ti:t] ADJ delicado, mignon
petition [pə'tɪʃən] N petição f; (list of signatures) abaixo-assinado ■ VT apresentar uma petição a ■ VI: **to** ~ **for divorce** requerer divórcio
pet name (Brit) N apelido carinhoso
petrified ['pɛtrɪfaɪd] ADJ (fig) petrificado, paralisado
petrify ['pɛtrɪfaɪ] VT paralisar; (frighten) petrificar
petrochemical [pɛtrə'kɛmɪkl] ADJ petroquímico
petrodollars ['pɛtrəʊdɔləz] NPL petrodólares mpl
petrol ['pɛtrəl] (Brit) N gasolina; **two/four star** ~ gasolina de duas/quatro estrelas; **petrol can** (Brit) N lata de gasolina; **petrol engine** (Brit) N motor m a gasolina
petroleum [pə'trəʊlɪəm] N petróleo; **petroleum jelly** N vaselina®
petrol pump (Brit) N (in car, at garage) bomba de gasolina
petrol station (Brit) N posto (BR) or bomba (PT) de gasolina

petrol tank (Brit) N tanque m de gasolina
petticoat ['pɛtɪkəʊt] N anágua; (slip) combinação f
pettifogging ['pɛtɪfɔgɪŋ] ADJ chicaneiro
pettiness ['pɛtɪnɪs] N mesquinharia f
petty ['pɛtɪ] ADJ (mean) mesquinho; (unimportant) insignificante; **petty cash** N fundo para despesas miúdas, caixa pequena, fundo de caixa; **petty officer** N suboficial m da marinha
petulant ['pɛtjulənt] ADJ irascível
pew [pju:] N banco (de igreja)
pewter ['pju:tə'] N peltre m
Pfc (US) ABBR (Mil) = **private first class**
PG N ABBR (Cinema: = parental guidance) aviso dos pais recomendado
PGA N ABBR = **Professional Golfers' Association**
PH (US) N ABBR (Mil: = Purple Heart) condecoração para feridos em combate
p & h (US) ABBR = **postage and handling**
PHA (US) N ABBR (= Public Housing Administration) órgão que supervisiona a construção
phallic ['fælɪk] ADJ fálico
phantom ['fæntəm] N fantasma m
Pharaoh ['fɛərəʊ] N faraó m
pharmaceutical [fɑ:mə'sju:tɪkl] ADJ farmacêutico
pharmaceuticals [fɑ:mə'sju:tɪklz] NPL farmacêuticos mpl
pharmacist ['fɑ:məsɪst] N farmacêutico(-a)
pharmacy ['fɑ:məsɪ] N farmácia
phase [feɪz] N fase f ■ VT: **to** ~ **sth in/out** introduzir/retirar algo por etapas
PhD N ABBR = **Doctor of Philosophy** ■ N = doutorado
pheasant ['fɛznt] N faisão m
phenomena [fə'nɔmɪnə] NPL of **phenomenon**
phenomenal [fə'nɔmɪnəl] ADJ fenomenal
phenomenon [fə'nɔmɪnən] (pl **phenomena**) N fenômeno
phew [fju:] EXCL ufa!
phial ['faɪəl] N frasco
philanderer [fɪ'lændərə'] N mulherengo
philanthropic [fɪlən'θrɔpɪk] ADJ filantrópico
philanthropist [fɪ'lænθrəpɪst] N filantropo(-a)
philatelist [fɪ'lætəlɪst] N filatelista m/f
philately [fɪ'lætəlɪ] N filatelia
Philippines ['fɪlɪpi:nz] NPL (also: **Philippine Islands**): **the** ~ as Filipinas
philosopher [fɪ'lɔsəfə'] N filósofo(-a)
philosophical [fɪlə'sɔfɪkl] ADJ filosófico; (fig) calmo, sereno
philosophy [fɪ'lɔsəfɪ] N filosofia
phishing ['fɪʃɪŋ] N phishing, golpe m de phishing
phlegm [flɛm] N fleuma
phlegmatic [flɛg'mætɪk] ADJ fleumático
phobia ['fəʊbjə] N fobia
phone [fəʊn] N telefone m ■ VT telefonar para, ligar para ■ VI telefonar, ligar; **to be on the** ~ ter telefone; (be calling) estar no telefone
  ▶ **phone back** VT, VI ligar de volta
  ▶ **phone up** VT telefonar para ■ VI telefonar

phone: phone book N lista telefônica; **phone booth** N cabine f telefônica; **phone box** (Brit) N cabine f telefônica; **phone call** N telefonema m, ligada

phone-in (Brit) N (Radio) programa com participação dos ouvintes; (TV) programa com participação dos espectadores

phone number N número de telefone

phonetics [fə'nɛtɪks] N fonética

phoney ['fəʊnɪ] ADJ falso; (person) fingido ■ N (person) impostor(a) m/f

phonograph ['fəʊnəgrɑːf] (US) N vitrola

phony ['fəʊnɪ] ADJ, N = **phoney**

phosphate ['fɒsfeɪt] N fosfato

phosphorus ['fɒsfərəs] N fósforo

photo ['fəʊtəʊ] N foto f

photo... ['fəʊtəʊ] PREFIX foto...

photocopier ['fəʊtəʊkɒpɪəʳ] N fotocopiadora f

photocopy ['fəʊtəʊkɒpɪ] N fotocópia, xerox® m ■ VT fotocopiar, xerocar

photoelectric [fəʊtəʊɪ'lɛktrɪk] ADJ fotoelétrico; ~ **cell** célula fotoelétrica

photogenic [fəʊtəʊ'dʒɛnɪk] ADJ fotogênico

photograph ['fəʊtəgrɑːf] N fotografia ■ VT fotografar; **to take a ~ of sb** bater or tirar uma foto de alguém

photographer [fə'tɒgrəfəʳ] N fotógrafo(-a)

photographic [fəʊtə'græfɪk] ADJ fotográfico

photography [fə'tɒgrəfɪ] N fotografia

Photostat® ['fəʊtəʊstæt] N cópia fotostática

photosynthesis [fəʊtəʊ'sɪnθəsɪs] N fotos síntese f

phrase [freɪz] N frase f ■ VT expressar; (letter) redigir; **phrase book** N livro de expressões idiomáticas (para turistas)

physical ['fɪzɪkl] ADJ físico; ~ **examination** exame m físico; ~ **exercise** exercício físico, movimento; **physical education** N educação f física

physically ['fɪzɪklɪ] ADV fisicamente

physician [fɪ'zɪʃən] N médico(-a)

physicist ['fɪzɪsɪst] N físico(-a)

physics ['fɪzɪks] N física

physiological [fɪzɪə'lɒdʒɪkl] ADJ fisiológico

physiology [fɪzɪ'ɒlədʒɪ] N fisiologia

physiotherapist [fɪzɪəʊ'θɛrəpɪst] N fisioterapeuta m/f

physiotherapy [fɪzɪəʊ'θɛrəpɪ] N fisioterapia

physique [fɪ'ziːk] N físico

pianist ['piːənɪst] N pianista m/f

piano [pɪ'ænəʊ] N piano; **piano accordion** (Brit) N acordeão m, sanfona

piccolo ['pɪkələʊ] N flautim m

pick [pɪk] N (tool: also: **pickaxe**) picareta ■ VT (select) escolher, selecionar; (gather) colher; (remove) tirar; (lock) forçar; **take your ~** escolha o que quiser; **the ~ of** o melhor de; **to ~ a bone** roer um osso; **to ~ one's nose** colocar o dedo no nariz; **to ~ one's teeth** palitar os dentes; **to ~ sb's brains** aproveitar os conhecimentos de alguém; **to ~ pockets** roubar or bater carteira; **to ~ a quarrel** or **a fight with sb** comprar

uma briga com alguém; **to ~ and choose** ser exigente

▶ **pick at** VT FUS (food) beliscar

▶ **pick off** VT (kill) matar de um tiro

▶ **pick on** VT FUS (person: criticize) criticar; (: treat badly) azucrinar, aporrinhar

▶ **pick out** VT escolher; (distinguish) distinguir

▶ **pick up** VI (improve) melhorar ■ VT (from floor, Aut) apanhar; (Police) prender; (telephone) atender, tirar do gancho; (collect) buscar; (for sexual encounter) paquerer; (learn) aprender; (Radio, TV, Tel) pegar; **to ~ up speed** acelerar; **to ~ o.s. up** levantar-se; **to ~ up where one left off** continuar do ponto onde se parou

pickaxe ['pɪkæks] (US **pickax**) N picareta

picket ['pɪkɪt] N (in strike) piquete m; (person) piqueteiro(-a) ■ VT formar piquete em frente de; **picket line** N piquete m

pickings ['pɪkɪŋz] NPL: **there are rich ~ to be had for investors in gold** os investidores em ouro vão se dar bem

pickle ['pɪkl] N (also: **pickles**: as condiment) picles mpl; (fig: mess) apuro ■ VT (in vinegar) conservar em vinagre; (in salt) conservar em sale água

pick-me-up N estimulante m

pickpocket ['pɪkpɒkɪt] N batedor(a) m/f de carteira (BR), carteirista m/f (PT)

pickup ['pɪkʌp] N (on record player) pick-up m; (small truck: also: **pickup truck, pickup van**) camioneta, pick-up m

picnic ['pɪknɪk] N piquenique m ■ VI fazer um piquenique

picnicker ['pɪknɪkəʳ] N pessoa que faz piquenique

pictorial [pɪk'tɔːrɪəl] ADJ pictórico; (magazine etc) ilustrado

picture ['pɪktʃəʳ] N quadro; (painting) pintura; (drawing) desenho; (etching) água-forte f; (photograph) foto(grafia) f; (TV) imagem f; (film) filme m; (fig: description) descrição f; (: situation) conjuntura ■ VT imaginar-se; (describe) retratar; **the pictures** NPL (Brit: inf) o cinema; **to take a ~ of sb/sth** tirar uma foto de alguém/ algo; **the overall ~** o quadro geral; **to put sb in the ~** pôr alguém a par da situação; **picture book** N livro de figuras

picturesque [pɪktʃə'rɛsk] ADJ pitoresco

picture window N janela panorâmica

piddling ['pɪdlɪŋ] (inf) ADJ irrisório

pidgin ['pɪdʒɪn] ADJ: ~ **English** forma achinesada do inglês usada entre comerciantes

pie [paɪ] N (vegetable) pastelão m; (fruit) torta; (meat) empadão m

piebald ['paɪbɔːld] ADJ malhado

piece [piːs] N pedaço; (portion) fatia; (of land) lote m, parcela; (Chess etc) peça; (item): **a ~ of clothing/furniture/advice** uma roupa/um móvel/um conselho ■ VT: **to ~ together** juntar; (Tech) montar; **in ~s** (broken) em pedaços; (not yet assembled) desmontado; **to fall to ~s** cair aos pedaços; **to take to ~s** desmontar; **in one ~** (object) inteiro; (person) ileso; **a 10p ~** (Brit) uma moeda de 10p; ~ **by** ~ pedaço por pedaço; **a six-~ band** um sexteto; **to say one's** ~ vender o seu peixe

piecemeal ['piːsmiːl] ADV pouco a pouco

piece rate N salário por peça

piecework ['piːswəːk] N trabalho por empreitada *or* peça

pie chart N gráfico de setores

pier [pɪəʳ] N cais *m*; (*jetty*) embarcadouro, molhe *m*; (*of bridge etc*) pilar *m*, pilastra

pierce [pɪəs] VT furar, perfurar; **to have one's ears ~d** furar as orelhas

piercing ['pɪəsɪŋ] ADJ (*cry*) penetrante, agudo; (*stare*) penetrante; (*wind*) cortante

piety ['paɪətɪ] N piedade *f*

piffling ['pɪflɪŋ] ADJ irrisório

pig [pɪg] N porco; (*fig*) porcalhão(-lhona) *m/f*; (*pej: unkind person*) grosseiro(-a); (: *greedy person*) ganancioso(-a)

pigeon ['pɪdʒən] N pombo

pigeonhole ['pɪdʒənhəul] N escaninho

pigeon-toed [-təud] ADJ com pé de pombo

piggy bank ['pɪgɪ-] N cofre em forma de porquinho

pig-headed [-'hɛdɪd] (*pej*) ADJ teimoso, cabeçudo

piglet ['pɪglɪt] N porquinho, leitão *m*

pigment ['pɪgmənt] N pigmento

pigmentation [pɪgmənˈteɪʃən] N pigmentação *f*

pigmy ['pɪgmɪ] N = **pygmy**

pigskin ['pɪgskɪn] N couro de porco

pigsty ['pɪgstaɪ] N chiqueiro

pigtail ['pɪgteɪl] N (*girl's*) rabo-de-cavalo, trança; (*Chinese*) rabicho

pike [paɪk] (*pl* **pikes**) N (*spear*) lança, pique *m*; (*fish*) lúcio

pilchard ['pɪltʃəd] N sardinha

pile [paɪl] N (*of books*) pilha; (*heap*) monte *m*; (*of carpet*) pêlo; (*of cloth*) lado felpudo; (*support: in building*) estaca ▪ VT (*also:* **pile up**) empilhar; (*heap*) amontoar; (*fig*) acumular ▪ VI (*also:* **pile up:** *objects*) empilhar-se; (: *problems, work*) acumular-se; **in a ~** numa pilha
▸ **pile into** VT FUS (*car*) apinhar-se
▸ **pile on** VT: **to ~ it on** (*inf*) exagerar

piles [paɪlz] NPL (*Med*) hemorróidas *fpl*

pile-up N (*Aut*) engavetamento

pilfer ['pɪlfəʳ] VT, VI furtar, afanar, surripiar

pilfering ['pɪlfərɪŋ] N furto

pilgrim ['pɪlgrɪm] N peregrino(-a)

pilgrimage ['pɪlgrɪmɪdʒ] N peregrinação *f*, romaria

pill [pɪl] N pílula; **the ~** a pílula; **to be on the ~** usar *or* tomar a pílula

pillage ['pɪlɪdʒ] N pilhagem *f* ▪ VT saquear, pilhar

pillar ['pɪləʳ] N pilar *m*; (*concrete*) coluna; **pillar box** (*Brit*) N caixa coletora (do correio) (BR), marco do correio (PT)

pillion ['pɪljən] N (*of motor cycle*) garupa; **to ride ~** andar na garupa

pillory ['pɪlərɪ] N pelourinho ▪ VT expor ao ridículo

pillow ['pɪləu] N travesseiro (BR), almofada (PT)

pillowcase ['pɪləukeɪs] N fronha

pillowslip ['pɪləuslɪp] N fronha

pilot ['paɪlət] N piloto(-a) ▪ CPD (*scheme etc*) piloto *inv* ▪ VT pilotar; (*fig*) guiar; **pilot boat** N barco-piloto; **pilot light** N piloto

pimento [pɪˈmɛntəu] N pimentão-doce *m*

pimp [pɪmp] N cafetão *m* (BR), cáften *m* (PT)

pimple ['pɪmpl] N espinha

pimply ['pɪmplɪ] ADJ espinhento

PIN N ABBR = **personal identification number**

pin [pɪn] N alfinete *m*; (*Tech*) cavilha; (*wooden, Brit: Elec: of plug*) pino ▪ VT alfinetar; **~s and needles** comichão *f*, sensação *f* de formigamento; **to ~ sb against** *or* **to** apertar alguém contra; **to ~ sth on sb** (*fig*) culpar alguém de algo
▸ **pin down** VT (*fig*): **to ~ sb down** conseguir que alguém se defina *or* tome atitude; **there's something strange here but I can't quite ~ it down** há alguma coisa estranha aqui, mas não consigo precisar o quê

pinafore ['pɪnəfɔːʳ] N (*also:* **pinafore dress**) avental *m*

pinball ['pɪnbɔːl] N fliper *m*, fliperama *m*

pincers ['pɪnsəz] NPL pinça, tenaz *f*

pinch [pɪntʃ] N beliscão *m*; (*of salt etc*) pitada ▪ VT beliscar; (*inf: steal*) afanar ▪ VI (*shoe*) apertar; **at a ~** em último caso; **to feel the ~** (*fig*) apertar o cinto, passar por um aperto

pinched [pɪntʃt] ADJ (*drawn*) abatido; **~ with cold** transido de frio; **~ for money** desprovido de dinheiro; **to be ~ for space** não dispor de muito espaço

pincushion ['pɪnkuʃən] N alfineteira

pine [paɪn] N (*also:* **pine tree**) pinho; (*wood*) madeira de pinho ▪ VI: **to ~ for** ansiar por
▸ **pine away** VI consumir-se, definhar

pineapple ['paɪnæpl] N abacaxi *m* (BR), ananás *m* (PT)

ping [pɪŋ] N (*noise*) silvo, sibilo

ping-pong® N pingue-pongue *m*

pink [pɪŋk] ADJ cor de rosa *inv* ▪ N (*colour*) cor *f* de rosa; (*Bot*) cravo, cravina

pinking scissors ['pɪŋkɪŋ-] NPL tesoura para picotar

pinking shears ['pɪŋkɪŋ-] NPL tesoura para picotar

pin money (*Brit*) N dinheiro extra

pinnacle ['pɪnəkl] N cume *m*; (*fig*) auge *m*

pinpoint ['pɪnpɔɪnt] VT (*discover*) descobrir; (*explain*) identificar; (*locate*) localizar com precisão

pinstripe ['pɪnstraɪp] N tecido listrado ▪ ADJ listrado

pint [paɪnt] N quartilho (*Brit:* = 568*cc*; *US:* = 473*cc*); **to go for a ~** (*Brit: inf*) ir tomar uma cerveja

pin-up N pin-up *f*, retrato de mulher atraente

pioneer [paɪəˈnɪəʳ] N pioneiro(-a) ▪ VT ser pioneiro de

pious ['paɪəs] ADJ pio, devoto

pip [pɪp] N (*seed*) caroço, semente *f*; **the pip**

NPL (Brit: time signal on radio) ≈ o toque de seis segundos

pipe [paɪp] N cano; (for smoking) cachimbo; (Mus) flauta ■ VT canalizar, encanar; **pipes** NPL (also: **bagpipes**) gaita de foles
▶ **pipe down** (inf) VI calar o bico, meter a viola no saco

pipe cleaner N limpa-cachimbo

piped music [paɪpt-] N música enlatada

pipe dream N sonho impossível, castelo no ar

pipeline ['paɪplaɪn] N (for oil) oleoduto; (for gas) gaseoduto; **it's in the ~** (fig) está na bica (inf)

piper ['paɪpər] N (gen) flautista m/f; (of bagpipes) gaiteiro(-a)

pipe tobacco N fumo (BR) or tabaco (PT) para cachimbo

piping ['paɪpɪŋ] ADV: **~ hot** chiando de quente

piquant ['piːkənt] ADJ picante

pique [piːk] N ressentimento, melindre m

piracy ['paɪrəsɪ] N pirataria

pirate ['paɪərət] N pirata m ■ VT (record, video, book) piratear; **pirate radio** (Brit) N rádio pirata

pirouette [pɪruˈɛt] N pirueta ■ VI fazer pirueta(s)

Pisces ['paɪsiːz] N Pisces m, Peixes mpl

piss [pɪs] (inf!) VI mijar; **~ off!** vai à merda (!)

pissed [pɪst] (inf!) ADJ (drunk) bêbado, de porre

pistol ['pɪstl] N pistola

piston ['pɪstən] N pistão m, êmbolo

pit [pɪt] N cova, fossa; (quarry, hole in surface of sth) buraco; (also: **coal pit**) mina de carvão; (also: **orchestra pit**) fosso ■ VT: **to ~ one's wits against sb** competir em conhecimento or inteligência contra alguém; **pits** NPL (Aut) box m; **to ~ A against B** opor A a B; **to ~ o.s. against** opor-se a

pitapat ['pɪtə'pæt] (Brit) ADV: **to go ~** (heart) disparar; (rain) tiquetaquear

pitch [pɪtʃ] N (throw) arremesso, lance m; (Mus) tom m; (of voice) altura; (fig: degree) intensidade f; (also: **sales pitch**) papo (de vendedor); (Brit: Sport) campo; (tar) piche m, breu m; (Naut) arfada; (in market etc) barraca ■ VT (throw) arremessar, lançar; (tent) armar; (set: price, message) adaptar ■ VI (fall forwards) tombar (para frente), cair; (Naut) jogar, arfar; **to be ~ed forward** ser jogado para frente; **at this ~** neste pique or ritmo; **to ~ one's aspirations too high** colocar as aspirações alto demais
▶ **pitch in** VI contribuir

pitch-black ADJ escuro como o breu

pitched battle [pɪtʃt-] N batalha campal

pitcher ['pɪtʃər] N jarro, cântaro; (US: Baseball) arremessador m

pitchfork ['pɪtʃfɔːk] N forcado

piteous ['pɪtɪəs] ADJ lastimável

pitfall ['pɪtfɔːl] N perigo (imprevisto), armadilha

pith [pɪθ] N (of orange) casca interna e branca; (fig) essência, parte f essencial

pithead ['pɪthɛd] (Brit) N boca do poço

pithy ['pɪθɪ] ADJ substancial

pitiable ['pɪtɪəbl] ADJ deplorável

pitiful ['pɪtɪful] ADJ (touching) comovente, tocante; (contemptible) desprezível, lamentável

pitifully ['pɪtɪfəlɪ] ADV lamentavelmente, deploravelmente

pitiless ['pɪtɪlɪs] ADJ impiedoso

pittance ['pɪtns] N ninharia, miséria

pitted ['pɪtɪd] ADJ: **~ with** (chickenpox) marcado com; (rust) picado de; **~ with potholes** esburacado

pity ['pɪtɪ] N (compassion) compaixão f, piedade f; (shame) pena ■ VT ter pena de, compadecer-se de; **what a ~!** que pena!; **it's a ~ (that) you can't come** é uma pena que você não possa vir; **to have** or **take ~ on sb** ter pena de alguém

pitying ['pɪtɪɪŋ] ADJ compassivo, compadecido

pivot ['pɪvət] N pino, eixo; (fig) pivô m ■ VI: **to ~ on** girar sobre; (fig) depender de

pixel ['pɪksl] N (Comput) píxel m

pixie ['pɪksɪ] N duende m

pizza ['piːtsə] N pizza

P&L ABBR = **profit and loss**

placard ['plækɑːd] N placar m; (in march etc) cartaz m

placate [pləˈkeɪt] VT apaziguar, aplacar

placatory [pləˈkeɪtərɪ] ADJ apaziguador(a), aplacador(a)

place [pleɪs] N lugar m; (rank, position) posição f; (post) posto; (role) papel m; (home): **at/to his ~** na/para a casa dele ■ VT (object) pôr, colocar; (identify) identificar, situar; (find a post for) colocar; **to ~** realizar-se; (occur) ocorrer; **from ~ to ~** de lugar em lugar; **all over the ~** em tudo quanto é lugar; **out of ~** (not suitable) fora de lugar, deslocado; **I feel out of ~ here** eu me sinto deslocado aqui; **in the first ~** em primeiro lugar; **to change ~s with sb** trocar de lugar com alguém; **to put sb in his ~** (fig) pôr alguém no seu lugar; **he's going ~s** (fig) ele vai se dar bem; **it's not my ~ to do it** não me compete fazê-lo; **to ~ an order with sb for sth** (Comm) encomendar algo a alguém; **to be ~d** (in race, exam) classificar-se; **how are you ~d next week?** você tem tempo na semana que vem?

placebo [pləˈsiːbəʊ] N placebo

place mat N descanso

placement ['pleɪsmənt] N (placing) colocação f; (job) cargo

place name N topônimo

placenta [pləˈsɛntə] N placenta

place of birth N local m de nascimento

placid ['plæsɪd] ADJ plácido, sereno

placidity [pləˈsɪdɪtɪ] N placidez f

plagiarism ['pleɪdʒərɪzm] N plágio

plagiarist ['pleɪdʒərɪst] N plagiário(-a)

plagiarize ['pleɪdʒəraɪz] VT plagiar

plague [pleɪg] N (Med) peste f; (fig) praga ■ VT (fig) atormentar, importunar; **to ~ sb with questions** importunar alguém com perguntas

plaice [pleɪs] N INV solha

plaid [plæd] N (material) tecido de xadrez; (pattern) xadrez m escocês

plain [pleɪn] ADJ (*unpatterned*) liso; (*clear*) claro, evidente; (*simple*) simples *inv*, despretensioso; (*frank*) franco, sem rodeios; (*not handsome*) sem atrativos; (*pure*) puro, natural ■ ADV claramente, com franqueza ■ N planície *f*, campina; **to make sth ~ to sb** dar claramente a entender algo a alguém; **plain chocolate** N chocolate *m* amargo

plain-clothes ADJ (*police officer*) à paisana

plainly ['pleɪnlɪ] ADV claramente, obviamente; (*hear, see*) facilmente; (*state*) francamente

plainness ['pleɪnnɪs] N clareza; (*simplicity*) simplicidade *f*; (*frankness*) franqueza

plaintiff ['pleɪntɪf] N querelante *m/f*, queixoso(-a)

plaintive ['pleɪntɪv] ADJ (*voice, tone*) queixoso; (*song*) lamentoso; (*look*) tristonho

plait [plæt] N trança, dobra ■ VT trançar

plan [plæn] N plano; (*scheme*) projeto; (*schedule*) programa *m* ■ VT planejar (BR), planear (PT) ■ VI fazer planos; **to ~ to do** pretender fazer; **how long do you ~ to stay?** quanto tempo você pretende ficar?

plane [pleɪn] N (*Aviat*) avião *m*; (*also*: **plane tree**) plátano; (*fig: level*) nível *m*; (*tool*) plaina; (*Art, Math*) plano ■ ADJ plano ■ VT (*with tool*) aplainar

planet ['plænɪt] N planeta *m*

planetarium [plænɪ'tɛərɪəm] N planetário

plank [plæŋk] N tábua; (*Pol*) item *m* da plataforma política

plankton ['plæŋktən] N plâncton *m*

planner ['plænəʳ] N planejador(a) *m/f* (BR), planeador(a) *m/f* (PT); (*chart*) agenda (*quadro*); (*town planner*) urbanista *m/f*; (*of TV programme, project*) programador(a) *m/f*

planning ['plænɪŋ] N planejamento (BR), planeamento (PT); **family ~** planejamento *or* planeamento familiar; **planning permission** (Brit) N autorização *f* para construir

plant [plɑːnt] N planta; (*machinery*) maquinaria; (*factory*) usina, fábrica ■ VT plantar; (*field*) semear; (*bomb*) colocar, pôr; (*inf*) pôr às escondidas; (*incriminating evidence*) incriminar

plantation [plæn'teɪʃən] N plantação *f*; (*estate*) fazenda; (*area of trees*) bosque *m*

plant hire N locação *f* de equipamentos

plant pot (Brit) N vaso para planta

plaque [plæk] N placa, insígnia; (*also*: **dental plaque**) placa dental

plasma ['plæzmə] N plasma *m*

plaster ['plɑːstəʳ] N (*for walls*) reboco; (*also*: **plaster of Paris**) gesso; (*Brit: also*: **sticking plaster**) esparadrapo, band-aid *m* ■ VT rebocar; (*cover*): **to ~ with** encher *or* cobrir de; **in ~** (*Brit: leg etc*) engessado; **~ of Paris** gesso; **plaster cast** N (*Med*) aparelho de gesso; (*Art*) molde *m* de gesso

plastered ['plɑːstəd] (*inf*) ADJ bêbado, de porre

plasterer ['plɑːstərəʳ] N rebocador(a) *m/f*, caiador(a) *m/f*

plastic ['plæstɪk] N plástico ■ ADJ de plástico; (*flexible*) plástico; (*art*) plástico; **plastic bag** N sacola de plástico

Plasticine® ['plæstɪsiːn] N plasticina®

plastic surgery N cirurgia plástica

plate [pleɪt] N prato, chapa; (*Phot, on door, dental*) chapa; (*Typ*) clichê *m*; (*in book*) gravura; (*Aut: number plate*) placa; **gold/silver ~** placa de ouro/prata

plateau ['plætəu] (*pl* **plateaux**) N planalto

plateaux ['plætəuz] NPL *of* **plateau**

plateful ['pleɪtful] N pratada

plate glass N vidro laminado

platen ['plætən] N (*on typewriter, printer*) rolo

plate rack N escorredor *m* de pratos

platform ['plætfɔːm] N (Rail) plataforma (BR), cais *m* (PT); (*stage*) estrado; (*at meeting*) tribuna; (*raised structure: for landing etc*) plataforma; (*Brit: of bus*) plataforma; (*Pol*) programa *m* partidário; **platform ticket** (Brit) N bilhete *m* de plataforma (BR) *or* cais (PT)

platinum ['plætɪnəm] N platina

platitude ['plætɪtjuːd] N lugar *m* comum, chavão *m*

platonic [plə'tɔnɪk] ADJ platônico

platoon [plə'tuːn] N pelotão *m*

platter ['plætəʳ] N travessa

plaudits ['plɔːdɪts] NPL aclamações *fpl*, aplausos *mpl*

plausible ['plɔːzɪbl] ADJ plausível; (*person*) convincente

play [pleɪ] N jogo; (Theatre) obra, peça ■ VT jogar; (*team, opponent*) jogar contra; (*instrument, music, record*) tocar; (Theatre) representar; (: *role*) fazer o papel de; (*fig*) desempenhar ■ VI (*sport, game*) jogar; (*music*) tocar; (*frolic*) brincar; **to bring** *or* **call into ~** (*plan*) acionar; (*emotions*) detonar; **~ on words** jogo de palavras, trocadilho; **to ~ a trick on sb** pregar uma peça em alguém; **they're ~ing at soldiers** eles estão brincando de soldados; **to ~ for time** (*fig*) tentar ganhar tempo, protelar; **to ~ into sb's hands** (*fig*) fazer o jogo de alguém; **to ~ the fool/innocent** bancar o tolo/inocente; **to ~ safe** não se arriscar, não correr riscos

▸ **play about** VI brincar

▸ **play along** VI (*fig*): **to ~ along with sb** fazer o jogo de alguém ■ VT (*fig*): **to ~ sb along** fazer alguém de criança

▸ **play around** VI brincar

▸ **play back** VT repetir

▸ **play down** VT minimizar

▸ **play on** VT FUS (*sb's feelings, credulity*) tirar proveito de, usar

▸ **play up** VI (*person*) dar trabalho; (*TV, car*) estar com defeito

playact ['pleɪækt] VI fazer fita

playboy ['pleɪbɔɪ] N playboy *m*

played-out [pleɪd-] ADJ gasto

player ['pleɪəʳ] N jogador(a) *m/f*; (Theatre) ator/atriz *m/f*; (Mus) músico(-a)

playful ['pleɪful] ADJ brincalhão(-lhona)

playgoer ['pleɪɡəuəʳ] N freqüentador(a) *m/f* de teatro

playground ['pleɪgraund] N (in park) playground m; (in school) pátio de recreio

playgroup ['pleɪgruːp] N espécie de jardim de infância

playing card ['pleɪɪŋ-] N carta de baralho

playing field ['pleɪɪŋ-] N campo de esportes (BR) or jogos (PT)

playmate ['pleɪmeɪt] N colega m/f, camarada m/f

play-off N (Sport) partida de desempate

playpen ['pleɪpen] N cercado para crianças

playroom ['pleɪruːm] N sala de jogos

plaything ['pleɪθɪŋ] N brinquedo; (fig) joguete m

playtime ['pleɪtaɪm] N (Sch) recreio

playwright ['pleɪraɪt] N dramaturgo(-a)

plc ABBR = **public limited company**

plea [pliː] N (request) apelo, petição f; (excuse) justificativa; (Law: defence) defesa

plead [pliːd] VT (Law) defender, advogar; (give as excuse) alegar ▪ VI (Law) declarar-se; (beg): **to ~ with sb (for sth)** suplicar or rogar (algo) a alguém; **to ~ guilty/not guilty** declarar-se culpado/inocente

pleasant ['pleznt] ADJ agradável; (person) simpático

pleasantly ['plezntlɪ] ADV agradavelmente

pleasantness ['plezntnɪs] N (of person) amabilidade f, simpatia; (of place) encanto

pleasantry ['plezntrɪ] N (joke) brincadeira; **pleasantries** NPL (polite remarks) amenidades fpl (na conversa)

please [pliːz] EXCL por favor ▪ VT (give pleasure to) agradar a, dar prazer a ▪ VI (think fit): **do as you ~** faça o que or como quiser; **~ yourself!** (inf) como você quiser!, você que sabe!

pleased [pliːzd] ADJ (happy) satisfeito, contente; **~ (with)** satisfeito (com); **~ to meet you** prazer (em conhecê-lo); **we are ~ to inform you that ...** temos a satisfação de informá-lo de que ...

pleasing ['pliːzɪŋ] ADJ agradável

pleasurable ['pleʒərəbl] ADJ agradável

pleasure ['pleʒə^r] N prazer m; **"it's a ~"** "não tem de quê"; **with ~** com muito prazer; **is this trip for business or ~?** esta viagem é de negócios ou de recreio?; **pleasure boat** N barco de recreio; **pleasure steamer** N vapor m de recreio

pleat [pliːt] N prega

plebiscite ['plebɪsɪt] N plebiscito

plebs [plebz] (pej) NPL plebe f

plectrum ['plektrəm] N plectro

pledge [pledʒ] N (object) penhor m; (promise) promessa ▪ VT (invest) empenhar; (promise) prometer; **to ~ support for sb** empenhar-se a apoiar alguém; **to ~ sb to secrecy** comprometer alguém a guardar sigilo

plenary ['pliːnərɪ] ADJ: **in ~ session** no plenário

plentiful ['plentɪful] ADJ abundante

plenty ['plentɪ] N abundância; **~ of** (food, money) bastante; (jobs, people) muitos(-as); **we've got ~ of time** temos tempo de sobra

pleurisy ['pluərɪsɪ] N pleurisia

Plexiglas® ['pleksɪglɑːs] (US) N Blindex® m

pliable ['plaɪəbl] ADJ flexível; (fig: person) adaptável, moldável

pliant ['plaɪənt] ADJ = **pliable**

pliers ['plaɪəz] NPL alicate m

plight [plaɪt] N situação f difícil, apuro

plimsolls ['plɪmsəlz] (Brit) NPL tênis mpl

plinth [plɪnθ] N peinto

PLO N ABBR (= Palestine Liberation Organization) OLP f

plod [plɔd] VI caminhar pesadamente; (fig) trabalhar laboriosamente

plodder ['plɔdə^r] N burro-de-carga m

plodding ['plɔdɪŋ] ADJ mourejador(a)

plonk [plɔŋk] (inf) N (Brit: wine) zurrapa ▪ VT: **to ~ sth down** deixar cair algo (pesadamente)

plot [plɔt] N (scheme) conspiração f, complô m; (of story, play) enredo, trama; (of land) lote m ▪ VT (mark out) traçar; (conspire) tramar, planejar (BR), planear (PT); (Aviat, Naut, Math) plotar ▪ VI conspirar; **a vegetable ~** (Brit) uma horta

plotter ['plɔtə^r] N conspirador(a) m/f; (instrument) plotadora; (Comput) plotter f, plotadora

plough [plau] (US **plow**) N arado ▪ VT (earth) arar; **to ~ money into** investir dinheiro em
  ▸ **plough back** VT (Comm) reinvestir
  ▸ **plough through** VT FUS (crowd) abrir caminho por; (snow) avançar penosamente por

ploughing ['plauɪŋ] (US **plowing**) N aradura

ploughman ['plaumən] (US **plowman**) (irreg) N lavrador m

ploughman's lunch (Brit) N lanche de pão, queijo e picles

plow etc [plau] (US) = **plough** etc

ploy [plɔɪ] N estratagema m

pluck [plʌk] VT (fruit) colher; (musical instrument) dedilhar; (bird) depenar ▪ N coragem f, puxão m; **to ~ one's eyebrows** fazer as sobrancelhas; **to ~ up courage** criar coragem

plucky ['plʌkɪ] ADJ corajoso, valente

plug [plʌg] N tampão m; (Elec) tomada (BR), ficha (PT); (in sink) tampa; (Aut: also: **spark(ing) plug**) vela (de ignição) ▪ VT (hole) tapar; (inf: advertise) fazer propaganda de; **to give sb/sth a ~** (inf) fazer propaganda de alguém/algo
  ▸ **plug in** VT (Elec) ligar

plughole ['plʌghəul] (Brit) N (in sink) escoadouro

plum [plʌm] N (fruit) ameixa ▪ CPD (inf): **a ~ job** um emprego jóia

plumage ['pluːmɪdʒ] N plumagem f

plumb [plʌm] ADJ vertical ▪ N prumo ▪ ADV (exactly) exatamente ▪ VT sondar; **to ~ the depths** (fig) chegar ao extremo
  ▸ **plumb in** VT (washing machine) instalar

plumber ['plʌmə^r] N bombeiro(-a) (BR), encanador(a) m/f (BR), canalizador(a) m/f (PT)

plumbing ['plʌmɪŋ] N (trade) ofício de encanador; (piping) encanamento

plumb line ['plʌmlaɪn] N fio de prumo

plume [pluːm] N pluma; (on helmet) penacho

plummet ['plʌmɪt] VI: **to ~ (down)** (bird, aircraft) cair rapidamente; (price) baixar rapidamente

plump [plʌmp] ADJ roliço, rechonchudo ▪ VT:

to ~ sth (down) on deixar cair algo em ■ vi: **to ~ for** (inf: choose) escolher, optar por

▶ **plump up** vt (cushion) afofar

plunder ['plʌndə^r] n pilhagem f; (loot) despojo ■ vt pilhar, espoliar

plunge [plʌndʒ] n (dive) salto; (submersion) mergulho; (fig) queda ■ vt (hand, knife) enfiar, meter ■ vi (fall, fig) cair; (dive) mergulhar; **to take the ~** topar a parada; **to ~ a room into darkness** mergulhar um aposento na escuridão

plunger ['plʌndʒə^r] n êmbolo; (for blocked sink) desentupidor m

plunging ['plʌndʒɪŋ] adj (neckline) decotado

pluperfect [pluː'pəːfɪkt] n mais-que-perfeito

plural ['pluərl] adj plural ■ n plural m

plus [plʌs] n (also: **plus sign**) sinal m de adição ■ prep mais; **ten/twenty ~** dez/vinte e tantos; **it's a ~** é uma vantagem; **plus fours** npl calça (BR) or calças fpl (PT) de golfe

plush [plʌʃ] adj de pelúcia; (car, hotel etc) suntuoso ■ n pelúcia

plutonium [pluː'təunɪəm] n plutônio

ply [plaɪ] n (of wool) fio; (of wood) espessura ■ vt (a trade) exercer ■ vi (ship) ir e vir; **three ~** (wool) de três fios; **to ~ sb with drink/questions** bombardear alguém com bebidas/perguntas

plywood ['plaɪwud] n madeira compensada

PM (Brit) n abbr = **Prime Minister**

p.m. adv abbr (= post meridiem) da tarde, da noite

PMT n abbr (= premenstrual tension) TPM f, tensão f pré-menstrual

pneumatic [njuː'mætɪk] adj pneumático; **pneumatic drill** n perfuratriz f

pneumonia [njuː'məunɪə] n pneumonia

PO n abbr = **Post Office**; (Mil) = **petty officer**

po abbr = **postal order**

POA (Brit) n abbr = **Prison Officers' Association**

poach [pəutʃ] vt (cook: fish) escaldar; (: eggs) fazer pochê (BR), escalfar (PT); (steal) furtar ■ vi caçar (or pescar) em propriedade alheia

poached [pəutʃt] adj (egg) pochê (BR), escalfado (PT)

poacher ['pəutʃə^r] n caçador m (or pescador m) furtivo

poaching ['pəutʃɪŋ] n caça (or pesca) furtiva

PO Box n abbr = **Post Office Box**

pocket ['pɔkɪt] n bolso; (fig: small area) pedaço; (Billiards) caçapa, ventanilha ■ vt meter no bolso; (steal) embolsar; (Billiards) encaçapar; **to be out of ~** (Brit) perder, ter prejuízo; **~ of resistance** foco de resistência

pocketbook ['pɔkɪtbuk] (US) n carteira

pocket calculator n calculadora de bolsa

pocket knife (irreg) n canivete m

pocket money n dinheiro para despesas miúdas; (for child) mesada

pockmarked ['pɔkmɑːkt] adj (face) com marcas de varíola

pod [pɔd] n vagem f ■ vt descascar

podcast [pɔdkɑːst] n podcast m

podcasting [pɔdkɑːstɪŋ] n podcasting m

podgy ['pɔdʒɪ] (inf) adj gorducho, rechanchudo

podiatrist [pɔ'diːətrɪst] (US) n pedicuro(-a)

podiatry [pɔ'diːətrɪ] (US) n podiatria

podium ['pəudɪəm] n pódio

POE n abbr = **port of embarkation**; **port of entry**

poem ['pəuɪm] n poema m

poet ['pəuɪt] n poeta/poetisa m/f

poetess ['pəuɪtɪs] n poetisa

poetic [pəu'ɛtɪk] adj poético

poet laureate [-'lɔːrɪət] n poeta m laureado

poetry ['pəuɪtrɪ] n poesia

poignant ['pɔɪnjənt] adj comovente; (sharp) agudo

point [pɔɪnt] n (gen) ponto; (of needle, knife etc) ponta; (purpose) finalidade f; (significant part) ponto principal; (position, place) lugar m, posição f; (moment) momento; (stage in development) estágio; (Brit: Elec: also: **power point**) tomada; (also: **decimal point**): **2 ~ 3 (2.3)** dois vírgula três ■ vt (show, mark) mostrar; (window, wall) tomar com argamassa; (gun etc): **to ~ sth at sb** apontar algo para alguém ■ vi apontar; **points** npl (Aut) platinado, contato; (Rail) agulhas fpl; **to ~ at** apontar para; **good ~s** qualidades; **to be on the ~ of doing sth** estar prestes a or a ponto de fazer algo; **to make a ~** fazer uma observação; **to make a ~ of** fazer questão de, insistir em; **to make one's ~** dar sua opinião; **you've made your ~** você já disse o que queria, você já falou (inf); **to get the ~** perceber; **to miss the ~** compreender mal; **to come to the ~** ir ao assunto; **when it comes to the ~** na hora; **there's no ~ (in doing)** não há razão (para fazer); **that's the whole ~!** aí é que está a questão!, aí é que 'tá! (inf); **to be beside the ~** estar fora do assunto; **you've got a ~ there!** você tem razão!; **in ~ of fact** na verdade, na realidade; **~ of departure** ponto de partida; **~ of sale** (Comm) ponto de venda; **~ of view** ponto de vista

▶ **point out** vt (indicate) indicar; (in debate etc) ressaltar

▶ **point to** vt fus apontar para; (fig) indicar

point-blank adv categoricamente; (also: **at point-blank range**) à queima-roupa ■ adj (fig) categórico

point duty (Brit) n: **to be on ~** estar de serviço no controle do trânsito

pointed ['pɔɪntɪd] adj (stick etc) pontudo; (remark) mordaz

pointedly ['pɔɪntɪdlɪ] adv sugestivamente

pointer ['pɔɪntə^r] n (on chart) indicador m; (on machine) ponteiro; (needle) agulha; (dog) pointer m; (fig) dica

pointless ['pɔɪntlɪs] adj (useless) inútil; (senseless) sem sentido; (motiveless) sem razão

poise [pɔɪz] n (composure) elegância; (balance) equilíbrio; (of head, body) porte m; (calmness) serenidade f ■ vt pôr em equilíbrio; **to be ~d for** (fig) estar pronto para

poison ['pɔɪzn] n veneno ■ vt envenenar

poisoning ['pɔɪznɪŋ] N envenenamento
poisonous ['pɔɪzənəs] ADJ venenoso; (*fumes etc*) tóxico; (*fig*) pernicioso
poke [pəuk] VT (*fire*) atiçar; (*jab with finger, stick etc*) cutucar; (*put*): **to ~ sth in(to)** enfiar *or* meter algo em ▪ N (*to fire*) remexida; (*jab*) cutucada; (*with elbow*) cotovelada; **to ~ one's nose into** meter o nariz em; **to ~ one's head out of the window** meter a cabeça para fora da janela; **to ~ fun at sb** ridicularizar *or* fazer troça de alguém
  ▸ **poke about** VI escarafunchar, espionar
poker ['pəukə'] N atiçador *m* (de brasas); (*Cards*) pôquer *m*
poker-faced [-feɪst] ADJ com rosto impassível
poky ['pəukɪ] (*pej*) ADJ apertado
Poland ['pəulənd] N Polônia
polar ['pəulə'] ADJ polar; **polar bear** N urso polar
polarize ['pəuləraɪz] VT polarizar
Pole [pəul] N polonês(-esa) *m/f*
pole [pəul] N vara; (*Geo*) pólo; (*telegraph pole*) poste *m*; (*flagpole*) mastro; (*tent pole*) estaca; **pole bean** (US) N feijão-trepador *m*
polecat ['pəulkæt] N furão-bravo
Pol. Econ. ['pɔlɪkɔn] N ABBR = **political economy**
polemic [pɔ'lemɪk] N polêmica
pole star N estrela Polar
pole vault N salto com vara
police [pə'li:s] N polícia ▪ VT policiar; **police car** N rádio-patrulha *f*; **police constable** (Brit) N policial *m/f* (BR), polícia *m/f* (PT); **police department** (US) N polícia; **police force** N polícia
policeman [pə'li:smən] (*irreg*) N policial *m* (BR), polícia *m* (PT)
police officer N policial *m/f* (BR), polícia *m/f* (PT)
police record N ficha na polícia
police state N estado policial
police station N delegacia (de polícia) (BR), esquadra (PT)
policewoman [pə'li:swumən] (*irreg*) N policial *f* (feminina) (BR), mulher *f* polícia (PT)
policy ['pɔlɪsɪ] N política; (*also:* **insurance policy**) apólice *f*; (*of newspaper, company*) orientação *f*; **to take out a ~** (*Insurance*) fazer uma apólice *or* um contrato de seguro; **policy holder** N segurado(-a)
polio ['pəulɪəu] N poliomielite *f*, polio *f*
Polish ['pəulɪʃ] ADJ polonês(-esa) ▪ N (*Ling*) polonês *m*
polish ['pɔlɪʃ] N (*for shoes*) graxa; (*for floor*) cera (para encerar); (*for nails*) esmalte *m*; (*shine*) brilho; (*fig: refinement*) refinamento, requinte *m* ▪ VT (*shoes*) engraxar; (*make shiny*) lustrar, dar brilho a; (*fig: improve*) refinar, polir
  ▸ **polish off** VT (*work*) dar os arremates a; (*food*) raspar
polished ['pɔlɪʃt] ADJ (*fig: person*) culto; (*: manners*) refinado
polite [pə'laɪt] ADJ educado; (*formal*) cortês; (*company, society*) retinado; **it's not ~ to do that**

é falta de educação fazer isso
politely [pə'laɪtlɪ] ADV educadamente
politeness [pə'laɪtnɪs] N gentileza, cortesia
politic ['pɔlɪtɪk] ADJ prudente
political [pə'lɪtɪkl] ADJ político; **political asylum** N asilo político; **to seek political asylum** pedir asilo político
politically [pə'lɪtɪklɪ] ADV politicamente
politician [pɔlɪ'tɪʃən] N político
politics ['pɔlɪtɪks] N, NPL política
polka ['pɔlkə] N polca; **polka dot** N bolinha
poll [pəul] N (*votes*) votação *f*; (*also:* **opinion poll**) pesquisa, sondagem *f* ▪ VT (*votes*) receber, obter; **to go to the ~s** (*voters*) ir às urnas; (*government*) convocar eleições
pollen ['pɔlən] N pólen *m*; **pollen count** N contagem *f* de pólen
pollination [pɔlɪ'neɪʃən] N polinização *f*
polling ['pəulɪŋ] N (*Brit: Pol*) votação *f*; (*Tel*) apuração *f*; **polling booth** (Brit) N cabine *f* de votar; **polling day** (Brit) N dia *m* de eleição; **polling station** (Brit) N centro eleitoral
pollute [pə'lu:t] VT poluir
pollution [pə'lu:ʃən] N poluição *f*
polo ['pəuləu] N (*sport*) pólo; **polo neck** N gola rulê ▪ ADJ: **polo-neck** de gola rulê
polo-necked [-nekt] ADJ de gola rulê
poltergeist ['pɔltəgaɪst] N espírito pertubador (*espécie de fantasma*)
poly ['pɔlɪ] (Brit) N ABBR = **polytechnic**
polyester [pɔlɪ'estə'] N poliéster *m*
polyethylene [pɔlɪ'eθɪli:n] (US) N polietileno
polygamy [pə'lɪgəmɪ] N poligamia
Polynesia [pɔlɪ'ni:zɪə] N Polinésia
Polynesian [pɔlɪ'ni:zɪən] ADJ, N polinésio(-a)
polyp ['pɔlɪp] N (*Med*) pólipo
polystyrene [pɔlɪ'staɪri:n] N isopor® *m*
polytechnic [pɔlɪ'teknɪk] N politécnico, escola politécnica
polythene ['pɔlɪθi:n] N politeno; **polythene bag** N bolsa de plástico
polyurethane [pɔlɪ'ju:rəθeɪn] N poliuretano
pomegranate ['pɔmɪgrænɪt] N romã *f*
pommel ['pɔml] N botão *m*; (*saddle*) maçaneta ▪ VT = **pummel**
pomp [pɔmp] N pompa, fausto
pompom ['pɔmpɔm] N pompom *m*
pompon ['pɔmpɔn] N = **pompom**
pompous ['pɔmpəs] (*pej*) ADJ pomposo
pond [pɔnd] N (*natural*) lago pequeno; (*artificial*) tanque *m*
ponder ['pɔndə'] VT, VI ponderar, meditar (sobre)
ponderous ['pɔndərəs] ADJ pesado
pong [pɔŋ] (Brit: inf) N fedor *m*, fartum *m* (inf), catinga (inf) ▪ VI feder
pontiff ['pɔntɪf] N pontífice *m*
pontificate [pɔn'tɪfɪkeɪt] VI (*fig*): **to ~ (about)** pontificar (sobre)
pontoon [pɔn'tu:n] N pontão *m*; (*Brit: card game*) vinte-e-um *m*
pony ['pəunɪ] N pônei *m*

ponytail ['pəʊnɪteɪl] N rabo-de-cavalo
pony trekking [-'trɛkɪŋ] (Brit) N excursão f em
pônei
poodle ['puːdl] N cão-d'água m
pooh-pooh [puːˈpuː] VT desprezar
pool [puːl] N (puddle) poça, charco; (pond) lago;
(also: **swimming pool**) piscina; (fig: of light) feixe
m; (: of liquid) poça; (Sport) sinuca; (sth shared)
fundo comum; (money at cards) bolo; (Comm:
consortium) consórcio, pool m; (US: monopoly trust)
truste m ▪ VT juntar; **(football) pools** NPL
(football pools) loteria esportiva (BR), totobola
(PT); **typing** (Brit) or **secretary** (US) ~ seção f de
datilografia
poor [puər] ADJ pobre; (bad) inferior, mau
▪ NPL: **the** ~ os pobres; ~ **in** (resources etc)
deficiente em
poorly ['puəlɪ] ADJ adoentado, indisposto ▪ ADV
mal
pop [pɔp] N (sound) estalo, estouro; (Mus) pop
m; (US: inf: father) papai m; (inf: fizzy drink) bebida
gasosa ▪ VT: **to** ~ **sth into/onto** etc (put) pôr
em/sobre etc ▪ VI estourar; (cork) saltar; **she**
~**ped her head out of the window** ela meteu a
cabeça fora da janela
▸ **pop in** VI dar um pulo
▸ **pop out** VI dar uma saída
▸ **pop up** VI surgir, aparecer inesperadamente
pop concert N concerto pop
popcorn ['pɔpkɔːn] N pipoca
pope [pəʊp] N papa m
poplar ['pɔplər] N álamo, choupo
poplin ['pɔplɪn] N popeline f
popper ['pɔpər] (Brit) N presilha
poppy ['pɔpɪ] N papoula
poppycock ['pɔpɪkɔk] (inf) N conversa fiada,
papo furado
Popsicle ® ['pɔpsɪkl] (US) N picolé m
pop star N pop star m/f
populace ['pɔpjʊləs] N povo
popular ['pɔpjʊlər] ADJ popular; (person) querido;
(fashionable) badalado; **to be** ~ **(with)** (person)
fazer sucesso (com); (decision) ser aplaudido
(por)
popularity [pɔpjʊ'lærɪtɪ] N popularidade f
popularize ['pɔpjʊləraɪz] VT popularizar;
(science) vulgarizar
populate ['pɔpjʊleɪt] VT povoar
population [pɔpjʊ'leɪʃən] N população f;
population explosion N explosão f
demográfica
populous ['pɔpjʊləs] ADJ populoso
porcelain ['pɔːslɪn] N porcelana
porch [pɔːtʃ] N pórtico; (US: verandah) varanda
porcupine ['pɔːkjʊpaɪn] N porco-espinho
pore [pɔːr] N poro ▪ VI: **to** ~ **over** examinar
minuciosamente
pork [pɔːk] N carne f de porco; **pork chop** N
costeleta de porco
pornographic [pɔːnə'græfɪk] ADJ pornográfico
pornography [pɔː'nɔgrəfɪ] N pornografia
porous ['pɔːrəs] ADJ poroso

porpoise ['pɔːpəs] N golfinho, boto
porridge ['pɔrɪdʒ] N mingau m (de aveia)
port [pɔːt] N (harbour) porto; (Naut: left side)
bombordo; (wine) vinho do Porto; (Comput) porta,
port m ▪ CPD portuário; **to** ~ (Naut) a bombordo;
~ **of call** porto de escala
portable ['pɔːtəbl] ADJ portátil
portal ['pɔːtl] N portal m
portcullis [pɔːt'kʌlɪs] N grade f levadiça
portend [pɔːˈtɛnd] VT pressagiar
portent ['pɔːtɛnt] N presságio, portento
porter ['pɔːtər] N (for luggage) carregador m;
(doorkeeper) porteiro
portfolio [pɔːtˈfəʊlɪəʊ] N (case) pasta; (Pol)
pasta ministerial; (Finance) carteira de ações ou
títulos; (of artist) pasta, portfólió
porthole ['pɔːthəʊl] N vigia
portico ['pɔːtɪkəʊ] N pórtico
portion ['pɔːʃən] N porção f, quinhão m; (of food)
ração f
portly ['pɔːtlɪ] ADJ corpulento
portrait ['pɔːtreɪt] N retrato
portray [pɔːˈtreɪ] VT retratar; (act) interpretar;
(in writing) descrever
portrayal [pɔːˈtreɪəl] N retrato; (actor's)
interpretação f; (in book, film) representação f
Portugal ['pɔːtjʊgl] N Portugal m (no article)
Portuguese [pɔːtjuˈgiːz] ADJ português(-esa)
▪ N INV português(-esa) m/f; (Ling) português m;
Portuguese man-of-war (irreg: like **man**) N
(jellyfish) urtiga-do-mar f, caravela
pose [pəʊz] N postura, pose f; (pej) pose, afetação
f ▪ VI posar; (pretend): **to** ~ **as** fazer-se passar por
▪ VT (question) fazer; (problem) causar; **to strike a**
~ fazer pose; **to** ~ **for** (painting) posar para
poser ['pəʊzər] N problema m, abacaxi m (BR)
(inf); (person) = **poseur**
poseur [pəʊˈzəːr] (pej) N posudo(-a), pessoa
afetada
posh [pɔʃ] (inf) ADJ fino, chique; (upper-class) de
classe alta; **to talk** ~ falar com sotaque fino
position [pə'zɪʃən] N posição f; (job) cargo;
(situation) situação f ▪ VT colocar, situar; **to be**
in a ~ **to do sth** estar em posição de fazer algo
positive ['pɔzɪtɪv] ADJ positivo; (certain) certo;
(definite) definitivo; **I'm** ~ tenho certeza
absoluta
posse ['pɔsɪ] (US) N pelotão m de civis armados
possess [pə'zɛs] VT possuir; **like one** ~**ed** como
um possuído do demônio; **whatever can have**
~**ed you?** o que é que te deu?
possession [pə'zɛʃən] N posse f, possessão
f; (object) bem m, posse; **possessions** NPL
(belongings) pertences mpl; **to take** ~ **of sth**
tomar posse de algo
possessive [pə'zɛsɪv] ADJ possessivo
possessively [pə'zɛsɪvlɪ] ADV possessivamente
possessor [pə'zɛsər] N possuidor(a) m/f
possibility [pɔsɪ'bɪlɪtɪ] N possibilidade f; (of sth
happening) probabilidade f
possible ['pɔsɪbl] ADJ possível; **it is** ~ **to do it**
é possível fazê-lo; **as far as** ~ tanto quanto

possível, na medida do possível; **if ~ se** for possível; **as big as ~ o** maior possível

possibly ['pɒsɪblɪ] ADV (*perhaps*) pode ser, talvez; **if you ~ can** se lhe for possível; **could you ~ come over?** será qué você podia vir para ca?; **I cannot ~ come** estou impossibilitado de vir

post [pəust] N (*Brit: mail*) correio; (*job, situation*) cargo, posto; (*pole*) poste *m*; (*Mil*) nomeação *f*; (*trading post*) entreposto comercial ▪ VT (*Brit: send by post*) pôr no correio; (: *Mil*) nomear; (*bills*) afixar, pregar; (*Brit: appoint*): **to ~ to** destinar a; **by ~** (*Brit*) pelo correio; **by return of ~** (*Brit*) na volta do correio; **to keep sb ~ed** manter alguém informado

post- [pəust] PREFIX pós...; **~1990** depois de 1990

postage ['pəustɪdʒ] N porte *m*, franquia; **~ paid** porte pago; **~ prepaid** (*US*) franquia de porte; **postage stamp** N selo postal

postal ['pəustəl] ADJ postal; **postal order** N vale *m* postal

postbag ['pəustbæg] (*Brit*) N mala de correio; (*postman's*) sacola

postbox ['pəustbɒks] (*Brit*) N caixa de correio

postcard ['pəustkɑːd] N cartão *m* postal

postcode ['pəustkəud] (*Brit*) N código postal, ≈ CEP *m* (BR)

postdate [pəust'deɪt] VT (*cheque*) pós-datar

poster ['pəustəʳ] N cartaz *m*; (*as decoration*) pôster *m*

poste restante [pəust'rɛstɑːnt] (*Brit*) N posta-restante *f*

posterior [pɒs'tɪərɪəʳ] (*inf*) N traseiro, nádegas *fpl*

posterity [pɒs'tɛrɪtɪ] N posteridade *f*

poster paint N guache *m*

post exchange (*US*) N (*Mil*) loja do exército

post-free (*Brit*) ADJ franco de porte

postgraduate [pəust'grædjuət] N pós-graduado(-a)

posthumous ['pɒstjuməs] ADJ póstumo

posthumously ['pɒstjuməslɪ] ADV postumamente

posting ['pəustɪŋ] (*Brit*) N nomeação *f*

postman ['pəustmən] (*irreg*) N carteiro

postmark ['pəustmɑːk] N carimbo do correio

postmaster ['pəustmɑːstəʳ] N agente *m* (BR) *or* chefe *m* (PT) do correio

Postmaster General N ≈ Superintendente *m* Geral dos Correios

postmen ['pəustmɛn] NPL *of* **postman**

postmistress ['pəustmɪstrɪs] N agente *f* (BR) *or* chefe *f* (PT) do correio

postmortem [pəust'mɔːtəm] N autópsia

postnatal [pəust'neɪtl] ADJ pós-natal

post office N (*building*) agência do correio, correio; (*organization*) ≈ Empresa Nacional dos Correios e Telégrafos (BR), ≈ Correios, Telégrafos e Telefones (PT)

post office box N caixa postal

post-paid (*Brit*) ADJ porte pago

postpone [pəs'pəun] VT adiar

postponement [pəs'pəunmənt] N adiamento

postscript ['pəustskrɪpt] N pós-escrito

postulate ['pɒstjuleɪt] VT postular

posture ['pɒstʃəʳ] N postura; (*fig*) atitude *f* ▪ VI posar

postwar [pəust'wɔː'] ADJ de após-guerra

posy ['pəuzɪ] N ramalhete *m*

pot [pɒt] N (*for cooking*) panela; (*for flowers*) vaso; (*container, teapot, coffee pot*) pote *m*; (*inf: marijuana*) maconha ▪ VT (*plant*) plantar em vaso; (*conserve*) pôr em conserva; **to go to ~** (*inf: country, economy*) arruinar-se, degringolar; **the town has gone to ~** a cidade mixou; **~s of ...** (*Brit: inf*) ... aos potes

potash ['pɒtæʃ] N potassa

potassium [pə'tæsɪəm] N potássio

potato [pə'teɪtəu] (*pl* **potatoes**) N batata; **potato crisps** (*US* **potato chips**) NPL batatinhas *fpl* fritas; **potato flour** N fécula (de batata); **potato peeler** N descascador *m* de batatas

potbellied ['pɒtbelɪd] ADJ barrigudo

potency ['pəutənsɪ] N potência; (*of drink*) teor *m* alcoólico

potent ['pəutnt] ADJ weapon, argument, poderoso; (*drink*) forte; (*man*) potente

potentate ['pəutnteɪt] N potentado

potential [pə'tɛnʃl] ADJ potencial ▪ N potencial *m*; **to have ~** ser promissor

potentially [pə'tɛnʃəlɪ] ADV potencialmente

pothole ['pɒthəul] N (*in road*) buraco; (*Brit: underground*) caldeirão *m*, cova

potholer ['pɒthəuləʳ] (*Brit*) N espeleologista *m/f*

potholing ['pɒthəulɪŋ] (*Brit*) N: **to go ~** dedicar-se à espeleologia

potion ['pəuʃən] N poção *f*

potluck [pɒt'lʌk] N: **to take ~** contentar-se com o que houver

potpourri [pəu'puːriː] N potpourri *m* (*de pétalas e folhas secas para perfumar o ambiente*)

pot roast N carne *f* assada

potshot ['pɒtʃɒt] N: **to take a ~ at sth** atirar em algo a esmo

potted ['pɒtɪd] ADJ (*food*) em conserva; (*plant*) de vaso; (*fig: shortened*) resumido

potter ['pɒtəʳ] N (*artistic*) ceramista *m/f*; (*artisan*) oleiro(-a) ▪ VI (*Brit*): **to ~ around, ~ about** ocupar-se com pequenos trabalhos; **~'s wheel** roda *or* torno do oleiro

pottery ['pɒtərɪ] N cerâmica; (*factory*) olaria; **a piece of ~** uma cerâmica

potty ['pɒtɪ] ADJ (*inf: mad*) maluco, doido ▪ N penico

potty-training N treino (da criança) para o uso do urinol

pouch [pautʃ] N (*Zool*) bolsa; (*for tobacco*) tabaqueira

pouf(fe) [puːf] N pufe *m*

poultice ['pəultɪs] N cataplasma

poultry ['pəultrɪ] N aves *fpl* domésticas; (*meat*) carne *f* de aves domésticas; **poultry farm** N granja avícola; **poultry farmer** N avicultor(a) *m/f*

pounce [pauns] VI: **to ~ on** lançar-se sobre;

(person) agarrar em; (fig: mistake etc) apontar ■ N salto, arremetida

pound [paund] N libra (weight = 453g, 16 ounces; money = 100 pence); (for dogs) canil m; (for cars) depósito ■ VT (beat) socar, esmurrar; (crush) triturar ■ VI (heart) bater; **half a ~ (of)** meia libra (de); **a five-~ note** uma nota de cinco libras

pounding ['paundɪŋ] N: **to take a ~** (fig) levar uma surra

pound sterling N libra esterlina

pour [pɔːʳ] VT despejar; (tea) servir ■ VI correr, jorrar; (rain) chover a cântaros; **to ~ sb a drink** servir uma bebida a alguém
> **pour away** VT esvaziar, decantar
> **pour in** VI (people) entrar numa enxurrada; (information) chegar numa enxurrada
> **pour off** VT esvaziar, decantar
> **pour out** VI (people) sair aos borbotões ■ VT (drink) servir; (water etc) esvaziar; (fig) extravasar

pouring ['pɔːrɪŋ] ADJ: **~ rain** chuva torrencial

pout [paut] VI fazer beicinho or biquinho

poverty ['pɔvətɪ] N pobreza, miséria

poverty-stricken ADJ muito pobre, carente

poverty trap (Brit) N armadilha da pobreza

POW N ABBR = **prisoner of war**

powder ['paudəʳ] N pó m; (face powder) pó-de-arroz m; (gunpowder) pólvora ■ VT pulverizar; (face) empoar, passar pó em; **to ~ one's nose** empoar-se; (euphemism) ir ao banheiro; **powder compact** N estojo (de pó-de-arroz)

powdered milk ['paudəd-] N leite m em pó

powder puff N esponja de pó-de-arroz

powder room N toucador m, banheiro de senhoras

powdery ['paudərɪ] ADJ poeirento

power ['pauəʳ] N poder m; (of explosion, engine) força, potência; (nation) potência; (ability, Pol: of party, leader) poder, poderio; (of speech, thought) faculdade f; (Math, Tech) potência; (electricity, strength) força ■ VT (Elec) alimentar; (engine, machine) acionar; (car, plane) propulsionar; **to do all in one's ~ to help sb** fazer tudo que tiver ao seu alcance para ajudar alguém; **the world ~s** as grandes potências; **to be in ~** estar no poder; **~ of attorney** procuração f

powerboat ['pauəbəut] (Brit) N barco a motor

power cut (Brit) N corte m de energia, blecaute m (BR)

power-driven ADJ movido a motor; (Elec) elétrico

powered ['pauəd] ADJ: **~ by** movido a; **nuclear-~ submarine** submarino nuclear

power failure N corte m de energia

powerful ['pauəful] ADJ poderoso; (engine) potente; (body) vigoroso; (blow) violento; (argument) convincente; (emotion) intenso

powerhouse ['pauəhaus] N (fig: person) poço de energia; **a ~ of ideas** um poço de idéias

powerless ['pauəlis] ADJ impotente

power line N fio de alta tensão

power point (Brit) N tomada

power station N central f elétrica

power steering N direção f hidráulica

powwow ['pauwau] N reunião f

pox [pɔks] (inf) N sífilis f; see also **chickenpox**; smallpox

pp ABBR (= per procurationem) p.p.; = **pages**

p&p (Brit) ABBR (= postage and packing) porte e embalagem

PPE (Brit) N ABBR (Sch) = **philosophy; politics and economics**

PPS N ABBR (= post postscriptum) PPS; (Brit: = parliamentary private secretary) parlamentário no serviço de um ministro

PQ (Canada) ABBR = **Province of Quebec**

PR N ABBR = **proportional representation**; **public relations** ■ ABBR (US: Post) = **Puerto Rico**

Pr. ABBR (= prince) Princ

practicability [præktɪkə'bɪlɪtɪ] N viabilidade f

practicable ['præktɪkəbl] ADJ (scheme) viável

practical ['præktɪkl] ADJ prático

practicality [præktɪ'kælɪtɪ] N (of plan) viabilidade f; (of person) índole f prática; **practicalities** NPL (of situation) aspectos mpl práticos

practical joke N brincadeira, peça

practically ['præktɪkəlɪ] ADV (almost) praticamente

practice ['præktɪs] N (habit, Rel) costume m, hábito; (exercise) prática; (of profession) exercício; (training) treinamento; (Med) consultório; (Law) escritório ■ VT, VI (US) = **practise; in ~** (in reality) na prática; **out of ~** destreinado; **it's common ~** é comum; **to put sth into ~** pôr algo em prática; **to set up in ~** abrir consultório; **practice match** N jogo de treinamento

practise ['præktɪs] (US **practice**) VT praticar; (profession) exercer; (sport) treinar ■ VI (doctor) ter consultório; (lawyer) ter escritório; (train) treinar, praticar

practised ['præktɪst] (Brit) ADJ (person) experiente, experimentado; (performance) competente; (liar) contumaz; **with a ~ eye** com olhar de entendedor

practising ['præktɪsɪŋ] ADJ (Christian etc) praticante; (lawyer) que exerce; (homosexual) assumido

practitioner [præk'tɪʃənəʳ] N praticante m/f; (Med) médico(-a)

pragmatic [præg'mætɪk] ADJ pragmático

Prague [prɑːg] N Praga

prairie ['prɛərɪ] N campina, pradaria

praise [preɪz] N (approval) louvor m; (admiration) elogio ■ VT elogiar, louvar

praiseworthy ['preɪzwəːðɪ] ADJ louvável, digno de elogio

pram [præm] (Brit) N carrinho de bebê

prance [prɑːns] VI: **to ~ about/up and down** etc (horse) curvetear, fazer cabriolas; (person) andar espalhafatosamente

prank [præŋk] N travessura, peça

prattle ['prætl] VI tagarelar; (child) balbuciar

prawn [prɔːn] N pitu m; (small) camarão m

pray [preɪ] vɪ: **to ~ for/that** rezar por/para que
prayer [preə^r] N (activity) reza; (words) oração f,
prece f; (entreaty) súplica, rogo; **prayer book** N
missal m, livro de orações
pre- ['priː] PREFIX pré-; **~1970** antes de 1970
preach [priːtʃ] vт pregar ▪ vɪ pregar; (pej:
moralize) catequizar; **to ~ at sb** fazer sermões a
alguém
preacher ['priːtʃə^r] N pregador(a) m/f; (US:
clergyman) pastor m
preamble [prɪ'æmbl] N preâmbulo
prearranged [priːə'reɪndʒd] ADJ combinado de
antemão
precarious [prɪ'kɛərɪəs] ADJ precário
precaution [prɪ'kɔːʃən] N precaução f
precautionary [prɪ'kɔːʃənrɪ] ADJ (measure) de
precaução
precede [prɪ'siːd] vт, vɪ preceder
precedence ['prɛsɪdəns] N precedência; (priority)
prioridade f
precedent ['prɛsɪdənt] N precedente m;
to establish or **set a ~** estabelecer or abrir
precedente
preceding [prɪ'siːdɪŋ] ADJ anterior
precept ['priːsɛpt] N preceito
precinct ['priːsɪŋkt] N (round church) recinto; (US:
district) distrito policial; **precincts** NPL (of large
building) arredores mpl; **pedestrian ~** (Brit) zona
para pedestres (BR) or peões (PT); **shopping ~**
(Brit) zona comercial
precious ['prɛʃəs] ADJ precioso; (stylized) afetado
▪ ADV (inf): **~ little** muito pouco, pouquíssimo;
your ~ dog (ironic) seu adorado cãozinho
precipice ['prɛsɪpɪs] N precipício
precipitate [adj prɪ'sɪpɪtɪt, vt prɪ'sɪpɪteɪt] ADJ
(hasty) precipitado, apressado ▪ vт (hasten)
precipitar, acelerar; (bring about) causar
precipitation [prɪsɪpɪ'teɪʃən] N precipitação f
precipitous [prɪ'sɪpɪtəs] ADJ (steep) íngreme,
escarpado
précis ['preɪsiː] N INV resumo, sumário
precise [prɪ'saɪs] ADJ exato, preciso; (plans)
detalhado; (person) escrupuloso, meticuloso
precisely [prɪ'saɪslɪ] ADV precisamente; (exactly)
exatamente
precision [prɪ'sɪʒən] N precisão f
preclude [prɪ'kluːd] vт excluir; **to ~ sb from
doing** impedir que alguém faça
precocious [prɪ'kəʊʃəs] ADJ precoce
preconceived [priːkən'siːvd] ADJ (idea)
preconcebido
preconception [priːkən'sɛpʃən] N preconceito
precondition [priːkən'dɪʃən] N condição f
prévia
precursor [priː'kɜːsə^r] N precursor(a) m/f
predate ['priːdeɪt] vт (precede) preceder
predator ['prɛdətə^r] N predador m
predatory ['prɛdətərɪ] ADJ predatório, rapace
predecessor ['priːdɪsɛsə^r] N predecessor(a) m/f,
antepassado(-a)
predestination [priːdɛstɪ'neɪʃən] N
predestinação f, destino

predetermine [priːdɪ'tɜːmɪn] vт
predeterminar, predispor
predicament [prɪ'dɪkəmənt] N situação f difícil,
apuro
predicate ['prɛdɪkɪt] N (Ling) predicado
predict [prɪ'dɪkt] vт prever, predizer,
prognosticar
predictable [prɪ'dɪktəbl] ADJ previsível
predictably [prɪ'dɪktəblɪ] ADV (behave, react) de
maneira previsível; **~ she didn't come** como
era de se esperar, ela não veio
prediction [prɪ'dɪkʃən] N previsão f,
prognóstico
predispose [priːdɪs'pəʊz] vт predispor
predominance [prɪ'dɔmɪnəns] N
predominância, preponderância
predominant [prɪ'dɔmɪnənt] ADJ
predominante, preponderante
predominantly [prɪ'dɔmɪnəntlɪ] ADV
predominantemente; (for the most part) na
maioria; (above all) sobretudo
predominate [prɪ'dɔmɪneɪt] vɪ predominar
pre-eminent ADJ preeminente
pre-empt [-ɛmt] (Brit) vт (obtain) adquirir por
preempção or de antemão; (fig): **to ~ sb/sth**
antecipar-se a alguém/antecipar algo
pre-emptive [-ɛmtɪv] ADJ: **~ strike** ataque m
preventivo
preen [priːn] vт: **to ~ itself** (bird) limpar e alisar
as penas (com o bico); **to ~ o.s.** enfeitar-se,
envaidecer-se
prefab ['priːfæb] N casa pré-fabricada
prefabricated [priː'fæbrɪkeɪtɪd] ADJ pré-
fabricado
preface ['prɛfəs] N prefácio
prefect ['priːfɛkt] N (Brit: Sch) monitor(a) m/f,
tutor(a) m/f; (in Brazil) prefeito(-a)
prefer [prɪ'fɜː^r] vт preferir; (Law): **to ~ charges**
intentar uma ação judicial; **to ~ coffee to tea**
preferir café a chá
preferable ['prɛfrəbl] ADJ preferível
preferably ['prɛfrəblɪ] ADV de preferência
preference ['prɛfrəns] N preferência; **in ~ to
sth** de preferência a algo; **preference shares**
(Brit) NPL ações fpl preferenciais
preferential [prɛfə'rɛnʃəl] ADJ preferencial; **~
treatment** preferência
preferred stock [prɪ'fɜːd-] (US) NPL ações fpl
preferenciais
prefix ['priːfɪks] N prefixo
pregnancy ['prɛgnənsɪ] N gravidez f; (animal)
prenhez f
pregnant ['prɛgnənt] ADJ grávida; (animal)
prenha; **3 months ~** grávida de 3 meses; **~ with**
rico de, cheio de
prehistoric [priːhɪs'tɔrɪk] ADJ pré-histórico
prehistory [priː'hɪstərɪ] N pré-história
prejudge [priː'dʒʌdʒ] vт fazer um juízo
antecipado de, prejulgar
prejudice ['prɛdʒʊdɪs] N (bias) preconceito;
(harm) prejuízo ▪ vт (predispose) predispor;
(harm) prejudicar; **to ~ sb in favour of/against**

predispor alguém a favor de/contra
prejudiced ['prɛdʒudɪst] ADJ *(person)* cheio de
preconceitos; *(view)* parcial, preconcebido;
to be ~ against sb/sth estar com prevenção
contra alguém/algo
prelate ['prɛlət] N prelado
preliminaries [prɪ'lɪmɪnərɪz] NPL preliminares
fpl
preliminary [prɪ'lɪmɪnərɪ] ADJ preliminar,
prévio
prelude ['prɛljuːd] N prelúdio
premarital [priː'mærɪtl] ADJ pré-nupcial
premature ['prɛmətʃuər] ADJ prematuro; **to be ~
(in doing sth)** precipitar-se (em fazer algo)
premeditated [priː'mɛdɪteɪtɪd] ADJ
premeditado
premeditation [priːmɛdɪ'teɪʃən] N
premeditação *f*
premenstrual [priː'mɛnstruəl] ADJ pré-
menstrual; **premenstrual tension** N tensão *f*
pré-menstrual
premier ['prɛmɪər] ADJ primeiro, principal ■ N
(Pol) primeiro-ministro/primeira-ministra
première ['prɛmɪɛər] N estréia
premise ['prɛmɪs] N premissa; **premises** NPL
(of business, institution) local *m*; *(house)* casa; *(shop)*
loja; **on the ~s** no local; **business ~s** local
utilizado para fins comerciais
premium ['priːmɪəm] N prêmio; **to be at a ~** ser
caro; **to sell at a ~** *(shares)* vender acima do par;
premium bond *(Brit)* N *obrigação qué dá direito a
prêmio mediante sorteio*; **premium deal** N *(Comm)*
oferta especial; **premium gasoline** *(US)* N
gasolina azul *or* super
premonition [prɛmə'nɪʃən] N presságio,
pressentimento
preoccupation [priːɔkju'peɪʃən] N
preocupação *f*
preoccupied [priː'ɔkjupaɪd] ADJ *(worried)*
preocupado, apreensivo; *(absorbed)* absorto
prep [prɛp] ADJ ABBR: **~ school**; **= preparatory
school** ■ N *(Sch: = study)* deveres *mpl*
prepackaged [priː'pækɪdʒd] ADJ embalado para
venda ao consumidor
prepaid [priː'peɪd] ADJ com porte pago
preparation [prɛpə'reɪʃən] N preparação *f*;
preparations NPL *(arrangements)* preparativos
mpl; **in ~ for** em preparação para
preparatory [prɪ'pærətərɪ] ADJ preparatório;
~ to antes de; **preparatory school** N *escola
particular para crianças até 11 ou 13 anod de idade*
prepare [prɪ'pɛər] VT preparar ■ VI: **to ~
for** preparar-se *or* aprontar-se para; *(make
preparations)* fazer preparativos para; **~d to**
disposto a; **~d for** pronto para
preponderance [prɪ'pɔndərns] N predomínio
preposition [prɛpə'zɪʃən] N preposição *f*
prepossessing [priːpə'zesɪŋ] ADJ atraente
preposterous [prɪ'pɔstərəs] ADJ absurdo,
disparatado
prep school N = **preparatory school**
prerecorded ['priːrɪ'kɔːdɪd] ADJ pré-gravado

prerequisite [priː'rɛkwɪzɪt] N pré-requisito,
condição *f* prévia
prerogative [prɪ'rɔgətɪv] N prerrogativa
presbyterian [prɛzbɪ'tɪərɪən] ADJ, N
presbiteriano(-a)
presbytery ['prɛzbɪtərɪ] N presbitério
preschool ['priː'skuːl] ADJ *(education, age)* pré-
escolar; *(child)* de idade pré-escolar
prescribe [prɪ'skraɪb] VT prescrever; *(Med)*
receitar; **~d books** *(Brit: Sch)* livros *mpl*
requisitados
prescription [prɪ'skrɪpʃən] N prescrição *f*,
ordem *f*; *(Med)* receita; **to make up** *(Brit) or* **fill**
(US) **a ~** aviar uma receita; **"only available on
~"** "venda exclusivamente mediante receita
médica"; **prescription charges** *(Brit)* NPL
participação *f* no preço das receitas médicas
prescriptive [prɪ'skrɪptɪv] ADJ prescritivo
presence ['prɛzns] N presença; *(spirit)* espectro;
presence of mind N presença de espírito
present [*adj, n* 'prɛznt, *vt* prɪ'zɛnt] ADJ *(in
attendance)* presente; *(current)* atual ■ N *(gift)*
presente *m*; *(actuality)*: **the ~ o** presente ■ VT
(give): **to ~ sth to sb, to ~ sb with sth** *(as gift)*
presentear alguém com algo; *(as prize)* entregar
algo a alguém; *(expound)* expor; *(information,
programme, person, difficulty, threat)* apresentar;
(describe) descrever; *(Theatre)* representar; **at ~** no
momento, agora; **for the ~** por enquanto; **to be
~ at** estar presente a, presenciar; **to give sb a ~**
presentear alguém
presentable [prɪ'zɛntəbl] ADJ apresentável
presentation [prɛzn'teɪʃən] N apresentação *f*;
(gift) presente *m*; *(ceremony)* entrega; *(of plan etc)*
exposição *f*; *(Theatre)* representação *f*; **on ~ of**
mediante apresentação
present-day ADJ atual, de hoje
presenter [prɪ'zɛntər] N *(Radio, TV)*
apresentador(a) *m/f*
presently ['prɛzntlɪ] ADV *(soon after)* logo após;
(soon) logo, em breve; *(now)* atualmente
preservation [prɛzə'veɪʃən] N conservação *f*,
preservação *f*
preservative [prɪ'zə:vətɪv] N preservativo
preserve [prɪ'zə:v] VT *(situation)* conservar,
manter; *(building, manuscript)* preservar; *(food)* pôr
em conserva; *(in salt)* conservar em sal, salgar
■ N *(for game)* reserva de caça, coutada; *(often pl:
jam)* geléia; *(: fruit)* compota, conserva
preshrunk ['priː'ʃrʌŋk] ADJ pré-encolhido
preside [prɪ'zaɪd] VI: **to ~ (over)** presidir
presidency ['prɛzɪdənsɪ] N presidência
president ['prɛzɪdənt] N presidente(-a) *m/f*
presidential [prɛzɪ'dɛnʃl] ADJ presidencial
press [prɛs] N *(tool, machine)* prensa; *(printer's)*
imprensa, prelo; *(newspapers)* imprensa; *(of
switch)* pressão *f*; *(crowd)* turba, apinhamento; *(of
hand)* apertão *m* ■ VT apertar; *(squeeze: fruit
etc)* espremer; *(clothes: iron)* passar; *(put pressure
on: person)* assediar; *(Tech)* prensar; *(harry)*
assediar; *(insist)*: **to ~ sth on sb** insistir para
que alguém aceite algo; *(urge)*: **to ~ sb to do or**

into doing sth impelir or pressionar alguém a fazer algo ■ vi (squeeze) apertar; (pressurize): **to ~ for** pressionar por; **we are ~ed for time/ money** estamos com pouco tempo/dinheiro; **to ~ for sth** pressionar por algo; **to ~ sb for an answer** pressionar alguém por uma resposta; **to ~ charges against sb** (Law) intentar ação judicial contra alguém; **to go to ~** (newspaper) ir para o prelo; **to be in the ~** estar no prelo; **to appear in the ~** sair no jornal

▶ **press on** vi continuar

press: **press agency** N agência de informações; **press clipping** N recorte m de jornal; **press conference** N entrevista coletiva (para a imprensa); **press cutting** N recorte m de jornal

press-gang N pelotão de recrutamento da marinha ■ vt: **to be ~ed into doing** ser impelido a fazer

pressing ['presɪŋ] ADJ urgente ■ N ação f (or serviço m) de passar roupa etc

pressman ['presmæn] (irreg) N jornalista m

press release N release m or comunicado à imprensa

press stud (Brit) N botão m de pressão

press-up (Brit) N flexão f

pressure ['preʃər] N pressão f ■ vt = **to put pressure on**; **to put ~ on sb (to do sth)** pressionar alguém (a fazer algo); **pressure cooker** N panela de pressão; **pressure gauge** N manômetro; **pressure group** N grupo de pressão

pressurize ['preʃəraɪz] vt pressurizar; (Brit: fig): **to ~ sb (into doing sth)** pressionar alguém (a fazer algo)

pressurized ['preʃəraɪzd] ADJ pressurizado

prestige [pres'tiːʒ] N prestígio

prestigious [pres'tɪdʒəs] ADJ prestigioso

presumably [prɪ'zjuːməblɪ] ADV presumivelmente, provavelmente; **~ he did it** é de se presumir que ele o fez

presume [prɪ'zjuːm] vt: **to ~ (that)** supor (que); **to ~ to do** (dare) ousar fazer, atrever-se a fazer; (set out to) pretender fazer

presumption [prɪ'zʌmpʃən] N suposição f; (pretension) presunção f; (boldness) atrevimento, audácia

presumptuous [prɪ'zʌmpʃəs] ADJ presunçoso

presuppose [priːsə'pəuz] vt pressupor

pre-tax ADJ antes de impostos

pretence [prɪ'tens] (US pretense) N (claim) pretensão f; (display) ostentação f; (pretext) pretexto; (make-believe) fingimento; **under false ~s** sob o pretexto de; **on the ~ of** sob o máscara de; **to make a ~ of doing** fingir fazer

pretend [prɪ'tend] vt fingir ■ vi (feign) fingir; (claim): **to ~ to sth** aspirar a or pretender a algo; **to ~ to do** fingir fazer

pretense [prɪ'tens] (US) N = **pretence**

pretension [prɪ'tenʃən] N (presumption) presunção f; (claim) pretensão f; **to have no ~s to sth/to being sth** não ter pretensão a algo/a ser algo

pretentious [prɪ'tenʃəs] ADJ pretensioso, presunçoso

preterite ['pretərɪt] N pretérito

pretext ['priːtekst] N pretexto; **on** or **under the ~ of doing sth** sob o or a pretexto de fazer algo

pretty ['prɪtɪ] ADJ bonito ■ ADV (quite) bastante

prevail [prɪ'veɪl] vi (gain acceptance) triunfar; (be current) imperar; (be usual) prevalecer, vigorar; (persuade): **to ~ (up)on sb to do sth** persuadir alguém a fazer algo

prevailing [prɪ'veɪlɪŋ] ADJ (wind) dominante; (fashion, attitude) predominante; (usual) corrente

prevalent ['prevələnt] ADJ (common) predominante; (usual) corrente; (fashionable) da moda

prevarication [prɪværɪ'keɪʃən] N embromação f

prevent [prɪ'vent] vt: **to ~ sb from doing sth** impedir alguém de fazer algo; **to ~ sth from happening** impedir que algo aconteça

preventable [prɪ'ventəbl] ADJ evitável

preventative [prɪ'ventətɪv] ADJ = **preventive**

prevention [prɪ'venʃən] N prevenção f

preventive [prɪ'ventɪv] ADJ preventivo

preview ['priːvjuː] N (of film etc) pré-estréia; (fig) antecipação f

previous ['priːvɪəs] ADJ (experience, notice) prévio; (earlier) anterior; **I have a ~ engagement** já tenho compromisso; **~ to doing** antes de fazer

previously ['priːvɪəslɪ] ADV (before) previamente; (in the past) anteriormente

prewar [priː'wɔː'] ADJ anterior à guerra

prey [preɪ] N presa ■ vi: **to ~ on** viver às custas de; (feed on) alimentar-se de; (plunder) saquear, pilhar; **it was ~ing on his mind** preocupava-o, atormentava-o

price [praɪs] N preço; (of shares) cotação f ■ vt fixar o preço de; **what is the ~ of ...?** qual é o preço de ...?, quanto é ...?; **to go up** or **rise in ~** subir de preço; **to put a ~ on sth** determinar o preço de algo; **to be ~d out of the market** (article) não ser competitivo; (producer, country) perder freguesia por causa de preços muito altos; **what ~ his promises now?** que valem suas promessas agora?; **he regained his freedom, but at a ~** ele recobrou a liberdade, mas pagou caro; **at any ~** por qualquer preço; **price control** N controle m de preços

price-cutting N corte m de preços

priceless ['praɪslɪs] ADJ inestimável; (inf: amusing) impagável

price list N lista or tabela de preços

price range N gama de preços; **it's within my ~** está dentro do meu preço

price tag N etiqueta de preço

price war N guerra de preços

pricey ['praɪsɪ] (inf) ADJ salgado

prick [prɪk] N picada; (with pin) alfinetada; (inf!: penis) pau m (!); (inf!: person) filho-da-puta m (!) ■ vt picar; (make holes in) furar; **to ~ up one's ears** aguçar os ouvidos

prickle ['prɪkl] N (sensation) comichão f,

ardência; (Bot) espinho
prickly ['prɪklɪ] ADJ espinhoso; (fig: person)
irritadiço; **prickly heat** N brotoeja; **prickly pear**
N opúncia
pride [praɪd] N orgulho; (pej) soberba ▪ VT:
to ~ o.s. on orgulhar-se de; **to take (a) ~ in**
orgulhar-se de, sentir orgulho em; **to have ~**
of place (Brit) ocupar o lugar de destaque, ter
destaque; **her ~ and joy** seu tesouro
priest [pri:st] N (Christian) padre m; (non-Christian)
sacerdote m
priestess ['pri:stɪs] N sacerdotisa
priesthood ['pri:sthud] N (practice) sacerdócio;
(priests) clero
prig [prɪg] N esnobe m/f
prim [prɪm] (pej) ADJ (formal) empertigado;
(affected) afetado; (easily shocked) pudico
prima facie ['praɪmə'feɪʃɪ] ADJ: **to have a ~ case**
(Law) ter uma causa convincente
primarily ['praɪmərɪlɪ] ADV (above all)
principalmente; (firstly) em primeiro lugar
primary ['praɪmərɪ] ADJ primário; (first in
importance) principal ▪ N (US: election) eleição f
primária; **primary colour** N cor f primária;
primary products NPL produtos mpl básicos;
primary school (Brit) N escola primária

● **PRIMARY SCHOOL**
●
● As primary schools da Grã-Bretanha acolhem
● crianças de 5 a 11 anos. Assinalam o início
● do ciclo escolar obrigatório e são compostas
● de duas partes: a pré-escola (infant school) e o
● primário junior school).

primate¹ ['praɪmɪt] N (Rel) primaz m
primate² ['praɪmeɪt] N (Zool) primata m
prime [praɪm] ADJ primeiro, principal; (basic)
fundamental, primário; (excellent) de primeira
▪ VT (wood) imprimar; (gun, pump) escorvar;
(fig) aprontar, preparar ▪ N: **in the ~ of life** na
primavera da vida; **~ example** exemplo típico;
prime minister N primeiro-ministro/primeira-
ministra
primer ['praɪmə'] N (book) livro de leitura; (paint)
pintura de base; (of gun) escorva
prime time N (Radio, TV) horário nobre
primeval [praɪ'mi:vl] ADJ primitivo
primitive ['prɪmɪtɪv] ADJ primitivo; (crude)
rudimentar; (uncivilized) grosseiro, inculto
primrose ['prɪmrəuz] N prímula, primavera
primus (stove)® ['praɪməs-] (Brit) N fogão m
portátil movido à parafina
prince [prɪns] N príncipe m
princess [prɪn'sɛs] N princesa
principal ['prɪnsɪpl] ADJ principal ▪ N (of school,
college) diretor(a) m/f; (in play) papel m principal;
(money) principal m
principality [prɪnsɪ'pælɪtɪ] N principado
principally ['prɪnsɪplɪ] ADV principalmente
principle ['prɪnsɪpl] N princípio; **in ~** em
princípio; **on ~** por princípio

print [prɪnt] N (impression) impressão f, marca;
(letters) letra de forma; (fabric) estampado;
(Art) estampa, gravura; (Phot) cópia; (footprint)
pegada; (fingerprint) impressão f digital ▪ VT
imprimir; (write in capitals) escrever em letra de
imprensa; **out of ~** esgotado
▸ **print out** VT (Comput) imprimir
printed circuit board ['prɪntɪd-] N placa de
circuito impresso
printed matter ['prɪntɪd-] N impressos mpl
printer ['prɪntə'] N (person) impressor(a) m/f;
(firm) gráfica; (machine) impressora
printhead ['prɪnthed] N cabeçote m de
impressão
printing ['prɪntɪŋ] N (art) imprensa; (act)
impressão f; (quantity) tiragem f; **printing press**
N prelo, máquina impressora
printout ['prɪntaut] N (Comput) cópia impressa
print wheel N margarida
prior ['praɪə'] ADJ anterior, prévio; (more
important) prioritário ▪ N (Rel) prior m; **~ to**
doing antes de fazer; **without ~ notice** sem
aviso prévio; **to have a ~ claim to sth** ter
prioridade na reivindicação de algo
priority [praɪ'ɔrɪtɪ] N prioridade f; **to have ~**
(over) ter prioridade (sobre)
priory ['praɪərɪ] N priorado
prise [praɪz] VT: **to ~ open** arrombar
prism ['prɪzəm] N prisma m
prison ['prɪzn] N prisão f ▪ CPD carcerário;
prison camp N campo de prisioneiros
prisoner ['prɪzənə'] N (in prison) preso(-a),
presidiário(-a); (under arrest) detido(-a); (in
dock) acusado(-a), réu(-ré) m/f; **to take sb ~**
aprisionar alguém, prender alguém; **prisoner**
of war N prisioneiro de guerra
prissy ['prɪsɪ] ADJ fresco, cheio de luxo
pristine ['prɪsti:n] ADJ imaculado
privacy ['prɪvəsɪ] N (seclusion) isolamento,
solidão f; (intimacy) intimidade f, privacidade f
private ['praɪvɪt] ADJ privado; (personal)
particular; (confidential) confidencial,
reservado; (lesson, car) particular; (personal:
belongings) pessoal; (: thoughts, plans) secreto,
íntimo; (place) isolado; (quiet: person) reservado;
(intimate) privado, íntimo; (sitting etc) a portas
fechadas ▪ N soldado raso; **"~"** (on envelope)
"confidencial"; (on door) "privativo"; **in ~**
em particular; **in (his) ~ life** em (sua) vida
particular; **he is a very ~ person** ele é uma
pessoa muito reservada; **to be in ~ practice**
ter clínica particular; **private enterprise** N
iniciativa privada; **private eye** N detetive m/f
particular
private hearing N (Law) audiência em segredo
da justiça; **private limited company** (Brit) N
sociedade f anônima fechada
privately ['praɪvɪtlɪ] ADV em particular; (in
oneself) no fundo
private parts NPL partes fpl (pudendas)
private property N propriedade f privada
private school N escola particular

privation [praɪ'veɪʃən] N privação f
privatize ['praɪvɪtaɪz] VT privatizar
privet ['prɪvɪt] N alfena
privilege ['prɪvɪlɪdʒ] N privilégio
privileged ['prɪvɪlɪdʒd] ADJ privilegiado
privy ['prɪvɪ] ADJ: **to be ~ to** estar inteirado de
Privy Council (Brit) N Conselho Privado
prize [praɪz] N prêmio ■ ADJ (bull, novel) premiado; (first class) de primeira classe; (example) perfeito ■ VT valorizar; **prize fight** N luta de boxe profissional
prize-giving [-'gɪvɪŋ] N distribuição f dos prêmios
prize money N dinheiro do prêmio
prizewinner ['praɪzwɪnəʳ] N premiado(-a)
prizewinning ['praɪzwɪnɪŋ] ADJ premiado
PRO N ABBR (= public relations officer) RP m/f inv
pro [prəu] N (Sport) profissional m/f ■ PREP a favor de; **the ~s and cons** os prós e os contras
pro- [prəu] PREFIX (in favour of) pró-
probability [prɔbə'bɪlɪtɪ] N: **~ of/that** probabilidade f de/de que; **in all ~** com toda a probabilidade
probable ['prɔbəbl] ADJ provável; (plausible) verossímil; **it is ~/hardly ~ that …** é provável/pouco provável que …
probably ['prɔbəblɪ] ADV provavelmente
probate ['prəubɪt] N (Law) homologação f, legitimação f
probation [prə'beɪʃən] N (in employment) estágio probatório; (Law) liberdade f condicional; (Rel) noviciado; **on ~** (employee) em estágio probatório; (Law) em liberdade condicional
probationary [prə'beɪʃənrɪ] ADJ (period) probatório
probe [prəub] N (Med, Space) sonda; (enquiry) pesquisa ■ VT investigar, esquadrinhar
probity ['prəubɪtɪ] N probidade f
problem ['prɔbləm] N problema m; **what's the ~?** qual é o problema?; **I had no ~ in finding her** não foi difícil encontrá-la; **no ~!** não tem problema!
problematic(al) [prɔblə'mætɪk(əl)] ADJ problemático
procedure [prə'siːdʒəʳ] N (Admin, Law) procedimento; (method) método, processo; **cashing a cheque is a simple ~** descontar um cheque é uma operação simples
proceed [prə'siːd] VI (do afterwards): **to ~ to do sth** passar a fazer algo; (continue): **to ~ (with)** continuar or prosseguir (com); (activity, event: carry on) continuar; (go) ir em direção a, dirigir-se a; **to ~ to** passar a; **to ~ to do** passar a fazer; **I am not sure how to ~** não sei como proceder; **to ~ against sb** (Law) processar alguém, instaurar processo contra alguém
proceeding [prə'siːdɪŋ] N processo; **proceedings** NPL (organized events) evento, acontecimento; (Law) processo
proceeds ['prəusiːdz] NPL produto, proventos mpl
process [n, vt 'prəusɛs, vi prə'sɛs] N processo

■ VT processar ■ VI (Brit: formal: go in procession) desfilar; **in ~** em andamento; **we are in the ~ of moving to Rio** estamos de mudança para o Rio
processed cheese ['prəusɛst-] N ≈ requeijão m
processing ['prəusɛsɪŋ] N processamento
procession [prə'sɛʃən] N desfile m, procissão f; **funeral ~** cortejo fúnebre
proclaim [prə'kleɪm] VT proclamar; (announce) anunciar
proclamation [prɔklə'meɪʃən] N proclamação f; (written) promulgação f
proclivity [prə'klɪvɪtɪ] N inclinação f
procrastinate [prəu'kræstɪneɪt] VI protelar
procrastination [prəukræstɪ'neɪʃən] N protelação f
procreation [prəukrɪ'eɪʃən] N procriação f
procure [prə'kjuəʳ] VT obter
procurement [prə'kjuəmənt] N obtenção f; (purchase) compra
prod [prɔd] VT (push) empurrar; (with elbow) acotovelar; (with finger, stick) cutucar; (jab) espetar ■ N empurrão m; cotovelada; espetada
prodigal ['prɔdɪgl] ADJ pródigo
prodigious [prə'dɪdʒəs] ADJ colossal, extraordinário
prodigy ['prɔdɪdʒɪ] N prodígio
produce [n 'prɔdjuːs, vt prə'djuːs] N (Agr) produtos mpl agrícolas ■ VT produzir; (profit) render; (cause) provocar; (evidence, argument) apresentar, monstrar; (show) apresentar, exibir; (Theatre) pôr em cena or em cartaz; (offspring) dar à luz
producer [prə'djuːsəʳ] N (Theatre) diretor(a) m/f; (Agr, Cinema, of record) produtor(a) m/f; (country) produtor m
product ['prɔdʌkt] N produto
production [prə'dʌkʃən] N produção f; (of electricity) geração f; (thing) produto; (Theatre) encenação f; **to put into ~** (goods) passar a fabricar; **production agreement** (US) N acordo sobre produtividade; **production control** N controle m de produção; **production line** N linha de produção or de montagem; **production manager** N gerente m/f de produção
productive [prə'dʌktɪv] ADJ produtivo
productivity [prɔdʌk'tɪvɪtɪ] N produtividade f; **productivity agreement** (Brit) N acordo sobre produtividade; **productivity bonus** N prêmio de produção
Prof. [prɔf] ABBR (= professor) Prof
profane [prə'feɪn] ADJ profano; (language etc) irreverente, sacrílego
profess [prə'fɛs] VT professar; (feeling, opinion) manifestar; **I do not ~ to be an expert** não me tenho na conta de entendido
professed [prə'fɛst] ADJ (self-declared) assumido
profession [prə'fɛʃən] N profissão f; (people) classe f; **the professions** NPL as profissões liberais

professional [prə'fɛʃənl] N profissional m/f
■ ADJ profissional; (work) de profissional; **he's a**
~ **man** ele exerce uma profissão liberal; **to take**
~ **advice** consultar um perito
professionalism [prə'fɛʃnəlɪzm] N
profissionalismo
professionally [prə'fɛʃnəlɪ] ADV
profissionalmente; (as a job) de profissão;
I only know him ~ eu só conheço ele pelo
trabalho
professor [prə'fɛsəʳ] N (Brit) catedrático(-a); (US,
Canada) professor(a) m/f
professorship [prə'fɛsəʃɪp] N cátedra
proffer ['prɔfəʳ] VT (hand) estender; (remark)
fazer; (apologies) apresentar
proficiency [prə'fɪʃənsɪ] N competência,
proficiência
proficient [prə'fɪʃənt] ADJ competente,
proficiente
profile ['prəufaɪl] N perfil m; **to keep a high** ~
destacar-se; **to keep a low** ~ sair de circulação
profit ['prɔfɪt] N (Comm) lucro; (fig) proveito,
vantagem f ■ VI: **to** ~ **by** or **from** (financially)
lucrar com; (benefit) aproveitar-se de, tirar
proveito de; ~ **and loss account** conta de lucros
e perdas; **to make a** ~ lucrar; **to sell sth at a** ~
vender algo com lucro
profitability [prɔfɪtə'bɪlɪtɪ] N rentabilidade f
profitable ['prɔfɪtəbl] ADJ (Econ) lucrativo,
rendoso; (useful) proveitoso
profit centre N centro de lucro
profiteering [prɔfɪ'tɪərɪŋ] N mercantilismo,
exploração f
profit-making ADJ com fins lucrativos
profit margin N margem f de lucro
profit-sharing [-'ʃɛərɪŋ] N participação f nos
lucros
profits tax (Brit) N imposto sobre os lucros
profligate ['prɔflɪgɪt] ADJ (behaviour, person)
devasso; (extravagant): ~ **(with)** pródigo (de)
pro forma [-'fɔ:mə] ADJ: ~ **invoice** fatura pro-
forma or simulada
profound [prə'faund] ADJ profundo
profuse [prə'fju:s] ADJ abundante
profusely [prə'fju:slɪ] ADV profusamente
profusion [prə'fju:ʒən] N profusão f,
abundância
progeny ['prɔdʒɪnɪ] N prole f, progênie f
prognoses [prɔg'nəusi:z] NPL of **prognosis**
prognosis [prɔg'nəusɪs] (pl **prognoses**) N
prognóstico
programme ['prəugræm] (US **program**) N
programa m ■ VT programar
program(m)er ['prəugræməʳ] N
programador(a) m/f
program(m)ing ['prəugræmɪŋ] N
programação f
program(m)ing language N linguagem f de
programação
progress [n 'prəugres, vi prə'gres] N progresso
■ VI progredir, avançar; **in** ~ em andamento; **to**
make ~ fazer progressos; **as the match ~ed** à

medida que o jogo se desenvolvia
progression [prə'grɛʃən] N progressão f
progressive [prə'grɛsɪv] ADJ progressivo;
(person) progressista
progressively [prə'grɛsɪvlɪ] ADV
progressivamente
progress report N (Med) boletim m médico;
(Admin) relatório sobre o andamento dos
trabalhos
prohibit [prə'hɪbɪt] VT proibir; **to** ~ **sb from**
doing sth proibir alguém de fazer algo;
"smoking ~ed" "proibido fumar"
prohibition [prəuɪ'bɪʃən] N proibição f; (US): **P~**
lei f seca
prohibitive [prə'hɪbɪtɪv] ADJ (price etc) proibitivo
project [n 'prɔdʒɛkt, vt, vi prə'dʒɛkt] N projeto;
(Sch: research) pesquisa ■ VT projetar; (figure)
estimar ■ VI (stick out) ressaltar, sobressair
projectile [prə'dʒɛktaɪl] N projétil m
projection [prə'dʒɛkʃən] N projeção f; (overhang)
saliência
projectionist [prə'dʒɛkʃənɪst] N operador(a) m/f
de projetor
projection room N (Cinema) sala de projeção
projector [prə'dʒɛktəʳ] N projetor m
proletarian [prəulɪ'tɛərɪən] ADJ, N
proletário(-a)
proletariat [prəulɪ'tɛərɪət] N proletariado
proliferate [prə'lɪfəreɪt] VI proliferar
proliferation [prəlɪfə'reɪʃən] N proliferação f
prolific [prə'lɪfɪk] ADJ prolífico
prologue ['prəulɔg] (US **prolog**) N prólogo
prolong [prə'lɔŋ] VT prolongar
prom [prɔm] N ABBR = **promenade**;
promenade concert; (US: ball) baile m de
estudantes
promenade [prɔmə'nɑ:d] N (by sea) passeio (à
orla marítima); **promenade concert** (Brit) N
concerto (de música clássica); **promenade deck**
N (Naut) convés m superior

⬤ **PROMENADE CONCERT**
⬤
⬤ Na Grã-Bretanha, um promenade concert (ou
⬤ prom) é um concerto de música clássica,
⬤ assim chamado porque originalmente o
⬤ público não ficava sentado, mas de pé ou
⬤ caminhando. Hoje em dia, uma parte do
⬤ público permanece de pé, mas há também
⬤ lugares sentados (mais caros). Os Proms
⬤ mais conhecidos são os londrinos. A
⬤ última sessão (the Last Night of the Proms) é
⬤ um acontecimento carregado de emoção,
⬤ quando são executadas árias tradicionais e
⬤ patrióticas. Nos Estados Unidos e no Canadá,
⬤ o prom, ou promenade, é um baile organizado
⬤ pelas escolas secundárias.

prominence ['prɔmɪnəns] N eminência,
importância
prominent ['prɔmɪnənt] ADJ (standing out)
proeminente; (important) eminente, notório; **he**

is ~ in the field of ... ele é muito conhecido no campo de ...
prominently ['prɒmɪnəntlɪ] ADV *(display, set)* bem à vista; **he figured ~ in the case** ele teve um papel importante no caso
promiscuity [prɒmɪ'skjuːɪtɪ] N promiscuidade f
promiscuous [prə'mɪskjuəs] ADJ promíscuo
promise ['prɒmɪs] N promessa ▪ VT: **to ~ sb sth**, **~ sth to sb** prometer a alguém algo, prometer algo a alguém ▪ VI prometer; **to make sb a ~** fazer uma promessa a alguém; **to ~ (sb) to do sth/that** prometer (a alguém) fazer algo/que; **a young man of ~** um jovem que promete; **to ~ well** prometer
promising ['prɒmɪsɪŋ] ADJ promissor(a), prometedor(a)
promissory note ['prɒmɪsərɪ-] N *(nota)* promissória
promontory ['prɒməntrɪ] N promontório
promote [prə'məut] VT promover; *(new product)* promover, fazer propaganda de; *(event)* patrocinar
promoter [prə'məutər] N *(of sporting event etc)* patrocinador(a) m/f; *(of cause etc)* partidário(-a)
promotion [prə'məuʃən] N promoção f
prompt [prɒmpt] ADJ pronto, rápido ▪ ADV *(exactly)* em ponto, pontualmente ▪ N *(Comput)* sinal m de orientação, prompt m ▪ VT *(urge)* incitar, impelir; *(cause)* provocar, ocasionar; *(Theatre)* servir de ponto a; **to ~ sb to do sth** induzir alguém a fazer algo; **he's very ~** *(punctual)* ele é pontual; **at 8 o'clock ~** às 8 horas em ponto; **he was ~ to accept** ele não hesitou em aceitar
prompter ['prɒmptər] N *(Theatre)* ponto
promptly ['prɒmptlɪ] ADV *(immediately)* imediatamente; *(exactly)* pontualmente; *(rapidly)* rapidamente
promptness ['prɒmptnɪs] N *(punctuality)* pontualidade f; *(rapidity)* rapidez f
promulgate ['prɒməlgeɪt] VT promulgar
prone [prəun] ADJ *(lying)* de bruços; **~ to** propenso a, predisposto a; **she is ~ to burst into tears if ...** ela tende a desatar a chorar se ...
prong [prɒŋ] N ponta; *(of fork)* dente m
pronoun ['prəunaun] N pronome m
pronounce [prə'nauns] VT pronunciar; *(verdict, opinion)* declarar ▪ VI: **to ~ (up)on** pronunciar-se sobre
pronounced [prə'naunst] ADJ *(marked)* pronunciado, marcado
pronouncement [prə'naunsmənt] N pronunciamento
pronunciation [prɪənʌnsɪ'eɪʃən] N pronúncia
proof [pruːf] N prova; *(of alcohol)* teor m alcoólico ▪ ADJ: **~ against** à prova de ▪ VT *(Brit: tent, anorak)* impermeabilizar; **to be 70° ~** ter 70° de gradação
proofreader ['pruːfriːdər] N revisor(a) m/f de provas
Prop. ABBR *(Comm)* = **proprietor**

prop [prɒp] N suporte m, escora; *(fig)* amparo, apoio ▪ VT *(also: prop up)* apoiar, escorar; *(lean)*: **to ~ sth against** apoiar algo contra
propaganda [prɒpə'gændə] N propaganda
propagate ['prɒpəgeɪt] VT propagar
propel [prə'pɛl] VT propelir, propulsionar; *(fig)* impelir
propeller [prə'pɛlər] N hélice f
propelling pencil [prə'pɛlɪŋ-] *(Brit)* N lapiseira
propensity [prə'pɛnsɪtɪ] N: **a ~ for/to/to do** uma propensão para/a/para fazer
proper ['prɒpər] ADJ *(correct)* correto; *(socially acceptable)* respeitável, digno; *(authentic)* genuíno, autêntico; *(referring to place)*: **the village ~** a cidadezinha propriamente dita; **physics ~** a física propriamente dita; **to go through the ~ channels** *(Admin)* seguir os trâmites oficiais
properly ['prɒpəlɪ] ADV *(eat, study)* bem; *(behave)* decentemente
proper noun N nome m próprio
property ['prɒpətɪ] N *(possessions, quality)* propriedade f; *(goods)* posses fpl, bens mpl; *(buildings)* imóveis mpl; *(estate)* propriedade f, fazenda; **it's their ~** é deles, pertence a eles; **property developer** *(Brit)* N empresário(-a) de imóveis; **property owner** N proprietário(-a); **property tax** N imposto predial e territorial
prophecy ['prɒfɪsɪ] N profecia
prophesy ['prɒfɪsaɪ] VT profetizar; *(fig)* predizer ▪ VI profetizar
prophet ['prɒfɪt] N profeta m/f
prophetic [prə'fɛtɪk] ADJ profético
proportion [prə'pɔːʃən] N proporção f; *(share)* parte f, porção f ▪ VT proporcionar; **in ~ to** or **with sth** em proporção or proporcional a algo; **out of ~** desproporcionado; **to see sth in ~** *(fig)* ter a visão adequada de algo
proportional [prə'pɔːʃənl] ADJ: **~ (to)** proporcional (a); **proportional representation** N *(Pol)* representação f proporcional
proportionate [prə'pɔːʃənɪt] ADJ: **~ (to)** proporcionado (a)
proposal [prə'pəuzl] N proposta; *(of marriage)* pedido
propose [prə'pəuz] VT propor; *(toast)* erguer ▪ VI propor casamento; **to ~ to do** propor-se fazer
proposer [prə'pəuzər] *(Brit)* N *(of motion etc)* apresentador(a) m/f
proposition [prɒpə'zɪʃən] N proposta, proposição f; *(offer)* oferta; **to make sb a ~** fazer uma proposta a alguém
propound [prə'paund] VT propor
proprietary [prə'praɪətrɪ] ADJ: **~ brand** marca registrada; **~ product** produto patenteado
proprietor [prə'praɪətər] N proprietário(-a), dono(-a)
propriety [prə'praɪətɪ] N propriedade f
propulsion [prə'pʌlʃən] N propulsão f
pro rata [-'rɑːtə] ADV pro rata,

proporcionalmente
prosaic [prəu'zeɪɪk] ADJ prosaico
Pros. Atty. (US) ABBR = **prosecuting attorney**
proscribe [prə'skraɪb] VT proscrever
prose [prəuz] N prosa
prosecute ['prɔsɪkjuːt] VT (Law) processar
prosecuting attorney ['prɔsɪkjuːtɪŋ-] (US) N promotor(a) m/f público(-a)
prosecution [prɔsɪ'kjuːʃən] N acusação f; (accusing side) autor m da demanda
prosecutor ['prɔsɪkjuːtər] N promotor(a) m/f; (also: **public prosecutor**) promotor(a) m/f público(-a)
prospect [n 'prɔspɛkt, vt, vi prə'spɛkt] N (chance) probabilidade f; (outlook, potential) perspectiva ■ VT explorar ■ VI: **to ~ (for)** prospectar (por); **prospects** NPL (for work etc) perspectivas fpl; **we are faced with the ~ of ...** nós estamos diante da perspectiva de ...; **there is every ~ of an early victory** há toda probabilidade de uma vitória rápida
prospecting [prə'spɛktɪŋ] N prospecção f
prospective [prə'spɛktɪv] ADJ (possible) provável; (future) futuro
prospector [prə'spɛktər] N garimpeiro(-a)
prospectus [prə'spɛktəs] N prospecto, programa m
prosper ['prɔspər] VI prosperar
prosperity [prɔ'spɛrɪtɪ] N prosperidade f
prosperous ['prɔspərəs] ADJ próspero
prostate ['prɔsteɪt] N (also: **prostate gland**) próstata
prostitute ['prɔstɪtjuːt] N prostituta; **male ~** prostituto
prostitution [prɔstɪ'tjuːʃən] N prostituição f
prostrate [adj 'prɔstreɪt, vt prɔ'streɪt] ADJ prostrado; (fig) abatido, aniquilado ■ VT: **to ~ o.s.** (before sb) prostrar-se (diante de alguém)
protagonist [prə'tægənɪst] N protagonista m/f; (leading participant) líder m/f
protect [prə'tɛkt] VT proteger
protection [prə'tɛkʃən] N proteção f; **to be under sb's ~** estar sob a proteção de alguém
protectionism [prə'tɛkʃənɪzm] N protecionismo
protection racket N extorsão f
protective [prə'tɛktɪv] ADJ protetor(a); **~ custody** (Law) prisão f preventiva
protector [prə'tɛktər] N protetor(a) m/f
protégé ['prəutɛʒeɪ] N protegido
protégée ['prəutɛʒeɪ] N protegida
protein ['prəutiːn] N proteína
pro tem [-tɛm] ADV ABBR (= pro tempore) provisoriamente
protest [n 'prəutɛst, vi, vt prə'tɛst] N protesto ■ VI: **to ~ about** or **against** or **at** protestar contra ■ VT (insist): **to ~ (that)** insistir (que)
Protestant ['prɔtɪstənt] ADJ, N protestante m/f
protester [prə'tɛstər] N manifestante m/f
protest march N passeata
protestor [prə'tɛstər] N = **protester**

protocol ['prəutəkɔl] N protocolo
prototype ['prəutətaɪp] N protótipo
protracted [prə'træktɪd] ADJ prolongado, demorado
protractor [prə'træktər] N (Geom) transferidor m
protrude [prə'truːd] VI projetar-se
protuberance [prə'tjuːbərəns] N protuberância
proud [praud] ADJ orgulhoso; (pej) vaidoso, soberbo; **to be ~ to do sth** sentir-se orgulhoso de fazer algo; **to do sb ~** (inf) fazer muita festa a alguém
proudly ['praudlɪ] ADV orgulhosamente
prove [pruːv] VT comprovar ■ VI: **to ~ (to be) correct** etc vir a ser correto etc; **to ~ o.s.** pôr-se à prova; **to ~ itself (to be) useful** etc revelar-se or mostrar-se útil etc; **he was ~d right in the end** no final deram-lhe razão
proverb ['prɔvəːb] N provérbio
proverbial [prə'vəːbɪəl] ADJ proverbial
provide [prə'vaɪd] VT fornecer, proporcionar; **to ~ sb with sth** fornecer alguém de algo, fornecer algo a alguém; **to be ~d with** estar munido de
▶ **provide for** VT FUS (person) prover à subsistência de; (emergency) prevenir
provided (that) [prə'vaɪdɪd-] CONJ contanto que (+ sub), sob condição de (que) (+ sub)
Providence ['prɔvɪdəns] N a Divina Providência
providing [prə'vaɪdɪŋ] CONJ: **~ (that)** contanto que (+ sub)
province ['prɔvɪns] N província; (fig) esfera
provincial [prə'vɪnʃəl] ADJ provincial; (pej) provinciano
provision [prə'vɪʒən] N provisão f; (supply) fornecimento; (supplying) abastecimento; (in contract) cláusula, condição f; **provisions** NPL (food) mantimentos mpl; **to make ~ for** fazer provisão para; **there's no ~ for this in the contract** não há cláusula nesse sentido no contrato
provisional [prə'vɪʒənəl] ADJ provisório, interino; (agreement, licence) provisório ■ N: **P~** (Ireland: Pol) militante do braço armado do IRA; **provisional licence** (Brit) N (Aut) licença prévia para aprendizagem
provisionally [prə'vɪʒnəlɪ] ADV provisoriamente
proviso [prə'vaɪzəu] N condição f; (reservation) ressalva; (Law) cláusula; **with the ~ that** com a ressalva que
Provo ['prɔvəu] (inf) N ABBR = **Provisional**
provocation [prɔvə'keɪʃən] N provocação f
provocative [prə'vɔkətɪv] ADJ provocante; (sexually) excitante
provoke [prə'vəuk] VT provocar; (cause) causar; **to ~ sb to sth/to do** or **into doing sth** provocar alguém a algo/a fazer algo
provoking [prə'vəukɪŋ] ADJ provocante
provost ['prɔvəst] N (Brit: of university) reitor(a)

m/f; (Scotland) prefeito(-a)

prow [prau] N proa

prowess ['prauɪs] N destreza, perícia

prowl [praul] VI *(also:* **prowl about, prowl around)** rondar, andar à espreita ■ N: **on the ~** de ronda, rondando

prowler ['praulə^r] N tarado(-a)

proximity [prɔk'sɪmɪtɪ] N proximidade *f*

proxy ['prɔksɪ] N procuração *f; (person)* procurador(a) *m/f;* **by ~** por procuração

prude [pruːd] N pudico(-a)

prudence ['pruːdns] N prudência

prudent ['pruːdənt] ADJ prudente

prudish ['pruːdɪʃ] ADJ pudico(-a)

prune [pruːn] N ameixa seca ■ VT podar

pry [praɪ] VI: **to ~ (into)** intrometer-se (em)

PS N ABBR *(= postscript)* PS *m*

psalm [sɑːm] N salmo

PSAT® *(US)* N ABBR = **Preliminary Scholastic Aptitude Test**

PSBR *(Brit)* N ABBR *(= public sector borrowing requirement)* necessidade *f* de empréstimos no setor público

pseud [sjuːd] *(Brit: inf)* N posudo(-a)

pseudo- [sjuːdəu] PREFIX pseudo-

pseudonym ['sjuːdənɪm] N pseudônimo

PST *(US)* N ABBR *(= Pacific Standard Time)* hora de inverno no Pacífico

PSV *(Brit)* N ABBR = **public service vehicle**

psyche ['saɪkɪ] N psiquismo

psychiatric [saɪkɪ'ætrɪk] ADJ psiquiátrico

psychiatrist [saɪ'kaɪətrɪst] N psiquiatra *m/f*

psychiatry [saɪ'kaɪətrɪ] N psiquiatria

psychic ['saɪkɪk] ADJ psíquico; *(also:* **psychical***: person)* sensível a forças psíquicas ■ N médium *m/f*

psychoanalyse [saɪkəu'ænəlaɪz] VT psicanalisar

psychoanalysis [saɪkəuə'nælɪsɪs] N psicanálise *f*

psychoanalyst [saɪkəu'ænəlɪst] N psicanalista *m/f*

psychological [saɪkə'lɔdʒɪkl] ADJ psicológico

psychologist [saɪ'kɔlədʒɪst] N psicólogo(-a)

psychology [saɪ'kɔlədʒɪ] N psicologia

psychopath ['saɪkəupæθ] N psicopata *m/f*

psychoses [saɪ'kəusiːz] NPL *of* **psychosis**

psychosis [saɪ'kəusɪs] *(pl* **psychoses***)* N psicose *f*

psychosomatic [saɪkəusə'mætɪk] ADJ psicossomático

psychotherapy [saɪkəu'θɛrəpɪ] N psicoterapia

psychotic [saɪ'kɔtɪk] ADJ, N psicótico(-a)

PT *(Brit)* N ABBR = **physical training**

Pt. ABBR *(in place names:* = *Point)* Pto

pt ABBR = **pint; point**

PTA N ABBR = **Parent-Teacher Association**

Pte. *(Brit)* ABBR *(Mil)* = **private**

PTO ABBR *(= please turn over)* v.v., vire

PTV *(US)* N ABBR = **pay television; public television**

pub [pʌb] N ABBR *(= public house)* pub *m*, bar *m*, botequim *m*

puberty ['pjuːbətɪ] N puberdade *f*

pubic ['pjuːbɪk] ADJ púbico, pubiano

public ['pʌblɪk] ADJ público ■ N público; **in ~** em público; **to make ~** tornar público; **the general ~** o grande público; **to be ~ knowledge** ser de conhecimento público; **to go ~** *(Comm)* tornar-se uma companhia de capital aberto, passar a ser cotado na Bolsa de Valores; **public address system** N sistema *m* (de reforço) de som

publican ['pʌblɪkən] N dono(-a) de pub

publication [pʌblɪ'keɪʃən] N publicação *f*

public company N sociedade *f* anônima aberta

public convenience *(Brit)* N banheiro público

public holiday N feriado

public house *(Brit)* N pub *m*, bar *m*, taberna

publicity [pʌb'lɪsɪtɪ] N publicidade *f*

publicize ['pʌblɪsaɪz] VT divulgar; *(product)* promover

public limited company N sociedade *f* anônima aberta

publicly ['pʌblɪklɪ] ADV publicamente

public opinion N opinião *f* pública

public ownership N: **to be taken into ~** ser estatizado

public relations N relações *fpl* públicas

public relations officer N relações-públicas *m/f inv*

public school N *(Brit)* escola particular; *(US)* escola pública

public sector N setor *m* público

public service vehicle *(Brit)* N veículo para o transporte público

public-spirited [-'spɪrɪtɪd] ADJ zeloso pelo bem-estar público

public transport *(US* **public transportation***)* N transporte *m* coletivo

public utility N (serviço de) utilidade *f* pública

public works NPL obras *fpl* públicas

publish ['pʌblɪʃ] VT publicar

publisher ['pʌblɪʃə^r] N editor(a) *m/f; (company)*

editora
publishing ['pʌblɪʃɪŋ] N (industry) a indústria
editorial;**publishing company** N editora
puce [pju:s] ADJ roxo
puck [pʌk] N (elf) duende m; (Ice Hockey) disco
pucker ['pʌkə'] VT (fabric) amarrotar; (brow etc)
franzir
pudding ['pudɪŋ] N (Brit: dessert) sobremesa;
(cake) pudim m, doce m; **black** (Brit) or **blood** (US)
~ morcela; **rice** ~ pudim de arroz
puddle ['pʌdl] N poça
puerile ['pjuəraɪl] ADJ infantil
Puerto Rican ['pwə:tə'ri:kən] ADJ, N porto-
riquenho(-a)
Puerto Rico ['pwə:təu'ri:kəu] N Porto Rico (no
article)
puff [pʌf] N sopro; (of cigarette) baforada; (of
air, smoke) lufada; (gust) rajada, lufada; (sound)
sopro; (also: **powder puff**) pompom m ■ VT: **to**
~ **one's pipe** tirar baforadas do cachimbo ■ VI
soprar; (pant) arquejar
▶ **puff out** VT (sails) enfunar; (cheeks) encher; **to**
~ **out smoke** lançar baforadas
▶ **puff up** VT inflar
puffed [pʌft] (inf) ADJ (out of breath) sem fôlego
puffin ['pʌfɪn] N papagaio-do-mar m
puff pastry (US **puff paste**) N massa folhada
puffy ['pʌfɪ] ADJ inchado, entumecido
pugnacious [pʌg'neɪʃəs] ADJ pugnaz,
brigão(-ona)
pull [pul] N (of magnet, sea etc) atração f; (influence)
influência; (tug): **to give sth a** ~ dar um puxão
em algo ■ VT puxar; (trigger) apertar; (curtain,
blind) fechar; (muscle) distender ■ VI puxar,
dar um puxão; **to** ~ **a face** fazer careta; **to** ~
to pieces picar em pedacinhos; **to** ~ **one's
punches** não usar toda a força; **to** ~ **one's
weight** fazer a sua parte; **to** ~ **o.s. together**
recompor-se; **to** ~ **sb's leg** (fig) brincar com
alguém, sacanear alguém (inf); **to** ~ **strings for
sb** mexer os pauzinhos para alguém
▶ **pull about** (Brit) VT (handle roughly) maltratar
▶ **pull apart** VT separar; (break) romper
▶ **pull down** VT abaixar; (building) demolir,
derrubar; (tree) abater, derrubar
▶ **pull in** VI (Aut: at the kerb) encostar; (Rail)
chegar (na plataforma)
▶ **pull off** VT tirar; (fig: deal etc) acertar
▶ **pull out** VI arrancar, partir; (withdraw) retirar-
se; (Aut: from kerb) sair; (Rail) partir ■ VT tirar,
arrancar; **to** ~ **out in front of sb** (Aut) dar uma
fechada em alguém
▶ **pull over** VI (Aut) encostar
▶ **pull round** VI (unconscious person) voltar a si;
(sick person) recuperar-se
▶ **pull through** VI sair-se bem (de um aperto);
(Med) sobreviver
▶ **pull up** VI (stop) deter-se, parar ■ VT
levantar; (uproot) desarraigar, arrancar; (stop)
parar
pulley ['pulɪ] N roldana
pull-out N (withdrawal) retirada; (section: in

magazine, newspaper) encarte m ■ CPD (magazine,
pages) destacável
pullover ['puləuvə'] N pulôver m
pulp [pʌlp] N (of fruit) polpa; (for paper) pasta,
massa; **to reduce sth to a** ~ amassar algo
pulpit ['pulpɪt] N púlpito
pulsate [pʌl'seɪt] VI pulsar, palpitar; (music)
vibrar;**pulse** [pʌls] N (Anat) pulso; (of music,
engine) cadência; (Bot) legume m; **to feel** or **take
sb's pulse** tomar o pulso de alguém
pulse rate ■ N freqüência de pulsos
pulverize ['pʌlvəraɪz] VT pulverizar; (fig)
esmagar, aniquilar
puma ['pju:mə] N puma, onça-parda
pumice ['pʌmɪs] N (also: **pumice stone**) pedra-
pomes f
pummel ['pʌml] VT esmurrar, socar
pump [pʌmp] N bomba; (shoe) sapatilha (de
dança) ■ VT bombear; (fig: inf) sondar; **to** ~ **sb
for information** tentar extrair informações
de alguém
▶ **pump up** VT encher
pumpkin ['pʌmpkɪn] N abóbora
pun [pʌn] N jogo de palavras, trocadilho
punch [pʌntʃ] N (blow) soco, murro; (tool)
punção m; (for tickets) furador m; (drink) ponche
m; (fig: force) vigor m, força ■ VT (make a hole in)
perfurar, picotar; (hit): **to** ~ **sb/sth** esmurrar or
socar alguém/algo
▶ **punch in** (US) VI assinar o ponto na
entrada
▶ **punch out** (US) VI assinar o ponto na saída
punch-drunk (Brit) ADJ estupidificado
punch(ed) card [pʌntʃ(t)-] N cartão m
perfurado
punch line N (of joke) remate m
punch-up (Brit: inf) N briga
punctual ['pʌŋktjuəl] ADJ pontual
punctuality [pʌŋktju'ælɪtɪ] N pontualidade f
punctually ['pʌŋktjuəlɪ] ADV pontualmente;
it will start ~ **at 6** começará às 6 horas em
ponto
punctuate ['pʌŋktjueɪt] VT pontuar
punctuation [pʌŋktju'eɪʃən] N pontuação f;
punctuation marks NPL sinais mpl de
pontuação
puncture ['pʌŋktʃə'] N picada; (flat tyre) furo
■ VT picar, furar; (tyre) furar; **I have a** ~ (Aut)
estou com um pneu furado
pundit ['pʌndɪt] N entendedor(a) m/f
pungent ['pʌndʒənt] ADJ (smell, taste) acre; (fig)
mordaz
punish ['pʌnɪʃ] VT punir, castigar; **to** ~ **sb for
sth/for doing sth** punir alguém por algo/por
ter feito algo
punishable ['pʌnɪʃəbl] ADJ punível, castigável
punishing ['pʌnɪʃɪŋ] ADJ (fig: exhausting)
desgastante ■ N punição f
punishment ['pʌnɪʃmənt] N castigo, punição f;
(fig: wear) desgaste m
punk [pʌŋk] N (also: **punk rocker**) punk m/f;
(also: **punk rock**) punk m; (US: inf: hoodlum) pinta-

brava m

punt [pʌnt] N (boat) chalana

punter ['pʌntə^r] N (Brit: gambler) jogador(a) m/f; (inf: client) cliente m/f

puny ['pju:nɪ] ADJ débil, fraco

pup [pʌp] N (dog) cachorrinho (BR), cachorro (PT); (seal etc) filhote m

pupil ['pju:pl] N aluno(-a); (of eye) pupila

puppet ['pʌpɪt] N marionete f, títere m; (fig) fantoche m; **puppet government** N governo fantoche or títere

puppy ['pʌpɪ] N cachorrinho (BR), cachorro (PT)

purchase ['pə:tʃɪs] N compra; (grip) ponto de apoio ■ VT comprar; **to get a ~ on** apoiar-se em; **purchase order** N ordem f de compra; **purchase price** N preço de compra

purchaser ['pə:tʃɪsə^r] N comprador(a) m/f

purchase tax (Brit) N ≈ imposto de circulação de mercadorias

purchasing power ['pə:tʃɪsɪŋ-] N poder m aquisitivo

pure [pjuə^r] ADJ puro; **a ~ wool jumper** um pulôver de pura lã; **~ and simple** puro e simples

purebred ['pjuəbrɛd] ADJ de sangue puro

purée ['pjuəreɪ] N purê m

purely ['pjuəlɪ] ADV puramente; (only) meramente

purgatory ['pə:gətərɪ] N purgatório; (fig) inferno

purge [pə:dʒ] N (Med) purgante m; (Pol) expurgo ■ VT purgar; (Pol) expurgar

purification [pjuərɪfɪ'keɪʃən] N purificação f, depuração f

purify ['pjuərɪfaɪ] VT purificar, depurar

purist ['pjuərɪst] N purista m/f

puritan ['pjuərɪtən] N puritano(-a)

puritanical [pjuərɪ'tænɪkl] ADJ puritano

purity ['pjuərɪtɪ] N pureza

purl [pə:l] N ponto reverso ■ VT fazer ponto de tricô

purloin [pə:'lɔɪn] VT surripiar

purple ['pə:pl] ADJ roxo, purpúreo

purport [pə:'pɔ:t] VI: **to ~ to be/do** dar a entender que é/faz

purpose ['pə:pəs] N propósito, objetivo; **on ~** de propósito; **for teaching ~s** para fins pedagógicos; **for the ~s of this meeting** para esta reunião; **to no ~** em vão

purpose-built (Brit) ADJ feito sob medida

purposeful ['pə:pəsful] ADJ decidido, resoluto

purposely ['pə:pəslɪ] ADV de propósito

purr [pə:^r] N ronrom m ■ VI ronronar

purse [pə:s] N (Brit) for money, carteira; (US: bag) bolsa ■ VT enrugar, franzir

purser ['pə:sə^r] N (Naut) comissário de bordo

purse snatcher [-'snætʃə^r] N trombadinha m/f

pursue [pə'sju:] VT perseguir; (fig: activity) exercer; (: interest, plan) dedicar-se a; (: result) lutar por

pursuer [pə'sju:ə^r] N perseguidor(a) m/f

pursuit [pə'sju:t] N (chase) caça; (persecution)

perseguição f; (fig) busca; (occupation) ocupação f, atividade f; (pastime) passatempo; **in (the) ~ of sth** em busca de algo

purveyor [pə'veɪə^r] N fornecedor(a) m/f

pus [pʌs] N pus m

push [puʃ] N empurrão m; (of button) aperto; (attack) ataque m, arremetida; (advance) avanço ■ VT empurrar; (button) apertar; (promote) promover; (thrust): **to ~ sth (into)** enfiar algo (em) ■ VI empurrar; (press) apertar; (fig): **to ~ for** reivindicar; **to ~ a door open/shut** abrir/fechar uma porta empurrando-a; **"~" (on door)** "empurre"; (on bell) "aperte"; **to be ~ed for time/money** estar com pouco tempo/dinheiro; **she is ~ing fifty** (inf) ela está beirando os 50; **at a ~** (Brit: inf) em último caso
  ▶ **push aside** VT afastar com a mão
  ▶ **push in** VI introduzir-se à força
  ▶ **push off** (inf) VI dar o fora
  ▶ **push on** VI (continue) prosseguir
  ▶ **push over** VT derrubar
  ▶ **push through** VI abrir caminho ■ VT (measure) forçar a aceitação de
  ▶ **push up** VT (total, prices) forçar a alta de

push-bike (Brit) N bicicleta

push-button ADJ por botões de pressão

pushchair ['puʃtʃɛə^r] (Brit) N carrinho

pusher ['puʃə^r] N (also: **drug pusher**) traficante m/f or passador(a) m/f de drogas

pushing ['puʃɪŋ] ADJ empreendedor(a)

pushover ['puʃəuvə^r] (inf) N: **it's a ~** é sopa

push-up (US) N flexão f

pushy ['puʃɪ] (pej) ADJ intrometido, agressivo

puss [pus] (inf) N gatinho

pussy(cat) ['pusɪ(kæt)] (inf) N gatinho

put [put] (pt, pp **put**) VT (place) pôr, colocar; (put into) meter; (person: in institution etc) internar; (say) dizer, expressar; (case, view) expor; (a question) fazer; (person: in situation) colocar; (estimate) avaliar, calcular; (write, type etc) colocar; **to ~ sb in a good/bad mood** deixar alguém de bom/mau humor; **to ~ sb to bed** pôr alguém para dormir; **to ~ sb to a lot of trouble** incomodar alguém; **how shall I ~ it?** como dizer?; **to ~ a lot of time into sth** investir muito tempo em algo; **to ~ money on a horse** apostar num cavalo; **I ~ it to you that ...** (Brit) eu gostaria de colocar que ...; **to stay ~** não se mexer
  ▶ **put about** VI (Naut) mudar de rumo ■ VT (rumour) espalhar
  ▶ **put across** VT (ideas etc) comunicar
  ▶ **put aside** VT deixar de lado
  ▶ **put away** VT (store) guardar
  ▶ **put back** VT (replace) repor; (postpone) adiar; (delay, also: watch, clock) atrasar
  ▶ **put by** VT (money etc) poupar, pôr de lado
  ▶ **put down** VT pôr em; (pay) pagar; (animal) sacrificar; (in writing) anotar, inscrever; (revolt etc) sufocar; (attribute: to put sth down to) atribuir algo a
  ▶ **put forward** VT (ideas) apresentar, propor;

(*date, clock*) adiantar
▶ **put in** VT (*application, complaint*) apresentar; (*time, effort*) investir, gastar; (*gas, electricity*) instalar
▶ **put in for** VT FUS (*job*) candidatar-se a; (*promotion, pay rise*) solicitar
▶ **put off** VT (*light*) apagar; (*postpone*) adiar, protelar; (*discourage*) desencorajar
▶ **put on** VT (*clothes, make-up, dinner*) pôr; (*light etc*) acender; (*play etc*) encenar; (*food, meal*) preparar; (*weight*) ganhar; (*brake*) aplicar; (*record, video, kettle*) ligar; (*attitude*) fingir, simular; (*accent, manner*) assumir; (*inf: tease*) fazer de criança; (*inform*): **to ~ sb on to sth** indicar algo a alguém
▶ **put out** VT (*take out*) colocar fora; (*fire, cigarette, light*) apagar; (*one's hand*) estender; (*news*) anunciar; (*rumour*) espalhar; (*tongue etc*) mostrar; (*person: inconvenience*) incomodar; (*Brit: dislocate*) deslocar; (*inf: person*): **to be ~ out** estar aborrecido ■ VI (*Naut*): **to ~ out to sea** fazer-se ao mar; **to ~ out from Plymouth** zarpar de Plymouth
▶ **put through** VT (*caller, call*) transferir; (*plan*) ser abrovado; **I'd like to ~ a call through to Brazil** eu gostaria de fazer uma ligação para o Brasil
▶ **put together** VT colocar junto(s); (*assemble*) montar; (*meal*) preparar
▶ **put up** VT (*raise*) levantar, erguer; (*hang*) prender; (*build*) construir, edificar; (*tent*) armar; (*increase*) aumentar; (*accommodate*) hospedar; **to ~ sb up to doing sth** incitar alguém a fazer algo; **to ~ sth up for sale** pôr algo à venda

▶ **put upon** VT FUS: **to be ~ upon** sofrer abusos
▶ **put up with** VT FUS suportar, agüentar
putrid ['pju:trɪd] ADJ pútrido, podre
putt [pʌt] VT (*Golf*) fazer um putt ■ N putt *m*, tacada leve
putter ['pʌtər] N (*Golf*) putter *m*
putting green ['pʌtɪŋ-] N campo de golfe em miniatura
putty ['pʌtɪ] N massa de vidraceiro, betume *m*
put-up ADJ: **~ job** (*Brit*) embuste *m*
puzzle ['pʌzl] N (*riddle*) charada; (*jigsaw*) quebra-cabeça *m*; (*also*: **crossword puzzle**) palavras cruzadas *fpl*; (*mystery*) mistério ■ VT desconcertar, confundir ■ VI: **to ~ over sth** tentar entender algo; **to be ~d about sth** estar perplexo com algo
puzzling ['pʌzlɪŋ] ADJ (*thing, action*) intrigante, confuso; (*mysterious*) enigmático, misterioso; (*unnerving*) desconcertante; (*incomprehensible*) incompreensível
PVC N ABBR (= *polyvinyl chloride*) PVC *m*
Pvt. (*US*) ABBR (*Mil*) = **private**
pw ABBR (= *per week*) por semana
PX (*US*) N ABBR (*Mil*) = **post exchange**
pygmy ['pɪgmɪ] N pigmeu(-méia) *m/f*
pyjamas [pɪ'dʒɑ:məz] (*US* **pajamas**) NPL pijama *m or f*
pylon ['paɪlən] N pilono, poste *m*, torre *f*
pyramid ['pɪrəmɪd] N pirâmide *f*
Pyrenees [pɪrə'ni:z] NPL: **the ~** os Pirineus
Pyrex® ['paɪrɛks] N Pirex® *m* ■ CPD: **a Pyrex dish** um pirex
python ['paɪθən] N pitão *m*

Qq

Q, q [kjuː] N (*letter*) Q, q *m*; **Q for Queen** Q de
Quinteta
Qatar [kæ'tɑːr] N Catar *m*
QC (*Brit*) N ABBR (= *Queen's Counsel*) título dado a
certos advogados
QED ABBR (= *quod erat demonstrandum*) QED
QM N ABBR = **quartermaster**
q.t. (*inf*) N ABBR = **quiet**; **on the q.t.** de fininho
qty ABBR (= *quantity*) quant
quack [kwæk] N (*of duck*) grasnido; (*pej: doctor*)
curandeiro(-a), charlatão(-tã) *m/f* ■ VI grasnar
quad [kwɔd] ABBR = **quadrangle**; **quadruplet**
quadrangle ['kwɔdræŋgl] N (*courtyard*) pátio
quadrangular
quadruped ['kwɔdrupɛd] N quadrúpede *m*
quadruple [kwɔ'drupl] ADJ quádruplo ■ N
quádruplo ■ VT, VI quadruplicar
quadruplets [kwɔː'druːplɪts] NPL
quadrigêmeos *mpl*, quádruplos *mpl*
quagmire ['kwægmaɪər] N lamaçal *m*, atoleiro
quail [kweɪl] N (*bird*) codorniz *f*, codorna (BR)
■ VI acovardar-se
quaint [kweɪnt] ADJ (*ideas*) curioso, esquisito;
(*village etc*) pitoresco
quake [kweɪk] VI (*with fear*) tremer ■ N ABBR
= **earthquake**
Quaker ['kweɪkər] N quacre *m/f*
qualification [kwɔlɪfɪ'keɪʃən] N (*skill, quality*)
qualificação *f*; (*reservation*) restrição *f*, ressalva;
(*modification*) modificação *f*; (*often pl: degree,
training*) título, qualificação; **what are your ~s?**
quais são as suas qualificações?
qualified ['kwɔlɪfaɪd] ADJ (*trained*) habilitado,
qualificado; (*professionally*) diplomado; (*fit*):
~ to apto para, capaz de; (*limited*) limitado;
(*professionally*) diplomado; **~ for/to do**
credenciado *or* qualificado para/para fazer
qualify ['kwɔlɪfaɪ] VT qualificar; (*modify*)
modificar; (*limit*) restringir, limitar ■ VI (*Sport*)
classificar-se; **to ~ (as)** VT classificar (como)
■ VI (*pass examination(s)*) formar-se *or* diplomar-
se (em); **to ~ (for)** reunir os requisitos (para)
qualifying ['kwɔlɪfaɪɪŋ] ADJ: **~ exam** exame *m* de
habilitação; **~ round** eliminatórias *fpl*
qualitative ['kwɔlɪteɪtɪv] ADJ qualitativo
quality ['kwɔlɪtɪ] N qualidade *f* ■ CPD de
qualidade; **of good/poor ~** de boa/má

qualidade; **quality control** N controle *m* de
qualidade; **quality papers** (*Brit*) NPL: **the
quality papers** os jornais de categoria

● QUALITY (NEWS)PAPERS
●
● Os *quality (news)papers* (ou *quality press*)
● englobam os jornais "sérios", diários
● ou semanais, em oposição aos jornais
● populares (*tabloid press*). Esses jornais visam
● a um público que procura informações
● detalhadas sobre uma grande variedade
● de assuntos e que está disposto a dedicar
● um bom tempo à leitura. Geralmente os
● *quality newspapers* são publicados em formato
● grande.

qualm [kwɑːm] N (*doubt*) dúvida; (*scruple*)
escrúpulo; **to have ~s about sth** ter dúvidas
sobre a retidão de algo
quandary ['kwɔndrɪ] N: **to be in a ~** estar num
dilema
quango ['kwæŋgəu] (*Brit*) N ABBR (= *quasi-
autonomous non-governmental organization*) comissão
nomeada pelo governo
quantitative ['kwɔntɪtətɪv] ADJ quantitativo
quantity ['kwɔntɪtɪ] N quantidade *f*; **in ~** em
quantidade; **quantity surveyor** N calculista
m/f de obra
quarantine ['kwɔrntiːn] N quarentena
quarrel ['kwɔrl] N (*argument*) discussão *f*; (*fight*)
briga ■ VI: **to ~ (with)** brigar (com); **to have a ~
with sb** ter uma briga *or* brigar com alguém; **I
have no ~ with him** não tenho nada contra ele;
I can't ~ with that não posso discordar disso
quarrelsome ['kwɔrlsəm] ADJ brigão(-gona)
quarry ['kwɔrɪ] N (*for stone*) pedreira; (*animal*)
presa, caça ■ VT (*marble etc*) extrair
quart [kwɔːt] N quarto de galão (1.136 l)
quarter ['kwɔːtər] N quarto, quarta parte *f*; (*of
year*) trimestre *m*; (*district*) bairro; (*US, Canada:
25 cents*) (moeda de) 25 centavos *mpl* de dólar
■ VT dividir em quatro; (*Mil: lodge*) aquartelar;
quarters NPL (*Mil*) quartel *m*; (*living quarters*)
alojamento; **a ~ of an hour** um quarto de hora;
it's a ~ to (*Brit*) *or* **of** (*US*) **3** são quinze para as
três (BR), são três menos um quarto (PT); **it's a**

~ past (*Brit*) *or* **after** (*US*) **3** são três e quinze (BR), são três e um quarto (PT); **from all ~s** de toda parte; **at close ~s** de perto
quarter-deck N (*Naut*) tombadilho superior
quarter final N quarta de final
quarterly ['kwɔːtəlɪ] ADJ trimestral ■ ADV trimestralmente ■ N (*Press*) revista trimestral
quartermaster ['kwɔːtəmɑːstəʳ] N (*Mil*) quartelmestre *m*; (*Naut*) contramestre *m*
quartet(te) [kwɔːˈtɛt] N quarteto
quarto ['kwɔːtəu] ADJ, N in-quarto *inv*
quartz [kwɔːts] N quartzo ■ CPD de quartzo
quash [kwɔʃ] VT (*verdict*) anular
quasi- ['kweɪzaɪ] PREFIX quase-
quaver ['kweɪvəʳ] N (*Brit: Mus*) colcheia ■ VI tremer
quay [kiː] N (*also:* **quayside**) cais *m*
queasy ['kwiːzɪ] ADJ (*sickly*) enjoado
Quebec [kwɪˈbɛk] N Quebec
queen [kwiːn] N rainha; (*also:* **queen bee**) abelha-mestra, rainha; (*Cards etc*) dama; **queen mother** N rainha-mãe *f*
queer [kwɪəʳ] ADJ (*odd*) esquisito, estranho; (*suspect*) suspeito, duvidoso; (*Brit: sick*): **I feel ~** não estou bem ■ N (*inf: homosexual*) bicha *m* (BR), maricas *m* (PT)
quell [kwɛl] VT (*opposition*) sufocar; (*fears*) abrandar, sufocar
quench [kwɛntʃ] VT apagar; **to ~ one's thirst** matar a sede
querulous ['kwɛruləs] ADJ lamuriante
query ['kwɪərɪ] N (*question*) pergunta; (*doubt*) dúvida; (*question mark*) ponto de interrogação ■ VT questionar
quest [kwɛst] N busca; (*journey*) expedição *f*
question ['kwɛstʃən] N pergunta; (*doubt*) dúvida; (*issue*) questão *f*; (*in text: problem*) problema *m* ■ VT (*doubt*) duvidar; (*interrogate*) interrogar, inquirir; **to ask sb a ~**, **to put a ~ to sb** fazer uma pergunta a alguém; **to bring** *or* **call sth into ~** colocar algo em questão, pôr algo em dúvida; **the ~ is ...** a questão é ...; **it is a ~ of** é questão de; **beyond ~** sem dúvida; **out of the ~** fora de cogitação, impossível
questionable ['kwɛstʃənəbl] ADJ discutível; (*doubtful*) duvidoso
questioner ['kwɛstʃənəʳ] N pessoa que faz uma pergunta (*or* que fez a pergunta *etc*)
questioning ['kwɛstʃənɪŋ] ADJ interrogador(a) ■ N interrogatório
question mark N ponto de interrogação
questionnaire [kwɛstʃəˈnɛəʳ] N questionário
queue [kjuː] (*Brit*) N fila (BR), bicha (PT) ■ VI (*also:* **queue up**) fazer fila (BR) *or* bicha (PT); **to jump the ~** furar a fila (BR), pôr-se à frente (PT)
quibble ['kwɪbl] VI: **to ~ about** *or* **over/with** tergiversar sobre/com
quiche [kiːʃ] N quiche *m*
quick [kwɪk] ADJ rápido; (*temper*) vivo; (*agile*) ágil; (*mind*) sagaz, despachado ■ ADV rápido ■ N: **to cut sb to the ~** ferir alguém; **be ~!** ande depressa!, vai rápido!; **to be ~ to act** agir

com rapidez; **she was ~ to see that ...** ela não tardou a ver que ...
quicken ['kwɪkən] VT apressar ■ VI apressar-se
quicklime ['kwɪklaɪm] N cal *f* viva
quickly ['kwɪklɪ] ADV rapidamente, depressa
quickness ['kwɪknɪs] N rapidez *f*; (*agility*) agilidade *f*; (*liveliness*) vivacidade *f*
quicksand ['kwɪksænd] N areia movediça
quickstep ['kwɪkstɛp] N dança de ritmo rápido
quick-tempered ADJ irritadiço, de pavio curto
quick-witted [-'wɪtɪd] ADJ perspicaz, vivo
quid [kwɪd] (*Brit: inf*) N INV libra; **quid pro quo** [-kwəu] N contrapartida
quiet ['kwaɪət] ADJ (*voice, music*) baixo; (*peaceful: place*) tranqüilo; (*person: calm*) calmo; (*not noisy: place*) silencioso; (*: person*) calado; (*silent*) silencioso; (*not busy: day, business*) calmo; (*ceremony, colour*) discreto ■ N (*peacefulness*) sossego; (*silence*) quietude *f* ■ VT, VI (*US*) = **quieten**; **keep ~!** cale-se!, fique quieto!; **on the ~** de fininho
quieten ['kwaɪətən] (*also:* **quieten down**) (*grow calm*) acalmar-se; (*grow silent*) calar-se ■ VT tranqüilizar; fazer calar
quietly ['kwaɪətlɪ] ADV tranqüilamente; (*silently*) silenciosamente; (*talk*) baixo
quietness ['kwaɪətnɪs] N (*silence*) quietude *f*; (*calm*) tranqüilidade *f*
quill [kwɪl] N pena (de escrever)
quilt [kwɪlt] N acolchoado, colcha; (**continental**) **~** (*Brit*) edredom *m* (BR), edredão *m* (PT)
quin [kwɪn] N ABBR = **quintuplet**
quince [kwɪns] N (*fruit*) marmelo; (*tree*) marmeleiro
quinine [kwɪˈniːn] N quinina
quintet(te) [kwɪnˈtɛt] N quinteto
quintuplets [kwɪnˈtjuːplɪts] NPL quíntuplos *mpl*
quip [kwɪp] N escárnio, dito espirituoso ■ VT: ... **he ~ped** ... soltou
quirk [kwəːk] N peculiaridade *f*; **by some ~ of fate** por uma singularidade do destino, por uma dessas coisas que acontecem
quit [kwɪt] (*pt, pp* **quitted**) VT (*smoking etc*) parar; (*job*) deixar (o emprego); (*premises*) desocupar ■ VI parar; (*give up*) desistir; (*resign*) demitir-se; **to ~ doing** parar *or* deixar de fazer; **~ stalling!** (*US: inf*) chega de evasivas!; **notice to ~** (*Brit*) aviso para desocupar (um imóvel)
quite [kwaɪt] ADV (*rather*) bastante; (*entirely*) completamente, totalmente; (*following a negative: almost*): **that's not ~ big enough** não é suficientemente grande; **~ new** novinho; **she's ~ pretty** ela é bem bonita; **I ~ understand** eu entendo completamente; **~ a few of them** um bom número deles; **that's not ~ right** não é bem assim; **not ~ as many as last time** um pouco menos do que da vez passada; **~ (so)!** exatamente!, isso mesmo!
Quito ['kiːtəu] N Quito
quits [kwɪts] ADJ: **~ (with)** quite (com); **let's call**

it ~ ficamos quites

quiver ['kwɪvəʳ] VI estremecer ∎ N (*for arrows*) carcás *m*, aljava

quiz [kwɪz] N (*game*) concurso (de cultura geral); (*in magazine etc*) questionário, teste *m* ∎ VT interrogar

quizzical ['kwɪzɪkəl] ADJ zombeteiro

quoits [kwɔɪts] NPL jogo de malha

quorum ['kwɔːrəm] N quorum *m*

quota ['kwəutə] N cota, quota

quotation [kwəu'teɪʃən] N citação *f*; (*estimate*) orçamento; (*of shares*) cotação *f*; **quotation**

marks NPL aspas *fpl*

quote [kwəut] N citação *f*; (*estimate*) orçamento ∎ VT (*sentence*) citar; (*price*) propor; (*figure, example*) citar, dar; (*shares*) cotar ∎ VI: **to ~ from** citar; **quotes** NPL (*quotation marks*) aspas *fpl*; **to ~ for a job** propor um preço para um trabalho; **in ~s** entre aspas; **~ ... un~** (*in dictation*) abre aspas ... fecha aspas

quotient ['kwəuʃənt] N quociente *m*

qv ABBR (= *quod vide*) vide

qwerty keyboard ['kwəːtɪ-] N teclado qwerty

Rr

R, r [ɑ:ʳ] N (letter) R, r m; **R for Robert** (Brit) or **Roger** (US) R de Roberto

R ABBR (= right) dir.; (: = river) R.; (: = Réaumur (scale)) R; (US: Cinema: = restricted) proibido para menores de 17 anos; (US: Pol) = **republican**; (Brit) = **Rex; Regina**

RA ABBR = **rear admiral** ∎ N ABBR (Brit) = **Royal Academy; Royal Academician**

RAAF N ABBR = **Royal Australian Air Force**

Rabat [rə'bɑːt] N Rabat

rabbi ['ræbaɪ] N rabino

rabbit ['ræbɪt] N coelho ∎ VI: **to ~ (on)** (Brit) tagarelar; **rabbit hole** N toca, lura; **rabbit hutch** N coelheira

rabble ['ræbl] (pej) N povinho, ralé f

rabid ['ræbɪd] ADJ raivoso

rabies ['reɪbiːz] N raiva

RAC (Brit) N ABBR (= Royal Automobile Club) ≈ TCB m (BR), ≈ ACP m (PT)

raccoon [rə'kuːn] N mão-pelada m, guaxinim m

race [reɪs] N (competition, rush) corrida; (species) raça ∎ VT (person) apostar corrida com; (horse) fazer correr; (engine) acelerar ∎ VI (compete) competir; (run) correr; (pulse) bater rapidamente; **the human ~** a raça humana; **to ~ in/out** etc entrar/sair correndo etc; **race car** (US) N = **racing car; race car driver** (US) N = **racing driver**

racecourse ['reɪskɔːs] N hipódromo

racehorse ['reɪshɔːs] N cavalo de corridas

race relations NPL relações fpl entre as raças

racetrack ['reɪstræk] N pista de corridas; (for cars) autódromo

racial ['reɪʃl] ADJ racial

racialism ['reɪʃəlɪzəm] N racismo

racialist ['reɪʃəlɪst] ADJ, N racista m/f

racing ['reɪsɪŋ] N corrida; **racing car** (Brit) N carro de corrida; **racing driver** (Brit) N piloto(-a) de corrida

racism ['reɪsɪzəm] N racismo

racist ['reɪsɪst] (pej) ADJ, N racista m/f

rack [ræk] N (also: **luggage rack**) bagageiro; (shelf) estante f; (also: **roof rack**) xalmas fpl, porta-bagagem m; (dish rack) secador m de prato; (clothes rack) cabide m ∎ VT (cause pain to) atormentar; **~ed by** (pain, anxiety) tomado por; **to ~ one's brains** quebrar a cabeça; **to go to ~ and**

ruin (building) cair aos pedaços; (business) falir
▶ **rack up** VT acumular

racket ['rækɪt] N (for tennis) raquete f (BR), raqueta (PT); (noise) barulheira, zoeira; (swindle) negócio ilegal, fraude f

racketeer [rækɪ'tɪəʳ] (esp US) N chantagista m/f

racoon [rə'kuːn] N = **raccoon**

racquet ['rækɪt] N raquete f (BR), raqueta (PT)

racy ['reɪsɪ] ADJ ousado, picante

RADA ['rɑːdə] (Brit) N ABBR = **Royal Academy of Dramatic Art**

radar ['reɪdɑːʳ] N radar m ∎ CPD de radar; **radar trap** N radar m rodoviário

radial ['reɪdɪəl] ADJ (also: **radial-ply**) radial

radiance ['reɪdɪəns] N brilho, esplendor m

radiant ['reɪdɪənt] ADJ radiante, brilhante; (Phys) radiante

radiate ['reɪdɪeɪt] VT (heat, emotion) irradiar; (emit) emitir ∎ VI (lines) difundir-se, estender-se

radiation [reɪdɪ'eɪʃən] N radiação f; **radiation sickness** N radiointoxicação f, intoxicação f radioativa

radiator ['reɪdɪeɪtəʳ] N radiador m; **radiator cap** N tampa do radiador; **radiator grill** N (Aut) grade f do radiador

radical ['rædɪkl] ADJ radical

radii ['reɪdɪaɪ] NPL of **radius**

radio ['reɪdɪəu] N rádio ∎ VI: **to ~ to sb** comunicar com alguém por rádio ∎ VT: **to ~ sb** comunicar-se por rádio com alguém; (information) transmitir por rádio; (position) comunicar por rádio; **on the ~** no rádio

radio... [reɪdɪəu] PREFIX radio...

radioactive [reɪdɪəu'æktɪv] ADJ radioativo

radioactivity [reɪdɪəuæk'tɪvɪtɪ] N radioatividade f

radio announcer N locutor(a) m/f de rádio

radio-controlled [-kən'trəuld] ADJ controlado por rádio

radiographer [reɪdɪ'ɔgrəfəʳ] N radiógrafo(-a)

radiography [reɪdɪ'ɔgrəfɪ] N radiografia

radiologist [reɪdɪ'ɔlədʒɪst] N radiologista m/f

radiology [reɪdɪ'ɔlədʒɪ] N radiologia

radio station N emissora, estação f de rádio

radio taxi N rádio-táxi m

radiotelephone [reɪdɪəu'tɛlɪfəun] N radiotelefone m

radiotherapist [reɪdɪəu'θɛrəpɪst] N radioterapeuta m/f

radiotherapy [reɪdɪəu'θɛrəpɪ] N radioterapia

radish ['rædɪʃ] N rabanete m

radium ['reɪdɪəm] N rádio

radius ['reɪdɪəs] (pl **radii**) N raio; (Anat) rádio; **within a 50-mile ~** dentro de um raio de 50 milhas

RAF (Brit) N ABBR = **Royal Air Force**

raffia ['ræfɪə] N ráfia

raffish ['ræfɪʃ] ADJ reles inv, ordinário

raffle ['ræfl] N rifa ■ VT rifar

raft [rɑːft] N (craft; also: **life raft**) balsa; (logs) flutuante m de árvores

rafter ['rɑːftə'] N viga, caibro

rag [ræg] N (piece of cloth) trapo; (torn cloth) farrapo; (pej: newspaper) jornaleco; (University: for charity) atividades estudantis beneficentes ■ VT (Brit) encarnar em, zombar de; **rags** NPL (torn clothes) trapos mpl, farrapos mpl; **in ~s** em farrapos

rag-and-bone man (Brit: irreg) N ~ **ragman**

ragbag ['rægbæg] N (fig) salada

rag doll N boneca de trapo

rage [reɪdʒ] N (fury) raiva, furor m ■ VI (person) estar furioso; (storm) assolar; (debate) continuar calorosamente; **to fly into a ~** enfurecer-se; **it's all the ~** é a última moda

ragged ['rægɪd] ADJ (edge) irregular, desigual; (clothes) puído, gasto; (appearance) esfarrapado, andrajoso; (coastline) acidentado

raging ['reɪdʒɪŋ] ADJ furioso; (fever, pain) violento; ~ **toothache** dor de dente alucinante; **in a ~ temper** enfurecido

ragman ['rægmæn] (irreg) N negociante m de trastes

rag trade (inf) N: **the ~** a confecção e venda de roupa

raid [reɪd] N (Mil) incursão f; (criminal) assalto; (attack) ataque m; (by police) batida ■ VT invadir, atacar; assaltar; atacar; fazer uma batida em

raider ['reɪdə'] N atacante m/f; (criminal) assaltante m/f

rail [reɪl] N (on stair) corrimão m; (on bridge, balcony) parapeito, anteparo; (of ship) amurada; **rails** NPL (for train) trilhos mpl; **by ~** de trem (BR), por caminho de ferro (PT)

railing(s) ['reɪlɪŋ(z)] N(PL) grade f

railroad ['reɪlrəud] (US) N = **railway**

railway ['reɪlweɪ] N estrada (BR) or caminho (PT) de ferro; **railway engine** N locomotiva (BR); **railway line** (Brit) N linha de trem (BR) or de comboio (PT)

railwayman ['reɪlweɪmən] (Brit: irreg) N ferroviário

railway station (Brit) N estação f ferroviária (BR) or de caminho de ferro (PT)

rain [reɪn] N chuva ■ VI chover; **in the ~** na chuva; **it's ~ing** está chovendo (BR), está a chover (PT); **it's ~ing cats and dogs** chove a cântaros

rainbow ['reɪnbəu] N arco-íris m inv

raincoat ['reɪnkəut] N impermeável m, capa de chuva

raindrop ['reɪndrɔp] N gota de chuva

rainfall ['reɪnfɔːl] N chuva; (measurement) pluviosidade f

rainproof ['reɪnpruːf] ADJ impermeável

rainstorm ['reɪnstɔːm] N chuvada torrencial

rainwater ['reɪnwɔːtə'] N água pluvial

rainy ['reɪnɪ] ADJ chuvoso; **a ~ day** um dia de chuva

raise [reɪz] N aumento ■ VT (lift) levantar; (end: siege, embargo) levantar, terminar; (build) erguer,. edificar; (salary, production) aumentar; (morale, standards) melhorar; (doubts) suscitar, despertar; (a question) fazer, expor; (cattle, family) criar; (crop) cultivar, plantar; (army) recrutar, alistar; (funds) angariar; (loan) levantar, obter; **to ~ one's voice** levantar a voz; **to ~ one's glass to sb/sth** brindar à saúde de alguém/brindar algo; **to ~ sb's hopes** dar esperanças a alguém; **to ~ a laugh/smile** provocar risada/sorrisos

raisin ['reɪzn] N passa, uva seca

Raj [rɑːdʒ] N: **the ~** o império (na Índia)

rajah ['rɑːdʒə] N rajá m

rake [reɪk] N (tool) ancinho; (person) libertino ■ VT (garden) revolver or limpar com o ancinho; (fire) remover as cinzas de; (with machine gun) varrer ■ VI: **to ~ through** (fig: search) vasculhar

rake-off (inf) N comissão f

rakish ['reɪkɪʃ] ADJ (dissolute) devasso, dissoluto; **at a ~ angle** de banda, inclinado

rally ['rælɪ] N (Pol etc) comício; (Aut) rally m, rali m; (Tennis) rebatida ■ VT reunir ■ VI reorganizar-se; (sick person, Stock Exchange) recuperar-se
▶ **rally round** VI dar apoio ■ VT FUS dar apoio a

rallying point ['rælɪŋ-] N (Pol, Mil) ponto de encontro

RAM [ræm] N ABBR (Comput: = random access memory) RAM f

ram [ræm] N carneiro; (Tech) êmbolo, aríete m ■ VT (push) cravar; (crash into) colidir com; (tread down) pisar, calcar

ramble ['ræmbl] N caminhada, excursão f a pé ■ VI caminhar; (talk: also: **ramble on**) divagar

rambler ['ræmblə'] N caminhante m/f; (Bot) roseira trepadeira

rambling ['ræmblɪŋ] ADJ (speech) desconexo, incoerente; (house) cheio de recantos; (plant) rastejante ■ N excursionismo

RAMC (Brit) N ABBR = **Royal Army Medical Corps**

ramification [ræmɪfɪ'keɪʃən] N ramificação f

ramp [ræmp] N (incline) rampa; (in road) lombada; **on/off ~** (US: Aut) entrada (para a rodovia) saída da rodovia

rampage [ræm'peɪdʒ] N: **to be on the ~** alvoroçar-se ■ VI: **they went rampaging through the town** correram feito loucos pela cidade

rampant ['ræmpənt] ADJ (disease etc) violento, implacável

rampart ['ræmpɑːt] N baluarte m; (wall) muralha

ramshackle ['ræmʃækl] ADJ caindo aos pedaços

RAN N ABBR = **Royal Australian Navy**
ran [ræn] PT of **run**
ranch [rɑːntʃ] N rancho, fazenda, estância
rancher ['rɑːntʃəʳ] N rancheiro(-a), fazendeiro(-a)
rancid ['rænsɪd] ADJ rançoso, rância
rancour ['ræŋkəʳ] (US **rancor**) N rancor m
random ['rændəm] ADJ ao acaso, casual, fortuito; (Comput, Math) aleatório ■ N: **at ~ a** esmo, aleatoriamente; **random access** N (Comput) acesso randômico or aleatório; **random access memory** N (Comput) memória de acesso randômico or aleatório
randy ['rændɪ] (Brit: inf) ADJ de fogo
rang [ræŋ] PT of **ring**
range [reɪndʒ] N (of mountains) cadeia, cordilheira; (of missile) alcance m; (of voice) extensão f; (series) série f; (of products) gama, sortimento; (Mil: also: **shooting range**) estande m; (also: **kitchen range**) fogão m ■ VT (place) colocar; (arrange) arrumar, ordenar ■ VI: **to ~ over** (wander) percorrer; (extend) estender-se por; **to ~ from ... to ...** variar de ... a ..., oscilar entre ... e ...; **do you have anything else in this price ~?** você tem outras coisas dentro desta faixa de preço?; **within (firing) ~** ao alcance de tiro; **~d left/right** (text) alinhado à esquerda/direita
ranger ['reɪndʒəʳ] N guarda-florestal m/f
Rangoon [ræŋ'guːn] N Rangum
rank [ræŋk] N (row) fila, fileira; (Mil) posto; (status) categoria, posição f; (Brit: also: **taxi rank**) ponto de táxi ■ VI: **I ~ him sixth** eu o coloco em sexto lugar ■ ADJ (stinking) fétido, malcheiroso; (hypocrisy, injustice) total; **the ranks** NPL (Mil) a tropa; **the ~ and file** (fig) a gente comum; **to close ~s** (Mil, fig) cerrar fileiras
rankle ['ræŋkl] VI (insult) doer, magoar
ransack ['rænsæk] VT (search) revistar; (plunder) saquear, pilhar
ransom ['rænsəm] N resgate m; **to hold sb to ~** (fig) encostar alguém contra a parede
rant [rænt] VI arengar
ranting ['ræntɪŋ] N palavreado oco
rap [ræp] N batida breve e seca, tapa ■ VT bater de leve
rape [reɪp] N estupro; (Bot) colza ■ VT violentar, estuprar
rape(seed) oil ['reɪp(siːd)-] N óleo de colza
rapid ['ræpɪd] ADJ rápido
rapidity [rə'pɪdɪtɪ] N rapidez f
rapidly ['ræpɪdlɪ] ADV rapidamente
rapids ['ræpɪdz] NPL (Geo) cachoeira
rapist ['reɪpɪst] N estuprador m
rapport [ræ'pɔːʳ] N harmonia, afinidade f
rapt [ræpt] ADJ absorvido; **to be ~ in contemplation** estar contemplando embevecido
rapture ['ræptʃəʳ] N êxtase m, arrebatamento; **to go into ~s over** extasiar-se com
rapturous ['ræptʃərəs] ADJ extático; (applause) entusiasta

rare [rɛəʳ] ADJ raro; (Culin: steak) mal passado
rarebit ['rɛəbɪt] N see **Welsh rarebit**
rarefied ['rɛərɪfaɪd] ADJ (air, atmosphere) rarefeito
rarely ['rɛəlɪ] ADV raramente
raring ['rɛərɪŋ] ADJ: **to be ~ to go** (inf) estar louco para começar
rarity ['rɛərɪtɪ] N raridade f
rascal ['rɑːskl] N maroto, malandro
rash [ræʃ] ADJ impetuoso, precipitado ■ N (Med) exantema m, erupção f cutânea; (of events) série f, torrente f; **he came out in a ~** apareceu-lhe uma irritação na pele
rasher ['ræʃəʳ] N fatia fina
rashness ['ræʃnɪs] N impetuosidade f
rasp [rɑːsp] N (tool) lima, raspadeira ■ VT (speak: also: **rasp out**) falar em voz áspera
raspberry ['rɑːzbərɪ] N framboesa; **raspberry bush** N framboeseira
rasping ['rɑːspɪŋ] ADJ: **a ~ noise** um ruído áspero or irritante
rat [ræt] N rato (BR), ratazana (PT)
ratable ['reɪtəbl] ADJ = **rateable**
ratchet ['rætʃɪt] N (Tech) roquete m, catraca
rate [reɪt] N (ratio) razão f; (percentage) percentagem f, proporção f; (price) preço, taxa; (: of hotel) diária; (of interest, change) taxa; (speed) velocidade f ■ VT (value) taxar; (estimate) avaliar; **rates** NPL (Brit) imposto predial e territorial; (fees) pagamento; **to ~ as** ser considerado como; **to ~ sb/sth as** considerar alguém/algo como; **to ~ sth among** considerar algo como um(a) dos/das; **to ~ sb/sth highly** valorizar alguém/algo; **at a ~ of 60 km/h** à velocidade de 60 km/h; **at any ~** de qualquer modo; **~ of exchange** taxa de câmbio; **~ of growth** taxa de crescimento; **~ of return** taxa de retorno
rateable value ['reɪtəbl-] (Brit) N valor m tributável (de um imóvel)
ratepayer ['reɪtpeɪəʳ] (Brit) N contribuinte m/f de imposto predial
rather ['rɑːðəʳ] ADV (somewhat) um tanto, meio; (to some extent) até certo ponto; (more accurately): **or ~** ou melhor; **it's ~ expensive** (quite) é meio caro; (too) é caro demais; **there's ~ a lot** há bastante or muito; **~ than** em vez de; **I would** or **I'd ~ go** preferiria or preferia ir; **I'd ~ not leave** eu preferiria or preferia não sair; **or ~** (more accurately) ou melhor; **I ~ think he won't come** eu estou achando que ele não vem
ratification [rætɪfɪ'keɪʃən] N ratificação f
ratify ['rætɪfaɪ] VT ratificar
rating ['reɪtɪŋ] N (assessment) avaliação f; (score) classificação f; (value) valor m; (standing) posição f; (Naut: category) posto; (: Brit: sailor) marinheiro; **ratings** NPL (Radio, TV) índice(s) m(pl) de audiência
ratio ['reɪʃɪəu] N razão f, proporção f; **in the ~ of 100 to 1** na proporção or razão de 100 para 1
ration ['ræʃən] N ração f ■ VT racionar; **rations** NPL (Mil) mantimentos mpl, víveres mpl
rational ['ræʃənl] ADJ racional; (solution, reasoning) lógico; (person) sensato, razoável

rationale [ræʃə'nɑ:l] N razão f fundamental
rationalization [ræʃnəlaɪ'zeɪʃən] N
racionalização f
rationalize ['ræʃənəlaɪz] VT racionalizar
rationally ['ræʃənəlɪ] ADV racionalmente;
(logically) logicamente
rationing ['ræʃnɪŋ] N racionamento
rat poison N raticida m
rat race N: **the** ~ a competição acirrada na vida
moderna
rattan [ræ'tæn] N rotim m
rattle ['rætl] N (of door) batida; (of train etc)
chocalhada; (of coins) chocalhar m; (of hail)
saraivada; (object: for baby) chocalho; (: of sports
fan) matraca; (of snake) guizo ■ VI chocalhar;
(small objects) tamborilar; (vehicle): **to** ~ **along**
mover-se ruidosamente ■ VT sacudir,
fazer bater; (unnerve) perturbar; (disconcert)
desconcertar; (annoy) encher
rattlesnake ['rætlsneɪk] N cascavel f
ratty ['rætɪ] (inf) ADJ rabugento
raucous ['rɔ:kəs] ADJ espalhafatoso, banelhento
raucously ['rɔ:kəslɪ] ADV em voz rouca
ravage ['rævɪdʒ] VT devastar, estragar
ravages ['rævɪdʒɪz] NPL estragos mpl
rave [reɪv] VI (in anger) encolerizar-se; (Med)
delirar; (with enthusiasm): **to** ~ **about** vibrar com
■ CPD: ~ **review** (inf) crítica estrondosa
raven ['reɪvən] N corvo
ravenous ['rævənəs] ADJ morto de fome,
esfomeado
ravine [rə'vi:n] N ravina, barranco
raving ['reɪvɪŋ] ADJ: ~ **lunatic** doido(-a)
varrido(-a)
ravings ['reɪvɪŋz] NPL delírios mpl
ravioli [rævɪ'əulɪ] N ravióli m
ravish ['rævɪʃ] VT arrebatar; (delight) encantar
ravishing ['rævɪʃɪŋ] ADJ encantador(a)
raw [rɔ:] ADJ (uncooked) cru(a); (not processed)
bruto; (sore) vivo; (inexperienced) inexperiente,
novato; (weather) muito frio; **raw deal** (inf) N:
to get a raw deal levar a pior; **raw material** N
matéria-prima
ray [reɪ] N raio; ~ **of hope** fio de esperança
rayon ['reɪɔn] N raiom m
raze [reɪz] VT (also: **raze to the ground**) arrasar,
aniquilar
razor ['reɪzəʳ] N (open) navalha; (safety razor)
aparelho de barbear; (electric) aparelho de
barbear elétrico; **razor blade** N gilete m (BR),
lâmina de barbear (PT)
razzle(-dazzle) ['ræzl-] (Brit: inf) N: **to go on the
razzle(-dazzle)** cair na farra
razzmatazz ['ræzmə'tæz] (inf) N alvoroço
R&B N ABBR = **rhythm and blues**
RC ABBR = **Roman Catholic**
RCAF N ABBR = **Royal Canadian Air Force**
RCMP N ABBR = **Royal Canadian Mounted
Police**
RCN N ABBR = **Royal Canadian Navy**
RD (US) ABBR (Post) = **rural delivery**
Rd ABBR = **road**

R&D N ABBR = **research and development**
RDC (Brit) N ABBR = **rural district council**
RE (Brit) N ABBR = **religious education**; (Mil)
= **Royal Engineers**
re [ri:] PREP referente a
reach [ri:tʃ] N alcance m; (Boxing) campo de
ação; (of river etc) extensão f ■ VT (be able to touch)
alcançar; (arrive at: place) chegar em; (: agreement,
conclusion) chegar a; (achieve) conseguir; (stretch
out) estender, esticar; (by telephone) conseguir
falar com ■ VI alcançar; (stretch out) esticar-se;
within ~ (object) ao alcance (da mão); **out of**
or **beyond** ~ fora de alcance; **within easy** ~ **of**
the shops/station perto das lojas/da estação;
"keep out of the ~ ~ of children" "manter
fora do alcance de crianças"; **to ~ out for sth**
estender or esticar a mão para pegar (em) algo;
to ~ sb by phone comunicar-se com alguém
por telefone; **can I ~ you at your hotel?** posso
entrar em contato com você no seu hotel?
▸ **reach out** VT (hand) esticar ■ VI: **to ~ out for
sth** estender or esticar a mão para pegar (em)
algo
react [ri:'ækt] VI reagir
reaction [ri:'ækʃən] N reação f; **reactions** NPL
(reflexes) reflexos mpl
reactionary [ri:'ækʃənrɪ] ADJ, N reacionário(-a)
reactor [ri:'æktəʳ] N (also: **nuclear reactor**)
reator m nuclear
read [ri:d] (pt, pp **read**) [rɛd] VI ler ■ VT ler;
(understand) compreender; (study) estudar;
to take sth as ~ (fig) considerar algo como
garantido; **do you** ~ **me?** (Tel) está me ouvindo?;
to ~ between the lines ler nas entrelinhas
▸ **read out** VT ler em voz alta
▸ **read over** VT reler
▸ **read through** VT (quickly) dar uma lida em;
(thoroughly) ler até o fim
▸ **read up (on)** VT FUS estudar
readable ['ri:dəbl] ADJ (writing) legível; (book) que
merece ser lido
reader ['ri:dəʳ] N leitor(a) m/f; (book) livro de
leituras; (Brit: at university) professor(a) m/f
adjunto(-a)
readership ['ri:dəʃɪp] N (of paper: readers) leitores
mpl; (: number of readers) número de leitores
readily ['rɛdɪlɪ] ADV (willingly) de boa vontade;
(easily) facilmente; (quickly) sem demora,
prontamente
readiness ['rɛdɪnɪs] N (willingness) boa vontade
f; (preparedness) prontidão f; **in** ~ (prepared)
preparado, pronto
reading ['ri:dɪŋ] N leitura; (understanding)
compreensão f; (on instrument) indicação f,
registro (BR), registo (PT); **reading lamp** N
lâmpada de leitura; **reading room** N sala de
leitura
readjust [ri:ə'dʒʌst] VT reajustar ■ VI (adapt): **to**
~ **to** reorientar-se para
ready ['rɛdɪ] ADJ pronto, preparado; (willing)
disposto; (available) disponível ■ ADV: ~-**cooked**
pronto para comer ■ N: **at the** ~ (Mil) pronto

para atirar; *(fig)* pronto; ~ **for use** pronto para o uso; **to be** ~ **to do sth** estar pronto *or* preparado para fazer algo; **to get** ~ VI preparar-se ▪ VT preparar; **ready cash** N dinheiro vivo
ready-made ADJ (já) feito; *(clothes)* pronto
ready-mix N *(for cakes etc)* massa pronta
ready money N dinheiro vivo *or* disponível
ready reckoner [-'rɛkənə^r] *(Brit)* N tabela de cálculos feitos
ready-to-wear ADJ pronto, prêt à porter *inv*
reaffirm [riːə'fəːm] VT reafirmar
reagent [riː'eɪdʒənt] N reagente *m*, reativo
real [rɪəl] ADJ real; *(genuine)* verdadeiro, autêntico; *(proper)* de verdade; *(for emphasis)*: **a ~ idiot/miracle** um verdadeiro idiota/milagre
▪ ADV *(US: inf: very)* bem; **in ~ life** na vida real; **in ~ terms** em termos reais; **real estate** N bens *mpl* imobiliários *or* de raiz
realism ['rɪəlɪzəm] N realismo
realist ['rɪəlɪst] N realista *m/f*
realistic [rɪə'lɪstɪk] ADJ realista
reality [riː'ælɪtɪ] N realidade *f*; **in ~** na verdade, na realidade; **reality TV** N reality TV *f*
realization [rɪəlaɪ'zeɪʃən] N *(fulfilment)* realização *f*; *(understanding)* compreensão *f*; *(Comm)* conversão *f* em dinheiro, realização
realize ['rɪəlaɪz] VT *(understand)* perceber; *(fulfil, Comm)* realizar; **I ~ that ...** eu concordo que ...
really ['rɪəlɪ] ADV *(for emphasis)* realmente; *(actually)*: **what ~ happened?** o que aconteceu na verdade?; **~?** *(interest)* é mesmo?; *(surprise)* verdade!; **~!** *(annoyance)* realmente!
realm [rɛlm] N reino
real-time ADJ *(Comput)* em tempo real
realtor® ['rɪəltə^r] *(US)* N corretor(a) *m/f* de imóveis (BR), agente *m/f* imobiliário(-a) (PT)
ream [riːm] N resma; **reams** NPL *(fig: inf)* páginas *fpl* e páginas
reap [riːp] VT segar, ceifar; *(fig)* colher
reaper ['riːpə^r] N segador(a) *m/f*, ceifeiro(-a); *(machine)* segadora
reappear [riːə'pɪə^r] VI reaparecer
reappearance [riːə'pɪərəns] N reaparição *f*
reapply [riːə'plaɪ] VI: **to ~ for** requerer de novo; *(job)* candidatar-se de novo a
reappraisal [riːə'preɪzl] N reavaliação *f*
rear [rɪə^r] ADJ traseiro, de trás ▪ N traseira; *(inf: bottom)* traseiro ▪ VT *(cattle, family)* criar ▪ VI *(also:* **rear up)** empinar-se
rear-engined [-'ɛndʒɪnd] ADJ *(Aut)* com motor traseiro
rearguard ['rɪəgɑːd] N retaguarda
rearm [riː'ɑːm] VT, VI rearmar
rearmament [riː'ɑːməmənt] N rearmamento *m*
rearrange [riːə'reɪndʒ] VT arrumar de novo, reorganizar
rear-view mirror N *(Aut)* espelho retrovisor
reason ['riːzn] N *(cause)* razão *f*; *(ability to think)* raciocínio; *(sense)* bom-senso ▪ VI: **to ~ with sb** argumentar com alguém, persuadir alguém; **the ~ for/why** a razão de/pela qual; **to have ~ to think** ter motivo para pensar; **it stands to ~**

that é razoável *or* lógico que; **she claims with good ~ that ...** ela afirma com toda a razão que **...;** **all the more ~ why you should not sell it** mais uma razão para você não vendê-lo
reasonable ['riːznəbl] ADJ *(fair)* razoável; *(sensible)* sensato
reasonably ['riːznəblɪ] ADV *(fairly)* razoavelmente; *(sensibly)* sensatamente; **one can ~ assume that ...** tudo indica que ...
reasoned ['riːzənd] ADJ *(argument)* fundamentado
reasoning ['riːzənɪŋ] N raciocínio
reassemble [riːə'sɛmbl] VT *(people)* reunir; *(machine)* montar de novo ▪ VI reunir-se de novo
reassert [riːə'səːt] VT reafirmar
reassurance [riːə'ʃuərəns] N garantia; *(comfort)* reconforto
reassure [riːə'ʃuə^r] VT tranqüilizar; **to ~ sb of** reafirmar a confiança de alguém acerca de
reassuring [riːə'ʃuərɪŋ] ADJ animador(a), tranqüilizador(a)
reawakening [riːə'weɪknɪŋ] N despertar *m*
rebate ['riːbeɪt] N *(on product)* abatimento; *(on tax etc)* devolução *f*; *(refund)* reembolso
rebel [*n* 'rɛbl, *vi* rɪ'bɛl] N rebelde *m/f* ▪ VI rebelar-se
rebellion [rɪ'bɛljən] N rebelião *f*, revolta
rebellious [rɪ'bɛljəs] ADJ insurreto; *(behaviour)* rebelde
rebirth [riː'bəːθ] N renascimento
rebound [*vi* rɪ'baund, *n* 'riːbaund] VI *(ball)* ressaltar ▪ N: **on the ~** ressalto; *(person)*: **she married him on the ~** ela casou com ele logo após o rompimento do casamento (*or* relacionamento) anterior
rebuff [rɪ'bʌf] N repulsa, recusa ▪ VT repelir
rebuild [riː'bɪld] *(irreg)* VT reconstruir; *(economy, confidence)* recuperar
rebuke [rɪ'bjuːk] N reprimenda, censura ▪ VT repreender
rebut [rɪ'bʌt] VT refutar
rebuttal [rɪ'bʌtl] N refutação *f*
recalcitrant [rɪ'kælsɪtrənt] ADJ recalcitrante, teimoso
recall [rɪ'kɔːl] VT *(remember)* recordar, lembrar; *(parliament)* reunir de volta; *(ambassador etc)* chamar de volta ▪ N *(memory)* recordação *f*, lembrança; *(of ambassador etc)* chamada (de volta); **it is beyond ~** caiu no esquecimento
recant [rɪ'kænt] VI retratar-se
recap ['riːkæp] VT sintetizar ▪ VI recapitular ▪ N recapitulação *f*
recapitulate [riːkə'pɪtjuleɪt] VT, VI = **recap**
recapture [riː'kæptʃə^r] VT *(town)* retomar, recobrar; *(atmosphere)* recriar
recd. ABBR = **received**
recede [rɪ'siːd] VI *(tide)* baixar; *(lights)* diminuir; *(memory)* enfraquecer; *(hair)* escassear
receding [rɪ'siːdɪŋ] ADJ *(forehead, chin)* metido *or* puxado para dentro; *(hair)* que está escasseando nas têmporas; **~ hairline** entradas *fpl* (no cabelo)

receipt [rɪ'siːt] N (document) recibo; (act of receiving) recebimento (BR), recepção f (PT); **receipts** NPL (Comm) receitas fpl; **on ~ of** ao receber; **to acknowledge ~ of** acusar o recebimento (BR) or a recepção (PT) de; **we are in ~ of ...** recebimos ...

receivable [rɪ'siːvəbl] ADJ (Comm) a receber

receive [rɪ'siːv] VT receber; (guest) acolher; (wound, criticism) sofrer; **"~d with thanks"** (Comm) "recebido"

receiver [rɪ'siːvəʳ] N (Tel) fone m (BR), auscultador m (PT); (Radio, TV) receptor m; (of stolen goods) receptador(a) m/f; (Comm) curador(a) m/f síndico(-a) de massa falida

recent ['riːsnt] ADJ recente; **in ~ years** nos últimos anos

recently ['riːsntlɪ] ADV (a short while ago) recentemente; (in recent times) ultimamente; **as ~ as yesterday** ainda ontem; **until ~** até recentemente

receptacle [rɪ'sɛptɪkl] N receptáculo, recipiente m

reception [rɪ'sɛpʃən] N recepção f; (welcome) acolhida; **reception centre** (Brit) N centro de recepção; **reception desk** N (mesa de) recepção f

receptionist [rɪ'sɛpʃənɪst] N recepcionista m/f

receptive [rɪ'sɛptɪv] ADJ receptivo

recess [rɪ'sɛs] N (in room) recesso, vão m; (for bed) nicho; (secret place) esconderijo; (Pol etc: holiday) férias fpl; (US: Law: short break) recesso; (Sch: esp US) recreio

recession [rɪ'sɛʃən] N recessão f

recharge [riː'tʃɑːdʒ] VT (battery) recarregar

rechargeable [riː'tʃɑːdʒəbl] ADJ recarregável

recipe ['rɛsɪpɪ] N receita

recipient [rɪ'sɪpɪənt] N recipiente m/f, recebedor(a) m/f; (of letter) destinatário(-a)

reciprocal [rɪ'sɪprəkl] ADJ recíproco

reciprocate [rɪ'sɪprəkeɪt] VT retribuir ■ VI (in hospitality etc) retribuir; (in aggression etc) revidar

recital [rɪ'saɪtl] N recital m

recite [rɪ'saɪt] VT (poem) recitar; (complaints etc) enumerar

reckless ['rɛkləs] ADJ (driver) imprudente; (speed) imprudente, excessivo; (spending) irresponsável

recklessly ['rɛkləslɪ] ADV temerariamente, sem prudência; (spend) irresponsavelmente

reckon ['rɛkən] VT (calculate) calcular, contar; (consider) considerar; (think): **I ~ that ...** acho que ... ■ VI: **he is somebody to be ~ed with** ele é alguém que não pode ser esquecido; **to ~ without sb/sth** não levar alguém/algo em conta, não contar com alguém/algo
▶ **reckon on** VT FUS contar com

reckoning ['rɛkənɪŋ] N (calculation) cálculo; **the day of ~** o dia do Juízo Final

reclaim [rɪ'kleɪm] VT (get back) recuperar; (demand back) reivindicar; (land) desbravar; (: from sea) aterrar; (waste materials) reaproveitar

reclamation [rɛklə'meɪʃən] N recuperação f; (of land from sea) aterro

recline [rɪ'klaɪn] VI reclinar-se; (lean) apoiar-se,

recostar-se

reclining [rɪ'klaɪnɪŋ] ADJ (seat) reclinável

recluse [rɪ'kluːs] N recluso(-a)

recognition [rɛkəg'nɪʃən] N reconhecimento; **transformed beyond ~** tão transformado que está irreconhecível; **in ~ of** em reconhecimento de; **to gain ~** ser reconhecido

recognizable ['rɛkəgnaɪzəbl] ADJ: **~ (by)** reconhecível (por)

recognize ['rɛkəgnaɪz] VT reconhecer; (accept) aceitar; **to ~ by/as** reconhecer por/como

recoil [vi rɪ'kɔɪl, n 'riːkɔɪl] VI recuar; (person): **to ~ from doing sth** recusar-se a fazer algo ■ N (of gun) coice m

recollect [rɛkə'lɛkt] VT lembrar, recordar

recollection [rɛkə'lɛkʃən] N (memory) recordação f; (remembering) lembrança; **to the best of my ~** se não me falha a memória

recommend [rɛkə'mɛnd] VT recomendar; **she has a lot to ~ her** ela tem muito a seu favor

recommendation [rɛkəmɛn'deɪʃən] N recomendação f

recommended retail price [rɛkə'mɛndɪd-] (Brit) N preço máximo consumidor

recompense ['rɛkəmpɛns] VT recompensar ■ N recompensa

reconcilable [rɛkən'saɪləbl] ADJ (ideas) conciliável

reconcile ['rɛkənsaɪl] VT (two people) reconciliar; (two facts) conciliar, harmonizar; **to ~ o.s. to sth** resignar-se a or conformar-se com algo

reconciliation [rɛkənsɪlɪ'eɪʃən] N reconciliação f

recondite [rɪ'kɔndaɪt] ADJ obscuro

recondition [riːkən'dɪʃən] VT recondicionar

reconnaissance [rɪ'kɔnɪsns] N (Mil) reconhecimento

reconnoitre [rɛkə'nɔɪtəʳ] (US **reconnoiter**) VT (Mil) reconhecer ■ VI fazer um reconhecimento

reconsider [riːkən'sɪdəʳ] VT reconsiderar

reconstitute [riː'kɔnstɪtjuːt] VT reconstituir

reconstruct [riːkən'strʌkt] VT reconstruir; (event) reconstituir

reconstruction [riːkən'strʌkʃən] N reconstrução f

record [n, adj 'rɛkɔːd, vt rɪ'kɔːd] N (Mus) disco; (of meeting etc) ata, minuta; (Comput, of attendance) registro (BR), registo (PT); (file) arquivo; (written) história; (also: **criminal record**) antecedentes mpl; (Sport) recorde m ■ VT (write down) anotar; (temperature, speed) registrar (BR), registar (PT); (relate) relatar, referir; (Mus: song etc) gravar ■ ADJ: **in ~ time** num tempo recorde; **public ~s** arquivo público; **to keep a ~ of** anotar; **to put the ~ straight** (fig) corrigir um equívoco; **he is on ~ as saying that ...** ele declarou publicamente que ...; **Italy's excellent ~** o excelente desempenho da Itália; **off the ~** ADJ confidencial ■ ADV confidencialmente; **record card** N (in file) ficha

recorded delivery letter [rɪ'kɔːdɪd-] (Brit) N (Post) ≈ carta registrada (BR) or registada (PT)

recorder [rɪ'kɔːdə'] N (Mus) flauta; (Tech) indicador m mecânico; (official) escrivão(-vã) m/f

record holder N (Sport) detentor(a) m/f do recorde

recording [rɪ'kɔːdɪŋ] N (Mus) gravação f; **recording studio** N estúdio de gravação

record library N discoteca

record player N toca-discos m inv (BR), gira-discos m inv (PT)

recount [rɪ'kaunt] VT relatar

re-count [n 'riːkaunt, vt riː'kaunt] N (Pol: of votes) nova contagem f, recontagem f ■ VT recontar

recoup [rɪ'kuːp] VT: **to ~ one's losses** recuperar-se dos prejuízos

recourse [rɪ'kɔːs] N recurso; **to have ~ to** recorrer a

recover [rɪ'kʌvə'] VT recuperar; (rescue) resgatar ■ VI (from illness) recuperar-se; (from shock) refazer-se

re-cover VT (chair etc) revestir

recovery [rɪ'kʌvərɪ] N recuperação f; (Med) recuperação, melhora

recreate [riː'krɪ'eɪt] VT recriar

recreation [rɛkrɪ'eɪʃən] N recreação f; (play) recreio

recreational [rɛkrɪ'eɪʃənl] ADJ recreativo; **recreational vehicle** (US) N kombi m

recrimination [rɪkrɪmɪ'neɪʃən] N recriminação f

recruit [rɪ'kruːt] N recruta m/f; (in company) novato(-a) ■ VT recrutar

recruiting office [rɪ'kruːtɪŋ-] N centro de recrutamento

recruitment [rɪ'kruːtmənt] N recrutamento

rectangle ['rɛktæŋgl] N retângulo

rectangular [rɛk'tæŋgjulə'] ADJ retangular

rectify ['rɛktɪfaɪ] VT retificar

rector ['rɛktə'] N (Rel) pároco; (Sch) reitor(a) m/f

rectory ['rɛktərɪ] N residência paroquial

rectum ['rɛktəm] N (Anat) reto

recuperate [rɪ'kuːpəreɪt] VI recuperar-se

recur [rɪ'kə:'] VI repetir-se, ocorrer outra vez; (opportunity) surgir de novo; (symptoms) reaparecer

recurrence [rɪ'kʌrəns] N repetição f; (of symptoms) reaparição f

recurrent [rɪ'kʌrənt] ADJ repetido, periódico

recurring [rɪ'kə:rɪŋ] ADJ (Math) periódico

recyclable [riː'saɪkləbl] ADJ reciclável

red [rɛd] N vermelho; (Pol: pej) vermelho(-a) ■ ADJ vermelho; (hair) ruivo; (wine) tinto; **to be in the ~** (person) estar no vermelho; (account) não ter fundos; **red carpet treatment** N: **she was given the red carpet treatment** ela foi recebida com todas as honras

Red Cross N Cruz f Vermelha

redcurrant ['rɛd'kʌrənt] N groselha

redden ['rɛdən] VT avermelhar ■ VI corar, ruborizar-se

reddish ['rɛdɪʃ] ADJ avermelhado; (hair) arruivado

redecorate [riː'dɛkəreɪt] VT decorar de novo, redecorar

redecoration [riːdɛkə'reɪʃən] N remodelação f

redeem [rɪ'diːm] VT (Rel) redimir; (sth in pawn) tirar do prego; (loan, fig: situation) salvar

redeemable [rɪ'diːməbl] ADJ resgatável

redeeming [rɪ'diːmɪŋ] ADJ: **~ feature** lado bom or que salva

redeploy [riːdɪ'plɔɪ] VT (resources, troops) redistribuir; **redeployment** [riːdɪ'plɔɪmənt] N redistribuição f

redevelop [riːdɪ'vɛləp] VT renovar

redevelopment [riːdɪ'vɛləpmənt] N renovação f

red-haired ADJ ruivo

red-handed [-'hændɪd] ADJ: **to be caught ~** ser apanhado em flagrante, ser flagrado

redhead ['rɛdhɛd] N ruivo(-a)

red herring N (fig) pista falsa

red-hot ADJ incandescente

redid [riː'dɪd] PT of **redo**

redirect [riːdaɪ'rɛkt] VT (mail) endereçar de novo

redistribute [riːdɪ'strɪbjuːt] VT redistribuir

red-letter day N dia m memorável

red light N: **to go through a ~** (Aut) avançar o sinal

red-light district N zona (de meretrício)

redness ['rɛdnɪs] N vermelhidão f

redo [riː'duː] (irreg) VT refazer

redolent ['rɛdələnt] ADJ: **~ of** que cheira a; (fig) que evoca

redone [riː'dʌn] PP of **redo**

redouble [riː'dʌbl] VT: **to ~ one's efforts** redobrar os esforços

redraft [riː'drɑːft] VT redigir de novo

redress [rɪ'drɛs] N compensação f ■ VT retificar; **to ~ the balance** restituir o equilíbrio

Red Sea N: **the ~** o mar Vermelho

redskin ['rɛdskɪn] N pele-vermelha m/f

red tape N (fig) papelada, burocracia

reduce [rɪ'djuːs] VT reduzir; (lower) rebaixar; **"~ speed now"** (Aut) "diminua a velocidade"; **to ~ sth by/to** diminuir algo em/reduzir algo a; **to ~ sb to** (silence, begging) levar alguém a; (tears) reduzir alguém a; **"greatly ~d prices"** "preços altamente reduzidos"; **at a ~d price** a preço reduzido

reduction [rɪ'dʌkʃən] N redução f; (of price) abatimento; (discount) desconto

redundancy [rɪ'dʌndənsɪ] N redundância; (Brit: dismissal) demissão f; (unemployment) desemprego; **compulsory ~** demissão; **voluntary ~** demissão voluntária; **redundancy payment** (Brit) N indenização paga aos empregados dispensados sem justa causa

redundant [rɪ'dʌndnt] ADJ (Brit: worker) desempregado; (detail, object) redundante, supérfluo; **to be made ~** ficar desempregado or sem trabalho

reed [riːd] N (Bot) junco; (Mus: of clarinet etc) palheta

reedy ['riːdɪ] ADJ (voice, instrument) agudo

reef [riːf] N (at sea) recife m

reek [riːk] VI: **to ~ (of)** cheirar (a), feder (a)

reel [riːl] N carretel m, bobina; (of film) rolo, filme m; (on fishing-rod) carretilha; (dance) dança típica da Escócia ■ VT (Tech) bobinar; (also: **reel up**) enrolar ■ VI (sway) cambalear, oscilar; **my head is ~ing** estou completamente confuso
▸ **reel in** VT puxar enrolando a linha
▸ **reel off** VT (say) enumerar, recitar
re-election N reeleição f
re-enter VT reentrar em
re-entry N reentrada
re-export [vt riːɪksˈpɔːt, n riːˈɛkspɔːt] VT reexportar ■ N reexportação f
ref [rɛf] (inf) N ABBR = **referee**
ref. ABBR (Comm: = reference) ref
refectory [rɪˈfɛktərɪ] N refeitório
refer [rɪˈfəːʳ] VT (matter, problem): **to ~ sth to** submeter algo à apreciação de; (person, patient): **to ~ sb to** encaminhar alguém a; (reader: to text): **to ~ sb to** remeter alguém a ■ VI: **to ~ to** (allude to) referir-se or aludir a; (apply to) aplicar-se a; (consult) recorrer a; **~ring to your letter** (Comm) com referência à sua carta
referee [rɛfəˈriː] N árbitro(-a); (Brit: for job application) referência ■ VT arbitrar; (football match) apitar
reference [ˈrɛfrəns] N referência; (mention) menção f; **with ~ to** com relação a; (Comm: in letter) com referência a; **"please quote this ~"** (Comm) "queira citar esta referência"; **reference book** N livro de consulta; **reference number** N número de referência
referenda [rɛfəˈrɛndə] NPL of **referendum**
referendum [rɛfəˈrɛndəm] (pl **referenda**) N referendum m, plebiscito
refill [vt riːˈfɪl, n ˈriːfɪl] VT reencher; (lighter etc) reabastecer ■ N (for pen) carga nova; (Comm) refill m
refine [rɪˈfaɪn] VT refinar
refined [rɪˈfaɪnd] ADJ (person, taste) refinado, culto
refinement [rɪˈfaɪnmənt] N (of person) cultura, refinamento, requinte m; (of system) refinamento
refinery [rɪˈfaɪnərɪ] N refinaria
refit [n ˈriːfɪt, vt riːˈfɪt] N (Naut) reequipamento ■ VT reequipar
reflate [riːˈfleɪt] VT (economy) reflacionar
reflation [riːˈfleɪʃən] N reflação f
reflationary [riːˈfleɪʃənrɪ] ADJ reflacionário
reflect [rɪˈflɛkt] VT refletir ■ VI (think) refletir, meditar; **it ~s badly/well on him** isso repercute mal/bem para ele
reflection [rɪˈflɛkʃən] N reflexo; (thought, act) reflexão f; (criticism): **~ on** crítica de; **on ~** pensando bem
reflector [rɪˈflɛktəʳ] N (Aut, on bicycle, for light) refletor m
reflex [ˈriːflɛks] ADJ, N reflexo
reflexive [rɪˈflɛksɪv] ADJ (Ling) reflexivo
reform [rɪˈfɔːm] N reforma ■ VT reformar
reformat [riːˈfɔːmæt] VT (Comput) reformatar
Reformation [rɛfəˈmeɪʃən] N: **the ~** a Reforma

reformatory [rɪˈfɔːmətərɪ] (US) N reformatório
reformed [rɪˈfɔːmd] ADJ emendado, reformado
reformer [rɪˈfɔːməʳ] N reformador(a) m/f
reformist [rɪˈfɔːmɪst] N reformista m/f
refrain [rɪˈfreɪn] VI: **to ~ from doing** abster-se de fazer ■ N estribilho, refrão m
refresh [rɪˈfrɛʃ] VT refrescar
refresher course [rɪˈfrɛʃəʳ-] (Brit) N curso de reciclagem
refreshing [rɪˈfrɛʃɪŋ] ADJ refrescante; (sleep) repousante; (change) agradável; (idea, thought) original
refreshment [rɪˈfrɛʃmənt] N (eating): **for some ~** para comer alguma coisa; (resting etc): **in need of ~** precisando se refazer, precisando refazer as suas forças; **refreshments** NPL (food and drink) bebidas fpl (não-alceólicas) e guloseimas
refrigeration [rɪfrɪdʒəˈreɪʃən] N refrigeração f
refrigerator [rɪˈfrɪdʒəreɪtəʳ] N refrigerador m, geladeira (BR), frigorífico (PT)
refuel [riːˈfjuəl] VT, VI reabastecer
refuge [ˈrɛfjuːdʒ] N refúgio; **to take ~ in** refugiar-se em
refugee [rɛfjuˈdʒiː] N refugiado(-a); **refugee camp** N campo de refugiados
refund [n ˈriːfʌnd, vt rɪˈfʌnd] N reembolso ■ VT devolver, reembolsar
refurbish [riːˈfəːbɪʃ] VT renovar
refurnish [riːˈfəːnɪʃ] VT colocar móveis novos em
refusal [rɪˈfjuːzəl] N recusa, negativa; **first ~** primeira opção
refuse¹ [rɪˈfjuːz] VT recusar; (order) recusar-se a ■ VI recusar-se, negar-se; (horse) recusar-se a pular a cerca; **to ~ to do sth** recusar-se a fazer algo
refuse² [ˈrɛfjuːs] N refugo, lixo; **refuse bin** N lata de lixo; **refuse collection** N remoção f de lixo; **refuse collector** N lixeiro(-a), gari m/f (BR); **refuse disposal** N destruição f de lixo; **refuse tip** N depósito de lixo
refute [rɪˈfjuːt] VT refutar
regain [rɪˈgeɪn] VT recuperar, recobrar
regal [ˈriːgl] ADJ real, régio
regale [rɪˈgeɪl] VT: **to ~ sb with sth** regalar alguém com algo
regalia [rɪˈgeɪlɪə] N, NPL insígnias fpl reais
regard [rɪˈgɑːd] N (gaze) olhar m firme; (aspect) respeito; (attention) atenção f; (esteem) estima, consideração f ■ VT (consider) considerar; **to give one's ~s to** dar lembranças a; **"with kindest ~s"** "cordialmente"; **as ~s, with ~ to** com relação a, com respeito a, quanto a
regarding [rɪˈgɑːdɪŋ] PREP com relação a
regardless [rɪˈgɑːdlɪs] ADV apesar de tudo; **~ of** apesar de
regatta [rɪˈgætə] N regata
regency [ˈriːdʒənsɪ] N regência
regenerate [rɪˈdʒɛnəreɪt] VT regenerar ■ VI regenerar-se
regent [ˈriːdʒənt] N regente m/f
régime [reɪˈʒiːm] N regime m
regiment [n ˈrɛdʒɪmənt, vt ˈrɛdʒɪmɛnt] N

regimento ■ VT regulamentar; (*children etc*)
subordinar a disciplina rígida
regimental [rɛdʒɪ'mɛntl] ADJ regimental
regimentation [rɛdʒɪmɛn'teɪʃən] N
organização *f*
region ['riːdʒən] N região *f*; **in the ~ of** (*fig*) por
volta de, ao redor de
regional ['riːdʒənl] ADJ regional; **regional
development** N desenvolvimento regional
register ['rɛdʒɪstər] N registro (BR), registo (PT);
(*Sch*) chamada; (*list*) lista ■ VT registrar (BR),
registar (PT); (*subj: instrument*) marcar, indicar
■ VI (*at hotel*) registrar-se (BR), registar-se (PT);
(*for work*) candidatar-se; (*as student*) inscrever-
se; (*make impression*) causar impressão; **to ~ for
a course** matricular-se num curso; **to ~ a
protest** registrar (BR) *or* registar (PT) uma
queixa
registered ['rɛdʒɪstəd] ADJ (*letter, parcel*)
registrado (BR), registado (PT); (*student*)
matriculado; (*voter*) inscrito; **registered
company** N sociedade *f* registrada (BR)
or registada (PT); **registered nurse** (*US*) N
enfermeiro(-a) formado(-a); **registered office**
N sede *f* social; **registered trademark** N marca
registrada (BR) *or* registada (PT)
registrar ['rɛdʒɪstrɑːʳ] N oficial *m/f* de registro
(BR) *or* registo (PT), escrivão(-vã) *m/f*; (*in college*)
funcionário(-a) administrativo(-a) sênior; (*in
hospital*) médico(-a) sênior
registration [rɛdʒɪs'treɪʃən] N (*act*) registro (BR),
registo (PT); (*Aut: also:* **registration number**)
número da placa
registry ['rɛdʒɪstrɪ] N registro (BR), registo (PT),
cartório; **registry office** (*Brit*) N registro (BR) *or*
registo (PT) civil, cartório; **to get married in a
registry office** casar-se no civil
regret [rɪ'grɛt] N desgosto, pesar *m*; (*remorse*)
remorso ■ VT (*deplore*) lamentar; (*repent of*)
arrepender-se de; **to ~ that ...** lamentar que ...
(+*sub*); **we ~ to inform you that ...**
lamentamos informá-lo de que ...
regretfully [rɪ'grɛtfulɪ] ADV com pesar,
pesarosamente
regrettable [rɪ'grɛtəbl] ADJ deplorável; (*loss*)
lamentável
regrettably [rɪ'grɛtəblɪ] ADV lamentavelmente;
~, he was unable ... infelizmente, ele não pôde ...
regroup [riː'gruːp] VT reagrupar ■ VI reagrupar-
se
regt ABBR = **regiment**
regular ['rɛgjuləʳ] ADJ (*verb, service, shape*) regular;
(*frequent*) freqüente; (*usual*) habitual; (*soldier*) de
linha; (*listener, reader*) assíduo; (*Comm: size*) médio
■ N (*client etc*) habitual *m/f*
regularity [rɛgju'lærɪtɪ] N regularidade *f*
regularly ['rɛgjulərlɪ] ADV regularmente; (*shaped*)
simetricamente; (*often*) freqüentemente
regulate ['rɛgjuleɪt] VT (*speed*) regular; (*spending*)
controlar; (*Tech*) regular, ajustar
regulation [rɛgju'leɪʃən] N (*rule*) regra,
regulamento; (*adjustment*) ajuste *m* ■ CPD

regulamentar
rehabilitation [riːhəbɪlɪ'teɪʃən] N reabilitação *f*
rehash [riː'hæʃ] (*inf*) VT retocar
rehearsal [rɪ'həːsəl] N ensaio; *see also* **dress**
rehearse [rɪ'həːs] VT, VI ensaiar
rehouse [riː'hauz] VT realojar
reign [reɪn] N reinado; (*fig*) domínio ■ VI reinar;
imperar
reigning ['reɪnɪŋ] ADJ (*monarch*) reinante;
(*champion*) atual
reimburse [riːɪm'bəːs] VT reembolsar
reimbursement [riːɪm'bəːsmənt] N reembolso
rein [reɪn] N (*for horse*) rédea; **to give ~ to** dar
rédeas a, dar rédea larga a; **to give sb free ~** (*fig*)
dar carta branca a alguém
reincarnation [riːɪnkɑː'neɪʃən] N
reencarnação *f*
reindeer ['reɪndɪəʳ] N INV rena
reinforce [riːɪn'fɔːs] VT reforçar
reinforced [riːɪn'fɔːst] ADJ (*concrete*) armado
reinforcement [riːɪn'fɔːsmənt] N reforço;
reinforcements NPL (*Mil*) reforços *mpl*
reinstate [riːɪn'steɪt] VT (*worker*) readmitir;
(*official*) reempossar; (*tax, law*) reintroduir
reinstatement [riːɪn'steɪtmənt] N readmissão *f*
reissue [riː'ɪʃuː] VT (*book*) reeditar; (*film*) relançar
reiterate [riː'ɪtəreɪt] VT reiterar, repetir
reject [*n* 'riːdʒɛkt, *vt* rɪ'dʒɛkt] N (*Comm*) artigo
defeituoso ■ VT rejeitar; (*offer of help*) recusar;
(*goods*) refugar
rejection [rɪ'dʒɛkʃən] N rejeição *f*; (*of offer of help*)
recusa
rejoice [rɪ'dʒɔɪs] VI: **to ~ at** *or* **over** regozijar-se *or*
alegrar-se de
rejoinder [rɪ'dʒɔɪndəʳ] N (*retort*) réplica
rejuvenate [rɪ'dʒuːvəneɪt] VT rejuvenescer
rekindle [riː'kɪndl] VT reacender; (*fig*) despertar,
reanimar
relapse [rɪ'læps] N (*Med*) recaída; (*into crime*)
reincidência
relate [rɪ'leɪt] VT (*tell*) contar, relatar; (*connect*):
to ~ sth to relacionar algo com ■ VI: **to ~ to**
relacionar-se com; **~d to** ligado a, relacionado a
relating [rɪ'leɪtɪŋ]: **~ to** PREP relativo a, acerca de
relation [rɪ'leɪʃən] N (*person*) parente *m/f*; (*link*)
relação *f*; **relations** NPL (*dealings*) relações
fpl; (*relatives*) parentes *mpl*; **diplomatic/
international ~s** relações diplomáticas;
internacionais; **in ~ to** em relação a; **to bear no
~ to** não ter relação com
relationship [rɪ'leɪʃənʃɪp] N relacionamento;
(*between two things*) relação *f*; (*also:* **family
relationship**) parentesco; (*affair*) caso
relative ['rɛlətɪv] N parente *m/f* ■ ADJ relativo;
(*respective*) respectivo
relatively ['rɛlətɪvlɪ] ADV relativamente
relax [rɪ'læks] VI (*rest*) descansar; (*unwind*)
descontrair-se; (*muscle*) relaxar-se; (*calm down*)
acalmar-se ■ VT (*grip*) afrouxar; (*control*) relaxar;
(*mind, person*) descansar; **~!** (*calm down*) calma!; **to
~ one's grip** *or* **hold** afrouxar um pouco
relaxation [riːlæk'seɪʃən] N (*rest*) descanso;

(of muscle, control) relaxamento; (of grip)
afrouxamento; (recreation) lazer m
relaxed [rɪ'lækst] ADJ relaxado; (tranquil)
descontraído
relaxing [rɪ'læksɪŋ] ADJ relaxante
relay ['riːleɪ] N (race) (corrida de) revezamento
■ VT (message) retransmitir
release [rɪ'liːs] N (from prison) libertação f; (from
obligation) liberação f; (of shot) disparo; (of gas)
escape m; (of water) despejo; (of film, book etc)
lançamento; (device) desengate m ■ VT (prisoner)
pôr em liberdade; (book, film) lançar; (report,
news) publicar; (gas etc) soltar; (free: from wreckage
etc) soltar; (Tech: catch, spring etc) desengatar,
desapertar; (let go) soltar; **to ~ one's grip** or **hold**
afrouxar; **to ~ the clutch** (Aut) desembrear
relegate ['rɛləgeɪt] VT relegar; (Sport): **to be ~d**
ser rebaixado
relent [rɪ'lent] VI abrandar-se; (yield) ceder
relentless [rɪ'lentlɪs] ADJ (unceasing) contínuo;
(determined) implacável
relevance ['rɛləvəns] N pertinência; (of question
etc) importância; **~ of sth to sth** relação de algo
com algo
relevant ['rɛləvənt] ADJ (fact, information)
pertinente; (apt) apropriado; (important)
relevante; **~ to** relacionado com
reliability [rɪlaɪə'bɪlɪtɪ] N (of person, firm)
confiabilidade f, seriedade f; (of method, machine)
segurança; (of news) fidedignidade f
reliable [rɪ'laɪəbl] ADJ (person, firm) digno de
confiança, confiável, sério; (method, machine)
seguro; (news) fidedigno
reliably [rɪ'laɪəblɪ] ADV: **to be ~ informed that ...**
saber através de fonte segura que ...
reliance [rɪ'laɪəns] N: **~ (on)** (trust) confiança
(em), esperança (em); (dependence) dependência
(de)
reliant [rɪ'laɪənt] ADJ: **to be ~ on sth/sb**
depender de algo/alguém
relic ['rɛlɪk] N (Rel) relíquia; (of the past) vestígio
relief [rɪ'liːf] N (from pain, anxiety) alívio; (help,
supplies) ajuda, socorro; (of guard) rendição f; (Art,
Geo) relevo; **by way of light ~** como forma de
diversão; **relief map** N mapa m em relevo; **relief
road** (Brit) N estrada alternativa
relieve [rɪ'liːv] VT (pain, fear) aliviar; (bring
help to) ajudar, socorrer; (burden) abrandar,
mitigar; (take over from: gen) substituir, revezar;
(: guard) render; **to ~ sb of sth** (load) tirar algo
de alguém; (duties) destituir alguém de algo;
to ~ sb of his command exonerar alguém,
destituir alguém de sua função; **to ~ o.s.** fazer
as necessidades
religion [rɪ'lɪdʒən] N religião f
religious [rɪ'lɪdʒəs] ADJ religioso
reline [riː'laɪn] VT (brakes) trocar o forro de
relinquish [rɪ'lɪŋkwɪʃ] VT abandonar; (plan,
habit) renunciar a
relish ['rɛlɪʃ] N (Culin) condimento, tempero;
(enjoyment) entusiasmo ■ VT (food etc) saborear;
(thought) ver com satisfação; **to ~ doing** gostar

de fazer
relive [riː'lɪv] VT reviver
reload [riː'ləud] VT recarregar
relocate [riː'ləu'keɪt] VT deslocar ■ VI deslocar-
se; **to ~ in** instalar-se em
reluctance [rɪ'lʌktəns] N relutância
reluctant [rɪ'lʌktənt] ADJ relutante; **to be ~ to
do sth** relutar em fazer algo
reluctantly [rɪ'lʌktəntlɪ] ADV relutantemente,
de má vontade
rely on [rɪ'laɪ-] VT FUS confiar em, contar com;
(be dependent on) depender de
remain [rɪ'meɪn] VI (survive) sobreviver; (stay)
ficar, permanecer; (be left) sobrar; (continue)
continuar; **to ~ silent** ficar calado; **I ~, yours
faithfully** (Brit: in letters) subscrevo-me
atenciosamente
remainder [rɪ'meɪndər] N resto, restante m
remaining [rɪ'meɪnɪŋ] ADJ restante
remains [rɪ'meɪnz] NPL (of body) restos mpl; (of
meal) sobras fpl; (of building) ruínas fpl
remand [rɪ'mɑːnd] N: **on ~** sob prisão preventiva
■ VT: **to be ~ed in custody** continuar sob
prisão preventiva, manter sob custódia;
remand home (Brit) N instituição f do juizado
de menores, reformatório
remark [rɪ'mɑːk] N observação f, comentário
■ VT comentar ■ VI: **to ~ on sth** comentar algo,
fazer um comentário sobre algo
remarkable [rɪ'mɑːkəbl] ADJ notável;
(outstanding) extraordinário
remarry [riː'mærɪ] VI casar-se de novo
remedial [rɪ'miːdɪəl] ADJ (tuition, classes) de
reforço; (exercise) terapêutico
remedy ['rɛmədɪ] N: **~ (for)** remédio (contra or a)
■ VT remediar
remember [rɪ'membər] VT lembrar-se de,
lembrar; (memorize) guardar; (bear in mind) ter
em mente; (send greetings): **~ me to her** dê
lembranças a ela; **I ~ seeing it, I ~ having seen
it** eu me lembro de ter visto aquilo; **she ~ed to
do it** ela se lembrou de fazer aquilo
remembrance [rɪ'membrəns] N (memory)
memória; (souvenir) lembrança, recordação f;
Remembrance Sunday N ver abaixo

● **REMEMBRANCE DAY**
●
●
● Remembrance Day ou Remembrance Sunday
● é o domingo mais próximo do dia 11 de
● novembro, dia em que a Primeira Guerra
● Mundial terminou oficialmente e no qual
● se homenageia as vítimas das duas guerras
● mundiais. Nessa ocasião são observados
● dois minutos de silêncio às 11 horas,
● horário da assinatura do armistício com
● a Alemanha em 1918. Nos dias anteriores,
● papoulas de papel são vendidas por
● associações de caridade e a renda é revertida
● aos ex-combatentes e suas famílias.

remind [rɪ'maɪnd] VT: **to ~ sb to do sth** lembrar

a alguém que tem de fazer algo; **to ~ sb of sth** lembrar algo a alguém, lembrar alguém de algo; **she ~s me of her mother** ela me lembra a mãe dela; **that ~s me, ...** falando nisso, ...

reminder [rɪ'maɪndə'] N lembrete *m*; (*souvenir*) lembrança; (*letter*) carta de advertência

reminisce [rɛmɪ'nɪs] VI relembrar velhas histórias; **to ~ about sth** relembrar algo

reminiscences [rɛmɪ'nɪsnsɪz] NPL recordações *fpl*, lembranças *fpl*

reminiscent [rɛmɪ'nɪsənt] ADJ: **to be ~ of sth** lembrar algo

remiss [rɪ'mɪs] ADJ negligente, desleixado; **it was ~ of him** foi um descuido dele

remission [rɪ'mɪʃən] N remissão *f*; (*of sentence*) diminuição *f*

remit [rɪ'mɪt] VT (*send: money*) remeter, enviar, mandar

remittance [rɪ'mɪtəns] N remessa

remnant ['rɛmnənt] N resto; (*of cloth*) retalho; **remnants** NPL (*Comm*) retalhos *mpl*

remonstrate ['rɛmənstreɪt] VI: **to ~ (with sb about sth)** reclamar (a alguém de algo)

remorse [rɪ'mɔːs] N remorso

remorseful [rɪ'mɔːsful] ADJ arrependido

remorseless [rɪ'mɔːslɪs] ADJ (*fig*) implacável

remote [rɪ'məut] ADJ (*distant*) remoto, distante; (*person*) reservado, afastado; (*slight*): **there is a ~ possibility that ...** existe uma possibilidade remota de que ...; **remote control** N controle *m* remoto

remote-controlled [-kən'trəuld] ADJ (*plane*) telecomandado; (*missile*) teleguiado

remotely [rɪ'məutlɪ] ADV remotamente; (*slightly*) levemente

remoteness [rɪ'məutnɪs] N afastamento, isolamento

remould ['riːməuld] (*Brit*) N (*tyre*) pneu *m* recauchutado

removable [rɪ'muːvəbl] ADJ (*detachable*) removível

removal [rɪ'muːvəl] N (*taking away*) remoção *f*; (*Brit: from house*) mudança; (*from office: sacking*) afastamento, demissão *f*; (*Med*) extração *f*; **removal man** (*irreg*) N homem *m* da companhia de mudanças; **removal van** (*Brit*) N caminhão *m* (BR) *or* camião *m* (PT) de mudanças

remove [rɪ'muːv] VT tirar, retirar; (*clothing*) tirar; (*stain*) remover; (*employee*) afastar, demitir; (*name from list, obstacle*) eliminar, remover; (*doubt, abuse*) afastar; (*Tech*) retirar, separar; (*Med*) extrair, extirpar; **first cousin once ~d** primo(-a) em segundo grau

remover [rɪ'muːvə'] N (*substance*) removedor *m*; **removers** NPL (*Brit: company*) companhia de mudanças

remunerate [rɪ'mjuːnəreɪt] VT remunerar

remuneration [rɪmjuːnə'reɪʃən] N remuneração *f*

Renaissance [rɪ'neɪsɔns] N: **the ~** a Renascença

rename [riː'neɪm] VT dar novo nome a

rend [rɛnd] (*pt, pp* **rent**) VT rasgar, despedaçar

render ['rɛndə'] VT (*give: thanks*) trazer; (: *service*) prestar; (: *account*) entregar; (*make*) fazer, tornar; (*translate*) traduzir; (*fat: also: render down*) clarificar; (*wall*) rebocar

rendering ['rɛndərɪŋ] N (*Mus etc*) interpretação *f*

rendezvous ['rɔndɪvuː] N encontro; (*place*) ponto de encontro ■ VI encontrar-se; **to ~ with sb** encontrar-se com alguém

renegade ['rɛnɪgeɪd] N renegado(-a)

renew [rɪ'njuː] VT renovar; (*resume*) retomar, recomeçar; (*loan etc*) prorrogar; (*negotiations, acquaintance*) reatar

renewable [rɪ'njuːəbl] ADJ renovável

renewal [rɪ'njuːəl] N (*of contract*) renovação *f*; (*resumption*) retomada; (*of loan*) prorrogação *f*

renounce [rɪ'nauns] VT renunciar a; (*disown*) repudiar, rejeitar

renovate ['rɛnəveɪt] VT renovar; (*house, room*) reformar

renovation [rɛnə'veɪʃən] N renovação *f*; (*of house etc*) reforma

renown [rɪ'naun] N renome *m*

renowned [rɪ'naund] ADJ renomado, famoso

rent [rɛnt] PT, PP *of* **rend** ■ N aluguel *m* (BR), aluguer *m* (PT) ■ VT (*also: rent out*) alugar

rental ['rɛntəl] N (*for television, car*) aluguel *m* (BR), aluguer *m* (PT)

renunciation [rɪnʌnsɪ'eɪʃən] N renúncia

reopen [riː'əupən] VT reabrir

reopening [riː'əupənɪŋ] N reabertura

reorder [riː'ɔːdə'] VT encomendar novamente; (*rearrange*) reorganizar

reorganize [riː'ɔːgənaɪz] VT reorganizar

Rep. (US) ABBR (*Pol*) = **representative**; **republican**

rep [rɛp] N ABBR (*Comm*) = **representative**; (*Theatre*) = **repertory**

repaid [riː'peɪd] PT, PP *of* **repay**

repair [rɪ'pɛə'] N reparação *f*, conserto; (*patch*) remendo ■ VT consertar; **beyond ~** irreparável; **in good/bad ~** em bom/mau estado; **under ~** no conserto; **repair kit** N caixa de ferramentas; **repair man** (*irreg*) N consertador *m*; **repair shop** N oficina de reparos

repartee [rɛpɑː'tiː] N resposta arguta e engenhosa; (*skill*) presteza em replicar

repast [rɪ'pɑːst] N (*formal*) repasto

repatriate [riː'pætrɪeɪt] VT repatriar

repay [riː'peɪ] (*irreg*) VT (*money*) reembolsar, restituir; (*person*) pagar de volta; (*debt*) saldar, liquidar; (*sb's efforts*) corresponder, retribuir; (*favour*) retribuir

repayment [riː'peɪmənt] N reembolso; (*of debt*) pagamento; (*of mortgage etc*) prestação *f*

repeal [rɪ'piːl] N (*of law*) revogação *f*; (*of sentence*) anulação *f* ■ VT revogar; anular

repeat [rɪ'piːt] N (*Radio, TV*) repetição *f* ■ VT repetir; (*Comm: order*) renovar ■ VI repetir-se

repeatedly [rɪ'piːtɪdlɪ] ADV repetidamente

repel [rɪ'pɛl] VT repelir; (*disgust*) repugnar

repellent [rɪ'pɛlənt] ADJ repugnante ■ N: **insect ~** repelente *m* de insetos

repent [rɪ'pɛnt] vi: **to ~ (of)** arrepender-se (de)
repentance [rɪ'pɛntəns] N arrependimento
repercussions [riːpə'kʌʃənz] NPL repercussões
fpl; **to have ~** repercutir
repertoire ['rɛpətwaː'] N repertório
repertory ['rɛpətərɪ] N (*also*: **repertory theatre**)
teatro de repertório; **repertory company** N
companhia teatral
repetition [rɛpɪ'tɪʃən] N repetição *f*
repetitious [rɛpɪ'tɪʃəs] ADJ (*speech*) repetitivo
repetitive [rɪ'pɛtɪtɪv] ADJ repetitivo
replace [rɪ'pleɪs] vt (*put back*) repor, devolver;
(*take the place of*) substituir; (*Tel*): **"~ the
receiver"** "desligue"
replacement [rɪ'pleɪsmənt] N (*substitution*)
substituição *f*; (*putting back*) reposição *f*;
(*substitute*) substituto(-a); **replacement part** N
peça sobressalente
replay [riː'pleɪ] N (*of match*) partida decisiva; (*TV*:
also: **action replay**) replay *m*
replenish [rɪ'plɛnɪʃ] vt (*glass*) reencher; (*stock etc*)
completar, prover; (*with fuel*) reabastecer
replete [rɪ'pliːt] ADJ repleto; (*well-fed*) cheio,
empanturrado
replica ['rɛplɪkə] N réplica, cópia, reprodução *f*
reply [rɪ'plaɪ] N resposta ■ vi responder; **in ~
(to)** em resposta (a); **there's no ~** (*Tel*) ninguém
atende; **reply coupon** N cartão-resposta *m*
report [rɪ'pɔːt] N relatório; (*Press etc*) reportagem
f; (*Brit*: *also*: **school report**) boletim *m* escolar;
(*of gun*) estampido, detonação *f* ■ vt informar
sobre; (*Press etc*) fazer uma reportagem sobre;
(*bring to notice*: *occurrence*) comunicar, anunciar;
(: *person*) denunciar ■ vi (*make a report*): **to ~ (on)**
apresentar um relatório (sobre); (*for newspaper*)
fazer uma reportagem (sobre); (*present o.s.*): **to ~
(to sb)** apresentar-se (a alguém); (*be responsible
to*): **to ~ to sb** obedecer as ordens de alguém; **it
is ~ed that** dizem que; **it is ~ed from Berlin
that** há notícias de Berlim de que; **report card**
(*US, Scottish*) N boletim *m* escolar
reportedly [rɪ'pɔːtɪdlɪ] ADV: **she is ~ living in
Spain** dizem que ela mora na Espanha
reported speech [rɪ'pɔːtɪd-] N (*Ling*) discurso
indireto
reporter [rɪ'pɔːtə'] N (*Press*) jornalista *m/f*,
repórter *m/f*; (*Radio, TV*) repórter
repose [rɪ'pəuz] N: **in ~** em repouso
repossess [riːpə'zɛs] vt retomar
reprehensible [rɛprɪ'hɛnsɪbl] ADJ repreensível,
censurável, condenável
represent [rɛprɪ'zɛnt] vt representar;
(*constitute*) constituir; (*Comm*) ser representante
de; (*describe*): **to ~ sth as** representar algo como;
(*explain*): **to ~ to sb that** explicar a alguém que
representation [rɛprɪzɛn'teɪʃən] N
representação *f*; (*picture, statue*) representação,
retrato; (*petition*) petição *f*; **representations**
NPL (*protest*) reclamação *f*, protesto
representative [rɛprɪ'zɛntətɪv] N
representante *m/f*; (*US: Pol*) deputado(-a) ■ ADJ:
~ (of) representativo (de)

repress [rɪ'prɛs] vt reprimir
repression [rɪ'prɛʃən] N repressão *f*
repressive [rɪ'prɛsɪv] ADJ repressivo
reprieve [rɪ'priːv] N (*Law*) suspensão *f*
temporária; (*fig*) adiamento ■ vt suspender
temporariamente; aliviar
reprimand ['rɛprɪmɑːnd] N reprimenda ■ vt
repreender, censurar
reprint [*n* 'riːprɪnt, *vt* riː'prɪnt] N reimpressão *f*
■ vt reimprimir
reprisal [rɪ'praɪzl] N represália; **reprisals** NPL
(*acts of revenge*) represálias *fpl*; **to take ~s** fazer *or*
exercer represálias
reproach [rɪ'prəutʃ] N repreensão *f*, censura
■ vt: **to ~ sb with sth** repreender alguém por
algo; **beyond ~** irrepreensível, impecável
reproachful [rɪ'prəutʃful] ADJ repreensivo,
acusatório
reproduce [riːprə'djuːs] vt reproduzir ■ vi
reproduzir-se
reproduction [riːprə'dʌkʃən] N reprodução *f*
reproductive [riːprə'dʌktɪv] ADJ reprodutivo
reproof [rɪ'pruːf] N reprovação *f*, repreensão *f*
reprove [rɪ'pruːv] vt (*action*) reprovar; **to ~ sb
for sth** repreender alguém por algo
reproving [rɪ'pruːvɪŋ] ADJ (*look*) de reprovação;
(*tone*) de censura
reptile ['rɛptaɪl] N réptil *m*
Repub. (*US*) ABBR (*Pol*) = **republican**
republic [rɪ'pʌblɪk] N república
republican [rɪ'pʌblɪkən] ADJ, N republicano(-a);
(*US: Pol*): **R~** membro(-a) do Partido
Republicano
repudiate [rɪ'pjuːdɪeɪt] vt (*accusation*)
rejeitar, negar; (*violence*) repudiar; (*obligation*)
desconhecer
repugnant [rɪ'pʌgnənt] ADJ repugnante,
repulsivo
repulse [rɪ'pʌls] vt repelir
repulsion [rɪ'pʌlʃən] N repulsa; (*Phys*) repulsão *f*
repulsive [rɪ'pʌlsɪv] ADJ repulsivo
reputable ['rɛpjutəbl] ADJ (*make etc*) bem
conceituado, de confiança; (*person*) honrado,
respeitável
reputation [rɛpju'teɪʃən] N reputação *f*; **to have
a ~ for** ter fama por; **he has a ~ for being cruel**
ele tem fama de ser cruel
repute [rɪ'pjuːt] N reputação *f*, renome *m*
reputed [rɪ'pjuːtɪd] ADJ suposto, pretenso; **he is
~ to be rich** dizem que ele é rico
reputedly [rɪ'pjuːtɪdlɪ] ADV segundo se diz,
supostamente
request [rɪ'kwɛst] N pedido; (*formal*) petição *f*
■ vt: **to ~ sth of *or* from sb** pedir algo a alguém;
(*formally*) solicitar algo a alguém; **on ~** a pedido;
at the ~ of a pedido de; **"you are ~ed not to
smoke"** "pede-se *or* favor não fumar"; **request
stop** (*Brit*) N (*for bus*) parada não obrigatória
requiem ['rɛkwɪəm] N réquiem *m*
require [rɪ'kwaɪə'] N (*need*: *subj*: *person*) precisar
de, necessitar; (: *thing, situation*) requerer, exigir;
(*want*) pedir; (*order*): **to ~ sb to do sth/sth of sb**

exigir que alguém faça algo/algo de alguém; **if ~d** se for necessário; **what qualifications are ~d?** quais são as qualificações necessárias?; **~d by law** exigido por lei

required [rɪ'kwaɪəd] ADJ (*necessary*) necessário; (*desired*) desejado

requirement [rɪ'kwaɪəmənt] N requisito; (*need*) necessidade *f*; (*want*) pedido

requisite ['rɛkwɪzɪt] N requisito ■ ADJ necessário, indispensável; **toilet ~s** artigos de toalete pessoal

requisition [rɛkwɪ'zɪʃən] N:~ **(for)** requerimento (para) ■ VT (*Mil*) requisitar, confiscar

reroute [riː'ruːt] VT (*train etc*) desviar

resale ['riːseɪl] N revenda; **resale price maintenance** N manutenção *f* de preços de revenda

rescind [rɪ'sɪnd] VT (*contract*) rescindir; (*law*) revogar; (*verdict*) anular

rescue ['rɛskjuː] N salvamento, resgate *m* ■ VT: **to ~ (from)** (*survivors, wounded etc*) resgatar (de); (*save, fig*) salvar (de); **to come to sb's ~** ir ao socorro de alguém; **rescue party** N grupo *or* expedição *f* de resgate

rescuer ['rɛskjuəʳ] N (*in disaster etc*) resgatador(a) *m/f*; (*fig*) salvador(a) *m/f*

research [rɪ'səːtʃ] N pesquisa ■ VT pesquisar ■ VI: **to ~ (into sth)** pesquisar (algo), fazer pesquisas (sobre algo); **a piece of ~** uma pesquisa; **~ and development** pesquisa e desenvolvimento

researcher [rɪ'səːtʃəʳ] N pesquisador(a) *m/f*

research work N trabalho de pesquisa

resell [riː'sɛl] (*irreg*) VT revender

resemblance [rɪ'zɛmbləns] N semelhança; **to bear a strong ~ to** ser muito parecido com

resemble [rɪ'zɛmbl] VT parecer-se com

resent [rɪ'zɛnt] VT (*attitude*) ressentir-se de; (*person*) estar ressentido com

resentful [rɪ'zɛntful] ADJ ressentido

resentment [rɪ'zɛntmənt] N ressentimento

reservation [rɛzə'veɪʃən] N (*booking, doubt, protected area*) reserva; (*Brit: Aut: also:* **central reservation**) canteiro divisor; **to make a ~** fazer reserva; **with ~s** (*doubts*) com reservas; **reservation desk** (*US*) N (*in hotel*) recepção *f*

reserve [rɪ'zəːv] N reserva; (*Sport*) suplente *m/f*, reserva *m/f* (BR) ■ VT reservar; **reserves** NPL (*Mil*) (tropas *fpl* da) reserva; (*Comm*) reserva; **in ~** de reserva; **reserve currency** N moeda de reserva

reserved [rɪ'zəːvd] ADJ reservado

reserve price (*Brit*) N preço mínimo de venda

reserve team (*Brit*) N time *m* reserva

reservist [rɪ'zəːvɪst] N reservista *m*

reservoir ['rɛzəvwɑːʳ] N (*large*) represa; (*small*) depósito

reset [riː'sɛt] (*irreg*) VT reajustar; (*Comput*) dar reset em, restabelecer

reshape [riː'ʃeɪp] VT (*policy*) reformar, remodelar

reshuffle [riː'ʃʌfl] N: **Cabinet ~** reforma

ministerial

reside [rɪ'zaɪd] VI residir

residence ['rɛzɪdəns] N residência; (*formal: home*) domicílio; **to take up ~** instalar-se; **in ~** (*monarch*) em residência; (*doctor*) residente; **residence permit** (*Brit*) N autorização *f* de residência

resident ['rɛzɪdənt] N (*of country, town*) habitante *m/f*; (*of house, area*) morador(a) *m/f*; (*in hotel*) hóspede *m/f* ■ ADJ (*population*) permanente; (*doctor*) interno, residente

residential [rɛzɪ'dɛnʃəl] ADJ residencial

residue ['rɛzɪdjuː] N resto; (*Comm*) montante *m* líquido; (*Chem, Phys*) resíduo

resign [rɪ'zaɪn] VT (*one's post*) renunciar a, demitir-se de ■ VI: **to ~ (from)** demitir-se (de); **to ~ o.s. to** (*endure*) resignar-se a

resignation [rɛzɪg'neɪʃən] N demissão *f*; (*state of mind*) resignação *f*; **to tender one's ~** pedir demissão

resigned [rɪ'zaɪnd] ADJ resignado

resilience [rɪ'zɪlɪəns] N (*of material*) elasticidade *f*; (*of person*) resistência

resilient [rɪ'zɪlɪənt] ADJ (*person*) forte; (*material*) resistente

resin ['rɛzɪn] N resina

resist [rɪ'zɪst] VT resistir a

resistance [rɪ'zɪstəns] N resistência

resistant [rɪ'zɪstənt] ADJ: ~ **(to)** resistente (a)

resold [riː'səuld] PT, PP *of* **resell**

resolute ['rɛzəluːt] ADJ resoluto, firme; (*refusal*) firme

resolution [rɛzə'luːʃən] N resolução *f*; (*of problem*) solução *f*; **to make a ~** tomar uma resolução

resolve [rɪ'zɔlv] N resolução *f*; (*purpose*) intenção *f* ■ VT resolver ■ VI: **to ~ to do** resolver-se a fazer

resolved [rɪ'zɔlvd] ADJ decidido

resonance ['rɛzənəns] N ressonância

resonant ['rɛzənənt] ADJ ressonante

resort [rɪ'zɔːt] N (*town*) local *m* turístico, estação *f* de veraneio; (*recourse*) recurso ■ VI: **to ~ to** recorrer a; **seaside/winter sports ~** balneário/ estação de inverno; **in the last ~** em último caso, em última instância

resound [rɪ'zaund] VI ressoar; **the room ~ed with shouts** os gritos ressoaram no quarto

resounding [rɪ'zaundɪŋ] ADJ retumbante

resource [rɪ'sɔːs] N (*raw material*) recurso naturel; **resources** NPL (*coal, money, energy*) recursos *mpl*; **natural ~s** recursos naturais

resourceful [rɪ'sɔːsful] ADJ engenhoso, habilidoso

resourcefulness [rɪ'sɔːsfəlnɪs] N desembaraço, engenho

respect [rɪs'pɛkt] N respeito ■ VT respeitar; **respects** NPL (*greetings*) cumprimentos *mpl*; **to pay one's ~s to sb** fazer visita de cortesia a alguém; **to pay one's last ~s to sb** prestar a última homenagem a alguém; **to have** *or* **show ~ for sb/sth** ter *or* mostrar respeito por alguém/ algo; **out of ~ for** por respeito a; **with ~ to** com respeito a; **in ~ of** a respeito de; **in this** ~ neste respeito; **in some ~s** em alguns pontos; **with all due ~, I ...** com todo respeito, eu ...

respectability [rɪspɛktə'bɪlɪtɪ] N respeitabilidade f

respectable [rɪs'pɛktəbl] ADJ respeitável; (large) considerável; (quite good: result, player) razoável

respectful [rɪs'pɛktful] ADJ respeitoso

respective [rɪs'pɛktɪv] ADJ respectivo

respectively [rɪs'pɛktɪvlɪ] ADV respectivamente

respiration [rɛspɪ'reɪʃən] N respiração f

respiratory [rɛs'pɪrətərɪ] ADJ respiratório

respite ['rɛspaɪt] N pausa, folga; (Law) adiamento, suspensão f

resplendent [rɪs'plɛndənt] ADJ resplandecente

respond [rɪs'pɔnd] VI (answer) responder; (react) reagir

respondent [rɪs'pɔndənt] N (in survey) respondedor(a) m/f; (Law) réu(-ré) m/f

response [rɪs'pɔns] N (answer) resposta; (reaction) reação f; **in ~ to** em resposta a

responsibility [rɪspɔnsɪ'bɪlɪtɪ] N responsabilidade f; (duty) dever m; **to take ~ for sth/sb** assumir a responsabilidade por algo/ alguém

responsible [rɪs'pɔnsɪbl] ADJ (character) sério, responsável; (job) de responsabilidade; (liable): ~ **(for)** responsável (por); **to be ~ to sb (for sth)** ser responsável diante de alguém (por algo); **to hold sb ~ (for sth)** responsabilizar alguém (por algo)

responsibly [rɪs'pɔnsɪblɪ] ADV com responsabilidade

responsive [rɪs'pɔnsɪv] ADJ receptivo

rest [rɛst] N descanso, repouso; (pause) pausa, intervalo; (support) apoio; (remainder) resto; (Mus) pausa ▪ VI descansar; (stop) parar; (be supported): **to ~ on** apoiar-se em ▪ VT descansar; (lean): **to ~ sth on/against** apoiar algo em or sobre/contra; **the ~ of them** os outros; **to set sb's mind at ~** tranqüilizar alguém; **it ~s with him to do it** cabe a ele fazê-lo; ~ **assured that ...** tenha certeza de que ...

restart [ri:'stɑ:t] VT (engine) arrancar de novo; (work) reiniciar, recomeçar

restaurant ['rɛstərɔŋ] N restaurante m; **restaurant car** (Brit) N vagão-restaurante m

rest cure N repouso forçado (para tratamento de saúde)

restful ['rɛstful] ADJ tranqüilo, repousante

rest home N asilo, casa de repouso

restitution [rɛstɪ'tjuːʃən] N: **to make ~ to sb for sth** indenizar alguém por algo

restive ['rɛstɪv] ADJ inquieto, impaciente; (horse) rebelão(-ona), teimoso

restless ['rɛstlɪs] ADJ desassossegado, irrequieto; **to get ~** impacientar-se

restlessly ['rɛstlɪslɪ] ADV inquietamente

restock [ri:'stɔk] VT reabastecer

restoration [rɛstə'reɪʃən] N restauração f

restorative [rɪ'stɔrətɪv] ADJ reconstituinte ▪ N reconstituinte m

restore [rɪ'stɔːʳ] VT (building, order) restaurar; (sth stolen) restituir; (peace, health) restabelecer

restorer [rɪ'stɔːrəʳ] N (Art etc) restaurador(a) m/f

restrain [rɪs'treɪn] VT (feeling) reprimir; (growth, inflation) refrear; (person): **to ~ (from doing)** impedir (de fazer)

restrained [rɪs'treɪnd] ADJ (style) moderado, comedido; (person) comedido

restraint [rɪs'treɪnt] N (restriction) restrição f; (moderation) moderação f, comedimento; (of style) sobriedade f; **wage ~** restrição salarial

restrict [rɪs'trɪkt] VT restringir, limitar; (people, animals) confinar; (activities) limitar

restricted area [rɪ'strɪktɪd-] N (Aut) zona com limite de velocidade

restriction [rɪs'trɪkʃən] N restrição f, limitação f; ~ **(on)** restrição (em)

restrictive [rɪs'trɪktɪv] ADJ restritivo; **restrictive practices** NPL (Industry) práticas fpl restritivas

rest room (US) N banheiro (BR), lavabo (PT)

restructure [ri:'strʌktʃəʳ] VT reestruturar

result [rɪ'zʌlt] N resultado ▪ VI: **to ~ (from)** resultar (de); **to ~ in** resultar em; **as a ~ of** como resultado or conseqüência de

resultant [rɪ'zʌltənt] ADJ resultante

resume [rɪ'zjuːm] VT (work, journey) retomar, recomeçar; (sum up) resumir ▪ VI recomeçar

résumé ['reɪzjuːmeɪ] N (summary) resumo; (US: curriculum vitae) curriculum vitae m, currículo

resumption [rɪ'zʌmpʃən] N retomada

resurgence [rɪ'səːdʒəns] N ressurgimento

resurrection [rɛzə'rɛkʃən] N ressurreição f

resuscitate [rɪ'sʌsɪteɪt] VT (Med) ressuscitar, reanimar

resuscitation [rɪsʌsɪ'teɪʃən] N ressuscitação f

retail ['riːteɪl] N varejo (BR), venda a retalho (PT) ▪ ADJ a varejo (BR), a retalho (PT) ▪ ADV a varejo (BR), a retalho (PT) ▪ VT vender no varejo (BR) or a retalho (PT) ▪ VI: **to ~ at $10** ser vendido no varejo (BR) or a retalho (PT) por $10

retailer ['riːteɪləʳ] N varejista m/f (BR), retalhista m/f (PT)

retail outlet N ponto de venda

retail price N preço no varejo (BR) or de venda a retalho (PT)

retail price index N ≈ índice m de preços ao consumidor

retain [rɪ'teɪn] VT (keep) reter, conservar; (employ) contratar

retainer [rɪ'teɪnəʳ] N (servant) empregado; (fee) adiantamento

retaliate [rɪ'tælɪeɪt] VI: **to ~ (against)** revidar (contra)

retaliation [rɪtælɪ'eɪʃən] N represálias fpl, vingança; **in ~ for** em retaliação por

retaliatory [rɪ'tælɪətərɪ] ADJ retaliativo, retaliatório

retarded [rɪ'tɑːdɪd] ADJ retardado

retch [rɛtʃ] VI fazer esforço para vomitar

retentive [rɪ'tɛntɪv] ADJ (memory) tenaz, de anjo

rethink ['riː'θɪŋk] (irreg) VT reconsiderar,

repensar

reticence ['rɛtɪsns] N reserva
reticent ['rɛtɪsnt] ADJ reservado
retina ['rɛtɪnə] N retina
retinue ['rɛtɪnjuː] N séquito, comitiva
retire [rɪ'taɪə^r] VI (give up work) aposentar-se; (withdraw) retirar-se; (go to bed) deitar-se
retired [rɪ'taɪəd] ADJ (person) aposentado (BR), reformado (PT)
retirement [rɪ'taɪəmənt] N (state, act) aposentadoria (BR), reforma (PT); **retirement age** N idade f de aposentadoria (BR) or de reforma (PT)
retiring [rɪ'taɪərɪŋ] ADJ (leaving) de saída; (shy) acanhado, retraído
retort [rɪ'tɔːt] N (reply) réplica; (container) retorta ■ VI replicar, retrucar
retrace [riː'treɪs] VT: **to ~ one's steps** voltar sobre (os) seus passos, refazer o mesmo caminho
retract [rɪ'trækt] VT (statement, offer) retirar, retratar; (claws) encolher; (undercarriage, aerial) recolher ■ VI retratar-se
retractable [rɪ'træktəbl] ADJ retrátil
retrain [riː'treɪn] VT reciclar ■ VI ser reciclado
retraining [riː'treɪnɪŋ] N readaptação f profissional, reciclagem f
retread [n 'riːtrɛd, vt riː'trɛd] N (tyre) pneu m recauchutado ■ VT recauchutar
retreat [rɪ'triːt] N (place) retiro; (act) retirada ■ VI retirar-se; (flood) retroceder; **to beat a hasty ~** bater em retirada
retrial [riː'traɪəl] N revisão f do processo
retribution [rɛtrɪ'bjuːʃən] N desforra, revide m, vingança
retrieval [rɪ'triːvəl] N recuperação f
retrieve [rɪ'triːv] VT (sth lost) reaver, recuperar; (situation, honour) salvar; (error, loss) reparar; (Comput) recuperar
retriever [rɪ'triːvə^r] N cão m de busca, perdigueiro
retroactive [rɛtrəu'æktɪv] ADJ retroativo
retrograde ['rɛtrəgreɪd] ADJ retrógrado
retrospect ['rɛtrəspɛkt] N: **in ~** retrospectivamente, em retrospecto
retrospective [rɛtrə'spɛktɪv] ADJ retrospectivo; (law) retroativo ■ N (Art) retrospectiva
return [rɪ'tɜːn] N (going or coming back) regresso, volta; (of sth stolen etc) devolução f; (recompense) recompensa; (Finance: from land, shares) rendimento; (report) relatório ■ CPD (journey) de volta; (Brit: ticket) de ida e volta; (match) de revanche ■ VI (person etc: come or go back) voltar, regressar; (symptoms etc) voltar; (regain): **to ~ to** (consciousness) recobrar; (power) retornar a ■ VT devolver; (favour, love etc) retribuir; (verdict) proferir, anunciar; (Pol: candidate) eleger; **returns** NPL (Comm) receita; (: returned goods) mercadorias fpl devolvidas; **in ~ (for)** em troca (de); **many happy ~s (of the day)!** parabéns!; **by ~ (of post)** por volta do correio
returnable [rɪ'tɜːnəbl] ADJ (bottle etc) restituível

return key N (Comput) tecla de retorno
reunion [riː'juːnɪən] N (family) reunião f; (two people, class) reencontro
reunite [riːjuː'naɪt] VT reunir; (reconcile) reconciliar
rev [rɛv] N ABBR (Aut: = revolution) revolução f ■ VT (also: **rev up**) aumentar a velocidade de ■ VI acelerar
revaluation [riːvæljuˈeɪʃən] N reavaliação f
revamp ['riːvæmp] VT dar um jeito em
rev counter (Brit) N tacômetro
Rev(d). ABBR = **reverend**
reveal [rɪ'viːl] VT revelar; (make visible) mostrar
revealing [rɪ'viːlɪŋ] ADJ revelador(a)
reveille [rɪ'vælɪ] N (Mil) toque m de alvorada
revel ['rɛvl] VI: **to ~ in sth/in doing sth** deleitar-se com algo/em fazer algo
revelation [rɛvəˈleɪʃən] N revelação f
reveller ['rɛvələ^r] N farrista m/f, folião(-liã) m/f
revelry ['rɛvəlrɪ] N festança, folia
revenge [rɪ'vɛndʒ] N vingança, desforra; (in sport) revanche f ■ VT vingar; **to take ~ on** vingar-se de
revengeful [rɪ'vɛndʒful] ADJ vingativo
revenue ['rɛvənjuː] N receita, renda; (on investment) rendimento
reverberate [rɪ'vəːbəreɪt] VI (sound) ressoar, repercutir, ecoar; (light) reverberar; (fig) repercutir
reverberation [rɪvəːbəˈreɪʃən] N repercussão f
revere [rɪ'vɪə^r] VT reverenciar, venerar
reverence ['rɛvərəns] N reverência
reverend ['rɛvərənd] ADJ reverendo; (in titles): **the R~ John Smith** o reverendo John Smith
reverent ['rɛvərənt] ADJ reverente
reverie ['rɛvərɪ] N devaneio, sonho
reversal [rɪ'vəːsl] N (of order) reversão f; (of direction) mudança em sentido contrário; (of decision) revogação f; (of opinion) reviravolta; (of roles) inversão f
reverse [rɪ'vəːs] N (opposite) contrário; (back: of cloth) avesso; (: of coin) reverso; (: of paper) dorso; (Aut: also: **reverse gear**) marcha a ré (BR), marcha atrás (PT); (setback) revés m, derrota ■ ADJ (order) inverso, oposto; (direction) contrário; (process) inverso ■ VT (turn over) virar do lado do avesso; (direction, roles) inverter; (position) mudar; (process, decision) revogar; (car) dar marcha-ré em ■ VI (Brit: Aut) dar (marcha à) ré (BR), fazer marcha atrás (PT); **to go into ~** dar ré (BR), fazer marcha atrás (PT); **in ~ order** na ordem inversa; **reverse-charge call** (Brit) N (Tel) ligação f a cobrar; **reverse video** N vídeo reverso
reversible [rɪ'vəːsəbl] ADJ reversível
reversing lights [rɪ'vəːsɪŋ-] (Brit) NPL luzes fpl de ré (BR), luzes fpl de marcha atrás (PT)
reversion [rɪ'vəːʃən] N volta
revert [rɪ'vəːt] VI: **to ~ to** voltar a; (Law) reverter a
review [rɪ'vjuː] N (magazine, Mil) revista; (of book, film) crítica, resenha; (examination) recapitulação f, exame m ■ VT (situation) rever,

examinar; (Mil) passar em revista; (book, film)
fazer a crítica or resenha de; **to come under ~**
ser estudado

reviewer [rɪ'vju:əʳ] N crítico(-a)

revile [rɪ'vaɪl] VT insultar

revise [rɪ'vaɪz] VT (manuscript) corrigir; (opinion,
procedure) alterar; (price) revisar; (study: subject)
recapitular; (look over) revisar, rever; **~d edition**
edição f revista

revision [rɪ'vɪʒən] N correção f; (for exam) revisão
f; (revised version) revisão f

revitalize [ri:'vaɪtəlaɪz] VT revitalizar,
revivificar

revival [rɪ'vaɪvəl] N (recovery) restabelecimento;
(of interest) renascença, renascimento; (Theatre)
reestréia; (of faith) despertar m

revive [rɪ'vaɪv] VT (person) reanimar, ressuscitar;
(economy) recuperar; (custom) restabelecer,
restaurar; (hope, courage) despertar; (play)
reapresentar ■ VI (person: from faint) voltar
a si, recuperar os sentidos; (: from ill-health)
recuperar-se; (activity, economy) reativar; (hope,
interest) renascer

revoke [rɪ'vəuk] VT revogar; (decision, promise)
voltar atrás com

revolt [rɪ'vəult] N revolta, rebelião f, insurreição
f ■ VI revoltar-se ■ VT causar aversão a,
repugnar

revolting [rɪ'vəultɪŋ] ADJ revoltante, repulsivo

revolution [rɛvə'lu:ʃən] N revolução f; (of wheel,
earth) rotação f

revolutionary [rɛvə'lu:ʃənərɪ] ADJ, N
revolucionário(-a)

revolutionize [rɛvə'lu:ʃənaɪz] VT revolucionar

revolve [rɪ'vɔlv] VI girar; (life): **to ~ (a)round**
girar em torno de

revolver [rɪ'vɔlvəʳ] N revólver m

revolving [rɪ'vɔlvɪŋ] ADJ (chair etc) giratório;
revolving credit N crédito rotativo; **revolving
door** N porta giratória

revue [rɪ'vju:] N (Theatre) revista

revulsion [rɪ'vʌlʃən] N aversão f, repugnância

reward [rɪ'wɔ:d] N recompensa ■ VT: **to ~ (for)**
recompensar or premiar (por)

rewarding [rɪ'wɔ:dɪŋ] ADJ (fig) gratificante,
compensador(a)

rewind [ri:'waɪnd] (irreg) VT (watch) dar corda
em; (tape) voltar para trás

rewire [ri:'waɪəʳ] VT (house) renovar a instalação
elétrica de

reword [ri:'wɔ:d] VT reformular, exprimir em
outras palavras

rewound [ri:'waund] PT, PP of **rewind**

rewrite [ri:'raɪt] (irreg) VT reescrever, escrever
de novo

Reykjavik ['reɪkjəvi:k] N Reikjavik

RFD (US) ABBR (Post) = **rural free delivery**

Rh ABBR (= rhesus) Rh

rhapsody ['ræpsədɪ] N (Mus) rapsódia; (fig)
elocução f exagerada or empolada

rhesus factor ['ri:səs-] N (Med) fator m Rh

rhetoric ['rɛtərɪk] N retórica

rhetorical [rɪ'tɔrɪkl] ADJ retórico

rheumatic [ru:'mætɪk] ADJ reumático

rheumatism ['ru:mətɪzəm] N reumatismo

rheumatoid arthritis ['ru:mətɔɪd-] N artrite f
reumatóide

Rhine [raɪn] N: **the ~** o (rio) Reno

rhinestone ['raɪnstəun] N diamante m postiço

rhinoceros [raɪ'nɔsərəs] N rinoceronte m

Rhodes [rəudz] N (ilha de) Rodes

Rhodesia [rəu'di:ʒə] N Rodésia

Rhodesian [rəu'di:ʒən] ADJ, N rodésio(-a)

rhododendron [rəudə'dɛndrən] N rododendro

Rhone [rəun] N: **the ~** o (rio) Ródano

rhubarb ['ru:bɑ:b] N ruibarbo

rhyme [raɪm] N rima; (verse) verso(s) m(pl)
rimado(s), poesia ■ VI: **to ~ (with)** rimar (com);
without ~ or reason sem pé nem cabeça

rhythm ['rɪðm] N ritmo

rhythmic(al) ['rɪðmɪk(l)] ADJ rítmico, com
passado

rhythmically ['rɪðmɪklɪ] ADV ritmicamente

RI N ABBR (Brit) = **religious instruction** ■ ABBR
(US: Post) = **Rhode Island**

rib [rɪb] N (Anat) costela ■ VT (mock) zombar de,
encarnar em

ribald ['rɪbəld] ADJ vulgarmente engraçado,
irreverente

ribbed [rɪbd] ADJ (knitting) em ponto de meia

ribbon ['rɪbən] N fita; (strip) faixa, tira; **in ~s**
(torn) em tirinhas, esfarrapado

rice [raɪs] N arroz m; **rice field** N arrozal m; **rice
pudding** N arroz m doce

rich [rɪtʃ] ADJ rico; (clothes) valioso; (banquet)
suntuoso, opulento; (soil) fértil; (food) suculento,
forte; (: sweet) rico; (colour) intenso; (voice) suave,
cheio ■ NPL: **the rich** os ricos; **riches** NPL
(wealth) riquezas fpl; **to be ~ in sth** ser rico em
algo

richly ['rɪtʃlɪ] ADV (decorated) ricamente;
(rewarded) generosamente; (deserved) bem

richness ['rɪtʃnɪs] N riqueza, opulência; (of soil
etc) fertilidade f

rickets ['rɪkɪts] N raquitismo

rickety ['rɪkɪtɪ] ADJ fraco, sem firmeza

rickshaw ['rɪkʃɔ:] N jinriquixá m

ricochet ['rɪkəʃeɪ] N ricochete m ■ VI
ricochetear

rid [rɪd] (pt, pp rid) VT: **to ~ sb of sth** livrar
alguém de algo; **to get ~ of** livrar-se de; (sth no
longer required) desfazer-se de

riddance ['rɪdns] N: **good ~!** bons ventos o
levem!

ridden ['rɪdn] PP of **ride**

riddle ['rɪdl] N (conundrum) adivinhação f;
(mystery) enigma m, charada ■ VT: **to be ~d
with** estar cheio de

ride [raɪd] (pt rode, pp ridden) N (gen) passeio; (on
horse) passeio a cavalo; (distance covered) percurso,
trajeto ■ VI (as sport) montar; (go somewhere: on
horse, bicycle) ir (a cavalo, de bicicleta); (journey:
on bicycle, motorcycle, bus) viajar ■ VT (a horse)
montar a; (bicycle, motorcycle) andar de; (distance)

percorrer; **to ~ a bicycle** andar de bicicleta; **can you ~ a bike?** você sabe andar de bicicleta?; **to ~ at anchor** (*Naut*) estar ancorado; **horse/car ~** passeio a cavalo/de carro; **to go for a ~** dar um passeio *or* uma volta (de carro *or* de bicicleta *etc*); **to take sb for a ~** (*fig*) enganar alguém
▶ **ride out** VT: **to ~ out the storm** (*fig*) superar as dificuldades

rider ['raɪdəʳ] N (*on horse: male*) cavaleiro; (: *female*) amazona; (*on bicycle*) ciclista *m/f*; (*on motorcycle*) motociclista *m/f*; (*in document*) cláusula adicional

ridge [rɪdʒ] N (*of hill*) cume *m*, topo; (*of roof*) cumeeira; (*wrinkle*) ruga

ridicule ['rɪdɪkjuːl] N escárnio, zombaria, mofa ■ VT ridicularizar, zombar de; **to hold sb/sth up to ~** ridicularizar alguém/algo

ridiculous [rɪ'dɪkjuləs] ADJ ridículo

riding ['raɪdɪŋ] N equitação *f*; **riding school** N escola de equitação

rife [raɪf] ADJ: **to be ~** ser comum; **to be ~ with** estar repleto de, abundar em

riffraff ['rɪfræf] N plebe *f*, ralé *f*, povinho

rifle ['raɪfl] N rifle *m*, fuzil *m* ■ VT saquear
▶ **rifle through** VT FUS vasculhar

rifle range N campo de tiro; (*at fair*) tiro ao alvo

rift [rɪft] N (*in ground*) fenda, fratura; (*in clouds*) brecha; (*fig: disagreement: between friends*) desentendimento; (: *in party*) rompimento, divergência

rig [rɪg] N (*also*: **oil rig**) torre *f* de perfuração ■ VT (*election etc*) adulterar *or* falsificar os resultados de
▶ **rig out** (*Brit*) VT: **to ~ out as/in** ataviar *or* vestir como/com
▶ **rig up** VT instalar, montar, improvisar

rigging ['rɪgɪŋ] N (*Naut*) cordame *m*

right [raɪt] ADJ (*true, correct*) certo, correto; (*suitable*) adequado, conveniente; (: *decision*) certo; (*just*) justo; (*morally good*) bom; (*not left*) direito ■ N direito; (*not left*) direita ■ ADV (*correctly*) bem, corretamente; (*fairly*) adequadamente, justamente; (*not on the left*) à direita; (*to the right*) para a direita; (*exactly*): **~ now** agora mesmo ■ VT colocar em pé; (*correct*) corrigir, indireitar ■ EXCL bom!; **all ~!** tudo bem!, está bem!; (*enough*) chega!, basta!; **the ~ time** (*precise*) a hora exata; (*not wrong*) a hora certa; **to be ~** (*person*) ter razão; (: *in guess etc*) acertar; (*answer, clock*) estar certo; **to get sth ~** acertar em algo; **let's get it ~ this time!** vamos acertar desta vez; **you did the ~ thing** você fez a coisa certa; **to put a mistake ~** (*Brit*) consertar um erro; **~ before/after** logo antes/depois; **~ against the wall** rente à parede; **to go ~ to the end of sth** ir até o finalzinho de algo; **by ~s** por direito; **on the ~** à direita; **to be in the ~** ter razão; **~ away** imediatamente, logo, já; **~ in the middle** bem no meio; **film ~s** direitos de adaptação para o cinema; **right angle** N ângulo reto

righteous ['raɪtʃəs] ADJ justo, honrado; (*anger*)

justificado

righteousness ['raɪtʃəsnɪs] N justiça

rightful ['raɪtful] ADJ (*heir*) legítimo; (*place*) justo, legítimo

rightfully ['raɪtfəlɪ] ADV legitimamente

right-hand ADJ à direita

right-handed [-'hændɪd] ADJ (*person*) destro

right-hand man N braço direito

right-hand side N lado direito

rightly ['raɪtlɪ] ADV corretamente, devidamente; (*with reason*) com razão; **if I remember ~** (*Brit*) se me lembro bem, se não me engano

right-minded ADJ sensato, ajuizado

right of way N prioridade *f* de passagem; (*Aut*) preferência

rights issue N (*Stock Exchange*) emissão *f* de bônus de subscrição

right wing N (*Pol*) direita; (*Sport*) ponta direita; (*Mil*) ala direita ■ ADJ: **right-wing** de direita

right-winger N (*Pol*) direitista *m/f*; (*Sport*) ponta-direita *m*

rigid ['rɪdʒɪd] ADJ rígido; (*principle*) inflexível

rigidity [rɪ'dʒɪdɪtɪ] N rigidez *f*, inflexibilidade *f*

rigidly ['rɪdʒɪdlɪ] ADV rigidamente; (*behave*) inflexivelmente

rigmarole ['rɪgmərəul] N (*process*) processo; (*story*) ladainha

rigor ['rɪgəʳ] (*US*) N = **rigour; rigor mortis** [-'mɔːtɪs] N rigidez *f* cadavérica

rigorous ['rɪgərəs] ADJ rigoroso

rigorously ['rɪgərəslɪ] ADV rigorosamente

rigour ['rɪgəʳ] (*US* **rigor**) N rigor *m*

rig-out (*Brit*: *inf*) N roupa, traje *m*

rile [raɪl] VT irritar, aborrecer

rim [rɪm] N borda, beira; (*of spectacles, wheel*) aro

rimless ['rɪmlɪs] ADJ (*spectacles*) sem aro

rind [raɪnd] N (*of bacon*) pele *f*; (*of lemon etc*) casca; (*of cheese*) crosta, casca

ring [rɪŋ] (*pt* **rang**, *pp* **rung**) N (*of metal*) aro; (*on finger*) anel *m*; (*also*: **wedding ring**) aliança; (*of people, objects*) círculo, grupo; (*of spies etc*) grupo; (*for boxing*) ringue *m*; (*of circus*) pista, picadeiro; (*bullring*) picadeiro, arena; (*of light, smoke*) círculo; (*sound: of small bell*) toque *m*; (: *of large bell*) badalada, repique *m*; (*telephone call*) chamada (telefônica), ligada ■ VI (*on telephone*) telefonar; (*bell*) tocar; (*also*: **ring out**: *voice, words*) soar; (*ears*) zumbir ■ VT (*Brit*: *Tel*) telefonar a, ligar para; (*bell etc*) badalar; (*doorbell*) tocar; **to give sb a ~** (*Brit*: *Tel*) dar uma ligada *or* ligar para alguém; **that has the ~ of truth about it** isso tem jeito de ser verdade; **the name doesn't ~ a bell (with me)** o nome não me diz nada
▶ **ring back** (*Brit*) VI (*Tel*) telefonar *or* ligar de volta ■ VT telefonar *or* ligar de volta para
▶ **ring off** (*Brit*) VI (*Tel*) desligar
▶ **ring up** (*Brit*) VT (*Tel*) telefonar a, ligar para

ring binder N fichário (*pasta*)

ring finger N dedo anelar

ringing ['rɪŋɪŋ] N (*of telephone*) toque *m*; (*of large bell*) repicar *m*; (*of doorbell*) tocar *m*; (*in ears*) zumbido; **ringing tone** (*Brit*) N (*Tel*) sinal *m* de chamada

ringleader ['rɪŋliːdəʳ] N (of gang) cabeça m/f, cérebro

ringlets ['rɪŋlɪts] NPL caracóis mpl, anéis mpl

ring road (Brit) N estrada periférica or perimetral

ringtone (Brit) N (on cellphone) toque m (de cellular)

rink [rɪŋk] N (also: **ice rink**) pista de patinação, rinque m; (for roller skating) rinque

rinse [rɪns] N enxaguada ■ VT enxaguar; (also: **rinse out**: mouth) bochechar

Rio (de Janeiro) ['riːəu(dədʒə'nɪərəu)] N o Rio (de Janeiro)

riot ['raɪət] N distúrbio, motim m, desordem f; (of colour) festival m, profusão f ■ VI provocar distúrbios, amotinar-se; **to run ~** desenfrear-se

rioter ['raɪətəʳ] N desordeiro(-a), amotinador(a) m/f

riotous ['raɪətəs] ADJ (crowd) desordeiro; (behaviour) turbulento; (party) tumultuado, barulhento; (uncontrolled) desenfreado

riotously ['raɪətəslɪ] ADV: **~ funny** hilariante

riot police N polícia anti-motim

RIP ABBR (= rest in peace) RIP

rip [rɪp] N rasgão m; (opening) abertura ■ VT rasgar ■ VI rasgar-se
  ▶ **rip up** VT rasgar

ripcord ['rɪpkɔːd] N corda de abertura (de pára-quedas)

ripe [raɪp] ADJ maduro; (ready) pronto

ripen ['raɪpən] VT, VI amadurecer

ripeness ['raɪpnɪs] N maturidade f, amadurecimento

rip-off (inf) N: **this is a ~** isso é roubo

riposte [rɪ'pɔst] N riposta

ripple ['rɪpl] N ondulação f, encrespação f; (of laughter etc) onda; (sound) murmúrio ■ VI encrespar-se ■ VT ondular

rise [raɪz] (pt **rose**, pp **risen**) N (slope) elevação f, ladeira; (hill) colina, rampa; (increase: in wages: Brit) aumento; (: in prices, temperature) subida; (fig: to power etc) ascensão f ■ VI (gen) levantar-se, erguer-se; (prices, waters) subir; (river) encher; (sun) nascer; (wind, person: from bed etc) levantar(-se); (sound, voice) aumentar, erguer-se; (also: **rise up**: building) erguer-se; (: rebel) sublevar-se; (in rank) ascender, subir; **to give ~ to** ocasionar, dar origem a; **to ~ to the occasion** mostrar-se à altura da situação

risen ['rɪzn] PP of **rise**

rising ['raɪzɪŋ] ADJ (increasing: prices) em alta; (: number) crescente, cada vez maior; (: unemployment) crescente; (tide) montante; (sun, moon) nascente ■ N (uprising) insurreição f; **rising damp** N umidade f que sobe

risk [rɪsk] N risco, perigo; (Insurance) risco ■ VT (endanger) pôr em risco; (chance) arriscar, aventurar; (dare) atrever-se a; **to take** or **run the ~ of doing** correr o risco de fazer; **at ~** em perigo; **at one's own ~** por sua própria conta e risco; **a fire/health/security ~** um risco de

incêndio/à saúde/à segurança; **I'll ~ it** eu vou me arriscar; **risk capital** N capital m de risco

risky ['rɪskɪ] ADJ perigoso

risqué ['riːskeɪ] ADJ (joke) picante

rissole ['rɪsəul] N rissole m

rite [raɪt] N rito; **funeral ~s** exéquias, cerimônia fúnebre; **last ~s** últimos sacramentos

ritual ['rɪtjuəl] ADJ ritual ■ N ritual m; (of initiation) rito

rival ['raɪvl] ADJ, N rival m/f; (in business) concorrente m/f ■ VT competir com; **to ~ sb/ sth in** rivalizar com alguém/algo em

rivalry ['raɪvlrɪ] N rivalidade f; (between companies) concorrência

river ['rɪvəʳ] N rio ■ CPD (port, traffic) fluvial; **up/ down ~** rio acima/abaixo

riverbank ['rɪvəbæŋk] N margem f (do rio)

riverbed ['rɪvəbed] N leito (do rio)

riverside ['rɪvəsaɪd] N beira, orla (do rio)

rivet ['rɪvɪt] N rebite m, cravo ■ VT rebitar; (fig) fixar

riveting ['rɪvɪtɪŋ] ADJ (fig) fascinante

Riviera [rɪvɪ'ɛərə] N: **the (French) ~** a Costa Azul (francesa), a Riviera francesa; **the Italian ~** a Riviera italiana

Riyadh [rɪ'jɑːd] N Riad

RN N ABBR (Brit) = **Royal Navy**; (US) = **registered nurse**

RNA N ABBR (= ribonucleic acid) ARN m

RNLI (Brit) N ABBR (= Royal National Lifeboat Institution) = Salvamar

RNZAF N ABBR = **Royal New Zealand Air Force**

RNZN N ABBR = **Royal New Zealand Navy**

road [rəud] N via; (motorway etc) estrada (de rodagem); (in town) rua; (fig) caminho ■ CPD rodoviário; **main ~** estrada principal; **major/ minor ~** via preferencial/secundária; **it takes four hours by ~** leva quatro horas de carro; **"~ up"** (Brit) "obras"; **road block** N barricada; **road haulage** N transportes mpl rodoviários; **road hog** N dono da estrada; **road map** N mapa m rodoviário; **road rage** N conduta agressiva dos motoristas no trânsito; **road safety** N segurança do trânsito

roadside ['rəudsaɪd] N beira da estrada ■ CPD à beira da estrada; **by the ~** à beira da estrada

road sign N placa de sinalização

road sweeper (Brit) N (person) gari m/f (BR), varredor(a) m/f (PT)

road transport N transportes mpl rodoviários

road user N usuário(-a) da via pública

roadway ['rəudweɪ] N pista, estrada

road works ['rəudwəːks] NPL obras fpl (na estrada)

roadworthy ['rəudwəːðɪ] ADJ (car) em bom estado de conservação e segurança

roam [rəum] VI vagar, perambular, errar ■ VT vagar or vadiar por

roar [rɔːʳ] N (of animal) rugido, urro; (of crowd) bramido; (of vehicle, storm) estrondo; (of laughter) barulho ■ VI rugir; (person, crowd) bradar; **to ~ with laughter** dar gargalhadas

roaring ['rɔ:rɪŋ] ADJ: **a ~ fire** labaredas; **a ~ success** um sucesso estrondoso; **to do a ~ trade** fazer um bom negócio

roast [rəust] N carne f assada, assado ◼ VT assar; (coffee) torrar; **roast beef** N rosbife m

rob [rɔb] VT roubar; (bank) assaltar; **to ~ sb of sth** roubar algo de alguém; (fig: deprive) despojar alguém de algo

robber ['rɔbəʳ] N ladrão/ladra m/f

robbery ['rɔbərɪ] N roubo

robe [rəub] N (for ceremony etc) toga, beca; (also: **bath robe**) roupão m (de banho) ◼ VT revestir

robin ['rɔbɪn] N pisco-de-peito-ruivo (BR), pintarroxo (PT)

robot ['rəubɔt] N robô m

robotics [rə'bɔtɪks] N robótica

robust [rəu'bʌst] ADJ robusto, forte; (appetite) sadio; (economy) forte

rock [rɔk] N rocha; (boulder) penhasco, rochedo; (US: small stone) cascalho; (Brit: sweet) pirulito ◼ VT (swing gently: cradle) balançar, oscilar; (: child) embalar, acalentar; (shake) sacudir ◼ VI (object) balançar-se; (person) embalar-se; (shake) sacudir-se; **on the ~s** (drink) com gelo; (marriage etc) arruinado, em dificuldades; **to ~ the boat** (fig) criar confusão; **rock and roll** N rock-and-roll m

rock-bottom ADJ (fig) mínimo, ínfimo ◼ N: **to hit** or **reach ~** (prices) chegar ao nível mais baixo; (person) chegar ao fundo do poço

rock climber N alpinista m/f

rock climbing N alpinismo

rockery ['rɔkərɪ] N jardim de plantas rasteiras entre pedras

rocket ['rɔkɪt] N foguete m ◼ VI (prices) disparar; **rocket launcher** [-'lɔ:ntʃəʳ] N dispositivo lança-foguetes

rock face N rochedo a pique

rock fall N queda de pedras

rocking chair ['rɔkɪŋ-] N cadeira de balanço

rocking horse ['rɔkɪŋ-] N cavalo de balanço

rocky ['rɔkɪ] ADJ rochoso; (unsteady: table) bambo, instável; (marriage, etc) instável

Rocky Mountains NPL: **the ~** as Montanhas Rochosas

rod [rɔd] N vara, varinha; (Tech) haste f; (also: **fishing rod**) vara de pescar

rode [rəud] PT of **ride**

rodent ['rəudnt] N roedor m

rodeo ['rəudɪəu] (US) N rodeio

roe [rəu] N (also: **roe deer**) corça, cerva; (of fish): **hard/soft ~** ova/esperma m de peixe

rogue [rəug] N velhaco, maroto

roguish ['rəugɪʃ] ADJ travesso, brincalhão(-lhona)

role [rəul] N papel m

roll [rəul] N rolo; (of banknotes) maço; (also: **bread roll**) pãozinho; (register) rol m, lista; (sound: of drums etc) rufar m; (movement: of ship) jogo ◼ VT rolar; (also: **roll up: string**) enrolar; (: sleeves) arregaçar; (cigarette) enrolar; (eyes) virar; (also: **roll out**: pastry) esticar; (lawn, road etc) aplanar

◼ VI rolar; (drum) rufar; (in walking) gingar; (vehicle) also; (roll along) rodar; (ship) balançar, jogar; **cheese ~** sanduíche de queijo (num pãozinho)

▶ **roll about** VI ficar rolando

▶ **roll around** VI = **roll about**

▶ **roll by** VI (time) passar

▶ **roll in** VI (mail, cash) chegar em grande quantidade

▶ **roll over** VI dar uma volta

▶ **roll up** VI (inf: arrive) pintar, chegar, aparecer ◼ VT (carpet etc) enrolar; (sleeves) arregaçar; **to ~ o.s. up into a ball** enrolar-se

roll call N chamada, toque m de chamada

rolled gold [rəuld-] N plaquê m

roller ['rəuləʳ] N (in machine) rolo, cilindro; (wheel) roda, roldana; (for lawn, road) rolo compressor; (for hair) rolo

Rollerblades® ['rəuləbleɪdz] N patins mpl em linha

roller blind (Brit) N estore m

roller coaster N montanha-russa

roller skates NPL patins mpl de roda

rollicking ['rɔlɪkɪŋ] ADJ alegre, brincalhão(-lhona), divertido

rolling ['rəulɪŋ] ADJ (landscape) ondulado; **rolling mill** N laminador m; **rolling pin** N rolo de pastel; **rolling stock** N (Rail) material m rodante

roll-on-roll-off (Brit) ADJ (ferry) para veículos

roly-poly ['rəulɪ'pəulɪ] (Brit) N (Culin) bolo de rolo

ROM [rɔm] N ABBR (Comput: = read-only memory) ROM m

Roman ['rəumən] ADJ, N romano(-a); **Roman Catholic** ADJ, N católico(-a) (romano(-a))

romance [rə'mæns] N (love affair) aventura amorosa, romance m; (book etc) história de amor; (charm) romantismo

Romania [ru:'meɪnɪə] N Romênia

Romanian [ru:'meɪnɪən] ADJ romeno ◼ N romeno(-a); (Ling) romeno

Roman numeral N número romano

romantic [rə'mæntɪk] ADJ romântico

romanticism [rə'mæntɪsɪzəm] N romantismo

Romany ['rəumənɪ] ADJ cigano ◼ N cigano(-a); (Ling) romani m

Rome [rəum] N Roma

romp [rɔmp] N brincadeira, travessura ◼ VI (also: **romp about**) brincar ruidosamente; **to ~ home** (horse) ganhar fácil

rompers ['rɔmpəz] NPL macacão m de bebê

rondo ['rɔndəu] N (Mus) rondó

roof [ru:f] N (of house) telhado; (of car) capota, teto; (of tunnel, cave) teto ◼ VT telhar, cobrir com telhas; **the ~ of the mouth** o céu da boca; **roof garden** N jardim m em terraço

roofing ['ru:fɪŋ] N cobertura

roof rack N (Aut) bagageiro

rook [ruk] N (bird) gralha; (Chess) torre f

room [ru:m] N (in house) quarto, aposento; (also: **bedroom**) quarto, dormitório; (in school etc) sala; (space) espaço, lugar m; (scope: for improvement) espaço; **rooms** NPL (lodging) alojamento; **"~s**

to let" (Brit), **"~s for rent"** (US) "alugam-se quartos or apartamentos"; **single ~** quarto individual; **double ~** quarto duplo or de casal or para duas pessoas; **is there ~ for this?** tem lugar para isto aqui?; **to make ~ for sb** dar lugar a alguém; **there is ~ for improvement** isso podia estar melhor

rooming house ['ruːmɪŋ-] (US) N casa de cômodos

roommate ['ruːmmeɪt] N companheiro(-a) de quarto

room service N serviço de quarto

room temperature N temperatura ambiente

roomy ['ruːmɪ] ADJ espaçoso; (garment) folgado

roost [ruːst] N poleiro ■ VI empoleirar-se, pernoitar

rooster ['ruːstər] N galo

root [ruːt] N raiz f; (fig: of problem, belief) origem f ■ VI (plant, belief) enraizar, arraigar; **roots** NPL (family origins) raízes fpl; **to take ~** (plant) enraizar; (idea) criar raízes

▸ **root about** VI (fig): **to ~ about in** (drawer) vasculhar; (house) esquadrinhar

▸ **root for** VT FUS torcer por

▸ **root out** VT extirpar

rope [rəup] N corda; (Naut) cabo ■ VT (tie) amarrar; (horse, cow) laçar; (climbers: also: **rope together**) amarrar or atar com uma corda; (area: also: **rope off**) isolar; **to know the ~s** (fig) estar por dentro (do assunto)

▸ **rope in** VT (fig): **to ~ sb in** persuadir alguém a tomar parte

rope ladder N escada de corda

rose [rəuz] PT of **rise** ■ N rosa; (also: **rosebush**) roseira; (on watering can) crivo ■ ADJ rosado, cor de rosa inv

rosé ['rəuzeɪ] N rosado, rosé m

rose bed N roseiral m

rosebud ['rəuzbʌd] N botão m de rosa

rosebush ['rəuzbuʃ] N roseira

rosemary ['rəuzmərɪ] N alecrim m

rosette [rəu'zɛt] N roseta

ROSPA ['rɔspə] (Brit) N ABBR = **Royal Society for the Prevention of Accidents**

roster ['rɔstər] N: **duty ~** lista de tarefas, escala de serviço

rostrum ['rɔstrəm] N tribuna

rosy ['rəuzɪ] ADJ rosado, rosáceo; (cheeks) rosado; (situation) cor-de-rosa inv; **a ~ future** um futuro promissor

rot [rɔt] N (decay) putrefação f, podridão f; (fig: pej) besteira ■ VT, VI apodrecer; **to stop the ~** (Brit: fig) acabar com a onda de fracassos; **dry ~** apodrecimento seco (de madeira); **wet ~** putrefação fungosa

rota ['rəutə] N lista de tarefas, escala de serviço; **on a ~ basis** em rodízio

rotary ['rəutərɪ] ADJ rotativo

rotate [rəu'teɪt] VT (revolve) fazer girar, dar voltas em; (change round: crops) alternar; (: jobs) alternar, revezar ■ VI (revolve) girar, dar voltas

rotating [rəu'teɪtɪŋ] ADJ (movement) rotativo

rotation [rəu'teɪʃən] N rotação f; **in ~** por turnos

rote [rəut] N: **by ~** de cor

rotor ['rəutər] N (also: **rotor blade**) rotor m

rotten ['rɔtn] ADJ (decayed) podre; (wood) carcomido; (fig) corrupto; (inf: bad) péssimo; **to feel ~** (ill) sentir-se podre

rotting ['rɔtɪŋ] ADJ podre

rotund [rəu'tʌnd] ADJ rotundo; (person) rechonchudo

rouble ['ruːbl] (US **ruble**) N rublo

rouge [ruːʒ] N rouge m, blush m, carmim m

rough [rʌf] ADJ (skin, surface) áspero; (terrain) acidentado; (road) desigual; (voice) áspero, rouco; (person, manner: coarse) grosseiro, grosso; (: violent) violento; (: brusque) rístido; (weather) tempestuoso; (treatment) brutal, mau(-má); (sea) agitado; (district) violento; (plan) preliminar; (work, cloth) grosseiro; (guess) aproximado ■ N (person) grosseirão m; (Golf): **in the ~** na grama crescida; **to have a ~ time (of it)** passar maus bocados; **~ estimate** estimativa aproximada; **to ~ it** passar aperto; **to play ~** jogar bruto; **to sleep ~** (Brit) dormir na rua; **to feel ~** (Brit) passar mal

▸ **rough out** VT (draft) rascunhar

roughage ['rʌfɪdʒ] N fibras fpl

rough-and-ready ADJ improvisado, feito às pressas

rough-and-tumble N luta, confusão f

roughcast ['rʌfkɑːst] N reboco

rough copy N rascunho

rough draft N rascunho

roughen ['rʌfən] VT (surface) tornar áspero

rough justice N justiça sumária

roughly ['rʌflɪ] ADV (handle) bruscamente; (make) toscamente; (speak) bruscamente; (approximately) aproximadamente

roughness ['rʌfnɪs] N aspereza; (rudeness) grosseria

roughshod ['rʌfʃɔd] ADV: **to ride ~ over** (person) tratar a pontapés; (objection) passar por cima de

rough work N (at school etc) rascunho

roulette [ruː'lɛt] N roleta

Roumania etc [ruː'meɪnɪə] N = **Romania etc**

round [raund] ADJ redondo ■ N círculo; (Brit: of toast) rodela; (of drinks) rodada; (of policeman) ronda; (of milkman) trajeto; (of doctor) visitas fpl; (game: of cards, golf, in competition) partida; (stage of competition) rodada, turno; (of ammunition) cartucho; (Boxing) rounde m, assalto; (of talks) ciclo ■ VT (corner) virar, dobrar; (bend) fazer; (cape) dobrar ■ PREP (surrounding): **~ his neck/the table** em volta de seu pescoço/ao redor da mesa; (in a circular movement): **to move ~ the room/~ the world** mover-se pelo quarto/dar a volta ao mundo; (in various directions) to move round a room/house, mover-se por um quarto/uma casa; (approximately): **~ about** aproximadamente ■ ADV: **all ~, right ~** por todos os lados; **the long way ~** o caminho mais comprido; **all the year ~** durante todo o ano; **in ~ figures** em números redondos; **it's just ~ the**

corner está logo depois de virar a esquina; (fig) está pertinho; ~ **the clock** ininterrupto; **to ask sb** ~ convidar alguém (para sua casa); **I'll be** ~ **at 6 o'clock** estarei aí às 6 horas; **to go** ~ dar a volta; **to go** ~ **to sb's (house)** dar um pulinho na casa de alguém; **to go** ~ **an obstacle** contornar um obstáculo; **to go** ~ **the back** passar por detrás; **to go** ~ **a house** visitar uma casa; **enough to go** ~ suficiente para todos; **she arrived** ~ **(about) noon** (Brit) ela chegou por volta do meio-dia; **to go the** ~**s** (story) divulgar-se; **the daily** ~ (fig) o cotidiano; **a** ~ **of applause** uma salva de palmas; **a** ~ **of drinks** uma rodada de bebidas; ~ **of sandwiches** sanduíche m (BR), sandes f inv (PT)
▸ **round off** VT (speech etc) terminar, completar
▸ **round up** VT (cattle) encurralar; (people) reunir; (price, figure) arredondar
roundabout ['raundəbaut] N (Brit: Aut) rotatória; (: at fair) carrossel m ■ ADJ (route, means) indireto
rounded ['raundɪd] ADJ arredondado; (style) expressivo
rounders ['raundəz] NPL (game) jogo semelhante ao beisebol
roundly ['raundlɪ] ADV (fig) energicamente, totalmente
round-shouldered [-'ʃəuldəd] ADJ encurvado
roundsman ['raundzmən] (Brit: irreg) N entregador m a domicílio
round trip N viagem f de ida e volta
roundup ['raundʌp] N (of news) resumo; (of animals) rodeio; (of criminals) batida
rouse [rauz] VT (wake up) despertar, acordar; (stir up) suscitar
rousing ['rauzɪŋ] ADJ emocionante, vibrante
rout [raut] N (Mil) derrota; (flight) fuga, debandada ■ VT derrotar
route [ru:t] N caminho, rota; (of bus) trajeto; (of shipping) rumo, rota; (of procession) rota; **"all ~s"** (Aut) "todas as direções"; **the best** ~ **to London** o melhor caminho para Londres; **en** ~ **for** a caminho de; **en** ~ **from ... to** a caminho de ... para; **route map** (Brit) N (for journey) mapa m rodoviário; (for trains etc) mapa da rede
routine [ru:'ti:n] ADJ (work) rotineiro; (procedure) de rotina ■ N rotina; (Theatre) número; **daily** ~ cotidiano
rove [rəuv] VT vagar por, perambular por
roving ['rəuvɪŋ] ADJ (wandering) errante; **roving reporter** N correspondente m/f
row¹ [rəu] N (line) fila, fileira; (in theatre, boat) fileira; (Knitting) carreira, fileira ■ VI, VT remar; **in a** ~ (fig) a fio, seguido
row² [rau] N (racket) barulho, balbúrdia; (dispute) discussão f, briga; (fuss) confusão f, bagunça; (scolding) repreensão f ■ VI brigar; **to have a** ~ ter uma briga
rowboat ['rəubəut] (US) N barco a remo
rowdiness ['raudɪnɪs] N barulheira; (fighting) brigas fpl
rowdy ['raudɪ] ADJ (person: noisy) barulhento;

(: quarrelsome) brigão(-ona); (occasion) tumultuado ■ N encrenqueiro, criador m de caso
rowdyism ['raudɪɪzəm] N violência
rowing ['rəuɪŋ] N remo; **rowing boat** (Brit) N barco a remo
rowlock ['rɔlək] (Brit) N toleteira, forqueta
royal ['rɔɪəl] ADJ real; **Royal Academy** (Brit) N ver abaixo; **Royal Air Force** (Brit) N força aérea britânica; **royal blue** ADJ azul vivo inv

● **ROYAL ACADEMY**
●
● A Royal Academy, ou Royal Academy of Arts,
● fundada em 1768 por George III para
● desenvolver a pintura, a escultura e a
● arquitetura, situa-se em Burlington House,
● Piccadilly. A cada verão há uma exposição de
● obras de artistas contemporâneos. A Royal
● Academy também oferece cursos de pintura,
● escultura e arquitetura.

royalist ['rɔɪəlɪst] ADJ, N monarquista m/f (BR), monárquico(-a) (PT)
Royal Navy (Brit) N marinha de guerra britânica
royalty ['rɔɪəltɪ] N (persons) família real, realeza; (payment: to author) direitos mpl autorais; (: to inventor) direitos mpl de exploração de patente
RP (Brit) N ABBR (= received pronunciation) norma de pronúncia
rpm ABBR (= revolutions per minute) rpm
RR (US) ABBR = **railroad**
R&R (US) N ABBR (Mil) = **rest and recreation**
RSA (Brit) N ABBR = **Royal Society of Arts; Royal Scottish Academy**
RSPB (Brit) N ABBR = **Royal Society for the Protection of Birds**
RSPCA (Brit) N ABBR = **Royal Society for the Prevention of Cruelty to Animals**
RSVP ABBR (= répondez s'il vous plaît) ER
Rt Hon. (Brit) ABBR (= Right Honourable) título honorífico de conselheiro do estado ou juiz
Rt Rev. ABBR (= Right Reverend) reverendíssimo
rub [rʌb] VT (part of body) esfregar; (object: with cloth, substance) friccionar ■ N esfregadela; (hard) fricção f; (touch) roçar m; **to give sth a** ~ dar uma esfregada em algo; **to** ~ **sb up** (Brit) or ~ **sb (US) the wrong way** irritar alguém
▸ **rub down** VT (person) esfregar; (horse) almofaçar
▸ **rub in** VT (ointment) esfregar
▸ **rub off** VI sair esfregando
▸ **rub off on** VT FUS transmitir-se para, influir sobre
▸ **rub out** VT apagar ■ VI apagar-se
rubber ['rʌbəʳ] N borracha; (Brit: eraser) borracha; **rubber band** N elástico, tira elástica; **rubber plant** N (tree) seringueira; (plant) figueira; **rubber ring** N (for swimming) bóia; **rubber stamp** N carimbo ■ VT: **to rubber-stamp** (fig) aprovar sem questionar
rubbery ['rʌbərɪ] ADJ elástico; (food) sem gosto

rubbish ['rʌbɪʃ] N (waste) refugo; (from household, in street) lixo; (junk) coisas fpl sem valor; (fig: pej: nonsense) disparates mpl, asneiras fpl ■ VT (Brit: inf) desprezar; **what you've just said is** ~ você acabou de dizer uma besteira; **~!** que nada!, nado disso!; **rubbish bin** (Brit) N lata de lixo; **rubbish dump** N (in town) depósito (de lixo)

rubbishy ['rʌbɪʃɪ] (Brit: inf) ADJ micha, chinfrim

rubble ['rʌbl] N (debris) entulho; (Constr) escombros mpl

ruble ['ru:bl] (US) N = **rouble**

ruby ['ru:bɪ] N rubi m

RUC (Brit) N ABBR = **Royal Ulster Constabulary**

rucksack ['rʌksæk] N mochila

ructions ['rʌkʃənz] NPL confusão f, tumulto

rudder ['rʌdəʳ] N leme m; (of plane) leme de direção

ruddy ['rʌdɪ] ADJ (face) corado, avermelhado; (inf: damned) maldito, desgraçado

rude [ru:d] ADJ (impolite: person) grosso, mal-educado; (: word, manners) grosseiro; (sudden) brusco; (shocking) obsceno, chocante; **to be ~ to sb** ser grosso com alguém

rudely ['ru:dlɪ] ADV grosseiramente

rudeness ['ru:dnɪs] N falta de educação

rudiment ['ru:dɪmənt] N rudimento; **rudiments** NPL (basics) primeiras noções fpl

rudimentary [ru:dɪ'mɛntərɪ] ADJ rudimentar

rue [ru:] VT arrepender-se de

rueful ['ru:ful] ADJ arrependido

ruff [rʌf] N rufo

ruffian ['rʌfɪən] N brigão m, desordeiro

ruffle ['rʌfl] VT (hair) despentear, desmanchar; (clothes) enrugar, amarrotar; (fig: person) perturbar, irritar

rug [rʌg] N tapete m; (Brit: for knees) manta (de viagem)

rugby ['rʌgbɪ] N (also: **rugby football**) rúgbi m (BR), râguebi m (PT)

rugged ['rʌgɪd] ADJ (landscape) acidentado, irregular; (features) marcado; (character) severo, austero; (determination) teimoso

rugger ['rʌgəʳ] (Brit: inf) N rúgbi m (BR), râguebi m (PT)

ruin ['ru:ɪn] N (of building) ruína; (destruction: of plans) destruição f; (downfall) queda; (bankruptcy) bancarrota ■ VT destruir; (future, person) arruinar; (spoil) estragar; **ruins** NPL (of building) ruínas fpl; **in ~s** em ruínas

ruination [ru:ɪ'neɪʃən] N ruína

ruinous ['ru:ɪnəs] ADJ desastroso

rule [ru:l] N (norm) regra; (regulation) regulamento; (government) governo, domínio; (ruler) régua ■ VT (country, person) governar; (decide) decidir; (draw: lines) traçar ■ VI (leader) governar; (monarch) reger; (Law): **to ~ in favour of/against** decidir oficialmente a favor de/contra; **to ~ that** (umpire, judge) decidir que; **under British** ~ sob domínio britânico; **it's against the ~s** não é permitido; **by ~ of thumb** empiricamente; **as a ~** por via de regra, geralmente

▶ **rule out** VT excluir

ruled [ru:ld] ADJ (paper) pautado

ruler ['ru:ləʳ] N (sovereign) soberano(-a); (for measuring) régua

ruling ['ru:lɪŋ] ADJ (party) dominante; (class) dirigente ■ N (Law) parecer m, decisão f

rum [rʌm] N rum m ■ ADJ (Brit: inf) esquisito

Rumania etc [ru:'meɪnɪə] N = **Romania** etc

rumble ['rʌmbl] N ruído surdo, barulho; (of thunder) estrondo, ribombo ■ VI ribombar, ressoar; (stomach) roncar; (pipe) fazer barulho; (thunder) ribombar

rumbustious [rʌm'bʌstʃəs] (Brit) ADJ (person) enérgico

rummage ['rʌmɪdʒ] VI vasculhar; **to ~ in** (drawer) vasculhar

rumour ['ru:məʳ] (US **rumor**) N rumor m, boato ■ VT: **it is ~ed that ...** corre o boato de que ...

rump [rʌmp] N (of animal) anca, garupa; **rump steak** N alcatra

rumple ['rʌmpl] VT (hair) despentear; (clothes) amarrotar

rumpus ['rʌmpəs] N barulho, confusão f, zorra; (quarrel) bate-boca m; **to kick up a** ~ fazer um escândalo

run [rʌn] (pt **ran**, pp **run**) N corrida; (in car) passeio (de carro); (distance travelled) trajeto, percurso; (journey) viagem f; (series) série f; (Theatre) temporada; (Ski) pista; (in stockings) fio puxado ■ VT (race) correr; (operate: business) dirigir; (: competition, course) organizar; (: hotel, house) administrar; (water) deixar correr; (bath) encher; (Press: feature) publicar; (Comput: program) rodar; (pass: hand, finger) passar ■ VI correr; (pass: road etc) passar; (work: machine) funcionar; (bus, train: operate) circular; (: travel) ir; (continue: play) continuar em cartaz; (: contract) ser válido; (slide: drawer) deslizar; (flow: river, bath) fluir, correr; (colours, washing) desbotar; (in election) candidatar-se; (nose) escorrer; **to go for a** ~ fazer cooper; (in car) dar uma volta (de carro); **to break into a** ~ pôr-se a correr; **a ~ of luck** um período de sorte; **to have the ~ of sb's house** ter a casa de alguém à sua disposição; **there was a ~ on** (meat, tickets) houve muita procura de; **in the long** ~ no final das contas, mais cedo ou mais tarde; **on the ~** em fuga, foragido; **to ~ for the bus** correr até o ônibus; **we'll have to ~ for it** vamos ter que correr atrás; **I'll ~ you to the station** vou te levar à estação; **to ~ a risk** correr um risco; **to ~ errands** fazer recados; **to make a ~ for it** fugir, dar no pé; **the train ~s between Gatwick and Victoria** o trem faz o percurso entre Gatwick e Victoria; **the bus ~s every 20 minutes** o ônibus passa a cada 20 minutos; **it's very cheap to ~** (car, machine) é muito econômico; **to ~ on petrol** (Brit) or **gas** (US)/**on diesel/off batteries** funcionar a gasolina/a óleo diesel/a pilhas; **to ~ for president** candidatar-se à presidência, ser presidenciável; **their losses ran into millions** suas perdas se elevaram a milhões; **to be ~ off one's feet**

(*Brit*) não ter descanso, não parar um minuto; **my salary won't ~ to a car** meu salário não é suficiente para comprar um carro
▶ **run about** VI (*children*) correr por todos os lados
▶ **run across** VT FUS (*find*) encontrar por acaso, topar com, dar com
▶ **run around** VI = **run about**
▶ **run away** VI fugir
▶ **run down** VI (*clock*) parar ■ VT (*Aut*) atropelar; (*production*) reduzir; (*factory*) reduzir a produção de; (*criticize*) criticar; **to be ~ down** (*tired*) estar enfraquecido *or* exausto
▶ **run in** (*Brit*) VT (*car*) rodar
▶ **run into** VT FUS (*meet: person*) dar com, topar com; (: *trouble*) esbarrar em; (*collide with*) bater em; **to ~ into debt** endividar-se
▶ **run off** VT (*water*) deixar correr; (*copies*) fotocopiar ■ VI fugir
▶ **run out** VI (*person*) sair correndo; (*liquid*) escorrer, esgotar-se; (*lease, passport*) caducar, vencer; (*money*) acabar
▶ **run out of** VT FUS ficar sem; **I've ~ out of petrol** (*Brit*) *or* **gas** (*US*) estou sem gasolina
▶ **run over** VT (*Aut*) atropelar ■ VT FUS (*revise*) recapitular
▶ **run through** VT FUS (*instructions*) examinar, recapitular; (*rehearse*) recapitular
▶ **run up** VT (*debt*) acumular ■ VI: **to ~ up against** (*difficulties*) esbarrar em
runaway ['rʌnəweɪ] ADJ (*horse*) desembestado; (*truck*) desgovernado; (*person*) fugitivo; (*inflation*) galopante
rundown ['rʌndaun] (*Brit*) N (*of industry etc*) redução *f* progressiva
rung [rʌŋ] PP *of* **ring** ■ N (*of ladder*) degrau *m*
run-in (*inf*) N briga, bate-boca *m*
runner ['rʌnəʳ] N (*in race: person*) corredor(a) *m/f*; (: *horse*) corredor *m*; (*on sledge*) patim *m*, lâmina; (*on curtain*) anel *m*; (*wheel*) roldana, roda; (*for drawer*) corrediça; (*carpet: in hall etc*) passadeira; **runner bean** (*Brit*) N (*Bot*) vagem *f* (BR), feijão *m* verde (PT)
runner-up N segundo(-a) colocado(-a)
running ['rʌnɪŋ] N (*sport, race*) corrida; (*of business*) direção *f*; (*of event*) organização *f*; (*of machine etc*) funcionamento ■ ADJ (*water*) corrente; (*commentary*) contínuo, seguido; **6 days ~** 6 dias seguidos *or* consecutivos; **to be in/out of the ~ for sth** disputar algo/estar fora da disputa por algo; **running costs** NPL (*of business*) despesas *fpl* operacionais; (*of car*) custos *mpl* de manutenção; **running head** N (*Typ, Word Processing*) título corrido; **running mate** (*US*) N (*Pol*) companheiro(-a) de chapa
runny ['rʌnɪ] ADJ (*sauce, paint*) aguado; (*egg*) mole; **to have a ~ nose** estar com coriza, estar com o nariz escorrendo

run-off N (*in contest, election*) segundo turno; (*extra race etc*) corrida decisiva
run-of-the-mill ADJ mediocre, ordinário
runt [rʌnt] N (*animal*) nanico; (*pej: person*) anão(-anã) *m/f*
run-through N ensaio
run-up N: **~ to sth** (*election etc*) período que antecede algo; **during** *or* **in the ~ to** nas vésperas de
runway ['rʌnweɪ] N (*Aviat*) pista (de decolagem *or* de pouso)
rupee [ruːˈpiː] N rupia
rupture ['rʌptʃəʳ] N (*Med*) hérnia ■ VT: **to ~ o.s.** provocar-se uma hérnia
rural ['ruərl] ADJ rural
ruse [ruːz] N ardil *m*, manha
rush [rʌʃ] N (*hurry*) pressa; (*Comm*) grande procura *or* demanda; (*Bot*) junco; (*current*) torrente *f*; (*of emotion*) ímpeto ■ VT apressar; (*work*) fazer depressa; (*attack: town etc*) assaltar; (*Brit: inf: charge*) cobrar ■ VI apressar-se, precipitar-se; (*air*) suprar impetuosamente; (*water*) afluir impetuosamente; **don't ~ me!** não me apresse!; **is there any ~ for this?** isso é urgente?; **to ~ sth off** (*do quickly*) fazer algo às pressas; (*send*) enviar depressa; **we've had a ~ of orders** recebimos uma enxurrada de pedidos; **to be in a ~** estar com pressa; **to do sth in a ~** fazer algo às pressas; **to be in a ~ to do sth** ter urgência em fazer algo
▶ **rush through** VT FUS (*work*) fazer às pressas ■ VT (*Comm: order*) executar com toda a urgência
rush:rush hour N rush *m* (BR), hora de ponta (PT); **rush job** N trabalho urgente; **rush matting** N tapete *m* de palha
rusk [rʌsk] N rosca
Russia ['rʌʃə] N Rússia
Russian ['rʌʃən] ADJ russo ■ N russo(-a); (*Ling*) russo
rust [rʌst] N ferrugem *f* ■ VI enferrujar
rustic ['rʌstɪk] ADJ rústico ■ N (*pej*) caipira *m/f*
rustle ['rʌsl] VI sussurrar ■ VT (*paper*) farfalhar; (*US: cattle*) roubar, afanar
rustproof ['rʌstpruːf] ADJ inoxidável, à prova de ferrugem
rustproofing ['rʌstpruːfɪŋ] N tratamento contra ferrugem
rusty ['rʌstɪ] ADJ enferrujado
rut [rʌt] N sulco; (*Zool*) cio; **to be in a ~** ser escravo da rotina
rutabaga [ruːtəˈbeɪgə] (*US*) N rutabaga
ruthless ['ruːθlɪs] ADJ implacável, sem piedade
ruthlessness ['ruːθlɪsnɪs] N crueldade *f*, desumanidade *f*, insensibilidade *f*
RV ABBR (= *revised version*) tradução inglesa da Bíblia de 1885 ■ N ABBR (*US*) = **recreational vehicle**
rye [raɪ] N centeio; **rye bread** N pão *m* de centeio

Ss

S, s [ɛs] N (*letter*) S, s *m*; (*US: Sch:* = *satisfactory*) satisfatório; **S for Sugar** S de Sandra

S ABBR (= *south*) S; (: = *saint*) S, S^{to}, Sta

SA N ABBR = **South Africa; South America**

Sabbath ['sæbəθ] N (*Christian*) domingo; (*Jewish*) sábado

sabbatical [sə'bætɪkl] N (*also:* **sabbatical year**) ano sabático *or* de licença

sabotage ['sæbətɑːʒ] N sabotagem *f* ■ VT sabotar

saccharin(e) ['sækərɪn] N sacarina

sachet ['sæʃeɪ] N sachê *m*

sack [sæk] N (*bag*) saco, saca ■ VT (*dismiss*) despedir; (*plunder*) saquear; **to get the ~** ser demitido; **to give sb the ~** pôr alguém no olho da rua, despedir alguém

sackful ['sækful] N: **a ~ of** um saco de

sacking ['sækɪŋ] N (*dismissal*) demissão *f*; (*material*) aniagem *f*

sacrament ['sækrəmənt] N sacramento

sacred ['seɪkrɪd] ADJ sagrado

sacrifice ['sækrɪfaɪs] N sacrifício ■ VT sacrificar; **to make ~s (for sb)** fazer um sacrifício (por alguém)

sacrilege ['sækrɪlɪdʒ] N sacrilégio

sacrosanct ['sækrəusæŋkt] ADJ sacrossanto

sad [sæd] ADJ triste; (*deplorable*) deplorável, triste

sadden ['sædn] VT entristecer

saddle ['sædl] N sela; (*of cycle*) selim *m* ■ VT (*horse*) selar; **to ~ sb with sth** (*inf: task, bill*) pôr algo nas costas de alguém; (: *responsibility*) sobrecarregar alguém com algo

saddlebag ['sædlbæg] N alforje *m*

sadism ['seɪdɪzm] N sadismo

sadist ['seɪdɪst] N sádico(-a)

sadistic [sə'dɪstɪk] ADJ sádico

sadly ['sædlɪ] ADV tristemente; (*regrettably*) infelizmente; (*mistaken, neglected*) gravemente; **~ lacking (in)** muito carente (de)

sadness ['sædnɪs] N tristeza

sae ABBR (= *stamped addressed envelope*) envelope selado e sobrescritado

safari [sə'fɑːrɪ] N safári *m*; **safari park** N parque com animais selvagens

safe [seɪf] ADJ seguro; (*out of danger*) fora de perigo; (*unharmed*) ileso, incólume; (*trustworthy*) digno de confiança ■ N cofre *m*, caixa-forte *f*;

~ from protegido de; **~ and sound** são e salvo; **(just) to be on the ~ side** por via das dúvidas; **to play ~** não correr riscos; **it is ~ to say that ...** posso afirmar que ...; **~ journey!** boa viagem!

safe-breaker (*Brit*) N arrombador *m* de cofres

safe-conduct N salvo-conduto

safe-cracker N arrombador *m* de cofres

safe-deposit N (*vault*) cofre *m* de segurança; (*box*) caixa-forte *f*

safeguard ['seɪfgɑːd] N salvaguarda, proteção *f* ■ VT proteger, defender

safekeeping [seɪf'kiːpɪŋ] N custódia, proteção *f*

safely ['seɪflɪ] ADV com segurança, a salvo; (*without mishap*) sem perigo; **I can ~ say ...** posso seguramente dizer ...

safety ['seɪftɪ] N segurança; **safety belt** N cinto de segurança; **safety curtain** N cortina de ferro; **safety net** N rede *f* de segurança; **safety pin** N alfinete *m* de segurança; **safety valve** N válvula de segurança

saffron ['sæfrən] N açafrão *m*

sag [sæg] VI (*breasts*) cair; (*roof*) afundar; (*hem*) desmanchar

saga ['sɑːgə] N saga; (*fig*) novela

sage [seɪdʒ] N (*herb*) salva; (*man*) sábio

Sagittarius [sædʒɪ'tɛərɪəs] N Sagitário

sago ['seɪgəu] N sagu *m*

Sahara [sə'hɑːrə] N: **the ~ (Desert)** o Saara

said [sɛd] PT, PP *of* **say**

sail [seɪl] N (*on boat*) vela; (*trip*): **to go for a ~** dar um passeio de barco a vela ■ VT (*boat*) governar ■ VI (*travel: ship*) navegar, velejar; (: *passenger*) ir de barco; (*Sport*) velejar; (*set off*) zarpar; **to set ~** zarpar; **they ~ed into Rio de Janeiro** entraram no porto do Rio de Janeiro

▶ **sail through** VT FUS (*fig*) fazer com facilidade ■ VI fazer de letra, fazer com um pé nas costas

sailboat ['seɪlbəut] (*US*) N barco a vela

sailing ['seɪlɪŋ] N (*Sport*) navegação *f* a vela, vela; **to go ~** ir velejar; **sailing boat** N barco a vela; **sailing ship** N veleiro

sailor ['seɪlə*] N marinheiro, marujo

saint [seɪnt] N santo(-a); **S~ John** São João

saintly ['seɪntlɪ] ADJ santo; (*life, expression*) de santo

sake [seɪk] N: **for the ~ of** por (causa de), em consideração a; **for sb's/sth's ~** pelo bem de alguém/algo; **for my ~** por mim; **arguing for arguing's ~** brigar por brigar; **for the ~ of argument** por exemplo; **for heaven's ~!** pelo amor de Deus!

salad ['sæləd] N salada; **salad bowl** N saladeira; **salad cream** (Brit) N maionese f; **salad dressing** N tempero or molho da salada; **salad oil** N azeite m de mesa

salami [sə'lɑːmɪ] N salame m

salaried ['sælərɪd] ADJ (staff) assalariado

salary ['sælərɪ] N salário; **salary scale** N escala salarial

sale [seɪl] N venda; (at reduced prices) liquidação f, saldo; (auction) leilão m; **sales** NPL (total amount sold) vendas fpl; **"for ~"** "vende-se"; **on ~** à venda; **on ~ or return** em consignação; **~ and lease back** venda com cláusula de aluguel ao vendedor do item vendido

saleroom ['seɪlrum] N sala de vendas

sales assistant (US **sales clerk**) N vendedor(a) m/f

sales conference N conferência de vendas

sales drive N campanha de vendas

sales force N equipe m de vendas

salesman ['seɪlzmən] (irreg) N vendedor m; (representative) vendedor m viajante

sales manager N gerente m/f de vendas

salesmanship ['seɪlzmənʃɪp] N arte f de vender

salesmen ['seɪlzmɛn] NPL of **salesman**

sales tax (US) N ≈ ICM m (BR), ≈ IVA m (PT)

saleswoman ['seɪlzwumən] (irreg) N vendedora; (representative) vendedora viajante

salient ['seɪlɪənt] ADJ saliente

saline ['seɪlaɪn] ADJ salino

saliva [sə'laɪvə] N saliva

sallow ['sæləu] ADJ amarelado

sally forth ['sælɪ-] VI partir, pôr-se em marcha

sally out ['sælɪ-] VI partir, pôr-se em marcha

salmon ['sæmən] N INV salmão m

salon ['sælɔn] N (hairdressing salon) salão m (de cabeleireiro); (beauty salon) salão (de beleza)

saloon [sə'luːn] N (US) bar m, botequim m; (Brit: Aut) sedã m; (ship's lounge) salão m

SALT [sɔːlt] N ABBR (= Strategic Arms Limitation Talks/Treaty) SALT m

salt [sɔːlt] N sal m ■ VT salgar ■ CPD de sal; (Culin) salgado; **an old ~** um lobo-do-mar
▶ **salt away** VT pôr de lado

salt cellar N saleiro

salt-free ADJ sem sal

saltwater ['sɔːltwɔːtər] ADJ de água salgada

salty ['sɔːltɪ] ADJ salgado

salubrious [sə'luːbrɪəs] ADJ salubre, sadio

salutary ['sæljutərɪ] ADJ salutar

salute [sə'luːt] N (greeting) saudação f; (of guns) salva; (Mil) continência ■ VT saudar; (guns) receber com salvas; (Mil) fazer continência a

salvage ['sælvɪdʒ] N (saving) salvamento, recuperação f; (things saved) salvados mpl ■ VT salvar; **salvage vessel** N navio de salvamento

salvation [sæl'veɪʃən] N salvação f

Salvation Army N Exército da Salvação

salve [sælv] N (cream etc) ungüento, pomada

salver ['sælvər] N bandeja, salva

salvo ['sælvəu] (pl **salvoes**) N salva

Samaritan [sə'mærɪtən] N: **the ~s** (or ganization) os Samaritanos

same [seɪm] ADJ mesmo ■ PRON: **the ~** o mesmo(-a) mesma; **the ~ book as** o mesmo livro que; **at the ~ time** ao mesmo tempo; **on the ~ day** no mesmo dia; **all** or **just the ~** apesar de tudo, mesmo assim; **it's all the ~** dá no mesmo, tanto faz; **they're one and the ~** (people) são os mesmos; (things) são idênticos; **to do the ~ (as sb)** fazer o mesmo (que alguém); **the ~ to you!** igualmente!; **~ here!** eu também!; **the ~ again!** (in bar etc) mais um ... por favor!

sample ['sɑːmpl] N amostra ■ VT (food, wine) provar, experimentar; **to take a ~** tirar uma amostra; **free ~** amostra grátis

sanatoria [sænə'tɔːrɪə] NPL of **sanatorium**

sanatorium [sænə'tɔːrɪəm] (pl **sanatoria**) N sanatório

sanctify ['sæŋktɪfaɪ] VT santificar

sanctimonious [sæŋktɪ'məunɪəs] ADJ carola, beato

sanction ['sæŋkʃən] N sançõo f ■ VT sancionar; **sanctions** NPL (severe measures) sanções fpl; **to impose economic ~s on** or **against** impor sanções econômicas a

sanctity ['sæŋktɪtɪ] N santidade f, divindade f; (inviolability) inviolabilidade f

sanctuary ['sæŋktjuərɪ] N (holy place) santuário; (refuge) refúgio, asilo; (for animals) reserva

sand [sænd] N areia; (beach: also: **sands**) praia ■ VT arear, jogar areia em; (also: **sand down**: wood etc) lixar

sandal ['sændl] N sandália; (wood) sândalo

sandbag ['sændbæg] N saco de areia

sandbank ['sændbæŋk] N banco de areia

sandblast ['sændblɑːst] VT limpar com jato de areia

sandbox ['sændbɔks] (US) N (for children) caixa de areia

sandcastle ['sændkɑːsl] N castelo de areia

sand dune N duna (de areia)

sandpaper ['sændpeɪpər] N lixa

sandpit ['sændpɪt] N (for children) caixa de areia

sandstone ['sændstəun] N arenito, grés m

sandstorm ['sændstɔːm] N tempestade f de areia

sandwich ['sændwɪtʃ] N sanduíche m (BR), sandes f inv (PT) ■ VT (also: **sandwich in**) intercalar; **~ed between** encaixado entre; **cheese/ham ~** sanduíche (BR) or sandes (PT) de queijo/presunto; **sandwich board** N cartaz m ambulante; **sandwich course** (Brit) N curso profissionalizante de teoria e prática alternadas

sandy ['sændɪ] ADJ arenoso; (colour) vermelho amarelado

sane [seɪn] ADJ são(-sã) do juízo; (sensible) ajuizado, sensato

sang [sæŋ] PT of **sing**

sanguine ['sæŋgwɪn] ADJ otimista

sanitaria [sænɪ'tɛərɪə] (US) NPL of **sanitarium**
sanitarium [sænɪ'tɛərɪəm] (US) (pl **sanitaria**) N
= **sanatorium**
sanitary ['sænɪtɪ] ADJ (system, arrangements)
sanitário; (clean) higiênico; **sanitary towel**
(US **sanitary napkin**) N toalha higiênica or
absorvente
sanitation [sænɪ'teɪʃən] N (in house) instalações
fpl sanitárias; (in town) saneamento; **sanitation
department** (US) N comissão f de limpeza
urbana
sanity ['sænɪtɪ] N sanidade f, equilíbrio mental;
(common sense) juízo, sensatez f
sank [sæŋk] PT of **sink**
San Marino ['sænmə'riːnəu] N San Marino (no
article)
Santa Claus [sæntə'klɔːz] N Papai Noel m
Santiago [sæntɪ'ɑːgəu] N (also: **Santiago de
Chile**) Santiago (do Chile)
sap [sæp] N (of plants) seiva ■ VT (strength)
esgotar, minar
sapling ['sæplɪŋ] N árvore f nova
sapphire ['sæfaɪər] N safira
sarcasm ['sɑːkæzm] N sarcasmo
sarcastic [sɑː'kæstɪk] ADJ sarcástico
sarcophagi [sɑː'kɔfəgaɪ] NPL of **sarcophagus**
sarcophagus [sɑː'kɔfəgəs] (pl **sarcophagi**) N
sarcófago
sardine [sɑː'diːn] N sardinha
Sardinia [sɑː'dɪnɪə] N Sardenha
Sardinian [sɑː'dɪnɪən] ADJ sardo ■ N sardo(-a);
(Ling) sardo
sardonic [sɑː'dɔnɪk] ADJ sardônico
sari ['sɑːrɪ] N sári m
sartorial [sɑː'tɔːrɪəl] ADJ indumentário
SAS (Brit) N ABBR (Mil) = **Special Air Service**
SASE (US) N ABBR (= self-addressed stamped envelope)
envelope selado e sobrescritado
sash [sæʃ] N faixa, banda; (belt) cinto; **sash
window** N janela de guilhotina
SAT (US) N ABBR = **Scholastic Aptitude Test**
Sat. ABBR (= Saturday) sáb
sat [sæt] PT, PP of **sit**
Satan ['seɪtn] N Satanás m, Satã m
satanic [sə'tænɪk] ADJ satânico, diabólico
satchel ['sætʃl] N sacola
sated ['seɪtɪd] ADJ saciado, farto
satellite ['sætəlaɪt] N satélite m; **satellite dish** N
antena parabólica
satiate ['seɪʃɪeɪt] VT saciar
satin ['sætɪn] N cetim m ■ ADJ acetinado; **with
a ~ finish** acetinado
satire ['sætaɪər] N sátira
satirical [sə'tɪrɪkl] ADJ satírico
satirist ['sætɪrɪst] N (writer) satirista m/f;
(cartoonist) chargista m/f
satirize ['sætɪraɪz] VT satirizar
satisfaction [sætɪs'fækʃən] N satisfação f;
(refund, apology etc) compensação f; **has it been
done to your ~?** você está satisfeito?
satisfactory [sætɪs'fæktərɪ] ADJ satisfatório
satisfy ['sætɪsfaɪ] VT satisfazer; (convince)

convencer, persuadir; **to ~ the requirements**
satisfazer as exigências; **to ~ sb (that)**
convencer alguém (de que); **to ~ o.s. of sth**
convencer-se de algo
satisfying ['sætɪsfaɪɪŋ] ADJ satisfatório
saturate ['sætʃəreɪt] VT: **to ~ (with)** saturar or
embeber (de)
saturation [sætʃə'reɪʃən] N saturação f
Saturday ['sætədɪ] N sábado; see also **Tuesday**
sauce [sɔːs] N molho; (sweet) calda; (fig: cheek)
atrevimento
saucepan ['sɔːspən] N panela (BR), caçarola (PT)
saucer ['sɔːsər] N pires m inv
saucy ['sɔːsɪ] ADJ atrevido, descarado; (flirtatious)
flertivo, provocante
Saudi ['saudɪ]: **~ Arabia** N Arábia Saudita; **Saudi
(Arabian)** ['saudɪ-] ADJ, N saudita m/f
sauna ['sɔːnə] N sauna
saunter ['sɔːntər] VI: **to ~ over/along/into**
andar devagar para/por/entrar devagar em
sausage ['sɔsɪdʒ] N salsicha, lingüiça; (cold
meat) frios mpl; **sausage roll** N folheado de
salsicha
sauté ['səuteɪ] ADJ (Culin: potatoes) sauté; (: onions)
frito rapidamente ■ VT fritar levemente
savage ['sævɪdʒ] ADJ (cruel, fierce) cruel, feroz;
(primitive) selvagem ■ N selvagem m/f ■ VT
(attack) atacar ferozmente
savagery ['sævɪdʒrɪ] N selvageria, ferocidade f
save [seɪv] VT (rescue, Comput) salvar; (money)
poupar, economizar; (time) ganhar; (put by: food)
guardar; (Sport) impedir; (avoid: trouble) evitar;
(keep: seat) guardar ■ VI (also: **save up**) poupar
■ N (Sport) salvamento ■ PREP salvo, exceto; **it
will ~ me an hour** vou ganhar uma hora; **to
~ face** salvar as aparências; **God ~ the Queen!**
Deus salve a Rainha!
saving ['seɪvɪŋ] N (on price etc) economia ■ ADJ:
the ~ grace of o único mérito de; **savings** NPL
(money) economias fpl; **to make ~s** economizar
savings account N (caderneta de) poupança
savings bank N caixa econômica, caderneta de
poupança
saviour ['seɪvjər] (US **savior**) N salvador(a) m/f
savour ['seɪvər] (US **savor**) N sabor m ■ VT
saborear; (experience) apreciar
savo(u)ry ['seɪvərɪ] ADJ saboroso; (dish: not sweet)
salgado
savvy ['sævɪ] (inf) N juízo
saw [sɔː] (pt **sawed**, pp **sawn**) PT of **see** ■ N (tool)
serra ■ VT serrar; **to ~ sth up** serrar algo em
pedaços
sawdust ['sɔːdʌst] N serragem f, pó m de serra
sawed-off shotgun [sɔːd-] (US) N = **sawn-off
shotgun**
sawmill ['sɔːmɪl] N serraria
sawn [sɔːn] PP of **saw**
sawn-off shotgun (Brit) N espingarda de cano
serrado
saxophone ['sæksəfəun] N saxofone m
say [seɪ] (pl, pp **said**) N: **to have one's ~** exprimir
sua opinião, vender seu peixe (inf) ■ VT dizer,

falar; **to have a** or **some ~ in sth** opinar sobre algo, ter que ver com algo; **~ after me ...** repita comigo ...; **to ~ yes/no** dizer (que) sim/não; **could you ~ that again?** poderia repetir?; **she said (that) I was to give you this** ela disse que eu deveria te dar isso; **my watch ~s 3 o'clock** meu relógio marca 3 horas; **shall we ~ Tuesday?** marcamos para terça?; **I should ~ it's worth about £100** acho que vale mais ou menos £100; **that doesn't ~ much for him** aquilo não o favorece; **when all is said and done** afinal das contas; **there is something** or **a lot to be said for it** isto tem muitas vantagens; **that is to ~** ou seja; **to ~ nothing of ...** por não falar em ...; **~ that ...** vamos supor que ...; **that goes without ~ing** é óbvio, nem é preciso dizer

saying ['seɪɪŋ] N ditado, provérbio

SBA (US) N ABBR (= *Small Business Administration*) *órgão de auxílio às pequenas empresas*

SC (US) N ABBR = **supreme court** ■ ABBR (*Post*) = **South Carolina**

s/c ABBR = **self-contained**

scab [skæb] N casca, crosta (de ferida); (*pej*) fura-greve *m/f inv*

scabby ['skæbɪ] ADJ cheio de casca or cicatrizes

scaffold ['skæfəuld] N (*for execution*) cadafalso, patíbulo

scaffolding ['skæfəuldɪŋ] N andaime *m*

scald [skɔ:ld] N escaldadura ■ VT escaldar, queimar

scalding ['skɔ:ldɪŋ] ADJ (*also*: **scalding hot**) escaldante

scale [skeɪl] N (*gen, Mus*) escala; (*of fish*) escama; (*of salaries, fees etc*) tabela; (*of map, also size, extent*) escala ■ VT (*mountain*) escalar; (*fish*) escamar; **scales** NPL (*for weighing*) balança; **pay ~** tabela de salários; **on a large ~** em grande escala; **~ of charges** tarifa, lista de preços; **to draw sth to ~** desenhar algo em escala; **small-~ model** modelo reduzido

▶ **scale down** VT reduzir

scale drawing N desenho em escala

scale model N maquete *f* em escala

scallion ['skæljən] N cebola

scallop ['skɔləp] N (*Zool*) vieira, venera; (*Sewing*) barra, arremate *m*

scalp [skælp] N couro cabeludo ■ VT escalpar

scalpel ['skælpl] N bisturi *m*

scalper ['skælpəʳ] (*US: inf*) N (*of tickets*) cambista *m/f*

scamp [skæmp] N moleque *m*

scamper ['skæmpəʳ] VI: **to ~ away** or **off** sair correndo

scampi ['skæmpɪ] NPL camarões *mpl* fritos

scan [skæn] VT (*examine*) esquadrinhar, perscrutar; (*glance at quickly*) passar uma vista de olhos por; (*TV, Radar*) explorar ■ N (*Med*) exame *m*

scandal ['skændl] N escândalo; (*gossip*) fofocas *fpl*; (*fig: disgrace*) vergonha

scandalize ['skændəlaɪz] VT escandalizar

scandalous ['skændələs] ADJ escandaloso; (*disgraceful*) vergonhoso; (*libellous*) difamatório, calunioso

Scandinavia [skændɪ'neɪvɪə] N Escandinávia

Scandinavian [skændɪ'neɪvɪən] ADJ, N escandinavo(-a)

scanner ['skænəʳ] N (*Radar*) antena; (*Med, Comput*) scanner *m*

scant [skænt] ADJ escasso, insuficiente

scantily ['skæntɪlɪ] ADV: **~ clad** or **dressed** precariamente vestido

scanty ['skæntɪ] ADJ (*meal*) insuficiente, pobre; (*underwear*) sumário

scapegoat ['skeɪpgəut] N bode *m* expiatório

scar [ska:] N cicatriz *f* ■ VT marcar (com uma cicatriz)

scarce [skɛəs] ADJ escasso, raro; **to make o.s. ~** (*inf*) dar o fora, cair fora

scarcely ['skɛəslɪ] ADV mal, quase não; (*with numbers: barely*) apenas; **~ anybody** quase ninguém; **I can ~ believe it** mal posso acreditar

scarcity ['skɛəsɪtɪ] N escassez *f*; **scarcity value** N valor *m* de escassez

scare [skɛəʳ] N susto; (*panic*) pânico ■ VT assustar; **to ~ sb stiff** deixar alguém morrendo de medo; **bomb ~** alarme de bomba

▶ **scare away** VT espantar

▶ **scare off** VT = **scare away**

scarecrow ['skɛəkrəu] N espantalho

scared [skɛəd] ADJ: **to be ~** estar assustado or com medo

scaremonger ['skɛəmʌŋgəʳ] N alarmista *m/f*

scarf [ska:f] (*pl* **scarves**) N (*long*) cachecol *m*; (*square*) lenço (de cabeça)

scarlet ['ska:lɪt] ADJ escarlate; **scarlet fever** N escarlatina

scarves [ska:vz] NPL *of* **scarf**

scary ['skɛərɪ] (*inf*) ADJ assustador(a)

scathing ['skeɪðɪŋ] ADJ mordaz; **to be ~ about sth** fazer uma crítica mordaz sobre algo

scatter ['skætəʳ] VT (*spread*) espalhar; (*put to flight*) dispersar ■ VI espalhar-se

scatterbrained ['skætəbreɪnd] (*inf*) ADJ desmiolado, avoado; (*forgetful*) esquecido

scattered ['skætəd] ADJ espalhado

scatty ['skætɪ] (*Brit: inf*) ADJ maluquinho

scavenge ['skævəndʒ] VI (*person*): **to ~ (for)** filar; **to ~ for food** (*hyenas etc*) procurar comida

scavenger ['skævəndʒəʳ] N (*person*) pessoa que procura comida no lixo; (*Zool*) animal *m* (or ave *f*) que se alimenta de carniça

SCE N ABBR = **Scottish Certificate of Education**

scenario [sɪ'na:rɪəu] N (*Theatre, Cinema*) sinopse *f*; (*fig*) quadro

scene [si:n] N (*Theatre, fig*) cena; (*of crime, accident*) cenário; (*sight*) vista, panorama *m*; (*fuss*) escândalo; **behind the ~s** nos bastidores; **to make a ~** (*inf: fuss*) fazer um escândalo; **to appear on the ~** entrar em cena; **the political ~** o panorama político

scenery ['si:nərɪ] N (*Theatre*) cenário; (*landscape*) paisagem *f*

scenic ['si:nɪk] ADJ pitoresco

scent [sɛnt] N perfume m; (smell) aroma; (track, fig) pista, rastro; (sense of smell) olfato ■ VT perfumar; **to put** or **throw sb off the ~** despistar alguém

scepter ['sɛptəʳ] (US) N = **sceptre**

sceptic ['skɛptɪk] (US **skeptic**) N cético(-a)

sceptical ['skɛptɪkl] (US **skeptical**) ADJ cético

scepticism ['skɛptɪsɪzm] (US **skepticism**) N ceticismo

sceptre ['sɛptəʳ] (US **scepter**) N cetro

schedule ['ʃɛdju:l, (US) 'skɛdju:l] N (of trains) horário; (of events) programa m; (plan) plano; (list) lista ■ VT (timetable) planejar; (visit) marcar (a hora de); **as ~d** como previsto; **the meeting is ~d for 7.00** a reunião está programada para as 7.00h; **on ~** na hora, sem atraso; **to be ahead of/behind ~** estar adiantado/atrasado; **we are working to a very tight ~** nosso horário está muito apertado; **everything went according to ~** tudo correu como planejado

scheduled ['ʃɛdju:ld, (US) 'skɛdju:ld] ADJ (date, time) marcado; (visit, event) programado; (train, bus, flight) de linha

schematic [skɪ'mætɪk] ADJ esquemático

scheme [ski:m] N (plan, plot) maquinação f; (method) método; (pension scheme etc) projeto; (trick) ardil m; (arrangement) arranjo ■ VI conspirar

scheming ['ski:mɪŋ] ADJ intrigante ■ N intrigas fpl

schism ['skɪzəm] N cisma m

schizophrenia [skɪtsəu'fri:nɪə] N esquizofrenia

schizophrenic [skɪtsə'frɛnɪk] ADJ esquizofrênico

scholar ['skɔləʳ] N (pupil) aluno(-a), estudante m/f; (learned person) sábio(-a), erudito(-a)

scholarly ['skɔləlɪ] ADJ erudito

scholarship ['skɔləʃɪp] N erudição f; (grant) bolsa de estudos

school [sku:l] N escola; (in university) faculdade f; (secondary school) colégio; (US: university) universidade f; (of fish) cardume m ■ CPD escolar ■ VT (animal) adestrar, treinar; **school age** N idade f escolar

schoolbook ['sku:lbuk] N livro escolar

schoolboy ['sku:lbɔɪ] N aluno

schoolchildren ['sku:ltʃɪldrən] NPL alunos mpl

schooldays ['sku:ldeɪz] NPL anos mpl escolares

schoolgirl ['sku:lgə:l] N aluna

schooling ['sku:lɪŋ] N educação f, ensino

school-leaving age [-'li:vɪŋ-] N idade f em que se termina a escola

schoolmaster ['sku:lmɑ:stəʳ] N professor m

schoolmistress ['sku:lmɪstrɪs] N professora

school report (Brit) N boletim m escolar

schoolroom ['sku:lrum] N sala de aula

schoolteacher ['sku:lti:tʃəʳ] N professor(a) m/f

schooner ['sku:nəʳ] N (ship) escuna; (glass) caneca, canecão m

sciatica [saɪ'ætɪkə] N ciática

science ['saɪəns] N ciência; **science fiction** N

ficção f científica

scientific [saɪən'tɪfɪk] ADJ científico

scientist ['saɪəntɪst] N cientista m/f

sci-fi ['saɪfaɪ] (inf) N ABBR = **science fiction**

Scillies ['sɪlɪz] NPL: **the ~** as ilhas Scilly

Scilly Isles ['sɪlɪ'aɪlz] NPL: **the ~** as ilhas Scilly

scintillating ['sɪntɪleɪtɪŋ] ADJ (wit etc) brilhante

scissors ['sɪzəz] NPL tesoura; **a pair of ~** uma tesoura

sclerosis [sklɪ'rəusɪs] N esclerose f

scoff [skɔf] VT (Brit: inf: eat) engolir ■ VI: **to ~ (at)** (mock) zombar (de)

scold [skəuld] VT ralhar

scolding ['skəuldɪŋ] N repreensão f

scone [skɔn] N bolinho de trigo

scoop [sku:p] N colherona; (for flour etc) pá f; (Press) furo (jornalístico)
  ▶ **scoop out** VT escavar
  ▶ **scoop up** VT recolher

scooter ['sku:təʳ] N (also: **motor scooter**) lambreta; (toy) patinete m

scope [skəup] N liberdade f de ação; (of plan, undertaking) âmbito; (reach) alcance m; (of person) competência; (opportunity) oportunidade f; **within the ~ of** dentro dos limites de; **there is plenty of ~ for improvement** (Brit) poderia ser muito melhor

scorch [skɔ:tʃ] VT (clothes) chamuscar; (earth, grass) secar, queimar

scorched earth policy [skɔ:tʃt-] N tática da terra arrasada

scorcher ['skɔ:tʃəʳ] (inf) N (hot day) dia m muito quente

scorching ['skɔ:tʃɪŋ] ADJ ardente

score [skɔ:ʳ] N (points etc) escore m, contagem f; (Mus) partitura; (reckoning) conta; (twenty) vintena ■ VT (goal, point) fazer; (mark) marcar, entalhar; (success) alcançar ■ VI (in game) marcar; (Football) marcar or fazer um gol; (keep score) marcar o escore; **on that ~** a esse respeito, por esse motivo; **to have an old ~ to settle with sb** (fig) ter umas contas a ajustar com alguém; **~s of** (fig) um monte de; **to keep (the) ~** marcar os pontos; **to ~ 6 out of 10** conseguir um escore de 6 num total de 10
  ▶ **score out** VT riscar

scoreboard ['skɔ:bɔ:d] N marcador m, placar m

scorecard ['skɔ:kɑ:d] N (Sport) cartão m de marcação

scorer ['skɔ:rəʳ] N marcador(a) m/f

scorn [skɔ:n] N desprezo ■ VT desprezar, rejeitar

scornful ['skɔ:nful] ADJ desdenhoso, zombador(a)

Scorpio ['skɔ:pɪəu] N Escorpião m

scorpion ['skɔ:pɪən] N escorpião m

Scot [skɔt] N escocês(-esa) m/f

Scotch [skɔtʃ] N uísque m (BR) or whisky m (PT) escocês

scotch [skɔtʃ] VT (rumour) desmentir; (plan) estragar

Scotch tape® N fita adesiva, durex® m (BR)

scot-free ADJ: **to get off ~** (*unpunished*) sair impune; (*unhurt*) sair ileso

Scotland ['skɔtlənd] N Escócia

Scots [skɔts] ADJ escocês(-esa)

Scotsman ['skɔtsmən] (*irreg*) N escocês *m*

Scotswoman ['skɔtswumən] (*irreg*) N escocesa

Scottish ['skɔtɪʃ] ADJ escocês(-esa)

scoundrel ['skaundrəl] N canalha *m/f*, patife *m*

scour ['skauər] VT (*clean*) limpar, esfregar; (*search*) esquadrinhar, procurar em

scourer ['skaurər] N esponja de aço, bombril® *m* (BR)

scourge [skə:dʒ] N flagelo, tormento

scout [skaut] N (*Mil*) explorador *m*, batedor *m*; (*also*: **boy scout**) escoteiro; **girl ~** (US) escoteira
▶ **scout around** VI explorar

scowl [skaul] VI franzir a testa; **to ~ at sb** olhar de cara feia para alguém

scrabble ['skræbl] VI (*claw*): **to ~ at** arranhar
■ N: **S~®** mexe-mexe *m*; **to ~ (around) for sth** (*search*) tatear procurando algo

scraggy ['skrægɪ] ADJ magricela, descarnado

scram [skræm] (*inf*) VI dar o fora, safar-se

scramble ['skræmbl] N (*climb*) escalada (difícil); (*struggle*) luta ■ VI: **to ~ out/through** conseguir sair com dificuldade; **to ~ for** lutar por

scrambled eggs ['skræmbld-] NPL ovos *mpl* mexidos

scrap [skræp] N (*of paper*) pedacinho; (*of material*) fragmento; (*fig: of truth*) mínimo; (*fight*) rixa, luta; (*also*: **scrap iron**) ferro velho, sucata ■ VT sucatar, jogar no ferro velho; (*fig*) descartar, abolir ■ VI brigar; **scraps** NPL (*leftovers*) sobras *fpl*, restos *mpl*; **to sell sth for ~** vender algo como sucata

scrapbook ['skræpbuk] N álbum *m* de recortes

scrap dealer N ferro-velho *m*, sucateiro(-a)

scrape [skreɪp] N (*fig*): **to get into a ~** meter-se numa enrascada ■ VT raspar; (*scrape against: hand, car*) arranhar, roçar ■ VI: **to ~ through** (*in exam*) passar raspando
▶ **scrape together** VT (*money*) juntar com dificuldade

scraper ['skreɪpər] N raspador *m*

scrap heap N (*fig*): **on the ~** rejeitado, jogado fora

scrap merchant (Brit) N sucateiro(-a)

scrap metal N sucata, ferro-velho

scrap paper N papel *m* de rascunho

scrappy ['skræpɪ] ADJ (*piece of work*) desconexo; (*speech*) incoerente, desconexo; (*bitty*) fragmentário

scrap yard N ferro-velho

scratch [skrætʃ] N arranhão *m*; (*from claw*) arranhadura ■ CPD: **~ team** time *m* improvisado, escrete *m* ■ VT (*rub: one's nose etc*) coçar; (*with claw, nail*) arranhar, unhar; (*damage: paint, car*) arranhar; (*Comput*) apagar ■ VI coçar(-se); **to start from ~** partir do zero; **to be up to ~** estar à altura (das circunstâncias); **scratch pad** (US) N bloco de rascunho

scrawl [skrɔ:l] N garrancho, garatujas *fpl* ■ VI garatujar, rabiscar

scrawny ['skrɔ:nɪ] ADJ magricela

scream [skri:m] N grito ■ VI gritar; **it was a ~** (*inf*) foi engraçadíssimo; **to ~ at sb** gritar com alguém

scree [skri:] N seixos *mpl*

screech [skri:tʃ] VI guinchar ■ N guincho

screen [skri:n] N (*Cinema, TV, Comput*) tela (BR), écran *m* (PT); (*movable*) biombo; (*wall*) tapume *m*; (*also*: **windscreen**) pára-brisa *m*; (*fig*) cortina ■ VT (*conceal*) esconder, tapar; (*from the wind etc*) proteger; (*film*) projetar; (*candidates etc, Med*) examinar; **screen editing** [-ˈɛdɪtɪŋ] N (*Comput*) edição *f* na tela

screening ['skri:nɪŋ] N (*Med*) exame *m* médico; (*of film*) exibição *f*; (*for security*) controle *m*

screen memory N (*Comput*) memória da tela

screenplay ['skri:npleɪ] N roteiro

screensaver ['skri:nseɪvər] N protetor *m* de tela

screen test N teste *m* de cinema

screw [skru:] N parafuso; (*propeller*) hélice *f* ■ VT aparafusar; (*also*: **screw in**) apertar, atarraxar; (*inf!: have sex with*) comer (!), trepar com (!); **to ~ sth to the wall** pregar algo na parede; **to have one's head ~ed on** (*fig*) ter juízo
▶ **screw up** VT (*paper etc*) amassar; (*inf: ruin*) estragar; **to ~ up one's eyes** franzir os olhos; **to ~ up one's face** contrair as feições

screwdriver ['skru:draɪvər] N chave *f* de fenda or de parafuso

screwy ['skru:ɪ] (*inf*) ADJ maluco, estranho

scribble ['skrɪbl] N garrancho ■ VT escrevinhar ■ VI rabiscar; **to ~ sth down** anotar algo apressadamente

scribe [skraɪb] N escriba *m/f*

script [skrɪpt] N (*Cinema etc*) roteiro, script *m*; (*writing*) escrita, caligrafia

scripted ['skrɪptɪd] ADJ (*Radio, TV*) com script

Scripture(s) ['skrɪptʃə(z)] N(PL) Sagrada Escritura

scriptwriter ['skrɪptraɪtər] N roteirista *m/f*

scroll [skrəul] N rolo de pergaminho ■ VT (*Comput*) passar na tela

scrotum ['skrəutəm] N escroto

scrounge [skraundʒ] (*inf*) VT: **to ~ sth off or from sb** filar algo de alguém ■ VI: **to ~ on sb** viver às custas de alguém ■ N: **on the ~** viver às custas de alguém (*or dos outros etc*)

scrounger ['skraundʒər] (*inf*) N filão(-lona) *m/f*

scrub [skrʌb] N (*clean*) esfregação *f*, limpeza; (*land*) mato, cerrado ■ VT esfregar; (*inf: reject*) cancelar, eliminar

scrubbing brush ['skrʌbɪŋ-] N escova de esfrega

scruff [skrʌf] N: **by the ~ of the neck** pelo cangote

scruffy ['skrʌfɪ] ADJ desmazelado

scrum(mage) ['skrʌm(ɪdʒ)] N rolo

scruple ['skru:pl] N escrúpulo; **to have no ~s about doing sth** não ter escrúpulos em fazer algo

scrupulous ['skru:pjuləs] ADJ escrupuloso

scrupulously ['skru:pjələslɪ] ADV

escrupulosamente

scrutinize ['skru:tınaɪz] vᴛ examinar minuciosamente; (*votes*) escrutinar

scrutiny ['skru:tɪnɪ] N escrutínio, exame *m* cuidadoso; **under the ~ of** vigiado por

scuba ['sku:bə] N equipamento de mergulho; **scuba diving** N mergulho

scuff [skʌf] vᴛ desgastar

scuffle ['skʌfl] N tumulto

scull [skʌl] N ginga

scullery ['skʌlərɪ] N copa

sculptor ['skʌlptər] N escultor(a) *m/f*

sculpture ['skʌlptʃər] N escultura

scum [skʌm] N (*on liquid*) espuma; (*pej: people*) ralé *f*, gentinha; (*fig*) escória

scupper ['skʌpər] (*Brit*) vᴛ (*ship*) afundar; (*inf: plans*) estragar

scurrilous ['skʌrɪləs] ADJ calunioso

scurry ['skʌrɪ] vɪ sair correndo
  ▸ **scurry off** vɪ sair correndo, dar no pé

scurvy ['skə:vɪ] N escorbuto

scuttle ['skʌtl] N (*also:* **coal scuttle**) balde *m* para carvão ■ vᴛ (*ship*) afundar voluntariamente, fazer ir a pique ■ vɪ (*scamper*): **to ~ away** *or* **off** sair em disparada

scythe [saɪð] N segadeira, foice *f* grande

SD (*US*) ABBR (*Post*) = **South Dakota**

SDI N ABBR (= *Strategic Defense Initiative*) IDE *f*

SDLP (*Brit*) N ABBR (*Pol*) = **Social Democratic and Labour Party**

SDP (*Brit*) N ABBR = **Social Democratic Party**

sea [si:] N mar *m* ■ CPD do mar, marino; **on the ~** (*boat*) no mar; (*town*) junto ao mar; **by** *or* **beside the ~** (*holiday*) na praia; (*village*) à beira-mar; **to go by ~** viajar por mar; **out to** *or* **at ~** em alto mar; **heavy** *or* **rough ~(s)** mar agitado; **a ~ of faces** (*fig*) uma grande quantidade de pessoas; **to be all at ~** (*fig*) estar confuso *or* desorientado; **sea anemone** N anêmona-do-mar *f*; **sea bed** N fundo do mar; **sea bird** N ave *f* marinha

seaboard ['si:bɔ:d] N costa, litoral *m*

sea breeze N brisa marítima, viração *f*

seafarer ['si:fɛərər] N marinheiro, homem *m* do mar

seafaring ['si:fɛərɪŋ] ADJ (*life*) de marinheiro; **~ people** povo navegante

seafood ['si:fu:d] N mariscos *mpl*

sea front N orla marítima

seagoing ['si:gəʊɪŋ] ADJ (*ship*) de longo curso

seagull ['si:gʌl] N gaivota

seal [si:l] N (*animal*) foca; (*stamp*) selo ■ vᴛ (*close*) fechar; (*: with seal*) selar; (*decide: sb's fate*) decidir; (*: bargain*) fechar; **~ of approval** aprovação *f*
  ▸ **seal off** vᴛ (*close*) fechar; (*cordon off*) isolar

sea level N nível *m* do mar

sealing wax ['si:lɪŋ-] N lacre *m*

sea lion N leão-marinho *m*

sealskin ['si:lskɪn] N pele *f* de foca

seam [si:m] N costura; (*where edges meet*) junta; (*of coal*) veio, filão *m*; **the hall was bursting at the ~s** a sala estava apinhada de gente

seaman ['si:mən] (*irreg*) N marinheiro

seamanship ['si:mənʃɪp] N náutica

seamen ['si:mɛn] NPL *of* **seaman**

seamless ['si:mlɪs] ADJ sem costura

seamstress ['sɛmstrɪs] N costureira

seamy ['si:mɪ] ADJ sórdido

seance ['seɪɒns] N sessão *f* espírita

seaplane ['si:pleɪn] N hidroavião *m*

seaport ['si:pɔ:t] N porto de mar

search [sə:tʃ] N (*for person, thing*) busca, procura; (*Comput*) procura; (*of drawer, pockets*) revista; (*inspection*) exame *m*, investigação *f* ■ vᴛ (*look in*) procurar em; (*examine*) examinar; (*person, place*) revistar ■ vɪ: **to ~ for** procurar; **in ~ of** à procura de; **"~ and replace"** (*Comput*) "procura e substituição"
  ▸ **search through** vᴛ ꜰᴜѕ dar busca em

search engine N (*on Internet*) ferramenta *f* de busca

searching ['sə:tʃɪŋ] ADJ penetrante, perscrutador(a); (*study*) minucioso

searchlight ['sə:tʃlaɪt] N holofote *m*

search party N equipe *f* de salvamento

search warrant N mandado de busca

searing ['sɪərɪŋ] ADJ (*heat*) ardente; (*pain*) agudo

seashore ['si:ʃɔ:r] N praia, beira-mar *f*, litoral *m*; **on the ~** na praia

seasick ['si:sɪk] ADJ enjoado, mareado; **to be** *or* **get ~** enjoar

seaside ['si:saɪd] N praia; **seaside resort** N balneário

season ['si:zn] N (*of year*) estação *f*; (*sporting etc*) temporada; (*of films etc*) série *f* ■ vᴛ (*food*) temperar; **to be in/out of ~** (*fruit*) estar na época/fora de época; **the busy ~** (*shops*) a época de muito movimento; (*hotels*) a temporada de férias; **the open ~** (*Hunting*) a temporada de caça

seasonal ['si:zənəl] ADJ sazonal

seasoned ['si:znd] ADJ (*wood*) tratado; (*fig: traveller*) experiente; (*: worker, troops*) calejado; **a ~ campaigner** um combatente experiente

seasoning ['si:zənɪŋ] N tempero

season ticket N bilhete *m* de temporada

seat [si:t] N (*in bus, train: place*) assento; (*chair*) cadeira; (*Pol*) lugar *m*, cadeira; (*of bicycle*) selim *m*; (*buttocks*) traseiro, nádegas *fpl*; (*of government*) sede *f*; (*of trousers*) fundilhos *mpl* ■ vᴛ sentar; (*have room for*) ter capacidade para; **to be ~ed** estar sentado; **are there any ~s left?** há algum lugar vago?; **to take one's ~** sentar-se; **please be ~ed** sentem-se; **seat belt** N cinto de segurança

seating ['si:tɪŋ] N lugares *mpl* sentados ■ CPD: **~ arrangements** distribuição *f* dos lugares sentados; **seating capacity** N lotação *f*

SEATO ['si:təʊ] N ABBR (= *Southeast Asia Treaty Organization*) OTSA *f*

sea urchin N ouriço-do-mar *m*

sea water N água do mar

seaweed ['si:wi:d] N alga marinha

seaworthy ['si:wə:ðɪ] ADJ em condições de navegar, resistente

SEC (US) N ABBR (= *Securities and Exchange Commission*) órgão que supervisiona o funcionamento da Bolsa de Valores

sec. ABBR (= *second*) seg

secateurs [sɛkə'təːz] NPL tesoura para podar plantas

secede [sɪ'siːd] VI separar-se

secluded [sɪ'kluːdɪd] ADJ (*place*) afastado; (*life*) solitário

seclusion [sɪ'kluːʒən] N reclusão f, isolamento

second¹ [sɪkɔnd] (*Brit*) VT (*employee*) transferir temporariamente

second² ['sɛkənd] ADJ segundo ■ ADV (*in race etc*) em segundo lugar ■ N segundo; (*Aut: also*: **second gear**) segunda; (*Comm*) artigo defeituoso; (*Brit: Sch: degree*) uma qualificação boa mas sem distinção ■ VT (*motion*) apoiar, secundar; **Charles the S~** Carlos II; **just a ~!** um minuto *or* minutinho!; **~ floor** (*Brit*) segundo andar; (*US*) primeiro andar; **to ask for a ~ opinion** (*Med*) querer uma segunda opinião

secondary ['sɛkəndərɪ] ADJ secundário;

secondary school N escola secundária, colégio

● **SECONDARY SCHOOL**
●
● Uma *secondary school* é um estabelecimento
● de ensino para alunos de 11 a 18 anos,
● alguns dos quais interrompem os estudos
● aos 16 anos. A maior parte dessas escolas
● é formada por *comprehensive schools*, mas
● algumas *secondary schools* ainda têm sistemas
● rigorosos de seleção.

second-best N segunda opção f

second-class ADJ de segunda classe ■ ADV em segunda classe; **to send sth ~** remeter algo em segunda classe; **to travel ~** viajar em segunda classe; **~ citizen** cidadão(-dã) da segunda classe

second cousin N primo(-a) em segundo grau

seconder ['sɛkəndər] N pessoa que secunda uma moção

secondhand [sɛkənd'hænd] ADJ de (BR) *or* em (PT) segunda mão, usado ■ ADV (*buy*) de (BR) *or* em (PT) segunda mão; **to hear sth ~** ouvir algo de fonte indireta

second hand N (*on clock*) ponteiro de segundos

second-in-command N suplente m/f

secondly ['sɛkəndlɪ] ADV em segundo lugar

secondment [sɪ'kɔndmənt] (*Brit*) N substituição f temporária

second-rate ADJ de segunda categoria

second thoughts (*US* second thought) NPL: **to have ~** (**about doing sth**) pensar duas vezes (antes de fazer algo); **on ~** pensando bem

secrecy ['siːkrəsɪ] N sigilo; **in ~** sob sigilo, sigilosamente

secret ['siːkrɪt] ADJ secreto ■ N segredo; **in ~** em segredo; **to keep sth ~ from sb** esconder algo de alguém; **keep it ~** não diz nada a ninguém; **to make no ~ of sth** não esconder algo de ninguém; **secret agent** N agente m/f

secreto(-a)

secretarial [sɛkrɪ'tɛərɪəl] ADJ de secretário(-a), secretarial

secretariat [sɛkrɪ'tɛərɪət] N secretaria, secretariado

secretary ['sɛkrətərɪ] N secretário(-a); (*Brit: Pol*): **S~ of State** Ministro(-a) de Estado; **Foreign S~** (*US: Pol*) Ministro(-a) das Relações Exteriores

secrete [sɪ'kriːt] VT (*Anat, Bio, Med*) secretar; (*hide*) esconder

secretion [sɪ'kriːʃən] N secreção f

secretive ['siːkrətɪv] ADJ sigiloso, reservado

secretly ['siːkrətlɪ] ADV secretamente

sect [sɛkt] N seita

sectarian [sɛk'tɛərɪən] ADJ sectário

section ['sɛkʃən] N seção f; (*part*) parte f, porção f; (*of document*) parágrafo, artigo; (*of opinion*) setor m; **cross-~** corte m transversal ■ VT secionar; **the business** *etc* **~** (*Press*) a seção de negócios *etc*

sector ['sɛktər] N setor m

secular ['sɛkjulər] ADJ (*priest*) secular; (*music, society*) leigo

secure [sɪ'kjuər] ADJ (*safe*) seguro; (*firmly fixed*) firme, rígido; (*in safe place*) a salvo, em segurança ■ VT (*fix*) prender; (*get*) conseguir, obter; (*Comm: loan*) garantir; **to make sth ~** firmar algo, segurar algo; **to ~ sth for sb** arranjar algo para alguém

secured creditor [sɪ'kjuəd-] N credor m com garantia

security [sɪ'kjurɪtɪ] N segurança; (*for loan*) fiança, garantia; (: *object*) penhor m; **securities** NPL (*Stock Exchange*) títulos mpl, valores mpl; **to increase** *or* **tighten ~** aumentar a segurança; **security forces** NPL forças fpl de segurança; **security guard** N (guarda m/f de) segurança m/f; **security risk** N risco à segurança

sedan [sɪ'dæn] (*US*) N (*Aut*) sedã m

sedate [sɪ'deɪt] ADJ calmo; (*calm*) sossegado, tranqüilo; (*formal*) sério, ponderado ■ VT sedar, tratar com calmantes

sedation [sɪ'deɪʃən] N (*Med*) sedação f; **to be under ~** estar sob o efeito de sedativos

sedative ['sɛdɪtɪv] N calmante m, sedativo

sedentary ['sɛdntrɪ] ADJ sedentário

sediment ['sɛdɪmənt] N sedimento

sedition [sɪ'dɪʃən] N sedição f

seduce [sɪ'djuːs] VT seduzir

seduction [sɪ'dʌkʃən] N sedução f

seductive [sɪ'dʌktɪv] ADJ sedutor(a)

see [siː] (*pt* saw, *pp* seen) VT ver; (*make out*) enxergar; (*understand*) entender; (*accompany*): **to ~ sb to the door** acompanhar *or* levar alguém até a porta ■ VI ver; (*find out*) achar ■ N sé f, sede f; **to ~ that** (*ensure*) assegurar que; **there was nobody to be ~n** não havia ninguém; **let me ~** deixa eu ver; **to go and ~ sb** ir visitar alguém; **~ for yourself** veja você mesmo, confira; **I don't know what she ~s in him** não sei o que ela vê nele; **as far as I can ~** que eu saiba; **~ you!** até logo! (BR), adeus! (PT); **~ you soon/later/tomorrow!** até logo/mais tarde/amanhã!

► **see about** VT FUS tratar de
► **see off** VT despedir-se de
► **see through** VT FUS enxergar através de
■ VT levar a cabo
► **see to** VT FUS providenciar
seed [si:d] N semente f; (*sperm*) esperma m; (*fig*: *gem pl*) germe m; (*Tennis*) pré-selecionado(-a); **to go to ~** produzir sementes; (*fig*) deteriorar-se
seedless ['si:dlɪs] ADJ sem caroças
seedling ['si:dlɪŋ] N planta brotada da semente, muda
seedy ['si:dɪ] ADJ (*shabby: place*) mal-cuidado; (*: person*) maltrapilho
seeing ['si:ɪŋ] CONJ: **~ (that)** visto (que), considerando (que)
seek [si:k] (*pt, pp* sought) VT procurar; (*post*) solicitar; **to ~ advice/help from sb** pedir um conselho a alguém/procurar ajuda de alguém
► **seek out** VT (*person*) procurar
seem [si:m] VI parecer; **there ~s to be ...** parece que há ...; **what ~s to be the trouble?** qual é o problema?; **I did what ~ed best** fiz o que me pareceu melhor
seemingly ['si:mɪŋlɪ] ADV aparentemente, pelo que aparenta
seen [si:n] PP *of* **see**
seep [si:p] VI filtrar-se, penetrar
seer [sɪə^r] N vidente m/f, profeta m/f
seersucker ['sɪəsʌkə^r] N tecido listrado de algodão
seesaw ['si:sɔ:] N gangorra, balanço
seethe [si:ð] VI ferver; **to ~ with anger** estar danado (da vida)
see-through ADJ transparente
segment ['sɛgmənt] N segmento; (*of orange*) gomo
segregate ['sɛgrɪgeɪt] VT segregar
segregation [sɛgrɪ'geɪʃən] N segregação f
Seine [seɪn] N: **the ~** o Sena
seismic ['saɪzmɪk] ADJ sísmico
seize [si:z] VT (*grasp*) agarrar, pegar; (*take possession of: power, hostage*) apoderar-se de, confiscar; (*: territory*) tomar posse de; (*opportunity*) aproveitar
► **seize up** VI (*Tech*) gripar
► **seize (up)on** VT FUS valer-se de
seizure ['si:ʒə^r] N (*Med*) ataque m, acesso; (*Law, of power*) confisco, embargo
seldom ['sɛldəm] ADV raramente
select [sɪ'lɛkt] ADJ seleto, fino ■ VT escolher, selecionar; (*Sport*) selecionar, escalar; **a ~ few** uns poucos escolhidos
selection [sɪ'lɛkʃən] N seleção f, escolha; (*Comm*) sortimento; **selection committee** N comissão f de seleção
selective [sɪ'lɛktɪv] ADJ seletivo
selector [sɪ'lɛktə^r] N (*person*) selecionador(a) m/f, seletor(a) m/f; (*Tech*) selecionador m
self [sɛlf] (*pl* selves) PRON *see* **herself; himself; itself; myself; oneself; ourselves; themselves; yourself** ■ N: **the ~** o eu
self... [sɛlf] PREFIX auto...

self-addressed [-ə'drɛst] ADJ: **~ envelope** envelope m endereçado ao remetente
self-adhesive ADJ auto-adesivo
self-appointed [-ə'pɔɪntɪd] ADJ auto-nomeado
self-assertive ADJ autoritário
self-assurance N autoconfiança
self-assured [-ə'ʃuəd] ADJ seguro de si
self-catering (*Brit*) ADJ (*flat*) com cozinha; (*holiday*) em casa alugada
self-centred [-'sɛntəd] (*US* **self-centered**) ADJ egocêntrico
self-cleaning ADJ de limpeza automática
self-coloured (*US* **self-colored**) ADJ de cor natural; (*of one colour*) de uma só cor
self-confessed [-kən'fɛst] ADJ assumido
self-confidence N autoconfiança, confiança em si
self-conscious ADJ inibido, constrangido
self-contained [-kən'teɪnd] (*Brit*) ADJ (*gen*) independente; (*flat*) completo, autônomo
self-control N autocontrole m, autodomínio
self-defeating [-dɪ'fi:tɪŋ] ADJ contraproducente
self-defence (*US* **self-defense**) N legítima defesa, autodefesa; **in ~** em legítima defesa
self-discipline N autodisciplina
self-employed [-ɪm'plɔɪd] ADJ autônomo
self-esteem N amor m próprio
self-evident ADJ patente
self-explanatory ADJ que se explica por si mesmo
self-governing [-'gʌvənɪs] ADJ autônomo
self-help N iniciativa própria, esforço pessoal
self-importance N presunção f
self-important ADJ presunçoso, que se dá muita importância
self-indulgent ADJ que se permite excessos
self-inflicted [-ɪn'flɪktɪd] ADJ infligido a si mesmo
self-interest N egoísmo
selfish ['sɛlfɪʃ] ADJ egoísta
selfishness ['sɛlfɪʃnɪs] N egoísmo
selfless ['sɛlflɪs] ADJ desinteressado
selflessly ['sɛlflɪslɪ] ADV desinteressadamente
self-made N: **~ man** homem m que se fez por conta própria
self-pity N pena de si mesmo
self-portrait N auto-retrato
self-possessed [-pə'zɛst] ADJ calmo, senhor(a) de si
self-preservation N auto-preservação f
self-raising [-'reɪzɪŋ] (*Brit*) ADJ: **~ flour** farinha de trigo com fermento acrescentado
self-reliant ADJ seguro de si, independente
self-respect N amor m próprio
self-respecting [-rɪs'pɛktɪŋ] ADJ que se respeita
self-righteous ADJ farisaico, santarrão(-rona)
self-rising (*US*) ADJ: **~ flour** farinha de trigo com fermento acrescentado
self-sacrifice N abnegação f, altruísmo
self-same ADJ mesmo
self-satisfied [-'sætɪsfaɪd] ADJ satisfeito consigo mesmo

self-sealing ADJ (envelope) auto-adesivo
self-service ADJ de auto-serviço ▪ N auto-serviço
self-styled [-staɪld] ADJ pretenso
self-sufficient ADJ auto-suficiente
self-supporting [-sə'pɔːtɪŋ] ADJ financeiramente independente
self-tanning ADJ autobronzeador
self-taught ADJ autodidata
self-test N (Comput) auto-teste m
sell [sɛl] (pt, pp sold) VT vender; (fig): **to ~ sb an idea** convencer alguém de uma idéia ▪ VI vender-se; **to ~ at** or **for £10** vender a or por £10
▸ **sell off** VT liquidar
▸ **sell out** VI vender todo o estoque ▪ VT: **the tickets are all sold out** todos os ingressos já foram vendidos; **to ~ out (to)** (Comm) vender o negócio (a); (fig) vender-se (a)
▸ **sell up** VI vender o negócio
sell-by date N vencimento
seller ['sɛlər] N vendedor(a) m/f; **~'s market** mercado de vendedor
selling price ['sɛlɪŋ-] N preço de venda
Sellotape® ['sɛləuteɪp] (Brit) N fita adesiva, durex® m (BR)
sellout ['sɛlaut] N traição f; (of tickets): **it was a ~** foi um sucesso de bilheteria
selves [sɛlvz] PL of **self**
semantic [sə'mæntɪk] ADJ semântico
semantics [sə'mæntɪks] N semântica
semaphore ['sɛməfɔːr] N semáforo
semblance ['sɛmbləns] N aparência
semen ['siːmən] N sêmen m
semester [sə'mɛstər] (esp US) N semestre m
semi ['sɛmɪ] (Brit: inf) N (casa) geminada
semi... [sɛmɪ] PREFIX semi..., meio...
semibreve ['sɛmɪbriːv] (Brit) N semibreve f
semicircle ['sɛmɪsəːkl] N semicírculo
semicircular [sɛmɪ'səːkjulər] ADJ semicircular
semicolon [sɛmɪ'kəulɔn] N ponto e vírgula
semiconductor [sɛmɪkən'dʌktər] N semicondutor m
semi-conscious ADJ semiconsciente
semidetached (house) [sɛmɪdɪtætʃt-] (Brit) N (casa) geminada
semifinal [sɛmɪfaɪnl] N semifinal f
seminar ['sɛmɪnɑːr] N seminário
seminary ['sɛmɪnərɪ] N (for priests) seminário
semiprecious [sɛmɪ'prɛʃəs] ADJ semiprecioso
semiquaver ['sɛmɪkweɪvər] (Brit) N semicolcheia
semiskilled [sɛmɪ'skɪld] ADJ (work, worker) semi-especializado
semi-skimmed milk [sɛmɪ'skɪmd-] N leite m semidesnatado
semitone ['sɛmɪtəun] N (Mus) semitom m
semolina [sɛmə'liːnə] N sêmola, semolina
SEN (Brit) N ABBR = **State Enrolled Nurse**
Sen. ABBR = **Senator; Senior**
sen. ABBR = **senator; senior**
senate ['sɛnɪt] N senado
senator ['sɛnətər] N senador(a) m/f

send [sɛnd] (pt, pp sent) VT mandar, enviar; (dispatch) expedir, remeter; (transmit) transmitir; (telegram) passar; **to ~ by post** (Brit) or **mail** (US) mandar pelo correio; **to ~ sb for sth** mandar alguém buscar algo; **to ~ word that ...** mandar dizer que ...; **she ~s (you) her love** ela lhe envia lembranças; **to ~ sb to Coventry** (Brit) colocar alguém em ostracismo; **to ~ sb to sleep** dar sono a alguém; **to ~ sb into fits of laughter** dar um ataque de riso a alguém; **to ~ sth flying** derrubar algo
▸ **send away** VT (letter, goods) expedir, mandar; (unwelcome visitor) mandar embora
▸ **send away for** VT FUS encomendar, pedir pelo correio
▸ **send back** VT devolver, mandar de volta
▸ **send for** VT FUS mandar buscar; (by post) pedir pelo correio, encomendar
▸ **send in** VT (report, application) entregar
▸ **send off** VT (goods) despachar, expedir; (Brit: Sport: player) expulsar
▸ **send on** VT (Brit: letter) remeter; (luggage etc: in advance) mandar com antecedência
▸ **send out** VT (invitation) distribuir; (signal) emitir
▸ **send round** VT (letter, document) circular
▸ **send up** VT (person, price) fazer subir; (Brit: parody) parodiar
sender ['sɛndər] N remetente m/f
send-off N: **a good ~** uma boa despedida
Senegal [sɛnɪ'gɔːl] N Senegal m
Senegalese [sɛnɪgə'liːz] ADJ, N INV senegalês(-esa) m/f
senile ['siːnaɪl] ADJ senil
senility [sɪ'nɪlɪtɪ] N senilidade f
senior ['siːnɪər] ADJ (old) mais velho or idoso; (on staff) mais antigo; (of higher rank) superior ▪ N o mais velho (a mais velha); (on staff) o mais antigo (a mais antiga); **P. Jones ~** P. Jones Sênior; **senior citizen** N idoso(-a); **senior high school** (US) N ≈ colégio
seniority [siːnɪ'ɔrɪtɪ] N antiguidade f; (in service) status m
sensation [sɛn'seɪʃən] N sensação f; **to cause a ~** causar sensação
sensational [sɛn'seɪʃənl] ADJ sensacional; (headlines, result) sensacionalista
sensationalism [sɛn'seɪʃənəlɪzəm] N sensacionalismo
sense [sɛns] N sentido; (feeling) sensação f; (good sense) bom senso ▪ VT sentir, perceber; **senses** NPL juízo; **it makes ~** faz sentido; **there is no ~ in (doing) that** não há sentido em (fazer) isso; **to come to one's ~s** (regain consciousness) recobrar os sentidos; (become reasonable) recobrar o juízo; **to take leave of one's ~s** enlouquecer
senseless ['sɛnslɪs] ADJ insensato, estúpido; (unconscious) sem sentidos, inconsciente
sense of humour N senso de humor
sensibility [sɛnsɪ'bɪlɪtɪ] N sensibilidade f; **sensibilities** NPL suscetibilidade f
sensible ['sɛnsɪbl] ADJ sensato, de bom senso;

(reasonable: price) razoável; (: advice, decision) sensato; (shoes etc) prático

sensitive ['sɛnsɪtɪv] ADJ sensível; (fig: touchy) suscetível

sensitivity [sɛnsɪ'tɪvɪtɪ] N sensibilidade f; (touchiness) suscetibilidade f

sensual ['sɛnsjuəl] ADJ sensual

sensuous ['sɛnsjuəs] ADJ sensual

sent [sɛnt] PT, PP of **send**

sentence ['sɛntəns] N (Ling) frase f, oração f; (Law: verdict) sentença; (: punishment) pena ■ VT: **to ~ sb to death/to 5 years** condenar alguém à morte/a 5 anos de prisão; **to pass ~ on sb** sentenciar alguém

sentiment ['sɛntɪmənt] N sentimento; (opinion: also pl) opinião f

sentimental [sɛntɪ'mɛntl] ADJ sentimental

sentimentality [sɛntɪmɛn'tælɪtɪ] N sentimentalismo

sentry ['sɛntrɪ] N sentinela f; **sentry duty** N: **to be on sentry duty** estar de guarda

Seoul [səul] N Seul

separable ['sɛprəbl] ADJ separável

separate [adj 'sɛprɪt, vt, vi 'sɛpəreɪt] ADJ separado; (distinct) diferente ■ VT separar; (part) dividir ■ VI separar-se; **~ from** separado de; **under ~ cover** (Comm) em separado; **to ~ into** dividir em

separated ['sɛpəreɪtɪd] ADJ (from spouse) separado

separately ['sɛprɪtlɪ] ADV separadamente

separates ['sɛprɪts] NPL (clothes) roupas fpl que fazem jogo

separation [sɛpə'reɪʃən] N separação f

Sept. ABBR (= September) set

September [sɛp'tɛmbəʳ] N setembro; see also **July**

septic ['sɛptɪk] ADJ sético; (wound) infeccionado

septicaemia [sɛptɪ'siːmɪə] (US **septicemia**) N septicemia

septic tank N fossa sética

sequel ['siːkwl] N conseqüência, resultado; (of film, story) continuação f

sequence ['siːkwəns] N série f, seqüência; (Cinema) série; **in ~** em seqüência

sequential [sɪ'kwɛnʃəl] ADJ: **~ access** (Comput) acesso seqüencial

sequin ['siːkwɪn] N lantejoula, paetê m

Serbo-Croat ['səː:bəu'krəuæt] N (Ling) serbo-croata m

serenade [sɛrə'neɪd] N serenata ■ VT fazer serenata para

serene [sɪ'riːn] ADJ sereno, tranqüilo

serenity [sə'rɛnɪtɪ] N serenidade f, tranqüilidade f

sergeant ['sɑːdʒənt] N sargento; **sergeant major** N sargento-ajudante m

serial ['sɪərɪəl] N (TV, Radio, magazine) seriado; (in newspaper) história em folhetim ■ ADJ (Comput: interface, printer) serial; (: access) seqüencial

serialize ['sɪərɪəlaɪz] VT (book) publicar em folhetim; (TV) seriar

serial number N número de série

series ['sɪəriːz] N INV série f

serious ['sɪərɪəs] ADJ sério; (matter) importante; (illness) grave; **are you ~ (about it)?** você está falando sério?

seriously ['sɪərɪəslɪ] ADV a sério, com seriedade; (hurt) gravemente; **to take sth/sb ~** levar algo/alguém a sério

seriousness ['sɪərɪəsnɪs] N (of manner) seriedade f; (importance) importância; (gravity) gravidade f

sermon ['səːmən] N sermão m

serrated [sɪ'reɪtɪd] ADJ serrado, dentado

serum ['sɪərəm] N soro

servant ['səːvənt] N empregado(-a); (fig) servidor(a) m/f

serve [səːv] VT servir; (customer) atender; (subj: train) passar por; (treat) tratar; (apprenticeship) fazer; (prison term) cumprir ■ VI (at table) servir-se; (Tennis) sacar; (be useful): **to ~ as/for/to do** servir como/para/para fazer ■ N (Tennis) saque m; **are you being ~d?** você já foi atendido?; **to ~ on a committee/jury** fazer parte de um comitê/júri; **it ~s him right** é bem feito para ele; **it ~s my purpose** isso me serve

▶ **serve out** VT (food) servir

▶ **serve up** VT = **serve out**

service ['səːvɪs] N serviço; (Rel) culto; (Aut) revisão f; (Tennis) saque m; (also: **dinner service**) aparelho de jantar ■ VT (car, washing machine) fazer a revisão de, revisar; (: repair) consertar; **the Services** NPL (army, navy etc) as Forças Armadas; **to be of ~ to sb, to do sb a ~** ser útil a alguém

serviceable ['səːvɪsəbl] ADJ aproveitável, prático, durável

service area N (on motorway) posto de gasolina com bar, restaurante etc

service charge (Brit) N serviço

service industries NPL setor m de serviços

serviceman ['səːvɪsmæn] (irreg) N militar m

service station N posto de gasolina (BR), estação f de serviço (PT)

serviette [səːvɪ'ɛt] (Brit) N guardanapo

servile ['səːvaɪl] ADJ servil

session ['sɛʃən] N (period of activity) sessão f; (Sch) ano letivo; **to be in ~** estar reunido em sessão

set [sɛt] (pt, pp **set**) N (collection of things) jogo; (radio set, TV set) aparelho; (of utensils) bateria de cozinha; (of cutlery) talher m; (of books) coleção f; (group of people) grupo; (Tennis) set m; (Theatre, Cinema) cenário; (Hairdressing) penteado; (Math) conjunto ■ ADJ (fixed) fixo; (ready) pronto; (resolved) decidido, estabelecido ■ VT (place) pôr, colocar; (table) pôr; (establish: price) fixar; (: rules etc) estabelecer, decidir; (record) estabelecer; (: time) marcar; (adjust) ajustar; (task, exam) passar; (Typ) compor ■ VI (sun) pôr-se; (jam, jelly, concrete) endurecer, solidificar-se; **to be ~ on doing sth** estar decidido a fazer algo; **to be all ~ to do** estar todo pronto para fazer; **to be (dead) ~ against** estar (completamente) contra; **he's ~ in his ways** ele tem opiniões fixas; **to ~ to music** musicar, pôr música em; **to ~ on fire**

botar fogo em, incendiar; **to ~ free** libertar; **to ~ sth going** pôr algo em movimento; **to ~ sail** zarpar, alçar velas; **~ phrase** frase *f* feita; **a ~ of false teeth** uma dentadura; **a ~ of dining-room furniture** um conjunto de salade jantar; **a film ~ in Rome** um filme ambientado em Roma
▶ **set about** VT FUS (*task*) começar com; **to ~ about doing sth** começar a fazer algo
▶ **set aside** VT deixar de lado
▶ **set back** VT (*cost*): **it ~ me back £5** me deu um prejuízo de £5; (*in time*): **to ~ sb back (by)** atrasar alguém (em); (*place*): **a house ~ back from the road** uma casa afastada da estrada
▶ **set in** VI (*infection*) manifestar-se; (*complications*) surgir; **the rain has ~ in for the day** vai chover o dia inteiro
▶ **set off** VI partir, ir indo ◼ VT (*bomb*) fazer explodir; (*alarm*) disparar; (*chain of events*) iniciar; (*show up well*) ressaltar
▶ **set out** VI partir ◼ VT (*arrange*) colocar, dispor; (*state*) expor, explicar; **to ~ out to do sth** pretender fazer algo; **to ~ out (from)** sair (de)
▶ **set up** VT (*organization*) fundar, estabelecer; **to ~ up shop** (*fig*) estabelecer-se
setback ['sɛtbæk] N (*hitch*) revés *m*, contratempo; (*in health*) piora
set menu N refeição *f* a preço fixo
set square N esquadro
settee [sɛ'tiː] N sofá *m*
setting ['sɛtɪŋ] N (*background*) cenário; (*position*) posição *f*; (*frame*) moldura; (*placing*) colocação *f*; (*of sun*) pôr(-do-sol) *m*; (*of jewel*) engaste *m*; **setting lotion** N loção *f* fixadora
settle ['sɛtl] VT (*argument, matter*) resolver, esclarecer; (*accounts*) ajustar, liquidar; (*land*) colonizar; (*Med: calm*) acalmar, tranqüilizar ◼ VI (*dust etc*) assentar; (*calm down: children*) acalmar-se; (*weather*) firmar, melhorar; (*also:* **settle down**) instalar-se, estabilizar-se; **to ~ sth** concentrar-se em algo; **to ~ for sth** concordar em aceitar algo; **to ~ on sth** optar por algo; **that's ~d then** está resolvido então; **to ~ one's stomach** acomodar o estômago
▶ **settle in** VI instalar-se
▶ **settle up** VI: **to ~ up with sb** ajustar as contas com alguém
settlement ['sɛtlmənt] N (*payment*) liquidação *f*; (*agreement*) acordo, convênio; (*village etc*) povoado, povoação *f*; **in ~ of our account** (*Comm*) em liquidação da nossa conta
settler ['sɛtlə'] N colono(-a), colonizador(a) *m/f*
setup ['sɛtʌp] N (*organization*) organização *f*; (*situation*) situação *f*
seven ['sɛvn] NUM sete; *see also* **five**
seventeen ['sɛvn'tiːn] NUM dezessete; *see also* **five**
seventh ['sɛvnθ] NUM sétimo; *see also* **fifth**
seventy ['sɛvntɪ] NUM setenta; *see also* **fifty**
sever ['sɛvə'] VT cortar; (*relations*) romper
several ['sɛvərl] ADJ, PRON vários(-as); **~ of us** vários de nós; **~ times** várias vezes

severance ['sɛvərəns] N (*of relations*) rompimento; **severance pay** N indenização *f* pela demissão
severe [sɪ'vɪə'] ADJ severo; (*serious*) grave; (*hard*) duro; (*pain*) intenso; (*dress*) austero
severely [sɪ'vɪəlɪ] ADV severamente; (*wounded, ill*) gravemente
severity [sɪ'vɛrɪtɪ] N severidade *f*; (*of pain*) intensidade *f*; (*of dress*) austeridade *f*
sew [səu] (*pt* **sewed**, *pp* **sewn**) VT, VI coser, costurar
▶ **sew up** VT coser, costurar; **it's all ~n up** (*fig*) está no papo
sewage ['suːɪdʒ] N detritos *mpl*
sewer ['suːə'] N (*cano do*) esgoto, bueiro
sewing ['səuɪŋ] N costura; **sewing machine** N máquina de costura
sewn [səun] PP *of* **sew**
sex [sɛks] N sexo; **to have ~ with sb** fazer sexo com alguém; **sex act** N ato sexual
sexism ['sɛksɪzm] N sexismo
sexist ['sɛksɪst] ADJ sexista
sextet [sɛks'tɛt] N sexteto
sexual ['sɛksjuəl] ADJ sexual; **~ assault** atentado ao pudor; **~ intercourse** relações *fpl* sexuais
sexy ['sɛksɪ] ADJ sexy
Seychelles [seɪ'ʃɛl(z)] NPL: **the ~** Seychelles (*no article*)
SF N ABBR = **science fiction**
SG (US) N ABBR = **Surgeon General**
Sgt ABBR (= *sergeant*) sarg
shabbiness ['ʃæbɪnɪs] N (*of clothes*) pobreza; (*of building*) mau estado de conservação
shabby ['ʃæbɪ] ADJ (*person*) esfarrapado, maltrapilho; (*clothes*) usado, surrado; (*behaviour*) indigno
shack [ʃæk] N choupana, barraca
shackles ['ʃæklz] NPL algemas *fpl*, grilhões *mpl*
shade [ʃeɪd] N sombra; (*for lamp*) quebra-luz *m*; (*for eyes*) viseira; (*of colour*) tom *m*, tonalidade *f*; (*US: window shade*) estore *m*; (*small quantity*): **a ~ (more/big)** um pouquinho (mais/grande) ◼ VT dar sombra a; (*eyes*) sombrear; **shades** NPL (*US: sunglasses*) óculos *mpl* escuros; **in the ~** à sombra
shadow ['ʃædəu] N sombra ◼ VT (*follow*) seguir de perto (sem ser visto); **without** *or* **beyond a ~ of doubt** sem sombra de dúvida; **shadow cabinet** (*Brit*) N (*Pol*) gabinete paralelo formado pelo partido da oposição
shadowy ['ʃædəuɪ] ADJ escuro; (*dim*) vago, indistinto
shady ['ʃeɪdɪ] ADJ à sombra; (*fig: dishonest: person*) suspeito, duvidoso; (: *deal*) desonesto
shaft [ʃɑːft] N (*of arrow, spear*) haste *f*; (*column*) fuste *m*; (*Aut, Tech*) eixo, manivela; (*of mine, of lift*) poço; (*of light*) raio
shaggy ['ʃægɪ] ADJ desgrenhado
shake [ʃeɪk] (*pt* **shook**, *pp* **shaken**) VT sacudir; (*building, confidence*) abalar; (*surprise*) surpreender ◼ VI tremer ◼ N (*movement*) sacudidela; (*violent*) safanão *m*; **to ~ hands with sb** apertar a mão

de alguém; **to ~ one's head** (in refusal etc) dizer
não com a cabeça; (in dismay) sacudir a cabeça
▶ **shake off** VT sacudir; (fig) livrar-se de
▶ **shake up** VT sacudir; (fig) reorganizar
shake-up N reorganização f
shakily ['ʃeɪkɪlɪ] ADV (reply) de voz trêmula; (walk)
vacilante; (write) de mão trêmula
shaky ['ʃeɪkɪ] ADJ (hand, voice) trêmulo; (table)
instável; (building) abalado; (person: in shock)
abalado; (: old) frágil; (knowledge) duvidoso
shale [ʃeɪl] N argila xistosa
shall [ʃæl] AUX VB: **I ~ go** irei; **~ I open the door?**
posso abrir a porta?; **I'll get some, ~ I?** eu vou
pegar algum, está bem?
shallot [ʃə'lɔt] (Brit) N cebolinha
shallow ['ʃæləu] ADJ raso; (breathing) fraco; (fig)
superficial
sham [ʃæm] N fraude f, fingimento ■ ADJ falso,
simulado ■ VT fingir, simular
shambles ['ʃæmblz] N confusão f; **the
economy is (in) a complete ~** a economia está
completamente desorganizada
shame [ʃeɪm] N vergonha; (pity) pena ■ VT
envergonhar; **it is a ~ (that/to do)** é (uma)
pena (que/fazer); **what a ~!** que pena!; **to put
sb/sth to ~** deixar alguém/algo envergonhado
shamefaced ['ʃeɪmfeɪst] ADJ envergonhado
shameful ['ʃeɪmful] ADJ vergonhoso
shameless ['ʃeɪmlɪs] ADJ sem vergonha,
descarado; (immodest) cínico, impudico
shampoo [ʃæm'pu:] N xampu m (BR), champô
m (PT) ■ VT lavar o cabelo (com xampu or
champô); **shampoo and set** N lavagem f e
penteado
shamrock ['ʃæmrɔk] N trevo
shandy ['ʃændɪ] N mistura de cerveja com refresco
gaseificado
shan't [ʃɑ:nt] = **shall not**
shanty town ['ʃæntɪ-] N favela
SHAPE [ʃeɪp] N ABBR (= Supreme Headquarters Allied
Powers, Europe) QG das forças aliadas na Europa
shape [ʃeɪp] N forma ■ VT (form) moldar; (clay,
stone) dar forma a; (sb's ideas) formar; (sb's life)
definir, determinar; **to take ~** tomar forma; **in
the ~ of a heart** em forma de coração; **I can't
bear gardening in any ~ or form** não suporto
jardinagem de forma alguma; **to get o.s. into ~**
ficar em forma
▶ **shape up** VI (events) desenrolar-se; (person)
tomar jeito
-shaped [ʃeɪpt] SUFFIX: **heart~** em forma de
coração
shapeless ['ʃeɪplɪs] ADJ informe, sem forma
definida
shapely ['ʃeɪplɪ] ADJ escultural
share [ʃeəʳ] N (part) parte f; (contribution) cota;
(Comm) ação f ■ VT dividir; (have in common)
compartilhar; **to ~ in** participar de; **to have a ~
in the profits** ter uma participação nos lucros
▶ **share out** VI: **to ~ out (among** or **between)**
distribuir (entre)
share capital N capital m em ações

share certificate N cautela de ação
shareholder ['ʃeəhəuldəʳ] N acionista m/f
share index N índice m da Bolsa de Valores
share issue N emissão f de ações
shark [ʃɑ:k] N tubarão m
sharp [ʃɑ:p] ADJ (razor, knife) afiado; (point, features)
pontiagudo; (outline) definido, bem marcado;
(pain, voice) agudo; (taste) acre; (curve, bend)
fechado; (Mus) desafinado; (contrast) marcado;
(person: quick-witted) perspicaz; (dishonest)
desonesto ■ N (Mus) sustenido ■ ADV: **at 2
o'clock ~** às 2 (horas) em ponto; **turn ~ left** vira
logo à esquerda; **to be ~ with sb** ser brusco com
alguém; **look ~!** rápido!
sharpen ['ʃɑ:pən] VT afiar; (pencil) apontar, fazer
a ponta de; (fig) aguçar
sharpener ['ʃɑ:pnəʳ] N (also: **pencil sharpener**)
apontador m (BR), apara-lápis m inv (PT)
sharp-eyed [-aɪd] ADJ de vista aguda
sharply ['ʃɑ:plɪ] ADV (abruptly) bruscamente;
(clearly) claramente; (harshly) severamente
sharp-tempered ADJ irascível
sharp-witted [-'wɪtɪd] ADJ perspicaz,
observador(a)
shatter ['ʃætəʳ] VT despedaçar, estilhaçar; (fig:
ruin) destruir, acabar com; (: upset) arrasar ■ VI
despedaçar-se, estilhaçar-se
shattered ['ʃætəd] ADJ (overwhelmed) arrasado;
(exhausted) exausto
shatterproof ['ʃætəpru:f] ADJ inestilhaçável
shave [ʃeɪv] VT barbear, fazer a barba de ■ VI
fazer a barba, barbear-se ■ N: **to have a ~** fazer
a barba
shaven ['ʃeɪvn] ADJ (head) raspado
shaver ['ʃeɪvəʳ] N barbeador m; **electric ~**
barbeador elétrico
shaving ['ʃeɪvɪŋ] N (action) barbeação f;
shavings NPL (of wood) aparas fpl; **shaving
brush** N pincel m de barba; **shaving cream** N
creme m de barbear; **shaving foam** N espuma
de barbear; **shaving soap** N sabão m de barba
shawl [ʃɔ:l] N xale m
she [ʃi:] PRON ela ■ PREFIX: **~-elephant** etc
elefante etc fêmea; **there ~ is** lá está ela
sheaf [ʃi:f] (pl **sheaves**) N (of corn) gavela; (of
arrows) feixe m; (of papers) maço
shear [ʃɪəʳ] (pt **sheared**, pp **shorn**) VT (sheep)
tosquiar, tosar
▶ **shear off** VT cercear ■ VI cisalhar
shears [ʃɪəz] NPL (for hedge) tesoura de jardim
sheath [ʃi:θ] N bainha; (contraceptive) camisa-de-
vênus f, camisinha
sheathe [ʃi:ð] VT embainhar
sheath knife (irreg) N faca com bainha
sheaves [ʃi:vz] NPL of **sheaf**
shed [ʃed] (pt, pp **shed**) N alpendre m, galpão
m; (Industry, Rail) galpão m ■ VT (skin) mudar;
(load, leaves, fur) perder; (tears, blood) derramar;
(workers) despedir; **to ~ light on** (problem, mystery)
esclarecer
she'd [ʃi:d] = **she had; she would**
sheen [ʃi:n] N brilho

sheep [ʃiːp] N INV ovelha
sheepdog ['ʃiːpdɔg] N cão m pastor
sheep farmer N criador(a) m/f de ovelhas
sheepish ['ʃiːpɪʃ] ADJ tímido, acanhado
sheepskin [ʃiːpskɪn] N pele f de carneiro, pelego; **sheepskin jacket** N casaco de pele de carneiro
sheer [ʃɪəʳ] ADJ (utter) puro, completo; (steep) íngreme, empinado; (almost transparent) fino, translúcido ∎ ADV a pique; **by ~ chance** totalmente por acaso
sheet [ʃiːt] N (on bed) lençol m; (of paper) folha; (of glass, metal) lâmina, chapa; (of ice) camada; **sheet feed** N (on printer) alimentação f de papel (em folhas soltas); **sheet lightning** N relâmpago difuso; **sheet metal** N metal m em chapa; **sheet music** N música
sheik(h) [ʃeɪk] N xeque m
shelf [ʃelf] (pl **shelves**) N prateleira; **set of shelves** estante f; **shelf life** N (Comm) validade f (de produtos perecíveis)
shell [ʃel] N (on beach) concha; (of egg, nut etc) casca; (explosive) obus m; (of building) armação f, esqueleto ∎ VT (peas) descascar; (Mil) bombardear
▶ **shell out** (inf) VI: **to ~ out (for)** pagar
she'll [ʃiːl] = **she will; she shall**
shellfish ['ʃelfɪʃ] N INV crustáceo; (as food) frutos mpl do mar, mariscos mpl
shelter ['ʃeltəʳ] N (building) abrigo; (protection) refúgio ∎ VT (protect) proteger; (give lodging to) abrigar; (hide) esconder ∎ VI abrigar-se, refugiar-se; **to take ~ from** abrigar-se de
sheltered ['ʃeltəd] ADJ (life) protegido; (spot) abrigado, protegido; **~ housing** acomodação para idosos e defeituosos
shelve [ʃelv] VT (fig) pôr de lado, engavetar
shelves [ʃelvz] NPL of **shelf**
shelving ['ʃelvɪŋ] N (shelves) prateleiras fpl
shepherd ['ʃepəd] N pastor m ∎ VT (guide) guiar, conduzir
shepherdess ['ʃepədɪs] N pastora
shepherd's pie (Brit) N empadão m de carne e batata
sherbet ['ʃəːbət] N (Brit: powder) pó doce e efervescente; (US: water ice) sorvete de frutas à base de água
sheriff ['ʃerɪf] (US) N xerife m
sherry ['ʃerɪ] N (vinho de) Xerez m
she's [ʃiːz] = **she is; she has**
Shetland ['ʃetlənd] N (also: **the Shetlands, the Shetland Isles**) as ilhas Shetland
shield [ʃiːld] N escudo; (Sport) escudo, brasão m; (protection) proteção f; (Tech) blindagem f ∎ VT: **to ~ (from)** proteger (contra)
shift [ʃɪft] N (change) mudança; (of place) transferência; (of work) turno; (of workers) turma ∎ VT transferir; (remove) tirar ∎ VI mudar; (change place) mudar de lugar; **the wind has ~ed to the south** o vento virou para o sul; **a ~ in demand** (Comm) um deslocamento de demanda; **shift key** N (on typewriter) tecla para maiúsculas

shiftless ['ʃɪftlɪs] ADJ indolente
shift work N trabalho em turnos; **to do ~** trabalhar em turnos
shifty ['ʃɪftɪ] ADJ esperto, trapaceiro; (eyes) velhaco, maroto
shilling ['ʃɪlɪŋ] (Brit) N xelim m (= 12 old pence; 20 in a pound)
shilly-shally ['ʃɪlɪʃælɪ] VI vacilar
shimmer ['ʃɪməʳ] N reflexo trêmulo ∎ VI cintilar, tremeluzir
shin [ʃɪn] N canela (da perna) ∎ VI: **to ~ up/ down a tree** subir em/descer de um árvore com mãos e pernas
shindig ['ʃɪndɪg] (inf) N arrasta-pé m
shine [ʃaɪn] (pt, pp **shone**) N brilho, lustre m ∎ VI brilhar ∎ VT (glasses) polir; (shoes) (pt, pp **shined**) lustrar; **to ~ a torch on sth** apontar uma lanterna para algo
shingle ['ʃɪŋgl] N (on beach) pedrinhas fpl, seixinhos mpl; (on roof) telha
shingles ['ʃɪŋglz] N (Med) herpes-zoster m
shining ['ʃaɪnɪŋ] ADJ brilhante
shiny ['ʃaɪnɪ] ADJ brilhante, lustroso
ship [ʃɪp] N barco; (large) navio ∎ VT (goods) embarcar; (send) transportar or mandar (por via marítima); **on board ~** a bordo
shipbuilder ['ʃɪpbɪldəʳ] N construtor m naval
shipbuilding ['ʃɪpbɪldɪŋ] N construção f naval
ship chandler [-'tʃændləʳ] N fornecedor m de provisões para navios
shipment ['ʃɪpmənt] N (act) embarque m; (goods) carregamento
shipowner ['ʃɪpəunəʳ] N armador(a) m/f
shipper ['ʃɪpəʳ] N exportador(a) m/f, expedidor(a) m/f
shipping ['ʃɪpɪŋ] N (ships) navios mpl; (cargo) transporte m de mercadorias (por via marítima); (traffic) navegação f; **shipping agent** N agente m/f marítimo(-a); **shipping company** N companhia de navegação; **shipping lane** N rota de navegação; **shipping line** N companhia de navegação
shipshape ['ʃɪpʃeɪp] ADJ em ordem
shipwreck ['ʃɪprek] N (event) malogro; (ship) naufrágio ∎ VT: **to be ~ed** naufragar
shipyard ['ʃɪpjɑːd] N estaleiro
shire ['ʃaɪəʳ] (Brit) N condado
shirk [ʃəːk] VT (work) esquivar-se de; (obligations) não cumprir, faltar a
shirt [ʃəːt] N (man's) camisa; (woman's) blusa; **in ~ sleeves** em manga de camisa
shirty ['ʃəːtɪ] (Brit: inf) ADJ chateado, sem graça
shit [ʃɪt] (inf!) EXCL merda (!)
shiver ['ʃɪvəʳ] N tremor m, arrepio ∎ VI tremer, estremecer, tiritar
shoal [ʃəul] N (of fish) cardume m; (fig: also: **shoals**) bando, multidão f
shock [ʃɔk] N (impact) choque m; (Elec) descarga; (emotional) comoção f, abalo; (start) susto, sobressalto; (Med) trauma m ∎ VT dar um susto em, chocar; (offend) escandalizar; **suffering from ~** (Med) traumatizado; **it gave us a ~**

ficamos chocados; **it came as a ~ to hear that ...** ficamos atônitos ao saber que ...; **shock absorber** [-əb'zɔːbəʳ] N amortecedor m

shocking ['ʃɔkɪŋ] ADJ (awful) chocante, lamentável; (outrageous) revoltante, chocante; (improper) escandaloso; (very bad) péssimo

shockproof ['ʃɔkpruːf] ADJ à prova de choque

shock therapy N terapia de choque

shock treatment N terapia de choque

shod [ʃɔd] PT, PP of **shoe** ■ ADJ calçado

shoddy ['ʃɔdɪ] ADJ de má qualidade

shoe [ʃuː] (pt, pp shod) N sapato; (for horse) ferradura; (also: **brake shoe**) sapata ■ VT (horse) ferrar; **shoe brush** N escova de sapato

shoehorn ['ʃuːhɔːn] N calçadeira

shoelace ['ʃuːleɪs] N cadarço, cordão m (de sapato)

shoemaker ['ʃuːmeɪkəʳ] N sapateiro(-a)

shoe polish N graxa de sapato

shoe rack N porta-sapatos m inv

shoeshop ['ʃuːʃɔp] N sapataria

shoestring ['ʃuːstrɪŋ] N (fig): **on a ~** com muito pouco dinheiro

shoetree ['ʃuːtriː] N fôrma de sapato

shone [ʃɔn] PT, PP of **shine**

shoo [ʃuː] EXCL xô! ■ VT (also: **shoo away, shoo off**) enxotar

shook [ʃuk] PT of **shake**

shoot [ʃuːt] (pt, pp shot) N (on branch, seedling) broto ■ VT disparar; (kill) matar à bala, balear; (wound) ferir à bala, balear; (execute) fuzilar; (film) filmar, rodar ■ VI (with gun, bow): **to ~ (at)** atirar (em); (Football) chutar; **to ~ past sb** passar disparado por alguém
  ▶ **shoot down** VT (plane) derrubar, abater
  ▶ **shoot in** VI entrar correndo
  ▶ **shoot out** VI sair correndo
  ▶ **shoot up** VI (fig) subir vertiginosamente

shooting ['ʃuːtɪŋ] N (shots) tiros mpl, tiroteio; (Hunting) caçada (com espingarda); (attack) tiroteio; (: murder) assassinato; (Cinema) filmagens fpl; **shooting range** N estande m; **shooting star** N estrela cadente

shop [ʃɔp] N loja; (workshop) oficina ■ VI (also: **go shopping**) ir fazer compras; **to talk ~** (fig) falar de negócios
  ▶ **shop around** VI comparar preços; (fig) estudar todas as possibilidades

shop assistant (Brit) N vendedor(a) m/f

shop floor (Brit) N operários mpl

shopkeeper ['ʃɔpkiːpəʳ] N lojista m/f

shoplift ['ʃɔplɪft] VI furtar (em lojas)

shoplifter ['ʃɔplɪftəʳ] N larápio(-a) de loja

shoplifting ['ʃɔplɪftɪŋ] N furto (em lojas)

shopper ['ʃɔpəʳ] N comprador(a) f

shopping ['ʃɔpɪŋ] N (goods) compras fpl; **shopping bag** N bolsa (de compras); **shopping centre** (US **shopping center**) N shopping (center) m

shop-soiled ADJ danificado (pelo tempo ou manuseio)

shop steward (Brit) N (Industry) representante

m/f sindical

shop window N vitrine f (BR), montra (PT)

shore [ʃɔːʳ] N (of sea) costa, praia; (of lake) margem f ■ VT: **to ~ (up)** reforçar, escorar; **on ~** em terra; **shore leave** N (Naut) licença para desembarcar

shorn [ʃɔːn] PP of **shear**

short [ʃɔːt] ADJ (not long) curto; (in time) breve, de curta duração; (person) baixo; (curt) seco, brusco; (insufficient) insuficiente, em falta ■ N (also: **short film**) curta-metragem m; **to be ~ of sth** estar em falta de algo; **to be in ~ supply** estar em falta; **I'm 3 ~** estão me faltando três; **in ~** em resumo; **~ of doing ...** a não ser fazer ...; **everything ~ of ...** tudo a não ser ...; **a ~ time ago** pouco tempo atrás; **in the ~ term** a curto prazo; **I'm ~ of time** tenho pouco tempo; **it is ~ for** é a abreviatura de; **to cut ~** (speech, visit) encurtar; (person) interromper; **to fall ~** ser deficiente; **to fall ~ of** não ser à altura de; **to run ~ of sth** ficar sem algo; **to stop ~** parar de repente; **to stop ~ of** chegar quase a

shortage ['ʃɔːtɪdʒ] N escassez f, falta

shortbread ['ʃɔːtbred] N biscoito amanteigado

short-change VT: **to ~ sb** roubar alguém no troco

short circuit N curto-circuito ■ VT provocar um curto-circuito ■ VI entrar em curto-circuito

shortcoming ['ʃɔːtkʌmɪŋ] N defeito, imperfeição f, falha

short(crust) pastry ['ʃɔːt(krʌst)-] (Brit) N massa amanteigada

shortcut ['ʃɔːtkʌt] N atalho

shorten ['ʃɔːtən] VT encurtar; (visit) abreviar

shortening ['ʃɔːtnɪŋ] N (Culin) gordura

shortfall ['ʃɔːtfɔːl] N déficit m

shorthand ['ʃɔːthænd] (Brit) N estenografia; **shorthand notebook** (Brit) N bloco para estenografia; **shorthand typist** (Brit) N estenodatilógrafo(-a)

short list (Brit) N (for job) lista dos candidatos escolhidos

short-lived [-lɪvd] ADJ de curta duração

shortly ['ʃɔːtlɪ] ADV em breve, dentro em pouco

shortness ['ʃɔːtnɪs] N (of distance) curteza; (of time) brevidade f; (manner) maneira brusca, secura

shorts NPL: (**a pair of**) **~** um calção (BR), um short (BR), uns calções (PT)

short-sighted (Brit) ADJ míope; (fig) imprevidente

short-staffed [-stɑːft] ADJ com falta de pessoal

short story N conto

short-tempered ADJ irritadiço

short-term ADJ (effect) a curto prazo

short time N: **to work ~, to be on ~** trabalhar em regime de semana reduzida

short wave N (Radio) onda curta

shot [ʃɔt] PT, PP of **shoot** ■ N (of gun) tiro; (pellets) chumbo; (person) atirador(a) m/f; (try, Football) tentativa; (injection) injeção f; (Phot) fotografia;

to be a good/bad ~ (*person*) ter boa/má pontaria; **to fire a ~ at sb/sth** atirar em alguém/algo; **to have a ~ at (doing) sth** tentar fazer algo; **like a ~** como um relâmpago, de repente; **to get ~ of sb/sth** (*inf*) livrar-se de alguém/algo; **a big ~** (*inf*) um mandachuva, um figurão

shotgun ['ʃɔtgʌn] N espingarda

should [ʃud] AUX VB: **I ~ go now** devo ir embora agora; **he ~ be there now** ele já deve ter chegado; **I ~ go if I were you** se eu fosse você eu iria; **I ~ like to** eu gostaria de; **~ he phone ...** caso ele telefone ...

shoulder ['ʃəuldəʳ] N ombro; (*Brit: of road*): **hard ~** acostamento (BR), berma (PT) ■ VT (*fig*) arcar com; **to look over one's ~** olhar para trás; **to rub ~s with sb** (*fig*) andar com alguém; **to give sb the cold ~** (*fig*) desprezar alguém, dar uma fria em alguém (*inf*); **shoulder bag** N sacola a tiracolo; **shoulder blade** N omoplata *m*; **shoulder strap** N alça

shouldn't ['ʃudnt] = **should not**

shout [ʃaut] N grito ■ VT gritar ■ VI (*also*: **shout out**) gritar, berrar; **to give sb a ~** chamar alguém
▶ **shout down** VT fazer calar com gritos

shouting N gritaria, berreiro

shove [ʃʌv] N empurrão *m* ■ VT empurrar; (*inf: put*): **to ~ sth in** botar algo em; **he ~d me out of the way** ele me empurrou para o lado
▶ **shove off** VI (*Naut*) zarpar, partir; (*inf*) dar o fora

shovel ['ʃʌvl] N pá *f*; (*mechanical*) escavadeira ■ VT cavar com pá

show [ʃəu] (*pt* **showed**, *pp* **shown**) N (*of emotion*) demonstração *f*; (*semblance*) aparência; (*exhibition*) exibição *f*; (*Theatre*) espetáculo, representação *f*; (*Cinema*) sessão *f* ■ VT mostrar; (*courage etc*) demonstrar, dar prova de; (*exhibit*) exibir, expor; (*depict*) ilustrar; (*film*) exibir ■ VI mostrar-se; (*appear*) aparecer; **it doesn't ~** não parece; **I've nothing to ~ for it** não consegui nada; **to ~ sb to his seat/to the door** levar alguém ao seu lugar/até a porta; **to ~ a profit/loss** (*Comm*) apresentar lucros/prejuízo; **it just goes to ~ (that)** ... isso só mostra (que) ...; **to ask for a ~ of hands** pedir uma votação pelo levantamento das mãos; **it's just for ~** isso é só para mostrar; **to be on ~** estar em exposição; **who's running the ~ here?** (*inf*) quem é que manda aqui?
▶ **show in** VT mandar entrar
▶ **show off** VI (*pej*) mostrar-se, exibir-se ■ VT (*display*) exibir, mostrar; (*pej*) fazer ostentação de
▶ **show out** VT levar até a porta
▶ **show up** VI (*stand out*) destacar-se; (*inf: turn up*) aparecer, pintar ■ VT descobrir; (*unmask*) desmascarar

show business N o mundo do espetáculo

showcase ['ʃəukeɪs] N vitrina

showdown ['ʃəudaun] N confrontação *f*

shower ['ʃauəʳ] N (*rain*) pancada de chuva; (*of stones etc*) chuva, enxurrada; (*also*: **shower bath**) chuveiro ■ VI tomar banho (de chuveiro) ■ VT: **to ~ sb with** (*gifts etc*) cumular alguém de; **to have** *or* **take a ~** tomar banho (de chuveiro);

shower cap N touca de banho

showerproof ['ʃauəpruːf] ADJ impermeável

showery ['ʃauərɪ] ADJ (*weather*) chuvoso

showground ['ʃəugraund] N recinto da feira

showing ['ʃəuɪŋ] N (*of film*) projeção *f*, exibição *f*

show jumping [-'dʒʌmpɪŋ] N hipismo

showman ['ʃəumən] (*irreg*) N artista *mf*; (*fig*) pessoa expansiva

showmanship ['ʃəumənʃɪp] N senso teatral

showmen ['ʃəumɛn] NPL *of* **showman**

shown [ʃəun] PP *of* **show**

show-off (*inf*) N (*person*) exibicionista *m/f*, faroleiro(-a)

showpiece ['ʃəupiːs] N (*of exhibition etc*) obra mais importante; **that hospital is a ~** aquele é um hospital modelo

showroom ['ʃəurum] N sala de exposição

showy ['ʃəuɪ] ADJ vistoso, chamativo

shrank [ʃræŋk] PT *of* **shrink**

shrapnel ['ʃræpnl] N estilhaços *mpl*

shred [ʃred] N (*gen pl*) tira, pedaço ■ VT rasgar em tiras, retalhar; (*Culin*) desfiar, picar; (*documents*) fragmentar; **not a ~ of evidence** prova alguma

shredder ['ʃredəʳ] N (*for vegetables*) ralador *m*; (*for documents*) fragmentadora

shrew [ʃruː] N (*Zool*) musaranho; (*pej: woman*) megera

shrewd [ʃruːd] ADJ perspicaz

shrewdness ['ʃruːdnɪs] N astúcia

shriek [ʃriːk] N grito ■ VT, VI gritar, berrar

shrift [ʃrɪft] N: **to give sb short ~** dar uma resposta a alguém sem maiores explicações

shrill [ʃrɪl] ADJ agudo, estridente

shrimp [ʃrɪmp] N camarão *m*

shrine [ʃraɪn] N santuário

shrink [ʃrɪŋk] (*pt* **shrank**, *pp* **shrunk**) VI encolher; (*be reduced*) reduzir-se; (*also*: **shrink away**) encolher-se ■ VT (*cloth*) fazer encolher ■ N (*inf: pej*) psicanalista *m/f*; **to ~ from doing sth** não se atrever a fazer algo

shrinkage ['ʃrɪŋkɪdʒ] N encolhimento, redução *f*

shrink-wrap VT embalar a vácuo

shrivel ['ʃrɪvl] VT (*also*: **shrivel up**: *dry*) secar; (*: crease*) enrugar ■ VI secar-se; enrugar-se, murchar

shroud [ʃraud] N mortalha ■ VT: **~ed in mystery** envolto em mistério

Shrove Tuesday [ʃrəuv-] N terça-feira gorda

shrub [ʃrʌb] N arbusto

shrubbery ['ʃrʌbərɪ] N arbustos *mpl*

shrug [ʃrʌg] N encolhimento dos ombros ■ VT, VI: **to ~ (one's shoulders)** encolher os ombros, dar de ombros (BR)
▶ **shrug off** VT negar a importância de

shrunk [ʃrʌŋk] PP *of* **shrink**

shrunken ['ʃrʌŋkn] ADJ encolhido

shudder ['ʃʌdəʳ] N estremecimento, tremor *m* ■ VI estremecer, tremer de medo

shuffle ['ʃʌfl] VT (*cards*) embaralhar ■ VI: **to ~ (one's feet)** arrastar os pés

shun [ʃʌn] VT evitar, afastar-se de

shunt [ʃʌnt] VT (*Rail*) manobrar, desviar; (*object*) desviar ■ VI: **to ~ (to and fro)** ir e vir

shunting ['ʃʌntɪŋ] N (*Rail*) manobras *fpl*; **shunting yard** N pátio de manobras

shush [ʃuʃ] EXCL psiu!

shut [ʃʌt] (*pt, pp* shut) VT fechar ■ VI fechar(-se)
  ► **shut down** VT fechar; (*machine*) parar ■ VI fechar
  ► **shut off** VT (*supply etc*) cortar, interromper
  ► **shut out** VT (*person, cold*) impedir que entre; (*noise*) abafar; (*memory*) reprimir
  ► **shut up** VI (*inf: keep quiet*) calar-se, calar a boca ■ VT (*close*) fechar; (*silence*) calar

shutdown ['ʃʌtdaun] N paralização *f*

shutter ['ʃʌtəʳ] N veneziana; (*Phot*) obturador *m*

shuttle ['ʃʌtl] N (*in weaving*) lançadeira; (*plane: also:* **shuttle service**) ponte *f* aérea; (*space shuttle*) ônibus *m* espacial ■ VI (*vehicle, person*) ir e vir ■ VT (*passengers*) transportar de ida e volta

shuttlecock ['ʃʌtlkɔk] N peteca

shy [ʃaɪ] ADJ tímido; (*reserved*) reservado ■ VI: **to ~ away from doing sth** (*fig*) não se atrever a fazer algo

shyness ['ʃaɪnɪs] N timidez *f*

Siam [saɪ'æm] N Sião *m*

Siamese [saɪə'miːz] ADJ: **~ cat** gato siamês; **~ twins** irmãos *mpl* siameses/irmãs *fpl* siamesas

Siberia [saɪ'bɪərɪə] N Sibéria *f*

sibling ['sɪblɪŋ] N irmão/irmã *m/f*

Sicilian [sɪ'sɪlɪən] ADJ, N siciliano(-a)

Sicily ['sɪsɪlɪ] N Sicília

sick [sɪk] ADJ (*ill*) doente; (*nauseated*) enjoado; (*humour*) negro; (*vomiting*): **to be ~** vomitar; **to feel ~** estar enjoado; **to fall ~** ficar doente; **to be (off) ~** estar ausente por motivo de doença; **to be ~ of** (*fig*) estar cheio *or* farto de; **he makes me ~** (*fig: inf*) ele me enche o saco

sickbay ['sɪkbeɪ] N enfermaria

sicken ['sɪkən] VT dar náuseas a; (*disgust*) enojar, repugnar ■ VI: **to be ~ing for sth** (*cold, flu etc*) estar no começo de algo

sickening ['sɪkənɪŋ] ADJ (*fig*) repugnante

sickle ['sɪkl] N foice *f*

sick leave N licença por doença

sickly ['sɪklɪ] ADJ doentio; (*causing nausea*) nauseante

sickness ['sɪknɪs] N doença, indisposição *f*; (*vomiting*) náusea, enjôo; **sickness benefit** N auxílio-enfermidade *m*, auxílio-doença *m*

sick pay N *salário pago em período de doença*

sickroom ['sɪkruːm] N enfermaria

side [saɪd] N (*gen*) lado; (*of body*) flanco; (*of lake*) margem *f*; (*aspect*) aspecto; (*team*) time *m* (BR), equipa (PT); (*of hill*) declive *m*; (*page*) página; (*of meat*) costela ■ CPD (*door, entrance*) lateral ■ VI: **to ~ with sb** tomar o partido de alguém; **by the ~ of** ao lado de; **~ by ~** lado a lado, juntos; **on this/that** *or* **the other ~** do lado de cá/do lado de lá; **they are on our ~** (*in game*) fazem parte

do nosso time; (*in discussion*) concordam com nós; **from ~ to ~** para lá e para cá; **from all ~s** de todos os lados; **to take ~s with** pôr-se ao lado de

sideboard ['saɪdbɔːd] N aparador *m*; **sideboards** NPL (*Brit*) = **sideburns**

sideburns ['saɪdbəːnz] NPL suiças *fpl*, costeletas *fpl*

sidecar ['saɪdkɑːʳ] N sidecar *m*

side dish N guarnição *f*

side drum N (*Mus*) caixa clara

side effect N efeito colateral

sidekick ['saɪdkɪk] (*inf*) N camarada *m/f*

sidelight ['saɪdlaɪt] N (*Aut*) luz *f* lateral

sideline ['saɪdlaɪn] N (*Sport*) linha lateral; (*fig*) linha adicional de produtos; (*: job*) emprego suplementar

sidelong ['saɪdlɔŋ] ADJ de soslaio

side plate N pequeno prato

side road N rua lateral

side-saddle ADV de silhão

sideshow ['saɪdʃəu] N (*stall*) barraca

sidestep ['saɪdstɛp] VT evitar ■ VI (*Boxing etc*) dar um passo para o lado

sidetrack ['saɪdtræk] VT (*fig*) desviar (do seu propósito)

sidewalk ['saɪdwɔːk] (*US*) N calçada

sideways ['saɪdweɪz] ADV de lado

siding ['saɪdɪŋ] N (*Rail*) desvio, ramal *m*

sidle ['saɪdl] VI: **to ~ up (to)** aproximar-se furtivamente (de)

siege [siːdʒ] N sítio, assédio; **to lay ~ to** assediar; **siege economy** N economia de guerra

Sierra Leone [sɪ'ɛrəlɪ'əun] N Serra Leoa (*no article*)

siesta [sɪ'ɛstə] N sesta

sieve [sɪv] N peneira ■ VT peneirar

sift [sɪft] VT peneirar; (*fig: information*) esquadrinhar, analisar minuciosamente ■ VI (*fig*): **to ~ through** examinar minuciosamente

sigh [saɪ] N suspiro ■ VI suspirar

sight [saɪt] N (*faculty*) vista, visão *f*; (*spectacle*) espetáculo; (*on gun*) mira ■ VT avistar; **in ~** à vista; **on ~** (*shoot*) no local; **out of ~** longe dos olhos; **at ~** (*Comm*) à vista; **at first ~** à primeira vista; **I know her by ~** conheço-a de vista; **to catch ~ of sb/sth** avistar alguém/algo; **to lose ~ of sb/sth** perder alguém/algo de vista; **to set one's ~s on sth** visar algo

sighted ['saɪtɪd] ADJ que enxerga; **partially ~** com vista parcial

sightseeing ['saɪtsiːɪŋ] N turismo; **to go ~** fazer turismo, passear

sightseer ['saɪtsiːəʳ] N turista *m/f*

sign [saɪn] N (*with hand*) sinal *m*, aceno; (*indication*) indício; (*trace*) vestígio; (*notice*) letreiro, tabuleta; (*also:* **road sign**) placa; (*written, of zodiac*) signo ■ VT assinar; **as a ~ of** como sinal de; **it's a good/bad ~** é um bom/mau sinal; **plus/minus ~** sinal de mais/menos; **there's no ~ of a change of mind** não há sinal *or* indícios de uma mudança de atitude; **he was showing ~s of improvement** ele

estava começando a melhorar; **to ~ one's name** assinar; **to ~ sth over to sb** assinar a transferência de algo para alguém
▶ **sign away** VT *(rights etc)* abrir mão de
▶ **sign off** VI *(Radio, TV)* terminar a transmissão
▶ **sign on** VI *(Mil)* alistar-se; *(Brit: as unemployed)* cadastrar-se para receber auxílio-desemprego; *(for course)* inscrever-se ■ VT *(Mil)* alistar; *(employee)* efetivar
▶ **sign out** VI assinar o registro na partida
▶ **sign up** VI *(Mil)* alistar-se; *(for course)* inscrever-se ■ VT recrutar
signal ['sɪgnl] N sinal *m*, aviso; *(US: Tel)* ruído discal ■ VI *(also: Aut)* sinalizar, dar sinal ■ VT *(person)* fazer sinais para; *(message)* transmitir; **to ~ a left/right turn** *(Aut)* dar sinal para esquerda/direita; **to ~ to sb (to do sth)** fazer sinais para alguém (fazer algo); **signal box** N *(Rail)* cabine *f* de sinaleiro
signalman ['sɪgnlmən] *(irreg)* N sinaleiro
signatory ['sɪgnətərɪ] N signatário(-a)
signature ['sɪgnətʃəʳ] N assinatura; **signature tune** N tema *m* (de abertura)
signet ring ['sɪgnət-] N anel *m* com o sinete *or* a chancela
significance [sɪg'nɪfɪkəns] N significado; *(importance)* importância; **that is of no ~** isto não tem importância alguma
significant [sɪg'nɪfɪkənt] ADJ significativo; *(important)* importante
significantly [sɪg'nɪfɪkəntlɪ] ADV *(improve, increase)* significativamente; *(smile)* sugestivamente; **and, ~, ... e,** significativamente, ...
signify ['sɪgnɪfaɪ] VT significar
sign language N mímica, linguagem *f* através de sinais
sign post N indicador *m*; *(traffic)* placa de sinalização
silage ['saɪlɪdʒ] N *(fodder)* silagem *f*; *(method)* ensilagem *f*
silence ['saɪləns] N silêncio ■ VT silenciar, impor silêncio a; *(guns)* silenciar
silencer ['saɪlənsəʳ] N *(on gun)* silenciador *m*; *(Brit: Aut)* silencioso
silent ['saɪlənt] ADJ silencioso; *(not speaking)* calado; *(film)* mudo; **to keep** *or* **remain ~** manter-se em silêncio
silently ['saɪləntlɪ] ADV silenciosamente
silent partner N *(Comm)* sócio(-a) comanditário(-a)
silhouette [sɪluː'ɛt] N silhueta ■ VT: **~d against** em silhueta contra
silicon ['sɪlɪkən] N silício; **silicon chip** N placa *or* chip *m* de silício
silicone ['sɪlɪkəun] N silicone *m*
silk [sɪlk] N seda ■ ADJ de seda
silky ['sɪlkɪ] ADJ sedoso
sill [sɪl] N *(also:* **window sill)** parapeito, peitoril *m*; *(Aut)* soleira
silly ['sɪlɪ] ADJ *(person)* bobo, idiota, imbecil; *(idea)* absurdo, ridículo; **to do something ~** fazer

uma besteira
silo ['saɪləu] N silo
silt [sɪlt] N sedimento, aluvião *m*
silver ['sɪlvəʳ] N prata; *(money)* moedas *fpl*; *(also:* **silverware)** prataria ■ ADJ de prata; **silver foil** N papel *m* de prata; **silver paper** *(Brit)* N papel *m* de prata
silver-plated [-'pleɪtɪd] ADJ prateado, banhado a prata
silversmith ['sɪlvəsmɪθ] N prateiro(-a)
silverware ['sɪlvəwɛəʳ] N prataria
silver wedding *(anniversary)* N bodas *fpl* de prata
silvery ['sɪlvərɪ] ADJ prateado
similar ['sɪmɪləʳ] ADJ: **~ to** parecido com, semelhante a
similarity [sɪmɪ'lærɪtɪ] N semelhança
similarly ['sɪmɪləlɪ] ADV da mesma maneira
simile ['sɪmɪlɪ] N símile *f*
simmer ['sɪməʳ] VI cozer em fogo lento, ferver lentamente
▶ **simmer down** *(inf)* VI *(fig)* acalmar-se
simper ['sɪmpəʳ] VI sorrir afetadamente
simpering ['sɪmpərɪŋ] ADJ idiota
simple ['sɪmpl] ADJ simples *inv*; *(foolish)* ingênuo; **the ~ truth** a pura verdade; **simple interest** N juros *mpl* simples
simple-minded ADJ simplório
simpleton ['sɪmpltən] N simplório(-a), pateta *m/f*
simplicity [sɪm'plɪsɪtɪ] N simplicidade *f*
simplification [sɪmplɪfɪ'keɪʃən] N simplificação *f*
simplify ['sɪmplɪfaɪ] VT simplificar
simply ['sɪmplɪ] ADV de maneira simples; *(merely)* simplesmente
simulate ['sɪmjuleɪt] VT simular
simulated ['sɪmjuleɪtɪd] ADJ simulado
simulation [sɪmju'leɪʃən] N simulação *f*
simultaneous [sɪməl'teɪnɪəs] ADJ simultâneo
simultaneously [sɪməl'teɪnɪəslɪ] ADV simultaneamente
sin [sɪn] N pecado ■ VI pecar
Sinai ['saɪneɪaɪ] N Sinai *m*
since [sɪns] ADV desde então, depois ■ PREP desde ■ CONJ *(time)* desde que; *(because)* porque, visto que, já que; **~ then** desde então; **~ Monday** desde segunda-feira; **(ever) ~ I arrived** desde que eu cheguei
sincere [sɪn'sɪəʳ] ADJ sincero
sincerely [sɪn'sɪəlɪ] ADV sinceramente; **yours ~** *(at end of letter)* atenciosamente
sincerity [sɪn'sɛrɪtɪ] N sinceridade *f*
sine [saɪn] N *(Math)* seno
sinew ['sɪnjuː] N tendão *m*
sinful ['sɪnful] ADJ *(thought)* pecaminoso; *(person)* pecador(a)
sing [sɪŋ] *(pt* **sang***, pp* **sung)** VT, VI cantar
Singapore [sɪŋgə'pɔːʳ] N Cingapura *(no article)*
singe [sɪndʒ] VT chamuscar
singer ['sɪŋəʳ] N cantor(a) *m/f*
Singhalese [sɪŋə'liːz] ADJ = **Sinhalese**
singing ['sɪŋɪŋ] N *(gen)* canto; *(songs)* canções *fpl*

(in the ears) zumbido

single ['sɪŋgl] ADJ único, só; *(unmarried)* solteiro; *(not double)* simples *inv* ■ N *(Brit: also:* **single ticket)** passagem *f* de ida; *(record)* compacto; **not a ~ one was left** não sobrou nenhum; **every ~ day** todo santo dia

▶ **single out** VT *(choose)* escolher; *(distinguish)* distinguir

single bed N cama de solteiro

single-breasted [-'brɛstɪd] ADJ não trespassado

single file N: **in ~** em fila indiana

single-handed [-'hændɪd] ADV sem ajuda, sozinho

single-minded ADJ determinado

single parent N pai *m* solteiro/mãe *f* solteira

single room N quarto individual

singles ['sɪŋglz] N *(Tennis)* partida simples ■ NPL *(US: people)* solteiros *mpl*

singlet ['sɪŋglɪt] N camiseta

singly ['sɪŋglɪ] ADV separadamente

singsong ['sɪŋsɔŋ] ADJ *(tone)* cantado ■ N *(songs)*: **to have a ~** cantar

singular ['sɪŋgjuləʳ] ADJ *(odd)* esquisito; *(outstanding)* extraordinário, excepcional; *(Ling)* singular ■ N *(Ling)* singular *m*; **in the feminine ~** no feminino singular

singularly ['sɪŋgjuləlɪ] ADV particularmente

Sinhalese [sɪnhə'liːz] ADJ cingalês(-esa)

sinister ['sɪnɪstəʳ] ADJ sinistro

sink [sɪŋk] *(pt* **sank,** *pp* **sunk)** N pia ■ VT *(ship)* afundar; *(foundations)* escavar ■ VI *(ship, ground)* afundar-se; *(heart)* partir; *(spirits)* ficar deprimido; *(also:* **sink back, sink down)** cair or mergulhar gradativamente; *(share prices)* cair; **to ~ sth into** *(teeth etc)* enterrar algo em; **he sank into a chair/the mud** ele afundou na cadeira/ na lama; **a ~ing feeling** um vazio no estômago

▶ **sink in** VI *(fig)* penetrar; **it took a long time to ~ in** demorou muito para ser entendido

sinking fund ['sɪŋkɪŋ-] N fundo de amortização

sink unit N pia

sinner ['sɪnəʳ] N pecador(a) *m/f*

sinuous ['sɪnjuəs] ADJ sinuoso

sinus ['saɪnəs] N *(Anat)* seio (paranasal)

sinusitis [saɪnə'saɪtəs] N sinusite *f*

sip [sɪp] N gole *m* ■ VT sorver, beberican

siphon ['saɪfən] N sifão *m*

▶ **siphon off** VT extrair com sifão; *(funds)* desviar

sir [səʳ] N senhor *m*; **S~ John Smith** Sir John Smith; **yes ~** sim, senhor; **Dear S~** *(in letter)* (Prezado) Senhor

siren ['saɪərn] N sirena

sirloin ['səːlɔɪn] N lombo de vaca; **sirloin steak** N filé *m* de alcatra

sisal ['saɪsəl] N sisal *m*

sissy ['sɪsɪ] *(inf)* N fresco

sister ['sɪstəʳ] N irmã *f*; *(Brit: nurse)* enfermeira-chefe *f*; *(nun)* freira ■ CPD: **~ ship** navio gêmeo

sister-in-law *(pl* **sisters-in-law)** N cunhada

sit [sɪt] *(pt, pp* **sat)** VI sentar-se; *(be sitting)* estar

sentado; *(assembly)* reunir-se; *(for painter)* posar; *(dress)* cair ■ VT *(exam)* prestar; **to ~ on a committee** ser membro de um comitê; **to ~ tight** não se mexer; *(fig)* esperar

▶ **sit about** VI ficar sentado não fazendo nada

▶ **sit around** VI ficar sentado não fazendo nada

▶ **sit back** VI acomodar-se num assento

▶ **sit down** VI sentar-se; **to be ~ting down** estar sentado

▶ **sit in on** VT FUS assistir a

▶ **sit up** VI *(after lying)* levantar-se; *(straight)* endireitar-se; *(not go to bed)* aguardar acordado, velar

sitcom ['sɪtkɔm] N ABBR (= *situation comedy*) comédia de costumes

sit-down ADJ: **~ strike** greve *f* de braços cruzados; **a ~ meal** uma refeição servida à mesa

site [saɪt] N local *m*, sítio; *(also:* **building site)** lote *m* (de terreno) ■ VT situar, localizar

sit-in N *(demonstration)* ocupação de um local como forma de protesto, manifestação *f* pacífica

siting ['saɪtɪŋ] N *(location)* localização *f*

sitter ['sɪtəʳ] N *(for painter)* modelo; *(also:* **babysitter)** baby-sitter *m/f*

sitting ['sɪtɪŋ] N *(of assembly etc)* sessão *f*; *(in canteen)* turno; **sitting member** N *(Pol)* parlamentar *m/f*; **sitting room** N sala de estar; **sitting tenant** *(Brit)* N inquilino(-a)

situate ['sɪtjueɪt] VT situar

situated ['sɪtjueɪtɪd] ADJ situado

situation [sɪtju'eɪʃən] N situação *f*; *(job)* posição *f*; *(location)* local *m*; **"~s vacant/wanted"** *(Brit)* "empregos oferecem-se/procurados"; **situation comedy** N *(Theatre, TV)* comédia de costumes

six [sɪks] NUM seis; *see also* **five**

sixteen ['sɪks'tiːn] NUM dezesseis; *see also* **five**

sixth [sɪksθ] NUM sexto; **the upper/lower ~** *(Brit: Sch)* os dois últimos anos do colégio; (:) *see also* **fifth**

sixty ['sɪkstɪ] NUM sessenta; *see also* **fifty**

size [saɪz] N *(gen)* tamanho; *(extent)* extensão *f*; *(of clothing)* tamanho, medida; *(of shoes)* número; *(glue)* goma; **I take ~ 14** *(of dress)* ≈ meu tamanho é 44; **the small/large ~** *(of soap powder etc)* o tamanho pequeno/grande; **what ~ do you take in shoes?** que número você calça?; **it's the ~ of** ... é do tamanho de ...

▶ **size up** VT avaliar, formar uma opinião sobre

sizeable ['saɪzəbl] ADJ considerável, importante

sizzle ['sɪzl] VI chiar

SK *(Canada)* ABBR = **Saskatchewan**

skate [skeɪt] N patim *m*; *(fish: pl inv)* arraia ■ VI patinar

▶ **skate around** VT FUS *(problem)* evitar

▶ **skate over** VT FUS = **skate around**

skateboard ['skeɪtbɔːd] N skate *m*, patim-tábua *m*

skater ['skeɪtəʳ] N patinador(a) *m/f*

skating ['skeɪtɪŋ] N patinação *f*; **skating rink** N rinque *m* de patinação

skeleton ['skɛlɪtn] N esqueleto; *(Tech)* armação

f; (outline) esquema m, esboço; **skeleton key**
N chave f mestra; **skeleton staff** N pessoal m
reduzido (ao mínimo)
skeptic etc ['skɛptɪk] (US) = **sceptic** etc
sketch [skɛtʃ] N (drawing) desenho; (outline)
esboço, croqui m; (Theatre) quadro, esquete m
■ VT desenhar, esboçar; (ideas: also: **sketch out**)
esboçar
sketchbook ['skɛtʃbuk] N caderno de rascunho
sketch pad N bloco de desenho
sketchy ['skɛtʃɪ] ADJ incompleto, superficial
skew [skjuː] (Brit) N: **on the ~** fora de esquadria
skewer ['skjuːəʳ] N espetinho
ski [skiː] N esqui m ■ VI esquiar; **ski boot** N bota
de esquiar
skid [skɪd] N derrapagem f ■ VI deslizar; (Aut)
derrapar; **skid mark** N marca de derrapagem
skier ['skiːəʳ] N esquiador(a) m/f
skiing ['skiːɪŋ] N esqui m; **to go ~** ir esquiar
ski instructor N instrutor(a) m/f de esqui
ski jump N pista para saltos de esqui; (event)
salto de esqui
skilful ['skɪlful] (US **skillful**) ADJ habilidoso,
jeitoso
skilfully ['skɪlfəlɪ] (US **skillfully**) ADV habilmente
ski lift N ski lift m
skill [skɪl] N habilidade f, perícia; (for work)
técnica
skilled [skɪld] ADJ hábil, perito; (worker)
especializado, qualificado
skillet ['skɪlɪt] N frigideira
skillful etc ['skɪlful] (US) = **skilful** etc
skim [skɪm] VT (milk) desnatar; (glide over) roçar
■ VI: **to ~ through** (book) folhear
skimmed milk [skɪmd-] N leite m desnatado
skimp [skɪmp] VT (work: also: **skimp on**)
atamancar; (cloth etc) economizar, regatear
skimpy ['skɪmpɪ] ADJ (meagre) escasso,
insuficiente; (skirt) sumário
skin [skɪn] N (gen) pele f; (of fruit, vegetable)
casca; (on pudding, paint) película ■ VT (fruit etc)
descascar; (animal) tirar a pele de; **wet or soaked
to the ~** encharcado, molhado como um pinto
skin-deep ADJ superficial
skin diver N mergulhador(a) m/f
skin diving N caça-submarina
skinflint ['skɪnflɪnt] N pão-duro m
skin graft N enxerto de pele
skinny ['skɪnɪ] ADJ magro, descarnado
skin test N cutirreação f
skintight ['skɪntaɪt] ADJ (dress etc) justo,
grudado (no corpo)
skip [skɪp] N salto, pulo; (Brit: container) balde m
■ VI saltar; (with rope) pular corda ■ VT (pass over)
omitir, saltar; (miss) deixar de; **to ~ school** (esp
US) matar aula
ski pants NPL calça (BR) or calças fpl (PT) de
esquiar
ski pole N vara de esqui
skipper ['skɪpəʳ] N (Naut, Sport) capitão m ■ VT
capitanear
skipping rope ['skɪpɪŋ-] (Brit) N corda (de pular)

ski resort N estação f de esqui
skirmish ['skəːmɪʃ] N escaramuça
skirt [skəːt] N saia ■ VT (surround) rodear; (go
round) orlar, circundar
skirting board ['skəːtɪŋ-] (Brit) N rodapé m
ski run N pista de esqui
ski slope N pista de esqui
ski suit N traje m de esqui
skit [skɪt] N paródia, sátira
ski tow N ski lift m
skittle ['skɪtl] N pau m; **skittles** N (game) (jogo
de) boliche m (BR), jogo da bola (PT)
skive [skaɪv] (Brit: inf) VI evitar trabalhar
skulk [skʌlk] VI esconder-se
skull [skʌl] N caveira; (Anat) crânio
skullcap ['skʌlkæp] N solidéu m; (worn by Pope)
barrete m
skunk [skʌŋk] N gambá m; (fig: person) cafajeste
m/f, pessoa vil
sky [skaɪ] N céu m; **to praise sb to the skies** pôr
alguém nas nuvens
sky-blue ADJ azul-celeste inv
sky-high ADV muito alto ■ ADJ: **prices are ~** os
preços dispararam
skylark ['skaɪlaːk] N (bird) cotovia
skylight ['skaɪlaɪt] N clarabóia, escotilha
skyline ['skaɪlaɪn] N (horizon) linha do horizonte;
(of city) silhueta
skyscraper ['skaɪskreɪpəʳ] N arranha-céu m
slab [slæb] N (stone) bloco; (flat) laje f; (of cake)
fatia grossa
slack [slæk] ADJ (loose) frouxo; (slow) lerdo;
(careless) descuidoso, desmazelado; (Comm:
market) inativo, frouxo; (: demand) fraco ■ N (in
rope) brando; **slacks** NPL (trousers) calça (BR),
calças fpl (PT); **business is ~** os negócios vão
mal
slacken ['slækən] VI (also: **slacken off**) afrouxar-
se ■ VT afrouxar; (speed) diminuir
slag [slæg] N escória, escombros mpl; **slag heap**
[slæg-] N monte m de escória or de escombros;
slag off [slæg-] (Brit: inf) VT malhar
slain [sleɪn] PP of **slay**
slake [sleɪk] VT (one's thirst) matar
slalom ['slaːləm] N slalom m
slam [slæm] VT (door) bater or fechar (com
violência); (throw) atirar violentamente;
(criticize) malhar, criticar ■ VI fechar-se (com
violência)
slander ['slaːndəʳ] N calúnia, difamação f ■ VT
caluniar, difamar
slanderous ['slaːndərəs] ADJ calunioso,
difamatório
slang [slæŋ] N gíria; (jargon) jargão m
slant [slaːnt] N declive m, inclinação f; (fig)
ponto de vista
slanted ['slaːntɪd] ADJ (roof) inclinado; (eyes)
puxado
slanting ['slaːntɪŋ] ADJ = **slanted**
slap [slæp] N tapa m or f ■ VT dar um(a) tapa em;
(paint etc): **to ~ sth on sth** passar algo em algo
descuidadamente ■ ADV (directly) diretamente,

slapdash | slip

exatamente
slapdash ['slæpdæʃ] ADJ impetuoso; (work) descuidado
slapstick ['slæpstɪk] N (comedy) (comédia-) pastelão m
slap-up (Brit) ADJ: **a ~ meal** uma refeição suntuosa
slash [slæʃ] VT cortar, talhar; (fig: prices) cortar
slat [slæt] N (of wood) ripa; (of plastic) tira
slate [sleɪt] N ardósia ■ VT (fig: criticize) criticar duramente, arrasar
slaughter ['slɔ:tər] N (of animals) matança; (of people) carnificina ■ VT abater; matar, massacrar
slaughterhouse ['slɔ:təhaus] N matadouro
Slav [slɑ:v] ADJ, N eslavo(-a)
slave [sleɪv] N escravo(-a) ■ VI (also: **slave away**) trabalhar como escravo; **to ~ (away) at sth/at doing sth** trabalhar feito condenado em algo/fazendo algo; **slave labour** N trabalho escravo
slaver ['slævər] VI (dribble) babar
slavery ['sleɪvərɪ] N escravidão f
Slavic ['slɑ:vɪk] ADJ eslavo
slavish ['sleɪvɪʃ] ADJ servil; (copy) descarado
Slavonic [slə'vɔnɪk] ADJ eslavo
slay [sleɪ] (pt **slew**, pp **slain**) VT (literary) matar
SLD (Brit) N ABBR (Pol) = **Social and Liberal Democratic Party**
sleazy ['sli:zɪ] ADJ (place) sórdido
sled [slɛd] (US) N trenó m
sledge [slɛdʒ] (Brit) N trenó m
sledgehammer ['slɛdʒhæmər] N marreta, malho
sleek [sli:k] ADJ (hair, fur) macio, lustroso; (car, boat) aerodinâmico
sleep [sli:p] (pt, pp **slept**) N sono ■ VI dormir
   ■ VT: **we can ~ 4** podemos acomodar 4 pessoas; **to go to ~** dormir, adormecer; **to have a good night's ~** ter uma boa noite de sono; **to put to ~** (patient) fazer dormir; (animal: euphemism: kill) sacrificar; **to ~ lightly** ter sono leve; **to ~ with sb** (euphemism) dormir com alguém
   ▶ **sleep around** VI ser promíscuo sexualmente
   ▶ **sleep in** VI (oversleep) dormir demais; (lie in) dormir até tarde
sleeper ['sli:pər] N (person) dorminhoco(-a); (Rail: on track) dormente m; (: train) vagão-leitos m (BR), carruagem-camas f (PT)
sleepily ['sli:pɪlɪ] ADV sonolentamente
sleeping ['sli:pɪŋ] ADJ adormecido, que dorme; **sleeping bag** N saco de dormir; **sleeping car** N vagão-leitos m (BR), carruagem-camas f (PT); **sleeping partner** (Brit) N (Comm) sócio comanditário; **sleeping pill** N pílula para dormir
sleepless ['sli:plɪs] ADJ: **a ~ night** uma noite em claro
sleeplessness ['sli:plɪsnɪs] N insônia
sleepwalker ['sli:pwɔ:kər] N sonâmbulo
sleepy ['sli:pɪ] ADJ sonolento; (fig) morto; **to be** or **feel ~** estar com sono
sleet [sli:t] N chuva com neve or granizo

sleeve [sli:v] N manga; (of record) capa
sleeveless ['sli:vlɪs] ADJ (garment) sem manga
sleigh [sleɪ] N trenó m
sleight [slaɪt] N: **~ of hand** prestidigitação f
slender ['slɛndər] ADJ esbelto, delgado; (means) escasso, insuficiente
slept [slɛpt] PT, PP of **sleep**
sleuth [slu:θ] (inf) N detetive m
slew [slu:] PT of **slay** ■ VI (Brit: also: **slew round**) virar
slice [slaɪs] N (of meat, bread) fatia; (of lemon) rodela; (of fish) posta; (utensil) pá f or espátula de bolo ■ VT cortar em fatias; **~d bread** pão m em fatias
slick [slɪk] ADJ (skilful) jeitoso, ágil, engenhoso; (quick) rápido; (clever) esperto, astuto ■ N (also: **oil slick**) mancha de óleo
slid [slɪd] PT, PP of **slide**
slide [slaɪd] N (downward movement) deslizamento, escorregão m; (in playground) escorregador m; (Phot) slide m; (Brit: also: **hair slide**) passador m; (microscope slide) lâmina; (in prices) queda, baixa ■ VT deslizar ■ VI (slip) escorregar; (glide) deslizar; **to let things ~** (fig) deixar tudo ir por água abaixo; **slide projector** N (Phot) projetor m de slides; **slide rule** N régua de cálculo
sliding ['slaɪdɪŋ] ADJ (door) corrediço; **~ roof** (Aut) teto deslizante; **sliding scale** N escala móvel
slight [slaɪt] ADJ (slim) fraco, franzino; (frail) delicado; (error, pain, increase) pequeno; (trivial) insignificante ■ N desfeita, desconsideração f ■ VT (offend) desdenhar, menosprezar; **not in the ~est** em absoluto, de maneira alguma; **the ~est** o(-a) menor; **a ~ improvement** uma pequena melhora
slightly ['slaɪtlɪ] ADV ligeiramente, um pouco; **~ built** magrinho
slim [slɪm] ADJ esbelto, delgado; (chance) pequeno ■ VI emagrecer
slime [slaɪm] N lodo, limo, lama
slimming ['slɪmɪŋ] N emagrecimento ■ ADJ (diet, pills) para emagrecer
slimy ['slaɪmɪ] ADJ pegajoso; (pond) lodoso; (fig) falso
sling [slɪŋ] (pt, pp **slung**) N (Med) tipóia; (for baby) bebêbag m; (weapon) estilingue m, funda ■ VT atirar, arremessar, lançar; **to have one's arm in a ~** estar com o braço na tipóia
slink [slɪŋk] (pt, pp **slunk**) VI: **to ~ away** or **off** escapulir
slip [slɪp] N (slide) tropeção m; (fall) escorregão m; (mistake) erro, lapso; (underskirt) combinação f; (of paper) tira ■ VT deslizar ■ VI (slide) deslizar; (lose balance) escorregar; (decline) decair; (move smoothly): **to ~ into/out of** entrar furtivamente em/sair furtivamente de; **to let a chance ~ by** deixar passar uma oportunidade; **to ~ sth on/off** enfiar/tirar algo; **it ~ped from her hand** escorregou da mão dela; **to give sb the ~** esgueirar-se de alguém; **a ~ of the tongue** um lapso da língua; see also **Freudian**

▶ **slip away** VI escapulir
▶ **slip in** VT meter ■ VI (*errors*) surgir
▶ **slip out** VI (*go out*) sair (um momento)
▶ **slip up** VI cometer um erro
slip-on ADJ sem fecho ou botões; ~ **shoes** mocassins *mpl*
slipped disc [slɪpt-] N disco deslocado
slipper ['slɪpəʳ] N chinelo
slippery ['slɪpərɪ] ADJ escorregadio
slip road (*Brit*) N (*to motorway*) entrada para a rodovia
slipshod ['slɪpʃɔd] ADJ descuidoso, desmazelado
slip-up N (*error*) equívoco, mancada; (*by neglect*) descuido
slipway ['slɪpweɪ] N carreira
slit [slɪt] (*pt, pp* **slit**) N fenda; (*cut*) corte *m* ■ VT (*cut*) rachar, cortar; (*open*) abrir; **to ~ sb's throat** cortar o pescoço de alguém
slither ['slɪðəʳ] VI escorregar, deslizar
sliver ['slɪvəʳ] N (*of glass, wood*) lasca; (*of cheese etc*) fatia fina
slob [slɔb] (*inf*) N (*in manners*) porco(-a); (*in appearance*) maltrapilho(-a)
slog [slɔg] (*Brit*) VI mourejar ■ N: **it was a ~** deu um trabalho louco
slogan ['sləʊgən] N lema *m*, slogan *m*
slop [slɔp] VI (*also*: **slop over**) transbordar, derramar ■ VT transbordar, entornar
slope [sləʊp] N ladeira; (*side of mountain*) encosta, vertente *f*; (*ski slope*) pista; (*slant*) inclinação *f*, declive *m* ■ VI: **to ~ down** estar em declive; **to ~ up** inclinar-se
sloping ['sləʊpɪŋ] ADJ inclinado, em declive; (*handwriting*) torto
sloppy ['slɔpɪ] ADJ (*work*) descuidado; (*appearance*) relaxado; (*film etc*) piegas *inv*
slosh [slɔʃ] (*inf*) VI: **to ~ about** or **around** (*children*) patinhar; (*liquid*) esparrinhar
sloshed [slɔʃt] (*inf*) ADJ (*drunk*) com a cara cheia
slot [slɔt] N (*in machine*) fenda; (*opening*) abertura; (*fig: in timetable, Radio, TV*) horário ■ VT: **to ~ into** encaixar em ■ VI encaixar-se em
sloth [sləʊθ] N (*vice, Zool*) preguiça
slot machine N (*for gambling*) caça-níqueis *m inv*; (*Brit: vending machine*) distribuidora automática
slot meter (*Brit*) N contador *m* (*de eletricidade ou gás*) operado por moedas
slouch [slautʃ] VI ter má postura
▶ **slouch about** VI vadiar
▶ **slouch around** VI = **slouch about**
slovenly ['slʌvənlɪ] ADJ (*dirty*) desalinhado, sujo; (*careless*) desmazelado
slow [sləʊ] ADJ lento; (*not clever*) bronco, de raciocínio lento; (*watch*): **to be ~** atrasar ■ ADV lentamente, devagar ■ VT (*also*: **slow down, slow up**: *vehicle*) ir (mais) devagar; (*business*) estar devagar ■ VI ir (mais) devagar; "**~**" (*road sign*) "devagar"; **at a ~ speed** devagar; **to be ~ to act/decide** ser lento nas ações/decisões, vacilar; **my watch is 20 minutes ~** meu relógio está atrasado vinte minutos; **business is ~** os negócios vão mal; **to go ~** (*driver*) dirigir

devagar; (*in industrial dispute*) fazer uma greve tartaruga; **the ~ lane** a faixa da direita; **bake for 2 hours in a ~ oven** asse durante 2 horas em fogo brando
slow-acting ADJ de ação lenta
slowdown (*US*) N greve *f* de trabalho lento, operação *f* tartaruga
slowly ['sləʊlɪ] ADV lentamente, devagar
slow motion N: **in ~** em câmara lenta
slowness ['sləʊnɪs] N lentidão *f*
sludge [slʌdʒ] N lama, lodo
slue [sluː] (*US*) VI = **slew**
slug [slʌg] N lesma; (*bullet*) bala
sluggish ['slʌgɪʃ] ADJ vagaroso; (*business*) lento
sluice [sluːs] N (*gate*) comporta, eclusa; (*channel*) canal *m* ■ VT: **to ~ down** or **out** lavar com jorro d'água
slum [slʌm] N (*area*) favela; (*house*) cortiço, barraco
slumber ['slʌmbəʳ] N sono
slump [slʌmp] N (*economic*) depressão *f*; (*Comm*) baixa, queda ■ VI (*person*) cair; (*prices*) baixar repentinamente; **he was ~ed over the wheel** estava caído sobre a direção
slung [slʌŋ] PT, PP *of* **sling**
slunk [slʌŋk] PT, PP *of* **slink**
slur [slɜːʳ] N calúnia ■ VT difamar, caluniar; (*word*) pronunciar indistintamente; **to cast a ~ on sb** manchar a reputação de alguém
slurred [sləːd] ADJ (*pronunciation*) indistinto, ininteligível
slush [slʌʃ] N neve *f* meio derretida; **slush fund** N verba para suborno
slushy ['slʌʃɪ] ADJ (*snow*) meio derretido; (*street*) lamacento; (*Brit: fig*) piegas *inv*
slut [slʌt] (*pej*) N mulher *f* desmazelada; (*whore*) prostituta
sly [slaɪ] ADJ (*person*) astuto; (*smile, remark*) malicioso, velhaco; **on the ~** às escondidas
smack [smæk] N (*slap*) palmada; (*blow*) tabefe *m* ■ VT bater; (*child*) dar uma palmada em; (*on face*) dar um tabefe em ■ VI: **to ~ of** cheirar a, saber a ■ ADV (*inf*): **it fell ~ in the middle** caiu exatamente no meio
smacker ['smækəʳ] (*inf*) N (*kiss*) beijoca; (*Brit: pound note*) libra; (*US: dollar bill*) dólar *m*
small [smɔːl] ADJ pequeno; (*short*) baixo; (*letter*) minúsculo ■ N: **the ~ of the back** os rins; **to get** or **grow ~er** diminuir; **to make ~er** diminuir; **a ~ shopkeeper** um pequeno comerciante; **small ads** (*Brit*) NPL classificados *mpl*; **small arms** NPL armas *fpl* leves; **small change** N trocado; **small fry** NPL gente *f* sem importância
smallholder ['smɔːlhəʊldəʳ] (*Brit*) N pequeno(-a) proprietário(-a)
smallholding ['smɔːlhəʊldɪŋ] (*Brit*) N minifúndio
small hours NPL: **in the ~** na madrugada, lá pelas tantas (*inf*)
smallish ['smɔːlɪʃ] ADJ de pequeno porte
small-minded ADJ mesquinho

smallpox ['smɔːlpɔks] N varíola
small print N tipo miúdo
small-scale ADJ (model, map) reduzido; (business, farming) de pequeno porte
small talk N conversa fiada
small-time ADJ (farmer etc) pequeno; **a ~ thief** um ladrão de galinha
smart [smɑːt] ADJ elegante; (clever) inteligente, astuto; (quick) vivo, esperto ■ VI sofrer; **the ~ set** a alta sociedade; **to look ~** estar elegante; **my eyes are ~ing** meus olhos estão ardendo; **smart card** N smart card m, cartão m inteligente
smarten up ['smɑːtən-] VI arrumar-se ■ VT arrumar
smash [smæʃ] N (also: **smash-up**) colisão f, choque m; (smash hit) sucesso de bilheteira; (sound) estrondo ■ VT (break) escangalhar, despedaçar; (car etc) bater com; (Sport: record) quebrar ■ VI despedaçar-se; (against wall etc) espatifar-se
▶ **smash up** VT destruir
smash hit N sucesso absoluto
smashing ['smæʃɪŋ] (inf) ADJ excelente
smattering ['smætərɪŋ] N: **a ~ of** um conhecimento superficial de
smear [smɪəʳ] N mancha, nódoa; (Med) esfregaço; (insult) difamação f ■ VT untar; (to make dirty) lambuzar; (fig) caluniar, difamar; **his hands were ~ed with oil/ink** as mãos dele estavam manchadas de óleo/tinta; **smear campaign** N campanha de desmoralização; **smear test** (Brit) N (Med) esfregaço
smell [smɛl] (pt, pp **smelled**) N cheiro; (sense) olfato ■ VT cheirar ■ VI (food etc) cheirar; (pej) cheirar mal; **to ~ of** cheirar a; **it ~s good** cheira bem, tem um bom cheiro
smelly ['smɛlɪ] (pej) ADJ fedorento, malcheiroso
smelt [smɛlt] PT, PP of **smell** ■ VT (ore) fundir
smile [smaɪl] N sorriso ■ VI sorrir
smiling ['smaɪlɪŋ] ADJ sorridente, risonho
smirk [smɜːk] (pej) N sorriso falso or afetado
smith [smɪθ] N ferreiro
smithy ['smɪðɪ] N forja, oficina de ferreiro
smitten ['smɪtn] ADJ: **~ with** (charmed by) encantado por; (grief etc) tomado por
smock [smɔk] N guarda-pó m; (children's) avental m
smog [smɔg] N nevoeiro com fumaça (BR) or fumo (PT)
smoke [sməuk] N fumaça (BR), fumo (PT) ■ VI fumar; (chimney) fumegar ■ VT (cigarettes) fumar; **to have a ~** fumar; **do you ~?** você fuma?; **to go up in ~** (house etc) queimar num incêndio; (fig) não dar em nada
smoked [sməukt] ADJ (bacon) defumado; (glass) fumée
smokeless fuel ['sməuklɪs-] N combustível m não poluente
smokeless zone ['sməuklɪs-] (Brit) N zona onde não é permitido o uso de combustíveis poluentes

smoker ['sməukəʳ] N (person) fumante m/f; (Rail) vagão m para fumantes
smokescreen ['sməukskriːn] N cortina de fumaça
smoke shop (US) N tabacaria, charutaria (BR)
smoking N: **"no ~"** (sign) "proibido fumar"; **he's given up ~** ele deixou de fumar; **smoking compartment** (US smoking car) N vagão m para fumantes
smoky ['sməukɪ] ADJ (room) enfumaçado; (taste) defumado
smolder ['sməuldəʳ] (US) VI = **smoulder**
smooth [smuːð] ADJ liso, macio; (sauce) cremoso; (sea) tranqüilo, calmo; (flat) plano; (flavour, movement) suave; (person) culto, refinado; (: pej) meloso; (flight, landing) tranqüilo; (cigarette) suave ■ VT (also: **smooth out**) alisar; (: difficulties) aplainar
▶ **smooth over** VT: **to ~ things over** (fig) arranjar as coisas
smoothly ['smuːðlɪ] ADV (easily) facilmente, sem problemas; **everything went ~** tudo correu muito bem
smother ['smʌðəʳ] VT (fire) abafar; (person) sufocar; (emotions) reprimir
smoulder ['sməuldəʳ] (US smolder) VI arder sem chamas; (fig) estar latente
smoulder ['sməuldəʳ] (US smolder) VI arder sem chamas; (fig) estar latente
SMS N ABBR (= short message service) SMS m
smug [smʌg] (pej) ADJ convencido
smuggle ['smʌgl] VT contrabandear; **to ~ in/ out** (goods etc) fazer entrar/sair de contrabando
smuggler ['smʌgləʳ] N contrabandista m/f
smuggling ['smʌglɪŋ] N contrabando
smut [smʌt] N (of soot) marca de fuligem; (mark) mancha; (in conversation etc) obscenidades fpl
smutty ['smʌtɪ] ADJ (fig) obsceno, indecente
snack [snæk] N lanche m (BR), merenda (PT); **to have a ~** fazer um lanche; **snack bar** N lanchonete f (BR), snackbar m (PT)
snag [snæg] N dificuldade f, obstáculo
snail [sneɪl] N caracol m; (water snail) caramujo
snake [sneɪk] N cobra
snap [snæp] N (sound) estalo; (of whip) estalido; (click) clique m; (photograph) foto f ■ ADJ repentino ■ VT (break) quebrar; (fingers, whip) estalar; (photograph) tirar uma foto de ■ VI quebrar; (fig: person) retrucar asperamente; (sound) estalar; **to ~ shut** fechar com um estalo; **to ~ one's fingers** estalar os dedos; **a cold ~** uma onda de frio
▶ **snap at** VT FUS (subj: person) retrucar bruscamente a; (: dog) tentar morder
▶ **snap off** VT (break) partir
▶ **snap up** VT arrebatar, comprar rapidamente
snap fastener N colchete m de mola
snappy ['snæpɪ] (inf) ADJ rápido; (slogan) vigoroso; **he's a ~ dresser** ele está sempre chique; **make it ~!** faça rápido!
snapshot ['snæpʃɔt] N foto f (instantânea)

snare [snɛəʳ] N armadilha, laço ▪ VT apanhar no laço *or* na armadilha

snarl [snɑːl] N grunhido ▪ VI grunhir ▪ VT: **to get ~ed up** (*wool, plans*) ficar embaralhado; (*traffic*) ficar engarrafado

snatch [snætʃ] N (*fig*) roubo; (*small piece*) trecho ▪ VT agarrar; (*fig: look*) roubar ▪ VI: **don't ~!** não tome as coisas dos outros!; **to ~ a sandwich** fazer um lanche rapidinho; **to ~ some sleep** dormir um pouco
▸ **snatch up** VT agarrar

sneak [sniːk] VI: **to ~ in/out** entrar/sair furtivamente ▪ VT: **to ~ a look at sth** olhar disfarçadamente para algo ▪ N (*inf*) dedo-duro; **to ~ up on sb** chegar de mausinho

sneakers ['sniːkəz] NPL tênis *m* (BR), sapatos *mpl* de treino (PT)

sneaking ['sniːkɪŋ] ADJ: **to have a ~ suspicion that ...** ter uma vaga suspeita de que ...

sneaky ['sniːkɪ] ADJ sorrateiro

sneer [snɪəʳ] N sorriso de desprezo ▪ VI rir-se com desdém; (*mock*): **to ~ at** zombar de, desprezar

sneeze [sniːz] N espirro ▪ VI espirrar

snide [snaɪd] ADJ sarcástico

sniff [snɪf] N fungada; (*of dog*) farejada; (*of person*) fungadela ▪ VI fungar ▪ VT fungar, farejar; (*glue, drug*) cheirar
▸ **sniff at** VT FUS: **it's not to be ~ed at** isso não deve ser desprezado

snigger ['snɪgəʳ] N riso dissimulado ▪ VI rir-se com dissimulação

snip [snɪp] N tesourada; (*piece*) pedaço, retalho; (*Brit: inf: bargain*) pechincha ▪ VT cortar com tesoura

sniper ['snaɪpəʳ] N franco-atirador(a) *m/f*

snippet ['snɪpɪt] N fragmento, trecho

snivelling ['snɪvlɪŋ] ADJ (*whimpering*) chorão(-rona), lamuriento

snob [snɔb] N esnobe *m/f*

snobbery ['snɔbərɪ] N esnobismo

snobbish ['snɔbɪʃ] ADJ esnobe

snooker ['snuːkəʳ] N sinuca

snoop [snuːp] VI: **to ~ about** bisbilhotar

snooper ['snuːpəʳ] N bisbilhoteiro(-a), xereta *m/f*

snooty ['snuːtɪ] ADJ arrogante

snooze [snuːz] N soneca ▪ VI tirar uma soneca, dormitar

snore [snɔːʳ] VI roncar ▪ N ronco

snoring ['snɔːrɪŋ] N roncadura, roncaria

snorkel ['snɔːkl] N tubo snorkel

snort [snɔːt] N bufo, bufido ▪ VI bufar ▪ VT (*drugs*) cheirar

snotty ['snɔtɪ] ADJ ranhoso; (*fig*) altivo, arrogante

snout [snaut] N focinho

snow [snəu] N neve *f* ▪ VI nevar ▪ VT: **to be ~ed under with work** estar atolado *or* sobrecarregado de trabalho

snowball ['snəubɔːl] N bola de neve ▪ VI acumular-se; (*fig*) aumentar (como bola de neve)

snowbound ['snəubaund] ADJ bloqueado pela neve

snow-capped [-kæpt] ADJ coberto de neve

snowdrift ['snəudrɪft] N monte *m* de neve (formado pelo vento)

snowdrop ['snəudrɔp] N campainha branca

snowfall ['snəufɔːl] N nevada

snowflake ['snəufleɪk] N floco de neve

snowman ['snəumæn] (*irreg*) N boneco de neve

snowplough ['snəuplau] (*US* **snowplow**) N máquina limpa-neve, removedor *m* de neve

snowshoe ['snəuʃuː] N raquete *f* de neve

snowstorm ['snəustɔːm] N nevasca, tempestade *f* de neve

snowy ['snəuɪ] ADJ nevoso

SNP (*Brit*) N ABBR (*Pol*) = **Scottish National Party**

snub [snʌb] VT desdenhar, menosprezar ▪ N repulsa

snub-nosed [-'nəuzd] ADJ de nariz arrebitado

snuff [snʌf] N rapé *m* ▪ VT (*also*: **snuff out**: *candle*) apagar

snug [snʌg] ADJ (*sheltered*) abrigado, protegido; (*fitted*) justo, cômodo

snuggle ['snʌgl] VI: **to ~ up to sb** aconchegar-se *or* aninhar-se a alguém

snugly ['snʌglɪ] ADV (*fit*) perfeitamente

SO ABBR (*Banking*) = **standing order**

○ KEYWORD

so [səu] ADV **1** (*thus, likewise*) assim, deste modo; **so saying he walked away** falou isto e foi embora; **if so** se for assim, se assim é; **I didn't do it — you did so** não fiz isso — você fez!; **so do I, so am I** *etc* eu também; **so it is!** é verdade!; **I hope/think so** espero/acho que sim; **so far** até aqui; **so far I haven't had any problems** até agora não tive nenhum problema
2 (*in comparisons etc: to such a degree*) tão; **so big/quickly (that)** tão grande/rápido(que); **she's not so clever as her brother** ela não é tão inteligente quanto o irmão
3: **so much** ▪ ADJ, ADV tanto; **I've got so much work** tenho tanto trabalho; **so many** tantos(-as); **there are so many people to see** tem tanta gente para ver
4 (*phrases*): **10 or so** 10 mais ou menos; **so long!** (*inf: goodbye*) tchau!
▪ CONJ **1** (*expressing purpose*): **so as to do** para fazer; **we hurried so as not to be late** nós nos apressamos para não chegarmos atrasados; **so (that)** para que, a fim de que
2 (*result*) de modo que; **he didn't arrive so I left** como ele não chegou, eu fui embora; **so I was right after all** então eu estava certo no final das contas

soak [səuk] VT (*drench*) embeber, ensopar; (*put*

in water) pôr de molho ■ vi estar de molho, impregnar-se

▶**soak in** vi infiltrar

▶**soak up** vt absorver

soaking ['səukɪŋ] ADJ (*also*: **soaking wet**) encharcado

so and so N fulano(-a)

soap [səup] N sabão *m*; **soap flakes** NPL flocos *mpl* de sabão; **soap opera** N novela; **soap powder** N sabão *m* em pó

soapsuds ['səupsʌdz] N água de sabão

soapy ['səupɪ] ADJ ensaboado

soar [sɔ:ʳ] vi (*on wings*) elevar-se em vôo; (*rocket, temperature*) subir; (*building etc*) levantar-se; (*price, production*) disparar; (*morale, spirits*) renascer

soaring ['sɔ:rɪŋ] ADJ (*flight*) a grande altura; (*prices, inflation*) disparado

sob [sɔb] N soluço ■ vi soluçar

s.o.b. (*US: inf!*) N ABBR (= *son of a bitch*) filho da puta (*!*)

sober ['səubəʳ] ADJ (*serious*) sério; (*sensible*) sensato; (*moderate*) moderado; (*not drunk*) sóbrio; (*colour, style*) discreto

▶**sober up** vi ficar sóbrio

sobriety [sə'braɪətɪ] N sobriedade *f*

Soc. ABBR = **society**

so-called [-kɔ:ld] ADJ chamado

soccer ['sɔkəʳ] N futebol *m*; **soccer pitch** N campo de futebol; **soccer player** N jogador *m* de futebol

sociable ['səuʃəbl] ADJ sociável

social ['səuʃl] ADJ social; (*sociable*) sociável ■ N reunião *f* social; **social climber** N arrivista *m/f*; **social club** N clube *m*; **Social Democrat** N democrata-social *m/f*; **social insurance** (US) N seguro social

socialism ['səuʃəlɪzəm] N socialismo

socialist ['səuʃəlɪst] ADJ, N socialista *m/f*

socialite ['səuʃəlaɪt] N socialite *m/f*, colunável *m/f*

socialize ['səuʃəlaɪz] vi: **to ~ (with)** socializar (com)

socially ['səuʃəlɪ] ADV socialmente

social science N ciências *fpl* sociais

social security (*Brit*) N previdência social; **Department of S~ S~** = Instituto Nacional de Assistência Médica e Previdência Social (BR)

social welfare N bem-estar *m* social

social work N assistência social, serviço social

social worker N assistente *m/f* social

society [sə'saɪətɪ] N sociedade *f*; (*club*) associação *f*; (*also*: **high society**) alta sociedade ■ CPD (*party, column*) da alta sociedade

socio-economic ['səusɪəu-] ADJ sócio-econômico

sociological [səusɪə'lɔdʒɪkl] ADJ sociológico

sociologist [səusɪ'ɔlədʒɪst] N sociólogo(-a)

sociology [səusɪ'ɔlədʒɪ] N sociologia

sock [sɔk] N meia (BR), peúga (PT) ■ vt (*inf: hit*) socar, dar um soco em; **to pull one's ~s up** (*fig*) tomar jeito

socket ['sɔkɪt] N bocal *m*, encaixe *m*; (*Brit: Elec*)

tomada

sod [sɔd] N (*of earth*) gramado, torrão *m*; (*Brit: inf!*) imbecil *m/f* ■ vt: **~ it!** (*inf!*) droga!

soda ['səudə] N (*Chem*) soda; (*also*: **soda water**) água com gás; (*US: also*: **soda pop**) soda

sodden ['sɔdn] ADJ encharcado

sodium ['səudɪəm] N sódio; **sodium chloride** N cloreto de sódio

sofa ['səufə] N sofá *m*

Sofia ['səufɪə] N Sófia

soft [sɔft] ADJ (*gen*) macio; (*not hard*) mole; (*voice, music, light*) suave; (*kind*) meigo, bondoso; (*weak*) fraco; (*stupid*) idiota; **soft-boiled egg** [-bɔɪld-] N ovo quente; **soft currency** N moeda fraca; **soft drink** N refrigerante *m*; **soft drugs** N drogas *fpl* leves

soften ['sɔfn] vt amolecer, amaciar; (*effect*) abrandar; (*expression*) suavizar ■ vi amolecer-se; (*voice, expression*) suavizar-se

softener ['sɔfnər] N amaciante *m*

soft fruit (Brit) N bagas *fpl*

soft furnishings NPL cortinas *fpl* e estofados *mpl*

soft-hearted ADJ bondoso, caridoso

softly ['sɔftlɪ] ADV suavemente; (*gently*) delicadamente

softness ['sɔftnɪs] N maciez *f*; (*gentleness*) suavidade *f*

soft sell N venda de forma não agressiva

soft spot N: **to have a ~ for sb** ter xodó por alguém

soft toy N brinquedo de pelúcia

software ['sɔftwɛəʳ] N software *m*; **software package** N soft *m*, pacote *m*

soggy ['sɔgɪ] ADJ ensopado, encharcado

soil [sɔɪl] N (*earth*) terra, solo; (*territory*) território ■ vt sujar, manchar

soiled [sɔɪld] ADJ sujo

sojourn ['sɔdʒə:n] N (*formal*) estada *f*

solace ['sɔlɪs] N consolo

solar ['səuləʳ] ADJ solar

solaria [sə'lɛərɪə] NPL *of* **solarium**

solarium [sə'lɛərɪəm] (*pl* **solaria**) N solário

solar plexus [-'plɛksəs] N plexo solar

sold [səuld] PT, PP *of* **sell** ■ ADJ: **~ out** (*Comm*) esgotado

solder ['səuldəʳ] vt soldar ■ N solda

soldier ['səuldʒəʳ] N soldado; (*army man*) militar *m*; **toy ~** soldado de chumbo

▶**soldier on** vi agüentar firme (*inf*), perseverar

sole [səul] N (*of foot, shoe*) sola; (*fish: pl inv*) solha, linguado ■ ADJ único; **the ~ reason** a única razão

solely ['səullɪ] ADV somente, unicamente; **I will hold you ~ responsible** vou apontar-lhe como o único responsável

solemn ['sɔləm] ADJ solene

sole trader N (*Comm*) comerciante *m/f* independente

solicit [sə'lɪsɪt] vt (*request*) solicitar ■ vi (*prostitute*) aliciar fregueses

solicitor [sə'lɪsɪtə^r] (Brit) N (for wills etc)
tabelião(-lioa) m/f; (in court) = advogado(-a)
solid ['sɔlɪd] ADJ sólido; (gold etc) maciço;
(person) sério; (line) contínuo; (vote) unânime
■ N sólido; **solids** NPL (food) comida sólida
(em contraste ao leite ou sopas); **we waited 2 ~
hours** esperamos durante 2 horas a fio; **to
be on ~ ground** estar em terra firme; (fig) ter
base
solidarity [sɔlɪ'dærɪtɪ] N solidariedade f
solidify [sə'lɪdɪfaɪ] VI solidificar-se
solidity [sə'lɪdɪtɪ] N solidez f
solid-state ADJ de estado sólido
soliloquy [sə'lɪləkwɪ] N monólogo
solitaire [sɔlɪ'tɛə^r] N (gem) solitário; (game)
solitário, jogo de paciência
solitary ['sɔlɪtərɪ] ADJ solitário, só; (walk) só;
(isolated) isolado, retirado; (single) único; **solitary
confinement** N prisão f celular, solitária
solitude ['sɔlɪtjuːd] N solidão f
solo ['səuləu] N, ADV solo
soloist ['səuləuɪst] N solista m/f
Solomon Islands ['sɔləmən-] NPL: **the ~** as ilhas
Salomão
solstice ['sɔlstɪs] N solstício
soluble ['sɔljubl] ADJ solúvel
solution [sə'luːʃən] N solução f
solve [sɔlv] VT resolver, solucionar
solvency ['sɔlvənsɪ] N (Comm) solvência
solvent ['sɔlvənt] ADJ (Comm) solvente ■ N
(Chem) solvente m; **solvent abuse** N abuso de
solventes alucinógenos
Somali [sə'mɑːlɪ] ADJ, N somaliano(-a)
Somalia [sə'mɑːlɪə] N Somália
sombre ['sɔmbə^r] (US **somber**) ADJ sombrio,
lúgubre

○ KEYWORD

some [sʌm] ADJ **1** (a certain number or amount):
some tea/water/biscuits um pouco de chá/
água/uns biscoitos; **some children came**
algumas crianças vieram; **there's some milk
in the fridge** há leite na geladeira; **I've got
some money, but not much** tenho algum
dinheiro, mas não muito
2 (certain: in contrasts) algum(a); **some people
say that ...** algumas pessoas dizem que ...
3 (unspecified) um pouco de; **some woman
was asking for you** uma mulher estava
perguntando por você; **some day** um dia
■ PRON **1** (a certain number) alguns/algumas; **I've
got some** (books etc) tenho alguns; **some went
for a taxi and some walked** alguns foram
pegar um táxi e outros foram andando
2 (a certain amount) um pouco; **I've got some**
(milk, money etc) tenho um pouco
■ ADV: **some 10 people** umas 10 pessoas

somebody ['sʌmbədɪ] PRON = **someone**
someday ['sʌmdeɪ] ADV algum dia
somehow ['sʌmhau] ADV de alguma maneira;

(for some reason) por uma razão ou outra

○ KEYWORD

someone ['sʌmwʌn] PRON alguém; **there's
someone coming** tem alguém vindo/
chegando

someplace ['sʌmpleɪs] (US) ADV = **somewhere**
somersault ['sʌməsɔːlt] N (deliberate) salto
mortal; (accidental) cambalhota ■ VI dar um
salto mortal or uma cambalhota

○ KEYWORD

something ['sʌmθɪŋ] PRON alguma coisa,
algo (BR); **something nice** alguma coisa boa;
something to do alguma coisa para fazer;
there's something wrong tem alguma coisa
errada; **would you like something to eat/
drink?** você gostaria de comer/beber alguma
coisa?

sometime ['sʌmtaɪm] ADV (in future) algum dia,
em outra oportunidade; (in past): **~ last month**
durante o mês passado; **I'll finish it ~** vou
terminar uma hora dessas
sometimes ['sʌmtaɪmz] ADV às vezes, de vez
em quando
somewhat ['sʌmwɔt] ADV um tanto

○ KEYWORD

somewhere ['sʌmwɛə^r] ADV (be) em algum
lugar; (go) para algum lugar; **I must have
lost it somewhere** devo ter perdido (isso)
em algum lugar; **it's somewhere or other
in Scotland** é em algum lugar na Escócia;
somewhere else (be) em outro lugar; (go) para
outro lugar

son [sʌn] N filho
sonar ['səunɑː^r] N sonar m
sonata [sə'nɑːtə] N sonata
song [sɔŋ] N canção f; (of bird) canto
songbook ['sɔŋbuk] N cancioneiro
songwriter ['sɔŋraɪtə^r] N compositor(a) m/f de
canções
sonic ['sɔnɪk] ADJ (boom) sônico
son-in-law ['sʌnɪnlɔː] (pl **sons-in-law**) N genro
sonnet ['sɔnɪt] N soneto
sonny ['sʌnɪ] (inf) N meu filho
soon [suːn] ADV logo, brevemente; (a short time
after) logo após; (early) cedo; **~ afterwards** pouco
depois; **very/quite ~** logo/daqui a pouco; **how ~
can you be ready?** quando você estará pronto?;
it's too ~ to tell é muito cedo para dizer; **see
you ~!** até logo!; see also **as**
sooner ['suːnə^r] ADV (time) antes, mais cedo;
(preference): **I would ~ do that** preferia fazer
isso; **~ or later** mais cedo ou mais tarde; **no ~
said than done** dito e feito; **the ~ the better**

quanto mais cedo melhor; **no - had we left than he ...** mal partimos, ele ...
soot [sut] N fuligem f
soothe [suːð] VT acalmar, sossegar; (pain) aliviar, suavizar
soothing ['suːðɪŋ] ADJ calmante
SOP N ABBR = **standard operating procedure**
sop [sɔp] N paliativo
sophisticated [sə'fɪstɪkeɪtɪd] ADJ sofisticado
sophistication [səfɪstɪ'keɪʃən] N sofisticação f
sophomore ['sɔfəmɔːʳ] (US) N segundanista m/f
soporific [sɔpə'rɪfɪk] ADJ soporífico
sopping ['sɔpɪŋ] ADJ: **- (wet)** encharcado
soppy ['sɔpɪ] (pej) ADJ piegas inv
soprano [sə'prɑːnəu] N soprano m/f
sorbet ['sɔːbeɪ] N sorvete de frutas à base de água
sorcerer ['sɔːsərəʳ] N feiticeiro
sordid ['sɔːdɪd] ADJ (dirty) imundo, sórdido; (wretched) miserável
sore [sɔːʳ] ADJ (painful) dolorido; (offended) magoado, ofendido ▪ N chaga, ferida; **it's a - point** é um ponto delicado; **my eyes are -, I've got - eyes** meus olhos estão doloridos
sorely ['sɔːlɪ] ADV: **I am - tempted (to)** estou muito tentado (a)
sore throat N dor f de garganta
sorrel ['sɔrəl] N azeda
sorrow ['sɔrəu] N tristeza, mágoa, dor f;
sorrows NPL (causes of grief) tristezas fpl
sorrowful ['sɔrəuful] ADJ (day) triste; (smile) aflito, magoado
sorry ['sɔrɪ] ADJ (regretful) arrependido; (condition, excuse) lamentável; **-!** desculpe!, perdão!, sinto muito!; **to feel - for sb** sentir pena de alguém; **I feel - for him** estou com pena dele; **I'm - to hear that ...** lamento saber que ...; **to be - about sth** arrepender-se de algo
sort [sɔːt] N tipo; (brand: of coffee etc) marca ▪ VT (also: **sort out**: papers) classificar; (: problems) solucionar, resolver; **what - do you want?** que tipo você quer?; **what - of car?** que tipo de carro?; **I'll do nothing of the -!** não farei nada do gênero!; **it's - of awkward** (inf) é meio difícil
sortie ['sɔːtɪ] N surtida
sorting office ['sɔːtɪŋ-] N departamento de distribuição
SOS N ABBR (= save our souls) S.O.S. m
so-so ADV mais ou menos, regular
soufflé ['suːfleɪ] N suflê m
sought [sɔːt] PT, PP of **seek**
sought-after ADJ desejado
soul [səul] N alma; (person) criatura; **I didn't see a -** não vi uma alma; **God rest his -** que a sua alma descanse em paz; **the poor - had nowhere to sleep** o pobre coitado não tinha onde dormir
soul-destroying [-dɪs'trɔɪɪŋ] ADJ desalentador(a)
soulful ['səulful] ADJ emocional, sentimental
soulless ['səullɪs] ADJ desalmado
soul mate N companheiro(-a) ideal
soul-searching N: **after much -** depois de

muita ponderação
sound [saund] ADJ (healthy) saudável, sadio; (safe, not damaged) sólido, completo; (secure) seguro; (reliable) confiável; (sensible) sensato; (argument, policy) válido; (move) acertado ▪ ADV: **- asleep** dormindo profundamente ▪ N (noise) som m, ruído, barulho; (volume: on TV etc) volume m; (Geo) estreito, braço (de mar) ▪ VT (alarm) soar ▪ VI soar, tocar; (fig: seem) parecer; **to be of - mind** estar em juízo perfeito; **I don't like the - of it** eu não estou gostando disso; **to - like** parecer; **it -s as if ...** parece que ...
▶ **sound off** (inf) VI: **to - off (about)** pontificar (sobre)
▶ **sound out** VI sondar
sound: sound barrier N barreira do som; **sound effects** NPL efeitos mpl sonoros; **sound engineer** N engenheiro(-a) de som
sounding ['saundɪŋ] N (Naut etc) sondagem f; **sounding board** N (Mus) caixa de ressonância; (fig): **to use sb as a sounding board for one's ideas** testar suas idéias em alguém
soundly ['saundlɪ] ADV (sleep) profundamente; (beat) completamente
soundproof ['saundpruːf] ADJ à prova de som ▪ VT insonorizar
soundtrack ['saundtræk] N (of film) trilha sonora
sound wave N onda sonora
soup [suːp] N (thick) sopa; (thin) caldo; **in the -** (fig) numa encrenca; **soup kitchen** N local onde se distribui comida aos pobres; **soup plate** N prato fundo (para sopa)
soupspoon ['suːpspuːn] N colher f de sopa
sour ['sauəʳ] ADJ azedo, ácido; (milk) talhado; (fig) mal-humorado, rabugento; **it's - grapes!** (fig) é despeito!; **to go or turn -** (milk, wine) azedar; (fig: relationship, plan) azedar, dar errado
source [sɔːs] N fonte f; **I have it from a reliable - that ...** uma fonte confiável me assegura que ...
south [sauθ] N sul m ▪ ADJ do sul, meridional ▪ ADV ao or para o sul; (to the) - of ao sul de; **the S- of France** o Sul da França; **to travel -** viajar para o sul
South Africa N África do Sul
South African ADJ, N sul-africano(-a)
South America N América do Sul
South American ADJ, N sul-americano(-a)
southbound ['sauθbaund] ADJ em direção ao sul
south-east N sudeste m ▪ ADJ do sudeste
South-East Asia N o Sudeste da Ásia
southerly ['sʌðəlɪ] ADJ para o sul; (from the south) do sul
southern ['sʌðən] ADJ (to the south) para o sul, em direção do sul; (from the south) do sul, sulista; **the - hemisphere** o Hemisfério Sul
South Pole N Pólo Sul
South Sea Islands NPL: **the -** as ilhas dos Mares do Sul
South Seas NPL: **the -** os Mares do Sul
southward(s) ['sauθwəd(z)] ADV para o sul

south-west N sudoeste *m*

souvenir [su:vəˈniəʳ] N lembrança

sovereign [ˈsɔvrɪn] ADJ, N soberano(-a)

sovereignty [ˈsɔvrɪntɪ] N soberania

soviet [ˈsəuvɪət] ADJ soviético; **the S~ Union** a União Soviética

sow¹ [sau] N porca

sow² [səu] (*pt* **sowed**, *pp* **sown**) VT semear; (*fig: spread*) disseminar, espalhar

sown [səun] PP *of* **sow²**; **soya** [ˈsɔɪə] (*US* **soy**) N soja

soya bean ▪ N semente *f* de soja

soya sauce ▪ N molho de soja

spa [spɑ:] N (*town*) estância hidro-mineral; (*US: also*: **health spa**) estância balnear

space [speɪs] N (*gen*) espaço; (*room*) lugar *m*; (*cpd*) espacial ▪ VT (*also*: **space out**) espaçar; **in a confined ~** num espaço confinado; **in a short ~ of time** num curto espaço de tempo; **(with)in the ~ of an hour** dentro do espaço de uma hora; **to clear a ~ for sth** abrir espaço para algo; **space bar** N tecla de espacejamento

spacecraft [ˈspeɪskrɑ:ft] N nave *f* espacial

spaceman [ˈspeɪsmæn] (*irreg*) N astronauta *m*, cosmonauta *m*

spaceship [ˈspeɪsʃɪp] N = **spacecraft**

space shuttle N ônibus *m* espacial

spacesuit [ˈspeɪssu:t] N traje *m* espacial

spacewoman [ˈspeɪswumən] (*irreg*) N astronauta, cosmonauta

spacing [ˈspeɪsɪŋ] N espacejamento, espaçamento; **single/double ~** espacejamento simples/duplo

spacious [ˈspeɪʃəs] ADJ espaçoso

spam [ˈspæm] N (*junk e-mail*) spam *m*

spade [speɪd] N pá *f*; **spades** NPL (*Cards*) espadas *fpl*

spadework [ˈspeɪdwə:k] N (*fig*) trabalho preliminar

spaghetti [spəˈgetɪ] N espaguete *m*

Spain [speɪn] N Espanha

span [spæn] N (*also*: **wingspan**) envergadura; (*of hand*) palma; (*of arch*) vão *m*; (*in time*) lapso, espaço ▪ VT estender-se sobre, atravessar; (*fig*) abarcar

Spaniard [ˈspænjəd] N espanhol(a) *m/f*

spaniel [ˈspænjəl] N spaniel *m*; **Spanish** [ˈspænɪʃ] ADJ espanhol(a) ▪ N (*Ling*) espanhol *m*, castelhano; **the Spanish** NPL os espanhóis

Spanish omelette ▪ N omelete *m* à espanhola

spank [spæŋk] VT bater, dar palmadas em

spanner [ˈspænəʳ] (*Brit*) N chave *f* inglesa

spar [spɑ:ʳ] N mastro, verga ▪ VI (*Boxing*) treinar

spare [speəʳ] ADJ (*free*) vago, desocupado; (*surplus*) de sobra, a mais; (*available*) disponível, de reserva ▪ N = **spare part** ▪ VT (*do without*) dispensar, passar sem; (*make available*) dispor de; (*afford to give*) dispor de, ter de sobra; (*refrain from hurting*) perdoar, poupar; (*be grudging with*) dar frugalmente; **to ~** (*surplus*) de sobra; **there are 2 going ~** (*Brit*) há 2 sobrando; **to ~ no expense** não poupar despesas; **can you ~ (me)**

£10? pode me ceder £10?; **can you ~ the time?** você tem tempo?; **there is no time to ~** não há tempo a perder; **I've a few minutes to ~** tenho alguns minutos de sobra; **spare part** N peça sobressalente; **spare room** N quarto de hóspedes; **spare time** N tempo livre; **spare tyre** N estepe *m*; **spare wheel** N estepe *m*

sparing [ˈspeərɪŋ] ADJ: **to be ~ with** ser econômico com

sparingly [ˈspeərɪŋlɪ] ADV frugalmente, com moderação

spark [spɑ:k] N chispa, faísca; (*fig*) centelha

spark(ing) plug [ˈspɑ:k(ɪŋ)-] N vela (de ignição)

sparkle [ˈspɑ:kl] N cintilação *f*, brilho ▪ VI cintilar; (*shine*) brilhar, faiscar

sparkling [ˈspɑ:klɪŋ] ADJ (*wine*) espumante; (*conversation*) animado; (*performance*) brilhante

sparrow [ˈspærəu] N pardal *m*

sparse [spɑ:s] ADJ escasso; (*hair*) ralo

spartan [ˈspɑ:tən] ADJ (*fig*) espartano

spasm [ˈspæzəm] N (*Med*) espasmo; (*fig*) acesso, ataque *m*

spasmodic [spæzˈmɔdɪk] ADJ espasmódico

spastic [ˈspæstɪk] N espástico(-a)

spat [spæt] PT, PP *of* **spit** ▪ N (*US*) bate-boca *m*

spate [speɪt] N série *f*; (*fig*): **a ~ of** uma enxurrada de; **in ~** (*river*) em cheia

spatial [ˈspeɪʃəl] ADJ espacial

spatter [ˈspætəʳ] N borrifo ▪ VT borrifar, salpicar ▪ VI borrifar

spatula [ˈspætjulə] N espátula

spawn [spɔ:n] VI desovar, procriar ▪ VT gerar; (*pej: create*) gerar, criar ▪ N ovas *fpl*

SPCA (*US*) N ABBR = **Society for the Prevention of Cruelty to Animals**

SPCC (*US*) N ABBR = **Society for the Prevention of Cruelty to Children**

speak [spi:k] (*pt* **spoke**, *pp* **spoken**) VT (*language*) falar; (*truth*) dizer ▪ VI falar; (*make a speech*) discursar; **to ~ to sb/of** *or* **about sth** falar com alguém/de *or* sobre algo; **~ up!** fale alto!; **~ing!** (*on phone*) é ele/ela mesmo!; **to ~ one's mind** desabafar; **he has no money to ~ of** ele quase não tem dinheiro

▶ **speak for** VT FUS: **to ~ for sb** falar por alguém; **that picture is already spoken for** aquele quadro já está vendido

speaker [ˈspi:kəʳ] N (*in public*) orador(a) *m/f*; (*also*: **loudspeaker**) alto-falante *m*; (*Pol*): **the S~** o Presidente da Câmara; **are you a Welsh ~?** você fala galês?

speaking [ˈspi:kɪŋ] ADJ falante; **Italian-~ people** pessoas de língua italiana

spear [spɪəʳ] N lança; (*for fishing*) arpão *m* ▪ VT lancear, arpoar

spearhead [ˈspɪəhɛd] N ponta-de-lança ▪ VT (*attack*) encabeçar

spearmint [ˈspɪəmɪnt] N hortelã *f*

spec [spɛk] (*inf*) N: **on ~** por acaso

special [ˈspɛʃl] ADJ especial; (*edition etc*) extra; (*delivery*) rápido ▪ N (*train*) trem *m* especial; **take ~ care** tome muito cuidado; **nothing ~** nada especial; **today's ~** (*at restaurant*) especialidade do dia, prato do dia; **special delivery** N: **by special delivery** por entrega rápida

specialist ['spɛʃəlɪst] N especialista *m/f*; **heart ~** especialista em doenças do coração

speciality [spɛʃɪ'ælɪtɪ] N especialidade *f*

specialize ['spɛʃəlaɪz] VI: **to ~ (in)** especializar-se (em)

specially ['spɛʃəlɪ] ADV especialmente

special offer N oferta especial

specialty ['spɛʃəltɪ] (*esp US*) N = **speciality**

species ['spiːʃiːz] N INV espécie *f*

specific [spə'sɪfɪk] ADJ específico

specifically [spə'sɪfɪklɪ] ADV especificamente

specification [spɛsɪfɪ'keɪʃən] N especificação *f*; (*requirement*) requinto; **specifications** NPL (*Tech*) ficha técnica; (*of building*) especificações *fpl*

specify ['spɛsɪfaɪ] VT, VI especificar; **unless otherwise specified** salvo indicação em contrário

specimen ['spɛsɪmən] N espécime *m*, amostra; (*for testing, Med*) espécime; (*fig*) exemplar *m*; **specimen copy** N exemplar *m* de amostra; **specimen signature** N modelo de assinatura

speck [spɛk] N mancha, pinta; (*particle*) grão *m*

speckled ['spɛkld] ADJ pintado

specs [spɛks] (*inf*) NPL óculos *mpl*

spectacle ['spɛktəkl] N espetáculo; **spectacles** NPL (*glasses*) óculos *mpl*; **spectacle case** N estojo de óculos

spectacular [spɛk'tækjulə^r] ADJ espetacular ■ N (*Cinema etc*) superprodução *f*

spectator [spɛk'teɪtə^r] N espectador(a) *m/f*

specter ['spɛktə^r] (*US*) N = **spectre**

spectra ['spɛktrə] NPL *of* **spectrum**

spectre ['spɛktə^r] (*US* **specter**) N espectro, aparição *f*

spectrum ['spɛktrəm] (*pl* **spectra**) N espectro

speculate ['spɛkjuleɪt] VI especular; (*try to guess*): **to ~ about** especular sobre

speculation [spɛkju'leɪʃən] N especulação *f*

speculative ['spɛkjulətɪv] ADJ especulativo

speculator ['spɛkjuleɪtə^r] N especulador(a) *m/f*

sped [spɛd] PT, PP *of* **speed**

speech [spiːtʃ] N (*faculty, Theatre*) fala; (*formal talk*) discurso; **speech day** (*Brit*) N (*Sch*) dia *m* de distribuição de prêmios; **speech impediment** N defeito *m* de articulação

speechless ['spiːtʃlɪs] ADJ estupefato, emudecido

speech therapy N ortofonia

speed [spiːd] (*pt, pp* **sped**) N (*fast travel*) velocidade *f*; (*rate*) rapidez *f*; (*haste*) pressa; (*promptness*) prontidão *f*; (*gear*) marcha ■ VI (*in car*) correr; **the years sped by** os anos voaram; **at full** *or* **top ~** a toda a velocidade; **at a ~ of 70 km/h** a uma velocidade de 70 km/h; **shorthand/typing ~** velocidade de estenografia/datilografia; **at ~** em alta velocidade; **a five-~ gearbox** uma caixa de mudanças com cinco marchas

▶ **speed up** (*pt , pp* **speeded up**) VT, VI acelerar

speedboat ['spiːdbəut] N lancha

speedily ['spiːdɪlɪ] ADV depressa, rapidamente

speeding ['spiːdɪŋ] N (*Aut*) excesso de velocidade

speed limit N limite *m* de velocidade, velocidade *f* máxima

speedometer [spɪ'dɔmɪtə^r] N velocímetro

speed trap N *área de fiscalização contra motoristas que dirigem em alta velocidade*

speedway ['spiːdweɪ] N (*Sport*) pista de corrida, rodovia de alta velocidade; (: *also*: **speedway racing**) corrida de motocicleta

speedy ['spiːdɪ] ADJ (*fast*) veloz, rápido; (*prompt*) pronto, imediato

speleologist [spiːlɪ'ɔlədʒɪst] N espeleologista *m/f*

spell [spɛl] (*pt, pp* **spelt**) N (*also*: **magic spell**) encanto, feitiço; (*period of time*) período, temporada ■ VT (*also*: **spell out**) soletrar; (*fig*) pressagiar, ser sinal de; **to cast a ~ on sb** enfeitiçar alguém; **he can't ~** não sabe escrever bem, comete erros de ortografia; **how do you ~ your name?** como você escreve o seu nome?; **can you ~ it for me?** pode soletrar isso para mim?

spellbound ['spɛlbaund] ADJ enfeitiçado, fascinado

spelling ['spɛlɪŋ] N ortografia; **spelling mistake** N erro ortográfico

spelt [spɛlt] PT, PP *of* **spell**

spend [spɛnd] (*pt, pp* **spent**) VT (*money*) gastar; (*time*) passar; **to ~ time/money on sth** gastar tempo/dinheiro em algo

spending ['spɛndɪŋ] N gastos *mpl*; **government ~** gastos públicos; **spending money** N dinheiro para pequenas despesas; **spending power** N poder *m* aquisitivo

spendthrift ['spɛndθrɪft] N esbanjador(a) *m/f*, perdulário(-a)

spent [spɛnt] PT, PP *of* **spend** ■ ADJ gasto

sperm [spə:m] N esperma; **sperm whale** N cachalote *m*

spew [spjuː] VT vomitar, lançar

sphere [sfɪə^r] N esfera

spherical ['sfɛrɪkl] ADJ esférico

sphinx [sfɪŋks] N esfinge *f*

spice [spaɪs] N especiaria ■ VT condimentar

spick-and-span [spɪk-] ADJ tudo arrumado

spicy ['spaɪsɪ] ADJ condimentado; (*fig*) picante

spider ['spaɪdə^r] N aranha; **~'s web** teia de aranha

spiel [spiːl] N lengalenga

spike [spaɪk] N (*point*) ponta, espigão *m*; (*Bot*) espiga; **spikes** NPL (*Sport*) ferrões *mpl*; **spike heel** (*US*) N salto alto e fino

spiky ['spaɪkɪ] ADJ espinhoso

spill [spɪl] (*pt, pp* **spilled**) VT entornar, derramar; (*blood*) derramar ■ VI derramar-se; **to ~ the beans** (*inf*) dar com a língua nos dentes

▶ **spill out** VI (*come out*) sair; (*fall out*) cair

▶ **spill over** VI transbordar

spin [spɪn] (*pt, pp* **spun**) N (*revolution of wheel*) volta, rotação f; (Aviat) parafuso; (trip in car) volta or passeio de carro; (ball): **to put ~ on** fazer rolar ■ VT (wool etc) fiar, tecer; (wheel) girar; (clothes) torcer ■ VI girar, rodar; (make thread) tecer; **the car spun out of control** o carro se desgovernou

▶ **spin out** VT prolongar; (money) fazer render

spinach ['spɪnɪtʃ] N espinafre m

spinal ['spaɪnl] ADJ espinhal; **spinal column** N coluna vertebral; **spinal cord** N espinha dorsal

spindly ['spɪndlɪ] ADJ longo e espigado

spin-dry VT torcer (na máquina)

spin-dryer (Brit) N secadora

spine [spaɪn] N espinha dorsal; (thorn) espinho

spine-chilling [-'tʃɪlɪŋ] ADJ arrepiante

spineless ['spaɪnlɪs] ADJ (fig) fraco, covarde

spinner ['spɪnər] N (of thread) fiandeiro(-a)

spinning ['spɪnɪŋ] N fiação f; **spinning top** N pião m; **spinning wheel** N roca de fiar

spin-off N subproduto

spinster ['spɪnstər] N solteira; (pej) solteirona

spiral ['spaɪərl] N espiral f ■ ADJ em espiral, helicoidal ■ VI (prices) disparar; **the inflationary ~** a espiral inflacionária; **spiral staircase** N escada em caracol

spire ['spaɪər] N flecha, agulha

spirit ['spɪrɪt] N espírito; (soul) alma; (ghost) fantasma m; (humour) humor m; (courage) coragem f, ânimo; (frame of mind) estado de espírito; (sense) sentido; **spirits** NPL (drink) álcool m; **in good ~s** alegre, de bom humor; **Holy S~** Espírito Santo; **community/public ~** espírito comunitário/público; **spirit duplicator** N duplicador m a álcool

spirited ['spɪrɪtɪd] ADJ animado, espirituoso

spirit level N nível m de bolha

spiritual ['spɪrɪtjuəl] ADJ espiritual ■ N (also: **Negro spiritual**) canto religioso dos negros

spiritualism ['spɪrɪtjuəlɪzəm] N espiritualismo

spit [spɪt] (pt, pp **spat**) N (for roasting) espeto; (Geog) restinga; (spittle) cuspe m, cusparada; (saliva) saliva ■ VI cuspir; (sound) escarrar; (rain) chuviscar

spite [spaɪt] N rancor m, ressentimento ■ VT contrariar; **in ~ of** apesar de, a despeito de

spiteful ['spaɪtful] ADJ maldoso, malévolo

spitting ['spɪtɪŋ] N: **"~ prohibited"** "proibido cuspir" ■ ADJ: **to be the ~ image of sb** ser a imagem escarrada de alguém

spittle ['spɪtl] N cuspe m

spiv [spɪv] (Brit: inf) N negocista m

splash [splæʃ] N (sound) borrifo, respingo; (of colour) mancha ■ VT: **to ~ (with)** salpicar (de) ■ VI (also: **splash about**) borrifar, respingar ■ EXCL pluft

splashdown ['splæʃdaun] N amerissagem f

spleen [spli:n] N (Anat) baço

splendid ['splɛndɪd] ADJ esplêndido; (impressive) impressionante

splendour ['splɛndər] (US **splendor**) N esplendor m; (of achievement) pompa, glória; **splendours** NPL (features) esplendores mpl

splice [splaɪs] VT juntar

splint [splɪnt] N tala

splinter ['splɪntər] N (of wood, glass) lasca; (in finger) farpa ■ VI lascar-se, estilhaçar-se, despedaçar-se; **splinter group** N grupo dissidente

split [splɪt] (pt, pp **split**) N fenda, brecha; (fig: division) rompimento; (: difference) diferença; (Pol) divisão f ■ VT partir, fender; (party, work) dividir; (profits) repartir ■ VI (divide) dividir-se, repartir-se; **the splits** NPL (Gymnastics): **to do the ~s** abrir or fazer espaguete; **to ~ sth down the middle** partir algo ao meio; (fig) dividir algo (pela metade)

▶ **split up** VI (couple) separar-se, acabar; (meeting) terminar

split-level ADJ em vários níveis

split peas NPL ervilhas secas fpl

split personality N dupla personalidade f

split second N fração f de segundo

splitting ['splɪtɪŋ] ADJ (headache) lancinante

splutter ['splʌtər] VI crepitar; (person) balbuciar, gaguejar

spoil [spɔɪl] (pt, pp **spoiled**) VT (damage) danificar; (mar) estragar, arruinar; (child) mimar; (ballot paper) violar ■ VI: **to be ~ing for a fight** estar querendo comprar uma briga

spoils [spɔɪlz] NPL desojo, saque m

spoilsport ['spɔɪlspɔːt] (pej) N desmancha-prazeres m/f inv

spoilt [spɔɪlt] PT, PP of **spoil** ■ ADJ (child) mimado; (ballot paper) violado

spoke [spəuk] PT of **speak** ■ N (of wheel) raio

spoken ['spəukn] PP of **speak**

spokesman ['spəuksmən] (irreg) N porta-voz m

spokeswoman ['spəukswumən] (irreg) N porta-voz f

sponge [spʌndʒ] N esponja; (cake) pão-de-ló m ■ VT lavar com esponja ■ VI: **to ~ on sb** viver às custas de alguém; **sponge bag** (Brit) N bolsa de toalete; **sponge cake** N pão-de-ló m

sponger ['spʌndʒər] (pej) N parasito(-a)

spongy ['spʌndʒɪ] ADJ esponjoso

sponsor ['sponsər] N patrocinador(a) m/f; (for membership) padrinho/madrinha; (Comm) fiador(a) m/f, financiador(a) m/f; (bill in parliament etc) responsável m/f ■ VT patrocinar; apadrinhar; fiar; (applicant, proposal) apoiar, defender; **I ~ed him at 3p a mile** eu o patrocinei à razão de 3p por milha

sponsorship ['sponsəʃɪp] N patrocínio

spontaneity [spontə'neɪtɪ] N espontaneidade f

spontaneous [spon'teɪnɪəs] ADJ espontâneo

spooky ['spu:kɪ] (inf) ADJ arrepiante

spool [spu:l] N carretel m; (of film) rolo; (for tape) bobina; (of sewing machine) bobina, novelo

spoon [spu:n] N colher f

spoon-feed ['spu:nfi:d] (irreg) VT dar de comer com colher; (fig) dar tudo mastigado a

spoonful ['spu:nful] N colherada

sporadic [spə'rædɪk] ADJ esporádico

sport [spɔːt] N esporte m (BR), desporto (PT);

(*person*) bom perdedor/boa perdedora *m/f* ■ VT
(*wear*) exibir; **indoor/outdoor ~s** esportes de
salão/ao ar livre; **to say sth in ~** dizer algo de
brincadeira

sporting ['spɔːtɪŋ] ADJ esportivo (BR),
desportivo (PT); (*generous*) nobre; **to give sb a ~
chance** dar uma grande chance a alguém

sport jacket (*US*) N = **sports jacket**

sports car N carro esporte (BR), carro de sport
(PT)

sports ground N campo de esportes (BR) *or* de
desportos (PT)

sports jacket (*Brit*) N casaco esportivo (BR) *or*
desportivo (PT)

sportsman ['spɔːtsmən] (*irreg*) N esportista *m*
(BR), desportista *m* (PT)

sportsmanship ['spɔːtsmənʃɪp] N espírito
esportivo (BR) *or* desportivo (PT)

sportsmen ['spɔːtsmɛn] NPL *of* **sportsman**

sports page N página de esportes

sportswear ['spɔːtswɛəʳ] N roupa esportiva (BR)
or desportiva (PT) *or* esporte

sportswoman ['spɔːtswumən] (*irreg*) N
esportista (BR), desportista (PT)

sporty ['spɔːtɪ] ADJ esportivo (BR), desportivo
(PT)

spot [spɔt] N (*mark*) marca; (*place*) lugar *m*, local
m; (*dot: on pattern*) mancha, ponto; (*on skin*)
espinha; (*Radio, TV*) hora; (*small amount*): **a ~ of**
um pouquinho de ■ VT (*notice*) notar; **on the ~**
(*at once*) na hora; (*there*) ali mesmo; (*in difficulty*)
em apuros; **spot check** N fiscalização *f* de
surpresa

spotless ['spɔtlɪs] ADJ sem mancha, imaculado

spotlight ['spɔtlaɪt] N holofote *m*, refletor *m*

spot-on (*Brit: inf*) ADJ acertado em cheio

spot price N preço à vista

spotted ['spɔtɪd] ADJ (*pattern*) com bolinhas

spotty ['spɔtɪ] ADJ (*face*) cheio de espinhas

spouse [spauz] N cônjuge *m/f*

spout [spaut] N (*of jug*) bico; (*of pipe*) cano ■ VI
jorrar

sprain [spreɪn] N distensão *f*, torcedura ■ VT:
to ~ one's ankle/wrist torcer o tornozelo/a
pulseira

sprang [spræŋ] PT *of* **spring**

sprawl [sprɔːl] VI esparramar-se ■ N: **urban
~** crescimento urbano; **to send sb ~ing** jogar
alguém no chão

spray [spreɪ] N borrifo; (*container*) spray *m*,
atomizador *m*; (*garden spray*) vaporizador *m*; (*of
paint*) pistola borrifadora; (*of flowers*) ramalhete
m ■ VT pulverizar; (*crops*) borrifar, regar ■ CPD
(*deodorant etc*) em spray

spread [sprɛd] N (*pt, pp* **spread**) N extensão *f*;
(*distribution*) expansão *f*, difusão *f*; (*Press, Typ: two
pages*) chapada; (*Culin*) pasta; (*inf: food*) banquete
m ■ VT espalhar; (*butter*) untar, passar;
(*wings, sails*) abrir, desdobrar; (*workload, wealth*)
distribuir; (*scatter*) disseminar; (*payments*)
espaçar ■ VI (*news, stain*) espalhar-se; (*disease*)
alastrar-se

▶ **spread out** VI dispersar-se

spread-eagled [-'iːgld] ADJ: **to be** *or* **lie ~** estar
estirado

spreadsheet ['sprɛdʃiːt] N (*Comput*) planilha

spree [spriː] N: **to go on a ~** cair na farra

sprig [sprɪg] N raminho

sprightly ['spraɪtlɪ] ADJ ativo, ágil

spring [sprɪŋ] (*pt* **sprang**, *pp* **sprung**) N (*leap*)
salto, pulo; (*coiled metal*) mola; (*bounciness*)
elasticidade *f*; (*season*) primavera; (*of water*)
fonte *f* ■ VI pular, saltar ■ VT: **to ~ a leak** (*pipe
etc*) furar; **he sprang the news on me** ele me
pegou de surpresa com a notícia; **in ~**, **in the
~** na primavera; **to ~ from** provir de; **to ~ into
action** partir para ação; **to walk with a ~ in
one's step** andar espevitado

▶ **spring up** VI aparecer de repente

springboard ['sprɪŋbɔːd] N trampolim *m*

spring-cleaning N limpeza total, faxina (geral)

spring onion (*Brit*) N cebolinha

springtime ['sprɪŋtaɪm] N primavera

springy ['sprɪŋɪ] ADJ elástico, flexível

sprinkle ['sprɪŋkl] VT (*liquid*) salpicar; (*salt, sugar*)
borrifar; **to ~ water on**, **~ with water** salpicar
de água; **~d with** (*fig*) salpicado *or* polvilhado de

sprinkler ['sprɪŋkləʳ] N (*for lawn etc*) regador *m*;
(*to put out fire*) sprinkler *m*

sprinkling ['sprɪŋklɪŋ] N (*of water*) borrifo; (*of
salt*) pitada; (*of sugar*) bocado

sprint [sprɪnt] N corrida de pequena distância
■ VI correr a toda velocidade

sprinter ['sprɪntəʳ] N corredor(a) *m/f*

sprite [spraɪt] N duende *m*, elfo

sprocket ['sprɔkɪt] N (*on printer etc*) dente *m* (de
roda)

sprout [spraut] VI brotar, germinar

sprouts [sprauts] NPL (*also*: **Brussels sprouts**)
couves-de-Bruxelas *fpl*

spruce [spruːs] N INV (*Bot*) abeto ■ ADJ
arrumado, limpo, elegante

▶ **spruce up** VT arrumar; **to ~ o.s. up** arrumar-
se

sprung [sprʌŋ] PP *of* **spring**

spry [spraɪ] ADJ ativo, ágil

SPUC N ABBR = **Society for the Protection of
Unborn Children**

spud [spʌd] (*inf*) N batata

spun [spʌn] PT, PP *of* **spin**

spur [spəːʳ] N espora; (*fig*) estímulo ■ VT (*also*:
spur on) incitar, estimular; **on the ~ of the
moment** de improviso, de repente

spurious ['spjuərɪəs] ADJ espúrio, falso

spurn [spəːn] VT desdenhar, desprezar

spurt [spəːt] N (*of energy*) acesso; (*of blood etc*) jorro
■ VI jorrar; **to put in** *or* **on a ~** (*runner*) dar uma
arrancada; (*fig: in work etc*) dar uma virada

sputter ['spʌtəʳ] VI crepitar; (*person*) balbuciar,
gaguejar

spy [spaɪ] N espião/espiã *m/f* ■ VI: **to ~ on** espiar,
espionar ■ VT (*see*) enxergar, avistar ■ CPD
(*film, story*) de espionagem

spying ['spaɪɪŋ] N espionagem *f*

Sq. ABBR (in address) = **square**

sq. ABBR (Math etc) = **square**

squabble ['skwɔbl] N briga, bate-boca m ■ vi brigar, discutir

squad [skwɔd] N (Mil, Police) pelotão m, esquadra; (Football) seleção f; **flying ~** (Police) polícia de prontidão; **squad car** (Brit) N (Police) radiopatrulha

squadron ['skwɔdrən] N (Mil) esquadrão m; (Aviat) esquadrilha; (Naut) esquadra

squalid ['skwɔlɪd] ADJ (conditions) esquálido; (story etc) sórdido

squall [skwɔ:l] N (storm) tempestade f; (wind) pé m (de vento), rajada

squalor ['skwɔlər] N sordidez f

squander ['skwɔndər] vt (money) esbanjar, dissipar; (chances) desperdiçar

square [skweər] N quadrado; (in town) praça; (Math: instrument) esquadro; (inf: person) quadrado(-a), careta m/f ■ ADJ quadrado; (inf: ideas, tastes) careta, antiquado ■ vt (arrange) ajustar, acertar; (Math) elevar ao quadrado; (reconcile) conciliar ■ vi (agree) ajustar-se; **all ~** igual, quite; **a ~ meal** uma refeição substancial; **2 metres ~** um quadrado de dois metros de lado; **2 ~ metres** 2 metros quadrados; **we're back to ~ one** voltamos à estaca zero
▸ **square up** (Brit) vi (settle) ajustar; **to ~ up with sb** acertar as contas com alguém

square bracket N (Typ) colchete m

squarely ['skweəlɪ] ADV em forma quadrada; (directly) diretamente; (fully) em cheio

square root N raiz f quadrada

squash [skwɔʃ] N (Brit: drink): **lemon/orange ~** limonada/laranjada concentrada; (Sport) squash m; (US: vegetable) abóbora ■ vt esmagar; **to ~ together** apinhar

squat [skwɔt] ADJ atarracado ■ vi (also: squat down) agachar-se, acocorar-se; (on property) ocupar ilegalmente

squatter ['skwɔtər] N posseiro(-a)

squawk [skwɔːk] vi grasnar

squeak [skwiːk] vi grunhir, chiar; (door) ranger; (mouse) guinchar ■ N grunhido, chiado; rangido; guincho

squeal [skwiːl] vi guinchar, gritar agudamente; (inf: inform) delatar

squeamish ['skwiːmɪʃ] ADJ melindroso, delicado

squeeze [skwiːz] N (gen, of hand) aperto; (in bus etc) apinhamento; (Econ) arrocho ■ vt comprimir, socar; (hand, arm) apertar ■ vi: **to ~ past/under sth** espremer-se para passar algo/ para passar por baixo de algo; **a ~ of lemon** umas gotas de limão
▸ **squeeze out** vt espremer; (fig) extorquir

squelch [skweltʃ] vi fazer ruído de passos na lama

squib [skwɪb] N busca-pé m

squid [skwɪd] (pl squid) N lula

squiggle ['skwɪgl] N garatuja

squint [skwɪnt] vi olhar or ser vesgo ■ N (Med) estrabismo; **to ~ at sth** olhar algo de soslaio or de esguelha

squire ['skwaɪər] (Brit) N proprietário rural

squirm [skwəːm] vi retorcer-se

squirrel ['skwɪrəl] N esquilo

squirt [skwəːt] vi, vt jorrar, esguichar

Sr ABBR = **senior**; (Rel) = **sister**

SRC (Brit) N ABBR = **Students' Representative Council**

Sri Lanka [srɪ'læŋkə] N Sri Lanka m

SRN (Brit) N ABBR = **State Registered Nurse**

SRO (US) ABBR = **standing room only**

SS ABBR = **steamship**

SSA (US) ABBR = **Social Security Administration**

SST (US) ABBR = **supersonic transport**

ST (US) ABBR = **Standard Time**

St ABBR (= saint) S.; = **street**

stab [stæb] N (with knife etc) punhalada; (of pain) pontada; (inf: try): **to have a ~ at (doing) sth** tentar (fazer) algo ■ vt apunhalar; **to ~ sb to death** matar alguém a facadas, esfaquear alguém

stabbing ['stæbɪŋ] N: **there's been a ~** houve um esfaqueamento ■ ADJ (pain) cortante

stability [stə'bɪlɪtɪ] N estabilidade f

stabilization [steɪbəlaɪ'zeɪʃən] N estabilização f

stabilize ['steɪbəlaɪz] vt estabilizar ■ vi estabilizar-se

stabilizer ['steɪbəlaɪzər] N estabilizador m

stable ['steɪbl] ADJ estável ■ N estábulo, cavalariça; **riding ~s** clube m de equitação

staccato [stə'kɑːtəu] ADV destacado, staccato ■ ADJ (Mus) destacado, staccato; (noise) interrupto; (voice) quebrado

stack [stæk] N montão m, pilha ■ vt amontoar, empilhar; **there's ~s of time** (Brit: inf) tem tempo de sobra

stadium ['steɪdɪəm] (pl stadiums) N estádio

staff [stɑːf] N (work force) pessoal m, quadro; (Brit: Sch: also: teaching staff) corpo docente; (stick) cajado, bastão m ■ vt prover de pessoal; **the office is ~ed by women** o escritório está composto de mulheres

staffroom ['stɑːfruːm] N sala dos professores

Staffs (Brit) ABBR = **Staffordshire**

stag [stæg] N veado, cervo

stage [steɪdʒ] N (in theatre) palco, cena; (point) etapa, fase f; (platform) plataforma, estrado; (profession): **the ~** o palco, o teatro ■ vt (play) pôr em cena, representar; (demonstration) montar, organizar; (fig: perform: recovery etc) realizar; **in ~s** por etapas; **to go through a difficult ~** passar por uma fase difícil; **in the early/final ~s** na fase inicial/final

stagecoach ['steɪdʒkəutʃ] N diligência

stage door N entrada dos artistas

stage fright N medo da platéia

stagehand ['steɪdʒhænd] N ajudante m/f de teatro

stage-manage vt (fig) orquestrar

stage manager N diretor(a) m/f de cena

stagger ['stægər] vi cambalear ■ vt (amaze)

surpreender, chocar; (*hours, holidays*) escalonar

staggering ['stægərɪŋ] ADJ (*amazing*) surpreendente, chocante

stagnant ['stægnənt] ADJ estagnado

stagnate [stæg'neɪt] VI estagnar

stagnation [stæg'neɪʃən] N estagnação *f*

stag party N despedida de solteiro

staid [steɪd] ADJ sério, sóbrio

stain [steɪn] N mancha; (*colouring*) tinta, tintura ▪ VT manchar; (*wood*) tingir

stained glass window [steɪnd-] N janela com vitral

stainless ['steɪnlɪs] ADJ (*steel*) inoxidável

stain remover N tira-manchas *m*

stair [stɛəʳ] N (*step*) degrau *m*; **stairs** NPL (*flight of steps*) escada

staircase ['stɛəkeɪs] N escadaria, escada

stairway ['stɛəweɪ] N = **staircase**

stairwell ['stɛəwɛl] N caixa de escada

stake [steɪk] N estaca, poste *m*; (*Comm: interest*) interesse *m*, participação *f*; (*Betting: gen pl*) aposta ▪ VT apostar; (*claim*) reivindicar; **to be at ~** estar em jogo; **to have a ~ in sth** ter interesse em algo; **to ~ a claim to sth** reivindicar algo

stalactite ['stæləktaɪt] N estalactite *f*

stalagmite ['stæləgmaɪt] N estalagmite *f*

stale [steɪl] ADJ (*bread*) dormido; (*food*) estragado; (*air*) viciado; (*smell*) mofado; (*beer*) velho

stalemate ['steɪlmeɪt] N empate *m*; (*fig*) impasse *m*, beco sem saída

stalk [stɔːk] N talo, haste *f* ▪ VT caçar de tocaia; **to ~ in/out** entrar/sair silenciosamente; **to ~ off** andar com arrogância

stall [stɔːl] N (*Brit: in market*) barraca; (*in stable*) baia ▪ VT (*Aut*) fazer morrer; (*fig: delay*) impedir, atrasar ▪ VI morrer; esquivar-se, ganhar tempo; **stalls** NPL (*Brit: in cinema, theatre*) platéia; **a newspaper/flower ~** uma banca de jornais/uma barraca de flores

stallholder ['stɔːlhəʊldəʳ] N feirante *m/f*

stallion ['stælɪən] N garanhão *m*

stalwart ['stɔːlwət] ADJ (*in build*) robusto; (*in spirit*) leal ▪ N partidário leal

stamen ['steɪmən] N estame *m*

stamina ['stæmɪnə] N resistência

stammer ['stæməʳ] N gagueira ▪ VI gaguejar, balbuciar

stamp [stæmp] N selo; (*rubber stamp*) carimbo, timbre *m*; (*mark, also fig*) marca, impressão *f* ▪ VI (*also:* **stamp one's foot**) bater com o pé ▪ VT (*letter*) selar; (*mark*) marcar; (*with rubber stamp*) carimbar; **~ed addressed envelope** envelope *m* selado e sobrescritado

▸ **stamp out** VT (*fire*) apagar com os pés; (*crime*) eliminar; (*opposition*) esmagar

stamp: stamp album N álbum *m* de selos; **stamp collecting** [-kə'lɛktɪŋ] N filatelia; **stamp duty** (*Brit*) N imposto de selo

stampede [stæm'piːd] N debandada, estouro (da boiada)

stamp machine N máquina de selos

stance [stæns] N postura, posição *f*

stand [stænd] (*pt, pp* **stood**) N (*position*) posição *f*, postura; (*for taxis*) ponto; (*also:* **hall stand**) pedestal *m*; (*also:* **music stand**) estante *f*; (*Sport*) tribuna, palanque *m*; (*stall*) barraca; (*also:* **news stand**) banca de jornais ▪ VI (*be*) estar, encontrar-se; (*be on foot*) estar em pé; (*rise*) levantar-se; (*remain: decision, offer*) estar de pé; (*in election*) candidatar-se ▪ VT (*place*) pôr, colocar; (*tolerate, withstand*) agüentar, suportar; (*cost*) pagar; **to make a ~** resistir; (*fig*) ater-se a um princípio; **to take a ~ on an issue** tomar posição definida sobre um assunto; **to ~ for parliament** (*Brit*) apresentar-se como candidato ao parlamento; **to ~ guard** *or* **watch** (*Mil*) montar guarda; **it ~s to reason** é lógico; **as things ~** como as coisas estão; **to ~ sb a drink/meal** pagar uma bebida/refeição para alguém; **I can't ~ him** não o agüento; **to ~ still** ficar parado

▸ **stand aside** VI pôr-se de lado

▸ **stand by** VI (*be ready*) estar a postos ▪ VT FUS (*opinion*) aferrar-se a; (*person*) ficar ao lado de

▸ **stand down** VI (*withdraw*) retirar-se; (*Mil*) deixar o serviço

▸ **stand for** VT FUS (*defend*) apoiar; (*signify*) significar; (*represent*) representar; (*tolerate*) tolerar, permitir

▸ **stand in for** VT FUS substituir

▸ **stand out** VI (*be prominent*) destacar-se

▸ **stand up** VI (*rise*) levantar-se

▸ **stand up for** VT FUS defender

▸ **stand up to** VT FUS enfrentar

stand-alone ADJ (*Comput*) autônomo, stand-alone

standard ['stændəd] N padrão *m*, critério; (*flag*) estandarte *m*; (*level*) nível *m* ▪ ADJ (*size etc*) padronizado, regular, normal; **standards** NPL (*morals*) valores *mpl* morais; **to be** *or* **come up to ~** alcançar os padrões exigidos; **to apply a double ~** ter dois pesos e duas medidas; **the gold ~** (*Comm*) o padrão ouro

standardization [stændədaɪ'zeɪʃən] N padronização *f*

standardize ['stændədaɪz] VT padronizar

standard lamp (*Brit*) N abajur *m* de pé

standard of living N padrão de vida

standard time N hora legal *or* oficial

stand-by ADJ de reserva ▪ N: **to be on ~** estar de sobreaviso *or* de prontidão; **stand-by ticket** N bilhete *m* de stand-by

stand-in N suplente *m/f*; (*Cinema*) dublê *m/f*

standing ['stændɪŋ] ADJ (*upright*) ereto vertical; (*on foot*) em pé; (*permanent*) permanente ▪ N posição *f*, reputação *f*; **of 6 months' ~** de 6 meses de duração; **of many years' ~** de muitos anos; **he was given a ~ ovation** ele foi ovacionado; **a man of some ~** um homem de posição; **standing joke** N piada conhecida; **standing order** N (*at bank*) instrução *f* permanente; **standing orders** NPL (*Mil*) regulamento geral; **standing room** N lugar *m* em pé

stand-offish [-'ɔfɪʃ] ADJ incomunicativo, reservado

standpat ['stændpæt] (US) ADJ inflexível, conservador(a)

standpipe ['stændpaɪp] N tubo de subida

standpoint ['stændpɔɪnt] N ponto de vista

standstill ['stændstɪl] N: **at a ~** paralisado, parado; **to come to a ~** (car) parar; (factory, traffic) ficar paralisado

stank [stæŋk] PT of **stink**

stanza ['stænzə] N estância, estrofe f

staple ['steɪpl] N (for papers) grampo; (chief product) produto básico ■ ADJ (food etc) básico ■ VT grampear

stapler ['steɪplə^r] N grampeador m

star [stɑː^r] N estrela; (celebrity) astro/estrela ■ VI: **to ~ in** ser a estrela em, estrelar ■ VT (Cinema) ser estrelado por; **the stars** NPL (horoscope) o horóscopo; **4-~ hotel** hotel 4 estrelas; **2-~ petrol** gasolina simples (BR) or normal (PT); **4-~ petrol** (Brit) gasolina azul (BR) or súper (PT); **star attraction** n atração f principal

starboard ['stɑːbəd] N estibordo; **to ~ a** estibordo

starch [stɑːtʃ] N (in food) amido, fécula; (for clothes) goma

starched ['stɑːtʃt] ADJ (collar) engomado

starchy ['stɑːtʃɪ] ADJ amiláceo

stardom ['stɑːdəm] N estrelato

stare [stɛə^r] N olhar m fixo ■ VI: **to ~ at** olhar fixamente, fitar

starfish ['stɑːfɪʃ] N INV estrela-do-mar f

stark [stɑːk] ADJ (bleak) severo, áspero; (colour) sóbrio; (reality, truth, simplicity) cru; (contrast) gritante ■ ADV: **~ naked** completamente nu, em pêlo

starlet ['stɑːlɪt] N (Cinema) vedete f

starlight ['stɑːlaɪt] N: **by ~** à luz das estrelas

starling ['stɑːlɪŋ] N estorninho

starlit ['stɑːlɪt] ADJ iluminado pelas estrelas

starry ['stɑːrɪ] ADJ estrelado

starry-eyed [-'aɪd] ADJ (innocent) deslumbrado

star-studded [-'stʌdɪd] ADJ: **a ~ cast** um elenco cheio de estrelas

start [stɑːt] N (beginning) princípio, começo; (departure) partida; (sudden movement) sobressalto, susto; (advantage) vantagem f ■ VT começar, iniciar; (cause) causar; (found) fundar; (engine) ligar; (fire) provocar ■ VI começar, iniciar; (with fright) sobressaltar-se, assustar-se; (train etc) sair; **to ~ doing** or **to do sth** começar a fazer algo; **at the ~** no início; **for a ~** para início de conversa; **to make an early ~** sair or começar cedo; **to ~ (off) with ...** (firstly) para começar ...; (at the beginning) no início ...; **to give sb a ~** dar um susto em alguém

▶ **start off** VI começar, principiar; (leave) sair, pôr-se a caminho

▶ **start over** (US) VI começar de novo

▶ **start up** VI começar; (car) pegar, pôr-se em marcha ■ VT começar; (car) ligar

starter ['stɑːtə^r] N (Aut) arranque m; (Sport: official) juiz/juíza m/f da partida; (: runner) corredor(a) m/f; (Brit: Culin) entrada

starting handle ['stɑːtɪŋ-] (Brit) N manivela de arranque

starting point ['stɑːtɪŋ-] N ponto de partida

starting price ['stɑːtɪŋ-] N preço inicial

startle ['stɑːtl] VT assustar, aterrar

startling ['stɑːtlɪŋ] ADJ surpreendente

star turn (Brit) N rei m /rainha f do show

starvation [stɑːˈveɪʃən] N fome f; (Med) inanição f

starve ['stɑːv] VI passar fome; (to death) morrer de fome ■ VT fazer passar fome; (fig): **to ~ (of)** privar (de); **I'm starving** estou morrendo de fome

starving ['stɑːvɪŋ] ADJ faminto, esfomeado

state [steɪt] N estado; (pomp): **in ~** com grande pompa ■ VT (say, declare) afirmar, declarar; (a case) expor, apresentar; **the States** NPL (Geo) os Estados Unidos; **to be in a ~** estar agitado; **~ of emergency** estado de emergência; **~ of mind** estado de espírito; **the ~ of the art** a última palavra; **to lie in ~** estar exposto em câmara ardente

State Department (US) N Departamento de Estado, = Ministério das Relações Exteriores

state education (Brit) N educação f pública

stateless ['steɪtlɪs] ADJ desnacionalizado

stately ['steɪtlɪ] ADJ majestoso, imponente

statement ['steɪtmənt] N declaração f; (Law) depoimento; (Econ) balanço; **official ~** comunicado oficial; **~ of account** extrato de conta, extrato bancário

state-owned [-əund] ADJ estatal

state secret N segredo de estado

statesman ['steɪtsmən] (irreg) N estadista m

statesmanship ['steɪtsmənʃɪp] N arte f de governar

statesmen ['steɪtsmɛn] NPL of **statesman**

static ['stætɪk] N (Radio, TV) interferência ■ ADJ estático; **static electricity** N (eletricidade f) estática

station ['steɪʃən] N estação f; (place) posto, lugar m; (Police) delegacia; (Radio) emissora; (rank) posição f social ■ VT colocar; **to be ~ed in** (Mil) estar estacionado em

stationary ['steɪʃnərɪ] ADJ estacionário

stationer ['steɪʃənə^r] N dono de papelaria

stationer's (shop) N papelaria

stationery ['steɪʃnərɪ] N artigos mpl de papelaria; (writing paper) papel m de carta

station master N (Rail) chefe m da estação

station wagon (US) N perua (BR), canadiana (PT)

statistic [stəˈtɪstɪk] N estatística

statistical [stəˈtɪstɪkl] ADJ estatístico

statistics [stəˈtɪstɪks] N (science) estatística

statue ['stætjuː] N estátua

statuesque [stætjuˈɛsk] ADJ escultural

statuette [stætjuˈɛt] N estatueta

stature ['stætʃə^r] N estatura, altura; (fig)

estatura, envergadura

status ['steɪtəs] N posição f; (official classification) categoria; (importance) status m; (Admin: also: **marital status**) estado civil; **status quo** [-kwəu] N: **the status quo** o status quo; **status symbol** N símbolo de prestígio

statute ['stætjuːt] N estatuto, lei f; **statutes** NPL (of club etc) estatuto; **statute book** N ≈ Código

statutory ['stætjutərɪ] ADJ (according to statutes) estatutário; (holiday etc) regulamentar

staunch [stɔːntʃ] ADJ fiel ■ VT estancar

stave [steɪv] N (Mus) pauta
  ▶ **stave off** VT (attack) repelir; (threat) evitar, protelar

stay [steɪ] N (period of time) estadia, estada; (Law): **~ of execution** adiamento de execução ■ VI (remain) ficar; (as guest) hospedar-se; (spend some time) demorar-se; **to ~ put** não se mexer; **to ~ the night** pernoitar
  ▶ **stay behind** VI ficar atrás
  ▶ **stay in** VI (at home) ficar em casa
  ▶ **stay on** VI ficar
  ▶ **stay out** VI (of house) ficar fora de casa; (strikers) continuar em greve
  ▶ **stay up** VI (at night) velar, ficar acordado

staying power ['steɪɪŋ-] N resistência, raça

STD N ABBR (Brit: = subscriber trunk dialling) DDD f; (: = sexually transmitted disease) DST f

stead [stɛd] N: **in sb's ~** em lugar de alguém; **to stand sb in good ~** prestar bons serviços a alguém

steadfast ['stɛdfɑːst] ADJ firme, estável, resoluto

steadily ['stɛdɪlɪ] ADV (firmly) firmemente; (unceasingly) sem parar, constantemente; (walk) regularmente; (drive) a uma velocidade constante

steady ['stɛdɪ] ADJ (job, boyfriend) constante; (speed) fixo; (unswerving) firme; (regular) regular; (person, character) sensato, equilibrado; (diligent) diligente; (calm) calmo, sereno ■ VT (hold) manter firme; (stabilize) estabilizar; (nerves) acalmar; **to ~ o.s. on** or **against sth** firmar-se em algo

steak [steɪk] N filé m; (beef) bife m

steakhouse ['steɪkhaus] N ≈ churrascaria

steal [stiːl] (pt **stole**, pp **stolen**) VT roubar ■ VI (move secretly) mover-se furtivamente
  ▶ **steal away** VI sair às escondidas
  ▶ **steal off** VI = **steal away**

stealth [stɛlθ] N: **by ~** furtivamente, às escondidas

stealthy ['stɛlθɪ] ADJ furtivo

steam [stiːm] N vapor m ■ VT (Culin) cozinhar no vapor ■ VI fumegar; (ship): **to ~ along** avançar or mover-se (a vapor); **under one's own ~** (fig) por esforço próprio; **to run out of ~** (fig: person) perder o pique; **to let off ~** (fig: inf) desabafar
  ▶ **steam up** VI (window) embaçar; **to get ~ed up about sth** irritar-se com algo

steam engine N máquina a vapor

steamer ['stiːmə'] N vapor m, navio (a vapor)

steam iron N ferro a vapor

steamroller ['stiːmrəulə'] N rolo compressor (a vapor)

steamy ['stiːmɪ] ADJ vaporoso; (room) cheio de vapor, úmido (BR), húmido (PT); (heat, atmosphere) vaporoso

steed [stiːd] N (literary) corcel m

steel [stiːl] N aço ■ ADJ de aço; **steel band** N banda de percussão do Caribe; **steel industry** N indústria siderúrgica; **steel mill** N (usina) siderúrgica

steelworks ['stiːlwəːks] N (usina) siderúrgica

steely ['stiːlɪ] ADJ (determination) inflexível; (gaze, eyes) duro, frio; **~-grey** cor de aço inv

steep [stiːp] ADJ íngreme; (increase) acentuada; (price) exorbitante ■ VT (food) colocar de molho; (cloth) ensopar, encharcar

steeple ['stiːpl] N campanário, torre f

steeplechase ['stiːpltʃeɪs] N corrida de obstáculos

steeplejack ['stiːpldʒæk] N consertador m de torres or de chaminés altas

steeply ['stiːplɪ] ADV escarpadamente, a pique

steer [stɪə'] N boi m ■ VT (person) guiar; (vehicle) dirigir ■ VI conduzir; **to ~ clear of sb/sth** (fig) evitar alguém/algo

steering ['stɪərɪŋ] N (Aut) direção f; **steering column** N (Aut) coluna da direção; **steering committee** N comitê m dirigente; **steering wheel** N volante m

stellar ['stɛlə'] ADJ estelar

stem [stɛm] N (of plant) caule m, haste f; (of glass) pé m; (of pipe) tubo ■ VT deter, reter; (blood) estancar
  ▶ **stem from** VT FUS originar-se de

stem cell N célula-tronco m

stench [stɛntʃ] (pej) N fedor m

stencil ['stɛnsl] N (pattern, design) estêncil m; (lettering) gabarito de letra ■ VT imprimir com estêncil

stenographer [stɛ'nɔgrəfə'] (US) N estenógrafo(-a)

stenography [stɛ'nɔgrəfɪ] (US) N estenografia

step [stɛp] N passo; (stair) degrau m; (action) medida, providência ■ VI: **to ~ forward** dar um passo a frente/atrás; **steps** NPL (Brit) = **stepladder**; **~ by ~** passo a passo; **to be in ~ (with)** (fig) manter a paridade (com); **to be out of ~ (with)** (fig) estar em disparidade (com); **to take ~s** tomar providências
  ▶ **step down** VI (fig) renunciar
  ▶ **step in** VI (fig) intervir
  ▶ **step off** VT FUS descer de
  ▶ **step on** VT FUS pisar
  ▶ **step over** VT FUS passar por cima de
  ▶ **step up** VT (increase) aumentar; (intensify) intensificar

stepbrother ['stɛpbrʌðə'] N meio-irmão m

stepchild ['stɛptʃaɪld] (irreg) N enteado(-a)

stepdaughter ['stɛpdɔːtə'] N enteada

stepfather ['stɛpfɑ:ðə^r] N padrasto
stepladder ['stɛplædə^r] (Brit) N escada portátil
  or de abrir
stepmother ['stɛpmʌðə^r] N madrasta
stepping stone ['stɛpɪŋ-] N pedra utilizada em
  passarelas; (fig) trampolim m
stepsister ['stɛpsɪstə^r] N meia-irmã f
stepson ['stɛpsʌn] N enteado
stereo ['stɛrɪəu] N estéreo; (record player)
  (aparelho de) som m ■ ADJ (also: **stereophonic**)
  estereofônico; **in** ~ em estéreo
stereotype ['stɪərɪətaɪp] N estereótipo ■ VT
  estereotipar
sterile ['stɛraɪl] ADJ (free from germs) esterelizado;
  (barren) estéril
sterility [stɛ'rɪlɪtɪ] N esterilidade f
sterilization [stɛrɪlaɪ'zeɪʃən] N esterilização f
sterilize ['stɛrɪlaɪz] VT esterilizar
sterling ['stə:lɪŋ] ADJ esterlino; (silver) de lei; (fig)
  genuíno, puro ■ N (currency) libra esterlina;
  one pound ~ uma libra esterlina; **sterling area**
  N zona esterlina
stern [stə:n] ADJ severo, austero ■ N (Naut)
  popa, ré f
sternum ['stə:nəm] N esterno
steroid ['stɪərɔɪd] N esteróide m
stethoscope ['stɛθəskəup] N estetoscópio
stevedore ['sti:vədɔ:^r] N estivador m
stew [stju:] N guisado, ensopado ■ VT, VI
  guisar, ensopar; (fruit) cozinhar; ~**ed tea** chá
  muito forte; ~**ed fruit** compota de frutas
steward ['stju:əd] N (Aviat) comissário de bordo;
  (also: **shop steward**) delegado(-a) sindical
stewardess ['stju:ədɪs] N aeromoça (BR),
  hospedeira de bordo (PT)
stewing steak ['stju:ɪŋ-] (US **stew meat**) N
  carne f para ensopado
St. Ex. ABBR = **stock exchange**
stg ABBR = **sterling**
stick [stɪk] (pt, pp **stuck**) N pau m; (as weapon)
  cacete m; (walking stick) bengala, cajado ■ VT
  (glue) colar; (thrust): **to ~ sth into** cravar or enfiar
  algo em; (inf: put) meter; (: tolerate) agüentar,
  suportar ■ VI (become attached) colar-se, aderir-
  se; (be unmoveable) emperrar; (in mind etc) gravar-
  se; **to get hold of the wrong end of the** ~ (Brit:
  fig) confundir-se; **to ~ to** (promise, principles)
  manter
  ▶ **stick around** (inf) VI ficar
  ▶ **stick out** VI estar saliente, projetar-se ■ VT:
  to ~ it out (inf) agüentar firme
  ▶ **stick up** VI estar saliente, projetar-se
  ▶ **stick up for** VT FUS defender
sticker ['stɪkə^r] N adesivo
sticking plaster ['stɪkɪŋ-] N esparadrapo
stickleback ['stɪklbæk] N espinhela
stickler ['stɪklə^r] N: **to be a ~ for** insistir em,
  exigir
stick-on ADJ adesivo
stick-up (inf) N assalto a mão armada
sticky ['stɪkɪ] ADJ pegajoso; (label) adesivo; (fig)
  delicado

stiff [stɪf] ADJ (strong) forte; (hard) duro; (difficult)
  difícil; (moving with difficulty: person) teso; (: door,
  zip) empenado; (formal) formal ■ ADV (bored,
  worried) extremamente; **to be** or **feel** ~ (person)
  ter dores musculares; ~ **upper lip** (Brit: fig)
  fleuma britânica
stiffen ['stɪfən] VT endurecer; (limb) entumecer
  ■ VI enrijecer-se; (grow stronger) fortalecer-se
stiff neck N torcicolo
stiffness ['stɪfnɪs] N rigidez f
stifle ['staɪfl] VT sufocar, abafar; (opposition)
  sufocar
stifling ['staɪflɪŋ] ADJ (heat) sufocante, abafado
stigma ['stɪgmə] (pl **stigmata**) N (Bot, Med, Rel)
  estigma m (pl **stigmas**) (fig) estigma m
stigmata [stɪg'mɑ:tə] NPL of **stigma**
stile [staɪl] N degraus para passar por uma cerca ou
  muro
stiletto [stɪ'lɛtəu] (Brit) N (also: **stiletto heel**)
  salto alto e fino
still [stɪl] ADJ parado; (motionless) imóvel; (calm)
  quieto; (Brit: orange drink etc) sem gás ■ ADV (up
  to this time) ainda; (even, yet) ainda; (nonetheless)
  entretanto, contudo ■ N (Cinema) still m; **to**
  stand ~ ficar parado; **keep** ~! não se mexa!; **he** ~
  hasn't arrived ele ainda não chegou
stillborn ['stɪlbɔ:n] ADJ nascido morto,
  natimorto
still life N natureza morta
stilt [stɪlt] N perna de pau; (pile) estaca,
  suporte m
stilted ['stɪltɪd] ADJ afetado
stimulant ['stɪmjulənt] N estimulante m
stimulate ['stɪmjuleɪt] VT estimular
stimulating ['stɪmjuleɪtɪŋ] ADJ estimulante
stimulation [stɪmju'leɪʃən] N estimulação f
stimuli ['stɪmjulaɪ] NPL of **stimulus**
stimulus ['stɪmjuləs] (pl **stimuli**) N estímulo,
  incentivo
sting [stɪŋ] (pt, pp **stung**) N (wound) picada; (pain)
  ardência; (of insect) ferrão m; (inf: confidence trick)
  conto-do-vigário ■ VT arguilhar ■ VI (insect,
  animal) picar; (eyes, ointment) queimar
stingy ['stɪndʒɪ] (pej) ADJ pão-duro, sovina
stink [stɪŋk] (pt **stank**, pp **stunk**) N fedor m,
  catinga ■ VI feder, cheirar mal
stinker ['stɪŋkə^r] (inf) N (problem, person) osso duro
  de roer
stinking ['stɪŋkɪŋ] ADJ fedorento, fétido; (inf: fig)
  maldito; ~ **rich** ricaço
stint [stɪnt] N tarefa, parte f ■ VI: **to ~ on** ser
  parco com; **to do one's** ~ fazer a sua parte
stipend ['staɪpɛnd] N (of vicar etc) estipêndio,
  remuneração f
stipendiary [staɪ'pɛndɪərɪ] ADJ: ~ **magistrate**
  juiz m estipendiário, juíza f estipendiário
stipulate ['stɪpjuleɪt] VT estipular
stipulation [stɪpju'leɪʃən] N estipulação f,
  cláusula
stir [stə:^r] N (fig: agitation) comoção f, rebuliço
  ■ VT (tea etc) mexer; (fig: emotions) comover ■ VI
  mover-se, remexer-se; **to give sth a** ~ mexer

algo; **to cause a ~** causar sensação or um rebuliço

▶ **stir up** VT excitar; (*trouble*) provocar

stirring ['stə:rɪŋ] ADJ comovedor(a)

stirrup ['stɪrəp] N estribo

stitch [stɪtʃ] N (*Sewing, Knitting, Med*) ponto; (*pain*) pontada ▪ VT costurar; (*Med*) dar pontos em, suturar

stoat [stəut] N arminho

stock [stɔk] N (*supply*) suprimento; (*Comm: reserves*) estoque *m*, provisão *f*; (*: selection*) sortimento; (*Agr*) gado; (*Culin*) caldo; (*lineage*) estirpe *f*, linhagem *f*; (*Finance*) valores *mpl*, títulos *mpl*; (*: shares*) ações *fpl*; (*Rail: also:* **rolling stock**) material *m* circulante ▪ ADJ (*fig: reply etc*) de sempre, costumeiro; (*: greeting*) habitual ▪ VT (*have in stock*) ter em estoque, estocar; (*sell*) vender; **well-~ed** bem sortido; **in ~** em estoque; **out of ~** esgotado; (*also:* **to take ~ of** (*fig*) fazer um balanço de; **~s and shares** valores e títulos mobiliários; **government ~** títulos do governo, fundos públicos

▶ **stock up** VI: **to ~ up (with)** abastecer-se (de)

stockade [stɔ'keɪd] N estacada

stockbroker ['stɔkbrəukə^r] N corretor(a) *m/f* de valores or da Bolsa

stock control N (*Comm*) controle *m* de estoque

stock cube (*Brit*) N (*Culin*) cubo de caldo

stock exchange N Bolsa de Valores

stockholder ['stɔkhəuldə^r] (*US*) N acionista *m/f*

Stockholm ['stɔkhəum] N Estocolmo

stocking ['stɔkɪŋ] N meia

stock-in-trade N (*tool*) instrumento de trabalho; (*fig*) arma

stockist ['stɔkɪst] (*Brit*) N estoquista *m/f*

stock market (*Brit*) N Bolsa, mercado de valores

stock phrase N frase *f* feita

stockpile ['stɔkpaɪl] N reservas *fpl*, estocagem *f* ▪ VT acumular reservas de, estocar

stockroom ['stɔkru:m] N almoxarifado

stocktaking ['stɔkteɪkɪŋ] (*Brit*) N (*Comm*) inventário

stocky ['stɔkɪ] ADJ (*strong*) robusto; (*short*) atarracado

stodgy ['stɔdʒɪ] ADJ pesado

stoic ['stəuɪk] N estóico(-a)

stoical ['stəuɪkəl] ADJ estóico

stoke [stəuk] VT atiçar, alimentar

stoker ['stəukə^r] N (*Rail, Naut etc*) foguista *m*

stole [stəul] PT of **steal** ▪ N estola

stolen ['stəuln] PP of **steal**

stolid ['stɔlɪd] ADJ fleumático

stomach ['stʌmək] N (*Anat*) estômago; (*belly*) barriga, ventre *m* ▪ VT suportar, tolerar; **stomach ache** N dor *f* de estômago; **stomach pump** N bomba gástrica; **stomach ulcer** N úlcera gástrica

stomp [stɔmp] VI: **to ~ in/out** entrar/sair como um furacão

stone [stəun] N pedra; (*pebble*) pedrinha; (*in fruit*) caroço; (*Med*) pedra, cálculo; (*Brit: weight*) = 6.348kg; 14 pounds ▪ ADJ de pedra ▪ VT apedrejar;

(*fruit*) tirar o(s) caroço(s) de; **within a ~'s throw of the station** pertinho da estação

Stone Age N: **the ~** a Idade da Pedra

stone-cold ADJ gelado

stoned [stəund] (*inf*) ADJ (*on drugs*) doidão(-dona), baratinado

stone-deaf ADJ surdo como uma porta

stonemason ['stəunmeɪsn] N pedreiro(-a)

stonework ['stəunwə:k] N cantaria

stony ['stəunɪ] ADJ pedregoso; (*fig*) glacial

stood [stud] PT, PP of **stand**

stool [stu:l] N tamborete *m*, banco

stoop [stu:p] VI (*also:* **have a stoop**) ser corcunda; (*also:* **stoop down**) debruçar-se, curvar-se; (*fig*): **to ~ to sth/doing sth** rebaixar-se para algo/fazer algo

stop [stɔp] N parada, interrupção *f*; (*for bus etc*) parada (BR), ponto (BR), paragem *f* (PT); (*also:* **full stop**) ponto ▪ VT parar, deter; (*break off*) interromper; (*pay, cheque*) sustar, suspender; (*also:* **put a stop to**) impedir ▪ VI parar, deter-se; (*watch, noise*) parar; (*end*) acabar; **to ~ doing sth** deixar de fazer algo; **to ~ sb (from) doing sth** impedir alguém de fazer algo; **~ it!** para com isso!

▶ **stop by** VI dar uma passada

▶ **stop dead** VI parar de repente

▶ **stop off** VI dar uma parada

▶ **stop up** VT (*hole*) tapar

stopcock ['stɔpkɔk] N torneira de passagem

stopgap ['stɔpgæp] N (*person*) tapa-buraco *m/f*; (*measure*) paliativo

stoplights ['stɔplaɪts] NPL (*Aut*) luzes *fpl* do freio (BR), faróis *mpl* de stop (PT)

stopover ['stɔpəuvə^r] N parada rápida; (*Aviat*) escala

stoppage ['stɔpɪdʒ] N (*strike*) greve *f*; (*temporary stop*) paralisação *f*; (*of pay*) suspensão *f*; (*blockage*) obstrução *f*

stopper ['stɔpə^r] N tampa, rolha

stop press N notícia de última hora

stopwatch ['stɔpwɔtʃ] N cronômetro

storage ['stɔ:rɪdʒ] N armazenagem *f*; **storage heater** (*Brit*) N *tipo de aquecimento que armazena calor durante a noite emitindo-o durante o dia*

store [stɔ:^r] N (*stock*) suprimento; (*depot*) armazém *m*; (*reserve*) estoque *m*; (*Brit: large shop*) loja de departamentos; (*US: shop*) loja ▪ VT armazenar; (*keep*) guardar; **stores** NPL (*provisions*) víveres *mpl*, provisões *fpl*; **who knows what is in ~ for us?** quem sabe o que nos espera?; **to set great/little ~ by sth** dar grande/pouca importância a algo

▶ **store up** VT acumular

storehouse ['stɔ:haus] N depósito, armazém *m*

storekeeper ['stɔ:ki:pə^r] (*US*) N lojista *m/f*

storeroom ['stɔ:ru:m] N depósito, almoxarifado

storey ['stɔ:rɪ] (*US* **story**) N andar *m*

stork [stɔ:k] N cegonha

storm [stɔ:m] N tempestade *f*; (*wind*) borrasca, vendaval *m*; (*fig*) tumulto ▪ VI (*fig*) enfurecer-se ▪ VT tomar de assalto, assaltar; **storm cloud** N nuvem f de tempestade; **storm door** N porta adicional

stormy ['stɔːmɪ] ADJ tempestuoso

story ['stɔːrɪ] N história, estória; (Press) matéria; (plot) enredo; (lie) mentira; (US) = **storey**

storybook ['stɔːrɪbuk] N livro de contos

storyteller ['stɔːrɪtɛləʳ] N contador(a) m/f de estórias

stout [staut] ADJ (strong) sólido, forte; (fat) gordo, corpulento; (resolute) decidido, resoluto ■ N cerveja preta

stove [stəuv] N (for cooking) fogão m; (for heating) estufa, fogareiro; **gas/electric** ~ (cooker) fogão a gás/elétrico

stow [stəu] VT guardar; (Naut) estivar

stowaway ['stəuəweɪ] N passageiro(-a) clandestino(-a)

straddle ['strædl] VT cavalgar

strafe [strɑːf] VT metralhar

straggle ['strægl] VI (houses) espalhar-se desordenadamente; (people) vagar, perambular; (lag behind) ficar para trás

straggler ['stræɡləʳ] N pessoa que fica para trás

straggling ['stræglɪŋ] ADJ (hair) rebelde, emaranhado

straggly ['stræglɪ] ADJ (hair) rebelde, emaranhado

straight [streɪt] ADJ reto; (back) esticado; (hair) liso; (honest) honesto; (frank) franco, direto; (simple) simples inv; (Theatre: part, play) sério; (inf: conventional) quadrado, careta (inf); (: heterosexual) heterossexual ■ ADV reto; (drink) puro ■ N: **the ~** (Sport) a reta; **to put** or **get sth ~** esclarecer algo; **let's get this ~** (explaining) então, vamos fazer assim; (warning) eu quero que isso fique bem claro; **10 ~ wins** 10 vitórias consecutivas; **to go ~ home** ir direto para casa; **~ away, ~ off** (at once) imediatamente; **~ off, ~ out** sem mais nem menos

straighten ['streɪtən] VT (skirt, bed) arrumar; **to ~ things out** arrumar as coisas

▸ **straighten out** VT endireitar; (fig) esclarecer

straight-faced [-feɪst] ADJ impassível ■ ADV com cara séria

straightforward [streɪt'fɔːwəd] ADJ (simple) simples inv, direto; (honest) honesto, franco

strain [streɪn] N tensão f; (Tech) esforço; (Med: back strain) distensão f; (: tension) luxação f; (breed) raça, estirpe f; (of virus) classe f ■ VT (back etc) forçar, torcer, distender; (tire) extenuar; (stretch) puxar, estirar; (Culin) coar; (filter) filtrar ■ VI esforçar-se; **strains** NPL (Mus) acordes mpl; **he's been under a lot of ~** ele tem estado sob muita tensão

strained [streɪnd] ADJ (muscle) distendido; (laugh) forçado; (relations) tenso

strainer ['streɪnəʳ] N (for tea, coffee) coador m; (sieve) peneira

strait [streɪt] N (Geo) estreito; **straits** NPL (fig): **to be in dire ~s** estar em apuros

straitjacket ['streɪtdʒækɪt] N camisa-de-força

strait-laced [-leɪst] ADJ puritano, austero

strand [strænd] N (of thread, hair) fio; (of rope) tira ■ VT (boat) encalhar

stranded ['strændɪd] ADJ desamparado; (holidaymakers) preso

strange [streɪndʒ] ADJ (not known) desconhecido; (odd) estranho, esquisito

strangely ['streɪndʒlɪ] ADV estranhamente

stranger ['streɪndʒəʳ] N desconhecido(-a); (from another area) forasteiro(-a)

strangle ['stræŋgl] VT estrangular; (fig: economy) sufocar

stranglehold ['stræŋglhəuld] N (fig) domínio total

strangulation [stræŋgjuˈleɪʃən] N estrangulação f

strap [stræp] N correia; (of slip, dress) alça ■ VT prender com correia

straphanging ['stræphæŋɪŋ] N viajar etc em pé (no metrô m)

strapless ['stræplɪs] ADJ (bra, dress) sem alças

strapping ['stræpɪŋ] ADJ corpulento, robusto, forte

Strasbourg ['stræzbɑːg] N Estrasburgo

strata ['strɑːtə] NPL of **stratum**

stratagem ['strætɪdʒəm] N estratagema m

strategic [strəˈtiːdʒɪk] ADJ estratégico

strategist ['strætɪdʒɪst] N estrategista m/f

strategy ['strætɪdʒɪ] N estratégia

stratosphere ['strætəsfɪəʳ] N estratosfera

stratum ['strɑːtəm] (pl **strata**) N camada

straw [strɔː] N palha; (drinking straw) canudo; **that's the last ~!** essa foi a última gota!

strawberry ['strɔːbərɪ] N morango; (plant) morangueiro

stray [streɪ] ADJ (animal) extraviado; (bullet) perdido; (scattered) espalhado ■ VI perder-se

streak [striːk] N listra, traço; (in hair) mecha; (fig: of madness etc) sinal m ■ VT listrar ■ VI: **to ~ past** passar como um raio; **to have ~s in one's hair** fazer mechas no cabelo; **a winning/losing ~** uma fase de sorte/azar

streaky ['striːkɪ] ADJ listrado; **streaky bacon** (Brit) N toicinho or bacon m em fatias (entremeado com gordura)

stream [striːm] N riacho, córrego; (current) fluxo, corrente f; (of people, vehicles) fluxo; (of smoke) rastro; (of questions etc) torrente f ■ VT (Sch) classificar ■ VI correr, fluir; **to ~ in/out** (people) entrar/sair em massa; **against the ~** contra a corrente; **on ~** (power plant etc) em funcionamento

streamer ['striːməʳ] N serpentina; (pennant) flâmula

stream feed N (on photocopier etc) alimentação f contínua

streamline ['striːmlaɪn] VT aerodinamizar; (fig) agilizar

streamlined ['striːmlaɪnd] ADJ aerodinâmico

street [striːt] N rua; **the back ~s** as ruelas; **to be on the ~s** (homeless) estar desabrigado; (as prostitute) fazer a vida

streetcar ['striːtkɑːʳ] (US) N bonde m (BR),

eléctrico (PT)
street lamp N poste m de iluminação
street lighting N iluminação f pública
street map N mapa m
street market N feira
street plan N mapa m
streetwise ['stri:twaɪz] (inf) ADJ malandro
strength [strɛŋθ] N força; (of girder, knot etc)
firmeza, resistência; (of chemical solution)
concentração f; (of wine) teor m alcoólico; (fig)
poder m; **on the ~ of** com base em; **at full ~**
completo; **below ~** desfalcado
strengthen ['strɛŋθən] VT fortificar; (fig)
fortalecer
strenuous ['strɛnjuəs] ADJ (tough) árduo,
estrênuo; (energetic) enérgico; (determined) tenaz
stress [strɛs] N (force, pressure) pressão f; (mental
strain) tensão f, stress m; (accent) acento;
(emphasis) ênfase f; (Tech) tensão ■ VT realçar,
dar ênfase a; (syllable) acentuar; **to lay great ~
on sth** dar muita ênfase a algo; **to be under ~**
estar com estresse
stressful ['strɛsful] ADJ (job) desgastante
stretch [strɛtʃ] N (of sand etc) trecho, extensão f;
(of time) período ■ VI espreguiçar-se; (extend): **to
~ to** or **as far as** estender-se até; (be enough: money,
food): **to ~ to** dar para ■ VT estirar, esticar; (fig:
subj: job, task) exigir o máximo de; **at a ~** sem
parar; **to ~ one's legs** esticar as pernas
▸ **stretch out** VI esticar-se ■ VT (arm etc)
esticar; (spread) estirar
stretcher ['strɛtʃəʳ] N maca, padiola
stretcher-bearer N padioleiro
stretch marks NPL estrias fpl
strewn [stru:n] ADJ: **~ with** coberto or cheio de
stricken ['strɪkən] ADJ (wounded) ferido;
(devastated) arrasado; (ill) acometido; **~ with**
tomado por
strict [strɪkt] ADJ (person) severo, rigoroso;
(meaning) exato, estrito; **in ~ confidence** muito
confidencialmente
strictly ['strɪktlɪ] ADV (severely) severamente;
(exactly) estritamente; (definitively)
rigorosamente; **~ confidential** estritamente
confidencial; **~ speaking** a rigor; **~ between
ourselves ...** cá entre nós ...
strictness ['strɪktnɪs] N rigor m, severidade f
stridden ['strɪdn] PP of **stride**
stride [straɪd] (pt **strode**, pp **stridden**) N passo
largo ■ VI andar a passos largos; **to take in
one's ~** (fig: changes etc) não se perturbar com
strident ['straɪdnt] ADJ estridente; (colour)
berrante
strife [straɪf] N conflito
strike [straɪk] (pt, pp **struck**) N greve f; (of oil etc)
descoberta; (attack) ataque m ■ VT bater em;
(fig): **the thought** or **it ~s me that ...** me ocorre
que ...; (oil etc) descobrir; (obstacle) esbarrar
em; (deal) fechar, acertar ■ VI estar em greve;
(attack: soldiers, illness) atacar; (: disaster) assolar;
(clock) bater; **on ~** em greve; **to call a ~** convocar
uma greve; **to ~ a match** acender um fósforo;

to ~ a balance (fig) encontrar um equilíbrio;
the clock struck nine o relógio bateu nove
horas
▸ **strike back** VI (Mil) contra-atacar; (fig)
revidar
▸ **strike down** VT derrubar
▸ **strike off** VT (from list) tirar, cortar; (doctor)
suspender
▸ **strike out** VT cancelar, rasurar
▸ **strike up** VT (Mus) começar a tocar;
(conversation, friendship) travar
strikebreaker ['straɪkbreɪkəʳ] N fura-greve m/f
inv
striker ['straɪkəʳ] N grevista m/f; (Sport) atacante
m/f
striking ['straɪkɪŋ] ADJ impressionante; (colour)
chamativo
string [strɪŋ] (pt, pp **strung**) N (cord) barbante m
(BR), cordel m (PT); (of beads) cordão m; (of onions)
réstia; (Mus) corda; (series) série f; (of people, cars)
fila (BR), bicha (PT); (Comput) string m ■ VT:
to ~ out esticar; **the strings** NPL (Mus) os
instrumentos de corda; **to ~ together** (words)
unir; (ideas) concatenar; **to get a job by pulling
~s** (fig) usar pistolão; **with no ~s attached** (fig)
sem condições; **string bean** N vagem f
string(ed) instrument [strɪŋ(d)-] N (Mus)
instrumento de corda
stringent ['strɪndʒənt] ADJ rigoroso
string quartet N quarteto de cordas
strip [strɪp] N tira; (of land) faixa; (of metal)
lâmina, tira; (Sport) cores fpl ■ VT despir; (fig): **to
~ sb of sth** despojar alguém de algo; (also: strip
down: machine) desmontar ■ VI despir-se; **strip
cartoon** N história em quadrinhos (BR), banda
desenhada (PT)
stripe [straɪp] N listra; (Mil) galão m
striped [straɪpt] ADJ listrado, com listras
strip light (Brit) N lâmpada fluorescente
strip lighting (Brit) N iluminação f fluorescente
stripper ['strɪpəʳ] N artista m/f de striptease
striptease ['strɪpti:z] N striptease m
strive [straɪv] (pt **strove**, pp **striven**) VI: **to ~ for
sth/to do sth** esforçar-se por or batalhar para
algo/para fazer algo
striven ['strɪvn] PP of **strive**
strode [strəud] PT of **stride**
stroke [strəuk] N (blow) golpe m; (Med) derrame
m cerebral; (caress) carícia; (of pen) traço; (of
paintbrush) pincelada; (Swimming: style) nado;
(: movement) braçada; (of piston) curso ■ VT
acariciar, afagar; **at a ~** de repente, de golpe; **on
the ~ of five** às cinco em ponto; **a ~ of luck** um
golpe de sorte; **a two-~ engine** um motor de
dois tempos
stroll [strəul] N volta, passeio ■ VI passear, dar
uma volta; **to go for a ~** dar uma volta
stroller ['strəuləʳ] (US) N carrinho (de criança)
strong [strɒŋ] ADJ forte; (imagination) fértil;
(personality) forte, dominante; (nerves) de aço;
(object, material) sólido; (chemical) concentrado
■ ADV: **to be going ~** (company) estar

prosperando; (person) estar com boa saúde; **they are 5o ~ são 5o**
strong-arm ADJ (tactics, methods) repressivo, violento
strongbox ['strɔŋbɔks] N cofre-forte m
strong drink N bebida alcoólica
stronghold ['strɔŋhəuld] N fortaleza; (fig) baluarte m
strong language N palavrões mpl
strongly ['strɔŋlɪ] ADV (construct) firmemente; (push, defend) vigorosamente; (believe) profundamente; **I feel ~ about it** tenho uma opinião firme sobre isso
strongman ['strɔŋmæn] (irreg) N homem m forte
strongroom ['strɔŋruːm] N casa-forte f
strove [strəuv] PT of **strive**
struck [strʌk] PT, PP of **strike**
structural ['strʌktʃərəl] ADJ estrutural
structurally ['strʌktʃrəlɪ] ADV estruturalmente
structure ['strʌktʃəʳ] N estrutura; (building) construção f
struggle ['strʌgl] N luta, contenda ■ VI (fight) lutar; (try hard) batalhar; **to have a ~ to do sth** ter que batalhar para fazer algo
strum [strʌm] VT (guitar) dedilhar
strung [strʌŋ] PT, PP of **string**
strut [strʌt] N escora, suporte m ■ VI pavonear-se, empertigar-se
strychnine ['strɪkniːn] N estricnina
stub [stʌb] N (of ticket etc) canhoto; (of cigarette) toco, ponta; **to ~ one's toe** dar uma topada
▶ **stub out** VT apagar
stubble ['stʌbl] N restolho; (on chin) barba por fazer
stubborn ['stʌbən] ADJ teimoso, cabeçudo, obstinado
stubby ['stʌbɪ] ADJ atarracado
stucco ['stʌkəu] N estuque
stuck [stʌk] PT, PP of **stick** ■ ADJ (jammed) emperrado; **to get ~** emperrar
stuck-up ADJ convencido, metido, esnobe
stud [stʌd] N (shirt stud) botão m; (earring) tarraxa, rosca; (of boot) cravo; (also: **stud farm**) fazenda de cavalos; (also: **stud horse**) garanhão m ■ VT (fig): **~ded with** salpicado de
student ['stjuːdənt] N estudante m/f ■ ADJ estudantil; **law/medical ~** estudante de direito/medicina; **student driver** (US) N aprendiz m/f
students' union (Brit) N (association) união f dos estudantes; (building) centro estudantil
studied ['stʌdɪd] ADJ estudado, calculado
studio ['stjuːdɪəu] N estúdio; (sculptor's) ateliê m; **studio flat** (US **studio apartment**) N (apartamento) conjugado
studious ['stjuːdɪəs] ADJ estudioso, aplicado; (careful) cuidadoso; (studied) calculado
studiously ['stjuːdɪəslɪ] ADV (carefully) com esmero
study ['stʌdɪ] N estudo; (room) sala de leitura or estudo ■ VT estudar; (examine) examinar,

investigar ■ VI estudar; **studies** NPL (subjects) estudos mpl, matérias fpl; **to make a ~ of sth** estudar algo; **to ~ for an exam** estudar para um exame
stuff [stʌf] N (substance) troço; (things) troços mpl, coisas fpl ■ VT encher; (Culin) rechear; (animals) empalhar; (inf: push) enfiar; **my nose is ~ed up** meu nariz está entupido; **get ~ed!** (inf!) vai tomar banho!; **~ed toy** brinquedo de pelúcia
stuffing ['stʌfɪŋ] N recheio
stuffy ['stʌfɪ] ADJ (room) abafado, mal ventilado; (person) rabujento, melindroso
stumble ['stʌmbl] VI tropeçar; **to ~ across or on** (fig) topar com
stumbling block ['stʌmblɪŋ-] N pedra no caminho
stump [stʌmp] N (of tree) toco; (of limb) coto ■ VT: **to be ~ed** ficar perplexo
stun [stʌn] VT (subj: blow) aturdir; (: news) pasmar
stung [stʌŋ] PT, PP of **sting**
stunk [stʌŋk] PP of **stink**
stunning ['stʌnɪŋ] ADJ (fig: news) atordoante; (: appearance) maravilhoso
stunt [stʌnt] N façanha sensacional; (Aviat) vôo acrobático; (publicity stunt) truque m publicitário ■ VT tolher
stunted ['stʌntɪd] ADJ atrofiado, retardado
stuntman ['stʌntmæn] (irreg) N dublê m
stupefaction [stjuːpɪ'fækʃən] N estupefação f, assombro
stupefy ['stjuːpɪfaɪ] VT deixar estupefato
stupendous [stjuː'pɛndəs] ADJ monumental
stupid ['stjuːpɪd] ADJ estúpido, idiota
stupidity [stjuː'pɪdɪtɪ] N estupidez f
stupidly ['stjuːpɪdlɪ] ADV estupidamente
stupor ['stjuːpəʳ] N estupor m
sturdy ['stəːdɪ] ADJ (person) robusto, firme; (thing) sólido
sturgeon ['stəːdʒən] N INV esturjão m
stutter ['stʌtəʳ] N gagueira, gaguez f ■ VI gaguejar
sty [staɪ] N (for pigs) chiqueiro
stye [staɪ] N (Med) terçol m
style [staɪl] N estilo; (elegance) elegância; (allure) charme m; **in the latest ~** na última moda; **hair ~** penteado
styli ['staɪlaɪ] NPL of **stylus**
stylish ['staɪlɪʃ] ADJ elegante, chique
stylist ['staɪlɪst] N (hair stylist) cabeleireiro(-a); (literary) estilista m/f
stylized ['staɪlaɪzd] ADJ estilizado
stylus ['staɪləs] (pl **styluses**) N (of record player) agulha
suave [swɑːv] ADJ suave, melífluo
sub [sʌb] N ABBR = **submarine; subscription**
sub... [sʌb] PREFIX sub...
subcommittee ['sʌbkəmɪtɪ] N subcomissão f
subconscious [sʌb'kɔnʃəs] ADJ do subconsciente ■ N subconsciente m
subcontinent [sʌb'kɔntɪnənt] N: **the (Indian) ~** o subcontinente (da Índia)
subcontract [n sʌb'kɔntrækt, vt sʌbkən'trækt] N

subcontrato ∎ VT subcontratar
subcontractor [sʌbkən'træktər] N
subempreiteiro(-a)
subdivide [sʌbdɪ'vaɪd] VT subdividir
subdivision [sʌbdɪ'vɪʒən] N subdivisão f
subdue [səb'dju:] VT subjugar; (passions)
dominar
subdued [səb'dju:d] ADJ (light) tênue; (person)
desanimado
subject [n 'sʌbdʒɪkt, vt səb'dʒɛkt] N (of king)
súdito(-a); (theme) assunto; (Sch) matéria;
(Ling) sujeito ∎ VT: **to ~ sb to sth** submeter
alguém a algo; **to be ~ to** estar sujeito
a; **~ to confirmation in writing** sujeito a
confirmação por escrito; **to change the ~**
mudar de assunto
subjection [səb'dʒɛkʃən] N submissão f,
dependência
subjective [səb'dʒɛktɪv] ADJ subjetivo
subject matter N assunto; (content) conteúdo
sub judice [-'dju:dɪsɪ] ADJ (Law) sob apreciação
judicial, sub judice
subjugate ['sʌbdʒugeɪt] VT subjugar, submeter
subjunctive [səb'dʒʌŋktɪv] ADJ, N subjuntivo
sublet [sʌb'lɛt] VT sublocar
sublime [sə'blaɪm] ADJ sublime
subliminal [sʌb'lɪmɪnl] ADJ subliminar
submachine gun ['sʌbməʃi:n-] N metralhadora
de mão
submarine ['sʌbməri:n] N submarino
submerge [səb'mə:dʒ] VT submergir; (flood)
inundar ∎ VI submergir-se
submersion [səb'mə:ʃən] N submersão f,
imersão f
submission [səb'mɪʃən] N submissão f; (to
committee) petição f; (of plan) apresentação f,
exposição f
submissive [səb'mɪsɪv] ADJ submisso
submit [səb'mɪt] VT submeter ∎ VI submeter-
se
subnormal [sʌb'nɔ:məl] ADJ anormal,
subnormal; (temperature) abaixo do normal;
(backward) atrasado
subordinate [sə'bɔ:dɪnət] ADJ, N
subordinado(-a)
subpoena [səb'pi:nə] N (Law) intimação f,
citação f judicial ∎ VT intimar a comparecer
judicialmente, citar
subroutine [sʌbru:'ti:n] N (Comput) sub-rotina
subscribe [səb'skraɪb] VI subscrever; **to ~ to**
(opinion) concordar com; (fund) contribuir para;
(newspaper) assinar
subscriber [səb'skraɪbər] N (to periodical,
telephone) assinante m/f
subscript ['sʌbskrɪpt] N (Typ) subscrito
subscription [səb'skrɪpʃən] N subscrição
f; (to magazine etc) assinatura; (to club) cota,
mensalidade f; **to take out a ~ to** fazer uma
assinatura de
subsequent ['sʌbsɪkwənt] ADJ subseqüente,
posterior; **~ to** posterior a
subsequently ['sʌbsɪkwəntlɪ] ADV

posteriormente, depois
subside [səb'saɪd] VI (feeling, wind) acalmar-se;
(flood) baixar
subsidence [səb'saɪdns] N baixa; (in road etc)
afundamento da superfície
subsidiary [səb'sɪdɪərɪ] ADJ secundário; (Brit:
Sch: subject) suplementar ∎ N (also: **subsidiary
company**) subsidiária
subsidize ['sʌbsɪdaɪz] VT subsidiar
subsidy ['sʌbsɪdɪ] N subsídio
subsist [səb'sɪst] VI: **to ~ on sth** subsistir de algo
subsistence [səb'sɪstəns] N subsistência;
(allowance) subsídio, ajuda de custo;
subsistence allowance N diária; **subsistence
level** N nível m de subsistência; **subsistence
wage** N salário de fome
substance ['sʌbstəns] N substância; (fig)
essência; **a man of ~** um homem de recursos;
to lack ~ não ter substância
substandard [sʌb'stændəd] ADJ (goods) de
qualidade inferior; (housing) inferior ao padrão
substantial [səb'stænʃl] ADJ (solid) sólido;
(reward, meal) substancial
substantially [səb'stænʃəlɪ] ADV
consideravelmente; (in essence)
substancialmente
substantiate [səb'stænʃɪeɪt] VT comprovar,
justificar
substitute ['sʌbstɪtju:t] N substituto(-a);
(person) suplente m/f ∎ VT: **to ~ A for B**
substituir B por A; **substitute teacher** (US) N
professor(a) m/f suplente
substitution [sʌbstɪ'tju:ʃən] N substituição f
subterfuge ['sʌbtəfju:dʒ] N subterfúgio
subterranean [sʌbtə'reɪnɪən] ADJ subterrâneo
subtitle ['sʌbtaɪtl] N (Cinema) legenda
subtle ['sʌtl] ADJ sutil
subtlety ['sʌtltɪ] N sutileza
subtly ['sʌtlɪ] ADV sutilmente
subtotal [sʌb'təutl] N total m parcial, subtotal m
subtract [səb'trækt] VT subtrair, deduzir
subtraction [səb'trækʃən] N subtração f
subtropical [sʌb'trɒpɪkl] ADJ subtropical
suburb ['sʌbə:b] N subúrbio
suburban [sə'bə:bən] ADJ suburbano; (train etc)
de subúrbio
suburbia [sə'bə:bɪə] N os subúrbios
subvention [səb'vɛnʃən] N subvenção f,
subsídio
subversion [səb'və:ʃən] N subversão f
subversive [səb'və:sɪv] ADJ subversivo
subway ['sʌbweɪ] N (Brit) passagem f
subterrânea; (US) metrô m (BR), metro(
politano) (PT)
sub-zero ADJ abaixo de zero
succeed [sək'si:d] VI (person) ser bem sucedido,
ter êxito; (plan) sair bem ∎ VT suceder a; **to ~ in
doing** conseguir fazer
succeeding [sək'si:dɪŋ] ADJ (following) sucessivo,
posterior
success [sək'sɛs] N êxito; (hit, person) sucesso;
(gain) triunfo

successful [sək'sɛsful] ADJ (*venture*) bem sucedido; (*writer*) de sucesso, bem sucedido; **to be ~ (in doing)** conseguir (fazer)

successfully [sək'sɛsfulɪ] ADV com sucesso, com êxito

succession [sək'sɛʃən] N (*series*) sucessão f, série f; (*to throne*) sucessão; (*descendants*) descendência; **in ~** em sucessão; **3 years in ~** três anos consecutivos

successive [sək'sɛsɪv] ADJ sucessivo; **on 3 ~ days** em 3 dias consecutivos

successor [sək'sɛsəʳ] N sucessor(a) *m/f*

succinct [sək'sɪŋkt] ADJ sucinto

succulent ['sʌkjulənt] ADJ suculento ■ N (*Bot*): **~s** suculentos *mpl*

succumb [sə'kʌm] VI sucumbir

such [sʌtʃ] ADJ tal, semelhante; (*of that kind: singular*): **~ a book** um livro parecido, tal livro; (: *plural*): **~ books** tais livros; (*so much*): **~ courage** tanta coragem ■ ADV tão; **~ a long trip** uma viagem tão longa; **~ good books** livros tão bons; **~ a lot of** tanto; **making ~ a noise that** fazendo tanto barulho que; **~ a long time ago** há tanto tempo atrás; **~ as** (*like*) tal como; **a noise ~ as to** um ruído tal que; **~ books as I have** os poucos livros que eu tenho; **I said no ~ thing** eu não disse tal coisa; **as ~** como tal; **until ~ time as** até que

such-and-such ADJ tal e qual

suchlike ['sʌtʃlaɪk] (*inf*) PRON: **and ~** e coisas assim

suck [sʌk] VT chupar; (*breast*) mamar; (*subj: pump, machine*) sugar

sucker ['sʌkəʳ] N (*Bot*) rebento; (*Zool*) ventosa; (*inf*) trouxa *m/f*, otário(-a)

suckle ['sʌkl] VT amamentar

sucrose ['su:krəuz] N sucrose f

suction ['sʌkʃən] N sucção f; **suction pump** N bomba de sucção

Sudan [su'dɑːn] N Sudão *m*

Sudanese [su:də'niːz] ADJ, N INV sudanês(-esa) *m/f*

sudden ['sʌdn] ADJ (*rapid*) repentino, súbito; (*unexpected*) imprevisto; **all of a ~** de repente; (*unexpectedly*) inesperadamente

suddenly ['sʌdnlɪ] ADV de repente; (*unexpectedly*) inesperadamente

suds [sʌdz] NPL água de sabão

sue [su:] VT processar ■ VI: **to ~ (for)** processar (por), promover ação (por); **to ~ for divorce** requerer divórcio; **to ~ sb for damages** intentar uma ação de perdas e danos contra alguém

suede [sweɪd] N camurça ■ CPD de camurça

suet ['suɪt] N sebo

Suez ['suːɪz] N: **the ~ Canal** o Canal de Suez

suffer ['sʌfəʳ] VT sofrer; (*bear*) agüentar, suportar ■ VI sofrer, padecer; **to ~ from** (*illness*) sofrer de, estar com; **to ~ from the effects of alcohol** sofrer os efeitos do álcool

sufferance ['sʌfrəns] N: **he was only there on ~** ele estava lá por tolerância

sufferer ['sʌfərəʳ] N sofredor(a) *m/f*; **a ~ from**

(*Med*) uma pessoa que sofre de

suffering ['sʌfərɪŋ] N sofrimento; (*pain*) dor f

suffice [sə'faɪs] VI bastar, ser suficiente

sufficient [sə'fɪʃənt] ADJ suficiente, bastante

sufficiently [sə'fɪʃəntlɪ] ADV suficientemente

suffix ['sʌfɪks] N sufixo

suffocate ['sʌfəkeɪt] VT sufocar, asfixiar ■ VI sufocar(-se), asfixiar(-se)

suffocation [sʌfə'keɪʃən] N sufocação f; (*Med*) asfixia

suffrage ['sʌfrɪdʒ] N sufrágio; (*vote*) direito de voto

suffused [sə'fju:zd] ADJ: **~ with** (*light etc*) banhado de

sugar ['ʃugəʳ] N açúcar *m* ■ VT pôr açúcar em, açucarar; **sugar beet** N beterraba (sacarina); **sugar bowl** N açucareiro; **sugar cane** N cana-de-açúcar f

sugar-coated [-'kəutɪd] ADJ cristalizado

sugar lump N torrão *m* de açúcar

sugar refinery N refinaria de açúcar

sugary ['ʃugərɪ] ADJ açucarado

suggest [sə'dʒɛst] VT sugerir; (*indicate*) indicar; (*advise*) aconselhar; **what do you ~ I do?** o que você sugere que eu faça?

suggestion [sə'dʒɛstʃən] N sugestão f; (*indication*) indicação f

suggestive [sə'dʒɛstɪv] ADJ sugestivo; (*pej*) indecente

suicidal [suɪ'saɪdl] ADJ suicida

suicide ['suɪsaɪd] N suicídio; (*person*) suicida *m/f*; *see also* **commit**; **suicide attack** N ataque *m* suicida, atentado suicida; **suicide attempt** N tentativa de suicídio; **suicide bid** N tentativa de suicídio; **suicide bomber** N bombardeio suicida

suit [su:t] N (*man's*) terno (BR), fato (PT); (*woman's*) conjunto; (*Law*) processo; (*Cards*) naipe *m* ■ VT (*gen*) convir a; (*clothes*) ficar bem a; (*adapt*): **to ~ sth to** adaptar *or* acomodar algo a; **to be ~ed to sth** ser apto para algo; **they are well ~ed** fazem um bom par; **to bring a ~ against sb** mover um processo contra alguém; **to follow ~** (*fig*) seguir o exemplo

suitable ['su:təbl] ADJ conveniente; (*appropriate*) apropriado; **would tomorrow be ~?** amanhã lhe convém?

suitably ['su:təblɪ] ADV (*dressed*) apropriadamente; (*impressed*) bem

suitcase ['su:tkeɪs] N mala

suite [swi:t] N (*of rooms*) conjunto de salas; (*Mus*) suite f; (*furniture*): **bedroom/dining room ~** conjunto de quarto/de sala de jantar; **a three-piece ~** um conjunto estofado (sofá e duas poltronas)

suitor ['su:təʳ] N pretendente *m*

sulfate ['sʌlfeɪt] (US) N = **sulphate**

sulfur *etc* ['sʌlfəʳ] (US) N = **sulphur** *etc*

sulk [sʌlk] VI ficar emburrado, fazer beicinho *or* biquinho (*inf*)

sulky ['sʌlkɪ] ADJ emburrado

sullen ['sʌlən] ADJ rabugento; (*silence*) pesado

sulphate ['sʌlfeɪt] (*US* **sulfate**) N sulfato; *see also* **copper sulphate**

sulphur ['sʌlfər] (*US* **sulfur**) N enxofre *m*

sulphuric [sʌl'fjuərɪk] (*US* **sulfuric**) ADJ: ~ **acid** ácido sulfúrico

sultan ['sʌltən] N sultão *m*

sultana [sʌl'tɑːnə] N (*Culin*) passa branca

sultry ['sʌltrɪ] ADJ (*weather*) abafado, mormacento; (*seductive*) sedutor(a)

sum [sʌm] N soma; (*calculation*) cálculo
▸ **sum up** VT sumariar, fazer um resumo de; (*describe*) resumir; (*evaluate*) avaliar ■ VI resumir

Sumatra [suˈmɑːtrə] N Sumatra

summarize ['sʌmməraɪz] VT resumir

summary ['sʌmərɪ] N resumo ■ ADJ (*justice*) sumário

summer ['sʌmər] N verão *m* ■ ADJ de verão; **in (the)** ~ no verão; **summer camp** (*US*) N colônia de férias

summerhouse ['sʌməhaus] N (*in garden*) pavilhão *m*

summertime ['sʌmətaɪm] N (*season*) verão *m*

summer time N (*by clock*) horário de verão

summery ['sʌmərɪ] ADJ estival, de verão

summing-up ['sʌmɪŋ-] N resumo, recapitulação *f*

summit ['sʌmɪt] N topo, cume *m*; (*also*: **summit conference**) (conferência de) cúpula

summon ['sʌmən] VT (*person*) mandar chamar; (*meeting*) convocar; (*Law: witness*) convocar
▸ **summon up** VT concentrar

summons ['sʌmənz] N (*Jur*) citação *f*, intimação *f*; (*fig*) chamada ■ VT citar, intimar; **to serve a ~ on sb** entregar uma citação a alguém

sump [sʌmp] (*Brit*) N (*Aut*) cárter *m*

sumptuous ['sʌmptjuəs] ADJ suntuoso

Sun. ABBR (= *Sunday*) dom

sun [sʌn] N sol *m*; **in the** ~ ao sol; **everything under the** ~ cada coisa

sunbathe ['sʌnbeɪð] VI tomar sol

sunbeam ['sʌnbiːm] N raio de sol

sunbed ['sʌnbed] N espreguiçadeira; (*with sunlamp*) cama para bronzeamento artificial

sunblock ['sʌnblblɔk] N bloqueador *m* solar

sunburn ['sʌnbəːn] N queimadura do sol

sunburned ['sʌnbəːnd] ADJ = **sunburnt**

sunburnt ['sʌnbəːnt] ADJ bronzeado; (*painfully*) queimado

sun cream N creme *m* solar

sundae ['sʌndeɪ] N sorvete *m* (BR) *or* gelado (PT) com frutas e nozes

Sunday ['sʌndɪ] N domingo; *see also* **Tuesday**; **Sunday school** N escola dominical

sundial ['sʌndaɪəl] N relógio de sol

sundown ['sʌndaun] N pôr *m* do sol

sundries ['sʌndrɪz] NPL gêneros *mpl* diversos

sundry ['sʌndrɪ] ADJ vários, diversos; **all and** ~ todos

sunflower ['sʌnflauər] N girassol *m*

sung [sʌŋ] PP *of* **sing**

sunglasses ['sʌnglɑːsɪz] NPL óculos *mpl* de sol

sunk [sʌŋk] PP *of* **sink**

sunken ['sʌŋkn] ADJ (*ship*) afundado; (*eyes, cheeks*) cavado; (*bath*) enterrado

sunlamp ['sʌnlæmp] N lâmpada ultravioleta

sunlight ['sʌnlaɪt] N (luz *f* do) sol *m*

sunlit ['sʌnlɪt] ADJ ensolarado, iluminado pelo sol

sunny ['sʌnɪ] ADJ cheio de sol; (*day*) ensolarado, de sol; (*fig*) alegre; **it's** ~ faz sol

sunrise ['sʌnraɪz] N nascer *m* do sol

sun roof N (*Aut*) teto solar

sunscreen ['sʌnskriːn] N protetor *m* solar

sunset ['sʌnset] N pôr *m* do sol

sunshade ['sʌnʃeɪd] N (*over table*) pára-sol *m*; (*on beach*) barraca

sunshine ['sʌnʃaɪn] N (luz *f* do) sol *m*

sunspot ['sʌnspɒt] N mancha solar

sunstroke ['sʌnstrəuk] N insolação *f*

suntan ['sʌntæn] N bronzeado; **suntan lotion** N loção *f* de bronzear

suntanned ['sʌntænd] ADJ bronzeado, moreno

suntan oil N óleo de bronzear, bronzeador *m*

suntrap ['sʌntræp] N lugar *m* muito ensolarado

super ['suːpər] (*inf*) ADJ bacana (BR), muito giro (PT)

superannuation [suːpərænjuˈeɪʃən] N pensão *f* de aposentadoria

superb [suːˈpəːb] ADJ excelente

supercilious [suːpəˈsɪliəs] ADJ (*disdainful*) arrogante, desdenhoso; (*haughty*) altivo

superficial [suːpəˈfɪʃəl] ADJ superficial

superficially [suːpəˈfɪʃəlɪ] ADV superficialmente

superfluous [suˈpəːfluəs] ADJ supérfluo, desnecessário

superhuman [suːpəˈhjuːmən] ADJ sobre-humano

superimpose [suːpərɪmˈpəuz] VT: **to** ~ **(on/with)** sobrepor (a)

superintend [suːpərɪnˈtend] VT superintender, dirigir

superintendent [suːpərɪnˈtendənt] N superintendente *m/f*; (*Police*) chefe *m/f* de polícia

superior [suˈpɪərɪər] ADJ superior; (*smug*) desdenhoso ■ N superior *m*; **Mother S~** (*Rel*) Madre Superiora

superiority [supɪərɪˈɒrɪtɪ] N superioridade *f*

superlative [suˈpəːlətɪv] ADJ superlativo ■ N superlativo

superman ['suːpəmæn] (*irreg*) N super-homem *m*

supermarket ['suːpəmɑːkɪt] N supermercado

supernatural [suːpəˈnætʃərəl] ADJ sobrenatural ■ N: **the** ~ o sobrenatural

superpower ['suːpəpauər] N (*Pol*) superpotência

supersede [suːpəˈsiːd] VT suplantar

supersonic [suːpəˈsɒnɪk] ADJ supersônico

superstar ['suːpəstɑːr] M superstar *m/f*

superstition [suːpəˈstɪʃən] N superstição *f*

superstitious [suːpəˈstɪʃəs] ADJ supersticioso

superstore ['suːpəstɔːr] (*Brit*) N hipermercado

supertanker ['suːpətæŋkər] N superpetroleiro

supertax ['suːpətæks] N sobretaxa

supervise ['su:pəvaɪz] VT supervisar, supervisionar

supervision [su:pə'vɪʒən] N supervisão f; **under medical** ~ a critério médico

supervisor ['su:pəvaɪzəʳ] N supervisor(a) m/f; (academic) orientador(a) m/f

supervisory [su:pə'vaɪzərɪ] ADJ fiscalizador(a)

supine ['su:paɪn] ADJ em supinação

supper ['sʌpəʳ] N jantar m; (late evening) ceia; **to have** ~ jantar

supplant [sə'plɑ:nt] VT suplantar

supple ['sʌpl] ADJ flexível

supplement [n 'sʌplɪmənt, vt sʌplɪ'mɛnt] N suplemento ▪ VT suprir, completar

supplementary [sʌplɪ'mɛntərɪ] ADJ suplementar; **supplementary benefit** (Brit) N auxílio suplementar pago aos de renda baixa

supplier [sə'plaɪəʳ] N abastecedor(a) m/f, fornecedor(a) m/f; (stockist) distribuidor(a) m/f

supply [sə'plaɪ] VT (provide): **to ~ sth (to sb)** fornecer algo (por alguém); (need) suprir a; (equip): **to ~ (with)** suprir (de) ▪ N fornecimento, provisão f; (stock) estoque m; (supplying) abastecimento ▪ ADJ (teacher etc) suplente; **supplies** NPL (food) víveres mpl; (Mil) apetrechos mpl; **office supplies** material m de escritório; **to be in short** ~ estar escasso; **the electricity/water/gas** ~ o abastecimento de força/água/gás; ~ **and demand** oferta e procura; **supply teacher** (Brit) N professor(a) m/f suplente

support [sə'pɔ:t] N (moral, financial etc) apoio; (Tech) suporte m ▪ VT apoiar; (financially) manter; (Tech: hold up) sustentar; (theory etc) defender; (Sport: team) torcer por; **to ~ o.s.** (financially) ganhar a vida

supporter [sə'pɔ:təʳ] N (Pol etc) partidário(-a); (Sport) torcedor(a) m/f

supporting [sə'pɔ:tɪŋ] ADJ (Theatre etc: role) secundário; (: actor) coadjuvante

suppose [sə'pəuz] VT supor; (imagine) imaginar; (duty): **to be ~d to do sth** dever fazer algo ▪ VI supor; imaginar; **he's ~d to be an expert** dizem que ele é um perito; **I don't ~ she'll come** eu acho que ela não virá

supposedly [sə'pəuzɪdlɪ] ADV supostamente, pretensamente

supposing [sə'pəuzɪŋ] CONJ caso, supondo-se que; **always ~ he comes** caso ele venha

supposition [sʌpə'zɪʃən] N suposição f

suppository [sə'pozɪtərɪ] N supositório

suppress [sə'prɛs] VT (information) suprimir; (feelings, revolt) reprimir; (yawn) conter; (scandal) abafar, encobrir

suppression [sə'prɛʃən] N (information) supressão f; (feelings, revolt) repressão f; (yawn) controle m; (scandal) abafamento

suppressor [sə'prɛsəʳ] N (Elec etc) supressor m

supremacy [su'prɛməsɪ] N supremacia

supreme [su'pri:m] ADJ supremo

Supreme Court (US) N Corte f Suprema

Supt. ABBR (Police) = **superintendent**

surcharge ['sə:tʃɑ:dʒ] N sobretaxa

sure [ʃuəʳ] ADJ (gen) seguro; (definite) certo; (aim) certeiro ▪ ADV (inf: esp US): **that ~ is pretty** é bonito mesmo; **to make ~ of sth/that** assegurar-se de algo/que; ~! (of course) claro que sim!; ~ **enough** efetivamente; **I'm not ~ how/ why/when** não tenho certeza como/por que/ quando; **to be ~ of sth** ter certeza de alguma coisa; **to be ~ of o.s.** estar seguro de si

sure-footed [-'futɪd] ADJ de andar seguro

surely ['ʃuəlɪ] ADV (certainly: US: also: sure) certamente; ~ **you don't mean that!** não acredito que você queira dizer isso

surety ['ʃuərətɪ] N garantia, fiança; (person) fiador(a) m/f; **to go** or **stand ~ for sb** afiançar alguém, prestar fiança por alguém

surf [sə:f] N (foam) espuma; (waves) ondas fpl, arrebentação f ▪ VI fazer surfe, pegar onda (inf)

surface ['sə:fɪs] N superfície f ▪ VT (road) revestir ▪ VI vir à superfície or à tona; (fig: news, feeling) vir à tona; **on the** ~ (fig) à primeira vista; **surface area** N área da superfície; **surface mail** N correio comum

surfboard ['sə:fbɔ:d] N prancha de surfe

surfeit ['sə:fɪt] N: **a ~ of** um excesso de

surfer ['sə:fəʳ] N surfista m/f; (on the Internet) internauta m/f

surfing ['sə:fɪŋ] N surfe m; **to go ~** fazer surfe, pegar onda (inf)

surge [sə:dʒ] N onda; (Elec) surto ▪ VI (sea) encapelar-se; (people, vehicles) precipitar-se; (feeling) aumentar repentinamente; **to ~ forward** avançar em tropel

surgeon ['sə:dʒən] N cirurgião(-giã) m/f

Surgeon General (US) N diretor(a) m/f nacional de saúde

surgery ['sə:dʒərɪ] N cirurgia; (Brit: room) consultório; (: also: **surgery hours**) horas fpl de consulta; **to undergo** ~ operar-se

surgical ['sə:dʒɪkl] ADJ cirúrgico; **surgical spirit** (Brit) N álcool m

surly ['sə:lɪ] ADJ malcriado, rude

surmise [sə'maɪz] VT conjeturar

surmount [sə'maunt] VT superar, sobrepujar, vencer

surname ['sə:neɪm] N sobrenome m (BR), apelido (PT)

surpass [sə:'pɑ:s] VT superar

surplus ['sə:pləs] N excedente m; (Comm) superávit m ▪ ADJ excedente, de sobra; ~ **to my requirements** que me sobram; ~ **stock** estoque m excedente

surprise [sə'praɪz] N surpresa; (astonishment) assombro ▪ VT surpreender; **to take by** ~ (person) pegar de surpresa; (Mil: town, fort) atacar de surpresa

surprising [sə'praɪzɪŋ] ADJ surpreendente; (unexpected) inesperado

surprisingly [sə'praɪzɪŋlɪ] ADV (easy, helpful) surpreendentemente; **(somewhat)** ~, **he agreed** para surpresa de todos, ele concordou

surrealism [sə'rɪəlɪzm] N surrealismo

surrealist [səˈrɪəlɪst] ADJ, N surrealista m/f

surrender [səˈrɛndəʳ] N rendição f, entrega ■ VI render-se, entregar-se ■ VT (claim, right) renunciar a; **surrender value** N valor m de resgate

surreptitious [sʌrəpˈtɪʃəs] ADJ clandestino, furtivo

surrogate [ˈsʌrəgɪt] N (Brit: substitute) substituto(-a) ■ ADJ substituto; **surrogate mother** N mãe f portadora

surround [səˈraund] VT circundar, rodear; (Mil etc) cercar

surrounding [səˈraundɪŋ] ADJ circundante, adjacente

surroundings [səˈraundɪŋz] NPL arredores mpl, cercanias fpl

surtax [ˈsəːtæks] N sobretaxa

surveillance [səːˈveɪləns] N vigilância

survey [n ˈsəːveɪ, vt səːˈveɪ] N (inspection) inspeção f, vistoria; (investigation: of habits etc) pesquisa, levantamento; (of house) inspeção f; (of land) levantamento ■ VT inspecionar, vistoriar; (look at) observar, contemplar; (land) fazer um levantamento de; (make inquiries about) pesquisar, fazer um levantamento de

surveying [səːˈveɪɪŋ] N agrimensura

surveyor [səːˈveɪəʳ] N (of land) agrimensor(a) m/f; (of building) inspetor(a) m/f

survival [səˈvaɪvl] N sobrevivência; (relic) remanescente m ■ CPD (course, kit) de sobrevivência

survive [səˈvaɪv] VI sobreviver; (custom etc) perdurar ■ VT sobreviver a

survivor [səˈvaɪvəʳ] N sobrevivente m/f

susceptible [səˈsɛptəbl] ADJ: ~ (to) (heat, injury) suscetível or sensível a(a); (flattery, pressure) vulnerável (a)

suspect [adj, n ˈsʌspɛkt, vt səsˈpɛkt] ADJ, N suspeito(-a) ■ VT suspeitar, desconfiar

suspend [səsˈpɛnd] VT suspender

suspended sentence [səsˈpɛndɪd-] N condenação f condicional

suspender belt [səsˈpɛndəʳ-] N cinta-liga

suspenders [səsˈpɛndəz] NPL (Brit) ligas fpl; (US) suspensórios mpl

suspense [səsˈpɛns] N incerteza, ansiedade f; (in film etc) suspense m; **to keep sb in** ~ manter alguém em suspense or na expectativa

suspension [səsˈpɛnʃən] N (gen, Aut) suspensão f; (of driving licence) cassação f; **suspension bridge** N ponte f pênsil

suspicion [səsˈpɪʃən] N suspeita; (trace) traço, vestígio; **to be under** ~ estar sob suspeita; **arrested on** ~ **of murder** preso sob suspeita de homicídio

suspicious [səsˈpɪʃəs] ADJ (suspecting) suspeitoso; (causing suspicion) suspeito; **to be** ~ **of** or **about sb/sth** desconfiar de alguém/algo

suss out [sʌs-] (Brit: inf) VT (discover) descobrir; (understand) sacar

sustain [səsˈteɪn] VT sustentar, manter; (subj: food, drink) sustenar; (suffer) sofrer

sustained [səsˈteɪnd] ADJ (effort) contínuo

sustenance [ˈsʌstɪnəns] N sustento

suture [ˈsuːtʃəʳ] N sutura

SUV N ABBR (= sports utility vehicle) SUV m

SW ABBR (= short wave) OC

swab [swɔb] N (Med) mecha de algodão ■ VT (Naut: also: **swab down**) lambazar

swagger [ˈswægəʳ] VI andar com ar de superioridade

swallow [ˈswɔləu] N (bird) andorinha; (of food etc) bocado; (of drink) trago ■ VT engolir, tragar; (fig: story) engolir; (pride) pôr de lado; (one's words) retirar

▶ **swallow up** VT (savings etc) consumir

swam [swæm] PT of **swim**

swamp [swɔmp] N pântano, brejo ■ VT atolar, inundar; (fig: person) assoberbar

swampy [ˈswɔmpɪ] ADJ pantanoso

swan [swɔn] N cisne m

swank [swæŋk] (inf) VI esnobar

swan song N (fig) canto do cisne

swap [swɔp] N troca, permuta ■ VT: **to** ~ **(for)** trocar (por); (replace (with)) substituir (por)

swarm [swɔːm] N (of bees) enxame m; (of people) multidão f ■ VI enxamear; aglomerar-se; (place): **to be ~ing with** estar apinhado de

swarthy [ˈswɔːðɪ] ADJ moreno

swashbuckling [ˈswɔʃbʌklɪŋ] ADJ (film) de capa e espada

swastika [ˈswɔstɪkə] N suástica

swat [swɔt] VT esmagar ■ N (Brit: also: **fly swat**) pá f para matar mosca

swathe [sweɪð] VT: **to** ~ **in** (bandages, blankets) enfaixar em, envolver em

swatter [ˈswɔtəʳ] N (also: **fly swatter**) pá f para matar mosca

sway [sweɪ] VI balançar-se, oscilar ■ VT (influence) influenciar ■ N (rule, power) domínio (sobre); **to hold** ~ **over sb** dominar alguém

Swaziland [ˈswɑːzɪlænd] N Suazilândia

swear [sweəʳ] (pt swore, pp sworn) VI (by oath) jurar; (curse) xingar ■ VT (promise) jurar; **to** ~ **an oath** prestar juramento; **to** ~ **to sth** afirmar algo sob juramento

▶ **swear in** VT (witness) ajuramentar; (president) empossar

swearword [ˈsweəwəːd] N palavrão m

sweat [swɛt] N suor m ■ VI suar

sweatband [ˈswɛtbænd] N (Sport) tira elástica (para o cabelo)

sweater [ˈswɛtəʳ] N suéter m or f (BR), camisola (PT)

sweatshirt [ˈswɛtʃəːt] N suéter m de malha de algodão

sweatshop [ˈswɛtʃɔp] N oficina onde os trabalhadores são explorados

sweaty [ˈswɛtɪ] ADJ suado

Swede [swiːd] N sueco(-a)

swede [swiːd] N tipo de nabo

Sweden [ˈswiːdən] N Suécia

Swedish [ˈswiːdɪʃ] ADJ sueco ■ N (Ling) sueco

sweep [swiːp] (pt, pp swept) N (act) varredura;

(of arm) movimento circular; (range) extensão f, alcance m; (also: **chimney sweep**) limpador m de chaminés ■ VT varrer; (with arm) empurrar; (subj: current) arrastar; (: fashion, craze) espalhar-se por; (: disease) arrasar ■ VI varrer; (person) passar majestosamente
▶ **sweep away** VT varrer; (rub out) apagar
▶ **sweep past** VI passar rapidamente; (brush by) roçar
▶ **sweep up** VT, VI varrer
sweeping ['swiːpɪŋ] ADJ (gesture) dramático; (reform) radical; (statement) generalizado
sweepstake ['swiːpsteɪk] N sweepstake m
sweet [swiːt] N (candy) bala (BR), rebuçado (PT); (Brit: pudding) sobremesa ■ ADJ doce; (sugary) açucarado; (fig: air) fresco; (: water, smell) doce; (: sound) suave; (: kind) meigo; (baby, kitten) bonitinho ■ ADV: **to smell ~** ter bom cheiro; **to taste ~** estar doce; **~ and sour** agridoce
sweetbread ['swiːtbrɛd] N moleja
sweetcorn ['swiːtkɔːn] N milho
sweeten ['swiːtən] VT pôr açúcar em; (temper) abrandar
sweetener ['swiːtnər] N (Culin) adoçante m
sweetheart ['swiːthɑːt] N namorado(-a); (as address) amor m
sweetly ['swiːtlɪ] ADV docemente; (gently) suavemente
sweetness ['swiːtnɪs] N doçura
sweet pea N ervilha-de-cheiro f
sweet potato (irreg) N batata doce
sweetshop ['swiːtʃɔp] N confeitaria
swell [swɛl] (pt swelled, pp swelled) N (of sea) vaga, onda ■ ADJ (US: inf: excellent) bacana ■ VT engrossar ■ VI (increase) aumentar; (get stronger) intensificar-se; (also: **swell up**) inchar(-se)
swelling ['swɛlɪŋ] N (Med) inchação f
sweltering ['swɛltərɪŋ] ADJ (heat) sufocante; (day) mormacento
swept [swɛpt] PT, PP of **sweep**
swerve [swəːv] VI desviar-se
swift [swɪft] N (bird) andorinhão m ■ ADJ rápido
swiftly ['swɪftlɪ] ADV rapidamente, velozmente
swiftness ['swɪftnɪs] N rapidez f, ligeireza
swig [swɪg] (inf) N (drink) trago, gole m
swill [swɪl] N lavagem f ■ VT (also: **swill out**, **swill down**) lavar, limpar com água
swim [swɪm] (pt swam, pp swum) N: **to go for a ~** ir nadar ■ VI nadar; (head, room) rodar; (fig): **my head/the room is ~ming** estou com a cabeça zonza/sinto o quarto rodar ■ VT atravessar a nado; (distance) percorrer (a nado); **to go ~ming** ir nadar; **to ~ a length** nadar uma volta
swimmer ['swɪmər] N nadador(a) m/f
swimming ['swɪmɪŋ] N natação f; **swimming baths** (Brit) NPL piscina; **swimming cap** N touca de natação; **swimming costume** (Brit) N (woman's) maiô m (BR), fato de banho (PT); (man's) calção m de banho (BR), calções mpl de banho (PT); **swimming pool** N piscina; **swimming trunks** NPL sunga (BR), calções mpl de banho (PT)

swimsuit ['swɪmsuːt] N maiô m (BR), fato de banho (PT)
swindle ['swɪndl] N fraude f ■ VT defraudar
swindler ['swɪndlər] N vigarista m/f
swine [swaɪn] N porcos mpl; (inf!) canalha m, calhorda m
swing [swɪŋ] (pt, pp swung) N (in playground) balanço; (movement) balanceio, oscilação f; (change: in opinion) mudança; (: of direction) virada; (rhythm) ritmo ■ VT balançar; (also: **swing round**) girar, rodar ■ VI oscilar; (on swing) balançar; (also: **swing round**) voltar-se bruscamente; **a ~ to the left** (Pol) uma guinada para a esquerda; **to be in full ~** estar a todo vapor; **to get into the ~ of things** familiarizar-se com tudo; **the road ~s south** a estrada vira em direção ao sul; **swing bridge** N ponte f giratória; **swing door** (US **swinging door**) N porta de vaivém
swingeing ['swɪndʒɪŋ] (Brit) ADJ esmagador(a); (cuts) devastador(a)
swinging ['swɪŋɪŋ] ADJ rítmico; (person) badalativo
swipe [swaɪp] N pancada violenta ■ VT (hit) bater com violência; (inf: steal) afanar, roubar
swirl [swəːl] VI redemoinhar ■ N redemoinho
swish [swɪʃ] ADJ (Brit: inf: smart) chique ■ N (of whip) silvo; (of skirt, grass) ruge-ruge m ■ VI (tail) abanar; (clothes) fazer ruge-ruge
Swiss [swɪs] ADJ, N INV suíço(-a); **Swiss roll** N bolo de rolo, rocambole m doce
switch [swɪtʃ] N (for light, radio etc) interruptor m; (change) mudança ■ VT (change) trocar
▶ **switch off** VT apagar; (engine) desligar; (Brit: gas, water) fechar
▶ **switch on** VT acender; ligar; abrir
switchback ['swɪtʃbæk] (Brit) N montanharussa
switchblade ['swɪtʃbleɪd] N (also: **switchblade knife**) canivete m de mola
switchboard ['swɪtʃbɔːd] N (Tel) mesa telefônica; **switchboard operator** N (Tel) telefonista m/f
Switzerland ['swɪtsələnd] N Suíça
swivel ['swɪvl] VI (also: **swivel round**) girar (sobre um eixo), fazer pião
swollen ['swəulən] PP of **swell** ■ ADJ inchado
swoon [swuːn] VI desmaiar
swoop [swuːp] N (by police etc) batida; (of bird) vôo picado ■ VI (also: **swoop down**) precipitar-se, cair
swop [swɔp] N, VT = **swap**
sword [sɔːd] N espada
swordfish ['sɔːdfɪʃ] N INV peixe-espada m
swore [swɔːr] PT of **swear**
sworn [swɔːn] PP of **swear** ■ ADJ (statement) sob juramento; (enemy) declarado
swot [swɔt] VI queimar as pestanas
swum [swʌm] PP of **swim**
swung [swʌŋ] PT, PP of **swing**
sycamore ['sɪkəmɔːr] N sicômoro
sycophant ['sɪkəfænt] N bajulador(a) m/f

sycophantic [sɪkə'fæntɪk] ADJ (person) bajulador(a); (behaviour) bajulatório

Sydney ['sɪdnɪ] N Sydney

syllable ['sɪləbl] N sílaba

syllabus ['sɪləbəs] N programa m de estudos; **on the ~** no roteiro

symbol ['sɪmbl] N símbolo

symbolic(al) [sɪm'bɔlɪk(l)] ADJ simbólico

symbolism ['sɪmbəlɪzəm] N simbolismo

symbolize ['sɪmbəlaɪz] VT simbolizar

symmetrical [sɪ'mɛtrɪkl] ADJ simétrico

symmetry ['sɪmɪtrɪ] N simetria

sympathetic [sɪmpə'θɛtɪk] ADJ (showing pity) compassivo; (understanding) compreensivo; (likeable) agradável; (supportive): **~ to(wards)** solidário com

sympathetically [sɪmpə'θɛtɪklɪ] ADV (with pity) com compaixão; (understandingly) compreensivamente

sympathize ['sɪmpəθaɪz] VI: **to ~ with** (person) compadecer-se de; (sb's feelings) compreender; (cause) simpatizar com

sympathizer ['sɪmpəθaɪzər] N (Pol) simpatizante m/f

sympathy ['sɪmpəθɪ] N (pity) compaixão f; **sympathies** NPL (tendencies) simpatia; **in ~ with** em acordo com; (strike) em solidariedade com; **with our deepest ~** com nossos mais profundos pêsames

symphonic [sɪm'fɔnɪk] ADJ sinfônico

symphony ['sɪmfənɪ] N sinfonia; **symphony orchestra** N orquestra sinfônica

symposium [sɪm'pəuzɪəm] (pl symposia) N simpósio

symptom ['sɪmptəm] N sintoma m; (sign) indício

symptomatic [sɪmptə'mætɪk] ADJ sintomático

synagogue ['sɪnəgɔg] N sinagoga

synchromesh ['sɪŋkrəumɛʃ] N (Aut) engrenagem f sincronizada

synchronize ['sɪŋkrənaɪz] VT sincronizar ■ VI: **to ~ with** sincronizar-se com

syncopated ['sɪŋkəpeɪtɪd] ADJ sincopado

syndicate ['sɪndɪkɪt] N sindicato; (of newspapers) cadeia

syndrome ['sɪndrəum] N síndrome f

synonym ['sɪnənɪm] N sinônimo

synonymous [sɪ'nɔnɪməs] ADJ: **~ (with)** sinônimo (de)

synopses [sɪ'nɔpsiːz] NPL of synopsis

synopsis [sɪ'nɔpsɪs] (pl synopses) N sinopse f, resumo

syntax ['sɪntæks] N sintaxe f

syntheses ['sɪnθəsiːz] NPL of synthesis

synthesis ['sɪnθəsɪs] (pl syntheses) N síntese f

synthesizer ['sɪnθəsaɪzə'] N (Mus) sintetizador m

synthetic [sɪn'θɛtɪk] ADJ sintético ■ N: **~s** matérias fpl sintéticas

syphilis ['sɪfɪlɪs] N sífilis f

syphon ['saɪfən] = **siphon**

Syria ['sɪrɪə] N Síria

Syrian ['sɪrɪən] ADJ, N sírio(-a)

syringe [sɪ'rɪndʒ] N seringa

syrup ['sɪrəp] N xarope m; (Brit: also: **golden syrup**) melaço

syrupy ['sɪrəpɪ] ADJ xaroposo

system ['sɪstəm] N sistema m; (method) método; (Anat) organismo

systematic [sɪstə'mætɪk] ADJ sistemático

system disk N (Comput) disco do sistema

systems analyst N analista m/f de sistemas

Tt

T, t [ti:] N (*letter*) T, t *m*; **T for Tommy** T de
Tereza
TA (*Brit*) N ABBR = **Territorial Army**
ta [tɑ:] (*Brit: inf*) EXCL obrigado(-a)
tab [tæb] N ABBR = **tabulator** ■ N lingüeta,
aba; (*label*) etiqueta; **to keep ~s on** (*fig*)
vigiar
tabby ['tæbɪ] N (*also:* **tabby cat**) gato malhado
or listrado
table ['teɪbl] N mesa; (*of statistics etc*) quadro,
tabela ■ VT (*motion etc*) apresentar; **to lay** *or* **set**
the ~ pôr a mesa; **to clear the ~** tirar a mesa;
league ~ (*Brit: Football*) classificação *f* dos times;
~ of contents índice *m*, sumário
tablecloth ['teɪblklɔθ] N toalha de mesa
table d'hôte [tɑ:bl'dəut] N refeição *f*
comercial
table lamp N abajur *m* (BR), candeeiro (PT)
tableland ['teɪbllænd] N planalto
table mat N descanso
table salt N sal *m* fino
tablespoon ['teɪblspu:n] N colher *f* de
sopa; (*also:* **tablespoonful**: *as measurement*)
colherada
tablet ['tæblɪt] N (*Med*) comprimido; (: *for*
sucking) pastilha; (*for writing*) bloco; (*of stone*)
lápide *f*; **~ of soap** (*Brit*) sabonete *m*
table tennis N pingue-pongue *m*, tênis *m* de
mesa
table wine N vinho de mesa
tabloid ['tæblɔɪd] N (*newspaper*) tablóide *m*;
the ~s os jornais populares; **tabloid press**
N *ver abaixo*

● **TABLOID PRESS**

● O termo *tabloid press* refere-se aos jornais
● populares de formato meio jornal que
● apresentam muitas fotografias e adotam
● um estilo bastante conciso. O público-alvo
● desses jornais é composto por leitores
● que se interessam pelos fatos do dia que
● contenham um certo toque de escândalo;
● veja *quality (news)papers*.

taboo [tə'bu:] N tabu *m* ■ ADJ tabu
tabulate ['tæbjuleɪt] VT (*data, figures*) dispor em
forma de tabela
tabulator ['tæbjuleɪtə'] N tabulador *m*
tachograph ['tækəgrɑ:f] N tacógrafo
tachometer [tæ'kɔmɪtə'] N tacômetro
tacit ['tæsɪt] ADJ tácito, implícito
taciturn ['tæsɪtə:n] ADJ taciturno
tack [tæk] N (*nail*) tachinha, percevejo; (*Brit:*
stitch) alinhavo; (*Naut*) amura ■ VT prender
com tachinha; alinhavar ■ VI virar de bordo;
to change ~ virar de bordo; (*fig*) mudar de
tática; **to ~ sth on to (the end of) sth** anexar
algo a algo
tackle ['tækl] N (*gear*) equipamento; (*also:* **fishing**
tackle) apetrechos *mpl*; (*for lifting*) guincho;
(*Football*) ato de tirar a bola de adversário ■ VT
(*difficulty*) atacar; (*challenge: person*) desafiar;
(*grapple with*) atracar-se com; (*Football*) tirar a
bola de
tacky ['tækɪ] ADJ pegajoso, grudento; (*inf:*
tasteless) cafona
tact [tækt] N tato, diplomacia
tactful ['tæktful] ADJ diplomático; **to be ~** ser
diplomata
tactfully ['tæktfulɪ] ADV discretamente, com
tato
tactical ['tæktɪkl] ADJ tático
tactics ['tæktɪks] N, NPL tática
tactless ['tæktlɪs] ADJ sem diplomacia
tactlessly ['tæktlɪslɪ] ADV indiscretamente
tadpole ['tædpəul] N girino
taffy ['tæfɪ] (*US*) N puxa-puxa *m* (BR), caramelo
(PT)
tag [tæg] N (*label*) etiqueta; **price/name ~**
etiqueta de preço/com o nome
▶ **tag along** VI seguir
Tahiti [tɑ:'hi:tɪ] N Taiti (*no article*)
tail [teɪl] N rabo; (*of bird, comet, plane*) cauda; (*of*
shirt, coat) aba ■ VT (*follow*) seguir bem de perto;
to turn ~ dar no pé; *see also* **head**
▶ **tail away** VI (*in size, quality etc*) diminuir
gradualmente
▶ **tail off** VI (*in size, quality etc*) diminuir
gradualmente
tailback ['teɪlbæk] (*Brit*) N fila (de carros)
tail coat N fraque *m*
tail end N (*of train*) cauda; (*of procession*) parte *f*
final

tailgate ['teɪlgeɪt] N (Aut) porta traseira

tailor ['teɪləʳ] N alfaiate m ▪ VT: **to ~ sth (to)** adaptar algo (a); **~'s (shop)** alfaiataria

tailoring ['teɪlərɪŋ] N (cut) feitio; (craft) ofício de alfaiate

tailor-made ADJ feito sob medida; (fig) especial

tailwind ['teɪlwɪnd] N vento de popa or de cauda

taint [teɪnt] VT (meat, food) estragar; (fig: reputation) manchar

tainted ['teɪntɪd] ADJ (food) estragado, passado; (water, air) poluído; (fig) manchado

Taiwan ['taɪ'wɑːn] N Taiuan (no article)

take [teɪk] (pt **took**, pp **taken**) VT (gen) tomar; (photo, holiday) tirar; (grab) pegar (em); (gain: prize) ganhar; (require: effort, courage) requerer, exigir; (tolerate) agüentar; (accompany, bring, carry: person) acompanhar, trazer; (: thing) trazer, carregar; (exam) fazer; (hold: passengers etc): **it ~s 50 people** cabem 50 pessoas ▪ VI (dye, fire) pegar ▪ N (Cinema) tomada; **to ~ sth from** (drawer etc) tirar algo de; (person) pegar algo de; **I ~ it that ...** suponho que ...; **I took him for a doctor** eu o tomei por médico; **to ~ sb's hand** pegar a mão de alguém; **to ~ for a walk** levar a passeio; **to be ~n ill** adoecer, ficar doente; **to ~ it upon o.s. to do sth** assumir a responsabilidade de fazer algo; **the first (street) on the left** pega a primeira (rua) à esquerda; **it won't ~ long** não vai demorar muito; **I was quite ~n with it/her** gostei muito daquilo/dela

▸ **take after** VT FUS parecer-se com

▸ **take apart** VT desmontar

▸ **take away** VT (extract) tirar; (carry off) levar; (subtract) subtrair ▪ VI: **to ~ away from** diminuir

▸ **take back** VT (return) devolver; (one's words) retirar

▸ **take down** VT (building) demolir; (dismantle) desmontar; (letter etc) tomar por escrito

▸ **take in** VT (deceive) enganar; (understand) compreender; (include) abranger; (lodger) receber; (orphan, stray dog) acolher; (dress etc) apertar

▸ **take off** VI (Aviat) decolar; (go away) ir-se ▪ VT (remove) tirar; (imitate) imitar

▸ **take on** VT (work) empreender; (employee) empregar; (opponent) desafiar

▸ **take out** VT tirar; (extract) extrair; (invite) acompanhar; (licence) tirar; **to ~ sth out of** tirar algo de; **don't ~ it out on me!** não descarregue em cima de mim!

▸ **take over** VT (business) assumir; (country) tomar posse de ▪ VI: **to ~ over from sb** suceder a alguém

▸ **take to** VT FUS (person) simpatizar com; (activity) afeiçoar-se a; **to ~ to doing sth** criar o hábito de fazer algo

▸ **take up** VT (dress) encurtar; (story) continuar; (occupy: time, space) ocupar; (engage in: hobby etc) dedicar-se a; (accept: offer, challenge) aceitar; (absorb: liquids) absorver ▪ VI: **to ~ up with sb** fazer amizade com alguém; **to ~ sb up on a**

---

suggestion/offer aceitar a oferta/sugestão de alguém sobre algo

takeaway ['teɪkəweɪ] (Brit) ADJ (food) para levar

take-home pay N salário líquido

taken ['teɪkən] PP of **take**

takeoff ['teɪkɔf] N (Aviat) decolagem f

takeout ['teɪkaut] (US) ADJ (food) para levar

takeover ['teɪkəuvəʳ] N (Comm) aquisição f de controle; **takeover bid** N oferta pública de aquisição de controle

takings ['teɪkɪŋz] NPL (Comm) receita, renda

talc [tælk] N (also: **talcum powder**) talco

tale [teɪl] N (story) conto; (account) narrativa; **to tell ~s** (fig: lie) dizer mentiras; (: sneak) dedurar

talent ['tælənt] N talento

talented ['tæləntɪd] ADJ talentoso

talent scout N caçador(a) m/f de talentos

talk [tɔːk] N conversa, fala; (gossip) mexerico, fofocas fpl; (conversation) conversa, conversação f ▪ VI (speak) falar; (chatter) bater papo, conversar; **talks** NPL (Pol etc) negociações fpl; **to give a ~** dar uma palestra; **to ~ about** falar sobre; **~ing of films, have you seen ...?** por falar em filmes, você viu ...?; **to ~ sb into doing sth** convencer alguém a fazer algo; **to ~ sb out of doing sth** dissuadir alguém de fazer algo; **to ~ shop** falar sobre negócios/questões profissionais

▸ **talk over** VT discutir

talkative ['tɔːkətɪv] ADJ loquaz, tagarela

talker ['tɔːkəʳ] N falador(a) m/f

talking point ['tɔːkɪŋ-] N assunto para discussão

talking-to ['tɔːkɪŋ-] N: **to give sb a good ~** passar um sabão em alguém

talk show N (TV, Radio) programa m de entrevistas

tall [tɔːl] ADJ alto; (tree) grande; **to be 6 feet ~** medir 6 pés, ter 6 pés de altura; **how ~ are you?** qual é a sua altura?

tallboy ['tɔːlbɔɪ] (Brit) N cômoda alta

tallness ['tɔːlnɪs] N altura

tall story N estória inverossímil

tally ['tælɪ] N conta ▪ VI: **to ~ (with)** conferir (com); **to keep a ~ of sth** fazer um registro de algo

talon ['tælən] N garra

tambourine [tæmbə'riːn] N tamborim m, pandeiro

tame [teɪm] ADJ (animal, bird) domesticado; (mild) manso; (fig: story, style) sem graça, insípido

tamper ['tæmpəʳ] VI: **to ~ with** mexer em

tampon ['tæmpən] N tampão m higiénico

tan [tæn] N (also: **suntan**) bronzeado ▪ VT bronzear ▪ VI bronzear-se ▪ ADJ (colour) bronzeado, marrom claro; **to get a ~** bronzear-se

tandem ['tændəm] N tandem m; **in ~** junto

tang [tæŋ] N sabor m forte

tangent ['tændʒənt] N (Math) tangente f; **to go off at a ~** (fig) sair pela tangente

tangerine [tændʒə'riːn] N tangerina, mexerica

tangible ['tændʒəbl] ADJ tangível; **~ assets** ativos mpl tangíveis

tangle ['tæŋgl] N emaranhado ■ VT emaranhar; **to get in(to) a ~** meter-se num rolo

tango ['tæŋgəu] N tango

tank [tæŋk] N (water tank) depósito, tanque m; (for fish) aquário; (Mil) tanque m

tankard ['tæŋkəd] N canecão m

tanker ['tæŋkə^r] N (ship) navio-tanque m; (: for oil) petroleiro; (truck) caminhão-tanque m

tanned [tænd] ADJ (skin) moreno, bronzeado

tannin ['tænɪn] N tanino

tanning ['tænɪŋ] N (of leather) curtimento

tannoy® ['tænɔɪ] (Brit) N alto-falante m; **over the tannoy** nos alto-falantes

tantalizing ['tæntəlaɪzɪŋ] ADJ tentador(a)

tantamount ['tæntəmaunt] ADJ: **~ to** equivalente a

tantrum ['tæntrəm] N chilique m, acesso (de raiva); **to throw a ~** ter um chilique or acesso

Tanzania [tænzə'nɪə] N Tanzânia

Tanzanian [tænzə'nɪən] ADJ, N tanzaniano(-a)

tap [tæp] N (on sink etc) torneira; (gentle blow) palmadinha; (gas tap) chave f ■ VT dar palmadinha em, bater de leve; (resources) utilizar, explorar; (telephone) grampear; **on ~** (beer) de barril; (resources) disponível

tap-dancing N sapateado

tape [teɪp] N fita; (also: **magnetic tape**) fita magnética; (sticky tape) fita adesiva ■ VT (record) gravar (em fita); (stick with tape) colar; **on ~** (song etc) em fita; **tape deck** N gravador m, toca-fitas m inv; **tape measure** N fita métrica, trena

taper ['teɪpə^r] N círio ■ VI afilar-se, estreitar-se

tape-record VT gravar (em fita)

tape recorder N gravador m

tape recording N gravação f (em fita)

tapered ['teɪpəd] ADJ afilado

tapering ['teɪpərɪŋ] ADJ afilado

tapestry ['tæpɪstrɪ] N (object) tapete m de parede; (art) tapeçaria

tapeworm ['teɪpwə:m] N solitária

tapioca [tæpɪ'əukə] N tapioca

tappet ['tæpɪt] N (Aut) tucho (BR), ponteiro de válvula (PT)

tar [tɑ:] N alcatrão m; (on road) piche m; **low-/ middle-~ cigarettes** cigarros com baixo/médio teor de alcatrão

tarantula [tə'ræntjulə] N tarântula

tardy ['tɑ:dɪ] ADJ tardio

target ['tɑ:gɪt] N alvo; (fig: objective) objetivo; **to be on ~** (project) progredir segundo as previsões; **target practice** N exercício de tiro ao alvo

tariff ['tærɪf] N tarifa; **tariff barrier** N barreira alfandegária

tarmac ['tɑ:mæk] N (Brit: on road) macadame m; (Aviat) pista ■ VT (Brit) asfaltar

tarnish ['tɑ:nɪʃ] VT empanar o brilho de

tarpaulin [tɑ:'pɔ:lɪn] N lona alcatroada

tarragon ['tærəgən] N estragão m

tart [tɑ:t] N (Culin) torta; (Brit: inf: pej: woman)

piranha ■ ADJ (flavour) ácido, azedo

▶ **tart up** (inf) VT arrumar, dar um jeito em; **to ~ o.s. up** arrumar-se; (pej) empetecar-se

tartan ['tɑ:tn] N pano escocês axadrezado, tartan m ■ ADJ axadrezado

tartar ['tɑ:tə^r] N (on teeth) tártaro

tartar(e) sauce ['tɑ:tə^r-] N molho tártaro

task [tɑ:sk] N tarefa; **to take to ~** repreender; **task force** N (Mil, Police) força-tarefa

taskmaster ['tɑ:skmɑ:stə^r] N: **he's a hard ~** ele é muito exigente

Tasmania [tæz'meɪnɪə] N Tasmânia f

tassel ['tæsl] N borla, pendão m

taste [teɪst] N gosto; (also: **aftertaste**) gosto residual; (sip) golinho; (sample, fig: glimpse, idea) amostra, idéia ■ VT (get flavour of) provar; (test) experimentar ■ VI: **to ~ of** or **like** (fish etc) ter gosto or sabor de; **you can ~ the garlic (in it)** sente-se o gosto de alho; **can I have a ~ of this wine?** posso provar o vinho?; **to have a ~ for** sentir predileção por; **in good/bad ~** de bom/mau gosto; **taste bud** N papila gustativa

tasteful ['teɪstful] ADJ de bom gosto

tastefully ['teɪstfulɪ] ADV com bom gosto

tasteless ['teɪstlɪs] ADJ (food) insípido, insosso; (remark) de mau gosto

tasty ['teɪstɪ] ADJ saboroso, delicioso

tattered ['tætəd] ADJ esfarrapado

tatters ['tætəz] NPL: **in ~** (clothes) em farrapos; (papers etc) em pedaços

tattoo [tə'tu:] N tatuagem f; (spectacle) espetáculo militar ■ VT tatuar

tatty ['tætɪ] (Brit: inf) ADJ (clothes) surrado; (shop, area) mal-cuidado

taught [tɔ:t] PT, PP of **teach**

taunt [tɔ:nt] N zombaria, escárnio ■ VT zombar de, mofar de

Taurus ['tɔ:rəs] N Touro

taut [tɔ:t] ADJ esticado

tavern ['tævən] N taverna

tawdry ['tɔ:drɪ] ADJ de mau gosto, espalhafatoso, berrante

tawny ['tɔ:nɪ] ADJ moreno, trigueiro

tax [tæks] N imposto ■ VT tributar; (fig: test) sobrecarregar; (: patience) esgotar; **before/after ~** antes/depois de impostos; **free of ~** isento de impostos

taxable ['tæksəbl] ADJ (income) tributável

tax allowance N abatimento da renda

taxation [tæk'seɪʃən] N (system) tributação f; (money paid) imposto; **system of ~** sistema fiscal

tax avoidance N evasão f de impostos

tax collector N cobrador(a) m/f de impostos

tax disc (Brit) N (Aut) = plaqueta

tax evasion N sonegação f fiscal

tax exemption N isenção f de impostos

tax exile N pessoa que se expatria para evitar impostos excessivos

tax-free ADJ isento de impostos

tax haven N refúgio fiscal

taxi ['tæksɪ] N táxi m ■ VI (Aviat) taxiar

taxidermist ['tæksɪdə:mɪst] N taxidermista m/f

taxi driver N motorista *m/f* de táxi
taximeter ['tæksɪmiːtəʳ] N taxímetro
tax inspector (*Brit*) N fiscal *m/f* de imposto de renda
taxi rank (*Brit*) N ponto de táxi
taxi stand N ponto de táxi
tax payer N contribuinte *m/f*
tax rebate N devolução *f* de imposto de renda
tax relief N isenção *f* de imposto
tax return N declaração *f* de rendimentos
tax year N ano fiscal, exercício
TB ABBR *of* **tuberculosis**
TD (*US*) N ABBR = **Treasury Department**; (*Football*) = **touchdown**
tea [tiː] N chá *m*; (*Brit*: *meal*) refeigão *f* à noite; **high ~** (*Brit*) ajantarado; **tea bag** N saquinho (*BR*) *or* carteira (*PT*) de chá; **tea break** (*Brit*) N pausa (para o chá)
teacake ['tiːkeɪk] (*Brit*) N pãozinho doce
teach [tiːtʃ] (*pt, pp* **taught**) VT: **to ~ sb sth**, **~ sth to sb** ensinar algo a alguém; (*in school*) lecionar ■ VI ensinar; (*be a teacher*) lecionar; **it taught him a lesson** (*fig*) isto lhe serviu de lição
teacher ['tiːtʃəʳ] N professor(a) *m/f*; **teacher training college** N faculdade *f* de formação de professores
teaching ['tiːtʃɪŋ] N ensino; (*as profession*) magistério; **teaching aids** NPL recursos *mpl* de ensino; **teaching hospital** (*Brit*) N hospital *m* escola; **teaching staff** (*Brit*) N corpo docente
tea cosy N coberta do bule, abafador *m*
teacup ['tiːkʌp] N xícara (*BR*) *or* chávena (*PT*) de chá
teak [tiːk] N (madeira de) teca ■ CPD de teca
tea leaves NPL folhas *fpl* de chá
team [tiːm] N (*Sport*) time *m* (*BR*), equipa (*PT*); (*group*) equipe *f* (*BR*), equipa (*PT*); (*of animals*) parelha
▶ **team up** VI: **to ~ up (with)** agrupar-se (com)
team games NPL jogos *mpl* de equipe
teamwork ['tiːmwəːk] N trabalho de equipe
tea party N chá *m* (*reunião*)
teapot ['tiːpɔt] N bule *m* de chá
tear¹ [tɪəʳ] N lágrima; **in ~s** chorando, em lágrimas; **to burst into ~s** romper em lágrimas
tear² [tɛəʳ] (*pt* **tore**, *pp* **torn**) N rasgão *m* ■ VT rasgar ■ VI rasgar-se; **to ~ to pieces** *or* **to bits** *or* **to shreds** despedaçar, estraçalhar; (*fig*) arrasar com
▶ **tear along** VI (*rush*) precipitar-se
▶ **tear apart** VT rasgar; (*fig*) arrasar
▶ **tear away** VT: **to ~ o.s. away (from sth)** desgrudar-se (de algo)
▶ **tear out** VT (*sheet of paper, cheque*) arrancar
▶ **tear up** VT rasgar
tearaway ['tɛərəweɪ] (*inf*) N bagunceiro(-a)
teardrop ['tɪədrɔp] N lágrima
tearful ['tɪəful] ADJ choroso
tear gas N gás *m* lacrimogênio
tearoom ['tiːruːm] N salão *m* de chá
tease [tiːz] N implicante *m/f* ■ VT implicar com

tea set N aparelho de chá
teashop ['tiːʃɔp] N salão *m* de chá
teaspoon ['tiːspuːn] N colher *f* de chá; (*also*: **teaspoonful**: *as measurement*) (conteúdo de) colher de chá
tea strainer N coador *m* (de chá)
teat [tiːt] N (*of bottle*) bico (de mamadeira)
teatime ['tiːtaɪm] N hora do chá
tea towel N pano de prato
tea urn N samovar *m*
tech [tɛk] (*inf*) N ABBR = **technology**; **technical college**
technical ['tɛknɪkl] ADJ técnico; **technical college** (*Brit*) N escola técnica
technicality [tɛknɪ'kælɪtɪ] N detalhe *m* técnico
technically ['tɛknɪklɪ] ADV tecnicamente
technician [tɛk'nɪʃn] N técnico(-a)
technique [tɛk'niːk] N técnica
technocrat ['tɛknəkræt] N tecnocrata *m/f*
technological [tɛknə'lɔdʒɪkl] ADJ tecnológico
technologist [tɛk'nɔlədʒɪst] N tecnólogo(-a)
technology [tɛk'nɔlədʒɪ] N tecnologia
teddy (*bear*) ['tɛdɪ-] N ursinho de pelúcia
tedious ['tiːdɪəs] ADJ maçante, chato
tedium ['tiːdɪəm] N tédio
tee [tiː] N (*Golf*) tee *m*
teem [tiːm] VI abundar, pulular; **to ~ with** abundar em; **it is ~ing (with rain)** está chovendo a cântaros
teenage ['tiːneɪdʒ] ADJ (*fashions etc*) de *or* para adolescentes
teenager ['tiːneɪdʒəʳ] N adolescente *m/f*, jovem *m/f*
teens [tiːnz] NPL: **to be in one's ~** estar entre os 13 e 19 anos, estar na adolescência
tee-shirt N = **T-shirt**
teeter ['tiːtəʳ] VI balançar-se
teeth [tiːθ] NPL *of* **tooth**
teethe [tiːð] VI começar a ter dentes
teething ring ['tiːðɪŋ-] N mastigador *m* para a dentição
teething troubles ['tiːðɪŋ-] NPL (*fig*) dificuldades *fpl* iniciais
teetotal ['tiː'təutl] ADJ (*person*) abstêmio
teetotaller ['tiː'təutləʳ] (*US* **teetotaler**) N abstêmio(-a)
TEFL ['tɛfl] N ABBR = **Teaching of English as a Foreign Language**
Teheran [tɛə'rɑːn] N Teerã (*BR*), Teerão (*PT*)
tel. ABBR (= *telephone*) tel
Tel Aviv ['tɛlə'viːv] N Telavive
telecast ['tɛlɪkɑːst] (*irreg: like* **cast**) VT televisionar, transmitir por televisão
telecommunications [tɛlɪkəmjuːnɪ'keɪʃənz] N telecomunicações *fpl*
teleconferencing ['tɛlɪkɔnfərənsɪŋ] N teleconferência *f*
telegram ['tɛlɪɡræm] N telegrama *m*
telegraph ['tɛlɪɡrɑːf] N telégrafo
telegraphic [tɛlɪ'ɡræfɪk] ADJ telegráfico
telegraph pole N poste *m* telegráfico
telegraph wire N fio telegráfico

telepathic [tɛlɪ'pæθɪk] ADJ telepático

telepathy [tə'lɛpəθɪ] N telepatia

telephone ['tɛlɪfəun] N telefone *m* ◼ VT (*person*) telefonar para; (*message*) telefonar; **to be on the ~** (*Brit*), **to have a ~** (*subscriber*) ter telefone; **to be on the ~** (*be speaking*) estar falando no telefone; **telephone booth** (BRIT **telephone box**) N cabine *f* telefônica; **telephone call** N telefonema *m*; **telephone directory** N lista telefônica, catálogo (BR); **telephone exchange** N estação *f* telefônica; **telephone kiosk** (*Brit*) N cabine *f* telefônica; **telephone number** N (número de) telefone *m*; **telephone operator** N telefonista *m/f*; **telephone tapping** [-'tæpɪŋ] N escuta telefônica

telephonist [tə'lɛfənɪst] (*Brit*) N telefonista *m/f*

telephoto ['tɛlɪfəutəu] ADJ: **~ lens** teleobjetivo

teleprinter ['tɛlɪprɪntəʳ] N teletipo

Teleprompter® ['tɛlɪprɔmptəʳ] (*US*) N ponto mecânico

telesales ['tɛlɪseɪlz] NPL televendas *fpl*

telescope ['tɛlɪskəup] N telescópio ◼ VT, VI abrir (*or* fechar) como um telescópio

telescopic [tɛlɪ'skɔpɪk] ADJ telescópico; (*legs, aerial*) desmontável

Teletext® ['tɛlətɛks] N (*Tel*) videotexto

televiewer ['tɛlɪvjuːəʳ] N telespectador(a) *m/f*

televise ['tɛlɪvaɪz] VT televisar, televisionar

television ['tɛlɪvɪʒən] N televisão *f*; **on ~** na televisão; **television licence** (*Brit*) N licença para utilizar um televisor; **television programme** N programa *m* de televisão; **television set** N (aparelho de) televisão *f*, televisor *m*

teleworking ['tɛlɪwɜːkɪŋ] N teletrabalho *m*

telex ['tɛlɛks] N telex *m* ◼ VT (*message*) enviar por telex, telexar; (*person*) mandar um telex para ◼ VI enviar um telex

tell [tɛl] (*pt, pp* **told**) VT dizer; (*relate: story*) contar; (*distinguish*): **to ~ sth from** distinguir algo de ◼ VI (*have effect*) ter efeito; (*talk*): **to ~ (of)** falar (de *or* em); **to ~ sb to do sth** dizer para alguém fazer algo; (*order*) mandar alguém fazer algo; **to ~ sb about sth** falar a alguém de algo; (*what happened*) contar algo a alguém; **to ~ the time** (*know how to*) dizer as horas; (*clock*) marcar as horas; **can you ~ me the time?** pode me dizer a hora?; **(I) ~ you what ...** escuta ...; **I can't ~ them apart** não consigo diferenciar um do outro; **to ~ the difference** sentir a diferença; **how can you ~?** como você sabe?
▶ **tell off** VT repreender
▶ **tell on** VT FUS (*inform against*) delatar, dedurar

teller ['tɛləʳ] N (*in bank*) caixa *m/f*

telling ['tɛlɪŋ] ADJ (*remark, detail*) revelador(a)

telltale ['tɛlteɪl] ADJ (*sign*) revelador(a)

telly ['tɛlɪ] (*Brit: inf*) N ABBR = **television**

temerity [tə'mɛrɪtɪ] N temeridade *f*

temp [tɛmp] (*Brit: inf*) ABBR = **temporary** ◼ N temporário(-a) ◼ VI trabalhar como temporário(-a)

temper ['tɛmpəʳ] N (*nature*) temperamento; (*mood*) humor *m*; (*bad temper*) mau gênio; (*fit*

of anger) cólera; (*of child*) birra ◼ VT (*moderate*) moderar; **to be in a ~** estar de mau humor; **to lose one's ~** perder a paciência *or* a calma, ficar zangado; **to keep one's ~** controlar-se

temperament ['tɛmprəmənt] N (*nature*) temperamento

temperamental [tɛmprə'mɛntl] ADJ temperamental

temperance ['tɛmpərəns] N moderação *f*; (*in drinking*) sobriedade *f*

temperate ['tɛmprət] ADJ moderado; (*climate*) temperado

temperature ['tɛmprətʃəʳ] N temperatura; **to have** *or* **run a ~** ter febre; **temperature chart** N (*Med*) tabela de temperatura

tempered ['tɛmpəd] ADJ (*steel*) temperado

tempest ['tɛmpɪst] N tempestade *f*

tempestuous [tɛm'pɛstjuəs] ADJ (*relationship*) tempestuoso

tempi ['tɛmpiː] NPL *of* **tempo**

template ['tɛmplɪt] N molde *m*

temple ['tɛmpl] N (*building*) templo; (*Anat*) têmpora

templet ['tɛmplɪt] N = **template**

tempo ['tɛmpəu] (*pl* **tempi**) N tempo; (*fig: of life etc*) ritmo

temporal ['tɛmpərəl] ADJ temporal

temporarily ['tɛmpərərɪlɪ] ADV temporariamente; (*closed*) provisoriamente

temporary ['tɛmpərərɪ] ADJ temporário; (*passing*) transitório; **~ secretary** secretária temporária; **~ teacher** professor suplente

temporize ['tɛmpəraɪz] VI temporizar

tempt [tɛmpt] VT tentar; **to ~ sb into doing sth** tentar *or* induzir alguém a fazer algo; **to be ~ed to do sth** ser tentado a fazer algo

temptation [tɛmp'teɪʃən] N tentação *f*

tempting ['tɛmptɪŋ] ADJ tentador(a)

ten [tɛn] NUM dez ◼ N: **~s of thousands** milhares *mpl* e milhares; *see also* **five**

tenable ['tɛnəbl] ADJ sustentável

tenacious [tə'neɪʃəs] ADJ tenaz

tenacity [tə'næsɪtɪ] N tenacidade *f*

tenancy ['tɛnənsɪ] N aluguel *m*; (*of house*) locação *f*

tenant ['tɛnənt] N inquilino(-a), locatário(-a)

tend [tɛnd] VT (*sick etc*) cuidar de; (*machine*) vigiar ◼ VI: **to ~ to do sth** tender a fazer algo

tendency ['tɛndənsɪ] N tendência

tender ['tɛndəʳ] ADJ (*person, heart, core*) terno; (*age*) tenro; (*delicate*) delicado; (*sore*) sensível, dolorido; (*meat*) macio ◼ N (*Comm: offer*) oferta, proposta; (*money*): **legal ~** moeda corrente *or* legal ◼ VT oferecer; **to ~ one's resignation** pedir demissão; **to put in a ~ (for)** apresentar uma proposta (para); **to put work out to ~** (*Brit*) abrir concorrência para uma obra

tenderize ['tɛndəraɪz] VT (*Culin*) amaciar

tenderly ['tɛndəlɪ] ADV afetuosamente

tenderness ['tɛndənɪs] N ternura; (*of meat*) maciez *f*

tendon ['tɛndən] N tendão *m*

tenement ['tɛnəmənt] N conjunto habitacional

Tenerife [tɛnə'riːf] N Tenerife (no article)

tenet ['tɛnət] N princípio

tenner ['tɛnər] (Brit: inf) N nota de dez libras

tennis ['tɛnɪs] N tênis m ■ CPD (match, racket etc) de tênis; **tennis ball** N bola de tênis; **tennis court** N quadra de tênis; **tennis elbow** N (Med) sinovite f do cotovelo; **tennis player** N jogador(a) m/f de tênis; **tennis racket** N raquete f de tênis; **tennis shoes** NPL tênis m

tenor ['tɛnər] N (Mus) tenor m; (of speech etc) teor m

tenpin bowling ['tɛnpɪn-] (Brit) N boliche m com 10 paus

tense [tɛns] ADJ tenso; (muscle) rígido, teso ■ N (Ling) tempo ■ VT (tighten: muscles) retesar

tenseness ['tɛnsnɪs] N tensão f

tension ['tɛnʃən] N tensão f

tent [tɛnt] N tenda, barraca

tentacle ['tɛntəkl] N tentáculo

tentative ['tɛntətɪv] ADJ (conclusion) provisório, tentativo; (person) hesitante, indeciso

tenterhooks ['tɛntəhuks] NPL: **on** ~ em suspense

tenth [tɛnθ] NUM décimo; see also **fifth**

tent peg N estaca

tent pole N pau m

tenuous ['tɛnjuəs] ADJ tênue

tenure ['tɛnjuər] N (of property) posse f; (of job) estabilidade f

tepid ['tɛpɪd] ADJ tépido, morno

term [tə:m] N (Comm) prazo; (word, expression) termo, expressão f; (period) período; (Sch) trimestre m; (Law) sessão f ■ VT denominar; **terms** NPL (conditions) condições fpl; (Comm) cláusulas fpl, termos mpl; **in ~s of ...** em função de ...; ~ **of imprisonment** pena de prisão; **his ~ of office** seu mandato; **in the short/long ~** a curto/longo prazo; **to be on good ~s with sb** dar-se bem com alguém; **to come to ~s with** (person) chegar a um acordo com; (problem) aceitar

terminal ['tə:mɪnl] ADJ incurável ■ N (Elec) borne m; (Brit: also: **air terminal**) terminal m; (for oil, ore etc, also: Comput) terminal m; (Brit: also: **coach terminal**) estação f rodoviária

terminate ['tə:mɪneɪt] VT terminar ■ VI: **to ~ in** acabar em; **to ~ a pregnancy** fazer um aborto

termination [tə:mɪ'neɪʃən] N término; (of contract) rescisão f; ~ **of pregnancy** (Med) interrupção da gravidez

termini ['tə:mɪnaɪ] NPL of **terminus**

terminology [tə:mɪ'nɔlədʒɪ] N terminologia

terminus ['tə:mɪnəs] (pl **termini**) N terminal m

termite ['tə:maɪt] N cupim m

Ter(r). ABBR = **terrace**

terrace ['tɛrəs] N terraço; (Brit: row of houses) lance m de casas; **the terraces** NPL (Brit: Sport) a arquibancada (BR), a geral (PT)

terraced ['tɛrəst] ADJ (house) ladeado por outras casas; (garden) em dois níveis

terracotta ['tɛrə'kɔtə] N terracota

terrain [tɛ'reɪn] N terreno

terrible ['tɛrɪbl] ADJ terrível, horroroso; (conditions) precário; (inf: awful) terrível

terribly ['tɛrɪblɪ] ADV terrivelmente; (very badly) pessimamente

terrier ['tɛrɪər] N terrier m

terrific [tə'rɪfɪk] ADJ terrível, magnífico; (wonderful) maravilhoso, sensacional

terrify ['tɛrɪfaɪ] VT apavorar

territorial [tɛrɪ'tɔ:rɪəl] ADJ territorial; **territorial waters** NPL águas fpl territoriais

territory ['tɛrɪtərɪ] N território

terror ['tɛrər] N terror m

terrorism ['tɛrərɪzəm] N terrorismo

terrorist ['tɛrərɪst] N terrorista m/f

terrorize ['tɛrəraɪz] VT aterrorizar

terse [tə:s] ADJ (style) conciso, sucinto; (reply) brusco

tertiary ['tə:ʃərɪ] ADJ terciário; ~ **education** (Brit) ensino superior

Terylene® ['tɛrɪliːn] (Brit) N tergal® m

TESL ['tɛsl] N ABBR = **Teaching of English as a Second Language**

test [tɛst] N (trial, check) prova, ensaio; (: of goods in factory) controle m; (of courage etc, Chem) prova; (Med) exame m; (exam) teste m, prova; (also: **driving test**) exame de motorista ■ VT testar, pôr à prova; **to put sth to the** ~ pôr algo à prova

testament ['tɛstəmənt] N testamento; **the Old/New T~** o Velho/Novo Testamento

test ban N (also: **nuclear test ban**) proibição f de testes nucleares

test case N (Law, fig) caso exemplar

test flight N teste m de vôo

testicle ['tɛstɪkl] N testículo

testify ['tɛstɪfaɪ] VI (Law) depor, testemunhar; **to** ~ **to sth** (Law) atestar algo; (gen) testemunhar algo

testimonial [tɛstɪ'məunɪəl] N (reference) carta de recomendação; (gift) obséquio, tributo

testimony ['tɛstɪmənɪ] N (Law) testemunho, depoimento; **to be (a)** ~ **to** ser uma prova de

testing ['tɛstɪŋ] ADJ (situation, period) difícil; **testing ground** N campo de provas

test match N (Cricket, Rugby) jogo internacional

test paper N (Sch) prova escrita

test pilot N piloto de prova

test tube N proveta, tubo de ensaio

test-tube baby N bebê m de proveta

testy ['tɛstɪ] ADJ rabugento, irritável

tetanus ['tɛtənəs] N tétano

tetchy ['tɛtʃɪ] ADJ irritável

tether ['tɛðər] VT amarrar ■ N: **at the end of one's** ~ a ponto de perder a paciência or as estribeiras

text [tɛkst] N texto; (also: **text message**) mensagem f de texto; (fam) torpedo

textbook ['tɛkstbuk] N livro didático, (Sch) livro escolar

textiles ['tɛkstaɪlz] NPL têxteis mpl; (textile industry) indústria têxtil

texture ['tɛkstʃəʳ] N textura
TGIF (inf) ABBR = **thank God it's Friday**
TGWU (Brit) N ABBR (= Transport and General Workers' Union) sindicato dos transportadores
Thai [taɪ] ADJ tailandês(-esa) ■ N tailandês(-esa) m/f; (Ling) tailandês m
Thailand ['taɪlænd] N Tailândia
thalidomide® [θəˈlɪdəmaɪd] N talidomida®
Thames [tɛmz] N: **the** ~ o Tâmisa (BR), o Tamisa (PT)

○ KEYWORD

than [ðæn, ðən] CONJ (in comparisons) do que; **more than 10** mais de 10; **I have more/less than you** tenho mais/menos do que você; **she has more apples than pears** ela tem mais maçãs do que peras; **she is older than you think** ela é mais velha do que você pensa; **than once** mais de uma vez

thank [θæŋk] VT agradecer; ~ **you (very much)** muito obrigado(-a); ~ **God** graças a Deus; **~s to** graças a; **to ~ sb for sth** agradecer a alguém (por) algo; **to say ~ you** agradecer
thankful ['θæŋkful] ADJ: ~ **(for)** agradecido (por); ~ **that** (relieved) aliviado que
thankfully ['θæŋkfəlɪ] ADV (gratefully) agradecidamente; (fortunately) felizmente
thankless ['θæŋklɪs] ADJ ingrato
thanks [θæŋks] NPL agradecimentos mpl; (to God etc) graças fpl ■ EXCL obrigado(-a)!; ~ **to** graças a
Thanksgiving (Day) ['θæŋksgɪvɪŋ-] N Dia m de Ação de Graças

● THANKSGIVING DAY

● O feriado de Ação de graças Thanksgiving
● Day nos Estados Unidos, quarta quinta-
● feira do mês de novembro, é o dia em que
● se comemora a boa colheita feita pelos
● peregrinos originários da Grã-Bretanha
● em 1621; tradicionalmente, é um dia em
● que se agradece a Deus e se organiza um
● grande banquete. Uma festa semelhante é
● celebrada no Canadá na segunda segunda-
● feira de outubro.

○ KEYWORD

that [ðæt, ðət] (pl **those**) ADJ (demonstrative) esse/essa; (more remote) aquele/aquela; **that man/woman/book** aquele homem/aquela mulher/aquele livro; **leave these books on the table** deixe aqueles livros na mesa; **that one** esse/essa; **that one over there** aquele lá; **I want this one, not that one** quero este, não esse ■ PRON **1** (demonstrative) esse/essa, aquele/aquela; (neuter) isso, aquilo; **who's/what's that?** quem é?/o que é isso?; **is that you?** é você?; **I prefer this to that** eu prefiro isto a aquilo; **that's my house** aquela é a minha

casa; **that's what he said** foi isso o que ele disse; **that is (to say)** isto é, quer dizer
2 (relative: direct: thing, person) que; (: person) quem; (relative: indirect: thing, person) o(-a) qual sg, os/as quais pl; (: person) quem; **the book (that) I read** o livro que eu li; **the books that are in the library** os livros que estão na biblioteca; **the man (that) I saw** o homem que eu vi; **all (that) I have** tudo o que eu tenho; **the box (that) I put it in** a caixa na qual eu botei-o; **the man (that) I spoke to** o homem com quem or o qual falei
3 (relative: of time): **on the day that he came** no dia em que ele veio
■ CONJ que; **she suggested that I phone you** ela sugeriu que eu telefonasse para você
■ ADV (demonstrative): **I can't work that much** não posso trabalhar tanto; **I didn't realize it was that bad** não pensei que fôsse tão ruim; **that high** dessa altura, até essa altura

thatched [θætʃt] ADJ (roof) de sapê; ~ **cottage** chalé m com telhado de sapê or de colmo
thaw [θɔ:] N degelo ■ VI (ice) derreter-se; (food) descongelar-se ■ VT (food) descongelar; **it's ~ing** (weather) degela

○ KEYWORD

the [ði:, ðə] DEF ART **1** (gen: singular) o (a); (: plural) os (as); **the history of France** a história da França; **the books/children are in the library** os livros/as crianças estão na biblioteca; **she put it on the table** ela colocou-o na mesa; **he took it from the drawer** ele tirou isto da gaveta; **to play the piano/violin** tocar piano/violino; **I'm going to the cinema** vou ao cinema
2 (+ adj to form n): **the rich and the poor** os ricos e os pobres; **to attempt the impossible** tentar o impossível
3 (in titles): **Richard the Second** Ricardo II; **Peter the Great** Pedro o Grande
4 (in comparisons: + adv): **the more he works the more he earns** quanto mais ele trabalha, mais ele ganha

theatre ['θɪətəʳ] (US **theater**) N teatro; (Med: also: operating theatre) sala de operação
theatre-goer ['θɪətəgəuəʳ] N freqüentador(a) m/f de teatro
theatrical [θɪˈætrɪkl] ADJ teatral; ~ **company** companhia de teatro
theft [θɛft] N roubo
their [ðɛəʳ] ADJ seu/sua, deles/delas
theirs [ðɛəz] PRON (o) seu/(a) sua; **a friend of ~** um amigo seu/deles; **it's ~** é deles
them [ðɛm, ðəm] PRON (direct) os/as; (indirect) lhes; (stressed, after prep) a eles(-a) elas; **I see ~** eu os vejo; **give ~ the book** dê o livro a eles; **give me some of ~** me dê alguns deles
theme [θi:m] N tema m; **theme song** N tema m

musical

themselves [ðəm'sɛlvz] PRON (*subject*) eles mesmos/elas mesmas; (*complement*) se; (*after prep*) si (mesmos/as)

then [ðɛn] ADV (*at that time*) então; (*next*) em seguida; (*later*) logo, depois; (*and also*) além disso ■ CONJ (*therefore*) então, nesse caso, portanto ■ ADJ: **the ~ president** o então presidente; **by ~** (*past*) até então; (*future*) até lá; **from ~ on** a partir de então; **before ~** antes (disso); **until ~** até lá; **and ~ what?** e então?, e daí?; **what do you want me to do ~?** (*afterwards*) o que você quer que eu faça depois?; (*in that case*) então, o que você quer que eu faça?

theologian [θɪə'laudʒən] N teólogo(-a)

theological [θɪə'lɔdʒɪkl] ADJ teológico

theology [θɪ'ɔlədʒɪ] N teologia

theorem ['θɪərəm] N teorema *m*

theoretical [θɪə'rɛtɪkl] ADJ teórico

theoretically [θɪə'rɛtɪklɪ] ADV teoricamente

theorize ['θɪəraɪz] VI teorizar, elaborar uma teoria

theory ['θɪərɪ] N teoria; **in ~** em teoria, teoricamente

therapeutic(al) [θɛrə'pju:tɪk(l)] ADJ terapêutico

therapist ['θɛrəpɪst] N terapeuta *m/f*

therapy ['θɛrəpɪ] N terapia

 KEYWORD

there [ðɛəʳ] ADV **1: there is, there are** há, tem; **there are 3 of them** (*people, things*) há 3 deles; **there is no-one here/no bread left** não tem ninguém aqui/não tem mais pão; **there has been an accident** houve um acidente **2** (*referring to place*) aí, ali, lá; **put it in/on/up/down there** põe isto lá dentro/cima/em cima/embaixo; **I want that book there** quero aquele livro lá; **there he is!** lá está ele! **3: there, there!** (*esp to child*) calma!

thereabouts ['ðɛərəbauts] ADV por aí; (*amount*) aproximadamente

thereafter [ðɛər'ɑ:ftəʳ] ADV depois disso

thereby ['ðɛəbaɪ] ADV assim, deste modo

therefore ['ðɛəfɔ:] ADV portanto

there's [ðɛəz] = **there is; there has**

thereupon [ðɛərə'pɔn] ADV (*at that point*) após o que; (*formal: on that subject*) a respeito

thermal ['θə:ml] ADJ térmico; **~ paper/printer** papel térmico/impressora térmica

thermodynamics [θə:mədaɪ'næmɪks] N termodinâmica

thermometer [θə'mɔmɪtəʳ] N termômetro

thermonuclear [θə:məu'nju:klɪəʳ] ADJ termonuclear

Thermos® ['θə:məs] N (*also:* **Thermos flask**) garrafa térmica (BR), termo (PT)

thermostat ['θə:məustæt] N termostato

thesaurus [θɪ'sɔ:rəs] N tesouro, dicionário de sinônimos

these [ði:z] PL ADJ, PRON estes/estas

theses ['θi:si:z] NPL *of* **thesis**

thesis ['θi:sɪs] (*pl* **theses**) N tese *f*

they [ðeɪ] PL PRON eles/elas; **~ say that ...** (*it is said that*) diz-se que ..., dizem que ...

they'd [ðeɪd] = **they had; they would**

they'll [ðeɪl] = **they shall; they will**

they're [ðeɪəʳ] = **they are**

they've [ðeɪv] = **they have**

thick [θɪk] ADJ (*in shape*) espesso; (*mud, fog, forest*) denso; (*sauce*) grosso; (*dense*) denso, compacto; (*stupid*) burro ■ N: **in the ~ of the battle** em plena batalha; **it's 20 cm ~** tem 20 cm de espessura

thicken ['θɪkən] VI (*fog*) adensar-se; (*plot etc*) complicar-se ■ VT (*sauce etc*) engrossar

thicket ['θɪkɪt] N matagal *m*

thickly ['θɪklɪ] ADV (*spread*) numa camada espessa; (*cut*) em fatias grossas

thickness ['θɪknɪs] N espessura, grossura

thickset [θɪk'sɛt] ADJ troncudo

thick-skinned [-'skɪnd] ADJ (*fig*) insensível, indiferente

thief |θi:f| (*pl* **thieves**) N ladrão/ladra *m/f*

thieves [θi:vz] NPL *of* **thief**

thieving ['θi:vɪŋ] N roubo, furto

thigh [θaɪ] N coxa

thighbone ['θaɪbəun] N fêmur *m*

thimble ['θɪmbl] N dedal *m*

thin [θɪn] ADJ magro; (*slice, line, book*) fino; (*light*) leve; (*hair*) ralo; (*crowd*) pequeno; (*fog*) pouco denso; (*soup, sauce*) aguado ■ VT (*also:* **thin down:** *sauce, paint*) diluir ■ VI (*fog*) rarefazer-se; (*also:* **thin out:** *crowd*) dispersar; **his hair is ~** o cabelo dele está caindo

thing [θɪŋ] N coisa; (*object*) negócio; (*matter*) assunto, negócio; (*mania*) mania; **things** NPL (*belongings*) pertences *mpl*; **to have a ~ about sb/sth** ser vidrado em alguém/algo; **the best ~ would be to ...** o melhor seria ...; **how are ~s?** como vai?, tudo bem?; **first ~ (in the morning)** de manhã, antes de mais nada; **last ~ (at night), he ...** logo antes de dormir, ele ...; **the ~ is ...** é que ..., o negócio é o seguinte ...; **for one ~** primeiro; **she's got a ~ about ...** ela detesta ...; **poor ~!** coitadinho(-a)!

think [θɪŋk] (*pt, pp* **thought**) VI pensar; (*believe*) achar ■ VT pensar, achar; (*imagine*) imaginar; **what did you ~ of them?** o que você achou deles?; **to ~ about sth/sb** pensar em algo/alguém; **I'll ~ about it** vou pensar sobre isso; **to ~ of doing sth** pensar em fazer algo; **I ~ so/not** acho que sim/não; **to ~ well of sb** fazer bom juízo de alguém; **~ again!** pensa bem!; **to ~ aloud** pensar em voz alta

▶ **think out** VT (*plan*) arquitetar; (*solution*) descobrir

▶ **think over** VT refletir sobre, meditar sobre; **I'd like to ~ things over** eu gostaria de pensar sobre isso com cuidado

▶ **think through** VT considerar todos os aspectos de

▶ **think up** VT inventar, bolar

thinking ['θɪŋkɪŋ] N: **to my (way of)** ~ na minha opinião

think tank N comissão f de peritos

thinly ['θɪnlɪ] ADV (cut) em fatias finas; (spread) numa camada fina

thinness ['θɪnnɪs] N magreza

third [θəːd] ADJ terceiro ■ N terceiro(-a); (fraction) terço; (Aut) terceira; (Sch: degree) terceira categoria; see also **fifth**

third-degree burns NPL queimaduras fpl de terceiro grau

thirdly ['θəːdlɪ] ADV em terceiro lugar

third party insurance N seguro contra terceiros

third-rate ADJ medíocre

Third World N: **the** ~ o Terceiro Mundo

thirst [θəːst] N sede f

thirsty ['θəːstɪ] ADJ (person) sedento, com sede; (work) que dá sede; **to be** ~ estar com sede

thirteen ['θəː'tiːn] NUM treze; see also **five**

thirteenth [θəː'tiːnθ] NUM décimo terceiro; see also **fifth**

thirtieth ['θəːtɪəθ] NUM trigésimo; see also **fifth**

thirty ['θəːtɪ] NUM trinta; see also **fifty**

O KEYWORD

this [ðɪs] (pl **these**) ADJ (demonstrative) este/esta; **this man/woman/book** este homem/esta mulher/este livro; **these people/children/ records** estas pessoas/crianças/estes discos; **this one** este aqui

■ PRON (demonstrative) este/esta; (neuter) isto; **who/what is this?** quem é esse?/o que é isso?; **this is where I live** é aqui que eu moro; **this is Mr Brown** (in photo, introduction) este é o Sr Brown; (on phone) aqui é o Sr Brown

■ ADV (demonstrative): **this high** desta altura; **this long** deste comprimento; **we can't stop now we've gone this far** não podemos parar agora que fomos tão longe

thistle ['θɪsl] N cardo

thong [θɒŋ] N correia, tira de couro

thorn [θɔːn] N espinho

thorny ['θɔːnɪ] ADJ espinhoso

thorough ['θʌrə] ADJ (search) minucioso; (knowledge, research: person: methodical) metódico, profundo; (work) meticuloso; (cleaning) completo

thoroughbred ['θʌrəbrɛd] ADJ (horse) de puro sangue

thoroughfare ['θʌrəfɛəʳ] N via, passagem f; **"no** ~**"** "passagem proibida"

thoroughly ['θʌrəlɪ] ADV (examine, study) minuciosamente; (search) profundamente; (wash) completamente; (very) muito; **he** ~ **agreed** concordou completamente

thoroughness ['θʌrənɪs] N (of person) meticulosidade f; (of search etc) minuciosidade f

those [ðəuz] PL PRON, ADJ esses/essas; (more remote) aqueles/aquelas

though [ðəu] CONJ embora, se bem que ■ ADV no entanto; **even** ~ mesmo que; **it's not easy,** ~ se bem que não é fácil

thought [θɔːt] PT, PP of **think** ■ N pensamento; (idea) idéia; (opinion) opinião f; (reflection) reflexão f; (intention) intenção f; **after much** ~ depois de muito pensar; **I've just had a** ~ acabei de pensar em alguma coisa; **to give sth some** ~ pensar sobre algo

thoughtful ['θɔːtful] ADJ pensativo; (serious) sério; (considerate) atencioso

thoughtfully ['θɔːtfəlɪ] ADV pensativamente; atenciosamente

thoughtless ['θɔːtlɪs] ADJ (behaviour) desatencioso; (words, person) inconseqüente

thoughtlessly ['θɔːtlɪslɪ] ADV desconsideradamente

thousand ['θauzənd] NUM mil; **two** ~ dois mil; ~**s (of)** milhares mpl (de)

thousandth ['θauzənθ] ADJ milésimo

thrash [θræʃ] VT surrar, malhar; (defeat) derrotar

▶ **thrash about** VI debater-se

▶ **thrash out** VT discutir exaustivamente

thrashing ['θræʃɪŋ] N: **to give sb a** ~ dar uma surra em alguém

thread [θrɛd] N fio, linha; (of screw) rosca ■ VT (needle) enfiar; **to** ~ **one's way between** passar por

threadbare ['θrɛdbɛəʳ] ADJ surrado, puído

threat [θrɛt] N ameaça; **to be under** ~ **of** estar sob ameaça de

threaten ['θrɛtən] VI ameaçar ■ VT: **to** ~ **sb with sth/to do** ameaçar alguém com algo/de fazer

threatening ['θrɛtnɪŋ] ADJ ameaçador(a)

three [θriː] NUM três; see also **five**

three-dimensional ADJ tridimensional, em três dimensões

threefold ['θriːfəuld] ADV: **to increase** ~ triplicar

three-piece suit N terno (3 peças) (BR), fato de 3 peças (PT)

three-piece suite N conjunto de sofá e duas poltronas

three-ply ADJ (wool) triple, com três fios; (wood) com três espessuras

three-quarters NPL três quartos mpl; ~ **full** cheio até os três quartos

three-wheeler N (car) carro de três rodas

thresh [θrɛʃ] VT (Agr) debulhar

threshing machine ['θrɛʃɪŋ-] N debulhadora

threshold ['θrɛʃhəuld] N limiar m; **to be on the** ~ **of** (fig) estar no limiar de; **threshold agreement** N (Econ) acordo sobre a indexação de salários

threw [θruː] PT of **throw**

thrift [θrɪft] N economia, poupança

thrifty ['θrɪftɪ] ADJ econômico, frugal

thrill [θrɪl] N (excitement) emoção f; (shudder) estremecimento ■ VI vibrar ■ VT emocionar, vibrar; **to be** ~**ed** (with gift etc) estar emocionado

thriller ['θrɪləʳ] N romance m (or filme m) de

suspense

thrilling ['θrılıŋ] ADJ (book, play etc) excitante; (news, discovery) emocionante

thrive [θraɪv] (pt **throve**, pp **thriven**) VI (grow) vicejar; (do well) prosperar, florescer; **to ~ on sth** realizar-se ao fazer algo

thriven ['θrɪvn] PP of **thrive**

thriving ['θraɪvɪŋ] ADJ próspero

throat [θrəut] N garganta; **to have a sore ~** estar com dor de garganta

throb [θrɔb] N (of heart) batida; (of engine) vibração f; (of pain) latejo ■ VI (heart) bater, palpitar; (pain) dar pontadas; (engine) vibrar; **my head is ~bing** minha cabeça está latejando

throes [θrəuz] NPL: **in the ~ of** no meio de

thrombosis [θrɔm'bəusıs] N trombose f

throne [θrəun] N trono

throng [θrɔŋ] N multidão f ■ VT apinhar, apinhar-se em

throttle ['θrɔtl] N (Aut) acelerador m ■ VT estrangular

through [θruː] PREP por, através de; (time) durante; (by means of) por meio de, de, intermédio de; (owing to) devido a ■ ADJ (ticket, train) direto ■ ADV através; **(from) Monday ~ Friday** (US) de segunda a sexta; **to let sb ~** deixar alguém passar; **to put sb ~ to sb** (Tel) ligar alguém com alguém; **to be ~** (Tel) estar na linha; (have finished) acabar; **"no ~ traffic"** (US) "trânsito proibido"; **"no ~ road"** "rua sem saída"; **I'm halfway ~ the book** estou na metade do livro

throughout [θruː'aut] PREP (place) por todo(-a); (time) durante todo(-a) ■ ADV por or em todas as partes

throughput ['θruːput] N (of goods, materials) quantidade f tratada; (Comput) capacidade f de processamento

throve [θrəuv] PT of **thrive**

throw [θrəu] (pt **threw**, pp **thrown**) N arremesso, tiro; (Sport) lançamento ■ VT jogar, atirar; (Sport) lançar; (rider) derrubar; (fig) desconcertar; (pot) afeiçoar; **to ~ a party** dar uma festa
▶ **throw about** VT (litter etc) esparramar
▶ **throw around** VT (litter etc) esparramar
▶ **throw away** VT (dispose of) jogar fora; (waste) desperdiçar
▶ **throw in** VT (Sport) pôr em jogo
▶ **throw off** VT desfazer-se de; (habit, cold) livrar-se
▶ **throw out** VT (person) expulsar; (rubbish) jogar fora; (idea) rejeitar
▶ **throw together** VT (clothes, meal etc) arranjar às pressas
▶ **throw up** VI vomitar, botar para fora

throwaway ['θrəuəweı] ADJ descartável; (line, remark) gratuito

throwback ['θrəubæk] N: **it's a ~ to** é um retrocesso a

throw-in N (Sport) lance m

thru [θruː] (US) PREP, ADJ, ADV = **through**

thrush [θrʌʃ] N (Zool) tordo; (Med) monília

thrust [θrʌst] (pt, pp **thrust**) N impulso; (Tech) empuxo ■ VT empurrar; (push in) enfiar, meter

thrusting ['θrʌstıŋ] ADJ dinâmico

thud [θʌd] N baque m, som m surdo

thug [θʌg] N (criminal) criminoso(-a); (pej) facínora m/f

thumb [θʌm] N (Anat) polegar m; (inf) dedão m ■ VT (book) folhear; **to ~ a lift** pegar carona (BR), arranjar uma boléia (PT); **to give sb/sth the ~s up** (approve) dar luz verde a alguém/algo
▶ **thumb through** VT FUS folhear

thumb index N índice m de dedo

thumbnail ['θʌmneıl] N unha do polegar; **thumbnail sketch** N descrição f resumida

thumbtack ['θʌmtæk] (US) N percevejo, tachinha

thump [θʌmp] N murro, pancada; (sound) baque m ■ VT dar um murro em ■ VI bater

thunder ['θʌndər] N trovão m; (sudden noise) trovoada; (of applause etc) estrondo ■ VI trovejar; (train etc): **to ~ past** passar como um raio

thunderbolt ['θʌndəbəult] N raio

thunderclap ['θʌndəklæp] N estampido do trovão

thunderous ['θʌndərəs] ADJ estrondoso

thunderstorm ['θʌndəstɔːm] N tempestade f com trovoada, temporal m

thunderstruck ['θʌndəstrʌk] ADJ estupefato

thundery ['θʌndərı] ADJ tempestuoso

Thur(s). ABBR (= Thursday) qui, 5ª

Thursday ['θəːzdı] N quinta-feira; see also **Tuesday**

thus [ðʌs] ADV assim, desta maneira; (consequently) conseqüentemente

thwart [θwɔːt] VT frustrar

thyme [taım] N tomilho

thyroid ['θaırɔıd] N tireóide f

tiara [tı'ɑːrə] N tiara, diadema m

Tibet [tı'bɛt] N Tibete m

Tibetan [tı'bɛtən] ADJ tibetano ■ N tibetano(-a); (Ling) tibetano

tibia ['tıbıə] N tíbia

tic [tık] N tique m

tick [tık] N (sound: of clock) tique-taque m; (mark) tique m, marca; (Zool) carrapato; (Brit: inf): **in a ~** num instante; (: credit): **to buy sth on ~** comprar algo a crédito ■ VI fazer tique-taque ■ VT marcar, ticar; **to put a ~ against sth** marcar or ticar algo
▶ **tick off** VT assinalar, ticar; (person) dar uma bronca em
▶ **tick over** (Brit) VI (engine) funcionar em marcha lenta; (fig) ir indo

ticker tape ['tıkər-] N fita de teleimpressor; (US: in celebrations) chuva de papel

ticket ['tıkıt] N (for bus, plane) passagem f; (for theatre, raffle) bilhete m; (for cinema) entrada; (in shop: on goods) etiqueta; (: receipt) ficha, nota fiscal; (parking ticket: fine) multa; (for library) cartão m; (US: Pol) chapa; **to get a (parking) ~** (Aut) ganhar uma multa (por estacionamento ilegal); **ticket agency** N agência de ingressos

teatrais; **ticket collector** N revisor(a) m/f;
ticket holder N portador(a) m/f de um bilhete
or ingresso; **ticket inspector** N revisor(a) m/f;
ticket office N bilheteria (BR), bilheteira (PT)
tickle ['tɪkl] N cócegas fpl ■ VT fazer cócegas em;
(captivate) encantar; (make laugh) fazer rir ■ VI
fazer cócegas
ticklish ['tɪklɪʃ] ADJ (person) coceguento; (problem)
delicado; (which tickles: blanket etc) que pica, que
faz cócegas; (: cough) irritante; **to be ~** (person)
ter cócegas
tidal ['taɪdl] ADJ de maré; **tidal wave** N macaréu
m, onda gigantesca
tidbit ['tɪdbɪt] (esp US) N = **titbit**
tiddlywinks ['tɪdlɪwɪŋks] N jogo de fichas
tide [taɪd] N maré f; (fig: of events) curso ■ VT: **to
~ sb over** dar para alguém agüentar; **high/low
~** maré alta/baixa; **the ~ of public opinion** a
corrente da opinião pública
▶ **tide over** VT (help out) ajudar num período
difícil
tidily ['taɪdɪlɪ] ADV com capricho
tidiness ['taɪdɪnɪs] N (good order) ordem f;
(neatness) asseio, limpeza
tidy ['taɪdɪ] ADJ (room) arrumado; (dress, work)
limpo; (person) bem arrumado; (mind) metódico
■ VT (also: **tidy up**) pôr em ordem, arrumar; **to ~
o.s. up** arrumar-se
tie [taɪ] N (string etc) fita, corda; (Brit: also:
necktie) gravata; (fig: link) vínculo, laço; (Sport:
draw) empate m; (US: Rail) dormente m ■ VT
amarrar ■ VI (Sport) empatar; **to ~ in a bow** dar
um laço em; **to ~ a knot in sth** dar um nó em
algo; **family ~s** laços de família; **"black/white
~"** "smoking/traje a rigor"
▶ **tie down** VT amarrar; (fig: person: restrict)
limitar, restringir; (to date, price etc) obrigar
▶ **tie in** VI: **to ~ in (with)** combinar com
▶ **tie on** (Brit) VT (label etc) prender (com
barbante)
▶ **tie up** VT (parcel) embrulhar; (dog) prender;
(boat, prisoner etc) amarrar; (arrangements)
concluir; **to be ~d up** (busy) estar ocupado
tie-break(er) N (Tennis) tie-break m; (in quiz etc)
decisão f de empate
tie-on (Brit) ADJ (label) para atar
tie-pin (Brit) N alfinete m de gravata
tier [tɪə r] N fileira; (of cake) camada
Tierra del Fuego [tɪ'ɛrədɛl'fweɪgəu] N Terra do
Fogo
tie tack (US) N alfinete m de gravata
tie-up (US) N engarrafamento
tiff [tɪf] N briga; (lover's tiff) arrufo
tiger ['taɪgə r] N tigre m
tight [taɪt] ADJ (rope) esticado, firme; (money)
escasso; (clothes, shoes) justo; (bend) fechado;
(budget, programme) rigoroso; (control) rigoroso;
(inf: drunk) bêbado ■ ADV (squeeze) bem forte;
(shut) hermeticamente; **to be packed ~** (suitcase)
estar abarrotado; (people) estar apinhado;
everybody hold ~! segurem firme!
tighten ['taɪtən] VT (rope) esticar; (screw, grip)

apertar; (security) aumentar ■ VI esticar-se;
apertar-se
tight-fisted [-'fɪstɪd] ADJ pão-duro
tightly ['taɪtlɪ] ADV (grasp) firmemente
tight-rope N corda (bamba); **tight-rope walker**
N funâmbulo(-a)
tights [taɪts] (Brit) NPL collant m
tigress ['taɪgrɪs] N tigre fêmea
tilde ['tɪldə] N til m
tile [taɪl] N (on roof) telha; (on floor) ladrilho; (on
wall) azulejo, ladrilho ■ VT (floor) ladrilhar;
(wall, bathroom) azulejar
tiled [taɪld] ADJ ladrilhado; (roof) de telhas
till [tɪl] N caixa (registradora) ■ VT (land)
cultivar ■ PREP, CONJ = **until**
tiller ['tɪlə r] N (Naut) cana do leme
tilt [tɪlt] VT inclinar ■ VI inclinar-se ■ N (slope)
inclinação f; **(at) full ~** a toda velocidade
timber ['tɪmbə r] N (material) madeira; (trees)
mata, floresta
time [taɪm] N tempo; (epoch: often pl) época; (by
clock) hora; (moment) momento; (occasion) vez
f; (Mus) compasso ■ VT calcular or medir o
tempo de; (fix moment for: visit etc) escolher o
momento para; (remark etc): **to ~ sth well/badly**
ser oportuno/não ser oportuno; **a long ~** muito
tempo; **4 at a ~** quatro de uma vez; **for the ~
being** por enquanto; **from ~ to ~** de vez em
quando; **at ~s** às vezes; **~ after ~, ~ and again**
repetidamente; **in ~** (soon enough) a tempo; (after
some time) com o tempo; (Mus) no compasso; **in a
week's ~** dentro de uma semana; **in no ~** num
abrir e fechar de olhos; **any ~** a qualquer hora;
on ~ na hora; **to be 30 minutes behind/ahead
of ~** estar atrasado/adiantado de 30 minutos;
by the ~ he arrived até ele chegar; **5 ~s 5 is 25**
5 vezes 5 são 25; **what ~ is it?** que horas são?;
what ~ do you make it? que horas você tem?;
to have a good ~ divertir-se; **we had a hard
~** foi difícil para nós; **he'll do it in his own
(good) ~** (without being hurried) ele vai fazer isso
quando tiver tempo; **he'll do it in** (Brit) or **on**
(US) **his own ~** (out of working hours) ele vai fazer
isso fora do expediente; **to be behind the ~s**
estar antiquado; **time-and-motion study** N
estudo de tempos e movimentos; **time bomb** N
bomba-relógio f; **time clock** N relógio de ponto;
time-consuming [-kən'sjuːmɪŋ] ADJ que exige
muito tempo; **time difference** N fuso horário;
time-honoured [-'ɔnəd] (US **time-honored**) ADJ
consagrado pelo tempo
timekeeper ['taɪmkiːpə r] N (Sport)
cronometrista m/f
time lag (Brit) N defasagem f; (in travel) fuso
horário
timeless ['taɪmlɪs] ADJ eterno
time limit N limite m de tempo; (Comm) prazo
timely ['taɪmlɪ] ADJ oportuno
time off N tempo livre
timer ['taɪmə r] N (in kitchen) cronômetro; (switch)
timer m
time-saving ADJ que economiza tempo

time scale N prazos *mpl*
time-sharing [-'ʃeərɪŋ] N (*Comput*) tempo compartilhado
time sheet N folha de ponto
time signal N tope *m*, sinal *m* horário
time switch (*Brit*) N interruptor *m* horário
timetable ['taɪmteɪbl] N horário; (*of project*) cronograma *m*
time zone N fuso horário
timid ['tɪmɪd] ADJ tímido
timidity [tɪ'mɪdɪtɪ] N timidez *f*
timing ['taɪmɪŋ] N escolha do momento; (*Sport*) cronometragem *f*; **the ~ of his resignation** o momento que escolheu para se demitir; **timing device** N (*on bomb*) dispositivo de retardamento
Timor ['ti:mɔːr] N Timor (*no article*)
timpani ['tɪmpənɪ] NPL tímbales *mpl*
tin [tɪn] N estanho; (*also*: **tin plate**) folha-de-flandres *f*; (*Brit*: *can*) lata; (: *for baking*) fôrma; **tin foil** N papel *m* de estanho
tinge [tɪndʒ] N (*of colour*) matiz *m*; (*of feeling*) toque *m* ■ VT: **~d with** tingido de
tingle ['tɪŋgl] N comichão *f* ■ VI formigar
tinker ['tɪŋkər] N funileiro(-a); (*gipsy*) cigano(-a)
▶ **tinker with** VT mexer com
tinkle ['tɪŋkl] VI tilintar, tinir ■ N (*inf*): **to give sb a ~** dar uma ligada para alguém
tin mine N mina de estanho
tinned [tɪnd] (*Brit*) ADJ (*food*) em lata, em conserva
tinny ['tɪnɪ] ADJ metálico
tin opener (*Brit*) N abridor *m* de latas (BR), abre-latas *m inv* (PT)
tinsel ['tɪnsl] N ouropel *m*
tint [tɪnt] N matiz *m*; (*for hair*) tintura, tinta ■ VT (*hair*) pintar
tinted ['tɪntɪd] ADJ (*hair*) pintado; (*spectacles, glass*) fumê *inv*
tiny ['taɪnɪ] ADJ pequenininho, minúsculo
tip [tɪp] N (*end*) ponta; (*gratuity*) gorjeta; (*Brit*: *for rubbish*) depósito; (*advice*) dica ■ VT (*waiter*) dar uma gorjeta a; (*tilt*) inclinar; (*winner*) apostar em; (*overturn*: *also*: **tip over**) virar, emborcar; (*empty*: *also*: **tip out**) esvaziar, entornar; **he ~ped out the contents of the box** esvaziou a caixa
▶ **tip off** VT avisar
tip-off N (*hint*) aviso, dica
tipped [tɪpt] ADJ (*Brit*: *cigarette*) com filtro; **steel-~** com ponta de aço
Tipp-Ex® ['tɪpɛks] (*Brit*) N líquido corretor
tipple ['tɪpl] (*Brit*) VT bebericar ■ N: **to have a ~** beber um gole
tipsy ['tɪpsɪ] ADJ embriagado, tocado, alto, alegre
tiptoe ['tɪptəu] N: **on ~** na ponta dos pés
tiptop ['tɪptɔp] ADJ: **in ~ condition** em perfeitas condições
tire ['taɪər] N (*US*) = **tyre** ■ VT cansar ■ VI cansar-se; (*become bored*) chatear-se
▶ **tire out** VT esgotar, exaurir
tired ['taɪəd] ADJ cansado; **to be ~ of sth** estar farto *or* cheio de algo

tiredness ['taɪədnɪs] N cansaço
tireless ['taɪəlɪs] ADJ incansável
tiresome ['taɪəsəm] ADJ enfadonho, chato
tiring ['taɪərɪŋ] ADJ cansativo
tissue ['tɪʃuː] N tecido; (*paper handkerchief*) lenço de papel; **tissue paper** N papel *m* de seda
tit [tɪt] N (*bird*) passarinho; (*inf*: *breast*) teta; **to give ~ for tat** pagar na mesma moeda
titanium [tɪ'teɪnɪəm] N titânio
titbit ['tɪtbɪt] N (*food*) guloseima; (*news*) boato, rumor *m*
titillate ['tɪtɪleɪt] VT titilar, excitar
titivate ['tɪtɪveɪt] VT arrumar
title ['taɪtl] N título; (*Law*: *right*): **~ (to)** direito (a); **title deed** N (*Law*) título de propriedade; **title page** N página de rosto; **title role** N papel *m* principal
titter ['tɪtər] VI rir-se com riso sufocado
tittle-tattle ['tɪtltætl] N fofocas *fpl* (BR), mexericos *mpl* (PT)
titular ['tɪtjulər] ADJ (*in name only*) nominal, titular
tizzy ['tɪzɪ] N: **to be in a ~** estar muito nervoso
T-junction N bifurcação *f* em T
TM N ABBR = **trademark**; **transcendental meditation**
TN (*US*) ABBR (*Post*) = **Tennessee**
TNT N ABBR (= *trinitrotoluene*) Tnt *m*, trotil *m*

 KEYWORD

to [tuː, tə] PREP **1** (*direction*) a, para; (*towards*) para; **to go to France/London/school/the station** ir à França/a Londres/ao colégio/à estação; **to go to Lígia's/the doctor's** ir à casa da Lígia/ao médico; **the road to Edinburgh** a estrada para Edinburgo; **to the left/right** à esquerda/direita
2 (*as far as*) até; **to count to 10** contar até 10; **from 40 to 50 people** de 40 a 50 pessoas
3 (*with expressions of time*): **a quarter to 5** quinze para as 5 (BR), 5 menos um quarto (PT)
4 (*for, or*) de, para; **the key to the front door** a chave da porta da frente; **a letter to his wife** uma carta para a sua mulher
5 (*expressing indirect object*): **to give sth to sb** dar algo a alguém; **to talk to sb** falar com alguém; **I sold it to a friend** vendi isto para um amigo; **to cause damage to sth** causar danos em algo; **to be a danger to sb/sth** ser um perigo para alguém/algo; **to carry out repairs to sth** fazer consertos em algo; **you've done something to your hair** você fêz algo no seu cabelo
6 (*in relation to*) para; **A is to B as C is to D** A está para B assim como C está para D; **3 goals to 2** 3 a 2; **8 apples to the kilo** 8 maçãs por quilo
7 (*purpose, result*) para; **to come to sb's aid** prestar ajuda a alguém; **to sentence sb to death** condenar alguém à morte; **to my surprise** para minha surpresa
■ WITH VB **1** (*simple infin*): **to go/eat** ir/comer
2 (*following another vb*): **to want/try to do** querer/

tentar fazer; **to start to do** começar a fazer
3 (with vb omitted): **I don't want to** eu não quero;
you ought to você deve
4 (purpose, result) para; **he did it to help you** ele
fez isso para ajudar você
5 (equivalent to relative clause) para, a; **I have
things to do** eu tenho coisas para fazer; **he has
a lot to lose** ele tem muito a perder; **the main
thing is to try** o principal é tentar
6 (after adj etc) para; **ready to go** pronto para ir;
too old/young to ... muito velho/jovem para ...
■ ADV: **pull/push the door to** puxar/empurrar
a porta

toad [təud] N sapo
toadstool ['təudstu:l] N chapéu-de-cobra m,
cogumelo venenoso
toady ['təudɪ] VI ser bajulador(a), puxar saco
(inf)
toast [təust] N (Culin) torradas fpl; (drink, speech)
brinde m ■ VT (Culin) torrar; (drink to) brindar; **a
piece** or **slice of ~** uma torrada
toaster ['təustəʳ] N torradeira
toastmaster ['təustmɑ:stəʳ] N mestre m de
cerimônias
toast rack N porta-torradas m inv
tobacco [tə'bækəu] N tabaco, fumo (BR)
tobacconist [tə'bækənɪst] N vendedor(a) m/f de
tabaco; **~'s (shop)** tabacaria, charutaria (BR)
Tobago [tə'beɪɡəu] N see **Trinidad**
toboggan [tə'bɔɡən] N tobogã m
today [tə'deɪ] ADV, N (fig) hoje m; **what day is
it ~?** que dia é hoje?; **what date is it ~?** qual é a
data de hoje?; **~ is the 4th of March** hoje é dia
4 de março; **a week ago ~** há uma semana atrás;
a fortnight ~ daqui a quinze dias; **~'s paper** o
jornal de hoje
toddler ['tɔdləʳ] N criança que começa a andar
toddy ['tɔdɪ] N ponche m quente
to-do N (fuss) rebuliço, alvoroço
toe [təu] N dedo do pé; (of shoe) bico ■ VT:
to ~ the line (fig) conformar-se, cumprir as
obrigações; **big ~** dedão m do pé; **little ~** dedo
mindinho do pé
toehold ['təuhəuld] N apoio
toenail ['təuneɪl] N unha do pé
toffee ['tɔfɪ] N puxa-puxa m (BR), caramelo (PT);
toffee apple (Brit) N maçã f do amor
toga ['təuɡə] N toga
together [tə'ɡɛðəʳ] ADV juntos; (at same time) ao
mesmo tempo; **~ with** junto com
togetherness [tə'ɡɛðənɪs] N companheirismo,
camaradagem f
toggle switch ['tɔɡl-] N (Comput: interruptor m)
teimoso
Togo ['təuɡəu] N Togo
togs [tɔɡz] (inf) NPL (clothes) roupa
toil [tɔɪl] N faina, labuta ■ VI labutar, trabalhar
arduamente
toilet ['tɔɪlət] N (apparatus) privada, vaso
sanitário; (Brit: lavatory) banheiro (BR), casa de
banho (PT) ■ CPD (bag, soap etc) de toalete; **to**

go to the ~ ir ao banheiro; **toilet bag** (Brit) N
bolsa de toucador; **toilet bowl** N vaso sanitário;
toilet paper N papel m higiênico
toiletries ['tɔɪlɪtrɪz] NPL artigos mpl de toalete;
(make-up etc) artigos de toucador
toilet roll N rolo de papel higiênico
toilet water N água de colônia
to-ing and fro-ing ['tu:ɪŋən'frəuɪŋ] (Brit) N
vaivém m
token ['təukən] N (sign) sinal m, símbolo, prova;
(souvenir) lembrança; (substitute coin) ficha;
(voucher) cupom m, vale m ■ CPD (fee, strike)
simbólico; **by the same ~** (fig) pela mesma
razão; **book/record ~** (Brit) vale para comprar
livros/discos
Tokyo ['təukjəu] N Tóquio
told [təuld] PT, PP of **tell**
tolerable ['tɔlərəbl] ADJ (bearable) suportável;
(fairly good) passável
tolerably ['tɔlərəblɪ] ADV: **~ good** razoável
tolerance ['tɔlərəns] N (also: Tech) tolerância
tolerant ['tɔlərənt] ADJ: **~ of** tolerante com
tolerate ['tɔləreɪt] VT suportar; (Med, Tech)
tolerar
toleration [tɔlə'reɪʃən] N tolerância
toll [təul] N (of casualties) número de baixas; (tax,
charge) pedágio (BR), portagem f (PT) ■ VI (bell)
dobrar, tanger
tollbridge ['təulbrɪdʒ] N ponte f de pedágio (BR)
or de portagem (PT)
tomato [tə'mɑ:təu] (pl **tomatoes**) N tomate m
tomb [tu:m] N tumba
tombola [tɔm'bəulə] N tômbola
tomboy ['tɔmbɔɪ] N menina moleque
tombstone ['tu:mstəun] N lápide f
tomcat ['tɔmkæt] N gato
tomorrow [tə'mɔrəu] ADV, N amanhã m; **the
day after ~** depois de amanhã; **~ morning**
amanhã de manhã
ton [tʌn] N (Brit) tonelada; (Naut: also: **register
ton**) tonelagem f de registro; **~s of** (inf) um
monte de
tonal ['təunl] ADJ tonal
tone [təun] N tom m; (Brit: Tel) sinal m ■ VI
harmonizar
  ▶ **tone down** VT (colour, criticism) suavizar;
  (sound) baixar; (Mus) entoar
  ▶ **tone up** VT (muscles) tonificar
tone-deaf ADJ que não tem ouvido
toner ['təunəʳ] N (for photocopier) tinta
Tonga ['tɔŋɡə] N Tonga (no article)
tongs [tɔŋz] NPL (for coal) tenaz f; (for hair) ferros
mpl de frisar cabelo
tongue [tʌŋ] N língua; **~ in cheek**
ironicamente
tongue-tied [-taɪd] ADJ (fig) calado
tongue-twister [-'twɪstəʳ] N trava-língua m
tonic ['tɔnɪk] N (Med) tônico; (Mus) tônica; (also:
tonic water) (água) tônica
tonight [tə'naɪt] ADV, N esta noite, hoje à noite;
(**I'll**) **see you ~!** até a noite!
tonnage ['tʌnɪdʒ] N (Naut) tonelagem f

tonne [tʌn] (Brit) N (metric ton) tonelada

tonsil ['tɒnsəl] N amígdala; **to have one's ~s out** tirar as amígdalas

tonsillitis [tɒnsɪ'laɪtɪs] N amigdalite f; **to have ~** estar com uma amigdalite

too [tu:] ADV (excessively) demais; (very) muito; (also) também; **~ much** ADV demais ■ ADJ demasiado; **~ many** ADJ muitos(-as), demasiados(-as); **~ sweet** doce demais; **I went ~** eu fui também

took [tuk] PT of **take**

tool [tu:l] N ferramenta; (fig: person) joguete m ■ VT trabalhar; **tool box** N caixa de ferramentas; **tool kit** N jogo de ferramentas

toot [tu:t] N (of horn) buzinada; (of whistle) apito ■ VI (with car horn) buzinar; (whistle) apitar

tooth [tu:θ] (pl teeth) N (Anat, Tech) dente m; (molar) molar m; **to have a ~ out** (Brit) or **pulled** (US) arrancar um dente; **to brush one's teeth** escovar os dentes; **by the skin of one's teeth** (fig) por um triz

toothache ['tu:θeɪk] N dor f de dente; **to have ~** estar com dor de dente

toothbrush ['tu:θbrʌʃ] N escova de dentes

toothpaste ['tu:θpeɪst] N pasta de dentes, creme m dental

toothpick ['tu:θpɪk] N palito

tooth powder N pó m dentifrício

top [tɒp] N (of mountain) cume m, cimo; (of tree) topo; (of head) cocuruto; (of cupboard, table) superfície f, topo; (of box, jar, bottle) tampa; (of ladder, page) topo; (of list etc) cabeça m; (toy) pião m; (Dress: blouse etc) top m, blusa; (: of pyjamas) paletó m ■ ADJ (highest: shelf, step) mais alto; (: marks) máximo; (in rank) principal, superior; (best) melhor ■ VT (exceed) exceder; (be first in) estar à cabeça de; **the ~ of the milk** (Brit) a nata do leite; **at the ~ of the stairs/page/street** no alto da escada/no alto da página/no começo da rua; **on ~ of** (above) sobre, em cima de; (in addition to) além de; **from ~ to toe** (Brit) da cabeça aos pés; **from ~ to bottom** de cima abaixo; **at the ~ of the list** à cabeça da lista; **at the ~ of one's voice** aos gritos; **at ~ speed** a toda velocidade; **a ~ surgeon** um dos melhores cirurgiões; **over the ~** (inf: behaviour etc) extravagante
  ▶ **top up** (US **top off**) VT completar; (mobile phone) recarregar

topaz ['təupæz] N topázio

topcoat ['tɒpkəut] N sobretudo

topflight ['tɒpflaɪt] ADJ de primeira categoria

top floor N último andar m

top hat N cartola

top-heavy ADJ (object) desequilibrado

topic ['tɒpɪk] N tópico, assunto

topical ['tɒpɪkl] ADJ atual

topless ['tɒplɪs] ADJ (bather etc) topless inv, sem a parte superior do biquíni

top-level ADJ (talks) de alto nível

topmost ['tɒpməust] ADJ o mais alto

topography [tə'pɒgrəfɪ] N topografia

topping ['tɒpɪŋ] N (Culin) cobertura

topple ['tɒpl] VT derrubar ■ VI cair para frente

top-ranking [-'ræŋkɪŋ] ADJ de alto escalão

top-secret ADJ ultra-secreto, supersecreto

top-security (Brit) ADJ de alta segurança

topsy-turvy ['tɒpsɪ'tə:vɪ] ADJ, ADV de pernas para o ar, confuso, às avessas

top-up N: **would you like a ~?** você quer mais?; (for mobile phone) recarga; **top-up card** N cartão de recarga (para celular)

torch [tɔ:tʃ] N tocha, archote m; (Brit: electric torch) lanterna

tore [tɔ:ʳ] PT of **tear**

torment [n 'tɔ:mɛnt, vt tɔ:'mɛnt] N tormento, suplício ■ VT atormentar; (fig: annoy) chatear, aborrecer

torn [tɔ:n] PP of **tear** ■ ADJ: **~ between** (fig) dividido entre

tornado [tɔ:'neɪdəu] (pl tornadoes) N tornado

torpedo [tɔ:'pi:dəu] (pl torpedoes) N torpedo ■ VT torpedear; **torpedo boat** N torpedeiro

torpor ['tɔ:pəʳ] N torpor m

torque [tɔ:k] N momento de torção

torrent ['tɔrənt] N torrente f

torrential [tɔ'rɛnʃl] ADJ torrencial

torrid ['tɔrɪd] ADJ tórrido; (fig) abrasador(a)

torso ['tɔ:səu] N torso

tortoise ['tɔ:təs] N tartaruga

tortoiseshell ['tɔ:təʃɛl] CPD de tartaruga

tortuous ['tɔ:tjuəs] ADJ tortuoso; (argument, mind) confuso

torture ['tɔ:tʃəʳ] N tortura ■ VT torturar; (fig) atormentar

torturer ['tɔ:tʃərəʳ] N torturador(a) m/f

Tory ['tɔ:rɪ] (Brit) ADJ, N (Pol) conservador(a) m/f

toss [tɒs] VT atirar, arremessar; (head) lançar para trás ■ N (of head) meneio; (of coin) lançamento ■ VI: **to ~ and turn in bed** virar de um lado para o outro na cama; **to ~ a coin** tirar cara ou coroa; **to ~ up for sth** (Brit) jogar cara ou coroa por algo; **to win/lose the ~** ganhar/perder no cara ou coroa; (Sport) ganhar/perder o sorteio

tot [tɒt] N (Brit: drink) copinho, golinho; (child) criancinha
  ▶ **tot up** (Brit) VT (figures) somar, adicionar

total ['təutl] ADJ total ■ N total m, soma ■ VT (add up) somar; (amount to) montar a; **in ~** em total

totalitarian [təutælɪ'tɛərɪən] ADJ totalitário

totality [təu'tælɪtɪ] N totalidade f

totally ['təutəlɪ] ADV totalmente

tote bag [təut-] N sacola

totem pole ['təutəm-] N mastro totêmico

totter ['tɒtəʳ] VI cambalear; (object, government) vacilar

touch [tʌtʃ] N (sense: also skill: of pianist etc) toque m; (contact) contato; (Football): **in ~** fora do campo ■ VT tocar (em); (tamper with) mexer com; (make contact with) fazer contato com; (emotionally) comover; **the personal ~** o toque pessoal; **to put the finishing ~es to sth** dar os últimos retoques em algo; **a ~ of** (fig) um traço

de; **to get in ~ with sb** entrar em contato com alguém; **to lose ~** (*friends*) perder o contato; **to be out of ~ with events** não estar a par dos acontecimentos; **no artist in the country can ~ him** nenhum artista no país se compara a ele
▶ **touch on** VT FUS (*topic*) tocar em, fazer menção de
▶ **touch up** VT (*paint*) retocar
touch-and-go ADJ arriscado; **it was ~ whether we did it** por pouco fizemos aquilo
touchdown ['tʌtʃdaun] N aterrissagem *f* (BR), aterragem *f* (PT); (*on sea*) amerissagem *f* (BR), amaragem *f* (PT); (US: *Football*) touchdown *m* (*colocação da bola no chão atrás da linha de gol*)
touched [tʌtʃt] ADJ comovido; (*inf*) tocado, muito louco
touching ['tʌtʃɪŋ] ADJ comovedor(a)
touchline ['tʌtʃlaɪn] N (*Sport*) linha de fundo
touch-type VI datilografar sem olhar para as teclas
touchy ['tʌtʃɪ] ADJ (*person*) suscetível, sensível
tough [tʌf] ADJ duro; (*difficult*) difícil; (*resistant*) resistente; (*person: physically*) forte; (: *mentally*) tenaz; (*exam, experience*) brabo; (*firm*) firme, inflexível ■ N (*gangster etc*) bandido, capanga *m*; ~ **luck!** azar!; **they got ~ with the workers** começaram a falar grosso com os trabalhadores
toughen ['tʌfən] VT (*sb's character*) fortalecer; (*glass etc*) tornar mais resistente
toughness ['tʌfnɪs] N dureza; (*difficulty*) dificuldade *f*; (*resistance*) resistência; (*of person*) tenacidade *f*
toupee ['tu:peɪ] N peruca
tour ['tuəʳ] N viagem *f*, excursão *f*; (*also*: **package tour**) excursão organizada; (*of town, museum*) visita; (*by artist*) turnê *f* ■ VT (*country, city*) excursionar por; (*factory*) visitar; **to go on a ~ of** (*museum, region*) visitar; **to go on ~** fazer turnê
touring ['tuərɪŋ] N viagens *fpl* turísticas, turismo
tourism ['tuərɪzm] N turismo
tourist ['tuərɪst] N turista *m/f* ■ CPD turístico; **the ~ trade** o turismo; **tourist office** N (*in country*) escritório de turismo; (*in embassy etc*) departamento de turismo
tournament ['tuənəmənt] N torneio
tourniquet ['tuənɪkeɪ] N (*Med*) torniquete *m*
tour operator (Brit) N empresa de viagens
tousled ['tauzld] ADJ (*hair*) despenteado
tout [taut] VI: **to ~ for** angariar clientes para ■ VT (Brit): **to ~ sth (around)** tentar vender algo ■ N (Brit: *ticket tout*) cambista *m/f*
tow [təu] N: **to give sb a ~** (*Aut*) rebocar alguém ■ VT rebocar; **"on ~"** (Brit), **"in ~"** (US) (*Aut*) "rebocado"; **with her husband in ~** com o marido a tiracolo
toward(s) [tə'wɔːd(z)] PREP em direção a; (*of attitude*) para com; (*of purpose*) para; **toward(s) noon/the end of the year** perto do meio-dia/ do fim do ano; **to feel friendly toward(s) sb** sentir amizade em relação a alguém

towel ['tauəl] N toalha; (*also*: **tea towel**) pano; **to throw in the ~** (*fig*) dar-se por vencido
towelling ['tauəlɪŋ] N (*fabric*) tecido para toalhas
towel rail (US **towel rack**) N toalheiro
tower ['tauəʳ] N torre *f* ■ VI (*building, mountain*) elevar-se; **to ~ above** *or* **over sb/sth** dominar alguém/algo; **tower block** (Brit) N prédio alto, espigão *m*, cortiço (BR)
towering ['tauərɪŋ] ADJ elevado; (*figure*) eminente
towline ['təulaɪn] N cabo de reboque
town [taun] N cidade *f*; **to go to ~** ir à cidade; (*fig*) fazer com entusiasmo, mandar brasa (BR); **in the ~** na cidade; **to be out of ~** (*person*) estar fora da cidade; **town centre** N centro (da cidade); **town clerk** N administrador(a) *m/f* municipal; **town council** N câmara municipal; **town hall** N prefeitura (BR), concelho (PT); **town plan** N mapa *m* da cidade; **town planner** N urbanista *m/f*; **town planning** N urbanismo
townspeople ['taunzpi:pl] NPL habitantes *mpl* da cidade
towpath ['təupɑːθ] N caminho de sirga
towrope ['təurəup] N cabo de reboque
tow truck (US) N reboque *m* (BR), pronto socorro (PT)
toxic ['tɔksɪk] ADJ tóxico
toxin ['tɔksɪn] N toxina
toy [tɔɪ] N brinquedo ■ CPD de brinquedo
▶ **toy with** VT FUS (*object, food*) brincar com; (*idea*) contemplar
toy shop N loja de brinquedos
trace [treɪs] N (*sign*) sinal *m*; (*small amount*) traço ■ VT (*through paper*) decalcar; (*draw*) traçar, esboçar; (*follow*) seguir a pista de; (*locate*) encontrar; **without ~** (*disappear*) sem deixar vestígios; **there was no ~ of it** não havia nenhum vestígio disso; **trace element** N elemento traço
trachea [trə'kɪə] N (*Anat*) traquéia
tracing paper ['treɪsɪŋ-] N papel *m* de decalque
track [træk] N (*mark*) pegada, vestígio; (*path: gen*) caminho, vereda; (: *of bullet etc*) trajetória; (: *of suspect, animal*) pista, rasto; (*Rail*) trilhos (BR), carris *mpl* (PT); (*on tape*) trilha; (*Sport*) pista; (*on record*) faixa ■ VT seguir a pista de; **to keep ~ of** não perder de vista; (*fig*) manter-se informado sobre; **to be on the right ~** (*fig*) estar no caminho certo
▶ **track down** VT (*prey*) seguir a pista de; (*sth lost*) procurar e encontrar
tracked [trækt] ADJ com lagarta
tracker dog ['trækə-] (Brit) N cão *m* policial
track events NPL (*Sport*) corridas *fpl*
tracking station ['trækɪŋ-] N (*Space*) estação *f* de rastreamento
track record N: **to have a good ~** (*fig*) ter uma boa folha de serviço
track suit N roupa de jogging
tract [trækt] N (*Geo*) região *f*; (*pamphlet*) folheto; **respiratory ~** (*Anat*) aparelho respiratório

traction ['trækʃən] N tração f; (Med): **in ~** em tração

tractor ['træktəʳ] N trator m; **tractor feed** N (on printer) alimentação f a trator

trade [treɪd] N comércio; (skill, job) ofício ■ vi negociar, comerciar ■ vt: **to ~ sth (for sth)** trocar algo (por algo); **to ~ with/in** comerciar com/em; **foreign ~** comércio exterior; **Department of T~ and Industry** (Brit) Ministério de Indústria e Comércio
▶ **trade in** vt dar como parte do pagamento

trade: trade barrier N barreira comercial; **trade deficit** N déficit m na balança comercial; **Trade Descriptions Act** (Brit) N lei contra a publicidade mentirosa; **trade discount** N desconto de revendedor; **trade fair** N feira industrial

trade-in N venda; **trade-in price** N valor de um objeto usado que se desconta do preço do outro novo

trademark ['treɪdmɑːk] N marca registrada

trade mission N missão f comercial

trade name N (of product) marca or nome comercial de um produto; (of company) razão f social

trader ['treɪdəʳ] N comerciante m/f

trade secret N segredo do ofício

tradesman ['treɪdzmən] (irreg) N (shopkeeper) lojista m

trade union N sindicato

trade unionism [-'juːnjənɪzəm] N sindicalismo

trade unionist [-'juːnjənɪst] N sindicalista m/f

trade wind N vento alísio

trading ['treɪdɪŋ] N comércio; **trading estate** (Brit) N parque m industrial; **trading stamp** N selo de bonificação

tradition [trə'dɪʃən] N tradição f

traditional [trə'dɪʃənl] ADJ tradicional

traffic ['træfɪk] N trânsito; (air traffic etc) tráfego; (illegal) tráfico ■ vi: **to ~ in** (pej: liquor, drugs) traficar com, fazer tráfico com; **traffic circle** (US) N rotatória; **traffic island** N refúgio de segurança (para pedestres); **traffic jam** N engarrafamento, congestionamento; **traffic lights** NPL sinal m luminoso

trafficker ['træfɪkəʳ] N traficante m/f

traffic offence (Brit) N infração f de trânsito

traffic sign N placa de sinalização

traffic violation (US) N infração f

traffic warden N guarda m/f de trânsito

tragedy ['trædʒədɪ] N tragédia

tragic ['trædʒɪk] ADJ trágico

trail [treɪl] N (tracks) rasto, pista; (path) caminho, trilha; (wake) esteira; (of smoke, dust) rasto, rastro ■ vt (drag) arrastar; (follow) seguir a pista de; (follow closely) vigiar ■ vi arrastar-se; (hang loosely) pender; (in game, contest) ficar para trás; **to be on sb's ~** estar no encalço de alguém
▶ **trail away** vi (sound, voice) ir-se perdendo; (interest) diminuir
▶ **trail behind** vi atrasar-se
▶ **trail off** vi (sound, voice) ir-se perdendo; (interest) diminuir

trailer ['treɪləʳ] N (Aut) reboque m; (US: caravan)

trailer m (BR), rulote f (PT); (Cinema) trailer; **trailer truck** (US) N caminhão-reboque m

train [treɪn] N trem m (BR), comboio (PT); (of dress) cauda; (series) seqüência, série f; (followers) séqüito, comitiva ■ vt (professionals etc) formar; (teach skills to) instruir; (Sport) treinar; (dog) adestrar, amestrar; (point: gun etc): **to ~ on** apontar para ■ vi (learn a skill) instruir; (Sport) treinar; (be educated) ser treinado; **to lose one's ~ of thought** perder o fio; **to go by ~** ir de trem; **to ~ sb to do sth** treinar alguém para fazer algo; **train attendant** (US) N revisor(a) m/f

trained [treɪnd] ADJ (worker) especializado; (teacher) formado; (animal) adestrado

trainee [treɪ'niː] N estagiário(-a); (in trade) aprendiz m/f

trainer ['treɪnəʳ] N (Sport) treinador(a) m/f; (of animals) adestrador(a) m/f; **trainers** NPL (shoes) tênis m

training ['treɪnɪŋ] N instrução f; (Sport, for occupation) treinamento; (professional) formação; **in ~** en treinamento; **training college** N (for teachers) Escola Normal; **training course** N curso de formação profissional; **training shoes** NPL tênis m

traipse [treɪps] vi perambular

trait [treɪt] N traço

traitor ['treɪtəʳ] N traidor(a) m/f

trajectory [trə'dʒɛktərɪ] N trajetória

tram [træm] (Brit) N (also: **tramcar**) bonde m (BR), eléctrico (PT)

tramline ['træmlaɪn] N trilho para bondes

tramp [træmp] N (person) vagabundo(-a); (inf: pej: woman) piranha ■ vi caminhar pesadamente ■ vt (walk through: town, streets) percorrer, andar por

trample ['træmpl] vt: **to ~ (underfoot)** calcar aos pés

trampoline ['træmpəliːn] N trampolim m

trance [trɑːns] N estupor m; (Med) transe m hipnótico; **to go into a ~** cair em transe

tranquil ['træŋkwɪl] ADJ tranqüilo

tranquillity [træŋ'kwɪlɪtɪ] N tranqüilidade f

tranquillizer ['træŋkwɪlaɪzəʳ] N (Med) tranqüilizante m

transact [træn'zækt] vt (business) negociar

transaction [træn'zækʃən] N transação f, negócio; **transactions** NPL (minutes) ata; **cash ~** transação à vista

transatlantic [trænzət'læntɪk] ADJ transatlântico

transcend [træn'sɛnd] vt transcender, exceder; (excel over) ultrapassar

transcendental [trænsɛn'dɛntl] ADJ: **~ meditation** meditação f transcendental

transcribe [træn'skraɪb] vt transcrever

transcript ['trænskrɪpt] N cópia, traslado

transcription [træn'skrɪpʃən] N transcrição f

transept ['trænsɛpt] N transepto

transfer [n 'trænsfəʳ, vt træns'fəːʳ] N transferência; (picture, design) decalcomania ■ vt transferir; **to ~ the charges** (Brit: Tel) ligar a cobrar; **by bank ~** por transferência bancária

transferable [træns'fəːrəbl] ADJ transferível; **not ~** intransferível

transfix [træns'fɪks] VT trespassar; (fig): **~ed with fear** paralisado de medo

transform [træns'fɔːm] VT transformar

transformation [trænsfə'meɪʃən] N transformação f

transformer [træns'fɔːmə^r] N (Elec) transformador m

transfusion [træns'fjuːʒən] N (also: **blood transfusion**) transfusão f (de sangue)

transgress [træns'grɛs] VT transgredir

transient ['trænziənt] ADJ transitório

transistor [træn'zɪstə^r] N (Elec: also: **transistor radio**) transistor m

transit ['trænzɪt] N: **in ~** em trânsito, de passagem; **transit camp** N campo de trânsito

transition [træn'zɪʃən] N transição f

transitional [træn'zɪʃənl] ADJ de transição, transicional

transitive ['trænzɪtɪv] ADJ (Ling) transitivo

transit lounge N salão m de trânsito

transitory ['trænzɪtərɪ] ADJ transitório

translate [trænz'leɪt] VT: **to ~ (from/into)** traduzir (do/para o)

translation [trænz'leɪʃən] N tradução f

translator [trænz'leɪtə^r] N tradutor(a) m/f

translucent [trænz'luːsnt] ADJ translúcido

transmission [trænz'mɪʃən] N transmissão f

transmit [trænz'mɪt] VT transmitir

transmitter [trænz'mɪtə^r] N transmissor m; (station) emissora

transparency [træns'pɛərnsɪ] N (of glass etc) transparência; (Brit: Phot) diapositivo

transparent [træns'pærnt] ADJ transparente

transpire [træns'paɪə^r] VI (turn out) tornar sabido; (happen) ocorrer, acontecer; (become known): **it finally ~d that ...** no final soube-se que ...

transplant [vt træns'plɑːnt, n 'trænsplɑːnt] VT transplantar ■ N (Med) transplante m; **to have a heart ~** ter um transplante de coração

transport [n 'trænspɔːt, vt træns'pɔːt] N transporte m ■ VT transportar; (carry) acarretar; **public ~** transportes coletivos; **Department of T~** (Brit) ministério dos Transportes

transportation [trænspɔː'teɪʃən] N transporte m; **Department of T~** (US) ministério da Infra-estrutura

transport café (Brit) N lanchonete f de estrada

transpose [træns'pəuz] VT transpor

transverse ['trænzvəːs] ADJ transversal

transvestite [trænz'vɛstaɪt] N travesti m/f

trap [træp] N (snare) armadilha, cilada; (trick) cilada; (carriage) aranha, charrete f ■ VT pegar em armadilha; (person: trick) armar; (: in bad marriage, fire) estar preso(-a); (immobilize) bloquear; (jam) emperrar; **to set** or **lay a ~ (for sb)** montar uma armadilha (para alguém); **to shut one's ~** (inf) calar a boca; **to ~ one's finger in the door** prender o dedo na porta; **trap door**

N alçapão m

trapeze [trə'piːz] N trapézio

trapper ['træpə^r] N caçador m de peles

trappings ['træpɪŋz] NPL adornos mpl, enfeites mpl

trash [træʃ] N (pej: goods) refugo, escória; (: nonsense) besteiras fpl; (US: rubbish) lixo; **trash can** (US) N lata de lixo

trauma ['trɔːmə] N trauma m

traumatic [trɔː'mætɪk] ADJ traumático

travel ['trævl] N viagem f ■ VI viajar; (sound) propagar-se; (news) levar; (wine): **this wine ~s well** este vinho não sofre alteração ao ser transportado; (move) deslocar-se ■ VT (distance) percorrer; **travels** NPL (journeys) viagens fpl; **travel agency** N agência de viagens; **travel agent** N agente m/f de viagens; **travel brochure** N prospecto turístico

traveller ['trævələ^r] (US **traveler**) N viajante m/f; (Comm) caixeiro(-a) viajante

traveller's cheque (US **traveler's check**) N cheque m de viagem

travelling ['trævəlɪŋ] (US **traveling**) N as viagens, viajar m ■ ADJ (circus, exhibition) itinerante; (salesman) viajante ■ CPD (bag, clock, expenses) de viagem

travel(l)ing salesman (irreg) N caixeiro viajante

travelogue ['trævəlɔg] N (book) livro de viagem; (film) documentário de viagem

travel sickness N enjôo

traverse ['trævəs] VT atravessar

travesty ['trævəstɪ] N paródia

trawler ['trɔːlə^r] N traineira

tray [treɪ] N bandeja; (on desk) cesta

treacherous ['trɛtʃərəs] ADJ traiçoeiro; (ground, tide) perigoso; **road conditions are ~** as estradas estão perigosas

treachery ['trɛtʃərɪ] N traição f

treacle ['triːkl] N melado

tread [trɛd] (pt **trod**, pp **trodden**) N (step) passo, pisada; (sound) passada; (of stair) piso; (of tyre) banda de rodagem ■ VI pisar

▶ **tread on** VT FUS pisar (em)

treadle ['trɛdl] N pedal m

treas. ABBR = **treasurer**

treason ['triːzn] N traição f

treasure ['trɛʒə^r] N tesouro; (person) jóia ■ VT (value) apreciar, estimar; **treasures** NPL (art treasures etc) preciosidades fpl; **treasure hunt** N caça ao tesouro

treasurer ['trɛʒərə^r] N tesoureiro(-a)

treasury ['trɛʒərɪ] N tesouraria; (Pol): **the T~** (Brit) or **T~ Department** (US); = **o Tesouro Nacional; treasury bill** N letra do Tesouro (Nacional)

treat [triːt] N (present) regalo, deleite m; (pleasure) prazer m ■ VT tratar; **to ~ sb to sth** convidar alguém para algo; **to give sb a ~** dar um prazer a alguém; **to ~ sth as a joke** não levar algo a sério

treatise ['triːtɪz] N tratado

treatment ['tri:tmənt] N tratamento; **to have ~ for sth** (*Med*) fazer tratamento para algo

treaty ['tri:tɪ] N tratado, acordo

treble ['trɛbl] ADJ tríplice ■ N (*Mus*) soprano ■ VT triplicar ■ VI triplicar(-se); **treble clef** N clave *f* de sol

tree [tri:] N árvore *f*

tree-lined ADJ ladeado de árvores

treetop ['tri:tɔp] N copa (de árvore)

tree trunk N tronco de árvore

trek [trɛk] N (*long journey*) jornada; (*walk*) caminhada; (*as holiday*) excursão *f* (a pé) ■ VI (*as holiday*) caminhar

trellis ['trɛlɪs] N grade *f* de ripas, latada

tremble ['trɛmbl] VI tremer

trembling ['trɛmblɪŋ] N tremor *m* ■ ADJ trêmulo, trepidante

tremendous [trɪ'mɛndəs] ADJ tremendo; (*enormous*) enorme; (*excellent*) sensacional, fantástico

tremendously [trɪ'mɛndəslɪ] ADV (*well, clever etc*) extraordinariamente; (*very much*) muitíssimo; (*very well*) muito bem

tremor ['trɛmə\'] N tremor *m*; (*also:* **earth tremor**) tremor de terra

trench [trɛntʃ] N trincheira; **trench coat** N capa (de chuva); **trench warfare** N guerra de trincheiras

trend [trɛnd] N (*tendency*) tendência; (*of events*) curso; (*fashion*) modismo, tendência; **~ towards/away from doing** tendência a/contra fazer; **to set the ~** dar o tom; **to set a ~** lançar uma moda

trendy ['trɛndɪ] ADJ (*idea*) de acordo com a tendência atual; (*clothes*) da última moda

trepidation [trɛpɪ'deɪʃən] N trepidação *f*; (*fear*) apreensão *f*

trespass ['trɛspəs] VI: **to ~ on** invadir; **"no ~ing"** "entrada proibida"

trespasser ['trɛspəsə\'] N intruso(-a); **"~s will be prosecuted"** "aqueles que invadirem esta área serão punidos"

tress [trɛs] N trança

trestle ['trɛsl] N cavalete *m*; **trestle table** N mesa de cavaletes

trial ['traɪəl] N (*Law*) processo; (*test: of machine etc*) prova, teste *m*; (*hardship*) provação *f*; **trials** NPL (*unpleasant experiences*) dissabores *mpl*; (*Sport*) eliminatórias *fpl*; **horse ~s** provas *fpl* de equitação; **by ~ and error** por tentativas; **~ by jury** julgamento por júri; **to be sent for ~** ser levado a julgamento; **to be on ~** ser julgado; **trial balance** N (*Comm*) balancete *m*; **trial basis** N: **on a trial basis** em experiência; **trial period** N período de experiência; **trial run** N ensaio

triangle ['traɪæŋgl] N (*Math, Mus*) triângulo

triangular [traɪ'æŋgjulə\'] ADJ triangular

tribal ['traɪbəl] ADJ tribal

tribe [traɪb] N tribo *f*

tribesman ['traɪbzmən] (*irreg*) N membro da tribo

tribulation [trɪbju'leɪʃən] N tribulação *f*, aflição *f*

tribunal [traɪ'bju:nl] N tribunal *m*

tributary ['trɪbju:tərɪ] N (*river*) afluente *m*

tribute ['trɪbju:t] N homenagem *f*; (*payment*) tributo; **to pay ~ to** prestar homenagem a, homenagear

trice [traɪs] N: **in a ~** num instante

trick [trɪk] N truque *m*; (*deceit*) fraude *f*, trapaça; (*joke*) peça, brincadeira; (*skill, knack*) habilidade *f*; (*Cards*) vaza ■ VT enganar; **to play a ~ on sb** pregar uma peça em alguém; **to ~ sb into doing sth** induzir alguém a fazer algo pela astúcia; **to ~ sb out of sth** obter algo de alguém pela astúcia; **it's a ~ of the light** é uma ilusão de ótica; **that should do the ~** (*inf*) isso deveria dar resultado

trickery ['trɪkərɪ] N trapaça, astúcia

trickle ['trɪkl] N (*of water etc*) fio (de água) ■ VI gotejar, pingar; **to ~ in/out** (*people*) ir entrando/ saindo aos poucos

trick question N pergunta capciosa

trickster ['trɪkstə\'] N vigarista *m/f*

tricky ['trɪkɪ] ADJ difícil, complicado

tricycle ['traɪsɪkl] N triciclo

trifle ['traɪfl] N (*small detail*) bobagem *f*, besteira; (*Culin*) tipo de bolo com fruta e creme ■ ADV: **a ~ long** um pouquinho longo ■ VI: **to ~ with** brincar com

trifling ['traɪflɪŋ] ADJ insignificante

trigger ['trɪgə\'] N (*of gun*) gatilho
▶ **trigger off** VT desencadear

trigonometry [trɪgə'nɔmətrɪ] N trigonometria

trilby ['trɪlbɪ] (*Brit*) N (*also:* **trilby hat**) chapéu *m* de feltro

trill [trɪl] N (*of bird, Mus*) trinado, trilo

trilogy ['trɪlədʒɪ] N trilogia

trim [trɪm] ADJ (*figure*) elegante; (*house*) arrumado; (*garden*) bem cuidado ■ N (*haircut etc*) aparada; (*on car*) estofamento; (*embellishment*) acabamento, remate *m* ■ VT (*cut*) aparar, cortar; (*decorate*): **to ~ (with)** enfeitar (com); (*Naut: sail*) ajustar; **to keep in (good) ~** manter em bom estado

trimmings ['trɪmɪŋz] NPL decoração *f*; (*extras: gen Culin*) acompanhamentos *mpl*

Trinidad and Tobago ['trɪnɪdæd-] N Trinidad e Tobago (*no article*)

Trinity ['trɪnɪtɪ] N: **the ~** a Trindade

trinket ['trɪŋkɪt] N buginganga; (*piece of jewellery*) berloque *m*, bijuteria

trio ['tri:əu] N trio

trip [trɪp] N viagem *f*; (*outing*) excursão *f*; (*stumble*) tropeção *m* ■ VI (*also:* **trip up**) tropeçar; (*go lightly*) andar com passos ligeiros ■ VT fazer tropeçar; **on a ~** de viagem
▶ **trip up** VI tropeçar ■ VT passar uma rasteira em

tripartite [traɪ'pɑ:taɪt] ADJ (*in three parts*) tripartido; (*Pol*) tripartidário

tripe [traɪp] N (*Culin*) bucho, tripa; (*pej: rubbish*) bobagem *f*

triple ['trɪpl] ADJ triplo, tríplice ■ ADV: **~ the distance/the speed** três vezes a distância/a velocidade

triplets ['trɪplɪts] NPL trigêmeos(-as) *m/fpl*

triplicate ['trɪplɪkət] N: **in ~** em triplicata, em três vias

tripod ['traɪpɔd] N tripé *m*

Tripoli ['trɪpəlɪ] N Trípoli

tripper ['trɪpəʳ] (*Brit*) N excursionista *m/f*

tripwire ['trɪpwaɪəʳ] N fio de disparo

trite [traɪt] ADJ gasto, banal

triumph ['traɪʌmf] N (*satisfaction*) satisfação *f*; (*great achievement*) triunfo ■ VI: **to ~ (over)** triunfar (sobre)

triumphal [traɪ'ʌmfl] ADJ triunfal

triumphant [traɪ'ʌmfənt] ADJ triunfante

trivia ['trɪvɪə] NPL trivialidades *fpl*

trivial ['trɪvɪəl] ADJ insignificante; (*commonplace*) trivial

triviality [trɪvɪ'ælɪtɪ] N trivialidade *f*

trivialize ['trɪvɪəlaɪz] VT banalizar, trivializar

trod [trɔd] PT *of* **tread**

trodden ['trɔdn] PP *of* **tread**

trolley ['trɔlɪ] N carrinho; (*table on wheels*) mesa volante; **trolley bus** N ônibus *m* elétrico (BR), trólei *m* (PT)

trollop ['trɔləp] N rameira

trombone [trɔm'bəun] N trombone *m*

troop [tru:p] N bando, grupo ■ VI: **to ~ in/out** entrar/sair em bando; **troops** NPL (*Mil*) tropas *fpl*; (: *men*) homens *mpl*; **~ing the colour** (*Brit: ceremony*) a saudação da bandeira; **troop carrier** N (*plane*) avião *m* de transporte de tropas; (*Naut: also:* **troopship**) navio-transporte *m*

trooper ['tru:pəʳ] N (*Mil*) soldado de cavalaria; (*US: policeman*) ≈ policial *m* militar, PM *m*

troopship ['tru:pʃɪp] N navio-transporte *m*

trophy ['trəufɪ] N troféu *m*

tropic ['trɔpɪk] N trópico; **in the ~s** nos trópicos; **T~ of Cancer/Capricorn** Trópico de Câncer/Capricórnio

tropical ['trɔpɪkl] ADJ tropical

trot [trɔt] N trote *m*; (*fast pace*) passo rápido ■ VI trotar; (*person*) andar rapidamente; **on the ~** (*fig: inf*) a fio

  ▶ **trot out** VT (*excuse, reason*) apresentar, dar; (*names, facts*) recitar

trouble ['trʌbl] N problema(s) *m(pl)*, dificuldade(s) *f(pl)*; (*worry*) preocupação *f*; (*bother, effort*) incômodo, trabalho; (*Pol*) distúrbios *mpl*; (*Med*): **stomach ~** *etc* problemas *mpl* gástricos *etc* ■ VT perturbar; (*worry*) preocupar, incomodar ■ VI: **to ~ to do sth** incomodar-se *or* preocupar-se de fazer algo; **troubles** NPL (*Pol etc*) distúrbios *mpl*; **to be in ~** (*in difficulty*) estar num aperto; (*for doing sth wrong*) estar numa encrenca; (*ship, climber etc*) estar em dificuldade; **to go to the ~ of doing sth** dar-se ao trabalho de fazer algo; **to have ~ doing sth** ter dificuldade em fazer algo; **it's no ~!** não tem problema!; **please don't ~ yourself** por favor, não se dê trabalho!; **the ~ is ...** o problema é ...; **what's the ~?** qual é o problema?

troubled ['trʌbld] ADJ (*person*) preocupado; (*epoch,*

life) agitado

trouble-free ADJ sem problemas

troublemaker ['trʌblmeɪkəʳ] N criador(a)-de-casos *m/f*; (*child*) encrenqueiro(-a)

troubleshooter ['trʌblʃu:təʳ] N (*in conflict*) conciliador(a) *m/f*; (*solver of problems*) solucionador(a) *m/f* de problemas

troublesome ['trʌblsəm] ADJ importuno; (*child: cough*) incômodo

trouble spot N área de conflito

trough [trɔf] N (*also:* **drinking trough**) bebedouro, cocho; (*also:* **feeding trough**) gamela; (*depression*) depressão *f*; (*channel*) canal *m*; **~ of low pressure** (*Meteorology*) cavado de baixa pressão

trounce [trauns] VT (*defeat*) dar uma surra *or* um banho em

troupe [tru:p] N companhia teatral

trouser press N passadeira de calças

trousers ['trauzəz] NPL calça (BR), calças *fpl* (PT)

trouser suit (*Brit*) N terninho (BR), conjunto de calças casaco (PT)

trousseau ['tru:səu] (*pl* **trousseaus** *or* **trousseaux**) N enxoval *m*

trousseaux ['tru:səuz] NPL *of* **trousseau**

trout [traut] N INV truta

trowel ['trauəl] N (*garden tool*) colher *f* de jardineiro; (*builder's tool*) colher *f* de pedreiro

truancy ['truənsɪ] N evasão *f* escolar

truant ['truənt] (*Brit*) N: **to play ~** matar aula (BR), fazer gazeta (PT)

truce [tru:s] N trégua, armistício

truck [trʌk] N caminhão *m* (BR), camião *m* (PT); (*Rail*) vagão *m*; **truck driver** N caminhoneiro(-a) (BR), camionista *m/f* (PT)

trucker ['trʌkəʳ] (*esp US*) N caminhoneiro (BR), camionista *m/f* (PT)

truck farm (*US*) N horta

trucking ['trʌkɪŋ] (*esp US*) N transporte *m* rodoviário; **trucking company** (*US*) N transportadora

truck stop (*US*) N bar *m* de estrada

truculent ['trʌkjulənt] ADJ agressivo

trudge [trʌdʒ] VI andar com dificuldade, arrastar-se

true [tru:] ADJ verdadeiro; (*accurate*) exato; (*genuine*) autêntico; (*faithful*) fiel, leal; (*wall*) aprumado; (*beam*) nivelado; (*wheel*) alinhado; **to come ~** realizar-se, tornar-se realidade; **~ to life** realista, fiel à realidade; **it's ~** é verdade

truffle ['trʌfl] N trufa; (*sweet*) docinho de chocolate *or* rum

truly ['tru:lɪ] ADV (*really*) realmente; (*truthfully*) verdadeiramente; (*faithfully*) fielmente; **yours ~** (*in letter*) atenciosamente

trump [trʌmp] N trunfo; **to turn** *or* **come up ~s** (*fig*) salvar a pátria; **trump card** N (*also:* **fig**) trunfo

trumped-up [trʌmpt-] ADJ inventado, forjado

trumpet ['trʌmpɪt] N trombeta

truncated [trʌŋ'keɪtɪd] ADJ truncado

truncheon ['trʌntʃən] N cassetete *m*

trundle ['trʌndl] VT (*push slowly: trolley etc*)

empurrar lentamente ■ vi: **to ~ along** rolar or rodar fazendo ruído

trunk [trʌŋk] N (of tree, person) tronco; (of elephant) tromba; (case) baú m; (US: Aut) mala (BR), portabagagens m (PT); **trunks** NPL (also: **swimming trunks**) sunga (BR), calções mpl de banho (PT); **trunk call** (Brit) N (Tel) ligação f interurbana; **trunk road** (Brit) N = rodovia nacional

truss [trʌs] N (Med) funda ■ vt: **to ~ (up)** atar, amarrar

trust [trʌst] N confiança; (responsibility) responsibilidade f; (Comm) truste m; (Law) fideicomisso ■ vt (rely on) confiar em; (entrust): **to ~ sth to sb** confiar algo a alguém; (hope): **to ~ (that)** esperar que; **to take sth on ~** aceitar algo sem verificação prévia; **in ~** (Law) em fideicomisso; **trust company** N companhia fiduciária

trusted ['trʌstɪd] ADJ de confiança

trustee [trʌs'tiː] N (Law) fideicomissário(-a), depositário(-a); (of school etc) administrador(a) m/f

trustful ['trʌstful] ADJ confiante

trust fund N fundo de fideicomisso

trusting ['trʌstɪŋ] ADJ confiante

trustworthy ['trʌstwə:ðɪ] ADJ digno de confiança

trusty ['trʌstɪ] ADJ fidedigno, fiel

truth [truː:θ, pl truː:ðz] N verdade f

truthful ['truː:θful] ADJ (person) sincero, honesto; (account) verídico

truthfully ['truː:θfulɪ] ADV sinceramente

truthfulness ['truː:θfulnɪs] N veracidade f

try [traɪ] N tentativa; (Rugby) ensaio ■ vt (Law) julgar; (test: sth new) provar, pôr à prova; (attempt) tentar; (food etc) experimentar; (strain) cansar ■ vi tentar; **to have a ~** fazer uma tentativa; **to ~ to do sth** tentar fazer algo; **to ~ one's (very) best** or **one's (very) hardest** fazer (todo) o possível; **to give sth a ~** tentar algo

▶ **try on** vt (clothes) experimentar, provar; **to ~ it on with sb** (fig: test sb's patience) testar a paciência de alguém; (: try to trick) tentar engambelar alguém

▶ **try out** vt experimentar, provar

trying ['traɪɪŋ] ADJ (person, experience) exasperante

tsar [zɑː'] N czar m

T-shirt N camiseta (BR), T-shirt f (PT)

T-square N régua em T

TT ADJ ABBR (Brit: inf) = **teetotal** ■ ABBR (US: Post) = **Trust Territory**

tub [tʌb] N tina; (bath) banheira

tuba ['tjuː:bə] N tuba

tubby ['tʌbɪ] ADJ gorducho

tube [tjuː:b] N tubo; (pipe) cano; (Brit: underground) metrô m (BR), metro(-politano) (PT); (for tyre) câmara-de-ar f

tubeless ['tjuː:blɪs] ADJ sem câmara

tuber ['tjuː:bə'] N (Bot) tubérculo

tuberculosis [tjubə:kjuˈləusɪs] N tuberculose f

tube station (Brit) N estação f de metrô

tubing ['tjuː:bɪŋ] N tubulação f, encanamento; **a piece of ~** um pedaço de tubo

tubular ['tjuː:bjulə'] ADJ tubular; (furniture) tubiforme

TUC (Brit) N ABBR (= Trades Union Congress) = CUT f

tuck [tʌk] N (Sewing) prega, dobra ■ vt (put) enfiar, meter

▶ **tuck away** vt esconder; **to be ~ed away** estar escondido

▶ **tuck in** vt enfiar para dentro; (child) aconchegar ■ vi (eat) comer com apetite

▶ **tuck up** vt (child) aconchegar

tuck shop N loja de balas

Tue(s). ABBR (= Tuesday) ter, 3ª

Tuesday ['tjuː:zdɪ] N terça-feira; (the date) **today is ~ 23rd March** hoje é terça-feira, 23 de março; **on ~** na terça(-feira); **on ~s** nas terças(-feiras); **every ~** todas as terças(-feiras); **every other ~** terça-feira sim, terça-feira não; **last/next ~** na terça-feira passada/na terça-feira que vem; **~ next** na terça-feira que vem; **the following ~** na terça-feira seguinte; **a week on ~** sem ser essa terça, a outra; **the ~ before last** na terça-feira retrasada; **the ~ after next** sem ser essa terça, a outra; **~ morning/lunchtime/afternoon/evening** na terça-feira de manhã/ao meio-dia/à tarde/à noite; **~ night** na terça-feira à noite; **~'s newspaper** o jornal de terça-feira

tuft [tʌft] N penacho; (of grass etc) tufo

tug [tʌg] N (ship) rebocador m ■ vt puxar

tug-of-war N cabo-de-guerra m; (fig) disputa

tuition [tjuː:'ɪʃən] N ensino; (private tuition) aulas fpl particulares; (US: fees) taxas fpl escolares

tulip ['tjuː:lɪp] N tulipa

tumble ['tʌmbl] N (fall) queda ■ vi cair, tombar ■ vt derrubar; **to ~ to sth** (inf) sacar algo

tumbledown ['tʌmbldaun] ADJ em ruínas

tumble dryer (Brit) N máquina de secar roupa

tumbler ['tʌmblə'] N copo

tummy ['tʌmɪ] (inf) N (belly) barriga; (stomach) estômago

tumour ['tjuː:mə'] (US tumor) N tumor m

tumult ['tjuː:mʌlt] N tumulto

tumultuous [tjuː:'mʌltjuəs] ADJ tumultuado

tuna ['tjuː:nə] N INV (also: **tuna fish**) atum m

tune [tjuː:n] N melodia ■ vt (Mus) afinar; (Radio, TV) sintonizar; (Aut) regular; **to be in/out of ~** (instrument) estar afinado/desafinado; (singer) cantar afinado/desafinar; **to be in/out of ~ with** (fig) harmonizar-se com/destoar de; **she was robbed to the ~ of £10,000** ela foi roubada em mais de £10,000

▶ **tune in** vi (Radio, TV): **to ~ in (to)** sintonizar (com)

▶ **tune up** vi (musician) afinar (seu instrumento)

tuneful ['tjuː:nful] ADJ melodioso

tuner ['tjuː:nə'] N (radio set) sintonizador m; **piano ~** afinador(a) m/f de pianos; **tuner amplifier** N sintonizador m amplificador

tungsten ['tʌŋstən] N tungstênio

tunic ['tjuːnɪk] N túnica
tuning ['tjuːnɪŋ] N (of radio) sintonia; (Mus) afinação f; (of car) regulagem f; **tuning fork** N diapasão m
Tunis ['tjuːnɪs] N Túnis
Tunisia [tjuː'nɪzɪə] N Tunísia
Tunisian [tjuː'nɪzɪən] ADJ, N tunisiano(-a)
tunnel ['tʌnl] N túnel m; (in mine) galeria ∎ VI abrir um túnel (or uma galeria)
tunny ['tʌnɪ] N atum m
turban ['təːbən] N turbante m
turbid ['təːbɪd] ADJ turvo
turbine ['təːbaɪn] N turbina
turbojet [təːbəu'dʒɛt] N turbojato (BR), turbojacto (PT)
turboprop [təːbəu'prɔp] N (engine) turboélice m
turbot ['təːbət] N INV rodovalho
turbulence ['təːbjuləns] N (Aviat) turbulência
turbulent ['təːbjulənt] ADJ turbulento
tureen [tə'riːn] N terrina
turf [təːf] N torrão m ∎ VT relvar, gramar; **the T~** o turfe
▸ **turf out** (inf) VT (thing) jogar fora; (person) pôr no olho da rua
turf accountant (Brit) N corretor m de apostas
turgid ['təːdʒɪd] ADJ (speech) pomposo
Turk [təːk] N turco(-a)
Turkey ['təːkɪ] N Turquia
turkey ['təːkɪ] N peru(a) m/f
Turkish ['təːkɪʃ] ADJ turco(-a) ∎ N (Ling) turco; **Turkish bath** N banho turco; **Turkish delight** N lokum m
turmeric ['təːmərɪk] N açafrão-da-terra m
turmoil ['təːmɔɪl] N tumulto, distúrbio, agitação f; **in ~** agitado, tumultuado
turn [təːn] N volta, turno; (in road) curva; (go) vez f, turno; (tendency: of mind, events) propensão f, tendência; (Theatre) número; (Med) choque m ∎ VT dar volta a, fazer girar; (collar) virar; (steak) virar; (milk) azedar; (shape: wood) tornear; (change): **to ~ sth into** converter algo em ∎ VI virar; (person: look back) voltar-se; (reverse direction) mudar de direção; (milk) azedar; (change) mudar; (become) tornar-se, virar; **to ~ nasty** engrossar; **to ~ forty** fazer quarenta anos; **to ~ into** converter-se em; **a good ~** um favor; **it gave me quite a ~** me deu um susto enorme; **"no left ~"** (Aut) "proibido virar à esquerda"; **it's your ~** é a sua vez; **in ~** por sua vez; **to take ~s (at)** revezar (em); **at the ~ of the year/century** no final do ano/século; **to take a ~ for the worse** (situation, patient) piorar; **to ~ left** (Aut) virar à esquerda; **she has no one to ~ to** ela não tem a quem recorrer
▸ **turn about** VI dar meia-volta
▸ **turn away** VI virar a cabeça ∎ VT (reject: person) rejeitar; (: business, applicants) recusar
▸ **turn back** VI voltar atrás ∎ VT voltar para trás; (clock) atrasar
▸ **turn down** VT (refuse) recusar; (reduce) baixar; (fold) dobrar, virar para baixo
▸ **turn in** VI (inf: go to bed) ir dormir ∎ VT (fold)

dobrar para dentro
▸ **turn off** VI (from road) virar, sair do caminho ∎ VT (light, radio etc) apagar; (engine) desligar
▸ **turn on** VT (light) acender; (engine, radio) ligar; (tap) abrir
▸ **turn out** VT (light, gas) apagar; (produce) produzir ∎ VI (troops) ser mobilizado; **to ~ out to be ...** revelar-se (ser) ..., resultar (ser) ..., vir a ser ...
▸ **turn over** VI (person) virar-se ∎ VT (object) virar
▸ **turn round** VI voltar-se, virar-se ∎ VT girar
▸ **turn up** VI (person) aparecer, pintar; (lost object) aparecer ∎ VT (collar) subir; (volume, radio etc) aumentar
turnabout ['təːnəbaut] N reviravolta
turnaround ['təːnəraund] N reviravolta
turncoat ['təːnkəut] N vira-casaca m/f
turned-up [təːnd-] ADJ (nose) arrebitado
turning ['təːnɪŋ] N (in road) via lateral; **the first ~ on the right** a primeira à direita; **turning circle** (Brit) N raio de viragem; **turning point** N (fig) momento decisivo, virada; **turning radius** (US) N raio de viragem
turnip ['təːnɪp] N nabo
turnout ['təːnaut] N assistência; (in election) comparecimento às urnas
turnover ['təːnəuvə] N (Comm: amount of money) volume m de negócios; (: of goods) movimento; (of staff) rotatividade f; (Culin) espécie de pastel
turnpike ['təːnpaɪk] (US) N estrada or rodovia com pedágio (BR) or portagem (PT)
turnstile ['təːnstaɪl] N borboleta (BR), torniquete m (PT)
turntable ['təːnteɪbl] N (on record player) prato
turn-up (Brit) N (on trousers) volta, dobra
turpentine ['təːpəntaɪn] N (also: **turps**) aguarrás f
turquoise ['təːkwɔɪz] N (stone) turquesa ∎ ADJ azul-turquesa inv
turret ['tʌrɪt] N torrinha
turtle ['təːtl] N tartaruga, cágado
turtleneck (sweater) ['təːtlnɛk-] N pulôver m (BR) or camisola (PT) de gola alta
tusk [tʌsk] N defesa (de elefante)
tussle ['tʌsl] N (fight) luta; (scuffle) contenda, rixa
tutor ['tjuːtə] N professor(a) m/f; (private tutor) professor(a) m/f particular
tutorial [tjuː'tɔːrɪəl] N (Sch) seminário
tuxedo [tʌk'siːdəu] (US) N smoking m
TV N ABBR (= television) TV f
twaddle ['twɔdl] N bobagens fpl, disparates mpl
twang [twæŋ] N (of instrument) dedilhado; (of voice) timbre m nasal or fanhoso ∎ VI vibrar ∎ VT (guitar) dedilhar
tweak [twiːk] VT (nose, ear) beliscar; (hair) puxar
tweed [twiːd] N tweed m, pano grosso de lã
tweezers ['twiːzəz] NPL pinça (pequena)
twelfth [twɛlfθ] NUM décimo segundo; see also **fifth**
Twelfth Night N noite f de Reis, Epifania
twelve [twɛlv] NUM doze; **at ~ (o'clock)** (midday)

ao meio-dia; (midnight) à meia-noite; see also **five**

twentieth ['twɛntɪɪθ] NUM vigésimo; see also **fifth**

twenty ['twɛntɪ] NUM vinte; see also **five**

twerp [twəːp] (inf) N imbecil m/f

twice [twaɪs] ADV duas vezes; ~ **as much** duas vezes mais; ~ **a week** duas vezes por semana; **she is** ~ **your age** ela tem duas vezes a sua idade

twiddle ['twɪdl] VT, VI: **to ~ (with) sth** mexer em algo; **to ~ one's thumbs** (fig) chupar o dedo

twig [twɪg] N graveto, varinha ■ VT, VI (inf) sacar

twilight ['twaɪlaɪt] N crepúsculo, meia-luz f; **in the ~** na penumbra

twill [twɪl] N sarja

twin [twɪn] ADJ (sister, brother, towers) gêmeo(-a); (beds) separado ■ N gêmeo(-a) ■ VT irmanar; **twin(-bedded) room** [-'bɛdɪd-] N quarto com duas camas; **twin beds** NPL camas fpl separadas

twin-carburettor ADJ de dois carburadores

twine [twaɪn] N barbante m (BR), cordel m (PT) ■ VI (plant) enroscar-se, enrolar-se

twin-engined [-'ɛndʒɪnd] ADJ bimotor; ~ **aircraft** (avião m) bimotor m

twinge [twɪndʒ] N (of pain) pontada; (of conscience) remorso

twinkle ['twɪŋkl] N cintilação f ■ VI cintilar; (eyes) pestanejar

twin town N cidade f irmã

twirl [twəːl] N giro, volta ■ VT fazer girar ■ VI girar rapidamente

twist [twɪst] N (action) torção f; (in road, coil) curva; (in wire, flex) virada; (in story) mudança imprevista ■ VT torcer, retorcer; (ankle) torcer; (weave) entrelaçar; (roll around) enrolar; (fig) deturpar ■ VI serpentear; **to ~ one's ankle/wrist** torcer o tornozelo/pulso

twisted ['twɪstɪd] ADJ (wire, rope, ankle) torcido; (fig: mind, logic) deturpado

twit [twɪt] (inf) N idiota m/f, bobo(-a)

twitch [twɪtʃ] N puxão m; (nervous) tique m nervoso ■ VI contrair-se

two [tuː] NUM dois; ~ **by** ~, **in ~s** de dois em dois; **to put ~ and ~ together** (fig) tirar conclusões; see also **five**

two-door ADJ (Aut) de duas portas

two-faced [-feɪst] (pej) ADJ (person) falso

twofold ['tuːfəuld] ADV: **to increase** ~ duplicar ■ ADJ (increase) em cem por cento; (reply) duplo

two-piece N (also: **two-piece suit**) traje m de duas peças; (also: **two-piece swimsuit**) maiô m de duas peças, biquíni m

two-seater [-'siːtəʳ] N (plane) avião m de dois lugares; (car) carro de dois lugares

twosome ['tuːsəm] N (people) casal m

two-stroke N (also: **two-stroke engine**) motor m de dois tempos ■ ADJ de dois tempos

two-tone ADJ em dois tons

two-way ADJ: ~ **radio** rádio emissor-receptor; ~ **traffic** trânsito em mão dupla

TX (US) ABBR (Post) = **Texas**

tycoon [taɪˈkuːn] N: (business) ~ magnata m

type [taɪp] N (category) tipo, espécie f; (model) modelo; (Typ) tipo, letra ■ VT (letter etc) datilografar, bater (à máquina); **what ~ do you want?** que tipo você quer?; **in bold/italic ~** em negrito/itálico

typecast ['taɪpkɑːst] ADJ que representa sempre o mesmo papel

typeface ['taɪpfeɪs] N tipo, letra

typescript ['taɪpskrɪpt] N texto datilografado

typeset ['taɪpsɛt] (irreg) VT compor (para imprimir)

typesetter ['taɪpsɛtəʳ] N compositor(a) m/f

typewriter ['taɪpraɪtəʳ] N máquina de escrever

typewritten ['taɪprɪtn] ADJ datilografado

typhoid ['taɪfɔɪd] N febre f tifóide

typhoon [taɪˈfuːn] N tufão m

typhus ['taɪfəs] N tifo

typical ['tɪpɪkl] ADJ típico

typify ['tɪpɪfaɪ] VT tipificar, simbolizar

typing ['taɪpɪŋ] N datilografia; **typing error** N erro de datilografia; **typing pool** N seção f de datilografia

typist ['taɪpɪst] N datilógrafo(-a) m/f

typo ['taɪpəu] (inf) N ABBR (= typographical error) erro tipográfico

typography [taɪˈpɔgrəfɪ] N tipografia

tyranny ['tɪrənɪ] N tirania

tyrant ['taɪərənt] N tirano(-a)

tyre ['taɪəʳ] (US tire) N pneu m; **tyre pressure** N pressão f dos pneus

Tyrrhenian Sea [tɪˈriːnɪən-] N: **the** ~ o mar Tirreno

tzar [zɑːʳ] N = **tsar**

Uu

U, u [ju:] N (*letter*) U, u *m*; **U for Uncle** U de Úrsula

U (Brit) N ABBR (*Cinema:* = *universal*) ≈ livre

UAW (US) N ABBR (= *United Automobile Workers*) sindicato dos trabalhadores na indústria automobilística

UB40 (Brit) N ABBR (= *unemployment benefit form 40*) carteira que comprova que o portador recebe o auxílio-desemprego

U-bend N (*in pipe*) curva em U

ubiquitous [ju:'bɪkwɪtəs] ADJ ubíquo, onipresente

UDA (Brit) N ABBR = **Ulster Defence Association**

UDC (Brit) N ABBR = **Urban District Council**

udder ['ʌdəʳ] N ubre f

UDI (Brit) N ABBR (*Pol*) = **unilateral declaration of independence**

UDR (Brit) N ABBR = **Ulster Defence Regiment**

UEFA [ju:'eɪfə] N ABBR (= *Union of European Football Associations*) UEFA f

UFO ['ju:fəu] N ABBR (= *unidentified flying object*) óvni *m*

Uganda [ju:'gændə] N Uganda (*no article*)

Ugandan [ju:'gændən] ADJ, N ugandense *m/f*

ugh [ə:h] EXCL uh!

ugliness ['ʌglɪnɪs] N feiúra

ugly ['ʌglɪ] ADJ feio; (*dangerous*) perigoso

UHF ABBR (= *ultra-high frequency*) UHF, frequência ultra-alta

UHT ADJ ABBR = **ultra-heat treated**; **~ milk** leite *m* longa-vida

UK N ABBR = **United Kingdom**

ulcer ['ʌlsəʳ] N úlcera; **mouth ~** afta

Ulster ['ʌlstəʳ] N Ulster *m*, Irlanda do Norte

ulterior [ʌl'tɪərɪəʳ] ADJ ulterior; **~ motive** segundas intenções *fpl*

ultimata [ʌltɪ'meɪtə] NPL *of* **ultimatum**

ultimate ['ʌltɪmət] ADJ último, final; (*authority*) máximo ■ N: **the ~ in luxury** o máximo em luxo

ultimately ['ʌltɪmətlɪ] ADV (*in the end*) no final, por último; (*fundamentally*) no fundo

ultimatum [ʌltɪ'meɪtəm] (*pl* **ultimata**) N ultimato

ultrasonic [ʌltrə'sɔnɪk] ADJ ultra-sônico

ultrasound ['ʌltrəsaund] N (*Med*) ultra-som *m*

ultraviolet [ʌltrə'vaɪəlɪt] ADJ ultravioleta

umbilical cord [ʌmbɪ'laɪkl-] N cordão *m* umbilical

umbrage ['ʌmbrɪdʒ] N: **to take ~** ofender-se

umbrella [ʌm'brɛlə] N guarda-chuva *m*; (*for sun*) guarda-sol *m*, barraca (da praia); (*fig*): **under the ~ of** sob a égide de

umpire ['ʌmpaɪəʳ] N árbitro ■ VT arbitrar

umpteen [ʌmp'ti:n] ADJ inúmeros(-as)

umpteenth [ʌmp'ti:nθ] ADJ: **for the ~ time** pela enésima vez

UMW N ABBR (= *United Mineworkers of America*) sindicato dos mineiros

UN N ABBR (= *United Nations*) ONU f

unabashed [ʌnə'bæʃt] ADJ imperturbado

unabated [ʌnə'beɪtɪd] ADJ sem diminuir

unable [ʌn'eɪbl] ADJ: **to be ~ to do sth** não poder fazer algo; (*be incapable*) ser incapaz de fazer algo

unabridged [ʌnə'brɪdʒd] ADJ integral

unacceptable [ʌnək'sɛptəbl] ADJ (*behaviour*) insuportável; (*price, proposal*) inaceitável

unaccompanied [ʌnə'kʌmpənɪd] ADJ desacompanhado; (*singing, song*) sem acompanhamento

unaccountably [ʌnə'kauntəblɪ] ADV inexplicavelmente

unaccounted [ʌnə'kauntɪd] ADJ: **two passengers are ~ for** dois passageiros estão desaparecidos

unaccustomed [ʌnə'kʌstəmd] ADJ desacostumado; **to be ~ to** não estar acostumado a

unacquainted [ʌnə'kweɪntɪd] ADJ: **to be ~ with** (*person*) não conhecer; (*facts etc*) não estar familiarizado com

unadulterated [ʌnə'dʌltəreɪtɪd] ADJ puro, natural

unaffected [ʌnə'fɛktɪd] ADJ (*person, behaviour*) natural, simples *inv*; (*emotionally*): **to be ~ by** não se comover com

unafraid [ʌnə'freɪd] ADJ: **to be ~** não ter medo

unaided [ʌn'eɪdɪd] ADJ sem ajuda, por si só

unanimity [ju:nə'nɪmɪtɪ] N unanimidade f

unanimous [ju:'nænɪməs] ADJ unânime

unanimously [ju:'nænɪməslɪ] ADV unanimemente

unanswered [ʌn'ɑ:nsəd] ADJ sem resposta

unappetizing [ʌn'æpɪtaɪzɪŋ] ADJ pouco apetitoso

unappreciative [ʌnə'pri:ʃɪətɪv] ADJ (*ungrateful*)
ingrato
unarmed [ʌn'ɑ:md] ADJ (*without a weapon*)
desarmado; (*defenceless*) indefeso
unashamed [ʌnə'ʃeɪmd] ADJ (*open*)
desembaraçado; (*pleasure, greed*) descarado;
(*impudent*) descarado
unassisted [ʌnə'sɪstɪd] ADJ, ADV sem ajuda
unassuming [ʌnə'sju:mɪŋ] ADJ modesto,
despretencioso
unattached [ʌnə'tætʃt] ADJ (*person*) livre; (*part
etc*) solto, separado
unattended [ʌnə'tɛndɪd] ADJ (*car, luggage*)
abandonado
unattractive [ʌnə'træktɪv] ADJ sem atrativos;
(*building, appearance, idea*) pouco atraente
unauthorized [ʌn'ɔ:θəraɪzd] ADJ não
autorizado, sem autorização
unavailable [ʌnə'veɪləbl] ADJ (*article, room, book*)
indisponível; (*person*) não disponível
unavoidable [ʌnə'vɔɪdəbl] ADJ inevitável
unavoidably [ʌnə'vɔɪdəblɪ] ADV
inevitavelmente
unaware [ʌnə'wɛəʳ] ADJ: **to be ~ of** ignorar, não
perceber
unawares [ʌnə'wɛəz] ADV improvisadamente,
de surpresa
unbalanced [ʌn'bælənst] ADJ desequilibrado
unbearable [ʌn'bɛərəbl] ADJ insuportável
unbeatable [ʌn'bi:təbl] ADJ (*team*) invencível;
(*price*) sem igual
unbeaten [ʌn'bi:tn] ADJ invicto; (*record*) não
batido
unbecoming [ʌnbɪ'kʌmɪŋ] ADJ (*unseemly:
language, behaviour*) inconveniente; (*unflattering:
garment*) que não fica bem
unbeknown(st) [ʌnbɪ'nəun(st)] ADV:
unbeknown(st) to me sem eu saber
unbelief [ʌnbɪ'li:f] N incredulidade *f*
unbelievable [ʌnbɪ'li:vəbl] ADJ inacreditável;
(*amazing*) incrível
unbelievingly [ʌnbɪ'li:vɪŋlɪ] ADV
incredulamente
unbend [ʌn'bɛnd] (*irreg*) VI relaxar-se ■ VT (*wire*)
desentortar
unbending [ʌn'bɛndɪŋ] ADJ inflexível
unbent [ʌn'bɛnt] PT, PP *of* **unbend**
unbiased [ʌn'baɪəst] ADJ imparcial
unblemished [ʌn'blɛmɪʃt] ADJ imaculado
unblock [ʌn'blɔk] VT (*pipe*) desentupir
unborn [ʌn'bɔ:n] ADJ por nascer
unbounded [ʌn'baundɪd] ADJ ilimitado,
infinito, imenso
unbreakable [ʌn'breɪkəbl] ADJ inquebrável
unbridled [ʌn'braɪdld] ADJ (*fig*) desenfreado
unbroken [ʌn'brəukən] ADJ (*seal*) intacto; (*line*)
contínuo; (*silence, series*) ininterrupto; (*record*)
mantido; (*spirit*) indômito
unbuckle [ʌn'bʌkl] VT desafivelar
unburden [ʌn'bə:dn] VT: **to ~ o.s.** desabafar
unbutton [ʌn'bʌtn] VT desabotoar
uncalled-for [ʌn'kɔ:ld-] ADJ desnecessário,

gratuito
uncanny [ʌn'kænɪ] ADJ (*silence, resemblance*)
estranho; (*knack*) excepcional
unceasing [ʌn'si:sɪŋ] ADJ contínuo
unceremonious [ʌnsɛrɪ'məunɪəs] ADJ (*abrupt*)
incerimonioso; (*rude*) rude
uncertain [ʌn'sə:tn] ADJ incerto; (*character*)
indeciso; (*unsure*): **~ about** inseguro sobre; **we
were ~ whether ...** não tínhamos certeza se ...;
in no ~ terms em termos precisos
uncertainty [ʌn'sə:tntɪ] N incerteza; (*also pl:
doubts*) dúvidas *fpl*
unchallenged [ʌn'tʃæləndʒd] ADJ incontestado;
to go ~ não ser contestado
unchanged [ʌn'tʃeɪndʒd] ADJ inalterado
uncharitable [ʌn'tʃærɪtəbl] ADJ sem caridade
uncharted [ʌn'tʃɑ:tɪd] ADJ inexplorado
unchecked [ʌn'tʃɛkt] ADV sem controle,
descontrolado
uncivilized [ʌn'sɪvəlaɪzd] ADJ (*country, people*)
primitivo; (*fig: behaviour*) incivilizado; (: *hour*) de
manhã bem cedo
uncle ['ʌŋkl] N tio
unclear [ʌn'klɪəʳ] ADJ (*not obvious*) pouco
evidente; (*confused*) confuso; (*indistinct*)
indistinto; **I'm still ~ about what I'm
supposed to do** ainda não sei exatamente o
que devo fazer
uncoil [ʌn'kɔɪl] VT desenrolar ■ VI desenrolar-
se
uncomfortable [ʌn'kʌmfətəbl] ADJ
incômodo; (*uneasy*) pouco à vontade; (*situation*)
desagradável
uncomfortably [ʌn'kʌmftəblɪ] ADV
desconfortavelmente; (*uneasily*) sem graça;
(*unpleasantly*) desagradavelmente
uncommitted [ʌnkə'mɪtɪd] ADJ não
comprometido
uncommon [ʌn'kɔmən] ADJ raro, incomum,
excepcional
uncommunicative [ʌnkə'mju:nɪkətɪv] ADJ
reservado
uncomplicated [ʌn'kɔmplɪkeɪtɪd] ADJ
descomplicado, simples *inv*
uncompromising [ʌn'kɔmprəmaɪzɪŋ] ADJ
intransigente, inflexível
unconcerned [ʌnkən'sə:nd] ADJ indiferente,
despreocupado; **to be ~ (about)** não estar
preocupado (com)
unconditional [ʌnkən'dɪʃənl] ADJ
incondicional
uncongenial [ʌnkən'dʒi:nɪəl] ADJ desagradável
unconnected [ʌnkə'nɛktɪd] ADJ não
relacionado
unconscious [ʌn'kɔnʃəs] ADJ sem sentidos,
desacordado; (*unaware*): **~ of** inconsciente de
■ N: **the ~** o inconsciente; **to knock sb ~** pôr
alguém nocaute, nocautear alguém
unconsciously [ʌn'kɔnʃəslɪ] ADV
inconscientemente
unconstitutional [ʌnkɔnstɪ'tju:ʃənl] ADJ
inconstitucional

uncontested [ʌnkən'tɛstɪd] ADJ incontestado
uncontrollable [ʌnkən'trəuləbl] ADJ
(temper) ingovernável; (child, animal, laughter)
incontrolável
uncontrolled [ʌnkən'trəuld] ADJ descontrolado
unconventional [ʌnkən'vɛnʃənl] ADJ (person)
inconvencional; (approach) heterodoxo
unconvinced [ʌnkən'vɪnst] ADJ: **to be ~** não
estar convencido
unconvincing [ʌnkən'vɪnsɪŋ] ADJ pouco
convincente
uncork [ʌn'kɔːk] VT desarrolhar
uncorroborated [ʌnkə'rɔbəreɪtɪd] ADJ não
confirmado
uncouth [ʌn'kuːθ] ADJ rude, grosseiro
uncover [ʌn'kʌvəʳ] VT descobrir; (take lid off)
destapar, destampar
unctuous [ˈʌŋktjuəs] ADJ untuoso, pegajoso
undamaged [ʌn'dæmɪdʒd] ADJ (goods) intacto;
(fig: reputation) incólume
undaunted [ʌn'dɔːntɪd] ADJ impávido,
inabalável
undecided [ʌndɪ'saɪdɪd] ADJ (character) indeciso;
(question) não respondido, pendente
undelivered [ʌndɪ'lɪvəd] ADJ não entregue
undeniable [ʌndɪ'naɪəbl] ADJ inegável
under [ˈʌndəʳ] PREP embaixo de (BR), debaixo
de (PT); (fig) sob; (in age, price: less than) menos
de; (according to) segundo, de acordo com ▪ ADV
embaixo; (movement) por baixo; **from ~ sth** de
embaixo de algo; **~ there** ali embaixo; **in ~ 2
hours** em menos de 2 horas; **~ anaesthetic** sob
anestesia; **~ discussion** em discussão; **~ the
circumstances** nas circunstâncias; **~ repair**
em conserto
under... [ˈʌndəʳ] PREFIX sub-
under-age ADJ menor de idade; **~ drinking**
consumo de bebidas alcoólicas por menores
de idade
underarm [ˈʌndərɑːm] ADV com a mão por
baixo ▪ ADJ (throw) com a mão por baixo;
(deodorant) para as axilas
undercapitalized [ʌndəˈkæpɪtəlaɪzd] ADJ
subcapitalizado
undercarriage [ˈʌndəkærɪdʒ] (Brit) N (Aviat)
trem m de aterrissagem
undercharge [ʌndəˈtʃɑːdʒ] VT não cobrar o
suficiente
underclothes [ˈʌndəkləuðz] NPL roupa de baixo,
roupa íntima
undercoat [ˈʌndəkəut] N (paint) primeira mão f
undercover [ˈʌndəkʌvəʳ] ADJ secreto,
clandestino
undercurrent [ˈʌndəkʌrənt] N (fig) tendência
undercut [ʌndəˈkʌt] (irreg) VT (person) prejudicar;
(prices) vender por menos que
underdeveloped [ʌndədɪˈvɛləpt] ADJ
subdesenvolvido
underdog [ˈʌndədɔg] N o mais fraco
underdone [ʌndəˈdʌn] ADJ (Culin) mal passado
under-employment N subemprego
underestimate [ʌndərˈɛstɪmeɪt] VT subestimar

underexposed [ʌndərɪk'spəuzd] ADJ (Phot) sem
exposição suficiente
underfed [ʌndəˈfɛd] ADJ subnutrido
underfoot [ʌndəˈfut] ADV sob os pés
undergo [ʌndəˈgəu] (irreg) VT sofrer; (test)
passar por; (operation, treatment) ser submetido
a; **the car is ~ing repairs** o carro está sendo
consertado
undergraduate [ʌndəˈgrædjuət] N
universitário(-a) ▪ CPD: **~ courses** profissões fpl
universitárias
underground [ˈʌndəgraund] N (Brit) metrô m
(BR), metro(-politano) (PT); (Pol) organização
f clandestina ▪ ADJ subterrâneo; (fig)
clandestina ▪ ADV (work) embaixo da terra; (fig)
na clandestinidade
undergrowth [ˈʌndəgrəuθ] N vegetação f
rasteira
underhand(ed) [ʌndəˈhænd(ɪd)] ADJ (fig)
secreto e desonesto
underinsured [ʌndərɪnˈʃuəd] ADJ segurado
abaixo do valor corrente
underlie [ʌndəˈlaɪ] (irreg) VT (fig) ser a base de
underline [ʌndəˈlaɪn] VT sublinhar
underling [ˈʌndəlɪŋ] (pej) N subalterno(-a)
underlying [ʌndəˈlaɪɪŋ] ADJ: **the ~ cause** a causa
subjacente
undermentioned [ʌndəˈmɛnʃənd] ADJ abaixo
mencionado
undermine [ʌndəˈmaɪn] VT minar, solapar
underneath [ʌndəˈniːθ] ADV embaixo, debaixo,
por baixo ▪ PREP embaixo de (BR), debaixo de
(PT)
undernourished [ʌndəˈnʌrɪʃt] ADJ subnutrido
underpaid [ʌndəˈpeɪd] ADJ mal pago
underpants [ˈʌndəpænts] (Brit) NPL cueca (BR),
cuecas fpl (PT)
underpass [ˈʌndəpɑːs] (Brit) N passagem f
inferior
underpin [ʌndəˈpɪn] VT (argument, case)
sustentar
underplay [ʌndəˈpleɪ] (Brit) VT minimizar
underpopulated [ʌndəˈpɔpjuleɪtɪd] ADJ de
população reduzida
underprice [ʌndəˈpraɪs] VT vender abaixo do
preço
underprivileged [ʌndəˈprɪvɪlɪdʒd] ADJ menos
favorecido
underrate [ʌndəˈreɪt] VT depreciar, subestimar
underscore [ʌndəˈskɔːʳ] VT sublinhar
underseal [ʌndəˈsiːl] (Brit) VT fazer bronzina em
undersecretary [ʌndəˈsɛkrətərɪ] N
subsecretário(-a)
undersell [ʌndəˈsɛl] (irreg) VT (competitors) vender
por preço mais baixo que
undershirt [ˈʌndəʃəːt] (US) N camiseta
undershorts [ˈʌndəʃɔːts] (US) NPL cueca (BR),
cuecas fpl (PT)
underside [ˈʌndəsaɪd] N parte f inferior
undersigned [ˈʌndəsaɪnd] ADJ, N abaixo
assinado(-a)
underskirt [ˈʌndəskəːt] (Brit) N anágua

understaffed [ʌndə'stɑːft] ADJ com falta de pessoal

understand [ʌndə'stænd] (irreg) VT entender, compreender ▪ VI (believe): **to ~ that** acreditar que; **I ~ that** ... (I hear) ouço dizer que ...; (I sympathize) eu compreendo que ...; **to make o.s. understood** fazer-se entender

understandable [ʌndə'stændəbl] ADJ compreensível

understanding [ʌndə'stændɪŋ] ADJ compreensivo ▪ N (in relationship) compreensão f; (knowledge) entendimento; (agreement) acordo; **to come to an ~** chegar a um acordo; **on the ~ that** ... sob condição que ..., contanto que ...

understate [ʌndə'steɪt] VT minimizar

understatement [ʌndə'steɪtmənt] N (quality) subestimação f; (euphemism) eufemismo; **it's an ~ to say that** ... é uma subestimação dizer que ...

understood [ʌndə'stud] PT, PP of **understand** ▪ ADJ entendido; (implied) subentendido, implícito

understudy ['ʌndəstʌdɪ] N ator m substituto/ atriz f substituta

undertake [ʌndə'teɪk] (irreg: like take) VT (job, project) empreender; (task, duty) incumbir-se de, encarregar-se de; **to ~ to do sth** comprometer-se a fazer algo

undertaker ['ʌndəteɪkər] N agente m/f funerário(-a)

undertaking ['ʌndəteɪkɪŋ] N empreendimento; (promise) promessa

undertone ['ʌndətəun] N (of criticism etc) sugestão f; (low voice): **in an ~** em meia voz

undertook [ʌndə'tuk] PT of **undertake**

undervalue [ʌndə'væljuː] VT subestimar

underwater [ʌndə'wɔːtər] ADV sob a água ▪ ADJ subaquático

underwear ['ʌndəwɛər] N roupa de baixo

underweight [ʌndə'weɪt] ADJ de peso inferior ao normal; (person) magro

underwent [ʌndə'wɛnt] PT of **undergo**

underworld ['ʌndəwɔːld] N (of crime) submundo

underwrite [ʌndə'raɪt] (irreg) VT (Comm) subscrever

underwriter ['ʌndəraɪtər] N (Insurance) subscritor(a) m/f (que faz resseguro)

underwritten [ʌndə'rɪtn] PP of **underwrite**

underwrote [ʌndə'rəut] PT of **underwrite**

undeserving [ʌndɪ'zəːvɪŋ] ADJ: **to be ~ of** não merecer

undesirable [ʌndɪ'zaɪərəbl] ADJ indesejável

undeveloped [ʌndɪ'vɛləpt] ADJ (land, resources) não desenvolvido

undid [ʌn'dɪd] PT of **undo**

undies ['ʌndɪz] (inf) NPL roupa de baixo, roupa íntima

undignified [ʌn'dɪgnɪfaɪd] ADJ sem dignidade, indecoroso

undiluted [ʌndaɪ'luːtɪd] ADJ não diluído, puro; (pleasure) puro

undiplomatic [ʌndɪplə'mætɪk] ADJ pouco diplomático, inábil

undischarged [ʌndɪs'tʃɑːdʒd] ADJ: **~ bankrupt** falido(-a) não reabilitado(-a)

undisciplined [ʌn'dɪsɪplɪnd] ADJ indisciplinado

undisguised [ʌndɪs'gaɪzd] ADJ (dislike etc) patente

undisputed [ʌndɪs'pjuːtɪd] ADJ incontestável

undistinguished [ʌndɪs'tɪŋgwɪʃt] ADJ medíocre, regular

undisturbed [ʌndɪs'təːbd] ADJ (sleep) tranqüilo; **to leave sth ~** não mexer em algo

undivided [ʌndɪ'vaɪdɪd] ADJ: **can I have your ~ attention?** quero a sua total atenção

undo [ʌn'duː] (irreg: like do) VT (unfasten) desatar; (spoil) desmanchar

undoing [ʌn'duːɪŋ] N ruína, desgraça

undone [ʌn'dʌn] PP of **undo** ▪ ADJ: **to come ~** desfazer-se

undoubted [ʌn'dautɪd] ADJ indubitável

undoubtedly [ʌn'dautɪdlɪ] ADV sem dúvida, indubitavelmente

undress [ʌn'drɛs] VI despir-se, tirar a roupa ▪ VT despir, tirar a roupa de

undrinkable [ʌn'drɪŋkəbl] ADJ (unpalatable) intragável; (poisonous) impotável

undue [ʌn'djuː] ADJ excessivo

undulating ['ʌndjuleɪtɪŋ] ADJ ondulante

unduly [ʌn'djuːlɪ] ADV excessivamente

undying [ʌn'daɪɪŋ] ADJ eterno

unearned [ʌn'əːnd] ADJ (praise, respect) imerecido; **~ income** rendimento não ganho com o trabalho individual

unearth [ʌn'əːθ] VT desenterrar; (fig) revelar

unearthly [ʌn'əːθlɪ] ADJ sobrenatural; **at an ~ hour of the night** na calada da noite

uneasy [ʌn'iːzɪ] ADJ (person) preocupado; (feeling) incômodo; (peace, truce) desconfortável; **to feel ~ about doing sth** estar apreensivo quanto a fazer algo

uneconomic(al) [ʌniːkə'nɔmɪk(l)] ADJ antieconômico; (unprofitable) não rentável

uneducated [ʌn'ɛdjukeɪtɪd] ADJ inculto, sem instrução, não escolarizado

unemployed [ʌnɪm'plɔɪd] ADJ desempregado ▪ NPL: **the ~** os desempregados

unemployment [ʌnɪm'plɔɪmənt] N desemprego; **unemployment benefit** (US **unemployment compensation**) N auxílio-desemprego

unending [ʌn'ɛndɪŋ] ADJ interminável

unenthusiastic [ʌnɪnθuːzɪ'æstɪk] ADJ sem entusiasmo

unenviable [ʌn'ɛnvɪəbl] ADJ nada invejável

unequal [ʌn'iːkwəl] ADJ desigual

unequalled [ʌn'iːkwəld] (US **unequaled**) ADJ inigualável, sem igual

unequivocal [ʌnɪ'kwɪvəkl] ADJ (answer) inequívoco; (person) categórico

unerring [ʌn'əːrɪŋ] ADJ infalível

UNESCO [juː'nɛskəu] N ABBR (= United Nations Educational, Scientific and Cultural Organization) UNESCO f

unethical [ʌn'ɛθɪkl] ADJ (methods) imoral;

(*professional behaviour*) contrário à ética
uneven [ʌn'iːvn] ADJ desigual; (*road etc*)
irregular, acidentado
uneventful [ʌnɪ'vɛntful] ADJ tranqüilo,
rotineiro
unexceptional [ʌnɪk'sɛpʃənl] ADJ regular,
corriqueiro
unexciting [ʌnɪk'saɪtɪŋ] ADJ monótono
unexpected [ʌnɪk'spɛktɪd] ADJ inesperado
unexpectedly [ʌnɪk'spɛktɪdlɪ] ADV
inesperadamente
unexplained [ʌnɪk'spleɪnd] ADJ inexplicado
unexploded [ʌnɪk'spləʊdɪd] ADJ não explodido
unfailing [ʌn'feɪlɪŋ] ADJ inexaurível
unfair [ʌn'fɛəʳ] ADJ: ~ (**to**) injusto (com); **it's ~
that** ... não é justo que ...; **unfair dismissal** N
demissão f injusta *or* infundada
unfairly [ʌn'fɛəlɪ] ADV injustamente
unfaithful [ʌn'feɪθful] ADJ infiel
unfamiliar [ʌnfə'mɪlɪəʳ] ADJ pouco familiar,
desconhecido; **to be ~ with** sth não estar
familiarizado com algo
unfashionable [ʌn'fæʃnəbl] ADJ fora da moda
unfasten [ʌn'fɑːsn] VT desatar; (*open*) abrir
unfathomable [ʌn'fæðəməbl] ADJ insondável
unfavourable [ʌn'feɪvərəbl] (US **unfavorable**)
ADJ desfavorável
unfavo(u)rably [ʌn'feɪvərəblɪ] ADV: **to look
unfavo(u)rably upon** não ser favorável a
unfeeling [ʌn'fiːlɪŋ] ADJ insensível
unfinished [ʌn'fɪnɪʃt] ADJ incompleto,
inacabado
unfit [ʌn'fɪt] ADJ (*physically*) sem preparo físico;
(*incompetent*) incompetente, incapaz; ~ **for work**
inapto para trabalhar
unflagging [ʌn'flægɪŋ] ADJ incansável
unflappable [ʌn'flæpəbl] ADJ imperturbável,
sereno
unflattering [ʌn'flætərɪŋ] ADJ (*dress, hairstyle*)
que não fica bem; (*remark*) pouco elogioso
unflinching [ʌn'flɪntʃɪŋ] ADJ destemido,
intrépido
unfold [ʌn'fəʊld] VT desdobrar; (*fig*) revelar ▪ VI
(*story, situation*) desdobrar-se
unforeseeable [ʌnfɔː'siːəbl] ADJ imprevisível
unforeseen [ʌnfɔː'siːn] ADJ imprevisto
unforgettable [ʌnfə'gɛtəbl] ADJ inesquecível
unforgivable [ʌnfə'gɪvəbl] ADJ imperdoável
unformatted [ʌn'fɔːmætɪd] ADJ (*disk, text*) não
formatado
unfortunate [ʌn'fɔːtʃənət] ADJ infeliz; (*event,
remark*) inoportuno
unfortunately [ʌn'fɔːtʃənətlɪ] ADV
infelizmente
unfounded [ʌn'faundɪd] ADJ infundado
unfriendly [ʌn'frɛndlɪ] ADJ antipático
unfulfilled [ʌnful'fɪld] ADJ (*ambition, prophecy*)
não realizado; (*desire*) não satisfeito; (*promise,
terms of contract*) não cumprido; (*person*) que não
se realizou
unfurl [ʌn'fəːl] VT desfraldar
unfurnished [ʌn'fəːnɪʃt] ADJ desmobiliado, sem

mobília
ungainly [ʌn'geɪnlɪ] ADJ desalinhado
ungodly [ʌn'gɔdlɪ] ADJ ímpio; **at an ~ hour** às
altas horas da madrugada
ungrateful [ʌn'greɪtful] ADJ mal-agradecido,
ingrato
unguarded [ʌn'gɑːdɪd] ADJ: ~ **moment**
momento de inatenção
unhappily [ʌn'hæpəlɪ] ADV tristemente;
(*unfortunately*) infelizmente
unhappiness [ʌn'hæpɪnɪs] N infelicidade f
unhappy [ʌn'hæpɪ] ADJ (*sad*) triste; (*unfortunate*)
desventurado; (*childhood*) infeliz; (*dissatisfied*):
~ **with** (*arrangements etc*) descontente com,
insatisfeito com
unharmed [ʌn'hɑːmd] ADJ ileso
unhealthy [ʌn'hɛlθɪ] ADJ insalubre; (*person*)
doentio; (*fig*) anormal
unheard-of [ʌn'həːd-] ADJ insólito; (*unknown*)
desconhecido
unhelpful [ʌn'hɛlpful] ADJ (*person*) imprestável;
(*advice*) inútil
unhesitating [ʌn'hɛzɪteɪtɪŋ] ADJ (*loyalty*) firme;
(*reply*) imediato
unhook [ʌn'huk] VT desenganchar; (*from wall*)
despendurar; (*dress*) abrir, soltar
unhurt [ʌn'həːt] ADJ ileso
unhygienic [ʌnhaɪ'dʒiːnɪk] ADJ anti-higiênico
UNICEF ['juːnɪsɛf] N ABBR (= *United Nations
International Children's Emergency Fund*) Unicef m
unicorn ['juːnɪkɔːn] N licorne m, unicórnio
unidentified [ʌnaɪ'dɛntɪfaɪd] ADJ não-
identificado; *see also* **UFO**
uniform ['juːnɪfɔːm] N uniforme m ▪ ADJ
uniforme
uniformity [juːnɪ'fɔːmɪtɪ] N uniformidade f
unify ['juːnɪfaɪ] VT unificar, unir
unilateral [juːnɪ'lætərəl] ADJ unilateral
unimaginable [ʌnɪ'mædʒɪnəbl] ADJ
inimaginável, inconcebível
unimaginative [ʌnɪ'mædʒɪnətɪv] ADJ sem
imaginação
unimpaired [ʌnɪm'pɛəd] ADJ inalterado
unimportant [ʌnɪm'pɔːtənt] ADJ sem
importância
unimpressed [ʌnɪm'prɛst] ADJ indiferente
uninhabited [ʌnɪn'hæbɪtɪd] ADJ inabitado
uninhibited [ʌnɪn'hɪbɪtɪd] ADJ sem inibições
uninjured [ʌn'ɪndʒəd] ADJ ileso
uninspired [ʌnɪn'spaɪəd] ADJ insípido
unintelligent [ʌnɪn'tɛlɪdʒənt] ADJ
ininteligente
unintentional [ʌnɪn'tɛnʃənəl] ADJ involuntário,
não intencional
unintentionally [ʌnɪn'tɛnʃənəlɪ] ADV sem
querer
uninvited [ʌnɪn'vaɪtɪd] ADJ (*guest*) não
convidado
uninviting [ʌnɪn'vaɪtɪŋ] ADJ (*place*) pouco
convidativo; (*food*) pouco apetitoso
union ['juːnjən] N união f; (*also:* **trade union**)
sindicato (de trabalhadores) ▪ CPD sindical

unionize ['ju:njənaɪz] VT sindicalizar

Union Jack N bandeira britânica

Union of Soviet Socialist Republics N União f das Repúblicas Socialistas Soviéticas

union shop N *empresa onde todos os trabalhadores têm que filiar-se ao sindicato*

unique [ju:'ni:k] ADJ único, sem igual

unisex ['ju:nɪsɛks] ADJ unissex *inv*

unison ['ju:nɪsn] N: **in ~** em harmonia, em uníssono

unit ['ju:nɪt] N unidade f; (*of furniture etc*) segão f; (*team, squad*) equipe f; **kitchen ~** armário de cozinha; **sink ~** pia de cozinha; **production ~** unidade de produção; **unit cost** N custo unitário

unite [ju:'naɪt] VT unir ■ VI unir-se

united [ju:'naɪtɪd] ADJ unido; (*effort*) conjunto

United Arab Emirates NPL Emirados *mpl* Árabes Unidos

United Kingdom N Reino Unido

United Nations (Organization) N (Organização f das) Nações *fpl* Unidas

United States (of America) N Estados Unidos *mpl* (da América)

unit price N preço unitário

unit trust (*Brit*) N (*Comm*) fundo de investimento

unity ['ju:nɪtɪ] N unidade f

Univ. ABBR = **university**

universal [ju:nɪ'və:sl] ADJ universal

universe ['ju:nɪvə:s] N universo

university [ju:nɪ'və:sɪtɪ] N universidade f, faculdade f ■ CPD universitário

unjust [ʌn'dʒʌst] ADJ injusto

unjustifiable [ʌndʒʌstɪ'faɪəbl] ADJ injustificável

unjustified [ʌn'dʒʌstɪfaɪd] ADJ injustificado; (*text*) não alinhado

unkempt [ʌn'kɛmpt] ADJ desleixado, descuidado; (*hair*) despenteado; (*beard*) mal tratado

unkind [ʌn'kaɪnd] ADJ maldoso; (*comment etc*) cruel

unkindly [ʌn'kaɪndlɪ] ADV (*treat, speak*) maldosamente

unknown [ʌn'nəun] ADJ desconhecido; **~ to me** sem eu saber; **~ quantity** (*Math, fig*) incógnita

unladen [ʌn'leɪdn] ADJ (*ship, weight*) sem carga

unlawful [ʌn'lɔ:ful] ADJ ilegal

unleash [ʌn'li:ʃ] VT (*fig*) desencadear

unleavened [ʌn'lɛvənd] ADJ sem fermento

unless [ʌn'lɛs] CONJ a menos que, a não ser que; **~ he comes** a menos que ele venha; **~ otherwise stated** salvo indicação contrária; **~ I am mistaken** se não me engano

unlicensed [ʌn'laɪsnst] (*Brit*) ADJ sem licença para a venda de bebidas alcoólicas

unlike [ʌn'laɪk] ADJ diferente ■ PREP diferentemente de, ao contrário de

unlikelihood [ʌn'laɪklɪhud] N improbabilidade f

unlikely [ʌn'laɪklɪ] ADJ (*not likely*) improvável;

(*unexpected*) inesperado

unlimited [ʌn'lɪmɪtɪd] ADJ ilimitado

unlisted [ʌn'lɪstɪd] ADJ (*Stock Exchange*) não cotado na Bolsa de Valores; (*US: Tel*): **an ~ number** um número que não consta na lista telefônica

unlit [ʌn'lɪt] ADJ (*room*) sem luz

unload [ʌn'ləud] VT descarregar

unlock [ʌn'lɔk] VT destrancar

unlucky [ʌn'lʌkɪ] ADJ infeliz; (*object, number*) de mau agouro; **to be ~** ser azarado, ter azar

unmanageable [ʌn'mænɪdʒəbl] ADJ (*unwieldy: tool*) de difícil manuseio, difícil de manejar; (*: situation*) difícil de controlar

unmanned [ʌn'mænd] ADJ não tripulado, sem tripulação

unmarked [ʌn'mɑ:kt] ADJ (*unstained*) sem marca; **~ police car** carro policial sem identificação

unmarried [ʌn'mærɪd] ADJ solteiro

unmask [ʌn'mɑ:sk] VT desmascarar

unmatched [ʌn'mætʃt] ADJ sem igual, inigualável

unmentionable [ʌn'mɛnʃnəbl] ADJ (*topic*) que não se deve mencionar; (*word*) que não se diz

unmerciful [ʌn'mə:sɪful] ADJ impiedoso

unmistak(e)able [ʌnmɪs'teɪkəbl] ADJ inconfundível

unmitigated [ʌn'mɪtɪgeɪtɪd] ADJ não mitigado, absoluto

unnamed [ʌn'neɪmd] ADJ (*nameless*) sem nome; (*anonymous*) anônimo

unnatural [ʌn'nætʃrəl] ADJ antinatural, artificial; (*manner*) afetado; (*habit*) depravado

unnecessary [ʌn'nɛsəsərɪ] ADJ desnecessário, inútil

unnerve [ʌn'nə:v] VT amedrontar

unnoticed [ʌn'nəutɪst] ADJ: **(to go** *or* **pass) ~** (passar) despercebido

UNO ['ju:nəu] N ABBR (= *United Nations Organization*) ONU f

unobservant [ʌnəb'zə:vənt] N desatento

unobtainable [ʌnəb'teɪnəbl] ADJ inacessível; (*Tel*) ocupado

unobtrusive [ʌnəb'tru:sɪv] ADJ discreto

unoccupied [ʌn'ɔkjupaɪd] ADJ (*seat etc*) desocupado, livre; (*house*) desocupado, vazio

unofficial [ʌnə'fɪʃl] ADJ não-oficial, informal; (*strike*) desautorizado

unopened [ʌn'əupənd] ADJ por abrir

unopposed [ʌnə'pəuzd] ADJ incontestado, sem oposição

unorthodox [ʌn'ɔ:θədɔks] ADJ pouco ortodoxo, heterodoxo

unpack [ʌn'pæk] VI desembrulhar ■ VT desfazer

unpaid [ʌn'peɪd] ADJ (*bill*) a pagar, não pago; (*holiday*) não pago, sem salário; (*work, worker*) não remunerado

unpalatable [ʌn'pælətəbl] ADJ desagradável

unparalleled [ʌn'pærəlɛld] ADJ (*unequalled*) sem paralelo; (*unique*) único, incomparável

unpatriotic [ʌnpætrɪˈɔtɪk] ADJ (*person*) antipatriota; (*speech, attitude*) antipatriótico

unplanned [ʌnˈplænd] ADJ (*visit*) imprevisto; (*baby*) não previsto

unpleasant [ʌnˈplɛznt] ADJ (*disagreeable*) desagradável; (*person, manner*) antipático

unplug [ʌnˈplʌg] VT desligar

unpolluted [ʌnpəˈluːtɪd] ADJ impoluído

unpopular [ʌnˈpɔpjuləʳ] ADJ impopular

unprecedented [ʌnˈprɛsɪdəntɪd] ADJ sem precedentes

unpredictable [ʌnprɪˈdɪktəbl] ADJ imprevisível

unprejudiced [ʌnˈprɛdʒudɪst] ADJ (*not biased*) imparcial; (*having no prejudices*) sem preconceitos

unprepared [ʌnprɪˈpɛəd] ADJ (*person*) despreparado; (*speech*) improvisado

unprepossessing [ʌnpriːpəˈzɛsɪŋ] ADJ pouco atraente

unpretentious [ʌnprɪˈtɛnʃəs] ADJ despretensioso

unprincipled [ʌnˈprɪnsɪpld] ADJ sem princípios

unproductive [ʌnprəˈdʌktɪv] ADJ improdutivo

unprofessional [ʌnprəˈfɛʃənl] ADJ (*conduct*) pouco profissional

unprofitable [ʌnˈprɔfɪtəbl] ADJ não lucrativo

unprovoked [ʌnprəˈvəukt] ADJ sem provocação

unpunished [ʌnˈpʌnɪʃt] ADJ ímpune

unqualified [ʌnˈkwɔlɪfaɪd] ADJ (*teacher*) não qualificado, inabilitado; (*success*) irrestrito, absoluto

unquestionably [ʌnˈkwɛstʃənəblɪ] ADV indubitavelmente

unquestioning [ʌnˈkwɛstʃənɪŋ] ADJ (*obedience, acceptance*) incondicional, total

unravel [ʌnˈrævl] VT desemaranhar; (*mystery*) desvendar

unreal [ʌnˈrɪəl] ADJ irreal, ilusório; (*extraordinary*) extraordinário

unrealistic [ʌnrɪəˈlɪstɪk] ADJ pouco realista

unreasonable [ʌnˈriːznəbl] ADJ insensato; (*demand*) absurdo

unrecognizable [ʌnrɛkəgˈnaɪzəbl] ADJ irreconhecível

unrecognized [ʌnˈrɛkəgnaɪzd] ADJ (*talent, genius*) não reconhecido

unrecorded [ʌnrəˈkɔːdɪd] ADJ não registrado

unrefined [ʌnrəˈfaɪnd] ADJ (*sugar, petroleum*) não refinado

unrehearsed [ʌnrɪˈhəːst] ADJ improvisado

unrelated [ʌnrɪˈleɪtɪd] ADJ sem relação; (*family*) sem parentesco

unrelenting [ʌnrɪˈlɛntɪŋ] ADJ implacável

unreliable [ʌnrɪˈlaɪəbl] ADJ (*person*) indigno de confiança; (*machine*) incerto, perigoso

unrelieved [ʌnrɪˈliːvd] ADJ (*monotony*) invariável

unremitting [ʌnrɪˈmɪtɪŋ] ADJ constante, incessante

unrepeatable [ʌnrɪˈpiːtəbl] ADJ (*offer*) irrepetível

unrepentant [ʌnrɪˈpɛntənt] ADJ convicto, impenitente

unrepresentative [ʌnrɛprɪˈzɛntətɪv] ADJ pouco representativo *or* característico

unreserved [ʌnrɪˈzəːvd] ADJ (*seat*) não reservado; (*approval, admiration*) total, integral

unreservedly [ʌnrɪˈzəːvɪdlɪ] ADV sem reserva, francamente

unresponsive [ʌnrɪsˈpɔnsɪv] ADJ indiferente, impassível

unrest [ʌnˈrɛst] N inquietação *f*, desassossego; (*Pol*) distúrbios *mpl*

unrestricted [ʌnrɪˈstrɪktɪd] ADJ irrestrito, ilimitado

unrewarded [ʌnrɪˈwɔːdɪd] ADJ sem sucesso

unripe [ʌnˈraɪp] ADJ verde, imaturo

unrivalled [ʌnˈraɪvəld] (*US* **unrivaled**) ADJ sem igual, incomparável

unroll [ʌnˈrəul] VT desenrolar

unruffled [ʌnˈrʌfld] ADJ (*person*) sereno, imperturbável; (*hair*) liso

unruly [ʌnˈruːlɪ] ADJ indisciplinado; (*hair*) desalinhado

unsafe [ʌnˈseɪf] ADJ perigoso; ~ **to eat/drink** não comestível/potável

unsaid [ʌnˈsɛd] ADJ: **to leave sth ~** deixar algo por dizer

unsaleable [ʌnˈseɪləbl] (*US* **unsalable**) ADJ invendável, invendível

unsatisfactory [ʌnsætɪsˈfæktərɪ] ADJ insatisfatório

unsatisfied [ʌnˈsætɪsfaɪd] ADJ descontente

unsavoury [ʌnˈseɪvərɪ] (*US* **unsavory**) ADJ (*fig*) repugnante, vil

unscathed [ʌnˈskeɪðd] ADJ ileso

unscientific [ʌnsaɪənˈtɪfɪk] ADJ não científico

unscrew [ʌnˈskruː] VT desparafusar

unscrupulous [ʌnˈskruːpjuləs] ADJ inescrupuloso, imoral

unsecured [ʌnsəˈkjuəd] ADJ: ~ **creditor** credor(a) *m/f* quirografário(-a)

unseemly [ʌnˈsiːmlɪ] ADJ inconveniente

unseen [ʌnˈsiːn] ADJ (*person*) despercebido; (*danger*) escondido

unselfish [ʌnˈsɛlfɪʃ] ADJ desinteressado

unsettled [ʌnˈsɛtld] ADJ (*uncertain*) incerto, duvidoso; (*weather*) instável; (*person*) inquieto

unsettling [ʌnˈsɛtlɪŋ] ADJ inquietador(a), inquietante

unshak(e)able [ʌnˈʃeɪkəbl] ADJ inabalável

unshaven [ʌnˈʃeɪvn] ADJ com a barba por fazer

unsightly [ʌnˈsaɪtlɪ] ADJ feio, disforme

unskilled [ʌnˈskɪld] ADJ não-especializado

unsociable [ʌnˈsəuʃəbl] ADJ anti-social

unsocial [ʌnˈsəuʃl] ADJ (*hours*) fora do horário normal

unsold [ʌnˈsəuld] ADJ não vendido

unsolicited [ʌnsəˈlɪsɪtɪd] ADJ não solicitado, espontâneo

unsophisticated [ʌnsəˈfɪstɪkeɪtɪd] ADJ simples *inv*, natural

unsound [ʌnˈsaund] ADJ (*health*) mau; (*floor, foundations*) em mau estado; (*policy, advice*) infundado

unspeakable [ʌn'spiːkəbl] ADJ indescritível; (*awful*) inqualificável

unspoken [ʌn'spəukən] ADJ (*agreement, approval*) tácito

unstable [ʌn'stɪbl] ADJ (*piece of furniture*) em falso; (*government, mentally*) instável; (*step, voice, hance*) trêmulo; (*ladder*) em falso

unsteady [ʌn'stɛdɪ] ADJ instável

unstinting [ʌn'stɪntɪŋ] ADJ (*support*) irrestrito, total; (*generosity*) ilimitado

unstuck [ʌn'stʌk] ADJ: **to come ~** despregar-se; (*fig*) fracassar

unsubstantiated [ʌnsəb'stænʃɪeɪtɪd] ADJ (*rumour*) que não foi confirmado; (*accusation*) sem provas

unsuccessful [ʌnsək'sɛsful] ADJ (*attempt*) frustrado, vão(-vã); (*writer, proposal*) sem êxito; **to be ~** (*in attempting sth*) ser mal sucedido, não conseguir; (*application*) ser recusado

unsuccessfully [ʌnsək'sɛsfulɪ] ADV em vão, debalde

unsuitable [ʌn'suːtəbl] ADJ (*clothes, person*) inadequado; (*time, moment*) inconveniente

unsuited [ʌn'suːtɪd] ADJ: **to be ~ for** or **to** ser inadequado or impróprio para

unsupported [ʌnsə'pɔːtɪd] ADJ (*claim*) não verificado; (*theory*) não sustentado

unsure [ʌn'ʃuəʳ] ADJ inseguro, incerto; **to be ~ of o.s.** não ser seguro de si

unsuspecting [ʌnsə'spɛktɪŋ] ADJ confiante, insuspeitado

unsweetened [ʌn'swiːtənd] ADJ não adoçado, sem açúcar

unswerving [ʌn'swəːvɪŋ] ADJ inabalável, firme, resoluto

unsympathetic [ʌnsɪmpə'θɛtɪk] ADJ insensível; (*unlikeable*) antipático; **~ to** indiferente a

untangle [ʌn'tæŋgl] VT desemaranhar, desenredar

untapped [ʌn'tæpt] ADJ (*resources*) inexplorado

untaxed [ʌn'tækst] ADJ (*goods*) isento de impostos; (*income*) não tributado

unthinkable [ʌn'θɪŋkəbl] ADJ impensável, inconcebível, incalculável

untidy [ʌn'taɪdɪ] ADJ (*room*) desarrumado, desleixado; (*appearance*) desmazelado, desalinhado

untie [ʌn'taɪ] VT desatar, desfazer; (*dog, prisoner*) soltar

until [ən'tɪl] PREP até ■ CONJ até que; **~ he comes** até que ele venha; **~ now** até agora; **~ then** até então; **from morning ~ night** de manhã à noite

untimely [ʌn'taɪmlɪ] ADJ inoportuno, intempestivo; (*death*) prematuro

untold [ʌn'təuld] ADJ (*story*) inédito; (*suffering*) incalculável; (*joy, wealth*) inestimável

untouched [ʌn'tʌtʃt] ADJ (*not used*) intacto; (*safe: person*) ileso; **~ by** indiferente a

untoward [ʌntə'wɔːd] ADJ desfavorável, inconveniente

untrammelled [ʌn'træmld] ADJ sem entraves

untranslatable [ʌntræns'leɪtəbl] ADJ impossível de traduzir, intraduzível

untrue [ʌn'truː] ADJ falso

untrustworthy [ʌn'trʌstwəːðɪ] ADJ indigno de confiança

unusable [ʌn'juːzəbl] ADJ inutilizável, imprestável

unused[1] [ʌn'juːzd] ADJ novo, sem uso

unused[2] [ʌn'juːst] ADJ: **to be ~ to sth/to doing sth** não estar acostumado com algo/a fazer algo

unusual [ʌn'juːʒuəl] ADJ (*strange*) estranho; (*rare*) incomum; (*exceptional*) extraordinário

unusually [ʌn'juːʒəlɪ] ADV extraordinariamente

unveil [ʌn'veɪl] VT (*statue*) desvelar, descobrir

unwanted [ʌn'wɒntɪd] ADJ não desejado, indesejável

unwarranted [ʌn'wɒrəntɪd] ADJ injustificado

unwary [ʌn'wɛərɪ] ADJ imprudente

unwavering [ʌn'weɪvərɪŋ] ADJ firme

unwelcome [ʌn'wɛlkəm] ADJ (*guest*) inoportuno; (*news*) desagradável; **to feel ~** não se sentir à vontade

unwell [ʌn'wɛl] ADJ: **to be ~** estar doente; **to feel ~** estar indisposto

unwieldy [ʌn'wiːldɪ] ADJ difícil de manejar, pesado

unwilling [ʌn'wɪlɪŋ] ADJ: **to be ~ to do sth** relutar em fazer algo, não querer fazer algo

unwillingly [ʌn'wɪlɪŋlɪ] ADV de má vontade

unwind [ʌn'waɪnd] (*irreg*) VT desenrolar ■ VI (*relax*) relaxar-se

unwise [ʌn'waɪz] ADJ imprudente

unwitting [ʌn'wɪtɪŋ] ADJ inconsciente, involuntário

unworkable [ʌn'wəːkəbl] ADJ (*plan etc*) inviável, inexequível

unworthy [ʌn'wəːðɪ] ADJ indigno

unwound [ʌn'waund] PT, PP *of* **unwind**

unwrap [ʌn'ræp] VT desembrulhar

unwritten [ʌn'rɪtən] ADJ (*agreement*) tácito

unzip [ʌn'zɪp] VT abrir (o fecho ecler de)

◯ **KEYWORD**

up [ʌp] PREP: **to go/be up sth** subir algo/estar em cima de algo; **we climbed/walked up the hill** nós subimos/andamos até em cima da colina; **they live further up the street** eles moram mais adiante nesta rua; **go up that road and turn left** vá por aquela rua e vire à esquerda

■ ADV **1** (*upwards, higher*) em cima, para cima; **up in the sky/the mountains** lá no céu/nas montanhas; **up there** lá em cima; **up above** em cima; **there's a village and up above, on the hill, a monastery** há uma aldeia e, mais acima na colina, um monastério

2: **to be up** (*out of bed*) estar de pé; (*prices, level*) estar elevado; (*building, tent*) estar erguido

3: up to (*as far as*) até; **the water came up to his knees** a água subiu até os seus joelhos; **up to now** até agora
4: to be up to (*depending on*): **it is up to you** você é quem sabe, você decide; **it's not up to me to decide** não sou eu quem decide
5: to be up to (*equal to*) estar à altura de; **he's not up to it** (*job, task etc*) ele não é capaz de fazê-lo; **his work is not up to the required standard** seu trabalho não atende aos padrões exigidos
6: to be up to (*inf: be doing*) estar fazendo (BR) *or* a fazer (PT); **what is he up to?** (*showing disapproval, suspicion*) o que ele está querendo?, o que ele está tramando?

■ N: **ups and downs** (*in life, career*) altos *mpl* e baixos; **we all have our ups and downs** todos nós temos nossos altos e baixos

up-and-coming ADJ prometedor(a)
upbeat ['ʌpbiːt] ADJ (*Mus*) movimentado; (*optimistic*) otimista
upbraid [ʌp'breɪd] VT repreender, censurar
upbringing ['ʌpbrɪŋɪŋ] N educação *f*, criação *f*
update [ʌp'deɪt] VT atualizar, pôr em dia; (*contract etc*) atualizar
upend [ʌp'ɛnd] VT colocar em pé
upgrade [ʌp'greɪd] VT (*person*) promover; (*job*) melhorar; (*house*) reformar; (*Comput*) fazer um upgrade de
upheaval [ʌp'hiːvl] N transtorno; (*unrest*) convulsão *f*
upheld [ʌp'hɛld] PT, PP of **uphold**
uphill [ʌp'hɪl] ADJ ladeira acima; (*fig: task*) trabalhoso, árduo ■ ADV: **to go ~** ir morro acima
uphold [ʌp'həʊld] (*irreg: like* **hold**) VT defender, preservar
upholstery [ʌp'həʊlstərɪ] N estofamento
upkeep ['ʌpkiːp] N manutenção *f*
up-market ADJ (*product*) requintado
upon [ə'pɔn] PREP sobre
upper ['ʌpəʳ] ADJ superior, de cima ■ N (*of shoe*) gáspea, parte *f* superior; **upper class** N: **the upper class** a classe alta ■ ADJ: **upper-class** de classe alta; **upper hand** N: **to have the upper hand** ter controle *or* domínio
uppermost ['ʌpəməʊst] ADJ mais elevado; **what was ~ in my mind** o que me preocupava mais
Upper Volta [-'vɔltə] N Alto Volta *m*
upright ['ʌpraɪt] ADJ vertical; (*straight*) reto; (*fig*) honesto ■ N viga vertical
uprising ['ʌpraɪzɪŋ] N revolta, rebelião *f*, sublevação *f*
uproar ['ʌprɔːʳ] N tumulto, algazarra
uproot [ʌp'ruːt] VT (*tree*) arrancar; (*fig*) desarraigar
upset [n 'ʌpsɛt, vt, adj ʌp'sɛt] (*irreg: like* **set**) N (*to plan etc*) revés *m*, reviravolta; (*stomach upset*) indisposição *f* ■ VT (*glass etc*) virar; (*spill*) derramar; (*plan*) perturbar; (*person: annoy*)

aborrecer; (*: sadden*) afligir ■ ADJ aborrecido, contrariado; (*sad*) aflito; (*stomach*) indisposto; **upset price** (*US, Scottish*) N preço mínimo
upsetting [ʌp'setɪŋ] ADJ desconcertante
upshot ['ʌpʃɔt] N resultado, conclusão *f*
upside down ['ʌpsaɪd-] ADV de cabeça para baixo; **to turn a place ~** (*fig*) deixar um lugar de cabeça para baixo
upstairs [ʌp'stɛəz] ADV (*be*) em cima; (*go*) lá em cima ■ ADJ (*room*) de cima ■ N andar *m* de cima
upstart ['ʌpstɑːt] (*pej*) N novo-rico, pessoa sem classe
upstream [ʌp'striːm] ADV rio acima
upsurge ['ʌpsəːdʒ] N (*of enthusiasm etc*) explosão *f*
uptake ['ʌpteɪk] N: **he is quick on the ~** ele vê longe; **he is slow on the ~** ele tem raciocínio lento
uptight [ʌp'taɪt] (*inf*) ADJ nervoso
up-to-date ADJ (*person*) moderno, atualizado; (*information*) atualizado; **to be ~ with the facts** estar a par dos fatos
upturn ['ʌptəːn] N (*in luck*) virada; (*in economy*) retomada
upturned ['ʌptəːnd] ADJ (*nose*) arrebitado
upward ['ʌpwəd] ADJ ascendente, para cima
upward(s) ['ʌpwəd(z)] ADV para cima; (*more than*): **upward(s) of** para cima de
URA (*US*) N ABBR = **Urban Renewal Administration**
Ural Mountains ['juərəl-] NPL: **the ~** (*also*: **the Urals**) as montanhas Urais, os Urais
uranium [juə'reɪnɪəm] N urânio
Uranus [juə'reɪnəs] N Urano
urban ['əːbən] ADJ urbano, da cidade
urbane [əː'beɪn] ADJ gentil, urbano
urbanization [əːbənaɪ'zeɪʃən] N urbanização *f*
urchin ['əːtʃɪn] (*pej*) N moleque *m*, criança maltrapilha
urge [əːdʒ] N (*force*) impulso; (*desire*) desejo ■ VT: **to ~ sb to do sth** incitar alguém a fazer algo
▶ **urge on** VT animar, encorajar
urgency ['əːdʒənsɪ] N urgência; (*of tone*) insistência
urgent ['əːdʒənt] ADJ urgente; (*tone, plea*) insistente
urgently ['əːdʒəntlɪ] ADV urgentemente
urinal ['juərɪnl] (*Brit*) N (*vessel*) urinol *m*; (*building*) mictório
urinate ['juərɪneɪt] VI urinar, mijar
urine ['juərɪn] N urina
URL ABBR (= *uniform resource locator*) URL *m*
urn [əːn] N urna; (*also*: **tea urn**) samovar *m*
Uruguay ['juərəgwaɪ] N Uruguai *m*
Uruguayan [juərə'gwaɪən] ADJ, N uruguaio(-a)
US N ABBR (= *United States*) EUA *mpl*
us [ʌs] PRON nos; (*after prep*) nós; *see also* **me**
USA N ABBR (= *United States (of America)*) EUA *mpl*; (*Mil*) = **United States Army**
usable ['juːzəbl] ADJ usável, utilizável

USAF N ABBR = United States Air Force
usage ['juːzɪdʒ] N uso
USCG N ABBR = United States Coast Guard
USDA N ABBR = United States Department of Agriculture
USDAW ['ʌzdɔː] (Brit) N ABBR (= Union of Shop,Distributive and Allied Workers) sindicato dos varejistas e distribuidores
USDI N ABBR = United States Department of the Interior
use [n juːs, vt juːz] N uso, emprego; (usefulness) utilidade f ■ VT usar, utilizar; (phrase) empregar; **in** ~ em uso; **out of** ~ fora de uso; **ready for** ~ pronto para ser usado; **to be of** ~ ser útil; **it's no** ~ (pointless) é inútil; (not useful) não serve; **to have** ~ **of** ter uso de; **to make** ~ **of** fazer uso de; **to be** ~**d to** estar acostumado a; **she** ~**d to do it** ela costumava fazê-lo
▸ **use up** VT esgotar, consumir; (money) gostar
used [juːzd] ADJ usado
useful ['juːsful] ADJ útil; **to come in** ~ serútil
usefulness ['juːsfəlnɪs] N utilidade f
useless ['juːslɪs] ADJ inútil; (person) incapaz
user ['juːzər] N usuário(-a) (BR), utente m/f (PT)
user-friendly ADJ de fácil utilização
USES N ABBR = United States Employment Service
usher ['ʌʃər] N (in cinema) lanterninha m (BR), arrumador m (PT); (at wedding) oficial m de justiça ■ VT: **to** ~ **sb in** fazer alguém entrar
usherette [ʌʃə'rɛt] N (in cinema) lanterninha (BR), arrumadora (PT)
USIA N ABBR = United States Information Agency

USM N ABBR = United States Mail; United States Mint
USN N ABBR = United States Navy
USPHS N ABBR = United States Public Health Service
USPO N ABBR = United States Post Office
USS N ABBR = United States Ship; United States Steamer
USSR N ABBR (= Union of Soviet Socialist Republics) URSS f
usual ['juːʒuəl] ADJ usual, habitual; **as** ~ como de hábito, como sempre
usually ['juːʒuəlɪ] ADV normalmente
usurer ['juːʒərər] N usurário(-a)
usurp [juː'zəːp] VT usurpar
UT (US) ABBR (Post) = Utah
utensil [juː'tensl] N utensílio; **kitchen** ~**s** utensílios de cozinha
uterus ['juːtərəs] N útero
utilitarian [juːtɪlɪ'tɛərɪən] ADJ utilitário
utility [juː'tɪlɪtɪ] N utilidade f; (public utility) utilidade f pública; **utility room** N área de serviço
utilization [juːtɪlaɪ'zeɪʃən] N utilização f
utilize ['juːtɪlaɪz] VT utilizar
utmost ['ʌtməust] ADJ maior ■ N: **to do one's** ~ fazer todo o possível; **of the** ~ **importance** da maior importância
utter ['ʌtər] ADJ total ■ VT (sounds) emitir; (words) proferir, pronunciar
utterance ['ʌtərəns] N declaração f
utterly ['ʌtəlɪ] ADV completamente, totalmente
U-turn N retorno; (fig) reviravolta

Vv

V, v [viː] N (letter) V, v m; **V for Victor** V de Vera
v ABBR = **verse**; (= vide: see) vide; (= versus) v; (= volt)
v
VA (US) ABBR (Post) = **Virginia**
vac [væk] (Brit: inf) N ABBR = **vacation**
vacancy ['veɪkənsɪ] N (Brit: job) vaga; (room)
quarto livre; **"no vacancies"** "cheio"
vacant ['veɪkənt] ADJ (house) vazio; (post) vago;
(seat etc) desocupado, livre; (expression) distraído;
vacant lot N terreno vago; (uncultivated) terreno
baldio
vacate [və'keɪt] VT (house) desocupar; (job)
deixar; (throne) renunciar a
vacation [və'keɪʃən] (esp US) N férias fpl; **to take
a ~** tirar férias; **on ~** de férias; **vacation course**
N curso de férias
vacationer [və'keɪʃənəʳ] (US) N veranista m/f
vaccinate ['væksɪneɪt] VT: **to ~ sb (against sth)**
vacinar alguém (contra algo)
vaccination [væksɪ'neɪʃən] N vacinação f
vaccine ['væksiːn] N vacina
vacuum ['vækjum] N vácuo m; **vacuum bottle**
(US) N garrafa térmica (BR), termo (PT);
vacuum cleaner N aspirador m de pó; **vacuum
flask** (Brit) N garrafa térmica (BR), termo (PT)
vacuum-packed ADJ embalado a vácuo
vagabond ['vægəbɔnd] N vagabundo(-a)
vagary ['veɪgərɪ] N extravagância, capricho
vagina [və'dʒaɪnə] N vagina
vagrancy ['veɪgrənsɪ] N vadiagem f
vagrant ['veɪgrənt] N vagabundo(-a), vadio(-a)
vague [veɪg] ADJ vago; (blurred: memory) fraco; **I
haven't the ~st idea** não tenho a mínima idéia
vaguely ['veɪglɪ] ADV vagamente
vain [veɪn] ADJ (conceited) vaidoso; (useless)
vão(-vã), inútil; **in ~** em vão
valance ['væləns] N sanefa
vale [veɪl] N vale m
valedictory [vælɪ'dɪktərɪ] ADJ de despedida
valentine ['væləntaɪn] N (also: **valentine
card**) cartão m do Dia dos Namorados; (person)
namorado; **V~'s Day** Dia m dos Namorados
valet ['vælɪt] N (of lord) criado pessoal; (in hotel)
camareiro; **valet parking** N estacionamento
por manobrista; **valet service** N (for clothes)
lavagem f a seco; (for car) limpeza completa
valiant ['vælɪənt] ADJ carajoso

valid ['vælɪd] ADJ válido
validate ['vælɪdeɪt] VT (contract, document)
validar, legitimar; (argument, claim) confirmar,
corroborar
validity [və'lɪdɪtɪ] N validade f
valise [və'liːz] N maleta
valley ['vælɪ] N vale m
valour ['væləʳ] (US **valor**) N valor m, valentia
valuable ['væljuəbl] ADJ (jewel) de valor; (time)
valioso; (help) precioso
valuables ['væljuəblz] NPL objetos mpl de valor
valuation [vælju'eɪʃən] N avaliação f; (of quality)
apreciação f
value ['væljuː] N valor m; (importance)
importância ■ VT (fix price of) avaliar; (appreciate)
valorizar, estimar; (cherish) apreciar; **values**
NPL (principles) valores mpl; **you get good ~ (for
money) in that shop** o seu dinheiro rende
mais naquela loja; **to lose (in) ~** desvalorizar-
se; **to gain (in) ~** valorizar-se; **to be of great ~
to sb** (fig) ser de grande utilidade para alguém;
to be ~d at $8 ser avaliado em $8; **value added
tax** [-'ædɪd-] (Brit) N imposto sobre a circulação
de mercadorias (BR), imposto sobre valor
acrescentado (PT)
valued ['væljuːd] ADJ (appreciated) valorizado
valuer ['væljuəʳ] N avaliador(a) m/f
valve [vælv] N válvula; (in radio) lâmpada
vampire ['væmpaɪəʳ] N vampiro(-a)
van [væn] N (Aut) camionete f (BR), camioneta
(PT)
V and A (Brit) N ABBR = **Victoria and Albert
Museum**
vandal ['vændl] N vândalo(-a)
vandalism ['vændəlɪzəm] N vandalismo
vandalize ['vændəlaɪz] VT destruir, depredar
vanguard ['vængɑːd] N: **in the ~ of** na
vanguarda de
vanilla [və'nɪlə] N baunilha ■ CPD (ice cream) de
baunilha
vanish ['vænɪʃ] VI desaparecer, sumir
vanity ['vænɪtɪ] N vaidade f; **vanity case** N
bolsa de maquilagem
vantage point ['vɑːntɪdʒ-] N posição f
estratégica
vapor etc ['veɪpəʳ] (US) N = **vapour** etc
vaporize ['veɪpəraɪz] VT vaporizar ■ VI

vaporizar-se

vapour ['veɪpə^r] (US **vapor**) N vapor m

variable ['vɛərɪəbl] ADJ variável ■ N variável f

variance ['vɛərɪəns] N: **to be at ~ (with)** estar em desacordo (com)

variant ['vɛərɪənt] N variante f

variation [vɛərɪ'eɪʃən] N variação f; (variant) variante f; (in opinion) mudança

varicose ['værɪkəus] ADJ: **~ veins** varizes fpl

varied ['vɛərɪd] ADJ variado

variety [və'raɪətɪ] N variedade f, diversidade f; (type, quantity) variedade; **for a ~ of reasons** por várias or diversas razões; **variety show** N espetáculo de variedades

various ['vɛərɪəs] ADJ vários(-as), diversos(-as); (several) vários(-as); **at ~ times** (different) em horas variadas; (several) várias vezes

varnish ['vɑːnɪʃ] N verniz m; (nail varnish) esmalte m ■ VT envernizar; (nails) pintar (com esmalte)

vary ['vɛərɪ] VT variar; (change) mudar ■ VI variar; (deviate) desviar-se; (become different): **to ~ with** or **according to** variar de acordo com

varying ['vɛərɪɪŋ] ADJ variado

vase [vɑːz] N vaso

vasectomy [væ'sɛktəmɪ] N vasectomia

Vaseline® ['væsɪliːn] N vaselina®

vast [vɑːst] ADJ enorme

vastly ['vɑːstlɪ] ADV (underestimate etc) enormemente; (different) completamente

vastness ['vɑːstnɪs] N imensidão f

VAT [væt] (Brit) N ABBR (= value added tax) ≈ ICM m (BR), IVA m (PT)

vat [væt] N tina, cuba

Vatican ['vætɪkən] N: **the ~** o Vaticano

vault [vɔːlt] N (of roof) abóbada; (tomb) sepulcro; (in bank) caixa-forte f; (jump) salto ■ VT (also: **vault over**) saltar (por cima de)

vaunted ['vɔːntɪd] ADJ: **much-~** tão alardeado

VC N ABBR = **vice-chairman**; (Brit: = Victoria Cross) distinção militar

VCR N ABBR = **video cassette recorder**

VD N ABBR = **venereal disease**

VDU N ABBR = **visual display unit**

veal [viːl] N carne f de vitela

veer [vɪə^r] VI virar

veg. [vɛdʒ] (Brit: inf) N ABBR = **vegetable(s)**

vegan ['viːgən] N vegetalista m/f

vegetable ['vɛdʒtəbl] N (Bot) vegetal m; (edible plant) legume m, hortaliça ■ ADJ vegetal; **vegetables** NPL (cooked) verduras fpl; **vegetable garden** N horta

vegetarian [vɛdʒɪ'tɛərɪən] ADJ, N vegetariano(-a)

vegetate ['vɛdʒɪteɪt] VI vegetar

vegetation [vɛdʒɪ'teɪʃən] N vegetação f

vehemence ['viːɪməns] N veemência, violência

vehement ['viːɪmənt] ADJ veemente; (impassioned) apaixonado; (attack) violento

vehicle ['viːɪkl] N veículo

vehicular [vɪ'hɪkjulə^r] ADJ: **"no ~ traffic"** "proibido trânsito de veículos automotores"

veil [veɪl] N véu m ■ VT velar; **under a ~ of**

secrecy (fig) sob um manto de sigilo

veiled [veɪld] ADJ velado

vein [veɪn] N veia; (of ore etc) filão m; (on leaf) nervura; (fig: mood) tom m

vellum ['vɛləm] N papel m velino

velocity [vɪ'lɔsɪtɪ] N velocidade f

velvet ['vɛlvɪt] N veludo ■ ADJ aveludado

vendetta [vɛn'dɛtə] N vendeta

vending machine ['vɛndɪŋ-] N vendedor m automático

vendor ['vɛndə^r] N vendedor(a) m/f; **street ~** camelô m

veneer [və'nɪə^r] N capa exterior, folheado; (wood) compensado; (fig) aparência

venerable ['vɛnərəbl] ADJ venerável

venereal [vɪ'nɪərɪəl] ADJ: **~ disease** doença venérea

Venetian blind [vɪ'niːʃən-] N persiana

Venezuela [vɛnɛ'zweɪlə] N Venezuela

Venezuelan [vɛnɛ'zweɪlən] ADJ, N venezuelano(-a)

vengeance ['vɛndʒəns] N vingança; **with a ~** (fig) para valer

vengeful ['vɛndʒful] ADJ vingativo

Venice ['vɛnɪs] N Veneza

venison ['vɛnɪsn] N carne f de veado

venom ['vɛnəm] N veneno; (bitterness) malevolência

venomous ['vɛnəməs] ADJ venenoso; (look, stare) malévolo

vent [vɛnt] N (opening, in jacket) abertura; (also: **air vent**) respiradouro; (in wall) abertura para ventilação ■ VT (fig: feelings) desabafar, descarregar

ventilate ['vɛntɪleɪt] VT ventilar

ventilation [vɛntɪ'leɪʃən] N ventilação f; **ventilation shaft** N poço de ventilação

ventilator ['vɛntɪleɪtə^r] N ventilador m

ventriloquist [vɛn'trɪləkwɪst] N ventríloquo

venture ['vɛntʃə^r] N empreendimento ■ VT aventurar; (opinion) arriscar ■ VI arriscar-se; **business ~** empreendimento comercial; **to ~ to do sth** aventurar-se or arriscar-se a fazer algo; **venture capital** N capital m de especulação

venue ['vɛnjuː] N local m; (meeting place) ponto de encontro; (theatre etc) espaço

Venus ['viːnəs] N (planet) Vênus f

veracity [və'ræsɪtɪ] N veracidade f

veranda(h) [və'rændə] N varanda

verb [vəːb] N verbo

verbal ['vəːbəl] ADJ verbal

verbally ['vəːbəlɪ] ADV verbalmente

verbatim [vəː'beɪtɪm] ADJ, ADV palavra por palavra

verbose [vəː'bəus] ADJ prolixo

verdict ['vəːdɪkt] N veredicto, decisão f; (fig) opinião f, parecer m; **~ of guilty/not guilty** veredicto de culpado/não culpado

verge [vəːdʒ] N beira, margem f; (on road) acostamento (BR), berma (PT); **"soft ~s"** (Brit: Aut) "acostamento mole"; **to be on the ~ of doing sth** estar a ponto or à beira de fazer algo

▶ **verge on** VT FUS beirar em

verger ['vəːdʒəʳ] N (Rel) sacristão m

verification [vɛrɪfɪ'keɪʃən] N verificação f

verify ['vɛrɪfaɪ] VT verificar

veritable ['vɛrɪtəbl] ADJ verdadeiro

vermin ['vəːmɪn] NPL (animals) bichos mpl; (insects, fig) insetos mpl nocivos

vermouth ['vəːməθ] N vermute m

vernacular [və'nækjuləʳ] N vernáculo; **in the ~** na língua corrente

versatile ['vəːsətaɪl] ADJ (person) versátil; (machine, tool etc) polivalente; (mind) ágil, flexível

verse [vəːs] N verso, poesia; (stanza) estrofe f; (in bible) versículo; **in ~** em verso

versed [vəːst] ADJ: **(well-)~ in** versado em

version ['vəːʃən] N versão f

versus ['vəːsəs] PREP contra, versus

vertebra ['vəːtɪbrə] (pl **vertebrae**) N vértebra

vertebrae ['vəːtɪbriː] NPL of **vertebra**

vertebrate ['vəːtɪbrɪt] N vertebrado

vertical ['vəːtɪkl] ADJ vertical ■ N vertical f

vertically ['vəːtɪklɪ] ADV verticalmente

vertigo ['vəːtɪgəu] N vertigem f; **to suffer from ~** ter vertigens

verve [vəːv] N garra, pique m

very ['vɛrɪ] ADV muito ■ ADJ: **the ~ book which** o mesmo livro que; **the ~ thought (of it)** ... só de pensar (nisso) ...; **at the ~ end** bem no final; **the ~ last** o último (de todos), bem o último; **at the ~ least** no mínimo; **~ much** muitíssimo; **~ little** muito pouco, pouquíssimo

vespers ['vɛspəz] NPL vésperas fpl

vessel ['vɛsl] N (Anat) vaso; (Naut) navio, barco; (container) vaso, vasilha

vest [vɛst] N (Brit) camiseta (BR), camisola interior (PT); (US: waistcoat) colete m ■ VT: **to ~ sb with sth, to ~ sth in sb** investir alguém de algo, conferir algo a alguém

vested interest ['vɛstɪd-] N: **to have a ~ in doing** ter um interesse em fazer; **vested interests** NPL (Comm) direitos mpl adquiridos

vestibule ['vɛstɪbjuːl] N vestíbulo

vestige ['vɛstɪdʒ] N vestígio

vestry ['vɛstrɪ] N sacristia

Vesuvius [vɪ'suːvɪəs] N Vesúvio

vet [vɛt] N ABBR (= veterinary surgeon) veterinário(-a) ■ VT examinar

veteran ['vɛtərn] N veterano(-a); (also: **war veteran**) veterano de guerra ■ ADJ: **she's a ~ campaigner for** ... ela é uma veterana nas campanhas de ...; **veteran car** N carro antigo

veterinarian [vɛtrɪ'nɛərɪən] (US) N veterinário(-a)

veterinary ['vɛtrɪnərɪ] ADJ veterinário; **veterinary surgeon** (Brit) N veterinário(-a)

veto ['viːtəu] (pl **vetoes**) N veto ■ VT vetar; **to put a ~ on** opor seu veto a

vex [vɛks] VT (irritate) irritar, apoquentar; (make impatient) impacientar

vexed [vɛkst] ADJ (question) controvertido, discutido

VFD (US) N ABBR = **voluntary fire department**

VG (Brit) N ABBR (Sch) = **very good**

VHF ABBR (= very high frequency) VHF, freqüência muito alta

VI (US) ABBR (Post) = **Virgin Islands**

via ['vaɪə] PREP por, via

viability [vaɪə'bɪlɪtɪ] N viabilidade f

viable ['vaɪəbl] ADJ viável

viaduct ['vaɪədʌkt] N viaduto

vibrant ['vaɪbrənt] ADJ (lively) entusiasmado; (colour) vibrante; (voice) ressonante

vibrate [vaɪ'breɪt] VI vibrar

vibration [vaɪ'breɪʃən] N vibração f

vicar ['vɪkəʳ] N vigário

vicarage ['vɪkərɪdʒ] N vicariato

vicarious [vɪ'kɛərɪəs] ADJ (pleasure, existence) indireto

vice [vaɪs] N (evil) vício; (Tech) torno mecânico

vice- [vaɪs] PREFIX vice-

vice-chairman (irreg) N vice-presidente m/f

vice-chancellor (Brit) N reitor(a) m/f

vice-president N vice-presidente m/f

vice squad N delegacia de costumes

vice versa ['vaɪsɪ'vəːsə] ADV vice-versa

vicinity [vɪ'sɪnɪtɪ] N (area: nearness) proximidade f

vicious ['vɪʃəs] ADJ (violent) violento; (depraved) depravado, vicioso; (cruel) cruel; (bitter) rancoroso; **vicious circle** N círculo vicioso

viciousness ['vɪʃəsnɪs] N violência; depravação f; crueldade f; rancor m

vicissitudes [vɪ'sɪsɪtjuːdz] NPL vicissitudes fpl

victim ['vɪktɪm] N vítima f

victimization [vɪktɪmaɪ'zeɪʃən] N perseguição f; (in strike) represálias fpl

victimize ['vɪktɪmaɪz] VT (strikers etc) fazer represália contra

victor ['vɪktəʳ] N vencedor(a) m/f

Victorian [vɪk'tɔːrɪən] ADJ vitoriano

victorious [vɪk'tɔːrɪəs] ADJ vitorioso

victory ['vɪktərɪ] N vitória; **to win a ~ over sb** conseguir uma vitória sobre alguém

video ['vɪdɪəu] N (video film) vídeo; (pop video) videoclipe m; (also: **video cassette**) videocassete m; (also: **video cassette recorder**) videocassete m ■ CPD de vídeo; **video cassette** N videocassete m; **video cassette recorder** N videocassete m; **video recording** N gravação f em vídeo; **video tape** N videoteipe m; (cassette) videocassete m

vie [vaɪ] VI: **to ~ (with sb) (for sth)** competir (com alguém) (por algo)

Vienna [vɪ'ɛnə] N Viena

Viet Nam ['vjɛt'næm] N = **Vietnam**

Vietnam ['vjɛt'næm] N Vietnã m (BR), Vietname m (PT)

Vietnamese [vjɛtnə'miːz] ADJ vietnamita ■ N INV vietnamita m/f; (Ling) vietnamita m

view [vjuː] N (sight) perspectiva; (landscape) paisagem f; (opinion) opinião f, parecer m ■ VT (look at, fig) olhar; (examine) examinar; **on ~** (in museum etc) em exposição; **in full ~ (of)** à plena vista (de); **an overall ~ of the situation** uma visão geral da situação; **in my ~** na minha opinião; **in ~ of the weather/the fact that** em vista do tempo/do fato de que; **with a ~ to doing sth** com a intenção de fazer algo

view-data ['vjuːdeɪtə] (*Brit*) N teletexto, videotexto

viewer ['vjuːəʳ] N (*small projector*) visor *m*; (*person*) telespectador(a) *m/f*

viewfinder ['vjuːfaɪndəʳ] N visor *m*

viewpoint ['vjuːpɔɪnt] N ponto de vista; (*place*) lugar *m*

vigil ['vɪdʒɪl] N vigília; **to keep ~** velar

vigilance ['vɪdʒɪləns] N vigilância

vigilant ['vɪdʒɪlənt] ADJ vigilante

vigor ['vɪgəʳ] (*US*) N = **vigour**

vigorous ['vɪgərəs] ADJ vigoroso; (*plant*) vigoso

vigour ['vɪgəʳ] (*US* **vigor**) N energia, vigor *m*

vile [vaɪl] ADJ (*action*) vil, infame; (*smell*) repugnante, repulsivo; (*temper*) violento

vilify ['vɪlɪfaɪ] VT vilipendiar

villa ['vɪlə] N (*country house*) casa de campo; (*suburban house*) vila, quinta

village ['vɪlɪdʒ] N aldeia, povoado

villager ['vɪlɪdʒəʳ] N aldeão/aldeã *m/f*

villain ['vɪlən] N (*scoundrel*) patife *m*; (*Brit: in novel etc*) vilão *m*; (*criminal*) marginal *m/f*

VIN (*US*) N ABBR = **vehicle identification number**

vindicate ['vɪndɪkeɪt] VT vingar; (*justify*) jusfificar

vindication [vɪndɪ'keɪʃən] N: **in ~ of** em defesa de

vindictive [vɪn'dɪktɪv] ADJ vingativo

vine [vaɪn] N vinha, videira; (*climbing plant*) planta trepadeira

vinegar ['vɪnɪgəʳ] N vinagre *m*

vine grower N vinhateiro(-a), viticultor(a) *m/f*

vine-growing ADJ vitícola ■ N viticultura

vineyard ['vɪnjɑːd] N vinha, vinhedo

vintage ['vɪntɪdʒ] N vindima; (*year*) safra, colheita ■ CPD (*comedy*) de época; (*performance*) clássico; **the 1970 ~** a safra de 1970; **vintage car** N carro antigo; **vintage wine** N vinho velho

vinyl ['vaɪnl] N vinil *m*

viola [vɪ'əʊlə] N viola

violate ['vaɪəleɪt] VT violar

violation [vaɪə'leɪʃən] N violação *f*; **in ~ of** (*rule, law*) em violação de

violence ['vaɪələns] N violência; (*strength*) força

violent ['vaɪələnt] ADJ violento; (*intense*) intenso; **a ~ dislike of sb/sth** uma forte aversão a alguém/algo

violently ['vaɪələntlɪ] ADV violentemente; (*ill, angry*) extremamente

violet ['vaɪələt] ADJ violeta ■ N (*colour, plant*) violeta

violin [vaɪə'lɪn] N violino

violinist [vaɪə'lɪnɪst] N violinista *m/f*

VIP N ABBR (= *very important person*) VIP *m/f*

viper ['vaɪpəʳ] N víbora

virgin ['vəːdʒɪn] N virgem *m/f* ■ ADJ virgem; **the Blessed V~** a Virgem Santíssima

virginity [vəː'dʒɪnɪtɪ] N virgindade *f*

Virgo ['vəːgəʊ] N Virgem *f*

virile ['vɪraɪl] ADJ viril

virility [vɪ'rɪlɪtɪ] N virilidade *f*

virtual ['vəːtjuəl] ADJ (*Comput, Phys*) virtual; (*in effect*): **it's a ~ impossibility** é praticamente impossível; **the ~ leader** o líder na prática

virtually ['vəːtjuəlɪ] ADV (*almost*) praticamente

virtue ['vəːtjuː] N virtude *f*; (*advantage*) vantagem *f*; **by ~ of** em virtude de

virtuoso [vəːtju'əʊzəu] (*pl* **virtuosi**) N virtuoso(-a)

virtuous ['vəːtjuəs] ADJ virtuoso

virulent ['vɪrulənt] ADJ virulento

virus ['vaɪərəs] N vírus *m*

visa ['viːzə] N visto

vis-à-vis [viːzə'viː] PREP com relação a

viscose ['vɪskəuz] N viscose *f*

viscount ['vaɪkaunt] N visconde *m*

viscous ['vɪskəs] ADJ viscoso

vise [vaɪs] (*US*) N (*Tech*) = **vice**

visibility [vɪzɪ'bɪlɪtɪ] N visibilidade *f*

visible ['vɪzəbl] ADJ visível; **~ exports/imports** exportações *fpl* /importações *fpl* visíveis

visibly ['vɪzəblɪ] ADV visivelmente

vision ['vɪʒən] N (*sight*) vista, visão *f*; (*foresight, in dream*) visão *f*

visionary ['vɪʒənərɪ] N visionário(-a)

visit ['vɪzɪt] N visita ■ VT (*person: US: also:* **visit with**) visitar, fazer uma visita a; (*place*) ir a, ir conhecer; **on a private/official ~** em visita particular/oficial

visiting ['vɪzɪtɪŋ] ADJ (*speaker, team*) visitante; **visiting card** N cartão *m* de visita; **visiting hours** NPL horário de visita; **visiting professor** N professor(a) *m/f* de outra faculdade

visitor ['vɪzɪtəʳ] N visitante *m/f*; (*to one's house*) visita; (*tourist*) turista *m/f*; (*tripper*) excursionista *m/f*

visitors' book N livro de visitas

visor ['vaɪzəʳ] N viseira

VISTA ['vɪstə] N ABBR (= *Volunteers in Service to America*) *programa de assistência às regiões pobres*

vista ['vɪstə] N vista

visual ['vɪzjuəl] ADJ visual; **visual aid** N recurso visual; **visual display unit** N terminal *m* de vídeo

visualize ['vɪzjuəlaɪz] VT visualizar; (*foresee*) prever

visually ['vɪzjuəlɪ] ADV visualmente; **~ handicapped** deficiente visual

vital ['vaɪtl] ADJ (*essential*) essencial, indispensável; (*important*) de importância vital; (*crucial*) crucial; (*person*) vivo; (*of life*) vital; **of ~ importance** de importância vital

vitality [vaɪ'tælɪtɪ] N energia, vitalidade *f*

vitally ['vaɪtəlɪ] ADV: **~ important** de importância vital

vital statistics NPL (*of population*) estatística demográfica; (*fig*) medidas *fpl*

vitamin ['vɪtəmɪn] N vitamina

vitiate ['vɪʃɪeɪt] VT viciar

vitreous ['vɪtrɪəs] ADJ vítreo

vitriolic [vɪtrɪ'ɔlɪk] ADJ (*fig*) mordaz

viva ['vaɪvə] N (also: **viva voce**) exame m oral

vivacious [vɪ'veɪʃəs] ADJ vivaz, animado

vivacity [vɪ'væsɪtɪ] N vivacidade f

vivid ['vɪvɪd] ADJ (account) vívido; (light) claro, brilhante; (imagination, colour) vivo

vividly ['vɪvɪdlɪ] ADV (describe) vividamente; (remember) distintamente

vivisection [vɪvɪ'sɛkʃən] N vivissecção f

vixen ['vɪksn] N raposa; (pej: woman) megera

viz ABBR (= videlicet) a saber

VLF ABBR = **very low frequency**

V-neck N (also: **V-neck jumper**, **V-neck pullover**) suéter f com decote em V

VOA N ABBR (= Voice of America) voz f da América, emissora que transmite para o estrangeiro

vocabulary [vəu'kæbjulərɪ] N vocabulário

vocal ['vəukl] ADJ vocal; (noisy) clamoroso; (articulate) claro, eloqüente; **vocal cords** NPL cordas fpl vocais

vocalist ['vəukəlɪst] N vocalista m/f, cantor(a) m/f

vocals ['vəuklz] NPL vozes fpl

vocation [vəu'keɪʃən] N vocação f

vocational [vəu'keɪʃənl] ADJ vocacional; ~ **guidance/training** orientação f vocacional/ ensino profissionalizante

vociferous [və'sɪfərəs] ADJ vociferante

vodka ['vɔdkə] N vodca

vogue [vəug] N voga, moda; **to be in** ~ estar na moda

voice [vɔɪs] N voz f ▪ VT (opinion) expressar; **in a low/loud** ~ em voz baixa/alta; **to give** ~ **to** dar voz a; **voice mail** N (Tel) correio m de voz

void [vɔɪd] N vazio; (hole) oco ▪ ADJ (null) nulo; (empty): ~ **of** destituido de

voile [vɔɪl] N voile m

vol. ABBR (= volume) vol

volatile ['vɔlətaɪl] ADJ volátil; (situation, person) imprevisível

volcanic [vɔl'kænɪk] ADJ vulcânico

volcano [vɔl'keɪnəu] (pl **volcanoes**) N vulcão m

volition [və'lɪʃən] N: **of one's own** ~ de livre vontade

volley ['vɔlɪ] N (of gunfire) descarga, salva; (of stones etc) chuva; (of questions etc) enxurrada, chuva; (Tennis etc) voleio

volleyball ['vɔlɪbɔːl] N voleibol m, vôlei m (BR)

volt [vəult] N volt m

voltage ['vəultɪdʒ] N voltagem f; **high/low** ~ alta/baixa tensão

voluble ['vɔljubl] ADJ (person) tagarela; (speech) loquaz

volume ['vɔljuːm] N volume m; (of tank) capacidade f; ~ **one/two** tomo um/dois; **his expression spoke** ~**s** sua expressão disse tudo; **volume control** N (Radio, TV) controle m de volume; **volume discount** N (Comm) desconto de volume

voluminous [və'luːmɪnəs] ADJ volumoso

voluntarily ['vɔləntrɪlɪ] ADV livremente, voluntariamente

voluntary ['vɔləntərɪ] ADJ voluntário; (unpaid) (a título) gratuito; **voluntary liquidation** N (Comm) liquidação f requerida pela empresa; **voluntary redundancy** (Brit) N demissão f voluntária

volunteer [vɔlən'tɪər] N voluntário(-a) ▪ VT oferecer voluntariamente ▪ VI (Mil) alistar-se voluntariamente; **to** ~ **to do** oferecer-se voluntariamente para fazer

voluptuous [və'lʌptjuəs] ADJ voluptuoso

vomit ['vɔmɪt] N vômito ▪ VT, VI vomitar

vote [vəut] N voto; (votes cast) votação f; (right to vote) direito de votar; (franchise) título de eleitor ▪ VT: **to be** ~**d chairman etc** ser eleito presidente etc; (propose): **to** ~ **that** propor que; (in election) votar ▪ VI votar; **to put sth to the** ~, **to take a** ~ **on sth** votar algo, submeter algo à votação; **to** ~ **for sb** votar em alguém; **to** ~ **for/against a proposal** votar a favor de/contra uma proposta; **to** ~ **to do sth** votar a favor de fazer algo; ~ **of censure** voto de censura; ~ **of confidence** voto de confiança; **vote of thanks** N agradecimento

voter ['vəutər] N votante m/f, eleitor(a) m/f

voting ['vəutɪŋ] N votação f; **voting paper** (Brit) N cédula eleitoral; **voting right** N direito de voto

voucher ['vautʃər] N (also: **luncheon voucher**) vale-refeição m; (with petrol etc) vale m; (gift voucher) vale m para presente; (receipt) comprovante m

vouch for [vautʃ-] VT FUS garantir, responder por

vow [vau] N voto ▪ VT: **to** ~ **to do/that** prometer solenemente fazer/que ▪ VI fazer votos; **to take** or **make a** ~ **to do sth** fazer voto de fazer algo

vowel ['vauəl] N vogal f

voyage ['vɔɪɪdʒ] N (journey) viagem f; (crossing) travessia

VP N ABBR = **vice-president**

vs ABBR (= versus) x

V-sign (Brit) N gesto grosseiro; **to give a** ~ **to sb** = dar uma banana para alguém

VSO (Brit) N ABBR = **Voluntary Service Overseas**

VT (US) ABBR (Post) = **Vermont**

vulgar ['vʌlgər] ADJ (rude) grosseiro, ordinário; (in bad taste) vulgar, baixo

vulgarity [vʌl'gærɪtɪ] N grosseria; (bad taste) vulgaridade f

vulnerability [vʌlnərə'bɪlɪtɪ] N vulnerabilidade f

vulnerable ['vʌlnərəbl] ADJ vulnerável

vulture ['vʌltʃər] N abutre m, urubu m

W, w ['dʌblju:] N (letter) W, w m; **W for William** W de William

W ABBR (= west) O; (Elec: = watt) W

WA (US) ABBR (Post) = **Washington**

wad [wɔd] N (of cotton wool) chumaço; (of paper) bola; (of banknotes etc) maço

wadding ['wɔdɪŋ] N enchimento

waddle ['wɔdl] VI andar gingando or bamboleando

wade [weɪd] VI: **to ~ through** andar em; (fig: a book) ler com dificuldade ■ VT vadear, atravessar (a vau)

wafer ['weɪfə⁷] N (biscuit) bolacha; (Rel) hóstia; (Comput) pastilha

wafer-thin ADJ fininho, finíssimo

waffle ['wɔfl] N (Culin) waffle m; (empty talk) lengalenga ■ VI encher linguiça; **waffle iron** N fôrma para fazer waffles

waft [wɔft] VT levar ■ VI flutuar

wag [wæg] VT (tail) sacudir; (finger) menear ■ VI acenar, abanar; **the dog ~ged its tail** o cachorro abanou o rabo

wage [weɪdʒ] N (also: **wages**) salário, ordenado ■ VT: **to ~ war** empreender or fazer guerra; **a day's ~s** uma diária; **wage claim** N reivindicação f salarial; **wage differential** N desnível m salarial, diferença de salário; **wage earner** ['weɪdʒ'ə:nə⁷] N assalariado(-a); **wage freeze** N congelamento de salários; **wage packet** (Brit) N envelope m de pagamento

wager ['weɪdʒə⁷] N aposta, parada ■ VT apostar

waggle ['wægl] VT mover

wag(g)on ['wægən] N (horse-drawn) carroça; (Brit: Rail) vagão m

wail [weɪl] N lamento, gemido ■ VI lamentar-se, gemer; (siren) tocar

waist [weɪst] N cintura

waistcoat ['weɪskəut] (Brit) N colete m

waistline ['weɪstlaɪn] N cintura

wait [weɪt] N espera ■ VI esperar; **to lie in ~ for** aguardar em emboscada; **I can't ~ to** (fig) estou morrendo de vontade de; **to ~ for sb/sth** esperar por alguém/algo; **to keep sb ~ing** deixar alguém esperando; **~ a minute!** espera aí!; **"repairs while you ~"** "conserta-se na hora"

▶ **wait behind** VI ficar para trás

▶ **wait on** VT FUS servir

▶ **wait up** VI esperar, não ir dormir; **don't ~ up for me** vá dormir, não espere por mim

waiter ['weɪtə⁷] N garçom m (BR), empregado (PT)

waiting ['weɪtɪŋ] N: **"no ~"** (Brit: Aut) "proibido estacionar"; **waiting list** ['weɪtɪŋ-] N lista de espera; **waiting room** N sala de espera

waitress ['weɪtrɪs] N garçonete f (BR), empregada (PT)

waive [weɪv] VT abrir mão de

waiver ['weɪvə⁷] N desistência

wake [weɪk] (pt **woke**, pp **woken**) VT (also: **wake up**) acordar ■ VI acordar ■ N (for dead person) velório; (Naut) esteira; **to ~ up to sth** (fig) abrir os olhos or acordar para algo; **in the ~ of** (fig) na esteira de; **to follow in sb's ~** (fig) seguir a esteira or o exemplo de alguém

waken ['weɪkən] VT, VI = **wake**

Wales [weɪlz] N País m de Gales; **the Prince of ~** o Príncipe de Gales

walk [wɔ:k] N passeio; (hike) excursão f a pé, caminhada; (gait) passo, modo de andar; (in park etc) alameda, passeio ■ VI andar; (for pleasure, exercise) passear ■ VT (distance) percorrer a pé, andar; (dog) levar para passear; **it's 10 minutes' ~ from here** daqui são 10 minutos a pé; **to go for a ~** (ir) dar uma volta; **I'll ~ you home** vou andar com você até a sua casa; **people from all ~s of life** pessoas de todos os níveis

▶ **walk out** VI (go out) sair; (audience) retirar-se; (strike) entrar em greve

▶ **walk out on** VT FUS (family etc) abandonar

walker ['wɔ:kə⁷] N (person) caminhante m/f

walkie-talkie ['wɔ:kɪ'tɔ:kɪ] N transmissor-receptor m portátil, walkie-talkie m

walking ['wɔ:kɪŋ] N o andar; **it's within ~ distance** dá para ir a pé; **walking holiday** N férias fpl fazendo excursões a pé; **walking shoes** NPL sapatos mpl para andar; **walking stick** N bengala

Walkman® N Walkman® m

walk-on ADJ (Theatre: part) de figurante

walkout ['wɔ:kaut] N (of workers) greve f branca

walkover ['wɔ:kəuvə⁷] (inf) N barbada

walkway ['wɔ:kweɪ] N passeio, passadiço

wall [wɔ:l] N parede f; (exterior) muro; (city wall

etc) muralha; **to go to the ~** (*fig: firm etc*) falir, quebrar
▶ **wall in** VT (*garden etc*) cercar com muros
wall cupboard N armário de parede
walled [wɔːld] ADJ (*city*) cercado por muralhas; (*garden*) murado, cercado
wallet ['wɔlɪt] N carteira
wallflower ['wɔːlflauəʳ] N goivo-amarelo; **to be a ~** (*fig*) tomar chá de cadeira
wall hanging N tapete *m*
wallop ['wɔləp] (*Brit: inf*) VT surrar, espancar
wallow ['wɔləu] VI (*in mud*) chafurdar; (*in water*) rolar; (*person: in guilt*) regozijar-se; **to ~ in one's own grief** regozijar-se na própria dor
wallpaper ['wɔːlpeɪpəʳ] N papel *m* de parede
■ VT colocar papel de parede em
wall-to-wall ADJ: **~ carpeting** carpete *m*
walnut ['wɔːlnʌt] N noz *f*; (*tree, wood*) nogueira
walrus ['wɔːlrəs] (*pl* **walruses**) N morsa, vaca marinha
waltz [wɔːlts] N valsa ■ VI valsar
wan [wɔn] ADJ pálido; (*smile*) amarelo
wand [wɔnd] N (*also*: **magic wand**) varinha de condão
wander ['wɔndəʳ] VI (*person*) vagar, perambular; (*thoughts*) divagar; (*get lost*) extraviar-se ■ VT perambular
wanderer ['wɔndərəʳ] N vagabundo(-a)
wandering ['wɔndərɪŋ] ADJ errante; (*thoughts*) distraído; (*tribe*) nômade; (*minstrel, actor*) itinerante
wane [weɪn] VI diminuir; (*moon*) minguar
wangle ['wæŋgl] (*Brit: inf*) VT: **to ~ sth** conseguir algo através de pistolão
want [wɔnt] VT (*wish for*) querer; (*demand*) exigir; (*need*) precisar de, necessitar; (*lack*) carecer de ■ N (*poverty*) pobreza, miséria; **wants** NPL (*needs*) necessidades *fpl*; **for ~ of** por falta de; **to ~ to do** querer fazer; **to ~ sb to do sth** querer que alguém faça algo; **"cook ~ed"** "precisa-se cozinheiro"; **want ads** (US) NPL classificados *mpl*
wanted ['wɔntɪd] ADJ (*criminal etc*) procurado (pela polícia); **"cook ~"** (*in advertisement*) "precisa-se cozinheiro"; **you're ~ on the phone** estão querendo falar com você no telefone
wanting ['wɔntɪŋ] ADJ falto, deficiente; **to be found ~** não estar à altura da situação; **to be ~ in** carecer de
wanton ['wɔntən] ADJ (*destruction*) gratuito, irresponsável; (*licentious*) libertino, lascivo
war [wɔːʳ] N guerra; **to make ~ (on)** fazer guerra (em); **to go to ~** entrar na guerra; **~ of attrition** guerra de atrição
warble ['wɔːbl] N gorjeio ■ VI gorjear
war cry N grito de guerra
ward [wɔːd] N (*in hospital*) ala; (*Pol*) distrito eleitoral; (*Law: child*) tutelado(-a), pupilo(-a)
▶ **ward off** VT desviar, aparar; (*attack*) repelir
warden ['wɔːdn] N (*Brit: of institution*) diretor(a) *m/f*; (*of park, game reserve*) administrador(a) *m/f*; (*Brit: also*: **traffic warden**) guarda *m/f*

warder ['wɔːdəʳ] (*Brit*) N carcereiro(-a)
wardrobe ['wɔːdrəub] N (*cupboard*) armário; (*clothes*) guarda-roupa *m*
warehouse ['wɛəhaus] N armazém *m*, depósito
wares [wɛəz] NPL mercadorias *fpl*
warfare ['wɔːfɛəʳ] N guerra, combate *m*
war game N jogo de estrategia militar
warhead ['wɔːhɛd] N ogiva
warily ['wɛərɪlɪ] ADV cautelosamente, com precaução
warlike ['wɔːlaɪk] ADJ guerreiro, bélico
warm [wɔːm] ADJ quente; (*thanks, welcome*) caloroso, cordial; (*supporter*) entusiasmado; **it's ~** está quente; **I'm ~** estou com calor; **to keep sth ~** manter algo aquecido
▶ **warm up** VI (*person, room*) esquentar; (*athlete*) fazer aquecimento; (*discussion*) esquentar-se ■ VT esquentar
warm-blooded [-'blʌdɪd] ADJ de sangue quente
war memorial N monumento aos mortos
warm-hearted [-'hɑːtɪd] ADJ afetuoso
warmly ['wɔːmlɪ] ADV calorosamente, afetuosamente
warmonger ['wɔːmʌŋgəʳ] N belicista *m/f*
warmongering ['wɔːmʌŋgərɪŋ] N belicismo
warmth [wɔːmθ] N calor *m*
warm-up N (*Sport*) aquecimento
warn [wɔːn] VT prevenir, avisar; **to ~ sb against sth** prevenir alguém contra algo; **to ~ sb that/ of/(not) not to do** prevenir alguém de que/de/ para (não) fazer
warning ['wɔːnɪŋ] N advertência; (*in writing*) aviso; (*signal*) sinal *m*; **without (any) ~** (*suddenly*) de improviso, inopinadamente; (*without notice*) sem aviso prévio, sem avisar; **gale ~** (*Meteorology*) aviso de vendaval; **warning light** N luz *f* de advertência; **warning triangle** N (*Aut*) triângulo de advertência
warp [wɔːp] N (*Textiles*) urdidura ■ VT deformar ■ VI empenar, deformar-se
warpath ['wɔːpɑːθ] N: **to be on the ~** (*fig*) estar disposto a brigar
warped [wɔːpt] ADJ (*wood*) empenado; (*fig: sense of humour*) pervertido, deformado
warrant ['wɔrnt] N (*guarantee*) garantia; (*voucher*) comprovante *m*; (*Law: to arrest*) mandado de prisão; (: *to search*) mandado de busca ■ VT (*justify*) justificar; **warrant officer** N (*Mil*) subtenente *m*; (*Naut*) suboficial *m*
warranty ['wɔrəntɪ] N garantia; **under ~** (*Comm*) sob garantia
warren ['wɔrən] N (*of rabbits*) lura; (*house*) coelheira; (*fig*) labirinto
warring ['wɔːrɪŋ] ADJ (*nations*) em guerra; (*interests etc*) antagônico
warrior ['wɔrɪəʳ] N guerreiro(-a)
Warsaw ['wɔːsɔː] N Varsóvia
warship ['wɔːʃɪp] N navio de guerra
wart [wɔːt] N verruga
wartime ['wɔːtaɪm] N: **in ~** em tempo de guerra
wary ['wɛərɪ] ADJ cauteloso, precavido; **to be ~ about *or* of doing sth** hesitar em fazer algo

was [wɔz] PT of **be**
wash [wɔʃ] VT lavar; (*sweep, carry: sea etc*) levar, arrastar; (: *ashore*) lançar ■ VI lavar-se; (*sea etc*): **to ~ over/against sth** bater/chocar-se contra algo ■ N (*clothes etc*) lavagem f; (*of ship*) esteira; **to have a ~** lavar-se; **to give sth a ~** lavar algo; **he was ~ed overboard** foi arrastado do navio pelas águas
 ▸ **wash away** VT (*stain*) tirar ao lavar; (*subj: river etc*) levar, arrastar
 ▸ **wash down** VT lavar; (*food*) regar
 ▸ **wash off** VT tirar lavando ■ VI sair ao lavar
 ▸ **wash up** VI (*Brit*) lavar a louça; (*US*) lavar-se
washable ['wɔʃəbl] ADJ lavável
washbasin ['wɔʃbeisn] N pia (BR), lavatório (PT)
washbowl ['wɔʃbəul] (*US*) N = **washbasin**
washcloth ['wɔʃklɔθ] (*US*) N taolhinha para lavar o rosto
washer ['wɔʃəʳ] N (*Tech*) arruela, anilha
wash-hand basin (*Brit*) N pia (BR), lavatório (PT)
washing ['wɔʃɪŋ] (*Brit*) N (*dirty*) roupa suja; (*clean*) roupa lavada; **washing line** (*Brit*) N corda de estender roupa, varal m; **washing machine** N máquina de lavar roupa, lavadora; **washing powder** (*Brit*) N sabão m em pó
Washington ['wɔʃɪŋtən] N (*city, state*) Washington
washing-up N: **to do the ~** lavar a louça; **washing-up liquid** (*Brit*) N detergente m
wash-out (*inf*) N fracasso, fiasco
washroom ['wɔʃruːm] (*US*) N banheiro (BR), casa de banho (PT)
wasn't ['wɔznt] = **was not**
WASP [wɔsp] (*US* **Wasp**) (*inf*) N ABBR (= *White Anglo-Saxon Protestant*) apelido, muitas vezes pejorativo, dado aos membros da classe dominante nos EUA
wasp [wɔsp] N vespa
waspish ['wɔspɪʃ] ADJ irritadiço
wastage ['weistidʒ] N desgaste m, desperdício; (*loss*) perda; **natural ~** desgaste natural
waste [weist] N desperdício, esbanjamento; (*wastage*) desperdício; (*of time*) perda; (*food*) sobras fpl; (*also:* **household waste**) detritos mpl domésticos; (*rubbish*) lixo ■ ADJ (*material*) de refugo; (*left over*) de sobra; (*land*) baldio ■ VT (*squander*) esbanjar, desperdiçar; (*time, opportunity*) perder; **wastes** NPL ermos mpl; **it's a ~ of money** é jogar dinheiro fora; **to go to ~** ser desperdiçado; **to lay ~** (*destroy*) devastar
 ▸ **waste away** VI definhar
waste bin (*Brit*) N lata de lixo
waste disposal (unit) (*Brit*) N triturador m de lixo
wasteful ['weistful] ADJ esbanjador(a); (*process*) anti-econômico
waste ground (*Brit*) N terreno baldio
wasteland ['weistlənd] N terra inculta; (*in town*) terreno baldio
wastepaper basket ['weistpeipəʳ-] N cesta de papéis

waste pipe N cano de esgoto
waste products N (*Industry*) resíduos mpl
watch [wɔtʃ] N (*clock*) relógio; (*also:* **wrist watch**) relógio de pulso; (*act of watching*) vigia; (*guard: Mil*) sentinela; (*Naut: spell of duty*) quarto ■ VT (*look at*) observar, olhar; (*programme, match*) assistir a; (*television*) ver; (*spy on, guard*) vigiar; (*be careful of*) tomar cuidado com ■ VI ver, olhar; (*keep guard*) montar guarda; **to keep a close ~ on sb/sth** vigiar alguém/algo, ficar de olho em alguém/algo; **~ what you're doing** presta atenção no que você está fazendo
 ▸ **watch out** VI ter cuidado
watchband ['wɔtʃbænd] (*US*) N pulseira de relógio
watchdog ['wɔtʃdɔg] N cão m de guarda; (*fig*) vigia m/f
watchful ['wɔtʃful] ADJ vigilante, atento
watchmaker ['wɔtʃmeikəʳ] N relojoeiro(-a)
watchman ['wɔtʃmən] (*irreg*) N vigia m; (*also:* **night watchman**) guarda m noturno; (: *in factory*) vigia m noturno
watch stem (*US*) N botão m de corda
watchstrap ['wɔtʃstræp] N pulseira de relógio
watchword ['wɔtʃwəːd] N lema m, divisa
water ['wɔːtəʳ] N água ■ VT (*plant*) regar ■ VI (*eyes*) lacrimejar; (*mouth*) salivar; **a drink of ~** um copo d'água; **in British ~s** nas águas territoriais britânicas; **to pass ~** urinar; **to make sb's mouth ~** dar água na boca de alguém
 ▸ **water down** VT (*milk*) aguar; (*fig*) diluir
water cannon N tanque de espirrar água para dispersar multidões
water closet (*Brit*) N privada
watercolour ['wɔːtəkʌləʳ] (*US* **watercolor**) N aquarela
water-cooled [-kuːld] ADJ refrigerado a água
watercress ['wɔːtəkres] N agrião m
waterfall ['wɔːtəfɔːl] N cascata, cachoeira
waterfront ['wɔːtəfrʌnt] N (*seafront*) orla marítima; (*docks*) zona portuária
water heater N aquecedor m de água, boiler m
water hole N bebedouro, poço
water ice (*Brit*) N sorvete de frutas à base de água
watering can ['wɔːtərɪŋ-] N regador m
water level N nível m d'água
water lily N nenúfar m
waterline ['wɔːtəlain] N (*Naut*) linha d'água
waterlogged ['wɔːtəlɔgd] ADJ alagado
water main N adutora
watermark ['wɔːtəmɑːk] N (*on paper*) filigrana
watermelon ['wɔːtəmelən] N melancia
water polo N pólo aquático
waterproof ['wɔːtəpruːf] ADJ impermeável; (*watch*) à prova d'água
water-repellent ADJ hidrófugo
watershed ['wɔːtəʃed] N (*Geo*) linha divisória das águas; (*fig*) momento crítico
water-skiing N esqui m aquático
water softener N abrandador m de água
water tank N depósito d'água

watertight['wɔ:tətaɪt] ADJ hermético, à prova d'água

water vapour N vapor *m* de água

waterway['wɔ:təweɪ] N hidrovia

waterworks['wɔ:təwə:ks] NPL usina hidráulica

watery['wɔ:tərɪ] ADJ (*colour*) pálido; (*coffee*) aguado; (*eyes*) húmido

watt[wɔt] N watt *m*

wattage['wɔtɪdʒ] N wattagem *f*

wattle['wɔtl] N caniçada

wave[weɪv] N (*on water, Radio, fig*) onda; (*of hand*) aceno, sinal *m*; (*in hair*) onda, ondulação *f* ∎ VI acenar com a mão; (*flag, grass, branches*) tremular ∎ VT (*hand*) acenar; (*handkerchief*) acenar com; (*weapon*) brandir; (*hair*) ondular; **to ~ goodbye to sb** despedir-se de alguém com um aceno; **short/medium/long ~** (*Radio*) ondas curtas/médias/longas; **the new ~** (*Cinema, Mus*) a nova onda

▸ **wave aside** VT (*fig: suggestion, objection*) rejeitar; (: *doubts*) pôr de lado; (*person*): **to ~ sb aside** fazer sinal para alguém pôr-se de lado

▸ **wave away** VT (*fig: suggestion, objection*) rejeitar; (: *doubts*) pôr de lado; (*person*): **to ~ sb away** fazer sinal para alguém pôr-se de lado

waveband['weɪvbænd] N faixa de onda

wavelength['weɪvleŋθ] N comprimento de onda; **to be on the same ~ as** ter os mesmos gostos e atitudes que

waver['weɪvəʳ] VI vacilar; (*voice, eyes, love*) hesitar

wavy['weɪvɪ] ADJ (*hair*) ondulado; (*line*) ondulante

wax[wæks] N cera ∎ VT encerar; (*car*) polir ∎ VI (*moon*) crescer

waxworks['wækswə:ks] N museu *m* de cera ∎ NPL (*models*) figuras *fpl* de cera

way[weɪ] N caminho; (*distance*) percurso; (*direction*) direção *f*, sentido; (*manner*) maneira, modo; (*habit*) costume *m*; (*condition*) estado; **which ~? — this ~** por onde? — por aqui; **to crawl one's ~ to ...** arrastar-se até ...; **to lie one's ~ out of it** mentir para livrar-se de apuros; **on the ~ (to)** a caminho (de); **to be on one's ~** estar a caminho; **to be in the ~** atrapalhar; **to keep out of sb's ~** evitar alguém; **it's a long ~ a~** é muito longe; **the village is rather out of the ~** o lugarejo é um pouco fora de mão; **to go out of one's ~ to do sth** (*fig*) dar-se ao trabalho de fazer algo; **to lose one's ~** perder-se; **to be under ~** (*work, project*) estar em andamento; **to make ~ (for sb/sth)** abrir caminho (para alguém/algo); **to get one's own ~** conseguir o que quer; **to put sth the right ~ up** (*Brit*) colocar algo na posição certa; **to be the wrong ~ round** estar às avessas; **he's in a bad ~** ele vai muito mal; **in a ~** de certo modo, até certo ponto; **in some ~s** a certos respeitos; **by the ~** a propósito; **"~ in"** (*Brit*) "entrada"; **"~ out"** (*Brit*) "saída"; **the ~ back** o caminho de volta; **"give ~"** (*Brit: Aut*) "dê a preferência"; **in the ~ of** em matéria de; **by ~**

of (*through*) por, via; (*as a sort of*) à guisa de; **no ~!** (*inf*) de jeito nenhum!

waybill['weɪbɪl] N (*Comm*) conhecimento

waylay[weɪ'leɪ] (*irreg*) VT armar uma cilada para; (*fig*): **I got waylaid** alguém me deteve

wayside['weɪsaɪd] N beira da estrada; **to fall by the ~** (*fig*) desistir; (*morally*) corromper-se

way station(US) N (*Rail*) apeadeiro; (*fig*) etapa

wayward['weɪwəd] ADJ (*behaviour, child*) caprichoso, voluntarioso

WC['dʌblju'si:] (*Brit*) N ABBR = **water closet**

WCC N ABBR = **World Council of Churches**

we[wi:] PL PRON nós

weak[wi:k] ADJ fraco, débil; (*morally, currency*) fraco; (*excuse*) pouco convincente; (*tea*) aguado, ralo; **to grow ~(er)** enfraquecer, ficar cada vez mais fraco

weaken['wi:kən] VI enfraquecer(-se); (*give way*) ceder; (*influence, power*) diminuir ∎ VT enfraquecer; (*lessen*) diminuir

weak-kneed[-ni:d] ADJ (*fig*) covarde

weakling['wi:klɪŋ] N pessoa fraca *or* delicada; (*morally*) pessoa de personalidade fraca

weakly['wi:klɪ] ADJ fraco ∎ ADV fracamente

weakness['wi:knɪs] N fraqueza; (*fault*) ponto fraco; **to have a ~ for** ter uma queda por

wealth[wɛlθ] N (*money, resources*) riqueza; (*of details*) abundância; **wealth tax** N imposto sobre fortunas

wealthy['wɛlθɪ] ADJ (*person, family*) rico, abastado; (*country*) rico

wean[wi:n] VT desmamar

weapon['wɛpən] N arma; **~s of mass destruction** armas de destruição em massa

wear[wɛəʳ] (*pt* **wore**, *pp* **worn**) N (*use*) uso; (*deterioration through use*) desgaste *m*; (*clothing*): **baby/sports ~** roupa infantil/de esporte ∎ VT (*clothes*) usar; (*shoes*) usar, calçar; (*put on*) vestir; (*damage: through use*) desgastar; (*beard etc*) ter ∎ VI (*last*) durar; (*rub through etc*) gastar-se; **town/evening ~** traje *m* de passeio/de moite; **to ~ a hole in sth** fazer um buraco em algo pelo uso

▸ **wear away** VT gastar ∎ VI desgastar-se

▸ **wear down** VT gastar; (*strength*) esgotar

▸ **wear off** VI (*pain etc*) passar

▸ **wear on** VI alongar-se

▸ **wear out** VT desgastar; (*person, strength*) esgotar

wearable['wɛərəbl] ADJ que se pode usar

wear and tear N desgaste *m*

wearily['wɪərɪlɪ] ADV de maneira cansada

weariness['wɪərɪnɪs] N cansaço, fadiga; (*boredom*) aborrecimento

wearisome['wɪərɪsəm] ADJ (*tiring*) cansativo; (*boring*) fastidioso

weary['wɪərɪ] ADJ (*tired*) cansado; (*dispirited*) deprimido ∎ VT aborrecer ∎ VI: **to ~ of** cansar-se de

weasel['wi:zl] N (*Zool*) doninha

weather['wɛðəʳ] N tempo ∎ VT (*storm, crisis*) resistir a; **what's the ~ like?** como está o tempo?; **under the ~** (*fig: ill*) doente

weather-beaten ADJ curtido; (building, stone) castigado, erodido

weathercock ['wɛðəkɔk] N cata-vento

weather forecast N previsão f do tempo

weatherman ['wɛðəmæn] (irreg: inf) N meteorologista m

weatherproof ['wɛðəpru:f] ADJ (garment) impermeável; (building) à prova de intempérie

weather report N boletim m meteorológico

weather vane [-veɪn] N = **weathercock**

weave [wi:v] (pt, pp **woven**) VT (cloth) tecer; (fig) compor, criar ▪ VI (fig) (pt, pp **weaved**) (move in and out) ziguezaguear

weaver ['wi:vər] N tecelão(-loa) m/f

weaving ['wi:vɪŋ] N tecelagem f

web [wɛb] N (of spider) teia; (on foot) membrana; (network) rede f; **the (World Wide) W~** a (World Wide) Web

webbed [wɛbd] ADJ (foot) palmípede

webbing ['wɛbɪŋ] N (on chair) tira de tecido forte

weblog ['wɛblɔg] N weblog m

webcam ['wɛbkæm] N webcam f

web page N página (da) web

website ['wɛbsaɪt] N site m, website m

wed [wɛd] (pt, pp **wedded**) VT casar ▪ VI casar-se ▪ N: **the newly-~s** os recém-casados

Wed. ABBR (= Wednesday) qua., 4ª a

we'd [wi:d] = **we had; we would**

wedded ['wɛdɪd] PT, PP of **wed**

wedding ['wɛdɪŋ] N casamento, núpcias fpl; **wedding anniversary** N aniversário de casamento; **silver/golden wedding anniversary** bodas fpl de prata/de ouro; **wedding day** N dia m de casamento; **wedding dress** N vestido de noiva; **wedding night** N noite f de núpcias; **wedding present** N presente m de casamento; **wedding ring** N anel m or aliança de casamento

wedge [wɛdʒ] N (of wood etc) cunha, calço; (of cake) fatia ▪ VT (pack tightly) apinhar; (door) pôr calço em

wedge-heeled shoes [-hi:ld-] NPL sapatos mpl tipo Annabella

wedlock ['wɛdlɔk] N matrimônio, casamento

Wednesday ['wɛdnzdɪ] N quarta-feira; see also **Tuesday**

wee [wi:] (Scottish) ADJ pequeno, pequenino

weed [wi:d] N erva daninha ▪ VT capinar

weedkiller ['wi:dkɪlər] N herbicida m

weedy ['wi:dɪ] ADJ (man) fraquinho

week [wi:k] N semana; **once/twice a ~** uma vez/duas vezes por semana; **in two ~s' time** daqui a duas semanas; **a ~ today** daqui a uma semana; **Tuesday ~, a ~ on Tuesday** sem ser essa terça-feira, a próxima; **every other ~** uma semana sim, uma semana não

weekday ['wi:kdeɪ] N dia m de semana; (Comm) dia útil; **on ~s** durante a semana

weekend ['wi:kɛnd] N fim m de semana; **weekend case** N maleta

weekly ['wi:klɪ] ADV semanalmente ▪ ADJ semanal ▪ N semanário

weep [wi:p] (pt, pp **wept**) VI (person) chorar; (Med: wound) supurar

weeping willow ['wi:pɪŋ-] N salgueiro chorão

weft [wɛft] N (Textiles) trama

weigh [weɪ] VT, VI pesar; **to ~ anchor** levantar ferro; **to ~ the pros and cons** pesar os prós e contras

▶ **weigh down** VT sobrecarregar; (fig: with worry) deprimir, acabrunhar

▶ **weigh out** VT (goods) pesar

▶ **weigh up** VT ponderar, avaliar

weighbridge ['weɪbrɪdʒ] N báscula automática

weighing machine ['weɪɪŋ-] N balança

weight [weɪt] N peso ▪ VT carregar com peso; (fig: statistic) ponderar; **to lose/put on ~** emagrecer/engordar; **sold by ~** vendido por peso; **~s and measures** pesos e medidas

weighting ['weɪtɪŋ] N (allowance) indenização f de residência

weightlessness ['weɪtlɪsnɪs] N ausência de peso

weightlifter ['weɪtlɪftər] N levantador m de pesos

weighty ['weɪtɪ] ADJ pesado; (matters) importante

weir [wɪər] N represa, açude m

weird [wɪəd] ADJ esquisito, estranho

welcome ['wɛlkəm] ADJ bem-vindo ▪ N acolhimento, recepção f ▪ VT dar as boas-vindas a; (be glad of) saudar; **you're ~** (after thanks) de nada; **to make sb ~** dar bom acolhimento a alguém; **you're ~ to try** pode tentar se quiser

welcoming ['wɛlkəmɪŋ] ADJ acolhedor(a); (speech) de boas-vindas

weld [wɛld] N solda ▪ VT soldar, unir

welder ['wɛldər] N (person) soldador(a) m/f

welding ['wɛldɪŋ] N soldagem f, solda

welfare ['wɛlfɛər] N bem-estar m; (social aid) assistência social; **welfare state** N país autofinanciador da sua assistência social; **welfare work** N trabalho social

well [wɛl] N poço; (pool) nascente f ▪ ADV bem ▪ ADJ: **to be ~** estar bem (de saúde) ▪ EXCL bem!, então!; **as ~** também; **as ~ as** assim como; **~ done!** muito bem!; **get ~ soon!** melhoras!; **to do ~** ir or sair-se bem; (business) ir bem; **to think ~ of sb** ter um bom conceito a respeito de alguém; **I don't feel ~** não estou me sentindo bem; **you might as ~ tell me** é melhor você me contar logo; **~, as I was saying ...** bem, como eu estava dizendo ...

▶ **well up** VI brotar

we'll [wi:l] = **we will; we shall**

well-behaved [-bɪ'heɪvd] ADJ bem comportado

well-being N bem-estar m

well-bred ADJ bem educado

well-built ADJ (person) robusto; (house) bem construído

well-chosen ADJ bem escolhido

well-deserved [-dɪ'zə:vd] ADJ bem merecido

well-developed [-dɪ'vɛləpt] ADJ bem desenvolvido

well-disposed ADJ: ~ **to(wards)** favorável a
well-dressed [-drɛst] ADJ bem vestido
well-earned ADJ (rest) bem merecido
well-groomed [-gru:md] ADJ bem tratado
well-heeled [-hi:ld] (inf) ADJ (wealthy) rico
well-informed ADJ bem informado, versado
wellingtons ['wɛlɪŋtənz] N (also: **wellington boots**) botas de borracha até os joelhos
well-kept ADJ (house, hands etc) bem tratado; (secret) bem guardado
well-known ADJ conhecido; **it's a ~ fact that ...** é sabido que ...
well-mannered [-'mænəd] ADJ bem educado
well-meaning ADJ bem intencionado
well-nigh [-naɪ] ADV: ~ **impossible** praticamente impossível
well-off ADJ próspero, rico
well-read ADJ lido, versado
well-spoken ADJ (person) bem-falante
well-stocked [-stɔkt] ADJ bem abastecido
well-timed [-taɪmd] ADJ oportuno
well-to-do ADJ abastado
well-wisher [-'wɪʃəʳ] N simpatizante m/f; (admirer) admirador(a) m/f
Welsh [wɛlʃ] ADJ galês/galesa ■ N (Ling) galês m; **the Welsh** NPL (people) os galeses
Welshman ['wɛlʃmən] (irreg) N galês m
Welsh rarebit N torradas com queijo derretido
Welshwoman ['wɛlʃwumən] (irreg) N galesa
welter ['wɛltəʳ] N tumulto
went [wɛnt] PT of **go**
wept [wɛpt] PT, PP of **weep**
were [wə:ʳ] PT of **be**
we're [wɪəʳ] = **we are**
weren't [wə:nt] = **were not**
werewolf ['wɪəwulf] (irreg) N lobisomem m
west [wɛst] N oeste m ■ ADJ ocidental, do oeste ■ ADV para o oeste or ao oeste; **the W~** (Pol) o Oeste, o Ocidente
westbound ['wɛstbaund] ADJ em direção ao oeste
West Country (Brit) N: **the ~** o sudoeste da Inglaterra
westerly ['wɛstəlɪ] ADJ (situation) ocidental; (wind) oeste
western ['wɛstən] ADJ ocidental ■ N (Cinema) western m, bangue-bangue (BR) (inf)
westernized ['wɛstənaɪzd] ADJ ocidentalizado
West German ADJ, N alemão(-ã) m/f ocidental
West Germany N Alemanha Ocidental
West Indian ADJ, N antilhano(-a)
West Indies [-'ɪndɪz] NPL Antilhas fpl
westward(s) ['wɛstwəd(z)] ADV para o oeste
wet [wɛt] (pt, pp **wetted**) ADJ molhado; (damp) úmido; (wet through) encharcado; (rainy) chuvoso ■ N (Brit: Pol) político de tendência moderada ■ VT molhar; **to ~ one's pants** or **o.s.** fazer xixi na calça; **to get ~** molhar-se; **"~ paint"** "tinta fresca"; **wet blanket** (pej) N (fig) desmancha-prazeres m/f inv
wetness ['wɛtnɪs] N umidade f
wetsuit ['wɛtsu:t] N roupa de mergulho

we've [wi:v] = **we have**
whack [wæk] VT bater
whacked [wækt] (inf) ADJ morto, esgotado
whale [weɪl] N (Zool) baleia
whaler ['weɪləʳ] N baleeiro
wharf [wɔ:f] (pl **wharves**) N cais m inv
wharves [wɔ:vz] NPL of **wharf**

 KEYWORD

what [wɔt] ADJ **1** (in direct/indirect questions) que, qual; **what size is it?** que tamanho é este?; **what colour/shape is it?** qual é a cor/o formato?; **what books do you need?** que livros você precisa?; **he asked me what books I needed** ele me perguntou de quais os livros eu precisava
2 (in exclamations) quê!, como!; **what a mess!** que bagunça!
■ PRON **1** (interrogative) que, o que; **what are you doing?** o que é que você está fazendo?; **what's happened?** o que aconteceu?; **what's in there?** o que é que tem lá dentro?; **what are you talking about?** sobre o que você está falando?; **what is it called?** como se chama?; **what about me?** e eu?; **what about doing ...?** que tal fazer ...?
2 (relative) o que; **I saw what you did/was on the table** eu vi o que você fez/estava na mesa; **he asked me what she had said** ele me perguntou o que ela tinha dito
■ EXCL (disbelieving): **what, no coffee!** o que, não tem café!; **I've crashed the car — what!** bati com o carro puxa!

whatever [wɔt'ɛvəʳ] ADJ: ~ **book you choose** qualquer livro que você escolha ■ PRON: **do ~ is necessary/you want** faça tudo o que for preciso/o que você quiser; ~ **happens** aconteça o que acontecer; **no reason ~** or **whatsoever** nenhuma razão seja qual for or em absoluto; **nothing ~** nada em absoluto
whatsoever [wɔt'səuevəʳ] ADJ = **whatever**
wheat [wi:t] N trigo
wheatgerm ['wi:tdʒə:m] N germe m de trigo
wheatmeal ['wi:tmi:l] N farinha de trigo
wheedle ['wi:dl] VT: **to ~ sb into doing sth** persuadir alguém a fazer algo; **to ~ sth out of sb** conseguir algo de alguém por meio de agrados
wheel [wi:l] N roda; (also: **steering wheel**) volante m; (Naut) roda do leme ■ VT (pram etc) empurrar ■ VI (birds) dar voltas; (also: **wheel round**) girar, dar voltas, virar-se
wheelbarrow ['wi:lbærəu] N carrinho de mão
wheelbase ['wi:lbeɪs] N distância entre os eixos
wheelchair ['wi:ltʃɛəʳ] N cadeira de rodas
wheel clamp N (Aut) grampo com que se imobiliza carros estacionados ilegalmente
wheeler-dealer ['wi:lə-] N negocista m/f
wheelhouse ['wi:lhaus] N casa do leme

wheeling ['wi:lɪŋ] N: ~ **and dealing** negociatas *fpl*

wheeze [wi:z] N respiração *f* difícil, chiado ■ VI respirar ruidosamente

○ KEYWORD

when [wɛn] ADV quando; **when are you going to Brazil?** quando você vai para o Brasil? ■ CONJ **1** (*at, during, after the time that*) quando; **she was reading when I came in** ela estava lendo quando eu entrei; **when you've read it, tell me what you think** depois que você tiver lido isto, diga-me o que acha; **that was when I needed you** foi quando eu precisei de você **2** (*on, at which*) quando, em que; **on the day when I met him** no dia em que o conheci; **one day when it was raining** um dia quando estava chovendo **3** (*whereas*) ao passo que; **you said I was wrong when in fact I was right** você disse que eu estava errado quando, na verdade, eu estava certo; **why did you buy it when you can't afford it?** por que você comprou isto se não tinha condições (de fazê-lo)

whenever [wɛn'ɛvəʳ] CONJ quando, quando quer que; (*every time that*) sempre que ■ ADV quando você quiser

where [wɛəʳ] ADV onde ■ CONJ onde, aonde; **this is ~ ...** aqui é onde ...; **~ are you from?** de onde você é?

whereabouts ['wɛərəbauts] ADV (por) onde ■ N: **nobody knows his ~** ninguém sabe o seu paradeiro

whereas [wɛər'æz] CONJ uma vez que, ao passo que

whereby [wɛə'baɪ] ADV (*formal*) pelo qual (*or* pela qual *etc*)

whereupon [wɛərə'pɔn] ADV depois do que

wherever [wɛər'ɛvəʳ] CONJ onde quer que ■ ADV (*interrogative*) onde?; **sit ~ you like** sente-se onde quiser

wherewithal ['wɛəwɪðɔ:l] N recursos *mpl*, meios *mpl*

whet [wɛt] VT afiar; (*appetite*) abrir

whether ['wɛðəʳ] CONJ se; **I don't know ~ to accept or not** não sei se aceito ou não; **~ you go or not** quer você vá quer não; **it's doubtful ~ ...** não é certo que ...

whey [weɪ] N soro (de leite)

○ KEYWORD

which [wɪtʃ] ADJ **1** (*interrogative: direct, indirect*) que, qual; **which picture do you want?** que quadro você quer?; **which books are yours?** quais são os seus livros?; **which one?** qual? **2**: **in which case** em cujo caso; **the train may be late, in which case don't wait up** o trem talvez esteja atrasado e, neste caso, não espere; **by which time** momento em que; **we got**

there at 8pm, by which time the cinema was full quando chegamos lá às 8 da noite, o cinema estava lotado ■ PRON **1** (*interrogative*) qual; **which (of these) are yours?** quais (destes) são seus?; **I don't mind which** não me importa qual **2** (*relative*) que, o que, o qual *etc*; **the apple which you ate** a maçã que você comeu; **the apple which is on the table** a maçã que está sobre a mesa; **the meeting (which) we attended** a reunião da qual participamos; **the chair on which you are sitting** a cadeira na qual você está sentado; **the book of which you spoke** o livro do qual você falou; **he said he knew, which is true** ele disse que sabia, o que é verdade; **after which** depois do que

whichever [wɪtʃ'ɛvəʳ] ADJ: **take ~ book you prefer** pegue o livro que preferir; **~ book you take** qualquer livro que você pegue

whiff [wɪf] N cheiro; **to catch a ~ of sth** tomar o cheiro de algo

while [waɪl] N tempo, momento ■ CONJ enquanto, ao mesmo tempo que; (*as long as*) contanto que; (*although*) embora; **for a ~** durante algum tempo; **in a ~** daqui a pouco; **all the ~** todo o tempo; **we'll make it worth your ~** faremos com que valha a pena para você
  ▶ **while away** VT (*time*) encher

whilst [waɪlst] CONJ = **while**

whim [wɪm] N capricho, veneta

whimper ['wɪmpəʳ] N (*weeping*) choradeira; (*moan*) lamúria ■ VI choramingar, soluçar

whimsical ['wɪmzɪkl] ADJ (*person*) caprichoso, de veneta; (*look*) excêntrico

whine [waɪn] N (*of pain*) gemido; (*of engine, siren*) zunido ■ VI (*person, animal*) gemer; zunir; (*fig*) lamuriar-se; (*dog*) ganir

whip [wɪp] N açoite *m*; (*for riding*) chicote *m*; (*Pol*) líder *m/f* da bancada ■ VT chicotear; (*snatch*) apanhar de repente; (*cream, eggs*) bater; (*move quickly*): **to ~ sth out/off/away** *etc* arrancar algo
  ▶ **whip up** VT (*cream*) bater; (*inf: meal*) arrumar; (*stir up: feeling*) atiçar; (*: support*) angariar

whiplash ['wɪplæʃ] N (*Med: also*: **whiplash injury**) golpe *m* de chicote, chicotinho

whipped cream [wɪpt-] N (*creme m*) chantilly *m*

whipping boy ['wɪpɪŋ-] N (*fig*) bode *m* expiatório

whip-round (*Brit*) N coleta, vaquinha

whirl [wə:l] N remoinho ■ VT fazer girar ■ VI (*dancers*) rodopiar; (*leaves, water etc*) redemoinhar

whirlpool ['wə:lpu:l] N remoinho

whirlwind ['wə:lwɪnd] N furacão *m*, remoinho

whirr [wə:ʳ] VI zumbir

whisk [wɪsk] N (*Culin*) batedeira ■ VT bater; **to ~ sth away from sb** arrebatar algo de alguém; **to ~ sb away** *or* **off** levar alguém rapidamente

whiskers ['wɪskəz] NPL (*of animal*) bigodes *mpl*; (*of man*) suíças *fpl*

whisky ['wɪskɪ] (*US, Ireland* **whiskey**) N uísque *m* (BR), whisky *m* (PT)

whisper ['wɪspəʳ] N sussurro, murmúrio;

(*rumour*) rumor *m* ■ VT, VI sussurrar; **to ~ sth to sb** sussurrar algo para alguém

whispering ['wɪspərɪŋ] N sussurros *mpl*

whist [wɪst] (*Brit*) N uíste *m* (BR), whist *m* (PT)

whistle ['wɪsl] N (*sound*) assobio; (*object*) apito ■ VT, VI assobiar

whistle-stop ADJ: **to make a ~ tour** (*Pol*) fazer uma viagem eleitoral

Whit [wɪt] N Pentecostes *m*

white [waɪt] ADJ branco; (*pale*) pálido ■ N branco; (*of egg*) clara; **the whites** NPL (*washing*) a roupa branca; **tennis ~s** traje *m* de tênis; **to turn** *or* **go ~** (*person*) ficar branco *or* pálido; (*hair*) ficar grisalho

whitebait ['waɪtbeɪt] N filhote *m* de arenque

white coffee (*Brit*) N café *m* com leite

white-collar worker N empregado(-a) de escritório

white elephant N (*fig*) elefante *m* branco

white goods N eletrodomésticos *mpl*

white-hot ADJ (*metal*) incandescente

White House N *ver abaixo*

○ **WHITE HOUSE**

● A *White House* é um grande edifício branco
● situado em Washington D.C. onde reside
● o presidente dos Estados Unidos. Por
● extensão, o termo se refere também ao
● poder executivo americano.

white lie N mentira inofensiva *or* social

whiteness ['waɪtnɪs] N brancura

white noise N ruído branco

whiteout ['waɪtaut] N resplendor *m* branco

White Paper N (*Pol*) relatório oficial sobre *determinado assunto*

whitewash ['waɪtwɔʃ] N (*paint*) cal *f* ■ VT caiar; (*fig*) encobrir

whiting ['waɪtɪŋ] N INV pescada-marlonga

Whit Monday N segunda-feira de Pentecostes

Whitsun ['wɪtsn] N Pentecostes *m*

whittle ['wɪtl] VT aparar; **to ~ away, ~ down** reduzir gradualmente, corroer

whizz [wɪz] VI zunir; **to ~ past** *or* **by** passar a toda velocidade; **whizz kid** (*inf*) N prodígio

WHO N ABBR (= *World Health Organization*) OMS *f*

○ KEYWORD

who [huː] PRON **1** (*interrogative*) quem?; **who is it?** quem é?; **who's there?** quem está aí?; **who are you looking for?** quem você está procurando?

2 (*relative*) que, o qual *etc*, quem; **my cousin, who lives in New York** meu primo que mora em Nova Iorque; **the man/woman who spoke to me** o homem/a mulher que falou comigo; **those who can swim** aqueles que sabem nadar

whodunit [huː'dʌnɪt] (*inf*) N romance *m* (*or*

filme *m*) policial

whoever [huː'ɛvəʳ] PRON: **~ finds it** quem quer que *or* seja quem for que o encontre; **ask ~ you like** pergunte a quem quiser; **~ he marries** não importa com quem se case; **~ told you that?** quem te disse isso pelo amor de Deus?

whole [həul] ADJ (*complete*) todo, inteiro; (*not broken*) intacto ■ N (*all*): **the ~ of the time** o tempo todo; (*entire unit*) conjunto; (*total*) total *m*; **the ~ lot (of it)** tudo; **the ~ lot (of them)** todos(-as); **the ~ of the town** toda a cidade, a cidade inteira; **~ villages were destroyed** lugarejos inteiros foram destruídos; **on the ~, as a ~** como um todo, no conjunto

wholefood(s) [həul'fuːd(z)] N comida integral

wholehearted [həul'hɑːtɪd] ADJ total

wholemeal ['həulmiːl] (*Brit*) ADJ (*flour, bread*) integral

whole note (*US*) N semibreve *f*

wholesale ['həulseɪl] N venda por atacado ■ ADJ por atacado; (*destruction*) em grande escala ■ ADV por atacado

wholesaler ['həulseɪləʳ] N atacadista *m/f*

wholesome ['həulsəm] ADJ saudável, sadio

wholewheat ['həulwiːt] ADJ = **wholemeal**

wholly ['həulɪ] ADV totalmente, completamente

○ KEYWORD

whom [huːm] PRON **1** (*interrogative*) quem?; **whom did you see?** quem você viu?; **to whom did you give it?** para quem você deu isto?

2 (*relative*) que, quem; **the man whom I saw/to whom I spoke** o homem que eu vi/com quem eu falei

whooping cough ['huːpɪŋ-] N coqueluche *f*

whoosh [wuʃ] N chio

whopper ['wɔpəʳ] (*inf*) N (*lie*) lorota; (*large thing*): **it was a ~** era enorme

whopping ['wɔpɪŋ] (*inf*) ADJ (*big*) imenso

whore [hɔːʳ] (*inf: pej*) N puta

○ KEYWORD

whose [huːz] ADJ **1** (*possessive: interrogative*): **whose book is this?, whose is this book?** de quem é este livro?; **I don't know whose it is** eu não sei de quem é isto

2 (*possessive: relative*): **the man whose son you rescued** o homem cujo filho você salvou; **the girl whose sister you were speaking to** a menina com cuja irmã você estava falando; **the woman whose car was stolen** a mulher de quem o carro foi roubado

■ PRON de quem; **whose is this?** de quem é isto?; **I know whose it is** eu sei de quem é; **whose are these?** de quem são estes?

Who's Who N Quem é quem

(registro de notabilidades)

🅾 **KEYWORD**

why [waɪ] ADV por que (BR), porque (PT); *(at end of sentence)* por quê (BR), porquê (PT); **why is he always late?** por que ele está sempre atrasado?; **I'm not coming — why not?** eu não vou — por que não?

▪ CONJ por que; **I wonder why he said that** eu me pergunto por que ele disse isso; **that's not why I'm here** não é por isso que estou aqui; **the reason why** a razão por que

▪ EXCL *(expressing surprise, shock, annoyance)* ora essa!; *(explaining)* bem!; **why, it's you!** ora, é você!

whyever [waɪˈɛvər] ADV mas por que
WI N ABBR *(Brit: = Women's Institute)* associação de mulheres ▪ ABBR *(Geo)* **= West Indies**; *(US: Post)* **= Wisconsin**
wick [wɪk] N mecha, pavio
wicked [ˈwɪkɪd] ADJ *(crime, man, witch)* perverso; *(smile)* malicioso; *(inf: terrible: prices, waste)* terrível
wicker [ˈwɪkər] N *(also: **wickerwork**)* (trabalho de) vime *m* ▪ ADJ de vime
wicket [ˈwɪkɪt] N *(Cricket)* arco; **wicket keeper** N *(Cricket)* guarda-meta *m* (no críquete)
wide [waɪd] ADJ largo; *(broad)* extenso, amplo; *(area, publicity, knowledge)* amplo ▪ ADV: **to open ~** abrir totalmente; **to shoot ~** atirar longe do alvo; **it is 4 metres ~** tem 4 metros de largura
wide-angle lens N lente *f* grande angular
wide-awake ADJ bem acordado; *(fig)* vivo, esperto
wide-eyed [-aɪd] ADJ de olhos arregalados; *(fig)* ingênuo
widely [ˈwaɪdlɪ] ADV *(different)* extremamente; *(travelled, spaced)* muito; *(believed, known)* amplamente; **it is ~ believed that ...** há uma convicção generalizada de que ...; **to be ~ read** ser muito lido
widen [ˈwaɪdən] VT *(road, river)* alargar; *(one's experience)* aumentar ▪ VI alargar-se
wideness [ˈwaɪdnɪs] N largura; *(breadth)* extensão *f*
wide open ADJ *(eyes)* arregalado; *(door)* escancarado
wide-ranging [-ˈreɪndʒɪŋ] ADJ *(survey, report)* abrangente; *(interests)* diversos
widespread [ˈwaɪdspred] ADJ *(belief etc)* difundido, comum
widow [ˈwɪdəu] N viúva
widowed [ˈwɪdəud] ADJ viúvo
widower [ˈwɪdəuər] N viúvo
width [wɪdθ] N largura; **it's 7 metres in ~** tem 7 metros de largura
widthways [ˈwɪdθweɪz] ADV transversalmente
wield [wiːld] VT *(sword)* brandir, empunhar; *(power)* exercer
wife [waɪf] *(pl **wives**)* N mulher *f*, esposa
wig [wɪg] N peruca

wigging [ˈwɪgɪŋ] *(Brit: inf)* N sabão *m*, descompostura
wiggle [ˈwɪgl] VT menear, agitar ▪ VI menear, agitar-se
wiggly [ˈwɪglɪ] ADJ *(line)* ondulado
wild [waɪld] ADJ *(animal)* selvagem; *(plant)* silvestre; *(rough)* violento, furioso; *(idea)* disparatado, extravagante; *(person)* insensato; *(enthusiastic)*: **to be ~ about** ser louco por ▪ N: **the ~** a natureza; **wilds** NPL *(remote area)* regiões *fpl* selvagens, terras *fpl* virgens; **wild card** N *(Comput)* carácter *m* de substituição
wildcat [ˈwaɪldkæt] N gato selvagem; *(US: lynx)* lince *m*; **wildcat strike** N *greve espontânea e não autorizada pelo sindicato*
wilderness [ˈwɪldənɪs] N ermo; *(in Brazil)* sertão *m*
wildfire [ˈwaɪldfaɪər] N: **to spread like ~** espalhar-se rapidamente
wild-goose chase N *(fig)* busca inútil
wildlife [ˈwaɪldlaɪf] N animais *mpl* (e plantas *fpl*) selvagens
wildly [ˈwaɪldlɪ] ADV *(behave)* freneticamente; *(hit, guess)* irrefletidamente; *(happy)* extremamente
wiles [waɪlz] NPL artimanhas *fpl*, estratagemas *mpl*
wilful [ˈwɪlful] *(US* **willful***)* ADJ *(person)* teimoso, voluntarioso; *(action)* deliberado, intencional; *(crime)* premeditado

🅾 **KEYWORD**

will [wɪl] *(vt)* *(pt, pp* **willed***)* AUX VB **1** *(forming future tense)*: **I will finish it tomorrow** vou acabar isto amanhã; **I will have finished it by tomorrow** até amanhã eu terei terminado isto; **will you do it? — yes I will/no I won't** você vai fazer isto? — sim, vou/não eu não vou
2 *(in conjectures, predictions)*: **he will come** ele virá; **he will** *or* **he'll be there by now** nesta altura ele está lá; **that will be the postman** deve ser o carteiro; **this medicine will/won't help you** este remédio vai/não vai fazer efeito em você
3 *(in commands, requests, offers)*: **will you be quiet!** fique quieto, por favor!; **will you come?** você vem?; **will you help me?** você pode me ajudar?; **will you have a cup of tea?** você vai querer uma xícara de chá *or* um chá?; **I won't put up with it** eu não vou tolerar isto

▪ VT: **to will sb to do sth** desejar que alguém faça algo; **he willed himself to go on** reuniu grande força de vontade para continuar

▪ N *(volition)* vontade *f*; *(testament)* testamento

willful [ˈwɪlful] *(US)* ADJ **= wilful**
willing [ˈwɪlɪŋ] ADJ *(with goodwill)* disposto, pronto; *(enthusiastic)* entusiasmado; *(submissive)* complacente ▪ N: **to show ~** mostrar boa vontade; **he's ~ to do it** ele é disposto a fazê-lo
willingly [ˈwɪlɪŋlɪ] ADV de bom grado, de boa

vontade
willingness ['wɪlɪŋnɪs] N boa vontade f,
　disposição f
will-o'-the-wisp N fogo-fátuo; (fig) quimera
willow ['wɪləu] N salgueiro
willpower ['wɪlpauə^r] N força de vontade
willy-nilly ['wɪlɪ'nɪlɪ] ADV quer queira ou não
wilt [wɪlt] VI (flower) murchar; (plant) morrer
Wilts [wɪlts] (Brit) ABBR = **Wiltshire**
wily ['waɪlɪ] ADJ esperto, astuto
wimp [wɪmp] (inf) N banana m
win [wɪn] (pt, pp **won**) N (in sports etc) vitória
　■ VT ganhar, vencer; (obtain) conseguir, obter;
　(support) alcançar ■ VI ganhar
　▶ **win over** VT conquistar
　▶ **win round** (Brit) VT = **win over**
wince [wɪns] VI encolher-se, estremecer ■ N
　estremecimento
winch [wɪntʃ] N guincho
Winchester disk ['wɪntʃɛstə-] N (Comput) (disco)
　Winchester m
wind[1] [wɪnd] N vento; (Med) gases mpl,
　flatulência; (breath) fôlego ■ VT (take breath
　away from) deixar sem fôlego; **the ~(s)** (Mus)
　instrumentos mpl de sopro; **into** or **against the**
　~ contra o vento; **to get ~ of sth** (fig) ter notícia
　de algo, tomar conhecimento de algo; **to break**
　~ soltar gases intestinais
wind[2] [waɪnd] (pt, pp **wound**) VT enrolar,
　bobinar; (wrap) envolver; (clock, toy) dar corda a
　■ VI (road, river) serpentear
　▶ **wind down** VT (car window) abaixar, abrir; (fig:
　production, business) diminuir gradativamente
　▶ **wind up** VT (clock) dar corda em; (debate)
　rematar, concluir
windbreak ['wɪndbreɪk] N quebra-ventos m
windbreaker ['wɪndbreɪkə^r] (US) N anoraque m
windcheater ['wɪndtʃi:tə^r] (Brit) N anoraque m
winder ['waɪndə^r] (Brit) N (on watch) botão m de
　corda
windfall ['wɪndfɔ:l] N golpe m de sorte
winding ['waɪndɪŋ] ADJ (road) sinuoso, tortuoso;
　(staircase) de caracol, em espiral
wind instrument N (Mus) instrumento de
　sopro
windmill ['wɪndmɪl] N moinho de vento
window ['wɪndəu] N janela; (in shop etc) vitrine
　f (BR), montra (PT); **window box** N jardineira
　(no peitoril da janela); **window cleaner** N
　(person) limpador(a) m/f de janelas; **window**
　dressing N decoração f de vitrines; **window**
　envelope N envelope m de janela; **window**
　frame N caixilho da janela; **window ledge** N
　peitoril m da janela; **window pane** N vidraça,
　vidro
window-shopping N: **to go ~** ir ver vitrines
windowsill ['wɪndəusɪl] N (inside) peitoril m;
　(outside) soleira
windpipe ['wɪndpaɪp] N traquéia
windscreen ['wɪndskri:n] (Brit) N pára-brisa m;
　windscreen washer (Brit) N lavador m de
　pára-brisa; **windscreen wiper** [-'waɪpə^r] (Brit) N

limpador m de pára-brisa
windshield etc ['wɪndʃi:ld] (US) N = **windscreen**
　etc
windswept ['wɪndswɛpt] ADJ varrido pelo
　vento
wind tunnel N túnel m aerodinâmico
windy ['wɪndɪ] ADJ com muito vento, batido
　pelo vento; **it's ~** está ventando (BR), faz vento
　(PT)
wine [waɪn] N vinho ■ VT: **to ~ and dine sb**
　levar alguém para jantar; **wine bar** N bar m
　para degustação de vinhos; **wine cellar** N
　adega; **wine glass** N cálice m (de vinho); **wine**
　list N lista de vinhos; **wine merchant** N
　negociante m/f de vinhos; **wine tasting**
　[-'teɪstɪŋ] N degustação f de vinhos; **wine**
　waiter N garçon m dos vinhos
wing [wɪŋ] N asa; (of building) ala; (Aut) aleta,
　pára-lamas m inv; **wings** NPL (Theatre)
　bastidores mpl
winger ['wɪŋə^r] N (Sport) ponta, extremo
wing mirror (Brit) N espelho lateral
wing nut N porca borboleta
wingspan ['wɪŋspæn] N envergadura
wingspread ['wɪŋsprɛd] N envergadura
wink [wɪŋk] N piscadela ■ VI piscar o olho; (light
　etc) piscar
winkle ['wɪŋkl] N búzio
winner ['wɪnə^r] N vencedor(a) m/f
winning ['wɪnɪŋ] ADJ (team) vencedor(a); (goal)
　decisivo; (smile) sedutor(a); **winning post** N
　meta de chegada
winnings ['wɪnɪŋz] NPL ganhos mpl
winsome ['wɪnsəm] ADJ encantador(a),
　cativante
winter ['wɪntə^r] N inverno ■ VI hibernar;
　winter sports NPL esportes mpl (BR) or
　desportos mpl (PT) de inverno
wintry ['wɪntrɪ] ADJ glacial, invernal
wipe [waɪp] N: **to give sth a ~** limpar algo com
　um pano; (rub) esfregar; (erase: tape) apagar ■ VT
　limpar; **to ~ one's nose** limpar o nariz
　▶ **wipe off** VT remover esfregando
　▶ **wipe out** VT (debt) liquidar; (memory) apagar;
　(destroy) exterminar
　▶ **wipe up** VT (mess) limpar; (dishes) enxugar
wire ['waɪə^r] N arame m; (Elec) fio (elétrico);
　(telegram) telegrama m ■ VT (house) instalar
　a rede elétrica em; (also: **wire up**) conectar;
　(telegram) telegrafar para; **wire brush** N escova
　de aço; **wire cutters** [-'kʌtəz] NPL alicate m
　corta-arame
wireless ['waɪəlɪs] (Brit) N rádio
wire netting N rede f de arame
wire-tapping [-'tæpɪŋ] N escuta telefônica
wiring ['waɪərɪŋ] N instalação f elétrica
wiry ['waɪərɪ] ADJ nervoso; (hair) grosso
wisdom ['wɪzdəm] N (of person) prudência; (of
　action, remark) bom-senso, sabedoria; **wisdom**
　tooth (irreg) N dente m do siso
wise [waɪz] ADJ (person) prudente; (action, remark)
　sensato; **I'm none the ~r** eu não entendi nada

▶ **wise up** (*inf*) VI: **to ~ up to** abrir os olhos para
...wise [waiz] SUFFIX: **time..wise** *etc* com relação ao tempo *etc*
wisecrack ['waizkræk] N piada
wish [wɪʃ] N desejo ■ VT desejar; (*want*) querer; **best ~es** (*on birthday etc*) parabéns *mpl*, felicidades *fpl*; **with best ~es** (*in letter*) cumprimentos; **give her my best ~es** dá um abraço para ela; **to ~ sb goodbye** despedir-se de alguém; **he ~ed me well** me desejou boa sorte; **to ~ to do/sb to do sth** querer fazer/que alguém faça algo; **to ~ for** desejar; **to ~ sth on sb** desejar algo a alguém
wishful ['wɪʃful] ADJ: **it's ~ thinking** é doce ilusão
wishy-washy ['wɪʃɪ'wɔʃɪ] (*inf*) ADJ (*colour*) indefinido; (*person*) sem caráter; (*ideas*) aguado
wisp [wɪsp] N mecha, tufo; (*of smoke*) fio
wistful ['wɪstful] ADJ melancólico
wit [wɪt] N (*wittiness*) presença de espírito, engenho; (*intelligence: also*: **wits**) entendimento; (*person*) espirituoso(-a); **to be at one's ~s' end** (*fig*) não saber para onde se virar; **to have one's ~s about one** ter uma presença de espírito; **to ~ a saber**
witch [wɪtʃ] N bruxa
witchcraft ['wɪtʃkrɑːft] N bruxaria
witch doctor N médico feiticeiro, pajé *m* (BR)
witch-hunt N caça às bruxas

○ KEYWORD

with [wɪð, wɪθ] PREP **1** (*accompanying, in the company of*) com; **I was with him** eu estava com ele; **to stay overnight with friends** dormir na casa de amigos; **we'll take the children with us** vamos levar as crianças conosco; **I'll be with you in a minute** vou vê-lo num minuto; **I'm with you** (*I understand*) compreendo; **to be with it** (*inf*) estar por dentro; (*aware*) estar a par da situação; (: *up-to-date*) estar atualizado com
2 (*descriptive*) com, de; **a room with a view** um quarto com vista; **the man with the grey hat/blue eyes** o homem do chapéu cinza/de olhos azuis
3 (*indicating manner, means, cause*) com, de; **with tears in her eyes** com os olhos cheios de lágrimas; **to walk with a stick** andar com uma bengala; **to tremble with fear** tremer de medo; **to fill sth with water** encher algo de água

withdraw [wɪð'drɔː] (*irreg*) VT tirar, remover; (*offer*) retirar ■ VI retirar-se; (*go back on promise*) voltar atrás; **to ~ money (from the bank)** retirar dinheiro (do banco); **to ~ into o.s.** introverter-se
withdrawal [wɪð'drɔːəl] N retirada; **withdrawal symptoms** NPL síndrome *f* de abstinência; **to have withdrawal symptoms** ter uma reação
withdrawn [wɪð'drɔːn] PP *of* **withdraw** ■ ADJ (*person*) reservado, introvertido

wither ['wɪðəʳ] VI murchar
withered ['wɪðəd] ADJ murcho
withhold [wɪð'həuld] (*irreg: like* **hold**) VT (*money*) reter; (*decision*) adiar; (*permission*) negar; (*information*) esconder
within [wɪð'ɪn] PREP dentro de ■ ADV dentro; **~ reach** ao alcance da mão; **~ sight** à vista; **~ the week** antes do fim da semana; **~ a mile of** a uma milha de; **~ an hour from now** daqui a uma hora; **to be ~ the law** estar dentro da lei
without [wɪð'aut] PREP sem; **~ anybody knowing** sem ninguém saber; **to go** *or* **do ~ sth** passar sem algo
withstand [wɪð'stænd] (*irreg: like* **stand**) VT resistir a
witness ['wɪtnɪs] N (*person*) testemunha; (*evidence*) testemunho ■ VT (*event*) testemunhar, presenciar; (*document*) legalizar; **to bear ~ to sth** (*fig*) testemunhar algo; **~ for the prosecution/defence** testemunha para acusação/defesa; **to ~ to sth/having seen sth** testemunhar algo/ter visto algo; **witness box** (US **witness stand**) N banco das testemunhas
witticism ['wɪtɪsɪzm] N observação *f* espirituosa, chiste *m*
witty ['wɪtɪ] ADJ espirituoso
wives [waɪvz] NPL *of* **wife**
wizard ['wɪzəd] N feiticeiro, mago
wizened ['wɪznd] ADJ encarquilhado
wk ABBR = **week**
Wm. ABBR = **William**
WO N ABBR = **warrant officer**
wobble ['wɔbl] VI oscilar; (*chair*) balançar
wobbly ['wɔblɪ] ADJ (*table*) balançante, bambo
woe [wəu] N dor *f*, mágoa
woke [wəuk] PT *of* **wake**
woken ['wəukən] PP *of* **wake**
wolf [wulf] (*pl* **wolves**) N lobo
wolves [wulvz] NPL *of* **wolf**
woman ['wumən] (*pl* **women**) N mulher *f*; **~ doctor** médica; **~ teacher** professora; **young ~** mulher jovem; **women's page** (*Press*) página da mulher
womanize ['wumənaɪz] VI paquerar as mulheres
womanly ['wumənlɪ] ADJ feminino
womb [wuːm] N (*Anat*) matriz *f*, útero
women ['wɪmɪn] NPL *of* **woman**
women's lib [-lɪb] (*inf*) N = **women's liberation movement**
women's liberation movement N movimento pela libertação da mulher
won [wʌn] PT, PP *of* **win**
wonder ['wʌndəʳ] N maravilha, prodígio; (*feeling*) espanto ■ VI: **to ~ whether/why** perguntar-se a si mesmo se/por quê; **to ~ at** admirar-se de; **to ~ about** pensar sobre *or* em; **it's no ~ that** não é de admirar que
wonderful ['wʌndəful] ADJ maravilhoso; (*miraculous*) impressionante
wonderfully ['wʌndəfulɪ] ADV maravilhosamente

wonky ['wɒŋkɪ] (*Brit*) ADJ errado, torto
won't [wəunt] = **will not**
woo [wu:] VT (*woman*) namorar, cortejar;
(*audience*) atrair
wood [wud] N (*timber*) madeira; (*forest*) floresta,
bosque *m*; (*firewood*) lenha ■ CPD de madeira;
wood carving N (*act*) escultura em madeira;
(*object*) entalhe *m*
wooded ['wudɪd] ADJ arborizado
wooden ['wudən] ADJ de madeira; (*fig*)
inexpressivo
woodland ['wudlənd] N floresta, bosque *m*
woodpecker ['wudpɛkəʳ] N pica-pau *m*
wood pigeon N pombo torcaz
woodwind ['wudwɪnd] N (*Mus*) instrumentos
mpl de sopro de madeira
woodwork ['wudwə:k] N carpintaria
woodworm ['wudwə:m] N carcoma, caruncho
woof [wuf] N (*of dog*) latido ■ VI latir; ~, ~! au-
au!
wool [wul] N lã *f*; **to pull the ~ over sb's eyes**
(*fig*) enganar alguém, vender a alguém gato
por lebre
woollen ['wulən] ADJ de lã
woollens ['wulənz] NPL artigos *mpl* de lã
woolly ['wulɪ] (*US* **wooly**) ADJ de lã; (*fig: ideas*)
confuso
word [wə:d] N palavra; (*news*) notícia; (*message*)
aviso ■ VT (*express*) expressar; (*document*) redigir;
in other ~s em outras palavras, ou seja; **to
break/keep one's ~** faltar à palavra/cumprir
a promessa; **~ for ~** ao pé da letra; **what's the ~
for "pen" in Portuguese?** como se fala "pen"
em português?; **to put sth into ~s** expressar
algo; **to have a ~ with sb** falar com alguém; **to
have ~s with sb** discutir com alguém; **I'll take
your ~ for it** acredito em você; **to send ~ that**
... mandar dizer que ...; **to leave ~ that** ... deixar
recado dizendo que ...
wording ['wə:dɪŋ] N fraseado
word-perfect ADJ: **he was ~ in his speech** *etc*
ele sabia o discurso *etc* de cor
word processing N processamento de textos
word processor [-'prəusɛsəʳ] N processador *m*
de textos
wordwrap ['wə:dræp] N (*Comput*) marginação *f*
automática
wordy ['wə:dɪ] ADJ prolixo, verboso
wore [wɔ:ʳ] PT *of* **wear**
work [wə:k] N trabalho; (*job*) emprego, trabalho;
(*Art, Literature*) obra ■ VI trabalhar; (*mechanism*)
funcionar; (*medicine etc*) surtir efeito, ser eficaz;
(*plan*) dar certo ■ VT (*clay*) moldar; (*wood etc*)
talhar; (*mine etc*) explorar; (*machine*) fazer
trabalhar, manejar; (*effect, miracle*) causar; **road
~s** obras *fpl* (na estrada); **to go to ~** ir trabalhar;
to set to ~, to start ~ começar a trabalhar; **to
be at ~ (on sth)** estar trabalhando (em algo);
to be out of ~ estar desempregado; **to ~ hard**
trabalhar muito; **to ~ loose** (*part*) soltar-se;
(*knot*) afrouxar-se
▶ **work on** VT FUS trabalhar em, dedicar-se a;

(*principle*) basear-se em
▶ **work out** VI (*plans etc*) dar certo, surtir efeito
■ VT (*problem*) resolver; (*plan*) elaborar, formular;
it ~s out at £100 monta *or* soma a £100
workable ['wə:kəbl] ADJ (*solution*) viável
workaholic [wə:kə'hɔlɪk] N burro de carga
workbench ['wə:kbɛntʃ] N banco, bancada
worked up [wə:kt-] ADJ: **to get ~** ficar exaltado
worker ['wə:kəʳ] N trabalhador(a) *m/f*,
operário(-a); **office ~** empregado(-a) de
escritório
work force N força de trabalho
work-in (*Brit*) N ocupação *f* de fábrica *etc* (*sem
paralisação da produção*)
working ['wə:kɪŋ] ADJ (*day, tools etc, conditions*)
de trabalha; (*wife*) que trabalha; (*population,
partner*) ativo; **a ~ knowledge of English** um
conhecimento prático do inglês; **working
capital** N (*Comm*) capital *m* de giro; **working
class** N proletariado, classe *f* operária ■ ADJ:
working-class do proletariado, da classe
operária; **working man** (*irreg*) N trabalhador *m*;
working model N modelo articulado; **working
order** N: **in working order** em perfeito estado;
working party (*Brit*) N grupo de trabalho;
working week N semana de trabalho
work-in-progress N (*Comm*) produção *f* em
curso
workload ['wə:kləud] N carga de trabalho
workman ['wə:kmən] (*irreg*) N operário,
trabalhador *m*
workmanship ['wə:kmənʃɪp] N (*art*)
acabamento; (*skill*) habilidade *f*
workmate ['wə:kmeɪt] N colega *m/f* de trabalho
workout ['wə:kaut] N treinamento, treino
work permit N permissão *f* de trabalho
works N (*Brit: factory*) fábrica, usina; (*of
clock, machine*) mecanismo; **works council** N
comissão *f* de operários
worksheet ['wə:kʃi:t] N registro das horas de
trabalho; (*Comput*) folha de trabalho
workshop ['wə:kʃɔp] N oficina; (*practical session*)
aula prática
work station N estação *f* de trabalho
work study N estudo de trabalho
work-to-rule (*Brit*) N paralisação *f* de trabalho
extraordinário (*forma de protesto*)
world [wə:ld] N mundo ■ CPD mundial; **to
think the ~ of sb** (*fig*) ter alguém em alto
conceito; **all over the ~** no mundo inteiro;
what in the ~ is he doing? o que é que ele está
fazendo, pelo amor de Deus?; **to do sb a ~ of
good** fazer muito bem a alguém; **W~ War One/
Two** Primeira/Segunda Guerra Mundial; **out of
this ~** sensacional
World Cup N: **the ~** (*Football*) a Copa do Mundo
world-famous ADJ de fama mundial
worldly ['wə:ldlɪ] ADJ mundano; (*knowledgeable*)
experiente
worldwide ['wə:ldwaɪd] ADJ mundial,
universal ■ ADV no mundo inteiro
worm [wə:m] N verme *m*; (*also:* **earthworm**)

minhoca, lombriga

worn [wɔ:n] PP of **wear** ▪ ADJ gasto

worn-out ADJ (object) gasto; (person) esgotado, exausto

worried ['wʌrɪd] ADJ preocupado; **to be ~ about sth** estar preocupado com algo

worrier ['wʌrɪə'] N: **he's a ~** ele se preocupa com tudo

worry ['wʌrɪ] N preocupação f ▪ VT preocupar, inquietar ▪ VI preocupar-se, afligir-se; **to ~ about** or **over sth/sb** preocupar-se com algo/ alguém

worrying ['wʌrɪɪŋ] ADJ inquietante, preocupante

worse [wə:s] ADJ, ADV pior ▪ N o pior; **a change for the ~** uma mudança para pior, uma piora; **to get ~** piorar; **he's none the ~ for it** não lhe fez mal; **so much the ~ for you!** pior para você!

worsen ['wə:sən] VT, VI piorar

worse off ADJ com menos dinheiro; (fig): **you'll be ~ this way** assim você ficará pior que nunca

worship ['wə:ʃɪp] N culto; (act) adoração f ▪ VT (god) adorar, venerar; (person, thing) adorar; **Your W~** (Brit: to mayor) vossa Excelência; (: to judge) senhor Juiz

worshipper ['wə:ʃɪpə'] N devoto(-a), venerador(a) m/f

worst [wə:st] ADJ (o/a) pior ▪ ADV pior ▪ N o pior; **at ~** na pior das hipóteses; **if the ~ comes to the ~** se o pior acontecer

worsted ['wə:stɪd] N: **(wool)** ~ lã f penteada

worth [wə:θ] N valor m, mérito ▪ ADJ: **to be ~** valer; **it's ~ it** vale a pena; **to be ~ one's while (to do)** valer a pena (fazer); **how much is it ~?** quanto vale?; **50 pence ~ of apples** maçãs no valor de 50 pence

worthless ['wə:θlɪs] ADJ sem valor; (person) imprestável; (thing) inútil

worthwhile [wə:θ'waɪl] ADJ (activity) que vale a pena; (cause) de mérito, louvável; **a ~ book** um livro que vale a pena ler

worthy ['wə:ðɪ] ADJ (person) merecedor(a), respeitável; (motive) justo; **~ of** digno de

○ KEYWORD

would [wud] AUX VB **1** (conditional tense): **if you asked him, he would do it** se você pedisse, ele faria isto; **if you had asked him, he would have done it** se você tivesse pedido, ele teria feito isto

2 (in offers, invitations, requests): **would you like a biscuit?** você quer um biscoito?; **would you ask him to come in?** pode pedir a ele para entrar?; **would you close the door, please?** quer fechar a porta por favor?

3 (in indirect speech): **I said I would do it** eu disse que eu faria isto; **he asked me if I would go with him** ele me perguntou se eu iria com ele

4 (emphatic): **it WOULD have to snow today!** tinha que nevar logo hoje!; **you WOULD say that, wouldn't you?** é lógico que você vai

dizer isso

5 (insistence): **she wouldn't behave** não houve jeito dela se comportar

6 (conjecture): **it would have been midnight** devia ser meia-noite; **it would seem so** parece que sim

7 (indicating habit): **he would go on Mondays** ele costumava ir às segundas-feiras

would-be ADJ aspirante, que pretende ser

wouldn't ['wudnt] = **would not**

wound¹ [waund] PT, PP of **wind**

wound² [wu:nd] N ferida ▪ VT ferir

wove [wəuv] PT of **weave**

woven ['wəuvən] PP of **weave**

WP N ABBR = **word processing; word processor** ▪ ABBR (Brit: inf) = **weather permitting**

WPC (Brit) N ABBR = **woman police constable**

wpm ABBR (= words per minute) palavras por minuto

WRAC (Brit) N ABBR = **Women's Royal Army Corps**

WRAF (Brit) N ABBR = **Women's Royal Air Force**

wrangle ['ræŋgl] N briga ▪ VI brigar

wrap [ræp] N (stole) xale m; (cape) capa ▪ VT (cover) envolver; (also: **wrap up**) embrulhar; **under ~s** (fig: plan, scheme) em sigilo

wrapper ['ræpə'] N (on chocolate) invólucro; (Brit: of book) capa

wrapping paper ['ræpɪŋ-] N papel m de embrulho; (fancy) papel de presente

wrath [rɔθ] N cólera, ira

wreak [ri:k] VT (destruction) causar; **to ~ havoc (on)** causar estragos (em); **to ~ vengeance on** vingar-se em, tirar vingança de

wreath [ri:θ, pl ri:ðz] N (funeral wreath) coroa; (of flowers) grinalda

wreathe [ri:ð] VT trançar, cingir

wreck [rɛk] N (vehicle) calhambeque m, lata-velha; (ship) restos mpl do naufrágio; (pej: person) ruína, caco ▪ VT destruir, danificar; (fig) arruinar, arrasar

wreckage ['rɛkɪdʒ] N (of car, plane) destroços mpl; (of ship) restos mpl; (of building) escombros mpl

wrecker ['rɛkə'] (US) N (breakdown van) reboque m (BR), pronto socorro (PT)

WREN [rɛn] (Brit) N ABBR membro do WRNS

wren [rɛn] N (Zool) carriça

wrench [rɛntʃ] N (Tech) chave f inglesa; (tug) puxão m; (fig) separação f penosa ▪ VT torcer com força; **to ~ sth from sb** arrancar algo de alguém

wrest [rɛst] VT: **to ~ sth from sb** extorquir algo de or a alguém

wrestle ['rɛsl] VI: **to ~ (with sb)** lutar (com or contra alguém); **to ~ with** (fig) lutar com

wrestler ['rɛslə'] N lutador m

wrestling ['rɛslɪŋ] N luta (livre); **wrestling match** N partida de luta romana

wretch [rɛtʃ] N desgraçado(-a); **little ~!** (often humorous) seu desgraçado!

wretched ['rɛtʃɪd] ADJ desventurado, infeliz;

(*inf*) maldito

wriggle ['rɪgl] N contorção *f* ■ VI (*also*: **wriggle about**) retorcer-se, contorcer-se

wring [rɪŋ] (*pt, pp* **wrung**) VT (*clothes, neck*) torcer; (*hands*) apertar; (*fig*): **to ~ sth out of sb** arrancar algo de alguém

wringer ['rɪŋə'] N máquina de espremer roupa

wringing ['rɪŋɪŋ] ADJ (*also*: **wringing wet**) encharcado, ensopado

wrinkle ['rɪŋkl] N (*on skin*) ruga; (*on paper*) prega ■ VT franzir ■ VI enrugar-se; (*cloth etc*) franzir-se

wrinkled ['rɪŋkld] ADJ (*fabric, paper*) franzido, pregueado; (*surface, skin*) enrugado

wrinkly ['rɪŋklɪ] ADJ (*fabric, paper*) franzido, pregueado; (*surface, skin*) enrugado

wrist [rɪst] N pulso

wristband ['rɪstbænd] (*Brit*) N (*of shirt*) punho; (*of watch*) pulseira

wristwatch ['rɪstwɔtʃ] N relógio *m* de pulso

writ [rɪt] N mandado judicial; **to issue a ~ against sb, serve a ~ on sb** demandar judicialmente alguém

write [raɪt] (*pt* **wrote**, *pp* **written**) VT letter; (*cheque, prescription*) passar ■ VI escrever; **to ~ to sb** escrever para alguém

▶ **write away** VI: **to ~ away for** (*information*) escrever pedindo; (*goods*) encomendar pelo correio

▶ **write down** VT escrever; (*note*) anotar; (*put on paper*) pôr no papel

▶ **write off** VT (*debt, plan*) cancelar; (*capital*) reduzir; (*smash up: car*) destroçar

▶ **write out** VT escrever por extenso; (*cheque etc*) passar; (*fair copy*) passar a limpo

▶ **write up** VT redigir

write-off N perda total; **the car is a ~** o carro virou sucata *or* está destroçado

write-protect VT (*Comput*) proteger de escrita *or* contra gravação

writer ['raɪtə'] N escritor(a) *m/f*

write-up N crítica

writhe [raɪð] VI contorcer-se

writing ['raɪtɪŋ] N escrita; (*handwriting*)

caligrafia, letra; (*of author*) obra; **in ~ por escrito; to put sth in ~** pôr algo no papel; **in my own ~** do próprio punho; **writing case** N pasta com material de escrita; **writing desk** N escrivaninha; **writing paper** N papel *m* para escrever

written ['rɪtn] PP *of* **write**

WRNS (*Brit*) N ABBR = **Women's Royal Naval Service**

wrong [rɔŋ] ADJ (*bad*) errado, mau; (*unfair*) injusto; (*incorrect*) errado, equivocado; (*inappropriate*) impróprio ■ ADV mal, errado ■ N mal *m*; (*injustice*) injustiça ■ VT ser injusto com; (*hurt*) ofender; **to be ~** estar errado; **you are ~ to do it** você se engana ao fazê-lo; **it's ~ to steal, stealing is ~** é errado roubar; **you are ~ about that, you've got it ~** você está enganado sobre isso; **to be in the ~** não ter razão; **what's ~?** o que é que há?; **there's nothing ~** não há nada de errado, não tem problema; **what's ~ with the car?** qual é o problema com o carro?; **to go ~** (*person*) desencaminhar-se; (*plan*) dar errado; (*machine*) sofrer uma avaria

wrongful ['rɔŋful] ADJ injusto; **~ dismissal** demissão *f* injusta

wrongly ['rɔŋlɪ] ADV (*treat*) injustamente; (*incorrectly*) errado

wrong number N (*Tel*): **you have the ~** o número está errado

wrong side N (*of cloth*) avesso

wrote [rəut] PT *of* **write**

wrought [rɔːt] ADJ: **~ iron** ferro forjado

wrung [rʌŋ] PT, PP *of* **wring**

WRVS (*Brit*) N ABBR (= *Women's Royal Voluntary Service*) instituição *de caridade*

wry [raɪ] ADJ (*humour, expression*) irônico; **to make a ~ face** fazer uma careta

wt. ABBR = **weight**

WV (*US*) ABBR (*Post*) = **West Virginia**

WWW N ABBR = **World Wide Web; the ~** a WWW

WY (*US*) ABBR (*Post*) = **Wyoming**

WYSIWYG ['wɪzɪwɪg] ABBR (*Comput*: = *what you see is what you get*) o documento sairá na impressora exatamente como aparece na tela

Xx

X, x [ɛks] N (*letter*) X, x *m*; (*Brit: Cinema: old*) (proibido para menores de) 18 anos; **X for Xmas** X de Xavier; **if you have ~ dollars a year ...** se você tem x dólares por ano ...

Xerox® [ˈzɪərɔks] N (*also:* **Xerox machine**) xerox® *m*; (*photocopy*) xerox® *m* ■ VT xerocar, tirar um xerox de

XL ABBR = **extra large**

Xmas [ˈɛksməs] N ABBR = **Christmas**

X-rated [-ˈreɪtɪd] (*US*) ADJ (*film*) proibido para menores de 18 anos

X-ray [ɛksˈreɪ] N radiografia ■ VT radiografar, tirar uma chapa de; **X-rays** NPL raios *mpl* X; **to have an ~** tirar *or* bater um raio x

xylophone [ˈzaɪləfəun] N xilofone *m*

Yy

Y, y [waɪ] N (letter) Y, y m; **Y for Yellow** (Brit) or **Yoke** (US) Y de Yolanda
yacht [jɔt] N iate m; (smaller) veleiro
yachting ['jɔtɪŋ] N (sport) iatismo
yachtsman ['jɔtsmən] (irreg) N iatista m
yam [jæm] N inhame m
Yank [jæŋk] (pej) N ianque m/f
yank [jæŋk] VT arrancar
Yankee ['jæŋkɪ] N = **Yank**
yap [jæp] VI (dog) ganir
yard [jɑːd] N pátio, quintal m; (US: garden) jardim m; (measure) jarda (914 mm; 3 feet); **builder's ~** depósito de material de construção
yardstick ['jɑːdstɪk] N (fig) critério, padrão m
yarn [jɑːn] N fio; (tale) história inverossímil
yawn [jɔːn] N bocejo ■ VI bocejar
yawning ['jɔːnɪŋ] ADJ (gap) enorme
yd ABBR = **yard(s)**
yeah [jeə] (inf) ADV é
year [jɪəʳ] N ano; **to be 8 ~s old** ter 8 anos; **every ~** todos os anos, todo ano; **this ~** este ano; **a** or **per ~** por ano; **~ in, ~ out** entra ano, sai ano; **an eight-~-old child** uma criança de oito anos (de idade)
yearbook ['jɪəbuk] N anuário, almanaque m
yearly ['jɪəlɪ] ADJ anual ■ ADV anualmente; **twice ~** duas vezes por ano
yearn [jəːn] VI: **to ~ to do/for sth** ansiar fazer/por algo
yearning ['jəːnɪŋ] N ânsia, desejo ardente
yeast [jiːst] N levedura, fermento
yell [jɛl] N grito, berro ■ VI gritar, berrar
yellow ['jɛləu] ADJ amarelo ■ N amarelo; **yellow fever** N febre f amarela
yellowish ['jɛləuɪʃ] ADJ amarelado
Yellow Sea N: **the ~** o mar Amarelo
yelp [jɛlp] N latido ■ VI latir
Yemen ['jɛmən] N Iêmen m (BR), Iémene m (PT)
yen [jen] N (currency) iene m; (craving): **~ for/to do** desejo de/de fazer
yeoman ['jəumən] (irreg) N: **Y~ of the Guard** membro da guarda real
yes [jɛs] ADV, N sim m; **do you speak English?** — ~ **I do** você fala inglês? — falo (sim); **does the plane leave at six?** — ~ o avião sai às seis? — é; **to say ~ to sth/sb** (approve) dar o sim a algo/alguém

yesterday ['jɛstədɪ] ADV, N ontem m; **the day before ~** anteontem; **~ morning/evening** ontem de manhã/à noite; **all day ~** ontem o dia inteiro
yet [jɛt] ADV ainda ■ CONJ porém, no entanto; **it is not finished ~** ainda não está acabado; **must you go just ~?** você já tem que ir?; **the best ~** o melhor até agora; **as ~** até agora, ainda; **a few days ~** mais alguns dias; **~ again** mais uma vez
yew [juː] N teixo
YHA (Brit) N ABBR = **Youth Hostels Association**
Yiddish ['jɪdɪʃ] N (i) ídiche m
yield [jiːld] N produção f; (Agr) colheita; (Comm) rendimento ■ VT (gen) produzir; (profit) render; (surrender) ceder ■ VI (give way) render-se, ceder; (US: Aut) ceder; **a ~ of 5%** um rendimento de 5%
YMCA N ABBR (= Young Men's Christian Association) ≈ ACM f
yob(bo) ['jɔb(əu)] (Brit: inf) N bagunçeiro
yodel ['jəudl] VI cantar tirolesa
yoga ['jəugə] N ioga
yog(h)ourt ['jəugət] N iogurte m
yog(h)urt ['jəugət] N = **yog(h)ourt**
yoke [jəuk] N canga, cangalha; (of oxen) junta; (on shoulders) balancim m; (fig) jugo ■ VT (also: **yoke together**) unir, ligar
yolk [jəuk] N gema (do ovo)
yonder ['jɔndəʳ] ADV além, acolá
Yorks [jɔːks] (Brit) ABBR = **Yorkshire**

○ KEYWORD

you [juː] PRON **1** (subj: singular) tu, você; (: plural) vós, vocês; **you French enjoy your food** vocês franceses gostam de comer; **you and I will go** nós iremos
2 (direct object: singular) te, o(-a); (: plural) vos, os/as; (indirect object: singular) te, lhe; (: plural) vos, lhes; **I know you** eu lhe conheço; **I gave it to you** dei isto para você
3 (stressed) você; **I told YOU to do it** eu disse para você fazer isto
4 (after prep, in comparisons: singular) ti, você; (: plural) vós, vocês; (polite form: singular) o senhor (a senhora); (: plural) os senhores (as senhoras); **it's for you** é para você; **can I come with you?**

posso ir com você?; **with you** contigo, com você; convosco, com vocês; com o senhor *etc*; **she's younger than you** ela é mais jovem do que você
5 (*impers: one*): **you never know** nunca se sabe; **apples do you good** as maçãs fazem bem à saúde; **you can't do that!** não se pode fazer isto!

you'd [juːd] = **you had; you would**
you'll [juːl] = **you will; you shall**
young [jʌŋ] ADJ jovem ■ NPL (*of animal*) filhotes *mpl*, crias *fpl*; (*people*): **the** ~ a juventude, os jovens; **a** ~ **man** um jovem; **a** ~ **lady** (*unmarried*) uma jovem, uma moça; (*married*) uma jovem senhora; **my** ~**er brother** o meu irmão mais novo
younger [ˈjʌŋər] ADJ (*brother etc*) mais novo; **the** ~ **generation** a geração mais jovem
youngish [ˈjʌŋɪʃ] ADJ bem novo
youngster [ˈjʌŋstər] N jovem *m/f*, moço(-a)
your [jɔːr] ADJ teu/tua, seu/sua; (*plural*) vosso, seu/sua; (*formal*) do senhor/da senhora; *see also* **my**
you're [juər] = **you are**
yours [jɔːz] PRON teu/tua, seu/sua; (*plural*) vosso, seu/sua; (*formal*) do senhor/da senhora; ~ **is blue** o teu(-a) tua *etc* é azul; **is it** ~? é teu *etc*?; ~ **sincerely** *or* **faithfully** atenciosamente; **a**

friend of ~ um amigo seu *etc*; *see also* **mine**
yourself [jɔːˈsɛlf] PRON (*emphatic*) tu mesmo, você mesmo; (*object, reflexive*) te, se; (*after prep*) ti mesmo, si mesmo; (*formal*) o senhor mesmo(-a) senhora mesma; **you** ~ **told me** você mesmo me falou; (**all**) **by** ~ sozinho(-a); *see also* **oneself**
yourselves [jɔːˈsɛlvz] PRON (*emphatic*) vós mesmos, vocês mesmos; (*object, reflexive*) vos, se; (*after prep*) vós mesmos, vôces mesmos; (*formal*) os senhores mesmos/as senhoras mesmas; *see also* **oneself**
youth [juːθ, *pl* juːðz] N mocidade *f*, juventude *f*; (*young man*) jovem *m*; **in my** ~ na minha juventude; **youth club** N associação *f* de juventude
youthful [ˈjuːθful] ADJ juvenil
youthfulness [ˈjuːθfəlnəs] N juventude *f*
youth hostel N albergue *m* da juventude
you've [juːv] = **you have**
yowl [jaul] N uivo ■ VI uivar
Yugoslav [ˈjuːɡəslɑːv] ADJ, N iugoslavo(-a)
Yugoslavia [juːɡəuˈslɑːvɪə] N Iugoslávia
Yugoslavian [juːɡəuˈslɑːvɪən] ADJ iugoslavo
Yule [juːl] N: ~ **log** acha de Natal
Yuletide [ˈjuːltaɪd] N época natalina *or* do Natal
yuppie [ˈjʌpɪ] (*inf*) ADJ, N yuppie *m/f*
YWCA N ABBR (= *Young Women's Christian Association*) ≈ ACM *f*

Zz

Z, z [zɛd, (US) ziː] N (letter) Z, z m; **Z for Zebra** Z
de Zebra
Zaire [zɑːˈiːəʳ] N Zaire m
Zambia [ˈzæmbɪə] N Zâmbia
Zambian [ˈzæmbɪən] ADJ, N zambiano(-a)
zany [ˈzeɪnɪ] ADJ tolo, bobo
zap [zæp] VT (Comput) apagar
zeal [ziːl] N entusiasmo; (religious) fervor m
zealot [ˈzɛlət] N fanático(-a)
zealous [ˈzɛləs] ADJ zeloso, entusiasta
zebra [ˈziːbrə] N zebra; **zebra crossing** (Brit) N
faixa (para pedestres) (BR), passadeira (PT)
zenith [ˈzɛnɪθ] N (Astronomy) zênite m; (fig)
apogeu m
zero [ˈzɪərəu] N zero ■ VI: **to ~ in on** fazer mira
em; **5°o below ~** 5 graus abaixo de zero; **zero
hour** N hora zero
zero-rated [-ˈreɪtɪd] (Brit) ADJ isento de IVA
zest [zɛst] N vivacidade f, entusiasmo; (of lemon
etc) zesto
zigzag [ˈzɪgzæg] N ziguezague m ■ VI
ziguezaguear
Zimbabwe [zɪmˈbɑːbwɪ] N Zimbábue m (BR),
Zimbabwe m (PT)
Zimbabwean [zɪmˈbɑːbwɪən] ADJ, N
zimbabuano(-a) (BR), zimbabweano(-a) (PT)
zinc [zɪŋk] N zinco
Zionism [ˈzaɪənɪzm] N sionismo
Zionist [ˈzaɪənɪst] ADJ, N sionista m/f
zip [zɪp] N (also: **zip fastener**) fecho ecler (BR)
or éclair (PT); (energy) vigor m ■ VT (also: **zip
up**) fechar o fecho ecler de, subir o fecho ecler
de; **zip code** (US) N código postal; **zip file** N
(Comput) arquivo zipado
zipper [ˈzɪpəʳ] (US) N = **zip**
zither [ˈzɪðəʳ] N citara
zodiac [ˈzəudɪæk] N zodíaco
zombie [ˈzɔmbɪ] N (fig): **like a ~** como um zumbi
zone [zəun] N zona
zoo [zuː] N (jardim m) zoológico
zoological [zuəˈlɔdʒɪkl] ADJ zoológico
zoologist [zuːˈɔlədʒɪst] N zoólogo(-a)
zoology [zuːˈɔlədʒɪ] N zoologia
zoom [zuːm] VI: **to ~ past** passar zunindo; **to ~
in (on sb/sth)** (Phot, Cinema) fechar a câmera
(em alguém/algo); **zoom lens** N zoom m,
zum m
zucchini [zuːˈkiːnɪ] (US) N(PL) abobrinha
Zulu [ˈzuːluː] ADJ, N zulu m/f
Zurich [ˈzjuərɪk] N Zurique

Aa

A, a [a] (*pl* **as**) M A, a; **A de Antônio** A for Andrew (*Brit*) *ou* Able (*US*)

⭕ PALAVRA CHAVE

a [a] (*a* + *o(s)* = *ao(s)*; *a* + *a(s)* = *à(s)*; *a* + *aquele/a(s)* = *àquele/a(s)*) ART DEF the; *v tb* **o**
■ PRON (*ela*) her; (*você*) you; (*coisa*) it; *v tb* **o**
■ PREP **1** (*direção*) to; **à direita/esquerda** to *ou* on the right/left
2 (*distância*): **está a 15 km daqui** it's 15 km from here
3 (*posição*): **ao lado de** beside, at the side of
4 (*tempo*) at; **a que horas?** at what time?; **às 5 horas** at 5 o'clock; **à noite** at night; **aos 15 anos** at 15 years of age
5 (*maneira*): **à francesa** in the French way; **a cavalo/pé** on horseback/foot
6 (*meio, instrumento*): **à força** by force; **a mão** by hand; **a lápis** in pencil; **fogão a gás** gas stove
7 (*razão*): **a R$300 o quilo** at R$300 a kilo; **a mais de 100 km/h** at over 100 km/h
8 (*depois de certos verbos*): **começou a nevar** it started snowing *ou* to snow; **passar a fazer** to become
9 (+ *infin*): **ao vê-lo, o reconheci imediatamente** when I saw him, I recognized him immediately; **ele ficou muito nervoso ao falar com o professor** he became very nervous while he was talking to the teacher
10 (*PT*: + *infin*: *gerúndio*): **a correr** running; **estou a trabalhar** I'm working

à [a] = **a** + **a**
(a) ABR (= *assinado*) signed
AAB ABR F (= *Aliança Anticomunista Brasileira*) terrorist group
aba ['aba] F (*de chapéu*) brim; (*de casaco*) tail; (*de montanha*) foot
abacate [aba'katʃi] M avocado (pear)
abacaxi [abaka'ʃi] (*BR*) M pineapple; (*col: problema*) pain
abade, ssa [a'badʒi, aba'desa] M/F abbot/abbess
Abadi [aba'dʒi] ABR F = **Associação Brasileira das Administradoras de Imóveis**
abadia [aba'dʒia] F abbey
abafadiço, -a [abafa'dʒisu, a] ADJ stifling; (*ar*) stuffy
abafado, -a [aba'fadu, a] ADJ (*ar*) stuffy; (*tempo*) humid, close; (*ocupado*) (extremely) busy; (*angustiado*) anxious
abafamento [abafa'mẽtu] M fug; (*sufocação*) suffocation
abafar [aba'fa^r] VT to suffocate; (*ocultar*) to suppress; (*som*) to muffle; (*encobrir*) to cover up; (*col*) to pinch ■ VI (*col: fazer sucesso*) to steal the show
abagunçado, -a [abagũ'sadu, a] ADJ messy
abagunçar [abagũ'sa^r] VT to make a mess of, mess up
abaixar [abaj'ʃa^r] VT to lower; (*luz, som*) to turn down; **abaixar-se** VR to stoop
abaixo [a'bajʃu] ADV down ■ PREP: ~ **de** below; ~ **o governo!** down with the government!; **morro** ~ downhill; **rio** ~ downstream; **mais** ~ further down; ~ **e acima** up and down; ~ **assinado** undersigned; **abaixo-assinado** [-asi'nadu] (*pl* **abaixo-assinados**) M (*documento*) petition
abajur [aba'ʒu^r] (*BR*) M (*cúpula*) lampshade; (*luminária*) table lamp
abalado, -a [aba'ladu, a] ADJ unstable, unsteady; (*fig*) shaken
abalar [aba'la^r] VT to shake; (*fig: comover*) to affect ■ VI to shake; **abalar-se** VR to be moved
abalizado, -a [abali'zadu, a] ADJ eminent, distinguished; (*opinião*) reliable
abalo [a'balu] M (*comoção*) shock; (*ação*) shaking; ~ **sísmico** earth tremor
abalroar [abawro'a^r] VT: **o carri foi abalroado pelo caminhão** the car was hit by the lorry
abanar [aba'na^r] VT to shake; (*rabo*) to wag; (*com leque*) to fan
abandalhar [abãda'ʎa^r] VT to debase
abandonar [abãdo'na^r] VT (*deixar*) to leave; (*idéia*) to reject; (*estudos*) to abandon; (*esperança*) to give up; (*descuidar*) to neglect; **abandonar-se** VR: **abandonar-se a** to abandon o.s. to

---

NB: *European Portuguese adds the following consonants to certain words:* **b** (sú(b)dito, su(b)til); **c** (a(c)ção, a(c)cionista, a(c)to); **m** (inde(m)ne); **p** (ado(p)çã, ado(p)tar); *for further details see p. xiii.*

abandono [abã'donu] M *(ato)* desertion; *(estado)* neglect

abarcar [abax'ka^r] VT *(abranger)* to comprise; *(conter)* to enclose

abarrotado, -a [abaxo'tadu, a] ADJ *(gaveta)* crammed full; *(lugar)* packed

abarrotar [abaxo'ta^r] VT: **~ de** to cram with

abastado, -a [abaʃ'tadu, a] ADJ wealthy

abastança [abaʃ'tãsa] F abundance, surfeit

abastardar [abaʃtax'da^r] VT to corrupt

abastecer [abaʃte'se^r] VT to supply; *(motor)* to fuel; *(Auto)* to fill up; *(Aer)* to refuel; **abastecer-se** VR: **abastecer-se de** to stock up with

abastecimento [abaʃtesi'mẽtu] M supply; *(comestíveis)* provisions pl; *(ato)* supplying; *(de avião)* refuelling (Brit), refueling (US); **abastecimentos** MPL *(suprimentos)* supplies

abater [aba'te^r] VT *(gado)* to slaughter; *(preço)* to reduce, lower; *(debilitar)* to weaken; *(desalentar)* to upset; **abatido, -a** [aba'tʃidu, a] ADJ depressed, downcast; *(fisionomia)* haggard;

abatimento [abatʃi'mẽtu] M *(fraqueza)* weakness; *(de preço)* reduction; *(prostração)* depression; **fazer um abatimento em** to give a discount on

abaulado, -a [abaw'ladu, a] ADJ convex; *(estrada)* cambered

abaular-se [abaw'laxsi] VR to bulge

ABBC ABR F = **Associação Brasileira dos Bancos Comerciais**

ABBR ABR F (= *Associação Brasileira Beneficente de Reabilitação) charity for the disabled*

abcesso [ab'sɛsu] M = **abcesso**

abdicação [abdʒika'sãw] *(pl -ões)* F abdication

abdicar [abdʒi'ka^r] VT, VI to abdicate

abdômen [ab'domẽ] M abdomen

á-bê-cê [abe'se] M alphabet; *(fig)* rudiments pl

abecedário [abese'darju] M alphabet, ABC

Abeenras ABR F = **Associação Brasileira das Empresas de Engenharia, Reparos e Atividades Subaquáticas**

abeirar [abej'ra^r] VT to bring near; **abeirar-se** VR: **abeirar-se de** to draw near to

abelha [a'beʎa] F bee

abelha-mestra *(pl* **abelhas-mestras)** F queen bee

abelhudo, -a [abe'ʎudu, a] ADJ nosy

abençoar [abẽ'swa^r] VT to bless

abendiçoar [abẽdʒi'swa^r] VT to bless

aberração [abexa'sãw] *(pl -ões)* F aberration

aberta [a'bɛxta] F opening; *(clareira)* clearing; *(intervalo)* break

aberto, -a [a'bɛxtu, a] PP de **abrir** ■ ADJ open; *(céu)* clear; *(sinal)* green; *(torneira)* on; *(desprotegido)* exposed; *(liberal)* open-minded

abertura [abex'tura] F opening; *(Foto)* aperture; *(ranhura)* gap, crevice; *(Pol)* liberalization

abestalhado, -a [abeʃta'ʎadu, a] ADJ stupid

ABH ABR F = **Associação Brasileira da Indústria de Hóteis**

ABI ABR F = **Associação Brasileira de Imprensa**

Abifarma ABR F = **Associação Brasileira da Industria Farmacêutica**

abilolado, -a [abilo'ladu, a] ADJ crazy

abismado, -a [abiʒ'madu, a] ADJ astonished

abismo [a'biʒmu] M abyss, chasm; *(fig)* depths pl

abjeção [abʒe'sãw] *(PT* **-cç-)** F baseness

abjeto, -a [ab'ʒetu, a] *(PT* **-ct-)** ADJ abject, contemptible

abjudicar [abʒudʒi'ka^r] VT to seize

ABL ABR F = **Academia Brasileira de Letras**

ABMU ABR F = **Associação Brasileira de Mulheres Universitárias**

abnegação [abnega'sãw] F self-denial

abnegado, -a [abne'gadu, a] ADJ self-sacrificing

abnegar [abne'ga^r] VT to renounce

abóbada [a'bɔbada] F vault; *(telhado)* arched roof

abobalhado, -a [aboba'ʎadu, a] ADJ *(criança)* simple

abóbora [a'bɔbora] F pumpkin

abobrinha [abo'briɲa] F courgette (Brit), zucchini (US)

abocanhar [aboka'ɲa^r] VT *(apanhar com a boca)* to seize with the mouth; *(morder)* to bite

abolição [aboli'sãw] F abolition

abolir [abo'li^r] VT to abolish

abominação [abomina'sãw] *(pl -ões)* F abomination

abominar [abomi'na^r] VT to loathe, detest

abominável [abomi'navew] *(pl -eis)* ADJ abominable

abonar [abo'na^r] VT to guarantee

abono [a'bɔnu] M guarantee; *(Jur)* bail; *(louvor)* praise; **~ de família** child benefit

abordagem [abox'daʒẽ] *(pl -ns)* F approach

abordar [abox'da^r] VT *(Náut)* to board; *(pessoa)* to approach; *(assunto)* to broach, tackle

aborígene [abo'riʒeni] ADJ aboriginal ■ M/F aborigine

aborrecer [aboxe'se^r] VT *(chatear)* to annoy; *(maçar)* to bore; **aborrecer-se** VR to get upset; to get bored; **aborrecido, -a** [aboxe'sidu, a] ADJ boring; *(chateado)* annoyed; **aborrecimento** [aboxesi'mẽtu] M boredom; *(chateação)* annoyance

abortar [abox'ta^r] VI *(Med)* to have a miscarriage; *(: de propósito)* to have an abortion ■ VT to abort; **aborto** [a'boxtu] M *(Med)* miscarriage; *(forçado)* abortion; **fazer/ter um aborto** to have an abortion/ a miscarriage

abotoadura [abotwa'dura] F cufflink

abotoar [abo'twa^r] VT to button up ■ VI *(Bot)* to bud

abr. ABR (= *abril*) Apr

abraçar [abra'sa^r] VT to hug; *(causa)* to embrace; **abraçar-se** VR to embrace; **ele abraçou-se a mim** he embraced me; **abraço** [a'brasu] M embrace, hug; **com um abraço** *(em carta)* with best wishes

abrandar [abrã'da^r] VT to reduce; *(suavizar)* to soften ■ VI to diminish; *(acalmar)* to calm down

abranger [abrã'ʒe^r] VT *(assunto)* to cover; *(alcançar)* to reach

abranjo etc [a'brãʒu] VB V **abranger**

abrasar [abra'za^r] VT to burn; (desbastar) to erode ■ VI to be on fire

abrasileirado, -a [abrazilej'radu, a] ADJ Brazilianized

ABRATES ABR F = **Associação Brasileira de Tradutores**

ABRATT ABR F = **Associação Brasileira dos Transportadores Exclusivos de Turismo**

abre-garrafas ['abri-] (PT) M INV bottle-opener

abre-latas ['abri-] (PT) M INV tin (Brit) ou can opener

abreugrafia [abrewgra'fia] F X-ray

abreviação [abrevja'sãw] (pl -ões) F abbreviation; (de texto) abridgement

abreviar [abre'vja^r] VT to abbreviate; (encurtar) to shorten; (texto) to abridge; **abreviatura** [abrevja'tura] F abbreviation

abridor [abri'do^r] (BR) M opener; ~ **(de lata)** tin (Brit) ou can opener; ~ **de garrafa** bottle-opener

abrigar [abri'ga^r] VT to shelter; (proteger) to protect; **abrigar-se** VR to take shelter

abrigo [a'brigu] M shelter, cover; ~ **anti-aéreo** air-raid shelter; ~ **anti-nuclear** fall-out shelter

abril [a'briw] (PT **Abril**) M April; V tb **juiho; 25 de Abril** (PT) see below

● **25 DE ABRIL**

● On 25 April 1974 in Portugal, the MAF
● (Armed Forces Movement) instigated the
● bloodless revolution that was to topple the
● 48-year-old dictatorship presided over until
● 1968 by António de Oliveira Salazar. The red
● carnation has come to symbolize the coup,
● as it is said that the Armed Forces took to
● the streets with carnations in the barrels of
● their rifles. 25 April is now a public holiday
● in Portugal.

abrilhantar [abriʎã'ta^r] VT to enhance

abrir [a'bri^r] VT to open; (fechadura) to unlock; (vestuário) to unfasten; (torneira) to turn on; (buraco, exceção) to make; (processo) to start ■ VI to open; (sinal) to go green; (tempo) to clear up; **abrir-se** VR: **~-se com alguém** to confide in sb, open up to sb

ab-rogação [abxoga'sãw] (pl -ões) F repeal, annulment

ab-rogar [abxo'ga^r] VT to repeal, annul

abrolho [a'broʎu] M thorn

abrupto, -a [a'bruptu, a] ADJ abrupt; (repentino) sudden

abrutalhado, -a [abruta'ʎadu, a] ADJ (pessoa) coarse; (sapatos) heavy

abscesso [ab'sɛsu] M abscess

absenteísta [absẽte'iʃta] M/F absentee

absentismo [absẽ'tʃiʒmu] M absenteeism

abside [ab'sidʒi] F apse; (relicário) shrine

absolutamente [absoluta'mẽtʃi] ADV absolutely; (em resposta) absolutely not, not at all

absolutismo [absolu'tʃiʒmu] M absolutism

absolutista [absolu'tʃiʃta] ADJ, M/F absolutist

absoluto, -a [abso'lutu, a] ADJ absolute; **em ~** absolutely not, not at all

absolver [absow've^r] VT to absolve; (Jur) to acquit

absolvição [absowvi'sãw] (pl -ões) F absolution; (Jur) acquittal

absorção [absox'sãw] F absorption

absorto, -a [ab'soxtu, a] PP de **absorver** ■ ADJ absorbed, engrossed

absorvente [absox'vẽtʃi] ADJ (papel etc) absorbent; (livro etc) absorbing

absorver [absox've^r] VT to absorb; **absorver-se** VR: **absorver-se em** to concentrate on

abstêmio, -a [abʃ'temju, a] ADJ abstemious; (álcool) teetotal ■ M/F abstainer; teetotaller (Brit), teetotaler (US)

abstenção [abʃtẽ'sãw] (pl -ões) F abstention

abstencionista [abʃtẽsjo'niʃta] ADJ abstaining ■ M/F abstainer

abstenções [abʃtẽ'sõjʃ] FPL de **abstenção**

abster-se [ab'ʃtexsi] (irreg) VR: **~ de** to abstain ou refrain from

abstinência [abʃtʃi'nẽsja] F abstinence; (jejum) fasting

abstinha etc [abʃ'tʃiɲa] VB V **abster-se**

abstive etc [abʃ'tʃivi] VB V **abster-se**

abstração [abʃtra'sãw] (PT -cç-) F abstraction; (concentração) concentration

abstracto, -a [abʃ'tratu, a] (PT) ADJ = **abstrato**

abstrair [abʃtra'i^r] VT to abstract; (omitir) to omit; (separar) to separate

abstrato, -a [abʃ'tratu, a] ADJ abstract

absurdo, -a [abi'suxdu, a] ADJ absurd ■ M nonsense

abulia [abu'lia] F apathy

abundância [abũ'dãsja] F abundance

abundante [abũ'dãtʃi] ADJ abundant; **abundar** [abũ'da^r] VI to abound

aburguesado, -a [abuxge'zadu, a] ADJ middle-class, bourgeois

abusar [abu'za^r] VI (exceder-se) to go too far; **~ de** to abuse

abuso [a'buzu] M abuse; (Jur) indecent assault; **~ de confiança** breach of trust

abutre [a'butri] M vulture

AC ABR = **Acre**

a.C. ABR (= antes de Cristo) B.C

a/c ABR (= aos cuidados de) c/o

acabado, -a [aka'badu, a] ADJ finished; (esgotado) worn out; (envelhecido) aged

acabamento [akaba'mẽtu] M finish

acabar [aka'ba^r] VT (terminar) to finish, complete; (levar a cabo) to accomplish; (aperfeiçoar) to complete; (consumir) to use up;

NB: European Portuguese adds the following consonants to certain words: **b** (sú(b)dito, su(b)til); **c** (a(c)ção, a(c)cionista, a(c)to); **m** (inde(m)ne); **p** (ado(p)çã, ado(p)tar); for further details see p. xiii.

(rematar) to finish off ■ vi to finish, end, come to an end; **acabar-se** vr *(terminar)* to be over; *(prazo)* to expire; *(esgotar-se)* to run out; ~ **com** to put an end to; *(destruir)* to do away with; *(namorado)* to finish with; ~ **de chegar** to have just arrived; ~ **por fazer** to end up (by) doing; **acabou-se!** it's all over!; *(basta!)* that's enough!; **ele acabou cedendo** he eventually gave in, he ended up giving in; ... **que não acaba mais** no end of ...; **quando acaba** *(no final)* in the end

acabrunhado, -a [akabru'ɲadu, a] ADJ *(abatido)* depressed; *(envergonhado)* embarrassed

acabrunhar [akabru'ɲaʳ] VT *(entristecer)* to distress; *(envergonhar)* to embarrass

acácia [a'kasja] F acacia

academia [akade'mia] F academy; ~ **(de ginástica)** gym; **Academia Brasileira de Letras**; *see below*; **acadêmico, -a** [aka'demiku, a] ADJ, M/F academic

● **ACADEMIA BRASILEIRA DE LETRAS**
●
● Founded in 1896 in Rio de Janeiro, on the
● initiative of the author Machado de Assis,
● the *Academia Brasileira de Letras*, or ABL, aims
● to preserve and develop the Portuguese
● language and Brazilian literature. Machado
● de Assis was its president until 1908. It is
● made up of forty life members known as the
● *imortais*. The Academia's activities include
● publication of reference books, promotion
● of literary prizes, and running a library,
● museum and archive.

açafrão [asa'frãw] M saffron

acalcanhar [akawka'ɲaʳ] VT *(sapato)* to put out of shape

acalentar [akalē'taʳ] VT to rock to sleep; *(esperanças)* to cherish

acalmar [akaw'maʳ] VT to calm ■ vi *(vento etc)* to abate; **acalmar-se** vr to calm down

acalorado, -a [akalo'radu, a] ADJ heated

acalorar [akalo'raʳ] VT to heat; *(fig)* to inflame; **acalorar-se** vr *(fig)* to get heated

acamado, -a [aka'madu, a] ADJ bedridden

açambarcar [asãbax'kaʳ] VT to monopolize; *(mercado)* to corner

acampamento [akãpa'mētu] M camping; *(Mil)* camp, encampment; **levantar** ~ to raise camp

acampar [akã'paʳ] vi to camp

acanhado, -a [aka'ɲadu, a] ADJ shy

acanhamento [akaɲa'mētu] M shyness

acanhar-se [aka'ɲaxsi] VR to be shy

ação [a'sãw] *(pl -ões)* F action; *(ato)* act, deed; *(Mil)* battle; *(enredo)* plot; *(Jur)* lawsuit; *(Com)* share; ~ **bonificada** *(Com)* bonus share; ~ **de graças** thanksgiving; ~ **integralizada/ diferida** *(Com)* fully paid-in/deferred share; ~ **ordinária/preferencial** *(Com)* ordinary/ preference share

acarajé [akara'ʒɛ] M *(Culin)* beans fried in palm oil

acareação [akarja'sãw] *(pl -ões)* F

confrontation

acarear [aka'rjaʳ] VT to confront

acariciar [akari'sjaʳ] VT to caress; *(fig)* to cherish

acarinhar [akari'ɲaʳ] VT to caress; *(fig)* to treat with tenderness

acarretar [akaxe'taʳ] VT to result in, bring about

acasalamento [akazala'mētu] M mating

acasalar [akaza'laʳ] VT to mate; **acasalar-se** VR to mate

acaso [a'kazu] M chance; **ao** ~ at random; **por** ~ by chance

acastanhado, -a [akaʃta'ɲadu, a] ADJ brownish; *(cabelo)* auburn

acatamento [akata'mētu] M respect, deference; *(de lei)* observance

acatar [aka'taʳ] VT *(respeitar)* to respect; *(honrar)* to honour *(Brit)*, honor *(US)*; *(lei)* to obey

acautelar [akawte'laʳ] VT to warn; **acautelar-se** VR to be cautious; ~**-se contra** to guard against

ACC ABR M = **adiantamento de contratos de câmbio**

acção [a'sãw] *(PT)* F = **ação**

accionar *etc* [asjo'naʳ] *(PT)* = **acionar** *etc*

acebolado, -a [asebo'ladu, a] ADJ *(Culin)* flavoured *(Brit)* ou flavored *(US)* with onion

aceder [ase'deʳ] vi: ~ **a** to agree to, accede to

aceitação [asejta'sãw] F acceptance; *(aprovação)* approval

aceitar [asej'taʳ] VT to accept; *(aprovar)* to approve; **você aceita uma bebida?** would you like a drink?; **aceitável** [asej'tavew] *(pl -eis)* ADJ acceptable

aceite [a'sejtʃi] *(PT)* PP *de* **aceitar** ■ ADJ accepted ■ M acceptance

aceito, -a [a'sejtu, a] PP *de* **aceitar** ■ ADJ accepted

aceleração [aselera'sãw] F acceleration; *(pressa)* haste

acelerado, -a [asele'radu, a] ADJ *(rápido)* quick; *(apressado)* hasty

acelerador [aselera'doʳ] M accelerator

acelerar [asele'raʳ] VT, vi to accelerate; ~ **o passo** to go faster

acenar [ase'naʳ] vi *(com a mão)* to wave; *(com a cabeça)* to nod; ~ **com** *(oferecer)* to offer, promise

acendedor [asēde'doʳ] M lighter

acender [asē'deʳ] VT *(cigarro, fogo)* to light; *(luz)* to switch on; *(fig)* to excite, inflame

aceno [a'sɛnu] M sign, gesture; *(com a mão)* wave; *(com a cabeça)* nod

acento [a'sētu] M accent; *(de intensidade)* stress; ~ **agudo/circunflexo** acute/circumflex accent

acentuação [asētwa'sãw] F accentuation; *(ênfase)* stress

acentuado, -a [asē'twadu, a] ADJ *(sílaba)* stressed; *(saliente)* conspicuous

acentuar [asē'twaʳ] VT *(marcar com acento)* to accent; *(salientar)* to stress, emphasize; *(realçar)* to enhance

acepção [asep'sãw] *(pl -ões)* F *(de uma palavra)*

sense

acepipe [ase'pipi] M titbit (*Brit*), tidbit (*US*), delicacy; **acepipes** MPL (*PT*) hors dœuvres

acerca [a'sexka]: **~ de** PREP about, concerning

acercar-se [asex'kaxsi] VR: **~ de** to approach, draw near to

acérrimo, -a [a'seximu, a] ADJ SUPERL *de* **acre**; (*acre*) (very) bitter; (*defensor*) staunch

acertado, -a [asex'tadu, a] ADJ (*certo*) right, correct; (*sensato*) sensible

acertar [asex'ta**ʳ**] VT (*ajustar*) to put right; (*relógio*) to set; (*alvo*) to hit; (*acordo*) to reach; (*pergunta*) to get right ■ VI to get it right, be right; **~ o caminho** to find the right way; **~ com** to hit upon

acervo [a'sexvu] M heap; (*Jur*) estate; (*de museu etc*) collection; **um ~ de** vast quantities of

aceso, -a [a'sezu, a] PP *de* **acender** ■ ADJ (*luz, gás, TV*) on; (*fogo*) alight; (*excitado*) excited; (*furioso*) furious

acessar [ase'sa**ʳ**] VT (*Comput*) to access

acessível [ase'sivew] (*pl* **-eis**) ADJ accessible; (*pessoa*) approachable; (*preço*) reasonable, affordable

acesso [a'sɛsu] M access; (*Med*) fit, attack; **um ~ de cólera** a fit of anger; **de fácil ~** easy to get to; **múltiplo ~** (*Comput*) multiple access; **tempo de ~** (*Comput*) access time

acessório, -a [ase'sɔrju, a] ADJ accessory ■ M accessory

ACET (*BR*) ABR F = **Agência Central dos Teatros**

acetona [ase'tɔna] F nail varnish remover; (*Quím*) acetone

achacar [aʃa'ka**ʳ**] (*col*) VT (*dinheiro*) to extort

achado, -a [a'ʃadu, a] ADJ: **não se dar por ~** to play dumb ■ M find, discovery; (*pechincha*) bargain; (*sorte*) godsend

achaque [a'ʃaki] M ailment

achar [a'ʃa**ʳ**] VT (*descobrir*) to find; (*pensar*) to think; **achar-se** VR (*considerar-se*) to think (that) one is; (*encontrar-se*) to be; **~ de fazer** (*resolver*) to decide to do; **o que é que você acha disso?** what do you think of it?; **acho que ...** I think (that) ...; **acho que sim** I think so; **~ algo bom/ estranho** *etc* to find sth good/strange *etc*; **~ ruim** to be cross

achatar [aʃa'ta**ʳ**] VT to squash, flatten; (*fig*) to talk round, convince

achegar-se [aʃe'gaxsi] VR: **~ a** *ou* **de** to approach, get closer to

acidentado, -a [asidẽ'tadu, a] ADJ (*terreno*) rough; (*estrada*) bumpy; (*viagem*) eventful; (*vida*) difficult ■ M/F injured person

acidental [asidẽ'taw] (*pl* **-ais**) ADJ accidental

acidente [asi'dẽtʃi] M accident; (*acaso*) chance; **por ~** by accident

acidez [asi'deʒ] F acidity

ácido, -a ['asidu, a] ADJ acid; (*azedo*) sour ■ M acid

acima [a'sima] ADV above; (*para cima*) up ■ PREP: **~ de** above; (*além de*) beyond; **mais ~** higher up; **rio ~** up river; **passar rua ~** to go up the street; **~ de 1000** more than 1000

acinte [a'sĩtʃi] M provocation ■ ADV deliberately, on purpose

acintosamente [asĩtoza'mẽtʃi] ADV on purpose

acinzentado, -a [asĩzẽ'tadu, a] ADJ greyish (*Brit*), grayish (*US*)

acionado, -a [asjo'nadu, a] M/F (*Jur*) defendant

acionar [asjo'na**ʳ**] VT to set in motion; (*máquina*) to operate; (*Jur*) to sue

acionista [asjo'niʃta] M/F shareholder; **~ majoritário/minoritário** majority/minority shareholder

acirrado, -a [asi'xadu, a] ADJ (*luta, competição*) tough

acirrar [asi'xa**ʳ**] VT to incite, stir up

aclamação [aklama'sãw] F acclamation; (*ovação*) applause

aclamar [akla'ma**ʳ**] VT to acclaim; (*aplaudir*) to applaud

aclarado, -a [akla'radu, a] ADJ clear

aclarar [akla'ra**ʳ**] VT to explain, clarify ■ VI to clear up; **aclarar-se** VR to become clear

aclimatação [aklimata'sãw] F acclimatization

aclimatar [aklima'ta**ʳ**] VT to acclimatize (*Brit*), acclimate (*US*); **aclimatar-se** VR to become acclimatized *ou* acclimated

aclive [a'klivi] M slope, incline

ACM ABR F (= *Associação Cristã de Moços*) YMCA

aço ['asu] M (*metal*) steel; **~ inox** stainless steel

acocorar-se [akoko'raxsi] VR to squat, crouch

acode *etc* [a'kɔdʒi] VB *V* **acudir**

ações [a'sõjʃ] FPL *de* **ação**

acoitar [akoj'ta**ʳ**] VT to shelter, give refuge to

açoitar [asoj'ta**ʳ**] VT to whip, lash

açoite [a'sojtʃi] M whip, lash

acolá [ako'la] ADV over there

acolchoado, -a [akow'ʃwadu, a] ADJ quilted ■ M quilt

acolchoar [akow'ʃwa**ʳ**] VT (*costurar*) to quilt; (*forrar*) to pad; (*estofar*) to upholster

acolhedor, a [akoʎe'do**ʳ**(a)] ADJ welcoming; (*hospitaleiro*) hospitable

acolher [ako'ʎe**ʳ**] VT to welcome; (*abrigar*) to shelter; (*aceitar*) to accept; **acolher-se** VR to shelter; **acolhida** [ako'ʎida] F (*recepção*) reception, welcome; (*refúgio*) refuge; **acolhimento** [ako'ʎimẽtu] M (*recepção*) reception, welcome; (*refúgio*) refuge

acometer [akome'te**ʳ**] VT (*atacar*) to attack; (*suj: doença*) to take hold of

acomodação [akomoda'sãw] (*pl* **-ões**) F accommodation; (*arranjo*) arrangement; (*adaptação*) adaptation

acomodar [akomo'da**ʳ**] VT (*alojar*) to accommodate; (*arrumar*) to arrange; (*tornar cômodo*) to make comfortable; (*adaptar*) to adapt

---

NB: *European Portuguese adds the following consonants to certain words:* **b** (sú(b)dito, su(b)til); **c** (a(c)ção, a(c)cionista, a(c)to); **m** (inde(m)ne); **p** (ado(p)çã, ado(p)tar); *for further details see p. xiii.*

acompanhamento [akõpaɲa'mẽtu] M attendance; (cortejo) procession; (Mús) accompaniment; (Culin) side dish

acompanhante [akõpa'ɲãtʃi] M/F companion; (Mús) accompanist

acompanhar [akõpa'ɲaᵣ] VT to accompany, go along with; (Mús) to accompany; (assistir) to watch; (eventos) to keep up with; ~ **alguém até a porta** to show sb to the door

aconchegado, -a [akõʃe'gadu, a] ADJ snug, cosy (Brit), cozy (US)

aconchegante [akõʃe'gãtʃi] ADJ cosy (Brit), cozy (US)

aconchegar [akõʃe'gaᵣ] VT to bring near; **aconchegar-se** VR (acomodar-se) to make o.s comfortable; ~-**se com** to snuggle up to

aconchego [akõ'ʃegu] M cuddle

acondicionamento [akõdʒisjona'mẽtu] M packaging

acondicionar [akõdʒisjo'naᵣ] VT to condition; (empacotar) to pack, wrap (up)

aconselhar [akõse'ʎaᵣ] VT to advise; (recomendar) to recommend; **aconselhar-se** VR: **aconselhar-se com** to consult; ~ **alguém a fazer** to advise sb to do

aconselhável [akõse'ʎavew] (pl -eis) ADJ advisable

acontecer [akõte'seᵣ] VI to happen;

acontecimento [akõtesi'mẽtu] M event

acoplador [akopla'doᵣ] M: ~ **acústico** (Comput) acoustic coupler

acordar [akox'daᵣ] VT (despertar) to wake (up); (concordar) to agree (on) ■ VI (despertar) to wake up

acorde [a'kɔrdʒi] M chord

acordeão [akox'dʒjãw] (pl -ões) M accordion

acordeonista [akoxdʒjo'niʃta] M/F accordionist

acordo [a'koxdu] M agreement; "**de ~!**" agreed; **de ~ com** (pessoa) in agreement with; (conforme) in accordance with; **estar de ~** to agree; ~ **de cavalheiros** gentlemen's agreement

Açores [a'soriʃ] MPL: **os ~** the Azores; **açoriano, -a** [aso'rjanu, a] ADJ, M/F Azorean

acorrentar [akoxẽ'taᵣ] VT to chain (up)

acorrer [ako'xeᵣ] VI: ~ **a alguém** to come to sb's aid

acossar [ako'saᵣ] VT (perseguir) to pursue; (atormentar) to harass

acostamento [akoʃta'mẽtu] M hard shoulder (Brit), berm (US)

acostar [akoʃ'taᵣ] VT to lean against; (Náut) to bring alongside; **acostar-se** VR to lean back

acostumado, -a [akoʃtu'madu, a] ADJ (habitual) usual, customary; **estar ~ to** be used to it; **estar ~ a algo** to be used to sth

acostumar [akoʃtu'maᵣ] VT to accustom; **acostumar-se** VR: **acostumar-se a** to get used to

acotovelar [akotove'laᵣ] VT to jostle; **acotovelar-se** VR to jostle

açougue [a'sogi] M butcher's (shop);

açougueiro [aso'gejru] M butcher

acovardado, -a [akovax'dadu, a] ADJ intimidated

acovardar-se [akovax'daxsi] VR (desanimar) to lose courage; (amedrontar-se) to flinch, cower

acre ['akri] ADJ (gosto) bitter; (cheiro) acrid; (fig) harsh

acreano, -a [a'krjanu, a] ADJ from Acre ■ M/F native of Acre

acreditado, -a [akredʒi'tadu, a] ADJ accredited

acreditar [akredʒi'taᵣ] VT to believe; (Com) to credit; (afiançar) to guarantee ■ VI: ~ **em** to believe in; (ter confiança em) to have faith in; "**acredite na sinalização**" "follow traffic signs"

acreditável [akredʒi'tavew] (pl -eis) ADJ credible

acre-doce ADJ (Culin) sweet and sour

acrescentar [akresẽ'taᵣ] VT to add

acrescer [akre'seᵣ] VT (aumentar) to increase; (juntar) to add ■ VI to increase; **acresce que** ... add to that the fact that ....

acréscimo [a'kresimu] M addition; (aumento) increase; (elevação) rise

acriançado, -a [akrjã'sadu, a] ADJ childish

acrílico [a'kriliku] M acrylic

acrimônia [akri'monja] F acrimony

acrobacia [akroba'sia] F acrobatics pl; **acrobacias** FPL: **acrobacias aéreas** aerobatics pl

acrobata [akro'bata] M/F acrobat

activo [a'tivu] (PT) = **ativo** etc

acto ['atu] (PT) M = **ato**

actor [a'toᵣ] (PT) M = **ator**

actriz [a'triʒ] (PT) F = **atriz**

actual etc [a'twaw] (PT) = **atual** etc

actuar etc [a'twaᵣ] (PT) = **atuar** etc

acuar [a'kwaᵣ] VT to corner

açúcar [a'sukaᵣ] M sugar

açucarado, -a [asuka'radu, a] ADJ sugary

açucarar [asuka'raᵣ] VT to sugar; (adoçar) to sweeten

açucareiro [asuka'rejru] M sugar bowl

açude [a'sudʒi] M dam

acudir [aku'dʒiᵣ] VT (irem socorro) to help, assist ■ VI (responder) to reply, respond; ~ **a** to come to the aid of

acuidade [akwi'dadʒi] F perceptiveness

açular [asu'laᵣ] VT (incitar) to incite; ~ **um cachorro contra alguém** to set a dog on sb

acumulação [akumula'sãw] (pl -ões) F accumulation

acumulado, -a [akumu'ladu, a] ADJ (Com: juros, despesas) accrued

acumular [akumu'laᵣ] VT to accumulate; (reunir) to collect; (amontoar) to pile up; (funções) to combine

acúmulo [a'kumulu] M accumulation

acusação [akuza'sãw] (pl -ões) F accusation, charge; (ato) accusation; (Jur) prosecution

acusado, -a [aku'zadu, a] M/F accused

acusar [aku'zaᵣ] VT to accuse; (revelar) to reveal; (culpar) to blame; ~ **o recebimento de** to acknowledge receipt of

acústica [a'kuʃtʃika] F (ciência) acoustics sg; (de

uma sala) acoustics *pl*
acústico, -a [a'kuʃtʃiku, a] ADJ acoustic
adaga [a'daga] F dagger
adágio [a'daʒu] M adage; (*Mús*) adagio
adaptabilidade [adaptabili'dadʒi] F adaptability
adaptação [adapta'sãw] (*pl* -ões) F adaptation
adaptado, -a [adap'tadu, a] ADJ (*criança*) well-adjusted
adaptar [adap'ta^r] VT (*modificar*) to adapt; (*acomodar*) to fit; **adaptar-se** VR: ~-**se a** to adapt to
ADECIF (BR) ABR F = **Associação de Diretores de Empresas de Créditos, Investimentos e Financiamento**
adega [a'dɛga] F cellar
adelgaçado, -a [adewga'sadu, a] ADJ thin; (*aguçado*) pointed
ademais [adʒi'majʃ] ADV (*além disso*) besides, moreover
ADEMI (BR) ABR F = **Associação de Dirigentes de Empresa do Mercado Imobiliário**
adentro [a'dẽtru] ADV inside, in; **mata** ~ into the woods
adepto, -a [a'dɛptu, a] M/F follower; (*de time*) supporter
adequado, -a [ade'kwadu, a] ADJ appropriate
adequar [ade'kwa^r] VT to adapt, make suitable
adereçar [adere'sa^r] VT to adorn, decorate; **adereçar-se** VR to dress up
adereço [ade'resu] M adornment; **adereços** MPL (*Teatro*) stage props
aderência [ade'rẽsja] F adherence
aderente [ade'rẽtʃi] ADJ adhesive, sticky ◾ M/F (*partidário*) supporter
aderir [ade'ri^r] VI to adhere; (*colar*) to stick; (*a uma moda etc*) to join in
adesão [ade'zãw] F adhesion; (*patrocínio*) support
adesivo, -a [ade'zivu, a] ADJ adhesive, sticky ◾ M adhesive tape; (*Med*) sticking plaster
adestrado, -a [adeʃ'tradu, a] ADJ skilful (*Brit*), skillful (*US*), skilled
adestrador, a [adeʃtra'do^r(a)] M/F trainer
adestramento [adeʃtra'mẽtu] M training
adestrar [adeʃ'tra^r] VT to train, instruct; (*cavalo*) to break in
adeus [a'dewʃ] EXCL goodbye!; **dizer** ~ to say goodbye, bid farewell
adiamento [adʒja'mẽtu] M postponement; (*de uma sessão*) adjournment
adiantado, -a [adʒjã'tadu, a] ADJ advanced; (*relógio*) fast; **chegar** ~ to arrive ahead of time; **pagar** ~ to pay in advance
adiantamento [adʒjãta'mẽtu] M progress; (*dinheiro*) advance (payment)
adiantar [adʒjã'ta^r] VT (*dinheiro, salário*) to advance, pay in advance; (*relógio*) to put forward; (*trabalho*) to advance; (*dizer*) to say

in advance ◾ VI (*relógio*) to be fast; (*conselho, violência etc*) to be of use; **adiantar-se** VR to advance, get ahead; **não adianta reclamar/ insistir** there's no point *ou* it's no use complaining/insisting; ~-**se a alguém** to get ahead of sb; ~-**se para** to go/come up to
adiante [a'dʒjãtʃi] ADV (*na frente*) in front; (*para a frente*) forward; **mais** ~ further on; (*no futuro*) later on
adiar [a'dʒja^r] VT to postpone, put off; (*sessão*) to adjourn
adição [adʒi'sãw] (*pl* -ões) F addition; (*Mat*) sum; **adicionar** [adʒisjo'na^r] VT to add
adições [adʒi'sõjʃ] FPL *de* **adição**
adido, -a [a'dʒidu, a] M/F attaché
adiro *etc* [a'diru] VB V **aderir**
Adis-Abeba [adʒiza'bɛba] N Addis Ababa
adivinhação [adʒiviɲa'sãw] F (*destino*) fortune-telling; (*conjectura*) guessing, guesswork
adivinhar [adʒivi'ɲa^r] VT to guess; (*ler a sorte*) to foretell ◾ VI to guess; ~ **o pensamento de alguém** to read sb's mind; **adivinho, -a** [adʒi'viɲu, a] M/F fortune-teller
adjacente [adʒa'sẽtʃi] ADJ adjacent
adjetivo [adʒe'tʃivu] M adjective
adjudicação [adʒudʒika'sãw] (*pl* -ões) F grant; (*de contratos*) award; (*Jur*) decision
adjudicar [adʒudʒi'ka^r] VT to award, grant
adjunto, -a [a'dʒũtu, a] ADJ joined, attached ◾ M/F assistant
administração [adʒiminiʃtra'sãw] (*pl* -ões) F administration; (*direção*) management; (*comissão*) board; ~ **de empresas** business administration, management; ~ **fiduciária** trusteeship
administrador, a [adʒiminiʃtra'do^r(a)] M/F administrator; (*diretor*) director; (*gerente*) manager
administrar [adʒiminiʃ'tra^r] VT to administer, manage; (*governar*) to govern; (*remédio*) to administer
admiração [adʒimira'sãw] F (*assombro*) wonder; (*estima*) admiration; **ponto de** ~ (*PT*) exclamation mark
admirado, -a [adʒimi'radu, a] ADJ astonished, surprised
admirador, a [adʒimira'do^r(a)] ADJ admiring
admirar [adʒimi'ra^r] VT to admire; **admirar-se** VR: **admirar-se de** to be astonished *ou* surprised at; **não me admiro!** I'm not surprised; **não é de se** ~ it's not surprising; **admirável** [adʒimi'ravew] (*pl* -eis) ADJ (*assombroso*) amazing
admissão [adʒimi'sãw] (*pl* -ões) F admission; (*consentimento para entrar*) admittance; (*de escola*) intake
admitir [adʒimi'tʃi^r] VT (*aceitar*) to admit; (*permitir*) to allow; (*funcionário*) to take on
admoestação [admweʃta'sãw] (*pl* -ões) F

admonition; (*repreensão*) reprimand

admoestar [admweʃ'ta'] VT to admonish

adoção [ado'sãw] F adoption

adoçar [ado'sa'] VT to sweeten

adocicado, -a [adosi'kadu, a] ADJ slightly sweet

adoecer [adoe'se'] VI to fall ill ∎ VT to make ill; ~ **de** *ou* **com** to fall ill with

adoidado, -a [adoj'dadu, a] ADJ crazy ∎ ADV (*col*) like mad *ou* crazy

adolescente [adole'sẽtʃi] ADJ, M/F adolescent

adoptar *etc* [ado'ta'] (PT) = **adotar** *etc*

adoração [adora'sãw] F adoration; (*veneração*) worship

adorar [ado'ra'] VT to adore; (*venerar*) to worship; (*col: gostar muito de*) to love

adorável [ado'ravew] (*pl* -**eis**) ADJ adorable

adormecer [adoxme'se'] VI to fall asleep; (*entorpecer-se*) to go numb; **adormecido, -a** [adoxme'sidu, a] ADJ sleeping ∎ M/F sleeper

adornar [adox'na'] VT to adorn, decorate

adorno [a'doxnu] M adornment

adotar [ado'ta'] VT to adopt; **adotivo, -a** [ado'tʃivu, a] ADJ (*filho*) adopted

adquirir [adʒiki'ri'] VT to acquire; (*obter*) to obtain

adrede [a'dredʒi] ADV on purpose, deliberately

Adriático, -a [a'drjatʃiku, a] ADJ: **o (mar)** ~ the Adriatic (Sea)

adro ['adru] M (church) forecourt; (*em volta da igreja*) churchyard

aduana [a'dwana] F customs *pl*, customs house

aduaneiro, -a [adwa'nejru, a] ADJ customs *atr* ∎ M customs officer

adubação [aduba'sãw] F fertilizing

adubar [adu'ba'] VT to manure; (*fertilizar*) to fertilize

adubo [a'dubu] M (*fertilizante*) fertilizer

adulação [adula'sãw] F flattery

adulador, a [adula'do'(a)] ADJ flattering ∎ M/F flatterer

adular [adu'la'] VT to flatter

adulteração [aduwtera'sãw] F adulteration; (*de contas*) falsification

adulterador, a [aduwtera'do'(a)] M/F adulterator

adulterar [aduwte'ra'] VT (*vinho*) to adulterate; (*contas*) to falsify ∎ VI to commit adultery

adultério [aduw'terju] M adultery

adúltero, -a [a'duwteru, a] M/F adulterer/adulteress

adulto, -a [a'duwtu, a] ADJ, M/F adult

adunco, -a [a'dũku, a] ADJ (*nariz*) hook

adveio *etc* [ad'veju] VB V **advir**

adventício, -a [advẽ'tʃisju, a] ADJ (*casual*) accidental; (*estrangeiro*) foreign ∎ M/F foreigner

advento [ad'vẽtu] M advent; **o A**~ Advent

advérbio [ad'vɛxbju] M adverb

adversário [adʒivex'sarju] M adversary, opponent, enemy

adversidade [adʒivexsi'dadʒi] F adversity, misfortune

adverso, -a [adʒi'vɛxsu, a] ADJ adverse,

unfavourable (*Brit*), unfavorable (*US*); (*oposto*): ~ **a** opposed to

advertência [adʒivex'tẽsja] F warning; (*repreensão*) (gentle) reprimand

advertido, -a [adʒivex'tʃidu, a] ADJ prudent; (*informado*) well-advised

advertir [adʒivex'tʃi'] VT to warn; (*repreender*) to reprimand; (*chamar a atenção a*) to draw attention to

advier *etc* [ad'vje'] VB V **advir**

advindo, -a [ad'vĩdu, a] ADJ: ~ **de** resulting from

advir [ad'vi'] (*irreg*) VI: ~ **de** to result from

advocacia [adʒivoka'sia] F legal profession, law

advogado, -a [adʒivo'gadu, a] M/F lawyer

advogar [adʒivo'ga'] VT (*promover*) to advocate; (*Jur*) to plead ∎ VI to practise (*Brit*) *ou* practice (*US*) law

aéreo, -a [a'erju, a] ADJ air *atr*; (*pessoa*) vague

aerobarco [aero'baxku] M hovercraft

aeroclube [aero'klubi] M flying club

aerodinâmica [aerodʒi'namika] F aerodynamics *sg*

aerodinâmico, -a [aerodʒi'namiku, a] ADJ aerodynamic

aeródromo [aero'drɔmu] M airfield

aeroespacial [aeroiʃpa'sjaw] (*pl* -**ais**) ADJ aerospace *atr*

aerofagia [aerofa'ʒia] F (*Med*) hyperventilation

aerofoto [aero'fɔtu] F aerial photograph

aeromoço, -a [aero'mosu, a] (*BR*) M/F steward/air hostess

aeromodelismo [aeromode'liʒmu] M aeromodelling

aeronauta [aero'nawta] M/F airman/woman

aeronáutica [aero'nawtʃika] F air force; (*ciência*) aeronautics *sg*; **Departamento de A**~ **Civil** ≈ Civil Aviation Authority

aeronave [aero'navi] F aircraft

aeroporto [aero'poxtu] M airport

aerossol [aero'sɔw] (*pl* -**óis**) M aerosol

afã [a'fã] M (*entusiasmo*) enthusiasm; (*diligência*) diligence; (*ânsia*) eagerness; (*esforço*) effort; (*faina*) task, job; **no seu** ~ **de agradar** in his eagerness to please

afabilidade [afabili'dadʒi] F friendliness, kindness

afaço *etc* [a'fasu] VB V **afazer**

afagar [afa'ga'] VT (*acariciar*) to caress; (*cabelo*) to stroke

afamado, -a [afa'madu, a] ADJ renowned

afanar [afa'na'] (*col*) VT to nick, pinch

afanoso, -a [afa'nozu, ɔza] ADJ laborious; (*meticuloso*) painstaking

afasia [afa'zia] F aphasia

afastado, -a [afaʃ'tadu, a] ADJ (*distante*) remote; (*isolado*) secluded; (*pernas*) apart; (*amigo*) distant; **manter-se** ~ to keep to o.s

afastamento [afaʃta'mẽtu] M removal; (*distância*) distance; (*de emprego solicitado*) rejection; (*de pessoal*) lay-off, sacking

afastar [afaʃ'ta'] VT to remove; (*amigo*) to distance; (*separar*) to separate; (*idéia*) to put out of one's mind; (*pessoal*) to lay off; **afastar-se** VR (*ir-se embora*) to move away, go away; (*de amigo*) to distance o.s; (*de cargo*) to step down; ~ **os olhos de** to take one's eyes off; **~-se do assunto** to stray from the subject

afável [a'favew] (*pl* -**eis**) ADJ friendly, genial

afazer [afa'ze^r] (*irreg*) VT to accustom; **afazer-se** VR: **afazer-se a** to get used to

afazeres [afa'zeriʃ] MPL business *sg*; (*dever*) duties, tasks; ~ **domésticos** household chores

afectar *etc* [afek'ta^r] (PT) = **afetar** *etc*

afegã [afe'] F *de* **afegão**

Afeganistão [afeganiʃ'tãw] M: **o** ~ Afghanistan

afegão, -gã [afe'gãw, 'gã] (*pl* -**ões/-s**) ADJ, M/F Afghan

afeição [afej'sãw] F (*amor*) affection, fondness; (*dedicação*) devotion; **afeiçoado, -a** [afej'swadu, a] ADJ: **afeiçoado a** (*amoroso*) fond of; (*devotado*) devoted to ■ M/F friend

afeiçoar-se [afej'swaxsi] VR: ~ **a** (*tomar gosto por*) to take a liking to

afeito, -a [a'fejtu, a] PP *de* **afazer** ■ ADJ: **afeito a** accustomed to, used to

afeminado, -a [afemi'nadu, a] ADJ effeminate

aferidor [aferi'do^r] M (*de pesos e medidas*) inspector; (*verificador*) checker; (*instrumento*) gauge (*Brit*), gage (*US*)

aferir [afe'ri^r] VT (*verificar*) to check, inspect; (*comparar*) to compare; (*conhecimentos, resultados*) to assess

aferrado, -a [afe'xadu, a] ADJ obstinate, stubborn

aferrar [afe'xa^r] VT (*prender*) to secure; (*Náut*) to anchor; (*agarrar*) to grasp; **aferrar-se** VR: **aferrar-se a** to cling to

aferrolhar [afexo'ʎa^r] VT to bolt; (*pessoa*) to imprison; (*coisas*) to hoard

aferventar [afexvẽ'ta^r] VT to bring to the (*Brit*) ou a (*US*) boil

afetação [afeta'sãw] F affectation

afetado, -a [afe'tadu, a] ADJ pretentious, affected

afetar [afe'ta^r] VT to affect; (*fingir*) to feign

afetividade [afetʃivi'dadʒi] F affection

afetivo, -a [afe'tʃivu, a] ADJ affectionate; (*problema*) emotional

afeto [a'fetu] M affection; **afetuoso, -a** [afe'twozu, ɔza] ADJ affectionate

afez *etc* [a'feʒ] VB *v* **afazer**

AFI ABR M (= *Alfabeto Fonético Internacional*) IPA

afiado, -a [a'fjadu, a] ADJ sharp; (*pessoa*) well-trained

afiançar [afjã'sa^r] VT (*Jur*) to stand bail for; (*garantir*) to guarantee

afiar [a'fja^r] VT to sharpen

aficionado, -a [afisjo'nadu, a] M/F enthusiast

afigurar-se [afigu'raxsi] VR to seem, appear; **afigura-se-me que ...** it seems to me that ...

afilado, -a [afi'ladu, a] ADJ (*nariz*) thin

afilhado, -a [afi'ʎadu, a] M/F godson/goddaughter

afiliação [afilja'sãw] (*pl* -**ões**) F affiliation

afiliada [afi'ljada] F affiliate, affiliated company

afiliado, -a [afi'ljadu, a] ADJ affiliated

afiliar [afi'lja^r] VT to affiliate; **afiliar-se** VR: **afiliar-se a** to join

afim [a'fĩ] (*pl* -**ns**) ADJ (*semelhante*) similar; (*consangüíneo*) related ■ M/F relative, relation; **estar** ~ **de** (*fazer*) **algo/alguém**; *v* **fim**

afinação [afina'sãw] F (*Mús*) tuning

afinado, -a [afi'nadu, a] ADJ in tune

afinal [afi'naw] ADV at last, finally; ~ (**de contas**) after all

afinar [afi'na^r] VT (*Mús*) to tune ■ VI (*adelgaçar*) to taper

afinco [a'fĩku] M tenacity, persistence; **com** ~ tenaciously

afinidade [afini'dadʒi] F affinity

afins [a'fĩʃ] PL *de* **afim**

afirmação [afixma'sãw] (*pl* -**ões**) F affirmation; (*declaração*) statement

afirmar [afix'ma^r] VT, VI to affirm, assert; (*declarar*) to declare

afirmativo, -a [afixma'tʃivu, a] ADJ affirmative

afiro *etc* [a'firu] VB *v* **aferir**

afivelar [afive'la^r] VT to buckle

afixar [afik'sa^r] VT (*cartazes*) to stick, post

afiz *etc* [a'fiʒ] VB *v* **afazer**

afizer *etc* [afi'ze^r] VB *v* **afazer**

aflição [afli'sãw] F (*sofrimento*) affliction; (*ansiedade*) anxiety; (*angústia*) anguish

afligir [afli'ʒi^r] VT to distress; (*atormentar*) to torment; (*inquietar*) to worry; **afligir-se** VR: **afligir-se com** to worry about

aflijo *etc* [a'fliʒu] VB *v* **afligir**

aflito, -a [a'flitu, a] PP *de* **afligir** ■ ADJ distressed, anxious

aflorar [aflo'ra^r] VI to emerge, appear

afluência [a'flwẽsja] F affluence; (*corrente copiosa*) flow; (*de pessoas*) stream; **afluente** [a'flwẽtʃi] ADJ copious; (*rico*) affluent ■ M tributary

afluir [a'flwi^r] VI to flow; (*pessoas*) to congregate

afobação [afoba'sãw] F fluster; (*ansiedade*) panic

afobado, -a [afo'badu, a] ADJ flustered; (*ansioso*) panicky, nervous

afobamento [afoba'mẽtu] M fluster; (*ansiedade*) panic

afobar [afo'ba^r] VT to fluster; (*deixar ansioso*) to make nervous *ou* panicky ■ VI to get flustered; to panic, get nervous; **afobar-se** VR to get flustered

afofar [afo'fa^r] VT to fluff

afogado, -a [afo'gadu, a] ADJ drowned

afogador [afoga'do^r] (BR) M (*Auto*) choke

afogar [afo'ga^r] VT to drown ■ VI (*Auto*) to flood; **afogar-se** VR to drown, be drowned

afoito, -a [aˈfojtu, a] ADJ bold, daring

afonia [afoˈnia] F voice loss

afônico, -a [aˈfoniku, a] ADJ: **estou ~** I've lost my voice

afora [aˈfɔra] PREP except for, apart from ■ ADV: **rua ~** down the street; **pelo mundo ~** throughout the world; **porta ~** out into the street

aforismo [afoˈriʒmu] M aphorism

aforrar [afoˈxaʳ] VT (roupa) to line; (poupar) to save; (liberar) to free

afortunado, -a [afoxtuˈnadu, a] ADJ fortunate, lucky

afrescalhado, -a [afreʃkaˈʎadu, a] (col) ADJ effeminate, camp

afresco [aˈfreʃku] M fresco

África [ˈafrika] F: **a ~** Africa; **a ~ do Sul** South Africa; **africano, -a** [afriˈkanu, a] ADJ, M/F African

AFRMM (BR) ABR M (= Adicional ao Frete para Renovação da Marinha Mercante) tax on goods imported by sea

afro-brasileiro, -a [ˈafru-] (pl -s) ADJ Afro-Brazilian

afrodisíaco [afrodʒiˈziaku] M aphrodisiac

afronta [aˈfrõta] F insult, affront

afrontado, -a [afrõˈtadu, a] ADJ (ofendido) offended; (com má digestão) too full

afrontar [afrõˈtaʳ] VT to insult; (ofender) to offend

afrouxar [afroˈʃaʳ] VT (desapertar) to slacken; (soltar) to loosen ■ VI (soltar-se) to come loose

afta [ˈafta] F (mouth) ulcer

afugentar [afuʒẽˈtaʳ] VT to drive away, put to flight

afundar [afũˈdaʳ] VT (submergir) to sink; (cavidade) to deepen; **afundar-se** VR to sink; (col: num exame) to do badly

agá [aˈga] M aitch, h

agachar-se [agaˈʃaxsi] VR (acaçapar-se) to crouch, squat; (curvar-se) to stoop; (fig) to cringe

agarração [agaxaˈsãw] (col) F necking

agarrado, -a [agaˈxadu, a] ADJ: **~ a** (preso) stuck to; (a uma pessoa) very attached to

agarramento [agaxaˈmẽtu] M (a uma pessoa) close attachment; (col: agarração) necking

agarrar [agaˈxaʳ] VT to seize, grasp; **agarrar-se** VR: **~ a** to cling to, hold on to

agasalhado, -a [agazaˈʎadu, a] ADJ warmly dressed, wrapped up

agasalhar [agazaˈʎaʳ] VT to dress warmly, wrap up; **agasalhar-se** VR to wrap o.s. up

agasalho [agaˈzaʎu] M (casaco) coat; (suéter) sweater

ágeis [ˈaʒejʃ] PL de **ágil**

agência [aˈʒẽsja] F agency; (escritório) office; (de banco etc) branch; **~ de correio** (BR) post office; **~ de viagens** travel agency; **~ publicitária** advertising agency

agenciar [aʒẽˈsjaʳ] VT (negociar) to negotiate; (obter) to procure; (ser agente de) to act as an agent for

agenda [aˈʒẽda] F diary; **~ eletrônica** personal organizer

agente [aˈʒẽtʃi] M/F agent; (de polícia) policeman/woman; **~ de seguros** (insurance) underwriter

agigantado, -a [aʒigãˈtadu, a] ADJ gigantic

ágil [ˈaʒiw] (pl -eis) ADJ agile

agilidade [aʒiliˈdadʒi] F agility

agilizar [aʒiliˈzaʳ] VT: **~ algo** (dar andamento a) to get sth moving; (acelerar) to speed sth up

ágio [ˈaʒju] M premium

agiota [aˈʒjɔta] M/F moneylender

agir [aˈʒiʳ] VI to act; **~ bem/mal** to do right/wrong

agitação [aʒitaˈsãw] (pl -ões) F agitation; (perturbação) disturbance; (inquietação) restlessness

agitado, -a [aʒiˈtadu, a] ADJ agitated, disturbed; (inquieto) restless

agitar [aʒiˈtaʳ] VT to agitate, disturb; (sacudir) to shake; (cauda) to wag; (mexer) to stir; (os braços) to swing, wave; **agitar-se** VR to get upset; (mar) to get rough

aglomeração [aglomeraˈsãw] (pl -ões) F gathering; (multidão) crowd

aglomerado [aglomeˈradu] M: **~ urbano** city

aglomerar [aglomeˈraʳ] VT to heap up, pile up; **aglomerar-se** VR (multidão) to crowd together

AGO ABR F (= assembléia geral ordinária) AGM

ago. ABR (= agosto) Aug

agonia [agoˈnia] F agony, anguish; (ânsia da morte) death throes pl; (indecisão) indecision

agoniado, -a [agoˈnjadu, a] ADJ anguished

agonizante [agoniˈzãtʃi] ADJ dying ■ M/F dying person

agonizar [agoniˈzaʳ] VI to be dying; (afligir-se) to agonize

agora [aˈgɔra] ADV now; (hoje em dia) now, nowadays; **e ~?** now what?; **~ mesmo** right now; (há pouco) a moment ago; **a partir de ~**, **de ~ em diante** from now on; **até ~** so far, up to now; **por ~** for now; **~ que** now that; **eu lhe disse ontem** I told him yesterday; **~, se ele esquecer ...** but if he forgets ...

agorinha [agoˈriɲa] ADV just now

agosto [aˈgoʃtu] (PT **Agosto**) M August; v tb **julho**

agourar [agoˈraʳ] VT to predict, foretell ■ VI to augur ill

agouro [aˈgoru] M omen; (mau agouro) bad omen

agraciar [agraˈsjaʳ] VT (condecorar) to decorate

agradabilíssimo, -a [agradabiˈlisimu, a] ADJ SUPERL de **agradável**

agradar [agraˈdaʳ] VT (deleitar) to please; (fazer agrados a) to be nice to ■ VI (ser agradável) to be pleasing; (satisfazer: show, piada etc) to go down well

agradável [agraˈdavew] (pl -eis) ADJ pleasant

agradecer [agradeˈseʳ] VT: **~ algo a alguém**, **~ a alguém por algo** to thank sb for sth; **agradecido, -a** [agradeˈsidu, a] ADJ grateful; **mal agradecido** ungrateful

agradecimento [agradesiˈmẽtu] M gratitude; **agradecimentos** MPL (gratidão) thanks

agrado [a'gradu] M: **fazer um ~ a alguém** (*afagar*) to be affectionate with sb; (*ser agradável*) to be nice to sb

agrário, -a [a'grarju, a] ADJ agrarian; **reforma agrária** land reform

agravação [agrava'sãw] (PT) F aggravation; (*piora*) worsening

agravamento [agrava'mẽtu] (BR) M aggravation

agravante [agra'vãtʃi] ADJ aggravating ■ F aggravating circumstance

agravar [agra'va ʳ] VT to aggravate, make worse; **agravar-se** VR (*piorar*) to get worse

agravo [a'gravu] M (*Jur*) appeal

agredir [agre'dʒi ʳ] VT to attack; (*insultar*) to insult

agregado, -a [agre'gadu, a] M/F (*lavrador*) tenant farmer; (BR) lodger ■ M aggregate, sum total

agregar [agre'ga ʳ] VT (*juntar*) to collect; (*acrescentar*) to add

agressão [agre'sãw] (*pl* -ões) F aggression; (*ataque*) attack; (*assalto*) assault

agressividade [agresivi'dadʒi] F aggressiveness

agressivo, -a [agre'sivu, a] ADJ aggressive

agressões [agre'sõjʃ] FPL *de* **agressão**

agressor, a [agre'so ʳ(a)] M/F aggressor

agreste [a'grɛʃtʃi] ADJ rural, rustic; (*terreno*) wild, uncultivated

agrião [a'grjãw] M watercress

agrícola [a'grikola] ADJ agricultural

agricultável [agrikuw'tavew] (*pl* -eis) ADJ arable

agricultor [agrikuw'to ʳ] M farmer

agricultura [agrikuw'tura] F agriculture, farming

agrido *etc* [a'gridu] VB V **agredir**

agridoce [agri'dosi] ADJ bittersweet

agronegócio [agrone'gɔsju] M agribusiness

agronomia [agrono'mia] F agronomy

agrônomo, -a [a'gronomu, a] M/F agronomist

agropecuária [agrope'kwarja] F farming, agriculture

agropecuário, -a [agrope'kwarju, a] ADJ farming *atr*, agricultural

agrotóxico [agro'tɔksiku] M pesticide

agrupamento [agrupa'mẽtu] M grouping

agrupar [agru'pa ʳ] VT to group; **agrupar-se** VR to group together

agrura [a'grura] F bitterness

água ['agwa] F water; **águas** FPL (*mar*) waters; (*chuvas*) rain *sg*; (*maré*) tides; **~ abaixo/acima** downstream/upstream; **até debaixo da ~** (*fig*) one thousand per cent; **dar ~ na boca** (*comida*) to be mouthwatering; **estar na ~** (*bêbado*) to be drunk; **fazer ~** (*Náut*) to leak; **ir nas ~s de alguém** (*fig*) to follow in sb's footsteps; **~ benta** holy water; **~ corrente** running water; **~ doce** fresh water; **~ dura/leve** hard/soft water; **~**

mineral mineral water; **~ oxigenada** peroxide; **~ salgada** salt water; **~ sanitária** household bleach; **jogar ~ na fervura** (*fig*) to put a damper on things; **mudar como da ~ para o vinho** to change radically; **desta ~ não beberei!** that won't happen to me!; **~s passadas não movem moinhos** it's all water under the bridge

aguaceiro [agwa'sejru] M (*chuva*) (heavy) shower, downpour; (*com vento*) squall

água-com-açúcar ADJ INV schmaltzy, mushy

água-de-coco F coconut milk

água-de-colônia (*pl* águas-de-colônia) F eau-de-cologne

aguado, -a [a'gwadu, a] ADJ watery

água-furtada [-fux'tada] (*pl* águas-furtadas) F garret, attic

água-marinha (*pl* águas-marinhas) F aquamarine

aguar [a'gwa ʳ] VT to water ■ VI: **~ por** (*salivar*) to drool over

aguardar [agwax'da ʳ] VT to wait for, await; (*contar com*) to expect ■ VI to wait

aguardente [agwax'dẽtʃi] M spirit

aguarrás [agwa'xajʃ] F turpentine

água-viva (*pl* águas-vivas) F jellyfish

aguçado, -a [agu'sadu, a] ADJ pointed; (*espírito, sentidos*) acute

aguçar [agu'sa ʳ] VT (*afiar*) to sharpen; (*estimular*) to excite; **~ a vista** to keep one's eyes peeled

agudeza [agu'deza] F sharpness; (*perspicácia*) perspicacity; (*de som*) shrillness

agudo, -a [a'gudu, a] ADJ sharp; (*som*) shrill; (*intenso*) acute

agüentar [agwẽ'ta ʳ] VT (*muro etc*) to hold up; (*dor, injustiças*) to stand, put up with; (*peso*) to withstand; (*resistir a*) to stand up to ■ VI to last, hold out; (*resistir a peso*) to hold; **agüentar-se** VR (*manter-se*) to remain, hold on; **~ com** to hold, withstand; **~ fazer algo** to manage to do sth; **não ~ de** not to be able to stand; **~ firme** to hold out

aguerrido, -a [age'xidu, a] ADJ warlike, bellicose; (*corajoso*) courageous

águia ['agja] F eagle; (*fig*) genius

agulha [a'guʎa] F (*de coser, tricô*) needle; (*Náut*) compass; (*Ferro*) points *pl* (Brit), switch (US); **trabalho de ~** needlework

agulheta [agu'ʎeta] F (*bico*) nozzle

ah [a] EXCL oh!

AI ABR F = **Anistia Internacional** ■ ABR M (BR) = **Ato Institucional**; **AI-5** *measure passed in 1968 suspending congress and banning opposition politicians*

ai [aj] EXCL (*suspiro*) oh!; (*de dor*) ouch! ■ M (*suspiro*) sigh; (*gemido*) groan; **ai de mim** poor me!

aí [a'i] ADV there; (*então*) then; **por aí** (*em lugar indeterminado*) somewhere over there, thereabouts; **espera aí!** wait!, hang on a minute!; **está aí!** (*col*) right!; **aí é que 'tá!** (*col*)

NB: *European Portuguese adds the following consonants to certain words:* **b** (sú(b)dito, su(b)til); **c** (a(c)ção, a(c)cionista, a(c)to); **m** (inde(m)ne); **p** (ado(p)çã, ado(p)tar); *for further details see p. xiii.*

that's just the point; **e por aí afora** *ou* **vai** and so on; **já não está aí quem falou** (*col*) I stand corrected; **e aí?** and then what?; **e aí (como vai)?** (*col*) how are things with you?

aiatolá [ajato'la] M ayatollah

aidético, -a [aj'dɛtʃiku, a] ADJ suffering from AIDS ■ M/F person with AIDS

AIDS ['ajdʒs] F AIDS

ainda [a'ĩda] ADV still; (*mesmo*) even; ~ **agora** just now; ~ **assim** even so, nevertheless; ~ **bem** just as well; ~ **por cima** on top of all that, in addition; ~ **não** not yet; ~ **que** even if; **maior** ~ even bigger

aipim [aj'pĩ] M cassava

aipo ['ajpu] M celery

airado, -a [aj'radu, a] ADJ (*frívolo*) frivolous; (*leviano*) dissolute

airoso, -a [aj'rozu, ɔza] ADJ graceful, elegant

ajantarado [aʒãta'radu] M lunch and dinner combined

ajardinar [aʒaxdʒi'na^r] VT to make into a garden

ajeitar [aʒej'ta^r] VT (*adaptar*) to fit, adjust; (*arranjar*) to arrange, fix; **ajeitar-se** VR to adapt; **aos poucos as coisas se ajeitam** things will gradually sort themselves out

ajo *etc* ['aʒu] VB V **agir**

ajoelhado, -a [aʒwe'ʎadu, a] ADJ kneeling

ajoelhar [aʒwe'ʎa^r] VI to kneel (down); **ajoelhar-se** VR to kneel down

ajuda [a'ʒuda] F help, aid; (*subsídio*) grant, subsidy; **sem** ~ unaided; **dar** ~ **a alguém** to lend *ou* give sb a hand; ~ **de custo** allowance; **ajudante** [aʒu'dãtʃi] M/F assistant, helper; (*Mil*) adjutant

ajudar [aʒu'da^r] VT to help

ajuizado, -a [aʒwi'zadu, a] ADJ (*sensato*) sensible; (*sábio*) wise; (*prudente*) discreet

ajuizar [aʒwi'za^r] VT to judge; (*calcular*) to calculate

ajuntamento [aʒũta'mẽtu] M gathering

ajuntar [aʒũ'ta^r] VT (*unir*) to join; (*documentos*) to attach; (*reunir*) to gather

ajustagem [aʒuʃ'taʒẽ] (BR) (*pl* -**ns**) F (*Tec*) adjustment

ajustagens [aʒuʃ'taʒẽʃ] FPL *de* **ajustagem**

ajustamento [aʒuʃta'mẽtu] M adjustment; (*de contas*) settlement

ajustar [aʒuʃ'ta^r] VT (*regular*) to adjust; (*conta, disputa*) to settle; (*acomodar*) to fit; (*roupa*) to take in; (*contratar*) to contract; (*estipular*) to stipulate; (*preço*) to agree on; **ajustar-se** VR: **ajustar-se a** to conform to; (*adaptar-se*) to adapt to

ajustável [aʒuʃ'tavew] (*pl* -**eis**) ADJ adjustable; (*aplicável*) applicable

ajuste [a'ʒuʃtʃi] M (*acordo*) agreement; (*de contas*) settlement; (*adaptação*) adjustment; ~ **final** (*Com*) settlement of account

AL ABR = **Alagoas** ■ ABR F (BR: = **Aliança Liberal**) former political party

al. ABR = **Alameda**

ala ['ala] F (*fileira*) row; (*passagem*) aisle; (*de edifício*,

exército, ave) wing

Alá [a'la] M Allah

ALADI ABR F = **Associação Latino-Americana de Desenvolvimento e Intercâmbio**

alagação [alaga'sãw] F flooding

alagadiço, -a [alaga'dʒisu, a] ADJ swampy, marshy ■ M swamp, marsh

alagamento [alaga'mẽtu] M flooding; (*arrasamento*) destruction

alagar [ala'ga^r] VT, VI to flood

alagoano, -a [ala'gwanu, a] ADJ from Alagoas ■ M/F native *ou* inhabitant of Alagoas

alambique [alã'biki] M still

alameda [ala'meda] F (*avenida*) avenue; (*arvoredo*) grove

álamo ['alamu] M poplar

alanhar [ala'ɲa^r] VT to slash; (*peixe*) to gut

alar [a'la^r] VT to haul, heave

alaranjado, -a [alarã'ʒadu, a] ADJ orangy

alarde [a'laxdʒi] M (*ostentação*) ostentation; (*jactância*) boasting; **fazer** ~ **de** to boast about; **alardear** [alax'dʒia^r] VT to show off; (*gabar-se de*) to boast of ■ VI to boast; **alardear-se** VR to boast; **alardear fazer** to boast of doing; **alardear(-se) de valente** to boast of being strong

alargamento [alaxga'mẽtu] M enlargement

alargar [alax'ga^r] VT (*ampliar*) to extend; (*fazer mais largo*) to widen, broaden; (*afrouxar*) to loosen, slacken

alarido [ala'ridu] M (*clamor*) outcry; (*tumulto*) uproar

alarma [a'laxma] F alarm; (*susto*) panic; (*tumulto*) tumult; (*vozearia*) outcry; **dar o sinal de** ~ to raise the alarm; ~ **de roubo** burglar alarm; **alarmante** [alax'mãtʃi] ADJ alarming; **alarmar** [alax'ma^r] VT to alarm; **alarmar-se** VR to be alarmed

alarme [a'laxmi] M = **alarma**

alarmista [alax'miʃta] ADJ, M/F alarmist

Alasca [a'laʃka] M: **o** ~ Alaska

alastrado, -a [alaʃ'tradu, a] ADJ: ~ **de** strewn with

alastrar [alaʃ'tra^r] VT (*espalhar*) to scatter; (*disseminar*) to spread; (*lastrar*) to ballast; **alastrar-se** VR (*epidemia, rumor*) to spread

alavanca [ala'vãka] F lever; (*pé-de-cabra*) crowbar; ~ **de mudanças** gear lever

albanês, -esa [awba'neʃ, eza] ADJ, M/F Albanian ■ M (*Ling*) Albanian

Albânia [aw'banja] F: **a** ~ Albania

albergar [awbex'ga^r] VT (*hospedar*) to provide lodging for; (*abrigar*) to shelter

albergue [aw'bexgi] M (*estalagem*) inn; (*refúgio*) hospice, shelter; ~ **noturno** hotel; ~ **para jovens** youth hostel

albino, -a [aw'binu, a] ADJ, M/F albino

albufeira [awbu'fejra] F lagoon

álbum ['awbũ] (*pl* -**ns**) M album; ~ **de recortes** scrapbook

alça ['awsa] F strap; (*asa*) handle; (*de fusil*) sight

alcácer [aw'kase^r] M fortress

alcachofra [awka'ʃofra] F artichoke
alcaçuz [awka'suʒ] M liquorice
alçada [aw'sada] F *(jurisdição)* jurisdiction; *(competência)* competence; **isso não é da minha ~** that is beyond my control
alcagüete [awka'gwetʃi] M/F informer
álcali ['awkali] M alkali
alcalino, -a [awka'linu, a] ADJ alkaline
alcançar [awkã'saʳ] VT to reach; *(estender)* to hand, pass; *(obter)* to obtain, get; *(atingir)* to attain; *(compreender)* to understand; *(desfalcar)*: **~ uma firma em $1 milhão** to embezzle $1 million from a firm ■ VI to reach; **alcançar-se** VR *(fazer um desfalque)* to embezzle funds
alcançável [awkã'savew] *(pl -eis)* ADJ *(acessível)* reachable; *(atingível)* attainable
alcance [aw'kãsi] M reach; *(competência)* power, competence; *(compreensão)* understanding; *(de tiro, visão)* range; *(desfalque)* embezzlement; **ao ~ de** within reach *ou* range of; **ao ~ da voz** within earshot; **de grande ~** far-reaching; **fora do ~ da mão** out of reach; **fora do ~ de alguém** beyond sb's grasp
alcantilado, -a [awkãtʃi'ladu, a] ADJ *(íngreme)* steep; *(penhascoso)* craggy
alçapão [awsa'pãw] *(pl -ões)* M trapdoor; *(urapuca)* trap
alcaparra [awka'paxa] F caper
alçapões [awsa'põjʃ] MPL *de* **alçapão**
alçaprema [awsa'prɛma] F *(alavanca)* crowbar
alçar [aw'saʳ] VT to lift (up); *(voz)* to raise; **~ vôo** to take off
alcaravia [awkara'via] F: **sementes de ~** caraway seeds
alcatéia [awka'tɛja] F *(de lobos)* pack; *(de ladrões)* gang
alcatra [aw'katra] F rump (steak)
alcatrão [awka'trãw] M tar
álcool ['awkɔw] M alcohol; **alcoólatra** [aw'kɔlatra] M/F alcoholic; **alcoólico, -a** [aw'kɔliku, a] ADJ, M/F alcoholic
alcoolismo [awko'liʒmu] M alcoholism
Alcorão [awko'rãw] M Koran
alcova [aw'kova] F bedroom
alcoviteiro, -a [awkovi'tejru, a] M/F pimp/procuress
alcunha [aw'kuɲa] F nickname
aldeão, -deã [aw'dʒãw, jã] *(pl -ões/-s)* M/F villager
aldeia [aw'deja] F village
aldeões [aw'dʒõjʃ] MPL *de* **aldeão**
aldraba [aw'draba] F (PT: *tranqueta*) latch; *(de bater)* door knocker
aleatório, -a [alea'tɔrju, a] ADJ random
alecrim [ale'krĩ] M rosemary
alegação [alega'sãw] *(pl -ões)* F allegation
alegado [ale'gadu] M *(Jur)* plea
alegar [ale'gaʳ] VT to allege; *(Jur)* to plead
alegoria [alego'ria] F allegory

alegórico, -a [ale'gɔriku, a] ADJ allegorical; **carro ~** float
alegrar [ale'graʳ] VT *(tornar feliz)* to cheer (up), gladden; *(ambiente)* to brighten up; *(animar)* to liven (up); **alegrar-se** VR to cheer up
alegre [a'lɛgri] ADJ *(jovial)* cheerful; *(contente)* happy, glad; *(cores)* bright; *(embriagado)* merry, tight; **alegria** [ale'gria] F joy, happiness
aleguei *etc* [ale'gej] VB *v* **alegar**
aléia [a'lɛja] F (tree-lined) avenue; *(passagem)* alley
aleijado, -a [alej'ʒadu, a] ADJ crippled ■ M/F cripple
aleijão [alej'ʒãw] *(pl -ões)* M deformity
aleijar [alej'ʒaʳ] VT *(mutilar)* to maim
aleijões [alej'ʒõjʃ] MPL *de* **aleijão**
aleitamento [alejta'mētu] M breast feeding
aleitar [alej'taʳ] VT, VI to breast-feed
além [a'lēj] ADV *(lá ao longe)* over there; *(mais adiante)* further on ■ M: **o ~** the hereafter ■ PREP: **~ de** beyond; *(no outro lado de)* on the other side of; *(para mais de)* over; *(ademais de)* apart from, besides; **~ disso** moreover; **mais ~** further
alemã [ale'mã] F *de* **alemão**
alemães [ale'mãjʃ] MPL *de* **alemão**
Alemanha [ale'maɲa] F: **a ~** Germany; **a ~ Ocidental/Oriental** West/East Germany
alemão, -mã [ale'mãw, 'mã] *(pl -ães/-s)* ADJ, M/F German ■ M *(Ling)* German
alentado, -a [alē'tadu, a] ADJ *(valente)* valiant; *(grande)* great; *(volumoso)* substantial
alentador, -a [alēta'doʳ(a)] ADJ encouraging
alentar [alē'taʳ] VT to encourage; **alentar-se** VR to cheer up
alentejano, -a [alēte'ʒanu, a] ADJ from Alentejo ■ M/F native *ou* inhabitant of Alentejo
alento [a'lētu] M *(fôlego)* breath; *(ânimo)* courage; **dar ~** to encourage; **tomar ~** to draw breath
alergia [alex'ʒia] F: **~ (a)** allergy (to); *(fig)* aversion (to); **alérgico, -a** [a'lɛxʒiku, a] ADJ: **alérgico (a)** allergic (to)
alerta [a'lɛxta] ADJ alert ■ ADV on the alert ■ M alert
alertar [alex'taʳ] VT to alert; **alertar-se** VR to be alerted
Alf. ABR = **Alferes**
alfabético, -a [awfa'bɛtʃiku, a] ADJ alphabetical
alfabetização [awfabetʃiza'sãw] F literacy
alfabetizado, -a [awfabetʃi'zadu, a] ADJ literate
alfabetizar [awfabetʃi'zaʳ] VT to teach to read and write; **alfabetizar-se** VR to learn to read and write
alfabeto [awfa'bɛtu] M alphabet
alface [aw'fasi] F lettuce
alfaia [aw'faja] F *(móveis)* furniture; *(utensílio)* utensil; *(enfeite)* ornament
alfaiataria [awfajata'ria] F tailor's shop
alfaiate [awfa'jatʃi] M tailor

NB: *European Portuguese adds the following consonants to certain words:* **b** (sú(b)dito, su(b)til); **c** (a(c)ção, a(c)cionista, a(c)to); **m** (inde(m)ne); **p** (ado(p)çã, ado(p)tar); *for further details see p. xiii.*

alfândega [aw'fãdʒiga] F customs pl, customs house; **alfandegário, -a** [awfãde'garju, a] ADJ customs atr ▪ M/F customs officer
alfanumérico, -a [awfanu'mɛriku, a] ADJ alphanumeric
alfavaca [awfa'vaka] F basil
alfazema [awfa'zɛma] F lavender
alfena [aw'fɛna] F privet
alfinetada [awfine'tada] F prick; (dor aguda) stabbing pain; (fig) dig
alfinetar [awfine'ta^r] VT to prick (with a pin); (costura) to pin; (fig) to needle
alfinete [awfi'netʃi] M pin; ~ **de chapéu** hat pin; ~ **de fralda** nappy (Brit) ou diaper (US) pin; ~ **de segurança** safety pin
alfineteira [awfine'tejra] F pin cushion; (caixa) pin box
alga ['awga] F seaweed; (Bot) alga
algarismo [awga'riʒmu] M numeral, digit; ~ **arábico/romano** Arabic/Roman numeral
Algarve [aw'gaxvi] M: **o** ~ the Algarve
algarvio, -a [awgax'viu, a] ADJ from the Algarve ▪ M/F native ou inhabitant of the Algarve
algazarra [awga'zaxa] F uproar, racket
álgebra ['awʒebra] F algebra
algemar [awʒe'ma^r] VT to handcuff
algemas [aw'ʒemaʃ] FPL handcuffs
algibeira [awʒi'bejra] F pocket
algo ['awgu] ADV somewhat, rather ▪ PRON something; (qualquer coisa) anything
algodão [awgo'dãw] M cotton; ~(-**doce**) candy floss; ~ (**hidrófilo**) cotton wool (Brit), absorbent cotton (US)
algodoeiro, -a [awgo'dwejru, a] ADJ (indústria) cotton atr ▪ M cotton plant
algoritmo [awgo'xitʃimu] M algorithm
algoz [aw'gɔʒ] M beast, cruel person
alguém [aw'gẽj] PRON someone, somebody; (em frases interrogativas ou negativas) anyone, anybody; **ser** ~ **na vida** to be somebody in life
algum, a [aw'gũ, 'guma] ADJ some; (em frases interrogativas ou negativas) any ▪ PRON one; (no plural) some; (negativa): **de modo** ~ in no way; **coisa ~a** nothing; ~ **dia** one day; ~ **tempo** for a while; ~**a coisa** something; ~**a vez** sometime
algures [aw'guriʃ] ADV somewhere
alheio, -a [a'ʎeju, a] ADJ (de outrem) someone else's; (estranho) alien; (estrangeiro) foreign; (impróprio) inappropriate; ~ **a** foreign to; (desatento) unaware of; ~ **de** (afastado) removed from, far from; (ignorante) unaware of
alho ['aʎu] M garlic; **confundir** ~**s com bugalhos** to get things mixed up
alho-poró [-po'rɔ] (pl **alhos-porós**) M leek
ali [a'li] ADV there; **até** ~ up to there; **por** ~ around there, somewhere there; (direção) that way; ~ **por** (tempo) round about; **de** ~ **por diante** from then on; ~ **dentro** in there
aliado, -a [a'ljadu, a] ADJ allied ▪ M/F ally
aliança [a'ljãsa] F alliance; (anel) wedding ring
aliar [a'lja^r] VT to ally; **aliar-se** VR to form an alliance

aliás [a'ljajʃ] ADV (a propósito) as a matter of fact; (ou seja) rather, that is; (contudo) nevertheless; (diga-se de passagem) incidentally
álibi ['alibi] M alibi
alicate [ali'katʃi] M pliers pl; ~ **de unhas** nail clippers pl
alicerçar [alisex'sa^r] VT (argumento etc) to base; (consolidar) to consolidate
alicerce [ali'sɛxsi] M (de edifício) foundation; (fig: base) basis
aliciar [ali'sja^r] VT (seduzir) to entice; (atrair) to attract
alienação [aljena'sãw] F alienation; (de bens) transfer (of property); ~ **mental** insanity
alienado, -a [alje'nadu, a] ADJ alienated; (demente) insane; (bens) transferred ▪ M/F lunatic
alienar [alje'na^r] VT (bens) to transfer; (afastar) to alienate; **alienar-se** VR to become alienated
alienígena [alje'niʒena] ADJ, M/F alien
alijar [ali'ʒa^r] VT to jettison; (livrar-se de): **to get rid of**; **alijar-se** VR: **alijar-se de** to free o.s. of
alimentação [alimẽta'sãw] F (alimentos) food; (ação) feeding; (nutrição) nourishment; (Elet) supply
alimentar [alimẽ'ta^r] VT to feed; (fig) to nurture ▪ ADJ (produto) food atr; (hábitos) eating atr; **alimentar-se** VR: **alimentar-se de** to feed on
alimentício, -a [alimẽ'tʃisju, a] ADJ nourishing; **gêneros** ~**s** foodstuffs
alimento [ali'mẽtu] M food; (nutrição) nourishment
alínea [a'linja] F opening line of a paragraph; (subdivisão de artigo) sub-heading
alinhado, -a [ali'ɲadu, a] ADJ (elegante) elegant; (texto) aligned; ~ **à esquerda/direita** (texto) ranged left/right
alinhamento [aliɲa'mẽtu] M alignment; ~ **da margem** justification
alinhar [ali'ɲa^r] VT to align; **alinhar-se** VR (enfileirar-se) to form a line
alinhavar [aliɲa'va^r] VT (Costura) to tack
alinhavo [ali'ɲavu] M tacking
alinho [a'liɲu] M (alinhamento) alignment; (elegância) neatness
alíquota [a'likwota] F bracket, percentage
alisar [ali'za^r] VT (tornar liso) to smooth; (cabelo) to straighten; (cariciar) to stroke
alistamento [aliʃta'mẽtu] M enlistment
alistar [aliʃ'ta^r] VT (Mil) to recruit; **alistar-se** VR to enlist
aliteração [alitera'sãw] F alliteration
aliviado, -a [ali'vj'adu, a] ADJ (pessoa, dor) relieved; (folgado) free; (carga) lightened
aliviar [ali'vja^r] VT to relieve; (carga etc) to lighten ▪ VI (diminuir) to diminish; (acalmar) to give relief; **aliviar-se** VR: **aliviar-se de** (libertar-se) to unburden o.s. of
alívio [a'livju] M relief
Alm. ABR = **Almirante**
alma ['awma] F soul; (entusiasmo) enthusiasm; (caráter) character; **eu daria a** ~ **para fazer** I

would give anything to do; **sua ~, sua palma** don't say I didn't warn you

almanaque [awma'naki] M almanac; **cultura de ~** superficial knowledge

almejar [awme'ʒaʳ] VT to long for, yearn for

almirantado [awmirã'tadu] M admiralty

almirante [awmi'rãtʃi] M admiral

almoçado, -a [awmo'sadu, a] ADJ: **ele está ~** he's had lunch

almoçar [awmo'saʳ] VI to have lunch ■ VT: **~ peixe** to have fish for lunch

almoço [aw'mosu] M lunch; **pequeno ~** (PT) breakfast

almofada [awmo'fada] F cushion; (PT: *travesseiro*) pillow

almofadado, -a [awmofa'dadu, a] ADJ cushioned

almofadinha [awmofa'dʒiɲa] F pin cushion

almôndega [aw'mõdega] F meat ball

almotolia [awmoto'lia] F oilcan

almoxarifado [awmoʃari'fadu] M storeroom

almoxarife [awmoʃa'rifi] M storekeeper

ALN (BR) ABR F (= *Ação Libertadora Nacional*) *former group opposed to junta*

alô [a'lo] (BR) EXCL (*Tel*) hullo

alocação [aloka'sãw] (*pl* -ões) F allocation

alocar [alo'kaʳ] VT to allocate

aloirado, -a [aloj'radu, a] ADJ = **alourado**

alojamento [aloʒa'mẽtu] M accommodation (*Brit*), accommodations *pl* (*US*); (*habitação*) housing; (*Mil*) billet

alojar [alo'ʒaʳ] VT to lodge; (*Mil*) to billet; **alojar-se** VR to stay

alongamento [alõga'mẽtu] M lengthening; (*prazo*) extension; (*ginástica*) stretching

alongar [alõ'gaʳ] VT (*fazer longo*) to lengthen; (*prazo*) to extend; (*prolongar*) to prolong; (*braço*) to stretch out; **alongar-se** VR (*sobre um assunto*) to dwell

aloprado, -a [alo'pradu, a] (*col*) ADJ nutty

alourado, -a [alo'radu, a] ADJ blondish

alpaca [aw'paka] F alpaca

alpendre [aw'pẽdri] M (*telheiro*) shed; (*pórtico*) porch

alpercata [awpex'kata] F sandal

Alpes ['awpiʃ] MPL: **os ~** the Alps

alpinismo [awpi'niʒmu] M mountaineering, climbing; **alpinista** [awpi'niʃta] M/F mountaineer, climber

alq. ABR = **alqueires**

alquebrar [awke'braʳ] VT to bend; (*enfraquecer*) to weaken ■ VI (*curvar*) to stoop, be bent double

alqueire [aw'kejri] M ≈ 4.84 hectares (*in São Paulo* = *2.42 hectares*)

alqueive [aw'kejvi] M fallow land

alquimia [awki'mia] F alchemy

alquimista [awki'miʃta] M/F alchemist

Alsácia [aw'sasja] F: **a ~** Alsace

alta ['awta] F (*de preços*) rise; (*de hospital*)

discharge; (*Bolsa*) high; **estar em ~** to be on the up; **pessoa da ~** high-class *ou* high-society person

alta-fidelidade F hi-fi, high fidelity

altaneiro, -a [awta'nejru, a] ADJ (*soberbo*) proud

altar [aw'taʳ] M altar

altar-mor [-mɔʳ] (*pl* **altares-mores**) M high altar

alta-roda F high society

alta-tensão F high tension

altear [aw'tʃaʳ] VT to raise; (*reputação*) to enhance ■ VI to spread out; **altear-se** VR to be enhanced

alteração [awtera'sãw] (*pl* -ões) F alteration; (*desordem*) disturbance; (*falsificação*) falsification

alterado, -a [awte'radu, a] ADJ (*de mau humor*) bad-tempered, irritated

alterar [awte'raʳ] VT (*mudar*) to alter; (*falsificar*) to falsify; **alterar-se** VR (*mudar-se*) to become altered; (*enfurecer-se*) to get angry, lose one's temper

altercar [awtex'kaʳ] VI to have an altercation ■ VT to argue for, advocate

alter ego [awter-] M alter ego

alternado, -a [awtex'nadu, a] ADJ alternate

alternância [awtex'nãsja] F (*Agr*) crop rotation

alternar [awtex'naʳ] VT, VI to alternate; **alternar-se** VR to alternate; (*por turnos*) to take turns

alternativa [awtexna'tʃiva] F alternative

alternativo, -a [awtexna'tʃivu, a] ADJ alternative; (*Elet*) alternating

alteroso, -a [awte'rozu, ɔza] ADJ towering; (*majestoso*) majestic

alteza [aw'teza] F highness

altissonante [awtʃiso'nãtʃi] ADJ high-sounding

altista [aw'tʃiʃta] M/F (*Bolsa*) bull ■ ADJ (*tendência*) bullish; **mercado ~** bull market

altitude [awtʃi'tudʒi] F altitude

altivez [awtʃi'veʒ] F (*arrogância*) haughtiness; (*nobreza*) loftiness

altivo, -a [aw'tʃivu, a] ADJ (*arrogante*) haughty; (*elevado*) lofty

alto, -a ['awtu, a] ADJ high; (*pessoa*) tall; (*som*) high, sharp; (*importância, luxo*) great; (*Geo*) upper ■ ADV (*falar*) loudly, loud; (*voar*) high ■ EXCL halt! ■ M (*topo*) top, summit; **~ lá!** just a minute!; **do ~** from above; **por ~** superficially; **estar ~** (*bêbado*) to be tipsy; **alta fidelidade** high fidelity, hi-fi; **alta noite** dead of night; **~s e baixos** ups and downs

alto-astral (*col*) M good vibes *pl*; **estar de ~** to be on good form

alto-falante (*pl* -s) M loudspeaker

altruísmo [awtru'iʒmu] M altruism

altruísta [awtru'iʃta] ADJ altruistic

altruístico, -a [awtru'iʃtʃiku, a] ADJ altruistic

altura [aw'tura] F height; (*momento*) point, juncture; (*altitude*) altitude; (*de um som*) pitch; (*lugar*) whereabouts; **em que ~ da Rio Branco**

NB: *European Portuguese adds the following consonants to certain words:* **b** (sú(b)dito, su(b)til); **c** (a(c)ção, a(c)cionista, a(c)to); **m** (inde(m)ne); **p** (ado(p)ção, ado(p)tar); *for further details see p. xiii.*

fica a livraria? whereabouts in Rio Branco is the bookshop?; **na ~ do banco** near the bank; **nesta ~** at this juncture; **estar à ~ de** (*ser capaz de*) to be up to; **pôr alguém nas ~s** (*fig*) to praise sb to the skies; **ter 1.80 metros de ~** to be 1.80 metres (*Brit*) *ou* meters (*US*) tall

alucinação [alusina'sãw] (*pl* -ões) F hallucination

alucinado, -a [alusi'nadu, a] ADJ (*maluco*) crazy; **~ por** crazy about

alucinante [alusi'nãtʃi] ADJ crazy; **o tráfego no Rio é ~** the traffic in Rio drives you crazy

aludir [alu'dʒiʳ] VI: **~ a** to allude to, hint at

alugar [alu'gaʳ] VT (*tomar de aluguel*) to rent, hire; (*dar de aluguel*) to let, rent out; **alugar-se** VR to let; **aluguel** [alu'gɛw] (*pl* -éis) (BR) M rent; (*ação*) renting; **aluguel de carro** car hire (*Brit*) *ou* rental (*US*)

aluguer [alu'gɛʳ] (PT) M = **aluguel**

aluir [a'lwiʳ] VT (*abalar*) to shake; (*derrubar*) to demolish; (*arruinar*) to ruin ■ VI to collapse; (*ameaçar ruína*) to crumble

alumiar [alu'mjaʳ] VT to light (up) ■ VI to give light

alumínio [alu'minju] M aluminium (*Brit*), aluminum (*US*)

alunissagem [aluni'saʒẽ] (*pl* -ns) F moon landing

alunissar [aluni'saʳ] VI to land on the moon

aluno, -a [a'lunu, a] M/F pupil, student; **~ excepcional** pupil with learning difficulties

alusão [alu'zãw] (*pl* -ões) F allusion, reference

alusivo, -a [alu'zivu, a] ADJ allusive

alusões [alu'zõjʃ] FPL *de* **alusão**

alvará [awva'ra] M permit

alvejante [awve'ʒãtʃi] M bleach

alvejar [awve'ʒaʳ] VT (*tomar como alvo*) to aim at; (*branquear*) to whiten, bleach ■ VI to whiten

alvenaria [awvena'ria] F masonry, brickwork; **de ~** brick *atr*, brick-built

alvéolo [aw'vɛolu] M cavity; (*de dentes*) socket

alvitrar [awvi'traʳ] VT to propose, suggest

alvitre [aw'vitri] M opinion

alvo, -a ['awvu, a] ADJ white ■ M target; **acertar no** *ou* **atingir o ~** to hit the mark; **ser ~ de críticas** *etc* to be the object of criticism *etc*

alvorada [awvo'rada] F dawn

alvorecer [awvore'seʳ] VI to dawn

alvoroçar [awvoro'saʳ] VT (*agitar*) to stir up; (*entusiasmar*) to excite; **alvoroçar-se** VR to get agitated

alvoroço [awvo'rosu] M (*agitação*) commotion; (*entusiasmo*) enthusiasm

alvura [aw'vura] F (*brancura*) whiteness; (*pureza*) purity

AM ABR = **Amazonas**; (*Rádio:* = *amplitude modulada*) AM

Amã [a'mã] N Amman

amabilidade [amabili'dadʒi] F kindness; (*simpatia*) friendliness

amabilíssimo, -a [amabi'lisimu, a] ADJ SUPERL *de* **amável**

amaciante [ama'sjãtʃi] M: **~ (de roupa)** (*fabric*) conditioner

amaciar [ama'sjaʳ] VT (*tornar macio*) to soften; (*carro*) to run in

ama-de-leite ['ama-] (*pl* **amas-de-leite**) F wet-nurse

amado, -a [a'madu, a] M/F beloved, sweetheart

amador, a [ama'do(a)] ADJ, M/F amateur

amadorismo [amado'riʒmu] M amateur status

amadorístico, -a [amado'riʃtʃiku, a] ADJ amateurish

amadurecer [amadure'seʳ] VT, VI (*frutos*) to ripen; (*fig*) to mature

âmago ['amagu] M (*centro*) heart, core; (*medula*) pith; (*essência*) essence

amainar [amaj'naʳ] VI (*tempestade*) to abate; (*cólera*) to calm down

amaldiçoar [amawdʒi'swaʳ] VT to curse, swear at

amálgama [a'mawgama] F amalgam

amalgamar [amawga'maʳ] VT to amalgamate; (*combinar*) to fuse (*Brit*), fuze (*US*), blend

amalucado, -a [amalu'kadu, a] ADJ crazy, whacky

amamentação [amamẽta'sãw] F breast-feeding

amamentar [amamẽ'taʳ] VT, VI to breast-feed

AMAN (BR) ABR F = **Academia Militar das Agulhas Negras**

amanhã [ama'ɲã] ADV, M tomorrow; **~ de manhã** tomorrow morning; **~ de tarde** tomorrow afternoon; **~ à noite** tomorrow night; **depois de ~** the day after tomorrow

amanhecer [amaɲe'seʳ] VI (*alvorecer*) to dawn; (*encontrar-se pela manhã*): **amanhecemos em Paris** we were in Paris at daybreak ■ M dawn; **ao ~** at daybreak

amansar [amã'saʳ] VT (*animais*) to tame; (*cavalos*) to break in; (*aplacar*) to placate ■ VI to grow tame

amante [a'mãtʃi] M/F lover

amanteigado, -a [amãtej'gadu, a] ADJ: **biscoito ~** shortbread

amapaense [amapa'ẽsi] ADJ from Amapá ■ M/F native *ou* inhabitant of Amapá

amar [a'maʳ] VT to love; **eu te amo** I love you

amarelado, -a [amare'ladu, a] ADJ yellowish; (*pele*) sallow

amarelar [amare'laʳ] VT, VI to yellow

amarelinha [amare'liɲa] F (*jogo*) hopscotch

amarelo, -a [ama'rɛlu, a] ADJ yellow ■ M yellow

amarfanhar [amaxfa'ɲaʳ] VT to screw up

amargar [amax'gaʳ] VT to make bitter; (*fig*) to embitter; (*sofrer*) to suffer; **ser de ~** to be murder

amargo, -a [a'maxgu, a] ADJ bitter; **amargura** [amax'gura] F bitterness; (*fig: sofrimento*) sadness, suffering

amargurado, -a [amaxgu'radu, a] ADJ sad

amargurar [amaxgu'raʳ] VT to embitter, sadden; (*sofrer*) to endure

amarração [amaxa'sãw] F: **ser uma ~** (*col*) to

be great

amarrado, -a [ama'xadu, a] ADJ *(cara)* scowling, angry; *(col: casado etc)* spoken for

amarrar [ama'xaʳ] VT to tie (up); *(Náut)* to moor; **amarrar-se** VR: **amarrar se em** to like very much; **~ a cara** to frown, scowl

amarronzado, -a [amaxõ'zadu, a] ADJ brownish

amarrotar [amaxo'taʳ] VT to crease

ama-seca ['ama-] *(pl* **amas-secas)** F nanny

amassado, -a [ama'sadu, a] ADJ *(roupa)* creased; *(papel)* screwed up; *(carro)* smashed in

amassar [ama'saʳ] VT *(pão)* to knead; *(misturar)* to mix; *(papel)* to screw up; *(roupa)* to crease; *(carro)* to dent

amável [a'mavew] *(pl* **-eis)** ADJ *(afável)* kind

amazona [ama'zɔna] F horsewoman

Amazonas [ama'zɔnaʃ] M: **o ~** the Amazon

amazonense [amazo'nẽsi] ADJ from Amazonas ■ M/F native *ou* inhabitant of Amazonas

Amazônia [ama'zonja] F: **a ~** the Amazon region

● **AMAZÔNIA**

Amazônia is the region formed by the basin of the river Amazon (the river with the largest volume of water in the world) and its tributaries. With a total area of almost 7 million square kilometres, it stretches from the Atlantic to the Andes. Most of *Amazônia* is in Brazilian territory, although it also extends into Peru, Colombia, Venezuela and Bolivia. It contains the richest biodiversity and largest area of tropical rainforest in the world.

amazônico, -a [ama'zoniku, a] ADJ Amazonian

âmbar ['ãbaʳ] M amber

ambição [ambi'sãw] *(pl* **-ões)** F ambition; **ambicionar** [ãbisjo'naʳ] VT *(ter ambição de)* to aspire to; *(desejar)* to crave for; **ambicioso, -a** [ãbi'sjozu, ɔza] ADJ ambitious

ambições [ãbi'sõjʃ] FPL *de* **ambição**

ambidestro, -a [ãbi'deʃtru, a] ADJ ambidextrous

ambiental [ãbjẽ'taw] *(pl* **-ais)** ADJ environmental

ambientalista [ãbjẽta'liʃta] M/F environmentalist

ambientar [ãbjẽ'taʳ] VT *(filme etc)* to set; *(adaptar)* to fit in; **ambientar-se** VR to fit in

ambiente [ã'bjẽtʃi] M atmosphere; *(meio, Comput)* environment; *(de uma casa)* ambience ■ ADJ surrounding; **meio ~** environment; **temperatura ~** room temperature

ambigüidade [ambigwi'dadʃi] F ambiguity

ambíguo, -a [ã'bigwu, a] ADJ ambiguous

âmbito ['ãbitu] M *(extensão)* extent; *(campo de ação)* scope, range; **no ~ nacional/**

internacional at (the) national/international level

ambivalência [ãbiva'lẽsja] F ambivalence

ambivalente [ãbiva'lẽtʃi] ADJ ambivalent

ambos, -as ['ãbuʃ, aʃ] ADJ PL both; **~ nós** both of us; **~ os lados** both sides

ambrosia [ãbro'zia] F egg custard

ambulância [ãbu'lãsja] F ambulance

ambulante [ãbu'lãtʃi] ADJ walking; *(errante)* wandering; *(biblioteca)* mobile

ambulatório [ãbula'tɔrju] M outpatient department

ameaça [ame'asa] F threat

ameaçador, a [ameasa'doʳ(a)] ADJ threatening, menacing

ameaçar [amea'saʳ] VT to threaten

ameba [a'mɛba] F amoeba *(Brit)*, ameba *(US)*

amedrontador, a [amedrõta'doʳ(a)] ADJ intimidating, frightening

amedrontar [amedrõ'taʳ] VT to scare, intimidate; **amedrontar-se** VR to be frightened

ameia [a'meja] F battlement

ameixa [a'mejʃa] F plum; *(passa)* prune

amélia [a'mɛlja] *(col)* F long-suffering wife *(ou* girlfriend)

amém [a'mẽj] EXCL amen; **dizer ~ a** *(fig)* to agree to

amêndoa [a'mẽdwa] F almond

amendoado, -a [amẽ'dwadu, a] ADJ *(olhos)* almond-shaped

amendoeira [amẽ'dwejra] F almond tree

amendoim [amẽdo'ĩ] *(pl* **-ns)** M peanut

amenidade [ameni'dadʒi] F wellbeing; **amenidades** FPL *(assuntos superficiais)* small talk *sg*

amenizar [ameni'zaʳ] VT *(abrandar)* to soften; *(tornar agradável)* to make pleasant; *(facilitar)* to ease; *(briga)* to settle

ameno, -a [a'mɛnu, a] ADJ *(agradável)* pleasant; *(clima)* mild, gentle

América [a'mɛrika] F: **a ~** America; **a ~ do Norte/do Sul** North/South America; **a ~ Central/Latina** Central/Latin America

americanizado, -a [amerikani'zadu, a] ADJ Americanized

americano, -a [ameri'kanu, a] ADJ, M/F American

amesquinhar [ameʃki'ɲaʳ] VT to belittle; **amesquinhar-se** VR to belittle o.s.; *(tornar-se avarento)* to become stingy

amestrar [ameʃ'traʳ] VT to train

ametista [ame'tʃiʃta] F amethyst

amianto [a'mjãtu] M asbestos

amicíssimo, -a [ami'sisimu, a] ADJ SUPERL *de* **amigo**

amido [a'midu] M starch

amigar-se [ami'gaxsi] VR: **~ (com)** to become friends (with)

amigável [ami'gavew] *(pl* -eis) ADJ amicable

amígdala [a'migdala] F tonsil; **amigdalite** [amigda'litʃi] F tonsillitis

amigo, -a [a'migu, a] ADJ friendly ■ M/F friend; **ser ~ de** to be friends with; **~ do peito** bosom friend

amigo, -a-da-onça *(pl* -s/as-da-onça) M/F false friend

amistoso, -a [amiʃ'tozu, ɔza] ADJ friendly, cordial ■ M *(jogo)* friendly

AMIU (BR) ABR F *(= Assistência Médica Infantil de Urgencia) emergency paediatric service*

amiudar [amju'daʳ] VT, VI to repeat; **~ as visitas** to make frequent visits

amiúde [a'mjudʒi] ADV often, frequently

amizade [ami'zadʒi] F *(relação)* friendship; *(simpatia)* friendliness; **fazer ~s** to make friends; **~ colorida** casual relationship

amnésia [am'nɛzja] F amnesia

amnistia [amniʃ'tia] (PT) F = **anistia**

amofinar [amofi'naʳ] VT to trouble; **amofinar-se (com)** VR to fret (over)

amolação [amola'sãw] *(pl* -ões) F bother, annoyance; *(desgosto)* upset

amolador, a [amola'doʳ(a)] M/F knife sharpener

amolante [amo'lãtʃi] (BR) ADJ bothersome

amolar [amo'laʳ] VT *(afiar)* to sharpen; *(aborrecer)* to annoy, bother ■ VI to be annoying; **amolar-se** VR *(aborrecer-se)* to get annoyed

amoldar [amow'daʳ] VT to mould *(Brit),* mold (US); **amoldar-se** VR: **amoldar-se a** *(conformar-se)* to conform to; *(acostumar-se)* to get used to

amolecer [amole'seʳ] VT to soften ■ VI to soften; *(abrandar-se)* to relent

amolecimento [amolesi'mẽtu] M softening

amônia [a'monja] F ammonia

amoníaco [amo'niaku] M ammonia

amontoado [amõ'twadu] M mass; *(de coisas)* pile

amontoar [amõ'twaʳ] VT to pile up, accumulate; **~ riquezas** to amass a fortune

amor [a'moʳ] M love; **por ~ de** for the sake of; **fazer ~** to make love; **ela é um ~ (de pessoa)** she's a lovely person; **~ próprio** self-esteem; *(orgulho)* conceit

amora [a'mɔra] F mulberry; **~ silvestre** blackberry

amoral [amo'raw] *(pl* -ais) ADJ amoral

amora-preta *(pl* amoras-pretas) F blackberry

amordaçar [amoxda'saʳ] VT to gag

amoreco [amo'rɛku] M: **ela é um ~** she's a lovely person

amorenado, -a [amore'nadu, a] ADJ darkish

amorfo, -a [a'mɔxfu, a] ADJ *(objeto)* amorphous; *(pessoa)* dull

amornar [amox'naʳ] VT to warm

amoroso, -a [amo'rozu, ɔza] ADJ loving, affectionate

amor-perfeito *(pl* amores-perfeitos) M pansy

amortecedor [amoxtese'doʳ] M shock absorber

amortecer [amoxte'seʳ] VT to deaden ■ VI to weaken, fade

amortecido, -a [amoxte'sidu, a] ADJ deadened; *(enfraquecido)* weak

amortização [amoxtʃiza'sãw] F payment in instalments *(Brit) ou* installments (US); *(Com)* amortization

amortizar [amoxtʃi'zaʳ] VT to pay in instalments *(Brit) ou* installments (US)

amostra [a'mɔʃtra] F sample

amostragem [amoʃ'traʒẽ] F sampling

amotinado, -a [amotʃi'nadu, a] ADJ mutinous, rebellious

amotinar [amotʃi'naʳ] VI to rebel, mutiny; **amotinar-se** VR to rebel, mutiny

amparar [ãpa'raʳ] VT to support; *(ajudar)* to assist; **amparar-se** VR: **amparar-se em/contra** *(apoiar-se)* to lean on/against

amparo [ã'paru] M *(apoio)* support; *(auxílio)* help, assistance

ampère [ã'pɛri] (BR) M ampere, amp

ampliação [amplja'sãw] *(pl* -ões) F *(aumento)* enlargement; *(extensão)* extension

ampliar [ã'pljaʳ] VT to enlarge; *(conhecimento)* to broaden

amplidão [ãpli'dãw] F vastness

amplificação [ãplifika'sãw] *(pl* -ões) F *(aumento)* enlargement; *(de som)* amplification

amplificador [ãplifika'doʳ] M amplifier

amplificar [ãplifi'kaʳ] VT to amplify

amplitude [ãpli'tudʒi] F *(Tec)* amplitude; *(espaço)* spaciousness; *(fig: extensão)* extent

amplo, -a ['ãplu, a] ADJ *(sala)* spacious; *(conhecimento, sentido)* broad; *(possibilidade)* ample

ampola [ã'pola] F ampoule *(Brit),* ampule (US)

amputação [ãputa'sãw] *(pl* -ões) F amputation

amputar [ãpu'taʳ] VT to amputate

Amsterdã [amiʃtex'dã] (BR) N Amsterdam

Amsterdão [amiʃtex'dãw] (PT) N = **Amsterdã**

amuado, -a [a'mwadu, a] ADJ sulky

amuar [a'mwaʳ] VI to sulk

amuleto [amu'letu] M charm

amuo [a'muu] M sulkiness

anã [a'nã] F *de* **anão**

anacrônico, -a [ana'kroniku, a] ADJ anachronistic

anacronismo [anakro'niʒmu] M anachronism

anagrama [ana'grama] M anagram

anágua [a'nagwa] F petticoat

ANAI ABR F = **Associação Nacional de Apoio ao Índio**

anais [a'najʃ] MPL annals

analfabetismo [anawfabe'tʃiʒmu] M illiteracy

analfabeto, -a [anawfa'bɛtu, a] ADJ, M/F illiterate

analgésico, -a [anaw'ʒɛziku, a] ADJ analgesic ■ M painkiller, analgesic

analisar [anali'zaʳ] VT to analyse; **análise** [a'nalizi] F analysis; **analista** [ana'liʃta] M/F analyst; **analista de sistemas** systems analyst

analítico, -a [ana'litʃiku, a] ADJ analytical

analogia [analo'ʒia] F analogy

análogo, -a [a'nalogu, a] ADJ analogous

ananás [ana'naʃ] *(pl* ananases) M (BR) *variety of*

pineapple; (PT) pineapple

anão, anã [a'nãw, a'nã] (*pl* -**ões/-s**) M/F dwarf

anarquia [anax'kia] F anarchy; (*fig*) chaos

anárquico, -a [a'naxkiku, a] ADJ anarchic

anarquista [anax'kiʃta] M/F anarchist

anarquizar [anaxki'za'] VT (*povo*) to incite to anarchy; (*desordenar*) to mess up; (*ridicularizar*) to ridicule

anátema [a'natema] M anathema

anatomia [anato'mia] F anatomy

anatômico, -a [ana'tomiku, a] ADJ anatomical

anavalhar [anava'ʎa'] VT to slash

Anbid (BR) ABR F = **Associação Nacional de Bancos de Investimentos e Desenvolvimento**

anca ['ãka] F (*de pessoa*) hip; (*de animal*) rump

Ancara [ã'kara] N Ankara

ancestrais [ãseʃ'trajʃ] MPL ancestors

anchova [ã'ʃova] F anchovy

ancião, anciã [ã'sjãw, ã'sjã] (*pl* -**ões/-s**) ADJ old ■ M/F old man/woman; (*de uma tribo*) elder

ancinho [ã'siɲu] M rake

anciões [a'sjõjʃ] MPL *de* **ancião**

âncora ['ãkora] F anchor

ancoradouro [ãkora'doru] M anchorage

ancorar [ãko'ra'] VT, VI to anchor

andada [ã'dada] F walk; **dar uma ~** to go for a walk

andaime [ã'dajmi] M (*Arq*) scaffolding

Andaluzia [ãdalu'zia] F: **a ~** Andalucia

andamento [ãda'mētu] M (*progresso*) progress; (*rumo*) course; (*Mús*) tempo; **em ~** in progress; **dar ~ a algo** to set sth in motion

andanças [ã'dãsaʃ] FPL wanderings

andar [ã'da'] VI (*ir a pé*) to walk; (*máquina*) to work; (*progredir*) to go, to progress; (*estar*): **ela anda triste** she's been sad lately ■ M (*modo de caminhar*) gait; (*pavimento*) floor, storey (*Brit*), story (*US*); **anda!** hurry up!; **~ com alguém** to have an affair with sb; **~ a cavalo** to ride; **~ de trem/avião/bicicleta** to travel by train/fly/ride a bike

andarilho, -a [ãda'riʎu, a] M/F good walker

ANDC (BR) ABR F = **Associação Nacional de Defesa do Consumidor**

Andes ['ãdʒiʃ] MPL: **os ~** the Andes

Andima (BR) ABR F = **Associação Nacional das Instituições de Mercado Aberto**

andorinha [ãdo'riɲa] F (*pássaro*) swallow

Andorra [ã'dɔxa] F Andorra

andrógino, -a [ã'drɔʒinu, a] ADJ androgynous

anedota [ane'dɔta] F anecdote

anedótico, -a [ane'dɔtʃiku, a] ADJ anecdotal

anel [a'nɛw] (*pl* -**éis**) M ring; (*elo*) link; (*de cabelo*) curl; **~ de casamento** wedding ring

anelado, -a [ane'ladu, a] ADJ curly

anemia [ane'mia] F anaemia (*Brit*), anemia (*US*)

anêmico, -a [a'nemiku, a] ADJ anaemic (*Brit*), anemic (*US*)

anestesia [aneʃte'zia] F anaesthesia (*Brit*),

anão | animalesco

anesthesia (*US*); (*anestésico*) anaesthetic (*Brit*), anesthetic (*US*)

anestesiar [aneʃte'zja'] VT to anaesthetize (*Brit*), anesthetize (*US*)

anestésico [aneʃ'teziku] M (*Med*) anaesthetic (*Brit*), anesthetic (*US*)

anestesista [aneʃte'ziʃta] M/F anaesthetist (*Brit*), anesthetist (*US*)

anexação [aneksa'sãw] (*pl* -**ões**) F annexation; (*de documento*) enclosure

anexar [anek'sa'] VT to annex; (*juntar*) to attach; (*documento*) to enclose; **anexo, -a** [a'nɛksu, a] ADJ attached ■ M annexe; (*de igreja*) hall; (*em carta*) enclosure; (*em e-mail*) attachment; **segue em anexo** please find enclosed

Anfavea (BR) ABR F = **Associação Nacional dos Fabricantes de Veículos Automotores**

anfetamina [ãfeta'mina] F amphetamine

anfíbio, -a [ã'fibju, a] ADJ amphibious ■ M amphibian

anfiteatro [ãfi'tʃatru] M amphitheatre (*Brit*), amphitheater (*US*); (*no teatro*) dress circle

anfitrião, -triã [ãfi'trjãw, 'trjã] (*pl* -**ões/-s**) M/F host/hostess

angariar [ãga'rja'] VT (*fundos, donativos*) to raise; (*adeptos*) to attract; (*reputação, simpatia*) to gain; **~ votos** to canvass (for votes)

angelical [ãʒeli'kaw] (*pl* -**ais**) ADJ angelic

angina [ã'ʒina] F: **~ do peito** angina (pectoris)

anglicano, -a [ãgli'kanu, a] ADJ, M/F Anglican

anglicismo [ãgli'siʒmu] M Anglicism

anglo-saxão, -saxôni(c)a [ãglosak'sãw, sak'soni(k)a] (*pl* -**ões/-s**) M/F Anglo-Saxon

anglo-saxônico, -a [ãglosak'soniku, a] ADJ Anglo-Saxon

Angola [ã'gɔla] F Angola

angolano, -a [ãgo'lanu, a] ADJ, M/F Angolan

angolense [ãgo'lẽsi] ADJ, M/F Angolan

angorá [ãgo'ra] ADJ angora

angra ['ãgra] F inlet, cove

angu [ã'gu] M corn-meal purée

angular [ãgu'la'] ADJ angular

ângulo ['ãgulu] M angle; (*canto*) corner; (*fig*) angle, point of view

angústia [ã'guʃtʃja] F anguish, distress

angustiado, -a [ãguʃ'tʃjadu, a] ADJ distressed

angustiante [ãguʃ'tʃjãtʃi] ADJ distressing; (*momentos*) anxious, nerve-racking

angustiar [ãguʃ'tʃja'] VT to distress

anil [a'niw] M (*cor*) indigo

animação [anima'sãw] F (*vivacidade*) liveliness; (*movimento*) bustle; (*entusiasmo*) enthusiasm

animado, -a [ani'madu, a] ADJ (*vivo*) lively; (*alegre*) cheerful; **~ com** enthusiastic about

animador, a [anima'do'(a)] ADJ encouraging ■ M/F (BR: TV) presenter

animal [ani'maw] (*pl* -**ais**) ADJ, M animal; **~ de estimação** pet (animal)

animalesco, -a [anima'leʃku, a] ADJ bestial,

NB: *European Portuguese adds the following consonants to certain words:* **b** (sú(b)dito, su(b)til); **c** (a(c)ção, a(c)cionista, a(c)to); **m** (inde(m)ne); **p** (ado(p)çã, ado(p)tar); *for further details see p. xiii.*

brutish

animar [aniˈmaʳ] VT (*dar vida*) to liven up; (*encorajar*) to encourage; **animar-se** VR (*alegrarse*) to cheer up; (*festa etc*) to liven up; ~**-se a** to bring o.s. to

ânimo [ˈanimu] M (*coragem*) courage; ~! cheer up!; **perder o** ~ to lose heart; **recobrar o** ~ to pluck up courage; (*alegrar-se*) to cheer up

animosidade [animoziˈdadʒi] F animosity

aninhar [aniˈɲaʳ] VT to nestle; **aninhar-se** VR to nestle

aniquilação [anikilaˈsãw] F annihilation

aniquilar [anikiˈlaʳ] VT to annihilate; (*destruir*) to destroy; (*prostrar*) to shatter; **aniquilar-se** VR to be annihilated; (*moralmente*) to be shattered

anis [aˈniʃ] M aniseed

anistia [aniʃˈtʃia] F amnesty

aniversariante [anivexsaˈrjãtʃi] M/F birthday boy/girl

aniversário [anivexˈsarju] M anniversary; (*de nascimento*) birthday; (: *festa*) birthday party; ~ **de casamento** wedding anniversary

anjo [ˈãʒu] M angel; ~ **da guarda** guardian angel

ANL (BR) ABR F (= *Aliança Nacional Libertadora*) *1930's left-wing movement*

ano [ˈanu] M year; **Feliz A~ Novo!** Happy New Year!; **o** ~ **passado** last year; **o** ~ **que vem** next year; **por** ~ per annum; **fazer** ~**s** to have a birthday; **ele faz** ~**s hoje** it's his birthday today; **ter dez** ~**s** to be ten (years old); **dia de** ~**s** (PT) birthday; ~ **civil** calendar year; ~ **corrente** current year; ~ **financeiro** financial year; ~ **letivo** academic year; (*da escola*) school year

ano-bom M New Year

anões [aˈnõjʃ] MPL *de* **anão**

anoitecer [anojteˈseʳ] VI to grow dark ■ M nightfall; **ao** ~ at nightfall

anomalia [anomaˈlia] F anomaly

anômalo, -a [aˈnomalu, a] ADJ anomalous

anonimato [anoniˈmatu] M anonymity

anônimo, -a [aˈnonimu, a] ADJ anonymous; (*Com*): **sociedade anônima** limited company (*Brit*), stock company (*US*)

anoraque [anoˈraki] M anorak

anorexia [anoˈreksja] F anorexia

anoréxico, -a [anoˈreksiku, a] ADJ anorexic

anormal [anoxˈmaw] (*pl* **-ais**) ADJ abnormal; (*incomum*) unusual; (*excepcional*) handicapped; **anormalidade** [anoxmaliˈdadʒi] F abnormality

anotação [anotaˈsãw] (*pl* **-ões**) F (*comentário*) annotation; (*nota*) note

anotar [anoˈtaʳ] VT (*tomar nota*) to note down; (*esclarecer*) to annotate

anseio *etc* [ãˈseju] VB *V* **ansiar**

ânsia [ˈãsja] F (*ansiedade*) anxiety; (*desejo*): ~ (**de**) longing (for); **ter** ~**s** (**de vômito**) to feel sick

ansiado, -a [ãˈsjadu, a] ADJ longed for

ansiar [ãˈsjaʳ] VI: ~ **por** (*desejar*) to yearn for; ~ **por fazer** to long to do

ansiedade [ãsjeˈdadʒi] F anxiety; (*desejo*) eagerness

ansioso, -a [ãˈsjozu, ɔza] ADJ anxious; (*desejoso*) eager

antagônico, -a [ãtaˈgoniku, a] ADJ antagonistic; (*rival*) opposing

antagonismo [ãtagoˈniʒmu] M (*hostilidade*) antagonism; (*oposição*) opposition

antagonista [ãtagoˈniʃta] M/F antagonist; (*adversário*) opponent

antártico, -a [ãˈtaxtʃiku, a] ADJ antarctic ■ M: **o A~** the Antarctic

ante [ˈãtʃi] PREP (*na presença de*) before; (*em vista de*) in view of, faced with

antebraço [ãtʃiˈbrasu] M forearm

antecedência [ãteseˈdẽsja] F: **com** ~ in advance; **3 dias de** ~ three days' notice

antecedente [ãteseˈdẽtʃi] ADJ (*anterior*) preceding ■ M antecedent; **antecedentes** MPL (*registro*) record *sg*; (*passado*) background *sg*; ~**s criminais** criminal record *sg ou* past *sg*

anteceder [ãteseˈdeʳ] VT to precede

antecessor, a [ãteseˈsoʳ(a)] M/F predecessor

antecipação [ãtesipaˈsãw] F anticipation; **com um mês de** ~ a month in advance; ~ **de pagamento** advance (payment)

antecipadamente [ãtesipadaˈmẽtʃi] ADV in advance, beforehand; **pagar** ~ to pay in advance

antecipado, -a [ãtesiˈpadu, a] ADJ (*pagamento*) (in) advance

antecipar [ãtesiˈpaʳ] VT to anticipate, forestall; (*adiantar*) to bring forward; **antecipar-se** VR (*adiantar-se*) to be previous

antegozar [ãtegoˈzaʳ] VT to anticipate

antemão [ãteˈmãw]: **de** ~ ADV beforehand

antena [ãˈtena] F (*Bio*) antenna, feeler; (*Radio, TV*) aerial; ~ **direcional** directional aerial; ~ **parabólica** satellite dish

anteontem [ãtʃiˈõtẽ] ADV the day before yesterday

anteparo [ãteˈparu] M (*proteção*) screen

antepassado [ãtʃipaˈsadu] M ancestor

antepor [ãteˈpoʳ] (*irreg*) VT (*pôr antes*) to put before; **antepor-se** VR to anticipate

anteprojeto [ãteproˈʒɛtu] (PT **-ect-**) M outline, draft; ~ **de lei** draft bill

antepunha *etc* [ãteˈpuɲa] VB *V* **antepor**

antepus *etc* [ãteˈpuʃ] VB *V* **antepor**

antepuser *etc* [ãtepuˈzeʳ] VB *V* **antepor**

anterior [ãteˈrjoʳ] ADJ (*prévio*) previous; (*antigo*) former; (*de posição*) front

antes [ˈãtʃiʃ] ADV before; (*antigamente*) formerly; (*ao contrário*) rather ■ PREP: ~ **de** before; **o quanto** ~ as soon as possible; ~ **de partir** before leaving; ~ **do tempo** ahead of time; ~ **de tudo** above all; ~ **que** before

ante-sala F ante-room

antever [ãteˈveʳ] (*irreg*) VT to anticipate, foresee

antevisto, -a [ãteˈviʃtu, a] PP *de* **antever**

anti- [ãtʃi] PREFIXO anti-

antiácido, -a [ãˈtʃjasidu, a] ADJ antacid ■ M antacid

antiaéreo, -a [ãtʃjaˈɛrju, a] ADJ anti-aircraft

antiamericano, -a [ãtʃjameriˈkanu, a] ADJ anti-American

antibiótico, -a [ãtʃi'bjɔtʃiku, a] ADJ antibiotic ∎ M antibiotic
anticaspa [ãtʃi'kaʃpa] ADJ INV anti-dandruff
anticiclone [ãtʃisi'klɔni] M anticyclone
anticlímax [ãtʃi'klimaks] M anticlimax
anticoncepcional [ãtʃikõsepsjo'naw] (*pl* -ais) ADJ, M contraceptive
anticongelante [ãtʃikõʒe'lãtʃi] M antifreeze
anticonstitucional [ãtʃikõʃtʃitusjo'naw] (*pl* -ais) ADJ unconstitutional
anticorpo [ãtʃi'koxpu] M antibody
antidemocrático, -a [ãtʃidemo'kratʃiku, a] ADJ undemocratic
antidepressivo, -a [ãtʃidepre'sivu, a] ADJ anti-depressant ∎ M anti-depressant
antiderrapante [ãtʃidexa'pãtʃi] ADJ (*pneu*) non-skid
antídoto [ã'tʃidotu] M antidote
antiestético, -a [ãtʃjeʃ'tɛtʃiku, a] ADJ tasteless
antiético, -a [ã'tʃjetʃiku, a] ADJ unethical
antigamente [ãtʃiga'mẽtʃi] ADV formerly; (*no passado*) in the past
antiglobalização [ãtʃiglobaliza'sãw] F antiglobalization
antigo, -a [ã'tʃigu, a] ADJ old; (*histórico*) ancient; (*de estilo*) antique; (*chefe etc*) former; **ele é muito ~ na firma** he's been with the firm for many years; **os ~s** (*gregos etc*) the ancients
Antígua [ã'tʃigwa] F Antigua
antiguidade [ãtʃigi'dadʒi] F antiquity, ancient times *pl*; (*de emprego*) seniority; **antiguidades** FPL (*monumentos*) ancient monuments; (*artigos*) antiques
anti-higiênico, -a ADJ unhygienic
anti-histamínico, -a [-iʃta'miniku, a] ADJ antihistamine ∎ M antihistamine
anti-horário, -a ADJ anticlockwise
antilhano, -a [ãtʃi'ʎanu, a] ADJ, M/F West Indian
Antilhas [ã'tʃiʎaʃ] FPL: **as ~** the West Indies
antílope [ã'tʃilopi] M antelope
antipatia [ãtʃipa'tʃia] F antipathy, dislike;
antipático, -a [ãtʃi'patʃiku, a] ADJ unpleasant, unfriendly
antipatizar [ãtʃipatʃi'za'] VI: **~ com alguém** to dislike sb
antipatriótico, -a [ãtʃipa'trjɔtʃiku, a] ADJ unpatriotic
antipoluente [ãtʃipo'lwẽtʃi] ADJ non-pollutant
antiquado, -a [ãtʃi'kwadu, a] ADJ antiquated; (*fora de moda*) out of date, old-fashioned
antiquário, -a [ãtʃi'kwarju, a] M/F antique dealer ∎ M (*loja*) antique shop
antiquíssimo, -a [ãtʃi'kisimu, a] ADJ SUPERL *de* **antigo**
anti-semita ADJ anti-Semitic
anti-semitismo [-semi'tʃiʒmu] M anti-Semitism
anti-séptico, -a ADJ antiseptic ∎ M antiseptic

anti-social (*pl* -ais) ADJ antisocial
antítese [ã'tʃitezi] F antithesis
antitruste [ãtʃi'truʃtʃi] ADJ: **legislação ~** (*Com*) antitrust legislation
antivírus [[˜]tʃi'viruʃ] M INV (*Comput*) antivirus
antolhos [ã'tɔʎuʃ] MPL (*pala*) eye-shade *sg*; (*de cavalo*) blinkers
antologia [ãtolo'ʒia] F anthology
antônimo [ã'tonimu] M antonym
antro ['ãtru] M cave, cavern; (*de animal*) lair; (*de ladrões*) den
antropofagia [ãtropofa'ʒia] F cannibalism
antropófago, -a [ãtro'pɔfagu, a] M/F cannibal
antropologia [ãtropolo'ʒia] F anthropology
antropólogo, -a [ãtro'pɔlogu, a] M/F anthropologist
ANTTUR (BR) ABR F = **Associação Nacional de Transportadores de Turismo e Agências de Viagens**
anual [a'nwaw] (*pl* -ais) ADJ annual, yearly
anuário [a'nwarju] M yearbook
anuidade [ãnwi'dadʒi] F annuity
anuir [a'nwi'] VI: **~ a** to agree to; **~ com** to comply with
anulação [anula'sãw] (*pl* -ões) F cancellation; (*de contrato, casamento*) annulment
anular [anu'la'] VT to cancel; (*contrato, casamento*) to annul; (*efeito*) to cancel out ∎ M ring finger
anunciante [anũ'sjãtʃi] M (*Com*) advertiser
anunciar [anũ'sja'] VT to announce; (*Com: produto*) to advertise
anúncio [a'nũsju] M announcement; (*Com*) advertisement, advert; (*cartaz*) notice; **~ luminoso** neon sign; **~s classificados** small *ou* classified ads
ânus ['anuʃ] M INV anus
anverso [ã'vexsu] M (*de moeda*) obverse
anzol [ã'zɔw] (*pl* -óis) M fish-hook
ao [aw] = **a + o**; *v* **a**
aonde [a'õdʒi] ADV where; **~ quer que** wherever
aos [awʃ] = **a + os**; *v* **a**
AP ABR = **Amapá**
Ap. ABR = **apartamento**
apadrinhar [apadri'ɲa'] VT (*ser padrinho*) to act as godfather to; (*: de noivo*) to be best man to; (*proteger*) to protect; (*patrocinar*) to support
apagado, -a [apa'gadu, a] ADJ (*fogo*) out; (*luz elétrica*) off; (*indistinto*) faint; (*pessoa*) dull
apagar [apa'ga'] VT (*fogo*) to put out; (*luz elétrica*) to switch off; (*vela*) to blow out; (*com borracha*) to rub out, erase; (*quadro-negro*) to clean; (*Comput*) to delete, erase; **apagar-se** VR to go out; (*desmaiar*) to pass out; (*col: dormir*) to nod off
apaguei *etc* [apa'gej] VB *v* **apagar**
apaixonante [apajʃo'nãtʃi] ADJ captivating
apaixonado, -a [apajʃo'nadu, a] ADJ (*pessoa*) in love; (*discurso*) impassioned; (*pessoa*): **ele está ~ por ela** he is in love with her; **ele é ~ por tênis** he's mad about tennis

---

NB: *European Portuguese adds the following consonants to certain words:* **b** (sú(b)dito, su(b)til); **c** (a(c)ção, a(c)cionista, a(c)to); **m** (inde(m)ne); **p** (ado(p)çã, ado(p)tar); *for further details see p. xiii.*

apaixonar-se [apajʃo'naxsi] VR: ~ **por** to fall in love with

Apalaches [apa'laʃiʃ] MPL: **os** ~ the Appalachians

apalermado, -a [apalex'madu, a] ADJ silly

apalpadela [apawpa'dɛla] F touch

apalpar [apaw'paʳ] VT to touch, feel; (Med) to examine

apanhado [apa'ɲadu] M (de flores) bunch; (resumo) summary; (pregas) gathering

apanhar [apa'ɲaʳ] VT to catch; (algo à mão, do chão) to pick up; (ir buscar, surra, táxi) to get; (flores, frutas) to pick; (agarrar) to grab ■ VI (ser espancado) to get a beating; (em jogo) to take a beating; ~ **sol/chuva** to sunbathe/get soaked

apaniguado, -a [apani'gwadu, a] M/F (protegido) protégé(e)

apapagaiado, -a [apapaga'jadu, a] ADJ loud, garish

apara [a'para] F (de madeira) shaving; (de papel) clipping

aparador [apara'doʳ] M sideboard

aparafusar [aparafu'zaʳ] VT to screw

apara-lápis [apara'lapiʃ] (PT) M pencil sharpener

aparar [apa'raʳ] VT (cabelo) to trim; (lápis) to sharpen; (algo arremessado) to catch; (pancada) to parry; (madeira) to plane

aparato [apa'ratu] M pomp; (coleção) array

aparatoso, -a [apara'tozu, ɔza] ADJ grand

aparecer [apare'seʳ] VI to appear; (apresentar-se) to turn up; (ser publicado) to be published; ~ **em casa de alguém** to call on sb; **aparecimento** [aparesi'mẽtu] M appearance; (publicação) publication

aparelhado, -a [apare'ʎadu, a] ADJ (preparado) ready, prepared; (madeira) planed

aparelhagem [apare'ʎaʒẽ] F equipment; (carpintaria) finishing; (Náut) rigging

aparelhar [apare'ʎaʳ] VT (preparar) to prepare, get ready; (Náut) to rig; **aparelhar-se** VR to get ready

aparelho [apa'reʎu] M apparatus; (equipamento) equipment; (Pesca) tackle, gear; (máquina) machine; (BR: fone) telephone; (Pol) hide-out; ~ **de barbear** electric shaver; ~ **de chá** tea set; ~ **de rádio/TV** radio/TV set; ~ **digestivo** digestive system; ~ **doméstico** domestic appliance; ~ **sanitário** bathroom suite

aparência [apa'rẽsja] F appearance; (aspecto) aspect; **na** ~ apparently; **sob a** ~ **de** under the guise of; **manter as** ~**s** to keep up appearances; **salvar as** ~**s** to save face; **as** ~**s enganam** appearances are deceptive

aparentado, -a [aparẽ'tadu, a] ADJ related; **bem** ~ well connected

aparentar [aparẽ'taʳ] VT (fingir) to feign; (parecer) to give the appearance of

aparente [apa'rẽtʃi] ADJ apparent; (concreto, madeira) exposed

aparição [apari'sãw] (pl -ões) F (visão) apparition; (fantasma) ghost

aparo [a'paru] (PT) M (de caneta) (pen) nib

apartamento [apaxta'mẽtu] M apartment, flat (Brit)

apartar [apax'taʳ] VT to separate; **apartar-se** VR to separate

aparte [a'paxtʃi] M (Teatro) aside

apartheid [apax'tajdʒi] M apartheid

aparvalhado, -a [apaxva'ʎadu, a] ADJ idiotic

apatetado, -a [apate'tadu, a] ADJ sluggish

apatia [apa'tʃia] F apathy

apático, -a [a'patʃiku, a] ADJ apathetic

apátrida [a'patrida] M/F stateless person

apavorado, -a [apavo'radu, a] ADJ terrified

apavoramento [apavora'mẽtu] M terror

apavorante [apavo'rãtʃi] ADJ terrifying

apavorar [apavo'raʳ] VT to terrify ■ VI to be terrifying; **apavorar-se** VR to be terrified

apaziguar [apazi'gwaʳ] VT to appease; **apaziguar-se** VR to calm down

apear-se [a'pjaxsi] VR: ~ **de** (cavalo) to dismount from

apedrejar [apedre'ʒaʳ] VT to stone

apegado, -a [ape'gadu, a] ADJ: **ser** ~ **a** (gostar de) to be attached to, attached

apegar-se [ape'gaxsi] VR: ~ **a** (afeiçoar-se) to become attached to

apego [a'pegu] M (afeição) attachment

apeguei etc [ape'gej] VB V **apegar**

apelação [apela'sãw] (pl -ões) F appeal

apelante [ape'lãtʃi] M/F appellant

apelar [ape'laʳ] VI to appeal; ~ **da sentença** (Jur) to appeal against the sentence; ~ **para** to appeal to; ~ **para a ignorância/violência** to resort to abuse/violence

apelidar [apeli'daʳ] VT (BR) to nickname; (PT) to give a surname to; **apelidar-se** VR: ~-**se de** to go by the name of; **Eduardo, apelidado de Dudu** Eduardo, nicknamed Dudu

apelido [ape'lidu] M (PT: nome de família) surname; (BR: alcunha) nickname; **feio é** ~! (col) ugly is not the word for it!

apelo [a'pelu] M appeal

apenas [a'penaʃ] ADV only

apêndice [a'pẽdʒisi] M appendix; (anexo) supplement

apendicite [apẽdʒi'sitʃi] F appendicitis

Apeninos [ape'ninuʃ] MPL: **os** ~ the Apennines

apenso, -a [a'pẽsu, a] ADJ (documento) attached

apequenar [apeke'naʳ] VT to belittle

aperceber-se [apexse'bexsi] VR: ~ **de** to notice, see

aperfeiçoamento [apexfejswa'mẽtu] M (perfeição) perfection; (melhoramento) improvement

aperfeiçoar [apexfej'swaʳ] VT to perfect; (melhorar) to improve; **aperfeiçoar-se** VR to improve o.s

aperitivo [aperi'tʃivu] M aperitif

aperreação [apexja'sãw] F annoyance

aperreado, -a [ape'xjadu, a] ADJ fed up

aperrear [ape'xjaʳ] VT to annoy

apertado, -a [apex'tadu, a] ADJ tight; (estreito)

narrow; (sem dinheiro) hard-up; (vida) hard

apertar [apex'ta^r] VT (agarrar) to hold tight; (roupa) to take in; (cinto) to tighten; (esponja) to squeeze; (botão) to press; (despesas) to limit; (vigilância) to step up; (coração) to break; (fig: pessoa) to put pressure on ■ VI (sapatos) to pinch; (chuva, frio) to get worse; (estrada) to narrow; **apertar-se** VR (com roupa) to corset o.s; (reduzir despesas) to cut down (on expenses); (ter problemas financeiros) to feel the pinch; ~ **em** (insistir) to insist on, press; ~ **a mão de alguém** (cumprimentar) to shake hands with sb

aperto [a'pextu] M (pressão) pressure; (situação difícil) spot of bother, jam; **um ~ de mãos** a handshake

apesar [ape'za^r] PREP: ~ **de** in spite of, despite; ~ **disso** nevertheless; ~ **de que** in spite of the fact that, even though

apetecer [apete'se^r] VI (comida) to be appetizing; **esse prato não me apetece** I don't fancy that dish

apetecível [apete'sivew] (pl -eis) ADJ tempting

apetite [ape'tʃitʃi] M appetite; (desejo) desire; (fig: ânimo) go; **abrir o ~** to get up an appetite; **bom ~!** enjoy your meal!

apetitoso, -a [apeti'tozu, ɔza] ADJ appetizing

apetrechar [apetre'ʃa^r] VT to fit out, equip

apetrechos [ape'treʃuʃ] MPL gear sg; (Pesca) tackle sg

ápice ['apisi] M (cume) summit, top; (vértice) apex; **num ~** (PT) in a trice

apicultura [apikuw'tura] F beekeeping, apiculture

apiedar-se [apje'daxsi] VR: ~ **de** (ter piedade) to pity; (compadecer-se) to take pity on

apimentado, -a [apimẽ'tadu, a] ADJ peppery

apimentar [apimẽ'ta^r] VT to pepper

apinhado, -a [api'ɲadu, a] ADJ crowded

apinhar [api'ɲa^r] VT to crowd, pack; **apinhar-se** VR (aglomerar-se) to crowd together; ~**se de** (gente) to be filled ou packed with

apitar [api'ta^r] VI to whistle; (col): **ele não apita em nada em casa** he doesn't have a say in anything at home ■ VT (jogo) to referee; **apito** [a'pitu] M whistle

aplacar [apla'ka^r] VT to placate ■ VI to calm down; **aplacar-se** VR to calm down

aplainar [aplaj'na^r] VT (madeira) to plane; (nivelar) to level out

aplanar [apla'na^r] VT (alisar) to smooth; (nivelar) to level; (dificuldades) to smooth over

aplaudir [aplaw'dʒi^r] VT to applaud

aplauso [a'plawzu] M applause; (apoio) support; (elogio) praise; (aprovação) approval; ~**s** applause sg

aplicação [aplika'sãw] (pl -ões) F application; (esforço) effort; (Costura) appliqué; (da lei) enforcement; (de dinheiro) investment; (de aluno) diligence; **pacote de aplicações** (Comput) applications package

aplicado, -a [apli'kadu, a] ADJ hard-working

aplicar [apli'ka^r] VT to apply; (lei) to enforce; (dinheiro) to invest; **aplicar-se** VR: ~**se a** to devote o.s. to, apply o.s. to

aplicativo, -a [aplika'tʃivu, a] ADJ: **pacote/ software** ~ applications package/software ■ M (Comput) applications program

aplicável [apli'kavew] (pl -eis) ADJ applicable

aplique [a'pliki] M (luz) wall light; (peruca) hairpiece

apliquei etc [apli'kej] VB V **aplicar**

apocalipse [apoka'lipsi] F apocalypse

apócrifo, -a [a'pɔkrifu, a] ADJ apocryphal

apoderar-se [apode'raxsi] VR: ~ **de** to seize, take possession of

apodrecer [apodre'se^r] VT to rot; (dente) to decay ■ VI to rot, decay

apodrecimento [apodresi'mẽtu] M rottenness, decay; (de dentes) decay

apogeu [apo'ʒew] M (Astronomia) apogee; (fig) height, peak

apoiar [apo'ja^r] VT to support; (basear) to base; (moção) to second; **apoiar-se** VR: ~**se em** to rest on

apoio [a'poju] M support; (financeiro) backing; ~ **moral** moral support

apólice [a'pɔlisi] F (certificado) policy, certificate; (ação) share, bond; ~ **de seguro** insurance policy

apologia [apolo'ʒia] F (elogio) eulogy; (defesa) defence (Brit), defense (US)

apologista [apolo'ʒiʃta] M/F apologist

apontador [apõta'do^r] M pencil sharpener

apontamento [apõta'mẽtu] M (nota) note

apontar [apõ'ta^r] VT (fusil) to aim; (erro) to point out; (com o dedo) to point at ou to; (razão) to put forward; (nomes) to name ■ VI (aparecer) to begin to appear; (brotar) to sprout; (com o dedo) to point; ~**!** take aim!; ~ **para** to point to; (com arma) to aim at

apoplético, -a [apo'plɛtʃiku, a] ADJ apoplectic

apoquentar [apokẽ'ta^r] VT to annoy, pester; **apoquentar-se** VR to get annoyed

aporrinhação [apoxiɲa'sãw] F annoyance

aporrinhar [apoxi'ɲa^r] VT to pester, annoy

aportar [apox'ta^r] VI to dock

aportuguesado, -a [apoxtuge'zadu, a] ADJ made Portuguese

após [a'pɔjʃ] PREP after

aposentado, -a [apozẽ'tadu, a] ADJ retired ■ M/ F retired person, pensioner; **ser** ~ to be retired; **aposentadoria** [apozẽtado'ria] F retirement; (dinheiro) pension

aposentar [apozẽ'ta^r] VT to retire; **aposentar-se** VR to retire

aposento [apo'zẽtu] M room

após-guerra M post-war period; **a Alemanha do** ~ post-war Germany

apossar-se [apo'saxsi] VR: ~ **de** to take possession of, seize

aposta [a'pɔʃta] F bet

apostar [apoʃ'taʳ] VT to bet ▪ VI: ~ **em** to bet on

a posteriori [apoʃte'rjɔri] ADV afterwards

apostila [apoʃ'tʃila] F students' notes pl, study aid

apóstolo [a'pɔʃtolu] M apostle

apóstrofo [a'pɔʃtrofu] M apostrophe

apoteose [apote'ɔzi] F apotheosis

aprazar [apra'zaʳ] VT to allow

aprazer [apra'zeʳ] VI to be pleasing; ~ **a alguém** to please sb; **ele faz o que lhe apraz** he does as he pleases; **aprazia-lhe escrever cartas** he liked to write letters

aprazível [apra'zivew] (pl -eis) ADJ pleasant

apreçar [apre'saʳ] VT to value, price

apreciação [apresja'sãw] F appreciation

apreciar [apre'sjaʳ] VT to appreciate; (gostar de) to enjoy

apreciativo, -a [apresja'tʃivu, a] ADJ appreciative

apreciável [apre'sjavew] (pl -eis) ADJ appreciable

apreço [a'presu] M (estima) esteem, regard; (consideração) consideration; **em** ~ in question

apreender [aprjē'deʳ] VT to apprehend; (tomar) to seize; (entender) to grasp

apreensão [aprjē'sãw] (pl -ões) F (percepção) perception; (tomada) seizure, arrest; (receio) apprehension

apreensivo, -a [aprjē'sivu, a] ADJ apprehensive

apreensões [aprjē'sõjʃ] FPL de **apreensão**

apregoar [apre'gwaʳ] VT to proclaim, announce; (mercadorias) to cry

aprender [aprē'deʳ] VT, VI to learn; ~ **a ler** to learn to read; ~ **de cor** to learn by heart

aprendiz [aprē'dʒiʒ] M apprentice; (condutor) learner

aprendizado [aprendʒi'zadu] M (num ofício) apprenticeship; (numa profissão) training; (escolar) learning

aprendizagem [aprēdʒi'zaʒē] F (num ofício) apprenticeship; (numa profissão) training; (escolar) learning

apresentação [aprezēta'sãw] (pl -ões) F presentation; (de peça, filme) performance; (de pessoas) introduction; (porte pessoal) appearance; ~ **de contas** (Com) rendering of accounts

apresentador, a [aprezēta'doʳ(a)] M/F presenter

apresentar [aprezē'taʳ] VT to present; (pessoas) to introduce; (entregar) to hand; (trabalho, documento) to submit; (queixa) to lodge; **apresentar-se** VR (identificar-se) to introduce o.s.; (problema) to present itself; (à polícia etc) to report; **quero ~-lhe** may I introduce you to

apresentável [aprezē'tavew] (pl -eis) ADJ presentable

apressado, -a [apre'sadu, a] ADJ hurried, hasty; **estar** ~ to be in a hurry

apressar [apre'saʳ] VT to hurry, hasten; **apressar-se** VR to hurry (up)

aprestar [apreʃ'taʳ] VT (aparelhar) to equip, fit out; (aprontar) to get ready; **aprestar-se** VR to get ready

aprestos [a'prɛʃtuʃ] MPL (preparativos) preparations

aprimorado, -a [aprimo'radu, a] ADJ (trabalho) polished; (pessoa) elegant

aprimorar [aprimo'raʳ] VT to improve; **aprimorar-se** VR (no vestir) to make o.s. look nice

a priori [a'prjɔri] ADV beforehand

aprisionamento [aprizjona'mētu] M imprisonment

aprisionar [aprizjo'naʳ] VT (cativar) to capture; (encarcerar) to imprison

aprofundar [aprofũ'daʳ] VT to deepen, make deeper; **aprofundar-se** VR: ~ **-se em** to go deeper into

aprontar [aprō'taʳ] VT to get ready, prepare; (briga) to pick ▪ VI (col) to play up; **aprontar-se** VR to get ready; ~ **alguma** (col) to be up to something

apropriação [aproprja'sãw] (pl -ões) F appropriation; (tomada) seizure; ~ **de custos** (Com) cost appropriation

apropriado, -a [apro'prjadu, a] ADJ appropriate, suitable

apropriar [apro'prjaʳ] VT to appropriate; **apropriar-se** VR: ~ **-se de** to seize, take possession of

aprovação [aprova'sãw] F approval; (louvor) praise; (num exame) pass

aprovado, -a [apro'vadu, a] ADJ approved; **ser** ~ **num exame** to pass an exam; **o índice de ~s** the pass rate

aprovar [apro'vaʳ] VT to approve of; (exame) to pass ▪ VI to make the grade, come up to scratch

aproveitador, a [aprovejta'doʳ(a)] M/F opportunist

aproveitamento [aprovejta'mētu] M use, utilization; (nos estudos) progress

aproveitar [aprovej'taʳ] VT (tirar proveito de) to take advantage of; (utilizar) to use; (não desperdiçar) to make the most of; (oportunidade) to take; (fazer bom uso de) to make good use of ▪ VI to make the most of it; (PT) to be of use; **não aproveita** it's no use; **aproveite!** enjoy yourself!, have a good time!

aproveitável [aprovej'tavew] (pl -eis) ADJ usable

aprovisionamento [aprovizjona'mētu] M supply, provision

aprovisionar [aprovizjo'naʳ] VT to supply; (estocar) to stock

aproximação [aprosima'sãw] (pl -ões) F (estimativa) approximation; (chegada) approach; (proximidade) nearness, closeness

aproximado, -a [aprosi'madu, a] ADJ (cálculo) approximate; (perto) nearby

aproximar [aprosi'maʳ] VT to bring near; (aliar) to bring together; **aproximar-se** VR: ~ **-se de** (acercar-se) to approach

aprumado, -a [apru'madu, a] ADJ vertical; (altivo) upright; (elegante) well-dressed

aprumo [a'prumu] M vertical position; (elegância) elegance; (altivez) haughtiness

aptidão [aptʃi'dãw] F aptitude, ability; (jeito) knack; ~ **física** physical fitness

aptitude [aptʃi'tudʒi] F aptitude, ability; (jeito) knack

apto, -a ['aptu, a] ADJ apt; (capaz) capable

apto. ABR = **apartamento**

APU (PT) ABR F (= Aliança Povo Unido) political party

apunhalar [apuɲa'laʳ] VT to stab

apuração [apura'sãw] F (de votos) counting; (descoberta) ascertainment; (averiguação) investigation; ~ **de contas** (Com) settlement of accounts; ~ **de custos** (Com) costing

apurado, -a [apu'radu, a] ADJ refined

apurar [apu'raʳ] VT (aperfeiçoar) to perfect; (descobrir) to find out; (averiguar) to investigate; (dinheiro) to raise, get; (votos) to count; **apurar-se** VR (no trajar) to dress up

apuro [a'puru] M (elegância) refinement, elegance; (dificuldade) difficulty; **estar em ~s** to be in trouble

aquarela [akwa'rɛla] F watercolour (Brit), watercolor (US)

aquário [a'kwarju] M aquarium; **A~** (Astrologia) Aquarius

aquartelar [akwaxte'laʳ] VT (Mil) to billet, quarter

aquático, -a [a'kwatʃiku, a] ADJ aquatic, water atr

aquecedor, a [akese'doʳ(a)] ADJ warming ■ M heater

aquecer [ake'seʳ] VT to heat ■ VI to heat up; **aquecer-se** VR to heat up; **aquecido, -a** [ake'sidu, a] ADJ heated; **aquecimento** [akesi'mẽtu] M heating; (da economia) acceleration; **aquecimento central** central heating; **aquecimento global** global warming

aqueduto [ake'dutu] M aqueduct

aquele, -ela [a'keli, ɛla] ADJ (sg) that; (pl) those ■ PRON (sg) that one; (pl) those; **sem mais aquela** (inesperadamente) all of a sudden; (sem cerimônia) without so much as a "by your leave"; **foi aquela confusão** it was a real mess

àquele, -ela [a'keli, ɛla] = **a + aquele**

aquém [a'kẽj] ADV on this side; ~ **de** on this side of

aqui [a'ki] ADV here; **eis** ~ here is/are; ~ **mesmo** right here; **até** ~ up to here; **por** ~ hereabouts; (nesta direção) this way; **por ~ e por ali** here and there; **estou por ~!** (col) I've had it up to here!; v tb **daqui**

aquiescência [akje'sẽsja] F consent

aquiescer [akje'seʳ] VI: ~ **(a)** to consent (to)

aquietar [akje'taʳ] VT to calm, quieten; **aquietar-se** VR to calm down

aquilatar [akila'taʳ] VT (metais) to value; (avaliar) to evaluate

aquilo [a'kilu] PRON that; ~ **que** what

àquilo [a'kilu] = **a + aquilo**

aquisição [akizi'sãw] (pl -ões) F acquisition

aquisitivo, -a [akizi'tʃivu, a] ADJ: **poder ~** purchasing power

ar [aʳ] M air; (aspecto) look; (brisa) breeze; (PT: Auto) choke; **ares** MPL (atitude) airs; (clima) climate sg; **ao ar livre** in the open air; **ir ao/sair do ar** (TV, Rádio) to go on/off the air; **no ar** (TV, Rádio) on air; (fig: planos) up in the air; **dar-se ares** to put on airs; **ir pelos ares** (explodir) to blow up; **tomar ar** to get some air; **ar condicionado** (aparelho) air conditioner; (sistema) air conditioning

árabe ['arabi] ADJ, M/F Arab ■ M (Ling) Arabic

Arábia [a'rabja] F: **A~ ~ Saudita** Saudi Arabia

arado [a'radu] M plough (Brit), plow (US)

aragem [a'raʒẽ] (pl -ns) F breeze

arame [a'rami] M wire; ~ **farpado** barbed wire

aranha [a'raɲa] F spider

aranha-caranguejeira [-karãge'ʒejra] (pl **aranhas-caranguejeiras**) F bird-eating spider

arapuca [ara'puka] F trap; (truque) trick

arar [a'raʳ] VT to plough (Brit), plow (US)

araque [a'raki] M: **de ~** (col) phony, bogus

arara [a'rara] F macaw; **estar/ficar uma ~** (fig) to be/get angry

arbitragem [axbi'traʒẽ] F arbitration; (Esporte) refereeing

arbitrar [axbi'traʳ] VT to arbitrate; (Esporte) to referee; (adjudicar) to award

arbitrariedade [axbitrarje'dadʒi] F arbitrariness; (ato) arbitrary act

arbitrário, -a [axbi'trarju, a] ADJ arbitrary

arbítrio [ax'bitrju] M decision; **ao ~ de** at the discretion of

árbitro ['axbitru] M (juiz) arbiter; (Jur) arbitrator; (Futebol) referee; (Tênis) umpire

arborizado, -a [axbori'zadu, a] ADJ green, wooded; (rua) tree-lined

arborizar [axbori'zaʳ] VT to plant with trees

arbusto [ax'buʃtu] M shrub, bush

arca ['axka] F chest, trunk; ~ **de Noé** Noah's Ark

arcabouço [axka'bosu] M outline(s)

arcada [ax'kada] F (série de arcos) arcade; (arco) arch, span; ~ **dentária** dental ridge

arcaico, -a [ax'kajku, a] ADJ archaic; (antiquado) antiquated

arcanjo [ax'kãʒu] M archangel

arcar [ax'kaʳ] VT: ~ **com** (responsabilidades) to shoulder; (despesas) to handle; (conseqüências) to take

arcebispo [axse'biʃpu] M archbishop

arco ['axku] M (Arq) arch; (Mil, Mús) bow; (Elet, Mat) arc; (de barril) hoop

arco-da-velha M: **coisa/história do ~** amazing thing/story

arco-íris M INV rainbow

NB: European Portuguese adds the following consonants to certain words: **b** (sú(b)dito, su(b)til); **c** (a(c)ção, a(c)cionista, a(c)to); **m** (inde(m)ne); **p** (ado(p)çã, ado(p)tar); for further details see p. xiii.

ardente [ax'dētʃi] ADJ burning; (*intenso*) fervent; (*apaixonado*) ardent

arder [ax'deʳ] VI to burn; (*pele, olhos*) to sting; ~ **de febre** to burn up with fever; ~ **de raiva** to seethe (with rage)

ardido, -a [ax'dʒidu, a] ADJ (*picante*) hot

ardil [ax'dʒiw] (*pl* -**is**) M trick, ruse

ardiloso, -a [axdʒi'lozu, ɔza] ADJ cunning

ardis [ax'dʒiʃ] MPL *de* **ardil**

ardor [ax'doʳ] M (*paixão*) ardour (*Brit*), ardor (*US*), passion; **ardoroso, -a** [axdo'rozu, ɔza] ADJ ardent

ardósia [ax'dɔzja] F slate

árduo, -a ['axdwu, a] ADJ arduous; (*difícil*) hard, difficult

área ['arja] F area; (*Esporte*) penalty area; (*fig*) field; ~ (**de serviço**) balcony (*for hanging washing etc*)

arear [a'rjaʳ] VT to polish

areia [a'reja] F sand; ~ **movediça** quicksand

arejado, -a [are'ʒadu, a] ADJ aired, ventilated

arejar [are'ʒaʳ] VT to air ■ VI to get some air; (*descansar*) to have a breather; **arejar-se** VR to get some air; to have a break

ARENA (BR) ABR F (= *Aliança Renovadora Nacional*) *former political party*

arena [a'rɛna] F arena; (*de circo*) ring

arenito [are'nitu] M sandstone

arenoso, -a [are'nozu, ɔza] ADJ sandy

arenque [a'rēki] M herring

aresta [a'rɛʃta] F edge

arfar [ax'faʳ] VI (*ofegar*) to pant, gasp for breath; (*Náut*) to pitch

argamassa [axga'masa] F mortar

argamassar [axgama'saʳ] VT to cement

Argel [ax'ʒɛw] N Algiers

Argélia [ax'ʒɛlja] F: **a** ~ Algeria

argelino, -a [axʒe'linu, a] ADJ, M/F Algerian

Argentina [axʒē'tʃina] F: **a** ~ Argentina

argentino, -a [axʒē'tʃinu, a] ADJ, M/F Argentinian

argila [ax'ʒila] F clay

argiloso, -a [axʒi'lozu, ɔza] ADJ (*terreno*) clay

argola [ax'gɔla] F ring; **argolas** FPL (*brincos*) hooped earrings; ~ (**de porta**) door-knocker

argúcia [ax'gusja] F (*sutileza*) subtlety; (*agudeza*) astuteness

argüição [axgwi'sãw] (*pl* -**ões**) F oral test

argüir [ax'gwiʳ] VT (*examinar*) to test, examine

argumentação [axgumēta'sãw] F line of argument

argumentador, a [axgumēta'doʳ(a)] ADJ argumentative ■ M/F arguer

argumentar [axgumē'taʳ] VT, VI to argue

argumento [axgu'mētu] M argument; (*de obra*) theme

arguto, -a [ax'gutu, a] ADJ (*sutil*) subtle; (*astuto*) shrewd

ária ['arja] F aria

ariano, -a [a'rjanu, a] ADJ, M/F Aryan; (*Astrologia*) Arian

aridez [ari'deʒ] F (*secura*) dryness; (*esterilidade*)

barrenness; (*falta de interesse*) dullness

árido, -a ['aridu, a] ADJ (*seco*) arid, dry; (*estéril*) barren; (*maçante*) dull, boring

Áries ['ariʃ] F Aries

arisco, -a [a'riʃku, a] ADJ unsociable

aristocracia [ariʃtokra'sia] F aristocracy

aristocrata [ariʃto'krata] M/F aristocrat

aristocrático, -a [ariʃto'kratʃiku, a] ADJ aristocratic

aritmética [aritʃ'mɛtʃika] F arithmetic

aritmético, -a [aritʃ'mɛtʃiku, a] ADJ arithmetical

arma ['axma] F weapon; **armas** FPL (*nucleares etc*) arms; (*brasão*) coat *sg* of arms; **de** ~**s e bagagem** with all one's belongings; **depor as** ~**s** to lay down arms; **passar pelas** ~**s** to shoot, execute; ~ **branca** cold steel; ~ **convencional/ nuclear** conventional/nuclear weapon; ~**s de destrui** firearm; ~**s de destruição em massa** weapons of mass destruction; ~ **de fogo** firearm

armação [axma'sãw] (*pl* -**ões**) F (*armadura*) frame; (*Pesca*) tackle; (*Náut*) rigging; (*de óculos*) frames *pl*

armada [ax'mada] F navy

armadilha [axma'dʒiʎa] F trap

armado, -a [ax'madu, a] ADJ armed; ~ **até os dentes** armed to the teeth

armador [axma'doʳ] M (*Náut*) shipowner

armadura [axma'dura] F armour (*Brit*), armor (*US*); (*Elet*) armature; (*Constr*) framework

armamento [axma'mētu] M (*armas*) armaments *pl*, weapons *pl*; (*Náut*) equipment; (*ato*) arming

armar [ax'maʳ] VT to arm; (*montar*) to assemble; (*barraca*) to pitch; (*um aparelho*) to set up; (*armadilha*) to set; (*maquinar*) to hatch; (*Náut*) to fit out; **armar-se** VR to arm o.s.; ~ **uma briga com** to pick a quarrel with; ~ **uma confusão** to cause chaos

armarinho [axma'riɲu] M haberdashery (*Brit*), notions *pl* (*US*)

armário [ax'marju] M cupboard; (*de roupa*) wardrobe

armazém [axma'zēj] (*pl* -**ns**) M (*depósito*) warehouse; (*loja*) grocery store

armazenagem [axmaze'naʒē] F storage

armazenamento [axmazena'mētu] M storage

armazenar [axmaze'naʳ] VT to store; (*provisões*) to stock; (*Comput*) to store

armazéns [axma'zēʃ] MPL *de* **armazém**

armeiro [ax'mejru] M gunsmith

Armênia [ax'menja] F: **a** ~ Armenia

arminho [ax'miɲu] M ermine

armistício [axmiʃ'tʃisju] M armistice

aro ['aru] M (*argola*) ring; (*de óculos, roda*) rim; (*de porta*) frame

aroma [a'rɔma] F (*de comida, café*) aroma; (*de perfume*) fragrance; **aromático, -a** [aro'matʃiku, a] ADJ (*comida*) aromatic; (*perfume*) fragrant

arpão [ax'pãw] (*pl* -**ões**) M harpoon

arpejo [ax'peʒu] M arpeggio

arpoar [ax'pwaʳ] VT to harpoon

arpões [ax'põjʃ] MPL de **arpão**

arqueado, -a [ax'kjadu, a] ADJ arched

arquear [ax'kjaʳ] VT to arch; **arquear-se** VR to bend, arch; (entortar-se) to warp

arquei etc [ax'kej] VB V **arcar**

arqueiro, -a [ax'kejru, a] M/F archer; (goleiro) goalkeeper

arquejar [axke'ʒaʳ] VI to pant, wheeze

arquejo [ax'keʒu] M panting, gasping

arqueologia [axkjolo'ʒia] F archaeology (Brit), archeology (US)

arqueológico, -a [axkjo'lɔʒiku, a] ADJ archaeological (Brit), archeological (US)

arqueólogo, -a [ax'kjɔlogu, a] M/F archaeologist (Brit), archeologist (US)

arquétipo [ax'kɛtʃipu] M archetype

arquibancada [axkibã'kada] F terrace

arquipélago [axki'pɛlagu] M archipelago

arquitetar [axkite'taʳ] (PT -ect-) VT to think up

arquiteto, -a [axki'tɛtu, a] (PT -ect-) M/F architect

arquitetónico, -a [axkite'toniku, a] (PT -ect-) ADJ architectural

arquitetura [axkite'tura] (PT -ect-) F architecture

arquivamento [axkiva'mẽtu] M filing; (de projeto) shelving

arquivar [axki'vaʳ] VT to file; (projeto) to shelve

arquivista [axki'viʃta] M/F archivist

arquivo [ax'kivu] M (ger, Comput) file; (lugar) archive; (de empresa) files pl; (móvel) filing cabinet; (Comput) file; **abrir/fechar um** ~ (Comput) to open/close a file; **nome do** ~ (Comput) file name; ~ **ativo** (Comput) active file; ~ **zipado** (Comput) zip file

arrabaldes [axa'bawdʒiʃ] MPL suburbs

arraia [a'xaja] F (peixe) ray

arraial [axa'jaw] (pl -ais) M (povoação) village; (PT: festa) fair

arraia-miúda F masses pl

arraigado, -a [axaj'gadu, a] ADJ deep-rooted; (fig) ingrained

arraigar [axaj'gaʳ] VI to root; **arraigar-se** VR (enraizar-se) to take root; (estabelecer-se) to settle

arrancada [axã'kada] F (puxão) pull, jerk; (partida) start; (investida) charge; (de atleta) burst of speed

arrancar [axã'kaʳ] VT to pull out; (botão etc) to pull off; (arrebatar) to snatch (away); (fig: confissão) to extract; (: aplausos) to get ■ VI to start (off); **arrancar-se** VR (partir) to leave; (fugir) to run off

arranco [a'xãku] M (puxão) pull, jerk; (partida) sudden start

arranha-céu [a'xaɲa-] (pl -s) M skyscraper

arranhadura [axaɲa'dura] F scratch

arranhão [axa'ɲãw] (pl -ões) M scratch

arranhar [axa'ɲaʳ] VT to scratch; ~ **(n)uma**
língua to know a smattering of a language

arranhões [axa'ɲõjʃ] MPL de **arranhão**

arranjador, a [axãʒa'doʳ(a)] M/F (Mús) arranger

arranjar [axã'ʒaʳ] VT to arrange; (emprego etc) to get, find; (doença) to get, catch; (namorado) to find; (questão) to settle; **arranjar-se** VR (virar-se) to manage; (conseguir emprego) to get a job; **~-se sem** to do without

arranjo [a'xãʒu] M arrangement; (negociata) shady deal; (col: caso) affair

arranque [a'xãki] M V **motor**

arranquei etc [axã'kej] VB V **arrancar**

arrasador, a [axaza'doʳ(a)] ADJ devastating

arrasar [axa'zaʳ] VT to devastate; (demolir) to demolish; (estragar) to ruin; (verbalmente) to lambast; **arrasar-se** VR to be devastated; (destruir-se) to destroy o.s; (arruinar-se) to lose everything; (nos exames) to do terribly

arrastado, -a [axaʃ'tadu, a] ADJ (rasteiro) crawling; (demorado) dragging; (voz) drawling

arrastão [axaʃ'tãw] (pl -ões) M tug, jerk; (rede) dragnet

arrasta-pé [a'xaʃta-] (pl -s) (col) M knees-up, shindig

arrastar [axaʃ'ta¹] VT to drag; (atrair) to draw ■ VI to trail; **arrastar-se** VR (rastejar) to crawl; (andar a custo) to drag o.s; (tempo) to drag; (processo) to drag on

arrasto [a'xaʃtu] M (ação) dragging; (rede) trawlnet; (Tec) drag

arrazoado, -a [axa'zwadu, a] ADJ (argumento) reasoned ■ M (Jur) defence (Brit), defense (US)

arrazoar [axa'zwaʳ] VI (discutir) to argue

arrear [a'xjaʳ] VT (cavalo etc) to bridle

arrebanhar [axeba'ɲaʳ] VT (gado) to herd; (juntar) to gather

arrebatado, -a [axeba'tadu, a] ADJ (impetuoso) rash, impetuous; (enlevado) entranced

arrebatador, a [axebata'doʳ(a)] ADJ enchanting

arrebatamento [axebata'mẽtu] M (impetuosidade) impetuosity; (enlevo) ecstasy

arrebatar [axeba'ta¹] VT (arrancar) to snatch (away); (levar) to carry off; (enlevar) to entrance; (enfurecer) to enrage; **arrebatar-se** VR (entusiasmar-se) to be entranced

arrebentação [axebẽta'sãw] F (na praia) surf

arrebentado, -a [axebẽ'tadu, a] ADJ (quebrado) broken; (vaso etc) smashed; (estafado) worn out

arrebentar [axebẽ'taʳ] VT to break; (porta) to break down; (corda) to snap, break ■ VI to break; to snap, break; (guerra) to break out; (bomba) to explode; (ondas) to break

arrebitado, -a [axebi'tadu, a] ADJ turned-up; (nariz) snub

arrebitar [axebi'taʳ] VT to turn up

arrecadação [axekada'sãw] F (de impostos etc) collection; (impostos arrecadados) tax revenue, taxes pl

arrecadar [axeka'daʳ] VT (impostos etc) to collect

NB: European Portuguese adds the following consonants to certain words: **b** (sú(b)dito, su(b)til); **c** (a(c)ção, a(c)cionista, a(c)to); **m** (inde(m)ne); **p** (ado(p)ção, ado(p)tar); for further details see p. xiii.

arrecife [axe'sifi] M reef
arredar [axe'da^r] VT to move away, move back;
arredar-se VR to move away; **não ~ pé** not to
budge, to stand one's ground
arredio, -a [axe'dʒiu, a] ADJ (pessoa) withdrawn
arredondado, -a [axedõ'dadu, a] ADJ round,
rounded
arredondar [axedõ'da^r] VT to round (off); (conta)
to round up
arredores [axe'dɔriʃ] MPL suburbs; (cercanias)
outskirts
arrefecer [axefe'se^r] VT to cool; (febre) to lower;
(desanimar) to discourage ■ VI to cool (off); to
get discouraged
arrefecimento [axefesi'mẽtu] M cooling
ar-refrigerado (pl ares-refrigerados) M
(aparelho) air conditioner; (sistema) air
conditioning
arregaçar [axega'sa^r] VT to roll up
arregalado, -a [axega'ladu, a] ADJ (olhos) wide;
com os olhos ~s pop-eyed
arregalar [axega'la^r] VT: ~ **os olhos** to stare in
amazement
arreganhar [axega'ɲa^r] VT (dentes) to bare;
(lábios) to draw back
arreios [a'xejuʃ] MPL harness sg
arrematar [axema'ta^r] VT (dizer concluindo) to
conclude; (comprar) to buy by auction; (vender) to
sell by auction; (Costura) to finish off
arremate [axe'matʃi] M (Costura) finishing off;
(conclusão) conclusion; (Futebol) finishing
arremedar [axeme'da^r] VT to mimic
arremedo [axe'medu] M mimicry
arremessar [axeme'sa^r] VT to throw, hurl;
arremessar-se VR to hurl o.s; **arremesso**
[axe'mesu] M (lançamento) throw; **arremesso
de peso** shot-put
arremeter [axeme'te^r] VI to lunge; ~ **contra**
(acometer) to attack, assail
arremetida [axeme'tʃida] F attack, onslaught
arrendador, a [axẽda'do^r(a)] M/F landlord/
landlady
arrendamento [axẽda'mẽtu] M (ação) leasing;
(contrato) lease
arrendar [axẽ'da^r] VT to lease
arrendatário, -a [axẽda'tarju, a] M/F tenant
arrepender-se [axepẽ'dexsi] VR to repent;
(mudar de opinião) to change one's mind;
~ **de** to regret, be sorry for; **arrependido,
-a** [axepẽ'dʒidu, a] ADJ (pessoa) sorry;
arrependimento [axepẽdʒi'mẽtu] M regret;
(Rel, de crime) repentance
arrepiado, -a [axe'pjadu, a] ADJ (cabelo)
standing on end; (pele, pessoa) goose-pimply;
(horrorizado) horrified
arrepiar [axe'pja^r] VT (amedrontar) to horrify;
(cabelo) to cause to stand on end; **arrepiar-se**
VR (sentir calafrios) to shiver; (cabelo) to stand on
end; **isso me arrepia** it gives me goose flesh;
(ser) de ~ **os cabelos** (to be) hair-raising
arrepio [axe'piu] M shiver; (de frio) chill; **isso me
dá ~s** it gives me the creeps

arresto [a'xɛʃtu] M (Jur) seizure, confiscation
arrevesado, -a [axeve'zadu, a] ADJ (obscuro)
obscure; (intricado) intricate
arrevesar [axeve'za^r] VT (complicar) to
complicate
arriado, -a [a'xjadu, a] ADJ (exausto) exhausted;
(por doença) very weak
arriar [a'xja^r] VT (baixar) to lower; (depor) to lay
down ■ VI (cair) to drop; (vergar) to sag; (desistir)
to give up; (fig) to collapse; (Auto: bateria) to go
flat
arribação [axiba'sãw] (BR) (pl -ões) F (de aves)
migration
arribar [axi'ba^r] VI (recuperar-se) to recuperate
arrimo [a'ximu] M support; ~ **de família**
breadwinner
arriscado, -a [axiʃ'kadu, a] ADJ risky; (audacioso)
daring
arriscar [axiʃ'ka^r] VT to risk; (pôr em perigo) to
endanger, jeopardize; **arriscar-se** VR to take a
risk; ~-**se a fazer** to risk doing
arrisquei etc [axiʃ'kej] VB V **arriscar**
arrivista [axi'viʃta] M/F upstart; (oportunista)
opportunist
arroba [a'xoba] (peso) F = 15 kg; (Comput) @ ('at'
symbol)
arrochado, -a [axo'ʃadu, a] ADJ (vestido) skin-
tight; (fig) tough
arrochar [axo'ʃa^r] VT (apertar) to tighten up ■ VI
(ser exigente) to be demanding
arrocho [a'xoʃu] M squeeze; (fig) predicament; ~
salarial/ao crédito wage/credit squeeze
arrogância [axo'gãsja] F arrogance,
haughtiness
arrogante [axo'gãtʃi] ADJ arrogant, haughty
arrogar-se [axo'gaxsi] VR (direitos, privilégios) to
claim
arroio [a'xɔju] M stream
arrojado, -a [axo'ʒadu, a] ADJ (design) bold;
(temerário) rash; (ousado) daring
arrojar [axo'ʒa^r] VT (lançar) to hurl
arrojo [a'xoʒu] M (ousadia) boldness
arrolamento [axola'mẽtu] M list
arrolar [axo'la^r] VT to list
arrolhar [axo'ʎa^r] VT to cork
arromba [a'xõba] F: **de** ~ great
arrombar [axõ'ba^r] VT (porta) to break down;
(cofre) to crack
arrotar [axo'ta^r] VI to belch ■ VT (alardear) to
boast of
arroto [a'xotu] M burp
arroubo [a'xobu] M ecstasy, rapture
arroz [a'xoʒ] M rice; ~ **doce** rice pudding
arrozal [axo'zaw] (pl -ais) M rice field
arruaça [a'xwasa] F street riot
arruaceiro, -a [axwa'sejru, a] M/F rioter
arruela [a'xwɛla] F (Tec) washer
arruinar [axwi'na^r] VT to ruin; (destruir) to
destroy; **arruinar-se** VR to be ruined; (perder a
saúde) to ruin one's health
arrulhar [axu'ʎa^r] VI (pombos) to coo
arrulho [a'xuʎu] M cooing

arrumação [axuma'sãw] F (arranjo)
arrangement; (de um quarto etc) tidying up; (de malas) packing

arrumadeira [axuma'dejra] F cleaning lady; (num hotel) chambermaid

arrumar [axu'ma^r] VT (pôr em ordem) to put in order, arrange; (quarto etc) to tidy up; (malas) to pack; (emprego) to get; (vestir) to dress up; (desculpa) to make up, find; (vida) to sort out; **arrumar-se** VR (aprontar-se) to get dressed, get ready; (na vida) to sort o.s out; (virar-se) to manage

arsenal [axse'naw] (pl -ais) M (Mil) arsenal; ~ **de Marinha** naval dockyard

arsênio [ax'senju] M arsenic

arte ['axtʃi] F art; (habilidade) skill; (ofício) trade, craft; **fazer** ~ (fig) to get up to mischief

artefato [axtʃi'fatu] (PT -act-) M (manufactured) article; **~s de couro** leather goods, leatherware sg

arteiro, -a [ax'tejru, a] ADJ (criança) mischievous

artéria [ax'tɛɪja] F (Anat) artery

arterial [axte'rjaw] (pl -ais) ADJ: **pressão** ~ blood pressure

arteriosclerose [axterjoʃkle'rɔzi] F hardening of the arteries, arteriosclerosis

artesã [axte'zã] F de **artesão**

artesanal [axteza'naw] (pl -ais) ADJ craft atr

artesanato [axteza'natu] M craftwork; **artigos de** ~ craft items

artesão, -sã [axte'zãw] (pl -s/-s) M/F artisan, craftsman/woman

ártico, -a ['axtʃiku, a] ADJ Arctic ◼ M: **o A**~ the Arctic

articulação [axtʃikula'sãw] (pl -ões) F articulation; (Med) joint

articulado, -a [axtʃiku'ladu, a] ADJ articulated, jointed

articular [axtʃiku'la^r] VT (pronunciar) to articulate; (ligar) to join together

artífice [ax'tʃifisi] M/F craftsman/woman; (inventor) inventor

artificial [axtʃifi'sjaw] (pl -ais) ADJ artificial; (pessoa) affected

artifício [axtʃi'fisju] M stratagem, trick

artificioso, -a [axtʃifi'sjozu, ɔza] ADJ (hábil) skilful (Brit), skillful (US); (astucioso) artful

artigo [ax'tʃigu] M article; (Com) item; **artigos** MPL (produtos) goods; ~ **definido/indefinido** (Ling) definite/indefinite article; ~ **de fundo** leading article, editorial; **~s de toucador** toiletries

artilharia [axtʃiʎa'ria] F artillery

artilheiro [axtʃi'ʎejru] M gunner, artilleryman; (Futebol) striker

artimanha [axtʃi'maɲa] F (ardil) stratagem; (astúcia) cunning

artista [ax'tʃiʃta] M/F artist; **artístico, -a** [ax'tʃiʃtʃiku, a] ADJ artistic

artrite [ax'tritʃi] F (Med) arthritis

arvorar [axvo'ra^r] VT (bandeira) to hoist; (elevar): ~ **alguém em** to promote ou elevate sb to; **arvorar-se** VR: **arvorar-se em** to set o.s. up as

árvore ['axvori] F tree; (Tec) shaft; ~ **de Natal** Christmas tree

arvoredo [axvo'redu] M grove

as [aʃ] ART DEF V **a**

ás [ajʃ] M ace

às [ajʃ] = **a** + **as**

asa ['aza] F wing; (de xícara etc) handle; **dar ~s à imaginação** to give free rein to one's imagination

asa-delta F hang-glider

asbesto [aʒ'bɛʃtu] M asbestos

ascendência [asẽ'dẽsja] F (antepassados) ancestry; (domínio) ascendancy, sway;

ascendente [asẽ'dẽtʃi] ADJ rising, upward

ascender [asẽ'de^r] VI (subir) to rise, ascend

ascensão [asẽ'sãw] (pl -ões) F ascent; (fig) rise; (Rel): **dia da A**~ Ascension Day

ascensor [asẽ'so^r] M lift (Brit), elevator (US)

ascensorista [asẽso'riʃta] M/F lift operator

asceta [a'seta] M/F ascetic

asco ['aʃku] M loathing, revulsion; **dar** ~ **a** to revolt, disgust

asfaltar [aʃfaw'ta^r] VT to asphalt

asfalto [aʃ'fawtu] M asphalt

asfixia [aʃfik'sia] F asphyxia, suffocation

asfixiar [aʃfik'sja^r] VT to asphyxiate, suffocate

Ásia ['azja] F: **a** ~ Asia

asiático, -a [a'zjatʃiku, a] ADJ, M/F Asian

asilar [azi'la^r] VT to give refuge to; **asilar-se** VR to take refuge

asilo [a'zilu] M (refúgio) refuge; (estabelecimento) home; ~ **político** political asylum

asma ['aʒma] F asthma

asmático, -a [aʒ'matʃiku, a] ADJ, M/F asthmatic

asneira [aʒ'nejra] F (tolice) stupidity; (ato, dito) stupid thing

asno ['aʒnu] M donkey; (fig) ass

aspargo [aʃ'paxgu] M asparagus

aspas ['aʃpaʃ] FPL inverted commas; **entre** ~ in inverted commas

aspecto [aʃ'pɛktu] M (de uma questão) aspect; (aparência) look, appearance; (característica) feature; (ponto de vista) point of view; **ter bom** ~ to look good; **tomar um** ~ to take on an aspect

aspereza [aʃpe'reza] F roughness; (severidade) harshness; (rudeza) rudeness

aspergir [aʃpex'ʒi^r] VT to sprinkle

áspero, -a ['aʃperu, a] ADJ rough; (severo) harsh; (rude) rude

asperso, -a [aʃ'pɛxsu, a] PP de **aspergir** ◼ ADJ scattered

aspiração [aʃpira'sãw] (pl -ões) F aspiration; (inalação) inhalation

aspirador [aʃpira'do^r] M: ~ **(de pó)** vacuum cleaner; **passar o** ~ **(em)** to vacuum

---

NB: *European Portuguese adds the following consonants to certain words:* **b** (sú(b)dito, su(b)til); **c** (a(c)ção, a(c)cionista, a(c)to); **m** (inde(m)ne); **p** (ado(p)çã, ado(p)tar); *for further details see p. xiii.*

aspirante [aʃpi'rãtʃi] ADJ aspiring ◼ M/F candidate; (Mil) cadet; (Náut) midshipman

aspirar [aʃpi'raʰ] VT to breathe in; (bombear) to suck up; (Ling) to aspirate ◼ VI to breathe; (soprar) to blow; (desejar): ~ **a algo** to aspire to sth

aspirina [aʃpi'rina] F aspirin

aspirjo etc [aʃ'pixʒu] VB V **aspergir**

asqueroso, -a [aʃke'rozu, ɔza] ADJ disgusting, revolting

assadeira [asa'dejra] F roasting tin

assado, -a [a'sadu, a] ADJ roasted; (Culin) roast ◼ M roast; **carne assada** roast beef

assadura [asa'dura] F rash; (em bebê) nappy rash

assalariado, -a [asala'rjadu, a] ADJ salaried ◼ M/F wage-earner

assaltante [asaw'tãtʃi] M/F assailant; (de banco) robber; (de casa) burglar; (na rua) mugger

assaltar [asaw'taʰ] VT (atacar) to attack; (casa) to break into; (banco) to rob; (pessoa na rua) to mug; **assalto** [a'sawtu] M (ataque) attack, raid; (a um banco etc) raid, robbery; (a uma casa) burglary, break-in; (a uma pessoa na rua) mugging; (Boxe) round

assanhado, -a [asa'ɲadu, a] ADJ excited; (criança) excitable; (desavergonhado) brazen; (namorador) amorous

assanhar [asa'ɲaʰ] VT to excite; **assanhar-se** VR to get excited

assar [a'saʰ] VT to roast; (na grelha) to grill

assassinar [asasi'naʰ] VT to murder, kill; (Pol) to assassinate; **assassinato** [asasi'natu] M murder, killing; (Pol) assassination

assassínio [asa'sinju] M murder, killing; (Pol) assassination

assassino, -a [asa'sinu, a] M/F murderer; (Pol) assassin

assaz [a'saʒ] ADV (suficientemente) sufficiently; (muito) rather

asseado, -a [a'sjadu, a] ADJ clean

assediar [ase'dʒjaʰ] VT (sitiar) to besiege; (importunar) to pester; **assédio** [a'sɛdʒu] M siege; (insistência) insistence

assegurar [asegu'raʰ] VT (tornar seguro) to secure; (garantir) to ensure; (afirmar) to assure; **assegurar-se** VR: ~-**se de** to make sure of

asseio [a'seju] M cleanliness

assembléia [asẽ'bleja] F assembly; (reunião) meeting; ~ **geral (ordinária)** annual general meeting; ~ **geral extraordinária** extraordinary general meeting

assemelhar [aseme'ʎaʰ] VT to liken; **assemelhar-se** VR (ser parecido) to be alike; ~-**se a** to resemble, look like

assenhorear-se [aseɲo'rjaxsi] VR: ~ **de** to take possession of

assentado, -a [asẽ'tadu, a] ADJ (firme) fixed, secure; (combinado) agreed; (ajuizado) sensible

assentamento [asẽta'mẽtu] M registration; (nota) entry, record

assentar [asẽ'taʰ] VT (fazer sentar) to seat; (colocar) to place; (tijolos) to lay; (estabelecer) to establish; (decidir) to decide upon; (determinar) to fix, settle; (soco) to land ◼ VI (pó etc) to settle; **assentar-se** VR to sit down; ~ **com** to go with; ~ **em** ou **a** (roupa) to suit

assente [a'sẽtʃi] PP de **assentar** ◼ ADJ agreed, decided

assentimento [asẽtʃi'mẽtu] M assent, agreement

assentir [asẽ'tʃiʰ] VI to agree; ~ **(em)** to consent ou agree (to); ~ **(a)** to accede (to)

assento [a'sẽtu] M seat; (base) base; **tomar** ~ (sentar) to take a seat; (pó) to settle

assertiva [asex'tʃiva] F assertion

assessor, a [ase'soʰ(a)] M/F adviser; (Pol) aide; (assistente) assistant

assessoramento [asesora'mẽtu] M assistance

assessorar [aseso'raʰ] VT to advise

assessoria [aseso'ria] F advisory body

assestar [aseʃ'taʰ] VT to aim, point

asseveração [asevera'sãw] (pl -ões) F assertion

asseverar [aseve'raʰ] VT to affirm, assert

assexuado, -a [asek'swadu, a] ADJ asexual

assiduidade [asidwi'dadʒi] F (às aulas etc) regular attendance; (diligência) assiduity

assíduo, -a [a'sidwu, a] ADJ (aluno) who attends regularly; (diligente) assiduous; (constante) constant; **ser** ~ **num lugar** to be a regular visitor to a place

assim [a'sĩ] ADV (deste modo) like this, in this way, thus; (portanto) therefore; (igualmente) likewise; ~ ~ so-so; ~ **mesmo** in any case; **e** ~ **por diante** and so on; ~ **como** as well as; **como** ~? how do you mean?; ~ **que** (logo que) as soon as; **nem tanto** ~ not as much as that

assimétrico, -a [asi'mɛtriku, a] ADJ asymmetrical

assimilação [asimila'sãw] F assimilation

assimilar [asimi'laʰ] VT to assimilate; (apreender) to take in; (assemelhar) to compare

assinalado, -a [asina'ladu, a] ADJ (marcado) marked; (notável) notable; (célebre) eminent

assin. ABR = **assinatura**

assinalar [asina'laʰ] VT (marcar) to mark; (distinguir) to distinguish; (especificar) to point out

assinante [asi'nãtʃi] M/F (de jornal etc) subscriber

assinar [asi'naʰ] VT to sign

assinatura [asina'tura] F (nome) signature; (de jornal etc) subscription; (Teatro) season ticket; **fazer a** ~ **de** (revista etc) to take out a subscription to

assinto etc [a'sĩtu] VB V **assentir**

assistência [asiʃ'tẽsja] F (presença) presence; (público) audience; (auxílio) aid, assistance; ~ **médica** medical aid; ~ **social** social work; (serviços) social services pl; ~ **técnica** technical back-up

assistente [asiʃ'tẽtʃi] ADJ assistant ◼ M/F (pessoa presente) spectator, onlooker; (ajudante) assistant; ~ **social** social worker

assistir [asiʃ'tʃiʰ] VT, VI: ~ **(a)** (Med) to attend (to); ~ **a** (auxiliar) to assist; (TV, filme, jogo) to watch; (reunião) to attend; (caber) to fall to

assoalho [aso'aʎu] M (wooden) floor

assoar [aso'aʳ] VT: ~ **o nariz** to blow one's nose; **assoar-se** VR (PT) to blow one's nose

assoberbado, -a [asobex'badu, a] ADJ (pessoa: de serviço) snowed under with work

assoberbar [asobex'baʳ] VT (de serviço) to overload

assobiar [aso'bjaʳ] VI to whistle

assobio [aso'biu] M whistle; (instrumento) whistle; (de vapor) hiss

associação [asosja'sãw] (pl -ões) F association; (organização) society; (parceria) partnership; ~ **de moradores** residents' association

associado, -a [aso'sjadu, a] ADJ associate ■ M/F associate, member; (Com) associate; (sócio) partner

associar [aso'sjaʳ] VT to associate; **associar-se** VR (Com) to form a partnership; ~**-se a** to associate with

assolador, a [asola'do'(a)] ADJ devastating

assolar [aso'laʳ] VT to devastate

assomar [aso'maʳ] VI (aparecer) to appear; ~ **a** (subir) to climb to the top of

assombração [asõbra'sãw] (pl -ões) F (fantasma) ghost

assombrado, -a [asõ'bradu, a] ADJ astonished, amazed

assombrar [asõ'braʳ] VT to astonish, amaze; **assombrar-se** VR to be amazed

assombro [a'sõbru] M amazement, astonishment; (maravilha) marvel; **assombroso, -a** [asõ'brozu, ɔza] ADJ (espantoso) astonishing, amazing

assoprar [aso'praʳ] VI to blow ■ VT to blow; (velas) to blow out

assoviar [aso'vjaʳ] VT = **assobiar**

assovio [aso'viu] M = **assobio**

assumir [asu'miʳ] VT to assume, take on; (reconhecer) to accept, admit ■ VI to take office

Assunção [asũ'sãw] N (no Paraguai) Asunción

assuntar [asũ'taʳ] VT (prestar atenção) to pay attention to; (verificar) to find out ■ VI (meditar) to cogitate

assunto [a'sũtu] M (tema) subject, matter; (enredo) plot

assustadiço, -a [asuʃta'dʒisu, a] ADJ timorous

assustador, a [asuʃta'do'(a)] ADJ (alarmante) startling; (amedrontador) frightening

assustar [asuʃ'taʳ] VT to frighten, scare, startle; **assustar-se** VR to be frightened

asteca [aʃ'tɛka] ADJ, M/F Aztec

asterisco [aʃte'riʃku] M asterisk

astigmatismo [aʃtʃigma'tʃiʒmu] M astigmatism

astral [aʃ'tɾaw] (pl -ais) M state of mind

astro ['aʃtru] M star

astrologia [aʃtrolo'ʒia] F astrology

astrólogo, -a [aʃ'trɔlogu, a] M/F astrologer

astronauta [aʃtro'nawta] M/F astronaut

astronave [aʃtro'navi] F spaceship

astronomia [aʃtrono'mia] F astronomy

astronômico, -a [aʃtro'nomiku, a] ADJ (preço) astronomical

astrônomo, -a [aʃ'tronomu, a] M/F astronomer

astúcia [aʃ'tusja] F cunning

astuto, -a [aʃ'tutu, a] ADJ astute; (esperto) cunning

ata ['ata] F (de reunião) minutes pl

atacadista [ataka'dʒiʃta] ADJ wholesale ■ M/F wholesaler

atacado, -a [ata'kadu, a] ADJ (col: pessoa) in a bad mood ■ M: **por** ~ wholesale

atacante [ata'kãtʃi] ADJ attacking ■ M/F attacker, assailant ■ M (Futebol) forward

atacar [ata'kaʳ] VT to attack; (problema etc) to tackle

atado, -a [a'tadu, a] ADJ (desajeitado) clumsy, awkward; (perplexo) puzzled

atadura [ata'dura] F bandage

atalaia [ata'laja] F lookout post

atalhar [ata'ʎaʳ] VT (impedir) to prevent; (abreviar) to shorten ■ VI (tomar um atalho) to take a short cut

atalho [a'taʎu] M (caminho) short cut

atapetar [atape'taʳ] VT to carpet

ataque [a'taki] M attack; **ter um** ~ **(de raiva)** to have a fit; **ter um** ~ **de riso** to burst out laughing; ~ **aéreo** air raid; ~ **suicida** suicide attack

ataquei etc [ata'kej] VB V **atacar**

atar [a'taʳ] VT to tie (up), fasten; **não** ~ **nem desatar** (pessoa) to waver; (negócio) to be in the air

atarantado, -a [atarã'tadu, a] ADJ (pessoa) flustered, in a flap

atarantar [atarã'taʳ] VT to fluster

atarefado, -a [atare'fadu, a] ADJ busy

atarracado, -a [ataxa'kadu, a] ADJ stocky

atarraxar [ataxa'ʃaʳ] VT to screw

ataúde [ata'udʒi] M coffin

ataviar [ata'vjaʳ] VT to adorn, decorate; **ataviar-se** VR to get dressed up

atavio [ata'viu] M adornment

atazanar [ataza'naʳ] VT to pester

até [a'tɛ] PREP (PT: +a: lugar) up to, as far as; (tempo etc) until, till ■ ADV (tb: **até mesmo**) even; ~ **agora** up to now; ~ **certo ponto** to a certain extent; ~ **em cima** to the top; ~ **já** see you soon; ~ **logo** bye!; ~ **onde** as far as; ~ **que** until; ~ **que enfim!** at last!

atear [ate'aʳ] VT (fogo) to kindle; (fig) to incite, inflame; **atear-se** VR (fogo) to blaze; (paixões) to flare up; ~ **fogo a** to set light to

atéia [a'teja] F de **ateu**

ateísmo [ate'iʒmu] M atheism

ateliê [ate'lje] M studio

atemorizador, a [atemoriza'do'(a)] ADJ frightening

NB: European Portuguese adds the following consonants to certain words: **b** (sú(b)dito, su(b)til); **c** (a(c)ção, a(c)cionista, a(c)to); **m** (inde(m)ne); **p** (ado(p)ção, ado(p)tar); for further details see p. xiii.

atemorizar [atemori'za^r] VT to frighten; (*intimidar*) to intimidate

Atenas [a'tenaʃ] N Athens

atenção [atẽ'sãw] (*pl* -ões) F attention; (*cortesia*) courtesy; (*bondade*) kindness; ~! be careful!; **chamar a ~** to attract attention; **chamar a ~ de alguém** to tell sb off; **atencioso, -a** [atẽ'sjozu, ɔza] ADJ considerate

atenções [atẽ'sõjʃ] FPL *de* **atenção**

atender [atẽ'de^r] VT: ~ (a) to attend to; (*receber*) to receive; (*em loja*) to serve; (*deferir*) to grant; (*telefone etc*) to answer; (*paciente*) to see ■ VI (*ao telefone, porta*) to answer; (*dar atenção*) to pay attention; **atendimento** [atẽdʒi'mẽtu] M service; (*recepção*) reception; **horário de atender** opening hours; (*em consultório*) surgery (*Brit*) *ou* office (*US*) hours

atenho *etc* [a'teɲu] VB *V* **ater-se**

atentado [atẽ'tadu] M (*ataque*) attack; (*crime*) crime; (*contra a vida de alguém*) attempt on sb's life; ~ **ao pudor** indecent exposure; ~ **suicida** suicide attack

atentar [atẽ'ta^r] VT (*empreender*) to undertake ■ VI to make an attempt; ~ **a** *ou* **em** *ou* **para** to pay attention to; ~ **contra a vida de alguém** to make an attempt on sb's life; ~ **contra a moral** to offend against morality

atento, -a [a'tẽtu, a] ADJ attentive; (*exame*) careful; **estar ~ a** to be aware *ou* mindful of

atenuação [atenwa'sãw] (*pl* -ões) F reduction, lessening

atenuante [ate'nwãtʃi] ADJ extenuating ■ M extenuating circumstance

atenuar [ate'nwa^r] VT (*diminuir*) to reduce, lessen

aterrador, a [atexa'do^r(a)] ADJ terrifying

aterragem [ate'xaʒẽj] (*PT*) (*pl* -ns) F (*Aer*) landing

aterrar [ate'xa^r] VT (*cobrir com terra*) to cover with earth; (*praia*) to reclaim; (*PT*) ■ VI (*Aer*) to land

aterrissagem [atexi'saʒẽ] (*BR*) (*pl* -ns) F (*Aer*) landing

aterrissar [atexi'sa^r] (*BR*) VI (*Aer*) to land

aterrizar [atexi'za^r] VI = **aterrissar**

aterro [a'texu] M landfill

aterrorizado, -a [atexori'zadu, a] ADJ terrified

aterrorizador, a [atexoriza'do^r(a)] ADJ terrifying

aterrorizante [atexori'zãtʃi] ADJ terrifying

aterrorizar [atexori'za^r] VT to terrorize

ater-se [a'texsi] (*irreg*) VR: ~ **a** (*prender-se*) to get caught up in; (*limitar-se*) to restrict o.s. to

atestado, -a [ateʃ'tadu, a] ADJ certified ■ M certificate; (*prova*) proof; (*Jur*) testimony

atestar [ateʃ'ta^r] VT (*certificar*) to certify; (*testemunhar*) to bear witness to; (*provar*) to prove

ateu, atéia [a'tew, a'teja] ADJ, M/F atheist

ateve *etc* [a'tevi] VB *V* **ater-se**

atiçador [atʃisa'do^r] M (*utensílio*) poker

atiçar [atʃi'sa^r] VT (*fogo*) to poke; (*incitar*) to incite; (*provocar*) to provoke; (*sentimento*) to induce

atilado, -a [atʃi'ladu, a] ADJ (*esperto*) clever

atinado, -a [atʃi'nadu, a] ADJ (*sensato*) wise, sensible

atinar [atʃi'na^r] VT (*acertar*) to guess correctly ■ VI: ~ **com** (*solução*) to find; ~ **em** to notice; ~ **a fazer algo** to succeed in doing sth

atingir [atʃi'ʒi^r] VT to reach; (*acertar*) to hit; (*afetar*) to affect; (*objetivo*) to achieve; (*compreender*) to grasp

atingível [atʃi'ʒivew] (*pl* -eis) ADJ attainable

atinha *etc* [a'tʃiɲa] VB *V* **ater-se**

atinjo *etc* [a'tʃĩʒu] VB *V* **atingir**

atípico, -a [a'tʃipiku, a] ADJ atypical, untypical

atirador, a [atʃira'do^r(a)] M/F marksman/woman; ~ **de tocaia** sniper

atirar [atʃi'ra^r] VT (*lançar*) to throw, fling, hurl ■ VI (*arma*) to shoot; **atirar-se** VR: ~-**se a** (*lançar-se a*) to hurl o.s. at; ~ (**em**) to shoot (at)

atitude [atʃi'tudʒi] F attitude; (*postura*) posture; **tomar uma ~** (*reagir*) to do something about it

ativa [a'tʃiva] F (*Mil*) active service

ativar [atʃi'va^r] VT to activate; (*apressar*) to hasten

ative *etc* [a'tʃivi] VB *V* **ater-se**

atividade [atʃivi'dadʒi] F activity

ativo, -a [a'tʃivu, a] ADJ active ■ M (*Com*) assets *pl*

atlântico, -a [at'lãtʃiku, a] ADJ Atlantic ■ M: **o (Oceano) A~** the Atlantic (Ocean)

atlas [a'tlaʃ] M INV atlas

atleta [at'lɛta] M/F athlete; **atlético, -a** [at'lɛtʃiku, a] ADJ athletic; **atletismo** [atle'tʃiʒmu] M athletics *sg*

atmosfera [atmoʃ'fera] F atmosphere

ato ['atu] M act; (*ação*) action; (*cerimônia*) ceremony; (*Teatro*) act; **em ~ contínuo** straight after; **no ~** on the spot; **no mesmo ~** at the same time; ~ **falho** Freudian slip; ~ **público** public ceremony

à-toa ADJ (*insignificante*) insignificant; (*simples*) simple, easy ■ ADV *vtb* **toa**

atoalhado, -a [atoa'ʎadu, a] ADJ: (*tecido*) ~ towelling

atolado, -a [ato'ladu, a] ADJ (*tb fig*) bogged down

atolar [ato'la^r] VT to bog down; **atolar-se** VR to get bogged down

atoleiro [ato'lejru] M bog, quagmire; (*fig*) quandary, fix

atômico, -a [a'tomiku, a] ADJ atomic

atomizador [atomiza'do^r] M atomizer

átomo ['atomu] M atom

atônito, -a [a'tonitu, a] ADJ astonished, amazed

ator [a'to^r] M actor

atordoado, -a [atox'dwadu, a] ADJ dazed

atordoador, a [atoxdwa'do^r(a)] ADJ stunning

atordoamento [atoxdwa'mẽtu] M daze

atordoar [atox'dwa^r] VT to daze, stun

atormentar [atoxmẽ'ta^r] VT to torment; (*importunar*) to plague

atracação [atraka'sãw] (*pl* -ões) F (*Náut*) mooring; (*briga*) fight; (*col: agarração*) necking

atração [atra'sãw] (*pl* -ões) F attraction

atracar [atra'ka^r] VT, VI (*Náut*) to moor; **atracar-**

se VR to grapple; (col: abraçar-se) to neck

atrações [atra'sõjʃ] FPL de **atração**

atractivo, -a [atra'tivu, a] (PT) ADJ = **atrativo**

atraente [atra'ẽtʃi] ADJ attractive

atraiçoar [atraj'swaʳ] VT to betray

atrair [atra'iʳ] VT to attract; (fascinar) to fascinate

atrapalhação [atrapaʎa'sãw] F (confusão) confusion

atrapalhar [atrapa'ʎaʳ] VT (confundir) to confuse; (perturbar) to disturb; (dificultar) to hinder ■ VI to be a nuisance; to be a hindrance; **atrapalhar-se** VR to get confused

atrás [a'trajʃ] ADV behind; (no fundo) at the back ■ PREP: ~ **de** behind; (no tempo) after; (em busca de) after; **um ~ de outro** one after the other; **dois meses ~** two months ago; **não ficar ~** (fig) not to be far behind

atrasado, -a [atra'zadu, a] ADJ late; (país etc) backward; (relógio etc) slow; (pagamento) overdue; (costumes, pessoa) antiquated; (número de revista) back; **estar ~ nos pagamentos** to be in arrears; **atrasados** [atra'zaduʃ] MPL (Com) arrears

atrasar [atra'zaʳ] VT to delay; (progresso, desenvolvimento) to hold back; (relógio) to put back; (pagamento) to be late with ■ VI (relógio etc) to be slow; (avião, pessoa) to be late; **atrasar-se** VR (chegar tarde) to be late; (num trabalho) to fall behind; (num pagamento) to get into arrears

atraso [a'trazu] M delay; (de país etc) backwardness; **atrasos** MPL (Com) arrears; **chegar com ~** to arrive late; **com 20 minutos de ~** 20 minutes late; **com um ~ de 6 meses** (Com: pagamento) six months in arrears; **um ~ de vida** a hindrance

atrativo, -a [atra'tʃivu, a] ADJ attractive ■ M attraction, appeal; (incentivo) incentive; **atrativos** MPL (encantos) charms

atravancar [atravã'kaʳ] VT to block, obstruct; (encher) to fill up

através [atra'vɛʃ] ADV across; ~ **de** (de lado a lado) across; (pelo centro de) through; (por meio de) through

atravessado, -a [atrave'sadu, a] ADJ (na garganta) stuck; **estar com alguém ~ na garganta** to be peeved with sb

atravessar [atrave'saʳ] VT (cruzar) to cross; (pôr ao través) to put ou lay across; (traspassar) to pass through; (crise etc) to go through

atrelar [atre'laʳ] VT (cão) to put on a leash; (cavalo) to harness; (duas viaturas) to couple up

atrever-se [atre'vexsi] VR: ~ **a** to dare to;

atrevido, -a [atre'vidu, a] ADJ (petulante) cheeky, impudent; (corajoso) bold; **atrevimento** [atrevi'mẽtu] M (ousadia) boldness; (insolência) cheek, insolence

atribuição [atribwi'sãw] (pl -ões) F attribution; **atribuições** FPL (direitos) rights; (poderes) powers

atribuir [atri'bwiʳ] VT: ~ **algo a** to attribute sth

to; (prêmios, regalias) to confer sth on

atribulação [atribula'sãw] (pl -ões) F tribulation

atribular [atribu'laʳ] VT to trouble, distress; **atribular-se** VR to be distressed

atributo [atri'butu] M attribute

átrio ['atrju] M hall; (pátio) courtyard

atrito [a'tritu] M (fricção) friction; (desentendimento) disagreement

atriz [a'triʒ] F actress

atrocidade [atrosi'dadʒi] F atrocity

atrofia [atro'fia] F atrophy

atrofiar [atro'fjaʳ] VT to atrophy; **atrofiar-se** VR to atrophy

atropeladamente [atropelada'mẽtʃi] ADV haphazardly

atropelamento [atropela'mẽtu] M (de pedestre) running over

atropelar [atrope'laʳ] VT to knock down, run over; (empurrar) to jostle

atropelo [atro'pelu] M bustle, scramble; (confusão) confusion

atroz [a'trɔʒ] ADJ (cruel) merciless; (crime) heinous; (dor, lembrança, feiúra) terrible, awful

attaché [ata'ʃe] M attaché

atuação [atwa'sãw] (pl -ões) F acting; (de ator etc) performance

atuado, -a [a'twadu, a] ADJ (pessoa) in a bad mood

atual [a'twaw] (pl -ais) ADJ current; (pessoa, carro) modern; **atualidade** [atwali'dadʒi] F present (time); **atualidades** FPL (notícias) news sg

atualização [atwaliza'sãw] (pl -ões) F updating

atualizado, -a [atwali'zadu, a] ADJ up-to-date

atualizar [atwali'zaʳ] VT to update; **atualizar-se** VR to bring o.s. up to date

atualmente [atwaw'mẽtʃi] ADV at present, currently; (hoje em dia) nowadays

atuante [a'twãtʃi] ADJ active

atuar [a'twaʳ] VI to act; ~ **para** to contribute to; ~ **sobre** to influence

atulhar [atu'ʎaʳ] VT (encher) to cram full; (meter) to stuff, cram

atum [a'tũ] (pl -ns) M tuna (fish)

aturar [atu'raʳ] VT (suportar) to endure, put up with

aturdido, -a [atux'dʒidu, a] ADJ stunned; (com barulho) deafened; (com confusão, movimento) bewildered

aturdimento [atuxdʒi'mẽtu] M bewilderment

aturdir [atux'dʒiʳ] VT to stun; (suj: barulho) to deafen; (: confusão, movimento) to bewilder

atxim [a'tʃĩ] EXCL achoo!

audácia [aw'dasja] F boldness; (insolência) insolence; **que ~!** what a cheek!; **audacioso, -a** [awda'sjozu, ɔza] ADJ daring; (insolente) insolent

audaz [aw'daʒ] ADJ daring; (insolente) insolent

audição [awdʒi'sãw] (pl -ões) F audition;

NB: European Portuguese adds the following consonants to certain words: **b** (sú(b)dito, su(b)til); **c** (a(c)ção, a(c)cionista, a(c)to); **m** (inde(m)ne); **p** (ado(p)çã, ado(p)tar); for further details see p. xiii.

(*concerto*) recital

audiência [aw'dʒjẽsja] F audience; (*de tribunal*) session, hearing

audiovisual [awdʒjovi'zwaw] (*pl* -ais) ADJ audiovisual

auditar [awdʒi'taʳ] VT (*Com*) to audit

auditivo, -a [awdʒi'tʃivu, a] ADJ hearing *atr*, auditory

auditor, a [awdʒi'toʳ(a)] M/F (*Com*) auditor; (*juiz*) judge; (*ouvinte*) listener

auditoria [awdʒito'ria] F auditing; **fazer a ~ de** to audit

auditório [awdʒi'tɔrju] M (*ouvintes*) audience; (*recinto*) auditorium; **programa de ~** program(me) recorded before a live audience

audível [aw'dʒivew] (*pl* -eis) ADJ audible

auferir [awfe'riʳ] VT (*lucro*) to derive

auge ['awʒi] M height, peak

augurar [awgu'raʳ] VT to augur; (*felicidades*) to wish

augúrio [aw'gurju] M omen

aula ['awla] F (*PT: sala*) classroom; (*lição*) lesson, class; **dar ~** to teach

aumentar [awmẽ'taʳ] VT to increase; (*salários, preços*) to raise; (*sala, casa*) to expand, extend; (*suj: lente*) to magnify; (*acrescentar*) to add ∎ VI to increase; (*preço, salário*) to rise, go up; **~ de peso** (*pessoa*) to put on weight

aumento [aw'mẽtu] M increase; (*de preços*) rise; (*ampliação*) enlargement; (*crescimento*) growth

áureo, -a ['awrju, a] ADJ golden

auréola [aw'rɛola] F halo

aurora [aw'rɔra] F dawn

auscultar [awʃkuw'taʳ] VT (*opinião pública*) to sound out; (*paciente*): **~ alguém** to sound sb's chest

ausência [aw'zẽsja] F absence

ausentar-se [awzẽ'taxsi] VR (*ir-se*) to go away; (*afastar-se*) to stay away

ausente [aw'zẽtʃi] ADJ absent ∎ M/F missing person

auspiciar [awʃpi'sjaʳ] VT to augur

auspício [aw'ʃpisju] M: **sob os ~s de** under the auspices of

auspicioso, -a [awʃpi'sjozu, ɔza] ADJ auspicious

austeridade [awʃteri'dadʒi] F austerity

austero, -a [awʃ'tɛru, a] ADJ austere

austral [awʃ'traw] (*pl* -ais) ADJ southern

Austrália [awʃ'tralja] F: **a ~** Australia; **australiano, -a** [awʃtra'ljanu, a] ADJ, M/F Australian

Áustria ['awʃtrja] F: **a ~** Austria; **austríaco, -a** [awʃ'triaku, a] ADJ, M/F Austrian

autarquia [awtax'kia] F non-governmental organization, ≈ quango (*Brit*)

autárquico, -a [aw'taxkiku, a] ADJ non-governmental

autenticar [awtẽtʃi'kaʳ] VT to authenticate; (*Com, Jur*) to certify

autenticidade [awtẽtʃisi'dadʒi] F authenticity

autêntico, -a [aw'tẽtʃiku, a] ADJ authentic; (*pessoa*) genuine; (*verdadeiro*) true, real

autismo [aw'tʃiʒmu] M autism

autista [aw'tʃiʃta] ADJ autistic ∎ M/F autistic person

auto ['awtu] M (*automóvel*) car; **autos** MPL (*Jur: processo*) legal proceedings; (*documentos*) legal papers

auto-adesivo, -a ADJ self-adhesive

auto-afirmação F self-assertion

autobiografia [awtobjogra'fia] F autobiography

autobiográfico, -a [awtobjo'grafiku, a] ADJ autobiographical

autocarro [awto'kaxu] (*PT*) M bus

autocontrole [awtokõ'troli] M self-control

autocrata [awto'krata] ADJ autocratic

autóctone [aw'tɔktoni] ADJ indigenous ∎ M/F native

autodefesa [awtode'feza] F self-defence (*Brit*), self-defense (*US*)

autodestruição [awtodeʃ'trwisãw] F self-destruction

autodeterminação [awtodetexmina'sãw] F self-determination

autodidata [awtodʒi'data] ADJ self-taught ∎ M/F autodidact

autodisciplina [awtodʒisi'plina] F self-discipline

autodomínio [awtodo'minju] M self-control

autódromo [aw'tɔdromu] M race track

auto-escola F driving school

auto-estrada F motorway (*Brit*), expressway (*US*)

autografar [awtogra'faʳ] VT to autograph

autógrafo [aw'tɔgrafu] M autograph

automação [awtoma'sãw] F automation; **~ de escritórios** office automation

automático, -a [awto'matʃiku, a] ADJ automatic

automatização [awtomatʃiza'sãw] F = **automação**

automatizar [awtomatʃi'zaʳ] VT to automate

autômato [aw'tomatu] M automaton

automedicar-se [awtomedʒi'kaxsi] VR to treat o.s.

automobilismo [awtomobi'liʒmu] M motoring; (*Esporte*) motor car racing

automóvel [awto'mɔvew] (*pl* -eis) M motor car (*Brit*), automobile (*US*)

autonomia [awtono'mia] F autonomy

autônomo, -a [aw'tonomu, a] ADJ autonomous; (*trabalhador*) self-employed ∎ M/F self-employed person

autopeça [awto'pesa] F car spare

autópsia [aw'tɔpsja] F post-mortem, autopsy

autor, a [aw'toʳ(a)] M/F author; (*de um crime*) perpetrator; (*Jur*) plaintiff

autoral [awto'raw] (*pl* -ais) ADJ: **direitos autorais** copyright *sg*

auto-retrato M self-portrait

autoridade [awtori'dadʒi] F authority

autoritário, -a [awtori'tarju, a] ADJ authoritarian

autoritarismo [awtorita'riʒmu] M authoritarianism

autorização [awtoriza'sãw] (*pl* -ões) F permission, authorization; **dar ~ a alguém para** to give sb permission to, authorize sb to

autorizar [awtori'za^r] VT to authorize

auto-serviço M self-service

auto-suficiente ADJ self-sufficient

auto-sugestão F autosuggestion

autuar [aw'twa^r] VT to sue

auxiliar [awsi'lja^r] ADJ auxiliary ■ M/F assistant ■ VT to help, assist; **auxílio** [aw'silju] M help, assistance, aid

auxílio-doença (*pl* auxílios-doença) M sickness benefit, sick pay

Av ABR (= *avenida*) Ave

avacalhado, -a [avaka'ʎadu, a] ADJ sloppy

avacalhar [avaka'ʎa^r] (*col*) VT to screw up

aval [a'vaw] (*pl* -ais) M guarantee; (*Com*) surety

avalancha [ava'lãʃa] F avalanche

avalanche [ava'lãʃi] F = **avalancha**

avaliação [avalja'sãw] (*pl* -ões) F valuation; (*apreciação*) assessment, evaluation

avaliador, a [avalja'do^r(a)] M/F: **~ de danos** loss adjuster

avaliar [ava'lja^r] VT to value; to assess, evaluate; (*imaginar*) to imagine; **~ algo em $100** to value sth at $100

avalista [ava'liʃta] M/F guarantor

avalizar [avali'za^r] VT to guarantee

avançada [avã'sada] F advance

avançado, -a [avã'sadu, a] ADJ advanced; (*idéias, pessoa*) progressive

avançar [avã'sa^r] VT to move forward ■ VI to advance; **avanço** [a'vãsu] M advancement; (*progresso*) progress; (*melhora*) improvement, advance

avantajado, -a [avãta'ʒadu, a] ADJ (*corpulento*) stout

avante [a'vãtʃi] ADV forward

avarento, -a [ava'rẽtu, a] ADJ mean ■ M/F miser

avareza [ava'reza] F meanness

avaria [ava'ria] F damage; (*Tec*) breakdown; **avariado, -a** [ava'rjadu, a] ADJ damaged; (*máquina*) out of order; (*carro*) broken down; **avariar** [ava'rja^r] VT to damage ■ VI to suffer damage; (*Tec*) to break down

avaro, -a [a'varu, a] ADJ mean ■ M/F miser

ave ['avi] F bird

aveia [a'veja] F oats *pl*

aveio *etc* [a'veju] VB V **avir-se**

avelã [ave'lã] F hazelnut

aveludado, -a [avelu'dadu, a] ADJ velvety; (*voz*) smooth

avenho *etc* [a'veɲu] VB V **avir-se**

avenida [ave'nida] F avenue

avental [avẽ'taw] (*pl* -ais) M apron; (*vestido*) pinafore dress (*Brit*), jumper (*US*)

aventar [avẽ'ta^r] VT (*idéia etc*) to put forward

aventura [avẽ'tura] F adventure; (*proeza*) exploit

aventurar [avẽtu'ra^r] VT (*ousar*) to risk, venture; **aventurar-se** VR: **aventurar-se a** to dare to

aventureiro, -a [avẽtu'rejru, a] ADJ adventurous ■ M/F adventurer

averiguação [averigwa'sãw] (*pl* -ões) F investigation, inquiry; (*verificação*) verification

averiguar [averi'gwa^r] VT (*inquirir*) to investigate; (*verificar*) to verify

avermelhado, -a [avexme'ʎadu, a] ADJ reddish

aversão [avex'sãw] (*pl* -ões) F aversion

averso, -a [a'vɛxsu, a] ADJ: **~ a** averse to

aversões [avex'sõjʃ] FPL *de* **aversão**

avesso, -a [a'vesu, a] ADJ (*lado*) opposite, reverse ■ M wrong side, reverse; **ao ~** inside out; **às avessas** (*inverso*) upside down; (*oposto*) the wrong way round; **virar pelo ~** to turn inside out

avestruz [aveʃ'truʒ] M ostrich

aviação [avja'sãw] F aviation, flying

aviado, -a [a'vjadu, a] ADJ (*executado*) ready; (*apressado*) hurried

aviador, a [avja'do^r(a)] M/F aviator, airman/woman

aviamento [avja'mẽtu] M (*Costura*) haberdashery (*Brit*), notions *pl* (*US*); (*de receita médica*) filling; (*Com*) goodwill

avião [a'vjãw] (*pl* -ões) M aeroplane; **~ a jato** jet

aviar [a'vja^r] VT (*receita médica*) to make up

avicultor, a [avikuw'to^r(a)] M/F poultry farmer

avicultura [avikuw'tura] F poultry farming

avidez [avi'deʒ] F (*cobiça*) greed; (*desejo*) eagerness

ávido, -a ['avidu, a] ADJ (*cobiçoso*) greedy; (*desejoso*) eager

aviltamento [aviwta'mẽtu] M debasement

aviltar [aviw'ta^r] VT to debase; **aviltar-se** VR to demean o.s

avim *etc* [a'vĩ] VB V **avir-se**

avinagrado, -a [avina'gradu, a] ADJ sour, acid

aviões [a'vjõjʃ] MPL *de* **avião**

avir-se [a'vixsi] (*irreg*) VR (*conciliar-se*) to reach an understanding

avisar [avi'za^r] VT (*advertir*) to warn; (*informar*) to tell, let know; **ele avisou que chega amanhã** he said he's arriving tomorrow; **aviso** [a'vizu] M (*comunicação*) notice; (*advertência*) warning; **aviso prévio** notice

avistar [aviʃ'ta^r] VT to catch sight of; **avistar-se** VR: **~-se com** (*ter entrevista*) to have an interview with

avitaminose [avitami'nɔzi] F vitamin deficiency

avivar [avi'va^r] VT (*intensificar*) to intensify, heighten; (*memória*) to bring back

avizinhar-se [avizi'ɲaxsi] VR (*aproximar-se*) to approach, come near

avo ['avu] M: **um doze ~s** one twelfth

NB: *European Portuguese adds the following consonants to certain words:* **b** (sú(b)dito, su(b)til); **c** (a(c)ção, a(c)cionista, a(c)to); **m** (inde(m)ne); **p** (ado(p)çã, ado(p)tar); *for further details see p. xiii.*

avô, avó [a'vo, a'vɔ] M/F grandfather/mother;
avós MPL grandparents
avoado, -a [avo'adu, a] ADJ (pessoa) absent-minded
avolumar [avolu'ma^r] VT (aumentar: em volume) to swell; (: em número) to accumulate; (ocupar espaço) to fill; **avolumar-se** VR to increase; to swell
avulso, -a [a'vuwsu, a] ADJ separate, detached ■ M single copy
avultado, -a [avuw'tadu, a] ADJ large, bulky
avultar [avuw'ta^r] VT to enlarge, expand ■ VI (sobressair) to stand out; (aumentar) to increase
axila [ak'sila] F armpit
axioma [a'sjɔma] M axiom
azáfama [a'zafama] F bustle; (pressa) hurry
azaléia [aza'lɛja] F azalea
azar [a'za^r] M bad luck; ~! too bad, bad luck!; **estar com** ~ to be unlucky; **ter** ~ to be unlucky
azarado, -a [aza'radu, a] ADJ (desafortunado) unlucky
azarento, -a [aza'rẽtu, a] ADJ (que dá azar) unlucky
azedar [aze'da^r] VT to turn sour; (pessoa) to put in a bad mood ■ VI to turn sour; (leite) to go off; **azedo, -a** [a'zedu, a] ADJ (sabor) sour; (leite) off; (fig) grumpy, bad-tempered
azedume [aze'dumi] M (sabor) sourness; (fig) grumpiness

azeitar [azej'ta^r] VT (untar) to grease; (lubrificar) to oil
azeite [a'zejtʃi] M oil; (de oliva) olive oil
azeitona [azej'tona] F olive
Azerbaijão [azexbaj'ʒãw] M: **o ~** Azerbaijan
azeviche [aze'viʃi] M (cor) jet black
azevinho [aze'viɲu] M holly
azia [a'zia] F heartburn
aziago, -a [a'zjagu, a] ADJ (de mau agouro) ominous
azinhaga [azi'ɲaga] F (country) lane
azinhavre [azi'ɲavri] M verdigris
azo ['azu] M (oportunidade) opportunity; (pretexto) pretext; **dar ~ a** to give occasion to
azougue [a'zogi] M quicksilver; (Quím) mercury; (fig: pessoa: inquieta) livewire; (: esperta) sharp person
azucrinar [azukri'na^r] VT to bother, pester
azul [a'zuw] (pl -uis) ADJ blue; **tudo** ~ (fig) everything's rosy
azular [azu'la^r] VI to flee
azulejar [azule'ʒa^r] VT to tile
azulejo [azu'leʒu] M (glazed) tile
azul-marinho ADJ INV navy blue
azul-turquesa ADJ INV turquoise

Bb

B, b [be] (pl **bs**) M B, b; **B de Beatriz** B for
Benjamin (Brit) ou Baker (US)
baba ['baba] F dribble
babá [ba'ba] F nanny
babaca [ba'baka] (col) ADJ stupid ▪ M/F idiot
baba-de-moça (pl **babas-de-moça**) F sweet made
with sugar, coconut milk and eggs
babado [ba'badu] M frill; (col) piece of gossip
babador [baba'do'] M bib
babaquice [baba'kisi] F stupidity; (ato, dito)
stupid thing
babar [ba'ba'] VT to dribble on ▪ VI to dribble;
babar-se VR to dribble; **~(-se) por** to drool over
babeiro [ba'bejru] (PT) M bib
babel [ba'bɛw] (pl **-éis**) F (fig) muddle
baby-sitter ['bejbisite'] (pl **-s**) M/F baby-sitter
bacalhau [baka'ʎaw] M (dried) cod
bacalhoada [bakaʎo'ada] F salt cod stew
bacana [ba'kana] (col) ADJ great
bacanal [baka'naw] (pl **-ais**) M orgy
bacharel [baʃa'rɛw] (pl **-éis**) M graduate
bacharelado [baʃare'ladu] M bachelor's degree
bacharelar-se [baʃare'laxsi] VR to graduate
bacia [ba'sia] F basin; (sanitária) bowl; (Anat)
pelvis
background [bɛk'grãwdʒi] (pl **-s**) M background
backup [ba'kapi] (pl **-s**) M (Comput) back-up;
tirar um ~ de to back up
baço, -a ['basu, a] ADJ dull; (metal) tarnished
▪ M (Anat) spleen
bacon ['bejkõ] M bacon
bactéria [bak'tɛrja] F germ, bacterium;
bactérias MPL (germes) bacteria pl
badalado, -a [bada'ladu, a] (col) ADJ talked
about, famous
badalar [bada'la'] VT, VI (sino) to ring ▪ VI to
ring; (col) to go out and about
badalativo, -a [badala'tʃivu, a] (col) ADJ fun-
loving
badalo [ba'dalu] M clapper
badejo [ba'deʒu] M sea bass
baderna [ba'dɛxna] F commotion
badulaque [badu'laki] M trinket; **badulaques**
MPL (coisas sem valor) junk sg

bafafá [bafa'fa] (col) M kerfuffle
bafejar [bafe'ʒa'] VT (aquecer com o bafo) to blow;
(fortuna) to smile upon
bafejo [ba'feʒu] M (sopro) whiff; **~ da sorte**
stroke of luck
bafio [ba'fiu] M musty smell
bafo ['bafu] M (hálito) (bad) breath; **isso é ~ dele**
(col) he's just making it up
bafômetro [ba'fometru] M Breathalyser®
baforada [bafo'rada] F (fumaça) puff
bagaço [ba'gasu] M (de frutos) pulp; (PT: cachaça)
brandy; **estar/ficar um ~** (fig: pessoa) to be/get
run down
bagageiro [baga'ʒejru] M (Auto) roof rack; (PT)
porter
bagagem [ba'gaʒẽ] F luggage; (fig) baggage,
luggage; **recebimento de ~** (Aer) baggage
reclaim
bagatela [baga'tɛla] F trinket; (fig) trifle
Bagdá [bagi'da] N Baghdad
bago ['bagu] M (fruto) berry; (uva) grape; (de
chumbo) pellet; (col!) ball (!)
bagulho [ba'guʎu] M (objeto) piece of junk;
(pessoa): **ser um ~** to be as ugly as sin
bagunça [ba'gũsa] F (confusão) mess, shambles
sg; **bagunçado, -a** [bagũ'sadu, a] ADJ in a mess;
bagunçar [bagũ'sa'] VT to mess up; **bagunceiro,
-a** [bagũ'sejru, a] ADJ messy
Bahamas [ba'amaʃ] FPL: **as ~** the Bahamas
baia ['baja] F bail
baía [ba'ia] F bay
baiano, -a [ba'janu, a] ADJ, M/F Bahian
baila ['bajla] F: **trazer/vir à ~** to bring/come up
bailado [baj'ladu] M dance; (balé) ballet
bailar [baj'la'] VT, VI to dance
bailarino, -a [bajla'rinu, a] M/F ballet dancer
baile ['bajli] M dance; (formal) ball; **dar um ~ em
alguém** to pull sb's leg; **~ à fantasia** fancy-
dress ball
bainha [ba'iɲa] F (de arma) sheath; (de costura)
hem
baioneta [bajo'neta] F bayonet; **~ calada** fixed
bayonet
bairrista [baj'xiʃta] ADJ loyal to one's

NB: European Portuguese adds the following consonants to certain words: **b** (sú(b)dito, su(b)til); **c** (a(c)ção,
a(c)cionista, a(c)to); **m** (inde(m)ne); **p** (ado(p)çã, ado(p)tar); for further details see p. xiii.

bairro | bananosa

neighbo(u)rhood ▪ M/F proud local
bairro ['bajxu] M district
baita ['bajta] ADJ huge; (gripe) bad
baixa ['bajʃa] F (abaixamento) decrease; (de preço) reduction, fall; (diminuição) drop; (Bolsa) low; (em combate) casualty; (do serviço) discharge; **dar** ou **ter** ~ to be discharged
baixada [baj'ʃada] F lowland
baixa-mar F low tide
baixar [baj'ʃaʳ] VT to lower; (bandeira) to take down; (ordem) to issue; (lei) to pass; (Comput) to download ▪ VI to go (ou come) down; (temperatura, preço) to drop, fall; (col: aparecer) to show up; ~ **ao hospital** to go into hospital
baixaria [bajʃa'ria] F vulgarity; (ação) cheap trick
baixela [baj'ʃɛla] F serving set
baixeza [baj'ʃeza] F meanness, baseness
baixinho [baj'ʃiɲu] ADV (falar) softly, quietly; (em segredo) secretly
baixio [baj'ʃiu] M sandbank, sandbar
baixista [baj'ʃiʃta] M/F (Bolsa) bear ▪ ADJ bear atr
baixo, -a ['bajʃu, a] ADJ low; (pessoa) short, small; (rio) shallow; (linguagem) common; (olhos) lowered; (atitude) mean, base; (metal) base ▪ ADV low; (em posição baixa) low down; (falar) softly ▪ M (Mús) bass; **em ~** below; (em casa) downstairs; **em voz baixa** in a quiet voice; **para** ~ down, downwards; (em casa) downstairs; **por ~ de** under, underneath; **altos e ~s** ups and downs; **estar por** ~ to be down on one's luck; **baixo-astral** (col) M bad vibes pl; **estar num baixo-astral** to be at a low ebb
baixote, -a [baj'ʃotʃi, ta] ADJ shortish
bajulador, a [baʒula'doʳ(a)] ADJ obsequious
bajular [baʒu'laʳ] VT to fawn over
bala ['bala] F bullet; (BR: doce) sweet; **estar em ponto de** ~ (fig) to be in tip-top condition; **estar/ficar uma** ~ (fig) to be/get furious
balada [ba'lada] F ballad
balaio [ba'laju] M straw basket
balança [ba'lãsa] F scales pl; **B~** (Astrologia) Libra; ~ **comercial** balance of trade; ~ **de pagamentos** balance of payments
balançar [balã'saʳ] VT (fazer oscilar) to swing; (pesar) to weigh (up) ▪ VI to swing; (carro, avião) to shake; (navio) to roll; (em cadeira) to rock; **balançar-se** VR to swing
balancear [balã'sjaʳ] VT to balance
balancete [balã'setʃi] M (Com) trial balance
balanço [ba'lãsu] M (movimento) swinging; (brinquedo) swing; (de navio) rolling; (de carro, avião) shaking; (Com: registro) balance (sheet); (: verificação) audit; **fazer um** ~ **de** (fig) to take stock of
balangandã [balãgã'dã] M bauble
balão [ba'lãw] (pl -ões) M balloon; (em história em quadrinhos) speech bubble; (Auto) turning area; ~ **de oxigênio** oxygen tank
balão-de-ensaio (pl balões-de-ensaio) M: **soltar um** ~ (fig) to put out feelers
balar [ba'laʳ] VI to bleat

balaustrada [balawʃ'trada] F balustrade
balaústre [bala'uʃtri] M ban(n)ister
balbuciar [bawbu'sjaʳ] VT, VI to babble
balbucio [bawbu'siu] M babbling
balbúrdia [baw'buxdʒja] F uproar, bedlam
balcão [baw'kãw] (pl -ões) M balcony; (de loja) counter; (Teatro) circle; **balconista** [bawko'niʃta] M/F shop assistant
baldado, -a [baw'dadu, a] ADJ unsuccessful, fruitless
baldar [baw'daʳ] VT to frustrate, foil
balde ['bawdʒi] M bucket, pail
baldeação [bawdʒja'sãw] (pl -ões) F transfer; **fazer** ~ to change
baldio, -a [baw'dʒiu, a] ADJ fallow, uncultivated; **(terreno)** ~ (piece of) waste ground
balé [ba'lɛ] M ballet
baleeira [bale'ejra] F whaler
baleia [ba'leja] F whale
baleiro, -a [ba'lejru, a] M/F confectioner
balido [ba'lidu] M bleating; (um só) bleat
balística [ba'liʃtʃika] F ballistics sg
balístico, -a [ba'liʃtʃiku, a] ADJ ballistic
baliza [ba'liza] F (estaca) post; (bóia) buoy; (luminosa) beacon; (Esporte) goal
balizar [bali'zaʳ] VT to mark out
balneário [baw'njarju] M bathing resort
balões [ba'lõjʃ] MPL de **balão**
balofo, -a [ba'lofu, a] ADJ (fofo) fluffy; (gordo) plump, tubby
baloiço [ba'lojsu] (PT) M (de criança) swing; (ação) swinging
balouçar [balo'saʳ] (PT) VT, VI to swing
balouço [ba'losu] (PT) M = **baloiço**
balsa ['bawsa] F raft; (barca) ferry
bálsamo ['bawsamu] M balm
báltico, -a ['bawtʃiku, a] ADJ Baltic ▪ M: **o B~** the Baltic
baluarte [ba'lwaxtʃi] M rampart, bulwark; (fig) supporter
balzaquiana [bawza'kjana] F woman in her thirties
bamba ['bãba] ADJ, M/F expert
bambear [bã'bjaʳ] VT to loosen ▪ VI to work loose; (pessoa) to grow weak
bambo, -a ['bãbu, a] ADJ slack, loose; (pernas) limp, wobbly
bambolê [bãbo'le] M hula hoop
bamboleante [bãbo'ljãtʃi] ADJ swaying; (sem firmeza) wobbly
bambolear [bãbo'ljaʳ] VT to sway ▪ VI (pessoa) to sway; (coisa) to wobble
bambu [bã'bu] M bamboo
banal [ba'naw] (pl -ais) ADJ banal
banalidade [banali'dadʒi] F banality
banana [ba'nana] F banana ▪ M/F (col) wimp; **dar uma** ~ = to stick two fingers up
bananada [bana'nada] F banana paste
bananeira [bana'nejra] F banana tree
bananosa [bana'nɔza] (col) F: **estar numa** ~ to be in a fix

banca ['bãka] F (de trabalho) bench; (escritório) office; (em jogo) bank; ~ **(de jornais)** newsstand; **botar ~** (col) to show off; **botar ~ em** ou **para cima de** (col) to lay down the law to; ~ **examinadora** examining body, examination board; **bancada** [bã'kada] F (banco, Pol) bench; (de cozinha) worktop

bancar [bã'ka^r] VT (financiar) to finance ■ VI (fingir): ~ **que** to pretend that; ~ **o idiota** etc to play the fool etc; ~ **que** to pretend that; **bancário, -a** [bã'karju, a] ADJ bank atr ■ M/F bank employee

bancarrota [bãka'xota] F bankruptcy; **ir à ~** to go bankrupt

banco ['bãku] M (assento) bench; (Com) bank; (de cozinha) stool; ~ **de areia** sandbank; ~ **de dados** (Comput) database

banda ['bãda] F band; (lado) side; (cinto) sash; **de ~** sideways; **pôr de ~** to put aside; **nestas ~s** in these parts; ~ **de percussão** steel band; ~ **desenhada** (PT) cartoon; ~ **larga** (Tel) broadband

bandear-se [bãde'axsi] VR: ~ **para** ou **a** to go over to

bandeira [bã'dejra] F flag; (estandarte, fig) banner; (de porta) fanlight; ~ **a meio pau** flag at half mast; **dar uma ~ em alguém** (col) to give sb the brush-off; **levar uma ~** to get the brush-off; **dar ~** (col) to give o.s. away

bandeirante [bãdej'rãtʃi] M pioneer ■ F girl guide

bandeirinha [bãdej'riɲa] M (Esporte) linesman

bandeja [bã'deʒa] F tray; **dar algo de ~ a alguém** (col) to give sb sth on a plate

bandido [bã'dʒidu, a] M bandit ■ M/F (fig) rascal

bando ['bãdu] M band; (grupo) group; (de malfeitores) gang; (de ovelhas) flock; (de gado) herd; (de livros etc) pile

bandô [bã'do] M pelmet

bandoleiro [bãdo'lejru] M bandit

bandolim [bãdo'lĩ] (pl -ns) M mandolin

bangalô [bãga'lo] M bungalow

Bangcoc [bãŋ'kɔki] N Bangkok

Bangladesh [bãgla'deʃ] M Bangladesh

bangue-bangue [bãgi'bãgi] M: **(filme de) ~** western

banguela [bã'gɛla] ADJ toothless

banha ['baɲa] F fat; (de porco) lard

banhar [ba'ɲa^r] VT (molhar) to wet; (mergulhar) to dip; (lavar) to wash, bathe; **banhar-se** VR (no mar) to bathe

banheira [ba'ɲejra] F bath

banheiro [ba'ɲejru] M bathroom; (PT) lifeguard

banhista [ba'ɲiʃta] M/F bather; (salva-vidas) lifeguard

banho ['baɲu] M (Tec, na banheira) bath; (mergulho) dip; **dar um ~ de cerveja** etc **em alguém** to spill beer etc all over sb; **tomar ~** to have a bath; (de chuveiro) to have a shower; **tomar um ~ de**

(fig) to have a heavy dose of; **vai tomar ~!** (col) get lost!; ~ **de chuveiro** shower; ~ **de espuma** bubble bath; **tomar ~ de mar** to have a swim (in the sea); ~ **de sol** sunbathing

banho-maria (pl banhos-marias) M (Culin) bain-marie

banimento [bani'mẽtu] M banishment

banir [ba'ni^r] VT to banish

banjo ['bãʒu] M banjo

banquei etc [bã'kej] VB v **bancar**

banqueiro, -a [bã'kejru, a] M/F banker

banqueta [bã'keta] F stool

banquete [bã'ketʃi] M banquet; (fig) feast

banquetear [bãke'tʃja^r] VT to feast; **banquetear-se** VR: **banquetear-se com** to feast on

banqueteiro, -a [bãke'tejru, a] M/F caterer

banzé [bã'zɛ] (col) M kerfuffle

baptismo etc [ba'tiʒmu] (PT) = **batismo** etc

baque ['baki] M thud, thump; (contratempo) setback; (queda) fall; **levar um ~** to be hard hit

baquear [ba'kja^r] VI to topple over

bar [ba^r] M bar

barafunda [bara'fũda] F confusion; (de coisas) hotch-potch

barafustar [barafuʃ'ta^r] VI: ~ **por** to burst through

baralhada [bara'ʎada] F muddle

baralhar [bara'ʎa^r] VT (fig) to mix up, confuse

baralho [ba'raʎu] M pack of cards

barão [ba'rãw] (pl -ões) M baron

barata [ba'rata] F cockroach; **entregue às ~s** (pessoa) gone to the dogs; (plano) gone out the window

baratear [bara'tʃja^r] VT to cut the price of; (menosprezar) to belittle

barateiro, -a [bara'tejru, a] ADJ cheap

baratinado, -a [baratʃi'nadu, a] (col) ADJ in a flap; (transtornado) shaken up

baratinar [baratʃi'na^r] (col) VT to drive crazy; (transtornar) to shake up

barato, -a [ba'ratu, a] ADJ cheap ■ ADV cheaply ■ M (col): **a festa foi um ~** the party was great

barba ['baxba] F beard; **barbas** FPL whiskers; **nas ~s de** (fig) under the nose of; **fazer a ~ to** shave; **pôr as ~s de molho** to take precautions

barbada [bax'bada] (col) F cinch, piece of cake; (Turfe) favourite

barbado, -a [bax'badu, a] ADJ bearded

Barbados [bax'baduʃ] M Barbados

barbante [bax'bãtʃi] (BR) M string

barbaramente [baxbara'mẽtʃi] ADV (muito) a lot

barbaridade [baxbari'dadʒi] F barbarity, cruelty; (disparate) nonsense; **que ~!** good heavens!

barbárie [bax'barie] F barbarism

barbarismo [baxba'riʒmu] M barbarism

bárbaro, -a [baxbaru, a] ADJ barbaric; (dor, calor) terrible; (maravilhoso) great

---

NB: European Portuguese adds the following consonants to certain words: **b** (sú(b)dito, su(b)til); **c** (a(c)ção, a(c)cionista, a(c)to); **m** (inde(m)ne); **p** (ado(p)ção, ado(p)tar); for further details see p. xiii.

barbatana [baxba'tana] F fin
barbeador [baxbja'do^r] M razor; (*tb*: **barbeador elétrico**) shaver
barbear [bax'bja^r] VT to shave; **barbear-se** VR to shave; **barbearia** [baxbja'ria] F barber's (shop)
barbeiragem [baxbej'raʒẽ] F bad driving; **fazer uma ~** to drive badly; (*fig*) to bungle it
barbeiro [bax'bejru] M barber; (*loja*) barber's; (*motorista*) bad driver, Sunday driver
barbitúrico [baxbi'turiku] M barbiturate
barbudo, -a [bax'budu, a] ADJ bearded
barca ['baxka] F barge; (*de travessia*) ferry
barcaça [bax'kasa] F barge
barco ['baxku] M boat; **estar no mesmo ~** (*fig*) to be in the same boat; **deixar o ~ correr** (*fig*) to let things take their course; **tocar o ~ para a frente** (*fig*) to struggle on; **~ a motor** motorboat; **~ a remo** rowing boat; **~ a vela** sailing boat
Barein [ba'rẽj] M: **o ~** Bahrain
barganha [bax'gaɲa] F bargain; **barganhar** [baxga'ɲa^r] VT, VI to negotiate
barítono [ba'ritonu] M baritone
barlavento [baxla'vẽtu] M (*Náut*) windward; **a ~** to windward
barman [bax'mã] (*pl* -**men**) M barman
barnabé [baxna'bɛ] (*col*) M petty civil servant
barões [ba'rõjʃ] MPL *de* **barão**
barômetro [ba'rometru] M barometer
baronesa [baro'neza] F baroness
barqueiro [bax'kejru] M boatman
barra ['baxa] F bar; (*faixa*) strip; (*traço*) stroke; (*alavanca*) lever; (*col*: *situação*) scene; **agüentar ou segurar a ~** to hold out; **forçar a ~** (*col*) to force the issue; **ser uma ~** (*pessoa, entrevista*) to be tough; **~ de direção** steering column; **~ fixa** high bar; **~s paralelas** parallel bars
barraca [ba'xaka] F (*tenda*) tent; (*de feira*) stall; (*de madeira*) hut; (*de praia*) sunshade; **barracão** [baxa'kãw] (*pl* -**ões**) M (*de madeira*) shed; **barraco** [ba'xaku] M shack, shanty
barracões [baxa'kõjʃ] MPL *de* **barracão**
barragem [ba'xaʒẽ] (*pl* -**ns**) F (*represa*) dam; (*impedimento*) barrier
barranco [ba'xãku] M ravine, gully; (*de rio*) bank
barra-pesada (*pl* **barras-pesadas**) M/F shady character ▪ ADJ INV (*lugar*) rough; (*pessoa*) shady; (*difícil*) difficult
barrar [ba'xa^r] VT to bar
barreira [ba'xejra] F barrier; (*cerca*) fence; (*Esporte*) hurdle; **pôr ~s a** to put obstacles in the way of; **~ do som** sound barrier
barrento, -a [ba'xẽtu, a] ADJ muddy
barrete [ba'xetʃi] (PT) M cap
barricada [baxi'kada] F barricade
barriga [ba'xiga] F belly; **estar de ~** to be pregnant; **falar ou chorar de ~ cheia** to complain for no reason; **fazer ~** to bulge; **~ da perna** calf; **barrigudo, -a** [baxi'gudu, a] ADJ paunchy, pot-bellied
barril [ba'xiw] (*pl* -**is**) M barrel, cask

barro ['baxu] M clay; (*lama*) mud
barroco, -a [ba'xoku, a] ADJ baroque; (*ornamentado*) extravagant
barrote [ba'xɔtʃi] M beam
barulhada [baru'ʎada] F racket, din
barulhento, -a [baru'ʎẽtu, a] ADJ noisy
barulho [ba'ruʎu] M (*ruído*) noise; (*tumulto*) din
base ['bazi] F base; (*fig*) basis; **sem ~** groundless; **com ~ em** based on; **na ~ de** (*por meio de*) by means of
baseado, -a [ba'zjadu, a] ADJ well-founded ▪ M (*col*) joint
basear [ba'zja^r] VT to base; **basear-se** VR: **basear-se em** to be based on
básico, -a ['baziku, a] ADJ basic
basquete [baʃ'kɛtʃi] M = **basquetebol**
basquetebol [baʃkete'bɔw] M basketball
basta ['baʃta] M: **dar um ~ em** to call a halt to
bastante [baʃ'tãtʃi] ADJ (*suficiente*) enough; (*muito*) quite a lot (of) ▪ ADV enough, a lot
bastão [baʃ'tãw] (*pl* -**ões**) M stick
bastar [baʃ'ta^r] VI to be enough, be sufficient; **bastar-se** VR to be self-sufficient; **basta!** (that's) enough!; **~ para** to be enough to
bastardo, -a [baʃ'taxdu, a] ADJ, M/F bastard
bastidor [baʃtʃi'do^r] M frame; **bastidores** MPL (*Teatro*) wings; **nos ~es** (*fig*) behind the scenes
basto, -a ['baʃtu, a] ADJ (*espesso*) thick; (*denso*) dense
bastões [baʃ'tõjʃ] MPL *de* **bastão**
bata ['bata] F (*de mulher*) smock; (*de médico*) overall
batalha [ba'taʎa] F battle; **batalhador, a** [bataʎa'do^r(a)] ADJ struggling ▪ M/F fighter
batalhão [bata'ʎãw] (*pl* -**ões**) M battalion
batalhar [bata'ʎa^r] VI to battle, fight; (*esforçar-se*) to make an effort, try hard ▪ VT (*emprego*) to go after
batalhões [bata'ʎõjʃ] MPL *de* **batalhão**
batata [ba'tata] F potato; **~ doce** sweet potato; **~ frita** chips *pl* (Brit), French fries *pl*; (*de pacote*) crisps *pl* (Brit), (potato) chips *pl* (US)
bate-boca ['batʃi-] (*pl* -**s**) M row, quarrel
bate-bola ['batʃi-] (*pl* -**s**) M kick around
batedeira [bate'dejra] F beater; (*de manteiga*) churn; **~ elétrica** mixer
batedor [bate'do^r] M beater; (*polícia*) escort; (*Criquete*) batsman; **~ de carteiras** pickpocket
bátega ['batega] F downpour
batelada [bate'lada] F: **uma ~ de** a whole bunch of
batente [ba'tẽtʃi] M doorpost; (*col*) job; **no ~** at work
bate-papo ['batʃi-] (*pl* -**s**) (BR) M chat
bater [ba'te^r] VT to beat; (*golpear*) to strike; (*horas*) to strike; (*pé*) to stamp; (*foto*) to take; (*datilografar*) to type; (*porta*) to slam; (*asas*) to flap; (*recorde*) to break; (*roupa: usar muito*) to wear all the time ▪ VI (*porta*) to slam; (*sino*) to ring; (*janela*) to bang; (*coração*) to beat; (*sol*) to beat down; **bater-se** VR: **bater-se para fazer/por** to fight to do/for; **~ (à porta)** to knock (at the door); **~ à**

maquina to type; **~ em** to hit; (*lugar*) to arrive in; (*assunto*) to harp on; **~ com o carro** to crash one's car; **~ com a cabeça** to bang one's head; **~ com o pé (em)** to kick; **ele não bate bem** (*col*) he is a bit crazy; **~ a carteira de alguém** (*col*) to nick sb's wallet

bateria [bate'ria] F battery; (*Mús*) drums *pl*; **~ de cozinha** kitchen utensils *pl*; **baterista** [bate'rifta] M/F drummer

batida [ba'tʃida] F beat; (*da porta*) slam; (*à porta*) knock; (*da polícia*) raid; (*Auto*) crash; (*bebida*) cocktail of *cachaça, fruit and sugar*; **dar uma ~ em** (*polícia*) to raid; (*colidir com*) to bump into; **dar uma ~ com o carro** to crash one's car; **dar uma ~ no carro de alguém** to crash into sb's car

batido, -a [ba'tʃidu, a] ADJ beaten; (*roupa*) worn; (*assunto*) hackneyed ■ M: **~ de leite** (PT) milkshake

batina [ba'tʃina] F (*Rel*) cassock

batismal [batʃiʒ'maw] (*pl* -**ais**) ADJ v **pia**

batismo [ba'tʃiʒmu] M baptism, christening

batizado [batʃi'zadu] M christening

batizar [batʃi'za^r] VT to baptize, christen; (*vinho*) to dilute

batom [ba'tõ] (*pl* -**ns**) M lipstick

batucada [batu'kada] F dance percussion group

batucar [batu'ka^r] VT, VI to drum

batuque [ba'tuki] M drumming

batuta [ba'tuta] F baton ■ ADJ (*col*) clever

baú [ba'u] M trunk

baunilha [baw'niʎa] F vanilla

bazar [ba'za^r] M bazaar; (*loja*) shop

bazófia [ba'zɔfja] F boasting, bragging

BB ABR M = **Banco do Brasil**

BBF ABR F = **Bolsa Brasileira de Futuros**

BC ABR M = **Banco Central do Brasil**

BCG ABR M (= *Bacilo Calmet-Guerin*) BCG

bê-á-bá [bea'ba] M ABC

beatitude [beatʃi'tudʒi] F bliss

beato, -a [be'atu, a] ADJ blessed; (*devoto*) overpious

bêbado, -a ['bebadu, a] ADJ, M/F drunk

bebê [be'be] M baby

bebedeira [bebe'dejra] F drunkenness; **tomar uma ~** to get drunk

bêbedo, -a ['bebedu, a] ADJ, M/F = **bêbado**

bebedor, a [bebe'do^r(a)] M/F drinker; (*ébrio*) drunkard

bebedouro [bebe'douru] M drinking fountain

beber [be'be^r] VT to drink; (*absorver*) to drink up, soak up ■ VI to drink

bebericar [beberi'ka^r] VT, VI to sip

bebida [be'bida] F drink

beca ['bɛka] F gown

beça ['bɛsa] (*col*) F: **à ~** (*com vb*) a lot; (*com n*) a lot of; (*com adj*) really

beco ['bɛku] M alley, lane; **~ sem saída** cul-de-sac; (*fig*) dead end

bedelho [be'deʎu] M kid; **meter o ~ em** to poke one's nose into

bege ['bɛʒi] ADJ INV beige

beicinho [bej'siɲu] M: **fazer ~** to sulk

beiço ['bejsu] M lip; **fazer ~** to pout

beiçudo, -a [bej'sudu, a] ADJ thick-lipped

beija-flor [bejʒa-] (*pl* -**es**) M hummingbird

beijar [bej'ʒa^r] VT to kiss; **beijar-se** VR to kiss (one another); **beijo** ['bejʒu] M kiss; **dar beijos em alguém** to kiss sb

beijoca [bej'ʒɔka] F kiss

beijocar [bejʒo'ka^r] VT to kiss

beira ['bejra] F (*borda*) edge; (*de rio*) bank; (*orla*) border; **à ~ de** on the edge of; (*ao lado de*) beside, by; (*fig*) on the verge of; **~ do telhado** eaves *pl*

beirada [bej'rada] F edge

beira-mar F seaside

beirar [bej'ra^r] VT (*ficar à beira de*) to be at the edge of; (*caminhar à beira de*) to skirt; (*desespero*) to be on the verge of; (*idade*) to approach, near ■ VI: **~ com** to border on; **~ por** (*idade*) to approach

Beirute [bej'rutʃi] N Beirut

beisebol [bejsi'bɔw] M baseball

belas-artes FPL fine arts

beldade [bew'dadʒi] F beauty

beleléu [bele'lɛw] (*col*) M: **ir para o ~** to go wrong

belenense [bele'nēsi] ADJ from Belém ■ M/F native *ou* inhabitant of Belém

beleza [be'leza] F beauty; **que ~!** how lovely!; **ser uma ~** to be lovely; **concurso de ~** beauty contest

belga ['bɛwga] ADJ, M/F Belgian

Bélgica ['bɛwʒika] F: **a ~** Belgium

Belgrado [bew'gradu] N Belgrade

beliche [be'liʃi] M bunk

bélico, -a ['bɛliku, a] ADJ war *atr*

belicoso, -a [beli'kozu, ɔza] ADJ warlike

beligerante [beliʒe'rātʃi] ADJ belligerent

beliscão [belif'kãw] (*pl* -**ões**) M pinch; **beliscar** [belif'ka^r] VT to pinch, nip; (*comida*) to nibble

beliscões [belif'kõjʃ] MPL *de* **beliscão**

Belize [be'lizi] M Belize

belo, -a ['bɛlu, a] ADJ beautiful

belo-horizontino, -a [-orizõ'tʃinu, a] ADJ from Belo Horizonte ■ M/F person from Belo Horizonte

bel-prazer [bɛw-] M: **a seu ~** at one's own convenience

beltrano [bew'tranu] M so-and-so

belvedere [bewve'deri] M lookout point

 PALAVRA CHAVE

bem [bēj] ADV **1** (*de maneira satisfatória, correta etc*) well; **trabalha/come bem** she works/eats well; **respondeu bem** he answered correctly; **me sinto/não me sinto bem** I feel fine/I don't feel very well; **tudo bem? — tudo bem** how's it going? — fine

NB: *European Portuguese adds the following consonants to certain words:* **b** (sú(b)dito, su(b)til); **c** (a(c)ção, a(c)cionista, a(c)to); **m** (inde(m)ne); **p** (ado(p)çã, ado(p)tar); *for further details see p. xiii.*

2 (*valor intensivo*) very; **um quarto bem quente** a nice warm room; **bem se vê que ...** it's clear that ...

3 (*bastante*) quite, fairly; **a casa é bem grande** the house is quite big

4 (*exatamente*): **bem ali** right there; **não é bem assim** it's not quite like that

5 (*estar bem*): **estou muito bem aqui** I feel very happy here; **está bem! vou fazê-lo** oh all right, I'll do it!

6 (*de bom grado*): **eu bem que iria mas ...** I'd gladly go but ...

7 (*cheirar*) good, nice

■ **M 1** (*bem-estar*) good; **estou dizendo isso para o seu bem** I'm telling you for your own good; **o bem e o mal** good and evil

2 (*posses*): **bens** goods, property *sg*; **bens de consumo** consumer goods; **bens de família** family possessions; **bens móveis/imóveis** moveable property *sg*/real estate *sg*

■ **EXCL 1** aprovação; **bem! OK!; muito bem!** well done!

2 (*desaprovação*): **bem feito!** it serves you right!

■ **ADJ INV** (*tom depreciativo*): **gente bem** posh people

■ **CONJ 1**: **nem bem** as soon as, no sooner than; **nem bem ela chegou começou a dar ordens** as soon as she arrived she started to give orders, no sooner had she arrived than she started to give orders

2: **se bem que** though; **gostaria de ir se bem que não tenho dinheiro** I'd like to go even though I've got no money

3: **bem como** as well as; **o livro bem como a peça foram escritos por ele** the book as well as the play was written by him

bem-agradecido, -a ADJ grateful
bem-apessoado, -a [-ape'swadu, a] ADJ smart, well-groomed
bem-arrumado, -a [-axu'madu, a] ADJ well-dressed
bem-casado, -a [-ka'zadu, a] ADJ happily married
bem-comportado, -a [-kõpox'tadu, a] ADJ well-behaved
bem-conceituado, -a ADJ highly regarded
bem-disposto, -a ADJ well, in good form
bem-educado, -a ADJ well-mannered
bem-estar M well-being
bem-humorado, -a [-umo'radu, a] ADJ good-tempered
bem-intencionado, -a ADJ well-intentioned
bem-me-quer (*pl* -es) M daisy
bem-passado, -a ADJ (*Culin*) well-done
bem-sucedido, -a ADJ successful
bem-vindo, -a ADJ welcome
bem-visto, -a ADJ well thought of
bênção ['bẽsãw] (*pl* -s) F blessing
bendigo *etc* [bẽ'dʒigu] VB *v* **bendizer**
bendisse *etc* [bẽ'dʒisi] VB *v* **bendizer**
bendito, -a [bẽ'dʒitu, a] PP *de* **bendizer** ■ ADJ blessed

bendizer [bẽdʒi'zeʳ] (*irreg*) VT (*louvar*) to praise; (*abençoar*) to bless
beneficência [benefi'sẽsja] F (*bondade*) kindness; (*caridade*) charity; **obra de ~** charity
beneficente [benefi'sẽtʃi] ADJ (*organização*) charitable; (*feira*) charity *atr*
beneficiado, -a [benefi'sjadu, a] M/F beneficiary
beneficiar [benefi'sjaʳ] VT (*favorecer*) to benefit; (*melhorar*) to improve; **beneficiar-se** VR to benefit
benefício [bene'fisju] M (*proveito*) benefit, profit; (*favor*) favour (*Brit*), favor (*US*); **em ~ de** in aid of; **em ~ próprio** for one's own benefit; **benéfico, -a** [be'nɛfiku, a] ADJ (*benigno*) beneficial; (*generoso*) generous
Benelux [bene'luks] M Benelux
benemérito, -a [bene'mɛritu, a] ADJ (*digno*) worthy
beneplácito [bene'plasitu] M consent, approval
benevolência [benevo'lẽsja] F benevolence, kindness
benévolo, -a [be'nɛvolu, a] ADJ benevolent, kind
Benfam [bẽ'fami] ABR F = **Sociedade Brasileira de Bem-Estar da Família**
benfazejo, -a [bẽfa'zeʒu, a] ADJ benevolent
benfeitor, a [bẽfej'toʳ(a)] M/F benefactor/benefactress
benfeitoria [bẽfejto'ria] F improvement
bengala [bẽ'gala] F walking stick
benigno, -a [be'nignu, a] ADJ (*bondoso*) kind; (*agradável*) pleasant; (*Med*) benign
Benin [be'nĩ] M: **o ~** Benin
benquisto, -a [bẽ'kiʃtu, a] ADJ well-loved, well-liked
bens [bẽjʃ] MPL *de* **bem**
bento, -a ['bẽtu, a] PP *de* **benzer** ■ ADJ blessed; (*água*) holy
benzedeiro, -a [bẽze'dejru, a] M/F sorcerer/sorceress
benzer [bẽ'zeʳ] VT to bless; **benzer-se** VR to cross o.s.
berçário [bex'sarju] M nursery
berço ['bexsu] M (*com balanço*) cradle; (*cama*) cot; (*origem*) birthplace; **nascer em ~ de ouro** (*fig*) to be born with a silver spoon in one's mouth; **ter ~** to be from a good family
berimbau [berĩ'baw] M *percussion instrument*
berinjela [berĩ'ʒela] F aubergine (*Brit*), eggplant (*US*)
Berlim [bex'lĩ] N Berlin
berlinda [bex'lĩda] F: **estar na ~** to be in the firing-line
berma ['bɛxma] (*PT*) F hard shoulder (*Brit*), berm (*US*)
Bermudas [bex'mudaʃ] FPL: **as ~** Bermuda *sg*
bermuda [bex'muda] F Bermuda shorts *pl*
Berna ['bɛxna] N Berne
berrante [be'xãtʃi] ADJ flashy, gaudy
berrar [be'xaʳ] VI to bellow; (*criança*) to bawl;

berreiro [be'xejru] M: **abrir o berreiro** to burst out crying
berro ['bɛxu] M yell
besouro [be'zoru] M beetle
besta ['beʃta] ADJ (tolo) stupid; (convencido) full of oneself; (pretensioso) pretentious ■ F (animal) beast; (pessoa) fool; **~ de carga** beast of burden; **ficar ~** (col: surpreso) to be amazed; **fazer alguém de ~** (col) to make a fool of sb
bestar [beʃ'taʳ] VI to laze around
besteira [beʃ'tejra] F (tolice) foolishness; (insignificância) small thing; **dizer ~s** to talk nonsense; **fazer uma ~** to do something silly
bestial [beʃ'tʃjaw] (pl -ais) ADJ bestial; (repugnante) repulsive
bestialidade [beʃtʃjali'dadʒi] F bestiality
bestificar [beʃtʃifi'kaʳ] VT to astonish, dumbfound
best-seller ['bɛst'sɛleʳ] (pl -s) M best seller
besuntar [bezũ'taʳ] VT to smear, daub
betão [be'tãw] (PT) M concrete
beterraba [bete'xaba] F beetroot
betoneira [beto'nejra] F cement mixer
betume [be'tumi] M asphalt
bexiga [be'ʃiga] F (órgão) bladder
bezerro, -a [be'zexu, a] M/F calf
BI ABR M see below

● **BI**

● All Portuguese citizens are required to carry
● an identity card, known as the BI or bilhete
● de identidade. The photocard, which gives
● the holder's name, date of birth, marital
● status, height and a fingerprint, can be used
● instead of a passport for travel within the
● European Union. Failure to produce a valid
● identity card when stopped by the police
● can result in a fine.

bianual [bja'nwaw] (pl -ais) ADJ biannual, twice yearly
bibelô [bibe'lo] M ornament
Bíblia ['biblja] F Bible
bíblico, -a ['bibliku, a] ADJ biblical
bibliografia [bibljogra'fia] F bibliography
biblioteca [bibljo'tɛka] F library; (estante) bookcase; **bibliotecário, -a** [bibljote'karju, a] M/F librarian
biblioteconomia [bibljotekono'mia] F librarianship
bica ['bika] F tap; (PT) black coffee, expresso; **suar em ~s** to drip with sweat
bicada [bi'kada] F peck
bicama [bi'kama] F pull-out bed
bicar [bi'kaʳ] VT to peck
bicarbonato [bikaxbo'natu] M bicarbonate
bíceps ['biseps] M INV biceps
bicha ['biʃa] F (lombriga) worm; (PT: fila) queue;

(BR: col, pej: homossexual) queer
bichado, -a [bi'ʃadu, a] ADJ eaten away
bicheiro [bi'ʃejru] M (illegal) bookie
bicho ['biʃu] M animal; (inseto) insect, bug; (col: pessoa: intratável) pain (in the neck); (: feio): **ela é um ~ (feio)** she's as ugly as sin; **virar ~** (col) to get mad; **ver que ~ dá** (col) to see what happens; **que ~ te mordeu?** what's got into you?
bicho-da-seda (pl bichos-da-seda) M silk worm
bicho-de-sete-cabeças M: **fazer um ~** to make a mountain out of a molehill
bicho-do-mato (pl bichos-do-mato) M extremely shy person
bicho-papão [-pa'pãw] (pl bichos-papões) M bogeyman
bicicleta [bisi'klɛta] F bicycle; (col) bike; **andar de ~** to cycle
bico ['biku] M (de ave) beak; (ponta) point; (de chaleira) spout; (boca) mouth; (de pena) nib; (do peito) nipple; (de gás) jet; (col: emprego) casual job; (chupeta) dummy; **calar o ~** to shut up; **não abrir o ~** not to say a word; **fazer ~** to sulk
bicudo, -a [bi'kudu, a] ADJ pointed; (difícil) tricky
BID ABR M = **Banco Interamericano de Desenvolvimento**
bidê [bi'de] M bidet
bidimensional [bidʒimẽsjo'naw] (pl -ais) ADJ two-dimensional
bidirecional [bidʒiresjo'naw] (pl -ais) ADJ bidirectional
biela ['bjɛla] F con(necting) rod
bienal [bje'naw] (pl -ais) ADJ biennial ■ F (biennial) art exhibition
bife ['bifi] M (~ beef) steak; **~ a cavalo** steak with fried eggs; **~ à milanesa** beef escalope; **~ de panela** beef stew
bifocal [bifo'kaw] (pl -ais) ADJ bifocal; **óculos bifocais** bifocals
bifurcação [bifuxka'sãw] (pl -ões) F fork
bifurcar-se [bifux'kaxsi] VR to fork, divide
bigamia [biga'mia] F bigamy
bígamo, -a ['bigamu, a] ADJ bigamous ■ M/F bigamist
bigode [bi'gɔdʒi] M moustache
bigodudo, -a [bigo'dudu, a] ADJ with a big moustache
bigorna [bi'gɔxna] F anvil
bijuteria [biʒute'ria] F (costume) jewellery (Brit) ou jewelry (US)
bilateral [bilate'raw] (pl -ais) ADJ bilateral
bilhão [bi'ʎãw] (pl -ões) M billion
bilhar [bi'ʎaʳ] M (jogo) billiards sg
bilhete [bi'ʎetʃi] M (entrada, loteria) ticket; (cartinha) note; **~ eletrônico** e-ticket; **~ de ida** single (Brit) ou one-way ticket; **~ de ida e volta** return (Brit) ou round-trip (US) ticket; **o ~ azul** (fig) the sack; **bilheteira** [biʎe'tejra] (PT) F ticket office; (Teatro) box office; **bilheteiro, -a** [biʎe'tejru, a] M/F ticket seller; **bilheteria**

[biʎete'ria] F ticket office; box office; **sucesso de bilheteria** box-office success

bilhões [bi'ʎõjʃ] MPL *de* **bilhão**

bilíngüe [bi'lĩgwi] ADJ bilingual

bilionário, -a [biljo'narju, a] ADJ, M/F billionaire

bilioso, -a [bi'ljozu, ɔza] ADJ bilious; (*fig*) bad-tempered

bílis ['biliʃ] M bile

bimensal [bimẽ'saw] (*pl* -ais) ADJ twice-monthly

bimestral [bimeʃ'traw] (*pl* -ais) ADJ two-monthly

bimotor [bimo'toʳ] ADJ twin-engined

binário, -a [bi'narju, a] ADJ binary

bingo ['bĩgu] M bingo

binóculo [bi'nɔkulu] M binoculars *pl*; (*para teatro*) opera glasses *pl*

biodegradável [bjodegra'davew] (*pl* -eis) ADJ biodegradable

biografia [bjogra'fia] F biography

biográfico, -a [bjo'grafiku, a] ADJ biographical

biógrafo, -a ['bjɔgrafu, a] M/F biographer

biologia [bjolo'ʒia] F biology

biológico, -a [bjo'lɔʒiku, a] ADJ biological

biólogo, -a ['bjɔlogu, a] M/F biologist

biombo ['bjõbu] M (*tapume*) screen

biônico, -a ['bjoniku, a] ADJ bionic; (*Pol: senador*) non-elected

biópsia ['bjɔpsja] F biopsy

bioquímica [bjo'kimika] F biochemistry

bioterrorismo [bjotexo'riʒmu] M bioterrorism

bipartidário, -a [bipaxtʃi'darju, a] ADJ two-party *atr*, bipartite

bipartidarismo [bipaxtʃida'riʒmu] M two-party system

biquíni [bi'kini] M bikini

BIRD ABR M = **Banco Internacional de Reconstrução e Desenvolvimento**

birita [bi'rita] (*col*) F drink

birmanês, -esa [bixma'neʃ, eza] ADJ, M/F Burmese ■ M (*Ling*) Burmese

Birmânia [bix'manja] F: **a ~** Burma

birô [bi'ro] M (*Comput*) bureau

birosca [bi'roʃka] F (*small*) shop

birra ['bixa] F (*teima*) wilfulness (*Brit*), willfulness (*US*), obstinacy; (*aversão*) aversion; **fazer ~** to have a tantrum; **ter ~ com** to dislike

birrento, -a [bi'xẽtu, a] ADJ stubborn, obstinate

biruta [bi'ruta] ADJ crazy ■ F windsock

bis [biʃ] EXCL encore!

bisar [bi'zaʳ] VT (*suj: público*) to ask for an encore of; (: *artista*) to do an encore of

bisavô, -ó [biza'vo, ɔ] M/F great-grandfather/great-grandmother; **bisavós** [biza'vɔʃ] MPL great-grandparents

bisbilhotar [biʒbiʎo'taʳ] VT to pry into ■ VI to snoop

bisbilhoteiro, -a [biʒbiʎo'tejru, a] ADJ prying ■ M/F snoop

bisbilhotice [biʒbiʎo'tʃisi] F prying

Biscaia [biʃ'kaja] F: **o golfo de ~** the Bay of Biscay

biscate [biʃ'katʃi] M odd job

biscateiro, -a [biʃka'tejru, a] M/F odd-job person

biscoito [biʃ'kojtu] M biscuit (*Brit*), cookie (*US*)

bisnaga [biʒ'naga] F (*tubo*) tube; (*pão*) French stick

bisneto, -a [biʒ'nɛtu, a] M/F great-grandson/great-granddaughter; **bisnetos** MPL (*filhos de neto*) great-grandchildren

bisonho, -a [bi'zɔɲu, a] ADJ inexperienced ■ M/F newcomer

bispado [biʃ'padu] M bishopric

bispo ['biʃpu] M bishop

bissemanal [bisema'naw] (*pl* -ais) ADJ twice-weekly

bissexto, -a [bi'seʃtu, a] ADJ: **ano ~** leap year

bissexual [bisek'swaw] (*pl* -ais) ADJ, M/F bisexual

bisturi [biʃtu'ri] M scalpel

bit ['bitʃi] M (*Comput*) bit

bitola [bi'tɔla] F gauge (*Brit*), gage (*US*); (*padrão*) pattern; (*estalão*) standard

bitolado, -a [bito'ladu, a] ADJ narrow-minded

bizarro, -a [bi'zaxu, a] ADJ bizarre

blablablá [blabla'bla] (*col*) M chitchat

black-tie ['blɛktaj] M evening dress

blasé [bla'ze] ADJ blasé

blasfemar [blaʃfe'maʳ] VT to curse ■ VI to blaspheme; **blasfêmia** [blaʃ'femja] F blasphemy; (*ultraje*) swearing

blasfemo, -a [blaʃ'femu, a] ADJ blasphemous ■ M/F blasphemer

blazer ['blejzeʳ] (*pl* -s) M blazer

blecaute [ble'kawtʃi] M power cut

blefar [ble'faʳ] VI to bluff

blefe ['blɛfi] M bluff

blindado, -a [blĩ'dadu, a] ADJ armoured (*Brit*), armored (*US*)

blindagem [blĩ'daʒẽ] F armour(-plating) (*Brit*), armor(-plating) (*US*)

blitz [blits] F police raid; (*na estrada*) police spot-check

bloco ['bloku] M block; (*Pol*) bloc; (*de escrever*) writing pad; **voto em ~** block vote; **~ de carnaval** carnival troupe; **~ de cilindros** cylinder block

blog, blogue ['bl gi] (*pl* -s) (*col*) M blog

blogueiro, -a [blo'gejru, a] (*col*) M/F blogger

bloquear [blo'kjaʳ] VT to blockade; (*obstruir*) to block; **bloqueio** [blo'keju] M (*Mil*) blockade; (*obstrução*) blockage; (*Psico*) mental block

blusa ['bluza] F (*de mulher*) blouse; (*de homem*) shirt; **~ de lã** jumper; **blusão** [blu'zãw] (*pl* -ões) M jacket

BMeF (BR) ABR F = **Bolsa Mercantil e de Futuros**

BMSP ABR F = **Bolsa de Mercadorias de São Paulo**

BNDES ABR M (= *Banco Nacional de Desenvolvimento Econômico e Social*) Brazilian development bank

BNH (BR) ABR M (= *Banco Nacional da Habitação*) home-funding bank

boa ['boa] ADJ F *de* **bom** ■ F boa constrictor

boa-gente ADJ INV nice
boa-pinta (pl **boas-pintas**) ADJ handsome
boa-praça (pl **boas-praças**) ADJ nice
boate ['bwatʃi] F nightclub
boateiro, -a [bwa'tejru, a] ADJ gossipy ▪ M/F gossip
boato ['bwatu] M rumour (Brit), rumor (US)
boa-vida (pl **boas-vidas**) M/F loafer
bobagem [bo'baʒẽ] (pl **-ns**) F silliness, nonsense; (dito, ato) silly thing; **deixe de bobagens!** stop being silly!
bobeada [bo'bjada] F slip-up
bobear [bo'bjaʳ] VI to miss out
bobice [bo'bisi] F silliness, nonsense; (dito, ato) silly thing
bobina [bo'bina] F reel, bobbin; (Elet) coil; (Foto) spool; (de papel) roll
bobo, -a ['bobu, a] ADJ silly, daft ▪ M/F fool ▪ M (de corte) jester; **fazer-se de ~** to act the fool
bobó [bo'bɔ] M beans, palm oil and manioc
boboca [bo'bɔka] ADJ silly ▪ M/F fool
boca ['boka] F mouth; (entrada) entrance; (de fogão) ring; **de ~** orally; **de ~ aberta** open-mouthed, amazed; **bater ~** to argue; **botar a ~ no mundo** (berrar) to scream; (revelar) to spill the beans; **falar da ~ para fora** to say one thing and mean another; **ser boa ~** to eat anything; **vira essa ~ para lá!** don't tempt providence!; **~ da noite** nightfall
boca-de-fumo (pl **bocas-de-fumo**) F drug den
boca-de-sino ADJ INV bell-bottomed
bocadinho [boka'dʒiɲu] M: **um ~** (pouco tempo) a little while; (pouquinho) a little bit
bocado [bo'kadu] M (quantidade na boca) mouthful, bite; (pedaço) piece, bit; **um ~ de tempo** quite some time
bocal [bo'kaw] (pl **-ais**) M (de vaso) mouth; (Mús, de aparelho) mouthpiece; (de cano) nozzle
boçal [bo'saw] (pl **-ais**) ADJ ignorant; (grosseiro) uncouth
boçalidade [bosali'dadʒi] F coarseness; (ignorância) ignorance
boca-livre (pl **bocas-livres**) F free meal
bocejar [bose'ʒaʳ] VI to yawn; **bocejo** [bo'seʒu] M yawn
bochecha [bo'ʃeʃa] F cheek
bochechar [boʃe'ʃaʳ] VI to rinse one's mouth
bochecho [bo'ʃeʃu] M mouthwash
bochechudo, -a [boʃe'ʃudu, a] ADJ puffy-cheeked
boda ['boda] F wedding; **bodas** FPL (aniversário de casamento) wedding anniversary sg; **~s de prata/ouro** silver/golden wedding sg
bode ['bɔdʒi] M goat; **~ expiatório** scapegoat; **vai dar ~** (col) there'll be trouble
bodega [bo'dɛga] F piece of rubbish
bodum [bo'dũ] M stink
boêmio, -a [bo'emju, a] ADJ, M/F Bohemian
bofetada [bofe'tada] F slap

bofetão [bofe'tãw] (pl **-ões**) M punch
Bogotá [bogo'ta] N Bogota
boi [boj] M ox; **pegar o ~ pelos chifres** (fig) to take the bull by the horns
bói [bɔj] M office boy
bóia ['bɔja] F buoy; (col) grub; (de braço) armband, water wing
boiada [bo'jada] F herd of cattle
bóia-fria (pl **bóias-frias**) M/F (itinerant) farm labourer (Brit) ou laborer (US)
boiar [bo'jaʳ] VT to float ▪ VI to float; (col) to be lost; **~ em** (inglês etc) to be hopeless at
boi-bumbá [-bũ'ba] N see below

● **BOI-BUMBÁ**
●
● The boi-bumbá, or bumba-meu-boi, is a
● traditional folk dance from north-eastern
● Brazil, which brings together human,
● animal and mythological characters in a
● theatrical performance. The ox, which the
● dance is named after, is played by a dancer
● wearing an iron frame covered in pieces
● of colourful fabric. Eventually the beast is
● "killed" and its meat is symbolically shared
● out before it comes back to life in the finale.

boicotar [bojko'taʳ] VT to boycott; **boicote** [boj'kɔtʃi] M boycott
boiler ['bɔjlaʳ] (pl **-s**) M boiler
boina ['bojna] F beret
bojo ['boʒu] M (saliência) bulge
bojudo, -a [bo'ʒudu, a] ADJ bulging; (arredondado) rounded
bola ['bɔla] F ball; (confusão) confusion; **dar ~ (para)** (col) to care (about); (dar atenção) to pay attention (to); **dar ~ para** (flertar) to flirt with; **não dar ~ para alguém** to ignore sb; **ela não dá a menor ~ (para isso)** she couldn't care less (about it); **pisar na ~** (fig) to make a mistake; **ser bom de ~** to be good at football; **não ser certo da ~** (col) not to be right in the head; **ser uma ~** (pessoa: gordo) to be fat; (: engraçado) to be a real character; **~ de futebol** football; **~ de gude** marble; **~ de neve** snowball
bolacha [bo'laʃa] F biscuit (Brit), cookie (US); (col: bofetada) wallop; (para chope) beer mat
bolada [bo'lada] F (dinheiro) lump sum
bolar [bo'laʳ] VT to think up; **bem bolado** clever
bole etc ['bɔli] VB V **bulir**
boleia [bo'leja] F driver's seat; **dar uma ~** (PT) to give a lift
boletim [bole'tʃĩ] (pl **-ns**) M report; (publicação) newsletter; (Educ) report; **~ meteorológico** weather forecast
bolha ['boʎa] F (na pele) blister; (de ar, sabão) bubble ▪ M/F (col) fool
boliche [bo'liʃi] M (jogo) bowling, skittles sg
bolinar [boli'naʳ] VT: **~ alguém** (col) to feel sb up

NB: European Portuguese adds the following consonants to certain words: **b** (sú(b)dito, su(b)til); **c** (a(c)ção, a(c)cionista, a(c)to); **m** (inde(m)ne); **p** (ado(p)çã, ado(p)tar); for further details see p. xiii.

bolinho [bo'liɲu] M: ~ **de carne** meat ball; ~ **de arroz/bacalhau** rice/dry cod cake

Bolívia [bo'livja] F: **a** ~ Bolivia

boliviano, -a [boli'vjanu, a] ADJ, M/F Bolivian

bolo ['bolu] M cake; (*monte: de gente*) bunch; (: *de papéis*) bundle; **dar o** ~ **em alguém** to stand sb up; **vai dar** ~ (*col*) there's going to be trouble

bolor [bo'lo^r] M mould (*Brit*), mold (*US*); (*nas plantas*) mildew; (*bafio*) mustiness

bolorento, -a [bolo'rētu, a] ADJ mouldy (*Brit*), moldy (*US*)

bolota [bo'lɔta] F acorn

bolsa ['bowsa] F bag; (*Com: tb*: bolsa de valores) stock exchange; ~ **(de estudos)** scholarship; ~ **de mercadorias** commodities market; ~ **de valores** stock exchange

bolsista [bow'siʃta] M/F scholarship holder

bolso ['bowsu] M pocket; **de** ~ pocket *atr*; **dicionário de** ~ pocket dictionary

 PALAVRA CHAVE

bom, boa [bõ, 'boa] (*pl* bons/boas) ADJ **1** (*ótimo*) good; **é um livro bom** *ou* **um bom livro** it's a good book; **a comida está boa** the food is delicious; **o tempo está bom** the weather's fine; **ele foi muito bom comigo** he was very nice *ou* kind to me

2 (*apropriado*): **ser bom para** to be good for; **acho bom você não ir** I think it's better if you don't go

3 (*irônico*): **um bom quarto de hora** a good quarter of an hour; **que bom motorista você é!** a fine *ou* some driver you are!; **seria bom que ...!** a fine thing it would be if ...!; **essa é boa!** what a cheek!

4 (*saudação*): **bom dia!** good morning!; **boa tarde!** good afternoon!; **boa noite!** good evening!; (*ao deitar-se*) good night!; **tudo bom?** how's it going?

5 (*outras frases*): **está bom?** OK?

■ EXCL: **bom!** all right!; **bom, ... right, ...**

bomba ['bõba] F (*Mil*) bomb; (*Tec*) pump; (*Culin*) éclair; (*fig*) bombshell; ~ **atômica/relógio/de fumaça** atomic/time/smoke bomb; ~ **de gasolina** petrol (*Brit*) *ou* gas (*US*) pump; ~ **de incêndio** fire extinguisher; **levar** ~ (*em exame*) to fail

bombada [bõ'bada] F (*prejuízo*) loss

Bombaim [bõba'ĩ] N Bombay

bombardear [bõbax'dʒja^r] VT to bomb, bombard; (*fig*) to bombard; **bombardeio** [bõbax'deju] M bombing, bombardment ■ M: **bombardeio suicida** suicide bombing

bomba-relógio (*pl* bombas-relógio) F time bomb

bombástico, -a [bõ'baʃtʃiku, a] ADJ pompous

bombear [bõ'bja^r] VT to pump

bombeiro [bõ'bejru] M fireman; (*BR: encanador*) plumber; **o corpo de** ~**s** fire brigade

bombom [bõ'bõ] (*pl* -ns) M chocolate

bombordo [bõ'bɔxdu] M (*Náut*) port

bonachão, -chona [bona'ʃãw, 'ʃona] (*pl* -ões/-s) ADJ simple and kind-hearted

bonança [bo'nãsa] F (*no mar*) fair weather; (*fig*) calm

bondade [bõ'dadʒi] F goodness, kindness; **tenha a** ~ **de vir** would you please come

bonde ['bõdʒi] (*BR*) M tram

bondoso, -a [bõ'dozu, ɔza] ADJ kind, good

boné [bo'nɛ] M cap

boneca [bo'nɛka] F doll

boneco [bo'neku] M dummy

bonificação [bonifika'sãw] (*pl* -ões) F bonus

bonina [bo'nina] (*PT*) F daisy

boníssimo, -a [bo'nisimu, a] ADJ SUPERL *de* **bom/boa**

bonitão, -tona [boni'tãw, 'tona] (*pl* -ões/-s) ADJ very attractive

bonito, -a [bo'nitu, a] ADJ (*belo*) pretty; (*gesto, dia*) nice ■ M (*peixe*) tuna (fish), tunny; **fazer um** ~ to do a good deed

bonitões [boni'tõjʃ] MPL *de* **bonitão**

bonitona [boni'tona] F *de* **bonitão**

bônus ['bonuʃ] M INV bonus

boquiaberto, -a [bokja'bɛxtu, a] ADJ dumbfounded, astonished

borboleta [boxbo'leta] F butterfly; (*BR: roleta*) turnstile

borboletear [boxbole'tʃja^r] VI to flutter, flit

borbotão [boxbo'tãw] (*pl* -ões) M gush, spurt; **sair aos borbotões** to gush out

borbulhante [boxbu'ʎãtʃi] ADJ bubbling

borbulhar [boxbu'ʎa^r] VI to bubble; (*jorrar*) to gush out

borco ['boxku] M: **de** ~ (*coisa*) upside down; (*pessoa*) face down

borda ['bɔxda] F edge; (*do rio*) bank; **à** ~ **de** on the edge of

bordado [box'dadu] M embroidery

bordão [box'dãw] (*pl* -ões) M staff; (*Mús*) bass string; (*arrimo*) support; (*frase*) catch phrase

bordar [box'da^r] VT to embroider

bordéis [box'd] MPL *de* **bordel**

bordejar [boxde'ʒa^r] VI (*Náut*) to tack

bordel [box'dɛw] (*pl* -éis) M brothel

bordo ['bɔxdu] M (*ao bordejar*) tack; (*de navio*) side; **a** ~ on board

bordoada [box'dwada] F blow

bordões [box'dõjʃ] MPL *de* **bordão**

borla ['bɔxla] F tassel

borocoxô [boroko'ʃo] ADJ dispirited

borra ['boxa] F dregs *pl*

borracha [bo'xaʃa] F rubber; **borracheiro** [boxa'ʃejru] M tyre (*Brit*) *ou* tire (*US*) specialist

borracho, -a [bo'xaʃu, a] ADJ drunk ■ M/F drunk(ard)

borrador [boxa'do^r] M (*Com*) day book

borrão [bo'xãw] (*pl* -ões) M (*rascunho*) rough draft; (*mancha*) blot

borrar [bo'xa^r] VT to blot; (*riscar*) to cross out; (*pintar*) to daub; (*sujar*) to dirty

borrasca [bo'xaʃka] F storm; (*no mar*) squall

borrifar[boxi'fa^r] VT to sprinkle; **borrifo** •
[bo'xifu] M spray
borrões[bo'xõjʃ] MPL *de* **borrão**
bosque['bɔʃki] M wood, forest
bossa['bɔsa] F (*charme*) charm; (*inchaço*)
swelling; (*no crânio*) bump; (*corcova*) hump; **ter ~
para** to have an aptitude for; **Bossa nova**(*Mús*)
see below

● **BOSSA NOVA**
●
● *Bossa nova* is a type of music invented by
● young, middle-class inhabitants of Rio
● de Janeiro at the end of the 1950s. It has
● an obvious jazz influence, an unusual,
● rhythmic beat and lyrics praising beauty
● and love. *Bossa nova* became known
● around the world through the work of the
● conductor and composer Antônio Carlos
● Jobim whose compositions, working with
● the poet Vinícius de Morais, include the
● famous song "The Girl from Ipanema".

bosta['bɔʃta] F dung; (*de humanos*) excrement
bota['bɔta] F boot; **~s de borracha** wellingtons;
bater as ~s (*col*) to kick the bucket
bota-fora(*pl* -s) F (*despedida*) send-off
botânica[bo'tanika] F botany; *v tb* **botânico**
botânico, -a[bo'taniku, a] ADJ botanical ■ M/F
botanist
botão[bo'tãw] (*pl* -ões) M button; (*flor*) bud;
dizer com os seus botões (*fig*) to say to o.s.
botar[bo'ta^r] VT to put; (*PT: lançar*) to throw;
(*roupa, sapatos*) to put on; (*mesa*) to set; (*defeito*) to
find; (*ovos*) to lay; **~ para quebrar** (*col*) to go for
broke, go all out; **~ em dia** to get up to date
bote['bɔtʃi] M (*barco*) boat; (*com arma*) thrust;
(*salto*) spring; (*de cobra*) strike
boteco[bo'tɛku] (*col*) M bar
botequim[botʃi'kĩ] (*pl* -ns) M bar
boticário, -a[botʃi'karju, a] M/F pharmacist,
chemist (*Brit*)
botija[bo'tʃiʒa] F (earthenware) jug
botina[bo'tʃina] F ankle boot
botoeira[bo'twejra] F buttonhole
botões[bo'tõjʃ] MPL *de* **botão**
Botsuana[bot'swana] F: **a ~** Botswana
Bovespa[bo'vɛʃpa] ABR F = **Bolsa de Valores do
Estado de São Paulo**
bovino, -a[bo'vinu, a] ADJ bovine
boxe['bɔksi] M boxing
boxeador[boksja'do^r] M boxer
boy[bɔj] M = **bói**
brabo, -a['brabu, a] ADJ (*feroz*) fierce; (*zangado*)
angry; (*ruim*) bad; (*calor*) unbearable; (*gripe*) bad
braça['brasa] F (*Náut*) fathom
braçada[bra'sada] F armful; (*Natação*) stroke
braçadeira[brasa'dejra] F armband; (*de cortina*)
tie-back; (*metálica*) bracket; (*Esporte*) sweatband

braçal[bra'saw] (*pl* -ais) ADJ manual
bracejar[brase'ʒa^r] VI to wave one's arms about
bracelete[brase'letʃi] M bracelet
braço['brasu] M arm; (*trabalhador*) hand;
~ direito (*fig*) right-hand man; **a ~s com**
struggling with; **de ~s cruzados** with arms
folded; (*fig*) without lifting a finger; **de ~ dado**
arm-in-arm; **cruzar os ~s** (*fig*) to down tools;
não dar o ~ a torcer (*fig*) not to give in; **meter o
~ em** (*col*) to clobber; **receber de ~s abertos** (*fig*)
to welcome with open arms
bradar[bra'da^r] VT, VI to shout, yell; **brado**
['bradu] M shout, yell
braguilha[bra'giʎa] F flies *pl*
braile['brajli] M braille
bramido[bra'midu] M roar
bramir[bra'mi^r] VI to roar
branco, -a['brãku, a] ADJ white ■ M/F white
man/woman ■ M (*espaço*) blank; **em ~** blank;
noite em ~ sleepless night; **deu um ~ nele**
he drew a blank; **brancura**[brã'kura] F
whiteness
brandir[brã'dʒi^r] VT to brandish
brando, -a['brãdu, a] ADJ gentle; (*mole*) soft
brandura[brã'dura] F gentleness; (*moleza*)
softness
branquear[brã'kja^r] VT to whiten; (*alvejar*) to
bleach ■ VI to turn white
brasa['braza] F hot coal; **em ~** red-hot; **pisar
em ~** to be on tenterhooks; **mandar ~** (*col*) to
go for it; **puxar a ~ para a sua sardinha** (*col*) to
look out for o.s.
brasão[bra'zãw] (*pl* -ões) M coat of arms
braseiro[bra'zejru] M brazier
Brasil[bra'ziw] M: **o ~** Brazil
brasileirismo[brazilej'riʒmu] M Brazilianism
brasileiro, -a[brazi'lejru, a] ADJ, M/F Brazilian
Brasília[bra'zilja] N Brasília
brasilianista[brazilja'niʃta] M/F Brazilianist
brasiliense[brazi'ljẽsi] ADJ from Brasília ■ M/F
person from Brasília
brasões[bra'zõjʃ] MPL *de* **brasão**
bravata[bra'vata] F bravado, boasting
bravatear[brava'tʃja^r] VI to boast, brag
bravio, -a[bra'viu, a] ADJ (*selvagem*) wild,
untamed; (*feroz*) ferocious
bravo, -a['bravu, a] ADJ (*corajoso*) brave; (*furioso*)
angry; (*mar*) rough, stormy ■ M brave man; **~!**
bravo!; **bravura**[bra'vura] F courage, bravery
breca['brɛka] F: **ser levado da ~** to be very
naughty
brecar[bre'ka^r] VT (*carro*) to stop; (*reprimir*) to
curb ■ VI to brake
brecha['brɛʃa] F breach; (*abertura*) opening;
(*dano*) damage; (*meio de escapar*) loophole; (*col*)
chance
brega['brɛga] (*col*) ADJ tacky
brejeiro, -a[bre'ʒejru, a] ADJ impish
brejo['brɛʒu] M marsh, swamp; **ir para o ~** (*fig*)

NB: *European Portuguese adds the following consonants to certain words:* **b** (sú(b)dito, su(b)til); **c** (a(c)ção,
a(c)cionista, a(c)to); **m** (inde(m)ne); **p** (ado(p)çã, ado(p)tar); *for further details see p. xiii.*

to go down the drain

brenha ['brɛɲa] F (*mata*) dense wood

breque ['brɛki] M (*freio*) brake

breu [brew] M tar, pitch; **escuro como ~ pitch** black

breve ['brɛvi] ADJ short; (*conciso, rápido*) brief ■ ADV soon; **em ~ soon, shortly; até ~ see you soon**

brevê [bre've] M pilot's licence (*Brit*) *ou* license (*US*)

brevidade [brevi'dadʒi] F brevity, shortness

bridge ['bridʒi] M bridge

briga ['briga] F (*luta*) fight; (*verbal*) quarrel

brigada [bri'gada] F brigade

brigadeiro [briga'dejru] M brigadier; (*doce*) chocolate truffle

brigão, -gona [bri'gãw, ɔna] (*pl -ões/-s*) ADJ quarrelsome ■ M/F troublemaker

brigar [bri'ga^r] VI (*lutar*) to fight; (*altercar*) to quarrel

brigões [bri'gõjʃ] MPL *de* **brigão**

brigona [bri'gɔna] F *de* **brigão**

briguei *etc* [bri'gej] VB V **brigar**

brilhante [bri'ʎãtʃi] ADJ brilliant ■ M diamond

brilhar [bri'ʎa^r] VI to shine

brilho ['briʎu] M (*luz viva*) brilliance; (*esplendor*) splendour (*Brit*), splendor (*US*); (*nos sapatos*) shine; (*de metais, olhos*) gleam

brincadeira [brĩka'dejra] F (*divertimento*) fun; (*gracejo*) joke; (*de criança*) game; **deixe de ~s!** stop fooling!; **de ~ for fun; fora de ~ joking apart; não é ~ it's no joke**

brincalhão, -lhona [brĩka'ʎãw, ɔna] (*pl -ões/-s*) ADJ playful ■ M/F joker, teaser

brincar [brĩ'ka^r] VI to play; (*gracejar*) to joke; **estou brincando I'm only kidding; ~ de soldados to play (at) soldiers; ~ com alguém** (*mexer com*) to tease sb

brinco ['brĩku] M (*jóia*) earring; **estar um ~ to be spotless**

brindar [brĩ'da^r] VT (*beber*) to drink to; (*presentear*) to give a present to; **brinde** ['brĩdʒi] M (*saudação*) toast; (*presente*) free gift

brinquedo [brĩ'kedu] M toy

brinquei *etc* [brĩ'kej] VB V **brincar**

brio ['briu] M self-respect, dignity

brioso, -a ['brjozu, ɔza] ADJ self-respecting

brisa ['briza] F breeze

britânico, -a [bri'taniku, a] ADJ British ■ M/F Briton

broca ['brɔka] F drill

broche ['brɔʃi] M brooch

brochura [bro'ʃura] F (*livro*) paperback; (*folheto*) brochure, pamphlet

brócolis ['brɔkoliʃ] MPL broccoli *sg*

brócolos ['brɔkoluʃ] (*PT*) MPL = **brócolis**

bronca ['brõka] (*col*) F telling off; **dar uma ~ em to tell off; levar uma ~ to get told off**

bronco, -a ['brõku, a] ADJ (*rude*) coarse; (*burro*) thick

bronquear [brõ'kja^r] (*col*) VI to get angry; **~ com**

to tell off

bronquite [brõ'kitʃi] F bronchitis

bronze ['brõzi] M bronze

bronzeado, -a [brõ'zjadu, a] ADJ (*da cor do bronze*) bronze *atr*; (*pelo sol*) suntanned ■ M suntan

bronzear [brõ'zja^r] VT to tan; **bronzear-se** VR to get a tan

brotar [bro'ta^r] VT to produce ■ VI (*manar*) to flow; (*Bot*) to sprout; (*nascer*) to spring up

brotinho, -a [bro'tʃiɲu, a] M/F teenager

broto ['brotu] M bud; (*fig*) youngster

broxa ['brɔʃa] F (*large*) paint brush

bruços ['brusuʃ]: **de ~** ADV face down

bruma ['bruma] F mist, haze

brumoso, -a [bru'mozu, ɔza] ADJ misty, hazy

brunido, -a [bru'nidu, a] ADJ polished

brunir [bru'ni^r] VT to polish

brusco, -a ['bruʃku, a] ADJ brusque; (*súbito*) sudden

brutal [bru'taw] (*pl -ais*) ADJ brutal

brutalidade [brutali'dadʒi] F brutality

brutamontes [bruta'mõtʃiʃ] M INV (*corpulento*) hulk; (*bruto*) brute

bruto, -a ['brutu, a] ADJ brutish; (*grosseiro*) coarse; (*móvel*) heavy; (*diamante*) uncut; (*petróleo*) crude; (*peso, Com*) gross; (*aggressivo*) aggressive ■ M brute; **em ~ raw, unworked; um ~ resfriado an awful cold**

bruxa ['bruʃa] F witch; (*velha feia*) hag; **bruxaria** [bruʃa'ria] F witchcraft

Bruxelas [bru'ʃelaʃ] N Brussels

bruxo ['bruʃu] M wizard

bruxulear [bruʃu'lja^r] VI to flicker

BTN (*BR*) ABR M (= *Bônus do Tesouro Nacional*) government bond used to quote prices

Bucareste [buka'rɛʃtʃi] N Bucharest

bucha ['buʃa] F (*para parafuso*) Rawlplug®; (*para buracos*) bung; **acertar na ~** (*fig*) to hit the nail on the head

bucho ['buʃu] (*col*) M gut; **ela é um ~** (*feio*) she's as ugly as sin

buço ['busu] M down

Budapest [buda'pɛʃtʃi] N Budapest

budismo [bu'dʒiʒmu] M Buddhism

budista [bu'dʒiʃta] ADJ, M/F Buddhist

bueiro [bu'ejru] M storm drain

Buenos Aires ['bwɛnuz'ajriʃ] N Buenos Aires

búfalo ['bufalu] M buffalo

bufante [bu'fãtʃi] ADJ (*manga etc*) puffed, full

bufar [bu'fa^r] VI to puff, pant; (*com raiva*) to snort; (*reclamar*) to moan, grumble

bufê [bu'fe] M (*móvel*) sideboard; (*comida*) buffet; (*serviço*) catering service

buffer ['bafe^r] (*pl -s*) M (*Comput*) buffer

bugiganga [buʒi'gãga] F trinket; **bugigangas** FPL (*coisas sem valor*) knicknacks

bujão [bu'ʒãw] (*pl -ões*) M (*Tec*) cap; **~ de gás gas cylinder**

bula ['bula] F (*Rel*) papal bull; (*Med*) directions *pl* for use

bulbo ['buwbu] M bulb

buldôzer [buw'dozeʳ] (pl -es) M bulldozer
bule ['buli] M (de chá) tea pot; (de café) coffeepot
Bulgária [buw'garja] F: **a** ~ Bulgaria; **búlgaro, -a** ['buwgaru, a] ADJ, M/F Bulgarian ■ M (Ling) Bulgarian
bulha ['buʎa] F row
bulhufas [bu'ʎufaʃ] (col) PRON nothing
bulício [bu'lisju] M (agitação) bustle; (sussurro) rustling
buliçoso, -a [buli'sozu, ɔza] ADJ (vivo) lively; (agitado) restless
bulir [bu'liʳ] VT to move ■ VI to move, stir; ~ **com** to tease; ~ **em** to touch, meddle with
bumbum [bũ'bũ] (pl -ns) (col) M bottom
bunda ['bũda] (col) F bottom, backside
buquê [bu'ke] M bouquet
buraco [bu'raku] M hole; (de agulha) eye; (jogo) rummy; **ser um** ~ (difícil) to be tough; ~ **da fechadura** keyhole
burburinho [buxbu'riɲu] M hubbub; (murmúrio) murmur
burguês, -guesa [bux'geʃ, 'geza] ADJ middle-class, bourgeois; **burguesia** [buxge'zia] F middle class, bourgeoisie
buril [bu'riw] (pl -is) M chisel
burilar [buri'laʳ] VT to chisel
buris [bu'riʃ] MPL de **buril**
Burkina [bux'kina] M: **o** ~ Burkina Faso
burla ['buxla] F trick, fraud; (zombaria) mockery
burlar [bux'laʳ] VT (enganar) to cheat; (defraudar) to swindle; (a lei, impostos) to evade
burlesco, -a [bux'leʃku, a] ADJ burlesque

burocracia [burokra'sia] F bureaucracy; (excessiva) red tape
burocrata [buro'krata] M/F bureaucrat
burocrático, -a [buro'kratʃiku, a] ADJ bureaucratic
burrice [bu'xisi] F stupidity
burro, -a ['buxu, a] ADJ stupid; (pouco inteligente) dim, thick ■ M/F (Zool) donkey; (pessoa) fool, idiot; **pra** ~ (col) a lot; (com adj) really; **dar com os** ~**s n'água** (fig) to come a cropper; ~ **de carga** (fig) hard worker
Burundi [burũ'dʒi] M: **o** ~ Burundi
busca ['buʃka] F search; **em** ~ **de** in search of; **dar** ~ **a** to search for
busca-pé [buʃka'pɛ] (pl -s) M banger
buscar [buʃ'kaʳ] VT to fetch; (procurar) to look **ou** search for; **ir** ~ to fetch, go for; **mandar** ~ to send for
busquei etc [buʃ'kej] VB v **buscar**
bússola ['busola] F compass
bustiê [buʃtʃi'eʳ] M boob tube
busto ['buʃtu] M bust
butique [bu'tʃiki] M boutique
buzina [bu'zina] F horn
buzinada [buzi'nada] F toot, hoot
buzinar [buzi'naʳ] VI to sound one's horn, toot the horn ■ VT to hoot; ~ **nos ouvidos de alguém** (fig) to hassle sb; ~ **algo nos ouvidos de alguém** (fig) to drum sth into sb
búzio ['buzju] M (concha) conch
BVRJ ABR F = **Bolsa de Valores do Rio de Janeiro**

NB: *European Portuguese adds the following consonants to certain words:* **b** (sú(b)dito, su(b)til); **c** (a(c)ção, a(c)cionista, a(c)to); **m** (inde(m)ne); **p** (ado(p)çã, ado(p)tar); *for further details see p. xiii.*

Cc

C, c [se] (*pl* **cs**) M C, c; **C de Carlos** C for Charlie
c/ ABR = **com**
Ca ABR (= *companhia*) Co
cá [ka] ADV here; **de cá** on this side; **para cá**
here, over here; **para lá e para cá** back and
forth; **de lá para cá** since then; **de um ano**
para cá in the last year; **cá entre nós** just
between us
caatinga [ka'tʃĩga] (BR) F scrub(-land)
cabal [ka'baw] (*pl* **-ais**) ADJ (*completo*) complete;
(*exato*) exact
cabala [ka'bala] F (*maquinação*) conspiracy,
intrigue
cabalar [kaba'la^r] VT (*votos etc*) to canvass (for)
■ VI to canvass
cabana [ka'bana] F hut
cabaré [kaba'rɛ] M (*boate*) night club
cabeça [ka'besa] F head; (*inteligência*) brain;
(*de uma lista*) top ■ M/F (*de uma revolta*) leader;
(*de uma organização*) brains *sg*; **cinqüenta ~s**
de gado fifty head of cattle; **de ~** off the top
of one's head; (*calcular*) in one's head; **de ~**
para baixo upside down; **por ~** per person,
per head; **deu-lhe na ~ de** he took it into his
head to; **esquentar a ~** (*col*) to lose one's cool;
não estar com a ~ para fazer not to feel like
doing; **fazer a ~ de alguém** (*col*) to talk sb into
it; **levar na ~** (*col*) to come a cropper; **meter**
na ~ to get into one's head; **tirar algo da ~** to
put sth out of one's mind; **perder a ~** to lose
one's head; **quebrar a ~** to rack one's brains;
subir à ~ (*sucesso etc*) to go to sb's head; **com a ~**
no ar absent-minded; **~ fria** cool-headedness;
cabeçada [kabe'sada] F (*pancada com cabeça*)
butt; (*Futebol*) header; (*asneira*) blunder; **dar**
uma cabeçada (em) to bang one's head (on);
dar uma cabeçada (*fazer asneira*) to make a
blunder; **dar uma cabeçada na bola** (*Futebol*)
to head the ball
cabeça-de-casal (*pl* **cabeças-de-casal**) M
dominant partner
cabeça-de-porco (*pl* **cabeças-de-porco**) (*col*) F
tenement building
cabeça-de-vento (*pl* **cabeças-de-vento**) M/F
scatterbrain
cabeçalho [kabe'saʎu] M (*de livro*) title page; (*de*
página, capítulo) heading

cabecear [kabe'sja^r] VT (*Futebol*) to head ■ VI to
nod; to head the ball
cabeceira [kabe'sejra] F (*de cama*) head; (*de mesa*)
end; **leitura de ~** bedtime reading
cabeçudo, -a [kabe'sudu, a] ADJ big-headed;
(*teimoso*) pigheaded
cabedal [kabe'daw] (*pl* **-ais**) M wealth
cabeleira [kabe'lejra] F head of hair; (*postiça*)
wig; **cabeleireiro, -a** [kabelej'rejru, a] M/F
hairdresser
cabelo [ka'belu] M hair; **cortar/fazer o ~** to
have one's hair cut/done; **ter ~ na venta** to be
short-tempered; **cabeludo, -a** [kabe'ludu, a]
ADJ hairy; (*difícil*) complicated; (*obsceno*) obscene
caber [ka'be^r] VI: **~ (em)** (*poder entrar*) to fit, go;
(*roupa*) to fit; (*ser compatível*) to be appropriate
(in); **~ a** (*em partilha*) to fall to; **cabe a alguém**
fazer it is up to sb to do; **~ por** to fit through;
não cabe aqui fazer comentários this is not
the time or place to comment; **acho que cabe**
exigir um explicação I think it is reasonable
to demand an explanation; **são fatos que**
cabe apurar they are facts which should be
investigated; **tua dúvida cabe perfeitamente**
your doubt is perfectly in order; **não ~ em si de**
to be beside o.s. with
cabide [ka'bidʒi] M (*coat*) hanger; (*móvel*) hat
stand; (*fixo à parede*) coat rack; **~ de empregos**
person who has several jobs
cabideiro [kabi'dejru] M hat stand; (*na parede*)
coat rack; (*para sapatos*) rack
cabimento [kabi'mẽtu] M suitability; **ter ~**
to be fitting *ou* appropriate; **não ter ~** to be
inconceivable
cabine [ka'bini] F cabin; (*em loja*) fitting room; **~**
do piloto (*Aer*) cockpit; **~ telefônica** telephone
box (*Brit*) *ou* booth
cabisbaixo, -a [kabiʒ'bajʃu, a] ADJ (*deprimido*)
dispirited, crestfallen; (*com a cabeça para baixo*)
head down
cabível [ka'bivew] (*pl* **-eis**) ADJ conceivable
cabo ['kabu] M (*extremidade*) end; (*de faca, vassoura*
etc) handle; (*corda*) rope; (*elétrico etc*) cable; (*Geo*)
cape; (*Mil*) corporal; **ao ~ de** at the end of; **de**
~ a rabo from beginning to end; **levar a ~** to
carry out; **dar ~ de** to do away with; **~ eleitoral**
canvasser

caboclo, -a [ka'boklu, a] (BR) ADJ copper-coloured (Brit), copper-colored (US) ■ M/F mestizo

cabotino, -a [kabo'tʃinu, a] ADJ ostentatious ■ M/F show-off

Cabo Verde M Cape Verde

cabo-verdiano, -a [-vex'dʒjanu, a] ADJ, M/F Cape Verdean

cabra ['kabra] F goat ■ M (BR: *sujeito*) guy; (: *capanga*) hired gun

cabra-cega F blind man's buff

cabra-macho (*pl* **cabras-machos**) M tough guy

cabreiro, -a [ka'brejru, a] (*col*) ADJ suspicious

cabresto [kab'reʃtu] M (*de cavalos*) halter

cabrito [ka'britu] M kid

cabrocha [ka'brɔʃa] F mulatto girl

caça ['kasa] F hunting; (*busca*) hunt; (*animal*) quarry, game ■ M (*Aer*) fighter (plane); **à ~ de** in pursuit of

caçada [ka'sada] F (*jornada de caçadores*) hunting trip

caçador, a [kasa'do'(a)] M/F hunter

caçamba [ka'sãba] F (*balde*) bucket

caça-minas M INV minesweeper

caça-níqueis M INV slot machine

cação [ka'sãw] (*pl* -ões) M shark

caçapa [ka'sapa] F pocket

caçar [ka'sa'] VT to hunt; (*com espingarda*) to shoot; (*procurar*) to seek ■ VI to hunt, go hunting

cacareco [kaka'rɛku] M piece of junk; **cacarecos** MPL (*coisas sem valor*) junk *sg*

cacarejar [kakare'ʒa'] VI (*galinhas etc*) to cluck

cacarejo [kaka'reʒu] M clucking

caçarola [kasa'rɔla] F (sauce)pan

cacau [ka'kaw] M cocoa; (*Bot*) cacao

cacaueiro [kaka'wejru] M cocoa tree

cacetada [kase'tada] F blow (with a stick)

cacete [ka'setʃi] ADJ tiresome, boring ■ M/F bore ■ M club, stick; **está quente pra ~** (*col!*) it's bloody hot (*!*)

caceteação [kasetʃja'sãw] F annoyance

cacetear [kase'tʃja'] VT to annoy

Cacex [ka'sɛks] ABR F (= *Carteira do Comércio Exterior*) *part of Banco do Brasil which helps to finance foreign trade*

cachaça [ka'ʃasa] F (white) rum

cachaceiro, -a [kaʃa'sejru, a] ADJ drunk ■ M/F drunkard

cachaço [ka'ʃasu] M neck

cachê [ka'ʃe] M fee

cachecol [kaʃe'kɔw] (*pl* **-óis**) M scarf

cachepô [kaʃe'po] M plant pot

cachimbo [ka'ʃĩbu] M pipe

cacho ['kaʃu] M bunch; (*de cabelo*) curl, lock; (*longo*) ringlet; (*col: caso*) affair

cachoeira [kaʃ'wejra] F waterfall

cachorra [ka'ʃoxa] F bitch, (female) puppy; **estar com a ~** (*col*) to be in a foul mood

cachorrada [kaʃo'xada] F pack of dogs; (*sujeira*) dirty trick

cachorrinho, -a [kaʃo'xiɲu, a] M/F puppy ■ M (*nado*) doggy paddle

cachorro [ka'ʃoxu] M dog, puppy; (*filhote de animal*) cub; (*patife*) rascal; **soltar os ~s em cima de alguém** (*fig*) to lash out at sb; **estar matando ~ a grito** (*col*) to be scraping the barrel; **cachorro-quente** (*pl* **cachorros-quentes**) M hot dog

cacilda [ka'siwda] EXCL wow!, crikey!

cacique [ka'siki] M (Indian) chief; (*mandachuva*) local boss

caco ['kaku] M bit, fragment; (*pessoa velha*) old relic; **chegamos ~s humanos** we arrived dead on our feet

caçoada [ka'swada] F jibe

caçoar [ka'swa'] VT to mock, make fun of ■ VI to mock

cações [ka'sõjʃ] MPL *de* **cação**

cacoete [ka'kwɛtʃi] M twitch, tic

cacto ['kaktu] M cactus

caçula [ka'sula] M/F youngest child

cada ['kada] ADJ INV each; (*todo*) every; **$10 ~** $10 each; **~ um** each one; **~ semana** each week; **a ~ 3 horas** every 3 hours; **em ~ 3 crianças, uma já teve sarampo** out of every 3 children, one has already had measles; **~ vez mais** more and more; **~ vez mais barato** cheaper and cheaper; **tem ~ museu um em Londres!** there are so many different museums in London; **tem ~ um!** it takes all sorts!

cadafalso [kada'fawsu] M (*forca*) gallows *sg*

cadarço [ka'daxsu] M shoelace

cadastrar [kadaʃ'tra'] VT (*Comput: banco de dados*) to set up

cadastro [ka'daʃtru] M (*registro*) register; (*ato*) registration; (*de criminosos*) criminal record; (*de banco etc*) client records *pl*; (*de imóveis*) land registry; **~ bancário** (*de pessoa*) credit rating

cadáver [ka'dave'] M corpse, (dead) body; **só passando por cima do meu ~** over my dead body; **ao chegar ao hospital, o motorista já era ~** the driver was dead on arrival at hospital

cadavérico, -a [kada'vɛriku, a] ADJ (*exame*) post-mortem; (*pessoa*) emaciated

CADE (BR) ABR M = **Conselho Administrativo de Defesa Econômica**

cadê [ka'de] (*col*) ADV: **~ ...?** where's/where are ...?, what's happened to ...?

cadeado [ka'dʒjadu] M padlock

cadeia [ka'deja] F chain; (*prisão*) prison; (*rede*) network

cadeira [ka'dejra] F (*móvel*) chair; (*disciplina*) subject; (*Teatro*) stall; (*função*) post; **cadeiras** FPL (*Anat*) hips; **~ cativa** private seat; **~ de balanço** rocking chair; **~ de rodas** wheelchair; **falar de ~** (*fig*) to speak with authority

cadeirudo, -a [kadej'rudu, a] ADJ big-hipped

NB: *European Portuguese adds the following consonants to certain words:* **b** (sú(b)dito, su(b)til); **c** (a(c)ção, a(c)cionista, a(c)to); **m** (inde(m)ne); **p** (ado(p)ção, ado(p)tar); *for further details see p. xiii.*

cadela [ka'dɛla] F (*cão*) bitch
cadência [ka'dẽsja] F cadence; (*ritmo*) rhythm
cadenciado, -a [kadẽ'sjadu, a] ADJ rhythmic;
(*pausado*) slow
cadente [ka'dẽtʃi] ADJ (*estrela*) falling
caderneta [kadex'neta] F notebook; ~ **de
poupança** savings account
caderno [ka'dɛxnu] M exercise book; (*de notas*)
notebook; (*de jornal*) section
cadete [ka'detʃi] M cadet
cadinho [ka'dʒiɲu] M crucible; (*fig*) melting pot
caducar [kadu'ka^r] VI (*documentos*) to lapse,
expire; (*pessoa*) to become senile; **caduco, -a**
[ka'duku, a] ADJ (*nulo*) invalid, expired; (*senil*)
senile; (*Bot*) deciduous
caduquice [kadu'kisi] F senility
cães [kãjʃ] MPL *de* **cão**
cafajeste [kafa'ʒɛʃtʃi] (*col*) ADJ roguish; (*vulgar*)
vulgar, coarse ▪ M/F rogue; rough customer
café [ka'fɛ] M coffee; (*estabelecimento*) café; ~ **com
leite** white coffee (*Brit*), coffee with cream
(*US*); ~ **preto** black coffee; ~ **da manhã** (*BR*)
breakfast; **é ~ pequeno** it's child's play
café-com-leite ADJ INV coffee-coloured (*Brit*),
coffee-colored (*US*)
cafeeiro, -a [kafe'ejru, a] ADJ coffee *atr* ▪ M
coffee plant
cafeicultor [kafejkuw'to^r] M coffee-grower
cafeicultura [kafejkuw'tura] F coffee-growing
cafeína [kafe'ina] F caffein(e)
cafetã [kafe'tã] M caftan
cafetão [kafe'tãw] (*pl* -**ões**) M pimp
cafeteira [kafe'tejra] F (*vaso*) coffee pot;
(*máquina*) percolator
cafetina [kafe'tʃina] F madam
cafetões [kafe'tõjʃ] MPL *de* **cafetão**
cafezal [kafe'zaw] (*pl* -**ais**) M coffee plantation
cafezinho [kafe'ziɲu] M *small black coffee*
cafona [ka'fona] ADJ tacky ▪ M/F tacky person
cafonice [kafo'nisi] F tackiness; (*coisa*) tacky
thing
cafundó-do-judas [kafũ'dɔ-] M: **no ~** out in the
sticks
cafuné [kafu'nɛ] M: **fazer ~ em alguém** to
stroke sb's hair
cagaço [ka'gasu] (*col!*) M shits *pl* (!)
cagada [ka'gada] (*col!*) F shit (!); (*coisa malfeita*)
cock-up (!)
cágado ['kagadu] M turtle; **a passos de ~** (*fig*) at
a snail's pace
caganeira [kaga'nejra] (*col*) F runs *pl*
cagão, -gona [ka'gãw, 'gɔna] (*pl* -**ões/-s**) (*col*)
M/F: **ser ~** to be a chicken
cagar [ka'ga^r] (*col!*) VI to (have a) shit (!) ▪ VT: ~
regras to tell others what to do; **cagar-se** VR: ~~
se de medo to be shit scared (!); ~ (**para**) not to
give a shit (about) (!)
cagões [ka'gõjʃ] MPL *de* **cagão**
cagona [ka'gɔna] F *de* **cagão**
cagüetar [kagwe'ta^r] VT to inform on; **cagüete**
[ka'gwetʃi] M informer
caiaque [ka'jaki] M kayak

caiar [kaj'a^r] VT to whitewash
caiba *etc* ['kajba] VB V **caber**
cãibra ['kãjbra] F (*Med*) cramp
caibro ['kajbru] M joist
caída [ka'ida] F = **queda**
caído, -a [ka'idu, a] ADJ (*deprimido*) dejected;
(*derrubado*) fallen; (*pendente*) droopy; ~ **por**
(*apaixonado*) in love with
câimbra ['kãjbra] F = **cãibra**
caimento [kaj'mẽtu] M hang, fall
caipira [kaj'pira] ADJ countrified; (*sem traquejo
social*) provincial ▪ M/F yokel
caipirinha [kajpi'riɲa] F *cocktail of cachaça, lemon
and sugar*
cair [ka'i^r] VI to fall; (*ser vítima de logro*) to be
taken in; ~ **bem/mal** (*roupa*) to fit well/badly;
(*col: pessoa*) to look good/bad; ~ **em si** to come to
one's senses; ~ **de quatro** to land on all fours;
estou caindo de sono I'm really sleepy; ~
para trás (*fig*) to be taken aback; **ao ~ da noite**
at nightfall; **o Natal caiu num domingo**
Christmas fell on a Sunday; **essa comida me
caiu mal** that food did not agree with me
Cairo ['kajru] M: **o ~** Cairo
cais [kajʃ] M (*Náut*) quay; (*PT: Ferro*) platform
caixa ['kajʃa] F box; (*cofre*) safe; (*de uma loja*)
cashdesk ▪ M/F (*pessoa*) cashier; **de alta/baixa
~** (*col*) well-off/poor; **fazer a ~** (*Com*) to cash up;
pequena ~ petty cash; ~ **acústica** loudspeaker;
~ **de correio** letter box; ~ **de mudanças** (*BR*) *ou*
de velocidades gear box; ~ **econômica** savings
bank; ~ **postal** P.O. box; ~ **registradora** cash
register
caixa-alta (*pl* **caixas-altas**) (*col*) ADJ rich ▪ M/F
fat cat
caixa-d'água (*pl* **caixas-d'água**) F water tank
caixa-forte (*pl* **caixas-fortes**) F vault
caixão [kaj'ʃãw] (*pl* -**ões**) M (*ataúde*) coffin; (*caixa
grande*) large box
caixa-preta (*pl* **caixas-pretas**) F (*Aer*) black box
caixeiro, -a [kaj'ʃejru] M/F shop assistant;
(*entregador*) delivery man/woman
caixeiro, -a-viajante (*pl* -**s/as-viajantes**) M/F
commercial traveller (*Brit*) *ou* traveler (*US*)
caixilho [kaj'ʃiʎu] M (*moldura*) frame
caixões [kaj'ʃõjʃ] MPL *de* **caixão**
caixote [kaj'ʃɔtʃi] M packing case; ~ **do lixo** (*PT*)
dustbin (*Brit*), garbage can (*US*)
caju [ka'ʒu] M cashew fruit
cajueiro [ka'ʒwejru] M cashew tree
cal [kaw] F lime; (*na água*) chalk; (*para caiar*)
whitewash
calabouço [kala'bosu] M dungeon
calada [ka'lada] F: **na ~ da noite** at dead of
night
calado, -a [ka'ladu, a] ADJ quiet
calafetar [kalafe'ta^r] VT to stop up
calafrio [kala'friu] M shiver; **ter ~s** to shiver
calamar [kala'ma^r] M squid
calamidade [kalami'dadʒi] F calamity, disaster
calamitoso, -a [kalami'tozu, ɔza] ADJ
disastrous

calão [ka'lãw] M: **(baixo)** ~ (BR) bad language; (PT) slang

calar [ka'la^r] VT (não dizer) to keep quiet about; (impor silêncio a) to silence ■ VI to go quiet; (manter-se calado) to keep quiet; **calar-se** VR to go quiet; to keep quiet; ~ **em** (penetrar) to mark; **cala a boca!** shut up!

calça ['kawsa] F (tb: **calças**) trousers pl (Brit), pants pl (US)

calçada [kaw'sada] F (PT: rua) roadway; (BR: passeio) pavement (Brit), sidewalk (US)

calçadão [kawsa'dãw] (pl -ões) M pedestrian precinct (Brit)

calçadeira [kawsa'dejra] F shoe-horn

calçado, -a [kaw'sadu, a] ADJ (rua) paved ■ M shoe; **calçados** MPL (para os pés) footwear sg

calçadões [kawsa'dõjʃ] MPL de **calçadão**

calçamento [kawsa'mẽtu] M paving

calcanhar [kawka'ɲa^r] M (Anat) heel

calcanhar-de-aquiles [-dʒia'kiliʃ] M Achilles' heel

calção [kaw'sãw] (pl -ões) M shorts pl; ~ **de banho** swimming trunks pl

calcar [kaw'ka^r] VT (pisar em) to tread on; (espezinhar) to trample (on); (comprimir) to press; (reprimir) to repress

calçar [kaw'sa^r] VT (sapatos, luvas) to put on; (pavimentar) to pave; (pôr calço) to wedge; **calçar-se** VR to put on one's shoes; **o sapato calça bem?** does the shoe fit?; **ela calça (número) 28** she takes size 28 (in shoes)

calcário, -a [kaw'karju, a] ADJ (água) hard ■ M limestone

calceiro, -a [kaw'sejru, a] M/F shoe-maker

calcinha [kaw'siɲa] F panties pl

cálcio ['kawsju] M calcium

calço ['kawsu] M (cunha) wedge

calções [kaw'sõjʃ] MPL de **calção**

calculadora [kawkula'dora] F calculator

calcular [kawku'la^r] VT to calculate; (imaginar) to imagine ■ VI to make calculations; ~ **que** to reckon that

calculável [kawku'lavew] (pl -eis) ADJ calculable

calculista [kawku'liʃta] ADJ calculating ■ M/F opportunist

cálculo ['kawkulu] M calculation; (Mat) calculus; (Med) stone

calda ['kawda] F (de doce) syrup; **caldas** FPL (águas termais) hot springs

caldeira [kaw'dejra] F (Tec) boiler

caldeirada [kawdej'rada] (PT) F (guisado) fish stew

caldeirão [kawdej'rãw] (pl -ões) M cauldron

caldo ['kawdu] M (sopa) broth; (de fruta) juice; ~ **de carne/galinha** beef/chicken stock; ~ **verde** potato and cabbage broth

calefação [kalefa'sãw] F heating

caleidoscópio [kalejdo'ʃkɔpju] M kaleidoscope

calejado, -a [kale'ʒadu, a] ADJ calloused; (fig:

experiente) experienced; (: endurecido) callous

calejar [kale'ʒa^r] VT (mãos) to callous; (pessoa) to harden; **calejar-se** VR (mãos) to get calluses; (insensibilizar-se) to become callous; (tornar-se experiente) to get experience

calendário [kalẽ'darju] M calendar

calha ['kaʎa] F (sulco) channel; (para água) gutter

calhamaço [kaʎa'masu] M tome

calhambeque [kaʎã'bɛki] (col) M old banger

calhar [ka'ʎa^r] VI: **calhou viajarmos no mesmo avião** we happened to travel on the same plane; **calhou que** it so happened that; **ele calhou de chegar** he happened to arrive; ~ **a** (cair bem) to suit; **vir a** ~ to come at the right time; **se** ~ (PT) perhaps, maybe

calhau [ka'ʎaw] M stone, pebble

calibrado, -a [kali'bradu, a] ADJ (meio bêbado) tipsy

calibrar [kali'bra^r] VT to gauge (Brit), gauge (US), calibrate

calibre [ka'libri] M (de cano) bore, calibre (Brit), caliber (US); (fig) calibre

cálice ['kalisi] M (copinho) wine glass; (Rel) chalice

calidez [kali'deʒ] F warmth

cálido, -a ['kalidu, a] ADJ warm

caligrafia [kaligra'fia] F (arte) calligraphy; (letra) handwriting

calista [ka'liʃta] M/F chiropodist (Brit), podiatrist (US)

calma ['kawma] F calm; **conservar/perder a** ~ to keep/lose one's temper; ~! take it easy!

calmante [kaw'mãtʃi] ADJ soothing ■ M (Med) tranquillizer

calmo, -a ['kawmu, a] ADJ calm, tranquil

calo ['kalu] M callus; (no pé) corn; **pisar nos ~s de alguém** (fig) to hit a (raw) nerve

calombo [ka'lõbu] M lump; (na estrada) bump

calor [ka'lo^r] M heat; (agradável) warmth; (fig) warmth; **está** ou **faz** ~ it is hot; **estar com** ~ to be hot

calorento, -a [kalo'rẽtu, a] ADJ (pessoa) sensitive to heat; (lugar) hot

caloria [calo'ria] F calorie

caloroso, -a [kalo'rozu, ɔza] ADJ warm; (entusiástico) enthusiastic; (protesto) fervent

calota [ka'lɔta] F (Auto) hubcap

calote [ka'lɔtʃi] (col) M (dívida) bad debt; **dar o** ~ to welsh (on one's debts)

caloteiro, -a [kalo'tejru, a] (col) ADJ unreliable ■ M/F bad payer

calouro, -a [ka'loru, a] M/F (Educ) fresher (Brit), freshman (US); (noviço) novice

calúnia [ka'lunja] F slander

caluniador, a [kalunja'do^r(a)] ADJ slanderous ■ M/F slanderer

caluniar [kalu'nja^r] VT to slander

calunioso, -a [kalu'njozu, ɔza] ADJ slanderous

NB: European Portuguese adds the following consonants to certain words: **b** (sú(b)dito, su(b)til); **c** (a(c)ção, a(c)cionista, a(c)to); **m** (inde(m)ne); **p** (ado(p)çã, ado(p)tar); for further details see p. xiii.

calvície [kaw'visi] F baldness

calvo, -a ['kawvu, a] ADJ bald

cama ['kama] F bed; **~ de casal** double bed; **~ de solteiro** single bed; **de ~** (*doente*) ill (in bed); **ficar de ~** to take to one's bed

cama-beliche (*pl* **camas-beliches**) F bunk bed

camada [ka'mada] F layer; (*de tinta*) coat

camafeu [kama'few] M cameo

câmara ['kamara] F chamber; (*Foto*) camera; **~ digital** digital camera; **~ municipal** (BR) town council; (PT) town hall; **em ~ lenta** in slow motion

câmara-ardente F: **estar exposto em ~** to lie in state

camarada [kama'rada] ADJ friendly, nice; (*preço*) good ■ M/F comrade; (*sujeito*) guy/woman

camaradagem [kamara'daʒẽ] F comradeship, camaraderie; **por ~** out of friendliness

câmara-de-ar (*pl* **câmaras-de-ar**) F inner tube

camarão [kama'rãw] (*pl* **-ões**) M shrimp; (*graúdo*) prawn

camareiro, -a [kama'rejru, a] M/F cleaner/ chambermaid

camarilha [kama'riʎa] F clique

camarim [kama'rĩ] (*pl* **-ns**) M (*Teatro*) dressing room

Camarões [kama'rõjʃ] M: **o ~** Cameroon

camarões [kama'rõjʃ] MPL *de* **camarão**

camarote [kama'rɔtʃi] M (*Náut*) cabin; (*Teatro*) box

cambada [kã'bada] F bunch, gang

cambaio, -a [kã'baju, a] ADJ (*mesa*) wobbly, rickety

cambalacho [kãba'laʃu] M scam

cambaleante [kãba'ljãtʃi] ADJ unsteady (on one's feet)

cambalear [kãba'ljaʳ] VI to stagger, reel

cambalhota [kãba'ʎɔta] F somersault

cambar [kã'baʳ] VI: **~ para** to lean on

cambial [kã'bjaw] (*pl* **-ais**) ADJ exchange *atr*

cambiante [kã'bjãtʃi] ADJ changing, variable ■ M (*cor*) shade

cambiar [kã'bjaʳ] VT to change; (*trocar*) to exchange

câmbio ['kãbju] M (*dinheiro etc*) exchange; (*preço de câmbio*) rate of exchange; **~ livre** free trade; **~ negro** black market; **~ oficial/paralelo** official/ black market

cambista [kã'biʃta] M (*de dinheiro*) money changer; (BR: *de ingressos*) (ticket-)tout

Camboja [kã'bɔja] M: **o ~** Cambodia

cambojano, -a [kãbo'ʒanu, a] ADJ, M/F Cambodian

camburão [kãbu'rãw] (*pl* **-ões**) M police van

camélia [ka'mɛlja] F camelia

camelo [ka'melu] M camel; (*fig*) dunce

camelô [kame'lo] M street pedlar

camião [ka'mjãw] (*pl* **-ões**) (PT) M lorry (Brit), truck (US)

caminhada [kami'ɲada] F walk

caminhante [kami'ɲãtʃi] M/F walker

caminhão [kami'ɲãw] (*pl* **-ões**) (BR) M lorry (Brit), truck (US)

caminhar [kami'ɲaʳ] VI (*ir a pé*) to walk; (*processo*) to get under way; (*negócios*) to go, progress

caminho [ka'miɲu] M way; (*vereda*) road, path; **~ de ferro** (PT) railway (Brit), railroad (US); **a meio ~** halfway (there); **ser meio ~ andado** (*fig*) to be halfway there; **a ~** on the way, en route; **cortar ~** to take a short cut; **ir pelo mesmo ~** to go the same way; **pôr-se a ~** to set off

caminhões [kami'ɲõjʃ] MPL *de* **caminhão**

caminhoneiro, -a [kamiɲo'nejru, a] M/F lorry driver (Brit), truck driver (US)

caminhonete [kamiɲo'nɛtʃi] M (*Auto*) van

camiões [ka'mjõjʃ] MPL *de* **camião**

camioneta [kamjo'neta] (PT) F (*para passageiros*) coach; (*comercial*) van

camionista [kamjo'niʃta] (PT) M/F lorry driver (Brit), truck driver (US)

camisa [ka'miza] F shirt; **~ de dormir** nightshirt; **~ esporte/pólo/social** sports/polo/ dress shirt; **mudar de ~** (*Esporte*) to change sides; **camisa-de-força** (*pl* **camisas-de-força**) F straitjacket

camisa-de-vênus (*pl* **camisas-de-vênus**) F condom

camiseta [kami'zeta] (BR) F T-shirt; (*interior*) vest

camisinha [kami'ziɲa] (*col*) F condom

camisola [kami'zɔla] F (BR) nightdress; (PT: *pulôver*) sweater; **~ interior** (PT) vest

camomila [kamo'mila] F camomile

campa ['kãpa] F (*de sepultura*) gravestone

campainha [kampa'iɲa] F bell

campal [kã'paw] (*pl* **-ais**) ADJ: **batalha ~** pitched battle; **missa ~** open-air mass

campanário [kãpa'narju] M (*torre*) church tower, steeple

campanha [kã'paɲa] F (*Mil etc*) campaign; (*planície*) plain

campeão, -peã [kã'pjãw, 'pjã] (*pl* **-ões/-s**) M/F champion; **campeonato** [kãpjo'natu] M championship

campestre [kã'pɛʃtri] ADJ rural, rustic

campina [kã'pina] F prairie, grassland

camping ['kãpĩŋ] (BR) (*pl* **-s**) M camping; (*lugar*) campsite

campismo [kã'piʒmu] M camping; **parque de ~** campsite

campista [kã'piʃta] M/F camper

campo ['kãpu] M field; (*fora da cidade*) countryside; (*Esporte*) ground; (*acampamento*) camp; (*âmbito*) field; (*Tênis*) court

camponês, -esa [kãpo'neʃ, eza] M/F countryman/woman; (*agricultor*) farmer

campus ['kãpuʃ] M INV campus

camuflagem [kamu'flaʒẽ] F camouflage

camuflar [kamu'flaʳ] VT to camouflage

camundongo [kamũ'dõgu] (BR) M mouse

camurça [ka'muxsa] F suede

CAN (BR) ABR M = **Correio Aéreo Nacional**
cana ['kana] F cane; (col: cadeia) nick; (de açúcar) sugar cane; **ir em** ~ to be put behind bars
Canadá [kana'da] M: **o** ~ Canada; **canadense** [kana'dēsi] ADJ, M/F Canadian
canal [ka'naw] (pl -ais) M channel; (de navegação) canal; (Anat) duct
canalha [ka'naʎa] F rabble, mob ■ M/F wretch, scoundrel
canalização [kanaliza'sāw] F (de água) plumbing; (de gás) piping
canalizador, a [kanaliza'do^r(a)] (PT) M/F plumber
canalizar [kanali'za^r] VT (água, esforços) to channel; (colocar canos) to lay pipes in
canapé [kana'pɛ] M sofa
canapê [kana'pe] M (Culin) canapé
canário [ka'narju] M canary
canastra [ka'naʃtra] F (big) basket; (jogo) canasta
canastrão, -trona [kanaʃ'trāw, 'trɔna] (pl -ões/-s) M/F ham actor/actress
canavial [kana'vjaw] (pl -ais) M cane field
canavieiro, -a [kana'vjejru, a] ADJ sugar cane atr
canção [kā'sāw] (pl -ões) F song; ~ **de ninar** lullaby
cancela [kā'sɛla] F gate
cancelamento [kāsela'mētu] M cancellation
cancelar [kāse'la^r] VT to cancel; (invalidar) to annul; (riscar) to cross out
câncer ['kāse^r] M cancer; **C~** (Astrologia) Cancer
canceriano, -a [kāse'rjanu, a] ADJ, M/F Cancerian
cancerígeno, -a [kāse'riʒenu, a] ADJ carcinogenic
cancerologista [kāserolo'ʒiʃta] M/F cancer specialist, oncologist
canceroso, -a [kāse'rozu, ɔza] ADJ (célula) cancerous ■ M/F cancer sufferer
canções [kā'sōjʃ] FPL de **canção**
cancro ['kākru] (PT) M cancer
candango, -a [kā'dāgu, a] M/F person from Brasília
candeeiro [kādʒi'ejru] M (BR: a óleo) oil-lamp; (a gás) gas-lamp; (PT) lamp
candelabro [kāde'labru] M (castiçal) candlestick; (lustre) chandelier
candente [kā'dētʃi] ADJ white hot; (fig) inflamed
candidatar-se [kādʒida'taxsi] VR: ~ **a** (vaga) to apply for; (presidência) to stand for
candidato, -a [kādʒi'datu, a] M/F candidate; (a cargo) applicant
candidatura [kādʒida'tura] F candidature; (a cargo) application
cândido, -a ['kādʒidu, a] ADJ (ingênuo) naive; (inocente) innocent
candomblé [kādō'blɛ] M candomblé (Afro-

Brazilian religion); (local) candomblé shrine

● **CANDOMBLÉ**
●
● Candomblé is Brazil's most influential
● Afro-Brazilian religion. Practised mainly
● in Bahia, it mixes catholicism and Yoruba
● tradition. According to candomblé, believers
● become possessed by spirits and thus
● become an instrument of communication
● between divine and mortal forces. Candomblé
● ceremonies are great spectacles of African
● rhythm and dance and are held in terreiros.

candura [kā'dura] F (simplicidade) simplicity; (inocência) innocence
caneca [ka'nɛka] F mug
caneco [ka'nɛku] M tankard; **pintar os ~s** (col) to play up
canela [ka'nɛla] F (especiaria) cinnamon; (Anat) shin
canelada [kane'lada] F kick in the shins; **dei uma ~ na mesa** I hit my shins on the table
caneta [ka'neta] F pen; ~ **esferográfica** ballpoint pen; ~ **pilot** felt-tip pen; ~ **seletora** (Comput) light pen
caneta-tinteiro (pl canetas-tinteiro) F fountain pen
canga ['kāga] F beach wrap
cangaceiro [kāga'sejru] (BR) M bandit
cangote [kā'gotʃi] M (back of the) neck
canguru [kāgu'ru] M kangaroo
cânhamo ['kaɲamu] M hemp
canhão [ka'ɲāw] (pl -ões) M (Mil) cannon; (Geo) canyon
canhestro, -a [ka'ɲeʃtru, a] ADJ awkward
canhões [ka'ɲōjʃ] MPL de **canhão**
canhoto, -a [ka'ɲotu, a] ADJ left-handed ■ M/F left-handed person ■ M (de cheque) stub
canibal [kani'baw] (pl -ais) M/F cannibal
canibalismo [kaniba'liʒmu] M cannibalism
caniço, -a [ka'nisu, a] ADJ (col) skinny ■ M reed
canícula [ka'nikula] F searing heat
canil [ka'niw] (pl -is) M kennel
caninha [ka'niɲa] (col) F rum
canino, -a [ka'ninu, a] ADJ canine; (fome) terrible ■ M canine
canis [ka'niʃ] MPL de **canil**
canivete [kani'vetʃi] M penknife; **nem que chovam ~s** whatever happens, come what may
canja ['kāʒa] F (sopa) chicken broth; (col) cinch, pushover
canjica [kā'ʒika] F maize porridge
cano ['kanʋ] M pipe; (tubo) tube; (de arma de fogo) barrel; (de bota) top; ~ **de esgoto** sewer; **entrar pelo ~** (col) to come off badly
canoa [ka'noa] F canoe
canoagem [ka'nwaʒe] F canoeing
canoeiro, -a [ka'nwejru, a] M/F canoeist

NB: European Portuguese adds the following consonants to certain words: **b** (sú(b)dito, su(b)til); **c** (a(c)ção, a(c)cionista, a(c)to); **m** (inde(m)ne); **p** (ado(p)çã, ado(p)tar); for further details see p. xiii.

canoísta [kano'iʃta] M/F canoeist

canonizar [kanoni'zaʳ] VT to canonize

cansaço [kã'sasu] M tiredness

cansado, -a [kã'sadu, a] ADJ tired

cansar [kã'saʳ] VT (*fatigar*) to tire; (*entediar*) to bore ■ VI (*ficar cansado*) to get tired; **cansar-se** VR to get tired; **cansativo, -a** [kãsa'tʃivu, a] ADJ tiring; (*tedioso*) tedious

canseira [kã'sejra] F (*cansaço*) weariness; (*trabalho árduo*) toil; **dar ~ em alguém** to wear sb out

cantada [kã'tada] (*col*) F sweet talk; **dar uma ~ em** to sweet-talk

cantado, -a [kã'tadu, a] ADJ (*missa*) sung; (*sotaque*) sing-song

cantar [kã'taʳ] VT to sing; (*respostas etc*) to sing out; (*col: seduzir*) to sweet-talk ■ VI to sing ■ M song

cantarolar [kãtaro'laʳ] VT to hum

canteiro [kã'tejru] M stonemason; (*de flores*) flower bed; (*de obra*) site office

cantiga [kã'tʃiga] F ballad; **~ de ninar** lullaby

cantil [kã'tʃĩw] (*pl* -**is**) M canteen, flask

cantina [kã'tʃina] F canteen

cantis [kã'tʃiʃ] MPL *de* **cantil**

canto ['kãtu] M corner; (*lugar*) place; (*canção*) song

cantor, a [kã'toʳ(a)] M/F singer

cantoria [kãto'ria] F singing

canudo [ka'nudu] M tube; (*para beber*) straw

cão [kãw] (*pl* **cães**) M dog; (*pessoa*) rascal; **ser** *ou* **estar um ~ de ruim** (*col*) to be awful

caolho, -a [ka'oʎu, a] ADJ cross-eyed

caos ['kaoʃ] M chaos

caótico, -a [ka'ɔtʃiku, a] ADJ chaotic

capa ['kapa] F (*roupa*) cape; (*cobertura*) cover; **livro de ~ dura/mole** hardback/paperback (book)

capacete [kapa'setʃi] M helmet

capacho [ka'paʃu] M door mat; (*fig*) toady

capacidade [kapasi'dadʒi] F capacity; (*aptidão*) ability, competence; **ser uma ~** (*pessoa*) to be brilliant; **~ ociosa** (*Com*) idle capacity

capacíssimo, -a [kapa'sisimu, a] ADJ SUPERL *de* **capaz**

capacitar [kapasi'taʳ] VT: **~ alguém a fazer/ para algo** to prepare sb to do/for sth; **capacitar-se** VR: **capacitar-se de/de que** to convince o.s. of/that

capar [ka'paʳ] VT to castrate, geld

capataz [kapa'taʒ] M foreman

capaz [ka'paʒ] ADJ able, capable; **ser ~ de** to be able to (*ou* capable of); **sou ~ de ...** (*talvez*) I might ...; **é ~ de chover hoje** it might rain today

capcioso, -a [kap'sjozu, ɔza] ADJ (*pergunta*) trick; (*pessoa*) tricky

capela [ka'pɛla] F chapel

capelão [kape'lãw] (*pl* -**ães**) M (*Rel*) chaplain

Capemi [kape'mi] (BR) ABR F (= *Caixa de Pecúlios, Pensões e Montepios dos Militares*) military pension fund

capenga [ka'pẽga] ADJ lame ■ M/F cripple

capengar [kapẽ'gaʳ] VI to limp

Capes (BR) ABR F (*Educ:* = *Coordenação de Aperfeiçoamento de Pessoal de Nível Superior*) grant-awarding body

capeta [ka'peta] M devil; **ele é um ~** he's a little devil

capilar [kapi'laʳ] ADJ hair *atr*

capim [ka'pĩ] M grass

capinar [kapi'naʳ] VT to weed ■ VI to weed; (*col*) to clear off

capitães [kapi'tãjʃ] MPL *de* **capitão**

capital [kapi'taw] (*pl* -**ais**) ADJ, M capital ■ F (*cidade*) capital; **~ circulante** (*Com*) circulating capital; **~ de giro** (*Com*) working capital; **~ investido** (*Com*) investment capital; **~ (em) ações** (*Com*) share capital; **~ imobilizado** *ou* **fixo** (*Com*) fixed capital; **~ integralizado** (*Com*) paid-up capital; **~ próprio** *ou* **social** (*Com*) equity capital; **~ de risco** (*Com*) venture capital

capitalismo [kapita'liʒmu] M capitalism; **capitalista** [kapita'liʃta] M/F capitalist

capitalizar [kapitali'zaʳ] VT (*tirar proveito de*) to capitalize on; (*Com*) to capitalize

capitanear [kapita'njaʳ] VT to command, head

capitania [kapita'nia] F: **~ do porto** port authority

capitão [kapi'tãw] (*pl* -**ães**) M captain

capitulação [kapitula'sãw] F capitulation, surrender

capitular [kapitu'laʳ] VT (*falhas, causas*) to list; (*descrever*) to characterize; (*rendição*) to fix the terms of ■ VI to capitulate; **~ alguém de algo** to brand sb (as) sth

capítulo [ka'pitulu] M chapter; (*de novela*) episode

capô [ka'po] M (*Auto*) bonnet (*Brit*), hood (*US*)

capoeira [ka'pwejra] F (*PT*) hencoop; (*mata*) brushwood; (*jogo*) capoeira (*foot-fighting dance*)

● **CAPOEIRA**

Capoeira is a fusion of martial arts and dance which originated among African slaves in colonial Brazil. It is danced in a circle to the sound of the *berimbau*, a percussion instrument of African origin. Opposed by the Brazilian authorities until the beginning of the twentieth century, today *capoeira* is regarded as a national sport.

capota [ka'pota] F (*Auto*) hood, top

capotar [kapo'taʳ] VI to overturn

capote [ka'pɔtʃi] M overcoat

caprichar [kapri'ʃaʳ] VI: **~ em** to take trouble over

capricho [ka'priʃu] M whim, caprice; (*teimosia*) obstinacy; (*apuro*) care; **caprichoso, -a** [kapri'ʃozu, ɔza] ADJ capricious; (*com apuro*) meticulous

capricorniano, -a [kaprikox'njanu, a] ADJ, M/F Capricorn

Capricórnio [kapri'kɔxnju] M Capricorn

cápsula ['kapsula] F capsule

captar [kap'taʳ] VT (*atrair*) to win; (*Rádio*) to pick

up; (*águas*) to collect, dam up; (*compreender*) to catch
captura [kap'tura] F capture; **capturar** [kaptu'ra^r] VT to capture, seize
capuz [ka'puʒ] M hood
caquético, -a [ka'kɛtʃiku, a] ADJ doddery
caqui [ka'ki] M persimmon
cáqui ['kaki] ADJ khaki
cara ['kara] F (*de pessoa*) face; (*aspecto*) appearance ■ M (*col*) guy; (*coragem*) courage, heart; ~ **ou coroa?** heads or tails?; **de ~** straightaway; **está na ~** it's obvious; **dar de ~ com** to bump into; **estar com boa ~** to look well; (*comida*) to look good; **não vou com a ~ dele** (*col*) I'm not very keen on him; **meter a ~** (*col*) to put one's back into it; **ser a ~ de** (*col*) to be the spitting image of; **ter ~ de** to look (like)
carabina [kara'bina] F rifle
Caracas [ka'rakaʃ] N Caracas
caracol [kara'kɔw] (*pl* -**óis**) M snail; (*de cabelo*) curl; **escada em ~** spiral staircase
caracteres [karak'tɛriʃ] MPL *de* **caráter**
característica [karakte'riʃtʃika] F characteristic, feature
característico, -a [karakte'riʃtʃiku, a] ADJ characteristic
caracterização [karakteriza'sãw] F characterization; (*de ator*) make-up
caracterizar [karakteri'za^r] VT to characterize, typify; (*ator*) to make up; **caracterizar-se** VR to be characterized; (*ator*) to get into character
cara-de-pau (*pl* **caras-de-pau**) ADJ brazen ■ M/F: **ele é ~** he's very forward
caraíba [kara'iba] ADJ Caribbean
caramanchão [karamã'ʃãw] (*pl* -**ões**) M summerhouse
caramba [ka'rãba] EXCL blimey (*Brit*), gee (*US*); **quente pra ~** (*col*) really hot
carambola [karã'bɔla] F carambole (*fruit*)
caramelo [kara'mɛlu] M caramel; (*bala*) toffee
cara-metade (*pl* **caras-metades**) F better half
caranguejo [karã'geʒu] M crab
carão [ka'rãw] (*pl* -**ões**) M telling-off; **passar/levar um ~** to give/get a telling-off
carapuça [kara'pusa] F cap; **enfiar a ~** to take the hint personally
caras-pintadas FPL *see below*

● **CARAS-PINTADAS**
●
● In 1992, during popular demonstrations
● calling for the impeachment of the
● then president Fernando Collor de Mello,
● students known as *caras-pintadas*, because
  they had the Brazilian flag painted on their
  faces, went through the streets shouting
  "Collor, out!" and similar slogans.

caratê [kara'te] M karate

caráter [ka'rate^r] (*pl* **caracteres**) M character; **de ~ social** of a social nature; **a ~** in character; **uma pessoa de ~** a person of hono(u)r
caravana [kara'vana] F caravan
carboidrato [kaxboi'dratu] M carbohydrate
carbônico, -a [kax'boniku, a] ADJ carbon *atr*
carbonizar [kaxboni'za^r] VT to carbonize; (*queimar*) to char
carbono [kax'bonu] M carbon
carburador [kaxbura'do^r] M carburettor (*Brit*), carburetor (*US*)
carcaça [kax'kasa] F (*esqueleto*) carcass; (*armação*) frame; (*de navio*) hull
carcamano, -a [kaxka'manu, a] M/F Italian-Brazilian
cárcere ['kaxseri] M prison
carcereiro, -a [kaxse'rejru, a] M/F jailer, warder
carcomido, -a [kaxko'midu, a] ADJ worm-eaten; (*rosto*) pock-marked, pitted
cardápio [kax'dapju] (*BR*) M menu
cardeal [kax'dʒjaw] (*pl* -**ais**) ADJ, M cardinal
cardíaco, -a [kax'dʒiaku, a] ADJ cardiac ■ M/F person with a heart condition; **ataque ~** heart attack; **parada cardíaca** cardiac arrest
cardigã [kaxdʒi'gã] M cardigan
cardinal [kaxdʒi'naw] (*pl* -**ais**) ADJ cardinal
cardiológico, -a [kaxdʒjo'lɔʒiku, a] ADJ heart *atr*
cardiologista [kaxdʒjolo'ʒiʃta] M/F heart specialist, cardiologist
cardume [kax'dumi] M (*peixes*) shoal
careca [ka'rɛka] ADJ bald ■ F baldness; **estar ~ de fazer/saber** (*col*) to be used to doing/know full well
carecer [kare'se^r] VI: ~ **de** (*ter falta*) to lack; (*precisar*) to need
careiro, -a [ka'rejru, a] ADJ expensive
carência [ka'rẽsja] F (*falta*) lack, shortage; (*necessidade*) need; (*privação*) deprivation; **carente** [ka'rẽtʃi] ADJ wanting; (*pessoa*) needy, deprived; (*de carinho*) in need of affection
carestia [kareʃ'tʃia] F high cost; (*preços altos*) high prices *pl*; (*escassez*) scarcity
careta [ka'reta] ADJ (*col*) straight, square ■ F grimace; **fazer uma ~** to pull a face
carga ['kaxga] F load; (*de navio, avião*) cargo; (*ato de carregar*) loading; (*Elet*) charge; (*fig: peso*) burden; (*Mil*) attack, charge; **dar ~ em** (*Comput*) to boot (up); **voltar à ~** to insist; ~ **d'água** heavy downpour; ~ **horária** workload; ~ **aérea** air cargo
cargo ['kaxgu] M (*responsabilidade*) responsibility; (*função*) post; **a ~ de** in charge of; **ter a ~** to be in charge of; **tomar a ~** to take charge of; ~ **honorífico** honorary post; ~ **de confiança** position of trust; ~ **público** public office
cargueiro [kax'gejru] M cargo ship
cariar [ka'rja^r] VT, VI to decay
Caribe [ka'ribi] M: **o** ~ the Caribbean (Sea)
caricatura [karika'tura] F caricature

caricatural [karikatu'raw] (pl -ais) ADJ (fig) grotesque

caricaturar [karikatu'ra^r] VT to caricature

caricaturista [karikatu'riʃta] M/F caricaturist

carícia [ka'risja] F caress

caridade [kari'dadʒi] F charity; **obra de ~** charity

caridoso, -a [kari'dozu, ɔza] ADJ charitable

cárie ['kari] F tooth decay; (Med) caries sg

carimbar [karĩ'ba^r] VT to stamp; (no correio) to postmark

carimbo [ka'rĩbu] M stamp; (postal) postmark

carinho [ka'riɲu] M affection, fondness; (carícia) caress; **fazer ~** to caress; **com ~** affectionately; (com cuidado) with care; **carinhoso, -a** [kari'ɲozu, ɔza] ADJ affectionate

carioca [ka'rjɔka] ADJ of Rio de Janeiro ■ M/F native of Rio de Janeiro ■ M (PT: café) type of weak coffee

carisma [ka'riʒma] M charisma

carismático, -a [kariʒ'matʃiku, a] ADJ charismatic

caritativo, -a [karita'tʃivu, a] ADJ charitable

carnal [kax'naw] (pl -ais) ADJ carnal; **primo ~** first cousin

carnaval [kaxna'vaw] (pl -ais) M carnival; (fig) mess; **conhecer alguém de outros carnavais** (col) to know sb from way back

● CARNAVAL

● In Brazil, Carnaval is the popular festival
● held each year in the four days before Lent.
● It is celebrated in very different ways in
● different parts of the country. In Rio de
● Janeiro, for example, the big attraction
● is the parades of the escolas de samba, in
● Salvador the trios elétricos, in Recife the frevo
● and, in Olinda, the giant figures, such as
● the Homem da meia-noite and Mulher do meio-dia.
● In Portugal, Carnaval is celebrated on Shrove
● Tuesday, with street parties and processions
● taking place throughout the country.

carnavalesco, -a [kaxnava'leʃku, a] ADJ (festa) carnival atr; (pessoa) keen on carnival; (fig) grotesque ■ M/F carnival organizer

carne ['kaxni] F flesh; (Culin) meat; **em ~ e osso** in the flesh; **ser de ~ e osso** to be human; **~ assada** roast beef

carnê [kax'ne] M (para compras) payment book

carneiro [kax'nejru] M sheep; (macho) ram; **perna/costeleta de ~** leg of lamb/lamb chop

carniça [kax'nisa] F carrion; **pular ~** to play leapfrog

carnificina [kaxnifi'sina] F slaughter

carnívoro, -a [kax'nivoru, a] ADJ carnivorous ■ M carnivore

carnudo, -a [kax'nudu, a] ADJ plump, fleshy; (col) beefy; (lábios) thick; (fruta) fleshy

caro, -a ['karu, a] ADJ dear, expensive; (estimado) dear; **sair ~** to work out expensive; **cobrar/**

pagar ~ to charge a lot/pay dearly

carochinha [karo'ʃiɲa] F: **conto da ~** fairy tale

caroço [ka'rosu] M (de frutos) stone; (endurecimento) lump

carões [ka'rõjʃ] MPL de **carão**

carola [ka'rɔla] (col) M/F pious person

carona [ka'rɔna] F lift; **viajar de ~** to hitchhike; **pegar uma ~** to get a lift

carpete [kax'pɛtʃi] M (fitted) carpet

carpintaria [kaxpĩta'ria] F carpentry

carpinteiro [kaxpĩ'tejru] M carpenter; (Teatro) stagehand

carranca [ka'xãka] F frown, scowl

carrancudo, -a [kaxã'kudu, a] ADJ (soturno) sullen; (semblante) scowling

carrapato [kaxa'patu] M (inseto) tick; (pessoa) hanger-on

carrapicho [kaxa'piʃu] M (do cabelo) bun

carrasco [ka'xaʃku] M executioner; (fig) tyrant

carrear [ka'xja^r] VT (transportar) to transport; (arrastar) to carry; (acarretar) to bring on

carreata [kaxe'ata] F motorcade

carregado, -a [kaxe'gadu, a] ADJ loaded, laden; (semblante) sullen; (céu) dark; (ambiente) tense

carregador [kaxega'do^r] M porter

carregamento [kaxega'mẽtu] M (ação) loading; (carga) load, cargo

carregar [kaxe'ga^r] VT to load; (levar) to carry; (bateria) to charge; (PT: apertar) to press; (levar para longe) to take away ■ VI: **~ em** (pôr em demasia) to overdo, put too much; (pôr enfase) to bring out

carreira [ka'xejra] F (ação de correr) run, running; (profissão) career; (Turfe) race; (Náut) slipway; (fileira) row; **às ~s** in a hurry; **dar uma ~** to go quickly; **fazer ~** to make a career; **arrepiar ~** to abandon one's career

carreirista [kaxej'riʃta] ADJ, M/F careerist

carreta [ka'xeta] F cart

carreteiro [kaxe'tejru] M cart driver

carretel [kaxe'tɛw] (pl -éis) M spool, reel

carreto [ka'xetu] M freight

carril [ka'xiw] (pl -is) (PT) M (Ferro) rail

carrilhão [kaxi'ʎãw] (pl -ões) M chime

carrinho [ka'xiɲu] M (para bagagem, compras) trolley; (brinquedo) toy car; **~ (de criança)** pram; **~ de mão** wheelbarrow; **~ de chá** tea trolley

carris [ka'xiʃ] MPL de **carril**

carro ['kaxo] M (automóvel) car; (de bois) cart; (de mão) handcart, barrow; (de máquina de escrever) carriage; **pôr o ~ adiante dos bois** (fig) to put the cart before the horse; **~ de corrida** racing car; **~ de passeio** saloon car; **~ de praça** cab; **~ de bombeiro** fire engine; **~ esporte** sports car

carroça [ka'xɔsa] F cart, waggon

carroçeria [kaxose'ria] F (Auto) bodywork

carro-chefe (pl carros-chefes) M (de desfile) main float; (fig) flagship, centrepiece (Brit), centerpiece (US)

carrocinha [kaxo'siɲa] F wagon

carro-forte (pl carros-fortes) M security van

carrossel [kaxo'sɛw] (pl -éis) M merry-go-round

carruagem [ka'xwaʒẽ] (pl -ns) F carriage, coach

carta ['kaxta] F letter; (de jogar) card; (mapa) chart; ~ **aberta** open letter; ~ **aérea** airmail letter; ~ **registrada** registered letter; ~ **de apresentação** letter of introduction; ~ **de crédito/intenção** letter of credit/intent; ~ **de condução** (PT) driving licence (Brit), driver's license (US); **dar as ~s** to deal; **dar/ter ~ branca** to give/have carte blanche; **pôr as ~s na mesa** (fig) to put one's cards on the table; ~ **magna** charter; ~ **patente** patent

carta-bomba (pl cartas-bomba) F letter bomb

cartada [kax'tada] F (fig) move

cartão [kax'tãw] (pl -ões) M card; (PT: material) cardboard; ~ **de visita** (calling) card; ~ **de crédito** credit card; ~ **comercial** business card; ~ **de recarga** (para celular) top-up card; **cartão-postal** (pl cartões-postais) M postcard

cartaz [kax'taʒ] M poster, bill (US); **ter ~** (ser famoso) to be well-known; (ter popularidade) to be popular; **(estar) em ~** (Teatro, Cinema) (to be) showing

cartear [kax'tʃjaʳ] VI to play cards ■ VT to play

carteira [kax'tejra] F (móvel) desk; (para dinheiro) wallet; (de ações) portfolio; ~ **de identidade** identity card; ~ **de motorista** driving licence (Brit), driver's license (US)

carteiro [kax'tejru] M postman (Brit), mailman (US)

cartel [kax'tɛw] (pl -éis) M cartel

cartilagem [kaxtʃi'laʒẽ] (pl -ns) F (Anat) cartilage

cartões [kax'tõjʃ] MPL de **cartão**

cartografia [kaxtogra'fia] F cartography

cartola [kax'tɔla] F top hat

cartolina [kaxto'lina] F card

cartomante [kaxto'mãtʃi] M/F fortune-teller

cartório [kax'tɔrju] M registry office

cartucho [kax'tuʃu] M cartridge; (saco de papel) packet

cartum [kax'tũ] (pl -ns) M cartoon

cartunista [kaxtu'niʃta] M/F cartoonist

cartuns [kax'tũʃ] MPL de **cartum**

caruncho [ka'rũʃu] M (inseto) woodworm

carvalho [kax'vaʎu] M oak

carvão [kax'vãw] (pl -ões) M coal; (de madeira) charcoal

carvoeiro [kaxvo'ejru] M coal merchant

carvões [kax'võjʃ] MPL de **carvão**

casa ['kaza] F house; (lar) home; (Com) firm; (Mat: decimal) place; **em/para ~** (at) home/home; ~ **de botão** buttonhole; ~ **de câmbio** bureau de change; ~ **de saúde** hospital; ~ **da moeda** mint; ~ **de banho** (PT) bathroom; ~ **e comida** board and lodging; **ser de ~** to be like one of the family; **ter dez anos de ~** (numa firma) to have ten years' service behind one; ~ **de campo** country house; ~ **de cômodos** tenement; ~ **de máquinas** engine room; ~ **popular** = council house

casaca [ka'zaka] F tails pl; **virar a ~** to become a turncoat

casacão [kaza'kãw] (pl -ões) M overcoat

casaco [ka'zaku] M coat; (paletó) jacket; ~ **de peles** fur coat

casacões [kaza'kõjʃ] MPL de **casacão**

casa-forte (pl casas-fortes) F vault

casa-grande (pl casas-grandes) F plantation owner's house

casal [ka'zaw] (pl -ais) M couple

casamenteiro, -a [kazamẽ'tejru, a] ADJ wedding atr

casamento [kaza'mẽtu] M marriage; (boda) wedding; (fig) combination

casar [ka'zaʳ] VT to marry; (combinar) to match (up); **casar-se** VR to get married; (harmonizar-se) to combine well

casarão [kaza'rãw] (pl -ões) M mansion

casca ['kaʃka] F (de árvore) bark; (de banana) skin; (de ferida) scab; (de laranja) peel; (de nozes, ovos) shell; (de milho etc) husk; (de pão) crust

casca-grossa (pl cascas-grossas) ADJ coarse, uneducated

cascalho [kaʃ'kaʎu] M gravel; (na praia) shingle

cascão [kaʃ'kãw] M crust; (sujeira) grime

cascata [kaʃ'kata] F waterfall; (col: mentira) tall story

cascateiro, -a [kaʃka'tejru, a] (col) ADJ big-mouthed ■ M/F storyteller

cascavel [kaʃka'vɛw] (pl -éis) M (serpente) rattlesnake

casco ['kaʃku] M (crânio) skull; (de animal) hoof; (de navio) hull; (para bebidas) empty bottle; (de tartaruga) shell

cascudo [kaʃ'kudu] M rap on the head

casebre [ka'zɛbri] M hovel, shack

caseiro, -a [ka'zejru, a] ADJ (produtos) home-made; (pessoa, vida) domestic ■ M/F housekeeper

caserna [ka'zɛxna] F barracks pl

casmurro, -a [kaʒ'muxu, a] ADJ introverted

caso ['kazu] M case; (tb: caso amoroso) affair; (estória) story ■ CONJ in case, if; **de ~ pensado** deliberately; **no ~ de** in case (of); **em todo ~** in any case; **neste ~** in that case; ~ **necessário** if necessary; **criar ~** to cause trouble; **fazer pouco ~ de** to belittle; **não fazer ~ de** to ignore; **vir ao ~** to be relevant; ~ **de emergência** emergency

casório [ka'zɔrju] (col) M wedding

caspa ['kaʃpa] F dandruff

casquinha [kaʃ'kiɲa] F (de sorvete) cone; (pele) skin

cassação [kasa'sãw] F withholding; (de políticos) banning

cassar [ka'saʳ] VT (direitos, licença) to cancel, withhold; (políticos) to ban

cassete [ka'sɛtʃi] M cassette

cassetete [kase'tɛtʃi] M truncheon (Brit),

NB: European Portuguese adds the following consonants to certain words: **b** (sú(b)dito, su(b)til); **c** (a(c)ção, a(c)cionista, a(c)to); **m** (inde(m)ne); **p** (ado(p)çã, ado(p)tar); for further details see p. xiii.

nightstick (US)

cassino [ka'sinu] M casino

casta ['kaʃta] F caste; (estirpe) lineage

castanha [kaʃ'taɲa] F chestnut; ~ **de caju** cashew nut; **castanha-do-pará** [-pa'ra] (pl **castanhas-do-pará**) F Brazil nut

castanheiro [kaʃta'ɲejru] M chestnut tree

castanho, -a [kaʃ'taɲu, a] ADJ brown

castanholas [kaʃta'ɲɔlaʃ] FPL castanets

castelo [kaʃ'tɛlu] M castle; **fazer ~s no ar** (fig) to build castles in the air

castiçal [kaʃtʃi'saw] (pl -ais) M candlestick

castiço, -a [kaʃ'tʃisu, a] ADJ pure; (de boa casta) of good stock, pedigree atr

castidade [kaʃtʃi'dadʒi] F chastity

castigar [kaʃtʃi'gaʳ] VT to punish; (aperfeiçoar) to perfect; (col: tocar) to play; **castigo** [kaʃ'tʃigu] M punishment; (fig: mortificação) pain; **estar/ficar de castigo** (criança) to be getting punished/be punished

casto, -a ['kaʃtu, a] ADJ chaste

castor [kaʃ'toʳ] M beaver

castrar [kaʃ'traʳ] VT to castrate

casual [ka'zwaw] (pl -ais) ADJ chance atr, accidental; (fortuito) fortuitous; **casualidade** [kazwali'dadʒi] F chance; (acidente) accident; **por casual** by chance, accidentally

casulo [ka'zulu] M (de sementes) pod; (de insetos) cocoon

cata ['kata] F: **à ~ de** in search of

cataclismo [kata'kliʒmu] M cataclysm

catacumbas [kata'kũbaʃ] FPL catacombs

catalizador, a [kataliza'doʳ(a)] ADJ catalytic ◾ M catalyst

catalogar [katalo'gaʳ] VT to catalogue (Brit), catalog (US)

catálogo [ka'talogu] M catalogue (Brit), catalog (US); ~ **(telefônico)** telephone directory

Catalunha [kata'luɲa] F: **a ~** Catalonia

catapora [kata'pɔra] (BR) F chickenpox

Catar [ka'taʳ] M: **o ~** Qatar

catar [ka'taʳ] VT to pick (up); (procurar) to look for, search for; (arroz) to clean; (recolher) to collect, gather

catarata [kata'rata] F waterfall; (Med) cataract

catarro [ka'taxu] M catarrh

catártico, -a [ka'taxtʃiku, a] ADJ cathartic

catástrofe [ka'taʃtrofi] F catastrophe

catastrófico, -a [kataʃ'trɔfiku, a] ADJ catastrophic

catatau [kata'tau] M: **um ~ de** a lot of

cata-vento M weathercock

catecismo [kate'siʒmu] M catechism

cátedra ['katedra] F chair

catedral [kate'draw] (pl -ais) F cathedral

catedrático, -a [kate'dratʃiku, a] M/F professor

categoria [katego'ria] F category; (social) rank; (qualidade) quality; **de alta ~** first-rate

categórico, -a [kate'gɔriku, a] ADJ categorical

categorizar [kategori'zaʳ] VT to categorize

catequizar [kateki'zaʳ] VT to talk round; (Rel) to catechize

catinga [ka'tʃĩga] F stench, stink

catinguento, -a [katʃi'gẽtu, a] ADJ smelly

catiripapo [katʃiri'papu] M punch

cativante [katʃi'vãtʃi] ADJ captivating; (atraente) charming

cativar [katʃi'vaʳ] VT (escravizar) to enslave; (fascinar) to captivate; (atrair) to charm

cativeiro [katʃi'vejru] M captivity; (escravidão) slavery; (cadeia) prison

cativo, -a [ka'tʃivu, a] M/F (escravo) slave; (prisioneiro) prisoner

catolicismo [katoli'siʒmu] M catholicism

católico, -a [ka'tɔliku, a] ADJ, M/F catholic

catorze [ka'toxzi] NUM fourteen; V tb **cinco**

catucar [katu'kaʳ] VT = **cutucar**

caturrice [katu'xisi] F obstinacy

caução [kaw'sãw] (pl -ões) F security, guarantee; (Jur) bail; **prestar ~** to give bail; **sob ~** on bail

caucionante [kawsjo'nãtʃi] M/F guarantor

caucionar [kawsjo'naʳ] VT to guarantee, stand surety for; (Jur) to stand bail for

cauções [kaw'sõjʃ] FPL de **caução**

cauda ['kawda] F tail; (de vestido) train

caudal [kaw'daw] (pl -ais) M torrent

caudaloso, -a [kawda'lozu, ɔza] ADJ torrential

caudilho [kaw'dʒiʎu] M leader, chief

caule ['kauli] M stalk, stem

causa ['kawza] F cause; (motivo) motive, reason; (Jur) lawsuit, case; **por ~ de** because of; **em ~ em question**; **causador, a** [kawza'doʳ(a)] ADJ which caused ◾ M cause

causar [kaw'zaʳ] VT to cause, bring about

cáustico, -a ['kawʃtʃiku, a] ADJ caustic

cautela [kaw'tɛla] F caution; (senha) ticket; (título) share certificate; ~ **(de penhor)** pawn ticket

cautelar [kawte'laʳ] ADJ precautionary

cauteloso, -a [kawte'lozu, ɔza] ADJ cautious, wary

cauterizar [kawteri'zaʳ] VT to cauterize

cava ['kava] F (de manga) armhole

cavação [kava'sãw] (col) F wheeling and dealing

cavaco [ka'vaku] M: **~s do ofício** occupational hazards

cavado, -a [ka'vadu, a] ADJ (olhos) sunken; (roupa) low-cut

cavador, a [kava'doʳ(a)] ADJ go-getting ◾ M/F go-getter

cavala [ka'vala] F mackerel

cavalar [kava'laʳ] ADJ (descomunal) enormous, huge

cavalaria [kavala'ria] F (Mil) cavalry; (instituição medieval) chivalry

cavalariça [kavala'risa] F stable

cavaleiro [kava'lejru] M rider, horseman; (medieval) knight

cavalete [kava'letʃi] M stand; (Foto) tripod; (de pintor) easel; (de mesa) trestle; (do violino) bridge

cavalgar [kavaw'gaʳ] VT to ride ◾ VI: ~ **em** to ride on; ~ **(sobre)** to jump over

cavalheiresco, -a [kavaʎej'refku, a] ADJ courteous, gallant, gentlemanly

cavalheiro, -a [kava'ʎejru, a] ADJ courteous, gallant ■ M gentleman; (*Dança*) partner

cavalinho-de-pau [kava'liɲu-] (*pl* **cavalinhos-de-pau**) M rocking horse

cavalo [ka'valu] M horse; (*Xadrez*) knight; (*pessoa*): **ser um ~** to be rude; **a ~** on horseback; **50 ~s(-vapor)** *ou* (**de força**) 50 horsepower; **quantos ~s tem esse carro?** how many horsepower is that car?; **fazer de algo um ~ de batalha** to make a mountain out of a molehill about sth; **tirar o ~ da chuva** (*fig*) to drop the idea; **~ de corrida** racehorse

cavalo-marinho (*pl* **cavalos-marinhos**) M seahorse

cavanhaque [kava'ɲaki] M goatee (beard)

cavaquinho [kava'kiɲu] M small guitar

cavar [ka'vaʳ] VT to dig; (*decote*) to lower; (*esforçar-se para obter*) to try to get ■ VI to dig; (*fig*) to delve; (*animal*) to burrow; (*esforçar-se*) to try hard; **~ a vida** to earn one's living

cave ['kavi] (PT) F wine-cellar

caveira [ka'vejra] F skull; **fazer a ~ de alguém** (*col*) to blacken sb's name

caverna [ka'vɛxna] F cavern

cavernoso, -a [kavex'nozu, ɔza] ADJ (*voz*) booming; (*pessoa*) horrible

caviar [ka'vjaʳ] M caviar

cavidade [kavi'dadʒi] F cavity

cavilha [ka'viʎa] F (*de madeira*) peg, dowel; (*de metal*) bolt

cavo, -a ['kavu, a] ADJ (*côncavo*) concave

caxias [ka'ʃiaʃ] ADJ INV overdisciplined ■ M/F INV stickler for discipline

caxumba [ka'ʃũba] F mumps *sg*

CBA ABR F = **Confederação Brasileira de Automobilismo**

CBAt ABR F = **Confederação Brasileira de Atletismo**

CBD ABR F = **Confederação Brasileira de Desportos**

CBF ABR F = **Confederação Brasileira de Futebol**

CBT ABR M = **Código Brasileiro de Telecomunicações**

CBTU ABR F = **Companhia Brasileira de Trens Urbanos**

c/c ABR (= *conta corrente*) c/a

CCT (BR) ABR M = **Conselho Científico e Tecnológico**

CDB ABR M = **Certificado de Depósito Bancário**

CDC (BR) ABR M = **Conselho de Desenvolvimento Comercial**

CDDPH (BR) ABR M = **Conselho de Defesa dos Direitos da Pessoa Humana**

CDI (BR) ABR M = **Certificado de Depósito Interbancário**; = **Conselho de Desenvolvimento Industrial**

cê [se] (*col*) PRON = **você**

cear [sja'ʳ] VT to have for supper ■ VI to dine

cearense [sea'rẽsi] ADJ from Ceará ■ M/F person from Ceará

cebola [se'bola] F onion; **cebolinha** [sebo'liɲa] F spring onion

Cebrae (BR) ABR F = **Centro de Apoio à Pequena e Média Empres**

Cebrap ABR M = **Centro Brasileiro de Análise e Planejamento**

cecear [se'sjaʳ] VI to lisp

cê-cedilha (*pl* **cês-cedilhas**) M c cedilla

ceceio [se'seju] M lisp

cê-dê-efe [-'ɛfi] (*col*) (*pl* -**s**) M/F swot

ceder [se'deʳ] VT to give up; (*dar*) to hand over; (*emprestar*) to lend ■ VI to give in, yield; (*porta etc*) to give (way); **~ a** to give in to

cedilha [se'dʒiʎa] F cedilla

cedo ['sedu] ADV early; (*em breve*) soon; **mais ~ ou mais tarde** sooner or later; **o mais ~ possível** as soon as possible

cedro ['sɛdru] M cedar

cédula ['sɛdula] F (*moeda-papel*) banknote; (*eleitoral*) ballot paper

CEE ABR F (= *Comunidade Econômica Européia*) EEC

CEF (BR) ABR F (= *Caixa Econômica Federal*) federal bank

cegar [se'gaʳ] VT to blind; (*ofuscar*) to dazzle; (*tesoura*) to blunt ■ VI (*ofuscar*) to be dazzling

cego, -a ['sɛgu, a] ADJ blind; (*total*) complete, total; (*tesoura*) blunt ■ M/F blind man/woman; **às cegas** blindly; **ser ~ por alguém** to be mad about sb

cegonha [se'goɲa] F stork

cegueira [se'gejra] F blindness

CEI (BR) ABR F (= *Comissão Especial de Inquérito*) commission of inquiry

ceia ['seja] F supper

ceifa ['sejfa] F harvest; (*fig*) destruction

ceifar [sej'faʳ] VT to reap, harvest; (*vidas*) to destroy

cela ['sɛla] F cell

celebração [selebra'sãw] (*pl* -**ões**) F celebration

celebrar [sele'braʳ] VT to celebrate; (*exaltar*) to praise; (*acordo*) to seal

célebre ['sɛlebri] ADJ famous, well-known

celebridade [selebri'dadʒi] F celebrity

celebrizar [selebri'zaʳ] VT to make famous; **celebrizar-se** VR to become famous

celeiro [se'lejru] M granary; (*depósito*) barn

célere ['sɛleri] ADJ swift, quick

celeste [se'lɛʃtʃi] ADJ celestial, heavenly

celeuma [se'lewma] F pandemonium, uproar

celibatário, -a [seliba'tarju, a] ADJ unmarried, single ■ M/F bachelor/spinster

celibato [seli'batu] M celibacy

celofane [selo'fani] M cellophane; **papel ~** cling film

celta ['sɛwta] ADJ Celtic ■ M/F Celt

célula ['sɛlula] F (*Bio, Elet*) cell; **celular** [selu'laʳ]

NB: *European Portuguese adds the following consonants to certain words:* **b** (sú(b)dito, su(b)til); **c** (a(c)ção, a(c)cionista, a(c)to); **m** (inde(m)ne); **p** (ado(p)çã, ado(p)tar); *for further details see p. xiii.*

ADJ cellular ■ N: **(telefone) celular** mobile (phone), cellphone (US); **celular com câmera** camera phone; **célula-tronco** ['sɛlula-'trõku] F stem cell

celulite [selu'litʃi] F cellulite

celulose [selu'lɔzi] F cellulose

cem [sẽ] NUM hundred; **ser ~ por cento** (fig) to be great; v tb **cinqüenta**

cemitério [semi'tɛrju] M cemetery, graveyard

cena ['sɛna] F scene; (palco) stage; **em ~** on the stage; **levar à ~** to stage; **fazer uma ~** to make a scene

cenário [se'narju] M (Teatro) scenery; (Cinema) scenario; (de um acontecimento) scene, setting; (panorama) view

cenho ['sɛɲu] M face

cênico, -a ['seniku, a] ADJ (Teatro) stage atr; (Cinema) set atr

cenografia [senogra'fia] F set design

cenógrafo, -a [se'nɔgrafu, a] M/F (Teatro) set designer

cenoura [se'nora] F carrot

censo ['sẽsu] M census

censor, a [sẽ'so^r(a)] M/F censor

censura [sẽ'sura] F (Pol etc) censorship; (reprovação) censure, criticism; (repreensão) reprimand; **censurar** [sẽsu'ra^r] VT (reprovar) to censure; (filme, livro etc) to censor

censurável [sẽsu'ravew] (pl -eis) ADJ reprehensible

centavo [sẽ'tavu] M cent; **estar sem um ~** to be penniless

centeio [sẽ'teju] M rye

centelha [sẽ'teʎa] F spark; (fig) flash

centena [sẽ'tɛna] F hundred; **às ~s** in hundreds

centenário, -a [sẽte'narju, a] ADJ centenary ■ M/F centenarian ■ M centenary, centennial

centésimo, -a [sẽ'tezimu, a] ADJ hundredth ■ M hundredth (part)

centígrado [sẽ'tʃigradu] M centigrade

centilitro [sẽtʃi'litru] M centilitre (Brit), centiliter (US)

centímetro [sẽ'tʃimetru] M centimetre (Brit), centimeter (US)

cento ['sẽtu] M: **~ e um** one hundred and one; **por ~** per cent

centopeia [sẽto'peja] F centipede

central [sẽ'traw] (pl -ais) ADJ central ■ F (de polícia etc) head office; **~ elétrica** (electric) power station; **~ telefônica** telephone exchange

centralização [sẽtraliza'sãw] F centralization

centralizar [sẽtrali'za^r] VT to centralize; **centralizar-se** VR to be centralized

centrar [sẽ'tra^r] VT to centre (Brit), center (US)

centro ['sẽtru] M centre (Brit), center (US); (de uma cidade) town centre; **~ das atenções** centre of attention; **~ de custo/lucro** (Com) cost/profit centre; **~ de mesa** centrepiece (Brit), centerpiece (US); **centroavante** [sẽtroa'vãtʃi] M (Futebol) centre forward

CEP ['sɛpi] (BR) ABR M (= Código de Endereçamento

Postal) postcode (Brit), zip code (US)

cepo ['sepu] M (toco) stump; (toro) log

céptico, -ca ['septiku] (PT) = **cético** etc

ceptro ['sɛtru] (PT) M = **cetro**

cera ['sera] F wax; **fazer ~** (fig) to dawdle, waste time

cerâmica [se'ramika] F pottery; (arte) ceramics sg

cerâmico, -a [se'ramiku, a] ADJ ceramic

ceramista [sera'miʃta] M/F potter

cerca ['sexka] F (de madeira, arame) fence ■ PREP: **~ de** (aproximadamente) around, about; **~ viva** hedge

cercado, -a [sex'kadu, a] ADJ surrounded; (com cerca) fenced in ■ M enclosure; (para animais) pen; (para crianças) playpen

cercanias [sexka'niaʃ] FPL (arredores) outskirts; (vizinhança) neighbourhood sg (Brit), neighborhood sg (US)

cercar [sex'ka^r] VT to enclose; (pôr cerca em) to fence in; (rodear) to surround; (assediar) to besiege

cercear [sex'sja^r] VT (liberdade) to curtail, restrict

cerco ['sexku] M encirclement; (Mil) siege; **pôr ~ a** to besiege

cereal [se'rjaw] (pl -ais) M cereal

cerebral [sere'braw] (pl -ais) ADJ cerebral, brain atr

cérebro ['sɛrebru] M brain; (fig) intelligence, brains pl

cereja [se'reʒa] F cherry

cerejeira [sere'ʒejra] F cherry tree

cerimônia [seri'monja] F ceremony; **de ~** formal; **sem ~** informal; **fazer ~** to stand on ceremony; **~ de posse** swearing-in ceremony, investiture

cerimonial [serimo'njaw] (pl -ais) ADJ, M ceremonial

cerimonioso, -a [serimo'njozu, ɔza] ADJ ceremonious

cerne ['sɛxni] M kernel

ceroulas [se'rolaʃ] FPL long johns

cerração [sexa'sãw] F (nevoeiro) fog

cerrado, -a [se'xadu, a] ADJ shut, closed; (punho) clenched; (denso) dense, thick ■ M (vegetação) scrub(land)

cerrar [se'xa^r] VT to close, shut; **cerrar-se** VR to close, shut

certame [sex'tami] M (concurso) contest, competition

certeiro, -a [sex'tejru, a] ADJ (tiro) accurate, well-aimed; (acertado) correct

certeza [sex'teza] F certainty; **com ~** certainly, surely; (provavelmente) probably; **ter ~ de** to be certain ou sure of; **ter ~ de que** to be sure that; **tem ~?** are you sure?

certidão [sextʃi'dãw] (pl -ões) F certificate

certificado [sextʃifi'kadu] M (garantia) certificate

certificar [sextʃifi'ka^r] VT to certify; (assegurar) to assure; **certificar-se** VR: **certificar-se de** to make sure of

certo, -a ['sɛxtu, a] ADJ certain, sure; (exato, direito) right; (um, algum) a certain ■ ADV correctly; na certa certainly; ao ~ for certain; dar ~ to work; está ~ okay, all right

cerveja [sex'veʒa] F beer; cervejaria [sexveʒa'ria] F (fábrica) brewery; (bar) bar, public house

cervical [sexvi'kaw] (pl -ais) ADJ cervical

cérvice ['sɛxvisi] F cervix

cervo ['sɛxvu] M deer

cerzir [sex'zir] VT to darn

cesariana [seza'rjana] F Caesarian (Brit), Cesarian (US)comin

cessação [sesa'sãw] F halting, ceasing

cessão [se'sãw] (pl -ões) F (cedência) surrender; (transferência) transfer

cessar [se'sar] VI to cease, stop; sem ~ continually; cessar-fogo M INV cease-fire

cessões [se'sõjʃ] FPL de cessão

cesta ['seʃta] F basket

cesto ['seʃtu] M basket; (com tampa) hamper

ceticismo [setʃi'siʒmu] M scepticism (Brit), skepticism (US)

cético, -a ['sɛtʃiku, a] ADJ sceptical (Brit), skeptical (US) ■ M/F sceptic (Brit), skeptic (US)

cetim [se'tʃĩ] M satin

cetro ['sɛtru] M sceptre (Brit), scepter (US)

céu [sɛw] M sky; (Rel) heaven; (da boca) roof; cair do ~ (fig) to come at the right time; mover ~s e terra (fig) to move heaven and earth

cevada [se'vada] F barley

cevar [se'var] VT (engordar) to fatten; (alimentar) to feed; (engodar) to bait

CGC (BR) ABR M (= Cadastro Geral de Contribuintes) roll of tax payers

CGT (BR) ABR F (= Central Geral dos Trabalhadores) trade union

chá [ʃa] M tea; (reunião) tea party; dar um ~ de sumiço (col) to disappear; tomar ~ de cadeira (fig) to be a wallflower

chacal [ʃa'kaw] (pl -ais) M jackal

chácara ['ʃakara] F (granja) farm; (casa de campo) country house

chacina [ʃa'sina] F slaughter; chacinar [ʃasi'nar] VT (matar) to slaughter

chacoalhar [ʃakwa'ʎar] VT to shake; (col: amolar) to bug ■ VI to shake about; to be annoying

chacota [ʃa'kɔta] F (zombaria) mockery

chacrinha [ʃa'kriɲa] (col) F get-together

Chade ['ʃadʒi] M: o ~ Chad

chã-de-dentro [ʃã-] (pl chãs-de-dentro) F round of beef

chá-de-panela M ≈ hen night, ≈ wedding shower (US)

chafariz [ʃafa'riʒ] M fountain

chafurdar [ʃafux'dar] VI: ~ em to wallow in; chafurdar-se VR: ~-se em to wallow in

chaga ['ʃaga] F (Med) wound; (fig) disease

chalé [ʃa'lɛ] M chalet

chaleira [ʃa'lejra] F kettle; (bajulador) crawler, toady

chaleirar [ʃalej'rar] VT to crawl to

chama ['ʃama] F flame; em ~s on fire

chamada [ʃa'mada] F call; (Mil) roll call; (Educ) register; (no jornal) headline; dar uma ~ em alguém (repreender) to tell sb off

chamar [ʃa'mar] VT to call; (convidar) to invite; (atenção) to attract ■ VI to call; (telefone) to ring; chamar-se VR to be called; chamo-me João my name is John; ~ alguém de idiota/Dudu to call sb an idiot/Dudu; mandar ~ to summon, send for

chamariz [ʃama'riʒ] M decoy; (fig) lure

chamativo, -a [ʃama'tʃivu, a] ADJ showy, flashy

chamego [ʃa'megu] M cuddle

chaminé [ʃami'nɛ] F chimney; (de navio) funnel

champanha [ʃã'paɲa] M OU F champagne

champanhe [ʃã'paɲi] M OU F = champanha

champu [ʃã'pu] (PT) M shampoo

chamuscar [ʃamuʃ'kar] VT to scorch, singe; chamuscar-se VR to scorch o.s.

chance ['ʃãsi] F chance

chancela [ʃã'sɛla] F seal, official stamp

chancelaria [ʃãsela'ria] F chancellery

chanceler [ʃãse'lɛr] M chancellor

chanchada [ʃã'ʃada] F second-rate film (ou play)

chantagear [ʃãta'ʒjar] VT to blackmail

chantagem [ʃã'taʒẽ] F blackmail

chantagista [ʃãta'ʒiʃta] M/F blackmailer

chão [ʃãw] (pl -s) M ground; (terra) soil; (piso) floor

chapa ['ʃapa] F (placa) plate; (eleitoral) list ■ M/F (col) mate, friend; ~ de matrícula (PT: Auto) number (Brit) ou license (US) plate; bife na ~ grilled steak; oi, meu ~! hi, mate!

chapa-branca (pl chapas-brancas) M civil service car

chapelaria [ʃapela'ria] F (loja) hat shop

chapeleira [ʃape'lejra] F hat box; v tb chapeleiro

chapeleiro, -a [ʃape'lejru, a] M/F milliner

chapéu [ʃa'pɛw] M hat

chapéu-coco (pl chapéus-cocos) M bowler (hat) (Brit), derby (US)

chapinha [ʃa'piɲa] F: ~ (de garrafa) (bottle) top

chapinhar [ʃapi'ɲar] VI to splash

charada [ʃa'rada] F (quebra-cabeça) puzzle

charco ['ʃaxku] M marsh, bog

charge ['ʃaxʒi] F (political) cartoon

chargista [ʃax'ʒiʃta] M/F (political) cartoonist

charlatão [ʃaxla'tãw] (pl -ães) M charlatan; (curandeiro) quack

charme ['ʃaxmi] M charm; fazer ~ to be nice, use one's charm; charmoso, -a [ʃax'mozu, ɔza] ADJ charming

charneca [ʃax'nɛka] F moor, heath

charrete [ʃa'xetʃi] F cart

charter ['tʃaxter] ADJ INV charter ■ M (pl -s) charter flight

charuto [ʃa'rutu] M cigar

NB: European Portuguese adds the following consonants to certain words: b (sú(b)dito, su(b)til); c (a(c)ção, a(c)cionista, a(c)to); m (inde(m)ne); p (ado(p)çã, ado(p)tar); for further details see p. xiii.

chassis [ʃa'si] M (Auto, Elet) chassis

chata ['ʃata] F (embarcação) barge; v tb **chato**

chateação [ʃatʃja'sãw] (pl -ões) F bother, upset; (maçada) bore

chatear [ʃa'tʃjaʳ] VT (aborrecer) to bother, upset; (importunar) to pester; (entediar) to bore; (irritar) to annoy ▪ VI to be upsetting; to be boring; to be annoying; **chatear-se** VR to get upset; to get bored; to get annoyed

chatice [ʃa'tʃisi] F nuisance

chato, -a ['ʃatu, a] ADJ (plano) flat, level; (pé) flat; (tedioso) boring; (irritante) annoying; (que fica mal) bad, rude ▪ M/F bore; (quem irrita) pain

chatura [ʃa'tura] (col) F pain (in the neck)

chauvinismo [ʃawvi'niʒmu] M chauvinism

chauvinista [ʃawvi'niʃta] ADJ chauvinistic ▪ M/F chauvinist

chavão [ʃa'vãw] (pl -ões) M cliché

chave ['ʃavi] F key; (Elet) switch; (Tip) curly bracket; ~ **de porcas** spanner; ~ **inglesa** (monkey) wrench; ~ **de fenda** screwdriver

-chave SUFIXO key atr

chaveiro [ʃa'vejru] M (utensílio) key ring; (pessoa) locksmith

chávena ['ʃavena] (PT) F cup

checar [ʃe'kaʳ] VT to check

check-up [tʃe'kapi] (pl -s) M check-up

chefatura [ʃefa'tura] F: ~ **de polícia** police headquarters sg

chefe ['ʃefi] M/F head, chief; (patrão) boss; ~ **de turma** foreman; ~ **de estação** stationmaster; **chefia** [ʃe'fia] F (liderança) leadership; (direção) management; (repartição) headquarters sg; **estar com a chefia de** to be in charge of

chefiar [ʃe'fjaʳ] VT to lead

chega ['ʃega] (col) M: **dar um ~ em alguém** to tell sb off ▪ PREP even

chegada [ʃe'gada] F arrival; **dar uma ~** to drop by

chegado, -a [ʃe'gadu, a] ADJ (próximo) near; (íntimo) close; **ser ~ a** (bebidas, comidas) to be keen on

chegar [ʃe'gaʳ] VT (aproximar) to bring near ▪ VI to arrive; (ser suficiente) to be enough; **chegar-se** VR: ~-**se a** to approach; **chega!** that's enough!; ~ **a** (atingir) to reach; (conseguir) to manage to; ~ **algo para cá/para lá** to bring sth closer/move sth over; **chega (mais) para cá/para lá!** come closer!/move over!; **vou chegando** I'm leaving

cheia ['ʃeja] F flood

cheio, -a ['ʃeju, a] ADJ full; (repleto) full up; (col: farto) fed up; ~ **de si** self-important; ~ **de dedos** all fingers and thumbs; (inibido) awkward; ~ **de frescura** (col) fussy; ~ **da nota** (col) rich, loaded; **acertar em ~** to be exactly right, hit the nail on the head; **estar ~ de algo** (col) to be fed up with sth

cheirar [ʃej'raʳ] VT, VI to smell; ~ **a** to smell of; **isto não me cheira bem** there's something fishy about this; **cheiro** ['ʃejru] M smell; **ter cheiro de** to smell of

cheiroso, -a [ʃej'rozu, ɔza] ADJ: **ser** ou **estar ~** to smell nice

cheiro-verde M bunch of parsley and spring onion

cheque ['ʃɛki] M cheque (Brit), check (US); (Xadrez) check; ~ **cruzado** crossed cheque; ~ **de viagem** traveller's cheque (Brit), traveler's check (US); ~ **em branco** blank cheque; ~ **sem fundos** uncovered cheque, rubber cheque (col); ~ **voador** rubber cheque

chequei etc [ʃe'kej] VB v **checar**

cheque-mate M checkmate

cherne ['ʃɛxni] M grouper

chiado ['ʃjadu] M squeak(ing); (de vapor) hiss(ing)

chiar [ʃjaʳ] VI to squeak; (porta) to creak; (vapor) to hiss; (fritura) to sizzle; (col: reclamar) to grumble

chibata [ʃi'bata] F (vara) cane

chiclete [ʃi'klɛtʃi] M chewing gum; ~ **de bola** bubble gum

chicória [ʃi'kɔrja] F chicory

chicote [ʃi'kɔtʃi] M whip

chicotear [ʃiko'tʃjaʳ] VT to whip, lash

chifrada [ʃi'frada] F (golpe) butt

chifrar [ʃi'fraʳ] VT to two-time

chifre ['ʃifri] M (corno) horn; **pôr ~ em alguém** (col) to be unfaithful to sb, cheat on sb

chifrudo, -a [ʃi'frudu, a] (col) ADJ cuckolded

Chile ['ʃili] M: **o ~** Chile

chileno, -a [ʃi'lenu, a] ADJ, M/F Chilean

chilique [ʃi'liki] (col) M fit

chilrear [ʃiw'xjaʳ] VI to chirp, twitter

chilreio [ʃiw'xeju] M chirping

chimarrão [ʃima'xãw] (pl -ões) M maté tea without sugar taken from a pipe-like cup

chimpanzé [ʃĩpã'zɛ] M chimpanzee

China ['ʃina] F: **a ~** China

chinelo [ʃi'nɛlu] M slipper; **botar no ~** (fig) to put to shame

chinês, -esa [ʃi'neʃ, eza] ADJ, M/F Chinese ▪ M (Ling) Chinese

chinfrim [ʃĩ'frĩ] (pl -ns) ADJ cheap and cheerful

chino, -a ['ʃinu, a] M/F Chinese

chio ['ʃiu] M squeak; (de rodas) screech

chip ['ʃipi] M (Comput) chip

Chipre ['ʃipri] F Cyprus

chique ['ʃiki] ADJ stylish, chic

chiqueiro [ʃi'kejru] M pigsty

chispa ['ʃiʃpa] F spark

chispada [ʃiʃ'pada] (BR) F dash

chispar [ʃiʃ'paʳ] VI (correr) to dash

chita ['ʃita] F printed cotton, calico

choça ['ʃɔsa] F shack, hut

chocalhar [ʃoka'ʎaʳ] VT, VI to rattle

chocalho [ʃo'kaʎu] M (Mús, brinquedo) rattle; (para animais) bell

chocante [ʃo'kãtʃi] ADJ shocking; (col) amazing

chocar [ʃo'kaʳ] VT (incubar) to hatch, incubate; (ofender) to shock, offend ▪ VI to shock; **chocar-se** VR to crash, collide; to be shocked

chocho, -a ['ʃoʃu, a] ADJ hollow, empty; (fraco) weak; (sem graça) dull

chocolate [ʃoko'latʃi] M chocolate

chofer [ʃo'feʳ] M driver
chofre ['ʃofri] M: **de ~** all of a sudden
chongas ['ʃõgaʃ] (col) PRON zilch, bugger all (!)
chopada [ʃo'pada] F drinking session
chope ['ʃopi] M draught beer
choque ['ʃɔki] M (abalo) shock; (colisão) collision; (Med, Elet) shock; (impacto) impact; (conflito) clash, conflict; **~ cultural** culture shock
choque etc [ʃo'kej] VB V **chocar**
choradeira [ʃora'dejra] F fit of crying
chorado, -a [ʃo'radu, a] ADJ (canto) sad; (gol) hard-won
choramingar [ʃoramĩ'gaʳ] VI to whine, whimper
choramingas [ʃora'mĩgaʃ] M/F INV crybaby
choramingo [ʃora'mĩgu] M whine, whimper
chorão, -rona [ʃo'rãw, rɔ] (pl **-ões/-s**) ADJ tearful ■ M/F crybaby ■ M (Bot) weeping willow
chorar [ʃo'raʳ] VT, VI to weep, cry
chorinho [ʃo'riɲu] M type of Brazilian music
choro ['ʃoru] M crying; (Mús) type of Brazilian music
choroso, -a [ʃo'rozu, ɔza] ADJ tearful
choupana [ʃo'pana] F shack, hut
chouriço [ʃo'risu] M (BR) black pudding; (PT) spicy sausage
chove-não-molha [ʃovinãw'mɔʎa] (col) M shilly-shallying
chover [ʃo've'ʳ] VI to rain; **~ a cântaros** to rain cats and dogs; **~am cartas** letters poured in
chuchu [ʃu'ʃu] M chayote (vegetable); **ele fala/ está quente pra ~** (col) he talks a lot/it's really hot
chucrute [ʃu'krutʃi] M sauerkraut
chué [ʃu'ɛ] (col) ADJ lousy
chulé [ʃu'lɛ] M foot odour (Brit) ou odor (US)
chulear [ʃu'ljaʳ] VT to hem
chulo, -a ['ʃulu, a] ADJ vulgar
chumaço [ʃu'masu] M (de papel, notas) wad; (material) wadding
chumbado, -a [ʃũ'badu, a] (col) ADJ (cansado) dog-tired; (doente) laid out
chumbar [ʃũ'baʳ] VT to fill with lead; (soldar) to solder; (atirar em) to fire at ■ VI (PT: reprovar) to fail
chumbo ['ʃũbu] M lead; (de caça) gunshot; (PT: de dente) filling; **esta mala está um ~** this case weighs a ton
chupado, -a [ʃu'padu, a] (col) ADJ (cara, pessoa) drawn
chupar [ʃu'paʳ] VT to suck; (absorver) to absorb
chupeta [ʃu'peta] F (para criança) dummy (Brit), pacifier (US)
churrascaria [ʃuxaʃka'ria] F barbecue restaurant
churrasco [ʃu'xaʃku] M barbecue
churrasqueira [ʃuxaʃ'kejra] F barbecue
churrasquinho [ʃuxaʃ'kiɲu] M kebab
chutar [ʃu'taʳ] VT to kick; (col: adivinhar) to guess at; (: dar o fora em) to dump ■ VI to kick; to guess;

(: mentir) to lie
chute ['ʃutʃi] M kick; (para o gol) shot; (col: mentira) lie; **dar o ~ em alguém** (col) to give sb the boot
chuteira [ʃu'tejra] F football boot; **pendurar as ~s** (col) to retire
chuva ['ʃuva] F rain; **tomar ~** to get caught in the rain; **estar na ~** (fig) to be drunk; **~ de pedra** hailstorm
chuvarada [ʃuva'rada] F torrential rain
chuveirada [ʃuvej'rada] F shower
chuveiro [ʃu'vejru] M shower
chuviscar [ʃuviʃ'kaʳ] VI to drizzle; **chuvisco** [ʃu'viʃku] M drizzle
chuvoso, -a [ʃu'vozu, ɔza] ADJ rainy
CIA ABR F (= Central Intelligence Agency) CIA
Cia. ABR (= companhia) Co.
cibercafé [sibexka'fɛ] M cybercafé
ciberespaço [sibexiʃ'pasu] M cyberspace
cibernética [sibex'nɛtʃika] F cybernetics sg
CIC (BR) ABR M = **Cartão de Identificação do Contribuinte**
cica ['sika] F sharpness
cicatriz [sika'triʒ] F scar
cicatrização [sikatriza'sãw] F scarring
cicatrizar [sikatri'zaʳ] VT (rosto) to scar; (ferida) to heal; (fig) to cure, heal ■ VI to heal; to scar
cicerone [sise'rɔni] M tourist guide
ciciar [si'sjaʳ] VI to whisper; (rumorejar) to murmur
cíclico, -a ['sikliku, a] ADJ cyclical
ciclismo [si'kliʒmu] M cycling
ciclista [si'kliʃta] M/F cyclist
ciclo ['siklu] M cycle; **~ básico** foundation year
ciclone [si'klɔni] M cyclone
ciclovia [siklo'via] F cycle path
cidadã [sida'dã] F de **cidadão**
cidadania [sidada'nia] F citizenship
cidadão, cidadã [sida'dãw] (pl **-s/-s**) M/F citizen
cidade [si'dadʒi] F town; (grande) city
cidadela [sida'dɛla] F citadel
cidra ['sidra] F citron
CIE (BR) ABR M = **Centro de Informações do Exército**
ciência ['sjẽsja] F science; (erudição) knowledge; **~s humanas/socias** business studies/social sciences
ciente ['sjẽtʃi] ADJ aware
científico, -a [sjẽ'tʃifiku, a] ADJ scientific
cientista [sjẽ'tʃiʃta] M/F scientist
CIEP (BR) ABR M (= Centro Integrado de Educação Popular) combined school and community centre
cifra ['sifra] F (escrita secreta) cipher; (algarismo) number, figure; (total) sum
cifrão [si'frãw] (pl **-ões**) M money sign
cifrar [si'fraʳ] VT to write in code
cifrões [si'frõjʃ] MPL de **cifrão**
cigano, -a [si'ganu, a] ADJ, M/F gypsy
cigarra [si'gaxa] F cicada; (Elet) buzzer
cigarreira [siga'xejra] F (estojo) cigarette case

NB: European Portuguese adds the following consonants to certain words: **b** (sú(b)dito, su(b)til); **c** (a(c)ção, a(c)cionista, a(c)to); **m** (inde(m)ne); **p** (ado(p)çã, ado(p)tar); for further details see p. xiii.

cigarrilha [siga'xiʎa] F cheroot
cigarro [si'gaxu] M cigarette
cilada [si'lada] F (*emboscada*) ambush; (*armadilha*) trap; (*embuste*) trick
cilíndrico, -a [si'lĩdriku, a] ADJ cylindrical
cilindro [si'lĩdru] M cylinder; (*rolo*) roller
cílio ['silju] M eyelash
cima ['sima] F: **de ~ para baixo** from top to bottom; **para ~** up; **em ~ de** on, on top of; **por ~ de** over; **de ~ from above; lá em ~** up there; (*em casa*) upstairs; **ainda por ~** on top of that; **estar por ~** to be better off; **dar em ~ de alguém** (*col*) to be after sb; **tudo em ~?** (*col*) how's it going?
cimeira [si'mejra] (PT) F summit
cimentar [simẽ'ta^r] VT to cement
cimento [si'mẽtu] M cement; (*chão*) concrete floor; (*fig*) foundation; **~ armado** reinforced concrete
cimo ['simu] M top, summit
cinco ['sĩku] NUM five; **somos ~** there are five of us; **ela tem ~ anos** she is five (years old); **aos ~ anos (de idade)** at the age of five; **são ~ horas** it's five o'clock; **às ~ (horas)** at five (o'clock); **hoje é dia ~ de julho** today is the fifth of July; **no dia ~ de julho** on the fifth of July, on July the fifth; **eles moram no número ~/na Barata Ribeiro número ~** they live at number five/number five Barata Ribeiro Street; **~ e um quarto/meio** five and a quarter/a half
Cindacta [sĩ'dakta] (BR) ABR M = **Centro Integrado de Defesa Aérea e Controle de Tráfego Aéreo**
cindir [sĩ'dʒi^r] VT to split; (*cortar*) to cut
cineasta [sine'aʃta] M/F film maker
cinegrafista [sinegra'fiʃta] M/F cameraman/woman
cinema [si'nɛma] F cinema
cinematográfico, -a [sinemato'grafiku, a] ADJ cinematographic
Cingapura [sĩga'pura] F Singapore
cingir [sĩ'ʒi^r] VT (*pôr à cintura*) to fasten round one's waist; (*prender em volta*) to tie round; (*cercar*) to encircle, ring; (*coroa, espada*) to put on; **cingir-se** VR: **cingir-se a** (*restringir-se*) to restrict o.s. to
cínico, -a ['siniku, a] ADJ cynical ■ M/F cynic
cinismo [si'niʒmu] M cynicism
cinjo *etc* ['sĩʒu] VB V **cingir**
cinqüenta [sĩ'kwẽta] NUM fifty; **umas ~ pessoas** about fifty people; **ele tem uns ~ anos** he's about fifty; **ele está na casa dos ~ anos** he's in his fifties; **nos anos ~** in the fifties; **ir a ~** (*Auto*) to do fifty (km/h)
cinqüentão, -tona [sĩkwẽ'tãw, 'tɔna] (*pl* -**tões/-s**) M/F person in his/her fifties ■ ADJ in his/her fifties
cinta ['sĩta] F (*faixa*) sash; (*de mulher*) girdle
cintado, -a [sĩ'tadu, a] ADJ gathered at the waist
cintilante [sĩtʃi'lãtʃi] ADJ sparkling
cintilar [sĩtʃi'la^r] VI to sparkle, glitter
cinto ['sĩtu] M belt; **~ de segurança** safety belt; (*Auto*) seatbelt
cintura [sĩ'tura] F waist; (*linha*) waistline

cinturão [sĩtu'rãw] (*pl* -ões) M belt; **~ verde** green belt
cinza ['sĩza] ADJ INV grey (*Brit*), gray (*US*) ■ F ash, ashes *pl*
cinzeiro [sĩ'zejru] M ashtray
cinzel [sĩ'zɛw] (*pl* -éis) M chisel
cinzelar [sĩze'la^r] VT to chisel; (*gravar*) to carve, engrave
cinzento, -a [sĩ'zẽtu, a] ADJ grey (*Brit*), gray (*US*)
cio [siu] M mating season; **no ~** on heat, in season
cioso, -a ['sjozu, ɔza] ADJ conscientious
CIP (BR) ABR M = **Conselho Interministerial de Preços**
cipreste [si'prɛʃtʃi] M cypress (tree)
cipriota [si'prjota] ADJ, M/F Cypriot
circense [six'sẽsi] ADJ circus *atr*
circo ['sixku] M circus
circuito [six'kwitu] M circuit
circulação [sixkula'sãw] F circulation
circular [sixku'la^r] ADJ circular, round ■ F (*carta*) circular ■ VI to circulate; (*girar, andar*) to go round ■ VT to circulate; (*estar em volta de*) to surround; (*percorrer em roda*) to go round
círculo ['sixkulu] M circle
circunavegar [sixkunave'ga^r] VT to circumnavigate, sail round
circuncidar [sixkũsi'da^r] VT to circumcise
circuncisão [sixkũsi'zãw] F circumcision
circundante [sixkũ'dãtʃi] ADJ surrounding
circundar [sixkũ'da^r] VT to surround
circunferência [sixkũfe'rẽsja] F circumference
circunflexo, -a [sixkũ'flɛksu, a] ADJ circumflex ■ M circumflex (accent)
circunlóquio [sixkũ'lɔkju] M circumlocution
circunscrever [sixkũʃkre've^r] VT to circumscribe, limit; (*epidemia*) to contain; (*abranger*) to cover; **circunscrever-se** VR to be limited
circunscrição [sixkũʃkri'sãw] (*pl* -ões) F district; **~ eleitoral** constituency
circunscrito, -a [sixkũʃ'kritu, a] PP *de* **circunscrever**
circunspecção [sixkũʃpe'sãw] F seriousness
circunspeto, -a [sixkũʃ'pɛtu, a] ADJ serious
circunstância [sixkũ'ʃtãsja] F circumstance; **~s atenuantes** mitigating circumstances
circunstanciado, -a [sixkũʃtãsi'sjadu, a] ADJ detailed
circunstancial [sixkũʃtã'sjaw] (*pl* -ais) ADJ circumstantial
circunstante [sixkũʃ'tãtʃi] M/F onlooker, bystander; **circunstantes** MPL (*audiência*) audience *sg*
cirrose [si'xɔzi] F cirrhosis
cirurgia [sirux'ʒia] F surgery; **~ plástica/estética** plastic/cosmetic surgery
cirurgião, -giã [sirux'ʒjãw, 'ʒjã] (*pl* -ões/-s) M/F surgeon
cirúrgico, -a [si'ruxʒiku, a] ADJ surgical
cirurgiões [sirux'ʒjõjʃ] MPL *de* **cirurgião**
cirzo *etc* ['sixzu] VB V **cerzir**

cisão [si'zãw] (pl -ões) F (divisão) split, division; (desacordo) disagreement

cisco ['siʃku] M speck

cisma ['siʒma] M schism ∎ F (mania) silly idea; (suspeita) suspicion; (antipatia) dislike; (devaneio) dream

cismado, -a [siʒ'madu, a] ADJ with fixed ideas

cismar [siʒ'ma^r] VI (pensar): ~ em to brood over; (antipatizar): ~ com to take a dislike to ∎ VT: ~ que to be convinced that; ~ de ou em fazer (meter na cabeça) to get into one's head to do; (insistir) to insist on doing

cisne ['siʒni] M swan

cisões [si'zõjʃ] FPL de **cisão**

cisterna [siʃ'texna] F cistern, tank

cistite [siʃ'tʃitʃi] F cystitis

citação [sita'sãw] (pl -ões) F quotation; (Jur) summons sg

citadino, -a [sita'dʒinu, a] ADJ town atr

citar [si'ta^r] VT to quote; (Jur) to summon

cítrico, -a ['sitriku, a] ADJ (fruta) citrus; (ácido) citric

ciumada [sju'mada] F fit of jealousy

ciúme ['sjumi] M jealousy; **ter ~s de** to be jealous of

ciumeira [sju'mejra] (col) F = **ciumada**

ciumento, -a [sju'mẽtu, a] ADJ jealous

cívico, -a ['siviku, a] ADJ civic

civil [si'viw] (pl -is) ADJ civil ∎ M/F civilian; **civilidade** [sivili'dadʒi] F politeness

civilização [siviliza'sãw] (pl -ões) F civilization

civilizador, a [siviliza'do^r(a)] ADJ civilizing

civilizar [sivili'za^r] VT to civilize

civis [si'viʃ] PL de **civil**

civismo [si'viʒmu] M public spirit

clamar [kla'ma^r] VT to clamour (Brit) ou clamor (US) for ∎ VI to cry out, clamo(u)r

clamor [kla'mo^r] M outcry, uproar

clamoroso, -a [klamo'rozu, ɔza] ADJ noisy

clandestino, -a [klãdeʃ'tʃinu, a] ADJ clandestine; (ilegal) underground

clara ['klara] F egg white

clarabóia [klara'bɔja] F skylight

clarão [kla'rãw] (pl -ões) M (cintilação) flash; (claridade) gleam

clarear [kla'rja^r] VI (dia) to dawn; (tempo) to clear up, brighten up ∎ VT to clarify

clareira [kla'rejra] F (na mata) clearing

clareza [kla'reza] F clarity

claridade [klari'dadʒi] F (luz) brightness

clarim [kla'rĩ] (pl -ns) M bugle

clarinete [klari'netʃi] M clarinet

clarinetista [klarine'tʃiʃta] M/F clarinet player

clarins [kla'rĩʃ] MPL de **clarim**

clarividente [klarivi'dẽtʃi] ADJ (prudente) far-sighted, prudent

claro, -a ['klaru, a] ADJ clear; (luminoso) bright; (cor) light; (evidente) clear, evident ∎ M (na escrita) space; (clareira) clearing ∎ ADV clearly; ~! of course!; ~ que sim!/não! of course!/of course not!; **às claras** openly; (publicamente) publicly; **dia ~** daylight; **passar a noite em ~** not to sleep a wink all night; ~ **como água** crystal clear

clarões [kla'rõjʃ] MPL de **clarão**

classe ['klasi] F class; ~ **média/operária** middle/working class

clássico, -a ['klasiku, a] ADJ classical; (fig) classic; (habitual) usual ∎ M classic

classificação [klasifika'sãw] (pl -ões) F classification; (Esporte) place, placing

classificado, -a [klasifi'kadu, a] ADJ (em exame) successful; (anúncio) classified; (Esporte) placed, qualified ∎ M (anúncio) classified ad

classificar [klasifi'ka^r] VT to classify; **classificar-se** VR: **classificar-se de algo** to call o.s. sth, describe o.s. as sth

classificatório, -a [klasifika'tɔrju, a] ADJ qualifying

classudo, -a [kla'sudu, a] (col) ADJ classy

claudicar [klawdʒi'ka^r] VI (mancar) to limp; (errar) to err

claustro ['klawʃtru] M cloister

claustrofobia [klawʃtrofo'bia] F claustrophobia

claustrofóbico, -a [klawʃtro'fɔbiku, a] ADJ claustrophobic

cláusula ['klawzula] F clause

clausura [klaw'zura] F (recinto) enclosure; (vida) cloistered existence

clave ['klavi] F (Mús) clef

clavícula [kla'vikula] F collar bone

clemência [kle'mẽsja] F mercy

clemente [kle'mẽtʃi] ADJ merciful

cleptomaníaco, -a [kleptoma'niaku, a] M/F kleptomaniac

clérigo ['klɛrigu] M clergyman

clero ['klɛru] M clergy

clicar [kli'ka^r] VI (Comput) to click

clichê [kli'ʃe] M (Foto) plate; (chavão) cliché

cliente ['kljẽtʃi] M client; (de loja) customer; (de médico) patient; **clientela** [kljẽ'tɛla] F clientele; (de loja) customers pl; (de médico) patients pl

clima ['klima] M climate

climático, -a [kli'matʃiku, a] ADJ climatic

clímax ['klimaks] M INV climax

clínica ['klinika] F clinic; ~ **geral** general practice; v tb **clínico**

clinicar [klini'ka^r] VI to have a practice

clínico, -a ['kliniku, a] ADJ clinical ∎ M/F doctor; ~ **geral** general practitioner, GP

clipe ['klipi] M clip; (para papéis) paper clip

clique ['kliki] M (Comput) click; **dar um ~ duplo em** to double-click on

clitóris [kli'tɔriʃ] M INV clitoris

clone ['klɔni] M clone

clorar [klo'ra^r] VT to chlorinate

cloro ['klɔru] M chlorine

clorofórmio [kloro'fɔxmju] M chloroform

close ['klɔzi] M close-up

NB: European Portuguese adds the following consonants to certain words: **b** (sú(b)dito, su(b)til); **c** (a(c)ção, a(c)cionista, a(c)to); **m** (inde(m)ne); **p** (ado(p)çã, ado(p)tar); for further details see p. xiii.

clube ['klubi] M club
CMB ABR F (= *Casa da Moeda do Brasil*) Brazilian National Mint
CMN (BR) ABR M = **Conselho Monetário Nacional**
CNA ABR M (= *Congresso Nacional Africano*) ANC; (BR) = **Conselho Nacional do Álcool**
CNB (BR) ABR M = **Conselho Nacional da Borracha**
CNBB ABR F = **Confederação Nacional dos Bispos do Brasil**
CNBV (BR) ABR F = **Comissão Nacional da Bolsa de Valores**
CND (BR) ABR M = **Conselho Nacional de Desportos**
CNDC (BR) ABR M = **Conselho Nacional de Defesa ao Consumidor**
CNDM (BR) ABR M = **Conselho Nacional dos Direitos da Mulher**
CNDU (BR) ABR M = **Conselho Nacional de Desenvolvimento Urbano**
CNEN (BR) ABR F (= *Comissão Nacional de Energia Nuclear*) ≈ AEA (*Brit*), ≈ AEC (US)
CNPq (BR) ABR M (= *Conselho Nacional de Desenvolvimento Científico*) organization supporting higher education
CNS (BR) ABR M = **Conselho Nacional de Saúde**
CNT (BR) ABR M = **Conselho Nacional de Transportes**
CNV (BR) ABR M = **Cadastro Nacional de Veículos**
coabitar [koabi'ta^r] VI to live together, cohabit
coação [koa'sãw] (PT **-çç-**) F coercion
coadjuvante [koadʒu'vãtʃi] ADJ supporting ■ M/F (*num crime*) accomplice; (*Teatro, Cinema*) co-star
coadjuvar [koadʒu'va^r] VT to aid; (*Teatro, Cinema*) to support
coador [koa'do^r] M strainer; (*de café*) filter bag; (*para legumes*) colander
coadunar [koadu'na^r] VT to combine; **coadunar-se** VR to combine
coagir [koa'ʒi^r] VT to coerce, compel
coagular [koagu'la^r] VT, VI to coagulate; (*sangue*) to clot; **coagular-se** VR to congeal
coágulo [ko'agulu] M clot
coajo *etc* [ko'aʒu] VB V **coagir**
coalhada [koa'ʎada] F curd
coalhado, -a [koa'ʎadu, a] ADJ curdled; **~ de gente** packed
coalhar [koa'ʎa^r] VT, VI (*leite*) to curdle; **coalhar-se** VR to curdle
coalizão [koali'zãw] (*pl* **-ões**) F coalition
coar [ko'a^r] VT (*líquido*) to strain
co-autor, a [ko-] M/F (*de livro*) co-author; (*de crime*) accomplice
coaxar [koa'ʃa^r] VI to croak ■ M croaking
COB ABR M = **Comité Olímpico Brasileiro**
cobaia [ko'baja] F guinea pig
cobalto [ko'bawtu] M cobalt
coberta [ko'bɛxta] F cover, covering; (*Náut*) deck
coberto, -a [ko'bɛxtu, a] PP *de* **cobrir** ■ ADJ covered

cobertor [kobex'to^r] M blanket
cobertura [kobex'tura] F covering; (*telhado*) roof; (*apartamento*) penthouse; (*TV, Rádio, Jornalismo*) coverage; (*Seguros*) cover; (*Tel*) network coverage; **aqui não tem ~** there's no network coverage here
cobiça [ko'bisa] F greed
cobiçar [kobi'sa^r] VT to covet
cobiçoso, -a [kobi'sozu, ɔza] ADJ covetous
cobra ['kɔbra] F snake ■ M/F (*col*) expert ■ ADJ (*col*) expert; **dizer ~s e lagartos de alguém** to say bad things about sb
cobrador, a [kobra'do^r(a)] M/F collector; (*em transporte*) conductor; **~ de impostos** tax collector
cobrança [ko'brãsa] F collection; (*ato de cobrar*) charging; **~ de pênalti/falta** penalty/free kick
cobrar [ko'bra^r] VT to collect; (*preço*) to charge; (*pênalti*) to take; **~ o prometido** to remind sb of what they promised; **~ uma falta** (*Futebol*) to take a free kick
cobre ['kɔbri] M copper; **cobres** MPL (*dinheiro*) money *sg*
cobrir [ko'bri^r] VT to cover; **cobrir-se** VR to cover o.s.
coca ['kɔka] F (*arbusto*) coca bush
coça ['kɔsa] (*col*) F wallop
cocada [ko'kada] F coconut sweet
cocaína [koka'ina] F cocaine
coçar [ko'sa^r] VT to scratch ■ VI (*comichar*) to itch; **coçar-se** VR to scratch o.s.; **não ter tempo nem para se ~** to have no time to breathe
cócegas ['kɔsegaʃ] FPL: **fazer ~ em** to tickle; **tenho ~ nos pés** my feet tickle; **sentir ~** to be ticklish; **estar em ~ para fazer** to be itching to do
coceira [ko'sejra] F itch; (*qualidade*) itchiness
cocheira [ko'ʃejra] F stable
cochichar [koʃi'ʃa^r] VI to whisper; **cochicho** [ko'ʃiʃu] M whispering
cochilada [koʃi'lada] F snooze; **dar uma ~** to have a snooze
cochilar [koʃi'la^r] VI to snooze, doze; **cochilo** [ko'ʃilu] M nap
coco ['koku] M coconut
cocô [ko'ko] (*col*) M pooh
cócoras ['kɔkoraʃ] FPL: **de ~** squatting; **ficar de ~** to squat (down)
cocoricar [kokori'ka^r] VI to crow
cocuruto [koku'rutu] M top
côdea ['kodʒa] F crust
codeína [kode'ina] F codeine
Codici [kodʒi'si] (BR) ABR F = **Comissão de Defesa dos Direitos do Cidadão**
codificador [kodʒifika'do^r] M (*Comput*) encoder
codificar [kodʒifi'ka^r] VT (*leis*) to codify; (*mensagem*) to encode, code
código ['kɔdʒigu] M code; **~ de barras** bar code; **~ de ética profissional** code of practice
codinome [kodʒi'nɔmi] M code name

codorna [ko'dɔxna] F quail

co-editar [ko-] VT to co-publish

coeficiente [koefi'sjẽtʃi] M (Mat) coefficient; (fig) factor

coelho [ko'eʎu] M rabbit; **matar dois ~s de uma cajadada só** (fig) to kill two birds with one stone

coentro [ko'ẽtru] M coriander

coerção [koex'sãw] F coercion

coerência [koe'rẽsja] F coherence; (consequência) consistency

coerente [koe'rẽtʃi] ADJ coherent; (consequente) consistent

coesão [koe'zãw] F cohesion

coeso, -a ['kwezu, a] ADJ cohesive

coexistência [koeziʃ'tẽsja] F coexistence

coexistir [koeziʃ'tʃiʳ] VI to coexist

Cofie (BR) ABR F = **Comissão de Fusão e Incorporação de Empresas**

cofre ['kɔfri] M safe; (caixa) strongbox; **os ~s públicos** public funds

cogitação [koʒita'sãw] F contemplation; **estar fora de** - to be out of the question

cogitar [koʒi'taʳ] VT, VI to contemplate

cognominar [kognomi'naʳ] VT to nickname

cogumelo [kogu'mɛlu] M mushroom; ~ **venenoso** toadstool

COHAB (BR) ABR F = **Companhia de Habitação Popular**

coibição [koibi'sãw] (pl -ões) F restraint, restriction

coibir [koi'biʳ] VT to restrain; **coibir-se** VR: **coibir-se de** to abstain from; ~ **de** to restrain from

coice ['kojsi] M kick; (de arma) recoil; **dar ~s em** to kick; (fig) to be aggressive with

coincidência [koĩsi'dẽsja] F coincidence

coincidir [koĩsi'dʒiʳ] VI to coincide; (concordar) to agree

coisa ['kojza] F thing; (assunto) matter; **coisas** FPL (objetos) things; (col: órgãos genitais) privates; ~ **de** about; **ser uma ~** (col) to be really something; (ruim) to be terrible; **que ~!** gosh!; **não dizer ~ com** ~ not to make any sense; **deu uma ~ nele** something strange got into him

coisíssima [koj'zisima] F: ~ **nenhuma** (nada) nothing; (de modo algum) not at all

coitado, -a [koj'tadu, a] ADJ poor, wretched; ~! poor thing!; ~ **do João** poor John

coito ['kojtu] M intercourse, coitus

cola ['kɔla] F glue; (BR: cópia) crib

colaboração [kolabora'sãw] (pl -ões) F collaboration; (num jornal etc) contribution

colaborador, a [kolabora'do(a)] M/F collaborator; (em jornal) contributor

colaborar [kolabo'raʳ] VI to collaborate; (ajudar) to help; (escrever artigos etc) to contribute

colagem [ko'laʒẽ] F collage

colante [ko'lãtʃi] ADJ (roupa) skin-tight

colapso [ko'lapsu] M collapse; ~ **cardíaco** heart failure

colar [ko'laʳ] VT to stick, glue; (BR: copiar) to crib ■ VI to stick; to cheat; (col: ser acreditado) to stand up, stick ■ M necklace; ~ **grau** to graduate

colarinho [kola'riɲu] M collar; (col: na cerveja) head

colarinho-branco (pl colarinhos-brancos) M white-collar worker

colateral [kolate'raw] (pl -ais) ADJ: **efeito ~** side effect

colcha ['kowʃa] F bedspread

colchão [kow'ʃãw] (pl -ões) M mattress

colcheia [kow'ʃeja] F (Mús) quaver

colchete [kow'ʃetʃi] M clasp, fastening; (parêntese) square bracket; ~ **de gancho** hook and eye; ~ **de pressão** press stud, popper

colchões [kow'ʃõjʃ] MPL de **colchão**

colchonete [kowʃo'nɛtʃi] M (portable) mattress

coleção [kole'sãw] (PT -cç-, pl -ões) F collection; **colecionador, a** [kolesjona'do(a)] (PT -cç-) M/F collector; **colecionar** [kolesjo'naʳ] (PT -cç-) VT to collect

coleções [kole'sõjʃ] FPL de **coleção**

colectar etc [kolek'taʳ] (PT) = **coletar** etc

colega [ko'lɛga] M/F (de trabalho) colleague; (de escola) classmate; (amigo) friend

colegial [kole'ʒjaw] (pl -ais) ADJ school atr ■ M/F schoolboy/girl

colégio [ko'lɛʒu] M school; ~ **eleitoral** electoral college

coleguismo [kole'ʒizmu] M loyalty to one's colleagues

coleira [ko'lejra] F collar

cólera ['kɔlera] F (ira) anger; (fúria) rage ■ M OU F (Med) cholera

colérico, -a [ko'lɛriku, a] ADJ (irado) angry; (furioso) furious ■ M/F (Med) cholera patient

colesterol [koleʃte'rɔw] M cholesterol

coleta [ko'lɛta] F collection; (imposto) levy

coletânea [kole'tanja] F collection

coletar [kole'taʳ] VT to tax; (arrecadar) to collect

colete [ko'letʃi] M waistcoat (Brit), vest (US); ~ **salva-vidas** life jacket (Brit), life preserver (US)

coletividade [koletʃivi'dadʒi] F community

coletivo, -a [kole'tʃivu, a] ADJ collective; (transportes) public ■ M bus

coletor, a [kole'to(a)] M/F collector

coletoria [koleto'ria] F tax office

colheita [ko'ʎejta] F harvest; (produto) crop

colher [ko'ʎeʳ] VT (recolher) to gather, pick; (dados) to gather ■ F spoon; ~ **de chá/sopa** teaspoon/tablespoon; **dar uma ~ de chá a alguém** (fig) to do sb a favo(u)r; **de ~** (col) on a silver platter

colherada [koʎe'rada] F spoonful

colibri [koli'bri] M hummingbird

cólica ['kɔlika] F colic

colidir [koli'dʒiʳ] VI: ~ **com** to collide with, crash into

---

coligação [koliga'sãw] (pl -ões) F coalition
coligar [koli'ga^r] VT to bring together, unite;
coligar-se VR to join forces
coligir [koli'ʒi^r] VT to collect
colina [ko'lina] F hill
colírio [ko'lirju] M eyewash
colisão [koli'zãw] (pl -ões) F collision
colis postaux [ko'li pos'to] MPL small packets
colite [ko'litʃi] F colitis
collant [ko'lã] (pl -s) M tights pl (Brit), pantihose (US); (blusa) leotard
colmeia [kow'meja] F beehive
colo ['kɔlu] M neck; (regaço) lap; **no ~ on** one's lap, in one's arms
colocação [koloka'sãw] (pl -ões) F placing; (emprego) job, position; (de pneus, tapete etc) fitting; (de uma questão, idéia) positing; (opinião) position
colocar [kolo'ka^r] VT to put, place; (empregar) to find a job for, place; (Com) to market; (pneus, tapetes) to fit; (questão, idéia) to put forward, state; **colocar-se** VR to place o.s.; **coloque-se no meu lugar** put yourself in my position
Colômbia [ko'lõbja] F: **a ~ Colombia**
colombiano, -a [kolõ'bjanu, a] ADJ, M/F Colombian
cólon ['kɔlõ] M colon
colônia [ko'lonja] F colony; (perfume) cologne;
colonial [kolo'njaw] (pl -ais) ADJ colonial
colonialismo [kolonja'liʒmu] M colonialism
colonização [koloniza'sãw] F colonization
colonizador, a [koloniza'do^r(a)] ADJ colonizing
■ M/F colonist, settler
colonizar [koloni'za^r] VT to colonize
colono, -a [ko'lɔnu, a] M/F settler; (cultivador) tenant farmer
coloquei etc [kolo'kej] VB V **colocar**
coloquial [kolo'kjaw] (pl -ais) ADJ colloquial
colóquio [ko'lɔkju] M conversation; (congresso) conference
coloração [kolora'sãw] F colouration (Brit), coloration (US)
colorido, -a [kolo'ridu, a] ADJ colourful (Brit), colorful (US) ■ M colouring (Brit), coloring (US)
colorir [kolo'ri^r] VT to colour (Brit), color (US)
colossal [kolo'saw] (pl -ais) ADJ colossal
colosso [ko'losu] M (pessoa) giant; (coisa) extraordinary thing
coluna [ko'luna] F column; (pilar) pillar;
~ dorsal ou **vertebral** spine; **colunável** [kolu'navew] (pl -eis) ADJ famous ■ M/F celebrity
colunista [kolu'niʃta] M/F columnist
com [kõ] PREP with; **estar ~ fome** to be hungry;
~ cuidado carefully; **estar ~ dinheiro/câncer** to have some money on one/have cancer; **"não ultrapasse ~ faixa contínua"** do not overtake when centre line is unbroken"
coma ['kɔma] F coma
comadre [ko'madri] F (urinol) bedpan; **minha ~** the godmother of my child (ou the mother of my godchild)

comandante [komã'dãtʃi] M commander; (Mil) commandant; (Náut) captain
comandar [komã'da^r] VT to command
comando [ko'mãdu] M command
combate [kõ'batʃi] M combat, fight; (fig) battle
combatente [kõba'tẽtʃi] M/F combatant
combater [kõba'te^r] VT to fight, combat; (opor-se a) to oppose ■ VI to fight; **combater-se** VR to fight
combinação [kõbina'sãw] (pl -ões) F combination; (Quím) compound; (acordo) arrangement; (plano) scheme; (roupa) slip
combinar [kõbi'na^r] VT to combine; (jantar etc) to arrange; (fuga etc) to plan ■ VI (roupas etc) to go together; **combinar-se** VR to combine; (pessoas) to get on well together; (temperamentos) to go well together; **~ com** (harmonizar-se) to go with; **~ de fazer** to arrange to do; **combinado!** agreed!
comboio [kõ'boju] M (PT) train; (de navios, carros) convoy
combustão [kõbuʃ'tãw] (pl -ões) F combustion
combustível [kõbuʃ'tʃivew] M fuel
combustões [kõbuʃ'tõjʃ] FPL de **combustão**
começar [kome'sa^r] VT, VI to begin, start; **~ a fazer** to begin ou start to do
começo [ko'mesu] M beginning, start
começo etc VB V **comedir-se**
comédia [ko'mɛdʒja] F comedy
comediante [kome'dʒjãtʃi] M/F (comic) actor/ actress
comedido, -a [kome'dʒidu, a] ADJ moderate; (prudente) prudent
comedir-se [kome'dʒixsi] VR to control o.s.
comedorias [komedo'riaʃ] FPL food sg
comemoração [komemora'sãw] (pl -ões) F commemoration
comemorar [komemo'ra^r] VT to commemorate; (celebrar: sucesso etc) to celebrate
comemorativo, -a [komemora'tʃivu, a] ADJ commemorative
comensal [komẽ'saw] (pl -ais) M/F diner
comentar [komẽ'ta^r] VT to comment on; (maliciosamente) to make comments about
comentário [komẽ'tarju] M comment, remark; (análise) commentary; **sem ~** no comment
comentarista [komẽta'riʃta] M/F commentator
comer [ko'me^r] VT to eat; (Damas, Xadrez) to take, capture; (dinheiro) to eat up; (corroer) to eat away ■ VI to eat; **comer-se** VR: **~-se (de)** to be consumed (with); **dar de ~ a** to feed; **~ por quatro** (fig) to eat like a horse; **~ fogo** (col) to go through hell
comercial [komex'sjaw] (pl -ais) ADJ commercial; (relativo ao negócio) business atr ■ M commercial
comercialização [komexsjaliza'sãw] F marketing
comercializar [komexsjali'za^r] VT to market
comercializável [komexsjali'zavew] (pl -eis) ADJ marketable
comerciante [komex'sjãtʃi] M/F trader
comerciar [komex'sja^r] VI to trade, do business

comerciário, -a [komex'sjarju, a] M/F employee in business

comércio [ko'mɛxsju] M commerce; (*tráfico*) trade; (*negócio*) business; (*lojas*) shops pl; **de fechar o ~** (*col*) really stunning; **~ eletrônico** e-commerce

comes ['kɔmiʃ] MPL: **~ e bebes** food and drink

comestíveis [komeʃ'tʃiveis] MPL foodstuffs, food sg

comestível [komeʃ'tʃivew] (*pl* -**eis**) ADJ edible

cometa [ko'meta] M comet

cometer [kome'te^r] VT to commit

cometimento [kometʃi'mẽtu] M undertaking, commitment

comichão [komi'ʃãw] F itch, itching

comichar [komi'ʃa^r] VT, VI to itch

comicidade [komisi'dadʒi] F comic quality

comício [ko'misju] M (*Pol*) rally, meeting; (*assembléia*) assembly

cômico, -a ['komiku, a] ADJ comic(al) ■ M comedian; (*de teatro*) actor

comida [ko'mida] F (*alimento*) food; (*refeição*) meal; **~ caseira** home cooking

comigo [ko'migu] PRON with me; (*reflexivo*) with myself

comilança [komi'lãsa] F overeating

comilão, -lona [komi'lãw] (*pl* -**ões/-s**) ADJ greedy ■ M/F glutton

cominho [ko'miɲu] M cumin

comiserar [komize'ra^r] VT to move to pity; **comiserar-se** VR: **comiserar-se (de)** to sympathize (with)

comissão [komi'sãw] (*pl* -**ões**) F commission; (*comitê*) committee

comissário [komi'sarju] M commissioner; (*Com*) agent; **~ de bordo** (*Aer*) steward; (*Náut*) purser

comissionar [komisjo'na^r] VT to commission

comissões [komi'sõjʃ] FPL **de comissão**

comitê [komi'te] M committee

comitiva [komi'tʃiva] F entourage

🔵 PALAVRA CHAVE

como ['kɔmu] ADV **1** (*modo*) as; **ela fez como eu pedi** she did as I asked; **como se** as if; **como quiser** as you wish; **seja como for** be that as it may

2 (*assim como*) like; **ela tem olhos azuis como o pai** she has blue eyes like her father's; **ela trabalha numa loja, como a mãe** she works in a shop, as does her mother

3 (*de que maneira*) how; **como?** pardon?; **como!** what!; **como assim?** what do you mean?; **como não!** of course!

■ CONJ (*porque*) as, since; **como estava tarde ele dormiu aqui** since it was late he slept here

comoção [komo'sãw] (*pl* -**ões**) F (*abalo*) distress;

---

comerciário | comparecimento

(*revolta*) commotion

cômoda ['komoda] F chest of drawers (*Brit*), bureau (*US*)

comodidade [komodʒi'dadʒi] F (*conforto*) comfort; (*conveniência*) convenience

comodismo [komo'dʒiʒmu] M complacency

comodista [komo'dʒiʃta] ADJ complacent

cômodo, -a ['komodu, a] ADJ (*confortável*) comfortable; (*conveniente*) convenient ■ M (*aposento*) room

comovedor, a [komove'do^r(a)] ADJ moving, touching

comovente [komo'vẽtʃi] ADJ moving, touching

comover [komo've^r] VT to move ■ VI to be moving; **comover-se** VR to be moved

comovido, -a [komo'vidu, a] ADJ moved

compacto, -a [kõ'paktu, a] ADJ (*pequeno*) compact; (*espesso*) thick; (*sólido*) solid ■ M (*disco*) single

compadecer-se [kõpade'sexsi] VR: **~-se de** to be sorry for, pity

compadecido, -a [kõpade'sidu, a] ADJ sympathetic

compadecimento [kõpadesi'mẽtu] M sympathy; (*piedade*) pity

compadre [kõ'padri] M (*col: companheiro*) buddy, pal, crony; **meu ~** the godfather of my child (*ou* the father of my godchild)

compaixão [kõpaj'ʃãw] M (*piedade*) compassion, pity; (*misericórdia*) mercy

companheirão, -rona [kõpaɲej'rãw, 'rɔna] (*pl* -**ões/-s**) M/F good friend

companheirismo [kõpaɲej'riʒmu] M companionship

companheiro, -a [kõpa'ɲejru, a] M/F companion; (*colega*) friend; (*col*) buddy, mate; **~ de viagem** fellow traveller (*Brit*) *ou* traveler (*US*), travelling (*Brit*) *ou* traveling (*US*) companion

companheirões [kõpaɲej'rõjʃ] MPL **de companheirão**

companheirona [kõpaɲej'rɔna] F **de companheirão**

companhia [kõpa'ɲia] F (*Com*) company, firm; (*convivência*) company; **fazer ~ a alguém** to keep sb company; **em ~ de** accompanied by; **dama de ~** companion

comparação [kõpara'sãw] (*pl* -**ões**) F comparison

comparar [kõpa'ra^r] VT to compare; **comparar-se** VR: **comparar-se com** to bear comparison with; **~ a** to liken to; **~ com** to compare with

comparativo, -a [kõpara'tʃivu, a] ADJ comparative

comparável [kõpa'ravew] (*pl* -**eis**) ADJ comparable

comparecer [kõpare'se^r] VI to appear, make an appearance; **~ a uma reunião** to attend a meeting

comparecimento [kõparesi'mẽtu] M (*presença*)

---

attendance

comparsa [kõ'paxsa] M/F (*Teatro*) extra; (*cúmplice*) accomplice

compartilhar [kõpaxtʃi'ʎaʳ] VT (*partilhar*) to share ■ VI: ~ **de** (*participar de*) to share in, participate in; ~ **com alguém** to share with sb

compartimentar [kõpaxtʃimẽ'taʳ] VT to compartmentalize

compartimento [kõpaxtʃi'mẽtu] M compartment; (*aposento*) room

compartir [kõpax'tʃiʳ] VT (*dividir*) to share out ■ VI: ~ **de** to share in

compassado, -a [kõpa'sadu, a] ADJ (*medido*) measured; (*moderado*) moderate; (*cadenciado*) regular; (*pausado*) slow

compassivo, -a [kõpa'sivu, a] ADJ compassionate

compasso [kõ'pasu] M (*instrumento*) a pair of compasses; (*Mús*) time; (*ritmo*) beat; **dentro do** ~ in time with the music; **fora do** ~ out of time

compatibilidade [kõpatʃibili'dadʒi] F compatibility

compatível [kõpa'tʃivew] (*pl* -**eis**) ADJ compatible; ~ **com o IBM-PC** IBM compatible

compatriota [kõpa'trjɔta] M/F fellow countryman/woman, compatriot

compelir [kõpe'liʳ] VT to force, compel

compêndio [kõ'pẽdʒju] M (*sumário*) compendium; (*livro de texto*) textbook

compenetração [kõpenetra'sãw] (*pl* -**ões**) F conviction

compenetrar [kõpene'traʳ] VT to convince; **compenetrar-se** VR to be convinced

compensação [kõpẽsa'sãw] (*pl* -**ões**) F compensation; (*de cheques*) clearance; **em** ~ **on** the other hand

compensado [kõpẽ'sadu] M hardboard

compensador, a [kõpẽsa'doʳ(a)] ADJ compensatory

compensar [kõpẽ'saʳ] VT (*reparar o dano*) to make up for, compensate for; (*equilibrar*) to offset, counterbalance; (*cheque*) to clear

competência [kõpe'tẽsja] F competence, ability; (*responsabilidade*) responsibility; **isto é de minha** ~ this is my responsibility; **competente** [kõpe'tẽtʃi] ADJ (*capaz*) competent, able; (*apropriado*) appropriate; (*responsável*) responsible

competição [kõpetʃi'sãw] (*pl* -**ões**) F competition

competidor, a [kõpetʃi'doʳ(a)] M/F competitor

competir [kõpe'tʃiʳ] VI to compete; ~ **a alguém** (*ser da competência de*) to be sb's responsibility; (*caber*) to be up to sb; ~ **com** to compete with

competitividade [kõpetʃitʃivi'dadʒi] F competitiveness

competitivo, -a [kõpetʃi'tʃivu, a] ADJ competitive

compilação [kõpila'sãw] (*pl* -**ões**) F compilation

compilar [kõpi'laʳ] VT to compile

compilo *etc* [kõ'pilu] VB V **compelir**

compito *etc* [kõ'pitu] VB V **competir**

complacência [kõpla'sẽsja] F complaisance

complacente [kõpla'sẽtʃi] ADJ obliging

compleição [kõplej'sãw] (*pl* -**ões**) F build

complementar [kõplemẽ'taʳ] ADJ complementary ■ VT to supplement

complemento [kõple'mẽtu] M complement

completamente [kõpleta'mẽtʃi] ADV completely, quite

completar [kõple'taʳ] VT to complete; (*água, gasolina*) to fill up, top up; ~ **dez anos** to be ten

completo, -a [kõ'plɛtu, a] ADJ complete; (*cheio*) full (up); **por** ~ completely

complexado, -a [kõplek'sadu, a] ADJ hung-up; **estar/ficar** ~ to have/get a complex

complexidade [kõpleksi'dadʒi] F complexity

complexo, -a [kõ'plɛksu, a] ADJ complex ■ M complex; ~ **de Édipo** Oedipus complex

complicação [kõplika'sãw] (*pl* -**ões**) F complication

complicado, -a [kõpli'kadu, a] ADJ complicated

complicar [kõpli'kaʳ] VT to complicate; **complicar-se** VR to become complicated; (*enredo*) to thicken

complô [kõ'plo] M plot, conspiracy

compõe *etc* [kõ'põʃ] VB V **compor**

compomos *etc* [kõ'pomoʃ] VB V **compor**

componente [kõpo'nẽtʃi] ADJ, M component

componho *etc* [kõ'poɲu] VB V **compor**

compor [kõ'poʳ] (*irreg*) VT to compose; (*discurso, livro*) to write; (*arranjar*) to arrange; (*Tip*) to set ■ VI to compose; **compor-se** VR (*controlar-se*) to compose o.s.; ~-**se de** to consist of

comporta [kõ'pɔxta] F floodgate; (*de canal*) lock

comportamento [kõpoxta'mẽtu] M behaviour (*Brit*), behavior (*US*); (*conduta*) conduct; **mau** ~ misbehavio(u)r

comportar [kõpox'taʳ] VT (*suportar*) to put up with, bear; (*conter*) to hold; **comportar-se** VR (*portar-se*) to behave; ~-**se mal** to misbehave, behave badly

compôs [kõ'poʃ] VB V **compor**

composição [kõpozi'sãw] (*pl* -**ões**) F composition; (*Tip*) typesetting; (*conciliação*) compromise

compositor, a [kõpozi'toʳ(a)] M/F composer; (*Tip*) typesetter

composto, -a [kõ'poʃtu, 'pɔʃta] PP *de* **compor** ■ ADJ (*sério*) serious; (*de muitos elementos*) composite, compound; ~ **de** made up of, composed of ■ M compound

compostura [kõpoʃ'tura] F composure

compota [kõ'pɔta] F fruit in syrup; ~ **de laranja** oranges in syrup

compra ['kõpra] F purchase; **fazer** ~**s** to go shopping; **comprador, a** [kõpra'doʳ(a)] M/F buyer, purchaser

comprar [kõ'praʳ] VT to buy; (*subornar*) to bribe; ~ **briga** to look for trouble; ~ **a briga de alguém** to fight sb's battle for him

comprazer-se [kõpra'zexsi] VR: ~ **com/em fazer** to take pleasure in/in doing

compreender [kõprjen'deʳ] VT (*entender*) to

understand; (constar de) to be comprised of, consist of; (abranger) to cover
compreensão [kõprjẽ'sãw] F understanding, comprehension
compreensível [kõprjẽ'sivew] (pl -eis) ADJ understandable, comprehensible
compreensivo, -a [kõprjẽ'sivu, a] ADJ understanding
compressa [kõ'presa] F compress
compressão [kõpre'sãw] (pl -ões) F compression
compressor, a [kõpre'so'(a)] ADJ v rolo
comprido, -a [kõ'pridu, a] ADJ long; (alto) tall; **ao ~** lengthways
comprimento [kõpri'mẽtu] M length
comprimido, -a [kõpri'midu, a] ADJ compressed ■ M (pílula) pill; (pastilha) tablet
comprimir [kõpri'mi'] VT to compress; (apertar) to squeeze
comprometedor, a [kõpromete'do'(a)] ADJ compromising
comprometer [kõprome'te'] VT to compromise; (envolver) to involve; (arriscar) to jeopardize; (empenhar) to pledge; **comprometer-se** VR to commit o.s.; **~-se a** to undertake to, promise to; **~-se com alguém** to make a commitment to sb
comprometido, -a [kõprome'tʃidu, a] ADJ (ocupado) busy; (noivo etc) spoken for
compromisso [kõpro'misu] M (promessa) promise; (obrigação) commitment; (hora marcada) appointment, engagement; (acordo) agreement; **sem ~** without obligation
comprovação [kõprova'sãw] (pl -ões) F proof, evidence; (Admin) receipts pl
comprovante [kõpro'vãtʃi] ADJ of proof ■ M receipt
comprovar [kõpro'va'] VT to prove; (confirmar) to confirm
compulsão [kõpuw'sãw] (pl -ões) F compulsion
compulsivo, -a [kõpuw'sivu, a] ADJ compulsive
compulsões [kõpuw'sõjʃ] FPL de compulsão
compulsório, -a [kõpuw'sɔrju, a] ADJ compulsory
compunção [kõpũ'sãw] F compunction
compungir [kõpũ'ʒi'] VT to pain ■ VI to be painful
compunha etc [kõ'puɲa] VB v compor
compus etc [kõ'puʃ] VB v compor
compuser etc [kõpu'ze'] VB v compor
computação [kõputa'sãw] F computation; (ciência, curso) computer science, computing
computador [kõputa'do'] M computer
computadorizar [kõputadori'za'] VT to computerize
computar [kõpu'ta'] VT to compute; (calcular) to calculate; (contar) to count
cômputo ['kõputu] M computation
comum [ko'mũ] (pl -ns) ADJ (pessoa) ordinary, common; (habitual) usual ■ M the usual thing;

em ~ in common; **o ~ é partirmos às 8** we usually set off at 8; **fora do ~** unusual
comuna [ko'muna] (col) M/F communist
comungar [komũ'ga'] VI to take communion
comunhão [komu'ɲãw] (pl -ões) F communion; (Rel) Holy Communion; **~ de bens** joint ownership
comunicação [komunika'sãw] (pl -ões) F communication; (mensagem) message; (curso) media studies sg; (acesso) access
comunicado [komuni'kadu] M notice; (oficial) communiqué
comunicar [komuni'ka'] VT to communicate; (unir) to join ■ VI to communicate; **comunicar-se** VR to communicate; **~ algo a alguém** to inform sb of sth; **~-se com** (entrar em contato) to get in touch with
comunicativo, -a [comunika'tʃivu, a] ADJ communicative; (riso) infectious
comunidade [komuni'dadʒi] F community; **C~ Econômica Européia** European (Economic) Community
comunismo [komu'niʒmu] M communism;
comunista [komu'niʃta] ADJ, M/F communist
comunitário, -a [komuni'tarju, a] ADJ community atr
comuns [ko'mũʃ] PL de comum
comutador [komuta'do'] M switch
comutar [komu'ta'] VT (Jur) to commute; (trocar) to exchange
concatenar [kõkate'na'] VT (idéias) to string together
côncavo, -a ['kõkavu, a] ADJ concave; (cavado) hollow ■ M hollow
conceber [kõse'be'] VT to conceive; (imaginar) to conceive of, imagine; (entender) to understand ■ VI to conceive, become pregnant
concebível [kõse'bivew] (pl -eis) ADJ conceivable
conceder [kõse'de'] VT (permitir) to allow; (outorgar) to grant, accord; (admitir) to concede; (dar) to give ■ VI: **~ em** to agree to
conceito [kõ'sejtu] M (idéia) concept, idea; (fama) reputation; (opinião) opinion; **conceituado, -a** [kõsej'twadu, a] ADJ well thought of, highly regarded
conceituar [kõsej'twa'] VT to conceptualize
concentração [kõsẽtra'sãw] (pl -ões) F concentration; (Esporte) training camp
concentrado, -a [kõsẽ'tradu, a] ADJ concentrated ■ M concentrate
concentrar [kõsẽ'tra'] VT to concentrate; (atenção) to focus; (reunir) to bring together; (molho) to thicken; **concentrar-se** VR to concentrate; **~-se em** to concentrate on
concepção [kõsep'sãw] (pl -ões) F (geração) conception; (noção) idea, concept; (opinião) opinion
concernente [kõsex'nẽtʃi] ADJ: **~ a** concerning
concernir [kõsex'ni'] VI: **~ a** to concern

NB: European Portuguese adds the following consonants to certain words: **b** (sú(b)dito, su(b)til); **c** (a(c)ção, a(c)cionista, a(c)to); **m** (inde(m)ne); **p** (ado(p)çã, ado(p)tar); for further details see p. xiii.

concertar[kõsex'taʳ] VT (endireitar) to adjust; (conciliar) to reconcile
concerto[kõ'sextu] M concert
concessão[kõse'sãw] (pl -ões) F concession; (permissão) permission
concessionária[kõsesjo'narja] F dealer, dealership
concessionário[kõsesjo'narju] M concessionaire
concessões[kõse'sõjʃ] FPL de **concessão**
concha['kõʃa] F (moluscos) shell; (para líquidos) ladle
conchavo[kõ'ʃavu] M conspiracy
conciliação[kõsilja'sãw] (pl -ões) F reconciliation
conciliador, a[kõsilja'doʳ(a)] ADJ conciliatory ■ M/F conciliator
conciliar[kõsi'ljaʳ] VT to reconcile; ~ o sono to get to sleep
conciliatório, -a[kõsilja'tɔrju, a] ADJ conciliatory
conciliável[kõsi'ljavew] (pl -eis) ADJ reconcilable
concílio[kõ'silju] M (Rel) council
concisão[kõsi'zãw] F concision, conciseness
conciso, -a[kõ'sizu, a] ADJ brief, concise
concitar[kõsi'taʳ] VT (estimular) to stir up, arouse; (incitar) to incite
conclamar[kõkla'maʳ] VT to shout; (aclamar) to acclaim; (convocar) to call together
Conclat[kõ'klatʃi] (BR) ABR F (= Conferência Nacional da Classe Trabalhadora) trade union
conclave[kõ'klavi] M conclave
concludente[kõklu'dẽtʃi] ADJ conclusive
concluir[kõ'klwiʳ] VT (terminar) to end, conclude ■ VI (deduzir) to conclude
conclusão[kõklu'zãw] (pl -ões) F (término) end; (dedução) conclusion; **chegar a uma** ~ to come to a conclusion; ~, **ele não veio** (col) the upshot is, he didn't come
conclusivo, -a[kõklu'zivu, a] ADJ conclusive
conclusões[kõklu'zõjʃ] FPL de **conclusão**
concomitante[kõkomi'tãtʃi] ADJ concomitant
concordância[kõkox'dãsja] F agreement
concordante[kõkox'dãtʃi] ADJ (fatos) concordant
concordar[kõkox'daʳ] VI, VT to agree; **não concordo!** I disagree!; ~ **com** to agree with; ~ **em** to agree to
concordata[kõkox'data] F liquidation agreement
concórdia[kõ'kɔxdʒja] F (acordo) agreement; (paz) peace
concorrência[kõko'xẽsja] F competition; (a um cargo) application
concorrente[kõko'xẽtʃi] M/F (competidor) contestant; (candidato) candidate
concorrer[kõko'xeʳ] VI (competir) to compete; ~ **a** (candidatar-se) to apply for; ~ **para** (contribuir) to contribute to
concorrido, -a[kõko'xidu, a] ADJ popular
concretização[kõkretʃiza'sãw] F realization

concretizar[kõkretʃi'zaʳ] VT to make real; **concretizar-se** VR (sonho) to come true; (ambições) to be realized
concreto, -a[kõ'krɛtu, a] ADJ concrete; (verdadeiro) real; (sólido) solid ■ M concrete; ~ **armado** reinforced concrete
concupiscência[kõkupi'sẽsja] F greed; (lascívia) lust
concurso[kõ'kuxsu] M contest; (exame) competition; ~ **público** open competition
concussão[kõku'sãw] F concussion; (desfalque) embezzlement
condado[kõ'dadu] M county
condão[kõ'dãw] M v **varinha**
conde['kõdʒi] M count
condecoração[kõdekora'sãw] (pl -ões) F decoration
condecorar[kõdeko'raʳ] VT to decorate
condenação[kõdena'sãw] (pl -ões) F condemnation; (Jur) conviction
condenar[kõde'naʳ] VT to condemn; (Jur: sentenciar) to sentence; (: declarar culpado) to convict
condenável[kõde'navew] (pl -eis) ADJ reprehensible
condensação[kõdẽsa'sãw] F condensation
condensar[kõdẽ'saʳ] VT to condense; **condensar-se** VR to condense
condescendência[kõdesẽ'dẽsja] F acquiescence
condescendente[kõdesẽ'dẽtʃi] ADJ condescending
condescender[kõdesẽ'deʳ] VI to acquiesce; ~ **a ou em** to condescend to, deign to
condessa[kõ'desa] F countess
condição[kõdʒi'sãw] (pl -ões) F condition; (social) status; (qualidade) capacity; **com a ~ de que** on condition that, provided that; **ter ~ ou condições para fazer** to be able to do; **em condições de fazer** (pessoa) able to do; (carro etc) in condition to do; **em sua ~ de líder** in his capacity as leader
condicionado, -a[kõdʒisjo'nadu, a] ADJ conditioned; v tb **ar**
condicional[kõdʒisjo'naw] (pl -ais) ADJ conditional
condicionamento[kõdʒisjona'mẽtu] M conditioning
condições[kõdʒi'sõjʃ] FPL de **condição**
condigno, -a[kõ'dʒignu, a] ADJ (apropriado) fitting; (merecido) deserved
condigo etc [kõ'dʒigu] VB v **condizer**
condimentar[kõdʒimẽ'taʳ] VT to season
condimento[kõdʒi'mẽtu] M seasoning
condisse etc [kõ'dʒisi] VB v **condizer**
condito[kõ'dʒitu] PP de **condizer**
condizente[kõdʒi'zẽtʃi] ADJ: ~ **com** in keeping with
condizer[kõdʒi'zeʳ] (irreg) VI: ~ **com** to match
condoer-se[kõdo'exsi] VR: ~ **de** to pity
condolência[kõdo'lẽsja] F condolence
condomínio[kõdo'minju] M condominium;

(contribuição) service charge
condução [kõdu'sãw] F (ato de conduzir) driving; (transporte) transport; (ônibus) bus; (Fís) conduction
conducente [kõdu'sētʃi] ADJ: ~ **a** conducive to
conduta [kõ'duta] F conduct, behaviour (Brit), behavior (US); **má** ~ misconduct
conduto [kõ'dutu] M (tubo) tube; (cano) pipe; (canal) channel
condutor, a [kõdu'to'(a)] M/F (de veículo) driver ▪ M (Elet) conductor
conduzir [kõdu'zi'] VT (PT: veículo) to drive; (levar) to lead; (negócio) to manage; (Fís) to conduct ▪ VI (PT) to drive; **conduzir-se** VR to behave; ~ **a** to lead to
cone ['kɔni] M cone
conectar [konek'ta'] VT to connect
cônego ['konegu] M (Rel) canon
conexão [konek'sãw] (pl -ões) F connection
conexo, -a [ko'nɛksu, a] ADJ connected
conexões [konek'sõjʃ] FPL de **conexão**
confabular [kõfabu'la'] VI to talk; ~ **com** to talk to
confecção [kõfek'sãw] (pl -ões) F (feitura) making; (de um boletim) production; (roupa) ready-to-wear clothes pl; (negócio) business selling ready-to-wear clothes
confeccionar [kõfeksjo'na'] VT (fazer) to make; (fabricar) to manufacture
confeccionista [kõfeksjo'niʃta] M/F maker of ready-to-wear clothes
confecções [kõfek'sõjʃ] FPL de **confecção**
confederação [kõfedera'sãw] (pl -ões) F confederation; (liga) league
confederar [kõfede'ra'] VT to unite; **confederar-se** VR to form an alliance
confeitar [kõfej'ta'] VT (bolo) to ice
confeitaria [kõfejta'ria] F patisserie
confeiteiro, -a [kõfej'tejru, a] M/F confectioner
conferência [kõfe'rēsja] F conference; (discurso) lecture; **fazer uma** ~ to give a lecture
conferencista [kõferē'siʃta] M/F (que fala) speaker
conferente [kõfe'rētʃi] M/F (verificador) checker
conferir [kõfe'ri'] VT (verificar) to check; (comparar) to compare; (outorgar) to grant; (título) to confer ▪ VI (estar certo) to tally; **confira!** see for yourself, check it out (col)
confessar [kõfe'sa'] VT, VI to confess; **confessar-se** VR to confess; ~ **alguém** (Rel) to hear sb's confession; --**se culpado** (Jur) to plead guilty
confessionário [kõfesjo'narju] M confessional
confessor [kõfe'so'] M confessor
confete [kõ'fɛtʃi] M confetti; **jogar** ~ (col) to be flattering
confiabilidade [kõfjabili'dadʒi] F reliability
confiado, -a [kõ'fjadu, a] (col) ADJ cheeky
confiança [kõ'fjãsa] F confidence; (fé) trust; (familiaridade) familiarity; **de** ~ reliable; **digno**

condução | confortante

de ~ trustworthy; **ter** ~ **em alguém** to trust sb; **dar** ~ **a alguém** (no tratamento) to be on informal terms with sb
confiante [kõ'fjãtʃi] ADJ confident; ~ **em** confident of
confiar [kõ'fja'] VT to entrust; (segredo) to confide ▪ VI: ~ **em** to trust; (ter fé) to have faith in
confiável [kõ'fjavew] (pl -eis) ADJ reliable
confidência [kõfi'dēsja] F secret; **em** ~ in confidence; **confidencial** [kõfidē'sjaw] (pl -ais) ADJ confidential
confidenciar [kõfidē'sja'] VT to tell in confidence
confidente [kõfi'dētʃi] M/F confidant(e)
configuração [kõfigura'sãw] (pl -ões) F configuration; (forma) shape, form
configurar [kõfigu'ra'] VT to shape, form; (representar) to represent; (Comput) to configure
confinamento [kõfina'mētu] M confinement
confinar [kõfi'na'] VT (limitar) to limit; (enclausurar) to confine ▪ VI: ~ **com** to border on; **confinar-se** VR: --**se a** to confine o.s. to
confins [kõ'fĩʃ] MPL limits, boundaries; **nos** ~ **de judas** (col) out in the sticks
confirmação [kõfixma'sãw] (pl -ões) F confirmation
confirmar [kõfix'ma'] VT to confirm; **confirmar-se** VR (Rel) to be confirmed; (realizar-se) to come true
confiro etc [kõ'firu] VB V **conferir**
confiscar [kõfiʃ'ka'] VT to confiscate, seize
confisco [kõ'fiʃku] M confiscation
confissão [kõfi'sãw] (pl -ões) F confession
conflagração [kõflagra'sãw] (pl -ões) F conflagration
conflagrar [kõfla'gra'] VT to inflame, set alight; (fig) to plunge into turmoil
conflitante [kõfli'tãtʃi] ADJ conflicting
conflito [kõ'flitu] M conflict; **entrar em** ~ **(com)** to clash (with)
confluente [kõ'flwētʃi] M tributary
conformação [kõfoxma'sãw] (pl -ões) F (resignação) resignation; (forma) form
conformado, -a [kõfox'madu, a] ADJ resigned
conformar [kõfox'ma'] VT (formar) to form ▪ VI: ~ **com** to conform to; **conformar-se** VR: **conformar-se com** to resign o.s. to; (acomodar-se) to conform to
conforme [kõ'fɔxmi] PREP according to; (dependendo de) depending on ▪ CONJ (logo que) as soon as; (como) as, according to what; (à medida que) as; (dependendo de) depending on; **você vai?** -- ~ are you going? -- it depends
conformidade [kõfoxmi'dadʒi] F agreement; **em** ~ **com** in accordance with
conformismo [kõfox'miʒmu] M conformity
conformista [kõfox'miʃta] M/F conformist
confortante [kõfox'tãtʃi] ADJ comforting

NB: European Portuguese adds the following consonants to certain words: **b** (sú(b)dito, su(b)til); **c** (a(c)ção, a(c)cionista, a(c)to); **m** (inde(m)ne); **p** (ado(p)çã, ado(p)tar); for further details see p. xiii.

confortar [kõfox'ta^r] VT (*consolar*) to comfort, console

confortável [kõfox'tavew] (*pl* -**eis**) ADJ comfortable

conforto [kõ'foxtu] M comfort

confraria [kõfra'ria] F fraternity

confraternizar [kõfratexni'za^r] VI to fraternize

confrontação [kõfrõta'sãw] (*pl* -**ões**) F (*acareação*) confrontation; (*comparação*) comparison

confrontar [kõfrõ'ta^r] VT (*acarear*) to confront; (*comparar*) to compare; **confrontar-se** VR to face each other

confronto [kõ'frõtu] M confrontation; (*comparação*) comparison

confundir [kõfũ'dʒi^r] VT to confuse; **confundir-se** VR to get mixed up, get confused

confusão [kõfu'zãw] (*pl* -**ões**) F confusion; (*tumulto*) uproar; (*problemas*) trouble; (*barafunda*) chaos; **isso vai dar tanta ~** this will cause so much trouble; **fazer ~** (*confundir-se*) to get mixed up *ou* confused

confuso, -a [kõ'fuzu, a] ADJ confused; (*problema*) confusing; **está tudo muito ~ aqui hoje** it's all very chaotic in here today

confusões [kõfu'zõjʃ] FPL *de* **confusão**

congelado, -a [kõʒe'ladu, a] ADJ frozen

congelador [kõʒela'do^r] M freezer, deep freeze

congelamento [kõʒela'mẽtu] M freezing; (*Econ*) freeze

congelar [kõʒe'la^r] VT to freeze; **congelar-se** VR to freeze

congênere [kõ'ʒeneri] ADJ similar

congênito, -a [kõ'ʒenitu, a] ADJ congenital

congestão [kõʒeʃ'tãw] F congestion; **congestionado, -a** [kõʒeʃtʃjo'nadu, a] ADJ (*trânsito*) congested; (*olhos*) bloodshot; (*rosto*) flushed; **congestionamento** [kõʒeʃtʃjona'mẽtu] M congestion; **um congestionamento (de tráfego)** a traffic jam

congestionar [kõʒeʃtʃjo'na^r] VT to congest; **congestionar-se** VR (*rosto*) to go red

conglomeração [kõglomera'sãw] (*pl* -**ões**) F conglomeration

conglomerado [kõglome'radu] M conglomerate

conglomerar [kõglome'ra^r] VT to heap together; **conglomerar-se** VR (*unir-se*) to join together, group together

Congo ['kõgu] M: **o ~** the Congo

congratular [kõgratu'la^r] VT: **~ alguém por** to congratulate sb on

congregação [kõgrega'sãw] (*pl* -**ões**) F (*Rel*) congregation; (*reunião*) gathering

congregar [kõgre'ga^r] VT to bring together; **congregar-se** VR to congregate

congressista [kõgre'siʃta] M/F congressman/ woman

congresso [kõ'grɛsu] M congress, conference

conhaque [ko'ɲaki] M cognac, brandy

conhecedor, a [koɲese'do^r(a)] ADJ knowing ■ M/F connoisseur, expert

conhecer [koɲe'se^r] VT to know; (*travar conhecimento com*) to meet; (*descobrir*) to discover; **conhecer-se** VR (*travar conhecimento*) to meet; (*ter conhecimento*) to know each other; **~ alguém de nome/vista** to know sb by name/sight; **quero ~ sua casa** I'd like to see your house; **você conhece Paris?** have you ever been to Paris?

conhecido, -a [koɲe'sidu, a] ADJ known; (*célebre*) well-known ■ M/F acquaintance

conhecimento [koɲesi'mẽtu] M knowledge; (*idéia*) idea; (*conhecido*) acquaintance; (*Com*) bill of lading; **conhecimentos** MPL (*informações*) knowledge *sg*; **levar ao ~ de alguém** to bring to sb's notice; **ter ~ de** to know; **tomar ~ de** to learn about; **não tomar ~ de** (*não dar atenção a*) to take no notice of; **é de ~ geral** it is common knowledge; **~ aéreo** air waybill

cônico, -a ['koniku, a] ADJ conical

conivência [koni'vẽsja] F connivance

conivente [koni'vẽtʃi] ADJ conniving; **ser ~ em** to connive in

conjetura [kõʒe'tura] (PT -**ct**-) F conjecture, supposition; **fazer ~ (sobre)** to guess (at)

conjeturar [kõʒetu'ra^r] (PT -**ct**-) VT to guess at ■ VI to conjecture

conjugação [kõʒuga'sãw] (*pl* -**ões**) F conjugation

conjugado [kõʒu'gadu] M studio

conjugal [kõʒu'gaw] (*pl* -**ais**) ADJ conjugal; **vida ~** married life

conjugar [kõʒu'ga^r] VT (*verbo*) to conjugate; (*unir*) to join; **conjugar-se** VR to join together

cônjuge ['kõʒuʒi] M spouse

conjunção [kõʒũ'sãw] (*pl* -**ões**) F (*união*) union; (*Ling*) conjunction

conjuntivite [kõʒũtʃi'vitʃi] F conjunctivitis

conjuntivo [kõʒũ'tʃivu] (PT) M (*Ling*) subjunctive

conjunto, -a [kõ'ʒũtu, a] ADJ joint ■ M (*totalidade*) whole; (*coleção*) collection; (*músicos*) group; (*roupa*) outfit; **em ~** together

conjuntura [kõʒũ'tura] F situation

conluio [kõ'luju] M collusion

conosco [ko'noʃku] PRON with us

conotação [konota'sãw] (*pl* -**ões**) F connotation

conotar [kono'ta^r] VT to connote

conquanto [kõ'kwãtu] CONJ although, though

conquista [kõ'kiʃta] F conquest; (*da ciência*) achievement; **conquistador, a** [kõkiʃta'do^r(a)] ADJ conquering ■ M conqueror; (*namorador*) ladies' man

conquistar [kõkiʃ'ta^r] VT (*subjugar*) to conquer; (*alcançar*) to achieve; (*ganhar*) to win, gain; (*pessoa*) to win over

consagração [kõsagra'sãw] (*pl* -**ões**) F (*Rel*) consecration; (*aclamação*) acclaim; (*exaltação*) praise; (*dedicação*) dedication; (*de uma expressão*) establishment

consagrado, -a [kõsa'gradu, a] ADJ (*estabelecido*) established

consagrar [kõsa'gra^r] VT (*Rel*) to consecrate; (*aclamar*) to acclaim; (*dedicar*) to dedicate; (*tempo*) to devote; (*expressão*) to establish; (*exaltar*) to glorify; **consagrar-se** VR: **consagrar-se a** to devote o.s. to

consangüíneo, -a [kõsã'gwinju, a] ADJ related by blood ■ M/F blood relation

consciência [kõ'sjẽsja] F (*moral*) conscience; (*percepção*) awareness; (*senso de responsabilidade*) conscientiousness; **estar com a ~ limpa/pesada** to have a clear/guilty conscience; **ter ~ de** to be conscious of

consciencioso, -a [kõsjẽ'sjozu, ɔza] ADJ conscientious

consciente [kõ'sjẽtʃi] ADJ conscious

conscientizar [kõsjẽtʃi'za^r] VT: **~ alguém** (*politicamente*) to raise sb's awareness; **conscientizar-se** VR to become more aware; **~ se de** to be aware of; **~ alguém de algo** to make sb aware of sth

cônscio, -a ['kõsju, a] ADJ aware

conscrição [kõʃkri'sãw] F conscription

consecução [kõseku'sãw] F attainment

consecutivo, -a [kõseku'tʃivu, a] ADJ consecutive

conseguinte [kõse'gĩtʃi] ADJ: **por ~** consequently

conseguir [kõse'gi^r] VT (*obter*) to get, obtain; **~ fazer** to manage to do, succeed in doing; **não consigo abrir a porta** I can't open the door

conselheiro, -a [kõse'ʎejru, a] M/F (*que aconselha*) counsellor (*Brit*), counselor (*US*), adviser; (*Pol*) councillor

conselho [kõ'seʎu] M piece of advice; (*corporação*) council; **conselhos** MPL (*advertência*) advice *sg*; **~ de guerra** court martial; **C~ de ministros** (*Pol*) Cabinet; **C~ de Diretoria** board of directors

consenso [kõ'sẽsu] M consensus, agreement

consensual [kõsẽ'swaw] (*pl* -ais) ADJ agreed

consentimento [kõsẽtʃi'mẽtu] M consent, permission

consentir [kõsẽ'tʃi^r] VT (*admitir*) to allow, permit; (*aprovar*) to agree to ■ VI: **~ em** to agree to

conseqüência [kõse'kwẽsja] F consequence; **por ~** consequently; **em ~ de** as a consequence of

conseqüente [kõse'kwẽtʃi] ADJ consequent; (*coerente*) consistent

consertar [kõsex'ta^r] VT to mend, repair; (*remediar*) to put right; **conserto** [kõ'sextu] M repair

conserva [kõ'sexva] F pickle; **em ~** pickled; **fábrica de ~s** cannery

conservação [kõsexva'sãw] F conservation; (*de vida, alimentos*) preservation

conservacionista [kõsexvasjo'niʃta] ADJ, M/F conservationist

conservado, -a [kõsex'vadu, a] ADJ (*pessoa*) well-preserved

conservador, a [kõsexva'do^r(a)] ADJ conservative ■ M/F (*Pol*) conservative

conservadorismo [kõsexvado'riʒmu] M conservatism

conservante [kõsex'vãtʃi] M preservative

conservar [kõsex'va^r] VT (*preservar*) to preserve, maintain; (*reter, manter*) to keep, retain; **conservar-se** VR to keep; "**conserve-se à direita**" "keep right"

conservatório [kõsexva'tɔrju] M conservatory

consideração [kõsidera'sãw] (*pl* -ões) F consideration; (*estima*) respect, esteem; (*reflexão*) thought; **levar em ~** to take into account

considerado, -a [kõside'radu, a] ADJ respected, well thought of

considerar [kõside'ra^r] VT to consider; (*prezar*) to respect ■ VI to consider; **considerar-se** VR to consider o.s.

considerável [kõside'ravew] (*pl* -eis) ADJ considerable

consignação [kõsigna'sãw] (*pl* -ões) F consignment; (*registro*) recording; (*de verbas*) assignment

consignar [kõsig'na^r] VT (*mercadorias*) to send, dispatch; (*registrar*) to record; (*verba etc*) to assign

consigo [kõ'sigu] PRON (*m*) with him; (*f*) with her; (*pl*) with them; (*com você*) with you

consigo *etc* VB V **conseguir**

consinto *etc* [kõ'sĩtu] VB V **consentir**

consistência [kõsiʃ'tẽsja] F consistency

consistente [kõsiʃ'tẽtʃi] ADJ (*sólido*) solid; (*espesso*) thick

consistir [kõsiʃ'tʃi^r] VI: **~ em** to be made up of, consist of

consoante [kõso'ãtʃi] F consonant ■ PREP according to ■ CONJ as; **~ prometera** as he had promised

consolação [kõsola'sãw] (*pl* -ões) F consolation

consolador, a [kõsola'do^r(a)] ADJ consoling

consolar [kõso'la^r] VT to console; **consolar-se** VR to console o.s.

console [kõ'sɔli] F (*Comput*) console

consolidar [kõsoli'da^r] VT to consolidate; (*fratura*) to knit ■ VI to become solid; to knit together

consolo [kõ'solu] M consolation

consome *etc* [kõ'somi] VB V **consumir**

consomê [kõso'me] M consommé

consonância [kõso'nãsja] F (*harmonia*) harmony; (*concordância*) agreement

consorciar [kõsox'sja^r] VT to join; (*combinar*) to combine ■ VI: **~ a** to unite with

consórcio [kõ'sɔxsju] M (*união*) partnership; (*Com*) consortium

consorte [kõ'sɔxtʃi] M/F consort

conspícuo, -a [kõʃ'pikwu, a] ADJ conspicuous

conspiração [kõʃpira'sãw] (*pl* -ões) F plot, conspiracy

conspirador, a [kõʃpira'do^r(a)] M/F plotter,

conspirator

conspirar [kõʃpi'ra^r] VT to plot ∎ VI to plot, conspire

constância [kõʃ'tãsja] F constancy; (estabilidade) steadiness

constante [kõʃ'tãtʃi] ADJ constant; (estável) steady ∎ F constant

constar [kõʃ'ta^r] VI to be in; **consta que** it says that; ~ **de** to consist of; **não me constava que** ... I was not aware that ...; **ao que me consta** as far as I know

constatação [kõʃtata'sãw] (pl -ões) F observation

constatar [kõʃta'ta^r] VT (estabelecer) to establish; (notar) to notice; (evidenciar) to show up; (óbito) to certify; **pudemos ~ que** we could see that

constelação [kõʃtela'sãw] (pl -ões) F constellation; (grupo) cluster

constelado, -a [kõʃte'ladu, a] ADJ (estrelado) starry

consternação [kõʃtexna'sãw] F (desalento) depression; (desolação) distress

consternado, -a [kõʃtex'nadu, a] ADJ (desalentado) depressed; (desolado) distressed

consternar [kõʃtex'na^r] VT (desolar) to distress; (desalentar) to depress; **consternar-se** VR to be distressed; to be depressed

constipação [kõʃtʃipa'sãw] (pl -ões) F constipation; (PT) cold

constipado, -a [kõʃtʃi'padu, a] ADJ: **estar ~** to be constipated; (PT) to have a cold

constipar-se [kõʃtʃi'paxsi] (PT) VR to catch a cold

constitucional [kõʃtʃitusjo'naw] (pl -ais) ADJ constitutional

constituição [kõʃtʃitwi'sãw] (pl -ões) F constitution

constituinte [kõʃtʃi'twĩtʃi] ADJ constituent ∎ M/F (deputado) member ∎ F: **a C~** the Constituent Assembly

constituir [kõʃtʃi'twi^r] VT (representar) to constitute; (formar) to form; (estabelecer) to establish, set up; (nomear) to appoint; **constituir-se** VR: **constituir-se em** to set o.s. up as; (representar) to constitute

constrangedor, a [kõʃtrãʒe'do^r(a)] ADJ restricting; (que acanha) embarrassing

constranger [kõʃtrã'ʒe^r] VT to constrain; (acanhar) to embarrass; **constranger-se** VR (acanhar-se) to feel embarrassed

constrangimento [kõʃtrãʒi'mẽtu] M constraint; (acanhamento) embarrassment

constranjo etc [kõʃ'trãʒu] VB V **constranger**

construção [kõʃtru'sãw] (pl -ões) F building, construction

construir [kõʃ'trwi^r] VT to build, construct

construtivo, -a [kõʃtru'tʃivu, a] ADJ constructive

construtor, a [kõʃtru'to^r(a)] ADJ building atr, construction atr ∎ M/F builder ∎ F building contractor

cônsul ['kõsuw] (pl -es) M consul; **consulado**

[kõsu'ladu] M consulate

consulesa [kõsu'leza] F (woman) consul; (esposa) consul's wife

consulta [kõ'suwta] F consultation; **livro de ~** reference book; **horário de ~** surgery hours pl (Brit), office hours pl (US); **consultar** [kõsuw'ta^r] VT to consult; **consultar alguém sobre** to ask sb's opinion about

consultivo, -a [kõsuw'tʃivu, a] ADJ advisory

consultor, a [kõsuw'to^r(a)] M/F adviser, consultant

consultoria [kõsuwto'ria] F consultancy

consultório [kõsuw'tɔrju] M surgery

consumação [kõsuma'sãw] (pl -ões) F consummation; (em restaurante etc) minimum order

consumado, -a [kõsu'madu, a] ADJ consummate; v tb **fato**

consumar [kõsu'ma^r] VT to consummate; **consumar-se** VR to be consummated

consumidor, a [kõsumi'do^r(a)] ADJ consumer atr ∎ M/F consumer

consumir [kõsu'mi^r] VT to consume; (devorar) to eat away; (gastar) to use up; **consumir-se** VR to waste away

consumismo [kõsu'miʒmu] M consumerism

consumista [kõsu'miʃta] ADJ, M/F consumerist

consumo [kõ'sumu] M consumption; **artigos de ~** consumer goods

conta ['kõta] F (cálculo) count; (em restaurante) bill; (fatura) invoice; (bancária) account; (de colar) bead; (responsabilidade) responsibility; **contas** FPL (Com) accounts; **à ~ de** to the account of; **ajustar ~s com** (fig) to settle an account with; **fazer de ~ que** to pretend that; **levar ou ter em ~** to take into account; **por ~ própria** of one's own accord; **trabalhar por ~ própria** to work for oneself; **prestar ~s de** to account for; **não é da sua ~** it's none of your business; **tomar ~ de** (criança etc) to look after; (encarregar-se de) to take care of; (dominar) to take hold of; **afinal de ~s** after all; **dar-se ~ de** to realize; (notar) to notice; **isso fica por sua ~** this is for you to deal with; **dar ~ de** (notar) to notice; (prestar contas de) to account for; (de tarefa) to handle, cope with; **ficar por ~** (furioso) to get mad; **ser a ~** to be just enough; **dar ~ do recado** (col) to deliver the goods; **~ bancária** bank account; **~ conjunta** joint account; **~ corrente** current account; **~ de e-mail** ou **de correio eletrônico** e-mail account

contábil [kõ'tabiw] (pl -eis) ADJ accounting atr

contabilidade [kõtabili'dadʒi] F book-keeping, accountancy; (departamento) accounts department; **~ de custos** cost accounting

contabilista [kõtabi'liʃta] (PT) M/F accountant

contabilizar [kõtabili'za^r] VT to write up, book; **valor contabilizado** (Com) book value

contacto etc [kõ'tatu] (PT) = **contato** etc

contado, -a [kõ'tadu, a] ADJ: **dinheiro de ~** (PT) cash payment; **estamos com dinheiro ~ para só três meses** we've got just enough money for three months

contador, a [kõta'do^r(a)] M/F (Com) accountant ■ M (Tec: medidor) meter; ~ **de estórias** story-teller

contadoria [kõtado'ria] F audit department

contagem [kõ'taʒẽ] (pl -ns) F (de números) counting; (escore) score; **abrir a** ~ (Futebol) to open the scoring

contagiante [kõta'ʒjãtʃi] ADJ (alegria) contagious

contagiar [kõta'ʒja^r] VT to infect; **contagiar-se** VR to become infected

contágio [kõ'taʒju] M infection

contagioso, -a [kõta'ʒjozu, ɔza] ADJ (doença) contagious

conta-gotas M INV dropper

contaminação [kõtamina'sãw] F contamination

contaminar [kõtami'na^r] VT to contaminate

contanto que [kõ'tãtu ki] CONJ provided that

conta-quilómetros (PT) M INV speedometer

contar [kõ'ta^r] VT to count; (narrar) to tell; (pretender) to intend; (imaginar) to think ■ VI to count; ~ **com** to count on; (esperar) to expect; **ela contava que a fossem ajudar** she expected them to help her; ~ **em fazer** to count on doing, expect to do

contatar [kõta'ta^r] VT to contact; **contato** [kõ'tatu] M contact; **entrar em contato com** to get in touch with, contact

contêiner [kõ'tejne^r] M container

contemplação [kõtẽpla'sãw] F contemplation

contemplar [kõtẽ'pla^r] VT to contemplate; (olhar) to gaze at ■ VI to meditate; **contemplar-se** VR to look at o.s.

contemplativo, -a [kõtẽpla'tʃivu, a] ADJ (pessoa) thoughtful; (vida, literatura) contemplative

contemporâneo, -a [kõtẽpo'ranju, a] ADJ, M/F contemporary

contemporizar [kõtẽpori'za^r] VT (situação) to ease ■ VI to ease the situation

contenção [kõtẽ'sãw] (pl -ões) F restriction, containment; ~ **de despesas** cutbacks pl

contencioso, -a [kõtẽ'sjozu, ɔza] ADJ contentious

contenções [kõtẽ'sõjʃ] FPL de **contenção**

contenda [kõ'tẽda] F quarrel, dispute

contenho etc [kõ'teɲu] VB v **conter**

contentamento [kõtẽta'mẽtu] M (felicidade) happiness; (satisfação) contentment

contentar [kõtẽ'ta^r] VT (dar prazer) to please; (dar satisfação) to satisfy; **contentar-se** VR to be satisfied

contente [kõ'tẽtʃi] ADJ (alegre) happy; (satisfeito) pleased, satisfied

contento [kõ'tẽtu] M: **a** ~ satisfactorily

conter [kõ'te^r] (irreg) VT (encerrar) to contain, hold; (refrear) to restrain, hold back; (gastos) to curb; **conter-se** VR to restrain o.s.

conterrâneo, -a [kõte'xanju, a] ADJ fellow ■ M/F compatriot, fellow countryman/woman

contestação [kõteʃta'sãw] (pl -ões) F challenge; (negação) denial

contestar [kõteʃ'ta^r] VT (contrariar) to dispute, contest, question; (impugnar) to challenge

contestável [kõteʃ'tavew] (pl -eis) ADJ questionable

conteúdo [kõte'udu] M contents pl; (de um texto) content

conteve etc [kõ'tevi] VB v **conter**

contexto [kõ'teʃtu] M context

contido, -a [kõ'tʃidu, a] PP de **conter** ■ ADJ contained; (raiva) repressed

contigo [kõ'tʃigu] PRON with you

contigüidade [kõtʃigwi'dadʒi] F proximity

contíguo, -a [kõ'tʃigwu, a] ADJ: ~ **a** next to

continência [kõtʃi'nẽsja] F (militar) salute; **fazer** ~ **a** to salute

continental [kõtʃinẽ'taw] (pl -ais) ADJ continental

continente [kõtʃi'nẽtʃi] M continent

contingência [kõtʃi'ʒẽsja] F contingency

contingente [kõtʃĩ'ʒẽtʃi] ADJ uncertain ■ M (Mil) contingent; (Com) contingency, reserve

continuação [kõtʃinwa'sãw] F continuation

continuar [kõtʃi'nwa^r] VT to continue ■ VI to continue, go on; ~ **falando** ou **a falar** to go on talking, continue talking ou to talk; **continue!** carry on!; **ela continua doente** she is still sick

continuidade [kõtʃinwi'dadʒi] F continuity

contínuo, -a [kõ'tʃinwu, a] ADJ (persistente) continual; (sem interrupção) continuous ■ M office boy

contista [kõ'tʃiʃta] M/F story writer

contive etc [kõ'tʃivi] VB v **conter**

contiver etc [kõtʃi've^r] VB v **conter**

conto ['kõtu] M story, tale; (PT: dinheiro) 1000 escudos; **de fadas** fairy tale

conto-do-vigário (pl contos-do-vigário) M confidence trick

contorção [kõtox'sãw] (pl -ões) F contortion; (dos músculos) twitch

contorcer [kõtox'se^r] VT to twist; **contorcer-se** VR to writhe

contorções [kõtox'sõjʃ] FPL de **contorção**

contornar [kõtox'na^r] VT (rodear) to go round; (ladear) to skirt; (fig: problema) to get round

contornável [kõtox'navew] (pl -eis) ADJ avoidable

contorno [kõ'toxnu] M outline; (da terra) contour; (do rosto) profile

contra ['kõtra] PREP against ■ M: **os prós e os** ~**s** the pros and cons; **dar o** ~ **(a)** to be opposed (to); **ser do** ~ to be against it

contra-almirante M rear-admiral

contra-argumento M counter-argument

contra-atacar VT to counterattack

contra-ataque M counterattack

NB: *European Portuguese adds the following consonants to certain words:* **b** (sú(b)dito, su(b)til); **c** (a(c)ção, a(c)cionista, a(c)to(to)); **m** (inde(m)ne); **p** (ado(p)çã, ado(p)tar); *for further details see p. xiii.*

contrabaixo [kõtra'bajʃu] M double bass

contrabalançar [kõtrabalã'saʳ] VT to counterbalance; (*compensar*) to compensate

contrabandear [kõtrabã'dʒjaʳ] VT, VI to smuggle; **contrabandista** [kõtrabã'dʒiʃta] M/F smuggler; **contrabando** [kõtra'bãdu] M smuggling; (*artigos*) contraband

contrabarra [kõtra'baxa] F (*Comput*) backslash

contração [kõtra'sãw] (*pl* -ões) F contraction

contracapa [kõtra'kapa] F inside cover

contracenar [kõtrase'naʳ] VI: ~ **com** to act alongside, star with

contraceptivo, -a [kõtrasep'tʃivu, a] ADJ contraceptive ■ M contraceptive

contracheque [kõtra'ʃɛki] M pay slip (*Brit*), check stub (*US*)

contrações [kõtra'sõjʃ] FPL *de* **contração**

contradição [kõtradʒi'sãw] (*pl* -ões) F contradiction

contradigo *etc* [kõtra'dʒigu] VB *v* **contradizer**

contradisse *etc* [kõtra'dʒisi] VB *v* **contradizer**

contradito [kõtra'dʒitu] PP *de* **contradizer**

contraditório, -a [kõtradʒi'tɔrju, a] ADJ contradictory

contradizer [kõtradʒi'zeʳ] (*irreg*) VT to contradict; **contradizer-se** VR (*pessoa*) to contradict o.s.; (*atitudes*) to be contradictory

contrafazer [kõtrafa'zeʳ] (*irreg*) VT to forge, counterfeit; (*pessoa*) to imitate, take off

contrafeito, -a [kõtra'fejtu, a] PP *de* **contrafazer** ■ ADJ constrained

contrafez *etc* [kõtra'feʒ] VB *v* **contrafazer**

contrafilé [kõtrafi'lɛ] M rump steak

contrafiz *etc* [kõtra'fiʒ] VB *v* **contrafazer**

contrafizer *etc* [kõtrafi'zeʳ] VB *v* **contrafazer**

contragosto [kõtra'goʃtu] M: **a** ~ against one's will, unwillingly

contraído, -a [kõtra'idu, a] ADJ (*tímido*) timid, shy

contra-indicação (*pl* -ões) F contra-indication

contra-indicado, -a ADJ contra-indicated

contrair [kõtra'iʳ] VT to contract; (*doença*) to contract, catch; (*hábito*) to form; **contrair-se** VR to contract; ~ **matrimônio** to get married

contralto [kõ'trawtu] M contralto

contramão [kõtra'mãw] ADJ one-way ■ F: **na** ~ the wrong way down a one-way street

contramestre, -tra [kõtra'mɛʃtri] M/F (*em fábrica*) supervisor ■ M (*Náut*) boatswain

Contran [kõ'trã] (BR) ABR M = **Conselho Nacional de Trânsito**

contra-ofensiva F counteroffensive

contra-oferta F counteroffer

contraparente, -a [kõtrapa'rẽtʃi, ta] M/F distant relative; (*afim*) in-law

contrapartida [kõtrapax'tʃida] F (*Com*) counterentry; (*fig*) compensation; **em** ~ **a** in the face of

contrapesar [kõtrape'zaʳ] VT to counterbalance; (*fig*) to offset

contrapeso [kõtra'pezu] M counterbalance; (*Tec*) counterweight; (*Com*) makeweight

contrapor [kõtra'poʳ] (*irreg*) VT (*comparar*) to compare; **contrapor-se** VR: **contrapor-se a** to be in opposition to; (*atitude*) to go against; ~ **algo a algo** to set sth against sth

contraproducente [kõtraprodu'sẽtʃi] ADJ counterproductive, self-defeating

contrapunha *etc* [kõtra'puɲa] VB *v* **contrapor**

contrapus *etc* [kõtra'puʃ] VB *v* **contrapor**

contrapuser *etc* [kõtrapu'zeʳ] VB *v* **contrapor**

contra-regra (*pl* -s) M/F stage manager

contra-revolução (*pl* -ões) F counter-revolution

contrariar [kõtra'rjaʳ] VT (*contradizer*) to contradict; (*aborrecer*) to annoy

contrariedade [kõtrarje'dadʒi] F (*aborrecimento*) annoyance, vexation

contrário, -a [kõ'trarju, a] ADJ (*oposto*) opposite; (*pessoa*) opposed; (*desfavorável*) unfavourable (*Brit*), unfavorable (*US*), adverse ■ M opposite; **do** ~ otherwise; **pelo** *ou* **ao** ~ on the contrary; **ao** ~ (*do outro lado*) the other way round; **muito pelo** ~ on the contrary, quite the opposite

contra-senso M nonsense

contrastante [kõtraʃ'tãtʃi] ADJ contrasting

contrastar [kõtraʃ'taʳ] VT to contrast; **contraste** [kõ'traʃtʃi] M contrast

contratação [kõtrata'sãw] F (*de pessoal*) employment

contratante [kõtra'tãtʃi] ADJ contracting ■ M/F contractor

contratar [kõtra'taʳ] VT (*serviços*) to contract; (*pessoal*) to employ, take on

contratempo [kõtra'tẽpu] M (*imprevisto*) setback; (*aborrecimento*) upset; (*dificuldade*) difficulty

contrato [kõ'tratu] M contract; (*acordo*) agreement

contratual [kõtra'twaw] (*pl* -ais) ADJ contractual

contravapor [kõtrava'poʳ] (*col*) M rebuff

contravenção [kõtravẽ'sãw] (*pl* -ões) F contravention, violation

contraventor, a [kõtravẽ'to'(a)] M/F offender

contribuição [kõtribwi'sãw] (*pl* -ões) F contribution; (*imposto*) tax

contribuinte [kõtri'bwĩtʃi] M/F contributor; (*que paga impostos*) taxpayer

contribuir [kõtri'bwiʳ] VT to contribute ■ VI to contribute; (*pagar impostos*) to pay taxes

contrição [kõtri'sãw] F contrition

contrito, -a [kõ'tritu, a] ADJ contrite

controlar [kõtro'laʳ] VT to control; **controlar-se** VR to control o.s.

controlável [kõtro'lavew] (*pl* -eis) ADJ controllable

controle [kõ'troli] M control; ~ **remoto** remote control; ~ **de crédito** (*Com*) credit control; ~ **de qualidade** (*Com*) quality control

controvérsia [kõtro'vɛxsja] F controversy; (*discussão*) debate; **controverso, -a** [kõtro'vɛxsu, a] ADJ controversial

contudo [kõ'tudu] CONJ nevertheless, however

contumácia [kõtu'masja] F obstinacy; (Jur) contempt of court

contumaz [kõtu'majʒ] ADJ obstinate, stubborn ■ M/F (Jur) defaulter

contundente [kõtũ'dẽtʃi] ADJ bruising; (argumento) cutting; instrumento ~ blunt instrument

contundir [kõtũ'dʒiʳ] VT to bruise; contundir-se VR to bruise o.s.

conturbação [kõtuxba'sãw] (pl -ões) F disturbance, unrest; (motim) riot

conturbado, -a [kõtux'badu, a] ADJ disturbed

conturbar [kõtux'baʳ] VT to disturb; (amotinar) to stir up

contusão [kõtu'zãw] (pl -ões) F bruise

contuso, -a [kõ'tuzu, a] ADJ bruised

contusões [kõtu'zõjʃ] FPL de contusão

convalescença [kõvale'sẽsa] F convalescence

convalescer [kõvale'seʳ] VI to convalesce

conveio etc [kõ'veju] VB v convir

convenção [kõvẽ'sãw] (pl -ões) F convention; (acordo) agreement

convencer [kõvẽ'seʳ] VT to convince; (persuadir) to persuade; convencer-se VR: convencer-se de to be convinced about; convencido, -a [kõvẽ'sidu, a] ADJ (convicto) convinced; (col: imodesto) conceited, smug

convencimento [kõvẽsi'mẽtu] M (convicção) conviction; (col: imodéstia) conceit, smugness

convencional [kõvẽsjo'naw] (pl -ais) ADJ conventional

convenções [kõvẽ'sõjʃ] FPL de convenção

convenha etc [kõ'veɲa] VB v convir

convencionar [kõvẽsjo'naʳ] VT to agree on; convencionar-se VR: convencionar-se em to agree to

conveniência [kõve'njẽsja] F convenience

conveniente [kõve'njẽtʃi] ADJ convenient, suitable; (vantajoso) advantageous

convênio [kõ'venju] M (reunião) convention; (acordo) agreement

convento [kõ'vẽtu] M convent

convergir [kõvex'ʒiʳ] VI to converge

conversa [kõ'vexsa] F conversation; (promessa falsa) hot air; ir na ~ de alguém (col) to be taken in by sb; ~ vai, ~ vem in the course of conversation; ele não tem muita ~ he hasn't got a lot to say for himself

conversação [kõvexsa'sãw] (pl -ões) F (ato) conversation

conversadeira [kõvexsa'dejra] F de conversador

conversado, -a [kõvex'sadu, a] ADJ (assunto) talked about; (pessoa) talkative, chatty; estamos ~s we've said all we had to say

conversador, -deira [kõvexsa'doʳ, 'dejra] ADJ talkative, chatty

conversa-fiada (pl conversas-fiadas) M/F: ser um ~ to be all talk

conversão [kõvex'sãw] (pl -ões) F conversion

conversar [kõvex'saʳ] VI to talk, to chat; (Internet) to chat

conversibilidade [kõvexsibili'dadʒi] F convertibility

conversível [kõvex'sivew] (pl -eis) ADJ convertible ■ M (Auto) convertible

conversões [kõvex'sõjʃ] FPL de conversão

converter [kõvex'teʳ] VT to convert; converter-se VR to be converted

convertido, -a [kõvex'tʃidu, a] ADJ converted ■ M/F convert

convés [kõ'vɛʃ] (pl -eses) M (Náut) deck

convexo, -a [kõ'veksu, a] ADJ convex

convicção [kõvik'sãw] (pl -ões) F conviction; (certeza) certainty

convicto, -a [kõ'viktu, a] ADJ (convencido) convinced; (réu) convicted; (patriota etc) staunch

convidado, -a [kõvi'dadu, a] ADJ invited ■ M/F guest

convidar [kõvi'daʳ] VT to invite; convidar-se VR to invite o.s.

convidativo, -a [kõvida'tʃivu, a] ADJ inviting

convier etc [kõ'vjeʳ] VB v convir

convincente [kõvĩ'sẽtʃi] ADJ convincing

convir [kõ'viʳ] (irreg) VI (ser conveniente) to suit, be convenient; (ficar bem) to be appropriate; (concordar) to agree; convém fazer isso o mais rápido possível we must do this as soon as possible; você há de ~ que ... you must agree that ....

convirjo etc [kõ'vixʒu] VB v convergir

convite [kõ'vitʃi] M invitation

conviva [kõ'viva] M/F guest

convivência [kõvi'vẽsja] F living together; (familiaridade) familiarity, intimacy

conviver [kõvi'veʳ] VI: ~ com (viver em comum) to live with; (ter familiaridade) to get on with; (familiaridade) familiarity

convívio [kõ'vivju] M (viver em comum) living together; (familiaridade) familiarity

convocar [kõvo'kaʳ] VT to summon, call upon; (reunião, eleições) to call; (para o serviço militar) to call up

convosco [kõ'voʃku] ADV with you

convulsão [kõvuw'sãw] (pl -ões) F convulsion; (fig) upheaval

convulsionar [kõvuwsjo'naʳ] VT (abalar) to shake; (excitar) to stir up

convulsivo, -a [kõvuw'sivu, a] ADJ convulsive

convulsões [kõvuw'sõjʃ] FPL de convulsão

cooper ['kupeʳ] M jogging, running; fazer ~ to go jogging ou running

cooperação [koopera'sãw] F cooperation

cooperante [koope'rãtʃi] ADJ cooperative, helpful

cooperar [koope'raʳ] VI to cooperate

cooperativa [koopera'tʃiva] F (Com) cooperative

cooperativo, -a [koopera'tʃivu, a] ADJ cooperative

NB: European Portuguese adds the following consonants to certain words: b (sú(b)dito, su(b)til); c (a(c)ção, a(c)cionista, a(c)to); m (inde(m)ne); p (ado(p)ção, ado(p)tar); for further details see p. xiii.

coordenação[kooxdena'sãw] F co-ordination
coordenada[kooxde'nada] F coordinate
coordenar[kooxde'na^r] VT to co-ordinate
copa['kɔpa] F *(de árvore)* top; *(dum chapéu)* crown; *(compartimento)* pantry; *(torneio)* cup; **copas** FPL *(Cartas)* hearts
copeira[ko'pejra] F kitchen maid
Copenhague[kope'ɲagi] N Copenhagen
cópia['kɔpja] F copy; **tirar ~ de** to copy;
copiadora[kopja'dora] F *(máquina)* duplicating machine
copiar[ko'pja^r] VT to copy
copidesque[kopi'dɛʃki] M copy editing ■ M/F copy editor
co-piloto[kopi'lotu] M co-pilot
copioso, -a[ko'pjozu, ɔza] ADJ abundant, numerous; *(refeição)* large; *(provas)* ample
copirraite[kopi'xajtʃi] M copyright
copo['kɔpu] M glass; **ser um bom ~** *(col)* to be a good drinker
copyright[kopi'xajtʃi] M = **copirraite**
coque['kɔki] M *(penteado)* bun
coqueiro[ko'kejru] M *(Bot)* coconut palm
coqueluche[koke'luʃi] F *(Med)* whooping cough; *(mania)* rage
coquete[ko'kɛtʃi] ADJ coquettish
coquetel[koke'tɛw] *(pl -éis)* M cocktail; *(festa)* cocktail party
cor[kɔ^r] M: **de ~** by heart
cor[kɔ^r] F colour *(Brit)*, color *(US)*; **de ~** colo(u)red
coração[kora'sãw] *(pl -ões)* M heart; **de bom ~** kind-hearted; **de todo o ~** wholeheartedly
corado, -a[ko'radu, a] ADJ ruddy
coragem[ko'raʒẽ] F courage; *(atrevimento)* nerve
corais[ko'rajʃ] MPL *de* **coral**
corajoso, -a[kora'ʒozu, ɔza] ADJ courageous
coral[ko'raw] *(pl -ais)* ADJ choral ■ M *(Mús)* choir; *(Zool)* coral
corante[ko'rãtʃi] ADJ, M colouring *(Brit)*, coloring *(US)*
corar[ko'ra^r] VT *(pintar)* to paint; *(roupa)* to bleach (in the sun) ■ VI *(ruborizar-se)* to blush; *(tornar-se branco)* to bleach
corbelha[kox'bɛʎa] F basket
corcova[kox'kɔva] F hump
corcunda[kox'kũda] ADJ hunchbacked ■ F hump ■ M/F *(pessoa)* hunchback
corda['kɔxda] F *(cabo)* rope, line; *(Mús)* string; *(varal)* clothes line; *(de relógio)* spring; **dar ~ em** to wind up; **roer a ~** to go back on one's word; **~s vocais** vocal chords; **estar com toda a ~** *(pessoa)* to be really wound up; **dar ~ a alguém** *(deixar falar)* to set sb off; *(flertar)* to flirt with sb
cordão[kox'dãw] *(pl -ões)* M string, twine; *(jóia)* chain; *(no carnaval)* group; *(Elet)* lead; *(fileira)* row; **~ de sapato** shoestring
cordeiro[kox'dejru] M lamb; *(fig)* sheep
cordel[kox'dew] *(pl -éis)* M string; **literatura de ~** pamphlet literature
cor-de-rosa ADJ INV pink
cordial[kox'dʒjaw] *(pl -ais)* ADJ cordial ■ M

(bebida) cordial
cordialidade[koxdʒjali'dadʒi] F warmth, cordiality
cordilheira[koxdʒi'ʎejra] F mountain range
cordões[kox'dõjʃ] MPL *de* **cordão**
coreano, -a[ko'rjanu, a] ADJ Korean ■ M/F Korean ■ M *(Ling)* Korean
Coréia[ko'reja] F: **a ~** Korea
coreografia[korjogra'fia] F choreography
coreógrafo, -a[ko'rjɔgrafu, a] M/F choreographer
coreto[ko'retu] M bandstand; **bagunçar o ~ (de alguém)** *(col)* to spoil things (for sb)
corisco[ko'riʃku] M *(faísca)* flash
corista[ko'riʃta] M/F chorister ■ F *(Teatro)* chorus girl
coriza[ko'riza] F runny nose
corja['kɔxʒa] F *(PT: canalha)* rabble; *(bando)* gang
córnea['kɔxnja] F cornea
córner['kɔxne^r] M *(Futebol)* corner
corneta[kox'neta] F cornet; *(Mil)* bugle
corneteiro[koxne'tejru] M bugler
cornetim[koxne'tʃĩ] *(pl -ns)* M *(Mús)* French horn
coro['koru] M chorus; *(conjunto de cantores)* choir; **em ~** in chorus
coroa[ko'roa] F crown; *(de flores)* garland ■ M/F *(BR: col)* old timer
coroação[korwa'sãw] *(pl -ões)* F coronation
coroar[koro'a^r] VT to crown; *(premiar)* to reward
coronel[koro'nɛw] *(pl -éis)* M colonel; *(político)* local political boss
coronha[ko'rɔɲa] F *(de um fuzil)* butt; *(de um revólver)* handle
corpete[kox'petʃi] M bodice
corpo['kɔxpu] M body; *(aparência física)* figure; (: *de homem)* build; *(de vestido)* bodice; *(Mil)* corps *sg*; **~ e alma** *(fig)* wholeheartedly; **lutar ~ a ~** to fight hand to hand; **fazer ~ mole** to get out of it; **tirar o ~ fora** *(col)* to duck out; **~ diplomático** diplomatic corps *sg*; **~ docente** teaching staff *(Brit)*, faculty *(US)*; **~ estranho** *(Med)* foreign body
corporal[koxpo'raw] *(pl -ais)* ADJ physical
corpulência[koxpu'lẽsja] F stoutness
corpulento, -a[koxpu'lẽtu, a] ADJ stout
correção[koxe'sãw] *(PT -cç-, pl -ões)* F correction; *(exatidão)* correctness; **casa de ~** reformatory; **~ salarial/monetária** wage/ monetary correction
corre-corre[kɔxi'kɔxi] *(pl -s)* M rush
correcto, -ta[ko'xektu] *(PT)* = **correto** *etc*
corrediço, -a[koxe'dʒisu, a] ADJ sliding
corredor, a[koxe'do^r(a)] M/F runner ■ M *(passagem)* corridor, passageway; *(em avião etc)* aisle; *(cavalo)* racehorse
córrego['kɔxegu] M stream, brook
correia[ko'xeja] F strap; *(de máquina)* belt; *(para cachorro)* leash
correio[ko'xeju] M mail, post; *(local)* post office; *(carteiro)* postman *(Brit)*, mailman *(US)*; **~ aéreo** air mail; **pôr no ~** to post; **pelo ~** by post; **~**

eletrônico e-mail; **~ de voz** voice mail
correlação [kokela'sãw] (pl -ões) F correlation
correlacionar [koxelasjo'na^r] VT to correlate
correlações [kokela'sõjʃ] FPL de **correlação**
correligionário, -a [koxeliʒjo'narju, a] M/F (Pol)
fellow party member
corrente [ko'xẽtʃi] ADJ (atual) current; (águas)
running; (fluente) flowing; (comum) usual,
common ■ F current; (cadeia, jóia) chain; **~ de ar**
draught (Brit), draft (US); **correnteza** [koxẽ'teza]
F (de ar) draught (Brit), draft (US); (de rio) current
correr [ko'xe^r] VT to run; (viajar por) to travel
across; (cortina) to draw; (expulsar) to drive
out ■ VI to run; (em carro) to drive fast, speed;
(líquido) to flow, run; (o tempo) to elapse; (boato) to
go round; (atuar com rapidez) to rush; **está tudo
correndo bem** everything is going well; **as
despesas ~ão por minha conta** I will handle
the expenses; **correria** [koxe'ria] F rush
correspondência [koxeʃpõ'dẽsja] F
correspondence; **correspondente**
[koxeʃpõ'dẽtʃi] ADJ corresponding ■ M
correspondent
corresponder [koxeʃpõ'de^r] VI: **~ a** to
correspond to; (ser igual) to match (up to);
(retribuir) to reciprocate; **corresponder-se** VR:
corresponder-se com to correspond with
corretagem [koxe'taʒẽ] F brokerage
corretivo, -a [koxe'tʃivu, a] ADJ corrective ■ M
punishment
correto, -a [ko'xɛtu, a] ADJ correct; (conduta)
right; (pessoa) straight, honest
corretor, a [koxe'to^r(a)] M/F broker ■ M (para
datilografia) correction strip; **~ de fundos** ou **de
bolsa** stockbroker; **~ de imóveis** estate agent
(Brit), realtor (US)
corrida [ko'xida] F (ato de correr) running;
(certame) race; (de taxi) fare; **~ de cavalos** horse
race; **~ armamentista** arms race
corrido, -a [ko'xidu, a] ADJ (rápido) quick;
(expulso) driven out ■ ADV quickly
corrigir [koxi'ʒi^r] VT to correct; (defeito, injustiça)
to put right
corrimão [koxi'mãw] (pl -s) M handrail
corriqueiro, -a [koxi'kejru, a] ADJ common;
(problema) trivial
corroa etc [ko'xoa] VB V **corroer**
corroboração [koxobora'sãw] (pl -ões) F
confirmation
corroborar [koxobo'ra^r] VT to corroborate,
confirm
corroer [koxo'e^r] VT (metais) to corrode; (fig) to
eat away; **corroer-se** VR to corrode; to be eaten
away
corromper [koxõ'pe^r] VT to corrupt; (subornar) to
bribe; **corromper-se** VR to be corrupted
corrosão [koxo'zãw] F (de metais) corrosion; (fig)
erosion
corrosivo, -a [koxo'zivu, a] ADJ corrosive

corrupção [koxup'sãw] F corruption
corrupto, -a [ko'xuptu, a] ADJ corrupt
Córsega ['kɔxsega] F: **a ~** Corsica
cortada [kox'tada] F (Esporte) smash; **dar uma ~
em alguém** (fig) to cut sb short
cortado [kox'tadu] M (aperto) tight spot; **trazer
alguém num ~** to keep sb under one's thumb
cortadura [koxta'dura] F (corte) cut; (entre
montes) gap
cortante [kox'tãtʃi] ADJ cutting
cortar [kox'ta^r] VT to cut; (eliminar) to cut out;
(água, telefone etc) to cut off; (efeito) to stop; (Auto)
to cut up ■ VI to cut; (encurtar caminho) to take a
short cut; **cortar-se** VR to cut o.s.; **~ o cabelo**
(no cabeleireiro) to have one's hair cut; **~ a palavra
de alguém** to interrupt sb
corte^1 ['kɔxtʃi] M cut; (gume) cutting edge; (de luz)
power cut; **sem ~** (tesoura etc) blunt; **~ de cabelo**
haircut
corte^2 ['kɔxtʃi] F (de um monarca) court; (de uma
pessoa) retinue; **cortes** FPL (PT) parliament sg
cortejar [koxte'ʒa^r] VT to court
cortejo [kox'teʒu] M (procissão) procession
cortês [kox'teʃ] (pl -eses) ADJ polite
cortesão, -tesã [koxte'zãw, te'zã] (pl -s/-s) ADJ
courtly ■ M/F courtier ■ F courtesan
cortesia [koxte'zia] F politeness; (de empresa)
free offer
cortiça [kox'tʃisa] F (matéria) cork
cortiço [kox'tʃisu] M (habitação) slum tenement
cortina [kox'tʃina] F curtain; **~ de rolo** roller
blind; **~ de voile** net curtain
cortisona [koxtʃi'zɔna] F cortisone
coruja [ko'ruʒa] ADJ: **pai/mãe ~** proud father/
mother ■ F owl; **sessão ~** late show
coruscar [koruʃ'ka^r] VI to sparkle, glitter
corvo ['koxvu] M crow
cós [kɔʃ] M INV waistband; (cintura) waist
cosca ['kɔʃka] F: **fazer ~** to tickle
coser [ko'ze^r] VT, VI to sew, stitch
cosmético, -a [koʒ'metʃiku, a] ADJ cosmetic
■ M cosmetic
cósmico, -a ['kɔʒmiku, a] ADJ cosmic
cosmo ['kɔʒmu] M cosmos
cosmonauta [koʒmo'nawta] M/F cosmonaut
cosmopolita [koʒmopo'lita] ADJ cosmopolitan
cospe etc ['kɔʃpi] VB V **cuspir**
costa ['kɔʃta] F coast; **costas** FPL (dorso) back sg;
dar as ~s a to turn one's back on; **ter ~s largas**
(fig) to be thick-skinned; **ter ~s quentes** (fig) to
have powerful backing, have friends in high
places
costado [koʃ'tadu] M back; **de quatro ~s**
through and through
Costa do Marfim F: **a ~** the Ivory Coast
Costa Rica F: **a ~** Costa Rica
costarriquenho, -a [koʃtaxi'keɲu, a] ADJ, M/F
Costa Rican
costear [koʃ'tʃja^r] VT (rodear) to go round; (gado)

NB: *European Portuguese adds the following consonants to certain words:* **b** (sú(b)dito, su(b)til); **c** (a(c)ção,
a(c)cionista, a(c)to); **m** (inde(m)ne); **p** (ado(p)çã, ado(p)tar); *for further details see p. xiii.*

to round up; (*Náut*) to follow ■ vi to follow the coast
costela [koʃ'tɛla] F rib
costeleta [koʃte'leta] F chop, cutlet; **costeletas** FPL (*suíças*) side-whiskers
costumar [koʃtu'ma^r] VT (*habituar*) to accustom ■ vi: **ele costuma chegar às 6.00** he usually arrives at 6.00; **costumava dizer ...** he used to say ...
costume [koʃ'tumi] M custom, habit; (*traje*) costume; **costumes** MPL (*comportamento*) behaviour *sg* (*Brit*), behavior *sg* (*US*); (*conduta*) conduct *sg*; (*de um povo*) customs; **de ~** usual; **como de ~** as usual; **ter o ~ de fazer** to have a habit of doing
costumeiro, -a [koʃtu'mejru, a] ADJ usual, habitual
costura [koʃ'tura] F sewing, needlework; (*sutura*) seam; **sem ~** seamless; **costurar** [koʃtu'ra^r] VT, vi to sew
costureira [koʃtu'rejra] F dressmaker; (*móvel*) sewing box
cota ['kɔta] F (*quinhão*) quota, share; (*Geo*) height
cotação [kota'sãw] (*pl* -ões) F (*de preços*) list, quotation; (*Bolsa*) price; (*consideração*) esteem; **~ bancária** bank rate
cotado, -a [ko'tadu, a] ADJ (*Com: ação*) quoted; (*bem-conceituado*) well thought of; (*num concurso*) fancied
cotar [ko'ta^r] VT (*ações*) to quote; **~ algo em** to value sth at
cotejar [kote'ʒa^r] VT to compare
cotejo [ko'teʒu] M comparison
cotidiano, -a [kotʃi'dʒjanu, a] ADJ daily, everyday ■ M: **o ~** daily life
cotoco [ko'toku] M (*do corpo*) stump; (*de uma vela etc*) stub
cotonete [koto'nɛtʃi] M cotton bud
cotovelada [kotove'lada] F (*pancada*) shove; (*cutucada*) nudge
cotovelo [koto'velu] M (*Anat*) elbow; (*curva*) bend; **falar pelos ~s** to talk non-stop
coube *etc* ['kobi] VB V **caber**
couraça [ko'rasa] F (*para o peito*) breastplate; (*de navio etc*) armour-plate (*Brit*), armor-plate (*US*); (*de animal*) shell
couraçado [kora'sadu] (*PT*) M battleship
couro ['koru] M leather; (*de um animal*) hide; **~ cabeludo** scalp
couve ['kovi] F spring greens *pl*
couve-de-bruxelas (*pl* couves-de-bruxelas) F Brussels sprout
couve-flor (*pl* couves-flores) F cauliflower
couvert [ku'vɛx] M cover charge
cova ['kɔva] F (*escavação*) pit; (*caverna*) cavern; (*sepultura*) grave
covarde [ko'vaxdʒi] ADJ cowardly ■ M/F coward; **covardia** [kovax'dʒia] F cowardice
coveiro [ko'vejru] M gravedigger
covil [ko'viw] (*pl* -is) M den, lair
covinha [ko'viɲa] F dimple
covis [ko'viʃ] MPL *de* **covil**

coxa ['koʃa] F thigh
coxear [ko'ʃja^r] VI to limp, hobble
coxia [ko'ʃia] F (*passagem*) aisle, gangway
coxo, -a ['koʃu, a] ADJ lame
cozer [ko'ze^r] VT, vi to cook
cozido [ko'zidu] M stew
cozinha [ko'ziɲa] F (*compartimento*) kitchen; (*arte*) cookery; (*modo de cozinhar*) cuisine
cozinhar [kozi'ɲa^r] VT to cook; (*remanchar*) to put off ■ vi to cook
cozinheiro, -a [kozi'ɲejru, a] M/F cook
CP ABR = **Caminhos de Ferro Portugueses** ■ ABR M (BR: = *certificado de privatização*) share in state company
CPF (BR) ABR M (= *Cadastro de Pessoa Física*) identification number
CPI (BR) ABR F = **Comissão Parlamentar de Inquérito**
CPJ (BR) ABR M (= *Cadastro de Pessoa Jurídica*) register of companies
CPLP ABR F *see below*

● **CPLP**
●
● The CPLP or *Comunidade de Países de Língua*
● *Portuguesa* was set up in 1996 to establish
● economic and diplomatic links between
● all countries where the official language
● is Portuguese. The members are Brazil,
● Portugal, Angola, Mozambique, Guinea-
● Bissau, Cape Verde and São Tomé e Príncipe.
● Portuguese is spoken by around 170 million
● people around the world today.

crachá [kra'ʃa] M badge
crânio ['kranju] M skull; **ser um ~** (*col*) to be a whizz kid
craque ['kraki] M/F ace, expert ■ M (*jogador de futebol*) soccer star
crasso, -a ['krasu, a] ADJ crass
cratera [kra'tera] F crater
cravar [kra'va^r] VT (*prego etc*) to drive (in); (*pedras*) to set; (*com os olhos*) to stare at; **cravar-se** VR to penetrate
cravejar [krave'ʒa^r] VT (*com cravos*) to nail; (*pedras*) to set; **~ alguém de balas** to spray sb with bullets
cravo ['kravu] M (*flor*) carnation; (*Mús*) harpsichord; (*especiaria*) clove; (*na pele*) blackhead; (*prego*) nail
creche ['krɛʃi] F crèche
Creci [kre'si] (BR) ABR M (= *Conselho Regional dos Corretores de Imóveis*) regulatory body of estate agents
credenciais [kredẽ'sjajʃ] FPL credentials
credenciar [kredẽ'sja^r] VT to accredit; (*habilitar*) to qualify
crediário [kre'dʒjarju] M credit plan
credibilidade [kredʒibili'dadʒi] F credibility
creditar [kredʒi'ta^r] VT to guarantee; (*Com*) to credit; **~ algo a alguém** (*quantia*) to credit sb with sth; (*garantir*) to assure sb of sth; **~ alguém em** to credit sb with; **~ uma quantia numa**

conta to deposit an amount into an account
crédito ['krɛdʒitu] M credit; **a** ~ on credit; **digno de** ~ reliable
credo ['krɛdu] M creed; ~! heavens!
credor, a [kre'do^r(a)] ADJ worthy, deserving; (Com: saldo) credit atr ■ M/F creditor
credulidade [kreduli'dadʒi] F credulity
crédulo, -a ['krɛdulu, a] ADJ credulous
creio etc ['kreju] VB V **crer**
cremação [krema'sãw] (pl -ões) F cremation
cremalheira [krema'ʎejra] F ratchet
cremar [kre'ma^r] VT to cremate
crematório [krema'tɔrju] M crematorium
creme ['krɛmi] ADJ INV cream ■ M cream; (Culin: doce) custard; ~ **dental** toothpaste; ~ **de leite** single cream; **cremoso, -a** [kre'mozu, ɔza] ADJ creamy
crença ['krẽsa] F belief
crendice [krẽ'dʒisi] F superstition
crente ['krẽtʃi] ADJ believing ■ M/F believer; (protestante) Protestant; **estar** ~ **que** to think (that)
creosoto [kreo'zotu] M creosote
crepitação [krepita'sãw] F crackling
crepitante [krepi'tãtʃi] ADJ crackling
crepitar [krepi'ta^r] VI to crackle
crepom [kre'põ] ADJ: **papel** ~ crêpe paper
crepuscular [krepuʃku'la^r] ADJ twilight atr
crepúsculo [kre'puʃkulu] M dusk, twilight
crer [kre^r] VT, VI to believe; **crer-se** VR to believe o.s. to be; ~ **em** to believe in; ~ **que** to think (that); **creio que sim** I think so
crescendo [kre'sẽdu] M crescendo
crescente [kre'sẽtʃi] ADJ growing; (forma) crescent ■ M crescent
crescer [kre'se^r] VI to grow; (Culin: massa) to rise
crescido, -a [kre'sidu, a] ADJ (pessoa) grown up
crescimento [kresi'mẽtu] M growth
crespo, -a ['krɛʃpu, a] ADJ (cabelo) curly
cretinice [kretʃi'nisi] F stupidity; (ato, dito) stupid thing
cretino [kre'tʃinu] M cretin, imbecile
cria ['kria] F (animal: sg) baby animal; (: pl) young pl
criação [krja'sãw] (pl -ões) F creation; (de animais) raising, breeding; (educação) upbringing; (animais domésticos) livestock pl; **filho de** ~ adopted child
criado, -a [ˈkrjadu, a] M/F servant
criado-mudo (pl criados-mudos) M bedside table
criador, a [krja'do^r(a)] M/F creator; ~ **de gado** cattle breeder
criança ['krjãsa] ADJ childish ■ F child; **ela é muito** ~ **para entender certas coisas** she's too young to understand certain things; **criançada** [krjã'sada] F: **a criançada** the kids
criancice [krjã'sisi] F (ato, dito) childish thing; (qualidade) childishness

criar [krja^r] VT to create; (crianças) to bring up; (animais) to raise, breed; (amamentar) to suckle; (planta) to grow; **criar-se** VR: ~-**se (com)** to grow up (with); ~ **fama/coragem** to achieve notoriety/pluck up courage; ~ **caso** to make trouble
criatividade [kriatʃivi'dadʒi] F creativity
criativo, -a [kria'tʃivu, a] ADJ creative
criatura [kria'tura] F creature; (indivíduo) individual
crime ['krimi] M crime; **criminal** [krimi'naw] (pl -ais) ADJ criminal; **criminalidade** [kriminali'dadʒi] F crime; **criminoso, -a** [krimi'nozu, ɔza] ADJ, M/F criminal
crina ['krina] F mane
crioulo, -a ['krjolu, a] ADJ creole ■ M/F creole; (BR: negro) Black (person)
críquete ['krikɛtʃi] M cricket
crisálida [kri'zalida] F chrysalis
crisântemo [kri'zãtemu] M chrysanthemum
crise ['krizi] F crisis; (escassez) shortage; (Med) attack, fit; ~ **de choro** fit of hysterical crying
crisma ['kriʒma] F (Rel) confirmation
crismar [kriʒ'ma^r] VT (Rel) to confirm; **crismar-se** VR to be confirmed
crista ['kriʃta] F (de serra, onda) crest; (de galo) cock's comb; **estar na** ~ **da onda** (fig) to enjoy a prominent position
cristal [kriʃ'taw] (pl -ais) M crystal; (vidro) glass; **cristais** MPL (copos) glassware sg; **cristalino, -a** [kriʃta'linu, a] ADJ crystal-clear
cristalizar [kriʃtali'za^r] VI to crystallize
cristandade [kriʃtã'dadʒi] F Christianity
cristão, -tã [kriʃ'tãw, 'tã] (pl -s/-s) ADJ, M/F Christian
cristianismo [kriʃtʃja'niʒmu] M Christianity
Cristo ['kriʃtu] M Christ
critério [kri'tɛrju] M (norma) criterion; (juízo) discretion, judgement; **deixo isso a seu** ~ I'll leave that to your discretion; **criterioso, -a** [krite'rjozu, ɔza] ADJ thoughtful, careful
crítica ['kritʃika] F criticism; (artigo) critique; (conjunto de críticos) critics pl; v tb **crítico**
criticar [kritʃi'ka^r] VT to criticize; (um livro) to review
crítico, -a ['kritʃiku, a] ADJ critical ■ M/F critic
critiquei etc [kritʃi'kej] VB V **criticar**
crivar [kri'va^r] VT (com balas etc) to riddle; (de perguntas, de insultos) to bombard
crível ['krivew] (pl -eis) ADJ credible
crivo ['krivu] M sieve; (fig) scrutiny
crocante [kro'kãtʃi] ADJ crunchy
crochê [kro'ʃe] M crochet
crocodilo [kroko'dʒilu] M crocodile
cromo ['krɔmu] M chrome
cromossomo [kromo'sɔmu] M chromosome
crônica ['kronika] F chronicle; (coluna de jornal) newspaper column; (texto jornalístico) feature; (conto) short story

NB: European Portuguese adds the following consonants to certain words: **b** (sú(b)dito, su(b)til); **c** (a(c)ção, a(c)cionista, a(c)to); **m** (inde(m)ne); **p** (ado(p)çã, ado(p)tar); for further details see p. xiii.

crônico, -a ['kroniku, a] ADJ chronic
cronista [kro'niʃta] M/F (de jornal) columnist; (historiógrafo) chronicler; (contista) short story writer
cronologia [kronolo'ʒia] F chronology
cronológico, -a [krono'lɔʒiku, a] ADJ chronological
cronometrar [kronome'traʳ] VT to time
cronômetro [kro'nometru] M stopwatch
croquete [kro'kɛtʃi] M croquette
croqui [kro'ki] M sketch
crosta ['krɔʃta] F crust; (Med) scab
cru, a [kru, 'krua] ADJ raw; (não refinado) crude; (ignorante) not very good; (realidade) harsh, stark
crucial [kru'sjaw] (pl -ais) ADJ crucial
crucificação [krusifika'sãw] (pl -ões) F crucifixion
crucificar [krusifi'kaʳ] VT to crucify
crucifixo [krusi'fiksu] M crucifix
crudelíssimo, -a [krude'lisimu, a] ADJ SUPERL de **cruel**
cruel [kru'ɛw] (pl -éis) ADJ cruel; **crueldade** [kruew'dadʒi] F cruelty
cruento, -a [kru'ẽtu, a] ADJ bloody
crupe ['krupi] M (Med) croup
crustáceos [kruʃ'tasjuʃ] MPL crustaceans
cruz [kruʒ] F cross; (infortúnio) undoing; ~ **gamada** swastika; **C~ Vermelha** Red Cross; **estar entre a ~ e a caldeirinha** (fig) to be between the devil and the deep (Brit), be between a rock and a hard place (US)
cruzada [kru'zada] F crusade
cruzado, -a [kru'zadu, a] ADJ crossed ■ M crusader; (moeda) cruzado
cruzador [kruza'doʳ] M (navio) cruiser
cruzamento [kruza'mẽtu] M (de estradas) crossroads; (mestiçagem) cross
cruzar [kru'zaʳ] VT to cross ■ VI (Náut) to cruise; (pessoas) to pass each other by; ~ **com** to meet
cruzeiro [kru'zejru] M (cruz) (monumental) cross; (moeda) cruzeiro; (viagem de navio) cruise
CSN (BR) ABR M = **Conselho de Segurança Nacional**
CTB ABR F = **Companhia Telefônica Brasileira**
cu [ku] (col!) M arse (!); **vai tomar no cu** fuck off (!)
Cuba ['kuba] F Cuba
cubano, -a [ku'banu, a] ADJ, M/F Cuban
cúbico, -a ['kubiku, a] ADJ cubic
cubículo [ku'bikulu] M cubicle
cubismo [ku'biʒmu] M cubism
cubo ['kubu] M cube; (de roda) hub
cubro etc ['kubru] VB V **cobrir**
cuca ['kuka] (col) F head; **fundir a ~** (quebrar a cabeça) to rack one's brain; (baratinar) to boggle the mind; (perturbar) to drive crazy
cuca-fresca (pl cucas-frescas) (col) M/F cool guy/girl
cuco ['kuku] M cuckoo
cucuia [ku'kuja] F: **ir para a ~** (col) to go down the drain
cu-de-ferro (pl cus-de-ferro) (col) M/F swot

cueca ['kwɛka] (BR) F underpants pl; ~**s** (para homens) underpants pl; (: para mulheres) panties pl
cueiro [ku'ejru] M wrap
cuíca ['kwika] F kind of musical instrument
cuidado [kwi'dadu] M care; **aos ~s de** in the care of; **ter** ~ to be careful; ~! watch out!, be careful!; **tomar** ~ **(de)** to be careful (of); ~ **para não se cortar** be careful you don't cut yourself; **cuidadoso, -a** [kwida'dozu, ɔza] ADJ careful
cuidar [kwi'daʳ] VI: ~ **de** to take care of, look after; **cuidar-se** VR to look after o.s.
cujo, -a ['kuʒu, a] PRON (de quem) whose; (de que) of which
culatra [ku'latra] F (de arma) breech
culinária [kuli'narja] F cookery
culinário, -a [kuli'narju, a] ADJ culinary
culminância [kuwmi'nãsja] F culmination
culminante [kuwmi'nãtʃi] ADJ: **ponto** ~ highest point; (fig) peak
culminar [kuwmi'naʳ] VI: ~ **(com)** to culminate (in)
culote [ku'lɔtʃi] M (calça) jodhpurs pl; (gordura) flab on the thighs
culpa ['kuwpa] F fault; (Jur) guilt; **ter** ~ **de** to be to blame for; **por** ~ **de** because of; **pôr a** ~ **em** to put the blame on; **sentimento de** ~ guilty conscience
culpabilidade [kuwpabili'dadʒi] F guilt
culpado, -a [kuw'padu, a] ADJ guilty ■ M/F culprit
culpar [kuw'paʳ] VT to blame; (acusar) to accuse; **culpar-se** VR to take the blame
culpável [kuw'pavew] (pl -eis) ADJ guilty
cultivar [kuwtʃi'vaʳ] VT to cultivate; (plantas) to grow
cultivável [kuwtʃi'vavew] (pl -eis) ADJ cultivable
cultivo [kuw'tʃivu] M cultivation
culto, -a ['kuwtu, a] ADJ cultured ■ M (homenagem) worship; (religião) cult
cultura [kuw'tura] F culture; (da terra) cultivation; **cultural** [kuwtu'raw] (pl -ais) ADJ cultural
cumbuca [kũ'buka] F pot
cume ['kumi] M top, summit; (fig) climax
cúmplice ['kũplisi] M/F accomplice
cumplicidade [kũplisi'dadʒi] F complicity
cumpridor, a [kũpri'doʳ(a)] ADJ punctilious, responsible
cumprimentar [kũprimẽ'taʳ] VT (saudar) to greet; (dar parabéns) to congratulate; **cumprimentar-se** VR to greet one another
cumprimento [kũpri'mẽtu] M (realização) fulfilment; (saudação) greeting; (elogio) compliment; **cumprimentos** MPL (sudações) best wishes; ~ **de uma lei/ordem** compliance with a law/an order
cumprir [kũ'priʳ] VT (desempenhar) to carry out; (promessa) to keep; (lei) to obey; (pena) to serve ■ VI (convir) to be necessary; **cumprir-se** VR to be fulfilled; ~ **a palavra** to keep one's word; **fazer** ~ to enforce
cumulativo, -a [kumula'tʃivu, a] ADJ

cumulative

cúmulo ['kumulu] M height; **é o ~!** that's the limit!

cunha ['kuɲa] F wedge

cunhado, -a [ku'ɲadu, a] M/F brother-in-law/sister-in-law

cunhar [ku'ɲaʳ] VT (*moedas*) to mint; (*palavras*) to coin

cunho ['kuɲu] M (*marca*) hallmark; (*caráter*) nature

cupê [ku'pe] M coupé

cupim [ku'pĩ] (*pl* **-ns**) M termite

cupincha [ku'pĩʃa] M/F mate, pal

cupins [ku'pĩʃ] MPL *de* **cupim**

cupom [ku'põ] (*pl* **-ns**) M coupon

cúpula ['kupula] F (*Arq*) dome; (*de abajur*) shade; (*de partido etc*) leadership; (**reunião de**) ~ summit (meeting)

cura ['kura] F (*ato de curar*) cure; (*tratamento*) treatment; (*de carnes etc*) curing, preservation ▪ M priest

curador, a [kura'doʳ(a)] M/F (*de menores, órfãos*) guardian; (*de instituição*) trustee

curandeiro [kurã'dejru] M (*feiticeiro*) healer, medicine man; (*charlatão*) quack

curar [ku'raʳ] VT (*doença*) to cure; (*ferida*) to treat; (*carne etc*) to cure, preserve; **curar-se** VR to get well

curativo [kura'tʃivu] M dressing

curável [ku'ravew] (*pl* **-eis**) ADJ curable

curetagem [kure'taʒẽ] F curettage

curinga [ku'rĩga] M wild card

curingão [kurĩ'gãw] (*pl* **-ões**) M joker

curiosidade [kurjozi'dadʒi] F curiosity; (*objeto raro*) curio

curioso, -a [ku'rjozu, ɔza] ADJ curious ▪ M/F snooper, inquisitive person; **curiosos** MPL (*espectadores*) onlookers; **o ~ é ...** the strange thing is ....

curitibano, -a [kuritʃi'banu, a] ADJ from Curitiba ▪ M/F person from Curitiba

curral [ku'xaw] (*pl* **-ais**) M pen, enclosure

currar [ku'xaʳ] (*col*) VT to rape

currículo [ku'xikulu] M curriculum; (*curriculum*) curriculum vitae, CV

curriculum vitae [ku'xikulũ 'vite] M curriculum vitae

cursar [kux'saʳ] VT (*aulas, escola*) to attend; (*cursos*) to follow; **ele está cursando História** he's studying *ou* doing history

cursivo [kux'sivu] M (*Tip*) script

curso ['kuxsu] M course; (*direção*) direction; **em ~** (*ano etc*) current; (*processo*) in progress; (*dinheiro*) in circulation; **~ primário/secundário/superior** primary school/secondary school/degree course; **~ normal** teacher-training course

cursor [kux'soʳ] M (*Comput*) cursor

curta ['kuxta] M (*Cinema*) short

curta-metragem (*pl* **curtas-metragens**) M short film

curtição [kuxtʃi'sãw] F (*col*) fun; (*de couro*) tanning

curtido, -a [kux'tʃidu, a] ADJ (*fig*) hardened

curtir [kux'tʃiʳ] VT (*couro*) to tan; (*tornar rijo*) to toughen up; (*padecer*) to suffer, endure; (*col*) to enjoy

curto, -a ['kuxtu, a] ADJ short; (*inteligência*) limited ▪ M (*Elet*) short (circuit); **curto-circuito** (*pl* **curtos-circuitos**) M short circuit

curva ['kuxva] F curve; (*de estrada, rio*) bend; **~ fechada** hairpin bend

curvar [kux'vaʳ] VT to bend, curve; (*submeter*) to put down; **curvar-se** VR (*abaixar-se*) to stoop; **~-se a** (*submeter-se*) to submit to

curvatura [kuxva'tura] F curvature

curvo, -a ['kuxvu, a] ADJ curved; (*estrada*) winding

cuscuz [kuʃ'kuʒ] M couscous

cusparada [kuʃpa'rada] F spit; **dar uma ~** to spit

cuspe ['kuʃpi] M spit, spittle

cuspido, -a [kuʃ'pidu, a] ADJ covered in spittle; **ele é o pai ~ e escarrado** (*col*) he's the spitting image of his father

cuspir [kuʃ'piʳ] VT, VI to spit; **~ no prato em que se come** to bite the hand that feeds one

custa ['kuʃta] F: **à ~ de** at the expense of; **custas** FPL (*Jur*) costs

custar [kuʃ'taʳ] VI to cost; (*ser difícil*) to be difficult; (*demorar*) to take a long time; **~ caro** to be expensive; **~ a fazer** (*ter dificuldade*) to have trouble doing; (*demorar*) to take a long time to do; **não custa nada perguntar** there's no harm in asking

custear [kuʃ'tʃjaʳ] VT to bear the cost of

custeio [kuʃ'teju] M funding; (*relação de custos*) costing

custo ['kuʃtu] M cost; **a ~** with difficulty; **a todo ~** at all costs

custódia [kuʃ'tɔdʒja] F custody

CUT (BR) ABR F (= *Central Única de Trabalhadores*) *trade union*

cutelaria [kutela'ria] F knife-making

cutelo [ku'tɛlu] M cleaver

cutícula [ku'tʃikula] F cuticle

cútis ['kutʃiʃ] F INV (*pele*) skin; (*tez*) complexion

cutucada [kutu'kada] F nudge; (*com o dedo*) prod

cutucar [kutu'kaʳ] VT (*com o dedo*) to prod, poke; (*com o cotovelo*) to nudge

CVV (BR) ABR M (= *Centro de Valorização da Vida*) *Samaritan organization*

Cz$ ABR = **cruzado**

czar [kza'ʳ] M czar

NB: *European Portuguese adds the following consonants to certain words:* **b** (sú(b)dito, su(b)til); **c** (a(c)ção, a(c)cionista, a(c)to); **m** (inde(m)ne); **p** (ado(p)çã, ado(p)tar); *for further details see p. xiii.*

Dd

D, d [de] (*pl* **ds**) D, d ABR = **Dom; Dona;**
 (= *direito*) r; (= *deve*) d; **D de dado** D for David
 (*Brit*) *ou* dog (*US*)
d/ ABR = **dia**
da [da] = **de + a**
dá [da] VB V **dar**
DAC (BR) ABR M = **Departamento de Aviação**
 Civil
dactilografar *etc* [datilogra'fa^r] (*PT*)
 = **datilografar** *etc*
dadaísmo [dada'iʒmu] M Dadaism
dádiva ['dadʒiva] F (*donativo*) donation; (*oferta*)
 gift
dadivoso, -a [dadʒi'vozu, ɔza] ADJ generous
dado, -a ['dadu, a] ADJ given; (*sociável*) sociable
 ▪ M (*em jogo*) die; (*fato*) fact; (*Comput*) piece of
 data; **dados** MPL (*em jogo*) dice; (*fatos, Comput*)
 data *sg*; **ser ~ a algo** to be prone *ou* given to sth;
 em ~ momento at a given moment; **~ que**
 (*suposto que*) supposing that; (*uma vez que*) given
 that
daí [da'ji] ADV = **de + aí**; (*desse lugar*) from there;
 (*desse momento*) from then; (*col: num relato*) then;
 ~ a um mês a month later; **~ por** *ou* **em diante**
 from then on; **e ~?** (*col*) so what?
dali [da'li] ADV = **de + ali** from there
dália ['dalja] F dahlia
daltônico, -a [daw'toniku, a] ADJ colour-blind
 (*Brit*), color-blind (*US*)
daltonismo [dawto'niʒmu] M colour (*Brit*) *ou*
 color (*US*) blindness
dama ['dama] F lady; (*Xadrez, Cartas*) queen;
 damas FPL (*jogo*) draughts (*Brit*), checkers (*US*);
 ~ de honra bridesmaid
Damasco [da'maʃku] N Damascus
damasco [da'maʃku] M (*fruta*) apricot; (*tecido*)
 damask
danação [dana'sãw] F damnation; (*travessura*)
 mischief, naughtiness
danado, -a [da'nadu, a] ADJ (*condenado*) damned;
 (*zangado*) furious, angry; (*menino*) mischievous,
 naughty; **cão ~** mad dog; **ela está com uma**
 fome/dor danada she's really hungry/got a
 terrible pain; **uma gripe danada/um susto ~**
 a really bad case of flu/a hell of a fright; **ele é ~**
 de bom (*col*) he's really good; **ser ~ em algo** to
 be really good at sth

danar-se [dã'naxsi] VR (*enfurecer-se*) to get
 furious; **dane-se!** (*col*) damn it!; **danou-se!** (*col*)
 oh, gosh!
dança ['dãsa] F dance; **entrar na ~** to get
 involved; **dançar** [dã'sa^r] VI to dance; (*col: pessoa:*
 sair-se mal) to lose out; (: *em exame*) to fail; (: *coisa*)
 to go by the board
dançarino, -a [dãsa'rinu, a] M/F dancer
danceteria [dãsete'ria] F disco(theque)
dancing ['dãsĩŋ] M dance hall
danificar [danifi'ka^r] VT (*objeto*) to damage
daninho, -a [da'niɲu, a] ADJ harmful; (*gênio*)
 nasty
dano ['danu] M (*tb*: **danos**) damage; (*moral*)
 harm; (*a uma pessoa*) injury
danoso, -a [da'nozu, ɔza] ADJ (*a uma pessoa*)
 harmful; (*a uma coisa*) damaging
dantes ['dãtʃiʃ] ADV before, formerly
Danúbio [da'nubju] M: **o ~** the Danube
daquele [da'kɛli] = **de + aquele**; V **aquele**
daqui [da'ki] ADV = **de + aqui**; (*deste lugar*) from
 here; **~ a pouco** soon, in a little while; **~ a uma**
 semana a week from now, in a week's time; **~**
 em diante from now on
daquilo [da'kilu] = **de + aquilo**

〇   **PALAVRA CHAVE**

dar [da^r] VT **1** (*ger*) to give; (*festa*) to hold;
 (*problemas*) to cause; **dar algo a alguém** to give
 sb sth, give sth to sb; **dar de beber a alguém**
 to give sb a drink; **dar aula de francês** to teach
 French
 2 (*produzir: fruta etc*) to produce
 3 (*notícias no jornal*) to publish
 4 (*cartas*) to deal
 5 (+ *n*: *perífrase de vb*): **me dá medo/pena** it
 frightens/upsets me
 ▪ VI **1**: **dar com** (*coisa*) to find; (*pessoa*) to meet
 2: **dar em** (*bater*) to hit; (*resultar*) to lead to; (*lugar*)
 to come to
 3: **dá no mesmo** it's all the same
 4: **dar de si** (*sapatos etc*) to stretch, give
 5: **dar para** (*impess: ser possível*): **dá para trocar**
 dinheiro aqui? can I change money here?;
 vai dar para eu ir amanhã I'll be able to go
 tomorrow; **dá para você vir amanhã — não,**

amanhã não vai dar can you come tomorrow? — no, I can't
6: **dar para** (*ser suficiente*): **dar para/para fazer** to be enough for/to do; **dá para todo mundo?** is there enough for everyone?
dar-se VR **1** (*sair-se*): **dar-se bem/mal** to do well/badly
2: **dar-se (com alguém)** to be acquainted (with sb); **dar-se bem (com alguém)** to get on well (with sb)
3: **dar-se por vencido** to give up

Dardanelos [daxda'nɛluʃ] MPL: **os** ~ the Dardanelles
dardo ['daxdu] M dart; (*grande*) spear
das [daʃ] = **de** + **as**
data ['data] F date; (*época*) time; **de longa** ~ of long standing
datação [data'sãw] F dating
datar [da'ta^r] VT to date ■ VI: ~ **de** to date from
datilografar [datʃilogra'fa^r] VT to type; **datilografia** [datʃilogra'fia] F typing; **datilógrafo, -a** [datʃi'lɔgrafu, a] M/F typist (*Brit*), stenographer (*US*)
dativo, -a [da'tʃivu, a] ADJ dative ■ M dative
d.C. ABR (= *depois de Cristo*) A.D.
DDD ABR F (= *discagem direta a distância*) STD (Brit), ≈ direct dialling
DDI ABR F (= *discagem direta internacional*) IDD

O **PALAVRA CHAVE**

de [dʒi] (*de* + *o(s)/a(s)* = *do(s)/da(s)*; + *ele(s)/a(s)* = *dele(s)/a(s)*; + *esse(s)/a(s)* = *desse(s)/a(s)*; + *isso* = *disso*; + *este(s)/a(s)* = *deste(s)/a(s)*; + *isto* = *disto*; + *aquele(s)/a(s)* = *daquele(s)/a(s)*; + *aquilo* = *daquilo*) PREP **1** (*posse*) of; **a casa de João/da irmã** João's/my sister's house; **é dele** it's his; **um romance de** a novel by
2 (*origem, distância, com números*) from; **sou de São Paulo** I'm from São Paulo; **de 8 a 20** from 8 to 20; **sair do cinema** to leave the cinema; **de dois em dois** two by two, two at a time
3 (*valor descritivo*): **um copo de vinho** a glass of wine; **um homem de cabelo comprido** a man with long hair; **o infeliz do homem** (*col*) the poor man; **um bilhete de avião** an air ticket; **uma criança de três anos** a three-year-old (child); **uma máquina de costurar** a sewing machine; **aulas de inglês** English lessons; **feito de madeira** made of wood; **vestido de branco** dressed in white
4 (*modo*): **de trem/avião** by train/plane; **de lado** sideways
5 (*hora, tempo*): **às 8 da manhã** at 8 o'clock in the morning; **de dia/noite** by day/night; **de hoje a oito dias** a week from now; **de dois em dois dias** every other day
6 (*comparações*): **mais/menos de cem pessoas** more/less than a hundred people; **é o mais caro da loja** it's the most expensive in the shop; **ela é mais bonita do que sua irmã** she's prettier than her sister; **gastei mais do que pretendia** I spent more than I intended
7 (*causa*): **estou morto de calor** I'm boiling hot; **ela morreu de câncer** she died of cancer
8 (*adj* + *de* + *infin*): **fácil de entender** easy to understand

dê *etc* [de] VB *v* **dar**
deão [dʒi'ãw] (*pl* -**s**) M dean
debaixo [de'bajʃu] ADV below, underneath ■ PREP: ~ **de** under, beneath
debalde [de'bawdʒi] ADV in vain
debandada [debã'dada] F stampede; **em** ~ in confusion
debandar [debã'da^r] VT to put to flight ■ VI to disperse
debate [de'batʃi] M (*discussão*) discussion, debate; (*disputa*) argument; **debater** [deba'te^r] VT to debate; (*discutir*) to discuss; **debater-se** VR to struggle
débeis ['debejʃ] PL *de* **débil**
debelar [debe'la^r] VT to put down, suppress; (*crise*) to overcome; (*doença*) to cure
debênture [de'bēturi] F (Com) debenture
debicar [debi'ka^r] VT (*caçoar*) to make fun of
débil ['debiw] (*pl* -**eis**) ADJ (*pessoa*) weak, feeble; (*Psico*) retarded ■ M: ~ **mental** mentally handicapped person; (*col: ofensivo*) moron; **debilidade** [debili'dadʒi] F weakness; **debilidade mental** mental handicap
debilitação [debilita'sãw] F weakening
debilitante [debili'tãtʃi] ADJ debilitating
debilitar [debili'ta^r] VT to weaken; **debilitar-se** VR to become weak, weaken
debilóide [debi'lɔjdʒi] (*col*) ADJ idiotic ■ M/F idiot
debique [de'biki] M mockery, ridicule
debitar [debi'ta^r] VT to debit; ~ **a conta de alguém em $40** to debit sb's account by $40; ~ **$40 à** *ou* **na conta de alguém** to debit $40 to sb's account; **débito** ['debitu] M debit
debochado, -a [debo'ʃadu, a] ADJ (*pessoa*) sardonic; (*jeito, tom*) mocking ■ M/F sardonic person
debochar [debo'ʃa^r] VT to mock ■ VI: ~ **de** to mock
deboche [de'bɔʃi] M gibe
debruar [de'brwa^r] VT (*roupa*) to edge; (*desenho*) to adorn
debruçar [debru'sa^r] VT to bend over; **debruçar-se** VR to bend over; (*inclinar-se*) to lean over; ~-**se na janela** to lean out of the window
debrum [de'brū] M edging
debulha [de'buʎa] F (*de trigo*) threshing
debulhar [debu'ʎa^r] VT (*grão*) to thresh; (*descascar*) to shell; **debulhar-se** VR: **debulhar-**

NB: *European Portuguese adds the following consonants to certain words:* **b** (sú(b)dito, su(b)til); **c** (a(c)ção, a(c)cionista, a(c)to); **m** (inde(m)ne); **p** (ado(p)çã, ado(p)tar); *for further details see p. xiii.*

se em lágrimas to burst into tears
debutante [debu'tãtʃi] F débutante
debutar [debu'ta^r] VI to appear for the first time, make one's début
década ['dɛkada] F decade
decadência [deka'dẽsja] F decadence
decadente [deka'dẽtʃi] ADJ decadent
decair [deka'i^r] VI to decline; (restaurante etc) to go downhill; (pressão, velocidade) to drop; (planta) to wilt
decalcar [dekaw'ka^r] VT to trace; (fig) to copy
decalque [de'kawki] M tracing
decano [de'kanu] M oldest member
decantar [dekã'ta^r] VT (líquido) to decant; (purificar) to purify
decapitar [dekapi'ta^r] VT to behead, decapitate
decatlo [de'katlu] M decathlon
decência [de'sẽsja] F decency
decênio [de'senju] M decade
decente [de'sẽtʃi] ADJ decent; (apropriado) proper; (honrado) honourable (Brit), honorable (US); (trabalho) neat, presentable; **decentemente** [desẽtʃi'mẽtʃi] ADV (com decoro) decently; (apropriadamente) properly; (honradamente) honourably (Brit), honorably (US)
decepar [dese'pa^r] VT to cut off, chop off
decepção [desep'sãw] (pl -ões) F disappointment; (desilusão) disillusionment; **decepcionar** [desepsjo'na^r] VT to disappoint, let down; (desiludir) to disillusion; **decepcionar-se** VR to be disappointed; to be disillusioned; **o filme decepcionou** the film was disappointing
decepções [desep'sõjʃ] FPL de **decepção**
decerto [dʒi'sextu] ADV certainly
decidido, -a [desi'dʒidu, a] ADJ (pessoa) determined; (questão) resolved
decidir [desi'dʒi^r] VT (determinar) to decide; (solucionar) to resolve; **decidir-se** VR: **decidir-se a** to make up one's mind to; **~-se por** to decide on, go for
decíduo, -a [de'sidwu, a] ADJ (Bot) deciduous
decifrar [desi'fra^r] VT to decipher; (futuro) to foretell; (compreender) to understand
decifrável (pl -eis) ADJ decipherable
decimal [desi'maw] (pl -ais) ADJ decimal ▪ M (número) decimal
décimo, -a ['dɛsimu, a] ADJ tenth ▪ M tenth; v tb **quinto**
decisão [desi'zãw] (pl -ões) F decision; (capacidade de decidir) decisiveness, resolution; **decisivo, -a** [desi'zivu, a] ADJ (fator) decisive; (jogo) deciding
decisões [desi'zõjʃ] FPL de **decisão**
declamação [deklama'sãw] F (de poema) recitation; (pej) ranting
declamar [dekla'ma^r] VT (poemas) to recite ▪ VI (pej) to rant
declaração [deklara'sãw] (pl -ões) F declaration; (depoimento) statement; (revelação) revelation; **~ de amor** proposal; **~ de imposto de renda** income tax return; **~ juramentada** affidavit

declarado, -a [dekla'radu, a] ADJ (intenção) declared; (opinião) professed; (inimigo) sworn; (alcoólatra) self-confessed; (cristão etc) avowed
declarante [dekla'rãtʃi] M/F (Jur) witness
declarar [dekla'ra^r] VT to declare; (confessar) to confess
Dec-lei [dek-] M = **decreto-lei**
declinação [deklina'sãw] (pl -ões) F (Ling) declension
declinar [dekli'na^r] VT (recusar) to decline, refuse; (nomes) to give; (Ling) to decline ▪ VI (sol) to go down; (terreno) to slope down; **declínio** [de'klinju] M decline
declive [de'klivi] M slope, incline
decô [de'ko] ADJ INV Art-Deco
decodificador [dekodʒifika'do^r] M (Comput) decoder
decodificar [dekodʒifi'ka^r] VT to decode
decolagem [deko'laʒẽ] (pl -ns) F (Aer) take-off
decolar [deko'la^r] VI (Aer) to take off
decompor [dekõ'po^r] (irreg) VT (analisar) to analyse; (apodrecer) to rot; (rosto) to contort; **decompor-se** VR to rot, decompose
decomposição [dekõpozi'sãw] (pl -ões) F (apodrecimento) decomposition; (análise) dissection; (do rosto) contortion
decomposto, -a [dekõ'poʃtu, a] PP de **decompor**
decompunha etc [dekõ'puɲa] VB v **decompor**
decompus etc [dekõ'puʃ] VB v **decompor**
decompuser etc [dekõpu'ze^r] VB v **decompor**
decoração [dekora'sãw] F decoration; (Teatro) scenery
decorar [deko'ra^r] VT to decorate; (aprender) to learn by heart; **decorativo, -a** [dekora'tʃivu, a] ADJ decorative
decoro [de'koru] M (decência) decency; (dignidade) decorum
decoroso, -a [deko'rozu, ɔza] ADJ decent, respectable
decorrência [deko'xẽsja] F consequence, result; **em ~ de** as a result of
decorrente [deko'xẽtʃi] ADJ: **~ de** resulting from
decorrer [deko'xe^r] VI (tempo) to pass; (acontecer) to take place, happen ▪ M: **no ~ de** in the course of; **~ de** to result from
decotado, -a [deko'tadu, a] ADJ (roupa) low-cut
decote [de'kɔtʃi] M (de vestido) low neckline
decrépito, -a [de'krɛpitu, a] ADJ decrepit
decrescente [dekre'sẽtʃi] ADJ decreasing, diminishing
decrescer [dekre'se^r] VI to decrease, diminish
decréscimo [de'krɛsimu] M decrease, decline
decretação [dekreta'sãw] (pl -ões) F announcement; (de estado de sítio) declaration
decretar [dekre'ta^r] VT to decree, order; (estado de sítio) to declare; (anunciar) to announce; (determinar) to determine; **decreto** [de'krɛtu] M decree, order; **nem por decreto** not for love nor money
decreto-lei (pl decretos-leis) M act, law
decúbito [de'kubitu] M: **em ~** recumbent
decurso [de'kuxsu] M (tempo) course; **no ~ de** in

the course of, during
dedal [de'daw] (pl -**ais**) M thimble
dedão [de'dãw] (pl -**ões**) M thumb; (do pé) big toe
dedetização [dedetʃiza'sãw] F spraying with insecticide
dedetizar [dedetʃi'za'] VT to spray with insecticide
dedicação [dedʒika'sãw] F dedication; (devotamento) devotion
dedicado, -a [dedʒi'kadu, a] ADJ (tb: Comput) dedicated
dedicar [dedʒi'ka'] VT (poema) to dedicate; (tempo, atenção) to devote; **dedicar-se** VR: **dedicar-se a** to devote o.s. to; **dedicatória** [dedʒika'tɔrja] F (de obra) dedication
dedilhar [dedʒi'ʎa'] VT (Mús: no braço) to finger; (: nas cordas) to pluck
dedo ['dedu] M finger; (do pé) toe; **dois ~s (de)** a little bit (of); **escolher a ~** to handpick; **~ anular** ring finger; **~ indicador** index finger; **~ mínimo** ou **mindinho** little finger; **~ polegar** thumb
dedo-duro (pl **dedos-duros**) (col) M (criminoso) grass; (criança) sneak, tell-tale
dedões [de'dõjʃ] MPL de **dedão**
dedução [dedu'sãw] (pl -**ões**) F deduction
dedurar [dedu'ra'] (col) VT: **~ alguém** (criminoso) to grass on sb; (colega etc) to drop sb in it
dedutivo, -a [dedu'tʃivu, a] ADJ deductive
deduzir [dedu'zi'] VT to deduct; (concluir): **~ (de)** to deduce, infer (from) ■ VI (concluir) to deduce, infer
defasado, -a [defa'zadu, a] ADJ: **~ (de)** out of step (with)
defasagem [defa'zaʒẽ] (pl -**ns**) F discrepancy
defecar [defe'ka'] VI to defecate
defecção [defek'sãw] (pl -**ões**) F defection; (deserção) desertion
defectivo, -a [defek'tʃivu, a] ADJ faulty, defective; (Ling) defective
defeito [de'fejtu] M defect, flaw; **pôr ~s em** to find fault with; **com ~** broken, out of order; **para ninguém botar ~** (col) perfect; **defeituoso, -a** [defej'twozu, ɔza] ADJ defective, faulty
defender [defẽ'de'] VT (ger, Jur) to defend; (proteger) to protect; **defender-se** VR to stand up for o.s.; (numa língua) to get by; **~-se de** (de ataque) to defend o.s. against; (do frio etc) to protect o.s. against
defensável [defẽ'savew] (pl -**eis**) ADJ defensible
defensiva [defẽ'siva] F defensive; **estar** ou **ficar na ~** to be on the defensive
defensor, a [defẽ'so'(a)] M/F defender; (Jur) defending counsel
deferência [defe'rẽsja] F (condescendência) deference; (respeito) respect
deferente [defe'rẽtʃi] ADJ deferential
deferimento [deferi'mẽtu] M (de dinheiro, pedido, petição) granting; (de prêmio, condecoração)

awarding; (aceitação) acceptance
deferir [defe'ri'] VT (pedido, petição) to grant; (prêmio, condecoração) to award ■ VI: **~ a** (pedido, petição) to concede to; (sugestão) to accept
defesa [de'feza] F defence (Brit), defense (US); (Jur) counsel for the defence ■ M (Futebol) back
deficiência [defi'sjẽsja] F deficiency
deficiente [defi'sjẽtʃi] ADJ (imperfeito) defective; (carente): **~ (em)** deficient (in)
déficit ['dɛfisitʃi] (pl -**s**) M deficit
deficitário, -a [defisi'tarju, a] ADJ in deficit
definhar [defi'ɲa'] VT to debilitate ■ VI (consumir-se) to waste away; (Bot) to wither
definição [defini'sãw] (pl -**ões**) F definition
definir [defi'ni'] VT to define; **definir-se** VR (decidir-se) to make a decision; (explicar-se) to make one's position clear; **~-se a favor de/ contra algo** to come out in favo(u)r of/against sth; **~-se como** to describe o.s. as
definitivamente [definitʃiva'mẽtʃi] ADV (finalmente) definitively; (permanentemente) for good; (sem dúvida) definitely
definitivo, -a [defini'tʃivu, a] ADJ (final) final, definitive; (permanente) permanent; (resposta, data) definite
definível (pl -**eis**) ADJ definable
defiro etc [de'firu] VB v **deferir**
deflação [defla'sãw] F deflation
deflacionar [deflasjo'na'] VT to deflate
deflacionário, -a [deflasjo'narju, a] ADJ deflationary
deflagração [deflagra'sãw] (pl -**ões**) F explosion; (fig) outbreak
deflagrar [defla'gra'] VI to explode; (fig) to break out ■ VT to set off; (fig) to trigger
deflorar [deflo'ra'] VT to deflower
deformação [defoxma'sãw] (pl -**ões**) F loss of shape; (de corpo) deformation; (de imagem, pensamento) distortion
deformar [defox'ma'] VT to put out of shape; (corpo) to deform; (imagem, pensamento) to distort; **deformar-se** VR to lose shape; to be deformed; to become distorted
deformidade [defoxmi'dadʒi] F deformity
defraudação [defrawda'sãw] (pl -**ões**) F fraud; (de dinheiro) embezzlement
defraudar [defraw'da'] VT (dinheiro) to embezzle; (uma pessoa) to defraud; **~ alguém de algo** to cheat sb of sth
defrontar [defrõ'ta'] VT to face ■ VI: **~ com** to face; (dar com) to come face to face with; **defrontar-se** VR to face each other
defronte [de'frõtʃi] ADV opposite ■ PREP: **~ de** opposite
defumado, -a [defu'madu, a] ADJ smoked
defumar [defu'ma'] VT (presunto) to smoke; (perfumar) to perfume
defunto, -a [de'fũtu, a] ADJ dead ■ M/F dead person

NB: *European Portuguese adds the following consonants to certain words:* **b** (sú(b)dito, su(b)til); **c** (a(c)ção, a(c)cionista, a(c)to); **m** (inde(m)ne); **p** (ado(p)çã, ado(p)tar); *for further details see p. xiii.*

degelar [deʒe'la^r] VT to thaw; (geladeira) to defrost ▪ VI to thaw out; to defrost
degelo [de'ʒelu] M thaw
degeneração [deʒenera'sãw] F (processo) degeneration; (estado) degeneracy
degenerar [deʒene'ra^r] VI: ~ (em) to degenerate (into); degenerar-se VR to become degenerate
deglutir [deglu'tʃi^r] VT, VI to swallow
degolação [degola'sãw] (pl -ões) F beheading, decapitation
degolar [dego'la^r] VT to decapitate
degradação [degrada'sãw] F degradation
degradante [degra'dãtʃi] ADJ degrading
degradar [degra'da^r] VT to degrade, debase; degradar-se VR to demean o.s.
dégradé [degra'de] ADJ INV (cor) shaded off
degrau [de'graw] M step; (de escada de mão) rung
degredar [degre'da^r] VT to exile
degredo [de'gredu] M exile
degringolar [degrĩgo'la^r] VI (cair) to tumble down; (fig) to collapse; (: deteriorar-se) to deteriorate; (desorganizar-se) to get messed up
degustação [deguʃta'sãw] (pl -ões) F tasting, sampling; (saborear) savouring (Brit), savoring (US)
degustar [deguʃ'ta^r] VT (provar) to taste; (saborear) to savour (Brit), savor (US)
dei etc [dej] VB V dar
deificar [dejfi'ka^r] VT to deify
deitada [dej'tada] (col) F: dar uma ~ to have a lie-down
deitado, -a [dej'tadu, a] ADJ (estendido) lying down; (na cama) in bed
deitar [dej'ta^r] VT to lay down; (na cama) to put to bed; (colocar) to put, place; (lançar) to cast; (PT: líquido) to pour; deitar-se VR to lie down; to go to bed; ~ sangue (PT) to bleed; ~ abaixo to knock down, flatten; ~ a fazer algo to start doing sth; ~ uma carta (PT) to post a letter; ~ fora (PT) to throw away ou out; ~ e rolar (col) to do as one likes
deixa ['dejʃa] F clue, hint; (Teatro) cue; (chance) chance
deixar [dej'ʃa^r] VT to leave; (abandonar) to abandon; (permitir) to let, allow ▪ VI: ~ de (parar) to stop; (não fazer) to fail to; não posso ~ de ir I must go; não posso ~ de rir I can't help laughing; ~ cair to drop; ~ alguém louco to drive sb crazy ou mad; ~ alguém cansado/ nervoso etc to make sb tired/nervous etc; ~ a desejar to leave something to be desired; deixa disso! (col) come off it!; deixa para lá! (col) forget it!
dela ['dɛla] = de + ela
delação [dela'sãw] (pl -ões) F (de pessoa: denúncia) accusation; (: traição) betrayal; (de abusos) disclosure
delatar [dela'ta^r] VT (pessoa) to inform on; (abusos) to reveal; (à polícia) to report; delator, a [dela'to^r(a)] M/F informer
délavé [dela've] ADJ INV (jeans) faded
dele ['deli] = de + ele

delegação [delega'sãw] (pl -ões) F delegation
delegacia [delega'sia] F office; ~ de polícia police station
delegado, -a [dele'gadu, a] M/F delegate, representative; ~ de polícia police chief
delegar [dele'ga^r] VT to delegate
deleitar [delej'ta^r] VT to delight; deleitar-se VR: deleitar-se com to delight in
deleite [de'lejtʃi] M delight
deleitoso, -a [delej'tozu, ɔza] ADJ delightful
deletar [dele'ta^r] VT (Comput) to delete
deletério, -a [dele'tɛrju, a] ADJ harmful
delével [de'lɛvew] (pl -eis) ADJ erasable
delgado, -a [dew'gadu, a] ADJ thin; (esbelto) slim, slender; (fino) fine
Délhi ['dɛli] N: (Nova) ~ (New) Delhi
deliberação [delibera'sãw] (pl -ões) F deliberation; (decisão) decision
deliberar [delibe'ra^r] VT to decide, resolve ▪ VI to deliberate
deliberativo, -a [delibera'tʃivu, a] ADJ (conselho) deliberative
delicadeza [delika'deza] F delicacy; (cortesia) kindness
delicado, -a [deli'kadu, a] ADJ delicate; (frágil) fragile; (cortês) polite; (sensível) sensitive
delícia [de'lisja] F delight; (prazer) pleasure; esse bolo é uma ~ this cake is delicious; que ~! how lovely!; deliciar [deli'sja^r] VT to delight; deliciar-se VR: deliciar-se com algo to take delight in sth
delicioso, -a [deli'sjozu, ɔza] ADJ lovely; (comida, bebida) delicious
delimitação [delimita'sãw] F delimitation
delimitar [delimi'ta^r] VT to delimit
delineador [delinja'do^r] M (de olhos) eyeliner
delinear [deli'nja^r] VT to outline
delinquência [delĩ'kwẽsja] F delinquency
delinquente [delĩ'kwẽtʃi] ADJ, M/F delinquent, criminal
delinquir [delĩ'kwi^r] VI to commit an offence (Brit) ou offense (US)
delir [de'li^r] VT to erase
delirante [deli'rãtʃi] ADJ delirious; (show, atuação) thrilling
delirar [deli'ra^r] VI (com febre) to be delirious; (de ódio, prazer) to go mad, go wild
delírio [de'lirju] M (Med) delirium; (êxtase) ecstasy; (excitação) excitement
delirium tremens [de'liriũ 'tremẽs] M delirium tremens
delito [de'litu] M (crime) crime; (falta) offence (Brit), offense (US)
delonga [de'lõga] F delay; sem mais ~s without more ado
delongar [delõ'ga^r] VT to delay; delongar-se VR (conversa) to wear on; ~-se em to dwell on
delta ['dɛwta] F delta
demagogia [demago'ʒia] F demagogy
demagógico, -a [dema'gɔʒiku, a] ADJ demagogic
demagogo [dema'gogu] M demagogue

demais [dʒi'majʃ] ADV (*em demasia*) too much; (*muitíssimo*) a lot, very much ■ PRON: **os/as** ~ the rest (of them); **já é ~!** this is too much!; **é bom ~** it's really good; **foi ~** (*col: bacana*) it was great

demanda [de'mãda] F (*Jur*) lawsuit; (*disputa*) claim; (*requisição*) request; (*Econ*) demand; **em ~ de** in search of; **demandar** [demã'da^r] VT (*Jur*) to sue; (*exigir, reclamar*) to demand; (*porto*) to head for

demão [de'mãw] (*pl -s*) F (*de tinta*) coat, layer

demarcação [demaxka'sãw] F demarcation

demarcar [demax'ka^r] VT (*delimitar*) to demarcate; (*fixar*) to mark out

demarcatório, -a [demaxka'tɔrju, a] ADJ: **linha demarcatória** demarcation line

demasia [dema'zia] F excess, surplus; (*imoderação*) lack of moderation; **em ~** (*dinheiro, comida etc*) too much; (*cartas, problemas etc*) too many

demasiadamente [demazjada'mẽtʃi] ADV too much; (*com adj*) too

demasiado, -a [dema'zjadu, a] ADJ too much; (*pl*) too many ■ ADV too much; (*com adj*) too

demência [de'mẽsja] F dementia

demente [de'mẽtʃi] ADJ insane, demented

demérito, -a [de'mɛritu, a] ADJ unworthy ■ M demerit

demissão [demi'sãw] (*pl -ões*) F dismissal; **pedido de ~** resignation; **pedir ~** to resign

demissionário, -a [demisjo'narju, a] ADJ resigning, outgoing

demissões [demi'sõjʃ] FPL *de* **demissão**

demitir [demi'tʃi^r] VT to dismiss; (*col*) to sack, fire; **demitir-se** VR to resign

democracia [demokra'sia] F democracy

democrata [demo'krata] M/F democrat

democrático, -a [demo'kratʃiku, a] ADJ democratic

democratização [demokratʃiza'sãw] F democratization

democratizar [demokratʃi'za^r] VT to democratize

démodé [demo'de] ADJ INV old-fashioned

demografia [demogra'fia] F demography

demográfico, -a [demo'grafiku, a] ADJ demographic

demolição [demoli'sãw] (*pl -ões*) F demolition

demolir [demo'li^r] VT to demolish, knock down; (*fig*) to destroy

demoníaco, -a [demo'niaku, a] ADJ devilish

demônio [de'monju] M devil, demon; (*col: criança*) brat

demonstração [demõʃtra'sãw] (*pl -ões*) F (*lição prática*) demonstration; (*de amizade*) show, display; (*prova*) proof; **~ de contas** (*Com*) statement of account; **~ de lucros e perdas** (*Com*) profit and loss statement

demonstrar [demõʃ'tra^r] VT (*mostrar*) to demonstrate; (*provar*) to prove; (*amizade etc*) to show

demonstrativo, -a [demõʃtra'tʃivu, a] ADJ demonstrative

demonstrável [demõ'ʃtravew] (*pl -eis*) ADJ demonstrable

demora [de'mɔra] F delay; (*parada*) stop; **sem ~** at once, without delay; **qual é a ~ disso?** how long will this take?; **demorado, -a** [demo'radu, a] ADJ slow; **demorar** [demo'ra^r] VT to delay, slow down ■ VI (*permanecer*) to stay; (*tardar a vir*) to be late; (*conserto*) to take (a long) time; **demorar-se** VR to stay for a long time, linger; **demorar a chegar** to be a long time coming; **vai demorar muito?** will it take long?; **não vou demorar** I won't be long

demover [demo've^r] VT: **~ alguém de algo** to talk sb out of sth; **demover-se** VR: **demover-se de algo** to be talked out of sth

Denatran [dena'trã] (BR) ABR M (= *Departamento Nacional de Trânsito*) ≈ Ministry of Transport

dendê [dẽ'de] M (*Culin: óleo*) palm oil; (*Bot*) oil palm

denegrir [dene'gri^r] VT to blacken; (*difamar*) to denigrate

dengo [dẽgu] M coyness; (*choro*) whimpering

dengoso, -a [dẽ'gozu, ɔza] ADJ coy; (*criança: choramingueiro*): **ser ~** to be a crybaby

dengue ['dẽgi] M (*Med*) dengue

denigro *etc* [de'nigru] VB *V* **denegrir**

denodado, -a [deno'dadu, a] ADJ brave, daring

denominação [denomina'sãw] (*pl -ões*) F (*Rel*) denomination; (*título*) name; (*ato*) naming

denominador [denomina'do^r] M: **~ comum** (*Mat, fig*) common denominator

denominar [denomi'na^r] VT: **~ algo/alguém ...** to call sth/sb ...; **denominar-se** VR to be called; (*a si mesmo*) to call o.s.

denotar [deno'ta^r] VT (*indicar*) to show, indicate; (*significar*) to signify

densidade [dẽsi'dadʒi] F density; **disco de alta ~** (*Comput*) high-density disk; **disco de ~ simples/dupla** (*Comput*) single-/double-density disk

denso, -a [dẽsu, a] ADJ (*cerrado*) dense; (*espesso*) thick; (*compacto*) compact

dentada [dẽ'tada] F bite

dentado, -a [dẽ'tadu, a] ADJ serrated

dentadura [dẽta'dura] F teeth *pl*, set of teeth; (*artificial*) dentures *pl*

dental [dẽ'taw] (*pl -ais*) ADJ dental

dentário, -a [dẽ'tarju, a] ADJ dental

dente ['dẽtʃi] M tooth; (*de animal*) fang; (*de elefante*) tusk; (*de alho*) clove; **falar entre os ~s** to mutter, mumble; **~ de leite/do siso** milk/wisdom tooth; **~s postiços** false teeth

dente-de-leão (*pl* dentes-de-leão) M dandelion

Dentel [dẽ'tew] (BR) ABR M = **Departamento Nacional de Telecomunicações**

dentição [dẽtʃi'sãw] F (*formação dos dentes*)

NB: *European Portuguese adds the following consonants to certain words*: **b** (sú(b)dito, su(b)til); **c** (a(c)ção, a(c)cionista, a(c)to); **m** (inde(m)ne); **p** (ado(p)çã, ado(p)tar); *for further details see p. xiii.*

teething; (*dentes*) teeth *pl*; **primeira ~** milk
teeth; **segunda ~** second teeth
dentifrício [dētʃiˈfrisju] M toothpaste
dentina [dēˈtʃina] F dentine
dentista [dēˈtʃiʃta] M/F dentist
dentre [ˈdētri] PREP (from) among
dentro [ˈdētru] ADV inside ◼ PREP: **~ de** inside;
(*tempo*) (with)in; **~ pouco** *ou* **em breve** soon,
before long; **de ~ para fora** inside out; **dar uma
~** (*col*) to get it right; **aí ~** in there; **por ~** on the
inside; **estar por ~** (*col*: *fig*) to be in the know;
estar por ~ de algo (*col*: *fig*) to know the ins and
outs of sth
dentuça [dēˈtusa] F buck teeth *pl*; *v tb* **dentuço**
dentuço, -a [dēˈtusu, a] ADJ buck-toothed ◼ M/F
buck-toothed person; **ser ~** to have buck teeth
denúncia [deˈnūsja] F denunciation; (*acusação*)
accusation; (*de roubo*) report; **denunciar**
[denūˈsjaʳ] VT (*acusar*) to denounce; (*delatar*) to
inform on; (*revelar*) to reveal
deparar [depaˈraʳ] VT (*revelar*) to reveal; (*fazer
aparecer*) to present ◼ VI: **~ com** to come across,
meet; **deparar-se** VR: **deparar-se com** to come
across, meet
departamental [depaxtamēˈtaw] (*pl* -**ais**) ADJ
departmental
departamento [depaxtaˈmētu] M department;
D~ de Marcas e Patentes Patent Office
depauperar [depawpeˈraʳ] VT: **~ algo/alguém** to
bleed sth/sb dry
depenar [depeˈnaʳ] VT to pluck; (*col*: *roubar*) to
clean out
dependência [depēˈdēsja] F dependence;
(*edificação*) annexe (*Brit*), annex (*US*); (*colonial*)
dependency; (*cômodo*) room
dependente [depēˈdētʃi] M/F dependant
depender [depēˈdeʳ] VI: **~ de** to depend on
dependurar [depēduˈraʳ] VI to hang
depilação [depilaˈsãw] (*pl* -**ões**) F depilation
depilador [depilaˈdoʳ(a)] M/F beauty
therapist
depilar [depiˈlaʳ] VT to wax; **~ as pernas** (*mandar
fazer*) to have one's legs done; (*fazer sozinho*) to
do one's legs; **depilatório** [depilaˈtɔrju] M hair-
remover
deplorar [deploˈraʳ] VT (*lamentar*) to regret;
(*morte, perda*) to lament
deplorável [deploˈravew] (*pl* -**eis**) ADJ
deplorable; (*lamentável*) regrettable
depoente [deˈpwētʃi] M/F witness
depoimento [depojˈmētu] M testimony,
evidence; (*na polícia*) statement
depois [deˈpojʃ] ADV afterwards ◼ PREP: **~ de**
after; **~ de comer** after eating; **~ que** after
depor [deˈpoʳ] (*irreg*) VT (*pôr*) to place; (*indicar*) to
indicate; (*rei*) to depose; (*governo*) to overthrow
◼ VI (*Jur*) to testify, give evidence; (*na polícia*) to
give a statement; **esses fatos depõem contra/
a favor dele** these facts speak against him/in
his favo(u)r
deportação [depoxtaˈsãw] (*pl* -**ões**) F
deportation

deportar [depoxˈtaʳ] VT to deport
deposição [depoziˈsãw] (*pl* -**ões**) F deposition;
(*governo*) overthrow
depositante [depoziˈtãtʃi] M/F depositor ◼ ADJ
depositing
depositar [depoziˈtaʳ] VT to deposit; (*voto*) to
cast; (*colocar*) to place; **depositar-se** VR (*líquido*)
to form a deposit; **~ confiança em** to place
one's confidence in
depositário, -a [depoziˈtarju, a] M/F trustee;
(*fig*) confidant(e)
depósito [deˈpɔzitu] M deposit; (*armazém*)
warehouse, depot; (*de lixo*) dump; (*reservatório*)
tank; **~ a prazo fixo** fixed-term deposit; **~ de
bagagens** left-luggage office (*Brit*), checkroom
(*US*)
depravação [depravaˈsãw] F depravity,
corruption
depravado, -a [depraˈvadu, a] ADJ depraved
◼ M/F degenerate
depravar [depraˈvaʳ] VT to deprave, corrupt;
(*estragar*) to ruin; **depravar-se** VR to become
depraved
deprecar [depreˈkaʳ] VT to beg for, pray for ◼ VI
to plead
depreciação [depresjaˈsãw] F depreciation
depreciador, a [depresjaˈdoʳ(a)] ADJ
deprecatory
depreciar [depreˈsjaʳ] VT (*desvalorizar*) to devalue;
(*Com*) to write down; (*menosprezar*) to belittle;
depreciar-se VR to depreciate, lose value;
(*menosprezar-se*) to belittle o.s.
depredação [depredaˈsãw] F depredation
depredador, a [depredaˈdoʳ(a)] ADJ destructive
◼ M/F vandal
depredar [depreˈdaʳ] VT to wreck
depreender [deprjēˈdeʳ] VT: **~ algo/que ... (de
algo)** to gather sth/that ... (from sth)
depressa [dʒiˈpresa] ADV fast, quickly; **vamos ~**
let's get a move on!
depressão [depreˈsãw] (*pl* -**ões**) F depression
depressivo, -a [depreˈsivu, a] ADJ depressive
depressões [depreˈsõjʃ] FPL *de* **depressão**
deprimente [depriˈmētʃi] ADJ depressing
deprimido, -a [depriˈmidu, a] ADJ depressed
deprimir [depriˈmiʳ] VT to depress; **deprimir-se**
VR to get depressed
depuração [depuraˈsãw] F purification
depurar [depuˈraʳ] VT to purify; (*Comput:
programa*) to debug
deputado, -a [depuˈtadu, a] M/F deputy; (*agente*)
agent; (*Pol*) ≈ Member of Parliament (*Brit*),
≈ Representative (*US*)
deputar [depuˈtaʳ] VT to delegate
deque [ˈdɛki] M deck
DER (*BR*) ABR M (= *Departamento de Estradas de
Rodagem*) state highways department
der *etc* [ˈdeʳ] VB *v* **dar**
deriva [deˈriva] F drift; **ir à ~** to drift; **ficar à ~** to
be adrift
derivação [derivaˈsãw] (*pl* -**ões**) F derivation
derivar [deriˈvaʳ] VT (*desviar*) to divert; (*Ling*) to

derive ▪ vi (ir à deriva) to drift; **derivar-se** vr (palavra) to be derived; (ir à deriva) to drift; (provir): **derivar(-se) (de)** to derive ou be derived (from)

dermatologia [dexmatolo'ʒia] f dermatology

dermatologista [dexmatolo'ʒiʃta] m/f dermatologist

dernier cri [dex'nje 'kri] m last word

derradeiro, -a [dexa'dejru, a] adj last, final

derramamento [dexama'mẽtu] m spilling; (de sangue, lágrimas) shedding

derramar [dexa'ma^r] vt (sem querer) to spill; (entornar) to pour; (sangue, lágrimas) to shed; **derramar-se** vr to pour out

derrame [de'xami] m haemorrhage (Brit), hemorrhage (US)

derrapagem [dexa'paʒẽ] (pl -ns) f skid; (ação) skidding

derrapar [dexa'pa^r] vi to skid

derredor [dexe'do^r] adv, prep: **em ~ (de)** around

derreter [dexe'te^r] vt to melt; **derreter-se** vr to melt; (coisa congelada) to thaw; (enternecer-se) to be touched; **~ alguém** to win sb's heart; **~-se por alguém** to fall for sb

derretido, -a [dexe'tʃidu, a] adj melted; (enternecido) touched; (apaixonado) smitten; **estar ~ por alguém** to be crazy about sb

derrocada [dexo'kada] f downfall; (ruína) collapse

derrogação [dexoga'sãw] (pl -ões) f amendment

derrota [de'xɔta] f defeat, rout; (Náut) route; **derrotar** [dexo'ta^r] vt (vencer) to defeat; (em jogo) to beat

derrubar [dexu'ba^r] vt to knock down; (governo) to bring down; (suj: doença) to lay low; (col: prejudicar) to put down

desabafar [dʒizaba'fa^r] vt (sentimentos) to give vent to ▪ vi: **~ (com)** to unburden o.s. (to); **desabafar-se** vr: **desabafar-se (com)** to unburden o.s. (to); **desabafo** [dʒiza'bafu] m confession

desabalado, -a [dʒizaba'ladu, a] adj: **correr/ sair ~** to run headlong/rush out

desabamento [dʒizaba'mẽtu] m collapse

desabar [dʒiza'ba^r] vi (edifício, ponte) to collapse; (chuva) to pour down; (tempestade) to break

desabilitar [dʒizabili'ta^r] vt: **~ alguém a ou para (fazer) algo** to bar sb from (doing) sth

desabitado, -a [dʒizabi'tadu, a] adj uninhabited

desabituar [dʒizabi'twa^r] vt: **~ alguém de (fazer) algo** to get sb out of the habit of (doing) sth; **desabituar-se** vr: **desabituar-se de (fazer) algo** to get out of the habit of (doing) sth

desabonar [dʒizabo'na^r] vt to discredit; **desabonar-se** vr to be discredited

desabotoar [dʒizabo'twa^r] vt to unbutton

desabrido, -a [dʒiza'bridu, a] adj rude, brusque

desabrigado, -a [dʒizabri'gadu, a] adj (sem casa) homeless; (exposto) exposed

desabrigar [dʒizabri'ga^r] vt to make homeless

desabrochar [dʒizabro'ʃa^r] vi (flores, fig) to blossom ▪ m blossoming

desabusado, -a [dʒizabu'zadu, a] adj (sem preconceitos) unprejudiced; (atrevido) impudent

desacatar [dʒizaka'ta^r] vt (desrespeitar) to have ou show no respect for; (afrontar) to defy; (desprezar) to scorn ▪ vi (col) to be amazing; **desacato** [dʒiza'katu] m (falta de respeito) disrespect; (desprezo) disregard; (col): **ele é um desacato** he's amazing

desaceleração [dʒizaselera'sãw] f (tb: Econ) slowing down

desacelerar [dʒizasele'ra^r] vt to slow down

desacerto [dʒiza'sextu] m mistake, blunder

desacomodar [dʒizakomo'da^r] vt to move out

desacompanhado, -a [dʒizakõpa'ɲadu, a] adj on one's own, alone

desaconselhar [dʒizakõse'ʎa^r] vt: **~ algo (a alguém)** to advise (sb) against sth

desaconselhável [dʒizakõse'ʎavew] (pl -eis) adj inadvisable

desacordado, -a [dʒizakox'dadu, a] adj unconscious

desacordo [dʒiza'koxdu] m (falta de acordo) disagreement; (desarmonia) discord

desacostumado, -a [dʒizakoʃtumadu, a] adj unaccustomed

desacostumar [dʒizakoʃtu'ma^r] vt: **~ alguém de algo** to get sb out of the habit of sth; **desacostumar-se** vr: **desacostumar-se de algo** to give sth up

desacreditado, -a [dʒizakredʒi'tadu, a] adj discredited

desacreditar [dʒizakredʒi'ta^r] vt to discredit; **desacreditar-se** vr to lose one's reputation

desafeto [dʒiza'fetu] m coldness

desafiador, a [dʒizafja'do^r(a)] adj challenging; (pessoa) defiant ▪ m/f challenger

desafiar [dʒiza'fja^r] vt (propor combate a) to challenge; (afrontar) to defy

desafinação [dʒizafina'sãw] f dissonance

desafinado, -a [dʒizafi'nadu, a] adj out of tune

desafinar [dʒizafi'na^r] vt to put out of tune ▪ vi to play out of tune; (cantor) to sing out of tune

desafio [dʒiza'fiu] m challenge; (PT: Esporte) match, game

desafivelar [dʒizafive'la^r] vt to unbuckle

desafogado, -a [dʒizafo'gadu, a] adj (desimpedido) clear; (desembaraçado) free

desafogar [dʒizafo'ga^r] vt (aliviar) to relieve; (desabafar) to give vent to; **desafogar-se** vr to free o.s.; (desabafar-se) to unburden o.s.

desafogo [dʒiza'fogu] m (alívio) relief; (folga) leisure

desaforado, -a [dʒizafo'radu, a] adj rude,

NB: European Portuguese adds the following consonants to certain words: **b** (sú(b)dito, su(b)til); **c** (a(c)ção, a(c)cionista, a(c)to); **m** (inde(m)ne); **p** (ado(p)çã, ado(p)tar); for further details see p. xiii.

insolent

desaforo [dʒiza'foru] M insolence, abuse

desafortunado, -a [dʒizafoxtu'nadu, a] ADJ unfortunate, unlucky

desafronta [dʒiza'frõta] F (satisfação) redress; (vingança) revenge

desagasalhado, -a [dʒizagaza'ʎadu, a] ADJ scantily clad

desagradar [dʒizagra'daʳ] VT to displease ■ VI: ~ **a alguém** to displease sb; **desagradável** [dʒizagra'davew] (pl -eis) ADJ unpleasant; **desagrado** [dʒiza'gradu] M displeasure

desagravar [dʒizagra'vaʳ] VT (insulta) to make amends for; (pessoa) to make amends to; **desagravar-se** VR to avenge o.s.

desagravo [dʒiza'gravu] M amends pl

desagregação [dʒizagrega'sãw] F (separação) separation; (dissolução) disintegration

desagregar [dʒizagre'gaʳ] VT (desunir) to break up, split; (separar) to separate; **desagregar-se** VR to break up, split; to separate

desaguar [dʒiza'gwaʳ] VT to drain ■ VI: ~ **(em)** to flow ou empty (into)

desairoso, -a [dʒizaj'rozu, ɔza] ADJ inelegant

desajeitado, -a [dʒizaʒej'tadu, a] ADJ clumsy, awkward

desajuizado, -a [dʒizaʒwi'zadu, a] ADJ foolish, unwise

desajustado, -a [dʒizaʒuʃ'tadu, a] ADJ (Psico) maladjusted; (peças) in need of adjustment ■ M/F maladjusted person

desajustamento [dʒizaʒuʃta'mẽtu] M (Psico) maladjustment

desajustar [dʒizaʒuʃ'taʳ] VT (peças) to mess up

desajuste [dʒiza'ʒuʃtʃi] M (Psico) maladjustment; (mecânico) problem

desalentado, -a [dʒizalẽ'tadu, a] ADJ disheartened

desalentar [dʒizalẽ'taʳ] VT to discourage; (deprimir) to depress; **desalento** [dʒiza'lẽtu] M discouragement

desalinhado, -a [dʒizali'ɲadu, a] ADJ untidy

desalinho [dʒiza'liɲu] M untidiness

desalmado, -a [dʒizaw'madu, a] ADJ cruel, inhuman

desalojar [dʒizalo'ʒaʳ] VT (expulsar) to oust; **desalojar-se** VR to move out

desamarrar [dʒizama'xaʳ] VT to untie ■ VI (Náut) to cast off

desamarrotar [dʒizamaxo'taʳ] VT to smooth out

desamassar [dʒizama'saʳ] VT (papel) to smooth out; (chapéu etc) to straighten out; (carro) to beat out

desambientado, -a [dʒizãbjē'tadu, a] ADJ unsettled

desamor [dʒiza'moʳ] M dislike

desamparado, -a [dʒizãpa'radu, a] ADJ (abandonado) abandoned; (sem apoio) helpless

desamparar [dʒizãpa'raʳ] VT to abandon

desamparo [dʒizã'paru] M helplessness

desandar [dʒizã'daʳ] VI (maionese, clara) to separate; ~ **a fazer** to begin to do; ~ **a correr** to break into a run; ~ **a chorar** to burst into tears

desanimação [dʒizanima'sãw] F dejection

desanimado, -a [dʒizani'madu, a] ADJ (pessoa) fed up, dispirited; (festa) dull; **ser** ~ (pessoa) to be apathetic

desanimar [dʒizani'maʳ] VT (abater) to dishearten; (desencorajar): ~ **(de fazer)** to discourage (from doing) ■ VI to lose heart; (ser desanimado) to be discouraging; ~ **de fazer algo** to lose the will to do sth; (desistir) to give up doing sth

desânimo [dʒi'zanimu] M dejection

desanuviado, -a [dʒizanu'vjadu, a] ADJ cloudless, clear

desanuviar [dʒizanu'vjaʳ] VT (céu) to clear; **desanuviar-se** VR to clear; (fig) to stop; ~ **alguém** to put sb's mind at rest

desapaixonado, -a [dʒizapajʃo'nadu, a] ADJ dispassionate

desaparafusar [dʒizaparafu'zaʳ] VT to unscrew

desaparecer [dʒizapare'seʳ] VI to disappear, vanish; **desaparecido, -a** [dʒizapare'sidu, a] ADJ lost, missing ■ M/F missing person

desaparecimento [dʒizaparesi'mẽtu] M disappearance; (falecimento) death

desapegado, -a [dʒizape'gadu, a] ADJ indifferent, detached

desapegar [dʒizape'gaʳ] VT to detach; **desapegar-se** VR: **desapegar-se de** to go off

desapego [dʒiza'pegu] M indifference, detachment

desapercebido, -a [dʒizapexse'bidu, a] ADJ unnoticed

desapertar [dʒizapex'taʳ] VT (afrouxar) to loosen; (livrar) to free

desapiedado, -a [dʒizapje'dadu, a] ADJ pitiless, ruthless

desapontador, a [dʒizapõta'do(ʳ)(a)] ADJ disappointing

desapontamento [dʒizapõta'mẽtu] M disappointment

desapontar [dʒizapõ'taʳ] VT to disappoint

desapossar [dʒizapo'saʳ] VT: ~ **alguém de algo** to take sth away from sb; **desapossar-se** VR: **desapossar-se de algo** to give sth up

desaprender [dʒizaprẽ'deʳ] VT to forget ■ VI: ~ **a fazer** to forget how to do

desapropriação [dʒizaproprja'sãw] F (de bens) expropriation; (de pessoa) dispossession

desapropriar [dʒizapro'prjaʳ] VT (bens) to expropriate; (pessoa) to dispossess

desaprovação [dʒizaprova'sãw] F disapproval

desaprovar [dʒizapro'vaʳ] VT (reprovar) to disapprove of; (censurar) to object to

desaproveitado, -a [dʒizaprovej'tadu, a] ADJ wasted; (terras) undeveloped

desaquecimento [dʒizakesi'mẽtu] M (Econ) cooling

desarmamento [dʒizaxma'mẽtu] M

disarmament

desarmar [dʒizax'ma^r] VT to disarm; (*desmontar*) to dismantle; (*bomba*) to defuse

desarmonia [dʒizaxmo'nia] F discord

desarraigar [dʒizaxaj'ga^r] VT to uproot

desarranjado, -a [dʒizaxã'ʒadu, a] ADJ (*intestino*) upset; (*Tec*) out of order; **estar ~** (*pessoa*) to have diarrhoea (*Brit*) *ou* diarrhea (*US*)

desarranjar [dʒizaxã'ʒa^r] VT (*transtornar*) to upset, disturb; (*desordenar*) to mess up

desarranjo [dʒizax'xãʒu] M (*desordem*) disorder; (*enguiço*) breakdown; (*diarréia*) diarrhoea (*Brit*), diarrhea (*US*)

desarregaçar [dʒizaxega'sa^r] VT (*mangas*) to roll down

desarrumado, -a [dʒizaxu'madu, a] ADJ untidy, messy

desarrumar [dʒizaxu'ma^r] VT to mess up; (*mala*) to unpack

desarticulado, -a [dʒizaxtʃiku'ladu, a] ADJ dislocated

desarticular [dʒizaxtʃiku'la^r] VT (*osso*) to dislocate

desarvorado, -a [dʒizaxvo'radu, a] ADJ (*desorientado*) disoriented

desassociar [dʒizaso'sja^r] VT to disassociate; **desassociar-se** VR: **desassociar-se de algo** to disassociate o.s. from sth

desassossego [dʒizaso'segu] M (*inquietação*) disquiet; (*perturbação*) restlessness

desastrado, -a [dʒizaʃ'tradu, a] ADJ clumsy

desastre [dʒi'zaʃtri] M disaster; (*acidente*) accident; (*de avião*) crash

desastroso, -a [dʒizaʃ'trozu, ɔza] ADJ disastrous

desatar [dʒiza'ta^r] VT (*nó*) to undo, untie ■ VI: **~ a fazer** to begin to do; **~ a chorar** to burst into tears; **~ a rir** to burst out laughing

desatarraxar [dʒizataxa'ʃa^r] VT to unscrew

desatencioso, -a [dʒizatẽ'sjozu, ɔza] ADJ inattentive; (*descortês*) impolite

desatender [dʒizatẽ'de^r] VT (*não fazer caso de*) to pay no attention to, ignore ■ VI: **~ a** to ignore

desatento, -a [dʒiza'tẽtu, a] ADJ inattentive

desatinado, -a [dʒizatʃi'nadu, a] ADJ crazy, wild ■ M/F lunatic

desatinar [dʒizatʃi'na^r] VI to behave foolishly

desatino [dʒiza'tʃinu] M (*loucura*) madness; (*ato*) folly

desativar [dʒizatʃi'va^r] VT (*firma, usina*) to shut down; (*veículos*) to withdraw from service; (*bomba*) to deactivate, defuse

desatracar [dʒizatra'ka^r] VT (*navio*) to unmoor; (*brigões*) to separate ■ VI (*navio*) to cast off

desatravancar [dʒizatravã'ka^r] VT to clear

desatrelar [dʒizatre'la^r] VT to unhitch

desatualizado, -a [dʒizatwali'zadu, a] ADJ out of date; (*pessoa*) out of touch

desautorizar [dʒizawtori'za^r] VT (*prática*) to disallow; (*desacreditar*) to discredit; **~ alguém** (*tirar a autoridade de*) to undermine sb's authority

desavença [dʒiza'vẽsa] F (*briga*) quarrel; (*discórdia*) disagreement; **em ~** at loggerheads

desavergonhado, -a [dʒizavexgo'ɲadu, a] ADJ insolent, impudent, shameless

desavir-se [dʒiza'vixsi] (*irreg*) VR: **~ (com alguém em algo)** to quarrel *ou* disagree (with sb about sth)

desavisado, -a [dʒizavi'zadu, a] ADJ careless

desbancar [dʒiʒbã'ka^r] VT: **~ alguém (em algo)** to outdo sb (in sth)

desbaratar [dʒiʒbara'ta^r] VT to ruin; (*desperdiçar*) to waste, squander; (*vencer*) to crush; (*pôr em desordem*) to mess up

desbarrigado, -a [dʒiʒbaxi'gadu, a] ADJ flat-bellied

desbastar [dʒiʒbaʃ'ta^r] VT (*cabelo, plantas*) to thin (out); (*vegetação*) to trim

desbocado, -a [dʒiʒbo'kadu, a] ADJ (*pessoa*) foul-mouthed, crude

desbotar [dʒiʒbo'ta^r] VT to discolour (*Brit*), discolor (*US*) ■ VI to fade

desbragadamente [dʒiʒbragada'mẽtʃi] ADV (*beber*) to excess; (*mentir*) blatantly

desbravador, a [dʒiʒbrava'do^r(a)] M/F explorer

desbravar [dʒiʒbra'va^r] VT (*terras desconhecidas*) to explore

desbundante [dʒiʒbũ'dãtʃi] (*col*) ADJ fantastic

desbundar [dʒiʒbũ'da^r] (*col*) VT to knock out ■ VI to flip, freak out

desbunde [dʒiʒ'bũdʒi] (*col*) M knockout

desburocratizar [dʒiʒburokratʃi'za^r] VT: **~ algo** to remove the bureaucracy from sth

descabelar [dʒiʃkabe'la^r] VT: **~ alguém** to mess up sb's hair; **descabelar-se** VR to get one's hair messed up

descabido, -a [dʒiʃka'bidu, a] ADJ (*impróprio*) improper; (*inoportuno*) inappropriate

descadeirado, -a [dʒiʃkadej'radu, a] ADJ (*cansado*) weary; **ficar ~** (*com dor*) to get backache

descalabro [dʒiʃka'labru] M disaster

descalçar [dʒiʃkaw'sa^r] VT (*sapatos*) to take off; **descalçar-se** VR to take off one's shoes

descalço, -a [dʒiʃ'kawsu, a] ADJ barefoot

descambar [dʒiʃkã'ba^r] VI: **~ (de algo) para algo** to sink *ou* deteriorate (from sth) to sth; **~ para** *ou* **em** to degenerate into

descampado [dʒiʃkã'padu] M open country

descansado, -a [dʒiʃkã'sadu, a] ADJ (*tranqüilo*) calm, quiet; (*vagaroso*) slow; **fique ~** don't worry; **pode ficar ~ que ...** you can rest assured that ..

descansar [dʒiʃkã'sa^r] VT to rest; (*apoiar*) to lean ■ VI to rest; to lean; **descanso** [dʒiʃ'kãsu] M (*repouso*) rest; (*folga*) break; (*para prato*) mat; **sem descanso** without a break

descapitalização [dʒiʃkapitaliza'sãw] F (*Com*)

decapitalization

descarado, -a [dʒiʃka'radu, a] ADJ cheeky, impudent

descaramento [dʒiʃkara'mẽtu] M cheek, impudence

descarga [dʒiʃ'kaxga] F unloading; (Mil) volley; (Elet) discharge; (de vaso sanitário): **dar a ~ to** flush the toilet

descarnado, -a [dʒiʃkax'nadu, a] ADJ scrawny, skinny

descaroçar [dʒiʃkaro'saʳ] VT (semente) to seed; (fruto) to stone, core; (algodão) to gin

descarregadouro [dʒiʃkaxega'doru] M wharf

descarregamento [dʒiʃkaxega'mẽtu] M (de carga) unloading; (Elet) discharge

descarregar [dʒiʃkaxe'gaʳ] VT (carga) to unload; (Elet) to discharge; (aliviar) to relieve; (raiva) to vent, give vent to; (arma) to fire ■ VI to unload; (bateria) to run out; **~ a raiva em alguém** to take it out on sb

descarrilhamento [dʒiʃkaxiʎa'mẽtu] M derailment

descarrilhar [dʒiʃkaxi'ʎaʳ] VT to derail ■ VI to run off the rails; (fig) to go off the rails

descartar [dʒiʃkax'taʳ] VT to discard; **descartar-se vR: descartar-se de** to get rid of

descartável [dʒiʃkax'tavew] (pl -eis) disposable

descascador [dʒiʃkaʃka'doʳ] M peeler

descascar [dʒiʃkaʃ'kaʳ] VT (fruta) to peel; (ervilhas) to shell ■ VI (depois do sol) to peel; (cobra) to shed its skin; **o feijão descascou** the skin came off the beans

descaso [dʒiʃ'kazu] M disregard

descendência [desẽ'dẽsja] F descendants pl, offspring pl

descendente [desẽ'dẽtʃi] ADJ descending, going down ■ M/F descendant

descender [desẽ'deʳ] VI: **~ de** to descend from

descentralização [dʒisẽtraliza'sãw] F decentralization

descentralizar [dʒisẽtrali'zaʳ] VT to decentralize

descer [de'seʳ] VT (escada) to go (ou come) down; (bagagem) to take down ■ VI (saltar) to get off; (baixar) to go (ou come) down; **~ a pormenores** to get down to details; **descida** [de'sida] F descent; (declive) slope; (abaixamento) fall, drop

desclassificação [dʒiʃklasifika'sãw] F disqualification

desclassificar [dʒiʃklasifi'kaʳ] VT (eliminar) to disqualify; (desacreditar) to discredit

descoberta [dʒiʃko'bɛxta] F discovery; (invenção) invention

descoberto, -a [dʒiʃko'bɛxtu, a] PP de **descobrir** ■ ADJ (nu) bare, naked; (exposto) exposed ■ M overdraft; **a ~** openly; **conta a ~** overdrawn account; **pôr** ou **sacar a ~** (conta) to overdraw

descobridor, a [dʒiʃkobri'doʳ(a)] M/F discoverer; (explorador) explorer

descobrimento [dʒiʃkobri'mẽtu] M discovery;

Descobrimentos MPL see below

● **DESCOBRIMENTOS**

● Portugal enjoyed a period of unrivalled
● overseas expansion during the 15th century,
● mainly due to the seafaring expertise of
● Henry the Navigator. He organized and
● financed several voyages to Africa, which
● eventually led to the rounding of the Cape
● of Good Hope in 1488 by Bartolomeu Dias.
● In 1497, Vasco da Gama became the first
● European to travel by sea to India, where
● he established a lucrative spice trade, and
● a few years later, in 1500, Pedro Álvares
● Cabral reached Brazil, which he claimed for
● Portugal. Brazil remained under Portuguese
● rule until 1822.

descobrir [dʒiʃko'briʳ] VT to discover; (tirar a cobertura de) to uncover; (panela) to take the lid off; (averiguar) to find out; (enigma) to solve

descolar [dʒiʃko'laʳ] VT to unstick; (col: arranjar) to get hold of; (: dar) to give ■ VI: **a criança não descola da mãe** the child won't leave its mother's side

descoloração [dʒiʃkolora'sãw] F discolouration (Brit), discoloration (US)

descolorante [dʒiʃkolo'rãtʃi] ADJ bleaching ■ M bleach

descolorar [dʒiʃkolo'raʳ] VT, VI = **descorar**

descolorir [dʒiʃkolo'riʳ] VT to discolour (Brit), discolor (US); (cabelo) to bleach ■ VI to fade

descomedimento [dʒiʃkomedʒi'mẽtu] M lack of moderation

descompassado, -a [dʒiʃkõpa'sadu, a] ADJ (exagerado) out of all proportion; (ritmo) out of step

descompor (irreg) VT to disarrange; (insultar) to abuse; (repreender) to scold, tell off; (fisionomia) to distort, twist; **descompor-se** VR (desordinar-se) to fall into disarray; (fisionomia) to be twisted; (desarrumar-se) to expose o.s.

descomposto, -a [dʒiʃkõ'poʃtu, 'pɔʃta] PP de **descompor** ■ ADJ (desalinhado) dishevelled; (fisionomia) twisted

descompostura [dʒiʃkõpoʃ'tura] F (repreensão) dressing-down; (insulto) abuse; **passar uma ~ em alguém** to give sb a dressing-down; to hurl abuse at sb

descompressão [dʒiʃkõpre'sãw] F decompression

descomprometido, -a [dʒiʃkõprome'tʃidu, a] ADJ (sem namorado) unattached

descomunal [dʒiʃkomu'naw] (pl -ais) ADJ (fora do comum) extraordinary; (colossal) huge, enormous

desconcentrar [dʒiʃkõsẽ'traʳ] VT to distract; **desconcentrar-se** VR to lose one's concentration

desconcertado, -a [dʒiʃkõsex'tadu, a] ADJ disconcerted

desconcertante [dʒiʃkõsex'tãtʃi] ADJ
disconcerting

desconcertar [dʒiʃkõsex'taʳ] VT (atrapalhar) to
confuse, baffle; **desconcertar-se** VR to get
upset

desconexo, -a [dʒiʃko'nɛksu, a] ADJ (desunido)
disconnected, unrelated; (incoerente) incoherent

desconfiado, -a [dʒiʃkõ'fjadu, a] ADJ suspicious,
distrustful ■ M/F suspicious person

desconfiança [dʒiʃkõ'fjãsa] F suspicion,
distrust

desconfiar [dʒiʃkõ'fjaʳ] VI to be suspicious; ~
de alguém (não ter confiança em) to distrust sb;
(suspeitar) to suspect sb; ~ **que ...** to have the
feeling that ....

desconforme [dʒiʃkõ'fɔxmi] ADJ disagreeing,
at variance

desconfortável [dʒiʃkõfox'tavew] (pl -eis) ADJ
uncomfortable

desconforto [dʒiʃkõ'foxtu] M discomfort

descongelar [dʒiʃkõʒe'laʳ] VT (degelar) to thaw
out; **descongelar-se** VR (derreter-se) to melt

descongestionante [dʒiʃkõʒeʃtʃjo'nãtʃi] ADJ, M
decongestant

descongestionar [dʒiʃkõʃeʃtʃjo'naʳ] VT
(cabeça, trânsito) to clear; (rua, cidade) to relieve
congestion in

desconhecer [dʒiʃkoɲe'seʳ] VT (ignorar) not to
know; (não reconhecer) not to recognize; (um
benefício) not to acknowledge; (não admitir) not to
accept; **desconhecido, -a** [dʒiʃkoɲe'sidu, a] ADJ
unknown ■ M/F stranger

desconhecimento [dʒiʃkoɲesi'mẽtu] M
ignorance

desconjuntado, -a [dʒiʃkõʒũ'tadu, a] ADJ
disjointed; (ossos) dislocated

desconjuntar [dʒiʃkõʒũ'taʳ] VT (ossos) to
dislocate; **desconjuntar-se** VR to come apart

desconsideração [dʒiʃkõsidera'sãw] F: ~ **(de
algo)** disregard (for sth)

desconsiderar [dʒiʃkõside'raʳ] VT: ~ **alguém** to
show a lack of consideration for sb; ~ **algo** to
fail to take sth into consideration

desconsolado, -a [dʒiʃkõso'ladu, a] ADJ
miserable, disconsolate

desconsolador, a [dʒiʃkõsola'doʳ(a)] ADJ
distressing

desconsolar [dʒiʃkõso'laʳ] VT to sadden,
depress; **desconsolar-se** VR to despair

descontar [dʒiʃkõ'taʳ] VT (abater) to deduct; (não
levar em conta) to discount; (não fazer caso de) to
make light of

descontentamento [dʒiʃkõtẽta'mẽtu] M
discontent; (desprazer) displeasure

descontentar [dʒiʃkõtẽ'taʳ] VT to displease

descontente [dʒiʃkõ'tẽtʃi] ADJ discontented,
dissatisfied

descontínuo, -a [dʒiʃkõ'tʃinwu, a] ADJ broken

desconto [dʒiʃ'kõtu] M discount; **com ~** at

a discount; **dar um ~ (para)** (fig) to make
allowances (for)

descontração [dʒiʃkõtra'sãw] F casualness

descontraído, -a [dʒiʃkõtra'idu, a] ADJ casual,
relaxed

descontrair [dʒiʃkõtra'iʳ] VT to relax;
descontrair-se VR to relax

descontrolar-se [dʒiʃkõtro'laxsi] VR (situação)
to get out of control; (pessoa) to lose one's self-
control

descontrole [dʒiʃkõ'troli] M lack of control

desconversar [dʒiʃkõvex'saʳ] VI to change the
subject

descorar [dʒiʃko'raʳ] VT to discolour (Brit),
discolor (US) ■ VI to pale, fade

descortês, -esa [dʒiʃkox'teʃ, teza] ADJ rude,
impolite

descortesia [dʒiʃkoxte'zia] F rudeness,
impoliteness

descortinar [dʒiʃkoxtʃi'naʳ] VT (retrato) to
unveil; (avistar) to catch sight of; (notar) to notice

descoser [dʒiʃko'zeʳ] VT (descosturar) to unstitch;
(rasgar) to rip apart; **descoser-se** VR to come
apart at the seams

descosturar [dʒiʃkoʃtu'raʳ] (BR) VT = **descoser**

descrédito [dʒiʃ'krɛdʒitu] M discredit

descrença [dʒiʃ'krẽsa] F disbelief, incredulity

descrente [dʒiʃ'krẽtʃi] ADJ sceptical (Brit),
skeptical (US) ■ M/F sceptic (Brit), skeptic (US)

descrer [dʒiʃ'kreʳ] (irreg) VT to disbelieve ■ VI: ~
de not to believe in

descrever [dʒiʃkre'veʳ] VT to describe

descrição [dʒiʃkri'sãw] (pl -ões) F description;
descritivo, -a [dʒiʃkri'tʃivu, a] ADJ descriptive

descrito, -a [dʒiʃ'kritu, a] PP de **descrever**

descubro etc [dʒiʃ'kubru] VB v **descobrir**

descuidado, -a [dʒiʃkwi'dadu, a] ADJ careless

descuidar [dʒiʃkwi'daʳ] VT to neglect ■ VI: ~ **de**
to neglect, disregard; **descuido** [dʒiʃ'kwidu]
M (falta de cuidado) carelessness; (negligência)
neglect; (erro) oversight, slip; **por descuido**
inadvertently

desculpa [dʒiʃ'kuwpa] F (pretexto, escusa) excuse;
(perdão) pardon; **pedir ~s a alguém por** ou
de algo to apologise to sb for sth; **desculpar**
[dʒiʃkuw'paʳ] VT (justificar) to excuse; (perdoar) to
pardon, forgive; **desculpar-se** VR to apologize;
desculpar algo a alguém to forgive sb for sth;
desculpe! (I'm) sorry, I beg your pardon

desculpável [dʒiʃkuw'pavew] (pl -eis) ADJ
forgivable

○ **PALAVRA CHAVE**

desde ['deʒdʒi] PREP **1** (lugar): **desde ... até ...**
from ... to ...; **andamos desde a praia até o
restaurante** we walked from the beach to the
restaurant

2 (tempo: + adv, n): **desde então** from then on,

NB: European Portuguese adds the following consonants to certain words: **b** (sú(b)dito, su(b)til); **c** (a(c)ção,
a(c)cionista, a(c)to); **m** (inde(m)ne); **p** (ado(p)çã, ado(p)tar); for further details see p. xiii.

ever since; **desde já** (*de agora*) from now on; (*imediatamente*) at once, right now; **desde o casamento** since the wedding

3 (*tempo*: + *vb*) since; for; **conhecemo-nos desde 1978/há 20 anos** we've known each other since 1978/for 20 years; **não o vejo desde 1983** I haven't seen him since 1983

4 (*variedade*): **desde os mais baratos até os mais luxuosos** from the cheapest to the most luxurious

■ CONJ: **desde que** since; **desde que comecei a trabalhar não o vi mais** I haven't seen him since I started work; **não saiu de casa desde que chegou** he hasn't been out since he arrived

desdém [deʒ'dẽ] M scorn, disdain

desdenhar [deʒde'ɲaʳ] VT to scorn, disdain

desdenhoso, -a [deʒdeɲozu, ɔza] ADJ disdainful, scornful

desdentado, -a [dʒizdẽ'tadu, a] ADJ toothless

desdigo *etc* [dʒiʒ'dʒigu] VB *v* **desdizer**

desdisse *etc* [dʒiʒ'dʒisi] VB *v* **desdizer**

desdita [dʒiʒ'dʒita] F (*desventura*) misfortune; (*infelicidade*) unhappiness

desdizer [dʒiʒdʒi'zeʳ] (*irreg*) VT to contradict; **desdizer-se** VR to go back on one's word

desdobramento [dʒiʒdobra'mẽtu] M (*de aventura, crise*) ramification; (*de obra etc*) spin-off; (Com: *de conta*) breakdown

desdobrar [dʒiʒdo'braʳ] VT (*abrir*) to unfold; (*esforços*) to increase, redouble; (*tropas*) to deploy; (Com: *conta*) to break down; (*bandeira*) to unfurl; (*dividir em grupos*) to split up; **desdobrar-se** VR to unfold; (*empenhar-se*) to work hard, make a big effort

deseducar [dʒizedu'kaʳ] VT: ~ **alguém** to neglect sb's education

desejar [dese'ʒaʳ] VT to want, desire; ~ **ardentemente** to long for; **que deseja?** what would you like?; ~ **algo a alguém** to wish sb sth

desejável [dese'ʒavew] (*pl* -**eis**) ADJ desirable

desejo [de'zeʒu] M wish, desire; **desejoso, -a** [deze'ʒozu, ɔza] ADJ: **desejoso de algo** wishing for sth; **desejoso de fazer** keen to do

deselegância [dʒizele'gãsja] F lack of elegance

deselegante [dʒizele'gãtʃi] ADJ inelegant

desemaranhar [dʒizimara'ɲaʳ] VT to disentangle

desembainhar [dʒizẽbaj'ɲaʳ] VT (*espada*) to draw

desembalar [dʒizẽba'laʳ] VT to unwrap

desembaraçado, -a [dʒizẽbara'sadu, a] ADJ (*livre*) free, clear; (*desinibido*) uninhibited, free and easy; (*expedito*) efficient; (*cabelo*) untangled

desembaraçar [dʒizẽbara'saʳ] VT (*livrar*) to free; (Com: *navio, remessa*) to clear; (*cabelo*) to untangle; **desembaraçar-se** VR (*desinibir-se*) to lose one's inhibitions; (*tornar-se expedito*) to show initiative; ~-**se de** to get rid of

desembaraço [dʒizẽba'rasu] M liveliness; (*facilidade*) ease; (*confiança*) self-assurance; ~

alfandegário customs clearance

desembarcar [dʒizẽbax'kaʳ] VT (*carga*) to unload; (*passageiros*) to let off ■ VI to disembark

desembargador, a [dʒizẽbaxga'do(a)] M/F High Court judge

desembarque [dʒizẽ'baxki] M landing, disembarkation; "~" (*no aeroporto*) "arrivals"

desembestado, -a [dʒizẽbeʃ'tadu, a] ADJ: **sair** ~ to rush off *ou* out

desembocadura [dʒizẽboka'dura] F mouth

desembocar [dʒizẽbo'kaʳ] VI: ~ **em** (*rio*) to flow into; (*rua*) to lead into

desembolsar [dʒizẽbow'saʳ] VT to spend

desembolso [dʒizẽ'bowsu] M expenditure

desembrulhar [dʒizẽbru'ʎaʳ] VT to unwrap

desembuchar [dʒizẽbu'ʃaʳ] (*col*) VT to get off one's chest ■ VI to get things off one's chest

desempacotar [dʒizẽpako'taʳ] VT to unpack

desempatar [dʒizẽpa'taʳ] VT to decide ■ VI to decide the match (*ou* race *etc*); **desempate** [dʒizẽ'patʃi] M: **partida de desempate** (*jogo*) play-off, decider

desempenar [dʒizẽpe'naʳ] VT (*endireitar*) to straighten; **desempenar-se** VR to stand up straight

desempenhar [dʒizẽpe'ɲaʳ] VT (*cumprir*) to carry out, fulfil (*Brit*), fulfill (*US*); (*papel*) to play; **desempenho** [dʒizẽ'peɲu] M performance; (*de obrigações etc*) fulfilment (*Brit*), fulfillment (*US*)

desemperrar [dʒizẽpe'xaʳ] VT, VI to loosen

desempregado, -a [dʒizẽpre'gadu, a] ADJ unemployed ■ M/F unemployed person

desempregar-se [dʒizẽpre'gaxsi] VR to lose one's job

desemprego [dʒizẽ'pregu] M unemployment

desencadear [dʒizẽka'dʒjaʳ] VT to unleash; (*despertar*) to provoke, trigger off ■ VI (*chuva*) to pour; **desencadear-se** VR to break loose; (*tempestade*) to break

desencaixado, -a [dʒizẽkaj'ʃadu, a] ADJ misplaced

desencaixar [dʒizẽkaj'ʃaʳ] VT to put out of joint; (*deslocar*) to dislodge; **desencaixar-se** VR to become dislodged

desencaixotar [dʒizẽkajʃo'taʳ] VT to unpack

desencalhar [dʒizẽka'ʎaʳ] VT (*navio*) to refloat ■ VI to be refloated; (*col*: *moça*) to find a husband

desencaminhar [dʒizẽkami'ɲaʳ] VT to lead astray; (*dinheiro*) to embezzle; **desencaminhar-se** VR to go astray

desencantar [dʒizẽkã'taʳ] VT to disenchant; (*desiludir*) to disillusion

desencardir [dʒizẽkax'dʒiʳ] VT to clean

desencargo [dʒizẽ'kaxgu] M fulfilment (*Brit*), fulfillment (*US*); **para** ~ **de consciência** to clear one's conscience

desencarregar-se [dʒizẽkaxe'gaxsi] VR (*de obrigação*) to discharge o.s.

desencavar [dʒizẽka'vaʳ] VT to unearth

desencontrar [dʒizẽkõ'traʳ] VT to keep apart; **desencontrar-se** VR (*não se encontrar*) to miss each other; (*perder-se um do outro*) to lose each

other; **~-se de** to miss; to get separated from
desencontro [dʒizē'kõtru] M failure to meet
desencorajar [dʒizẽkora'ʒaʳ] VT to discourage
desencostar [dʒizēkoʃ'taʳ] VT to move away;
desencostar-se VR: **desencostar-se de** to
move away from
desenfastiar [dʒizẽfaʃ'tʃjaʳ] VT to amuse;
desenfastiar-se VR to amuse o.s.
desenferrujar [dʒizẽfexu'zaʳ] VT (metal) to clean
the rust off; (pernas) to stretch; (língua) to brush
up
desenfreado, -a [dʒizē'frjadu, a] ADJ wild
desenganado, -a [dʒizẽga'nadu, a] ADJ (sem
cura) incurable; (desiludido) disillusioned
desenganar [dʒizẽga'naʳ] VT: **~ alguém** to
disillusion sb; (de falsas crenças) to open sb's eyes;
(doente) to give up hope of curing; **desenganar-
se** VR to become disillusioned; (sair de erro)
to realize the truth; **desengano** [dʒizē'ganu]
M disillusionment; (desapontamento)
disappointment
desengarrafar [dʒizẽgaxa'faʳ] VT (trânsito) to
unblock; (vinho) to pour out
desengatar [dʒizẽga'taʳ] VT to unhitch; (Ferro)
to uncouple
desengonçado, -a [dʒizẽgõ'sadu, a] ADJ (mal-
seguro) rickety; (pessoa) ungainly
desengrenado, -a [dʒizẽgre'nadu, a] ADJ (Auto)
out of gear, in neutral
desengrenar [dʒizẽgre'naʳ] VT to disengage;
(carro) to put in neutral
desengrossar [dʒizẽgro'saʳ] VT to thin
desenhar [deze'ɲaʳ] VT to draw; (Tec) to design;
desenhar-se VR (destacar-se) to stand out;
(figurar-se) to take shape; **desenhista** [deze'ɲiʃta]
M/F (Tec) designer
desenho [de'zeɲu] M drawing; (modelo) design;
(esboço) sketch; (plano) plan; **~ animado** cartoon;
~ industrial industrial design
desenlace [dʒizē'lasi] M outcome
desenredar [dʒizẽxe'daʳ] VT to disentangle;
(mistério) to unravel; (questão) to sort out, resolve;
(dúvida) to clear up; (explicação) to clarify;
desenredar-se VR: **desenredar-se de algo**
to extricate o.s. from sth; **~ alguém de algo** to
extricate sb from sth
desenrolar [dʒizẽxo'laʳ] VT to unroll; (narrativa)
to develop; **desenrolar-se** VR to unfold
desentender [dʒizẽtẽ'deʳ] VT (não entender)
to misunderstand; **desentender-se** VR:
desentender-se com to have a disagreement
with; **desentendido, -a** [dʒizẽtẽ'dʒidu, a] ADJ:
fazer-se de desentendido to pretend not to
understand
desentendimento [dʒizẽtẽdʒi'mẽtu] M
misunderstanding
desenterrar [dʒizẽte'xaʳ] VT (cadáver) to
exhume; (tesouro) to dig up; (descobrir) to bring
to light

desentoado, -a [dʒizē'twadu, a] ADJ (desafinado)
out of tune
desentranhar [dʒizẽtra'ɲaʳ] VT to disembowel;
(raiz) to draw out; (lembranças) to dredge up;
(mistério) to fathom
desentrosado, -a [dʒizẽtro'zadu, a] ADJ
unintegrated
desentupir [dʒizẽtu'piʳ] VT to unblock
desenvolto, -a [dʒizē'vowtu, a] ADJ
(desembaraçado) self-assured, confident;
(desinibido) uninhibited
desenvoltura [dʒizẽvow'tura] F (desembaraço)
self-confidence
desenvolver [dʒizẽvow've ʳ] VT to develop;
desenvolver-se VR to develop
desenvolvido, -a [dʒizẽvow'vidu, a] ADJ
developed
desenvolvimento [dʒizẽvowvi'mẽtu] M
development; (crescimento) growth; **país em ~**
developing country
desenxabido, -a [dʒizẽʒa'bidu, a] ADJ dull
desequilibrado, -a [dʒizekili'bradu, a] ADJ
unbalanced
desequilibrar [dʒizekili'braʳ] VT (pessoa) to
throw off balance; (objeto) to tip over; (fig) to
unbalance; **desequilibrar-se** VR to lose one's
balance; to tip over
desequilíbrio [dʒizeki'librju] M imbalance
deserção [dezex'sãw] F desertion
desertar [desex'taʳ] VT to desert, abandon ■ VI
to desert; **deserto, -a** [de'zɛxtu, a] ADJ deserted
■ M desert
desertor, a [dezex'to ʳ(a)] M/F deserter
desesperado, -a [dʒizeʃpe'radu, a] ADJ
desperate; (furioso) furious
desesperador, a [dʒizeʃpera'doʳ(a)] ADJ
desperate; (enfurecedor) maddening
desesperança [dʒizeʃpe'rãsa] F despair
desesperançar [dʒizeʃperã'saʳ] VT: **~ alguém** to
make sb despair
desesperar [dʒizeʃpe'raʳ] VT to drive to despair;
(enfurecer) to infuriate; **desesperar-se** VR to
despair; (enfurecer-se) to become infuriated;
desespero [dʒizeʃ'peru] M despair, desperation;
(raiva) fury; **levar ao desespero** to drive to
despair
desestabilizar [dʒizeʃtabili'zaʳ] VT to
destabilize
desestimulador, a [dʒizeʃtʃimula'doʳ(a)] ADJ
discouraging
desestimular [dʒizeʃtʃimu'laʳ] VT to discourage
desfaçatez [dʒiʃfasa'teʒ] F impudence, cheek
desfalcar [dʒiʃfaw'kaʳ] VT (dinheiro) to embezzle;
(reduzir): **~ (de)** to reduce (by); **~ uma firma em
$400** to embezzle $400 from a firm; **o jogo está
desfalcado** the game is incomplete
desfalecer [dʒiʃfale'seʳ] VT (enfraquecer) to
weaken ■ VI (enfraquecer) to weaken; (desmaiar)
to faint

NB: *European Portuguese adds the following consonants to certain words*: **b** (sú(b)dito, su(b)til); **c** (a(c)ção,
   a(c)cionista, a(c)to); **m** (inde(m)ne); **p** (ado(p)çã, ado(p)tar); *for further details see p. xiii.*

desfalecimento [dʒiʃfalesi'mẽtu] M (*enfraquecimento*) weakening; (*desmaio*) faint
desfalque [dʒiʃ'fawki] M (*de dinheiro*) embezzlement; (*diminuição*) reduction
desfavor [dʒiʃfa'voʳ] M disfavour (*Brit*), disfavor (*US*)
desfavorável [dʒiʃfavo'ravew] (*pl* -**eis**) ADJ unfavourable (*Brit*), unfavorable (*US*)
desfavorecer [dʒiʃfavore'seʳ] VT to discriminate against
desfazer [dʒiʃfa'zeʳ] (*irreg*) VT (*costura*) to undo; (*dúvidas*) to dispel; (*agravo*) to redress; (*grupo*) to break up; (*contrato*) to dissolve; (*noivado*) to break off ▪ VI: ~ **de alguém** to belittle sb; **desfazer-se** VR (*desaparecer*) to vanish; (*tecido*) to come to pieces; (*grupo*) to break up; (*vaso*) to break; ~-**se de** (*livrar-se*) to get rid of; ~-**se em lágrimas/ gentilezas** to burst into tears/go out of one's way to please
desfechar [dʒiʃfe'ʃaʳ] VT (*disparar*) to fire; (*setas*) to shoot; (*golpe*) to deal; (*insultos*) to hurl
desfecho [dʒiʃ'feʃu] M ending, outcome
desfeita [dʒiʃ'fejta] F affront, insult
desfeito, -a [dʒiʃ'fejtu, a] PP *de* **desfazer** ▪ ADJ (*desmanchado*) undone; (*cama*) unmade; (*contrato*) broken
desferir [dʒiʃfe'riʳ] VT (*golpe*) to strike; (*sons*) to emit; (*lançar*) to throw
desfiar [dʒiʃ'fjaʳ] VT (*tecido*) to unravel; (*Culin: galinha*) to tear into thin shreds; **desfiar-se** VR to become frayed; ~ **o rosário** to say one's rosary
desfiguração [dʒiʃfigura'sãw] F distortion
desfigurar [dʒiʃfigu'raʳ] VT (*pessoa, cidade*) to disfigure; (*texto*) to mutilate; **desfigurar-se** VR to be disfigured
desfiladeiro [dʒiʃfila'dejru] M (*de montanha*) pass
desfilar [dʒiʃfi'laʳ] VI to parade; **desfile** [dʒiʃ'fili] M parade, procession
desflorestamento [dʒiʃfloreʃta'mẽtu] M deforestation
desflorestar [dʒiʃfloreʃ'taʳ] VT to clear of forest
desforra [dʒiʃ'foxa] F (*vingança*) revenge; (*reparação*) redress; **tirar** ~ to get even
desfraldar [dʒiʃfraw'daʳ] VT to unfurl
desfranzir [dʒiʃfrã'ziʳ] VT to smooth out
desfrutar [dʒiʃfru'taʳ] VT to enjoy ▪ VI: ~ **de** to enjoy; ~ **de bom conceito** to have a good reputation, be well thought of
desfrute [dʒiʃ'frutʃi] M (*deleite*) enjoyment; (*desplante*): **ter o** ~ **de fazer algo** to have the nerve to do sth
desgarrado, -a [dʒiʒga'xadu, a] ADJ stray; (*navio*) off course
desgarrar-se [dʒiʒga'xaxsi] VR: ~ **de** to stray from
desgastante [dʒiʒgaʃ'tãtʃi] ADJ (*fig*) stressful
desgastar [dʒiʒgaʃ'taʳ] VT to wear away, erode; (*pessoa*) to wear out, get down; **desgastar-se** VR to be worn away; (*pessoa*) to get worn out
desgaste [dʒiʒ'gaʃtʃi] M wear and tear; (*mental*) stress

desgostar [dʒiʒgoʃ'taʳ] VT to upset ▪ VI: ~ **de** to dislike; **desgostar-se** VR: **desgostar-se de** to go off; ~-**se com** to take offence at
desgosto [dʒiʒ'goʃtu] M (*desprazer*) displeasure; (*pesar*) sorrow, unhappiness
desgostoso, -a [dʒiʒgoʃ'tozu, ɔza] ADJ sad, sorrowful
desgraça [dʒiʒ'grasa] F (*desventura*) misfortune; (*miséria*) misery; (*desfavor*) disgrace
desgraçado, -a [dʒiʒgra'sadu, a] ADJ poor; (*col: admirável*) amazing ▪ M/F wretch; **estou com uma gripe desgraçada** (*col*) I've got a hell of a cold
desgraçar [dʒiʒgra'saʳ] VT to disgrace
desgraceira [dʒiʒgra'sejra] F series of misfortunes
desgravar [dʒiʒgra'vaʳ] VT (*música*) to wipe, rub off
desgrenhado, -a [dʒiʒgre'ɲadu, a] ADJ dishevelled, tousled
desgrenhar [dʒiʒgre'ɲaʳ] VT to tousle; **desgrenhar-se** VR to get tousled
desgrudar [dʒiʒgru'daʳ] VT to unstick ▪ VI: ~ **de** to tear o.s. away from; ~ **algo de algo** to take sth off sth
desguarnecer [dʒiʒgwaxne'seʳ] VT to strip
desidratação [dʒizidrata'sãw] F dehydration
desidratante [dʒizidra'tãtʃi] ADJ dehydrating
desidratar [dʒizidra'taʳ] VT to dehydrate
design [dʒi'zãjn] M design
designação [dezigna'sãw] (*pl* -**ões**) F designation; (*nomeação*) appointment
designar [dezig'naʳ] VT to designate; (*nomear*) to name, appoint; (*dia, data*) to fix
designer [dʒi'zajneʳ] (*pl* -**s**) M/F designer
desígnio [de'zignju] M (*propósito*) purpose; (*intenção*) intention
desigual [dezi'gwaw] (*pl* -**ais**) ADJ unequal; (*terreno*) uneven; **desigualdade** [dʒizigwaw'dadʒi] F inequality
desiludir [dʒizilu'dʒiʳ] VT (*desenganar*) to disillusion; (*causar decepção a*) to disappoint; **desiludir-se** VR to lose one's illusions
desilusão [dʒizilu'zãw] F disillusionment, disenchantment
desimpedido, -a [dʒizĩpe'dʒidu, a] ADJ free
desimpedir [dʒizĩpe'dʒiʳ] VT (*desobstruir*) to unblock; (*trânsito*) to ease
desinchar [dʒizin'ʃaʳ] VT (*Med*) to get rid of the swelling on ▪ VI: **meu pé desinchou** the swelling in my foot went down
desincumbir-se [dʒizĩkũ'bixsi] VR: ~ **de algo** to carry sth out
desinfeccionar [dʒizĩfeksjo'naʳ] VT to disinfect
desinfetante [dʒizĩfe'tãtʃi] (PT -**ct**-) ADJ, M disinfectant
desinfetar [dʒizĩfe'taʳ] (PT -**ct**-) VT to disinfect
desinflamar [dʒizĩfla'maʳ] VT to remove *ou* get rid of the inflammation on; **desinflamar-se** VR to become less inflamed
desinibido, -a [dʒizini'bidu, a] ADJ uninhibited
desinibir [dʒizini'biʳ] VT to make less inhibited;

desinibir-se VR to lose one's inhibitions

desintegração[dʒizintegra'sãw] F disintegration, break-up

desintegrar[dʒizĩte'gra^r] VT to separate; **desintegrar-se** VR to disintegrate, fall to pieces

desinteressado, -a[dʒizĩtere'sadu, a] ADJ disinterested

desinteressar[dʒizĩtere'sa^r] VT: ~ **alguém de algo** to make sb lose interest in sth; **desinteressar-se** VR to lose interest

desinteresse[dʒizĩte'resi] M (falta de interesse) lack of interest

desintoxicar[dʒizĩtoksi'ka^r] VT to detoxify

desistência[deziʃ'tẽsja] F giving up; (cancelamento) cancellation

desistir[deziʃ'tʃi^r] VI to give up; ~ **de fumar** to stop smoking; **ele ia, mas no final desistiu** he was going, but in the end he gave up the idea ou he decided not to

desjejum[dʒiʒe'ʒũ] M breakfast

deslanchar[dʒiʒlã'ʃa^r] VI (carro) to move off; (projeto) to get off the ground, take off

deslavado, -a[dʒiʒla'vadu, a] ADJ (pessoa, atitude) shameless; (mentira) blatant

desleal[dʒiʒle'aw] (pl -ais) ADJ disloyal

deslealdade[dʒiʒleaw'dadʒi] F disloyalty

desleixado, -a[dʒiʒlej'ʃadu, a] ADJ sloppy

desleixo[dʒiʒ'lejʃu] M sloppiness

desligado, -a[dʒiʒli'gadu, a] ADJ (eletricidade) off; (pessoa) absent-minded; **estar** ~ to be miles away

desligar[dʒiʒli'ga^r] VT (Tec) to disconnect; (luz, TV, motor) to switch off; (telefone) to hang up; **desligar-se** VR: **desligar-se de algo** (afastar-se) to leave sth; (problemas etc) to turn one's back on sth; **não desligue** (Tel) hold the line

deslizante[dʒiʒli'zãtʃi] ADJ slippery

deslizar[dʒiʒli'za^r] VI to slide; (por acidente) to slip; (passar de leve) to glide; **deslize**[dʒiʒ'lizi] M (lapso) lapse; (escorregadela) slip

deslocado, -a[dʒiʒlo'kadu, a] ADJ (membro) dislocated; (desambientado) out of place

deslocamento[dʒiʒloka'mẽtu] M moving; (de membro) dislocation; (de funcionário) transfer

deslocar[dʒiʒlo'ka^r] VT (mover) to move; (articulação) to dislocate; (funcionário) to transfer; **deslocar-se** VR to move; to be dislocated; **eu me desloquei até lá à toa** I went all the way there for nothing

deslumbrado, -a[dʒiʒlũ'bradu, a] ADJ (ofuscado) dazzled; (maravilhado) amazed ■ M/F impressionable person

deslumbramento[dʒiʒlũbra'mẽtu] M dazzle; (fascinação) fascination

deslumbrante[dʒiʒlũ'brãtʃi] ADJ (ofuscante) dazzling; (casa, festa) amazing

deslumbrar[dʒiʒlũ'bra^r] VT (ofuscar) to dazzle; (maravilhar) to amaze; (fascinar) to fascinate ■ VI

to be dazzling; to be amazing; **deslumbrar-se** VR: **deslumbrar-se com** to be fascinated by

deslustrar[dʒiʒluʃ'tra^r] VT to tarnish

desmaiado, -a[dʒiʒma'jadu, a] ADJ (sem sentidos) unconscious; (cor) pale

desmaiar[dʒiʒma'ja^r] VI to faint; **desmaio** [dʒiʒ'maju] M faint

desmamar[dʒiʒma'ma^r] VT to wean

desmancha-prazeres[dʒiʒ'manʃa-] M/F INV kill-joy, spoilsport

desmanchar[dʒiʒman'ʃa^r] VT (costura) to undo; (contrato) to break; (noivado) to break off; (penteado) to mess up; **desmanchar-se** VR (costura) to come undone

desmantelar[dʒiʒmãte'la^r] VT (demolir) to demolish; (desmontar) to dismantle, take apart

desmarcar[dʒiʒmax'ka^r] VT (compromisso) to cancel

desmascarar[dʒiʒmaʃka'ra^r] VT to unmask

desmatamento[dʒiʒmata'mẽtu] M deforestation

desmatar[dʒiʒma'ta^r] VT to clear the forest from

desmazelado, -a[dʒiʒmaze'ladu, a] ADJ slovenly, untidy

desmazelar-se[dʒiʒmaze'laxsi] VR to get untidy

desmedido, -a[dʒiʒme'dʒidu, a] ADJ excessive

desmembramento[dʒiʒmẽbra'mẽtu] M dismemberment

desmembrar[dʒiʒmẽ'bra^r] VT to dismember

desmemoriado, -a[dʒiʒmemo'rjadu, a] ADJ forgetful

desmentido[dʒiʒmẽ'tʃidu] M (negação) denial; (contradição) contradiction

desmentir[dʒiʒmẽ'tʃi^r] VT (contradizer) to contradict; (negar) to deny

desmerecer[dʒiʒmere'se^r] VT (não merecer) not to deserve; (desfazer de) to belittle

desmesurado, -a[dʒiʒmezu'radu, a] ADJ immense, enormous

desmilinguido, -a[dʒiʒmilĩ'gwidu, a] (col) ADJ spent

desmiolado, -a[dʒiʒmjo'ladu, a] ADJ brainless; (esquecido) forgetful

desmistificar[dʒiʒmiʃtʃifi'ka^r] VT to demystify; ~ **alguém** to remove the mystery surrounding sb

desmitificar[dʒiʒmitʃifi'ka^r] VT: ~ **algo/alguém** to dispel the myth(s) surrounding sth/sb

desmontar[dʒiʒmõ'ta^r] VT (máquina) to take to pieces ■ VI (do cavalo) to dismount, get off

desmoralização[dʒiʒmoraliza'sãw] F demoralization

desmoralizante[dʒiʒmorali'zãtʃi] ADJ demoralizing

desmoralizar[dʒiʒmorali'za^r] VT to demoralize

desmoronamento[dʒiʒmorona'mẽtu] M collapse

NB: European Portuguese adds the following consonants to certain words: **b** (sú(b)dito, su(b)til); **c** (a(c)ção, a(c)cionista, a(c)to); **m** (inde(m)ne); **p** (ado(p)çã, ado(p)tar); for further details see p. xiii.

desmoronar [dʒiʒmoro'na^r] VT to knock down ■ VI to collapse

desmotivado, -a [dʒiʒmotʃi'vadu, a] ADJ despondent

desmunhecar [dʒiʒmuɲe'ka^r] (col) VI (declarar-se homossexual) to come out; (fazer gestos efeminados) to be camp

desnatado, -a [dʒiʒna'tadu, a] ADJ (leite) skimmed

desnaturado, -a [dʒiʒnatu'radu, a] ADJ inhumane ■ M/F monster

desnecessário, -a [dʒiʒnese'sarju, a] ADJ unnecessary

desnível [dʒiʒ'nivew] M unevenness; (fig) difference

desnorteado, -a [dʒiʒnox'tʃjadu, a] ADJ (perturbado) bewildered, confused; (desorientado) off course

desnortear [dʒiʒnox'tʃja^r] VT (desorientar) to throw off course; (perturbar) to bewilder; **desnortear-se** VR to lose one's way; (perturbar-se) to become confused

desnudar [dʒiʒnu'da^r] VT to strip; (revelar) to expose; **desnudar-se** VR to undress

desnutrição [dʒiʒnutri'sãw] F malnutrition

desnutrido, -a [dʒiʒnu'tridu, a] ADJ malnourished

desobedecer [dʒizobede'se^r] VT to disobey; **desobediência** [dʒizobe'dʒjẽsja] F disobedience; **desobediente** [dʒizobe'dʒjẽtʃi] ADJ disobedient

desobrigar [dʒizobri'ga^r] VT: ~ **(de)** to free (from); ~ **de fazer algo** to free from doing sth

desobstruir [dʒizobiʃ'trwi^r] VT to unblock

desocupação [dʒizokupa'sãw] F (de casa) vacating; (falta de ocupação) leisure; (desemprego) unemployment

desocupado, -a [dʒizoku'padu, a] ADJ (casa) empty, vacant; (disponível) free; (sem trabalho) unemployed

desocupar [dʒizoku'pa^r] VT (casa) to vacate; (liberar) to free

desodorante [dʒizodo'rãtʃi] (PT -dorizante) M deodorant

desodorizar [dʒizodori'za^r] VT to deodorize

desolação [dezola'sãw] F (consternação) grief; (de um lugar) desolation; **desolado, -a** [dezo'ladu, a] ADJ (consternado) distressed; (lugar) desolate

desolar [dezo'la^r] VT (consternar) to distress; (lugar) to devastate

desonestidade [dezoneʃtʃi'dadʒi] F dishonesty

desonesto, -a [dezo'nɛʃtu, a] ADJ dishonest

desonra [dʒi'zõʃa] F dishonour (Brit), dishonor (US); (descrédito) disgrace

desonrar [dʒizõ'xa^r] VT (infamar) to disgrace; (mulher) to seduce; **desonrar-se** VR to disgrace o.s.

desonroso, -a [dʒizõ'xozu, ɔza] ADJ dishonourable (Brit), dishonorable (US)

desopilar [dʒizopi'la^r] VT (Med) to flush out; (mente) to clear

desoprimir [dʒizopri'mi^r] VT to relieve;

desoprimir-se VR to be relieved

desordeiro, -a [dʒizox'dejru, a] ADJ troublemaking ■ M/F troublemaker, hooligan

desordem [dʒi'zoxdẽ] F disorder, confusion; **em ~** (casa) untidy

desordenar [dʒizoxde'na^r] VT (tirar da ordem) to put out of order; (desarrumar) to mess up

desorganização [dʒizoxganiza'sãw] F disorganization

desorganizar [dʒizoxgani'za^r] VT to disorganize; (dissolver) to break up; **desorganizar-se** VR to become disorganized; to break up

desorientação [dʒizorjẽta'sãw] F bewilderment, confusion

desorientar [dʒizorjẽ'ta^r] VT (desnortear) to throw off course; (perturbar) to confuse; (desvairar) to unhinge; **desorientar-se** VR (perder-se) to lose one's way; to get confused; to go mad

desossar [dʒizo'sa^r] VT (galinha) to bone

desovar [dʒizo'va^r] VT to lay; (peixe) to spawn

despachado, -a [dʒiʃpa'ʃadu, a] ADJ (pessoa) efficient

despachante [dʒiʃpa'ʃãtʃi] M/F (de mercadorias) forwarding agent; (de documentos) agent (who handles official bureaucracy)

despachar [dʒiʃpa'ʃa^r] VT (expedir) to dispatch, send off; (atender, resolver) to deal with; (despedir) to sack ■ VI (funcionário) to work; **despachar-se** VR to hurry (up); **despacho** [dʒiʃ'paʃu] M dispatch; (de negócios) handling; (nota em requerimento) ruling; (reunião) consultation; (macumba) witchcraft

desparafusar [dʒiʃparafu'sa^r] VT to unscrew

despeço etc [dʒiʃ'pesu] VB V **despedir**

despedaçar [dʒiʃpeda'sa^r] VT (quebrar) to smash; (rasgar) to tear apart; **despedaçar-se** VR to smash; to tear

despedida [dʒiʃpe'dʒida] F (adeus) farewell; (de trabalhador) dismissal

despedir [dʒiʃpe'dʒi^r] VT (de emprego) to dismiss, sack; **despedir-se** VR: **despedir-se (de)** to say goodbye (to)

despeitado, -a [dʒiʃpej'tadu, a] ADJ spiteful; (ressentido) resentful

despeito [dʒiʃ'pejtu] M spite; **a ~ de** in spite of, despite

despejar [dʒiʃpe'ʒa^r] VT (água) to pour; (esvaziar) to empty; (inquilino) to evict; **despejo** [dʒiʃ'peʒu] M (de casa) eviction; **quarto de despejo** junk room

despencar [dʒiʃpẽ'ka^r] VI to fall down, tumble down

despender [dʒiʃpẽ'de^r] VT (dinheiro) to spend; (energia) to expend

despenhadeiro [dʒiʃpeɲa'dejro] M cliff, precipice

despensa [dʒiʃ'pẽsa] F larder

despentear [dʒiʃpẽ'tʃja^r] VT (cabelo: sem querer) to mess up; (: de propósito) to let down; **despentear-se** VR to mess one's hair up; to let one's hair down

despercebido, -a [dʒiʃpexse'bidu, a] ADJ
unnoticed

desperdiçar [dʒiʃpexdʒi'saʳ] VT to waste;
(*dinheiro*) to squander; **desperdício**
[dʒiʃpex'dʒisju] M waste

despersonalizar [dʒiʃpexsonali'zaʳ] VT to
depersonalize

despersuadir [dʒiʃpexswa'dʒiʳ] VT: ~ **alguém de**
fazer algo to dissuade sb from doing sth

despertador [dʒiʃpexta'doʳ] M (*tb:* **relogio**
despertador) alarm clock

despertar [dʒiʃpex'taʳ] VT (*pessoa*) to wake;
(*suspeitas, interesse*) to arouse; (*reminiscências*) to
revive; (*apetite*) to whet ■ VI to wake up, awake
■ M awakening; **desperto, -a** [dʒiʃ'pɛxtu, a] ADJ
awake

despesa [dʒiʃ'peza] F expense; **despesas** FPL (*de*
uma empresa) expenses, costs; **~s antecipadas**
prepayments; **~s gerais** (*Com*) overheads; **~s**
mercantis sales and marketing expenses; **~s**
não-operacionais non-operating expenses
ou costs; **~s operacionais** operating expenses
ou costs; **~s tributárias** (*de uma empresa*)
corporation tax *sg*

despido, -a [dʒiʃ'pidu, a] ADJ (*nu*) naked, bare;
(*livre*) free

despir [dʒiʃ'piʳ] VT (*roupa*) to take off; (*pessoa*)
to undress; (*despojar*) to strip; **despir-se** VR to
undress

despistar [dʒiʃpiʃ'taʳ] VT to throw off the scent

desplante [dʒiʃ'plãtʃi] M (*fig*) nerve

despojado, -a [dʒiʃpo'ʒadu, a] ADJ (*pessoa*)
unambitious; (*lugar*) spartan, basic

despojar [dʒiʃpo'ʒaʳ] VT (*casas*) to loot, sack;
(*pessoas*) to rob; **~ alguém de algo** to strip sb
of sth

despojo [dʒiʃ'poʒu] M loot, booty; **despojos**
MPL: **despojo s mortais** (*restos*) mortal remains

despoluir [dʒiʃpo'lwiʳ] VT to clean up

despontar [dʒiʃpõ'taʳ] VI to emerge; (*sol*) to
come out; (: *ao amanhecer*) to come up; **ao ~ do**
dia at daybreak

desporto [dʒiʃ'poxtu] M sport

déspota ['dɛʃpota] M/F despot

despotismo [deʃpo'tʃiʒmu] M despotism

despovoado, -a [dʒiʃpo'vwadu, a] ADJ
uninhabited ■ M wilderness

despovoar [dʒiʃpo'vwaʳ] VT to depopulate

desprazer [dʒiʃpra'zeʳ] M displeasure

desprecavido, -a [dʒiʃpreka'vidu, a] ADJ
unprepared, careless

despregar [dʒiʃpre'gaʳ] VT to take off, detach;
despregar-se VR to come off; **~ os olhos de**
algo to take one's eyes off sth

desprender [dʒiʃprẽ'deʳ] VT (*soltar*) to
loosen; (*desatar*) to unfasten; (*emitir*) to emit;
desprender-se VR (*botão*) to come off; (*cheiro*)
to be given off; **~-se dos braços de alguém** to

extricate o.s. from sb's arms

desprendido, -a [dʒiʃprẽ'dʒidu, a] ADJ (*abnegado*)
disinterested

despreocupado, -a [dʒiʃpreoku'padu, a] ADJ
carefree, unconcerned; **com a notícia ele**
ficou mais ~ after hearing the news he was
less concerned *ou* worried

despreocupar [dʒiʃpreoku'paʳ] VT: **~ alguém**
(de algo) to set sb's mind at rest (about sth);
despreocupar-se VR: **despreocupar-se (de**
algo) to stop worrying (about sth)

despreparado, -a [dʒiʃprepa'radu, a] ADJ
unprepared

despretensioso, -a [dʒiʃpretẽ'sjozu, ɔza] ADJ
unpretentious, modest

desprestigiar [dʒiʃpreʃtʃi'ʒjaʳ] VT to discredit;
desprestigiar-se VR to lose prestige

desprevenido, -a [dʒiʃpreve'nidu, a] ADJ
unprepared, unready; **apanhar ~** to catch
unawares

desprezar [dʒiʃpre'zaʳ] VT (*desdenhar*) to despise,
disdain; (*não dar importância a*) to disregard,
ignore; **desprezível** [dʒiʃpre'zivew] (*pl* **-eis**) ADJ
despicable; **desprezo** [dʒiʃ'prezu] M scorn,
contempt; **dar ao desprezo** to ignore

desproporção [dʒiʃpropox'sãw] F disproportion

desproporcionado, -a [dʒiʃpropoxsjo'nadu, a]
ADJ disproportionate; (*desigual*) unequal

desproporcional [dʒiʃpropoxsjo'naw] ADJ
disproportionate

despropositado, -a [dʒiʃpropozi'tadu, a] ADJ
(*absurdo*) preposterous

despropósito [dʒiʃpro'pɔzitu] M nonsense

desproteger [dʒiʃprote'ʒeʳ] VT to leave
unprotected

desprover [dʒiʃpro'veʳ] VT: **~ alguém (de algo)**
to deprive sb (of sth)

desprovido, -a [dʒiʃpro'vidu, a] ADJ deprived; **~**
de without

despudorado, -a [dʒiʃpudo'radu, a] ADJ
shameless

desqualificar [dʒiʃkwalifi'kaʳ] VT (*Esporte etc*) to
disqualify; (*tornar indiguo*) to disgrace, lower

desquitar-se [dʒiʃki'taxsi] VR to get a legal
separation

desquite [dʒiʃ'kitʃi] M legal separation

desregrado, -a [dʒiʒxe'gradu, a] ADJ
(*desordenado*) disorderly, unruly; (*devasso*)
immoderate

desregrar-se [dʒiʒxe'graxsi] VR to run riot

desregular [dʒiʒxegu'laʳ] VT (*mercado*) to
deregulate

desrespeitar [dʒiʒxeʃpej'taʳ] VT to have no
respect for

desrespeito [dʒiʒxe'ʃpejtu] M disrespect

desrespeitoso, -a [dʒiʒxeʃpej'tozu, ɔza] ADJ
disrespectful

desse *etc* ['desi] = **de + esse**

desse *etc* VB V **dar**

NB: *European Portuguese adds the following consonants to certain words:* **b** (sú(b)dito, su(b)til); **c** (a(c)ção,
a(c)cionista, a(c)to); **m** (inde(m)ne); **p** (ado(p)çã, ado(p)tar); *for further details see p. xiii.*

destacado, -a [dʒiʃta'kadu, a] ADJ outstanding; *(separado)* detached
destacamento [dʒiʃtaka'mẽtu] M *(Mil)* detachment
destacar [dʒiʃta'kaʳ] VT *(Mil)* to detail; *(separar)* to detach; *(fazer sobressair)* to highlight; *(enfatizar)* to emphasize ■ VI to stand out; **destacar-se** VR to stand out; *(pessoa)* to be outstanding
destampar [dʒiʃtã'paʳ] VT to take the lid off
destapar [dʒiʃta'paʳ] VT to uncover
destaque [dʒiʃ'taki] M distinction; *(pessoa, coisa)* highlight; *(do noticiário)* main point; **pessoa de ~** distinguished person
deste *etc* ['deʃtʃi] = **de + este**; *v* **este**
destemido, -a [deʃte'midu, a] ADJ fearless, intrepid
destemperar [dʒiʃtẽpe'raʳ] VT *(diluir)* to dilute, weaken ■ VI *(perder a cabeça)* to go mad
desterrar [dʒiʃte'xaʳ] VT *(exilar)* to exile; *(fig)* to banish
desterro [dʒiʃ'texu] M exile
destilação [deʃtʃila'sãw] F distillation
destilar [deʃtʃi'laʳ] VT to distil *(Brit)*, distill *(US)*
destilaria [deʃtʃila'ria] F distillery
destinação [deʃtʃina'sãw] *(pl -ões)* F destination
destinar [deʃ'tʃinaʳ] VT to destine; *(dinheiro)*: **~ (para)** *(dinheiro)* to set aside (for); **destinar-se** VR: **destinar-se a** to be intended for, be addressed to
destinatário, -a [deʃtʃina'tarju, a] M/F addressee
destino [deʃ'tʃinu] M destiny, fate; *(lugar)* destination; **com ~ a** bound for; **sem ~** ADJ aimless ■ ADV aimlessly
destituição [deʃtʃitwi'sãw] *(pl -ões)* F *(demissão)* dismissal
destituir [deʃtʃi'twiʳ] VT *(demitir)* to dismiss; **~ de** *(privar de)* to deprive of; *(demitir de)* to dismiss from
destoante [dʒiʃto'ãtʃi] ADJ *(som)* discordant; *(opiniões)* diverging
destoar [dʒiʃto'aʳ] VI *(som)* to jar; **~ (de)** *(não condizer)* to be out of keeping (with); *(traje, cor)* to clash (with); *(pessoa: discordar)* to disagree (with)
destorcer [dʒiʃtox'seʳ] VT to straighten out
destrambelhado, -a [dʒiʃtrãbe'ʎadu, a] ADJ scatterbrained
destrancar [dʒiʃtrã'kaʳ] VT to unlock
destratar [dʒiʃtra'taʳ] VT to abuse, insult
destravar [dʒiʃtra'vaʳ] VT *(veículo)* to take the brake off; *(fechadura)* to unlatch
destreza [deʃ'treza] F *(habilidade)* skill; *(agilidade)* dexterity
destrinchar [dʒiʃtrĩ'ʃaʳ] VT *(desenredar)* to unravel; *(esmiuçar)* to treat in detail; *(problema)* to solve, resolve
destro, -a ['dɛʃtru, a] ADJ *(hábil)* skilful *(Brit)*, skillful *(US)*; *(ágil)* agile; *(não canhoto)* right-handed
destrocar [dʒiʃtro'kaʳ] VT to give back, return
destroçar [dʒiʃtro'saʳ] VT *(destruir)* to destroy; *(quebrar)* to smash, break; *(devastar)* to ruin,

wreck; **destroços** [dʒiʃ'trɔsuʃ] MPL wreckage *sg*
destróier [dʒiʃ'trɔjeʳ] M destroyer
destronar [dʒiʃtro'naʳ] VT to depose
destroncar [dʒiʃtrõ'kaʳ] VT to dislocate
destruição [dʒiʃtrwi'sãw] F destruction
destruidor, a [dʒiʃtrwi'doʳ(a)] ADJ destructive
destruir [dʒiʃ'trwiʳ] VT to destroy
desumano, -a [dʒizu'manu, a] ADJ inhuman; *(bárbaro)* cruel
desunião [dʒizun'jãw] F disunity; *(separação)* separation
desunir [dʒizu'niʳ] VT *(separar)* to separate; *(Tec)* to disconnect; *(fig: desavir)* to cause a rift between
desusado, -a [dʒizu'zadu, a] ADJ *(não usado)* disused; *(incomum)* unusual
desuso [dʒi'zuzu] M disuse; **em ~** outdated
desvairado, -a [dʒiʒvaj'radu, a] ADJ *(louco)* crazy, demented; *(desorientado)* bewildered
desvairar [dʒiʒvaj'raʳ] VT to drive mad
desvalido, -a [dʒiʒva'lidu, a] ADJ *(desamparado)* helpless; *(miserável)* destitute
desvalorização [dʒiʒvaloriza'sãw] *(pl -ões)* F devaluation
desvalorizar [dʒiʒvalori'zaʳ] VT to devalue; **desvalorizar-se** VR *(pessoa)* to undervalue o.s.; *(carro)* to depreciate; *(moeda)* to lose value
desvanecer [dʒiʒvane'seʳ] VT *(envaidecer)* to make proud; *(sentimentos)* to dispel; **desvanecer-se** VR *(envaidecer-se)* to feel proud; *(sentimentos)* to vanish
desvanecido, -a [dʒiʒvane'sidu, a] ADJ proud
desvantagem [dʒiʒvã'taʒẽ] *(pl -ns)* F disadvantage
desvantajoso, -a [dʒiʒvãta'ʒozu, ɔza] ADJ disadvantageous
desvão [dʒiʒ'vãw] *(pl -s)* M loft
desvario [dʒiʒva'riu] M madness, folly
desvelar [dʒiʒve'laʳ] VT *(noiva, estátua)* to unveil; *(corpo, trama)* to uncover; *(segredo)* to reveal; *(problema)* to clarify; **desvelar-se** VR: **desvelar-se em fazer algo** to go to a lot of trouble to do sth
desvelo [dʒiʒ'velu] M *(cuidado)* care; *(dedicação)* devotion
desvencilhar [dʒiʒvẽsi'ʎaʳ] VT to free, extricate; **desvencilhar-se** VR to free o.s., extricate o.s.
desvendar [dʒiʒvẽ'daʳ] VT *(tirar a venda)* to remove the blindfold from; *(revelar)* to disclose; *(mistério)* to solve
desventura [dʒiʒvẽ'tura] F *(infortúnio)* misfortune; *(infelicidade)* unhappiness
desventurado, -a [dʒiʒvẽtu'radu, a] ADJ *(desafortunado)* unfortunate; *(infeliz)* unhappy ■ M/F wretch
desviar [dʒiʒ'vjaʳ] VT to divert; *(golpe)* to deflect; *(dinheiro)* to embezzle; **desviar-se** VR *(afastar-se)* to turn away; **~-se de** *(evitar)* to avoid; **~-se do assunto** to digress; **~ os olhos** to look away; **desviei o carro para a direita** I pulled the car over to the right; **tentei desviá-lo do assunto** I tried to get *ou* steer him off the subject

desvincular [dʒiʒvĩ'ku'la^r] vt: ~ **algo de algo to divest** sth of sth; **desvincular-se** vr: **desvincular-se de algo** to disassociate o.s. from sth

desvio [dʒiʒ'viu] m diversion, detour; (curva) bend; (fig) deviation; (de dinheiro) embezzlement; (de mercadorias) misappropriation; (Ferro) siding; (da coluna vertebral) dislocation

desvirar [dʒiʒvi'ra^r] vt to turn back

desvirginar [dʒiʒvixʒi'na^r] vt to deflower

desvirtuar [dʒiʒvix'twa^r] vt (fatos) to misrepresent

detalhadamente [detaʎada'mẽtʃi] adv in detail

detalhado, -a [deta'ʎadu, a] adj detailed

detalhar [deta'ʎa^r] vt to (give in) detail

detalhe [de'taʎi] m detail; **entrar em** ~ to go into detail

detalhista [deta'ʎiʃta] adj painstaking, meticulous

detectar [detek'ta^r] vt to detect

detective [detek'tivə] (PT) m = **detetive**

detector [detek'to^r] m detector

detenção [detẽ'sãw] (pl -ões) f detention

détente [de'tãtʃi] f détente

detento, -a [de'tẽtu, a] m/f detainee

detentor, a [detẽ'to^r(a)] m/f (de título, recorde) holder

deter [de'te^r] (irreg) vt (fazer parar) to stop; (prender) to arrest, detain; (reter) to keep; (conter: riso) to contain; **deter-se** vr (parar) to stop; (ficar) to stay; (conter-se) to restrain o.s.; **~-se em minúcias** etc to get bogged down in details etc

detergente [detex'ʒẽtʃi] m detergent

deterioração [deterjora'sãw] f deterioration

deteriorar [deterjo'ra^r] vt to spoil, damage; **deteriorar-se** vr to deteriorate; (relações) to worsen

determinação [detexmina'sãw] f (firmeza) determination; (decisão) decision; (ordem) order; **por** ~ **de** by order of

determinado, -a [detexmi'nadu, a] adj (resoluto) determined; (certo) certain, given

determinar [detexmi'na^r] vt (fixar, precisar) to determine; (decretar) to order; (resolver) to decide (on); (causar) to cause; (fronteiras) to mark out

detestar [deteʃ'ta^r] vt to hate, detest

detestável [deteʃ'tavew] (pl -eis) adj horrible, hateful

detetive [dete'tʃivi] m detective

detidamente [detʃida'mẽtʃi] adv carefully, thoroughly

detido, -a [de'tʃidu, a] adj (preso) under arrest; (minucioso) thorough ▪ m/f person under arrest, prisoner

detonação [detona'sãw] (pl -ões) f explosion

detonar [deto'na^r] vi to detonate, go off ▪ vt to detonate

Detran [de'trã] (BR) abr m (= Departamento de Trânsito) state traffic department

detrás [de'trajʃ] adv behind ▪ prep: ~ **de** behind; **por** ~ (from) behind

detrimento [detri'mẽtu] m: **em** ~ **de** to the detriment of

detrito [de'tritu] m debris sg; (de comida) remains pl; (resíduo) dregs pl

deturpação [detuxpa'sãw] f corruption; (de palavras) distortion

deturpar [detux'pa^r] vt to corrupt; (desfigurar) to disfigure; (palavras) to twist; **você deturpou minhas palavras** you twisted my words

deu [dew] vb v **dar**

deus, a [dewʃ(sa)] m/f god/goddess; **D~ me livre!** God forbid!; **graças a D~** thank goodness; **se D~ quiser** God willing; **meu D~!** good Lord!; **D~ e o mundo** everybody

deus-dará [-da'ra] adv: **viver ao** ~ to live from hand to mouth; **estar ao** ~ (casa) to be unattended

deus-nos-acuda [-a'kuda] m commotion

devagar [dʒiva'ga^r] adv slowly ▪ adj inv (col): **ele é um cara tão** ~ he's such an old fogey

devagarinho [dʒivaga'riɲu] adv nice and slowly

devanear [deva'nja^r] vt to imagine, dream of ▪ vi to daydream; (divagar) to wander, digress

devaneio [deva'neju] m daydream

devassa [de'vasa] f investigation, inquiry

devassado, -a [deva'sadu, a] adj (casa) exposed

devassidão [devasi'dãw] f debauchery

devasso, -a [de'vasu, a] adj dissolute

devastar [devaʃ'ta^r] vt (destruir) to devastate; (arruinar) to ruin

deve ['dɛvi] m (débito) debit; (coluna) debit column

devedor, a [deve'do^r(a)] adj (pessoa) in debt ▪ m/f debtor; **saldo** ~ debit balance

dever [de've^r] m duty ▪ vt to owe ▪ vi (suposição): **deve (de) estar doente** he must be ill; (obrigação): **devo partir às oito** I must go at eight; **você devia ir ao médico** you should go to the doctor; **ele devia ter vindo** he should have come; **que devo fazer?** what shall I do?

deveras [dʒi'veraʃ] adv really, truly

devidamente [devida'mẽtʃi] adv properly; (preencher formulário etc) duly

devido, -a [de'vidu, a] adj (maneira) proper; (respeito) due; ~ **a** due to, owing to; **no** ~ **tempo** in due course

devoção [devo'sãw] f devotion

devolução [devolu'sãw] f devolution; (restituição) return; (reembolso) refund; ~ **de impostos** tax rebate

devolver [devow've^r] vt to give back, return; (Com) to refund

devorar [devo'ra^r] vt to devour; (destruir) to destroy

devotar [devo'ta^r] vt to devote; **devotar-se** vr:

NB: European Portuguese adds the following consonants to certain words: **b** (sú(b)dito, su(b)til); **c** (a(c)ção, a(c)cionista, a(c)to); **m** (inde(m)ne); **p** (ado(p)çã, ado(p)tar); for further details see p. xiii.

devotar-se a to devote o.s. to

devoto, -a [de'vɔtu, a] ADJ devout ∎ M/F devotee

dez [dɛʒ] NUM ten; v tb **cinco**

dez. ABR (= *dezembro*) Dec

dezanove [deza'nɔvə] (PT) NUM = **dezenove**

dezasseis [deza'sejʃ] (PT) NUM = **dezesseis**

dezassete [deza'setə] (PT) NUM = **dezessete**

dezembro [de'zēbru] (PT D-) M December; v tb **julho**

dezena [de'zena] F: **uma ~** ten

dezenove [deze'nɔvi] NUM nineteen; v tb **cinco**

dezesseis [deze'sejʃ] NUM sixteen; v tb **cinco**

dezessete [dezi'setʃi] NUM seventeen; v tb **cinco**

dezoito [dʒi'zojtu] NUM eighteen; v tb **cinco**

DF (BR) ABR = **Distrito Federal**

dia ['dʒia] M day; (*claridade*) daylight; **~ a ~** day by day; **~ de folga** day off; **~ santo** holy day; **~ útil** weekday; **estar** ou **andar em ~** (*com*) to be up to date (with); **de ~** in the daytime, by day; **mais ~ menos ~** sooner or later; **todo ~, todos os ~s** every day; **o ~ inteiro** all day (long); **~ sim, ~ não** every other day; **de dois em dois ~s** every two days; **no ~ seguinte** the next day; **~ após ~** day after day; **do ~ para a noite** (*fig*) overnight; **bom ~** good morning; **um ~ desses** one of these days; **~s a fio** days on end; **~ cheio/morto** busy/quiet ou slow day; **todo santo ~** (*col*) every single day, day after day; **recebo por ~** I'm paid by the day; **um bebê de ~s** a newborn baby; **ele está com os ~s contados** his days are numbered; **dia-a-dia** M daily life, everyday life

diabete, diabetes [dʒja'betʃi(ʃ)] F diabetes *sg*; **diabético, -a** [dʒja'betʃiku, a] ADJ, M/F diabetic

diabo ['dʒjabu] M devil; **que ~!** (*col*) damn it!; **por que ~ ...?** why on earth ...?; **o ~ é que ...** (*col*) the darnedest thing is that ...; **o ~ do eletricista não apareceu** (*col*) the damned electricity man didn't turn up; **está um calor do ~** (*col*) it's damned ou bloody (*!*) hot; **deu um trabalho dos ~s** (*col*) it was a hell of a job; **quente pra ~** (*col*) damned hot; **dizer o ~ de alguém** (*col*) to slag sb off

diabólico, -a [dʒja'bɔliku, a] ADJ diabolical

diabrete [dʒja'bretʃi] M imp

diabrura [dʒja'brura] F prank; **diabruras** FPL (*travessura*) mischief *sg*

diacho ['dʒjaʃu] (*col*) EXCL hell!

diadema [dʒja'dema] M diadem; (*jóia*) tiara

diáfano, -a ['dʒjafanu, a] ADJ (*tecido*) diaphanous; (*águas*) clear

diafragma [dʒja'fragma] M diaphragm; (*anticoncepcional*) diaphragm, cap

diagnosticar [dʒjagnoʃtʃi'ka'] VT to diagnose

diagnóstico [dʒjag'nɔʃtʃiku] M diagnosis

diagonal [dʒjago'naw] (*pl* -ais) ADJ, F diagonal

diagrama [dʒja'grama] M diagram

diagramador, a [dʒjagrama'do'(a)] M/F designer

diagramar [dʒjagra'ma'] VT to design

dialecto [dja'lɛktu] (PT) M = **dialeto**

dialética [dʒja'lɛtʃika] F dialectics *sg*

dialeto [dʒja'lɛtu] M dialect

dialogar [dʒjalo'ga'] VI: **~ (com alguém)** to talk (to sb); (*Pol*) to have ou hold talks (with sb)

diálogo ['dʒjalogu] M dialogue; (*conversa*) talk, conversation

diamante [dʒja'mãtʃi] M diamond

diâmetro ['dʒjametru] M diameter

diante ['dʒjātʃi] PREP: **~ de** before; (*na frente de*) in front of; (*problemas etc*) in the face of; **e assim por ~** and so on; **para ~** forward

dianteira [dʒjã'tejra] F front, vanguard; **tomar a ~** to get ahead

dianteiro, -a [dʒjã'tejru, a] ADJ front

diapasão [dʒjapa'zãw] (*pl* -ões) M (*afinador*) tuning fork; (*tom*) pitch; (*extensão de voz ou instrumento*) range

diapositivo [dʒjapozi'tʃivu] M (*Foto*) slide

diária ['dʒjarja] F (*de hotel*) daily rate

diário, -a ['dʒjarju, a] ADJ daily ∎ M diary; (*jornal*) (daily) newspaper; (*Com*) daybook; **~ de bordo** (*Aer*) logbook

diarista [dʒja'riʃta] M/F casual worker, worker paid by the day; (*em casa*) cleaner

diarréia [dʒja'xɛja] F diarrhoea (*Brit*), diarrhea (US)

dica ['dʒika] (*col*) F hint

dicção [dʒik'sãw] F diction

dicionário [dʒisjo'narju] M dictionary

dicionarista [dʒisjona'riʃta] M/F lexicographer

dicotomia [dʒikoto'mia] F dichotomy

didata [dʒi'data] (PT -ct-) M/F teacher

didática [dʒi'datʃika] (PT -ct-) F education, teaching

didático, -a [dʒi'datʃiku, a] (PT -ct-) ADJ (*livro*) educational; (*métoda*) teaching *atr*; (*modo*) didactic

diesel ['dʒizew] M: **motor a ~** diesel engine

dieta [dʒi'eta] F diet; **fazer ~** to go on a diet

dietético, -a [dʒje'tetʃiku, a] ADJ dietetic

dietista [dʒje'tʃiʃta] M/F dietician

difamação [dʒifama'sãw] F (*falada*) slander; (*escrita*) libel

difamador, a [dʒifama'do'(a)] ADJ defamatory ∎ M/F slanderer

difamar [dʒifa'ma'] VT to slander; (*por escrito*) to libel

difamatório, -a [dʒifama'tɔrju, a] ADJ defamatory

diferença [dʒife'rēsa] F difference; **ela tem uma ~ comigo** she's got something against me

diferenciação [dʒiferēsja'sãw] F (*tb: Mat*) differentiation

diferenciar [dʒiferē'sja'] VT to differentiate

diferente [dʒife'rētʃi] ADJ different; **estar ~ com alguém** to be at odds with sb

diferimento [dʒiferi'mētu] M deferment

diferir [dʒife'ri'] VI: **~ (de)** to differ (from) ∎ VT (*adiar*) to defer

difícil [dʒi'fisiw] (*pl* -eis) ADJ (*trabalho, vida*) difficult, hard; (*problema, situação*) difficult; (*pessoa: intratável*) difficult; (: *exigente*) hard to please; (*improvável*) unlikely; **o ~ é que ...** the ...

difficult thing is ...; **acho ~ ela aceitar nossa proposta** I think it's unlikely she will accept our proposal; **falar ~** to use big words; **bancar o ~** to play hard to get

dificílimo, -a [dʒifi'silimu, a] ADJ SUPERL de **difícil**

dificilmente [dʒifisiw'mẽtʃi] ADV with difficulty; *(mal)* hardly; *(raramente)* hardly ever; **~ ele poderá ...** it won't be easy for him to ....

dificuldade [dʒifikuw'dadʒi] F difficulty; *(aperto)* trouble; **em ~s** in trouble

dificultar [dʒifikuw'ta⁴] VT to make difficult; *(complicar)* to complicate

difteria [dʒifte'ria] F diphtheria

difundir [dʒifũ'dʒi⁴] VT *(luz)* to diffuse; *(boato, rumor)* to spread; *(notícia)* to spread, circulate; *(idéias)* to disseminate

difusão [dʒifu'zãw] F *(de luz)* diffusion; *(espalhamento)* spreading; *(de notícias)* circulation; *(de idéias)* dissemination

difuso, -a [dʒi'fuzu, a] ADJ diffuse

digerir [dʒiʒe'ri⁴] VT, VI to digest

digestão [dʒiʒeʃ'tãw] F digestion

digital [dʒiʒi'taw] *(pl -ais)* ADJ digital; **impressão ~** fingerprint

digitar [dʒiʒi'ta⁴] VT *(Comput: dados)* to key (in)

dígito ['dʒiʒitu] M digit

digladiar [dʒigla'dʒja⁴] VI to fight, fence; **digladiar-se** VR: **digladiar (com alguém)** to do battle (with sb)

dignar-se [dʒig'naxsi] VR: **~ de** to deign to, condescend to

dignidade [dʒigni'dadʒi] F dignity

dignificar [dʒignifi'ka⁴] VT to dignify

digno, -a ['dʒignu, a] ADJ *(merecedor)* worthy; *(nobre)* dignified

digo etc ['dʒigu] VB V **dizer**

digressão [dʒigre'sãw] *(pl -ões)* F digression

dilaceração [dʒilasera'sãw] *(pl -ões)* F laceration

dilacerante [dʒilase'rãtʃi] ADJ *(dor)* excruciating; *(cruel)* cruel

dilacerar [dʒilase'ra⁴] VT to tear to pieces, lacerate; **dilacerar-se** VR to tear one another to pieces

dilapidação [dʒilapida'sãw] F *(de casas etc)* demolition; *(de dinheiro)* squandering

dilapidar [dʒilapi'da⁴] VT *(fortuna)* to squander; *(casa)* to demolish

dilatação [dʒilata'sãw] F dilation

dilatar [dʒila'ta⁴] VT to dilate, expand; *(prolongar)* to prolong; *(retardar)* to delay

dilatório, -a [dʒila'tɔrju, a] ADJ dilatory

dilema [dʒi'lɛma] M dilemma

diletante [dʒile'tãtʃi] ADJ, M/F amateur; *(pej)* dilettante

diletantismo [dʒiletã'tʃiʒmu] M amateurism; *(pej)* dilettantism

diligência [dʒili'ʒẽsja] F diligence; *(pesquisa)* inquiry; *(veículo)* stagecoach

---

diligenciar [dʒiliʒẽ'sja⁴] VT to strive for; **~ (por)** fazer to strive to do

diligente [dʒili'ʒẽtʃi] ADJ hardworking, industrious

diluição [dʒilwi'sãw] F dilution

diluir [dʒi'lwi⁴] VT to dilute

dilúvio [dʒi'luvju] M flood

dimensão [dʒimẽ'sãw] *(pl -ões)* F dimension; **dimensões** FPL *(medidas)* measurements

dimensionar [dʒimẽsjo'na⁴] VT: **~ algo** to calculate the size of sth; *(fig)* to assess the extent of sth

diminuição [dʒiminwi'sãw] F reduction

diminuir [dʒimi'nwi⁴] VT to reduce; *(som)* to turn down; *(interesse)* to lessen ■ VI to lessen, diminish; *(preço)* to go down; *(dor)* to wear off; *(barulho)* to die down

diminutivo, -a [dʒiminu'tʃivu, a] ADJ diminutive ■ M *(Ling)* diminutive

diminuto, -a [dʒimi'nutu, a] ADJ minute, tiny

Dinamarca [dʒina'maxka] F Denmark;

dinamarquês, -quesa [dʒinamax'keʃ, 'keza] ADJ Danish ■ M/F Dane ■ M *(Ling)* Danish

dinâmico, -a [dʒi'namiku, a] ADJ dynamic

dinamismo [dʒina'miʒmu] M *(fig)* energy, drive

dinamitar [dʒinami'ta⁴] VT to blow up

dinamite [dʒina'mitʃi] F dynamite

dínamo ['dʒinamu] M dynamo

dinastia [dʒinaʃ'tʃia] F dynasty

dinda ['dʒĩda] *(col)* F godmother

dinheirão [dʒiɲej'rãw] M: **um ~** loads pl of money

dinheiro [dʒi'ɲejru] M money; **~ à vista** cash for paying in cash; **sem ~** penniless; **em ~** in cash; **~ em caixa** money in the till; **~ em espécie** cash; **~ vivo** hard cash

dinossauro [dʒino'sawru] M dinosaur

diocese [dʒjo'sɛzi] F diocese

dióxido ['dʒjɔksidu] M dioxide; **~ de carbono** carbon dioxide

DIP (BR) ABR M = **Departamento de Imprensa e Propaganda**

diploma [dʒip'lɔma] M diploma

diplomacia [dʒiploma'sia] F diplomacy; *(fig)* tact

diplomando, -a [dʒiplo'mãdu, a] M/F diploma candidate

diplomar [dʒiplo'ma⁴] VT to give a diploma *(ou* degree) to; **diplomar-se** VR: **diplomar-se (em algo)** to get one's diploma (in sth)

diplomata [dʒiplo'mata] M/F diplomat;

diplomático, -a [dʒiplo'matʃiku, a] ADJ diplomatic; *(discreto)* tactful

dique ['dʒiki] M dam; *(Geo)* dyke

direção [dʒire'sãw] *(PT -cç-, pl -ões)* F direction; *(endereço)* address; *(Auto)* steering; *(administração)* management; *(comando)* leadership; *(diretoria)* board of directors; **em ~ a** towards

---

NB: *European Portuguese adds the following consonants to certain words:* **b** (sú(b)dito, su(b)til); **c** (a(c)ção, a(c)cionista, a(c)to); **m** (inde(m)ne); **p** (ado(p)çã, ado(p)tar); *for further details see p. xiii.*

directo, -a [di'rɛktu,a] (PT) = **direto** etc
direi etc [dʒi'rej] vb v **dizer**
direita [dʒi'rejta] f (mão) right hand; (lado) right-hand side; (Pol) right wing; **à ~** on the right; **"mantenha-se à ~"** "keep right"
direitinho [dʒirej'tʃiɲu] ADV properly, just right; (diretamente) directly
direitista [dʒirej'tʃiʃta] ADJ right-wing ▪ M/F right-winger
direito, -a [dʒi'rejtu,a] ADJ (lado) right-hand; (mão) right; (honesto) honest; (devido) proper; (justo) right, just ▪ M (prerrogativa) right; (Jur) law; (de tecido) right side ▪ ADV (em linha reta) straight; (bem) right; (de maneira certa) properly; **direitos** MPL (humanos) rights; (alfandegários) duty sg; **~ civil** civil law; **~s civis** civil rights; **~s de importação** import duty; **~s humanos** human rights; **livre de ~s** duty-free; **ter ~ a** to have a right to, be entitled to; **minha roupa está direita?/meu cabelo está ~?** are my clothes/is my hair all right?
diretas [dʒi'retaʃ] FPL (Pol) direct elections
direto, -a [dʒi'rɛtu,a] ADJ direct ▪ ADV straight; **transmissão direta** (TV) live broadcast; **ir ~ ao assunto** to get straight to the point
diretor, a [dʒire'to'(a)] ADJ directing, guiding ▪ M/F (Com, de cinema) director; (de jornal) editor; (de escola) head teacher
diretor, a (pl directores/as-gerentes) M/F managing director; **diretoria** [dʒireto'ria] f (cargo) directorship; (: em escola) headship; (direção: Com) management; (sala) boardroom
diretório [dʒire'tɔrju] M directorate; (Comput) directory; **~ acadêmico** students' union
diretriz [dʒire'triʒ] f directive
dirigente [dʒiri'ʒẽtʃi] ADJ (classe) ruling ▪ M/F (de país, partido) leader; (diretor) director; (gerente) manager
dirigir [dʒiri'ʒi'] vt to direct; (Com) to manage, run; (veículo) to drive; (atenção) to turn ▪ vi to drive; **dirigir-se** VR: **dirigir-se a** (falar com) to speak to, address; (ir, recorrer) to go to; (esforços) to be directed towards
dirimir [dʒiri'mi'] vt (dúvida, contenda) to settle, clear up
discagem [dʒiʃ'kaʒẽ] f (Tel) dialling; **~ direta** direct dialling
discar [dʒiʃ'ka'] vt to dial
discente [dʒi'sẽtʃi] ADJ: **corpo ~** student body
discernimento [dʒisexni'mẽtu] M discernment
discernir [dʒisex'ni'] vt (perceber) to discern, perceive; (diferenciar) to discriminate, distinguish
discernível [dʒisex'nivew] (pl -eis) ADJ discernible
disciplina [dʒisi'plina] f discipline
disciplinador, a [dʒisiplina'do'(a)] ADJ disciplinary
disciplinar [dʒisipli'na'] vt to discipline; **disciplinar-se** VR to discipline o.s.
discípulo, -a [dʒi'sipulu,a] M/F disciple; (aluno) pupil

disc-jóquei [dʒiʃk-] M/F disc jockey, DJ
disco ['dʒiʃku] M disc; (Comput) disk; (Mús) record; (de telefone) dial; **~ laser** (máquina) compact disc player, CD player; (disco) compact disc, CD; **~ flexível/rígido** (Comput) floppy/hard disk; **~ mestre** (Comput) master disk; **~ do sistema** system disk; **~ voador** flying saucer; **mudar o ~** (col) to change the subject
discordância [dʒiʃkox'dasja] f disagreement; (de opiniões) difference
discordante [dʒiʃkox'dãtʃi] ADJ divergent, conflicting
discordar [dʒiʃkox'da'] vi: **~ de alguém em algo** to disagree with sb on sth
discórdia [dʒiʃ'kɔxdʒja] f discord, strife
discorrer [dʒiʃko'xe'] vi: **~ (sobre)** (falar) to talk (about)
discoteca [dʒiʃko'tɛka] f (boate) discotheque, disco (col); (coleção de discos) record library
discotecário, -a [dʒiʃkote'karju,a] M/F disc jockey, DJ
discrepância [dʒiʃkre'pãsja] f discrepancy; (desacordo) disagreement; **discrepante** [dʒiʃkre'pãtʃi] ADJ conflicting
discrepar [dʒiʃkre'pa'] vi: **~ de** to differ from
discreto, -a [dʒiʃ'kretu,a] ADJ discreet; (modesto) modest; (prudente) shrewd; (roupa) plain, sober; **discrição** [dʒiʃkri'sãw] f discretion, good sense
discricionário, -a [dʒiʃkrisjo'narju,a] ADJ discretionary
discriminação [dʒiʃkrimina'sãw] f discrimination; (especificação) differentiation; **~ racial** racial discrimination
discriminar [dʒiʃkrimi'na'] vt to distinguish ▪ vi: **~ entre** to discriminate between
discriminatório, -a [dʒiʃkrimina'tɔrju,a] ADJ discriminatory
discursar [dʒiʃkux'sa'] vi (em público) to make a speech; (falar) to speak
discurso [dʒiʃ'kuxsu] M speech; (Ling) discourse
discussão [dʒiʃku'sãw] (pl -ões) f (debate) discussion, debate; (contenda) argument
discutir [dʒiʃku'tʃi'] vt to discuss ▪ vi: **~ (sobre algo)** (debater) to talk (about sth); (contender) to argue (about sth)
discutível [dʒiʃku'tʃivew] (pl -eis) ADJ debatable
disenteria [dʒizẽte'ria] f dysentery
disfarçar [dʒiʃfax'sa'] vt to disguise ▪ vi to pretend; **disfarçar-se** VR: **disfarçar-se em ou de algo** to disguise o.s. as sth; **disfarce** [dʒiʃ'faxsi] M disguise; (máscara) mask
disfasia [dʒiʃfa'zia] f (Med) speech defect
disforme [dʒiʃ'fɔxmi] ADJ deformed; (monstruoso) hideous
disfunção [dʒiʃfũ'sãw] (pl -ões) f (Med) dysfunction
dislético, -a [dʒiʒ'lɛtʃiku,a] ADJ, M/F dyslexic
dislexia [dʒiʒlek'sia] f dyslexia
disléxico, -a [dʒiʒ'lɛksiku,a] ADJ, M/F dyslexic
díspar ['dʒiʃpa'] ADJ dissimilar
disparada [dʒiʃpa'rada] f: **dar uma ~** to surge ahead; **em ~** at full tilt

disparado, -a [dʒiʃpaˈradu, a] ADJ very fast
■ ADV by a long way
disparar [dʒiʃpaˈraʳ] VT to shoot, fire ■ VI to
fire; (arma) to go off; (correr) to shoot off, bolt
disparatado, -a [dʒiʃparaˈtadu, a] ADJ silly,
absurd
disparate [dʒiʃpaˈratʃi] M nonsense, rubbish;
(ação) blunder
disparidade [dʒiʃpariˈdadʒi] F disparity
dispêndio [dʒiʃˈpẽdʒu] M expenditure
dispendioso, -a [dʒiʃpẽˈdʒozu, ɔza] ADJ costly,
expensive
dispensa [dʒiʃˈpẽsa] F exemption; (Rel)
dispensation
dispensar [dʒiʃpẽˈsaʳ] VT (desobrigar) to excuse;
(prescindir de) to do without; (conferir) to grant
dispensário [dʒiʃpẽˈsarju] M dispensary
dispensável [dʒiʃpẽˈsavew] (pl -eis) ADJ
expendable
dispepsia [dʒiʃpepˈsia] F dyspepsia
dispersão [dʒiʃpexˈsãw] F dispersal
dispersar [dʒiʃpexˈsaʳ] VT, VI to disperse
dispersivo, -a [dʒiʃpexˈsivu, a] ADJ (pessoa)
scatterbrained
disperso, -a [dʒiʃˈpɛxsu, a] ADJ scattered
displicência [dʒiʃpliˈsensja] (BR) F (descuido)
negligence, carelessness; **displicente**
[dʒiʃpliˈsẽtʃi] ADJ careless
dispo etc [ˈdʒiʃpu] VB V **despir**
disponibilidade [dʒiʃponibiliˈdadʒi] F
availability; (finanças) liquid ou available assets
pl; ~ **de caixa** cash in hand
disponível [dʒiʃpoˈnivew] (pl -eis) ADJ available
dispor [dʒiʃˈpoʳ] (irreg) VT (arranjar) to arrange;
(colocar em ordem) to put in order ■ VI: ~ **de** (usar)
to have the use of; (ter) to have, own; (pessoas) to
have at one's disposal; **dispor-se** VR: **dispor-se**
a (estar pronto a) to be prepared to, be willing to;
(decidir) to decide to; ~ **sobre** to talk about; **não**
disponho de tempo para ... I can't afford the
time to ...; **disponha!** feel free!
disposição [dʒiʃpoziˈsãw] (pl -ões) F
arrangement; (humor) disposition; (inclinação)
inclination; **à sua** ~ at your disposal
dispositivo [dʒiʃpoziˈtʃivu] M (mecanismo)
gadget, device; (determinação de lei) provision;
(conjunto de meios): ~ **de segurança** security
operation; ~ **intra-uterino** intra-uterine
device
disposto, -a [dʒiʃˈpoftu, ˈpɔʃta] PP de **dispor**
■ ADJ (arranjado) arranged; **estar** ~ **a** to be
willing to; **estar bem** ~ to look well; **sentir-se** ~
a fazer algo to feel like doing sth
disputa [dʒiʃˈputa] F (contenda) dispute,
argument; (competição) contest; **disputar**
[dʒiʃpuˈtaʳ] VT to dispute; (concorrer a) to
compete for; (lutar por) to fight over ■ VI
(discutir) to quarrel, argue; to compete; **disputar**
uma corrida to run a race

disquete [dʒiʃˈketʃi] M (Comput) floppy disk,
diskette
dissabor [dʒisaˈboʳ] M (desgosto) sorrow;
(aborrecimento) annoyance
disse etc [ˈdʒisi] VB V **dizer**
dissecar [dʒiseˈkaʳ] VT to dissect
disseminação [dʒisiseminaˈsãw] F (de pólen etc)
spread(ing); (de idéias) dissemination
disseminar [dʒisemiˈnaʳ] VT to disseminate;
(espalhar) to spread
dissensão [dʒisẽˈsãw] F dissension, discord
dissentir [dʒisẽˈtʃiʳ] VI: ~ **de alguém** (em algo)
to be in disagreement with sb (over sth); ~ **de**
algo (não combinar) to be at variance with sth
disse-que-disse M gossip, tittle-tattle
dissertação [dʒisextaˈsãw] (pl -ões) F
dissertation; (discurso) lecture
dissertar [dʒisexˈtaʳ] VI to speak
dissidência [dʒisiˈdẽsja] F (divergência)
dissension; (dissidentes) dissidents pl; (cisão)
difference of opinion
dissidente [dʒisiˈdẽtʃi] ADJ, M/F dissident
dissídio [dʒiˈsidʒu] M (Jur): ~ **coletivo/**
individual collective/individual dispute
dissimilar [dʒisimiˈlaʳ] ADJ dissimilar
dissimulação [dʒisimulaˈsãw] F (fingimento)
pretence (Brit), pretense (US); (disfarce) disguise
dissimular [dʒisimuˈlaʳ] VT (ocultar) to hide;
(fingir) to feign ■ VI to dissemble
dissinto etc [dʒiˈsĩtu] VB V **dissentir**
dissipação [dʒisipaˈsãw] F waste, squandering
dissipar [dʒisiˈpaʳ] VT (dispersar) to disperse,
dispel; (malgastar) to squander, waste; **dissipar-**
se VR to vanish
disso [ˈdʒisu] = **de** + **isso**
dissociar [dʒisoˈsjaʳ] VT: ~ **algo (de/em algo)**
to separate sth (from sth)/break sth up (into
sth); **dissociar-se** VR: **dissociar-se de algo** to
dissociate o.s. from sth
dissolução [dʒisoluˈsãw] F (dissolvência)
dissolving; (libertinagem) debauchery; (de
casamento) dissolution
dissoluto, -a [dʒisoˈlutu, a] ADJ dissolute,
debauched
dissolver [dʒisowˈveʳ] VT to dissolve; (dispersar)
to disperse; (motim) to break up
dissonância [dʒisoˈnãsja] F dissonance;
(discordância) discord
dissonante [dʒisoˈnãtʃi] ADJ (som) dissonant,
discordant; (fig) discordant
dissuadir [dʒiswaˈdʒiʳ] VT to dissuade; ~
alguém de fazer algo to talk sb out of doing
sth, dissuade sb from doing sth
dissuasão [dʒiswaˈzãw] F dissuasion
dissuasivo, -a [dʒiswaˈzivu, a] ADJ dissuasive
distância [dʒiʃˈtãsja] F distance; **a grande** ~ far
away; **a 3 quilômetros de** ~ 3 kilometres (Brit)
ou kilometers (US) away
distanciamento [dʒiʃtãsjaˈmẽtu] M distancing

distanciar [dʒiʃtã'sjaʳ] VT (afastar) to distance, set apart; (colocar por intervalos) to space out; **distanciar-se** VR to move away; (fig) to distance o.s.

distante [dʒiʃ'tãtʃi] ADJ distant, far-off; (fig) aloof

distar [dʒiʃ'taʳ] VI to be far away; **o aeroporto dista 10 quilômetros da cidade** the airport is 10 km away from the city

distender [dʒiʃtẽ'deʳ] VT (estender) to expand; (estirar) to stretch; (dilatar) to distend; (músculo) to pull; **distender-se** VR to expand; to distend

distinção [dʒiʃtʃĩ'sãw] (pl -ões) F distinction; **fazer ~** to make a distinction

distinguir [dʒiʃtʃĩ'giʳ] VT (diferenciar) to distinguish, differentiate; (avistar, ouvir) to make out; (enobrecer) to distinguish; **distinguir-se** VR to stand out; **~ algo de algo/entre** to distinguish sth from sth/between

distintivo, -a [dʒiʃtʃĩ'tʃivu, a] ADJ distinctive ■ M (insígnia) badge; (emblema) emblem

distinto, -a [dʒiʃ'tʃĩtu, a] ADJ (diferente) different; (eminente) distinguished; (claro) distinct; (refinado) refined

disto ['dʒiʃtu] = **de + isto**

distorção [dʒiʃtox'sãw] (pl -ões) F distortion

distorcer [dʒiʃtox'seʳ] VT to distort

distorções [dʒiʃtox'sõjʃ] FPL de **distorção**

distração [dʒiʃtra'sãw] (PT -cç-, pl -ões) F (alheamento) absent-mindedness; (divertimento) pastime; (descuido) oversight

distraído, -a [dʒiʃtra'idu, a] ADJ absent-minded; (não atento) inattentive

distrair [dʒiʃtra'iʳ] VT (tornar desatento) to distract; (divertir) to amuse; **distrair-se** VR to amuse o.s.

distribuição [dʒiʃtribwi'sãw] F distribution; (de cartas) delivery

distribuidor, a [dʒiʃtribwi'doʳ(a)] M/F distributor ■ M (Auto) distributor ■ F (Com) distribution company, distributor

distribuir [dʒiʃtri'bwiʳ] VT to distribute; (repartir) to share out; (cartas) to deliver

distrito [dʒiʃ'tritu] M district; (delegacia) police station; **~ eleitoral** constituency; **~ federal** federal area

distúrbio [dʒiʃ'tuxbju] M disturbance; **distúrbios** MPL (Pol) riots

ditado [dʒi'tadu] M dictation; (provérbio) saying

ditador [dʒita'doʳ] M dictator; **ditadura** [dʒita'dura] F dictatorship

ditame [dʒi'tami] M (da consciência) dictate; (regra) rule

ditar [dʒi'taʳ] VT to dictate; (impor) to impose

ditatorial [dʒitato'rjaw] (pl -ais) ADJ dictatorial

dito, -a ['dʒitu, a] PP de **dizer** ■ M: **~ espirituoso** witticism; **~ e feito** no sooner said than done

dito-cujo (pl ditos-cujos) (col) M said person

ditongo [dʒi'tõgu] M diphthong

ditoso, -a [dʒi'tozu, ɔza] ADJ (feliz) happy; (venturoso) lucky

DIU ABR M (= dispositivo intra-uterino) IUD

diurético, -a [dʒju'rɛtʃiku, a] ADJ diuretic ■ M diuretic

diurno, -a ['dʒjuxnu, a] ADJ daytime atr

divã [dʒi'vã] M couch, divan

divagação [dʒivaga'sãw] (pl -ões) F (andança) wandering; (digressão) digression; (devaneio) rambling

divagar [dʒiva'gaʳ] VI (vaguear) to wander; (falar sem nexo) to ramble (on); **~ do assunto** to wander off the subject, digress

divergência [dʒivex'ʒẽsja] F divergence; (desacordo) disagreement

divergente [dʒivex'ʒẽtʃi] ADJ divergent

divergir [dʒivex'ʒiʳ] VI to diverge; (discordar): **~ (de alguém)** to disagree (with sb)

diversão [dʒivex'sãw] (pl -ões) F (divertimento) amusement; (passatempo) pastime

diversidade [dʒivexsi'dadʒi] F diversity

diversificação [dʒivexsifika'sãw] F diversification

diversificar [dʒivexsifi'kaʳ] VT to diversify ■ VI to vary

diverso, -a [dʒi'vɛxsu, a] ADJ (diferente) different; (pl) various

diversões [divex'sõjʃ] FPL de **diversão**

diversos, -as [dʒi'vɛxsuʃ] ADJ several ■ MPL (na contabilidade) sundries

divertido, -a [dʒivex'tʃidu, a] ADJ amusing, funny

divertimento [dʒivextʃi'mẽtu] M amusement, entertainment

divertir [dʒivex'tʃiʳ] VT to amuse, entertain; **divertir-se** VR to enjoy o.s., have a good time

dívida ['dʒivida] F debt; (obrigação) indebtedness; **contrair ~s** to run into debt; **~ externa** foreign debt

dividendo [dʒivi'dẽdu] M dividend

dividido, -a [dʒivi'dʒidu, a] ADJ divided; **sentir-se ~ entre duas coisas** to feel torn between two things

dividir [dʒivi'dʒiʳ] VT to divide; (despesas, lucro, comida etc) to share; (separar) to separate ■ VI (Mat) to divide; **dividir-se** VR to divide, split up; **as opiniões se dividem** opinions are divided; **ele tem que se ~ entre a família e o trabalho** he has to divide his time between the family and work; **~ 21 por 7** to divide 21 by 7; **~ algo em 3 partes** to split sth into 3 parts; **~ algo pela metade** to divide sth in half ou in two

divindade [dʒivĩ'dadʒi] F divinity

divino, -a [dʒi'vinu, a] ADJ divine; (col) gorgeous ■ M Holy Ghost

divirjo etc [dʒi'vixʒu] VB V **divergir**

divisa [dʒi'viza] F (emblema) emblem; (frase) slogan; (fronteira) border; (Mil) stripe; **divisas** FPL (câmbio) foreign exchange sg, foreign currency sg

divisão [dʒivi'zãw] (pl -ões) F division; (discórdia) split; (partilha) sharing

divisar [dʒivi'zaʳ] VT (avistar) to see, make out

divisível [dʒivi'zivew] (pl -eis) ADJ divisible

divisões [dʒivi'zõjʃ] FPL *de* **divisão**
divisória [dʒivi'zɔrja] F partition
divisório, -a [dʒivi'zɔrju, a] ADJ *(linha)* dividing
divorciado, -a [dʒivox'sjadu, a] ADJ divorced
■ M/F divorcé(e)
divorciar [dʒivox'sja^r] VT to divorce; **divorciar-se** VR to get divorced; **divórcio** [dʒi'vɔxsju] M divorce
divulgação [dʒivuwga'sãw] F *(de notícias)* spread; *(de segredo)* divulging; *(de produto)* marketing
divulgar [dʒivuw'ga^r] VT *(notícias)* to spread; *(segredo)* to divulge; *(produto)* to market; *(livro)* to publish; **divulgar-se** VR to leak out
dizer [dʒi'ze^r] VT to say ■ M saying; **dizer-se** VR to claim to be; **diz-se** *ou* **dizem que ...** it is said that ...; **diga-se de passagem** by the way; **~ algo a alguém** *(informar, avisar)* to tell sb sth; *(falar)* to say sth to sb; **~ a alguém que ...** to tell sb that ...; **o que você diz da minha sugestão?** what do you think of my suggestion?; **~ para alguém fazer** to tell sb to do; **o filme não me disse nada** *(não interessou)* the film left me cold; **o nome não me diz nada** *(não significa)* the name means nothing to me; **~ bem com** to go well with; **querer ~** to mean; **quer ~** that is to say; **nem é preciso ~** that goes without saying; **não ~ coisa com coisa** to make no sense; **digo** *(ou seja)* I mean; **diga!** what is it?; **não diga!** you don't say!; **digamos** let's say; **bem que eu te disse, eu não disse?** I told you so; **ele tem dificuldade em acordar às sete, que dirá às cinco** he finds it difficult to wake at seven, let alone *ou* never mind five; **por assim ~** so to speak; **até ~ chega** as much as possible
dizimar [dʒizi'ma^r] VT to decimate; *(herança)* to fritter away
Djibuti [dʒibu'tʃi] M: **o ~** Djibouti
DNER (BR) ABR M (= *Departamento Nacional de Estradas de Rodagem*) national highways department
DNOCS (BR) ABR M = **Departamento Nacional de Obras contra as Secas**
DNPM (BR) ABR M = **Departamento Nacional de Produção Mineral**
do [du] = **de + o**
dó [dɔ] M *(lástima)* pity; *(Mús)* do; **ter dó de** to feel sorry for
doação [doa'sãw] *(pl* -ões) F donation, gift
doador, a [doa'do^r(a)] M/F donor
doar [do'a^r] VT to donate, give
dobra ['dɔbra] F fold; *(prega)* pleat; *(de calças)* turn-up
dobradiça [dobra'dʒisa] F hinge
dobradiço, -a [dobra'dʒisu, a] ADJ flexible
dobradinha [dobra'dʒiɲa] F *(Culin)* tripe stew; *(col: dupla)* pair, partnership
dobrar [do'bra^r] VT *(duplicar)* to double; *(papel)* to fold; *(joelho)* to bend; *(esquina)* to turn, go round; *(fazer ceder)*: **~ alguém** to talk sb round ■ VI to

double; *(sino)* to toll; *(vergar)* to bend; **dobrar-se** VR to double (up)
dobro ['dobru] M double
DOC (BR) ABR F = **Diretoria de Obras de Cooperação**
doca ['dɔka] F *(Náut)* dock
doce ['dosi] ADJ sweet; *(terno)* gentle ■ M sweet; **ele é um ~** he's a sweetie; **fazer ~** *(col)* to play hard to get
doce-de-coco *(pl* **doces-de-coco**) M *(pessoa)* sweetie
doceiro, -a [do'sejru, a] M/F sweet-seller
dôceis ['dɔsejʃ] ADJ PL *de* **dócil**
docemente [dose'mẽtʃi] ADV gently
docência [do'sẽsja] F teaching *atr*
docente [do'sẽtʃi] ADJ teaching *atr*; **o corpo ~** teaching staff
dócil ['dɔsiw] *(pl* -**eis**) ADJ docile
documentação [dokumẽta'sãw] F documentation; *(documentos)* papers *pl*
documentar [dokumẽ'ta^r] VT to document
documentário, -a [dokumẽ'tarju, a] ADJ documentary ■ M documentary
documento [doku'mẽtu] M document; **não é ~** *(col)* it doesn't mean a thing
doçura [do'sura] F sweetness; *(brandura)* gentleness
Dodecaneso [dodeka'nεzu] M: **o ~** the Dodecanese
dodói [do'dɔj] *(col)* M: **você tem ~?** does it hurt? ■ ADJ INV ill, under the weather
doença [do'ẽsa] F illness
doente [do'ẽtʃi] ADJ ill, sick ■ M/F sick person; *(cliente)* patient
doentio, -a [doẽ'tʃiu, a] ADJ *(pessoa)* sickly; *(clima)* unhealthy; *(curiosidade)* morbid
doer [do'e^r] VI to hurt, ache; **~ a alguém** *(pesar)* to grieve sb; **dói ver tanta pobreza** it's sad to see so much poverty
dogma ['dɔgma] M dogma
dogmático, -a [dog'matʃiku, a] ADJ dogmatic
DOI (BR) ABR M (= *Destacamento de Operações Internas*) *military secret police*
Doi-Codi ['dɔi-'kɔdʒi] (BR) ABR M (= *Departamento de Operações e Informações -- Centro de Operação e Defesa Interna*) *secret police HQ during the military dictatorship*
doidão, -dona [doj'dãw, 'dɔna] *(pl* -ões/-s) ADJ: **(ser) ~** *(to be)* completely crazy; **(estar) ~** *(to be)* high
doideira [doj'dejra] F madness, foolishness
doidice [doj'dʒisi] F madness, foolishness
doidivanas [dojdʒi'vanaʃ] M/F INV hothead
doido, -a ['dojdu, a] ADJ mad, crazy ■ M/F madman/woman; **~ por** mad *ou* crazy about; **~ varrido** *ou* **de pedras** *(col)* raving loony
doído, -a [do'idu, a] ADJ sore, painful; *(moralmente)* hurt; *(que causa dor)* painful
doidões [doj'dõjʃ] MPL *de* **doidão**

NB: *European Portuguese adds the following consonants to certain words:* **b** (sú(b)dito, su(b)til); **c** (a(c)ção, a(c)cionista, a(c)to); **m** (inde(m)ne); **p** (ado(p)çã, ado(p)tar); *for further details see p. xiii.*

doidona [doj'dɔna] F de **doidão**

doirar [doj'ra^r] VT = **dourar**

dois [dojʃ] NUM two; **conversa a ~ tête-à-tête;** v tb **cinco**

dólar ['dɔla^r] M dollar; **~ oficial/paralelo** dollar at the official/black-market rate; **~-turismo** dollar at the special tourist rate; **doleiro, -a** [do'lejru, a] M/F (black market) dollar dealer

dolo ['dɔlu] M fraud

dolorido, -a [dolo'ridu, a] ADJ painful, sore; (fig) sorrowful

dolorosa [dolo'rɔza] F bill

doloroso, -a [dolo'rozu, ɔza] ADJ painful

dom [dõ] M gift; (aptidão) knack; **o ~ da palavra** the gift of the gab

dom. ABR (= domingo) Sun

domador, a [domado^r(a)] M/F tamer

domar [do'ma^r] VT to tame

doméstica [do'mɛʃtʃika] F maid

domesticado, -a [domeʃtʃi'kadu, a] ADJ domesticated; (manso) tame

domesticar [domeʃtʃi'ka^r] VT to domesticate; (povo) to tame

doméstico, -a [do'mɛʃtʃiku, a] ADJ domestic; (vida) home atr

domiciliar [domisi'lja^r] ADJ home atr

domicílio [domi'silju] M home, residence; **vendas/entrega a ~** home sales/delivery; **"entregamos a ~"** "we deliver"

dominação [domina'sãw] F domination

dominador, a [domina'do^r(a)] ADJ (pessoa) domineering; (olhar) imposing ■ M/F ruler

dominante [domi'nãtʃi] ADJ dominant; (predominante) predominant

dominar [domi'na^r] VT to dominate; (reprimir) to overcome ■ VI to dominate, prevail; **dominar-se** VR to control o.s.

domingo [do'mĩgu] M Sunday; v tb **terça-feira**

domingueiro, -a [domĩ'gejru, a] ADJ Sunday atr; **traje ~** Sunday best

Dominica [domi'nika] F Dominica

dominicano, -a [domini'kanu, a] ADJ, M/F Dominican; **República Dominicana** Dominican Republic

domínio [do'minju] M (poder) power; (dominação) control; (território) domain; (esfera) sphere; **~ próprio** self-control

dom-juan [-'jwã] M ladies' man, Don Juan

domo ['dɔmu] M dome

dona ['dɔna] F (proprietária) owner; (col: mulher) lady; **~ de casa** housewife; **D~ Lígia** Lígia; **D~ Luísa Souza** Mrs Luísa Souza

donatário, -a [dona'tarju, a] M/F recipient

donde ['dõda] (PT) ADV from where; (daí) thus; **~ vem?** where do you come from?

dondoca [dõ'dɔka] (col) F society lady, lady of leisure

dono ['donu] M (proprietário) owner

donzela [dõ'zɛla] F (mulher) maiden

dopar [do'pa^r] VT (cavalo) to dope; **dopar-se** VR (atleta) to take drugs

DOPS (BR) ABR M (= Departamento de Ordem Política

e Social) internal security agency

dor [do^r] F ache; (aguda) pain; (fig) grief, sorrow; **~ de cabeça** headache; **~ de dentes** toothache; **~ de estômago** stomach ache

doravante [dora'vãtʃi] ADV henceforth

dor-de-cotovelo (col) M jealousy; **estar com ~** to be jealous

dormência [dox'mẽsja] F numbness

dormente [dox'mẽtʃi] ADJ numb ■ M (Ferro) sleeper

dormida [dox'mida] F sleep; (lugar) place to sleep; **dar uma ~** to have a sleep

dormideira [doxmi'dejra] F drowsiness

dorminhoco, -a [doxmi'ɲoku, a] ADJ dozy ■ M/F sleepyhead

dormir [dox'mi^r] VI to sleep; **~ como uma pedra** ou **a sono solto** to sleep like a log ou soundly; **hora de ~** bedtime; **~ no ponto** (fig) to miss the boat; **~ fora** to spend the night away

dormitar [doxmi'ta^r] VI to doze

dormitório [doxmi'tɔrju] M bedroom; (coletivo) dormitory

dorsal [dox'saw] (pl -ais) ADJ: **coluna ~** spine

dorso ['doxsu] M back

dos [duʃ] = **de + os**

dosagem [do'zaʒẽ] M dosage

dosar [do'za^r] VT (medicamento) to judge the correct dosage of; (graduar) to give in small doses; **você tem que ~ bem o que diz para ele** you have to be careful what you say to him

dose ['dɔzi] F dose; **~ cavalar** huge dose; **~ excessiva** overdose; **é ~ para leão** ou **cavalo** (col) it's too much

dossiê [do'sje] M dossier, file

dotação [dota'sãw] (pl -ões) F endowment, allocation

dotado, -a [do'tadu, a] ADJ gifted; **~ de** endowed with

dotar [do'ta^r] VT to endow; (filha) to give a dowry to; **~ alguém de algo** to endow sb with sth

dote ['dɔtʃi] M dowry; (fig) gift

DOU ABR M (= Diário Oficial da União) official journal of Brazilian government

dou [do] VB v **dar**

dourado, -a [do'radu, a] ADJ golden; (com camada de ouro) gilt, gilded ■ M gilt; (cor) golden colour (Brit) ou color (US)

dourar [do'ra^r] VT to gild

douto, -a ['dotu, a] ADJ learned

doutor, a [do'to^r(a)] M/F doctor; **D~** (forma de tratamento) Sir; **D~ Eduardo Souza** Mr Eduardo Souza

doutorado [doto'radu] M doctorate

doutrina [do'trina] F doctrine

doze ['dozi] NUM twelve; v tb **cinco**

DP (BR) ABR F = **delegacia policial**

DPF (BR) ABR M = **Departamento de Polícia Federal**

DPNRE (BR) ABR M = **Departamento de Parques Nacionais e Reservas Equivalentes**

Dr(a). ABR (= Doutor(a)) Dr

dracma ['drakma] F drachma

draga ['draga] F dredger
dragagem [dra'gaʒẽ] F dredging
dragão [dra'gãw] (pl -ões) M dragon; (Mil)
dragoon
dragar [dra'gaʳ] VT to dredge
drágea ['draʒja] F tablet
dragões [dra'gõjʃ] MPL de **dragão**
drama ['drama] M (teatro) drama; (peça) play;
fazer ~ (col) to make a scene; **ser um ~** (col) to
be an ordeal
dramalhão [drama'ʎãw] (pl -ões) M melodrama
dramático, -a [dra'matʃiku, a] ADJ dramatic
dramatização [dramatʃiza'sãw] (pl -ões) F
dramatization
dramatizar [dramatʃi'zaʳ] VT, VI to dramatize
dramaturgo, -a [drama'tuxgu, a] M/F
playwright, dramatist
drapeado, -a [dra'pjadu, a] ADJ draped ■ M
hang
drástico, -a ['draʃtʃiku, a] ADJ drastic
drenagem [dre'naʒẽ] F drainage
drenar [dre'naʳ] VT to drain
dreno ['drɛnu] M drain
driblar [dri'blaʳ] VT (Futebol) to dribble; (fig) to get
round ■ VI to dribble
drinque ['drĩki] M drink
drive ['drajvi] M (Comput) (disk) drive
droga ['drɔga] F drug; (fig) rubbish ■ EXCL: ~ !
damn!, blast!; **ser uma ~** (col: filme, caneta etc) to
be a dead loss; (obrigação, atividade) to be a drag;
drogado, -a [dro'gadu, a] M/F drug addict;
drogar [dro'gaʳ] VT to drug; **drogar-se** VR to
take drugs
drogaria [droga'ria] F chemist's shop (Brit),
drugstore (US)
dromedário [drome'darju] M dromedary
duas ['duaʃ] F de **dois**
duas-peças M INV two-piece
dúbio, -a ['dubju, a] ADJ dubious; (vago)
uncertain
dublagem [du'blaʒẽ] F (de filme) dubbing
dublar [du'blaʳ] VT to dub
dublê [du'ble] M/F double
ducentésimo, -a [dusẽ'tɛzimu, a] NUM two-
hundredth
ducha ['duʃa] F shower; (Med) douche
ducto ['duktu] M duct
duelo ['dwɛlu] M duel
duende ['dwẽdʒi] M elf
dueto ['dwetu] M duet
dulcíssimo, -a [duw'sisimu, a] ADJ SUPERL de
doce
dumping ['dãpĩŋ] M (Econ) dumping
duna ['duna] F dune
duodécimo, -a [dwo'dɛsimu, a] NUM twelfth
duodeno [dwo'dɛnu] M duodenum

dupla ['dupla] F pair; (Esporte): **~ masculina/**
feminina/mista men's/women's/mixed
doubles
dúplex ['dupleks] ADJ INV two-storey (Brit), two-
story (US) ■ M INV luxury maisonette, duplex
duplicação [duplika'sãw] F (repetição)
duplication; (aumento) doubling
duplicar [dupli'kaʳ] VT (repetir) to duplicate
■ VI (dobrar) to double; **duplicata** [dupli'kata] F
(cópia) duplicate; (título) trade note, bill
duplicidade [duplisi'dadʒi] F (fig) duplicity
duplo, -a ['duplu, a] ADJ double ■ M double
duque ['duki] M duke
duquesa [du'keza] F duchess
durabilidade [durabili'dadʒi] F durability
duração [dura'sãw] F duration; **de pouca ~**
short-lived
duradouro, -a [dura'doru, a] ADJ lasting
durante [du'rãtʃi] PREP during; **~ uma hora** for
an hour
durão, -rona [du'rãw, 'rɔna] (col) (pl -ões/-s) ADJ
strict, tough
durar [du'raʳ] VI to last
durável [du'ravew] (pl -eis) ADJ lasting
durex® [du'rɛks] ADJ: **fita durex** adhesive tape,
Sellotape® (Brit), Scotchtape® (US)
dureza [du'reza] F hardness; (severidade)
harshness; (col: falta de dinheiro) lack of funds
durmo etc ['duxmu] VB V **dormir**
duro, -a ['duru, a] ADJ hard; (severo) harsh;
(resistente, fig) tough; (sentença, palavras) harsh,
tough; (inverno) hard, harsh; (fig: difícil) hard,
tough; **ser ~ com alguém** to be hard on sb;
estar ~ (col) to be broke; **dar um ~** (col: trabalhar)
to work hard; **dar um ~ em alguém** (col) to
come down hard on sb; **~ de roer** (fig) hard to
take; **no ~** (col) really; **a praia estava dura de**
gente the beach was packed
durões [du'rõjʃ] MPL de **durão**
durona [du'rɔna] F de **durão**
DUT (BR) ABR M (= documento único de trânsito)
vehicle licensing document
dúvida ['duvida] F doubt; **sem ~** undoubtedly,
without a doubt; **duvidar** [duvi'daʳ] VT to doubt
■ VI to have one's doubts; **duvidar de alguém/**
algo to doubt sb/sth; **duvidar que ...** to doubt
that ...; **duvido!** I doubt it!; **duvido que você**
consiga correr a maratona I bet you don't
manage to run the marathon
duvidoso, -a [duvi'dozu, ɔza] ADJ (incerto)
doubtful; (suspeito) dubious
duzentos, -tas [du'zẽtuʃ] NUM two hundred
dúzia ['duzja] F dozen; **meia ~** half a dozen
DVD ABR M (= disco digital versátil) DVD
dz. ABR = **dúzia**

NB: European Portuguese adds the following consonants to certain words: **b** (sú(b)dito, su(b)til); **c** (a(c)ção,
a(c)cionista, a(c)to)); **m** (inde(m)ne); **p** (ado(p)çã, ado(p)tar); for further details see p. xiii.

Ee

E, e [ɛ] M (pl **es**) E, e ■ ABR (= *esquerda*) L.; (= *este*) E; (= *editor*) Ed.; **E de Eliane** E for Edward (*Brit*) *ou* easy (*US*)

e [i] CONJ and; **e a bagagem?** what about the luggage?

é [ɛ] VB V **ser**

EAPAC (BR) ABR F (= *Escola de Aperfeiçoamento e Preparação Civil*) civil service training school

ébano ['ɛbanu] M ebony

EBN ABR F = **Empresa Brasileira de Notícias**

ébrio, -a ['ɛbrju, a] ADJ drunk ■ M/F drunkard

EBTU ABR F = **Empresa Brasileira de Transportes Urbanos**

ebulição [ebuli'sãw] F boiling; (*fig*) ferment

ebuliente [ebu'ljẽtʃi] ADJ boiling

ECEME (BR) ABR F (= *Escola de Comando e Estado-Maior do Exército*) officer training school

eclesiástico, -a [ekle'zjastʃiku, a] ADJ ecclesiastical, church *atr* ■ M clergyman

eclético, -a [e'klɛtʃiku, a] ADJ eclectic

eclipsar [eklip'sa^r] VT (*tb fig*) to eclipse

eclipse [e'klipsi] M eclipse

eclodir [eklo'dʒi^r] VI (*aparecer*) to emerge; (*revolução*) to break out; (*flor*) to open

eclusa [e'kluza] F (*de canal*) lock; (*comporta*) floodgate

eco ['ɛku] M echo; **ter ~** to catch on; **ecoar** [e'kwa^r] VT to echo ■ VI (*ressoar*) to echo; (*fig: repercutir*) to have repercussions

ecologia [ekolo'ʒia] F ecology

ecológico, -a [eko'lɔʒiku, a] ADJ ecological

ecologista [ekolo'ʒiʃta] M/F ecologist

economia [ekono'mia] F economy; (*ciência*) economics *sg*; **economias** FPL (*poupanças*) savings; **fazer ~ (de)** to economize (with)

econômico, -a [eko'nomiku, a] ADJ (*barato*) cheap; (*que consome pouco*) economical; (*pessoa*) thrifty; (*Com*) economic

economista [ekono'miʃta] M/F economist

economizar [ekonomi'za^r] VT (*gastar com economia*) to economize on; (*poupar*) to save (up) ■ VI to economize; to save up

écran ['ɛkrã] (PT) M screen

ECT ABR F = **Empresa Brasileira de Correios e Telégrafos**

ecumênico, -a [eku'meniku, a] ADJ ecumenical

eczema [eg'zema] M eczema

Ed. ABR = **edifício**

ed. ABR = **edição**

éden ['ɛdẽ] M paradise

edição [edʒi'sãw] (pl -ões) F (*publicação*) publication; (*conjunto de exemplares*) edition; (TV, Cinema) editing; **~ atualizada/revista** updated/revised edition; **~ extra** special edition; **~ de imagem** video editing

edicto [e'ditu] (PT) M = **edito**

edificação [edʒifika'sãw] F construction, building; (*fig: moral*) edification

edificante [edʒifi'kãtʃi] ADJ edifying

edificar [edʒifi'ka^r] VT (*construir*) to build; (*fig*) to edify ■ VI to be edifying

edifício [edʒi'fisju] M building; **~ garagem** multistorey car park (*Brit*), multistory parking lot (US)

Edimburgo [edʒĩ'buxgu] N Edinburgh

Édipo ['ɛdʒipu] M V **complexo**

edital [edʒi'taw] (pl -ais) M announcement

editar [edʒi'ta^r] VT to publish; (*Comput etc*) to edit

edito [e'dʒitu] M edict, decree

editor, a [edʒi'to^r(a)] ADJ publishing *atr* ■ M/F publisher; (*redator*) editor ■ F publishing company; **casa ~a** publishing house; **~ de imagem** video editor; **~ de texto** (*Comput*) text editor

editoração [edʒitora'sãw] F: **~ eletrônica** desktop publishing

editoria [edʒito'ria] F section; **~ de esportes** (*em jornal*) sports desk

editorial [edʒitor'jaw] (pl -ais) ADJ publishing *atr* ■ M editorial

edredão [ədrə'dãw] (pl -ões) (PT) M = **edredom**

edredom [edre'dõ] (pl -ns) M eiderdown

educação [eduka'sãw] F (*ensino*) education; (*criação*) upbringing; (*de animais*) training; (*maneiras*) good manners *pl*; **é falta de ~ falar com a boca cheia** it's rude to talk with your mouth full; **educacional** [edukasjo'naw] (pl -ais) ADJ education *atr*

educado, -a [edu'kadu, a] ADJ (*bem-educado*) polite

educador, a [eduka'do^r(a)] M/F educator

educandário [edukã'darju] M educational establishment

educar [edu'ka^r] VT (*instruir*) to educate; (*criar*) to bring up; (animal) to train

educativo, -a [eduka'tʃivu, a] ADJ educational

efectivo, -va [efek'tivu] (PT) ADJ = **efetivo** etc

efectuar [efek'twaʳ] (PT) VT = **efetuar**

efeito [e'fejtu] M effect; **fazer ~** to work; **levar a ~** to put into effect; **com ~** indeed; **para todos os ~s** to all intents and purposes; **~ estufa** greenhouse effect

efêmero, -a [e'femeru, a] ADJ ephemeral, short-lived

efeminado [efemi'nadu] ADJ effeminate ■ M effeminate man

efervescência [efexve'sẽsja] F effervescence; (fig) ferment

efervescente [efexve'sẽtʃi] ADJ fizzy

efervescer [efexve'seʳ] VI to fizz; (fig) to hum

efetivamente [efetʃiva'mẽtʃi] ADV effectively; (realmente) really, in fact

efetivar [efetʃi'vaʳ] VT (mudanças, cortes) to carry out; (professor, estagiário) to take on permanently

efetividade [efetʃivi'dadʒi] F effectiveness; (realidade) reality

efetivo, -a [efe'tʃivu, a] ADJ effective; (real) actual, real; (cargo, funcionário) permanent ■ M (Com) liquid assets pl

efetuar [efe'twaʳ] VT to carry out; (soma) to do, perform

eficácia [efi'kasja] F (de pessoa) efficiency; (de tratamento) effectiveness

eficacíssimo, -a [efika'sisimu, a] ADJ SUPERL de **eficaz**

eficaz [efi'kaʒ] ADJ (pessoa) efficient; (tratamento) effective

eficiência [efi'sjẽsja] F efficiency; **eficiente** [efi'sjẽtʃi] ADJ efficient, competent

efígie [e'fiʒi] F effigy

efusão [efu'zãw] (pl -ões) F effusion

efusivo, -a [efu'zivu, a] ADJ effusive; (sentimentos) warmest

efusões [efu'zõjʃ] FPL de **efusão**

Egeu [e'ʒew] M: **o (mar) ~** the Aegean (Sea)

EGF (BR) ABR M = **empréstimo do governo federal**

égide ['ɛʒidʒi] F: **sob a ~ de** under the aegis (Brit) ou egis (US) of

egípcio, -a [e'ʒipsju, a] ADJ, M/F Egyptian

Egito [e'ʒitu] (PT -pt-) M: **o ~** Egypt

ego ['ɛgu] M ego

egocêntrico, -a [ego'sẽtriku, a] ADJ self-centred (Brit); self-centered (US), egocentric

egoísmo [ego'iʒmu] M selfishness, egoism; **egoísta** [ego'iʃta] ADJ selfish, egoistic ■ M/F egoist ■ M earplug

egolatria [egola'tria] F self-admiration

egotismo [ego'tʃiʒmu] M egotism

egotista [ego'tʃiʃta] M/F egotist ■ ADJ egotistical

egrégio, -a [e'greʒju, a] ADJ distinguished

egresso [e'grɛsu] M (preso) ex-prisoner; (frade)

former monk; (universidade) graduate

égua ['ɛgwa] F mare

ei [ej] EXCL hey!

ei-lo etc = **eis + o**; v **eis**

eira ['ejra] (PT) F threshing floor; **sem ~ nem beira** down and out

eis [ejʃ] ADV (sg) here is; (pl) here are; **~ aí** there is; there are

eivado, -a [ej'vadu, a] ADJ (fig) full

eixo ['ejʃu] M (de rodas) axle; (Mat) axis; (de máquina) shaft; **~ de transmissão** drive shaft; **entrar nos ~s** (pessoa) to get back on the straight and narrow; (situação) to get back to normal; **pôr algo/alguém nos ~s** to set sth/sb straight; **sair dos ~s** to step out of line; **o ~ Rio-São Paulo** the Rio-São Paulo area

ejacular [eʒaku'laʳ] VT (sêmen) to ejaculate; (líquido) to spurt ■ VI to ejaculate

ejetar [eʒe'taʳ] VT to eject

ela ['ɛla] PRON (pessoa) she; (coisa) it; (com prep) her; it; **elas** FPL they; (com prep) them; **~s por ~s** (col) tit for tat; **aí é que são ~s** (col) that's just the point

elã [c'lã] M enthusiasm, drive

elaboração [elabora'sãw] (pl -ões) F (de uma teoria) working out; (preparo) preparation

elaborador, a [elabora'do(a)] M/F maker

elaborar [elabo'raʳ] VT (preparar) to prepare; (fazer) to make

elasticidade [elaʃtʃisi'dadʒi] F elasticity; (flexibilidade) suppleness

elástico, -a [e'laʃtʃiku, a] ADJ elastic; (flexível) flexible; (colchão) springy ■ M elastic band

ele ['eli] PRON he; (coisa) it; (com prep) him; it; **eles** MPL they; (com prep) them

electri... etc [elektri] (PT) = **eletri...** etc

eléctrico, -a [e'lɛktriku, a] (PT) ADJ = **elétrico** ■ M tram (Brit), streetcar (US)

electro... etc [elektru] (PT) = **eletro...** etc

eléctrodo [e'lɛktrodu] (PT) M = **eletrodo**

elefante, -ta [ele'fãtʃi] M/F elephant; (col: pessoa gorda) fatso, fatty; **~ branco** (fig) white elephant

elefantino, -a [elefã'tʃinu, a] ADJ elephantine

elegância [ele'gãsja] F elegance

elegante [ele'gãtʃi] ADJ elegant; (da moda) fashionable

eleger [ele'ʒeʳ] VT (por votação) to elect; (escolher) to choose

elegia [ele'ʒia] F elegy

elegibilidade [eleʒibili'dadʒi] F eligibility

elegível [ele'ʒivɛw] (pl -eis) ADJ eligible

eleição [elej'sãw] (pl -ões) F (por votação) election; (escolha) choice

eleito, -a [e'lejtu, a] PP de **eleger** ■ ADJ (por votação) elected; (escolhido) chosen

eleitor, a [elej'to(a)] M/F voter

eleitorado [elejto'radu] M electorate; **conhecer o seu ~** (fig: col) to know what one is up against

eleitoral [elejto'raw] (pl -ais) ADJ electoral

NB: European Portuguese adds the following consonants to certain words: **b** (sú(b)dito, su(b)til); **c** (a(c)ção, a(c)cionista, a(c)to); **m** (inde(m)ne); **p** (ado(p)ção, ado(p)tar); for further details see p. xiii.

elejo *etc* [eleˈʒu] VB V **eleger**
elementar [elemẽˈtaʳ] ADJ (*simples*) elementary; (*fundamental*) basic, fundamental
elemento [eleˈmẽtu] M element; (*parte*) component; (*recurso*) means; (*informação*) grounds *pl*; **elementos** MPL (*rudimentos*) rudiments; **ele é mau** ~ he's a bad lot
elenco [eˈlẽku] M list; (*de atores*) cast
elepê [eliˈpe] M LP, album
eletivo, -a [eleˈtʃivu, a] ADJ elective
eletricidade [eletrisiˈdadʒi] F electricity
eletricista [eletriˈsiʃta] M/F electrician
elétrico, -a [eˈlɛtriku, a] ADJ electric; (*fig*: *agitado*) worked up
eletrificar [eletrifiˈkaʳ] VT to electrify
eletrizar [eletriˈzaʳ] VT to electrify; (*fig*) to thrill
eletro [eˈletru] M (*Med*) ECG
eletro... [eletru] PREFIXO electro...
Eletrobrás [eletroˈbraʃ] ABR F *Brazilian state electricity company*
eletrocutar [eletrokuˈtaʳ] VT to electrocute
eletrodo [eleˈtrodu] M electrode
eletrodomésticos [eletrodoˈmʃtʃikuʃ] (BR) MPL (electrical) household appliances
eletrônica [eleˈtronika] F electronics *sg*
eletrônico, -a [eleˈtroniku, a] ADJ electronic
elevação [elevaˈsãw] (*pl* -ões) F (*Arq*) elevation; (*aumento*) rise; (*ato*) raising; (*altura*) height; (*promoção*) elevation, promotion; (*ponto elevado*) bump
elevado, -a [eleˈvadu, a] ADJ high; (*pensamento, estilo*) elevated ■ M (*via*) elevated road
elevador [elevaˈdoʳ] M lift (*Brit*), elevator (*US*); ~ **de serviço** service lift
elevar [eleˈvaʳ] VT (*levantar*) to lift up; (*voz, preço*) to raise; (*exaltar*) to exalt; (*promover*) to elevate, promote; **elevar-se** VR to rise
eliminação [eliminaˈsãw] F elimination
eliminar [elimiˈnaʳ] VT to remove, eliminate; (*suprimir*) to delete; (*possibilidade*) to rule out; (*Med, banir*) to expel; (*Esporte*) to eliminate; **eliminatória** [eliminaˈtɔrja] F (*Esporte*) heat, preliminary round; (*exame*) test
eliminatório, -a [eliminaˈtɔrju, a] ADJ eliminatory
elipse [eˈlipsi] F ellipse; (*Ling*) ellipsis
elite [eˈlitʃi] F elite
elitismo [eliˈtʃiʒmu] M elitism
elitista [eliˈtʃiʃta] ADJ, M/F elitist
elitizar [elitʃiˈzaʳ] VT (*arte, ensino*) to make elitist
elixir [elikˈsiʳ] M elixir
elo [ˈɛlu] M link
elocução [elokuˈsãw] F elocution
elogiar [eloˈʒjaʳ] VT to praise; ~ **alguém por algo** to compliment sb on sth; **elogio** [eloˈʒiu] M praise; (*cumprimento*) compliment
elogioso, -a [eloˈʒozu, ɔza] ADJ complimentary
eloqüência [eloˈkwẽsja] F eloquence
eloqüente [eloˈkwẽtʃi] ADJ eloquent; (*persuasivo*) persuasive
El Salvador [ew-] N El Salvador
elucidação [elusidaˈsãw] F elucidation

elucidar [elusiˈdaʳ] VT to elucidate, clarify
elucidativo, -a [elusidaˈtʃivu, a] ADJ elucidatory
elucubração [elukubraˈsãw] (*pl* -ões) F cogitation, musing

🅞 **PALAVRA CHAVE**

em [ẽ] (*em* + *o*(*s*)/*a*(*s*) = *no*(*s*)/*na*(*s*); + *ele*(*s*)/*a*(*s*) = *nele*(*s*)/*a*(*s*); + *esse*(*s*)/*a*(*s*) = *nesse*(*s*)/*a*(*s*); + *isso* = *nisso*; + *este*(*s*)/*a*(*s*) = *neste*(*s*)/*a*(*s*); + *isto* = *nisto*; + *aquele*(*s*)/*a*(*s*) = *naquele*(*s*)/*a*(*s*); + *aquilo* = *naquilo*) PREP **1** (*posição*) in; (: *sobre*) on; **está na gaveta/no bolso** it's in the drawer/pocket; **está na mesa/no chão** it's on the table/floor
2 (*lugar*) in; (: *casa, escritório etc*) at; (: *andar, meio de transporte*) on; **no Brasil/em São Paulo** in Brazil/São Paulo; **em casa/no dentista** at home/the dentist; **no avião** on the plane; **no quinto andar** on the fifth floor
3 (*ação*) into; **ela entrou na sala de aula** she went into the classroom; **colocar algo na bolso** to put sth into one's bag
4 (*tempo*) in; on; **em 1962/3 semanas** in 1962/3 weeks; **no inverno** in the winter; **em janeiro, no mês de janeiro** in January; **nessa ocasião/altura** on that occasion/at that time; **em breve** soon
5 (*diferença*): **reduzir/aumentar em um 20%** to reduce/increase by 20%
6 (*modo*): **escrito em inglês** written in English
7 (*após vb que indica gastar etc*) on; **a metade do seu salário vai em comida** he spends half his salary on food
8 (*tema, ocupação*): **especialista no assunto** expert on the subject; **ele trabalha na construção civil** he works in the building industry

emaecer [iʒmajeˈseʳ] VI to fade
Emaer [emaˈeʳ] (BR) ABR M = **Estado-Maior da Aeronáutica**
emagrecer [imagreˈseʳ] VT to make thin ■ VI to grow thin; (*mediante regime*) to slim; **emagrecimento** [imagresiˈmẽtu] M (*mediante regime*) slimming
e-mail [iˈmew] M e-mail; **mandar um ~ para** to e-mail; **mandar por** ~ to e-mail
emanar [emaˈnaʳ] VI: ~ **de** to come from, emanate from
emancipação [imãsipaˈsãw] (*pl* -ões) F emancipation; (*atingir a maioridade*) coming of age
emancipar [imãsiˈpaʳ] VT to emancipate; **emancipar-se** VR (*atingir a maioridade*) to come of age
emaranhado, -a [imaraˈɲadu, a] ADJ tangled ■ M tangle
emaranhar [imaraˈɲaʳ] VT to tangle; (*complicar*) to complicate; **emaranhar-se** VR to get entangled; (*fig*) to get mixed up
emassar [emaˈsaʳ] VT (*parede*) to plaster; (*janela*) to putty

Emater [ema'tɛʳ] (BR) ABR F (= *Empresa de Assistência Técnica e Extensão Rural*) *company giving aid to farmers*

embaçado, -a [ēba'sadu, a] ADJ (*vidro*) steamed up

embaçar [ēba'saʳ] VT to steam up

embaciado, -a [ēba'sjadu, a] ADJ dull; (*vidro*) misted; (*janela*) steamed up; (*olhos*) misty

embaciar [ēba'sjaʳ] VT (*vidro*) to steam up; (*olhos*) to cloud ▪ VI to steam up; (*olhos*) to grow misty

embainhar [ēbaj'ɲaʳ] VT (*espada*) to put away, sheathe; (*calça etc*) to hem

embaixada [ēbaj'ʃada] F embassy

embaixador, a [ēbajʃa'doʳ(a)] M/F ambassador

embaixatriz [ēbajʃa'triʒ] F ambassador; (*mulher de embaixador*) ambassador's wife

embaixo [ē'bajʃu] ADV below, underneath ▪ PREP: ~ **de** under, underneath; (**lá**) ~ (*em andar inferior*) downstairs

embalado, -a [ēba'ladu, a] ADJ (*acelerado*) fast; (*drogado*) high; **ir** ~ to race (along)

embalagem [ēba'laʒē] F packing; (*de produto: caixa etc*) packaging

embalar [ēba'laʳ] VT to pack; (*balançar*) to rock

embalo [ē'balu] M (*balanço*) rocking; (*impulso*) rush; (*col: com drogas*) high; **aproveitar o** ~ to take the opportunity

embalsamar [ēbawsa'maʳ] VT (*perfumar*) to perfume; (*cadáver*) to embalm

embananado, -a [ēbana'nadu, a] (*col*) ADJ (*confuso*) muddled; (*em dificuldades*) in trouble

embananamento [ēbanana'mētu] (*col*) M muddle; (*bananosa*) jam

embananar [ēbana'naʳ] (*col*) VT (*tornar confuso*) to muddle up; (*complicar*) to complicate; (*meter em dificuldades*) to get into trouble; **embananar-se** VR to get tied up in knots

embaraçar [ēbara'saʳ] VT (*impedir*) to hinder; (*complicar*) to complicate; (*encabular*) to embarrass; (*confundir*) to confuse; (*obstruir*) to block; **embaraçar-se** VR to become embarrassed

embaraço [ēba'rasu] M (*estorvo*) hindrance; (*cábula*) embarrassment; **embaraçoso, -a** [ēbara'sozu, ɔza] ADJ embarrassing

embarafustar [ēbarafuʃ'taʳ] VI: ~ **por** to burst *ou* barge into

embaralhar [ēbara'ʎaʳ] VT (*confundir*) to muddle up; (*cartas*) to shuffle; **embaralhar-se** VR to get mixed up

embarcação [ēbaxka'sāw] (*pl* -**ões**) F vessel

embarcadiço [ēbaxka'dʒisu] M seafarer

embarcadouro [ēbaxka'doru] M wharf

embarcar [ēbax'kaʳ] VT to embark, put on board; (*mercadorias*) to ship, stow ▪ VI to go on board, embark; ~ **em algo** (*fig: col*) to fall for sth

embargar [ēbax'gaʳ] VT (*Jur*) to seize; (*pôr obstáculos a*) to hinder; (*reprimir: voz*) to keep down; (*impedir*) to forbid

embargo [ē'baxgu] M (*de navio*) embargo; (*Jur*) seizure; (*impedimento*) impediment; **sem** ~ nevertheless

embarque [ē'baxki] M (*de pessoas*) boarding, embarkation; (*de mercadorias*) shipment

embasamento [ēbaza'mētu] M (*Arq*) foundation; (*de coluna*) base; (*fig*) basis

embasbacado, -a [ēbaʒba'kadu, a] ADJ gaping, open-mouthed

embasbacar [ēbaʒba'kaʳ] VT to leave open-mouthed; **embasbacar-se** VR to be taken aback, be dumbfounded

embate [ē'batʃi] M clash; (*choque*) shock

embatucar [ēbatu'kaʳ] VT to dumbfound ▪ VI to be speechless

embebedar [ēbebe'daʳ] VT to make drunk ▪ VI: **o vinho embebeda** wine makes you drunk; **embebedar-se** VR to get drunk

embeber [ēbe'beʳ] VT to soak up, absorb; **embeber-se** VR: **embeber-se em** to become absorbed in

embelezador, a [ēbeleza'doʳ(a)] ADJ cosmetic

embelezar [ēbele'zaʳ] VT to make beautiful; (*casa*) to brighten up; **embelezar-se** VR to make o.s. beautiful

embevecer [ēbeve'seʳ] VT to captivate; **embevecer-se** VR to be captivated

embicar [ēbi'kaʳ] VI (*Náut*) to enter port, dock; (*fig*): ~ **para** to head for; ~ **com alguém** to quarrel with sb

embirrar [ēbi'xaʳ] VI to sulk; ~ **em** to insist on; ~ **com** to dislike

emblema [ē'blɛma] M emblem; (*na roupa*) badge

embocadura [ēboka'dura] F (*de rio*) mouth; (*Mús*) mouthpiece; (*de freio*) bit

emboço [ē'bosu] M roughcast, render

embolar [ēbo'laʳ] VT (*confundir*) to confuse ▪ VI: ~ **com** to grapple with; **embolar-se** VR: **embolar-se (com)** to grapple (with)

êmbolo [ē'bolu] M piston

embolorar [ēbolo'raʳ] VI to go musty

embolsar [ēbow'saʳ] VT to pocket; (*herança etc*) to come by; (*indenizar*) to refund

embonecar [ēbone'kaʳ] VT to doll up; **embonecar-se** VR to doll o.s. up, get dolled up

embora [ē'bɔra] CONJ though, although ▪ EXCL even so, what of it?; **ir(-se)** ~ to go away

emborcar [ēbox'kaʳ] VT to turn upside down

emboscada [ēboʃ'kada] F ambush

embotar [ēbo'taʳ] VT (*lâmina*) to blunt; (*fig*) to deaden, dull

embrabecer [ēbrabe'seʳ] VI = **embravecer**

Embraer [ēbra'ɛʳ] ABR F (= *Empresa Brasileira de Aeronáutica SA*) *aerospace company*

embranquecer [ēbrāke'seʳ] VT, VI to turn white

Embratur [ēbra'tuʳ] ABR F (= *Empresa Brasileira de Turismo*) *state tourist board*

embravecer [ēbrave'seʳ] VR to get furious; **embravecer-se** VR to get furious

---

NB: *European Portuguese adds the following consonants to certain words:* **b** (sú(b)dito, su(b)til); **c** (a(c)ção, a(c)cionista, a(c)to); **m** (inde(m)ne); **p** (ado(p)ção, ado(p)tar); *for further details see p. xiii.*

embreagem [ēb'rjaʒē] (pl -ns) F (Auto) clutch

embrear [ē'brjaʳ] VT (Auto) to disengage ■ VI to let in the clutch

embrenhar [ēbre'ɲaʳ] VT to penetrate; **embrenhar-se** VR: **embrenhar-se (em/por)** to make one's way (into/through)

embriagante [ēbrja'gãtʃi] ADJ intoxicating

embriagar [ēbrja'gaʳ] VT to make drunk, intoxicate; **embriagar-se** VR to get drunk; **embriaguez** [ēbrja'geʒ] F drunkenness; (fig) rapture; **embriaguez no volante** drunk(en) driving

embrião [e'brjãw] (pl -ões) M embryo

embrionário, -a [ēbrjo'narju, a] ADJ (tb fig) embryonic

embromação [ēbroma'sãw] (pl -ões) F stalling; (trapaça) con

embromador, a [ēbroma'doʳ(a)] ADJ (remanchador) slow; (trapaçeiro) dishonest, bent ■ M/F (remanchador) staller; (trapaçeiro) con merchant

embromar [ēbro'maʳ] VT (adiar) to put off; (enganar) to con, cheat ■ VI (prometer e não cumprir) to make empty promises, be all talk (and no action); (protelar) to stall; (falar em rodeios) to beat about the bush

embrulhada [ēbru'ʎada] F muddle, mess

embrulhar [ēbru'ʎaʳ] VT (pacote) to wrap; (enrolar) to roll up; (confundir) to muddle up; (enganar) to cheat; (estômago) to upset; **embrulhar-se** VR to get into a muddle; **ao contar a estória, ele embrulhou tudo** when he told the story he got everything mixed up

embrulho [ē'bruʎu] M (pacote) package, parcel; (confusão) mix-up

embrutecer [ēbrute'seʳ] VT, VI to brutalize; **embrutecer-se** VR to be brutalized

emburrar [ēbu'xaʳ] VI to sulk

embuste [ē'buʃtʃi] M (engano) deception; (ardil) trick

embusteiro, -a [ēbuʃ'tejru, a] ADJ deceitful ■ M/F cheat; (mentiroso) liar; (impostor) impostor

embutido, -a [ēbu'tʃidu, a] ADJ (armário) built-in, fitted

embutir [ēbu'tʃiʳ] VT to build in; (marfim etc) to inlay

emenda [e'mēda] F correction; (Jur) amendment; (de uma pessoa) improvement; (ligação) join; (sambladura) joint; (Costura) seam

emendar [emē'daʳ] VT (corrigir) to correct; (reparar) to mend; (injustiças) to make amends for; (Jur) to amend; (ajuntar) to put together; **emendar-se** VR to mend one's ways

ementa [e'mēta] (PT) F menu

emergência [imex'ʒēsja] F (nascimento) emergence; (crise) emergency

emergente [imex'ʒētʒi] ADJ emerging

emergir [imex'ʒiʳ] VI to emerge, appear; (submarino) to surface

EMFA (BR) ABR M = **Estado-maior das Forças Armadas**

emigração [imigra'sãw] (pl -ões) F emigration;

(de aves) migration

emigrado, -a [emi'gradu, a] ADJ emigrant

emigrante [emi'grãtʃi] M/F emigrant

emigrar [emi'graʳ] VI to emigrate; (aves) to migrate

eminência [emi'nēsja] F eminence; (altura) height; **eminente** [emi'nētʃi] ADJ eminent, distinguished; (Geo) high

Emirados Árabes Unidos [emi'raduʃ-] MPL: **os ~** the United Arab Emirates

emirjo etc [e'mixʒu] VB **v emergir**

emissão [emi'sãw] (pl -ões) F emission; (Rádio) broadcast; (de moeda, ações) issue

emissário, -a [emi'sarju, a] M/F emissary ■ M outlet

emissões [emi'sõjʃ] FPL de **emissão**

emissor, a [emi'soʳ(a)] ADJ (de moeda-papel) issuing ■ M (Rádio) transmitter ■ F (estação) broadcasting station; (empresa) broadcasting company

emitente [emi'tētʃi] ADJ (Com) issuing ■ M/F issuer

emitir [emi'tʃiʳ] VT (som) to give out; (cheiro) to give off; (moeda, ações) to issue; (Rádio) to broadcast; (opinião) to express ■ VI (emitir moeda) to print money

emoção [emo'sãw] (pl -ões) F emotion; (excitação) excitement; **emocional** [imosjo'naw] (pl -ais) ADJ emotional; **emocionante** [imosjo'nãtʃi] ADJ (comovente) moving; (excitante) exciting; **emocionar** [imosjo'naʳ] VT (comover) to move; (perturbar) to upset; (excitar) to excite, thrill ■ VI to be exciting; (comover) to be moving; **emocionar-se** VR to get emotional

emoções [emo'sõjʃ] FPL de **emoção**

emoldurar [emowdu'raʳ] VT to frame

emotividade [emotʃivi'dadʒi] F emotions pl

emotivo, -a [emo'tʃivu, a] ADJ emotional

empacar [ēpa'kaʳ] VI (cavalo) to baulk; (fig: negócios etc) to grind to a halt; (orador) to dry up; **~ numa palavra** to get stuck on a word

empachado, -a [ēpa'ʃadu, a] ADJ full up

empacotar [ēpako'taʳ] VT to pack, wrap up ■ VI (col: morrer) to pop one's clogs

empada [ē'pada] F pie

empadão [ēpa'dãw] (pl -ões) M pie

empalhar [ēpa'ʎaʳ] VT (animal) to stuff; (louça, fruta) to pack with straw

empalidecer [ēpalide'seʳ] VT, VI to turn pale

empanar [ēpa'naʳ] VT (fig) to tarnish; (Culin) to batter

empanturrar [ēpãtu'xaʳ] VT: **~ alguém de algo** to stuff sb full of sth; **empanturrar-se** VR to gorge o.s., stuff o.s. (col)

empanzinado, -a [ēpãzi'nadu, a] ADJ full

empapar [ēpa'paʳ] VT to soak; **empapar-se** VR to get soaked

empapuçado, -a [ēpapu'sadu, a] ADJ (olhos) puffy; (blusa) full

emparedar [ēpare'daʳ] VT to wall in; (pessoa) to shut up

emparelhar [ēpare'ʎaʳ] VT to pair; (equiparar) to

match ∎ VI: ~ **com** to be equal to

empastado, -a [ẽpaʃ'tadu, a] ADJ (cabelo) plastered down

empastar [ẽpaʃ'ta^r] VT: ~ **algo de algo** to plaster sth with sth

empatar [ẽpa'ta^r] VT (embaraçar) to hinder; (dinheiro) to tie up; (no jogo) to draw; (corredores) to tie; (tempo) to take up ∎ VI (no jogo): ~ (**com**) to draw (with); **empate** [ẽ'patʃi] M (no jogo) draw; (numa corrida etc) tie; (Xadrez) stalemate; (em negociações) deadlock

empatia [ẽpa'tʃia] F empathy

empavonar-se [ẽpavo'naxsi] VR to strut

empecilho [ẽpe'siʎu] M obstacle; (col) snag

empedernido, -a [ẽpedex'nidu, a] ADJ hardhearted

empedrar [ẽpe'dra^r] VT to pave

empenar [ẽpe'na^r] VT, VI (curvar) to warp

empenhar [ẽpe'ɲa^r] VT (objeto) to pawn; (palavra) to pledge; (empregar) to exert; (compelir) to oblige; **empenhar-se** VR: **empenhar-se em fazer** to strive to do, do one's utmost to do; **empenho** [ẽ'peɲu] M (de um objeto) pawning; (palavra) pledge; (insistência): **empenho (em)** commitment (to); **ele pôs todo seu empenho neste projeto** he committed himself wholeheartedly to this project

emperiquitar-se [ẽperiki'taxsi] VR to get done up to the nines

emperrar [ẽpe'xa^r] VT (máquina) to jam; (porta, junta) to make stiff; (fazer calar) to cut short ∎ VI to jam; (gaveta, porta) to stick; (junta) to go stiff; (calar) to go quiet

empertigado, -a [ẽpextʃi'gadu, a] ADJ upright

empertigar-se [ẽpextʃi'gaxsi] VR to stand up straight

empestar [ẽpeʃ'ta^r] VT (infetar) to infect; (tornar desagradável) to pollute, stink out (col)

empetecar [ẽpete'ka^r] VT to doll up; **empetecar-se** VR to doll o.s. up

empilhar [ẽpi'ʎa^r] VT to pile up

empinado, -a [ẽpi'nadu, a] ADJ (direito) upright; (cavalo) rearing; (colina) steep

empinar [ẽpi'na^r] VT to raise, uplift; (ressaltar) to thrust out; (papagaio) to fly; (copo) to empty

empipocar [ẽpipo'ka^r] VI to come out in spots

empírico, -a [ẽ'piriku, a] ADJ empirical

empistolado, -a [ẽpiʃto'ladu, a] ADJ wellconnected

emplacar [ẽpla'ka^r] VT (col: anos, sucessos) to notch up; (carro) to put number (Brit) ou license (US) plates on; ~ **o ano 2000** to make it to the year 2000

emplastrar [ẽplaʃ'tra^r] VT to put in plaster

emplastro [ẽ'plaʃtru] M (Med) plaster

empobrecer [ẽpobre'se^r] VT to impoverish ∎ VI to become poor; **empobrecimento** [ẽpobresi'mẽtu] M impoverishment

empoeirar [ẽpoej'ra^r] VT to cover in dust

empola [ẽ'pola] F (na pele) blister; (de água) bubble

empolado, -a [ẽpo'ladu, a] covered with blisters; (estilo) pompous, bombastic

empolgação [ẽpowga'sãw] F excitement; (entusiasmo) enthusiasm

empolgante [ẽpow'gãtʃi] ADJ exciting

empolgar [ẽpow'ga^r] VT to stimulate, fill with enthusiasm; (prender a atenção de): ~ **alguém** to keep sb riveted

emporcalhar [ẽpoxka'ʎa^r] VT to dirty; **emporcalhar-se** VR to get dirty

empório [ẽ'pɔrju] M (mercado) market; (armazém) department store

empossar [ẽpo'sa^r] VT to appoint

empreendedor, a [ẽprjẽde'do^r(a)] ADJ enterprising ∎ M/F entrepreneur

empreender [ẽprjẽ'de^r] VT to undertake; **empreendimento** [ẽprjẽdʒi'mẽtu] M undertaking

empregada [ẽpre'gada] F (BR: doméstica) maid; (PT: de restaurante) waitress; v tb **empregado**

empregado, -a [ẽpre'gadu, a] M/F employee; (em escritório) clerk ∎ M (PT: de restaurante) waiter

empregador, a [ẽprega'do^r(a)] M/F employer

empregar [ẽpre'ga^r] VT (pessoa) to employ; (coisa) to use; **empregar-se** VR to get a job

empregatício, -a [ẽprega'tʃisju, a] ADJ v **vínculo**

emprego [ẽ'pregu] M (ocupação) job; (uso) use

empreguismo [ẽpre'giʒmu] M patronage, nepotism

empreitada [ẽprej'tada] F (Com) contract job; (tarefa) enterprise, venture

empreiteira [ẽprej'tejra] F (firma) contractor

empreiteiro [ẽprej'tejru] M contractor

empresa [ẽ'preza] F undertaking; (Com) enterprise, firm; ~ **pontocom** dotcom

empresariado [ẽpreza'rjadu] M business community

empresarial [ẽpreza'rjaw] (pl -**ais**) ADJ business atr

empresário, -a [ẽpre'zarju, a] M/F businessman/woman; (de cantor, boxeador etc) manager; ~ **teatral** impresario

emprestado, -a [ẽpreʃ'tadu, a] ADJ on loan; **pedir** ~ to borrow; **tomar algo** ~ to borrow sth

emprestar [ẽpreʃ'ta^r] VT to lend; **empréstimo** [ẽ'prɛʃtʃimu] M loan

emproado, -a [ẽpro'adu, a] ADJ arrogant

empulhação [ẽpuʎa'sãw] (pl -**ões**) F (ato) trickery; (embuste) con

empulhar [ẽpu'ʎa^r] VT to trick, con

empunhar [ẽpu'ɲa^r] VT to grasp, seize

empurrão [ẽpu'xãw] (pl -**ões**) M push, shove; **aos empurrões** jostling

empurrar [ẽpu'xa^r] VT to push

empurrões [ẽpu'xõjʃ] MPL de **empurrão**

emudecer [emude'se^r] VT to silence ∎ VI to fall silent, go quiet

emular [emu'la^r] VT to emulate

NB: European Portuguese adds the following consonants to certain words: **b** (sú(b)dito, su(b)til); **c** (a(c)ção, a(c)cionista, a(c)to); **m** (inde(m)ne); **p** (ado(p)çã, ado(p)tar); for further details see p. xiii.

enaltecer[enawte'se^r] VT (fig) to elevate

enamorado, -a[enamo'radu, a] ADJ (encantado) enchanted; (apaixonado) in love

ENAP(BR) ABR F (= Escola Nacional de Administração Pública) civil service training school

encabeçar[ēkabe'sa^r] VT to head

encabulação[ēkabula'sãw] F (vergonha) embarrassment; (acanhamento) shyness

encabulado, -a[ēkabu'ladu, a] ADJ shy

encabular[ēkabu'la^r] VT to embarrass ▪ VI (fato, situação) to be embarrassing; (pessoa) to get embarrassed; **não se encabule!** don't be shy!

encaçapar[ēkasa'pa^r] VT (bola) to sink; (col: surrar) to bash

encadeamento[ēkadʒja'mētu] M (série) chain; (conexão) link

encadear[ēka'dʒja^r] VT to chain together, link together

encadernação[ēkadexna'sãw] (pl -ões) F (de livro) binding

encadernado, -a[ēkadex'nadu, a] ADJ bound; (de capa dura) hardback

encadernador, a[ēkadexna'do^r(a)] M/F bookbinder

encadernar[ēkadex'na^r] VT to bind

encafuar[ēka'fwa^r] VT to hide; **encafuar-se** VR to hide

encaixar[ēkaj'ʃa^r] VT (colocar) to fit in; (inserir) to insert ▪ VI to fit; **encaixe**[ē'kajʃi] M (ato) fitting; (ranhura) groove; (buraco) socket

encaixotar[ēkajʃo'ta^r] VT to pack into boxes

encalacrar[ēkala'kra^r] VT: ~ **alguém** to get sb into trouble; **encalacrar-se** VR to get into debt

encalço[ē'kawsu] M pursuit; **ir no ~ de** to pursue

encalhado, -a[ēka'ʎadu, a] ADJ stranded; (mercadoria) unsaleable; (col: solteiro) unmarried

encalhar[ēka'ʎa^r] VI (embarcação) to run aground; (fig: processo) to grind to a halt; (: mercadoria) to be returned, not to sell; (col: ficar solteiro) to be left on the shelf

encalorado, -a[ēkalo'radu, a] ADJ hot

encaminhar[ēkami'ɲa^r] VT (dirigir) to direct; (no bom caminho) to put on the right path; (processo) to set in motion; **encaminhar-se** VR: **encaminhar-se para/a** to set out for/to; **eu encaminhei-os para a seção devida** I referred them to the appropriate department; **~ uma petição a alguém** to refer an application to sb; **foi minha mãe quem me encaminhou para as letras** it was my mother who steered me towards literature; **as coisas se encaminham bem no momento** things are going well at the moment

encampar[ēkã'pa^r] VT (empresa) to expropriate; (opinião, medida) to adopt

encanador[ēkana'do^r] (BR) M plumber

encanamento[ēkana'mētu] (BR) M plumbing

encanar[ēka'na^r] VT to channel; (BR: col: prender) to throw in jail

encanecido, -a[ēkane'sidu, a] ADJ grey (Brit), gray (US); (cabelo) white

encantado, -a[ēkã'tadu, a] ADJ (contente) delighted; (castelo etc) enchanted; (fascinado): ~ **(por alguém/algo)** to be smitten (with sb/sth)

encantador, a[ēkãta'do^r(a)] ADJ delightful, charming ▪ M/F enchanter/enchantress

encantamento[ēkãta'mētu] M (magia) spell; (fascinação) charm

encantar[ēkã'ta^r] VT (enfeitiçar) to bewitch; (cativar) to charm; (deliciar) to delight

encanto[ē'kãtu] M (delícia) delight; (fascinação) charm

encapar[ēka'pa^r] VT (livro, sofá) to cover; (envolver) to wrap

encapelar[ēkape'la^r] VT (mar) to swell ▪ VI (mar) to turn rough

encapetado, -a[ēkape'tadu, a] ADJ (criança) mischievous

encapotar[ēkapo'ta^r] VT to wrap up; **encapotar-se** VR to wrap o.s. up

encaracolar[ēkarako'la^r] VT, VI to curl; **encaracolar-se** VR to curl up

encarangar[ēkarā'ga^r] VT to cripple ▪ VI (pessoa) to be crippled; (reumatismo) to be crippling

encarapinhado, -a[ēkarapi'ɲadu, a] ADJ (cabelo) frizzy

encarapitar[ēkarapi'ta^r] VT to perch; **encarapitar-se** VR: **encarapitar-se em algo** to climb on top of sth; (num cargo etc) to get o.s. fixed up in sth

encarar[ēka'ra^r] VT to face; (olhar) to look at; (considerar) to consider

encarcerar[ēkaxse'ra^r] VT to imprison

encardido, -a[ēkax'dʒidu, a] ADJ (roupa, casa) grimy; (pele) sallow

encardir[ēkax'dʒi^r] VT to make grimy ▪ VI to get grimy

encarecer[ēkare'se^r] VT (subir o preço) to raise the price of; (louvar) to praise; (exagerar) to exaggerate ▪ VI to go up in price, get dearer

encarecidamente[ēkaresida'mētʃi] ADV insistently

encarecimento[ēkaresi'mētu] M (preço) increase

encargo[ē'kaxgu] M (responsabilidade) responsibility; (ocupação) job, assignment; (oneroso) burden; **dar a alguém o ~ de fazer algo** to give sb the job of doing sth

encarnação[ēkaxna'sãw] (pl -ões) F incarnation

encarnado, -a[ēkax'nadu, a] ADJ red, scarlet

encarnar[ēkax'na^r] VT to embody, personify; (Teatro) to play ▪ VI to be embodied; **encarnar-se** VR to be embodied; **~ em alguém** (col) to pick on sb

encarneirado, -a[ēkaxnej'radu, a] ADJ (mar) choppy

encaroçar[ēkaro'sa^r] VI (molho) to go lumpy; (pele) to come up in bumps

encarquilhado, -a[ēkaxki'ʎadu, a] ADJ (fruta) wizened; (rosto) wrinkled

encarregado, -a[ēkaxe'gadu, a] ADJ: ~ **de** in charge of ▪ M/F person in charge ▪ M (de

operários) foreman; ~ **de negócios** chargé d'affaires
encarregar [ēkaxe'ga^r] vT: ~ **alguém de algo** to put sb in charge of sth; **encarregar-se** vR: **encarregar-se de fazer** to undertake to do
encarreirar [ēkaxej'ra^r] vT to guide; (negócios) to run; (moralmente): ~ **alguém** to put sb on the right track
encarrilhar [ēkaxi'ʎa^r] vT to put back on the rails; (fig) to put on the right track
encartar [ēkax'ta^r] vT to insert
encarte [ē'kaxtʃi] M insert
encasacar-se [ēkaza'kaxsi] vR to put on one's coat
encasquetar [ēkaʃke'ta^r] vT: ~ **uma idéia** to get an idea into one's head
encatarrado, -a [ēkata'xadu, a] ADJ congested
encenação [ēsena'sãw] (pl -ões) F (de peça) staging, putting on; (produção) production; (fingimento) play-acting; (atitude fingida) put-on, put-up job (col); **fazer** ~ (col) to put it on
encenador, a [ēsena'do^r(a)] M/F (Teatro) director
encenar [ēse'na^r] vT (Teatro: pôr em cena) to stage, put on; (: produzir) to produce; (fingir) to put on
enceradeira [ēsera'dejra] F floor-polisher
encerar [ēse'ra^r] vT to wax
encerramento [ēsexa'mētu] M (término) close, end
encerrar [ēse'xa^r] vT (confinar) to shut in, lock up; (conter) to contain; (concluir) to close
encestar [ēseʃ'ta^r] vT (Basquete) to put in the basket ■ vI to score a basket
encetar [ēse'ta^r] vT to start, begin
encharcar [ēʃax'ka^r] vT (alagar) to flood; (ensopar) to soak, drench; **encharcar-se** vR to get soaked ou drenched; ~-**se de algo** (beber muito) to drink gallons of sth
encheção [ēʃe'sãw] (col) F annoyance
enchente [ē'ʃētʃi] F flood
encher [ē'ʃe^r] vT to fill (up); (balão) to blow up; (tempo) to fill, take up ■ vI (col) to be annoying; **encher-se** vR to fill up; ~-**se (de)** (col) to get fed up (with); ~ **de** ou **com** to fill up with; ~ **o saco de alguém** (col) to bug sb, piss sb off (!); **ela enche o filho de presentes** she showers her son with presents; **enchimento** [ēʃi'mētu] M filling
enchova [ē'ʃova] F anchovy
enciclopédia [ēsiklo'pɛdʒja] F encyclopedia, encyclopaedia (Brit)
enciumar [ēsju'ma^r] vT to make jealous; **enciumar-se** vR to get jealous
enclausurar [ēklawzu'ra^r] vT to shut away; **enclausurar-se** vR to shut o.s. away
encoberto, -a [ēko'bextu, a] PP de **encobrir** ■ ADJ (escondido) concealed; (tempo) overcast
encobrir [ēko'bri^r] vT to conceal, hide
encolerizar [ēkoleri'za^r] vT to irritate, annoy; **encolerizar-se** vR to get angry

encolher [ēko'ʎe^r] vT (pernas) to draw up; (os ombros) to shrug; (roupa) to shrink ■ vI to shrink; **encolher-se** vR (de frio) to huddle; (para dar lugar) to hunch up
encomenda [ēko'mēda] F order; **feito de** ~ made to order, custom-made; **vir de** ~ (fig) to come just at the right time; **encomendar** [ēkomē'da^r] vT: **encomendarr algo a alguém** to order sth from sb
encompridar [ēkōpri'da^r] vT to lengthen
encontrão [ēkō'trãw] (pl -ões) M (esbarrão) collision, impact; (empurrão) shove; **dar um** ~ **em** to bump into; **ir aos encontrões pela multidão** to jostle one's way through the crowd
encontrar [ēkō'tra^r] vT (achar) to find; (inesperadamente) to come across, meet; (dar com) to bump into ■ vI: ~ **com** to bump into; **encontrar-se** vR (achar-se) to be; (ter encontro): **encontrar-se (com alguém)** to meet (sb)
encontro [ē'kōtru] M (de pessoas) meeting; (Mil) encounter; ~ **marcado** appointment; **ir/vir ao** ~ **de** to go/come and meet; **ir ou vir ao** ~ **de** (aspirações) to meet, fulfil (Brit), fulfill (US); **ir de** ~ **a** to go against, run contrary to; **meu carro foi de** ~ **ao muro** my car ran into the wall
encontrões [ēkō'trōjʃ] MPL de **encontrão**
encorajamento [ēkoraʒa'mētu] M encouragement
encorajar [ēkora'ʒa^r] vT to encourage
encorpado, -a [ēkox'padu, a] ADJ stout; (vinho) full-bodied; (tecido) closely-woven; (papel) thick
encorpar [ēkox'pa^r] vT (ampliar) to expand ■ vI (criança) to fill out
encosta [ē'kɔʃta] F slope
encostar [ēkoʃ'ta^r] vT (cabeça) to put down; (carro) to park; (pôr de lado) to put to one side; (pôr junto) to put side by side; (porta) to leave ajar ■ vI to pull in; **encostar-se** vR: **encostar-se em** to lean against; (deitar-se) to lie down on; ~ **em** to lean against; ~ **a mão em** (bater) to hit; **ele está sempre se encostando nos outros** he's always depending on others
encosto [ē'koʃtu] M (arrimo) support; (de cadeira) back
encouraçado, -a [ēkora'sadu, a] ADJ armoured (Brit), armored (US) ■ M (Náut) battleship
encravado, -a [ēkra'vadu, a] ADJ (unha) ingrowing
encravar [ēkra'va^r] vT: ~ **algo em algo** to stick sth into sth; (diamante num anel) to mount sth in sth
encrenca [ē'krēka] (col) F (problema) fix, jam; (briga) fight; **meter-se numa** ~ to get into trouble
encrencar [ēkrē'ka^r] (col) vT (situação) to complicate; (pessoa) to get into trouble ■ vI (complicar-se) to get complicated; (carro) to break down; **encrencarse** vR to get complicated; to get into trouble; ~ **(com alguém)** to fall out

NB: European Portuguese adds the following consonants to certain words: **b** (sú(b)dito, su(b)til); **c** (a(c)ção, a(c)cionista, a(c)to); **m** (inde(m)ne); **p** (ado(p)ção, ado(p)tar); for further details see p. xiii.

(with sb)

encrenqueiro, -a [ẽkrẽ'kejru, a] (col) M/F troublemaker ▪ ADJ troublemaking

encrespado, -a [ẽkreʃ'padu, a] ADJ (cabelo) curly; (mar) choppy; (água) rippling

encrespar [ẽkreʃ'paʳ] VT (o cabelo) to curl; **encrespar-se** VR (o cabelo) to curl; (água) to ripple; (o mar) to get choppy

encruar [ẽkru'aʳ] VI (negócio) to grind to a halt

encruzilhada [ẽkruzi'ʎada] F crossroads sg

encucação [ẽkuka'sãw] (pl -ões) F fixation

encucado, -a [ẽku'kadu, a] (col) ADJ: ~ **(com)** hung up (about)

encucar [ẽku'kaʳ] (col) VT: ~ **alguém** to give sb a hang-up ▪ VI: ~ **com** ou **em algo/alguém** to be hung up about sth/sb

encurralar [ẽkura'laʳ] VT (gado, pessoas) to herd; (cercar) to corner

encurtar [ẽkux'taʳ] VT to shorten

endêmico, -a [ẽ'demiku, a] ADJ endemic

endemoninhado, -a [ẽdemoni'ɲadu, a] ADJ (pessoa) possessed; (espíritu) demoniac; (fig: criança) naughty

endentar [ẽdẽ'taʳ] VT to engage

endereçamento [ẽderesa'mẽtu] M (tb: Comput) addressing; (endereço) address

endereçar [ẽdere'saʳ] VT (carta) to address; (encaminhar) to direct

endereço [ẽde'resu] M address; ~ **absoluto/ relativo** (Comput) absolute/relative address; ~ **eletrônico** ou **de e-email** e-mail address; ~ **de site** web address

endeusar [ẽdew'zaʳ] VT to deify; (amado) to worship

endiabrado, -a [ẽdʒja'bradu, a] ADJ devilish; (travesso) mischievous

endinheirado, -a [ẽdʒiɲej'radu, a] ADJ rich, wealthy, well-off

endireitar [ẽdʒirej'taʳ] VT (objeto) to straighten; (retificar) to put right; (fig) to straighten out; **endireitar-se** VR to straighten up

endividado, -a [ẽdʒivi'dadu, a] ADJ in debt

endividamento [ẽdʒivida'mẽtu] M debt

endividar [ẽdʒivi'daʳ] VT to put into debt; **endividar-se** VR to run into debt

endócrino, -a [ẽ'dɔkrinu, a] ADJ: **glândula endócrina** endocrine gland

endoidecer [ẽdojde'seʳ] VT to madden ▪ VI to go mad

endoscopia [ẽdoʃko'pia] F (Med) endoscopy

endossante [ẽdo'sãtʃi] M/F endorser

endossar [ẽdo'saʳ] VT to endorse

endossável [ẽdo'savew] (pl -eis) ADJ endorsable

endosso [ẽ'dosu] M endorsement

endurecer [ẽdure'seʳ] VT, VI to harden

endurecido, -a [ẽdure'sidu, a] ADJ hardened

endurecimento [ẽduresi'mẽtu] M hardening

ENE ABR (= és-nordeste) ENE

enegrecer [enegre'seʳ] VT to darken; (fig: nome) to blacken ▪ VI to darken

enema [e'nema] M enema

energético, -a [enex'ʒɛtʃiku, a] ADJ energy atr

▪ M energy source

energia [enɛx'ʒia] F (vigor) energy, drive; (Tec) power, energy; **enérgico, -a** [e'nɛxʒiku, a] ADJ energetic, vigorous; **ele é enérgico com os filhos** he is hard on his children

enervação [enexva'sãw] F annoyance, irritation

enervante [enex'vãtʃi] ADJ annoying

enervar [enex'vaʳ] VT to annoy, irritate ▪ VI to be irritating; **enervar-se** VR to get annoyed

enevoado, -a [ene'vwadu, a] ADJ misty, hazy

enfadar [ẽfa'daʳ] VT (entediar) to bore; (incomodar) to annoy; **enfadar-se** VR: **enfadar-se de** to get tired of; **~-se com** (aborrecer-se) to get fed up with

enfado [ẽ'fadu] M annoyance

enfadonho, -a [ẽfa'doɲu, a] ADJ (cansativo) tiresome; (aborrecido) boring

enfaixar [ẽfaj'ʃaʳ] VT (perna) to bandage, bind; (bebê) to wrap up

enfarte [ẽ'faxtʃi] M (Med) coronary

ênfase [ˈẽfazi] F emphasis, stress

enfastiado, -a [ẽfaʃ'tʃjadu, a] ADJ bored

enfastiar [ẽfaʃ'tʃjaʳ] VT (cansar) to weary; (aborrecer) to bore; **enfastiar-se** VR: **enfastiar-se de** ou **com** to get tired of; to get bored with

enfático, -a [ẽ'fatʃiku, a] ADJ emphatic

enfatizar [ẽfatʃi'zaʳ] VT to emphasize

enfear [ẽfe'aʳ] VT (pessoa etc) to make ugly; (deturpar) to distort ▪ VI to become ugly

enfeitar [ẽfej'taʳ] VT to decorate; **enfeitar-se** VR to dress up; **enfeite** [ẽ'fejtʃi] M decoration

enfeitiçante [ẽfejtʃi'sãtʃi] ADJ enchanting, charming

enfeitiçar [ẽfejtʃi'saʳ] VT to bewitch, cast a spell on

enfermagem [ẽfex'maʒẽ] F nursing

enfermaria [ẽfexma'ria] F ward

enfermeiro, -a [ẽfex'mejru, a] M/F nurse

enfermidade [ẽfexmi'dadʒi] F illness

enfermo, -a [ẽ'fexmu, a] ADJ ill, sick ▪ M/F sick person, patient

enferrujar [ẽfexu'ʒaʳ] VT to rust, corrode ▪ VI to go rusty

enfezado, -a [ẽfe'zadu, a] ADJ (irritadiço) irritable; (irritado) angry, mad

enfezar [ẽfe'zaʳ] VT (irritar) to make angry; **enfezar-se** VR to become angry

enfiada [ẽ'fjada] F (de pérolas) string; (fila) row

enfiar [ẽ'fjaʳ] VT (meter) to put; (agulha) to thread; (pérolas) to string together; (vestir) to slip on; **enfiar-se** VR: **enfiar-se em** to slip into

enfileirar [ẽfilej'raʳ] VT to line up

enfim [ẽ'fi] ADV finally, at last; (em suma) in short; **até que ~!** at last!

enfocar [ẽfo'kaʳ] VT (assunto) to tackle

enfoque [ẽ'fɔki] M approach

enforcamento [ẽfoxka'mẽtu] M hanging

enforcar [ẽfox'kaʳ] VT to hang; (trabalho, aulas) to skip; **enforcar-se** VR to hang o.s.; ~ **a sexta-feira** to take the Friday off

enfraquecer [ẽfrake'seʳ] VT to weaken ▪ VI to

grow weak

enfraquecimento [ẽfrakesi'mẽtu] M weakening

enfrentar [ẽfrẽ'ta^r] VT (encarar) to face; (confrontar) to confront; (problemas) to face up to

enfronhado, -a [ẽfro'ɲadu, a] ADJ: **estar bem ~ num assunto** to be well versed in a subject

enfronhar [ẽfro'ɲa^r] VI: **~ alguém em algo** to instruct sb in sth; **enfronhar-se** VR: **enfronhar-se em algo** to learn about sth, become well versed in sth

enfumaçado, -a [ẽfuma'sadu, a] ADJ full of smoke, smoky

enfumaçar [ẽfuma'sa^r] VT to fill with smoke

enfurecer [ẽfure'se^r] VT to infuriate; **enfurecer-se** VR to get furious

enfurnar [ẽfux'na^r] VT to hide away; (meter) to stow away; **enfurnar-se** VR to hide (o.s.) away

eng^a ABR (= engenheira) Eng.

eng° ABR (= engenheiro) Eng.

engaiolar [ẽgajo'la^r] (col) VT to jail

engajamento [ẽgaʒa'mẽtu] M (empenho, Pol) commitment; (de trabalhadores) hiring; (Mil) enlistment

engajar [ẽga'ʒa^r] VT (trabalhadores) to take on, hire; **engajar-se** VR to take up employment; (Mil) to enlist; **~se em algo** to get involved in sth; (Pol) to be committed to sth

engalfinhar-se [ẽgawfi'ɲaxsi] VR (atacar-se) to fight; (discutir) to argue

engambelar [ẽgãbe'la^r] VT to con, trick

enganado, -a [ẽga'nadu, a] ADJ (errado) mistaken; (traído) deceived

enganador, a [ẽgana'do^r(a)] ADJ (mentiroso) deceitful; (artificioso) fake; (conselho) misleading; (aspecto) deceptive

enganar [ẽga'na^r] VT to deceive; (desonrar) to seduce; (cônjuge) to be unfaithful to; (fome) to stave off; **enganar-se** VR (cair em erro) to be wrong, be mistaken; (iludir-se) to deceive o.s.; **as aparências enganam** appearances are deceptive

enganchar [ẽgã'ʃa^r] VT: **~ algo (em algo)** to hook sth up (to sth)

engano [ẽ'gãnu] M (error) mistake; (ilusão) deception; (logro) trick; **é ~** (Tel) I've (ou you've) got the wrong number

engarrafado, -a [ẽgaxa'fadu, a] ADJ bottled; (trânsito) blocked

engarrafamento [ẽgaxafa'mẽtu] M bottling; (de trânsito) traffic jam

engarrafar [ẽgaxa'fa^r] VT to bottle; (trânsito) to block

engasgar [ẽgaʒ'ga^r] VT to choke ■ VI to choke; (máquina) to splutter; **engasgar-se** VR to choke

engasgo [ẽ'gaʒgu] M choking

engastar [ẽgaʃ'ta^r] VT (jóias) to set, mount

engaste [ẽ'gaʃtʃi] M meeting, mounting

engatar [ẽga'ta^r] VT (vagões) to couple, hitch up;

(Auto) to put into gear

engatilhar [ẽgatʃi'Aa^r] VT (revólver) to cock; (fig: resposta etc) to prepare

engatinhar [ẽgatʃi'ɲa^r] VI to crawl; (fig) to be feeling one's way

engavetamento [ẽgaveta'mẽtu] M (de carros) pile-up

engavetar [ẽgave'ta^r] VT (fig: projeto) to shelve; **engavetar-se** VR to crash into one another; **~se em algo** to crash into (the back of) sth

engelhar [ẽʒe'Aa^r] VT, VI (pele) to wrinkle

engendrar [ẽʒẽ'dra^r] VT to dream up

engenharia [ẽʒeɲa'ria] F engineering; **engenheiro, -a** [ẽʒe'ɲejru, a] M/F engineer

engenho [ẽ'ʒeɲu] M (talento) talent; (destreza) skill; (máquina) machine; (moenda) mill; (fazenda) sugar plantation

engenhoso, -a [ẽʃe'ɲozu, ɔza] ADJ clever, ingenious

engessar [ẽʒe'sa^r] VT (perna) to put in plaster; (parede) to plaster

englobar [ẽglo'ba^r] VT to include

engodar [ẽgo'da^r] VT to lure, entice

engodo [ẽ'godu] M (para peixe) bait; (para pessoas) lure, enticement

engolir [ẽgo'li^r] VT to swallow; **até hoje não engoli o que ele me fez** I still haven't forgiven him for what he did to me

engomar [ẽgo'ma^r] VT to starch; (passar) to iron

engonço [ẽ'gõsu] M hinge

engordar [ẽgox'da^r] VT to fatten ■ VI to put on weight; **o açúcar engorda** sugar is fattening

engordurado, -a [ẽgoxdu'radu, a] ADJ (comida) fatty; (mãos) greasy

engordurar [ẽgoxdu'ra^r] VT to cover with grease

engraçado, -a [ẽgra'sadu, a] ADJ funny, amusing

engraçar-se [ẽgra'saxsi] (col) VR: **~ com alguém** to take advantage of sb

engradado [ẽgra'dadu] M crate

engrandecer [ẽgrãde'se^r] VT to elevate ■ VI to grow; **engrandecer-se** VR to become great

engravatar-se [ẽgrava'taxsi] VR to put on a tie; (vestir-se bem) to dress smartly

engravidar [ẽgravi'da^r] VT: **~ alguém** to get sb pregnant; (Med) to impregnate sb ■ VI to get pregnant

engraxador [ẽgraʃa'do^r] (PT) M shoe shiner

engraxar [ẽgra'ʃa^r] VT to polish

engraxate [ẽgra'ʃatʃi] M shoe shiner

engrenagem [ẽgre'naʒẽ] (pl -ns) F (Auto) gear

engrenar [ẽgre'na^r] VT (Auto) to put into gear; (fig: conversa) to strike up ■ VI: **~ com alguém** to get on with sb

engrolado, -a [ẽgro'ladu, a] ADJ (voz) slurred

engrossar [ẽgro'sa^r] VT (sopa) to thicken; (aumentar) to swell; (voz) to raise ■ VI to thicken; to swell; to rise; (col: pessoa, conversa) to turn nasty

---

NB: European Portuguese adds the following consonants to certain words: **b** (sú(b)dito, su(b)til); **c** (a(c)ção, a(c)cionista, a(c)to); **m** (inde(m)ne); **p** (ado(p)çã, ado(p)tar); for further details see p. xiii.

engrupir [ēgru'piʳ] (col) VT to con, trick

enguia [ē'gia] F eel

enguiçar [ēgi'saʳ] VI (máquina) to break down ■ VT to cause to break down; **enguiço** [ē'gisu] M (empecilho) snag; (desarranjo) breakdown

engulho [ē'guʎu] M nausea

enigma [e'nigima] M enigma; (mistério) mystery

enigmático, -a [enigi'matʃiku, a] ADJ enigmatic

enjaular [ēʒaw'laʳ] VT (fera) to cage, cage up; (prender: pessoa) to imprison

enjeitado, -a [ēʒej'tadu, a] M/F foundling, waif

enjeitar [ēʒej'taʳ] VT (rejeitar) to reject; (abandonar) to abandon; (condenar) to condemn

enjoado, -a [ē'ʒwadu, a] ADJ sick; (enfastiado) bored; (enfadonho) boring; (mal-humorado) in a bad mood

enjoar [ē'ʒwaʳ] VT to make sick; (enfastiar) to bore ■ VI (pessoa) to be sick; (remédio, comida) to cause nausea; **enjoar-se** VR: **enjoarse de** to get sick of; **eu enjôo com o cheiro de fritura** the smell of frying makes me sick; **eu enjoei de ir ao cinema** I'm sick of going to the cinema

enjoativo, -a [ēʒwa'tʃivu, a] ADJ (comida) revolting; (tedioso) boring

enjôo [ē'ʒou] M sickness; (em carro) travel sickness; (em navio) seasickness; (aborrecimento) boredom; **que ~!** what a bore!

enlaçar [ēla'saʳ] VT (atar) to tie, bind; (abraçar) to hug; (unir) to link, join; (bois) to hitch; (cingir) to wind around; **enlaçar-se** VR to be linked

enlace [ē'lasi] M link, connection; (casamento) marriage, union

enlamear [ēla'mjaʳ] VT to cover in mud; (reputação) to besmirch

enlatado, -a [ēla'tadu, a] ADJ tinned (Brit), canned ■ M (pej: filme) foreign import; **enlatados** MPL (comida) tinned (Brit) ou canned foods

enlatar [ēla'taʳ] VT (comida) to can

enlevar [ēle'vaʳ] VT (extasiar) to enrapture; (absorver) to absorb

enlevo [ē'levu] M (êxtase) rapture; (deleite) delight

enlouquecer [ēloke'seʳ] VT to drive mad ■ VI to go mad

enluarado, -a [ēlua'rado, a] ADJ moonlit

enlutado, -a [ēlu'tadu, a] ADJ in mourning

enlutar-se [ēlu'taxsi] VR to go into mourning

enobrecer [enobre'seʳ] VT to ennoble ■ VI to be ennobling

enojar [eno'jaʳ] VT to disgust, sicken

enorme [e'nɔxmi] ADJ enormous, huge; **enormidade** [enoxmi'dadʒi] F enormity; **uma enormidade (de)** (col) a hell of a lot (of)

enovelar [enove'laʳ] VT to wind into a ball; (enrolar) to roll up

enquadrar [ēkwa'draʳ] VT to fit; (gravura) to frame ■ VI: **~ com** (condizer) to fit ou tie in with

enquanto [ē'kwātu] CONJ while; (considerado como) as; **~ isso** meanwhile; **por ~** for the time being; **~ ele não vem** until he comes; **~ que** whereas

enquête [ā'kɛtʒi] F survey

enrabichar-se [ēxabi'ʃaxsi] VR: **~ por alguém** to fall for sb

enraivecer [ēxajve'seʳ] VT to enrage

enraizar [ēxaj'zaʳ] VI to take root; **enraizar-se** VR (pessoa) to settle down

enrascada [ēxaʃ'kada] F tight spot, predicament; **meter-se numa ~** to get into a spot of bother

enrascar [ēxaʃ'kaʳ] VT to embroil; **enrascar-se** VR to get embroiled

enredar [ēxe'daʳ] VT (emaranhar) to entangle; (complicar) to complicate; **enredar-se** VR to get entangled

enredo [ē'xedu] M (de uma obra) plot; (intriga) intrigue; **ele faz tanto ~** (fig) he makes such a fuss

enregelado, -a [ēxeʒe'ladu, a] ADJ (pessoa, mão) frozen; (muito frio) freezing

enrijecer [ēxiʒe'seʳ] VT to stiffen; **enrijecer-se** VR to stiffen; (fortalecer) to get stronger

enriquecer [ēxike'seʳ] VT to make rich; (fig) to enrich ■ VI to get rich; **enriquecer-se** VR to get rich

enriquecimento [ēxikesi'mētu] M enrichment

enrolado, -a [ēxo'ladu, a] (col) ADJ complicated

enrolar [ēxo'laʳ] VT to roll up; (agasalhar) to wrap up; (col: enganar) to con ■ VI (col) to waffle; **enrolar-se** VR to roll up; to wrap up; (col: confundir-se) to get mixed ou muddled up

enroscar [ēxoʃ'kaʳ] VT (torcer) to twist, wind (round); **enroscar-se** VR to coil up

enrouquecer [ēxoke'seʳ] VT to make hoarse ■ VI to go hoarse

enrubescer [ēxube'seʳ] VT to redden, colour (Brit), color (US) ■ VI (por vergonha) to blush, go red

enrugar [ēxu'gaʳ] VT (pele) to wrinkle; (testa) to furrow; (tecido) to crease ■ VI (pele, mãos) to go wrinkly; (pessoa) to get wrinkles

enrustido, -a [ēxuʃ'tʃido, a] (col) ADJ withdrawn

ensaboar [ēsa'bwaʳ] VT to wash with soap; **ensaboar-se** VR to soap o.s.

ensaiar [ēsa'jaʳ] VT (provar) to test, try out; (treinar) to practise (Brit), practice (US); (Teatro) to rehearse

ensaio [ē'saju] M (prova) test; (tentativa) attempt; (treino) practice; (Teatro) rehearsal; (literário) essay

ensaísta [ēsaj'iʃta] M/F essayist

ensangüentado, -a [ēsāgwē'tadu, a] ADJ bloody

ensangüentar [ēsāgwē'taʳ] VT to stain with blood

enseada [ē'sjada] F inlet, cove; (baía) bay

ensebado, -a [ēse'badu, a] ADJ greasy; (sujo) soiled

ensejar [ēse'ʒaʳ] VT: **~ algo (a alguém)** to provide (sb with) an opportunity for sth

ensejo [ē'seʒu] M chance, opportunity

ensimesmado, -a [ēsimeʒ'madu, a] ADJ lost in

thought

ensimesmar-se [ēsimeʒ'maxsi] VR to be lost in thought; **~ em** to be lost in

ensinamento [ēsina'mētu] M teaching; (*exemplo*) lesson

ensinar [ēsi'na^r] VT, VI to teach; **~ alguém a patinar** to teach sb to skate; **~ algo a alguém** to teach sb sth; **~ o caminho a alguém** to show sb the way; **você quer ~ o padre a rezar missa?** are you trying to teach your grandmother to suck eggs?

ensino [ē'sinu] M teaching, tuition; (*educação*) education

ensolarado, -a [ēsola'radu, a] ADJ sunny

ensombrecido, -a [ēsōbre'sidu, a] ADJ darkened

ensopado, -a [ēso'padu, a] ADJ soaked ■ M stew

ensopar [ēso'pa^r] VT to soak, drench

ensurdecedor, a [ēsuxdese'do^r(a)] ADJ deafening

ensurdecer [ēsuxde'se^r] VT to deafen ■ VI to go deaf

entabular [ētabu'la^r] VT (*negociação*) to start, open; (*empreender*) to undertake; (*assunto*) to broach; (*conversa*) to strike up

entalado, -a [ēta'ladu, a] ADJ (*apertado*) wedged, jammed; (*enrascado*) embroiled, involved; (*engasgado*) choking

entalar [ēta'la^r] VT (*encravar*) to wedge, jam; (*fig*) to put in a fix; (*encher*): **ela me entalou de comida** she stuffed me full of food

entalhador, a [ētaʎa'do^r(a)] M/F woodcarver

entalhar [ēta'ʎa^r] VT to carve; **entalhe** [ē'taʎi] M groove, notch

entalho [ē'taʎu] M woodcarving

entanto [ē'tãtu]: **no ~** ADV yet, however

então [ē'tãw] ADV then; **até ~** up to that time; **desde ~** ever since; **e ~?** well then?; **para ~** so that; **pois ~** in that case; **~, você vai ou não?** so, are you going or not?

entardecer [ētaxde'se^r] VI to get late ■ M sunset

ente ['ētʃi] M being

enteado, -a [ē'tʃjadu, a] M/F stepson/ stepdaughter

entediante [ēte'dʒjātʃi] ADJ boring, tedious

entediar [ēte'dʒja^r] VT to bore; **entediar-se** VR to get bored

entendedor, a [ētēde'do^r(a)] ADJ knowledgeable ■ M: **a bom ~ meia palavra basta** a word to the wise is enough

entender [ētē'de^r] VT (*compreender*) to understand; (*pensar*) to think; (*ouvir*) to hear; **entender-se** VR (*compreender-se*) to understand one another; **dar a ~** to imply; **no meu ~** in my opinion; **~ de música** to know about music; **~ de fazer** to decide to do; **~-se por** to be meant by; **~-se com alguém** to get along with sb;

(*dialogar*) to sort things out with sb

entendido, -a [ētē'dʒidu, a] ADJ (*col*) gay; (*conhecedor*): **~ em** good at ■ M expert; (*col*) homosexual, gay; **bem ~** that is

entendimento [ētēdʒi'mētu] M (*compreensão*) understanding; (*opinião*) opinion; (*combinação*) agreement

enternecedor, a [ētexnese'do^r(a)] ADJ touching

enternecer [ētexne'se^r] VT to move, touch; **enternecer-se** VR to be moved

enterrar [ēte'xa^r] VT to bury; (*faca*) to plunge; (*lever à ruina*) to ruin; (*assunto*) to close; **~ o chapéu na cabeça** to put one's hat on

enterro [ē'texu] M burial; (*funeral*) funeral

entidade [ētʃi'dadʒi] F (*ser*) being; (*corporação*) body; (*coisa que existe*) entity

entoação [ētoa'sãw] F singing

entoar [ē'twa^r] VT (*cantar*) to chant

entonação [ētona'sãw] (*pl* **-ões**) F intonation

entontecer [ētōtʃe'se^r] VT to make dizzy; (*enlouquecer*) to drive mad ■ VI to become ou get dizzy; to go mad; **o vinho entontece** wine makes you dizzy

entornar [ētox'na^r] VT to spill; (*fig: copo*) to drink ■ VI to drink a lot

entorpecente [ētoxpe'sētʃi] M narcotic

entorpecer [ētoxpe'se^r] VT (*paralisar*) to numb, stupefy; (*retardar*) to slow down

entorpecimento [ētoxpesi'mētu] M numbness; (*torpor*) lethargy

entorse [ē'tɔxsi] F sprain

entortar [ētox'ta^r] VT (*curvar*) to bend; (*empenar*) to warp; **~ os olhos** to squint

entourage [ātu'raʒi] M entourage

entrada [ē'trada] F (*ato*) entry; (*lugar*) entrance; (*Tec*) inlet; (*de casa*) doorway; (*começo*) beginning; (*bilhete*) ticket; (*Culin*) starter, entrée; (*Comput*) input; (*pagamento inicial*) down payment; (*corredor de casa*) hall; (*no cabelo*) receding hairline; **~ gratuita** admission free; **"~ proibida"** "no entry", "no admittance"; **meia ~** half-price ticket; **dar ~ a** (*requerimento*) to submit; (*processo*) to institute; **dar uma ~** to go in; **~ de serviço** service entrance

entrado, -a [ē'tradu, a] ADJ: **~ em anos** (PT) elderly

entra-e-sai ['ētrai'saj] M comings and goings *pl*

entranhado, -a [ētra'ɲadu, a] ADJ deep-rooted

entranhar-se [ētra'ɲaxsi] VT to penetrate

entranhas [ē'traɲaʃ] FPL bowels, entrails; (*sentimentos*) feelings; (*centro*) heart *sg*

entrar [ē'tra^r] VI to go (ou come) in, enter; (*conseguir entrar*) to get in; **deixar ~** to let in; **~ com** (*Comput: dados etc*) to enter; **eu entrei com £10** I contributed £10; **~ de férias/licença** to start one's holiday (Brit) ou vacation (US) / leave; **~ em** (*casa etc*) to go (ou come) into, enter; (*assunto*) to get onto; (*comida, bebida*) to start in on; (*universidade*) to enter; **~ em detalhes** to go

---

NB: *European Portuguese adds the following consonants to certain words:* **b** (sú(b)dito, su(b)til); **c** (a(c)ção, a(c)cionista, a(c)to); **m** (inde(m)ne); **p** (ado(p)çã, ado(p)tar); *for further details see p. xiii.*

into details; ~ **em vigor** to come into force;
ele entra às 9 no trabalho he starts work at
9.00; **o que entra nesta receita?** what goes
into this recipe?; ~ **para um clube** to join a
club; **quando a primavera entra** when spring
comes; ~ **bem** (col) to get into trouble

entravar [ētra'va^r] VT to obstruct, impede

entrave [ē'travi] M (fig) impediment

entre ['ētri] PREP (dois) between; (mais de dois)
among(st); ~ **si** amongst themselves

entreaberto, -a [ētrja'bɛxtu, a] PP de **entreabrir**
■ ADJ half-open; (porta) ajar

entreabrir [ētrja'bri^r] VT to half open;
entreabrir-se VR (flores) to open up

entrechocar-se [ētriʃo'kaxsi] VR to collide,
crash; (fig) to clash

entrecortado, -a [ētrikox'tadu, a] ADJ
intermittent; **região entrecortada de
estradas** region intersected by roads

entrecosto [ētri'koʃtu] M (Culin) entrecôte

entrega [ē'trega] F (de mercadorias) delivery; (a
alguém) handing over; (rendição) surrender;
caminhão/serviço de ~ delivery van/service;
pronta ~ speedy delivery; ~ **rápida** special
delivery; ~ **a domicílio** home delivery

entregar [ētre'ga^r] VT (dar) to hand over;
(mercadorias) to deliver; (denunciar) to hand over;
(confiar) to entrust; (devolver) to return; **entregar-
se** VR (render-se) to give o.s. up; (dedicar-se) to
devote o.s.; ~ **os pontos** to give up, throw in
the towel; ~-**se à dor/bebida** to be overcome by
grief/take to drink; ~-**se a um homem** to sleep
with a man

entregue [ē'tregi] PP de **entregar**

entrelaçar [ētrila'sa^r] VT to entwine

entrelinha [ētre'liɲa] F line spacing; **ler nas ~s**
to read between the lines

entremear [ētri'mja^r] VT to intermingle

entremostrar [ētrimoʃ'tra^r] VT to give a
glimpse of

entreolhar-se [ētrio'ʎaxsi] VR to exchange
glances

entrepernas [ētri'pɛxnaʃ] ADV between one's
legs

entrepor [ētripo^r] (irreg) VT to insert; **entrepor-
se** VR: **entrepor-se entre** to come between

entressafra [ētri'safra] F time between
harvests; (fig): **as ~s de algo** the periods
without sth

entretanto [ētri'tātu] CONJ however

entretela [ētri'tɛla] F (Costura) interlining,
buckram

entretenimento [ētriteni'mētu] M
entertainment; (distração) pastime

entreter [ētri'te^r] (irreg) VT (divertir) to entertain,
amuse; (ocupar) to occupy; (manter) to keep
up; (esperanças) to cherish; **entreter-se** VR to
amuse o.s.; to occupy o.s.

entrevar [ētre'va^r] VT to paralyse, cripple

entrever [ētri've^r] (irreg) VT to glimpse, catch a
glimpse of

entrevista [ētre'viʃta] F interview; ~ **coletiva** (à

imprensa) press conference

entrevistador, a [ētreviʃta'do^r(a)] M/F
interviewer

entrevistar [ētreviʃ'ta^r] VT to interview;
entrevistar-se VR to have an interview

entrevisto, -a [ētre'viʃtu, a] PP de **entrever**

entristecedor, a [ētriʃtese'do^r(a)] ADJ
saddening, sad

entristecer [ētriʃte'se^r] VT to sadden, grieve
■ VI to feel sad; **entristecer-se** VR to feel sad

entroncamento [ētrōka'mētu] M junction

entrosado, -a [ētro'zadu, a] ADJ (fig) integrated

entrosamento [ētroza'mētu] M (fig)
integration

entrosar [ētro'za^r] VT (rodas) to mesh; (peças) to
fit; (fig) to integrate ■ VI to mesh; to fit; ~ **com**
(fig) to fit in with; ~ **em** (adaptar-se) to settle into

entrudo [ē'trudu] (PT) M carnival; (Rel)
Shrovetide

entulhar [ētu'ʎa^r] VT to cram full; (suj: multidão)
to pack

entulho [ē'tuʎu] M rubble, debris sg

entupido, -a [ētu'pidu, a] ADJ blocked; **estar ~**
(col: congestionado) to have a blocked-up nose; (de
comida) to be fit to burst, be full up

entupimento [ētupi'mētu] M blockage

entupir [ētu'pi^r] VT to block, clog; **entupir-se**
VR to become blocked; (de comida) to stuff o.s.

entupitivo, -a [ētupi'tʃivu, a] ADJ filling

enturmar-se [ētux'maxsi] VR: ~ (**com**) to make
friends (with)

entusiasmar [ētuzjaʒ'ma^r] VT to fill with
enthusiasm; (animar) to excite; **entusiasmar-
se** VR to get excited

entusiasmo [ētu'zjaʒmu] M enthusiasm;
(júbilo) excitement

entusiasta [ētu'zjaʃta] ADJ enthusiastic ■ M/F
enthusiast

entusiástico, -a [ētu'zjaʃtʃiku, a] ADJ
enthusiastic

enumeração [enumera'sāw] (pl -ões) F
enumeration; (numeração) numbering

enumerar [enume'ra^r] VT to enumerate; (com
números) to number

enunciar [enū'sja^r] VT to express, state

envaidecer [ēvajde'se^r] VT to make conceited;
envaidecer-se VR to become conceited

envelhecer [ēveʎe'se^r] VT to age ■ VI to grow
old, age

envelhecimento [ēveʎesi'mētu] M aging

envelope [ēve'lɔpi] M envelope

envenenado, -a [ēvene'nadu, a] ADJ poisoned;
(col: festa, roupa) wild, great; (: carro) souped-up

envenenamento [ēvenena'mētu] M poisoning;
~ **do sangue** blood poisoning

envenenar [ēvene'na^r] VT to poison; (fig) to
corrupt; (: declaração, palavras) to distort, twist;
(tornar amargo) to sour; (col: carro) to soup up ■ VI
to be poisonous; **envenenar-se** VR to poison
o.s.

enverdecer [ēvexde'se^r] VT to turn green

enveredar [ēvere'da^r] VI: ~ **por um caminho** to follow a road; **~ para** to head for

envergadura [ẽvexga'dura] F (*asas, velas*) spread; (*de avião*) wingspan; (*fig*) scope; **de grande ~** large-scale

envergar [ẽvex'ga^r] VT (*arquear*) to bend; (*vestir*) to wear

envergonhado, -a [ẽvexgo'ɲadu, a] ADJ ashamed; (*tímido*) shy

envergonhar [ẽvexgo'ɲa^r] VT to shame; (*degradar*) to disgrace; **envergonhar-se** VR to be ashamed

envernizar [ẽvexni'za^r] VT to varnish

enviado, -a [ẽ'vjadu, a] M/F envoy, messenger

enviar [ẽ'vja^r] VT to send

envidar [ẽvi'da^r] VT: **~ esforços (para fazer algo)** to endeavour (*Brit*) *ou* endeavor (*US*) (to do sth)

envidraçado, -a [ẽvidra'sadu, a] ADJ: **varanda envidraçada** conservatory

envidraçar [ẽvidra'sa^r] VT to glaze

enviesado, -a [ẽvje'zadu, a] ADJ slanting

envilecer [ẽvile'se^r] VT to debase, degrade

envio [ẽ'viu] M sending; (*expedição*) dispatch; (*remessa*) remittance; (*de mercadorias*) consignment

enviuvar [ẽvju'va^r] VI to be widowed

envolto, -a [ẽ'vowtu, a] PP *de* **envolver**

envoltório [ẽvow'tɔrju] M cover

envolvente [ẽvow'vẽtʃi] ADJ compelling

envolver [ẽvow've^r] VT (*embrulhar*) to wrap (up); (*cobrir*) to cover; (*comprometer, acarretar*) to involve; (*nos braços*) to embrace; **envolver-se** VR (*intrometer-se*) to become involved; (*cobrir-se*) to wrap o.s. up; **envolvimento** [ẽvowvi'mẽtu] M involvement

enxada [ẽ'ʃada] F hoe

enxadrista [ẽʃa'driʃta] M/F chess player

enxaguada [ẽʃa'gwada] F rinse

enxaguar [ẽʃa'gwa^r] VT to rinse

enxame [ẽ'ʃami] M swarm

enxaqueca [ẽʃa'keka] F migraine

enxergão [ẽʃex'gãw] (*pl* -ões) M (straw) mattress

enxergar [ẽʃex'ga^r] VT (*avistar*) to catch sight of; (*divisar*) to make out; (*notar*) to observe, see; **enxergar-se** VR: **ele não se enxerga** he doesn't know his place

enxergões [ẽʃex'gõjʃ] MPL *de* **enxergão**

enxerido, -a [ẽʃe'ridu, a] ADJ nosy, interfering

enxertar [ẽʃex'ta^r] VT to graft; (*fig*) to incorporate

enxerto [ẽ'ʃextu] M graft

enxó [ẽ'ʃɔ] M adze

enxofre [ẽ'ʃofri] M sulphur (*Brit*), sulfur (*US*)

enxota-moscas [ẽ'ʃota-] (PT) M fly swatter

enxotar [ẽʃo'ta^r] VT (*expulsar*) to drive out

enxoval [ẽʃo'vaw] (*pl* -ais) M (*de noiva*) trousseau; (*de recém-nascido*) layette

enxovalhar [ẽʃova'ʎa^r] VT (*sujar*) to soil;

(*amarrotar*) to crumple; (*reputação*) to blacken; (*insultar*) to insult; **enxovalhar-se** VR to disgrace o.s.

enxugador [ẽʃuga'do^r] M clothes drier

enxugar [ẽʃu'ga^r] VT to dry; (*fig: texto*) to tidy up; **~ as lágrimas** to dry one's eyes

enxurrada [ẽʃu'xada] F (*de água*) torrent; (*fig*) spate

enxuto, -a [ẽ'ʃutu, a] ADJ dry; (*corpo*) shapely; (*bonito*) good-looking

enzima [ẽ'zima] F enzyme

epicentro [epi'sẽtru] M epicentre (*Brit*), epicenter (*US*)

épico, -a ['ɛpiku, a] ADJ epic ▪ M epic poet

epidemia [epide'mia] F epidemic

epidêmico, -a [epi'demiku, a] ADJ epidemic

Epifania [epifa'nia] F Epiphany

epilepsia [epile'psia] F epilepsy

epiléptico, -a [epi'lɛptʃiku, a] ADJ, M/F epileptic

epílogo [e'pilogu] M epilogue

episcopado [epiʃko'padu] M bishopric

episódio [epi'zɔdʒu] M episode

epístola [e'piʃtola] F epistle; (*carta*) letter

epitáfio [epi'tafju] M epitaph

epítome [e'pitomi] M summary; (*fig*) epitome

época ['ɛpoka] F time, period; (*da história*) age, epoch; **~ da colheita** harvest time; **naquela ~** at that time; **fazer ~** to be epoch-making; **fazer segunda ~** to resit one's exams

epopéia [epo'pɛja] F epic

equação [ekwa'sãw] (*pl* -ões) F equation

equacionar [ekwasjo'na^r] VT to set out

equações [ekwa'sõjʃ] FPL *de* **equação**

Equador [ekwa'do^r] M: **o ~** Ecuador

equador [ekwa'do^r] M equator

equânime [e'kwanimi] ADJ fair; (*caráter*) unbiassed, neutral

equatorial [ekwato'rjaw] (*pl* -ais) ADJ equatorial

equatoriano, -a [ekwato'rjanu, a] ADJ, M/F Ecuadorian

eqüestre [e'kwɛstri] ADJ equestrian

eqüidade [ekwi'dadʒi] F equity

eqüidistante [ekwidʒiʃ'tãtʃi] ADJ equidistant

eqüilátero, -a [ekwi'lateru, a] ADJ equilateral

equilibrado, -a [ekili'bradu, a] ADJ balanced; (*pessoa*) level-headed

equilibrar [ekili'bra^r] VT to balance; **equilibrar-se** VR to balance; **equilíbrio** [eki'librju] M balance; **perder o equilíbrio** to lose one's balance

eqüino, -a [e'kwinu, a] ADJ equine

equipa [e'kipa] (PT) F team

equipamento [ekipa'mẽtu] M equipment, kit

equipar [eki'pa^r] VT (*navio*) to fit out; (*prover*) to equip

equiparação [ekipara'sãw] (*pl* -ões) F comparison

equiparar [ekipa'ra^r] VT (*comparar*) to equate; **equiparar-se** VR: **equiparar-se a** to equal

---

NB: *European Portuguese adds the following consonants to certain words:* **b** (sú(b)dito, su(b)til); **c** (a(c)ção, a(c)cionista, a(c)to); **m** (inde(m)ne); **p** (ado(p)çã, ado(p)tar); *for further details see p. xiii.*

equiparável [ekipa'ravew] (*pl* -**eis**) ADJ comparable, equitable

equipe [e'kipi] (BR) F team

equitação [ekita'sãw] F (*ato*) riding; (*arte*) horsemanship

eqüitativo, -a [ekwita'tʃivu, a] ADJ fair, equitable

equivalência [ekiva'lẽsja] F equivalence

equivalente [ekiva'lẽtʃi] ADJ, M equivalent

equivaler [ekiva'le^r] VI: ~ **a** to be the same as, equal

equivocado, -a [ekivo'kadu, a] ADJ mistaken, wrong

equivocar-se [ekivo'kaxsi] VR to make a mistake, be wrong

equívoco, -a [e'kivoku, a] ADJ ambiguous ■ M (*engano*) mistake

ER ABR (= *espera resposta*) RSVP

era ['ɛra] F era, age

era *etc* VB *V* **ser**

erário [e'rarju] M exchequer

ereção [ere'sãw] (PT -**cç**-, *pl* -**ões**) (*tb: Fisiol*) erection

erecto, -a [e'rɛktu, a] (PT) ADJ = **ereto**

eremita [ere'mita] M/F hermit

eremitério [eremi'tɛrju] M hermitage

ereto, -a [e'rɛtu, a] ADJ upright, erect

erguer [ex'ge^r] VT (*levantar*) to raise, lift; (*edificar*) to build, erect; **erguer-se** VR to rise; (*pessoa*) to stand up

eriçado, -a [eri'sadu, a] ADJ bristling; (*cabelos*) (standing) on end

eriçar [eri'sa^r] VT: ~ **o cabelo de alguém** to make sb's hair stand on end; **eriçar-se** VR to bristle; (*cabelos*) to stand on end

erigir [eri'ʒi^r] VT to erect

ermo, -a ['ɛxmu, a] ADJ (*solitário*) lonely; (*desabitado*) uninhabited ■ M wilderness

erógeno, -a [e'rɔʒenu, a] ADJ erogenous

erosão [ero'zãw] F erosion

erótico, -a [e'rɔtʃiku, a] ADJ erotic

erotismo [ero'tʃiʒmu] M eroticism

erradicar [exadʒi'ka^r] VT to eradicate

errado, -a [e'xadu, a] ADJ wrong; **dar** ~ to go wrong

errante [e'xãtʃi] ADJ wandering

errar [e'xa^r] VT (*o alvo*) to miss; (*a conta*) to get wrong ■ VI (*vaguear*) to wander, roam; (*enganar-se*) to be wrong, make a mistake; ~ **o caminho** to lose one's way

errata [e'xata] F errata

erro ['exu] M mistake; **salvo** ~ unless I am mistaken; ~ **de imprensa** misprint; ~ **de programa** (*Comput*) bug; ~ **de pronúncia** mispronunciation

errôneo, -a [e'xonju, a] ADJ wrong, mistaken; (*falso*) false, untrue

erudição [erudʒi'sãw] F erudition, learning

erudito, -a [eru'dʒitu, a] ADJ learned, scholarly ■ M scholar

erupção [erup'sãw] (*pl* -**ões**) F eruption; (*na pele*) rash; (*fig*) outbreak

erva ['ɛxva] F herb; ~ **daninha** weed; (*col: dinheiro*) dosh; (: *maconha*) dope

erva-cidreira [-si'drejra] (*pl* **ervas-cidreiras**) F lemon verbena

erva-doce (*pl* **ervas-doces**) F fennel

erva-mate (*pl* **ervas-mates**) mate

ervilha [ex'viʎa] F pea

ES (BR) ABR = **Espírito Santo**

ESAO [e'saw] (BR) ABR F (= *Escola Superior de Aperfeiçoamento de Oficiais*) officer training school

esbaforido, -a [iʒbafo'ridu, a] ADJ breathless, panting

esbaldar-se [iʒbaw'daxsi] VR to have a great time, really enjoy o.s.

esbandalhado, -a [iʒbãda'ʎadu, a] ADJ (*pessoa*) scruffy; (*casa, jardim*) untidy

esbanjador, a [iʒbãʒa'do^r(a)] ADJ extravagant, spendthrift ■ M/F spendthrift

esbanjamento [iʒbãʒa'mẽtu] M (*ato*) squandering; (*qualidade*) extravagance

esbanjar [iʒbã'ʒa^r] VT to squander, waste; **estar esbanjando saúde** to be bursting with health

esbarrão [iʒba'xãw] (*pl* -**ões**) M collision

esbarrar [iʒba'xa^r] VI: ~ **em** to bump into; (*obstáculo, problema*) to come up against

esbarrões [iʒba'xõjʃ] MPL *de* **esbarrão**

esbeltez [iʒbew'teʒ] F slenderness

esbelto, -a [iʒ'bɛwtu, a] ADJ slim, slender

esboçar [iʒbo'sa^r] VT to sketch; (*delinear*) to outline; (*plano*) to draw up; ~ **um sorriso** to give a little smile; **esboço** [iʒ'bosu] M sketch; (*primeira versão*) draft; (*fig: resumo*) outline

esbodegado, -a [iʒbode'gadu, a] ADJ tatty; (*cansado*) worn out

esbodegar [iʒbode'ga^r] (*col*) VT to ruin

esbofar [iʒbo'fa^r] VT to tire out; **esbofar-se** VR to be worn out

esbofetear [iʒbofe'tʃja^r] VT to slap, hit

esbórnia [iʒ'bɔxnja] F orgy

esborrachar [iʒboxa'ʃa^r] VT to squash; (*esbofetear*) to hit; **esborrachar-se** VR to go sprawling

esbranquiçado, -a [iʒbrãki'sadu, a] ADJ whitish; (*lábios*) pale

esbravejar [iʒbrave'ʒa^r] VT, VI to shout

esbregue [iʒ'brɛgi] (*col*) M (*descompostura*) telling-off, dressing-down (*Brit*); (*rolo*) punch-up, brawl

esbugalhado, -a [iʒbuga'ʎadu, a] ADJ: **olhos ~s** goggle eyes

esbugalhar-se [iʒbuga'ʎaxsi] VR to goggle, boggle

esburacado, -a [iʒbura'kadu, a] ADJ full of holes, holey; (*rua*) full of potholes

esburacar [iʒbura'ka^r] VT to make holes (*ou* a hole) in

esc (PT) ABR = **escudo**

escabeche [iʃka'bɛʃi] M (*Culin*) marinade, *sauce of spiced vinegar and onion*

escabroso, -a [iʃka'brozu, ɔza] ADJ (*difícil*) tough; (*indecoroso*) indecent

escada [iʃ'kada] F (*dentro da casa*) staircase, stairs *pl*; (*fora da casa*) steps *pl*; (*de mão*) ladder; ~

de incêndio fire escape; **~ rolante** escalator; **escadaria** [iʃkada'ria] F staircase

escafandrista [iʃkafã'driʃta] M/F deep-sea diver

escafandro [iʃka'fãdru] M diving suit

escafeder-se [iʃkafe'dexsi] (col) VI to sneak off

escala [iʃ'kala] F scale; (Náut) port of call; (parada) stop; **fazer ~ em** to call at; **sem ~** non-stop; **~ móvel** sliding scale

escalação [iʃkala'sãw] F climbing; (designação) selection

escalada [iʃka'lada] F (de guerra) escalation

escalafobético, -a [iʃkalafo'bɛtʃiku, a] (col) ADJ weird, strange

escalão [eʃka'lãw] (pl -ões) M step; (Mil) echelon; **o primeiro ~ do governo** the highest level of government

escalar [iʃka'laʳ] VT (montanha) to climb; (muro) to scale; (designar) to select

escalavrar [iʃkala'vraʳ] VT (pele) to graze; (parede) to damage

escaldado, -a [iʃkaw'dadu, a] ADJ (fig) cautious, wary

escaldar [iʃkaw'daʳ] VT to scald; (Culin) to blanch; **escaldar-se** VR to scald o.s.

escaler [iʃka'leʳ] M launch

escalfar [iʃkaw'faʳ] (PT) VT (ovos) to poach

escalões [eʃka'lõjʃ] MPL de **escalão**

escalonamento [iʃkalona'mẽtu] M (Com: de dívida) scheduling

escalonar [iʃkalo'naʳ] VT (argumentos, opiniões) to set out; (dívida) to spread, schedule

escalope [iʃka'lɔpi] M escalope (Brit), cutlet (US)

escama [iʃ'kama] F (de peixe) scale; (de pele) flake

escamar [iʃka'maʳ] VT to scale

escamotear [iʃkamo'tʃjaʳ] VT (furtar) to pilfer, pinch (Brit); (empalmar) to make disappear (by sleight of hand)

escancarado, -a [iʃkãka'radu, a] ADJ wide open

escancarar [iʃkãka'raʳ] VT to open wide

escandalizar [iʃkãdali'zaʳ] VT to shock; **escandalizar-se** VR to be shocked; (ofender-se) to be offended

escândalo [iʃ'kãdalu] M scandal; (indignação) outrage; **fazer** ou **dar um ~** to make a scene; **escandaloso, -a** [iʃkãdalozu, ɔza] ADJ shocking, scandalous

Escandinávia [iʃkãdʒi'navja] F: **a ~** Scandinavia; **escandinavo, -a** [iʃkãdʒi'navu, a] ADJ, M/F Scandinavian

escangalhar [iʃkãga'ʎaʳ] VT to break, smash (up); (a saúde) to ruin; **escangalhar-se** VR: **escangalhar-se de rir** to split one's sides laughing

escaninho [iʃka'niɲu] M (na secretária) pigeonhole

escanteio [iʃkã'teju] M (Futebol) corner

escapada [iʃka'pada] F escape; (ato leviano) escapade

escapar [iʃka'paʳ] VI: **~ a** ou **de** to escape from;

(fugir) to run away from; **escapar-se** VR to run away, flee; **deixar ~** (uma oportunidade) to miss; (palavras) to blurt out; **~ da morte/de uma incumbência** to escape death/get out of a task; **ele escapou de ser atropelado** he escaped being run over; **o vaso escapou-lhe das mãos** the vase slipped out of his hands; **nada lhe escapa** (passar desapercebido) nothing escapes him, he doesn't miss a thing; **o nome me escapa no momento** the name escapes me for the moment; **não está bom, mas escapa** it's not good, but it'll do; **~ de boa** (col) to have a close shave

escapatória [iʃkapa'tɔrja] F (saída) way out; (desculpa) excuse

escape [iʃ'kapi] M (de gás) leak; (Auto) exhaust

escapismo [iʃka'piʒmu] M escapism

escapulida [iʃkapu'lida] F escape

escapulir [iʃkapu'liʳ] VI: **~ (de)** to get away (from); (suj: coisa) to slip (from)

escarafunchar [iʃkarafũ'ʃaʳ] VT: **~ algo** (remexer em) to rummage in sth; (com as unhas) to scratch at sth; (investigar) to pore over sth

escaramuça [iʃkara'musa] F skirmish

escaravelho [iʃkara'veʎu] M beetle

escarcéu [iʃkax'sɛw] M (fig): **fazer um ~** to make a scene

escarlate [iʃkax'latʃi] ADJ scarlet

escarlatina [iʃkaxla'tʃina] F scarlet fever

escarnecer [iʃkaxne'seʳ] VT to mock, make fun of ■ VI: **~ de** to mock, make fun of

escárnio [iʃ'kaxnju] M mockery; (desprezo) derision

escarpa [iʃ'kaxpa] F steep slope

escarpado, -a [iʃkax'padu, a] ADJ steep

escarrado, -a [iʃka'xadu, a] ADJ (fig): **ela é o pai ~** she's the spitting image of her father

escarrapachar-se [iʃkaxapa'ʃaxsi] VR to sprawl

escarrar [iʃka'xaʳ] VT to spit, cough up ■ VI to spit

escarro [iʃ'kaxu] M phlegm, spit

escasseamento [iʃkasja'mẽtu] M (Com) shortage

escassear [iʃka'sjaʳ] VT to skimp on ■ VI to become scarce

escassez [iʃka'seʒ] F (falta) shortage

escasso, -a [iʃ'kasu, a] ADJ scarce

escavação [iʃkava'sãw] (pl -ões) F digging, excavation

escavadeira [iʃkava'dejra] F digger

escavar [iʃka'vaʳ] VT to excavate

esclarecedor, a [iʃklarese'doʳ(a)] ADJ explanatory; (que alarga o conhecimento) informative

esclarecer [iʃklare'seʳ] VT (situação) to explain; (mistério) to clear up, explain; **esclarecer-se** VR: **esclarecer-se (sobre algo)** to find out (about sth); **~ alguém sobre algo** to explain to sb about sth

---

NB: *European Portuguese adds the following consonants to certain words:* **b** (sú(b)dito, su(b)til); **c** (a(c)ção, a(c)cionista, a(c)to); **m** (inde(m)ne); **p** (ado(p)çã, ado(p)tar); *for further details see p. xiii.*

esclarecido, -a [iʃklareˈsidu, a] ADJ (pessoa) enlightened

esclarecimento [iʃklaresiˈmẽtu] M explanation; (informação) information

esclerosado, -a [iʃkleroˈzadu, a] (col) ADJ (pessoa) batty, nutty

esclerótica [iʃkleˈrɔtʃika] F white of the eye

escoadouro [iʃkoaˈdoru] M drain; (cano) drainpipe

escoar [iʃkoˈaʳ] VT to drain off ■ VI to drain away; **escoar-se** VR to seep out

escocês, -esa [iʃkoˈseʃ, seza] ADJ Scottish, Scots ■ M/F Scot, Scotsman/woman

Escócia [iʃˈkɔsja] F Scotland

escoicear [iʃkojˈsjaʳ] VT to kick; (fig) to ill-treat ■ VI to kick

escol [iʃˈkɔw] M best; **de ~** of excellence

escola [iʃˈkɔla] F school; **~ de línguas** language school; **~ naval** naval college; **~ primária/ secundária** primary (Brit) ou elementary (US) /secondary (Brit) ou high (US) school; **~ particular/pública** private/state (Brit) ou public (US) school; **~ superior** college; **fazer ~** to win converts; **Escola de samba** see below

● **ESCOLAS DE SAMBA**
●
● Escolas de samba are musical and recreational
● associations made up, among others, of
● samba dancers, percussionists and carnival
● dancers. Although they exist throughout
● Brazil, the most famous schools are in Rio
● de Janeiro. The schools in Rio rehearse all
● year long for the carnaval, where they appear
● for two days in the Sambódromo, the samba
● parade, and compete for the samba school
● championship. Characterised by their
● extravagance, the biggest schools have up to
● 4,000 members and are one of Brazil's major
● tourist attractions.

escolado, -a [iʃkoˈladu, a] ADJ (esperto) shrewd; (experiente) experienced

escolar [iʃkoˈlaʳ] ADJ school atr ■ M/F schoolboy/ girl; **escolares** MPL (alunos) schoolchildren

escolaridade [iʃkolariˈdadʒi] F schooling

escolarização [iʃkolarizaˈsãw] F education, schooling

escolarizar [iʃkolariˈzaʳ] VT to educate (in school)

escolha [iʃˈkoʎa] F choice

escolher [iʃkoˈʎeʳ] VT to choose, select

escolho [iʃˈkoʎu] M (recife) reef; (rocha) rock

escolta [iʃˈkɔwta] F escort; **escoltar** [iʃkowˈtaʳ] VT to escort

escombros [iʃˈkõbruʃ] MPL ruins, debris sg

esconde-esconde [iʃkõdʃiʃˈkõdʒi] M hide-and-seek

esconder [iʃkõˈdeʳ] VT to hide, conceal; **esconder-se** VR to hide; **brincar de ~** to play hide-and-seek

esconderijo [iʃkõdeˈriʒu] M hiding place; (de

bandidos) hideout

escondidas [iʃkõˈdʒidaʃ] FPL: **às ~** secretly

esconjurar [iʃkõʒuˈraʳ] VT (o Demônio) to exorcize; (afastar) to keep off; (amaldiçoar) to curse; **esconjurar-se** VR (lamentar-se) to complain

escopo [iʃˈkopu] M aim, purpose

escora [iʃˈkɔra] F prop, support; (cilada) ambush

escorar [iʃkoˈraʳ] VT to prop (up); (amparar) to support; (esperar de espreita) to lie in wait for ■ VI to lie in wait; **escorar-se** VR: **escorar-se em** (fundamentar-se) to go by; (amparar-se) to live off

escorbuto [iʃkoxˈbutu] M scurvy

escore [iʃˈkɔri] M score

escória [iʃˈkɔrja] F (de metal) dross; **a ~ da humanidade** the scum of the earth

escoriação [iʃkorjaˈsãw] (pl -ões) F abrasion, scratch

escorpiano, -a [iʃkoxˈpjanu, a] ADJ, M/F (Astrologia) Scorpio

escorpião [iʃkoxpiˈãw] (pl -ões) M scorpion; **E~** (Astrologia) Scorpio

escorraçar [iʃkoxaˈsaʳ] VT (tratar mal) to ill-treat; (expulsar) to throw out; **~ alguém de casa** ou **para fora de casa** to throw sb out of the house

escorrega [iʃkoˈxɛga] F slide; **escorregadela** [iʃkoxegaˈdɛla] F slip

escorregadio, -a [iʃkoxegaˈdʒi(s)u, a] ADJ slippery

escorregador [iʃkoxegaˈdoʳ] M slide

escorregão [iʃkoxeˈgãw] (pl -ões) M slip; (fig) slip(-up)

escorregar [iʃkoxeˈgaʳ] VI to slip; (errar) to slip up

escorregões [iʃkoxeˈgõjʃ] MPL de **escorregão**

escorrer [iʃkoˈxeʳ] VT (fazer correr) to drain (off); (verter) to pour out ■ VI (pingar) to drip; (correr em fio) to trickle

escoteiro [iʃkoˈtejru] M scout

escotilha [iʃkoˈtʃiʎa] F hatch, hatchway

escova [iʃˈkova] F brush; (penteado) blow-dry; **~ de dentes** toothbrush; **fazer ~ no cabelo** to blow-dry one's hair; (por outra pessoa) to have a blow-dry; **escovar** [iʃkoˈvaʳ] VT to brush

escovinha [iʃkoˈviɲa] F v **cabelo**; **cabelo à ~** crew cut

escrachado, -a [iʃkraˈʃadu, a] (col) ADJ (desleixado) scruffy; **estar** ou **ser ~** (ter ficha na polícia) to have a criminal record

escravatura [iʃkravaˈtura] F (tráfico) slave trade; (escravidão) slavery

escravidão [iʃkraviˈdãw] F slavery

escravização [iʃkravizaˈsãw] F enslavement

escravizar [iʃkraviˈzaʳ] VT to enslave; (cativar) to captivate

escravo, -a [iʃˈkravu, a] ADJ captive ■ M/F slave; **ele é um ~ do amigo/trabalho** he's a slave to his friend/work

escrete [iʃˈkrɛtʃi] M team

escrevente [iʃkreˈvẽtʃi] M/F clerk

escrever [iʃkreˈveʳ] VT, VI to write; **escrever-se** VR to write to each other; **~ à máquina** to type

escrevinhador, a [iʃkreviɲaˈdoʳ(a)] (col) M/F

hack (writer)

escrevinhar [iʃkrevi'ɲaʳ] vт to scribble

escrita [eʃ'krita] ғ writing; (pessoal) handwriting; **pôr a ~ em dia** to bring one's correspondence up to date

escrito, -a [eʃ'kritu, a] pp de **escrever** ■ adj written ■ m piece of writing; **~ à mão** handwritten; **dar por ~** to put in writing; **ela é o pai ~** she's the spitting image of her father

escritor, a [iʃkri'toʳ(a)] m/ғ writer; (autor) author

escritório [iʃkri'tɔrju] m office; (em casa) study

escritura [iʃkri'tura] ғ (Jur) deed; (ato na compra de imóveis) ≈ exchange of contracts; **as Sagradas E~s** the Scriptures

escrituração [iʃkritura'sãw] ғ book-keeping; (de transações, quantias) entering, recording; **~ por partidas simples/dobradas** (Com) single-entry/double-entry book-keeping

escriturar [iʃkritu'raʳ] vт (contas) to register, enter up; (documento) to draw up

escriturário, -a [iʃkritu'rarju, a] m/ғ clerk

escrivã [iʃkri'vã] ғ de **escrivão**

escrivaninha [iʃkriva'niɲa] ғ writing desk

escrivão, -vã [iʃkri'vãw, vã] (pl -ões/-s) m/ғ registrar, recorder

escroque [iʃ'krɔki] m swindler, con man

escroto, -a [iʃ'krotu, a] m scrotum ■ adj (col!: pessoa) vile, gross; (: filme etc) crappy (!), shitty (!)

escrúpulo [iʃ'krupulu] m scruple; (cuidado) care; **sem ~** unscrupulous

escrupuloso, -a [iʃkrupu'lozu, ɔza] adj scrupulous; (cuidadoso) careful

escrutinar [iʃkrutʃina'ʳ] vi to act as a scrutineer

escrutínio [iʃkru'tʃinju] m (votação) poll; (apuração de votos) counting; (exame atento) scrutiny; **~ secreto** secret ballot

escudar [iʃku'daʳ] vт to shield; **escudar-se** vr to shield o.s.; (apoiar-se): **escudar-se em algo** to rely on sth

escudeiro [iʃku'dejru] m squire

escudo [iʃ'kudu] m shield; (moeda) escudo

esculachado, -a [iʃkula'ʃadu, a] (col) adj sloppy

esculachar [iʃkula'ʃaʳ] (col) vт (bagunçar) to mess up; (espancar) to beat up; (criticar) to get at; (repreender) to tick off

esculacho [iʃku'laʃu] (col) m mess; (repreensão) telling-off

esculhambação [iʃkuʎãba'sãw] (pl -ões) (col!) ғ mess; (repreensão) telling-off, bollocking (!)

esculhambado, -a [iʃkuʎã'badu, a] (col!) adj (descuidado) shabby, slovenly; (estragado) messed up, knackered

esculhambar [iʃkuʎã'baʳ] (col!) vт to mess up, fuck up (!); **~ alguém** (criticar) to give sb stick; (descompor) to give sb a bollocking (!)

esculpir [iʃkuw'piʳ] vт to carve, sculpt; (gravar) to engrave

escultor, a [iʃkuw'toʳ(a)] m/ғ sculptor

escultura [iʃkuw'tura] ғ sculpture

escultural [iʃkuwtu'raw] (pl -ais) adj sculptural; (corpo) statuesque

escuma [iʃ'kuma] (PT) ғ foam; (em cerveja) froth

escumadeira [iʃkuma'dejra] ғ skimmer

escuna [iʃ'kuna] ғ (Náut) schooner

escuras [iʃ'kuraʃ] ғpl: **às ~** in the dark

escurecer [iʃkure'seʳ] vт to darken ■ vi to get dark; **ao ~** at dusk

escurecimento [iʃkuresi'mẽtu] m darkening

escuridão [iʃkuri'dãw] ғ (trevas) dark

escuro, -a [iʃ'kuru, a] adj (sombrio) dark; (dia) overcast; (pessoa) swarthy; (negócios) shady ■ m darkness

escusa [iʃ'kuza] ғ excuse

escusado, -a [iʃku'zadu, a] adj unnecessary; **é ~ fazer isso** there's no need to do that

escusar [iʃku'zaʳ] vт (desculpar) to excuse, forgive; (justificar) to vindicate; (dispensar) to exempt; (não precisar de) not to need; **escusar-se** vr (desculpar-se) to apologise; **~-se de fazer** to refuse to do; **escuso-me de dar maiores explicações** I need not explain further

escuta [iʃ'kuta] ғ listening; **à ~** listening out; **ficar na ~** to stand by; **~ eletrônica/telefônica** bugging/phone tapping

escutar [iʃku'taʳ] vт to listen to; (sem prestar atenção) to hear ■ vi to listen; to hear; **escuta!** listen!; **ele não escuta bem** he is hard of hearing; **o médico escutou o paciente** the doctor listened to the patient's chest

esdrúxulo, -a [iʒ'druʃulu, a] adj weird, odd

esfacelar [iʃfase'laʳ] vт (destruir) to destroy

esfaimado, -a [iʃfaj'madu, a] adj famished, ravenous

esfalfar [iʃfaw'faʳ] vт to tire out, exhaust; **esfalfar-se** vr to tire o.s. out

esfaquear [iʃfaki'aʳ] vт to stab

esfarelar [iʃfare'laʳ] vт to crumble; **esfarelar-se** vr to crumble

esfarrapado, -a [iʃfaxa'padu, a] adj ragged, in tatters

esfarrapar [iʃfaxa'paʳ] vт to tear to pieces

esfera [iʃ'fera] ғ sphere; (globo) globe; (Tip, Comput) golf ball

esférico, -a [iʃ'feriku, a] adj spherical

esferográfico, -a [iʃfero'grafiku, a] adj: **caneta esferográfica** ballpoint pen

esfiapar [iʃfja'paʳ] vт to fray; **esfiapar-se** vr to fray

esfinge [iʃ'fĩʒi] ғ sphinx

esfogueado, -a [iʃfo'gjadu, a] adj impatient

esfolar [iʃfo'laʳ] vт to skin; (arranhar) to graze; (cobrar demais a) to overcharge, fleece

esfomeado, -a [iʃfo'mjadu, a] adj famished, starving

esforçado, -a [iʃfox'sadu, a] adj committed, dedicated

esforçar-se [iʃfox'saxsi] vr: **~ para** to try hard to, strive to

---

NB: European Portuguese adds the following consonants to certain words: **b** (sú(b)dito, su(b)til); **c** (a(c)ção, a(c)cionista, a(c)to); **m** (inde(m)ne); **p** (ado(p)çã, ado(p)tar); for further details see p. xiii.

esforço [iʃ'foxsu] M effort; **fazer ~** to try hard, make an effort

esfregação [iʃfrega'sãw] F rubbing; (col) necking, petting

esfregaço [iʃfre'gasu] M smear

esfregar [iʃfre'gaʳ] VT to rub; (com água) to scrub

esfriamento [iʃfrja'mẽtu] M cooling

esfriar [iʃ'frjaʳ] VT to cool, chill ■ VI to get cold; (fig) to cool off

esfumaçar [iʃfuma'saʳ] VT to fill with smoke

esfumar [iʃfu'maʳ] VT to disperse; **esfumar-se** VR to fade away

esfuziante [iʃfu'zjãtʃi] ADJ (pessoa) bubbly; (alegria) irrepressible

ESG (BR) ABR F (= Escola Superior de Guerra) military training school

esganado, -a [iʒga'nadu, a] ADJ (sufocado) choked; (voraz) greedy; (avaro) grasping

esganar [iʒga'naʳ] VT to strangle, choke

esganiçado, -a [iʒgani'sadu, a] ADJ (voz) shrill

esgaravatar [iʒgarava'taʳ] VT (fig) to delve into

esgarçar [iʒgax'saʳ] VT, VI to tear; (com o uso) to wear into a hole

esgazeado, -a [iʒga'zjadu, a] ADJ (olhos, olhar) crazed

esgoelar [iʒgoe'laʳ] VT to yell; (estrangular) to choke; **esgoelar-se** VR to yell, scream

esgotado, -a [iʒgo'tadu, a] ADJ (exausto) exhausted; (consumido) used up; (livros) out of print; **os ingressos estão ~s** the tickets are sold out

esgotamento [iʒgota'mẽtu] M exhaustion

esgotar [iʒgo'taʳ] VT (vazar) to drain, empty; (recursos) to use up; (pessoa, assunto) to exhaust; **esgotar-se** VR (cansar-se) to become exhausted; (mercadorias, edição) to be sold out; (recursos) to run out

esgoto [iʒ'gotu] M drain; (público) sewer

esgrima [iʒ'grima] F (Esporte) fencing

esgrimir [iʒgri'miʳ] VI to fence

esgrouvinhado, -a [iʒgrovi'ɲadu, a] ADJ dishevelled

esgueirar-se [iʒgej'raxsi] VR to slip away, sneak off

esguelha [iʒ'geʎa] F slant; **olhar alguém de ~** to look at sb out of the corner of one's eye

esguichar [iʒgi'ʃaʳ] VT to squirt ■ VI to squirt out

esguicho [iʒ'giʃu] M (jacto) jet; (de mangueira etc) spout

esguio, -a [eʒ'giu, a] ADJ slender

eslavo, -a [iʃ'lavu, a] ADJ Slavic ■ M/F Slav

esmagador, a [iʒmagado'ʳ(a)] ADJ crushing; (provas) irrefutable; (maioria) overwhelming

esmagar [iʒma'gaʳ] VT to crush

esmaltado, -a [iʒmaw'tadu, a] ADJ enamelled (Brit), enameled (US)

esmalte [iʒ'mawtʃi] M enamel; (de unhas) nail polish

esmerado, -a [iʒme'radu, a] ADJ careful, neat; (bem acabado) polished

esmeralda [iʒme'rawda] F emerald

esmerar-se [iʒme'raxsi] VR: **~ em** to take great care to

esmero [iʒ'meru] M (great) care

esmigalhar [iʒmiga'ʎaʳ] VT to crumble; (despedaçar) to shatter; (esmagar) to crush; **esmigalhar-se** VR (pão etc) to crumble; (vaso) to smash, shatter

esmirrado, -a [iʒmi'xadu, a] ADJ (roupa) skimpy, tight

esmiuçar [iʒmju'saʳ] VT (pão) to crumble; (examinar) to examine in detail

esmo ['eʒmu] M: **a ~** at random; **andar a ~** to walk aimlessly; **falar a ~** to prattle

esmola [iʒ'mɔla] F alms pl; (col: surra) thrashing; **pedir ~s** to beg

esmolar [iʒmo'laʳ] VT, VI: **~ (algo a alguém)** to beg (sth from sb)

esmorecer [iʒmore'seʳ] VT to discourage ■ VI (desanimar-se) to lose heart

esmorecimento [iʒmoresi'mẽtu] M dismay, discouragement; (enfraquecimento) weakening

esmurrar [iʒmu'xaʳ] VT to punch

Esni [eʒ'ni] (BR) ABR F (= Escola Nacional de Informações) training school for intelligence services

esnobação [iʒnoba'sãw] F snobbishness

esnobar [iʒno'baʳ] VI to be snobbish ■ VT: **~ alguém** to give sb the cold shoulder

esnobe [iʒ'nɔbi] ADJ snobbish; (col) stuck-up ■ M/F snob

esnobismo [iʒno'biʒmu] M snobbery

esôfago [e'zofagu] M oesophagus (Brit), esophagus (US)

esotérico, -a [ezo'tɛriku, a] ADJ esoteric

espaçado, -a [iʃpa'sadu, a] ADJ spaced out

espaçar [iʃpa'saʳ] VT to space out; **~ visitas/saídas** etc to visit/go out etc less often

espacejamento [iʃpaseʒa'mẽtu] M (Tip) spacing; **~ proporcional** proportional spacing

espacial [iʃpa'sjaw] (pl -ais) ADJ spatial, space atr; **nave ~** spaceship

espaço [iʃ'pasu] M space; (tempo) period; **~ para 3 pessoas** room for 3 people; **a ~s** from time to time; **sujeito a ~** (em avião) stand-by; **espaçoso, -a** [iʃpa'sozu, ɔza] ADJ spacious, roomy

espada [iʃ'pada] F sword; **espadas** FPL (Cartas) spades; **estar entre a ~ e a parede** to be between the devil and the deep blue sea

espadachim [iʃpada'ʃĩ] (pl -ns) M swordsman

espadarte [iʃpa'daxtʃi] M swordfish

espádua [iʃ'padwa] F shoulder blade

espairecer [iʃpajre'seʳ] VT to amuse, entertain ■ VI to relax; **espairecer-se** VR to relax

espairecimento [iʃpajresi'mẽtu] M recreation

espaldar [iʃpaw'daʳ] M (chair) back

espalha-brasas [iʃpaʎa'-] M/F INV troublemaker

espalhafato [iʃpaʎa'fatu] M din, commotion

espalhafatoso, -a [iʃpaʎafa'tozu, ɔza] ADJ (pessoa) loud, rowdy; (roupa) loud, garish

espalhar [iʃpa'ʎaʳ] VT to scatter; (boato, medo) to spread; (luz) to shed; **espalhar-se** VR (fogo, boato) to spread; (refestelar-se) to lounge

espanador [iʃpana'doʳ] M duster

espanar [iʃpa'naʳ] VT to dust

espancamento [iʃpãka'mẽtu] M beating

espancar [iʃpã'kaʳ] VT to beat up

espandongado, -a [iʃpãdõ'gadu, a] ADJ (no vestir) scruffy; (estragado) tatty

Espanha [iʃ'paɲa] F: **a ~** Spain; **espanhol, a** [iʃpa'ɲow, ola] (pl -óis/espanhols) ADJ Spanish ▪ M/F Spaniard ▪ M (Ling) Spanish; **os espanhóis** MPL the Spanish

espantado, -a [iʃpã'tadu, a] ADJ astonished; (cor) loud, garish

espantalho [iʃpã'taʎu] M scarecrow

espantar [iʃpã'taʳ] VT (causar medo a) to frighten; (admirar) to amaze, astonish; (afugentar) to frighten away ▪ VI to be amazing; **espantar-se** VR to be amazed; (assustar-se) to be frightened

espanto [iʃ'pãtu] M (medo) fright, fear; (admiração) amazement; **espantoso, -a** [iʃpã'tozu, ɔza] ADJ amazing

esparadrapo [iʃpara'drapu] M (sticking) plaster (Brit), bandaid® (US)

espargir [iʃpax'ʒiʳ] VT (líquido) to sprinkle; (flores) to scatter; (luz) to shed

esparramar [iʃpaxa'maʳ] VT (líquido) to splash; (espalhar) to scatter

esparso, -a [iʃ'paxsu, a] ADJ scattered; (solto) loose

espartano, -a [iʃpax'tanu, a] ADJ (fig) spartan

espartilho [iʃpax'tʃiʎu] M corset

espasmo [iʃ'paʒmu] M spasm, convulsion

espasmódico, -a [iʃpaʒ'mɔdʒiku, a] ADJ spasmodic

espatifar [iʃpatʃi'faʳ] VT to smash; **espatifar-se** VR to smash; (avião) to crash

espavorir [iʃpavo'riʳ] VT to terrify

EsPCEx (BR) ABR F = **Escola Preparatória de Cadetes do Exército**

especial [iʃpe'sjaw] (pl -ais) ADJ special; **em ~** especially; **especialidade** [iʃpesjali'dadʒi] F speciality (Brit), specialty (US); (ramo de atividades) specialization; **especialista** [iʃpesja'liʃta] M/F specialist; (perito) expert

especialização [iʃpesjaliza'sãw] (pl -ões) F specialization

especializado, -a [iʃpesjali'zadu, a] ADJ specialized; (operário, mão de obra) skilled

especializar-se [iʃpesjali'zaxsi] VR: **~ (em)** to specialize (in)

especiaria [iʃpesja'ria] F spice

espécie [iʃ'pɛsi] F (Bio) species; (tipo) sort, kind; **causar ~** to be surprising; **pagar em ~** to pay in cash

especificação [iʃpesifika'sãw] (pl -ões) F specification

especificar [iʃpesifi'kaʳ] VT to specify; **específico, -a** [iʃpe'sifiku, a] ADJ specific

espécime [iʃ'pɛsimi] M specimen

espécimen [iʃ'pɛsimẽ] (pl -s) M = **espécime**

espectáculo etc [iʃpek'takulu] (PT) M = **espetáculo** etc

espectador, a [iʃpekta'doʳ(a)] M/F (testemunha) onlooker; (TV) viewer; (Esporte) spectator; (Teatro) member of the audience; **espectadores** MPL audience sg

espectro [iʃ'pɛktru] M spectre (Brit), specter (US); (Fís) spectrum; (pessoa) gaunt figure

especulação [iʃpekula'sãw] (pl -ões) F speculation

especulador, a [iʃpekula'doʳ(a)] ADJ speculating ▪ M/F (na Bolsa etc) speculator; (explorador) opportunist

especular [iʃpeku'laʳ] VI: **~ (sobre)** to speculate (on)

especulativo, -a [iʃpekula'tʃivu, a] ADJ speculative

espelhar [iʃpe'ʎaʳ] VT to mirror; **espelhar-se** VR to be mirrored; **seus olhos espelham malícia, espelha-se malícia nos seus olhos** there is malice in his eyes

espelho [iʃ'peʎu] M mirror; (fig) model; **~ retrovisor** (Auto) rear-view mirror

espelunca [iʃpe'lũka] (col) F (bar) dive; (casa) dump, hole

espera [iʃ'pɛra] F (demora) wait; (expectativa) expectation; **à ~ de** waiting for; **à minha ~** waiting for me

espera-marido (pl -s) M (Culin) sweet made with burnt sugar and eggs

esperança [iʃpe'rãsa] F (confiança) hope; (expectativa) expectation; **dar ~s a alguém** to get sb's hopes up; **que ~!** (col) no chance!

esperançar [iʃperã'saʳ] VT: **~ alguém** to give sb hope

esperançoso, -a [iʃperã'sozu, ɔza] ADJ hopeful

esperar [iʃpe'raʳ] VT (aguardar) to wait for; (desejar) to hope for; (contar com, bebê) to expect ▪ VI to wait; to hope; to expect; **espero que sim/não** I hope so/not; **fazer alguém ~** to keep sb waiting; **espera aí!** hold on!; (col: não vem) come off it!

esperável [iʃpe'ravew] (pl -eis) ADJ expected, probable

esperma [iʃ'pɛxma] F sperm

espernear [iʃpex'njaʳ] VI to kick out; (protestar) to protest

espertalhão, -lhona [iʃpexta'ʎãw, ʎɔna] (pl -ões/-s) ADJ crafty, shrewd ▪ M/F shrewd operator

esperteza [iʃpex'teza] F cleverness; (astúcia) cunning

esperto, -a [iʃ'pɛxtu, a] ADJ clever; (espertalhão) crafty; (col: bacana) great

espesso, -a [iʃ'pesu, a] ADJ thick

espessura [iʃpe'sura] F thickness

espetacular [iʃpetaku'laʳ] ADJ spectacular

espetáculo [iʃpe'takulu] M (Teatro) show; (vista)

NB: European Portuguese adds the following consonants to certain words: **b** (sú(b)dito, su(b)til); **c** (a(c)ção, a(c)cionista, a(c)to); **m** (inde(m)ne); **p** (ado(p)çã, ado(p)tar); for further details see p. xiii.

sight; (*cena ridícula*) spectacle; **dar** ~ to make a spectacle of o.s.; **ela/a casa é um** ~ (*col*) she/the house is fabulous

espetada [iʃpe'tada] F prick

espetar [iʃpe'ta^r] VT (*carne*) to put on a spit; (*cravar*) to stick; **espetar-se** VR to prick o.s.; ~ **algo em algo** to pin sth to sth

espetinho [iʃpe'tʃiɲu] M skewer

espeto [iʃ'petu] M spit; (*pau*) pointed stick; (*fig: pessoa magra*) beanpole; **ser um** ~ (*ser difícil*) to be awkward

espevitado, -a [iʃpevi'tadu, a] ADJ (*fig: vivo*) lively

espezinhar [iʃpezi'ɲa^r] VT to trample (on); (*humilhar*) to treat like dirt

espia [iʃ'pia] M/F spy

espiã [iʃ'pjã] F *de* **espião**

espiada [iʃ'pjada] F: **dar uma** ~ to have a look

espião, -piã [iʃ'pjãw, 'pjã] (*pl* -ões/-s) M/F spy

espiar [iʃ'pja^r] VT (*espionar*) to spy on; (*uma ocasião*) to watch out for; (*olhar*) to watch ■ VI to spy; (*olhar*) to peer

espicaçar [iʃpika'sa^r] VT to trouble, torment

espichar [iʃpi'ʃa^r] VT (*couro*) to stretch out; (*pescoço, pernas*) to stretch ■ VI (*col: crescer*) to shoot up; **espichar-se** VR to stretch out

espiga [iʃ'piga] F (*de milho*) ear

espigado, -a [iʃpigadu, a] ADJ (*milho*) fully-grown; (*ereto*) upright

espigueiro [iʃpi'gejru] M granary

espinafração [iʃpinafra'sãw] (*pl* -ões) (*col*) F telling-off

espinafrar [iʃpina'fra^r] (*col*) VT: ~ **alguém** (*repreender*) to give sb a telling-off; (*criticar*) to get at sb; (*ridicularizar*) to jeer at sb

espinafre [iʃpi'nafri] M spinach

espingarda [iʃpĩ'gaxda] F shotgun, rifle; ~ **de ar comprimido** air rifle

espinha [iʃ'piɲa] F (*de peixe*) bone; (*na pele*) spot, pimple; (*coluna vertebral*) spine

espinhar [iʃpi'ɲa^r] VT (*picar*) to prick; (*irritar*) to irritate, annoy

espinheiro [iʃpi'ɲejru] M bramble bush

espinhento, -a [iʃpi'ɲẽtu, a] ADJ spotty, pimply

espinho [iʃ'piɲu] M thorn; (*de animal*) spine; (*fig: dificuldade*) snag; **espinhoso, -a** [iʃpi'ɲozu, ɔza] ADJ (*planta*) prickly, thorny; (*fig: difícil*) difficult; (: *problema*) thorny

espinotear [iʃpino'tʃja^r] VI (*cavalo*) to buck; (*pessoa*) to leap about

espiões [iʃ'pjõjʃ] MPL *de* **espião**

espionagem [iʃpio'naʒẽ] F spying, espionage

espionar [iʃpjo'na^r] VT to spy on ■ VI to spy, snoop

espiral [iʃpi'raw] (*pl* -ais) ADJ, F spiral

espírita [iʃ'pirita] ADJ, M/F spiritualist

espiritismo [iʃpiri'tʃiʒmu] M spiritualism

espírito [iʃ'piritu] M spirit; (*pensamento*) mind; ~ **de porco** wet blanket; ~ **esportivo** sense of humo(u)r; ~ **forte/fraco** (*fig: pessoa*) freethinker/sheep; **E~ Santo** Holy Spirit

espiritual [iʃpiri'twaw] (*pl* -ais) ADJ spiritual

espirituoso, -a [iʃpiri'twozu, ɔza] ADJ witty

espirrar [iʃpi'xa^r] VI to sneeze; (*jorrar*) to spurt out ■ VT (*água*) to spurt; **espirro** [iʃ'pixu] M sneeze

esplanada [iʃpla'nada] F esplanade

esplêndido, -a [iʃ'plẽdʒidu, a] ADJ splendid

esplendor [iʃplẽ'do^r] M splendour (*Brit*), splendor (*US*)

espocar [iʃpo'ka^r] VI to explode

espoleta [iʃpo'leta] F (*de arma*) fuse

espoliar [iʃpo'lja^r] VT to plunder

espólio [iʃ'polju] M (*herança*) estate, property; (*roubado*) booty, spoils *pl*

esponja [iʃ'põʒa] F sponge; (*de pó de arroz*) powder puff; (*parasita*) sponger; (*col: ébrio*) boozer

esponjoso, -a [iʃpõ'ʒozu, ɔza] ADJ spongy

espontaneidade [iʃpõtanei'dadʒi] F spontaneity

espontâneo, -a [iʃpõ'tanju, a] ADJ spontaneous; (*pessoa: natural*) straightforward

espora [iʃ'pora] F spur

esporádico, -a [iʃpo'radʒiku, a] ADJ sporadic

esporão [iʃpo'rãw] (*pl* -ões) M (*de galo*) spur

esporear [iʃpo'rja^r] VT (*picar*) to spur on; (*fig*) to incite

esporões [iʃpo'rõjʃ] MPL *de* **esporão**

esporte [iʃ'pɔxtʃi] (BR) M sport; **esportista** [iʃpox'tʃiʃta] ADJ sporting ■ M/F sportsman/woman

esportiva [iʃpox'tʃiva] F sense of humour (*Brit*) *ou* humor (*US*); **perder a** ~ to lose one's sense of humo(u)r

esportivo, -a [iʃpox'tʃivu, a] ADJ sporting

esposa [iʃ'poza] F wife

esposar [iʃpo'za^r] VT to marry; (*causa*) to defend

esposo [iʃ'pozu] M husband

espoucar [iʃpo'ka^r] VT = **espocar**

espraiar [iʃpra'ja^r] VT, VI to spread; (*dilatar*) to expand; **espraiar-se** VR (*mar*) to wash across the beach; (*rio*) to spread out; (*fig: epidemia*) to spread

espreguiçadeira [iʃpregisa'dejra] F deck chair; (*com lugar para as pernas*) lounger

espreguiçar-se [iʃpregi'saxsi] VR to stretch

espreita [iʃ'prejta] F: **ficar à** ~ to keep watch

espreitar [iʃprej'ta^r] VT (*espiar*) to spy on; (*observar*) to observe, watch

espremedor [iʃpreme'do^r] M squeezer

espremer [iʃpre'me^r] VT (*fruta*) to squeeze; (*roupa molhada*) to wring out; (*pessoas*) to squash; **espremer-se** VR (*multidão*) to be squashed together; (*uma pessoa*) to squash up

espuma [iʃ'puma] F foam; (*de cerveja*) froth, head; (*de sabão*) lather; (*de ondas*) surf; **colchão de** ~ foam mattress; ~ **de borracha** foam rubber; **espumante** [iʃpu'mãtʃi] ADJ frothy, foamy; (*vinho*) sparkling

espumar [iʃpu'ma^r] VI to foam; (*fera, cachorro*) to foam at the mouth

espúrio, -a [iʃ'purju, a] ADJ spurious, bogus

esputinique [iʃputʃi'niki] M satellite, sputnik

esq. ABR (= *esquerdo*) l.; = **esquina**

esq° ABR = **esquerdo**

esquadra [iʃ'kwadra] F (*Náut*) fleet; (*PT*: *da polícia*) police station

esquadrão [iʃkwa'drãw] (*pl* -ões) M squadron

esquadrilha [iʃkwa'driʎa] F squadron

esquadrinhar [iʃkwadri'ɲaʳ] VT (*casa, área*) to search, scour; (*fatos*) to scrutinize

esquadro [iʃ'kwadru] M set square

esquadrões [iʃkwa'drõjʃ] MPL *de* **esquadrão**

esqualidez [iʃkwali'deʃ] F squalor

esquálido, -a [iʃ'kwalidu, a] ADJ squalid, filthy

esquartejar [iʃkwaxte'ʒaʳ] VT to quarter

esquecer [iʃke'seʳ] VT, VI to forget; **esquecer-se** VR: **esquecer-se de** to forget; **~-se de fazer algo** to forget to do sth; **~-se (de) que** ... to forget that ..; **esquecido, -a** [iʃke'sidu, a] ADJ forgotten; (*pessoa*) forgetful

esquecimento [iʃkesi'mẽtu] M (*falta de memória*) forgetfulness; (*olvido*) oblivion; **cair no ~** to fall into oblivion

esquelético, -a [iʃke'lɛtʃiku, a] ADJ (*Anat*) skeletal; (*pessoa*) scrawny

esqueleto [iʃke'letu] M skeleton; (*arcabouço*) framework; **ser um ~** (*fig: pessoa*) to be just skin and bone

esquema [iʃ'kɛma] M (*resumo*) outline; (*plano*) scheme; (*diagrama*) diagram, plan; **~ de segurança** security operation

esquemático, -a [iʃke'matʃiku, a] ADJ schematic

esquematizar [iʃkematʃi'zaʳ] VT to represent schematically; (*planejar*) to plan

esquentado, -a [iʃkẽ'tadu, a] ADJ (*fig: irritado*) annoyed; (: *irritadiço*) irritable

esquentar [iʃkẽ'taʳ] VT to heat (up), warm (up); (*fig: irritar*) to annoy ▪ VI to warm up; (*casaco*) to be warm; **esquentar-se** VR to get annoyed; **~ a cabeça** (*col*) to get worked up; **não esquenta!** don't worry!

esquerda [iʃ'kexda] F (*tb: Pol*) left; **à ~** on the left; **dobrar à ~** to turn left; **políticos de ~** left-wing politicians; **a ~ festiva** the trendy left

esquerdista [iʃkex'dʒiʃta] ADJ left-wing ▪ M/F left-winger

esquerdo, -a [iʃ'kexdu, a] ADJ left

esquete [iʃ'ketʃi] M (*Teatro, TV*) sketch

esqui [iʃ'ki] M (*patim*) ski; (*esporte*) skiing; **~ aquático** water skiing; **fazer ~** to go skiing

esquiador, a [iʃkja'do'(a)] M/F skier

esquiar [iʃ'kjaʳ] VI to ski

esquilo [iʃ'kilu] M squirrel

esquina [iʃ'kina] F corner; **fazer ~ com** to join

esquisitão, -ona [iʃkizi'tãw, ɔna] (*pl* -ões/-s) ADJ odd, peculiar

esquisitice [iʃkizi'tʃisi] F oddity, peculiarity; (*ato, dito*) strange thing

esquisito, -a [iʃki'zitu, a] ADJ strange, odd

esquisitões [iʃkizi'tõjʃ] MPL *de* **esquisitão**

esquisitona [iʃkizi'tɔna] F *de* **esquisitão**

esquiva [iʃ'kiva] F dodge

esquivar-se [iʃki'vaxsi] VR: **~ de** to escape from, get away from; (*deveres*) to get out of

esquivo, -a [iʃ'kivu, a] ADJ aloof, standoffish

esquizofrenia [iʃkizofre'nia] F schizophrenia

esquizofrênico, -a [iʃkizo'freniku, a] ADJ, M/F schizophrenic

essa ['ɛsa] PRON: **~ é/foi boa** that is/was a good one; **~ não, sem ~** come off it!; **vamos nessa** let's go!; **ainda mais ~!** that's all I need!; **corta ~!** cut it out!; **gostei dessa** I like that; **estou nessa** count me in, I'm game; **por ~s e outras** for these and other reasons; **~ de fazer** ... this business of doing ..

esse ['esi] ADJ (*sg*) that; (*pl*) those; (*BR*: *este*: *sg*) this; (: *pl*) these ▪ PRON (*sg*) that one; (*pl*) those; (*BR*: *este*: *sg*) this one; (: *pl*) these

essência [e'sẽsja] F essence; **essencial** [esẽ'sjaw] (*pl* -ais) ADJ essential; (*principal*) main ▪ M: **o essencial** the main thing

Est. ABR (= *Estação*) Stn.; (= *Estrada*) ≈ Rd.

esta ['ɛʃta] F *de* **este**

estabanado, -a [iʃtaba'nadu, a] ADJ clumsy

estabelecer [iʃtabele'seʳ] VT to establish; (*fundar*) to set up; **estabelecer-se** VR to establish o.s., set o.s. up; **estabeleceu-se que** ... it was established that ...; **o governo estabeleceu que** ... the government decided that ...

estabelecimento [iʃtabelesi'mẽtu] M establishment; (*casa comercial*) business

estabilidade [iʃtabili'dadʒi] F stability

estabilização [iʃtabiliza'sãw] F stabilization

estabilizar [iʃtabili'zaʳ] VT to stabilize; **estabilizar-se** VR to stabilize

estábulo [iʃ'tabulu] M cow-shed

estaca [iʃ'taka] F post, stake; (*de barraca*) peg; **voltar à ~ zero** to go back to square one

estacada [iʃta'kada] F (*defensiva*) stockade; (*fileira de estacas*) fencing

estação [iʃta'sãw] (*pl* -ões) F station; (*do ano*) season; **~ de águas** spa; **~ balneária** seaside resort; **~ emissora** broadcasting station

estacar [iʃta'kaʳ] VT to prop up ▪ VI to stop short, halt

estacionamento [iʃtasjona'mẽtu] M (*ato*) parking; (*lugar*) car park (*Brit*), parking lot (*US*)

estacionar [iʃtasjo'naʳ] VT to park ▪ VI to park; (*não mover*) to remain stationary

estacionário, -a [iʃtasjo'narju, a] ADJ (*veículo*) stationary; (*Com*) slack

estações [iʃta'sõjʃ] FPL *de* **estação**

estada [iʃ'tada] F stay

estadia [iʃta'dʒia] F = **estada**

estádio [iʃ'tadʒu] M stadium

estadista [iʃta'dʒiʃta] M/F statesman/woman

estado [i'ʃtadu] M state; **E~s Unidos (da América)** United States (of America), USA; **~ civil** marital status; **~ de espírito** state of

NB: *European Portuguese adds the following consonants to certain words*: **b** (sú(b)dito, su(b)til); **c** (a(c)ção, a(c)cionista, a(c)to); **m** (inde(m)ne); **p** (ado(p)çã, ado(p)tar); *for further details see p. xiii.*

mind; ~ **de saúde** condition; ~ **maior** staff; **em bom** ~ in good condition; **estar em** ~ **interessante** to be expecting; **estar em** ~ **de fazer** to be in a position to do; **estadual** [iʃta'dwaw] (*pl* **-ais**) ADJ state *atr*

estadunidense [iʃtaduni'dẽsi] ADJ (North) American, US *atr*

estafa [iʃ'tafa] F fatigue; (*esgotamento*) nervous exhaustion

estafante [iʃta'fãtʃi] ADJ exhausting

estafar [iʃta'faʳ] VT to tire out, fatigue; **estafar-se** VR to tire o.s. out

estafermo [iʃta'fɛxmu] (PT) M scarecrow; (*col*) nincompoop

estagiar [iʃta'ʒjaʳ] VI to work as a trainee, do a traineeship

estagiário, -a [iʃta'ʒjarju, a] M/F probationer, trainee; (*professor*) student teacher; (*médico*) junior doctor

estágio [iʃ'taʒu] M (*aprendizado*) traineeship; (*fase*) stage

estagnação [iʃtagna'sãw] F stagnation

estagnado, -a [iʃtag'nadu, a] ADJ stagnant

estagnar [iʃtag'naʳ] VT to make stagnant; (*país*) to bring to a standstill ■ VI to stagnate; **estagnar-se** VR to stagnate

estalagem [iʃta'laʒẽ] (*pl* **-ns**) F inn

estalar [iʃta'laʳ] VT (*quebrar*) to break; (*os dedos*) to snap ■ VI (*fender-se*) to split, crack; (*crepitar*) to crackle; **estou estalando de dor de cabeça** I've got a splitting headache

estaleiro [iʃta'lejru] M shipyard

estalido [iʃta'lidu] M pop

estalo [iʃ'talu] M (*do chicote*) crack; (*dos dedos*) snap; (*dos lábios*) smack; (*de foguete*) bang; ~ **de trovão** thunderclap; **de** ~ suddenly; **me deu um** ~ it clicked, the penny dropped

estampa [iʃ'tãpa] F (*figura impressa*) print; (*ilustração*) picture; **ter uma bela** ~ (*fig*) to be beautiful

estampado, -a [iʃtã'padu, a] ADJ printed ■ M (*tecido*) print; (*num tecido*) pattern; **sua angústia estava estampada no rosto** his anxiety was written on his face

estampar [iʃtã'paʳ] VT (*imprimir*) to print; (*marcar*) to stamp

estamparia [iʃtãpa'ria] F (*oficina*) print shop; (*tecido, figura*) print

estampido [iʃtã'pidu] M bang

estancar [iʃtã'kaʳ] VT (*sangue, água*) to staunch; (*fazer cessar*) to stop; **estancar-se** VR (*parar*) to stop

estância [iʃ'tãsja] F (*fazenda*) ranch, farm; (*versos*) stanza; ~ **hidromineral** spa resort

estandardizar [iʃtãdaxdʒi'zaʳ] VT to standardize

estandarte [iʃtã'daxtʃi] M standard, banner

estande [iʃ'tãdʒi] M stand

estanho [iʃ'taɲu] M (*metal*) tin

estanque [iʃ'tãki] ADJ watertight

estante [iʃ'tãtʃi] F (*armário*) bookcase; (*suporte*) stand

estapafúrdio, -a [iʃtapa'fuxdʒu, a] ADJ outlandish, odd

○ **PALAVRA CHAVE**

estar [iʃ'taʳ] VI **1** (*lugar*) to be; (*em casa*) to be in; (*no telefone*): **a Lúcia está?** — **não, ela não está** is Lúcia there? — no, she's not here

2 (*estado*) to be; **estar doente** to be ill; **estar bem** (*de saúde*) to be well; (*financeiramente*) to be well off; **estar calor/frio** to be hot/cold; **estar com fome/sede/medo** to be hungry/thirsty/ afraid

3 (*ação contínua*): **estar fazendo** (BR) *ou* **a fazer** (PT) to be doing

4 (+ *pp*: = *adj*): **estar sentado/cansado** to be sitting down/tired

5 (+ *pp*: *uso passivo*): **está condenado à morte** he's been condemned to death; **o livro está emprestado** the book's been borrowed

6: **estar de, estar de férias/licença** to be on holiday (Brit) *ou* vacation (US)/leave; **ela estava de chapéu** she had a hat on, she was wearing a hat

7: **estar para, estar para fazer** to be about to do; **ele está para chegar a qualquer momento** he'll be here any minute; **não estar para conversas** not to be in the mood for talking

8: **estar por fazer** to be still to be done

9: **estar sem, estar sem dinheiro** to have no money; **estar sem dormir** not to have slept; **estou sem dormir há três dias** I haven't slept for three days; **está sem terminar** it isn't finished yet

10 (*frases*): **está bem, tá (bem)** (*col*) OK; **estar bem com** to be on good terms with

estardalhaço [iʃtaxda'ʎasu] M fuss; (*ostentação*) ostentation

estarrecer [iʃtaxe'seʳ] VT to petrify ■ VI to be petrified

estas ['ɛʃtaʃ] FPL *de* **este**

estatal [iʃta'taw] (*pl* **-ais**) ADJ nationalized, state-owned ■ F state-owned company

estatelado, -a [iʃtate'ladu, a] ADJ (*cair*) sprawling

estatelar [iʃtate'laʳ] VT to send sprawling; (*estarrecer*) to stun; **estatelar-se** VR (*cair*) to go sprawling

estática [iʃ'tatʃika] F (*Tec*) static

estático, -a [iʃ'tatʃiku, a] ADJ static

estatística [iʃta'tʃiʃtʃika] F statistic; (*ciência*) statistics *sg*

estatístico, -a [iʃta'tʃiʃtʃiku, a] ADJ statistical

estatização [iʃtatʃiza'sãw] (*pl* **-ões**) F nationalization

estatizar [iʃtatʃi'zaʳ] VT to nationalize

estátua [iʃ'tatwa] F statue

estatueta [iʃta'tweta] F statuette

estatura [iʃta'tura] F stature

estatuto [iʃta'tutu] M (*Jur*) statute; (*de cidade*)

bye-law; (de associação) rule; **-s sociais** ou **da empresa** (Com) articles of association

estável [iʃ'tavew] (pl **-eis**) ADJ stable

este ['ɛʃtʃi] M east ■ ADJ INV (região) eastern; (vento, direção) easterly

este, -ta ['eʃtʃi, 'ɛʃta] ADJ (sg) this; (pl) these ■ PRON this one; (pl) these; (a quem/que se referiu por último) the latter; **esta noite** (noite passada) last night; (noite de hoje) tonight

esteio [iʃ'teju] M prop, support; (Náut) stay

esteira [iʃ'tejra] F mat; (de navio) wake; (rumo) path

esteja etc [iʃ'teʒa] VB v **estar**

estelionato [iʃteljo'natu] M fraud

estêncil [iʃ'tẽsiw] (pl **-eis**) M stencil

estender [iʃtẽ'de'] VT to extend; (mapa) to spread out; (pernas) to stretch; (massa) to roll out; (conversa) to draw out; (corda) to pull tight; (roupa molhada) to hang out; **estender-se** VR (no chão) to lie down; (fila, terreno) to stretch, extend; **~-se sobre algo** to dwell on sth, expand on sth; **esta lei estende-se a todos** this law applies to all; **o conferencista estendeu-se demais** the speaker went on too long; **~ a mão** to hold out one's hand; **~ uma cadeira para alguém** to offer sb a chair; **~ uma crítica a todos** to extend a criticism to everyone

estenodatilógrafo, -a [iʃtenodatʃi'lɔgrafu, a] M/F shorthand typist (Brit), stenographer (US)

estenografar [iʃtenogra'fa'] VT to write in shorthand

estenografia [iʃtenogra'fia] F shorthand

estepe [iʃ'tɛpi] M spare wheel

esterco [iʃ'texku] M manure, dung

estéreis [iʃ'terejʃ] ADJ PL de **estéril**

estereo... [iʃterju] PREFIXO stereo...;

estereofônico, -a [iʃterjo'foniku, a] ADJ stereo(phonic)

estereotipado, -a [iʃterjotʃi'padu, a] ADJ stereotypical

estereotipar [iʃterjotʃi'pa'] VT to stereotype

estereótipo [iʃte'rjɔtʃipu] M stereotype

estéril [iʃ'teriw] (pl **-eis**) ADJ sterile; (terra) infertile; (fig) futile

esterilidade [iʃterili'dadʒi] F sterility; (de terra) infertility; (escassez) dearth

esterilização [iʃteriliza'sãw] F sterilization

esterilizar [iʃterili'za'] VT to sterilize

esterlino, -a [iʃtex'linu, a] ADJ sterling ■ M sterling; **libra esterlina** pound sterling

esteróide [iʃte'rɔjdʒi] M steroid

esteta [iʃ'tɛta] M/F aesthete (Brit), esthete (US)

estética [iʃ'tɛtʃika] F aesthetics sg (Brit), esthetics sg (US)

esteticista [iʃtetʃi'siʃta] M/F beautician

estético, -a [iʃ'tɛtʃiku, a] ADJ aesthetic (Brit), esthetic (US)

estetoscópio [iʃteto'skopju] M stethoscope

esteve [iʃ'tevi] VB v **estar**

estiagem [iʃ'tʃjaʒẽ] (pl **-ns**) F (depois da chuva) calm after the storm; (falta de chuva) dry spell

estiar [iʃ'tʃja'] VI (não chover) to stop raining; (o tempo) to clear up

estibordo [iʃtʃi'bɔxdu] M starboard

esticada [iʃtʃi'kada] F: **dar uma ~** (esticar-se) to stretch, have a stretch; **dar uma ~ numa boate** (col) to go on to a nightclub

esticar [iʃtʃi'ka'] VT (uma corda) to stretch, tighten; (a perna) to stretch; **esticar-se** VR to stretch out; **~ as canelas** (col) to pop one's clogs, kick the bucket; **depois da festa esticamos numa boate** (col) after the party we went on to a nightclub

estigma [iʃ'tʃigima] M (marca) mark, scar; (fig) stigma

estigmatizar [iʃtʃigimatʃi'za'] VT to brand; **~ alguém de algo** to brand sb (as) sth

estilhaçar [iʃtʃiʎa'sa'] VT to splinter; (despedaçar) to shatter; **estilhaçar-se** VR to shatter;

estilhaço [iʃtʃi'ʎasu] M fragment; (de pedra) chip; (de madeira, metal) splinter

estilista [iʃtʃi'liʃta] M/F stylist; (de moda) designer

estilística [iʃtʃi'liʃtʃika] F stylistics sg

estilístico, -a [iʃtʃi'liʃtʃiku, a] ADJ stylistic

estilizar [iʃtʃili'za'] VT to stylize

estilo [iʃ'tʃilu] M style; (Tec) stylus; **~ de vida** way of life; **móveis de ~** stylish furniture; **o vestido não é do meu ~** ou **não faz o meu ~** the dress isn't my style

estima [iʃ'tʃima] F esteem; (afeto) affection

estimação [iʃtʃima'sãw] F: **... de ~** favourite (Brit) ..., favorite (US) ....

estimado, -a [iʃtʃi'madu, a] ADJ respected; (em cartas): **E~ Senhor** Dear Sir

estimar [iʃtʃi'ma'] VT (apreciar) to appreciate; (avaliar) to value; (ter estima a) to have a high regard for; (calcular aproximadamente) to estimate; **estimar-se** VR: **eles se estimam muito** they have a high regard for one another; **estima-se o número de ouvintes em 3 milhões** the number of listeners is estimated to be 3 million; **~ em** (avaliar) to value at; (população) to estimate to be; **estimo que você tenha exito** I wish you success

estimativa [iʃtʃima'tʃiva] F estimate; **fazer uma ~ de algo** to estimate sth; **~ de custo** estimate, costing

estimável [iʃtʃi'mavew] (pl **-eis**) ADJ (digno de estima) decent; **prejuízo ~ em 3 milhões** loss estimated at 3 million

estimulação [iʃtʃimula'sãw] F stimulation

estimulante [iʃtʃimu'lãtʃi] ADJ stimulating ■ M stimulant

estimular [iʃtʃimu'la'] VT to stimulate; (incentivar) to encourage; **~ alguém a fazer algo** to encourage sb to do sth; **estímulo** [iʃ'tʃimulu] M stimulus; (ânimo) encouragement; **falta**

NB: European Portuguese adds the following consonants to certain words: **b** (sú(b)dito, su(b)til); **c** (a(c)ção, a(c)cionista, a(c)to); **m** (inde(m)ne); **p** (ado(p)ção, ado(p)tar); for further details see p. xiii.

de estímulo lack of incentive; **ele não tem estímulo para nada no momento** he has got no incentive to do anything at the moment
estio [iʃˈtʃiu] M summer
estipêndio [iʃtʃiˈpẽdʒu] M pay
estipulação [iʃtʃipulaˈsãw] (pl -ões) F stipulation, condition
estipular [iʃtʃipuˈlaʳ] VT to stipulate
estirar [iʃtʃiˈraʳ] VT to stretch (out); **estirar-se** VR to stretch
estirpe [iʃˈtʃixpi] F stock, lineage
estivador, a [iʃtʃivaˈdoʳ(a)] M/F docker
estive etc [iʃˈtʃivi] VB v **estar**
estocada [iʃtoˈkada] F stab, thrust
estocado, -a [iʃtoˈkadu, a] ADJ (Com) in stock
estocagem [iʃtoˈkaʒẽ] F (estocar) stockpiling; (estoque) stock
estocar [iʃtoˈkaʳ] VT to stock
Estocolmo [iʃtoˈkɔwmu] N Stockholm
estofador, a [iʃtofaˈdoʳ(a)] M/F upholsterer
estofar [iʃtoˈfaʳ] VT to upholster; (acolchoar) to pad, stuff
estofo [iʃˈtofu] M (tecido) material; (para acolchoar) padding, stuffing
estóico, -a [iʃˈtɔjku, a] ADJ stoic(al) ▪ M/F stoic
estojo [iʃˈtoʒu] M case; **~ de ferramentas** tool kit; **~ de óculos** glasses case; **~ de tintas** paintbox; **~ de unhas** manicure set
estola [iʃˈtɔla] F stole
estólido, -a [iʃˈtɔlidu, a] ADJ stupid
estômago [iʃˈtomagu] M stomach; **ter ~ para (fazer) algo** to be up to (doing) sth; **estar com o ~ embrulhado** to have an upset stomach; **forrar o ~** to have a little bite to eat
Estônia [iʃˈtonja] F: **a ~** Estonia
estoniano, -a [iʃtoˈnjanu, a] ADJ, M/F Estonian
estonteante [iʃtõˈtʃjãtʃi] ADJ stunning
estontear [iʃtõˈtʃjaʳ] VT to stun, daze
estoque [iʃˈtɔki] M (Com) stock; **em ~** in stock
estore [iʃˈtɔri] M blind
estória [iʃˈtɔrja] F story
estorninho [iʃtoxˈniɲu] M starling
estorricar [iʃtoxiˈkaʳ] VT, VI = **esturricar**
estorvar [iʃtoxˈvaʳ] VT to hinder, obstruct; (fig: importunar) to bother, disturb; **~ alguém de fazer** to prevent sb from doing
estorvo [iʃˈtoxvu] M hindrance, obstacle; (amolação) bother, nuisance
estourado, -a [iʃtoˈradu, a] ADJ (temperamental) explosive; (col: cansado) knackered, worn out
estoura-peito [iʃtora-ˈ] (col: pl estoura-peitos) M strong cigarette
estourar [iʃtoˈraʳ] VI to explode; (pneu) to burst; (escândalo) to blow up; (guerra) to break out; (BR: chegar) to turn up, arrive; **~ (com alguém)** (zangar-se) to blow up (at sb); **estou estourando de dor de cabeça** I've got a splitting headache; **eu devo chegar às 9.00, estourando, 9 e meia** I should get there at 9 o'clock, or 9.30 at the latest
estouro [iʃˈtoru] M explosion; **ser um ~** (col) to be great; **dar o ~** (fig: zangar-se) to blow up, blow

one's top
estouvado, -a [iʃtoˈvadu, a] ADJ rash, foolhardy
estrábico, -a [iʃˈtrabiku, a] ADJ cross-eyed
estrabismo [iʃtraˈbiʒmu] M squint
estraçalhar [iʃtrasaˈʎaʳ] VT (livro, objeto) to pull to pieces; (pessoa) to tear to pieces; **estraçalhar-se** VR to mutilate one another
estrada [iʃˈtrada] F road; **~ de contorno** ring road (Brit), beltway (US); **~ de ferro** (BR) railway (Brit), railroad (US); **~ de terra** dirt road; **~ principal** main road (Brit), state highway (US); **~ secundária** minor road
estrado [iʃˈtradu] M (tablado) platform; (de cama) base
estragado, -a [iʃtraˈgadu, a] ADJ ruined, wrecked; (saúde) ruined; (fruta) rotten; (muito mimado) spoiled, spoilt (Brit)
estragão [iʃtraˈgãw] M tarragon
estraga-prazeres [iʃtraga-] M/F INV spoilsport
estragar [iʃtraˈgaʳ] VT to spoil; (arruinar) to ruin, wreck; (desperdiçar) to waste; (saúde) to damage; (mimar) to spoil; **estrago** [iʃˈtragu] M (destruição) destruction; (desperdício) waste; (dano) damage; **os estragos da guerra** the ravages of war
estrangeiro, -a [iʃtrãˈʒejru, a] ADJ foreign ▪ M/F foreigner; **no ~** abroad
estrangulação [iʃtrãgulaˈsãw] F strangulation
estrangulador [iʃtrãgulaˈdoʳ] M strangler
estrangular [iʃtrãguˈlaʳ] VT to strangle; **esta suéter está me estrangulando** this sweater is too tight for me
estranhar [iʃtraˈɲaʳ] VT (surpreender-se de) to be surprised at; (achar estranho): **~ algo** to find sth strange; **estranhei o clima** the climate did not agree with me; **minha filha estranhou a visita/a cama nova** my daughter was shy with the visitor/found it hard to get used to the new bed; **não é de se ~** it's not surprising; **você não quer um chocolate? — estou te estranhando** you don't want a chocolate? — that's not like you
estranho, -a [iʃˈtraɲu, a] ADJ strange, odd; (influências) outside ▪ M/F (desconhecido) stranger; (de fora) outsider; **o nome não me é ~** the name rings a bell
Estrasburgo [iʃtraʒˈbuxgu] N Strasbourg
estratagema [iʃrataˈʒema] M (Mil) stratagem; (ardil) trick
estratégia [iʃtraˈtɛʒa] F strategy
estratégico, -a [iʃtraˈtɛʒiku, a] ADJ strategic
estratificar-se [iʃtratʃifiˈkaxsi] VR (fig: idéias, opiniões) to become entrenched
estrato [iʃˈtratu] M layer, stratum
estratosfera [iʃtratoʃˈfera] F stratosphere
estreante [iʃˈtrjãtʃi] ADJ new ▪ M/F newcomer
estrear [iʃˈtrjaʳ] VT (vestido) to wear for the first time; (peça de teatro) to perform for the first time; (veículo) to use for the first time; (filme) to show for the first time, première; (iniciar): **~ uma carreira** to embark on ou begin a career ▪ VI (ator, jogador) to make one's first appearance; (filme, peça) to open

estrebaria [iʃtreba'ria] F stable
estrebuchar [iʃtrebu'ʃaʳ] VI to struggle; (ao morrer) to shake (in death throes)
estréia [iʃ'treja] F (de artista) debut; (de uma peça) first night; (de um filme) première, opening; **é a ~ do meu carro** it's the first time I've used my car
estreitamento [iʃtrejta'mẽtu] M (diminuição) narrowing; (aperto) tightening; (de relações) strengthening
estreitar [iʃtrej'taʳ] VT (reduzir) to narrow; (roupa) to take in; (abraçar) to hug; (laços de amizade) to strengthen ■ VI (estrada) to narrow; **estreitar-se** VR (laços de amizade) to deepen
estreiteza [iʃtrej'teza] F narrowness; (de regulamento) strictness; **~ de pontos de vista** narrow-mindedness
estreito, -a [iʃ'trejtu, a] ADJ narrow; (saia) straight; (vínculo, relação) close; (medida) strict ■ M strait; **ter convivência estreita com alguém** to live at close quarters with sb
estrela [iʃ'trela] F star; **~ cadente** falling star; **~ de cinema** film (Brit) ou movie (US) star; **ter boa ~** to be lucky; **estrelado, -a** [iʃtre'ladu, a] ADJ (céu) starry; (ovo) fried; **um filme estrelado por Marilyn Monroe** a film starring Marilyn Monroe
estrela-do-mar (pl estrelas-do-mar) F starfish
estrelar [iʃtre'laʳ] VT (PT: ovos) to fry; (filme, peça) to star in; **estrelar-se** VR (céu) to fill with stars
estrelato [iʃtre'latu] M: **o ~** stardom
estrelinha [iʃtre'liɲa] F (fogo de artifício) sparkler
estrelismo [iʃtre'liʒmu] M star quality
estremadura [iʃtrema'dura] F frontier
estremecer [iʃtreme'seʳ] VT (sacudir) to shake; (amizade) to strain; (fazer tremer): **~ alguém** to make sb shudder ■ VI (vibrar) to shake; (tremer) to tremble; (horrorizar-se) to shudder; (amizade) to be strained; **ela estremeceu de susto, o susto estremeceu-a** the fright made her jump
estremecido, -a [iʃtreme'sidu, a] ADJ (sacudido) shaken; (sobressaltado) startled; (amizade) strained
estremecimento [iʃtremesi'mẽtu] M (sacudida) shaking, trembling; (tremor) tremor; (abalo numa amizade) tension
estremunhado, -a [iʃtremu'ɲadu, a] ADJ half-asleep
estrepar-se [iʃtre'paxsi] VR (fig) to come unstuck
estrepe [iʃ'trɛpi] (col) M (mulher) dog
estrépito [iʃ'trɛpitu] M din, racket; **com ~** with a lot of noise, noisily; **fazer ~** to make a din
estrepitoso, -a [iʃtrepitozu, ɔza] ADJ noisy, rowdy; (fig) sensational
estressante [iʃtre'sãtʃi] ADJ stressful
estressar [iʃtre'saʳ] VT to stress
estresse [iʃ'tresi] M stress
estria [iʃ'tria] F groove; (na pele) stretch mark

estribar [iʃtri'baʳ] VT to base; **estribar-se** VR: **estribar-se em** to be based on
estribeira [iʃtri'bejra] F: **perder as ~s** (col) to fly off the handle, lose one's temper
estribilho [iʃtri'biʎu] M (Mús) chorus
estribo [iʃ'tribu] M (de cavalo) stirrup; (degrau) step; (fig: apoio) support
estricnina [iʃtrik'nina] F strychnine
estridente [iʃtri'dẽtʃi] ADJ shrill, piercing
estrilar [iʃtri'laʳ] (col) VI (zangar-se) to get mad; (reclamar) to moan
estrilo [iʃ'trilu] M: **dar um ~** to blow one's top
estripulia [iʃtripu'lia] F prank
estrito, -a [iʃ'tritu, a] ADJ (rigoroso) strict; (restrito) restricted; **no sentido ~ da palavra** in the strict sense of the word
estrofe [iʃ'trɔfi] F stanza
estrogonofe [iʃtrogo'nɔfi] M (Culin) stroganoff
estrompado, -a [iʃtrõ'padu, a] ADJ worn out; (pessoa) exhausted
estrondar [iʃtrõ'daʳ] VI to boom; (fig) to resound
estrondo [iʃ'trõdu] M (de trovão) rumble; (de armas) din; **~ sônico** sonic boom
estrondoso, -a [iʃtrõ'dozu, ɔza] ADJ (ovação) tumultuous, thunderous; (sucesso) resounding; (notícia) sensational
estropiar [iʃtro'pjaʳ] VT (aleijar) to maim, cripple; (fatigar) to wear out, exhaust; (texto) to mutilate; (pronunciar mal) to mispronounce
estrumar [iʃtru'maʳ] VT to spread manure on
estrume [iʃ'trumi] M manure
estrutura [iʃtru'tura] F structure; (armação) framework; (de edifício) fabric
estrutural [iʃtrutu'raw] (pl -ais) ADJ structural
estruturalismo [iʃtrutura'liʒmu] M structuralism
estruturar [iʃtrutu'raʳ] VT to structure
estuário [iʃtu'arju] M estuary
estudado, -a [iʃtu'dadu, a] ADJ (fig) studied, affected
estudantada [iʃtudã'tada] F students pl
estudante [iʃtu'dãtʃi] M/F student; **estudantil** [iʃtudã'tʃiw] (pl -is) ADJ student atr
estudar [iʃtu'daʳ] VT, VI to study
estúdio [iʃ'tudʒu] M studio
estudioso, -a [iʃtudʒozu, ɔza] ADJ studious ■ M/F student
estudo [iʃ'tudu] M study; **~ de caso** case study; **~ de viabilidade** feasibility study
estufa [iʃ'tufa] F (fogão) stove; (de plantas) greenhouse; (de fogão) plate warmer; **este quarto é uma ~** this room is like an oven
estufado [iʃtu'fadu] (PT) M stew
estufar [iʃtu'faʳ] VT (peito) to puff up; (almofada) to stuff
estulto, -a [iʃ'tuwtu, a] ADJ foolish, silly
estupefação [iʃtupefa'sãw] (PT -cç-) F amazement, astonishment
estupefato, -a [iʃtupe'fatu, a] (PT -ct-) ADJ

dumbfounded; **ele me olhou ~** he looked at me in astonishment

estupendo, -a [iʃtu'pẽdu, a] ADJ wonderful; (col) fantastic, terrific

estupidamente [iʃtupida'mẽtʃi] ADV stupidly; **uma cerveja ~ gelada** (col) an ice-cold beer

estupidez [iʃtupi'deʒ] F stupidity; (ato, dito) stupid thing; (grosseria) rudeness; **que ~!** what a stupid thing to do! (ou to say!)

estúpido, -a [iʃ'tupidu, a] ADJ stupid; (grosseiro) rude, churlish ■ M/F idiot; (grosseiro) oaf; **calor ~** incredible heat

estupor [iʃtu'poʳ] M stupor; (fig: pessoa de mau caráter) bad lot; (: pessoa feia) fright

estuporado, -a [iʃtupo'radu, a] ADJ (estragado) ruined; (cansado) tired out; (ferido) seriously injured

estuporar-se [iʃtupo'raxsi] (col) VR (num acidente) to be seriously injured

estuprador [iʃtupra'doʳ] M rapist

estuprar [iʃtu'praʳ] VT to rape; **estupro** [iʃ'tupru] M rape

estuque [iʃ'tuki] M stucco; (massa) plaster

esturricado, -a [iʃtuxi'kadu, a] ADJ (seco) shrivelled, dried out; (roupa) skimpy, tight

esturricar [iʃtuxi'kaʳ] VT, VI to shrivel, dry out

esvaecer-se [iʒvaje'sexsi] VR to fade away, vanish

esvair-se [iʒva'jixsi] VR to vanish, disappear; **~ em sangue** to lose a lot of blood

esvaziamento [iʒvazja'mẽtu] M emptying

esvaziar [iʒva'zjaʳ] VT to empty; **esvaziar-se** VR to empty

esverdeado, -a [iʒvex'dʒjado, a] ADJ greenish

esvoaçante [iʒvwa'sãtʃi] ADJ billowing

esvoaçar [iʒvoa'saʳ] VI to flutter

ETA ['ɛta] ABR M: **Euskadi Ta Askatasuna** ETA

eta ['eta] (col) EXCL: **~ filme chato!** what a boring film!; **~ ferro!** gosh!

etapa [e'tapa] F (fase) stage; **por ~s** in stages

etário, -a [e'tarju, a] ADJ age atr

etc. ABR (= et cetera) etc

éter ['ɛteʳ] M ether

eternidade [etexni'dadʒi] F eternity

eternizar [etexni'zaʳ] VT (fazer eterno) to make eternal; (nome, pessoa) to immortalize; (discussão, processo) to drag out; **eternizar-se** VR to be immortalized; to drag on

eterno, -a [e'texnu, a] ADJ eternal

ética ['ɛtʃika] F ethics pl

ético, -a ['ɛtʃiku, a] ADJ ethical

etimologia [etʃimolo'ʒia] F etymology

etíope [e'tʃjopi] ADJ, M/F Ethiopian

Etiópia [e'tʃjɔpja] F: **a ~** Ethiopia

etiqueta [etʃi'keta] F (maneiras) etiquette; (rótulo, em roupa) label; (que se amarra) tag; **~ adesiva** adhesive ou stick-on label

etiquetar [etʃike'taʳ] VT to label

étnico, -a ['ɛtʃniku, a] ADJ ethnic

etnocêntrico, -a [etʃno'sẽtriku, a] ADJ ethnocentric

etnografia [etʃnogra'fia] F ethnography

etnologia [etʃnolo'ʒia] F ethnology

etos ['ɛtuʃ] M INV ethos

eu [ew] PRON I ■ M self; **sou eu** it's me; **eu mesmo** I myself; **eu, hein?** I don't know ... (how strange!)

EUA ABR MPL (= Estados Unidos da América) USA; **nos ~** in the USA

eucalipto [ewka'liptu] M eucalyptus

eucaristia [ewkariʃ'tʃia] F Holy Communion

eufemismo [ewfe'miʒmu] M euphemism

eufonia [ewfo'nia] F euphony

euforia [ewfo'ria] F euphoria

eunuco [ew'nuku] M eunuch

euro ['ewru] M (moeda) euro

Europa [ew'rɔpa] F: **a ~** Europe

européia [euro'pɛja] F de **europeu**

europeizar [ewropeji'zaʳ] VT to Europeanize; **europeizar-se** VR to become Europeanized

europeu, -péia [ewro'peu, 'pɛ] ADJ, M/F European

eutanásia [ewta'nazja] F euthanasia

evacuação [evakwa'sãw] (pl -ões) F evacuation

evacuar [eva'kwaʳ] VT to evacuate; (sair de) to leave; (Med) to discharge ■ VI to defecate

evadir [eva'dʒiʳ] VT to evade; (col) to dodge; **evadir-se** VR to escape

evanescente [evane'sẽtʃi] ADJ fading, vanishing

evangelho [evã'ʒeʎu] M gospel

evangélico, -a [evã'ʒɛliku, a] ADJ evangelical

evaporação [evapora'sãw] F evaporation

evaporar [evapo'raʳ] VT, VI to evaporate; **evaporar-se** VR to evaporate; (desaparecer) to vanish

evasão [eva'zãw] (pl -ões) F escape, flight; (fig) evasion; **~ de impostos** tax avoidance

evasê [eva'ze] ADJ (saia) flared

evasiva [eva'ziva] F excuse

evasivo, -a [eva'zivu, a] ADJ evasive

evasões [eva'zõjʃ] FPL de **evasão**

evento [e'vẽtu] M (acontecimento) event; (eventualidade) eventuality

eventual [evẽ'tuaw] (pl -ais) ADJ fortuitous, accidental; **eventualidade** [evẽtwali'dadʒi] F eventuality

evicção [evik'sãw] (pl -ões) F (Jur) eviction

evidência [evi'dẽsja] F evidence, proof; **evidenciar** [evidẽ'sjaʳ] VT (comprovar) to prove; (mostrar) to show; **evidenciar-se** VR to be evident, be obvious

evidente [evi'dẽtʃi] ADJ obvious, evident

evitar [evi'taʳ] VT to avoid; **~ de fazer algo** to avoid doing sth

evitável [evi'tavew] (pl -eis) ADJ avoidable

evocação [evoka'sãw] (pl -ões) F evocation; (de espíritos) invocation

evocar [evo'kaʳ] VT to evoke; (espíritos) to invoke

evolução [evolu'sãw] (pl -ões) F (desenvolvimento) development; (Mil) manoeuvre (Brit), maneuver (US); (movimento) movement; (Bio) evolution

evoluído, -a [evo'lwidu, a] ADJ advanced; (pessoa) broad-minded

evoluir [evo'lwiʳ] vi to evolve; ~ **para** to evolve into; **ela não evoluiu com os tempos** she hasn't moved with the times

ex- [eʃ-, eʒ-] PREFIXO ex-, former

Ex.ª ABR = **Excelência**

exacerbação [ezasexba'sãw] F worsening; (*exasperação*) irritation

exacerbante [ezasex'bãtʃi] ADJ exacerbating

exacerbar [ezasex'baʳ] VT (*irritar*) to irritate, annoy; (*agravar*) to aggravate, worsen; (*revolta, indignação*) to deepen

exacto, -cta [e'zatu, a] (*PT*) = **exato** etc

exagerado, -a [ezaʒe'radu, a] ADJ (*relato*) exaggerated; (*maquilagem etc*) overdone; (*pessoa*): **ele é** ~ (*na maneira de falar*) he exaggerates; (*nos gestos*) he overdoes it ou things

exagerar [ezaʒe'raʳ] VT to exaggerate ■ VI to exaggerate; (*agir com exagero*) to overdo it; **exagero** [eza'ʒeru] M exaggeration

exalações [ezala'zõjʃ] FPL fumes

exalar [eza'laʳ] VT (*odor*) to give off

exaltação [ezawta'sãw] F (*de virtudes etc*) exaltation; (*excitamento*) excitement; (*irritação*) annoyance

exaltado, -a [ezaw'tadu, a] ADJ (*fanático*) fanatical; (*apaixonado*) overexcited

exaltar [ezaw'taʳ] VT (*elevar: pessoa, virtude*) to exalt; (*louvar*) to praise; (*excitar*) to excite; (*irritar*) to annoy; **exaltar-se** VR (*irritar-se*) to get worked up; (*arrebatar-se*) to get carried away

exame [e'zami] M (*Educ*) examination, exam; (*Med etc*) examination; **fazer um** ~ (*Educ*) to take an exam; (*Med*) to have an examination; ~ **de direção** driving test; ~ **de sangue** blood test; ~ **médico** medical (examination); (~) **vestibular** university entrance exam

examinador, a [ezamina'doʳ(a)] M/F examiner ■ ADJ examining

examinando, -a [ezami'nãdu, a] M/F (exam) candidate

examinar [ezami'naʳ] VT to examine

exangue [e'zãgi] ADJ (*sem sangue*) bloodless

exasperação [ezaʃpera'sãw] F exasperation

exasperador, a [ezaʃpera'doʳ(a)] ADJ exasperating

exasperante [ezaʃpe'rãtʃi] ADJ exasperating

exasperar [ezaʃpe'raʳ] VT to exasperate; **exasperar-se** VR to get exasperated

exatidão [ezatʃi'dãw] F (*precisão*) accuracy; (*perfeição*) correctness

exato, -a [e'zatu, a] ADJ (*certo*) right, correct; (*preciso*) exact; ~! exactly!

exaurir [ezaw'riʳ] VT to exhaust, drain; **exaurir-se** VR to become exhausted

exaustão [ezaw'ʃtãw] F exhaustion

exaustar [ezaw'ʃtaʳ] VT to exhaust, drain; **exaustar-se** VR to become exhausted

exaustivo, -a [ezaw'ʃtʃivu, a] ADJ (*tratado*) exhaustive; (*trabalho*) exhausting

exausto, -a [e'zawʃtu, a] PP de **exaurir** ■ ADJ exhausted

exaustor [ezaw'ʃtoʳ] M extractor fan

exceção [ese'sãw] (*pl -ões*) F exception; **com** ~ **de** with the exception of; **abrir** ~ to make an exception

excedente [ese'dētʃi] ADJ excess; (*Com*) surplus ■ M (*Com*) surplus; (**aluno**) ~ *pupil who cannot be given a place because the school is full*

exceder [ese'deʳ] VT to exceed; (*superar*) to surpass; **exceder-se** VR (*cometer excessos*) to go too far; (*cansar-se*) to overdo things; ~ **em peso/brilho** to outweigh/outshine

excelência [ese'lēsja] F excellence; **por** ~ par excellence; **Vossa E~** Your Excellency; **excelente** [ese'lētʃi] ADJ excellent

excelentíssimo, -a [eselē'tʃisimu, a] ADJ SUPERL de **excelente**; (*tratamento*) honourable (*Brit*), honorable (*US*)

excelso, -a [e'sewsu, a] ADJ (*sublime*) sublime; (*excelente*) excellent

excentricidade [esẽtrisi'dadʒi] F eccentricity

excêntrico, -a [e'sẽtriku, a] ADJ, M/F eccentric

excepção [ese'sãw] (*PT*) F = **exceção**

excepcional [esepsjo'naw] (*pl -ais*) ADJ (*extraordinário*) exceptional; (*especial*) special; (*Med*) handicapped

excepcionalidade [esepsjonali'dadʒi] F exceptional nature

excepto etc [e'setu] (*PT*) = **exceto** etc

excerto [e'sextu] M fragment, excerpt

excessivo, -a [ese'sivu, a] ADJ excessive

excesso [e'sesu] M excess; (*Com*) surplus; **em** ~ in excess; ~ **de peso** excess weight; ~ **de velocidade** excessive speed

exceto [e'setu] PREP except (for), apart from

excetuar [ese'twaʳ] VT to except, make an exception of; **todos, excetuando você** everyone except you

excitação [esita'sãw] F excitement

excitado, -a [esi'tadu, a] ADJ excited; (*estimulado*) aroused

excitante [esi'tãtʃi] ADJ exciting

excitar [esi'taʳ] VT to excite; (*estimular*) to arouse; **excitar-se** VR to get excited

excitável [esi'tavew] (*pl -eis*) ADJ excitable

exclamação [iʃklama'sãw] (*pl -ões*) F exclamation

exclamar [iʃkla'maʳ] VI to exclaim

exclamativo, -a [iʃklama'tʃivu, a] ADJ exclamatory; *v tb* **ponto**

excluir [iʃ'klwiʳ] VT to exclude, leave out; (*eliminar*) to rule out; (*ser incompatível com*) to preclude; **exclusão** [iʃklu'zãw] F exclusion

exclusividade [iʃkluzivi'dadʒi] F exclusiveness; (*Com*) exclusive rights *pl*; **com** ~ **no "Globo"** only in the "Globo"

exclusivo, -a [iʃklu'zivu, a] ADJ exclusive; **para uso** ~ **de** for the sole use of

---

NB: *European Portuguese adds the following consonants to certain words:* **b** (sú(b)dito, su(b)til); **c** (a(c)ção, a(c)cionista, a(c)to); **m** (inde(m)ne); **p** (ado(p)ção, ado(p)tar); *for further details see p. xiii.*

excluso, -a [iʃ'kluzu, a] ADJ excluded
excomungar [iʃkomũ'ga^r] VT to excommunicate
excremento [iʃkre'mẽtu] M excrement
excruciante [iʃkru'sjātʃi] ADJ excruciating
excursão [iʃkux'sãw] (*pl* -ões) F trip, outing; (*em grupo*) excursion; ~ **a pé** hike
excursionar [iʃkuxsjo'na^r] VI to go on a trip; ~ **pela Europa** *etc* to tour Europe *etc*
excursionista [iʃkuxsjo'niʃta] M/F tourist; (*para o dia*) day-tripper; (*a pé*) hiker
excursões [iʃkux'sõjʃ] FPL *de* **excursão**
execrável [eze'kravew] (*pl* -eis) ADJ execrable, deplorable
execução [ezeku'sãw] (*pl* -ões) F execution; (*de música*) performance; ~ **de hipoteca** (*Com*) foreclosure
executante [ezeku'tātʃi] M/F player, performer
executar [ezeku'ta^r] VT to execute; (*Mús*) to perform; (*plano*) to carry out; (*papel teatral*) to play; ~ **uma hipoteca** (*Com*) to foreclose on a mortgage
executivo, -a [ezeku'tʃivu, a] ADJ, M/F executive
executor, a [ezeku'to^r(a)] M/F executioner
exemplar [ezẽ'pla^r] ADJ exemplary ■ M model, example; (*Bio*) specimen; (*livro*) copy; (*peça*) piece
exemplificar [ezẽplifi'ka^r] VT to exemplify
exemplo [e'zẽplu] M example; **por** ~ for example; **dar o** ~ to set an example; **servir de** ~ **a alguém** to be an example to sb; **a** ~ **de** just like; **a** ~ **do que** just as; **ela é um** ~ **de bondade** she's a model of kindness
exéquias [e'zɛkjaʃ] FPL funeral rites
exeqüível [eze'kwivew] (*pl* -eis) ADJ feasible
exercer [ezex'se^r] VT to exercise; (*influência, pressão*) to exert; (*função*) to perform; (*profissão*) to practise (*Brit*), practice (*US*); (*obrigações*) to carry out
exercício [ezex'sisju] M (*ginástica, Educ*) exercise; (*de medicina*) practice; (*de direitos*) exercising; (*Mil*) drill; (*Com*) financial year; **em** ~ (*funcionário*) in office; (*professor etc*) in service; **em pleno** ~ **de suas faculdades mentais** in full command of one's mental faculties; ~ **anterior/corrente** (*Com*) previous/current (financial) year
exercitar [ezexsi'ta^r] VT (*profissão*) to practise (*Brit*), practice (*US*); (*direitos, músculos*) to exercise; (*adestrar*) to train
exército [e'zɛxsito] M army
exibição [ezibi'sãw] (*pl* -ões) F show, display; (*de filme*) showing
exibicionismo [ezibisjo'niʒmu] M flamboyance; (*Psico*) exhibitionism
exibicionista [ezibisjo'niʃta] ADJ flamboyant; (*Psico*) exhibitionist ■ M/F flamboyant character; exhibitionist
exibições [ezibi'sõjʃ] FPL *de* **exibição**
exibido, -a [ezi'bidu, a] ADJ (*exibicionista*) flamboyant ■ M/F show-off
exibidor, a [ezibi'do^r(a)] M/F exhibitor; (*Cinema*) cinema owner
exibir [ezi'bi^r] VT to show; (*alardear*) to

show off; (*filme*) to show, screen; **exibir-se** VR to show off; (*indecentemente*) to expose o.s.
exigência [ezi'ʒẽsja] F demand; (*o necessário*) requirement; **exigente** [ezi'ʒẽtʃi] ADJ demanding; **ser exigente com alguém** to be hard on sb
exigibilidades [eziʒibili'dadʒiʃ] FPL (*Com*) liabilities
exigir [ezi'ʒi^r] VT to demand; ~ **que alguém faça algo** to demand that sb do sth; **o médico exigiu-lhe repouso absoluto** the doctor ordered him to have complete rest
exigível [ezi'ʒivew] (*pl* -eis) ADJ (*Com: passivo*): ~ **a curto/longo prazo** current/long-term liabilities *pl*
exíguo, -a [e'zigwu, a] ADJ (*diminuto*) small; (*escasso*) scanty
exilado, -a [ezi'ladu, a] ADJ exiled ■ M/F exile
exilar [ezi'la^r] VT to exile; (*pessoa indesejável*) to deport; **exilar-se** VR to go into exile; **exílio** [e'zilju] M exile; (*forçado*) deportation
exímio, -a [e'zimju, a] ADJ (*eminente*) famous, distinguished; (*excelente*) excellent
eximir [ezi'mi^r] VT: ~ **de** to exempt from; (*obrigação*) to free from; (*culpa*) to clear of; **eximir-se** VR: **eximir-se de** to avoid, shun
existência [eziʃ'tẽsja] F existence; (*vida*) life
existencial [eziʃtẽ'sjaw] (*pl* -ais) ADJ existential
existencialismo [eziʃtẽsja'liʒmu] M existentialism
existencialista [eziʃtẽsja'liʃta] ADJ, M/F existentialist
existente [eziʃ'tẽtʃi] ADJ extant; (*vivente*) living
existir [eziʃ'tʃi^r] VI to exist; **existe/existem ...** (*há*) there is/are ...; **ela não existe** (*col*) she's incredible
êxito ['ezitu] M (*resultado*) result; (*sucesso*) success; (*música, filme etc*) hit; **ter** ~ **(em)** to succeed (in), be successful (in); **não ter** ~ **(em)** to fail (in), be unsuccessful (in)
Exmo(s), -a(s) ABR (= *Excelentíssimo(s)*) Dear
êxodo ['ezodu] M exodus
exoneração [ezonera'sãw] (*pl* -ões) F dismissal
exonerar [ezone'ra^r] VT (*demitir*) to dismiss; ~ **de uma obrigação** to free from an obligation
exorbitante [ezoxbi'tātʃi] ADJ (*preço*) exorbitant; (*pretensões*) extravagant; (*exigências*) excessive
exorcismo [ezox'siʒmu] M exorcism
exorcista [ezox'siʃta] M/F exorcist
exorcizar [ezoxsi'za^r] VT to exorcise
exortação [ezoxta'sãw] (*pl* -ões) F exhortation
exortar [ezox'ta^r] VT: ~ **alguém a fazer algo** to urge sb to do sth
exortativo, -a [ezoxta'tʃivu, a] ADJ (*tom*) encouraging
exótico, -a [e'zɔtʃiku, a] ADJ exotic
exotismo [ezo'tʃiʒmu] M exoticism, exotic nature
expandir [iʃpã'dʒi^r] VT to expand; (*espalhar*) to spread; **expandir-se** VR (*dilatar-se*) to expand; ~~**se com alguém** to be frank with sb
expansão [iʃpã'sãw] F expansion, spread; (*de*

alegria) effusiveness

expansividade [iʃpãsivi'dadʒi] F outgoing nature

expansivo, -a [iʃpã'sivu, a] ADJ (*pessoa*) outgoing

expatriação [iʃpatrja'sãw] F expatriation

expatriado, -a [iʃpa'trjadu, a] ADJ, M/F expatriate

expatriar [iʃpa'trjaʳ] VT to expatriate

expeça *etc* [iʃ'pesa] VB *v* **expedir**

expectativa [iʃpekta'tʃiva] F (*esperança*) expectation; **na ~ de** in expectation of; **estar na ~** to be expectant; (*em suspense*) to be in suspense; **~ de vida** life expectancy

expectorante [iʃpekto'rãtʃi] ADJ, M expectorant

expectorar [iʃpekto'raʳ] VT to cough up ■ VI to expectorate

expedição [iʃpedʒi'sãw] (*pl* -ões) F (*viagem*) expedition; (*de mercadorias*) despatch; (*por navio*) shipment; (*de passaporte etc*) issue

expediência [iʃpe'dʒjẽsja] F (*desembaraço*) efficiency

expediente [iʃpe'dʒjẽtʃi] M means; (*serviço*) working day; (*correspondência*) correspondence ■ ADJ expedient; **~ bancário** banking hours *pl*; **~ do escritório** office hours *pl*; **meio ~** part-time working; **só trabalho meio ~** I only work part-time; **viver de ~s** to live on one's wits; **ser** *ou* **ter ~** (*pessoa*) to be resourceful, have initiative

expedir [iʃpe'dʒiʳ] VT (*enviar*) to send, despatch; (*bilhete, passaporte, decreto*) to issue

expedito, -a [iʃpe'dʒitu, a] ADJ prompt, speedy; (*pessoa*) efficient

expelir [iʃpe'liʳ] VT (*expulsar*) to expel; (*sangue*) to spit

experiência [iʃpe'rjẽsja] F (*prática*) experience; (*prova*) experiment, test; **em ~** on trial

experienciar [iʃperjẽ'sjaʳ] VT to experience

experiente [iʃpe'rjẽtʃi] ADJ experienced

experimentação [iʃperimẽta'sãw] F experimentation

experimentado, -a [iʃperimẽ'tadu, a] ADJ (*experiente*) experienced; (*testado*) tried; (*provado*) tested

experimental [iʃperimẽ'taw] (*pl* -ais) ADJ experimental

experimentar [iʃperimẽ'taʳ] VT (*comida*) to taste; (*vestido*) to try on; (*pôr à prova*) to try out, test; (*conhecer pela experiência*) to experience; (*sofrer*) to suffer, undergo; **~ fazer algo** to try doing sth, have a go at doing sth; **experimento** [iʃperi'mẽtu] M (*científico*) experiment

expiar [iʃ'pjaʳ] VT to atone for

expiatório, -a [iʃpja'tɔrju, a] ADJ *v* **bode**

expilo *etc* [iʃ'pilu] VB *v* **expelir**

expiraçao [iʃpira'sãw] (*pl* -ões) F (*de ar*) exhalation; (*termo*) expiry

expirar [iʃpi'raʳ] VT (*ar*) to exhale, breathe out ■ VI (*morrer*) to die; (*terminar*) to end

explanação [iʃplana'sãw] (*pl* -ões) F explanation

explanar [iʃpla'naʳ] VT to explain

explicação [iʃplika'sãw] (*pl* -ões) F explanation; (*PT: lição*) private lesson

explicar [iʃpli'kaʳ] VT, VI to explain; **explicar-se** VR to explain o.s.; **isto não se explica** this does not make sense

explicável [iʃpli'kavew] (*pl* -eis) ADJ explicable, explainable

explícito, -a [iʃ'plisitu, a] ADJ explicit, clear

explodir [iʃplo'dʒiʳ] VT (*bomba*) to explode ■ VI to explode, blow up

exploração [iʃplora'sãw] F (*de um país*) exploration; (*abuso*) exploitation; (*de uma mina*) running

explorador, a [iʃplora'doʳ(a)] ADJ exploitative ■ M/F (*descobridor*) explorer; (*de outros*) exploiter

explorar [iʃplo'raʳ] VT (*região*) to explore; (*mina*) to work, run; (*ferida*) to probe; (*trabalhadores etc*) to exploit

explosão [iʃplo'zãw] (*pl* -ões) F explosion, blast; (*fig*) outburst; **explosivo, -a** [iʃplo'zivu, a] ADJ explosive; (*pessoa*) hot-headed ■ M explosive

explosões [iʃplo'sõjʃ] FPL *de* **explosão**

Expoagro [eʃpu'agru] ABR F = **Exposição Agropecuária Internacional do Rio de Janeiro**

expor [iʃ'poʳ] (*irreg*) VT to expose; (*a vida*) to risk; (*teoria*) to explain; (*revelar*) to reveal; (*mercadorias*) to display; (*quadros*) to exhibit; **expor-se** VR to expose o.s.; **~(-se) a algo** to expose (o.s.) to sth; **seu rosto expõe sinais de cansaço** his face shows signs of tiredness

exportação [iʃpoxta'sãw] F (*ato*) export(ing); (*mercadorias*) exports *pl*

exportador, a [iʃpoxta'doʳ(a)] ADJ exporting ■ M/F exporter

exportar [iʃpox'taʳ] VT to export

expôs *etc* [iʃ'poʃ] VB *v* **expor**

exposição [iʃpozi'sãw] (*pl* -ões) F (*exibição*) exhibition; (*explicação*) explanation; (*declaração*) statement; (*narração*) account; (*Foto*) exposure

expositor, a [iʃpozi'toʳ(a)] M/F exhibitor

exposto, -a [iʃ'poʃtu, 'poʃta] PP *de* **expor** ■ ADJ (*lugar*) exposed; (*quadro, mercadoria*) on show *ou* display ■ M: **o acima ~** the above; **estar ~ a algo** to be open *ou* exposed to sth

expressão [iʃpre'sãw] (*pl* -ões) F expression

expressar [iʃpre'saʳ] VT to express; **expressar-se** VR to express o.s.

expressividade [iʃpresivi'dadʒi] F expressiveness

expressivo, -a [iʃpre'sivu, a] ADJ expressive; (*pessoa*) demonstrative

expresso, -a [iʃ'prɛsu, a] PP *de* **exprimir** ■ ADJ (*manifesto*) definite, clear; (*trem, ordem, carta*) express ■ M express

expressões [iʃpre'sõjʃ] FPL *de* **expressão**

exprimir [iʃpri'miʳ] VT to express; **exprimir-se** VR to express o.s.

expropriar [iʃpro'prjaʳ] VT to expropriate

expugnar [iʃpugi'naʳ] VT to take by storm

expulsado, -a [iʃpuw'sadu, a] PP *de* **expulsar**

expulsão [iʃpul'sãw] (*pl* -ões) F expulsion; (*Esporte*) sending off

expulsar [iʃpuw'saʳ] VT to expel; (*de uma festa, clube etc*) to throw out; (*inimigo*) to drive out; (*estrangeiro*) to expel, deport; (*jogador*) to send off

expulso, -a [iʃ'puwsu, a] PP *de* **expulsar**

expulsões [iʃpul'sõjʃ] FPL *de* **expulsão**

expunha *etc* [iʃ'puɲa] VB V **expor**

expurgar [iʃpux'gaʳ] VT to expurgate

expus *etc* [iʃ'puʃ] VB V **expor**

expuser *etc* [iʃpu'zeʳ] VB V **expor**

êxtase ['eʃtazi] M ecstasy; (*transe*) trance; **estar em ~** to be in a trance

extasiado, -a [iʃta'zjadu, a] ADJ entranced

extensão [iʃtẽ'sãw] (*pl* -ões) F (*ger, Tel*) extension; (*de uma empresa*) expansion; (*terreno*) expanse; (*tempo*) length, duration; (*de conhecimentos*) extent

extensivo, -a [iʃtẽ'sivu, a] ADJ extensive; **ser ~ a** to extend to

extenso, -a [iʃ'tẽsu, a] ADJ (*amplo*) extensive, wide; (*comprido*) long; (*conhecimentos*) extensive; (*artigo*) full, comprehensive; **por ~** in full

extensões [iʃtẽ'sõjʃ] FPL *de* **extensão**

extenuado, -a [iʃte'nwadu, a] ADJ (*esgotado*) worn out

extenuante [iʃte'nwãtʃi] ADJ exhausting; (*debilitante*) debilitating

extenuar [iʃte'nwaʳ] VT to exhaust; (*debilitar*) to weaken

exterior [iʃte'rjoʳ] ADJ (*de fora*) outside, exterior; (*aparência*) outward; (*comércio*) foreign ▪ M (*da casa*) outside; (*aspecto*) outward appearance; **do ~** (*do estrangeiro*) from abroad; **no ~** abroad

exteriorizar [iʃterjori'zaʳ] VT to show, manifest

exteriormente [iʃterjox'mẽtʃi] ADV on the outside

exterminação [iʃtexmina'sãw] F extermination

exterminar [iʃtexmi'naʳ] VT (*inimigo*) to wipe out, exterminate; (*acabar com*) to do away with

extermínio [iʃtex'minju] M extermination, wiping out

externato [iʃtex'natu] M day school

externo, -a [iʃ'tɛxnu, a] ADJ external; (*aparente*) outward; **aluno ~** day pupil; **"para uso ~"** "external use only"

extinção [iʃtʃĩ'sãw] F extinction

extinguir [iʃtʃĩ'giʳ] VT (*fogo*) to put out, extinguish; (*um povo*) to wipe out; **extinguir-se** VR (*fogo, luz*) to go out; (*Bio*) to become extinct

extinto, -a [iʃ'tʃĩtu, a] ADJ (*fogo*) extinguished; (*língua*) dead; (*animal, vulcão*) extinct; (*associação etc*) defunct; (*pessoa*) dead; **extintor** [iʃtʃĩ'toʳ] M (fire) extinguisher

extirpar [iʃtix'paʳ] VT (*desarraigar*) to uproot; (*corrupção*) to eradicate; (*tumor*) to remove

extorquir [iʃtox'kiʳ] VT to extort

extorsão [iʃtox'sãw] F extortion

extorsivo, -a [iʃtox'sivu, a] ADJ extortionate

extra ['eʃtra] ADJ extra ▪ M/F extra person; (*Teatro*) extra; v *tb* **hora**

extração [iʃtra'sãw] (PT -cç-, *pl* -ões) F extraction; (*de loteria*) draw

extraconjugal [eʃtrakõʒu'gaw] (*pl* -ais) ADJ extramarital

extracto [iʃ'tratu] (PT) M = **extrato**

extracurricular [eʃtrakuxiku'laʳ] ADJ extracurricular

extradição [eʃtradʒi'sãw] F extradition

extraditar [eʃtradʒi'taʳ] VT to extradite

extrafino, -a [eʃtra'finu, a] ADJ extra high-quality

extrair [iʃtra'jiʳ] VT to extract, take out

extra-oficial (*pl* -ciais) ADJ unofficial

extraordinário, -a [iʃtraoxdʒi'narju, a] ADJ extraordinary; (*despesa*) extra; (*reunião*) special; **nada de ~** nothing out of the ordinary

extrapolar [iʃtrapo'laʳ] VT to extrapolate

extraterrestre [eʃtrate'xeʃtri] ADJ extraterrestrial

extrato [iʃ'tratu] M extract; (*resumo*) summary; **~ (bancário)** (bank) statement

extravagância [iʃtrava'gãsja] F extravagance; **extravagante** [iʃtrava'gãtʃi] ADJ extravagant; (*roupa*) outlandish; (*conduta*) wild

extravasar [iʃtrava'zaʳ] VI to overflow

extraviado, -a [iʃtra'vjadu, a] ADJ lost, missing

extraviar [iʃtra'vjaʳ] VT (*perder*) to mislay; (*pessoa*) to lead astray; (*dinheiro*) to embezzle; **extraviar-se** VR to get lost; **extravio** [iʃtra'viu] M (*perda*) loss; (*roubo*) embezzlement; (*fig*) deviation

extremado, -a [iʃtre'madu, a] ADJ extreme

extremar-se [iʃtre'maxsi] VR to do one's utmost, make every effort; (*distinguir-se*) to distinguish o.s.; **~ em gentilezas** to show extreme kindness

extrema-unção (*pl* extrema-unções) F (*Rel*) extreme unction

extremidade [iʃtremi'dadʒi] F extremity; (*do dedo*) tip; (*ponta*) end; (*beira*) edge

extremo, -a [iʃ'trɛmu, a] ADJ extreme ▪ M extreme; **extremos** MPL (*carinho*) doting *sg*; (*descomedimento*) extremes; **ao ~** extremely; **de um ~ a outro** from one extreme to another

extremoso, -a [iʃtre'mozu, ɔza] ADJ doting

extroversão [eʃtrovex'sãw] F extroversion

extroverso, -a [eʃtro'vɛxsu, a] ADJ extrovert

extroverter-se [eʃtrovex'texsi] VR to be outgoing

extrovertido, -a [eʃtrovex'tʃidu, a] ADJ extrovert, outgoing ▪ M/F extrovert

exu [e'ʃu] M devil (*in voodoo rituals*)

exuberância [ezube'rãsja] F exuberance

exuberante [ezube'rãtʃi] ADJ exuberant

exultação [ezuwta'sãw] F joy, exultation

exultante [ezuw'tãtʃi] ADJ jubilant, exultant

exultar [ezuw'taʳ] VI to rejoice

exumar [ezu'maʳ] VT (*corpo*) to exhume; (*fig*) to dig up

ex-voto M votive offering

F, f ['ɛfi] (pl **fs**) M F, f; **F de Francisco** F for Frederick (Brit) ou fox (US)

f ABR = **folha**

F-1 ABR = **Fórmula Um**

fá [fa] M (Mús) F

fã [fã] (col) M/F fan

FAB ['fabi] ABR F = **Força Aérea Brasileira**

fábrica ['fabrika] F factory; ~ **de cerveja** brewery; ~ **de conservas** cannery; ~ **de papel** paper mill; **a preço de** ~ wholesale

fabricação [fabrika'sãw] F manufacture; **de** ~ **caseira/própria** home-made/own-brand; ~ **em série** mass production

fabricante [fabri'kãtʃi] M/F manufacturer

fabricar [fabri'ka^r] VT to manufacture, make; (inventar) to fabricate

fabrico [fa'briku] M production

fabril [fa'briw] (pl -**is**) ADJ: **indústria** ~ manufacturing industry

fábula ['fabula] F fable; (conto) tale; (BR: grande quantia) fortune

fabuloso, -a [fabu'lozu, ɔza] ADJ fabulous

faca ['faka] F knife; **é uma** ~ **de dois gumes** (fig) it's a two-edged sword; **entrar na** ~ (col) to be operated on, to go under the knife; **ter a** ~ **e o queijo na mão** (fig) to have things in hand

facada [fa'kada] F stab, cut; **dar uma facada em alguém** to stab sb; (fig: col) to touch sb for money

façanha [fa'saɲa] F exploit, deed

facão [fa'kãw] (pl -**ões**) M carving knife; (para cortar o mato) machete

facção [fak'sãw] (pl -**ões**) F faction

faccioso, -a [fak'ajozu, ɔza] ADJ factious

facções [fak'sõjʃ] FPL de **facção**

face ['fasi] F (rosto, de moeda) face; (bochecha) cheek; **em** ~ **de** in view of; **fazer** ~ **a** to face up to; ~ **a** ~ face to face; **disquete de** ~ **simples/dupla** (Comput) single-/double-sided disk

faceiro, -a [fa'sejru, a] ADJ (elegante) smart; (alegre) cheerful

fáceis ['fasejʃ] ADJ PL de **fácil**

faceta [fa'seta] F facet

fachada [fa'ʃada] F façade, front; (col: rosto) face, mug (col)

facho ['faʃu] M beam

facial [fa'sjaw] (pl -**ais**) ADJ facial

fácil ['fasiw] (pl -**eis**) ADJ easy; (temperamento, pessoa) easy-going; (mulher) easy ■ ADV easily; **facilidade** [fasili'dadʒi] F ease; (jeito) facility; **facilidades** FPL (recursos) facilities; **ter facilidade para algo** to have a talent ou a facility for sth; **com facilidade** easily

facílimo, -a [fa'silimu, a] ADJ SUPERL de **fácil**

facilitação [fasilita'sãw] F facilitation; (fornecimento) provision

facilitar [fasili'ta^r] VT to facilitate, make easy; (fornecer): ~ **algo a alguém** to provide sb with sth ■ VI (agir sem cautela) to be careless

facinora [fa'sinora] M criminal

fã-clube (pl **fãs-clubes**) M fan club

faço etc ['fasu] VB V **fazer**

facões [fa'kõjʃ] FPL de **facão**

fac-símile [fak-] (pl -**s**) M (cópia) facsimile; (carta) fax; (máquina) fax (machine); **enviar por** ~ to fax

factício, -a [fak'tʃisju, a] ADJ unnatural

facto ['faktu] (PT) M = **fato**

factor [fak'to^r] (PT) M = **fator**

factótum [fak'tɔtũ] M factotum

factual [fak'twaw] (pl -**ais**) ADJ factual

factura etc [fak'tura] (PT) = **fatura** etc

faculdade [fakuw'dadʒi] F faculty; (poder) power; (BR: escola) university, college; (corpo docente) teaching staff (Brit), faculty (US); **fazer** ~ to go to university ou college

facultar [fakuw'ta^r] VT (permitir) to allow; (conceder) to grant

facultativo, -a [fakuwta'tʃivu, a] ADJ optional ■ M/F doctor

fada ['fada] F fairy; **conto de** ~**s** fairy tale

fadado, -a [fa'dadu, a] ADJ destined

fada-madrinha (pl **fadas-madrinhas**) F fairy godmother

fadiga [fa'dʒiga] F fatigue

fadista [fa'dʒiʃta] M/F "fado" singer ■ M (PT) ruffian

NB: European Portuguese adds the following consonants to certain words: **b** (sú(b)dito, su(b)til); **c** (a(c)ção, a(c)cionista, a(c)to); **m** (inde(m)ne); **p** (ado(p)çã, ado(p)tar); for further details see p. xiii.

fado ['fadu] M fate; (canção) traditional song of Portugal

● **FADO**
●
● The best-known musical form in Portugal is
● the melancholic fado, which is traditionally
● sung by a soloist (known as a fadista)
● accompanied by the Portuguese guitarra.
● There are two main types of fado: Coimbra
● fado is traditionally sung by men, and is
● considered to be more cerebral than the fado
● from Lisbon, which is sung by both men
● and women. The theme is nearly always one
● of deep nostalgia known as saudade, and the
● harsh reality of life.

Faferj [fa'fɛxʒi] ABR F = **Federação das Associaçes das Favelas do Estado do Rio de Janeiro**
fagueiro, -a [fa'gejru, a] ADJ (contente) happy; (agradável) pleasant
fagulha [fa'guʌa] F spark
fahrenheit [farẽ'ajtʃi] ADJ INV Fahrenheit
faia ['faja] F beech (tree)
faina ['fajna] F toil, work; (tarefa) task, job
fair-play ['fɛxplej] M fair play
faisão [faj'zãw] (pl -ães) M pheasant
faísca [fa'iʃka] F spark; (brilho) flash
faiscante [faj'ʃkãtʃi] ADJ flashing; (fogo) flickering
faiscar [fajʃ'ka'] VI to sparkle; (brilhar) to flash
faisões [faj'zõjʃ] MPL de **faisão**
faixa ['fajʃa] F (cinto, Judô) belt; (tira) strip; (área) zone; (Auto: pista) lane; (BR: para pedestres) zebra crossing (Brit), crosswalk (US); (Med) bandage; (num disco) track; ~ **etária** age group
faixa-título (pl faixas-títulos) F (Mús) title track
fajuto, -a [fa'ʒutu, a] (col) ADJ (pão) rough; (falso: nota) fake
fala ['fala] F speech; **chamar às ~s** to call to account; **sem ~** speechless; **perder a ~** to be struck dumb
falação [fala'sãw] (pl -ões) F (ato) talk; (discurso) speech
falácia [fa'lasja] F fallacy
falações [fala'sõjʃ] FPL de **falação**
faladeira [fala'dejra] F de **falador**
falado, -a [fa'ladu, a] ADJ (caso etc) talked about, much discussed; (famoso) well-known; (de má fama) notorious; (Cinema) talking
falador, -deira [fala'do'] ADJ talkative ■ M/F chatterbox
falante [fa'lãtʃi] ADJ talkative
falar [fa'la'] VT (língua) to speak; (besteira etc) to talk; (dizer) to say; (verdade, mentira) to tell ■ VI to speak, talk; (discursar) to speak; **falar-se** VR to talk to one another; ~ **algo a alguém** to tell sb sth; ~ **que** to say that; ~ **de** ou **em algo** to talk about sth; ~ **com alguém** to talk to sb; **por ~ em speaking of; por ~ nisso** by the way; **sem ~ em** not to mention; ~ **alto** to talk loudly; ~ **alto**

com alguém (fig) to give sb a good talking-to; **sua consciência falou mais alto** his conscience got the better of him; **falou!**, **'tá falado!** (col) OK!; **falando sério** ... but seriously ...; ~ **sozinho** to talk to o.s.; **ele está falando da boca para fora** (col) he's just saying that, he doesn't mean it; **ele falou por** ~ he was just saying that; **dar que** ~ to cause a stir; ~ **para dentro** to talk into one's beard; ~ **pelos cotovelos** to talk one's head off; **eles não se falam** (estão de mal) they are not speaking to one another; **nem se fala!** definitely not!
falatório [fala'tɔrju] M (ruído de vozes) voices pl, talking; (falar demorado) diatribe; (maledicência) rumour (Brit), rumor (US)
falaz [fa'laʒ] ADJ deceptive, misleading; (falso) false
falcão [faw'kãw] (pl -ões) M falcon
falcatrua [fawka'trua] F fraud
falcões [faw'kõjʃ] MPL de **falcão**
falecer [fale'se'] VI to die
falecido, -a [fale'sidu, a] ADJ dead, late ■ M/F deceased
falecimento [falesi'mẽtu] M death
falência [fa'lẽsja] F bankruptcy; **abrir** ~ to declare o.s. bankrupt; **ir à** ~ to go bankrupt; **levar à** ~ to bankrupt
falésia [fa'lɛzja] F cliff
falha ['faʌa] F (defeito, Geo etc) fault; (lacuna) omission; (de caráter) flaw
falhar [fa'ʌa'] VI to fail; (não acertar) to miss; (errar) to be wrong; **o motor está falhando** the engine is missing; (ao telefone) break up; **sua voz está falhando** you're breaking up
falho, -a ['faʌu, a] ADJ faulty; (deficiente) wanting
fálico, -a ['faliku, a] ADJ phallic
falido, -a [fa'lidu, a] ADJ, M/F bankrupt
falir [fa'li'] VI to fail; (Com) to go bankrupt
falível [fa'livew] (pl -eis) ADJ fallible
falo ['falu] M phallus
falsário, -a [faw'sarju, a] M/F forger
falsear [faw'sja'] VT (forjar) to forge; (falsificar) to falsify; (verdade) to twist; **o pé** to blunder
falseta [faw'seta] (col) F dirty trick
falsete [faw'setʃi] M falsetto
falsidade [fawsi'dadʒi] F falsehood; (fingimento) pretence (Brit), pretense (US); (mentira) lie
falsificação [fawsifika'sãw] (pl -ões) F (ato) falsification; (efeito) forgery; (falsa interpretação) misrepresentation
falsificador, a [fawsifika'do'(a)] M/F forger
falsificações [fawsifika'sõjʃ] FPL de **falsificação**
falsificar [fawsifi'ka'] VT (forjar) to forge; (falsear) to falsify; (adulterar) to adulterate; (desvirtuar) to misrepresent
falso, -a ['fawsu, a] ADJ false; (fraudulento) dishonest; (errôneo) wrong; (jóia, moeda, quadro) fake; (pessoa: insincero) two-faced; **pisar em** ~ to blunder
falta ['fawta] F (carência) lack; (ausência) absence; (defeito, culpa) fault; (Futebol) foul; **por** ou **na** ~ **de** for lack of; **sem** ~ without fail; **cometer/**

cobrar uma ~ (*Futebol*) to commit a foul/take a free kick; **estar em** ~ **com alguém** to feel guilty about sb; **fazer** ~ to be lacking, be needed; **ela faz** ~ she is missed; **este livro não vai te fazer** ~? won't you need this book?; **sentir** ~ **de alguém/algo** to miss sb/sth; **ter** ~ **de** to lack, be in need of; ~ **de água** water shortage; ~ **de ânimo** lack of enthusiasm; ~ **de educação** *ou* **modos** rudeness; ~ **de tato** tactlessness

faltar [faw'ta^r] VI (*escassear*) to be lacking, be wanting; (*pessoa*) to be absent; (*falhar*) to fail; ~ **ao trabalho** to be absent from work; ~ **à palavra** to break one's word; **falta pouco para ... it won't be long until ...; falta uma semana para nossas férias** it's only a week until our holidays; **faltam 10 minutos para as 3** it's ten minutes to three; **faltam 3 páginas (para eu acabar)** there are 3 pages to go (before I finish); **faltam chegar duas pessoas** two people are still to come; **falta fazermos mais algumas coisas** there are still a few things for us to do; **só faltava essa!** that's all I (*ou* we *etc*) needed!; **nada me falta** I have all I need

falto, -a ['fawtu, a] ADJ: ~ **de** lacking in, deficient in

faltoso, -a [faw'tozu, ɔza] ADJ (*culpado*) at fault; (*que costuma faltar*) frequently absent

fama ['fama] F (*renome*) fame; (*reputação*) reputation; **ter** ~ **de (ser) generoso** to be said to be generous; **de** ~ famous; **de má** ~ notorious, of ill repute

Famerj [fa'mɛxʒi] ABR F = **Federação das Associações de Moradores do Estado do Rio de Janeiro**

famigerado, -a [famiʒe'radu, a] ADJ (*malfeitor*) notorious; (*autor etc*) famous

família [fa'milja] F family; (*Comput*) font ■ ADJ INV (*col: pessoa*) decent; (*: festa*) well-behaved; **de boa** ~ from a good family; **estar em** ~ to be one of the family, be among friends; **isso é de** ~ this runs in the family, this is a family trait

familiar [fami'lja^r] ADJ (*da família*) family *atr*; (*conhecido*) familiar ■ M/F relation, relative; **familiaridade** [familjari'dadʒi] F familiarity; (*sem-cerimônia*) informality

familiarização [familjariza'sãw] F familiarization

familiarizar [familjari'za^r] VT to familiarize; **familiarizar-se** VR: **familiarizar-se com algo** to familiarize o.s. with sth

faminto, -a [fa'mĩtu, a] ADJ hungry; (*fig*): ~ **de** eager for

famoso, -a [fa'mozu, ɔza] ADJ famous

fanático, -a [fa'natʃiku, a] ADJ fanatical ■ M/F fanatic

fanatismo [fana'tʃiʒmu] M fanaticism

fanhoso, -a [fa'ɲozu, ɔza] ADJ (*pessoa*) with a nasal voice; (*voz*) nasal; **falar** *ou* **ser** ~ to talk through one's nose

faniquito [fani'kitu] (*col*) M attack of nerves

fantasia [fãta'zia] F fantasy; (*imaginação*) imagination; (*capricho*) fancy; (*traje*) fancy dress; **jóia (de)** ~ (piece of) costume jewellery (*Brit*) *ou* jewelry (*US*)

fantasiar [fãta'zja^r] VT to imagine ■ VI to daydream; **fantasiar-se** VR to dress up (in fancy dress)

fantasioso, -a [fãta'zjozu, ɔza] ADJ imaginative

fantasista [fãta'ziʃta] ADJ imaginative

fantasma [fã'taʒma] M ghost; (*alucinação*) illusion

fantasmagórico, -a [fãtazma'gɔriku, a] ADJ ghostly

fantástico, -a [fã'taʃtʃiku, a] ADJ fantastic; (*ilusório*) imaginary; (*incrível*) unbelievable

fantoche [fã'toʃi] M puppet

fanzoca [fã'zɔka] (*col*) M/F great fan

faqueiro [fa'kejru] M (*jogo de talheres*) set of cutlery; (*pessoa*) cutler

faquir [fa'ki^r] M fakir

faraó [fara'ɔ] M pharaoh

faraônico, -a [fara'oniku, a] ADJ (*fig: obra*) large-scale

farda ['faxda] F uniform

fardar [fax'da^r] VT to dress in uniform

fardo ['faxdu] M bundle; (*carga*) load; (*fig*) burden

farei *etc* [fa'rej] VB V **fazer**

farejar [fare'ʒa^r] VT to sniff around ■ VI to sniff

farelo [fa'rɛlu] M (*de pão*) crumb; (*de madeira*) sawdust; ~ **de trigo** bran

farfalhante [faxfa'ʎãtʃi] ADJ rustling

farfalhar [faxfa'ʎa^r] VI to rustle

farfalhudo, -a [faxfa'ʎudu, a] ADJ ostentatious

farináceo, -a [fari'nasju, a] ADJ (*alimento*) starchy; (*molho etc*) floury

farináceos [fari'nasjuʃ] MPL (*alimentos*) starchy foods

faringe [fa'rĩʒi] F pharynx

faringite [farĩ'ʒitʃi] F pharyngitis

farinha [fa'riɲa] F: ~ **(de mesa)** (manioc) flour; ~ **de arroz** rice flour; ~ **de osso** bone meal; ~ **de rosca** breadcrumbs *pl*; ~ **de trigo** plain flour

farmacêutico, -a [faxma'sewtʃiku, a] ADJ pharmaceutical ■ M/F pharmacist, chemist (*Brit*)

farmácia [fax'masja] F pharmacy, chemist's (shop) (*Brit*); (*ciência*) pharmacy

farnel [fax'nɛw] (*pl* **-éis**) M (*provisões*) provisions *pl*; (*saco*) food parcel

faro ['faru] M sense of smell; (*fig*) flair

faroeste [fa'rwɛʃtʃi] M (*filme*) western; (*região*) wild west

farofa [fa'rɔfa] F (*Culin*) side dish based on manioc flour

farofeiro, -a [faro'fejru, a] M/F picnicker (*who comes to the beach from far away*)

NB: *European Portuguese adds the following consonants to certain words*: **b** (sú(b)dito, su(b)til); **c** (a(c)ção, a(c)cionista, a(c)to); **m** (inde(m)ne); **p** (ado(p)çã, ado(p)tar); *for further details see p. xiii.*

farol [fa'rɔw] (pl **-óis**) M lighthouse; (Auto)
headlight; (col) bragging; **~ alto** (Auto) full (Brit)
ou high (US) beam; **~ baixo** dipped headlights
pl (Brit), dimmed beam (US); **contar ~** (col) to
brag

faroleiro [faro'lejru] M lighthouse keeper; (col)
braggart

farolete [faro'letʃi] M (Auto: dianteiro) sidelight;
(tb: **farolete traseiro**) tail-light

farpa ['faxpa] F barb; (estilha) splinter

farpado, -a [fax'padu, a] ADJ: **arame ~** barbed
wire

farra ['faxa] F binge, spree; **cair na ~** to go on
the razzle; **só de** ou **por ~** just for the fun of it

farrapo [fa'xapu] M rag; **ela parecia um ~** she
looked like a tramp; **esta blusa está um ~** this
blouse is a sight

farrear [fa'xja^r] VI to go on a spree

farripas [fa'xipaʃ] FPL wisps of hair

farrista [fa'xiʃta] ADJ fun-loving ■ M/F party
animal (col)

farsa ['faxsa] F farce; **farsante** [fax'sãtʃi] M/F
joker; (pessoa sem palavra) smooth operator

farta ['faxta] F: **comer à ~** to eat one's fill

fartar [fax'ta^r] VT (saciar) to satiate; (encher) to fill
up; **fartar-se** VR to gorge o.s.; **~-se de** (cansar-se)
to get fed up with; **me fartei (de comer)** I'm
full up

farto, -a ['faxtu, a] ADJ full, satiated; (abundante)
plentiful; (aborrecido) fed up; **cabeleira farta**
full head of hair, shock of hair

fartum [fax'tũ] (pl **-ns**) M stench

fartura [fax'tura] F abundance, plenty

fascículo [fa'sikulu] M (de publicação) instalment
(Brit), installment (US)

fascinação [fasina'sãw] F fascination; **ter ~ por
alguém** to be infatuated with sb

fascinante [fasi'nãtʃi] ADJ fascinating

fascinar [fasi'na^r] VT to fascinate; (encantar) to
charm; **fascínio** [fa'sinju] M fascination

fascismo [fa'siʒmu] M fascism

fascista [fa'siʃta] ADJ, M/F fascist

fase ['fazi] F phase; (etapa) stage

fashion ['fɛʃjõ] (col) ADJ trendy

fastidioso, -a [faʃtʃi'dʒjozu, ɔza] ADJ tedious;
(enfadonho) annoying

fastígio [faʃ'tʃiʒju] M (fig) height

fastio [faʃ'tʃiu] M lack of appetite; (tédio)
boredom

fatal [fa'taw] (pl **-ais**) ADJ (mortal) fatal; (inevitável)
fateful; **fatalidade** [fatali'dadʒi] F (destino) fate;
(desgraça) disaster

fatalista [fata'liʃta] ADJ fatalistic ■ M/F
fatalist

fatalmente [fataw'mẽtʃi] ADV (de modo fatal)
fatally; (certamente) inevitably

fatia [fa'tʃia] F slice

fatídico, -a [fa'tʃidʒiku, a] ADJ fateful

fatigante [fatʃi'gãtʃi] ADJ tiring; (aborrecido)
tiresome

fatigar [fatʃi'ga^r] VT to tire; (aborrecer) to bore;
fatigar-se VR to get tired

Fátima ['fatima] F see below

fato ['fatu] M fact; (acontecimento) event; (PT:
traje) suit; **~ de banho** (PT) swimming costume
(Brit), bathing suit (US); **~ consumado** fait
accompli; **de ~** in fact, really; **o ~ é que ...** the
fact remains that ...; **chegar às vias de ~** to
come to blows

fator [fa'to^r] M factor

fatura [fa'tura] F bill, invoice

faturamento [fatura'mẽtu] M (Com: volume de
negócios) turnover; (faturar) invoicing

faturar [fatu'ra^r] VT to invoice; (dinheiro) to
make; (col: gol) to score, notch up ■ VI (col:
ganhar dinheiro): **~ (alto)** to rake it in; **~ algo a
alguém** to invoice sb for sth

fauna ['fawna] F fauna

fausto, -a ['fawʃtu, a] ADJ lucky ■ M luxury

fava ['fava] F (broad) bean; **mandar alguém às
~s** to send sb packing

favela [fa'vɛla] F slum, shanty town

favelado, -a [fave'ladu, a] M/F slum-dweller

favo ['favu] M honeycomb

favor [fa'vo^r] M favour (Brit), favor (US); **a ~ de** in
favo(u)r of; **em ~ de** on behalf of; **por ~** please;
fazer um ~ para alguém to do sb a favo(u)r;
faça ou **faz o ~ de ...** would you be so good
as to ..., kindly ...; **faça-me o ~!** (col) do me a
favo(u)r!; **ter a seu ~** to have to one's credit;
favorável [favo'ravew] (pl **-eis**) ADJ: **favorável
(a)** favourable (Brit) ou favorable (US) (to)

favorecer [favore'se^r] VT to favour (Brit), favor
(US); (beneficiar) to benefit; (suj: vestido) to suit;
(: retrato) to flatter

favoritismo [favori'tʃizmu] M favouritism (Brit),
favoritism (US)

favorito, -a [favo'ritu, a] ADJ, M/F favourite
(Brit), favorite (US)

faxina [fa'ʃina] F: **fazer ~** to clean up; **faxineiro,
-a** [faʃi'nejru, a] M/F (pessoa) cleaner

faz-de-conta [fajʒ-] M: **o ~** make-believe

fazedor, a [faze'do^r(a)] M/F maker

fazenda [fa'zẽda] F farm; (de café) plantation; (de
gado) ranch; (pano) cloth, fabric; (Econ) treasury,
exchequer (Brit); **fazendeiro** [fazẽ'dejru] M
farmer; (de café) plantation-owner; (de gado)
rancher, ranch-owner

 PALAVRA CHAVE

fazer [fa'ze^r] VT **1** (fabricar, produzir) to make;
(construir) to build; (pergunta) to ask; (poema,
música) to write; **fazer um filme/ruído** to make

a film/noise; **eu fiz o vestido** I made the dress **2** (*executar: trabalho etc*) to do; **o que você está fazendo?** what are you doing?; **fazer a comida** to do the cooking; **fazer o papel de** (*Teatro*) to play **3** (*estudos, alguns esportes*) to do; **fazer medicina/direito** to do *ou* study medicine/law; **fazer ioga/ginástica** to do yoga/keep-fit **4** (*transformar, tornar*): **sair o fará sentir melhor** going out will make him feel better; **sua partida fará o trabalho mais difícil** his departure will make work more difficult **5** (*como sustituto de vb*): **ele bebeu e eu fiz o mesmo** he drank and I did likewise **6: fazer anos, ele faz anos hoje** it's his birthday today; **fiz 30 anos ontem** I was 30 yesterday

■ VI **1** (*portar-se*) to act, behave; **fazer bem/mal** to do the right/wrong thing; **não fiz por mal** I didn't mean it; **faz como quem não sabe** act as if you don't know anything **2: fazer com que alguém faça algo** to make sb do sth

■ VB IMPESS **1: faz calor/frio** it's hot/cold **2** (*tempo*): **faz um ano** a year ago; **faz dois anos que ele se formou** it's two years since he graduated; **faz três meses que ele está aqui** he's been here for three months **3: não faz mal** never mind; **tanto faz** it's all the same

fazer-se VR **1: fazer-se de desentendido** to pretend not to understand **2: faz-se com ovos e leite** it's made with eggs and milk; **isso não se faz** that's not done

faz-tudo [faʒ-] M/F INV jack-of-all-trades
FBI ABR M (= *Federal Bureau of Investigation*) FBI
FC ABR M (= *Futebol Clube*) FC
FDLP ABR F (= *Frente Democrática para a Libertação da Palestina*) PFLP
fé [fɛ] F faith; (*crença*) belief; (*confiança*) trust; **de boa/má fé** in good/bad faith; **dar fé de** to bear witness to; **fazer fé em** to have faith in; **fé em Deus e pé na tábua** go for it
fealdade [feaw'dadʒi] F ugliness
FEB ['fɛbi] ABR F (= *Força Expedicionária Brasileira*) *force sent out in World War II*
FEBEM [fe'bẽ] (BR) ABR F (= *Fundação Estadual do Bem-Estar do Menor*) *reform school*
febrão [fe'brãw] (*pl* -ões) M raging fever
febre ['fɛbri] F fever; (*fig*) excitement; **~ amarela** yellow fever; **~ do feno** hay fever; **~ do poder** *etc* hunger for power *etc*; **febril** [fe'briw] (*pl* -is) ADJ feverish
febrões [fe'brõjʃ] MPL *de* **febrão**
fecal [fe'kaw] (*pl* -ais) ADJ V **matéria**
fechada [fe'ʃada] F: **dar uma ~ em alguém** (*Auto*) to cut sb up; **levar uma ~** to be cut up
fechado, -a [fe'ʃadu, a] ADJ shut, closed; (*pessoa*)

reserved; (*sinal*) red; (*luz, torneira*) off; (*tempo*) overcast; (*cara*) stern; **noite fechada** well into the night
fechadura [feʃa'dura] F (*de porta*) lock
fechamento [feʃa'mẽtu] M closure
fechar [fe'ʃaʳ] VT to close, shut; (*concluir*) to finish, conclude; (*luz, torneira*) to turn off; (*rua*) to close off; (*ferida*) to close up; (*bar, loja*) to close down; (*negócio*) to make; (*Auto*) to cut up ■ VI to close (up), shut; (*ferida*) to heal; (*sinal*) to turn red; to close down; (*tempo*) to cloud over; **fechar-se** VR to close, shut; (*pessoa*) to withdraw; **~-se no quarto** *etc* to shut o.s. away in one's room *etc*; **~ à chave** to lock; **~ a cara** to look annoyed; **ser de ~ o comércio** (*col*) to be a real show-stopper
fecho ['feʃu] M fastening; (*trinco*) latch; (*término*) close, closing; **~ ecler** zip fastener (*Brit*), zipper (*US*)
fécula ['fɛkula] F starch
fecundação [fekũda'sãw] F fertilization
fecundar [fekũ'daʳ] VT to fertilize, make fertile
fecundidade [fekũdʒi'dadʒi] F fertility
fecundo, -a [fe'kũdu, a] ADJ fertile; (*produtivo*) fruitful; (*fig*) prolific
fedelho, -a [fe'deʎu, a] M/F kid
feder [fe'deʳ] VI to stink; **não ~ nem cheirar** (*fig*) to be wishy-washy
federação [federa'sãw] (*pl* -ões) F federation
federal [fede'raw] (*pl* -ais) ADJ federal; (*col: grande*) huge
federativo, -a [federa'tʃivu, a] ADJ federal
fedor [fe'doʳ] M stench
fedorento, -a [fedo'rẽtu, a] ADJ stinking
FEEM (BR) ABR F (= *Fundação Estadual de Educação do Menor*) *children's home*
Feema (BR) ABR F (= *Fundação Estadual de Engenharia do Meio Ambiente*) *environmental protection agency*
feérico, -a [fe'ɛriku, a] ADJ magical
feição [fej'sãw] (*pl* -ões) F form, shape; (*caráter*) nature; (*modo*) manner; **feições** FPL (*face*) features; **à ~ de** in the manner of
feijão [fej'ʒãw] (*pl* -ões) M bean(s) (*pl*); (*preto*) black bean(s) (*pl*)
feijão-fradinho [-fra'dʒiɲu] (*pl* **feijões-fradinhos**) M black-eyed bean(s) (*pl*)
feijão-mulatinho [-mula'tʃiɲu] (*pl* **feijões-mulatinhos**) M red kidney bean(s) (*pl*)
feijão-preto (*pl* **feijões-pretos**) M black bean(s) (*pl*)
feijão-soja (*pl* **feijões-sojas**) M soya bean(s) (*pl*) (US), soybean(s) (*pl*) (US)
feijão-tropeiro [-tro'pejru] (*pl* **feijões-tropeiros**) M (*Culin*) bean stew
feijoada [fej'ʒwada] F (*Culin*) meat, rice and black beans
feijoeiro [fej'ʒwejru] M bean plant

NB: *European Portuguese adds the following consonants to certain words:* **b** (sú(b)dito, su(b)til); **c** (a(c)ção, a(c)cionista, a(c)to); **m** (inde(m)ne); **p** (ado(p)çã, ado(p)tar); *for further details see p. xiii.*

feijões [fej'ʒõjʃ] MPL *de* **feijão**

feio, -a ['feju, a] ADJ ugly; *(situação)* grim; *(atitude)* bad; *(tempo)* horrible ▪ ADV *(perder)* badly; **olhar ~** to give a filthy look; **fazer ~** to make a bad impression; **ficar ~** *(dar má impressão)* to look bad; *(situação)* to turn nasty; **quem ama o ~, bonito lhe parece** love is blind

feioso, -a [fe'jozu, ɔza] ADJ plain

feira ['fejra] F fair; *(mercado)* market; **fazer a ~** to go to market; **~ livre** market

feirante [fej'rãtʃi] M/F market trader, stallholder

feita ['fejta] F: **certa ~** once, on one occasion; **de uma ~** once and for all

feitiçaria [fejtʃisa'ria] F witchcraft, magic

feiticeira [fejtʃi'sejra] F witch

feiticeiro, -a [fejtʃi'sejru, a] ADJ bewitching, enchanting ▪ M wizard

feitiço [fej'tʃisu] M charm, spell; **virou o ~ contra o feiticeiro** *(fig)* the tables were turned

feitio [fej'tʃiu] M shape, pattern; *(caráter)* nature, manner; *(Tec)* workmanship

feito, -a ['fejtu, a] PP *de* **fazer** ▪ ADJ *(terminado)* finished, ready ▪ M act, deed; *(façanha)* feat ▪ CONJ like; **~ a mão** hand-made; **homem ~** grown man; **que é ~ dela?** what has become of her?; **bem ~ (por você)!** (it) serves you right!; **dito e ~** no sooner said than done; **estar ~** *(pessoa: ter dinheiro etc)* to have it made

feitor, a [fej'to'(a)] M/F administrator; *(capataz)* supervisor

feitura [fej'tura] F work

feiúra [fe'jura] F ugliness

feixe ['fejʃi] M bundle, bunch; *(Tec)* beam

fel [few] M bile, gall; *(fig)* bitterness; **esse remédio é um ~** that medicine is really bitter

felicidade [felisi'dadʒi] F happiness; *(sorte)* good luck; *(êxito)* success; **felicidades** FPL *(congratulações)* congratulations

felicíssimo, -a [feli'sisimu, a] ADJ SUPERL *de* **feliz**

felicitações [felisita'sõjʃ] FPL congratulations, best wishes

felicitar [felisi'ta'] VT: **~ alguém (por)** to congratulate sb (on)

felino, -a [fe'linu, a] ADJ feline; *(fig: traiçoeiro)* treacherous ▪ M feline

feliz [fe'liʒ] ADJ happy; *(afortunado)* lucky; *(idéia, sugestão)* timely; *(próspero)* successful; *(expressão)* fortunate; **~ aniversário/Natal!** happy birthday/Christmas!; **dar-se por ~** to think o.s. lucky

felizardo, -a [feli'zaxdu, a] M/F lucky devil

felizmente [feliʒ'mẽtʃi] ADV fortunately

felonia [felo'nia] F *(traição)* treachery

felpa ['fewpa] F *(de animais)* down; *(de tecido)* nap

felpudo, -a [few'pudu, a] ADJ *(penujento)* fuzzy; *(peludo)* downy

feltro ['fewtru] M felt

fêmea ['femja] F *(Bio, Bot)* female

feminil [femi'niw] *(pl* **-is***)* ADJ feminine

feminilidade [feminili'dadʒi] F femininity

feminino, -a [femi'ninu, a] ADJ feminine; *(sexo)* female; *(equipe, roupas)* women's ▪ M *(Ling)* feminine

feminis [femi'niʃ] ADJ PL *de* **feminil**

feminismo [femi'niʒmu] M feminism

feminista [femi'niʃta] ADJ, M/F feminist

fêmur ['femu'] M *(Anat)* femur

fenda ['fẽda] F slit, crack; *(Geo)* fissure

fender [fẽ'de'] VT, VI to split, crack

fenecer [fene'se'] VI to die; *(terminar)* to come to an end

feno ['fenu] M hay

fenomenal [fenome'naw] *(pl* **-ais***)* ADJ phenomenal; *(espantoso)* amazing; *(pessoa)* brilliant

fenômeno [fe'nomenu] M phenomenon

fera ['fɛra] F wild animal; *(fig: pessoa cruel)* beast; *(: pessoa severa)* hothead; **ser ~ em algo** to be brilliant at sth; **ficar uma ~ (com alguém)** *(fig)* to get mad (with sb)

féretro ['feretru] M coffin

feriado [fe'rjadu] M holiday *(Brit)*, vacation *(US)*; **~ bancário** bank *(Brit)* ou public holiday

férias ['fɛrjaʃ] FPL holidays, vacation *sg*; **de ~** on holiday; **tirar ~** to have ou take a holiday

ferida [fe'rida] F wound, injury; **tocar na ~** *(fig)* to hit home; *v tb* **ferido**

ferido, -a [fe'ridu, a] ADJ injured; *(em batalha)* wounded; *(magoado)* hurt ▪ M/F casualty

ferimento [feri'mẽtu] M injury; *(em batalha)* wound

ferino, -a [fe'rinu, a] ADJ *(cruel)* cruel; *(crítica, ironia)* biting

ferir [fe'ri'] VT to injure; *(tb fig)* to hurt; *(em batalha)* to wound; *(ofender)* to offend

fermentar [fexmẽ'ta'] VT to ferment; *(fig)* to excite ▪ VI to ferment

fermento [fex'mẽtu] M yeast; **~ em pó** baking powder

ferocidade [ferosi'dadʒi] F fierceness, ferocity

ferocíssimo, -a [fero'sisimu, a] ADJ SUPERL *de* **feroz**

feroz [fe'roʒ] ADJ fierce, ferocious; *(cruel)* cruel

ferrado, -a [fe'xadu, a] ADJ *(cavalo)* shod; *(col: sem saída)* done for; **~ no sono** sound asleep

ferradura [fexa'dura] F horseshoe

ferragem [fe'xaʒẽ] *(pl* **-ns***)* F *(peças)* hardware; *(guarnição)* metalwork; **loja de ferragens** ironmonger's *(Brit)*, hardware store

ferramenta [fexa'mẽta] F tool; **~ de busca** *(Comput)* search engine; *(caixa de ferramentas)* tool kit

ferrão [fe'xãw] *(pl* **-ões***)* M goad; *(de inseto)* sting

ferrar [fe'xa'] VT to spike; *(cavalo)* to shoe; *(gado)* to brand; **ferrar-se** VR *(col)* to fail

ferreiro [fe'xejru] M blacksmith

ferrenho, -a [fe'xeɲu, a] ADJ *(vontade)* iron; *(marxista etc)* staunch

férreo, -a ['fɛxju, a] ADJ iron *atr*; *(Quím)* ferrous; *(vontade)* iron; *(disciplina)* strict; **via férrea** railway *(Brit)*, railroad *(US)*

ferrete [fe'xetʃi] M branding iron; (fig) stigma

ferro ['fɛxu] M iron; **ferros** MPL (algemas) shackles, chains; ~ **batido** wrought iron; ~ **de passar** iron; ~ **fundido** cast iron; ~ **ondulado** corrugated iron; **a ~ e fogo** at all costs; **ninguém é/não sou de ~** (fig) we're all/I'm only human

ferrões [fe'xõjʃ] MPL de **ferrão**

ferrolho [fe'xoʎu] M (trinco) bolt

ferro-velho (pl **ferros-velhos**) M (pessoa) scrap metal dealer; (lugar) scrap metal yard; (sucata) scrap metal

ferrovia [fexo'via] F railway (Brit), railroad (US); **ferroviário, -a** [fexo'vjarju, a] ADJ railway atr (Brit), railroad atr (US) ■ M/F railway ou railroad worker

ferrugem [fe'xuʒẽ] F rust; (Bot) blight

fértil ['fɛxtʃiw] (pl **-eis**) ADJ fertile

fertilidade [fextʃili'dadʒi] F fertility; (abundância) fruitfulness

fertilizante [fextʃili'zãtʃi] ADJ fertilizing ■ M fertilizer

fertilizar [fextʃili'zaʳ] VT to fertilize

fervente [fex'vẽtʃi] ADJ boiling

ferver [fex'veʳ] VT, VI to boil; ~ **de raiva/ indignação** to seethe with rage/indignation; ~ **em fogo baixo** (Culin) to simmer

fervilhar [fexvi'ʎaʳ] VI (ferver) to simmer; (com excitação) to hum; (pulular): ~ **de** to swarm with

fervor [fex'voʳ] M fervour (Brit), fervor (US)

fervoroso, -a [fexvo'rozu, ɔza] ADJ fervent

fervura [fex'vura] F boiling

festa ['fɛʃta] F (reunião) party; (conjunto de ceremônias) festival; **festas** FPL (carícia) embrace; **boas ~s** Merry Christmas and a Happy New Year; **dia de ~** public holiday; **fazer ~ a alguém** to make a fuss of sb; **fazer ~(s) em alguém** to caress sb; **fazer a ~** (fig) to have a ball, have a whale of a time; ~ **caipira** hoedown; ~ **de arromba** (col) big party; ~ **de embalo** (col) wild party

festança [feʃ'tãsa] F big party

festeiro, -a [feʃ'tejru, a] ADJ party-going

festejar [feʃte'ʒaʳ] VT (celebrar) to celebrate; (acolher) to welcome, greet; **festejo** [feʃ'teʒu] M (festividade) festivity; (ato) celebration

festim [feʃ'tʃĩ] (pl **-ns**) M feast

festival [feʃtʃi'vaw] (pl **-ais**) M festival

festividade [feʃtʃivi'dadʒi] F festivity

festivo, -a [feʃ'tʃivu, a] ADJ festive

fetiche [fe'tʃiʃi] M fetish

fetichismo [fetʃi'ʃiʒmu] M fetishism

fetichista [fetʃi'ʃiʃta] ADJ fetishistic ■ M/F fetishist

fétido, -a ['fɛtʃidu, a] ADJ foul

feto ['fɛtu] M (Med) foetus (Brit), fetus (US); (Bot) fern

feudal [few'daw] (pl **-ais**) ADJ feudal

feudalismo [fewda'liʒmu] M feudalism

fev. ABR = **fevereiro**

fevereiro [feve'rejru] (PT **F-**) M February; v tb **julho**

fez [feʒ] VB v **fazer**

fezes ['fɛziʃ] FPL faeces (Brit), feces (US)

FGTS (BR) ABR M (= Fundo de Garantia por Tempo de Serviço) pension fund

FGV (BR) ABR F (= Fundação Getúlio Vargas) economic research agency

fiação [fja'sãw] (pl **-ões**) F spinning; (fábrica) textile mill; (Elet) wiring; **fazer a ~ da casa** to rewire the house

fiada ['fjada] F (fileira) row, line

fiado, -a ['fjadu, a] ADJ (a crédito) on credit ■ ADV: **comprar/vender ~** to buy/sell on credit

fiador, a [fja'doʳ(a)] M/F (Jur) guarantor; (Com) backer

fiambre ['fjãbri] M cold meat; (presunto) ham

fiança ['fjãsa] F guarantee; (Jur) bail; **prestar ~ por** to stand bail for; **sob ~** on bail

fiapo ['fjapu] M thread

fiar ['fjaʳ] VT (algodão etc) to spin; (confiar) to entrust; (vender a crédito) to sell on credit; **fiar-se** VR: **fiar-se em** to trust

fiasco ['fjaʃku] M fiasco

FIBGE ABR F = **Fundação do Instituto Brasileiro de Geografia e Estatística**

fibra ['fibra] F fibre (Brit), fiber (US); (fig): **pessoa de ~** person of character; ~ **ótica** optical fibre ou fiber

O PALAVRA CHAVE

ficar [fi'kaʳ] VI **1** (permanecer) to stay; (sobrar) to be left; **ficar perguntando/olhando** etc to keep asking/looking etc; **ficar por fazer** to have still to be done; **ficar para trás** to be left behind

2 (tornar-se) to become; **ficar cego/surdo/ louco** to go blind/deaf/mad; **fiquei contente ao saber da notícia** I was happy when I heard the news; **ficar com raiva/medo** to get angry/ frightened; **ficar de bem/mal com alguém** (col) to make up/fall out with sb

3 (posição) to be; **a casa fica ao lado da igreja** the house is next to the church; **ficar sentado/deitado** to be sitting down/lying down

4 (tempo: durar): **ele ficou duas horas para resolver** he took two hours to decide; (: ser adiado): **a reunião ficou para amanhã** the meeting was postponed until the following day

5: **ficar bem** (comportamento): **sua atitude não ficou bem** his (ou her etc) behaviour was inappropriate; (cor): **você fica bem em azul** blue suits you, you look good in blue; (roupa): **ficar bem para** to suit

6: **ficar bom** (de saúde) to be cured; (trabalho, foto

NB: European Portuguese adds the following consonants to certain words: **b** (sú(b)dito, su(b)til); **c** (a(c)ção, a(c)cionista, a(c)to); **m** (inde(m)ne); **p** (ado(p)çã, ado(p)tar); for further details see p. xiii.

etc) to turn out well
7: ficar de fazer algo (*combinar*) to arrange to
do sth; (*prometer*) to promise to do sth
8: ficar de pé to stand up

ficção [fik'sãw] F fiction
ficcionista [fiksjo'niʃta] M/F author, fiction
writer
ficha ['fiʃa] F (*tb*: ficha de telefone) token; (*tb*:
ficha de jogo) chip; (*de fichário*) (index) card;
(*Polícia*) record; (*PT*: Elet) plug; (*em loja, lanchonete*)
ticket; **dar a ~ de alguém** (*fig*: *col*) to give the
low-down on sb; **ter ~ na polícia** to have a
criminal record; **ter ~ limpa** (*col*) to have a
clean record; **~ de identidade** means *sg* of
identification, ID
fichar [fi'ʃaʳ] VT to file, index
fichário [fi'ʃarju] M (*móvel*) filing cabinet; (*caixa*)
card index; (*caderno*) file
ficheiro [fi'ʃejru] (PT) M = **fichário**
fictício, -a [fik'tʃisju, a] ADJ fictitious
FIDA (BR) ABR M = **Fundo Internacional para o
Desenvolvimento Agrícola**
fidalgo [fi'dawgu] M nobleman
fidedigno, -a [fide'dʒignu, a] ADJ trustworthy
fidelidade [fideli'dadʒi] F (*lealdade*) fidelity,
loyalty; (*exatidão*) accuracy
fidelíssimo, -a [fide'lisimu, a] ADJ SUPERL *de* **fiel**
fiduciário, -a [fidu'sjarju, a] ADJ (*companhia*)
trust *atr* ■ M/F trustee
fiéis [fjεjʃ] ADJ PL *de* **fiel** ■ MPL: **os ~** the faithful
fiel [fjεw] (*pl* -**éis**) ADJ (*leal*) faithful, loyal;
(*acurado*) accurate; (*que não falha*) reliable
Fiesp [fi'εʃpi] ABR F = **Federação das Indústrias
do Estado de São Paulo**
FIFA ['fifa] ABR F (= *Fédération Internationale de
Football Association*) FIFA
figa ['figa] F talisman; **fazer uma ~** to make
a *figa*, ≈ cross one's fingers; **de uma ~** (*col*)
damned
figada [fi'gada] F fig jelly
fígado ['figadu] M liver; **de maus ~s** (*genioso*)
bad-tempered; (*vingativo*) vindictive
figo ['figu] M fig; **figueira** [fi'gejra] F fig tree
figura [fi'gura] F figure; (*forma*) form, shape;
(*Ling*) figure of speech; (*aspecto*) appearance;
(*Cartas*) face card; (*ilustração*) picture; (*col*: *pessoa*)
character; **fazer ~** to cut a figure; **fazer má ~** to
make a bad impression; **mudar de ~** to take
on a new aspect; **ser uma ~ difícil** (*col*) to be
difficult to get hold of; **ele é uma ~** (*col*) he's a
real character
figura-chave (*pl* figuras-chave) F key figure
figurado, -a [figu'radu, a] ADJ figurative
figurante [figu'rãtʃi] M/F (*Cinema*) extra
figurão [figu'rãw] (*pl* -ões) M big shot
figurar [figu'raʳ] VI (*ator*) to appear; (*fazer parte*):
~ (entre/em) to figure *ou* appear (among/in)
■ VT (*imaginar*) to imagine; **ela figura ter
menos de 30 anos** she looks younger than 30
figurinha [figu'riɲa] F sticker; **~ difícil** (*col*)
person who is difficult to get hold of

figurinista [figuri'niʃta] M/F fashion designer
figurino [figu'rinu] M model; (*revista*) fashion
magazine; (*Cinema, Teatro*) costume design;
(*exemplo*) example; **como manda o ~** as it
should be
figurões [figu'rõjʃ] MPL *de* **figurão**
Fiji [fi'ʒi] M Fiji
fila ['fila] F row, line; (BR: *fileira de pessoas*) queue
(*Brit*), line (US); (*num teatro, cinema*) row ■ M (*cão*)
Brazilian mastiff; **em ~** in a row; **fazer ~** to
form a line, queue; **~ indiana** single file
Filadélfia [fila'dεwfja] F Philadelphia
filamento [fila'mẽtu] M filament
filante [fi'lãtʃi] M/F sponger ■ ADJ sponging
filantropia [filãtro'pia] F philanthropy
filantrópico, -a [filã'trɔpiku, a] ADJ
philanthropic
filantropo [filã'tropu] M philanthropist
filão [fi'lãw] (*pl* -ões) M (*Jornalismo*) lead
filar [fi'laʳ] VT (*agarrar*) to seize; (*col*: *pedir/obter
gratuitamente*) to scrounge
filarmônica [filax'monika] F philharmonic
filarmônico, -a [filax'moniku, a] ADJ
philharmonic
filatelia [filate'lia] F stamp collecting
filé [fi'lε] M (*bife*) steak; (*peixe*) fillet; **~ mignon**
filet mignon
fileira [fi'lejra] F row, line; **fileiras** FPL (*serviço
militar*) military service *sg*
filete [fi'letʃi] M fillet; (*de parafuso*) thread
filharada [fiʎa'rada] F gang of children
filhinho, -a [fi'ʎiɲu, a] M/F little son/daughter; **~
de mamãe** mummy's boy; **~ de papai** rich kid
filho, -a [fi'ʎu, a] M/F son/daughter; **filhos** MPL
children; (*de animais*) young; **minha filha/meu
~** (*col*) dear, darling; **ter um ~** to have a child;
(*fig*: *col*) to have kittens, have a fit; **ele também
é ~ de Deus** he is just as good as anyone else; **~
adotivo** adoptive child; **~ da mãe, ~ da puta**
(*col!*) wanker (!), bastard (!); **~ de criação** foster
child; **~ ilegítimo/natural** illegitimate/
natural child; **~ único** only child; **~ único de
mãe viúva** (*fig*) one in a million
filhote [fi'ʎɔtʃi] M (*de leão, urso etc*) cub; (*cachorro*)
pup(py)
filiação [filja'sãw] (*pl* -ões) F affiliation
filial [fi'ljaw] (*pl* -ais) F (*sucursal*) branch ■ ADJ
filial; **gerente de ~** branch manager
filigrana [fili'grana] F filigree
Filipinas [fili'pinaʃ] FPL: **as ~** the Philippines
filipino, -a [fili'pinu, a] ADJ, M/F Filipino ■ M
(*Ling*) Filipino
filmagem [fiw'maʒẽ] F filming
filmar [fiw'maʳ] VT, VI to film
filme ['fiwmi] M film (*Brit*), movie (US); **~ (de)
bangue-bangue** *ou* **faroeste** western; **~ (de)
curta/longa metragem** short/feature film;
~ de época period film; **~ de capa e espada**
swashbuckling film
filmoteca [fiwmo'tεka] F (*lugar*) film library;
(*coleção*) film collection
filó [fi'lɔ] M tulle

filões [fi'lõjʃ] MPL *de* **filão**

filologia [filolo'ʒia] F philology

filólogo, -a [fi'lɔlogu, a] M/F philologist

filosofar [filozo'fa^r] VI to philosophize

filosofia [filozo'fia] F philosophy

filosófico, -a [filo'zɔfiku, a] ADJ philosophical

filósofo, -a [fi'lɔzofu, a] M/F philosopher

filtrar [fiw'tra^r] VT to filter; **filtrar-se** VR (*líquidos*) to filter; (*infiltrar-se*) to infiltrate

filtro ['fiwtru] M (*Tec*) filter

fim [fĩ] (*pl* **-ns**) M end; (*motivo*) aim, purpose; (*de história, filme*) ending; **a ~ de** in order to; **estar a ~ de (fazer) algo** to feel like (doing) sth, fancy (doing) sth; **estar a ~ de alguém** (*col*) to fancy sb; **no ~ das contas** after all; **por ~** finally; **sem ~** endless; **ter por ~** to aim at; **levar ao ~** to carry through; **pôr** *ou* **dar ~ a** to put an end to; **ter ~** to come to an end; **~ de mundo** (*fig*) hole; **ele mora no ~ do mundo** he lives miles from anywhere; **é o ~ (do mundo** *ou* **da picada)** (*fig*) it's the pits; **~ de semana** weekend

finado, -a [fi'nadu, a] ADJ, M/F deceased

● **DIA DOS FINADOS**

The *dia dos Finados*, 2 November, a holiday throughout Brazil, is dedicated to remembering the dead. On this day, people usually gather in cemeteries to remember their family dead, and also to worship at the graves of popular figures from Brazilian culture and society, such as singers, actors and other personalities. It is popularly believed that these people can work miracles.

final [fi'naw] (*pl* **-ais**) ADJ final, last ■ M end; (*Mús*) finale ■ F (*Esporte*) final; **finalista** [fina'liʃta] M/F finalist

finalização [finaliza'sãw] (*pl* **-ões**) F conclusion

finalizar [finali'za^r] VT to finish, conclude ■ VI (*Futebol*) to finish; **finalizar-se** VR to end

Finam [fi'nã] ABR M (= *Fundo de Investimento da Amazônia*) regional development fund

Finame [fi'nami] (BR) ABR M = **Agência Especial de Financiamento Industrial**

finanças [fi'nãsaʃ] FPL finance *sg*; **financeiro, -a** [finã'sejru, a] ADJ financial ■ M/F financier

financiamento [finãsja'mẽtu] M financing

financiar [finã'sja^r] VT to finance

financista [finã'siʃta] M/F financier

finar-se [fi'naxsi] VR (*consumir-se*) to waste away; (*morrer*) to die

fincar [fĩ'ka^r] VT (*cravar*) to drive in; (*fixar*) to fix; (*apoiar*) to lean

findar [fĩ'da^r] VT, VI to end, finish

findo, -a ['fĩdu, a] ADJ (*ano*) past; (*assunto*) closed

fineza [fi'neza] F fineness; (*gentileza*) kindness

fingido, -a [fĩ'ʒidu, a] ADJ pretend; (*pessoa*) two-faced, insincere ■ M/F hypocrite

fingimento [fĩʒi'mẽtu] M pretence (*Brit*), pretense (*US*)

fingir [fĩ'ʒi^r] VT (*simular*) to feign ■ VI to pretend; **fingir-se** VR: **fingir-se de** to pretend to be; **~ fazer/que** to pretend to do/that

finito, -a [fi'nitu, a] ADJ finite

finlandês, -esa [fĩlã'deʃ, eza] ADJ Finnish ■ M/F Finn ■ M (*Ling*) Finnish

Finlândia [fĩ'lãdʒia] F: **a ~** Finland

fino, -a ['finu, a] ADJ fine; (*delgado*) slender; (*educado*) polite; (*som, voz*) shrill; (*elegante*) refined ■ ADV: **falar ~** to talk in a high voice; **ser o ~** (*col*) to be the business; **tirar um ~ em alguém** to almost drive into sb

Finor [fi'nɔ^r] (BR) ABR M (= *Fundo de Investimento do Nordeste*) regional development fund

finório, -a [fi'nɔrju, a] ADJ crafty, sly

fins [fĩʃ] MPL *de* **fim**

Finsocial [fĩso'sjaw] (BR) ABR M = **Fundo de Investimento Social**

finura [fi'nura] F fineness; (*elegância*) finesse

fio ['fiu] M thread; (*Bot*) fibre (*Brit*), fiber (*US*); (*Elet*) wire; (*Tel*) line; (*de líquido*) trickle; (*gume*) edge; (*encadeamento*) series; **horas/dias a ~** hours/days on end; **de ~ a pavio** from beginning to end; **por um ~** (*fig: escapar*) by the skin of one's teeth; **bater um ~** (*col*) to make a call; **estar por um ~** to be on one's last legs; **perder o ~ (da meada)** (*fig*) to lose one's thread; **retomar o ~ perdido** (*fig*) to take up the thread again; **~ condutor** (*fig*) connecting thread

fiorde ['fjoxdʒi] M fjord

firewall [fajau'aw] M firewall

Firjan [fix'ʒã] ABR F = **Federação das Indústrias do Rio do Janeiro**

firma ['fixma] F (*assinatura*) signature; (*Com*) firm, company

firmamento [fixma'mẽtu] M firmament

firmar [fix'ma^r] VT (*tornar firme*) to secure, make firm; (*assinar*) to sign; (*estabelecer*) to establish; (*basear*) to base ■ VI (*tempo*) to settle; **firmar-se** VR: **firmar-se em** (*basear-se*) to rest on, be based on

firme ['fixmi] ADJ firm; (*estável*) stable; (*sólido*) solid; (*tempo*) settled ■ ADV firmly; **agüentar ~** to hang on; **pisar ~** to stride out; **firmeza** [fix'meza] F firmness; (*estabilidade*) stability; (*solidez*) solidity

FISA ['fiza] ABR F (= *Federação Internacional de Automobilismo Esportivo*) FISA

fiscal [fiʃ'kaw] (*pl* **-ais**) M/F supervisor; (*aduaneiro*) customs officer; (*de impostos*) tax inspector

fiscalização [fiʃkaliza'sãw] (*pl* **-ões**) F inspection

fiscalizar [fiʃkali'za^r] VT (*supervisionar*) to supervise; (*examinar*) to inspect, check

fisco ['fiʃku] M: **o ~** ≈ the Inland Revenue (*Brit*), ≈ the Internal Revenue Service (*US*)

NB: *European Portuguese adds the following consonants to certain words:* **b** (sú(b)dito, su(b)til); **c** (a(c)ção, a(c)cionista, a(c)to); **m** (inde(m)ne); **p** (ado(p)çã, ado(p)tar); *for further details see p. xiii.*

Fiset [fi'sɛtʃi] (BR) ABR M = **Fundo de Investimentos Setoriais**

fisgada [fiʒ'gada] F stabbing pain

fisgar [fiʒ'gaʳ] VT to catch

física ['fizika] F physics *sg*; ~ **nuclear** nuclear physics; *v tb* **físico**

físico, -a ['fiziku, a] ADJ physical ∎ M/F (*cientista*) physicist ∎ M (*corpo*) physique

fisiologia [fizjolo'ʒia] F physiology

fisionomia [fizjono'mia] F (*rosto*) face; (*ar*) expression, look; (*aspecto de algo*) appearance; (*conjunto de caracteres*) make-up

fisionomista [fizjono'miʃta] M/F person with a good memory for faces

fisioterapeuta [fizjotera'pewta] M/F physiotherapist

fisioterapia [fizjotera'pia] F physiotherapy

fissura [fi'sura] F crack; (*col: ansia*) craving

fissurado, -a [fisu'radu, a] ADJ cracked; **estar ~ em** (*col*) to be wild about

fissurar [fisu'raʳ] VT to crack

fita ['fita] F (*tira*) strip, band; (*de seda, algodão*) ribbon, tape; (*filme*) film; (*para máquina de escrever*) ribbon; (*magnética, adesiva*) tape; ~ **durex®** adhesive tape, Sellotape® (*Brit*), Scotchtape® (*US*); ~ **isolante** insulating tape; ~ **métrica** tape measure; **fazer ~** (*col*) to put on an act; **isso é ~ dela** (*col*) it's just an act

fitar [fi'taʳ] VT (*com os olhos*) to stare at, gaze at; **fitar-se** VR to stare at each other

fiteiro, -a [fi'tejru, a] ADJ melodramatic

fito, -a ['fitu, a] ADJ fixed ∎ M aim, intention

fivela [fi'vɛla] F buckle

fixação [fiksa'sãw] (*pl* -ões) F fixation

fixador [fiksa'doʳ] M hair gel; (: *líquido*) setting lotion

fixar [fik'saʳ] VT to fix; (*colar, prender*) to stick; (*data, prazo, regras*) to set; (*atenção*) to concentrate; **fixar-se** VR: **fixar-se em** (*assunto*) to concentrate on; (*detalhe*) to fix on; (*apegar-se a*) to be attached to; ~ **os olhos em** to stare at; ~ **residência** to set up house, settle down; ~ **algo na memória** to fix sth in one's mind

fixo, -a ['fiksu, a] ADJ fixed; (*firme*) firm; (*permanente*) permanent; (*cor*) fast

fiz *etc* [fiʒ] VB *v* **fazer**

flacidez [flasi'deʒ] F softness, flabbiness

flácido, -a ['flasidu, a] ADJ flabby

Fla-Flu [fla-] M local derby (*football match between rivals Flamengo and Fluminense*)

flagelado, -a [flaʒe'ladu, a] M/F: **os ~s** the afflicted, the victims

flagrante [fla'grãtʃi] ADJ flagrant; **apanhar em ~ (delito)** to catch red-handed *ou* in the act

flagrar [fla'graʳ] VT to catch

flambar [flã'baʳ] VT (*Culin*) to flambé

flamejante [flame'ʒãtʃi] ADJ flaming

flamejar [flame'ʒaʳ] VI to blaze

flamengo, -a [fla'mẽgu, a] ADJ Flemish ∎ M (*Ling*) Flemish

flamingo [fla'mĩgu] M flamingo

flâmula ['flamula] F pennant

flanco ['flãku] M flank

Flandres ['flãdriʃ] F Flanders

flanela [fla'nɛla] F flannel

flanquear [flã'kjaʳ] VT to flank; (*Mil*) to outflank

flash [flaʃ] M (*Foto*) flash

flash-back [flaʃ'baki] (*pl* -s) M flashback

flatulência [flatu'lẽsja] F flatulence

flauta ['flawta] F flute; **ele leva tudo na ~** (*col*) he doesn't take anything seriously; ~ **doce** (*Mús*) recorder

flautista [flaw'tʃiʃta] M/F flautist

flecha ['flɛʃa] F arrow

flechada [fle'ʃada] F (*golpe*) shot; (*ferimento*) arrow wound

flertar [flex'taʳ] VI: ~ **(com alguém)** to flirt (with sb)

flerte ['flextʃi] M flirtation

fleuma ['flewma] F phlegm

flexão [flek'sãw] (*pl* -ões) F flexing; (*exercício*) press-up; (*Ling*) inflection

flexibilidade [fleksibili'dadʒi] F flexibility

flexionar [fleksjo'naʳ] VT, VI (*Ling*) to inflect

flexível [flek'sivew] (*pl* -eis) ADJ flexible

flexões [flek'sõjʃ] FPL *de* **flexão**

fliperama [flipe'rama] M pinball machine

floco ['flɔku] M flake; ~ **de milho** cornflake; ~ **de neve** snowflake; **sorvete de ~s** chocolate chip ice-cream

flor [floʳ] F flower; (*o melhor*) cream, pick; **em ~** in bloom; **a fina ~** the elite; **a ~ de** on the surface of; **ele não é ~ que se cheire** (*col*) he's a bad lot

flora ['flɔra] F flora

floreado, -a [flo'rjadu, a] ADJ (*jardim*) full of flowers; (*relevo*) ornate; (*estilo*) florid

floreio [flo'reju] M clever turn of phrase

florescente [flore'sẽtʃi] ADJ (*Bot*) in flower; (*próspero*) flourishing

florescer [flore'seʳ] VI (*Bot*) to flower; (*prosperar*) to flourish

floresta [flo'rɛʃta] F forest; **florestal** [floreʃ'taw] (*pl* -ais) ADJ forest *atr*

florianopolitano, -a [florjanopoli'tanu, a] ADJ from Florianópolis ∎ M/F native of Florianópolis

Flórida ['flɔrida] F: **a ~** Florida

florido, -a [flo'ridu, a] ADJ (*jardim*) in flower; (*mesa*) decorated with flowers

florir [flo'riʳ] VI to flower

flotilha [flo'tʃiʎa] F flotilla

flozô [flo'zo] (*col*) M: **ficar de ~** to lounge around; **viver de ~** to lead a life of leisure

Flu [flu] ABR M = **Fluminense Futebol Clube**

fluência [flu'ẽsja] F fluency

fluente [flu'ẽtʃi] ADJ fluent

fluidez [flui'deʒ] F fluidity

fluido, -a ['flwidu, a] ADJ fluid ∎ M fluid

fluir [flwiʳ] VI to flow

fluminense [flumi'nẽsi] ADJ from the state of Rio de Janeiro ∎ M/F native *ou* inhabitant of the state of Rio de Janeiro

fluorescente [flwore'sẽtʃi] ADJ fluorescent

flutuação [flutwa'sãw] (*pl* -ões) F fluctuation

flutuante [flu'twãtʃi] ADJ floating; (bandeira) fluttering; (fig: vacilante) hesitant, wavering; (Com: câmbio) floating

flutuar [flu'twaʳ] VI to float; (bandeira) to flutter; (fig: vacilar) to waver

fluvial [flu'vjaw] (pl -ais) ADJ river atr

fluxo ['fluksu] M (corrente) flow; (Elet) flux; ~ **de caixa** (Com) cash flow

fluxograma [flukso'grama] M flow chart

FM ABR (Rádio: freqüência modulada) FM ■ F (pl **fluxogramas**) FM (radio) station

FMI ABR M (= Fundo Monetário Internacional) IMF

FMS ABR F = **Federação Mundial dos Sindicatos**

FN (BR) ABR M = **Fuzileiro Naval**

FND (BR) ABR M = **Fundo Nacional de Desenvolvimento**

fobia [fo'bia] F phobia

foca ['fɔka] F (animal) seal ■ M/F (col: jornalista) cub reporter

focalização [fokaliza'sãw] F focusing

focalizar [fokali'zaʳ] VT to focus (on)

focinho [fo'siɲu] M snout; (col: cara) face, mug (col)

foco ['fɔku] M focus; (Med, fig) seat, centre (Brit), center (US); **fora de** ~ out of focus

fofo, -a ['fofu, a] ADJ soft; (col: pessoa) cute

fofoca [fo'fɔka] F piece of gossip; **fofocas** (mexericos) gossip sg; **fazer** ~ to gossip; **fofocar** [fofo'kaʳ] VI to gossip

fofoqueiro, -a [fofo'kejru, a] ADJ gossipy ■ M/F gossip

fofura [fo'fura] (col) F cutie

fogão [fo'gãw] (pl -ões) M stove, cooker

fogareiro [foga'rejru] M stove

foge etc ['fɔʒi] VB V **fugir**

fogo ['fogu] M fire; (fig) ardour (Brit), ardor (US); **você tem** ~? have you got a light?; **~s de artifício** fireworks; **a** ~ **lento** on a low flame; **à prova de** ~ fireproof; **abrir** ~ to open fire; **brincar com** ~ (fig) to play with fire; **cessar** ~ (Mil) to cease fire; **estar com** ~ (col: pessoa) to be randy; **estar de** ~ (col: bêbado) to be drunk; **pegar** ~ to catch fire; (estar com febre) to burn up; **pôr** ~ **a** to set fire to; **ser bom para o** ~ (fig) to be useless; **ser** ~ (na roupa) (col: pessoa) to be a pain; (: trabalho etc) to be murder; (: ser incrível) to be amazing

fogões [fo'gõjʃ] MPL de **fogão**

fogo-fátuo (pl **fogos-fátuos**) M will-o'-the-wisp

fogoso, -a [fo'gozu, ɔza] ADJ fiery; (libidinoso) lustful

fogueira [fo'gejra] F bonfire

foguete [fo'getʃi] M rocket; (pessoa) live wire; **soltar os ~s antes da festa** (fig) to jump the gun

foi [foj] VB V ir; ser

foice ['fojsi] F scythe

folclore [fowk'lɔri] M folklore

folclórico, -a [fowk'lɔriku, a] ADJ (música etc) folk

atr; (comida, roupa) ethnic

fole ['fɔli] M bellows sg

fôlego ['folegu] M breath; (folga) breathing space; **perder o** ~ to get out of breath; **tomar** ~ to pause for breath

folga [ˈfowga] F (descanso) rest, break; (espaço livre) clearance; (ócio) inactivity; (col: atrevimento) cheek; **dia de** ~ day off; **que** ~! what a cheek!;

folgado, -a [fow'gadu, a] ADJ (roupa) loose; (vida) leisurely; (col: atrevido) cheeky; (: boa vida) easy-living ■ M/F (col: atrevido) cheeky devil; (: boa vida) loafer

folgar [fow'gaʳ] VT to loosen, slacken ■ VI (descansar) to rest, relax; (divertir-se) to have fun, amuse o.s.; ~ **em saber que ...** to be pleased to hear that ...

folgazão, -zona [fowga'zãw, 'zona] (pl -ões/-s) ADJ (pessoa) fun-loving; (gênio) lively

folha ['foʎa] F leaf; (de papel, de metal) sheet; (página) page; (de faca) blade; (jornal) paper; **novo em** ~ brand new; ~ **de estanho** tinfoil (Brit), aluminum foil (US); ~ **de exercícios** worksheet; ~ **de pagamento** payroll; ~ **de rosto** imprint page; **~s soltas** (Comput) single sheets, cut sheets

folhagem [fo'ʎaʒē] F foliage

folha-seca (pl **folhas-secas**) F (Futebol) swerving shot

folheado, -a [fo'ʎjadu, a] ADJ veneered; ~ **a ouro** gold-plated

folhear [fo'ʎjaʳ] VT to leaf through

folheto [fo'ʎetu] M booklet, pamphlet

folhinha [fo'ʎiɲa] F tear-off calendar

folhudo, -a [fo'ʎudu, a] ADJ leafy

folia [fo'lia] F revelry, merriment

folião, -liona [fo'ʎjãw, 'jona] (pl -ões/-s) M/F reveller (in carnival)

folículo [fo'likulu] M follicle

foliões [fo'ʎõjʃ] MPL de **folião**

foliona [fo'ʎjona] F de **folião**

fome ['fɔmi] F hunger; (escassez) famine; (fig: avidez) longing; **passar** ~ to go hungry; **estar com** ou **ter** ~ to be hungry; **varado de** ~ starving, ravenous

fomentar [fomē'taʳ] VT to instigate, incite; (discórdia) to sow, cause

fomento [fo'mētu] M (Med) fomentation; (estímulo) incitement; (de discórdia, ódio etc) stirring up

fominha [fo'miɲa] (col) ADJ stingy ■ M/F skinflint

fonador, a [fona'doʳ(a)] ADJ: **aparelho** ~ vocal track

fone ['fɔni] M telephone, phone; (peça do telefone) receiver

fonema [fo'nɛma] M (Ling) phoneme

fonética [fo'nɛtʃika] F phonetics sg

fonético, -a [fo'nɛtʃiku, a] ADJ phonetic

fonfom [fõ'fõ] (pl -ns) M toot

NB: European Portuguese adds the following consonants to certain words: **b** (sú(b)dito, su(b)til); **c** (a(c)ção, a(c)cionista, a(c)to); **m** (inde(m)ne); **p** (ado(p)çã, ado(p)tar); for further details see p. xiii.

fonologia [fonolo'ʒia] F phonology
fonte ['fõtʃi] F (*nascente*) spring; (*chafariz*) fountain; (*origem*) source; (*Anat*) temple; **de ~ limpa** from a reliable source; **retido/tributado na ~** (*Com*) deducted/taxed at source
footing ['futʃiŋ] M jogging
for *etc* [fo'ʳ] VB V **ir; ser**
fora ['fɔra] ADV out, outside ■ PREP (*além de*) apart from ■ M: **dar o ~** (*bateria, radio*) to give out; (*pessoa*) to leave, be off; **dar um ~** to slip up; **dar um ~ em alguém** (*namorado*) to chuck sb, dump sb; (*esnobar*) to snub sb; **levar um ~** (*de namorado*) to be given the boot; (*ser esnobado*) to get the brush-off; **~ de** outside; **~ de si** beside o.s.; **estar ~** (*viajando*) to be away; **estar ~ (de casa)** to be out; **lá ~** outside; (*no exterior*) abroad; **jantar ~** to eat out; **com os braços de ~** with bare arms; **ser de ~** to be from out of town; **ficar de ~** not to join in; **lá para ~** outside; **ir para ~** (*viajar*) to go out of town; **com a cabeça para ~ da janela** with one's head sticking out of the window; **costurar/cozinhar para ~** to do sewing/cooking for other people; **por ~** on the outside; **cobrar por ~** to charge extra; **~ de dúvida** beyond doubt; **~ de propósito** irrelevant
fora *etc* VB V **ir; ser**
fora-de-lei M/F INV outlaw
foragido, -a [fora'ʒidu, a] ADJ, M/F (*fugitivo*) fugitive
foragir-se [fora'ʒixsi] VR to go into hiding
forasteiro, -a [foraʃ'tejru, a] ADJ (*estranho*) alien ■ M/F outsider, stranger; (*de outro país*) foreigner
forca ['foxka] F gallows *sg*
força ['foxsa] F (*energia física*) strength; (*Tec, Elet*) power; (*esforço*) effort; (*coerção*) force; **à ~** by force; **à ~ de** by dint of; **com ~** hard; **por ~** of necessity; **dar (uma) ~ a** to back up, encourage; **fazer ~ to try (hard); como vai essa ~?** (*col*) how's it going?; **F~ Aérea** Air Force; **~ de trabalho** workforce; **~ maior** (*Com*) act of God
forcado [fox'kadu] M pitchfork
forçado, -a [fox'sadu, a] ADJ forced; (*afetado*) false
forçar [fox'saʳ] VT to force; (*olhos, voz*) to strain; **forçar-se** VR: **forçar-se a** to force o.s. to
força-tarefa (*pl* forças-tarefa) F task force
forcejar [foxse'ʒaʳ] VI (*esforçar-se*) to strive; (*lutar*) to struggle
fórceps ['fɔxsipʃ] M INV forceps *pl*
forçoso, -a [fox'sozu, ɔza] ADJ (*necessário*) necessary; (*obrigatório*) obligatory
forja ['fɔxʒa] F forge
forjar [fox'ʒaʳ] VT to forge; (*pretexto*) to invent
forma ['fɔxma] F form; (*de um objeto*) shape; (*físico*) figure; (*maneira*) way; (*Med*) fitness; **desta ~** in this way; **de (tal) ~ que** in such a way that; **de qualquer ~** anyway; **da mesma ~** likewise; **de outra ~** otherwise; **de ~ alguma** in no way whatsoever; **em ~ de pêra/comprimido** pear-shaped/in tablet form; **estar fora de/em ~** (*pessoa*) to be unfit/fit; **manter a ~** to keep fit; **~**

de pagamento means of payment
fôrma ['foxma] F (*Culin*) cake tin; (*molde*) mould (*Brit*), mold (*US*); (*para sapatos*) last
formação [foxma'sãw] (*pl* -ões) F formation; (*antecedentes*) background; (*caráter*) make-up; (*profissional*) training
formado, -a [fox'madu, a] ADJ (*modelado*): **ser ~ de** to consist of ■ M/F graduate; **ser ~ em** to be a graduate in
formal [fox'maw] (*pl* -ais) ADJ formal;
formalidade [foxmali'dadʒi] F formality
formalizar [foxmali'zaʳ] VT to formalize
formando, -a [fox'mãdu, a] M/F graduating student, graduand
formão [fox'mãw] (*pl* -ões) M chisel
formar [fox'maʳ] VT to form; (*constituir*) to constitute, make up; (*educar*) to train, educate; (*soldados*) to form up ■ VI to form up; **formar-se** VR (*tomar forma*) to form; (*Educ*) to graduate
formatar [foxma'taʳ] VT (*Comput*) to format
formato [fox'matu] M format; (*de papel*) size
formatura [foxma'tura] F (*Mil*) formation; (*Educ*) graduation
fórmica® ['fɔxmika] F Formica®
formidável [foxmi'davew] (*pl* -eis) ADJ tremendous, great
formiga [fox'miga] F ant
formigar [foxmi'gaʳ] VI (*ser abundante*) to abound; (*sentir comichão*) to itch; **~ de algo** to swarm with sth
formigueiro [foxmi'gejru] M ants' nest; (*multidão*) throng, swarm
formões [fox'mõjʃ] MPL *de* **formão**
Formosa [fox'mɔza] F Taiwan
formoso, -a [fox'mozu, ɔza] ADJ (*belo*) beautiful; (*esplêndido*) superb
formosura [foxmo'zura] F beauty
fórmula ['fɔxmula] F formula
formulação [foxmula'sãw] (*pl* -ões) F formulation
formular [foxmu'laʳ] VT to formulate; (*queixas*) to voice; **~ votos** to express one's hopes/wishes
formulário [foxmu'larju] M form; **formulários** MPL: **~s contínuos** (*Comput*) continuous stationery *sg*
fornalha [fox'naʎa] F furnace; (*fig: lugar quente*) oven
fornecedor, a [foxnese'doʳ(a)] M/F supplier ■ F (*empresa*) supplier ■ ADJ supply *atr*
fornecer [foxne'seʳ] VT to supply, provide; **~ algo a alguém** to supply sb with sth; **fornecimento** [foxnesi'mẽtu] M supply
fornicar [foxni'kaʳ] VI to fornicate
forno ['foxnu] M (*Culin*) oven; (*Tec*) furnace; (*para cerâmica*) kiln; **alto ~** blast furnace; **cozinheiro/a de ~ e fogão** expert cook
foro ['foru] M forum; (*Jur*) Court of Justice; **foros** MPL (*privilégios*) privileges; **de ~ íntimo** personal, private
forra ['fɔxa] F: **ir à ~** (*col*) to get one's own back
forragem [fo'xaʒẽ] F fodder
forrar [fo'xaʳ] VT (*cobrir*) to cover; (: *interior*) to

line; (*de papel*) to paper

forro ['foxu] M (*cobertura*) covering; (*interior*) lining; **com ~ de pele** fur-lined

forró [fo'xɔ] (*col*) M dance

fortalecer [foxtale'se ͬ] VT to strengthen

fortalecimento [foxtalesi'mẽtu] M strengthening

fortaleza [foxta'leza] F (*forte*) fortress; (*força*) strength; (*moral*) fortitude; **ser uma ~** to be as strong as an ox

fortalezense [foxtale'zẽsi] ADJ from Fortaleza ■ M/F native *ou* inhabitant of Fortaleza

forte ['fɔxtʃi] ADJ strong; (*pancada*) hard; (*chuva*) heavy; (*som*) loud; (*dor*) sharp, strong; (*filme*) powerful; (*pessoa: musculoso*) muscular ■ ADV strongly; (*som*) loud(ly) ■ M (*fortaleza*) fort; (*talento*) strength; **ser ~ em algo** (*versado*) to be good at sth *ou* strong in sth

fortificação [foxtʃifika'sãw] (*pl* -ões) F fortification; (*fortaleza*) fortress

fortificante [foxtʃifi'kãtʃi] ADJ fortifying ■ M fortifier

fortificar [foxtʃifi'ka ͬ] VT to fortify; **fortificar-se** VR to build o.s. up

fortuitamente [foxtwita'mẽtʃi] ADV (*imprevisivelmente*) by chance, unexpectedly; (*ocasionalmente*) casually

fortuito, -a [fox'twitu, a] ADJ accidental

fortuna [fox'tuna] F fortune, (good) luck; (*riqueza*) fortune, wealth; **custar uma ~** to cost a fortune

fosco, -a ['foʃku, a] ADJ (*sem brilho*) dull; (*opaco*) opaque

fosfato [foʃ'fatu] M phosphate

fosforescente [foʃfore'sẽtʃi] ADJ phosphorescent

fósforo ['fɔʃforu] M match; (*Quím*) phosphorus

fossa ['fɔsa] F pit; (*col*) blues *pl*; **estar/ficar na ~** (*col*) to be/get depressed *ou* down in the dumps; **tirar alguém da ~** (*col*) to cheer sb up; **~ séptica** septic tank

fosse *etc* ['fosi] VB *v* **ir**; **ser**

fóssil ['fɔsiw] (*pl* -eis) M fossil

fosso ['fosu] M trench, ditch; (*de uma fortaleza*) moat

foto ['fɔtu] F photo

fotocópia [foto'kɔpja] F photocopy; **fotocopiadora** [fotokopja'dora] F photocopier; **fotocopiar** [fotoko'pja ͬ] VT to photocopy

fotogênico, -a [foto'ʒeniku, a] ADJ photogenic

fotografar [fotogra'fa ͬ] VT to photograph

fotografia [fotogra'fia] F photography; (*uma foto*) photograph

fotográfico, -a [foto'grafiku, a] ADJ photographic; *v tb* **máquina**

fotógrafo, -a [fo'tɔgrafu, a] M/F photographer

fotonovela [fotono'vɛla] F photo story

fotossíntese [foto'sĩtezi] F (*Biol*) photosynthesis

foxtrote [foks'trɔtʃi] M foxtrot

foyer [fua'je] M foyer

foz [fɔʒ] F river mouth

FP-25 ABR FPL (= *Forças Populares do 25 de Abril*) Portuguese terrorist group

fração [fra'sãw] (*pl* -ões) F fraction

fracassar [fraka'sa ͬ] VI to fail; **fracasso** [fra'kasu] M failure

fracção [fra'sãw] (PT) F = **fração**

fracionar [frasjo'na ͬ] VT to break up; **fracionar-se** VR to break up, fragment

fraco, -a ['fraku, a] ADJ weak; (*sol, som*) faint ■ M weakness; **estar ~ em algo** to be poor at sth; **ter um ~ por algo** to have a weakness for sth

frações [fra'sõjʃ] FPL *de* **fração**

fractura *etc* [fra'tura] (PT) F = **fratura** *etc*

frade ['fradʒi] M (*Rel*) friar; (*: monge*) monk

fraga ['fraga] F crag, rock

fragata [fra'gata] F (*Náut*) frigate

frágil ['fraʒiw] (*pl* -eis) ADJ (*débil*) fragile; (*Com*) breakable; (*pessoa*) frail; (*saúde*) delicate, poor

fragilidade [fraʒili'dadʒi] F fragility; (*de uma pessoa*) frailty

fragílimo, -a [fra'ʒilimu, a] ADJ SUPERL *de* **frágil**

fragmentar [fragmẽ'ta ͬ] VT to break up; **fragmentar-se** VR to break up

fragmento [frag'mẽtu] M fragment

fragrância [fra'grãsja] F fragrance, perfume

fragrante [fra'grãtʃi] ADJ fragrant

frajola [fra'ʒɔla] (*col*) ADJ smart

fralda ['frawda] F (*da camisa*) shirt tail; (*para bebê*) nappy (Brit), diaper (US); (*de montanha*) foot; **mal saído das ~s** (*fig*) still wet behind the ears

framboesa [frã'beza] F raspberry

França ['frãsa] F France

francamente [fråka'mẽtʃi] ADV (*abertamente*) frankly; (*realmente*) really

francês, -esa [frã'seʃ, eza] ADJ French ■ M/F Frenchman/woman ■ M (*Ling*) French

franco, -a ['fråku, a] ADJ (*sincero*) frank; (*isento de pagamento*) free; (*óbvio*) clear ■ M franc; **entrada franca** free admission

frangalho [frã'gaʎu] M (*trapo*) rag, tatter; (*pessoa*) wreck; **em ~s** in tatters

frango ['frãgu] M chicken; (*Futebol*) easy goal

franja ['frãʒa] F fringe (Brit), bangs *pl* (US)

franquear [frã'kja ͬ] VT (*caminho*) to clear; (*isentar de imposto*) to exempt from duties; (*carta*) to frank; **~ algo a alguém** (*facultar*) to make sth available to sb

franqueza [frã'keza] F frankness

franquia [frã'kia] F (*Com*) franchise; (*isenção*) exemption; **~ de bagagem** baggage allowance; **~ diplomática** diplomatic immunity; **~ postal** Freepost®

franzido [frã'zidu] M pleat

franzino, -a [frã'zinu, a] ADJ skinny

franzir [frã'zi ͬ] VT (*preguear*) to pleat; (*enrugar*) to wrinkle, crease; (*lábios*) to curl; **~ as**

NB: *European Portuguese adds the following consonants to certain words:* **b** (sú(b)dito, su(b)til); **c** (a(c)ção, a(c)cionista, a(c)to); **m** (inde(m)ne); **p** (ado(p)ção, ado(p)tar); *for further details see p. xiii.*

sobrancelhas to frown
fraque ['fraki] M morning suit
fraquejar [frake'ʒaʳ] VI to grow weak; (vontade) to weaken
fraqueza [fra'keza] F weakness
frasco ['fraʃku] M (de remédio, perfume) bottle
frase ['frazi] F sentence; ~ **feita** set phrase
fraseado [fra'zjadu] M wording
frasqueira [fraʃ'kejra] F vanity case
fraternal [fratex'naw] (pl -ais) ADJ fraternal, brotherly
fraternidade [fratexni'dadʒi] F fraternity
fraternizar [fratexni'zaʳ] VT to bring together ■ VI to fraternize
fraterno, -a [fra'tɛxnu, a] ADJ fraternal, brotherly
fratura [fra'tura] F fracture, break; **fraturar** [fratu'raʳ] VT to fracture
fraudar [fraw'daʳ] VT to defraud; (expectativa, esperanças) to dash
fraude ['frawdʒi] F fraud
fraudulento, -a [frawdu'lẽtu, a] ADJ fraudulent
freada [fre'ada] (BR) F: **dar uma** ~ to slam on the brakes
frear [fre'aʳ] (BR) VT (conter) to curb, restrain; (veículo) to stop ■ VI (veículo) to brake
freelance [fri'lãs] M/F freelancer
freezer ['frizeʳ] M freezer
frege ['freʒi] M mess
freguês, -guesa [fre'geʃ, 'geza] M/F (cliente) customer; (PT) parishioner; **freguesia** [frege'zia] F customers pl; (PT) parish
frei [frej] M friar, monk; (título) Brother
freio ['freju] M (BR: veículo) brake; (de cavalo) bridle; (bocado do freio) bit; (fig) check; ~ **de mão** handbrake
freira ['frejra] F nun
freixo ['frejʃu] M (Bot) ash
Frelimo [fre'limo] ABR F (= Frente de Libertação de Moçambique) Frelimo
fremente [fre'mẽtʃi] ADJ (fig) rousing
fremir [fre'miʳ] VI (bramar) to roar; (tremer) to tremble
frêmito ['fremitu] M (fig: de alegria etc) wave
frenesi [frene'zi] M frenzy; **frenético, -a** [fre'nɛtʃiku, a] ADJ frantic, frenzied
frente ['frẽtʃi] F (de objeto, Pol, Mil) front; (rosto) face; (fachada) façade; ~ **a** ~ face to face; **à** ~ **de** at the front of; **de** ~ **para** facing; **em** ~ **de** in front of; (de fronte a) opposite; **para a** ~ ahead, forward; **de trás para** ~ from back to front; **porta da** ~ front door; **apartamento de** ~ apartment at the front; **seguir em** ~ to go straight on; **a casa em** ~ the house opposite; **na minha** (ou sua etc) ~ in front of me (ou you etc); **sair da** ~ to get out of the way; **sai da minha** ~! get out of my sight!; **pela** ~ ahead; **pra** ~ (col) fashionable, trendy; **fazer** ~ **a algo** to face sth; **ir para a** ~ (progredir) to progress; **levar à** ~ to carry through; ~ **de combate** (Mil) front; ~ **de trabalho** area of employment; ~ **fria/quente** (Meteorologia) cold/warm front

freqüência [fre'kwẽsja] F frequency; **com** ~ often, frequently
freqüentador, a [frekwẽta'doʳ(a)] M/F regular visitor; (de restaurante etc) regular customer
freqüentar [frekwẽ'taʳ] VT to frequent; ~ **a casa de alguém** to go to sb's house a lot; ~ **um curso** to attend a course
freqüente [fre'kwẽtʃi] ADJ frequent
fresca ['freʃka] F cool breeze
frescão [freʃ'kãw] (pl -ões) M air-conditioned coach
fresco, -a ['freʃku, a] ADJ fresh; (vento, tempo) cool; (col: efeminado) camp; (: afetado) pretentious; (: cheio de luxo) fussy ■ M (ar) fresh air; (Arte) fresco
frescobol [freʃko'bɔw] M (kind of) racketball (played mainly on the beach)
frescões [freʃ'kõjʃ] MPL de **frescão**
frescor [freʃ'koʳ] M freshness
frescura [freʃ'kura] F freshness; (frialdade) coolness; (col: luxo) fussiness; (: afetaçao) pretentiousness; **que** ~! how fussy!; **how pretentious!**
fresta ['freʃta] F gap, slit
fretar [fre'taʳ] VT (avião, navio) to charter; (caminhão) to hire
frete ['frɛtʃi] M (carregamento) freight, cargo; (tarifa) freightage; **a** ~ for hire
freudiano, -a [frɔj'dʒjanu, a] ADJ Freudian
frevo ['frevu] M improvised Carnival dance
fria ['fria] F: **dar uma** ~ **em alguém** to give sb the cold shoulder; **estar/entrar numa** ~ (col) to be in/get into a mess; **levar uma** ~ **de alguém** to get the cold shoulder from sb
friagem ['frjaʒẽ] F cold weather
frialdade [frjaw'dadʒi] F coldness; (indiferença) indifference, coolness
fricção [frik'sãw] F friction; (ato) rubbing; (Med) massage; **friccionar** [friksjo'naʳ] VT to rub
fricote [fri'kɔtʃi] (col) M finickiness
fricoteiro, -a [fiko'tejru, a] (col) ADJ finicky ■ M/F fusspot
frieira ['frjejra] F chilblain
frieza ['frjeza] F coldness; (indiferença) coolness
frigideira [friʒi'dejra] F frying pan
frigidez [friʒi'deʒ] F frigidity
frígido, -a ['friʒidu, a] ADJ frigid
frigir [fri'ʒiʳ] VT to fry
frigorífico [frigo'rifiku] M refrigerator; (congelador) freezer
frincha ['frĩʃa] F chink, slit
frio, -a ['friu, a] ADJ cold; (col) forged ■ M coldness; **frios** MPL (Culin) cold meats; **estou com** ~ I'm cold; **faz** ou **está** ~ it's cold
friorento, -a [frjo'rẽtu, a] ADJ (pessoa) sensitive to the cold; (lugar) chilly
frisar [fri'zaʳ] VT (encrespar) to curl; (salientar) to emphasize
Frísia ['frizja] F: **a** ~ Frisia
friso ['frizu] M border; (na parede) frieze; (Arq) moulding (Brit), molding (US)
fritada [fri'tada] F fry-up; **dar uma** ~ **em algo**

to fry sth

fritar [fri'ta^r] VT to fry

fritas ['fritaʃ] FPL chips (Brit), French fries (US)

frito, -a ['fritu, a] ADJ fried; (col): **estar ~** to be done for

fritura [fri'tura] F fried food

frivolidade [frivoli'dadʒi] F frivolity

frívolo, -a ['frivolu, a] ADJ frivolous

fronha ['froɲa] F pillowcase

front [frõ] (pl **-s**) M (Mil, fig) front

fronte ['frõtʃi] F (Anat) forehead, brow

fronteira [frõ'tejra] F frontier, border

fronteiriço, -a [frõtej'risu, a] ADJ frontier atr

fronteiro, -a [frõ'tejru, a] ADJ front

frontispício [frõtʃiʃ'pisju] M (de edifício) main façade; (de livro) frontispiece; (rosto) face

frota ['frota] F fleet

frouxo, -a ['froʃu, a] ADJ loose; (corda) slack; (fraco) weak; (indolente) slack; (col: condescendente) soft

frufru [fru'fru] M (enfeite) ruff

frugal [fru'gaw] (pl **-ais**) ADJ frugal

fruição [frwi'sãw] F enjoyment

fruir ['frwi^r] VT to enjoy ■ VI: **~ de algo** to enjoy sth

frustração [fruʃtra'sãw] F frustration

frustrado, -a [fruʃ'tradu, a] ADJ frustrated; (planos) thwarted

frustrante [fruʃ'trãtʃi] ADJ frustrating

frustrar [fruʃ'tra^r] VT to frustrate

fruta ['fruta] F fruit

fruta-de-conde (pl **frutas-de-conde**) F sweetsop

fruta-pão (pl **frutas-pães**) F breadfruit

fruteira [fru'tejra] F fruit bowl

frutífero, -a [fru'tʃiferu, a] ADJ (proveitoso) fruitful; (árvore) fruit-bearing

fruto ['frutu] M (Bot) fruit; (resultado) result, product; **dar ~** (fig) to bear fruit

fubá [fu'ba] M corn meal

fubeca [fu'bɛka] (col) F thrashing

fubica [fu'bika] (col) F heap, jalopy

fuçar [fu'sa^r] VI: **~ em algo** (remexer) to rummage in sth; (meter-se) to meddle in sth

fuças ['fusaʃ] (col) FPL face sg, chops

fuga ['fuga] F flight, escape; (de gás etc) leak; (da prisão) escape; (de namorados) elopement; (Mús) fugue

fugacíssimo, -a [fuga'sisimu, a] ADJ SUPERL de **fugaz**

fugaz [fu'gaʒ] ADJ fleeting

fugida [fu'ʒida] F sortie; **dar uma ~** ou **fugidinha** to pop out for a moment

fugir [fu'ʒi^r] VI to flee, escape; (prisioneiro) to escape; (criança: de casa) to run away; (namorados) to elope; **~ a algo** to avoid sth

fugitivo, -a [fuʒi'tʃivu, a] ADJ, M/F fugitive

fui [fuj] VB V **ir**; **ser**

fulano, -a [fu'lanu, a] M/F so-and-so; **~ de**

tal what's-his-name/what's-her-name; **~, beltrano e sicrano** Tom, Dick and Harry

fulcro ['fuwkru] M fulcrum

fuleiro, -a [fu'lejru, a] ADJ tacky

fúlgido, -a ['fuwʒidu, a] ADJ brilliant

fulgir [fuw'ʒi^r] VI to shine

fulgor [fuw'go^r] M brilliance

fuligem [fu'liʒẽ] F soot

fulminante [fuwmi'nãtʃi] ADJ (devastador) devastating; (palavras) scathing

fulminar [fuwmi'na^r] VT (ferir, matar) to strike down; (petrificar) to stop dead; (aniquilar) to annihilate ■ VI to flash with lightning; **fulminado por um raio** struck by lightning

fulo, -a ['fulu, a] ADJ: **estar** ou **ficar ~ de raiva** to be furious

fumaça [fu'masa] (BR) F (de fogo) smoke; (de gás) fumes pl; **500 e lá vai ~** (col) 500 and then some

fumador, a [fuma'do^r(a)] (PT) M/F smoker

fumante [fu'mãtʃi] M/F smoker

fumar [fu'ma^r] VT, VI to smoke

fumê [fu'me] ADJ INV (vidro) smoked

fumo ['fumu] M (PT: de fogo) smoke; (: de gás) fumes pl; (BR: tabaco) tobacco; (fumar) smoking; (BR: col: maconha) dope; **~ louro** Virginia tobacco; **puxar ~** (col) to smoke dope

FUNABEM [funa'bẽ] (BR) ABR F (= Fundação Nacional do Bem-Estar do Menor) children's home

Funai [fu'naj] (BR) ABR F = **Fundação Nacional do Índio**

Funarte [fu'naxtʃi] (BR) ABR F = **Fundação Nacional de Arte**

função [fũ'sãw] (pl **-ões**) F function; (ofício) duty; (papel) role; (espetáculo) performance

Funcep [fũ'sepi] (BR) ABR F (= Fundação Centro de Formação do Servidor Público) civil service training centre

funcho ['fũʃu] M (Bot) fennel

funcional [fũsjo'naw] (pl **-ais**) ADJ functional

funcionalismo [fũsjona'liʒmu] M: **~ público** civil service

funcionamento [fũsjona'mẽtu] M functioning, working; **pôr em ~** to set going, start

funcionar [fũsjo'na^r] VI to function; (máquina) to work, run; (dar bom resultado) to work

funcionário, -a [fũsjo'narju, a] M/F official; **~ (público)** civil servant

funções [fũ'sõjʃ] FPL de **função**

fundação [fũda'sãw] (pl **-ões**) F foundation

fundador, a [fũda'do^r(a)] M/F founder ■ ADJ founding

fundamental [fũdamẽ'taw] (pl **-ais**) ADJ fundamental, basic

fundamentar [fũdamẽ'ta^r] VT (argumento) to substantiate; (basear): **~ (em)** to base (on)

fundamento [fũda'mẽtu] M (fig) foundation, basis; (motivo) motive; **sem ~** groundless

fundar [fũ'da^r] VT to establish, found; (basear) to base; **fundar-se** VR: **fundar-se em** to be

NB: European Portuguese adds the following consonants to certain words: **b** (sú(b)dito, su(b)til); **c** (a(c)ção, a(c)cionista, a(c)to); **m** (inde(m)ne); **p** (ado(p)ção, ado(p)tar); for further details see p. xiii.

based on

fundear [fũ'dʒiaʳ] vi to anchor

fundição [fũdʒi'sãw] (pl -ões) F fusing; (fábrica) foundry

fundilho [fũ'dʒiʎu] M (da calça) seat

fundir [fũ'dʒiʳ] vt to fuse; (metal) to smelt, melt down; (Com: empresas) to merge; (em molde) to cast; **fundir-se** vr (derreter-se) to melt; (juntar-se) to merge, fuse; (Com) to merge; ~ **a cuca** to crack up

fundo, -a ['fũdu, a] adj deep; (fig) profound; (col: ignorante) ignorant; (: despreparado) hopeless ■ M (do mar, jardim) bottom; (profundidade) depth; (base) basis; (da loja, casa, do papel) back; (de quadro) background; (de dinheiro) fund ■ adv deeply; **fundos** MPL (Com) funds; (da casa etc) back sg; **a ~** thoroughly; **ao ~** in the background; **ir ao ~** (navio) to sink, go down; **no ~** (de caixa etc) at the bottom; (de casa etc) at the back; (de quadro) in the background; (fig) basically, at bottom; **sem ~** (poço) bottomless; **dar ~s para** (casa etc) to back on to; ~ **de contingência** contingency fund; ~ **de investimento** investment fund; **F~ Monetário Internacional** International Monetary Fund

fundura [fũ'dura] F depth; (col) ignorance

fúnebre ['funebri] adj funeral atr, funereal; (fig: triste) gloomy, lugubrious

funeral [fune'raw] (pl -ais) M funeral

funerário, -a [fune'rarju, a] adj funeral atr; **casa funerária** undertakers pl

funesto, -a [fu'nɛʃtu, a] adj (fatal) fatal; (infausto) disastrous; (notícia) fateful

fungar [fũ'gaʳ] vt, vi to sniff

fungo ['fũgu] M (Bot) fungus

funil [fu'niw] (pl -is) M funnel

Funrural [fũxu'raw] (BR) ABR M = **Fundo de Assistência e Previdência ao Trabalhador Rural**

Funtevê [fũte've] ABR F = **Fundação Centro-Brasileira de TV Educativa**

fura-bolo ['fura-] (pl -s) (col) M index finger

furacão [fura'kãw] (pl -ões) M hurricane; **entrar/sair como um ~** to stomp in/out

furado, -a [fu'radu, a] adj perforated; (pneu) flat; (orelha) pierced; (col: programa) crummy

furão, -rona [fu'rãw, 'rɔna] (pl -ões/-s) M ferret ■ M/F (col) go-getter ■ adj (col) hard-working, dynamic

furar [fu'raʳ] vt (perfurar) to bore, perforate; (penetrar) to penetrate; (greve) to break; (frustrar) to foil; (fila) to jump ■ vi (col: programa) to fall through

furdúncio [fux'dũsju] (col) M commotion

furgão [fux'gãw] (pl -ões) M van

furgoneta [fuxgo'neta] (PT) F van

fúria ['furja] F fury, rage; **estar uma ~** to be furious

furibundo, -a [furi'bũdu, a] adj furious

furioso, -a [fu'rjozu, ɔza] adj furious

furo ['furu] M hole; (num pneu) puncture; ~ **jornalístico** scoop; **dar um ~** (col) to make a

blunder; **estar muitos ~s acima de algo** (fig) to be a cut above sth, be a lot better than sth

furões [fu'rõjʃ] MPL de **furão**

furona [fu'rɔna] F de **furão**

furor [fu'roʳ] M fury, rage; **causar ~** to cause a furore; **fazer ~** to be all the rage

furta-cor ['fuxta-] (pl -es) adj iridescent ■ M iridescence

furtar [fux'taʳ] vt, vi to steal; **furtar-se** vr: **furtar-se a** to avoid, evade

furtivo, -a [fux'tʃivu, a] adj furtive, stealthy

furto ['fuxtu] M theft

furúnculo [fu'rũkulu] M (Med) boil

fusão [fu'zãw] (pl -ões) F fusion; (Com) merger; (derretimento) melting; (união) union

fusca ['fuʃka] (col) M (VW) beetle

fusco, -a ['fuʃku, a] adj dark, dusky

fuselagem [fuze'laʒē] (pl -ns) F fuselage

fusível [fu'zivew] (pl -eis) M (Elet) fuse

fuso ['fuzu] M (Tec) spindle; ~ **horário** time zone

fusões [fu'zõjʃ] FPL de **fusão**

fustão [fuʃ'tãw] M corduroy

fustigar [fuʃtʃi'gaʳ] vt (açoitar) to flog, whip; (suj: vento) to lash; (maltratar) to lash out at

futebol [futʃi'bɔw] M football; ~ **de salão** five-a-side football; ~ **totó** table football; **fazer um ~ de algo** (col) to get sth all mixed up

Futevôlei [futʃi'volej] M see below

⬤ **FUTEVÔLEI**

⬤ Futevôlei is a type of volleyball in which the
⬤ ball is allowed to touch only the feet, legs,
⬤ trunk and head of the players. It is very
⬤ popular on the beaches of Rio de Janeiro,
⬤ where tournaments take place during the
⬤ summer, in which many famous footballers
⬤ take part.

fútil ['futʃiw] (pl -eis) adj (pessoa) superficial, shallow; (insignificante) trivial

futilidade [futʃili'dadʒi] F (de pessoa) shallowness; (insignificância) triviality; (coisa fútil) trivial thing

futurismo [futu'riʒmu] M futurism

futuro, -a [fu'turu, a] adj future ■ M future; **no ~** in the future; **num ~ próximo** in the near future

fuxicar [fuʃi'kaʳ] vi to gossip

fuxico [fu'ʃiku] M piece of gossip

fuxiqueiro, -a [fuʃi'kejru, a] M/F gossip ■ adj gossipy

fuzil [fu'ziw] (pl -is) M rifle

fuzilamento [fuzila'mētu] M shooting

fuzilante [fuzi'lãtʃi] adj (olhos) blazing

fuzilar [fuzi'laʳ] vt to shoot ■ vi (olhos) to blaze; (pessoa) to fume

fuzileiro, -a [fuzi'lejru, a] M/F: ~ **naval** (Mil) marine

fuzis [fu'ziʃ] MPL de **fuzil**

fuzuê [fu'zwe] M commotion

Gg

G, g [ʒe] (pl **gs**) M G, g; **G de Gomes** G for George
g. ABR (= grama) gr.; (= grau) deg
Gabão [ga'bãw] M: **o ~** Gabon
gabar [ga'baʳ] VT to praise; **gabar-se** VR: **gabar-se de** to boast about
gabardine [gabax'dʒini] F gabardine
gabaritado, -a [gabari'tadu, a] ADJ (pessoa) well-qualified
gabarito [gaba'ritu] M (fig): **ter ~ para** to have the ability to; **de ~** (of) high calibre atr (Brit) ou caliber atr (US)
gabinete [gabi'netʃi] M (Com) office; (escritório) study; (Pol) cabinet
gado ['gadu] M livestock; (bovino) cattle; **~ leiteiro** dairy cattle; **~ suíno** pigs pl
gaélico, -a [ga'ɛliku, a] ADJ Gaelic ■ M (Ling) Gaelic
gafanhoto [gafa'ɲotu] M grasshopper
gafe ['gafi] F gaffe, faux pas; **dar** ou **cometer uma ~** to make a faux pas
gafieira [ga'fjejra] (col) F (lugar) dive; (baile) knees-up
gagá [ga'ga] ADJ senile
gago, -a ['gagu, a] ADJ stuttering ■ M/F stutterer
gagueira [ga'gejra] F stutter
gaguejar [gage'ʒaʳ] VI to stammer, stutter ■ VT (resposta) to stammer
gaiato, -a [ga'jatu, a] ADJ funny
gaiola [ga'jɔla] F (para pássaro) cage; (cadeia) jail ■ M (barco) riverboat
gaita ['gajta] F harmonica; (col: dinheiro) cash, dough; **cheio/a da ~** (col) loaded; **solta a ~!** (col) hand over your cash!; **~ de foles** bagpipes pl
gaivota [gaj'vɔta] F seagull
gajo ['gaʒu] (PT: col) M guy, fellow
gala ['gala] F: **traje de ~** full dress; **festa de ~** gala
galã [ga'lã] M (ator) leading man; (fig) ladies' man
galalau [gala'law] M giant
galante [ga'lãtʃi] ADJ (gracioso) graceful; (gentil) gallant
galanteador [galãtʃja'doʳ] M suitor, admirer

galantear [galã'tʃjaʳ] VT to court, woo
galanteio [galã'teju] M wooing
galantina [galã'tʃina] F (Culin): **~ de galinha** chicken galantine
galão [ga'lãw] (pl **-ões**) M (Mil) stripe; (medida) gallon; (PT: café) white coffee; (passamanaria) braid
Galápagos [ga'lapaguʃ]: **(as) Ilhas** FPL (the) Galapagos Islands
galardão [galax'dãw] (pl **-ões**) M reward
galardoar [galax'dwaʳ] VT: **~ alguém (com algo)** to reward sb (with sth)
galardões [galax'dõjʃ] MPL de **galardão**
galáxia [ga'laksja] M galaxy
galé [ga'lɛ] F (Náut) galley ■ M galley slave
galego, -a [ga'legu, a] ADJ Galician ■ M/F Galician; (col: pej) Portuguese ■ M (Ling) Galician
galera [ga'lɛra] F (Náut) galley; (col: pessoas, público) crowd
galeria [gale'ria] F gallery; (Teatro) circle; (para águas pluviais) storm drain
Gales ['galiʃ] M: **País de ~** Wales
galês, -esa [ga'leʃ, eza] ADJ Welsh ■ M/F Welshman/woman ■ M (Ling) Welsh; **os galeses** MPL the Welsh
galeto [ga'letu] M spring chicken
galgar [gaw'gaʳ] VT (saltar) to leap over; (subir) to climb up
galgo ['gawgu] M greyhound
galhardia [gaʎax'dʒia] F (elegância) elegance; (bravura, gentileza) gallantry; **com ~** gallantly
galhardo, -a [ga'ʎaxdu, a] ADJ (elegante) elegant; (bravo, gentil) gallant
galheteiro [gaʎe'tejru] M cruet
galho ['gaʎu] M (de árvore) branch; (col: bico) part-time job; (: problema): **dar o ~** to cause trouble; **quebrar um** ou **o ~** to sort it out
galicismo [gali'siʒmu] M Gallicism
galináceos [gali'nasjuʃ] MPL poultry sg
galinha [ga'liɲa] F hen; (Culin; fig: covarde) chicken; (fig: puta) slut; **a ~ do vizinho é sempre mais gorda** (fig) the grass is always greener (on the other side of the fence); **matar**

NB: European Portuguese adds the following consonants to certain words: **b** (sú(b)dito, su(b)til); **c** (a(c)ção, a(c)cionista, a(c)to); **m** (inde(m)ne); **p** (ado(p)çã, ado(p)tar); for further details see p. xiii.

a ~ dos ovos de ouro (*fig*) to kill the goose that lays the golden egg

galinha-d'angola (*pl* galinhas-d'angolas) F guinea fowl

galinha-morta (*pl* galinhas-mortas) (*col*) F (*pechincha*) bargain; (*coisa fácil*) piece of cake ■ M/ F (*pessoa*) weakling

galinheiro [gali'ɲejru] M (*lugar*) hen-house

galo ['galu] M cock, rooster; (*inchação*) bump; **missa do ~** midnight mass; **ouvir cantar o ~ e não saber onde** (*fig*) to jump to conclusions; **~ de briga** fighting cock; (*fig: pessoa*) troublemaker

galocha [ga'lɔʃa] F (*bota*) Wellington (boot)

galões [ga'lõjʃ] MPL *de* **galão**

galopante [galo'pãtʃi] ADJ (*fig: inflação*) galloping; (: *doença*) rampant

galopar [galo'paʳ] VI to gallop; **galope** [ga'lɔpi] M gallop

galpão [gaw'pãw] (*pl* -ões) M shed

galvanizar [gawvani'zaʳ] VT to galvanize

gama ['gama] F (*Mús*) scale; (*fig*) range; (*Zool*) doe

gamado, -a [ga'madu, a] (*col*) ADJ: **ser** *ou* **estar ~ por** to be crazy about

gamão [ga'mãw] M backgammon

gamar [ga'maʳ] (*col*) VI: **~ (por)** to fall in love (with)

gambá [gã'ba] M (*Zool*) opossum; **bêbado como um ~** (*col*) pissed as a newt

Gâmbia ['gãbja] M: **o ~** (the) Gambia

gambito [gã'bitu] M (*Xadrez* etc) gambit; (*col: perna*) pin

gamo ['gamu] M (*fallow*) deer

Gana ['gana] M Ghana

gana ['gana] F (*desejo*) craving, desire; (*ódio*) hate; **ter ~s de (fazer) algo** to feel like (doing) sth; **ter ~ de alguém** to hate sb

ganância [ga'nãsja] F greed; **ganancioso, -a** [ganã'sjozu, ɔza] ADJ greedy

gancho ['gãʃu] M hook; (*de calça*) crotch

gandaia [gã'daja] F (*vadiagem*) idling; (*farra*) living it up; **viver na ~** to lead the life of Riley; **cair na ~** to live it up

Ganges ['gãʒiʃ] M: **o ~** the Ganges

gânglio ['gãglju] M (*Med*) ganglion

gangorra [gã'goxa] F seesaw

gangrena [gã'grena] F gangrene

gangrenar [gãgre'naʳ] VI to go gangrenous

gângster ['gãʃteʳ] M gangster

gangue ['gãgi] (*col*) F gang

ganhador, a [gaɲa'doʳ(a)] ADJ winning ■ M/F winner

ganha-pão ['gaɲa-] (*pl* -ães) M living, livelihood

ganhar [ga'ɲaʳ] VT to win; (*salário*) to earn; (*adquirir*) to get; (*lugar*) to reach; (*lucrar*) to gain ■ VI to win; **~ de alguém** (*num jogo*) to beat sb; **~ a alguém em algo** to outdo sb in sth; **~ tempo** to gain time; **~ a vida** to earn a living; **sair ganhando** to come out better off, come off better; **ganhei o dia** (*fig*) it made my day; **ganho, -a** ['gaɲu, a] PP *de* **ganhar** ■ M (*lucro*) profit, gain; **ganhos** MPL (*ao jogo*) winnings;

ganho de capital (*Com*) capital gain

ganido [ga'nidu] M (*de cão*) yelp; (*de pessoa*) squeal

ganir [ga'niʳ] VI (*cão*) to yelp; (*pessoa*) to squeal ■ VT (*gemido, gritos*) to let out

ganso, -a ['gãsu, a] M/F gander/goose

garagem [ga'raʒẽ] (*pl* -ns) F garage

garagista [gara'ʒiʃta] M/F garage owner

garanhão [gara'ɲãw] (*pl* -ões) M stallion; (*col: homem*) stud

garantia [garã'tʃia] F guarantee; (*de dívida*) surety; **estar na ~** (*compra*) to be under guarantee; **empréstimo sem ~** (*Com*) unsecured loan

garantir [garã'tʃiʳ] VT to guarantee; **garantir-se** VR: **garantir-se contra algo** to defend o.s. against sth; **~ algo (a alguém)** (*prometer*) to promise (sb) sth; **~ que ...** to maintain that ...; **~ a alguém que ...** to assure sb that ...; **~ alguém contra algo** to defend sb against sth

garatujar [garatu'ʒaʳ] VT to scribble, scrawl

garbo ['gaxbu] M (*elegância*) elegance; (*distinção*) distinction

garboso, -a [gax'bozu, ɔza] ADJ (*elegante*) elegant; (*distinto*) distinguished

garça ['gaxsa] F heron

garçom [gax'sõ] (BR) (*pl* -ns) M waiter

garçonete [gaxso'netʃi] (BR) F waitress

garçonnière [gaxso'njeʳ] F love nest

garçons [gax'sõʃ] MPL *de* **garçom**

garfada [gax'fada] F forkful

garfo ['gaxfu] M fork; **ser um bom ~** (*fig*) to enjoy one's food

gargalhada [gaxga'ʎada] F burst of laughter; **rir às ~s** to roar with laughter; **dar** *ou* **soltar uma ~** to burst out laughing; **~ homérica** guffaw

gargalo [gax'galu] M (*tb fig*) bottleneck

garganta [gax'gãta] F (*Anat*) throat; (*Geo*) gorge, ravine ■ M/F (*col*) braggart, loudmouth ■ ADJ (*col*) loudmouth(ed); **limpar a ~** to clear one's throat; **molhar a ~** (*col*) to wet one's whistle; **aquilo não me passou pela ~** (*fig*) that stuck in my craw

gargantilha [gaxgã'tʃiʎa] F choker

gargarejar [gaxgare'ʒaʳ] VI to gargle

gargarejo [gaxga'reʒu] M (*ato*) gargling; (*líquido*) gargle

gari ['gari] M/F (*na rua*) roadsweeper (*Brit*), streetsweeper (*US*); (*lixeiro*) dustman (*Brit*), garbage man (*US*)

garimpar [garĩ'paʳ] VI to prospect

garimpeiro [garĩ'pejru] M prospector

garoa [ga'roa] F drizzle; **garoar** [ga'rwaʳ] VI to drizzle

garota [ga'rota] (BR: *col*) F (*cerveja*) beer; *v tb* **garoto**

garotada [garo'tada] F: **a ~** the kids *pl*

garota-de-programa (*pl* garotas-de-programa) (*col*) F good-time girl

garoto, -a [ga'rotu, a] M/F boy/girl; (*namorado*) boyfriend/girlfriend; (PT: *café*) coffee with milk

garoto, -ta-propaganda (pl -s/as-propaganda) M/F boy/girl who advertises products on television

garoupa [ga'ropa] F (peixe) grouper

garra ['gaxa] F claw; (de ave) talon; (fig: entusiasmo) enthusiasm, drive; **garras** FPL (fig) clutches

garrafa [ga'xafa] F bottle

garrafada [gaxa'fada] F: **dar uma ~ em alguém** to hit sb with a bottle

garrafão [gaxa'fãw] (pl -ões) M flagon

garrancho [ga'xãʃu] M scrawl

garrido, -a [ga'xidu, a] ADJ (elegante) smart; (alegre) lively; (vistoso) showy; (gracioso) pretty

garrote [ga'xɔtʃi] M (Med) tourniquet; (tortura) garrote

garupa [ga'rupa] F (de cavalo) hindquarters pl; (de moto) back seat; **andar na ~** (de moto) to ride pillion

gás [gajʃ] M gas; **gases** MPL (do intestino) wind sg; **~ natural** natural gas

gaseificar [gazejfi'kaʳ] VT to vapourize (Brit), vaporize (US); **gaseificar-se** VR to vapo(u)rize

gasoduto [gazo'dutu] M gas pipeline

gasóleo [ga'zɔlju] M diesel oil

gasolina [gazo'lina] F petrol (Brit), gas(oline) (US)

gasômetro [ga'zometru] M gasometer

gasosa [ga'zɔza] F fizzy drink, soda pop (US)

gasoso, -a [ga'zozu, ɔza] ADJ (Quím) gaseous; (água) sparkling; (bebida) fizzy

gáspea ['gaʃpja] F (de sapato) upper

gastador, -deira [gaʃta'doʳ, 'dejra] ADJ, M/F spendthrift

gastar [gaʃ'taʳ] VT (dinheiro, tempo) to spend; (gasolina, electricidade) to use; (roupa, sapato) to wear out; (salto, piso etc) to wear down; (saúde) to damage; (desperdiçar) to waste ■ VI to spend; to wear out; to wear down; **gastar-se** VR to wear out; to wear down

gasto, -a ['gaʃtu, a] PP de **gastar** ■ ADJ (dinheiro, tempo, energias) spent; (frase) trite; (sapato etc, fig: pessoa) worn out; (salto, piso) worn down ■ M (despesa) expense; **gastos** MPL (Com) expenses, expenditure sg; **~s públicos** public spending sg; **dar para o ~** (col) to do, be OK

gastrenterite [gaʃtrẽte'ritʃi] F (Med) gastroenteritis

gástrico, -a ['gaʃtriku, a] ADJ gastric

gastrite [gaʃ'tritʃi] F (Med) gastritis

gastronomia [gaʃtrono'mia] F gastronomy

gastronômico, -a [gaʃtro'nomiku, a] ADJ gastronomic

gata ['gata] F (she-)cat; (col: mulher) sexy lady; **andar de ~s** (PT) to go on all fours; **~ borralheira** Cinderella; (mulher) stay-at-home

gatão [ga'tãw] (col) (pl -ões) M (homem) hunk

gatilho [ga'tʃiʎu] M trigger

gatinha [ga'tʃiɲa] (col) F (mulher) sexy lady

gatinhas [ga'tʃiɲaʃ] FPL: **andar de ~** (BR) to go

on all fours

gato ['gatu] M cat; (col: homem) dish, hunk; **ter um ~** (col) to have kittens; **~ escaldado tem medo de água fria** once bitten, twice shy; **~ montês** wild cat

gatões [ga'tõjʃ] MPL de **gatão**

gato-sapato M: **fazer alguém de ~** to walk all over sb, treat sb as a doormat

gatos-pingados MPL stalwarts

GATT ABR M (= Acordo Geral sobre Tarifas Aduaneiras e Comércio) GATT

gatuno, -a [ga'tunu, a] ADJ thieving ■ M/F thief

gaúcho, -a [ga'uʃu, a] ADJ from Rio Grande do Sul ■ M/F native of Rio Grande do Sul

gaveta [ga'veta] F drawer

gavetão [gave'tãw] (pl -ões) M big drawer

gavião [ga'vjãw] (pl -ões) M hawk

Gaza ['gaza] F: **a faixa de ~** the Gaza Strip

gaza ['gaza] F = **gaze**

gaze ['gazi] F gauze

gazela [ga'zela] F gazelle

gazeta [ga'zeta] F (jornal) newspaper, gazette; **fazer ~** to play truant

gazua [ga'zua] F skeleton key

GB ABR (= Guanabara) former state, now Rio de Janeiro

geada ['ʒjada] F frost

geladeira [ʒela'dejra] (BR) F refrigerator, icebox (US)

gelado, -a [ʒe'ladu, a] ADJ frozen ■ M (PT: sorvete) ice cream

gelar [ʒe'laʳ] VT to freeze; (vinho etc) to chill ■ VI to freeze

gelatina [ʒela'tʃina] F gelatine; (sobremesa) jelly (Brit), jello (US)

gelatinoso, -a [ʒelatʃi'nozu, ɔza] ADJ gooey

geléia [ʒe'lɛja] F jam

geleira [ʒe'lejra] F (Geo) glacier

gélido, -a ['ʒɛlidu, a] ADJ chill, icy

gelo ['ʒelu] ADJ INV light grey (Brit) ou gray (US) ■ M ice; (cor) light grey (Brit) ou gray (US); **quebrar o ~** (fig) to break the ice; **hoje está um ~** it's freezing today; **dar o ~ em alguém** (col) to give sb the cold shoulder

gelo-seco M dry ice

gema ['ʒema] F (de ovo) yolk; (pedra preciosa) gem; **ser da ~** to be genuine; **ela é paulista da ~** she's a real Paulista

gemada [ʒe'mada] F eggnog

gêmeo, -a ['ʒemju, a] ADJ, M/F twin; **Gêmeos** MPL (Astrologia) Gemini sg

gemer [ʒe'meʳ] VT (canção) to croon ■ VI (de dor) to groan, moan; (lamentar-se) to wail, howl; (animal) to whine; (vento) to howl; **gemido** [ʒe'midu] M groan, moan; (lamento) wail; (de animal) whine

gen. ABR (= general) Gen

gene ['ʒeni] M gene

genealogia [ʒenjalo'ʒia] F genealogy

genealógico, -a [ʒenja'lɔʒiku, a] ADJ genealogical; **árvore genealógica** family tree
Genebra [ʒe'nɛbra] N Geneva
genebra [ʒe'nɛbra] (PT) F gin
general [ʒene'raw] (pl -ais) M (Mil) general
generalidade [ʒenerali'dadʒi] F generality; (maioria) majority; **generalidades** FPL (princípios) basics, principles
generalização [ʒeneraliza'sãw] (pl -ões) F generalization
generalizar [ʒenerali'za^r] VT (propagar) to propagate ▪ VI to generalize; **generalizar-se** VR to become general, spread
genérico, -a [ʒe'nɛriku, a] ADJ generic
gênero ['ʒeneru] M (espécie) type, kind; (Literatura) genre; (Bio) genus; (Ling) gender; **gêneros** MPL (produtos) goods; **~s alimentícios** foodstuffs; **~s de primeira necessidade** essentials; **~ de vida** way of life; **~ humano** humankind, human race; **essa roupa/ele não faz o meu ~** this outfit is not my style/he is not my type
generosidade [ʒenerozi'dadʒi] F generosity
generoso, -a [ʒene'rozu, ɔza] ADJ generous
gênese ['ʒenezi] F origin, beginning; **G~** (Rel) Genesis
genética [ʒe'nɛtʃika] F genetics sg
genético, -a [ʒe'nɛtʃiku, a] ADJ genetic
gengibre [ʒẽ'ʒibri] M ginger
gengiva [ʒẽ'ʒiva] F (Anat) gum
genial [ʒe'njaw] (pl -ais) ADJ inspired; (idéia) brilliant; (col) terrific, fantastic
gênio ['ʒenju] M (temperamento) nature; (irascibilidade) temper; (talento, pessoa) genius; **de bom ~** good-natured; **de mau ~** bad-tempered; **um cientista de ~** a scientific genius, a genius at science
genioso, -a [ʒe'njozu, ɔza] ADJ bad-tempered
genital [ʒeni'taw] (pl -ais) ADJ: **órgãos genitais** genitals pl
genitivo [ʒeni'tʃivu] M (Ling) genitive
genitora [ʒeni'tora] F mother
genocídio [ʒeno'sidʒju] M genocide
genro ['ʒẽxu] M son-in-law
gentalha [ʒẽ'taʎa] F rabble
gente ['ʒẽtʃi] F (pessoas) people pl; (col) folks pl; (família) folks pl, family; (col: alguém): **tem ~ batendo à porta** there's somebody knocking at the door; **a ~** (nós: suj) we; (: obj) us; **~!** (exprime admiração, surpresa) gosh!; **vai com a ~** come with us; **a casa da ~** our house; **toda a ~** everybody; **ficar ~** to grow up; **ser ~** (ser alguém) to be somebody; **também ser ~** (col) to be as good as anyone else; **ser ~ boa** ou **fina** (col) to be a nice person; **a ~ bem** the upper crust; **~ grande** grown-ups pl; **oi/tchau, ~!** hi/bye, folks!
gentil [ʒẽ'tʃiw] (pl -is) ADJ kind; **gentileza** [ʒẽtʃi'leza] F kindness; **por gentileza** if you please; **tenha a gentileza de fazer ...?** would you be so kind as to do ...?
gentinha [ʒẽ'tʃiɲa] F rabble
gentio, -a [ʒẽ'tʃiu, a] ADJ, M/F heathen

gentis [ʒe'tʃiʃ] ADJ PL de gentil
genuflexão [ʒenuflek'sãw] (pl -ões) F (Rel) genuflection
genuíno, -a [ʒe'nwinu, a] ADJ genuine
geofísica [ʒeo'fizika] F geophysics sg
geografia [ʒeogra'fia] F geography
geográfico, -a [ʒeo'grafiku, a] ADJ geographical
geógrafo, -a [ʒe'ɔgrafu, a] M/F geographer
geologia [ʒeolo'ʒia] F geology
geólogo, -a [ʒe'ɔlogu, a] M/F geologist
geometria [ʒeome'tria] F geometry
geométrico, -a [ʒeo'mɛtriku, a] ADJ geometrical
geopolítico, -a [ʒeopo'litʃiku, a] ADJ geopolitical
Geórgia ['ʒɔxʒa] F: **a ~** Georgia
georgiano, -a [ʒox'ʒanu, a] ADJ, M/F Georgian
geração [ʒera'sãw] (pl -ões) F (tb: Comput) generation; **linguagem de quarta ~** (Comput) fourth-generation language
gerador, a [ʒera'do^r(a)] ADJ: **~ de algo** causing sth ▪ M/F (produtor) creator ▪ M (Tec) generator
geral [ʒe'raw] (pl -ais) ADJ general ▪ F (Teatro) gallery; (revisão) general overhaul; **dar uma ~ em algo** (col) to have a blitz on sth; **em ~** in general, generally; **de um modo ~** on the whole; **geralmente** [ʒeraw'mẽtʃi] ADV generally, usually
gerânio [ʒe'ranju] M geranium
gerar [ʒe'ra^r] VT (produzir) to produce; (filhos) to beget; (causar: ódios etc) to engender, cause; (eletricidade) to generate
gerativo, -a [ʒera'tʃivu, a] ADJ generative
gerência [ʒe'rẽsja] F management
gerenciador [ʒerẽsja'do^r] M: **~ de banco de dados** (Comput) database manager
gerencial [ʒerẽ'sjaw] (pl -ais) ADJ management atr
gerenciar [ʒerẽ'sja^r] VT, VI to manage
gerente [ʒe'rẽtʃi] ADJ managing ▪ M/F manager
gergelim [ʒexʒe'lĩ] M (Bot) sesame
geriatria [ʒerja'tria] F geriatrics sg
geriátrico, -a [ʒe'rjatriku, a] ADJ geriatric
geringonça [ʒerĩ'gõsa] F contraption
gerir [ʒe'ri^r] VT to manage, run
germânico, -a [ʒex'maniku, a] ADJ Germanic
germe ['ʒexmi] M (embrião) embryo; (micróbio) germ; (fig) origin; **o ~ de uma idéia** the germ of an idea
germicida [ʒexmi'sida] ADJ germicidal ▪ M germicide
germinação [ʒexmina'sãw] F germination
germinar [ʒexmi'na^r] VI (semente) to germinate; (fig) to develop
gerontologia [ʒerõtolo'ʒia] F gerontology
gerúndio [ʒe'rũdʒju] M (Ling) gerund
gesso ['ʒesu] M plaster (of Paris)
gestação [ʒeʃta'sãw] F gestation
gestante [ʒeʃ'tãtʃi] F pregnant woman
gestão [ʒeʃ'tãw] F management
gesticular [ʒeʃtʃiku'la^r] VI to make gestures,

gesture ■ VT: ~ **um adeus** to wave goodbye

gesto ['ʒɛʃtu] M gesture; **fazer ~s** to gesture

gibi [ʒi'bi] (col) M comic; **não estar no ~** (fig) to be incredible ou amazing

Gibraltar [ʒibraw'ta^r] F Gibraltar

gigante, -a [ʒi'gãtʃi] ADJ gigantic, huge ■ M giant; **gigantesco, -a** [ʒigã'teʃku, a] ADJ gigantic

gigolô [ʒigo'lo] M gigolo

gilete [ʒi'lɛtʃi] (BR) F (*lâmina*) razor blade; (col) bisexual, bi

gim [ʒĩ] (*pl* -ns) M gin

ginásio [ʒi'nazju] M (*para ginástica*) gymnasium; (*escola*) secondary (Brit) ou high (US) school

ginasta [ʒi'naʃta] M/F gymnast

ginástica [ʒi'naʃtʃika] F (*competitiva*) gymnastics sg; (*para fortalecer o corpo*) keep-fit

ginecologia [ʒinekolo'ʒia] F gynaecology (Brit), gynecology (US)

ginecologista [ʒinekolo'ʒiʃta] M/F gynaecologist (Brit), gynecologist (US)

ginete [ʒi'netʃi] M thoroughbred

gingar [ʒĩ'ga^r] VI to sway

ginja ['ʒĩʒa] (PT) F morello cherry

ginjinha [ʒĩ'ʒiɲa] (PT) F cherry brandy

gins [ʒĩʃ] MPL *de* **gim**

gira ['ʒira] ADJ crazy

gira-discos (PT) M INV record-player

girafa [ʒi'rafa] F giraffe; (col: *pessoa*) giant

girar [ʒi'ra^r] VT to turn, rotate; (*como pião*) to spin ■ VI to go round; to spin; (*vaguear*) to wander; **ele não gira bem** (col) he's not all there

girassol [ʒira'sɔw] (*pl* -óis) M sunflower

giratório, -a [ʒira'tɔrju, a] ADJ revolving; (*cadeira*) swivel atr

gíria ['ʒirja] F (*calão*) slang; (*jargão*) jargon

giro ['ʒiru] M turn; **dar um ~** to go for a wander; (*em veículo*) to go for a spin; **que ~!** (PT) terrific!

giro etc VB V **gerir**

giz [ʒiʒ] M chalk

glacê [gla'se] M icing

glacial [gla'sjaw] (*pl* -ais) ADJ icy

gladiador [gladʒja'do^r] M gladiator

glamouroso, -a [glamu'rozu, ɔza] ADJ glamorous

glândula ['glãdula] F gland

glandular [glãdu'la^r] ADJ glandular

gleba ['glɛba] F field

glicerina [glise'rina] F glycerine

glicose [gli'kɔzi] F glucose

global [glo'baw] (*pl* -ais) ADJ (*da terra*) global; (*total*) overall; **quantia ~** lump sum; **globalização** [globaliza'sãw] (*pl* **globalizações**) F globalization

globo ['globu] M globe; **~ ocular** eyeball

globular [globu'la^r] ADJ (*forma*) rounded

glóbulo ['glɔbulu] M (tb: **glóbulo sanguíneo**) corpuscle

glória ['glɔrja] F glory

gloriar-se [glo'rjaxsi] VR: ~ **de** to boast of

glorificar [glorifi'ka^r] VT to glorify

glorioso, -a [glo'rjozu, ɔza] ADJ glorious

glosa ['glɔza] F comment

glosar [glo'za^r] VT to comment on; (*conta*) to cancel

glossário [glo'sarju] M glossary

glote ['glɔtʃi] F (Anat) glottis

gluglu [glu'glu] M (*de peru*) gobble-gobble; (*de água*) glug-glug

glutão, -tona [glu'tãw] (*pl* -ões/-s) ADJ greedy ■ M/F glutton

glúten ['glutẽ] (*pl* -s) M gluten

glutões [glu'tõjʃ] MPL *de* **glutão**

glutona [glu'tɔna] F *de* **glutão**

gnomo ['gnomu] M gnome

GO ABR = **Goiás**

Goa ['goa] N Goa

godê [go'de] ADJ (*saia*) flared

goela ['gwɛla] F throat

goela-de-pato (*pl* **goelas-de-pato**) F (Culin) pasta strand

gogó [go'gɔ] (col) M Adam's apple

goiaba [go'jaba] F guava; **goiabada** [goja'bada] F guava jelly

goiabeira [goja'bejra] F guava tree

goianense [goja'n(j)ẽsi] ADJ from Goiânia ■ M/F native of Goiânia

goiano, -a [go'janu, a] ADJ from Goiás ■ M/F native of Goiás

gol [gow] (*pl* -s) M goal; **marcar um ~** to score a goal

gola ['gɔla] F collar

golaço [go'lasu] M (Futebol) great goal

Golan [go'lã] M: **as colinas de ~** the Golan heights

gole ['gɔli] M gulp, swallow; (*pequeno*) sip; **de um só ~** at one gulp; **dar um ~** to have a sip

goleada [go'ljada] F (Futebol) convincing win

golear [go'lja^r] VT to thrash ■ VI to win convincingly

goleiro [go'lejru] (BR) M goalkeeper

golfada [gow'fada] F (*jacto*) spurt

golfar [gow'fa^r] VT (*vomitar*) to spit up; (*lançar*) to throw out ■ VI (*sair*) to spurt out; (*bebê*) to bring up some milk

golfe ['gowfi] M golf; **campo de ~** golf course

golfinho [gow'fiɲu] M (Zool) dolphin

golfista [gow'fiʃta] M/F golfer

golfo ['gowfu] M gulf

golinho [go'liɲu] M sip; **beber algo aos ~s** to sip sth

golo ['golu] (PT) M = **gol**

golpe ['gɔwpi] M (tb fig) blow; (*de mão*) smack; (*de punho*) punch; (*manobra*) ploy; (*de vento*) gust; **de um só ~** at a stroke; **dar um ~ em alguém** (*golpear*) to hit sb; (fig: *trapacear*) to trick sb; **o ~ é fazer ...** the clever thing is to do ...; **dar o ~ do baú** (fig) to marry for money; **~ baixo** (fig, col)

NB: *European Portuguese adds the following consonants to certain words:* **b** (sú(b)dito, su(b)til); **c** (a(c)ção, a(c)cionista, a(c)to); **m** (inde(m)ne); **p** (ado(p)çã, ado(p)tar); *for further details see p. xiii.*

dirty trick; ~ **(de estado)** coup (d'état); ~ **de mestre** masterstroke; ~ **de vista** (olhar) glance; (de motorista) eye for distances; ~ **mortal** death blow; **golpear** [gow'pja^r] VT to hit; (com navalha) to stab; (com o punho) to punch

golpista [gow'piʃta] ADJ tricky

golquíper [gow'kipe^r] M goalkeeper

goma ['gɔma] F (cola) gum, glue; (de roupa) starch; ~ **de mascar** chewing gum

gomo ['gomu] M (de laranja) slice

gôndola ['gõdola] F (Náut) gondola; (em supermercado) basket

gondoleiro [gõdo'lejru] M gondolier

gongo ['gõgu] M gong; (sineta) bell

gonorréia [gono'xɛja] F (Med) gonorrhea

gonzo ['gõzu] M hinge

gorar [go'ra^r] VT to frustrate, thwart ▪ VI (plano) to fail, go wrong

gordo, -a ['goxdu, a] ADJ (pessoa) fat; (gordurento) greasy; (carne) fatty; (fig: quantia) considerable, ample ▪ M/F fat man/woman; **nunca vi mais ~** (col) I've never seen him (ou her, them etc) before in my life

gorducho, -a [gox'duʃu, a] ADJ plump, tubby ▪ M/F plump person

gordura [gox'dura] F fat; (derretida) grease; (obesidade) fatness

gordurento, -a [goxdu'rẽtu, a] ADJ (ensebado) greasy; (gordo) fatty

gorduroso, -a [goxdu'rozu, ɔza] ADJ (pele) greasy; (comida) fatty

gorgolejar [goxgole'ʒa^r] VI to gurgle

gorila [go'rila] M gorilla

gorjear [gox'ʒja^r] VI to chirp, twitter

gorjeio [gox'ʒeju] M twittering, chirping

gorjeta [gox'ʒeta] F tip, gratuity

gororoba [goro'rɔba] (col) F (comida) grub; (comida ruim) muck

gorro ['goxu] M cap; (de lã) hat

gosma ['gɔʒma] F spittle; (fig) slime

gosmento, -a [goʒ'mẽtu, a] ADJ slimy

gostar [goʃ'ta^r] VI: ~ **de** to like; (férias, viagem etc) to enjoy; **gostar-se** VR to like each other; ~ **de fazer algo** to like ou enjoy doing sth; **eu ~ia de ir** I would like to go; **gosto de sua companhia** I enjoy your company; **gosto de nadar** I like ou enjoy swimming; **gostei muito de falar com você** it was very nice talking to you; ~ **mais de ...** to prefer ..., to like ... better

gosto ['goʃtu] M taste; (prazer) pleasure; **falta de ~** lack of taste; **a seu ~** to your liking; **com ~** willingly; (vestir-se) tastefully; (comer) heartily; **de bom/mau ~** in good/bad taste; **para o meu ~** for my liking; **ter ~ de** to taste of; **tenho muito ~ em ...** it gives me a lot of pleasure to ...; **tomar ~ por** to take a liking to

gostosão, -sona [goʃto'zaw, 'zɔna] (col) (pl -ões/-s) M/F stunner

gostoso, -a [goʃ'tozu, ɔza] ADJ (comida) tasty; (agradável) pleasant; (cheiro) lovely; (risada) good; (col: pessoa) gorgeous ▪ M/F (col) cracker; **é ~ viajar** it's really nice to travel

gostosões [goʃto'zõjʃ] MPL de **gostosão**

gostosona [goʃto'zɔna] F de **gostosão**

gostosura [goʃto'zura] F: **ser uma ~** (comida) to be delicious; (bebê, jogo etc) to be lovely

gota ['gota] F drop; (de suor) bead; (Med) gout; ~ **a** ~ drop by drop; **ser a ~ d'água** ou **a última ~** (fig) to be the last straw; **ser uma ~ d'água no oceano** (fig) to be a drop in the ocean

goteira [go'tejra] F (cano) gutter; (buraco) leak

gotejante [gote'ʒãtʃi] ADJ dripping

gotejar [gote'ʒa^r] VT to drip ▪ VI to drip; (telhado) to leak

gótico, -a ['gɔtʃiku, a] ADJ Gothic

gotícula [go'tʃikula] F droplet

gourmet [gux'me] (pl -s) M/F gourmet

governador, a [govexnado^r(a)] M/F governor

governamental [govexnamẽ'taw] (pl -ais) ADJ government atr

governanta [govex'nãta] F (de casa) housekeeper; (de criança) governess

governante [govex'nãtʃi] ADJ ruling ▪ M/F ruler ▪ F governess

governar [govex'na^r] VT (Pol) to govern, rule; (barco) to steer

governista [govex'niʃta] ADJ pro-government ▪ M/F government supporter

governo [go'vexnu] M government; (controle) control; (Náut) steering; **para o seu ~** (col) for the record, for your information

gozação [goza'sãw] (pl -ões) F (desfrute) enjoyment; (zombaria) teasing; (uma gozação) joke

gozada [go'zada] F: **dar uma ~ em alguém** to pull sb's leg

gozado, -a [go'zadu, a] ADJ funny; (estranho) strange, odd

gozador, a [goza'do^r(a)] ADJ (caçoador) comical; (boa-vida) happy-go-lucky ▪ M/F joker; loafer

gozar [go'za^r] VT to enjoy; (col: rir de) to make fun of ▪ VI to enjoy o.s.; (ao fazer sexo) to have an orgasm; ~ **de** to enjoy; to make fun of; **gozo** ['gozu] M (prazer) pleasure; (uso) enjoyment, use; (orgasmo) orgasm; **estar em pleno gozo de suas faculdades mentais** to be in full possession of one's faculties; **ser um gozo** (ser engraçado) to be a laugh

G/P ABR (Com) = **ganhos e perdas**

gr. ABR = **grátis**; (= grau) deg.; (= gross) gr

Grã-Bretanha [grã-bre'taɲa] F Great Britain

graça ['grasa] F (Rel) grace; (charme) charm; (gracejo) joke; (Jur) pardon; **de ~** (grátis) for nothing; (sem motivo) for no reason; **sem ~** dull, boring; **fazer** ou **ter ~** to be funny; **ficar sem ~** to be embarrassed; ~**s a** thanks to; **não tem ~ fazer** (é chato) it's no fun to do; (não é certo) it's not right to do; **deixa de ~** don't be cheeky; **não sei que ~ você vê nele/nisso** I don't know what you see in him/it; **ser uma ~** to be lovely

gracejar [grase'ʒa^r] VI to joke; **gracejo** [gra'seʒu] M joke

gracinha [gra'siɲa] F: **ser uma ~** to be sweet ou cute; **que ~!** how sweet!

gracioso, -a [gra'sjozu, ɔza] ADJ (*pessoa*)
charming; (*gestos*) gracious

gradação [grada'sãw] (*pl* -ões) F gradation

gradativo, -a [grada'tʃivu, a] ADJ gradual

grade ['gradʒi] F (*no chão*) grating; (*grelha*) grill;
(*na janela*) bars *pl*; (*col*: *cadeia*) prison

gradear [gra'dʒjaʳ] VT (*janela*) to put bars up at;
(*jardim*) to fence off

grado, -a ['gradu, a] ADJ (*importante*) important
■ M: **de bom/mau** ~ willingly/unwillingly

graduação [gradwa'sãw] (*pl* -ões) F gradation;
(*classificação*) grading; (*Educ*) graduation; (*Mil*)
rank; **curso de** ~ degree course

graduado, -a [gra'dwadu, a] ADJ (*dividido em
graus*) graduated; (*diplomado*) graduate; (*eminente*)
highly thought of

gradual [gra'dwaw] (*pl* -ais) ADJ gradual

graduando, -a [gra'dwandu, a] M/F graduating
student, graduand

graduar [gra'dwaʳ] VT (*termômetro*) to graduate;
(*classificar*) to grade; (*luz, fogo*) to regulate;
graduar-se VR to graduate; ~ **alguém em algo**
(*Educ*) to confer a degree in sth on sb; ~ **alguém
em coronel** *etc* (*Mil*) to make sb a colonel *etc*

graduável [gra'dwavew] (*pl* -eis) ADJ adjustable

grafia [gra'fia] F (*escrita*) writing; (*ortografia*)
spelling

gráfica ['grafika] F (*arte*) graphics *sg*;
(*estabelecimento*) printer's; (*seção*: *de jornal etc*)
production department; *v tb* **gráfico**

gráfico, -a ['grafiku, a] ADJ graphic ■ M/F
printer ■ M (*Mat*) graph; (*diagrama*) diagram,
chart; **gráficos** MPL (*Comput*) graphics; ~ **de
barras** bar chart

grã-finagem [grãfi'naʒẽ] F: **a** ~ the upper crust

grã-finismo [grãfi'niʒmu] M (*qualidade*)
poshness; (*ato*) thing which posh people do; **o** ~
(*pessoas*) the upper crust

grã-fino, -a [grã-] (*col*) ADJ posh ■ M/F nob, toff

grafite [gra'fitʃi] F (*lápis*) lead; (*pichação*) (piece
of) graffiti

grafologia [grafolo'ʒia] F graphology

grama ['grama] M (*peso*) gramme ■ F (BR: *capim*)
grass

gramado [gra'madu] (BR) M lawn; (*Futebol*)
pitch

gramar [gra'maʳ] VT to plant *ou* sow with grass;
(PT: *col*) to be fond of ■ VI (PT: *col*) to cry out

gramática [gra'matʃika] F grammar; *v tb*
gramático

gramatical [gramatʃi'kaw] (*pl* -ais) ADJ
grammatical

gramático, -a [gra'matʃiku, a] ADJ
grammatical ■ M/F grammarian

gramofone [gramo'fɔni] M gramophone

grampeador [grãpja'doʳ] M stapler

grampear [grã'pjaʳ] VT to staple; (BR: *Tel*) to tap;
(*col*: *prender*) to nick

grampo ['grãpu] M staple; (*no cabelo*) hairgrip;

(*de carpinteiro*) clamp; (*de chapéu*) hatpin

grana ['grana] (*col*) F cash

Granada [gra'nada] F Grenada

granada [gra'nada] F (*Mil*) shell; (*pedra*) garnet; ~
de mão hand grenade

grandalhão, -lhona [grãda'ʎãw, 'ʎɔna] (*pl* -ões/-
s) ADJ enormous

grandão, -dona [grã'dãw, 'dɔna] (*pl* -ões/-s) ADJ
huge

grande ['grãdʒi] ADJ big, large; (*alto*) tall; (*notável,
intenso*) great; (*longo*) long; (*adulto*) grown-up; ~
mulher ~ big woman; ~ **mulher** great woman;
a G~ Londres Greater London

grandessíssimo, -a [grãdʒi'sisimu, a] ADJ
SUPERL *de* **grande**

grandeza [grã'deza] F (*tamanho*) size; (*fig*)
greatness; (*ostentação*) grandeur; **ter mania de** ~
to have delusions of grandeur

grandiloqüente [grãdʒilo'kwẽtʃi] ADJ
grandiloquent

grandiosidade [grãdʒjozi'dadʒi] F grandeur,
magnificence

grandioso, -a [grã'dʒjozu, ɔza] ADJ magnificent,
grand

grandíssimo, -a [grã'dʒisimu, a] ADJ SUPERL *de*
grande

grandões [grã'dõjʃ] MPL *de* **grandão**

grandona [grã'dɔna] F *de* **grandão**

granel [gra'nɛw] M: **a** ~ (*Com*) in bulk; **compra a**
~ bulk buying

granfa ['grãfa] (*col*) ADJ posh ■ M/F nob, toff

granito [gra'nitu] M (*Geo*) granite

granizo [gra'nizu] M hailstone; **chover** ~ to
hail; **chuva de** ~ hailstorm

granja ['grãʒa] F farm; (*de galinhas*) chicken farm

granjear [grã'ʒjaʳ] VT (*simpatia, amigos*) to win,
gain; (*bens, fortuna*) to procure; ~ **algo a** *ou* **para
alguém** to win sb sth

granulado, -a [granu'ladu, a] ADJ grainy;
(*açúcar*) granulated

grânulo ['granulu] M granule

grão ['grãw] (*pl* -s) M grain; (*semente*) seed; (*de
café*) bean; **grão-de-bico** (*pl* grãos-de-bico) M
chick pea

grapefruit [greip'frutʃi] (*pl* -s) M grapefruit

grasnar [graʒ'naʳ] VI (*corvo*) to caw; (*pato*) to
quack; (*rã*) to croak

gratidão [gratʃi'dãw] F gratitude

gratificação [gratʃifika'sãw] (*pl* -ões) F (*gorjeta*)
gratuity, tip; (*bônus*) bonus; (*recompensa*) reward

gratificado, -a [gratʃifi'kadu, a] ADJ (*grato*)
grateful

gratificante [gratʃifi'kãtʃi] ADJ gratifying

gratificar [gratʃifi'kaʳ] VT (*dar gorjeta a*) to tip;
(*dar bônus a*) to give a bonus to; (*recompensar*) to
reward

gratinado, -a [gratʃi'nadu, a] ADJ (*Culin*) au
gratin ■ M (*prato*) gratin; (*crosta*) crust

grátis ['gratʃiʃ] ADJ free

NB: *European Portuguese adds the following consonants to certain words:* **b** (sú(b)dito, su(b)til); **c** (a(c)ção,
a(c)cionista, a(c)to); **m** (inde(m)ne); **p** (ado(p)çã, ado(p)tar); *for further details see p. xiii.*

grato, -a ['gratu, a] ADJ (*agradecido*) grateful; (*agradável*) pleasant; **ficar ~ a alguém por** to be grateful to sb for

gratuidade [gratwi'dadʒi] F gratuity

gratuito, -a [gra'twitu, a] ADJ (*grátis*) free; (*infundado*) gratuitous

grau [graw] M degree; (*nível*) level; (*Educ*) class; **a temperatura é de 38 ~s** the temperature is 38 degrees; **primo/a em segundo** ~ second cousin; **em alto** ~ to a high degree; **primeiro/ segundo** ~ (*Educ*) primary/secondary level; **ensino de primeiro/segundo** ~ primary (*Brit*) *ou* elementary (*US*) /secondary education; **estar no 1°/2°** ~ (*Educ*) to be at primary/secondary (*Brit*) *ou* high (*US*) school

graúdo, -a [gra'udu, a] ADJ (*grande*) big; (*pessoa: influente*) important ■ M/F bigwig

gravação [grava'sãw] F (*em madeira*) carving; (*em disco, fita*) recording

gravador, a [grava'do'(a)] M tape recorder ■ M/ F engraver ■ F (*empresa*) record company; **~ de CD/DVD** CD/DVD burner, CD/DVD writer

gravame [gra'vami] M (*imposto*) duty; (*Jur*) lien

gravar [gra'va'] VT (*madeira*) to carve; (*metal, pedra*) to engrave; (*na memória*) to fix; (*disco, fita*) to record; **~ algo/alguém com impostos** to mark sth up/burden sb with taxes; **aquele dia ficou gravado na minha mente/memória** that day remained fixed in my mind/memory

gravata [gra'vata] F tie; **dar** *ou* **aplicar uma ~ em alguém** to get sb in a stranglehold; **~ borboleta** bow tie

grave ['gravi] ADJ (*situação, falta*) serious, grave; (*doença*) serious; (*tom*) deep; (*Ling*) grave; **gravemente** [grave'mẽtʃi] ADV (*doente, ferido*) seriously

graveto [gra'vetu] M piece of kindling

grávida ['gravida] ADJ pregnant

gravidade [gravi'dadʒi] F (*Fís*) gravity; (*de doença, situação*) seriousness

gravidez [gravi'deʒ] F pregnancy

gravitação [gravita'sãw] F gravitation

gravura [gra'vura] F (*em madeira*) engraving; (*estampa*) print

Grécia ['grɛsja] F: **a ~** Greece

grega ['grega] F (*galão*) braid; *v tb* **grego**

gregário, -a [gre'garju, a] ADJ gregarious

grego, -a ['gregu, a] ADJ, M/F Greek ■ M (*Ling*) Greek

grei [grej] F flock

grelar [gre'la'] VT to stare at

grelha ['grɛʎa] F grill; (*de fornalha*) grate; **bife na ~** grilled steak; **grelhado, -a** [gre'ʎadu, a] ADJ grilled ■ M (*prato*) grill

grelhar [gre'ʎa'] VT to grill

grêmio ['gremju] M (*associação*) guild; (*clube*) club

grená [gre'na] ADJ, M dark red

greta ['greta] F crack

gretado, -a [gre'tadu, a] ADJ cracked

greve ['grɛvi] F strike; **fazer ~** to go on strike;

~ de fome hunger strike; **~ branca** go-slow; **grevista** [gre'viʃta] M/F striker

grifado, -a [gri'fadu, a] ADJ in italics

grifar [gri'fa'] VT to italicize; (*sublinhar*) to underline; (*fig*) to emphasize

griffe ['grifi] M designer label

grifo ['grifu] M italics *pl*

grilado, -a [gri'ladu, a] (*col*) ADJ full of hang-ups; **estar ~ com algo** to be hung-up about sth

grilar [gri'la'] (*col*) VT: **~ alguém** to get sb worked up; **grilar-se** VR to get worked up

grilhão [gri'ʎãw] (*pl* -ões) M chain; **grilhões** MPL (*fig*) fetters

grilo ['grilu] M cricket; (*Auto*) squeak; (*col: de pessoa*) hang-up; **qual é o ~?** what's the matter?; **dar ~** (*col*) to cause problems; **se der ~** (*impess*) if there's a problem; **não tem ~!** (*col*) (there's) no problem!

grimpar [grĩ'pa'] VI to climb

grinalda [gri'nawda] F garland

gringada [grĩ'gada] F (*grupo*) bunch of foreigners; (*gringos*) foreigners *pl*

gringo, -a ['grĩgu, a] (*col: pej*) M/F foreigner

gripado, -a [gri'padu, a] ADJ: **estar/ficar ~** to have/get a cold

gripar-se [gri'paxsi] VR to catch flu

gripe ['gripi] F flu, influenza

grisalho, -a [gri'zaʎu, a] ADJ (*cabelo*) grey (*Brit*), gray (*US*)

grita ['grita] F uproar

gritante [gri'tãtʃi] ADJ (*hipocrisia*) glaring; (*desigualdade*) gross; (*mentira*) blatant; (*cor*) loud, garish

gritar [gri'ta'] VT to shout, yell ■ VI to shout; (*de dor, medo*) to scream; (*protestar*) to speak out; **~ com alguém** to shout at sb; **gritaria** [grita'ria] F shouting, din; **grito** ['gritu] M shout; (*de medo*) scream; (*de dor*) cry; (*de animal*) call; **dar um grito** to cry out; **falar/protestar aos gritos** to shout/shout protests; **no grito** (*col*) by force

Groenlândia [grwẽ'lãdʒja] F: **a ~** Greenland

grogue ['grɔgi] ADJ groggy

groom [grũ] (*pl* -s) M groom

grosa ['grɔza] F gross

groselha [gro'zeʎa] F (red)currant

grosseiro, -a [gro'sejru, a] ADJ (*pessoa, comentário*) rude; (*piada*) crude; (*modos*) coarse; (*tecido*) coarse, rough; (*móvel*) roughly-made; **grosseria** [grose'ria] F rudeness; (*ato*): **fazer uma grosseria** to be rude; (*dito*): **dizer uma grosseria** to be rude, say something rude

grosso, -a ['grosu, 'grɔsa] ADJ (*tamanho, consistência*) thick; (*áspero*) rough; (*voz*) deep; (*col: pessoa, piada*) rude ■ M: **o ~ de** the bulk of ■ ADV: **falar ~** to talk in a deep voice; **falar ~ com alguém** (*fig*) to get tough with sb; **a ~ modo** roughly; **grossura** [gro'sura] F thickness

grotão [gro'tãw] (*pl* -ões) M gorge

grotesco, -a [gro'teʃku, a] ADJ grotesque

grotões [gro'tõjʃ] MPL *de* **grotão**

grua ['grua] F (*Constr*) crane

grudado, -a [gru'dadu, a] ADJ (*fig*): **ser ~ com ou**

em alguém to be very attached to sb
grudar [gru'da'] VT to glue, stick ■ VI to stick
grude ['grudʒi] F glue; (*col: comida*) grub; (*ligação entre pessoas*): **ficar numa** ~ to cling to sb;
grudento, -a [gru'dẽtu, a] ADJ sticky
gruja ['gruʒa] (*col*) F tip
grunhido [gru'ɲidu] M grunt
grunhir [gru'ɲi'] VI (*porco*) to grunt; (*tigre*) to growl; (*resmungar*) to grumble
grupo ['grupu] M group; (*Tec*) unit, set
gruta ['gruta] F grotto
guache ['gwaʃi] M gouache
guapo, -a ['gwapu, a] ADJ beautiful
guaraná [gwara'na] M guarana; (*bebida*) soft drink flavoured with guarana
guarani [gwara'ni] ADJ, M/F Guarani ■ M (*Ling*) Guarani; (*moeda*) guarani
guarda ['gwaxda] M/F policeman/woman ■ F (*vigilância*) guarding; (*de objeto*) safekeeping ■ M (*Mil*) guard; **estar de** ~ to be on guard; **pôr-se em** ~ to be on one's guard; **a velha** ~ the old guard; **a G-** **Civil** the Civil Guard; **guarda-chuva** (*pl* **guarda-chuvas**) M umbrella
guarda-civil (*pl* **guardas-civis**) M/F civil guard
guarda-costas M INV (*Náut*) coastguard boat; (*capanga*) bodyguard
guardador, a [gwaxda'do'(a)] M/F car attendant
guardados [gwax'daduʃ] MPL keepsakes, valuables
guarda-florestal (*pl* **guardas-florestais**) M/F forest ranger
guarda-fogo (*pl* -s) M fireguard
guarda-louça [gwaxda-'losa] (*pl* -s) M sideboard
guarda-marinha (*pl* **guardas-marinha(s)**) M naval ensign
guarda-mor [-mɔ'] (*pl* **guardas-mores**) M inspector of customs
guardamoria [gwaxdamo'ria] F customs authorities *pl*
guarda-móveis M INV furniture storage warehouse
guardanapo [gwaxda'napu] M napkin
guarda-noturno (*pl* **guardas-noturnos**) M night watchman
guardar [gwax'da'] VT (*pôr em algum lugar*) to put away; (*zelar por*) to guard; (*lembrança, segredo*) to keep; (*vigiar*) to watch over; (*gravar na memória*) to remember; **guardar-se** VR (*defender-se*) to protect o.s.; ~ **silêncio** to keep quiet; ~ **o lugar para alguém** to keep sb's seat; **vou** ~ **este resto de bolo para ele** I'll keep this last piece of cake for him; ~**-se de** (*acautelar-se*) to guard against
guarda-redes (PT) M INV goalkeeper
guarda-roupa (*pl* -s) M wardrobe
guarda-sol (*pl* -óis) M sunshade, parasol
guardião, -diã [gwax'dʒjãw, 'dʒjã] (*pl* -ães) M/F guardian
guarida [gwa'rida] F refuge
guarita [gwa'rita] F (*casinha*) sentry box; (*torre*) watch tower
guarnecer [gwaxne'se'] VT (*Mil: fronteira*) to garrison; (*comida*) to garnish; (*Náut: tripular*) to crew; ~ **alguém (de algo)** to equip sb (with sth); ~ **a despensa** *etc* **(de algo)** to stock the pantry *etc* (with sth)
guarnição [gwaxni'sãw] (*pl* -ões) F (*Mil*) garrison; (*Náut*) crew; (*Culin*) garnish
Guatemala [gwate'mala] F: **a** ~ Guatemala
guatemalteco, -a [gwatemaw'tɛku, a] ADJ, M/F Guatemalan
gude ['gudʒi] M: **bola de** ~ marble; (*jogo*) marbles *pl*
gueixa ['gejʃa] F geisha
guelra ['gɛwxa] F (*de peixe*) gill
guerra ['gɛxa] F war; **em** ~ at war; **declarar** ~ **(a alguém)** to declare war (on sb); **estar em pé de** ~ **(com)** (*países, facções*) to be at war (with); (*vizinhos, casal*) to be at loggerheads (with); **fazer** ~ to wage war; ~ **atômica** *ou* **nuclear** nuclear war; ~ **civil** civil war; ~ **de nervos** war of nerves; ~ **fria** cold war; ~ **mundial** world war; ~ **santa** holy war
guerrear [ge'xja'] VI to wage war
guerreiro, -a [ge'xejru, a] ADJ (*espírito*) fighting; (*belicoso*) warlike ■ M warrior
guerrilha [ge'xiʎa] F (*luta*) guerrilla warfare; (*tropa*) guerrilla band
guerrilhar [gexi'ʎa'] VI to engage in guerrilla warfare
guerrilheiro, -a [gexi'ʎejru, a] ADJ guerrilla *atr* ■ M/F guerrilla
gueto ['getu] M ghetto
guia ['gia] F (*orientação*) guidance; (*Com*) permit, bill of lading; (*formulário*) advice slip ■ M (*livro*) guide(book) ■ M/F (*pessoa*) guide; **para que lhe sirva de** ~ as a guide
Guiana ['gjana] F: **a** ~ Guyana; **a** ~ **Francesa** French Guyana
guiar [gja'] VT (*orientar*) to guide; (*Auto*) to drive; (*cavalos*) to steer ■ VI (*Auto*) to drive; **guiar-se** VR: **guiar-se por** to go by
guichê [gi'ʃe] M ticket window; (*em banco, repartição*) window, counter
guidão [gi'dãw] (*pl* -ões) M = **guidom**
guidões [gi'dõjʃ] MPL *de* **guidão**
guidom [gi'dõ] (*pl* -ns) M handlebar
guidons [gi'dõʃ] MPL *de* **guidom**
guilder [giw'de'] M guilder
guilhotina [giʎo'tʃina] F guillotine
guimba ['gĩba] (*col*) F (cigarette) butt
guinada [gi'nada] F (*Náut*) lurch; (*virada*) swerve; **dar uma** ~ (*com o carro*) to swerve; (*fig: governo etc*) to do a U-turn
guinchar [gĩ'ʃa'] VT (*carro*) to tow
guincho ['gĩʃu] M (*de animal, rodas*) squeal; (*de pessoa*) shriek
guindar [gĩ'da'] VT to hoist, lift; (*fig*): ~ **alguém a** to promote sb to

---

NB: *European Portuguese adds the following consonants to certain words:* **b** (sú(b)dito, su(b)til); **c** (a(c)ção, a(c)cionista, a(c)to); **m** (inde(m)ne); **p** (ado(p)çã, ado(p)tar); *for further details see p. xiii.*

guindaste [gĩ'daʃtʃi] M hoist, crane
Guiné [gi'nɛ] F: a ~ Guinea
Guiné-Bissau [-bi'saw] F: a ~ Guinea-Bissau
guisa ['giza] F: à ~ de like, by way of
guisado [gi'zadu] M stew
guisar [gi'za'] VT to stew
guitarra [gi'taxa] F (electric) guitar
guitarrista [gita'xiʃta] M/F guitarist; (col) forger
(of money)
guizo ['gizu] M bell
gula ['gula] F gluttony, greed

gulodice [gulo'dʒisi] F greed
guloseima [gulo'zejma] F delicacy, titbit
guloso, -a [gu'lozu, ɔza] ADJ greedy
gume ['gumi] M cutting edge; (fig) sharpness
guri, a [gu'ri(a)] M/F kid ▪ F (namorada)
girlfriend
gurizote [guri'zɔtʃi] M lad
guru [gu'ru] M/F guru
gustação [guʃta'sãw] F tasting
gutural [gutu'raw] (pl -ais) ADJ guttural

Hh

H, h [a'ga] (*pl* **hs**) M H, h; **H de Henrique** H for Harry (*Brit*) *ou* How (*US*)

há [a] VB *v* **haver**

hã [ã] EXCL aha!

habeas-corpus ['abjas-'kɔxpus] M habeas corpus

hábil ['abiw] (*pl* **-eis**) ADJ (*competente*) competent, capable; (*com as mãos*) clever; (*astucioso, esperto*) clever, shrewd; (*sutil*) diplomatic; (*Jur*) qualified; **em tempo ~** in reasonable time; **habilidade** [abill'dadʒi] F (*aptidão, competência*) skill, ability; (*astúcia, esperteza*) shrewdness; (*tato*) discretion; (*Jur*) qualification; **ele não teve a menor habilidade com ela** (*tato*) he wasn't at all tactful with her; **ela não tem a menor habilidade com crianças** (*jeito*) she's hopeless with children; **ter habilidade manual** to be good with one's hands

habilidoso, -a [abili'dozu, ɔza] ADJ skilful (*Brit*), skillful (*US*), clever

habilitação [abilita'sãw] (*pl* **-ões**) F (*aptidão*) competence; (*ato*) qualification; (*Jur*) attestation; **habilitações** FPL (*conhecimentos*) qualifications

habilitado, -a [abili'tadu, a] ADJ qualified; (*manualmente*) skilled

habilitar [abili'ta^r] VT (*tornar apto*) to enable; (*dar direito a*) to qualify, entitle; (*preparar*) to prepare; (*Jur*) to qualify

habitação [abita'sãw] (*pl* **-ões**) F dwelling, residence; (*Pol: alojamento*) housing

habitacional [abitasjo'naw] (*pl* **-ais**) ADJ housing *atr*

habitações [abita'sõjʃ] FPL *de* **habitação**

habitante [abi'tãtʃi] M/F inhabitant

habitar [abi'ta^r] VT (*viver em*) to live in; (*povoar*) to inhabit ■ VI to live

hábitat ['abitatʃi] M habitat

habitável [abi'tavew] (*pl* **-eis**) ADJ (in)habitable

hábito ['abitu] M habit; (*social*) custom; (*Rel: traje*) habit; **adquirir/perder o ~ de (fazer) algo** to get into/out of the habit of (doing) sth; **ter o ~ de (fazer) algo** to be in the habit of (doing) sth; **por força do ~** by force of habit

habituação [abitwa'sãw] F acclimatization (*Brit*), acclimatation (*US*), adjustment

habituado, -a [abi'twadu, a] ADJ: **~ a (fazer) algo** used to (doing) sth

habitual [abi'twaw] (*pl* **-ais**) ADJ usual

habituar [abi'twa^r] VT: **~ alguém a** to get sb used to, accustom sb to; **habituar-se** VR: **habituar-se a** to get used to

habitué [abi'twe] M habitué

hacker ['ake^r] (*pl* **-s**) M (*Comput*) hacker

hadoque [a'dɔki] M haddock

Haia ['aja] N the Hague

Haiti [aj'tʃi] M: **o ~** Haiti

haitiano, -a [aj'tʃjanu, a] ADJ, M/F Haitian

haja *etc* ['aʒa] VB *v* **haver**

hálito ['alitu] M breath; **mau ~** bad breath

halitose [ali'tɔzi] F halitosis

hall [xɔw] (*pl* **-s**) M hall; (*de teatro, hotel*) foyer; **~ de entrada** entrance hall

halo ['alu] M halo

haltere [aw'tɛri] M dumbbell

halterofilismo [awterofi'liʒmu] M weightlifting

halterofilista [awterofi'liʃta] M/F weightlifter

hambúrguer [ã'buxge^r] M hamburger

handicap [ãdʒi'kapi] M handicap

hangar [ã'ga^r] M hangar

hão [ãw] VB *v* **haver**

haras ['araʃ] M INV stud

hardware ['xadwe^r] M (*Comput*) hardware

harém [a'rɛ̃] (*pl* **-ns**) M harem

harmonia [axmo'nia] F harmony

harmônica [ax'monika] F concertina

harmonioso, -a [axmo'njozu, ɔza] ADJ harmonious

harmonizar [axmoni'za^r] VT (*Mús*) to harmonize; (*conciliar*): **~ algo (com algo)** to reconcile sth with sth; **harmonizar-se** VR: **harmonizar(-se) (com algo)** (*idéias etc*) to coincide (with sth); (*pessoas*) to be in agreement (with sth); (*música*) to fit in (with sth); (*tapete*) to match (sth)

harpa ['axpa] F harp

harpista [ax'piʃta] M/F harpist

NB: *European Portuguese adds the following consonants to certain words*: **b** (sú(b)dito, su(b)til); **c** (a(c)ção, a(c)cionista, a(c)to); **m** (inde(m)ne); **p** (ado(p)çã, ado(p)tar); *for further details see p. xiii.*

hasta ['aʃta] F: ~ **pública** auction
haste ['aʃtʃi] F (*de bandeira*) flagpole; (*Tec*) shaft, rod; (*Bot*) stem
hastear [aʃ'tʃjaʳ] VT to raise, hoist
Havaí [avaj'i] M: **o ~** Hawaii
havaiano, -a [avaj'anu, a] ADJ, M/F Hawaiian
■ M (*Ling*) Hawaiian
Havana [a'vana] N Havana
havana [a'vana] ADJ INV light brown ■ M (*charuto*) Havana cigar

◯ **PALAVRA CHAVE**

haver [a'veʳ] VB AUX 1 (*ter*) to have; **ele havia saído/comido** he had left/eaten
2: **haver de, quem haveria de dizer que ...** who would have thought that ...
■ VB IMPESS 1 (*existência*): **há** (*sg*) there is; (*pl*) there are; **o que é que há?** what's the matter?; **o que é que houve?** what happened?, what was that?; **não há de quê** don't mention it, you're welcome; **haja o que houver** come what may
2 (*tempo*): **há séculos/cinco dias que não o vejo** I haven't seen him for ages/five days; **há um ano que ela chegou** it's a year since she arrived; **há cinco dias (atrás)** five days ago
haver-se VR: **haver-se com alguém** to sort things out with sb
■ M (*Com*) credit
haveres MPL (*pertences*) property *sg*, possessions; (*riqueza*) wealth *sg*

haxixe [a'ʃiʃi] M hashish
hebraico, -a [e'brajku, a] ADJ, M/F Hebrew ■ M (*Ling*) Hebrew
hebreu, -bréia [e'brew, 'brɛja] M/F Hebrew
Hébridas ['ɛbridaʃ] FPL: **as (ilhas) ~** the Hebrides
hecatombe [eka'tõbi] F (*fig*) massacre
hectare [ek'tari] M hectare
hectograma [ekto'grama] M hectogram
hectolitro [ekto'litru] M hectolitre (*Brit*), hectoliter (*US*)
hediondo, -a [e'dʒjõdu, a] ADJ (*repulsivo*) vile, revolting; (*crime*) heinous; (*horrendo*) hideous
hedonista [edo'niʃta] ADJ hedonistic ■ M/F hedonist
hegemonia [eʒemo'nia] F hegemony
hei [ej] VB V**haver**
hein [ẽj] EXCL eh?; (*exprimindo indignação*) hmm
hélice ['ɛlisi] F propeller
helicóptero [eli'kɔpteru] M helicopter
hélio ['ɛlju] M helium
heliporto [eli'poxtu] M heliport
Helsinque [ew'sĩki] N Helsinki
hem [ẽj] EXCL = **hein**
hematologia [ematolo'ʒia] F haematology (*Brit*), hematology (*US*)
hematoma [ema'tɔma] M bruise
hemisférico, -a [emiʃ'fɛriku, a] ADJ hemispherical

hemisfério [emiʃ'fɛrju] M hemisphere
hemofilia [emofi'lia] F haemophilia (*Brit*), hemophilia (*US*)
hemofílico, -a [emo'filiku, a] ADJ, M/F haemophiliac (*Brit*), hemophiliac (*US*)
hemoglobina [emoglo'bina] F haemoglobin (*Brit*), hemoglobin (*US*)
hemograma [emo'grama] M blood count
hemorragia [emoxa'ʒia] F haemorrhage (*Brit*), hemorrhage (*US*); ~ **nasal** nosebleed
hemorróidas [emo'xɔjdaʃ] FPL haemorrhoids (*Brit*), hemorrhoids (*US*), piles
hena ['ɛna] F henna
henê [e'ne] M = **hena**
hepatite [epa'tʃitʃi] F hepatitis
heptágono [ep'tagonu] M heptagon
hera ['ɛra] F ivy
heráldica [e'rawdʒika] F heraldry
herança [e'rãsa] F inheritance; (*fig*) heritage
herbáceo, -a [ex'basju, a] ADJ herbaceous
herbicida [exbi'sida] M weedkiller, herbicide
herbívoro, -a [ex'bivoru, a] ADJ herbivorous
■ M/F herbivore
herdade [ex'dadʒi] (*PT*) F large farm
herdar [ex'daʳ] VT: ~ **algo (de)** to inherit sth (from); ~ **a** to bequeath to
herdeiro, -a [ex'dejru, a] M/F heir(ess)
hereditário, -a [eredʒi'tarju, a] ADJ hereditary
herege [e'reʒi] M/F heretic
heresia [ere'zia] F heresy
herético, -a [e'rɛtʃiku, a] ADJ heretical
hermafrodita [exmafro'dʒita] M/F hermaphrodite
hermético, -a [ex'mɛtʃiku, a] ADJ airtight; (*fig*) obscure, impenetrable
hérnia ['ɛxnja] F hernia; ~ **de hiato** hiatus hernia
herói [e'rɔj] M hero
heróico, -a [e'rɔjku, a] ADJ heroic
heroína [ero'ina] F heroine; (*droga*) heroin
heroísmo [ero'iʒmu] M heroism
herpes ['ɛxpiʃ] M INV herpes *sg*
herpes-zoster [-'zɔsteʳ] M (*Med*) shingles *sg*
hertz ['ɛxtzi] M INV hertz
hesitação [ezita'sãw] F (*pl* -ões) hesitation
hesitante [ezi'tãtʃi] ADJ hesitant
hesitar [ezi'taʳ] VI to hesitate; ~ **em (fazer) algo** to hesitate in (doing) sth
heterodoxo, -a [etero'dɔksu, a] ADJ unorthodox
heterogêneo, -a [etero'ʒenju, a] ADJ heterogeneous
heterônimo [ete'ronimu] M pen name, nom de plume
heterossexual [eterosek'swaw] (*pl* -ais) ADJ, M/F heterosexual
heterossexualidade [eterosekswali'dadʒi] F heterosexuality
hexagonal [eksago'naw] (*pl* -ais) ADJ hexagonal
hexágono [ek'sagonu] M hexagon
hiato ['jatu] M hiatus
hibernação [ibexna'sãw] F hibernation
hibernar [ibex'naʳ] VI to hibernate

hibisco [i'biʃku] M (Bot) hibiscus
híbrido, -a ['ibridu, a] ADJ hybrid
hidramático, -a [idra'matʃiku, a] ADJ (mudança) hydraulic; (carro) with hydraulic transmission
hidratante [idra'tãtʃi] ADJ moisturizing ■ M moisturizer
hidratar [idra'ta'] VT to hydrate; (pele) to moisturize
hidrato [i'dratu] M: ~ **de carbono** carbohydrate
hidráulica [i'drawlika] F hydraulics sg
hidráulico, -a [i'drawliku, a] ADJ hydraulic; **força hidráulica** hydraulic power
hidrelétrica [idre'lɛtrika] (PT -ct-) F (usina) hydroelectric power station; (empresa) hydroelectric power company
hidreletricidade [idreletrisi'dadʒi] (PT -ct-) F hydroelectric power
hidrelétrico, -a [idre'lɛtriku, a] (PT -ct-) ADJ hydroelectric
hidro... [idru] PREFIXO hydro..., water... atr
hidroavião [idrua'vjãw] (pl -ões) M seaplane
hidrocarboneto [idrokaxbo'netu] M hydrocarbon
hidrófilo, -a [i'drɔfilu, a] ADJ absorbent; **algodão ~** cotton wool (Brit), absorbent cotton (US)
hidrofobia [idrofo'bia] F rabies sg
hidrogênio [idro'ʒenju] M hydrogen
hidroterapia [idrotera'pia] F hydrotherapy
hidrovia [idro'via] F waterway
hiena ['jena] F hyena
hierarquia [jerax'kia] F hierarchy
hierárquico, -a [je'raxkiku, a] ADJ hierarchical
hierarquizar [jeraxki'za'] VT to place in a hierarchy
hieroglífico, -a [jero'glifiku, a] ADJ hieroglyphic
hieróglifo [je'rɔglifu] M hieroglyph(ic)
hífen ['ifē] (pl -s) M hyphen
higiene [i'ʒjeni] F hygiene; ~ **mental** (mental) rest; **higiênico, -a** [i'ʒjeniku, a] ADJ hygienic; (pessoa) clean; **papel higiênico** toilet paper
hilariante [ila'rjãtʃi] ADJ hilarious
Himalaia [ima'laja] M: **o ~** the Himalayas pl
hímen ['imē] (pl -s) M (Anat) hymen
hindi [ĩ'dʒi] M (Ling) Hindi
hindu [ĩ'du] ADJ, M/F Hindu; (indiano) Indian
hinduismo [ĩ'dwiʒmu] M Hinduism
hino ['inu] M hymn; ~ **nacional** national anthem
hinterlândia [ĩtex'lãdʒja] F hinterland
hiper... [ipe'] PREFIXO hyper...; (col) really
hipérbole [i'pɛxboli] F hyperbole
hipermercado [ipexmex'kadu] M hypermarket
hipersensível [ipexsē'sivew] (pl -eis) ADJ hypersensitive
hipertensão [ipextē'sãw] F high blood pressure
hípico, -a ['ipiku, a] ADJ riding atr; **clube ~** riding club

hipismo [i'piʒmu] M (turfe) horse racing; (equitação) (horse) riding
hipnose [ip'nɔzi] F hypnosis
hipnótico, -a [ip'nɔtʃiku, a] ADJ hypnotic; (substância) sleep-inducing ■ M sleeping drug
hipnotismo [ipno'tʃiʒmu] M hypnotism
hipnotizador, a [ipnotʃizado'(a)] M/F hypnotist
hipnotizar [ipnotʃi'za'] VT to hypnotize
hipocondríaco, -a [ipokõ'driaku, a] ADJ, M/F hypochondriac
hipocrisia [ipokri'sia] F hypocrisy; **hipócrita** [i'pɔkrita] ADJ hypocritical ■ M/F hypocrite
hipodérmico, -a [ipo'dɛxmiku, a] ADJ hypodermic
hipódromo [i'pɔdromu] M racecourse
hipopótamo [ipo'pɔtamu] M hippopotamus
hipoteca [ipo'tɛka] F mortgage; **hipotecar** [ipote'ka'] VT to mortgage
hipotecário, -a [ipote'karju, a] ADJ mortgage atr; **credor/devedor ~** mortgagee/mortgager
hipotermia [ipotex'mia] F hypothermia
hipótese [i'pɔtezi] F hypothesis; **na ~ de** in the event of; **em ~ alguma** under no circumstances; **na melhor/pior das ~s** at best/worst
hipotético, -a [ipo'tɛtʃiku, a] ADJ hypothetical
hirsuto, -a [ix'sutu, a] ADJ (cabeludo) hairy, hirsute; (barba) spiky; (fig: ríspido) harsh
hirto, -a ['ixtu, a] ADJ stiff, rigid; **ficar ~** (pessoa) to stand stock still
hispânico, -a [iʃ'paniku, a] ADJ Hispanic
hispanista [iʃpa'niʃta] M/F Hispanist
hispano-americano, -a [iʃ'pano-] ADJ Spanish American
histamina [iʃta'mina] F histamine
histerectomia [iʃterekto'mia] F hysterectomy
histeria [iʃte'ria] F hysteria; ~ **coletiva** mass hysteria; **histérico, -a** [iʃ'tɛriku, a] ADJ hysterical
histerismo [iʃte'riʒmu] M hysteria
história [iʃ'tɔrja] F (estudo, ciência) history; (conto) story; **histórias** FPL (chateação) bother sg, fuss sg; **a mesma ~ de sempre** the same old story; **isso é outra ~** that's a different matter; **é tudo ~ dela** she's making it all up; **deixe de ~!** come off it!; **que ~ é essa?** what's going on?; **essa ~ de ...** (col: troço) this business of ...; **~ antiga/natural** ancient/natural history; ~ **da carochinha** fairy story; **historiador, a** [iʃtorja'do'(a)] M/F historian
historiar [iʃto'rja'] VT to recount
histórico, -a [iʃ'tɔriku, a] ADJ (personagem, pesquisa etc) historical; (fig: notável) historic ■ M history
historieta [iʃto'rjeta] F anecdote, very short story
histrionismo [iʃtrjo'niʒmu] M histrionics pl
hobby ['xɔbi] (pl -bies) M hobby
hodierno, -a [o'dʒjɛxnu, a] ADJ today's, present

NB: European Portuguese adds the following consonants to certain words: **b** (sú(b)dito, su(b)til); **c** (a(c)ção, a(c)cionista, a(c)to); **m** (inde(m)ne); **p** (ado(p)ção, ado(p)tar); for further details see p. xiii.

hoje ['oʒi] ADV today; (*atualmente*) now(adays); ~ **à noite** tonight; **de ~ a uma semana** in a week's time; **de ~ em diante** from now on; ~ **em dia** nowadays; ~ **faz uma semana** a week ago today; **ainda** ~ (before the end of) today; **de ~ para amanhã** in one day; **por ~ é só** that's all for today

Holanda [o'lãda] F: **a ~** Holland; **holandês, -esa** [olã'deʃ, eza] ADJ Dutch ■ M/F Dutchman/ woman ■ M (*Ling*) Dutch

holding ['xowdiŋ] (*pl* -s) M holding company

holocausto [olo'kawʃtu] M holocaust

holofote [olo'fɔtʃi] M searchlight; (*em campo de futebol etc*) floodlight

holograma [olo'grama] M hologram

homem ['omẽ] (*pl* -ns) M man; (*a humanidade*) mankind; **uma conversa de ~ para ~** a man-to-man talk; **ser o ~ da casa** (*fig*) to wear the trousers; **ser outro ~** (*fig*) to be a changed man; ~ **de ação** man of action; ~ **de bem** honest man; ~ **de empresa** *ou* **negócios** businessman; ~ **de estado** statesman; ~ **da lei** lawyer; ~ **de letras** man of letters; ~ **de palavra** man of his word; ~ **de peso** influential man; ~ **da rua** man in the street; ~ **de recursos** man of means; ~ **público** public servant; **homem-bomba** (*pl* **homens-bomba**) M suicide bomber; **homem-feito** (*pl* **homens-feitos**) M grown man; **homem-rã** (*pl* **homens-rã(s)**) M frogman; **homem-sanduíche** (*pl* **homens-sanduíche**) M sandwich board man

homenageado, -a [omena'ʒjadu, a] ADJ honoured (*Brit*), honored (*US*) ■ M/F person hono(u)red

homenageante [omena'ʒjãtʃi] ADJ respectful

homenagear [omena'ʒjaʳ] VT (*pessoa*) to pay tribute to, honour (*Brit*), honor (*US*)

homenagem [ome'naʒẽ] F tribute; (*Rel*) homage; **prestar ~ a alguém** to pay tribute to sb; **em ~ a** in honour (*Brit*) *ou* honor (*US*) of

homenzarrão [omẽza'xãw] (*pl* -ões) M hulk (of a man)

homens ['omẽʃ] MPL *de* **homem**

homenzinho [omẽ'ziɲu] M little man; (*jovem*) young man

homeopata [omjo'pata] M/F homoeopath(ic) doctor (*Brit*), homeopath(ic doctor) (*US*)

homeopatia [omjopa'tʃia] F homoeopathy (*Brit*), homeopathy

homeopático, -a [omjo'patʃiku, a] ADJ homoeopathic (*Brit*), homeopathic (*US*); (*fig*): **em doses homeopáticas** in tiny quantities

homérico, -a [o'mɛriku, a] ADJ (*fig*) phenomenal

homicida [omi'sida] ADJ (*pessoa*) homicidal ■ M/F murderer; **homicídio** [omi'sidʒju] M murder; **homicídio involuntário** manslaughter

homiziado, -a [omi'zjadu, a] ADJ in hiding ■ M/F fugitive

homiziar [omi'zjaʳ] VT (*esconder*) to hide; **homiziar-se** VR to hide

homogeneidade [omoʒenej'dadʒi] F homogeneity

homogeneizado, -a [omoʒenej'zadu, a] ADJ: **leite ~** homogenized milk

homogêneo, -a [omo'ʒenju, a] ADJ homogeneous; (*Culin*) blended

homologar [omolo'gaʳ] VT to ratify

homólogo, -a [o'mɔlogu, a] ADJ homologous; (*fig*) equivalent ■ M/F opposite number

homônimo [o'monimu] M (*de pessoa*) namesake; (*Ling*) homonym

homossexual [omosek'swal] (*pl* -ais) ADJ, M/F homosexual

homossexualismo [omosekswa'liʒmu] M homosexuality

Honduras [õ'duraʃ] F Honduras

hondurenho, -a [õdu'rɛɲu, a] ADJ, M/F Honduran

honestidade [oneʃtʃi'dadʒi] F honesty; (*decência*) decency; (*justeza*) fairness

honesto, -a [o'nɛʃtu, a] ADJ honest; (*decente*) decent; (*justo*) fair, just

Hong Kong [oŋ'koŋ] F Hong Kong

honorário, -a [ono'rarju, a] ADJ honorary; **honorários** [ono'rarjuʃ] MPL fees

honorífico, -a [ono'rifiku, a] ADJ honorific

honra ['õxa] F honour (*Brit*), honor (*US*); **honras** FPL: **honras fúnebres** funeral rites; **convidado de ~** guest of hono(u)r; **em ~ de** in hono(u)r of; **por ~ da firma** (*por obrigação*) out of a sense of duty; (*para salvar as aparências*) to save face; **fazer as ~s da casa** to do the hono(u)rs, attend to the guests

honradez [õxa'deʒ] F honesty; (*de pessoa*) integrity

honrado, -a [õ'xadu, a] ADJ honest; (*respeitado*) honourable (*Brit*), honorable (*US*)

honrar [õ'xaʳ] VT to honour (*Brit*), honor (*US*); **honrar-se** VR: **honrar-se em fazer** to be hono(u)red to do

honraria [õxa'ria] F honour (*Brit*), honor (*US*)

honroso, -a [õ'xozu, ɔza] ADJ honourable (*Brit*), honorable (*US*)

hóquei ['ɔkej] M hockey; ~ **sobre gelo** ice hockey

hora ['ɔra] F (*60 minutos*) hour; (*momento*) time; **a que ~s?** (at) what time?; **que ~s são?** what time is it?; **são duas ~s** it's two o'clock; **você tem as ~s?** have you got the time?; **isso são ~s?** what time do you call this?; **dar as ~s** (*relógio*) to strike the hour; **fazer ~** to kill time; **fazer ~ com alguém** (*col*) to tease sb; **marcar ~** to make an appointment; **perder a ~** to be late; **não vejo a ~ de ...** I can't wait to ...; **às altas ~s da noite ou da madrugada** in the small hours; **de ~ em ~** every hour; **em boa/má ~** at the right/wrong time; **chegar em cima da ~** to arrive just in time *ou* on the dot; **fora de ~** at the wrong moment; **na ~** (*no ato, em seguida*) on the spot; (*em boa hora*) at the right moment; (*na hora H*) at the moment of truth; **na ~ H** (*no momento certo*) in the nick of time; (*na hora crítica*) at the moment of truth, when it comes (*ou* came) to it; **está na ~ de ...** it's time to ...; **bem na ~** just

in time; **chegar na** ~ to be on time; **de última** ~
ADJ last-minute ∎ ADV at the last minute; ~ **de
dormir** bedtime; **meia** ~ half an hour; ~ **local**
local time; **~s extras** overtime *sg*; **trabalhei
2 ~s extras** I worked 2 hours overtime; **você
recebe por ~ extra?** do you get paid overtime?;
~s vagas spare time *sg*; **horário, -a** [o'rarju, a]
ADJ: **100 km horários** 100 km an hour ∎ M
(*tabela*) timetable; (*hora*) time; **horário de
expediente** working hours *pl*; (*de um escritório*)
office hours *pl*; **horário de verão** summer
time; **horário integral** full time; **horário
nobre** (TV) prime time

horda ['ɔxda] F horde

horista [o'riʃta] ADJ paid by the hour ∎ M/F
hourly-paid worker

horizontal [orizõ'taw] (*pl* -ais) ADJ horizontal
∎ F: **estar na** ~ (*col*) to be lying down

horizonte [ori'zõtʃi] M horizon

hormonal [oxmo'naw] (*pl* -ais) ADJ hormonal

hormônio [ox'monju] M hormone

horóscopo [o'rɔʃkopu] M horoscope

horrendo, -a [o'xẽdu, a] ADJ horrendous,
frightful

horripilante [oxipi'lãtʃi] ADJ horrifying, hair-
raising

horripilar [oxipi'la^r] VT to horrify; **horripilar-
se** VR to be horrified

horrível [o'xivew] (*pl* -eis) ADJ awful, horrible

horror [o'xo^r] M horror; **que ~!** how awful!; **ser
um ~** to be awful; **ter ~ a algo** to hate sth; **um
~ de** (*porção*) a lot of; **dizer/fazer ~es** to say/do
terrible things; **~es de** (*muitos*) loads of; **ele está
faturando ~es** he's raking it in, he's making
a fortune; **horrorizar** [oxori'za^r] VT to horrify,
frighten ∎ VI: **cenas de horrorizar** horrifying
scenes; **horrorizar-se** VR to be horrified

horroroso, -a [oxo'rozu, ɔza] ADJ horrible,
ghastly

horta ['ɔxta] F vegetable garden

hortaliças [oxta'lisaʃ] FPL vegetables

hortelã [oxte'lã] F mint; ~ **pimenta** peppermint

hortelão, -loa [oxte'lãw] (*pl* -s) (PT) M/F
(market) gardener

hortênsia [ox'tẽsja] F hydrangea

horticultor, a [oxtʃikuw'to^r(a)] M/F market
gardener (*Brit*), truck farmer (*US*)

horticultura [oxtʃikuw'tura] F horticulture

hortifrutigranjeiros [oxtʃifrutʃigrã'ʒejruʃ] MPL
fruit and vegetables

hortigranjeiros [oxtʃigrã'ʒejruʃ] MPL garden
vegetables

horto ['oxtu] M market garden (*Brit*), truck farm
(*US*)

hospedagem [oʃpe'daʒẽ] F guest house

hospedar [oʃpe'da^r] VT to put up; **hospedar-se**
VR to stay, lodge; **hospedaria** [oʃpeda'ria] F
guest house

hóspede ['ɔʃpedʒi] M (*amigo*) guest; (*estranho*)

lodger

hospedeira [oʃpe'dejra] F landlady; (PT: *de bordo*)
stewardess, air hostess (*Brit*)

hospedeiro, -a [oʃpe'dejru, a] ADJ hospitable
∎ M (*dono*) landlord

hospício [oʃ'pisju] M mental hospital

hospital [oʃpi'taw] (*pl* -ais) M hospital

hospitalar [oʃpita'la^r] ADJ hospital *atr*

hospitaleiro, -a [oʃpita'lejru, a] ADJ hospitable

hospitalidade [oʃpitali'dadʒi] F hospitality

hospitalização [oʃpitaliza'sãw] (*pl* -ões) F
hospitalization

hospitalizar [oʃpitali'za^r] VT to hospitalize,
admit to hospital

hostess [oʃ'tes] (*pl* -es) F hostess

hóstia ['ɔʃtʃia] F Host, wafer

hostil [oʃ'tʃiw] (*pl* -is) ADJ hostile

hostilidade [oʃtʃili'dadʒi] F hostility

hostilizar [oʃtʃili'za^r] VT to antagonize; (*Mil*) to
wage war on

hostis [oʃ'tʃiʃ] PL *de* **hostil**

hotel [o'tew] (*pl* -éis) M hotel; ~ **de alta
rotatividade** motel *for sexual encounters*

hotelaria [otela'ria] F (*curso*) hotel
management; (*conjunto de hotéis*) hotels *pl*

hoteleiro, -a [ote'lejru, a] ADJ hotel *atr* ∎ M/F
hotelier; **rede hoteleira** hotel chain

houve *etc* ['ovi] VB *v* **haver**

h(s). ABR (= *hora(s)*) o'clock

hui [wi] EXCL (*de dor*) ow!; (*de susto, surpresa*) ah!;
(*de repugnância*) ugh!

humanidade [umani'dadʒi] F (*os homens*)
man(kind); (*compaixão*) humanity;
humanidades FPL (*Educ*) humanities

hum [ũ] EXCL hmm

humanismo [uma'niʒmu] M humanism

humanista [uma'niʃta] ADJ, M/F humanist

humanitário, -a [umani'tarju, a] ADJ
humanitarian; (*benfeitor*) humane ∎ M/F
humanitarian

humanizar [umani'za^r] VT to humanize;
humanizar-se VR to become more human

humano, -a [u'manu, a] ADJ human; (*bondoso*)
humane

humanos [u'manuʃ] MPL humans

húmido, -a (PT) ADJ = **úmido**

humildade [umiw'dadʒi] F humility; (*pobreza*)
poverty

humilde [u'miwdʒi] ADJ humble; (*pobre*) poor

humildes [u'miwdʒiʃ] M/FPL: **os** (*ou* **as**) ~ the
poor

humilhação [umiʎa'sãw] F humiliation

humilhante [umi'ʎãtʃi] ADJ humiliating

humilhar [umi'ʎa^r] VT to humiliate ∎ VI to be
humiliating; **humilhar-se** VR to humble o.s.

humor [u'mo^r] M (*disposição*) mood, temper;
(*graça*) humour (*Brit*), humor (*US*); **de bom/mau
~** in a good/bad mood

humorismo [umo'riʒmu] M humour (*Brit*),

NB: *European Portuguese adds the following consonants to certain words*: **b** (sú(b)dito, su(b)til); **c** (a(c)ção,
a(c)cionista, a(c)to); **m** (inde(m)ne); **p** (ado(p)çã, ado(p)tar); *for further details see p. xiii.*

humor (US)

humorista [umoˈriʃta] M/F (escritor) humorist; (na TV, no palco) comedian

humorístico, -a [umoˈriʃtʃiku, a] ADJ humorous

húmus [ˈumuʃ] M INV humus

húngaro, -a [ˈũgaru, a] ADJ, M/F Hungarian

Hungria [ũˈgria] F: a ~ Hungary

hurra [ˈuxa] M cheer ▪ EXCL hurrah!

Hz ABR (= hertz) Hz

I i

I, i [i:] (*pl* **is**) M I, i; **I de Irene** I for Isaac (*Brit*) *ou* item (*US*)

ia *etc* ['ia] VB V **ir**

IAB ABR M = **Instituto dos Advogados do Brasil; Instituto dos Arquitetos do Brasil**

ialorixá [jalori'ʃa] F macumba priestess

IAPAS (BR) ABR M = **Instituto de Administração da Previdência e Assistência Social**

iate ['jatʃi] M yacht; **~ clube** yacht club

iatismo [ja'tʃiʒmu] M yachting

iatista [ja'tʃiʃta] M/F yachtsman/woman

IBAM ABR M = **Instituto Brasileiro de Administração Municipal**

IBDF ABR M = **Instituto Brasileiro de Desenvolvimento Florestal**

ibérico, -a [i'bɛriku, a] ADJ, M/F Iberian

ibero, -a [i'bɛru, a] ADJ, M/F Iberian

ibero-americano, -a ADJ, M/F Ibero-American

IBGE ABR M = **Instituto Brasileiro de Geografia e Estatística**

IBMC ABR M = **Instituto Brasileiro do Mercado de Capitais**

Ibope [i'bɔpi] ABR M = **Instituto Brasileiro de Opinião Pública e Estatística; dar ibope** (TV) to get high ratings; (*fig*) to be popular

IBV ABR M = **Índice da Bolsa de Valores (do Rio de Janeiro)**

içar [i'saʳ] VT to hoist, raise

iceberg [ajs'bɛxgi] (*pl* **-s**) M iceberg

ICM (BR) ABR M (= *Imposto sobre Circulação de Mercadorias*) ≈ VAT

icone ['ikoni] M icon

iconoclasta [ikono'klaʃta] ADJ iconoclastic ■ M/F iconoclast

icterícia [ikte'risja] F jaundice

ida ['ida] F going, departure; **~ e volta** round trip, return; **a (viagem de) ~** the outward journey; **na ~** on the way there; **~s e vindas** comings and goings; **comprei só a ~** I only bought a single *ou* one-way (*US*) (ticket)

idade [i'dadʒi] F age; **ter cinco anos de ~** to be five (years old); **de meia ~** middle-aged; **qual é a ~ dele?** how old is he?; **na minha ~** at my age; **ser menor/maior de ~** to be under/of age; **pessoa de ~** elderly person; **estar na ~ de trabalhar** to be (of) working age; **já não estou mais em ~ de fazer** I'm past doing; **~ atômica** atomic age; **~ da pedra** Stone Age; **I~ Média** Middle Ages *pl*

ideação [idea'sãw] (*pl* **-ões**) F conception

ideal [ide'jaw] (*pl* **-ais**) ADJ, M ideal

idealismo [idea'liʒmu] M idealism

idealista [idea'liʃta] ADJ idealistic ■ M/F idealist

idealização [idealiza'sãw] (*pl* **-ões**) F idealization; (*planejamento*) creation

idealizar [ideali'zaʳ] VT to idealize; (*planejar*) to devise, create

idear [ide'aʳ] VT (*imaginar*) to imagine, think up; (*idealizar*) to create

ideário [i'dʒjarju] M ideas *pl*, thinking

idéia [i'dɛja] F idea; (*mente*) mind; **mudar de ~** to change one's mind; **não ter a mínima ~** to have no idea; **não faço ~** I can't imagine; **estar com ~ de fazer** to plan to do; **fazer uma ~ errada de algo** to get the wrong idea about sth; **~ fixa** obsession; **~ genial** brilliant idea

idem ['idɛ] PRON ditto

idêntico, -a [i'dɛtʃiku, a] ADJ identical

identidade [idɛtʃi'dadʒi] F identity; **carteira de ~** identity (*Brit*) *ou* identification (*US*) card

identificação [idɛtʃifika'sãw] F identification

identificar [idɛtʃifi'kaʳ] VT to identify; **identificar-se** VR: **identificar-se com** to identify with

ideologia [ideolo'ʒia] F ideology

ideológico, -a [ideo'lɔʒiku, a] ADJ ideological

ideólogo, -a [ide'ɔlogu, a] M/F ideologue

ídiche ['idiʃi] M = **iídiche**

idílico, -a [i'dʒiliku, a] ADJ idyllic

idílio [i'dʒilju] M idyll

idioma [i'dʒɔma] M language

idiomático, -a [idʒo'matʃiku, a] ADJ idiomatic

idiossincrasia [idʒosĩkra'zia] F character

idiota [i'dʒɔta] ADJ idiotic ■ M/F idiot

idiotice [idʒo'tʃisi] F idiocy

ido, -a ['idu, a] ADJ past

idólatra [i'dɔlatra] ADJ idolatrous ■ M/F

NB: *European Portuguese adds the following consonants to certain words:* **b** (sú(b)dito, su(b)til); **c** (a(c)ção, a(c)cionista, a(c)to); **m** (inde(m)ne); **p** (ado(p)çã, ado(p)tar); *for further details see p. xiii.*

idolater/tress

idolatrar [idola'tra^r] VT to idolize

idolatria [idola'tria] F idolatry

ídolo ['idolu] M idol

idoneidade [idonej'daʒi] F suitability; (competência) competence; ~ **moral** moral probity

idôneo, -a [i'donju, a] ADJ (adequado) suitable, fit; (pessoa) able, capable

idos ['iduʃ] MPL bygone days

idoso, -a [i'dozu, ɔza] ADJ elderly, old

Iemanjá [jemã'ʒa] F Iemanjá (Afro-Brazilian sea goddess)

lêmen ['jemẽ] M: **o** ~ Yemen

iemenita [jeme'nita] ADJ, M/F Yemeni

iene ['jɛni] M yen

IGC (BR) ABR M = **Imposto sobre Ganhos de Capital**

iglu [i'glu] M igloo

ignaro, -a [igi'naru, a] ADJ ignorant

ignição [igni'sãw] (pl -ões) F ignition

ignóbil [ig'nɔbiw] (pl -eis) ADJ ignoble

ignomínia [igno'minja] F disgrace, ignominy

ignominioso, -a [ignomi'njozu, ɔza] ADJ ignominious

ignorado, -a [igno'radu, a] ADJ unknown

ignorância [igno'rãsja] F ignorance; **apelar para a** ~ (col) to lose one's rag; **ignorante** [igno'rãtʃi] ADJ ignorant, uneducated ▪ M/F ignoramus

ignorar [igno'ra^r] VT not to know; (não dar atenção a) to ignore

ignoto, -a [ig'nɔtu, a] ADJ (formal) unknown

IGP (BR) ABR M = **Índice Geral de Preços**

igreja [i'greʒa] F church

igual [i'gwaw] (pl -ais) ADJ equal; (superfície) even ▪ M/F equal; **em partes iguais** in equal parts; **ser** ~ **to be the same; ser** ~ **a** to be the same as, be like; ~ **se ... as if ...; por** ~ equally; **sem** ~ unequalled, without equal; **de** ~ **para** ~ on equal terms; **tratar alguém de** ~ **para** ~ to treat sb as an equal; **nunca vi coisa** ~ I've never seen anything like it

igualar [igwa'la^r] VT (ser igual a) to equal; (fazer igual) to make equal; (nivelar) to level ▪ VI: ~ **a ou com** to be equal to, be the same as; (ficar no mesmo nível) to be level with; **igualar-se** VR: **igualar-se a alguém** to be sb's equal; ~ **algo com ou a algo** to equal sth to sth; ~ **algo com algo** (terreno etc) to level sth with sth

igualdade [igwaw'dadʒi] F (paridade) equality; (uniformidade) uniformity

igualitário, -a [igwali'tarju, a] ADJ egalitarian

igualmente [igwaw'mẽtʃi] ADV equally; (também) likewise, also; ~! (saudação) the same to you!

iguana [i'gwana] M iguana

iguaria [igwa'ria] F (Culin) delicacy

ih [i:] EXCL (de admiração, surpresa) cor (Brit), gee (US); (de perigo próximo) eek!

iídiche ['jidiʃi] M (Ling) Yiddish

ilação [ila'sãw] (pl -ões) F inference, deduction

I.L. Ano (BR) ABR (Com) = **Índice de Lucratividade no Ano**

ilegal [ile'gaw] (pl -ais) ADJ illegal

ilegalidade [ilegali'dadʒi] F illegality

ilegítimo, -a [ile'ʒitʃimu, a] ADJ illegitimate; (ilegal) unlawful

ilegível [ile'ʒivew] (pl -eis) ADJ illegible

ileso, -a [i'lɛzu, a] ADJ unhurt; **sair** ~ to escape unhurt

iletrado, -a [ile'tradu, a] ADJ, M/F illiterate

ilha ['iʎa] F island

ilhar [i'ʎa^r] VT to cut off, isolate

ilharga [i'ʎaxga] F (Anat) side

ilhéu, ilhoa [i'ʎɛw, i'ʎoa] M/F islander

ilhós [i'ʎɔʃ] (pl ilhoses) M eyelet

ilhota [i'ʎɔta] F small island

ilícito, -a [i'lisitu, a] ADJ illicit

ilimitado, -a [ilimi'tadu, a] ADJ unlimited

ilógico, -a [i'lɔʒiku, a] ADJ illogical; (absurdo) absurd

iludir [ilu'dʒi^r] VT to delude; (enganar) to deceive; (a lei) to evade; **iludir-se** VR to delude o.s.

iluminação [ilumina'sãw] (pl -ões) F lighting; (fig) enlightenment

iluminado, -a [ilumi'nadu, a] ADJ illuminated, lit; (estádio) floodlit; (fig) enlightened

iluminante [ilumi'nãtʃi] ADJ bright

iluminar [ilumi'na^r] VT to light up; (estádio etc) to floodlight; (fig) to enlighten

ilusão [ilu'zãw] (pl -ões) F illusion; (quimera) delusion; ~ **de ótica** optical illusion; **viver de ilusões** to live in a dream-world

ilusionista [iluzjo'niʃta] M/F conjurer; (que escapa) escapologist

ilusões [ilu'zõjʃ] FPL de **ilusão**

ilusório, -a [ilu'zɔrju, a] ADJ (enganoso) deceptive

ilustração [iluʃtra'sãw] (pl -ões) F (figura, exemplo) illustration; (saber) learning

ilustrado, -a [iluʃ'tradu, a] ADJ (com gravuras) illustrated; (instruído) learned

ilustrador, a [iluʃtra'do^r(a)] M/F illustrator

ilustrar [iluʃ'tra^r] VT (com gravuras) to illustrate; (instruir) to instruct; (exemplificar) to illustrate; **ilustrar-se** VR (distinguir-se) to excel; (instruir-se) to inform o.s.

ilustrativo, -a [iluʃtra'tʃivu, a] ADJ illustrative

ilustre [i'luʃtri] ADJ famous, illustrious; **um** ~ **desconhecido** a complete stranger

ilustríssimo, -a [iluʃ'trisimu, a] ADJ SUPERL de **ilustre**; (tratamento): ~ **senhor** dear Sir

ímã ['imã] M magnet

imaculado, -a [imaku'ladu, a] ADJ immaculate

imagem [i'maʒẽ] (pl -ns) F image; (semelhança) likeness; (TV) picture; **imagens** FPL (Literatura) imagery sg; **ela é a** ~ **do pai** she's the image of her father

imaginação [imaʒina'sãw] (pl -ões) F imagination

imaginar [imaʒi'na^r] VT to imagine; (supor) to suppose; **imaginar-se** VR to imagine o.s.; **imagine só!** just imagine!; **obrigado -- imagina!** thank you -- don't worry about it!;

imaginário, -a [imaʒi'narju, a] ADJ imaginary

imaginativo, -a [imaʒina'tʃivu, a] ADJ imaginative

imaginável [imaʒi'navew] (pl -eis) ADJ imaginable

imaginoso, -a [imaʒi'nozu, ɔza] ADJ (pessoa) imaginative

íman ['imã] (PT) M = **ímã**

imanente [ima'nẽtʃi] ADJ: ~ **(a)** inherent (in)

imantar [imã'taʳ] VT to magnetize

imaturidade [imaturi'dadʒi] F immaturity

imaturo, -a [ima'turu, a] ADJ immature

imbatível [ĩba'tʃivew] (pl -eis) ADJ invincible

imbecil [ĩbe'siw] (pl -is) ADJ stupid ▪ M/F imbecile, half-wit; **imbecilidade** [ĩbesili'dadʒi] F stupidity

imbecis [ĩbe'siʃ] PL de **imbecil**

imberbe [ĩ'bɛxbi] ADJ (sem barba) beardless; (jovem) youthful

imbricar [ĩbri'kaʳ] VT to overlap; **imbricar-se** VR to overlap

imbuir [ĩ'bwiʳ] VT: ~ **alguém de** (sentimentos) to imbue sb with

IME (BR) ABR M = **Instituto Militar de Engenharia**

imediações [imedʒa'sõjʃ] FPL vicinity sg, neighbourhood sg (Brit), neighborhood sg (US)

imediatamente [imedʒata'mẽtʃi] ADV immediately, right away

imediato, -a [ime'dʒatu, a] ADJ immediate; (seguinte) next ▪ M second-in-command; ~ **a** next to; **de ~** straight away

imemorial [imemo'rjaw] (pl -ais) ADJ immemorial

imensidade [imẽsi'dadʒi] F immensity

imensidão [imẽsi'dãw] F hugeness, enormity

imenso, -a [i'mẽsu, a] ADJ immense, huge; (ódio, amor) great

imensurável [imẽsu'ravew] (pl -eis) ADJ immeasurable

imerecido, -a [imere'sidu, a] ADJ undeserved

imergir [imex'ʒiʳ] VT to immerse; (fig) to plunge ▪ VI to be immersed; to plunge

imersão [imex'sãw] (pl -ões) F immersion

imerso, -a [i'mɛxsu, a] ADJ (tb fig) immersed

imersões [imex'sõjʃ] FPL de **imersão**

imigração [imigra'sãw] (pl -ões) F immigration

imigrante [imi'grãtʃi] ADJ, M/F immigrant

imigrar [imi'graʳ] VI to immigrate

iminência [imi'nẽsja] F imminence

iminente [imi'nẽtʃi] ADJ imminent

imiscuir-se [imiʃ'kwixsi] VR: ~ **em** to meddle (in), interfere (in)

imitação [imita'sãw] (pl -ões) F imitation, copy; **jóia de ~** imitation jewel

imitador, a [imita'do¹(a)] ADJ imitative ▪ M/F imitator

imitar [imi'taʳ] VT to imitate; (assinatura) to copy

imobiliária [imobi'ljarja] F estate agent's (Brit),

imobiliário, -a [imobi'ljarju, a] ADJ property atr, real estate atr

imobilidade [imobili'dadʒi] F immobility

imobilizar [imobili'zaʳ] VT to immobilize; (fig: economia, progresso) to bring to a standstill; (Com: capital) to tie up

imoderação [imodera'sãw] F lack of moderation

imoderado, -a [imode'radu, a] ADJ immoderate

imodéstia [imo'dɛʃtʃja] F immodesty

imodesto, -a [imo'dɛʃtu, a] ADJ immodest

imódico, -a [i'mɔdʒiku, a] ADJ exorbitant

imolar [imo'laʳ] VT (sacrificar) to sacrifice; (prejudicar) to harm

imoral [imo'raw] (pl -ais) ADJ immoral

imoralidade [imorali'dadʒi] F immorality

imortal [imox'taw] (pl -ais) ADJ immortal ▪ M/F (membro da ABL) member of the Brazilian Academy of Letters

imortalidade [imoxtali'dadʒi] F immortality

imortalizar [imoxtali'zaʳ] VT to immortalize

imóvel [i'mɔvew] (pl -eis) ADJ (parado) motionless, still; (não movediço) immovable ▪ M property; (edifício) building; **imóveis** MPL (propriedade) real estate sg, property sg

impaciência [ĩpa'sjẽsja] F impatience; **impacientar-se** [ĩpasjẽ'taxsi] VR to lose one's patience; **impaciente** [ĩpa'sjẽtʃi] ADJ impatient; (inquieto) anxious

impacto [ĩ'paktu] (PT -cte) M impact

impagável [ĩpa'gavew] (pl -eis) ADJ (fig) priceless

impaludismo [ĩpalu'dʒiʒmu] M malaria

ímpar ['ĩpaʳ] ADJ (número) odd; (sem igual) unique, unequalled

imparcial [ĩpax'sjaw] (pl -ais) ADJ fair, impartial

imparcialidade [ĩpaxsjali'dadʒi] F impartiality

impasse [ĩ'pasi] M impasse, deadlock

impassível [ĩpa'sivew] (pl -eis) ADJ impassive

impávido, -a [ĩ'pavidu, a] ADJ (formal) fearless, intrepid

impecável [ĩpe'kavew] (pl -eis) ADJ perfect, impeccable

impeço etc [ĩ'pɛsu] VB V **impedir**

impedido, -a [ĩpe'dʒidu, a] ADJ (estrada) blocked; (Futebol) offside; (PT: Tel) engaged (Brit), busy (US)

impedimento [ĩpedʒi'mẽtu] M impediment; (Futebol) offside; (Pol) impeachment

impedir [ĩpe'dʒiʳ] VT to obstruct; (estrada, passagem, tráfego) to block; (movimento, execução, progresso) to impede; ~ **alguém de fazer** to prevent sb from doing; (proibir) to forbid sb from doing; ~ **(que aconteça) algo** to prevent sth (happening)

impelir [ĩpe'liʳ] VT (tb fig) to drive (on); (obrigar) to force

impenetrável [ĩpene'travew] (pl -eis) ADJ

---

impenitência | impor

impenetrable

impenitência [ĩpeni'tẽsja] F unrepentance
impenitente [ĩpeni'tẽtʃi] ADJ unrepentant
impensado, -a [ĩpẽ'sadu, a] ADJ *(imprevidente)*
thoughtless; *(não calculado)* unpremeditated;
(imprevisto) unforeseen
impensável [ĩpẽ'savew] *(pl -eis)* ADJ
unthinkable
imperador [ĩpera'doʳ] M emperor
imperar [ĩpe'raʳ] VI to reign; *(fig: prevalecer)* to
prevail
imperativo, -a [ĩpera'tʃivu, a] ADJ *(tb: Ling)*
imperative ■ M absolute necessity; imperative
imperatriz [ĩpera'triʒ] F empress
imperceptível [ĩpexsep'tʃivew] *(pl -eis)* ADJ
imperceptible
imperdível [ĩpex'dʒivew] *(pl -eis)* ADJ *(eleição)*
that cannot be lost; *(filme)* unmissable; *(questão)*:
**o ordem público é uma questão ~ para o
partido** the party's onto a winner with law
and order
imperdoável [ĩpex'dwavew] *(pl -eis)* ADJ
unforgivable, inexcusable
imperecível [ĩpere'sivew] *(pl -eis)* ADJ
imperishable
imperfeição [ĩmpexfej'sãw] *(pl -ões)* F
imperfection; *(falha)* flaw
imperfeito, -a [ĩpex'fejtu, a] ADJ imperfect ■ M
(Ling) imperfect (tense)
imperial [ĩpe'rjaw] *(pl -ais)* ADJ imperial
imperialismo [ĩperja'liʒmu] M imperialism
imperialista [ĩperja'liʃta] ADJ, M/F imperialist
imperícia [ĩpe'risja] F *(inabilidade)* inability;
(inexperiência) inexperience
império [ĩ'pɛrju] M empire
imperioso, -a [ĩpe'rjozu, ɔza] ADJ *(dominador)*
domineering; *(necessidade)* pressing, urgent;
(tom, olhar) imperious
impermeabilidade [ĩpexmjabili'dadʒi] F
imperviousness
impermeabilizar [ĩpexmjabili'zaʳ] VT to
waterproof
impermeável [ĩpex'mjavew] *(pl -eis)* ADJ: **~ a**
(tb fig) impervious to; *(à água)* waterproof ■ M
raincoat
impertinência [ĩpextʃi'nẽsja] F impertinence;
(irrelevância) irrelevance
impertinente [ĩpextʃi'nẽtʃi] ADJ *(alheio)*
irrelevant; *(insolente)* impertinent
imperturbável [ĩpextux'bavew] *(pl -eis)* ADJ
imperturbable; *(impassível)* impassive
impessoal [ĩpe'swaw] *(pl -ais)* ADJ impersonal
impetigo [ĩpe'tʃigo] M impetigo
ímpeto ['ĩpetu] M *(Tec: força)* impetus; *(movimento
súbito)* start; *(de cólera)* fit; *(de emoção)* surge; *(de
chamas)* fury; **agir com ~** to act on impulse;
levantar-se num ~ to get up with a start; **senti
um ~ de sair correndo** I felt an urge to run
away
impetrante [ĩpe'trãtʃi] M/F *(Jur)* petitioner
impetrar [ĩpe'traʳ] VT *(Jur)*: **~ algo** to petition
for sth

586 PORTUGUÊS - INGLÊS

impetuosidade [ĩpetwozi'dadʒi] F impetuosity
impetuoso, -a [ĩpe'twozu, ɔza] ADJ *(pessoa)*
headstrong, impetuous; *(ato)* rash, hasty; *(rio)*
fast-moving
impiedade [ĩpje'dadʒi] F irreverence; *(crueldade)*
cruelty
impiedoso, -a [ĩpje'dozu, ɔza] ADJ merciless,
cruel
impilo *etc* [ĩ'pilu] VB V **impelir**
impingir [ĩpĩ'ʒiʳ] VT: **~ algo a alguém** *(mentiras,
mercadorias)* to palm sth off on sb; **~ algo em
alguém** *(bofetada, pontapé etc)* to land sth on sb
implacável [ĩpla'kavew] *(pl -eis)* ADJ *(pessoa)*
unforgiving; *(destino, doença, perseguição)*
relentless
implantação [ĩplãta'sãw] *(pl -ões)* F
introduction; *(Med)* implant
implantar [ĩplã'taʳ] VT to introduce; *(Med)* to
implant
implante [ĩ'plãtʃi] M *(Med)* implant
implausível [ĩplaw'zivew] *(pl -eis)* ADJ
implausible
implementação [ĩplemẽta'sãw] *(pl -ões)* F
implementation
implementar [ĩpleme'taʳ] VT to implement
implemento [ĩple'mẽtu] M implement
implicação [ĩplika'sãw] *(pl -ões)* F implication;
(envolvimento) involvement
implicância [ĩpli'kãsja] F *(ato de chatear)* teasing;
(antipatia) nastiness; **estar de ~ com alguém** to
pick on sb, have it in for sb
implicante [ĩpli'kãtʃi] ADJ bullying ■ M/F
stirrer
implicar [ĩpli'kaʳ] VT *(envolver)* to implicate;
(pressupor) to imply ■ VI: **~ com alguém**
(antipatizar) to be horrible to sb; *(chatear)* to tease
sb, pick on sb; **implicar-se** VR *(envolver-se)* to get
involved; **~ (em) algo** to involve sth
implícito, -a [ĩ'plisitu, a] ADJ implicit
impliquei *etc* [ĩpli'kej] VB V **implicar**
implodir [ĩplo'dʒiʳ] VI to implode
imploração [ĩplora'sãw] F begging
implorar [ĩplo'raʳ] VT: **~ (algo a alguém)** to beg
ou implore (sb for sth)
impõe *etc* [ĩ'põj] VB V **impor**
impoluto, -a [ĩpo'lutu, a] ADJ immaculate;
(pessoa) beyond reproach
impomos [ĩ'pomoʃ] VB V **impor**
imponderado, -a [ĩpõde'radu, a] ADJ rash
imponderável [ĩpõde'ravew] *(pl -eis)* ADJ
imponderable
imponência [ĩpo'nẽsja] F impressiveness
imponente [ĩpo'nẽtʃi] ADJ impressive,
imposing
imponho *etc* [ĩ'poɲu] VB V **impor**
impontual [ĩpõ'twaw] *(pl -ais)* ADJ unpunctual
impopular [ĩpopu'laʳ] ADJ unpopular;
impopularidade [ĩpopulari'dadʒi] F
unpopularity
impor [ĩ'poʳ] *(irreg)* VT to impose; *(respeito)* to
command; **impor-se** VR to assert o.s.; **~ algo a
alguém** to impose sth on sb

importação [ĩpoxta'sãw] (pl -ões) F (ato) importing; (mercadoria) import

importador, a [ĩpoxta'do^r(a)] ADJ import atr ■ M/F importer ■ F (empresa) import company; (loja) shop selling imported goods

importância [ĩpox'tãsja] F importance; (de dinheiro) sum, amount; **dar ~ a algo/alguém** to attach importance to sth/show consideration for sb; **não dê ~ ao que ele disse** take no notice of what he said; **não tem ~** it doesn't matter, never mind; **ter ~** to be important; **de certa ~** of some importance; **sem ~** unimportant; **importante** [ĩpox'tãtʃi] ADJ important; (arrogante) self-important ■ M: **o (mais) importante** the (most) important thing

importar [ĩpox'ta^r] VT (Com) to import; (trazer) to bring in; (causar: prejuízos etc) to cause; (implicar) to imply, involve ■ VI to matter, be important; **importar-se** VR: **importar-se com algo** to mind sth; **não** ou **pouco importa!** it doesn't matter!; **~ em** (preço) to add up to, amount to; (resultar) to lead to; **não me importo** I don't care; **eu pouco me importo que ela venha ou não** I don't care whether she comes or not

importe [ĩ'pɔxtʃi] M (soma) amount; (custo) cost

importunação [ĩpoxtuna'sãw] (pl -ões) annoyance

importunar [ĩpoxtu'na^r] VT to bother, annoy

importuno, -a [ĩpox'tunu, a] ADJ (maçante) annoying; (inoportuno) inopportune ■ M/F nuisance

impôs [ĩ'poʃ] VB V **impor**

imposição [ĩpozi'sãw] (pl -ões) F imposition

impossibilidade [ĩposibili'dadʒi] F impossibility

impossibilitado, -a [ĩposibili'tadu, a] ADJ: **~ de fazer** unable to do

impossibilitar [ĩposibili'ta^r] VT: **~ algo** to make sth impossible; **~ alguém de fazer, ~ a alguém fazer** to prevent sb doing; **~ algo a alguém, ~ alguém para algo** to make sth impossible for sb

impossível [ĩpo'sivew] (pl -eis) ADJ impossible; (insuportável: pessoa) insufferable; (incrível) incredible

impostação [ĩpoʃta'sãw] F (da voz) diction, delivery

impostar [ĩpoʃ'ta^r] VT (voz) to throw

imposto, -a [ĩ'poʃtu, 'poʃta] PP de **impor** ■ M tax; **antes/depois de ~s** before/after tax; **~ de renda** (BR) income tax; **~ predial** rates pl; **~ sobre ganhos de capital** capital transfer tax (Brit), inheritance tax (US); **~ sobre os lucros** profits tax; **~ sobre transferência de capital** capital transfer tax; **I~ sobre Circulação de Mercadorias (e Serviços)** (BR), **~ sobre valor agregado** value added tax (Brit), sales tax (US)

impostor, a [ĩpoʃ'to^r(a)] M/F impostor

impostura [ĩpoʃ'tura] F deception

impotência [ĩpo'tẽʃja] F impotence

impotente [ĩpo'tẽtʃi] ADJ powerless; (Med) impotent

impraticabilidade [ĩpratʃikabili'dadʒi] F impracticability

impraticável [ĩpratʃi'kavew] (pl -eis) ADJ impracticable; (rua, rio etc) impassable

imprecisão [ĩpresi'zãw] (pl -ões) F inaccuracy

impreciso, -a [ĩpre'sizu, a] ADJ vague; (falto de rigor) inaccurate

imprecisões [ĩpresi'zõjʃ] FPL de **imprecisão**

impregnar [ĩpreg'na^r] VT to impregnate; **~ algo de** to impregnate sth with; (fig: mente etc) to fill sth with

imprensa [ĩ'prẽsa] F (a arte) printing; (máquina, jornais) press; **~ marrom** tabloid press, gutter press

imprensar [ĩprẽ'sa^r] VT (no prelo) to stamp; (apertar) to squash; (fig): **~ alguém (contra a parede)** to press sb

imprescindível [ĩpresĩ'dʒivew] (pl -eis) ADJ essential, indispensable

impressão [ĩpre'sãw] (pl -ões) F impression; (de livros) printing; (marca) imprint; **causar boa ~** to make a good impression; **ficar com/ter a ~ (de) que** to get/have the impression that; **ter má ~ de algo** to have a bad impression of sth; **~ digital** fingerprint

impressionante [ĩpresjo'nãtʃi] ADJ impressive; (abalador) amazing

impressionar [ĩpresjo'na^r] VT to impress; (abalar) to affect ■ VI to be impressive; (pessoa) to make an impression; **impressionar-se** VR: **impressionar-se (com algo)** (comover-se) to be moved (by sth)

impressionável [ĩpresjo'navew] (pl -eis) ADJ impressionable

impressionismo [ĩpresjo'niʒmu] M impressionism

impressionista [ĩpresjo'niʃta] ADJ, M/F impressionist

impresso, -a [ĩ'presu, a] PP de **imprimir** ■ ADJ printed ■ M (para preencher) form; (folheto) leaflet; **impressos** MPL (formulário) printed matter sg

impressões [ĩpre'sõjʃ] FPL de **impressão**

impressor [ĩpre'so^r] M printer

impressora [ĩpre'sora] F printing machine; (Comput) printer; **~ a laser** laser printer; **~ de linha** line printer; **~ margarida** daisywheel printer; **~ matricial** dot-matrix printer

imprestável [ĩpreʃ'tavew] (pl -eis) ADJ (inútil) useless; (pessoa) unhelpful

impreterível [ĩprete'rivew] (pl -eis) ADJ (compromisso) essential; (prazo) final

imprevidente [ĩprevi'dẽtʃi] ADJ short-sighted

imprevisão [ĩprevi'zãw] F lack of foresight, short-sightedness

---

NB: European Portuguese adds the following consonants to certain words: **b** (sú(b)dito, su(b)til); **c** (a(c)ção, a(c)cionista, a(c)to); **m** (inde(m)ne); **p** (ado(p)ção, ado(p)tar); for further details see p. xiii.

imprevisível [ĩprevi'zivew] (pl -eis) ADJ
unforeseeable
imprevisto, -a [ĩpre'viʃtu, a] ADJ unexpected,
unforeseen ■ M: **um ~** something unexpected
imprimir [ĩpri'mi^r] VT to print; (marca) to stamp;
(infundir) to instil (Brit), instill (US); (Comput) to
print out; **imprimir-se** VR to be stamped, be
impressed; **~-se na memória** to impress o.s. on
the memory; **~ algo a algo** to stamp sth on sth
improbabilidade [ĩprobabili'dadʒi] F
improbability
improcedente [ĩprose'dẽtʃi] ADJ groundless,
unjustified
improdutivo, -a [ĩprodu'tʃivu, a] ADJ
unproductive
improfícuo, -a [impro'fikwu, a] ADJ useless,
futile
impropério [ĩpro'pɛrju] M insult; **dizer ~s** to
swear
impropriedade [ĩproprje'dadʒi] F
inappropriateness; (moral) impropriety
impróprio, -a [ĩ'prɔprju, a] ADJ (inadequado)
inappropriate; (indecente) improper; **filme ~
para menores de 18 anos** X-certificate ou X-
rated film
improrrogável [ĩproxo'gavew] (pl -eis) ADJ non-
extendible
improvável [ĩpro'vavew] (pl -eis) ADJ unlikely
improvidência [ĩprovi'dẽsja] F lack of foresight
improvidente [ĩprovi'dẽtʃi] ADJ short-sighted
improvisação [ĩproviza'sãw] (pl -ões) F
improvisation
improvisado, -a [ĩprovi'zadu, a] ADJ
improvised, impromptu
improvisar [ĩprovi'za^r] VT, VI to improvise;
(Teatro) to ad-lib
improviso [ĩpro'vizu] M impromptu talk; **de
~** (de repente) suddenly; (sem preparação) without
preparation; **falar de ~** to talk off the cuff
imprudência [ĩpru'dẽsja] F rashness; (descuido)
carelessness
imprudente [ĩpru'dẽtʃi] ADJ (irrefletido) rash;
(motorista) careless
impudico, -a [ĩpu'dʒiku, a] ADJ shameless
impugnar [ĩpug'na^r] VT (refutar) to refute; (opor-
se a) to oppose
impulsionar [ĩpuwsjo'na^r] VT (impelir) to drive,
impel; (fig: estimular) to urge
impulsividade [ĩpuwsivi'dadʒi] F
impulsiveness
impulsivo, -a [ĩpuw'sivu, a] ADJ impulsive
impulso [ĩ'puwsu] M impulse; (fig: estímulo) urge,
impulse; **tomar ~** (fig: empresa, negócio) to take
off; **compra por ~** (ato) impulse buying
impune [ĩ'puni] ADJ unpunished
impunemente [ĩpune'mẽtʃi] ADV with
impunity
impunha etc [ĩ'puɲa] VB V **impor**
impunidade [ĩpuni'dadʒi] F impunity
impureza [ĩpu'reza] F impurity
impuro, -a [ĩ'puru, a] ADJ impure
impus etc [ĩ'puʃ] VB V **impor**

impuser etc [ĩpu'ze^r] VB V **impor**
imputação [imputa'sãw] (pl -ões) F accusation
imputar [ĩpu'ta^r] VT: **~ algo a** (atribuir) to
attribute sth to; **~ algo a alguém** to blame sb
for sth
imputável [ĩpu'tavew] (pl -eis) ADJ attributable
imundice [imũ'dʒisi] F = **imundície**
imundície [imũ'dʒisji] F filth; **imundo, -a**
[i'mũdu, a] ADJ filthy; (obsceno) dirty
imune [i'muni] ADJ: **~ a** immune to; **imunidade**
[imuni'dadʒi] F immunity
imunizar [imuni'za^r] VT: **~ alguém (contra
algo)** (Med) to immunize sb (against sth); (fig)
to protect sb (from sth)
imutável [imu'tavew] (pl -eis) ADJ (idéia) fixed;
(decisão: firme) firm; (: irreversível) irreversible;
(pessoa): **ele tem um comportamento ~** he's
very set in his ways
inabalável [inaba'lavew] (pl -eis) ADJ
unshakeable
inábil [i'nabiw] (pl -eis) ADJ (incapaz) incapable;
(desajeitado) clumsy
inabilidade [inabili'dadʒi] F (incompetência)
incompetence; (falta de destreza) clumsiness
inabilidoso, -a [inabili'dozu, ɔza] ADJ clumsy,
awkward
inabilitação [inabilita'sãw] (pl -ões) F
disqualification
inabilitar [inabili'ta^r] VT (incapacitar) to
incapacitate; (em exame) to disqualify
inabitado, -a [inabi'tadu, a] ADJ uninhabited
inabitável [inabi'tavew] (pl -eis) ADJ
uninhabitable
inacabado, -a [inaka'badu, a] ADJ unfinished
inacabável [inaka'bavew] (pl -eis) ADJ
interminable, unending
inação [ina'sãw] (PT -cç-) F (inércia) inactivity;
(irresolução) indecision
inaceitável [inasej'tavew] (pl -eis) ADJ
unacceptable
Inacen [ina'sẽ] (BR) ABR M = **Instituto Nacional
de Artes Cênicas**
inacessível [inase'sivew] (pl -eis) ADJ
inaccessible
inacreditável [inakredʒi'tavew] (pl -eis) ADJ
unbelievable, incredible
inactivo, -va [ina'tivu] (PT) = **inativo** etc
inadaptado, -a [inadap'tadu, a] ADJ
maladjusted
inadequação [inadekwa'sãw] (pl -ões) F
inadequacy; (impropriedade) unsuitability
inadequado, -a [inade'kwadu, a] ADJ
inadequate; (impróprio) unsuitable
inadiável [ina'dʒjavew] (pl -eis) ADJ pressing
inadimplência [inadʒĩ'plẽsja] F (Jur) breach of
contract, default
inadimplente [inadʒĩ'plẽtʃi] ADJ (Jur) in breach
of contract, at fault
inadimplir [inadʒĩ'pli^r] VT, VI: **~ (algo)** to default
(on sth)
inadmissível [inadʒimi'sivew] (pl -eis) ADJ
inadmissible

inadquirível [inadʒiki'rivew] (*pl* -eis) ADJ unobtainable

inadvertência [inadʒivex'tẽsja] F oversight; **por** ~ by mistake

inadvertido, -a [inadʒivex'tʃidu, a] ADJ inadvertent

inalação [inala'sãw] (*pl* -ões) F inhalation

inalar [ina'laʳ] VT to inhale, breathe in

inalcançável [inawkã'savew] (*pl* -eis) ADJ out of reach; (*sucesso, ambição*) unattainable

inalterado, -a [inawte'radu, a] ADJ unchanged; (*sereno*) unperturbed

inalterável [inawte'ravew] (*pl* -eis) ADJ unchangeable; (*impassível*) imperturbable

Inamps [i'nãps] (BR) ABR M = **Instituto Nacional de Assistência Médica e Previdência Social**

inanição [inani'sãw] (*pl* -ões) F starvation

inanimado, -a [inani'madu, a] ADJ inanimate

inapetência [inape'tẽsja] F loss of appetite

inapetente [inape'tẽtʃi] ADJ off one's food

inaplicado, -a [inapli'kadu, a] ADJ (*aluno*) idle, lazy

inaplicável [inapli'kavew] (*pl* -eis) ADJ inapplicable

inapreciável [inapre'sjavew] (*pl* -eis) ADJ invaluable

inaproveitável [inaprovej'tavew] (*pl* -eis) ADJ useless

inaptidão [inaptʃi'dãw] (*pl* -ões) F inability

inapto, -a [i'naptu, a] ADJ (*incapaz*) unfit, incapable; (*inadequado*) unsuited

inarticulado, -a [inaxtʃiku'ladu, a] ADJ inarticulate

inatacável [inata'kavew] (*pl* -eis) ADJ unassailable

inatenção [inatẽ'sãw] F inattention

inatingido, -a [inatʃi'ʒidu, a] ADJ unconquered

inatingível [inatʃi'ʒivew] (*pl* -eis) ADJ unattainable

inatividade [inatʃivi'dadʒi] F inactivity; (*aposentadoria*) redundancy (*Brit*), dismissal (*US*); (*Mil: reforma*) retirement (on health grounds)

inativo, -a [ina'tʃivu, a] ADJ inactive; (*aposentado, reformado*) retired

inato, -a [i'natu, a] ADJ innate, inborn

inaudito, -a [inaw'dʒitu, a] ADJ unheard-of

inaudível [inaw'dʒivew] (*pl* -eis) ADJ inaudible

inauguração [inawgura'sãw] (*pl* -ões) F inauguration; (*de exposição*) opening; (*de estátua*) unveiling; **inaugural** [inawgu'raw] (*pl* -ais) ADJ inaugural; **inaugurar** [inawgu'raʳ] VT to inaugurate; (*exposição*) to open; (*estátua*) to unveil

inca ['ĩka] ADJ, M/F Inca

incabível [ĩka'bivew] (*pl* -eis) ADJ unacceptable

incalculável [ĩkawku'lavew] (*pl* -eis) ADJ incalculable

incandescente [ĩkãde'sẽtʃi] ADJ incandescent

incansável [ĩkã'savew] (*pl* -eis) ADJ tireless, untiring

incapacidade [ĩkapasi'dadʒi] F incapacity; (*incompetência*) incompetence; ~ **de fazer** inability to do

incapacitado, -a [ĩkapasi'tadu, a] ADJ (*inválido*) disabled, handicapped ■ M/F handicapped person; **estar** ~ **de fazer** to be unable to do

incapacitar [ĩkapasi'taʳ] VT: ~ **alguém (para)** to make sb unable (to)

incapaz [ĩka'pajʒ] ADJ, M/F incompetent; ~ **de fazer** incapable of doing; ~ **para** unfit for

incauto, -a [in'kawtu, a] ADJ (*imprudente*) rash

incendiar [ĩsẽ'dʒjaʳ] VT to set fire to; (*fig*) to inflame; **incendiar-se** VR to catch fire

incendiário, -a [ĩsẽ'dʒjarju, a] ADJ incendiary; (*fig*) inflammatory ■ M/F arsonist; (*agitador*) agitator

incêndio [ĩ'sẽdʒju] M fire; ~ **criminoso** *ou* **premeditado** arson

incenso [ĩ'sẽsu] M incense

incentivador, a [ĩsẽtʃiva'do'(a)] ADJ stimulating, encouraging

incentivar [ĩsẽtʃi'vaʳ] VT to stimulate, encourage

incentivo [ĩse'tʃivu] M incentive; ~ **fiscal** tax incentive

incerteza [ĩsex'teza] F uncertainty

incerto, -a [ĩ'sextu, a] ADJ uncertain

incessante [ĩse'sãtʃi] ADJ incessant

incesto [ĩ'seʃtu] M incest

incestuoso, -a [ĩseʃ'twozu, ɔza] ADJ incestuous

inchação [ĩʃa'sãw] (*pl* -ões) F swelling

inchado, -a [ĩ'ʃadu, a] ADJ swollen; (*fig*) conceited

inchar [ĩ'ʃaʳ] VT, VI to swell; **inchar-se** VR to swell (up); (*fig*) to become conceited

incidência [ĩsi'dẽsja] F incidence, occurrence

incidente [ĩsi'dẽtʃi] M incident

incidir [ĩsi'dʒiʳ] VI: ~ **em erro** to go wrong; ~ **em** *ou* **sobre algo** (*luz*) to fall on sth; (*influir*) to affect sth; (*imposto*) to be payable on sth

incinerar [ĩsine'raʳ] VT to burn

incipiente [ĩsi'pjẽtʃi] ADJ incipient

incisão [ĩsi'zãw] (*pl* -ões) F cut; (*Med*) incision

incisivo, -a [ĩsi'zivu, a] ADJ cutting, sharp; (*fig*) incisive ■ M incisor

incisões [ĩsi'zõjʃ] FPL *de* **incisão**

incitação [ĩsita'sãw] (*pl* -ões) F incitement

incitamento [ĩsita'mẽtu] M incitement

incitar [ĩsi'taʳ] VT to incite; (*pessoa, animal*) to drive on; (*instigar*) to rouse; ~ **alguém a (fazer) algo** to urge sb on to (do) sth, incite sb to (do) sth

incivil [ĩsi'viw] (*pl* -is) ADJ rude, ill-mannered

incivilidade [ĩsivili'dadʒi] F rudeness

incivilizado, -a [ĩsivili'zadu, a] ADJ uncivilized

incivis [ĩsi'viʃ] ADJ PL *de* **incivil**

inclemência [ĩkle'mẽsja] F harshness, rigour (*Brit*), rigor (*US*); (*tempo*) inclemency

---

NB: *European Portuguese adds the following consonants to certain words:* **b** (sú(b)dito, su(b)til); **c** (a(c)ção, a(c)cionista, a(c)to); **m** (inde(m)ne); **p** (ado(p)çã, ado(p)tar); *for further details see p. xiii.*

inclemente [ĩkle'mẽtʃi] ADJ severe, harsh; (*tempo*) inclement

inclinação [ĩklina'sãw] (*pl -ões*) F inclination; (*da terra*) slope; (*simpatia*) liking; ~ **da cabeça** nod

inclinado, -a [ĩkli'nadu, a] ADJ (*terreno, estrada*) sloping; (*corpo, torre*) leaning; **estar ~/pouco ~ a** to be inclined/loath to

inclinar [ĩkli'naʳ] VT (*objeto*) to tilt; (*cabeça*) to nod ■ VI (*terra*) to slope; (*objeto*) to tilt; **inclinar-se** VR (*objeto*) to tilt; (*dobrar o corpo*) to bow, stoop; ~ **para** (*propensão*) to lean towards; ~-**se sobre algo** (*debruçar-se*) to lean over sth; ~(-**se**) **para trás** to lean back

ínclito, -a [ˈĩklitu, a] ADJ illustrious, renowned

incluir [ĩˈklwiʳ] VT to include; (*em carta*) to enclose; **incluir-se** VR to be included; **tudo incluído** (*Com*) all in

inclusão [ĩkluˈzãw] F inclusion; **inclusive** [ĩkluˈzivi] PREP including ■ ADV inclusive; (*até mesmo*) even; **de segunda à sexta inclusive** from Monday to Friday inclusive; **e inclusive falou que ...** and furthermore he said that ....

incluso, -a [ĩˈkluzu, a] ADJ included; (*em carta*) enclosed

incobrável [ĩkoˈbravew] (*pl -eis*) ADJ (*Com*): **dívida** ~ bad debt

incoercível [ĩkoexˈsivew] (*pl -eis*) ADJ uncontrollable

incoerência [ĩkoeˈrẽsja] F incoherence; (*contradição*) inconsistency

incoerente [ĩkoeˈrẽtʃi] ADJ incoherent; (*contraditório*) inconsistent

incógnita [ĩˈkɔgnita] F (*Mat*) unknown; (*fato incógnito*) mystery; **incógnito, -a** [ĩˈkɔgnitu, a] ADJ unknown ■ ADV incognito

incolor [ĩkoˈloʳ] ADJ colourless (*Brit*), colorless (US)

incólume [ĩˈkɔlumi] ADJ safe and sound; (*ileso*) unharmed

incomensurável [ĩkomẽsuˈravew] (*pl -eis*) ADJ immense

incomodada [ĩkomoˈdada] ADJ (*menstruada*) having one's period

incomodar [ĩkomoˈdaʳ] VT (*importunar*) to bother, trouble; (*aborrecer*) to annoy ■ VI to be bothersome; **incomodar-se** VR to bother, put o.s. out; ~-**se com algo** to be bothered by sth, mind sth; **não se incomode!** don't worry!; **você se incomoda se eu abrir a janela?** do you mind if I open the window?

incômodo, -a [ĩˈkomodu, a] ADJ (*desconfortável*) uncomfortable; (*incomodativo*) troublesome; (*inoportuno*) inconvenient ■ M (*menstruação*) period; (*maçada*) nuisance, trouble; (*amolação*) inconvenience

incomparável [ĩkopaˈravew] (*pl -eis*) ADJ incomparable

incompatibilidade [ĩkopatʃibiliˈdadʒi] F incompatibility

incompatibilizar [ĩkopatʃibiliˈzaʳ] VT: ~ **alguém (com alguém)** to alienate sb (from sb); **incompatibilizar-se** VR: **incompatibilizar-se (com alguém)** to alienate o.s. (from sb)

incompatível [ĩkopaˈtʃivew] (*pl -eis*) ADJ incompatible

incompetência [ĩkopeˈtẽsja] F incompetence

incompetente [ĩkopeˈtẽtʃi] ADJ, M/F incompetent

incompleto, -a [ĩkõˈplɛtu, a] ADJ incomplete, unfinished

incompreendido, -a [ĩkõprjẽˈdʒidu, a] ADJ misunderstood

incompreensão [ĩkõprjẽˈsãw] F incomprehension

incompreensível [ĩkõprjẽˈsivew] (*pl -eis*) ADJ incomprehensible

incompreensivo, -a [ĩkõprjẽˈsivu, a] ADJ uncomprehending

incomum [ĩkoˈmũ] ADJ uncommon

incomunicável [ĩkomuniˈkavew] (*pl -eis*) ADJ cut off; (*privado de comunicação, fig*) incommunicado; (*preso*) in solitary confinement

inconcebível [ĩkõseˈbivew] (*pl -eis*) ADJ inconceivable; (*incrível*) incredible

inconciliável [ĩkõsiˈljavew] (*pl -eis*) ADJ irreconcilable

inconcludente [ĩkõkluˈdẽtʃi] ADJ inconclusive

inconcluso, -a [ĩkõˈkluzu, a] ADJ unfinished

incondicional [ĩkõdʒisjoˈnaw] (*pl -ais*) ADJ unconditional; (*apoio*) wholehearted; (*partidário*) staunch; (*amizade, fã*) loyal

inconfesso, -a [ĩkõˈfɛsu, a] ADJ closet *atr*

inconfidência [ĩkõfiˈdẽsja] F disloyalty; (*Jur*) treason

inconfidente [ĩkõfiˈdẽtʃi] ADJ disloyal ■ M conspirator

inconformado, -a [ĩkõfoxˈmadu, a] ADJ bitter; ~ **com** unreconciled to

inconfundível [ĩkõfũˈdʒivew] (*pl -eis*) ADJ unmistakeable

incongruência [ĩkõˈgrwẽsja] F: **ser uma** ~ to be incongruous

incongruente [ĩkõˈgrwẽtʃi] ADJ incongruous

incôngruo, -a [ĩˈkõgrwu, a] ADJ incongruous

inconsciência [ĩkõˈsjẽsja] F (*Med*) unconsciousness; (*irreflexão*) thoughtlessness

inconsciente [ĩkõˈsjẽtʃi] ADJ (*Med, Psico*) unconscious; (*involuntário*) unwitting; (*irresponsável*) irresponsible ■ M (*Psico*) unconscious ■ M/F (*irresponsável*) irresponsible person

inconseqüência [ĩkõseˈkwẽsja] F (*irresponsabilidade*) irresponsibility; (*incoerência*) inconsistency

inconseqüente [ĩkõseˈkwẽtʃi] ADJ (*incoerente*) inconsistent; (*contraditório*) illogical; (*irresponsável*) irresponsible

inconsistência [ĩkõsiʃˈtẽsja] F inconsistency; (*falta de solidez*) runny consistency

inconsistente [ĩkõsiʃˈtẽtʃi] ADJ inconsistent; (*sem solidez*) runny

inconsolável [ĩkõsoˈlavew] (*pl -eis*) ADJ inconsolable

inconstância [ĩkõʃ'tãsja] F fickleness; (do tempo) changeability

inconstante [ĩkõʃ'tãtʃi] ADJ fickle; (tempo) changeable

inconstitucional [ĩkõʃtʃitusjo'naw] (pl -ais) ADJ unconstitutional

incontável [ĩkõ'tavew] (pl -eis) ADJ countless

incontestável [ĩkõteʃ'tavew] (pl -eis) ADJ undeniable

incontinência [ĩkõtʃi'nẽsja] F (Med) incontinence; (sensual) licentiousness

incontinente [ĩkõtʃi'nẽtʃi] ADJ (Med) incontinent; (sensual) licentious

incontinenti [ĩkõtʃi'nẽtʃi] ADV immediately

incontrolável [ĩkõtro'lavew] (pl -eis) ADJ uncontrollable

incontroverso, -a [ĩkõtro'vɛxsu, a] ADJ incontrovertible

inconveniência [ĩkõve'njẽsja] F (inadequação) inconvenience; (impropriedade) inappropriateness; (descortesia) impoliteness; (ato, dito) indiscretion

inconveniente [ĩkõve'njẽtʃi] ADJ (incômodo) inconvenient; (inoportuno) awkward; (grosseiro) rude; (importuno) annoying ■ M (desvantagem) disadvantage; (obstáculo) difficulty, problem

Incor [ĩ'koɾ] ABR M (= Instituto do Coração) hospital in São Paulo

incorporação [ĩkoxpora'sãw] (pl -ões) F (tb: Com) incorporation; (no espiritismo) embodiment, incorporation

incorporado, -a [ĩkoxpo'radu, a] ADJ (Tec) built-in

incorporar [ĩkoxpo'raɾ] VT to incorporate; (juntar) to add; (Com) to merge; **incorporar-se** VR (espírito) to be embodied; **~-se a** ou **em** to join

incorreção [ĩkoxe'sãw] (PT -cç-, pl -ões) F (erro) inaccuracy

incorrecto, -a [ĩko'xɛktu, a] (PT) ADJ = **incorreto**

incorrer [ĩko'xeɾ] VI: **~ em** to incur

incorreto, -a [ĩko'xɛtu, a] ADJ incorrect; (desonesto) dishonest

incorrigível [ĩkoxi'ʒivew] (pl -eis) ADJ incorrigible

incorruptível [ĩkoxup'tʃivew] (pl -eis) ADJ incorruptible

incorrupto, -a [ĩko'xuptu, a] ADJ incorrupt

INCRA [ĩ'kra] (BR) ABR M = **Instituto Nacional de Colonização e Reforma Agrária**

incredulidade [ĩkreduli'dadʒi] F incredulity; (ceticismo) scepticism (Brit), skepticism (US)

incrédulo, -a [ĩ'kredulu, a] ADJ incredulous; (cético) sceptical (Brit), skeptical (US) ■ M/F sceptic (Brit), skeptic (US)

incrementado, -a [ĩkremẽ'tadu, a] ADJ (indústria) well-developed; (col: festa) lively; (: roupa) trendy; (: carro) expensive

incrementar [ĩkremẽ'taɾ] VT (agricultura, economia, turismo) to develop; (aumentar) to

increase; (col: festa, roupa) to liven up

incremento [ĩkre'mẽtu] M (desenvolvimento) growth; (aumento) increase

incriminação [ĩkrimina'sãw] F criminalization

incriminar [ĩkrimi'naɾ] VT to criminalize; **~ alguém de algo** to accuse sb of sth

incrível [ĩ'krivew] (pl -eis) ADJ incredible

incrustar [ĩkruʃ'taɾ] VT to encrust; (móveis etc) to inlay

incubadora [ĩkuba'dora] F incubator

incubar [ĩku'baɾ] VT (ovos, doença) to incubate; (plano) to hatch ■ VI (ovos) to incubate

inculpar [ĩkuw'paɾ] VT: **~ alguém de algo** (culpar) to blame sb for sth; (acusar) to accuse sb of sth; **inculpar-se** VR: **inculpar-se de algo** to blame o.s. for sth

inculto, -a [ĩ'kuwtu, a] ADJ (pessoa) uncultured, uneducated; (terreno) uncultivated

incumbência [ĩkũ'bẽsja] F task, duty; **não é da minha ~** it is not part of my duty

incumbir [ĩkũ'biɾ] VT: **~ alguém de algo** ou **algo a alguém** to put sb in charge of sth ■ VI: **~ a alguém** to be sb's duty; **incumbir-se** VR: **incumbir-se de** to undertake, take charge of

incurável [ĩku'ravew] (pl -eis) ADJ incurable

incúria [ĩ'kurja] F carelessness

incursão [ĩkux'sãw] (pl -ões) F (invasão) raid, attack; (penetração) foray

incursionar [ĩkuxsjo'naɾ] VI: **~ por algo** to make forays into sth

incursões [ĩkux'sõjʃ] FPL de **incursão**

incutir [ĩku'tʃiɾ] VT: **~ algo (em** ou **a alguém)** to instil (Brit) ou instill (US) ou inspire sth (in sb)

inda [ˈĩda] ADV = **ainda**

indagação [ĩdaga'sãw] (pl -ões) F (investigação) investigation; (pergunta) inquiry, question

indagar [ĩda'gaɾ] VT (investigar) to investigate, inquire into ■ VI to inquire; **indagar-se** VR: **indagar-se a si mesmo** to ask o.s.; **~ algo de alguém** to ask sb about sth; **~ (de alguém) sobre** ou **de algo** to inquire (of sb) about sth

indébito, -a [ĩ'dɛbitu, a] ADJ undue; (queixa) unfounded

indecência [ĩde'sẽsja] F indecency; (ato, dito) vulgar thing

indecente [ĩde'sẽtʃi] ADJ indecent, improper; (obsceno) rude, vulgar

indecifrável [ĩdesi'fravew] (pl -eis) ADJ indecipherable; (pessoa) inscrutable

indecisão [ĩdesi'zãw] F indecision

indeciso, -a [ĩde'sizu, a] ADJ undecided; (hesitante) indecisive; (indistinto) vague; (hesitante) hesitant, indecisive

indeclinável [ĩdekli'navew] (pl -eis) ADJ indeclinable

indecoroso, -a [ĩdeko'rozu, ɔza] ADJ indecent, improper

indefensável [ĩdefẽ'savew] (pl -eis) ADJ indefensible

NB: *European Portuguese adds the following consonants to certain words:* **b** (sú(b)dito, su(b)til); **c** (a(c)ção, a(c)cionista, a(c)to); **m** (inde(m)ne); **p** (ado(p)çã, ado(p)tar); *for further details see p. xiii.*

indeferido | indispor

indeferido, -a [ĩdefe'ridu, a] ADJ refused, rejected
indeferir [ĩdefe'ri'] VT (desatender) to reject; (requerimento) to turn down
indefeso, -a [ĩde'fezu, a] ADJ undefended; (população) defenceless (Brit), defenseless (US)
indefinição [ĩdefini'sãw] (pl -ões) F (de pessoa) vague stance
indefinido, -a [ĩdefi'nidu, a] ADJ indefinite; (vago) vague, undefined; **por tempo** ~ indefinitely
indefinível [ĩdefi'nivew] (pl -eis) ADJ indefinable
indefiro etc [ĩde'firu] VB V **indeferir**
indelével [ĩde'lεvew] (pl -eis) ADJ indelible
indelicadeza [ĩdelika'deza] F impoliteness; (ação, dito) rude thing
indelicado, -a [ĩdeli'kadu, a] ADJ impolite, rude
indene [ĩ'dεni] (PT -mn-) ADJ (pessoa) unharmed; (objeto) undamaged
indenização [indeniza'sãw] (PT -mn-, pl -ões) F compensation; (Com) indemnity; (de demissão) redundancy (Brit) ou severance (US) payment
indenizar [ĩdeni'za'] (PT -mn-) VT: ~ **alguém por** ou **de algo** (compensar) to compensate sb for sth; (por gastos) to reimburse sb for sth
independência [ĩdepẽ'dẽsja] F independence;
independente [ĩdepẽ'dẽtʃi] ADJ independent; (auto-suficiente) self-sufficient; **quarto independente** room with private entrance
independer [ĩdepẽ'de'] VI: ~ **de algo** not to depend on sth
indescritível [ĩdeʃkri'tʃivew] (pl -eis) ADJ indescribable
indesculpável [ĩdʒiʃkuw'pavew] (pl -eis) ADJ inexcusable
indesejável [ĩdeze'ʒavew] (pl -eis) ADJ undesirable
indestrutível [ĩdʒiʃtru'tʃivew] (pl -eis) ADJ indestructible
indeterminado, -a [ĩdetexmi'nadu, a] ADJ indeterminate
indevassável [ĩdeva'savew] (pl -eis) ADJ impenetrable
indevido, -a [ĩde'vidu, a] ADJ (imerecido) unjust; (impróprio) inappropriate
índex ['ĩdeks] (pl índices) M = **índice**
indexar [ĩdek'sa'] VT to index
Índia ['ĩdʒa] F: **a** ~ India; **as** ~s **Ocidentais** the West Indies; **indiano, -a** [ĩ'dʒanu, a] ADJ, M/F Indian
indicação [indʒika'sãw] (pl -ões) F indication; (de termômetro) reading; (para um cargo, prêmio) nomination; (recomendação) recommendation; (de um caminho) directions pl
indicado, -a [ĩdʒi'kadu, a] ADJ (apropriado) appropriate
indicador, a [ĩdʒika'do'(a)] ADJ: ~ **de** indicative of ■ M indicator; (Tec) gauge; (dedo) index finger; (ponteiro) pointer; ~ **econômico** economic indicator
indicar [ĩdʒi'ka'] VT (mostrar) to indicate;

(apontar) to point to; (temperatura) to register; (recomendar) to recommend; (para um cargo) to nominate; (determinar) to determine; ~ **o caminho a alguém** to give sb directions; **ao que tudo indica** ... by the looks of things ...
indicativo, -a [ĩdʒika'tʃivu, a] ADJ (tb: Ling) indicative ■ M indicative
índice ['ĩdʒisi] M (de livro) index; (dedo) index finger; (taxa) rate; ~ **do custo de vida** cost of living index; ~ **de audiência** (TV) rating
índices ['ĩdʒisiʃ] MPL de **índice**
indiciado, -a [ĩdʒi'sjadu, a] M/F defendant
indiciar [ĩdʒi'sja'] VT (Jur: acusar) to charge; (submeter a inquérito) to investigate
indício [in'dʒisju] M (sinal) sign; (vestígio) trace; (Jur) clue
indiferença [ĩdʒife'rẽsa] F indifference;
indiferente [ĩdʒife'rẽtʃi] ADJ: **indiferente (a)** indifferent (to); **isso me é indiferente** it's all the same to me
indígena [ĩ'dʒiʒena] ADJ, M/F native; (índio: da América) Indian
indigência [ĩdʒi'ʒẽsja] F poverty; (fig) lack, need
indigente [ĩdʒi'ʒẽtʃi] ADJ destitute, indigent
indigestão [ĩdʒiʒeʃ'tãw] F indigestion
indigesto, -a [ĩdʒi'ʒeʃtu, a] ADJ indigestible; (fig: aborrecido) dull, boring; (: obscuro) turgid
indignação [ĩdʒigna'sãw] F indignation;
indignado, -a [ĩdʒig'nadu, a] ADJ indignant
indignar [ĩdʒig'na'] VT to anger, incense; **indignar-se** VR to get angry; ~-**se com** to get indignant about
indignidade [ĩdʒigni'dadʒi] F indignity; (ultraje) outrage
indigno, -a [ĩ'dʒignu, a] ADJ (não merecedor) unworthy; (desprezível) disgraceful, despicable
índio, -a ['ĩdʒju, a] ADJ, M/F (da América) Indian; **o Oceano Í**~ the Indian Ocean
indiquei etc [ĩdʒi'kej] VB V **indicar**
indireta [ĩdʒi'rεta] (PT -ct-) F insinuation; **dar uma** ~ to drop a hint
indireto, -a [ĩdʒi'rεtu, a] (PT -ct-) ADJ indirect; (olhar) sidelong; (procedimento) roundabout
indisciplina [ĩdʒisi'plina] F indiscipline
indisciplinado, -a [ĩdʒisipli'nadu, a] ADJ undisciplined
indiscreto, -a [ĩdʒiʃ'krεtu, a] ADJ indiscreet
indiscrição [ĩdʒiʃkri'sãw] (pl -ões) F indiscretion
indiscriminado, -a [ĩdʒiʃkrimi'nadu, a] ADJ indiscriminate
indiscutível [ĩdʒiʃku'tʃivew] (pl -eis) ADJ indisputable
indispensável [ĩdʒiʃpẽ'savew] (pl -eis) ADJ essential, vital ■ M: **o** ~ the essentials pl
indispõe etc [ĩdʒiʃ'põj] VB V **indispor**
indispomos etc [ĩdʒiʃ'pomoʃ] VB V **indispor**
indisponho etc [ĩdʒiʃ'poɲu] VB V **indispor**
indisponível [ĩdʒiʃpo'nivew] (pl -eis) ADJ unavailable
indispor [ĩdʒiʃ'po'] (irreg) VT (de saúde) to make ill; (aborrecer) to upset; **indispor-se** VR: **indispor-se com alguém** to fall out with sb; ~ **alguém**

com *ou* contra alguém to turn sb against sb;
~-se com *ou* contra alguém (*governo etc*) to turn
against sb
indisposição [ĩdʒiʃpozi'sãw] (*pl* -ões) F illness
indisposto, -a [ĩdʒiʃ'poʃtu, 'poʃta] PP *de* **indispor**
■ ADJ (*doente*) unwell, poorly
indispunha *etc* [ĩdʒiʃ'puɲa] VB V **indispor**
indispus *etc* [ĩdʒiʃ'puʃ] VB V **indispor**
indispuser *etc* [ĩdʒiʃpu'zeʳ] VB V **indispor**
indisputável [ĩdʒiʃpu'tavew] (*pl* -eis) ADJ
indisputable
indissolúvel [ĩdʒiso'luvew] (*pl* -eis) ADJ (*material*)
insoluble; (*contrato*) indissoluble
indistinguível [ĩdʒiʃtʃĩ'givew] (*pl* -eis) ADJ
indistinguishable
indistinto, -a [ĩdʒiʃ'tʃĩtu, a] ADJ indistinct
individual [ĩdʒivi'dwaw] (*pl* -ais) ADJ individual
individualidade [ĩdʒividwali'dadʒi] F
individuality
individualismo [ĩdʒividwa'liʒmu] M
individualism
individualista [ĩdʒividwa'liʃta] ADJ
individualist(ic) ■ M/F individualist
individualizar [ĩdʒividwali'zaʳ] VT to
individualize
indivíduo [ĩdʒi'vidwu] M individual; (*col: sujeito*)
person
indivisível [ĩdʒivi'zivew] (*pl* -eis) ADJ indivisible
indiviso, -a [ĩdʒi'vizu, a] ADJ undivided;
(*propriedade*) joint
indizível [ĩdʒi'zivew] (*pl* -eis) ADJ unspeakable;
(*indescritível*) indescribable
Ind. Lucr. (BR) ABR (*Com*) = **Índice de Lucrativide**
indóceis [ĩ'dɔsejʃ] ADJ PL *de* **indócil**
Indochina [ĩdo'ʃina] F: **a** ~ Indochina
indócil [ĩ'dɔsiw] (*pl* -eis) ADJ (*rebelde*) unruly,
wayward; (*impaciente*) restless
indo-europeu, -péia [ĩdu-] ADJ Indo-European
índole ['ĩdoli] F (*temperamento*) nature; (*tipo*) sort,
type
indolência [ĩdo'lẽsja] F laziness, indolence;
(*apatia*) apathy
indolente [ĩdo'lẽtʃi] ADJ indolent; (*apático*)
apathetic
indolor [ĩdo'loʳ] ADJ painless
indomável [ĩdo'mavew] (*pl* -eis) ADJ (*animal*)
untameable; (*coragem*) indomitable; (*criança*)
unmanageable; (*paixão*) consuming
indômito, -a [ĩ'domitu, a] ADJ untamed, wild
Indonésia [ĩdo'nɛzja] F: **a** ~ Indonesia
indonésio, -a [ĩdo'nɛzju, a] ADJ, M/F Indonesian
indoor [ĩ'doʳ] ADJ INV (*Esporte*) indoor
indubitável [ĩdubi'tavew] (*pl* -eis) ADJ
indubitable
indução [ĩdu'sãw] (*pl* -ões) F induction;
(*persuasão*) inducement
indulgência [ĩduw'ʒẽsja] F indulgence;
(*tolerância*) leniency; (*Jur*) clemency
indulgente [ĩduw'ʒẽtʃi] ADJ (*juiz, atitude*)

lenient; (*atitude*) indulgent
indultar [ĩduw'taʳ] VT (*Jur*) to reprieve
indulto [ĩ'duwtu] M (*Jur*) reprieve
indumentária [ĩdumẽ'tarja] F costume
indústria [ĩ'duʃtrja] F industry; "~ **brasileira**"
"made in Brazil"; ~ **automobilística** car
industry; ~ **de consumo** *ou* **de ponta** *ou* **leve**
light industry; ~ **de base** key industry; ~
pesada heavy industry; ~ **de transformação**
process industry; **industrial** [ĩduʃ'trjaw] (*pl* -ais)
ADJ industrial ■ M/F industrialist
industrialização [ĩduʃtrjaliza'sãw] F
industrialization
industrializado, -a [ĩduʃtrjali'zadu, a] ADJ (*país*)
industrialized; (*produto*) manufactured; (*gêneros*)
processed; (*pão*) sliced
industrializar [ĩduʃtrjali'zaʳ] VT (*país*)
to industrialize; (*aproveitar*) to process;
industrializar-se VR to become industrialized
industriar [ĩduʃ'trjaʳ] VT (*orientar*) to instruct;
(*amestrar*) to train
industrioso, -a [ĩduʃ'trjozu, ɔza] ADJ
(*trabalhador*) hard-working, industrious; (*hábil*)
clever, skilful (*Brit*), skillful (*US*)
indutivo, -a [ĩdu'tʃivu, a] ADJ inductive
induzir [ĩdu'ziʳ] VT to induce; (*persuadir*): ~
alguém a fazer to persuade sb to do; ~ **alguém
em erro** to mislead sb; ~ **(algo de algo)** to infer
(sth from sth)
inebriante [ine'brjãtʃi] ADJ intoxicating
inebriar [ine'brjaʳ] VT (*fig*) to intoxicate;
inebriar-se VR to be intoxicated
inédito, -a [i'nɛdʒitu, a] ADJ (*livro*) unpublished;
(*incomum*) unheard-of, rare
inefável [ine'favew] (*pl* -eis) ADJ indescribable
ineficácia [inefi'kasja] F (*de remédio, medida*)
ineffectiveness; (*de empregado, máquina*)
inefficiency
ineficaz [inefi'kajʒ] ADJ (*remédio, medida*)
ineffective; (*empregado, máquina*) inefficient
ineficiência [inefi'sjẽsja] F inefficiency
ineficiente [inefi'sjẽtʃi] ADJ inefficient
inegável [ine'gavew] (*pl* -eis) ADJ undeniable
inelutável [inelu'tavew] (*pl* -eis) ADJ
inescapable
inépcia [i'nɛpsja] F ineptitude
inepto, -a [i'nɛptu, a] ADJ inept, incompetent
inequívoco, -a [ine'kivoku, a] ADJ (*evidente*)
clear; (*inconfundível*) unmistakable
inércia [i'nɛxsja] F (*torpor*) lassitude, lethargy;
(*Fís*) inertia
inerente [ine'rẽtʃi] ADJ; ~ **a** inherent in *ou* to
inerme [i'nɛxmi] ADJ (*formal: não armado*)
unarmed; (*indefeso*) defenceless (*Brit*),
defenseless (US)
inerte [i'nɛxtʃi] ADJ lethargic; (*Fís*) inert
INES (BR) ABR M = **Instituto Nacional de
Educação dos Surdos**
inescrupuloso, -a [ineʃkrupu'lozu, ɔza] ADJ

NB: *European Portuguese adds the following consonants to certain words:* **b** (sú(b)dito, su(b)til); **c** (a(c)ção,
a(c)cionista, a(c)to); **m** (inde(m)ne); **p** (ado(p)ção, ado(p)tar); *for further details see p. xiii.*

unscrupulous
inescrutável [ineʃkru'tavew] (*pl* -eis) ADJ
inscrutable
inescusável [ineʃku'zavew] (*pl* -eis) ADJ
(*indesculpável*) inexcusable; (*indispensável*)
essential
inesgotável [ineʒgo'tavew] (*pl* -eis) ADJ
inexhaustible; (*superabundante*) boundless
inesperado, -a [ineʃpe'radu, a] ADJ unexpected,
unforeseen ■ M: **o** ~ the unexpected
inesquecível [ineʃke'sivew] (*pl* -eis) ADJ
unforgettable
inestimável [ineʃtʃi'mavew] (*pl* -eis) ADJ
invaluable
inevitável [inevi'tavew] (*pl* -eis) ADJ inevitable
inexatidão [inezatʃi'dãw] (PT -ct-, *pl* -ões) F
inaccuracy
inexato, -a [ine'zatu, a] (PT -ct-) ADJ inaccurate
inexaurível [inezaw'rivew] (*pl* -eis) ADJ
inexhaustible
inexcedível [inese'dʒivew] (*pl* -eis) ADJ
unsurpassed
inexeqüível [ineze'kwivew] (*pl* -eis) ADJ
impracticable, unworkable
inexistência [ineziʃ'tẽsja] F lack
inexistente [ineziʃ'tẽtʃi] ADJ non-existent
inexistir [ineziʃ'tʃir] VI not to exist
inexorável [inezo'ravew] (*pl* -eis) ADJ
implacable
inexperiência [ineʃpe'rjẽsja] F inexperience,
lack of experience; **inexperiente** [ineʃpe'rjẽtʃi]
ADJ inexperienced; (*ingênuo*) naive
inexplicável [ineʃpli'kavew] (*pl* -eis) ADJ
inexplicable
inexplorado, -a [ineʃplo'radu, a] ADJ
unexplored
inexpressivo, -a [ineʃpre'sivu, a] ADJ
expressionless
inexpugnável [ineʃpug'navew] (*pl* -eis) ADJ
(*fortaleza*) impregnable; (*invencível*) invincible
inextinto, -a [ineʃ'tʃĩtu, a] ADJ unextinguished
inextricável [ineʃtri'kavew] (*pl* -eis) ADJ
inextricable
infalível [ĩfa'livew] (*pl* -eis) ADJ infallible;
(*sucesso*) guaranteed
infame [ĩ'fami] ADJ (*pessoa, procedimento*) mean,
nasty; (*comida, trabalho*) awful
infâmia [ĩ'famja] F (*desonra*) disgrace; (*vileza*)
vicious behaviour; (*dito*) nasty thing
infância [ĩ'fãsja] F childhood; **primeira ~**
infancy, early childhood
infantaria [ĩfãta'ria] F infantry
infante, -a [ĩ'fãtʃi, a] M/F (*filho dos reis*) prince/
princess ■ M (*soldado*) foot soldier
infanticídio [ĩfãtʃi'sidʒu] M infanticide
infantil [ĩfã'tʃiw] (*pl* -is) ADJ (*ingênuo*) childlike;
(*pueril*) childish; (*para crianças*) children's
infantilidade [ĩfãtʃili'dadʒi] F childishness;
(*dito, ação*) childish thing
infantis [ĩfã'tʃiʃ] ADJ PL *de* **infantil**
infanto-juvenil [ĩfãto-] (*pl* -is) ADJ children's
infarto [ĩ'faxtu] M heart attack

infatigável [ĩfatʃi'gavew] (*pl* -eis) ADJ untiring
infausto, -a [ĩ'fawʃtu, a] ADJ unlucky
infecção [ĩfek'sãw] (*pl* -ões) F infection;
(*contaminação*) contamination; **infeccionar**
[ĩfeksjo'na r] VT (*ferida*) to infect; (*contaminar*) to
contaminate; **infeccioso, -a** [ĩfek'sjozu, ɔza]
ADJ infectious
infecções [ĩfek'sõjʃ] FPL *de* **infecção**
infectar [ĩfek'ta r] (PT) VT = **infetar**
infelicidade [ĩfelisi'dadʒi] F unhappiness;
(*desgraça*) misfortune
infelicíssimo, -a [ĩfeli'sisimu, a] ADJ SUPERL *de*
infeliz
infeliz [ĩfe'liʒ] ADJ (*triste*) unhappy; (*infausto*)
unlucky; (*ação, medida*) unfortunate; (*sugestão,
idéia*) inappropriate ■ M/F unhappy person;
como um ~ (*col*) like there's no tomorrow;
infelizmente [ĩfeliʒ'mẽtʃi] ADV unfortunately
infenso, -a [ĩ'fẽsu, a] ADJ adverse
inferior [ĩfe'rjo r] ADJ: ~ **(a)** (*em valor, qualidade*)
inferior (to); (*mais baixo*) lower (than)
■ M/F inferior, subordinate; **inferioridade**
[ĩferjori'dadʒi] F inferiority
inferiorizar [ĩferjori'za r] VT to put down;
inferiorizar-se VR to become inferior
inferir [ĩfe'ri r] VT to infer, deduce
infernal [ĩfex'naw] (*pl* -ais) ADJ infernal; (*col:
excepcional*) amazing
inferninho [ĩfex'niɲu] M club
infernizar [ĩfexni'za r] VT: ~ **a vida de alguém** to
make sb's life hell
inferno [ĩ'fexnu] M hell; **é um ~** (*fig*) it's hell; **vá
pro ~!** piss off! (*col*)
infértil [ĩ'fextʃiw] (*pl* -eis) ADJ infertile
infertilidade [ĩfextʃili'dadʒi] F infertility
infestar [ĩfeʃ'ta r] VT to infest
infetar [ĩfe'ta r] VT to infect; (*contaminar*) to
contaminate
infidelidade [ĩfideli'dadʒi] F infidelity,
unfaithfulness; (*Rel*) disbelief; ~ **conjugal**
marital infidelity
infidelíssimo, -a [ĩfide'lisimu, a] ADJ SUPERL *de*
infiel
infiel [ĩ'fjew] (*pl* -éis) ADJ (*desleal*) disloyal;
(*marido*) unfaithful; (*texto*) inaccurate ■ M/F
(*Rel*) non-believer
infiltração [ĩfiwtra'sãw] (*pl* -ões) F infiltration
infiltrar [ĩfiw'tra r] VT to permeate; **infiltrar-se**
VR (*água, luz, odor*) to permeate; ~**-se em algo**
(*pessoas*) to infiltrate sth
ínfimo, -a [ĩ'fimu, a] ADJ lowest; (*qualidade*)
poorest
infindável [ĩfĩ'davew] (*pl* -eis) ADJ unending,
constant
infinidade [ĩfini'dadʒi] F infinity; **uma ~ de**
countless
infinitesimal [ĩfinitezi'maw] (*pl* -ais) ADJ
infinitesimal
infinitivo, -a [ĩfini'tʃivu, a] ADJ (*Ling*) infinitive
■ M infinitive
infinito, -a [ĩfi'nitu, a] ADJ infinite ■ M
infinity

infiro etc [ĩ'firu] VB V **inferir**

inflação [ĩfla'sãw] F inflation

inflacionar [ĩflasjo'na^r] VT (Econ) to inflate

inflacionário, -a [ĩflasjo'narju, a] ADJ inflationary

inflacionista [ĩflasjo'niʃta] ADJ, M/F inflationist

inflamação [ĩflama'sãw] (pl -ões) F (Med) inflammation; (de madeira etc) combustion; **inflamado, -a** [ĩfla'madu, a] ADJ (Med) inflamed; (discurso) heated

inflamar [ĩfla'ma^r] VT (madeira, pólvora) to set fire to; (Med, fig) to inflame; **inflamar-se** VR to catch fire; (fig) to get worked up; ~-**se de algo** to be consumed with sth

inflamatório, -a [ĩflama'tɔrju, a] ADJ inflammatory

inflamável [ĩfla'mavew] (pl -eis) ADJ inflammable

inflar [ĩ'fla^r] VT to inflate, blow up; **inflar-se** VR to swell (up); ~ **algo de algo** to inflate sth (ou fill sth up) with sth

inflexibilidade [ĩfleksibili'dadʒi] F inflexibility

inflexível [ĩflek'sivew] (pl -eis) ADJ stiff, rigid; (fig) unyielding

infligir [ĩfli'ʒi^r] VT: ~ **algo (a alguém)** to inflict sth (upon sb)

influência [ĩ'flwẽsja] F influence; **sob a ~ de** under the influence of; **influenciar** [ĩflwẽ'sja^r] VT to influence ▪ VI: **influenciar em algo** to influence sth, have an influence on sth; **influenciar-se** VR: **influenciar-se por** to be influenced by

influenciável [ĩflwẽ'sjavew] (pl -eis) ADJ easily influenced

influente [ĩ'flwẽtʃi] ADJ influential

influir [ĩ'flwi^r] VI (importar) to matter, be important; ~ **em** ou **sobre** to influence, have an influence on

influxo [ĩ'fluksu] M influx; (maré-cheia) high tide

informação [ĩfoxma'sãw] (pl -ões) F (piece of) information; (notícia) news; (Mil) intelligence; (Jur) inquiry; (Comput) piece of data; (instrução) instruction; **informações** FPL (detalhes) information sg; **Informações** (Tel) directory enquiries (Brit), information (US); **pedir informações sobre** to ask about, inquire about; **serviço de ~** intelligence service

informado, -a [ĩfox'madu, a] ADJ informed

informal [ĩfox'maw] (pl -ais) ADJ informal

informalidade [ĩfoxmali'dadʒi] F informality

informante [ĩfox'mãtʃi] M informant; (Jur) informer

informar [ĩfox'ma^r] VT: ~ **alguém (de/sobre algo)** to inform sb (of/about sth) ▪ VI to inform, be informative; **informar-se** VR: **informar-se de** to find out about, inquire about; ~ **de** to report on; ~ **algo a alguém** to tell sb sth

informática [ĩfox'matʃika] F (ciência) computer science; (ramo) computing, computers pl

informativo, -a [ĩfoxma'tʃivu, a] ADJ informative

informatização [ĩfoxmatʃiza'sãw] F computerization

informatizar [ĩfoxmatʃi'za^r] VT to computerize

informe [ĩ'foxmi] M (piece of) information; (Mil) briefing; **informes** MPL (informações) information sg

infortúnio [ĩfox'tunju] M misfortune

infração [ĩfra'sãw] (PT -cç-, pl -ões) F breach, infringement; (Esporte) foul; ~ **de trânsito** traffic offence (Brit) ou violation (US)

infractor, a [ĩfra'to^r(a)] (PT) M/F = **infrator(a)**

infra-estrutura [ĩfra-] F infrastructure

infrator, a [ĩfra'to^r(a)] M/F offender

infravermelho, -a [ĩfravex'meʎu, a] ADJ infra-red

infreqüente [ĩfre'kwẽtʃi] ADJ infrequent

infringir [ĩfrĩ'ʒi^r] VT to infringe, contravene

infrutífero, -a [ĩfru'tʃiferu, a] ADJ fruitless

infundado, -a [ĩfũ'dadu, a] ADJ groundless, unfounded

infundir [ĩfũ'dʒi^r] VT to infuse; (terror) to strike; (incutir) to instil (Brit), instill (US)

infusão [ĩfu'zãw] (pl -ões) F infusion

ingenuidade [ĩʒenwi'dadʒi] F ingenuousness

ingênuo, -a [ĩ'ʒenwu, a] ADJ ingenuous, naïve; (comentário) harmless ▪ M/F naïve person

ingerência [ĩʒe'rẽsja] F interference

ingerir [ĩʒe'ri^r] VT to ingest; (engolir) to swallow; **ingerir-se** VR: **ingerir-se em algo** to interfere in sth

Inglaterra [ĩgla'texa] F: **a ~** England; **inglês, -esa** [ĩ'gleʃ, eza] ADJ English ▪ M/F Englishman/woman ▪ M (Ling) English; **os ingleses** MPL the English; **(só) para inglês ver** (col) (just) for show

inglesar [ĩgle'za^r] VT to Anglicize; **inglesar-se** VR to become Anglicized

inglório, -a [ĩ'glɔrju, a] ADJ inglorious

ingovernável [ĩgovex'navew] (pl -eis) ADJ ungovernable

ingratidão [ĩgratʃi'dãw] F ingratitude

ingrato, -a [ĩ'gratu, a] ADJ ungrateful

ingrediente [ĩgre'dʒjẽtʃi] M ingredient

íngreme ['ĩgremi] ADJ steep

ingressar [ĩgre'sa^r] VI: ~ **em** to enter, go into; (um clube) to join

ingresso [ĩ'gresu] M (entrada) entry; (admissão) admission; (bilhete) ticket

inhaca [i'ɲaka] (col) F (fedor) stink

inhame [i'ɲami] M yam

inibição [inibi'sãw] (pl -ões) F inhibition

inibido, -a [ini'bidu, a] ADJ inhibited

inibidor, a [inibi'do^r(a)] ADJ inhibiting

inibir [ini'bi^r] VT: ~ **alguém (de fazer)** to inhibit sb (from doing); **inibir-se** VR: **inibir-se (de**

fazer) to be inhibited (from doing)

iniciação [inisja'sãw] (*pl* **-ões**) F initiation

iniciado, -a [ini'sjadu, a] M/F initiate

iniciador, a [inisja'do'(a)] ADJ initiating ■ M/F initiator

inicial [ini'sjaw] (*pl* **-ais**) ADJ initial, first ■ F initial

inicializar [inisjali'za'] VT (*Comput*) to initialize

iniciar [ini'sja'] VT, VI (*começar*) to begin, start; ~ **alguém em algo** (*arte, seita*) to initiate sb into sth

iniciativa [inisja'tʃiva] F initiative; **tomar a ~** to take the initiative; **por ~ própria** on one's own initiative, off one's own bat (*Brit*); **a ~ privada** (*Econ*) private enterprise; **não ter ~** to lack initiative

início [i'nisju] M beginning, start; **no ~** at the start

inigualável [inigwa'lavev] (*pl* **-eis**) ADJ unequalled

inimaginável [inimaʒi'navew] (*pl* **-eis**) ADJ unimaginable

inimigo, -a [ini'migu, a] ADJ, M/F enemy

inimizade [inimi'zadʒi] F enmity, hatred

inimizar [inimi'za'] VT: ~ **alguém com alguém** to set sb against sb; **inimizar-se** VR: **inimizar-se com** to fall out with

ininteligível [inĩteli'ʒivew] (*pl* **-eis**) ADJ unintelligible

ininterrupto, -a [inĩte'xuptu, a] ADJ continuous; (*esforço*) unstinting; (*vôo*) non-stop; (*serviço*) 24-hour

iniqüidade [inikwi'dadʒi] F iniquity

iníquo, -a [i'nikwu, a] ADJ iniquitous

injeção [inʒe'sãw] (*PT* **-cç-**, *pl* **-ões**) F injection

injetado, -a [ĩʒe'tadu, a] (*PT* **-ct-**) ADJ (*olhos*) bloodshot

injetar [ĩʒe'ta'] (*PT* **-ct-**) VT to inject

injunção [ĩʒũ'sãw] (*pl* **-ões**) F (*ordem*) order; (*pressão*) pressure

injúria [ĩ'ʒurja] F (*insulto*) insult

injuriar [ĩʒu'rja'] VT to insult

injurioso, -a [ĩʒu'rjozu, ɔza] ADJ insulting; (*ofensivo*) offensive

injustiça [ĩʒuʃ'tʃisa] F injustice

injustiçado, -a [ĩʒuʃtʃi'sadu, a] ADJ wronged ■ M/F victim of injustice

injustificável [ĩʒuʃtʃifi'kavew] (*pl* **-eis**) ADJ unjustifiable

injusto, -a [ĩ'ʒuʃtu, a] ADJ unfair, unjust

INM (*BR*) ABR M = **Instituto Nacional de Meteorologia**

inobservado, -a [inobizex'vadu, a] ADJ unobserved; (*nunca visto*) never witnessed

inobservância [inobizex'vãsja] F non-observance

inobservante [inobizex'vãtʃi] ADJ inobservant

inocência [ino'sẽsja] F innocence

inocentar [inosẽ'ta'] VT: ~ **alguém (de algo)** to clear sb (of sth)

inocente [ino'sẽtʃi] ADJ innocent ■ M/F innocent man/woman; **os ~s** the innocent

inoculação [inokula'sãw] (*pl* **-ões**) F inoculation

inocular [inoku'la'] VT to inoculate

inócuo, -a [i'nɔkwu, a] ADJ harmless

inodoro, -a [ino'dɔru, a] ADJ odourless (*Brit*), odorless (*US*)

inofensivo, -a [inofẽ'sivu, a] ADJ harmless, inoffensive

inolvidável [inowvi'davew] (*pl* **-eis**) ADJ unforgettable

inoperante [inope'rãtʃi] ADJ inoperative

inopinado, -a [inopi'nadu, a] ADJ unexpected

inoportuno, -a [inopox'tunu, a] ADJ inconvenient, inopportune

inorgânico, -a [inox'ganiku, a] ADJ inorganic

inóspito, -a [i'nɔʃpitu, a] ADJ inhospitable

inovação [inova'sãw] (*pl* **-ões**) F innovation

inovar [ino'va'] VT to innovate

inoxidável [inoksi'davew] (*pl* **-eis**) ADJ: **aço ~** stainless steel

INPC (*BR*) ABR M (= *Índice Nacional de Preços ao Consumidor*) RPI

INPS (*BR*) ABR M (= *Instituto Nacional de Previdência Social*) ≈ DSS (*Brit*), ≈ Welfare Dept (*US*)

inqualificável [ĩkwalifi'kavew] (*pl* **-eis**) ADJ incalculable; (*vil*) unacceptable

inquebrantável [ĩkebrã'tavew] (*pl* **-eis**) ADJ unbreakable; (*fig*) unshakeable

inquérito [ĩ'kɛritu] M inquiry; (*Jur*) inquest

inquestionável [ĩkeʃtʃjo'navew] (*pl* **-eis**) ADJ unquestionable

inquietação [ĩkjeta'sãw] F (*preocupação*) anxiety, uneasiness; (*agitação*) restlessness

inquietador, a [ĩkjeta'do'(a)] ADJ worrying, disturbing

inquietante [ĩkje'tãtʃi] ADJ worrying, disturbing

inquietar [ĩkje'ta'] VT to worry, disturb; **inquietar-se** VR to worry, bother; **inquieto, -a** [ĩ'kjɛtu, a] ADJ (*ansioso*) anxious, worried; (*agitado*) restless

inquietude [ĩkje'tudʒi] F (*preocupação*) anxiety, uneasiness; (*agitação*) restlessness

inquilino, -a [ĩki'linu, a] M/F tenant

inquirição [ĩkiri'sãw] (*pl* **-ões**) F investigation; (*Jur*) cross-examination

inquirir [ĩki'ri'] VT (*investigar*) to investigate; (*perguntar*) to question; (*Jur*) to cross-examine ■ VI to enquire

inquisição [ĩkizi'sãw] (*pl* **-ões**) F: **a I~** the Inquisition

inquisitivo, -a [ĩkizi'tʃivu, a] ADJ inquisitive

insaciável [ĩsa'sjavew] (*pl* **-eis**) ADJ insatiable

insalubre [ĩsa'lubri] ADJ unhealthy

insanidade [ĩsani'dadʒi] F madness, insanity; **insano, -a** [ĩ'sanu, a] ADJ insane; (*fig: trabalho*) exhaustive

insatisfação [ĩsatʃiʃfa'sãw] F dissatisfaction

insatisfatório, -a [ĩsatʃiʃfa'tɔrju, a] ADJ unsatisfactory

insatisfeito, -a [ĩsatʃiʃ'fejtu, a] ADJ dissatisfied, unhappy

inscrever [ĩʃkre've'] VT (*gravar*) to inscribe;

(aluno) to enrol (Brit), enroll (US); (em registro) to register; **inscrever-se** VR to enrol(l); to register
inscrição [ĩʃkri'sãw] (pl -ões) F (legenda) inscription; (Educ) enrolment (Brit), enrollment (US); (em lista etc) registration
inscrito, -a [ĩ'ʃkritu, a] PP de **inscrever**
insecto etc [ĩ'sɛktu] (PT) = **inseto** etc
insegurança [ĩsegu'rāsa] F insecurity;
inseguro, -a [ĩse'guru, a] ADJ insecure
inseminação [ĩsemina'sãw] F: ~ **artificial** artificial insemination
inseminar [ĩsemi'naʳ] VT to inseminate
insensatez [ĩsēsa'teȝ] F folly, madness
insensato, -a [ĩsē'satu, a] ADJ unreasonable, foolish
insensibilidade [ĩsēsibili'dadȝi] F insensitivity; (dormência) numbness
insensível [ĩsē'sivew] (pl -eis) ADJ insensitive; (dormente) numb
inseparável [ĩsepa'ravew] (pl -eis) ADJ inseparable
inserção [ĩsex'sãw] (pl -ões) F insertion; (Comput) entry
inserir [ĩse'riʳ] VT to insert, put in; (Comput: dados) to enter; **inserir-se** VR: **inserir-se em** to become part of
inseticida [ĩsetʃi'sida] M insecticide
inseto [ĩ'setu] M insect
insidioso, -a [ĩsi'dȝjozu, ɔza] ADJ insidious
insigne [ĩ'signi] ADJ distinguished, eminent
insígnia [ĩ'signia] F (sinal distintivo) badge; (emblema) emblem
insignificância [ĩsignifi'kãsja] F insignificance
insignificante [ĩsignifi'kãtʃi] ADJ insignificant
insinceridade [ĩsĩseri'dadȝi] F insincerity
insincero, -a [ĩsĩ'sɛru, a] ADJ insincere
insinuação [ĩsinwa'sãw] (pl -ões) F insinuation; (sugestão) hint
insinuante [ĩsi'nwãtʃi] ADJ ingratiating
insinuar [ĩsi'nwaʳ] VT to insinuate, imply ■ VI to make insinuations; **insinuar-se** VR: **insinuar-se por** ou **entre** to slip through; **~-se na confiança de alguém** to worm one's way into sb's confidence
insípido, -a [ĩ'sipidu, a] ADJ insipid; (fig) dull
insiro etc [ĩ'siru] VB v **inserir**
insistência [ĩsiʃ'tēsja] F: **~ (em)** insistence (on); (obstinação) persistence (in); **insistente** [ĩsiʃ'tētʃi] ADJ (pessoa) insistent; (apelo) urgent
insistir [ĩsiʃ'tʃiʳ] VI: **~ (em)** (exigir) to insist (on); (perseverar) to persist (in); **~ por algo** to stand up for sth; **~ sobre algo** to dwell on sth; **~ (para) que alguém faça** to insist that sb do ou on sb doing; **~ (em) que** to insist that
insociável [ĩso'sjavew] (pl -eis) ADJ unsociable, antisocial
insofismável [ĩsofiȝ'mavew] (pl -eis) ADJ simple
insofrido, -a [ĩso'fridu, a] ADJ impatient, restless

insolação [insola'sãw] F sunstroke; **pegar uma ~** to get sunstroke
insolência [ĩso'lēsja] F insolence
insolente [ĩso'lētʃi] ADJ insolent
insólito, -a [ĩ'sɔlitu, a] ADJ unusual
insolúvel [ĩso'luvew] (pl -eis) ADJ insoluble
insolvência [ĩsow'vēsja] F insolvency
insolvente [ĩsow'vētʃi] ADJ insolvent
insondável [ĩsõ'davew] (pl -eis) ADJ unfathomable
insone [ĩ'sɔni] ADJ (pessoa) insomniac; (noite) sleepless
insônia [ĩ'sonja] F insomnia
insosso, -a [ĩ'sosu, a] ADJ unsalted; (sem sabor) tasteless; (pessoa) uninteresting, dull
inspeção [ĩʃpe'sãw] (PT -cç-, pl -ões) F inspection, check; (departamento) inspectorate;
inspecionar [ĩʃpesjo'naʳ] (PT -cc-) VT to inspect
inspeções [ĩʃpe'sõjʃ] FPL de **inspeção**
inspetor, a [ĩʃpe'toʳ(a)] (PT -ct-) M/F inspector
inspetoria [ĩʃpeto'ria] (PT -ct-) F inspectorate
inspiração [ĩʃpira'sãw] (pl -ões) F inspiration; (nos pulmões) inhalation
inspirador, a [ĩʃpira'doʳ(a)] ADJ inspiring
inspirar [ĩʃpi'raʳ] VT to inspire; (Med) to inhale; **inspirar-se** VR to be inspired; **ele não me inspira confiança** he does not inspire me with confidence
instabilidade [ĩʃtabili'dadȝi] F instability
instalação [ĩʃtala'sãw] (pl -ões) F installation; **~ elétrica** (de casa) wiring; **~ hidráulica** waterworks sg
instalar [ĩʃta'laʳ] VT (equipamento) to install; (estabelecer) to set up; (alojar) to accommodate, put up; (num cargo) to place; **instalar-se** VR (numa cadeira) to settle down; (alojar-se) to settle in; (num cargo) to take up office
instância [ĩʃ'tãsja] F (insistência) persistence; (súplica) entreaty; (legislativa) authority; (Jur): **tribunal de primeira ~** = magistrate's court (Brit), = district court (US); **em última ~** = as a last resort
instantâneo, -a [ĩʃtã'tanju, a] ADJ instant, instantaneous; (café) instant ■ M (Foto) snap
instante [ĩʃ'tãtʃi] ADJ urgent ■ M moment; **nesse ~** just a moment ago; **num ~** in an instant, quickly; **a cada ~** (at) any moment; **só um ~!** just a moment!
instar [ĩʃ'taʳ] VT to urge ■ VI to insist; **~ com alguém para que faça algo** to urge sb to do sth
instauração [ĩʃtawra'sãw] F setting-up; (de processo, inquérito) institution
instaurar [ĩʃtaw'raʳ] VT to establish, set up; (processo, inquérito) to institute
instável [ĩʃ'tavew] (pl -eis) ADJ unstable; (tempo) unsettled
instigação [ĩʃtʃiga'sãw] F instigation; **por ~ de alguém** at sb's instigation
instigar [ĩʃtʃi'gaʳ] VT (incitar) to urge; (provocar)

NB: European Portuguese adds the following consonants to certain words: **b** (sú(b)dito, su(b)til); **c** (a(c)ção, a(c)cionista, a(c)to); **m** (inde(m)ne); **p** (ado(p)çã, ado(p)tar); for further details see p. xiii.

to provoke; ~ **alguém contra alguém** to set sb
against sb

instilar [ĩʃtʃi'la'] VT: ~ **algo em algo** (veneno) to
inject sth into sth; ~ **algo em alguém** (fig: ódio
etc) to instil (Brit) ou instill (US) sth in sb

instintivo, -a [ĩʃtʃĩ'tʃivu, a] ADJ instinctive

instinto [ĩʃ'tʃĩtu] M instinct; **por** ~ instinctively;
~ **de conservação** survival instinct

institucional [ĩʃtʃitusjo'naw] (pl -ais) ADJ
institutional

instituição [ĩʃtʃitwi'sãw] (pl -ões) F institution

instituir [ĩʃtʃi'twi'] VT to institute; (fundar) to
establish, found; (prazo) to set

instituto [ĩʃtʃi'tutu] M (escola) institute;
(instituição) institution; ~ **de beleza** beauty
salon; **I~ de Pesos e Medidas** ≈ British
Standards Institution

instrução [ĩʃtru'sãw] (PT -cç-, pl -ões) F
education; (erudição) learning; (diretriz)
instruction; (Mil) training; **instruções** FPL
(para o uso) instructions (for use); **manual de
instruções** instruction manual

instructor, a [ĩʃtru'to'(a)] (PT) M/F
= **instrutor(a)**

instruído, -a [ĩʃ'trwidu, a] ADJ educated

instruir [ĩʃ'trwi'] VT to instruct; (Mil) to train;
(Jur: processo) to prepare; **instruir-se** VR:
instruir-se em algo to learn sth; ~ **alguém de**
ou **sobre algo** to inform sb about sth

instrumentação [ĩʃtrumẽta'sãw] F (Mús)
instrumentation

instrumental [ĩʃtrumẽ'taw] (pl -ais) ADJ
instrumental ■ M instruments pl

instrumentar [ĩʃtrumẽ'ta'] VT (Mús) to score

instrumentista [ĩʃtrumẽ'tʃiʃta] M/F
instrumentalist

instrumento [ĩʃtru'mẽtu] M instrument;
(ferramenta) implement; (Jur) deed, document;
~ **de cordas/percussão/sopro** stringed/
percussion/wind instrument; ~ **de trabalho**
tool

instrutivo, -a [ĩʃtru'tʃivu, a] ADJ instructive

instrutor, a [ĩʃtru'to'(a)] M/F instructor; (Esporte)
coach

insubordinação [ĩsuboxdʒina'sãw] F rebellion;
(Mil) insubordination

insubordinado, -a [ĩsuboxdʒi'nadu, a] ADJ
unruly; (Mil) insubordinate

insubordinar-se [ĩsuboxdʒi'naxsi] VR to rebel;
(Náut) to mutiny

insubstituível [ĩsubiʃtʃi'twivew] (pl -eis) ADJ
irreplaceable

insucesso [ĩsu'sesu] M failure

insuficiência [ĩsufi'sjẽsja] F inadequacy;
(carência) shortage; (Med) deficiency; ~ **cardíaca**
heart failure; **insuficiente** [ĩsufi'sjẽtʃi] ADJ (não
bastante) insufficient; (Educ: nota) ≈ fail; (pessoa)
incompetent

insuflar [ĩsu'fla'] VT to blow up, inflate; (ar) to
blow; (fig): ~ **algo (em** ou **a alguém)** to instil
(Brit) ou instill (US) sth (in sb)

insular [ĩsu'la'] ADJ insular ■ VT (Tec) to

insulate

insulina [ĩsu'lina] F insulin

insultar [ĩsuw'ta'] VT to insult; **insulto**
[ĩ'suwtu] M insult

insultuoso, -a [ĩsuw'twozu, ɔza] ADJ insulting

insumo [ĩ'sumu] M raw materials pl; (Econ)
input

insuperável [ĩsupe'ravew] (pl -eis) ADJ
(dificuldade) insuperable; (qualidade)
unsurpassable

insuportável [ĩsupox'tavew] (pl -eis) ADJ
unbearable

insurgente [ĩsux'ʒẽtʃi] ADJ rebellious ■ M/F
rebel

insurgir-se [ĩsux'ʒixsi] VR to rebel, revolt

insurreição [ĩsuxej'sãw] (pl -ões) F rebellion,
insurrection

insurreto, -a [ĩsu'xɛtu, a] ADJ rebellious ■ M/F
insurgent

insuspeito, -a [ĩsuʃ'pejtu, a] ADJ unsuspected;
(imparcial) impartial

insustentável [ĩsuʃtẽ'tavew] (pl -eis) ADJ
untenable

intacto, -a [ĩ'tatu, a] (PT) ADJ = **intato**

intangível [ĩtã'ʒivew] (pl -eis) ADJ intangible

intato, -a [ĩ'tatu, a] ADJ intact; (ileso)
unharmed; (fig) pure

íntegra ['ĩtegra] F: **na** ~ in full

integração [ĩtegra'sãw] F integration

integral [ĩte'graw] (pl -ais) ADJ whole ■ F (Mat)
integral; **arroz** ~ brown rice; **pão** ~ wholemeal
(Brit) ou wholewheat (US) bread

integralismo [ĩtegra'liʒmu] M Brazilian fascism

integralmente [ĩtegraw'mẽtʃi] ADV in full,
fully

integrante [ĩte'grãtʃi] ADJ integral ■ M/F
member

integrar [ĩte'gra'] VT to unite, combine;
(completar) to form, make up; (Mat, raças) to
integrate; **integrar-se** VR to become complete;
~-**se em** ou **a algo** (juntar-se) to join sth; (adaptar-
se) to integrate into sth

integridade [ĩtegri'dadʒi] F (totalidade) entirety;
(fig: de pessoa) integrity

íntegro, -a ['ĩtegru, a] ADJ entire; (honesto)
upright, honest

inteiramente [ĩtejra'mẽtʃi] ADV completely

inteirar [ĩtej'ra'] VT (completar) to complete;
inteirar-se VR: **inteirar-se de** to find out
about; ~ **alguém de** to inform sb of

inteireza [ĩtej'reza] F entirety; (moral) integrity

inteiriçado, -a [ĩtejri'sadu, a] ADJ stiff

inteiriço, -a [ĩtej'risu, a] ADJ (pedaço de pano)
single; (vestido) one-piece

inteiro, -a [ĩ'tejru, a] ADJ (todo) whole, entire;
(ileso) unharmed; (não quebrado) undamaged;
(completo, ilimitado) complete; (vestido) one-piece;
(fig: caráter) upright

intelecto [ĩte'lɛktu] M intellect; **intelectual**
[ĩtelek'twaw] (pl -ais) ADJ, M/F intellectual

intelectualidade [ĩtelektwali'dadʒi] F
(qualidade) intellect; (pessoas) intellectuals pl

inteligência [īteli'ʒēsja] F intelligence; (*interpretação*) interpretation; (*pessoa*) intellect, thinker; ~ **artificial** artificial intelligence; **inteligente** [īteli'ʒētʃi] ADJ (*pessoa*) intelligent, clever; (*decisão, romance, filme etc*) clever

inteligível [īteli'ʒivew] (*pl -eis*) ADJ intelligible

intempérie [ītẽ'pɛri] F bad weather

intempestivo, -a [ītẽpeʃ'tʃivu, a] ADJ ill-timed

intenção [ītẽ'sãw] (*pl -ões*) F intention; **segundas intenções** ulterior motives; **ter a ~ de** to intend to; **com boa ~** with good intent; **com má ~** maliciously; (*Jur*) with malice aforethought; **intencionado, -a** [ītẽsjo'nadu, a] ADJ: **bem intencionado** well-meaning; **mal intencionado** spiteful

intencional [ītẽsjo'naw] (*pl -ais*) ADJ intentional, deliberate

intencionar [ītẽsjo'naʳ] VT: ~ **fazer** to intend to do

intenções [ītẽ'sõjʃ] FPL *de* **intenção**

intendência [ītẽ'dẽsja] (PT) F management, administration

intendente [ītẽ'dẽtʃi] M/F manager; (*Mil*) quartermaster

intensidade [ītẽsi'dadʒi] F intensity

intensificação [ītẽsifika'sãw] F intensification

intensificar [ītẽsifi'kaʳ] VT to intensify; **intensificar-se** VR to intensify

intensivo, -a [ītẽ'sivu, a] ADJ intensive

intenso, -a [ī'tẽsu, a] ADJ intense; (*emoção*) deep; (*impressão*) vivid; (*vida social*) full

intentar [ītẽ'taʳ] VT (*obra*) to plan; (*assalto*) to commit; (*tentar*) to attempt; ~ **fazer** to intend to do; ~ **uma ação contra** (*Jur*) to sue

intento [ī'tẽtu] M aim, purpose

intentona [ītẽ'tɔna] F (*Pol*) plot, conspiracy

interação [ītera'sãw] (PT **-cç-**) F interaction

interagir [ītera'ʒiʳ] VI: ~ **(com)** to interact (with)

interamericano, -a [īter-] ADJ inter-American

interativo, -a [ītera'tʃivu, a] ADJ (*Comput*) interactive

intercalar [ītexka'laʳ] VT to insert; (*Comput: arquivos*) to merge

intercâmbio [ītex'kãbju] M exchange

interceder [ītexse'deʳ] VI: ~ **por** to intercede on behalf of

interceptar [ītexsep'taʳ] VT to intercept; (*fazer parar*) to stop; (*ligação telefônica*) to cut off; (*ser obstáculo a*) to hinder

intercessão [ītexse'sãw] (*pl -ões*) F intercession

interconexão [ītexkonek'sãw] (*pl -ões*) F interconnection

intercontinental [ītexkõtʃinẽ'taw] (*pl -ais*) ADJ intercontinental

intercostal [ītexkoʃ'taw] (*pl -ais*) ADJ (*Med*) intercostal

interdependência [ītexdepẽ'dẽsja] F interdependence

interdição [ītexdʒi'sãw] (*pl -ões*) F (*de estrada,*

porta) closure; (*Jur*) injunction; ~ **de direitos civis** removal of civil rights

interdisciplinar [ītexdʒisipli'naʳ] ADJ interdisciplinary

interditado, -a [ītexdʒi'tadu, a] ADJ closed, sealed off

interditar [ītexdʒi'taʳ] VT (*importação etc*) to ban; (*estrada, praia*) to close off; (*cinema etc*) to close down; (*Jur*) to interdict

interdito, -a [ītex'dʒitu, a] ADJ (*Jur*) interdicted ■ M (*Jur: interdição*) injunction

interessado, -a [ītere'sadu, a] ADJ interested; (*amizade*) self-seeking ■ M/F interested party

interessante [ītere'sãtʃi] ADJ interesting; **estar em estado ~** to be expecting *ou* pregnant

interessar [ītere'saʳ] VT to interest, be of interest to ■ VI to be interesting; **interessar-se** VR: **interessar-se em** *ou* **por** to take an interest in, be interested in; **a quem possa ~** to whom it may concern

interesse [īte'resi] M interest; (*próprio*) self-interest; (*proveito*) advantage; **no ~ de** for the sake of; **por ~ (próprio)** for one's own ends; **interesseiro, -a** [ītere'sejru, a] ADJ self-seeking

interestadual [ītereʃta'dwaw] (*pl -ais*) ADJ interstate

interface [ītex'fasi] F (*Comput*) interface

interferência [ītexfe'rẽsja] F interference

interferir [ītexfe'riʳ] VI: ~ **em** to interfere in; (*rádio*) to jam

interfone [ītex'fɔni] M intercom

ínterim ['īterĩ] M interim; **nesse ~** in the meantime

interino, -a [īte'rinu, a] ADJ temporary, interim

interior [īte'rjoʳ] ADJ inner, inside; (*vida*) inner; (*Com*) domestic, internal ■ M inside, interior; (*coração*) heart; (*do país*): **no ~** inland; **Ministério do I~** ≈ Home Office (*Brit*), ≈ Department of the Interior (*US*); **Ministro do I~** Home Secretary (*Brit*), Secretary of the Interior (*US*); **na parte ~** inside

interiorizar [īterjori'zaʳ] VT to internalize

interjeição [ītexʒej'sãw] (*pl -ões*) F interjection

interligar [ītexli'gaʳ] VT to interconnect; **interligar-se** VR to be interconnected

interlocutor, a [ītexloku'toʳ(a)] M/F speaker; **meu ~** the person I was speaking to

interlúdio [ītex'ludʒu] M interlude

intermediário, -a [ītexme'dʒjarju, a] ADJ intermediary ■ M/F (*Com*) middleman; (*mediador*) intermediary, mediator

intermédio [ītex'mɛdʒu] M: **por ~ de** through

interminável [ītexmi'navew] (*pl -eis*) ADJ endless

interministerial [ītexminiʃte'rjaw] (*pl -ais*) ADJ interministerial

intermissão [ītexmi'sãw] (*pl -ões*) F interval

intermitente [ītexmi'tẽtʃi] ADJ intermittent

internação [ītexna'sãw] (*pl -ões*) F (*de doente*)

NB: *European Portuguese adds the following consonants to certain words:* **b** (sú(b)dito, su(b)til); **c** (a(c)ção, a(c)cionista, a(c)to); **m** (inde(m)ne); **p** (ado(p)çã, ado(p)tar); *for further details see p. xiii.*

internacional | intransitável

admission; *(de aluno)* sending to boarding school

internacional [ĩtexnasjo'naw] *(pl* -**ais***)* ADJ international

internacionalismo [ĩtexnasjona'liʒmu] M internationalism

internacionalizar [ĩtexnasjonali'za^r] VT to internationalize; **internacionalizar-se** VR to become international

internações [ĩtexna'sõjʃ] FPL *de* **internação**

internar [ĩtex'na^r] VT *(aluno)* to put into boarding school; *(doente)* to take into hospital; *(Mil, Pol)* to intern

internato [ĩtex'natu] M boarding school

internauta [ĩtex'nawta] M/F Internet user, web ou net surfer *(col)*

Internet [ĩtex'nɛtʃi] F Internet

interno, -a [ĩ'tɛxnu, a] ADJ internal, interior; *(Pol)* domestic ▪ M/F *(tb:* **aluno interno**) boarder; *(Med: estudante)* houseman *(Brit)*, intern *(US)*; **de uso ~** *(Med)* for internal use

interpelação [ĩtexpela'sãw] *(pl* -**ões**) F questioning; *(Jur)* summons *sg*

interpelar [ĩtexpe'la^r] VT: **~ alguém sobre algo** to question sb about sth; *(pedir explicações)* to challenge sb about sth

interplanetário, -a [ĩtexplane'tarju, a] ADJ interplanetary

interpõe *etc* [ĩtex'põj] VB *v* **interpor**

interpolar [ĩtexpo'la^r] VT to interpolate

interpor [ĩtex'po^r] *(irreg)* VT to put in, interpose; **interpor-se** VR to intervene; **~-se a algo** *(contrapor-se)* to militate against sth; **~ A (a B)** *(argumentos etc)* to counter (B) with A

interposto, -a [ĩtex'poʃtu, 'pɔʃta] PP *de* **interpor**

interpretação [ĩtexpreta'sãw] *(pl* -**ões***)* F interpretation; *(Teatro)* performance; **má ~** misinterpretation

interpretar [ĩtexpre'ta^r] VT to interpret; *(um papel)* to play; **~ mal** to misinterpret; **intérprete** [ĩ'tɛxpretʃi] M/F *(Ling)* interpreter; *(Teatro)* performer, artist

interpunha *etc* [ĩtex'puɲa] VB *v* **interpor**

interpus *etc* [ĩtex'puʃ] VB *v* **interpor**

interpuser *etc* [ĩtexpu'ze^r] VB *v* **interpor**

inter-racial [ĩtex-] *(pl* -**ais***)* ADJ interracial

interrogação [ĩtexoga'sãw] *(pl* -**ões***)* F questioning, interrogation; **ponto de ~** question mark

interrogador, a [ĩtexoga'do^r(a)] M/F interrogator

interrogar [ĩtexo'ga^r] VT to question, interrogate; *(Jur)* to cross-examine

interrogativo, -a [ĩtexoga'tʃivu, a] ADJ interrogative

interrogatório [ĩtexoga'tɔrju] M cross-examination

interromper [ĩtexõ'pe^r] VT to interrupt; *(parar)* to stop; *(Elet)* to cut off

interrupção [ĩtexup'sãw] *(pl* -**ões***)* F interruption; *(intervalo)* break

interruptor [ĩtexup'to^r] M *(Elet)* switch

interseção [ĩtexse'sãw] *(PT* -**cç**-, *pl* -**ões***)* F intersection

interstício [ĩtexʃ'tʃisju] M gap

interurbano, -a [ĩterux'banu, a] ADJ *(Tel)* long-distance ▪ M long-distance *ou* trunk call

intervalado, -a [ĩtexva'ladu, a] ADJ spaced out

intervalo [ĩtex'valu] M interval; *(descanso)* break; **a ~s** every now and then

interveio *etc* [ĩtex'veju] VB *v* **intervir**

intervenção [ĩtexvẽ'sãw] *(pl* -**ões***)* F intervention; **~ cirúrgica** *(Med)* operation

interventor, a [ĩtexvẽ'to^r(a)] M/F inspector ▪ M OU F *(Pol)* caretaker governor

intervir [ĩtex'vi^r] *(irreg)* VI to intervene; *(sobrevir)* to come up

intestinal [ĩteʃtʃi'naw] *(pl* -**ais***)* ADJ intestinal

intestino [ĩteʃ'tʃinu] M intestine; **~ delgado/grosso** small/large intestine; **~ solto** diarrhoea *(Brit)*, diarrhea *(US)*

inti [ĩ'tʃi] M inti *(Peruvian currency)*

intimação [ĩtʃima'sãw] *(pl* -**ões***)* F *(ordem)* order; *(Jur)* summons

intimar [ĩtʃi'ma^r] VT *(Jur)* to summon; **~ alguém a fazer** *ou* **a alguém que faça** to order sb to do

intimidação [ĩtʃimida'sãw] F intimidation

intimidade [ĩtʃimi'dadʒi] F intimacy; *(vida privada)* private life; *(familiaridade)* familiarity; **ter ~ com alguém** to be close to sb; **ela é pessoa de minha ~** she's a close friend of mine

intimidar [ĩtʃimi'da^r] VT to intimidate; **intimidar-se** VR to be intimidated

íntimo, -a [ĩ'tʃimu, a] ADJ intimate; *(sentimentos)* innermost; *(amigo)* close; *(vida)* private ▪ M/F close friend; **no ~** at heart; **festa íntima** small gathering

intitular [ĩtʃitu'la^r] VT *(livro)* to title; **intitular-se** VR to be called; *(livro)* to be entitled; *(a si mesmo)* to call oneself; **~ algo de algo** to call sth sth

intocável [ĩto'kavew] *(pl* -**eis***)* ADJ untouchable

intolerância [ĩtole'rãsja] F intolerance

intolerante [ĩtole'rãtʃi] ADJ intolerant

intolerável [ĩtole'ravew] *(pl* -**eis***)* ADJ intolerable, unbearable

intoxicação [ĩtoksika'sãw] F poisoning; **~ alimentar** food poisoning

intoxicar [ĩtoksi'ka^r] VT to poison

intraduzível [ĩtradu'zivew] *(pl* -**eis***)* ADJ untranslateable

intragável [ĩtra'gavew] *(pl* -**eis***)* ADJ unpalatable; *(pessoa)* unbearable

intranet [ĩtra'nɛtʃi] F intranet

intranqüilidade [ĩtrãkwili'dadʒi] F disquiet

intranqüilo, -a [ĩtrã'kwilu, a] ADJ *(aflito)* worried; *(desassossegado)* restless

intransferível [ĩtrãʃfe'rivew] *(pl* -**eis***)* ADJ non-transferable

intransigência [ĩtrãsi'ʒẽsja] F intransigence

intransigente [ĩtrãsi'ʒẽtʃi] ADJ uncompromising; *(fig: rígido)* strict

intransitável [ĩtrãsi'tavew] *(pl* -**eis***)* ADJ impassable

intransitivo, -a [ĩtrãsi'tʃivu, a] ADJ intransitive

intransponível [ĩtrãʃpo'nivew] (*pl* -**eis**) ADJ (*rio*) impossible to cross; (*problema*) insurmountable

intratável [ĩtra'tavew] (*pl* -**eis**) ADJ (*pessoa*) contrary, awkward; (*doença*) untreatable; (*problema*) insurmountable

intra-uterino, -a ['ĩtra-] ADJ: **dispositivo ~** intra-uterine device

intravenoso, -a [ĩtrave'nozu, ɔza] ADJ intravenous

intrepidez [ĩtrepi'deʒ] F courage, bravery

intrépido, -a [ĩ'trɛpidu, a] ADJ daring, intrepid

intriga [ĩ'triga] F intrigue; (*enredo*) plot; (*fofoca*) piece of gossip; **intrigas** (*fofocas*) gossip *sg*; ~ **amorosa** (PT) love affair; **intrigante** [ĩtri'gãtʃi] M/F troublemaker ■ ADJ intriguing

intrigar [ĩtri'gaʳ] VT to intrigue ■ VI to be intriguing

intrincado, -a [ĩtrĩ'kadu, a] ADJ intricate

intrínseco, -a [ĩ'trĩseku, a] ADJ intrinsic

introdução [ĩtrodu'sãw] (*pl* -**ões**) F introduction

introdutório, -a [ĩtrodu'tɔrju, a] ADJ introductory

introduzir [ĩtrodu'ziʳ] VT to introduce; (*prego*) to insert

intróito [ĩ'trɔjtu] M beginning; (*Rel*) introit

intrometer-se [ĩtrome'texsi] VR to interfere, meddle; **intrometido, -a** [ĩtrome'tʃidu, a] ADJ interfering; (*col*) nosey ■ M/F busybody

intromissão [ĩtromi'sãw] (*pl* -**ões**) F interference, meddling

introspecção [ĩtroʃpek'sãw] F introspection

introspectivo, -a [ĩtroʃpek'tʃivu, a] ADJ introspective

introversão [ĩtrovex'sãw] F introversion

introvertido, -a [ĩtrovex'tʃidu, a] ADJ introverted ■ M/F introvert

intrujão, -jona [ĩtru'ʒãw, 'ʒona] (*pl* -**ões**/-**s**) M/F swindler

intrujar [ĩtru'ʒaʳ] VT to trick, swindle

intrujões [ĩtru'ʒõjʃ] MPL *de* **intrujão**

intrujona [ĩtru'ʒona] F *de* **intrujão**

intruso, -a [ĩ'truzu, a] M/F intruder

intuição [ĩtwi'sãw] (*pl* -**ões**) F intuition; (*pressentimento*) feeling; **por ~** by intuition, intuitively

intuir [ĩ'twiʳ] VT, VI to intuit

intuitivo, -a [ĩtwi'tʃivu, a] ADJ intuitive

intuito [ĩ'tuito] M (*intento*) intention, aim

intumescência [ĩtume'sẽsja] F swelling

intumescer-se [ĩtume'sexsi] VR to swell (up)

intumescido, -a [ĩtume'sidu, a] ADJ swollen

inumano, -a [inu'manu, a] ADJ inhuman

inumerável [inume'ravew] (*pl* -**eis**) ADJ countless, innumerable

inúmero, -a [i'numeru, a] ADJ countless, innumerable

inundação [inũda'sãw] (*pl* -**ões**) F (*enchente*) flood; (*ato*) flooding

inundar [inũ'daʳ] VT to flood; (*fig*) to inundate ■ VI (*rio*) to flood

inusitado, -a [inuzi'tadu, a] ADJ unusual

inútil [i'nutʃiw] (*pl* -**eis**) ADJ useless; (*esforço*) futile; (*desnecessário*) pointless ■ M/F good-for-nothing; **ser ~** to be of no use, be no good

inutilidade [inutʃili'dadʒi] F uselessness

inutilizar [inutʃili'zaʳ] VT to make useless, render useless; (*incapacitar*) to put out of action; (*danificar*) to ruin; (*esforços*) to thwart; **inutilizar-se** (*pessoa*) to become incapacitated

inutilizável [inutʃili'zavew] (*pl* -**eis**) ADJ unusable

inutilmente [inutʃiw'mẽtʃi] ADV in vain

invadir [ĩva'dʒiʳ] VT to invade; (*suj*: *água*) to overrun; (: *sentimento*) to overcome

invalidação [ĩvalida'sãw] F invalidation

invalidar [ĩvali'daʳ] VT to invalidate; (*pessoa*) to make an invalid

invalidez [ĩvali'deʒ] F disability

inválido, -a [ĩ'validu, a] ADJ, M/F invalid; ~ **de guerra** wounded war veteran

invariável [ĩva'rjavew] (*pl* -**eis**) ADJ invariable

invasão [ĩva'zãw] (*pl* -**ões**) F invasion

invasor, a [ĩva'zoʳ(a)] ADJ invading ■ M/F invader

inveja [ĩ'veʒa] F envy; **invejar** [ĩve'ʒaʳ] VT to envy; (*cobiçar*: *bens*) to covet ■ VI to be envious

invejável [ĩve'ʒavew] (*pl* -**eis**) ADJ enviable

invejoso, -a [ĩve'ʒozu, ɔza] ADJ envious ■ M/F envious person

invenção [ĩvẽ'sãw] (*pl* -**ões**) F invention

invencível [ĩvẽ'sivew] (*pl* -**eis**) ADJ invincible

invenções [ĩvẽ'sõjʃ] FPL *de* **invenção**

inventar [ĩvẽ'taʳ] VT to invent; (*história, desculpa*) to make up; (*nome*) to think up ■ VI to make things up; ~ **de fazer** to take it into one's head to do

inventariação [ĩvẽtarja'sãw] (*pl* -**ões**) F (*Com*) stocktaking

inventariar [ĩvẽta'rjaʳ] VT: ~ **algo** to make an inventory of sth

inventário [ĩvẽ'tarju] M inventory

inventiva [ĩvẽ'tʃiva] F inventiveness

inventivo, -a [ĩvẽ'tʃivu, a] ADJ inventive

inventor, a [ĩvẽ'toʳ(a)] M/F inventor

inverdade [ĩvex'dadʒi] F untruth

inverificável [ĩverifi'kavew] (*pl* -**eis**) ADJ impossible to verify

invernada [ĩvex'nada] F winter pasture

invernar [ĩvex'naʳ] VI to spend the winter

inverno [ĩ'vɛxnu] M winter

inverossímil [ĩvero'simiw] (PT -**osí-**, *pl* -**eis**) ADJ (*improvável*) unlikely, improbable; (*inacreditável*) implausible

inversão [ĩvex'sãw] (*pl* -**ões**) F reversal, inversion

inverso, -a [ĩ'vɛxsu, a] ADJ inverse; (*oposto*) opposite; (*ordem*) reverse ■ M opposite, reverse;

NB: *European Portuguese adds the following consonants to certain words:* **b** (sú(b)dito, su(b)til); **c** (a(c)ção, a(c)cionista, a(c)to); **m** (inde(m)ne); **p** (ado(p)ção, ado(p)tar); *for further details see p. xiii.*

ao ~ de contrary to

inversões [ĩvex'sõjʃ] FPL *de* **inversão**

invertebrado, -a [ĩvexte'bradu, a] ADJ
invertebrate ▪ M invertebrate

inverter [ĩvex'te^r] VT (*mudar*) to alter; (*ordem*) to
invert, reverse; (*colocar às avessas*) to turn upside
down, invert

invés [ĩ'vεʃ] M: **ao ~ de** instead of

investida [ĩveʃ'tʃida] F attack; (*tentativa*) attempt

investidura [ĩveʃtʃi'dura] F investiture

investigação [ĩveʃtʃiga'sãw] (*pl* -**ões**) F
investigation; (*pesquisa*) research

investigar [ĩveʃtʃi'ga^r] VT to investigate;
(*examinar*) to examine; (*pesquisar*) to research
into

investimento [ĩveʃtʃi'mẽtu] M investment

investir [ĩveʃ'tʃi^r] VT (*dinheiro*) to invest ▪ VI to
invest; **~ contra** *ou* **para alguém** (*atacar*) to
attack sb; **~ alguém no cargo de presidente** to
install sb in the presidency; **~ para algo** (*atirar-
se*) to rush towards sth

inveterado, -a [ĩvete'radu, a] ADJ (*mentiroso*)
inveterate; (*criminoso*) hardened; (*hábito*) deep-
rooted

inviabilidade [ĩvjabili'dadʒi] F impracticality

inviabilizar [ĩvjabili'za^r] VT: **~ algo** to make sth
impracticable

inviável [ĩ'vjavew] (*pl* -**eis**) ADJ impracticable

invicto, -a [ĩ'viktu, a] ADJ unconquered;
(*invencível*) unbeatable

inviolabilidade [ĩvjolabili'dadʒi] F
inviolability; (*Jur*) immunity

inviolável [ĩvjo'lavew] (*pl* -**eis**) ADJ inviolable;
(*Jur*) immune

invisível [ĩvi'zivew] (*pl* -**eis**) ADJ invisible

invisto *etc* [ĩ'viʃtu] VB V **investir**

invocado, -a [ĩvo'kadu, a] ADJ: **estar/ficar ~
com alguém** to dislike/take a dislike to sb

invocar [ĩvo'ka^r] VT to invoke; (*col: irritar*) to
provoke; (: *impressionar*) to have a profound effect
on ▪ VI: **~ com alguém** (*col: antipatizar*) to take a
dislike to sb

invólucro [ĩ'vɔlukru] M (*cobertura*) covering;
(*envoltório*) wrapping; (*caixa*) box

involuntário, -a [ĩvolũ'tarju, a] ADJ (*movimento*)
involuntary; (*ofensa*) unintentional

invulnerável [ĩvuwne'ravew] (*pl* -**eis**) ADJ
invulnerable

iodo ['jodu] M iodine

IOF (BR) ABR M = **Imposto sobre Operações
Financeiras**

ioga ['jɔga] F yoga

iogurte [jo'guxtʃi] M yogurt

ioiô [jo'jo] M yoyo

íon ['iõ] (*pl* -**s**) M ion

iônico, -a ['joniku, a] ADJ ionic

IPC (BR) ABR M (= *Índice de Preços ao Consumidor*) RPI

IPEA (BR) ABR M = **Instituto de Planejamento
Econômico Social**

ipecacuanha [ipeka'kwaɲa] F ipecac

IPI (BR) ABR M = **Imposto sobre Produtos
Industrializados**

IPM (BR) ABR M = **Inquérito Policial-Militar**

IPT (BR) ABR M = **Instituto de Pesquisas
Tecnológicas**

IPTU (BR) ABR M (= *Imposto Predial e Territorial
Urbano*) ≈ rates *pl* (Brit), ≈ property tax (US)

IPVA (BR) ABR M (= *Imposto Sobre Veículos
Automóveis*) road (Brit) *ou* motor-vehicle (US) tax

IR (BR) ABR M = **Imposto de Renda**

 PALAVRA CHAVE

ir [i^r] VI **1** to go; (*a pé*) to walk; (*a cavalo*) to ride;
(*viajar*) to travel; **ir caminhando** to walk; **fui
de trem** I went *ou* travelled by train; **vamos!,
vamos nessa!** (*col*): **vamos embora!** let's go!; **já
vou!** I'm coming!; **ir atrás de alguém** (*seguir*) to
follow sb; (*confiar*) to take sb's word for it
2 (*progredir: pessoa, coisa*) to go; **o trabalho vai
muito bem** work is going very well; **como vão
as coisas?** how are things going?; **vou muito
bem** I'm very well; (*na escola etc*) I'm getting on
very well
▪ VB AUX **1** (+*infin*): **vou fazer** I will do, I am
going to do
2 (+*gerúndio*): **ir fazendo** to keep on doing
ir-se VR to go away, leave

IRA ABR M (= *Irish Republican Army*) IRA

ira ['ira] F anger, rage

Irã [i'rã] M: **o ~** Iran

irado, -a [i'radu, a] ADJ angry, irate

iraniano, -a [ira'njanu, a] ADJ, M/F Iranian

Irão [i'rãw] (PT) M = **Irã**

Iraque [i'raki] M: **o ~** Iraq; **iraquiano, -a**
[ira'kjanu, a] ADJ, M/F Iraqi

irascibilidade [irasibili'dadʒi] F irritability

irascível [ira'sivew] (*pl* -**eis**) ADJ irritable, short-
tempered

ir-e-vir (*pl* **ires-e-vires**) M comings and goings *pl*

íris ['iriʃ] F INV iris

Irlanda [ix'lãda] F: **a ~** Ireland; **a ~ do Norte**
Northern Ireland; **irlandês, -esa** [ixlã'deʃ, eza]
ADJ Irish ▪ M/F Irishman/woman ▪ M (*Ling*)
Irish

irmã [ix'mã] F sister ▪ ADJ (*empresa etc*) sister;
almas ~s kindred souls; **~ Paula** (*fig*) good
Samaritan; **~ gêmea** twin sister; **~ de criação**
half sister

irmanar [ixma'na^r] VT to join together, unite

irmandade [ixmã'dadʒi] F (*associação*)
brotherhood; (*confraternidade*) fraternity

irmão [ix'mãw] (*pl* -**s**) M brother; (*fig: similar*)
twin; (*col: companheiro*) mate; **~ de criação** half-
brother; **~ gêmeo** twin brother; **~s siameses**
Siamese twins

ironia [iro'nia] F irony; (*sarcasmo*) sarcasm; **com ~**
ironically; (*com sarcasmo*) sarcastically; **por ~ do
destino** by a quirk of fate

irônico, -a [i'roniku, a] ADJ ironic(al); (*sarcástico*)
sarcastic

ironizar [ironi'za^r] VT to be ironic about ▪ VI to
be ironic

IRPF (BR) ABR M (= *Imposto de Renda Pessoa Física*) personal income tax

IRPJ (BR) ABR M (= *Imposto de Renda Pessoa Jurídica*) corporation tax

irra! ['ixa] (PT) EXCL damn!

irracional [ixasjo'naw] (*pl* **-ais**) ADJ irrational

irracionalidade [ixasjonali'dadʒi] F irrationality

irradiação [ixadʒja'sãw] (*pl* **-ões**) F (*de luz*) radiation; (*espalhamento*) spread; (*Rádio*) broadcasting; (*Med*) radiation treatment

irradiar [ixa'dʒjaʳ] VT (*luz*) to radiate; (*espalhar*) to spread; (*Rádio*) to broadcast, transmit; (*simpatia*) to radiate, exude ▪ VI to radiate; (*Rádio*) to be on the air; **irradiar-se** VR to spread; to be transmitted

irreais [ixe'ajʃ] ADJ PL *de* **irreal**

irreajustável [ixeaʒuʃ'tavew] (*pl* **-eis**) ADJ fixed

irreal [ixe'aw] (*pl* **-ais**) ADJ unreal

irrealizado, -a [ixeali'zadu, a] ADJ (*pessoa*) unfulfilled; (*sonhos*) unrealized

irrealizável [ixeali'zavew] (*pl* **-eis**) ADJ unrealizable

irreconciliável [ixekõsi'ljavew] (*pl* **-eis**) ADJ irreconcilable

irreconhecível [ixekõɲe'sivew] (*pl* **-eis**) ADJ unrecognizable

irrecorrível [ixeko'xivew] (*pl* **-eis**) ADJ (*Jur*) unappealable

irrecuperável [ixekupe'ravew] (*pl* **-eis**) ADJ irretrievable

irrecusável [ixeku'zavew] (*pl* **-eis**) ADJ (*incontestável*) irrefutable; (*convite*) which cannot be turned down

irrefletido, -a [ixefle'tʃidu, a] ADJ rash; **de maneira irrefletida** rashly

irrefreável [ixe'frjavew] (*pl* **-eis**) ADJ uncontrollable

irrefutável [ixefu'tavew] (*pl* **-eis**) ADJ irrefutable

irregular [ixegu'laʳ] ADJ irregular; (*vida*) unconventional; (*feições*) unusual; (*aluno, gênio*) erratic

irregularidade [ixegulari'dadʒi] F irregularity

irrelevância [ixele'vãsja] F irrelevance

irrelevante [ixele'vãtʃi] ADJ irrelevant

irremediável [ixeme'dʒjavew] (*pl* **-eis**) ADJ irremediable; (*sem remédio*) incurable

irreparável [ixepa'ravew] (*pl* **-eis**) ADJ irreparable

irrepreensível [ixeprjẽ'sivew] (*pl* **-eis**) ADJ irreproachable, impeccable

irreprimível [ixepri'mivew] (*pl* **-eis**) ADJ irrepressible

irrequietação [ixekjeta'sãw] F restlessness

irrequieto, -a [ixe'kjɛtu, a] ADJ restless

irresgatável [ixeʒga'tavew] (*pl* **-eis**) ADJ (*Com*) irredeemable

irresistível [ixeziʃ'tʃivew] (*pl* **-eis**) ADJ irresistible; (*desejo*) overwhelming

irrevogável [ixevo'gavew] (*pl* **-eis**) ADJ irrevocable

irresoluto, -a [ixezo'lutu, a] ADJ (*pessoa*) irresolute, indecisive; (*problema*) unresolved

irresponsabilidade [ixeʃpõsabili'dadʒi] F irresponsibility

irresponsável [ixeʃpõ'savew] (*pl* **-eis**) ADJ irresponsible

irrestrito, -a [ixeʃ'tritu, a] ADJ unrestricted

irreverente [ixeve'rẽtʃi] ADJ irreverent

irreversível [ixevex'sivew] (*pl* **-eis**) ADJ irreversible

irrigação [ixiga'sãw] F irrigation

irrigar [ixi'gaʳ] VT to irrigate

irrisório, -a [ixi'zɔrju, a] ADJ derisory, ludicrous; (*quantia*) derisory, paltry

irritabilidade [ixitabili'dadʒi] F irritability

irritação [ixita'sãw] (*pl* **-ões**) F irritation

irritadiço, -a [ixita'dʒisu, a] ADJ irritable

irritante [ixi'tãtʃi] ADJ irritating, annoying

irritar [ixi'taʳ] VT to irritate, annoy; (*Med*) to irritate; **irritar-se** VR to get angry, get annoyed

irritável [ixi'tavew] (*pl* **-eis**) ADJ irritable

irromper [ixõ'peʳ] VI (*epidemia*) to break out; (*surgir*) to emerge; (*lágrimas*) to well; (*voz*) to be heard; (*entrar subitamente*): **~ (em)** to burst in(to)

irrupção [ixup'sãw] (*pl* **-ões**) F invasion; (*de idéias*) emergence; (*de doença*) outbreak

isca ['iʃka] F (*Pesca*) bait; (*fig*) lure, bait

iscambau [iʃkã'baw] (*col*) M: **e o ~** and what not

isenção [izẽ'sãw] (*pl* **-ões**) F exemption; **~ de impostos** tax exemption

isentar [izẽ'taʳ] VT (*dispensar*) to exempt; (*livrar*) to free

isento, -a [i'zẽtu, a] ADJ (*dispensado*) exempt; (*livre*) free; **~ de taxas** duty-free; **~ de impostos** tax-free

Islã [iʒ'lã] M Islam

islâmico, -a [iʒ'lamiku, a] ADJ Islamic

islamismo [iʒla'miʒmu] M Islam

islamita [iʒla'mita] ADJ, M/F Muslim

islandês, -esa [iʒlã'deʃ, eza] ADJ Icelandic ▪ M/F Icelander ▪ M (*Ling*) Icelandic

Islândia [iʒ'lãdʒa] F: **a ~** Iceland

isolado, -a [izo'ladu, a] ADJ (*separado*) isolated; (*solitário*) lonely; (*Elet*) insulated

isolamento [izola'mẽtu] M isolation; (*Med*) isolation ward; (*Elet*) insulation; **~ acústico** soundproofing

isolante [izo'lãtʃi] ADJ (*Elet*) insulating

isolar [izo'laʳ] VT to isolate; (*Elet*) to insulate ▪ VI (*afastar mau agouro*) to touch wood (*Brit*), knock on wood (*US*); **isolar-se** VR to isolate o.s., cut o.s. off

isonomia [izono'mia] F equality

isopor® [izo'poʳ] M polystyrene

isqueiro [iʃ'kejru] M (cigarette) lighter

NB: *European Portuguese adds the following consonants to certain words:* **b** (sú(b)dito, su(b)til); **c** (a(c)ção, a(c)cionista, a(c)to); **m** (inde(m)ne); **p** (ado(p)çã, ado(p)tar); *for further details see p. xiii.*

Israel [iʒxa'ɛw] M Israel; **israelense** [iʒxae'lẽsi] ADJ, M/F Israeli
israelita [iʒxae'lita] ADJ, M/F Israelite
ISS (BR) ABR M = **Imposto Sobre Serviços**
isso ['isu] PRON that; (col: isto) this; ~ **mesmo** exactly; **por** ~ therefore, so; **por** ~ **mesmo** for that very reason; **só** ~? is that all?; ~! that's it!; **é** ~, **é** ~ **aí** (col: você tem razão) that's right; (é tudo) that's it, that's all; **é** ~ **mesmo** exactly, that's right; **não seja por** ~ that's no big deal; **eu não tenho nada com** ~ it's got nothing to do with me; **que é** ~? (exprime indignação) what's going on?, what's all this?; ~ **de fazer** ... this business of doing....
Istambul [iʃtã'buw] N Istanbul
istmo ['iʃtʃimu] M isthmus
isto ['iʃtu] PRON this; ~ **é** that is, namely
ITA (BR) ABR M = **Instituto Tecnológico da Aeronáutica**
Itália [i'talja] F: **a** ~ Italy; **italiano, -a** [ita'ljanu, a] ADJ, M/F Italian ■ M (Ling) Italian
itálico [i'taliku] M italics pl

Itamarati [itamara'tʃi] M: **o** ~ the Brazilian Foreign Ministry

⬤ **ITAMARATI**
⬤
⬤ The Palace of Itamarati was built in 1855
⬤ in Rio de Janeiro. It became the seat of
⬤ government when Brazil became a republic
⬤ in 1889, and was later the Foreign Ministry.
⬤ It ceased to be this when the Brazilian
⬤ capital was transferred to Brasília, but
⬤ Itamarati is still used to refer to the Foreign
⬤ Ministry.

item ['itẽ] (pl -ns) M item
iterar [ite'ra'] VT to repeat
itinerante [itʃine'rãtʃi] ADJ, M/F itinerant
itinerário [itʃine'rarju] M (plano) itinerary; (caminho) route
Iugoslávia [jugoʒ'lavja] F: **a** ~ Yugoslavia
iugoslavo, -a [jugoʒ'lavu, a] ADJ, M/F Yugoslav(ian)

J j

J, j ['ʒɔta] (pl **js**) M J, j; **J de José** J for Jack (Brit) ou jig (US)

já [ʒa] ADV already; (em perguntas) yet; (agora) now; (imediatamente) right now; (agora mesmo) right away ■ CONJ on the other hand; **até já** bye; **desde já** from now on; **desde já lhe agradeço** thanking you in anticipation; **é para já** it won't be a minute; **já esteve na Inglaterra?** have you ever been to England?; **já não** no longer; **ele já não vem mais aqui** he doesn't come here any more; **já que** as, since; **já se vê** of course; **já vou** I'm coming; **já até** even; **já, já** right away; **já era** (col) it's been and gone; **você já viu o filme?** — **já** have you seen the film? — yes

jabaculê [ʒabaku'le] (col) M backhander

jabota [ʒa'bɔta] F giant tortoise

jabuti [ʒabu'tʃi] M giant tortoise

jabuticaba [ʒabutʃi'kaba] F jaboticaba (type of berry)

jaca ['ʒaka] F jack fruit

jacarandá [ʒakarã'da] M jacaranda

jacaré [ʒaka'rɛ] (BR) M alligator; **fazer** ou **pegar ~** to body-surf

Jacarta [ʒa'kaxta] N Jakarta

jacente [ʒa'sẽtʃi] ADJ lying; (herança) unclaimed

jacinto [ʒa'sĩtu] M hyacinth

jactância [ʒak'tãsja] F boasting

jactar-se [ʒak'taxsi] VR: **~ de** to boast about

jacto ['ʒaktu] (PT) M = **jato**

jade ['ʒadʒi] M jade

jaez [ʒa'ɛʒ] M harness; (fig: categoria) sort

jaguar [ʒa'gwaɾ] M jaguar

jaguatirica [ʒagwatʃi'rika] F leopard cat

jagunço [ʒa'gũsu] M hired gun(man)

jaleco [ʒa'lɛku] M jacket

Jamaica [ʒa'majka] F: **a ~** Jamaica

jamais [ʒa'majʃ] ADV never; (com palavra negativa) ever; **ninguém ~ o tratou assim** nobody ever treated him like that

jamaicano, -a [ʒamaj'kanu, a] ADJ, M/F Jamaican

jamanta [ʒa'mãta] F juggernaut (Brit), truck-trailer (US)

jamegão [ʒame'gãw] (pl **-ões**) (col) M signature

jan. ABR = **janeiro**

janeiro [ʒa'nejru] (PT **J-**) M January; v tb **julho**

janela [ʒa'nɛla] F window; **(~) basculante** louvre (Brit) ou louver (US) window

janelão [ʒane'lãw] (pl **-ões**) M picture window

jangada [ʒã'gada] F raft

jangadeiro [ʒãga'dejru] M jangada fisherman

janota [ʒa'nɔta] ADJ foppish ■ M dandy

janta ['ʒãta] (col) F dinner

jantar [ʒã'taɾ] M dinner ■ VT to have for dinner ■ VI to have dinner; **~ americano** buffet dinner; **~ dançante** dinner dance

jantarado [ʒãta'radu] M tea

Japão [ʒa'pãw] M: **o ~** Japan

japona [ʒa'pɔna] F (casaco) three-quarter length coat ■ M/F (col) Japanese

japonês, -esa [ʒapo'neʃ, eza] ADJ, M/F Japanese ■ M (Ling) Japanese

jaqueira [ʒa'kejra] F jack tree

jaqueta [ʒa'keta] F jacket

jaquetão [ʒake'tãw] (pl **-ões**) M double-breasted coat

jararaca [ʒara'raka] F (cobra) jararaca (snake); (fig: mulher) shrew

jarda ['ʒaxda] F yard

jardim [ʒax'dʒĩ] (pl **-ns**) M garden; **~ zoológico** zoo; **jardim-de-infância** (pl **jardins-de-infância**) M kindergarten

jardim-de-inverno (pl **jardins-de-inverno**) M conservatory

jardinagem [ʒaxdʒi'naʒẽ] F gardening

jardinar [ʒaxdʒi'naɾ] VT to cultivate ■ VI to garden

jardineira [ʒaxdʒi'nejra] F (móvel) plant-stand; (caixa) trough; (ônibus) open bus; (calça) dungarees pl; (vestido) pinafore dress (Brit), jumper (US); v tb **jardineiro**

jardineiro, -a [ʒaxdʒi'nejru, a] M/F gardener

jardins [ʒax'dʒĩʃ] MPL de **jardim**

jargão [ʒax'gãw] M jargon

jarra ['ʒaxa] F pot

jarro ['ʒaxu] M jug

jasmim [ʒaʒ'mĩ] M jasmine

NB: European Portuguese adds the following consonants to certain words: **b** (sú(b)dito, su(b)til); **c** (a(c)ção, a(c)cionista, a(c)to); **m** (inde(m)ne); **p** (ado(p)çã, ado(p)tar); for further details see p. xiii.

jato ['ʒatu] M jet; (de luz) flash; (de ar) blast; **a ~ at top speed**
jaula ['ʒawla] F cage
Java ['ʒava] F Java
javali [ʒava'li] M wild boar
jazer [ʒa'zeʳ] VI to lie
jazida [ʒa'zida] F deposit
jazigo [ʒa'zigu] M grave; (monumento) tomb; **~ de família** family tomb
jazz [dʒɛz] M jazz
jazzista [dʒa'ziʃta] M/F (músico) jazz artist; (fā) jazz fan
jazzístico, -a [dʒa'ziʃtʃiku, a] ADJ jazzy
JB ABR M = **Jornal do Brasil**
JEC (BR) ABR F = **Juventude Estudantil Católica**
jeca ['ʒɛka] ADJ rustic; (cafona) tacky ■ M/F Brazilian hillbilly
jeca-tatu (pl **jecas-tatus**) M/F Brazilian hillbilly
jeitão [ʒej'tãw] (col) (pl -ões) M (aspecto) look; (modo de ser) style, way
jeitinho [ʒej'tʃiɲu] M knack
jeito ['ʒejtu] M (maneira) way; (aspecto) appearance; (aptidão, habilidade) skill, knack; (modos pessoais) manner; **falta de ~** clumsiness; **ter ~ de** to look like; **ter um ~ para** to have a gift for, be good at; **não ter ~** (pessoa) to be awkward; (situação) to be hopeless; **dar um ~ em algo** (pé) to twist sth; (quarto, casa, papéis) to tidy sth up; (consertar) to fix sth; **dar um ~ em alguém** to sort sb out; **dar um ~** to find a way; **tomar ~** to pull one's socks up; **o ~ é ... the thing to do is ...; é o ~** it's the best way; **ao ~ de** in the style of; **com ~** tactfully; **daquele ~** (in) that way; (col: em desordem, mal) anyhow; **de qualquer ~** anyway; **de ~ nenhum!** no way!; **ficar sem ~** to feel awkward
jeitões [ʒej'tõjʃ] MPL de **jeitão**
jeitoso, -a [ʒej'tozu, ɔza] ADJ (hábil) skilful (Brit), skillful (US); (elegante) handsome; (apropriado) suitable
jejuar [ʒe'ʒwaʳ] VI to fast
jejum [ʒe'ʒũ] (pl -ns) M fast; **em ~** fasting
Jeová [ʒeo'va] M: **testemunha de ~** Jehovah's witness
jequice [ʒe'kisi] F country ways pl; (cafonice) tackiness
jerico [ʒe'riku] M donkey; **idéia de ~** stupid idea
jérsei ['ʒɛxsej] M jersey
Jerusalém [ʒeruza'lẽ] N Jerusalem
jesuíta [ʒe'zwita] M Jesuit
Jesus [ʒe'zuʃ] M Jesus ■ EXCL heavens!
jetom [ʒe'tõ] (pl -ns) M (ficha) token; (remuneração) fee
jibóia [ʒi'bɔja] F boa (constrictor)
jiboiar [ʒibo'jaʳ] VI to let one's dinner go down
jiló [ʒi'lɔ] M kind of vegetable
jingle ['dʒĩgew] M jingle
jipe ['ʒipi] M jeep
jirau [ʒi'raw] M (na cozinha) rack; (palanque) platform
jiu-jitsu [ʒu'ʒitsu] M jiu-jitsu
joalheiro, -a [ʒoa'ʎejru, a] M/F jeweller (Brit),

jeweler (US)
joalheria [ʒoaʎe'ria] F jeweller's (shop) (Brit), jewelry store (US)
joanete [ʒwa'netʃi] M bunion
joaninha [ʒwa'niɲa] F ladybird (Brit), ladybug (US)
joão-ninguém M nonentity
JOC (BR) ABR F = **Juventude Operária Católica**
joça ['ʒɔsa] (col) F thing, contraption
jocoso, -a [ʒo'kozu, ɔza] ADJ jocular, humorous
joelhada [ʒoe'ʎada] F: **dar uma ~ em alguém** to knee sb
joelheira [ʒoe'ʎejra] F (Esporte) kneepad
joelho [ʒo'eʎu] M knee; **de ~s** kneeling; **ficar de ~s** to kneel down
jogada [ʒo'gada] F (num jogo) move; (lanço) throw; (negócio) scheme; (col: modo de agir) move; **a ~ é a seguinte** (col) this is the situation; **morar na ~** (col) to catch on
jogado, -a [ʒo'gadu, a] ADJ (prostrado) flat out; (abandonado) abandoned
jogador, a [ʒoga'doʳ(a)] M/F player; (de jogo de azar) gambler; **~ de futebol** footballer
jogão [ʒo'gãw] (pl -ões) M great game
jogar [ʒo'gaʳ] VT to play; (em jogo de azar) to gamble; (atirar) to throw; (indiretas) to drop ■ VI to play; to gamble; (barco) to pitch; **jogar-se** VR to throw o.s.; **~ fora** to throw away; **~ na Bolsa** to play the markets; **~ no bicho** to play the numbers game; **~ com** (combinar) to match
jogatina [ʒoga'tʃina] F gambling
jogging ['ʒɔgĩ] M jogging; (roupa) track suit; **fazer ~** to go jogging, jog
jogo ['ʒogu] M game; (jogar) play; (de azar) gambling; (conjunto) set; (artimanha) trick; **abrir o ~** (fig) to lay one's cards on the table, come clean; **esconder o ~** to play one's cards close to one's chest; **estar em ~** (fig) to be at stake; **fazer o ~ de alguém** to play sb's game, go along with sb; **ter ~ de cintura** (fig) to be flexible; **~ de armar** construction set; **~ de cartas** card game; **~ de damas** draughts sg (Brit), checkers sg (US); **~ de luz** lighting effects pl; **~ de salão** indoor game; **~ do bicho** (illegal) numbers game; **J~s Olímpicos** Olympic Games; **~ limpo/sujo** fair play/dirty tricks pl; **o ~ político** political manoeuvring (Brit) ou maneuvering (US)
jogo-da-velha M noughts and crosses sg
jogões [ʒo'gõjʃ] MPL de **jogão**
joguei etc [ʒo'gej] VB V **jogar**
joguete [ʒo'getʃi] M plaything; **fazer alguém de ~** to toy with sb
jóia ['ʒɔja] F jewel; (taxa) entry fee ■ ADJ (col) great; **tudo ~?** (col) how's things?
jóquei ['ʒɔkej] M (clube) jockey club; (cavaleiro) jockey
jóquei-clube (pl **jóqueis-clubes**) M jockey club
Jordânia [ʒox'danja] F: **a ~** Jordan
jordaniano, -a [ʒoxda'njanu, a] ADJ, M/F Jordanian
Jordão [ʒox'dãw] M: **o (rio) ~** the Jordan (River)
jornada [ʒox'nada] F (viagem) journey; (percurso

diário) day's journey; ~ **de trabalho** working day

jornal [ʒox'naw] (*pl* -**ais**) M newspaper; (*TV, Rádio*) news *sg*; **jornaleiro, -a** [ʒoxna'lejru, a] M/F newsagent (*Brit*), newsdealer (*US*)

jornalismo [ʒoxna'liʒmu] M journalism; **jornalista** [ʃoxna'liʃta] M/F journalist

jornalístico, -a [ʒoxna'liʃtʃiku, a] ADJ journalistic

jorrante [ʒo'xãtʃi] ADJ gushing

jorrar [ʒo'xaʳ] VI to gush, spurt out

jorro ['ʒoxu] M jet; (*de sangue*) spurt; (*fig*) stream, flood

jovem ['ʒovẽ] (*pl* -**ns**) ADJ young; (*aspecto*) youthful; (*música*) youth *atr* ■ M/F young person

jovial [ʒo'vjaw] (*pl* -**ais**) ADJ jovial, cheerful

jovialidade [ʒovjali'dadʒi] F joviality

JPCCC (BR) ABR F = **Justiça de Pequenas Causas Civis e Criminais**

Jr ABR = **Júnior**

JT (BR) ABR M = **Jornal da Tarde**

juba ['ʒuba] F (*de leão*) mane; (*col: cabelo*) mop

jubilação [ʒubila'sãw] F (*aposentadoria*) retirement; (*de estudante*) sending down

jubilar [ʒubi'laʳ] VT (*aposentar*) to retire, pension off; (*aluno*) to send down

jubileu [ʒubi'lew] M jubilee; ~ **de prata** silver jubilee

júbilo ['ʒubilu] M rejoicing; **com** ~ jubilantly

jubiloso, -a [ʒubi'lozu, ɔza] ADJ jubilant

JUC (BR) ABR F = **Juventude Universitária Católica**

judaico, -a [ʒu'dajku, a] ADJ Jewish

judaísmo [ʒuda'iʒmu] M Judaism

judas ['ʒudaʃ] M (*fig*) Judas; (*boneco*) effigy; **onde J~ perdeu as botas** (*col*) at the back of beyond

judeu, judia [ʒu'dew, ʒu'dʒia] ADJ Jewish ■ M/F Jew

judiação [ʒudʒja'sãw] F ill-treatment

judiar [ʒu'dʒjaʳ] VI: ~ **de alguém/algo** to ill-treat sb/sth

judiaria [ʒudʒja'ria] F ill-treatment; **que ~!** how cruel!

judicatura [ʒudʒika'tura] F (*cargo*) office of judge; (*magistratura*) judicature

judicial [ʒudʒi'sjaw] (*pl* -**ais**) ADJ judicial

judiciário, -a [ʒudʒi'sjarju, a] ADJ judicial; **o (poder)** ~ the judiciary

judicioso, -a [ʒudʒi'sjozu, ɔza] ADJ judicious, wise

judô [ʒu'do] M judo

jugo ['ʒugu] M yoke

juiz, -íza [ʒwiʒ, 'iza] M/F judge; (*em jogos*) referee; ~ **de menores** juvenile judge; ~ **de paz** justice of the peace; **julgado** [ʒwi'zado] M court; **Juizado de Menores** Juvenile Court; **Juizado de Pequenas Causas** small claims court

juízo ['ʒwizu] M judgement; (*parecer*) opinion;

(*siso*) common sense; (*foro*) court; **J~ Final** Day of Judgement, doomsday; **perder o** ~ to lose one's mind; **não ter** ~ to be foolish; **tomar** *ou* **criar** ~ to come to one's senses; **chamar/levar a** ~ to summon/take to court; **~!** behave yourself!

jujuba [ʒu'ʒuba] F (*Bot*) jujube; (*bala*) jujube sweet

jul. ABR = **julho**

julgador, a [ʒuwga'doʳ(a)] ADJ judging ■ M/F judge

julgamento [ʒuwga'mẽtu] M judgement; (*audiência*) trial; (*sentença*) sentence

julgar [ʒuw'gaʳ] VT to judge; (*achar*) to think; (*Jur: sentenciar*) to sentence; **julgar-se** VR: **julgar-se algo** to consider o.s. sth, think of o.s. as sth

julho ['ʒuʎu] (PT **J~**) M July; **dia primeiro de** ~ the first of July (*Brit*), July first (*US*); **dia dois/ onze de** ~ the second/eleventh of July (*Brit*), July second/eleventh (*US*); **ele chegou no dia cinco de** ~ he arrived on 5th July *ou* July 5th; **em** ~ in July; **no começo/fim de** ~ at the beginning/end of July; **em meados de** ~ in mid July; **todo ano em** ~ every July; **em** ~ **do ano que vem/do ano passado** next/last July

jumento, -a [ʒu'mẽtu, a] M/F donkey

jun. ABR = **junho**

junção [ʒũ'sãw] (*pl* -**ões**) F (*ato*) joining; (*junta*) join

junco ['ʒũku] M reed, rush

junções [ʒũ'sõjʃ] FPL *de* **junção**

junho ['ʒuɲu] (PT **J~**) M June; *v tb* **julho**

junino, -a [ʒu'ninu, a] ADJ June; **festa junina** St John's day party

júnior ['ʒunjoʳ] (*pl* **juniores**) ADJ younger, junior ■ M/F (*Esporte*) junior; **Eduardo Autran J~** Eduardo Autran Junior

junta ['ʒũta] F (*comissão*) board, committee; (*Pol*) junta; (*articulação, juntura*) joint; ~ **comercial** board of trade; ~ **médica** medical team

juntar [ʒũ'taʳ] VT (*por junto*) to join; (*reunir*) to bring together; (*aglomerar*) to gather together; (*recolher*) to collect up; (*acrescentar*) to add; (*dinheiro*) to save up ■ VI to gather; **juntar-se** VR to gather; (*associar-se*) to join up; **~-se a alguém** to join sb; **~-se com alguém** to (go and) live with sb

junto, -a ['ʒũtu, a] ADJ (*chegado*) near; **ir ~s** to go together; ~ **a/de** near/next to; **segue** ~ (*Com*) please find enclosed

juntura [ʒũ'tura] F join; (*articulação*) joint

Júpiter ['ʒupiteʳ] M Jupiter

jura ['ʒura] F vow

jurado, -a [ʒu'radu, a] ADJ sworn ■ M/F juror

juramentado, -a [ʒuramẽ'tadu, a] ADJ accredited, legally certified

juramento [ʒura'mẽtu] M oath

jurar [ʒu'raʳ] VT, VI to swear; **jura?** really?

júri ['ʒuri] M jury

jurídico, -a [ʒu'ridʒiku, a] ADJ legal

NB: *European Portuguese adds the following consonants to certain words:* **b** (sú(b)dito, su(b)til); **c** (a(c)ção, a(c)cionista, a(c)to); **m** (inde(m)ne); **p** (ado(p)çã, ado(p)tar); *for further details see p. xiii.*

jurisconsulto, -a [ʒuriʃkõ'suwtu, a] M/F legal advisor

jurisdição [ʒuriʃdʒi'sãw] F jurisdiction

jurisprudência [ʒuriʃpru'dẽsja] F jurisprudence

jurista [ʒu'riʃta] M/F jurist

juros ['ʒuruʃ] MPL (Econ) interest sg; **a/sem ~** at interest/interest-free; **render ~** to yield ou bear interest; **~ fixos/variáveis** fixed/variable interest; **~ simples/compostos** simple/compound interest

jururu [ʒuru'ru] ADJ melancholy, wistful

jus [ʒuʃ] M: **fazer ~ a algo** to live up to sth

jusante [ʒu'zãtʃi] F: **a ~ (de)** downstream (from)

justamente [ʒuʃta'mẽtʃi] ADV (com justiça) fairly, justly; (precisamente) exactly

justapor [ʒuʃta'poʳ] (irreg) VT to juxtapose; **justapor-se** VR to be juxtaposed; **~ algo a algo** to juxtapose sth with sth

justaposição [ʒuʃtapozi'sãw] (pl -ões) F juxtaposition

justaposto [ʒuʃta'poʃtu] PP de **justapor**

justapunha etc [ʒuʃta'puɲa] VB v **justapor**

justapus etc [ʒuʃta'puʃ] VB v **justapor**

justapuser etc [ʒuʃtapu'zeʳ] VB v **justapor**

justeza [ʒuʃ'teza] F fairness; (precisão) precision

justiça [ʒuʃ'tʃisa] F justice; (poder judiciário)

judiciary; (eqüidade) fairness; (tribunal) court; **com ~** justly, fairly; **ir à ~** to go to court; **fazer ~ a** to do justice to; **J~ Eleitoral** Electoral Court; **J~ do Trabalho** ≈ industrial tribunal (Brit), ≈ labor relations board (US)

justiceiro, -a [ʒuʃtʃi'sejru, a] ADJ righteous; (inflexível) inflexible

justificação [ʒuʃtʃifika'sãw] (pl -ões) F justification

justificar [ʒuʃtʃifi'kaʳ] VT to justify; **justificar-se** VR to justify o.s.

justificativa [ʒuʃtʃifika'tʃiva] F (Jur) justification

justificável [ʒuʃtʃifi'kavew] (pl -eis) ADJ justifiable

justo, -a ['ʒuʃtu, a] ADJ just, fair; (legítimo: queixa) legitimate, justified; (exato) exact; (apertado) tight ■ ADV just

juta ['ʒuta] F jute

juvenil [ʒuve'niw] (pl -is) ADJ (ar) youthful; (roupa) young; (livro) for young people; (Esporte: equipe, campeonato) youth atr, junior ■ M (Esporte) junior championship

juventude [ʒuvẽ'tudʒi] F youth; (jovialidade) youthfulness; (jovens) young people pl, youth

Kk

K, k [ka] (*pl* **ks**) M K, k; **K de Kátia** K for king
kanga ['kãga] F beach wrap
karaokê [karao'ke] M karaoke; (*lugar*) karaoke bar
kart ['kaxtʃi] (*pl* -**s**) M go-kart
ketchup [ke'tʃupi] M ketchup
kg ABR (= *quilograma*) kg
KGB ABR F KGB
kHz ABR (= *quilohertz*) kHz
kibutz [ki'butz] M INV kibbutz
kilt ['kiwtʃi] (*pl* -**s**) M kilt
kirsch [kixʃ] M kirsch

kit ['kitʃi] (*pl* -**s**) M kit; ~ **de sobrevivência** survival kit
kitchenette [kitʃe'netʃi] F studio flat
kitsch [kitʃ] ADJ INV, M kitsch
kl ABR (= *quilolitro*) kl
km ABR (= *quilômetro*) km
km/h ABR (= *quilômetros por hora*) km/h
know-how ['now'haw] M know-how
Kremlin [krẽ'lĩ] M: **o** ~ the Kremlin
Kuweit [ku'wejtʃi] M: **o** ~ Kuwait
kW ABR (= *quilowatt*) kW
kwh ABR (= *quilowatt-hora*) kwh

NB: *European Portuguese adds the following consonants to certain words:* **b** (sú(b)dito, su(b)til); **c** (a(c)ção, a(c)cionista, a(c)to); **m** (inde(m)ne); **p** (ado(p)ção, ado(p)tar); *for further details see p. xiii.*

Ll

L, L ['eli] (pl **ls**) M L, l; **L de Lúcia** L for Lucy (Brit)
ou love (US)

L ABR = **Largo**

-la [la] PRON her; (você) you; (coisa) it

lá [la] ADV there ■ M (Mús) A; **lá fora** outside; **lá
em baixo** down there; **por lá** (direção) that way;
(situação) over there; **até lá** (no espaço) there; (no
tempo) until then; **lá pelas tantas** in the small
hours; **para lá de** (mais do que) more than; **diga
lá** ... come on and say ...; **sei lá!** don't ask me!;
ela sabe lá she's got no idea; **ele pode lá pagar
um aluguel tão caro** there's no way he can
pay such a high rent; **o apartamento não é lá
essas coisas** the apartment is nothing special;
estar mais para lá do que para cá (de cansaço)
to be dead on one's feet; (prestes a morrer) to be at
death's door

lã [lã] F wool; **de lã** woollen (Brit), woolen (US);
de pura lã pure wool; **lã de camelo** camel hair

labareda [laba'reda] F flame; (fig) ardour (Brit),
ardor (US)

labia ['labja] F (astúcia) cunning; **ter ~** to have
the gift of the gab

labial [la'bjaw] (pl **-ais**) ADJ lip atr; (Ling) labial
■ F (Ling) labial

lábio ['labju] M lip

labirinto [labi'rĩtu] M labyrinth, maze

labor [la'boʳ] M work, labour (Brit), labor (US)

laborar [labo'raʳ] VI: **~ em erro** to labour (Brit) ou
labor (US) under a misconception

laboratório [labora'tɔrju] M laboratory

laborioso, -a [labo'rjozu, ɔza] ADJ (diligente)
hard-working; (árduo) laborious

LABRE ABR F = **Liga de Amadores Brasileiros de
Radio Emissão**

labuta [la'buta] F toil, drudgery

labutar [labu'taʳ] VI to toil; (esforçar-se) to
struggle, strive

laca ['laka] F lacquer

laçada [la'sada] F (nó) slipknot; (no tricô) loop

laçar [la'saʳ] VT to bind, tie; (boi) to rope

laçarote [lasa'rɔtʃi] M big bow

laço ['lasu] M bow; (de gravata) knot; (armadilha)
snare; (fig) bond, tie; **dar um ~** to tie a bow; **~s
de família** family ties

lacônico, -a [la'koniku, a] ADJ laconic

lacraia [la'kraja] F centipede

lacrar [la'kraʳ] VT to seal (with wax); **lacre**
['lakri] M sealing wax

lacrimal [lakri'maw] (pl **-ais**) ADJ (canal) tear atr

lacrimejante [lakrime'ʒãtʃi] ADJ weeping

lacrimejar [lakrime'ʒaʳ] VI (olhos) to water;
(chorar) to weep

lacrimogêneo, -a [lakrimo'ʒenju, a] ADJ tear-
jerking; **gás ~** tear gas

lacrimoso, -a [lakri'mozu, ɔza] ADJ tearful

lactação [lakta'sãw] F lactation; (amamentação)
breastfeeding

lácteo, -a ['laktju, a] ADJ milk atr; **Via Láctea**
Milky Way

lacticínio [laktʃi'sinju] M dairy product

lactose [lak'tɔzi] F lactose

lacuna [la'kuna] F gap; (omissão) omission;
(espaço em branco) blank

ladainha [lada'iɲa] F litany; (fig) rigmarole

ladear [la'dʒjaʳ] VT to flank; (problema) to get
round; **o rio ladeia a estrada** the river runs by
the side of the road

ladeira [la'dejra] F slope

ladino, -a [la'dʒinu, a] ADJ cunning, crafty

lado ['ladu] M side; (Mil) flank; (rumo) direction;
ao ~ (perto) close by; **a casa ao ~** the house next
door; **ao ~ de** beside; **de ~** sideways; **deixar de
~** to set aside; (fig) to leave out; **de um ~ para
outro** back and forth; **do ~ de dentro/fora** on
the inside/outside; **do ~ de cá/lá** on this/that
side; **no outro ~ da rua** across the road; **ela foi
para aqueles ~s** she went that way; **por um ~
... por outro ~** on the one hand ... on the other
hand; **por todos os ~s** all around; **~ a ~** side by
side; **o meu ~** (col: interesses) my interests

ladra ['ladra] F thief, robber; (picareta) crook

ladrão, -ona [la'drãw, ɔna] (pl **-ões/-s**) ADJ
thieving ■ M/F thief, robber; (picareta) crook
■ M (tubo) overflow pipe; **pega ~!** stop thief!

ladrar [la'draʳ] VI to bark

ladrilhar [ladri'ʎaʳ] VT, VI to tile

ladrilheiro, -a [ladri'ʎejru, a] M/F tiler

ladrilho [la'driʎu] M tile; (chão) tiled floor,
tiles pl

ladro ['ladru] M (latido) bark; (ladrão) thief

ladroagem [la'drwaʒẽ] (pl **-ns**) F robbery

ladroeira [la'drwejra] F robbery

ladrões [la'drõjʃ] MPL de **ladrão**

ladrona [la'drɔna] F de **ladrão**
lagarta [la'gaxta] F caterpillar
lagartixa [lagax'tʃiʃa] F gecko
lagarto [la'gaxtu] M lizard; (carne) silverside
lago ['lagu] M lake; (de jardim) pond; (de sangue) pool
lagoa [la'goa] F pool, pond; (lago) lake
lagosta [la'goʃta] F lobster
lagostim [lagoʃ'tʃĩ] (pl -ns) M crayfish
lágrima ['lagrima] F tear; **~s de crocodilo** crocodile tears; **chorar ~s de sangue** to cry bitterly
laguna [la'guna] F lagoon
laia ['laja] F kind, sort, type
laico, -a ['lajku, a] ADJ (pessoa) lay; (ensino etc) secular
laivos ['lajvuʃ] MPL hints, traces
laje ['laʒi] F paving stone, flagstone
lajear [la'ʒjaʳ] VT to pave
lajedo [la'ʒedu] M rock
lajota [la'ʒɔta] F paving stone
lama ['lama] F mud; **tirar alguém da ~** (fig) to rescue sb from poverty
lamaçal [lama'saw] (pl -ais) M quagmire; (pântano) bog, marsh
lamaceiro [lama'sejru] M = **lamaçal**
lamacento, -a [lama'sẽtu, a] ADJ muddy
lambança [lã'bãsa] F mess
lambão, -bona [lam'bãw, 'bɔna] (pl -ões/-s) ADJ (guloso) greedy; (no trabalho) sloppy; (lambuzado) messy; (tolo) idiotic
lamber [lã'beʳ] VT to lick; **de ~ os beiços** (comida) delicious; **lambida** [lã'bida] F lick; **dar uma lambida em algo** to lick sth
lambido, -a [lã'bidu, a] ADJ (cara) without make-up; (cabelo) plastered down
lambiscar [lãbiʃ'kaʳ] VT, VI to nibble
lambisgóia [lãbiʒ'gɔja] F haggard person
lambões [lã'bõjʃ] MPL de **lambão**
lambona [lã'bɔna] F de **lambão**
lambreta [lã'breta] F scooter
lambri(s) [lã'bri(ʃ)] M(PL) panelling sg (Brit), paneling sg (US)
lambuja [lã'buʒa] F start, advantage
lambujem [lã'buʒẽ] (pl -ns) F start, advantage
lambuzar [lãbu'zaʳ] VT to smear
lambuzeira [lãbu'zejra] F sticky mess
lamentação [lamẽta'sãw] (pl -ões) F lamentation
lamentar [lamẽ'taʳ] VT to lament; (sentir) to regret; **lamentar-se** VR: **lamentar-se (de algo)** to lament (sth); **~ (que)** to be sorry (that); **lamentável** [lamẽ'tavew] (pl -eis) ADJ regrettable; (deplorável) deplorable
lamentavelmente [lamẽtavew'mẽtʃi] ADV regrettably
lamento [la'mẽtu] M lament; (gemido) moan
lamentoso, -a [lamẽ'tozu, ɔza] ADJ (voz, som) sorrowful; (lamentável) lamentable

lâmina ['lamina] F (chapa) sheet; (placa) plate; (de faca) blade; (de persiana) slat
laminado, -a [lami'nadu, a] ADJ laminated ■ M laminate
laminar [lami'naʳ] VT to laminate
lâmpada ['lãpada] F lamp; (tb: **lâmpada elétrica**) light bulb; **~ de mesa** table lamp; **~ fluorescente** fluorescent light
lamparina [lãpa'rina] F lamp
lampejante [lãpe'ʒãtʃi] ADJ flashing, glittering
lampejar [lãpe'ʒaʳ] VI to glisten, flash ■ VT to give off
lampejo [lã'peʒu] M flash
lampião [lã'pjãw] (pl -ões) M lantern; (de rua) street lamp
lamúria [la'murja] F whining, lamentation
lamuriante [lamu'rjãtʃi] ADJ whining
lamuriar-se [lamu'rjaxsi] VR: **~ de algo** to moan about sth
lança ['lãsa] F lance, spear
lançadeira [lãsa'dejra] F shuttle
lançador, a [lãsa'do'(a)] M/F (Esporte) thrower; (em leilão) bidder; (Com) company or person launching a product
lançamento [lãsa'mẽtu] M throwing; (Com: em livro) entry; (Náut, Com: de produto, campanha) launch; (: de disco, filme) release; **novo ~** (livro) new title; (filme, disco) new release; (produto) new product; **~ do dardo** (Esporte) javelin; **~ do disco** (Esporte) discus; **~ do martelo** (Esporte) hammer
lança-perfume (pl -s) M ether spray (used as a drug in carnival)
lançar [lã'saʳ] VT to throw; (Náut, Com) to launch; (disco, filme) to release; (em livro comercial) to enter; (em leilão) to bid; (imposto) to assess; **lançar-se** VR to throw o.s.; **~ ações no mercado** to float shares on the market; **~ mão de algo** to make use of sth
lance ['lãsi] M (arremesso) throw; (incidente) incident; (história) story; (situação) position; (fato) fact; (Esporte: jogada) shot; (em leilão) bid; (de escada) flight; (de casas) row; (episódio) moment; (de muro, estrada) stretch
lancha ['lãʃa] F launch; (col: sapato, pé) clodhopper; **~ torpedeira** torpedo boat
lanchar [lã'ʃaʳ] VI to have a snack ■ VT to have as a snack; **lanche** ['lãʃi] M snack
lanchonete [lãʃo'netʃi] (BR) F snack bar
lancinante [lãsi'nãtʃi] ADJ (dor) stabbing; (grito) piercing
langanho [lã'gaɲu] M rake
languidez [lãgi'deʒ] F languor, listlessness
lânguido, -a ['lãgidu, a] ADJ languid, listless
lanhar [la'ɲaʳ] VT to slash, gash; (peixe) to gut; **lanhar-se** VR to cut o.s.
lanho ['laɲu] M slash, gash
lanígero, -a [la'niʒeru, a] ADJ (gado) wool-producing; (planta) downy
lanolina [lano'lina] F lanolin

NB: European Portuguese adds the following consonants to certain words: **b** (sú(b)dito, su(b)til); **c** (a(c)ção, a(c)cionista, a(c)to); **m** (inde(m)ne); **p** (ado(p)ção, ado(p)tar); for further details see p. xiii.

lantejoula [lãte'ʒola] F sequin
lanterna [lã'tɛxna] F lantern; (portátil) torch (Brit), flashlight (US)
lanternagem [lãtex'naʒẽ] (pl -ns) F (Auto) panel-beating; (oficina) body shop
lanterneiro, -a [lãtex'nejru, a] M/F panel-beater
lanterninha [lãtex'niɲa] (BR) M/F usher(ette)
lanugem [la'nuʒẽ] F down, fluff
Laos ['lawʃ] M: o ~ Laos
lapão, -pona [la'pãw, 'pɔna] (pl -ões/-s) ADJ, M/F Lapp
lapela [la'pɛla] F lapel
lapidador, a [lapida'do'(a)] M/F cutter
lapidar [lapi'da'] VT (jóias) to cut; (fig) to polish, refine ■ ADJ (fig) masterful
lápide ['lapidʒi] F (tumular) tombstone; (comemorativa) memorial stone
lápis ['lapiʃ] M INV pencil; **escrever a ~** to write in pencil; **~ de cor** coloured (Brit) ou colored (US) pencil, crayon; **~ de olho** eyebrow pencil; **lapiseira** [lapi'zejra] F propelling (Brit) ou mechanical (US) pencil; (caixa) pencil case
lápis-lazúli [-la'zuli] M lapis-lazuli
lapões [la'põjʃ] MPL de **lapão**
lapona [la'pɔna] F de **lapão**
Lapônia [la'ponja] F: **a ~** Lappland
lapso ['lapsu] M lapse; (de tempo) interval; (erro) slip
laquê [la'ke] M lacquer
laquear [la'kja'] VT to lacquer
lar [la'] M home
laranja [la'rãʒa] ADJ INV orange ■ F orange ■ M (cor) orange; **laranjada** [larã'ʒada] F orangeade
laranjal [larã'ʒaw] (pl -ais) M orange grove
laranjeira [larã'ʒejra] F orange tree
larápio [la'rapju] M thief
lardo ['laxdu] M bacon
lareira [la'rejra] F hearth, fireside
larga ['laxga] F: **à ~** lavishly; **dar ~s a** to give free rein to; **viver à ~** to lead a lavish life
largada [lax'gada] F start; **dar a ~** to start; (fig) to make a start
largado, -a [lax'gadu, a] ADJ spurned; (no vestir) scruffy
largar [lax'ga'] VT (soltar) to let go of, release; (deixar) to leave; (deixar cair) to drop; (risada) to let out; (velas) to unfurl; (piada) to tell; (pôr em liberdade) to let go ■ VI (Náut) to set sail; **largar-se** VR (desprender-se) to free o.s.; (ir-se) to go off; (pôr-se) to proceed; **ele não a larga** ou **não larga dela um instante** he won't leave her alone for a moment; **me larga!** leave me alone!; **~ a mão em alguém** to wallop sb; **~ de fazer** to stop doing; **largue de besteira** stop being stupid
largo, -a ['laxgu, a] ADJ wide, broad; (amplo) extensive; (roupa) loose, baggy; (conversa) long ■ M (praça) square; (alto-mar) open sea; **ao ~** at a distance, far off; **fazer-se ao ~** to put out to sea; **passar de ~ sobre um assunto** to gloss over a subject; **passar ao ~ de algo** (fig) to sidestep sth
larguei etc [lax'gej] VB V **largar**
largueza [lax'geza] F largesse

largura [lax'gura] F width, breadth
laringe [la'rĩʒi] F larynx
laringite [larĩ'ʒitʃi] F laryngitis
larva ['laxva] F larva, grub
lasanha [la'zaɲa] F lasagna
lasca ['laʃka] F (de madeira, metal) splinter; (de pedra) chip; (fatia) slice
lascado, -a [laʃ'kadu, a] (col) ADJ in a hurry ou rush
lascar [laʃ'ka'] VT to chip; (pergunta) to throw in; (tapa) to let go ■ VI to chip; **ser** ou **estar de ~** to be horrible
lascívia [la'sivja] F lewdness
lascivo, -a [la'sivu, a] ADJ lewd; (movimentos) sensual
laser ['lejze'] M laser; **raio ~** laser beam
lassidão [lasi'dãw] F lassitude, weariness
lassitude [lasi'tudʒi] F lassitude, weariness
lasso, -a ['lasu, a] ADJ lax; (cansado) weary
lástima ['laʃtʃima] F pity, compassion; (infortúnio) misfortune; **é uma ~ (que)** it's a shame (that); **lastimar** [laʃtʃi'ma'] VT to lament; **lastimar-se** VR to complain, be sorry for o.s.
lastimável [laʃtʃi'mavew] (pl -eis) ADJ lamentable
lastimoso, -a [laʃtʃi'mozu, ɔza] ADJ (lamentável) pitiful; (plangente) mournful
lastro ['laʃtru] M ballast
lata ['lata] F tin, can; (material) tin-plate; **~ de lixo** rubbish bin (Brit), garbage can (US); **~ velha** (col: carro) old banger (Brit) ou clunker (US)
latada [la'tada] F trellis
latão [la'tãw] M brass
lataria [lata'ria] F (Auto) bodywork; (enlatados) canned food
látego ['lategu] M whip
latejante [late'ʒãtʃi] ADJ throbbing
latejar [late'ʒa'] VI to throb
latejo [la'teʒu] M throbbing, beat
latente [la'tẽtʃi] ADJ latent, hidden
lateral [late'raw] (pl -ais) ADJ side, lateral ■ F (Futebol) sideline ■ M (Futebol) throw-in
látex ['lateks] M INV latex
laticínio [latʃi'sinju] M = **lacticínio**
latido [la'tʃidu] M bark(ing), yelp(ing)
latifundiário, -a [latʃifũ'dʒjarju, a] ADJ land-owning ■ M/F landowner
latifúndio [latʃi'fũdʒju] M large estate
latim [la'tʃĩ] M (Ling) Latin; **gastar o seu ~ to** waste one's breath
latino, -a [la'tʃinu, a] ADJ Latin; **latino-americano, -a** ADJ, M/F Latin-American
latir [la'tʃi'] VI to bark, yelp
latitude [latʃi'tudʒi] F latitude; (largura) breadth; (fig) scope
lato, -a ['latu, a] ADJ broad
latrina [la'trina] F latrine
latrocínio [latro'sinju] M armed robbery
lauda ['lawda] F page
laudatório, -a [lawda'tɔrju, a] ADJ laudatory
laudo ['lawdu] M (Jur) decision; (resultados)

findings pl; (peça escrita) report
laureado, -a [law'rjadu, a] ADJ honoured (Brit),
honored (US) ■ M laureate
laurear [law'rja^r] VT to honour (Brit), honor (US)
laurel [law'rɛw] (pl -éis) M laurel wreath; (fig)
prize, reward
lauto, -a ['lawtu, a] ADJ sumptuous; (abundante)
lavish, abundant
lava ['lava] F lava
lavabo [la'vabu] M toilet
lavadeira [lava'dejra] F washerwoman
lavadora [lava'dora] F washing machine
lavadouro [lava'doru] M washing place
lavagem [la'vaʒē] F washing; ~ **a seco** dry
cleaning; ~ **cerebral** brainwashing; **dar uma ~
em alguém** (col: Esporte) to thrash sb
lavanda [la'vāda] F (Bot) lavender; (colônia)
lavender water; (para lavar os dedos) finger bowl
lavanderia [lavāde'ria] F laundry; (aposento)
laundry room
lavar [la'va^r] VT to wash; (culpa) to wash away; ~
a seco to dry clean; ~ **a égua** (col: Esporte) to win
hands down; ~ **as mãos de algo** (fig) to wash
one's hands of sth
lavatório [lava'tɔrju] M washbasin; (aposento)
toilet
lavoura [la'vora] F tilling; (agricultura) farming;
(terreno) plantation
lavra ['lavra] F ploughing (Brit), plowing (US);
(de minerais) mining; (mina) mine; **ser da ~ de** to
be the work of
lavradio, -a [lavra'dʒiu, a] ADJ workable, arable
■ M farming
lavrador, a [lavra'do^r(a)] M/F farmhand, farm
labourer (Brit) ou laborer (US)
lavrar [la'vra^r] VT to work; (esculpir) to carve;
(redigir) to draw up
laxante [la'ʃātʃi] ADJ, M laxative
laxativo, -a [laʃa'tʃivu, a] ADJ laxative ■ M
laxative
lazer [la'ze^r] M leisure
LBA ABR F (= Legião Brasileira de Assistência) charity
LBC (BR) ABR F = **Letra do Banco Central**
leal [le'aw] (pl -ais) ADJ loyal; **lealdade**
[leaw'dadʒi] F loyalty
leão [le'ãw] (pl -ões) M lion; **L~** (Astrologia) Leo;
o L~ (BR: fisco) = the Inland Revenue (Brit), the
IRS (US)
leão-de-chácara (pl leões-de-chácara) M
bouncer
lebre ['lebri] F hare
lecionar [lesjo'na^r] (PT -cc-) VT, VI to teach
lecitina [lesi'tʃina] F lecithin
lectivo, -a [lek'tivu, a] (PT) ADJ = **letivo**
legação [lega'sāw] (pl -ões) F legation
legado [le'gadu] M envoy, legate; (herança)
legacy, bequest
legal [le'gaw] (pl -ais) ADJ legal, lawful; (col)
fine; (: pessoa) nice ■ ADV (col) well; **(tá)** ~! OK!;

---

legalidade [legali'dadʒi] F legality, lawfulness
legalização [legaliza'sāw] F legalization; (de
documento) authentication
legalizar [legali'za^r] VT to legalize; (documento) to
authenticate
legar [le'ga^r] VT to bequeath, leave
legatário, -a [lega'tarju, a] M/F legatee
legenda [le'ʒēda] F inscription; (texto explicativo)
caption; (Cinema) subtitle; (Pol) party
legendário, -a [leʒē'darju, a] ADJ legendary
legião [le'ʒjāw] (pl -ões) F legion; **a L~
Estrangeira** the Foreign Legion
legionário, -a [leʒjo'narju, a] ADJ legionary ■ M
legionary
legislação [leʒiʒla'sāw] F legislation
legislador, a [leʒiʒla'do^r(a)] M/F legislator
legislar [leʒiʒ'la^r] VI to legislate ■ VT to pass
legislativo, -a [leʒiʒla'tʃivu, a] ADJ legislative
■ M legislature
legislatura [leʒiʒla'tura] F legislature; (período)
term of office
legista [le'ʒiʃta] ADJ: **médico** ~ expert in medical
law ■ M/F legal expert; (médico) expert in
medical law
legitimar [leʒitʃi'ma^r] VT to legitimize; (justificar)
to legitimate; (filho) to legally adopt
legitimidade [leʒitʃimi'dadʒi] F legitimacy
legítimo, -a [le'ʒitʃimu, a] ADJ legitimate; (justo)
rightful; (autêntico) genuine; **legítima defesa**
self-defence (Brit), self-defense (US)
legível [le'ʒivew] (pl -eis) ADJ legible, readable; ~
por máquina machine readable
légua ['lɛgwa] F league
legume [le'gumi] M vegetable
lei [lej] F law; (regra) rule; (metal) standard; **prata
de** ~ sterling silver; **ditar a** ~ to lay down the
law
leiaute [lej'awtʃi] M layout
leigo, -a ['lejgu, a] ADJ (Rel) lay, secular ■ M
layman; **ser** ~ **em algo** (fig) to be no expert at
sth, be unversed in sth
leilão [lej'lāw] (pl -ões) M auction; **vender em** ~
to sell by auction, auction off
leiloamento [lejlwa'mētu] M auctioning
leiloar [lej'lwa^r] VT to auction
leiloeiro, -a [lej'lwejru, a] M/F auctioneer
leilões [lej'lõjʃ] MPL de **leilão**
leio etc ['leju] VB v **ler**
leitão, -toa [lej'tāw, 'toa] (pl -ões/-s) M/F
sucking (Brit) ou suckling (US) pig
leite ['lejtʃi] M milk; ~ **em pó** powdered milk;
~ **desnatado** ou **magro** skimmed milk; ~ **de
magnésia** milk of magnesia; ~ **condensado**/
evaporado condensed/evaporated milk; ~ **de
vaca** cow's milk
leite-de-onça M milk with cachaça
leiteira [lej'tejra] F (para ferver) milk pan; (para
servir) milk jug; v tb **leiteiro**
leiteiro, -a [lej'tejru, a] ADJ (vaca, gado) dairy;

NB: European Portuguese adds the following consonants to certain words: **b** (sú(b)dito, su(b)til); **c** (a(c)ção,
a(c)cionista, a(c)to)); **m** (inde(m)ne); **p** (ado(p)çã, ado(p)tar); for further details see p. xiii.

(*trem*) milk *atr* ∎ M/F milkman/woman
leiteria [lejte'ria] F dairy
leito ['lejtu] M bed
leitoa [lej'toa] F *de* **leitão**
leitões [lej'tõjʃ] MPL *de* **leitão**
leitor, a [lej'to'(a)] M/F reader; (*professor*) lector
leitoso, -a [lej'tozu, ɔza] ADJ milky
leitura [lej'tura] F reading; (*livro etc*) reading matter; **pessoa de muita ~** well-read person; **~ dinâmica** speed reading
lelé [le'lɛ] (*col*) ADJ nuts, crazy; **~ da cuca** out of one's mind
lema ['lɛma] M motto; (*Pol*) slogan
lembrança [lẽ'brãsa] F recollection, memory; (*presente*) souvenir; **lembranças** FPL: **~s a sua mãe!** (*recomendações*) regards to your mother!
lembrar [lẽ'bra'] VT, VI to remember; **lembrar-se** VR: **lembrar(-se) de** to remember; **~(-se) (de) que** to remember that; **~ algo a alguém, ~ alguém de algo** to remind sb of sth; **~ alguém de que, ~ a alguém que** to remind sb that; **esta rua lembra a rua onde eu ...** this street reminds me of the street where I ...; **ele lembra meu irmão** he reminds me of my brother, he is like my brother; **lembrete** [lẽ'bretʃi] M reminder
leme ['lɛmi] M rudder; (*Náut*) helm; (*fig*) control
lenço ['lẽsu] M handkerchief; (*de pescoço*) scarf; (*de cabeça*) headscarf; **~ de papel** tissue
lençol [lẽ'sɔw] (*pl* -óis) M sheet; **estar em maus lençóis** to be in a fix; **~ de água** water table
lenda ['lẽda] F legend; (*fig: mentira*) lie; **lendário, -a** [lẽ'darju, a] ADJ legendary
lengalenga [lẽga'lẽga] F rigmarole
lenha ['lɛɲa] F firewood; **fazer ~** (*de carro*) to have a race; **meter a ~ em alguém** (*col: surrar*) to give sb a beating; (: *criticar*) to run sb down; **ser uma ~** (*col*) to be tough; **botar ~ no fogo** (*fig*) to fan the flames, make things worse
lenhador [lɛɲa'do'] M woodcutter
lenho ['lɛɲu] M (*tora*) log; (*material*) timber
Leningrado [lenĩ'gradu] N Leningrad
leninista [leni'niʃta] ADJ, M/F Leninist
lenitivo, -a [leni'tʃivu, a] ADJ soothing ∎ M palliative; (*fig: alívio*) relief
lenocínio [leno'sinju] M living off immoral earnings
lente ['lẽtʃi] F lens *sg*; **~ de aumento** magnifying glass; **~s de contato** contact lenses
lentidão [lẽtʃi'dãw] F slowness
lentilha [lẽ'tʃiʎa] F lentil
lento, -a ['lẽtu, a] ADJ slow
leoa [le'oa] F lioness
leões [le'õjʃ] MPL *de* **leão**
leopardo [ljo'paxdu] M leopard
lépido, -a ['lɛpidu, a] ADJ (*alegre*) sprightly, bright; (*ágil*) nimble, agile
leporino, -a [lepo'rinu, a] ADJ: **lábio ~** hare lip
lepra ['lɛpra] F leprosy
leprosário [lepro'zarju] M leprosy hospital
leproso, -a [le'prozu, ɔza] ADJ leprous ∎ M/F leper

leque ['lɛki] M fan; (*fig*) array
ler [le'] VT, VI to read; **~ a sorte de alguém** to tell sb's fortune; **~ nas entrelinhas** (*fig*) to read between the lines
lerdeza [lex'deza] F sluggishness
lerdo, -a ['lɛxdu, a] ADJ slow, sluggish
lero-lero [lɛru'lɛru] (*col*) M chit-chat, idle talk
lés [lɛʃ] (*PT*) M: **de ~ a ~** from one end to the other
lesão [le'zãw] (*pl* -ões) F harm, injury; (*Jur*) violation; (*Med*) lesion; **~ corporal** (*Jur*) bodily harm
lesar [le'za'] VT to harm, damage; (*direitos*) to violate; **~ alguém** (*financeiramente*) to leave sb short; **o fisco** to withhold one's taxes
lesbianismo [leʒbja'niʒmu] M lesbianism
lésbica ['lɛʒbika] F lesbian
lesco-lesco [lɛʃku'lɛʃku] (*col*) M daily grind; **estar no ~** to be on the go *ou* hard at it
leseira [le'zejra] F lethargy
lesionar [lezjo'na'] VT to injure
lesivo, -a [le'zivu, a] ADJ harmful
lesma ['leʒma] F slug; (*fig: pessoa*) slowcoach
lesões [le'zõjʃ] FPL *de* **lesão**
Lesoto [le'zotu] M: **o ~** Lesotho
lesse *etc* ['lesi] VB V **ler**
leste ['lɛʃtʃi] M east
letal [le'taw] (*pl* -ais) ADJ lethal
letargia [letax'ʒia] F lethargy
letárgico, -a [le'taxʒiku, a] ADJ lethargic
letivo, -a [le'tʃivu, a] ADJ school *atr*; **ano ~** academic year
Letônia [le'tonja] F: **a ~** Latvia
letra ['letra] F letter; (*caligrafia*) handwriting; (*de canção*) lyrics *pl*; **Letras** FPL (*curso*) language and literature; **à ~** literally; **seguir à ~** to follow to the letter; **ao pé da ~** literally, word for word; **fazer** *ou* **tirar algo de ~** (*col*) to be able to do sth standing on one's head; **~ de câmbio** (*Com*) bill of exchange; **~ de fôrma** block letter; **~ de imprensa** print; **~ de médico** (*fig*) scrawl; **~ maiúscula/minúscula** capital/small letter; **letrado, -a** [le'tradu, a] ADJ learned, erudite ∎ M/F scholar; **ser letrado em algo** to be well-versed in sth
letreiro [le'trejru] M sign, notice; (*inscrição*) inscription; (*Cinema*) subtitle; **~ luminoso** neon sign
leu *etc* [lew] VB V **ler**
léu [lɛw] M: **ao ~** (*à toa*) aimlessly; (*à mostra*) uncovered
leucemia [lewse'mia] F leukaemia (*Brit*), leukemia (*US*)
leva ['lɛva] F (*de pessoas*) group
levadiço, -a [leva'dʒisu, a] ADJ: **ponte levadiça** drawbridge
levado, -a [le'vadu, a] ADJ mischievous; (*criança*) naughty; **~ da breca** naughty
leva-e-traz [-'trajʒ] M/F INV gossip, stirrer
levantador, a [levãta'do'(a)] ADJ lifting ∎ M/F: **~ de pesos** weightlifter
levantamento [levãta'mẽtu] M lifting, raising; (*revolta*) uprising, rebellion; (*arrolamento*) survey;

|

~ de pesos weightlifting

levantar [levãˈtaʳ] VT to lift, raise; (*voz, capital*) to raise; (*apanhar*) to pick up; (*suscitar*) to arouse; (*ambiente*) to brighten up ∎ VI to stand up; (*da cama*) to get up; (*dar vida*) to brighten; **levantar-se** VR to stand up; (*da cama*) to get up; (*rebelar-se*) to rebel; **~ vôo** to take off; **~ a mão** to raise *ou* put up one's hand

levante [leˈvãtʃi] M east; (*revolta*) revolt

levar [leˈvaʳ] VT to take; (*portar*) to carry; (*tempo*) to pass, spend; (*roupa*) to wear; (*lidar com*) to handle; (*induzir*) to lead; (*filme*) to show; (*peça teatral*) to do, put on ∎ VI to get a beating; **~ a** to lead to; **~ a mal** to take amiss; **~ a cabo** to carry out; **~ adiante** to go ahead with; **~ uma vida feliz** to lead a happy life; **~ a melhor/pior** to get a good/raw deal; **~ pancadas/um susto/ uma bronca** to get hit/a fright/told off; **~ a educação a todos** to bring education to all; **deixar-se ~ por** to be carried along by

leve [ˈlɛvi] ADJ light; (*insignificante*) slight; **de ~** lightly, softly

levedo [leˈvedu] M yeast

levedura [leveˈdura] F **= levedo**

leveza [leˈveza] F lightness

levezinho [leveˈziɲu] ADJ: **de ~** very lightly

leviandade [levjãˈdadʒi] F frivolity

leviano, -a [leˈvjanu, a] ADJ frivolous

levitação [levitaˈsãw] F levitation

levitar [leviˈtaʳ] VI to levitate

lexical [leksiˈkaw] (*pl* **-ais**) ADJ lexical

léxico, -a [ˈlɛksiku, a] ADJ lexical ∎ M lexicon

lexicografia [leksikograˈfia] F lexicography

lexicógrafo, -a [leksiˈkɔgrafu, a] M/F lexicographer

leziria [leˈzirja] (*PT*) F marshland

LFT (*BR*) ABR F **= Letra Financeira do Tesouro**

lhama [ˈʎama] M llama

lha(s) [ʎa(ʃ)] **= lhe + a(s)**

lhaneza [ʎaˈneza] F amiability

lhano, -a [ˈʎanu, a] ADJ amiable

lhe [ʎi] PRON (*a ele*) to him; (*a ela*) to her; (*a você*) to you

lhes [ʎiʃ] PRON PL (*a eles/elas*) to them; (*a vocês*) to you

lho(s) [ʎu(ʃ)] **= lhe + o(s)**

lhufas [ˈʎufaʃ] (*col*) PRON nothing, bugger all (*!*)

li *etc* [li] VB v **ler**

lia [ˈlia] F dregs *pl*, sediment

liame [ˈljami] M tie, bond

libanês, -esa [libaˈneʃ, eza] ADJ Lebanese

Líbano [ˈlibanu] M: **o ~** (*the*) Lebanon

libelo [liˈbɛlu] M satire, lampoon; (*Jur*) formal indictment

libélula [liˈbɛlula] F dragonfly

liberação [liberaˈsãw] F liberation

liberal [libeˈraw] (*pl* **-ais**) ADJ, M/F liberal

liberalidade [liberaliˈdadʒi] F liberality

liberalismo [liberaˈliʒmu] M liberalism

liberalização [liberalizaˈsãw] F liberalization

liberalizante [liberaliˈzãtʃi] ADJ liberalizing

liberalizar [liberaliˈzaʳ] VT to liberalize

liberar [libeˈraʳ] VT to release; (*libertar*) to free; (*Comput: dados*) to output

liberdade [libexˈdadʒi] F freedom; **liberdades** FPL (*direitos*) liberties; **estar em ~** to be free; **pôr alguém em ~** to set sb free; **tomar a ~ de fazer** to take the liberty of doing; **tomar ~s com alguém** to take liberties with sb; **~ condicional** probation; **~ de cultos** freedom of worship; **~ de expressão** freedom of expression; **~ de imprensa** press freedom; **~ de palavra** freedom of speech; **~ de pensamento** freedom of thought; **~ sob palavra** parole

Libéria [liˈbɛrja] F: **a ~** Liberia

líbero [ˈliberu] M (*Futebol*) sweeper

libérrimo, -a [liˈbɛximu, a] ADJ SUPERL *de* **livre**

libertação [libextaˈsãw] F release

libertador, a [libextaˈdoʳ(a)] M/F liberator

libertar [libexˈtaʳ] VT to free, release

libertinagem [libextʃiˈnaʒẽ] F licentiousness, loose living

libertino, -a [libexˈtʃinu, a] ADJ loose-living ∎ M/F libertine

liberto, -a [liˈbextu, a] PP *de* **libertar**

Líbia [ˈlibja] F: **a ~** Libya

libidinoso, -a [libidʒiˈnozu, ɔza] ADJ lecherous, lustful

libido [liˈbidu] F libido

líbio, -a [ˈlibju, a] ADJ, M/F Libyan

libra [ˈlibra] F pound; **L~** (*Astrologia*) Libra; **~ esterlina** pound sterling

librar [liˈbraʳ] VT to support

libreto [liˈbretu] M libretto

libriano, -a [liˈbrjanu, a] ADJ, M/F Libran

lição [liˈsãw] (*pl* **-ões**) F lesson; **que isto lhe sirva de ~** let this be a lesson to you

licença [liˈsẽsa] F licence (*Brit*), license (*US*); (*permissão*) permission; (*do trabalho, Mil*) leave; **com ~** excuse me; **estar de ~** to be on leave; **sob ~** under licence; **dá ~?** may I?; **tirar ~** to go on leave; **~ poética** poetic licence

licença-prêmio (*pl* **licenças-prêmio**) F long paid leave

licenciado, -a [lisẽˈsjadu, a] M/F graduate

licenciar [lisẽˈsjaʳ] VT to license; **licenciar-se** VR (*Educ*) to graduate; (*ficar de licença*) to take leave; **~ alguém** to give sb leave; **licenciatura** [lisẽsjaˈtura] F (*título*) degree; (*curso*) degree course

licencioso, -a [lisẽˈsjozu, ɔza] ADJ licentious

liceu [liˈsew] (*PT*) M secondary (*Brit*) *ou* high (*US*) school

licitação [lisitaˈsãw] (*pl* **-ões**) F auction; (*concorrência*) tender; **abrir ~** to put out to tender

licitante [lisiˈtãtʃi] M/F bidder

licitar [lisiˈtaʳ] VT (*pôr em leilão*) to put up for auction ∎ VI to bid

lícito, -a ['lisitu, a] ADJ (Jur) lawful; (justo) fair, just; (permissível) permissible

lições [li'sõjʃ] FPL de **lição**

licor [li'koʳ] M liqueur

licoroso, -a [liko'rozu, ɔza] ADJ (vinho) fortified

lida ['lida] F toil; (col: leitura): **dar uma ~ em** to have a read of

lidar [li'daʳ] VI: ~ **com** (ocupar-se) to deal with; (combater) to struggle against; ~ **em algo** to work in sth

lide ['lidʒi] F (trabalho) work, chores pl; (luta) fight; (Jur) case

líder ['lideʳ] M/F leader; **liderança** [lide'rãsa] F leadership; (Esporte) lead; **liderar** [lide'raʳ] VT to lead

lido, -a ['lidu, a] PP de **ler** ■ ADJ (pessoa) well-read

lifting ['liftĩŋ] (pl -**s**) M face lift

liga ['liga] F league; (de meias) suspender (Brit), garter (US); (metal) alloy

ligação [liga'sãw] (pl -**ões**) F connection; (fig: de amizade) bond; (Tel) call; (relação amorosa) liaison; **fazer uma ~ para alguém** to call sb; **não consigo completar a ~** (Tel) I can't get through; **caiu a ~** (Tel) I (ou he etc.) was cut off

ligada [li'gada] F (Tel) ring, call; **dar uma ~ para alguém** (col) to give sb a ring

ligado, -a [li'gadu, a] ADJ (Tec) connected; (luz, rádio etc) on; (metal) alloy; **estar ~ (em)** (col: absorto) to be wrapped up in (in); (: em droga) to be hooked (on); (afetivamente) to be attached (to)

ligadura [liga'dura] F bandage; (Mús) ligature

ligamento [liga'mẽtu] M ligament

ligar [li'gaʳ] VT to tie, bind; (unir) to join, connect; (luz, TV) to switch on; (afetivamente) to bind together; (carro) to start (up) ■ VI (telefonar) to ring; **ligar-se** VR to join; ~-**se com alguém** to join with sb; ~-**se a algo** to be connected with sth; ~ **para alguém** to ring sb up; ~ **para fora** to ring out; ~ **para** ou **a algo** (dar atenção) to take notice of sth; (dar importância) to care about sth; **eu nem ligo** it doesn't bother me; **não ligo a mínima (para)** I couldn't care less (about)

ligeireza [liʒej'reza] F lightness; (rapidez) swiftness; (agilidade) nimbleness

ligeiro, -a [li'ʒejru, a] ADJ light; (ferimento) slight; (referência) passing; (conhecimentos) scant; (rápido) quick, swift; (ágil) nimble ■ ADV swiftly, nimbly

liguei etc [li'gej] VB V **ligar**

lilás [li'laʃ] ADJ, M lilac

lima ['lima] F (laranja) type of (very sweet) orange; (ferramenta) file; ~ **de unhas** nailfile

limão [li'mãw] (pl -**ões**) M lime; **limão(-galego)** (pl **limões(-galegos)**) M lemon

limar [li'maʳ] VT to file

limbo ['lĩbu] M: **estar no ~** to be in limbo

limeira [li'mejra] F lime tree

limiar [li'mjaʳ] M threshold

liminar [limi'naʳ] F (Jur) preliminary verdict

limitação [limita'sãw] (pl -**ões**) F limitation, restriction

limitado, -a [limi'tadu, a] ADJ limited; **ele é**

meio ou **bem ~** he's not very bright

limitar [limi'taʳ] VT to limit, restrict; **limitar-se** VR: **limitar-se a** to limit o.s. to; ~(-**se**) **com** to border on; **ele limitava-se a dizer ...** he did nothing more than say ....; **limite** [li'mitʃi] M (de terreno etc) limit, boundary; (fig) limit; **passar dos limites** to go too far; **limite de crédito** credit limit; **limite de idade** age limit

limo ['limu] M (Bot) water weed; (lodo) slime

limoeiro [li'mwejru] M lemon tree

limões [li'mõjʃ] MPL de **limão**

limonada [limo'nada] F lemonade (Brit), lemon soda (US)

limpa ['lĩpa] (col) F clean; (roubo): **fazer uma ~ em** to clean out

limpação [lĩpa'sãw] F cleaning

limpador [lĩpa'doʳ] M: ~ **de pára-brisas** windscreen wiper (Brit), windshield wiper (US)

limpa-pés M INV shoe scraper

limpar [lĩ'paʳ] VT to clean; (lágrimas, suor) to wipe away; (polir) to shine, polish; (fig) to clean up; (arroz, peixe) to clean; (roubar) to rob

limpa-trilhos M INV cowcatcher

limpeza [lĩ'peza] F cleanliness; (esmero) neatness; (ato) cleaning; (fig) clean-up; (roubo): **fazer uma ~ em** to clean out; ~ **de pele** facial; ~ **pública** rubbish (Brit) ou garbage (US) collection, sanitation

límpido, -a ['lĩpidu, a] ADJ limpid

limpo, -a ['lĩpu, a] PP de **limpar** ■ ADJ clean; (céu, consciência) clear; (Com) net, clear; (fig) pure; (col: pronto) ready; **passar a ~** to make a fair copy; **tirar a ~** to find out the truth about, clear up; **estar ~ com alguém** (col) to be in with sb

limusine [limu'zini] F limousine

lince ['lĩsi] M lynx; **ter olhos de ~** to have eyes like a hawk

linchar [lĩ'ʃaʳ] VT to lynch

lindeza [lĩ'deza] F beauty

lindo, -a ['lĩdu, a] ADJ lovely; ~ **de morrer** (col) stunning

linear [li'njaʳ] ADJ linear

linfático, -a [lĩ'fatʃiku, a] ADJ lymphatic

lingerie [lĩʒe'ri] M lingerie

lingote [lĩ'gɔtʃi] M ingot

língua ['lĩgwa] F tongue; (linguagem) language; **botar a ~ para fora** to stick out one's tongue; **dar com a ~ nos dentes** to let the cat out of the bag; **dobrar a ~** to bite one's tongue; **estar na ponta da ~** to be on the tip of one's tongue; **ficar de ~ de fora** (exausto) to be pooped; **pagar pela ~** to live to regret one's words; **saber algo na ponta da ~** to know sth inside out; **ter uma ~ comprida** (fig) to have a big mouth; **em ~ da gente** (col) ≈ in plain English; ~ **franca** lingua franca; ~ **materna** mother tongue

linguado [lĩ'gwadu] M (peixe) sole

linguagem [lĩ'gwaʒẽ] (pl -**ns**) F (tb: Comput) language; (falada) speech; ~ **de alto nível** (Comput) high-level language; ~ **de máquina** (Comput) machine language; ~ **de montagem** (Comput) assembly language; ~

de programação (*Comput*) programming language

linguajar [lĩgwa'ʒaʳ] M speech, language

linguarudo, -a [lĩgwa'rudu, a] ADJ gossiping ■ M/F gossip

lingüeta [lĩ'gweta] F (*fechadura*) bolt; (*balança*) pointer

lingüiça [lĩ'gwisa] F sausage; **encher ~** (*col*) to waffle on

lingüista [lĩ'gwista] M/F linguist

lingüística [lĩ'gwistʃika] F linguistics *sg*

lingüístico, -a [lĩ'gwistʃiku, a] ADJ linguistic

linha ['liɲa] F line; (*para costura*) thread; (*barbante*) string, cord; (*fila*) row; **linhas** FPL (*carta*) letter *sg*; **as ~s gerais de um projeto** the outlines of a project; **em ~** in line, in a row; (*Comput*) on line; **fora de ~** (*Comput*) off line; **andar na ~** (*fig*) to toe the line; **sair da ~** (*fig*) to step out of line; **comportar-se com muita ~** to behave very correctly; **manter/perder a ~** to keep/lose one's cool; **o telefone não deu ~** the line was dead; **~ aérea** airline; **~ de ataque** (*Futebol*) forward line, forwards *pl*; **~ de conduta** course of action; **~ de crédito** (*Com*) credit line; **~ de fogo** firing line; **~ de mira** sights *pl*; **~ de montagem** assembly line; **~ de partido** party line; **~ de saque** (*Tênis*) baseline; **~ férrea** railway (*Brit*), railroad (*US*)

linhaça [li'ɲasa] F linseed

linha-dura (*pl* **linhas-duras**) M/F hardliner

linhagem [li'ɲaʒē] F lineage

linho ['liɲu] M linen; (*planta*) flax

linóleo [li'nɔlju] M linoleum

lipoaspiração [lipuaʃpira'sãw] F liposuction

liquefazer [likefa'zeʳ] (*irreg*) VT to liquefy

líquen ['likē] M lichen

liquidação [likida'sãw] (*pl* -**ões**) F liquidation; (*em loja*) (clearance) sale; (*de conta*) settlement; **em ~** on sale; **entrar em ~** to go into liquidation

liquidante [liki'dãtʃi] M/F liquidator

liquidar [liki'daʳ] VT to liquidate; (*conta*) to settle; (*mercadoria*) to sell off; (*assunto*) to lay to rest ■ VI (*loja*) to have a sale; **liquidar-se** VR (*destruir-se*) to be destroyed; **~ (com) alguém** (*fig: arrasar*) to destroy sb; (: *matar*) to do away with sb

liquidez [liki'deʒ] F (*Com*) liquidity

liqüidificador [likwidʒifika'doʳ] M liquidizer

liqüidificar [likwidʒifi'kaʳ] VT to liquidize

líquido, -a ['likidu, a] ADJ liquid, fluid; (*Com*) net ■ M liquid

lira ['lira] F lyre; (*moeda*) lira

lírica ['lirika] F (*Mús*) lyrics *pl*; (*poesia*) lyric poetry

lírico, -a ['liriku, a] ADJ lyric(al)

lírio ['lirju] M lily

lírio-do-vale (*pl* **lírios-do-vale**) M lily of the valley

lirismo [li'riʒmu] M lyricism

Lisboa [liʒ'boa] N Lisbon; **lisboeta** [liʒ'bweta] ADJ Lisbon *atr* ■ M/F inhabitant *ou* native of Lisbon

liso, -a ['lizu, a] ADJ smooth; (*tecido*) plain; (*cabelo*) straight; (*col: sem dinheiro*) broke; **estar ~, leso e louco** (*col*) to be flat broke

lisonja [li'zõʒa] F flattery

lisonjeador, a [lizõʒja'doʳ(a)] ADJ flattering ■ M/F flatterer

lisonjear [lizõ'ʒjaʳ] VT to flatter

lisonjeiro, -a [lizõ'ʒejru, a] ADJ flattering

lista ['liʃta] F list; (*listra*) stripe; (*PT: menu*) menu; **~ civil** civil list; **~ negra** black list; **~ telefônica** telephone directory

listado, -a [li'ʃtadu, a] ADJ = **listrado**

listagem [liʃ'taʒē] (*pl* -**ns**) F (*Comput*) listing

listar [liʃ'taʳ] VT (*Comput*) to list

listra ['liʃtra] F stripe; **listrado, -a** [liʃ'tradu, a] ADJ striped

literal [lite'raw] (*pl* -**ais**) ADJ literal

literário, -a [lite'rarju, a] ADJ literary

literato [lite'ratu] M man of letters

literatura [litera'tura] F literature; **Literatura de cordel**; *see below*

● **LITERATURA DE CORDEL**
●
● *Literatura de cordel* is a type of literature
● typical of the north-east of Brazil, published
● in the form of cheaply printed booklets.
● Their authors hang these booklets from
● wires attached to walls in the street so that
● people can look at them. While they do
● this, the authors sing their stories aloud.
● *Literatura de cordel* deals both with local events
● and people, and with everyday public life,
● almost always in an irreverent manner.

litigante [litʃi'gãtʃi] M/F (*Jur*) litigant

litigar [litʃi'gaʳ] VT to contend ■ VI to go to law

litígio [li'tʃiʒju] M (*Jur*) lawsuit; (*contenda*) dispute

litigioso, -a [litʃi'ʒozu, ɔza] ADJ (*Jur*) disputed

litografia [litogra'fia] F (*processo*) lithography; (*gravura*) lithograph

litogravura [litogra'vura] F lithograph

litoral [lito'raw] (*pl* -**ais**) ADJ coastal ■ M coast, seaboard

litorâneo, -a [lito'ranju, a] ADJ coastal

litro ['litru] M litre (*Brit*), liter (*US*)

Lituânia [li'twanja] F: **a ~** Lithuania

liturgia [litux'ʒia] F liturgy

litúrgico, -a [li'tuxʒiku, a] ADJ liturgical

lívido, -a ['lividu, a] ADJ livid

living ['livĩ] (*pl* -**s**) M living room

livramento [livra'mētu] M release; **~ condicional** parole

livrar [li'vraʳ] VT to release, liberate; (*salvar*) to

NB: *European Portuguese adds the following consonants to certain words:* **b** (sú(b)dito, su(b)til); **c** (a(c)ção, a(c)cionista, a(c)to); **m** (inde(m)ne); **p** (ado(p)çã, ado(p)tar); *for further details see p. xiii.*

save; **livrar-se** VR to escape; **~-se de** to get rid of; (*compromisso*) to get out of; **Deus me livre!** Heaven forbid!

livraria [livra'ria] F bookshop (*Brit*), bookstore (*US*)

livre ['livri] ADJ free; (*lugar*) unoccupied; (*desimpedido*) clear, open; **~ de impostos** tax-free; **estar ~ de algo** to be free of sth; **de ~ e espontânea vontade** of one's own free will; **livre-arbítrio** M free will

livreiro, -a [liv'rejru, a] M/F bookseller

livresco, -a [li'vreʃku, a] ADJ book *atr*; (*pessoa*) bookish

livrete [li'vretʃi] M booklet

livro ['livru] M book; **~ brochado** paperback; **~ caixa** (*Com*) cash book; **~ de bolso** pocket-sized book; **~ de cabeceira** favo(u)rite book; **~ de cheques** cheque book (*Brit*), check book (*US*); **~ de consulta** reference book; **~ de cozinha** cookery book (*Brit*), cookbook (*US*); **~ de mercadorias** stock book; **~ de registro** catalogue (*Brit*), catalog (*US*); **~ de texto** *ou* **didático** text book; **~ encadernado** *ou* **de capa dura** hardback

lixa ['liʃa] F sandpaper; (*de unhas*) nailfile; (*peixe*) dogfish

lixadeira [liʃa'dejra] F sander

lixar [li'ʃaʳ] VT to sand; **lixar-se** VR (*col*): **estou me lixando com isso** I couldn't care less about it

lixeira [li'ʃejra] F dustbin (*Brit*), garbage can (*US*)

lixeiro [li'ʃejru] M dustman (*Brit*), garbage man (*US*)

lixo ['liʃu] M rubbish, garbage (*US*); **ser um ~** (*col*) to be rubbish; **~ atômico** nuclear waste

Lj. ABR = **loja**

lj. ABR = **loja**

-lo [lu] PRON him; (*você*) you; (*coisa*) it

lobby ['lɔbi] (*pl* -**ies**) M (*Pol*) lobby

lóbi ['lɔbi] M = **lobby**

lobinho [lo'biɲu] M (*Zool*) wolf cub; (*escoteiro*) cub

lobisomem [lobi'somẽ] (*pl* -**ns**) M werewolf

lobista [lo'biʃta] M/F lobbyist

lobo ['lobu] M wolf

lobo-do-mar (*pl* **lobos-do-mar**) M old salt

lobo-marinho (*pl* **lobos-marinhos**) M sea lion

lobrigar [lobri'gaʳ] VT to glimpse

lóbulo ['lɔbulu] M lobe

locação [loka'sãw] (*pl* -**ões**) F lease; (*de vídeo etc*) rental

locador, a [loka'doʳ(a)] M/F (*de casa*) landlord; (*de carro, filme*) rental agent ■ F rental company; **~ de vídeo** video rental shop

local [lo'kaw] (*pl* -**ais**) ADJ local ■ M site, place ■ F (*notícia*) story; **localidade** [lokali'dadʒi] F (*lugar*) locality; (*povoação*) town; **localização** [lokaliza'sãw] (*pl* -**ões**) F location; **localizar** [lokali'zaʳ] VT to locate; (*situar*) to place; **localizar-se** VR (*estabelecer-se*) to be located; (*orientar-se*) to get one's bearings

loção [lo'sãw] (*pl* -**ões**) F lotion; **~ após-barba** aftershave (lotion)

locatário, -a [loka'tarju, a] M/F (*de casa*) tenant; (*de carro, filme*) hirer

locaute [lo'kawtʃi] M lockout

loções [lo'sõjʃ] FPL *de* **loção**

locomoção [lokomo'sãw] (*pl* -**ões**) F locomotion

locomotiva [lokomo'tʃiva] F railway (*Brit*) *ou* railroad (*US*) engine, locomotive

locomover-se [lokomo'vexsi] VR to move around

locução [loku'sãw] (*pl* -**ões**) F (*Ling*) phrase; (*dicção*) diction

locutor, a [loku'toʳ(a)] M/F (*TV, Rádio*) announcer

lodacento, -a [loda'sẽtu, a] ADJ muddy

lodo ['lodu] M (*lama*) mud; (*limo*) slime

lodoso, -a [lo'dozu, ɔza] ADJ (*lamacento*) muddy; (*limoso*) slimy

logaritmo [loga'ritʃimo] M logarithm

lógica ['lɔʒika] F logic; **lógico, -a** ['lɔʒiku, a] ADJ logical; (**é**) **lógico!** of course!

logística [lo'ʒiʃtʃika] F logistics *sg*

logo ['lɔgu] ADV (*imediatamente*) right away, at once; (*em breve*) soon; (*justamente*) just, right; (*mais tarde*) later; **~**, **~** straightaway, without delay; **~ mais** later; **~ no começo** right at the start; **~ que, tão ~** as soon as; **até ~!** bye!; **~ antes/depois** just before/shortly afterwards; **~ de saída** *ou* **de cara** straightaway, right away

logopedia [logope'dʒia] F speech therapy

logopedista [logope'dʒiʃta] M/F speech therapist

logotipo [logo'tʃipu] M logo

logradouro [logra'doru] M public area

lograr [lo'graʳ] VT (*alcançar*) to achieve; (*obter*) to get, obtain; (*enganar*) to cheat; **~ fazer** to manage to do

logro ['logru] M fraud

loiro, -a ['lojru, a] ADJ = **louro**

loja ['lɔʒa] F shop; (*maçônica*) lodge; **~ de antiguidades** antique shop; **~ de brinquedos** toy shop; **~ de departamentos** department store; **~ de produtos naturais** health food shop; **lojista** [lo'ʒiʃta] M/F shopkeeper

lomba ['lõba] F ridge; (*ladeira*) slope

lombada [lõ'bada] F (*de animal*) back; (*de livro*) spine; (*na estrada*) ramp

lombar [lõ'baʳ] ADJ lumbar

lombeira [lõ'bejra] F listlessness

lombinho [lõ'biɲu] M (*carne*) tenderloin

lombo ['lõbu] M back; (*carne*) loin

lombriga [lõ'briga] F ringworm

lona ['lɔna] F canvas; **estar na última ~** (*col*) to be broke

Londres ['lõdriʃ] N London; **londrino, -a** [lõ'drinu, a] ADJ London *atr* ■ M/F Londoner

longa-metragem (*pl* **longas-metragens**) M: (**filme de**) **~** feature (film)

longe ['lõʒi] ADV far, far away ■ ADJ distant; **ao ~** in the distance; **de ~** from far away; (*sem dúvida*) by a long way; **~ dos olhos, ~ do coração** out of sight, out of mind; **~ de** a long way *ou* far from; **~ disso** far from it; **ir ~ demais** (*fig*) to go too far; **essa sua mania vem de ~** he's had this habit

for a long time; **ver** ~ *(fig)* to have vision
longevidade [lõʒevi'dadʒi] F longevity
longínquo, -a [lõ'ʒĩkwu, a] ADJ distant, remote
longíquo, -a [lõ'ʒikwu, a] ADJ = **longínquo**
longitude [lõʒi'tudʒi] F *(Geo)* longitude
longitudinal [lõʒitudʒi'naw] *(pl* **-ais)** ADJ
longitudinal
longo, -a ['lõgu, a] ADJ long ■ M *(vestido)* long
dress, evening dress; **ao** ~ **de** along, alongside
lontra ['lõtra] F otter
loquacidade [lokwasi'dadʒi] F loquacity
loquaz [lo'kwaʒ] ADJ talkative
lorde ['lɔxdʒi] M lord
lorota [lo'rɔta] *(col)* F fib
losango [lo'zãgu] M lozenge, diamond
lotação [lota'sãw] F capacity; *(vinho)* blending;
(de funcionários) complement; (BR: *ônibus)* bus; ~
completa *ou* **esgotada** *(Teatro)* sold out
lotado, -a [lo'tadu, a] ADJ *(Teatro)* full; *(ônibus)*
full up; *(bar, praia)* packed, crowded
lotar [lo'ta'] VT to fill, pack; *(funcionário)* to place
■ VI to fill up
lote ['lɔtʃi] M *(porção)* portion, share; *(em leilão)*
lot; *(terreno)* plot; *(de ações)* parcel, batch
loteamento [lotʃja'mẽtu] M division into lots
lotear [lo'tʃja'] VT to divide into lots
loteca [lu'tɛka] *(col)* F pools *pl* (Brit), lottery (US)
loteria [lote'ria] F lottery; **ganhar na** ~ to win
the lottery; ~ **esportiva** football pools *pl* (Brit),
lottery (US)
loto¹ ['lotu] M lotus
loto² ['lotu] M bingo
lótus ['lɔtuʃ] M INV lotus
louça ['losa] F china; *(conjunto)* crockery; *(tb:*
louça sanitária) bathroom suite; **de** ~ china *atr*;
~ **de barro** earthenware; ~ **de jantar** dinner
service; **lavar a** ~ to do the washing up (Brit) *ou*
the dishes
louçaria [losa'ria] F china; *(loja)* china shop
louco, -a ['loku, a] ADJ crazy, mad; *(sucesso)*
runaway; *(frio)* freezing ■ M/F lunatic;
~ **varrido** raving mad; ~ **de fome/raiva**
ravenous; **por** crazy about; ~ **por** crazy about;
deixar alguém ~ to drive sb crazy; **ser uma**
coisa de ~ *(col)* to be really something; **estar/**
ficar ~ **da vida (com)** to be/get mad (at); ~ **de**
pedra *(col)* stark staring mad; **deu uma louca**
nele e ... something strange came over him
and ...; **cada** ~ **com sua mania** whatever turns
you on; **loucura** [lo'kura] F madness; *(ato)* crazy
thing; **ser loucura (fazer)** to be crazy (to do);
ser uma loucura to be crazy; *(col: ser muito bom)*
to be fantastic; **ter loucura por** to be crazy
about
louquice [lo'kisi] F madness; *(ato, dito)* crazy
thing
louro, -a ['loru, a] ADJ blond, fair ■ M laurel;
(Culin) bay leaf; *(cor)* blondness; *(papagaio)* parrot;
louros MPL *(fig)* laurels

lousa ['loza] F flagstone; *(tumular)* gravestone;
(quadro-negro) blackboard
louva-a-deus ['lova-] M INV praying mantis
louvação [lova'sãw] *(pl* **-ões)** F praise
louvar [lo'va'] VT, VI: ~ **(a) Deus** to praise God;
louvável [lo'vavew] *(pl* **-eis)** ADJ praiseworthy
louvor [lo'vo'] M praise
LP ABR M LP
lpm ABR (= *linhas por minuto)* lpm
Ltda. ABR ≈ Limitada, Ltd
lua ['lua] F moon; **estar** *ou* **viver no mundo da**
~ to have one's head in the clouds; **estar de** ~
(col) to be in a mood; **ser de** ~ *(col)* to be moody;
~ **cheia/nova** full/new moon; **lua-de-mel** F
honeymoon
Luanda ['lwãda] N Luanda
luar ['lwa'] M moonlight; **banhado de** ~ moonlit
luarento, -a [lwa'rẽtu, a] ADJ moonlit
lubrificação [lubrifika'sãw] *(pl* **-ões)** F
lubrication
lubrificante [lubrifi'kãtʃi] M lubricant ■ ADJ
lubricating
lubrificar [lubrifi'ka'] VT to lubricate
lucidez [lusi'deʒ] F lucidity, clarity
lúcido, -a ['lusidu, a] ADJ lucid
lúcio ['lusju] M *(peixe)* pike
lucrar [lu'kra'] VT *(tirar proveito)* to profit from
ou by; *(dinheiro)* to make; *(gozar)* to enjoy ■ VI to
make a profit; ~ **com** *ou* **em** to profit by
lucratividade [lukratʃivi'dadʒi] F profitability
lucrativo, -a [lukra'tʃivu, a] ADJ lucrative,
profitable
lucro ['lukru] M gain; *(Com)* profit; ~ **bruto/**
líquido *(Com)* gross/net profit; **participação**
nos ~**s** *(Com)* profit-sharing; ~**s e perdas** *(Com)*
profit and loss
lucubração [lukubra'sãw] *(pl* **-ões)** F
meditation, pondering
ludibriar [ludʒi'brja'] VT *(enganar)* to dupe,
deceive; *(escarnecer)* to mock, deride
lúdico, -a ['ludʒiku, a] ADJ playful
lufada [lu'fada] F gust (of wind)
lugar [lu'ga'] M place; *(espaço)* space, room; *(para*
sentar) seat; *(emprego)* job; *(ocasião)* opportunity;
em ~ instead of; **dar** ~ **a** *(causar)* to give rise
to; ~ **comum** commonplace; **em primeiro** ~ in
the first place; **em algum/nenhum/outro/**
todo ~ somewhere/nowhere/somewhere else
ou elsewhere/everywhere; **ter** ~ *(acontecer)* to
take place; **ponha-se em meu** ~ put yourself in
my position; **ponha-se no seu** ~ don't get ideas
above your station; **ele foi no meu** ~ he went
instead of me *ou* in my place; **tirar o primeiro**
~ to come first; **conhecer o seu** ~ to know one's
place; ~ **de nascimento** place of birth; **lugarejo**
[luga'reʒu] M village
lúgubre ['lugubri] ADJ mournful; *(escuro)*
gloomy
lula ['lula] F squid

NB: *European Portuguese adds the following consonants to certain words:* **b** (sú(b)dito, su(b)til); **c** (a(c)ção,
a(c)cionista, a(c)to); **m** (inde(m)ne); **p** (ado(p)çã, ado(p)tar); *for further details see p. xiii.*

lumbago [lũˈbagu] M lumbago
lume [ˈlumi] M fire; (*luz*) light
luminária [lumiˈnarja] F lamp; **luminárias** FPL (*iluminações*) illuminations
luminosidade [luminoziˈdadʒi] F brightness
luminoso, -a [lumiˈnozu, ɔza] ADJ luminous; (*fig: raciocínio*) clear; (: *idéia, talento*) brilliant; (*letreiro*) illuminated
lunar [luˈnaʳ] ADJ lunar ▪ M (*na pele*) mole
lunático, -a [luˈnatʃiku, a] ADJ mad
luneta [luˈneta] F eye-glass; (*telescópio*) telescope
lupa [ˈlupa] F magnifying glass
lúpulo [ˈlupulu] M (*Bot*) hop
lusco-fusco [ˈluʃku-] M twilight
lusitano, -a [luziˈtanu, a] ADJ Portuguese, Lusitanian
luso, -a [ˈluzu, a] ADJ Portuguese; **luso-brasileiro, -a** (*pl* luso-brasileiros) ADJ Luso-Brazilian
lustra-móveis [ˈluʃtra-] M INV furniture polish
lustrar [luʃˈtraʳ] VT to polish, clean
lustre [ˈluʃtri] M gloss, sheen; (*fig*) lustre (*Brit*), luster (*US*); (*luminária*) chandelier
lustroso, -a [luʃˈtrozu, ɔza] ADJ shiny
luta [ˈluta] F fight, struggle; ~ **armada** armed combat; ~ **de boxe** boxing; ~ **de classes** class struggle; ~ **livre** wrestling; **foi uma ~ convencê-lo** it was a struggle to convince him; **lutador, a** [lutaˈdoʳ(a)] M/F fighter; (*atleta*) wrestler; **lutar** [luˈtaʳ] VI to fight, struggle; (*luta livre*) to wrestle ▪ VT (*caratê, judô*) to do; **lutar contra/por algo** to fight against/for sth; **lutar para fazer algo** to fight *ou* struggle to do sth;

lutar com (*dificuldades*) to struggle against; (*competir*) to fight with
luto [ˈlutu] M mourning; (*tristeza*) grief; **de ~ in mourning; pôr ~** to go into mourning
luva [ˈluva] F glove; **luvas** FPL (*pagamento*) payment *sg*; (*ao locador*) fee *sg*; **caber como uma ~** to fit like a glove
luxação [luʃaˈsãw] (*pl* -ões) F dislocation
luxar [luˈʃaʳ] VI to show off
Luxemburgo [luʃẽˈbuxgu] M: **o ~** Luxembourg
luxento, -a [luˈʃẽtu, a] ADJ fussy, finnicky
luxo [ˈluʃu] M luxury; **de ~** luxury *atr*; **dar-se ao ~ de** to allow o.s. to; **poder dar-se ao ~ de** to be able to afford to; **cheio de ~** (*col*) prissy, finicky; **deixe de ~** (*col*) don't come it; **fazer ~** (*col*) to play hard to get; **com ~** luxurious(ly); (*vestir-se*) fancily
luxuosidade [luʃwoziˈdadʒi] F luxuriousness
luxuoso, -a [luˈʃwozu, ɔza] ADJ luxurious
luxúria [luˈʃurja] F lust
luxuriante [luʃuˈrjãtʃi] ADJ lush
luz [luʒ] F light; (*eletricidade*) electricity; **à ~ de** by the light of; (*fig*) in the light of; **a meia ~** with subdued lighting; **dar à ~ (um filho)** to give birth (to a son); **deu-me uma ~** I had an idea; ~ **artificial/natural** artificial/natural light; ~ **de vela** candlelight; **pessoa de muita ~** enlightened person
luzidio, -a [luziˈdʒiu, a] ADJ shining, glossy
luzir [luˈziʳ] VI to shine, gleam; (*fig*) to be successful
Lx.a ABR = **Lisboa**
Lycra® [ˈlajkra] F Lycra®

Mm

M, m ['emi] (pl ms) M M, m; **M de Maria** M for Mike

MA ABR = **Maranhão**

ma [ma] PRON = **me + a**

má [ma] ADJ F de **mau**

maca ['maka] F stretcher

maçã [ma'sã] F apple; ~ **do rosto** cheekbone

macabro, -a [ma'kabru, a] ADJ macabre

macaca [ma'kaka] F: **estar com a ~** (col) to be in a foul mood; v tb **macaco**

macacada [maka'kada] F (turma): **a ~** (família, amigos) the gang

macacão [maka'kãw] (pl -ões) M (de trabalhador) overalls pl (Brit), coveralls pl (US); (da moda) jump-suit

macaco, -a [ma'kaku, a] M/F monkey ■ M (Mecânica) jack; **(fato)** ~ (PT) overalls pl (Brit), coveralls pl (US); (pessoa feia) ugly mug; (tb: **macaco de imitação**) copycat; ~ **velho** (fig) old hand; ~**s me mordam** (col) blow me down

macacões [maka'kõjʃ] MPL de **macacão**

maçada [ma'sada] F bore

macadame [maka'dami] M asphalt, tarmac (Brit)

maçador, a [masa'do'(a)] (PT) ADJ boring

macambúzio, -a [makã'buzju, a] ADJ sullen

maçaneta [masa'neta] F knob

maçante [ma'sãtʃi] (BR) ADJ boring

macaquear [maka'kja'] VT to ape

macaquice [maka'kisi] F: **fazer ~s** to clown around

maçar [ma'sa'] VT to bore

maçarico [masa'riku] M (tubo) blowpipe; (ave) curlew

maçaroca [masa'rɔka] F wad

macarrão [maka'xãw] M pasta; (em forma de canudo) spaghetti; **macarronada** [makaxo'nada] F pasta with cheese and tomato sauce

macarrônico, -a [maka'xoniku, a] ADJ (francês etc) broken, halting

Macau [ma'kaw] N Macau

maceioense [masej'wẽsi] ADJ from Maceió ■ M/F person from Maceió

macerado, -a [mase'radu, a] ADJ (rosto) haggard

macerar [mase'ra'] VT (amolecer) to soften; (fig: mortificar) to mortify; (: rosto) to make haggard

macérrimo, -a [ma'sɛximu, a] ADJ SUPERL de **magro**

macete [ma'setʃi] M mallet; (col) trick; **dar o ~ a alguém** (col) to show sb the way

maceteado, -a [mase'tʃjadu, a] (col) ADJ (plano) clever; (casa) well-designed

machadada [maʃa'dada] F blow with an axe (Brit) ou ax (US)

machado [ma'ʃadu] M axe (Brit), ax (US)

machão, -ona [ma'ʃãw, ɔ] (pl -ões/-s) ADJ tough; (mulher) butch ■ M macho man; (valentão) tough guy

machê [ma'ʃe] ADJ: **papel ~** papier-mâché

machete [ma'ʃetʃi] M machete

machismo [ma'ʃiʒmu] M male chauvinism, machismo; (col) toughness

machista [ma'ʃiʃta] ADJ chauvinistic, macho ■ M male chauvinist

macho ['maʃu] ADJ male; (fig) virile, manly; (valentão) tough ■ M male; (Tec) tap

machões [ma'ʃõjʃ] MPL de **machão**

machona [ma'ʃona] ADJ F de **machão** ■ F butch woman; (col: ofensivo: lésbica) dyke

machucado, -a [maʃu'kadu, a] ADJ hurt; (pé, braço) bad ■ M injury; (área machucada) sore patch

machucar [maʃu'ka'] VT to hurt; (produzir contusão) to bruise ■ VI to hurt; **machucar-se** VR to hurt o.s.; (col: estrepar-se) to come a cropper

maciço, -a [ma'sisu, a] ADJ solid; (espesso) thick; (quantidade) massive ■ M (Geo) massif; **ouro ~** solid gold; **uma dose maciça** a massive dose

macieira [ma'sjejra] F apple tree

maciez [ma'sjeʒ] F softness

macilento, -a [masi'lẽtu, a] ADJ gaunt, haggard

macio, -a [ma'siu, a] ADJ soft; (liso) smooth

maciota [ma'sjɔta] F: **na ~** without problems

maço ['masu] M (de folhas, notas) bundle; (de cigarros) packet

maçom [ma'sõ] (pl -ns) M (free)mason

maçonaria [masona'ria] F (free)masonry

maconha [ma'kɔɲa] F dope; **cigarro de ~** joint

NB: *European Portuguese adds the following consonants to certain words:* **b** (sú(b)dito, su(b)til); **c** (a(c)ção, a(c)cionista, a(c)to); **m** (inde(m)ne); **p** (ado(p)çã, ado(p)tar); *for further details see p. xiii.*

maconhado, -a [makoˈɲadu, a] ADJ stoned
maconheiro, -a [makoˈɲejru, a] (col) M/F
(viciado) dope fiend; (vendedor) dope peddler
maçônico, -a [maˈsoniku, a] ADJ masonic; **loja**
maçônica masonic lodge
maçons [maˈsõʃ] MPL de **maçom**
má-criação (pl -ões) F rudeness; (ato, dito) rude
thing
macrobiótica [makroˈbjɔtʃika] F (dieta)
macrobiotic diet
macrobiótico, -a [makroˈbjɔtʃiku, a] ADJ
macrobiotic
macroeconomia [makroekonoˈmia] F
macroeconomics sg
mácula [ˈmakula] F stain, blemish
macumba [maˈkũba] F ≈ voodoo; (despacho)
macumba offering; **macumbeiro, -a**
[makũˈbejru, a] ADJ ≈ voodoo atr ■ M/F
follower of macumba
madama [maˈdama] F = **madame**
madame [maˈdami] F (senhora) lady; (col: dona-
de-casa) lady of the house; (: esposa) missus; (: de
bordel) madame
Madeira [maˈdejra] F: **a ~** Madeira
madeira [maˈdejra] F wood ■ M Madeira
(wine); **de ~** wooden; **bater na ~** (fig) to touch
(Brit) ou knock on (US) wood; **~ compensada**
plywood; **~ de lei** hardwood
madeira-branca (pl madeiras-brancas) F
softwood
madeiramento [madejraˈmẽtu] M woodwork
madeirense [madejˈrẽsi] ADJ, M/F Madeiran
madeiro [maˈdejru] M (lenho) log; (viga) beam
madeixa [maˈdejʃa] F (de cabelo) lock
madona [maˈdɔna] F madonna
madrasta [maˈdraʃta] F stepmother; (fig)
heartless mother
madre [ˈmadri] F (freira) nun; (superiora) mother
superior
madrepérola [madreˈpɛrola] F mother of pearl
madressilva [madreˈsiwva] F honeysuckle
Madri [maˈdri] N Madrid
Madrid [maˈdrid] (PT) N Madrid
madrinha [maˈdriɲa] F godmother; (fig:
patrocinadora) patron
madrugada [madruˈgada] F (early) morning;
(alvorada) dawn, daybreak; **duas horas da ~** two
in the morning
madrugador, a [madrugaˈdo(a)] M/F early
riser; (fig) early bird ■ ADJ early-rising
madrugar [madruˈga(r)] VI to get up early;
(aparecer cedo) to be early
madurar [maduˈra(r)] VT, VI (fruta) to ripen; (fig)
to mature
madureza [maduˈreza] F (de pessoa) maturity
maduro, -a [maˈduro, a] ADJ (fruta) ripe; (fig)
mature; (: prudente) prudent
mãe [mãj] F mother; **~ adotiva/de criação**
adoptive mother; **~ de família** wife and mother
mãe-benta (pl mães-bentas) F (Culin) coconut
cookie
mãe-de-santo (pl mães-de-santo) F voodoo

priestess
MAer (BR) ABR M = **Ministério da Aeronáutica**
maestria [majʃˈtria] F mastery; **com ~** in a
masterly way
maestro, -trina [maˈɛʃtru, ˈtrina] M/F
conductor
má-fé F malicious intent
máfia [ˈmafja] F mafia
mafioso, -a [maˈfjozu, ɔza] ADJ gangsterish
■ M mobster
mafuá [maˈfwa] M fair; (bagunça) mess
magarefe [magaˈrefi] (PT) M butcher
magazine [magaˈzini] M magazine; (loja)
department store
magia [maˈʒia] F magic; **~ negra** black magic
mágica [ˈmaʒika] F magic; (truque) magic trick;
v tb **mágico**
mágico, -a [ˈmaʒiku, a] ADJ magic ■ M/F
magician
magistério [maʒiʃˈtɛrju] M (ensino) teaching;
(profissão) teaching profession; (professorado)
teachers pl
magistrado [maʒiʃˈtradu] M magistrate
magistral [maʒiʃˈtraw] (pl -ais) ADJ magisterial;
(fig) masterly
magistratura [maʒiʃtraˈtura] F magistracy
magnanimidade [magnanimiˈdadʒi] F
magnanimity
magnânimo, -a [magˈnanimu, a] ADJ
magnanimous
magnata [magˈnata] M magnate, tycoon
magnésia [magˈnɛzja] F magnesia
magnésio [magˈnɛzju] M magnesium
magnético, -a [magˈnɛtʃiku, a] ADJ magnetic
magnetismo [magneˈtʃizmu] M magnetism
magnetizar [magnetʃiˈza(r)] VT to magnetize;
(fascinar) to mesmerize
magnificência [magnifiˈsẽsja] F magnificence,
splendour (Brit), splendor (US)
magnífico, -a [magˈnifiku, a] ADJ splendid,
magnificent
magnitude [magniˈtudʒi] F magnitude
magno, -a [ˈmagnu, a] ADJ (grande) great;
(importante) important
magnólia [magˈnɔlja] F magnolia
mago [ˈmagu] M magician; **os reis ~s** the Three
Wise Men, the Three Kings
mágoa [ˈmagwa] F (tristeza) sorrow, grief; (fig:
desagrado) hurt
magoado, -a [maˈgwadu, a] ADJ hurt
magoar [maˈgwa(r)] VT, VI to hurt; **magoar-se**
VR: **magoar-se com algo** to be hurt by sth
MAgr (BR) ABR M = **Ministério da Agricultura**
magreza [maˈgreza] F slimness; (de carne)
leanness; (fig) meagreness (Brit), meagerness
(US)
magricela [magriˈsɛla] ADJ skinny
magrinho, -a [maˈgriɲu, a] ADJ thin
magro, -a [ˈmagru, a] ADJ (pessoa) slim; (carne)
lean; (fig: parco) meagre (Brit), meager (US); (leite)
skimmed; **ser ~ como um palito** to be like a
beanpole

mai. ABR = **maio**

mainframe [mẽj'frejm] M mainframe

maio ['maju] (PT M-) M May; v tb **julho**

maiô [ma'jo] (BR) M swimsuit

maionese [majo'nezi] F mayonnaise

maior [ma'jɔʳ] ADJ (compar: de tamanho) bigger; (: de importância) greater; (superl: de tamanho) biggest; (: de importância) greatest ▪ M/F adult; **tive a ~ discussão com ela** I had a real argument with her; **foi o ~ barato** (col) it was really great; **tenho a ~ para te contar, não te conto a ~** the best is yet to come; **~ de idade** of age, adult; **~ de 21 anos** over 21; **ser de ~** (col) to be of age ou grown up; **ser ~ e vacinado** (col) to be one's own master

maioral [majo'raw] (pl -ais) M boss; **o ~** the greatest

Maiorca [maj'ɔxka] F Majorca

maioria [majo'ria] F majority; **a ~ de** most of; **~ absoluta** absolute majority

maioridade [majori'daʒi] F adulthood; **atingir a ~** to come of age

○ **PALAVRA CHAVE**

mais [majʃ] ADV 1 (compar): **mais magro/inteligente (do que)** thinner/more intelligent (than); **ele trabalha mais (do que eu)** he works more (than me)
2 (superl): **o mais ... the most ...; o mais magro/inteligente** the thinnest/most intelligent
3 (negativo): **ele não trabalha mais aqui** he doesn't work here any more; **nunca mais** never again
4 + ADJ (valor intensivo): **que livro mais chato!** what a boring book!
5: **por mais que** however much; **por mais que se esforce ...** no matter how hard you try ...; **por mais que eu quisesse ...** much as I should like to ...
6: **a mais, temos um a mais** we've got one extra
7 (tempo): **mais cedo ou mais tarde** sooner or later; **a mais tempo** sooner; **logo mais** later on; **no mais tardar** at the latest
8 (frases): **mais ou menos** more or less; **mais uma vez** once more; **cada vez mais** more and more; **sem mais nem menos** out of the blue
▪ ADJ 1 (compar): **mais (do que)** more (than); **ele tem mais dinheiro (do que o irmão)** he's got more money (than his brother)
2 (superl): **ele é quem tem mais dinheiro** he's got most money
3 (+ números): **ela tem mais de dez bolsas** she's got more than ten bags
4 (negativo): **não tenho mais dinheiro** I haven't got any more money
5 (adicional) else; **mais alguma coisa?**

anything else?; **nada/ninguém mais** nothing/no-one else
▪ PREP: **2 mais 2 são 4** 2 and 2 ou plus 2 are 4
▪ M: **o mais** the rest

maisena [maj'zena] F cornflour

mais-valia (pl -s) F surplus value

maître ['metrə] M head waiter

maiúscula [ma'juʃkula] F capital letter

majestade [maʒeʃ'tadʒi] F majesty; **Sua/Vossa M~** His (ou Her)/Your Majesty; **majestoso, -a** [maʒeʃ'tozu, ɔza] ADJ majestic

major [ma'ʒɔʳ] M (Mil) major

majoritário, -a [maʒori'tarju, a] ADJ majority atr

mal [maw] (pl -es) M harm; (Med) illness ▪ ADV badly; (quase não) hardly ▪ CONJ hardly; **~ desliguei o fone, a campainha tocou** I had hardly put the phone down when the doorbell rang; **o bem e o ~** good and bad; **o ~ é que ...** the bad thing is that ...; **falar ~ de alguém** to speak ill of sb, run sb down; **desejar ~ a alguém** to wish sb ill; **fazer ~ a alguém** to harm sb; (deflorar) to deflower sb; **fazer ~ à saúde de alguém** to damage sb's health; **fazer ~ em** fazer to be wrong to do; **não faz ~** never mind; **não fiz por ~** I meant no harm, I didn't mean it; **levar algo a ~** to take offence (Brit) ou offense (US) at sth; **querer ~ a alguém** to wish sb ill; **estar ~** (doente) to be ill; **passar ~** to be sick; **estar ~ da vida** to be in a bad way; **viver ~ com alguém** not to get on with sb; **~ e porcamente** in a slapdash way; **estar de ~ com alguém** not to be speaking to sb; **dos ~es o menor** the lesser of two evils

mal- [mal-] PREFIXO badly

mala ['mala] F suitcase; (BR: Auto) boot, trunk (US); **malas** FPL (bagagem) luggage sg; **fazer as ~s** to pack; **~ aérea** air courier; **~s de mão** hand luggage sg; **~ direta** (Com) direct mail; **~ postal** mail bag

malabarismo [malaba'riʒmu] M juggling; (fig) shrewd manoeuvre (Brit) ou maneuver (US); **malabarista** [malaba'riʃta] M/F juggler; (fig) smooth operator

mal-acabado, -a ADJ badly finished; (pessoa) deformed

mal-acostumado, -a ADJ maladjusted

mal-afamado, -a ADJ notorious; (mal-visto) of ill repute

malagradecido, -a [malagrade'sidu, a] ADJ ungrateful

malagueta [mala'geta] F chilli pepper

malaio, -a [ma'laju, a] ADJ, M/F Malay ▪ M (Ling) Malay

Malaísia [mala'izja] F: **a ~** Malaysia

malaísio, -a [mala'izju, a] ADJ, M/F Malaysian

mal-ajambrado, -a [-aʒã'bradu, a] ADJ scruffy

mal-amada ADJ unloved ▪ F single woman

NB: European Portuguese adds the following consonants to certain words: **b** (sú(b)dito, su(b)til); **c** (a(c)ção, a(c)cionista, a(c)to); **m** (inde(m)ne); **p** (ado(p)çã, ado(p)tar); for further details see p. xiii.

malandragem [malã'draʒẽ] F (*patifaria*) double-dealing; (*preguiça*) idleness; (*esperteza*) cunning

malandrear [malã'drjaʳ] vi to loaf about *ou* around

malandrice [malã'drisi] F = **malandragem**

malandro, -a [ma'lãdru, a] ADJ (*patife*) double-dealing; (*preguiçoso*) idle; (*esperto*) wily, cunning ■ M/F crook; idler, layabout; streetwise person

mal-apanhado, -a ADJ unpleasant-looking

mal-apessoado, -a [-ape'swadu, a] ADJ unpleasant-looking

malária [ma'larja] F malaria

mal-arrumado, -a [-axu'madu, a] ADJ untidy

mal-assombrado, -a ADJ haunted

Malavi [mala'vi] M: **o ~ Malawi**

mal-avisado, -a [-avi'zadu, a] ADJ rash

malbaratar [mawbara'taʳ] vt (*dinheiro*) to squander, waste

malcasado, -a [mawka'zadu, a] ADJ unhappily married; (*com pessoa inferior*) married to sb below one's class

malcheiroso, -a [mawʃej'rozu, ɔza] ADJ evil-smelling

malcomportado, -a [mawkõpox'tadu, a] ADJ badly behaved

malconceituado, -a [mawkõsej'twadu, a] ADJ badly thought of

malcriado, -a [maw'krjadu, a] ADJ rude ■ M/F slob

maldade [maw'dadʒi] F cruelty; (*malícia*) malice; **é uma ~** it is cruel

maldição [mawdʒi'sãw] (*pl* -ões) F curse

maldigo *etc* [maw'dʒigu] vb v **maldizer**

maldisposto, -a [mawdʒiʃ'poʃtu, 'poʃta] ADJ indisposed

maldisse *etc* [maw'dʒisi] vb v **maldizer**

maldito, -a [maw'dʒitu, a] PP *de* **maldizer** ■ ADJ damned

Maldivas [maw'dʒivaʃ] FPL: **as (ilhas) ~ the Maldives**

maldiz *etc* [maw'dʒiʒ] vb v **maldizer**

maldizente [mawdʒi'zẽtʃi] M/F slanderer

maldizer [mawdʒi'zeʳ] (*irreg*) vt to curse

maldoso, -a [maw'dozu, ɔza] ADJ wicked; (*malicioso*) malicious

maldotado, -a [mawdo'tadu, a] ADJ untalented

maleável [ma'ljavew] (*pl* -eis) ADJ malleable

maledicência [maledʒi'sẽsja] F slander

maledicente [maledʒi'sẽtʃi] M/F slanderer

mal-educado, -a ADJ rude ■ M/F slob

malefício [male'fisju] M harm; **maléfico, -a** [ma'lɛfiku, a] ADJ (*pessoa*) malicious; (*prejudicial*) harmful; (*efeito*) injurious

mal-empregado, -a ADJ wasted

mal-encarado, -a [-ẽka'radu, a] ADJ shady, shifty

mal-entendido, -a ADJ misunderstood ■ M misunderstanding

mal-estar M (*indisposição*) indisposition, discomfort; (*embaraço*) uneasiness

maleta [ma'leta] F small suitcase, grip

malevolência [malevo'lẽsja] F malice, spite

malevolente [malevo'lẽtʃi] ADJ malicious, spiteful

malévolo, -a [ma'lɛvolu, a] ADJ malicious, spiteful

malfadado, -a [mawfa'dadu, a] ADJ unlucky; (*viagem*) ill-fated

malfeito, -a [mal'fejtu, a] ADJ (*roupa*) poorly made; (*corpo*) misshapen; (*fig: injusto*) wrong, unjust

malfeitor, -a [mawfej'toʳ(a)] M/F wrong-doer

malgastar [mawgaʃ'taʳ] vt to waste

malgasto, -a [maw'gaʃtu, a] ADJ wasted

malgrado [maw'gradu] PREP despite

malha ['maʎa] F (*de rede*) mesh; (*tecido*) jersey; (*suéter*) sweater; (*de ginástica*) leotard; **fazer ~** (PT) to knit; **artigos de ~** knitwear; **~ perdida** ladder (Brit), run (US); **vestido de ~** jersey dress

mal-habituado, -a ADJ maladjusted

malhado, -a [ma'ʎadu, a] ADJ mottled; (*roque*) heavy

malhar [ma'ʎaʳ] vt (*bater*) to beat; (*cereais*) to thresh; (*col: criticar*) to knock, run down ■ vi (*col: fazer ginástica*) to work out

malharia [maʎa'ria] F (*fábrica*) mill; (*artigos de malha*) knitted goods *pl*

malho ['maʎu] M (*maço*) mallet; (*grande*) sledgehammer

mal-humorado, -a [-umo'radu, a] ADJ grumpy, sullen

Mali [ma'li] M: **o ~ Mali**

malícia [ma'lisja] F malice; (*astúcia*) slyness; (*espeteza*) cleverness; **pôr ~ em algo** to give sth a double meaning

maliciar [mali'sjaʳ] vt (*ação*) to see malice in; (*palavras*) to misconstrue

malicioso, -a [mali'sjozu, ɔza] ADJ malicious; (*astuto*) sly; (*esperto*) clever; (*mente suja*) dirty-minded

malignidade [maligni'dadʒi] F malice, spite; (*Med*) malignancy

maligno, -a [ma'lignu, a] ADJ (*maléfico*) evil, malicious; (*danoso*) harmful; (*Med*) malignant

má-língua (*pl* **más-línguas**) F backbiting ■ M/F backbiter

mal-intencionado, -a ADJ malicious

malmequer [mawme'keʳ] M marigold

maloca [ma'lɔka] F (*casa*) communal hut; (*aldeia*) (Indian) village; (*esconderijo*) bolt hole

malocar [malo'kaʳ] (*col*) vt to hide

malogrado, -a [malo'gradu, a] ADJ (*plano*) abortive, frustrated; (*sem êxito*) unsuccessful

malograr [malo'graʳ] vt (*planos*) to spoil, upset; (*frustrar*) to thwart, frustrate ■ vi (*planos*) to fall through; (*fracassar*) to fail; **malograr-se** VR to fall through; to fail

malogro [ma'logru] M failure

malote [ma'lɔtʃi] M pouch; (*serviço*) express courier

mal-passado, -a ADJ underdone; (*bife*) rare

malproporcionado, -a [mawpropoxsjo'nadu, a] ADJ ill-proportioned

malquerença [mawke'rẽsa] F ill will, enmity

malquisto | mandões

malquisto, -a [maw'kiʃtu, a] ADJ disliked

malsão, -sã [maw'sãw, 'sã] (pl -s) ADJ (insalubre) unhealthy; (nocivo) harmful

malsucedido, -a [mawsuse'dʒidu, a] ADJ unsuccessful

Malta ['mawta] F Malta

malta ['mawta] (PT) F gang, mob

malte ['mawtʃi] M malt

maltês, -esa [maw'teʃ, eza] ADJ, M/F Maltese

maltrapilho, -a [mawtra'piʎu, a] ADJ in rags, ragged ▪ M/F ragamuffin

maltratar [mawtra'taʳ] VT to ill-treat; (com palavras) to abuse; (estragar) to ruin, damage

maluco, -a [ma'luku, a] ADJ crazy, daft ▪ M/F madman/woman

maluquice [malu'kisi] F madness; (ato, dito) crazy thing

malvadez [mawva'deʒ] F = **malvadeza**

malvadeza [mawva'deza] F wickedness; (ato) wicked thing

malvado, -a [maw'vadu, a] ADJ wicked

malversação [mawvexsa'sãw] F (de dinheiro) embezzlement; (má administração) mismanagement

malversar [mawvex'saʳ] VT (administrar mal) to mismanage; (dinheiro) to embezzle

Malvinas [maw'vinaʃ] FPL: **as (ilhas)** ~ the Falklands, the Falkland Islands

MAM (BR) ABR M (= Museu de Arte Moderna (no Rio))

mama ['mama] F breast

mamada [ma'mada] F breastfeeding

mamadeira [mama'dejra] (BR) F feeding bottle

mamãe [ma'mãj] F mum, mummy

mamão [ma'mãw] (pl -ões) M papaya

mamar [ma'maʳ] VT to suck; (dinheiro) to extort, get; (empresa) to milk (dry) ▪ VI (bebê) to be breastfed; ~ **numa empresa** to get a rake-off from a company; **dar de** ~ **a um bebê** to (breast)feed a baby

mamata [ma'mata] F (negociata) racket; (boa vida) cushy number

mambembe [mã'bẽbi] M/F amateur thespian ▪ ADJ shoddy, second-rate

mameluco, -a [mame'luku, a] M/F half-breed (of Indian and white)

mamífero [ma'miferu] M mammal

mamilo [ma'milu] M nipple

mamoeiro [ma'mwejru] M papaya tree

mamões [ma'mõjʃ] MPL de **mamão**

mana ['mana] F sister

manada [ma'nada] F herd, drove

Manágua [ma'nagwa] N Managua

manancial [manã'sjaw] (pl -ais) M spring; (fig: fonte) source; (: abundância) wealth

manar [ma'naʳ] VT, VI to pour

manauense [manaw'ẽsi] ADJ from Manaus ▪ M/F person from Manaus

mancada [mã'kada] F (erro) mistake; (gafe) blunder; **dar uma** ~ to blunder

mancar [mã'kaʳ] VT to cripple ▪ VI to limp; **mancar-se** VR (col) to get the message, take the hint

manceba [mã'seba] F young woman; (concubina) concubine

mancebo [mã'sebu] M young man, youth

Mancha ['mãʃa] F: **o canal da** ~ the English Channel

mancha ['mãʃa] F (nódoa) stain; (na pele) mark, spot; (em pintura) blotch; **sem ~s** (reputação) spotless; **manchado, -a** [mã'ʃadu, a] ADJ (sujo) soiled; (malhado) mottled, spotted; **manchar** [mã'ʃaʳ] VT to stain, mark; (reputação) to soil

manchete [mã'ʃetʃi] F headline; **virar** ~ to make ou hit (col) the headlines

manco, -a ['mãku, a] ADJ crippled, lame ▪ M/F cripple

mancomunar [mãkomu'naʳ] VT to contrive; **mancomunar-se** VR: **mancomunar-se (com)** to conspire (with)

mandachuva [mãda'ʃuva] M (figurão) big shot; (chefe) boss

mandado [mã'dadu] M (ordem) order; (Jur) writ; (: tb: **mandado de segurança**) injunction; ~ **de arresto** repossession order; ~ **de prisão/busca** warrant for sb's arrest/search warrant; ~ **de segurança** injunction

mandamento [mãda'mẽtu] M order, command; (Rel) commandment

mandante [mã'dãtʃi] M/F instigator; (dirigente) person in charge; (Com) principal

mandão, -dona [mã'dãw, 'dɔna] (pl -ões/-s) ADJ bossy, domineering ▪ M/F bossy person

mandar [mã'daʳ] VT (ordenar) to order; (enviar) to send ▪ VI to be in charge; **mandar-se** VR (col: partir) to make tracks, get going; (fugir) to take off; ~ **buscar** ou **chamar** to send for; ~ **dizer** to send word; ~ **embora** to send away; ~ **fazer um vestido** to have a dress made; ~ **que alguém faça**, ~ **alguém fazer** to tell sb to do; ~ **alguém passear** (fig) to send sb packing; ~ **alguém para o inferno** to tell sb to go to hell; **o que é que você manda?** (col) what can I do for you?; ~ **em alguém** to boss sb around; **manda!** (col) fire away!; ~ **ver** (col) to go to town; ~ **a mão**, ~ **um soco (em alguém)** to hit (sb); **aqui quem manda sou eu** I give the orders around here

mandarim [mãda'rĩ] (pl -ns) M (Ling) Mandarin; (fig) mandarin

mandatário, -a [mãda'tarju, a] M/F (delegado) delegate; (representante) representative, agent

mandato [mã'datu] M (autorização) mandate; (ordem) order; (Pol) term of office

mandíbula [mã'dʒibula] F jaw

mandinga [mã'dʒĩga] F witchcraft

mandioca [mã'dʒɔka] F cassava, manioc

mando ['mãdu] M (comando) command; (poder) power; **a** ~ **de** by order of

mandões [mã'dõjʃ] MPL de **mandão**

NB: *European Portuguese adds the following consonants to certain words:* **b** (sú(b)dito, su(b)til); **c** (a(c)ção, a(c)cionista, a(c)to); **m** (inde(m)ne); **p** (ado(p)ção, ado(p)tar); *for further details see p. xiii.*

mandona [mã'dɔna] F de **mandão**
mandrião, -driona [mã'drjãw, 'drjɛna] (pl -ões/
-s) (PT) ADJ lazy ■ M/F idler, lazybones sg
mandriar [mã'drjaʳ] VI to idle, loaf about
mandriões [mã'drjõjʃ] MPL de **mandrião**
mandriona [mã'drjɔna] F de **mandrião**
maneira [ma'nejra] F (modo) way; (estilo) style,
manner; **maneiras** FPL (modos) manners;
à ~ de like; de ~ que so that; de ~ alguma ou
nenhuma not at all; desta ~ in this way; de
qualquer ~ anyway; não houve ~ de convencê-
lo it was impossible to convince him
maneirar [manej'raʳ] (col) VT to sort out, fix ■ VI
to sort things out; **maneira!** take it easy!
maneiro, -a [ma'nejru, a] ADJ (ferramenta, roupa)
manageable; (trabalho) easy; (pessoa) capable;
(col: bacana) great, brilliant
manejar [mane'ʒaʳ] VT (instrumento) to handle;
(máquina) to work
manejável [mane'ʒavew] (pl -eis) ADJ
manageable
manejo [ma'neʒu] M handling
manequim [mane'kĩ] (pl -ns) M (boneco) dummy
■ M/F model
maneta [ma'neta] ADJ one-handed ■ M/F one-
handed person
manga ['mãga] F sleeve; (fruta) mango; (filtro)
filter; em ~s de camisa in (one's) shirt sleeves
manganês [mãga'neʃ] M manganese
mangue ['mãgi] M mangrove swamp; (planta)
mangrove; (col: zona) red-light district
mangueira [mã'gejra] F hose(pipe); (árvore)
mango tree
manguinha [mã'giɲa] F: **botar as ~s de fora**
(col) to let one's hair down
manha ['maɲa] F (malícia) guile, craftiness;
(destreza) skill; (ardil) trick; (birra) tantrum; **fazer**
~ to have a tantrum
manhã [ma'ɲã] F morning; de ou pela ~ in the
morning; **amanhã/hoje de ~** tomorrow/this
morning; de ~ cedo early in the morning; 4 hs
da ~ 4 o'clock in the morning
manhãzinha [maɲã'ziɲa] F: de ~ early in the
morning
manhoso, -a [ma'ɲozu, ɔza] ADJ (ardiloso) crafty,
sly; (criança) whining
mania [ma'nia] F (Med) mania; (obsessão) craze;
ela é cheia de ~s she's very compulsive;
estar com ~ de ... to have a thing about ...; ~
de grandeza delusions pl of grandeur; ~ de
perseguição persecution complex; **maníaco,
-a** [ma'niaku, a] ADJ manic ■ M/F maniac
maníaco-depressivo (pl -s) ADJ, M/F manic
depressive
manicômio [mani'komju] M asylum, mental
hospital
manicura [mani'kura] F (tratamento) manicure;
(pessoa) manicurist
manicure [mani'kuri] F = **manicura**
manifestação [manifeʃta'sãw] (pl -ões) F show,
display; (expressão) expression, declaration;
(política) demonstration

manifestante [manifeʃ'tãtʃi] M/F demonstrator
manifestar [manifeʃ'taʳ] VT (revelar) to
show, display; (declarar) to express, declare;
manifestar-se VR to manifest o.s.; (pronunciar-
se) to express an opinion
manifesto, -a [mani'fɛʃtu, a] ADJ obvious, clear
■ M manifesto
manilha [ma'niʎa] F (ceramic) drainpipe
manipulação [manipula'sãw] F handling; (fig)
manipulation
manipular [manipu'laʳ] VT to manipulate;
(manejar) to handle
manivela [mani'vela] F (ferramenta) crank
manjado, -a [mã'ʒadu, a] (col) ADJ well-known
manjar [mã'ʒaʳ] M (iguaria) delicacy, titbit
(Brit), tidbit (US) ■ VT (col: conhecer) to know;
(: entender) to grasp; (: observar) to check out ■ VI
(col) to catch on; ~ de algo to know about sth;
manjou? (col) get it?, see?
manjar-branco M blancmange
manjedoura [mãʒe'dora] F manger, crib
manjericão [mãʒeri'kãw] M basil
mano ['manu] M brother
manobra [ma'nɔbra] F (de carro, barco)
manoeuvre (Brit), maneuver (US); (de
mecanismo) operation; (de trens) shunting; (fig)
move; (: artimanha) manoeuvre ou maneuver,
trick; **manobras** FPL (Mil) manoeuvres ou
maneuvers; **manobrar** [mano'braʳ] VT to
manoeuvre (Brit), maneuver (US); (mecanismo)
to operate, work; (governar) to take charge of;
(manipular) to manipulate ■ VI to manoeuvre ou
maneuver; (tomar medidas) to make moves
manobreiro, -a [mano'brejru, a] M/F operator
manobrista [mano'briʃta] M/F parking
attendant
manquejar [mãke'ʒaʳ] VI to limp
mansão [mã'sãw] (pl -ões) F mansion
mansidão [mãsi'dãw] F gentleness, meekness;
(do mar) calmness; (de animal) tameness
mansinho [mã'siɲu]: de ~ ADV (devagar) slowly;
(de leve) gently; (sorrateiramente): sair/entrar de ~
to creep out/in
manso, -a ['mãsu, a] ADJ (brando) gentle; (mar)
calm; (animal) tame
mansões [mã'sõjʃ] FPL de **mansão**
manta ['mãta] F (cobertor) blanket; (xale) shawl;
(agasalho) cloak; (de viajar) travelling rug
manteiga [mã'tejga] F butter; ~ derretida (fig,
col) cry-baby; ~ de cacau cocoa butter
manteigueira [mãtej'gejra] F butter dish
mantém etc [mã'tẽ] VB V **manter**
mantenedor, a [mãtene'doʳ(a)] M/F (da família)
breadwinner; (de opinião, princípio) holder; (de
ordem, Esporte) retainer
manter [mã'teʳ] (irreg) VT to maintain; (num
lugar) to keep; (uma família) to support; (a palavra)
to keep; (princípios) to abide by; **manter-se**
VR (sustentar-se) to support o.s.; (permanecer) to
remain; ~-se firme to stand firm
mantilha [mã'tʃiʎa] F mantilla; (véu) veil
mantimento [mãtʃi'mẽtu] M maintenance;

mantimentos MPL (alimentos) provisions

mantinha etc [mã'tʃiɲa] VB V **manter**

mantive etc [mã'tʃivi] VB V **manter**

mantiver etc [mãtʃi've^r] VB V **manter**

manto ['mãtu] M cloak; (de cerimônia) robe

mantô [mã'to] M coat

manual [ma'nwaw] (pl -ais) ADJ manual ■ M handbook, manual; **ter habilidade** ~ to be good with one's hands

manufatura [manufa'tura] (PT -ct-) F manufacture

manufaturados [manufatu'raduʃ] (PT -ct-) MPL manufactured products

manufaturar [manufatu'ra^r] (PT -ct-) VT to manufacture

manuscrever [manuʃkre've^r] VT to write by hand

manuscrito, -a [manuʃ'kritu, a] ADJ handwritten ■ M manuscript

manusear [manu'zja^r] VT (manejar) to handle; (livro) to leaf through

manuseio [manu'zeju] M handling

manutenção [manutẽ'sãw] F maintenance; (da casa) upkeep

mão [mãw] (pl -s) F hand; (de animal) paw; (de pintura) coat; (de direção) flow of traffic; **à ~** by hand; (perto) at hand; **feito à ~** handmade; **de ~s dadas** hand in hand; **de** ou **em primeira ~** first-hand; **de segunda ~** second-hand; **em ~** by hand; **fora de ~** out of the way; **abrir ~ de algo** (fig) to give sth up; **agüentar a ~** (col: suportar) to hold out; (: esperar) to hang on; **dar a ~ à palmatória** to admit one's mistake; **dar a ~ a alguém** to hold sb's hand; (cumprimentar) to shake hands with sb; **dar uma ~ a alguém** to give sb a hand, help sb out; **ficar na ~** (col) to be stood up; **forçar a ~** to go overboard; **lançar ~ de algo** to have recourse to sth; **largar algo de ~** to give sth up; **uma ~ lava a outra** (fig) one good turn deserves another; **meter a ~ em alguém** to hit sb; **meter** ou **passar a ~ em algo** (col) to nick sth; **passar a ~ pela cabeça de alguém** (fig) to let sb off; **pôr a ~ no fogo por alguém** (fig) to vouch for sb; **pôr ~s à obra** to set to work; **ser uma ~ na roda** (fig) to be a great help; **ter ~ leve** (bater facilmente) to be violent; (ser ladrão) to be light-fingered; **ter a ~ pesada** to be heavy-handed; **ter uma boa ~ para** to be good at; **vir com as ~s abanando** (fig) to come back empty-handed; **~ única/dupla** one-way/two-way traffic; **esta rua dá ~ para o centro** this street goes to the centre (Brit) ou center (US); **rua de duas ~s** two-way street; **~s ao alto!** hands up!; **de ~ beijada** (fig) for nothing

mão-aberta (pl mãos-abertas) ADJ generous ■ M/F generous person

mão-cheia F: **de ~** first-rate

mão-de-obra F (trabalho) workmanship; (trabalhadores) labour (Brit), labor (US); (coisa difícil) tricky thing; **~ especializada** skilled labo(u)r

maoísta [maw'iʃta] ADJ, M/F Maoist

mão-leve (pl mãos-leves) M/F pilferer

mãozinha [mãw'ziɲa] F: **dar uma ~ a alguém** to give sb a hand, help sb out

mapa ['mapa] M map; (gráfico) chart; **não estar no ~** (fig, col) to be extraordinary; **sair do ~** (col) to disappear

mapa-múndi [-'mũdʒi] (pl mapas-múndi) M world map

Maputo [ma'putu] N Maputo

maquete [ma'kɛtʃi] F model

maquiador, a [makja'do^r(a)] M/F make-up artist

maquiagem [ma'kjaʒẽ] F = **maquilagem**

maquiar [ma'kja^r] VT to make up; (fig) to touch up; **maquiar-se** VR to make o.s. up, put on one's make-up

maquiavélico, -a [makja'vɛliku, a] ADJ Machiavellian

maquilagem [maki'laʒẽ] (PT -lha-) F make-up; (ato) making up

maquilar [makila^r] (PT -iha-) VT to make up; **maquilar-se** VR to make o.s. up, put on one's make-up

máquina ['makina] F machine; (de trem) engine; (de relógio) movement; (fig) machinery; **~ a vapor** steam engine; **~s agrícolas** agricultural machinery; **~ de calcular** calculator; **~ de costura** sewing machine; **~ fotográfica** ou **de filmar** camera; **~ de escrever** typewriter; **~ de lavar (roupa)** washing machine; **~ de lavar pratos** dishwasher; **~ de tricotar** knitting machine; **costurar/escrever à ~** to machine-sew/type; **escrito à ~** typewritten; **preencher um formulário à ~** to fill in a form on the typewriter

maquinação [makina'sãw] (pl -ões) F machination, plot

maquinal [maki'naw] (pl -ais) ADJ mechanical, automatic

maquinar [maki'na^r] VT to plot ■ VI to conspire

maquinaria [makina'ria] F machinery

maquinismo [maki'niʒmu] M mechanism; (máquinas) machinery; (Teatro) stage machinery

maquinista [maki'niʃta] M (Ferro) engine driver; (Náut) engineer

mar [ma^r] M sea; **por ~** by sea; **cair no ~** to fall overboard; **fazer-se ao ~** to set sail; **~ aberto** open sea; **pleno ~, ~ alto** high sea; **um ~ de** (fig) a sea of; **~ de rosas** calm sea; (fig) bed of roses; **nem tanto ao ~ nem tanto à terra** (fig) somewhere in between; **o ~ Cáspio** the Caspian Sea; **o ~ Morto** the Dead Sea; **o ~ Negro** the Black Sea; **o ~ Vermelho** the Red Sea

maraca [ma'raka] F maraca

maracujá [maraku'ʒa] M passion fruit; **pé de ~** passion flower

---

NB: European Portuguese adds the following consonants to certain words: **b** (sú(b)dito, su(b)til); **c** (a(c)ção, a(c)cionista, a(c)to); **m** (inde(m)ne); **p** (ado(p)çã, ado(p)tar); for further details see p. xiii.

maracujazeiro [maraku3a'zejru] M passion-fruit plant

maracutaia [maraku'taja] F dirty trick

marafa [ma'rafa] (col) F loose living

marafona [mara'fɔna] (col) F whore

marajá [mara'3a] M maharaja; (BR: Pol) civil service fat-cat

maranhense [mara'ɲẽsi] ADJ from Maranhão ∎ M/F person from Maranhão

marasmo [ma'ra3mu] M (inatividade) stagnation; (apatia) apathy

maratona [mara'tona] F marathon

maratonista [marato'niʃta] M/F marathon runner

maravilha [mara'viʎa] F marvel, wonder; **às mil ~s** wonderfully

maravilhar [maravi'ʎaʳ] VT to amaze, astonish ∎ VI to be amazing; **maravilhar-se** VR: **maravilhar-se de** to be astonished ou amazed at

maravilhoso, -a [maravi'ʎozu, ɔza] ADJ marvellous (Brit), marvelous (US), wonderful

marca ['maxka] F mark; (Com) make, brand; (carimbo) stamp; (da prata) hallmark; (fig: categoria) calibre (Brit), caliber (US); **de ~ maior** (fig) of the first order; **~ de fábrica** trademark; **~ registrada** registered trademark

marcação [maxka'sãw] (pl -ões) F marking; (em jogo) scoring; (de instrumento) reading; (Teatro) action; (PT: Tel) dialling; **estar de ~ com alguém** (col) to pick on sb constantly

marcador [maxka'doʳ] M marker; (de livro) bookmark; (Esporte: quadro) scoreboard; (: jogador) scorer

marcante [max'kãtʃi] ADJ outstanding

marcapasso [maxka'pasu] M (Med) pacemaker

marcar [max'kaʳ] VT to mark; (hora, data) to fix, set; (PT: discar) to dial; (animal) to brand; (delimitar) to demarcate; (observar) to keep an eye on; (gol, ponto) to score; (Futebol: jogador) to mark; (produzir impressão em) to leave one's mark on ∎ VI (impressionar) to make one's mark; **~ uma consulta, ~ hora** to make an appointment; **~ um encontro com alguém** to arrange to meet sb; **~ uma reunião/um jantar para sexta-feira** to arrange a meeting/a dinner for Friday; **~ época** to make history; **~ o ponto** to punch the clock; **ter hora marcada com alguém** to have an appointment with sb; **~ o tempo de algo** to time sth

marcenaria [maxsena'ria] F joinery; (oficina) joiner's

marceneiro [maxse'nejru] M cabinet-maker, joiner

marcha ['maxʃa] F march; (ato) marching; (de acontecimentos) course; (passo) pace; (Auto) gear; (progresso) progress; **~ à ré** (BR), **~ atrás** (PT) reverse (gear); **primeira (~)** first (gear); **pôr-se em ~** to set off

marchar [max'ʃaʳ] VI (ir) to go; (andar a pé) to walk; (Mil) to march

marcha-rancho (pl **marchas-rancho**) F carnival march

marchetar [maxʃe'taʳ] VT to inlay

marcial [max'sjaw] (pl -ais) ADJ martial; **corte ~** court martial; **lei ~** martial law

marciano, -a [max'sjanu, a] ADJ, M Martian

marco ['maxku] M landmark; (de janela) frame; (fig) frontier; (moeda) mark

março ['maxsu] (PT **M-**) M March; v tb **julho**

maré [ma'rɛ] F tide; (fig: oportunidade) chance; **~ alta/baixa** high/low tide; **estar de boa ~ ou de ~ alta** to be in a good mood; **remar contra a ~** (fig) to swim against the tide

marear [ma'rjaʳ] VT to make seasick; (oxidar) to dull, stain ∎ VI to be seasick

marechal [mare'ʃaw] (pl -ais) M marshal

marejar [mare'3aʳ] VT to wet ∎ VI to get wet

maremoto [mare'mɔtu] M tidal wave

maresia [mare'zia] F smell of the sea, sea air

marfim [max'fĩ] M ivory

margarida [maxga'rida] F daisy; (Comput) daisy wheel

margarina [maxga'rina] F margarine

margear [max'3jaʳ] VT to border

margem ['max3ẽ] (pl -ns) F (borda) edge; (de rio) bank; (litoral) shore; (de impresso) margin; (fig: tempo) time; (: lugar) space; (: oportunidade) chance; **à ~ de** alongside; **dar ~ a alguém** to give sb a chance; **~ de erro** margin of error; **~ de lucro** profit margin

marginal [max3i'naw] (pl -ais) ADJ marginal ∎ M/F delinquent

marginalidade [max3inali'dad3i] F delinquency

marginalizar [max3inali'zaʳ] VT to marginalize

maria-fumaça [ma'ria-] (pl **marias-fumaças**) F steam train

maria-sem-vergonha [ma'ria-] (pl **marias-sem-vergonha**) F (Bot) busy lizzie

maria-vai-com-as-outras [ma'ria-] M/F INV sheep, follower

maricas [ma'rikaʃ] (ofensivo) M INV queer, poof

marido [ma'ridu] M husband

marimbondo [marĩ'bõdu] M hornet

marina [ma'rina] F marina

marinha [ma'riɲa] F (tb: marinha de guerra) navy; (pintura) seascape; **~ mercante** merchant navy; **marinheiro** [mari'ɲejru] M seaman, sailor; **marinheiro de primeira viagem** (fig) beginner

marinho, -a [ma'riɲu, a] ADJ sea atr, marine

marionete [marjo'netʃi] F puppet

mariposa [mari'poza] F moth

marisco [ma'riʃku] M shellfish

marital [mari'taw] (pl -ais) ADJ marital

maritalmente [maritaw'mẽtʃi] ADV: **viver ~ (com alguém)** to live (with sb) as man and wife

marítimo, -a [ma'ritʃimu, a] ADJ sea atr, maritime; **pesca marítima** sea fishing

marketing ['maxketʃĩ] M marketing

marmanjo [max'mã3u] M grown man

marmelada [maxme'lada] F quince jam; (col)

double-dealing
marmelo [max'mɛlu] M quince
marmita [max'mita] F (*vasilha*) pot
mármore ['maxmori] M marble
marmóreo, -a [max'mɔrju, a] ADJ marble atr; (*fig*) cold
marola [ma'rɔla] F wave, roller
maroto, -a [ma'rotu, a] M/F rogue, rascal; (*criança*) naughty boy/girl ▪ ADJ roguish; naughty
marquei etc [max'kej] VB V **marcar**
marquês, -quesa [max'keʃ, 'keza] M/F marquis/ marchioness
marquise [max'kizi] F awning, canopy
marra ['maxa] F: **na ~** (*à força*) forcibly; (*a qualquer preço*) whatever the cost
marreco [ma'xeku] M duck
Marrocos [ma'xɔkuʃ] M: **o ~** Morocco
marrom [ma'xõ] (*pl* **-ns**) ADJ, M brown
marroquino, -a [maxo'kinu, a] ADJ, M/F Moroccan
Marte ['maxtʃi] M Mars ◆
martelada [maxte'lada] F (*pancada*) blow (with a hammer); (*ruído*) hammering sound
martelar [maxte'la^r] VT to hammer; (*amolar*) to bother ▪ VI to hammer; (*insistir*): **~ (em algo)** to keep ou harp on (about sth); **martelo** [max'tɛlu] M hammer
martíni® [max'tʃini] M martini®
Martinica [maxtʃi'nika] F: **a ~** Martinique
mártir ['maxtʃi^r] M/F martyr; **martírio** [max'tʃirju] M martyrdom; (*fig*) torment
martirizante [maxtʃiri'zãtʃi] ADJ agonizing
martirizar [maxtʃiri'za^r] VT to martyr; (*atormentar*) to afflict; **martirizar-se** VR to agonize
marujo [ma'ruʒu] M sailor
marulhar [maru'ʎa^r] VI (*mar*) to surge; (*ondas*) to lap; (*produzir ruído*) to roar
marulho [ma'ruʎu] M (*do mar*) surge; (*das ondas*) lapping
marxismo [max'ksiʒmu] M Marxism
marxista [max'ksiʃta] ADJ, M/F Marxist
marzipã [maxzi'pã] M marzipan
mas [ma(j)ʃ] CONJ but ▪ PRON = **me + as**
mascar [maʃ'ka^r] VT to chew
máscara ['maʃkara] F mask; (*para limpeza de pele*) face-pack; **sob a ~ de** under the guise of; **tirar a ~ de alguém** (*fig*) to unmask sb; **baile de ~s** masked ball; **~ de oxigênio** oxygen mask
mascarado, -a [maʃka'radu, a] ADJ masked; (*convencido*) conceited
mascarar [maʃka'ra^r] VT to mask; (*disfarçar*) to disguise; (*encobrir*) to cover up
mascate [maʃ'katʃi] M peddler, hawker (Brit)
mascavo, -a [maʃ'kavu, a] ADJ: **açúcar ~** brown sugar
mascote [maʃ'kɔtʃi] F mascot
masculinidade [maʃkulini'dadʒi] F

---

masculinity
masculino, -a [maʃku'linu, a] ADJ masculine; (Bio) male ▪ M (Ling) masculine; **roupa masculina** men's clothes pl
másculo, -a ['maʃkulu, a] ADJ masculine; (viril) manly
masmorra [maʒ'mɔxa] F dungeon; (fig) black hole
masoquismo [mazo'kiʒmu] M masochism
masoquista [mazo'kiʃta] ADJ masochistic ▪ M/F masochist
MASP ABR M = **Museu de Arte de São Paulo**
massa ['masa] F (Fís, fig) mass; (de tomate) paste; (Culin: de pão) dough; (: macarrão etc) pasta; **as ~s** the masses; **em ~** en masse; **~ de vidraceiro** putty; **estar com as mãos na ~** (fig) to be about ou at it
massacrante [masa'krãtʃi] ADJ annoying
massacrar [masa'kra^r] VT to massacre; (fig: chatear) to annoy; (: torturar) to tear apart; **massacre** [ma'sakri] r massacre; (fig) annoyance
massagear [masa'ʒja^r] VT to massage ▪ VI to do massage; **massagem** [ma'saʒẽ] (pl **-ns**) F massage
massagista [masa'ʒiʃta] M/F masseur/ masseuse
massificar [masifi'ka^r] VT to influence (through mass communication)
massudo, -a [ma'sudu, a] ADJ bulky; (espesso) thick; (com aspecto de massa) doughy
mastectomia [maʃtekto'mia] F mastectomy
mastigado, -a [maʃtʃi'gadu, a] ADJ (fig) well-planned
mastigar [maʃtʃi'ga^r] VT to chew; (pronunciar mal) to mumble, mutter; (fig: refletir) to mull over
mastim [maʃ'tʃĩ] (pl **-ns**) M watchdog
mastodonte [maʃto'dõtʃi] M (fig: pessoa gorda) hulk, lump
mastro ['maʃtru] M (Náut) mast; (para bandeira) flagpole
masturbação [maʃtuxba'sãw] F masturbation
masturbar [maʃtux'ba^r] VT to masturbate; **masturbar-se** VR to masturbate
mata ['mata] F forest, wood; **~ virgem** virgin forest
mata-bicho M tot of brandy, snifter
mata-borrão M blotting paper
matacão [mata'kãw] (pl **-ões**) M lump; (pedra) boulder
matado, -a [ma'tadu, a] ADJ (trabalho) badly done
matador, a [mata'do^r(a)] M/F killer ▪ M (em tourada) matador
matadouro [mata'doru] M slaughterhouse
matagal [mata'gaw] (pl **-ais**) M bush; (brenha) thicket, undergrowth
mata-moscas M INV fly-killer
mata-mosquito (pl **-s**) M mosquito

NB: *European Portuguese adds the following consonants to certain words:* **b** (sú(b)dito, su(b)til); **c** (a(c)ção, a(c)cionista, a(c)to); **m** (inde(m)ne); **p** (ado(p)çã, ado(p)tar); *for further details see p. xiii.*

exterminator

matança[ma'tãsa] F massacre; (*de reses*) slaughter(ing)

mata-piolho(*pl* -s)(*col*) M thumb

matar[ma'ta^r] VT to kill; (*sede*) to quench; (*fome*) to satisfy; (*aula*) to skip; (*trabalho: não aparecer*) to skive off; (: *fazer rápido*) to dash off; (*tempo*) to kill; (*adivinhar*) to guess, get ∎ VI to kill; **matar-se** VR to kill o.s.; (*esfalfar-se*) to wear o.s. out; **um calor/uma dor de ~** stifling heat/excruciating pain; **~ saudades** to catch up

mata-rato(*pl* -s) M (*veneno*) rat poison; (*cigarro*) throat-scraper

mate['matʃi] ADJ matt ∎ M (*chá*) maté tea; (*xeque-mate*) checkmate

matelassê[matela'se] ADJ quilted ∎ M quilting

matemática[mate'matʃika] F mathematics *sg*, maths *sg* (*Brit*), math (*US*); *v tb* **matemático**;

matemático, -a[mate'matʃiku, a] ADJ mathematical ∎ M/F mathematician

matéria[ma'tɛrja] F matter; (*Tec*) material; (*Educ*: *assunto*) subject; (*tema*) topic; (*jornalística*) story, article; **em ~ de** on the subject of; **~ fecal** faeces *pl* (*Brit*), feces *pl* (*US*); **~ plástica** plastic

material[mate'rjaw] (*pl* -ais) ADJ material; (*físico*) physical ∎ M material; (*Tec*) equipment; (*col*: *corpo*) body; **~ humano** manpower; **~ bélico** armaments *pl*; **~ de construção** building materials *pl*; **~ de limpeza** cleaning materials *pl*; **~ escolar** school materials *pl*

materialismo[materja'liʒmu] M materialism

materialista[materja'liʃta] ADJ materialistic ∎ M/F materialist

materializar[materjali'za^r] VT to materialize; **materializar-se** VR to materialize

matéria-prima(*pl* **matérias-primas**) F raw material

maternal[matex'naw] (*pl* -ais) ADJ motherly, maternal; **escola ~** nursery (school); **maternidade**[matexni'dadʒi] F motherhood, maternity; (*hospital*) maternity hospital

materno, -a[ma'tɛxnu, a] ADJ motherly, maternal; (*língua*) native; (*avô*) maternal

matilha[ma'tʃiʎa] F (*cães*) pack; (*fig*: *corja*) rabble

matina[ma'tʃina] F morning

matinal[matʃi'naw] (*pl* -ais) ADJ morning *atr*

matinê[matʃi'ne] F matinée

matiz[ma'tʃiʒ] M (*de cor*) shade; (*fig*: *de ironia*) tinge; (*cor política*) colouring (*Brit*), coloring (*US*)

matizar[matʃi'za^r] VT (*colorir*) to tinge, colour (*Brit*), color (*US*); (*combinar cores*) to blend; **~ algo de algo** (*fig*) to tinge sth with sth

mato['matu] M scrubland, bush; (*plantas agrestes*) scrub; (*o campo*) country; **ser ~** (*col*) to be there for the taking; **estar num ~ sem cachorro** (*col*) to be up the creek without a paddle

mato-grossano, -a[-gro'sanu, a] ADJ, M/F = **mato-grossense**

mato-grossense[-gro'sẽsi] ADJ from Mato Grosso ∎ M/F person from Mato Grosso

matraca[ma'traka] F rattle; (*pessoa*) chatterbox;

falar como uma ~ to talk nineteen to the dozen (*Brit*) *ou* a blue streak (*US*)

matraquear[matra'kja^r] VI to rattle, clatter; (*tagarelar*) to chatter, rabbit on

matreiro, -a[ma'trejru, a] ADJ cunning, crafty

matriarca[ma'trjaxka] F matriarch

matriarcal[matrjax'kaw] (*pl* -ais) ADJ matriarchal

matrícula[ma'trikula] F (*lista*) register; (*inscrição*) registration; (*pagamento*) enrolment (*Brit*) *ou* enrollment (*US*) fee; (*PT*: *Auto*) registration number (*Brit*), license number (*US*); **fazer a ~** to enrol (*Brit*), enroll (*US*)

matricular[matriku'la^r] VT to enrol (*Brit*), enroll (*US*), register; **matricular-se** VR to enrol(l), register

matrimonial[matrimo'njaw] (*pl* -ais) ADJ marriage *atr*, matrimonial

matrimônio[matri'monju] M marriage; **contrair ~ (com alguém)** to be joined in marriage (with sb)

matriz[ma'triʒ] F (*Med*) womb; (*fonte*) source; (*molde*) mould (*Brit*), mold (*US*); (*Com*) head office; (*col*) wife; **igreja ~** mother church

matrona[ma'trona] F matron

maturação[matura'sãw] F maturing; (*de fruto*) ripening

maturidade[maturi'dadʒi] F maturity

matusquela[matuʃ'kɛla] (*col*) M/F lunatic

matutar[matu'ta^r] VT (*planejar*) to plan ∎ VI: **~ em** *ou* **sobre algo** to turn sth over in one's mind

matutino, -a[matu'tʃinu, a] ADJ morning *atr* ∎ M morning paper

matuto, -a[ma'tutu, a] ADJ, M/F (*caipira*) rustic; (*provinciano*) provincial

mau, má[maw, ma] ADJ bad; (*malvado*) evil, wicked ∎ M bad; (*Rel*) evil; **os ~s** bad people; (*num filme*) the baddies

mau-caráter(*pl* **maus-carateres**) ADJ shady ∎ M bad lot

mau-olhado[-o'ʎadu] M evil eye

Maurício[maw'risju] M Mauritius

Mauritânia[mawri'tanja] F: **a ~** Mauritania

mausoléu[mawzo'lɛw] M mausoleum

maus-tratos MPL ill-treatment *sg*

mavioso, -a[ma'vjozu, ɔza] ADJ tender, soft; (*som*) sweet

máx. ABR (= *máximo*) max

máxi['maksi] ADJ INV (*saia*) maxi

maxidesvalorização[maksidʒiʒvaloriza'sãw] (*pl* -ões) F large-scale devaluation

maxila[mak'sila] F jawbone

maxilar[maksi'la^r] ADJ jaw *atr* ∎ M jawbone

máxima['masima] F maxim, saying

máxime['maksime] ADV especially

maximizar[masimi'za^r] VT to maximize; (*superestimar*) to play up

máximo, -a['masimu, a] ADJ (*maior que todos*) greatest; (*o maior possível*) maximum ∎ M maximum; (*o cúmulo*) peak; (*temperature*) high; **o ~ cuidado** the greatest of care; **no ~** at most; **ao ~**

to the utmost; **chegar ao ~** (*fig*) to reach a peak; **ele acha-a o ~** (*col*) he thinks she is the greatest

maxixe [ma'ʃiʃi] M gherkin; (BR: *dança*) 19th-century dance

mazela [ma'zɛla] F (*ferida*) sore spot; (*doença*) illness; (*fig*) blemish

MCE ABR M = **Mercado Comum Europeu**

MCom (BR) ABR M = **Ministério das Comunicações**

MCT (BR) ABR M = **Ministério de Ciência e Tecnologia**

MD (BR) ABR M = **Ministério da Desburocratização**

MDB ABR M (*antes*) = **Movimento Democrático Brasileiro**

me [mi] PRON (*direto*) me; (*indireto*) (to) me; (*reflexivo*) (to) myself

meada ['mjada] F skein, hank

meado ['mjadu] M middle; **em ~s** *ou* **no(s) ~(s) de julho/do ano** in mid-July/in the middle of the year

meandro ['mjãdru] M meander; **os ~s** (*fig*) the ins and outs

MEC (BR) ABR M = **Ministério de Educação e Cultura**

Meca ['mɛka] N Mecca

mecânica [me'kanika] F (*ciência*) mechanics *sg*; (*mecanismo*) mechanism; *v tb* **mecânico**

mecânico, -a [me'kaniku, a] ADJ mechanical ▪ M/F mechanic; **broca mecânica** power drill

mecanismo [meka'niʒmu] M mechanism; **~ de busca** (BR: *Comput*) search engine

mecanização [mekaniza'sãw] F mechanization

mecanizar [mekani'zaʳ] VT to mechanize

mecenas [me'sɛnaʃ] M INV patron

mecha ['mɛʃa] F (*de vela*) wick; (*cabelo*) tuft; (*no cabelo*) highlight; (*Med*) swab; **fazer ~ no cabelo** to put highlights in one's hair, to highlight one's hair

mechado, -a [me'ʃadu, a] ADJ highlighted

meço *etc* ['mɛsu] VB *v* **medir**

méd. (= *médio*) av

medalha [me'daʎa] F medal; **medalhão** [meda'ʎãw] (*pl* -ões) M medallion; (*fig: figurão*) big name; (*jóia*) locket

média ['mɛdʒja] F average; (*café*) coffee with milk; **em ~** on average; **fazer ~** to ingratiate o.s.

mediação [medʒja'sãw] F mediation; **por ~ de** through

mediador, a [medʒja'doʳ(a)] M/F mediator

mediano, -a [me'dʒjanu, a] ADJ medium, average; (*medíocre*) mediocre

mediante [me'dʒjãtʃi] PREP by (means of), through; (*a troco de*) in return for

mediar [me'dʒjaʳ] VT to mediate (for) ▪ VI (*ser mediador*) to mediate; **a distância que medeia entre** the distance between

medicação [medʒika'sãw] (*pl* -ões) F treatment;

(*medicamentos*) medication

medicamento [medʒika'mẽtu] M medicine

medição [medʒi'sãw] (*pl* -ões) F measurement

medicar [medʒi'kaʳ] VT to treat ▪ VI to practise (Brit) *ou* practice (US) medicine; **medicar-se** VR to take medicine, doctor o.s. up

medicina [medʒi'sina] F medicine; **~ legal** forensic medicine

medicinal [medʒisi'naw] (*pl* -ais) ADJ medicinal

médico, -a ['mɛdʒiku, a] ADJ medical ▪ M/F doctor; **receita médica** prescription

médico-cirurgião, médica-cirurgiã (*pl* **médicos-cirurgiões/médicas-cirurgiãs**) M/F surgeon

medições [medʒi'sõjʃ] FPL *de* **medição**

médico-hospitalar (*pl* -es) ADJ hospital and medical

médico-legal (*pl* -ais) ADJ forensic

médico-legista, -a-legista (*pl* **médicos/as-legistas**) M/F forensic expert (Brit), medical examiner (US)

medida [me'dʒida] F measure; (*providência*) step; (*medição*) measurement; (*moderação*) prudence; **à ~ que** while, as; **na ~ em que** in so far as; **feito sob ~** made to measure; **software sob ~** bespoke software; **encher as ~s** (*satisfazer*) to fit the bill; **encher as ~s de alguém** (*chatear*) to get on sb's wick; **ir além da ~** to go too far; **tirar as ~s de alguém** to take sb's measurements; **tomar ~s** to take steps; **tomar as ~s de** to measure; **~ de emergência/urgência** emergency/urgent measure

medidor [medʒi'doʳ] M: **~ de pressão** pressure gauge; **~ de gás** gas meter

medieval [medʒje'vaw] (*pl* -ais) ADJ medieval

médio, -a ['mɛdʒju, a] ADJ (*dedo, classe*) middle; (*tamanho, estatura*) medium; (*mediano*) average; **a ~ prazo** in the medium term; **ensino ~** secondary education; **o brasileiro ~** the average Brazilian

medíocre [me'dʒiokri] ADJ mediocre

mediocridade [medʒjokri'dadʒi] F mediocrity

mediocrizar [medʒjokri'zaʳ] VT to make mediocre

medir [me'dʒiʳ] VT to measure; (*atos, palavras*) to weigh; (*avaliar: conseqüências, distâncias*) to weigh up ▪ VI to measure; **medir-se** VR to measure o.s.; **~-se (com alguém)** (*comparar-se*) to be on a par (with sb); **quanto você mede?** -- **meço 1.60 m** how tall are you? -- I'm 1.60 m (tall); **a saia mede 80 cm de comprimento** the skirt is 80 cm long; **meça suas palavras!** watch your language!; **~ alguém dos pés à cabeça** (*fig*) to eye sb up; **não ter mãos a ~** (*fig*) to have one's hands full

meditação [medʒita'sãw] (*pl* -ões) F meditation

meditar [medʒi'taʳ] VI to meditate; **~ sobre algo** to ponder (on) sth

meditativo, -a [medʒita'tʃivu, a] ADJ

NB: *European Portuguese adds the following consonants to certain words:* **b** (sú(b)dito, su(b)til); **c** (a(c)ção, a(c)cionista, a(c)to); **m** (inde(m)ne); **p** (ado(p)çã, ado(p)tar); *for further details see p. xiii.*

thoughtful, reflective
mediterrâneo, -a [medʒite'xanju, a] ADJ
Mediterranean ■ M: **o M~** the Mediterranean
médium ['mɛdʒjũ] (pl **-ns**) M (pessoa) medium
mediunidade [medʒjuni'dadʒi] F second sight
médiuns ['mɛdʒjũʃ] MPL de **médium**
medo ['medu] M fear; **com ~** afraid; **com ~ que**
for fear that; **ficar com ~** to get frightened;
meter ~ to be frightening; **meter ~ em**
alguém to frighten sb; **ter ~ de** to be afraid of;
ter um ~ que se péla (fig) to be frightened out
of one's wits
medonho, -a [me'doɲu, a] ADJ terrible, awful
medrar [me'draʳ] VI to thrive, flourish; (col: ter
medo) to get frightened
medroso, -a [me'drozu, ɔza] ADJ (com medo)
frightened; (tímido) timid
medula [me'dula] F marrow
megabyte [mega'bajtʃi] M megabyte
megalomania [megaloma'nia] F megalomania
megalomaníaco, -a [megaloma'niaku, a] ADJ,
M/F megalomaniac
megaton [mega'tõ] M megaton
megera [me'ʒɛra] F shrew; (mãe) cruel mother
meia ['meja] F stocking; (curta) sock; (meia-
entrada) half-price ticket ■ NUM six; **(ponto de)**
~ stocking stitch
meia-calça (pl **meias-calças**) F tights pl (Brit),
panty hose (US)
meia-direita (pl **meias-direitas**) F (Futebol)
inside right ■ M (jogador) inside right
meia-entrada (pl **meias-entradas**) F half-price
ticket
meia-esquerda (pl **meias-esquerdas**) F (Futebol)
inside left ■ M (jogador) inside left
meia-estação F: **roupa de ~** spring ou autumn
clothing
meia-idade F middle age; **pessoa de ~** middle-
aged person
meia-lua F half moon; (formato) semicircle
meia-luz F half light
meia-noite F midnight
meia-tigela F: **de ~** two-bit
meia-volta (pl **meias-voltas**) F (tb: Mil) about-
turn (Brit), about-face (US)
meigo, -a ['mejgu, a] ADJ sweet
meiguice [mej'gisi] F sweetness
meio, -a ['meju, a] ADJ half ■ ADV a bit, rather
■ M (centro) middle; (social, profissional) milieu;
(tb: **meio ambiente**) environment; (meios)
means pl; (maneira) way; **meios** MPL (recursos)
means pl; **~ quilo** half a kilo; **um mês e ~** one
and a half months; **cortar ao ~** to cut in half;
deixar algo pelo ~ to leave sth half-finished;
dividir algo ~ a ~ to divide sth in half ou fifty-
fifty; **o quarto do ~** the middle room, the room
in the middle; **em ~ a** amid; **no ~ (de)** in the
middle (of); **nos ~s financeiros** in financial
circles; **~s de comunicação (de massa)**
(mass) media pl; **~s de produção** means pl
of production; **~ de transporte** means sg of
transport; **por ~ de** through; **por todos os ~s** by

all available means; **não há ~ de chover/de ela**
chegar cedo there is no way it's going to rain/
she will arrive early; **embolar o ~ de campo**
(fig) to foul things up
meio-de-campo (pl **meios-de-campo**) M
(Futebol) centre (Brit) ou center (US) forward;
(: posição) midfield
meio-dia M midday, noon
meio-feriado (pl **meios-feriados**) M half-day
holiday
meio-fio M kerb (Brit), curb (US)
meio-termo (pl **meios-termos**) M (fig)
compromise
meio-tom (pl **meios-tons**) M (Mús) semitone;
(nuança) half-tone
mel [mɛw] M honey
melaço [me'lasu] M treacle (Brit), molasses pl
(US)
melado, -a [me'ladu, a] ADJ (pegajoso) sticky ■ M
(melaço) treacle (Brit), molasses pl (US)
melancia [melã'sia] F watermelon
melancieira [melã'sjejra] F watermelon plant
melancolia [melãko'lia] F melancholy,
sadness; **melancólico, -a** [melã'kɔliku, a] ADJ
melancholy, sad
Melanésia [mela'nɛzja] F: **a ~** Melanesia
melão [me'lãw] (pl **-ões**) M melon
melar [me'laʳ] VT to dirty ■ VI (gorar) to flop;
melar-se VR to get messy
meleca [me'lɛka] (col) F snot; (uma meleca) bogey;
tirar ~ to pick one's nose; **que ~!** (col) what crap!
meleira [me'lejra] F sticky mess
melena [me'lena] F long hair
melhor [me'ʎɔʳ] ADJ, ADV (compar) better;
(superl) best; **~ que nunca** better than ever;
quanto mais ~ the more the better; **seria ~**
começarmos we had better begin; **tanto ~** so
much the better; **~ ainda** even better; **bem ~**
much better; **o ~ é ...** the best thing is ...; **levar**
a ~ to come off best; **ou ~ ...** (ou antes) or rather
...; **fiz o ~ que pude** I did the best I could; **no ~ da**
festa (fig: no melhor momento) when things are
(ou were) in full swing; (: inesperadamente) all of
a sudden; **melhora** [me'ʎɔra] F improvement;
melhoras! get well soon!
melhorada [meʎo'rada] (col) F: **dar uma ~** to
get better
melhoramento [meʎora'mẽtu] M
improvement
melhorar [meʎo'raʳ] VT to improve, make
better; (doente) to cure ■ VI to improve,
get better; **~ de vida** to improve one's
circumstances; **~ no emprego** to get better at
one's job
meliante [me'ljãtʃi] M scoundrel; (vagabundo)
tramp
melindrar [melĩ'draʳ] VT to offend, hurt;
melindrar-se VR to take offence (Brit) ou
offense (US), be hurt
melindre [me'lĩdri] M sensitivity
melindroso, -a [melĩ'drozu, ɔza] ADJ (sensível)
sensitive, touchy; (problema, situação) tricky;

(operação) delicate
melodia [melo'dʒia] F melody; (composição) tune
melódico, -a [me'lɔdʒiku, a] ADJ melodic
melodrama [melo'drama] M melodrama
melodramático, -a [melodra'matʃiku, a] ADJ melodramatic
meloeiro [me'lwejru] M melon plant
melões [me'lõjʃ] MPL de **melão**
meloso, -a [me'lozu, ɔza] ADJ sweet; (voz) mellifluous; (fig: pessoa) sweet-talking
melro ['mewxu] M blackbird
membrana [mẽ'brana] F membrane
membro ['mẽbru] M member; (Anat: braço, perna) limb
membrudo, -a [mẽ'brudu, a] ADJ big; (fig) robust
memento [me'mẽtu] M reminder; (caderneta) jotter
memorando [memo'rãdu] M (aviso) note; (Com: comunicação) memorandum
memorável [memo'ravew] (pl -eis) ADJ memorable
memória [me'mɔrja] F memory; **memórias** FPL (de autor) memoirs; **de ~** by heart; **em ~ de** in memory of; **~ fraca** bad memory; **falta de ~** loss of memory; **digno de ~** memorable; **vir à ~** to come to mind; **varrer da ~** (fig) to wipe sth from one's memory; **~ RAM** RAM memory; **~ não-volátil** non-volatile memory
memorial [memo'rjaw] (pl -ais) M memorial; (Jur) brief
memorizar [memori'za'] VT to memorize
menção [mẽ'sãw] (pl -ões) F mention, reference; **~ honrosa** honours (Brit), honors (US), distinction; **fazer ~ de algo** to mention sth; **fazer ~ de sair** to make as if to leave, begin to leave
mencionar [mẽsjo'na'] VT to mention; **para não ~ ...** not to mention ...; **sem ~ ...** let alone ....
menções [mẽ'sõjʃ] FPL de **menção**
mendicância [mẽdʒi'kãsja] F begging
mendicante [mẽdʒi'kãtʃi] ADJ mendicant
■ M/F beggar
mendigar [mẽdʒi'ga'] VT to beg for ■ VI to beg;
mendigo, -a [mẽ'dʒigu, a] M/F beggar
menear [me'nja'] VT (corpo, cabeça) to shake; (quadris) to swing; **~ a cabeça de modo afirmativo** to nod (one's head)
meneio [me'neju] M (balanço) swaying
menina [me'nina] F: **~ do olho** pupil; **ser a ~ dos olhos de alguém** (fig) to be the apple of sb's eye; v tb **menino**
meninada [meni'nada] F kids pl
meningite [meni'ʒitʃi] F meningitis
meninice [meni'nisi] F (infância) childhood; (modos de criança) childishness; (ato, dito) childish thing
menino, -a [me'ninu, a] M/F boy/girl; **seu sorriso de ~** his boyish smile

meninote, -a [meni'nɔtʃi, ta] M/F boy/girl
menopausa [meno'pawza] F menopause
menor [me'nɔ'] ADJ (mais pequeno: compar) smaller; (: superl) smallest; (mais jovem: compar) younger; (: superl) youngest; (o mínimo) least, slightest; (tb: **menor de idade**) under age
■ M/F juvenile, young person; (Jur) minor; **~ abandonado** abandoned child; **proibido para ~es** over 18s only; (filme) X-certificate (Brit), X-rated (US); **um ~ de 10 anos** a child of ten; **não tenho a ~ idéia** I haven't the slightest idea
menoridade [menori'dadʒi] F under-age status

O **PALAVRA CHAVE**

menos ['menuʃ] ADJ **1** (compar): **menos (do que)** (quantidade) less (than); (número) fewer (than); **com menos entusiasmo** with less enthusiasm; **menos gente** fewer people
2 (superl) least; **é o que tem menos culpa** he is the least to blame
■ ADV **1** (compar): **menos (do que)** less (than); **gostei menos do que do outro** I liked it less than the other one
2 (superl): **é o menos inteligente da classe** he is the least bright in his class; **de todas elas é a que menos me agrada** out of all of them she's the one I like least; **pelo menos** at (the very) least
3 (frases): **temos sete a menos** we are seven short; **não é para menos** it's no wonder; **isso é o de menos** that's nothing
■ PREP (exceção) except; (números) minus; **todos menos eu** everyone except (for) me; **5 menos 2** 5 minus 2
■ CONJ: **a menos que** unless; **a menos que ele venha amanhã** unless he comes tomorrow
■ M: **o menos** the least

menosprezar [menuʃpre'za'] VT (subestimar) to underrate; (desprezar) to despise, scorn
menosprezível [menuʃpre'zivew] (pl -eis) ADJ despicable
menosprezo [menuʃ'prezu] M contempt, disdain
mensageiro, -a [mẽsa'ʒejru, a] ADJ messenger atr ■ M/F messenger
mensagem [mẽ'saʒẽ] (pl -ns) F message; **~ de erro** (Comput) error message; **~ de texto** text (message); **mandar uma ~ de texto para** to text; **eu te mando uma ~ de texto quando voltar** I'll text you when I get back; **~s** (fpl) **instantâneas** ou **sistema** (m) **de ~s instantâneas** instant messaging
mensal [mẽ'saw] (pl -ais) ADJ monthly; **ele ganha £1000 mensais** he earns £1000 a month; **mensalidade** [mẽsali'dadʒi] F monthly payment; **mensalmente** [mẽsaw'mẽtʃi] ADV monthly

---

NB: European Portuguese adds the following consonants to certain words: **b** (sú(b)dito, su(b)til); **c** (a(c)ção, a(c)cionista, a(c)to); **m** (inde(m)ne); **p** (ado(p)ção, ado(p)tar); for further details see p. xiii.

menstruação [mẽ∫trwa'sãw] F period, menstruation

menstruada [mẽ∫'trwada] ADJ having one's period; (*Med*) menstruating

menstrual [mẽ∫'trwaw] (*pl* -ais) ADJ menstrual

menstruar [mẽ∫'trwaʳ] VI to menstruate, have a period

mênstruo ['mẽ∫tru] M period, menstruation

menta ['mẽta] F mint

mental [mẽ'taw] (*pl* -ais) ADJ mental; **mentalidade** [mẽtali'dadʒi] F mentality

mentalizar [mẽtali'zaʳ] VT (*plano*) to conceive; ~ **alguém de algo** to make sb realize sth

mente ['mẽt∫i] F mind; **de boa** ~ willingly; **ter em** ~ to bear in mind

mentecapto, -a [mẽt∫i'kaptu, a] ADJ mad, crazy ▪ M/F fool, idiot

mentir [mẽ't∫iʳ] VI to lie; **minto!** (I) tell a lie!

mentira [mẽ't∫ira] F lie; (*ato*) lying; **parece** ~ **que** it seems incredible that; **de** ~ not for real; ~! (*acusação*) that's a lie!, you're lying; (*de surpresa*) you don't say!, no!; **mentiroso, -a** [mẽt∫i'rozu, ɔza] ADJ lying; (*enganoso*) deceitful; (*falso*) deceptive ▪ M/F liar

mentol [mẽ'tow] (*pl* -óis) M menthol

mentolado, -a [mẽto'ladu, a] ADJ mentholated

mentor [mẽ'toʳ] M mentor

menu [me'nu] M (*tb: Comput*) menu

mercadinho [mexka'dʒiɲu] M local market

mercado [mex'kadu] M market; ~ **à vista** spot market; **M~ Comum** Common Market; ~ **de capitais** capital market; ~ **das pulgas** flea market; ~ **de trabalho** labo(u)r market; ~ **externo/interno** foreign/domestic *ou* home market; ~ **negro** *ou* **paralelo** black market

mercadologia [mexkadolo'ʒia] F marketing

mercador [mexka'doʳ] M merchant, trader

mercadoria [mexkado'ria] F commodity; **mercadorias** (*produtos*) FPL goods

mercante [mex'kãt∫i] ADJ merchant *atr*

mercantil [mexkã't∫iw] (*pl* -is) ADJ mercantile, commercial

mercê [mex'se] F (*favor*) favour (Brit), favor (US); (*perdão*) mercy; **à** ~ **de** at the mercy of

mercearia [mexsja'ria] F grocer's (shop) (Brit), grocery store

merceeiro [mex'sjejru] M grocer

mercenário, -a [mexse'narju, a] ADJ mercenary ▪ M mercenary

mercúrio [mex'kurju] M mercury; **M~** Mercury

merda ['mɛxda] (*col!*) F shit (!) ▪ M/F (*pessoa*) jerk; **a** ~ **do carro** the bloody (Brit) *ou* goddamn (US) car (!); **mandar alguém à** ~ to tell sb to piss off (!); **estar numa** ~ to be fucked up (!); ~ **nenhuma** fuck all (!); **ser uma** ~ (*viagem, filme*) to be crap (!)

merecedor, a [merese'doʳ(a)] ADJ deserving

merecer [mere'seʳ] VT to deserve; (*consideração*) to merit; (*valer*) to be worth ▪ VI to be worthy; **merecido, -a** [mere'sidu, a] ADJ deserved; (*castigo, prêmio*) just

merecimento [meresi'mẽtu] M desert; (*valor,*

talento) merit

merenda [me'rẽda] F packed lunch; ~ **escolar** free school meal

merendar [merẽ'daʳ] VI to have school dinner

merendeira [merẽ'dejra] F (*maleta*) lunch-box; (*funcionária*) dinner-lady

merengue [me'rẽgi] M meringue

meretrício [mere'trisju] M prostitution

meretriz [mere'triʒ] F prostitute

mergulhador, a [mexguʎa'doʳ(a)] ADJ diving ▪ M/F diver

mergulhar [mexgu'ʎaʳ] VI (*para nadar*) to dive; (*penetrar*) to plunge ▪ VT: ~ **algo em algo** (*num líquido*) to dip sth into sth; (*na terra etc*) to plunge sth into sth; ~ **no trabalho/na floresta** to immerse o.s. in one's work/go deep into the forest; **mergulho** [mex'guʎu] M dip(ping), immersion; (*em natação*) dive; (*vôo*) nose-dive; **dar um mergulho** (*na praia*) to go for a dip

meridiano [meri'dʒjanu] M meridian

meridional [meridʒjo'naw] (*pl* -ais) ADJ southern

mérito ['meritu] M merit

meritório, -a [meri'tɔrju, a] ADJ meritorious

merluza [mex'luza] F hake

mero, -a ['mɛru, a] ADJ mere

mertiolate® [mext∫jo'latʒi] M antiseptic

mês [me∫] M month; **pago por** ~ paid by the month; **duas vezes por** ~ twice a month; ~ **corrente** this month

mesa ['meza] F table; (*de trabalho*) desk; (*comitê*) board; (*numa reunião*) panel; **pôr/tirar a** ~ to lay/clear the table; **à** ~ at the table; **por baixo da** ~ (*tb fig*) under the table; ~ **de bilhar** billiard table; ~ **de centro** coffee table; ~ **de cozinha/ jantar** kitchen/dining table; ~ **de jogo** card table; ~ **de toalete** dressing table; ~ **telefônica** switchboard

mesada [me'zada] F monthly allowance; (*de criança*) pocket-money

mesa-de-cabeceira (*pl* mesas-de-cabeceira) F bedside table

mesa-redonda (*pl* mesas-redondas) F discussion panel

mescla ['me∫kla] F mixture, blend

mesclar [me∫'klaʳ] VT to mix (up); (*cores*) to blend

meseta [me'zeta] F plateau, tableland

mesmice [meʒ'misi] F sameness

mesmo, -a ['meʒmu, a] ADJ same; (*enfático*) very ▪ ADV (*exatamente*) right; (*até*) even; (*realmente*) really ▪ M/F: **o ~/a mesma** the same (one); **o** ~ (*a mesma coisa*) the same (thing); **eu** ~ I myself; **este** ~ **homem** this very man; **ele** ~ **o fez** he did it himself; **o Rei** ~ the King himself; **continuar na mesma** to be just the same; **dá no** ~ *ou* **na mesma** it's all the same; **aqui/agora/hoje** ~ right here/right now/this very day; ~ **que** even if; **é** ~ it's true; **é** ~? really?; (**é**) **isso** ~! exactly!, that's right!; **por isso** ~ that's why; ~ **assim** even so; **nem** ~ not even; ~ **quando** even when; **só** ~ only; **por si** ~ by one's self; ..., **e estive com o** ~ **ontem** (*referindo-se a pessoa já mencionada*)

..., and I was with him yesterday; **ficar na mesma** (*não entender*) to be none the wiser; **isto para mim é o ~** it's all the same to me; **o ~, por favor!** (*num bar etc*) the same again, please

mesquinharia [meʃki'ɲa'ria] F meanness; (*ato, dito*) mean thing

mesquinho, -a [meʃ'kiɲu, a] ADJ mean

mesquita [meʃ'kita] F mosque

messias [me'siaʃ] M Messiah

mestiçar-se [meʃtʃi'saxsi] VR: **~ (com)** to interbreed (with)

mestiço, -a [meʃ'tʃisu, a] ADJ half-caste, of mixed race; (*animal*) crossbred ■ M/F half-caste; half-breed

mestrado [meʃ'trado] M master's degree; **fazer/ tirar o ~** to do/get one's master's (degree)

mestre, -a ['mɛʃtri, a] ADJ (*chave, viga*) master; (*linha, estrada*) main; (*qualidade*) masterly ■ M/F master/mistress; (*professor*) teacher; **de ~** masterly; **obra mestra** masterpiece; **ele é ~ em mentir** he's an expert liar

mestre-cuca (*pl* mestres-cucas) (*col*) M chef

mestre-de-cerimônias (*pl* mestres-de- cerimônias) M master of ceremonies, MC

mestre-de-obras (*pl* mestres-de-obras) M foreman

mestria [meʃ'tria] F mastery; (*habilidade*) expertise; **com ~** to perfection

mesura [me'zura] F (*cumprimento*) bow; (*cortesia*) courtesy; **cheio de ~s** cap in hand

meta ['mɛta] F (*em corrida*) finishing post; (*regata*) finishing line; (*gol*) goal; (*objetivo*) aim, goal

metabolismo [metabo'liʒmu] M metabolism

metade [me'tadʒi] F half; (*meio*) middle; **~ de uma laranja** half an orange; **pela ~** halfway through

metafísica [meta'fizika] F metaphysics *sg*

metafísico, -a [meta'fiziku, a] ADJ metaphysical

metáfora [me'tafora] F metaphor

metafórico, -a [meta'foriku, a] ADJ metaphorical

metal [me'taw] (*pl* -ais) M metal; **metais** MPL (*Mús*) brass *sg*; **metálico, -a** [me'taliku, a] ADJ metallic; (*de metal*) metal

metalinguagem [metali'gwaʒẽ] (*pl* -ns) F metalanguage

metalizado, -a [metali'zadu, a] ADJ (*papel etc*) metallic

metalurgia [metalux'ʒia] F metallurgy

metalúrgica [meta'luxʒika] F metal works *sg*; *v tb* **metalúrgico**

metalúrgico, -a [meta'luxʒiku, a] ADJ metallurgical ■ M/F metalworker

metamorfose [metamox'fozi] F metamorphosis

metamorfosear [metamoxfo'zjaʳ] VT: **~ alguém em algo** to transform sb into sth

metano [me'tanu] M methane

meteórico, -a [mete'ɔriku, a] ADJ meteoric

meteorito [meteo'ritu] M meteorite

meteoro [me'tjɔru] M meteor

meteorologia [meteorolo'ʒia] F meteorology

meteorológico, -a [meteoro'lɔʒiku, a] ADJ meteorological

meteorologista [meteorolo'ʒiʃta] M/F meteorologist; (*TV, Rádio*) weather forecaster

meter [me'teʳ] VT (*colocar*) to put; (*envolver*) to involve; (*introduzir*) to introduce; **meter-se** VR (*esconder-se*) to hide; (*retirar-se*) to closet o.s.; **~-se a fazer algo** to decide to have a go at sth; **~-se a médico** fraudulently, to act as a doctor; **~-se com** (*provocar*) to pick a quarrel with; (*associar- se*) to get involved with; **meta-se com a sua vida** mind your own business; **~-se em** to get involved in; (*intrometer-se*) to interfere in; **~ na cabeça** to take it into one's head; **~-se na cama** to get into bed; **~-se onde não é chamado** to poke one's nose in(to other people's business)

meticulosidade [metʃikulozi'dadʒi] F meticulousness

meticuloso, -a [metʃiku'lozu, ɔza] ADJ meticulous

metido, -a [me'tʃidu, a] ADJ (*envolvido*) involved; (*intrometido*) meddling; **~ na** snobbish

metódico, -a [me'tɔdʒiku, a] ADJ methodical

metodismo [meto'dʒiʒmu] M (*Rel*) Methodism

metodista [meto'dʒiʃta] ADJ, M/F Methodist

método ['mɛtodu] M method

metodologia [metodolo'ʒia] F methodology

metragem [me'traʒẽ] F length (in metres (*Brit*) *ou* meters (*US*)); (*Cinema*) footage, length; **filme de longa/curta ~** feature *ou* full-length/short film

metralhadora [metraʎa'dora] F sub-machine gun

metralhar [metra'ʎaʳ] VT (*ferir, matar*) to shoot; (*fazer fogo contra*) to spray with machine-gun fire

métrica ['mɛtrika] F (*em poesia*) metre (*Brit*), meter (*US*)

métrico, -a ['mɛtriku, a] ADJ metric

metro ['mɛtru] M metre (*Brit*), meter (*US*); (*PT: metropolitano*) underground (*Brit*), subway (*US*); **~ quadrado/cúbico** square/cubic metre

metrô [me'tro] (*BR*) M underground (*Brit*), subway (*US*)

metrópole [me'trɔpoli] F metropolis; (*capital*) capital

metropolitano, -a [metropoli'tanu, a] ADJ metropolitan ■ M (*PT*) underground (*Brit*), subway (*US*)

metroviário, -a [metro'vjarju, a] ADJ underground *atr* (*Brit*), subway *atr* (*US*) ■ M/F underground (*Brit*) *ou* subway (*US*) worker

meu, minha [mew, 'miɲa] ADJ my ■ PRON mine; **os meus** MPL (*minha família*) my family *ou* folks (*col*); **um amigo ~** a friend of mine; **este livro é ~** this book is mine; **estou na minha**

NB: *European Portuguese adds the following consonants to certain words:* **b** (sú(b)dito, su(b)til); **c** (a(c)ção, a(c)cionista, a(c)to); **m** (inde(m)ne); **p** (ado(p)ção, ado(p)tar); *for further details see p. xiii.*

I'm doing my own thing

MEx (BR) ABR M = **Ministério do Exército**

mexer [me'ʃeʳ] VT (*mover*) to move; (*cabeça: dizendo sim*) to nod; (: *dizendo não*) to shake; (*misturar*) to stir; (*ovos*) to scramble ■ VI (*mover*) to move; **mexer-se** VR to move; (*apressar-se*) to get a move on; ~ **com algo** (*trabalhar*) to work with sth; (*comerciar*) to deal in sth; ~ **com alguém** (*provocar*) to tease sb; (*comover*) to have a profound effect on sb, get to sb (*col*); ~ **em algo** to touch sth; **mexa-se!** get going!, move yourself!

mexerica [meʃe'rika] F tangerine

mexericar [meʃeri'kaʳ] VI to gossip

mexerico [meʃe'riku] M piece of gossip; **mexericos** MPL (*fofocas*) gossip *sg*

mexeriqueiro, -a [meʃeri'kejru, a] ADJ gossiping ■ M/F gossip, busybody

mexicano, -a [meʃi'kanu, a] ADJ, M/F Mexican

México ['meʃiku] M: **o** ~ Mexico; **a Cidade do ~** Mexico City

mexida [me'ʃida] F mess, disorder

mexido, -a [me'ʃidu, a] ADJ (*papéis*) mixed up; (*ovos*) scrambled

mexilhão [meʃi'ʎãw] (*pl* -ões) M mussel

mezanino [meza'ninu] M mezzanine (floor)

MF (BR) ABR M = **Ministério da Fazenda**

MG (BR) ABR = **Minas Gerais**

mg ABR (= *miligrama*) mg

mi [mi] M (*Mús*) E

miado ['mjadu] M miaow

miar [mjaʳ] VI to miaow; (*vento*) to whistle

miasma ['mjaʒma] M (*fig*) decay

miau [mjaw] M miaow

MIC (BR) ABR M = **Ministério de Indústria e Comércio**

miçanga [mi'sãga] F beads *pl*

micção [mik'sãw] F urination

mico ['miku] M capuchin monkey

micose [mi'kɔzi] F mycosis

micrão [mi'krãw] (*pl* -ões) M (*Comput*) supermicro

micro... [mikru] PREFIXO micro...

micróbio [mi'krɔbju] M germ, microbe

microcirurgia [mikrosirux'ʒia] F microsurgery

microcomputador [mikro'kõputa'doʳ)] M micro(computer)

microcosmo [mikro'kɔʒmu] M microcosm

microempresa [mikroẽ'preza] F small business

micrões [mi'krõjʃ] MPL *de* **micrão**

microfilme [mikro'fiwmi] M microfilm

microfone [mikro'fɔni] M microphone

microinformática [mikroĩfox'matʃika] F microcomputing

Micronésia [mikro'nɛzja] F: **a** ~ Micronesia

microonda [mikro'õda] F microwave

microondas [mikro'õdaʃ] M INV (*tb*: **forno de microondas**) microwave (oven)

microônibus [mikro'onibuʃ] M INV minibus

microplaqueta [mikropla'keta] F microchip; ~ **de silicone** silicon chip

microprocessador [mikroprosesa'doʳ] M

microprocessor

microrganismo [mikroxga'niʒmu] M microorganism

microscópico, -a [mikro'ʃkɔpiku, a] ADJ microscopic

microscópio [mikro'ʃkɔpju] M microscope

mídi ['midʒi] ADJ INV midi

mídia ['midʒja] F media *pl*

migalha [mi'gaʎa] F crumb; **migalhas** FPL (*restos, sobras*) scraps

migração [migra'sãw] (*pl* -ões) F migration

migrar [mi'graʳ] VI to migrate

migratório, -a [migra'tɔrju, a] ADJ migratory; **aves migratórias** birds of passage

miguel [mi'gɛw] (*pl* -eis) (*col*) M (*banheiro*) loo (*Brit*), john (*US*)

mijada [mi'ʒada] (*col*) F pee; **dar uma** ~ to have a pee

mijar [mi'ʒaʳ] (*col*) VI to pee; **mijar-se** VR to wet o.s.

mijo ['miʒu] (*col*) M pee

mil [miw] NUM thousand; **dois** ~ two thousand; **estar a** ~ (*col*) to be buzzing

milagre [mi'lagri] M miracle; **por** ~ miraculously; **milagroso, -a** [mila'grozu, ɔza] ADJ miraculous

milenar [mile'naʳ] ADJ thousand-year-old; (*fig*) ancient

milênio [mi'lenju] M millennium

milésimo, -a [mi'lezimu, a] NUM thousandth

mil-folhas F INV (*massa*) millefeuille pastry; (*doce*) cream slice

milha ['miʎa] F mile; (*col*: *mil cruzeiros*): **dez** ~**s** ten grand; ~ **marítima** nautical mile

milhão [mi'ʎãw] (*pl* -ões) M million; **um** ~ **de vezes** hundreds of times; **adorei milhões!** (*col*) I loved it!

milhar [mi'ʎaʳ] M thousand; **turistas aos** ~**es** tourists in their thousands

milharal [miʎa'raw] (*pl* -ais) M maize (*Brit*) *ou* corn (*US*) field

milho ['miʎu] M maize (*Brit*), corn (*US*)

milhões [mi'ʎõjs] MPL *de* **milhão**

miliardário, -a [miljax'darju, a] ADJ, M/F billionaire

milícia [mi'lisja] F (*Mil*) militia; (: *vida*) military life; (: *força*) military force

milico [mi'liku] (*col*) M military type

miligrama [mili'grama] M milligram

mililitro [mili'litru] M millilitre (*Brit*), milliliter (*US*)

milímetro [mi'limetru] M millimetre (*Brit*), millimeter (*US*)

milionário, -a [miljo'narju, a] ADJ, M/F millionaire

militância [mili'tãsja] F militancy

militante [mili'tãtʃi] ADJ, M/F militant

militar [mili'taʳ] ADJ military ■ M soldier ■ VI to fight; ~ **em** (*Mil*: *regimento*) to serve in; (*Pol*: *partido*) to belong to, be active in; (*profissão*) to work in

militarismo [milita'riʒmu] M militarism

militarista [milita'riʃta] ADJ, M/F militarist
militarizar [militari'za'] VT to militarize
mil-réis M INV *former unit of currency in Brazil and Portugal*
mim [mĩ] PRON me; (*reflexivo*) myself; de ~ para ~ to myself
mimado, -a [mi'madu, a] ADJ spoiled, spoilt (*Brit*)
mimar [mi'ma'] VT to pamper, spoil
mimeógrafo [mime'ɔgrafu] M duplicating machine
mimetismo [mime'tʃiʒmu] M (*Bio*) mimicry
mímica ['mimika] F mime; (*jogo*) charades; *v tb* mímico
mímico, -a ['mimiku, a] M/F mime artist
mimo ['mimu] M (*presente*) gift; (*pessoa, coisa encantadora*) delight; (*carinho*) tenderness; (*gentileza*) kindness; cheio de ~s (*criança*) spoiled, spoilt (*Brit*); mimoso, -a [mi'mozu, ɔza] ADJ (*delicado*) delicate; (*carinhoso*) tender, loving; (*encantador*) delightful
MIN (BR) ABR M = Ministério do Interior
min. ABR (= *mínimo*) min
mina ['mina] F mine; (*fig: de riquezas*) gold mine; (: *de informações*) mine of information; (*col: garota*) girl; ~ de carvão coal mine; ~ de ouro (*tb fig*) gold mine
minar [mi'na'] VT to mine; (*fig*) to undermine
minarete [mina'retʃi] M minaret
Minc (BR) ABR M = Ministério da Cultura
mindinho [mĩ'dʒiɲu] M (*tb: dedo mindinho*) little finger
mineiro, -a [mi'nejru, a] ADJ mining *atr*; (*de Minas Gerais*) from Minas Gerais ■ M/F miner; person from Minas Gerais
mineração [minera'sãw] F mining
mineral [mine'raw] (*pl -ais*) ADJ, M mineral
mineralogia [mineralo'ʒia] F mineralogy
minerar [mine'ra'] VT, VI to mine
minério [mi'nɛrju] M ore; ~ de ferro iron ore
mingau [mĩ'gaw] M (*tb: mingau de aveia*) porridge; (*fig*) slop
míngua ['mĩgwa] F lack; à ~ de for want of; viver à ~ to live in poverty; minguado, -a [mĩ'gwadu, a] ADJ scant; (*criança*) stunted; minguado de algo short of sth
minguante [mĩ'gwãtʃi] ADJ waning; (quarto) ~ (*Astronomia*) last quarter
minguar [mĩ'gwa'] VI (*diminuir*) to decrease, dwindle; (*faltar*) to run short
minha ['miɲa] F *de* meu
minhoca [mi'nɔka] F (earth)worm; (*col: bobagem*) daft idea; ~ da terra (*fig: caipira*) country person
míni ['mini] ADJ INV mini ■ M minicomputer
mini... [mini] PREFIXO mini...
miniatura [minja'tura] ADJ, F miniature
minicomputador [minikõputa'do'] M minicomputer

---

mínima ['minima] F (*temperatura*) low; (*Mús*) minim
minimalista [minima'liʃta] ADJ (*fig*) stark
minimizar [minimi'za'] VT to minimize; (*subestimar*) to play down
mínimo, -a ['minimu, a] ADJ minimum ■ M minimum; (*tb: dedo mínimo*) little finger; não dou *ou* ligo a mínima para isso I couldn't care less about it; a mínima importância/idéia the slightest importance/idea; o ~ que podem fazer the least they can do; no ~ at least; no ~ às 11 horas at 11.00 at the earliest
minissaia [mini'saja] F miniskirt
ministerial [miniʃte'rjaw] (*pl -ais*) ADJ ministerial
ministeriável [miniʃte'rjavew] (*pl -eis*) ADJ eligible to be a minister
ministério [mini'ʃterju] M ministry; ~ da Fazenda = Treasury (*Brit*), = Treasury Department (*US*); M~ do Interior = Home Office (*Brit*), = Department of the Interior (*US*); M~ da Marinha/Educação/Saúde = Admiralty/Ministry of Education/Health; M~ das Relações Exteriores = Foreign Office (*Brit*), = State Department (*US*); M~ do Trabalho = Department of Employment (*Brit*) *ou* Labor (*US*); ~ público public prosecution service
ministrar [mini'ʃtra'] VT (*dar*) to supply; (*remédio*) to administer; (*aulas*) to give ■ VI to serve as a minister
ministro, -a [mi'niʃtru, a] M/F minister; ~ da Fazenda = Chancellor of the Exchequer (*Brit*), = Head of the Treasury Department (*US*); ~ do Interior = Home Secretary (*Brit*); ~ das Relações Exteriores = Foreign Secretary (*Brit*), = Head of the State Department (*US*); ~ sem pasta minister without portfolio
minorar [mino'ra'] VT to lessen, reduce
Minorca [mi'nɔrka] F Menorca
minoria [mino'ria] F minority
minoritário, -a [minori'tarju, a] ADJ minority *atr*
minto *etc* ['mĩtu] VB V mentir
minúcia [mi'nusja] F detail
minucioso, -a [minu'sjozu, ɔza] ADJ (*indivíduo, busca*) thorough; (*explicação*) detailed
minúsculo, -a [mi'nuʃkulu, a] ADJ minute, tiny; letra minúscula lower case
minuta [mi'nuta] F (*rascunho*) rough draft; (*Culin*) dish cooked to order; ~ de contrato draft contract
minutar [minu'ta'] VT to draft
minuto [mi'nutu] M minute
miolo ['mjolu] M inside; (*polpa*) pulp; (*de maçã*) core; miolos MPL (*cérebro, inteligência*) brains
míope ['miopi] ADJ short-sighted ■ M/F myopic
miopia [mjo'pia] F short-sightedness, myopia
miosótis [mjo'zɔtʃiʃ] M INV (*Bot*) forget-me-not
mira ['mira] F (*de fuzil*) sight; (*pontaria*) aim; (*fig*)

NB: *European Portuguese adds the following consonants to certain words*: b (sú(b)dito, su(b)til); c (a(c)ção, a(c)cionista, a(c)to); m (inde(m)ne); p (ado(p)çã, ado(p)tar); *for further details see p. xiii*.

aim, purpose; **à ~ de** on the lookout for; **ter em ~** to have one's eye on
mirabolante [mirabo'lãtʃi] ADJ (*roupa*) showy, loud; (*plano*) ambitious; (*surpreendente*) amazing
mirada [mi'rada] F look
miradouro [mira'doru] M viewpoint, belvedere
miragem [mi'raʒẽ] (*pl* **-ns**) F mirage
miramar [mira'maʳ] M sea view
mirante [mi'rãtʃi] M viewpoint, belvedere
mirar [mi'raʳ] VT to look at; (*observar*) to watch; (*apontar para*) to aim at ■ VI: **~ em** to aim at; **mirar-se** VR to look at o.s.; **~ para** to look onto
miríade [mi'riadʒi] F myriad
mirim [mi'rĩ] (*pl* **-ns**) ADJ little
mirrado, -a [mi'xadu, a] ADJ (*planta*) withered; (*pessoa*) haggard
mirrar-se [mi'xaxsi] VR (*planta*) to wither, dry up; (*pessoa*) to waste away
misantropo, -a [mizã'tropu, a] ADJ misanthropic ■ M/F misanthrope
miscelânea [mise'lanja] F miscellany; (*confusão*) muddle
miscigenação [misiʒena'sãw] F interbreeding
mise-en-plis [mizã'pli] M shampoo and set
miserável [mize'ravew] (*pl* **-eis**) ADJ (*digno de compaixão*) wretched; (*pobre*) impoverished; (*avaro*) stingy, mean; (*insignificante*) paltry; (*lugar*) squalid; (*infame*) despicable ■ M (*indigente*) wretch; (*coitado*) poor thing; (*pessoa infame*) rotter
miserê [mize're] (*col*) M poverty, pennilessness
miséria [mi'zɛrja] F (*estado lastimável*) misery; (*pobreza*) poverty; (*avareza*) stinginess; **chorar ~** to complain that one is hard up; **fazer ~s** (*col*) to do wonders; **ganhar/custar uma ~** to earn/cost a pittance; **ser uma ~** (*col*) to be awful
misericórdia [mizeri'kɔxdʒja] F (*compaixão*) pity, compassion; (*graça*) mercy
misógino, -a [mi'zɔʒinu, a] ADJ misogynistic ■ M misogynist
missa ['misa] F (*Rel*) mass; **não saber da ~ a metade** (*col*) not to know the half of it
missal [mi'saw] (*pl* **-ais**) M missal
missão [mi'sãw] (*pl* **-ões**) F mission; (*dever*) duty; (*incumbência*) job
misse ['misi] F beauty queen
míssil ['misiw] (*pl* **-eis**) M missile; **~ balístico/guiado** ballistic/guided missile; **~ de curto/médio/longo alcance** short-/medium-/long-range missile
missionário, -a [misjo'narju, a] M/F missionary
missiva [mi'siva] F missive
missões [mi'sõjʃ] FPL *de* **missão**
mister [miʃ'teʳ] M (*ocupação*) occupation; (*trabalho*) job; **ser ~** to be necessary; **ter-se ~ de algo** to need sth; **não há ~ de** there's no need for
mistério [miʃ'terju] M mystery; **fazer ~ de algo** to make a mystery of sth; **não ter ~** to be straightforward; **misterioso, -a** [miʃte'rjozu, ɔza] ADJ mysterious
misticismo [miʃtʃi'siʒmu] M mysticism
místico, -a ['miʃtʃiku, a] ADJ, M/F mystic

mistificar [miʃtʃifi'kaʳ] VT, VI to fool
misto, -a ['miʃtu, a] ADJ mixed; (*confuso*) mixed up; (*escola*) mixed ■ M mixture; **misto-quente** (*pl* **mistos-quentes**) M toasted cheese and ham sandwich
mistura [miʃ'tura] F mixture; (*ato*) mixing
misturada [miʃtu'rada] F jumble
misturar [miʃtu'raʳ] VT to mix; (*confundir*) to mix up; **misturar-se** VR: **misturar-se com** to mix in with, mingle with
mítico, -a ['mitʃiku, a] ADJ mythical
mitificar [mitʃifi'kaʳ] VT to mythicize; (*mulher, estrela*) to idolize
mitigar [mitʃi'gaʳ] VT (*raiva*) to temper; (*dor*) to relieve; (*sede*) to lessen
mito ['mitu] M myth
mitologia [mitolo'ʒia] F mythology
mitológico, -a [mito'lɔʒiku, a] ADJ mythological
miudezas [mju'dezaʃ] FPL minutiae; (*bugigangas*) odds and ends; (*objetos pequenos*) trinkets
miúdo, -a ['mjudu, a] ADJ (*pequeno*) tiny, minute ■ M/F (PT: *criança*) youngster, kid; **miúdos** MPL (*dinheiro*) change *sg*; (*de aves*) giblets; **dinheiro ~** small change; **trocar em ~s** (*fig*) to spell it out
mixa ['miʃa] (*col*) ADJ (*insignificante*) measly; (*de má qualidade*) crummy; (*festa*) dull
mixagem [mik'saʒẽ] F mixing
mixar¹ [mi'ʃaʳ] VT to mess up ■ VI (*gorar*) to go down the drain; (*acabar*) to finish
mixar² [mik'saʳ] VT (*sons*) to mix
mixaria [miʃa'ria] (*col*) F (*coisa sem valor*) trifle; (*insignificância*) trivial matter
mixórdia [mi'ʃɔxdʒja] F mess, jumble
MJ ABR M = **Ministério da Justiça**
MM ABR M = **Ministério da Marinha**
mm ABR (= *milímetro*) mm
MME (BR) ABR M = **Ministério de Minas e Energia**
mnemônico, -a [mne'moniku, a] ADJ mnemonic
mo [mu] PRON = **me + o**
mó [mɔ] F (*de moinho*) millstone; (*para afiar*) grindstone
moa *etc* ['moa] VB V **moer**
moagem ['mwaʒẽ] F grinding
móbil ['mɔbiw] (*pl* **-eis**) ADJ = **móvel**
mobilar [mobi'laʳ] (PT) VT to furnish
móbile ['mɔbili] M mobile
mobília [mo'bilja] F furniture; **mobiliar** [mobi'ljaʳ] (BR) VT to furnish
mobiliária [mobi'ljarja] F furniture shop
mobiliário [mobi'ljarju] M furnishings *pl*
mobilidade [mobili'dadʒi] F mobility; (*fig: de espírito*) changeability
mobilização [mobiliza'sãw] F mobilization
mobilizar [mobili'zaʳ] VT to mobilize; (*movimentar*) to move
Mobral [mo'braw] ABR M = **Movimento Brasileiro de Alfabetização**
moça ['mosa] F girl, young woman

moçada [mo'sada] F (*moços*) boys pl; (*moças*) girls pl

moçambicano, -a [mosãbi'kanu, a] ADJ, M/F Mozambican

Moçambique [mosã'biki] M Mozambique

moção [mo'sãw] (pl -ões) F motion

mocassim [moka'sĩ] (pl -ns) M moccasin; (*sapato esporte*) slip-on

mochila [mo'ʃila] F rucksack

mocidade [mosi'dadʒi] F youth; (*os moços*) young people pl

mocinho, -a [mo'siɲu, a] M/F little boy/girl ■ M (*herói*) hero, good guy

moço, -a ['mosu, a] ADJ young ■ M young man, lad; ~ **de bordo** ordinary seaman; ~ **de cavalariça** groom

moções [mo'sõjʃ] FPL de **moção**

mocorongo, -a [moko'rõgu, a] (*col*) M/F country bumpkin

moda ['mɔda] F fashion; **estar na** ~ to be in fashion, be all the rage; **fora da** ~ old-fashioned; **sair da** *ou* **cair de** ~ to go out of fashion; **a última** ~ the latest fashion; **à brasileira** in the Brazilian way; **ele faz tudo à sua** ~ he does everything his own way; **fazer** ~ to make up stories

modalidade [modali'dadʒi] F kind; (*Esporte*) event

modelagem [mode'laʒẽ] F modelling; ~ **do corpo** bodybuilding

modelar [mode'la'] VT to model; (*assinalar os contornos de*) to shape, highlight; **modelar-se** VR: **modelar(-se) a algo** to model o.s. on sth

modelista [mode'liʃta] M/F designer

modelo [mo'delu] M model; (*criação de estilista*) design

moderação [modera'sãw] (pl -ões) F moderation

moderado, -a [mode'radu, a] ADJ moderate; (*clima*) mild

moderar [mode'ra'] VT to moderate; (*violência*) to control, restrain; (*velocidade*) to reduce; (*voz*) to lower; (*gastos*) to cut down; **moderar-se** VR to control o.s.

modernidade [modexni'dadʒi] F modernity

modernismo [modex'niʒmu] M modernism

modernização [modexniza'sãw] (pl -ões) F modernization

modernizar [modexni'za'] VT to modernize; **modernizar-se** VR to modernize

moderno, -a [mo'dɛxnu, a] ADJ modern; (*atual*) present-day

modernoso, -a [modex'nozu, ɔza] ADJ newfangled

módess® [mɔdeʃ] (*col*) M INV sanitary towel (*Brit*) *ou* napkin (US)

modéstia [mo'dɛʃtʃja] F modesty

modesto, -a [mo'dɛʃtu, a] ADJ modest; (*simples*) simple, plain; (*vida*) frugal

módico, -a ['mɔdʒiku, a] ADJ moderate; (*preço*) reasonable; (*bens*) scant

modificação [modʒifika'sãw] (pl -ões) F modification

modificar [modʒifi'ka'] VT to modify, alter

modinha [mo'dʒiɲa] F popular song, tune

modismo [mo'dʒiʒmu] M idiom

modista [mo'dʒiʃta] F dressmaker

modo ['mɔdu] M (*maneira*) way, manner; (*método*) way; (*Ling*) mood; (*Mús*) mode; **modos** MPL (*comportamento*) manners; ~ **de pensar** way of thinking; **de (tal)** ~ **que** so (that); **de** ~ **nenhum** in no way; **de qualquer** ~ anyway, anyhow; **tenha** ~**s!** behave yourself!; **de** ~ **geral** in general; ~ **de andar** way of walking, walk; ~ **de escrever** style of writing; ~ **de emprego** instructions pl for use; ~ **de ser** way (of being), manner; ~ **de vida** way of life

modorra [mo'doxa] F (*sonolência*) drowsiness; (*letargia*) lethargy

modulação [modula'sãw] (pl -ões) F modulation; ~ **de freqüência** frequency modulation

modular [modu'la'] VT to modulate ■ ADJ modular

módulo ['mɔdulu] M module; ~ **lunar** lunar module

moeda ['mwɛda] F (*uma moeda*) coin; (*dinheiro*) currency; **uma** ~ **de 10p** a 10p piece; ~ **corrente** currency; **pagar na mesma** ~ to give tit for tat; **Casa da M**~ ≈ the Mint (*Brit*), ≈ the (US) Mint; ~ **falsa** forged money; ~ **forte** hard currency

moedor [moe'do'] M (*de café*) grinder; (*de carne*) mincer

moenda ['mwẽda] F grinding equipment

moer [mwe'] VT (*café*) to grind; (*cana*) to crush; (*bater*) to beat; (*cansar*) to tire out

mofado, -a [mo'fadu, a] ADJ mouldy (*Brit*), moldy (US)

mofar [mo'fa'] VI to go mouldy (*Brit*) *ou* moldy (US); (*na prisão*) to rot; (*ficar esperando*) to hang around; (*zombar*) to mock, scoff ■ VT to cover in mo(u)ld

mofo ['mofu] M (*Bot*) mould (*Brit*), mold (US); **cheiro de** ~ musty smell

mogno ['mɔgnu] M mahogany

mói *etc* [mɔj] VB V **moer**

moía *etc* [mo'ia] VB V **moer**

moído, -a [mo'idu, a] PP de **moer** ■ ADJ (*café*) ground; (*carne*) minced; (*cansado*) tired out; (*corpo*) aching

moinho ['mwiɲu] M mill; (*de café*) grinder; ~ **de vento** windmill

moisés [moj'zɛʃ] M INV carry-cot

moita ['mɔjta] F thicket; ~**!** mum's the word!; **na** ~ (*fig*) on the quiet; **ficar na** ~ (*fazer segredo*) to keep quiet, not say a word; (*ficar na expectativa*) to stand by

mola ['mɔla] F (*Tec*) spring; (*fig*) motive,

NB: *European Portuguese adds the following consonants to certain words:* **b** (sú(b)dito, su(b)til); **c** (a(c)ção, a(c)cionista, a(c)to); **m** (inde(m)ne); **p** (ado(p)çã, ado(p)tar); *for further details see p. xiii.*

motivation

molambo [mo'lãbu] M rag

molar [mo'laʳ] M molar (tooth)

moldar [mow'daʳ] VT to mould (Brit), mold (US); (metal) to cast; (fig) to mo(u)ld, shape

Moldávia [mow'davja] F: **a ~** Moldavia

molde ['mɔwdʒi] M mould (Brit), mold (US); (de papel) pattern; (fig) model; **~ de vestido** dress pattern

moldura [mow'dura] F (de pintura) frame; (ornato) moulding (Brit), molding (US)

moldurar [mowdu'raʳ] VT to frame

mole ['mɔli] ADJ (macio, fofo) soft; (sem energia) listless; (carnes) flabby; (col: fácil) easy; (pessoa: sentimental) soft; (lento) slow; (preguiçoso) sluggish ■ ADV (facilmente) easily; (lentamente) slowly

moleca [mo'lɛka] F urchin; (menina) youngster

molecada [mole'kada] F urchins pl

molecagem [mole'kaʒẽ] (pl -ns) F (de criança) prank; (sujeira) dirty trick; (brincadeira) joke

molécula [mo'lɛkula] F molecule

molecular [moleku'laʳ] ADJ molecular

molejo [mo'leʒu] M (de carro) suspension; (col: de pessoa) wiggle

moleque [mo'lɛki] M (de rua) urchin; (menino) youngster; (pessoa sem palavra) unreliable person; (canalha) scoundrel ■ ADJ (levado) mischievous; (brincalhão) funny

molestar [moleʃ'taʳ] VT (ofender) to upset; (enfadar) to annoy; (importunar) to bother

moléstia [mo'lɛʃtʃja] F illness

molesto, -a [mo'lɛʃtu, a] ADJ tiresome; (prejudicial) unhealthy

moletom [mole'tõ] (pl -ns) M (de lã) fleece; (de algodão) sweatshirt material; **blusa de ~** sweatshirt

moleza [mo'leza] F softness; (falta de energia) listlessness; (falta de força) weakness; **ser (uma) ~** (col) to be easy; **na ~** without exerting oneself

molhada [mo'ʎada] F soaking

molhado, -a [mo'ʎadu, a] ADJ wet, damp

molhar [mo'ʎaʳ] VT to wet; (de leve) to moisten, dampen; (mergulhar) to dip; **molhar-se** VR to get wet; (col: urinar) to wet o.s.

molhe ['moʎi] (PT) M jetty; (cais) wharf, quay

molheira [mo'ʎejra] F sauce boat; (para carne) gravy boat

molho[1] ['mɔʎu] M (de chaves) bunch; (de trigo) sheaf

molho[2] ['moʎu] M (Culin) sauce; (: de salada) dressing; (: de carne) gravy; **pôr de ~** to soak; **estar/deixar de ~** (roupa etc) to be/leave to soak; **estar/ficar de ~** (fig) to be/stay in bed; **~ branco** white sauce; **~ inglês** Worcester sauce

molinete [moli'netʃi] M reel; (caniço) fishing rod

molóide [mo'lɔjdʒi] (col) ADJ slow ■ M/F lazy-bones

molusco [mo'luʃku] M mollusc (Brit), mollusk (US)

momentâneo, -a [momẽ'tanju, a] ADJ momentary

momento [mo'mẽtu] M moment; (Tec)

momentum; **a todo ~** constantly; **de um ~ para outro** suddenly; **no ~ em que** just as; **no/neste ~** at the/this moment; **a qualquer ~** at any moment

Mônaco ['monaku] M Monaco

monarca [mo'naxka] M/F monarch, ruler

monarquia [monax'kia] F monarchy

monarquista [monax'kiʃta] ADJ, M/F monarchist

monastério [monaʃ'tɛrju] M monastery

monástico, -a [mo'naʃtʃiku, a] ADJ monastic

monção [mõ'sãw] (pl -ões) F monsoon

mondar [mõ'daʳ] (PT) VT (ervas daninhas) to pull up; (árvores) to prune; (fig) to weed out

monetário, -a [mone'tarju, a] ADJ monetary; **correção monetária** currency adjustment

monetarismo [moneta'riʒmu] M monetarism

monetarista [moneta'riʃta] ADJ, M/F monetarist

monge ['mõʒi] M monk

mongol [mõ'gɔw] (pl -óis) ADJ, M/F Mongol, Mongolian

Mongólia [mõ'gɔlja] F: **a ~** Mongolia

mongolismo [mõgo'liʒmu] M (Med) mongolism

mongolóide [mõgo'lɔjdʒi] ADJ, M/F (ofensivo) mongol

monitor [moni'toʳ] M monitor

monitorar [monito'raʳ] VT to monitor

monitorizar [monitori'zaʳ] VT = **monitorar**

monja ['mõʒa] F nun

monocromo, -a [mono'krɔmu, a] ADJ monochrome

monóculo [mo'nɔkulu] M monocle

monocultura [monokuw'tura] F monoculture

monogamia [monoga'mia] F monogamy

monógamo, -a [mo'nɔgamu, a] ADJ monogamous

monograma [mono'grama] M monogram

monologar [monolo'gaʳ] VI to talk to o.s.; (Teatro) to speak a monologue ■ VT to say to o.s.

monólogo [mo'nɔlogu] M monologue

monoplano [mono'planu] M monoplane

monopólio [mono'pɔlju] M monopoly; **monopolizar** [monopoli'zaʳ] VT to monopolize

monossilábico, -a [monosi'labiku, a] ADJ monosyllabic

monossílabo [mono'silabu] M monosyllable; **responder por ~s** to reply in monosyllables

monotonia [monoto'nia] F monotony;

monótono, -a [mo'nɔtonu, a] ADJ monotonous

monotrilho [mono'triʎu] M monorail

monóxido [mo'nɔksidu] M: **~ de carbono** carbon monoxide

monsenhor [mõse'ɲoʳ] M monsignor

monstro, -a ['mõʃtru, a] ADJ INV giant ■ M (tb fig) monster; **~ sagrado** superstar

monstruosidade [mõʃtrwozi'dadʒi] F monstrosity

monstruoso, -a [mõ'ʃtrwozu, ɔza] ADJ monstrous; (enorme) gigantic, huge

monta ['mõta] F: **de pouca ~** trivial, of little account

montador, a [mõta'do^r(a)] M/F (Cinema) editor
montagem [mõ'taʒẽ] (pl -ns) F assembly; (Arq) erection; (Cinema) editing; (Teatro) production
montanha [mõ'taɲa] F mountain; **montanha-russa** F roller coaster
montanhês, -esa [mõta'ɲeʃ, eza] ADJ mountain atr ■ M/F highlander
montanhismo [mõta'ɲiʒmu] M mountaineering
montanhista [mõta'ɲiʃta] M/F mountaineer ■ ADJ mountaineering
montanhoso, -a [mõta'ɲozu, ɔza] ADJ mountainous
montante [mõ'tãtʃi] M amount, sum ■ ADJ (maré) rising; **a ~** (nadar) upstream
montão [mõ'tãw] (pl -ões) M heap, pile
montar [mõ'ta^r] VT (cavalo) to mount, get on; (colocar em) to put on; (cavalgar) to ride; (peças) to assemble, put together; (loja, máquina) to set up; (casa) to put up; (peça teatral) to put on ■ VI to ride; **~ a** ou **em** (animal) to get on; (cavalgar) to ride; (despesa) to come to
montaria [mõta'ria] F (cavalgadura) mount
monte ['mõtʃi] M hill; (pilha) heap, pile; **um ~ de** (muitos) a lot of, lots of; **gente aos ~s** loads of people
montepio [mõtʃi'piu] M (pensão) pension; (fundo) trust fund
montês [mõ'teʃ] ADJ: **cabra ~** mountain goat
Montevidéu [mõtʃivi'dɛw] N Montevideo
montoeira [mõ'twejra] F stack
montões [mõ'tõjʃ] MPL de **montão**
montra ['mõtra] (PT) F shop window
monumental [monumẽ'taw] (pl -ais) ADJ monumental; (fig) magnificent, splendid
monumento [monu'mẽtu] M monument
moqueca [mo'kɛka] F fish or seafood simmered in coconut cream and palm oil; **~ de camarão** prawn moqueca
morada [mo'rada] F home, residence; (PT: endereço) address; **moradia** [mora'dʒia] F home, dwelling; **morador, a** [mora'do^r(a)] M/F (de casa, bairro) resident; (de casa alugada) tenant
moral [mo'raw] (pl -ais) ADJ moral ■ F (ética) ethics pl; (conclusão) moral ■ M (de pessoa) sense of morality; (ânimo) morale; **levantar o ~** to raise morale; **estar de ~ baixa** to be demoralized; **~ da história** moral of the story; **moralidade** [morali'dadʒi] F morality
moralista [mora'liʃta] ADJ moralistic ■ M/F moralist
moralizar [morali'za^r] VI to moralize ■ VT to preach at
morango [mo'rãgu] M strawberry
morangueiro [morã'gejru] M strawberry plant
morar [mo'ra^r] VI to live, reside; (col: entender) to catch on; **~ em algo** (col) to grasp sth; **morou?** got it?, see?
moratória [mora'tɔrja] F moratorium

morbidez [moxbi'deʒ] F morbidness
mórbido, -a ['mɔxbidu, a] ADJ morbid
morcego [mox'segu] M (Bio) bat
morcela [mox'sɛla] (PT) F black pudding (Brit), blood sausage (US)
mordaça [mox'dasa] F (de animal) muzzle; (fig) gag
mordaz [mox'daʒ] ADJ scathing
morder [mox'de^r] VT to bite; (corroer) to corrode; **morder-se** VR to bite o.s.; **~ a língua** to bite one's tongue; **~-se de inveja** to be green with envy; **mordida** [mox'dʒida] F bite
mordomia [moxdo'mia] F (de executivos) perk; (col: regalia) luxury, comfort
mordomo [mox'dɔmu] M butler
morenaço, -a [more'nasu, a] M/F dark beauty
moreno, -a [mo'renu, a] ADJ dark(-skinned); (de cabelos) dark(-haired); (de tomar sol) brown ■ M/F dark person; **ela é loura ou morena?** is she a blonde or a brunette?
morfina [mox'fina] F morphine
morfologia [moxfolo'ʒia] F morphology
morgada [mox'gada] (PT) F heiress
morgado [mox'gadu] (PT) M (herdeiro) heir; (filho mais velho) eldest son; (propriedade) entailed estate
moribundo, -a [mori'būdu, a] ADJ dying
morigerado, -a [moriʒe'radu, a] ADJ upright
moringa [mo'rĩga] F water-cooler
mormacento, -a [moxma'sẽtu, a] ADJ sultry
mormaço [mox'masu] M sultry weather
mormente [mox'mẽtʃi] ADV chiefly, especially
mórmon ['mɔxmõ] M/F Mormon
morno, -a ['moxnu, 'mɔxna] ADJ lukewarm, tepid
morosidade [morozi'dadʒi] F slowness
moroso, -a [mo'rozu, ɔza] ADJ slow, sluggish
morrer [mo'xe^r] VI to die; (luz, cor) to fade; (fogo) to die down; (Auto) to stall; **~ de rir** to kill o.s. laughing; **estou morrendo de fome/inveja/medo/saudades** I'm starving/green with envy/scared stiff/really missing you (ou him, home etc); **~ de amores por alguém** to be mad about sb; **estou morrendo de vontade de fazer** I'm dying to do; **~ atropelado/afogado** to be knocked down and killed/drown; **lindo de ~** (col) stunning; **~ em** (col: pagar) to fork out
morrinha [mo'xiɲa] F (fedor) stench ■ M/F (col: chato) pain (in the neck) ■ ADJ (col) boring
morro ['moxu] M hill; (favela) shanty town, slum
mortadela [moxta'dɛla] F salami
mortal [mox'taw] (pl -ais) ADJ mortal; (letal, insuportável) deadly ■ M mortal; **restos mortais** mortal remains
mortalha [mox'taʎa] F shroud
mortalidade [moxtali'dadʒi] F mortality; **~ infantil** infant mortality
mortandade [moxtã'dadʒi] F slaughter

NB: European Portuguese adds the following consonants to certain words: **b** (sú(b)dito, su(b)til); **c** (a(c)ção, a(c)cionista, a(c)to); **m** (inde(m)ne); **p** (ado(p)çã, ado(p)tar); for further details see p. xiii.

morte ['mɔxtʃi] F death; **pena de ~** death penalty; **ser de ~** (fig) to be impossible; **estar às portas da ~** to be at death's door; **pensar na ~ da bezerra** (fig) to be miles away

morteiro [mox'tejru] M mortar

mortiço, -a [mox'tʃisu, a] ADJ (olhar) dull; (desanimado) lifeless; (luz) dimming

mortífero, -a [mox'tʃiferu, a] ADJ deadly, lethal

mortificar [moxtʃifi'kaʳ] VT (torturar) to torture; (afligir) to annoy, torment

morto, -a ['moxtu, 'mɔxta] PP de **matar**; **morrer** ■ ADJ (cor) dull; (exausto) exhausted; (inexpressivo) lifeless ■ M/F dead man/woman; **cem/os ~s** a hundred/the dead; **estar ~** to be dead; **ser ~** to be killed; **estar ~ de inveja** to be green with envy; **estar ~ de vontade de** to be dying to; **~ de medo/cansaço** scared stiff/dead tired; **nem ~!** not on your life!, no way!; **~ da silva** (col) dead as a doornail

mos [muʃ] PRON = **me + os**

mosaico [mo'zajku] M mosaic

mosca ['moʃka] F fly; **estar às ~s** (bar etc) to be deserted

mosca-morta (pl **moscas-mortas**) (col) M/F (pessoa) stiff

Moscou [moʃ'ku] (BR) N Moscow

Moscovo [moʃ'kovu] (PT) N Moscow

mosquitada [moʃki'tada] F load of mosquitos

mosquiteiro [moʃki'tejru] M mosquito net

mosquito [moʃ'kitu] M mosquito

mossa ['mɔsa] F dent; (fig) impression

mostarda [moʃ'taxda] F mustard

mosteiro [moʃ'tejru] M monastery; (de monjas) convent

mosto ['moʃtu] M (do vinho) must

mostra ['mɔʃtra] F (exibição) display; (sinal) sign, indication; **dar ~s de** to show signs of

mostrador [moʃtra'doʳ] M (de relógio) face, dial

mostrar [moʃ'traʳ] VT to show; (mercadorias) to display; (provar) to demonstrate, prove; **mostrar-se** VR to show o.s. to be; (exibir-se) to show off

mostruário [moʃ'trwarju] M display case

mote ['mɔtʃi] M motto

motéis [mo'tɛw] MPL de **motel**

motejar [mote'ʒaʳ] VI: **~ de** (zombar) to jeer at, make fun of

motejo [mo'teʒu] M mockery, derision

motel [mo'tɛw] (pl **-éis**) M motel

motilidade [motʃili'dadʒi] F mobility

motim [mo'tʃĩ] (pl **-ns**) M riot, revolt; (militar) mutiny

motivação [motʃiva'sãw] (pl **-ões**) F motivation

motivado, -a [motʃi'vadu, a] ADJ (causado) caused; (pessoa) motivated

motivar [motʃi'vaʳ] VT (causar) to cause, bring about; (estimular) to motivate; **motivo** [mo'tʃivu] (causa): **motivo (de** ou **para)** cause (of), ~on (for); (fim) motive; (Arte, Mús) motif; **ser ~o de riso** etc to be a cause of laughter etc; **~tivo de algo a alguém** to give sb cause **~r motivo de** because of, owing to;

sem motivo for no reason

moto ['mɔtu] F motorbike ■ M (lema) motto; **de ~ próprio** of one's own accord

motoca [mo'tɔka] (col) F motorbike, bike

motocicleta [motosi'kleta] F motorcycle, motorbike

motociclismo [motosi'kliʒmu] M motorcycling

motociclista [motosi'kliʃta] M/F motorcyclist

motociclo [moto'siklu] (PT) M = **motocicleta**

motoneta [moto'neta] F (motor-)scooter

motoniveladora [motonivela'dora] F bulldozer

motoqueiro, -a [moto'kejru, a] (col) M/F biker, motorcyclist

motor, -triz [mo'toʳ] ADJ (Tec) driving; (Anat) motor ■ M motor; (de carro, avião) engine; **~ de arranque** starter (motor); **~ de explosão** internal combustion engine; **~ de popa** outboard motor; **~ diesel** diesel engine; **com ~ motorizado**; **~ de pesquisa** (PT: Comput) search engine

motorista [moto'riʃta] M/F driver

motorizado, -a [motori'zadu, a] ADJ motorized; (col: com carro) motorized, driving

motorizar [motori'zaʳ] VT to motorize; **motorizar-se** VR to get a car

motorneiro, -a [motox'nejru, a] M/F tram (Brit) ou streetcar (US) driver

motosserra [moto'sɛxa] F chain-saw

motriz [mo'triʒ] F de **motor**; **força motriz** driving force

mouco, -a ['moku, a] ADJ deaf, hard of hearing; **fazer ouvido ~** to pretend not to hear

movediço, -a [move'dʒisu, a] ADJ easily moved; (instável) unsteady; v tb **areia**

móvel ['mɔvew] (pl **-eis**) ADJ movable ■ M (peça de mobília) piece of furniture; **móveis** MPL (mobília) furniture sg; **bens móveis** personal property; **móveis e utensílios** (Com) fixtures and fittings

mover [mo'veʳ] VT to move; (cabeça) to shake; (mecanismo: acionar) to drive; (campanha) to start (up); **mover-se** VR to move; **~ uma ação** to start a lawsuit; **~ alguém a fazer** to move sb to do

movido, -a [mo'vidu, a] ADJ moved; (impelido) powered; (causado) caused; **~ a álcool** alcohol-powered

movimentação [movimẽta'sãw] (pl **-ões**) F movement; (na rua) bustle

movimentado, -a [movimẽ'tadu, a] ADJ (rua, lugar) busy; (pessoa) active; (show, música) up-tempo

movimentar [movimẽ'taʳ] VT to move; (animar) to liven up

movimento [movi'mẽtu] M movement; (Tec) motion; (na rua) activity, bustle; **de muito ~** (loja, rua etc) busy; **pôr algo em ~** to set sth in motion

movível [mo'vivew] (pl **-eis**) ADJ movable

MPAS (BR) ABR M = **Ministério da Previdência e Assistência Social**

MPB ABR F = **Música Popular Brasileira**

MPlan (BR) ABR M = **Ministério do Planejamento**

MRE(BR) ABR M = **Ministério das Relações Exteriores**
MS(BR) ABR = **Mato Grosso do Sul** ■ ABR M = **Ministério da Saúde**
MT(BR) ABR M = **Mato Grosso** ■ ABR M = **Ministério dos Transportes**
MTb(BR) ABR M = **Ministério do Trabalho**
muamba['mwãba] (col) F (contrabando) contraband; (objetos roubados) loot
muambeiro, -a[mwã'bejru, a] M/F smuggler; (de objetos roubados) fence
muar[mwa⁣ʳ] M/F mule
muco['muku] M mucus
mucosa[mu'kɔza] F (Anat) mucous membrane
muçulmano, -a[musuw'manu, a] ADJ, M/F Moslem
muda['muda] F (planta) seedling; (vestuário) outfit; ~ **de roupa** change of clothes
mudança[mu'dãsa] F change; (de casa) move; (Auto) gear
mudar[mu'da⁣ʳ] VT to change; (deslocar) to move ■ VI to change; (ave) to moult (Brit), molt (US); **mudar-se** VR (de casa) to move (away); ~ **de roupa/de assunto** to change clothes/the subject; ~ **de casa** to move (house); ~ **de idéia** to change one's mind
mudez[mu'deʒ] F muteness; (silêncio) silence
mudo, -a['mudu, a] ADJ dumb; (calado, Cinema) silent; (telefone) dead ■ M/F mute
mugido[mu'ʒidu] M moo
mugir[mu'ʒi⁣ʳ] VI (vaca) to moo, low
mugunzá[mugũ'za] M = **munguzá**

O PALAVRA CHAVE

muito, -a['mwĩtu, a] ADJ (quantidade) a lot of; (: em frase negativa ou interrogativa) much; (número) lots of, a lot of; many; **muito esforço** a lot of effort; **faz muito calor** it's very hot; **muito tempo** a long time; **muitas amigas** lots ou a lot of friends; **muitas vezes** often
■ PRON a lot; (em frase negativa ou interrogativa: sg) much; (: pl) many; **tenho muito que fazer** I've got a lot to do; **muitos dizem que ...** a lot of people say that ...
■ ADV **1** a lot; (+ adj) very; (+ compar): **muito melhor** much ou far ou a lot better; **gosto muito disto** I like it a lot; **sinto muito** I'm very sorry; **muito interessante** very interesting
2 (resposta) very; **está cansado? — muito** are you tired? — very
3 (tempo): **muito depois** long after; **há muito** a long time ago; **não demorou muito** it didn't take long

mula['mula] F mule
mulato, -a[mu'latu, a] ADJ, M/F mulatto
muleta[mu'leta] F crutch; (fig) support
mulher[mu'ʎe⁣ʳ] F woman; (esposa) wife; ~ **da**

vida prostitute
mulheraço[muʎe'rasu] M fantastic woman
mulherão[muʎe'rãw] (pl -ões) M = **mulheraço**
mulher-bomba(pl mulheres-bomba) F suicide bomber
mulherengo[muʎe'rẽgu] M womanizer ■ ADJ womanizing
mulherio[muʎe'riu] M women pl
multa['muwta] F fine; **levar uma** ~ to be fined; **multar**[muw'ta⁣ʳ] VT to fine; **multar alguém em $1000** to fine sb $1000
multi...[muwtʃi] PREFIXO multi...
multicolor[muwtʃiko'lo⁣ʳ] ADJ multicoloured (Brit), multicolored (US)
multidão[muwtʃi'dãw] (pl -ões) F crowd; **uma** ~ **de** (muitos) lots of
multiforme[muwtʃi'fɔxme] ADJ manifold, multifarious
multilateral[muwtʃilate'raw] (pl -ais) ADJ multilateral
multimídia[muwtʃi'midʒia] ADJ multimedia
multimilionário, -a[muwtʃimiljo'narju, a] ADJ, M/F multimillionaire
multinacional[muwtʃinasjo'naw] (pl -ais) ADJ, F multinational
multiplicação[muwtʃiplika'sãw] F multiplication
multiplicar[muwtʃipli'ka⁣ʳ] VT (Mat) to multiply; (aumentar) to increase
multiplicidade[muwtʃiplisi'dadʒi] F multiplicity
múltiplo, -a['muwtʃiplu, a] ADJ multiple ■ M multiple; **múltipla escolha** multiple choice
multirracial[muwtʃixa'sjaw] (pl -ais) ADJ multiracial
multiusuário, -a[muwtʃju'zwarju, a] ADJ (Comput) multiuser
múmia['mumja] F mummy; (fig) plodder
mundano, -a[mũ'danu, a] ADJ worldly
mundial[mũ'dʒjaw] (pl -ais) ADJ worldwide; (guerra, recorde) world atr ■ M (campeonato) world championship; **o** ~ **de futebol** the World Cup
mundo['mũdu] M world; **todo o** ~ everybody; **um** ~ **de** lots of, a great many; **correr** ~ to see the world; **vir ao** ~ to come into the world; **como este** ~ **é pequeno!** (what a) small world!; **desde que o** ~ **é** ~ since time immemorial; **~s e fundos** (quantia altíssima) the earth; **prometer** **~s e fundos** to promise the earth; **tinha meio** ~ **no comício** there were loads of people at the rally; **com esta notícia meu** ~ **veio abaixo** the news shattered my world; **abarcar o** ~ **com as pernas** (fig) to take on too much; **Novo/Velho/ Terceiro M**~ New/Old/Third World
munguzá[mũgu'za] M corn meal
munheca[mu'ɲeka] F wrist
munição[muni'sãw] (pl -ões) F (de armas) ammunition; (chumbo) shot; (Mil) munitions pl, supplies pl

NB: European Portuguese adds the following consonants to certain words: **b** (sú(b)dito, su(b)til); **c** (a(c)ção, a(c)cionista, a(c)to); **m** (inde(m)ne); **p** (ado(p)çã, ado(p)tar); for further details see p. xiii.

municipal | MVR

municipal [munisi'paw] (pl -ais) ADJ municipal
municipalidade [munisipali'dadʒi] F local authority
município [muni'sipju] M local authority; (cidade) town; (condado) county
munições [muni'sõjʃ] FPL de **munição**
munir [mu'ni^r] VT: ~ **de** to provide with, supply with; **munir-se** VR: **munir-se de** (provisões) to equip o.s. with; (paciência) to arm o.s. with
mural [mu'raw] (pl -ais) ADJ, M mural
muralha [mu'raʎa] F (de fortaleza) rampart; (muro) wall
murchar [mux'ʃa^r] VT (Bot) to wither; (sentimentos) to dull; (pessoa) to sadden ■ VI (Bot) to wither, wilt; (fig) to fade; (: pessoa) to grow sad
murcho, -a ['muxʃu, a] ADJ (planta) wilting; (esvaziado) shrunken; (fig) languid, resigned
murmuração [muxmura'sãw] F muttering; (maledicência) gossiping
murmurante [muxmu'rãtʃi] ADJ murmuring
murmurar [muxmu'ra^r] VI (segredar) to murmur, whisper; (queixar-se) to mutter, grumble; (água) to ripple; (folhagem) to rustle ■ VT to murmur
murmurinho [muxmu'riɲu] M (de vozes) murmuring; (som confuso) noise; (de folhas) rustling; (de água) trickling
murmúrio [mux'murju] M murmuring, whispering; (queixa) grumbling; (de água) rippling; (de folhagem) rustling
muro ['muru] M wall
murro ['muxu] M punch, sock; **dar um ~ em alguém** to punch sb; **levar um ~ de alguém** to be punched by sb; **dar ~ em ponta de faca** (fig) to bash one's head against a brick wall
musa ['muza] F muse
musculação [muʃkula'sãw] F body-building
muscular [muʃku'la^r] ADJ muscular
musculatura [muʃkula'tura] F musculature

músculo ['muʃkulu] M muscle; **musculoso, -a** [muʃku'lozu, ɔza] ADJ muscular
museu [mu'zew] M museum; (de pintura) gallery
musgo ['muʒgu] M moss
musgoso, -a [muʒ'gozu, ɔza] ADJ mossy
música ['muzika] F music; (canção) song; **dançar conforme a ~** (fig) to play the game; **~ de câmara** chamber music; **~ de fundo** background music; **~ erudita** classical music; v tb **músico**
musicado, -a [muzi'kadu, a] ADJ set to music
musical [muzi'kaw] (pl -ais) ADJ, M musical; **fundo ~** background music
musicalidade [muzikali'dadʒi] F musicality
músico, -a ['muziku, a] ADJ musical ■ M/F musician
musse ['musi] F mousse
musselina [muse'lina] F muslin
mutação [muta'sãw] (pl -ões) F change, alteration; (Bio) mutation
mutável [mu'tavew] (pl -eis) ADJ changeable
mutilação [mutʃila'sãw] F mutilation; (de texto) cutting
mutilado, -a [mutʃi'ladu, a] ADJ mutilated; (pessoa) maimed ■ M/F cripple
mutilar [mutʃi'la^r] VT to mutilate; (pessoa) to maim; (texto) to cut; (árvore) to strip
mutirão [mutʃi'rãw] (pl -ões) M collective effort
mútua ['mutwa] F loan company
mutuante [mu'twãtʃi] M/F lender
mutuário, -a [mu'twarju, a] M/F borrower
mútuo, -a ['mutwu, a] ADJ mutual
muxiba [mu'ʃiba] F (pelancas) wrinkled flesh; (carne para cães) dog meat; (seios) drooping breasts pl
muxoxo [mu'ʃoʃu] M tutting; **fazer ~** to tut
MVR (BR) ABR M = **Maior Valor de Referência**

Nn

N, n ['eni] (pl **ns**) M N, n; **N de Nair** N for Nelly
(Brit) ou Nan (US)

N ABR (= norte) N

n. ABR (= nascido) b; (: = nome) name

ñ ABR = **não**

na [na] = **em + a**

-na [na] PRON her; (coisa) it

nabo ['nabu] M turnip

nac. ABR (= nacional) nat

nação [na'sãw] (pl -ões) F nation; **as Nações Unidas** the United Nations

nácar ['naka^r] M mother-of-pearl; (cor) pink

nacional [nasjo'naw] (pl -ais) ADJ national; (carro, vinho etc) domestic, home-produced;
nacionalidade [nasjonali'dadʒi] F nationality;
nacionalismo [nasjona'liʒmu] M nationalism;
nacionalista [nasjona'liʃta] ADJ, M/F nationalist

nacionalização [nasjonaliza'sãw] (pl -ões) F nationalization

nacionalizar [nasjonali'za^r] VT to nationalize

naco ['naku] M piece, chunk

nações [na'sõjʃ] FPL de **nação**

nada ['nada] PRON nothing ■ M nothingness; (pessoa) nonentity ■ ADV at all; **não dizer ~** to say nothing, not to say anything; **antes de mais ~** first of all; **não é ~ difícil** it's not at all hard, it's not hard at all; **~ mais** nothing else; **quase ~** hardly anything; **~ de novo** nothing new; **~ feito** nothing doing; **~ mau** not bad (at all); **obrigado -- de ~** thank you -- not at all ou don't mention it; **(que) ~!**, **~ disso!** nonsense!, not at all!; **não foi ~** it was nothing; **por ~ nesse mundo** (not) for love nor money; **ele fez o que você pediu? -- fez ~!** did he do as you asked? -- no, he did not!; **não ser de ~** (col) to be a dead loss; **é uma coisinha de ~** it's nothing; **de ~ (à-toa)** trifling; **discutimos por um ~** we argued over nothing

nadada [na'dada] F swim; **dar uma ~** to go for a swim

nadadeira [nada'dejra] F (de peixe) fin; (de golfinho, foca, mergulhador) flipper

nadador, a [nada'do^r(a)] ADJ swimming

■ M/F swimmer

nadar [na'da^r] VI to swim; **~ em** to be dripping with; **estar ou ficar nadando** (fig) to be out of it, be out of one's depth; **ele está nadando em dinheiro** he's rolling in money

nádegas ['nadegaʃ] FPL buttocks

nadinha [na'dʒiɲa] PRON absolutely nothing

nado ['nadu] M: **a ~** swimming; **atravessar a ~** to swim across; **~ borboleta** butterfly (stroke); **~ de cachorrinho** doggy paddle; **~ de costas** backstroke; **~ de peito** breastroke; **~ livre** freestyle

naftalina [nafta'lina] F naphthaline

náilon ['najilõ] M nylon

naipe ['najpi] M (cartas) suit; (fig: categoria) order

Nairobi [naj'rɔbi] N Nairobi

namoradeira [namora'dejra] ADJ flirtatious

■ F flirt

namorado, -a [namo'radu, a] M/F boyfriend/girlfriend

namorador, a [namora'do^r(a)] ADJ flirtatious

■ M ladies' man

namorar [namo'ra^r] VT (ser namorado de) to be going out with; (cobiçar) to covet; (fitar) to stare longingly at ■ VI (casal) to go out together; (homem, mulher) to have a boyfriend (ou girlfriend)

namoricar [namori'ka^r] VT to flirt with ■ VI to flirt

namoro [na'moru] M relationship

nanar [na'na^r] (col) VI to sleep, kip

nanico, -a [na'niku, a] ADJ tiny

nanquim [nã'kĩ] M Indian ink

não [nãw] ADV not; (resposta) no ■ M no; **~ sei** I don't know; **~ muito** not much; **~ só ... mas também** not only ... but also; **agora ~** not now; **~ tem de quê** don't mention it; **~ é?** isn't it?, won't you? (etc, segundo o verbo precedente); **eles são brasileiros, ~ é?** they're Brazilian, aren't they?

não- [nãw-] PREFIXO non-

não-agressão F: **pacto de ~** non-aggression treaty

não-alinhado, -a ADJ non-aligned

NB: European Portuguese adds the following consonants to certain words: **b** (sú(b)dito, su(b)til); **c** (a(c)ção, a(c)cionista, a(c)to); **m** (inde(m)ne); **p** (ado(p)çã, ado(p)tar); for further details see p. xiii.

não-conformista ADJ, M/F non-conformist
não-intervenção F non-intervention
napa ['napa] F napa leather
naquele(s), -la(s) [na'keli(ʃ), na'kɛla(ʃ)] = **em +**
aquele(s)
naquilo [na'kilu] = **em + aquilo**
narcisismo [naxsi'ziʒmu] M narcissism
narcisista [naxsi'ziʃta] ADJ narcissistic
narciso [nax'sizu] M (Bot) narcissus; ~ **dos**
prados daffodil
narcótico, -a [nax'kɔtʃiku, a] ADJ narcotic ■ M
narcotic
narcotizar [naxkotʃi'zaʳ] VT to drug; (fig) to bore
narigudo, -a [nari'gudu, a] ADJ with a big nose;
ser ~ to have a big nose
narina [na'rina] F nostril
nariz [na'riʒ] M nose; ~ **adunco/arrebitado**
hook/snub nose; **meter o ~ em** to poke one's
nose into; **torcer o ~ para** to turn one's nose
up at; **ser dono/a do seu** ~ to know one's own
mind; **dar com o ~ na porta** (fig) to find (the)
doors closed to one
narração [naxa'sãw] (pl -ões) F narration;
(relato) account
narrador, a [naxa'doʳ(a)] M/F narrator
narrar [na'xaʳ] VT to narrate, recount
narrativa [naxa'tʃiva] F narrative; (história) story
narrativo, -a [naxa'tʃivu, a] ADJ narrative
nas [naʃ] = **em + as**
-nas [naʃ] PRON them
NASA ['naza] ABR F NASA
nasal [na'zaw] (pl -ais) ADJ nasal
nasalado, -a [naza'ladu, a] ADJ nasalized, nasal
nasalização [nazaliza'sãw] F nasalization
nascença [na'sẽsa] F birth; **de** ~ by birth; **ele é**
surdo de ~ he was born deaf
nascente [na'sẽtʃi] ADJ nascent ■ M East,
Orient ■ F (fonte) spring
nascer [na'seʳ] VI to be born; (plantas) to sprout;
(o sol) to rise; (ave) to hatch; (dente) to come
through; (fig: ter origem) to come into being
■ M: ~ **do sol** sunrise; ~ **de** (descender) to be born
of; (fig: originar-se) to be born out of; ~ **de novo**
(fig) to have a narrow escape, escape with
one's life; **não nasci ontem** I wasn't born
yesterday; ~ **em berço de ouro** to be born with
a silver spoon in one's mouth; **ele nasceu para**
médico etc he's a born doctor etc; **não nasci**
para fazer isto I wasn't cut out to do this
nascido, -a [na'sidu, a] ADJ born; **bem** ~ from a
good family
nascimento [nasi'mẽtu] M birth; (fig) origin;
(estirpe) descent
Nassau [na'saw] N Nassau
nata ['nata] F (Culin) cream; (elite) élite
natação [nata'sãw] F swimming
natais [na'tajʃ] ADJ PL de **natal**
Natal [na'taw] M Christmas; **Feliz** ~! Merry
Christmas!
natal [na'taw] (pl -ais) ADJ (relativo ao nascimento)
natal; (país) native; **cidade** ~ home town
natalício, -a [nata'lisju, a] ADJ: **aniversário** ~

birthday ■ M birthday
natalidade [natali'dadʒi] F: (índice de) ~ birth
rate
natalino, -a [nata'linu, a] ADJ Christmas atr
natividade [natʃivi'dadʒi] F nativity
nativo, -a [na'tʃivi, a] ADJ, M/F native
NATO ['natu] ABR F NATO
nato, -a ['natu, a] ADJ born
natural [natu'raw] (pl -ais) ADJ natural; (nativo)
native ■ M/F (nativo) native; **de tamanho**
~ full-scale; **ao** ~ (Culin) fresh, uncooked;
naturalidade [naturali'dadʒi] F naturalness;
falar com naturalidade to talk openly; **agir**
com a maior naturalidade to act as if nothing
had happened; **de naturalidade paulista** etc
born in São Paulo etc
naturalismo [natura'liʒmu] M naturalism
naturalista [natura'liʃta] ADJ, M/F naturalist
naturalização [naturaliza'sãw] F
naturalization
naturalizado, -a [naturali'zadu, a] ADJ
naturalized ■ M/F naturalized citizen
naturalizar [naturali'zaʳ] VT to naturalize;
naturalizar-se VR to become naturalized
naturalmente [naturaw'mẽtʃi] ADV naturally;
~! of course!
natureza [natu'reza] F nature; (espécie) kind,
type; ~ **morta** still life; **por** ~ by nature
naturismo [natu'riʒmu] M naturism
naturista [natu'riʃta] ADJ, M/F naturist
nau [naw] F (literário) ship
naufragar [nawfra'gaʳ] VI (navio) to be wrecked;
(marinheiro) to be shipwrecked; (fig: malograr-se)
to fail
naufrágio [naw'fraʒu] M shipwreck; (fig) failure
náufrago, -a ['nawfragu, a] M/F castaway
náusea ['nawzea] F nausea; **dar ~s a alguém** to
make sb feel sick; **sentir ~s** to feel sick
nauseabundo, -a [a nawzja'bũdu, a] ADJ
nauseating, sickening
nauseante [naw'zjãtʃi] ADJ nauseating,
sickening
nausear [naw'zjaʳ] VT to nauseate, sicken ■ VI
to feel sick
náutica ['nawtʃika] F seamanship
náutico, -a ['nawtʃiku, a] ADJ nautical
naval [na'vaw] (pl -ais) ADJ naval; **construção** ~
shipbuilding
navalha [na'vaʎa] F (de barba) razor; (faca) knife
navalhada [nava'ʎada] F cut (with a razor)
navalhar [nava'ʎaʳ] VT to cut ou slash with a
razor
nave ['navi] F (de igreja) nave; ~ **espacial**
spaceship
navegação [navega'sãw] F navigation, sailing;
~ **aérea** air traffic; ~ **costeira** coastal shipping;
fluvial river traffic; **companhia de** ~ shipping
line
navegador, a [navega'doʳ(a)] M/F navigator
navegante [nave'gãtʃi] M seafarer
navegar [nave'gaʳ] VT to navigate; (mares) to sail
■ VI to sail; (dirigir o rumo) to navigate

navegável [nave'gavew] (pl -eis) ADJ navigable
navio [na'viu] M ship; ~ **aeródromo** aircraft
carrier; ~ **cargueiro** cargo ship, freighter;
~ **de carreira** liner; ~ **de guerra** warship; ~
escola training ship; ~ **fábrica** factory ship;
~ **mercante** merchant ship; ~ **petroleiro** oil
tanker; ~ **tanque** tanker; **ficar a ver ~s** to be
left high and dry
Nazaré [naza'rɛ] N Nazareth
nazi [na'zi] (PT) ADJ, M/F = **nazista**
nazismo [na'ziʒmu] M Nazism
nazista [na'ziʃta] (BR) ADJ, M/F Nazi
NB ABR (= note bem) NB
n/c ABR (= nossa carta) our letter; (: = nossa conta)
our account; (: = nossa casa) our firm
N da R ABR = **nota da redação**
N do A ABR = **nota do autor**
N do E ABR = **nota do editor**
N do T ABR = **nota do tradutor**
NE ABR (= nordeste) NE
neblina [ne'blina] F fog, mist
nebulosa [nebu'lɔza] F (Astronomia) nebula
nebulosidade [nebulozi'dadʒi] F cloud
nebuloso, -a [nebu'lozu, ɔza] ADJ foggy, misty;
(céu) cloudy; (fig) vague
neca ['nɛka] (col) PRON nothing ■ EXCL nope
necessaire [nese'sɛr] M toilet bag
necessário, -a [nese'sarju, a] ADJ necessary
■ M: **o** ~ the necessities pl; **se for** ~ if necessary
necessidade [nesesi'dadʒi] F need, necessity; (o
que se necessita) need; (pobreza) poverty, need; **ter**
~ **de** to need; **não há** ~ **de algo/de fazer algo**
there is no need for sth/to do sth; **em caso de**
~ if need be
necessitado, -a [nesesi'tadu, a] ADJ needy, poor
■ M/F person in need; **os necessitados** MPL
the needy pl; ~ **de** in need of
necessitar [nesesi'ta'] VT to need, require ■ VI
to be in need; ~ **de** to need
necrológio [nekro'lɔʒu] M obituary
necrópole [ne'krɔpoli] F cemetery
necrose [ne'krɔzi] F necrosis
necrotério [nekro'tɛrju] M mortuary, morgue
(US)
néctar ['nɛkta'] M nectar
nectarina [nekta'rina] F nectarine
nédio, -a ['nɛdʒu, a] ADJ (luzidio) glossy, sleek;
(rechonchudo) plump
neerlandês, -esa [neexlã'deʃ, eza] ADJ Dutch
■ M/F Dutchman/woman
Neerlândia [neex'lãdʒa] F the Netherlands pl
nefando, -a [ne'fãdu, a] ADJ atrocious, heinous
nefasto, -a [ne'faʃtu, a] ADJ (de mau agouro)
ominous; (trágico) tragic
negaça [ne'gasa] F lure, bait; (engano) deception;
(recusa) refusal; (desmentido) denial
negação [nega'sãw] (pl -ões) F negation; (recusa)
refusal; (desmentido) denial; **ele é uma ~ em
matéria de cozinha** he's hopeless at cooking

negacear [nega'sja'] VT (atrair) to entice;
(enganar) to deceive; (recusar) to refuse ■ VI
(cavalo) to balk; (Hipismo) to refuse
negações [nega'sõjʃ] FPL de **negação**
negar [ne'ga'] VT (desmentir, não permitir) to deny;
(recusar) to refuse; **negar-se** VR: **negar-se a** to
refuse to
negativa [nega'tʃiva] F (Ling) negative; (recusa)
denial
negativo, -a [nega'tʃivu, a] ADJ negative ■ M
(Tec, Foto) negative ■ EXCL (col) nope!
negável [ne'gavew] ADJ (pl -eis) deniable
negligé [negli'ʒe] M negligee
negligência [negli'ʒẽsja] F negligence,
carelessness
negligenciar [negliʒẽ'sja'] VT to neglect
negligente [negli'ʒẽtʃi] ADJ negligent, careless
nego, -a ['negu, a] (col) M/F (negro) Black;
(camarada): **tudo bem, (meu) ~?** how are you,
mate?; (querido): **tchau, (meu) ~** bye, dear ou
darling
negociação [negosja'sãw] (pl -ões) F
negotiation; (transação) transaction
negociador, a [negosja'do'(a)] ADJ negotiating
■ M/F negotiator
negociante [nego'sjãtʃi] M/F businessman/
woman; (comerciante) merchant
negociar [nego'sja'] VT (Pol etc) to negotiate;
(Com) to trade ■ VI: ~ **(com)** to trade ou deal (in);
to negotiate (with)
negociata [nego'sjata] F crooked deal;
negociatas MPL (negócios escusos) wheeling and
dealing sg
negociável [nego'sjavew] (pl -eis) ADJ
negotiable
negócio [ne'gɔsju] M (Com) business; (transação)
deal; (questão) matter; (col: troço) thing; (assunto)
affair, business; **homem de ~s** businessman; **a
~s** on business; **fazer um bom ~** (pessoa) to get a
good deal; (loja etc) to do good business; **fechar
um ~** to make a deal; ~ **fechado!** it's a deal!;
isso não é ~ it's not worth it; **a casa dela é um
~** (col) her house is really something; **tenho um
~ para te contar** I've got something to tell you;
aconteceu um ~ estranho comigo something
strange happened to me; **mas que ~ é esse?**
(col) what's the big idea?; **meu ~ é outro** (col)
this isn't my thing; **o ~ é o seguinte ...** (col) the
thing is ..
negocista [nego'siʃta] ADJ crooked ■ M/F
wheeler-dealer
negridão [negri'dãw] F blackness
negrito [ne'gritu] M (Tip) bold (face)
negritude [negri'tudʒi] F (Pol etc) Black
awareness
negro, -a ['negru, a] ADJ black; (raça) Black;
(fig: lúgubre) black, gloomy ■ M/F Black man/
woman; **a situação está negra** the situation
is bad; **humor ~** black humo(u)r; **magia negra**

NB: European Portuguese adds the following consonants to certain words: **b** (sú(b)dito, su(b)til); **c** (a(c)ção,
a(c)cionista, a(c)to); **m** (inde(m)ne); **p** (ado(p)ção, ado(p)tar); for further details see p. xiii.

black magic
negrume [ne'grumi] M black, darkness
negrura [ne'grura] F blackness
neguei etc [ne'gej] VB V **negar**
nele, -la ['neli, 'nɛla] = **em + ele**
neles, -las ['neliʃ, 'nɛlaʃ] = **em + eles**
nem [nẽj] CONJ nor, neither; ~ **(sequer)** not
even; ~ **que** even if; ~ **bem** hardly; ~ **um só** not
a single one; ~ **estuda** ~ **trabalha** he neither
studies nor works; ~ **eu** nor me; **sem** ~ without
even; ~ **todos** not all; ~ **tanto** not so much; ~
sempre not always; ~ **por isso** nonetheless;
ele fala português que ~ **brasileiro** he speaks
Portuguese like a Brazilian; ~ **vem (que não
tem)** (col) don't give me that
nenê [ne'ne] M/F baby
neném [ne'nẽj] (pl -ns) M/F = **nenê**
nenhum, a [ne'ɲũ, 'ɲuma] ADJ no, not any
■ PRON (nem um só) none, not one; (de dois)
neither; ~ **professor** no teacher; **não vi
professor** ~ I didn't see any teachers; ~ **dos
professores** none of the teachers; ~ **dos dois**
neither of them; ~ **lugar** nowhere; **ele não fez** ~
comentário he didn't make any comments, he
made no comments; **não vou a** ~ **lugar** I'm not
going anywhere; **estar a** ~ (col) to be flat broke
neofascismo [neofa'siʒmu] M neofascism
neolatino, -a [neola'tʃinu, a] ADJ: **línguas
neolatinas** Romance languages
neolítico, -a [neo'litʃiku, a] ADJ neolithic
neologismo [neolo'ʒiʒmu] M neologism
néon ['nɛõ] M neon
neônio [ne'onju] M = **néon**
neo-realismo ['neo-] M new realism
neozelandês, -esa [neozelã'deʃ, deza] ADJ New
Zealand atr ■ M/F New Zealander
Nepal [ne'paw] M: **o** ~ Nepal
nepotismo [nepo'tʃiʒmu] M nepotism
nervo ['nexvu] M (Anat) nerve; (fig) energy,
strength; (em carne) sinew; **ser** ou **estar
uma pilha de ~s** to be a bundle of nerves;
nervosismo [nexvo'ziʒmu] M (nervosidade)
nervousness; (irritabilidade) irritability; **nervoso,
-a** [nex'vozu, ɔza] ADJ nervous; (irritável) touchy,
on edge; (exaltado) worked up; **isso/ele me
deixa nervoso** he gets on my nerves; **sistema
nervoso** nervous system
nervudo, -a [ner'vudu, a] (PT) ADJ (robusto)
robust
nervura [nex'vura] F rib; (Bot) vein
néscio, -a ['nɛsju, a] ADJ (idiota) stupid;
(insensato) foolish
nesga ['neʒga] F (Costura) gore; (porção: de comida)
portion; (: de mesa, terra) corner, patch
nesse(s), -ssa(s) ['nesi(ʃ), 'nɛ] = **em + esse(s)**
neste(s), -ta(s) ['neʃtʃi(ʃ), 'nɛʃta(ʃ)] = **em +
este(s)**
neto, -a ['nɛtu, a] M/F grandson/daughter;
netos MPL grandchildren
neuralgia [newraw'ʒia] F neuralgia
neurastênico, -a [newraʃ'teniku, a] ADJ (Psico)
neurasthenic; (col: irritadiço) irritable

neurite [new'ritʃi] F (Med) neuritis
neurocirurgião, -giã [newrosirux3jãw, 3jã] (pl
-ões/-s) M/F neurosurgeon
neurologia [newrolo'ʒia] F neurology
neurológico, -a [newro'lɔʒiku, a] ADJ
neurological
neurologista [newrolo'ʒiʃta] M/F neurologist
neurose [new'rɔzi] F neurosis; **neurótico, -a**
[new'rɔtʃiku, a] ADJ, M/F neurotic
neutralidade [newtrali'dadʒi] F neutrality
neutralização [newtraliza'sãw] F
neutralization
neutralizar [newtrali'zaʳ] VT to neutralize;
(anular) to counteract
neutrão [new'trãw] (pl) (PT) M = **nêutron**
neutro, -a ['newtru, a] ADJ (Ling: imparcial)
neutral, neuter
neutrões [new'trõjs] MPL de **neutrão**
nêutron ['newtrõ] (pl -s) M neutron; **bomba de
~s** neutron bomb
nevada [ne'vada] F snowfall
nevado, -a [ne'vadu, a] ADJ snow-covered;
(branco) snow-white
nevar [ne'vaʳ] VI to snow; **nevasca** [ne'vaʃka]
F snowstorm; **neve** ['nɛvi] F snow; **clara em
neve** (Culin) beaten egg-white
névoa ['nɛvoa] F fog; **nevoeiro** [nevo'ejru] M
thick fog
nevralgia [nevraw'ʒia] F neuralgia
nexo ['nɛksu] M connection, link; **sem** ~
disconnected, incoherent
nhenhenhém [ɲeɲe'ɲẽj] M (conversa fiado) idle
talk; (reclamação) whingeing
nhoque ['ɲɔki] M (Culin) gnocchi
Nicarágua [nika'ragwa] F: **a** ~ Nicaragua
nicaragüense [nikara'gwẽsi] ADJ, M/F
Nicaraguan
nicho ['niʃu] M niche
Nicósia [ni'kɔzja] N Nicosia
nicotina [niko'tʃina] F nicotine
Níger ['niʒeʳ] M: **o** ~ Niger
Nigéria [ni'ʒɛrja] F: **a** ~ Nigeria
nigeriano, -a [niʒe'rjanu, a] ADJ, M/F Nigerian
niilista [nii'liʃta] ADJ nihilistic ■ M/F nihilist
Nilo ['nilu] M: **o** ~ the Nile
nimbo ['nĩbu] M (nuvem) rain cloud; (Geo) halo
ninar [ni'naʳ] VT to sing to sleep; **ninar-se** VR:
ninar-se para algo to ignore sth
ninfeta [nĩ'feta] F nymphette
ninfomaníaca [nĩfoma'niaka] F
nymphomaniac
ninguém [nĩ'gẽj] PRON nobody, no-one; ~ **o
conhece** no-one knows him; **não vi** ~ I saw no-
one, I didn't see anybody; ~ **mais** nobody else
ninhada [ni'ɲada] F brood
ninharia [niɲa'ria] F trifle
ninho ['niɲu] M (de aves) nest; (toca) lair; (lar)
home; ~ **de rato** (col) mess, tip
níquel ['nikew] M nickel; **estar sem um** ~ to be
penniless
niquelar [nike'laʳ] VT (Tec) to nickel-plate
nirvana [nix'vana] F nirvana

nisei [ni'zej] ADJ, M/F second-generation Japanese Brazilian

nisso ['nisu] = **em** + **isso**

nisto ['niʃtu] = **em** + **isto**

nitidez [nitʃi'deʒ] F (clareza) clarity; (brilho) brightness; (imagem) sharpness

nítido, -a ['nitʃidu, a] ADJ clear, distinct; (brilhante) bright; (imagem) sharp, clear

nitrato [ni'tratu] M nitrate

nítrico, -a ['nitriku, a] ADJ: **ácido** ~ nitric acid

nitrogênio [nitro'ʒenju] M nitrogen

nitroglicerina [nitroglise'rina] F nitroglycerine

nível ['nivew] (pl -eis) M level; (fig: padrão) level, standard; (: ponto) point, pitch; ~ **de vida** standard of living; ~ **do mar** sea level; **a** ~ **de** in terms of; **ao** ~ **de** level with

nivelamento [nivela'mẽtu] M levelling (Brit), leveling (US)

nivelar [nive'la[r]] VT (terreno etc) to level ■ VI: **nivelar com** to be level with; **nivelar-se** VR: **nivelar-se com** to be equal to; **a morte nivela os homens** death is the great leveller (Brit) ou leveler (US)

NO ABR (= nordeste) NW

no [nu] = **em** + **o**

-no [nu] PRON him; (coisa) it

n° ABR (= número) no

n/o ABR = **nossa ordem**

nó M knot; (de uma questão) crux; **nó corredio** slipknot; **nó na garganta** lump in the throat; **nós dos dedos** knuckles; **dar um nó** to tie a knot

nobilíssimo, -a [nobi'lisimu, a] ADJ SUPERL de **nobre**

nobilitar [nobili'ta[r]] VT to ennoble

nobre ['nɔbri] ADJ noble; (bairro etc) exclusive ■ M/F noble; **horário** ~ prime time; **nobreza** [no'breza] F nobility

noção [no'sãw] (pl -ões) F notion; **noções** FPL (rudimentos) rudiments, basics; ~ **vaga** inkling; **não ter a menor** ~ **de algo** not to have the slightest idea about sth

nocaute [no'kawtʃi] M knockout; (soco) knockout blow ■ ADV: **pôr alguém** ~ to knock sb out

nocautear [nokaw'tʃja[r]] VT to knock out

nocivo, -a [no'sivu, a] ADJ harmful

noções [no'sõjʃ] FPL de **noção**

nocturno, -a [no'tuxnu, a] (PT) ADJ = **noturno**

nódoa ['nɔdwa] F spot; (mancha) stain

nódulo ['nɔdulu] M nodule

nogueira [no'gejra] F (árvore) walnut tree; (madeira) walnut

noitada [noj'tada] F (noite inteira) whole night; (noite de divertimento) night out

noite ['nojtʃi] F night; (início da noite) evening; **à** ou **de** ~ at night, in the evening; **ontem/hoje/amanhã à** ~ last night/tonight/tomorrow night; **boa** ~ good evening; (despedida) good night; **da** ~ **para o dia** overnight; **tarde da** ~ late at night; **passar a** ~ **em claro** to have a sleepless night; **a** ~ **carioca** Rio nightlife; ~ **de estréia** opening night

noitinha [noj'tʃiɲa] F: **à** ~**s** at nightfall

noivado [noj'vadu] M engagement

noivar [noj'va[r]] VI: ~ **(com)** (ficar noivo) to get engaged (to); (ser noivo) to be engaged (to)

noivo, -a ['nojvu, a] M/F (prometido) fiancé/fiancée; (no casamento) bridegroom/bride; **os noivos** MPL (prometidos) the engaged couple; (no casamento) the bride and groom; (recém-casados) the newly-weds

nojeira [no'ʒejra] F disgusting thing; (trabalho) filthy job

nojento, -a [no'ʒẽtu, a] ADJ disgusting

nojo ['noʒu] M (náusea) nausea; (repulsão) disgust, loathing; **ela é um** ~ she's horrible; **este trabalho está um** ~ this work is messy

no-la(s) = **nos** + **a(s)**

no-lo(s) = **nos** + **o(s)**

nômade ['nomadʒi] ADJ nomadic ■ M/F nomad

nome ['nomi] M name; (fama) fame; **de** ~ by name; **escritor de** ~ famous writer; **um restaurante de** ~ a restaurant with a good reputation; **em** ~ **de** in the name of; **dar** ~ **aos bois** to call a spade a spade; **esse** ~ **não me é estranho** the name rings a bell; ~ **comercial** trade name; ~ **completo** full name; ~ **de batismo** Christian name; ~ **de família** family name; ~ **de guerra** nickname; ~ **feio** swearword; ~ **próprio** (Ling) proper name

nomeação [nomja'sãw] (pl -ões) F nomination; (para cargo) appointment

nomeada [no'mjada] F fame

nomeadamente [nomjada'mẽtʃi] ADV namely

nomear [no'mja[r]] VT to nominate; (conferir um cargo) to appoint; (dar nome a) to name

nomenclatura [nomẽkla'tura] F nomenclature

nominal [nomi'naw] (pl -ais) ADJ nominal

nonagésimo, -a [nona'ʒezimu, a] NUM ninetieth

nono, -a ['nonu, a] NUM ninth; v tb **quinto**

nora ['nɔra] F daughter-in-law

nordeste [nox'dɛʃtʃi] M, ADJ northeast; **o N~** the Northeast

nordestino, -a [noxdeʃ'tʃinu, a] ADJ north-eastern ■ M/F North-easterner

nórdico, -a ['nɔxdʒiku, a] ADJ, M/F Nordic

norma ['nɔxma] F standard, norm; (regra) rule; **como** ~ as a rule

normal [nox'maw] (pl -ais) ADJ normal; (habitual) usual; **escola** ~ ≈ teacher training college; **curso** ~ primary (Brit) ou elementary (US) school teacher training; **está um calor que não é** ~ it's incredibly hot

normalidade [noxmali'dadʒi] F normality

normalista [noxma'liʃta] M/F trainee primary (Brit) ou elementary (US) school teacher

---

NB: European Portuguese adds the following consonants to certain words: **b** (sú(b)dito, su(b)til); **c** (a(c)ção, a(c)cionista, a(c)to); **m** (inde(m)ne); **p** (ado(p)ção, ado(p)tar); for further details see p. xiii.

normalização [noxmaliza'sãw] F
normalization
normalizar [noxmali'za^r] VT to bring back
to normal; (Pol: relações etc) to normalize;
normalizar-se VR to return to normal
normativo, -a [noxma'tʃivu, a] ADJ prescriptive
noroeste [nor'wɛʃtʃi] ADJ northwest,
northwestern ■ M northwest
norte ['nɔxtʃi] ADJ northern, north; (vento,
direção) northerly ■ M north; **ao ~ de** to the
north of
norte-africano, -a ADJ, M/F North African
norte-americano, -a ADJ, M/F (North)
American
nortear [nox'tʃia^r] VT to orientate; **nortear-se**
VR to orientate o.s.
norte-coreano, -a ADJ, M/F North Korean
norte-vietnamita ADJ, M/F North Vietnamese
nortista [nox'tʃiʃta] ADJ northern ■ M/F
Northerner
Noruega [nor'wega] F Norway; **norueguês,
-esa** [norwe'geʃ, geza] ADJ, M/F Norwegian ■ M
(Ling) Norwegian
nos¹ [nuʃ] = **em + os**
nos² [nuʃ] PRON (direto) us; (indireto) us, to us, for
us; (reflexivo) (to) ourselves; (recíproco) (to) each
other
-nos [nuʃ] PRON them
nós [nɔʃ] PRON we; **~ mesmos** we ourselves;
para ~ for us; **~ dois** we two, both of us; **cá**
entre ~ between the two (ou three etc) of us
nossa ['nɔsa] EXCL: ~! my goodness!
nosso, -a ['nɔsu, a] ADJ our ■ PRON ours; **um**
amigo ~ a friend of ours; **Nossa Senhora** (Rel)
Our Lady; **os ~s** (família) our family sg
nostalgia [noʃtaw'ʒia] F nostalgia; (saudades
da pátria etc) homesickness; **nostálgico, -a**
[noʃ'tawʒiku, a] ADJ nostalgic; (saudoso)
homesick
nota ['nɔta] F note; (Educ) mark; (conta) bill;
(cédula) banknote; **digno de ~** noteworthy;
cheio da ~ (col) flush; **custar uma ~ (preta)**
(col) to cost a bomb; **tomar ~** to make a note;
~ de venda sales receipt; **~ fiscal** receipt; (~)
promissória promissory note
notabilidade [notabili'dadʒi] F notability;
(pessoa) notable
notabilizar [notabili'za^r] VT to make known;
notabilizar-se VR to become known
notação [nota'sãw] (pl -ões) F notation
notadamente [notada'mẽtʃi] ADV especially
notar [no'ta^r] VT (reparar em) to notice, note;
notar-se VR to be obvious; **é de ~ que** it is to be
noted that; **fazer ~** to call attention to; **notável**
[no'tavew] (pl -eis) ADJ notable, remarkable
notícia [no'tʃisja] F (uma notícia) piece of news;
(TV etc) news item; **notícias** FPL (informações)
news sg; **pedir ~s de** to inquire about; **ter ~s de**
to hear from
noticiar [notʃi'sja^r] VT to announce, report
noticiário [notʃi'sjarju] M (de jornal) news
section; (Cinema) newsreel; (TV, Rádio) news

bulletin
noticiarista [notʃisja'riʃta] M/F news writer,
reporter; (TV, Rádio) newsreader, newscaster
noticioso, -a [notʃi'sjozu, ɔza] ADJ news atr
notificação [notʃifika'sãw] (pl -ões) F
notification
notificar [notʃifi'ka^r] VT to notify, inform
notívago, -a [no'tʃivagu, a] ADJ nocturnal
■ M/F sleepwalker; (pessoa que gosta da noite)
night bird
notoriedade [notorje'dadʒi] F renown, fame
notório, -a [no'tɔrju, a] ADJ well-known
noturno, -a [no'tuxnu, a] ADJ nocturnal,
nightly; (trabalho) night atr ■ M (trem) night
train
nouveau-riche [nuvo'xiʃi] (pl nouveaux-riches)
M/F nouveau-riche
nov. ABR (= novembro) Nov
nova ['nɔva] F piece of news; **novas** FPL
(novidades) news sg
novamente [nova'mẽtʃi] ADV again
novato, -a [no'vatu, a] ADJ inexperienced, raw
■ M/F (principiante) beginner, novice; (Educ)
fresher
nove ['nɔvi] NUM nine; v tb **cinco**
novecentos, -tas [nove'sẽtuʃ] NUM nine
hundred
novela [no'vɛla] F short novel, novella; (Rádio,
TV) soap opera
novelista [nove'liʃta] M/F novella writer
novelo [no'velu] M ball of thread
novembro [no'vẽbru] (PT N-) M November; v tb
julho
novena [no'vena] F (Rel) novena
noventa [no'vẽta] NUM ninety; v tb **cinqüenta**
noviciado [novi'sjadu] M (Rel) novitiate
noviço, -a [no'visu, a] M/F (Rel, fig) novice
novidade [novi'dadʒi] F novelty; (notícia) piece
of news; **novidades** FPL (notícias) news sg; **sem ~**
without incident
novidadeiro, -a [novida'dejru, a] ADJ chatty
■ M/F gossip
novilho, -a [no'viʎu, a] M/F young bull/heifer
novo, -a ['novu, 'nɔva] ADJ new; (jovem) young;
(adicional) further; **de ~** again; **~ em folha**
brand new; **o que há de ~?** what's new?; **~ rico**
nouveau riche
noz [nɔʒ] F (de várias árvores) nut; (da nogueira)
walnut; **~ moscada** nutmeg
nu, a [nu, 'nua] ADJ (corpo, pessoa) naked; (braço,
arvore, sala, parede) bare ■ M nude; **a olho nu**
with the naked eye; **a verdade nua e crua** the
stark truth ou reality; **pôr a nu** (fig) to expose
nuança [nu'ãsa] F nuance
nubente [nu'bẽtʃi] ADJ, M/F betrothed
nublado, -a [nu'bladu, a] ADJ cloudy, overcast
nublar [nu'bla^r] VT to darken; **nublar-se** VR to
cloud over
nuca ['nuka] F nape (of the neck)
nuclear [nu'klja^r] ADJ nuclear; **energia/usina ~**
nuclear energy/power station
núcleo ['nuklju] M nucleus sg; (centro) centre

(Brit), center (US)

nudez [nu'deʒ] F nakedness, nudity; (de paredes etc) bareness

nudismo [nu'dʒiʒmu] M nudism

nudista [nu'dʒiʃta] ADJ, M/F nudist

nulidade [nuli'dadʒi] F nullity, invalidity; (pessoa) nonentity

nulo, -a ['nulu, a] ADJ (Jur) null, void; (nenhum) non-existent; (sem valor) worthless; (esforço) vain, useless; **ele é ~ em matemática** he's useless at maths (Brit) ou math (US)

num [nũ] = **em + um** ADV (col: não) not

numa(s) ['numa(ʃ)] = **em + uma(s)**

numeração [numera'sãw] F (ato) numbering; (números) numbers pl; (de sapatos etc) sizes pl

numerado, -a [nume'radu, a] ADJ numbered; (em ordem numérica) in numerical order

numeral [nume'raw] (pl -ais) M numeral ■ ADJ numerical

numerar [nume'ra'] VT to number

numerário [nume'rarju] M cash, money

numérico, -a [nu'meriku, a] ADJ numerical

número ['numeru] M number; (de jornal) issue; (Teatro etc) act; (de sapatos, roupa) size; **sem ~** countless; **um sem ~ de vezes** hundreds ou thousands of times; **amigo/escritor ~ um** number one friend/writer; **fazer ~** to make up the numbers; **ele é um ~** (col) he's a riot; **~**

cardinal/ordinal cardinal/ordinal number; **~ de matrícula** registration (Brit) ou license plate (US) number; **~ primo** prime number; **numeroso, -a** [nume'rozu, ɔza] ADJ numerous

nunca ['nũka] ADV never; **~ mais** never again; **como ~** as never before; **quase ~** hardly ever; **mais que ~** more than ever

nuns [nũʃ] = **em + uns**

nupcial [nup'sjaw] ADJ (pl -ais) wedding atr

núpcias ['nupsjaʃ] FPL nuptials, wedding sg

nutrição [nutri'sãw] F nutrition

nutricionista [nutrisjo'niʃta] M/F nutritionist

nutrido, -a [nu'tridu, a] ADJ (bem alimentado) well-nourished; (robusto) robust

nutrimento [nutri'mẽtu] M nourishment

nutrir [nu'tri'] VT (sentimento) to harbour (Brit), harbor (US); (alimentar-se): **~ (de)** to nourish (with), feed (on); (fig) to feed (on) ■ VI to be nourishing

nutritivo, -a [nutri'tʃivu, a] ADJ nourishing; **valor ~** nutritional value

nuvem ['nuvẽj] (pl -ns) F cloud; (de insetos) swarm; **cair das nuvens** (fig) to be astounded; **estar nas nuvens** to be daydreaming, be miles away; **pôr nas nuvens** to praise to the skies; **o aniversário passou em brancas nuvens** the birthday went by without any celebration

NB: European Portuguese adds the following consonants to certain words: **b** (sú(b)dito, su(b)til); **c** (a(c)ção, a(c)cionista, a(c)to); **m** (inde(m)ne); **p** (ado(p)çã, ado(p)tar); for further details see p. xiii.

Oo

O, o [ɔ] (*pl* **os**) M O, o; **O de Osvaldo** O for Oliver (*Brit*) *ou* oboe (*US*)

⭕ **PALAVRA CHAVE**

o, a [u, a] ART DEF **1** the; **o livro/a mesa/os estudantes** the book/table/students **2** (*com n abstrato: não se traduz*): **o amor/a juventude** love/youth **3** (*posse: traduz-se muitos vezes por adj possessivo*): **quebrar o braço** to break one's arm; **ele levantou a mão** he put his hand up; **ela colocou o chapéu** she put her hat on **4** (*valor descritivo*): **ter a boca grande/os olhos azuis** to have a big mouth/blue eyes
■ PRON DEMOSTRATIVO: **meu livro e o seu** my book and yours; **as de Pedro são melhores** Pedro's are better; **não a(s) branca(s) mas a(s) cinza(s)** not the white one(s) but the grey one(s)
■ PRON RELATIVO: **o que** *etc* **1** (*indef*): **o(s) que quiser(em) pode(m) sair** anyone who wants to can leave; **leve o que mais gostar** take the one you like best **2** (*def*): **o que comprei ontem** the one I bought yesterday; **os que sairam** those who left **3**: **o que** what; **o que eu acho/mais gosto** what I think/like most
■ PRON PESSOAL **1** (*pessoa: m*) him; (: *f*) her; (: *pl*) them; **não posso vê-lo(s)** I can't see him/them; **vemo-la todas as semanas** we see her every week **2** (*animal, coisa: sg*) it; (: *pl*) them; **não posso vê-lo(s)** I can't see it/them; **acharam-nos na praia** they found us on the beach

ó [ɔ] EXCL oh!; (*olha*) look!; **ó Pedro** hey Pedro
ô [o] EXCL oh!; **ô Pedro** hey Pedro; **ô de casa!** anyone at home?; **ô criança difícil!** oh, what a difficult child!
OAB ABR F = **Ordem dos Advogados do Brasil**
oásis [o'asiʃ] M INV oasis
oba ['oba] EXCL wow!, great!; (*saudação*) hi!
obcecado, -a [obise'kadu, a] ADJ obsessed
obcecar [obise'kaᵗ] VT to obsess
obedecer [obede'seᵗ] VI: ~ **a** to obey; **obedeça!** (*a criança*) do as you're told!; **obediência**

[obe'dʒẽsja] F obedience; **obediente** [obe'dʒẽtʃi] ADJ obedient
obelisco [obe'liʃku] M obelisk
obesidade [obezi'dadʒi] F obesity
obeso, -a [o'bɛzu, a] ADJ obese
óbice ['ɔbisi] M obstacle
óbito ['ɔbitu] M death; **atestado de ~** death certificate
obituário [obi'twarju] M obituary
objeção [obʒe'sãw] (*PT* **-çç-**, *pl* **-ões**) F objection; (*obstáculo*) obstacle; **fazer** *ou* **pôr objeções a** to object to
objetar [obʒe'taᵗ] (*PT* **-ct-**) VT to object ■ VI: ~ **(a algo)** to object (to sth)
objetiva [obʒe'tʃiva] (*PT* **-ct-**) F lens; **sem ~** aimlessly
objetivar [obʒetʃi'vaᵗ] (*PT* **-ct-**) VT (*visar*) to aim at; ~ **fazer** to aim to do, set out to do
objetividade [obʒetʃivi'dadʒi] (*PT* **-ct-**) F objectivity
objetivo, -a [obʒe'tʃivu, a] (*PT* **-ct-**) ADJ objective ■ M objective, aim
objeto [ob'ʒɛtu] (*PT* **-ct-**) M object; ~ **de uso pessoal** personal effect
oblíqua [o'blikwa] F oblique
oblíquo, -a [o'blikwu, a] ADJ oblique, slanting; (*olhar*) sidelong; (*Ling*) oblique
obliterar [oblite'raᵗ] VT to obliterate; (*Med*) to close off
oblongo, -a [ob'lõgu, a] ADJ oblong
oboé [o'bwɛ] M oboe
oboísta [o'bwiʃta] M/F oboe player
obra ['ɔbra] F work; (*Arq*) building, construction; (*Teatro*) play; **em ~s** under repair; **ser ~ de alguém** to be the work of sb; **ser ~ de algo** to be the result of sth; ~ **de arte** work of art; ~ **de caridade** charity; ~**s completas** complete works; ~**s públicas** public works
obra-mestra (*pl* **obras-mestras**) F masterpiece
obra-prima (*pl* **obras-primas**) F masterpiece
obreiro, -a [o'brejru, a] ADJ working ■ M/F worker
obrigação [obriga'sãw] (*pl* **-ões**) F obligation, duty; (*Com*) bond; **cumprir (com) suas obrigações** to fulfil(l) one's obligations; **dever obrigações a alguém** to owe sb favo(u)rs; ~ **ao portador** bearer bond

obrigado, -a [obri'gadu, a] ADJ (*compelido*) obliged, compelled ■ EXCL thank you; (*recusa*) no, thank you

obrigar [obri'ga^r] VT to oblige, compel; **obrigar-se** VR: **obrigar-se a fazer algo** to undertake to do sth

obrigatoriedade [obrigatorje'dadʒi] F compulsory nature

obrigatório, -a [obriga'tɔrju, a] ADJ compulsory, obligatory

obscenidade [obiseni'dadʒi] F obscenity

obsceno, -a [obi'sɛnu, a] ADJ obscene

obscurecer [obiʃkure'se^r] VT to darken; (*entendimento, verdade etc*) to obscure; (*prestígio*) to dim ■ VI to get dark

obscuridade [obiʃkuri'dadʒi] F (*falta de luz*) darkness; (*fig*) obscurity

obscuro, -a [obi'ʃkuru, a] ADJ dark; (*fig*) obscure

obsequiar [obse'kja^r] VT (*presentear*) to give presents to; (*tratar com agrados*) to treat kindly

obséquio [ob'sɛkju] M favour (*Brit*), favor (*US*), kindness; **faça o ~ de ...** would you be kind enough to ....

obsequioso, -a [obse'kjozu, ɔza] ADJ obliging, courteous

observação [obisexva'sãw] (*pl* -ões) F observation; (*comentário*) remark, comment; (*de leis, regras*) observance

observador, a [obisexva'do^r(a)] ADJ observant ■ M/F observer

observância [obisex'vãsja] F observance

observar [obisex'va^r] VT to observe; (*notar*) to notice; (*replicar*) to remark; **~ algo a alguém** to point sth out to sb

observatório [obisexva'tɔrju] M observatory

obsessão [obise'sãw] (*pl* -ões) F obsession; **obsessivo, -a** [obise'sivu, a] ADJ obsessive

obsessões [obise'sõjʃ] FPL *de* **obsessão**

obsoleto, -a [obiso'lɛtu, a] ADJ obsolete

obstáculo [obi'ʃtakulu] M obstacle; (*dificuldade*) hindrance, drawback

obstante [obi'ʃtãtʃi]: **não ~** CONJ nevertheless, however ■ PREP in spite of, notwithstanding

obstar [obi'ʃta^r] VI: **~ a** to hinder; (*opor-se*) to oppose

obstetra [obi'ʃtetra] M/F obstetrician

obstetrícia [obiʃte'trisja] F obstetrics *sg*

obstétrico, -a [obi'ʃtetriku, a] ADJ obstetric

obstinação [obiʃtʃina'sãw] F obstinacy

obstinado, -a [obiʃtʃi'nadu, a] ADJ obstinate, stubborn

obstinar-se [obiʃtʃi'naxsi] VR to be obstinate; **~ em** (*insistir em*) to persist in

obstrução [obiʃtru'sãw] (*pl* -ões) F obstruction; **obstruir** [obi'ʃtrwi^r] VT to obstruct; (*impedir*) to impede

obtêm *etc* [obi'tẽ] VB *v* **obter**

obtemperar [obitẽpe'ra^r] VT to reply respectfully ■ VI: **~ (a algo)** to demur (at sth)

obtenção [obitẽ'sãw] (*pl* -ões) F acquisition; (*consecução*) attainment

obtenho *etc* [ob'teɲu] VB *v* **obter**

obtenível [obite'nivew] (*pl* -eis) ADJ obtainable

obter [obi'te^r] (*irreg*) VT to obtain, get; (*alcançar*) to gain

obturação [obitura'sãw] (*pl* -ões) F (*de dente*) filling

obturador [obitura'do^r] M (*Foto*) shutter

obturar [obitu'ra^r] VT to stop up, plug; (*dente*) to fill

obtuso, -a [obi'tuzu, a] ADJ (*ger*) obtuse; (*fig: pessoa*) thick, slow

obviedade [obvje'dadʒi] F obviousness; (*coisa óbvia*) obvious fact

óbvio, -a ['ɔbvju, a] ADJ obvious; **(é) ~!** of course!; **é o ~ ululante** it's glaringly *ou* screamingly (*col*) obvious

OC ABR (= *onda curta*) SW

ocasião [oka'zjãw] (*pl* -ões) F (*oportunidade*) opportunity, chance; (*momento, tempo*) occasion, time

ocasional [okazjo'naw] (*pl* -ais) ADJ chance *atr*

ocasionar [okazjo'na^r] VT to cause, bring about

ocaso [o'kazu] M (*do sol*) sunset; (*ocidente*) west; (*decadência*) decline

Oceania [osja'nia] F: **a ~** Oceania

oceânico, -a [o'sjaniku, a] ADJ ocean *atr*

oceano [o'sjanu] M ocean; **O~ Atlântico/ Pacífico/Índico** Atlantic/Pacific/Indian Ocean

oceanografia [osjanogra'fia] F oceanography

ocidental [osidẽ'taw] (*pl* -ais) ADJ western ■ M/F westerner

ocidente [osi'dẽtʃi] M west; **o O~** (*Pol*) the West

ócio ['ɔsju] M (*lazer*) leisure; (*inação*) idleness

ociosidade [osjozi'dadʒi] F idleness

ocioso, -a [o'sjozu, ɔza] ADJ idle; (*vaga*) unfilled

oco, -a ['oku, a] ADJ hollow, empty

ocorrência [oko'xẽsja] F incident, event; (*circunstância*) circumstance

ocorrer [oko'xe^r] VI to happen, occur; (*vir ao pensamento*) to come to mind; **~ a alguém** to happen to sb; (*vir ao pensamento*) to occur to sb

ocre ['ɔkri] ADJ, M ochre (*Brit*), ocher (*US*)

octogenário, -a [oktoʒe'narju, a] ADJ eighty-year-old ■ M/F octogenarian

octogonal [oktogo'naw] (*pl* -ais) ADJ octagonal

octógono [ok'tɔgonu] M octagon

ocular [oku'la^r] ADJ ocular; **testemunha ~** eye witness

oculista [oku'liʃta] M/F optician

óculo ['ɔkulu] M spyglass; **óculos** MPL glasses, spectacles; **~s de proteção** goggles

ocultar [okuw'ta^r] VT to hide, conceal

ocultas [o'kuwtaʃ] FPL: **às ~** in secret

oculto, -a [o'kuwtu, a] ADJ hidden; (*desconhecido*) unknown; (*secreto*) secret; (*sobrenatural*) occult

ocupação [okupa'sãw] (*pl* -ões) F occupation

ocupacional [okupasjo'naw] (*pl* -ais) ADJ

NB: *European Portuguese adds the following consonants to certain words:* **b** (sú(b)dito, su(b)til); **c** (a(c)ção, a(c)cionista, a(c)to); **m** (inde(m)ne); **p** (ado(p)çã, ado(p)tar); *for further details see p. xiii.*

occupational

ocupações [okupa'sõjʃ] FPL *de* **ocupação**

ocupado, -a [oku'padu, a] ADJ (*pessoa*) busy; (*lugar*) taken, occupied; (*BR: telefone*) engaged (*Brit*), busy (*US*); **sinal de ~** (*BR: Tel*) engaged tone (*Brit*), busy signal (*US*)

ocupar [oku'paʳ] VT to occupy; (*tempo*) to take up; (*pessoa*) to keep busy; **ocupar-se** VR to keep o.s. occupied; **~-se com** *ou* **de** *ou* **em algo** (*dedicar-se a*) to deal with sth; (*cuidar de*) to look after sth; (*passar seu tempo com*) to occupy o.s. with sth; **posso ~ esta mesa/cadeira?** can I take this table/chair?

ode ['ɔdʒi] F ode

odiar [o'dʒjaʳ] VT to hate

odiento, -a [o'dʒjẽtu, a] ADJ hateful

ódio ['ɔdʒju] M hate, hatred; **que ~!** (*col*) I'm (*ou* was) furious!

odioso, -a [o'dʒjozu, ɔza] ADJ hateful

odontologia [odõtolo'ʒia] F dentistry

odor [o'doʳ] M smell

OEA ABR F (= *Organização dos Estados Americanos*) OAS

oeste ['wɛʃtʃi] M west ■ ADJ INV (*região*) western; (*direção, vento*) westerly; **ao ~ de** to the west of; **em direção ao ~** westwards

ofegante [ofe'gãtʃi] ADJ breathless, panting

ofegar [ofe'gaʳ] VI to pant, puff

ofender [ofẽ'deʳ] VT to offend; **ofender-se** VR to take offence (*Brit*) *ou* offense (*US*)

ofensa [o'fẽsa] F insult; (*à lei, moral*) offence (*Brit*), offense (*US*); **ofensiva** [ofẽ'siva] F (*Mil*) offensive; **tomar a ofensiva** to go on to the offensive

ofensivo, -a [ofẽ'sivu, a] ADJ offensive; (*agressivo*) aggressive; **~ à moral** morally offensive

oferecer [ofere'seʳ] VT to offer; (*dar*) to give; (*jantar*) to give; (*propor*) to propose; (*dedicar*) to dedicate; **oferecer-se** VR (*pessoa*) to offer o.s., volunteer; (*oportunidade*) to present itself, arise; **~-se para fazer** to offer to do

oferecido, -a [ofere'sidu, a] ADJ (*intrometido*) pushy

oferecimento [oferesi'mẽtu] M offer

oferenda [ofe'rẽda] F (*Rel*) offering

oferta [o'fɛxta] F (*oferecimento*) offer; (*dádiva*) gift; (*Com*) bid; (*em loja*) special offer; **a ~ e a demanda** (*Econ*) supply and demand; **em ~** (*numa loja*) on special offer

ofertar [ofex'taʳ] VT to offer

office-boy [ɔfis'bɔj] (*pl* -s) M messenger

oficial [ofi'sjaw] (*pl* -ais) ADJ official ■ M/F official; (*Mil*) officer; **~ de justiça** bailiff

oficializar [ofisjali'zaʳ] VT to make official

oficiar [ofi'sjaʳ] VI (*Rel*) to officiate ■ VT: **~ (algo) a alguém** to report (sth) to sb

oficina [ofi'sina] F workshop; **~ mecânica** garage

ofício [o'fisju] M (*profissão*) profession, trade; (*Rel*) service; (*carta*) official letter; (*função*) function; (*encargo*) job, task; **bons ~s** good

offices; **~ de notas** notary public

oficioso, -a [ofi'sjozu, ɔza] ADJ (*não oficial*) unofficial

ofsete [of'sɛtʃi] M offset printing

oftálmico, -a [of'tawmiku, a] ADJ ophthalmic

oftalmologia [oftawmolo'ʒia] F ophthalmology

ofuscante [ofuʃ'kãtʃi] ADJ dazzling

ofuscar [ofuʃ'kaʳ] VT (*obscurecer*) to blot out; (*deslumbrar*) to dazzle; (*entendimento*) to colour (*Brit*), color (*US*); (*suplantar em brilho*) to outshine ■ VI to be dazzling

ogro ['ɔgru] M ogre

ogum [o'gũ] M *Afro-Brazilian god of war*

oh [ɔ] EXCL oh

oi [ɔj] EXCL oh; (*saudação*) hi; (*resposta*) yes?

oitava-de-final (*pl* oitavas-de-final) F round before the quarter finals

oitavo, -a [oj'tavu, a] ADJ eighth ■ M eighth; *v* **quinto**

oitenta [oj'tẽta] NUM eighty; *v tb* **cinqüenta**

oito ['ojtu] NUM eight; **ou ~ ou** oitenta all or nothing; *v tb* **cinco**

oitocentos, -tas [ojtu'sẽtuʃ] NUM eight hundred; **os O~** the nineteenth century

ojeriza [oʒe'riza] F dislike; **ter ~ a alguém** to dislike sb

o.k. [o'ke] EXCL, ADV OK, okay

olá [o'la] EXCL hello!

olaria [ola'ria] F (*fáa: de louças de barro*) pottery; (*: de tijolos*) brickworks *sg*

oleado [o'ljadu] M oilcloth

oleiro [o'lejru, a] M/F potter; (*de tijolos*) brick maker

óleo ['ɔlju] M (*lubricante*) oil; **pintura a ~** oil painting; **tinta a ~** oil paint; **~ combustível** fuel oil; **~ de bronzear** suntan oil; **~ diesel** diesel oil

oleoduto [oljo'dutu] M (oil) pipeline

oleoso, -a [o'ljozu, ɔza] ADJ oily; (*gorduroso*) greasy

olfato [ow'fatu] M sense of smell

olhada [o'ʎada] F glance, look; **dar uma ~** to have a look

olhadela [oʎa'dɛla] F peep

olhar [o'ʎaʳ] VT to look at; (*observar*) to watch; (*ponderar*) to consider; (*cuidar de*) to look after ■ VI to look ■ M look; **olhar-se** VR to look at o.s.; (*duas pessoas*) to look at each other; **olha!** look!; **~ fixamente** to stare at; **~ para** to look at; **~ por** to look after; **~ alguém de frente** to look sb straight in the eye; **e olha lá** (*col*) and that's pushing it; **olha lá o que você vai me arranjar!** careful you don't make things worse for me!; **~ fixo** stare

olheiras [o'ʎejraʃ] FPL dark rings under the eyes

olho ['oʎu] M (*Anat, de agulha*) eye; (*vista*) eyesight; (*de queijo*) hole; **~ nele!** watch him!; **~ vivo!** keep your eyes open!; **a ~** (*medir, calcular etc*) by eye; **a ~ nu** with the naked eye; **a ~s vistos** visibly; **abrir os ~s de alguém** (*fig*) to open sb's eyes; **andar** *ou* **estar de ~ em algo** to have one's eyes on sth; **custar/pagar os ~s da cara** to cost/pay the earth; **ficar de ~** to keep an eye out; **ficar de ~ em algo** to keep an eye on sth; **ficar de ~ comprido em algo** to look longingly at sth; **passar os ~s por algo** to scan over sth; **pôr alguém nos ~s da rua** to put sb on the street; (de emprego) to fire sb; **não pregar o ~** not to sleep a wink; **ter bom ~ para** to have a good eye for; **ver com bons ~s** to approve of; **~ clínico** sharp ou keen eye; **~ de lince** sharp eye; **ter ~ de peixe morto** to be glassy-eyed; **~ grande** (fig) envy; **estar de ~ grande em algo** to covet sth; **ter ~ grande** to be envious; **~ mágico** (na porta) peephole, magic eye; **~ roxo** black eye; **~ por ~** an eye for an eye; **num abrir e fechar de ~s** in a flash; **longe dos ~s, longe do coração** out of sight, out of mind; **ele tem o ~ maior que a barriga** his eyes are bigger than his belly

oligarquia [oligax'kia] F oligarchy

olimpíada [oli'piada] F: **as O~s** the Olympics

olimpicamente [olĩpika'mẽtʃi] ADJ blissfully

olímpico, -a [o'lĩpiku, a] ADJ (jogos, chama) Olympic

olival [oli'vaw] (pl -ais) M olive grove

olivedo [oli'vedu] M = **olival**

oliveira [oli'vejra] F olive tree

olmeiro [ow'mejru] M = **olmo**

olmo ['ɔwmu] M elm

OLP ABR F (= Organização para a Libertação da Palestina) PLO

OM ABR (= onda média) MW

Omã [o'mã] M: (o) ~ Oman

ombreira [õ'brejra] F (de porta) doorpost; (de roupa) shoulder pad

ombro ['õbru] M shoulder; **encolher os ~s** ou **dar de ~s** to shrug one's shoulders; **chorar no ~ de alguém** to cry on sb's shoulder

omeleta [ome'leta] (PT) F = **omelete**

omelete [ome'letʃi] (BR) F omelette (Brit), omelet (US)

omissão [omi'sãw] (pl -ões) F omission; (negligência) negligence; (ato de não se manifestar) failure to appear

omisso, -a [o'misu, a] ADJ omitted; (negligente) negligent; (que não se manifesta) absent

omissões [omi'sõjʃ] FPL de **omissão**

omitir [omi'tʃiʳ] VT to omit; **omitir-se** VR to fail to appear

OMM ABR F (= Organização Meteorológica Mundial) WMO

omnipotente etc [omnipo'tẽtə] (PT) = **onipotente** etc

omnipresente [omnipre'zẽtə] (PT) ADJ = **onipresente**

omnisciente [omni'sjẽtə] (PT) ADJ = **onisciente**

omnívoro, -a [om'nivoru, a] (PT) ADJ = **onívoro**

omoplata [omo'plata] F shoulder blade

OMS ABR F (= Organização Mundial da Saúde) WHO

ON ABR (Com: de ações) = **ordinária nominativa**

onça ['õsa] F (peso) ounce; (animal) jaguar; **ser do tempo da ~** to be as old as the hills; **ficar uma ou virar ~** (col) to get furious; **estou numa ~ danada** (col) I'm flat broke

onça-parda (pl onças-pardas) F puma

onda ['õda] F wave; (moda) fashion; (confusão) commotion; **~ sonora/luminosa** sound/light wave; **~ curta/média/longa** short/medium/ long wave; **~ de calor** heat wave; **pegar ~** to go surfing; **ir na ~** (col) to follow the crowd; **ir na ~ de alguém** (col) to be taken in by sb; **estar na ~** to be in fashion; **fazer ~** (col) to make a fuss; **deixa de ~!** (col) cut the crap!; **isso é ~ dela** (col) that's just something she's made up; **tirar uma ~ de algo** to act like sth

onde ['õdʒi] ADV where ■ CONJ where, in which; **de ~ você é?** where are you from?; **por ~ through which; **por ~?** which way?; **~ quer que** wherever; **não ter ~ cair morto** (fig) to have nothing to call one's own; **fazer por ~** to work for it

ondeado, -a [õ'dʒjadu, a] ADJ wavy ■ M (de cabelo) wave

ondeante [õ'dʒjãtʃi] ADJ waving, undulating

ondear [õ'dʒjaʳ] VT to wave ■ VI to wave; (água) to ripple; (serpear) to meander, wind

ondulação [õdula'sãw] (pl -ões) F undulation

ondulado, -a [õdu'ladu, a] ADJ wavy

ondulante [õdu'lãtʃi] ADJ wavy

onerar [one'raʳ] VT to burden; (Com) to charge

oneroso, -a [one'rozu, ɔza] ADJ onerous; (dispendioso) costly

ônibus ['onibuʃ] (BR) M INV bus; **ponto de ~** bus-stop

onipotência [onipo'tẽsja] F omnipotence

onipotente [onipo'tẽtʃi] ADJ omnipotent

onipresente [onipre'zẽtʃi] ADJ omnipresent, ever-present

onírico, -a [o'niriku, a] ADJ dreamlike

onisciente [oni'sjẽtʃi] ADJ omniscient

onívoro, -a [o'nivoru, a] ADJ omnivorous

onomástico, -a [ono'maʃtʃiku, a] ADJ: **índice ~** index of proper names; **dia ~** name day

ônix ['oniks] M onyx

onomatopéia [onomato'pɛja] F onomatopoeia

ontem ['õtẽ] ADV yesterday; **~ à noite** last night; **~ à tarde/de manhã** yesterday afternoon/ morning

ONU ['onu] ABR F (= Organização das Nações Unidas) UNO

ônus ['onuʃ] M INV onus; (obrigação) obligation; (Com) charge; (encargo desagradável) burden; (imposto) tax burden

onze ['õzi] NUM eleven; v tb **cinco**

OP ABR (Com: ações) = **ordinária ao portador**

opa ['opa] EXCL (de admiração) wow!; (de espanto) oops!; (saudação) hi!

opacidade [opasi'dadʒi] F opaqueness; (escuridão) blackness

NB: European Portuguese adds the following consonants to certain words: **b** (sú(b)dito, su(b)til); **c** (a(c)ção, a(c)cionista, a(c)to); **m** (inde(m)ne); **p** (ado(p)çã, ado(p)tar); for further details see p. xiii.

opaco, -a [o'paku, a] ADJ opaque; (*obscuro*) dark
opala [o'pala] F opal; (*tecido*) fine muslin
opalino, -a [opa'linu, a] ADJ bluish white
opção [op'sãw] (*pl -ões*) F option, choice;
(*preferência*) first claim, right
open market ['opẽ('maxkitʃ)] M open market
OPEP [o'pepɪ] ABR F (= *Organização dos Países
Exportadores de Petróleo*) OPEC
ópera ['ɔpera] F opera; ~ **bufa** comic opera
operação [opera'sãw] (*pl -ões*) F operation;
(*Com*) transaction
operacional [operasjo'naw] (*pl -ais*) ADJ
operational; (*sistema, custos*) operating
operações [opera'sõjʃ] FPL *de* **operação**
operado, -a [ope'radu, a] ADJ (*Med*) who has (*ou
have*) had an operation ■ M/F person who has
had an operation
operador, a [opera'doᵣ(a)] M/F operator;
(*cirurgião*) surgeon; (*num cinema*) projectionist
operante [ope'rãtʃi] ADJ effective
operar [ope'raᵣ] VT to operate; (*produzir*) to
effect, bring about; (*Med*) to operate on ■ VI
to operate; (*agir*) to act, function; **operar-se**
VR (*suceder*) to take place; (*Med*) to have an
operation
operariado [opera'rjadu] M: **o** ~ the working
class
operário, -a [ope'rarju, a] ADJ working ■ M/F
worker; **classe operária** working class
opereta [ope'reta] F operetta
opinar [opi'naᵣ] VT (*julgar*) to think ■ VI (*dar o seu
parecer*) to give one's opinion
opinião [opi'njãw] (*pl -ões*) F opinion; **na
minha** ~ in my opinion; **ser de** *ou* **da** ~ **(de) que**
to be of the opinion that; **ser da** ~ **de alguém** to
think the same as sb, share sb's view; **mudar
de** ~ to change one's mind; ~ **pública** public
opinion
ópio ['ɔpju] M opium
opíparo, -a [o'piparu, a] ADJ (*formal*) splendid,
lavish
opõe *etc* [o'põj] VB *V* **opor**
opomos [o'pomoʃ] VB *V* **opor**
oponente [opo'nẽtʃi] ADJ opposing ■ M/F
opponent
opor [o'poᵣ] (*irreg*) VT to oppose; (*resistência*) to put
up, offer; (*objeção, dificuldade*) to raise; **opor-se**
VR: **opor-se a** (*fazer objeção*) to object to; (*resistir*)
to oppose; ~ **algo a algo** (*colocar em contraste*) to
contrast sth with sth
oportunamente [opoxtuna'mẽtʃi] ADV at an
opportune moment
oportunidade [opoxtuni'dadʒi] F opportunity;
na primeira ~ at the first opportunity
oportunismo [opoxtu'niʒmu] M opportunism
oportunista [opoxtu'niʃta] ADJ, M/F
opportunist
oportuno, -a [opox'tunu, a] ADJ (*momento*)
opportune, right; (*oferta de ajuda*) well-timed;
(*conveniente*) convenient, suitable
opôs [o'poʃ] VB *V* **opor**
oposição [opozi'sãw] F opposition; **em** ~ **a**

against; **fazer** ~ **a** to oppose
oposicionista [opozisjo'niʃta] ADJ opposition
atr ■ M/F member of the opposition
oposto, -a [o'poʃtu, 'pɔʃta] PP *de* **opor** ■ ADJ
(*contrário*) opposite; (*em frente*) facing, opposite;
(*opiniões*) opposing, opposite ■ M opposite
opressão [opre'sãw] (*pl -ões*) F oppression;
(*sufocação*) feeling of suffocation, tightness
in the chest; **opressivo, -a** [opre'sivu, a] ADJ
oppressive
opressões [opre'sõjʃ] FPL *de* **opressão**
opressor, a [opre'soᵣ(a)] M/F oppressor
oprimido, -a [opri'midu, a] ADJ oppressed ■ M:
os ~**s** the oppressed
oprimir [opri'miᵣ] VT to oppress; (*comprimir*) to
press ■ VI to be oppressive
opróbrio [o'prɔbrju] M (*infâmia*) ignominy;
(*formal: desonra*) shame
optar [op'taᵣ] VI to choose; ~ **por** to opt for; ~ **por
fazer** to opt to do; ~ **entre** to choose between
optativo, -a [opta'tʃivu, a] ADJ optional; (*Ling*)
optative
óptico, -ta ['ɔtiku, a] (PT) = **ótico** *etc*
óptimo, -a ['ɔtimu] (PT) ADJ = **ótimo** *etc*
opulência [opu'lẽsja] F opulence
opulento, -a [opu'lẽtu, a] ADJ opulent
opunha *etc* [o'puɲa] VB *V* **opor**
opus *etc* [o'puʃ] VB *V* **opor**
opúsculo [o'puʃkulu] M (*livreto*) booklet; (*pequena
obra*) pamphlet
opuser *etc* [opu'zeᵣ] VB *V* **opor**
ora ['ɔra] ADV now ■ CONJ well; **por** ~ for the
time being; ~ ..., ~ ... one moment ..., the next
...; ~ **sim**, ~ **não** first yes, then no; ~ **essa!** the
very idea!, come off it!; ~ **bem** now then; ~ **viva!**
hello there!; ~, **que besteira!** well, how stupid!;
~ **bolas!** (*col*) for heaven's sake!
oração [ora'sãw] (*pl -ões*) F (*reza*) prayer; (*discurso*)
speech; (*Ling*) clause
oráculo [o'rakulu] M oracle
orador, a [ora'doᵣ(a)] M/F (*aquele que fala*) speaker
oral [o'raw] (*pl -ais*) ADJ oral ■ F oral (exam)
orangotango [orãgu'tãgu] M orang-utan
orar [o'raᵣ] VI (*Rel*) to pray
oratória [ora'tɔrja] F public speaking, oratory
oratório, -a [ora'tɔrju, a] ADJ oratorical ■ M
(*Mús*) oratorio; (*Rel*) oratory
orbe ['ɔxbi] M globe
órbita ['ɔxbita] F orbit; (*do olho*) socket; **entrar/
colocar em** ~ to go/put into orbit; **estar em** ~ to
be in orbit
orbital [oxbi'taw] (*pl -ais*) ADJ orbital
Órcades ['ɔxkadʒiʃ] FPL: **as** ~ the Orkneys
orçamentário, -a [oxsamẽ'tarju, a] ADJ budget
atr
orçamento [oxsa'mẽtu] M (*do estado etc*) budget;
(*avaliação*) estimate; ~ **sem compromisso**
estimate with no obligation
orçar [ox'saᵣ] VT to value, estimate ■ VI: ~ **em**
(*gastos etc*) to be valued at, be put at; ~ **a** to reach,
go up to; **ele orça por 20 anos** he is around 20;
um projeto orçado em $100 a project valued

at $100

ordeiro, -a [ox'dejru, a] ADJ orderly

ordem ['oxdẽ] (pl -ns) F order; **às suas ordens**
at your service; **um lucro da ~ de $60 milhões**
a profit in the order of $60 million; **até nova ~**
until further notice; **de primeira ~** first-rate;
estar em ~ to be tidy; **pôr em ~** to arrange,
tidy; **tudo em ~?** (col) everything OK?; **por
~** in order, in turn; **dar/receber ordens** to
give/take orders; **dar uma ~ na casa** to tidy the
house; **~ alfabética/cronológica** alphabetical/
chronological order; **~ bancária** banker's
order; **~ de grandeza** order of magnitude; **~ de
pagamento** (Com) banker's draft; **~ de prisão**
(Jur) prison order; **~ do dia** agenda; **O~ dos
Advogados** Bar Association; **~ pública** public
order, law and order; **~ social** social order

ordenação [oxdena'sãw] (pl -ões) F (Rel)
ordination; (ordem) order; (arrumação) tidiness,
orderliness

ordenado, -a [oxde'nadu, a] ADJ (posto em ordem)
in order; (metódico) orderly; (Rel) ordained ▪ M
salary, wages pl

ordenança [oxde'nãsa] M (Mil) orderly ▪ F
(regulamento) ordinance

ordenar [oxde'na'] VT to arrange, put in order;
(determinar) to order; (Rel) to ordain; **ordenar-se**
VR (Rel) to be ordained; **~ que alguém faça** to
order sb to do; **~ algo a alguém** to order sth
from sb

ordenhar [oxde'ɲa'] VT to milk

ordens ['oxdẽʃ] FPL de **ordem**

ordinariamente [oxdʒinarja'mẽte] ADV
ordinarily, usually

ordinário, -a [oxdʒi'narju, a] ADJ ordinary;
(comum) usual; (medíocre) mediocre; (grosseiro)
coarse, vulgar; (de má qualidade) inferior; (sem
caráter) rough; **de ~** usually

orégano [o'rɛganu] M oregano

orelha [o'reʎa] F (Anat) ear; (aba) flap; **de ~s em
pé** (col) on one's guard; **endividado até as ~s** up
to one's ears in debt; **~s de abano** flappy ears

orelhada [ore'ʎada] (col) F: **de ~** through the
grapevine

orelhão [ore'ʎãw] (pl -ões) M open telephone
booth

órfã ['oxfã] F de **órfão**

orfanato [oxfa'natu] M orphanage

órfão, -fã ['oxfãw] (pl -s) ADJ, M/F orphan; **~ de
pai** with no father; **~ de** (fig) starved of

orfeão [ox'fjãw] (pl -ões) M choral society

orgânico, -a [ox'ganiku, a] ADJ organic

organismo [oxga'niʒmu] M organism; (entidade)
organization

organista [oxga'niʃta] M/F organist

organização [oxganiza'sãw] (pl -ões) F
organization; **~ de caridade** charity; **~ de
fachada** front; **~ sem fins lucrativos** non-
profit-making organization

organizador, a [oxganiza'do'(a)] M/F organizer
▪ ADJ (comitê) organizing

organizar [oxgani'za'] VT to organize

organograma [oxgano'grama] M flow chart

órgão ['oxgãw] (pl -s) M organ; (governamental
etc) institution, body; **~ de imprensa** news
publication

orgasmo [ox'gaʒmu] M orgasm

orgia [ox'ʒia] F orgy

orgulhar [oxgu'ʎa'] VT to make proud; **orgulhar-
se** VR: **orgulhar-se de** to be proud of

orgulho [ox'guʎu] M pride; (arrogância)
arrogance; **orgulhoso, -a** [oxgu'ʎozu, ɔza] ADJ
proud; (arrogante) haughty

orientação [orjẽta'sãw] F (direção) direction; (de
tese) supervision; (posição) position; (tendência)
tendency; **~ educacional** training, guidance; **~
vocacional** careers guidance

orientador, a [orjẽta'do'(a)] M/F advisor; (de
tese) supervisor ▪ ADJ guiding; **~ profissional**
careers advisor

oriental [orjẽ'taw] (pl -ais) ADJ eastern; (do
Extremo Oriente) oriental ▪ M/F oriental

orientar [orjẽ'ta'] VT (situar) to orientate; (indicar
o rumo) to direct; (aconselhar) to guide; **orientar-
se** VR to get one's bearings; **~-se por algo** to
follow sth

oriente [o'rjẽtʃi] M: **o O~** the East; **Extremo O~**
Far East; **O~ Médio/Próximo** Middle/Near East

orifício [ori'fisju] M orifice

origem [o'riʒẽ] (pl -ns) F origin; (ascendência)
lineage, descent; **lugar de ~** birthplace; **pessoa
de ~ brasileira/humilde** person of Brazilian
origin/of humble origins; **dar ~ a** to give rise to;
país de ~ country of origin; **ter ~** to originate

original [oriʒi'naw] (pl -ais) ADJ original;
(estranho) strange, odd ▪ M original;
(na datilografia) top copy; **originalidade**
[oriʒinali'dadʒi] F originality; (excentricidade)
eccentricity

originar [oriʒi'na'] VT to give rise to, start;
originar-se VR to arise; **~-se de** to originate
from

originário, -a [oriʒi'narju, a] ADJ (natural)
native; **~ de** (proveniente) originating from; **um
pássaro ~ do Brasil** a bird native to Brazil

oriundo, -a [o'rjũdu, a] ADJ: **~ de** (procedente)
arising from; (natural) native of

orixá [ori'ʃa] M Afro-Brazilian deity

orla ['oxla] F (borda) edge, border; (de roupa) hem;
(faixa) strip; **~ marítima** seafront

orlar [ox'la'] VT: **~ algo de algo** to edge sth with
sth

ornamentação [oxnamẽta'sãw] F
ornamentation

ornamental [oxnamẽ'taw] (pl -ais) ADJ
ornamental

ornamentar [oxnamẽ'ta'] VT to decorate, adorn

ornamento [oxna'mẽtu] M adornment,

decoration
ornar [ox'na^r] VT to adorn, decorate
ornato [ox'natu] M adornment, decoration
ornitologia [oxnitolo'ʒia] F ornithology
ornitologista [oxnitolo'ʒiʃta] M/F ornithologist
orquestra [ox'kɛʃtra] (PT -esta) F orchestra;
~sinfônica/de câmara symphony/chamber
orchestra
orquestração [oxkeʃtra'sãw] (PT -esta-) F (Mús)
orchestration; (fig) harmonization
orquestrar [oxkeʃ'tra^r] (PT -estar) VT (Mús) to
orchestrate; (fig) to harmonize
orquídea [ox'kidʒia] F orchid
ortodoxia [oxtodok'sia] F orthodoxy
ortodoxo, -a [oxto'dɔksu, a] ADJ orthodox
ortografia [oxtogra'fia] F spelling
ortopedia [oxtope'dʒia] F orthopaedics sg (Brit),
orthopedics sg (US)
ortopédico, -a [oxto'pɛdʒiku, a] ADJ
orthopaedic (Brit), orthopedic (US)
ortopedista [oxtope'dʒiʃta] M/F orthopaedic
(Brit) ou orthopedic (US) specialist
orvalhar [ox'vaʎa^r] VT to sprinkle with dew
orvalho [ox'vaʎu] M dew
os [uʃ] ART DEF V **o**
Osc. ABR (= oscilação) change in price from previous day
oscilação [osila'sãw] (pl -ões) F (movimento)
oscillation; (flutuação) fluctuation; (hesitação)
hesitation
oscilante [osi'lãtʃi] ADJ oscillating; (fig: hesitante)
hesitant
oscilar [osi'la^r] VI to oscillate; (balançar-se) to
sway, swing; (variar) to fluctuate; (hesitar) to
hesitate
ossatura [osa'tura] F skeleton, frame
ósseo, -a ['ɔsju, a] ADJ bony; (Anat: medula etc)
bone atr
osso ['osu] M bone; (dificuldade) predicament;
um ~ duro de roer a hard nut to crack; **~s do
ofício** occupational hazards
ossudo, -a [o'sudu, a] ADJ bony
ostensivo, -a [oʃtẽ'sivu, a] ADJ ostensible,
apparent; (com alarde) ostentatious
ostentação [oʃtẽta'sãw] (pl -ões) F ostentation;
(exibição) display, show
ostentar [oʃtẽ'ta^r] VT to show; (alardear) to show
off, flaunt
ostentoso, -a [oʃtẽ'tozu, ɔza] ADJ ostentatious,
showy
osteopata [oʃtʃjo'pata] M/F osteopath
ostra ['oʃtra] F oyster
ostracismo [oʃtra'siʒmu] M ostracism
OTAN ['otã] ABR F (= Organização do Tratado do
Atlântico Norte) NATO
otário [o'tarju] (col) M fool, idiot
OTE (BR) ABR F = **Obrigação do Tesouro
Estadual**
ótica ['ɔtʃika] F optics sg; (loja) optician's; (fig:
ponto de vista) viewpoint; v tb **ótico**
ótico, -a ['ɔtʃiku, a] ADJ optical ■ M/F optician
otimismo [otʃi'miʒmu] M optimism
otimista [otʃi'miʃta] ADJ optimistic ■ M/F

optimist
otimizar [otʃimi'za^r] VT to optimize
ótimo, -a ['ɔtʃimu, a] ADJ excellent, splendid
■ EXCL great!, super!
OTN (BR) ABR F = **Obrigação do Tesouro
Nacional**
otorrino [oto'xinu] M/F ear, nose and throat
specialist
ou [o] CONJ or; **ou este ou aquele** either this
one or that one; **ou seja** in other words
OUA ABR F (= Organização da Unidade Africana) OAU
ouço etc ['osu] VB V **ouvir**
ourela [o'rela] F edge, border
ouriçado, -a [ori'sadu, a] (col) ADJ excited
ouriçar [ori'sa^r] VT (col: animar) to liven up;
(: excitar) to excite; **ouriçar-se** VR to bristle; (col)
to get excited
ouriço [o'risu] M (europeu) hedgehog; (casca)
shell; (col: animação) riot
ouriço-cacheiro [-ka'ʃejru] (pl **ouriços-
cacheiros**) M coendou
ouriço-do-mar (pl **ouriços-do-mar**) M sea
urchin
ourives [o'riviʃ] M/F INV (fabricante) goldsmith;
(vendedor) jeweller (Brit), jeweler (US)
ourivesaria [oriveza'ria] F (arte) goldsmith's
art; (loja) jeweller's (shop) (Brit), jewelry store
(US)
ouro ['oru] M gold; **ouros** MPL (Cartas)
diamonds; **de ~** golden; **nadar em ~** to be
rolling in money; **valer ~s** to be worth one's
weight in gold
ousadia [oza'dʒia] F daring; (lance ousado)
daring move; **ter a ~ de fazer** to have the
cheek to do; **ousado, -a** [o'zadu, a] ADJ daring,
bold
ousar [o'za^r] VT, VI to dare
out. ABR (= Outubro) Oct
outdoor [awt'dɔ^r] (pl -s) M billboard
outeiro [o'tejru] M hill
outonal [oto'naw] (pl -ais) ADJ autumnal
outono [o'tɔnu] M autumn
outorga [o'tɔxga] F granting, concession
outorgante [otox'gãtʃi] M/F grantor
outorgar [otox'ga^r] VT to grant
outrem [o'trẽ] PRON INV (sg) somebody else's; (pl)
other people

○ **PALAVRA CHAVE**

outro, -a ['otru, a] ADJ **1** (distinto: sg) another;
(: pl) other; **outra coisa** something else; **de
outro modo, de outra maneira** otherwise; **no
outro dia** the next day; **ela está outra** (mudada)
she's changed
2 (adicional): **traga-me outro café, por favor**
can I have another coffee please; **outra vez**
again
■ PRON **1: o outro** the other one; **(os) outros**
(the) others; **de outro** somebody else's
2 (recíproco): **odeiam-se uns aos outro** they
hate one another ou each other

3: outro tanto the same again; **comer outro tanto** to eat the same *ou* as much again; **ele recebeu uma dezena de telegramas e outras tantas chamadas** he got about ten telegrams and as many calls

outrora [o'trɔra] ADV formerly

outrossim [otro'sī] ADV likewise, moreover

outubro [o'tubru] (PT O-) M October; *v tb* julho

ouvido [o'vidu] M (*Anat*) ear; (*sentido*) hearing; **de ~** by ear; **dar ~s a** to listen to; **entrar por um ~ e sair pelo outro** to go in one ear and out the other; **fazer ~s moucos** *ou* **de mercador** to turn a deaf ear, pretend not to hear; **ser todo ~s** to be all ears; **ter bom ~ para música** to have a good ear for music; **se isso chegar aos ~s dele, ...** if he gets to hear about it, ...

ouvinte [o'vītʃi] M/F listener; (*estudante*) auditor

ouvir [o'vi'] VT to hear; (*com atenção*) to listen to; (*missa*) to attend ■ VI to hear; to listen; (*levar descompostura*) to catch it; **~ dizer que ...** to hear that ...; **~ falar de** to hear of

ova ['ɔva] F roe; **uma ~!** (*col*) my eye!, no way!

ovação [ova'sãw] (*pl* -ões) F ovation, acclaim

ovacionar [ovasjo'na'] VT to acclaim; (*pessoa no palco*) to give a standing ovation to

ovações [ova'sõjʃ] FPL *de* **ovação**

oval [o'vaw] (*pl* -ais) ADJ, F oval

ovalado, -a [ova'ladu, a] ADJ oval

ovário [o'varju] M ovary

ovelha [o'veʎa] F sheep; **~ negra** (*fig*) black sheep

over ['ove'] ADJ overnight ■ M overnight market

overnight [ovex'najtʃi] = **over**

óvni ['ɔvni] ABR M (= *objeto voador não identificado*) UFO

ovo ['ovu] M egg; **~s cozidos duros** hard-boiled eggs; **~s escaldados** (PT) *ou* **pochê** (BR) poached eggs; **~s estrelados** *ou* **fritos** fried eggs; **~s mexidos** scrambled eggs; **~s quentes** soft-boiled eggs; **~s de granja** free-range eggs; **~ de Páscoa** Easter egg; **estar/acordar de ~ virado** (*col*) to be/wake up in a bad mood; **pisar em ~s** (*fig*) to tread carefully; **ser um ~** (*apartamento etc*) to be a shoebox

ovulação [ovula'sãw] F ovulation

óvulo ['ɔvulu] M egg, ovum

oxalá [oʃa'la] EXCL let's hope ...; **~ a situação melhore em breve** let's hope the situation improves soon

oxidação [oksida'sãw] F (*Quím*) oxidation; (*ferrugem*) rusting

oxidado, -a [oksi'dadu, a] ADJ rusty; (*Quím*) oxidized

oxidar [oksi'da'] VT to rust; (*Quím*) to oxidize; **oxidar-se** VR to rust, go rusty; to oxidize

óxido ['ɔksidu] M oxide

oxigenado, -a [oksiʒe'nadu, a] ADJ (*cabelo*) bleached; (*Quím*) oxygenated; **água oxigenada** peroxide; **uma loura oxigenada** a peroxide blonde

oxigenar [oksiʒe'na'] VT to oxygenate; (*cabelo*) to bleach

oxigênio [oksi'ʒenju] M oxygen

oxum [o'ʃũ] M *Afro-Brazilian river god*

ozônio [o'zonju] M ozone; **camada de ~** ozone layer

NB: *European Portuguese adds the following consonants to certain words:* **b** (sú(b)dito, su(b)til); **c** (a(c)ção, a(c)cionista, a(c)to); **m** (inde(m)ne); **p** (ado(p)çã, ado(p)tar); *for further details see p. xiii.*

Pp

P, p [pe] (*pl* ps) M P, p; **P de Pedro** P for Peter
P. ABR (= *Praça*) Sq.; = **Padre**
p. ABR (= *página*) p.; (: = *parte*) pt; = **por**;
= **próximo**
p/ ABR = **para**
PA ABR = **Pará** ■ ABR (*Com: de ações*)
= **preferencial, classe A**
p.a. ABR (= *por ano*) p.a
pá [pa] F shovel; (*de remo, hélice*) blade; (*de moinho*)
sail ■ M (PT) pal, mate; **pá de lixo** dustpan; **pá
mecânica** bulldozer; **uma pá de** lots of; **da pá
virada** (*col*) wild
paca ['paka] F (*Zool*) paca ■ M/F fool ■ ADJ
stupid ■ ADV (*col*): **'tá quente ~** it's bloody hot
pacatez [paka'teʒ] F (*de pessoa*) quietness; (*de
lugar, vida*) peacefulness
pacato, -a [pa'katu, a] ADJ (*pessoa*) quiet; (*lugar*)
peaceful
pachorra [pa'ʃoxa] F phlegm, impassiveness;
ter a ~ de fazer to have the gall to do
pachorrento, -a [paʃo'xẽtu, a] ADJ slow,
sluggish
paciência [pa'sjẽsja] F patience; (*Cartas*)
patience; **ter ~** to be patient; **~!** we'll (*ou* you'll
etc) just have to put up with it!; **perder a ~** to
lose one's patience; **paciente** [pa'sjẽtʃi] ADJ, M/F
patient
pacificação [pasifika'sãw] F pacification
pacificador, a [pasifika'do^r(a)] ADJ calming
■ M/F peacemaker
pacificar [pasifi'ka^r] VT to pacify, calm (down);
pacificar-se VR to calm down
pacífico, -a [pa'sifiku, a] ADJ (*pessoa*) peace-
loving; (*aceito sem discussão*) undisputed;
(*sossegado*) peaceful; **o (Oceano) P~** the Pacific
(Ocean); **ponto ~** undisputed point
pacifismo [pasi'fiʒmu] M pacifism
pacifista [pasi'fiʃta] M/F pacifist
paço ['pasu] M palace; (*fig*) court
paçoca [pa'sɔka] F (*doce*) peanut fudge; (*fig:
misturada*) jumble, hotchpotch; (: *coisa amassada*)
crumpled mess
pacote [pa'kɔtʃi] M packet; (*embrulho*) parcel;
(*Econ, Comput, Turismo*) package
pacto ['paktu] M pact; (*ajuste*) agreement; **~ de
não-agressão** non-aggression treaty; **~ de
sangue** blood pact; **P~ de Varsóvia** Warsaw

Pact
pactuar [pak'twa^r] VT to agree on ■ VI: **~ (com)**
to make a pact *ou* an agreement with
padaria [pada'ria] F bakery, baker's (shop)
padecer [pade'se^r] VT to suffer; (*suportar*) to put
up with, endure ■ VI: **~ de** to suffer from
padecimento [padesi'mẽtu] M suffering; (*dor*)
pain
padeiro [pa'dejru] M baker
padiola [pa'dʒɔla] F stretcher
padrão [pa'drãw] (*pl* -ões) M standard; (*medida*)
gauge; (*desenho*) pattern; (*fig: modelo*) model; **~ de
vida** standard of living
padrasto [pa'draʃtu] M stepfather
padre ['padri] M priest; **O Santo P~** the Holy
Father
padrinho [pa'driɲu] M (*Rel*) godfather; (*de noivo*)
best man; (*patrono*) sponsor; (*paraninfo*) guest of
honour
padroeiro, -a [pa'drwejru, a] M/F patron; (*santo*)
patron saint
padrões [pa'drõjʃ] MPL *de* **padrão**
padronização [padroniza'sãw] F
standardization
padronizado, -a [padroni'zadu, a] ADJ
standardized, standard
padronizar [padroni'za^r] VT to standardize
pães [pãjʃ] MPL *de* **pão**
paetê [pae'te] M sequin
pág. ABR (= *página*) p
paga ['paga] F payment; (*salário*) pay; **em ~ de** in
return for
pagã [pa'gã] F *de* **pagão**
pagador, a [paga'do^r(a)] ADJ paying ■ M/F
(*quem paga*) payer; (*de salário*) pay clerk; (*de banco*)
teller
pagadoria [pagado'ria] F payment office
pagamento [paga'mẽtu] M payment; **~ a prazo**
ou **em prestações** payment in instal(l)ments; **~
à vista** cash payment; **~ contra entrega** (*Com*)
COD, cash on delivery
pagão, -gã [pa'gãw] (*pl* -s/-s) ADJ, M/F pagan
pagar [pa'ga^r] VT to pay; (*compras, pecados*) to
pay for; (*o que devia*) to pay back; (*retribuir*) to
repay ■ VI to pay; **~ por algo** (*tb fig*) to pay for
sth; **~ a prestações** to pay in instal(l)ments; **~
à vista** (BR), **~ a pronto** to pay on the spot, pay

at the time of purchase; ~ **de contado** (PT) to pay cash; **a** ~ unpaid; ~ **caro** (fig) to pay a high price; ~ **a pena** to pay the penalty; ~ **na mesma moeda** (fig) to give tit for tat; ~ **para ver** (fig) to call sb's bluff, demand proof; **você me paga!** you'll pay for this!

página ['paʒina] F page; ~ **de rosto** frontispiece, title page; ~ **em branco** blank page; ~ **(da) web** web page

paginação [paʒina'sãw] F pagination

paginar [paʒi'na^r] VT to paginate

pago, -a ['pagu, a] PP de **pagar** ■ ADJ paid; (fig) even ■ M pay

pagode [pa'gɔdʒi] M pagoda; (fig) fun, high jinks pl; (festa) knees-up

pagto. ABR = **pagamento**

paguei etc [pa'gej] VB V **pagar**

pai [paj] M father; **pais** MPL parents; ~ **adotivo** adoptive father; ~ **de família** family man; **um idiota de ~ e mãe** (col) a complete idiot

pai-de-santo (pl pais-de-santo) M macumba priest

pai-de-todos (pl pais-de-todos) (col) M middle finger

pai-dos-burros (pl pais-dos-burros) (col) M dictionary

painel [paj'nɛw] (pl -éis) M (numa parede) panel; (quadro) picture; (Auto) dashboard; (de avião) instrument panel; (reunião de especialistas) panel (of experts)

paio ['paju] M pork sausage

paiol [pa'jɔw] (pl -óis) M storeroom; (celeiro) barn; (de pólvora) powder magazine; ~ **de carvão** coal bunker

pairar [paj'ra^r] VI to hover ■ VT (embarcação) to lie to

país [pa'jiʃ] M country; (região) land; ~ **encantado** fairyland; ~ **natal** native land

paisagem [paj'zaʒẽ] (pl -ns) F scenery, landscape; (pintura) landscape

paisano, -a [paj'zanu, a] ADJ civilian ■ M/F (não militar) civilian; (compatriota) fellow countryman; **à paisana** (soldado) in civvies; (policial) in plain clothes

Países Baixos MPL: **os** ~ the Netherlands

paixão [paj'ʃãw] (pl -ões) F passion

paixonite [pajʃo'nitʃi] (col) F: ~ **(aguda)** crush, infatuation

pajé [pa'ʒɛ] M medicine man

pajear [pa'ʒja^r] VT (cuidar) to look after; (paparicar) to mollycoddle

pajem ['paʒẽ] (pl -ns) M (moço) page

pala ['pala] F (de boné) peak; (em automóvel) sun visor; (de vestido) yoke; (de sapato) strap; (col: dica) tip

palacete [pala'setʃi] M small palace

palácio [pa'lasju] M palace; ~ **da justiça** courthouse; ~ **real** royal palace; **Palácio do**

Planalto; see below

● **PALÁCIO DO PLANALTO**
●
● Palácio de Planalto is the seat of the Brazilian
● government, in Brasília. The name comes
● from the fact that the Brazilian capital is
● situated on a plateau. It has come to be a
● byword for central government.

paladar [pala'da^r] M taste; (Anat) palate

paladino [pala'dʒinu] M (medieval, fig) champion

palafita [pala'fita] F (estacaria) stilts pl; (habitação) stilt house

palanque [pa'lãki] M (estrado) stand

palatável [pala'tavew] (pl -eis) ADJ palatable

palato [pa'latu] M palate

palavra [pa'lavra] F word; (fala) speech; (promessa) promise; (direito de falar) right to speak; ~! honestly!; **pessoa de/sem** ~ reliable/unreliable person; **em outras ~s** in other words; **em poucas ~s** briefly; **cumprir a/faltar com a** ~ to keep/break one's word; **dar a ~ a alguém** to give sb the chance to speak; **não dar uma** ~ not to say a word; **dirigir a ~ a** to address; **estar com a** ~ **na boca** to have the word on the tip of one's tongue; **pedir a** ~ to ask permission to speak; **ter** ~ (pessoa) to be reliable; **tirar a** ~ **da boca de alguém** to take the words right out of sb's mouth; **tomar a** ~ to take the floor; **a última** ~ (tb fig) the last word; ~ **de honra** word of honour; ~ **de ordem** watchword, formula; ~**s cruzadas** crossword (puzzle) sg

palavra-chave (pl palavras-chaves) F key word

palavrão [pala'vrãw] (pl -ões) M (obsceno) swearword

palavreado [pala'vrjadu] M babble, gibberish; (loquacidade) smooth talk

palavrões [pala'vrõjʃ] MPL de **palavrão**

palco ['palku] M (Teatro) stage; (fig: local) scene

paleontologia [paljõtolo'ʒia] F palaeontology (Brit), paleontology (US)

palerma [pa'lɛxma] ADJ silly, stupid ■ M/F fool

Palestina [paleʃ'tʃina] F: a ~ Palestine; **palestino, -a** [paleʃ'tʃinu, a] ADJ, M/F Palestinian

palestra [pa'lɛʃtra] F (conversa) chat, talk; (conferência) lecture, talk

palestrar [paleʃ'tra^r] VI to chat, talk

paleta [pa'leta] F palette

paletó [pale'tɔ] M jacket; **abotoar o** ~ (col) to kick the bucket

palha ['paʎa] F straw; **chapéu de** ~ straw hat; **não mexer ou levantar uma** ~ (col) not to lift a finger

palhaçada [paʎa'sada] F (ato, dito) joke; (cena) farce

palhaço [pa'ʎasu] M clown

palheiro [pa'ʎejru] M hayloft; (monte de feno) haystack

NB: European Portuguese adds the following consonants to certain words: **b** (sú(b)dito, su(b)til); **c** (a(c)ção, a(c)cionista, a(c)to); **m** (inde(m)ne); **p** (ado(p)çã, ado(p)tar); for further details see p. xiii.

palheta [pa'ʎeta] F (*de veneziana*) slat; (*de turbina*) blade; (*de pintor*) palette

palhoça [pa'ʎɔsa] F thatched hut

paliar [pa'ljaʳ] VT (*disfarçar*) to disguise, gloss over; (*atenuar*) to mitigate, extenuate

paliativo, -a [palja'tʃivu, a] ADJ palliative

paliçada [pali'sada] F fence; (*militar*) stockade; (*para torneio*) enclosure

palidez [pali'deʒ] F paleness

pálido, -a ['palidu, a] ADJ pale

pálio ['palju] M canopy

palitar [pali'taʳ] VT to pick ■ VI to pick one's teeth

paliteiro [pali'tejru] M toothpick holder

palito [pa'litu] M stick; (*para os dentes*) toothpick; (*col: pessoa*) beanpole; (: *perna*) pin

palma ['pawma] F (*folha*) palm leaf; (*da mão*) palm; **bater ~s** to clap; **conhecer algo como a ~ da mão** to know sth like the back of one's hand; **trazer alguém nas ~s da mão** (*fig*) to pamper sb; **palmada** [paw'mada] F slap

palmatória [pawma'tɔrja] F: **~ do mundo** self-righteous person; v tb **mão**

palmeira [paw'mejra] F palm tree

palmilha [paw'miʎa] F inner sole

palmilhar [pawmi'ʎaʳ] VT, VI to walk

palmito [paw'mitu] M palm heart

palmo ['pawmu] M (*hand*) span; **~ a ~** inch by inch; **não enxerga um ~ adiante do nariz** he can't see further than the nose on his face

palpável [paw'pavew] (*pl* -**eis**) ADJ tangible; (*fig*) obvious

pálpebra ['pawpebra] F eyelid

palpitação [pawpita'sãw] (*pl* -**ões**) F beating, throbbing; **palpitações** FPL (*batimentos cardíacos*) palpitations

palpitante [pawpi'tãtʃi] ADJ beating, throbbing; (*fig: emocionante*) thrilling; (: *de interesse atual*) sensational

palpitar [pawpi'taʳ] VI (*coração*) to beat; (*comover-se*) to shiver; (*dar palpite*) to stick one's oar in

palpite [paw'pitʃi] M (*intuição*) hunch; (*Jogo, Turfe*) tip; (*opinião*) opinion; **dar ~** to give one's two cents' worth, stick one's oar in

palpiteiro, -a [pawpi'tejru, a] ADJ meddling ■ M/F meddler

palude [pa'ludʒi] M marsh, swamp

paludismo [palu'dʒiʒmu] M malaria

palustre [pa'luʃtri] ADJ (*terra*) marshy; (*aves*) marsh-dwelling

pamonha [pa'mɔɲa] ADJ idiotic ■ M/F nitwit

pampa ['pãpa] F pampas; **às ~s** (+n: *col*) loads of; (+ *adj, adv*) really

panaca [pa'naka] ADJ stupid ■ M/F fool

panacéia [pana'sɛja] F panacea

Panamá [pana'ma] M: **o ~** Panama; **o canal do ~** the Panama Canal

panamenho, -a [pana'mɛɲu, a] ADJ, M/F Panamanian

pan-americano, -a [pan-] ADJ Pan-American

pança ['pãsa] F belly, paunch

pancada [pã'kada] F (*no corpo*) blow, hit; (*choque*) knock; (*de relógio*) stroke ■ M/F (*col*) loony ■ ADJ crazy; **~ d'água** downpour; **dar uma ~ com a cabeça** to bang one's head; **dar ~ em alguém** to get hit; **pancadaria** [pãkada'ria] F (*surra*) beating; (*tumulto*) fight

pâncreas ['pãkrjaʃ] M INV pancreas

pançudo, -a [pã'sudu, a] ADJ fat, potbellied

panda ['pãda] F panda

pandarecos [pãda'rɛkuʃ] MPL: **em ~** in pieces; (*fig: exausto*) worn out; (: *moralmente*) devastated

pândega ['pãdega] F merrymaking, good time

pândego, -a ['pãdegu, a] ADJ (*farrista*) merrymaking; (*engraçado*) jolly ■ M/F merrymaker; joker

pandeiro [pã'dejru] M tambourine

pandemônio [pãde'monju] M pandemonium

pane ['pani] F breakdown

panegírico [pane'ʒiriku] M panegyric

panejar [pane'ʒaʳ] VI to flap

panela [pa'nɛla] F (*de barro*) pot; (*de metal*) pan; (*de cozinhar*) saucepan; (*no dente*) large cavity, hole; **~ de pressão** pressure cooker

panelinha [pane'liɲa] F clique

panfletar [pãfle'taʳ] VI to distribute pamphlets

panfleto [pã'fletu] M pamphlet

pangaré [pãga'rɛ] M (*cavalo*) nag

pânico ['paniku] M panic; **em ~** panic-stricken; **entrar em ~** to panic

panificação [panifika'sãw] (*pl* -**ões**) F (*fabricação*) bread-making; (*padaria*) bakery

panificadora [panifika'dora] F baker's

pano ['panu] M cloth; (*Teatro*) curtain; (*largura de tecido*) width; (*vela*) sheet, sail; **~ de chão** floor cloth; **~ de pratos** tea-towel; **~ de pó** duster; **~ de fundo** (*tb fig*) backdrop; **a todo o ~** at full speed; **por baixo do ~** (*fig*) under the counter; **dar ~ para mangas** (*fig*) to give food for thought; **pôr ~s quentes em algo** (*fig*) to dampen sth down

panorama [pano'rama] M (*vista*) view; (*fig: observação*) survey

panorâmica [pano'ramika] F (*exposição*) survey

panorâmico, -a [pano'ramiku, a] ADJ panoramic

panqueca [pã'kɛka] F pancake

pantalonas [pãta'lɔnaʃ] FPL baggy trousers

pantanal [pãta'naw] (*pl* -**ais**) M swampland

pântano ['pãtanu] M marsh, swamp

pantanoso, -a [pãta'nozu, ɔza] ADJ marshy, swampy

panteão [pã'tjãw] (*pl* -**ões**) M pantheon

pantera [pã'tɛra] F panther

pantomima [pãto'mima] F pantomime

pantufa [pã'tufa] F slipper

pão [pãw] (*pl* **pães**) M bread; **o P~ de Açúcar** (*no Rio*) Sugarloaf Mountain; **~ de carne** meat loaf; **~ de centeio** rye bread; **~ de fôrma** sliced loaf; **~ caseiro** home-made bread; **~ francês** French bread; **~ integral** wholemeal (*Brit*) ou wholewheat (*US*) bread; **~ preto** black bread; **~ torrado** toast; **ganhar o ~** to earn a living; **~ dormido** day-old bread; **dizer ~, ~, queijo,**

queijo (col) to call a spade a spade, pull no punches; **comer o ~ que o diabo amassou** (fig) to have it tough; **tirar o ~ da boca de alguém** (fig) to take the food out of sb's mouth

pão-de-ló [-lɔ] M sponge cake

pão-durismo [-du'riʒmu] (col) M meanness, stinginess

pão-duro (pl **pães-duros**) (col) ADJ mean, stingy ■ M/F miser

pãozinho [pãw'ziɲu] M roll

papa ['papa] M Pope; (fig) spiritual leader ■ F mush, pap; (mingau) porridge; **não ter ~s na língua** to be outspoken, not to mince one's words

papada [pa'pada] F double chin

papagaiada [papagaj'ada] (col) F showing off

papagaio [papa'gaju] M parrot; (pipa) kite; (Com) accommodation bill; (Auto) provisional licence (Brit), student driver's license (US) ■ EXCL (col) heavens!

papai [pa'paj] M dad, daddy; **P~ Noel** Santa Claus, Father Christmas; **o ~ aqui** (col) yours truly

papal [pa'paw] (pl **-ais**) ADJ papal

papa-moscas F INV (Bio) flycatcher

papar [pa'paʳ] (col) VT (comer) to eat; (extorquir): **~ algo a alguém** to get sth out of sb ■ VI to eat

paparicar [papari'kaʳ] VT to pamper

paparicos [papa'rikuʃ] MPL (mimos) pampering sg

papear [pa'pjaʳ] VI to chat

papel [pa'pew] (pl **-éis**) M paper; (Teatro) part, role; (função) role; **fazer o ~ de** to play the part of; **fazer ~ de idiota** etc to play the fool etc; **~ aéreo** airmail paper; **~ de embrulho** wrapping paper/tinfoil; **~ higiênico** toilet paper; **~ de parede** wallpaper; **~ de seda/transparente** tissue paper/tracing paper; **~ laminado** ou **lustroso** coated paper; **~ ofício** foolscap; **~ pardo** brown paper; **~ timbrado** headed paper; **~ usado** waste paper; **~ yes®** tissue, kleenex®; **ficar no ~** (fig) to stay on the drawing board; **pôr no ~** to put down on paper ou in writing; **de ~ passado** officially; **papelada** [pape'lada] F pile of papers; (burocracia) paperwork, red tape; **papelão** [pape'lãw] M cardboard; (fig) fiasco; **fazer um papelão** to make a fool of o.s.

papelaria [papela'ria] F stationer's (shop)

papel-carbono M carbon paper

papeleta [pape'leta] F (cartaz) notice; (papel avulso) piece of paper; (Med) chart

papel-moeda (pl **papéis-moeda(s)**) M paper money, banknotes pl

papel-pergaminho M parchment

papelzinho [papew'ziɲu] M scrap of paper

papiro [pa'piru] M papyrus

papo ['papu] M (de ave) crop; (col: de pessoa) double chin; (: conversa) chat; (: chute) hot air; (numa

roupa) tuck; **ele é um bom ~** (col) he's a good talker; **bater** ou **levar um ~** (col) to have a chat; **ficar de ~ para o ar** (fig) to laze around; **~ firme** (col: verdade) gospel (truth); (: pessoa) straight talker

papo-de-anjo (pl **papos-de-anjo**) M sweet made of egg yolks

papo-firme (pl **papos-firmes**) (col) ADJ reliable ■ M/F reliable sort

papo-furado (pl **papos-furados**) (col) ADJ unreliable ■ M/F: **ele é um ~** he never comes up with the goods

papoula [pa'pola] F poppy

páprica ['paprika] F paprika

Papua Nova Guiné [pa'pua-] F Papua New Guinea

papudo, -a [pa'pudu, a] ADJ fat in the face, double-chinned

paqueração [pakera'sãw] (col) (pl **-ões**) F pick-up

paquerador, a [pakera'do(a)] (col) ADJ flirtatious ■ M/F flirt

paquerar [pake'raʳ] (col) VI to flirt ■ VT to chat up

paquete [pa'ketʃi] M steamship

paquistanês, -esa [pakiʃta'neʃ, eza] ADJ, M/F Pakistani

Paquistão [pakiʃ'tãw] M: **o ~** Pakistan

par [paʳ] ADJ (igual) equal; (número) even ■ M pair; (casal) couple; (pessoa na dança) partner; **~ a ~** side by side, level; **ao ~** (Com) at par; **sem ~** incomparable; **abaixo de ~** (Com, Golfe) below par; **estar/ficar a ~ de algo** to be/get up to date with sth

para ['para] PREP for; (direção) to, towards; **bom ~ comer** good to eat; **~ não ser ouvido** so as not to be heard; **~ que** so that, in order that; **~ quê?** what for?, why?; **ir ~ São Paulo** to go to São Paulo; **ir ~ casa** to go home; **~ com** (atitude) towards; **de lá ~ cá** since then; **~ a semana** next week; **estar ~** to be about to; **é ~ nós ficarmos aqui?** should we stay here?

parabenizar [parabeni'zaʳ] VT: **~ alguém por algo** to congratulate sb on sth

parabéns [para'bẽjʃ] MPL congratulations; (no aniversário) happy birthday; **dar ~ a** to congratulate; **você está de ~** you are to be congratulated

parábola [pa'rabola] F parable; (Mat) parabola

pára-brisa ['para-] (pl **-s**) M windscreen (Brit), windshield (US)

pára-choque ['para-] (pl **-s**) M (Auto) bumper

parada [pa'rada] F stop; (Com) stoppage; (militar, colegial) parade; (col: coisa difícil) ordeal; **ser uma ~** (col: pessoa: difícil) to be awkward; (: ser bonito) to be gorgeous; **agüentar a ~** (col) to stick it out; **topar a ~** (col) to accept the challenge; **topar qualquer ~** (col) to be game for anything; **~ cardíaca** heart failure

NB: European Portuguese adds the following consonants to certain words: **b** (sú(b)dito, su(b)til); **c** (a(c)ção, a(c)cionista, a(c)to); **m** (inde(m)ne); **p** (ado(p)ção, ado(p)tar); for further details see p. xiii.

paradeiro [para'dejru] M whereabouts
paradigma [para'dʒigma] M paradigm
paradisíaco, -a [paradʒi'ʒiaku, a] ADJ (fig) idyllic
parado, -a [pa'radu, a] ADJ (pessoa: imóvel) standing still; (: sem vida) lifeless; (carro) stationary; (máquina) out of action; (olhar) fixed; (trabalhador, fábrica) idle; **fiquei ~ uma hora no ponto de ônibus** I stood for an hour at the bus stop; **não fique aí ~!** don't just stand there!
paradoxal [paradok'saw] (pl -ais) ADJ paradoxical
paradoxo [para'dɔksu] M paradox
paraense [para'ẽsi] ADJ from Pará ■ M/F person from Pará
parafernália [parafex'nalja] F (de uso pessoal) personal items pl; (equipamento) equipment; (tralha) paraphernalia
parafina [para'fina] F paraffin
paráfrase [pa'rafrazi] F paraphrase
parafrasear [parafra'zjaʳ] VT to paraphrase
parafusar [parafu'zaʳ] VT to screw in ■ VI (meditar) to ponder
parafuso [para'fuzu] M screw; **entrar em ~** (col) to get into a state; **ter um ~ de menos** (col) to have a screw loose
paragem [pa'raʒẽ] (pl -ns) F stop; **~ de eléctrico** (PT) tram (Brit) ou streetcar (US) stop; **paragens** FPL (lugares) places, parts
parágrafo [pa'ragrafu] M paragraph
Paraguai [para'gwaj] M: **o ~** Paraguay; **paraguaio, -a** [para'gwaju, a] ADJ, M/F Paraguayan
paraíba [para'iba] (col) M (operário) labourer (Brit), laborer (US) ■ F (mulher macho) butch woman
paraibano, -a [paraj'banu, a] ADJ from Paraíba ■ M/F person from Paraíba
paraíso [para'izu] M paradise
pára-lama ['para-] (pl -s) M wing (Brit), fender (US); (de bicicleta) mudguard
paralela [para'lɛla] F parallel line; **paralelas** FPL (Esporte) parallel bars
paralelamente [paralela'mẽtʃi] ADV in parallel; (ao mesmo tempo) at the same time
paralelepípedo [paralele'pipedu] M paving stone
paralelo, -a [para'lɛlu, a] ADJ (tb: Comput) parallel ■ M (Geo, comparação) parallel
paralisação [paraliza'sãw] (pl -ões) F (suspensão) stoppage
paralisar [parali'zaʳ] VT to paralyse; (trabalho) to bring to a standstill; **paralisar-se** VR to become paralysed; (fig) to come to a standstill
paralisia [parali'zia] F paralysis
paralítico, -a [para'litʃiku, a] ADJ, M/F paralytic
paramédico, -a [para'mɛdʒiku, a] ADJ paramedical
paramentado, -a [paramẽ'tadu, a] ADJ smart
paramento [para'mẽtu] M (adorno) ornament; **paramentos** MPL (vestes) vestments; (de igreja) hangings
parâmetro [pa'rametru] M parameter

paramilitar [paramili'taʳ] ADJ paramilitary
paranaense [parana'ẽsi] ADJ from Paraná ■ M/F person from Paraná
paraninfo [para'nĩfu] M patron; (pessoa homenageada) guest of honour (Brit) ou honor (US)
paranóia [para'nɔja] F paranoia
paranóico, -a [para'nɔjku, a] ADJ, M/F paranoid
paranormal [paranox'maw] (pl -ais) ADJ paranormal
parapeito [para'pejtu] M (muro) wall, parapet; (da janela) windowsill
parapente [para'pẽtʃi] M (Esporte) paragliding; (equipamento) paraglider
paraplégico, -a [para'plɛʒiku, a] ADJ, M/F paraplegic
pára-quedas ['para-] M INV parachute; **saltar de ~** to parachute
pára-quedismo [parake'dʒiʒmu] M parachuting, sky-diving
pára-quedista [parake'dʒiʃta] M/F parachutist ■ M (Mil) paratrooper
parar [pa'raʳ] VI to stop; (ficar) to stay ■ VT to stop; **fazer ~** (deter) to stop; **~ na cadeia** to end up in jail; **~ de fazer** to stop doing
pára-raios ['para-] M INV lightning conductor
parasita [para'zita] ADJ parasitic ■ M parasite
parasitar [parazi'taʳ] VT to sponge ■ VT: **~ alguém** to sponge off sb
parasito [para'zitu] M parasite
parceiro, -a [pax'sejru, a] ADJ matching ■ M/F partner
parcela [pax'sɛla] F piece, bit; (de pagamento) instalment (Brit), installment (US); (de terra) plot; (do eleitorado etc) section; (Mat) item
parcelado, -a [paxse'ladu, a] ADJ (pagamento) in instalments (Brit) ou installments (US)
parcelar [paxse'laʳ] VT (pagamento, dívida) to schedule in instalments (Brit) ou installments (US)
parceria [paxse'ria] F partnership
parcial [pax'sjaw] (pl -ais) ADJ (incompleto) partial; (feito por partes) in parts; (pessoa) biased; (Pol) partisan; **parcialidade** [paxsjali'dadʒi] F bias, partiality; (Pol) partisans pl
parcimonioso, -a [paxsimo'njozu, ɔza] ADJ parsimonious
parco, -a ['paxku, a] ADJ (escasso) scanty; (econômico) thrifty; (refeição) frugal
pardal [pax'daw] (pl -ais) M sparrow
pardieiro [pax'dʒjejru] M ruin, heap
pardo, -a ['paxdu, a] ADJ (cinzento) grey (Brit), gray (US); (castanho) brown; (mulato) mulatto
parecença [pare'sẽsa] F resemblance
parecer [pare'seʳ] M (opinião) opinion ■ VI (ter a aparência de) to look, seem; **parecer-se** VR to look alike, resemble each other; **~ de auditoria** (Com) auditors' report; **~ (com)** (ter semelhança com) to look (like); **ao que parece** apparently; **parece-me que** I think that, it seems to me that; **que lhe parece?** what do you think?; **parece que** it looks as if; **~-se com alguém** to

look like sb

parecido, -a [pare'sidu, a] ADJ alike, similar; ~ **com** like

paredão [pare'dãw] (pl-ões) M (de serra) face

parede [pa'redʒi] F wall; **imprensar** ou **pôr alguém contra a** ~ to put sb on the spot, buttonhole sb; ~ **divisória** partition wall

paredões [pare'dõjʃ] MPL de **paredão**

parelha [pa'reʎa] F (de cavalos) team; (par) pair

parente, -a [pa'rẽtʃi] M/F relative, relation; **ser** ~ **de alguém** to be related to sb

parentela [parẽ'tɛla] F relations pl

parentesco [parẽ'teʃku] M relationship; (fig) connection

parêntese [pa'rẽtezi] M parenthesis; (na escrita) bracket; (fig: digressão) digression

páreo ['parju] M race; (fig) competition; **ser um** ~ **duro** to be a hard nut to crack

pareô [pa'rjo] M beach wrap

pária ['parja] M pariah

paridade [pari'dadʒi] F (igualdade) equality; (de câmbio, remuneração) parity; **abaixo/acima da** ~ below/above par

parir [pa'ri'] VT to give birth to ■ VI to give birth; (mulher) to have a baby

Paris [pa'riʃ] N Paris; **parisiense** [pari'zjẽsi] ADJ, M/F Parisian

parlamentar [paxlamẽ'ta'] ADJ parliamentary ■ M/F member of parliament, MP ■ VI to parley

parlamentarismo [paxlamẽta'riʒmu] M parliamentary democracy

parlamentarista [paxlamẽta'riʃta] ADJ in favo(u)r of parliamentary democracy ■ M/F supporter of the parliamentary system

parlamento [paxla'mẽtu] M parliament

parmesão [paxme'zãw] ADJ: **(queijo)** ~ Parmesan (cheese)

pároco ['paroku] M parish priest

paródia [pa'rɔdʃja] F parody

parodiar [paro'dʒja'] VT (fazer paródia de) to parody; (imitar) to mimic, copy

paróquia [pa'rɔkja] F (Rel) parish; (col: localidade) neighbourhood (Brit), neighborhood (US)

paroquial [paro'kjaw] (pl-ais) ADJ parochial

paroquiano, -a [paro'kjanu, a] M/F parishioner

paroxismo [parok'siʒmu] M fit, attack; **paroxismos** MPL (de moribundo) death throes

parque ['paxki] M park; ~ **industrial** industrial estate; ~ **infantil** children's playground; ~ **nacional** national park

parqueamento [paxkja'mẽtu] M parking

parquear [pax'kja'] VT to park

parreira [pa'xejra] F trellised vine

parrudo, -a [pa'xudu, a] ADJ muscular, well-built

part. ABR (= particular) priv

parte ['paxtʃi] F part; (quinhão) share; (lado) side; (ponto) point; (Jur) party; (papel) role; ~ **interna**

---

inside; **a maior** ~ **de** most of; **a maior** ~ **das vezes** most of the time; **à** ~ aside; (separado) separate; (separadamente) separately; (além de) apart from; **da** ~ **de alguém** on sb's part; **de** ~ **a** ~ each other; **em** ~ in part, partly; **em grande** ~ to a great extent; **em alguma/qualquer** ~ somewhere/anywhere; **em** ~ **alguma** nowhere; **por toda (a)** ~ everywhere; **por -s** in parts; **por** ~ **da mãe** on one's mother's side; **pôr de** ~ to set aside; **tomar** ~ **em** to take part in; **dar** ~ **de alguém à polícia** to report sb to the police; **fazer** ~ **de algo** to be part of sth; **mandar alguém àquela** ~ (col!) to tell sb to go to hell

parteira [pax'tejra] F midwife

partição [paxtʃi'sãw] F division; (Pol) partition

participação [paxtʃisipa'sãw] F participation; (Com) stake, share; (comunicação) announcement, notification

participante [paxtʃisi'pãtʃi] M/F participant ■ ADJ participating

participar [paxtʃisi'pa'] VT to announce, notify of ■ VI: ~ **de** ou **em** (tomar parte) to participate in, take part in; (compartilhar) to share in

particípio [paxtʃi'sipju] M participle

partícula [pax'tʃikula] F particle

particular [paxtʃiku'la'] ADJ (especial) particular, special; (privativo, pessoal) private ■ M particular; (indivíduo) individual; **particulares** MPL (pormenores) details; **em** ~ in private

particularidade [paxtʃikulari'dadʒi] F peculiarity

particularizar [paxtʃikulari'za'] VT (especificar) to specify; (detalhar) to give details of; **particularizar-se** VR to distinguish o.s.

particularmente [paxtʃikulax'mẽtʃi] ADV privately; (especialmente) particularly

partida [pax'tʃida] F (saída) departure; (Esporte) game, match; (Com: quantidade) lot; (: remessa) shipment; (em corrida) start; **dar** ~ **em** to start; **perder a** ~ to lose

partidário, -a [paxtʃi'darju, a] ADJ supporting ■ M/F supporter, follower

partido, -a [pax'tʃidu, a] ADJ (dividido) divided; (quebrado) broken ■ M (Pol) party; (em jogo) handicap; **tirar** ~ **de** to profit from; **tomar o** ~ **de** to side with

partilha [pax'tʃiʎa] F share

partilhar [paxtʃi'ʎa'] VT to share; (distribuir) to share out

partir [pax'tʃi'] VT (quebrar) to break; (dividir) to divide, split ■ VI (pôr-se a caminho) to set off, set out; (ir-se embora) to leave, depart; **partir-se** VR (quebrar-se) to break; ~ **de** (começar, tomar por base) to start from; (originar) to arise from; **a** ~ **de** (starting) from; **a** ~ **de agora** from now on, starting from now; ~ **ao meio** to split down the middle; **eu parto do princípio que ...** I am working on the principle that ...; ~ **para** (col: recorrer a) to resort to; ~ **para outra** (col) to

---

NB: European Portuguese adds the following consonants to certain words: **b** (sú(b)dito, su(b)til); **c** (a(c)ção, a(c)cionista, a(c)to); **m** (inde(m)ne); **p** (ado(p)ção, ado(p)tar); for further details see p. xiii.

change tack

partitura [paxtʃi'tura] F score

parto ['paxtu] M (child)birth; **estar em trabalho de** ~ to be in labour (*Brit*) *ou* labor (*US*); ~ **induzido** induced labo(u)r; ~ **prematuro** premature birth

parturiente [paxtu'rjẽtʃi] F woman about to give birth

parvo, -a ['paxvu, a] ADJ stupid, silly ■ M/F fool, idiot

parvoíce [pax'vwisi] F silliness, stupidity

Pasart [pa'zaxtʃi] (BR) ABR M = **Partido Socialista Agrário e Renovador Trabalhista**

Páscoa ['paʃkwa] F Easter; (*dos judeus*) Passover; **a ilha da** ~ Easter Island

Pasep [pa'zɛpi] (BR) ABR M = **Programa de Formação do Patrimônio do Servidor Público**

pasmaceira [paʒma'sejra] F (*apatia*) indolence

pasmado, -a [paʒ'madu, a] ADJ amazed, astonished

pasmar [paʒ'maʳ] VT to amaze, astonish; **pasmar-se** VR: **pasmar-se com** to be amazed at

pasmo, -a ['paʒmu, a] ADJ astonished ■ M amazement

paspalhão, -lhona [paʃpa'ʎãw, 'ʎɔna] (*pl* -ões/ -s) ADJ stupid ■ M/F fool

paspalho [paʃ'paʎu] M simpleton

paspalhões [paʃpa'ʎõjʃ] MPL *de* **paspalhão**

paspalhona [paʃpa'ʎɔna] F *de* **paspalhão**

pasquim [paʃ'kĩ] (*pl* -ns) M (*jornal*) satirical newspaper

passa ['pasa] F raisin

passada [pa'sada] F (*passo*) step; **dar uma** ~ **em** to call in at

passadeira [pasa'dejra] F (*tapete*) stair carpet; (*mulher*) ironing lady; (*PT: para peões*) zebra crossing (*Brit*), crosswalk (*US*)

passadiço, -a [pasa'dʒisu, a] ADJ passing ■ M walkway; (*Náut*) bridge

passado, -a [pa'sadu, a] ADJ (*decorrido*) past; (*antiquado*) old-fashioned; (*fruta*) bad; (*peixe*) off ■ M past; **o ano** ~ last year; **bem/mal passada** (*carne*) well done/rare; **ficar** ~ (*encabulado*) to be very embarrassed

passageiro, -a [pasa'ʒejru, a] ADJ (*transitório*) passing ■ M/F passenger

passagem [pa'saʒẽ] (*pl* -ns) F passage; (*preço de condução*) fare; (*bilhete*) ticket; ~ **de ida e volta** return ticket, round trip ticket (*US*); ~ **de nível** level (*Brit*) *ou* grade (*US*) crossing; ~ **de pedestres** pedestrian crossing (*Brit*), crosswalk (*US*); ~ **subterrânea** underpass, subway (*Brit*); **de** ~ in passing; **estar de** ~ to be passing through

passamanaria [pasamana'ria] F trimming

passamento [pasa'mẽtu] M (*morte*) passing

passaporte [pasa'pɔxtʃi] M passport

passar [pa'saʳ] VT to pass; (*ponte, rio*) to cross; (*exceder*) to go beyond, exceed; (*coar: farinha*) to sieve; (: *líquido*) to strain; (: *café*) to percolate; (*a ferro*) to iron; (*tarefa*) to set; (*telegrama*) to send;

(*o tempo*) to spend; (*bife*) to cook; (*a outra pessoa*) to pass on; (*pomada*) to put on; (*contrabandear*) to smuggle ■ VI to pass; (*na rua*) to go past; (*tempo*) to go by; (*dor*) to wear off; (*terminar*) to be over; (*ser razoável*) to pass, be passable; (*mudar*) to change; **passar-se** VR (*acontecer*) to go on, happen; (*desertar*) to go over; (*tempo*) to go by; ~ **bem** (*de saúde*) to be well; **como está passando?** how are you?; ~ **a** (*questão*) to move on to; (*suj: propriedade*) to pass to; ~ **a fazer** to start to do; ~ **a ser** to become; **passava das dez horas** it was past ten o' clock; **ele passa dos 50 anos** he's over 50; **não** ~ **de** to be only; ~ **na frente** to go ahead; ~ **alguém para trás** to con sb; (*cônjuge*) to cheat on sb; ~ **pela casa de** to call in on; ~ **pela cabeça de** to occur to; ~ **por algo** (*sofrer*) to go through sth; (*transitar: estrada*) to go along sth; (*ser considerado como*) to be thought of as sth; ~ **por cima de algo** to overlook sth; ~ **algo por algo** to put *ou* pass sth through sth; ~ **sem** q do without

passarela [pasa'rɛla] F footbridge; (*para modelos*) catwalk

pássaro ['pasaru] M bird

passatempo [pasa'tẽpu] M pastime; **como** ~ for fun

passável [pa'savew] (*pl* -eis) ADJ passable

passe ['pasi] M (*licença*) pass; (*Futebol: ato*) pass; (: *contrato*) contract; ~ **de mágica** sleight of hand

passear [pa'sjaʳ] VT to take for a walk ■ VI (*a pé*) to go for a walk; (*sair*) to go out; ~ **a cavalo** (*ou* **de carro**) to go for a ride; **não moro aqui, estou passeando** I don't live here, I'm on holiday (*Brit*) *ou* vacation (*US*); **mandar alguém** ~ (*col*) to send sb packing; **passeata** [pa'sjata] F (*marcha coletiva*) protest march; (*passeio*) stroll; **passeio** [pa'seju] M walk; (*de carro*) drive, ride; (*excursão*) outing; (*calçada*) pavement (*Brit*), sidewalk (*US*); **dar um passeio** to go for a walk; (*de carro*) to go for a drive *ou* ride; **passeio público** promenade

passional [pasjo'naw] (*pl* -ais) ADJ passionate; **crime** ~ crime of passion

passista [pa'siʃta] M/F dancer (*in carnival parade*)

passível [pa'sivew] (*pl* -eis) ADJ: ~ **de** (*dor etc*) susceptible to; (*pena, multa*) subject to

passividade [pasivi'dadʒi] F passivity

passivo, -a [pa'sivu, a] ADJ passive ■ M (*Com*) liabilities *pl*

passo ['pasu] M step; (*medida*) pace; (*modo de andar*) walk; (*ruído dos passos*) footstep; (*sinal de pé*) footprint; ~ **a** ~ one step at a time; **a cada** ~ constantly; **a um** ~ **de** (*fig*) on the verge of; **a dois** ~**s de** (*perto de*) a stone's throw away from; **ao** ~ **que** while; **apertar o** ~ to hurry up; **ceder o** ~ **a** to give way to; **dar um** ~ to take a step; **dar um mau** ~ to slip up; **marcar** ~ (*fig*) to mark time; **seguir os** ~**s de alguém** (*fig*) to follow in sb's footsteps; ~ **de cágado** snail's pace

pasta ['paʃta] F paste; (*de couro*) briefcase; (*de cartolina*) folder; (*de ministro*) portfolio; ~

dentifrícia ou **de dentes** toothpaste; **~ de galinha** chicken pâté

pastagem [paʃ'taʒē] (pl -ns) F pasture

pastar [paʃ'ta^r] VT to graze on ▪ VI to graze

pastel [paʃ'tɛw] (pl -éis) ADJ INV (cor) pastel ▪ M samosa; (desenho) pastel drawing

pastelão [paʃte'lãw] M (comédia) slapstick

pastelaria [paʃtela'ria] F (loja) cake shop; (comida) pastry

pasteurizado, -a [paʃtewri'zadu, a] ADJ pasteurized

pastiche [paʃ'tʃiʃi] M pastiche

pastilha [paʃ'tʃiʎa] F (Med) tablet; (doce) pastille; (Comput) chip

pastio [paʃ'tʃiu] M pasture; (ato) grazing

pasto ['paʃtu] M (erva) grass; (terreno) pasture; **casa de ~** (PT) cheap restaurant, diner

pastor, a [paʃ'to^r(a)] M/F shepherd(ess) ▪ M (Rel) clergyman, pastor

pastoral [paʃto'raw] (pl -ais) ADJ pastoral

pastorear [paʃto'rja^r] VT (gado) to watch over

pastoril [paʃto'riw] (pl -is) ADJ pastoral

pastoso, -a [paʃ'tozu, ɔza] ADJ pasty

pata ['pata] F (pé de animal) foot, paw; (ave) duck; (col: pé) foot; **meter a ~** to put one's foot in it

pata-choca (pl patas-chocas) F lump

patada [pa'tada] F kick; **dar uma ~** to kick; (fig: col) to behave rudely; **levar uma ~** (fig) to be treated rudely

Patagônia [pata'gonja] F: **a ~** Patagonia

patamar [pata'ma^r] M (de escada) landing; (fig) level

patavina [pata'vina] PRON nothing, (not) anything

patê [pa'te] M pâté

patente [pa'tẽtʃi] ADJ obvious, evident ▪ F (Com) patent; (Mil: título) commission; **altas ~s** high-ranking officers

patentear [patẽ'tʃja^r] VT to show, reveal; (Com) to patent; **patentear-se** VR to be shown, be evident

paternal [patex'naw] (pl -ais) ADJ paternal, fatherly

paternalista [patexna'liʃta] ADJ paternalistic

paternidade [patexni'dadʒi] F paternity

paterno, -a [pa'tɛxnu, a] ADJ paternal, fatherly; **casa paterna** family home

pateta [pa'tɛta] ADJ stupid, daft ▪ M/F idiot

patetice [pate'tʃisi] F stupidity; (ato, dito) daft thing

patético, -a [pa'tɛtʃiku, a] ADJ pathetic, moving

patíbulo [pa'tʃibulu] M gallows sg

patifaria [patʃifa'ria] F roguishness; (ato) nasty thing

patife [pa'tʃifi] M scoundrel, rogue

patim [pa'tʃĩ] (pl -ns) M skate; **~ de rodas** roller skate

patinação [patʃina'sãw] (pl -ões) F skating; (lugar) skating rink

patinador, a [patʃinado^r(a)] M/F skater

patinar [patʃi'na^r] VI to skate; (Auto: derrapar) to skid

patinete [patʃi'netʃi] F skateboard

patinhar [patʃi'ɲa^r] VI (como um pato) to dabble; (em lama) to splash about, slosh

patinho [pa'tʃiɲu] M duckling; (carne) leg of beef; (urinol) bedpan; **cair como um ~** to be taken in

patins [pa'tʃĩʃ] MPL de **patim**

pátio ['patʃju] M (de uma casa) patio, backyard; (espaço cercado de edifícios) courtyard; (tb: pátio de recreio) playground; (Mil) parade ground

pato ['patu] M duck; (macho) drake; (col: otário) sucker; **pagar o ~** (col) to carry the can

patologia [patolo'ʒia] F pathology; **patológico, -a** [pato'lɔʒiku, a] ADJ pathological

patologista [patolo'ʒiʃta] M/F pathologist

patota [pa'tɔta] (col) F gang

patrão [pa'trãw] (pl -ões) M (Com) boss; (dono de casa) master; (proprietário) landlord; (Náut) skipper; (col: tratamento) sir

pátria ['patrja] F homeland; **lutar pela ~** to fight for one's country; **salvar a ~** (fig) to save the day

patriarca [pa'trjaxka] M patriarch

patriarcal [patrjax'kaw] (pl -ais) ADJ patriarchal

patrício, -a [pa'trisju, a] ADJ, M/F patrician

patrimonial [patrimo'njaw] (pl -ais) ADJ (bens) family atr; (imposto) wealth atr

patrimônio [patri'monju] M (herança) inheritance; (fig) heritage; (bens) property; **~ líquido** equity

patriota [pa'trjɔta] M/F patriot

patriótico, -a [pa'trjɔtʃiku, a] ADJ patriotic

patriotismo [patrjo'tʃiʒmu] M patriotism

patroa [pa'troa] F (mulher do patrão) boss's wife; (dona de casa) lady of the house; (proprietária) landlady; (col: esposa) missus, wife; (: tratamento) madam

patrocinador, a [patrosina'do^r(a)] ADJ sponsoring ▪ M/F sponsor, backer

patrocinar [patrosi'na^r] VT to sponsor; (proteger) to support; **patrocínio** [patro'sinju] M sponsorship, backing; (proteção) support

patrões [pa'trõjʃ] MPL de **patrão**

patrono [pa'trɔnu] M patron; (advogado) counsel

patrulha [pa'truʎa] F patrol; **patrulhar** [patru'ʎa^r] VT, VI to patrol

pau [paw] M (madeira) wood; (vara) stick; (col: briga) punch-up; (: cruzeiro) cruzeiro; (col!: pênis) cock (!); **paus** MPL (Cartas) clubs; **~ a ~** neck and neck; **a meio ~** (bandeira) at half-mast; **o ~ comeu** (col) all hell broke loose; **estar/ficar ~ da vida** (col) to be/get mad; **ir ao** ou **levar ~ (em exame)** to fail; **meter o ~ em alguém** (col: espancar) to beat sb up; (: criticar) to run sb down; **mostrar a alguém com quantos ~s se faz uma canoa** (fig) to teach sb a lesson; **ser ~** (col:

NB: *European Portuguese adds the following consonants to certain words:* **b** (sú(b)dito, su(b)til); **c** (a(c)ção, a(c)cionista, a(c)to); **m** (inde(m)ne); **p** (ado(p)çã, ado(p)tar); *for further details see p. xiii.*

maçante) to be a drag; **ser ~ para toda obra** to
be a jack of all trades; **comida a dar com um ~**
tons of food; **~ de bandeira** flagpole
pau-a-pique M wattle and daub
pau-d'água (pl paus-d'água) M drunkard
pau-de-arara (pl paus-de-arara) M (tortura)
upside-down torture ▪ M/F migrant (from
North-East); (pej) North-Easterner
pau-de-cabeleira (pl paus-de-cabeleira) M
chaperon
paulada [paw'lada] F blow (with a stick)
paulatinamente [pawlatʃina'mētʃi] ADV
gradually
paulatino, -a [pawla'tʃinu, a] ADJ slow, gradual
Paulicéia [pawli'sɛja] F: **a ~** São Paulo
paulificante [pawlifi'kātʃi] ADJ annoying
paulificar [pawlifi'ka^r] VT to annoy, bother
paulista [paw'liʃta] ADJ from (the state of) São
Paulo ▪ M/F person from São Paulo
paulistano, -a [pawliʃi'tanu, a] ADJ from (the
city of) São Paulo ▪ M/F person from São Paulo
pau-mandado (pl paus-mandados) M yes man
paupérrimo, -a [paw'pɛximu, a] ADJ poverty-
stricken
pausa ['pawza] F pause; (intervalo) break;
(descanso) rest
pausado, -a [paw'zadu, a] ADJ (lento) slow; (sem
pressa) leisurely; (cadenciado) measured ▪ ADV
(falar) in measured tones
pauta ['pawta] F (linha) (guide)line; (Mús) stave;
(lista) list; (folha) ruled paper; (de programa deTV)
running order; (ordem do dia) agenda; (indicações)
guidelines pl; **sem ~** (papel) plain; **em ~** on the
agenda
pautado, -a [paw'tadu, a] ADJ (papel) ruled
pautar [paw'ta^r] VT (papel) to rule; (assuntos) to
put in order, list; (conduta) to regulate
pauzinho [paw'ziɲu] M: **mexer os ~s** to pull
strings
pavão, -voa [pa'vãw, 'voa] (pl -ões/-s) M/F
peacock/peahen
pavê [pa've] M (Culin) cream cake
pavilhão [pavi'ʎãw] (pl -ões) M (tenda) tent;
(de madeira) hut; (no jardim) summerhouse;
(em exposição) pavilion; (bandeira) flag; **~ de
isolamento** isolation ward
pavimentação [pavimēta'sãw] F (da rua)
paving; (piso) flooring
pavimentar [pavimē'ta^r] VT to pave
pavimento [pavi'mētu] M (chão, andar) floor; (da
rua) road surface
pavio [pa'viu] M wick
pavoa [pa'voa] F de **pavão**
pavões [pa'võjʃ] MPL de **pavão**
pavonear [pavo'nja^r] VT (ostentar) to show off
▪ VI (caminhar) to strut; **pavonear-se** VR to
show off
pavor [pa'vo^r] M dread, terror; **ter ~ de** to be
terrified of; **pavoroso, -a** [pavo'rozu, ɔza] ADJ
dreadful, terrible
paz [pajʒ] F peace; **fazer as ~es** to make up, be
friends again; **estar em ~** to be at peace; **deixar**

alguém em ~ to leave sb alone; **ser de boa ~** to
be easy-going
PB ABR F = **Paraíba** ▪ ABR (Com: de ações)
= **preferencial, classe B**
PC ABR M = **Partido Comunista**; = personal
computer
Pça. ABR (= Praça) Sq
PCB ABR M = **Partido Comunista Brasileiro**
PCBR ABR M = **Partido Comunista Brasileiro
Revolucionário**
PCC ABR M = **Partido Comunista Chinês**
PC do B ABR M = **Partido Comunista do Brasil**
PCN (BR) ABR M = **Partido Comunitário
Nacional**
PCUS ABR M = **Partido Comunista da União
Soviética**
PDC (BR) ABR M = **Partido Demócrata-Cristão**
PDI (BR) ABR M = **Partido Democrático
Independente**
PDS (BR) ABR M = **Partido Democrático Social**
PDT (BR) ABR M = **Partido Democrático
Trabalhista**
PE ABR M = **Pernambuco**
pé [pɛ] M foot; (da mesa) leg; (fig: base) footing;
(de alface) head; (de milho, café) plant; **ir a pé** to
walk, go on foot; **ao pé de** near, by; **ao pé da
letra** literally; **ao pé do ouvido** in secret; **pé
ante pé** on tip-toe; **com um pé nas costas**
(com facilidade) standing on one's head; **estar
de pé** (festa etc) to be on; **estar de pé no chão**
to be barefoot; **em** ou **de pé** standing (up); **em
pé de guerra/igualdade** on a war/an equal
footing; **dar no pé** (col) to run away, take off;
pôr-se em pé, ficar de pé to stand up; **arredar
pé** to move; **bater o pé** (fig) to dig one's heels
in; **não chegar aos pés de** (fig) to be nowhere
near as good as; **a água dá pé** (Natação) you can
touch the bottom; **ficar com o pé atrás** to be
suspicious; **ficar no pé de alguém** to keep on
at sb; **larga meu pé!** leave me alone!; **levantar-
se** ou **acordar com o pé direito/esquerdo**
to wake up in a good mood/get out of bed on
the wrong side; **meter os pés pelas mãos** to
mess up; **perder o pé** (no mar) to get out of one's
depth; **pôr os pés em** to set foot in; **não ter pé
nem cabeça** (fig) to make no sense; **ter os pés
na terra** (fig) to be down-to-earth, have one's
feet firmly on the ground
peão [pjãw] (pl -ões) M (PT) pedestrian; (Mil)
foot soldier; (Xadrez) pawn; (trabalhador) farm
labourer (Brit) ou laborer (US)
peça ['pɛsa] F (pedaço) piece; (Auto) part; (aposento)
room; (Teatro) play; **(serviço) pago por ~**
piecework; **~ de reposição** spare part; **~ de
roupa** garment; **pregar uma ~ em alguém** to
play a trick on sb
pecado [pe'kadu] M sin; **~ mortal** deadly sin
pecador, a [peka'do^r(a)] M/F sinner, wrongdoer
pecaminoso, -a [pekami'nozu, ɔza] ADJ sinful
pecar [pe'ka^r] VI to sin; (cometer falta) to do
wrong; **~ por excesso de zelo** to be over-
zealous

pechincha [pe'ʃiʃa] F (vantagem) godsend; (coisa barata) bargain; **pechinchar** [peʃi'ʃaʳ] vi to bargain, haggle

pechincheiro, -a [peʃi'ʃejru, a] M/F bargain hunter

peço etc ['pɛsu] VB V **pedir**

peçonha [pe'sɔɲa] F poison

pectina [pek'tʃina] F pectin

pecuária [pe'kwarja] F cattle-raising

pecuário, -a [pe'kwarju, a] ADJ cattle atr

pecuarista [pekwa'riʃta] M/F cattle farmer

peculiar [peku'ljaʳ] ADJ (especial) special, peculiar; (particular) particular; **peculiaridade** [pekuljari'dadʒi] F peculiarity

pecúlio [pe'kulju] M (acumulado) savings pl; (bens) wealth

pecuniário, -a [pecu'njarju, a] ADJ money atr, financial

pedaço [pe'dasu] M piece; (fig: trecho) bit; **aos ~s** in pieces; **caindo aos ~s** (objeto, carro) tatty, broken-down; (casa) tumbledown; (pessoa) worn out

pedágio [pe'daʒju] (BR) M (pagamento) toll; (posto) tollbooth

pedagogia [pedago'ʒia] F pedagogy; (curso) education

pedagógico, -a [peda'gɔʒiku, a] ADJ educational, teaching atr

pedagogo, -a [peda'gogu, a] M/F educationalist

pé-d'água (pl **pés-d'água**) M shower, downpour

pedal [pe'daw] (pl **-ais**) M pedal

pedalada [peda'lada] F turn of the pedals; **dar uma ~** to pedal

pedalar [peda'laʳ] VT, VI to pedal

pedalinho [peda'liɲu] M pedalo (boat)

pedante [pe'dãtʃi] ADJ pretentious ■ M/F pseud

pedantismo [pedã'tʃiʒmu] M pretentiousness

pé-de-atleta M athlete's foot

pé-de-galinha (pl **pés-de-galinha**) M crow's foot

pé-de-meia (pl **pés-de-meia**) M nest egg, savings pl

pé-de-moleque (pl **pés-de-moleque**) M (doce) nut brittle; (calçamento) crazy paving

pé-de-pato (pl **pés-de-pato**) M flipper

pederneira [pedex'nejra] F flint

pedestal [pedeʃ'taw] (pl **-ais**) M pedestal

pedestre [pe'dɛʃtri] (BR) M pedestrian

pé-de-vento (pl **pés-de-vento**) M gust of wind

pediatra [pe'dʒjatra] M/F paediatrician (Brit), pediatrician (US)

pediatria [pedʒja'tria] F paediatrics sg (Brit), pediatrics sg (US)

pedicuro, -a [pedʒi'kuru, a] M/F chiropodist (Brit), podiatrist (US)

pedida [pe'dʒida] F: **boa ~** (col) good idea

pedido [pe'dʒidu] M (solicitação) request; (Com) order; **a ~ de alguém** at sb's request; **~ de casamento** proposal (of marriage); **~ de**

---

demissão resignation; **~ de desculpa** apology; **~ de informação** inquiry

pedigree [pedʒi'gri] M pedigree

pedinte [pe'dʒĩtʃi] ADJ begging ■ M/F beggar

pedir [pe'dʒiʳ] VT to ask for; (Com, comida) to order; (exigir) to demand ■ VI to ask; (num restaurante) to order; **~ algo a alguém** to ask sb for sth; **~ a alguém que faça, ~ para alguém fazer** to ask sb to do; **~ $100 por algo** to ask $100 for sth; **~ alguém em casamento** ou **a mão de alguém** to ask for sb's hand in marriage, propose to sb

pedra ['pɛdra] F stone; (rochedo) rock; (de granizo) hailstone; (de açúcar) lump; (quadro-negro) slate; **~ de amolar** grindstone; **~ de gelo** ice cube; **~ preciosa** precious stone; **~ falsa** (Med) stone; **~ de toque** (fig) touchstone, benchmark; **doido de ~s** raving mad; **dormir como uma ~** to sleep like a log; **pôr uma ~ em cima de algo** (fig) to consider sth dead and buried; **ser de ~** (fig) to be hard-hearted; **ser uma ~ no sapato de alguém** (fig) to be a thorn in sb's side; **vir** ou **responder com quatro ~s na mão** (fig) to be aggressive; **uma ~ no caminho** (fig) a stumbling block, a hindrance

pedrada [pe'drada] F blow with a stone; **dar ~s em** to throw stones at

pedra-mármore F polished marble

pedra-pomes [-pɔmiʃ] F pumice stone

pedregal [pedre'gaw] (pl **-ais**) M stony ground

pedregoso, -a [pedre'gozu, ɔza] ADJ stony, rocky

pedregulho [pedre'guʎu] M gravel

pedreira [pe'drejra] F quarry

pedreiro [pe'drejru] M stonemason

pedúnculo [pe'dũkulu] M stalk

pê-eme [pe'ɛmi] (pl **-s**) F military police ■ M/F military policeman/woman

pé-frio (pl **pés-frios**) (col) M jinx

pega¹ ['pɛga] M (briga) quarrel

pega² ['pega] F magpie; (PT: col: moça) bird; (: meretriz) tart

pegada [pe'gada] F (de pé) footprint; (Futebol) save; **ir nas ~s de alguém** (fig) to follow in sb's footsteps

pegado, -a [pe'gadu, a] ADJ (colado) stuck; (unido) together; **a casa pegada** the house next door

pega-gelo (pl **-s**) M ice tongs pl

pegajoso, -a [pega'ʒozu, ɔza] ADJ sticky

pega-pra-capar (col) M INV scuffle

pegar [pe'gaʳ] VT to catch; (selos) to stick (on); (segurar) to take hold of; (hábito, mania) to get into; (compreender) to take in; (trabalho) to take on; (estação de rádio) to pick up, get ■ VI (aderir) to stick; (planta) to take; (moda) to catch on; (doença) to be catching; (motor) to start; (vacina) to take; (mentira) to stand up, stick; (fogueira) to catch; **pegar-se** VR (brigar) to have a fight, quarrel; **~ com** (casa) to be next door to; **~ a fazer** to start to do; **~ em** (começar) to start on; (segurar) to

---

NB: European Portuguese adds the following consonants to certain words: **b** (sú(b)dito, su(b)til); **c** (a(c)ção, a(c)cionista, a(c)to)); **m** (inde(m)ne); **p** (ado(p)çã, ado(p)tar); for further details see p. xiii.

grab, pick up; **ir** ~ (*buscar*) to go and get; ~ **um emprego** to get a job; ~ **uma rua** to take a street; ~ **fogo a algo** to set fire to sth; ~ **3 anos de cadeia** to get 3 years in prison; ~ **alguém fazendo** to catch sb doing; **pega, ladrão!** stop thief!; ~ **no sono** to fall asleep; **ele pegou e disse ...** he upped and said ...; **pegue e pague** cash and carry; ~ **bem/mal** (*col*) to go down well/badly

pega-rapaz (*pl* **-es**) M kiss curl

pego, -a ['pɛgu, a] PP *de* **pegar**

peguei *etc* [pe'gej] VB V **pegar**

peidar [pej'da^r] (*col!*) VI to fart (!)

peido ['pejdu] (*col!*) M fart (!)

peitilho [pej'tʃiʎu] M shirt front

peito ['pejtu] M (*Anat*) chest; (*de ave, mulher*) breast; (*fig*) courage; **dar o ~ a um bebê** to breastfeed a baby; **largar o ~** to be weaned; **meter os ~s** (*col*) to put one's heart into it; **no ~ (e na raça)** (*col*) whatever it takes; ~ **do pé** instep; **amigo do ~** bosom pal, close friend

peitoril [pejto'riw] (*pl* **-is**) M windowsill

peitudo, -a [pej'tudu, a] ADJ big-chested; (*valente*) feisty

peixada [pej'ʃada] F *fish cooked in a seafood sauce*

peixaria [pejʃa'ria] F fish shop, fishmonger's (*Brit*)

peixe ['pejʃi] M fish; **Peixes** MPL (*Astrologia*) Pisces *sg*; **como ~ fora d'água** like a fish out of water; **filho de ~, peixinho é** like father, like son; **não ter nada com o ~** (*fig*) to have nothing to do with the matter; **vender seu ~** (*ver seus interesses*) to feather one's nest; (*falar*) to say one's piece, have one's say

peixeira [pej'ʃejra] F fishwife; (*faca*) fish knife

peixeiro [pej'ʃejru] M fishmonger

pejar-se [pe'ʒaxsi] VR to be ashamed

pejo ['peʒu] M shame; **ter ~** to be ashamed

pejorativo, -a [peʒora'tʃivu, a] ADJ pejorative

pela ['pɛla] = **por + a**

pelada [pe'lada] F football game

● **PELADA**

● *Pelada* is an improvised, generally short,
● game of football, which in the past was
● played with a ball made out of socks, or an
● inflatable rubber ball. It is still played today
● on any piece of open land, or even in the
● street.

pelado, -a [pe'ladu, a] ADJ (*sem pele*) skinned; (*sem pêlo, cabelo*) shorn; (*nu*) naked, in the nude; (*sem dinheiro*) broke

pelanca [pe'lãka] F fold of skin; (*de carne*) lump

pelancudo, -a [pelã'kudu, a] ADJ (*pessoa*) flabby

pelar [pe'la^r] VT (*tirar a pele*) to skin; (*tirar o pêlo*) to shear; (*col*) to fleece; **pelar-se** VR: **pelar-se por** to be crazy about, adore; ~**-se de medo** to be scared stiff

pelas ['pɛlaʃ] = **por + as**

pele ['pɛli] F (*de pessoa, fruto*) skin; (*couro*) leather;

(*como agasalho*) fur (coat); (*de animal*) hide; **cair na ~ de alguém** (*col*) to pester sb; **arriscar/salvar a ~** (*col*) to risk one's neck/save one's skin; **sentir algo na ~** (*fig*) to feel sth at first hand; **estar na ~ de alguém** (*fig*) to be in sb's shoes; **ser** *ou* **estar ~ e osso** to be all skin and bone

peleja [pe'leʒa] F (*luta*) fight; (*briga*) quarrel

pelejar [pele'ʒa^r] VI (*lutar*) to fight; (*discutir*) to quarrel; ~ **pela paz** to fight for peace; ~ **para fazer/para que alguém faça** to fight to do/to fight to get sb to do

pelerine [pele'rini] F cape

peleteiro, -a [pele'tejru, a] M/F furrier

peleteria [pelete'ria] F furrier's

pele-vermelha (*pl* **peles-vermelhas**) M/F redskin

pelica [pe'lika] F kid (leather)

pelicano [peli'kanu] M pelican

película [pe'likula] F film; (*de pele*) film of skin

pelintra [pe'lĩtra] (*PT*) ADJ shabby; (*pobre*) penniless

pelo ['pɛlu] = **por + o**

pêlo ['pelu] M hair; (*de animal*) fur, coat; **nu em ~** stark naked; **montar em ~** to ride bareback

Peloponeso [pelopo'nɛzu] M: **o ~** the Peloponnese

pelos ['pɛluʃ] = **por + os**

pelota [pe'lɔta] F ball; (*num molho*) lump; (*na pele*) bump; **dar ~ para** (*col*) to pay attention to

pelotão [pelo'tãw] (*pl* **-ões**) M platoon

pelúcia [pe'lusja] F plush

peludo, -a [pe'ludu, a] ADJ hairy; (*animal*) furry

pélvico, -a ['pɛwviku, a] ADJ pelvic

pélvis ['pɛwviʃ] F INV pelvis

pena ['pena] F (*pluma*) feather; (*de caneta*) nib; (*escrita*) writing; (*Jur*) penalty, punishment; (*sofrimento*) suffering; (*piedade*) pity; **que ~!** what a shame!; **a duras ~s** with great difficulty; **sob ~ de** under penalty of; **cumprir ~** to serve a term in jail; **dar ~** to be upsetting; **é uma ~ que ...** it is a pity that ...; **ter ~ de** to feel sorry for; **valer a ~** to be worthwhile; **não vale a ~** it's not worth it; ~ **capital** capital punishment

penacho [pe'naʃu] M plume; (*crista*) crest

penal [pe'naw] (*pl* **-ais**) ADJ penal

penalidade [penali'dadʒi] F (*Jur*) penalty; (*castigo*) punishment; **impor uma ~ a** to penalize

penalizar [penali'za^r] VT (*causar pena a*) to trouble; (*castigar*) to penalize

pênalti ['penawtʃi] M (*Futebol*) penalty (kick); **cobrar um ~** to take a penalty

penar [pe'na^r] VT to grieve ■ VI to suffer

penca ['pẽka] F bunch; **gente em ~** lots of people

pence ['pẽsi] F dart

pendão [pẽ'dãw] (*pl* **-ões**) M pennant; (*fig*) banner; (*do milho*) blossom

pendência [pẽ'dẽsja] F dispute, quarrel

pendente [pẽ'dẽtʃi] ADJ (*pendurado*) hanging; (*por decidir*) pending; (*inclinado*) sloping; (*dependente*): ~

de dependent on ∎ M pendant
pender [pẽ'de^r] VT to hang ∎ VI to hang; (*estar para cair*) to sag, droop; ~ **de** (*depender de*) to depend on, hang on; (*estar pendurado*) to hang from; ~ **para** (*inclinar*) to lean towards; (*ter tendência para*) to tend towards; ~ **a** (*estar disposto a*) to be inclined to
pendões [pẽ'dõjʃ] MPL *de* **pendão**
pendor [pẽ'do^r] M inclination, tendency
pêndulo ['pẽdulu] M pendulum
pendura [pẽ'dura] F: **estar na ~** (*col*) to be broke
pendurado, -a [pẽdu'radu, a] ADJ hanging; (*col: compra*) on tick
pendurar [pẽdu'ra^r] VT to hang; (*col: conta*) to put on tick ∎ VI: ~ **de** to hang from; **não estou com dinheiro hoje, posso ~?** (*col*) I haven't got any money today, can I pay you later?
penduricalho [pẽduri'kaʎu] M pendant
pendurucalho [pẽduru'kaʎu] M = **penduricalho**
penedo [pe'nedu] M rock, boulder
peneira [pe'nejra] F (*da cozinha*) sieve; **peneirar** [penej'ra^r] VT to sift, sieve ∎ VI (*chover*) to drizzle
penetra [pe'nɛtra] (*col*) M/F gatecrasher; **entrar de ~** to gatecrash
penetração [penetra'sãw] F penetration; (*perspicácia*) insight, sharpness
penetrante [pene'trãtʃi] ADJ (*olhar*) searching; (*ferida*) deep; (*frio*) biting; (*som, análise*) penetrating, piercing; (*dor, arma*) sharp; (*inteligência, idéias*) incisive
penetrar [pene'tra^r] VT to get into, penetrate; (*em segredo*) to steal into; (*compreender*) to understand ∎ VI: ~ **em** *ou* **por** *ou* **entre** to penetrate
penha ['peɲa] F (*rocha*) rock; (*penhasco*) cliff
penhasco [pe'ɲaʃku] M cliff, crag
penhoar [pe'ɲwa^r] M dressing gown
penhor [pe'ɲo^r] M pledge; **casa de ~es** pawnshop; **dar em ~** to pawn
penhora [pe'ɲɔra] F (*Jur*) seizure
penhoradamente [peɲorada'mẽtʃi] ADV gratefully
penhorado, -a [peɲo'radu, a] ADJ pawned
penhorar [peɲo'ra^r] VT (*dar em penhor*) to pledge, pawn; (*apreender*) to confiscate; (*fig*) to put under an obligation; **a ajuda do amigo penhorou-a bastante** she was very grateful for her friend's help
pêni ['peni] M penny
penicilina [penisi'lina] F penicillin
penico [pe'niku] M (*col*) potty; **pedir ~** (*col*) to chicken out
Peninos [pe'ninuʃ] MPL: **os ~** the Pennines
península [pe'nĩsula] F peninsula
peninsular [penĩsu'la^r] ADJ peninsular
pênis ['peniʃ] M INV penis
penitência [peni'tẽsja] F (*contrição*) penitence; (*expiação*) penance

penitenciar [penitẽ'sja^r] VT to impose penance on; (*crime etc*) to pay for; **penitenciar-se** VR to castigate o.s.
penitenciária [penitẽ'sjarja] F prison; *vtb* **penitenciário**
penitenciário, -a [penitẽ'sjarju, a] ADJ prison *atr* ∎ M/F prisoner, inmate
penitente [peni'tẽtʃi] ADJ repentant ∎ M/F penitent
penosa [pe'noza] (*col*) F chicken
penoso, -a [pe'nozu, ɔza] ADJ (*assunto, tratamento*) painful; (*trabalho*) hard
pensado, -a [pẽ'sadu, a] ADJ deliberate, intentional
pensador, a [pẽsa'do^r(a)] M/F thinker
pensamento [pẽsa'mẽtu] M thought; (*ato*) thinking; (*mente*) mind; (*opinião*) way of thinking; (*idéia*) idea
pensante [pẽ'sãtʃi] ADJ thinking
pensão [pẽ'sãw] (*pl* **-ões**) F (*pequeno hotel: tb:* **casa de pensão**) boarding house; (*comida*) board; ~ **completa** full board; ~ **de aposentadoria** (retirement) pension; ~ **alimentícia** alimony, maintenance; ~ **de invalidez** disability allowance
pensar [pẽ'sa^r] VI to think; (*imaginar*) to imagine ∎ VT to think about; (*ferimento*) to dress; ~ **em** to think of *ou* about; ~ **fazer** (*ter intenção*) to intend to do, be thinking of doing; ~ **sobre** (*meditar*) to ponder over; **pensando bem** on second thoughts; ~ **alto** to think out loud; ~ **melhor** to think better of it; **pensativo, -a** [pẽsa'tʃivu, a] ADJ thoughtful, pensive
Pensilvânia [pẽsiw'vanja] F: **a ~** Pennsylvania
pensionato [pẽsjo'natu] M boarding school
pensionista [pẽsjo'niʃta] M/F pensioner; (*que mora em pensão*) boarder
penso, -a ['pẽsu, a] ADJ leaning ∎ M (*curativo*) dressing
pensões [pẽ'sõjʃ] FPL *de* **pensão**
pentágono [pẽ'tagonu] M pentagon; **o P~** the Pentagon
pentatlo [pẽ'tatlu] M pentathlon
pente ['pẽtʃi] M comb
penteadeira [pẽtʃja'dejra] F dressing table
penteado, -a [pẽ'tʃjadu, a] ADJ (*cabelo*) in place; (*pessoa*) smart ∎ M hairdo, hairstyle
pentear [pẽ'tʃja^r] VT to comb; (*arranjar o cabelo*) to do, style; **pentear-se** VR to comb one's hair; to do one's hair
Pentecostes [pẽtʃi'kɔʃtʃiʃ] M Whitsun
pente-fino [pẽtʃi'finu] (*pl* **pentes-finos**) M fine-tooth comb
penugem [pe'nuʒẽ] F (*de ave*) down; (*pêlo*) fluff
penúltimo, -a [pe'nuwtʃimu, a] ADJ last but one, penultimate
penumbra [pe'nũbra] F (*ao cair da tarde*) twilight, dusk; (*sombra*) shadow; (*meia-luz*) half-light
penúria [pe'nurja] F poverty

NB: *European Portuguese adds the following consonants to certain words:* **b** (sú(b)dito, su(b)til); **c** (a(c)ção, a(c)cionista, a(c)to); **m** (inde(m)ne); **p** (ado(p)çã, ado(p)tar); *for further details see p. xiii.*

peões [pjõjʃ] MPL *de* **peão**
pepino [pe'pinu] M cucumber
pepita [pe'pita] F *(de ouro)* nugget
pequena [pe'kena] F girl; *(namorada)* girlfriend
pequenez [peke'neʒ] F smallness; *(fig:
mesquinhez)* meanness; **~ de sentimentos**
pettiness
pequenininho, -a [pekeni'niɲu, a] ADJ tiny
pequenino, -a [peke'ninu, a] ADJ little
pequeninos [peke'ninuʃ] MPL: **os ~** the little
children
pequeno, -a [pe'kenu, a] ADJ small; *(mesquinho)*
petty ▪ M boy; **em ~ eu fazia ...** when I was
small I used to do ....
pequeno-burguês, -esa *(pl* -eses/-s) ADJ petty
bourgeois
pequerrucho, -a [peke'xuʃu, a] ADJ tiny ▪ M
thimble
Pequim [pe'kĩ] N Peking
pequinês [peki'neʃ] M *(cão)* Pekinese
pêra ['pera] F pear
peralta [pe'rawta] ADJ naughty ▪ M/F *(menino)*
naughty child
perambular [perãbu'la**r**] VI to wander
perante [pe'rãtʃi] PREP before, in the presence
of
pé-rapado [-xa'padu] *(pl* **pés-rapados***)* M
nobody
percalço [pex'kawsu] M *(de uma tarefa)* difficulty;
(de profissão, matrimônio etc) pitfall
per capita [pex'kapita] ADV, ADJ per capita
perceber [pexse'be**r**] VT *(notar)* to realize; *(por
meio dos sentidos)* to perceive; *(compreender)* to
understand; *(ver)* to see; *(ouvir)* to hear; *(ver ao
longe)* to make out; *(dinheiro: receber)* to receive
percentagem [pexsẽ'taʒẽ] F percentage
percentual [pexsẽ'twaw] *(pl* -ais*)* ADJ
percentage *atr* ▪ M percentage
percepção [pexsep'sãw] F perception;
(compreensão) understanding; **perceptível**
[pexsep'tʃivew] *(pl* -eis*)* ADJ perceptible,
noticeable; *(som)* audible
perceptividade [pexseptʃivi'dadʒi] F
perceptiveness, perception
perceptivo, -a [pexsep'tʃivu, a] ADJ perceptive
percevejo [pexse'veʒu] M *(inseto)* bug; *(prego)*
drawing pin *(Brit)*, thumbtack *(US)*
perco *etc* ['pexku] VB V **perder**
percorrer [pexko'xe**r**] VT *(viajar por)* to travel
(across *ou* over); *(passar por)* to go through,
traverse; *(investigar)* to search through
percurso [pex'kuxsu] M *(espaço percorrido)*
distance (covered); *(trajeto)* route; *(viagem)*
journey; **fazer o ~ entre** to travel between
percussão [pexku'sãw] F *(Mús)* percussion
percussionista [pexkusjo'niʃta] M/F
percussionist, percussion player
percutir [pexku'tʃi**r**] VT to strike ▪ VI to
reverberate
perda ['pexda] F loss; *(desperdício)* waste; **~ de
tempo** waste of time; **~s e danos** damages,
losses

perdão [pex'dãw] M pardon, forgiveness; **~!**
sorry!, I beg your pardon!; **pedir ~ a alguém** to
ask sb for forgiveness; **~ da dívida** cancellation
of the debt; **~ da pena** *(Jur)* pardon
perder [pex'de**r**] VT to lose; *(tempo)* to waste; *(trem,
show, oportunidade)* to miss ▪ VI to lose; **perder-
se** VR *(extraviar-se)* to get lost; *(arruinar-se)* to be
ruined; *(desaparecer)* to disappear; *(em reflexões)* to
be lost; *(num discurso)* to lose one's thread; **~-se
de alguém** to lose sb; **~ algo de vista** to lose
sight of sth; **a ~ de vista** *(fig)* as far as the eye
can see; **pôr tudo a ~** to risk losing everything;
saber ~ to be a good loser
perdição [pexdʒi'sãw] F perdition, ruin;
(desonra) depravity; **ser uma ~** *(col)* to be
irresistible
perdido, -a [pex'dʒidu, a] ADJ lost; *(pervertido)*
depraved; **~ por** *(apaixonado)* desperately in
love with; **~s e achados** lost and found, lost
property
perdigão [pexdʒi'gãw] *(pl* -ões*)* M *(macho)*
partridge
perdigueiro [pexdʒi'gejru] M *(cachorro)* gundog
perdiz [pex'dʒiʒ] F partridge
perdoar [pex'dwa**r**] VT *(desculpar)* to forgive;
(pena) to lift; *(dívida)* to cancel; **~ (algo) a alguém**
to forgive sb (for sth)
perdoável [pex'dwavew] *(pl* -eis*)* ADJ forgivable
perdulário, -a [pexdu'larju, a] ADJ wasteful
▪ M/F spendthrift
perdurar [pexdu'ra**r**] VI *(durar muito)* to last a
long time; *(continuar a existir)* to still exist
pereba [pe'rɛba] F *(ferida pequena)* scratch
perecer [pere'se**r**] VI to perish; *(morrer)* to die;
(acabar) to come to nothing
perecível [pere'sivew] *(pl* -eis*)* ADJ perishable
peregrinação [peregrina'sãw] *(pl* -ões*)* F
(viagem) travels pl; *(Rel)* pilgrimage
peregrinar [peregri'na**r**] VI *(viajar)* to travel; *(Rel)*
to go on a pilgrimage
peregrino, -a [pere'grinu, a] ADJ *(beleza)* rare
▪ M/F pilgrim
pereira [pe'rejra] F pear tree
peremptório, -a [perẽp'tɔrju, a] ADJ *(final)* final;
(decisivo) decisive
perene [pe'rɛni] ADJ *(perpétuo)* everlasting; *(Bot)*
perennial
perereca [pere'rɛka] F tree frog
perfazer [pexfa'ze**r**] *(irreg)* VT *(completar o número
de)* to make up; *(concluir)* to complete
perfeccionismo [pexfeksjo'niʒmu] M
perfectionism
perfeccionista [pexfeksjo'niʃta] ADJ, M/F
perfectionist
perfeição [pexfej'sãw] F perfection; **à ~** to
perfection
perfeitamente [pexfejta'mẽtʃi] ADV perfectly
▪ EXCL exactly!
perfeito, -a [pex'fejtu, a] ADJ perfect; *(carro etc)*
in perfect condition ▪ M *(Ling)* perfect
perfez [pex'feʒ] VB V **perfazer**
perfídia [pex'fidʒja] F treachery

pérfido | pernambucano

pérfido, -a ['pɛxfidu, a] ADJ treacherous

perfil [pex'fiw] (*pl* **-is**) M (*do rosto, fig*) profile; (*silhueta*) silhouette, outline; (*Arq*) (*cross*) section; **de ~** in profile

perfilar [perfi'laʳ] VT (*soldados*) to line up; (*aprumar*) to straighten up; **perfilar-se** VR to stand to attention

perfilhar [pexfi'ʎaʳ] VT (*Jur*) to legally adopt; (*princípio, teoria*) to adopt

perfis [pex'fiʃ] MPL *de* **perfil**

perfiz [pex'fiʒ] VB *V* **perfazer**

perfizer *etc* [pexfi'zeʳ] VB *V* **perfazer**

performance [pex'fɔxmãs] F performance

perfumado, -a [pexfu'madu, a] ADJ sweet-smelling; (*pessoa*) wearing perfume

perfumar [pexfu'maʳ] VT to perfume; **perfumar-se** VR to put perfume on

perfumaria [pexfuma'ria] F perfumery; (*col*) idle talk

perfume [pex'fumi] M perfume; (*cheiro*) scent

perfunctório, -a [pexfũk'tɔrju, a] ADJ perfunctory

perfurado, -a [pexfu'radu, a] ADJ (*cartão*) punched

perfurador [pexfura'doʳ] M punch

perfurar [pexfu'raʳ] VT (*o chão*) to drill a hole in; (*papel*) to punch (a hole in)

perfuratriz [pexfura'triʒ] F drill

pergaminho [pexga'miɲu] M parchment; (*diploma*) diploma

pérgula ['pɛxgula] F arbour (*Brit*), arbor (*US*)

pergunta [pex'gũta] F question; **fazer uma ~ a alguém** to ask sb a question

perguntador, a [pexgũta'doʳ(a)] ADJ inquiring, inquisitive ■ M/F questioner

perguntar [pexgũ'taʳ] VT to ask; (*interrogar*) to question ■ VI: **~ por alguém** to ask after sb; **perguntar-se** VR to wonder; **~ algo a alguém** to ask sb sth

perícia [pe'risja] F (*conhecimento*) expertise; (*destreza*) skill; (*exame*) investigation; **~ (criminal)** criminal investigation; (*os peritos criminais*) criminal investigators *pl*

pericial [peri'sjaw] (*pl* **-ais**) ADJ expert

periclitante [perikli'tãtʃi] ADJ (*situação*) perilous; (*saúde*) shaky

periclitar [perikli'taʳ] VI to be in danger; (*negócio etc*) to be at risk

periculosidade [perikulozi'dadʒi] F dangerousness; (*Jur*) risk factor

peridural [peridu'raw] (*pl* **-ais**) F (*Med*) epidural

periferia [perife'ria] F periphery; (*da cidade*) outskirts *pl*

periférico, -a [peri'fɛriku, a] ADJ peripheral ■ M (*Comput*) peripheral; **estrada periférica** ring road

perífrase [pe'rifrazi] F circumlocution

perigar [peri'gaʳ] VI to be at risk; **~ ser ... to** risk being ..., be in danger of being ....

perigo [pe'rigu] M danger; **correr ~** to be in danger; **fora de ~** safe, out of danger; **pôr em ~** to endanger; **o carro dele é um ~** his car is a deathtrap; **ser um ~** (*col: pessoa*) to be a tease; **estar a ~** (*col: sem dinheiro*) to be broke; (: *em situação difícil*) to be in a bad way; **perigoso, -a** [peri'gozu, ɔza] ADJ dangerous; (*arriscado*) risky

perímetro [pe'rimetru] M perimeter; **~ urbano** city limits *pl*

periódico, -a [pe'rjɔdʒiku, a] ADJ periodic; (*chuvas*) occasional; (*doença*) recurrent ■ M (*revista*) magazine, periodical; (*jornal*) (news)paper

período [pe'riodu] M period; (*estação*) season; **~ letivo** term (time)

peripécia [peri'pɛsja] F (*aventura*) adventure; (*incidente*) turn of events

periquito [peri'kitu] M parakeet

periscópio [periʃ'kɔpju] M periscope

perito, -a [pe'ritu, a] ADJ expert ■ M/F expert; (*quem faz perícia*) investigator; **~ em** (*atividade*) expert at, clever at; (*matéria*) highly knowledgeable in; **~ em matéria de** expert in

peritonite [perito'nitʃi] F peritonitis

perjurar [pexʒu'raʳ] VI to commit perjury

perjúrio [pex'ʒurju] M perjury

perjuro, -a [pex'ʒuru, a] M/F perjurer

permanecer [pexmane'seʳ] VI to remain; (*num lugar*) to stay; (*continuar a ser*) to remain, keep; **~ parado** to keep still

permanência [pexma'nẽsja] F permanence; (*estada*) stay; **permanente** [pexma'nẽtʃi] ADJ (*dor*) constant; (*cor*) fast; (*residência, pregas*) permanent ■ M (*cartão*) pass ■ F perm; **fazer uma permanente** to have a perm

permeável [pex'mjavew] (*pl* **-eis**) ADJ permeable

permeio [pex'meju]: **de ~** ADV in between

permissão [pexmi'sãw] F permission, consent

permissível [pexmi'sivew] (*pl* **-eis**) ADJ permissible

permissivo, -a [pexmi'sivu, a] ADJ permissive

permitir [pexmi'tʃiʳ] VT to allow, permit; (*conceder*) to grant; **~ a alguém fazer** to let sb do, allow sb to do

permuta [pex'muta] F exchange; (*Com*) barter

permutação [pexmuta'sãw] (*pl* **-ões**) F (*Mat*) permutation; (*troca*) exchange

permutar [pexmu'taʳ] VT to exchange; (*Com*) to barter

perna ['pɛxna] F leg; **de ~(s) para o ar** upside down, topsy turvy; **em cima da ~** (*col*) sloppily, in a slapdash way; **bater ~s** (*col*) to wander; **passar a ~ em alguém** (*col*) to put one over on sb; **trocar as ~s** (*col*) to stagger; **~ de pau** wooden leg; **~ mecânica** artificial leg; **~s tortas** bow legs

perna-de-pau (*pl* **pernas-de-pau**) M/F pegleg; (*Futebol*) bad player

pernambucano, -a [pexnãbu'kanu, a] ADJ from

NB: *European Portuguese adds the following consonants to certain words:* **b** (sú(b)dito, su(b)til); **c** (a(c)ção, a(c)cionista, a(c)to); **m** (inde(m)ne); **p** (ado(p)çã, ado(p)tar); *for further details see p. xiii.*

Pernambuco ■ M/F person from Pernambuco
perneira [pex'nejra] F (de dançarina etc)
legwarmer
perneta [pex'neta] M/F one-legged person
pernicioso, -a [pexni'sjozu, ɔza] ADJ pernicious;
(Med) malignant
pernil [pex'niw] (pl -is) M (de animal) haunch;
(Culin) leg
pernilongo [pexni'lõgu] M mosquito
pernis [pex'niʃ] MPL de **pernil**
pernoitar [pexnoj'ta'] VI to spend the night
pernóstico, -a [pex'nɔʃtʃiku, a] ADJ pedantic
■ M/F pedant
pérola ['pɛrola] F pearl
perpassar [pexpa'sa'] VI (tempo) to go by; ~ **(por)**
to pass (by); ~ **a mão em/por** to run one's hand
through/over
perpendicular [pexpẽdʒiku'la'] ADJ, F
perpendicular; **ser** ~ **a** to be at right angles to
perpetração [pexpetra'sãw] F perpetration
perpetrar [pexpe'tra'] VT to perpetrate, commit
perpetuar [pexpe'twa'] VT to perpetuate
perpetuidade [pexpetwi'dadʒi] F eternity
perpétuo, -a [pex'petwu, a] ADJ perpetual;
(eterno) eternal; **prisão perpétua** life
imprisonment
perplexidade [pexpleksi'dadʒi] F confusion,
bewilderment
perplexo, -a [pex'plɛksu, a] ADJ (confuso)
bewildered, puzzled; (indeciso) uncertain; **ficar** ~
(atônito) to be taken aback
perquirir [pexki'ri'] VT to probe, investigate
persa ['pɛxsa] ADJ, M/F Persian
perscrutar [pexʃkru'ta'] VT to scrutinize,
examine
perseguição [pexsegi'sãw] F pursuit; (Rel, Pol)
persecution
perseguidor, a [pexsegi'do'(a)] M/F pursuer;
(Rel, Pol) persecutor
perseguir [pexse'gi'] VT (seguir) to pursue; (correr
atrás) to chase (after); (Rel, Pol) to persecute;
(importunar) to harass, pester
perseverança [pexseve'rãsa] F (insistência)
persistence; (constância) perseverance
perseverante [pexseve'rãtʃi] ADJ persistent
perseverar [pexseve'ra'] VI to persevere; ~ **em**
(conservar-se firme) to persevere in, persist in; ~
corajoso to keep one's courage up; ~ **em erro**
to persist in doing wrong
Pérsia ['pɛxsja] F: **a** ~ Persia
persiana [pex'sjana] F blind
Pérsico, -a ['pɛxsiku, a] ADJ: **o golfo** ~ the
Persian Gulf
persignar-se [pexsig'naxsi] VR to cross o.s.
persigo etc [pex'sigu] VB V **perseguir**
persistência [pexsiʃ'tẽsja] F persistence
persistente [pexsiʃ'tẽtʃi] ADJ persistent
persistir [pexsiʃ'tʃi'] VI to persist; ~ **em** to persist
in; ~ **calado** to keep quiet
personagem [pexso'naʒẽ] (pl -ns) M/F famous
person, celebrity; (num livro, filme) character
personalidade [pexsonali'dadʒi] F personality;

~ **dupla** dual personality
personalizado, -a [pexsonali'zadu, a] ADJ
personalized; (móveis etc) custom-made
personalizar [pexsonali'za'] VT to personalize;
(personificar) to personify; (nomear) to name
personificação [pexsonifika'sãw] F
personification
personificar [pexsonifi'ka'] VT to personify
perspectiva [pexʃpek'tʃiva] F (na pintura)
perspective; (panorama) view; (probabilidade)
prospect; (ponto de vista) point of view; **em** ~ in
prospect
perspicácia [pexʃpi'kasja] F insight,
perceptiveness; **perspicaz** [pexʃpi'kaʒ] ADJ (que
observa) observant; (sagaz) shrewd
persuadir [pexswa'dʒi'] VT to persuade;
persuadir-se VR to convince o.s.; ~ **alguém**
de que/alguém a fazer to persuade sb that/sb
to do; **persuasão** [pexswa'zãw] F persuasion;
(convicção) conviction; **persuasivo, -a**
[pexswa'zivu, a] ADJ persuasive
pertencente [pextẽ'sẽtʃi] ADJ belonging; ~ **a**
(pertinente) pertaining to
pertencer [pextẽ'se'] VI: ~ **a** to belong to; (referir-
se) to concern
pertences [pex'tẽsiʃ] MPL (de uma pessoa)
belongings
pertinácia [pextʃi'nasja] F (persistência)
persistence; (obstinação) obstinacy
pertinaz [pextʃi'naʒ] ADJ (persistente) persistent;
(obstinado) obstinate
pertinência [pextʃi'nẽsja] F relevance;
pertinente [pextʃi'nẽtʃi] ADJ relevant;
(apropriado) appropriate
perto, -a ['pɛxtu, a] ADJ nearby ■ ADV near; ~
de near to; (em comparação com) next to; ~ **da casa**
near ou close to the house; ~ **de 100 cruzeiros**
about 100 cruzeiros; **estar** ~ **de fazer** (a ponto de)
to be close to doing; **de** ~ closely; (ver) close up;
(conhecer) very well
perturbação [pextuxba'sãw] (pl -ões) F
disturbance; (desorientação) perturbation; (Med)
trouble; (Pol) disturbance; ~ **da ordem** breach
of the peace
perturbado, -a [pextux'badu, a] ADJ perturbed;
(desvairado) unbalanced
perturbador, a [pextuxba'do'(a)] ADJ (pessoa)
disruptive; (notícia) perturbing, disturbing
perturbar [pextux'ba'] VT to disturb; (abalar) to
upset, trouble; (atrapalhar) to put off; (andamento,
trânsito) to disrupt; (envergonhar) to embarrass;
(alterar) to affect; **não perturba!** do not disturb!;
~ **a ordem** to cause a breach of the peace
Peru [pe'ru] M: **o** ~ Peru
peru, a [pe'ru(a)] M/F turkey ■ M (col!: pênis)
cock (!)
perua [pe'rua] F (carro) estate (car) (Brit), station
wagon (US)
peruada [pe'rwada] (col) F (palpite) tip
peruano, -a [pe'rwanu, a] ADJ, M/F Peruvian
peruar [pe'rwa'] VT (jogo) to watch ■ VI to hang
around

peruca [pe'ruka] F wig
perversão [pexvex'sãw] (pl -ões) F perversion
perversidade [pexvexsi'dadʒi] F perversity
perverso, -a [pex'vɛxsu, a] ADJ perverse;
(malvado) wicked
perversões [pexvex'sõjʃ] FPL de **perversão**
perverter [pexvex'teʳ] VT (corromper) to corrupt,
pervert; **perverter-se** VR to become corrupt;
pervertido, -a [pexvex'tʃidu, a] ADJ perverted
■ M/F pervert
pesada [pe'zada] F weighing
pesadelo [peza'delu] M nightmare
pesado, -a [pe'zadu, a] ADJ heavy; (ambiente)
tense; (trabalho) hard; (estilo) dull, boring; (andar)
slow; (piada) coarse; (comida) stodgy; (tempo)
sultry ■ ADV heavily; **pegar no** ~ (col) to work
hard; **da pesada** (col: legal) great; (: barra-pesada)
rough, violent
pesagem [pe'zaʒẽ] F weighing
pêsames ['pesamiʃ] MPL condolences,
sympathy sg
pesar [pe'zaʳ] VT to weigh; (fig) to weigh up ■ VI
to weigh; (ser pesado) to be heavy; (influir) to carry
weight; (causar mágoa): ~ **a** to hurt, grieve ■ M
grief; **sobre** (recair) to fall upon; **em que pese
a** despite; **apesar dos -es** despite everything
pesaroso, -a [peza'rozu, ɔza] ADJ (triste)
sorrowful, sad; (arrependido) regretful, sorry
pesca ['pɛʃka] F (ato) fishing; (os peixes) catch; **ir à**
~ to go fishing; ~ **submarina** skin diving
pescada [peʃ'kada] F whiting
pescado [peʃ'kadu] M fish
pescador, a [peʃka'doʳ(a)] M/F fisherman/
woman; ~ **à linha** angler
pescar [peʃ'kaʳ] VT (peixe) to catch; (tentar
apanhar) to fish for; (retirar da água) to fish out;
(um marido) to catch, get ■ VI to fish; (BR: col) to
understand; ~ **de algo** (col) to know about sth;
pescou? got it?, see?
pescoção [peʃko'sãw] (pl -ões) M slap
pescoço [peʃ'kosu] M neck; **até o** ~ (endividado)
up to one's neck
pescoções [peʃko'sõjʃ] MPL de **pescoção**
pescoçudo, -a [peʃko'sudu, a] ADJ bull-necked
peso ['pezu] M weight; (fig: ônus) burden;
(importância) importance; **pessoa/argumento
de** ~ important person/weighty argument;
de pouco ~ lightweight; **em** ~ in full force;
~ **atômico** atomic weight; ~ **bruto/líquido**
gross/net weight; ~ **morto** dead weight; **ter
dois -s e duas medidas** (fig) to have double
standards
pespontar [peʃpõ'taʳ] VT to backstitch
pesponto [peʃ'põtu] M backstitch
pesquei etc [peʃ'kej] VB V **pescar**
pesqueiro, -a [peʃ'kejru, a] ADJ fishing atr
pesquisa [peʃ'kiza] F inquiry, investigation;
(científica) research; ~ **de campo** field
work; ~ **de mercado** market research; ~ **e**

desenvolvimento research and development
pesquisador, a [peʃkiza'doʳ(a)] M/F
investigator; (científico, de mercado) researcher; ~
no Google® to google
pesquisar [peʃki'zaʳ] VT, VI to investigate; (nas
ciências etc) to research
pêssego ['pesegu] M peach
pessegueiro [pese'gejru] M peach tree
pessimismo [pesi'miʒmu] M pessimism
pessimista [pesi'miʃta] ADJ pessimistic ■ M/F
pessimist
péssimo, -a ['pɛsimu, a] ADJ very bad, awful;
estar ~ (pessoa) to be in a bad way
pessoa [pe'soa] F person; **pessoas** FPL people;
em ~ personally; ~ **de bem** honest person; ~
física/jurídica (Jur) individual/legal entity;
pessoal [pe'swaw] (pl -ais) ADJ personal ■ M
personnel pl, staff pl; (col) people pl, folks pl; **oi,
pessoal!** (col) hi, everyone!, hi, folks!
pestana [peʃ'tana] F eyelash; **tirar uma** ~ (col)
to have a nap
pestanejar [peʃtane'ʒaʳ] VI to blink; **sem** ~ (fig)
without batting an eyelid
peste ['pɛʃtʃi] F (opidemia) epidemic; (bubônica)
plague; (fig) pest, nuisance
pesticida [peʃtʃi'sida] M pesticide
pestífero, -a [peʃ'tʃiferu, a] ADJ (fig) pernicious
pestilência [peʃtʃi'lẽsja] F plague; (epidemia)
epidemic; (fedor) stench
pestilento, -a [peʃtʃi'lẽtu, a] ADJ pestilential,
plague atr; (malcheiroso) putrid
pétala ['petala] F petal
peteca [pe'tɛka] F (kind of) shuttlecock; **fazer
alguém de** ~ to make a fool of sb; **não deixar a** ~
cair (col) to keep the ball rolling
peteleco [pete'lɛku] M flick; **dar um** ~ **em algo**
to flick sth
petição [petʃi'sãw] (pl -ões) F (rogo) request;
(documento) petition; **em** ~ **de miséria** in a
terrible state
peticionário, -a [petʃisjo'narju, a] M/F
petitioner; (Jur) plaintiff
petições [petʃi'sõjʃ] FPL de **petição**
petiscar [petʃiʃ'kaʳ] VT to nibble at, peck at ■ VI
to have a nibble
petisco [pe'tʃiʃku] M savoury (Brit), savory (US),
titbit (Brit), tidbit (US)
petit-pois [petʃi'pwa] M INV pea
petiz [pe'tʃiʒ] (PT) M boy
petrechos [pe'treʃuʃ] MPL equipment sg; (Mil)
stores, equipment sg; (de cozinha) utensils
petrificar [petrifi'kaʳ] VT to petrify; (empedernir)
to harden; (assombrar) to stun; **petrificar-se** VR
to be petrified; to be stunned; to become hard
Petrobrás [petro'brajʃ] ABR F Brazilian state oil
company
petrodólar [petro'dɔlaʳ] M petrodollar
petroleiro, -a [petro'lejru, a] ADJ oil atr,
petroleum atr ■ M (navio) oil tanker

NB: European Portuguese adds the following consonants to certain words: **b** (sú(b)dito, su(b)til); **c** (a(c)ção,
a(c)cionista, a(c)to); **m** (inde(m)ne); **p** (ado(p)çã, ado(p)tar); for further details see p. xiii.

petróleo [pe'trɔlju] M oil, petroleum; ~ **bruto** crude oil

petrolífero, -a [petro'liferu, a] ADJ oil-producing

petroquímica [petro'kimika] F petrochemicals pl; (*ciência*) petrochemistry

petroquímico, -a [petro'kimiku, a] ADJ petrochemical

petulância [petu'lãsja] F impudence

petulante [petu'lãtʃi] ADJ impudent

petúnia [pe'tunja] F petunia

peúga ['pjuga] (*PT*) F sock

pevide [pe'vidʒi] (*PT*) F (*de melão*) seed; (*de maçã*) pip

p. ex. ABR (= *por exemplo*) e.g

pexote [pe'ʃotʃi] M/F (*criança*) little kid; (*novato*) beginner, novice

PF (*BR*) ABR F = **Polícia Federal**

PFL (*BR*) ABR M = **Partido da Frente Liberal**

PH (*BR*) ABR M = **Partido Humanitário**

PI ABR = **Piauí**

pia ['pia] F wash basin; (*da cozinha*) sink; ~ **batismal** font

piada ['pjada] F joke

piadista [pja'dʒiʃta] M/F joker

pianista [pja'niʃta] M/F pianist

piano ['pjanu] M piano; ~ **de cauda** grand piano

pião [pjãw] (*pl* -ões) M (*brinquedo*) top

piar [pjaʳ] VI (*pinto*) to cheep; (*coruja*) to hoot; **não** ~ not to say a word

piauiense [pjaw'jẽsi] ADJ from Piauí ■ M/F person from Piauí

PIB ABR M (= *Produto Interno Bruto*) GNP

picada [pi'kada] F (*de agulha etc*) prick; (*de abelha*) sting; (*de mosquito, cobra*) bite; (*de avião*) dive; (*de navalha*) stab; (*atalho*) path, trail; (*de droga*) shot

picadeiro [pika'dejru] M (*circo*) ring

picadinho [pika'dʒiɲu] M stew

picado, -a [pi'kadu, a] ADJ (*por agulha*) pricked; (*por abelha*) stung; (*por cobra, mosquito*) bitten; (*papel*) shredded; (*carne*) minced; (*legumes*) chopped

picante [pi'kãtʃi] ADJ (*tempero*) hot; (*piada*) risqué, blue; (*comentário*) saucy

pica-pau ['pika-] (*pl* -s) M woodpecker

picar [pi'kaʳ] VT (*com agulha*) to prick; (*suj: abelha*) to sting; (: *mosquito*) to bite; (: *pássaro*) to peck; (*um animal*) to goad; (*carne*) to mince; (*papel*) to shred; (*fruta*) to chop up; (*comichar*) to prickle ■ VI (*a isca*) to take the bait; (*comichar*) to prickle; (*avião*) to dive; **picar-se** VR to prick o.s.

picardia [pikax'dʒia] F (*implicância*) spitefulness; (*esperteza*) craftiness

picaresco, -a [pika'reʃku, a] ADJ comic, ridiculous

picareta [pika'reta] F pickaxe (*Brit*), pickax (*US*) ■ M/F crook

picaretagem [pikare'taʒẽ] (*pl* -ns) F con

pícaro, -a ['pikaru, a] ADJ crafty, cunning

pichação [piʃa'sãw] (*pl* -ões) F (*ato*) spraying; (*grafite*) piece of graffiti

pichar [pi'ʃaʳ] VT (*dizeres, muro*) to spray; (*aplicar*

piche *em*) to cover with pitch; (*col*: *espinafrar*) to run down ■ VI (*col*) to criticize

piche ['piʃi] M pitch

piclés ['pikliʃ] MPL pickles

pico ['piku] M (*cume*) peak; (*ponta aguda*) sharp point; (*PT*: *um pouco*) a bit; **mil e** ~ just over a thousand; **meio-dia e** ~ just after midday

picolé [piko'lɛ] M lolly

picotar [piko'taʳ] VT to perforate; (*bilhete*) to punch

picote [pi'kɔtʃi] M perforation

pictórico, -a [pik'tɔriku, a] ADJ pictorial

picuinha [pi'kwiɲa] F: **estar de** ~ **com alguém** to have it in for sb

piedade [pje'dadʒi] F (*devoção*) piety; (*compaixão*) pity; **ter** ~ **de** to have pity on; **piedoso, -a** [pje'dozu, ɔza] ADJ (*Rel*) pious; (*compassivo*) merciful

piegas ['pjɛgaʃ] ADJ INV sentimental; (*col*) soppy ■ M/F INV softy

pieguice [pje'gisi] F sentimentality

píer ['pieʳ] M pier

piercing ['pixs[~i]] (*pl* ~s) M piercing

pifa ['pifa] (*col*) M booze-up; **tomar um** ~ to get smashed

pifado, -a [pi'fadu, a] (*col*) ADJ (*carro*) broken down; (*TV etc*) broken

pifar [pi'faʳ] (*col*) VI (*carro*) to break down; (*rádio etc*) to go wrong; (*plano, programa*) to fall through

pigarrear [piga'xjaʳ] VI to clear one's throat

pigarro [pi'gaxu] (*col*) M frog in the throat

pigméia [pig'mɛja] F *de* **pigmeu**

pigmentação [pigmẽta'sãw] F pigmentation, colouring (*Brit*), coloring (*US*)

pigmento [pig'mẽtu] M pigment

pigmeu, -méia [pig'mew, 'mɛ] ADJ, M/F pigmy

pijama [pi'ʒama] M pyjamas pl

pilantra [pi'lãtra] (*col*) M/F crook

pilantragem [pilã'traʒẽ] (*pl* -ns) (*col*) F rip-off

pilão [pi'lãw] (*pl* -ões) M mortar

pilar [pi'laʳ] VT to pound, crush ■ M pillar

pilastra [pi'laʃtra] F pilaster

pileque [pi'lɛki] (*col*) M booze-up; **tomar um** ~ to get smashed *ou* plastered; **estar de** ~ to be smashed *ou* plastered

pilha ['piʎa] F (*Elet*) battery; (*monte*) pile, heap; (*Comput*) stack; **às** ~**s** in vast quantities; **estar uma** ~ **(de nervos)** to be a bundle of nerves

pilhagem [pi'ʎaʒẽ] F (*ato*) pillage; (*objetos*) plunder, booty

pilhar [pi'ʎa] VT (*saquear*) to plunder, pillage; (*roubar*) to rob; (*surpreender*) to catch

pilhéria [pi'ʎɛrja] F joke

pilheriar [piʎe'rjaʳ] VI to joke, jest

pilões [pi'lõjʃ] MPL *de* **pilão**

pilotagem [pilo'taʒẽ] F flying; **escola de** ~ flying school

pilotar [pilo'taʳ] VT (*avião*) to fly; (*carro de corrida*) to drive ■ VI to fly

pilotis [pilo'tʃiʃ] MPL stilts

piloto [pi'lotu] M (*de avião*) pilot; (*de navio*) first mate; (*motorista*) (*racing*) driver; (*bico de gás*) pilot light ■ ADJ INV (usina, plano) pilot; (peça) sample atr; ~ automático automatic pilot; ~ de prova test pilot

pílula ['pilula] F pill; a ~ (anticoncepcional) the pill

pimba ['pĩba] EXCL wham!

pimenta [pi'mẽta] F (Culin) pepper; ~ de Caiena cayenne pepper; pimenta-do-reino F black pepper; pimenta-malagueta (pl pimentas-malagueta) F chilli (Brit) ou chili (US) pepper; pimentão [pimẽ'tãw] (pl -ões) M (Bot) pepper; pimentão verde green pepper

pimenteira [pimẽ'tejra] F (Bot) pepper plant; (à mesa) pepper pot; (: moedor) pepper mill

pimpão, -pona [pĩ'pãw, 'pɔna] (PT) (pl -ões/-s) ADJ smart, flashy ■ M/F show-off

pimpolho [pĩ'poʎu] M (criança) youngster

pimpona [pĩ'pɔna] F de pimpão

PIN (BR) ABR M = Plano de Integração Nacional

pinacoteca [pinako'tɛka] F art gallery; (coleção de quadros) art collection

pináculo [pi'nakulu] M (tb fig) pinnacle

pinça ['pĩsa] F (de sobrancelhas) tweezers pl; (de casa) tongs pl; (Med) callipers pl (Brit), calipers pl (US)

pinçar [pĩ'saˈ] VT to pick up; (sobrancelhas) to pluck; (fig: exemplos, defeitos) to pick out

píncaro ['pĩkaru] M summit, peak

pincel [pĩ'sɛw] (pl -éis) M brush; (para pintar) paintbrush; ~ de barba shaving brush

pincelada [pĩse'lada] F (brush) stroke

pincelar [pĩse'laˈ] VT to paint

pincenê [pĩse'ne] M pince-nez

pindaíba [pĩda'iba] F: estar na ~ (col) to be broke

pinel [pi'nɛw] (pl -éis) (col) M/F: ser/ficar ~ to be/go crazy

pinga ['pĩga] F (cachaça) rum; (PT: trago) drink

pingado, -a [pĩ'gadu, a] ADJ: ~ de covered in drops of

pingar [pĩ'gaˈ] VI to drip; (começar a chover) to start to rain

pingente [pĩ'ʒẽtʃi] M pendant

pingo ['pĩgu] M (gota) drop; (pingo do i) dot; ~ de gente (col) slip of a child; um ~ de (comida etc) a spot of; (educação etc) a scrap of

pingue-pongue® [pĩgi-'põgi] M Ping-Pong®

pingüim [pĩ'gwĩ] (pl -ns) M penguin

pinguinho [pĩ'giɲu] M little drop; (pouquinho): um ~ a tiny bit

pingüins [pĩ'gwĩʃ] MPL de pingüim

pinha ['piɲa] F pine cone

pinheiral [piɲej'raw] (pl -ais) M pine wood

pinheiro [pi'ɲejru] M pine (tree)

pinho ['piɲu] M pine

pinicada [pini'kada] F (beliscão) pinch; (cutucada) poke; (de pássaro) peck

pinicar [pini'kaˈ] VT (pele) to prickle; (como o bico) to peck; (beliscar) to pinch; (cutucar) to poke

pinimba [pi'nĩba] (col) F: estar de ~ com

alguém to have it in for sb

pino ['pinu] M (peça) pin; (Auto: na porta) lock; a ~ upright; sol a ~ noon-day sun; bater ~ (Auto) to knock; (col) to be in a bad way

pinóia [pi'nɔja] (col) F piece of trash; que ~! what a drag!

pinote [pi'nɔtʃi] M buck

pinotear [pino'tʃjaˈ] VI to buck

pinta ['pĩta] F (mancha) spot; (col: aparência) appearance, looks pl; (: sujeito) guy; dar na ~ (col) to give o.s. away; ela tem ~ de (ser) inglesa she looks English; está com ~ de chover it looks like rain

pinta-braba [pĩta'braba] (pl pintas-brabas) M/F hoodlum, shady character

pintado, -a [pĩ'tadu, a] ADJ painted; (cabelo) dyed; (olhos, lábios) made up; é o avô ~ he's the image of his grandfather; não querer ver alguém nem ~ (col) to hate the sight of sb

pintar [pĩ'taˈ] VT to paint; (cabelo) to dye; (rosto) to make up; (descrever) to describe; (imaginar) to picture ■ VI to paint; (col: aparecer) to appear, turn up; (: problemas, oportunidade) to crop up; pintar-se VR to make o.s. up; ~ (o sete) to paint the town red

pintarroxo [pĩta'xoʃu] M linnet, robin

pinto ['pĩtu] M chick; (col!) prick (!); como um ~ (molhado) like a drowned rat; ser ~ to be a piece of cake

pintor, a [pĩ'toˈ(a)] M/F painter

pintura [pĩ'tura] F painting; (maquiagem) make-up; ~ a óleo oil painting

pio, -a ['piu, a] ADJ (devoto) pious; (caridoso) charitable ■ M cheep, chirp; não dar um ~ not to make a sound

piões [pjõjʃ] MPL de pião

piolho ['pjoʎu] M louse

pioneiro, -a [pjo'nejru, a] ADJ pioneering ■ M pioneer

piopio [pju'pju] (col) M birdie, dicky bird

pior ['pjɔˈ] ADJ, ADV (comparativo) worse; (superlativo) worst ■ M: o ~ worst of all ■ F: estar na ~ (col) to be in a jam

piora ['pjɔra] F worsening

piorar [pjo'raˈ] VT to make worse, worsen ■ VI to get worse

pipa ['pipa] F barrel, cask; (de papel) kite

piparote [pipa'rɔtʃi] M (com o dedo) flick

pipi [pi'pi] (col) M (urina) pee; fazer ~ to have a pee, pee

pipilar [pipi'laˈ] VI to chirp

pipoca [pi'pɔka] F popcorn; (col: na pele) blister; ~s! blast!

pipocar [pipo'kaˈ] VI to go pop, pop; (aparecer) to spring up

pipoqueiro, -a [pipo'kejru, a] M/F popcorn seller

pique ['piki] M (corte) nick; (auge) peak; (grande disposição) keenness, enthusiasm; a ~ vertically,

---

NB: European Portuguese adds the following consonants to certain words: b (sú(b)dito, su(b)til); c (a(c)ção, a(c)cionista, a(c)to); m (inde(m)ne); p (ado(p)çã, ado(p)tar); for further details see p. xiii.

steeply; **a ~ de** on the verge of; **ir/pôr a ~ to** sink; **perder o ~ to** lose one's momentum; **estou no maior ~ no momento** I'm really in the mood *ou* keen at the moment

piquei *etc* [pi'kej] VB V **picar**

piquenique [piki'niki] M picnic; **fazer ~ to have** a picnic

piquete [pi'ketʃi] M (*Mil*) squad; (*em greve*) picket

pira ['pira] (*col*) F: **dar o ~ to** take off

pirado, -a [pi'radu, a] (*col*) ADJ crazy

pirâmide [pi'ramidʒi] F pyramid

piranha [pi'raɲa] F piranha (fish); (*col: mulher*) tart

pirão [pi'rãw] M manioc meal

pirar [pi'raʳ] (*col*) VI to go mad; (*com drogas*) to get high; (*ir embora*) to take off

pirata [pi'rata] M pirate; (*namorador*) lady-killer; (*vigarista*) crook ■ ADJ pirate

pirataria [pirata'ria] F piracy; (*patifaria*) crime

pires ['piriʃ] M INV saucer

pirilampo [piri'lãpu] M glow worm

Pirineus [piri'newʃ] MPL: **os ~** the Pyrenees

piriri [piri'ri] (*col*) M (*diarréia*) the runs *pl*

pirotecnia [pirotek'nia] F pyrotechnics *sg*, art of making fireworks

pirraça [pi'xasa] F spiteful thing; **fazer ~ to be** spiteful

pirracento, -a [pixa'sẽtu, a] ADJ (*vingativo*) spiteful; (*perverso*) bloody-minded

pirralho, -a [pi'xaʎu, a] M/F child

pirueta [pi'rweta] F pirouette

pirulito [piru'litu] (BR) M lollipop

PISA (BR) ABR F = **Papel de Imprensa SA**

pisada [pi'zada] F (*passo*) footstep; (*rastro*) footprint

pisar [pi'zaʳ] VT (*andar por cima de*) to tread on; (*uvas*) to tread, press; (*esmagar, subjugar*) to crush; (*café*) to grind; (*assunto*) to harp on ■ VI (*andar*) to step, tread; (*acelerar*) to put one's foot down; **~ em** (*grama, pé*) to step *ou* tread on; (*casa de alguém, pátria*) to set foot in; **"não pise na grama"** "do not walk on the grass"; **~ forte** to stomp; **pisa mais leve!** don't stamp your feet!

piscadela [piʃka'dɛla] F (*involuntária*) blink; (*sinal*) wink

pisca-pisca [piʃka-'piʃka] (*pl -s*) M (*Auto*) indicator

piscar [piʃ'kaʳ] VT to blink; (*dar sinal*) to wink; (*estrelas*) to twinkle ■ M: **num ~ de olhos** in a flash

piscicultor, a [pisikuw'toʳ(a)] M/F fish farmer

piscicultura [pisikuw'tura] F fish farming

piscina [pi'sina] F swimming pool; (*para peixes*) fish pond

piscoso, -a [piʃ'kozu, ɔza] ADJ rich in fish

piso ['pizu] M floor; **~ salarial** wage floor, lowest wage

pisotear [pizo'tʃiaʳ] VT to trample (on); (*fig*) to ride roughshod over

pisquei *etc* [piʃ'kej] VB V **piscar**

píssico, -a ['pisiku, a] ADJ crazy, mad

pista ['piʃta] F (*vestígio*) trace; (*indicação*) clue; (*de*

corridas) track; (*Aviat*) runway; (*de equitação*) ring; (*de estrada*) lane; (*de dança*) (dance) floor

pistache [piʃ'taʃi] M pistachio (nut)

pistacho [piʃ'taʃu] M = **pistache**

pistão [piʃ'tãw] (*pl -ões*) M = **pistom**

pistola [piʃ'tɔla] F (*arma*) pistol; (*para tinta*) spray gun

pistolão [piʃto'lãw] (*pl -ões*) M contact

pistoleiro [piʃto'lejru] M gunman

pistolões [piʃto'lõjʃ] MPL *de* **pistolão**

pistom [piʃ'tõ] (*pl -ns*) M piston

pitada [pi'tada] F (*porção*) pinch

pitanga [pi'tãga] F Surinam cherry

pitar [pi'taʳ] VT, VI to smoke

piteira [pi'tejra] F cigarette-holder

pito ['pitu] M (*cachimbo*) pipe; (*col: repreensão*) telling-off; **sossegar o ~ to** calm down

pitonisa [pito'niza] F fortune-teller

pitoresco, -a [pito'reʃku, a] ADJ picturesque

pituitário, -a [pitwi'tarju, a] ADJ (*glândula*) pituitary

pivete [pi'vɛtʃi] M child thief

pivô [pi'vo] M (*Tec*) pivot; (*fig*) central figure, prime mover

pixaim [piʃa'ĩ] ADJ (*cabelo*) frizzy ■ M frizzy hair

pixote [pi'ʃɔtʃi] M/F = **pexote**

pizza ['pitsa] F pizza

pizzaria [pitsa'ria] F pizzeria

PJ (BR) ABR M = **Partido da Juventude**

PL (BR) ABR M = **Partido Liberal**

plá [pla] (*col*) M (*dica*) tip; (*papo*) chat

placa ['plaka] F plate; (*Auto*) number plate (*Brit*), license plate (*US*); (*comemorativa*) plaque; (*Comput*) board; (*na pele*) blotch ■ F: **~ de memória** (*Comput*) memory card; **~ de sinalização** roadsign; **~ fria** false number *ou* license plate

placar [pla'kaʳ] M scoreboard; **abrir o ~ to open** the scoring

placebo [pla'sɛbu] M placebo

placenta [pla'sẽta] F placenta

placidez [plasi'deʒ] F peacefulness, serenity

plácido, -a ['plasidu, a] ADJ (*sereno*) calm; (*manso*) placid

plagiador, a [plaʒja'doʳ(a)] M/F = **plagiário**

plagiar [pla'ʒjaʳ] VT to plagiarize

plagiário, -a [pla'ʒjarju, a] M/F plagiarist

plágio ['plaʒu] M plagiarism

plaina ['plajna] F (*instrumento*) plane

plana ['plana] F: **de primeira ~** first-class

planador [plana'doʳ] M glider

planalto [pla'nawtu] M tableland, plateau

planar [pla'naʳ] VI to glide

planear [pla'njaʳ] (PT) VT = **planejar**

planejador, a [planeʒa'doʳ(a)] M/F planner

planejamento [planeʒa'mẽtu] M planning; (*Arq*) design; **~ familiar** family planning

planejar [plane'ʒaʳ] (BR) VT to plan; (*edifício*) to design

planeta [pla'neta] M planet

planetário, -a [plane'tarju, a] ADJ planetary ■ M planetarium

plangente [plã'ʒētʃi] ADJ plaintive, mournful
planície [pla'nisi] F plain
planificar [planifi'ka^r] VT (*programar*) to plan
out; (*uma região*) to make a plan of
planilha [pla'niʎa] F (*Comput*) spreadsheet
plano, -a ['planu, a] ADJ (*terreno*) flat, level;
(*liso*) smooth ▪ M plan; (*Mat*) plane; **~ diretor**
master plan; **em primeiro/em último ~** in the
foreground/background; **Plano Real**; *see below*

● **PLANO REAL**

● The *Plano Real*, launched in 1994, was a plan
● for the economic stabilization of Brazil. In
● an attempt to contain inflation without
● resorting to measures such as a price and
● wage freeze, the government changed
● the Brazilian currency from the *cruzeiro*
● to the *real*. In addition, it speeded up the
● privatization of state-owned companies,
● reduced public spending and raised interest
● rates to rein in consumer demand.

planta ['plãta] F (*Bio*) plant; (*de pé*) sole; (*Arq*) plan
plantação [plãta'sãw] F (*ato*) planting; (*terreno*)
planted land; (*safra*) crops *pl*
plantado, -a [plã'tadu, a] ADJ: **deixar alguém/**
ficar ~ em algum lugar (*col*) to leave sb/be left
standing somewhere
plantão [plã'tãw] (*pl* -ões) M duty; (*noturno*)
night duty; (*plantonista*) person on duty; (*Mil*:
serviço) sentry duty; (: *pessoa*) sentry; **estar de**
~ to be on duty; **médico/farmácia de ~** duty
doctor/pharmacy *ou* chemist's (*Brit*)
plantar [plã'ta^r] VT to plant; (*semear*) to sow;
(*estaca*) to drive in; (*estabelecer*) to set up; **plantar-**
se VR to plant o.s.
plantio [plã'tʃiu] M planting; (*terreno*) planted
land
plantões [plã'tõjʃ] MPL *de* **plantão**
plantonista [plãto'niʃta] M/F person on duty
planura [pla'nura] F plain
plaquê [pla'ke] (PT) M gold plate
plaqueta [pla'keta] F plaque; (*Auto*) licensing
badge (*attached to number plate*); (*Comput*) chip
plasma ['plaʒma] M plasma
plasmar [plaʒ'ma^r] VT to mould (*Brit*), mold (*US*),
shape
plástica ['plaʃtʃika] F (*cirurgia*) piece of plastic
surgery; (*do corpo*) build; **fazer uma ~** to have
plastic surgery
plástico, -a ['plaʃtʃiku, a] ADJ plastic ▪ M
plastic
plastificado, -a [plaʃtʃifi'kadu, a] ADJ plastic-
coated
plataforma [plata'fɔxma] F platform; **~**
de exploração de petróleo oil rig; **~ de**
lançamento launch pad
plátano ['platanu] M plane tree

platéia [pla'tɛja] F (*Teatro etc*) stalls *pl* (*Brit*),
orchestra (*US*); (*espectadores*) audience
platina [pla'tʃina] F platinum
platinado, -a [platʃi'nadu, a] ADJ platinum *atr*;
loura platinada platinum blonde
platinados [platʃi'naduʃ] MPL (*Auto*) points
platinar [platʃi'na^r] VT (*cabelo*) to dye platinum
blonde
platô [pla'to] M plateau
platônico, -a [pla'toniku, a] ADJ platonic
plausibilidade [plawzibili'dadʒi] F plausibility
plausível [plaw'zivew] (*pl* -eis) ADJ credible,
plausible
playboy [plej'bɔi] (*pl* -s) M playboy
playground [plej'grãwdʒi] (*pl* -s) M children's
playground
PLB ABR M = **Partido Liberal Brasileiro**
plebe ['plɛbi] F common people *pl*, populace
plebeu, -béia [ple'bew, 'bɛja] ADJ plebeian
▪ M/F pleb
plebiscito [plebi'situ] M referendum, plebiscite
plectro ['plɛktru] M (*Mús*) plectrum
pleitear [plej'tʃja^r] VT (*Jur*: *causa*) to plead;
(*contestar*) to contest; (*tentar conseguir*) to go after;
(*concorrer a*) to compete for
pleito ['plejtu] M lawsuit, case; (*fig*) dispute; **~**
(eleitoral) election
plenamente [plena'mētʃi] ADV fully,
completely
plenário, -a [ple'narju, a] ADJ plenary ▪ M
plenary session; (*local*) chamber
plenipotência [plenipo'tēsja] F full powers *pl*
plenipotenciário, -a [plenipotē'sjarju, a] ADJ,
M/F plenipotentiary
plenitude [pleni'tudʒi] F plenitude, fullness
pleno, -a ['plenu, a] ADJ full; (*completo*) complete;
em ~ dia in broad daylight; **em plena rua/**
Londres in the middle of the street/London;
em ~ inverno in the middle *ou* depths of
winter; **em ~ mar** out at sea; **ter plena certeza**
to be completely sure; **~s poderes** full powers
pleonasmo [pljo'naʒmu] M pleonasm
pletora [ple'tɔra] F plethora
pleurisia [plewri'zia] F pleurisy
plinto ['plĩtu] M plinth
plissado, -a [pli'sadu, a] ADJ pleated
pluma ['pluma] F feather
plumagem [plu'maʒē] F plumage
plural [plu'raw] (*pl* -ais) ADJ, M plural
pluralismo [plura'liʒmu] M pluralism
pluralista [plura'liʃta] ADJ, M/F pluralist
Plutão [plu'tãw] M Pluto
plutocrata [pluto'krata] M/F plutocrat
plutônio [plu'tonju] M plutonium
pluvial [plu'vjaw] (*pl* -ais) ADJ pluvial, rain *atr*
PM (BR) ABR F, M = **Polícia Militar**
PMB ABR M = **Partido Municipalista Brasileiro**
PMC (BR) ABR M = **Partido Municipalista**
Comunitário

NB: *European Portuguese adds the following consonants to certain words:* **b** (sú(b)dito, su(b)til); **c** (a(c)ção,
a(c)cionista, a(c)to); **m** (inde(m)ne); **p** (ado(p)ção, ado(p)tar); *for further details see p. xiii.*

PMDB ABR M = **Partido do Movimento Democrático Brasileiro**

PMN (BR) ABR M = **Partido da Mobilização Nacional**

PN ABR M (BR) = **Partido Nacionalista** ▪ ABR F (*Com: de ações*) = **preferencial nominativa**

PNA (BR) ABR M = **Plano Nacional de Álcool**

PNB ABR M (= *Produto Nacional Bruto*) GNP

PNC (BR) ABR M = **Partido Nacionalista Comunitário**

PND (BR) ABR M = **Plano Nacional de Desenvolvimento**; = **Partido Nacionalista Democrático**

pneu ['pnew] M tyre (*Brit*), tire (*US*)

pneumático, -a [pnew'matʃiku, a] ADJ pneumatic ▪ M tyre (*Brit*), tire (*US*)

pneumonia [pnewmo'nia] F pneumonia

PNR (BR) ABR M = **Partido da Nova República**

pó [pɔ] M (*partículas*) powder; (*sujeira*) dust; (*col: cocaína*) coke; **pó de arroz** face powder; **ouro/ sabão em pó** gold dust/soap powder; **tirar o pó (de algo)** to dust (sth)

pô [po] (*col*) EXCL (*dando ênfase*) blimey; (*mostrando desagrado*) damn it!

pobre ['pɔbri] ADJ poor ▪ M/F poor person; **os ~s** the poor; **~ de espírito** simple, dull; **um Sinatra dos ~s** a poor man's Sinatra

pobre-diabo (*pl* pobres-diabos) M poor devil

pobretão, -tona [pobre'tãw, 'tɔna] (*pl* -ões/-s) M/F pauper

pobreza [po'breza] F poverty; **~ de espírito** simplicity

poça ['pɔsa] F puddle, pool; **~ de sangue** pool of blood

poção [po'sãw] (*pl* -ões) F potion

pocilga [po'siwga] F pigsty

poço ['posu] M well; (*de mina, elevador*) shaft; **ser um ~ de ciência/bondade** (*fig*) to be a fount of knowledge/kindness; **~ de petróleo** oil well

poções [po'sõjʃ] FPL *de* **poção**

poda ['pɔda] F pruning

podadeira [poda'dejra] F pruning knife

podar [po'daʳ] VT to prune

pôde *etc* ['podʒi] VB V **poder**

pó-de-arroz M face powder

○ **PALAVRA CHAVE**

poder [po'deʳ] VI **1** (*capacidade*) can, be able to; **não posso fazê-lo** I can't do it, I'm unable to do it

2 (*ter o direito de*) can, may, be allowed to; **posso fumar aqui?** can I smoke here?; **pode entrar?** (*posso?*) can I come in?

3 (*possibilidade*) may, might, could; **pode ser** maybe; **pode ser que** it may be that; **ele poderá vir amanhã** he might come tomorrow

4: **não poder com, não posso com ele** I cannot cope with him

5 (*col: indignação*): **pudera!** no wonder!; **como é que pode?** you're joking!

▪ M power; (*autoridade*) authority; **poder aquisitivo** purchasing power; **estar no poder** to be in power; **em poder de alguém** in sb's hands

poderio [pode'riu] M might, power

poderoso, -a [pode'rozu, ɔza] ADJ mighty, powerful; (*Comput*) powerful

pódio ['pɔdʒju] M podium

podre ['podri] ADJ rotten, putrid; (*fig*) rotten, corrupt; **sentir-se ~** (*col: mal*) to feel grotty; **~ de rico/cansaço** filthy rich/dog tired

podres ['podriʃ] MPL faults

podridão [podri'dãw] F decay, rottenness; (*fig*) corruption

põe *etc* [põj] VB V **pôr**

poeira ['pwejra] F dust; **~ radioativa** fall-out

poeirada [pwej'rada] F pile of dust

poeirento, -a [pwej'rẽtu, a] ADJ dusty

poema ['pwema] M poem

poente ['pwẽtʃi] M west; (*do sol*) setting

poesia [poe'zia] F poetry; (*poema*) poem

poeta ['pweta] M poet

poética ['pwetʃika] F poetics *sg*

poético, -a ['pwetʃiku, a] ADJ poetic

poetisa [pwe'tʃiza] F (woman) poet

poetizar [pwetʃi'zaʳ] VT to set to poetry ▪ VI to write poetry

pogrom [po'grõ] (*pl* -s) M pogrom

pois [pojʃ] ADV (*portanto*) so; (*PT: assentimento*) yes ▪ CONJ as, since, because; (*mas*) but; **~ bem** well then; **~ é** that's right; **~ não!** (BR) of course!; **~ não?** (*numa loja*) what can I do for you?, isn't it?, aren't you?, didn't they? *etc*; **~ sim!** certainly not!; **~ (então)** then

polaco, -a [po'laku, a] ADJ Polish ▪ M/F Pole ▪ M (*Ling*) Polish

polainas [po'lajnaʃ] FPL gaiters

polar [po'laʳ] ADJ polar

polaridade [polari'dadʒi] F polarity

polarizar [polari'zaʳ] VT to polarize

polca ['pɔwka] F polka

poldro, -a ['powdru, a] M/F colt/filly

polegada [pole'gada] F inch

polegar [pole'gaʳ] M (*tb:* **dedo polegar**) thumb

poleiro [po'lejru] M perch

polêmica [po'lemika] F controversy; **polêmico, -a** [po'lemiku, a] ADJ controversial

polemista [pole'miʃta] ADJ argumentative ▪ M/F debater

polemizar [polemi'zaʳ] VI to debate, argue

pólen ['pɔlẽ] M pollen

polia [po'lia] F pulley

poliamida [polja'mida] F polyamide

polichinelo [poliʃi'nɛlu] M Mr Punch

polícia [po'lisja] F police, police force ▪ M/F policeman/woman; **agente ~** police officer; **~ aduaneira** border police; **~ militar** military police; **~ rodoviária** traffic police; **policial** [poli'sjaw] (*pl* -ais) ADJ police *atr* ▪ M/F (BR) policeman/woman; **novela** *ou* **romance policial** detective novel

policial-militar (*pl* policiais-militares) ADJ military police *atr*

policiamento [polisja'mẽtu] M policing

policiar [poli'sja^r] VT to police; (*instintos, modos*) to control, keep in check; **policiar-se** VR to control o.s.

policlínica [poli'klinika] F general hospital

policultura [polikuw'tura] F mixed farming

polidez [poli'deʒ] F good manners *pl*, politeness

polido, -a [po'lidu, a] ADJ (*lustrado*) polished, shiny; (*cortês*) well-mannered, polite

poliéster [po'ljɛfte^r] M polyester

poliestireno [poljeftʃi'rɛnu] M polystyrene

polietileno [poljetʃi'lenu] M polythene (*Brit*), polyethylene (US)

poligamia [poliga'mia] F polygamy

polígamo, -a [po'ligamu, a] ADJ polygamous

poliglota [poli'glɔta] ADJ, M/F polyglot

polígono [po'ligonu] M polygon

polimento [poli'mẽtu] M (*lustração*) polishing; (*finura*) refinement

Polinésia [poli'nɛzja] F: a ~ Polynesia

polinésio, -a [poli'nɛzju, a] ADJ, M/F Polynesian

polinização [poliniza'sãw] F pollination

polinizar [polini'za^r] VT, VI to pollinate

pólio ['pɔlju] F polio

poliomielite [poljomje'litʃi] F poliomyelitis

pólipo ['pɔlipu] M polyp

polir [po'li^r] VT to polish

polissílabo, -a [poli'silabu, a] ADJ polysyllabic ■ M polysyllable

politécnica [poli'tɛknika] F (*Educ*) polytechnic

política [po'litʃika] F politics *sg*; (*programa*) policy; (*diplomacia*) tact; (*astúcia*) cunning; *v tb* **político**

politicagem [politʃi'kaʒẽ] F politicking

politicar [politʃi'ka^r] VI to be involved in politics; (*discorrer*) to talk politics

político, -a [po'litʃiku, a] ADJ political; (*astuto*) crafty ■ M/F politician

politiqueiro, -a [politʃi'kejru, a] M/F political wheeler-dealer ■ ADJ politicking

politizar [politʃi'za^r] VT to politicize; (*trabalhadores*) to mobilize politically; **politizar-se** VR to become politically aware

pólo ['pɔlu] M pole; (*Esporte*) polo; ~ **aquático** water polo; ~ **petroquímico** petrochemical complex; **P~ Norte/Sul** North/South Pole

polonês, -esa [polo'nef, eza] ADJ Polish ■ M/F Pole ■ M (*Ling*) Polish

Polônia [po'lonja] F: a ~ Poland

polpa ['powpa] F pulp

polpudo, -a [pow'pudu, a] ADJ (*fruta*) fleshy; (*negócio*) profitable, lucrative; (*quantia*) sizeable, considerable

poltrão, -trona [pow'trãw, 'trɔna] (*pl* -ões/-s) ADJ cowardly ■ M/F coward

poltrona [pow'trɔna] F armchair; (*em teatro, cinema*) upholstered seat; *v tb* **poltrão**

poluente [po'lwẽtʃi] ADJ, M pollutant

poluição [polwi'sãw] F pollution

poluidor, a [polwi'do^r(a)] ADJ pollutant

poluir [po'lwi^r] VT to pollute

polvilhar [powvi'ʎa^r] VT to sprinkle, powder

polvilho [pow'viʎu] M powder; (*farinha*) manioc flour

polvo ['powvu] M octopus

pólvora ['pɔwvora] F gunpowder

polvorosa [powvo'rɔza] (*col*) F uproar; **em ~** (*apressado*) in a flap; (*desarrumado*) in a mess

pomada [po'mada] F ointment

pomar [po'ma^r] M orchard

pomba ['põba] F dove; **~(s)!** for heaven's sake!

pombal [põ'baw] (*pl* -ais) M dovecote

pombo ['põbu] M pigeon

pombo-correio (*pl* pombos-correios) M carrier pigeon

pomo ['pomu] M: ~ **de discórdia** bone of contention

pomo-de-Adão [-a'dãw] (BR) M Adam's apple

pomos ['pomoʃ] VB V **pôr**

pompa ['põpa] F pomp

Pompéia [põ'pɛja] N Pompeii

pompom [põ'põ] (*pl* -ns) M pompom

pomposo, -a [põ'pozu, ɔza] ADJ ostentatious, pompous

ponche ['põʃi] M punch

poncheira [põ'ʃejra] F punchbowl

poncho ['põʃu] M poncho

ponderação [põdera'sãw] F consideration, meditation; (*prudência*) prudence

ponderado, -a [põ'dɛradu, a] ADJ prudent

ponderar [põde'ra^r] VT to consider, weigh up ■ VI to meditate, muse; ~ **que** (*alegar*) to point out that

pônei ['ponej] M pony

ponho *etc* ['poɲu] VB V **pôr**

ponta ['põta] F tip; (*de faca*) point; (*de sapato*) toe; (*extremidade*) end; (*Teatro, Cinema*) walk-on part; (*Futebol: posição*) wing; (: *jogador*) winger; **uma ~ de** (*um pouco*) a touch of; ~ **de cigarro** cigarette end; ~ **do dedo** fingertip; **na ~ da língua** on the tip of one's tongue; **na(s) ~(s) dos pés** on tiptoe; **de ~ a ~** from one end to the other; (*do princípio ao fim*) from beginning to end; ~ **de terra** point; **estar de ~ com alguém** to be at odds with sb; **agüentar as ~s** (*col*) to hold on

ponta-cabeça F: **de ~** upside down; (*cair*) head first

pontada [põ'tada] F (*dor*) twinge

ponta-de-lança (*pl* pontas-de-lança) M/F (*fig*) spearhead

ponta-direita (*pl* pontas-direitas) M (*Futebol*) right winger

ponta-esquerda (*pl* pontas-esquerdas) M (*Futebol*) left winger

pontal [põ'taw] (*pl* -ais) M (*de terra*) point, promontory

NB: *European Portuguese adds the following consonants to certain words:* **b** (sú(b)dito, su(b)til); **c** (a(c)ção, a(c)cionista, a(c)to); **m** (inde(m)ne); **p** (ado(p)çã, ado(p)tar); *for further details see p. xiii.*

pontão [põ'tãw] M pontoon
pontapé [põta'pɛ] M kick; **dar ~s em alguém** to kick sb
pontaria [põta'ria] F aim; **fazer ~** to take aim
ponte ['põtʃi] F bridge; **~ aérea** air shuttle, airlift; **~ de safena** (heart) bypass operation; **~ móvel** swing bridge; **~ suspensa** *ou* **pênsil** suspension bridge
ponteado, -a [põ'tʃjadu, a] ADJ stippled, dotted ∎ M stipple
pontear [põ'tʃjaʳ] VT (*pontilhar*) to dot, stipple; (*dar pontos*) to sew, stitch
ponteira [põ'tejra] F ferrule, tip
ponteiro [põ'tejru] M (*indicador*) pointer; (*de relógio*) hand; (*Mús: plectro*) plectrum
pontiagudo, -a [põtʃja'gudu, a] ADJ sharp, pointed
pontificado [põtʃifi'kadu] M pontificate
pontificar [põtʃifi'kaʳ] VI to pontificate
pontífice [põ'tʃifisi] M pontiff, Pope
pontilhado, -a [põtʃi'ʎadu, a] ADJ dotted ∎ M dotted area
pontilhar [põtʃi'ʎaʳ] VT to dot, stipple
pontinha [põ'tʃiɲa] F: **uma ~ de** a bit *ou* touch of
ponto ['põtu] M point; (*Med, Costura, Tricô*) stitch; (*pequeno sinal, do i*) dot; (*na pontuação*) full stop (Brit), period (US); (*na pele*) spot; (*Teatro*) prompter; (*de ônibus*) stop; (*de táxi*) rank (Brit), stand (US); (*tb:* **ponto cantado**) *macumba* chant; (*matéria escolar*) subject; (*boca-de-fumo*) drug den; **estar a ~ de fazer** to be on the point of doing; **ao ~** (*bife*) medium; **até certo ~** to a certain extent; **às cinco em ~** at five o'clock on the dot; **em ~ de bala** (*col*) all set; **assinar o ~** to sign in; (*fig*) to put in an appearance; **dar ~s** (*Med*) to put in stitches; **não dar ~ sem nó** (*fig*) to look out for one's own interests; **entregar os ~s** (*fig*) to give up; **fazer ~ em** to hang out at; **pôr um ~ em algo** (*fig*) to put a stop to sth; **dois ~s** colon *sg*; **~ cardeal** cardinal point; **~ de admiração** (PT) exclamation mark; **~ de equilíbrio** (*Com*) break-even point; **~ de exclamação/interrogação** exclamation/question mark; **~ de meia/de tricô** stocking/plain stitch; **~ de mira** bead; **~ de partida** starting point; **~ de referência** point of reference; **~ de vista** point of view, viewpoint; **~ facultativo** optional day off; **~ final** (*fig*) end; (*de ônibus*) terminus; **~ fraco** weak point
ponto-de-venda (*pl* **pontos-de-venda**) M (*Com*) point of sale, outlet
ponto-e-vírgula (*pl* **~-s**) M semicolon
pontuação [põtwa'sãw] F punctuation
pontual [põ'twaw] (*pl* -ais) ADJ punctual
pontualidade [põtwali'dadʒi] F punctuality
pontuar [põ'twaʳ] VT to punctuate
pontudo, -a [põ'tudu, a] ADJ pointed
poodle ['pudw] M poodle
pool [puw] M pool
popa ['popa] F stern, poop; **à ~** astern, aft
popelina [pope'lina] F poplin
população [popula'sãw] (*pl* -ões) F population

populacional [populasjo'naw] (*pl* -ais) ADJ population *atr*
populações [popula'sõjʃ] FPL *de* **população**
popular [popu'laʳ] ADJ popular; **popularidade** [populari'dadʒi] F popularity
popularizar [populari'zaʳ] VT to popularize, make popular; **popularizar-se** VR to become popular
populista [popu'liʃta] ADJ populist
populoso, -a [popu'lozu, oza] ADJ populous
pôquer ['pokeʳ] M poker

○ **PALAVRA CHAVE**

por [poʳ] (*por + o(s)/a(s) = pelo(s)/a(s)*) PREP
1 (*objetivo*) for; **lutar pela pátria** to fight for one's country
2 (*+ infin*): **está por acontecer** it is about to happen, it is yet to happen; **está por fazer** it is still to be done
3 (*causa*) out of, because of; **por falta de fundos** through lack of funds; **por hábito/natureza** out of habit/by nature; **faço isso por ela** I do it for her; **por isso** therefore; **a razão pela qual ... the** reason why ...; **pelo amor de Deus!** for Heaven's sake!
4 (*tempo*): **pela manhã** in the morning; **por volta das duas horas** at about two o'clock; **ele vai ficar por uma semana** he's staying for a week
5 (*lugar*): **por aqui** this way; **viemos pelo parque** we came through the park; **passar por São Paulo** to pass through São Paulo; **por fora/dentro** outside/inside
6 (*troca, preço*) for; **trocar o velho pelo novo** to change old for new; **comprei o livro por dez libras** I bought the book for ten pounds
7 (*valor proporcional*): **por cento** per cent; **por hora/dia/semana/mês/ano** hourly/daily/weekly/monthly/yearly; **por cabeça** a *ou* per head; **por mais difícil** *etc* **que seja** however difficult *etc* it is
8 (*modo, meio*) by; **por correio/avião** by post/air; **por sí** by o.s.; **por escrito** in writing; **entrar pela entrada principal** to go in through the main entrance
9: **por que** (BR: *por causa*) because; (PT) why; **por quê?** (BR) why?
10: **por mim tudo bem** as far as I'm concerned that's OK

○ **PALAVRA CHAVE**

pôr [poʳ] VT 1 (*colocar*) to put; (*roupas*) to put on; (*objeções, dúvidas*) to raise; (*ovos, mesa*) to lay; (*defeito*) to find; **põe mais forte** turn it up; **você põe açúcar?** do you take sugar?; **pôr de lado** to set aside
2 (*+ adj*) to make; **você está me pondo nervoso** you're making me nervous; **pôr-se** VR 1 (*sol*) to set
2 (*colocar-se*): **pôr-se de pé** to stand up; **ponha-**

se no meu lugar put yourself in my position
3: pôr-se a to start to; **ela pôs-se a chorar** she
started crying M: **o pôr do sol** sunset

porão [po'rãw] (pl -ões) M (Náut) hold; (de casa)
basement; (: armazém) cellar
porca ['pɔxka] F (animal) sow; (Tec) nut
porcalhão, -lhona [poxka'ʎãw, 'ʎɔna] (pl -ões/
-s) ADJ filthy ■ M/F pig
porção [pox'sãw] (pl -ões) F portion, piece; **uma**
~ de a lot of
porcaria [poxka'ria] F filth; (dito sujo) obscenity;
(coisa ruim) piece of junk ■ EXCL damn!; **o filme**
era uma ~ the film was a load of rubbish
porcelana [poxse'lana] F porcelain, china
porcentagem [poxsẽ'taʒẽ] (pl -ns) F percentage
porco, -a ['poxku, 'pɔxka] ADJ filthy
■ M (animal) pig, hog (US); (carne) pork; **~**
chauvinista male chauvinist pig
porções [pox'sõjʃ] FPL de **porção**
porco-espinho (pl porcos-espinhos) M
porcupine
porco-montês [-mõ'teʃ] (pl porcos-monteses)
M wild boar
porejar [pore'ʒaʳ] VT to exude ■ VI to be exuded
porém [po'rẽ] CONJ however
porfia [pox'fia] F (altercação) dispute, wrangle;
(rivalidade) rivalry
pormenor [poxme'nɔʳ] M detail
pormenorizar [poxmenori'zaʳ] VT to detail
pornô [pox'no] (col) ADJ INV porn ■ M (filme)
porn film
pornochanchada [poxnoʃã'ʃada] F (filme) soft
porn movie
pornografia [poxnogra'fia] F pornography
pornográfico, -a [poxno'grafiku, a] ADJ
pornographic
poro ['pɔru] M pore
porões [po'rõjs] MPL de **porão**
pororoca [poro'rɔka] F bore
poroso, -a [po'rozu, ɔza] ADJ porous
porquanto [pox'kwãtu] CONJ since, seeing that
porque ['pɔxke] CONJ because; (interrogativo: PT)
why
porquê [pox'ke] ADV why ■ M reason, motive;
~? (PT) why?
porquinho-da-índia [pox'kiɲu-] (pl porquinhos-
da-índia) M guinea pig
porra ['poxa] (col!) F come (!), spunk (!) ■ EXCL
fuck (!), fucking hell (!); **para quê ~?** what the
fuck for? (!)
porrada [po'xada] F (col: pancada) beating; **uma ~**
de (col!) fucking loads of (!)
porra-louca (pl porras-loucas) (col!) M/F fucking
maniac (!) ■ ADJ fucking crazy (!)
porre ['pɔxi] (col) M booze-up; **tomar um ~** to
get plastered; **estar de ~** to be plastered; **ser**
um ~ (ser chato) to be boring, be a drag
porretada [poxe'tada] F clubbing

porrete [po'xetʃi] M club
porta ['pɔxta] F door; (vão da porta) doorway; (de
um jardim) gate; (Comput) port; **a ~s fechadas**
behind closed doors; **de ~ em ~** from door to
door; **~ corrediça** sliding door; **~ da rua/da**
frente/dos fundos street/front/back door; **~**
de entrada entrance door; **~ de vaivém** swing
door; **~ giratória** revolving door; **~ sanfonada**
folding door
porta-aviões M INV aircraft carrier
porta-bandeira (pl -s) M/F standard-bearer
porta-chaves M INV keyring
portador, a [poxta'doʳ(a)] M/F bearer; **ao ~** (Com)
payable to the bearer
porta-espada (pl -s) M sheath
porta-estandarte (pl -s) M/F standard-bearer
porta-fólio [-'fɔlju] (pl -s) M portfolio
portagem [pox'taʒẽ] (PT) (pl -ns) F toll
porta-jóias M INV jewellery (Brit) ou jewelry
(US) box
portal [pox'taw] (pl -ais) M doorway
porta-lápis M INV pencil box
portaló [poxta'lɔ] M (Náut) gangway
porta-luvas M INV (Auto) glove compartment
porta-malas M INV (Auto) boot (Brit), trunk (US)
porta-moedas (PT) M purse
porta-níqueis M INV purse
portanto [pox'tãtu] CONJ so, therefore
portão [pox'tãw] (pl -ões) M gate
porta-partitura (pl -s) M music stand
portar [pox'taʳ] VT to carry; **portar-se** VR to
behave
porta-retratos M INV photo frame
porta-revistas M INV magazine rack
portaria [poxta'ria] F (de um edifício) entrance
hall; (recepção) reception desk; (do governo) edict,
decree; **baixar uma ~** to issue a decree
porta-seios M INV bra, brassiere
portátil [pox'tatʃiw] (pl -eis) ADJ portable
porta-toalhas M INV towel rail
porta-voz (pl -es) M/F (pessoa) spokesman/
woman
porte ['pɔxtʃi] M (transporte) transport; (custo)
freight charge, carriage; (Náut) tonnage,
capacity; (atitude) bearing; **~ pago** post paid; **de**
grande ~ far-reaching, important; **empresa**
de ~ medio medium-sized enterprise; **um**
autor do ~ de ... an author of the calibre (Brit)
ou caliber (US) of ....
porteiro, -a [pox'tejru, a] M/F caretaker; **~**
eletrônico entry phone
portenho, -a [pox'teɲu, a] ADJ from Buenos
Aires ■ M/F person from Buenos Aires
portento [pox'tẽtu] M wonder, marvel
portentoso, -a [poxtẽ'tozu, ɔza] ADJ amazing,
marvellous (Brit), marvelous (US)
pórtico ['pɔxtʃiku] M porch, portico
portinhola [poxtʃi'ɲɔla] F small door; (de
carruagem) door

NB: European Portuguese adds the following consonants to certain words: **b** (sú(b)dito, su(b)til); **c** (a(c)ção,
a(c)cionista, a(c)to); **m** (inde(m)ne); **p** (ado(p)ção, ado(p)tar); for further details see p. xiii.

porto ['poxtu] M (*do mar*) port, harbour (*Brit*), harbor (*US*); (*vinho*) port; **o P~** Oporto; **~ de escala** port of call; **~ franco** freeport
porto-alegrense [-ale'grẽsi] ADJ from Porto Alegre ▪ M/F person from Porto Alegre
portões [pox'tõjʃ] MPL *de* **portão**
Porto Rico M Puerto Rico
porto-riquenho, -a [poxtuxi'keɲu, a] ADJ, M/F Puertorican
portuense [pox'twẽsi] ADJ from Oporto ▪ M/F person from Oporto
portuga [pox'tuga] (*pej*) M/F Portuguese
Portugal [poxtu'gaw] M Portugal; **português, -guesa** [portu'geʃ, 'geza] ADJ Portuguese ▪ M/F Portuguese ▪ M (*Ling*) Portuguese; **português de Portugal/do Brasil** European/Brazilian Portuguese
portunhol [poxtu'ɲɔw] M *mixture of Spanish and Portuguese*
porventura [poxvẽ'tura] ADJ by chance; **se ~ você ...** if you happen to ....
porvir [pox'viʳ] M future
pôs [poʃ] VB V **pôr**
pós- [pɔjʃ-] PREFIXO post-
posar [po'zaʳ] VI (*Foto*) to pose
pós-datado, -a [-da'tadu, a] ADJ post-dated
pós-datar VT to postdate
pose ['pozi] F pose
pós-escrito M postscript
pós-graduação F postgraduation; **curso de ~** postgraduate course
pós-graduado, -a ADJ, M/F postgraduate
pós-guerra M post-war period; **o Brasil do ~** post-war Brazil
posição [pozi'sãw] (*pl* -**ões**) F position; (*social*) standing, status; (*de esportista no mundo*) ranking; **tomar uma ~** to take a stand; **posicionar** [pozisjo'naʳ] VT to position; **posicionar-se** VR to position o.s.; (*tomar atitude*) to take a position
positivo, -a [pozi'tʃivu, a] ADJ positive ▪ M positive ▪ EXCL (*col*) yeah! sure!
posologia [pozolo'ʒia] F dosage
pós-operatório, -a [-opera'tɔrju, a] ADJ postoperative
pospor [poʃ'poʳ] (*irreg*) VT to put after; (*adiar*) to postpone
possante [po'sãtʃi] ADJ powerful, strong; (*carro*) flashy
posse ['pɔsi] F possession, ownership; (*investidura*) swearing in; **posses** FPL (*pertences*) possessions, belongings; **tomar ~** to take office; **tomar ~ de** to take possession of; **cerimônia de ~** swearing in ceremony; **pessoa de ~s** person of means; **viver de acordo com suas ~s** to live according to one's means
posseiro, -a [po'sejru, a] ADJ leaseholding ▪ M/F leaseholder
possessão [pose'sãw] F possession; **possessivo, -a** [pose'sivu, a] ADJ possessive
possesso, -a [po'sɛsu, a] ADJ possessed; (*furioso*) furious
possibilidade [posibili'dadʒi] F possibility;

(*oportunidade*) chance; **possibilidades** FPL (*recursos*) means
possibilitar [posibili'taʳ] VT to make possible, permit
possível [po'sivew] (*pl* -**eis**) ADJ possible; **fazer todo o ~ to** do one's best; **não é ~!** (*col*) you're joking!
posso *etc* ['posu] VB V **poder**
possuidor, a [poswi'do(ʳ)(a)] M/F (*de casa, livro etc*) owner; (*de dinheiro, talento etc*) possessor; **ser ~ de** to be the owner/possessor of
possuir [po'swiʳ] VT (*casa, livro etc*) to own; (*dinheiro, talento*) to possess; (*dominar*) to possess, grip; (*sexualmente*) to take, have
posta ['pɔʃta] F (*pedaço*) piece, slice
postal [poʃ'taw] (*pl* -**ais**) ADJ postal ▪ M postcard
postar [poʃ'taʳ] VT to place, post; **postar-se** VR to position o.s.
posta-restante (*pl* **postas-restantes**) F poste-restante (*Brit*), general delivery (*US*)
poste ['pɔʃtʃi] M pole, post
pôster ['poʃteʳ] M poster
postergar [poʃtex'gaʳ] VT (*adiar*) to postpone; (*amigos*) to pass over; (*interesse pessoal*) to set *ou* put aside; (*lei, norma*) to disregard
posteridade [poʃteri'dadʒi] F posterity
posterior [poʃte'rjoʳ] ADJ (*mais tarde*) subsequent, later; (*traseiro*) rear, back ▪ M (*col*) posterior, bottom; **posteriormente** [poʃterjox'mẽtʃi] ADV later, subsequently
postiço, -a [poʃ'tʃisu, a] ADJ false, artificial
postigo [poʃ'tʃigu] M (*em porta*) peephole
posto, -a ['poʃtu, 'pɔʃta] PP *de* **pôr** ▪ M post, position; (*emprego*) job; (*de diplomata: local*) posting; **~ de comando** command post; **~ de gasolina** service *ou* petrol station; **~ que** although; **a ~s** at action stations; **~ do corpo de bombeiros** fire station; **~ de saúde** health centre *ou* center
posto-chave (*pl* **postos-chaves**) M key position *ou* post
postulado [poʃtu'ladu] M postulate, assumption
postulante [poʃtu'lãtʃi] M/F petitioner; (*candidato*) candidate
postular [poʃtu'laʳ] VT (*pedir*) to request; (*teoria*) to postulate
póstumo, -a ['poʃtumu, a] ADJ posthumous
postura [poʃ'tura] F (*posição*) posture, position; (*aspecto físico*) appearance; (*fig*) posture
posudo, -a [po'zudu, a] ADJ poseurish
potassa [po'tasa] F potash
potássio [po'tasju] M potassium
potável [po'tavew] (*pl* -**eis**) ADJ drinkable; **água ~** drinking water
pote ['pɔtʃi] M jug, pitcher; (*de geléia*) jar; (*de creme*) pot; **chover a ~s** (*PT*) to rain cats and dogs; **dinheiro aos ~s** (*fig*) pots of money
potência [po'tẽsja] F power; (*força*) strength; (*nação*) power; (*virilidade*) potency
potencial [potẽ'sjaw] (*pl* -**ais**) ADJ potential, latent ▪ M potential; **riquezas** *etc* **em ~**

potential wealth etc
potentado [potẽ'tadu] M potentate
potente [po'tẽtʃi] ADJ powerful, potent
pot-pourri [popu'xi] M (Mús) medley; (fig) pot-
pourri
potro, -a ['potru, a] M/F (cavalo) colt/filly, foal
pouca-vergonha (pl poucas-vergonhas) F
(ato) shameful act, disgrace; (falta de vergonha)
shamelessness

○ **PALAVRA CHAVE**

pouco, -a ['poku, a] ADJ **1** (sg) little, not much;
pouco tempo little ou not much time; **de
pouco interesse** of little interest, not very
interesting; **pouca coisa** not much
2 (pl) few, not many; **uns poucos** a few, some;
poucas vezes rarely; **poucas crianças comem
o que devem** few children eat what they
should
▪ ADV **1** little, not much; **custa pouco/a** it
doesn't cost much; **dentro em pouco, daqui a
pouco** shortly; **pouco antes** shortly before
2 (+ adj: = negativo): **ela é pouco inteligente/
simpática** she's not very bright/friendly
3: por pouco eu não morri I almost died
4: pouco a pouco little by little
5: aos poucos gradually
▪ M: **um pouco** a little, a bit; **nem um pouco**
not at all

pouco-caso M scorn
poupador, a [popa'do'(a)] ADJ thrifty
poupança [po'pãsa] F thrift; (economias) savings
pl; (tb: **caderneta de poupança**) savings bank
poupar [po'pa'] VT to save; (vida) to spare; ~
alguém (de sofrimentos) to spare sb; ~ **algo a
alguém**, ~ **alguém de algo** (trabalho etc) to save
sb sth; (aborrecimentos) to spare sb sth
pouquinho [po'kiɲu] M: **um ~ (de)** a little
pouquíssimo, -a [po'kisimu, a] ADJ, ADV SUPERL
de pouco
pousada [po'zada] F (hospedagem) lodging;
(hospedaria) inn
pousar [po'za'] VT to place; (mão) to rest, place
▪ VI (avião, pássaro) to land; (pernoitar) to spend
the night
pouso ['pozu] M landing; (lugar) resting place
povão [po'vãw] M ordinary people pl
povaréu [pova'rɛw] M crowd of people
povo ['povu] M people; (raça) people pl, race;
(plebe) common people pl; (multidão) crowd
povoação [povwa'sãw] (pl -ões) F (aldeia) village,
settlement; (habitantes) population; (ato de
povoar) settlement, colonization
povoado, -a [po'vwadu, a] ADJ populated ▪ M
village
povoamento [povwa'mẽtu] M settlement
povoar [po'vwa'] VT (de habitantes) to people,

populate; (de animais etc) to stock
poxa ['poʃa] EXCL gosh!
PP ABR (Com: de ações) = **preferencial ao portador**
PPB ABR M = **Partido do Povo Brasileiro**
PR (BR) ABR = **Paraná** ▪ ABR F = **Polícia
Rodoviária**
pra [pra] (col) PREP = **para; para a**
praça ['prasa] F (largo) square; (mercado)
marketplace; (soldado) soldier; (cidade) town
▪ M (Mil) private; (polícia) constable; **sentar ~** to
enlist; ~ **de touros** bullring; ~ **forte** stronghold
praça-d'armas (pl praças-d'armas) M officers'
mess
pracinha [pra'siɲa] M GI
prado ['pradu] M meadow, grassland; (BR:
hipódromo) racecourse
pra-frente (col) ADJ INV trendy
prafrentex [prafrẽ'tɛks] (col) ADJ INV trendy
Praga ['praga] N Prague
praga ['praga] F (maldição) curse; (coisa, pessoa
importuna) nuisance; (desgraça) misfortune; (erva
daninha) weed; **rogar ~ a alguém** to curse sb
pragmático, -a [prag'matʃiku, a] ADJ (prático)
pragmatic
pragmatismo [pragma'tʃiʒmu] M pragmatism
pragmatista [pragma'tʃiʃta] ADJ, M/F
pragmatist
praguejar [prage'ʒa'] VT, VI to curse
praia ['praja] F beach, seashore
pralina [pra'lina] F praline
prancha ['prãʃa] F plank; (Náut) gangplank; (de
surfe) board
prancheta [prã'ʃeta] F (mesa) drawing board
prantear [prã'tʃja'] VT to mourn ▪ VI to weep
pranto ['prãtu] M weeping; **debulhar-se em ~**
to weep bitterly
Prata ['prata] F: **o rio da ~** the River Plate
prata ['prata] F silver; (col: cruzeiro) ≈ quid (Brit),
≈ buck (US); **de ~** silver atr; ~ **de lei** sterling silver
prataria [prata'ria] F silverware; (pratos)
crockery
pratarrão [prata'xãw] (pl -ões) M large plate
prateado, -a [pra'tʃjadu, a] ADJ silver-plated;
(brilhante) silvery; (cor) silver ▪ M (cor) silver; (de
um objeto) silver-plating; **papel ~** silver paper
pratear [pra'tʃja'] VT to silver-plate; (fig) to turn
silver
prateleira [prate'lejra] F shelf
prática ['pratʃika] F (ato de praticar) practice;
(experiência) experience, know-how; (costume)
habit, custom; **na ~** in practice; **pôr em ~** to put
into practice; **aprender com a ~** to learn with
practice; v tb **prático**
praticagem [pratʃi'kaʒẽ] F (Náut) pilotage
praticante [pratʃi'kãtʃi] ADJ practising (Brit),
practicing (US) ▪ M/F apprentice; (de esporte)
practitioner
praticar [pratʃi'ka'] VT to practise (Brit), practice
(US); (profissão, medicina) to practise ou practice;

NB: European Portuguese adds the following consonants to certain words: **b** (sú(b)dito, su(b)til); **c** (a(c)ção,
a(c)cionista, a(c)to); **m** (inde(m)ne); **p** (ado(p)çã, ado(p)tar); for further details see p. xiii.

(*roubo, operação*) to carry out
praticável [pratʃiˈkavew] (*pl* **-eis**) ADJ practical, feasible
prático, -a [ˈpratʃiku, a] ADJ practical ■ M/F expert ■ M (*Náut*) pilot
prato [ˈpratu] M (*louça*) plate; (*comida*) dish; (*de uma refeição*) course; (*de toca-discos*) turntable; **pratos** MPL (*Mús*) cymbals; **~ raso/fundo/de sobremesa** dinner/soup/dessert plate; **~ do dia** dish of the day; **cuspir no ~ em que comeu** (*fig*) to bite the hand that feeds one; **pôr algo em ~s limpos** to get to the bottom of sth; **~ de resistência** pièce de résistance
praxe [ˈpraksi] F custom, usage; **de ~** usually; **ser de ~** to be the norm

● **PRAXE**
●
● Student life in Portugal follows the
● traditions set out in a written set of rules
● known as the 'código da praxe'. It begins in
● freshers' week, where freshers are jeered
● at by their seniors, and are subjected to a
● number of humiliating practical jokes, such
■ as having their hair cut against their will
● and being made to walk around town in
● fancy dress.

prazenteiro, -a [prazẽˈtejru, a] ADJ cheerful, pleasant
prazer [praˈzeʳ] M pleasure ■ VI: **~ a alguém** to please sb; **muito ~ em conhecê-lo** pleased to meet you
prazeroso, -a [prazeˈrozu, ɔza] ADJ (*pessoa*) pleased; (*viagem*) pleasurable
prazo [ˈprazu] M term, period; (*vencimento*) expiry date, time limit; **a curto/médio/longo ~** in the short/medium/long term; **comprar a ~** to buy on hire purchase (*Brit*) *ou* on the installment plan (*US*); **último ~** *ou* **~ final** deadline
pre- [pri-] PREFIXO pre-
pré- [prɛ-] PREFIXO pre-
preamar [preaˈmaʳ] (*BR*) F high tide water
preâmbulo [preˈãbulu] M preamble, introduction; **sem mais ~s** without further ado
preaquecer [prjakeˈseʳ] VT to preheat
pré-aviso M (*prior*) notice
precário, -a [preˈkarju, a] ADJ precarious, insecure; (*escasso*) failing; (*estado de saúde*) delicate
precatado, -a [prekaˈtadu, a] ADJ cautious
precatar-se [prekaˈtaxsi] VR to take precautions; **~-se contra** to be wary of; **precate-se para o pior** prepare yourself for the worst
precatória [prekaˈtɔrja] F (*Jur*) writ, prerogative order
precaução [prekawˈsãw] (*pl* **-ões**) F precaution
precaver-se [prekaˈvexsi] VR: **~ (contra** *ou* **de)** to be on one's guard (against); **~ para algo/fazer algo** to prepare o.s. for sth/be prepared to do

sth; **precavido, -a** [prekaˈvidu, a] ADJ cautious
prece [ˈprɛsi] F prayer; (*súplica*) entreaty
precedência [preseˈdẽsja] F precedence; **ter ~ sobre** to take precedence over
precedente [preseˈdẽtʃi] ADJ preceding ■ M precedent; **sem ~(s)** unprecedented
preceder [preseˈdeʳ] VT, VI to precede; **~ a algo** to precede sth; (*ter primazia*) to take precedence over sth
preceito [preˈsejtu] M precept, ruling
preceituar [presejˈtwaʳ] VT to set down, prescribe
preceptor [presepˈtoʳ] M mentor
preciosidade [presjoziˈdadʒi] F (*qualidade*) preciousness; (*coisa*) treasure
preciosismo [presjoˈziʒmu] M preciosity
precioso, -a [preˈsjozu, ɔza] ADJ precious; (*de grande importância*) invaluable
precipício [presiˈpisju] M precipice; (*fig*) abyss
precipitação [presipitaˈsãw] F haste; (*imprudência*) rashness
precipitado, -a [presipiˈtadu, a] ADJ hasty; (*imprudente*) rash
precipitar [presipiˈtaʳ] VT (*atirar*) to hurl; (*acontecimentos*) to precipitate ■ VI (*Quím*) to precipitate; **precipitar-se** VR (*atirar-se*) to hurl o.s.; (*contra, para*) to rush; (*agir com precipitação*) to be rash, act rashly; **~ alguém/~-se em** (*situação*) to plunge sb/be plunged into; (*aventuras, perigos*) to sweep sb/be swept into
precisado, -a [presiˈzadu, a] ADJ needy, in need
precisamente [presizaˈmẽtʃi] ADV precisely
precisão [presiˈzãw] F (*exatidão*) precision, accuracy; **ter ~ de** to need
precisar [presiˈzaʳ] VT to need; (*especificar*) to specify ■ VI to be in need; **precisar-se** VR: **"precisa-se"** "needed"; **~ de** to need; (*uso impess*): **não precisa você se preocupar** you needn't worry; **precisa de um passaporte** a passport is necessary *ou* needed; **preciso ir** I have to go; **~ que alguém faça** to need sb to do
preciso, -a [preˈsizu, a] ADJ (*exato*) precise, accurate; (*necessário*) necessary; (*claro*) concise; **é ~ você ir** you must go
preclaro, -a [preˈklaru, a] ADJ famous, illustrious
preço [ˈpresu] M price; (*custo*) cost; (*valor*) value; **por qualquer ~** at any price; **a ~ de banana** (*BR*) *ou* **de chuva** (*PT*) dirt cheap; **não ter ~** (*fig*) to be priceless; **~ por atacado/a varejo** wholesale/retail price; **~ de custo** cost price; **~ de venda** sale price; **~ de fábrica/de revendedor** factory/trade price; **~ à vista** cash price; (*de commodities*) spot price; **~ pedido** asking price
precoce [preˈkɔsi] ADJ precocious; (*antecipado*) early; (*calvície*) premature
precocidade [prekosiˈdadʒi] F precociousness
preconcebido, -a [prekõseˈbidu, a] ADJ preconceived
preconceito [prekõˈsejtu] M prejudice
preconizar [prekoniˈzaʳ] VT to extol; (*aconselhar*) to advocate

precursor, a [prekux'so^r(a)] M/F (*predecessor*) predecessor, forerunner; (*mensageiro*) herald

predador [preda'do^r] M predator

pré-datado, -a [-da'tadu, a] ADJ predated

pré-datar VT to predate

predatório, -a [preda'tɔrju, a] ADJ predatory

predecessor [predese'so^r] M predecessor

predestinado, -a [predeʃtʃi'nadu, a] ADJ predestined

predestinar [predeʃtʃi'na^r] VT to predestine

predeterminado, -a [predetexmi'nadu, a] ADJ predetermined

predeterminar [predetexmi'na^r] VT to predetermine

predial [pre'dʒjaw] (*pl* -ais) ADJ property *atr*, real-estate *atr*; **imposto** ~ domestic rates

prédica ['predʒika] F sermon

predicado [predʒi'kadu] M predicate

predição [predʒi'sãw] (*pl* -ões) F prediction, forecast

predigo *etc* [pre'dʒigu] VB V **predizer**

predileção [predʒile'sãw] (PT -cç-, *pl* -ões) F preference, predilection

predileto, -a [predʒi'lɛtu, a] (PT -ct-) ADJ favourite (*Brit*), favorite (*US*)

prédio ['predʒju] M building; ~ **de apartamentos** block of flats (*Brit*), apartment house (*US*)

predispor [predʒiʃ'po^r] (*irreg*) VT: ~ **alguém contra** to prejudice sb against; **predispor-se** VR: **predispor-se a/para** to get o.s. in the mood to/for; **a natação me predispõe para o trabalho** swimming puts me in the mood for work; **a notícia os predispôs para futuros problemas** the news prepared them for future problems

predisposição [predʒiʃpozi'sãw] F predisposition

predisposto, -a [predʒiʃ'poʃtu, 'pɔʃta] PP *de* **predispor** ■ ADJ predisposed

predispunha *etc* [predʒiʃ'puɲa] VB V **predispor**

predispus *etc* [predʒiʃ'puʃ] VB V **predispor**

predispuser *etc* [predʒiʃpu'ze^r] VB V **predispor**

predizer [predʒi'ze^r] (*irreg*) VT to predict, forecast

predominância [predomi'nãsja] F predominance, prevalence

predominante [predomi'nãtʃi] ADJ predominant

predominar [predomi'na^r] VI to predominate, prevail

predomínio [predo'minju] M predominance, supremacy

pré-eleitoral (*pl* -ais) ADJ pre-election

preeminência [preemi'nẽsja] F pre-eminence, superiority

preeminente [preemi'nẽtʃi] ADJ pre-eminent, superior

preencher [preẽ'ʃe^r] VT (*formulário*) to fill in (*Brit*) *ou* out, complete; (*requisitos*) to fulfil (*Brit*),

fulfill (*US*), meet; (*espaço, vaga, tempo, cargo*) to fill; ~ **à máquina** (*formulário*) to complete on a typewriter

preenchimento [preẽʃi'mẽtu] M completion; (*de requisitos*) meeting; (*de vaga*) filling

pré-escolar ADJ pre-school

preestabelecer [preeʃtabele'se^r] VT to prearrange

pré-estréia F preview

preexistir [preeziʃ'tʃi^r] VI to preexist; ~ **a algo** to exist before sth

pré-fabricado, -a [-fabri'kadu, a] ADJ prefabricated

prefaciar [prefa'sja^r] VT to preface

prefácio [pre'fasju] M preface

prefeito, -a [pre'fejtu, a] M/F mayor; **prefeitura** [prefej'tura] F town hall

preferência [prefe'rẽsja] F preference; (*Auto*) priority; **de** ~ preferably; **ter** ~ **por** to have a preference for

preferencial [preferẽ'sjaw] (*pl* -ais) ADJ (*rua*) main; (*ação*) preference *atr* ■ F main road (*with priority*)

preferido, -a [prefe'ridu, a] ADJ favourite (*Brit*), favorite (*US*)

preferir [prefe'ri^r] VT to prefer; ~ **algo a algo** to prefer sth to sth

preferível [prefe'rivew] (*pl* -eis) ADJ: ~ **(a)** preferable (to)

prefigurar [prefigu'ra^r] VT to prefigure

prefiro *etc* [pre'firu] VB V **preferir**

prefixo [pre'fiksu] M (*Ling*) prefix; (*Tel*) code

prega ['prega] F pleat, fold

pregado, -a [pre'gadu, a] ADJ exhausted

pregador [prega'do^r] M preacher; (*de roupa*) peg

pregão [pre'gãw] (*pl* -ões) M proclamation, cry; **o** ~ (*na Bolsa*) trading; (*em leilão*) bidding

pregar¹ [prɛ'ga^r] VT (*sermão*) to preach; (*anunciar*) to proclaim; (*idéias, virtude*) to advocate ■ VI to preach

pregar² [pre'ga^r] VT (*com prego*) to nail; (*fixar*) to pin, fasten; (*cosendo*) to sew on ■ VI to give out; ~ **uma peça** to play a trick; ~ **os olhos em** to fix one's eyes on; **não** ~ **olho** not to sleep a wink; ~ **mentiras em alguém** to fob sb off with lies; ~ **um susto em alguém** to give sb a fright

prego ['pregu] M nail; (*col: casa de penhor*) pawn shop; **dar o** ~ (*pessoa, carro*) to give out; **pôr algo no** ~ to pawn sth; **não meter** ~ **sem estopa** (*fig*) to be out for one's own advantage

pregões [pre'gõjʃ] MPL *de* **pregão**

pré-gravado, -a [-gra'vadu, a] ADJ prerecorded

pregresso, -a [pre'gresu, a] ADJ past, previous

preguear [pre'gja^r] VT to pleat, fold

preguiça [pre'gisa] F laziness; (*animal*) sloth; **estar com** ~ to feel lazy; **estou com** ~ **de cozinhar** I can't be bothered to cook

preguiçar [pregi'sa^r] VI to laze around

preguiçoso, -a [pregi'sozu, ɔza] ADJ lazy ■ M/F

NB: *European Portuguese adds the following consonants to certain words:* **b** (sú(b)dito, su(b)til); **c** (a(c)ção, a(c)cionista, a(c)to); **m** (inde(m)ne); **p** (ado(p)ção, ado(p)tar); *for further details see p. xiii.*

lazybones
pré-história F prehistory
pré-histórico, -a ADJ prehistoric
preia ['prɛja] F prey
preia-mar (PT) F high tide
preito ['prejtu] M homage, tribute; **render ~ a** to pay homage to
prejudicar [preʒudʒi'ka^r] VT to damage; (*atrapalhar*) to hinder; **prejudicar-se** VR (*pessoa*) to do o.s. no favours (Brit) *ou* favors (US)
prejudicial [preʒudʒi'sjaw] (*pl* -**ais**) ADJ damaging; (*à saúde*) harmful
prejuízo [pre'ʒwizu] M (*dano*) damage, harm; (*em dinheiro*) loss; **com ~** (Com) at a loss; **em ~ de** to the detriment of
prejulgar [preʒuw'ga^r] VT to prejudge
prelado [pre'ladu] M prelate
preleção [prele'sãw] (PT -**cç**-, *pl* -**ões**) F lecture
preliminar [prelimi'na^r] ADJ preliminary ■ F (*partida*) preliminary ■ M (*condição*) preliminary
prelo ['prelu] M (printing) press; **no ~** in the press
prelúdio [pre'ludʒju] M prelude
prematuro, -a [prema'turu, a] ADJ premature
premeditação [premedʒita'sãw] F premeditation
premeditado, -a [premedʒi'tadu, a] ADJ premeditated
premeditar [premedʒi'ta^r] VT to premeditate
premência [pre'mẽsja] F urgency, pressing nature
pré-menstrual (*pl* -**ais**) ADJ premenstrual
premente [pre'mẽtʃi] ADJ pressing
premer [pre'me^r] VT to press
premiado, -a [pre'mjadu, a] ADJ prize-winning; (*bilhete*) winning ■ M/F prize-winner
premiar [pre'mja^r] VT to award a prize to; (*recompensar*) to reward
premiê [pre'mje] M (Pol) premier
premier [pre'mje] M = **premiê**
prêmio ['premju] M prize; (*recompensa*) reward; (Seguros) premium; **Grande P~** Grand Prix; **~ de consolação** consolation prize
premir [pre'mi^r] VT = **premer**
premissa [pre'misa] F premise
pré-moldado, -a [-mow'dadu, a] ADJ precast ■ M breeze block
premonição [premoni'sãw] (*pl* -**ões**) F premonition
premonitório, -a [premoni'tɔrju, a] ADJ premonitory
pré-natal [prɛ-] (*pl* -**ais**) ADJ antenatal (Brit), prenatal (US)
prenda ['prẽda] F gift, present; (*em jogo*) forfeit; **prendas** FPL (*aptidões*) talents; **~s domésticas** housework *sg*
prendado, -a [prẽ'dadu, a] ADJ gifted, talented; (*homem: em afazeres domésticos*) domesticated
prendedor [prẽde'do^r] M fastener; (*de cabelo, gravata*) clip; **~ de roupa** clothes peg; **~ de papéis** paper clip
prender [prẽ'de^r] VT (*pregar*) to fasten, fix; (*roupa,*

cabelo) to clip; (*capturar*) to arrest; (*atar, ligar*) to tie; (*atenção*) to catch; (*afetivamente*) to tie, bind; (*reter: doença, compromisso*) to keep; (*movimentos*) to restrict; **prender-se** VR to get caught, stick; **~-se a alguém** (*por amizade*) to be attached to sb; (*casar-se*) to tie o.s. down to sb; **~-se a algo** (*detalhes, maus hábitos*) to get caught up in sth; **~-se com algo** to be connected with sth
prenhe ['prẽɲi] ADJ pregnant
prenhez [pre'ɲeʒ] F pregnancy
prenome [pre'nɔmi] M first name, Christian name
prensa ['prẽsa] F (ger) press
prensar [prẽ'sa^r] VT to press, compress; (*fruta*) to squeeze; (*uvas*) to press; **~ alguém contra a parede** to push sb up against the wall
prenunciar [prenũ'sja^r] VT to predict, foretell; **as nuvens prenunciam chuva** the clouds suggest rain
prenúncio [pre'nũsju] M forewarning, sign
preocupação [preokupa'sãw] (*pl* -**ões**) F (*idéia fixa*) preoccupation; (*inquietação*) worry, concern
preocupante [preoku'pãtʃi] ADJ worrying
preocupar [preoku'pa^r] VT (*absorver*) to preoccupy; (*inquietar*) to worry; **preocupar-se** VR: **preocupar-se com** to worry about, be worried about
preparação [prepara'sãw] (*pl* -**ões**) F preparation
preparado [prepa'radu] M preparation
preparar [prepa'ra^r] VT to prepare; **preparar-se** VR to get ready; **~-se para algo/para fazer** to prepare for sth/to do; **preparativos** [prepa'tʃivuʃ] MPL preparations, arrangements
preparo [pre'paru] M preparation; (*instrução*) ability; **~ físico** physical fitness
preponderância [prepõde'rãsja] F preponderance, predominance
preponderante [prepõde'rãtʃi] ADJ predominant
preponderar [prepõde'ra^r] VI: **~ (sobre)** to prevail (over)
preposição [prepozi'sãw] (*pl* -**ões**) F preposition
preposto, -a [pre'poʃtu, 'pɔʃta] M/F person in charge; (*representante*) representative
prepotência [prepo'tẽsja] F superiority; (*despotismo*) absolutism
prepotente [prepo'tẽtʃi] ADJ (*poderoso*) predominant; (*despótico*) despotic; (*atitude*) overbearing
prerrogativa [prexoga'tʃiva] F prerogative, privilege
presa ['preza] F (*na guerra*) spoils *pl*; (*vítima*) prey; (*dente de animal*) fang
presbiteriano, -a [preʒbite'rjanu, a] ADJ, M/F Presbyterian
presbitério [preʒbi'terju] M presbytery
presciência [pre'sjẽsja] F foreknowledge, foresight
presciente [pre'sjẽtʃi] ADJ far-sighted, prescient

prescindir [presī'dʒir] vi: ~ **de algo** to do without sth
prescindível [presī'dʒivew] (*pl* -*eis*) ADJ dispensable
prescrever [preʃkre've^r] vt to prescribe; (*prazo*) to set ■ vi (*Jur: crime, direito*) to lapse; (*cair em desuso*) to fall into disuse
prescrição [preʃkri'sãw] (*pl* -*ões*) F order, rule; (*Med*) instruction; (: *de um remédio*) prescription; (*Jur*) lapse
prescrito, -a [preʃ'kritu, a] PP *de* **prescrever**
presença [pre'zēsa] F presence; (*freqüência*) attendance; ~ **de espírito** presence of mind; **ter boa** ~ to be presentable; **na ~ de** in the presence of; **presenciar** [prezē'sja^r] vt to be present at; (*testemunhar*) to witness
presente [pre'zētʃi] ADJ present; (*fig: interessado*) attentive; (: *evidente*) clear, obvious ■ M present ■ F (*Com: carta*): **a** ~ this letter; **os presentes** MPL (*pessoas*) those present; **ter algo** ~ to bear sth in mind; **dar/ganhar de** ~ to give/get as a present; ~ **de grego** undesirable gift, mixed blessing; **anexamos à** ~ we enclose herewith; **pela** ~ hereby; **presentear** [prezē'tʃja^r] vt: **presentear alguém (com algo)** to give sb (sth as) a present
presentemente [prezētʃe'mētʃi] ADV at present
presepada [preze'pada] F (*fanfarrice*) boasting; (*atitude, espetáculo ridículo*) joke
presépio [pre'zεpju] M Nativity scene, crib
preservação [prezexva'sãw] F preservation
preservar [prezex'va^r] vt to preserve, protect
preservativo [prezexva'tʃivu] M preservative; (*anticoncepcional*) condom
presidência [prezi'dēsja] F (*de um país*) presidency; (*de uma assembléia*) chair, presidency; **assumir a** ~ (*Pol*) to become president
presidencial [prezidē'sjaw] (*pl* -*ais*) ADJ presidential
presidencialismo [prezidēsja'liʒmu] M presidential system
presidenciável [prezidē'sjavew] (*pl* -*eis*) ADJ eligible for the presidency ■ M/F presidential candidate
presidente, -a [prezi'dētʃi, ta] M/F (*de um país*) president; (*de uma assembléia, Com*) chair, president; **o P~ da República** the President (of Brazil)
presidiário, -a [prezi'dʒjarju, a] M/F convict
presídio [prezi'dʒju] M prison
presidir [prezi'dʒi^r] vt, vi: ~ **(a)** to preside over; (*reunião*) to chair; (*suj: leis, critérios*) to govern
presilha [pre'ziʎa] F fastener; (*para o cabelo*) slide
preso, -a ['prezu, a] ADJ (*em prisão*) imprisoned; (*capturado*) under arrest, captured; (*atado*) bound, tied; (*moralmente*) bound ■ M/F prisoner; **ficar** ~ **a detalhes** to get bogged down in detail(s); **ficar** ~ **em casa** (*com filhos pequenos etc*) to be stuck at home; **estar** ~ **a alguém** to be attached

to sb; **você está** ~! you're under arrest!; **com a greve dos ônibus, fiquei** ~ **na cidade** with the bus strike I got stuck in town
pressa ['prεsa] F haste, hurry; (*rapidez*) speed; (*urgência*) urgency; **às** ~**s** hurriedly; **estar com** ~ to be in a hurry; **sem** ~ unhurriedly; **não tem** ~ there's no hurry; **ter** ~ **de** *ou* **em fazer** to be in a hurry to do
pressagiar [presa'ʒja^r] vt to foretell, presage
presságio [pre'saʒu] M omen, sign; (*pressentimento*) premonition
pressago, -a [pre'sagu, a] ADJ (*comentário*) portentous
pressão [pre'sãw] (*pl* -*ões*) F pressure; **(colchete de)** ~ press stud, popper; **fazer** ~ **(sobre alguém/algo)** to put pressure on (sb/sth); ~ **arterial** *ou* **sanguínea** blood pressure
pressentimento [presētʃi'mētu] M premonition, presentiment
pressentir [presē'tʃi^r] vt (*pressagiar*) to foresee; (*suspeitar*) to sense; (*inimigo*) to preempt
pressionar [presjo'na^r] vt (*botão*) to press; (*coagir*) to pressure ■ vi to press, put on pressure
pressões [pre'sõjʃ] FPL *de* **pressão**
pressupor [presu'po^r] (*irreg*) vt to presuppose
pressuposto, -a [presu'poʃtu, 'pɔʃta] PP *de* **pressupor** ■ M (*conjetura*) presupposition
pressupunha *etc* [presu'puɲa] VB V **pressupor**
pressupus *etc* [presu'puʃ] VB V **pressupor**
pressupuser *etc* [presu'puze^r] VB V **pressupor**
pressurização [presuriza'sãw] F pressurization
pressurizado, -a [presuri'zadu, a] ADJ pressurized
pressuroso, -a [presu'rozu, ɔza] ADJ (*apressado*) hurried, in a hurry; (*zeloso*) keen, eager
prestação [preʃta'sãw] (*pl* -*ões*) F instalment (*Brit*), installment (*US*); (*por uma casa*) repayment; **à** ~, **a prestações** in instal(l)ments; ~ **de contas/serviços** accounts/services rendered
prestamente [preʃta'mētʃi] ADV promptly
prestamista [preʃta'miʃta] M/F moneylender; (*comprador*) person paying hire purchase (*Brit*) *ou* on the installment plan (*US*)
prestar [preʃ'ta^r] vt (*cuidados*) to give; (*favores, serviços*) to do; (*contas*) to render; (*informações*) to supply; (*uma qualidade a algo*) to lend ■ vi: ~ **a alguém para algo** to be of use to sb for sth; **prestar-se** VR: **prestar-se a** (*servir*) to be suitable for; (*admitir*) to lend o.s. to; (*dispor-se*) to be willing to; ~ **atenção** to pay attention; ~ **juramento** to take an oath; **isto não presta para nada** it's absolutely useless; **ele não presta** he's good for nothing; ~ **homenagem/culto a** to pay tribute to/worship
prestativo, -a [preʃta'tʃivu, a] ADJ helpful, obliging
prestável [preʃ'tavew] (*pl* -*eis*) ADJ serviceable

NB: *European Portuguese adds the following consonants to certain words:* **b** (sú(b)dito, su(b)til); **c** (a(c)ção, a(c)cionista, a(c)to); **m** (inde(m)ne); **p** (ado(p)çã, ado(p)tar); *for further details see p. xiii.*

prestes ['prɛʃtʃiʃ] ADJ INV (pronto) ready; (a ponto de): ~ **a partir** about to leave

presteza [preʃ'teza] F (prontidão) promptness; (rapidez) speed; **com** ~ promptly

prestidigitação [preʃtʃidʒiʒita'sãw] F sleight of hand, conjuring, magic tricks pl

prestidigitador [preʃtʃidʒiʒita'do^r] M conjurer, magician

prestigiar [preʃtʃi'ʒja^r] VT to give prestige to

prestígio [preʃ'tʃiʒu] M prestige

prestigioso, -a [preʃtʃi'ʒozu, ɔza] ADJ prestigious, eminent

préstimo ['prɛʃtʃimu] M use, usefulness; **préstimos** MPL (obséquios) favours (Brit), favors (US), services; **sem** ~ useless, worthless

presto, -a ['prɛʃtu, a] ADJ swift

presumido, -a [prezu'midu, a] ADJ vain, self-important

presumir [prezu'mi^r] VT to presume

presunção [prezũ'sãw] (pl -ões) F (suposição) presumption; (vaidade) conceit, self-importance; **presunçoso, -a** [prezũ'sozu, ɔza] ADJ vain, self-important

presunto [pre'zũtu] M ham; (col; cadáver) stiff

pret-à-porter [prɛtapox'te] ADJ INV ready to wear

pretendente [pretẽ'dẽtʃi] M/F claimant; (candidato) candidate, applicant ■ M (de uma mulher) suitor

pretender [pretẽ'de^r] VT to claim; (cargo, emprego) to go for; ~ **fazer** to intend to do

pretensamente [pretẽsa'mẽtʃi] ADV supposedly

pretensão [pretẽ'sãw] (pl -ões) F (reivindicação) claim; (vaidade) pretension; (propósito) aim; (aspiração) aspiration; **pretensões** FPL (presunção) pretentiousness; **pretensioso, -a** [pretẽ'sjozu, ɔza] ADJ pretentious

pretenso, -a [pre'tẽsu, a] ADJ alleged, supposed

pretensões [pretẽ'sõjʃ] FPL de **pretensão**

preterir [prete'ri^r] VT (desprezar) to ignore; (deixar de promover) to pass over; (ocupar cargo de) to displace; (ser usado em lugar de) to usurp; (omitir) to disregard

pretérito, -a [pre'tɛritu, a] ADJ past ■ M (Ling) preterite

pretextar [preteʃ'ta^r] VT to give as an excuse

pretexto [pre'teʃtu] M pretext, excuse; **a** ~ **de** on the pretext of

preto, -a ['pretu, a] ADJ black ■ M/F Black (man/woman); **pôr o** ~ **no branco** to put it down in writing

preto-e-branco ADJ INV (filme, TV) black and white

pretume [pre'tumi] M blackness

prevalecente [prevale'sẽtʃi] ADJ prevalent

prevalecer [prevale'se^r] VI to prevail; **prevalecer-se** VR: **prevalecer-se de** (aproveitar-se) to take advantage of; ~ **sobre** to outweigh

prevaricar [prevari'ka^r] VI (faltar ao dever) to fail in one's duty; (proceder mal) to behave badly; (cometer adultério) to commit adultery

prevê etc [pre've] VB V **prever**

prevejo etc [pre'veʒu] VB V **prever**

prevenção [prevẽ'sãw] (pl -ões) F (ato de evitar) prevention; (preconceito) prejudice; (cautela) caution; **estar de** ~ **com** ou **contra alguém** to be bias(s)ed against sb

prevenido, -a [preve'nidu, a] ADJ (cauteloso) cautious, wary; (avisado) forewarned; **estar** ~ (com dinheiro) to have cash on one

prevenir [preve'ni^r] VT (evitar) to prevent; (avisar) to warn; (preparar) to prepare; **prevenir-se** VR: **prevenir-se contra** (acautelar-se) to be wary of; ~**-se de** (equipar-se) to equip o.s. with; ~**-se para** to prepare (o.s.) for

preventivo, -a [prevẽ'tʃivu, a] ADJ preventive

prever [pre've^r] (irreg) VT to predict, foresee; (pressupor) to presuppose

pré-vestibular [-veʃtʃibu'la^r] ADJ (curso) preparing for university entry ■ M preparation for university entry

previa etc [pre'via] VB V **prever**

prévia ['prɛvja] F opinion poll

previamente [prevja'mẽtʃi] ADJ previously

previdência [previ'dẽsja] F (previsão) foresight; (precaução) precaution; ~ **social** social welfare; (instituição) ≈ DSS (Brit), ≈ Welfare Department (US)

previdente [previ'dẽtʃi] ADJ: **ser** ~ to show foresight

previno etc [pre'vinu] VB V **prevenir**

prévio, -a ['prɛvju, a] ADJ prior; (preliminar) preliminary

prever etc [pre'vi^r] VB V **prever**

previsão [previ'zãw] (pl -ões) F (antevisão) foresight; (prognóstico) prediction, forecast; ~ **do tempo** weather forecast

previsível [previ'zivew] (pl -eis) ADJ predictable

previsões [previ'zõjʃ] FPL de **previsão**

previsto, -a [pre'viʃtu, a] PP de **prever** ■ ADJ predicted; (na lei etc) prescribed

prezado, -a [pre'zadu, a] ADJ esteemed; (numa carta) dear

prezar [pre'za^r] VT (amigos) to value highly; (autoridade) to respect; (gostar de) to appreciate; **prezar-se** VR (ter dignidade) to have self-respect; ~**-se de** (orgulhar-se) to pride o.s. on

primado [pri'madu] M (primazia) primacy

prima-dona (pl -s) F leading lady

primar [pri'ma^r] VI to excel, stand out

primário, -a [pri'marju, a] ADJ primary; (elementar) basic, rudimentary; (primitivo) primitive ■ M (curso) elementary education

primata [pri'mata] M (Zool) primate

primavera [prima'vera] F spring; (planta) primrose

primaveril [primave'riw] (pl -is) ADJ spring atr; (pessoa) youthful, young

primaz [pri'majʒ] M primate

primazia [prima'zia] F primacy; (prioridade) priority; (superioridade) superiority

primeira [pri'mejra] F (Auto) first gear

primeira-dama (pl primeiras-damas) F (Pol)

first lady
primeiranista [primejra'niʃta] M/F first-year (student)
primeiro, -a [pri'mejru, a] ADJ first; (*fundamental*) fundamental, prime ■ ADV first; **de primeira** (*pessoa, restaurante*) first-class; (*carne*) prime; **viajar de primeira** to travel first class; **à primeira vista** at first sight; **em ~ lugar** first of all; **de ~** first; **primeira página** (*de jornal*) front page; **ele foi o ~ que disse isso** he was the first to say this
primeiro-de-abril (*pl* primeiros-de-abril) M April fool
primeiro-time (*col*) ADJ INV top-notch, first-rate
primitivo, -a [primi'tʃivu, a] ADJ primitive; (*original*) original
primo, -a ['primu, a] M/F cousin; **~ irmão** first cousin; **~ em segundo grau** second cousin; (**número**) **~** prime number
primogênito, -a [primo'ʒenitu, a] ADJ, M/F first-born
primor [pri'mo'] M excellence, perfection; (*beleza*) beauty; **com ~** to perfection; **é um ~** it's perfect
primordial [primox'dʒjaw] (*pl* -ais) ADJ (*primitivo*) primordial, primeval; (*principal*) principal, fundamental
primórdio [pri'mɔxdʒju] M origin
primoroso, -a [primo'rozu, ɔza] ADJ (*excelente*) excellent; (*belo*) exquisite
princesa [prĩ'seza] F princess
principado [prĩsi'padu] M principality
principal [prĩsi'paw] (*pl* -ais) ADJ principal; (*entrada, razão, rua*) main ■ M (*chefe*) head, principal; (*essencial, de dívida*) principal ■ F (*Ling*) main clause
príncipe ['prĩsipi] M prince
principiante [prĩsi'pjãtʃi] M/F beginner
principiar [prĩsi'pja'] VT, VI to begin; **~ a fazer** to begin to do
princípio [prĩ'sipju] M (*começo*) beginning, start; (*origem*) origin; (*legal, moral*) principle; **princípios** MPL (*de matéria*) rudiments; **em ~** in principle; **no ~** in the beginning; **por ~** on principle; **do ~ ao fim** from beginning to end; **uma pessoa de ~s** a person of principle
prior [prjo'] M (*sacerdote*) parish priest; (*de convento*) prior
prioridade [prjori'dadʒi] F priority; **ter ~ sobre** to have priority over
prioritário, -a [prjori'tarju, a] ADJ priority *atr*
prisão [pri'zãw] (*pl* -ões) F (*encarceramento*) imprisonment; (*cadeia*) prison, jail; (*detenção*) arrest; **ordem de ~** warrant for arrest; **~ perpétua** life imprisonment; **~ preventiva** protective custody; **~ de ventre** constipation; **~**
prisioneiro, -a [prizjo'nejru, a] M/F prisoner
prisma ['priʒma] M prism; **sob esse ~** (*fig*) in

this light, from this angle
prisões [pri'zõjʃ] FPL *de* **prisão**
privação [priva'sãw] (*pl* -ões) F deprivation; **privações** FPL (*penúria*) hardship *sg*
privacidade [privasi'dadʒi] F privacy
privações [priva'sõjʃ] FPL *de* **privação**
privada [pri'vada] F toilet
privado, -a [pri'vadu, a] ADJ (*particular*) private; (*carente*) deprived
privar [pri'va'] VT: **~ alguém de algo** to deprive sb of sth; **privar-se** VR: **privar-se de algo** to deprive o.s. of sth
privativo, -a [priva'tʃivu, a] ADJ (*particular*) private; **~ de** peculiar to
privatização [privatʃiza'sãw] (*pl* -ões) F privatization
privatizar [privatʃi'za'] VT to privatize
privilegiado, -a [privile'ʒjadu, a] ADJ privileged; (*excepcional*) unique, exceptional
privilegiar [privile'ʒja'] VT to privilege; (*favorecer*) to favour (*Brit*), favor (*US*)
privilégio [privi'lɛʒu] M privilege
pro [pru] (*col*) = **para + o**
pró [prɔ] ADV for, in favour (*Brit*) *ou* favor (*US*); ■ M advantage; **os ~s e os contras** the pros and cons; **em ~ de** in favo(u)r of
pró- [prɔ] PREFIXO pro-; **~soviético** pro-Soviet
proa ['proa] F prow, bow
probabilidade [probabili'dadʒi] F probability, likelihood; **probabilidades** FPL (*chances*) odds; **segundo todas as ~s** in all probability
probabilíssimo, -a [probabi'lisimu, a] ADJ SUPERL *de* **provável**
problema [prob'lema] M problem
problemática [proble'matʃika] F problematics *sg*; (*problemas*) problems *pl*
problemático, -a [proble'matʃiku, a] ADJ problematic
procedência [prose'dẽsja] F (*origem*) origin, source; (*lugar de saída*) point of departure
procedente [prose'dẽtʃi] ADJ (*oriundo*) derived, rising; (*lógico*) logical
proceder [prose'de'] VI (*ir adiante*) to proceed; (*comportar-se*) to behave; (*agir*) to act; (*Jur*) to take legal action ■ M conduct; **~ a** to carry out; **~ de** (*originar-se*) to originate from; (*descender*) to be descended from; **procedimento** [prosedʒi'mẽtu] M (*comportamento*) conduct, behaviour (*Brit*), behavior (*US*); (*processo*) procedure; (*Jur*) proceedings *pl*
procela [pro'sɛla] F storm, tempest
proceloso, -a [prose'lozu, ɔza] ADJ stormy
prócer ['prɔse'] M chief, leader
processador [prosesa'do'] M processor; **~ de texto** word processor
processamento [prosesa'mẽtu] M (*de requerimentos, Comput*) processing; (*Jur*) prosecution; (*verificação*) verification; (*de depoimentos*) taking down; **~ de dados** data

processing; ~ **por lotes** batch processing; ~ **de texto** word processing
processar [prose'sa^r] VT (Jur) to take proceedings against, prosecute; (verificar) to check, verify; (depoimentos) to take down; (requerimentos, Comput) to process
processo [pro'sɛsu] M process; (procedimento) procedure; (Jur) lawsuit, legal proceedings pl; (: autos) record; (conjunto de documentos) documents pl; (de uma doença) course, progress; **abrir um ~ (contra alguém)** to start legal proceedings (against sb); ~ **inflamatório** (Med) inflammation
procissão [prosi'sãw] (pl -ões) F procession
proclamação [proklama'sãw] (pl -ões) F proclamation; **Proclamação da República** (BR) see below

● **PROCLAMAÇÃO DA REPÚBLICA**
●
● Commemorated on 15 November, which
● is a public holiday, the proclamation of
● the republic in 1889 was a military coup,
● led by Marshal Deodoro da Fonseca. It
● brought down the empire which had
● been established after independence and
● installed a federal republic in Brazil.

proclamar [prokla'ma^r] VT to proclaim
proclamas [pro'klamaʃ] MPL banns
procrastinar [prokraʃtʃi'na^r] VT to put off ■ VI to procrastinate
procriação [prokrja'sãw] F procreation
procriar [pro'krja^r] VT, VI to procreate
procura [pro'kura] F search; (Com) demand; **em ~ de** in search of
procuração [prokura'sãw] (pl -ões) F power of attorney; (documento) letter of attorney; **por ~** by proxy
procurado, -a [proku'radu, a] ADJ sought after, in demand
procurador, a [prokura'do^r(a)] M/F (advogado) attorney; (mandatário) proxy; **P~ Geral da República** Attorney General
procurar [proku'ra^r] VT to look for, seek; (emprego) to apply for; (ir visitar) to call on, go and see; (contatar) to get in touch with; ~ **fazer** to try to do
prodigalizar [prodʒigali'za^r] VT (gastar excessivamente) to squander; (dar com profusão) to lavish
prodígio [pro'dʒiʒu] M prodigy
prodigioso, -a [prodʒi'ʒozu, ɔza] ADJ prodigious, marvellous (Brit), marvelous (US)
pródigo, -a ['prɔdʒigu, a] ADJ (perdulário) wasteful; (generoso) lavish; **filho ~** prodigal son
produção [produ'sãw] (pl -ões) F production; (volume de produção) output; (produto) product; ~ **em massa** ou **série** mass production
produtividade [produtʃivi'dadʒi] F productivity
produtivo, -a [produ'tʃivu, a] ADJ productive;

(rendoso) profitable
produto [pro'dutu] M product; (renda) proceeds pl, profit; ~**s alimentícios** foodstuffs; ~**s agrícolas** agricultural produce sg; **ser ~ de** to be a product of; ~ **nacional bruto** gross national product; ~**s acabados/semi-acabados** finished/semi-finished products
produtor, a [produ'to^r(a)] ADJ producing ■ M/F producer
produzido, -a [produ'zidu, a] ADJ trendy
produzir [produ'zi^r] VT to produce; (ocasionar) to cause, bring about; (render) to bring in ■ VI to be productive; (Econ) to produce
proeminência [proemi'nẽsja] F prominence; (protuberância) protuberance; (elevação de terreno) elevation
proeminente [proemi'nẽtʃi] ADJ prominent
proeza [pro'eza] F achievement, feat
profanação [profana'sãw] F sacrilege, profanation
profanar [profa'na^r] VT to desecrate, profane;
profano, -a [pro'fanu, a] ADJ profane; (secular) secular ■ M/F layman/woman
profecia [profe'sia] F prophecy
proferir [profe'ri^r] VT to utter; (sentença) to pronounce; ~ **um discurso** to make a speech
professar [profe'sa^r] VT to profess; (profissão) to practise (Brit), practice (US) ■ VI (Rel) to take religious vows
professo, -a [pro'fɛsu, a] ADJ (católico etc) confirmed; (político etc) seasoned
professor, a [profe'so^r(a)] M/F teacher; (universitário) lecturer; ~ **titular** ou **catedrático** (university) professor; ~ **associado** reader
professorado [profeso'radu] M (professores) teachers pl; (magistério) teaching profession
profeta, -isa [pro'fɛta, profe'tʃiza] M/F prophet
profético, -a [pro'fɛtʃiku, a] ADJ prophetic
profetisa [profe'tʃiza] F de **profeta**
profetizar [profetʃi'za^r] VT, VI to prophesy, predict
proficiência [profi'sjẽsja] F proficiency, competence
proficiente [profi'sjẽtʃi] ADJ proficient, competent
profícuo, -a [pro'fikwu, a] ADJ useful, advantageous
profiro etc [pro'firu] VB V **proferir**
profissão [profi'sãw] (pl -ões) F (ofício) profession; (de fé) declaration; ~ **liberal** liberal profession; **profissional** [profisjo'naw] (pl -ais) ADJ, M/F professional
profissionalizante [profisjonali'zãtʃi] ADJ (ensino) vocational
profissionalizar [profisjonali'za^r] VT to professionalize; **profissionalizar-se** VR to turn professional; (atividade) to become professional
profissões [profi'sõjʃ] FPL de **profissão**
profundas [pro'fũdaʃ] FPL depths
profundidade [profũdʒi'dadʒi] F depth; (fig) profoundness, depth; **tem 4 metros de ~** it is 4

metres *ou* meters deep

profundo, -a [pro'fūdu, a] ADJ deep; (*fig*) profound

profusão [profu'zãw] F profusion, abundance

profuso, -a [pro'fuzu, a] ADJ (*abundante*) profuse, abundant

progênie [pro'ʒeni] F (*ascendência*) lineage; (*prole*) offspring, progeny

progenitor, a [proʒeni'to'(a)] M/F ancestor; (*pai/ mãe*) father/mother

prognosticar [prognoʃtʃi'ka'] VT to predict, forecast ▪ VI (*Med*) to make a prognosis

prognóstico [prog'nɔʃtʃiku] M prediction, forecast; (*Med*) prognosis

programa [pro'grama] M programme (*Brit*), program (*US*); (*Comput*) program; (*plano*) plan; (*diversão*) thing to do; (*de um curso*) syllabus; **fazer um ~** to go out; **~ de índio** (*col*) boring thing to do; **programação** [programa'sãw] F planning; (*TV, Rádio, Comput*) programming; **programação visual** graphic design

programador, a [programa'do'(a)] M/F programmer; **~ visual** graphic designer

programar [progra'ma'] VT to plan; (*Comput*) to program

programável [progra'mavew] (*pl* -**eis**) ADJ programmable

progredir [progre'dʒi'] VI to progress, make progress; (*avançar*) to move forward; (*infecção*) to progress

progressão [progre'sãw] F progression

progressista [progre'siʃta] ADJ, M/F progressive

progressivo, -a [progre'sivu, a] ADJ progressive; (*gradual*) gradual

progresso [pro'gresu] M progress

progrido *etc* [pro'gridu] VB V **progredir**

proibição [proibi'sãw] (*pl* -**ões**) F prohibition, ban

proibir [proi'bi'] VT to prohibit, forbid; (*livro, espetáculo*) to ban; **" é proibido fumar"** "no smoking"; **~ alguém de fazer, ~ que alguém faça** to forbid sb to do

proibitivo, -a [proibi'tʃivu, a] ADJ prohibitive

projeção [proʒe'sãw] (PT -**cç**-, *pl* -**ões**) F projection; (*arremesso*) throwing; (*proeminência*) prominence; **tempo de ~** (*de filme*) running time

projetar [proʒe'ta'] (PT -**ct**-) VT to project; (*arremessar*) to throw; (*planejar*) to plan; (*Arq, Tec*) to design; **projetar-se** VR (*lançar-se*) to hurl o.s.; (*sombra etc*) to fall; (*delinear-se*) to jut out; **~ fazer** to plan to do

projétil [pro'ʒetʃiw] (PT -**ct**-, *pl* -**eis**) M projectile, missile; (*Mil*) missile

projetista [proʒe'tʃiʃta] (PT -**ct**-) ADJ design *atr* ▪ M/F designer

projeto [pro'ʒetu] (PT -**ct**-) M (*empreendimento*) project; (*plano, Arq*) plan; (*Tec*) design; (*de tese etc*) draft; **~ de lei** bill; **~ assistido por**

computador computer-aided design

projetor [proʒe'to'] (PT -**ct**-) M (*Cinema*) projector; (*holofote*) searchlight

prol [prɔw] M advantage; **em ~ de** on behalf of, for the benefit of

pró-labore [-la'bɔri] M remuneration, fee

prolapso [pro'lapsu] M (*Med*) prolapse

prole ['prɔli] F offspring, progeny

proletariado [proleta'rjadu] M proletariat

proletário, -a [prole'tarju, a] ADJ, M/F proletarian

proliferação [prolifera'sãw] F proliferation

proliferar [prolife'ra'] VI to proliferate

prolífico, -a [pro'lifiku, a] ADJ prolific

prolixo, -a [pro'liksu, a] ADJ long-winded, tedious

prólogo ['prɔlogu] M prologue

prolongação [prolõga'sãw] F extension

prolongado, -a [prolõ'gadu, a] ADJ (*demorado*) prolonged; (*alongado*) extended

prolongamento [prolõga'mẽtu] M extension

prolongar [prolõ'ga'] VT (*tornar mais longo*) to extend, lengthen; (*decisão etc*) to postpone; (*vida*) to prolong; **prolongar-se** VR to extend; (*durar*) to last

promessa [pro'mɛsa] F promise; (*compromisso*) pledge

prometedor, a [promete'do'(a)] ADJ promising

prometer [prome'te'] VT to promise ▪ VI to promise; (*ter potencial*) to show promise; **~ fazer/ que** to promise to do/that

prometido, -a [prome'tʃidu, a] ADJ promised ▪ M: **o ~** what one promised; **cumprir o ~** to keep one's promise

promiscuidade [promiʃkwi'dadʒi] F (*sexual*) promiscuity; (*desordem*) untidiness

promiscuir-se [promiʃ'kwixsi] VR: **~ (com)** to mix (with)

promíscuo, -a [pro'miʃkwu, a] ADJ (*misturado*) disorderly, mixed up; (*comportamento sexual*) promiscuous

promissor, a [promi'so'(a)] ADJ promising

promissório, -a [promi'sɔrju, a] ADJ, F: (**nota**) **promissória** promissory note

promoção [promo'sãw] (*pl* -**ões**) F promotion; **fazer ~ de alguém/algo** to promote sb/sth

promontório [promõ'tɔrju] M headland, promontory

promotor, a [promo'to'(a)] ADJ promoting ▪ M/F promoter; (*Jur*) prosecutor; **~ público** public prosecutor

promover [promo've'] VT (*dar impulso a*) to promote; (*causar*) to cause; (*elevar a cargo superior*) to promote; (*reunião, encontro*) to bring about

promulgação [promuwga'sãw] F promulgation

promulgar [promuw'ga'] VT (*lei etc*) to promulgate; (*tornar público*) to declare publicly

pronome [pro'nɔmi] M pronoun

NB: *European Portuguese adds the following consonants to certain words:* **b** (sú(b)dito, su(b)til); **c** (a(c)ção, a(c)cionista, a(c)to); **m** (inde(m)ne); **p** (ado(p)çã, ado(p)tar); *for further details see p. xiii.*

pronta-entrega (*pl* -s) F immediate delivery department
prontidão [prõtʃi'dãw] F (*estar preparado*) readiness; (*rapidez*) promptness, speed; **estar de ~** to be at the ready
prontificar [prõtʃifi'ka^r] VT to have ready; **prontificar-se** VR: **prontificar-se a fazer/para algo** to volunteer to do/for sth
pronto, -a [prõtu, a] ADJ ready; (*rápido*) quick, speedy; (*imediato*) prompt; (*col: sem dinheiro*) broke ■ ADV promptly; **de ~** promptly; **estar ~ a** ... to be prepared *ou* willing to ...; **(e) ~!** (and) that's that!; **pronto-socorro** (*pl* prontos-socorros) M emergency hospital; (PT: *reboque*) tow truck
prontuário [prõ'twarju] M (*manual*) handbook; (*policial*) record
pronúncia [pro'nũsja] F pronunciation; (*Jur*) indictment
pronunciação [pronũsja'sãw] (*pl* -ões) F pronouncement; (*Ling*) pronunciation
pronunciamento [pronũsja'mẽtu] M proclamation, pronouncement
pronunciar [pronũ'sja^r] VT to pronounce; (*discurso*) to make, deliver; (*Jur: réu*) to indict; (: *sentença*) to pass; **pronunciar-se** VR (*expressar opinião*) to express one's opinion; **~ mal** to mispronounce
propagação [propaga'sãw] F propagation; (*fig: difusão*) dissemination
propaganda [propa'gãda] F (*Pol*) propaganda; (*Com*) advertising; (: *uma propaganda*) advert, advertisement; **fazer ~ de** to advertise
propagar [propa'ga^r] VT to propagate; (*fig: difundir*) to disseminate
propender [propẽ'de^r] VI to lean; **~ para algo** (*fig*) to incline *ou* tend towards sth
propensão [propẽ'sãw] (*pl* -ões) F inclination, tendency; **propenso, -a** [pro'pẽsu, a] ADJ: **propenso a** inclined to, with a tendency to; **ser propenso a** to be inclined to, have a tendency to
propensões [propẽ'sõjʃ] FPL *de* **propensão**
propiciar [propi'sja^r] VT (*tornar favorável*) to favour (*Brit*), favor (*US*); (*permitir*) to allow; (*proporcionar*) to provide
propício, -a [pro'pisju, a] ADJ (*favorável*) favourable (*Brit*), favorable (*US*), propitious; (*apropriado*) appropriate
propina [pro'pina] F (*gorjeta*) tip; (PT: *cota*) fee
propor [pro'po^r] (*irreg*) VT to propose; (*oferecer*) to offer; (*um problema*) to pose; (*Jur: ação*) to start, move; **propor-se** VR: **propor-se (a) fazer** (*pretender*) to intend to do; (*visar*) to aim to do; (*dispor-se*) to decide to do; (*oferecer-se*) to offer to do; **~-se** *ou* **para governador** *etc* to stand for governor *etc*
proporção [propox'sãw] (*pl* -ões) F proportion; **proporções** FPL (*dimensões*) dimensions; **à ~ que** as
proporcionado, -a [propoxsjo'nadu, a] ADJ proportionate
proporcional [propoxsjo'naw] (*pl* -ais) ADJ proportional

proporcionar [propoxsjo'na^r] VT (*dar*) to provide, give; (*adaptar*) to adjust, adapt
proporções [propox'sõjʃ] FPL *de* **proporção**
propôs [pro'poʃ] VB V **propor**
proposição [propozi'sãw] (*pl* -ões) F proposition, proposal
propositado, -a [propozi'tadu, a] ADJ intentional
proposital [propozi'taw] (*pl* -ais) ADJ intentional
propósito [pro'pɔzitu] M (*intenção*) purpose; (*objetivo*) aim; **a ~** by the way; (*oportunamente*) at an opportune moment; **a ~ de** with regard to; **com o ~ de** with the purpose of; **de ~** on purpose; **fora de ~** irrelevant
proposta [pro'pɔʃta] F proposal; (*oferecimento*) offer
proposto, -a [pro'poʃtu, 'pɔʃta] PP *de* **propor**
propriamente [proprja'mẽtʃi] ADV properly, exactly; **~ falando** *ou* **dito** strictly speaking; **a Igreja ~ dita** the Church proper
propriedade [proprje'dadʒi] F property; (*direito de proprietário*) ownership; (*o que é apropriado*) appropriateness, propriety; **~ imobiliária** real estate
proprietário, -a [proprje'tarju, a] M/F owner, proprietor; (*de casa alugada*) landlord/lady; (*de jornal*) publisher
próprio, -a ['proprju, a] ADJ (*possessivo*) own, of one's own; (*mesmo*) very, selfsame; (*hora, momento*) opportune, right; (*nome*) proper; (*característico*) characteristic; (*sentido*) proper, true; (*depois de pronome*) -self; **~ (para)** suitable (for); **eu ~** I myself; **ele ~** he himself; **mora em casa própria** he lives in a house of his own; **por si ~** of one's own accord; **o ~ homem** the very man; **ele é o ~ inglês** he's a typical Englishman; **é o ~** it's him himself
propulsão [propuw'sãw] F propulsion; **~ a jato** jet propulsion
propulsor, a [propuw'so^r(a)] ADJ propelling ■ M propellor
propus *etc* [pro'puʃ] VB V **propor**
propuser *etc* [propu'ze^r] VB V **propor**
prorrogação [proxoga'sãw] (*pl* -ões) F extension; (*Com*) deferment; (*Jur*) stay; (*Futebol*) extra time
prorrogar [proxo'ga^r] VT to extend, prolong
prorrogável [proxo'gavel] (*pl* -eis) ADJ extendible
prorromper [proxo'pe^r] VI (*águas, lágrimas*) to burst forth, break out; **~ em choro/gargalhadas** to burst into tears/burst out laughing
prosa ['proza] F prose; (*conversa*) chatter; (*fanfarrice*) boasting, bragging ■ ADJ full of oneself; **ter boa ~** to have the gift of the gab
prosador, a [proza'do^r(a)] M/F prose writer
prosaico, -a [pro'zajku, a] ADJ prosaic
proscênio [pro'senju] M proscenium
proscrever [proʃkre've^r] VT to prohibit, ban;

(*expulsar*) to ban, exile; (*vícios, usos*) to do away with

proscrição [proʃkri'sãw] (*pl* -ões) F proscription; (*proibição*) prohibition, ban; (*desterro*) exile; (*abolição*) abolition

proscrito, -a [proʃ'kritu, a] PP *de* **proscrever** ■ M/F (*desterrado*) exile

prosear [pro'zjaʳ] VI to chat

prosélito [pro'zɛlitu] M convert

prosódia [pro'zɔdʒja] F prosody

prosopopéia [prozopo'pɛja] F (*fig*) diatribe; (*col: pose*) pose

prospecto [proʃ'pɛktu] M (*desdobrável*) leaflet; (*em forma de livro*) brochure

prospector [proʃpek'toʳ] M prospector

prosperar [proʃpe'raʳ] VI to prosper, thrive; **prosperidade** [proʃperi'dadʒi] F prosperity; (*bom êxito*) success; **próspero, -a** ['prɔʃperu, a] ADJ prosperous; (*bem sucedido*) successful; (*favorável*) favourable (*Brit*), favorable (*US*)

prosseguimento [prosegi'mētu] M continuation

prosseguir [prose'giʳ] VT to continue ■ VI to continue, go on; ~ **em** to continue (with)

próstata ['prɔʃtata] F prostate

prostíbulo [proʃ'tʃibulu] M brothel

prostituição [proʃtʃitwi'sãw] F prostitution

prostituir [proʃtʃi'twiʳ] VT to prostitute; (*fig: desonrar*) to debase; **prostituir-se** VR (*tornar-se prostituta*) to become a prostitute; (*ser prostituta*) to be a prostitute; (*no trabalho*) to prostitute o.s.; (*corromper-se*) to be corrupted; (*desonrar-se*) to debase o.s.

prostituta [proʃti'tuta] F prostitute

prostração [proʃtra'sãw] F (*cansaço*) exhaustion; (*moral*) desolation

prostrado, -a [proʃ'tradu, a] ADJ prostrate

prostrar [proʃ'traʳ] VT (*derrubar*) to knock down, throw down; (*extenuar*) to tire out; (*abater*) to lay low; **prostrar-se** VR to prostrate o.s.

protagonista [protago'niʃta] M/F protagonist

protagonizar [protagoni'zaʳ] VT to play the lead role in; (*fig*) to be at the centre (*Brit*) *ou* center (*US*) of

proteção [prote'sãw] (PT -cç-) F protection; (*amparo*) support, backing

protecionismo [protesjo'niʒmu] (PT -cç-) M protectionism

protector, a [protek'toʳ(a)] (PT) = **protetor**

proteger [prote'ʒeʳ] VT to protect; **protegido, -a** [prote'ʒidu, a] ADJ protected ■ M/F protégé(e)

proteína [prote'ina] F protein

protejo *etc* [pro'teʒu] VB V **proteger**

protelar [prote'laʳ] VT to postpone, put off

PROTERRA (BR) ABR M = **Programa de Redistribuição da Terra e de Estímulo Agro-Industrial do Norte e Nordeste**

protestante [proteʃ'tãtʃi] ADJ, M/F Protestant

protestantismo [proteʃtã'tʃiʒmu] M

Protestantism

protestar [proteʃ'taʳ] VT to protest; (*declarar*) to declare, affirm ■ VI to protest; **protesto** [pro'tɛʃtu] M protest; (*declaração*) affirmation

protetor, a [prote'toʳ(a)] ADJ protective ■ M/F protector; ~ **solar** sunscreen; ~ **de tela** (*Comput*) screensaver

protocolar [protoko'laʳ] ADJ protocol *atr* ■ VT to record

protocolo [proto'kɔlu] M protocol; (*recibo*) record slip

protótipo [pro'tɔtʃipu] M prototype

protuberância [protube'rãsja] F bump; **protuberante** [protube'rãtʃi] ADJ sticking out

prova ['prɔva] F proof; (*Tec: teste*) test, trial; (*Educ: exame*) examination; (*sinal*) sign; (*de comida, bebida*) taste; (*de roupa*) fitting; (*Esporte*) competition; (*Tip*) proof; **prova(s)** F(PL) (*Jur*) evidence *sg*; **à** ~ on trial; **à** ~ **de bala/fogo/água** bulletproof/fireproof/water proof; **pôr à** ~ to put to the test; ~ **circunstancial/documental** (piece of) circumstantial/documentary evidence

provação [prova'sãw] F (*sofrimento*) trial

provado, -a [pro'vadu, a] ADJ proven

provar [pro'vaʳ] VT to prove; (*comida*) to taste, try; (*roupa*) to try on ■ VI to try

provável [pro'vavew] (*pl* -eis) ADJ probable, likely; **é** ~ **que não venha** he probably won't come

provê *etc* [pro've] VB V **prover**

provedor, a [prove'doʳ(a)] M/F provider; ~ **de acesso à Internet** Internet service provider

proveio *etc* [pro'veju] VB V **provir**

proveito [pro'vejtu] M (*vantagem*) advantage; (*ganho*) profit; **em** ~ **de** for the benefit of; **fazer** ~ **de** to make use of; **tirar** ~ **de** to benefit from; **proveitoso, -a** [provej'tozu, ɔza] ADJ profitable, advantageous; (*útil*) useful

provejo *etc* [pro'veʒu] VB V **prover**

proveniência [prove'njẽsja] F source, origin

proveniente [prove'njẽtʃi] ADJ: ~ **de** originating from; (*que resulta de*) arising from

proventos [pro'vẽtuʃ] MPL proceeds *pl*

prover [pro'veʳ] (*irreg*) VT (*fornecer*) to provide, supply; (*vaga*) to fill ■ VI: ~ **a** to take care of, see to; **prover-se** VR: **prover-se de algo** to provide o.s. with sth; ~ **alguém de algo** to provide sb with sth; (*dotar*) to endow sb with sth

provérbio [pro'vɛxbju] M proverb

proveta [pro'veta] F test tube; **bebê de** ~ test-tube baby

provi *etc* [pro'vi] VB V **prover**

provia *etc* [pro'via] VB V **prover**

providência [provi'dẽsja] F providence; **providências** FPL (*medidas*) measures, steps; **tomar** ~**s** to take steps; **providencial** [providẽ'sjaw] (*pl* -ais) ADJ opportune; **providenciar** [providẽ'sjaʳ] VT (*prover*) to provide; *(tomar providências)* to arrange ■ VI *(tomar providências)* to make arrangements, take steps; *(prover)*: **providenciar a** to make provision for; **providenciar para que** to see to it that

providente [provi'dēt∫i] ADJ provident; *(prudente)* prudent, careful

provido, -a [pro'vidu, a] ADJ *(fornecido)* supplied, provided; *(cheio)* full up, fully stocked

provier *etc* [pro'vjeʳ] VB V **provir**

provim *etc* [pro'vĩ] VB V **provir**

provimento [provi'mētu] M provision; **dar ~** *(Jur)* to grant a petition

província [pro'vīsja] F province; **provinciano, -a** [provĩ'sjanu, a] ADJ provincial

provindo, -a [pro'vĩdu, a] PP *de* **provir** ■ ADJ: **~ de** coming from, originating from

provir [pro'viʳ] *(irreg)* VI: **~ de** to come from, derive from

provir *etc* VB V **prover**

provisão [provi'zãw] *(pl -ões)* F provision, supply; **provisões** FPL *(suprimentos)* provisions

provisoriamente [provizorja'mēt∫i] ADV provisionally

provisório, -a [provi'zɔrju, a] ADJ provisional, temporary

provisto, -a [pro'vi∫tu, a] PP *de* **prover**

provocação [provoka'sãw] *(pl -ões)* F provocation

provocador, a [provoka'doʳ(a)] ADJ provocative ■ M/F provoker

provocante [provo'kãt∫i] ADJ provocative

provocar [provo'kaʳ] VT to provoke; *(ocasionar)* to cause; *(atrair)* to tempt, attract; *(estimular)* to rouse, stimulate ■ VI to provoke, be provocative

proximidade [prosimi'dadʒi] F proximity, nearness; *(iminência)* imminence; **proximidades** FPL *(vizinhança)* neighbourhood *sg* (Brit), neighborhood *sg* (US), vicinity *sg*

próximo, -a ['prɔsimu, a] ADJ *(no espaço)* near, close; *(no tempo)* close; *(seguinte)* next; *(amigo, parente)* close; *(vizinho)* neighbouring (Brit), neighboring (US) ■ ADV near ■ M fellow man; **~ a** *ou* **de** near to, close to; **futuro ~** near future; **até a próxima!** see you again soon!

PRP (BR) ABR M = **Partido Renovador Progressista**

PRT (BR) ABR M = **Partido Reformador Trabalhista**

prudência [pru'dēsja] F *(comedimento)* care, prudence; *(cautela)* care, caution; **prudente** [pru'dēt∫i] ADJ sensible, prudent; *(cauteloso)* cautious

prumo ['prumu] M plumb line; *(Náut)* lead; **a ~** perpendicularly, vertically

prurido [pru'ridu] M itch

Prússia ['prusja] F: **a ~** Prussia

PS (BR) ABR M = **Partido Socialista**

PSB ABR M = **Partido Socialista Brasileiro**

PSC (BR) ABR M = **Partido Social Cristão**

PSD (BR) ABR M = **Partido Social Democrático.**

PSDB ABR M = **Partido Social-Democrata Brasileiro**

pseudônimo [psew'donimu] M pseudonym

psicanálise [psika'nalizi] F psychoanalysis

psicanalista [psikana'li∫ta] M/F psychoanalyst

psicanalítico, -a [psikana'lit∫iku, a] ADJ psychoanalytic(al)

psicodélico, -a [psiko'dɛliku, a] ADJ psychedelic

psicologia [psikolo'ʒia] F psychology; **psicológico, -a** [psiko'lɔʒiku, a] ADJ psychological; **psicólogo, -a** [psi'kɔlogu, a] M/F psychologist

psicopata [psiko'pata] M/F psychopath

psicose [psi'kɔzi] F psychosis; **estar com ~ de** to be obsessed with *ou* by

psicossomático, -a [psikoso'matʃiku, a] ADJ psychosomatic

psicoterapeuta [psikotera'pewta] M/F psychotherapist

psicoterapia [psikotera'pia] F psychotherapy

psicótico, -a [psi'kɔtʃiku, a] ADJ psychotic

psique ['psiki] F psyche

psiquiatra [psi'kjatra] M/F psychiatrist

psiquiatria [psikja'tria] F psychiatry

psiquiátrico, -a [psi'kjatriku, a] ADJ psychiatric

psíquico, -a ['psikiku, a] ADJ psychological

psiu [psiw] EXCL hey!

PST (BR) ABR M = **Partido Social Trabalhista**

PT (BR) ABR M = **Partido dos Trabalhadores**

PTN (BR) ABR M = **Partido Tancredista Nacional**

PTR (BR) ABR M = **Partido Trabalhista Renovador**

PUA (BR) ABR M = (= *Pacto de Unidade e Ação*) workers' movement

pua ['pua] F *(de broca)* bit; **sentar a ~ em alguém** *(col)* to give sb a beating

puberdade [pubex'dadʒi] F puberty

púbere ['puberi] ADJ pubescent

púbis ['pubiʃ] M INV pubis

publicação [publika'sãw] F publication

publicar [publi'kaʳ] VT *(editar)* to publish; *(divulgar)* to divulge; *(proclamar)* to announce

publicidade [publisi'dadʒi] F publicity; *(Com)* advertising; **publicitário, -a** [publisi'tarju, a] ADJ publicity *atr*; *(Com)* advertising *atr* ■ M/F *(Com)* advertising executive

público, -a ['publiku, a] ADJ public ■ M public; *(Cinema, Teatro etc)* audience; **em ~** in public; **o grande ~** the general public

PUC (BR) ABR F = **Pontifícia Universidade Católica**

púcaro ['pukaru] (PT) M jug, mug

pude *etc* [pudʒi] VB V **poder**

pudera *etc* [pu'dɛra] VB V **poder**

pudicícia [pudi'sisja] F modesty

pudico, -a [pu'dʒiku, a] ADJ bashful; *(pej)* prudish

pudim [pu'dʒĩ] *(pl -ns)* M pudding; **~ de leite** crème caramel

pudim-flã [pudĩ'flã] (PT) M crème caramel

pudins [pu'dʒĩʃ] MPL *de* **pudim**

pudor [pu'doʳ] M bashfulness, modesty; *(moral)*

decency; **atentado ao ~** indecent assault
puerícia [pwe'risʒa] F childhood
puericultura [pwerikuw'tura] F child care
pueril [pwe'riw] (pl -is) ADJ puerile
puerilidade [pwerili'dadʒi] F childishness, foolishness
pueris [pwe'riʃ] ADJ PL de **pueril**
pufe ['pufi] M pouf(fe)
pugilismo [puʒi'liʒmu] M boxing
pugilista [puʒi'liʃta] M boxer
pugna ['pugna] F fight, struggle
pugnar [pug'naʳ] VI to fight
pugnaz [pug'najʒ] ADJ pugnacious
puído, -a ['pwidu, a] ADJ worn
puir [pwiʳ] VT to wear thin
pujança [pu'ʒãsa] F vigour (Brit), vigor (US), strength; (de vegetação) lushness; **na ~ da vida** in the prime of life
pujante [pu'ʒãtʃi] ADJ powerful; (saúde) robust
pular [pu'laʳ] VI to jump; (no Carnaval) to celebrate ▪ VT (muro) to jump (over); (páginas, trechos) to skip; **~ de alegria** to jump for joy; **~ Carnaval** to celebrate Carnival; **~ corda** to skip
pulga ['puwga] F flea; **estar/ficar com a ~ atrás da orelha** to smell a rat
pulgão [puw'gãw] (pl -ões) M greenfly
pulha ['puʎa] (col) M rat, creep
pulmão [puw'mãw] (pl -ões) M lung
pulmonar [puwmo'naʳ] ADJ pulmonary, lung atr
pulo ['pulu] M jump; **dar ~ s (de contente)** to be delighted; **dar um ~ em** to stop off at; **aos ~ s** by leaps and bounds; **a um ~ de** a stone's throw away from; **num ~** in a flash
pulo etc VB V **polir**
pulôver [pu'loveʳ] (BR) M pullover
púlpito ['puwpitu] M pulpit
pulsação [puwsa'sãw] F pulsation, beating; (Med) pulse
pulsar [puw'saʳ] VI (palpitar) to pulsate, throb
pulseira [puw'sejra] F bracelet; (de sapato) strap
pulso ['puwsu] M (Anat) wrist; (Med) pulse; (fig) vigour (Brit), vigor (US), energy; **obra de ~** work of great importance; **homem de ~** energetic man; **tomar o ~ de alguém** to take sb's pulse; **tomar o ~ de algo** (fig) to look into sth, sound sth out; **a ~** by force
pulular [pulu'laʳ] VI to abound; (surgir) to spring up; **~ de** to teem with; (de turistas, mendigos) to be crawling with
pulverizador [puwveriza'doʳ] M (para líquidos etc) spray, spray gun
pulverizar [puwveri'zaʳ] VT to pulverize; (líquido) to spray; (polvilhar) to dust
pum [pũ] EXCL bang! ▪ M (col) fart (!)
pumba ['pũba] EXCL zoom!
punção [pũ'sãw] (pl -ões) M (instrumento) punch ▪ F (Med) puncture
Pundjab [pũ'dʒabi] M: **o ~** the Punjab

pundonor [pũdo'noʳ] M dignity, self-respect
pungente [pũ'ʒẽtʃi] ADJ painful
pungir [pũ'ʒiʳ] VT to afflict ▪ VI to be painful
punguear [pũ'gjaʳ] (col) VT (bolso) to pick; (bolsa) to snatch
punguista [pũ'giʃta] M pickpocket
punha etc ['puɲa] VB V **pôr**
punhado [pu'ɲadu] M handful
punhal [pu'ɲaw] (pl -ais) M dagger
punhalada [puɲa'lada] F stab
punho ['puɲu] M (Anat) fist; (de manga) cuff; (de espada) hilt; **de (seu) próprio ~** in one's own hand(writing)
punição [puni'sãw] (pl -ões) F punishment
punir [pu'niʳ] VT to punish
punitivo, -a [puni'tʃivu, a] ADJ punitive
punja etc ['pũʒa] VB V **pungir**
pupila [pu'pila] F (Anat) pupil; V tb **pupilo**
pupilo, -a [pu'pilu, a] M/F (tutelado) ward; (aluno) pupil
purê [pu're] M purée; **~ de batatas** mashed potatoes
pureza [pu'reza] F purity
purgação [puxga'sãw] (pl -ões) F purge; (purificação) purification
purgante [pux'gãtʃi] M purgative; (col: pessoa) bore
purgar [pux'gaʳ] VT to purge; (purificar) to purify
purgativo, -a [puxga'tʃivu, a] ADJ purgative ▪ M purgative
purgatório [puxga'tɔrju] M purgatory
purificação [purifika'sãw] F purification
purificar [purifi'kaʳ] VT to purify
purista [pu'riʃta] M/F purist
puritanismo [purita'niʒmu] M puritanism
puritano, -a [puri'tanu, a] ADJ (atitude) puritanical; (seita) puritan ▪ M/F puritan
puro, -a ['puru, a] ADJ pure; (uísque) neat; (verdade) plain; (intenções) honourable (Brit), honorable (US); (estilo) clear; **isto é pura imaginação sua** it's pure imagination on your part, you're just imagining it; **~ e simples** pure and simple
puro-sangue (pl puros-sangues) ADJ, M thoroughbred
púrpura ['puxpura] F purple
purpúreo, -a [pux'purju, a] ADJ (cor) crimson
purpurina [puxpu'rina] F metallic paint
purulento, -a [puru'lẽtu, a] ADJ festering, suppurating
pus [puʃ] M pus, matter
pus etc [puʃ] VB V **pôr**
puser etc [pu'zeʳ] VB V **pôr**
pusilânime [puzi'lanimi] ADJ fainthearted; (covarde) cowardly
pústula ['puʃtula] F pustule; (fig) rotter
puta ['puta] (col!) F whore; **~ que pariu!** fucking hell! (!); **mandar alguém para a ~ que (o) pariu** to tell sb to fuck off (!); V tb **puto**

NB: *European Portuguese adds the following consonants to certain words:* **b** (sú(b)dito, su(b)til); **c** (a(c)ção, a(c)cionista, a(c)to); **m** (inde(m)ne); **p** (ado(p)ção, ado(p)tar); *for further details see p. xiii.*

putativo, -a [puta'tʃivu, a] ADJ supposed
puto, -a ['putu, a] (col!) M/F (sem-vergonha)
bastard ■ ADJ (zangado) furious; (incrível): **um ~**
... a hell of a ...; **o ~ de** ... the bloody ..
putrefação [putrefa'sãw] F rotting,
putrefaction
putrefato, -a [putre'fatu, a] ADJ rotten
putrefazer [putrefa'ze ͬ] (irreg) VT to rot ■ VI to
putrefy, rot; **putrefazer-se** VR to putrefy, rot
pútrido, -a ['putridu, a] ADJ putrid, rotten
puxa ['puʃa] EXCL gosh; **~ vida!** gosh!
puxada [pu'ʃada] F pull; (puxão) tug; **dar uma ~**
(nos estudos) to make an effort
puxado, -a [pu'ʃadu, a] ADJ (col: aluguel) steep,

high; (: curso) tough; (: trabalho) hard
puxador [puʃa'do ͬ] M handle, knob
puxão [pu'ʃãw] (pl -ões) M tug, jerk
puxa-puxa (pl -s) M toffee
puxar [pu'ʃa ͬ] VT to pull; (sacar) to pull out;
(assunto) to bring up; (conversa) to strike up;
(briga) to pick ■ VI: **~ de uma perna** to limp; **~
a** to take after; **~ por** (alunos etc) to push; **uma
coisa puxa a outra** one thing leads to another;
os paulistas puxam pelo esse the s is very
pronounced in São Paulo
puxa-saco (pl -s) M creep, crawler
puxo ['puʃu] M (em parto) push
puxões [pu'ʃõjʃ] MPL de **puxão**

Qq

Q, q [ke] (*pl* **qs**) M Q, q; **Q de Quintela** Q for
Queen
q. ABR (= *quartel*) 60 kg
QG ABR M (= *Quartel-General*) HQ
QI ABR M (= *Quociente de Inteligência*) IQ
ql. ABR (= *quilate*) ct
qtd. ABR (= *quantidade*) qty
qua. ABR (= *quarta-feira*) Weds
quadra ['kwadra] F (*quarteirão*) block; (*de tênis etc*)
court; (*período*) time, period; (*jogos*) four; (*estrofe*)
quatrain
quadrado, -a [kwa'dradu, a] ADJ square;
(*col: antiquado*) square ▪ M square ▪ M/F (*col*)
square
quadragésimo, -a [kwadra'ʒɛzimu, a] NUM
fortieth; *v tb* **quinto**
quadrangular [kwadrãgu'laᴿ] ADJ
quadrangular
quadrângulo [kwa'drãgulu] M quadrangle
quadrar [kwa'draᴿ] VT to square, make square
▪ VI: **~ a** (*ser conveniente*) to suit; **~ com** (*condizer*)
to square with
quadriculado, -a [kwadriku'ladu, a] ADJ
checked; **papel ~** squared paper
quadril [kwa'driw] (*pl* -**is**) M hip
quadrilátero, -a [kwadri'lateru, a] ADJ
quadrilateral
quadrilha [kwa'driʎa] F gang; (*dança*) square
dance
quadrimotor [kwadrimo'toᴿ] ADJ four-engined
▪ M four-engined plane
quadrinho [kwa'driɲu] M (*de tira*) frame;
história em ~s (BR) cartoon, comic strip
quadris [kwa'driʃ] MPL *de* **quadril**
quadro ['kwadru] M (*pintura*) painting; (*gravura,
foto*) picture; (*lista*) list; (*tabela*) chart, table;
(*Tec: painel*) panel; (*pessoal*) staff; (*time*) team;
(*Teatro, fig*) scene; (*fig: Med*) patient's condition;
~ de avisos bulletin board; **~ de reserva** (*Mil*)
reserve list; **~ clínico** clinical picture; **o ~
político** (*fig*) the political scene; **~ social** (*de
um clube*) members pl; (*de uma empresa*) partners
pl; **quadro-negro** (*pl* **quadros-negros**) M
blackboard

quadrúpede [kwa'drupedʒi] ADJ, M quadruped
▪ M/F (*fig*) blockhead
quadruplicar [kwadrupli'kaᴿ] VT, VI to
quadruple
quádruplo, -a ['kwadruplu, a] ADJ quadruple
▪ M quadruple ▪ M/F (*quadrigêmeo*) quad
qual [kwaw] (*pl* -**ais**) PRON which ▪ CONJ as,
like ▪ EXCL what!; **~ deles** which of them;
~ é o problema/o seu nome? what's the
problem/your name?; **o ~** which; (*pessoa: suj*)
who; (*pessoa: objeto*) whom; **seja ~ for** whatever
ou whichever it may be; **cada ~** each one; **~ é?**
ou **é a tua?** (*col*) what are you up to?; **~ seja**
such as; **tal ~** just like; **~ nada!, ~ o quê!** no
such thing!
qual. ABR (= *qualidade*) qual
qualidade [kwali'dadʒi] F quality; **na ~ de** in
the capacity of; **produto de ~** quality product;
Q~ Carta (*Comput*) letter quality
qualificação [kwalifika'sãw] (*pl* -**ões**) F
qualification
qualificado, -a [kwalifi'kadu, a] ADJ qualified;
não ~ unqualified
qualificar [kwalifi'kaᴿ] VT to qualify; (*avaliar*) to
evaluate; **qualificar-se** VR to qualify; **~ de** *ou*
como to classify as
qualificativo, -a [kwalifika'tʃivu, a] ADJ
qualifying ▪ M qualifier
qualitativo, -a [kwalita'tʃivu, a] ADJ
qualitative
qualquer [kwaw'keᴿ] (*pl* **quaisquer**) ADJ, PRON
any; **~ pessoa** anyone, anybody; **~ um dos dois**
either; **~ outro** any other; **~ dia** any day; **~ que**
seja whichever it may be; **um disco ~** any
record at all, any record you like; **a ~ momento**
at any moment; **a ~ preço** at any price; **de ~
jeito** *ou* **maneira** anyway; (*a qualquer preço*) no
matter what; (*sem cuidado*) anyhow; **um(a) ~** (*pej*)
any old person
quando ['kwãdu] ADV when ▪ CONJ when;
(*interrogativo*) when?; (*ao passo que*) whilst; **~
muito** at most; **~ quer que** whenever; **de ~ em
~, de vez em ~** now and then; **desde ~?** how
long?, since when?; **~ mais não seja** if for no

NB: *European Portuguese adds the following consonants to certain words:* **b** (sú(b)dito, su(b)til); **c** (a(c)ção,
a(c)cionista, a(c)to); **m** (inde(m)ne); **p** (ado(p)ção, ado(p)tar); *for further details see p. xiii.*

other reason; ~ **de** on the occasion of; ~ **menos se esperava** when we (*ou* they, I *etc*) least expected (it)
quant. ABR (= *quantidade*) quant
quantia [kwã'tʃia] F sum, amount
quantidade [kwãtʃi'dadʒi] F quantity, amount; **uma ~ de** a large amount of; **em ~** in large amounts
quantificar [kwãtʃifi'kaʳ] VT to quantify
quantitativo, -a [kwãtʃita'tʃivu, a] ADJ quantitative

○ PALAVRA CHAVE

quanto, -a ['kwãtu, a] ADJ **1** (*interrogativo: sg*) how much?; (: *pl*) how many?; **quanto tempo?** how long?
2 (*o* (*que for*) *necessário*) all that, as much as; **daremos quantos exemplares ele precisar** we'll give him as many copies as *ou* all the copies he needs
3: **tanto/tantos ... quanto** as much/many ... as
■ PRON **1** how much?; how many?; **quanto custa?** how much?; **a quanto está o jogo?** what's the score?
2: **tudo quanto** everything that, as much as
3: **tanto/tantos quanto ...** as much/as many as ...
4: **um tanto quanto** somewhat, rather
■ ADV **1**: **quanto a** as regards; **quanto a mim** as for me
2: **quanto antes** as soon as possible
3: **quanto mais** (*principalmente*) especially; (*muito menos*) let alone; **quanto mais cedo melhor** the sooner the better
4: **tanto quanto possível** as much as possible; **tão ... quanto ...** as ... as ...
■ CONJ: **quantoa mais trabalha, mais ele ganha** the more he works, the more he earns; **quanto mais, (tanto) melhor** the more, the better

quão [kwãw] ADV how
quarenta [kwa'rēta] NUM forty; *v tb* **cinqüenta**
quarentão, -tona [kware'tãw, 'tɔna] (*pl* -ões/ -s) ADJ in one's forties ■ M/F man/woman in his/her forties
quarentena [kwarē'tena] F quarantine
quarentões [kware'tõjʃ] MPL *de* **quarentão**
quarentona [kware'tɔna] F *de* **quarentão**
quaresma [kwa'reʒma] F Lent
quart. ABR = **quarteirão**
quarta ['kwaxta] F (*tb*: **quarta-feira**) Wednesday; (*parte*) quarter; (*Auto*) fourth (gear); (*Mús*) fourth
quarta-de-final (*pl* quartas-de-final) F quarter final
quarta-feira ['kwaxta-'fejra] (*pl* quartas-feiras) F Wednesday; ~ **de cinzas** Ash Wednesday; *v tb* **terça-feira**
quartanista [kwaxta'niʃta] M/F fourth-year
quarteirão [kwaxtej'rãw] (*pl* -ões) M (*de casas*)

block
quartel [kwax'tɛw] (*pl* -éis) M barracks *sg*; **quartel-general** (*pl* quartéis-generais) M headquarters *pl*
quarteto [kwax'tetu] M (*Mús*) quartet(te); ~ **de cordas** string quartet
quarto, -a ['kwaxtu, a] NUM fourth ■ M (*quarta parte*) quarter; (*aposento*) room; (*Mil*) watch; (*anca*) haunch; ~ **de banho** bathroom; ~ **de dormir** bedroom; ~ **de casal** double bedroom; ~ **de solteiro** single room; ~ **crescente/ minguante** (*Astro*) first/last quarter; **três ~s de hora** three quarters of an hour; **passar um mau ~ de hora** (*fig*) to have a rough time; *v tb* **quinto**
quarto-e-sala (*pl* -s) M two-room apartment
quartzo ['kwaxtsu] M quartz
quase ['kwazi] ADV almost, nearly; ~ **nada** hardly anything; ~ **nunca** hardly ever; ~ **sempre** nearly always
quaternário, -a [kwatex'narju, a] ADJ quaternary
quatorze [kwa'toxzi] NUM fourteen; *v tb* **cinco**
quatro ['kwatru] NUM four; **estar/ficar de ~ to** be/get down on all fours; *v tb* **cinco**
quatrocentos, -tas [kwatro'sētuʃ] NUM four hundred

○ PALAVRA CHAVE

que [ki] CONJ **1** (*com oração subordinada: muitas vezes não se traduz*) that; **ele disse que viria** he said (that) he would come; **não há nada que fazer** there's nothing to be done; **espero que sim/não** I hope so/not; **dizer que sim/não** to say yes/no
2 (*consecutivo: muitas vezes não se traduz*) that; **é tão pesado que não consigo levantá-lo** it's so heavy (that) I can't lift it
3 (*comparações*): (**do**) **que** than; *v tb* **mais; menos; mesmo**
■ PRON **1** (*coisa*) which, that; (+ *prep*) which; **o chapéu que você comprou** the hat (that *ou* which) you bought
2 (*pessoa: suj*) who, that; (: *complemento*) whom, that; **o amigo que me levou ao museu** the friend who took me to the museum; **a moça que eu convidei** the girl (that *ou* whom) I invited
3 (*interrogativo*) what?; **o que você disse?** what did you say?
4 (*exclamação*) what!; **que pena!** what a pity!; **que lindo!** how lovely!

quê [ke] (*col*) M something ■ PRON what; **~!** what!; **não tem de ~** don't mention it; **para ~?** what for?; **por ~?** why?; **sem ~ nem por ~** for no good reason, all of a sudden
Quebec [ke'bɛk] N Quebec
quebra ['kɛbra] F break, rupture; (*falência*) bankruptcy; (*de energia elétrica*) cut; (*de disciplina*) breakdown; **de ~** in addition; ~ **de página**

(*Comput*) page break; **quebra-cabeça** (*pl* **quebra-cabeças**) M puzzle, problem; (*jogo*) jigsaw puzzle

quebrada [ke'brada] F (*vertente*) slope; (*barranco*) ravine, gully

quebradiço, -a [kebra'dʒisu, a] ADJ fragile, breakable

quebrado, -a [ke'bradu, a] ADJ broken; (*cansado*) exhausted; (*falido*) bankrupt; (*carro, máquina*) broken down; (*telefone*) out of order; (*col: pronto*) broke

quebrados [ke'braduʃ] MPL loose change *sg*

quebra-galho (*pl* -s) (*col*) M lifesaver

quebra-gelos M INV (*Náut*) icebreaker

quebra-mar (*pl* -es) M breakwater, sea wall

quebra-molas M INV speed bump, sleeping policeman

quebra-nozes M INV nutcrackers *pl* (*Brit*), nutcracker (*US*)

quebrantar [kebrã'taʳ] VT to break; (*entusiasmo, ânimo*) to dampen; (*debilitar*) to weaken, wear out; **quebrantar-se** VR (*tornar-se fraco*) to grow weak

quebranto [ke'brãtu] M (*fraqueza*) weakness; (*mau-olhado*) evil eye

quebra-pau (*pl* -s) (*col*) M row

quebra-quebra (*pl* -s) M riot

quebrar [ke'braʳ] VT to break; (*entusiasmo*) to dampen; (*espancar*) to beat; (*dobrar*) to bend ■ VI to break; (*carro*) to break down; (*Com*) to go bankrupt; (*ficar sem dinheiro*) to go broke

quebra-vento (*pl* -s) M (*Auto*) fanlight

quéchua ['keʃwa] M (*Ling*) Quechua

queda ['kɛda] F fall; (*fig: ruína*) downfall; **ter ~ para algo** to have a bent for sth; **ter uma ~ por alguém** to have a soft spot for sb; **~ de barreira** landslide; **queda-d'água** (*pl* **quedas-d'água**) F waterfall

queda-de-braço F arm wrestling

quedê [ke'de] (*col*) ADV where is/are?

queijada [kej'ʒada] F cheesecake

queijadinha [kejʒa'dʒiɲa] F coconut sweet

queijeira [kej'ʒejra] F cheese dish

queijo ['kejʒu] M cheese; **~ prato** ≈ cheddar cheese; **~ ralado** grated cheese

queijo-de-minas M white cheese, ≈ Cheshire cheese

queijo-do-reino M ≈ Edam cheese

queima ['kejma] F burning; (*Com*) clearance sale

queimada [kej'mada] F burning (of forests)

queimado, -a [kej'madu, a] ADJ burnt; (*de sol: machucado*) sunburnt; (: *bronzeado*) brown, tanned; (*plantas, folhas*) dried up; **cheiro/gosto de ~** smell of burning/burnt taste

queimadura [kejma'dura] F burn; (*de sol*) sunburn; **~ de primeiro/terceiro grau** first-/third-degree burn

queimar [kej'maʳ] VT to burn; (*roupa*) to scorch;

(*com líquido*) to scald; (*bronzear a pele*) to tan; (*planta, folha*) to wither; (*calorias*) to burn off ■ VI to burn; (*estar quente*) to be burning hot; (*lâmpada, fusível*) to blow; **queimar-se** VR (*pessoa*) to burn o.s.; to tan; (*zangar-se*) to get angry

queima-roupa F: **à ~** point-blank, at point-blank range

queira *etc* ['kejra] VB V **querer**

queixa ['kejʃa] F complaint; (*lamentação*) lament; **fazer ~ de alguém** to complain about sb; **ter ~ de alguém** to have a problem with sb

queixa-crime (*pl* **queixas-crime(s)**) F (*Jur*) citation

queixada [kej'ʃada] F (*de animal*) jaw; (*queixo grande*) prominent chin

queixar-se [kej'ʃaxsi] VR to complain; **~ de** to complain about; (*dores etc*) to complain of

queixo ['kejʃu] M chin; (*maxilar*) jaw; **ficar de ~ caído** to be open-mouthed; **bater o ~** to shiver

queixoso, -a [kej'ʃozu, ɔza] ADJ complaining; (*magoado*) doleful ■ M/F (*Jur*) plaintiff

queixume [kej'ʃumi] M complaint; (*lamentação*) lament

quem [kẽj] PRON who; (*como objeto*) who(m); **~ quer que** whoever; **seja ~ for** whoever it may be; **de ~ é isto?** whose is this?; **~ é?** who is it?; **a pessoa com ~ trabalha** the person he works with; **para ~ você deu o livro?** who did you give the book to?; **convide ~ você quiser** invite whoever you want; **~ disse isso, se enganou** whoever said that was wrong; **~ fez isso fui eu** it was me who did it, the person who did it was me; **~ diria!** who would have thought (it)!; **~ me dera ser rico** if only I were rich; **~ me dera que isso não fosse verdade** I wish it weren't true; **~ sabe** (*talvez*) perhaps; **~ sou eu para negar?** who am I to deny it?

Quênia ['kenja] M: **o ~** Kenya

queniano, -a [ke'njanu, a] ADJ, M/F Kenyan

quentão [kẽ'tãw] M ≈ mulled wine

quente ['kẽtʃi] ADJ hot; (*roupa*) warm; (*notícia*) reliable, solid; **o ~ agora é ...** (*col*) the big thing now is ..

quentinha [kẽ'tʃiɲa] F heatproof carton (*for food*)

quentura [kẽ'tura] F heat, warmth

quer [keʳ] CONJ: **~ ... ~ ...** whether ... or ...; **~ chova ~ não** whether it rains or not; **~ você queira, ~ não** whether you like it or not; **onde ~ que** wherever; **quando ~ que** whenever; **quem ~ que** whoever; **o que ~ que seja** whatever it is; **~ chova, ~ faça sol** come rain or shine

quer VB V **querer**

querela [ke'rela] F dispute; (*Jur*) complaint, accusation

querelado [kere'ladu] M (*Jur*) defendant

querelado, a [kerela'dɔʳ(a)] M/F (*Jur*) plaintiff

querelante [kere'lãtʃi] M/F (*Jur*) plaintiff

querelar [kere'laʳ] VT (*Jur*) to prosecute, sue ■ VI:

~ **contra** ou **de** (*queixar-se*) to lodge a complaint against

🔵 PALAVRA CHAVE

querer [ke're^r] VT 1 (*desejar*) to want; **quero mais dinheiro** I want more money; **queria um chá** I'd like a cup of tea; **quero ajudar/ que vá** I want to help/you to go; **você vai querer sair amanhã?** do you want to go out tomorrow?; **eu vou querer uma cerveja** (*num bar etc*) I'd like a beer; **por/sem querer** intentionally/unintentionally; **como queira** as you wish

2 (*perguntas para pedir algo*): **você quer fechar a janela?** will you shut the window?; **quer me dar uma mão?** can you give me a hand?

3 (*amar*) to love

4 (*convite*): **quer entrar/sentar** do come in/sit down

5: **querer dizer** (*significar*) to mean; (*pretender dizer*) to mean to say; **quero dizer** I mean; **quer dizer** (*com outras palavras*) in other words

■ VI: **querer bem a** to be fond of; **querer-se**
■ VR to love one another
■ M (*vontade*) wish; (*afeto*) affection

querido, -a [ke'ridu, a] ADJ dear ■ M/F darling; ~ **no grupo/por todos** prized in the group/by all; **o ator ~ das mulheres** the women's favo(u)rite actor; **Q~ João** Dear John

quermesse [kex'mɛsi] F fête

querosene [kero'zɛni] M kerosene

querubim [keru'bĩ] (*pl* -**ns**) M cherubim

quesito [ke'zitu] M (*questão*) query, question; (*requisito*) requirement

questão [keʃ'tãw] (*pl* -**ões**) F (*pergunta*) question, inquiry; (*problema*) matter, question; (*Jur*) case; (*contenda*) dispute, quarrel; **fazer ~ (de)** to insist (on); **em ~** in question; **há ~ de um ano** about a year ago; ~ **de tempo/de vida ou morte** question of time/matter of life and death; ~ **de ordem** point of order; ~ **fechada** point of principle; **questionar** [keʃtʃjo'na^r] VI to question ■ VT to question, call into question

questionário [keʃtʃjo'narju] M questionnaire

questionável [keʃtʃjo'navew] (*pl* -**eis**) ADJ questionable

questões [keʃ'tõjʃ] FPL *de* **questão**

qui. ABR (= **quinta-feira**) Thurs

quiabo ['kjabu] M okra

quibe ['kibi] M *deep-fried mince with flour and mint*

quibebe [ki'bɛbi] M pumpkin purée

quicar [ki'ka^r] VT (*bola*) to bounce ■ VI to bounce; (*col: pessoa*) to go mad

quiche ['kiʃi] F quiche

quieto, -a ['kjɛtu, a] ADJ quiet; (*imóvel*) still; **fica ~!** be quiet!; **quietude** [kje'tudʒi] F calm, tranquility

quilate [ki'latʃi] M carat; (*fig*) calibre (*Brit*), caliber (*US*)

quilha ['kiʎa] F (*Náut*) keel

quilo ['kilu] M kilo; **quilobyte** [kilo'bajtʃi] M kilobyte; **quilograma** [kilo'grama] M kilogram

quilohertz [kilo'hɛxts] M kilohertz

quilometragem [kilome'traʒẽ] F number of kilometres ou kilometers travelled, = mileage

quilometrar [kilome'tra^r] VT to measure in kilometres ou kilometers

quilométrico, -a [kilo'mɛtriku, a] ADJ (*distância*) in kilometres ou kilometers; (*fig: fila etc*) = mile-long

quilômetro [ki'lometru] M kilometre (*Brit*), kilometer (*US*)

quilowatt [kilo'watʃi] M kilowatt

quimbanda [kĩ'bãda] M (*ritual*) macumba ceremony; (*feiticeiro*) medicine man; (*local*) macumba site

quimera [ki'mɛra] F chimera

quimérico, -a [ki'mɛriku, a] ADJ fantastic

química ['kimika] F chemistry; *v tb* **químico**

químico, -a ['kimiku, a] ADJ chemical ■ M/F chemist

quimioterapia [kimjotera'pia] F chemotherapy

quimono [ki'mɔnu] M kimono; (*penhoar*) robe

quina ['kina] F (*canto*) corner; (*de mesa etc*) edge; **de** ~ edgeways (*Brit*), edgewise (*US*)

quindim [kĩ'dʒĩ] M *sweet made of egg yolks, coconut and sugar*

quinhão [ki'ɲãw] (*pl* -**ões**) M share, portion

quinhentista [kiɲẽ'tʃiʃta] ADJ sixteenth century *atr*

quinhentos, -tas [ki'ɲẽtuʃ] NUM five hundred; **isso são outros** ~ (*col*) that's a different matter, that's a different kettle of fish

quinhões [ki'ɲõjʃ] MPL *de* **quinhão**

quinina [ki'nina] F quinine

qüinquagésimo, -a [kwĩkwa'ʒɛzimu, a] NUM fiftieth

quinquilharias [kĩkiʎa'riaʃ] FPL odds and ends; (*miudezas*) knicknacks, trinkets

quinta ['kĩta] F (*tb*: **quinta-feira**) Thursday; (*propriedade*) estate; (*PT*) farm

quinta-essência (*pl* -**s**) F quintessence

quinta-feira ['kĩta-'fejra] (*pl* **quintas-feiras**) F Thursday; *v tb* **terça-feira**

quintal [kĩ'taw] (*pl* -**ais**) M back yard

quintanista [kĩta'niʃta] M/F fifth-year

quinteiro [kĩ'tejru] (*PT*) M farmer

quinteto [kĩ'tetu] M quintet(te)

quinto, -a ['kĩtu, a] NUM fifth; **ele tirou o ~ lugar** he came fifth; **eu fui o ~ a chegar** I was the fifth to arrive, I arrived fifth; (*numa corrida*) I came fifth

quintuplo, -a [kĩ'tuplu, a] ADJ, M quintuple ■ M/F: ~**s** (*crianças*) quins, quintuplets

quinze ['kĩzi] NUM fifteen; **duas e** ~ a quarter past (*Brit*) ou after (*US*) two; ~ **para as sete** a quarter to (*Brit*) ou of (*US*) seven; *v tb* **cinco**

quinzena [kĩ'zɛna] F two weeks, fortnight (*Brit*); (*salário*) two weeks' wages; **quinzenal** [kĩze'naw] (*pl* -**ais**) ADJ fortnightly; **quinzenalmente** [kĩzenaw'mẽtʃi] ADV

fortnightly
quiosque ['kjɔʃki] M kiosk; (de jardim) gazebo
qüiproquó [kwipro'kwɔ] M misunderstanding,
mix-up
quiromante [kiro'mãtʃi] M/F palmist, fortune
teller
quis etc [kiʒ] VB V **querer**
quiser etc [ki'zeʳ] VB V **querer**
quisto ['kiʃtu] M cyst
quitação [kita'sãw] (pl -ões) F (remissão)
discharge, remission; (pagamento) settlement;
(recibo) receipt
quitanda [ki'tãda] F (loja) grocer's (shop) (Brit),
grocery store (US)
quitandeiro, -a [kitã'dejru, a] M/F grocer;

(vendedor de hortaliças) greengrocer (Brit), produce
dealer (US)
quitar [ki'taʳ] VT (dívida: pagar) to pay off;
(: perdoar) to cancel; (devedor) to release
quite ['kitʃi] ADJ (livre) free; (com um credor)
squared up; (igualado) even; **estar ~ (com
alguém)** to be quits (with sb)
quitute [ki'tutʃi] N titbit (Brit), tidbit (US)
quizumba [ki'zũba] (col) F punch-up, brawl
quociente [kwo'sjẽtʃi] M quotient; **~ de
inteligência** intelligence quotient
quorum ['kwɔrũ] M quorum
quota ['kwota] F quota; (porção) share, portion
quotidiano, -a [kwotʃi'dʒjanu, a] ADJ everyday
q.v. ABR (= queira ver) q.v

Rr

R, r ['ɛxi] (pl **rs**) M R, r; **R de Roberto** R for Robert (Brit) ou Roger (US)

R ABR (= rua) St

R$ ABR = **real**

rã [xã] F frog

rabada [xa'bada] F (rabo) tail; (fig) tail end; (Culin) oxtail stew

rabanada [xaba'nada] F (Culin) cinnamon toast; (golpe) blow with the tail; **dar uma ~ em alguém** (col) to give sb the brush-off

rabanete [xaba'netʃi] M radish

rabear [xa'bjaʳ] VI (cão) to wag its tail; (navio) to wheel around; (carro) to skid round

rabecão [xabe'kãw] (pl -ões) M mortuary wagon

rabicho [xa'biʃu] M ponytail

rabino [xa'binu] M rabbi

rabiscar [xabiʃ'kaʳ] VT (escrever) to scribble; (papel) to scribble on ■ VI to doodle; (escrever mal) to scribble; **rabisco** [xa'biʃku] M scribble

rabo ['xabu] M (cauda) tail; (col!) arse (!); **meter o ~ entre as pernas** (fig) to be left with one's tail between one's legs; **olhar alguém com o ~ do olho** to look at sb out of the corner of one's eye; **pegar em ~ de foguete** (col) to stick one's neck out; **ser ~ de foguete** (col) to be a minefield

rabo-de-cavalo (pl **rabos-de-cavalo**) M ponytail

rabo-de-saia (pl **rabos-de-saia**) (col) M woman; **não poder ver ~** to be a womanizer

rabugento, -a [xabu'ʒẽtu, a] ADJ grumpy

rabugice [xabu'ʒisi] F grumpiness

rabujar [xabu'ʒaʳ] VI to be grumpy; (criança) to have a tantrum

raça ['xasa] F breed; (grupo étnico) race; **cão/cavalo de ~** pedigree dog/thoroughbred horse; **(no peito e) na ~** (col) by sheer effort; **ter ~** to have guts; (ter ascendência africana) to be of African origin

ração [xa'sãw] (pl -ões) F ration; (para animal) food; **~ de cachorro** dog food

racha ['xaʃa] F (fenda) split; (greta) crack ■ M (col) scrap; **rachadura** [xaʃa'dura] F crack; **rachar** [xa'ʃaʳ] VT to crack; (objeto, despesas) to split; (lenha) to chop ■ VI to split; (cristal) to crack; **rachar-se** VR to split; to crack; **frio de rachar** bitter cold; **sol de rachar** scorching sun; **ou vai ou racha** it's make or break

racial [xa'sjaw] (pl -ais) ADJ racial; **preconceito ~** racial prejudice

raciocinar [xasjosi'naʳ] VI to reason

raciocínio [xasjo'sinju] M reasoning

racional [xasjo'naw] (pl -ais) ADJ rational

racionalização [xasjonaliza'sãw] F rationalization

racionalizar [xasjonali'zaʳ] VT to rationalize

racionamento [xasjona'mẽtu] M rationing

racionar [xasjo'naʳ] VT (distribuir) to ration out; (limitar a venda de) to ration

racismo [xa'siʒmu] M racism; **racista** [xa'siʃta] ADJ, M/F racist

raçoes [xa'sõjʃ] FPL de **ração**

radar [xa'daʳ] M radar

radiação [xadʒja'sãw] (pl -ões) F radiation; (raio) ray

radiador [xadʒja'doʳ] M radiator

radialista [xadʒja'liʃta] M/F radio announcer; (na produção) radio producer

radiante [xa'dʒjãtʃi] ADJ radiant; (de alegria) overjoyed

radical [xadʒi'kaw] (pl -ais) ADJ radical ■ M radical; (Ling) root

radicalismo [xadʒika'liʒmu] M radicalism

radicalizar [xadʒikali'zaʳ] VT to radicalize; **radicalizar-se** VR to become radical

radicar-se [xadʒi'kaxsi] VR to take root; (fixar residência) to settle

rádio ['xadʒu] M radio; (Quím) radium ■ F radio station

radioactivo, -tiva [xadjua'tivu] (PT) ADJ = **radioativo** etc

radioamador, a [xadʒjuama'doʳ(a)] M/F radio ham

radioatividade [xadʒjuatʃivi'dadʒi] F radioactivity

radioativo, -a [xadʒjua'tʃivu, a] ADJ radioactive

radiodifusão [xadʒjodʒifu'zãw] F broadcasting

radiodifusora [xadʒjodʒifu'zora] F radio station

radioemissora [xadʒjuemi'sora] F radio station

radiografar [xadʒjogra'faʳ] VT (Med) to X-ray; (notícia) to radio

radiografia [xadʒjogra'fia] F X-ray

radiograma [xadʒjo'grama] M cablegram

radiogravador [xadʒjograva'doʳ] M radio cassette

radiojornal [xadʒjoʒox'naw] (pl -**ais**) M radio news sg

radiologia [xadʒjolo'ʒia] F radiology

radiologista [xadʒjolo'ʒiʃta] M/F radiologist

radionovela [xadʒjono'vɛla] F radio serial

radiooperador, a [xadʒjoopera'doʳ(a)] M/F radio operator

radiopatrulha [xadʒjopa'truʎa] F (viatura) patrol car

radiorrepórter [xadʒjoxe'pɔxteʳ] M/F radio reporter

radioso, -a [xa'dʒjozu, ɔza] ADJ radiant, brilliant

radiotáxi [xadʒjo'taksi] M radio taxi ou cab

radioterapia [xadʒjotera'pia] F radiotherapy

radiouvinte [xadʒjo'vītʃi] M/F (radio) listener

ragu [xa'gu] M stew, ragoût

raia ['xaja] F (risca) line; (fronteira) boundary; (limite) limit; (de corrida) lane; (peixe) ray; **chegar às ~s** to reach the limit

raiado, -a [xa'jadu, a] ADJ striped

raiar [xa'jaʳ] VI (brilhar) to shine; (madrugada) to dawn; (aparecer) to appear

rainha [xa'iɲa] F queen; **ela é a ~ da preguiça** (col) she's the world's worst for laziness

rainha-mãe (pl **rainhas-mães**) F queen mother

raio ['xaju] M (de sol) ray; (de luz) beam; (de roda) spoke; (relâmpago) flash of lightning; (distância) range; (Mat) radius; **~s X** X-rays; **~ de ação** range; **onde está o ~ da chave?** (col) where's the blasted key?

raiva ['xajva] F rage, fury; (Med) rabies sg; **estar/ficar com ~ (de)** to be/get angry (with); **estar morto de ~** to be furious; **ter ~ de** to hate; **tomar ~ de** to begin to hate; **que ~!** I am (ou was etc) furious!; **raivoso, -a** [xaj'vozu, ɔza] ADJ furious; (Med) rabid, mad

raiz [xa'iʒ] F root; (origem) source; **~ quadrada** square root; **criar raízes** to put down roots

rajada [xa'ʒada] F (vento) gust; (de tiros) burst

ralado, -a [xa'ladu, a] ADJ grated; (esfolado) grazed; **ralador** [xala'doʳ] M grater

ralar [xa'laʳ] VT to grate; (esfolar) to graze

ralé [xa'lɛ] F common people pl, rabble

ralhar [xa'ʎaʳ] VI to scold; **~ com alguém** to tell sb off

rali [xa'li] M rally

ralo, -a ['xalu, a] ADJ (cabelo) thinning; (tecido) thin, flimsy; (vegetação) sparse; (sopa) thin, watery; (café) weak ▪ M (de regador) rose, nozzle; (de pia, banheiro) drain

rama ['xama] F branches pl, foliage; **algodão em ~** raw cotton; **pela ~** superficially; **ramagem** [xa'maʒē] F branches pl, foliage; (num tecido) floral pattern; **ramal** [xa'maw] (pl -**ais**) M (Ferro) branch line; (Tel) extension; (Auto) side road

ramalhete [xama'ʎetʃi] M bouquet, posy

rameira [xa'mejra] F prostitute

ramerrão [xame'xãw] (pl -**ões**) M routine, round

ramificação [xamifika'sãw] (pl -**ões**) F (tb: Comput) branching; (ramo) branch

ramificar-se [xamifi'kaxsi] VR to branch out

ramo ['xamu] M branch; (profissão, negócios) line; (de flores) bunch; **Domingo de R~s** Palm Sunday; **um perito do ~** an expert in the field

rampa ['xãpa] F ramp; (ladeira) slope

rançar [xã'saʳ] VI to go rancid

rancheiro [xã'ʃejru] M cook

rancho ['xãʃu] M (grupo) group, band; (cabana) hut; (refeição) meal

rancor [xã'koʳ] M (ressentimento) bitterness; (ódio) hatred

rancoroso, -a [xãko'rozu, ɔza] ADJ bitter, resentful; (odiento) hateful

rançoso, -a [xã'sozu, ɔza] ADJ rancid; (cheiro) musty

randevu [xãde'vu] M brothel

ranger [xã'ʒeʳ] VI to creak ▪ VT: **~ os dentes** to grind one's teeth

rangido [xã'ʒidu] M creak

rango ['xãgu] (col) M grub

Rangum [xã'gũ] N Rangoon

ranheta [xa'ɲeta] ADJ sullen, surly

ranhetice [xaɲe'tʃisi] F sullenness; (ato) surly thing

ranho ['xaɲu] (col) M snot

ranhura [xa'ɲura] F groove; (para moeda) slot

ranjo etc ['xãʒu] VB V **ranger**

ranzinza [xã'zīza] ADJ peevish

rapa ['xapa] M (de comida) remains pl; (carro) illegal trading patrol car; (policial) policeman concerned with illegal street trading

rapadura [xapa'dura] F (doce) raw brown sugar

rapagão [xapa'gãw] (pl -**ões**) M hunk

rapapé [xapa'pɛ] M touch of the forelock; **rapapés** MPL (bajulação) bowing and scraping; (lisonja) flattery sg; **fazer ~s a alguém** to bow and scrape to sb

rapar [xa'paʳ] VT to scrape; (barbear) to shave; (o cabelo) to crop; **~ algo a alguém** (roubar) to steal sth from sb

rapariga [xapa'riga] F girl

rapaz [xa'pajʒ] M boy; (col) lad; **ô, ~, tudo bem?** hi, mate, how's it going?

rapaziada [xapa'zjada] F (grupo) lads pl

rapazote [xapa'zɔtʃi] M little boy

rapé [xa'pɛ] M snuff

rapidez [xapi'deʒ] F speed, rapidity; **com ~** quickly, fast

rápido, -a ['xapidu, a] ADJ quick, fast ▪ ADV fast, quickly ▪ M (trem) express

rapina [xa'pina] F robbery; **ave de ~** bird of prey

raposo, -a [xa'pozu, ɔza] M/F fox/vixen; (fig) crafty person

rapsódia [xap'sɔdʒja] F rhapsody

raptado, -a [xap'tadu, a] M/F kidnap victim

raptar [xap'taʳ] VT to kidnap; **rapto** ['xaptu] M

NB: European Portuguese adds the following consonants to certain words: **b** (sú(b)dito, su(b)til); **c** (a(c)ção, a(c)cionista, a(c)to); **m** (inde(m)ne); **p** (ado(p)çã, ado(p)tar); for further details see p. xiii.

kidnapping; **raptor** [xap'to^r] M kidnapper

raqueta [xa'keta] (PT) F = **raquete**

raquetada [xake'tada] F stroke with a (ou the) racquet

raquete [xa'ketʃi] F (de tênis) racquet; (de pingue-pongue) bat

raquidiana [xaki'dʒjana] F (anestesia) epidural

raquítico, -a [xa'kitʃiku, a] ADJ (Med) suffering from rickets; (franzino) puny; (vegetação) poor

raquitismo [xaki'tʃiʒmu] M (Med) rickets sg

raramente [xara'mẽtʃi] ADV rarely, seldom

rarear [xa'rja^r] VT to make rare; (diminuir) to thin out ■ VI to become rare; (cabelos) to thin; (casas etc) to thin out

rarefazer [xarefa'ze^r] (irreg) VT, VI to rarefy; (nuvens) to disperse, blow away; (multidão) to thin out

rarefeito, -a [xare'fejtu, a] PP de **rarefazer** ■ ADJ rarefied; (multidão, população) sparse

rarefez [xare'feʒ] VB V **rarefazer**

rarefizer etc [xarefi'ze^r] VB V **rarefazer**

raridade [xari'dadʒi] F rarity

raro, -a ['xaru, a] ADJ rare ■ ADV rarely, seldom; **não ~** often

rasante [xa'zãtʃi] ADJ (avião) low-flying; (vôo) low

rascunhar [xaʃku'ɲa^r] VT to draft, make a rough copy of

rascunho [xaʃ'kuɲu] M rough copy, draft

rasgado, -a [xaʒ'gadu, a] ADJ (roupa) torn, ripped; (cumprimentos, elogio, gesto) effusive

rasgão [xaʒ'gãw] (pl -ões) M tear, rip

rasgar [xaʒ'ga^r] VT to tear, rip; (destruir) to tear up, rip up; **rasgar-se** VR to split; **rasgo** ['xaʒgu] M (rasgão) tear, rip; (risco) stroke; (ação) feat; (ímpeto) burst; (da imaginação) flight

rasgões [xaʒ'gõjʃ] MPL de **rasgão**

rasguei etc [xaʒ'gej] VB V **rasgar**

raso, -a ['xazu, a] ADJ (liso) flat, level; (sapato) flat; (não fundo) shallow; (baixo) low; (colher: como medida) level ■ M: **o ~** the shallow water; **soldado ~** private

raspa ['xaʃpa] F (de madeira) shaving; (de metal) filing

raspadeira [xaʃpa'dejra] F scraper

raspão [xaʃ'pãw] (pl -ões) M scratch, graze; **tocar de ~** to graze

raspar [xaʃ'pa^r] VT (limpar, tocar) to scrape; (alisar) to file; (tocar de raspão) to graze; (arranhar) to scratch; (pêlos, cabeça) to shave; (apagar) to rub out ■ VI: **~ em** to scrape; **passar raspando (num exame)** to scrape through (an exam)

raspões [xaʃ'põjʃ] MPL de **raspão**

rasteira [xaʃ'tejra] F (pernada) trip; **dar uma ~ em alguém** to trip sb up

rasteiro, -a [xaʃ'tejru, a] ADJ (que se arrasta) crawling; (planta) creeping; (a pouca altura) low-lying; (ordinário) common

rastejante [xaʃte'ʒãtʃi] ADJ trailing; (arrastando-se) creeping; (voz) slurred

rastejar [xaʃte'ʒa^r] VI to crawl; (furtivamente) to creep; (fig: rebaixar-se) to grovel ■ VT (fugitivo etc)

to track

rastilho [xaʃ'tʃiʎu] M (de pólvora) fuse

rasto ['xaʃtu] M (pegada) track; (de veículo) trail; (fig) sign, trace; **de ~s** crawling; **andar de ~s** to crawl; **levar de ~s** to drag along

rastrear [xaʃ'trja^r] VT to track; (investigar) to scan ■ VI to track

rastro ['xaʃtru] M = **rasto**

rasura [xa'zura] F deletion

rasurar [xazu'ra^r] VT to delete items from

rata ['xata] F rat; (pequena) mouse; **dar uma ~** to slip up

ratão [xa'tãw] (pl -ões) M rat

rataplã [xata'plã] M drum roll

ratazana [xata'zana] F rat

ratear [xa'tʃja^r] VT (dividir) to share ■ VI (motor) to miss

rateio [xa'teju] M (de custos) sharing, spreading

ratificação [xatʃifika'sãw] F ratification

ratificar [xatʃifi'ka^r] VT to confirm, ratify

rato ['xatu] M rat; (rato pequeno) mouse; **~ de biblioteca** bookworm; **~ de hotel/praia** hotel/beach thief; **ratoeira** [xa'twejra] F rat trap; (pequena) mousetrap

ratões [xa'tõjʃ] MPL de **ratão**

ravina [xa'vina] F ravine

ravióli [xa'vjɔli] M ravioli

razão [xa'zãw] (pl -ões) F reason; (bom senso) common sense; (argumento) reasoning, argument; (conta) account; (Mat) ratio ■ M (Com) ledger; **à ~ de** at the rate of; **com/sem ~** with good reason/for no reason; **em ~ de** on account of; **dar ~ a alguém** to support sb; **ter/não ter ~** to be right/wrong; **ter toda ~** (em fazer) to be quite right (to do); **estar coberto de ~** to be quite right; **a ~ pela qual ...** the reason why ...; **~ demais para você ficar aqui** all the more reason for you to stay here; **~ de Estado** reason of State; **razoável** [xa'zwavew] (pl -eis) ADJ reasonable

razões [xa'zõjʃ] FPL de **razão**

r/c (PT) ABR = **rés-do-chão**

RDA ABR F (antes: = República Democrática Alemã) GDR

ré [xɛ] F (Auto) reverse (gear); **dar (marcha à) ré** to reverse, back up; v tb **réu**

reá [xe'a] VB V **reaver**

reabastecer [xeabaʃte'se^r] VT (avião) to refuel; (carro) to fill up; **reabastecer-se** VR: **reabastecer-se de** to replenish one's supply of

reabastecimento [xeabaʃtesi'mẽtu] M (de avião) refuelling; (de uma cidade) reprovisioning

reaberto, -a [xea'bɛxtu, a] PP de **reabrir**

reabertura [xeabex'tura] F reopening

reabilitação [xeabilita'sãw] F rehabilitation; **~ motora** physiotherapy

reabilitar [xeabili'ta^r] VT to rehabilitate; (falido) to discharge, rehabilitate

reabrir [xea'bri^r] VT to reopen

reaça [xe'asa] (col) M/F reactionary

reação [xea'sãw] (PT -cç-, pl -ões) F reaction; **~ em cadeia** chain reaction

reacender [xease'de'] VT to relight; (*fig*) to rekindle

reacionário, -a [xeasjo'narju, a] ADJ reactionary

reações [xea'sõjʃ] FPL *de* **reação**

reactor [xea'to'] (PT) M = **reator**

readaptar [xeadap'ta'] VT to readapt

readmitir [xeadʒimi'tʃi'] VT to readmit; (*funcionário*) to reinstate

readquirir [xeadʒiki'ri'] VT to reacquire

reafirmar [xeafix'ma'] VT to reaffirm

reagir [xea'ʒi'] VI to react; (*doente, time perdedor*) to fight back; ~ **a** (*resistir*) to resist; (*protestar*) to rebel against

reais [xe'ajʃ] ADJ PL *de* **real**

reaja *etc* [xe'aʒa] VB V **reagir; reaver**

reajustar [xeaʒuʃ'ta'] VT to readjust; (*Mecânica*) to regulate; (*salário, preço*) to adjust (*in line with inflation*)

reajuste [xea'ʒuʃtʃi] M adjustment; ~ **salarial/ de preços** wage/price adjustment (*in line with inflation*)

real [xe'aw] (*pl* **-ais**) ADJ real; (*relativo à realeza*) royal ■ M (*moeda*) real

realçar [xeaw'sa'] VT to highlight; **realce** [xe'awsi] M (*destaque*) emphasis; (*mais brilho*) highlight; **dar realce a** to enhance

realejo [xea'leʒu] M barrel organ

realeza [xea'leza] F royalty

realidade [xeali'dadʒi] F reality; **na** ~ actually, in fact

realimentação [xealimẽta'sãw] F (*Elet*) feedback

realismo [xea'liʒmu] M realism

realista [xea'liʃta] ADJ realistic ■ M/F realist

reality TV [xe'alitʃite've] F reality TV

realização [xealiza'sãw] F fulfilment (*Brit*), fulfillment (*US*), realization; (*de projeto*) execution, carrying out; (*transformação em dinheiro*) conversion into cash

realizado, -a [xeali'zadu, a] ADJ (*pessoa*) fulfilled

realizador, a [xealiza'do'(a)] ADJ (*pessoa*) enterprising

realizar [xeali'za'] VT (*um objetivo*) to achieve; (*projeto*) to carry out; (*ambições, sonho*) to fulfil (*Brit*), fulfill (*US*), realize; (*negócios*) to transact; (*perceber, convertir en dinheiro*) to realize; **realizar-se** VR (*acontecer*) to take place; (*ambições*) to be realized; (*sonhos*) to come true; (*pessoa*) to fulfil(l) o.s.; **o congresso será realizado em Lisboa** the conference will be held in Lisbon

realizável [xeali'zavew] (*pl* **-eis**) ADJ realizable

realmente [xeaw'mẽtʃi] ADV really; (*de fato*) actually

reanimar [xeani'ma'] VT to revive; (*encorajar*) to encourage; **reanimar-se** VR (*pessoa*) to cheer up

reão [xe'ãw] VB V **reaver**

reaparecer [xeapare'se'] VI to reappear

reaprender [xeaprẽ'de'] VT to relearn

reapresentar [xeaprezẽ'ta'] VT (*espetáculo*) to put on again

reaproximação [xeaprosima'sãw] (*pl* **-ões**) F (*entre pessoas, países*) rapprochement

reaproximar [xeaprosi'ma'] VT to bring back together; **reaproximar-se** VR to be brought back together

reaquecer [xeake'se'] VT to reheat

reassumir [xeasu'mi'] VT, VI to take over again

reatar [xea'ta'] VT (*continuar*) to resume, take up again; (*nó*) to retie

reativar [xeatʃi'va'] VT to reactivate; (*organização, lei*) to revive

reator [xea'to'] M reactor

reavaliação [xeavalja'sãw] F revaluation

reaver [xea've'] VT to recover, get back

reavivar [xeavi'va'] VT (*cor*) to brighten up; (*lembrança*) to revive; (*sofrimento, dor*) to bring back

rebaixa [xe'bajʃa] F reduction

rebaixar [xebaj'ʃa'] VT (*tornar mais baixo*) to lower; (*o preço de*) to lower the price of; (*humilhar*) to put down, humiliate ■ VI to drop; **rebaixar-se** VR to demean o.s.

rebanho [xe'baɲu] M (*de carneiros, fig*) flock; (*de gado, elefantes*) herd

rebarbar [xebax'ba'] VT (*opor-se a*) to oppose ■ VI (*reclamar*) to complain

rebarbativo, -a [xebaxba'tʃivu, a] ADJ (*pessoa*) disagreeable, unpleasant

rebate [xe'batʃi] M (*sinal*) alarm; (*Com*) discount; ~ **falso** false alarm

rebater [xeba'te'] VT (*golpe*) to ward off; (*acusações, argumentos*) to refute; (*bola*) to knock back; (*à máquina*) to retype

rebelar [xebe'la'] VT to cause to rebel; **rebelar-se** VR to rebel

rebelde [xe'bɛwdʒi] ADJ rebellious; (*indisciplinado*) unruly, wild ■ M/F rebel

rebeldia [xebew'dʒia] F rebelliousness; (*fig: obstinação*) stubbornness; (*: oposição*) defiance

rebelião [xebe'ljãw] (*pl* **-ões**) F rebellion

rebentar [xebẽ'ta'] VI (*guerra*) to break out; (*louça*) to smash; (*corda*) to snap; (*represa*) to burst; (*ondas*) to break ■ VT (*louça*) to smash; (*corda*) to snap; (*porta, ponte*) to break down

rebento [xe'bẽtu] M (*filho*) offspring

rebite [xe'bitʃi] M (*Tec*) rivet

reboar [xe'bwa'] VI to resound, echo

rebobinar [xebobi'na'] VT (*vídeo*) to rewind

rebocador [xeboka'do'] M (*Náut*) tug(boat)

rebocar [xebo'ka'] VT (*paredes*) to plaster; (*veículo mal estacionado*) to tow away; (*dar reboque a*) to tow

reboco [xe'boku] M plaster

rebolar [xebo'la'] VT to swing ■ VI to sway; (*fig*) to work hard; **rebolar-se** VR to sway

rebolo [xe'bolu] M (*mó*) grindstone; (*cilindro*) cylinder

NB: *European Portuguese adds the following consonants to certain words:* **b** (sú(b)dito, su(b)til); **c** (a(c)ção, a(c)cionista, a(c)to); **m** (inde(m)ne); **p** (ado(p)ção, ado(p)tar); *for further details see p. xiii.*

reboque [xe'bɔki] M (ato) tow; (veículo: tb: **carro reboque**) trailer; (cabo) towrope; (BR: de socorro) towtruck; **a ~ on ou ou in** (US) tow

reboque etc VB V **rebocar**

rebordo [xe'boxdu] M rim, edge; **~ da lareira** mantelpiece

rebordosa [xebox'dɔza] F (situação difícil) difficult situation; (doença grave) serious illness; (reincidência de moléstia) recurrence; (pancadaria) commotion

rebu [xe'bu] (col) M commotion, rumpus

rebuçado [xebu'sadu] (PT) M sweet, candy (US)

rebuliço [xebu'lisu] M commotion, hubbub

rebuscado, -a [xebuʃ'kadu, a] ADJ affected

recado [xe'kadu] M message; **menino de ~s** errand boy; **dar o ~, dar conta do ~** (fig) to deliver the goods; **deixar ~** to leave a message; **mandar ~** to send word

recaída [xeka'ida] F relapse

recair [xeka'iʳ] VI (doente) to relapse; **~ em erro** ou **falta** to go wrong again; **a culpa recaiu nela** she got the blame; **o acento recai na última sílaba** the accent falls on the last syllable

recalcado, -a [xekaw'kadu, a] ADJ repressed

recalcar [xekaw'kaʳ] VT to repress

recalcitrante [xekawsi'trãtʃi] ADJ recalcitrant

recalque [xe'kawki] M repression

recalque etc VB V **recalcar**

recamado, -a [xeka'madu, a] ADJ embroidered

recambiar [xekã'bjaʳ] VT to send back

recanto [xe'kãtu] M (lugar aprazível) corner, nook; (esconderijo) hiding place

recapitulação [xekapitula'sãw] F (resumo) recapitulation; (rememorar) revision

recapitular [xekapitu'laʳ] VT (resumir) to sum up, recapitulate; (fatos) to review; (matéria escolar) to revise

recarga [xe'kaxga] F (de celular) top-up; **preciso fazer a ~ do meu celular** I need to get a top-up for my mobile

recarregar [xekaxe'gaʳ] VT (celular) to top up; (bateria) recharge; (cartucho) refill

recatado, -a [xeka'tadu, a] ADJ (modesto) modest; (reservado) reserved

recatar-se [xeka'taxsi] VR to become withdrawn; (ocultar-se) to hide

recato [xe'katu] M (modéstia) modesty

recauchutado, -a [xekawʃu'tadu, a] ADJ (fig) revamped; (col: pessoa) having had cosmetic surgery; **pneu ~** (Auto) retread, remould (Brit)

recauchutagem [xekawʃu'taʒē] (pl -ns) F (de pneu) retreading; (fig) face-lift

recauchutar [xekawʃu'taʳ] VT (pneu) to retread; (fig) to give a face-lift to

recear [xe'sjaʳ] VT to fear ■ VI: **~ por** to fear for; **~ fazer/que** to be afraid to do/that

recebedor, a [xesebe'doʳ(a)] M/F recipient; (de impostos) collector

receber [xese'beʳ] VT to receive; (ganhar) to earn, get; (hóspedes) to take in; (convidados) to entertain; (acolher bem) to welcome ■ VI (receber convidados) to entertain; (ser pago) to be paid; **a ~**

(Com) receivable; **recebimento** [xesebi'mētu] (BR) M reception; (de uma carta) receipt; **acusar o recebimento de** to acknowledge receipt of

receio [xe'seju] M fear; **não tenha ~** never fear; **ter ~ de que** to fear that

receita [xe'sejta] F (renda) income; (do Estado) revenue; (Med) prescription; (culinária) recipe; **~ pública** tax revenue; **R~ Federal** ≈ Inland Revenue (Brit), ≈ IRS (US); **receitar** [xesej'taʳ] VT to prescribe ■ VI to write prescriptions

recém [xe'sē] ADV recently, newly; **recém-casado, -a** ADJ newly-married; **os recém-casados** the newlyweds

recém-chegado, -a M/F newcomer

recém-nascido, -a M/F newborn child

recém-publicado, -a ADJ newly ou recently published

recender [xesē'deʳ] VT: **~ um cheiro** to give off a smell ■ VI to smell; **~ a** to smell of

recenseamento [xesēsja'mētu] M census

recensear [xesē'sjaʳ] VT to take a census of

recente [xe'sētʃi] ADJ recent; (novo) new ■ ADV recently; **recentemente** [xesētʃi'mētʃi] ADV recently

receoso, -a [xe'sjozu, ɔza] ADJ (medroso) frightened, fearful; (apreensivo) afraid; **estar ~ de (fazer)** to be afraid of (doing)

recepção [xesep'sãw] (pl -ões) F reception; (PT: de uma carta) receipt; **acusar a ~ de** (PT) to acknowledge receipt of

recepcionar [xesepsjo'naʳ] VT to receive

recepcionista [xesepsjo'niʃta] M/F receptionist

recepcões [xesep'sõjʃ] FPL de **recepção**

receptáculo [xesep'takulu] M receptacle

receptador, a [xesepta'doʳ(a)] M/F fence, receiver of stolen goods

receptar [xesep'taʳ] VT to fence, receive

receptivo, -a [xesep'tʃivu, a] ADJ receptive; (acolhedor) welcoming

receptor [xesep'toʳ] M (Tec) receiver

recessão [xese'sãw] (pl -ões) F recession

recesso [xe'sɛsu] M recess

recessões [xese'sõjʃ] FPL de **recessão**

rechaçar [xeʃa'saʳ] VT (ataque) to repel; (idéias, argumentos) to oppose; (oferta) to turn down

réchaud [xe'ʃo] M (pl -s) plate-warmer

recheado, -a [xe'ʃjadu, a] ADJ (ave, carne) stuffed; (empada, bolo) filled; (cheio) full, crammed

rechear [xe'ʃjaʳ] VT to fill; (ave, carne) to stuff; **recheio** [xe'ʃeju] M (para carne assada) stuffing; (de empada, de bolo) filling; (o conteúdo) contents pl

rechonchudo, -a [xeʃõ'ʃudu, a] ADJ chubby, plump

recibo [xe'sibu] M receipt

reciclagem [xesi'klaʒē] F (de papel etc) recycling; (de professores, funcionários) retraining

reciclável [xesi'klavew] (pl -eis) ADJ recyclable

reciclar [xesi'klaʳ] VT (papel etc) to recycle; (professores, funcionários) to retrain

recidiva [xesi'dʒiva] F recurrence

recife [xe'sifi] M reef

recifense [xesi'fēsi] ADJ from Recife ■ M/F

person from Recife

recinto [xe'sĩtu] M (*espaço fechado*) enclosure; (*lugar*) area

recipiente [xesi'pjẽtʃi] M container, receptacle

recíproca [xe'siproka] F reverse

reciprocar [xesipro'ka^r] VT to reciprocate

reciprocidade [xesiprosi'dadʒi] F reciprocity

recíproco, -a [xe'siproku, a] ADJ reciprocal

récita ['xɛsita] F (*teatral*) performance

recitação [xesita'sãw] (*pl* -ões) F recitation

recital [xesi'taw] (*pl* -ais) M recital

recitar [xesi'ta^r] VT (*declamar*) to recite

reclamação [xeklama'sãw] (*pl* -ões) F (*queixa*) complaint; (*Jur*) claim

reclamante [xekla'mãtʃi] M/F claimant

reclamar [xekla'ma^r] VT (*exigir*) to demand; (*herança*) to claim ▪ VI: ~ **(de)** (*comida etc*) to complain (about); (*dores etc*) to complain (of); ~ **contra** to complain about

reclame [xe'klami] M advertisement

reclinado, -a [xekli'nadu, a] ADJ (*inclinado*) leaning; (*recostado*) lying back

reclinar [xekli'na^r] VT to rest, lean; **reclinar-se** VR to lie back; (*deitar-se*) to lie down

reclinável [xekli'navew] (*pl* **-eis**) ADJ (*cadeira*) reclinable

reclusão [xeklu'zãw] F (*isolamento*) seclusion; (*encarceramento*) imprisonment

recluso, -a [xe'kluzu, a] ADJ reclusive ▪ M/F recluse; (*prisioneiro*) prisoner

recobrar [xeko'bra^r] VT to recover, get back; **recobrar-se** VR to recover

recolher [xeko'ʎe^r] VT to collect; (*coisas dispersas*) to collect up; (*gado, roupa do varal*) to bring in; (*juntar*) to gather together; (*abrigar*) to give shelter to; (*notas antigas*) to withdraw; (*encolher*) to draw in; **recolher-se** VR (*ir para casa*) to go home; (*deitar-se*) to go to bed; (*ir para o quarto*) to retire; (*em meditações*) to meditate; ~ **alguém a algum lugar** to take sb somewhere; **recolhido, -a** [xeko'ʎidu, a] ADJ (*lugar*) secluded; (*pessoa*) withdrawn; **recolhimento** [xekoʎi'mẽtu] M (*vida retraída*) retirement; (*arrecadação*) collection; (*ato de levar*) taking

recomeçar [xekome'sa^r] VT, VI to restart; ~ **a fazer** to start to do again

recomeço [xeko'mesu] M restart

recomendação [xekomẽda'sãw] (*pl* -ões) F recommendation; **recomendações** FPL (*cumprimentos*) regards; **carta de** ~ letter of recommendation

recomendar [xekomẽ'da^r] VT to recommend; (*confiar*) to entrust; ~ **alguém a alguém** (*enviar cumprimentos*) to remember sb to sb, give sb's regards to sb; (*pedir favor*) to put in a word for sb with sb; ~ **algo a alguém** (*confiar*) to entrust sth to sb; ~ **que alguém faça** to recommend that sb do; (*lembrar, pedir*) to urge that sb do; **recomendável** [xekomẽ'davew] (*pl* **-eis**) ADJ

advisable

recompensa [xekõ'pẽsa] F (*prêmio*) reward; (*indenização*) recompense; **recompensar** [xekõpẽ'sa^r] VT (*premiar*) to reward; **recompensar alguém de algo** (*indenizar*) to compensate sb for sth

recompor [xekõ'po^r] (*irreg*) VT (*reorganizar*) to reorganize; (*restabelecer*) to restore

recôncavo [xe'kõkavu] M (*enseada*) bay area

reconciliação [xekõsilja'sãw] (*pl* -ões) F reconciliation

reconciliar [xekõsi'lja^r] VT to reconcile; **reconciliar-se** VR to become reconciled

recondicionar [xekõdʒisjo'na^r] VT to recondition

recôndito, -a [xe'kõdʒitu, a] ADJ (*escondido*) hidden; (*lugar*) secluded

reconfortar [xekõfox'ta^r] VT to invigorate; **reconfortar-se** VR to be invigorated

reconhecer [xekoɲe'se^r] VT to recognize; (*admitir*) to admit; (*Mil*) to reconnoitre (*Brit*), reconnoiter (*US*); (*assinatura*) to witness; **reconhecido, -a** [xekoɲe'sidu, a] ADJ recognized; (*agradecido*) grateful, thankful; **reconhecimento** [xekoɲesi'mẽtu] M recognition; (*admissão*) admission; (*gratidão*) gratitude; (*Mil*) reconnaissance; (*de assinatura*) witnessing; **reconhecível** [xekoɲe'sivew] (*pl* **-eis**) ADJ recognizable

reconquista [xekõ'kiʃta] F reconquest

reconsiderar [xekõside'ra^r] VT, VI to reconsider

reconstituinte [xekõʃtʃi'twĩtʃi] M tonic

reconstituir [xekõʃtʃi'twi^r] VT to reconstitute; (*doente*) to build up; (*crime*) to piece together

reconstrução [xekõʃtru'sãw] F reconstruction

reconstruir [xekõʃ'trwi^r] VT to rebuild, reconstruct

recontar [xekõ'ta^r] VT (*objetos, pessoas*) to recount; (*história*) to retell

recordação [xekoxda'sãw] (*pl* -ões) F (*reminiscência*) memory; (*objeto*) memento

recordar [xekox'da^r] VT (*relembrar*) to remember; (*parecer*) to look like; (*lição*) to revise; **recordar-se** VR: **recordar-se de** to remember; ~ **algo a alguém** to remind sb of sth

recorde [xe'kɔxdʒi] ADJ INV record *atr* ▪ M record; **em tempo** ~ in record time; **bater um** ~ to break a record

recordista [xekox'dʒiʃta] ADJ record-breaking ▪ M/F record-breaker; (*quem detém o recorde*) record-holder; ~ **mundial** world record-holder

recorrer [xeko'xe^r] VI: ~ **a** (*para socorro*) to turn to; (*valer-se de*) to resort to; ~ **da sentença/decisão** to appeal against the sentence/decision

recortar [xekox'ta^r] VT to cut out; **recorte** [xe'kɔxtʃi] M (*ato*) cutting out; (*de jornal*) cutting, clipping

recostar [xekoʃ'ta^r] VT to lean, rest; **recostar-se** VR to lean back; (*deitar-se*) to lie down

NB: *European Portuguese adds the following consonants to certain words:* **b** (sú(b)dito, su(b)til); **c** (a(c)ção, a(c)cionista, a(c)to); **m** (inde(m)ne); **p** (ado(p)çã, ado(p)tar); *for further details see p. xiii.*

recosto [xe'koʃtu] M back(rest)
recreação [xekrja'sãw] F recreation
recrear [xe'krja^r] VT to entertain, amuse;
recrear-se VR to have fun
recreativo, -a [xekrja'tʃivu, a] ADJ recreational
recreio [xe'kreju] M recreation; (Educ) playtime;
viagem de ~ trip, outing; **hora do ~** break
recriar [xe'krja^r] VT to recreate
recriminação [xekrimina'sãw] (pl -ões) F
recrimination
recriminador, a [xekrimina'do^r(a)] ADJ
reproving
recriminar [xekrimi'na^r] VT to reproach,
reprove
recrudescência [xekrude'sẽsja] F
= **recrudescimento**
recrudescer [xekrude'se^r] VI to grow worse,
worsen
recrudescimento [xekrudesi'mẽtu] M
worsening
recruta [xe'kruta] M/F recruit
recrutamento [xekruta'mẽtu] M recruitment
recrutar [xekru'ta^r] VT to recruit
rectângulo etc [xek'tãgulu] (PT) = **retângulo** etc
rectificar etc [xektifi'ka^r] (PT) = **retificar** etc
recto, -a ['xɛkto] (PT) = **reto** etc
récua ['xɛkwa] F (de mulas) pack, train; (de cavalos)
drove
recuado, -a [xe'kwadu, a] ADJ (prédio) set back
recuar [xe'kwa^r] VT to move back ■ VI to move
back; (exército) to retreat; (num intento) to back
out; (num compromisso) to backpedal; (ciência)
to regress; **~ a** ou **para** (no tempo) to return ou
regress to; (numa decisão, opinião) to back down to;
~ de (lugar) to move back from; (intenções, planos)
to back out of
recuo [xe'kuu] M retreat; (de ciência) regression;
(de intento) climbdown; (de um prédio) frontage
recuperação [xekupera'sãw] F recovery
recuperar [xekupe'ra^r] VT to recover; (tempo
perdido) to make up for; (reabilitar) to rehabilitate;
recuperar-se VR to recover; **~-se de** to recover
ou recuperate from
recurso [xe'kuxsu] M (meio) resource; (Jur)
appeal; **recursos** MPL (financeiros) resources;
em último ~ as a last resort; **o ~ à violência**
resorting to violence; **não há outro ~ contra a**
fome there is no other solution to famine; **~s**
próprios (Com) own resources
recusa [xe'kuza] F refusal; (negação) denial;
recusar [xeku'za^r] VT to refuse; (negar) to deny;
recusar-se VR: **recusar-se a** to refuse to;
recusar fazer to refuse to do; **recusar algo a**
alguém to refuse ou deny sb sth
redação [xeda'sãw] (PT -cç-, pl -ões) F (ato)
writing; (Educ) composition, essay; (redatores)
editorial staff; (lugar) editorial office
redactor, a [xeda'to^r(a)] (PT) M/F = **redator(a)**
etc
redargüir [xedax'gwi^r] VI to retort
redator, a [xeda'to^r(a)] M/F journalist; (editor)
editor; (quem redige) writer

redator, a M/F editor in chief
rede ['xedʒi] F net; (de salvamento) safety net; (de
cabelos) hairnet; (de dormir) hammock; (cilada)
trap; (Ferro, Tec, fig) network; **a R~** (a Internet) the
Net; **~ bancária** banking system; **~ de esgotos**
drainage system; **comunicar-se em ~ (com)**
(Comput) to network (with); **operação em ~**
(Comput) networking
rédea ['xɛdʒja] F rein; **dar ~ larga a** to give free
rein to; **tomar as ~s** (fig) to take control, take
over; **falar à ~ solta** to talk nineteen to the
dozen
redenção [xedē'sãw] F redemption
redentor, a [xedē'to^r(a)] ADJ redeeming ■ M/F
redeemer
redigir [xedʒi'ʒi^r] VT, VI to write
redime etc [xe'dʒimi] VB V **remir**
redimir [xedʒi'mi^r] VT (livrar) to free; (Rel) to
redeem
redobrar [xedo'bra^r] VT (dobrar de novo) to
fold again; (aumentar) to increase; (esforços)
to redouble; (sinos) to ring ■ VI to increase;
(intensificar) to intensify; to ring out
redoma [xe'dɔma] F glass dome
redondamente [xedõda'mẽtʃi] ADV
(completamente) completely
redondeza [xedõ'deza] F roundness;
redondezas FPL (arredores) surroundings
redondo, -a [xe'dõdu, a] ADJ round; (gordo)
plump
redor [xe'do^r] M: **ao** ou **em ~ (de)** around, round
about
redução [xedu'sãw] (pl -ões) F reduction;
(conversão: de moeda) conversion
redundância [xedũ'dãsja] F redundancy;
redundante [xedũ'dãtʃi] ADJ redundant
redundar [xedũ'da^r] VI: **~ em** (resultar em) to
result in
reduto [xe'dutu] M stronghold; (refúgio) haven
reduzido, -a [xedu'zidu, a] ADJ reduced;
(limitado) limited; (pequeno) small; **ficar ~ a** to be
reduced to
reduzir [xedu'zi^r] VT to reduce; (converter: dinheiro)
to convert; (abreviar) to abridge; **reduzir-se** VR:
reduzir-se a to be reduced to; (fig: resumir-se
em) to come down to; **"reduza a velocidade"**
"reduce speed now"
reedificar [xeedʒifi'ka^r] VT to rebuild
reeditar [xeedʒi'ta^r] VT (livro) to republish;
(repetir) to repeat
reeducar [xeedu'ka^r] VT to reeducate
reeleger [xeele'ʒe^r] VT to re-elect; **reeleger-se**
VR to be re-elected
reeleição [xeelej'sãw] F re-election
reelejo etc [xee'leʒu] VB V **reeleger**
reembolsar [xeẽbow'sa^r] VT (reaver) to recover;
(restituir) to reimburse; (depósito) to refund; **~**
alguem de algo ou **algo a alguém** to reimburse
sb for sth; **reembolso** [xeẽ'bowsu] M (de depósito)
refund; (de despesa) reimbursement; **reembolso**
postal cash on delivery
reencarnação [xeẽkaxna'sãw] F reincarnation

reencarnar [xeẽkax'na^r] VI to be reincarnated

reencontrar [xeẽkõ'tra^r] VT to meet again;
reencontrar-se VR: **reencontrar-se (com)** to
meet up (with)

reencontro [xeẽ'kõtru] M reunion

reentrância [xeẽ'trãsja] F recess

reescalonamento [xeeʃkalona'mẽtu] M
rescheduling

reescalonar [xeeʃkalo'na^r] VT (*dívida*) to
reschedule

reescrever [xeeʃkre've^r] VT to rewrite

reexaminar [xeezami'na^r] VT to re-examine

refaço etc [xe'fasu] VB V **refazer**

refastelado, -a [xefaʃte'ladu, a] ADJ stretched
out

refastelar-se [xefaʃte'laxsi] VR to stretch out,
lounge

refazer [xefa'ze^r] (*irreg*) VT (*trabalho*) to redo;
(*consertar*) to repair, fix; (*forças*) to restore;
(*finanças*) to recover; (*vida*) to rebuild; **refazer-
se** VR (*Med etc*) to recover; **~-se de despesas** to
recover one's expenses

refeição [xefej'sãw] (*pl* -ões) F meal; **na hora da
~** at mealtimes

refeito, -a [xe'fejtu, a] PP *de* **refazer**

refeitório [xefej'tɔrju] M dining hall, refectory

refém [xe'fẽ] (*pl* -ns) M hostage

referência [xefe'rẽsja] F reference; **referências**
FPL (*informaçoes para emprego*) references; **com ~
a** with reference to, about; **fazer ~ a** to make
reference to, refer to

referendar [xeferẽ'da^r] VT to countersign,
endorse; (*aprovar: tratado etc*) to ratify

referendum [xefe'rẽdũ] M (*Pol*) referendum

referente [xefe'rẽtʃi] ADJ: **~ a** concerning,
regarding

referido, -a [xefe'ridu, a] ADJ aforesaid, already
mentioned

referir [xefe'ri^r] VT (*contar*) to relate, tell; **referir-
se** VR: **referir-se a** to refer to

REFESA F (= *Rede Ferroviária SA*) ≈ BR

refestelar-se [xefeʃte'laxsi] VR = **refastelar-se**

refez [xe'feʒ] VB V **refazer**

refil [xe'fiw] (*pl* -is) M refill

refiz [xe'fiʒ] VB V **refazer**

refinado, -a [xefi'nadu, a] ADJ refined

refinamento [xefina'mẽtu] M refinement

refinanciamento [xefinãsja'mẽtu] M
refinancing

refinanciar [xefinã'sja^r] VT to refinance

refinar [xefi'na^r] VT to refine

refinaria [xefina'ria] F refinery

refiro etc [xe'firu] VB V **referir**

refis [xe'fiʃ] MPL *de* **refil**

refizer etc [xefi'ze^r] VB V **refazer**

refletido, -a [xefle'tʃidu, a] (PT -**ct**-) ADJ
reflected; (*prudente*) thoughtful; (*ação*) prudent,
shrewd

refletir [xefle'tʃi^r] (PT -**ct**-) VT (*espelhar*) to reflect;

(*som*) to echo; (*fig: revelar*) to reveal ■ VI: **~ em** *ou*
sobre (*pensar*) to consider, think about; **refletir-
se** VR to be reflected; **~-se em** (*repercutir-se*) to
have implications for

refletor, a [xefle'to^r(a)] (PT -**ct**-) ADJ reflecting
■ M reflector

reflexão [xeflek'sãw] (*pl* -ões) F reflection;
(*meditação*) thought, reflection

reflexivo, -a [xeflek'sivu, a] ADJ reflexive

reflexo, -a [xe'flɛksu, a] ADJ (*luz*) reflected; (*ação*)
reflex ■ M reflection; (*Anat*) reflex; (*no cabelo*)
streak

reflexões [xeflek'sõjʃ] FPL *de* **reflexão**

reflito etc [xe'flitu] VB V **refletir**

refluxo [xe'fluksu] M ebb

refogado, -a [xefo'gadu, a] ADJ sautéed ■ M
(*molho*) tomatoes, onion, garlic and herbs fried together;
(*prato*) stew

refogar [xefo'ga^r] VT to sauté

reforçado, -a [xefox'sadu, a] ADJ reinforced;
(*pessoa*) strong; (*café da manhã, jantar*) hearty

reforçar [xefox'sa^r] VT to reinforce; (*revigorar*) to
invigorate; **reforço** [xe'foxsu] M reinforcement

reforma [xe'fɔxma] F reform; (*Arq*) renovation;
(*Rel*) reformation; (*Mil*) retirement; **fazer ~s em
casa** to have building work done in the house;
o banheiro está em ~ the bathroom is being
done up; **~ agrária** land reform; **~ ministerial**
cabinet reshuffle; **reformado, -a** [xefox'madu,
a] ADJ reformed; (*Arq*) renovated; (*Mil*) retired;
reformar [xefox'ma^r] VT to reform; (*Arq*) to
renovate; (*Mil*) to retire; (*sentença*) to commute;
reformar-se VR (*militar*) to retire; (*criminoso*) to
reform, mend one's ways

reformatar [xefoxma'ta^r] VT to reformat

reformatório [xefoxma'tɔrju] M reformatory,
approved school (*Brit*)

refractário, -a [xefra'tarju, a] (PT) ADJ
= **refratário**

refrão [xe'frãw] (*pl* -ãos) M (*cantado*) chorus,
refrain; (*provérbio*) saying

refratário, -a [xefra'tarju, a] ADJ (*rebelde*)
difficult, unmanageable; (*Tec*) heat-resistant;
(*Culin*) ovenproof; **ser ~ a** (*admoestações etc*) to be
impervious to

refrear [xefre'a^r] VT (*cavalo*) to rein in; (*inimigo*)
to contain, check; (*paixões, raiva*) to control;
refrear-se VR to restrain o.s.; **~ a língua** to
mind one's language

refrega [xe'frega] F fight

refrescante [xefreʃ'kãtʃi] ADJ refreshing

refrescar [xefreʃ'ka^r] VT (*ar, ambiente*) to cool;
(*pessoa*) to refresh ■ VI to cool down; **refrescar-
se** VR to refresh o.s.

refresco [xe'freʃku] M cool fruit drink, squash;
refrescos MPL (*refrigerantes*) refreshments

refrigeração [xefriʒera'sãw] F cooling;
(*de alimentos*) refrigeration; (*de casa*) air
conditioning

NB: *European Portuguese adds the following consonants to certain words:* **b** (sú(b)dito, su(b)til); **c** (a(c)ção,
a(c)cionista, a(c)to); **m** (inde(m)ne); **p** (ado(p)çã, ado(p)tar); *for further details see p. xiii.*

refrigerado, -a [xefriʒe'radu, a] ADJ cooled; (*casa*) air-conditioned; (*alimentos*) refrigerated; ~ **a ar** air-cooled

refrigerador [xefriʒera'doʳ] M refrigerator, fridge (*Brit*)

refrigerante [xefriʒe'rãtʃi] M soft drink

refrigerar [xefriʒe'raʳ] VT to keep cool; (*com geladeira*) to refrigerate; (*casa*) to air-condition

refrigério [xefri'ʒɛrju] M solace, consolation

refugar [xefu'gaʳ] VT (*alimentos*) to reject; (*proposta, conselho*) to reject, dismiss ▪ VI (*cavalo*) to balk; (*Hipismo*) to refuse

refugiado, -a [xefu'ʒjadu, a] ADJ, M/F refugee

refugiar-se [xefu'ʒjaxsi] VR to take refuge; ~ **na leitura** *etc* to seek solace in reading *etc*; **refúgio** [xe'fuʒju] M refuge

refugo [xe'fugu] M rubbish, garbage (*US*); (*mercadoria*) reject

refulgência [xefuw'ʒẽsja] F brilliance

refulgir [xefuw'ʒiʳ] VI to shine

refutação [xefuta'sãw] (*pl* -ões) F refutation

refutar [xefu'taʳ] VT to refute

reg ABR = **regimento**; = **regular**

rega ['xɛga] F watering; (*PT*: *irrigação*) irrigation

regaço [xe'gasu] M (*colo*) lap

regador [xega'doʳ] M watering can

regalado, -a [xega'ladu, a] ADJ (*encantado*) delighted; (*confortável*) comfortable ▪ ADV comfortably

regalar [xega'laʳ] VT (*causar prazer*) to delight; **regalar-se** VR (*divertir-se*) to enjoy o.s.; (*alegrar-se*) to be delighted; ~ **alguém com algo** to give sb sth, present sb with sth

regalia [xega'lia] F privilege

regalo [xe'galu] M (*presente*) present; (*prazer*) pleasure, treat

regar [xe'gaʳ] VT (*plantas, jardim*) to water; (*umedecer*) to sprinkle; ~ **o jantar a vinho** to wash one's dinner down with wine

regata [xe'gata] F regatta

regatear [xega'tʃjaʳ] VT (*o preço*) to haggle over, bargain for ▪ VI to haggle

regateio [xega'teju] M haggling

regato [xe'gatu] M brook, stream

regência [xe'ʒẽsja] F regency; (*Ling*) government; (*Mús*) conducting

regeneração [xeʒenera'sãw] F regeneration; (*de criminosos*) reform

regenerar [xeʒene'raʳ] VT to regenerate; (*criminoso*) to reform; **regenerar-se** VR to regenerate; to reform

regente [xe'ʒẽtʃi] M (*Pol*) regent; (*de orquestra*) conductor; (*de banda*) leader

reger [xe'ʒeʳ] VT to govern, rule; (*regular, Ling*) to govern; (*orquestra*) to conduct; (*empresa*) to run ▪ VI (*governar*) to rule; (*maestro*) to conduct; ~ **uma cadeira** (*Educ*) to hold a chair

região [xe'ʒjãw] (*pl* -ões) F region; (*de uma cidade*) area

regime [xe'ʒimi] M (*Pol*) regime; (*dieta*) diet; (*maneira*) way; **meu ~ agora é levantar cedo** my routine now is to get up early; **fazer ~** to diet;

estar de ~ to be on a diet; **o ~ das prisões/dos hospitais** the prison/hospital system; ~ **de vida** way of life

regimento [xeʒi'mẽtu] M regiment; (*regras*) regulations *pl*, rules *pl*; ~ **interno** (*de empresa*) company rules *pl*

régio, -a ['xɛʒju, a] ADJ (*real*) royal; (*digno do rei*) regal; (*suntuoso*) princely

regiões [xe'ʒjõjʃ] FPL *de* **região**

regional [xeʒjo'naw] (*pl* -ais) ADJ regional

registrador, a [xeʒiʃtra'doʳ(a)] (PT -ista-) M/F registrar, recorder ▪ F: (**caixa**) ~**a** cash register, till

registrar [xeʒiʃ'traʳ] (PT -ista-) VT to register; (*anotar*) to record; (*com máquina registradora*) to ring up

registro [xe'ʒiʃtru] (PT -to-) M (*ato*) registration; (: *anotação*) recording; (*livro, Ling*) register; (*histórico, Comput*) record; (*relógio*) meter; (*Mús*) range; (*torneira*) stopcock; ~ **civil** registry office

rego ['xegu] M (*para água*) ditch; (*de arado*) furrow; (*col!*) crack

reg° ABR = **regulamento**

regozijar [xegozi'ʒaʳ] VT to gladden; **regozijar-se** VR to be delighted, rejoice

regozijo [xego'ziʒu] M joy, delight

regra ['xɛgra] F rule; **regras** FPL (*Med*) periods; **sair da** ~ to step out of line; **em** ~ as a rule, usually; **por via de** ~ as a rule

regrado, -a [xe'gradu, a] ADJ (*sensato*) sensible

regravável [xegra'vavew] (*pl* -eis) ADJ rewritable

regredir [xegre'dʒiʳ] VI to regress; (*doença*) to retreat

regressão [xegre'sãw] F regression

regressar [xegre'saʳ] VI to come (*ou* go) back, return

regressivo, -a [xegre'sivu, a] ADJ regressive; **contagem regressiva** countdown

regresso [xe'grɛsu] M return

regrido *etc* [xe'gridu] VB V **regredir**

régua ['xɛgwa] F ruler; ~ **de calcular** slide rule

regulador, a [xegula'doʳ(a)] ADJ regulating ▪ M regulator

regulagem [xegu'laʒẽ] F (*de motor, carro*) tuning

regulamentação [xegulamẽta'sãw] F regulation; (*regras*) regulations *pl*

regulamento [xegula'mẽtu] M rules *pl*, regulations *pl*

regular [xegu'laʳ] ADJ regular; (*estatura*) average, medium; (*tamanho*) normal; (*razoável*) not bad ▪ VT to regulate; (*reger*) to govern; (*máquina*) to adjust; (*carro, motor*) to tune; (*relógio*) to put right ▪ VI to work, function; **regular-se** VR: **regular-se por** to be guided by; **ele não regula (bem)** he's not quite right in the head; ~ **por** to be about; ~ **com alguém** to be about the same age as sb; **regularidade** [xegulari'dadʒi] F regularity

regularizar [xegulari'zaʳ] VT to regularize

regurgitar [xeguxʒi'taʳ] VT, VI to regurgitate

rei [xej] M king; **ele é o** ~ **da bagunça** (*col*)

he's the world's worst for untidiness; **ter o ~ na barriga** to be full of oneself; **Dia de R-s** Epiphany; **R~ Momo** carnival king

reimprimir [xeĩpri'mi^r] vt to reprint

reinado [xej'nadu] м reign

reinar [xej'na^r] vi to reign; (fig) to reign, prevail

reincidência [xeĩsi'dẽsja] ϝ backsliding; (de criminoso) recidivism

reincidir [xeĩsi'dʒi^r] vi to relapse; (criminoso) to re-offend; **~ em erro** to do wrong again

reingressar [xeĩgre'sa^r] vi: **~ (em)** to re-enter

reiniciar [xejni'sja^r] vt to restart

reino ['xejnu] м kingdom; (fig) realm; **~ animal** animal kingdom; **o R~ Unido** the United Kingdom

reintegrar [xeĩte'gra^r] vt (em emprego) to reinstate; (reconduzir) to return, restore

reiterar [xeite'ra^r] vt to reiterate, repeat

reitor, a [xej'to^r(a)] м/ϝ (de uma universidade) vicechancellor (Brit), president (US) ■ м (PT: pároco) rector

reitoria [xejto'ria] ϝ (de universidade: cargo) vicechancellorship (Brit), presidency (US); (gabinete) vice-chancellor's (Brit) ou president's (US) office

reivindicação [xejvĩdʒika'sãw] (pl -ões) ϝ claim, demand

reivindicar [rejvĩdʒi'ka^r] vt to claim; (aumento salarial, direitos) to demand

rejeição [xeʒej'sãw] (pl -ões) ϝ rejection

rejeitar [xeʒej'ta^r] vt to reject; (recusar) to refuse

rejo etc ['xeju] vb v **reger**

rejubilar [xeʒubi'la^r] vt to fill with joy ■ vi to rejoice; **rejubilar-se** vr to rejoice

rejuvenescedor, a [xeʒuvenese'do^r(a)] ADJ rejuvenating

rejuvenescer [xeʒuvene'se^r] vt to rejuvenate ■ vi to be rejuvenated; **rejuvenescer-se** vr to be rejuvenated

relação [xela'sãw] (pl -ões) ϝ relation; (conexão) connection, relationship; (relacionamento) relationship; (Mat) ratio; (lista) list; **com** ou **em ~ a** regarding, with reference to; **ter relações com alguém** to have intercourse with sb; **relações públicas** public relations

relacionado, -a [xelasjo'nadu, a] ADJ (listado) listed; (ligado) related, connected; **uma pessoa bem** ou **muito relacionada** a well-connected person

relacionamento [xelasjona'mẽtu] м relationship

relacionar [xelasjo'na^r] vt (listar) to make a list of; (ligar): **~ algo com algo** to connect sth with sth, relate sth to sth; **relacionar-se** vr to be connected ou related; **~ alguém com alguém** to bring sb into contact with sb; **~-se com** (ligar-se) to be connected with, have to do with; (conhecer) to become acquainted with

relaçoes [xela'sõjʃ] FPL de **relação**

relações-públicas м/ϝ INV PR person

relâmpago [xe'lãpagu] м flash of lightning ■ ADJ INV (visita) lightning atr; **relâmpagos** MPL (clarões) lightning sg; **passar como um ~** to flash past; **como um ~** like lightning, as quick as a flash

relampejar [xelãpe'ʒa^r] vi to flash; **relampejou** the lightning flashed

relance [xe'lãsi] м glance; **olhar de ~** to glance at

relapso, -a [xe'lapsu, a] ADJ (reincidente) recidivous; (negligente) negligent

relatar [xela'ta^r] vt to give an account of

relativo, -a [xela'tʃivu, a] ADJ relative

relato [xe'latu] м account

relator, a [xela'to^r(a)] м/ϝ storyteller

relatório [xela'tɔrju] м report; **~ anual** (Com) annual report

relaxado, -a [xela'ʃadu, a] ADJ relaxed; (desleixado) slovenly, sloppy; (relapso) negligent

relaxamento [xelaʃa'mẽtu] м relaxation; (de moral, costumes) debasement; (desleixo) slovenliness; (de relapsos) negligence

relaxante [xela'ʃãtʃi] ADJ relaxing ■ м tranquillizer

relaxar [xela'ʃa^r] vt to relax; (moral, costumes) to debase ■ vi to relax; (tornar-se negligente): **~ (em)** to grow complacent (in); **~ com** (transigir) to acquiesce in

relaxe [xe'laʃi] м relaxation

relê [xe'le] vb v **reler**

relegar [xele'ga^r] vt to relegate

releio etc [xe'leju] vb v **reler**

relembrar [xelẽ'bra^r] vt to recall

relento [xe'lẽtu] м: **ao ~** out of doors

reler [xe'le^r] (irreg) vt to reread

reles ['xɛliʃ] ADJ INV (gente) common, vulgar; (comportamento) despicable; (mero) mere

relevância [xele'vãsja] ϝ relevance

relevante [xele'vãtʃi] ADJ relevant

relevar [xele'va^r] vt (tornar saliente) to emphasize; (atenuar) to relieve; (desculpar) to pardon, forgive

relevo [xe'levu] м relief; (fig) prominence, importance; **pôr em ~** to emphasize

reli [xe'li] vb v **reler**

relicário [xeli'karju] м reliquary, shrine

relido, -a [xe'lido, a] PP de **reler**

religião [xeli'ʒãw] (pl -ões) ϝ religion; **religioso, -a** [xeli'ʒozu, ɔza] ADJ religious; (casamento) church atr ■ м/ϝ religious person; (frade/freira) monk/nun ■ м (casamento) church wedding

relinchar [xelĩ'ʃa^r] vt to neigh

relincho [xe'lĩʃu] м (som) neigh; (ato) neighing

relíquia [xe'likja] ϝ relic; **~ de família** family heirloom

relógio [xe'lɔʒu] м clock; (de gás) meter; **~ de pé** grandfather clock; **~ de ponto** time clock; **~ (de pulso)** (wrist)watch; **~ de sol** sundial; **corrida contra o ~** race against the clock

NB: European Portuguese adds the following consonants to certain words: **b** (sú(b)dito, su(b)til); **c** (a(c)ção, a(c)cionista, a(c)to); **m** (inde(m)ne); **p** (ado(p)çã, ado(p)tar); for further details see p. xiii.

relojoaria [xeloʒwa'ria] F watchmaker's, watch shop

relojoeiro, -a [xelo'ʒwejru, a] M/F watchmaker, clockmaker

relutância [xelu'tãsja] F reluctance

relutante [xelu'tãtʃi] ADJ reluctant

relutar [xelu'ta'] VI: ~ **(em fazer)** to be reluctant (to do); ~ **contra algo** to be reluctant to accept sth

reluzente [xelu'zẽtʃi] ADJ brilliant, shining

reluzir [xelu'zi'] VI to gleam, shine

relva ['xɛwva] F grass; (terreno gramado) lawn

relvado [xew'vadu] (PT) M lawn

rem ABR (= remetente) sender

remador, a [xema'do'(a)] M/F rower, oarsman/woman

remanchar [xemã'ʃa'] VI to delay, take one's time

remanescente [xemane'sẽtʃi] ADJ remaining ■ M remainder; (excesso) surplus

remanescer [xemane'se'] VI to remain

remanso [xe'mãsu] M (pausa) pause, rest; (sossego) stillness, quiet; (água) backwater

remar [xe'ma'] VT to row; (canoa) to paddle ■ VI to row; ~ **contra a maré** (fig) to swim against the tide

remarcação [xemaxka'sãw] F (de preços) changing; (de artigos) repricing; (artigos remarcados) repriced goods pl

remarcar [xemax'ka'] VT (preços) to adjust; (artigos) to reprice

rematado, -a [xema'tadu, a] ADJ (concluído) completed

rematar [xema'ta'] VT to finish off; **remate** [xe'matʃi] M (fim) end; (acabamento) finishing touch; (Arq) coping; (fig: cume) peak; (de piada) punch line

remedeio etc [xeme'deju] VB V **remediar**

remediado, -a [xeme'dʒjadu, a] ADJ comfortably off

remediar [xeme'dʒja'] VT (corrigir) to put right, remedy

remediável [xeme'dʒjavew] (pl -eis) ADJ rectifiable

remédio [xe'mɛdʒju] M (medicamento) medicine; (recurso, solução) remedy; (Jur) recourse; **não tem** ~ there's no way; **que ~?** what else can one do?; ~ **caseiro** home remedy

remela [xe'mɛla] F (nos olhos) sleep

remelento, -a [xeme'lẽtu, a] ADJ bleary-eyed

remelexo [xeme'leʃu] M (requebro) swaying

rememorar [xememo'ra'] VT to remember

rememorável [xememo'ravew] (pl -eis) ADJ memorable

remendar [xemẽ'da'] VT to mend; (com pano) to patch; **remendo** [xe'mẽdu] M repair; (de pano) patch

remessa [xe'mɛsa] F (Com) shipment; (de dinheiro) remittance

remetente [xeme'tẽtʃi] M/F (de carta) sender; (Com) shipper

remeter [xeme'te'] VT (expedir) to send, dispatch;

(dinheiro) to remit; (entregar) to hand over; **remeter-se** VR: **remeter-se a** (referir-se) to refer to

remexer [xeme'ʃe'] VT (papéis) to shuffle; (sacudir: braços) to wave; (folhas) to shake; (revolver: areia, lama) to stir up ■ VI: ~ **em** to rummage through; **remexer-se** VR (mover-se) to move around; (rebolar-se) to sway

remição [xemi'sãw] F redemption

reminiscência [xemini'sẽsja] F reminiscence

remir [xe'mi'] VT (coisa penhorada, Rel) to redeem; (livrar) to free; (danos, perdas) to make good; **remir-se** VR (pecador) to redeem o.s.

remissão [xemi'sãw] (pl -ões) F (Com, Rel) redemption; (compensação) payment; (num livro) cross-reference

remisso, -a [xe'misu, a] ADJ remiss; ~ **em fazer** (lento) slow to do

remissões [xemi'sõjʃ] FPL de **remissão**

remível [xe'mivew] (pl -eis) ADJ redeemable

remo ['xɛmu] M oar; (de canoa) paddle; (Esporte) rowing

remoa etc [xe'moa] VB V **remoer**

remoção [xemo'sãw] F removal

remoçar [xemo'sa'] VT to rejuvenate ■ VI to be rejuvenated

remoer [xe'mwe'] VT (café) to regrind; (no pensamento) to turn over in one's mind; (amofinar) to eat away; **remoer-se** VR (amofinar-se) to be consumed ou eaten away

remoinho [xemo'iɲu] M = **rodamoinho**

remontar [xemõ'ta'] VT (elevar) to raise; (tornar a armar) to re-assemble ■ VI (em cavalo) to remount; ~ **ao passado** to return to the past; ~ **ao século XV** etc to date back to the 15th century etc; ~ **o vôo** to soar

remoque [xe'mɔki] M gibe, taunt

remorso [xe'mɔxsu] M remorse

remoto, -a [xe'mɔtu, a] ADJ remote, far off; (controle, Comput) remote

remover [xemo've'] VT (mover) to move; (transferir) to transfer; (demitir) to dismiss; (retirar, afastar) to remove; (terra) to churn up

remuneração [xemunera'sãw] (pl -ões) F remuneration; (salário) wage

remunerador, a [xemunera'do'(a)] ADJ remunerative; (recompensador) rewarding

remunerar [xemune'ra'] VT to remunerate; (premiar) to reward

rena ['xɛna] F reindeer

renal [xe'naw] (pl -ais) ADJ renal, kidney atr

Renamo [xe'namu] ABR F = **Resistência Nacional Moçambicana**

Renascença [xena'sẽsa] F: **a** ~ the Renaissance

renascer [xena'se'] VI to be reborn; (fig) to revive

renascimento [xenasi'mẽtu] M rebirth; (fig) revival; **o R**~ the Renaissance

Renavam (BR) ABR M = **Registro Nacional de Veículos Automotores**

renda ['xẽda] F income; (nacional) revenue; (de aplicação, locação) yield; (tecido) lace; ~ **bruta/líquida** gross/net income; **imposto de** ~ (BR) income tax; ~ **per capita** per capita income

rendado, -a [xẽ'dadu, a] ADJ lace-trimmed; (*com aspecto de renda*) lacy ■ M lacework

rendeiro, -a [xẽ'dejru, a] M/F lacemaker

render [xẽ'de^r] VT (*lucro, dinheiro*) to bring in, yield; (*preço*) to fetch; (*homenagem*) to pay; (*graças*) to give; (*serviços*) to render; (*armas*) to surrender; (*guarda*) to relieve; (*causar*) to bring ■ VI (*dar lucro*) to pay; (*trabalho*) to be productive; (*comida*) to go a long way; (*conversa, caso*) to go on, last; **render-se** VR to surrender

rendez-vous [xãde'vu] M INV = **randevu**

rendição [xẽdʒi'sãw] F surrender

rendido, -a [xẽ'dʒidu, a] ADJ subdued

rendimento [xẽdʒi'mẽtu] M (*renda*) income; (*lucro*) profit; (*juro*) yield, interest; (*produtividade*) productivity; (*de máquina*) efficiency; (*de um produto*) value for money; ~ **por ação** (*Com*) earnings per share, earnings yield; ~ **de capital** (*Com*) return on capital

rendoso, -a [xẽ'dozu, ɔza] ADJ profitable

renegado, -a [xene'gadu, a] ADJ, M/F renegade

renegar [xene'ga^r] VT (*crença*) to renounce; (*detestar*) to hate; (*trair*) to betray; (*negar*) to deny; (*desprezar*) to reject

renhido, -a [xe'ɲidu, a] ADJ hard-fought; (*batalha*) bloody

renitência [xeni'tẽsja] F obstinacy

renitente [xeni'tẽtʃi] ADJ obstinate, stubborn

Reno ['xenu] M: **o** ~ the Rhine

renomado, -a [xeno'madu, a] ADJ renowned

renome [xe'nɔmi] M fame, renown; **de** ~ renowned

renovação [xenova'sãw] (*pl* -ões) F renewal; (*Arq*) renovation

renovar [xeno'va^r] VT to renew; (*Arq*) to renovate; (*ensino, empresa*) to revamp ■ VI to be renewed

renque ['xẽki] M row

rentabilidade [xẽtabili'dadʒi] F profitability

rentável [xẽ'tavew] (*pl* -eis) ADJ profitable

rente ['xẽtʃi] ADJ (*cabelo*) close-cropped; (*casa*) nearby ■ ADV close; (*muito curto*) very short; ~ **a** close by

renúncia [xe'nũsja] F renunciation; (*de cargo*) resignation; ~ **a um direito** waiver (of a right)

renunciar [xenũ'sja^r] VT to give up, renounce ■ VI to resign; (*abandonar*): ~ **a algo** to give sth up; (*direito*) to surrender sth; (*fé, crença*) to renounce sth

reorganizar [xeoxgani'za^r] VT to reorganize

reouve *etc* [xe'ovi] VB V **reaver**

reouver *etc* [xeo've^r] VB V **reaver**

reparação [xepara'sãw] (*pl* -ões) F (*conserto*) mending, repairing; (*de mal, erros*) remedying; (*de prejuizos, ofensa*) making amends; (*fig*) amends *pl*, reparation

reparar [xepa'ra^r] VT (*consertar*) to repair; (*forças*) to restore; (*mal, erros*) to remedy; (*prejuizo, danos,*

ofensa) to make amends for; (*notar*) to notice ■ VI: ~ **em** to notice; **não repare em** pay no attention to; **repare em** (*olhe*) look at; **reparo** [xe'paru] M (*conserto*) repair; (*crítica*) criticism; (*observação*) observation

repartição [xepaxtʃi'sãw] (*pl* -ões) F (*ato*) distribution; (*seção*) department; (*escritório*) office; ~ (**pública**) government department

repartir [xepax'tʃi^r] VT (*distribuir*) to distribute; (*dividir entre vários*) to share out; (*dividir em várias porções*) to divide up; (*cabelo*) to part; **repartir-se** VR (*dividir-se*) to divide

repassar [xepa'sa^r] VT (*ponte, fronteira*) to go over again; (*lição*) to revise, go over ■ VI to go by again; **passar e** ~ to go back and forth

repasto [xe'paʃtu] M (*refeição*) meal, repast; (*banquete*) feast

repatriar [xepa'trja^r] VT to repatriate; **repatriar-se** VR to go back home

repelão [xepe'lãw] (*pl* -ões) M push, shove; **de** ~ brusquely

repelente [xepe'lẽtʃi] ADJ, M repellent

repelir [xepe'li^r] VT to repel; (*curiosos*) to drive away; (*idéias, atitudes*) to reject, repudiate; **seu estômago repele certos alimentos** his stomach cannot take certain foods

repelões [xepe'lõjʃ] FPL **de repelão**

repensar [xepẽ'sa^r] VI to reconsider, rethink

repente [xe'pẽtʃi] M outburst; **de** ~ suddenly; (*col: talvez*) maybe

repentino, -a [xepẽ'tʃinu, a] ADJ sudden

repercussão [xepexku'sãw] (*pl* -ões) F repercussion

repercutir [xepexku'tʃi^r] VT (*som*) to echo ■ VI (*som*) to reverberate, echo; (*fig*): ~ (**em**) to have repercussions (on)

repertório [xepex'tɔrju] M (*lista*) list; (*coleção*) collection; (*Mús*) repertoire

repetição [xepetʃi'sãw] (*pl* -ões) F repetition

repetidamente [xepetʃida'mẽtʃi] ADJ repeatedly

repetido, -a [xepe'tʃidu, a] ADJ repeated; **repetidas vezes** repeatedly, again and again

repetir [xepe'tʃi^r] VT to repeat; (*vestido*) to wear again ■ VI (*ao comer*) to have seconds; **repetir-se** VR (*acontecer de novo*) to happen again; (*pessoa*) to repeat o.s.; **repetitivo, -a** [xepetʃi'tʃivu, a] ADJ repetitive

repicar [xepi'ka^r] VT (*sinos*) to ring ■ VI to ring (out)

repilo *etc* [xe'pilu] VB V **repelir**

repimpado, -a [xepĩ'padu, a] ADJ (*refestelado*) lolling; (*satisfeito*) full up

repique [xe'piki] M (*de sinos*) peal; ~ **falso** false alarm

repique *etc* VB V **repicar**

repisar [xepi'za^r] VT (*repetir*) to repeat; (*uvas*) to tread ■ VI: ~ **em** (*assunto*) to keep on about, harp on

---

NB: *European Portuguese adds the following consonants to certain words:* **b** (sú(b)dito, su(b)til); **c** (a(c)ção, a(c)cionista, a(c)to); **m** (inde(m)ne); **p** (ado(p)çã, ado(p)tar); *for further details see p. xiii.*

716

repito etc [xe'pitu] VB V **repetir**
replay [xe'plei] (pl-s) M (TV) (action) replay
repleto, -a [xe'plɛtu, a] ADJ replete, full up
réplica ['xeplika] F (cópia) replica; (contestação) reply, retort
replicar [xepli'ka^r] VT to answer, reply to ■ VI to reply, answer back
repõe etc [xe'põj] VB V **repor**
repolho [xe'poʎu] M cabbage
repomos [xe'pomoʃ] VB V **repor**
reponho etc [xe'poɲu] VB V **repor**
repontar [xepõ'ta^r] VI (aparecer) to appear
repor [xe'po^r] (irreg) VT to put back, replace; (restituir) to return; **repor-se** VR (pessoa) to recover
reportagem [xepox'taʒẽ] (pl-ns) F (ato) reporting; (notícia) report; (repórteres) reporters pl
reportar [xepox'ta^r] VT: ~ **a** (o pensamento) to take back to; (atribuir) to attribute to; **reportar-se** VR: **reportar-se a** to refer to; (relacionar-se a) to be connected with
repórter [xe'pɔxte^r] M/F reporter
repôs [xe'poʃ] VB V **repor**
reposição [xepozi'sãw] (pl-ões) F replacement; (restituição) return; ~ **salarial** wage adjustment
repositório [xepozi'tɔrju] M repository
reposto, -a [xe'poʃtu, 'poʃta] PP de **repor**
repousar [xepo'za^r] VI to rest; **repouso** [xe'pozu] M rest
repreender [xeprjẽ'de^r] VT to reprimand
repreensão [xeprjẽ'sãw] (pl-ões) F rebuke, reprimand
repreensível [xeprjẽ'sivew] (pl-eis) ADJ reprehensible
repreensões [xeprjẽ'sõjʃ] FPL de **repreensão**
represa [xe'preza] F dam
represália [xepre'zalja] F reprisal
representação [xeprezẽta'sãw] (pl-ões) F representation; (representantes) representatives pl; (Teatro) performance; (atuação do ator) acting; **representante** [xeprezẽ'tãtʃi] M/F representative
representar [xeprezẽ'ta^r] VT to represent; (Teatro: papel) to play; (: encenar) to put on ■ VI (ator) to act; (tb: Jur) to make a complaint; **representativo, -a** [xeprezẽta'tʃivu, a] ADJ representative
repressão [xepre'sãw] (pl-ões) F repression
repressivo, -a [xepre'sivu, a] ADJ repressive
repressões [xepre'sõjʃ] FPL de **repressão**
reprimido, -a [xepri'midu, a] ADJ repressed
reprimir [xepri'mi^r] VT to repress; (lágrimas) to keep back
reprise [xe'prizi] F reshowing
réprobo, -a ['xɛprobu, a] ADJ, M/F reprobate
reprodução [xeprodu'sãw] (pl-ões) F reproduction
reprodutor, a [xeprodu'to^r(a)] ADJ reproductive
reproduzir [xeprodu'zi^r] VT to reproduce; (repetir) to repeat; **reproduzir-se** VR to breed, multiply; to be repeated
reprovação [xeprova'sãw] (pl-ões) F

disapproval; (em exame) failure
reprovado, -a [xepro'vadu, a] M/F failed candidate, failure; **taxa de ~s** failure rate
reprovador, a [xeprova'do^r(a)] ADJ (olhar) disapproving, reproving
reprovar [xepro'va^r] VT (condenar) to disapprove of; (aluno) to fail
réptil ['xɛptʃiw] (pl-eis) M reptile
repto ['xɛptu] M challenge, provocation
república [xe'publika] F republic; ~ **de estudantes** students' house; ~ **popular** people's republic; **republicano, -a** [xepubli'kanu, a] ADJ, M/F republican
repudiar [xepu'dʒja^r] VT to repudiate, reject; (abandonar) to disown; **repúdio** [xe'pudʒju] M rejection, repudiation
repugnância [xepug'nãsja] F repugnance; (por comida etc) disgust; (aversão) aversion; (moral) abhorrence
repugnante [xepug'nãtʃi] ADJ repugnant, repulsive
repugnar [xepug'na^r] VT to oppose ■ VI to be repulsive; ~ **a alguém** to disgust sb; (moralmente) to be repugnant to sb
repulsa [xe'puwsa] F (ato) rejection; (sentimento) repugnance; (física) repulsion
repulsão [xepuw'sãw] (pl-ões) F repulsion; (rejeição) rejection
repulsivo, -a [xepuw'sivu, a] ADJ repulsive
repulsões [xepuw'sõjʃ] FPL de **repulsão**
repunha etc [xe'puɲa] VB V **repor**
repus etc [xe'puʃ] VB V **repor**
repuser etc [xepu'ze^r] VB V **repor**
reputação [reputa'sãw] (pl-ões) F reputation
reputado, -a [xepu'tadu, a] ADJ renowned
reputar [xepu'ta^r] VT to consider, regard as
repuxado, -a [xepu'ʃadu, a] ADJ (pele) tight, firm; (olhos) slanted
repuxar [xepu'ʃa^r] VT (puxar) to tug; (esticar) to pull tight
repuxo [xe'puʃu] M (de água) fountain; **agüentar o ~** (col) to bear up
requebrado [reke'bradu] M (rebolado) swing, sway
requebrar [xeke'bra^r] VT to wiggle, swing; **requebrar-se** VR to wiggle, swing
requeijão [xekej'ʒãw] M cheese spread
requeira etc [xe'kejra] VB V **requerer**
requentar [xekẽ'ta^r] VT to reheat, warm up
requer [xe'ke^r] VB V **requerer**
requerente [xeke'rẽtʃi] M/F (Jur) petitioner
requerer [xeke're^r] VT (emprego) to apply for; (pedir) to request, ask for; (exigir) to require; (Jur) to petition for; **requerimento** [xekeri'mẽtu] M application; (pedido) request; (petição) petition
réquiem ['xɛkjẽ] (pl-ns) M requiem
requintado, -a [xekĩ'tadu, a] ADJ refined, elegant
requintar [xekĩ'ta^r] VT to refine ■ VI: ~ **em** to be refined in
requinte [xe'kĩtʃi] M refinement, elegance; (cúmulo) height

requisição [xekizi'sãw] (*pl* -ões) F request, demand

requisitado, -a [xekizi'tadu, a] ADJ (*requerido*) required; (*muito procurado*) sought after

requisitar [xekizi'ta^r] VT to make a request for; (*Mil*) to requisition

requisito [xeki'zitu] M requirement

rês [xeʃ] F head of cattle; **reses** FPL (*gado*) cattle, livestock *sg*

rescindir [xesĩ'dʒi^r] VT (*contrato*) to rescind

rescrever [xeʃkre've^r] VT = **reescrever**

rés-do-chão [xɛʒ-] (PT) M INV (*andar térreo*) ground floor (*Brit*), first floor (*US*)

resenha [xe'zeɲa] F (*relatório*) report; (*resumo*) summary; (*de livro*) review; **fazer a ~ de** (*livro*) to review

reserva [xe'zɛxva] F reserve; (*para hotel, fig: ressalva*) reservation; (*discrição*) discretion ◼ M/F (*Esporte*) reserve; **~ de mercado** (*Com*) protected market; **~ de petróleo** oil reserve; **~ natural** nature reserve; **~ em dinheiro** cash reserve

reservado, -a [xezex'vadu, a] ADJ reserved; (*pej: retraído*) standoffish

reservar [xezex'va^r] VT to reserve; (*guardar de reserva*) to keep; (*forças*) to conserve; **reservar-se** VR to save o.s.; **~ se o direito de fazer** to reserve the right to do; **ele não sabe o que o futuro lhe reserva** he does not know what the future has in store for him

reservatório [xezexva'tɔrju] M (*lago*) reservoir

reservista [xezex'viʃta] M/F (*Mil*) member of the reserves

resfolegar [xeʃfole'ga^r] VI to pant

resfriado, -a [xeʃ'frjadu, a] (BR) ADJ: **estar ~ to** have a cold ◼ M cold, chill; **ficar ~** to catch (a) cold

resfriar [xeʃ'frja^r] VT to cool, chill ◼ VI (*pessoa*) to catch (a) cold; **resfriar-se** VR to catch (a) cold

resgatar [xeʒga'ta^r] VT (*salvar*) to rescue; (*retomar*) to get back, recover; (*dívida*) to pay off; (*Com: ação, coisa penhorada*) to redeem

resgatável [xeʒga'tavew] (*pl* -eis) ADJ redeemable

resgate [xeʒ'gatʃi] M (*salvamento*) rescue; (*para livrar reféns*) ransom; (*Com: de ações, coisa penhorada*) redemption; (*retomada*) recovery

resguardar [xeʒgwax'da^r] VT to protect; **resguardar-se** VR: **resguardar-se de** to guard against

resguardo [xeʒ'gwaxdu] M protection; (*cuidado*) care; (*convalescência*): **estar** *ou* **ficar de ~** to take *ou* be taking things easy

residência [xezi'dẽsja] F residence; **residencial** [xezidẽ'sjaw] (*pl* -ais) ADJ (*zona, edifício*) residential; (*computador, telefone etc*) home *atr*; **residente** [xezi'dẽtʃi] ADJ, M/F resident; **residente na memória** (*Comput*) memory-resident

residir [xezi'dʒi^r] VI to live, reside; (*achar-se*) to reside

resíduo [xe'zidwu] M residue

resignação [xezigna'sãw] (*pl* -ões) F resignation

resignadamente [xezignada'mẽtʃi] ADJ with resignation

resignado, -a [xezig'nadu, a] ADJ resigned

resignar-se [xezig'naxsi] VR: **~ com** to resign o.s. to

resiliente [xezi'ljẽtʃi] ADJ resilient

resina [xe'zina] F resin

resistência [xeziʃ'tẽsja] F resistance; (*de atleta*) stamina; (*de material, objeto*) strength; (*moral*) morale

resistente [xeziʃ'tẽtʃi] ADJ resistant; (*material, objeto*) hard-wearing, strong; **~ a traças** mothproof

resistir [xeziʃ'tʃi^r] VI (*suporte*) to hold; (*pessoa*) to hold out; **~ a** (*não ceder*) to resist; (*sobreviver*) to survive; **~ ao uso** to wear well; **~ (ao tempo)** to endure, stand the test of time

resma ['xeʒma] F ream

resmungar [xeʒmũ'ga^r] VT, VI to mutter, mumble

resmungo [xeʒ'mũgu] M grumbling

resolução [xezolu'sãw] (*pl* -ões) F resolution; (*coragem*) courage; (*de um problema*) solution; **de alta ~ (gráfica)** (*Comput*) high-resolution; **resoluto, -a** [xezo'lutu, a] ADJ decisive; **resoluto a fazer** resolved to do

resolver [xezow've^r] VT to sort out; (*problema*) to solve; (*questão*) to resolve; (*decidir*) to decide; **resolver-se** VR: **resolver-se (a fazer)** to make up one's mind (to do), decide (to do); **chorar não resolve** crying doesn't help, it's no use crying; **~-se por** to decide on

resolvido, -a [xezow'vidu, a] ADJ (*pessoa*) decisive

respaldo [xeʃ'pawdu] M (*de cadeira*) back; (*fig*) support, backing

respectivo, -a [xeʃpek'tʃivu, a] ADJ respective

respeitador, a [xeʃpejta'do^r(a)] ADJ respectful

respeitante [xeʃpej'tãtʃi] ADJ: **~ a** concerning, with regard to

respeitar [xeʃpej'ta^r] VT to respect; **respeitável** [xeʃpej'tavew] (*pl* -eis) ADJ respectable; (*considerável*) considerable

respeito [xeʃ'pejtu] M: **~ (a** *ou* **por)** respect (for); **respeitos** MPL (*cumprimentos*) regards; **a ~ de, com ~ a** as to, as regards; (*sobre*) about; **dizer ~ a** to concern; **faltar ao ~ a** to be rude to; **em ~ a** with respect to; **dar-se ao ~** to command respect; **pessoa de ~** respected person; **ela não me disse nada a seu ~** she didn't tell me anything about you; **não sei nada a ~ (disso)** I know nothing about it

respeitoso, -a [xeʃpej'tozu, ɔza] ADJ respectful

respingar [xeʃpĩ'ga^r] VT, VI to splash, spatter

respingo [xeʃ'pĩgu] M splash

respiração [xeʃpira'sãw] F breathing; (*Med*)

NB: *European Portuguese adds the following consonants to certain words:* **b** (sú(b)dito, su(b)til); **c** (a(c)ção, a(c)cionista, a(c)to); **m** (inde(m)ne); **p** (ado(p)çã, ado(p)tar); *for further details see p. xiii.*

respirador | reta

respiration
respirador [xeʃpira'doʳ] M respirator
respirar [xeʃpi'raʳ] VT to breathe; (*revelar*) to reveal, show ▪ VI to breathe; (*descansar*) to have a respite
respiratório, -a [xeʃpira'tɔrju, a] ADJ respiratory
respiro [xeʃ'piru] M breath; (*descanso*) respite; (*abertura*) vent
resplandecente [xeʃplãde'sētʃi] ADJ resplendent
resplandecer [xeʃplãde'seʳ] VI to gleam, shine (out)
resplendor [xeʃplē'doʳ] M brilliance; (*fig*) glory
respondão, -dona [xeʃpõ'dãw, 'dɔna] (*pl* -ões/-s) ADJ cheeky, insolent
responder [xeʃpõ'deʳ] VT to answer ▪ VI to answer; (*ser respondão*) to answer back; ~ **a** (*tratamento, agressão*) to respond to; (*processo, inquérito*) to undergo; ~ **por** to be responsible for, answer for; (*Com*) to be liable for
respondões [xeʃpõ'dõjʃ] MPL *de* **respondão**
respondona [xeʃpõ'dɔna] F *de* **respondão**
responsabilidade [xeʃpõsabili'dadʒi] F responsibility; (*Jur*) liability
responsabilizar [xeʃpõsabili'zaʳ] VT: ~ **alguém** (**por algo**) to hold sb responsible (for sth); **responsabilizar-se** VR: **responsabilizar-se por** to take responsibility for
responsável [xeʃpõ'savew] (*pl* -eis) ADJ: ~ (**por**) responsible (for) ▪ M person responsible *ou* in charge; ~ **a** answerable to, accountable to
resposta [xeʃ'pɔʃta] F answer, reply
resquício [xeʃ'kisju] M (*vestígio*) trace
ressabiado, -a [xesa'bjadu, a] ADJ (*desconfiado*) wary; (*ressentido*) resentful
ressaca [xe'saka] F (*refluxo*) undertow; (*mar bravo*) rough sea; (*fig: de quem bebeu*) hangover; **estar de** ~ (*mar*) to be rough; (*pessoa*) to have a hangover
ressaibo [xe'sajbu] M (*mau sabor*) unpleasant taste; (*fig: indício*) trace; (: *ressentimento*) ill feeling
ressaltar [xesaw'taʳ] VT to emphasize ▪ VI to stand out
ressalva [xe'sawva] F (*proteção*) safeguard; (*Mil*) exemption certificate; (*correção*) correction; (*restrição*) reservation, proviso; (*exceção*) exception
ressarcir [xesax'siʳ] VT (*pagar*) to compensate; (*compensar*) to compensate for; ~ **alguém de** to compensate sb for
ressecado, -a [xese'kadu, a] ADJ (*terra, lábios*) parched; (*pele, planta*) very dry
ressecar [xese'kaʳ] VT, VI to dry up
resseguro [xese'guru] M reinsurance
ressentido, -a [xesē'tʃidu, a] ADJ resentful
ressentimento [xesētʃi'mētu] M resentment
ressentir-se [xesē'tʃixsi] VR: ~ **de** (*ofender-se*) to resent; (*magoar-se*) to be hurt by; (*sofrer*) to suffer from, feel the effects of
ressequido, -a [xese'kidu, a] ADJ = **ressecado**
ressinto *etc* [xe'sĩtu] VB V **ressentir-se**
ressoar [xe'swaʳ] VI to resound; (*ecoar*) to echo

PORTUGUÊS - INGLÊS

ressonância [xeso'nãsja] F resonance; (*eco*) echo
ressonante [xeso'nãtʃi] ADJ resonant
ressurgimento [xesux3i'mētu] M resurgence, revival
ressurreição [xesuxej'sãw] (*pl* -ões) F resurrection
ressuscitar [xesusi'taʳ] VT to revive, resuscitate; (*costumes etc*) to revive ▪ VI to revive
restabelecer [xeʃtabele'seʳ] VT to re-establish; (*ordem, forças*) to restore; (*doente*) to restore to health; **restabelecer-se** VR to recover, recuperate; **restabelecimento** [xeʃtabelesi'mētu] M re-establishment; (*da ordem*) restoration; (*Med*) recovery
restante [xeʃ'tãtʃi] ADJ remaining ▪ M rest
restar [xeʃ'taʳ] VI to remain, be left; (*esperança, dúvida*) to remain; **não lhe resta nada** he has nothing left; **resta-me fechar o negócio** I still have to close the deal; **não resta dúvida de que** there is no longer any doubt that
restauração [xeʃtawra'sãw] (*pl* -ões) F restoration; (*de doente*) restoring to health; (*de costumes, usos*) revival
restaurante [xeʃtaw'rãtʃi] M restaurant
restaurar [xeʃtaw'raʳ] VT to restore; (*recuperar*) *doente*) to restore to health; (*costumes, usos*) to revive, restore
réstia ['xɛʃtʃja] F (*de cebolas*) string; (*luz*) ray
restinga [xeʃ'tʃĩga] F spit
restituição [xeʃtʃitwi'sãw] (*pl* -ões) F restitution, return; (*de dinheiro*) repayment; (*a cargo*) reinstatement
restituir [xeʃtʃi'twiʳ] VT to return; (*dinheiro*) to repay; (*forças, saúde*) to restore; (*usos*) to revive; (*reempossar*) to reinstate
resto ['xɛʃtu] M rest; (*Mat*) remainder; **restos** MPL (*sobras*) remains; (*de comida*) scraps; ~**s mortais** mortal remains; **de** ~ apart from that
restrição [xeʃtri'sãw] (*pl* -ões) F restriction
restringir [xeʃtrĩ'3iʳ] VT to restrict; **restringir-se** VR: ~-**se a** to be restricted to; (*pessoa*) to restrict o.s. to
restrito, -a [xeʃ'tritu, a] ADJ restricted
resultado [xezuw'tadu] M result; **dar** ~ to work, be effective; ~ ... (*col*) the upshot being ....
resultante [xezuw'tãtʃi] ADJ resultant; ~ **de** resulting from
resultar [xezuw'taʳ] VI: ~ (**de/em**) (*from/in*) ▪ VI (*vir a ser*) to turn out to be
resumido, -a [xezu'midu, a] ADJ abbreviated, abridged; (*curto*) concise
resumir [xezu'miʳ] VT to summarize; (*livro*) to abridge; (*reduzir*) to reduce; (*conter em resumo*) to sum up; **resumir-se** VR: **resumir-se a** *ou* **em** to consist in *ou* of; **resumo** [xe'zumu] M summary, résumé; **em resumo** in short, briefly
resvalar [xe3va'laʳ] VT to slide, slip
resvés [xeʃ'vɛʃ] ADJ tight ▪ ADV closely; ~ **a** right by; (*na conta*) just
reta ['xɛta] F (*linha*) straight line; (*trecho de estrada*) straight; ~ **final** *ou* **de chegada** home

straight; **na ~ final** (*tb fig*) on the home straight
retaguarda [xeta'gwaxda] F rearguard; (*posição*) rear
retalhar [xeta'ʎaʳ] VT to cut up; (*separar*) to divide; (*despedaçar*) to shred; (*ferir*) to slash
retalho [xe'taʎu] M (*de pano*) scrap, remnant; **vender a ~** (*PT*) to sell retail; **colcha de ~s** patchwork quilt
retaliação [xetalja'sãw] (*pl -ões*) F retaliation
retaliar [xeta'ljaʳ] VT to repay ▪ VI to retaliate
retangular [xetãgu'laʳ] ADJ rectangular
retângulo [xe'tãgulu] M rectangle
retardado, -a [xetax'dadu, a] ADJ (*Psico*) retarded
retardar [xetax'daʳ] VT to hold up, delay; (*adiar*) to postpone
retardatário, -a [xetaxda'tarju, a] M/F latecomer
retardo [xe'taxdu] M (*Psico*) retardedness
retenção [xetẽ'sãw] F retention
reter [xe'teʳ] (*irreg*) VT (*guardar, manter*) to keep; (*deter*) to stop, detain; (*segurar*) to hold; (*ladrão, suspeito*) to detain, hold; (*na memória*) to retain; (*lágrimas, impulsos*) to hold back; (*impedir de sair*) to keep back; **reter-se** VR to restrain o.s.
retesado, -a [xete'zadu, a] ADJ taut
retesar [xete'zaʳ] VT (*músculo*) to flex; (*corda*) to pull taut
reteve [xe'tevi] VB Vreter
reticência [xetʃi'sẽsja] F reticence, reserve; **reticências** FPL (*Ling*) suspension points
reticente [xetʃi'sẽtʃi] ADJ reticent
retidão [xetʃi'dãw] F (*integridade*) rectitude; (*de linha*) straightness
retificar [xetʃifi'kaʳ] VT to rectify
retinha *etc* [xe'tʃiɲa] VB Vreter
retinir [xetʃi'niʳ] VI (*ferros*) to clink; (*campainha*) to ring, jingle; (*ressoar*) to resound
retirada [xetʃi'rada] F (*Mil*) withdrawal, retreat; (*salário, saque*) withdrawal; **bater em ~** to beat a retreat
retirado, -a [xetʃi'radu, a] ADJ (*vida*) solitary; (*lugar*) isolated
retirante [xetʃi'rãtʃi] M/F migrant (*from the NE of Brazil*)
retirar [xetʃi'raʳ] VT to withdraw; (*tirar*) to take out; (*afastar*) to take away, remove; (*fazer sair*) to get out; (*ganhar*) to make; **retirar-se** VR to withdraw; (*de uma festa etc*) to leave; (*da política etc*) to retire; (*recolher-se*) to retire, withdraw; (*Mil*) to retreat
retiro [xe'tʃiru] M retreat
retitude [xetʃi'tudʒi] F rectitude
retive *etc* [xe'tʃivi] VB Vreter
retiver *etc* [xetʃi've'ʳ] VB Vreter
reto, -a ['xɛtu, a] ADJ straight; (*fig: justo*) fair; (*: honesto*) honest, upright ▪ M (*Anat*) rectum
retocar [xeto'kaʳ] VT (*pintura*) to touch up; (*texto*) to tidy up

retomar [xeto'maʳ] VT to take up again; (*reaver*) to get back
retoque [xe'tɔki] M finishing touch
retoque *etc* VB Vretocar
retorcer [xetox'seʳ] VT to twist; **retorcer-se** VR to wriggle, writhe; **~-se de dor** to writhe in pain
retórica [xe'tɔrika] F rhetoric; (*pej*) affectation
retórico, -a [xe'tɔriku, a] ADJ rhetorical; (*pej*) affected
retornar [xetox'naʳ] VI to return, go back; **retorno** [xe'toxnu] M return; (*Com*) barter, exchange; (*em rodovia*) turning area; **dar retorno** to do a U-turn; **retorno sobre investimento** return on investment; **retorno (do carro)** (*Comput*) (carriage) return
retorquir [xetox'kiʳ] VT to answer, say in reply ▪ VI to retort, reply; **ela não retorquiu nada** she said nothing in reply
retractação [xetrata'sãw] (*PT*) F = **retratação**
retraído, -a [xetra'idu, a] ADJ retracted; (*tímido*) reserved, timid
retraimento [xetraj'mẽtu] M withdrawal; (*contração*) contraction; (*fig: de pessoa*) timidity, shyness
retrair [xetra'iʳ] VT to withdraw; (*contrair*) to contract; (*pessoa*) to make reserved; **retrair-se** VR to withdraw; (*encolher-se*) to retract
retrasado, -a [xetra'zadu, a] ADJ: **a semana retrasada** the week before last
retratação [xetrata'sãw] (*pl -ões*) F retraction
retratar [xetra'taʳ] VT to portray, depict; (*mostrar*) to show; (*dito*) to retract; **retratar-se** VR: **~-se (de algo)** to retract (sth)
retrátil [xe'tratʃiw] (*pl -eis*) ADJ retractable; **cinto de segurança ~** inertia-reel seat belt
retratista [xetra'tʃiʃta] M/F portrait painter
retrato [xe'tratu] M portrait; (*Foto*) photo; (*fig: efígie*) likeness; (*: representação*) portrayal; **ela é o ~ da mãe** she's the image of her mother; **tirar um ~ (de alguém)** to take a photo (of sb); **~ a meio corpo/de corpo inteiro** half/full-length portrait; **~ falado** Identikit® picture
retribuição [xetribwi'sãw] (*pl -ões*) F reward, recompense; (*pagamento*) remuneration; (*de hospitalidade, favor*) return, reciprocation
retribuir [xetri'bwiʳ] VT (*recompensar*) to reward, recompense; (*pagar*) to remunerate; (*hospitalidade, favor, sentimento, visita*) to return
retroactivo, -a [xetroa'tivu, a] (*PT*) ADJ = **retroativo**
retroagir [xetroa'ʒiʳ] VI (*lei*) to be retroactive; (*modificar o que está feito*) to change what has been done
retroativo, -a [xetroa'tʃivu, a] ADJ retroactive; (*pagamento*) ~ **(a)** backdated (to)
retroceder [xetrose'deʳ] VI to retreat, fall back; (*decair*) to decline; (*num intento*) to back down; **retrocesso** [xetro'sɛsu] M retreat; (*ao passado*)

NB: *European Portuguese adds the following consonants to certain words:* **b** (sú(b)dito, su(b)til); **c** (a(c)ção, a(c)cionista, a(c)to); **m** (inde(m)ne); **p** (ado(p)çã, ado(p)tar); *for further details see p. xiii.*

return; (*decadência*) decline; (*tecla*) backspace (key); (*da economia*) slowdown
retrógrado, -a [xe'trɔgradu, a] ADJ retrograde; (*reacionário*) reactionary
retroprojetor [xetroproʒe'to^r] M overhead projector
retrospectiva [xetroʃpek'tʃiva] F retrospective
retrospectivamente [xetroʃpektʃiva'mētʃi] ADV in retrospect
retrospectivo, -a [xetroʃpek'tʃivu, a] ADJ retrospective
retrospecto [xetro'ʃpɛktu] M retrospective look; **em ~** in retrospect
retrovisor [xetrovi'zo^r] ADJ, M: **(espelho) ~** (*rearview*) mirror
retrucar [xetru'ka^r] VT to answer ▪ VI to retort, reply
retumbância [xetũ'bãsja] F resonance
retumbante [xetũ'bãtʃi] ADJ (*tb fig*) resounding
retumbar [xetũ'ba^r] VI to resound, echo; (*ribombar*) to rumble, boom
returco *etc* [xe'tuxku] VB V **retorquir**
réu, ré [xɛw, xɛ] M/F defendant; (*culpado*) culprit, criminal; **~ de morte** condemned man
reumático, -a [xew'matʃiku, a] ADJ rheumatic
reumatismo [xewma'tʃiʒmu] M rheumatism
reumatologista [xewmatolo'ʒiʃta] M/F rheumatologist
reunião [xeu'njãw] (*pl* **-ões**) F meeting; (*ato, reencontro*) reunion; (*festa*) get-together, party; **~ de cúpula** summit (meeting); **~ de diretoria** board meeting
reunir [xeu'ni^r] VT (*pessoas*) to bring together; (*partes*) to join, unite; (*qualidades*) to combine; **reunir-se** VR to meet; (*amigos*) to meet, get together; **~-se a** to join
reutilizar [xeutʃili'za^r] VT to re-use
revalorizar [xevalori'za^r] VT (*moeda*) to revalue
revanche [xe'vãʃi] F revenge; (*Esporte*) return match
revê *etc* [xe've] VB V **rever**
reveillon [xeve'jõ] M New Year's Eve
revejo *etc* [xe'veʒu] VB V **rever**
revelação [xevela'sãw] (*pl* **-ões**) F revelation; (*Foto*) development; (*novo cantor, ator etc*) promising newcomer
revelar [xeve'la^r] VT to reveal; (*mostrar*) to show; (*Foto*) to develop; **revelar-se** VR to turn out to be; **ela se revelou nessa crise** she showed her true colo(u)rs in this crisis
revelia [xeve'lia] F default; **à ~** by default; **à ~ de** without the knowledge *ou* consent of
revendedor, a [xevẽde'do^r(a)] M/F dealer
revender [xevẽ'de^r] VT to resell
rever [xe've^r] (*irreg*) VT to see again; (*examinar*) to check; (*revisar*) to revise; (*provas tipográficas*) to proofread
reverberar [xevexbe'ra^r] VT (*luz*) to reflect ▪ VI to be reflected
reverdecer [xevexde'se^r] VT, VI to turn green again
reverência [xeve'rẽsja] F reverence, respect;

(*ato*) bow; (: *de mulher*) curtsey; **fazer uma ~** to bow; to curtsey
reverenciar [xeverẽ'sja^r] VT to revere, venerate; (*obedecer*) to obey
reverendo, -a [xeve'rẽdu, a] ADJ reverend ▪ M priest, clergyman
reverente [xeve'rẽtʃi] ADJ reverential
reversão [xevex'sãw] (*pl* **-ões**) F reversion
reversível [xevex'sivew] (*pl* **-eis**) ADJ reversible
reverso [xe'vɛxsu] M reverse; **o ~ da medalha** (*fig*) the other side of the coin
reversões [xevex'sõjʃ] FPL *de* **reversão**
reverter [xevex'te^r] VT to revert; (*a questão*) to return; **~ em benefício de** to benefit
revertério [xevex'tɛrju] M: **dar o ~** (*col*) to go wrong
revés [xe'vɛʃ] M reverse; (*infortúnio*) setback, mishap; **ao ~** (*roupa*) inside out; **de ~** (*olhar*) askance
revestimento [xeveʃtʃi'mētu] M (*da parede*) covering; (*de sofá*) cover; (*de caixa*) lining
revestir [xeveʃ'tʃi^r] VT (*traje*) to put on; (*cobrir: paredes etc*) to cover; (*interior de uma caixa etc*) to line; **revestir-se** VR: **revestir-se de** (*poderes*) to assume, take on; (*paciência*) to arm o.s. with; (*coragem*) to take, pluck up; **~ alguém de poderes** *etc* to invest sb with powers *etc*
revezamento [xeveza'mētu] M alternation
revezar [xeve'za^r] VT to alternate ▪ VI to take turns, alternate; **revezar-se** VR to take turns, alternate
revi [xe'vi] VB V **rever**
revia *etc* [xe'via] VB V **rever**
revidar [xevi'da^r] VT (*soco, insulto*) to return; (*retrucar*) to answer; (*crítica*) to rise to, respond to ▪ VI to hit back; (*retrucar*) to respond
revide [xe'vidʒi] M response
revigorar [xevigo'ra^r] VT to reinvigorate ▪ VI to regain one's strength; **revigorar-se** VR to regain one's strength
revir *etc* [xe'vi^r] VB V **rever**
revirado, -a [xevi'radu, a] ADJ (*casa*) untidy, upside-down
revirar [xevi'ra^r] VT to turn round; (*gaveta*) to turn out, go through; **revirar-se** VR (*na cama*) to toss and turn; **~ os olhos** to roll one's eyes
reviravolta [xevira'vɔwta] F about-turn, U-turn; (*mudança da situação*) turn
revisão [xevi'zãw] (*pl* **-ões**) F revision; (*de máquina*) overhaul; (*de carro*) service; (*Jur*) appeal; **~ de provas** proofreading
revisar [xevi'za^r] VT to revise; (*prova tipográfica*) to proofread
revisões [xevi'zõjʃ] FPL *de* **revisão**
revisor, a [xevi'zo^r(a)] M/F (*Ferro etc*) ticket inspector; (*de provas*) proofreader
revista [xe'viʃta] F (*busca*) search; (*Mil, exame*) inspection; (*publicação*) magazine; (: *profissional, erudita*) journal; (*Teatro*) revue; **passar ~ a** to review; (*Mil*) to inspect, review; **~ em quadrinhos** comic; **~ literária** literary review; **~ para mulheres** women's magazine

revistar [xeviʃ'ta^r] vt to search; (tropa) to review; (examinar) to examine

revisto etc [xe'viʃtu] vb v **revestir**

revisto, -a [xe'viʃtu, a] pp de **rever**

revitalizar [xevitali'za^r] vt to revitalize

reviu [xe'viu] vb v **rever**

reviver [xevi've^r] vt to relive; (costumes, palavras) to revive ■ vi to revive; (doente) to pick up

revocar [xevo'ka^r] vt (o passado) to evoke; (mandar voltar) to recall; ~ **alguém a/de** to bring sb back to/from

revogação [xevoga'sãw] (pl -ões) f (de lei) repeal; (de ordem) reversal

revogar [xevo'ga^r] vt to revoke

revolta [xe'vɔwta] f revolt; (fig: indignação) disgust; **Revolta da vacina;** see below; **revoltado, -a** [xevow'tadu, a] adj in revolt; (indignado) disgusted; (amargo) bitter; **revoltante** [xevow'tãtʃi] adj disgusting; (repugnante) revolting

● **REVOLTA DA VACINA**
●
● This was a popular movement of opposition
● to the government which took place
● in Rio de Janeiro in 1904, following the
● passing of a law which made vaccination
● against smallpox compulsory. It was the
● culmination of general dissatisfaction
● with health reforms undertaken at that
● time by the scientist Osvaldo Cruz, and
● the relocation programme of the prefect
● Pereira Passos, as a result of which part of
● the population of Rio had been moved from
● the slums and shanty towns of the central
● region to suburbs much further out.

revoltar [xevow'ta^r] vt to disgust; (insurgir) to incite to revolt ■ vi to cause indignation; **revoltar-se** vr to rebel, revolt; (indignar-se) to be disgusted

revolto, -a [xe'vowtu, a] pp de **revolver** ■ adj (década) turbulent; (mundo) troubled; (cabelo) dishevelled; (mar) rough; (desarrumado) untidy

revoltoso, -a [xevow'tozu, ɔza] adj in revolt

revolução [xevolu'sãw] (pl -ões) f revolution; **revolucionar** [xevolusjo'na^r] vt to revolutionize; **revolucionário, -a** [xevolusjo'narju, a] adj, m/f revolutionary

revoluções [xevolu'sõjʃ] fpl de **revolução**

revolver [xevow've^r] vt (terra) to turn over, dig over; (gaveta) to rummage through; (olhos) to roll; (suj: vento) to blow around ■ vi (girar) to revolve, rotate

revólver [xe'vɔwve^r] m revolver, gun

reza ['xeza] f prayer; **rezar** [xe'za^r] vt (missa, prece) to say ■ vi to pray; **rezar (que)** (contar, dizer) to state (that)

RFA abr f (antes: = República Federal Alemã) FRG

RFFSA (BR) abr f = **Rede Ferroviária Federal SA**

RG (BR) abr m (= Registro Geral) identity document

rh abr: **factor rezar** Rh. ou rhesus (Brit) factor; **rh negativo/positivo** rhesus negative/positive

riacho ['xjaʃu] m stream, brook

ribalta [xi'bawta] f footlights pl; (fig) boards pl

ribanceira [xibã'sejra] f (margem) steep river bank; (rampa) steep slope; (precipício) cliff

ribeira [xi'bejra] f riverside; (riacho) river

ribeirão [xibej'rãw] (BR) (pl -ões) m stream

ribeirinho, -a [xibej'riɲu, a] adj riverside atr

ribeiro [xi'bejru] m brook, stream

ribeirões [xibej'rõjʃ] mpl de **ribeirão**

ribombar [xibõ'ba^r] vi (trovão) to rumble, boom; (ressoar) to resound

ricaço [xi'kasu] m plutocrat, very rich man

rícino ['xisinu] m castor-oil plant; **óleo de ~** castor oil

rico, -a ['xiku, a] adj rich; (PT: lindo) beautiful; (: excelente) splendid ■ m/f rich man/woman

ricochetear [xikoʃe'tʃja^r] vi to ricochet

ricota [xi'kɔta] f cream cheese

ridicularizar [xidʒikulari'za^r] vt to ridicule

ridículo, -a [xi'dʒikulu, a] adj ridiculous

rifa ['xifa] f raffle

rifão [xi'fãw] (pl -ões) m proverb, saying

rifar [xi'fa^r] vt to raffle; (col: abandonar) to dump

rififi [xifi'fi] (col) m fight, brawl

rifle ['xifli] m rifle

rifões [xi'fõjʃ] mpl de **rifão**

rigidez [xiʒi'deʒ] f rigidity, stiffness; (austeridade) severity, strictness; (inflexibilidade) inflexibility

rígido, -a ['xiʒidu, a] adj rigid, stiff; (fig) strict

rigor [xi'go^r] m rigidity; (meticulosidade) rigour (Brit), rigor (US); (severidade) harshness, severity; (exatidão) precision; **a ~** strictly speaking; **vestido a ~** in full evening dress; **ser de ~** to be essential ou obligatory; **no ~ do inverno** in the depths of winter; **rigoroso, -a** [xigo'rozu, -ɔza] adj rigorous, strict; (severo) strict; (exigente) demanding; (minucioso) precise, accurate; (inverno) hard, harsh

rijo, -a ['xiʒu, a] adj tough, hard; (severo) harsh, severe; (músculos, braços) firm

rim [xĩ] (pl -ns) m kidney; **rins** mpl (parte inferior das costas) small sg of the back

rima ['xima] f rhyme; (poema) verse, poem; **rimar** [xi'ma^r] vt, vi to rhyme; **rimar com** (condizer) to agree with, tally with

rímel® ['ximew] (pl -eis) m mascara

rinçagem [xĩ'saʒẽ] (pl -ns) f rinse

rinçar [xĩ'sa^r] vt to rinse

rinchar [xĩ'ʃa^r] vi to neigh, whinny

rincho ['xĩʃu] m neigh(ing)

ringue ['xĩgi] m ring

rinha ['xĩɲa] f cock-fight

rinoceronte [xinose'rõtʃi] m rhinoceros

rinque ['xĩki] m rink

NB: European Portuguese adds the following consonants to certain words: **b** (sú(b)dito, su(b)til); **c** (a(c)ção, a(c)cionista, a(c)to); **m** (inde(m)ne); **p** (ado(p)ção, ado(p)tar); for further details see p. xiii.

rins [xĩʃ] MPL *de* **rim**

Rio ['xiu] M: **o ~ (de Janeiro)** Rio (de Janeiro)

rio ['xiu] M river

ripa ['xipa] F lath, slat

riqueza [xi'keza] F wealth, riches *pl*; *(qualidade)* richness; *(fartura)* abundance; *(fecundidade)* fertility

rir [xiʳ] VI to laugh; **~ de** to laugh at; **morrer de ~** to laugh one's head off

risada [xi'zada] F *(riso)* laughter; *(gargalhada)* guffaw

risca ['xiʃka] F stroke; *(listra)* stripe; *(no cabelo)* parting; **à ~** to the letter, exactly

riscar [xiʃ'kaʳ] VT *(papel)* to draw lines on; *(marcar)* to mark; *(apagar)* to cross out; *(desenhar)* to outline; *(fósforo)* to strike; *(expulsar: sócios)* to expel, throw out; *(eliminar)* to do away with; *(amigo)* to write off

risco ['xiʃku] M *(marca)* mark, scratch; *(traço)* stroke; *(desenho)* drawing, sketch; *(perigo)* risk; **sob o ~ de** at the risk of; **correr o ~ de** to run the risk of; **correr ~s** to take risks; **pôr em ~** to put at risk, risk

risível [xi'zivew] *(pl* -eis) ADJ laughable, ridiculous

riso ['xizu] M laughter; **não ser motivo de ~** to be no laughing matter; **risonho, -a** [xi'zɔɲu, a] ADJ smiling; *(contente)* cheerful; **estar muito risonho** to be all smiles

risoto [xi'zotu] M risotto

rispidez [xiʃpi'deʒ] F brusqueness; *(aspereza)* harshness

ríspido, -a ['xiʃpidu, a] ADJ brusque; *(áspero)* harsh

risquei *etc* [xiʃ'kej] VB V **riscar**

rissole [xi'sɔli] M rissole

riste ['xiʃtʃi] M: **em ~** *(dedo)* pointing; *(orelhas)* pointed

rítmico, -a ['xitʃmiku, a] ADJ rhythmic(al)

ritmo ['xitʃmu] M rhythm

rito ['xitu] M rite; *(seita)* cult

ritual [xi'twaw] *(pl* -ais) ADJ, M ritual

rival [xi'vaw] *(pl* -ais) ADJ, M/F rival; **rivalidade** [xivali'dadʒi] F rivalry; **rivalizar** [xivali'zaʳ] VT to rival ■ VI: **rivalizar com** to compete with, vie with

rixa ['xiʃa] F quarrel, fight

RJ ABR = **Rio de Janeiro**

RN ABR = **Rio Grande do Norte**

RNVA (BR) ABR M = **Registro Nacional de Veículos Automotores**

RO ABR = **Rondônia**

roa *etc* ['xoa] VB V **roer**

robalo [xo'balu] M snook *(type of fish)*

robô [xo'bo] M robot

robustecer [xobuʃte'seʳ] VT to strengthen ■ VI to become stronger; **robustecer-se** VR to become stronger

robustez [xobuʃ'teʒ] F strength

robusto, -a [xo'buʃtu, a] ADJ strong, robust

roça ['xɔsa] F plantation; *(no mato)* clearing; *(campo)* country

roçado [xo'sadu] M clearing

rocambole [xokã'bɔli] M roll

roçar [xo'saʳ] VT *(terreno)* to clear; *(tocar de leve)* to brush against ■ VI: **~ em** *ou* **por** to brush against

roceiro, -a [xo'sejru, a] M/F *(lavrador)* peasant; *(caipira)* country bumpkin

rocha ['xɔʃa] F rock; *(penedo)* crag

rochedo [xo'ʃedu] M crag, cliff

rock ['xɔki] M = **roque**

rock-and-roll [-ã'xɔw] M rock and roll

roda ['xɔda] F wheel; *(círculo, grupo de pessoas)* circle; *(de saia)* width, fullness; **~ dentada** cog(wheel); **alta ~** high society; **em** *ou* **à ~ de** round, around; **~ de direção** steering wheel; **~ do leme** ship's wheel, helm; **brincar de ~** to play in the round

rodada [xo'dada] F *(de bebidas, Esporte)* round

roda-d'água *(pl* rodas-d'água) F water wheel

rodado, -a [xo'dadu, a] ADJ *(saia)* full, wide; **o carro tem 5000 km ~s** the car has 5000 km on the clock

rodagem [xo'daʒẽ] *(pl* -ns) F: **estrada de ~** *(trunk)* road *(Brit)*

roda-gigante *(pl* rodas-gigantes) F big wheel

rodamoinho [xodamo'iɲu] M *(na água)* whirlpool; *(de vento)* whirlwind; *(no cabelo)* swirl

Ródano ['xɔdanu] M: **o ~** the Rhône

rodapé [xoda'pɛ] M skirting board *(Brit)*, baseboard *(US)*; *(de página)* foot

rodar [xo'daʳ] VT *(fazer girar)* to turn, spin; *(viajar por)* to tour, travel round; *(quilômetros)* to do; *(filme)* to make; *(imprimir)* to print; *(Comput: programa)* to run ■ VI *(girar)* to turn round; *(Auto)* to drive around; *(col: ser reprovado)* to fail; *(: sair)* to make o.s. scarce; *(: ser excluído)* to be ruled out; **~ por** *(a pé)* to wander around; *(de carro)* to drive around

roda-viva *(pl* rodas-vivas) F bustle, commotion; **estou numa ~ danada** I'm in a real flap

rodear [xo'dʒjaʳ] VT to go round; *(circundar)* to encircle, surround; *(pessoa)* to surround

rodeio [xo'deju] M *(em discurso)* circumlocution; *(subterfúgio)* subterfuge; *(de gado)* round-up; **fazer ~s** to beat about the bush; **sem ~s** plainly, frankly

rodela [xo'dɛla] F *(pedaço)* slice

rodízio [xo'dʒizju] M rota; **à ~** *(em restaurante)* at discretion; **em ~** on a rota basis

rodo ['xodu] M rake; *(para puxar água)* water rake; **a ~** in abundance

rododendro [xodo'dẽtru] M rhododendron

rodoferroviário, -a [xodofexo'vjarju, a] ADJ road and rail *atr*

rodopiar [xodo'pjaʳ] VI to whirl around, swirl

rodopio [xodo'piu] M spin

rodovia [xodo'via] F highway, ≈ motorway *(Brit)*, ≈ interstate *(US)*

rodoviária [xodo'vjarja] F *(tb:* **estação rodoviária)** bus station; *v tb* **rodoviário**

rodoviário, -a [xodo'vjarju, a] ADJ road *atr*; *(polícia)* traffic *atr* ■ M/F roadworker

roedor, a [xwe'do^r(a)] ADJ gnawing ∎ M rodent
roer [xwe^r] VT to gnaw, nibble; (*enferrujar*) to corrode; (*afligir*) to eat away; **ser duro de** ~ to be a hard nut to crack
rogado [xo'gadu] ADJ: **fazer-se de** ~ to play hard to get
rogar [xo'ga^r] VI to ask, request; ~ **a alguém que faça** to beg sb to do
rogo ['xogu] M request; **a** ~ **de** at the request of
rói [xɔj] VB V **roer**
roía *etc* [xo'ia] VB V **roer**
róis [xɔjʃ] MPL *de* **rol**
rojão [xo'ʒãw] (*pl* -ões) M (*foguete*) rocket; (*fig: ritmo intenso*) hectic pace; **agüentar o** ~ (*fig*) to stick it out
rol [xɔw] (*pl* **róis**) M roll, list
rolagem [xo'laʒẽ] F (*de uma dívida*) snowball ing
rolar [xo'la^r] VT to roll; (*dívida*) to run up ∎ VI to roll; (*na cama*) to toss and turn; (*col: vinho etc*) to flow; (: *estender-se*) to roll on
roldana [xow'dana] F pulley
roleta [xo'leta] F roulette; (*borboleta*) turnstile
roleta-paulista F: **fazer uma** ~ (*Auto*) to go through a red light
roleta-russa F Russian roulette
rolha ['xoʎa] F cork; (*fig*) gag (on free speech)
roliço, -a [xo'lisu, a] ADJ (*pessoa*) plump, chubby; (*objeto*) round, cylindrical
rolo ['xolu] M (*de papel etc*) roll; (*para nivelar o solo, para pintura*) roller; (*almofada*) bolster; (*para cabelo*) curler; (*col: briga*) brawl, fight; ~ **compressor** steamroller; ~ **de massa** *ou* **pastel** rolling pin
Roma ['xoma] N Rome
romã [xo'mã] F pomegranate
romance [xo'mãsi] M (*livro*) novel; (*caso amoroso*) romance; (*fig: história*) complicated story; ~ **policial** detective story; **fazer um** ~ **(de algo)** (*exagerar*) to dramatize (sth)
romanceado, -a [xomã'sjadu, a] ADJ (*biografia*) in the style of a novel; (*exagerado*) exaggerated, fanciful
romancear [xomã'sja^r] VT (*biografia*) to write in the style of a novel; (*exagerar*) to exaggerate, embroider ∎ VI (*inventar histórias*) to tell tales
romancista [xomã'siʃta] M/F novelist
românico, -a [xo'maniku, a] ADJ (*Ling*) Romance; (*Arq*) romanesque
romano, -a [xo'manu, a] ADJ, M/F Roman
romântico, -a [xo'mãtʃiku, a] ADJ romantic
romantismo [xomã'tʃiʒmu] M romanticism; (*romance*) romance
romaria [xoma'ria] F (*peregrinação*) pilgrimage; (*festa*) festival
rombo ['xõbu] M (*buraco*) hole; (*Mat*) rhombus; (*fig: desfalque*) embezzlement; (: *prejuízo*) loss, shortfall
rombudo, -a [xõ'budu, a] ADJ very blunt
romeiro, -a [xo'mejru, a] M/F pilgrim
Romênia [xo'menja] F: **a** ~ Romania; **romeno,**

-a [xo'mɛnu, a] ADJ, M/F Rumanian ∎ M (*Ling*) Rumanian
romeu-e-julieta [xo'mewiʒu'ljeta] M (*Culin*) guava jelly with cheese
rompante [xõ'pãtʃi] M outburst
romper [xõ'pe^r] VT to break; (*rasgar*) to tear; (*relações*) to break off ∎ VI (*sol, manhã*) to break through; ~ **com** to break with; ~ **de** (*jorrar*) to well up from; ~ **em pranto** *ou* **lágrimas** to burst into tears; ~ **em soluços** to sob; **rompimento** [xõpi'mẽtu] M (*ato*) breakage; (*fenda*) break; (*de relações*) breaking off
roncar [xõ'ka^r] VI to snore; **ronco** ['xõku] M snore; (*de motor*) roar; (*de porco*) grunt
ronda ['xõda] F patrol, beat; **fazer a** ~ to go the rounds; **rondar** [xõ'da^r] VT to patrol, go the rounds of; (*espreitar*) to prowl, hang around; (*rodear*) to go round ∎ VI to prowl, lurk; (*fazer a ronda*) to patrol, do the rounds; **a inflação ronda os 30% ao mês** inflation is in the region of 30% a month
rondoniano, -a [xõdo'njanu, a] ADJ from Rondônia ∎ M/F person from Rondônia
ronquei *etc* [xõ'kej] VB V **roncar**
ronqueira [xõ'kejra] F wheeze
ronrom [xõ'xõ] M purr
ronronar [xõxo'na^r] VI to purr
roque ['xɔki] M (*Xadrez*) rook, castle; (*Mús*) rock
roqueiro, -a [xo'kejru, a] M/F rock musician
roraimense [xoraj'mẽsi] ADJ from Roraima ∎ M/F person from Roraima
rosa ['xɔza] ADJ INV pink ∎ F rose; **a vida não é feita de ~s** life is not a bed of roses; **rosado, -a** [xo'zadu, a] ADJ rosy, pink
rosa-dos-ventos F INV compass
rosário [xo'zarju] M rosary
rosa-shocking [-'ʃɔkĩ] ADJ INV shocking pink
rosbife [xoʒ'bifi] M roast beef
rosca ['xoʃka] F spiral, coil; (*de parafuso*) thread; (*pão*) ring-shaped loaf
roseira [xo'zejra] F rosebush
róseo, -a ['xɔzju, a] ADJ rosy
roseta [xo'zeta] F rosette
rosetar [xoze'ta^r] VI to loaf around
rosnar [xoʒ'na^r] VI (*cão*) to growl, snarl; (*murmurar*) to mutter, mumble
rossio [xo'siu] (PT) M large square
rosto ['xoʃtu] M (*cara*) face; (*frontispício*) title page
rota ['xɔta] F route, course
rotação [xota'sãw] (*pl* -ões) F rotation; ~ **de estoques** turnover of stock
rotativa [xota'tʃiva] F rotary printing press
rotatividade [xotatʃivi'dadʒi] F rotation; **hotel de alta** ~ hotel renting rooms by the hour, love hotel
rotativo, -a [xota'tʃivu, a] ADJ rotary
roteirista [xotej'riʃta] M/F scriptwriter
roteiro [xo'tejru] M (*itinerário*) itinerary; (*ordem*) schedule; (*guia*) guidebook; (*de filme*) script; (*de*

NB: *European Portuguese adds the following consonants to certain words:* **b** (sú(b)dito, su(b)til); **c** (a(c)ção, a(c)cionista, a(c)to); **m** (inde(m)ne); **p** (ado(p)çã, ado(p)tar); *for further details see p. xiii.*

discussão, trabalho escrito) list of topics; (*fig: norma*) norm

rotina [xo'tʃina] F (*tb: Comput*) routine; **rotineiro, -a** [xotʃi'nejru, a] ADJ routine

roto, -a ['xotu, a] ADJ broken; (*rasgado*) torn; (*maltrapilho*) scruffy; **o ~ rindo do esfarrapado** the pot calling the kettle black

rótula ['xɔtula] F (*Anat*) kneecap

rotular [xotu'laʳ] VT (*tb fig*) to label; **~ alguém/ algo de** to label sb/sth as; **rótulo** ['xɔtulu] M label, tag; (*fig*) label

rotunda [xo'tũda] F (*Arq*) rotunda

rotundo, -a [xo'tũdu, a] ADJ (*redondo*) round; (*gorducho*) rotund

roubalheira [xoba'ʎejra] F (*do Estado, de empresa*) embezzlement

roubar [xo'baʳ] VT to steal; (*loja, casa, pessoa*) to rob ■ VI to steal; (*em jogo, no preço*) to cheat; **~ algo a alguém** to steal sth from sb; **roubo** ['xobu] M theft, robbery; **$100 é roubo** $100 is daylight robbery

rouco, -a ['ʀoku, a] ADJ hoarse

round ['xãwdʒi] (*pl* -s) M (*Boxe*) round

roupa ['xopa] F clothes *pl*, clothing; **~ de baixo** underwear; **~ de cama** bedclothes *pl*, bed linen

roupagem [xo'paʒẽ] (*pl* -ns) F clothes *pl*, apparel; (*fig*) appearance

roupão [xo'pãw] (*pl* -ões) M dressing gown

rouquidão [xoki'dãw] F hoarseness

rouxinol [xoʃi'nɔw] (*pl* -óis) M nightingale

roxo, -a ['xoʃu, a] ADJ purple, violet; **~ por** (*col*) mad about; **~ de saudades** pining away

royalty ['xɔjawtʃi] (*pl* -ies) M royalty

RR ABR = **Roraima**

RS ABR = **Rio Grande do Sul**

rua ['xua] F street ■ EXCL: **~! get out!**, clear off!; **botar alguém na ~** to put sb out on the street; **ir para a ~** to go out; (*ser despedido*) to get the sack; **viver na ~** to be out all the time; **estar na ~ da amargura** to be going through hell; **~ principal** main street; **~ sem saída** no through road, cul-de-sac

Ruanda ['xwãda] F Rwanda

rubéola [xu'bɛola] F (*Med*) German measles

rubi [xu'bi] M ruby

rublo ['xublu] M rouble (*Brit*), ruble (*US*)

rubor [xu'boʳ] M blush; (*fig*) shyness, bashfulness

ruborizar [xubori'zaʳ] VT to make blush; **ruborizar-se** VR to blush

rubrica [xu'brika] F (*signed*) initials *pl*

rubricar [xubri'kaʳ] VT to initial

rubro, -a ['xubru, a] ADJ ruby-red; (*faces*) rosy, ruddy

rubro-negro, -a ADJ of Flamengo FC

ruço, -a ['xusu, a] ADJ grey (*Brit*), gray (*US*), dun; (*desbotado*) faded; (*col*) tough, tricky

rude ['xudʒi] ADJ (*povo*) simple, primitive;

(*ignorante*) simple; (*grosseiro*) rude

rudeza [xu'deza] F simplicity; (*grosseria*) rudeness

rudimentar [xudʒimẽ'taʳ] ADJ rudimentary

rudimento [xudʒi'mẽtu] M rudiment; **rudimentos** MPL (*noções básicas*) rudiments, first principles

ruela ['xwɛla] F lane, alley

rufar [xu'faʳ] VT (*tambor*) to roll ■ M roll

rufião [xu'fjãw] (*pl* -ães) M pimp

ruflar [xuf'laʳ] VT, VI to rustle

ruga ['xuga] F (*na pele*) wrinkle; (*na roupa*) crease

rúgbi ['xugbi] M rugby

ruge ['xuʒi] M rouge

rugido [xu'ʒidu] M roar

rugir [xu'ʒiʳ] VI to roar, bellow

ruibarbo [xwi'baxbu] M rhubarb

ruído ['xwidu] M noise, din; (*Elet, Tec*) noise; **ruidoso, -a** [xwi'dozu, ɔza] ADJ noisy

ruim [xu'ĩ] (*pl* -ns) ADJ bad; (*defeituoso*) defective; **achar ~** (*col*) to get upset

ruína ['xwina] F ruin; (*decadência*) downfall; **levar alguém à ~** to ruin sb, be sb's downfall

ruindade [xwĩ'dadʒi] F wickedness, evil; (*ação*) bad thing

ruins [xu'ĩʃ] ADJ PL *de* **ruim**

ruir ['xwiʳ] VI to collapse, go to ruin

ruivo, -a ['xwivu, a] ADJ red-haired ■ M/F redhead

rujo *etc* ['xuju] VB V **rugir**

rulê [xu'le] ADJ: **gola ~** polo neck

rum [xũ] M rum

rumar [xu'maʳ] VT (*barco*) to steer ■ VI: **~ para** to head for

rumba ['xũba] F rumba

ruminação [xumina'sãw] (*pl* -ões) F rumination

ruminante [xumi'nãtʃi] ADJ, M ruminant

ruminar [xumi'naʳ] VT to chew; (*fig*) to ponder ■ VI (*tb fig*) to ruminate

rumo ['xumu] M course, bearing; (*fig*) course; **~ a** bound for; **sem ~** adrift

rumor [xu'moʳ] M (*ruído*) noise; (*notícia*) rumour (*Brit*), rumor (*US*), report

rumorejar [xumore'ʒaʳ] VI to murmur; (*folhas*) to rustle; (*água*) to ripple

rupia [xu'pia] F rupee

ruptura [xup'tura] F break, rupture

rural [xu'raw] (*pl* -ais) ADJ rural

rusga ['xuʒga] F (*briga*) quarrel, row

rush [xaʃ] M rush; (**a hora do**) **~** rush hour; **o ~ imobiliário** the rush to buy property

Rússia ['xusja] F: **a ~** Russia; **russo, -a** ['xusu, a] ADJ, M/F Russian ■ M (*Ling*) Russian

rústico, -a ['xuʃtʃiku, a] ADJ rustic; (*pessoa*) simple; (*utensílio, objeto*) rough; (*casa*) rustic-style; (*lugar*) countrified

Ss

S, s [ˈɛsi] (*pl* **ss**) M S, s; **S de Sandra** S for Sugar
S. ABR (= *Santo ou São*) St
SA ABR (= *Sociedade Anônima*) Ltd., Inc. (US)
sã [sã] F *de* **são**
Saara [saˈara] M: **o ~** the Sahara
sáb. ABR (= *sábado*) Sat
sábado [ˈsabadu] M Saturday; (*dos judeus*)
  Sabbath; **~ de aleluia** Easter Saturday; *v tb*
  terça-feira
sabão [saˈbãw] (*pl* **-ões**) M soap; (*descompostura*):
  passar um ~ em alguém/levar um ~ to give sb
  a telling-off/get a telling-off; **~ de coco** coconut
  soap; **~ em pó** soap powder
sabatina [sabaˈtʃina] F revision test
sabedor, a [sabeˈdo(ʀ)(a)] ADJ informed
sabedoria [sabedoˈria] F wisdom; (*erudição*)
  learning
saber [saˈbe(ʀ)] VT, VI to know; (*descobrir*) to find
  out ■ M knowledge; **a ~** namely; **~ fazer** to
  know how to do, be able to do; **ele sabe nadar?**
  can he swim?; **~ de cor (e salteado)** to know off
  by heart; **que eu saiba** as far as I know; **sei** (*col*)
  I see; **sei lá** (*col*) I've got no idea, heaven knows;
  sabe de uma coisa? (*col*) you know what?; **você**
  é quem sabe, você que sabe (*col*) it's up to you
Sabesp [saˈbɛʃpi] ABR M = **Saneamento Básico**
  do Estado de São Paulo
sabiá [saˈbja] M/F thrush
sabichão, -chona [sabiˈʃãw, ˈʃɔna] (*pl* **-ões/-s**)
  M/F know-it-all, smart aleck
sabido, -a [saˈbidu, a] ADJ (*versado*)
  knowledgeable; (*esperto*) shrewd, clever
sábio, -a [ˈsabju, a] ADJ wise; (*erudito*) learned
  ■ M/F wise person; (*erudito*) scholar
sabões [saˈbõjʃ] MPL *de* **sabão**
sabonete [saboˈnetʃi] M toilet soap
saboneteira [saboneˈtejra] F soap dish
sabor [saˈbo(ʀ)] M taste, flavour (*Brit*), flavor (*US*);
  ao ~ de at the mercy of; **saborear** [saboˈrja(ʀ)]
  VT to taste, savour (*Brit*), savor (*US*); (*fig*) to
  relish; **saboroso, -a** [saboˈrozu, ɔza] ADJ tasty,
  delicious
sabotador, a [sabotaˈdo(ʀ)(a)] M/F saboteur
sabotagem [saboˈtaʒẽ] F sabotage

sabotar [saboˈta(ʀ)] VT to sabotage
saburrento, -a [saburˈxẽtu, a] ADJ (*língua*) furry
saca [ˈsaka] F sack
sacada [saˈkada] F balcony; *v tb* **sacado**
sacado, -a [saˈkadu, a] M/F (*Com*) drawee
sacador, a [sakaˈdo(ʀ)(a)] M/F (*Com*) drawer
sacal [saˈkaw] (*col*) (*pl* **-ais**) ADJ boring; **ser ~** to
  be a pain
sacana [saˈkana] (*col!*) ADJ (*canalha*) crooked;
  (*lascivo*) randy
sacanagem [sakaˈnaʒẽ] (*col*) (*pl* **-ns**) F (*sujeira*)
  dirty trick; (*libidinagem*) screwing; **fazer uma**
  ~ com alguém (*sujeira*) to screw sb; **filme de ~**
  blue movie
sacanear [sakaˈnja(ʀ)] (*col!*) VT: **~ alguém** (*fazer*
  sujeira) to screw sb; (*amolar*) to take the piss out
  of sb (!)
sacar [saˈka(ʀ)] VT to take out, pull out; (*dinheiro*)
  to withdraw; (*arma, cheque*) to draw; (*Esporte*)
  to serve; (*col: entender*) to understand ■ VI (*col:*
  entender) to understand; (: *mentir*) to tell fibs;
  (: *dar palpites*) to talk off the top of one's head;
  ~ de um revólver to pull a gun; **~ sobre um**
  devedor to borrow money from sb
saçaricar [sasariˈka(ʀ)] VI to have fun, fool
  around
sacarina [sakaˈrina] F saccharine (*Brit*),
  saccharin (US)
saca-rolhas M INV corkscrew
sacerdócio [sasexˈdɔsju] M priesthood
sacerdote [sasexˈdɔtʃi] M priest
sachê [saˈʃe] M sachet
saci [saˈsi] M (*in Brazilian folklore*) one-legged Black
  man who ambushes travellers
saciar [saˈsja(ʀ)] VT (*fome etc*) to satisfy; (*sede*) to
  quench
saco [ˈsaku] M bag; (*enseada*) inlet; (*col: testículos*)
  balls *pl* (!); **~!** (BR: *col*) damn!; **que ~!** (BR: *col*)
  how boring!; **encher o ~ de alguém** (BR: *col*)
  to annoy sb, get on sb's nerves; **estar de ~**
  cheio (de) to be fed up (with); **haja ~!** give me
  strength!; **puxar o ~ de alguém** (*col*) to suck
  up to sb; **ser um ~** (*col*) to be a drag; **ter ~** (*col*)
  to have patience; **ter ~ de fazer algo** to be

NB: *European Portuguese adds the following consonants to certain words:* **b** (sú(b)dito, su(b)til); **c** (a(c)ção,
  a(c)cionista, a(c)to); **m** (inde(m)ne); **p** (ado(p)çã, ado(p)tar); *for further details see p. xiii.*

bothered to do sth; **~ de água quente** hot water
bottle; **~ de café** coffee filter; **~ de dormir**
sleeping bag
sacode etc [sa'kɔdʒi] vb v **sacudir**
sacola [sa'kɔla] F bag
sacolejar [sakole'ʒaʳ] vt, vi to shake
sacramentar [sakramẽ'taʳ] vt (documento etc)
to legalize
sacramento [sakra'mẽtu] M sacrament
sacrificar [sakrifi'kaʳ] vt to sacrifice; (consagrar)
to dedicate; (submeter) to subject; (animal) to
have put down; **sacrificar-se** vr to sacrifice
o.s.; **sacrifício** [sakri'fisju] M sacrifice
sacrilégio [sakri'lɛʒu] M sacrilege
sacrílego, -a [sa'krilegu, a] ADJ sacrilegious
sacristão [sakri'ʃtãw] (pl -s) M sacristan, sexton
sacristia [sakriʃ'tʃia] F sacristy
sacristões [sakriʃ'tõjʃ] MPL de **sacristão**
sacro, -a ['sakru, a] ADJ sacred; (santo) holy;
(música) religious
sacrossanto, -a [sakro'sãtu, a] ADJ sacrosanct
sacudida [saku'dʒida] F shake
sacudidela [sakudʒi'dela] F shake, jolt
sacudido, -a [saku'dʒidu, a] ADJ shaken;
(movimento) rapid, quick; (robusto) sturdy
sacudir [saku'dʒiʳ] vt to shake; **sacudir-se** vr
to shake
sádico, -a ['sadʒiku, a] ADJ sadistic ■ M/F sadist
sadio, -a [sa'dʒiu, a] ADJ healthy
sadismo [sa'dʒiʒmu] M sadism
sadomasoquista [sadomazo'kiʃta] ADJ
sadomasochistic ■ M/F sadomasochist
safadeza [safa'deza] F (vileza) meanness;
(imoralidade) crudity; (travessura) mischief
safado, -a [sa'fadu, a] ADJ (descarado) shameless,
barefaced; (imoral) dirty; (travesso) mischievous
■ M rogue; **estar/ficar ~ (da vida) com** to be/
get furious with
safanão [safa'nãw] (pl -ões) M (puxão) tug; (tapa)
slap
safári [sa'fari] M safari
safira [sa'fira] F sapphire
safo, -a ['safu, a] ADJ (livre) clear; (col: esperto)
quick, clever
safra ['safra] F harvest; (fig: de músicos etc) crop
saga ['saga] F saga
sagacidade [sagasi'dadʒi] F sagacity,
shrewdness
sagaz [sa'gajʒ] ADJ sagacious, shrewd
sagitariano, -a [saʒita'rjanu, a] ADJ, M/F
Sagittarian
Sagitário [saʒi'tarju] M Sagittarius
sagrado, -a [sa'gradu, a] ADJ sacred, holy
saguão [sa'gwãw] (pl -ões) M (pátio) yard, patio;
(entrada) foyer, lobby; (de estação) entrance hall
saia ['saja] F skirt; (col: mulher) woman; **viver
agarrado às ~s de alguém** (fig) to be tied to sb's
apron strings; **~ escocesa** kilt
saia-calça (pl saias-calças) F culottes pl
saiba etc ['sajba] vb v **saber**
saibro ['sajbru] M gravel
saída [sa'ida] F (porta) exit, way out; (partida)

departure; (ato: de pessoa) going out; (fig: solução)
way out; (Comput: de programa) exit; (: de dados)
output; **de ~** (primeiro) first; (de cara) straight
away; **estar de ~** to be on one's way out; **na
~ do cinema** on the way out of the cinema;
(não) ter boa ~ (produto) (not) to sell well; **uma
mercadoria de muita** ~ a commodity which
sells well; **dar uma ~** to go out; **ter boas ~s**
(réplicas) to be witty; **não tem ~** (fig) there is no
escaping it; **~ de emergência** emergency exit
saideira [saj'dejra] F last drink
saidinha [saj'dʒinha] F: **dar uma ~** to pop out
saiote [sa'jɔtʃi] M short skirt
sair [sa'iʳ] vi to go (ou come) out; (partir) to leave;
(realizar-se) to turn out; (Comput) to exit; **sair-se**
vr: **sair-se bem/mal de** to be successful/
unsuccessful in; **~-se com** (dito) to come out
with; **~ caro/barato** to work out expensive/
cheap; **~ ganhando/perdendo** to come out
better/worse off; **~ a alguém** (parecer-se) to take
after sb; **~ de** (casa etc) to leave; (situação difícil)
to get out of; (doença) to come out of; **a notícia
saiu na TV/no jornal** the news was on TV/in
the paper
sal [saw] (pl sais) M salt; **sem ~** (comida) salt-free;
(pessoa) lacklustre (Brit), lackluster (US); **~ de
banho** bath salts pl; **~ de cozinha** cooking salt
sala ['sala] F room; (num edifício público) hall;
(classe, turma) class; **fazer ~ a alguém** to
entertain sb; **~ de audiências** (Jur) courtroom;
~ (de aula) classroom; **~ de bate-papo** (Internet)
chatroom; **~ de conferências** conference room;
~ de embarque departure lounge; **~ de espera**
waiting room; **~ de espetáculo** concert hall;
~ (de estar) living room, lounge; **~ de jantar**
dining room; **~ de operação** (Med) operating
theatre (Brit) ou theater (US); **~ de parto** delivery
room
salada [sa'lada] F salad; (fig) confusion, jumble;
~ de frutas fruit salad; **~ russa** (Culin) Russian
salad; (fig) hotchpotch
saladeira [sala'dejra] F salad bowl
sala-e-quarto M two-room flat ou apartment
salafra [sa'lafra] (col) M/F rat
salafrário [sala'frarju] (col) M crook
salame [sa'lami] M (Culin) salami
salaminho [sala'miɲu] M pepperoni (sausage)
salão [sa'lãw] (pl -ões) M large room, hall;
(exposição) show; (cabeleireiro) hairdressing salon;
de ~ (jogos) indoor; (anedota) proper, acceptable; **~
de baile** dance studio; **~ de beleza** beauty salon
salarial [sala'rjaw] (pl -ais) ADJ wage atr, pay atr
salário [sa'larju] M wages pl, salary; **~ mínimo**
minimum wage
salário-família (pl salários-família) M family
allowance
saldar [saw'daʳ] vt (contas) to settle; (dívida) to
pay off
saldo ['sawdu] M balance; (sobra) surplus; (fig:
resultado) result; **~ anterior/credor/devedor**
opening balance/credit balance/debit balance
saleiro [sa'lejru] M salt cellar; (moedor) salt mill

salgadinho [sawga'dʒiɲu] M savoury (Brit), savory (US), snack

salgado, -a [saw'gadu, a] ADJ salty, salted; (preço) exorbitant

salgar [saw'ga'] VT to salt

salgueiro [saw'gejru] M willow; ~ **chorão** weeping willow

saliência [sa'ljẽsja] F projection; (assanhamento) forwardness

salientar [saljẽ'ta'] VT to point out; (acentuar) to stress, emphasise; **salientar-se** VR (pessoa) to distinguish o.s.; **saliente** [sa'ljẽtʃi] ADJ jutting out, prominent; (evidente) clear, conspicuous; (importante) outstanding; (assanhado) forward

salina [sa'lina] F salt bed; (empresa) salt company

salino, -a [sa'linu, a] ADJ saline

salitre [sa'litri] M saltpetre (Brit), saltpeter (US), nitre (Brit), niter (US)

saliva [sa'liva] F saliva; **gastar** ~ (col) to waste one's breath

salivar [sali'va'] VI to salivate

salmão [saw'mãw] (pl -ões) M salmon ■ ADJ INV salmon-pink

salmo ['sawmu] M psalm

salmões [saw'mõjʃ] MPL de **salmão**

salmonela [sawmo'nɛla] F salmonella

salmoura [saw'mora] F brine

salobro, -a [sa'lobru, a] ADJ salty, brackish

salões [sa'lõjʃ] MPL de **salão**

saloio [sa'loju] (PT) M (camponês) country bumpkin

Salomão [salo'mãw]: **(as) ilhas** FPL: **(as) ilhas de** ~ (the) Solomon Islands

salpicão [sawpi'kãw] (pl -ões) M (paio) pork sausage; (prato) fricassee

salpicar [sawpi'ka'] VT to splash; (polvilhar, fig) to sprinkle

salpicões [sawpi'kõjʃ] MPL de **salpicão**

salsa ['sawsa] F parsley

salsicha [saw'siʃa] F sausage; **salsichão** [sawsi'ʃãw] (pl -ões) M sausage

saltado, -a [saw'tadu, a] ADJ (saliente) protruding

saltar [saw'ta'] VT to jump (over), leap (over); (omitir) to skip ■ VI to jump, leap; (sangue) to spurt out; (de ônibus, cavalo): ~ **de** to get off; ~ **à vista** ou **aos olhos** to be obvious

salteado, -a [saw'tʃjadu, a] ADJ broken up; (Culin) sautéed

salteador [sawtʃja'do'] M highwayman

saltear [saw'tʃja'] VT (trechos de um livro) to skip; (Culin) to sauté

saltimbanco [sawtʃĩ'bãku] M travelling (Brit) ou traveling (US) player

saltitante [sawtʃi'tãtʃi] ADJ: ~ **de alegria** as pleased as punch

saltitar [sawtʃi'ta'] VI (pássaros) to hop; (fig: de um assunto a outro) to skip

salto ['sawtu] M jump, leap; (de calçado) heel;

dar um ~ to jump, leap; **dar ~s de alegria** ou **de contente** to jump for joy; ~ **de vara** pole vault; ~ **em altura** high jump; ~ **em distância** long jump

salto-mortal (pl saltos-mortais) M somersault

salubre [sa'lubri] ADJ healthy, salubrious

salutar [salu'ta'] ADJ salutary, beneficial

salva ['sawva] F salvo; (bandeja) tray, salver; (Bot) sage; ~ **de palmas** round of applause; ~ **de tiros** round of gunfire

salvação [sawva'sãw] F salvation; ~ **da pátria** ou **da lavoura** (col) lifesaver

salvador [sawva'do'] M saviour (Brit), savior (US)

salvados [saw'vaduʃ] MPL salvage sg; (Com) salvaged goods

salvaguarda [sawva'gwaxda] F protection, safeguard

salvaguardar [sawvagwax'da'] VT to safeguard

salvamento [sawva'mẽtu] M rescue; (de naufrágio) salvage

salvar [saw'va'] VT (tb: Comput) to save; (resgatar) to rescue; (objetos, de ruína) to salvage; (honra) to defend; **salvar-se** VR to escape

salva-vidas M INV (bóia) lifebuoy; (pessoa) lifeguard; **barco** ~ lifeboat

salve ['sawvi] EXCL hooray (for)!

salvo, -a ['sawvu, a] ADJ safe ■ PREP except, save; **a** ~ in safety; **pôr-se a** ~ to run to safety; **todos** ~ **ele** all except him

salvo-conduto (pl -s) M safe-conduct

samambaia [samã'baja] F fern

samaritano [samari'tanu] M: **bom** ~ good Samaritan; (pej) do-gooder

samba ['sãba] M samba; **cueca** ~ boxer shorts pl

● SAMBA

The greatest form of musical expression of the Brazilian people, the samba is a type of music and dance of African origin. It embraces a number of rhythmic styles, such as samba de breque, samba-enredo, samba-canção and pagode, among others. Officially, the first samba, entitled Pelo telefone", was written in Rio in 1917.

samba-canção (pl sambas-canção) M slow samba

sambar [sã'ba'] VI to dance the samba

sambista [sã'biʃta] M/F (dançarino) samba dancer; (compositor) samba composer

sambódromo [sã'bɔdromu] M carnival parade ground

Samoa [sa'moa] M: ~ **Ocidental** Western Samoa

samovar [samo'va'] M tea urn

sanar [sa'na'] VT to cure; (remediar) to remedy

sanatório [sana'tɔrju] M sanatorium (Brit), sanitorium (US)

sanável [sa'navew] (pl -eis) ADJ curable;

NB: European Portuguese adds the following consonants to certain words: **b** (sú(b)dito, su(b)til); **c** (a(c)ção, a(c)cionista, a(c)to); **m** (inde(m)ne); **p** (ado(p)çã, ado(p)tar); for further details see p. xiii.

(*remediável*) remediable

sanca ['sãka] F cornice, moulding (*Brit*), molding (*US*)

sanção [sã'sãw] (*pl* -ões) F sanction; **sancionar** [sansjo'na^r] VT to sanction; (*autorizar*) to authorize

sanções [sã'sõjʃ] FPL *de* **sanção**

sandália [sã'dalja] F sandal

sândalo ['sãdalu] M sandalwood

sandes ['sãdəʃ] (*PT*) F INV sandwich

sanduíche [sand'wiʃi] (*BR*) M sandwich; ~ **americano** ham and egg sandwich; ~ **misto** ham and cheese sandwich; ~ **natural** wholemeal sandwich

saneamento [sanja'mẽtu] M sanitation; (*de governo etc*) clean-up

sanear [sa'nja^r] VT to clean up; (*pântanos*) to drain

sanfona [sã'fɔna] F (*Mús*) accordion; (*Tricô*) ribbing

sanfonado, -a [sãfo'nadu, a] ADJ (*porta*) folding; (*suéter*) ribbed

sangrar [sã'gra^r] VT, VI to bleed; ~ **alguém** (*fig*) to bleed sb dry; **sangrento, -a** [sã'grẽtu, a] ADJ bloody; (*ensanguentado*) bloodstained; (*Culin: carne*) rare

sangria [sã'gria] F bloodshed; (*extorsão*) extortion; (*bebida*) sangria

sangue ['sãgi] M blood; ~ **pisado** bruise

sangue-frio M cold-bloodedness

sanguessuga [sãgi'suga] F leech

sanguinário, -a [sãgi'narju, a] ADJ bloodthirsty, cruel

sanguíneo, -a [sã'ginju, a] ADJ blood *atr*; **grupo** ~ blood group; **pressão sanguínea** blood pressure; **vaso** ~ blood vessel

sanha ['saɲa] F rage, fury

sanidade [sani'dadʒi] F (*saúde*) health; (*mental*) sanity

sanita [sa'nita] (*PT*) F toilet, lavatory

sanitário, -a [sani'tarju, a] ADJ sanitary; **vaso** ~ toilet, lavatory (bowl); **sanitários** [sani'tarjuʃ] MPL toilets

sanitarista [sanita'riʃta] M/F health worker

Santiago [sã'tʃjagu] F: ~ **(do Chile)** Santiago (de Chile)

santidade [sãtʃi'dadʒi] F holiness, sanctity; **Sua S~** His Holiness (the Pope)

santificar [sãtʃifi'ka^r] VT to sanctify, make holy

santinho [sãt'ʃiɲu] M (*imagem*) holy picture; (*col: pessoa*) saint

santista [sã'tʃiʃta] ADJ from Santos ■ M/F person from Santos

santo, -a ['sãtu, a] ADJ holy, sacred; (*pessoa*) saintly; (*remédio*) effective ■ M/F saint; **todo** ~ **dia** every single day; **ter** ~ **forte** (*col*) to have good backing

santuário [sã'twarju] M shrine, sanctuary

São [sãw] M Saint

são, sã [sãw] (*pl* -s/-s) ADJ healthy; (*conselho*) sound; (*atitude*) wholesome; (*mentalmente*) sane; ~ **e salvo** safe and sound

São Lourenço [-lo'rẽsu] M: **o (rio)** ~ the St. Lawrence river

São Marinho M San Marino

São Paulo [-'pawlu] N São Paulo

são-tomense [-to'mẽsi] ADJ from São Tomé e Príncipe ■ M/F native *ou* inhabitant of São Tomé e Príncipe

sapata [sa'pata] M (*do freio*) shoe

sapatão [sapa'tãw] (*pl* -ões) M big shoe; (*col: lésbica*) lesbian

sapataria [sapata'ria] F shoe shop

sapateado [sapa'tʃjadu] M tap dancing

sapateador, a [sapatʃja'do^r(a)] M/F tap dancer

sapatear [sapa'tʃja^r] VI to tap one's feet; (*dançar*) to tap-dance

sapateiro [sapa'tejru] M shoemaker; (*vendedor*) shoe salesman; (*que conserta*) shoe repairer; (*loja*) shoe repairer's

sapatilha [sapa'tʃiʎa] F (*de balé*) shoe; (*sapato*) pump; (*de atleta*) running shoe

sapato [sa'patu] M shoe

sapatões [sapa'tõjʃ] MPL *de* **sapatão**

sapé [sa'pɛ] M = **sapê**

sapê [sa'pe] M thatch; **teto de** ~ thatched roof

sapeca [sa'pɛka] ADJ flirtatious; (*criança*) cheeky

sapecar [sape'ka^r] VT (*tapa, pontapé*) to land ■ VI (*flertar*) to flirt

sapiência [sa'pjẽsja] F wisdom, learning

sapiente [sa'pjẽtʃi] ADJ wise

sapinho [sa'piɲu] M (*Med*) thrush

sapo ['sapu] M toad; **engolir** ~**s** (*fig*) to sit back and take it

saque ['saki] M (*de dinheiro*) withdrawal; (*Com*) draft, bill; (*Esporte*) serve; (*pilhagem*) plunder, pillage; (*col: mentira*) fib; ~ **a descoberto** (*Com*) overdraft

saque *etc* VB V **sacar**

saquear [sa'kja^r] VT to pillage, plunder

saracotear [sarako'tʃja^r] VI to wiggle one's hips; (*vaguear*) to wander around ■ VT to shake

Saragoça [sara'gɔsa] N Zaragoza

saraiva [sa'rajva] F hail

saraivada [sarai'vada] F hailstorm; **uma** ~ **de** (*fig*) a hail of

saraivar [sarai'va^r] VI to hail; (*fig*) to spray

sarampo [sa'rãpu] M measles *sg*

sarapintado, -a [sarapĩ'tadu, a] ADJ spotted, speckled

sarar [sa'ra^r] VT to cure; (*ferida*) to heal ■ VI to recover, be cured

sarau [sa'raw] M soirée

sarcasmo [sax'kaʒmu] M sarcasm

sarcástico, -a [sax'kaʃtʃiku, a] ADJ sarcastic

sarda ['saxda] F freckle

Sardenha [sax'deɲa] F: **a** ~ Sardinia

sardento, -a [sax'dẽtu, a] ADJ freckled, freckly

sardinha [sax'dʒiɲa] F sardine; **como** ~ **em lata** (*apertado*) like sardines

sardônico, -a [sax'doniku, a] ADJ sardonic, sarcastic

sargento [sax'ʒẽtu] M sergeant

sári ['sari] M sari

sarjeta [sax'ʒeta] F gutter

sarna ['saxna] F scabies sg

sarrafo [sa'xafu] M: **baixar o ~ em alguém** (col) to let sb have it

sarro ['saxu] M (de vinho, nos dentes) tartar; (na língua) fur, coating; (col) laugh; **tirar um ~** (col) to pet, neck

Satã [sa'tã] M Satan, the Devil

Satanás [sata'naʃ] M Satan, the Devil

satânico, -a [sa'taniku, a] ADJ satanic; (fig) devilish

satélite [sa'tɛlitʃi] ADJ satellite atr ■ M satellite

sátira ['satʃira] F satire

satírico, -a [sa'tʃiriku, a] ADJ satirical

satirizar [satʃiri'za^r] VT to satirize

satisfação [satʃiʃfa'sãw] (pl -ões) F satisfaction; (recompensa) reparation; **dar uma ~ a alguém** to give sb an explanation; **ela não dá satisfações a ninguém** she answers to no-one; **tomar satisfações de alguém** to ask sb for an explanation

satisfaço etc [satʃiʃ'fasu] VB V **satisfazer**

satisfações [satʃiʃfa'sõjʃ] FPL de **satisfação**

satisfatório, -a [satʃiʃfa'tɔrju, a] ADJ satisfactory

satisfazer [satʃiʃfa'ze^r] (irreg) VT to satisfy; (dívida) to pay off ■ VI (ser satisfatório) to be satisfactory; **satisfazer-se** VR to be satisfied; (saciar-se) to fill o.s. up; **~ a** to satisfy; **~ com** to fulfil (Brit), fulfill (US); **satisfeito, -a** [satʃiʃ'fejtu, a] PP de **satisfazer** ■ ADJ satisfied; (alegre) content; (saciado) full; **dar-se por satisfeito com algo** to be content with sth; **dar alguém por satisfeito** to make sb happy

satisfez [satʃiʃ'feʒ] VB V **satisfazer**

satisfiz etc [satʃiʃ'fiʒ] VB V **satisfazer**

saturado, -a [satu'radu, a] ADJ (de comida) full; (aborrecido) fed up; (Com: mercado) saturated

saturar [satu'ra^r] VT to saturate; (de comida, aborrecimento) to fill

Saturno [sa'tuxnu] M Saturn

saudação [sawda'sãw] (pl -ções) F greeting

saudade [saw'dadʒi] F (desejo ardente) longing, yearning; (lembrança nostálgica) nostalgia; **deixar ~s** to be greatly missed; **matar as ~s de alguém/algo** to catch up with sb/cure one's nostalgia for sth; **ter ~s de** (desejar) to long for; (sentir falta de) to miss; **~s (de casa** ou **da família** ou **dada pátria)** homesickness sg

saudar [saw'da^r] VT (cumprimentar) to greet; (dar as boas vindas) to welcome; (aclamar) to acclaim

saudável [saw'davew] (pl -eis) ADJ healthy; (moralmente) wholesome

saúde [sa'udʒi] F health; (brinde) toast; **~!** (brindando) cheers!; (quando se espirra) bless you!; **à sua ~!** your health!; **beber à ~ de** to drink to, toast; **estar bem/mal de ~** to be well/ill; **não ter mais ~ para fazer** not to be up to doing; **vender ~** to be bursting with health; **~ pública**

public health; (órgão) health service

saudosismo [sawdo'ziʒmu] M nostalgia

saudoso, -a [saw'dozu, ɔza] ADJ (nostálgico) nostalgic; (da família ou terra natal) homesick; (de uma pessoa) longing; (que causa saudades) much-missed

sauna ['sawna] F sauna; **fazer ~** to have ou take a sauna

saveiro [sa'vejru] M sailing boat

saxofone [sakso'fɔni] M saxophone

saxofonista [saksofo'niʃta] M/F saxophonist

sazonado, -a [sazo'nadu, a] ADJ ripe, mature

sazonal [sazo'naw] (pl -ais) ADJ seasonal

SBPC ABR F = **Sociedade Brasileira para o Progresso da Ciência**

SBT ABR M (= Sistema Brasileiro de Televisão) television station

SC ABR = **Santa Catarina**

SCDF ABR F = **Sagrada Congregação para a Doutrina da Fé**

SE ABR = **Sergipe**

○ **PALAVRA CHAVE**

se [si] PRON **1** (reflexivo: impess) oneself; (: m) himself; (: f) herself; (: coisa) itself; (: você) yourself; (: pl) themselves; (: vocês) yourselves; **ela está se vestindo** she's getting dressed; (usos léxicos del pron) v o vb em questão p. ex. **arrepender-se**

2 (uso recíproco) each other, one another; **olharam-se** they looked at each other

3 (impess): **come-se bem aqui** you can eat well here; **sabe-se que ...** it is known that ...; **vende(m)-se jornais naquela loja** they sell newspapers in that shop

■ CONJ if; (em pergunta indireta) whether; **se bem que** even though

sé [sɛ] F cathedral; **Santa Sé** Holy See

sê [se] VB V **ser**

Seade [se'adʒi] (BR) ABR M = **Sistema Estadual de Análise de Dados**

seara ['sjara] F (campo de cereais) wheat (ou corn) field; (campo cultivado) tilled field

sebe ['sɛbi] (PT) F fence; **~ viva** hedge

sebento, -a [se'bẽtu, a] ADJ greasy; (sujo) dirty, filthy

sebo ['sebu] M tallow; (livraria) secondhand bookshop

seborréia [sebo'xɛja] F seborrhoea (Brit), seborrhea (US)

seboso, -a [se'bozu, ɔza] ADJ greasy; (sujo) dirty; (col) stuck-up

seca ['sɛka] F (estiagem) drought

secador [seka'do^r] M dryer; **~ de cabelo/roupa** hairdryer/clothes horse

secagem [se'kaʒẽ] F drying

seção [se'sãw] (pl -ões) F section; (em loja,

NB: European Portuguese adds the following consonants to certain words: **b** (sú(b)dito, su(b)til); **c** (a(c)ção, a(c)cionista, a(c)to); **m** (inde(m)ne); **p** (ado(p)çã, ado(p)tar); for further details see p. xiii.

repartição) department; ~ **rítmica** rhythm section

secar [se'ka^r] VT to dry; (*planta*) to parch; (*rio*) to dry up ■ VI to dry; (*oo*) to wither; (*fonte*) to dry up

secção [sek'sãw] (PT) = **seção**

seccionar [seksjo'na^r] VT to split up

secessão [sese'sãw] (*pl* -ões) F secession

seco, -a ['seku, a] ADJ dry; (*árido*) arid; (*fruta, carne*) dried; (*ríspido*) curt, brusque; (*pancada, ruído*) dull; (*magro*) thin; (*pessoa: frio*) cold; (: *sério*) serious; **em ~** (*barco*) aground; **estar ~ por algo/para fazer algo** (*col*) to be dying for sth/to do sth

seções [se'sõjʃ] FPL *de* **seção**

secreção [sekre'sãw] (*pl* -ões) F secretion

secretaria [sekreta'ria] F (*escritório geral*) general office; (*de secretário*) secretary's office; (*ministério*) ministry

secretária [sekre'tarja] F (*mesa*) writing desk; ~ **eletrônica** (telephone) answering machine; *v tb* **secretário**

secretariar [sekreta'rja^r] VT to work as a secretary to ■ VI to work as a secretary

secretário, -a [sekre'tarju, a] M/F secretary; ~ **particular** private secretary; **S~ de Estado de** ... Secretary of State for ..

secretário, -ria-geral (*pl* -s/as-gerais) M/F secretary-general

secreto, -a [se'krɛtu, a] ADJ secret

sectário, -a [sek'tarju, a] ADJ sectarian ■ M/F follower

sectarismo [sekta'riʒmu] M sectarianism

sector [sek'to^r] (PT) M = **setor**

secular [seku'la^r] ADJ (*leigo*) secular, lay; (*muito antigo*) age-old

secularizar [sekulari'za^r] VT to secularize

século ['sɛkulu] M (*cem anos*) century; (*época*) age; **há ~s** (*fig*) for ages; (: *atrás*) ages ago

secundar [sekũ'da^r] VT (*apoiar*) to second, support; (*ajudar*) to help; (*pedido*) to follow up

secundário, -a [sekũ'darju, a] ADJ secondary

secura [se'kura] F dryness; (*fig*) coldness; (*col: desejo*) keenness

seda ['seda] F silk; **ser** *ou* **estar uma ~** to be nice; **bicho da ~** silkworm

sedã [se'dã] M (*Auto*) saloon (car) (*Brit*), sedan (US)

sedativo, -a [seda'tʃivu, a] ADJ sedative ■ M sedative

SEDE (BR) ABR M = **Sistema Estadual de Empregos**

sede¹ ['sɛdʒi] F (*de empresa, instituição*) headquarters *sg*; (*de governo*) seat; (*Rel*) see, diocese; ~ **social** head office

sede² ['sedʒi] F thirst; (*fig*): ~ **(de)** craving (for); **estar com** *ou* **ter ~** to be thirsty; **matar a ~ to** quench one's thirst

sedentário, -a [sedẽ'tarju, a] ADJ sedentary

sedento, -a [se'dẽtu, a] ADJ thirsty; (*fig*): ~ **(de)** eager (for)

sediar [se'dʒja^r] VT to base

sedição [sedʒi'sãw] F sedition

sedicioso, -a [sedʒi'sjozu, ɔza] ADJ seditious

sedimentar [sedʒimẽ'ta^r] VI to silt up

sedimento [sedʒi'mẽtu] M sediment

sedoso, -a [se'dozu, ɔza] ADJ silky

sedução [sedu'sãw] (*pl* -ões) F seduction; (*atração*) allure, charm

sedutor, a [sedu'to^r(a)] ADJ seductive; (*oferta etc*) tempting ■ M/F seducer

seduzir [sedu'zi^r] VT to seduce; (*fascinar*) to fascinate; (*desencaminhar*) to lead astray

Sefiti [sefi'tʃi] (BR) ABR M = **Serviço de Fiscalização de Trânsito Interestadual e Internacional**

seg. ABR (= *segunda-feira*) Mon

segmentar [segmẽ'ta^r] VT to segment

segmento [seg'mẽtu] M segment

segredar [segre'da^r] VT, VI to whisper

segredo [se'gredu] M secret; (*sigilo*) secrecy; (*de fechadura*) combination; **em ~** in secret; ~ **de estado** state secret

segregação [segrega'sãw] F segregation

segregar [segre'ga^r] VT to segregate, separate

seguidamente [segida'mẽtʃi] ADV (*sem parar*) continuously; (*logo depois*) soon afterwards

seguido, -a [se'gidu, a] ADJ following; (*contínuo*) continuous, consecutive; ~ **de** *ou* **por** followed by; **três dias ~s** three days running; **horas seguidas** for hours on end; **em seguida** next; (*logo depois*) soon afterwards; (*imediatamente*) immediately, right away

seguidor, a [segi'do^r(a)] M/F follower

seguimento [segi'mẽtu] M continuation; **dar ~ a** to proceed with; **em ~ de** after

seguinte [se'gĩtʃi] ADJ following, next; **(o negócio) é o ~** (*col*) the thing is; **eu lhe disse o ~** this is what I said to him; **pelo ~** hereby

seguir [se'gi^r] VT to follow; to continue ■ VI to follow; (*continuar*) to continue, carry on; (*ir*) to go; **seguir-se** VR: **seguir-se (a)** to follow; **logo a ~** next; ~ **-se (de)** to result (from); **ao jantar seguiu-se uma reunião** the dinner was followed by a meeting

segunda [se'gũda] F (*tb*: **segunda-feira**) Monday; (*Mús*) second; (*Auto*) second (gear); **de ~** second-rate; **segunda-feira** (*pl* **segundas-feiras**) F Monday; *v tb* **terça-feira**

segundanista [segũda'niʃta] M/F second year (student)

segundo, -a [se'gũdu, a] ADJ second ■ PREP according to ■ CONJ as, from what ■ ADV secondly ■ M second; **de segunda mão** second-hand; **de segunda (classe)** second-class; ~ **ele disse** according to what he said; ~ **dizem** apparently; ~ **me consta** as far as I know; ~ **se afirma** according to what is said, from what is said; **segundas intenções** ulterior motives; ~ **tempo** (*Futebol*) second half; *v tb* **quinto**

segundo-time ADJ INV (*pessoa*) second-rate

segurado, -a [segu'radu, a] ADJ, M/F (*Com*) insured

segurador, a [segura'do^r(a)] M/F insurer ■ F

insurance company

seguramente [segura'mētʃi] ADV (com certeza) certainly; (muito provavelmente) surely

segurança [segu'rãsa] F security; (ausência de perigo) safety; (confiança) confidence; (convicção) assurance ■ M/F security guard; **com ~** assuredly; **~ nacional** national security

segurar [segu'ra^r] VT to hold; (amparar) to hold up; (Com: bens) to insure ■ VI: **~ em** to hold; **segurar-se** VR (Com: fazer seguro) to insure o.s.; **~-se em** to hold on to

seguro, -a [se'guru, a] ADJ (livre de perigo) safe; (livre de risco, firme) secure; (certo) certain, assured; (confiável) reliable; (de si mesmo) secure, confident; (tempo) settled ■ ADV confidently ■ M (Com) insurance; **~ de si** self-assured; **~ morreu de velho** better safe than sorry; **estar ~ de/de que** to be sure of/that; **fazer ~** to take out an insurance policy; **companhia de ~s** insurance company; **~ contra acidentes/ incêndio** accident/fire insurance; **~ de vida/ automóvel** life/car insurance; **seguro-saúde** (pl seguros-saúde) M health insurance

SEI (BR) ABR F = **Secretaria Especial da Informática**

sei [sej] VB V **saber**

seio ['seju] M breast, bosom; (âmago) heart; (seio paranasal) sinus; **no ~ de** in the heart of

seis [sejʃ] NUM six; V tb **cinco**

seiscentos, -tas [sejʃ'sētuʃ] NUM six hundred

seita ['sejta] F sect

seiva ['sejva] F sap; (fig) vigour (Brit), vigor (US), vitality

seixo ['sejʃu] M pebble

seja etc ['seʒa] VB V **ser**

SELA ABR M = **Sistema Econômico Latino-Americano**

sela ['sɛla] F saddle

selagem [se'laʒē] F (de cartas) franking; **máquina de ~** franking machine

selar [se'la^r] VT (carta) to stamp; (documento oficial, pacto) to seal; (cavalo) to saddle; (fechar) to shut, seal; (concluir) to conclude

seleção [sele'sãw] (PT -cç-, pl -ões) F selection; (Esporte) team

selecionado [selesjo'nadu] (PT -cc-) M (Esporte) team

selecionador, a [selesjona'do^r(a)] (PT -cc-) M/F selector

selecionar [selesjo'na^r] (PT -cc-) VT to select

seleções [sele'sõjʃ] FPL de **seleção**

seleta [se'leta] (PT -ct-) F anthology

seletivo, -a [sele'tʃivu, a] (PT -ct-) ADJ selective

seleto, -a [se'lɛtu, a] (PT -ct-) ADJ select

selim [se'lĩ] (pl -ns) M saddle

selo ['selu] M stamp; (carimbo, sinete) seal; (fig) stamp, mark

selva ['sɛwva] F jungle

selvagem [sew'vaʒē] (pl -ns) ADJ (silvestre) wild; (feroz) fierce; (povo) savage; (fig: indivíduo, maneiras) coarse; **selvageria** [sewvaʒe'ria] F savagery

sem [sē] PREP without ■ CONJ: **~ que eu peça** without my asking; **a casa está ~ limpar há duas semanas** the house hasn't been cleaned for two weeks; **estar/ficar ~ dinheiro/ gasolina** to have no/have run out of money/ petrol; **~ quê nem para quê** for no apparent reason

SEMA (BR) ABR F = **Secretaria Especial do Meio Ambiente**

semáforo [se'maforu] M (Auto) traffic lights pl; (Ferro) signal

semana [se'mana] F week

semanada [sema'nada] F (weekly) wages pl; (mesada) weekly allowance

semanal [sema'naw] (pl -ais) ADJ weekly; **ganha $200 semanais** he earns $200 a week

semanário [sema'narju] M weekly (publication)

semântica [se'mãtʃika] F semantics sg

semântico, -a [se'mãtʃiku, a] ADJ semantic

semblante [sē'blãtʃi] M face; (fig) appearance, look

semeadura [semja'dura] F sowing

semear [se'mja^r] VT to sow; (fig) to spread; (espalhar) to scatter

semelhança [seme'ʎãsa] F similarity, resemblance; **a ~ de** like; **ter ~ com** to resemble

semelhante [seme'ʎãtʃi] ADJ similar; (tal) such ■ M fellow creature

semelhar [seme'ʎa^r] VI: **~ a** to look like, resemble ■ VT to look like, resemble; **semelhar-se** VR to be alike

sêmen ['semē] M semen

semente [se'mētʃi] F seed

sementeira [semē'tejra] F sowing, spreading

semestral [semeʃ'traw] (pl -ais) ADJ half-yearly, bi-annual

semestralmente [semeʃtraw'mētʃi] ADV every six months

semestre [se'mɛʃtri] M six months; (Educ) semester

sem-fim M: **um ~ de perguntas** etc endless questions etc

semi... [semi] PREFIXO semi..., half..

semi-aberto, -a ADJ half-open

semi-analfabeto, -a ADJ semiliterate

semibreve [semi'brɛvi] F (Mús) semibreve

semicírculo [semi'sixkulu] M semicircle

semicondutor [semikõdu'to^r] M semiconductor

semiconsciente [semikõ'sjētʃi] ADJ semiconscious

semifinal [semi'finaw] (pl -ais) F semi-final

semifinalista [semifina'liʃta] M/F semi-finalist

semi-internato M day school

semi-interno, -a M/F (tb: aluno semi-interno) day pupil

NB: European Portuguese adds the following consonants to certain words: **b** (sú(b)dito, su(b)til); **c** (a(c)ção, a(c)cionista, a(c)to); **m** (inde(m)ne); **p** (ado(p)çã, ado(p)tar); for further details see p. xiii.

seminal [semi'naw] (*pl* -ais) ADJ seminal
seminário [semi'narju] M (*Educ, congresso*) seminar; (*Rel*) seminary
seminarista [semina'riʃta] M seminarist
seminu, a [semi'nu(a)] ADJ half-naked
semiótica [se'mjɔtʃika] F semiotics *sg*
semiprecioso, -a [semipre'sjozu, ɔza] ADJ semi-precious
semita [se'mita] ADJ Semitic
semítico, -a [se'mitʃiku, a] ADJ Semitic
semitom [semi'tõ] M (*Mús*) semitone
sem-lar M/F INV homeless person
sem-número M: **um ~ de coisas** loads of things
semolina [semo'lina] F semolina
sem-par ADJ INV unequalled, unique
sempre ['sẽpri] ADV always; **você ~ vai?** (*PT*) are you still going?; **~ que** whenever; **como ~ as usual**; **a comida/hora** *etc* **de ~** the usual food/time *etc*; **a mesma história de ~** the same old story; **para ~** forever; **para todo o ~** for ever and ever; **quase ~** nearly always
sem-sal ADJ INV insipid
sem-terra M/F INV landless labourer (*Brit*) *ou* laborer (*US*)
sem-teto M/F INV: **os ~** the homeless
sem-vergonha ADJ INV shameless ■ M/F INV (*pessoa*) rogue
Sena ['sɛna] M: **o ~** the Seine
Senac [se'naki] (*BR*) ABR M = **Serviço Nacional de Aprendizagem Comercial**
senado [se'nadu] M senate; **senador, a** [sena'do'(a)] M/F senator
Senai [se'naj] (*BR*) ABR M = **Serviço Nacional de Aprendizagem Industrial**
senão [se'nãw] (*pl* -ões) CONJ (*do contrário*) otherwise; (*mas sim*) but, but rather ■ PREP (*exceto*) except ■ M flaw, defect; **~ quando** suddenly
Senav [se'navi] (*BR*) ABR F = **Superintendência Estadual de Navegação**
senda ['sẽda] F path
Senegal [sene'gaw] M: **o ~** Senegal
senha ['sɛɲa] F (*sinal*) sign; (*palavra de passe, Comput*) password; (*de caixa automática*) PIN number; (*recibo*) receipt; (*bilhete*) ticket, voucher
senhor, a [se'ɲo'(a)] M (*homem*) man; (*formal*) gentleman; (*homem idoso*) elderly man; (*Rel*) lord; (*dono*) owner; (*tratamento*) Mr(.); (*tratamento respeitoso*) sir ■ F (*mulher*) lady; (*esposa*) wife; (*mulher idosa*) elderly lady; (*dona*) owner; (*tratamento*) Mrs(.), Ms(.); (*tratamento respeitoso*) madam ■ ADJ marvellous (*Brit*), marvelous (*US*); **uma ~a gripe** a bad case of flu; **o ~/a ~a** (*você*) you; **nossa ~a!** (*col*) gosh; **sim, ~(a)!** yes indeed; **estar ~ de si** to be cool *ou* collected; **estar ~ da situação** to be in control of the situation; **ser ~ do seu nariz** to be one's own boss; **~ de engenho** plantation owner
senhoria [seɲo'ria] F (*proprietária*) landlady; **Vossa S~** (*em cartas*) you

senhoril [seɲo'riw] (*pl* -is) ADJ (*roupa etc*) gentlemen's/ladies'; (*distinto*) lordly
senhorio [seɲo'riu] M (*proprietário*) landlord; (*posse*) ownership
senhoris [seɲo'riʃ] ADJ PL *de* **senhoril**
senhorita [seɲo'rita] F young lady; (*tratamento*) Miss, Ms(.); **a ~** (*você*) you
senil [se'niw] (*pl* -is) ADJ senile
senilidade [senili'dadʒi] F senility
senilizar [senili'za'] VT to age
senis [se'niʃ] ADJ PL *de* **senil**
senões [se'nõjʃ] MPL *de* **senão**
sensação [sẽsa'sãw] (*pl* -ões) F sensation; **a ~ de que/uma ~ de** the feeling that/a feeling of; **causar ~** to cause a sensation; **sensacional** [sẽsasjo'naw] (*pl* -ais) ADJ sensational
sensacionalismo [sẽsasjona'liʒmu] M sensationalism
sensacionalista [sẽsasjona'liʃta] ADJ sensationalist
sensações [sẽsa'sõjʃ] FPL *de* **sensação**
sensatez [sẽsa'teʒ] F good sense
sensato, -a [sẽ'satu, a] ADJ sensible
sensibilidade [sẽsibili'dadʒi] F sensitivity; (*artística*) sensibility; (*física*) feeling; **estou com muita ~ neste dedo** this finger is very sensitive
sensibilizar [sẽsibili'za'] VT to touch, move; (*opinião pública*) to influence; **sensibilizar-se** VR to be moved
sensitivo, -a [sẽsi'tʃivu, a] ADJ sensory; (*pessoa*) sensitive
sensível [sẽ'sivew] (*pl* -eis) ADJ sensitive; (*visível*) noticeable; (*considerável*) considerable; (*dolorido*) tender
sensivelmente [sẽsivew'mẽtʃi] ADV perceptibly, markedly
senso ['sẽsu] M sense; (*juízo*) judgement; **~ comum** *ou* **bom ~** common sense; **~ de humor/responsabilidade** sense of humour (*Brit*) *ou* humor (*US*) /responsibility
sensorial [sẽso'rjaw] (*pl* -ais) ADJ sensory
sensual [sẽ'swaw] (*pl* -ais) ADJ sensual, sensuous
sensualidade [sẽswali'dadʒi] F sensuality, sensuousness
sentado, -a [sẽ'tadu, a] ADJ sitting; (*almoço*) sit-down
sentar [sẽ'ta'] VT to seat ■ VI to sit; **sentar-se** VR to sit down
sentença [sẽ'tẽsa] F (*Jur*) sentence; **~ de morte** death sentence; **sentenciar** [sẽtẽ'sja'] VT (*julgar*) to pass judgement on; (*condenar por sentença*) to sentence ■ VI to pass judgement; to pass sentence
sentidamente [sẽtʃida'mẽtʃi] ADV (*chorar*) bitterly; (*desculpar-se*) abjectly
sentido, -a [sẽ'tʃidu, a] ADJ (*magoado*) hurt; (*choro, queixa*) heartfelt ■ M sense; (*significação*) sense, meaning; (*direção*) direction; (*atenção*) attention; (*aspecto*) respect; **~!** (*Mil*) attention!; **em certo ~** in a sense; **sem ~** meaningless;

fazer ~ to make sense; **perder/recobrar os** ~**s** to lose/recover consciousness; **(não) ter** ~ (not) to be acceptable; ~ **figurado** figurative sense; "**~ único**" (PT: *sinal*) "one-way"

sentimental [sē'tʃimē'taw] (*pl* -**ais**) ADJ sentimental; **aventura** ~ romance; **vida** ~ love life

sentimentalismo [sētʃimēta'liʒmu] M sentimentality

sentimento [sētʃi'mētu] M feeling; (*senso*) sense; **sentimentos** MPL (*pêsames*) condolences; **fazer algo com** ~ to do sth with feeling; **ter bons** ~**s** to be good-natured

sentinela [sētʃi'nɛla] F sentry, guard; **estar de** ~ to be on guard duty; **render** ~ to relieve the guard

sentir [sē'tʃir] VT to feel; (*perceber, pressentir*) to sense; (*ser afetado por*) to be affected by; (*magoar-se*) to be upset by ■ VI to feel; (*sofrer*) to suffer; **sentir-se** VR to feel; (*julgar-se*) to consider o.s. (to be); ~ **(a) falta de** to miss; ~ **cheiro/gosto (de)** to smell/taste; ~ **tristeza** to feel sad; ~ **vontade de** to feel like; **você sente a diferença?** can you tell the difference?; **sinto muito** I am very sorry

senzala [sē'zala] F slave quarters *pl*

separação [separa'sãw] (*pl* -**ões**) F separation

separado, -a [sepa'radu, a] ADJ separate; (*casal*) separated; **em** ~ separately, apart

separar [sepa'rar] VT to separate; (*dividir*) to divide; (*pôr de lado*) to put aside; **separar-se** VR to separate; to be divided; ~-**se de** to separate from

separata [sepa'rata] F offprint

separatismo [separa'tʃiʒmu] M separatism

séptico, -a ['sɛptʃiku, a] ADJ septic

septuagésimo, -a [septwa'ʒɛzimu, a] (PT) NUM seventieth; = **setuagésimo**

sepulcro [se'puwkru] M tomb

sepultamento [sepuwta'mētu] M burial

sepultar [sepuw'tar] VT to bury; (*esconder*) to hide, conceal; (*segredo*) to keep quiet; **sepultura** [sepuw'tura] F grave, tomb

sequei *etc* [se'kej] VB V **secar**

seqüela [se'kwɛla] F sequel; (*consequência*) consequence; (*Med*) after-effect

seqüência [se'kwēsja] F sequence

seqüencial [sekwē'sjaw] (*pl* -**ais**) ADJ (*Comput*) sequential

sequer [se'kɛr] ADV at least; (**nem**) ~ not even

seqüestrador, a [sekweʃtra'dor(a)] M/F (*raptor*) kidnapper; (*de avião etc*) hijacker

seqüestrar [sekweʃ'trar] VT (*bens*) to seize, confiscate; (*raptar*) to kidnap; (*avião etc*) to hijack; **seqüestro** [se'kwɛʃtru] M seizure; (*rapto*) abduction, kidnapping; (*de avião etc*) hijack

sequidão [seki'dãw] F dryness; (*de pessoa*) coldness

sequioso, -a [se'kjozu, ɔza] ADJ (*sedento*)

thirsty; (*fig: desejoso*) eager

séquito ['sɛkitu] M retinue

○ **PALAVRA CHAVE**

ser [ser] VI **1** (*descrição*) to be; **ela é médica/ muito alta** she's a doctor/very tall; **é Ana** (*Tel*) Ana speaking *ou* here; **ela é de uma bondade incrível** she's incredibly kind; **ele está é danado** he's really angry; **ser de mentir/briga** to be the sort to lie/fight

2 (*horas, datas, números*): **é uma hora** it's one o'clock; **são seis e meia** it's half past six; **é dia 1° de junho** it's the first of June; **somos/são seis** there are six of us/them

3 (*origem, material*): **ser de** to be *ou* come from; (*feito de*) to be made of; (*pertencer*) to belong to; **sua família é da Bahia** his (*ou* her *etc*) family is from Bahia; **a mesa é de mármore** the table is made of marble; **é de Pedro** it's Pedro's, it belongs to Pedro

4 (*em orações passivas*): **já foi descoberto** it had already been discovered

5 (*locuções com subjun*): **ou seja** that is to say; **seja quem for** whoever it may be; **se eu fosse você** if I were you; **se não fosse você, ...** if it hadn't been for you ...

6 (*locuções*): **a não ser** except; **a não ser que** unless; **é** (*resposta afirmativa*) yes; **..., não é?** isn't it?, don't you? *etc*; **ah, é?** really?; **que foi?** (*o que aconteceu?*) what happened?; (*qual é o problema?*) what's the problem?; **será que ...?** I wonder if ...?

■ M being

seres MPL (*criaturas*) creatures

serão [se'rãw] (*pl* -**ões**) M (*trabalho noturno*) night work; (*horas extraordinárias*) overtime; **fazer** ~ to work late; (*dormir tarde*) to go to bed late

sereia [se'reja] F mermaid

serelepe [sere'lɛpi] ADJ frisky

serenar [sere'nar] VT to calm ■ VI (*pessoa*) to calm down; (*mar*) to grow calm; (*dor*) to subside

serenata [sere'nata] F serenade

serenidade [sereni'dadʒi] F serenity, tranquillity

sereno, -a [se'rɛnu, a] ADJ calm; (*olhar*) serene; (*tempo*) fine, clear ■ M (*relento*) damp night air; **no** ~ in the open

seresta [se'rɛʃta] F serenade

SERFA (BR) ABR M = **Serviço de Fiscalização Agrícola**

sergipano, -a [sexʒi'panu, a] ADJ from Sergipe ■ M/F person from Sergipe

seriado, -a [se'rjadu, a] ADJ (*número*) serial; (*publicação, filme*) serialized

serial [se'rjaw] (*pl* -**ais**) ADJ (*Comput*) serial

série ['sɛri] F series; (*seqüência*) sequence, succession; (*Educ*) grade; (*categoria*) category;

NB: *European Portuguese adds the following consonants to certain words:* **b** (sú(b)dito, su(b)til); **c** (a(c)ção, a(c)cionista, a(c)to); **m** (inde(m)ne); **p** (ado(p)ção, ado(p)tar); *for further details see p. xiii.*

fora de ~ out of order; *(fig)* extraordinary; **fabricar em ~** to mass-produce

seriedade [serje'dadʒi] F seriousness; *(honestidade)* honesty

seringa [se'rĩga] F syringe

seringal [serĩ'gaw] *(pl* **-ais)** M rubber plantation

seringalista [serĩga'liʃta] M rubber plantation owner

seringueira [serĩ'gejra] F rubber tree; *v tb* **seringueiro**

seringueiro, -a [serĩ'gejru, a] M/F rubber tapper

sério, -a ['sɛrju, a] ADJ serious; *(honesto)* honest, decent; *(responsável)* responsible; *(confiável)* reliable; *(roupa)* sober ■ ADV seriously; **a ~** seriously; **falando ~ ...** seriously ...; **~?** really?

sermão [sex'mãw] *(pl* **-ões)** M sermon; *(fig)* telling-off; **levar um ~ de alguém** to get a telling-off from sb; **passar um ~ em alguém** to give sb a telling-off

serões [se'rõjʃ] MPL *de* **serão**

serpeante [sex'pjãtʃi] ADJ wriggling; *(fig: caminho, rio)* winding, meandering

serpear [sex'pjaʳ] VI *(como serpente)* to wriggle; *(fig: caminho, rio)* to wind, meander

serpente [sex'pẽtʃi] F snake; *(pessoa)* snake in the grass

serpentear [sexpẽ'tʃjaʳ] VI = **serpear**

serpentina [sexpẽ'tʃina] F *(conduto)* coil; *(fita de papel)* streamer

serra ['sexa] F *(montanha)* mountain range; *(Tec)* saw; **~ circular** circular saw; **~ de arco** hacksaw; **~ de cadeia** chain saw; **~ tico-tico** fret saw

serrado, -a [se'xadu, a] ADJ serrated

serragem [se'xaʒẽ] F *(pó)* sawdust

Serra Leoa F Sierra Leone

serralheiro, -a [sexa'ʎejru, a] M/F locksmith

serrania [sexa'nia] F mountain range

serrano, -a [se'xanu, a] ADJ highland *atr* ■ M/F highlander

serrar [se'xaʳ] VT to saw

serraria [sexa'ria] F sawmill

serrote [se'xɔtʃi] M handsaw

sertanejo, -a [sexta'neʒu, a] ADJ rustic, country ■ M/F inhabitant of the "sertão"

sertão [sex'tãw] *(pl* **-ões)** M backwoods *pl*, bush (country)

servente [sex'vẽtʃi] M/F *(criado)* servant; *(operário)* labourer (Brit), laborer *(US)*; **~ de pedreiro** bricklayer's mate

serventuário, -a [sexvẽ'twarju, a] M/F *(Jur)* legal official

serviçal [sexvi'saw] *(pl* **-ais)** ADJ obliging, helpful ■ M/F *(criado)* servant; *(trabalhador)* wage earner

serviço [sex'visu] M service; *(de chá etc)* set; **o ~** *(emprego)* work; **um ~** *(trabalho)* a job; **não brincar em ~** not to waste time; **dar o ~** *(col: confessar)* to blab; **estar de ~** to be on duty; **matar o ~** to cut corners; **prestar ~** to help; **~ doméstico** housework; **~ ativo** *(Mil)* active duty; **~ de informações** *(Mil)* intelligence

service; **~ militar** military service; **S~ Nacional de Saúde** National Health Service; **S~ Público** Civil Service; **~s públicos** public utilities

servidão [sexvi'dãw] F servitude, serfdom; *(Jur: de passagem)* right of way

servidor, a [sexvi'doʳ(a)] M/F *(criado)* servant; *(funcionário)* employee; **~ público** civil servant

servil [sex'viw] *(pl* **-is)** ADJ servile

servir [sex'viʳ] VT to serve ■ VI to serve; *(ser útil)* to be useful; *(ajudar)* to help; *(roupa: caber)* to fit; **servir-se** VR: **servir-se (de)** *(comida, café)* to help o.s. (to); **~-se de** *(meios)* to use, make use of; **~ de** *(prover)* to supply with, provide with; **você está servido?** *(num bar)* are you all right for a drink?; **~ de algo** to serve as sth; **para que serve isto?** what is this for?; **ele não serve para trabalhar aqui** he's not suitable to work here; **qualquer ônibus serve** any bus will do

servis [sex'viʃ] ADJ PL *de* **servil**

servível [sex'vivew] *(pl* **-eis)** ADJ serviceable; *(roupa)* wearable

servo, -a ['sɛxvu, a] M/F *(feudal)* serf; *(criado)* servant

servo-croata [sɛxvu'krwata] M *(Ling)* Serbo-Croat

Sesc ['sɛʃki] (BR) ABR M = **Serviço Social do Comércio**

Sesi [sɛ'zi] (BR) ABR M = **Serviço Social da Indústria**

sessão [se'sãw] *(pl* **-ões)** F *(do parlamento etc)* session; *(reunião)* meeting; *(de cinema)* showing; **primeira/segunda ~** first/second show; **~ coruja** late show; **~ da tarde** matinée

sessenta [se'sẽta] NUM sixty; *v tb* **cinqüenta**

sessões [se'sõjʃ] FPL *de* **sessão**

sesta ['sɛʃta] F siesta, nap

set ['sɛtʃi] M *(Tênis)* set

set. ABR (= *setembro*) Sept

seta ['sɛta] F arrow

sete ['sɛtʃi] NUM seven; **pintar o ~** *(fig)* to get up to all sorts; *v tb* **cinco**

setecentos, -as [sete'sẽtuʃ, aʃ] NUM seven hundred

sete-e-meio M seven-and-a-half *(card game similar to pontoon)*

setembro [se'tẽbru] (PT S-) M September; *v tb* **julho; 7 de setembro;** *see below*

● **7 DE SETEMBRO**

● Brazil's independence from Portugal
● is commemmorated on 7 September.
● Independence was declared in 1822 by the
● Portuguese prince regent, Dom Pedro,
● who rebelled against several orders from
● the Portuguese crown, among them the
● order to swear loyalty to the Portuguese
● constitution. It is a national holiday and
● the occasion for processions and military
● parades through the main cities.

setenta [se'tẽta] NUM seventy; *v tb* **cinqüenta**

setentrional [setẽtrjo'naw] (pl -ais) ADJ northern

sétima ['sɛtʃima] F (Mús) seventh

sétimo, -a ['sɛtʃimu, a] NUM seventh; v tb **quinto**

setor [se'to^r] M sector

setuagésimo, -a [setwa'ʒɛzimu, a] NUM seventieth; v tb **quinto**

seu, sua [sew, 'sua] ADJ (dele) his; (dela) her; (de coisa) its; (deles, delas) their; (de você, vocês) your ■ PRON (dele) his; (dela) hers; (deles, delas) theirs; (de você, vocês) yours ■ M (senhor) Mr(.); **um homem de ~s 60 anos** a man of about sixty; **~ idiota!** you idiot!

Seul [se'uw] N Seoul

severidade [severi'dadʒi] F severity, harshness

severo, -a [se'vɛru, a] ADJ severe, harsh

seviciar [sevi'sja^r] VT to ill-treat; (mulher, criança) to batter

sevícias [se'visjaʃ] FPL (maus tratos) ill treatment sg; (desumanidade) inhumanity sg, cruelty sg

Sevilha [se'viʎa] N Seville

sex. ABR (= sexta-feira) Fri

sexagésimo, -a [seksa'ʒɛzimu, a] NUM sixtieth; v tb **quinto**

sexo ['sɛksu] M sex; **de ~ feminino/masculino** female/male

sexta ['seʃta] F (tb: **sexta-feira**) Friday; (Mús) sixth; **sexta-feira** (pl **sextas-feiras**) F Friday; **Sexta-feira Santa** Good Friday; v tb **terça-feira**

sexto, -a ['seʃtu, a] NUM sixth; v tb **quinto**

sexual [se'kswaw] (pl -ais) ADJ sexual; (vida, ato) sex atr

sexualidade [sekswali'dadʒi] F sexuality

sexy ['sɛksi] (pl -s) ADJ sexy

Seychelles [sej'ʃɛliʃ] F OU FPL: **a(s) ~ the** Seychelles

sezão [se'zãw] (pl -ões) F (febre) (intermittent) fever; (malária) malaria

s.f.f. (PT) ABR = **se faz favor**

SFH (BR) ABR M = **Sistema Financeiro de Habitação**

shopping center ['ʃopĩŋ('sẽte^r)] M shopping centre (Brit), (shopping) mall (US)

short ['ʃoxtʃi] M (pair of) shorts pl

show [ʃow] (pl -s) M show; (de cantor, conjunto) concert, gig; **dar um ~** (fig) to put on a real show; (dar escândalo) to make a scene; **ser um ~** (col) to be a sensation

showroom [ʃow'rũ] (pl -s) M showroom

si [si] PRON oneself; (ele) himself; (ela) herself; (coisa) itself; (PT: você) yourself, you; (: vocês) yourselves; (eles, elas) themselves; **em si** in itself; **fora de si** beside oneself; **cheio de si** full of oneself; **voltar a si** to come round

siamês, -esa [sja'meʃ, eza] ADJ Siamese

Sibéria [si'bɛrja] F: **a ~ Siberia**

sibilar [sibi'la^r] VI to hiss

sicário [si'karju] M hired assassin

Sicília [si'silja] F: **a ~ Sicily**

sicrano [si'kranu] M: **fulano e ~ so-and-so**

SIDA ['sida] (PT) ABR F: **síndrome de deficiência imunológica adquirida, a sicrano** AIDS

siderúrgica [side'ruxʒika] F steel industry

siderúrgico, -a [side'ruxʒiku, a] ADJ iron and steel atr; **(usina) siderúrgica** steelworks sg

sidra ['sidra] F cider

SIF (BR) ABR M = **Serviço de Inspeção Federal**

sifão [si'fãw] (pl -ões) M syphon

sífilis ['sifiliʃ] F syphilis

sifões [si'fõjʃ] MPL de **sifão**

sigilo [si'ʒilu] M secrecy; **guardar ~ sobre algo** to keep quiet about sth

sigiloso, -a [siʒi'lozu, ɔza] ADJ secret

sigla ['sigla] F acronym; (abreviação) abbreviation

signatário, -a [signa'tarju, a] M/F signatory

significação [signifika'sãw] F significance

significado [signifi'kadu] M meaning

significante [signifi'kãtʃi] ADJ significant

significar [signifi'ka^r] VT to mean, signify; **significativo, -a** [signifika'tʃivu, a] ADJ significant

signo ['signu] M sign; **~ do zodíaco** sign of the zodiac

sigo etc ['sigu] VB v **seguir**

sílaba ['silaba] F syllable

silenciar [silẽ'sja^r] VT (pessoa) to silence; (escândalo) to hush up ■ VI to remain silent

silêncio [si'lẽsju] M silence, quiet; **~!** silence!; **ficar em ~** to remain silent; **silencioso, -a** [silẽ'sjozu, ɔza] ADJ silent, quiet ■ M (Auto) silencer (Brit), muffler (US)

silhueta [si'ʎweta] F silhouette

silício [si'lisju] M silicon; **plaqueta de ~ silicon chip**

silicone [sili'kɔni] M silicone

silo ['silu] M silo

silvar [siw'va^r] VI to hiss; (assobiar) to whistle

silvestre [siw'veʃtri] ADJ wild

silvícola [siw'vikola] ADJ wild

silvicultura [siwvikuw'tura] F forestry

sim [sĩ] ADV yes; **creio que ~ I think so; isso ~ that's it!; pelo ~, pelo não** just in case; **dar ou dizer o ~** to consent, say yes

simbólico, -a [sĩ'bɔliku, a] ADJ symbolic

simbolismo [sĩbo'liʒmu] M symbolism

simbolizar [sĩboli'za^r] VT to symbolise

símbolo ['sĩbolu] M symbol

simetria [sime'tria] F symmetry

simétrico, -a [si'mɛtriku, a] ADJ symmetrical

similar [simi'la^r] ADJ similar

similaridade [similari'dadʒi] F similarity

símile ['simili] M simile

similitude [simili'tudʒi] F similarity

simpatia [sĩpa'tʃia] F (por alguém, algo) liking; (afeto) affection; (afinidade, solidariedade) sympathy; **simpatias** FPL (inclinações) sympathies; **com ~ sympathetically; ser uma ~** to be very nice; **ter ou sentir ~ por** to

---

NB: European Portuguese adds the following consonants to certain words: **b** (sú(b)dito, su(b)til); **c** (a(c)ção, a(c)cionista, a(c)to); **m** (inde(m)ne); **p** (ado(p)ção, ado(p)tar); for further details see p. xiii.

like; **simpático, -a** [sī'patʃiku, a] ADJ (*pessoa, decoração etc*) nice; (*lugar*) pleasant, nice; (*amável*) kind ■ M (*Anat*) nervous system; **ser simpático a** to be sympathetic to
simpatizante [sīpatʃi'zātʃi] ADJ sympathetic
■ M/F sympathizer
simpatizar [sīpatʃi'za^r] VI: ~ **com** (*pessoa*) to like; (*causa*) to sympathize with
simples ['sīpliʃ] ADJ INV simple; (*único*) single; (*fácil*) easy; (*mero*) mere; (*ingênuo*) naïve ■ ADV simply; **simplicidade** [sīplisi'dadʒi] F simplicity; (*ingenuidade*) naïvety; (*modéstia*) plainness; (*naturalidade*) naturalness
simplicíssimo, -a [sīpli'sisimu, a] ADJ SUPERL *de* **simples**
simplificação [sīplifika'sāw] (*pl* -ões) F simplification
simplificar [sīplifi'ka^r] VT to simplify
simplíssimo, -a [sī'plisimu, a] ADJ SUPERL *de* **simples**
simplista [sī'pliʃta] ADJ simplistic
simplório, -a [sī'plɔrju, a] ADJ simple ■ M/F simple person
simpósio [sī'pɔzju] M symposium
simulação [simula'sāw] (*pl* -ões) F simulation; (*fingimento*) pretence (*Brit*), pretense (*US*), sham
simulacro [simu'lakru] M (*imitação*) imitation; (*fingimento*) pretence (*Brit*), pretense (*US*)
simulado, -a [simu'ladu, a] ADJ simulated
simular [simu'la^r] VT to simulate
simultaneamente [simuwtanja'mētʃi] ADV simultaneously
simultâneo, -a [simuw'tanju, a] ADJ simultaneous
sina ['sina] F fate, destiny
sinagoga [sina'gɔga] F synagogue
Sinai [sina'i] M Sinai
sinal [si'naw] (*pl* -ais) M (*ger*) sign; (*gesto, Tel*) signal; (*na pele*) mole; (: *de nascença*) birthmark; (*depósito*) deposit; (*tb*: **sinal de tráfego luminoso**) traffic light; ~ **rodoviário** road sign; **dar de** ~ to give as a deposit; **em** ~ **de** (*fig*) as a sign of; **por** ~ (*por falar nisso*) by the way; (*aliás*) as a matter of fact; **avançar o** ~ (*Auto*) to jump the lights; (*fig*) to jump the gun; **dar** ~ **de vida** to show up; **fazer** ~ to signal; ~ **de alarma** alarm; ~ **de chamada** (*Tel*) ringing tone; **de discar** (*BR*) *ou* **de marcar** (*PT*) dialling tone (*Brit*), dial tone (*US*); ~ **de ocupado** (*BR*) *ou* **de impedido** (*PT*) engaged tone (*Brit*), busy signal (*US*); ~ **de mais/ menos** (*Mat*) plus/minus sign; ~ **de perigo** danger signal; ~ **de pontuação** punctuation mark; ~ **verde** *ou* **aberto/vermelho** *ou* **fechado** green/red light
sinal-da-cruz M sign of the cross; **fazer o** ~ to cross o.s.
sinaleiro [sina'lejru] M (*Ferro*) signalman; (*aparelho*) traffic lights *pl*
sinalização [sinaliza'sāw] F (*ato*) signalling; (*para motoristas*) traffic signs *pl*; (*Ferro*) signals *pl*
sinalizar [sinali'za^r] VI to signal
sinceridade [sīseri'dadʒi] F sincerity

sincero, -a [sī'sɛru, a] ADJ sincere; (*opinião, confissão*) honest
sincopado, -a [sīko'padu, a] ADJ (*Mús*) syncopated
síncope ['sīkopi] F fainting fit
sincronizar [sīkroni'za^r] VT to synchronize
sindical [sīdʒi'kaw] (*pl* -ais) ADJ (trade) union *atr*
sindicalismo [sīdʒika'liʒmu] M trade unionism
sindicalista [sīdʒika'liʃta] M/F trade unionist
sindicalizar [sīdʒikali'za^r] VT to unionize; **sindicalizar-se** VR to become unionized
sindicância [sīdʒi'kāsja] F inquiry, investigation
sindicato [sīdʒi'katu] M (*de trabalhadores*) trade union; (*financeiro*) syndicate
síndico, -a ['sīdʒiku, a] M/F (*de condomínio*) manager; (*de massa falida*) receiver
síndrome ['sīdromi] F syndrome; ~ **de deficiência imunológica adquirida** acquired immune deficiency syndrome
SINE (*BR*) ABR M = **Sistema Nacional de Empregos**
sinecura [sine'kura] F sinecure
sineta [si'neta] F bell
sinfonia [sīfo'nia] F symphony
sinfônica [sī'fonika] F (*tb*: **orquestra sinfônica**) symphony orchestra
sinfônico, -a [sī'foniku, a] ADJ symphonic
singeleza [sīʒe'leza] F simplicity
singelo, -a [sī'ʒɛlu, a] ADJ simple
singular [sīgu'la^r] ADJ singular; (*extraordinário*) exceptional; (*bizarro*) odd, peculiar
singularidade [sīgulari'dadʒi] F peculiarity
singularizar [sīgulari'za^r] VT (*distinguir*) to single out; **singularizar-se** VR to stand out, distinguish o.s.
sinistrado, -a [siniʃ'tradu, a] ADJ damaged
sinistro, -a [si'niʃtru, a] ADJ sinister ■ M disaster, accident; (*prejuízo*) damage
sino ['sinu] M bell
sinônimo, -a [si'nonimu, a] ADJ synonymous ■ M synonym
sinopse [si'nɔpsi] F synopsis
sintático, -a [sī'tatʃiku, a] ADJ syntactic
sintaxe [sī'tasi] F syntax
síntese ['sītezi] F synthesis; **em** ~ in short; **sintético, -a** [sī'tetʃiku, a] ADJ synthetic; (*resumido*) brief; **sintetizar** [sītetʃi'za^r] VT to synthesize; (*resumir*) to summarize
sinto *etc* ['sītu] VB V **sentir**
sintoma [sī'tɔma] M symptom
sintomático, -a [sīto'matʃiku, a] ADJ symptomatic
sintonizador [sītoniza'do^r] M tuner
sintonizar [sītoni'za^r] VT (*Rádio*) to tune ■ VI to tune in; ~ (**com**) (*pessoa*) to get on (with); (*opinião*) to coincide (with)
sinuca [si'nuka] F snooker; (*mesa*) snooker table; **estar numa** ~ (*col*) to be snookered
sinuoso, -a [si'nwozu, ɔza] ADJ (*caminho*) winding; (*linha*) wavy
sinusite [sinu'zitʃi] F sinusitis

sionismo [sjo'niʒmu] M Zionism
sionista [sjo'niʃta] ADJ, M/F Zionist
sirena [si'rɛna] F siren
sirene [si'rɛni] F = **sirena**
siri [si'ri] M crab; **casquinha de ~** (Culin) crab au gratin
sirigaita [siri'gajta] (col) F floozy
Síria ['sirja] F: **a ~** Syria
sírio, -a ['sirju, a] ADJ, M/F Syrian
sirvo etc ['sixvu] VB V **servir**
siso ['sizu] M good sense; **dente de ~** wisdom tooth
sísmico, -a ['siʒmiku, a] ADJ seismic
sismógrafo [siʒ'mɔgrafu] M seismograph
sistema [siʃ'tɛma] M system; (método) method; **~ operacional** (Comput) operating system; **~ solar** solar system
sistemático, -a [siʃte'matʃiku, a] ADJ systematic
sistematizar [siʃtematʃi'za'] VT to systematize
sisudo, -a [si'zudu, a] ADJ serious, sober
site ['sajtʃi] M (na Internet) website
sitiar [si'tʃja'] VT to besiege
sítio ['sitʃju] M (Mil) siege; (propriedade rural) small farm; (PT: lugar) place; **estado de ~** state of siege
situação [sitwa'sãw] (pl -ões) F situation; (posição) position; (social) standing
situado, -a [si'twadu, a] ADJ situated; **estar** ou **ficar ~** to be situated
situar [si'twa'] VT (pôr) to place, put; (edifício) to situate, locate; **situar-se** VR (pôr-se) to position o.s.; (estar situado) to be situated
SL ABR = **sobreloja**
sl ABR = **SL**
slogan [iʃ'lɔgã] (pl -s) M slogan
smoking [iʒ'mokĩʃ] (pl -s) M dinner jacket (Brit), tuxedo (US)
SMTU (BR) ABR F = **Superintendência Municipal de Transportes Urbanos**
SNI (BR) ABR M (antes: = Serviço Nacional de Informações) state intelligence service
só [sɔ] ADJ alone; (único) single; (solitário) solitary ■ ADV only; **um só** only one; **a sós** alone; **por si só** by himself (ou herself, itself); **é só!** that's all!; **é só discar** all you have to do is dial; **veja/imagine só** just look/imagine; **não só ... mas também ...** not only ... but also ...; **que** ou **como só ele** etc like nobody else; **só isso?** is that all?
soalho ['swaʎu] M = **assoalho**
soar [swa'] VI to sound; (cantar) to sing; (sinos, clarins) to ring; (apito) to blow; (boato) to go round ■ VT (horas) to strike; (instrumento) to play; **~ a** to sound like; **~ bem/mal** (fig) to go down well/badly
sob [sob] PREP under; **~ emenda** subject to correction; **~ juramento** on oath; **~ medida** (roupa) made to measure; (software) bespoke; **~ minha palavra** on my word; **~ pena de** on pain of

sobe etc ['sɔbi] VB V **subir**
sobejar [sobe'ʒa'] VI (superabundar) to abound; (restar) to be left over
sobejos [so'beʒuʃ] MPL remains, leftovers
soberania [sobera'nia] F sovereignty
soberano, -a [sobe'ranu, a] ADJ sovereign; (fig: supremo) supreme; (: altivo) haughty ■ M/F sovereign
soberba [so'bexba] F haughtiness, arrogance
soberbo, -a [so'bexbu, a] ADJ (arrogante) haughty, arrogant; (magnífico) magnificent, splendid
sobra ['sɔbra] F surplus, remnant; **sobras** FPL remains; (de tecido) remnants; (de comida) leftovers; **ter algo de ~** to have sth extra; (tempo, comida, motivos) to have plenty of sth; **ficar de ~** to be left over
sobraçar [sobra'sa'] VT (levar debaixo do braço) to carry under one's arm; (meter debaixo do braço) to put under one's arm
sobrado [so'bradu] M (andar) floor; (casa) house (of two or more storeys)
sobrancelho, -a [sobrã'sejru, a] ADJ (que está acima de) lofty, towering; (proeminente) prominent; (arrogante) haughty, arrogant
sobrancelha [sobrã'seʎa] F eyebrow
sobrar [so'bra'] VI to be left; (dúvidas) to remain; **ficar sobrando** (pessoa) to be left out; (: não ter parceiro) to be the odd one out; **sobram-me cinco** I have five left; **isto dá e sobra** this is more than enough
sobre ['sobri] PREP on; (por cima de) over; (acima de) above; (a respeito de) about; **ser meio ~ o chato** (col) to be a bit boring
sobreaviso [sobrja'vizu] M warning; **estar de ~** to be alert, be on one's guard
sobrecapa [sobri'kapa] F cover
sobrecarga [sobri'kaxga] F overload
sobrecarregar [sobrikaxe'ga'] VT to overload
sobreestimar [sobreʃtʃi'ma'] VT to overestimate
sobre-humano, -a ADJ superhuman
sobrejacente [sobriʒa'sẽtʃi] ADJ: **~ a** over
sobreloja [sobri'lɔʒa] F mezzanine (floor)
sobremaneira [sobrema'nejra] ADV exceedingly
sobremesa [sobri'meza] F dessert
sobremodo [sobri'mɔdu] ADV exceedingly
sobrenatural [sobrinatu'raw] (pl -ais) ADJ supernatural; (esforço) superhuman ■ M: **o ~** the supernatural
sobrenome [sobri'nɔmi] (BR) M surname, family name
sobrepairar [sobripaj'ra'] VI: **~ a** to hover above; (crise) to rise above
sobrepor [sobri'po'] (irreg) VT: **~ algo a algo** (pôr em cima) to put sth on top of sth; (adicionar) to add sth to sth; (dar preferência) to put sth before sth; **sobrepor-se** VR: **sobrepor-se a** (pôr-se sobre) to cover, go on top of; (sobrevir) to succeed

---

NB: European Portuguese adds the following consonants to certain words: **b** (sú(b)dito, su(b)til); **c** (a(c)ção, a(c)cionista, a(c)to); **m** (inde(m)ne); **p** (ado(p)ça, ado(p)tar); for further details see p. xiii.

sobrepujar[sobripu'ʒaʳ] VT (exceder em altura) to rise above; (superar) to surpass; (obstáculos, perigos) to overcome; (inimigo) to overwhelm

sobrepunhaetc [sobri'puɲa] VB v **sobrepor**

sobrepusetc [sobri'pujʃ] VB v **sobrepor**

sobrepuseretc [sobripu'zeʳ] VB v **sobrepor**

sobrescritar[sobreʃkri'taʳ] VT to address

sobrescrito[sobreʃ'kritu] M address

sobressair[sobrisa'iʳ] VI to stand out; **sobressair-se** VR to stand out

sobressalente[sobrisa'lẽtʃi] ADJ, M spare

sobressaltado, -a [sobrisaw'tadu, a] ADJ: **viver ~** to live in fear; **acordar ~** to wake up with a start

sobressaltar[sobrisaw'taʳ] VT to startle, frighten; **sobressaltar-se** VR to be startled

sobressalto[sobri'sawtu] M (movimento brusco) start; (temor) trepidation; **de ~** suddenly; **o seu ~ com aquele estrondo/aquela notícia** his fright at that noise/his shock at that news; **ter um ~** to get a fright

sobretaxa[sobri'taʃa] F surcharge

sobretudo[sobri'tudu] M overcoat ■ ADV above all, especially

sobrevir[sobri'viʳ] (irreg) VI to occur, arise; **~ a** (seguir) to follow (on from); **sobreveio-lhe uma doença** he was struck down by illness

sobrevivência[sobrivi'vẽsja] F survival; **sobrevivente**[sobrivi'vẽtʃi] ADJ surviving ■ M/F survivor

sobreviver[sobrivi'veʳ] VI: **~ (a)** to survive

sobrevoar[sobrivo'aʳ] VT, VI to fly over

sobriedade[sobrje'dadʒi] F soberness; (comedimento) moderation, restraint

sobrinho, -a [so'briɲu, a] M/F nephew/niece

sóbrio, -a ['sɔbrju, a] ADJ sober; (moderado) moderate, restrained

socado, -a [so'kadu, a] ADJ (alho) crushed; (escondido) hidden; (pessoa) stout

socador[soka'doʳ] M crusher; **~ de alho** garlic press

soçaite [so'sajtʃi] (col) M high society

socapa [so'kapa] F: **à ~** furtively, on the sly

socar[so'kaʳ] VT (esmurrar) to hit, strike; (calcar) to crush, pound; (massa de pão) to knead

social [so'sjaw] (pl -ais) ADJ social; (entrada, elevador) private; (camisa) dress atr

socialismo[sosja'liʒmu] M socialism

socialista[sosja'liʃta] ADJ, M/F socialist

socialite[sosja'lajtʃi] M/F socialite

socializar[sosjali'zaʳ] VT to socialize

sociável[so'sjavew] (pl -eis) ADJ sociable

sociedade[sosje'dadʒi] F society; (Com: empresa) company; (: de sócios) partnership; (associação) association; **~ anônima** limited company (Brit), incorporated company (US); **~ anônima aberta/fechada** public/private limited company

sócio, -a ['sɔsju, a] M/F (Com) partner, associate; (de clube) member; **~ comanditário** (Com) silent partner

socio-econômico, -a ADJ socio-economic

sociolinguística[sosjolĩ'gwiʃtʃika] F

sociolinguistics sg

sociologia[sosjolo'ʒia] F sociology

sociológico, -a[sosjo'lɔʒiku, a] ADJ sociological

sociólogo, -a[so'sjɔlogu, a] M/F sociologist

socio-político, -a ADJ socio-political

soco['soku] M punch; **dar um ~ em** to punch

soçobrar[soso'braʳ] VT (afundar) to sink ■ VI to sink; (esperanças) to founder; **~ em** (fig: no vício etc) to sink into

soco-inglês(pl **socos-ingleses**) M knuckleduster

socorrer[soko'xeʳ] VT (ajudar) to help, assist; (salvar) to rescue; **socorrer-se** VR: **socorrer-se de** to resort to, have recourse to; **socorro** [so'koxu] M help, assistance; (reboque) breakdown (Brit) ou tow (US) truck; **socorro!** help!; **ir em socorro de** to come to the aid of; **primeiros socorros** first aid sg; **equipe de socorro** rescue team

soda ['sɔda] F soda (water); **pedir ~** (col) to back off, back down; **~ cáustica** caustic soda

sódio ['sɔdʒju] M sodium

sodomia[sodo'mia] F sodomy

sofá [so'fa] M sofa, settee; **sofá-cama**(pl **sofás-camas**) M sofa-bed

Sófia ['sɔfja] N Sofia

sofisma [so'fiʒma] M sophism; (col) trick

sofismar[sofiʒ'maʳ] VT (fatos) to twist; (enganar) to swindle, cheat

sofisticação[sofiʃtʃika'sãw] F sophistication

sofisticado, -a[sofiʃtʃi'kadu, a] ADJ sophisticated; (afetado) pretentious

sofisticar[sofiʃtʃi'kaʳ] VT to refine

sôfrego, -a['sofregu, a] ADJ (ávido) keen; (impaciente) impatient; (no comer) greedy

sofreguidão[sofregi'dãw] F keenness; (impaciência) impatience; (no comer) greed

sofrer[so'freʳ] VT to suffer; (acidente) to have; (agüentar) to bear, put up with; (experimentar) to undergo, experience ■ VI to suffer; **~ de reumatismo/do fígado** to suffer from rheumatism/with one's liver; **sofrido, -a** [so'fridu, a] ADJ long-suffering; **sofrimento** [sofri'mẽtu] M suffering

sofrível[so'frivew] (pl -eis) ADJ bearable; (razoável) reasonable

soft ['sɔftʃi] (pl -s) M (Comput) piece of software, software package

software[sof'tweʳ] (pl -s) M (Comput) software; **um ~** a piece of software

sogro, -a ['sogru, 'sɔgra] M/F father-in-law/mother-in-law

sóis [sɔjʃ] MPL de **sol**

soja ['sɔʒa] F soya (Brit), soy (US); **leite de ~** soya ou soy milk

sol [sɔw] (pl **sóis**) M sun; (luz) sunshine, sunlight; **ao** ou **no ~** in the sun; **fazer ~** to be sunny; **pegar ~** to sunbathe; **tomar (banho de) ~** to sunbathe

sola ['sɔla] F sole

solado, -a[so'ladu, a] ADJ (bolo) flat

solão[so'lãw] M very hot sun

solapar[sola'pa^r] VT (escavar) to dig into; (abalar) to shake; (fig: arruinar) to destroy

solar[so'la^r] ADJ solar ∎ M manor house ∎ VT (sapato) to sole ∎ VI (bolo) not to rise; (cantor, músico) to sing (ou play) solo

solavanco[sola'vãku] M jolt, bump; **andar aos ~s** to jog along

solda['sɔwda] F solder

soldado[sow'dadu] M soldier; **~ de chumbo** toy soldier; **~ raso** private soldier

soldador, a[sowda'do^r(a)] M/F welder

soldadura[sowda'dura] F (ato) welding; (parte soldada) weld

soldagem[sow'daʒẽ] F welding

soldar[sow'da^r] VT to weld; (fig) to unite, amalgamate

soldo['sowdu] M (Mil) pay

soleira[so'lejra] F doorstep

solene[so'lɛni] ADJ solemn; **solenidade** [soleni'dadʒi] F solemnity; (cerimônia) ceremony

solenizar[soleni'za^r] VT to solemnize

solércia[so'lɛxsja] F ploy

soletração[soletra'sãw] F spelling

soletrar[sole'tra^r] VT to spell; (ler devagar) to read out slowly

solicitação[solisita'sãw] (pl -ões) F request; **solicitações** FPL (apelo) appeal sg

solicitar[solisi'ta^r] VT to ask for; (requerer: emprego etc) to apply for; (amizade, atenção) to seek; **~ algo a alguém** to ask sb for sth

solícito, -a[so'lisitu, a] ADJ helpful

solicitude[solisi'tudʒi] F (zelo) care; (boa vontade) concern, thoughtfulness; (empenho) commitment

solidão[soli'dãw] F solitude, isolation; (sensação) loneliness; (de lugar) desolation; **sentir ~** to feel lonely

solidariedade[solidarje'dadʒi] F solidarity

solidário, -a[soli'darju, a] ADJ (pessoas) who show solidarity; (a uma causa etc) sympathetic; (Jur: obrigação) mutually binding; (: devedores) jointly liable; **ser ~ com** to stand by

solidarizar[solidari'za^r] VT to bring together; **solidarizar-se** VR to join forces

solidez[soli'deʒ] F solidity, strength

solidificar[solidʒifi'ka^r] VT to solidify; (fig) to consolidate; **solidificar-se** VR to solidify; to be consolidated

sólido, -a['sɔlidu, a] ADJ solid

solilóquio[soli'lɔkju] M soliloquy

solista[so'liʃta] M/F soloist

solitária[soli'tarja] F (verme) tapeworm; (cela) solitary confinement

solitário, -a[soli'tarju, a] ADJ lonely, solitary ∎ M hermit; (jóia) solitaire

solo['sɔlu] M ground, earth; (Mús) solo

soltar[sow'ta^r] VT (tornar livre) to set free; (desatar) to loosen, untie; (afrouxar) to slacken,

loosen; (largar) to let go of; (emitir) to emit; (grito, risada) to let out; (foguete, fogos de artifício) to set ou let off; (cabelo) to let down; (freio, animais) to release; (piada) to tell; **soltar-se** VR (desprender-se) to come loose; (desinibir-se) to let o.s. go; **~ palavrão** to swear

solteira[sol'tejra] F single woman, spinster

solteirão[sowtej'rãw] (pl -ões) M bachelor

solteiro, -a[sow'tejru, a] ADJ unmarried, single ∎ M bachelor

solteirões[sowtej'rõjʃ] MPL de **solteirão**

solteirona[sowtej'rona] F old maid

solto, -a['sowtu, a] PP de **soltar** ∎ ADJ loose; (livre) free; (sozinho) alone; (arroz) fluffy; **à solta** freely

soltura[sow'tura] F looseness; (liberdade) release, discharge

solução[solu'sãw] (pl -ões) F solution

soluçar[solu'sa^r] VI (chorar) to sob; (Med) to hiccup

solucionar[solusjo'na^r] VT to solve; (decidir) to resolve

soluço[so'lusu] M (pranto) sob; (Med) hiccup

soluções[solu'sõjʃ] FPL de **solução**

solúvel[so'luvew] (pl -eis) ADJ soluble

solvência[sow'vẽsja] F solvency

solvente[sow'vẽtʃi] ADJ, M solvent

som[sõ] (pl -ns) M sound; (Mús) tone; (BR: equipamento) hi-fi, stereo; (: música) music; **ao ~ de** (Mús) to the accompaniment of

soma['sɔma] F sum

Somália[so'malja] F: **a ~** Somalia

somar[so'ma^r] VT (adicionar) to add (up); (chegar a) to add up to, amount to ∎ VI to add up

somatório[soma'tɔrju] M sum; (fig) sum total

sombra['sõbra] F shadow; (proteção) shade; (indício) trace, sign; **à ~ de** in the shade of; (fig) under the protection of; **sem ~ de dúvida** without a shadow of a doubt; **querer ~ e água fresca** (fig) to want the good things in life

sombreado, -a[sõ'brjadu, a] ADJ shady ∎ M shading

sombrear[sõ'brja^r] VT to shade

sombreiro[sõ'brejru] M (chapéu) sombrero

sombrinha[sõ'briɲa] F parasol, sunshade; (BR) lady's umbrella

sombrio, -a[sõ'briu, a] ADJ (escuro) shady, dark; (triste) gloomy; (rosto) grim

some etc ['sɔmi] VB V **sumir**

somenos[so'menuʃ] ADJ inferior, poor; **de ~ importância** unimportant

somente[sɔ'mẽtʃi] ADV only; **tão ~** only

somos['sɔmoʃ] VB V **ser**

sonambulismo[sonãbu'liʒmu] M sleepwalking

sonâmbulo, -a[so'nãbulu, a] ADJ sleepwalking ∎ M/F sleepwalker

sonante[so'nãtʃi] ADJ: **moeda ~** cash

sonata[so'nata] F sonata

NB: European Portuguese adds the following consonants to certain words: **b** (sú(b)dito, su(b)til); **c** (a(c)ção, a(c)cionista, a(c)to); **m** (inde(m)ne); **p** (ado(p)çã, ado(p)tar); for further details see p. xiii.

sonda ['sõda] F (*Náut*) plummet, sounding lead; (*Med*) probe; (*de petróleo*) drill; (*de alimentação*) drip; ~ **espacial** space probe

sondagem [sõ'daʒẽ] (*pl* -**ns**) F (*Náut*) sounding; (*de terreno, opinião*) survey; (*para petróleo*) drilling; (*para minerais*) boring; (*atmosférica*) testing

sondar [sõ'daʳ] VT to probe; (*opinião etc*) to sound out

soneca [so'nɛka] F nap, snooze; **tirar uma** ~ to have a nap

sonegação [sonega'sãw] F withholding; (*furto*) theft; ~ **de impostos** tax evasion

sonegar [sone'gaʳ] VT (*dinheiro, valores*) to conceal, withhold; (*furtar*) to steal, pilfer; (*impostos*) to dodge, evade; (*informações, dados*) to withhold

soneto [so'netu] M sonnet

sonhador, a [soɲa'doʳ(a)] ADJ dreamy ■ M/F dreamer

sonhar [so'ɲaʳ] VT, VI to dream; ~ **com** to dream about; ~ **em fazer** to dream of doing; ~ **acordado** to daydream; **nem sonhando** *ou* ~! (*col*) no way!; **sonho** ['sõɲu] M dream; (*Culin*) doughnut

sono ['sonu] M sleep; **estar caindo de** ~ to be half-asleep; **estar com** *ou* **ter** ~ to be sleepy; **estar sem** ~ not to be sleepy; **ferrar no** ~ to fall into a deep sleep; **pegar no** ~ to fall asleep; **ter o** ~ **leve/pesado** to be a light/heavy sleeper

sonolência [sono'lẽsja] F drowsiness

sonolento, -a [sono'lẽtu, a] ADJ sleepy, drowsy

sonoridade [sonori'dadʒi] F sound quality

sonoro, -a [so'nɔru, a] ADJ resonant; (*consoante*) voiced

sonoterapia [sonotera'pia] F hypnotherapy

sons [sõʃ] MPL *de* **som**

sonso, -a ['sõsu, a] ADJ sly, artful

sopa ['sopa] F soup; (*col*) pushover, cinch; **dar** ~ (*abundar*) to be plentiful; (*estar disponível*) to go spare; (*descuidar-se*) to be careless; **essa** ~ **vai acabar** (*col*) all good things come to an end; ~ **de legumes** vegetable soup

sopapear [sopa'pjaʳ] VT to slap

sopapo [so'papu] M slap, cuff; **dar um** ~ **em** to slap

sopé [so'pɛ] M foot, bottom

sopeira [so'pejra] F (*Culin*) soup dish

sopitar [sopi'taʳ] VT (*conter*) to curb, repress

soporífero, -a [sopo'riferu, a] ADJ soporific ■ M sleeping drug

soporífico, -a [sopo'rifiku, a] ADJ, M = **soporífero**

soprano [so'pranu] ADJ, M/F soprano

soprar [so'praʳ] VT to blow; (*balão*) to blow up; (*vela*) to blow out; (*dizer em voz baixa*) to whisper ■ VI to blow; **sopro** ['sopru] M blow, puff; (*de vento*) gust; (*no coração*) murmur; **instrumento de sopro** wind instrument

soquei *etc* [so'kej] VB *V* **socar**

soquete [so'kɛtʃi] F ankle sock

sordidez [soxdʒi'deʒ] F sordidness; (*imundície*) squalor

sórdido, -a ['sɔxdʒidu, a] ADJ sordid; (*imundo*)

squalid; (*obsceno*) indecent, dirty

soro ['soru] M (*Med*) serum; (*do leite*) whey

sóror ['sɔrɔʳ] F (*Rel*) sister

sorrateiro, -a [soxa'tejru, a] ADJ sly, sneaky

sorridente [soxi'dẽtʃi] ADJ smiling

sorrir [so'xiʳ] VI to smile; **sorriso** [so'xizu] M smile; **sorriso amarelo** forced smile

sorte ['sɔxtʃi] F luck; (*casualidade*) chance; (*destino*) fate, destiny; (*condição*) lot; (*espécie*) sort, kind; **de** ~ (*pessoa etc*) lucky; **desta** ~ so, thus; **de** ~ **que** so that; **por** ~ luckily; **dar** ~ (*trazer sorte*) to bring good luck; (*ter sorte*) to be lucky; **estar com** *ou* **ter** ~ to be lucky; **tentar a** ~ to try one's luck; **ter a** ~ **de** to be lucky enough to; **tirar a** ~ to draw lots; **tirar a** ~ **grande** (*tb fig*) to hit the jackpot; ~ **grande** big prize

sorteado, -a [sox'tʃjadu, a] ADJ (*pessoa, bilhete*) winning; (*Mil*) conscripted

sortear [sox'tʃjaʳ] VT to draw lots for; (*rifar*) to raffle; (*Mil*) to draft; **sorteio** [sox'teju] M draw; (*rifa*) raffle; (*Mil*) draft

sortido, -a [sox'tʃidu, a] ADJ (*abastecido*) supplied, stocked; (*variado*) assorted; (*loja*) well-stocked

sortilégio [soxtʃi'lɛʒu] M (*bruxaria*) sorcery; (*encantamento*) charm, fascination

sortimento [soxtʃi'mẽtu] M assortment, stock

sortir [sox'tʃiʳ] VT (*abastecer*) to supply, stock; (*variar*) to vary, mix

sortudo, -a [sox'tudu, a] (*col*) ADJ lucky ■ M/F lucky beggar

sorumbático, -a [sorũ'batʃiku, a] ADJ gloomy, melancholy

sorvedouro [soxve'doru] M whirlpool; (*abismo*) chasm; **um** ~ **de dinheiro** (*fig*) a drain on resources

sorver [sox'veʳ] VT (*beber*) to sip; (*inalar*) to inhale; (*tragar*) to swallow up; (*absorver*) to soak up, absorb

sorvete [sox'vetʃi] (BR) (*feito com leite*) ice cream; (*feito com água*) sorbet; ~ **de chocolate/creme** chocolate/dairy ice cream

sorveteiro [soxve'tejru] M ice-cream man

sorveteria [soxvete'ria] F ice-cream parlour (*Brit*) *ou* parlor (US)

sorvo ['soxvu] M sip

SOS ABR SOS

sósia ['sɔzja] M/F double

soslaio [soʒ'laju]: **de** ~ ADV sideways, obliquely; **olhar algo de** ~ to squint at sth

sossegado, -a [sose'gadu, a] ADJ peaceful, calm

sossegar [sose'gaʳ] VT to calm, quieten ■ VI to quieten down

sossego [so'segu] M peace (and quiet)

sotaina [so'tajna] F cassock, soutane

sótão ['sɔtãw] (*pl* -**s**) M attic, loft

sotaque [so'taki] M accent

sotavento [sota'vẽtu] M (*Náut*) lee; **a** ~ to leeward

soterrar [sote'xaʳ] VT to bury

soturno, -a [so'tuxnu, a] ADJ sad, gloomy

sou [so] VB *V* **ser**

soube *etc* ['sobi] VB *V* **saber**

soutien [su'tʃjã] M = **sutiã**

sova ['sɔva] F beating, thrashing; **dar uma ~ em alguém** to beat sb up; **levar uma ~ (de alguém)** to be beaten up (by sb)

sovaco [so'vaku] M armpit

sovaqueira [sova'kejra] F body odour (Brit) ou odor (US)

sovar [so'va^r] VT (surrar) to beat, thrash; (massa) to knead; (uva) to tread; (roupa) to wear out; (couro) to soften up

soviético, -a [so'vjetʃiku, a] ADJ, M/F Soviet

sovina [so'vina] ADJ mean, stingy ■ M/F miser, skinflint

sovinice [sovi'nisi] F meanness

sozinho, -a [sɔ'ziɲu, a] ADJ (all) alone, by oneself; (por si mesmo) by oneself

SP ABR = **São Paulo**

spam [iʃpã] (pl -s) M (Comput) spam

SPI (BR) ABR M = **Serviço de Proteção ao Índio**

spot [iʃ'pɔtʃi] (pl -s) M spotlight

spray [iʃ'prej] (pl -s) M spray

spread [iʃ'predʒi] M (Com) spread

SPU (BR) ABR M = **Serviço de Patrimônio da União**; = **Serviço Psiquiátrico de Urgência**

squash [iʃ'kweʃ] M squash

Sr. ABR (= senhor) Mr(.)

Sr.ª ABR (= senhora) Mrs

Sri Lanka [ʃri'lãka] M: **o ~** Sri Lanka

Sr.ª ABR: **senhorita** Miss

SSP (BR) ABR F = **Secretaria de Segurança Pública**

staff [iʃ'tafi] M staff

standard [iʃ'tãdaxdʒi] ADJ INV standard

status [iʃ'tatus] M status

STF (BR) ABR M = **Supremo Tribunal Federal**

STM (BR) ABR M = **Supremo Tribunal Militar**

sua ['sua] F de **seu**

suado, -a ['swadu, a] ADJ sweaty; (fig: dinheiro etc) hard-earned

suadouro [swa'doru] M sweat; (lugar) sauna

suar [swa^r] VT to sweat ■ VI to sweat; (fig): **~ por algo/para conseguir algo** to sweat blood for sth/to get sth; **~ em bicas** to sweat buckets; **~ frio** to come out in a cold sweat

suástica ['swaʃtʃika] F swastika

suave ['swavi] ADJ gentle; (música, voz) soft; (sabor, vinho) smooth; (cheiro) delicate; (dor) mild; (trabalho) light; (prestações) easy; **suavidade** [suavi'dadʒi] F gentleness; (de voz) softness

suavizar [swavi'za^r] VT to soften; (dor, sofrimento) to alleviate

subalimentado, -a [subalimẽ'tadu, a] ADJ undernourished

subalterno, -a [subaw'tɛxnu, a] ADJ inferior, subordinate ■ M/F subordinate

subalugar [subalu'ga^r] VT to sublet

subarrendar [subaxẽ'da^r] (PT) VT = **subalugar**

subconsciência [subkõ'sjẽsja] F subconscious

subconsciente [subkõ'sjẽtʃi] ADJ, M subconscious

subdesenvolvido, -a [subdʒizẽvow'vidu, a] ADJ underdeveloped ■ M/F (pej) degenerate

subdesenvolvimento [subdʒizẽvowvi'mẽtu] M underdevelopment

súbdito ['subditu] (PT) M = **súdito**

subdividir [subdʒivi'dʒi^r] VT to subdivide; **subdividir-se** VR to subdivide

subeditor, a [subedʒi'to^r(a)] M/F subeditor

subemprego [subẽ'pregu] M low-paid unskilled job

subentender [subẽtẽ'de^r] VT to understand, assume; **subentendido, -a** [subẽtẽ'dʒidu, a] ADJ implied ■ M implication

subestimar [subeʃtʃi'ma^r] VT to underestimate

subida [su'bida] F ascent, climb; (ladeira) slope; (de preços) rise

subido, -a [su'bidu, a] ADJ high

subir [su'bi^r] VI to go up; (preço, de posto etc) to rise ■ VT (levantar) to raise; (ladeira, escada, rio) to climb, go up; **~ em** (morro, árvore) to climb, go up; (cadeira, palanque) to climb onto, get up onto; (ônibus) to get on

súbito, -a ['subitu, a] ADJ sudden ■ ADV (tb: **de súbito**) suddenly

subjacente [subʒa'sẽtʃi] ADJ (tb fig) underlying

subjetivo, -a [subʒe'tʃivu, a] (PT -ct-) ADJ subjective

subjugar [subʒu'ga^r] VT to subjugate, subdue; (inimigo) to overpower; (moralmente) to dominate

subjuntivo, -a [subʒũ'tʃivu, a] ADJ subjunctive ■ M subjunctive

sublevação [subleva'sãw] (pl -ões) F (up)rising, revolt

sublevar [suble'va^r] VT to stir up (to revolt), incite (to revolt); **sublevar-se** VR to revolt, rebel

sublimar [subli'ma^r] VT (pessoa) to exalt; (desejos) to sublimate

sublime [su'blimi] ADJ sublime; (nobre) noble; (música, espetáculo) marvellous (Brit), marvelous (US)

sublinhado [subli'ɲadu] M underlining

sublinhar [subli'ɲa^r] VT (pôr linha debaixo de) to underline; (destacar) to emphasize, stress

sublocar [sublo'ka^r] VT, VI to sublet

sublocatário, -a [subloka'tarju, a] M/F sub-tenant

submarino, -a [subma'rinu, a] ADJ underwater ■ M submarine

submergir [submex'ʒi^r] VT to submerge; **submergir-se** VR to submerge

submerso, -a [sub'mexsu, a] ADJ submerged; (absorto): **~ em** immersed ou engrossed in

submeter [subme'te^r] VT (povos, inimigo) to subdue; (plano) to submit; (sujeitar): **~ a** to subject to; **submeter-se** VR: **submeter-se a** to submit to; (operação) to undergo

submirjo etc [sub'mixʒu] VB V **submergir**

NB: European Portuguese adds the following consonants to certain words: **b** (sú(b)dito, su(b)til); **c** (a(c)ção, a(c)cionista, a(c)to); **m** (inde(m)ne); **p** (ado(p)ção, ado(p)tar); for further details see p. xiii.

submissão [submi'sãw] F submission

submisso, -a [sub'misu, a] ADJ submissive, docile

submundo [sub'mũdu] M underworld

subnutrição [subnutri'sãw] F malnutrition

subnutrido, -a [subnu'tridu, a] ADJ undernourished

subordinar [suboxdʒi'na^r] VT to subordinate

subornar [subox'na^r] VT to bribe; **suborno** [su'boxnu] M bribery

subproduto [subpro'dutu] M by-product

sub-reptício, -a [subxep'tʃisju, a] ADJ surreptitious

subrotina [subxo'tʃina] F (Comput) subroutine

subscrever [subʃkre've^r] VT to sign; (opinião, Com: ações) to subscribe to; (contribuir) to put in ■ VI: ~ **a** to endorse; **subscrever-se** VR to sign one's name; ~ **para** to contribute to; **subscrevemos** **nos ...** (Com: em cartas) ≈ we remain ..

subscrição [subʃkri'sãw] (pl -ões) F subscription; (contribuição) contribution

subscritar [subʃkri'ta^r] VT to sign

subscrito, -a [sub'ʃkritu, a] PP de **subscrever**

subsecretário, -a [subsekre'tarju, a] M/F undersecretary

subseqüente [subse'kwẽtʃi] ADJ subsequent

subserviente [subsex'vjẽtʃi] ADJ obsequious, servile

subsidiar [subsi'dʒja^r] VT to subsidize

subsidiária [subsi'dʒjarja] F (Com) subsidiary (company)

subsidiário, -a [subsi'dʒjarju, a] ADJ subsidiary

subsídio [sub'sidʒu] M subsidy; (ajuda) aid; **subsídios** MPL (informações) data sg, information sg

subsistência [subsiʃ'tẽsja] F (sustento) subsistence; (meio de vida) livelihood

subsistir [subsiʃ'tʃi^r] VI (existir) to exist; (viver) to subsist, live; (estar em vigor) to be in force; (perdurar) to remain, survive

subsolo [sub'sɔlu] M subsoil; (de prédio) basement

substabelecer [subiʃtabele'se^r] VT to delegate

substância [sub'ʃtãsja] F substance; **substancial** [subʃtã'sjaw] (pl -ais) ADJ substantial

substantivo, -a [subʃtã'tʃivu, a] ADJ substantive ■ M noun

substituição [subʃtʃitwi'sãw] (pl -ões) F substitution, replacement

substituir [subʃtʃi'twi^r] VT to substitute, replace

substituto, -a [subʃti'tutu, a] ADJ, M/F substitute

subterfúgio [subtex'fuʒu] M subterfuge

subterrâneo, -a [subite'xanju, a] ADJ subterranean, underground

subtil etc [sub'tiw] (PT) = **sutil** etc

subtítulo [subi'tʃitulu] M subtitle

subtrair [subtra'i^r] VT (furtar) to steal; (deduzir) to subtract ■ VI to subtract

subumano, -a [subu'manu, a] ADJ subhuman; (desumano) inhuman

suburbano, -a [subux'banu, a] ADJ suburban; (pej) uncultivated

subúrbio [su'buxbju] M suburb

subvenção [subvẽ'sãw] (pl -ões) F subsidy, grant

subvencionar [subvẽsjo'na^r] VT to subsidize

subvenções [subvẽ'sõjʃ] FPL de **subvenção**

subversivo, -a [subvex'sivu, a] ADJ, M/F subversive

subverter [subvex'te^r] VT to subvert; (povo) to incite (to revolt); (planos) to upset

Sucam ['sukã] (BR) ABR F = **Superintendência da Campanha de Saúde Pública**

sucata [su'kata] F scrap metal

sucatar [suka'ta^r] VT to scrap

sucção [suk'sãw] F suction

sucedâneo, -a [suse'danju, a] ADJ substitute ■ M (substância) substitute

suceder [suse'de^r] VI to happen ■ VT to succeed; **suceder-se** VR to succeed one another; ~ **a** (num cargo) to succeed; (seguir) to follow; ~ **com** to happen to; **-se a** to follow

sucedido [suse'dʒidu] M event, occurrence

sucessão [suse'sãw] (pl -ões) F succession; **sucessivo, -a** [suse'sivu, a] ADJ successive

sucesso [su'sesu] M success; (música, filme) hit; **com/sem ~** successfully/unsuccessfully; **de ~** successful; **fazer** ou **ter ~** to be successful

sucessor, a [suse'so^r(a)] M/F successor

súcia ['susja] F gang, band

sucinto, -a [su'sĩtu, a] ADJ succinct

suco ['suku] (BR) M juice; ~ **de laranja** orange juice

suculento, -a [suku'lẽtu, a] ADJ succulent, juicy; (substancial) substantial

sucumbir [sukũ'bi^r] VI (render) to succumb, yield; (morrer) to die, perish

sucursal [sukux'saw] (pl -ais) F (Com) branch

Sudam ['sudã] ABR F = **Superintendência de Desenvolvimento da Amazônia**

Sudão [su'dãw] M: **o ~** (the) Sudan

Sudeco [su'dɛku] (BR) ABR F = **Superintendência de Desenvolvimento do Centro-Oeste**

Sudene [su'dɛni] (BR) ABR F = **Superintendência de Desenvolvimento do Nordeste**

Sudepe [su'dɛpi] (BR) ABR F = **Superintendência de Desenvolvimento da Pesca**

sudeste [su'dɛʃtʃi] ADJ southeast ■ M southeast

Sudhevea [sude'vɛa] (BR) ABR F = **Superintendência da Borracha**

súdito ['sudʒitu] M (de rei etc) subject

sudoeste [sud'weʃtʃi] ADJ southwest ■ M southwest

Suécia ['swɛsja] F: **a ~** Sweden; **sueco, -a** ['swɛku, a] ADJ Swedish ■ M/F Swede ■ M (Ling) Swedish

suéter ['swete^r] (BR) M ou F sweater

Suez [swɛʒ]: **o canal de ~** the Suez canal

suficiência [sufi'sjẽsja] F sufficiency

suficiente [sufi'sjẽtʃi] ADJ sufficient, enough; **o ~** enough

sufixo [su'fiksu] M suffix

suflê [su'fle] M soufflé
sufocante [sufo'kãtʃi] ADJ suffocating; (calor) sweltering, oppressive
sufocar [sufo'kaʳ] VT to suffocate; (revolta) to put down ■ VI to suffocate
sufoco [su'foku] M (afã) eagerness; (ansiedade) anxiety; (dificuldade) hassle
sufrágio [su'fraʒu] M (direito de voto) suffrage; (voto) vote; ~ **universal** universal suffrage
sugar [su'gaʳ] VT to suck; (fig) to extort
sugerir [suʒe'riʳ] VT to suggest
sugestão [suʒeʃ'tãw] (pl -ões) F suggestion; **dar uma ~** to make a suggestion
sugestionar [suʒeʃtʃjo'naʳ] VT to influence; **sugestionar-se** VR to be influenced
sugestionável [suʒeʃtʃjo'navew] (pl -eis) ADJ impressionable
sugestivo, -a [suʒeʃ'tʃivu, a] ADJ suggestive
sugestões [suʒeʃ'tõjʃ] FPL de **sugestão**
sugiro etc [su'ʒiru] VB V **sugerir**
suguei etc [su'gej] VB V **sugar**
Suíça ['swisa] F: **a ~** Switzerland
suíças ['swisaʃ] FPL sideburns; v tb **suiço**
suicida [swi'sida] ADJ suicidal ■ M/F suicidal person; (morto) suicide; **suicidar-se** [swisi'daxsi] VR to commit suicide; **suicídio** [swi'sidʒju] M suicide
suíço, -a ['swisu, a] ADJ, M/F Swiss
sui generis [swi'ʒeneris] ADJ INV in a class of one's own, unique
suíno ['swinu] M pig, hog ■ ADJ v **gado**
Suipa ['swipa] (BR) ABR F = **Sociedade União Internacional Protetora dos Animais**
suíte ['switʃi] F (Mús, em hotel) suite; (em residência) maid's quarters pl
sujar [su'ʒaʳ] VT to dirty; (fig: honra) to sully ■ VI to make a mess; **sujar-se** VR to get dirty; (fig) to sully o.s.
sujeição [suʒej'sãw] F subjection
sujeira [su'ʒejra] F dirt; (estado) dirtiness; (col) dirty trick; **fazer uma ~ com alguém** to do the dirty on sb
sujeitar [suʒej'taʳ] VT to subject; **sujeitar-se** VR to submit
sujeito, -a [su'ʒejtu, a] ADJ: ~ **a** subject to ■ M (Ling) subject ■ M/F man/woman; ~ **a espaço** (Aer) stand-by
sujidade [suʒi'dadʒi] (PT) F dirt; (estado) dirtiness
sujo, -a ['suʒu, a] ADJ dirty; (fig: desonesto) nasty, dishonest ■ M dirt; **estar/ficar ~ com alguém** to be/get into sb's bad books
sul [suw] ADJ INV south, southern ■ M: **o ~** the south; **sul-africano, -a** ADJ, M/F South African
sul-americano, -a ADJ, M/F South American
sulcar [suw'kaʳ] VT to plough (Brit), plow (US); (rosto) to line, furrow
sulco [suw'ku] M furrow
sulfato [suw'fatu] M sulphate (Brit), sulfate (US)

sulfúrico, -a [suw'furiku, a] ADJ: **ácido ~** sulphuric (Brit) ou sulfuric (US) acid
sulista [su'liʃta] ADJ Southern ■ M/F Southerner
sultão, -tana [suw'tãw, 'tana] (pl -ões/-s) M/F sultan(a)
suma ['suma] F: **em ~** in short
sumamente [suma'mẽtʃi] ADV extremely
sumário, -a [su'marju, a] ADJ (breve) brief, concise; (Jur) summary; (biquíni) brief, skimpy ■ M summary
sumiço [su'misu] M disappearance; **dar ~ a** ou **em** to do away with; (comida) to put away
sumidade [sumi'dadʒi] F (pessoa) genius
sumido, -a [su'midu, a] ADJ (apagado) faint, indistinct; (voz) low; (desaparecido) vanished; (escondido) hidden; **ela anda sumida** she's not around much
sumir [su'miʳ] VI to disappear, vanish
sumo, -a ['sumu, a] ADJ (importância) extreme; (qualidade) supreme ■ M (PT) juice
sumptuoso, -a [sũ'twozu, ɔza] (PT) ADJ = **suntuoso**
Sunab [su'nabi] (BR) ABR F = **Superintendência Nacional de Abastecimento**
Sunamam [suna'mami] (BR) ABR F = **Superintendência Nacional da Marinha Mercante**
sundae ['sãdej] M sundae
sunga ['sũga] F swimming trunks pl
sungar [sũ'gaʳ] VT to hitch up
suntuoso, -a [sũ'twozu, ɔza] ADJ sumptuous
suor [swɔʳ] M sweat; (fig): **com o meu ~** by the sweat of my brow
super- [supeʳ-] PREFIXO super-; (col) really
superabundante [superabũ'dãtʃi] ADJ overabundant
superado, -a [supe'radu, a] ADJ (idéias) outmoded
superalimentar [superalimẽ'taʳ] VT to overfeed
superaquecer [superake'seʳ] VT to overheat
superar [supe'raʳ] VT (rival) to surpass; (inimigo, dificuldade) to overcome; (expectativa) to exceed
superávit [supe'ravitʃi] M (Com) surplus
superdose [supex'dɔzi] F overdose
superdotado, -a [supexdo'tadu, a] ADJ exceptionally gifted
superestimar [supereʃtʃi'maʳ] VT to overestimate
superestrutura [supereʃtru'tura] F superstructure
superficial [supexfi'sjaw] (pl -ais) ADJ superficial; (pessoa) shallow
superfície [supex'fisi] F (parte externa) surface; (extensão) area; (fig: aparência) appearance
superfino, -a [supex'finu, a] ADJ (de largura) extra fine; (de qualidade) excellent quality
supérfluo, -a [su'pexflwu, a] ADJ superfluous, unnecessary

NB: European Portuguese adds the following consonants to certain words: **b** (sú(b)dito, su(b)til); **c** (a(c)ção, a(c)cionista, a(c)to); **m** (inde(m)ne); **p** (ado(p)çã, ado(p)tar); for further details see p. xiii.

super-homem (*pl* -ns) M superman
superintendência [superĩtē'dēsja] F (*órgão*)
bureau
superintendente [superĩtē'dētʃi] M
superintendent; (*de empresa*) chief executive
superintender [superĩtē'deʳ] VT to superintend
superior [supe'rjoʳ] ADJ superior; (*mais elevado*)
higher; (*quantidade*) greater; (*mais acima*) upper
■ M superior; (*Rel*) superior, abbot; ~ **a** superior
to; **um número** ~ **a 10** a number greater *ou*
higher than 10; **curso/ensino** ~ degree course/
higher education; **lábio** ~ upper lip
superiora [supe'rjora] ADJ, F: (**madre**) ~ mother
superior
superioridade [superjori'dadʒi] F superiority
superlativo, -a [supexla'tʃivu, a] ADJ
superlative ■ M superlative
superlotação [supexlota'sãw] F overcrowding
superlotado, -a [supexlo'tadu, a] ADJ (*cheio*)
crowded; (*excessivamente cheio*) overcrowded
supermercado [supexmex'kadu] M
supermarket
supermicro [supex'mikru] M (*Comput*)
supermicro
supermíni [supex'mini] M (*Comput*) supermini
superpor [supex'poʳ] (*irreg*) VT: ~ **algo a algo** to
put sth before sth
superpotência [supexpo'tēsja] F superpower
superpovoado, -a [supexpo'vwadu, a] ADJ
overpopulated
superprodução [supexprodu'sãw] F
overproduction
superproteger [supexprote'ʒeʳ] VT to
overprotect
superpunha *etc* [supex'puɲa] VB V **superpor**
superpus *etc* [supex'puʃ] VB V **superpor**
superpuser *etc* [supexpu'zeʳ] VB V **superpor**
supersecreto, -a [supexse'kretu, a] ADJ top
secret
supersensível [supexsē'sivew] (*pl* -eis) ADJ
oversensitive
supersimples [supex'sĩpliʃ] ADJ INV extremely
simple
supersônico, -a [supex'soniku, a] ADJ
supersonic
superstição [supexʃtʃi'sãw] (*pl* -ões) F
superstition; **supersticioso, -a** [supexʃtʃi'sjozu,
ɔza] ADJ superstitious
superstições [supexʃtʃi'sõjʃ] FPL *de* **superstição**
supervisão [supexvi'zãw] F supervision;
supervisionar [supexvizjo'naʳ] VT to supervise;
supervisor, a [supexvi'zoʳ(a)] M/F supervisor
supetão [supe'tãw] M: **de** ~ all of a sudden
suplantar [suplã'taʳ] VT to supplant, supersede
suplementar [suplemē'taʳ] ADJ supplementary
■ VT to supplement
suplemento [suple'mētu] M supplement
suplente [su'plētʃi] M/F substitute
súplica ['suplika] F supplication, plea
suplicante [supli'kãtʃi] M/F supplicant; (*Jur*)
plaintiff
suplicar [supli'kaʳ] VT, VI to plead, beg; ~ **algo a**

ou **de alguém** to beg sb for sth; ~ **a alguém que
faça** to beg sb to do
suplício [su'plisju] M torture; (*experiência penosa*)
trial
supor [su'poʳ] (*irreg*) VT to suppose; (*julgar*) to
think; **suponhamos que** let us suppose that;
vamos ~ let us suppose *ou* say; **suponho que**
sim I suppose so; **era de** ~ **que** one could
assume that
suportar [supox'taʳ] VT to hold up, support;
(*tolerar*) to bear, tolerate; **suportável**
[supox'tavew] (*pl* -eis) ADJ bearable, tolerable;
suporte [su'pɔxtʃi] M support, stand; **suporte
atlético** athletic support
suposição [supozi'sãw] (*pl* -ões) F supposition,
presumption
supositório [supozi'tɔrju] M suppository
supostamente [supoʃta'mētʃi] ADV supposedly
suposto, -a [su'poʃtu, 'pɔʃta] PP *de* **supor** ■ ADJ
supposed ■ M assumption, supposition
supracitado, -a [suprasi'tadu, a] ADJ foregoing
■ M foregoing
supra-sumo ['supra-] M: **o** ~ **da beleza** *etc* the
pinnacle of beauty *etc*
supremacia [suprema'sia] F supremacy
supremo, -a [su'premu, a] ADJ supreme ■ M:
o S ~ the Supreme Court; **S** ~ **Tribunal Federal**
(BR) Federal Supreme Court
supressão [supre'sãw] (*pl* -ões) F suppression;
(*omissão*) omission; (*abolição*) abolition
suprimento [supri'mētu] M supply
suprimir [supri'miʳ] VT to suppress; (*frases de um
texto*) to delete; (*abolir*) to abolish
suprir [su'priʳ] VT (*fazer as vezes de*) to take the
place of; ~ **alguém de** to provide *ou* supply sb
with; ~ **algo por algo** to substitute sth with
sth; ~ **uma quantia** to make up an amount;
~ **a falta de alguém/algo** to make up for sb's
absence/the lack of sth; ~ **as necessidades/
uma família** to provide for needs/a family
supunha *etc* [su'puɲa] VB V **supor**
supus *etc* [su'puʃ] VB V **supor**
supuser *etc* [supu'zeʳ] VB V **supor**
supurar [supu'raʳ] VI to go septic, suppurate
surdez [sux'deʒ] F deafness; **aparelho para a** ~
hearing aid
surdina [sux'dʒina] F (*Mús*) mute; **em** ~
stealthily, on the quiet
surdo, -a ['suxdu, a] ADJ deaf; (*som*) muffled,
dull; (*consoante*) voiceless ■ M/F deaf person; ~
como uma porta as deaf as a post
surdo, -a-mudo/a ADJ deaf and dumb ■ M/F
deaf-mute
surfe ['suxfi] M surfing
surfista [sux'fiʃta] M/F surfer
surgir [sux'ʒiʳ] VI to appear; (*problema, dificuldade*)
to arise, crop up; (*oportunidade*) to arise, come up;
~ **de** (*proceder*) to come from; ~ **à mente** to come
ou spring to mind
Suriname [suri'nami] M: **o** ~ Surinam
surjo *etc* ['suxju] VB V **surgir**
surpreendente [suxprjē'dētʃi] ADJ surprising

surpreender [suxprjẽ'de^r] VT to surprise; (*pegar de surpresa*) to take unawares ◼ VI to be surprising; **surpreender-se** VR: **surpreender-se (de)** to be surprised (at); **surpresa** [sux'preza] F surprise; **de surpresa** by surprise

surpreso, -a [sux'prezu, a] PP *de* **surpreender** ◼ ADJ surprised

surra ['suxa] F (*ger, Esporte*) thrashing; **dar uma ~ em** to thrash; **levar uma ~ (de)** to get thrashed (by)

surrado, -a [su'xadu, a] ADJ (*espancado*) beaten up; (*roupa*) worn out

surrar [su'xa^r] VT to beat, thrash; (*roupa*) to wear out

surrealismo [suxea'liʒmu] M surrealism

surrealista [suxea'liʃta] ADJ, M/F surrealist

surrupiar [suxu'pja^r] VT to steal

sursis [sux'si] M INV (*Jur*) suspended sentence

surte *etc* ['suxtʃi] VB V **sortir**

surtir [sux'tʃi^r] VT to produce, bring about ◼ VI: **~ bem** to turn out well; **~ efeito** to have an effect

surto ['suxtu] M (*de doença*) outbreak; (*de progresso*) surge

suscetibilidade [susetʃibili'dadʒi] F susceptibility; (*sensibilidade*) sensitivity

suscetível [suse'tʃivew] (*pl* -**eis**) ADJ susceptible; **~ de** liable to

suscitar [susi'ta^r] VT to arouse; (*admiração*) to cause; (*dúvidas*) to raise; (*obstáculos*) to throw up

Susep [su'zɛpi] (*BR*) ABR F = **Superintendência de Seguros Privados**

suspeição [suʃpej'sãw] (*pl* -**ões**) F suspicion

suspeita [suʃ'pejta] F suspicion; **suspeitar** [suʃpej'ta^r] VT to suspect ◼ VI: **suspeitar de algo** to suspect sth; **suspeitar de alguém** to be suspicious of sb

suspeito, -a [suʃ'pejtu, a] ADJ suspect, suspicious ◼ M/F suspect

suspeitoso, -a [suʃpej'tozu, ɔza] ADJ suspicious

suspender [suʃpẽ'de^r] VT (*levantar*) to lift; (*pendurar*) to hang; (*trabalho, pagamento etc*) to suspend, stop; (*funcionário, aluno*) to suspend; (*jornal*) to suspend publication of; (*encomenda*) to cancel; (*sessão*) to adjourn, defer; (*viagem*) to put off; **suspensão** [suʃpẽ'sãw] (*pl* -**ões**) F (*ger, Auto*) suspension; (*de trabalho, pagamento*) stoppage; (*de viagem, sessão*) deferment; (*de encomenda*) cancellation; **suspense** [suʃ'pẽsi] M suspense; **filme de suspense** thriller

suspenso, -a [suʃ'pẽsu, a] PP *de* **suspender**

suspensões [suʃpẽ'sõjʃ] FPL *de* **suspensão**

suspensórios [suʃpẽ'sɔrjuʃ] MPL braces (*Brit*), suspenders (*US*)

suspicácia [suʃpi'kasja] F distrust, suspicion

suspicaz [suʃpi'kaj3] ADJ (*suspeito*) suspect; (*desconfiado*) suspicious

suspirar [suʃpi'ra^r] VI to sigh; **~ por algo** to long for sth; **suspiro** [suʃ'piru] M sigh; (*doce*) meringue

sussurrar [susu'xa^r] VT, VI to whisper; **sussurro** [su'suxu] M whisper

sustância [suʃ'tãsja] F (*força*) strength; (*de comida*) nourishment

sustar [suʃ'ta^r] VT, VI to stop

sustenho *etc* [suʃ'teɲu] VB V **suster**

sustentáculo [suʃtẽ'takulu] M (*tb fig*) support

sustentar [suʃtẽ'ta^r] VT to sustain; (*prédio*) to hold up; (*padrão*) to maintain; (*financeiramente, acusação*) to support; **sustentar-se** VR (*alimentar-se*) to sustain o.s.; (*financeiramente*) to support o.s.; (*equilibrar-se*) to balance; **~ que** to maintain that; **sustento** [suʃ'tẽtu] M sustenance; (*subsistência*) livelihood; (*amparo*) support

suster [suʃ'te^r] (*irreg*) VT to support, hold up; (*reprimir*) to restrain, hold back

susto ['suʃtu] M fright, scare; **tomar** *ou* **levar um ~** to get a fright; **que ~!** what a fright!

sutiã [su'tʃjã] M bra(ssiere)

sutil [su'tʃiw] (*pl* -**is**) ADJ subtle; (*fino*) fine, delicate; **sutileza** [sutʃi'leza] F subtlety; (*finura*) fineness, delicacy

sutilizar [sutʃili'za^r] VT to refine

sutis [su'tʃiʃ] ADJ PL *de* **sutil**

sutura [su'tura] F (*Med*) suture

suturar [sutu'ra^r] VT, VI to suture

NB: *European Portuguese adds the following consonants to certain words*: **b** (sú(b)dito, su(b)til); **c** (a(c)ção, a(c)cionista, a(c)to); **m** (inde(m)ne); **p** (ado(p)çã, ado(p)tar); *for further details see p. xiii.*

Tt

T, t [te] (*pl* **ts**) M T, t; **T de Tereza** T for Tommy
ta [ta] = **te + a**
tá [ta] (*col*) = **está** EXCL OK; **tá bom** OK, fine
tabacaria [tabaka'ria] F tobacconist's (shop)
tabaco [ta'baku] M tobacco
tabefe [ta'bɛfi] (*col*) M slap
tabela [ta'bɛla] F table, chart; (*lista*) list; **por**
~ indirectly; **estar caindo pelas ~s** (*fig*) to be
feeling low; ~ **de preços** price table
tabelado, -a [tabe'ladu, a] ADJ (*produto*) price-
controlled; (*preço*) controlled
tabelar [tabe'la^r] VT (*produto*) to fix the price of;
(*preço*) to fix; (*dados*) to tabulate
tabelião [tabe'ljãw] (*pl* -**ães**) M notary public
taberna [ta'bɛxna] F tavern, bar
tabique [ta'biki] M partition
tablado [ta'bladu] M platform; (*para espectadores*)
grandstand
tablete [ta'bletʃi] M (*de chocolate*) bar; (*de
manteiga*) pat
tablóide [ta'blɔjdʒi] M tabloid
tabu [ta'bu] ADJ, M taboo
tábua ['tabwa] F (*de madeira*) plank, board; (*Mat*)
list, table; (*de mesa*) leaf; ~ **de passar roupa**
ironing board; ~ **de salvação** (*fig*) last resort
tabuada [ta'bwada] F times table; (*livro*) tables
book
tabulador [tabula'do^r] M tab(ulator key)
tabular [tabu'la^r] VT to tabulate
tabuleiro [tabu'lejru] M tray; (*Xadrez*) board
tabuleta [tabu'leta] F (*letreiro*) sign, signboard
taça ['tasa] F cup; ~ **de champanhe** champagne
glass *ou* flute
tacada [ta'kada] F shot; **de uma** ~ in one go
tacanho, -a [ta'kaɲu, a] ADJ mean; (*de idéias
curtas*) narrow-minded; (*baixo*) small
tacar [ta'ka^r] VT (*bola*) to hit; (*col: jogar*) to chuck; ~
a mão *ou* **um soco em alguém** to punch sb
tacha ['taʃa] F (*prego*) tack; (*em calça jeans*) stud
tachar [ta'ʃa^r] VT: ~ **algo de** to brand sth as
tachinha [ta'ʃiɲa] F drawing pin (*Brit*), thumb
tack (*US*)
tácito, -a ['tasitu, a] ADJ tacit, implied
taciturno, -a [tasi'tuxnu, a] ADJ taciturn,
reserved
taco ['taku] M (*Bilhar*) cue; (*Golfe*) club; (*Hóquei*)
stick; (*bucha*) plug, wad; (*de assoalho*) parquet
block

táctico, -ca ['tatiku] (*PT*) = **tático** *etc*
táctil ['tatiw] (*PT*) ADJ = **tátil**
tacto ['tatu] (*PT*) M = **tato**
tadinho, -a [ta'dʒiɲu, a] (*col*) EXCL poor thing!; ~
dele! poor him!
tafetá [tafe'ta] M taffeta
tagarela [taga'rɛla] ADJ talkative ■ M/F
chatterbox; **tagarelar** [tagare'la^r] VI to chatter
tagarelice [tagare'lisi] F chat, chatter, gossip
tailandês, -esa [tajlã'deʃ, eza] ADJ, M/F Thai ■ M
(*Ling*) Thai
Tailândia [taj'lãdʒia] F: **a** ~ Thailand
tailleur [taj'e^r] M suit
tainha [ta'iɲa] F mullet
taipa ['tajpa] F: **parede de** ~ mud wall
tais [tajʃ] ADJ PL *de* **tal**
Taiti [taj'tʃi] M: **o** ~ Tahiti
tal [taw] (*pl* **tais**) ADJ such; ~ **e coisa** this and
that; **um** ~ **de Sr. X** a certain Mr. X; **que** ~? what
do you think?; (*PT*) how are things?; **que** ~ **um
cafezinho?** what about a coffee?; **que** ~ **nós
irmos ao cinema?** what about (us) going to
the cinema?; ~ **pai,** ~ **filho** like father, like son;
~ **como** such as; (*da maneira que*) just as; ~ **qual**
just like; **o** ~ **professor** that teacher; **a** ~ **ponto**
to such an extent; **de** ~ **maneira** in such a way;
e ~ and so on; **o/a** ~ (*col*) the greatest; **o Pedro
de** ~ Peter what's-his-name; **na rua** ~ in such
and such a street; **foi um** ~ **de gente ligar lá
para casa** there were people ringing home
non-stop
tala ['tala] F (*Med*) splint
talão [ta'lãw] (*pl* -**ões**) M (*de recibo*) stub; ~ **de
cheques** cheque book (*Brit*), check book (*US*)
talco ['tawku] M talcum powder; **pó de** ~ (*PT*)
talcum powder
talento [ta'lẽtu] M talent; (*aptidão*) ability
talentoso, -a [talẽ'tozu, ɔza] ADJ talented
talha ['taʎa] F (*corte*) carving; (*vaso*) pitcher;
(*Náut*) tackle
talhado, -a [ta'ʎadu, a] ADJ (*apropriado*)
appropriate, right; (*leite*) curdled
talhar [ta'ʎa^r] VT to cut; (*esculpir*) to carve ■ VI
(*coalhar*) to curdle
talharim [taʎa'rĩ] M tagliatelle
talhe ['taʎi] M cut, shape; (*de rosto*) line

talher[ta'ʎeˢ] M set of cutlery; **talheres** MPL cutlery sg

talho['taʎu] M (corte) cutting, slicing; (PT: açougue) butcher's (shop)

talismã[taliʒ'mã] M talisman

talo['talu] M stalk, stem; (Arq) shaft

talões[ta'lõjʃ] MPL de **talão**

talude[ta'ludʒi] M slope, incline

taludo, -a[ta'ludu, a] ADJ stocky

talvez[taw'veʒ] ADV perhaps, maybe; ~ **tenha razão** maybe you're right

tamanco[ta'mãku] M clog, wooden shoe

tamanduá[tamã'dwa] M anteater

tamanho, -a[ta'maɲu, a] ADJ such (a) great ■ M size; **em ~ natural** life-size; **de que ~ é?** what size is it?; **uma casa que não tem ~** (col) a huge house; **do ~ de um bonde** (col) enormous

tamanho-família ADJ INV family-size; (fig) giant-size

tamanho-gigante ADJ INV giant-size

tâmara['tamara] F date

tamarindo[tama'rĩdu] M tamarind

também[tã'bẽj] ADV also, too, as well; (além disso) besides; ~ **não** not ... either, nor; **eu ~ me too**; **eu ~ não** nor me, neither do (ou did ou am ou have etc) I

tambor[tã'boˢ] M drum

tamborilar[tãbori'laˢ] VI (com os dedos) to drum; (chuva) to pitter-pat

tamborim[tãbo'rĩ] (pl -ns) M tambourine

Tâmisa['tamiza] M: **o ~** the Thames

tampa['tãpa] F lid; (de garrafa) cap

tampão[tã'pãw] (pl -ões) M tampon; (para curativos) compress; (rolha) stopper, plug

tampar[tã'paˢ] VT (lata, garrafa) to put the lid on; (cobrir) to cover

tampinha[tã'piɲa] F lid, top ■ M/F (col) shorty

tampo['tãpu] M lid; (Mús) sounding board

tampões[tã'põjʃ] MPL de **tampão**

tampouco[tã'poku] ADV nor, neither

tanga['tãga] F loincloth; (biquíni) bikini

tangente[tã'ʒẽtʃi] F tangent; (trecho retilíneo) straight section; **pela ~** (fig) narrowly

tanger[tã'ʒeˢ] VT (Mús) to play; (sinos) to ring; (cordas) to pluck ■ VI (sinos) to ring; ~ **a** (dizer respeito a) to concern; **no que tange a** as regards, with respect to

tangerineira[tãʒeri'nejra] F tangerine tree

tangerina[tãʒe'rina] F tangerine

tangível[tã'ʒivew] (pl -eis) ADJ tangible

tango['tãgu] M tango

tanjo etc ['tãʒu] VB v **tanger**

tanque['tãki] M (reservatório, Mil) tank; (de lavar roupa) sink

tantã[tã'tã] (col) ADJ crazy

tanto, -a['tãtu, a] ADJ, PRON (sg) so much; (: + interrogativa/negativa) as much; (pl) so many; (: + interrogativa/negativa) as many ■ ADV so much; ~ **melhor/pior** so much the better/

more's the pity; ~ ... **como** ... both ... and ...; ~ **mais** ... **quanto mais** ... the more ... the more ...; ~ ... **quanto** ... as much ... as ...; ~**s** ... **quanto** ... as many ... as ...; ~ **tempo** so long; **quarenta e ~s anos** forty-odd years; **vinte e tantas pessoas** twenty-odd people; ~ **a Lúcia, quanto o Luís** both Lúcia and Luís; ~ **faz** it's all the same to me, I don't mind; **um ~ de vinho** some wine; **um outro ~ de vinho** a little more wine; **um ~ (quanto)** (como adv) rather, somewhat; **as tantas** the small hours; **lá para as tantas** late, in the small hours; **um médico e ~** quite a doctor; **não é para ~** it's not such a big deal; **não** ou **nem ~ assim** not as much as all that; ~ **(assim) que** so much so that

Tanzânia[tã'zanja] F: **a ~** Tanzania

tão[tãw] ADV so; ~ **rico quanto** as rich as; **tão-só** ADV only

tapa['tapa] M ou F slap; **no ~** (col) by force

tapado, -a[ta'padu, a] ADJ (col: bobo) stupid

tapar[ta'paˢ] VT to cover; (garrafa) to cork; (caixa) to put the lid on; (ouvidos) to block; (orifício) to block up; (encobrir) to block out

tapeação[tapja'sãw] F cheating

tapear[ta'pjaˢ] VT, VI to cheat

tapeçaria[tapesa'ria] F tapestry; (loja) carpet shop

tapetar[tape'taˢ] VT to carpet

tapete[ta'petʃi] M carpet, rug

tapioca[ta'pjɔka] F tapioca

tapume[ta'pumi] M fencing, boarding

taquicardia[takikax'dʒia] F palpitations pl

taquigrafar[takigra'faˢ] VT, VI to write in shorthand

taquigrafia[takigra'fia] F shorthand

taquígrafo, -a[ta'kigrafu, a] M/F shorthand typist (Brit), stenographer (US)

tara['tara] F fetish, mania; (Com) tare

tarado, -a[ta'radu, a] ADJ, M/F sex maniac; **ser ~ por** to be mad about

tarar[ta'raˢ] VI: ~ **(por)** to be smitten (with)

tardança[tax'dãsa] F delay, slowness

tardar[tax'daˢ] VI to delay, be slow; (chegar tarde) to be late ■ VT to delay; **sem mais ~** without delay; ~ **a** ou **em fazer** to take a long time to do; **o mais ~** at the latest

tarde['taxdʒi] F afternoon ■ ADV late; **ele chegou ~ (demais)** he got there too late; **mais cedo ou mais ~** sooner or later; **antes ~ do que nunca** better late than never; **boa ~!** good afternoon!; **hoje à ~** this afternoon; **à** ou **de ~** in the afternoon; **às três da ~** at three in the afternoon; ~ **da noite** late at night; **ontem/sexta à ~** yesterday/(on) Friday afternoon

tardinha[tax'dʒiɲa] F late afternoon; **de ~** late in the afternoon

tardio, -a[tax'dʒiu, a] ADJ late

tarefa[ta'refa] F task, job; (faina) chore

tarifa[ta'rifa] F tariff; (para transportes) fare; (lista

de preços) price list; ~ **alfandegária** customs
duty; ~ **de embarque** (*Aer*) airport tax
tarimba [ta'rĩba] F bunk; (*fig*) army life;
(: *experiência*) experience; **ter** ~ to be an old hand
tarimbado, -a [tarĩ'badu, a] ADJ experienced
tartamudear [taxtamu'dʒjaʳ] VI, VT to
mumble; (*gaguejar*) to stammer, stutter
tartamudo, -a [taxta'mudu, a] M/F mumbler;
(*gago*) stammerer, stutterer
tártaro ['taxtaru] M tartar
tartaruga [taxta'ruga] F turtle; **pente de ~**
tortoiseshell comb
tasca ['taʃka] (PT) F cheap eating place
tascar [taʃ'kaʳ] VT (*tapa, beijo*) to plant
tasco ['taʃku] (*col*) M bit, mouthful
Tasmânia [taʒ'manja] F: **a ~** Tasmania
tatear [ta'tʃjaʳ] VT to touch, feel; (*fig*) to sound
out ▪ VI to feel one's way
táteis ['tatejʃ] ADJ PL *de* **tátil**
tática ['tatʃika] F tactics *pl*
tático, -a ['tatʃiku, a] ADJ tactical
tátil ['tatʃiw] (*pl* -**eis**) ADJ tactile
tato ['tatu] M touch; (*fig: diplomacia*) tact
tatu [ta'tu] M armadillo
tatuador, a [tatwa'doʳ(a)] M/F tattooist
tatuagem [ta'twaʒẽ] (*pl* -**ns**) F tattoo
tatuar [ta'twaʳ] VT to tattoo
tauromaquia [tawroma'kia] F bullfighting
tautologia [tawtolo'ʒia] F tautology
tautológico, -a [tawto'lɔʒiku, a] ADJ
tautological
taxa ['taʃa] F (*imposto*) tax; (*preço*) fee; (*índice*)
rate; ~ **de câmbio** exchange rate; ~ **de juros**
interest rate; ~ **bancária** bank rate; ~ **de**
desconto discount rate; ~ **de matrícula** *ou*
inscrição enrollment *ou* registration fee; ~ **de**
exportação export duty; ~ **rodoviária** road
tax; ~ **fixa** (*Com*) flat rate; ~ **de retorno** (*Com*)
rate of return; ~ **de crescimento** growth rate;
taxação [taʃa'sãw] F taxation; (*de preços*) fixing;
taxar [ta'ʃaʳ] VT (*fixar o preço de*) to fix the price
of; (*lançar impostos sobre*) to tax
taxativo, -a [taʃa'tʃivu, a] ADJ categorical, firm
táxi ['taksi] M taxi, cab; ~ **aéreo** air taxi
taxímetro [tak'simetru] M taxi meter
tchã [tʃã] (*col*) M (*toque*) special touch; (*charme*)
charm
tchau [tʃaw] EXCL bye!
tcheco, -a ['tʃɛku, a] ADJ, M/F Czech
Tcheco-Eslováquia [tʃɛkuiʒlo'vakja] F
= **Tchecoslováquia**
Tchecoslováquia [tʃekoʒlo'vakja] F: **a ~**
Czechoslovakia
TCU (BR) ABR M = **Tribunal de Contas da União**
te [tʃi] PRON you; (*para você*) (to) you
té [tɛ] PREP ABR *de* **até**
tear [tʃjaʳ] M loom
teatral [tʃja'traw] (*pl* -**ais**) ADJ theatrical; (*grupo*)
theatre *atr* (*Brit*), theater *atr* (*US*); (*obra, arte*)
dramatic
teatralizar [tʃjatrali'zaʳ] VT to dramatize
teatro ['tʃjatru] M theatre (*Brit*), theater (*US*);

(*obras*) plays *pl*, dramatic works *pl*; (*gênero,*
curso) drama; **peça de ~** play; **fazer ~** (*fig*) to be
dramatic; ~ **de arena** theatre-in-the-round;
~ **de bolso** small theatre; ~ **de marionetes**
puppet theatre; ~ **de variedades** vaudeville
theatre; ~ **rebolado** burlesque theatre
teatrólogo, -a [tʃja'trɔlogu, a] M/F playwright,
dramatist
teatro-revista (*pl* **teatros-revista**) M review
theatre (*Brit*) *ou* theater (*US*)
tecelão, -lã [tese'lãw, 'lã] (*pl* -**ões/-s**) M/F weaver
tecer [te'seʳ] VT to weave; (*fig: intrigas*) to weave;
(*disputas*) to cause ▪ VI to weave; **tecido** [te'sidu]
M cloth, material; (*Anat*) tissue
tecla ['tɛkla] F key; **bater na mesma ~** (*fig*)
to harp on the same subject; ~ **de controle**
(*Comput*) control key; ~ **de função** (*Comput*)
function key; ~ **de saída** (*Comput*) exit key
tecladista [tekla'dʒiʃta] M/F (*Mús*) keyboards
player; (*Comput*) keyboard operator
teclado [tek'ladu] M keyboard; ~
complementar (*Comput*) keypad
teclar [tek'laʳ] VT (*dados*) to key (in)
tecnicalidade [teknikali'dadʒi] F technicality
técnica ['tɛknika] F technique; *v tb* **técnico**
técnico, -a ['tɛkniku, a] ADJ technical ▪ M/F
technician; (*especialista*) expert
tecnicolor [tekniko'loʳ] ADJ Technicolour®
(*Brit*), Technicolor® (*US*) ▪ M: **em ~** in
technicolo(u)r
tecnocrata [tekno'krata] M/F technocrat
tecnologia [teknolo'ʒia] F technology; ~ **de**
ponta leading edge technology; **tecnológico,**
-a [tekno'lɔʒiku, a] ADJ technological
teco ['tɛku] M hit; (*tiro*) shot; (*peteleco*) flick
teco-teco (*pl* -**s**) M small plane, light aircraft
tecto ['tɛktu] (PT) M = **teto**
tédio ['tɛdʒju] M tedium, boredom; **tedioso, -a**
[te'dʒjozu, ɔza] ADJ tedious, boring
Teerã [tee'rã] N Teheran
teia ['teja] F web; (*fig: enredo*) intrigue, plot;
(: *série*) series; ~ **de aranha** cobweb; ~ **de**
espionagem spy ring, web of espionage
teima ['tejma] F insistence
teimar [tej'maʳ] VI to insist, keep on; ~ **em** to
insist on
teimosia [tejmo'zia] F stubbornness; ~ **em**
fazer insistence on doing
teimoso, -a [tej'mozu, ɔza] ADJ obstinate;
(*criança*) wilful (*Brit*), willful (*US*)
teixo ['tejʃu] M yew
Tejo ['teʒu] M: **o (rio) ~** the (river) Tagus
tel. ABR (= *telefone*) tel.
tela ['tɛla] F (*tecido*) fabric, material; (*de pintar*)
canvas; (*Cinema, TV*) screen
telão [te'lãw] (*pl* -**ões**) M big screen
Telavive [tela'vivi] N Tel Aviv
tele... ['tele] PREFIXO tele..
telecomandar [telekomã'daʳ] VT to operate by
remote control
telecomando [teleko'mãdu] M remote control
telecomunicaçãos [telekomunika'sõjʃ] FPL

telecommunications

teleconferência [telekõfe'rẽsja] F teleconference

teleférico [tele'fɛriku] M cable car

telefonar [telefo'na^r] VI to (tele)phone, phone; **~ para alguém** to (tele)phone sb

telefone [tele'fɔni] M phone, telephone; (*número*) (tele)phone number; (*telefonema*) phone call; **estar/falar no ~** to be/talk on the phone; **~ público** public phone; **~ sem fio** cordless (tele)phone; **telefonema** [telefo'nɛma] M phone call; **dar um telefonema** to make a phone call

telefônico, -a [tele'foniku, a] ADJ telephone *atr*

telefonista [telefo'niʃta] M/F telephonist; (*na companhia telefônica*) operator

telegrafar [telegra'fa^r] VT, VI to telegraph, wire

telegrafia [telegra'fia] F telegraphy

telegráfico, -a [tele'grafiku, a] ADJ telegraphic

telegrafista [telegra'fiʃta] M/F telegraph operator

telégrafo [te'lɛgrafu] M telegraph

telegrama [tele'grama] M telegram, cable; **passar um ~** to send a telegram; **~ fonado** telemessage

teleguiado, -a [tele'gjadu, a] ADJ remote-controlled

teleguiar [tele'gja^r] VT to operate by remote control

teleimpressor [teleĩpre'so^r] M teleprinter

telejornal [teleʒox'naw] (*pl* -ais) M television news *sg*

telêmetro [te'lemetru] M rangefinder

telemóvel [tɛle'mɔvel] (*pl* -eis) M (PT) mobile (phone) (*Brit*), cellphone (*US*)

telenovela [teleno'vɛla] F (TV) soap opera

teleobjetiva [teleobʒe'tʃiva] (PT -ct-) F telephoto lens

telepatia [telepa'tʃia] F telepathy

telepático, -a [tele'patʃiku, a] ADJ telepathic

teleprocessamento [teleprosesa'mẽtu] M teleprocessing

Telerj [te'lɛxʒi] ABR F *Rio telephone company*

telescópico, -a [tele'skɔpiku, a] ADJ telescopic

telescópio [tele'skɔpju] M telescope

Telesp [te'lɛʃpi] ABR F *São Paulo telephone company*

telespectador, a [teleʃpekta'do^r(a)] M/F viewer ■ ADJ (*público*) viewing

teletexto [tele'teʃtu] M teletext

teletipista [teletʃi'piʃta] M/F teletypist

teletipo [tele'tʃipu] M teletype

teletrabalho [teletra'baʎu] M teleworking

televendas [tele'vẽdaʃ] FPL telesales

televisão [televi'zãw] F television; **~ por assinatura** pay television; **~ a cores** colo(u)r television; **~ a cabo** cable television; **~ digital** digital television; **aparelho de ~** television set

televisar [televi'za^r] VT = **televisionar**

televisionar [televizjo'na^r] VT to televise

televisivo, -a [televi'zivu, a] ADJ television *atr*

televisor [televi'zo^r] M (*aparelho*) television (set), TV (set)

telex [te'lɛks] M telex; **enviar por ~** to telex

telexar [telɛks'a^r] VT to telex

telha [te'ʎa] F tile; (*col*: *cabeça*) head; **ter uma ~ de menos** to have a screw loose; **não estar bom da ~** not to be right in the head; **deu-lhe na ~ (de) viajar** he got it into his head to go travel(l)ing

telhado [te'ʎadu] M roof

telões [te'lõjʃ] MPL *de* **telão**

tema ['tema] M theme; (*assunto*) subject; **temática** [te'matʃika] F theme

temático, -a [te'matʃiku, a] ADJ thematic

temer [te'me^r] VT to fear, be afraid of ■ VI to be afraid; **~ por** to fear for; **~ que** to be afraid that; **~ fazer** to be afraid of doing

temerário, -a [teme'rarju, a] ADJ reckless; (*arriscado*) risky; (*juízo*) unfounded

temeridade [temeri'dadʒi] F recklessness

temeroso, -a [teme'rozu, ɔza] ADJ fearful, afraid; (*pavoroso*) dreadful

temido, -a [te'midu, a] ADJ fearsome, frightening

temível [te'mivew] (*pl* -eis) ADJ = **temido**

temor [te'mo^r] M fear

tempão [tẽ'pãw] (*col*) M: **um ~** a long time, ages *pl*

têmpera ['tẽpera] F (*de metais*) tempering; (*caráter*) temperament; (*pintura*) distemper, tempera

temperado, -a [tẽpe'radu, a] ADJ (*metal*) tempered; (*clima*) temperate; (*comida*) seasoned

temperamental [tẽperamẽ'taw] (*pl* -ais) ADJ temperamental

temperamento [tẽpera'mẽtu] M temperament, nature

temperança [tẽpe'rãsa] F temperance

temperar [tẽpe'ra^r] VT (*metal*) to temper, harden; (*comida*) to season

temperatura [tẽpera'tura] F temperature

tempero [tẽ'peru] M seasoning, flavouring (*Brit*), flavoring (*US*)

tempestade [tẽpeʃ'tadʒi] F storm, tempest; **fazer uma ~ em copo de água** to make a mountain out of a molehill; **tempestuoso, -a** [tẽpeʃ'twozu, ɔza] ADJ stormy; (*fig*) tempestuous

templo ['tẽplu] M temple; (*igreja*) church

tempo ['tẽpu] M time; (*meteorológico*) weather; (*Ling*) tense; **o ~ todo** the whole time; **a ~** on time; **ao mesmo ~** at the same time; **a um ~** at once; **a ~ e a hora** at the appropriate time; **antes do ~** before time; **com ~** in good time; **de ~ em ~** from time to time; **nesse ~** at that time; **nesse meio ~** in the meantime; **em ~ de fazer** about to do; **em ~ recorde** in record time; **em seu devido ~** in due course; **quanto ~?** how

---

NB: *European Portuguese adds the following consonants to certain words:* **b** (sú(b)dito, su(b)til); **c** (a(c)ção, a(c)cionista, a(c)to); **m** (inde(m)ne); **p** (ado(p)çã, ado(p)tar); *for further details see p. xiii.*

long?; **muito/pouco** ~ a long/short time; **mais** ~ longer; **ganhar/perder** ~ to gain/waste time; **já era** ~ it's about time; **não dá** ~ there isn't time; **dar** ~ **ao** ~ to bide one's time, wait and see; **matar o** ~ to kill time; **nos bons** ~**s** in the good old days; **o maior de todos os** ~**s** the greatest of all time; **há** ~**s** for ages; (*atrás*) ages ago; **com o passar do** ~ in time; **primeiro/segundo** ~ (*Esporte*) first/second half; ~ **integral** full time; ~ **real** (*Comput*) real time

tempo-quente M fight, set-to

têmpora ['tɛpora] F (*Anat*) temple

temporada [tẽpo'rada] F season; (*tempo*) spell; ~ **de ópera** opera season

temporal [tẽpo'raw] (*pl* **-ais**) ADJ worldly ▪ M storm, gale

temporário, -a [tẽpo'rarju, a] ADJ temporary, provisional

tenacidade [tenasi'dadʒi] F tenacity

tenaz [te'najʒ] ADJ tenacious ▪ F tongs *pl*

tenção [tẽ'sãw] (*pl* **-ões**) F intention; **fazer** ~ **de fazer** to decide to do

tencionar [tẽsjo'na'] VT to intend, plan

tenções [tẽ'sõjʃ] FPL *de* **tenção**

tenda ['tẽda] F (*barraca*) tent; ~ **de oxigênio** oxygen tent

tendão [tẽ'dãw] (*pl* **-ões**) M tendon; ~ **de Aquiles** Achilles tendon

tendência [tẽ'dẽsja] F tendency; (*da moda etc*) trend; **a** ~ **de** *ou* **em** *ou* **a fazer** the tendency to do

tendencioso, -a [tẽdẽ'sjozu, ɔza] ADJ tendentious, bias(s)ed

tendente [tẽ'dẽtʃi] ADJ: ~ **a** tending to

tender [tẽ'de'] VI: ~ **para** to tend towards; ~ **a fazer** to tend *ou* have a tendency to do; (*encaminhar-se*) to head towards doing; (*visar*) to aim to do

tendinha [tẽ'dʒiɲa] F (*botequim*) bar; (*birosca*) (small) shop

tendões [tẽ'dõjʃ] MPL *de* **tendão**

tenebroso, -a [tene'brozu, ɔza] ADJ dark, gloomy; (*fig*) horrible

tenente [te'nẽtʃi] M lieutenant

tenho *etc* ['teɲu] VB *v* **ter**

tênis ['teniʃ] M INV (*jogo*) tennis; (*sapatos*) training shoes *pl*; (*um sapato*) training shoe; ~ **de mesa** table tennis; **tenista** [te'niʃta] M/F tennis player

tenor [te'no'] ADJ, M (*Mús*) tenor

tenro, -a ['tẽxu, a] ADJ tender; (*macio*) soft; (*delicado*) delicate; (*novo*) young

tensão [tẽ'sãw] F tension; (*pressão*) pressure, strain; (*rigidez*) tightness; (*Tec*) stress; (*Elet: voltagem*) voltage; ~ **nervosa** nervous tension; ~ **pré-menstrual** premenstrual tension

tenso, -a ['tẽsu, a] ADJ tense; (*sob pressão*) under stress, strained

tentação [tẽta'sãw] F temptation

tentáculo [tẽ'takulu] M tentacle

tentado, -a [tẽ'tadu, a] ADJ (*pessoa*) tempted; (*crime*) attempted

tentador, a [tẽta'do'(a)] ADJ tempting; (*sedutor*) inviting ▪ M/F tempter/temptress

tentar [tẽ'ta'] VT to try; (*seduzir*) to tempt, entice ▪ VI to try; ~ **fazer** to try to do; **tentativa** [tẽta'tʃiva] F attempt; **tentativa de fazer** attempt to do; **tentativa de homicídio/suicídio/roubo** (*Jur*) attempted murder/suicide/robbery; **por tentativas** by trial and error

tentativo, -a [tẽta'tʃivu, a] ADJ tentative

tentear [tẽ'tʃja'] VT (*tentar*) to try

tênue ['tenwi] ADJ tenuous; (*fino*) thin; (*delicado*) delicate; (*luz, voz*) faint; (*pequeníssimo*) minute

tenuidade [tenwi'dadʒi] F tenuousness

teologia [teolo'ʒia] F theology

teológico, -a [teo'lɔʒiku, a] ADJ theological

teólogo, -a [te'ɔlogu, a] M/F theologian

teor [te'o'] M (*conteúdo*) tenor; (*sentido*) meaning, drift; (*fig: norma*) system; (: *modo*) way; (*Quím*) grade; ~ **alcoólico** alcoholic content; **baixo** ~ **de nicotina** low tar

teorema [teo'rema] M theorem

teoria [teo'ria] F theory; **teoricamente** [teorika'mẽtʃi] ADV theoretically, in theory; **teórico, -a** [te'ɔriku, a] ADJ theoretical ▪ M/F theoretician

teorizar [teori'za'] VI to theorize

tépido, -a ['tɛpidu, a] ADJ tepid, lukewarm

○ **PALAVRA CHAVE**

ter [te'] VT **1** (*possuir, ger*) to have; (*na mão*) to hold; **você tem uma caneta?** have you got a pen?; **ela vai ter neném** she is going to have a baby **2** (*idade, medidas, estado*) to be; **ela tem 7 anos** she's 7 (years old); **a mesa tem 1 metro de comprimento** the table is 1 metre long; **ter fome/sorte** to be hungry/lucky; **ter frio/calor** to be cold/hot

3 (*conter*) to hold, contain; **a caixa tem um quilo de chocolates** the box holds one kilo of chocolates

4: **ter que** *ou* **de fazer** to have to do

5: **ter a ver com** to have to do with

6: **ir ter com** to (go and) meet

▪ VB IMPESS **1**: **tem** (*sg*) there is; (*pl*) there are; **tem 3 dias que não saio de casa** I haven't been out for 3 days

2: **não tem de quê** don't mention it

ter. ABR (= **terça-feira**) Tues

terapeuta [tera'pewta] M/F therapist

terapêutica [tera'pewtʃika] F therapeutics *sg*

terapêutico, -a [tera'pewtʃiku, a] ADJ therapeutic

terapia [tera'pia] F therapy; ~ **ocupacional** occupational therapy; ~ **de reposição de estrogênio** hormone replacement therapy

terça ['texsa] F (*tb*: **terça-feira**) Tuesday; **terça-feira** (*pl* **terças-feiras**) F Tuesday; **terça-feira gorda** Shrove Tuesday; **terça-feira que vem** next Tuesday; **terça-feira passada/retrasada**

last Tuesday/Tuesday before last; **hoje é terça-feira dia 12 de junho** today is Tuesday the 12th of June; **na terça-feira** on Tuesday; **nas terças-feiras** on Tuesdays; **todas as terças-feiras** every Tuesday; **terça-feira sim, terça-feira não** every other Tuesday; **na terça-feira de manhã** on Tuesday morning; **o jornal da terça-feira** Tuesday's newspaper

terceiranista [texsejra'niʃta] M/F third-year

terceiro, -a [tex'sejru, a] NUM third ■ M (Jur) third party; **terceiros** MPL (os outros) outsiders; **o T~ Mundo** the Third World; v tb **quinto**

terciário, -a [tex'sjarju, a] ADJ tertiary

terço ['texsu] M third (part)

terçol [tex'sɔw] (pl -óis) M stye

tergal® [tex'gaw] M Terylene®

tergiversar [texʒivex'sa^r] VI to prevaricate, evade the issue

termal [tex'maw] (pl -ais) ADJ thermal

termas ['texmaʃ] FPL bathhouse sg

térmico, -a ['texmiku, a] ADJ thermal; **garrafa térmica** (Thermos®) flask; **impressora térmica/papel ~** (Comput) thermal printer/paper

terminação [texmina'sãw] (pl -ões) F (Ling) ending

terminal [texmi'naw] (pl -ais) ADJ terminal ■ M (de rede, Elet, Comput) terminal ■ F terminal; **~ (de vídeo)** monitor, visual display unit

terminante [texmi'nãtʃi] ADJ final; (categórico) categorical, firm; (decisivo) decisive

terminantemente [texminãtʃi'mẽtʃi] ADV categorically, expressly

terminar [texmi'na^r] VT to finish ■ VI (pessoa) to finish; (coisa) to end; **~ de fazer** to finish doing; (ter feito há pouco) to have just done; **~ por algo/fazer algo** to end with sth/end up doing sth

término ['texminu] M (fim) end, termination

terminologia [texminolo'ʒia] F terminology

termo ['texmu] M term; (fim) end, termination; (limite) limit, boundary; (prazo) period; (PT: garrafa) (Thermos®) flask; **pôr ~ a** to put an end to; **meio ~** compromise; **em ~s (de)** in terms (of)

termodinâmica [texmodʒi'namika] F thermodynamics sg

termômetro [tex'mometru] M thermometer

termonuclear [texmonukle'a^r] ADJ thermonuclear ■ F nuclear power station

termostato [texmoʃ'tatu] M thermostat

terninho [tex'niɲu] M trouser suit (Brit), pantsuit (US)

terno, -a ['texnu, a] ADJ gentle, tender ■ M (BR: roupa) suit; **ternura** [tex'nura] F gentleness, tenderness

terra ['texa] F (mundo) earth, world; (Agr, propriedade) land; (pátria) country; (chão) ground; (Geo) soil, earth; (pó) dirt; (Elet) earth; **~ firme**

dry land; **por ~** on the ground; **nunca viajei por essas ~s** I've never been to those parts; **ela não é da ~** she's not from these parts; **caminho de ~ batida** dirt road; **~ de ninguém** no man's land; **~ natal** native land; **~ prometida** promised land; **a T~ Santa** the Holy Land; **~ vegetal** black earth; **soltar em ~** to disembark

terraço [te'xasu] M terrace

terracota [texa'kɔta] F terracotta

Terra do Fogo F Tierra del Fuego

terramoto [texa'mɔtu] (PT) M earthquake

Terra Nova F: **a ~** Newfoundland

terraplenagem [texaple'naʒẽ] F earth-moving

terreiro [te'xejru] M yard, square; (de macumba) shrine

terremoto [texe'mɔtu] M earthquake

terreno, -a [te'xɛnu, a] M ground, land; (porção de terra) plot of land; (Geo) terrain ■ ADJ earthly; **ganhar/perder ~** (fig) to gain/lose ground; **sondar o ~** (fig) to test the ground

térreo, -a ['tɛxju, a] ADJ ground level atr; **andar ~** (BR) ground floor (Brit), first floor (US)

terrestre [te'xɛʃtri] ADJ land atr; **globo ~** globe, Earth

terrificante [texifi'kãtʃi] ADJ terrifying

terrífico, -a [te'xifiku, a] ADJ terrifying

terrina [te'xina] F tureen

territorial [texito'rjaw] (pl -ais) ADJ territorial

território [texi'tɔrju] M territory; (distrito) district, region

terrível [te'xivew] (pl -eis) ADJ terrible, dreadful

terror [te'xo^r] M terror, dread

terrorismo [texo'riʒmu] M terrorism

terrorista [texo'riʃta] ADJ, M/F terrorist; **~ suicida** suicide bomber

tertúlia [tex'tulja] F gathering (of friends)

tesão [te'zãw] (pl -ões) (col!) M randiness; (pessoa, coisa) turn-on; (ereção) hard-on; **sentir ~ por alguém** to fancy sb; **estar de ~** to feel randy; (ter ereção) to have a hard-on

tese ['tɛzi] F proposition, theory; (Educ) thesis; **em ~** in theory

teso, -a ['tezu, a] ADJ (cabo) taut; (rígido) stiff; **estar ~** (col) to be broke ou skint

tesões [te'zõjʃ] MPL de **tesão**

tesoura [te'zora] F scissors pl; (fig) backbiter; **uma ~** a pair of scissors

tesourar [tezo'ra^r] VT to cut; (col) to run down

tesouraria [tezora'ria] F treasury

tesoureiro, -a [tezo'rejru, a] M/F treasurer

tesouro [te'zoru] M treasure; (erário) treasury, exchequer; (livro) thesaurus; **um ~ (de informações)** a treasure trove of information

testa ['tɛʃta] F brow, forehead; **à ~ de** at the head of

testa-de-ferro (pl **testas-de-ferro**) F figurehead, dummy

testamentário, -a [teʃtamẽ'tarju, a] ADJ of a will

NB: European Portuguese adds the following consonants to certain words: **b** (sú(b)dito, su(b)til); **c** (a(c)ção, a(c)cionista, a(c)to); **m** (inde(m)ne); **p** (ado(p)ção, ado(p)tar); for further details see p. xiii.

testamento [teʃta'mẽtu] M will, testament; (*Rel*): **Velho/Novo T~** Old/New Testament

testar [teʃ'ta^r] VT to test; (*deixar em testamento*) to bequeath

teste ['tɛʃtʃi] M test; **~ de aptidão** aptitude test

testemunha [teʃte'muɲa] F witness; **~ ocular** eyewitness; **~ de acusação** prosecution witness; **~s de Jeová** Jehovah's witnesses; **testemunhar** [teʃtemu'ɲa^r] VI to testify ■ VT to give evidence about; (*presenciar*) to witness; (*confirmar*) to demonstrate

testemunho [teʃte'muɲu] M evidence, testimony; (*prova*) evidence; **dar ~** to give evidence

testículo [teʃ'tʃikulu] M testicle

testificar [teʃtʃifi'ka^r] VT to testify to; (*comprovar*) to attest; (*assegurar*) to maintain

testudo, -a [teʃ'tudu, a] ADJ big-headed

teta ['tɛta] F teat, nipple

tétano ['tɛtanu] M tetanus

tête-à-tête [tɛta'tɛtʃi] M tête-à-tête

tetéia [te'tɛja] F (*pessoa*) gem

teto ['tɛtu] M ceiling; (*telhado*) roof; (*habitação*) home; (*para preço etc*) ceiling; **~ solar** sun roof

tetracampeão [tetrakã'pjãw] (*pl* -ões) M four-times champion

tétrico, -a ['tɛtriku, a] ADJ (*lúgubre*) gloomy, dismal; (*horrível*) horrible

teu, tua [tew, 'tua] ADJ your ■ PRON yours

teve ['tevi] VB V **ter**

tevê [te've] F telly (*Brit*), TV

têxtil ['teʃtʃiw] (*pl* -eis) M textile

texto ['teʃtu] M text

textual [teʃ'twaw] (*pl* -ais) ADJ textual; **estas são suas palavras textuais** these are his exact words

textualmente [teʃtwaw'mẽtʃi] ADV (*exatamente*) exactly, to the letter

textura [teʃ'tura] F texture

texugo [te'ʃugu] M badger

tez [teʒ] F complexion; (*pele*) skin

TFR (*BR*) ABR M = **Tribunal Federal de Recursos**

thriller ['srila^r] (*pl* -s) M thriller

ti [tʃi] PRON you

tia ['tʃia] F aunt

tia-avó (*pl* tias-avós) F great aunt

tiara ['tʃjara] F tiara

Tibete [tʃi'bɛtʃi] M: **o ~** Tibet

tíbia ['tʃibja] F shinbone

ticar [tʃi'ka^r] VT to tick

tico ['tʃiku] M: **um ~ (de)** a little bit (of)

tido, -a ['tʃidu, a] PP *de* **ter** ■ ADJ: **~ como** *ou* **por** considered to be

tiete ['tʃjetʃi] (*col*) M/F fan

tifo ['tʃifu] M typhus

tifóide [tʃi'ɔidʒi] ADJ: **febre ~** typhoid (fever)

tigela [tʃi'ʒɛla] F bowl; **de meia ~** (*fig, col*) second-rate, small-time

tigre ['tʃigri] M tiger

tigresa [tʃi'greza] F tigress

tijolo [tʃi'ʒolu] M brick; **~ furado** air brick

til [tʃiw] (*pl* tis) M tilde

tilintar [tʃilĩ'ta^r] VT, VI to jingle ■ M jingling

timaço [tʃi'masu] (*col*) M great team

timão [tʃi'mãw] (*pl* -ões) M (*Náut*) helm, tiller; (*time*) great team

timbre ['tʃibri] M insignia, emblem; (*selo*) stamp; (*Mús*) tone, timbre; (*de voz*) tone; (*Ling: de vogal*) quality; (*em papel de carta*) heading

time ['tʃimi] (*BR*) M team; **de segundo ~** (*fig*) second-rate; **tirar o ~ de campo** (*col*) to get going

timer ['tajme^r] (*pl* -s) M timer

timidez [tʃimi'deʒ] F shyness, timidity

tímido, -a ['tʃimidu, a] ADJ shy, timid

timões [tʃi'mõjʃ] MPL *de* **timão**

timoneiro [tʃimo'nejru] M helmsman, coxswain

tímpano ['tʃipanu] M eardrum; (*Mús*) kettledrum

tina ['tʃina] F vat

tingimento [tʃiʒi'mẽtu] M dyeing

tingir [tʃi'ʒi^r] VT to dye; (*fig*) to tinge

tinha *etc* ['tʃiɲa] VB V **ter**

tinhoso, -a [tʃi'ɲozu, ɔza] ADJ single-minded

tinido [tʃi'nidu] M jingle

tinir [tʃi'ni^r] VI to jingle, tinkle; (*ouvidos*) to ring; (*de frio, febre*) to shiver; (*de raiva, fome*) to tremble; **estar tinindo** (*carro, atleta*) to be in tip-top condition

tinjo *etc* ['tʃiʒu] VB V **tingir**

tino ['tʃinu] M (*juízo*) discernment, judgement; (*intuição*) intuition; (*prudência*) prudence; **perder o ~** to lose one's senses; **ter ~ para algo** to have a flair for sth

tinta ['tʃita] F (*de pintar*) paint; (*de escrever*) ink; (*para tingir*) dye; (*fig: vestígio*) shade, tinge; **carregar nas ~s** (*fig*) to exaggerate, embroider; **~ de impressão** printing ink

tinteiro [tʃi'tejru] M inkwell

tintim [tʃi'tʃi] EXCL cheers! ■ M: **~ por ~** blow by blow

tinto, -a ['tʃitu, a] ADJ dyed; (*fig*) stained; **vinho ~** red wine

tintura [tʃi'tura] F dye; (*ato*) dyeing; (*fig*) tinge, hint

tinturaria [tʃitura'ria] F (*lavanderia a seco*) dry-cleaner's

tintureiro, -a [tʃitu'rejru, a] (*col*) M/F dry cleaner ■ M police van

tio ['tʃiu] M uncle; **meus ~s** my uncle and aunt

tio-avô (*pl* tios-avôs) M great uncle

tipa ['tʃipa] (*col: pej*) F dolly bird

tipão [tʃi'pãw] (*col*) (*pl* -ões) M good looker

típico, -a ['tʃipiku, a] ADJ typical

tipificar [tʃipifi'ka^r] VT to typify

tipo ['tʃipu] M type; (*de imprensa*) print; (*de impressora*) typeface; (*classe*) kind; (*col: sujeito*) guy, chap; (*pessoa*) person

tipões [tʃi'põjʃ] MPL *de* **tipão**

tipografia [tʃipogra'fia] F printing, typography; (*estabelecimento*) printer's

tipógrafo, -a [tʃi'pɔgrafu, a] M/F printer

tipóia [tʃi'pɔja] F (*tira de pano*) sling

tique ['tʃiki] M (*Med*) twitch, tic; (*sinal*) tick

tique-taque [-'taki] (*pl* -s) M tick-tock

tíquete ['tʃiketʃi] M ticket

tiquinho [tʃi'kiɲu] M: **um ~ (de)** a little bit (of)

tira ['tʃira] F strip ▪ M (BR: *col*) cop

tiracolo [tʃira'kɔlu] M: **a ~** slung from the shoulder; **com o marido a ~** with her husband in tow

tirada [tʃi'rada] F (*dito*) tirade

tiragem [tʃi'raʒē] F (*de livro*) print run; (*de jornal, revista*) circulation; (*de chaminé*) draught (*Brit*), draft (US)

tira-gosto (*pl* -s) M snack, savoury (*Brit*)

tira-manchas M INV stain remover

tirania [tʃira'nia] F tyranny

tirânico, -a [tʃi'raniku, a] ADJ tyrannical

tiranizar [tʃirani'za^r] VT to tyrannize

tirano, -a [tʃi'ranu, a] ADJ tyrannical ▪ M/F tyrant

tirante [tʃi'rātʃi] M (*de arreio*) brace; (*Mecânica*) driving rod; (*viga*) tie beam ▪ PREP except; **uma cor ~ a vermelho** *etc* a reddish *etc* colo(u)r

tirar [tʃi'ra^r] VT to take away; (*de dentro*) to take out; (*de cima*) to take off; (*roupa, sapatos*) to take off; (*arrancar*) to pull out; (*férias*) to take, have; (*boas notas*) to get; (*salário*) to get, earn; (*curso*) to do, take; (*mancha*) to remove; (*foto, cópia*) to take; (*radiografia*) to have; (*mesa*) to clear; (*música, letra*) to take down; (*libertar*) to get out; **~ algo a alguém** to take sth from sb; **sem ~ nem pôr** exactly, precisely; **~ proveito/conclusões de** to benefit/draw conclusions from; **~ alguém para dançar** to ask sb to dance; **~ a tampa de** to take the lid off

tiririca [tʃiri'rika] (*col*) ADJ hopping mad

tiritante [tʃiri'tātʃi] ADJ shivering

tiritar [tʃiri'ta^r] VI to shiver

tiro ['tʃiru] M (*disparo*) shot; (*ato de disparar*) shooting, firing; **~ ao alvo** target practice; **trocar ~s** to fire at one another; **o ~ saiu pela culatra** (*fig*) the plan backfired; **dar um ~ no escuro** (*fig*) to take a shot in the dark; **ser ~ e queda** (*fig*) to be a dead cert

tirocínio [tʃiro'sinju] M apprenticeship, training

tiroteio [tʃiro'teju] M shooting, exchange of shots

tis [tʃiʃ] MPL *de* **til**

tísica ['tʃizika] F consumption; *v tb* **tísico**

tísico, -a ['tʃiziku, a] ADJ, M/F consumptive

tisnar [tʃiʒ'na^r] VT (*enegrecer*) to blacken; (*tostar*) to brown

titânico, -a [tʃi'taniku, a] ADJ titanic

titânio [tʃi'taɲju] M titanium

títere ['tʃiteri] M (*tb fig*) puppet

titia [tʃi'tʃia] F aunty; **ficar para ~** to be left on the shelf

titica [tʃi'tʃika] (*col*) F (piece of) junk ▪ M/F good-for-nothing

titio [tʃi'tʃiu] M uncle

tititi [tʃitʃi'tʃi] M (*tumulto*) hubbub; (*falatório*) gossip, talk

titubeante [tʃitu'bjātʃi] ADJ tottering; (*vacilante*) hesitant

titubear [tʃitu'bja^r] VI (*cambalear*) to totter, stagger; (*vacilar*) to hesitate

titular [tʃitu'la^r] ADJ titular ▪ M/F holder; (*Pol*) minister ▪ VT to title

título ['tʃitulu] M title; (*Com*) bond; (*universitário*) degree; **a ~ de** by way of, as; **a ~ de que você fez isso?** what was your reason for doing that?; **a ~ de curiosidade** out of curiosity; **~ ao portador** (*Com*) bearer bond; **~ de propriedade** title deed; **~ de câmbio** (*Com*) bill of exchange

tive *etc* ['tʃivi] VB *v* **ter**

TJ (BR) ABR M = **Tribunal do Júri; Tribunal de Justiça**

tlim [tʃlĩ] M ring

TO ABR = **Tocantins**

to [tu] = **te + o**

toa ['toa] F towrope; **à ~** (*sem reflexão*) at random; (*sem motivo*) for no reason; (*inutilmente*) in vain, for nothing; (*sem ocupação*) with nothing to do; (*sem mais nem menos*) out of the blue; **andar à ~** to wander aimlessly; **não é à ~ que** it is not for nothing *ou* without reason that

toada [to'ada] F tune, melody

toalete [twa'letʃi] F washing and dressing ▪ M (*banheiro*) toilet; (*traje*) outfit; **fazer a ~** to have a wash

toalha [to'aʎa] F towel; **~ de mesa** tablecloth; **~ de banho** bath towel; **~ de rosto** hand towel

toar [to'a^r] VI to sound, resound

tobogã [tobo'gã] M toboggan

toca ['tɔka] F burrow, hole; (*fig: refúgio*) bolt-hole; (: *casebre*) hovel

toca-discos (BR) M INV record-player

tocado, -a [to'kadu, a] ADJ (*col: alegre*) tipsy; (*expulso*) thrown out

tocador [toka'do^r] M player; **~ MP3** MP3 player

toca-fitas M INV cassette player

tocaia [to'kaja] F ambush

tocante [to'kātʃi] ADJ moving, touching; **no ~ a** regarding, concerning

tocar [to'ka^r] VT to touch; (*Mús*) to play; (*campainha*) to ring; (*comover*) to touch; (*programa, campanha*) to conduct; (*ônibus, gado*) to drive; (*expulsar*) to drive out; (*chegar a*) to reach ▪ VI to touch; (*Mús*) to play; (*campainha, sino, telefone*) to ring; (*em carro*) to drive; **tocar-se** VR to touch (each other); (*ir-se*) to head off; (*perceber*) to realize; **~ a** (*dizer respeito a*) to concern, affect; **~ em** to touch; (*assunto*) to touch upon; (*Náut*) to call at; **~ para alguém** (*telefonar*) to ring sb (up), call sb (up); **~ (o bonde) para frente** (*fig*) to get going, get a move on; **pelo que me toca** as far as I am concerned

tocha ['tɔʃa] F torch

NB: *European Portuguese adds the following consonants to certain words:* **b** (sú(b)dito, su(b)til); **c** (a(c)ção, a(c)cionista, a(c)to); **m** (inde(m)ne); **p** (ado(p)çã, ado(p)tar); *for further details see p. xiii.*

toco ['toku] M (de cigarro) stub; (de árvore) stump
todavia [toda'via] ADV yet, still, however

○ **PALAVRA CHAVE**

todo, -a ['todu, 'tɔda] ADJ **1** (com artigo sg) all; **toda a carne** all the meat; **toda a noite** all night, the whole night; **todo o Brasil** the whole of Brazil; **a toda (velocidade)** at full speed; **todo o mundo** (BR), **toda a gente** (PT) everybody, everyone; **em toda (a) parte** everywhere **2** (com artigo pl) all; (: cada) every; **todos os livros** all the books; **todos os dias/todas as noites** every day/night; **todos os que querem sair** all those who want to leave; **todos nós** all of us ▪ ADV: **ao todo** altogether; (no total) in all; **de todo** completely ▪ PRON: **todo/as** ▪ MPL everybody sg, everyone sg

todo-poderoso, -a ADJ almighty, all-powerful
▪ M: **o T~** the Almighty
tofe ['tɔfi] M toffee
toga ['tɔga] F toga; (Educ, de magistrado) gown
toicinho [toj'siɲu] M bacon fat
toldo ['towdu] M awning, sun blind
toleima [to'lejma] F folly, stupidity
tolerância [tole'rãsja] F tolerance; **tolerante** [tole'rãtʃi] ADJ tolerant
tolerar [tole'ra'] VT to tolerate; **tolerável** [tole'ravew] (pl -eis) ADJ tolerable, bearable; (satisfatório) passable; (falta) excusable
tolher [to'ʎe'] VT to impede, hinder; (voz) to cut off; ~ **alguém de fazer** to stop sb doing
tolice [to'lisi] F stupidity, foolishness; (ato, dito) stupid thing
tolo, -a ['tolu, a] ADJ foolish, silly, stupid ▪ M/F fool; **fazer alguém/fazer-se de ~** to make a fool of sb/o.s.
tom [tõ] (pl -ns) M tone; (Mús: altura) pitch; (: escala) key; (cor) shade; **ser de bom ~** to be good manners; ~ **agudo/grave** high/low note; ~ **maior/menor** (Mús) major/minor key
tomada [to'mada] F capture; (Elet) socket; (Cinema) shot; ~ **de posse** investiture; ~ **de preços** tender
tomar [to'ma'] VT to take; (capturar) to capture, seize; (decisão) to make; (bebida) to drink; **tomar-se** VR: **tomar-se de** to be overcome with; ~ **alguém por algo** to take sb for sth; ~ **algo como** to take sth as; **toma!** here you are!; **quer ~ alguma coisa?** do you want something to drink?; ~ **café** (de manhã) to have breakfast; **toma lá, dá cá** give and take
tomara [to'mara] EXCL: ~! if only!; ~ **que venha hoje** I hope he comes today
tomara-que-caia ADJ INV: (vestido) ~ strapless dress
tomate [to'matʃi] M tomato
tombadilho [tõba'dʒiʎu] M deck
tombar [tõ'ba'] VI to fall down, tumble down

▪ VT to knock down, knock over; (conservar: edifício) to list; **tombo** ['tõbu] M (queda) tumble, fall; (registro) archives pl, records pl
tomilho [to'miʎu] M thyme
tomo ['tɔmu] M tome, volume
tona ['tɔna] F surface; **vir à ~** to come to the surface; (fig) to emerge; **trazer à ~** to bring up; (recordações) to bring back
tonalidade [tonali'dadʒi] F (de cor) shade; (Mús) tonality; (: tom) key
tonel [to'nɛw] (pl -éis) M cask, barrel
tonelada [tone'lada] F ton; **uma ~ de** (fig) tons of
tonelagem [tone'laʒẽ] F tonnage
toner ['tone'] M toner
tônica ['tonika] F (água) tonic (water); (Mús) tonic; (Ling) stressed syllable; (fig) keynote
tônico, -a ['toniku, a] ADJ tonic; (sílaba) stressed ▪ M tonic; **acento ~** stress
tonificante [tonifi'kãtʃi] ADJ invigorating
tonificar [tonifi'ka'] VT to tone up
tons [tõʃ] MPL de **tom**
tontear [tõ'tʃja'] VT: ~ **alguém** to make sb dizzy; (suj: barulheira) to get sb down, give sb a headache; (: alvoroço, notícia) to stun sb ▪ VI (pessoa: com bebida) to get dizzy; (: com barulho) to get a headache; (: com alvoroço) to be dazed; (barulho) to be wearing; (alvoroço) to be upsetting; ~ **de sono** to be half-asleep
tonteira [tõ'tejra] F dizziness
tontice [tõ'tʃisi] F stupidity, nonsense
tonto, -a ['tõtu, a] ADJ (tolo) stupid, silly; (zonzo) dizzy, lightheaded; (atarantado) flustered; **às tontas** impulsively
tontura [tõ'tura] F dizziness, light-headedness
topada [to'pada] F trip; **dar uma ~ em** to stub one's toe on
topar [to'pa'] VT to agree to ▪ VI: ~ **com** to come across; **topar-se** VR (duas pessoas) to run into one another; ~ **em** (tropeçar) to stub one's toe on; (esbarrar) to run into; (tocar) to touch; **você topa ir ao cinema?** do you fancy going to the cinema?; ~ **que alguém faça** to agree that sb should do
topa-tudo ['tɔpa-] M INV person who can't say no
topázio [to'pazju] M topaz
tope ['tɔpi] M top
topete [to'petʃi] M quiff; **ter o ~ de fazer** (fig) to have the cheek to do
tópico, -a ['tɔpiku, a] ADJ topical ▪ M topic
topless [tɔp'les] ADJ INV topless ▪ M INV (na praia) topless bikini
topo ['topu] M top; (extremidade) end, extremity
topografia [topogra'fia] F topography
topográfico, -a [topo'grafiku, a] ADJ topographical
topônimo [to'ponimu] M place name, toponym
toque ['tɔkɪ] M touch; (de instrumento musical) playing; (de campainha) ring; (fig: vestígio) touch; (de celular) ringtone; (retoque) finishing touch; **os últimos ~s** the finishing touches; **dar um**

~ em alguém (col: avisar) to let sb know; (: falar com) to have a word with sb; **a ~ de caixa** in all haste

toque etc VB V **tocar**

Tóquio ['tɔkju] N Tokyo

tora ['tɔra] F (pedaço) piece; (de madeira) log; (sesta) nap; **tirar uma ~** to have a nap

toranja [to'rãʒa] F grapefruit

tórax ['tɔraks] M INV thorax

torção [tox'sãw] (pl -ões) M twist, twisting; (Med) sprain

torcedor, a [toxse'do'(a)] M/F supporter, fan

torcedura [toxse'dura] F twist; (Med) sprain

torcer [tox'se'] VT to twist; (Med) to sprain; (desvirtuar) to distort, misconstrue; (roupa: espremer) to wring; (: na máquina) to spin; (vergar) to bend ■ VI: **~ por** (time) to support; (amigo etc) to keep one's fingers crossed for; **torcer-se** VR (contorcer-se) to squirm, writhe; **~ para** ou **por** to cheer for; **~ para que tudo dê certo** to keep one's fingers crossed that everything works out right

torcicolo [toxsi'kɔlu] M stiff neck

torcida [tox'sida] F (pavio) wick; (Esporte: ato de torcer) cheering; (: torcedores) supporters pl; **dar uma ~ em algo** to twist sth; (roupa) to wring sth out

torções [tox'sõjʃ] MPL de **torção**

tormenta [tox'mẽta] F storm; (fig) upset

tormento [tox'mẽtu] M torment, torture; (angústia) anguish

tormentoso, -a [toxmẽ'tozu, ɔza] ADJ stormy, tempestuous

tornado [tox'nadu] M tornado

tornar [tox'na'] VI (voltar) to return, go back ■ VT: **~ algo em algo** to turn ou make sth into sth; **tornar-se** VR to become; **~ a fazer algo** to do sth again

torneado, -a [tox'njadu, a] ADJ: **bem ~** (pernas, pescoço) shapely

tornear [tox'nja'] VT to turn (on a lathe), shape

torneio [tox'neju] M tournament

torneira [tox'nejra] F tap (Brit), faucet (US)

torniquete [toxni'ketʃi] M (Med) tourniquet; (PT: roleta) turnstile

torno ['toxnu] M lathe; (Cerâmica) wheel; **em ~ de** (ao redor de) around; (sobre) about; **em ~ de 5 milhões** around 5 million

tornozeleira [toxnoze'lejra] F ankle support

tornozelo [toxno'zelu] M ankle

toró [to'rɔ] M (chuva) downpour, shower; **caiu um ~** there was a sudden downpour

torpe ['toxpi] ADJ vile

torpedear [toxpe'dʒja'] VT to torpedo

torpedo [tox'pedu] M torpedo; (col: mensagem) text (message)

torpeza [tox'peza] F vileness

torpor [tox'po'] M torpor; (Med) numbness

torrada [to'xada] F toast; **uma ~** a piece of toast;

torradeira [toxa'dejra] F toaster

torrão [to'xãw] (pl -ões) M turf, sod; (terra) soil, land; (de açúcar) lump; **~ natal** native land

torrar [to'xa'] VT (pão) to toast; (café) to roast; (plantação) to parch; (dinheiro) to blow, squander; (vender) to sell off cheap; **~ (alguém)** (col) to get on sb's nerves; **~ a paciência** ou **o saco** (col) **de alguém** to try sb's patience

torre ['toxi] F tower; (Xadrez) castle, rook; (Elet) pylon; **~ de controle** (Aer) control tower; **~ de vigia** watchtower

torreão [to'xjãw] (pl -ões) M turret

torrefação [toxefa'sãw] (PT -çç-, pl -ões) F coffee-roasting house

torrencial [toxẽ'sjaw] (pl -ais) ADJ torrential

torrente [to'xẽtʃi] F (tb fig) torrent

torreões [to'xjõjʃ] MPL de **torreão**

torresmo [to'xeʒmu] M crackling

tórrido, -a ['tɔxidu, a] ADJ torrid

torrinha [to'xiɲa] F (Teatro) gallery; **as ~s** the gods

torrões [to'xõjʃ] MPL de **torrão**

torrone [to'xɔni] M nougat

torso ['toxsu] M torso, trunk

torta ['tɔxta] F pie, tart; **~ de maçã** apple pie

torto, -a ['toxtu, 'tɔxta] ADJ twisted, crooked; **a ~ e a direito** indiscriminately; **cometer erros a ~ e a direito** to make mistakes left, right and centre

tortuoso, -a [tox'twozu, ɔza] ADJ winding

tortura [tox'tura] F torture; (fig) anguish, agony

torturador, a [toxtura'do'(a)] M/F torturer

torturante [toxtu'rãtʃi] ADJ (sonhos) haunting; (dor) excruciating

torturar [toxtu'ra'] VT to torture; (fig: afligir) to torment

torvelinho [toxve'liɲu] M (de vento) whirlwind; (de água) whirlpool; (fig: de pensamentos) swirl

tos [tuʃ] = **te + os**

tosão [to'zãw] (pl -ões) M fleece

tosar [to'za'] VT (ovelha) to shear; (cabelo) to crop

tosco, -a ['toʃku, a] ADJ rough, unpolished; (grosseiro) coarse, crude

tosões [to'zõjʃ] MPL de **tosão**

tosquiar [toʃ'kja'] VT (ovelha) to shear, clip

tosse ['tɔsi] F cough; **~ de cachorro** whooping cough; **~ seca** dry ou tickly cough; **tossir** [to'si'] VI to cough ■ VT to cough up

tosta ['tɔʃta] (PT) F toast; **~ mista** toasted cheese and ham sandwich

tostado, -a [toʃ'tadu, a] ADJ toasted; (pessoa) tanned; (carne) browned

tostão [toʃ'tãw] M (dinheiro) cash; **estar sem um ~** to be completely penniless

tostar [toʃ'ta'] VT to toast; (pele, pessoa) to tan; (carne) to brown; **tostar-se** VR to get tanned

total [to'taw] (pl -ais) ADJ, M total

totalidade [totali'dadʒi] F totality, entirety; **em sua ~** in its entirety; **a ~ da população/dos**

NB: European Portuguese adds the following consonants to certain words: **b** (sú(b)dito, su(b)til); **c** (a(c)ção, a(c)cionista, a(c)to); **m** (inde(m)ne); **p** (ado(p)çã, ado(p)tar); for further details see p. xiii.

políticos the entire population/all politicians
totalitário, -a [totali'tarju, a] ADJ totalitarian
totalitarismo [totalita'riʒmu] M totalitarianism
totalizar [totali'zaʳ] VT to total up
totalmente [totaw'mētʃi] ADV totally, completely
touca ['toka] F bonnet; (de freira) veil; ~ **de banho** bathing cap
toucador [toka'doʳ] M (penteadeira) dressing table
toucinho [to'siɲu] M = **toicinho**
toupeira [to'pejra] F mole; (fig) numbskull, idiot
tourada [to'rada] F bullfight
tourear [to'rjaʳ] VI to fight bulls
toureiro [to'rejru] M bullfighter
touro ['toru] M bull; **T~** (Astrologia) Taurus; **pegar o ~ à unha** to take the bull by the horns
toxemia [tokse'mia] F blood poisoning
tóxico, -a ['tɔksiku, a] ADJ poisonous, toxic ■ M (veneno) poison; (droga) drug; **toxicômano, -a** [toksi'komanu, a] M/F drug addict
toxina [tok'sina] F toxin
trabalhadeira [trabaʎa'dejra] F: **ela é ~** she's a hard worker
trabalhador, a [trabaʎa'doʳ(a)] ADJ (laborioso) hard-working, industrious; (Pol: classe) working ■ M/F worker; ~ **braçal** manual worker
trabalhão [traba'ʎãw] (pl -ões) M big job
trabalhar [traba'ʎaʳ] VI to work; (Teatro) to act ■ VT (terra) to till, work; (madeira, metal) to work; (texto) to work on; ~ **com** (comerciar) to deal in; ~ **de** ou **como** to work as
trabalheira [traba'ʎejra] F big job
trabalhista [traba'ʎiʃta] ADJ labour atr (Brit), labor atr (US) ■ M/F Labour Party member (Brit); **Partido T~** (Pol) Labour Party (Brit)
trabalho [tra'baʎu] M work; (emprego, tarefa) job; (Econ) labour (Brit), labor (US); (Educ: tarefa) assignment; ~ **braçal** manual work; ~**s forçados** hard labo(u)r, forced labo(u)r; **estar sem** ~ to be out of work; **dar** ~ to need work; **dar** ~ **a alguém** to cause sb trouble; **dar-se o ~ de fazer** to take the trouble to do; **um** ~ **ingrato** a thankless task; ~ **doméstico** housework; ~ **de parto** labo(u)r
trabalhões [traba'ʎõjʃ] MPL de **trabalhão**
trabalhoso, -a [traba'ʎozu, ɔza] ADJ laborious, arduous
traça ['trasa] F moth
traçado [tra'sadu] M sketch, plan
tração [tra'sãw] F traction
traçar [tra'saʳ] VT to draw; (determinar) to set out, outline; (limites, fronteiras) to mark out; (planos) to draw up; (escrever) to compose; (col: comer, beber) to guzzle down
traccçao [tra'sãw] (PT) F = **tração**
traço ['trasu] M (linha) line, dash; (de lápis) stroke; (vestígio) trace, vestige; (aspecto) feature, trait; **traços** MPL (do rosto) features; ~ **(de união)** hyphen; (entre frases) dash
tractor [tra'toʳ] (PT) M = **trator**

tradição [tradʒi'sãw] (pl -ões) F tradition;
tradicional [tradʒisjo'naw] (pl -ais) ADJ traditional
tradições [tradʒi'sõjʃ] FPL de **tradição**
tradução [tradu'sãw] (pl -ões) F translation
tradutor, a [tradu'toʳ(a)] M/F translator; ~ **juramentado** legally recognized translator
traduzir [tradu'ziʳ] VT to translate; **traduzir-se** VR to come across; ~ **do inglês para o português** to translate from English into Portuguese
trafegar [trafe'gaʳ] VI to move, go
trafegável [trafe'gavew] (pl -eis) ADJ (rua) open to traffic
tráfego ['trafegu] M (trânsito) traffic; ~ **aéreo/marítimo** air/sea traffic
traficante [trafi'kãtʃi] M/F trafficker, dealer; ~ **de drogas** drug trafficker, pusher (col)
traficar [trafi'kaʳ] VI: ~ **(com)** to deal (in), traffic (in)
tráfico ['trafiku] M traffic; ~ **de drogas** drug trafficking
tragada [tra'gada] F (em cigarro) drag, puff
tragar [tra'gaʳ] VT to swallow; (fumaça) to inhale; (suportar) to tolerate ■ VI to inhale
tragédia [tra'ʒedʒja] F tragedy; **fazer ~ de algo** to make a drama out of sth; **trágico, -a** ['traʒiku, a] ADJ tragic; (dado a fazer tragédia) dramatic
tragicomédia [traʒiko'medʒja] F tragicomedy
tragicômico, -a [traʒi'komiku, a] ADJ tragicomic
trago ['tragu] M mouthful; (em cigarro) drag, puff; **tomar um** ~ to have a mouthful; to have a drag; **de um** ~ in one gulp
trago etc VB V **trazer**
traguei etc [tra'gej] VB V **tragar**
traição [traj'sãw] (pl -ões) F treason, treachery; (deslealdade) disloyalty; (infidelidade) infidelity; **alta** ~ high treason
traiçoeiro, -a [traj'swejru, a] ADJ treacherous; (infiel) disloyal
traições [traj'sõjʃ] FPL de **traição**
traidor, a [traj'doʳ(a)] M/F traitor
trailer ['trejlaʳ] (pl -s) M trailer; (tipo casa) caravan (Brit), trailer (US)
traineira [traj'nejra] F trawler
training ['trejnĩŋ] (pl -s) M track suit
trair [tra'iʳ] VT to betray; (mulher, marido) to be unfaithful to; (esperanças) not to live up to; **trair-se** VR to give o.s. away
trajar [tra'ʒaʳ] VT to wear; **trajar-se** VR: **trajar-se de preto** to be dressed in black
traje ['traʒi] M dress, clothes pl; ~ **de banho** swimsuit; ~ **de noite** evening gown; ~ **a rigor** evening dress; ~ **de passeio** smart dress; **em** ~**s de Adão** in one's birthday suit; ~**s menores** smalls, underwear sg
trajeto [tra'ʒetu] (PT -ct-) M course, path
trajetória [traʒe'tɔrja] (PT -ct-) F trajectory; path; (fig) course
tralha ['traʎa] F fishing net; (col) junk
trama ['trama] F (tecido) weft (Brit), woof (US);

(*enredo, conspiração*) plot

tramar [tra'ma^r] VT (*tecer*) to weave; (*maquinar*) to plot ■ VI: **~ contra** to conspire against

trambicar [trãbi'ka^r] (*col*) VT to con

trambique [trã'biki] (*col*) M con

trambiqueiro, -a [trãbi'kejru, a] M/F con merchant ■ ADJ slippery

trambolhão [trambo'ʎãw] (*pl -ões*) M tumble; **andar aos trambolhões** to stumble along

trambolho [trã'boʎu] M encumbrance

trambolhões [trambo'ʎõjʃ] MPL *de* **trambolhão**

tramitar [trami'ta^r] VI to go through the procedure

trâmites ['tramitʃiʃ] MPL procedure *sg*, channels

tramóia [tra'mɔja] F (*fraude*) swindle, trick; (*trama*) plot, scheme

trampolim [trãpo'lĩ] (*pl -ns*) M trampoline; (*de piscina*) diving board; (*fig*) springboard

trampolinagem [trãpoli'naʒẽ] (*pl -ns*) F trick, swindle

trampolineiro [trãpoli'nejru] M trickster, swindler

trampolinice [trãpoli'nisi] F trick, swindle

trampolins [trãpo'lĩʃ] MPL *de* **trampolim**

tranca ['trãka] F (*de porta*) bolt; (*de carro*) lock

trança ['trãsa] F (*cabelo*) plait; (*galão*) braid

trançado, -a [trã'sadu, a] ADJ (*cesto*) woven

trancafiar [trãka'fja^r] VT to lock up

trancão [trã'kãw] (*pl -ões*) M bump

trancar [trã'ka^r] VT to lock; (*matrícula*) to suspend; (*Futebol*) to shove; **trancar-se** VR (*mostrar-se fechado*) to clam up; **~-se no quarto** to lock o.s. (away) in one's room

trançar [trã'sa^r] VT to weave; (*cabelo*) to plait, braid ■ VI (*col*) to wander around

tranco ['trãku] M (*solavanco*) jolt; (*esbarrão*) bump; (*de cavalo*) walk; (*col: admoestação*) put-down; **aos ~s** jolting; **aos ~s e barrancos** with great difficulty; (*aos saltos*) jolting

trancões [trã'kõjʃ] MPL *de* **trancão**

tranqüilamente [trãkwila'mẽtʃi] ADV calmly; (*facilmente*) easily; (*seguramente*) for sure

tranqüilidade [trãkwili'dadʒi] F tranquillity; (*paz*) peace

tranqüilizador, a [trãkwiliza'do^r(a)] ADJ reassuring; (*música*) soothing

tranqüilizante [trãkwili'zãtʃi] ADJ = **tranqüilizador** ■ M (*Med*) tranquillizer

tranqüilizar [trãkwili'za^r] VT to calm, quieten; (*despreocupar*): **~ alguém** to reassure sb, put sb's mind at rest; **tranqüilizar-se** VR to calm down; (*pessoa preocupada*) to be reassured

tranqüilo, -a [trã'kwilu, a] ADJ peaceful; (*mar, pessoa*) calm; (*criança*) quiet; (*consciência*) clear; (*seguro*) sure, certain ■ ADV with no problems

transa ['trãza] (*BR: col*) F (*namoro*) affair; (*combinação*) arrangement; (*trama, negócios*) business; (*ligação*) relationship; (*assunto*) matter; **combinar altas ~s** to be into all sorts of things

transação [trãza'sãw] (*PT -cç-*, *pl -ões*) F (*Com*) transaction, deal; (*combinação*) arrangement; (*col: maquinação*) business

transada [trã'zada] F: **dar uma ~** (*col*) to have sex

transado, -a [trã'zadu, a] ADJ: **bem ~** (*col: objeto*) well made; (*relacionamento*) healthy; (*pessoa, casa*) classy

Transamazônica [trãzama'zonika]: **a ~** the trans-Amazonian highway

transamazônico, -a [trãzama'zoniku, a] ADJ trans-Amazonian

transar [trã'za^r] (*col*) VT (*combinar*) to arrange; (*arranjar*) to fix up; (*tramar*) to plan; (*drogas*) to do ■ VI (*namorar*) to go out; (*ter relação sexual*) to have sex; **~ com** (*relacionar-se*) to hang out with; (*negociar*) to deal in

transatlântico, -a [trãzat'lãtʃiku, a] ADJ transatlantic ■ M (transatlantic) liner

transbordar [trãʒbox'da^r] VI to overflow; **~ de alegria** to burst with happiness

transbordo [trãʒ'boxdu] M (*de viajantes*) change, transfer

transcendental [trãsẽdẽ'taw] (*pl -ais*) ADJ transcendental

transcender [trãsẽ'de^r] VT, VI: **~ (a)** to transcend

transcorrer [trãʃko'xe^r] VI to elapse, go by; (*evento*) to pass off

transcrever [trãʃkre've^r] VT to transcribe

transcrição [trãʃkri'sãw] (*pl -ões*) F transcription

transcrito, -a [trãʃ'kritu, a] PP *de* **transcrever** ■ M transcript

transe ['trãzi] M ordeal; (*lance*) plight; (*hipnótico*) trance; **a todo ~** at all costs

transeunte [trã'zjũtʃi] M/F passer-by

transferência [trãʃfe'rẽsja] F transfer; (*Jur*) conveyancing

transferir [trãʃfe'ri^r] VT to transfer; (*adiar*) to postpone

transferível [trãʃfe'rivew] (*pl -eis*) ADJ transferable

transfigurar [trãʃfigu'ra^r] VT to transfigure, transform; **transfigurar-se** VR to transform

transfiro *etc* [trãʃ'firu] VB *v* **transferir**

transformação [trãʃfoxma'sãw] (*pl -ões*) F transformation

transformador [trãʃfoxma'do^r] M (*Elet*) transformer

transformar [trãʃfox'ma^r] VT to transform, turn; **transformar-se** VR to turn; **~ algo em algo** to turn *ou* transform sth into sth

trânsfuga ['trãʃfuga] M (*desertor*) deserter; (*político*) turncoat; (*da Rússia etc*) defector

transfusão [trãʃfu'zãw] (*pl -ões*) F transfusion; **~ de sangue** blood transfusion

transgredir [trãʒgre'dʒi^r] VT to infringe

transgressão [trãʒgre'sãw] (*pl -ões*) F transgression, infringement

transgrido *etc* [trãʒ'gridu] VB *v* **transgredir**

NB: *European Portuguese adds the following consonants to certain words:* **b** (sú(b)dito, su(b)til); **c** (a(c)ção, a(c)cionista, a(c)to); **m** (inde(m)ne); **p** (ado(p)ção, ado(p)tar); *for further details see p. xiii.*

transição [trãzi'sãw] (pl -ões) F transition; **período** ou **fase de** ~ transition period

transicional [trãzisjo'naw] (pl -ais) ADJ transitional

transições [trãzi'sõjʃ] FPL de **transição**

transido, -a [trã'zidu, a] ADJ numb

transigente [trãzi'ʒẽtʃi] ADJ willing to compromise

transigir [trãzi'ʒiʳ] VI to compromise, make concessions; ~ **com alguém** to compromise with sb, meet sb halfway

transistor [trãziʃ'toʳ] M transistor

transitar [trãzi'taʳ] VI: ~ **por** to move through; (rua) to go along

transitável [trãzi'tavew] (pl -eis) ADJ (caminho) passable

transitivo, -a [trãzi'tʃivu, a] ADJ (Ling) transitive

trânsito ['trãzitu] M (ato) transit, passage; (na rua: veículos) traffic; (: pessoas) flow; **em** ~ in transit; **sinal de** ~ traffic signal; **transitório, -a** [trãzi'tɔrju, a] ADJ transitory, passing; (período) transitional

transladar [trãʒla'daʳ] VT = **trasladar**

translado [trãʒ'ladu] M = **traslado**

translúcido, -a [trãʒ'lusidu, a] ADJ translucent

transmissão [trãʒmi'sãw] (pl -ões) F transmission; (Rádio, TV) transmission, broadcast; (transferência) transfer; ~ **ao vivo** live broadcast; ~ **de dados** data transmission

transmissível [trãʒmi'sivew] (pl -eis) ADJ transmittable

transmissões [trãʒmi'sõjʃ] FPL de **transmissão**

transmissor, a [trãʒmi'soʳ(a)] ADJ transmitting ▪ M transmitter

transmitir [trãʒmi'tʃiʳ] VT to transmit; (Rádio, TV) to broadcast, transmit; (transferir) to transfer; (recado, notícia) to pass on; (aroma, som) to carry; **transmitir-se** VR (doença) to be transmitted; ~ **algo a alguém** (paz etc) to bring sb sth

transparecer [trãʃpare'seʳ] VI to be visible, appear; (revelar-se) to be apparent

transparência [trãʃpa'rẽsja] F transparency; (de água) clarity

transparente [trãʃpa'rẽtʃi] ADJ transparent; (roupa) see-through; (água) clear; (evidente) clear, obvious

transpassar [trãʃpa'saʳ] VT = **traspassar**

transpiração [trãʃpira'sãw] F perspiration

transpirar [trãʃpi'raʳ] VI (suar) to perspire; (divulgar-se) to become known; (verdade) to come out ▪ VT to exude

transplantar [trãʃplã'taʳ] VT to transplant

transplante [trãʃ'plãtʃi] M transplant

transpor [trãʃ'poʳ] (irreg) VT to cross; (inverter) to transpose

transportação [trãʃpoxta'sãw] F transportation

transportadora [trãʃpoxta'dora] F haulage company

transportar [trãʃpox'taʳ] VT to transport; (levar)

to carry; (enlevar) to entrance, enrapture; (fig: remontar) to take back; **transportar-se** VR to be entranced; (remontar) to be transported back; **a** ~ (Com: quantia) carry forward, c/f

transporte [trãʃ'poxtʃi] M transport; (Com) haulage; (em contas) amount carried forward; (fig: êxtase) rapture, delight; **despesas de** ~ transport costs; **Ministério dos T~s** Ministry of Transport (Brit), Department of Transportation (US); ~ **rodoviário** road transport; ~**s coletivos** public transport sg

transposição [trãʃpozi'sãw] F transposition; (de rio) crossing

transpôs [trãʃ'poʃ] VB V **transpor**

transposto, -a [trãʃ'poʃtu, 'pɔʃta] PP de **transpor**

transpunha etc [trãʃ'puɲa] VB V **transpor**

transpus etc [trãʃ'puʃ] VB V **transpor**

transpuser etc [trãʃpu'zeʳ] VB V **transpor**

transtornar [trãʃtox'naʳ] VT to upset; (rotina, reunião) to disrupt; **transtornar-se** VR to get upset; to be disrupted

transtorno [trãʃ'toxnu] M upset, disruption; (contrariedade) hardship; (mental) distraction

transversal [trãʒvex'saw] (pl -ais) ADJ transverse, cross; (rua) ~ cross street

transverso, -a [trãʒ'vexsu, a] ADJ transverse, cross

transviado, -a [trãʒ'vjadu, a] ADJ wayward, erring

transviar [trãʒ'vjaʳ] VT to lead astray; **transviar-se** VR to go astray

trapaça [tra'pasa] F swindle, fraud

trapacear [trapa'sjaʳ] VT, VI to swindle

trapaceiro, -a [trapa'sejru, a] ADJ crooked, cheating ▪ M/F swindler, cheat

trapalhada [trapa'ʎada] F confusion, mix-up

trapalhão, -lhona [trapa'ʎãw, 'ʎ] (pl -ões/-s) M/F bungler, blunderer

trapézio [tra'pɛzju] M trapeze; (Mat) trapezium

trapezista [trape'ziʃta] M/F trapeze artist

trapo ['trapu] M rag; **ser** ou **estar um** ~ (pessoa) to be washed up

traquéia [tra'kɛja] F windpipe

traquejo [tra'keʒu] M experience

traqueotomia [trakjoto'mia] F tracheotomy

traquinas [tra'kinaʃ] ADJ INV mischievous

trarei etc [tra'rej] VB V **trazer**

trás [trajʃ] PREP, ADV: **para** ~ backwards; **por** ~ **de** behind; **de** ~ from behind; **a luz de** ~ the back light; **de** ~ **para frente** back to front; **ano** ~ **ano** year after year; **dar para** ~ (fig: pessoa) to go wrong

traseira [tra'zejra] F rear; (Anat) bottom

traseiro, -a [tra'zejru, a] ADJ back, rear ▪ M (Anat) bottom, behind

trasladar [traʒla'daʳ] VT to remove, transfer; (copiar) to transcribe

traslado [traʒ'ladu] M (cópia) transcript; (deslocamento) removal, transference

traspassar [traʃpa'saʳ] VT (rio etc) to cross; (penetrar) to pierce, penetrate; (exceder) to exceed, overstep; (transferir) to transmit, transfer; (PT:

sublocar) to sublet

traspasse [traʃ'pasi] M transfer; (*sublocação*) sublease

traste ['traʃtʃi] M thing; (*coisa sem valor*) piece of junk; (*patife*) rogue, rascal; **estar** *ou* **ficar um ~** to be devastated

tratado [tra'tadu] M treaty; (*Literatura*) treatise; **~ de paz** peace treaty

tratador, a [trata'do^r(a)] M/F: **~ de cavalos** groom

tratamento [trata'mẽtu] M treatment; (*título*) title; **forma de ~** form of address; **~ de choque** shock treatment

tratante [tra'tãtʃi] M/F rogue

tratar [tra'ta^r] VT to treat; (*tema*) to deal with, cover; (*combinar*) to agree ■ VI: **~ com** to deal with; (*combinar*) to agree with; **tratar-se** VR (*Med*) to take treatment; (*cuidar-se*) to take care of o.s.; **~ de** to deal with; **~ por** *ou* **de** to address as; **de que se trata?** what is it about?; **trata-se de** it is a question of; **~ de fazer** (*esforçar-se*) to try to do; (*resolver*) to resolve to do; **trate da sua vida!** mind your own business!; **~-se a pão e água** to live on bread and water

tratável [tra'tavew] (*pl* **-eis**) ADJ treatable; (*afável*) approachable, amenable

trato ['tratu] M (*tratamento*) treatment; (*contrato*) agreement, contract; **tratos** MPL (*relações*) dealings; **maus ~s** ill-treatment; **pessoa de fino ~** refined person; **dar ~s à bola** to rack one's brains

trator [tra'to^r] M tractor

traulitada [trawli'tada] F beating

trauma ['trawma] M trauma

traumático, -a [traw'matʃiku, a] ADJ traumatic

traumatizante [trawmatʃi'zãtʃi] ADJ traumatic, harrowing

traumatizar [trawmatʃi'za^r] VT to traumatize

travada [tra'vada] F: **dar uma ~** to put on the brake

travão [tra'vãw] (*PT*) (*pl* **-ões**) M brake

travar [tra'va^r] VT (*roda*) to lock; (*iniciar*) to engage in; (*conversa*) to strike up; (*luta*) to wage; (*carro*) to stop; (*passagem*) to block; (*movimentos*) to hinder ■ VI (*PT*) to brake; **~ amizade com** to become friendly with, make friends with

trave ['travi] F beam, crossbeam; (*Esporte*) crossbar; **foi na ~** (*col: resposta etc*) (it was) close

través [tra'vεʃ] M slant, incline; **de ~** across, sideways; **olhar de ~** to look sideways (at)

travessa [tra'vesa] F crossbeam, crossbar; (*rua*) lane, alley; (*prato*) dish; (*para o cabelo*) comb, slide

travessão [trave'sãw] (*pl* **-ões**) M (*de balança*) bar, beam; (*pontuação*) dash

travesseiro [trave'sejru] M pillow; **consultar o ~** to sleep on it

travessia [trave'sia] F (*viagem*) journey, crossing

travesso, -a¹ [tra'vεsu, a] ADJ cross, transverse

travesso, -a² [tra'vesu, a] ADJ mischievous, naughty

travessões [trave'sõjʃ] MPL *de* **travessão**

travessura [trave'sura] F mischief, prank; **fazer ~s** to get up to mischief

travesti [traveʃ'tʃi] M/F transvestite; (*artista*) drag artist

travões [tra'võjʃ] MPL *de* **travão**

trazer [tra'ze^r] VT to bring; (*roupa*) to wear; (*nome, marcas*) to bear; **~ à memória** to bring to mind; **o jornal traz uma notícia sobre isso** the newspaper has an item about that; **~ de volta** to bring back

TRE (*BR*) ABR M = **Tribunal Regional Eleitoral**

trecho ['treʃu] M passage; (*de rua, caminho*) stretch; (*espaço*) space

treco ['treku] (*col*) M (*tralha*) thing; (*indisposição*) bad turn; **trecos** MPL (*bugigangas*) stuff *sg*; **ter um ~** (*sentir-se mal*) to be taken bad; (*zangar-se*) to have a fit

trégua ['tregwa] F truce; (*descanso*) respite, rest; **não dar ~ a** to give no respite to

treinado, -a [trej'nadu, a] ADJ (*atleta*) fit; (*animal*) trained; (*acostumado*) practised (*Brit*), practiced (*US*)

treinador, a [trejna'do^r(a)] M/F trainer

treinamento [trejna'mẽtu] M training

treinar [trej'na^r] VT to train; **treinar-se** VR to train; **~ seu inglês** to practise (*Brit*) *ou* practice (*US*) one's English; **treino** ['trejnu] M training

trejeito [tre'ʒejtu] M (*gesto*) gesture; (*careta*) grimace, face

trela ['trεla] F (*correia*) lead, leash; (*col: conversa*) chat; **dar ~ a** (*col: conversar*) to chat with; (*encorajar*) to lead on

treliça [tre'lisa] F trellis

trem [trẽj] (*pl* **-ns**) M train; (*PT: carruagem*) carriage, coach; **ir de ~** to go by train; **mudar de ~** to change trains; **pegar um ~** to catch a train; **puxar o ~** (*col*) to make tracks; **trens** MPL (*col: coisas, objetos*) gear *sg*, belongings; **~ de carga/passageiros** freight/passenger train; **~ correio** mail train; **~ de aterrissagem** (*avião*) landing gear; **~ da alegria** (*Pol*) jobs *pl* for the boys, nepotism

trema ['trema] M di(a)eresis

tremedeira [treme'dejra] F trembling

tremelicante [tremeli'kãtʃi] ADJ trembling

tremelicar [tremeli'ka^r] VI to tremble, shiver

tremelique [treme'liki] M trembling

tremeluzir [tremelu'zi^r] VI to twinkle, glimmer

tremendo, -a [tre'mẽdu, a] ADJ tremendous; (*terrível*) terrible, awful

tremer [tre'me^r] VI to shudder, quake; (*terra*) to shake; (*de frio, medo*) to shiver

tremor [tre'mo^r] M tremor, trembling; **~ de terra** (*earth*) tremor

tremular [tremu'la^r] VI (*bandeira*) to flutter,

NB: *European Portuguese adds the following consonants to certain words:* **b** (sú(b)dito, su(b)til); **c** (a(c)ção, a(c)cionista, a(c)to); **m** (inde(m)ne); **p** (ado(p)çã, ado(p)tar); *for further details see p. xiii.*

wave; (*luz*) to glimmer, flicker
trêmulo, -a ['tremulu, a] ADJ shaky, trembling; (*voz*) faltering
trena ['trɛna] F tape measure
trenó [tre'nɔ] M sledge, sleigh (*Brit*), sled (*US*)
trens [trējʃ] MPL *de* **trem**
trepadeira [trepa'dejra] F (*Bot*) creeper
trepada [tre'pada] (*col!*) F screw, fuck (*!*)
trepar [tre'pa\]] VT to climb ▪ VI: ~ **em** to climb; ~ (**com alguém**) (*col!*) to screw (sb)
trepidação [trepida'sãw] F shaking
trepidar [trepi'da\] VI to tremble, shake
trépido, -a ['trɛpidu, a] ADJ fearful
três [treʃ] NUM three; **a ~ por dois** every five minutes, all the time; *v tb* **cinco**
tresloucado, -a [treʒlo'kadu, a] ADJ crazy, deranged
três-quartos ADJ INV (*saia, manga*) three-quarter-length ▪ M INV (*apartamento*) three-room flat (*Brit*) *ou* apartment
trespassar [treʃpa'sa\] VT = **traspassar**
trespasse [treʃ'pasi] M = **traspasse**
trevas ['trɛvaʃ] FPL darkness *sg*
trevo ['trevu] M clover; (*de vias*) intersection
treze ['trezi] NUM thirteen; *v tb* **cinco**
trezentos, -as [tre'zẽtuʃ] NUM three hundred
tríade ['triadʒi] F triad
triagem ['trjaʒẽ] F selection; (*separação*) sorting; **fazer uma ~ de** to make a selection of, sort out
triangular [trjãgu'la\] ADJ triangular
triângulo ['trjãgulu] M triangle
tribal [tri'baw] (*pl* -**ais**) ADJ tribal
tribo ['tribu] F tribe
tribulação [tribula'sãw] (*pl* -**ões**) F tribulation, affliction
tribuna [tri'buna] F platform, rostrum; (*Rel*) pulpit
tribunal [tribu'naw] (*pl* -**ais**) M court; (*comissão*) tribunal; ~ **de apelação** *ou* **de recursos** court of appeal; **T~ de Justiça/Contas** Court of Justice/Accounts; **T~ do Trabalho** Industrial Tribunal
tributação [tributa'sãw] F taxation
tributar [tribu'ta\] VT (*impor impostos a*) to tax; (*pagar*) to pay
tributário, -a [tribu'tarju, a] ADJ tax *atr* ▪ M (*de rio*) tributary
tributável [tribu'tavew] (*pl* -**eis**) ADJ taxable
tributo [tri'butu] M tribute; (*imposto*) tax
tricampeão, -peã [trikã'pjãw, 'pjã] (*pl* -**ões/-s**) M/F three-times champion
tricô [tri'ko] M knitting; **artigos de ~** knitted goods, knitwear *sg*; **ponto de ~** plain stitch
tricolor [triko'lo\] ADJ three-coloured (*Brit*), three-colored (*US*)
tricotar [triko'ta\] VT, VI to knit
tridimensional [tridimẽsjo'naw] (*pl* -**ais**) ADJ three-dimensional
triênio ['trjenju] M three-year period
trigal [tri'gaw] (*pl* -**ais**) M wheat field
trigêmeo, -a [tri'ʒemju, a] M/F triplet
trigésimo, -a [tri'ʒezimu, a] ADJ thirtieth; *v tb*

quinto
trigo ['trigu] M wheat
trigonometria [trigonome'tria] F trigonometry
trigueiro, -a [tri'gejru, a] ADJ dark, swarthy
trilátero, -a [tri'lateru, a] ADJ trilateral
trilha ['triʎa] F (*caminho*) path; (*rasto*) track, trail; (*Comput*) track; ~ **sonora** soundtrack
trilhado, -a [tri'ʎadu, a] ADJ (*pisado*) well-worn, well-trodden; (*percorrido*) covered
trilhão [tri'ʎãw] (*pl* -**ões**) M billion (*Brit*), trillion (*US*)
trilhar [tri'ʎa\] VT (*vereda*) to tread, wear
trilho ['triʎu] M (*BR: Ferro*) rail; (*vereda*) path, track
trilhões [tri'ʎõjʃ] MPL *de* **trilhão**
trilíngue [tri'lĩgwi] ADJ trilingual
trilogia [trilo'ʒia] F trilogy
trimestral [trimeʃ'traw] (*pl* -**ais**) ADJ quarterly
trimestralidade [trimeʃtrali'dadʒi] F quarterly payment
trimestralmente [trimeʃtraw'mētʃi] ADV quarterly
trimestre [tri'meʃtri] M (*Educ*) term; (*Com*) quarter
trinca ['trĩka] F set of three; (*col: trio*) threesome
trincar [trĩ'ka\] VT to crunch; (*morder*) to bite; (*dentes*) to grit ▪ VI to crunch
trinchar [trĩ'ʃa\] VT to carve
trincheira [trĩ'ʃejra] F trench
trinco ['trĩku] M latch
trindade [trĩ'dadʒi] F: **a T~** the Trinity; **trindades** FPL (*sino*) angelus *sg*
Trinidad e Tobago [trinidadʒito'bagu] M Trinidad and Tobago
trinta ['trĩta] NUM thirty; *v tb* **cinquenta**
trio ['triu] M trio; **trio elétrico** music float; *see below*

● **TRIO ELÉTRICO**
●
● *Trios elétricos* are lorries, carrying floats
● equipped for sound and/or live music,
● which parade through the streets during
● *carnaval*, especially in Bahia. Bands and
● popular performers on the floats draw
● crowds by giving frenzied performances of
● various types of music.

tripa ['tripa] F gut, intestine; **tripas** FPL (*intestinos*) bowels; (*vísceras*) guts; (*Culin*) tripe *sg*; **fazer das ~s coração** to make a great effort
tripé [tri'pɛ] M tripod
tríplex ['tripleks] ADJ INV three-storey (*Brit*), three-story (*US*) ▪ M INV three-stor(e)y apartment
triplicar [tripli'ka\] VT, VI to treble; **triplicar-se** VR to treble
Trípoli ['tripoli] N Tripoli
tripulação [tripula'sãw] (*pl* -**ões**) F crew
tripulante [tripu'lãtʃi] M/F crew member

tripular [tripu'la^r] VT to man

trisavô, -vó [triza'vo, 'vɔ] M/F great-great-grandfather/mother

triste ['triʃtʃi] ADJ sad; (*lugar*) depressing

tristeza [triʃ'teza] F sadness; (*de lugar*) gloominess; **esse professor é uma ~** (*col*) this teacher is awful

tristonho, -a [triʃ'tɔɲu, a] ADJ sad, melancholy

triturar [tritu'ra^r] VT (*moer*) to grind; (*espancar*) to beat to a pulp; (*afligir*) to beset

triunfal [trjū'faw] (*pl* -ais) ADJ triumphal

triunfante [trjū'fātʃi] ADJ triumphant

triunfar [trjū'fa^r] VI to triumph; **triunfo** ['trjūfu] M triumph

trivial [tri'vjaw] (*pl* -ais) ADJ (*comum*) common(place), ordinary; (*insignificante*) trivial, trifling ■ M (*pratos*) everyday food

trivialidade [trivjali'dadʒi] F triviality; **trivialidades** FPL (*futilidades*) trivia *sg*

triz [triʒ] M: **por um ~** by a hair's breadth; **escapar por um ~** to have a narrow escape

troca ['trɔka] F exchange, swap; **em ~ de** in exchange for

troça ['trɔsa] F ridicule, mockery; **fazer ~ de** to make fun of

trocadilho [troka'dʒiʎu] M pun, play on words

trocado, -a [tro'kadu, a] ADJ mixed up ■ M: **~(s)** (*small*) change

trocador, a [troka'do^r(a)] M/F (*em ônibus*) conductor

trocar [tro'ka^r] VT to exchange, swap; (*mudar*) to change; (*inverter*) to change *ou* swap round; (*confundir*) to mix up; **trocar-se** VR to change; **~ dinheiro** to change money; **~ algo por algo** to exchange *ou* swap sth for sth; **~ algo de lugar** to move sth; **~ de roupa/lugar** to change (clothes)/places; **~ de bem/mal** to make up/fall out

troçar [tro'sa^r] VI: **~ de** to ridicule, make fun of

troca-troca (*pl* -s) M swap

trocista [tro'siʃta] M/F joker

troco ['troku] M (*dinheiro*) change; (*revide*) retort, rejoinder; **a ~ de** at the cost of; (*por causa de*) because of; **em ~ de** in exchange for; **dar o ~ a alguém** (*fig*) to pay sb back

troço ['trɔsu] (*BR: col*) M (*coisa inútil*) piece of junk; (*coisa*) thing; **ser ~** (*pessoa*) to be a big-shot; **ser um ~** to be amazing; **ter um ~** (*sentir-se mal*) to be taken bad; (*zangar-se*) to get mad; **senti** *ou* **me deu um ~** I felt bad; **ele é um ~ de feio** he's incredibly ugly; **meus ~s** my things

troféu [tro'fɛw] M trophy

tromba ['trōba] F (*do elefante*) trunk; (*de outro animal*) snout; (*col*) poker face; **estar de ~** (*col*) to be poker-faced

trombada [trō'bada] F crash; **dar uma ~** to have a crash

tromba-d'água (*pl* trombas-d'água) F waterspout; (*chuva*) downpour

trombadinha [trōba'dʒiɲa] F child thief

trombeta [trō'beta] F (*Mús*) trumpet

trombone [trō'bɔni] M (*Mús*) trombone; **botar a boca no ~** (*fig: col*) to tell the world

trombose [trō'bɔzi] F thrombosis

trombudo, -a [trō'budu, a] ADJ (*fig*) poker-faced

trompa ['trōpa] F (*Mús*) horn; **~ de Falópio** (*Anat*) Fallopian tube

tronchar [trō'ʃa^r] VT to cut off, chop off

troncho, -a ['trōʃu, a] ADJ (*torto*) crooked; **~ de uma perna** one-legged

tronco ['trōku] M (*caule*) trunk; (*ramo*) branch; (*de corpo*) torso, trunk; (*de família*) lineage; (*Tel*) trunkline

troncudo, -a [trō'kudu, a] ADJ stocky

trono ['trɔnu] M throne

tropa ['trɔpa] F troop, gang; (*Mil*) troop; (*exército*) army; **ir para a ~** (*PT*) to join the army; **~ de choque** riot police, riot squad

tropeção [trope'sãw] (*pl* -ões) M trip-up; (*fig*) faux pas, slip-up; **dar um ~ (em)** to stumble (on)

tropeçar [trope'sa^r] VI to stumble, trip; (*fig*) to blunder; **~ em dificuldades** to meet with difficulties

tropeço [tro'pesu] M stumbling block

tropeções [trope'sõjʃ] MPL *de* **tropeção**

trôpego, -a ['tropegu, a] ADJ shaky, unsteady

tropel [tro'pεw] (*pl* -éis) M (*ruído*) uproar, tumult; (*confusão*) confusion; (*estrépito de pés*) stamping of feet; (*turbamulta*) mob

tropical [tropi'kaw] (*pl* -ais) ADJ tropical

trópico ['trɔpiku] M tropic; **T~ de Câncer/Capricórnio** Tropic of Cancer/Capricorn

troquei *etc* [tro'kej] VB *v* **trocar**

trotar [tro'ta^r] VI to trot; **trote** ['trɔtʃi] M trot; (*por telefone etc*) hoax call; (: *obsceno*) obscene call; (*em calouro*) trick; **passar um trote** to play a hoax

trottoir [tro'twa^r] M: **fazer ~** to go on the streets (as a prostitute)

trouxa ['troʃa] ADJ (*col*) gullible ■ F bundle of clothes ■ M/F (*col: pessoa*) sucker

trouxe *etc* ['trosi] VB *v* **trazer**

trova ['trɔva] F ballad, folksong

trovador [trova'do^r] M troubadour, minstrel

trovão [tro'vãw] (*pl* -ões) M clap of thunder; (*trovoada*) thunder; **trovejar** [trove'ʒa^r] VI to thunder; **trovoada** [tro'vwada] F thunderstorm

trovoar [tro'vwa^r] VI to thunder

trovões [tro'võjʃ] MPL *de* **trovão**

TRT (*BR*) ABR M = **Tribunal Regional do Trabalho**

TRU (*BR*) ABR F = **Taxa Rodoviária Única**

trucidar [trusi'da^r] VT to butcher, slaughter

truculência [truku'lẽsja] F cruelty, barbarism

truculento, -a [truku'lẽtʃi] ADJ cruel, barbaric

trufa ['trufa] F (*Bot*) truffle

NB: *European Portuguese adds the following consonants to certain words:* **b** (sú(b)dito, su(b)til); **c** (a(c)ção, a(c)cionista, a(c)to)); **m** (inde(m)ne); **p** (ado(p)çã, ado(p)tar); *for further details see p. xiii.*

truísmo [tru'iʒmu] M truism

trumbicar-se [trũbi'kaxsi] (col) VR to come a cropper

truncar [trũ'kaᵣ] VT to chop off, cut off; (texto) to garble

trunfo ['trũfu] M trump (card)

truque ['truki] M trick; (publicitário) gimmick

truste ['truʃtʃi] M trust, monopoly

truta ['truta] F trout

TSE (BR) ABR M = **Tribunal Superior Eleitoral**

TST (BR) ABR M = **Tribunal Superior do Trabalho**

tu [tu] (PT) PRON you

tua ['tua] F de **teu**

tuba ['tuba] F tuba

tubarão [tuba'rãw] (pl -ões) M shark

tubário, -a [tu'barju, a] ADJ: **gravidez tubária** ectopic pregnancy

tubarões [tuba'rõjʃ] MPL de **tubarão**

tuberculose [tubexku'lɔzi] F tuberculosis, TB

tuberculoso, -a [tubexku'lozu, ɔza] ADJ suffering from tuberculosis ■ M/F TB sufferer

tubinho [tu'biɲu] M tube dress

tubo ['tubu] M tube, pipe; ~ **de ensaio** test tube; **gastar/custar os ~s** (col) to spend/cost a bomb

tubulação [tubula'sãw] F piping, plumbing; **entrar pela** ~ to come a cropper

tubular [tubu'laᵣ] ADJ tubular

tucano [tu'kanu] M toucan

tudo ['tudu] PRON everything; ~ **quanto** everything that; **antes de** ~ first of all; **apesar de** ~ despite everything; **acima de** ~ above all; **depois de** ~ after all; ~ **ou nada** all or nothing; **estar com** ~ to be sitting pretty

tufão [tu'fãw] (pl -ões) M typhoon

tugúrio [tu'gurju] M (cabana) hut, shack; (refúgio) shelter

tulipa [tu'lipa] F tulip; (copo) tall glass

tumba ['tũba] F (sepultura) tomb; (lápide) tombstone

tumido, -a [tu'midu, a] ADJ (inchado) swollen

tumular [tumu'laᵣ] ADJ (pedra) tomb atr; (silêncio) like the grave

túmulo ['tumulu] M tomb; (sepultura) burial; **ser um** ~ (pessoa) to be very discreet

tumor [tu'moᵣ] M tumour (Brit), tumor (US); ~ **benigno/maligno** benign/malignant tumo(u)r; ~ **cerebral** brain tumo(u)r

tumulto [tu'muwtu] M (confusão) uproar, trouble; (grande movimento) bustle; (balbúrdia) hubbub; (motim) riot; **tumultuado, -a** [tumuw'twadu, a] ADJ riotous, heated; **tumultuar** [tumuw'twaᵣ] VT (fazer tumulto em) to disrupt; (amotinar) to rouse, incite

tumultuoso, -a [tumuw'twozu, ɔza] ADJ tumultuous; (revolto) stormy

tunda ['tũda] F thrashing, beating; (fig) dressing-down

túnel ['tunew] (pl -eis) M tunnel

túnica ['tunika] F tunic

Tunísia [tu'nizja] F: **a** ~ Tunisia

tupi [tu'pi] M Tupi (tribe); (Ling) Tupi ■ M/F Tupi Indian

tupi-guarani [-gwara'ni] M (Ling) see below

● **TUPI-GUARANI**

● This is an important branch of indigenous
● languages from the tropical region of South
● America. It takes in thirty indigenous
● peoples and includes Tupi, Guarani,
● and other languages. Before Brazil was
● discovered by the Portuguese it had 1,300
● indigenous languages, 87% of which are
● now extinct due to the extermination of
● indigenous peoples and the loss of territory.

tupiniquim [tupini'kĩ] (pej) (pl -ns) ADJ Brazilian (Indian)

turba ['tuxba] F throng; (em desordem) mob

turbamulta [tuxba'muwta] F mob

turbante [tux'bãtʃi] M turban

turbar [tux'baᵣ] VT (escurecer) to darken, cloud; (perturbar) to perturb; **turbar-se** VR to be perturbed

turbilhão [tuxbi'ʎãw] (pl -ões) M (de vento) whirlwind; (de água) whirlpool; **um** ~ **de** a whirl of

turbina [tux'bina] F turbine

turbulência [tuxbu'lẽsja] F turbulence; **turbulento, -a** [tuxbu'lẽtu, a] ADJ turbulent, stormy; (pessoa) disorderly

turco, -a ['tuxku, a] ADJ Turkish ■ M/F Turk ■ M (Ling) Turkish

turfa ['tuxfa] F peat

turfe ['tuxfi] M horse-racing

túrgido, -a ['tuxʒidu, a] ADJ swollen, bloated

turíbulo [tu'ribulu] M incense-burner

turismo [tu'riʒmu] M tourism; (indústria) tourist industry; **fazer** ~ to go sightseeing; **agência de** ~ travel agency; **turista** [tu'riʃta] M/F tourist; (aluno) persistent absentee ■ ADJ (classe) tourist atr

turístico, -a [tu'riʃtʃiku, a] ADJ tourist atr; (viagem) sightseeing atr

turma ['tuxma] F group; (Educ) class; **a** ~ **da pesada** (col) the in crowd

turnê [tux'ne] F tour

turnedô [tuxne'do] M (Culin) tournedos

turno ['tuxnu] M shift; (vez) turn; (Esporte, de eleição) round; **por** ~s alternately, by turns, in turn; ~ **da noite** night shift

turquesa [tux'keza] ADJ INV turquoise

Turquia [tux'kia] F: **a** ~ Turkey

turra ['tuxa] F (disputa) argument, dispute; **andar** ou **viver às** ~s to be at loggerheads

turvar [tux'vaᵣ] VT to cloud; (escurecer) to darken; **turvar-se** VR to become clouded; to darken

turvo, -a ['tuxvu, a] ADJ clouded

tusso etc ['tusu] VB V **tossir**

tusta ['tuʃta] (col) M: **nem um** ~ not a penny

tutano [tu'tanu] M (Anat) marrow

tutela [tu'tɛla] F protection; (Jur) guardianship;

estar sob a ~ de (*fig*) to be under the protection of
tutelar [tute'la^r] ADJ protective; (*Jur*) guardian
■ VT to protect; to act as a guardian to
tutor, a [tu'to^r(a)] M/F guardian
tutu [tu'tu] M (*Culin*) beans, bacon and manioc flour;

(*de balé*) tutu; (*col: dinheiro*) cash
TV [te've] ABR F (= *televisão*) TV
TVE (BR) ABR F (= *Televisão Educativa*) educational television station
TVS (BR) ABR F = **Televisão Stúdio Sílvio Santos**
tweed ['twidʒi] M tweed

NB: *European Portuguese adds the following consonants to certain words:* **b** (sú(b)dito, su(b)til); **c** (a(c)ção, a(c)cionista, a(c)to); **m** (inde(m)ne); **p** (ado(p)çã, ado(p)tar); *for further details see p. xiii.*

Uu

U, u [u] (*pl* **us**) M U, u; **U de Úrsula** U for Uncle
uai [waj] EXCL ah
UBE ABR F = **União Brasileira de Empresários**
úbere ['uberi] ADJ fertile ■ M udder
ubérrimo, -a [u'bɛximu, a] ADJ SUPERL *de* **úbere**
ubiqüidade [ubikwi'dadʒi] F ubiquity
ubíquo, -a [u'bikwu, a] ADJ ubiquitous
Ucrânia [u'kranja] F: **a ~** the Ukraine
UD (BR) ABR F = **Feira de Utilidades Domésticas**
UDN ABR F (= *União Democrática Nacional*) *former Brazilian political party*
UE ABR F (= *União Européia*) EU
ué [wɛ] EXCL what?, just a minute!
UERJ ['wɛxʒi] ABR F = **Universidade Estadual do Rio de Janeiro**
ufa ['ufa] EXCL phew!
ufanar-se [ufa'naxsi] VR: **~ de** to take pride in, pride o.s. on
ufanismo [ufa'niʒmu] (BR) M boastful nationalism, chauvinism
Uferj [u'fɛxʒi] ABR F = **Unidade Fiscal do Estado do Rio de Janeiro**
UFF ABR F = **Universidade Federal Fluminense**
UFMG ABR F = **Universidade Federal de Minas Gerais**
UFPE ABR F = **Universidade Federal de Pernambuco**
UFRJ ABR F = **Universidade Federal do Rio de Janeiro**
Uganda [u'gãda] M Uganda
ugandense [ugã'dẽsi] ADJ, M/F Ugandan
uh [uh] EXCL ooh!; (*de repugnância*) ugh!
ui [ui] EXCL (*de dor*) ouch, ow; (*de surpresa*) oh; (*de repugnância*) ugh
uísque ['wiʃki] M whisky (*Brit*), whiskey (*US*)
uisqueria [wiʃke'ria] F whisk(e)y bar
uivada [wi'vada] F howl
uivante [wi'vãtʃi] ADJ howling
uivar [wi'vaʳ] VI to howl; (*berrar*) to yell; **uivo** ['wivu] M howl; (*fig*) yell
úlcera ['uwsera] F ulcer
ulceração [uwsera'sãw] F ulceration
ulcerar [uwse'raʳ] VT, VI to ulcerate; **ulcerar-se** VR to ulcerate
ulceroso, -a [uwse'rozu, ɔza] ADJ ulcerous
ulterior [ulte'rjoʳ] ADJ (*além*) further, farther; (*depois*) later, subsequent

ulteriormente [uwteriox'mẽtʃi] ADV later on, subsequently
ultimamente [uwtʃima'mẽtʃi] ADV lately
ultimar [uwtʃi'maʳ] VT to finish; (*negócio, compra*) to complete
ultimato [uwtʃi'matu] M ultimatum
ultimátum [uwtʃi'matũ] M = **ultimato**
último, -a ['uwtʃimu, a] ADJ last; (*mais recente*) latest; (*qualidade*) lowest; (*fig*) final; **por ~** finally; **fazer algo por ~** to do sth last; **nos ~s anos** in recent years; **em ~ caso** if the worst comes to the worst; **pela última vez** (for) the last time; **a última** (*notícia*) the latest (news); (*absurdo*) the latest folly; **dizer as últimas a alguém** to insult sb; **estar nas últimas** (*na miséria*) to be down and out; (*agonizando*) to be on one's last legs
ultra- [uwtra-] PREFIXO ultra-
ultracheio, -a [uwtra'ʃeju, a] ADJ packed
ultrajante [uwtra'ʒãtʃi] ADJ outrageous; (*que insulta*) insulting
ultrajar [uwtra'ʒaʳ] VT to outrage; (*insultar*) to insult, offend; **ultraje** [uw'traʒi] M outrage; (*insulto*) insult, offence (*Brit*), offense (*US*)
ultraleve [uwtra'lɛvi] ADJ ultralight ■ M microlite
ultramar [uwtra'maʳ] M overseas
ultramarino, -a [uwtrama'rinu, a] ADJ overseas
ultramoderno, -a [uwtramo'dɛxnu, a] ADJ ultramodern
ultrapassado, -a [uwtrapa'sadu, a] ADJ (*idéias etc*) outmoded
ultrapassagem [uwtrapa'saʒẽ] F overtaking (*Brit*), passing (*US*)
ultrapassar [uwtrapa'saʳ] VT (*atravessar*) to cross, go beyond; (*ir além de*) to exceed; (*transgredir*) to overstep; (*Auto*) to overtake (*Brit*), pass (*US*); (*ser superior a*) to surpass ■ VI (*Auto*) to overtake (*Brit*), pass (*US*)
ultra-secreto, -a ADJ top secret
ultra-sensível (*pl* **-eis**) ADJ hypersensitive
ultra-som M ultrasound
ultra-sônico, -a [-'soniku, a] ADJ ultrasonic; (*Med*) ultrasound *atr*
ultra-sonografia [-sonogra'fia] F ultrasound scanning
ultravioleta [uwtravjo'leta] ADJ ultraviolet

ululante [ulu'lãtʃi] ADJ howling; (*mentira, óbvio*) blatant

ulular [ulu'la^r] VI to howl, wail ■ M howling, wailing

🔘 **PALAVRA CHAVE**

um(a) [ũ, 'uma] (*pl* uns/um(a)s) NUM one; **um(a) e outro** both; **um(a) a um(a)** one by one; **à uma (hora)** at one (o'clock)
■ ADJ: **uns cinco** about five; **uns poucos** a few
■ ART INDEF **1** (*sg*) a; (*: antes de vogal ou `h' mudo*) an; (*pl*) some; **ela é de uma beleza incrível** she's incredibly beautiful
2 (*dando ênfase*): **estou com uma fome!** I'm so hungry!
3: **um ao outro** one another; (*entre dois*) each other

umbanda [ũ'bãda] M umbanda (*Afro-Brazilian cult*)

umbigo [ũ'bigu] M navel

umbilical [ũbili'kaw] (*pl* -ais) ADJ: **cordão ~** umbilical cord

umbral [ũ'braw] (*pl* -ais) M (*limiar*) threshold

umedecer [umede'se^r] VT to moisten, wet; **umedecer-se** VR to get wet

umedecido, -a [umede'sidu, a] ADJ damp

umidade [umi'dadʒi] F dampness; (*clima*) humidity

úmido, -a ['umidu, a] ADJ wet, moist; (*roupa*) damp; (*clima*) humid

unânime [u'nanimi] ADJ unanimous

unanimidade [unanimi'dadʒi] F unanimity

unção [ũ'sãw] F anointing; (*Rel*) unction

UNE (BR) ABR F = **União Nacional de Estudantes**

UNESCO [u'nɛʃku] ABR F UNESCO

ungir [ũ'ʒi^r] VT to rub with ointment; (*Rel*) to anoint

ungüento [ũ'gwẽtu] M ointment

unha ['uɲa] F nail; (*garra*) claw; **com ~s e dentes** tooth and nail; **ser ~ e carne (com)** to be hand in glove (with); **fazer as ~s** to do one's nails; (*por outra pessoa*) to have one's nails done; **~ encravada** (*no pé*) ingrowing toenail; **unhada** [u'ɲada] F scratch

unha-de-fome (*pl* **unhas-de-fome**) ADJ mean ■ M/F miser

unhar [u'ɲa^r] VT to scratch

união [u'njãw] (*pl* -ões) F union; (*ato*) joining; (*unidade, solidariedade*) unity; (*casamento*) marriage; (*Tec*) joint; **a U~ Soviética** the Soviet Union; **a ~ faz a força** unity is strength; **a U~** (*no Brasil*) the Union, the Federal Government

unicamente [unika'mẽtʃi] ADV only

único, -a ['uniku, a] ADJ only; (*sem igual*) unique; (*um só*) single; **ele é o ~ que ...** he is the only one who ...; **ela é filha única** she's an only child; **um caso ~** a one-off; **preço ~** one price

unicórnio [uni'kɔxnju] M unicorn

unidade [uni'dadʒi] F unity; (*Tec, Com*) unit; **~ central de processamento** (*Comput*) central processing unit; **~ de disco** (*Comput*) disk drive; **~ de fita** (*Comput*) tape streamer

unido, -a [u'nidu, a] ADJ joined, linked; (*fig*) united; **manter-se ~s** to stick together

Unif [u'nifi] (BR) ABR F = **Unidade Fiscal**

unificação [unifika'sãw] F unification

unificar [unifi'ka^r] VT to unite; **unificar-se** VR to join together

uniforme [uni'fɔxmi] ADJ uniform; (*semelhante*) alike, similar; (*superfície*) even ■ M uniform; **de ~** uniformly

uniformidade [unifoxmi'dadʒi] F uniformity

uniformizado, -a [unifoxmi'zadu, a] ADJ (*uniforme*) uniform, standardized; (*vestido de uniforme*) in uniform

uniformizar [unifoxmi'za^r] VT to standardize; (*pessoa*) to put into uniform; **uniformizar-se** VR to put on one's uniform

unilateral [unilate'raw] (*pl* -ais) ADJ unilateral

unilíngüe [uni'lĩgwi] ADJ monolingual

uniões [u'njõjʃ] FPL *de* **união**

unir [u'ni^r] VT (*juntar*) to join together; (*ligar*) to link; (*pessoas, fig*) to unite; (*misturar*) to mix together; (*atar*) to tie together; **unir-se** VR to come together; (*povos etc*) to unite; **~-se a alguém** to join forces with sb

unissex [uni'sɛks] ADJ INV unisex

uníssono [u'nisonu] M: **em ~** in unison

Unita [u'nita] ABR F (= *União Nacional pela Libertação de Angola*) Unita

unitário, -a [uni'tarju, a] ADJ (*preço*) unit *atr*; (*Pol*) unitarian ■ M/F (*Pol, Rel*) unitarian

universal [univex'saw] (*pl* -ais) ADJ universal; (*geral*) general; (*mundial*) worldwide; (*espírito*) broad

universalidade [univexsali'dadʒi] F universality

universalizar [univexsali'za^r] VT to universalize

universidade [univexsi'dadʒi] F university; **universitário, -a** [univexsi'tarju, a] ADJ university *atr* ■ M/F (*professor*) lecturer; (*aluno*) university student

universo [uni'vexsu] M universe; (*mundo*) world

unjo *etc* ['ũʒu] VB V **ungir**

uno, -a ['unu, a] ADJ one

uns [ũʃ] MPL *de* **um**

untar [ũ'ta^r] VT (*esfregar*) to rub; (*com óleo, manteiga*) to grease

upa ['upa] EXCL (*quando algo cai*) whoops!; (*para animar a se levantar*) up you get!; (*de espanto*) wow!

UPC (BR) ABR F = **Unidade Padrão de Capital**

Urais [u'rajʃ] MPL: **os ~** the Urals

urânio [u'ranju] M uranium

Urano [u'ranu] M Uranus

urbanidade [uxbani'dadʒi] F courtesy,

NB: *European Portuguese adds the following consonants to certain words:* **b** (sú(b)dito, su(b)til); **c** (a(c)ção, a(c)cionista, a(c)to); **m** (inde(m)ne); **p** (ado(p)çã, ado(p)tar); *for further details see p. xiii.*

politeness

urbanismo [uxba'niʒmu] M town planning

urbanista [uxba'niʃta] M/F town planner

urbanístico, -a [uxba'niʃtʃiku, a] ADJ town planning *atr*

urbanização [uxbaniza'sãw] F urbanization

urbanizado, -a [uxbani'zadu, a] ADJ (*zona*) built-up

urbanizar [uxbani'za'] VT to urbanize; (*pessoa*) to refine

urbano, -a [ux'banu, a] ADJ (*da cidade*) urban; (*fig*) urbane

urbe ['uxbi] F city

urdir [ux'dʒi'] VT to weave; (*fig: maquinar*) to weave, hatch

urdu [ux'du] M (*Ling*) Urdu

uretra [u'retra] F urethra

urgência [ux'ʒẽsja] F urgency; **com toda ~ as** quickly as possible; **de ~ urgent; pedir algo com ~** to ask for sth insistently; **urgente** [ux'ʒẽtʃi] ADJ urgent

urgir [ux'ʒi'] VI to be urgent; (*tempo*) to be pressing ■ VT to require urgently; **são providências que urge sejam tomadas** they are steps which urgently need to be taken; **urge fazermos** we must do

urina [u'rina] F urine

urinado, -a [uri'nadu, a] ADJ (*molhado*) soaked with urine; (*manchado*) urine-stained

urinar [uri'na'] VI to urinate ■ VT (*sangue*) to pass; (*cama*) to wet; **urinar-se** VR to wet o.s.

urinário, -a [uri'narju, a] ADJ urinary

urinol [uri'nɔw] (*pl* -óis) M chamber pot

urna ['uxna] F urn; **as urnas** FPL (*eleições*) the polls; **~ eleitoral** ballot box

urologia [urolo'ʒia] F urology

urologista [urolo'ʒiʃta] M/F urologist

URP (BR) ABR F = **Unidade de Referência de Preços**

URPE (BR) ABR FPL = **Urgências Pediátricas**

urrar [u'xa'] VT, VI to roar; (*de dor*) to yell

urro ['uxu] M roar; (*de dor*) yell

ursa ['uxsa] F bear; **U~ Maior/Menor** Ursa Major/Minor

urso ['uxsu] M bear

urso-branco (*pl* ursos-brancos) M polar bear

URSS ABR F = **União das Repúblicas Socialistas Soviéticas**; **a urso-branco** the USSR

urticária [uxtʃi'karja] F nettle rash

urtiga [ux'tʃiga] F nettle

urubu [uru'bu] M vulture

urubusservar [urubusex'va'] (*col*) VT, VI to watch

urucubaca [uruku'baka] F bad luck; **estar com uma ~** to be unlucky

Uruguai [uru'gwaj] M: **o ~** Uruguay

uruguaio, -a [uru'gwaju, a] ADJ, M/F Uruguayan

urze ['uxzi] M heather

usado, -a [u'zadu, a] ADJ used; (*comum*) common; (*roupa*) worn; (*gasto*) worn out; (*de segunda mão*) second-hand; **~ a** (*acostumado*) accustomed to

usar [u'za'] VT (*servir-se de*) to use; (*vestir*) to wear; (*gastar com o uso*) to wear out; (*barba, cabelo curto*) to have, wear ■ VI: **~ de** to use; **~ fazer** to be in the habit of doing; **modo de ~** directions *pl*

usina [u'zina] F (*fábrica*) factory; (*de energia*) plant; **~ de açúcar** sugar mill; **~ de aço** steelworks; **~ hidrelétrica** hydroelectric power station; **~ termonuclear** nuclear power plant

usineiro, -a [uzi'nejru, a] ADJ plant *atr* ■ M/F sugar mill owner

uso ['uzu] M (*emprego*) use; (*utilização*) usage; (*prática*) practice; (*moda*) fashion; (*costume*) custom; (*vestir*) wearing; **~ e desgaste normal** (*Com*) fair wear and tear

USP ['uʃpi] ABR F = **Universidade de São Paulo**

usual [u'zwaw] (*pl* -ais) ADJ usual; (*comum*) common

usuário, -a [u'zwarju, a] M/F user; **~ do telefone** telephone subscriber

usucapião [uzuka'pjãw] M (*Jur*) prescription

usufruir [uzu'frwi'] VT to enjoy ■ VI: **~ de** to enjoy

usufruto [uzu'frutu] M (*Jur*) usufruct

usura [u'zura] F (*juro*) interest; (*avareza*) avarice

usurário, -a [uzu'rarju, a] M/F (*avaro*) miser; (*col: agiota*) loan shark ■ ADJ avaricious

usurpar [uzux'pa'] VT to usurp

úteis ['utejʃ] ADJ PL *de* útil

utensílio [utẽ'silju] M utensil

uterino, -a [ute'rinu, a] ADJ uterine

útero ['uteru] M womb, uterus

UTI ['utʃi] ABR F (= *Unidade de Terapia Intensiva*) intensive care (unit), ICU

útil ['utʃiw] (*pl* -eis) ADJ useful; (*vantajoso*) profitable, worthwhile; (*tempo*) working; (*prazo*) stipulated; **dias úteis** weekdays, working days; **em que lhe posso ser ~?** how can I be of assistance (to you)?; **utilidade** [utʃili'dadʒi] F usefulness; (*vantagem*) advantage; (*utensílio*) utility

utilitário, -a [utʃili'tarju, a] ADJ utilitarian, practical; (*pessoa*) matter-of-fact, pragmatic; (*veículo*) general purpose *atr*; **programa ~** (*Comput*) utilities program

utilização [utʃiliza'sãw] F use

utilizar [utʃili'za'] VT to use; **utilizar-se** VR: **utilizar-se de** to make use of

utilizável [utʃili'zavew] (*pl* -eis) ADJ usable

utopia [uto'pia] F Utopia

utópico, -a [u'tɔpiku, a] ADJ Utopian

uva ['uva] F grape; (*col: mulher*) peach; (: *coisa*) lovely thing; **ser uma ~** (*pessoa, objeto*) to be lovely; **uma ~ de pessoa/broche** a lovely person/brooch

úvula ['uvula] F uvula

Vv

V, v [ve] (*pl* **vs**) M V, v; **V de Vera** V for Victor
V ABR (= *volt*) v
vá *etc* [va] VB V **ir**
vã [vã] F *de* **vão**
vaca ['vaka] F cow; **carne de ~** beef; **tempo das ~s magras** (*fig*) lean period; **a ~ foi para o brejo** (*fig*) everything went wrong; **voltar à ~ fria** to get back to the subject
vacância [va'kãsja] F vacancy
vacante [va'kãtʃi] ADJ vacant
vaca-preta (*pl* **vacas-pretas**) F *coca-cola with ice cream*
vacilação [vasila'sãw] F (*hesitação*) hesitation; (*balanço*) swaying
vacilada [vasi'lada] F slip-up; **dar uma ~** (*col*) to slip up
vacilante [vasi'lãtʃi] ADJ (*hesitante*) hesitant; (*pouco firme*) unsteady; (*luz*) flickering
vacilar [vasi'la'] VI (*hesitar*) to hesitate; (*balançar*) to sway; (*cambalear*) to stagger; (*luz*) to flicker; (*col*) to slip up
vacina [va'sina] F vaccine
vacinação [vasina'sãw] (*pl* -**ões**) F vaccination
vacinar [vasi'na'] VT to vaccinate; (*fig*) to immunize; **vacinar-se** VR to take vaccine
vacuidade [vakwi'dadʒi] F emptiness
vacum [va'kũ] ADJ: **gado ~** cattle
vácuo ['vakwu] M vacuum; (*fig*) void; (*espaço*) space; **empacotado a ~** vacuum-packed
vadear [va'dʒja'] VT to wade through
vadiação [vadʒja'sãw] F vagrancy
vadiagem [va'dʒjaʒẽ] F = **vadiação**
vadiar [va'dʒja'] VI to lounge about; (*não trabalhar*) to idle about; (*não estudar*) to skive; (*perambular*) to wander
vadio, -a [va'dʒiu, a] ADJ (*ocioso*) idle, lazy; (*vagabundo*) vagrant ■ M/F idler; vagabond, vagrant
vaga ['vaga] F (*onda*) wave; (*em hotel, trabalho*) vacancy; (*em estacionamento*) parking place; **ser bom de ~** to be good at parking
vagabundear [vagabũ'dʒja'] VI to wander about, roam about; (*vadiar*) to laze around
vagabundo, -a [vaga'bũdu, a] ADJ vagrant; (*vadio*) lazy, idle; (*de má qualidade*) shoddy; (*canalha*) rotten; (*mulher*) easy ■ M/F tramp; (*canalha*) bum
vagalhão [vaga'ʎãw] (*pl* -**ões**) M big wave, breaker
vaga-lume [vaga'lumi] (*pl* -**s**) M (*Zool*) glow-worm; (*no cinema*) usher
vagão [va'gãw] (*pl* -**ões**) M (*de passageiros*) carriage; (*de cargas*) wagon; **vagão-leito** (*pl* **vagões-leitos**) (PT) M sleeping car; **vagão-restaurante** (*pl* **vagões-restaurantes**) M buffet car
vagar [va'ga'] VI to wander about, roam about; (*barco*) to drift; (*ficar vago*) to be vacant ■ M slowness; **fazer algo com mais ~** to do sth at a more leisurely pace
vagareza [vaga'reza] F slowness; **com ~** slowly
vagaroso, -a [vaga'rozu, ɔza] ADJ slow
vagem ['vaʒẽ] (*pl* -**ns**) F green bean
vagido [va'ʒidu] M wail
vagina [va'ʒina] F vagina
vaginal [vaʒi'naw] (*pl* -**ais**) ADJ vaginal
vago, -a ['vagu, a] ADJ (*indefinido*) vague; (*desocupado*) vacant, free; **tempo ~, horas vagas** spare time
vagões [va'gõjʃ] MPL *de* **vagão**
vaguear [va'gja'] VI to wander, roam; (*passear*) to ramble
vai *etc* [vaj] VB V **ir**
vaia ['vaja] F booing; **vaiar** [va'ja'] VT, VI to boo, hiss
vaidade [vaj'dadʒi] F vanity; (*futilidade*) futility
vai-da-valsa M: **ir no ~** to take life as it comes, go with the flow
vaidoso, -a [vaj'dozu, ɔza] ADJ vain
vai-e-vem M INV = **vaivém**
vai-não-vai M INV shilly-shallying
vaivém [vaj'vẽj] M to-ing and fro-ing
vala ['vala] F ditch; **~ comum** pauper's grave
vale ['vali] M valley; (*poético*) vale; (*escrito*) voucher; (*reconhecimento de dívida*) I O U; **~ postal** postal order
valentão, -tona [valẽ'tãw, 'tɔna] (*pl* -**ões/-s**) ADJ tough ■ M/F tough nut

NB: *European Portuguese adds the following consonants to certain words:* **b** (sú(b)dito, su(b)til); **c** (a(c)ção, a(c)cionista, a(c)to); **m** (inde(m)ne); **p** (ado(p)çã, ado(p)tar); *for further details see p. xiii.*

valente [va'lẽtʃi] ADJ brave

valentia [valẽ'tʃia] F courage, bravery; (*proeza*) feat

valentões [valẽ'tõjʃ] MPL *de* **valentão**

valentona [valẽ'tɔna] F *de* **valentão**

valer [va'le^r] VI to be worth; (*ser válido*) to be valid; (*ter influência*) to carry weight; (*servir*) to serve; (*ser proveitoso*) to be useful; **valer-se** VR: **valer-se de** to use, make use of; **~ a pena** to be worthwhile; **não vale a pena** it isn't worth it; **vale a pena fazer** it is worth doing; **~ a** (*ajudar*) to help; **~ por** (*equivaler*) to be worth the same as; **para ~** (*muito*) very much, a lot; (*realmente*) for real, properly; **vale dizer** in other words; **fazer ~ os seus direitos** to stand up for one's rights; **vale examinar os detalhes** we should examine the details; **mais vale ... (do que ...)** it would be better to ... (than ...); **não vale empurrar** (*Esporte etc*) you're not allowed to push; **assim não vale!** that's not fair!; **vale tudo** anything goes; **ser para ~** (*col*) to be for real; **ou coisa que o valha** or something like it; **valeu!** (*col*) you bet!

valeta [va'leta] F gutter

valete [va'letʃi] M (*Cartas*) jack

vale-tudo M INV (*Esporte*) all-in wrestling; (*fig*) "anything goes" principle

valha *etc* ['vaʎa] VB V **valer**

valia [va'lia] F value; **de grande ~** valuable

validação [valida'sãw] F validation

validade [vali'dadʒi] F validity

validar [vali'da^r] VT to validate, make valid; **válido, -a** ['validu, a] ADJ valid

valioso, -a [va'ljozu, ɔza] ADJ valuable

valise [va'lizi] F case, grip

valor [va'lo^r] M value; (*mérito*) merit; (*coragem*) courage; (*preço*) price; (*importância*) importance; **valores** MPL (*morais*) values; (*num exame*) marks; (*Com*) securities; **dar ~ a** to value; **sem ~** worthless; **no ~ de** to the value of; **objetos de ~** valuables; **~ nominal** face value; **~ contábil** *ou* **contabilizado** (*Com*) book value; **~ ao par** (*Com*) par value

valorização [valoriza'sãw] F increase in value

valorizar [valori'za^r] VT to value; (*aumentar o valor*) to raise the value of; **valorizar-se** VR to go up in value; (*pessoa*) to value o.s.

valoroso, -a [valo'rozu, ɔza] ADJ brave

valsa ['vawsa] F waltz

válvula ['vawvula] F valve

vampe ['vãpi] F vamp, femme fatale

vampiro, -a [vã'piru, a] M/F vampire

vandalismo [vãda'liʒmu] M vandalism

vândalo, -a ['vãdalu, a] M/F vandal

vangloriar-se [vãglo'rjaxsi] VR: **~ de** to boast of *ou* about

vanguarda [vã'gwaxda] F vanguard, forefront; (*arte*) avant-garde; **artista de ~** avant-garde artist

vantagem [vã'taʒẽ] (*pl* **-ns**) F advantage; (*ganho*) profit, benefit; **contar ~** (*col*) to brag, boast; **levar ~** to get the upper hand; **tirar ~ de** to take

advantage of; **vantajoso, -a** [vãta'ʒozu, ɔza] ADJ advantageous; (*lucrativo*) profitable; (*proveitoso*) beneficial

vão[1] [vãw] VB V **ir**

vão[2], **vã** [vãw, vã] (*pl* **-s, vãs**) ADJ vain; (*fútil*) futile ■ M (*intervalo*) space; (*de porta etc*) opening; (*Arq*) empty space; **em ~** in vain

vapor [va'po^r] M steam; (*navio*) steamer; (*de gás*) vapour (*Brit*), vapor (*US*); **cozer no ~** to steam; **ferro a ~** steam iron; **a todo o ~** at full speed

vaporizador [vaporiza'do^r] M vaporizer; (*de perfume*) spray

vaporizar [vapori'za^r] VT to vaporize; (*perfume*) to spray

vaporoso, -a [vapo'rozu, ɔza] ADJ steamy, misty; (*transparente*) transparent, see-through

vaqueiro [va'kejru] M cowboy, cowhand

vaquinha [va'kiɲa] F: **fazer uma ~** to have a whip-round

vara ['vara] F (*pau*) stick; (*Tec*) rod; (*Jur*) jurisdiction; (*de porcos*) herd; **salto de ~** pole vault; **~ de condão** magic wand

varal [va'raw] (*pl* **-ais**) M clothes line

varanda [va'rãda] F verandah; (*balcão*) balcony

varão, -roa [va'rãw, 'roa] (*pl* **-ões/-s**) ADJ male ■ M man, male; (*de ferro*) rod

varapau [vara'paw] (*col*) M (*pessoa*) beanpole

varar [va'ra^r] VT (*furar*) to pierce; (*passar*) to cross ■ VI to beach, run aground

varejar [vare'ʒa^r] VT (*com vara*) to beat; (*revistar*) to search

varejeira [vare'ʒejra] F bluebottle

varejista [vare'ʒiʃta] (BR) M/F retailer ■ ADJ (*mercado*) retail

varejo [va'reʒu] (BR) M (*Com*) retail trade; **loja de ~** retail store; **a ~** retail; **preço no ~** retail price

variação [varja'sãw] (*pl* **-ões**) F variation, change

variado, -a [va'rjadu, a] ADJ varied; (*sortido*) assorted

variante [va'rjãtʃi] ADJ, F variant

variar [va'rja^r] VT, VI to vary; **para ~** for a change; **variável** [va'rjavew] (*pl* **-eis**) ADJ variable; (*tempo, humor*) changeable ■ F variable

varicela [vari'sɛla] F chickenpox

variedade [varje'dadʒi] F variety; **variedades** FPL (*Teatro*) variety *sg*; **espetáculo/teatro de ~s** variety show/theatre (*Brit*) *ou* theater (*US*)

Varig ['varigi] ABR F (= *Viação Aérea Rio-Grandense*) *Brazilian national airline*

varinha [va'riɲa] F wand; **~ de condão** magic wand

vário, -a ['varju, a] ADJ (*diverso*) varied; (*pl*) various, several; (*Com*) sundry

varíola [va'riola] F smallpox

varizes [va'riziʃ] FPL varicose veins

varoa [va'roa] F *de* **varão**

varões [va'rõjʃ] MPL *de* **varão**

varonil [varo'niw] (*pl* **-is**) ADJ manly, virile

VAR-Palmares ABR F (= *Vanguarda Armada Revolucionária*) *former Brazilian terrorist movement*

varredor, a [vaxe'do^r(a)] ADJ sweeping ■ M/F sweeper; **~ de rua** road sweeper

varrer [va'xe^r] VT to sweep; (*sala*) to sweep out; (*folhas*) to sweep up; (*fig*) to sweep away

varrido, -a [va'xidu, a] ADJ: **um doido ~** a raving lunatic

Varsóvia [vax'sɔvja] N Warsaw; **pacto de ~** Warsaw Pact

várzea ['vaxzja] F meadow, field

vascular [vaʃku'la^r] ADJ vascular

vasculhar [vaʃku'ʎa^r] VT (*pesquisar*) to research; (*remexer*) to rummage through

vasectomia [vazekto'mia] F vasectomy

vaselina® [vaze'lina] F Vaseline®; (*col: pessoa*) smooth talker

vasilha [va'ziʎa] F (*para líquidos*) jug; (*para alimentos*) dish, container; (*barril*) barrel

vaso ['vazu] M pot; (*para flores*) vase; **~ (sanitário)** toilet (bowl); **~ sanguíneo** blood vessel

Vasp ['vaʃpi] ABR F (= *Viação Aérea de São Paulo*) Brazilian internal airline

vassoura [va'sora] F broom

vastidão [vaʃtʃi'dãw] F vastness, immensity

vasto, -a ['vaʃtu, a] ADJ vast

vatapá [vata'pa] M *fish or chicken with coconut milk, shrimps, peanuts, palm oil and spices*

Vaticano [vatʃi'kanu] M: **o ~** the Vatican; **a Cidade do ~** the Vatican City

vaticinar [vatʃisi'na^r] VT to foretell, prophesy

vaticínio [vatʃi'sinju] M prophecy

vau [vaw] M ford, river crossing; (*Náut*) beam

vazamento [vaza'mẽtu] M leak

vazante [va'zãtʃi] F ebb tide

vazão [va'zãw] (*pl* **-ões**) F flow; (*venda*) sale; **dar ~ a** (*expressar*) to give vent to; (*Com*) to clear; (*atender*) to deal with; (*resolver*) to attend to

vazar [va'za^r] VT (*tornar vazio*) to empty; (*derramar*) to spill; (*verter*) to pour out ■ VI to leak; (*maré*) to go out; (*notícia*) to leak; **ser vazado em** (*moldado*) to be modelled on

vazio, -a [va'ziu, a] ADJ empty; (*pessoa*) empty-headed, frivolous; (*cidade*) deserted ■ M (*tb fig*) emptiness; (*deixado por alguém/algo*) void; **~ de** (*fig: sem*) devoid of

vazões [va'zõjʃ] FPL *de* **vazão**

VBC (BR) ABR M = **Valor Básico de Custeio**

vê *etc* [ve] VB V **ver**

veado ['vjadua] M deer; (*BR: col: ofensivo*) poof (*Brit*), fag (*US*); **carne de ~** venison

vedado, -a [ve'dadu, a] ADJ (*proibido*) forbidden; (*fechado*) enclosed

vedar [ve'da^r] VT (*proibir*) to ban, prohibit; (*sangue*) to stop (the flow of); (*buraco*) to stop up; (*garrafa*) to cork; (*entrada, passagem*) to block; (*terreno*) to close off

vedete [ve'detʃi] F star

veemência [vje'mẽsja] F vehemence

veemente [vje'mẽtʃi] ADJ vehement

vegetação [veʒeta'sãw] F vegetation

vegetal [veʒe'taw] (*pl* **-ais**) ADJ vegetable *atr*; (*reino, vida*) plant *atr* ■ M vegetable;

medicamento ~ herbal remedy

vegetar [veʒe'ta^r] VI to vegetate

vegetariano, -a [veʒeta'rjanu, a] ADJ, M/F vegetarian

vegetativo, -a [veʒeta'tʃivu, a] ADJ: **vida vegetativa** (*fig*) insular life

veia ['veja] F (*Med, Bot*) vein; (*fig: pendor*) bent

veicular [vejku'la^r] VT to convey; (*anúncios*) to distribute

veículo [ve'ikulu] M vehicle; (*fig: meio*) means *sg*; **~ com tração nas quatro rodas, ~ 4x4** sports utility vehicle; **~ de propaganda** advertising medium

veio ['veju] M (*de rocha*) vein; (*na mina*) seam; (*de madeira*) grain; (*eixo*) shaft

veio VB V **vir**

vejo *etc* ['veʒu] VB V **ver**

vela ['vela] F candle; (*Auto*) spark plug; (*Náut*) sail; **fazer-se à** *ou* **de ~** to set sail; **segurar a ~** (*col*) to play gooseberry; **barco à ~** sailing boat; **~ mestra** mainsail

velar [ve'la^r] VT (*cobrir*) to veil; (*ocultar*) to hide; (*vigiar*) to keep watch over; (*um doente*) to sit up with ■ VI (*não dormir*) to stay up; (*vigiar*) to keep watch; **~ por** to look after

veleidade [velej'dadʒi] F (*capricho*) whim, fancy; (*inconstância*) fickleness

veleiro [ve'lejru] M (*barco*) sailing boat

velejar [vele'ʒa^r] VI to sail

velhaco, -a [ve'ʎaku, a] ADJ crooked ■ M/F crook

velha-guarda F old guard

velharia [veʎa'ria] F (*os velhos*) old people *pl*; (*coisa*) old thing

velhice [ve'ʎisi] F old age

velho, -a ['vɛʎu, a] ADJ old ■ M/F old man/ woman; (*col: pai/mãe*) old man/lady; **meus ~s** (*col: pais*) my folks; **meu ~!** (*col*) old chap

velhote, -ta [ve'ʎɔtʃi] ADJ elderly ■ M/F elderly man/woman

velocidade [velosi'dadʒi] F speed, velocity; (PT: *Auto*) gear; **a toda ~** at full speed; **trem de alta ~** high-speed train; **"diminua a ~"** "reduce speed now"; **~ máxima** (*em estrada*) speed limit; **~ de processamento** (*Comput*) processing speed

velocímetro [velo'simetru] M speedometer

velocíssimo, -a [velo'sisimu, a] ADJ SUPERL *de* **veloz**

velocista [velo'siʃta] M/F sprinter

velódromo [ve'lɔdromu] M cycle track

velório [ve'lɔrju] M wake

veloz [ve'lɔʒ] ADJ fast

velozmente [veloʒ'mẽtʃi] ADV fast

veludo [ve'ludu] M velvet; **~ cotelê** corduroy

vem [vẽj] VB V **vir**

vêm [vẽj] VB V **vir**

vencedor, a [vẽse'do^r(a)] ADJ winning ■ M/F winner

vencer [vẽ'se^r] VT (*num jogo*) to beat; (*competição*) to win; (*inimigo*) to defeat; (*exceder*) to surpass;

NB: *European Portuguese adds the following consonants to certain words:* **b** (sú(b)dito, su(b)til); **c** (a(c)ção, a(c)cionista, a(c)to); **m** (inde(m)ne); **p** (ado(p)çã, ado(p)tar); *for further details see p. xiii.*

(obstáculos) to overcome; *(percorrer)* to pass ■ VI *(num jogo)* to win; **vencer(-se)** VR *(prazo)* to run out; *(promissória)* to become due; *(apólice)* to mature; **vencido, -a** [vẽ'sidu, a] ADJ: **dar-se por vencido** to give in

vencimento [vẽsi'mẽtu] M *(Com)* expiry; (: *de letra, dívida)* maturation; *(data)* expiry date; (: *de promissória)* due date; *(salário)* salary; *(de gêneros alimentícios etc)* sell-by date; **vencimentos** MPL *(ganhos)* earnings

venda ['vẽda] F sale; *(pano)* blindfold; *(mercearia)* general store; **à ~** on sale, for sale; **pôr algo à ~** to put sth up for sale; **preço de ~** selling price; **~ a crédito** credit sale; **~ a prazo** *ou* **prestação** sale in instal(l)ments; **~ à vista** cash sale; **~ por atacado** wholesale; **~ pelo correio** mail-order

vendar [vẽ'da[ᵣ]] VT to blindfold

vendaval [vẽda'vaw] *(pl* **-ais)** M gale

vendável [vẽ'davew] *(pl* **-eis)** ADJ marketable

vendedor, a [vẽde'do[ᵣ](a)] M/F seller; *(de imóvel)* vendor; **~ ambulante** street vendor

vender [vẽ'de[ᵣ]] VT, VI to sell; **vender-se** VR *(pessoa)* to allow o.s. to be bribed; **~ por atacado/ a varejo** to sell wholesale/retail; **~ fiado/a prestações** *ou* **a prazo** to sell on credit/in instal(l)ments; **~ à vista** to sell for cash; **ela está vendendo saúde** she's bursting with health

vendeta [vẽ'deta] F vendetta

vendinha [vẽ'dʒiɲa] F corner shop

veneno [ve'nɛnu] M poison; *(fig, de serpente)* venom; **ser um ~ para** *(fig)* to be very bad for; **venenoso, -a** [vene'nozu, ɔza] ADJ poisonous; *(fig)* venomous

veneração [venera'sãw] F reverence

venerar [vene'ra[ᵣ]] VT to revere; *(Rel)* to worship

venéreo, -a [ve'nɛrju, a] ADJ: **doença venérea** venereal disease

veneta [ve'neta] F: **ser de ~** *(pessoa)* to be moody; **deu-lhe na ~ (que)** he got it into his head (that)

Veneza [ve'neza] N Venice

veneziana [vene'zjana] F *(porta)* louvre *(Brit) ou* louvre *(US)* door; *(janela)* louvre *ou* louvre window

Venezuela [vene'zwɛla] F: **a ~** Venezuela

venezuelano, -a [venezwe'lanu, a] ADJ, M/F Venezuelan

venha *etc* ['vɛɲa] VB V **vir**

vênia ['venja] F *(desculpa)* forgiveness; *(licença)* permission

venial [ve'njaw] *(pl* **-ais)** ADJ venial, forgiveable

venta ['vẽta] F nostril; **ventas** FPL *(nariz)* nose *sg*

ventania [vẽta'nia] F gale

ventar [vẽ'ta[ᵣ]] VI: **está ventando** it is windy

ventarola [vẽta'rɔla] F fan

ventilação [vẽtʃila'sãw] F ventilation

ventilador [vẽtʃila'do[ᵣ]] M ventilator; *(elétrico)* fan

ventilar [vẽtʃi'la[ᵣ]] VT to ventilate; *(roupa, sala)* to air; *(fig)* to discuss; (: *hipótese, possibilidade)* to entertain

vento ['vẽtu] M wind; *(brisa)* breeze; **de ~ em**

popa *(fig)* swimmingly, very well; **ventoinha** [vẽ'twiɲa] F *(cata-vento)* weathercock, weather vane; *(PT: Auto)* fan

ventoso, -a [vẽ'tozu, ɔza] ADJ windy

ventre ['vẽtri] M belly; *(literário: útero)* womb

ventríloquo, -a [vẽ'trilokwu, a] M/F ventriloquist

ventura [vẽ'tura] F fortune; *(felicidade)* happiness; **se por ~** if by any chance

venturoso, -a [vẽtu'rozu, ɔza] ADJ happy

Vênus ['venuʃ] F Venus

ver [ve[ᵣ]] VT to see; *(olhar para, examinar)* to look at; *(resolver)* to see to; *(televisão)* to watch ■ VI to see ■ M: **a meu ~** in my opinion; **ver-se** VR *(achar-se)* to be, find o.s.; *(no espelho)* to see o.s.; *(duas pessoas)* to see each other; **vai ~ que ...** maybe ...; **viu?** *(col)* OK?; **deixa eu ~** let me see; **ele tem um carro que só vendo** *(col)* he's got a car like you wouldn't believe; **não tem nada a ~ (com)** it has nothing to do (with); **não tenho nada que ~ com isto** it is nothing to do with me, it is none of my concern; **~-se com** to settle accounts with; **bem se vê que** it's obvious that; **já se vê** of course; **pelo que se vê** apparently

veracidade [verasi'dadʒi] F truthfulness

veranear [vera'nja[ᵣ]] VI to spend the summer; *(tirar férias)* to take summer holidays *(Brit) ou* a summer vacation *(US)*

veraneio [vera'neju] M summer holidays *pl (Brit) ou* vacation *(US)*

veranista [vera'niʃta] M/F holidaymaker *(Brit)*, (summer) vacationer *(US)*

verão [ve'rãw] *(pl* **-ões)** M summer

veraz [ve'rajʒ] ADJ truthful

verba ['vexba] F allowance; **verba(s)** FPL *(recursos)* funds *pl*

verbal [vex'baw] *(pl* **-ais)** ADJ verbal

verbalizar [vexbali'za[ᵣ]] VT, VI to verbalize

verbete [vex'betʃi] M *(num dicionário)* entry

verbo ['vexbu] M verb; **deitar o ~** *(col)* to say a few words; **soltar o ~** *(col)* to start talking

verborragia [vexboxa'ʒia] F verbiage, waffle

verboso, -a [vex'bozu, ɔza] ADJ wordy, verbose

verdade [vex'dadʒi] F truth; **na ~** in fact; **é ~** it's true; **é ~?** *(col)* really?; **uma princesa de ~** a real princess; **de ~** *(falar)* truthfully; *(ameaçar etc)* really; **dizer umas ~s a alguém** to tell sb a few home truths; **a ~ nua e crua** the plain truth; **para falar a ~** to tell the truth; **..., não é ~?** *(col)* ..., isn't that so?

verdadeiramente [vexdadejra'mẽtʃi] ADV really

verdadeiro, -a [vexda'dejru, a] ADJ true; *(genuíno)* real; *(pessoa)* truthful; **foi um ~ desastre** it was a real disaster

verde [ve'xdʒi] ADJ green; *(fruta)* unripe; *(fig)* inexperienced ■ M green; *(plantas etc)* greenery; **~ de medo** pale with fear; **~ de fome/raiva** terribly hungry/angry; **jogar ~ (para colher maduro)** to fish, ask leading questions; **Partido V~** Green Party

verde-abacate ADJ INV avocado (green)

verde-garrafa ADJ INV bottle-green

verdejar [vexde'ʒaʳ] VI to turn green

verdor [vex'doʳ] M greenness; (Bot) greenery; (fig) inexperience

verdugo [vex'dugu] M executioner; (fig) beast

verdura [vex'dura] F (hortaliça) greens pl; (Bot) greenery; (cor verde) greenness

verdureiro, -a [verdu'rejru, a] M/F greengrocer (Brit), produce dealer (US)

vereador, a [verja'doʳ(a)] M/F councillor (Brit), councilor (US)

vereda [ve'reda] F path

veredicto [vere'dʒiktu] M verdict

verga ['vexga] F (vara) stick; (de metal) rod

vergão [vex'gãw] (pl -ões) M weal

vergar [vex'gaʳ] VT (curvar) to bend ■ VI to bend; (com um peso) to sag

vergões [vex'gõjʃ] MPL de vergão

vergonha [vex'gɔɲa] F shame; (timidez) embarrassment; (humilhação) humiliation; (ato indecoroso) indecency; (brio) self-respect; **é uma ~** it's disgraceful; **ter ~** to be ashamed; **ter ~ de fazer** to be ashamed of doing; (ser tímido) to be too shy to do; **não ter ~ na cara** to have a cheek, have no shame; **vergonhoso, -a** [vexgo'ɲozu, ɔza] ADJ (infame) shameful; (indecoroso) disgraceful

verídico, -a [ve'ridʒiku, a] ADJ true, truthful

verificação [verifika'sãw] F (exame) checking; (confirmação) verification

verificar [verifi'kaʳ] VT to check; (confirmar, Comput) to verify; **verificar-se** VR (acontecer) to happen; (realizar-se) to come true; **~ se ...** to check that ..

verme ['vɛxmi] M worm

vermelhidão [vexmeʎi'dãw] F redness; (da pele) rosiness

vermelho, -a [vex'meʎu, a] ADJ red ■ M red; **estar no ~** to be in the red; **ficar ~** to go red

vermute [vex'mutʃi] M vermouth

vernáculo, -a [vex'nakulu, a] ADJ: **língua vernácula** vernacular ■ M vernacular

vernissage [vexni'saʒ] M opening, vernissage

verniz [vex'niʒ] M varnish; (couro) patent leather; (fig) whitewash; (: polidez) veneer; **sapatos de ~** patent shoes

verões [ve'rõjʃ] MPL de verão

verossímil [vero'simiw] (PT -osí, pl -eis) ADJ (provável) likely, probable; (crível) credible

verossimilhança [verosimi'ʎãsa] (PT -osi-) F probability

verruga [ve'xuga] F wart

versado, -a [vex'sadu, a] ADJ: **~ em** clever at, good at

versão [vex'sãw] (pl -ões) F version; (tradução) translation

versar [vex'saʳ] VI: **~ sobre** to be about, concern

versátil [vex'satʃiw] (pl -eis) ADJ versatile

versatilidade [vexsatʃili'dadʒi] F versatility

versículo [vex'sikulu] M (Rel) verse; (de artigo) paragraph

verso ['vɛxsu] M verse; (linha) line of poetry; (da página) other side, reverse; **vide ~** see over; **~ solto** blank verse; **~s brancos** blank verse sg

versões [vex'sõjʃ] FPL de versão

vértebra ['vɛxtebra] F vertebra

vertebrado, -a [vexte'bradu, a] ADJ vertebrate ■ M vertebrate

vertebral [vexte'braw] (pl -ais) ADJ: **coluna ~** spine

vertente [vex'tẽtʃi] F slope

verter [vex'teʳ] VT to pour; (por acaso) to spill; (traduzir) to translate; (lágrimas, sangue) to shed ■ VI: **~ de** to spring from; **~ em** (rio) to flow into

vertical [vextʃi'kaw] (pl -ais) ADJ vertical; (de pé) upright, standing ■ F vertical

vértice ['vɛxtʃisi] M apex

vertigem [vex'tʃiʒẽ] F (medo de altura) vertigo; (tonteira) dizziness

vertiginoso, -a [vextʃiʒi'nozu, ɔza] ADJ dizzy, giddy; (velocidade) frenetic

verve ['vɛxvi] F verve

vesgo, -a ['veʒgu, a] ADJ cross-eyed

vesícula [ve'zikula] F: **~ (biliar)** gall bladder

vespa ['veʃpa] F wasp

véspera ['veʃpera] F: **a ~** the day before; **vésperas** FPL (Rel) vespers; **a ~ de Natal** Christmas Eve; **nas ~s de** on the eve of; (de eleição etc) in the run-up to; **estar nas ~s de** to be about to

vesperal [veʃpe'raw] (pl -ais) ADJ afternoon atr ■ F matinée

vespertino, -a [veʃpex'tʃinu, a] ADJ evening atr

veste ['veʃtʃi] F garment; (Rel) vestment, robe

vestiário [veʃ'tʃjarju] M (em casa, teatro) cloakroom; (Esporte) changing room; (de ator) dressing room

vestibular [veʃtʃibu'laʳ] M college entrance exam

vestíbulo [veʃ'tʃibulu] M hall(way), vestibule; (Teatro) foyer

vestido, -a [veʃ'tʃidu, a] ADJ: **~ de branco** etc dressed in white etc ■ M dress; **~ de baile** ball gown; **~ de noiva** wedding dress

vestidura [veʃtʃi'dura] F (Rel) robe

vestígio [veʃ'tʃiʒju] M (rastro) track; (fig) sign, trace

vestimenta [veʃtʃi'mẽta] F (roupa) garment; (Rel) vestment

vestir [veʃ'tʃiʳ] VT (uma criança) to dress; (pôr sobre si) to put on; (trajar) to wear; (comprar, dar roupa para) to clothe; (fazer roupa para) to make clothes for; **vestir-se** VR to dress; (pôr roupa) to get dressed; **~-se de algo** to dress up as sth; **ela se veste naquela butique** she buys her clothes in that boutique; **~-se de preto** etc to dress in black etc; **este terno veste bem** this suit is a good fit

vestuário [veʃ'twarju] M clothing

NB: European Portuguese adds the following consonants to certain words: **b** (sú(b)dito, su(b)til); **c** (a(c)ção, a(c)cionista, a(c)to); **m** (inde(m)ne); **p** (ado(p)çã, ado(p)tar); for further details see p. xiii.

vetar [ve'ta^r] VT to veto; *(proibir)* to forbid
veterano, -a [vete'ranu, a] ADJ, M/F veteran
veterinário, -a [veteri'narju, a] ADJ veterinary
■ M/F vet(erinary surgeon)
veto ['vɛtu] M veto
véu [vɛw] M veil; ~ **do paladar** *(Anat)* soft palate, velum
vexame [ve'ʃami] F *(vergonha)* shame, disgrace; *(tormento)* affliction; *(humilhação)* humiliation; *(afronta)* insult; **passar um** ~ to be disgraced; **dar um** ~ to make a fool of o.s.
vexaminoso, -a [veʃami'nozu, ɔza] ADJ shameful, disgraceful
vexar [ve'ʃa^r] VT *(atormentar)* to upset; *(envergonhar)* to put to shame; **vexar-se** VR to be ashamed
vez [veʒ] F time; *(turno)* turn; **uma** ~ once; **duas** ~**es** twice; **alguma** ~ ever; **algumas** ~**es, às** ~**es** sometimes; ~ **por outra** sometimes; **cada** ~ **(que)** every time; **cada** ~ **mais/menos** more and more/less and less; **desta** ~ this time; **de** ~ once and for all; **de uma** ~ *(ao mesmo tempo)* at once; *(de um golpe)* in one go; **de** ~ **em quando** from time to time; **em** ~ **de** instead of; **fazer as** ~**es de** *(pessoa)* to stand in for; *(coisa)* to replace; **mais uma** ~, **outra** ~ again, once more; **raras** ~**es** seldom; **uma** ~ **que** since; **3** ~**es 6** 3 times 6; **de uma** ~ **por todas** once and for all; **ter** ~ *(pessoa)* to have a chance; *(argumento etc)* to apply; **muitas** ~**es** many times; *(freqüentemente)* often; **mais** ~**es** more often; **na maioria das** ~**es** most times; **toda** ~ **que** every time; **um de cada** ~ one at a time; **repetidas** ~**es** repeatedly; **uma** ~ **ou outra** once in a while; **uma** ~ **na vida, outra na morte** once in a blue moon; **era uma** ~ ... once upon a time there was ....
vi [vi] VB V **ver**
via ['via] F road, route; *(meio)* way; *(documento)* copy; *(conduto)* channel ■ PREP via, by way of; ~ **aérea** airmail; ~ **de acesso** access road; **V~ Láctea** Milky Way; **primeira** ~ *(de documento)* top copy; **chegar às** ~ **s de fato** to come to blows; **em** ~ **s de** about to; **por** ~ **aérea** by airmail; **por** ~ **das dúvidas** just in case; **por** ~ **de regra** generally, as a rule; **por** ~ **terrestre/ marítima** by land/sea
via *etc* VB V **ver**
viabilidade [vjabili'dadʒi] F feasibility, viability
viação [vja'sãw] *(pl* -**ões)** F transport; *(companhia de ônibus)* bus *(ou* coach) company; *(conjunto de estradas)* roads *pl*
viaduto [vja'dutu] M viaduct
viageiro, -a [vja'ʒejru, a] ADJ travelling *(Brit),* traveling *(US)*
viagem ['vjaʒẽ] *(pl* -**ns)** F journey, trip; *(o viajar)* travel; *(Náut)* voyage; *(com droga)* trip; **viagens** FPL *(jornadas)* travels; ~ **de ida e volta** return trip, round trip; ~ **de núpcias** honeymoon; ~ **de ida** outward trip; ~ **de negócios** business trip; ~ **inaugural** *(Náut)* maiden voyage; **boa** ~! bon voyage!, have a good trip!
viajado, -a [vja'ʒadu, a] ADJ well-travelled *(Brit),*

well-traveled *(US)*
viajante [vja'ʒãtʃi] ADJ travelling *(Brit),* traveling *(US)* ■ M traveller *(Brit),* traveler *(US); (Com)* commercial travel(l)er
viajar [vja'ʒa^r] VI to travel; ~ **por** to travel, tour
viário, -a ['vjarju, a] ADJ road *atr*
viatura [vja'tura] F vehicle
viável ['vjavew] *(pl* -**eis)** ADJ feasible, viable
víbora ['vibora] F viper; *(fig: pessoa)* snake in the grass
vibração [vibra'sãw] *(pl* -**ões)** F vibration; *(fig)* thrill
vibrante [vi'brãtʃi] ADJ vibrant; *(discurso)* stirring
vibrar [vi'bra^r] VT *(brandir)* to brandish; *(fazer estremecer)* to vibrate; *(cordas)* to strike ■ VI to vibrate; *(som)* to echo; *(col)* to be thrilled
vice ['visi] M/F deputy
vice- [visi-] PREFIXO vice-
vice-campeão, -peã *(pl* -**ões/-s)** M/F runner-up
vicejar [vise'ʒa^r] VI to flourish
vice-presidente, -a M/F vice president
vice-rei M viceroy
vice-reitor, a M/F deputy head
vice-versa [-'vɛxsa] ADV vice versa
viciado, -a [vi'sjadu, a] ADJ addicted; *(ar)* foul ■ M/F addict; **um** ~ **em entorpecentes** a drug addict; ~ **em algo** addicted to sth
viciar [vi'sja^r] VT *(criar vício em)* to make addicted; *(falsificar)* to falsify; *(taxímetro etc)* to fiddle; **viciar-se** VR to become addicted; ~/~**-se em algo** to make/become addicted to sth
vicinal [visi'naw] *(pl* -**ais)** ADJ local
vício ['visju] M vice; *(defeito)* failing; *(costume)* bad habit; *(em entorpecentes)* addiction
vicioso, -a [vi'sjozu, ɔza] ADJ corrupt, defective; **círculo** ~ vicious circle
vicissitude [visisi'tudʒi] F vicissitude; **vicissitudes** FPL ups and downs
viço ['visu] M vigour *(Brit),* vigor *(US); (da pele)* freshness
viçoso, -a [vi'sozu, ɔza] ADJ *(plantas)* luxuriant; *(fig)* exuberant
vida ['vida] F life; *(duração)* lifetime; *(fig)* vitality; **com** ~ alive; **modo de** ~ way of life; **para toda a** ~ forever; **sem** ~ dull, lifeless; **na** ~ **real** in real life; **cair na** ~ *(col)* to go on the game; **dar** ~ **a** *(festa, ambiente)* to liven up; **dar a** ~ **por algo/por fazer algo** to give one's right arm for sth/to do sth; **estar bem de** ~ to be well off; **estar entre a** ~ **e a morte** to be at death's door; **mete-se com a sua** ~ mind your own business; **é a** ~! that's life!; **danado/feliz da** ~ really angry/ happy; **siga essa rua toda a** ~ follow this street as far as you can go; **ele trabalha que não é** ~ *(col)* he works really hard; **a** ~ **mansa** the easy life; ~ **civil/privada/pública/sentimental/ sexual/social** civilian/private/public/love/sex/ social life; ~ **conjugal/doméstica** married/ home life; ~ **útil** *(Com)* useful life
vidão [vi'dãw] M good life
vide ['vidʒi] VT see; ~ **verso** see over
videira [vi'dejra] F grapevine

vidente [vi'dētʃi] M/F clairvoyant; (no mundo antigo) seer

vídeo ['vidʒju] M video; (televisão) TV; (tela) screen

videocâmara [vidʒju'kamara] F video camera

videocassete [vidʒjuka'sɛtʃi] M (fita) video cassette ou tape; (aparelho) video (recorder)

videoclipe [vidʒju'klipi] M video

videoclube [vidʒju'klubi] M video club

videodisco [vidʒju'dʒiʃku] M video disk

vídeo game ['gejmi] (pl -s) M video game

videoteipe [vidʒju'tejpi] M (fita) video tape; (processo) (video-)taping

videotexto [vidʒju'teʃtu] M Teletext®

vidraça [vi'drasa] F window pane

vidraçaria [vidrasa'ria] F glazier's; (fábrica) glass factory; (conjunto de vidraças) glasswork

vidraceiro [vidra'sejru] M glazier

vidrado, -a [vi'dradu, a] ADJ glazed; (porta) glass atr; (olhos) glazed, glassy; **estar** ou **ser ~ em** ou **por** (col) to be crazy about

vidrar [vi'dra'] VT to glaze ■ VI: **~ em** ou **por** (col) to fall in love with

vidreiro [vi'drejru] M glazier, glassmaker

vidro ['vidru] M glass; (frasco) bottle; **fibra de ~** fibreglass (Brit), fiberglass (US); **~ fosco** frosted glass; **~ fumê** tinted glass; **~ de aumento** magnifying glass

viela ['vjɛla] F alley

Viena ['vjɛna] N Vienna

vier etc [vje'] VB v **vir**

viés [vjɛʃ] M slant; (Costura) bias strip; **ao** ou **de ~** diagonally

vieste ['vjeʃtʃi] VB v **vir**

viga ['viga] F beam; (de ferro) girder

Vietnã [vjet'nã] (BR) M: **o ~** Vietnam; **vietnamita** [vjetna'mita] ADJ, M/F Vietnamese

vigarice [viga'risi] F swindle

vigário [vi'garju] M vicar

vigarista [viga'riʃta] M swindler, confidence trickster

vigência [vi'ʒẽsja] F validity; **durante a ~ da lei** while the law is in force

vigente [vi'ʒẽtʃi] ADJ in force, valid

viger [vi'ʒe'] VI to be in force

vigésimo, -a [vi'ʒezimu, a] NUM twentieth; v tb **quinto**

vigia [vi'ʒia] F (ato) watching; (Náut) porthole ■ M night watchman; **de ~** on watch

vigiar [vi'ʒja'] VT to watch, keep an eye on; (ocultamente) to spy on; (velar por) to keep watch over; (presos, fronteira) to guard ■ VI to be on the lookout

vigilância [viʒi'lãsja] F vigilance; **vigilante** [viʒi'lãtʃi] ADJ vigilant; (atento) alert

vigília [vi'ʒilja] F (falta de sono) wakefulness; (vigilância) vigilance

vigor [vi'go'] M energy; **em ~** in force; **entrar/pôr em ~** to take effect/put into effect

vigorar [vigo'ra'] VI to be in force; **a ~ a partir**

de effective as of

vigoroso, -a [vigo'rozu, ɔza] ADJ vigorous

vil [viw] (pl **vis**) ADJ vile, low

vila ['vila] F town; (casa) villa; (conjunto de casas) group of houses round a courtyard; **~ militar** military base

vilã [vi'lã] F de **vilão**

vilania [vila'nia] F villainy

vilão, -lã [vi'lãw, 'lã] (pl **-s/-s**) M/F villain

vilarejo [vila'reʒu] M village

vileza [vi'leza] F vileness; (ação) mean trick

vilipendiar [vilipē'dʒja'] VT to revile; (desprezar) to despise

vim [vĩ] VB v **vir**

vime ['vimi] M wicker

vinagre [vi'nagri] M vinegar

vinagrete [vina'grɛtʃi] M vinaigrette

vincar [vĩ'ka'] VT to crease; (produzir sulco em) to furrow; (rosto) to line

vinco ['vĩku] M crease; (sulco) furrow; (no rosto) line

vincular [vĩku'la'] VT to link, tie; **vincular-se** VR to be linked ou tied; **vínculo** ['vĩkulu] M bond, tie; (relação) link; **vínculo de parentesco** blood tie; **vínculo empregatício** contract of employment

vinda ['vĩda] F arrival; (ato de vir) coming; (regresso) return; **dar as boas ~s a** to welcome

vindicar [vĩdʒi'ka'] VT to vindicate

vindima [vĩ'dʒima] F grape harvest

vindique etc [vĩ'dʒiki] VB v **vindicar**

vindouro, -a [vĩ'doru, a] ADJ future, coming

vingador, a [vĩga'do'(a)] ADJ avenging ■ M/F avenger

vingança [vĩ'gãsa] F vengeance, revenge; **vingar** [vĩ'ga'] VT to avenge ■ VI (ter êxito) to be successful; (planta) to grow; **vingar-se** VR: **vingar-se de** to take revenge on

vingativo, -a [vĩga'tʃivu, a] ADJ vindictive

vingue etc ['vĩgi] VB v **vingar**

vinha ['viɲa] F vineyard; (planta) vine

vinha etc VB v **vir**

vinha-d'alho (pl **vinhas d'alho**) F marinade

vinhedo [vi'ɲedu] M vineyard

vinho ['viɲu] M wine ■ ADJ INV maroon; **~ branco/rosado/tinto** white/rosé/red wine; **~ seco/doce** dry/sweet wine; **~ espumante/de mesa** sparkling/table wine; **~ do Porto** port

vinícola [vi'nikola] ADJ INV wine-producing

vinicultor, a [vinikuw'to'(a)] M/F wine grower

vinicultura [vinikuw'tura] F wine growing, viticulture

vinil [vi'niw] M vinyl

vinte ['vĩtʃi] NUM twenty; **o século ~** the twentieth century; **as ~** (col: de cigarro, bebida) the last bit; v tb **cinqüenta**

vintém [vĩ'tẽj] M: **sem um ~** penniless

vintena [vĩ'tɛna] F: **uma ~** twenty, a score

viola ['vjɔla] F viola

NB: European Portuguese adds the following consonants to certain words: **b** (sú(b)dito, su(b)til); **c** (a(c)ção, a(c)cionista, a(c)to); **m** (inde(m)ne); **p** (ado(p)çã, ado(p)tar); for further details see p. xiii.

violação [vjola'sãw] (*pl* -ões) F violation; ~ **da lei** lawbreaking; ~ **de domicílio** housebreaking

violão [vjo'lãw] (*pl* -ões) M guitar

violar [vjo'la^r] VT to violate; (*a lei*) to break

violência [vjo'lẽsja] F violence; **violentar** [vjolẽ'ta^r] VT to force; (*mulher*) to rape; (*fig*: *sentido*) to distort; **violento, -a** [vjo'lẽtu, a] ADJ violent; (*furioso*) furious

violeta [vjo'leta] F violet ■ ADJ INV violet

violinista [vjoli'niʃta] M/F violinist, violin player

violino [vjo'linu] M violin

violões [vjo'lõjʃ] MPL *de* **violão**

violoncelista [vjolõse'liʃta] M/F 'cellist

violoncelo [vjolõ'sɛlu] M 'cello

VIP ['vipi] M/F VIP ■ ADJ (*sala*) VIP *atr*

vir [vi^r] VI to come; ~ **a ser** to turn out to be; **a semana que vem** next week; ~ **abaixo** to collapse; **mandar** ~ to send for; ~ **fazendo algo** to have been doing sth; ~ **fazer** to come to do; ~ **buscar** to come for; ~ **com** (*alegar*) to come up with; **isso não vem ao caso** that's irrelevant; **veio-lhe uma idéia** he had an idea, an idea came to him; ~ **a saber** to come to know; **venha o que vier** come what may; **vem cá!** come here!; (*col*: *escuta*) listen!; **não vem que não tem!** (*col*) come off it!

vir *etc* VB V **ver**

viração [vira'sãw] (*pl* -ões) F breeze

vira-casaca ['vira-] (*pl* -s) M/F turncoat

virada [vi'rada] F turning; (*guinada*) swerve; (*Esporte*) turnaround; **dar uma** ~ (*col*) to put on a last burst

virado, -a [vi'radu, a] ADJ (*às avessas*) upside down ■ M (*Culin*): ~ (**de feijão**) *fried beans with sausage and eggs*; ~ **para** facing

vira-lata ['vira-] (*pl* -s) M (*cão*) mongrel; (*pessoa*) bum

virar [vi'ra^r] VT to turn; (*página, disco, barco*) to turn over; (*esquina*) to turn; (*bolsos*) to turn inside out; (*copo*) to empty; (*despejar*) to tip; (*opinião*) to turn round; (*transformar-se em*) to become ■ VI to turn; (*barco*) to turn over, capsize; (*mudar*) to change; **virar-se** VR to turn; (*voltar-se*) to turn round; (*defender-se*) to fend for o.s.; ~ **de cabeça para baixo** to turn upside down; ~ **do avesso** to turn inside out; ~ **para** to face; **vira e mexe** every so often; ~(-**se**) **contra** to turn against; ~-**se para** (*recorrer a*) to turn to; ~-**se de bruços** to turn onto one's stomach

viravolta [vira'vɔwta] F (*fig*) turnabout; (*volta completa*) complete turn; (*giro sobre si mesmo*) about-turn; (*cambalhota*) somersault

virgem ['vixʒẽ] (*pl* -ns) ADJ (*puro*) pure; (*mata*) virgin; (*não usado*) unused; (: *fita*) blank ■ F virgin; **V**~ (*Astrologia*) Virgo; ~ **de** free of

virgindade [vixʒĩ'dadʒi] F virginity

vírgula ['vixgula] F comma; (*decimal*) point; **uma** ~! (*col*) my eye!

virgular [vixgu'la^r] VT: ~ **com** *ou* **de** (*entremear*) to punctuate with

viril [vi'riw] (*pl* -is) ADJ virile

virilha [vi'riʎa] F groin

virilidade [virili'dadʒi] F virility

viris [vi'riʃ] ADJ PL *de* **viril**

virose [vi'rɔzi] F viral illness

virtual [vix'twaw] (*pl* -ais) ADJ virtual; (*potencial*) potential

virtualmente [vixtwaw'mẽtʃi] ADV virtually

virtude [vix'tudʒi] F virtue; **em** ~ **de** owing to, because of

virtuosidade [vixtwozi'dadʒi] F virtuosity

virtuosismo [vixtwo'ziʒmu] M = **virtuosidade**

virtuoso, -a [vix'twozu, ɔza] ADJ virtuous ■ M virtuoso

virulência [viru'lẽsja] F virulence

virulento, -a [viru'lẽtu, a] ADJ virulent

vírus ['viruʃ] M INV virus

vis [viʃ] ADJ PL *de* **vil**

visado, -a [vi'zadu, a] ADJ stamped; (*pessoa*: *pela polícia, imprensa*) under observation

visão [vi'zãw] (*pl* -ões) F vision; (*Anat*) eyesight; (*vista*) sight; (*maneira de perceber*) view; ~ **de conjunto** overall view

visar [vi'za^r] VT (*alvo*) to aim at; (*ter em vista*) to have in view; (*ter como objetivo*) to aim for; (*passaporte, cheque*) to stamp ■ VI: ~ **a** to have in view; to aim for; ~ **fazer** to aim to do

Visc. ABR = **Visconde**

vísceras ['viseraʃ] FPL innards, bowels; (*fig*) heart *sg*

visconde [viʃ'kõdʒi] M viscount

viscondessa [viʃkõ'desa] F viscountess

viscoso, -a [viʃ'kozu, ɔza] ADJ sticky, viscous

viseira [vi'zejra] F visor

visibilidade [vizibili'dadʒi] F visibility

visionário, -a [vizjo'narju, a] ADJ, M/F visionary

visita [vi'zita] F visit, call; (*pessoa*) visitor; (*na Internet*) hit; **fazer uma** ~ **a** to visit; **ter** ~**s** to have company; ~ **de médico** (*col*) flying visit; **horário de** ~**s** visiting hours *pl*; **visitante** [vizi'tãtʃi] ADJ visiting ■ M/F visitor

visitar [vizi'ta^r] VT to visit; (*inspecionar*) to inspect

visível [vi'zivew] (*pl* -eis) ADJ visible

vislumbrar [viʒlũ'bra^r] VT to glimpse, catch a glimpse of; **vislumbre** [viʒ'lũbri] M glimpse

visões [vi'zõjʃ] FPL *de* **visão**

visom [vi'zõ] (*pl* -ns) M mink; **casaco de** ~ mink coat

visor [vi'zo^r] M (*Foto*) viewfinder

visse *etc* ['visi] VB V **ver**

vista ['viʃta] F sight; (*Med*) eyesight; (*panorama*) view; (*braguilha*) fly, flies *pl*; **à** *ou* **em** ~ **de** in view of; **conhecer de** ~ to know by sight; **dar na** ~ to attract attention; **dar uma** ~ **de olhos em** to glance at; **fazer** ~ **grossa (a)** to turn a blind eye (to); **pôr à** ~ to show; **ter em** ~ to have in mind; **à primeira** ~ at first sight; **à** ~ visible, showing; (*Com*) in cash; **até à** ~! see you!; **na** ~ **de todos** in view of everyone; **perder de** ~ to lose sight of; **a perder de** ~ as far as the eye can (*ou* could) see; (*pagamento*) over a long period; **saltar à** ~ to be obvious; **fazer** ~ to look nice; ~ **cansada/curta** eye strain/shortsightedness

vista-d'olhos F glance, quick look; **dar uma vista-d'olhos em** to have a quick look at
visto, -ta ['viʃtu] PP de **ver** ▪ ADJ seen ▪ M (em passaporte) visa; (em documento) stamp; **hoya ~** witness; **pelo ~** by the looks of things
visto VB v **vestir**
vistoria [viʃto'ria] F inspection
vistoriar [viʃto'rjaʳ] VT to inspect
vistoso, -a [viʃ'tozu, ɔza] ADJ eye-catching
visual [vi'zwaw] (pl -ais) ADJ visual ▪ M (col: de pessoa) look; (aparência) appearance; (vista) view;
visualizar [vizwali'zaʳ] VT to visualize
vital [vi'taw] (pl -ais) ADJ vital; (essencial) essential; **vitalício, -a** [vita'lisju, a] ADJ for life
vitalidade [vitali'dadʒi] F vitality
vitalizar [vitali'zaʳ] VT to revitalize
vitamina [vita'mina] F vitamin; (para beber) fruit crush
vitaminado, -a [vitami'nadu, a] ADJ with added vitamins
vitamínico, -a [vita'miniku, a] ADJ vitamin atr
vitela [vi'tɛla] F calf; (carne) veal
viticultura [vitʃikuw'tura] F wine growing
vítima ['vitʃima] F victim; **fazer-se de ~** to play the martyr
vitimar [vitʃi'maʳ] VT to sacrifice; (matar) to kill, claim the life of; (danificar) to damage
vitória [vi'tɔrja] F victory; (Esporte) win
vitória-régia (pl **vitórias-régias**) F giant water lily
vitorioso, -a [vito'rjozu, ɔza] ADJ victorious; (time) winning
vitral [vi'traw] (pl -ais) M stained glass window
vítreo, -a ['vitrju, a] ADJ (feito de vidro) glass atr; (com o aspecto de vidro) glassy; (água) clear
vitrina [vi'trina] F = **vitrine**
vitrine [vi'trini] F shop window; (armário) display case
vitrola [vi'trɔla] F record player
viuvez [vju'veʒ] F widowhood
viúvo, -a ['vjuvu, a] ADJ widowed ▪ M/F widower/widow
viva ['viva] M cheer; **~!** hurray!; **~ o rei!** long live the king!
vivacidade [vivasi'dadʒi] F vivacity; (energia) vigour (Brit), vigor (US)
vivalma [vi'vawma] F: **não ver ~** not to see a (living) soul
vivamente [viva'mētʃi] ADV animatedly; (descrever, sentir) vividly; (protestar) loudly
vivar [vi'vaʳ] VT, VI to cheer
viva-voz [viva'vɔʃ] M (BR: Tel: em telefone) speakerphone; (para celular) hands-free kit
vivaz [vi'vajʒ] ADJ (animado) lively
viveiro [vi'vejru] M nursery
vivência [vi'vēsja] F existence; (experiência) experience
vivenda [vi'vēda] F (casa) residence
vivente [vi'vētʃi] ADJ living ▪ M/F living being;

os ~s the living
vívido, -a [vi'vidu, a] ADJ experienced in life
vívido, -a ['vividu, a] ADJ vivid
viver [vi've ʳ] VI to live; (estar vivo) to be alive ▪ VT (vida) to live; (experimentar) to have, experience ▪ M life; **~ de** to live on; **~ à custa de** to live off; **ela vive viajando/cansada** she's always travel(l)ing/tired; **ele vive resfriado/com dor de estômago** he's always got a cold/stomach ache; **vivendo e aprendendo** live and learn
víveres ['vivereʃ] MPL provisions
vivificar [vivifi'kaʳ] VT to bring to life
vivissecção [vivisek'sãw] F vivisection
vivo, -a ['vivu, a] ADJ living; (esperto) clever; (cor) bright; (criança, debate) lively ▪ M: **os ~s** the living; **televisionar ao ~** to televise live; **estar ~** to be alive
vizinhança [vizi'ɲãsa] F neighbourhood (Brit), neighborhood (US)
vizinho, -a [vi'ziɲu, a] ADJ neighbouring (Brit), neighboring (US); (perto) nearby ▪ M/F neighbour (Brit), neighbor (US)
voador, a [vwa'doʳ(a)] ADJ flying
voar [vo'aʳ] VI to fly; (explodir) to blow up, explode; **fazer ~ (pelos ares)** (dinamitar) to blow up, blast; **~ para cima de alguém** to fly at sb; **estar voando** (col) to be in the dark; **~ alto** (fig) to aim high; **fazer algo voando** to do sth in a hurry
vocabulário [vokabu'larju] M vocabulary
vocábulo [vo'kabulu] M word
vocação [voka'sãw] (pl -ões) F vocation
vocacional [vokasjo'naw] (pl -ais) ADJ vocational; (orientação) careers atr
vocações [voka'sõjʃ] FPL de **vocação**
vocal [vo'kaw] (pl -ais) ADJ vocal
você [vo'se] PRON you
vocês [vo'seʃ] PRON PL you
vociferação [vosifera'sãw] (pl -ões) F shouting; (censura) harangue
vociferar [vosife'raʳ] VT, VI to shout, yell; **~ contra** to decry
vodca ['vodʒka] F vodka
voga ['vɔga] F (Náut) rowing; (moda) fashion; (popularidade) popularity; **em ~** popular, fashionable
vogal [vo'gaw] (pl -ais) F (Ling) vowel ▪ M/F (votante) voting member
vogar [vo'gaʳ] VI to sail; (boiar) to float; (importar) to matter; (estar na moda) to be popular; (lei) to be in force; (palavra) to be in use
voile ['vwali] M voile; **cortina de ~** net curtain
vol. ABR (= volume) vol
volante [vo'lãtʃi] M (Auto) steering wheel; (piloto) racing driver; (impresso para apostas) betting slip; (roda) flywheel
volátil [vo'latʃiw] (pl -eis) ADJ volatile
vôlei ['volej] M volleyball
voleibol [volej'bow] M = **vôlei**

NB: European Portuguese adds the following consonants to certain words: **b** (sú(b)dito, su(b)til); **c** (a(c)ção, a(c)cionista, a(c)to); **m** (inde(m)ne); **p** (ado(p)çã, ado(p)tar); for further details see p. xiii.

volt ['vɔwtʃi] (*pl* -s) M volt

volta ['vɔwta] F turn; (*regresso*) return; (*curva*) bend, curve; (*circuito*) lap; (*resposta*) retort; **passagem de ida e ~** return ticket (*Brit*), round trip ticket (*US*); **dar uma ~** (*a pé*) to go for a walk; (*de carro*) to go for a drive; **dar ~s** *ou* **uma ~ (a)** to go round; **estar de ~** to be back; **na ~ do correio** by return (post); **por ~ de** about, around; **à** *ou* **em ~ de** around; **na ~** (*no caminho de volta*) on the way back; **vou resolver isso na ~** I'll sort this out when I get back; **estar** *ou* **andar às ~s com** to be tied up with; **fazer a ~**, **dar meia ~** (*Auto*) to do a U-turn; **dar meia ~** (*Mil*) to do an about-turn; **dar a ~ por cima** (*fig*) to get over it, pick o.s. up; **~ e meia** every so often

voltado, -a [vow'tadu, a] ADJ: **estar ~ para** to be concerned with

voltagem [vowl'taʒẽ] F voltage

voltar [vow'taʳ] VT to turn ■ VI to return, go (*ou* come) back; **voltar-se** VR to turn round; **~ uma arma contra** to turn a weapon on; **~ a fazer** to do again; **~ a si** to come to; **~ atrás** (*fig*) to backtrack; **~-se para** to turn to; **~-se contra** to turn against

voltear [vow'tʃaʳ] VT to go round; (*manivela*) to turn ■ VI to spin; (*borboleta*) to flit around

volubilidade [volubili'dadʒi] F fickleness

volume [vo'lumi] M volume; (*tamanho*) bulk; (*pacote*) package; **volumoso, -a** [volu'mozu, ɔza] ADJ bulky, big; (*som*) loud

voluntário, -a [volũ'tarju, a] ADJ voluntary ■ M/F volunteer

voluntarioso, -a [volũta'rjozu, ɔza] ADJ headstrong

volúpia [vo'lupja] F pleasure, ecstasy

voluptuoso, -a [volup'twozu, ɔza] ADJ voluptuous

volúvel [vo'luvew] (*pl* -eis) ADJ fickle, changeable

volver [vow'veʳ] VT to turn ■ VI to go (*ou* come) back

vomitar [vomi'taʳ] VT, VI to vomit; (*fig*) to pour out; **vômito** ['vomitu] M (*ato*) vomiting; (*efeito*) vomit

vontade [võ'tadʒi] F will; (*desejo*) wish; **boa/má ~** good/ill will; **de boa/má ~** willingly/grudgingly; **frutas à ~** fruit galore; **coma à ~** eat as much as you like; **fique** *ou* **esteja à ~** make yourself at home; **não estar à ~** to be uncomfortable *ou* ill at ease; **com ~** (*com prazer*) with pleasure; (*com gana*) with gusto; **estar com** *ou* **ter ~ de fazer** to feel like doing; **dar ~ a alguém de fazer** to make sb want to do; **essa música dá ~ de bailar** this music makes you want to dance; **fazer a ~ de alguém** to do what sb wants; **de livre e espontânea ~** of one's own free will; **por ~ própria** off one's own bat; **força de ~** will power; **ser cheio de ~s** to be spoilt

vôo ['vou] (*PT* voo) M flight; **levantar ~** to take off; **~ cego** flying blind, instrument flying; **~ livre** (*Esporte*) hang-gliding; **~ picado** nose dive

voragem [vo'raʒẽ] (*pl* -ns) F abyss, gulf; (*de águas*) whirlpool; (*fig: de paixões*) maelstrom

voraz [vo'raʒ] ADJ voracious, greedy

vórtice ['vɔxtʃisi] M vortex

vos [vuʃ] PRON you; (*a vós*) to you

vós [vɔʃ] PRON you

vosso, -a ['vɔsu, a] ADJ your ■ PRON: **(o)** ~ yours

votação [vota'sãw] (*pl* -ões) F vote, ballot; (*ato*) voting; **submeter algo a ~** to put sth to the vote; **~ secreta** secret ballot

votado, -a [vo'tadu, a] ADJ: **o deputado mais ~** the MP (*Brit*) *ou* Member of Congress (*US*) with the highest number of votes

votante [vo'tãtʃi] M/F voter

votar [vo'taʳ] VT (*eleger*) to vote for; (*aprovar*) to pass; (*submeter a votação*) to vote on; (*dedicar*) to devote ■ VI to vote; **votar-se** VR: **votar-se a** to devote o.s. to; **~ em** to vote for; **~ por/contra** to vote for/against; **voto** ['vɔtu] M vote; (*promessa*) vow; **votos** MPL (*desejos*) wishes; **fazer votos por** to wish for; **fazer votos que** to hope that; **fazer voto de castidade** to take a vow of chastity; **voto nulo** *ou* **em branco** blank vote; **voto de confiança** vote of confidence; **voto secreto** secret ballot

vou [vo] VB V ir

vovó [vo'vɔ] F grandma

vovô [vo'vo] M grandad

voz [vɔʒ] F voice; (*clamor*) cry; **a meia ~** in a whisper; **dar ~ de prisão a alguém** to tell sb he is under arrest; **de viva ~** orally; **ter ~ ativa** to have a say; **em ~ baixa** in a low voice; **em ~ alta** aloud; **levantar a ~ para alguém** to raise one's voice to sb; **~ de cana rachada** (*col*) screeching voice; **~ de comando** command, order

vozearia [vozja'ria] F = **vozerio**

vozeirão [vozej'rãw] (*pl* -ões) M loud voice

vozerio [voze'riu] M hullabaloo

VPR ABR F (= *Vanguarda Popular Revolucionária*) *former Brazilian revolutionary movement*

vulcânico, -a [vuw'kaniku, a] ADJ volcanic

vulcão [vuw'kãw] (*pl* -s) M volcano

vulgar [vuw'gaʳ] ADJ (*comum*) common; (*reles*) cheap; (*pej: pessoa etc*) vulgar

vulgaridade [vuwgari'dadʒi] F commonness; (*pej*) vulgarity

vulgarizar [vuwgari'zaʳ] VT to popularize; (*abandalhar*) to cheapen

vulgarmente [vuwgax'mẽtʃi] ADV commonly, popularly

vulgo ['vuwgu] M common people *pl* ■ ADV commonly known as

vulnerabilidade [vuwnerabili'dadʒi] F vulnerability

vulnerável [vuwne'ravew] (*pl* -eis) ADJ vulnerable

vulto ['vuwtu] M figure; (*volume*) mass; (*fig*) importance; (*pessoa importante*) important person; **obras de ~** important works; **tomar ~** to take shape

vultoso, -a [vuw'tozu, ɔza] ADJ bulky; (*importante*) important; (*quantia*) considerable

vulva ['vuwva] F vulva

vupt ['vuptʃi] EXCL wham!

Ww

W, w ['dablju] (*pl* **ws**) ᴍ W, w; **W de William** W
  for William
w. ᴀʙʀ (= *watt*) w
walkie-talkie [wɔki'tɔki] (*pl* **-s**) ᴍ walkie-talkie
watt ['wɔtʃi] (*pl* **-s**) ᴍ watt
watt-hora (*pl* **watts-horas**) ᴍ watt-hour
Web [u'ɛbi] ꜰ (*Comput*) web

webcam [wɛb'cã] ꜰ webcam
weblog [wɛb'lɔgui] ᴍ weblog
western ['wɛʃtexn] (*pl* **-s**) ᴍ western
windsurfe [wĩ'suxfi] ᴍ windsurfing
windsurfista [wĩsux'fiʃta] ᴍ/ꜰ windsurfer
WWW ᴀʙʀ ꜰ (= *World Wide Web*) WWW

NB: *European Portuguese adds the following consonants to certain words:* **b** (sú(b)dito, su(b)til); **c** (a(c)ção,
  a(c)cionista, a(c)to); **m** (inde(m)ne); **p** (ado(p)çã, ado(p)tar); *for further details see p. xiii.*

Xx

X, x [ʃiʃ] *(pl* **xs)** M X, x; **o ~ do problema** the crux of the problem; **X de Xavier** X for Xmas
xá [ʃa] M shah
xadrez [ʃa'dreʒ] M *(jogo)* chess; *(tabuleiro)* chessboard; *(tecido)* checked cloth; *(col: cadeia)* clink ■ ADJ INV check(ered); **tecido de ~** check material
xale ['ʃali] M shawl
xampu [ʃã'pu] M shampoo
Xangai [ʃã'gaj] N Shanghai
xangô [ʃã'go] M *(orixá)* Afro-Brazilian deity; *(culto)* Afro-Brazilian religion
xará [ʃa'ra] M/F namesake; *(companheiro)* mate
xaropada [ʃaro'pada] *(col)* F bore; *(conversa)* boring talk
xarope [ʃa'rɔpi] M syrup; *(para a tosse)* cough syrup
xavante [ʃa'vãtʃi] ADJ, M/F Shavante Indian
xaveco [ʃa'vɛku] M *(coisa sem valor)* piece of junk
xaxim [ʃa'ʃĩ] M plant fibre *(Brit)* ou fiber *(US)* *(used to plant indoor plants)*
xelim [ʃe'lĩ] *(pl* **-ns)** M shilling
xenofobia [ʃenofo'bia] F xenophobia
xenófobo, -a [ʃe'nɔfobu, a] ADJ xenophobic ■ M/F xenophobe
xepa ['ʃepa] *(col)* F leftovers *pl*
xepeiro, -a [ʃe'pejru, a] M/F rubbish *(Brit)* ou garbage *(US)* picker
xeque ['ʃɛki] M *(Xadrez)* check; *(soberano)* sheikh; **pôr em ~** *(fig)* to call into question; **xeque-mate** *(pl* **xeques-mate)** M checkmate
xereta [ʃe'reta] M/F busybody ■ ADJ nosy
xeretar [ʃere'tar] VI to poke one's nose in
xerez [ʃe'reʒ] M sherry
xerife [ʃe'rifi] M sheriff
xerocar [ʃero'kar] VT to photocopy, Xerox®
xerocópia [ʃero'kɔpja] F photocopy
xerocopiar [ʃeroko'pjar] VT = **xerocar**
xerox® [ʃe'rɔks] M *(copia)* photocopy; *(máquina)* photocopier
xexelento, -a [ʃeʃe'lẽtu, a] *(col)* ADJ scruffy ■ M/F scruff
xexéu [ʃe'ʃɛw] M stink
xi [ʃi] EXCL cor! *(Brit),* gee! *(US)*
xícara ['ʃikara] *(BR)* F cup
xicrinha [ʃi'kriɲa] *(BR)* F little cup
xiita [ʃi'ita] ADJ, M/F Shiite
xilindró [ʃili'drɔ] *(col)* M clink
xilofone [ʃilo'fɔni] M xylophone
xilografia [ʃilogra'fia] F woodcut
xingação [ʃĩga'sãw] *(pl* **-ões)** F curse
xingamento [ʃĩga'mẽtu] M = **xingação**
xingar [ʃĩ'gar] VT to swear at ■ VI to swear; **~ alguém de algo** to call sb sth
xingatório [ʃĩga'tɔrju] M stream of invectives
Xingu [ʃĩ'gu] M *see below*

■ XINGU

The *Xingu* National Park was created in 1961 by the federal government and directed by the brothers Orlando and Cláudio Vilasboas, who were known internationally for their efforts to preserve Brazil's indigenous people. Situated in the north of the state of Mato Grosso, it aims to preserve indigenous culture. It brings together sixteen communities, a total of two thousand Indians.

xinxim [ʃĩ'ʃĩ] M *(tb:* **xinxim de galinha)** chicken ragout
xixi [ʃi'ʃi] *(col)* M wee, pee; **fazer ~** to wee, have a wee
xô [ʃo] EXCL shoo
xodó [ʃo'dɔ] M *(pessoa)* sweetheart; *(coisa)* passion; **ter ~ por alguém/algo** to have a soft spot for sb/sth

Zz

Z, z [ze] (pl **zs**) M Z, z; **Z de Zebra** Z for Zebra
zaga ['zaga] F (Futebol) fullback position
zagueiro [za'gejru] M (Futebol) fullback
Zaire ['zajri] M: **o ~** Zaire
Zâmbia ['zãbja] F Zambia
zanga ['zãga] F (raiva) anger; (irritação) annoyance
zangado, -a [zã'gadu, a] ADJ angry; (irritado) annoyed; (irritadiço) bad-tempered; **ele está ~ comigo** (de relações cortadas) he's not speaking to me
zangão [zã'gãw] (pl **-s**) M (inseto) drone
zangar [zã'gaʳ] VT to annoy, irritate ■ VI to get angry; **zangar-se** VR (aborrecer-se) to get annoyed; **~-se com** to get cross with
zangões [zã'gõjʃ] MPL de **zangão**
zanzar [zã'zaʳ] VI to wander
zarolho, -a [za'roʌu, a] ADJ blind in one eye
zarpar [zax'paʳ] VI (navio) to set sail; (ir-se) to set off; (fugir) to run away
Zé [zɛ] ABR (= José) Joe
zebra ['zebra] F zebra; (col: pessoa) silly ass; (jogo) upset, turn-up for the books; **deu ~** (col) there was an upset
zebrar [ze'braʳ] VI to be a turn-up for the books
zelador, a [zela'doʳ(a)] M/F caretaker ■ ADJ caring
zelar [ze'laʳ] VT, VI: **~ (por)** to look after
zelo ['zelu] M devotion, zeal; **~ por alguém/algo** devotion to sb/sth
zeloso, -a [ze'lozu, ɔza] ADJ zealous; (diligente) hard-working
zen-budismo [zɛ̃-] M Zen (Buddhism)
zênite ['zenitʃi] M zenith
zé-povinho [-po'viɲu] (pl **-s**) M the man in the street; (o povo) the masses pl; (ralé) riff raff
zerar [ze'raʳ] VT (conta, inflação) to reduce to zero; (déficit) to pay off, wipe out; (aluno) to give no marks to ■ VI: **~ em** (aluno) to get no marks in
zerinho, -a [ze'riɲu, a] (col) ADJ brand new
zero ['zɛru] M zero; (Esporte) nil; **ser um ~ à esquerda** to be useless; **8 graus abaixo/acima de ~** 8 degrees below/above zero; **reduzir alguém a ~** to clean sb out; **ficar a ~** to lose

everything; **começar do ~** (fig) to start from nothing; **zero-quilômetro** ADJ INV brand new ■ M INV brand new car
ziguezague [zigi'zagi] M zigzag
ziguezagueante [zigiza'gjãtʃi] ADJ zigzag
ziguezaguear [zigiza'gjaʳ] VI to zigzag
Zimbábue [zĩ'babwi] M: **o ~** Zimbabwe
zinco ['zĩku] M zinc; **folha de ~** corrugated iron
-zinho, -a [-'ziɲu, a] SUFIXO little; **florzinha** little flower
zipe ['zipi] M = **zíper**
zíper ['zipeʳ] M zip (Brit), zipper (US)
ziquizira [ziki'zira] (col) F lurgy
zoada ['zwada] F = **zoeira**
zodíaco [zo'dʒiaku] M zodiac
zoeira ['zwejra] F din
zombador, a [zõba'doʳ(a)] ADJ mocking ■ M/F mocker
zombar [zõ'baʳ] VI to mock; **~ de** to make fun of;
zombaria [zõba'ria] F mockery, ridicule
zona ['zɔna] F area; (de cidade) district; (Geo) zone; (col: local de meretrício) red-light district; (: confusão) mess; (: tumulto) free-for-all; **fazer a ~** to be on the game; **fazer uma ~** to raise hell, make a fuss; **~ eleitoral** electoral district, constituency; **~ franca** free-trade area; **Z~ Norte/Sul** (do Rio, São Paulo etc) Northern/ Southern District; **a Z~ Sul carioca** the fashionable middle-class suburbs along the beaches in Rio
zonear [zo'njaʳ] VT to divide into districts; (col) to make a mess in ■ VI (col) to raise hell
zonzeira [zõ'zejra] F dizziness; **dar/sentir ~** to make/feel dizzy
zonzo, -a ['zõzu, a] ADJ dizzy
zôo ['zou] M zoo
zoologia [zolo'ʒia] F zoology
zoológico, -a [zo'lɔʒiku, a] ADJ zoological; **jardim ~** zoo
zoólogo, -a [zo'ɔlogu, a] M/F zoologist
zoom [zũ] M = **zum**
zorra ['zoxa] (col) F mess
zuarte ['zwaxtʃi] M denim
zulu [zu'lu] ADJ, M/F Zulu ■ M (Ling) Zulu

NB: European Portuguese adds the following consonants to certain words: **b** (sú(b)dito, su(b)til); **c** (a(c)ção, a(c)cionista, a(c)to); **m** (inde(m)ne); **p** (ado(p)ção, ado(p)tar); for further details see p. xiii.

zum | zurro

zum [zũ] M zoom lens

zumbido [zũ'bidu] M buzz(ing); (de tráfego) hum; **um ~ no ouvido** a ringing in one's ear

zumbir [zũ'biʳ] VI to buzz; (ouvido) to ring ■ M buzzing; ringing

zunido [zu'nidu] M (de vento) whistling; (de inseto) buzz

zunir [zu'niʳ] VI (vento) to whistle; (seta) to whizz; (bala) to zip; (inseto) to buzz

zunzum [zũ'zũ] M buzz(ing); (boato) rumour

(Brit), rumor (US)

zunzunzum [zũzũ'zũ] M rumour (Brit), rumour (US)

zura ['zura] M/F INV miser ■ ADJ INV mean, stingy

zureta [zu'reta] (col) M/F loony

Zurique [zu'riki] N Zurich

zurrapa [zu'xapa] F rough wine, plonk (col)

zurrar [zu'xaʳ] VI to bray

zurro ['zuxu] M bray